The Roug.

Canada

written and researched by

Tim Jepson, Phil Lee, Tania Smith
and Christian Williams

with additional contributions by

Emma Rose Rees and John Shandy Watson

ROUGH GUIDES

NEW YORK • LONDON • DELHI

www.roughguides.com

EASTERN
STANDARD
TIME

ATLANTIC
STANDARD
TIME

N

Ellesmere Island

GREENLAND
(DENMARK)

Davis Strait

Arctic Circle

Baffin Island

**CANADA'S PROVINCES
AND TERRITORIES**
Alberta (AB)
British Columbia (BC)
Manitoba (MB)
New Brunswick (NB)
Newfoundland & Labrador (NL)
Northwest Territories (NT)
Nova Scotia (NS)
Nunavut (NU)
Ontario (ON)
Prince Edward Island (PE)
Québec (QC)
Saskatchewan (SK)
Yukon Territory (YT)

Metres	Feet
5000	16000
4000	13000
3000	10000
2000	6500
1000	3300
500	1600
200	650
0	0

Iqaluit

Hudson Strait

Labrador Sea

Hudson Bay

Schefferville

Goose Bay

Labrador

NEWFOUNDLAND & LABRADOR

Newfoundland

Gander

Big Trout Lake

QUÉBEC

St John's

Gaspé *Gulf of St Lawrence*

Sydney

NEWFOUNDLAND STANDARD TIME

ONTARIO

Lake Nipigon

Saguenay

St Lawrence

PRINCE EDWARD ISLAND

Charlottetown

NEW BRUNSWICK

Rivière-du-Loup

Moncton

Thunder Bay

Lake Superior

Sault Ste Marie

Québec City

Fredericton

Halifax

Trois-Rivières

Sudbury

Montréal

Sherbrooke

NOVA SCOTIA

Ottawa

Lake Huron

Toronto

Lake Ontario

Boston

ATLANTIC OCEAN

Lake Michigan

Niagara Falls

Detroit

Lake Erie

Windsor

Chicago

New York

0	200 miles

iii

△ Banff National Park

Introduction to

Canada

Canada is almost unimaginably vast. It stretches from the Atlantic to the Pacific and from the latitude of Rome to beyond the Magnetic North Pole. Its archetypal landscapes are the Rockies' lakes and peaks, the endless forests and the prairie wheatfields, but Canada holds landscapes that defy expectations: rainforest and desert lie close together in the southwest corner of the country, while in the east a short drive can take you from fjords to lush orchards. Better still, great tracts of Canada are completely unspoiled: ninety percent of Canadians live within 160km of the US border.

Like its neighbour to the south, Canada is a spectrum of cultures, a hotchpotch of immigrant groups who supplanted the continent's many native peoples. There's a crucial difference, though, between the two countries. Whereas citizens of the US are encouraged to perceive themselves as Americans above all else, Canada's concertedly multicultural approach has done more to acknowledge the origins of its people, creating an ethnic mosaic, rather than a US-style melting-pot. Alongside the French and British majorities live a host of communities who maintain many of the traditions of their homelands – Chinese, Ukrainians, Portuguese, Indians, Dutch, Polish, Greek and Spanish, to name just the most numerous.

For the visitor, the mix that results from Canada's mostly exemplary tolerance is an exhilarating experience, offering such widely differing environments as Vancouver's huge Chinatown and the austere religious enclaves of Manitoba. Canadians themselves, however, are often troubled by the lack of

Fact file

• Canada is the world's second-largest country (after the Russian Federation), covering almost ten million square kilometres. About a quarter of it comprises an Inuit homeland, Nunavut. Canada extends across six time zones, and shares a border with the US of 8900km. The highest point is Mount Logan (5959m).

• The population is around 30 million. Almost a half claim British ancestry, a quarter French ancestry and just under a million (3.3 percent) claim some aboriginal ancestry. Canada ranks first in the world for literacy and fourth for life expectancy (almost 80 years).

• Canada has colossal natural resources: it's the world's largest exporter of timber and the largest producer of zinc and uranium. Almost two-thirds of its power is hydroelectric.

• Canada is a confederation comprising ten provinces and three territories (see list on p.iii). It has been self-governing since 1867, but retains ties to Britain: the Canadian head of state is Queen Elizabeth II, represented by a Governor General. The bicameral parliament consists of the elected House of Commons and the appointed Senate. The official languages are English and French.

a clear self-image, tending to emphasize the ways in which they are different from the US as a means of self-description. The question "What is a Canadian?" has acquired a new immediacy with the interminable and acrimonious debate over Québec and its possible secession, but ultimately there can be no simple characterization of a people whose country is not so much a single nation as a committee on a continental scale. Pierre Berton, one of Canada's finest writers, wisely ducked the issue: Canadians, he quipped, are "people who know how to make love in a canoe".

"The typical Canadian" might be an elusive concept, but you'll find there's a distinctive feel to the country. Some towns might seem a touch too well regulated, but against this there's the overwhelming sense of Canadian pride in their history and pleasure in the beauty of their land. Canada embraces its own clichés with an energy that's irresistible, promoting everything from the Calgary

▽ Autumn colours

Stampede to maple-syrup festivals and lumberjack contests with an extraordinary zeal and openness. As John Buchan, writer and former Governor General of Canada, once said, "You have to know a man awfully well in Canada to know his surname."

Where to go

The time and expense involved in covering Canada's immense distances means that most visitors confine their trips to the area around one of the main cities – usually Toronto, Montréal, Vancouver or Calgary for arrivals by air. The attractions of these centres vary widely, but they have one thing in common with each other and all other Canadian towns: they are within easy reach of the great outdoors.

Great journeys

A country the size of Canada lends itself to epic journeys. Travelling by car or bus, you can enjoy some of the world's greatest wilderness drives, from the Icefields Parkway through the heart of the Rockies to routes that push some of North America's last frontiers: the Alaska and Cassiar highways in British Columbia, for example, or the Dempster Highway in the Yukon, the only public road on the continent to cross the Arctic Circle. Trains, too, offer superlative rides, whether it's the northbound route to Churchill or the classic transcontinental odyssey from Toronto to Vancouver. At sea, ferries also ply routes that provide a dramatic window on glorious scenery, none more so than the boats running up the Inside Passage from Vancouver Island towards Alaska.

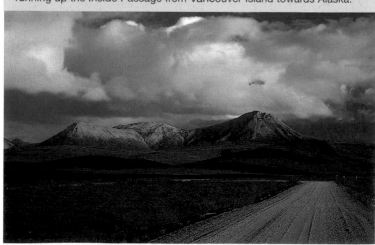

△ The Dempster Highway

Canada's most southerly region, south **Ontario**, contains not only the country's manufacturing heart and its largest city, **Toronto**, but also **Niagara Falls**, the premier tourist sight. North of Toronto there's the far less packaged scenic attraction of **Georgian Bay**, a beautiful waterscape of pine-studded islets set against crystal-blue waters. Like the forested Algonquin park, the bay is also accessible from the Canadian capital, **Ottawa**, not as dynamic a city as Toronto, but still well worth a stay for its galleries and museums.

Québec, set apart by the depth of its French tradition, focuses on its biggest city, **Montréal**, which is for many people the most vibrant place in the country, a fascinating mix of old-world style and commercial dynamism. The pace of life is more relaxed in the historic provincial capital **Québec City**, and more easygoing still in the villages dotted along the St Lawrence lowlands, where glittering spires attest to the enduring influence of the Catholic Church. For something more bracing, you could continue north to **Tadoussac**, where whales can be seen near the mouth of the splendid **Saguenay fjord** – and if you're really prepared for the wilds, forge on through to **Labrador**, as inhospitable a zone as you'll find in the east.

Across the mouth of the St Lawrence, the pastoral **Gaspé** peninsula – the easternmost part of Québec – borders **New Brunswick**, a mild-mannered introduction to the three **Maritime Provinces**, whose people have long been dependent on timber and the sea for their livelihood. Here, the tapering **Bay of Fundy** boasts amazing tides – rising and falling by nine metres or more – whilst the region's tiny fishing villages are at their most beguiling near **Halifax**, the bustling capital of **Nova Scotia**. Perhaps even prettier, and certainly more austere, are the land and seascapes of **Cape Breton Island**, whose rugged topography anticipates that of the

▽ Banff

Aboriginal peoples

The British, French and Spanish were latecomers to Canada, a country that for countless thousands of years was home to a vast aboriginal population. Today, almost a million Canadians claim descent from these first peoples, from the so-called "Indians" of the central and western heartlands, to the Inuit, inhabitants of the great sweep of Canada's north. A third

group, the Métis – descendants of mixed unions of white and aboriginal people – also have a distinct culture, part of a rich cultural, social and artistic mosaic which provides a beguiling complement to the mainstream. You'll find evidence of Canada's former aboriginal life in many museums and galleries, and plenty of areas nurturing living aboriginal cultures, though there's no escaping the fact that many aboriginal people are among the poorest and most marginalized of all Canadians.

island of **Newfoundland** to the north. Newfoundland's isolation has spawned a distinctive culture that's at its most lively in **St John's**, where the local folk-music scene is Canada's best. The island also boasts some of the Atlantic seaboard's finest landscapes, particularly the flat-topped peaks and glacier-gouged lakes of Gros Morne.

Back on the mainland, separating Ontario from Alberta and the Rockies, the "prairie provinces" of **Manitoba** and **Saskatchewan** have a reputation for dullness that's unfair: even in the flat southern parts there's the diversion of **Winnipeg**, whose traces of its early days make it a good place

△ Blueberry pancakes with maple syrup

▽ Flowerpot Island, near Tobermory, ON

to break a trans-Canadian journey. To the north, myriad lakes and gigantic forests offer magnificent canoeing and hiking, especially within **Prince Albert** National Park. In the far north, beside Hudson Bay, the settlement of **Churchill** – remote, but accessible by train – is famous for its polar bears, who gather near town from the end of June waiting to move out over the ice as soon as the bay freezes.

Moving west, the wheatfields of **Alberta** ripple into ranching country on the approach to the **Canadian Rockies**, whose reputation for natural drama is more than borne out by the reality. The provincial capital, **Edmonton**, is overshadowed by **Calgary**, an exuberant city grown fat on the region's oil and gas fields, and the most useful springboard for a venture into the mountains – most popularly to the resorts of **Banff**, **Lake Louise** and **Jasper**. Further west **British Columbia** embodies the popular picture of Canada to perfection: a land of snow-capped summits, rivers and forests, pioneer villages, gold-rush ghost towns, and some of the greatest hiking, skiing, fishing and canoeing in the world. Its urban focus, **Vancouver**, is the country's third city, known for its spectacular natural setting and a laid-back West Coast hedonism. Off the coast lies **Vancouver Island**, a microcosm of the province's immense natural riches and home to **Victoria**, a devotedly anglophile little city.

North of British Columbia, wedged alongside Alaska, is the **Yukon Territory**, half grandiose mountains, half subarctic tundra, and full of evocative echoes of the Klondike gold rush. **Whitehorse**, its capital, and **Dawson City**, a gold-rush relic, are virtually the only towns here, each accessed by dramatic frontier highways. The **Northwest Territories** and **Nunavut**, covering the Canadian Arctic, are an immensity of stunted forest, lakes, tundra and ice, the realm of Dene and Inuit aboriginal bands whose traditional way of life is being threatened as oil and gas exploration reaches ever-northwards. Roads are

Canada embraces its own clichés with an energy that's irresistible, promoting everything from maple syrup festivals to lumberjack contests

△ Polar bear

virtually non-existent in the deep north, and only **Yellowknife**, a bizarre frontier city, plus a handful of ramshackle villages, offer the air links and resources necessary to explore this wilderness.

Outdoor activities

Few countries compare with Canada when it comes to the great outdoors. Almost every settlement has lakes, mountains, rivers and forest on its doorstep, a vast natural playground where you can indulge in just about any outdoor activity. Hiking and mountain-biking are the most obvious, with thousands of kilometres of well-kept and well-marked trails to suit all abilities in countless national and provincial parks. In winter skiing and snow sports take over, most notably in Banff National Park, Mont-Tremblant and Whistler, the last regarded as one of North America's top ski and snowboard resorts. Calmer pleasures include golf and some of the world's finest salmon fishing, along with water-bound activities that range from gentle rafting to kayaking on some of the continent's most ferocious rivers.

△ Climbers, Milk River Valley, AB

xi

When to go

Canada's **climate** is hugely varied, but it's a safe generalization to say that the areas near the coast or the Great Lakes have milder winters and cooler summers than the interior. **July and August** are reliably warm throughout the country, even in the far north, making these the busiest months to visit. **November to March**, by contrast, is an ordeal of sub-zero temperatures almost everywhere except on the west coast, though winter days in many areas are clear and dry, and all large Canadian towns are geared to the challenge of cold conditions, with covered walkways and indoor malls protecting their inhabitants from the worst of the weather.

More specifically, the **Maritime Provinces** and **eastern Canada** have four distinct seasons: chill, snowy winters; short, mild springs; warm summers (which are shorter and colder in northern and inland regions); and long, crisp autumns. Summer is the key season in the resorts, though late September and October, particularly in New Brunswick, are also popular for the autumn colours. Coasts year-round can be blanketed in mist or fog.

In **Ontario** and **Québec** the seasons are also marked and the extremes intense, with cold, damp and grey winters in southern Ontario (drier and colder in Québec) and a long temperate spring from about April to June. Summers can be hot, but often uncomfortably humid, with the cities often empty of locals but full of visitors. The long autumn can be the best time to visit, with equable temperatures and few crowds.

The central provinces of **Manitoba**, **Saskatchewan** and **Alberta** experience the country's wildest climatic extremes, suffering the longest, harshest winters but also some of the finest, clearest summers, punctuated by fierce thunderstorms. Winter skiing brings a lot of people to the **Rockies**, but summer is still the busiest time, when July and August offer the best walking weather and the least chance of

▽ Café in Montréal

rain – though this often falls in heavy downpours, the mirror of winter's raging blizzards.

The southwestern parts of **British Columbia** enjoy some of Canada's best weather: the extremes are less marked and the overall temperatures generally milder than elsewhere. Much of the province, though, bears the brunt of Pacific depressions, so this is one of the country's damper regions: visiting between late spring and early autumn offers the best chance of missing the rain.

Across the **Yukon**, the **Northwest Territories** and **Nunavut** winters are bitterly cold, with temperatures rarely above freezing for months on end, though precipitation year-round is among the country's lowest. Summers, by contrast, are short but surprisingly warm. Spring – though late – can produce outstanding displays of wild flowers across the tundra.

Average temperatures and snowfall

	Average daily maximum temperatures				Annual snowfall	Duration of snow cover
	Jan	April	July	Oct		
Banff, AB	-7°C/19°F	8°C/46°F	22°C/72°F	10°C/50°F	251cm/99in	149 days
Calgary, AB	-6°C/21°F	9°C/48°F	23°C/73°F	12°C/54°F	153cm/60in	116 days
Charlottetown, PE	-3°C/27°F	7°C/45°F	23°C/73°F	12°C/54°F	275cm/108in	122 days
Edmonton, AB	-17°C/1°F	9°C/48°F	22°C/72°F	11°C/52°F	136cm/54in	133 days
Goose Bay, NL	-12°C/10°F	3°C/37°F	21°C/70°F	7°C/45°F	445cm/175in	188 days
Halifax, NS	-1°C/30°F	9°C/48°F	23°C/73°F	14°C/57°F	217cm/85in	99 days
Inuvik, NT	-25°C/-13°F	-8°C/18°F	19°C/66°F	-5°C/23°F	177cm/70in	232 days
Montréal, QC	-6°C/21°F	11°C/52°F	26°C/79°F	13°C/56°F	243cm/96in	116 days
Ottawa, ON	-6°C/21°F	11°C/52°F	26°C/79°F	13°C/56°F	206cm/81in	121 days
Regina, SK	-13°C/9°F	9°C/48°F	26°C/79°F	12°C/54°F	87cm/34in	134 days
Saint John, NB	-3°C/27°F	8°C/46°F	22°C/72°F	12°C/54°F	224cm/88in	104 days
St John's, NL	0°C/32°F	5°C/41°F	21°C/70°F	11°C/52°F	322cm/127in	109 days
Thunder Bay, ON	-9°C/16°F	8°C/46°F	24°C/75°F	11°C/52°F	213cm/84in	132 days
Vancouver, BC	5°C/41°F	13°C/56°F	22°C/72°F	14°C/57°F	51cm/20in	11 days
Whitehorse, YT	-16°C/3°F	6°C/43°F	20°C/68°F	4°C/39°F	78cm/31in	170 days
Winnipeg, MB	-14°C/7°F	9°C/48°F	26°C/79°F	12°C/54°F	126cm/50in	135 days
Yellowknife, NT	-25°C/-13°F	-1°C/30°F	21°C/70°F	1°C/34°F	135cm/53in	210 days

things not to miss

It's not possible to see everything that Canada has to offer in one trip – and we don't suggest you try. What follows is a selective and subjective taste of the country's highlights: beautiful landscapes, alluring cities, great activities and spectacular events. They're arranged in five colour-coded categories to help you find the very best things to see, do and experience. All entries have a page reference to take you straight into the guide, where you can find out more.

01 **Yoho** Page **744** • This national park holds some of the most spectacular scenery in western Canada.

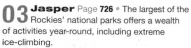

03 **Jasper** Page **726** • The largest of the Rockies' national parks offers a wealth of activities year-round, including extreme ice-climbing.

02 **Vancouver** Page **777** • Totems adorn Stanley Park in this famously relaxed, attractive western city.

04 **Prince Edward Island** Page **451** • The reddish sands of PEI's National Park band the island's northern shore.

05 **Bay of Fundy** Page **441** • These rugged Nova Scotian sea cliffs and sheltered coves experience the highest tides in the world.

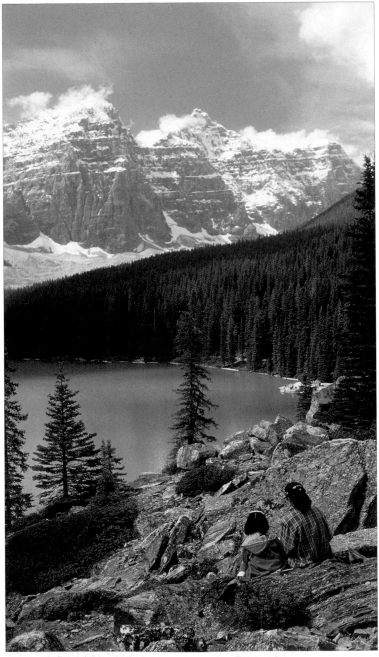

06 **Banff** Page **684** • Moraine Lake is the starting point for several excellent hikes in Banff National Park.

07 **Montréal** Page **224** • The startling Biosphere exemplifies vibrant, cultured Montréal – urban Canada at its best.

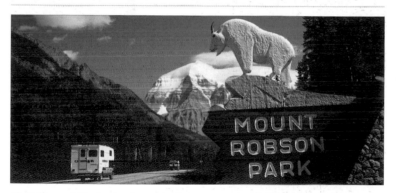

08 **Mount Robson** Page **742** • The highest peak in the Canadian Rockies, set amidst stunning scenery on the Alberta/BC border.

09 **Ottawa** Page **172** •
Canada's agreeable capital has benefited from wads of federal cash, one result being first-rate museums, such as the Museum of Civilization.

10 **Niagara Falls** Page **120** • Millions come to see the falls – two great sheets of water thundering over a 50m precipice.

11 **Churchill** Page **613** • Bleak and solitary, this northern town bills itself as "polar bear capital of the world" – with justification.

12 **Haida Gwaii** Page **983** • Explore this west-coast archipelago of 200 islets for its vibrant aboriginal culture, unique fauna and deep, mossy forests.

13 **Emily Carr** Page **798** • One of the most memorable of Canadian artists, Carr loved the forests and villages of the West Coast: this painting, *Totem Poles, Kitseukla 1912*, hangs in the Vancouver Art Gallery.

14 **Québec City** Page **277** • With its clutch of fine old buildings, handsome location and great restaurant scene, Québec City is an outstanding attraction.

xix

15 **Lunenburg** Page **394** • Of all the old fishing towns along the Nova Scotian coast, Lunenburg is the prettiest.

16 **Dawson City** Page **1017** • Dawson City was at the centre of the great 1898 Klondike gold rush.

17 **Calgary Stampede** Page **644** • This annual rodeo attracts hundreds of thousands of visitors to the city.

18 **Whale-watching** Page **1074** • On both the east and west coasts, venturing out to view whales at close quarters is a popular activity.

19 Newfoundland Page **502** • Every spring hundreds of icebergs break free from the Arctic pack-ice and drift south past Labrador and Newfoundland.

20 Toronto Page **73** • Big-city Toronto offers just about everything, from a spirited nightlife through to fine museums and winter skating.

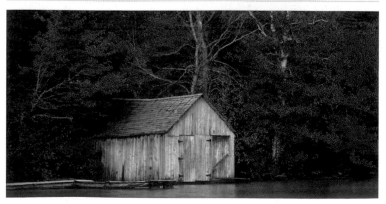

21 The Laurentians Page **266** • Some of the finest and most diverse scenery in Québec, from rolling farmland to a vast coniferous forest.

22 **The far north** Page **969** • One of the most remote spots in Canada's northern wilderness is the Kaskawulsh glacier in the Yukon's St Elias Mountains.

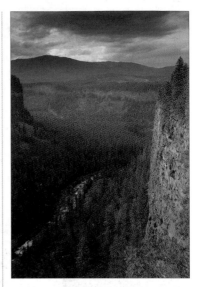

23 **Wells Gray** Page **924** • With the stunning Helmcken Falls, this is among the most appealing of British Columbia's many provincial parks.

24 **Whistler** Page **902** • This popular mountain resort has a wealth of outdoor activities, including some outstanding skiing.

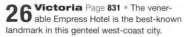

26 Victoria Page **831** • The venerable Empress Hotel is the best-known landmark in this genteel west-coast city.

25 Wildlife Page **1074** • In every province, Canada's vast landscapes are world famous for their wildlife – not least the salmon-catching grizzly bears.

27 Kayaking Page **56** • Kayaking on rivers and lakes is popular all over Canada, from British Columbia in the west to Newfoundland in the east.

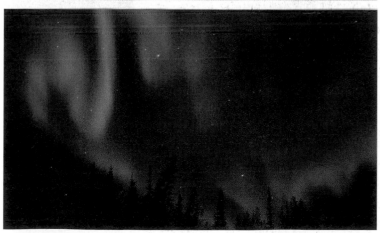

28 Aurora borealis Page **974** • The disconcertingly beautiful Northern Lights, swirling sheets of iridescent colour, can often be seen all across Canada's north.

29 Long Beach Page **876** • The majestic centrepiece of Vancouver Island's Pacific Rim National Park.

30 Skiing Page **676** • The many resorts of the Canadian Rockies offer some of the best powder skiing in North America.

31 St John's Page **475** • The dramatic approach to St John's old sea port is through a slender channel called The Narrows.

32 Algonquin Provincial Park Page **161** • The wild tracts of this enormous park, the largest in Ontario, are best explored by canoe; just watch out for the local moose!

Contents

Using this Rough Guide

We've tried to make this Rough Guide a good read and easy to use. The book is divided into six main sections, and you should be able to find whatever you want in one of them.

Colour section

The front colour section offers a quick tour of Canada. The **introduction** aims to give you a feel for the country, with suggestions on where to go. We also tell you what the weather is like and include a basic fact file. Next, our authors round up their favourite aspects of Canada in the **things not to miss** section – whether it's great cities, amazing natural sights or special events.

Basics

The Basics sections covers all the **pre-departure** nitty-gritty to help you plan your trip. This is where to find out which airlines fly to your destination, what paperwork you'll need, what to do about money and insurance, about Internet access, food, public transport, car rental – in fact, just about every piece of **general practical information** you might need.

Guide

This is the heart of the Rough Guide, divided into user-friendly chapters, each of which covers a specific area. Every chapter starts with a list of **highlights** and an **introduction** that helps you to decide where to go, depending on your time and budget. Likewise, introductions to the various towns and smaller regions within each chapter should help you plan your itinerary. We start most town accounts with information on arrival and accommodation, followed by a tour of the sights, and finally reviews of places to eat and drink, and details of nightlife. Longer accounts also have a directory of practical listings. Each chapter concludes with **public transport details** for that region.

Contexts

Read Contexts to get a deeper understanding of what makes Canada tick. We include a brief **history** of the country, articles about **aboriginal peoples** and the Canadian **natural environment**, and a detailed further reading section that reviews dozens of **books**.

Language

The **language** section gives useful guidance for speaking French in Canada's francophone areas, and pulls together all the vocabulary you might need on a trip, including a comprehensive **menu reader**.

Index + small print

Apart from a **full index**, which includes entries for maps as well as places, this section covers publishing information, credits and acknowledgements, and also has our contact details in case you want to send in updates or corrections to the book – or suggestions as to how we might improve it.

Chapter list and map

Contents

Contexts

1053–1090

Language

1091–1100

Small print and index

1113–1136

Basics

Basics

Getting there

US travellers are spoilt for choice when it comes to deciding how to get to Canada. There are flights from many US airports to the three big Canadian cities, Toronto, Vancouver and Montréal, as well as to a string of smaller Canadian towns and cities, whilst many US citizens live within driving distance of the border. It's also easy to reach Canada from the US by bus, train and – on some routes on the west and east coasts – by ferry. Other travellers, including those from the UK, Australia and New Zealand, have little choice but to fly.

Airfares from the UK, Australia and New Zealand to Canada depend on the **season**, with the highest prices applying from around mid-June to early September, the peak tourist season. You'll get the best prices during the low season, mid-November through to April (excluding Christmas and New Year, when seats are at a premium and prices are hiked up). Note also that flying on the weekend is generally more expensive. If you're flying from the US, the same general strictures apply, though the market is more unpredictable, with airlines constantly moving their prices up and down.

Airfare costs can often be cut by going through a **specialist flight agent** rather than an airline. These agents come in two main flavours: there are **consolidators**, who buy up blocks of tickets from the airlines and sell them at a discount, and **discount agents**, who in addition to dealing with discounted flights may also offer special student and youth fares, plus a range of other travel-related services such as travel insurance, car rentals and the like. Some agents specialize in **charter flights**, which may be cheaper than anything available on a scheduled flight – though be aware that departure dates are fixed and withdrawal penalties high.

Package deals from **tour operators** are rarely going to save you money in getting to Canada. That said, several of the best provide an excellent range of options, from city breaks to wilderness adventures, at competitive prices.

Booking flights online

Many airlines and discount travel websites offer you the opportunity to **book tickets online**, cutting out the costs of agents and middlemen. Good deals can also often be found through **discount or auction sites**, as well as through the airlines' own websites.

Online booking agents and general travel sites

Ⓦ **www.aircanadascanada.com** Canadian holiday packages for US travellers.
Ⓦ **www.airgorilla.com** Easy-to-use site posts the most economical, direct flights from major US cities to Canadian destinations.
Ⓦ **www.cheapflights.co.uk** (in UK & Ireland),
Ⓦ **www.cheapflights.com** (in US),
Ⓦ **www.cheapflights.ca** (in Canada),
Ⓦ **www.cheapflights.com.au** (in Australia), Flight deals, travel agents, plus links to other travel sites.
Ⓦ **www.cheaptickets.com** Discount flight specialists (US only). Also at ☎ 1-888/922-8849.
Ⓦ **www.ebookers.com** Efficient, easy to use flight finder, with competitive fares.
Ⓦ **www.etn.nl/discount.htm** A hub of consolidator and discount agent links, maintained by the nonprofit European Travel Network.
Ⓦ **www.expedia.co.uk** (in UK),
Ⓦ **www.expedia.com** (in US),
Ⓦ **www.expedia.ca** (in Canada). Discount airfares, all-airline search engine and daily deals.
Ⓦ **www.flyaow.com** "Airlines of the Web" – online air travel info and reservations.
Ⓦ **www.gaytravel.com** US gay travel agent, offering accommodation, cruises, tours and more. Also at ☎ 1-800/GAY-TRAVEL.
Ⓦ **www.geocities.com/thavery2000** An extensive list of airline websites and US toll-free numbers.
Ⓦ **www.kelkoo.co.uk** Useful UK-only price-comparison site, checking several sources of

low-cost flights (and other goods and services) according to specific criteria.

ⓦ **www.lastminute.com** (in UK),
ⓦ **www.lastminute.com.au** (in Australia),
ⓦ **www.lastminute.co.nz** (in New Zealand). Good last-minute holiday package and flight-only deals.
ⓦ **www.opodo.co.uk** Popular and reliable source of low UK airfares. Owned by, and run in conjunction with, nine major European airlines.
ⓦ **www.priceline.co.uk** (in UK),
ⓦ **www.priceline.com** (in US). Name-your-own-price website that has deals at around forty percent off standard fares.
ⓦ **www.skyauction.com** Bookings from the US only. Auctions tickets and travel packages to destinations worldwide.
ⓦ **www.travelocity.co.uk** (in UK),
ⓦ **www.travelocity.com** (in US),
ⓦ **www.travelocity.ca** (in Canada),
ⓦ **www.zuji.com.au** (in Australia). Destination guides, hot fares and great deals for car rental, accommodation and lodging.
ⓦ **www.travelshop.com.au** Australian site offering discounted flights, packages, insurance, and online bookings. Also on ☎1800/108 108.
ⓦ **travel.yahoo.com** Incorporates some Rough Guides material in its coverage of destination countries and cities across the world, with information about places to eat and sleep.

From Britain

Most nonstop scheduled flights **from Britain** to Canada depart from London Heathrow, with some nonstop scheduled departures from airports around Britain supplemented by holiday charter flights. The main gateways are Montréal, Toronto and Vancouver, but there are also nonstop scheduled flights from Britain to Calgary, Edmonton, Ottawa, Halifax and St John's. Connecting flights from these airports delve into every corner of the country.

As an illustration of potential **fares**, a standard return from London to Toronto with Air Canada can cost anywhere between £400 and £1200 (low/high season), and not much more to Vancouver. With restrictions – commonly having to book in advance for a minimum stay of seven nights – this can, however, easily be trimmed to a very affordable £250–300. In 2004, Canadian carrier Zoom began nonstop flights from London Gatwick and Glasgow to six Canadian cities for bargain rates: fares to eastern destinations are just £250–270, to western cities about £350. Most airlines also offer good-value **open-jaw** (or "multi-city") deals that enable you to fly into one Canadian city and back from another – a useful idea if you want to make your own way across the country.

Package holidays (whether fly-drive, flight-accommodation, flight-guided tour or a combination of all three) can work out cheaper than arranging the same trip yourself, though they do have drawbacks, chiefly the loss of flexibility and the fact that you'll probably have to stay in nondescript – and sometimes relatively expensive – chain hotels. Short-stay **city breaks** start from around £400 per person for a transatlantic return flight and accommodation in a downtown Montréal or Toronto hotel for four nights; you'll pay more like £600 for seven nights. **Fly-drive** deals, which give cut-price car rental when buying a transatlantic ticket from an airline or tour operator, are nearly always cheaper than renting a car on the spot and give great value if you intend to do a lot of travelling: a return flight to Vancouver and a fortnight's car rental might cost as little as £700 per person. A typical **flight-guided tour** might comprise a fourteen-day trans-Canadian holiday taking in Toronto, Niagara Falls, Ottawa, Montréal, Calgary, the Rockies and Vancouver, including an outbound flight to Toronto, a domestic flight, coach trips, middle-range hotel accommodation and some sightseeing tours, at a cost of around £2300.

To see a chunk of Canada's great outdoors without being hassled by too many practical considerations, you could take a specialist **touring** or **adventure package**, which usually includes transport in Canada, accommodation, food and a guide – but not flights. Some of the more adventurous carry small groups around on minibuses and use a combination of budget hotels and camping, providing all equipment. These deals are not cheap, however: a typical package of thirteen days' hiking and camping in the Rockies will cost from £650 plus flights. Operators offering a range of Canadian adventure holidays are listed below; we've listed local companies specializing in the more extreme locations – for example, Labrador – in the appropriate section of the Guide.

Airlines in Britain

Air Canada ☎ 0871/220 1111,
🌐 www.aircanada.com. London Heathrow nonstop to Calgary, Halifax, Montréal, Ottawa, St John's, Toronto and Vancouver. Manchester and Glasgow to Toronto (April–Oct only). Many onward connections.

American Airlines ☎ 0845/778 9789,
🌐 www.aa.com. London Heathrow to: Montréal via New York or Chicago; Ottawa via Chicago; Toronto via Boston or Chicago. London Gatwick to: Calgary via Dallas; Vancouver via Dallas.

bmi ☎ 0870/607 0555, 🌐 www.flybmi.com. London Heathrow to Toronto; Manchester to Toronto (April–Oct only). Flies in conjunction with Air Canada.

British Airways ☎ 0870/850 9850, 🌐 www
.ba.com. London Heathrow nonstop to Montréal, Toronto and Vancouver. Connections into Heathrow from a string of UK airports, including Birmingham, Edinburgh, Glasgow, Manchester and Newcastle.

Continental ☎ 0845/607 6760,
🌐 www.continental.com. Birmingham, Glasgow, London Gatwick and Manchester to Toronto via Newark, plus to a string of east Canada destinations via New York, and to west Canadian cities via Houston.

Delta ☎ 0800/414 767, 🌐 www.delta.com. London Gatwick to Toronto via Cincinnati.

KLM/Northwest ☎ 0870/507 4074,
🌐 www.klm.com. Aberdeen, Birmingham, Edinburgh, Glasgow, Humberside, Leeds-Bradford, London City, London Heathrow, Manchester and Norwich to Montréal, Toronto and Vancouver (all via Amsterdam).

Lufthansa ☎ 0845/773 7747,
🌐 www.lufthansa.com. Flights from several UK airports to Toronto via Frankfurt.

United ☎ 0845/844 4777, 🌐 www
.unitedairlines.co.uk. London Heathrow to Toronto via Chicago or Washington DC.

Zoom ☎ 0870/240 0055, 🌐 www.flyzoom.com. Canadian carrier flying from London Gatwick nonstop to Toronto, Ottawa, Halifax, Edmonton, Calgary and Vancouver. Also Glasgow nonstop to all those except Edmonton.

Travel agents in Britain

Bridge the World ☎ 0870/444 7474,
🌐 www.bridgetheworld.com. Specializing in round-the-world tickets, with good deals aimed at the backpacker market.

Citybreaks4Less ☎ 0871/222 3423,
🌐 www.citybreaks4less.co.uk. Bargain global city-break deals. Part of Lastminute.com.

Co-op Travel Care ☎ 0870/112 0099,
🌐 www.travelcareonline.com. Flights and holidays around the world.

Destination Group ☎ 020/7400 7045,
🌐 www.destination-group.com. Good discount airfares.

ebookers ☎ 0870/010 7000,
🌐 www.ebookers.com. Low fares on an extensive selection of scheduled flights and package deals.

Flightcentre ☎ 0870/890 8099, 🌐 www
.flightcentre.co.uk. Rock-bottom fares worldwide.

Flights4Less ☎ 0871/222 3423,
🌐 www.flights4less.co.uk. Good discount airfares. Part of Lastminute.com.

Flynow ☎ 0870/444 0045, 🌐 www.flynow.com. Large range of discounted tickets.

Holidays4Less UK ☎ 0871/222 3423,
🌐 www.holidays4less.co.uk. Discounted package deals worldwide. Part of Lastminute.com.

North South Travel ☎ 01245/608 291,
🌐 www.northsouthtravel.co.uk. Friendly, competitive travel agency, offering discounted fares worldwide – profits are used to support projects in the developing world, especially the promotion of sustainable tourism.

STA Travel ☎ 0870/160 0599,
🌐 www.statravel.co.uk. Worldwide specialists in low-cost flights and tours for students and under-26s, though other customers welcome.

Top Deck ☎ 020/7244 8000,
🌐 www.topdecktravel.co.uk. Long-established agent dealing in discount flights.

Trailfinders ☎ 020/7628 7628,
🌐 www.trailfinders.co.uk. One of the best-informed and most efficient agents for independent travellers; produces a very useful quarterly magazine worth scrutinizing for round-the-world routes.

Travel Cuts ☎ 020/7255 2082 or 7255 1944,
🌐 www.travelcuts.co.uk. Canadian company specializing in budget, student and youth travel and round-the-world tickets.

Tour operators in Britain

Abercrombie & Kent ☎ 0845/070 0610,
🌐 www.abercrombiekent.co.uk. Classy operator with a strong reputation.

All Canada Travel & Holidays 🌐 www
.all-canada.co.uk. Comprehensive Canada agent. Runs everything from escorted coach tours to adventure holidays and city breaks. Bookings through appointed travel agents.

Australian Pacific Touring ☎ 020/8879 7444,
🌐 www.aptours.com. Long-established, award-winning operator running package tours and independent travel to Canada.

Bales Worldwide ☎0870/241 3208, ⊛www.balesworldwide.com. Family-owned company offering high-quality escorted tours to Canada, as well as tailor-made itineraries.

British Airways Holidays ☎0870/240 0747, ⊛www.baholidays.co.uk. An exhaustive range of package and tailor-made holidays around the world.

Canada's Best ☎01502/565648, ⊛www .best-in-travel.com. Canada specialist offering a wide range of holiday options. Deals in cottages, resorts and inns, as well as hotels. Package and tailor-made holidays.

Contiki ☎020/8290 6777, ⊛www.contiki.co.uk. Tours and trips for 18–35-year-old party animals.

Exodus ☎020/8675 5550, ⊛www.exodus.co.uk. Adventure tour operators taking small groups on specialist programmes that take in walking, biking, overlanding, adventure and cultural trips.

Experience Canada ☎01323/416699, ⊛www.experienceholidays.co.uk. Extensive range of tours and tailor-made holidays in every region of the country.

Explore Worldwide ☎01252/760 000, ⊛www.explore.co.uk. Big range of small-group tours, treks and expeditions, staying mostly in small local hotels.

Frontier Ski ☎020/8776 8709, ⊛www .frontier-ski.co.uk. Leading Canadian ski holiday specialist, with trips to the Rockies and Québec.

Go Fishing Worldwide ☎020/8742 8299, ⊛www.go-fishingworldwide.com. Fishing trips to Labrador, New Brunswick, Québec, the Yukon, Alberta, BC, Ontario and NWT.

Great Rail Journeys ☎01904/521900, ⊛www .greatrail.com. From Toronto to the Rockies by train.

Headwater ☎01606/720 099, ⊛www.headwater.com. Walking, cycling and canoeing holidays in off-the-beaten-track locations.

Kuoni Travel ☎01306/747 002, ⊛www.kuoni.co.uk. Award-winning major tour operator running flexible package holidays to long-haul destinations worldwide. Especially good deals for families.

Momentum Travel ☎020/7371 9111, ⊛www.momentum.uk.com. Ski specialist, with the Rockies as one of its destinations.

MyTravel ☎0870/238 7788, ⊛www.uk.mytravel.com. Large tour company offering trips worldwide.

Ramblers Holidays ☎01707/331133, ⊛www.ramblersholidays.co.uk. Walking and hiking specialist offering West Coast and Rockies guided holidays.

Ski Independence ☎0870/555 0555, ⊛www.ski-independence.co.uk. Wide range of ski packages, mostly to the Rockies.

Ski Safari ☎01273/223 680, ⊛www.skisafari.com. Sixteen Canadian resorts in the Rockies and Québec.

Thomas Cook ☎0870/750 0512, ⊛www.thomascook.co.uk. Long-established one-stop travel agency for package holidays, city breaks or flights, with bureau de change issuing Thomas Cook branded travellers' cheques, plus travel insurance and car rental.

Trek America ☎01295/256 777, ⊛www.trekamerica.com. Walking and soft adventure tours all over Canada, year-round. Three concepts: "Trek America" (1–9-week camping adventure trips for 18–38-year-olds), "Footloose" (camping trips for all ages, softer walking and hiking trips, plus tours using hotel lodging), "WinterSun" (off-season trips).

Viator ⊛www.viator.com. Bookings for local tours and sightseeing trips in destinations around the world.

Wildlife Encounters ☎01737/218 802, ⊛www.wildlife-encounters.co.uk. Top-rated wildlife-watching tours around the world, including whale-watching and polar-bear tracking in Canada.

Wildlife Worldwide ☎020/8667 9158, ⊛www.wildlifeworldwide.com. Tailor-made trips for wildlife and wilderness enthusiasts, ranging from classic whale-watching trips to specialist Canadian itineraries covering bears, the Bay of Fundy, seals, sea-kayaking, Wilderness Québec and Wild Newfoundland.

From Ireland

From **Ireland**, the only daily nonstop flights are in the summer season (mid-April to mid-Oct) with Air Canada from Dublin and Shannon to Toronto. Otherwise both Air Canada and British Airways will quote you through fares from Ireland to most Canadian destinations on one-stop flights. Aer Lingus does not fly to Canada. **Fares** on nonstop Dublin–Toronto flights (7hr) are around €725. From Dublin or Belfast to Toronto via London with Air Canada costs slightly more, from €750/£450. BA has a standard fare of €680 Dublin–Toronto in the summer (€480 in low season). Flying to Montréal costs much the same, while you can expect to add around €100 if you're flying to Vancouver. **Students and under-26s** should consult Usit, which can usually offer the best deals: their return fares from Dublin or Belfast to Toronto are priced from €480/£330, to Vancouver €720/£500.

It's often possible to save money by **flying independently** to London on one of several no-frills airlines and then taking a separate flight from Heathrow to Canada with BA or Air Canada. From Dublin, Ryanair flies seven times daily to London Stansted, for €35–50 return if you book weeks in advance; don't forget to factor in time and money to get across London to Heathrow for your onward flight. From Belfast, easyJet flies to London Luton, Gatwick and Stansted many times a day, from as little as £30–40, but the most convenient option is to fly straight into Heathrow with bmi from £64 or BA from £89.

Airlines in Ireland

Air Canada UK ☎0871/220 1111, Republic of Ireland ☎01/679 3958, ⓦwww.aircanada.com.
bmi UK ☎0870/607 0555, Republic of Ireland ☎01/407 3036, ⓦwww.flybmi.com.
British Airways UK ☎0870/850 9850, Republic of Ireland ☎1800/626 747, ⓦwww.ba.com.
easyJet UK ☎0871/750 0100, ⓦwww.easyjet.com.
Ryanair UK ☎0871/246 0000, Republic of Ireland ☎0818/30 30 30, ⓦwww.ryanair.com.

Travel agents in Ireland

American Holidays Belfast ☎028/9023 8762, Dublin ☎01/673 3840, ⓦwww.american-holidays .com. Full range of package deals from Ireland to all parts of the US and Canada.
Apex Travel Republic of Ireland ☎01/241 8000, ⓦwww.apextravel.ie. Specialists in flights to North America.
Aran Travel International Republic of Ireland ☎091/562 595, ⓦhomepages.iol.ie/~arantvl/aranmain.htm. Good-value flights worldwide.
CIE Tours International Republic of Ireland ☎01/703 1888, ⓦwww.cietours.ie. Wide range of escorted bus tours in Canada.
ebookers UK ☎0870/010 7000, ⓦwww.ebookers.com, Republic of Ireland ☎01/241 5689, ⓦwww.ebookers.ie. Low fares on an extensive selection of scheduled flights and package deals.
Go Holidays Republic of Ireland ☎01/874 4126, ⓦwww.goholidays.ie. City breaks and package tours.
Joe Walsh Tours Republic of Ireland ☎01/676 0991, ⓦwww.joewalshtours.ie. Long-established general budget fares and holidays agent.

Lee Travel Republic of Ireland ☎021/427 7111, ⓦwww.leetravel.ie. Flights and holidays worldwide.
Maxwells Travel Republic of Ireland ☎01/677 9749. Agent for a wide array of deals from adventure operators worldwide.
McCarthys Travel Republic of Ireland ☎021/427 0127, ⓦwww.mccarthystravel.ie. General flight agent.
Neenan Travel Republic of Ireland ☎01/607 9900, ⓦwww.neenantrav.ie. Specialists in city breaks.
Premier Travel UK ☎028/7126 3333, ⓦwww.premiertravel.uk.com. Discount flight specialists in Derry.
Rosetta Travel UK ☎028/9064 4996, ⓦwww.rosettatravel.com. Flight and holiday agent, specializing in deals direct from Belfast.
Trailfinders UK ☎020/7938 3939, ⓦwww.trailfinders.com, Republic of Ireland ☎01/677 7888, ⓦwww.trailfinders.ie. One of the best-informed and most efficient agents for independent travellers.
Twohigs Republic of Ireland ☎01/677 2666. North America specialists.
USIT Northern Ireland ☎028/9032 7111, ⓦwww.usitnow.com, Republic of Ireland ☎0818/200 020, ⓦwww.usit.ie. Specialists in student, youth and independent travel – flights, trains, study tours, TEFL, visas and more.
World Travel Centre Republic of Ireland ☎01/416 7007, ⓦwww.worldtravel.ie. Excellent fares worldwide.

From the US

Crossing the longest undefended border in the world – between **the US** and Canada – is straightforward. Many visitors from the northern US just **drive**, since the major cities (Montréal and Toronto in the east, Winnipeg and Calgary in the middle and Vancouver in the west) are all within an hour's drive north of the border. However, if you're coming from Florida or southern California, say, or want to go from New York to British Columbia, **flying** is obviously a lot quicker. Travelling by **train** is another alternative, at least if you're not in a hurry and want to see something of the landscapes along the way, and there are a few **bus** and **ferry** options too.

By car from the US

The **US highway** system leads into Canada at thirteen points along the border. The busiest corridors are from Blaine, WA to

White Rock, BC; from Detroit, MI to Windsor, ON; from Buffalo, NY to Fort Erie, ON; and at Niagara Falls. You may encounter traffic jams at the border and long lines, particularly at the weekends, in the summer months and on US or Canadian holidays. For an idea of **journey times**, from New York to Montréal (383 miles) reckon on eight hours' driving; from San Francisco to Vancouver (954 miles), around nineteen hours. For route advice in the US, check with the AAA (ⓦwww.aaa.com). It has offices in most major cities, but you probably won't find them much help unless you're a member. For more detailed route enquiries within Canada, try the Canadian Automobile Association (ⓦwww.caa.ca).

At customs you will probably be asked to declare your citizenship, place of residence and proposed length of stay. Vehicle insurance, with minimum liability coverage of US$200,000, is compulsory; it is also advisable to obtain a yellow Non-Resident Inter-Province Motor Vehicle Liability Card from your insurance company before you go. Make sure you have your driver's licence, documents establishing proof of insurance and proof of vehicle ownership with you at all times while driving in Canada. If you are renting a car in the US you should mention that you intend to travel to Canada, though this is rarely a problem. Fill the car with gas before going, as US prices are still less than those over the border.

By bus from the US

The scope of North America's **Greyhound bus** service (ⓣ1-800/229-9424, ⓦwww.greyhound.com) is as vast as the continent itself. The network extends into Canada from three points on the East Coast and one each from the West and Midwest; prices below are approximate. Note also that some of the bus passes (see p.32) are valid in both the US and Canada.

Travelling overland from San Diego to Montréal, say, is no problem: it's an epic, three-day-plus journey, but if you're on a tight budget, the US$238 fare (purchased a week in advance) may be compelling – though be sure to factor in three days worth

of food and drink. Plus, of course, you get to see a whole lot of country in between. Buses of both Greyhound and Adirondack Trailways (ⓣ1-800/858-8555, ⓦwww.trailways.com) compete on the popular run **from New York** to Montréal, offering half a dozen trips per day. Fares for the eight-hour journey are US$109 return. Most trips **from Boston** to Montréal are made by Greyhound subsidiary Vermont Transit Lines (ⓣ1-800/552-8737, ⓦwww.vermonttransit.com); tickets cost US$111 ($98 if bought a week in advance) and the journey takes around seven hours. Other cross-border connections include **from Buffalo** to Toronto (around 8 daily; 2hr 30min–3hr; US$19 one-way, $37 return); **from Burlington**, VT, to Montréal (5 daily; 2hr 30min–3hr; US$21 one-way, $39 return); **from Seattle** to Vancouver (6 daily; 3hr 30min–4hr 30min; US$23 one-way, $41 return); and **from Fargo**, ND, to Winnipeg (1 daily; 6hr 10min; US$43 one-way, $83 return). Be sure to arrive at the terminal one hour before departure.

Green Tortoise (ⓣ1-800/227-4766, ⓦwww.greentortoise.com) – the alternative to long-distance bus hell, with its foam cushions, bunks, fridges and rock music – no longer runs a regular service into Canada, but it does still offer a month-long trip from San Francisco north to Alaska, which includes a ferry ride along the Inside Passage and side-trips into the Canadian Rockies (US$1500, plus $250 for food).

By air from the US

From the US to Canada, there are plenty of nonstop **flights** on Air Canada and most US airlines. Montréal, Toronto and Vancouver are the most popular destinations, but there are also services to Halifax, Calgary, Winnipeg and many other cities. Low-cost Canadian carrier **Jetsgo** offers connections from Newark, Florida and Las Vegas. Connecting flights within Canada serve some 75 additional destinations.

Flying to Canada from major cities in the US is straightforward: flights run on a business schedule and tend to be more expensive during the weekdays, with special fares – usually available at the last minute – to capture the "weekend getaway" crowd. There are dozens of fare options, to match the various types of aircraft (from little commuter planes to charters) – and there are frequent specials. Sometimes businesses buy up blocks of tickets they don't use, so occasionally you can fly standby. Sample budget **return** fares quoted by the major airlines are: New York to Toronto US$195; New York to Montréal US$225; New York to Halifax US$275; Chicago to Winnipeg US$310; LA to Calgary US$260; LA to Vancouver US$220. If you plan only a long weekend trip, you can often find special fares: NY–Toronto for US$120 or Chicago–Winnipeg for US$190.

Even more than with other international flights, you really need to **shop around** to get the very best deals on the busy US–Canada routes. In addition to fares with the usual Apex restrictions (21-day advance booking, Sat night stay, midweek travel, etc), you might find special offers which require you to book before a particular date, limit your stay, fly at a certain time of day or, perversely, allow you more flexibility than on a higher fare. Your best bet is to first try a **discount agent**, who may be able to dig up scheduled return fares for as little as New York–Toronto US$90, New York–Montréal US$155 or LA–Vancouver US$199.

Domestic flights wholly within the US or Canada generally cost less than flights between the two countries, so you may make savings by crossing the border before or after your flight: flying from New York to Buffalo and taking the bus the short distance to Toronto, for instance, rather than flying NY–Toronto direct. This is especially true of long-haul flights: a transcontinental flight from New York to Vancouver can be considerably more expensive than a similar flight to Seattle (which lies only a hundred miles south of Vancouver). Sample budget return fares within Canada are Toronto to Montréal C$235; Montréal to Vancouver C$379; Vancouver to Winnipeg C$350; Winnipeg to Toronto C$279. If your main destination is somewhere upcountry you can often save money by buying a separate, domestic flight from the nearest major Canadian destination, rather than treating that leg of the journey as part of an international itinerary.

As for **flight times**, flying north/south is reasonably quick: from New York to Montréal takes around 1hr 15min; New York to Toronto 1hr 30min; New York to Halifax 1hr 50min; Chicago to Winnipeg 2hr 10min; LA to Vancouver 2hr 45min; LA to Calgary 3hr. Flying east/west on domestic routes is fairly painless, too: New York–LA or Montréal–Vancouver takes around 5hr. However, flying east/west between countries usually involves a stopover or onward connection, so New York–Vancouver can take 7–8hr.

Airlines in North America

Air Canada ☎1-888/247-2262, Ⓦwww.aircanada.com..
American Airlines ☎1-800/624-6262, Ⓦwww.aa.com.
ATA ☎1-800/435-9282, Ⓦwww.ata.com.
British Airways ☎1-800/AIRWAYS, Ⓦwww.ba.com.
Continental ☎1-800/231-0856, Ⓦwww.continental.com.
Delta ☎1-800/241-4141, Ⓦwww.delta.com.
HMY Airways ☎1-866/868-6789, Ⓦwww.hmyairways.com.
JetBlue ☎1-800/JET-BLUE, Ⓦwww.jetblue.com.
Jetsgo ☎1-866/440-0441, Ⓦwww.jetsgo.net.
Northwest ☎1-800/447-4747, Ⓦwww.nwa.com.
United ☎1-800/538-2929, Ⓦwww.united.com.
US Airways ☎1-800/622-1015, Ⓦwww.usair.com.
USA 3000 ☎1-877/USA-3000, Ⓦwww.usa3000airlines.com.
WestJet ☎1-888/WEST-JET, Ⓦwww.westjet.com.
Zip ☎1-866/4321-ZIP, Ⓦwww.4321zip.com.

Travel agents in North America

Air Brokers International ☎1-800/883-3273, Ⓦwww.airbrokers.com. Consolidator.
Airtech ☎212/219-7000, Ⓦwww.airtech.com. Standby seat broker; also deals in consolidator fares.
Educational Travel Center ☎1-800/747-5551 or 608/256-5551, Ⓦwww.edtrav.com. Low-cost fares worldwide, student/youth discount offers, car rental and tours.
Flightcentre US ☎1-866/WORLD-51, Ⓦwww.flightcentre.us, Canada ☎1-888/WORLD-55, Ⓦwww.flightcentre.ca. Rock-bottom fares.
New Frontiers ☎1-800/677-0720, Ⓦwww.newfrontiers.com. Discount firm.
STA Travel US ☎1-800/329-9537, Canada ☎1-888/427-5639, Ⓦwww.statravel.com. Specialists

in independent travel; also student IDs, travel insurance, car rental, rail passes, and more.

Student Flights ☎1-800/255-8000 or 480/951-1177, ⓦ www.isecard.com/studentflights. Student/youth fares, plus student IDs.

TFI Tours ☎1-800/745-8000 or 212/736-1140, ⓦ www.lowestairprice.com. Consolidator.

Travel Avenue ☎1-800/333-3335, ⓦ www.travelavenue.com. Full-service travel agent that offers discounts in the form of rebates.

Travel Cuts US ☎1-800/592-CUTS, Canada ☎1-888/246-9762, ⓦ www.travelcuts.com. Popular, long-established student-travel organization.

Travelers Advantage ☎1-877/259-2691, ⓦ www.travelersadvantage.com. Discount travel club, with cashback deals and discounted car rental. Membership required ($1 for 3 months' trial).

Travelosophy ☎1-800/332-2687, ⓦ www.itravelosophy.com. Good range of discounted and student fares.

By train from the US

For specific journeys, the **train** is usually more expensive than the bus (and often the plane), though special deals, especially in off-peak periods, can bring the round-trip cost down considerably. There are discounts available on trains for "Student Advantage" pass-holders, senior citizens and travellers with disabilities. Children from 2 to 15 who are accompanied by an adult go for half-fare; children under 2 travel free.

Three routes on **Amtrak** (☎1-800/USA-RAIL, ⓦ www.amtrak.com) from the north-eastern US have direct connections with **VIA Rail**, Canada's national rail company: the "Maple Leaf" from New York to Toronto via Buffalo and Niagara Falls (1 daily; 12hr; US$65/99 one-way in low/high season); the "Adirondack" from New York to Montréal via Albany and Plattsburgh (1 daily; 9hr 30min; US$53/66 one-way) and the "International" from Chicago to Toronto (1 daily; 14hr; US$98 one-way). Sleeping cars have been discontinued on these trains, but they may be reintroduced. In the northwest, the "Mount Baker International" runs from Seattle to Vancouver (1 daily; 4hr; US$21/33 one-way). All these fares are for travel in economy (the cheapest) class, where pillows are provided for overnight journeys.

You should always **reserve** as far as possible in advance, as it is compulsory to have a seat and some of the eastern-seaboard trains in particular get booked up solid. Some rail passes for the US network are also valid as far as a Canadian gateway like Vancouver or Montréal. For more on these, and train travel within Canada, see p.34.

By ferry from the US

There are five US–Canada **ferry** services: three on the West Coast and two on the East. Quite apart from the enjoyment of the ride, the boats can save you hours of driving on some cross-country routes. You should always **book ahead**.

On the **West Coast**, the *Victoria Clipper* catamaran for foot passengers runs between Seattle and Victoria on Vancouver Island, three times daily from mid-May to mid-September and once daily in spring and fall (2hr 30min; US$60 one-way; ☎1-800/888-2535 or 206/448-5000, ⓦ www.victoriaclipper.com). Further north, Alaska Marine Highway ferries link several Alaskan towns with Prince Rupert. The Juneau service, for instance, operates on alternate days from May to late September (24hr; US$132 one-way, cars US$293; in US ☎1-800/526-6731, in Yukon and BC ☎1-800/478-2268, ⓦ www.akferry.com). The most useful West Coast ferry is the Washington State Ferries service from Anacortes to Sidney, on Vancouver Island. The ferry travels twice daily in summer, once in winter via Washington's beautiful San Juan archipelago (average-sized vehicle with driver $28.75 each way, extra adult passengers $10 each; 3hr; ☎206/464-6400 or 1-800/84-FERRY in WA only, ⓦ www.wsdot.wa.gov). Disabled travellers and senior citizens can get discounts of around fifty percent; children from 5 to 11 can get discounts of around seventy percent; under-5s travel free. There are no student discounts.

On the **East Coast**, a car ferry, the *Scotia Prince* (☎1-800/482-0955 in Maine, ☎1-800/341-7540 elsewhere, ⓦ www.princeoffundy.com), runs almost nightly (early May to mid-Oct) from Portland, ME to Yarmouth, NS for US$63/83 per person one-way in low/high season (cars US$83/101; cabins US$21–64/33–98). Journey time is around eleven hours. Five- to

14-year-olds pay half one-way fare and under-5s travel free. Also worth looking into are return discount packages for two adults and car in spring, summer and fall. In addition, the *Cat* ferry (☎1-888/249-7245, ☯www.catferry.com) runs from Bar Harbor, ME to Yarmouth, NS daily from May to October (takes 4hr). Prices vary seasonally: US$48/57 one-way, cars US$72/82.

Package deals from the US

US **tour operators** offer a variety of options, from all-inclusive packages combining plane tickets, bus or train travel, hotel accommodation, meals, transfers and sightseeing tours to land-only deals based around a single specialized activity (bird-watching, for instance). These kind of holidays may not sound too appealing to an independent traveller, but one reason why a package could be your best bet is if you're travelling into the wilderness for backcountry adventure. Local guides and training (for example, in whitewater canoeing) are commonly available as well as the normal flights and lodgings.

Abercrombie & Kent ☎1-800/323-7308 or 630/954-2944, ☯www.abercrombiekent.com. Classy operator with a strong reputation.

Adventure Center ☎1-800/228-8747 or 510/654-1879, ☯www.adventurecenter.com. Hiking and "soft adventure" specialists worldwide. They offer a 10-day trip to Québec City and its hinterland, including four days canoeing, from US$980.Their 8-day "Newfoundland, Naturally" package runs from $1575 (land only). The 15-day "Rocky Mountains and the Pacific" starts at $990 (land only).

Adventures Abroad ☎1-800/665-3998, ☯www.adventures-abroad.com. Adventure specialists with a 9-day tour of Montréal, Québec City and Charlevoix (whose only real adrenaline rush is a whale-watching trip). From US$1310.

American Airlines Vacations ☎1-800/321-2121, ☯www.aavacations.com. City breaks and more extensive packages. Five nights in Québec City, with 3-star hotel accommodation, car rental and return flight out of New York would cost from around $800.

Australian Pacific Touring ☎1-800/290-8687, ☯www.aptours.com. Long-established, award-winning operator running package tours and independent travel.

Backroads ☎1-800/GO-ACTIVE or 510/527-1555, ☯www.backroads.com. Cycling, hiking and

multi-sport tours designed for the young at heart, with the emphasis on going at your own pace. Accommodation ranges from campsites to luxury hotels. Also family-friendly options and singles trips. Camping/cycling holidays from $998 (6 days; land only) and hotel/cycling holidays from $1698 (6 days; land only).

Classic Journeys ☎1-800/200-3887 or 858/454-5004, ☯www.classicjourneys.com. Walking trips with an emphasis on culture. Example itinerary includes Québec City, small towns and countryside in Charlevoix and the inevitable whale-watching cruise in the Saguenay. Six days for US$2095.

Contiki ☎1-888/CONTIKI, ☯www.contiki.com. 18- to 35-year-olds-only tour operator.

Cosmos ☎1-800/276-1241, ☯www.cosmosvacations.com. Planned vacation packages with an independent focus.

Delta Vacations ☎1-800/654-6559, ☯www.deltavacations.com. City breaks (such as a foodie tour of Montréal) and some last-minute deals on air and hotel packages.

Different Strokes Tours ☎1-800/668 3301. Customized tours for gay/lesbian travellers.

Ecosummer Expeditions ☎1-800/465-8884 or 250/674-0102, ☯www.ecosummer.com. Wilderness expeditions and ecotourism.

Far and Wide ☎1-866/FAR-WIDE, ☯www.farandwide.com. Very broad array of deals, from customized trips to group tours. Offerings include a 9-day bus tour of Ontario and Québec's major cities for US$1700 plus flights and a 3-day trip to Montréal that concludes with a 10-day cruise down the St Lawrence and along the Atlantic coast to Boston (from US$2650 including flights).

Globus ☎1-866/755-8581, ☯www.globusjourneys.com. Planned vacations, particularly bus tours: 9-days for US$1200–1450.

Maupintour ☎1-800/255-4266, ☯www.maupintour.com. Luxury independent and escorted tours: 7-day "Rocky Mountain Escape" from $1850; 12-day "Trans Canada by Train" from $3685.

Moose Travel Network ☎905/853-4762 or 1-888/816-6673, ☯www.moosenetwork.com. Outfit that runs hop-on and hop-off backpacker mini-coach tours in British Columbia, Alberta, Ontario and Quebec. See also p.32.

Real Traveller ☎1-866/REAL-TVL, ☯www.realtraveller.com. Canadian agent for a multitude of adventure companies all over the world, taking small groups on specialist programmes that include walking, biking, overlanding, adventure and cultural trips.

REI Adventures ☎1-800/622-2236, ☯www.rei.com. Climbing, cycling, hiking, cruising, paddling, kayaking and multisport tours in BC, the Rockies and Nova Scotia.

Rod and Reel Adventures ☎1-800/356-6982, ⓦwww.rodreeladventures.com. Fishing holidays.

Saga Holidays ☎1-877/265-6862, ⓦwww.sagaholidays.com. Specialists in group travel for seniors, with a variety of Canada tours.

Suntrek Tours ☎1-800/SUNTREK, ⓦwww.suntrek.com. Soft adventure specialists who offer camping tours that allow some time in cities: 3 weeks costs around US$1300.

Trek America ☎1-800/221-0596, ⓦwww.trekamerica.com. Walking and soft adventure tours all over the US, Canada and Mexico, year-round. Three concepts: "Trek America" (1–9 week camping adventure trips for 18–38-year-olds), "Footloose" (camping trips for all ages, softer walking and hiking trips, plus tours using hotel lodging), and "WinterSun" (off-season trips).

Trek Holidays Canada ☎1-800/661-7265, ⓦwww.trekholidays.com. Agent for a vast array of deals from adventure companies. An example 10-day trip to Québec City includes four days back-country canoeing starts at $1500.

United Vacations Ski ☎1-800/328-6877, ⓦwww.unitedvacations.com. Ski trips to Whistler or Banff from $888 (return flights from New York, 3 nights 2-star accommodation, transfers).

VIA Rail ⓦwww.viarail.ca. Although they don't organize tours, VIA's website does provide a lengthy list of US and Canadian operators who offer rail and sightseeing trips.

Viator ⓦwww.viator.com. Bookings for local tours and sightseeing trips in destinations around Canada.

Worldwide Quest International ☎1-800/387-1483 or 416/633-5666, ⓦwww.worldwidequest.com. A wide range of exotic all-inclusive nature tours: "Hiking in the Canadian Rockies" ($900, 7 days); "Kayaking in Québec" ($800, 8 days).

From Australia and New Zealand

There are no direct flights **from Australia or New Zealand** to Canada. However Air Canada, Qantas and Air New Zealand have daily connecting flights from all major Australasian cities to Vancouver via Los Angeles or Hawaii. These are the most convenient and economical routes and, if you're heading to other parts of Canada, all these airlines will quote you through-fares via Vancouver to your chosen destination.

From **Australia**, Air Canada flies daily to Vancouver from Sydney via Hawaii, for around A$2263/2754 in low/high season. Qantas has daily flights to Vancouver from Sydney, Melbourne and Brisbane via LA, as well as to Toronto from Sydney via LA; their fares start at A$2280 from Sydney. Through fares from Perth and Darwin start at A$3000. Expect to pay an extra A$400 to Edmonton or Calgary, or A$600 to Toronto or Montréal. United Airlines flies to several Canadian cities – Calgary, Edmonton, Montréal and Toronto – from Sydney via LA or San Francisco with similar fares, as does American Airlines. Many Asian airlines have frequent special deals which make flights via Asia very competitive – although, with overnight stopovers, the journey takes much longer. Fares start at A$1749, and as an incentive JAL offers free stopovers (up to 30 days) in either Tokyo or Osaka.

From **New Zealand**, Air NZ/Air Canada (via LA or Hawaii) and both United and American (via LA) provide daily connections to Vancouver (NZ$2488/2579 in low/high season), Edmonton and Calgary (NZ$2784/2876) and Toronto and Montréal (NZ$3010/3352), as well as other major cities in Canada. It's also possible to fly with Qantas (via Sydney and LA) for similar fares. JAL has daily flights from Auckland to Tokyo, with an overnight connection on to LA and Vancouver (NZ$2450/2530).

If you intend to to do a fair amount of flying around within Canada, you'd be well advised to take advantage of **Air Canada's Airpass** which costs between A$683/NZ$772 and A$1511/NZ$1707 for a minimum of three flights (or coupons) and a maximum of eight in both Canada and the USA. Air Canada also regularly has special deals which tack on other domestic cities in various combinations to standard return flights from as little as A$1839/NZ$2078.

If you intend to take in Canada as part of a world trip, then **round-the-world** (RTW) tickets and **circle** fares offer the best value for money, often working out just a little more than an all-in ticket. Star Alliance (ⓦwww.star-alliance.com) and One World (ⓦwww.oneworld.com) are the best known airline groupings and have the most comprehensive and flexible routes. Student travel agents are especially knowledgeable about these kinds of tickets. There are numerous combinations to choose from: the Midi Star Alliance costs from A$2279/NZ$2575 for a maximum of 26,000 miles with no more than 5 stops – one sample route is Brisbane–Vancouver–Toronto–London–Glasgow–Bangkok–Brisbane. The One World Explorer starts at A$3420/NZ$3864 and takes in six continents with up to 15 stops. Another option that enables you to visit some of the Pacific Islands on your way to and from Vancouver is Air New Zealand's "Circle Pacific Fare", starting at A$2839/NZ$2939 for up to 22,000 miles, which allows stopovers in Auckland, Apia, Nadi, Rarotonga, Papeete, Honolulu and LA.

Airlines in Australia and New Zealand

Air Canada Australia ☎ 1300/655 747 or 02/8248 5757, New Zealand ☎ 09/379 3371, ⓦ www.aircanada.com. Several daily flights from Australia and NZ to Vancouver and Toronto via Hawaii. Special deals on airpasses and multi-stop domestic travel.
Air New Zealand Australia ☎ 13 24 76, ⓦ www.alrnz.com.au, New Zealand ☎ 0800/737 000, ⓦ www.alrnz.co.nz. Daily flights to Vancouver and Toronto from major Australasian cities via Auckland and either Honolulu or LA. Onward connections to other cities with Air Canada.
American Airlines Australia ☎ 1300/130 757, New Zealand ☎ 0800/887 997, ⓦ www.aa.com. Daily flights from Sydney and Auckland to Vancouver via LA.
Cathay Pacific Australia ☎ 13 17 47, New Zealand ☎ 0508/800 454 or 09/379 0861, ⓦ www.cathaypacific.com. To Vancouver from major Australasian cities via Hong Kong.
JAL Japan Airlines Australia ☎ 02/9272 1111, New Zealand ☎ 09/379 9906, ⓦ www.jal.com. Flights to Vancouver from Sydney and Auckland via Tokyo or Osaka.
Korean Air Australia ☎ 02/9262 6000, New Zealand ☎ 09/914 2000, ⓦ www.koreanair.com.au. To Vancouver from Australia via Seoul.
Qantas Australia ☎ 13 13 13, New Zealand ☎ 0800/808 767 or 09/357 8900, ⓦ www.qantas.com. Daily to Vancouver and Toronto via LA, with onward connections.
Singapore Airlines Australia ☎ 13 10 11, New Zealand ☎ 0800/808 909, ⓦ www.singaporeair.com. Flights from major Australian cities to Vancouver via Singapore.

United Airlines Australia ☎ 13 17 77, New Zealand ☎ 09/379 3800, ⓦ www.united.com. Daily to Vancouver, Edmonton, Calgary, Montréal and Toronto from Sydney, Melbourne and Auckland, via LA or San Francisco.

Travel agents in Australia and New Zealand

Flight Centre Australia ☎ 13 31 33, ⓦ www.flightcentre.com.au, New Zealand ☎ 0800 243 544, ⓦ www.flightcentre.co.nz. Rock-bottom fares worldwide.
Holiday Shoppe New Zealand ☎ 0800/808 480, ⓦ www.holidayshoppe.co.nz. Great deals on flights, hotels and holidays.
OTC Australia ☎ 1300/855 118, ⓦ www.otctravel.com.au. Deals on flights, hotels and holidays.
STA Travel Australia ☎ 1300/733 035, New Zealand ☎ 0508/782 872, ⓦ www.statravel.com. Worldwide specialists in low-cost flights, overlands and holiday deals. Good discounts for students and under-26s.
Student Uni Travel Australia ☎ 02/9232 8444, ⓦ www.sut.com.au, New Zealand ☎ 09/379 4224, ⓦ www.sut.co.nz. Great deals for students.
Trailfinders Australia ☎ 02/9247 7666, ⓦ www.trailfinders.com.au. One of the best-informed and most efficient agents for independent travellers.
travel.com.au and **travel.co.nz** Australia ☎ 1300/130 482 or 02/9249 5444, ⓦ www.travel.com.au, New Zealand ☎ 0800/468 332, ⓦ www.travel.co.nz. Comprehensive online travel company, with discounted fares.

Tour operators in Australia and New Zealand

Abercrombie & Kent Australia ☎ 1300/851 800, New Zealand ☎ 0800/441 638, ⓦ www.abercrombiekent.com.au. Classy operator with a strong reputation.
Adventure World Australia ☎ 02/8913 0755, ⓦ www.adventureworld.com.au, New Zealand ☎ 09/524 5118, ⓦ www.adventureworld.co.nz. Agents for a vast array of international adventure travel companies that operate trips to every continent.
Australian Pacific Touring Australia ☎ 1800/675 222 or 03/9277 8555, New Zealand ☎ 09/279 6077, ⓦ www.aptours.com. Long-established, award-winning operator running package tours and independent travel.
Canada & America Travel Specialists Australia ☎ 02/9922 4600, ⓦ www.canada-americatravel.com.au. North American specialists –

accommodation, train travel, adventure sports, car and motorhome rentals, Greyhound and other long-distance bus passes, cruises, escorted tours, independent travel, and more.

Contiki Australia ℡ 02/9511 2200, New Zealand ℡ 09/309 8824, ⓦ www.contiki.com. Frenetic trips for 18- to 35-year-old party animals.

Eastern Eurotours Australia ℡ 1800/242 353 or 07/5526 2855, ⓦ www.easterneurotours.com.au. Sightseeing holidays to Canada, plus winter packages.

Explore Holidays Australia ℡ 02/9423 8080, ⓦ www.exploreholidays.com.au. Accommodation and package tours to Canada.

Peregrine Adventures Australia ℡ 03/9663 8611, ⓦ www.peregrine.net.au. Agent for a multitude of adventure companies all over the world, taking small groups on specialist programmes that include walking, biking, overlanding, adventure and cultural trips. In New

Zealand, contact Adventure Travel Company ℡ 09/379 9755.

Ski and Snowboard Travel Company Australia ℡ 1300/766 938, ⓦ www.skiandsnowboard.com.au. Customized skiing holidays.

Snow Bookings Only ℡ 1800/623 266, ⓦ www.snowbookingsonly.com.au. Skiing packages.

Travelplan Australia ℡ 1300/130 754 or 02/9958 1888, ⓦ www.travelplan.com.au. Holidays in the snow worldwide, plus extreme heli-skiing trips.

USA Travel Australia ℡ 02/9250 9320, ⓦ www.usatravel.com. Good deals on flights, accommodation, city stays, car rental and trip packages to the US and Canada.

Viator ⓦ www.viator.com. Bookings for local tours and sightseeing trips in destinations around the world.

Red tape and visas

Citizens of the EU, Norway, Iceland and most Commonwealth countries, including Australia and New Zealand, only need a valid passport to enter Canada. US citizens simply need some form of photo identification plus proof of US citizenship (see box for more details).

All visitors to Canada have to complete a **customs declaration form**, which you'll be given on the plane or at the US–Canadian border. On the form you'll have to give details of where you intend to stay during your trip. If you don't know, write "touring", but be prepared to give an idea of your schedule and destinations to the immigration officer.

At point of entry, the Canadian immigration officer decides the **length of stay permitted** – usually not more than three months. The officers rarely refuse entry, but they may launch into an impromptu investigation, asking how much money you have and what job you do; they may also ask to see a return or onward ticket. If they ask where you're staying and you give the name and address of friends, don't be surprised if they check. Note also that although passing

overland between the US and Canada is usually straightforward, there can sometimes be long delays.

For visits of more than six months, study trips and stints of temporary employment, contact the nearest Canadian embassy, consulate or high commission for authorization prior to departure. Once inside Canada, if you need an extension of your stay, you must make a written application to the nearest Canada Immigration Centre well before the expiry of the authorized visit.

Canadian embassies abroad

Australia High Commission, Commonwealth Ave, Canberra, ACT 2600 ℡ 02/6273 3285, ⓦ www.dfait-maeci.gc.ca/australia. Consulates in Perth & Sydney.

Entry to Canada for US citizens

If you're a **US citizen**, you don't need a visa to enter Canada as a tourist. All you need is one ID card with your photo, plus proof of US citizenship. This can be a valid US passport, an original US birth certificate (or certified copy), or original US naturalization papers. Note that a US driver's licence alone is **not** sufficient proof of citizenship.

Visitors with **children** must show identification for each child similar to that required by adults and a letter of permission from the parents of any children for whom they don't have legal custody. Divorced parents with shared custody rights should carry legal documents that establish their status. Unaccompanied children should have a letter of permission from their parents or a legal guardian. Contrary to expectations, since the signing of the North American Free Trade Agreement (NAFTA), entering and exiting Canada has become a particularly sensitive issue – on both sides of the border. You would be well advised, where documentation is involved, to always err on the side of caution.

All US citizens wishing to **work** in Canada, including those exempted from the validation process by the terms of NAFTA, must have employment authorization from a Canadian embassy or consulate before entering the country. **Students** who are US citizens, permanent residents of the US, or Green Card holders, who have already been accepted by a school in Canada and have sufficient funds to cover all expenses, must apply for student authorization at a port of entry or a Canadian consulate four months before entering the country.

Ireland Embassy, 65 St Stephen's Green, Dublin 2 ☎01/417 4100, ⓦwww.canadaeuropa .gc.ca/ireland.
New Zealand High Commission, PO Box 12049, Thorndon, Wellington ☎04/473 9577, ⓦwww.wellington.gc.ca. Consulate in Auckland.
UK High Commission, Macdonald House, 1 Grosvenor Sq, London W1X 4AB ☎020/7258 6600, ⓦwww.dfait-maeci.gc.ca/london. Consulates in Belfast, Birmingham, Cardiff & Edinburgh.
USA Embassy, 501 Pennsylvania Ave NW, Washington DC 20001 ☎202/682-7726, ⓦwww.can-am.gc.ca/washington. Consulates in Atlanta, Boston, Buffalo, Chicago, Dallas, Detroit, Los Angeles, Miami, Minneapolis, New York, San Francisco, San Jose & Seattle.

Embassies in Canada

Australian High Commission, Suite 710, 50 O'Connor St, Ottawa, ON, K1P 6L2 ☎613/236-0841, ⓦwww.ahc-ottawa.org. Consulates in Toronto & Vancouver.
Irish Embassy, Suite 1105, 130 Albert St, Ottawa, ON, K1P 5G4 ☎613/233-6281, ⓔembassyofireland@rogers.com. Consulates in Calgary, Vancouver, Toronto, St John's NL & St Albert AB.
New Zealand High Commission, Suite 727, 99 Bank St, Ottawa, ON, K1P 6G3 ☎613/238-5991, ⓦwww.nzembassy.com. Consulates in Toronto & Vancouver.
UK High Commission, 80 Elgin St, Ottawa, ON, K1P 5K7 ☎613/237-1530, ⓦwww.britainincanada .org. Consulates in Montréal, Toronto, Vancouver, St John's NL, Winnipeg, Halifax & Québec City.
US Embassy, 490 Sussex Drive, Ottawa, ON, K1N 1G8 ☎613/238-5335, ⓦwww.usembassycanada .gov. Consulates in Halifax, Montréal, Québec City, Toronto, Winnipeg, Calgary & Vancouver.

Customs

Bear in mind that if you cross the border in your car, the trunk and passenger compartment are subject to spot searches by the **customs** personnel of both the US and Canada. Officers at the more obscure entry points on the border can be real sticklers, so expect to be delayed. Americans who visit Canada for at least 48 hours and haven't made an international trip in the previous thirty days can bring back goods to the value of US$400. Non-residents of Canada are also entitled to a tax refund on goods worth more than C$50 purchased at one establishment at one time and totalling more than $200. The refund is given at the border when exiting the country, provided you are able to supply original itemized receipts; ask the customs official for information before entering Canada or check ⓦwww .ccra-adrc.gc.ca ahead of time.

Gifts valued at less than C$60 that do not contain tobacco or alcohol can be brought into Canada; those valued at more than C$60 are subject to regular import duty on the excess amount. The US Customs Service (☎202/927-6724) and the Canada Customs and Revenue Agency (☎902/432-5608 or 1-800/668-4748, ⓦwww.ccra-adrc .gc.ca/visitors) can help with any queries.

Information, websites and maps

You'll find there's no shortage of tourist information handed out by the Canadians – not least at ⓦwww.travelcanada.ca. The most useful sources of information before you go are the various provincial tourist offices in Canada: if you contact them well in advance of your departure, and are as specific as possible about your intentions, they should be able to provide you with everything you need to know.

Most of Canada's provinces have at least one **toll-free visitor information number** for use within mainland North America. These lines are staffed by tourist office employees trained to answer all manner of queries and to advise on room reservations.

Outside Canada, the consulates, embassies and high commissions usually have tourist information departments, though these cannot match the specific detailed advice dispensed in Canada.

Tourist information

The main source of tourist information before you depart is the encyclopedic national tourist commission website ⓦ**www.travelcanada.ca**. In Canada, there are often seasonal **provincial tourist information centres** along the main highways, especially at provincial boundaries and along the US border. The usual **opening hours** for the seasonal centres are daily in July and August 9am–9pm, and Monday to Friday in May, June, September and October 9am to 5 or 6pm. These dispense all sorts of glossy material and, most usefully, have details of local provincial and national parks. The parks themselves (see "Outdoor pursuits", p.55) have offices that sell fishing and backcountry permits and give help on the specifics of hiking, canoeing, wildlife watching and so forth. At Canada's **airports** general information is harder to come by, though there's usually a city tourist desk or a complimentary phone to help arrange accommodation.

All of Canada's large cities have their own **tourist offices**, with the services of the main branch complemented by summertime booths, kiosks and offices. Smaller towns nearly always have a seasonal **tourist office, infocentre** or **visitors' centre**, frequently operated by the municipal chamber of commerce, holding local maps and information. The usual opening hours in summer are daily 9am–6pm; in winter, tourist information is often dispensed from the city hall or chamber of commerce (Mon–Fri 9am–5pm). Many larger towns have a **free newspaper** or broadsheet, carrying local reviews and entertainment listings.

In the UK, you can order tourist brochures 24 hours a day from ☎0906/871 5000 (premium rate).

Provincial tourist offices in Canada

Alberta ⓦwww.discoveralberta.com. Travel Alberta, Visitor Sales and Service, 3rd Floor,

10155–102nd St, Edmonton, AB, T5J 4G8
☎403/427-4321, or toll-free ☎1-800/661-8888.
British Columbia ⊛www.tbc.gov.bc.ca. Tourism
BC, Box 9830, Parliament Buildings, Victoria,
BC, V8W 9W5 ☎250/356-6363, or toll-free
☎1-800/663-6000.
Manitoba ⊛www.gov.mb.ca/travel-manitoba.
Travel Manitoba, 7th Floor, 155 Carlton St,
Winnipeg, MB, R3C 3H8 ☎204/945-3777,
or toll-free ☎1-800/665-0040.
New Brunswick ⊛www.gov.nb.ca/tourism. Dept
of Tourism, PO Box 12345, Woodstock, NB, E0J
2B0. Toll-free ☎1-800/561-0123.
Newfoundland and Labrador ⊛www.public
.gov.nf.ca/tourism. Dept of Tourism, Culture and
Recreation, PO Box 8730, St John's, NL, A1B 4K2
☎709/729-2830, or toll free ☎1-800/563-6353.
Northwest Territories ⊛www.nwttravel.nt.ca.
NWT Arctic Tourism, PO Box 610, Yellowknife,
NT, X1A 2N5 ☎867/873-7200, or toll-free
☎1-800/661-0788.
Nova Scotia ⊛www.explorens.com. Dept of
Tourism and Culture, PO Box 456, Halifax, NS,
B3J 2R5 ☎902/424-5000, or toll-free
☎1-800/565-0000.
Nunavut ⊛www.nunavut.com/~nunatour. Nunavut
Tourism, PO Box 1450, Iqaluit, NU, X0A 0H0
☎867/979-6551, or toll-free ☎1-800/491-7910.
Ontario ⊛www.tourism.gov.on.ca. Ontario
Travel, Queens Park, Toronto, ON, M7A 2E5
☎416/314-0944, or toll-free ☎1-800/668-2746.
Prince Edward Island ⊛www.peiplay.com.
Tourism PEI, PO Box 940, Charlottetown, PE,
C1A 7M5 ☎902/629-2400, or toll-free
☎1-888/743-7529.
Québec ⊛www.tourisme-quebec.org. Tourisme
Québec, PO Box 979, Montréal, PQ, G1R 2B5
☎514/873-2015, or toll-free ☎1-800/363-7777.
Saskatchewan ⊛www.sasktourism.com.
Tourism Saskatchewan, 500-1900 Albert St,
Regina, SK, S4P 4L9 ☎306/787-2300, or toll-free
☎1-877/667-7191.
Yukon ⊛www.touryukon.com. Tourism Yukon,
PO Box 2703, Whitehorse, YK, Y1A 2C6
☎867/667-5340.

Websites

There's a vast quantity of useful information
on the **Internet**. Aside from the official website ⊛www.travelcanada.ca, you'll come
across endless quantities of material on any
given destination, both official and not. What
follows is a personal selection.
Assembly of First Nations ⊛www.afn.ca.
Lobbying organization of Canada's native peoples,

with plenty to get you briefed on the latest
circumstances.
Canada.Com ⊛www.canada.com. Canada's
number one online news and information service,
with content from newspapers, TV, city sites and
classified ads.
Canada Eh? Net Directory ⊛www.canadianeh
.com. Impressive array of links to every conceivable
Canada-related site.
Canada Worldweb ⊛Canada.worldweb.com.
Travel and tourism site with online hotel reservations,
maps and detailed tourist information.
Canadian Hockey Association ⊛www
.hockeycanada.ca. The official site of the amateur
governing body for the national obsession.
Canadian Parks ⊛parkscanada.pch.gc.ca/parks.
A good site by Canadian Heritage detailing opening
times, camping facilities and how to get there, to all
major Canadian parks.
Canadian Tourism Commission ⊛www
.travelcanada.ca. Official site of the Canadian
Tourism Commission with featured destinations,
information on special events and festivals and
listings of tour operators.
Gateway to the Arts ⊛artscanadian.com. Good
arts information.
The Globe and Mail ⊛www.theglobeandmail
.com. Canada's premier newspaper online.
Government of Canada ⊛www.canada.gc.ca.
Official sites of provincial governments and various
Canadian businesses.
Infospace ⊛infospace.com. Exhaustive Yellow
Pages-like listings. If you want to find a vet in Labrador
or a body piercer in Prince Albert, this will have it.
MacLean's ⊛www.macleans.ca. Top stories and
the editor's pick from past issues of Canada's
premier news magazine.
National Atlas of Canada Online
⊛www.atlas.gc.ca. Maps, stats and plenty of
details on Canada's geographic features.
National Library of Canada ⊛www.nlc-bnc.ca.
Information on all things Canadian, ordered by
subject. Includes Canadian arts, literature, history.
The Native Trail ⊛www.nativetrail.com. Insight
into the First Nations and Québec's Inuit peoples.
Northern Stars ⊛www.northernstars.ca. Tracks
the progress of all Canada's film stars, with short
bios and lists of credits.
Slam! Sport ⊛www.canoe.ca. A very thorough
Canadian site on all matters sporting.
Statistics Canada ⊛www.statcan.ca. A national
agency that gives you all the numerical data and
analysis on population, economic trends, and more.
Tickets ⊛www.ticketmaster.ca. Ticket booking
service for shows, gigs and sporting events
across Canada.

Trains ⓦ www.viarail.ca. VIA Rail's page with times and tickets for Canada's train services.
Yahoo! Canada ⓦ ca.yahoo.ca. The canuck section of the useful Web directory provides good avenues of investigation.

Maps

The **free maps** issued by each provincial tourist office are excellent for general driving and route planning, especially as they provide the broad details of ferry connections. The best of the commercially produced maps are those published by Rand McNally, also available bound together in their *Rand McNally Road Atlas of North America*.

In the case of **hiking** and **canoe** routes, all the national and most of the provincial parks have visitors' centres, which provide free parkland maps indicating hiking and canoe trails. Many of them also sell proper local survey maps, as do lots of outfitters and some of the provincial parks' departments, whose details are given in the guide or can be obtained through the toll-free numbers.

If you want to be absolutely sure of getting the maps you need for independent wilderness travel, check with the **Canada Map Office** (ⓣ 1-800/465 6277, ⓦ maps.nrcan.gc.ca). While the map office, a department of Natural Resources Canada, no longer distributes maps directly to the public, Its website can locate your nearest map dealer and has a useful online service to help you determine which topographic map covers the area you're heading for. The map office also produces a useful brochure entitled *Topographic Basics* and publishes two main series of maps, at 1:250,000 and 1:50,000.

Map outlets

In the UK and Ireland

Stanfords 12–14 Long Acre, London WC2 ⓣ 020/7836 1321, ⓦ www.stanfords.co.uk. Also at 39 Spring Gardens, Manchester ⓣ 0161/831 0250, and 29 Corn St, Bristol ⓣ 0117/929 9966.
Blackwell's Map Centre 50 Broad St, Oxford ⓣ 01865/793 550, ⓦ maps.blackwell.co.uk.

Branches in Bristol, Cambridge, Cardiff, Leeds, Liverpool, Newcastle, Reading & Sheffield.
The Map Shop 30a Belvoir St, Leicester ⓣ 0116/247 1400, ⓦ www.mapshopleicester.co.uk.
National Map Centre 22–24 Caxton St, London SW1 ⓣ 020/7222 2466, ⓦ www.mapsnmc.co.uk.
National Map Centre Ireland 34 Aungier St, Dublin ⓣ 01/476 0471, ⓦ www.mapcentre.ie.
The Travel Bookshop 13–15 Blenheim Crescent, London W11 ⓣ 020/7229 5260, ⓦ www.thetravelbookshop.co.uk.
Traveller 55 Grey St, Newcastle-upon-Tyne ⓣ 0191/261 5622, ⓦ www.newtraveller.com.

In the US and Canada

110 North Latitude US ⓣ 336/369-4171, ⓦ www.110nlatitude.com.
Book Passage 51 Tamal Vista Blvd, Corte Madera, CA 94925 ⓣ 1-800/999-7909, ⓦ www.bookpassage.com.
Distant Lands 56 S Raymond Ave, Pasadena, CA 91105 ⓣ 1-800/310-3220, ⓦ www.distantlands.com.
Globe Corner Bookstore 28 Church St, Cambridge, MA 02138 ⓣ 1-800/358-6013, ⓦ www.globecorner.com.
Longitude Books 115 W 30th St #1206, New York, NY 10001 ⓣ 1-800/342-2164, ⓦ www.longitudebooks.com.
Map Town 400 5 Ave SW #100, Calgary, AB, T2P 0L6 ⓣ 1-877/921-6277, ⓦ www.maptown.com.
Travel Bug Bookstore 3065 W Broadway, Vancouver, BC, V6K 2G9 ⓣ 604/737-1122, ⓦ www.travelbugbooks.ca.
World of Maps 1235 Wellington St, Ottawa, ON, K1Y 3A3 ⓣ 1-800/214-8524, ⓦ www.worldofmaps.com.

In Australia and New Zealand

Map Centre ⓦ www.mapcentre.co.nz.
Mapland 372 Little Bourke St, Melbourne ⓣ 03/9670 4383, ⓦ www.mapland.com.au.
Map Shop 6–10 Peel St, Adelaide ⓣ 08/8231 2033, ⓦ www.mapshop.net.au.
Map World 371 Pitt St, Sydney ⓣ 02/9261 3601, ⓦ www.mapworld.net.au. Also at 900 Hay St, Perth ⓣ 08/9322 5733.
Map World 173 Gloucester St, Christchurch ⓣ 0800/627 967, ⓦ www.mapworld.co.nz.

Insurance and health

Prior to travelling, you should take out an insurance policy to cover against theft, loss and illness or injury. Before paying for a new policy, however, it's worth checking whether you already have some degree of coverage: some all-risks home insurance policies may cover your possessions when overseas; many private medical schemes include cover when abroad; and bank and credit cards often have certain levels of medical or other insurance included if you use one of them to pay for your trip. In addition, holders of official student/teacher/youth cards in the US may be entitled to meagre accident coverage and hospital in-patient benefits. Students will often find that their student health coverage extends during vacations and for one term beyond the date of last enrolment.

After exhausting the possibilities above, you'll probably want to contact a **specialist travel insurance company,** or consider the travel insurance deal we offer (see box, p.28). A typical travel insurance policy usually provides cover for the loss of baggage, tickets and – up to a certain limit – cash or cheques, as well as cancellation or curtailment of your journey. Most of them exclude so-called dangerous sports unless an extra premium is paid: in Canada this can mean white-water rafting, mountain climbing, and so on. Many policies can be chopped and changed to exclude coverage you don't need: for example, sickness and accident benefits can often be excluded or included at will. If you do take medical coverage, ascertain whether benefits will be paid as treatment proceeds or only after return home, and whether there is a 24-hour medical emergency number. When securing baggage cover, make sure that the per-article limit will cover your most valuable possession. If you need to make a claim, you should keep receipts for medicines and medical treatment, and in the event you have anything stolen, you must obtain an official statement from the police.

Health

It is vital to have travel insurance against potential **medical** expenses. Canada has an excellent health service, but non-residents are not entitled to free health care, and medical costs can be astronomical. If you have

an accident, medical services will get to you quickly and charge you later.

Doctors and **dentists** can be found listed in the Yellow Pages. If you are carrying medicine prescribed by your doctor, also bring a copy of the prescription – first, to avoid problems at customs and immigration and, second, for renewing medication with Canadian doctors, if needed. **Pharmacies** are often well equipped to advise on **minor ailments** and to distinguish between unfamiliar brand names. Most larger towns and cities should have a 24hr pharmacy; many stay open late as a matter of course.

Specific health problems

Health problems can kick in when you're walking or camping in the backcountry. Tap water is generally safe to drink, though it's always prudent to ask, and at campgrounds water is sometimes good for washing only. You should, however, **always boil backcountry water** for at least ten minutes to protect against the Giardia parasite (or "beaver fever"), which thrives in warm water, so equally be careful about swimming in hot springs – if possible, keep nose, eyes and mouth above water. Symptoms are intestinal cramps, flatulence, fatigue, weight loss and vomiting, all of which can appear up to a

> In a medical **emergency,**
> call T911.

Rough Guides travel insurance

Rough Guides offers its own low-cost **travel insurance**, especially customized for our statistically low-risk readers. There are five main plans: No Frills, the bare minimum for secure travel; Essential, which provides decent all-round cover; Premier, for comprehensive cover with a wide range of benefits; Extended Stay, for cover lasting between four months and a year; and Annual Multi-Trip, a cost-effective way of getting Premier cover if you travel more than once a year. Premier, Annual Multi-Trip and Extended Stay policies can be supplemented by a "Hazardous Pursuits Extension" if you plan to indulge in sports considered dangerous, such as white-water rafting.

For a quote, check ⓦ www.roughguides.com/insurance or call the Rough Guide Insurance Line: toll-free in the UK on ☏ 0800/015 0906, or at usual international rates from elsewhere on ☏ +44 1392/314665. Rough Guides insurance is underwritten by a leading British broker, provided by the American International Group (AIG) and registered with the British regulatory body GISC (the General Insurance Standards Council).

week after infection. If left untreated, more unpleasant complications can arise, so see a doctor immediately if you think you've contracted it.

Blackfly and **mosquitoes** are notorious for the problems they cause walkers and campers, and are especially bad in areas near standing water and throughout most of northern Canada. **Horseflies** are another pest. Late April to June is the blackfly season, and the mosquito season is from June until about October. If you're planning an expedition into the wilderness, you'd be well advised to take three times the recommended daily dosage of vitamin B complex for two weeks before you go, and to take the recommended dosage while you're in Canada; this cuts down bites by up to 75 percent.

Once you're there, **repellent creams** and **sprays** may help: the best are those containing DEET. The ointment version of Deep-Woods Off is the best brand, with 95 percent DEET. If you're camping or picnicking you'll find that burning coils or candles containing allethrin or citronella can help. If you're walking in an area that's rife with pests, it's well worth taking a gauze mask to protect your head and neck; wearing white clothes and no perfumed products also makes you less attractive to the insects. Once bitten, an **antihistamine cream** like phenergan is the best antidote. On no account go anywhere near an area marked as a blackfly mating ground – people have

died from bites sustained when the creatures are in heat. Also dangerous is **West Nile virus**, a mosquito-born affliction with life-threatening properties; the virus has appeared in a few places as far west as Ontario and will probably spread – so pay attention to local advice.

If you develop a large rash and flu-like symptoms, you may have been bitten by a tick carrying lyme borreliosis (or **"lyme tick disease"**). This is easily curable, but if left untreated can lead to nasty complications, so again see a doctor as soon as possible. It's spreading in Canada, especially in the more southerly and wooded parts of the country; you should check on its prevalence with the local tourist authority. It also may be advisable to buy a strong **tick repellent** and to wear long socks, trousers and sleeved shirts when walking.

In backcountry areas, look out for **poison ivy**, which grows in most places, but particularly in a belt across southern Ontario and Quebec, where poison-ivy ointment is widely available. If you're likely to be walking in affected areas, ask at tourist offices for tips on where it is and how to recognize it. The ivy causes itchy open blisters and lumpy sores up to ten days after contact. If you do come into contact with poison ivy, wash your body and clothes as soon as possible, smother yourself in calamine lotion and try not to scratch. In serious cases, hospital emergency rooms can give antihistamine or adrenalin jabs.

Also keep an eye open for **snakes** in certain western areas; pharmacists and wilderness outfitters can advise on snakebite kits, and park wardens can give useful preventive advice. Should you get bitten without an antidote on you, get a good look at the culprit so that the doctor can identify the species and administer the right medicine.

If walking or climbing, go properly equipped and be prepared for sudden changes of weather. Watch out for signs of **exposure** – mild delirium, exhaustion, inability to get warm – and on snow or in high country during summer take a good **sunblock**.

Costs, money and banks

By western European standards, Canada is very reasonably priced, with most basic items – from maps through to food and clothing – costing significantly less than back home. US residents, Australians and New Zealanders, on the other hand, will find prices about the same – maybe a little higher, but not by much. As for dining and drinking, the sheer plethora of restaurants and bars keeps prices down except in the far north, where the high cost of transporting foodstuffs is necessarily passed on to the customer. Accommodation, almost certainly your major outlay, can be very pricey in the country's cities and towns – especially if you're after a degree of comfort – though to be fair there are plenty of bargains to be had, not least in the burgeoning B&B market.

Currency

Canadian currency is the **dollar** ($), made up of 100 cents (¢). Coins come as 1¢ (penny), 5¢ (nickel), 10¢ (dime), 25¢ (quarter), $1 and $2. The $1 coin is known as a "loonie", after the bird on one face; no one's come up with a suitable name for the newer $2 coin – "twoonie" has been tried but hasn't really caught on. There are notes of $5, $10, $20, $50 and $100.

Approximate **exchange rates** at the time of writing are £1=C$2.25, US$1=C$1.30, €1=C$1.60, A$1=C$0.95, NZ$1=C$0.85. For the most up-to-date rates, check ⓦwww.oanda.com.

US dollars are widely accepted, but you'll generally be able to pay only on a one-for-one basis. Since the US dollar is usually worth more than its Canadian counterpart, it makes sense to change US currency.

Carrying and changing money

All but the tiniest of settlements in Canada has a **bank** or **savings bank**, the vast majority of which will change foreign currency and travellers' cheques. Many will also give cash advances on credit cards. **Banking hours** are a minimum of Monday to Friday 10am–3pm, but many have late opening – till 6pm – on one night a week, others open on Saturday mornings. The main nationwide banks include the Toronto Dominion, the Royal Bank of Canada and the Bank of Montréal.

ATMs are commonplace. Most accept a host of **debit cards**, including all those carrying the Cirrus coding. If in doubt, check with your bank to find out whether the card you wish to use will be accepted – and if you need a new (international) PIN. You'll rarely be charged a transaction fee, as the banks make their profits from applying different exchange rates. **Credit cards** can be used in ATMs too, but in this case transactions are treated as loans, with interest accruing daily from the date of withdrawal. All major credit and charge cards, including American

27

Express, Visa and Mastercard, are widely accepted.

Though a lot more hassle, old-fashioned **travellers' cheques** are still the safest way to carry your money. The usual fee for buying them is one or two percent, though this may be waived if you buy the cheques through a bank where you have an account. It pays to get a selection of denominations. Make sure to keep the purchase agreement and a record of cheque serial numbers safe and separate from the cheques themselves. All well-known brands of traveller's cheque in all major currencies are widely accepted in Canada, with US dollar and Canadian dollar cheques being the most common. When you cash your cheques, almost all banks make a percentage charge per transaction on top of a basic minimum charge.

A compromise between travellers' cheques and plastic is **Visa TravelMoney** (Ⓦ international.visa.com/ps), a disposable pre-paid debit card with a PIN which works in all ATMs that take Visa cards. You load up your account with funds before leaving home, and when they run out you simply throw the card away. You can buy up to nine cards to access the same funds – useful for couples or families travelling together – and it's a good idea to buy at least one extra as a

back-up in case of loss or theft. The 24-hour toll-free customer assistance service centre is on ☏1-800/847-2399 from the whole of North America.

Average costs

For an idea of **costs**, if you're prepared to buy your own picnic lunch, stay in hostels, and stick to the least expensive bars and restaurants, you could get by on around £25/US$40/C$60 a day. Staying in a good B&B, eating out in medium-range restaurants most nights and drinking regularly in bars, you'll get through at least £65/US$100/C$150 a day, with the main variable being the cost of your room. On £100/$150/C$230 a day and upwards, you'll be limited only by your energy reserves – though if you're planning to stay in the best hotels and make every night a big night out, this still won't be enough.

As always, if you're travelling alone you'll spend much more on accommodation than you would in a group of two or more: most hotels do have single rooms, but they're fixed at about sixty-five percent of the price of a double.

Restaurants don't come cheap, but costs remain manageable if you avoid the extras and concentrate on the main courses, which

---

Taxes – GST, PST and HST

Virtually all prices in Canada, for everything from bubble-gum to hotel rooms, are quoted **without tax**, which means that the price you see quoted is not the price you'll end up paying. There are both national and provincial taxes to take into account. The Goods and Services Tax (**GST**) – the equivalent of sales tax or VAT – is a nationwide seven-percent charge levied on most goods and services, including hotel and restaurant bills. In addition, all provinces except Alberta, the Yukon, Nunavut and NWT levy a Provincial Sales Tax (**PST**) of six to ten percent on most goods and services, again including hotel accommodation and restaurant bills. The net result is that you can end up paying seventeen percent over the listed price for hotel rooms and a mixed bag of services, with precise rates varying between the provinces. In Newfoundland, Labrador, Nova Scotia and New Brunswick, PST and GST have been merged into the so-called Harmonized Sales Tax (**HST**) of fifteen percent.

As a small mercy, visitors can claim a **GST rebate** on certain goods and short-term accommodation over the value of C$50 and up to C$200 per night. Claim forms are available at many hotels, shops and airports, and from any Canadian embassy. Return it, with **all original receipts**, to the address given on the form. If you're returning overland to the US, you can claim your rebate on the border at selected duty-free shops. For more information, call ☏902/432-5608 outside Canada or ☏1-800/668-4748 within Canada, or consult Ⓦ www.ccra.gc.ca/visitors.

start at around £5/US$8/C$12 – though you can, of course, pay a lot more. Obviously enough, **tipping** is optional, but a fifteen percent tip is expected by restaurant waiters and anticipated by taxi drivers. **Museum admission prices** are mostly in the £3/US$5/C$7 range, but discounts of at least fifty percent are routinely available for children, seniors and students. Indeed, concessionary fares and rates are offered on all sorts of things, from boat tours and public transport through to extra beds in rooms.

Wiring money

Wiring money from home using Thomas Cook (@www.thomascook.com), Travelers Express MoneyGram (@www.moneygram.com) or Western Union (@www.westernunion.com) is never convenient or cheap, and should be considered a last resort. It's also possible to have money wired directly from a bank in your home country to a bank in Canada, although this is somewhat less reliable because it involves two separate institutions. If you go this route, your home bank will need the address of the branch bank where you want to pick up the money and the address and telex number of the head office, which will act as the clearing house; money wired this way normally takes two working days to arrive, and costs around £25/US$40 per transaction. If you can last out the week, then arrange for friends or family to post you an **international money order**; these are exchangeable at any post office and are by far the cheapest way of sending money. If you're in really dire straits, you can get in touch with your embassy or High Commission, who will usually let you make one phone call home free of charge, and may – in worst cases only – repatriate you, but will never, under any circumstances, lend money.

Getting around

To get the most out of a visit, you'd be well advised to plan carefully how you'll get around. With VIA Rail services now skeletal, province-wide bus companies provide the main surface links between major cities, though in isolated areas you may be thrown back on more sporadic local bus services. Flying is of course more expensive, but competition in the skies can lead to some decent bargains.

On most forms of public transport there are **discounted fares** for children under 12, for people between 13 and 21, and over-60s. It has to be said, however, that things are always easier if you have a **car**: even if a bus can take you to the general vicinity of a provincial park, for example, it can prove impossible to explore the interior without your own vehicle.

All prices given in this section are in **Canadian dollars**, excluding tax, unless otherwise indicated.

By bus

If you're travelling on your own, **buses** are by far the cheapest way to get around. Greyhound Canada runs most of the long-distance buses west of Toronto, including a service along the Trans-Canada Highway from Toronto to Vancouver. The major centres in the east of the country are served by a network of smaller lines and by a wide range of different companies. Long-distance buses run to a fairly full timetable (at least during the day), stopping only for meal breaks and driver changeovers. Nearly all are non-smoking, have toilets and coffee-making facilities and are less uncomfortable than you might expect – it's feasible, if you're on the tightest of budgets, to save on a

The Moose Travel Network

The **Moose Travel Network** (eastern office ☎905/853-4762 or 1-888/816-6673, western office ☎604/944-3007 or 1-888/388-4881, ⓦwww.moosenetwork.com) provides a completely different experience from regular buses, aimed at backpackers. Their mini-coaches (seating 14–24 people) hit the major destinations on the travellers' circuit in both western and eastern Canada (but not the centre) between May and mid-October; there are some additional winter packages, and also links by VIA Rail trains. The jump-on, jump-off service stops three days a week in the major cities and interesting smaller towns. You don't need to book your own accommodation, since Moose ensures that a hostel dorm bed is available for every passenger at all major stopovers (if you want to stay elsewhere, you must make your own arrangements). There's no time limit, so you can take as long as you like to complete the circuit, and you get picked up and dropped off at the door of your hostel. There's also no age limit, although most travellers tend to be in the 19–34 age bracket; to match this, there's an array of adventure activities offered as add-ons, including white-water rafting, bungee jumping and sea kayaking.

They have a range of **bus passes**: you'd need a full month to do justice to the Mega Moose Pass ($750), which covers the country, while two weeks is recommended for either the East Pass ($399) or West Pass (also $399). There's a handful of other deals, such as the "Loonie Pass" ($239), which covers Montréal, the Laurentians, Québec City and as far east as Tadoussac (for whale-watching). As for **train passes**, options include the Prairie Rail Link ($440), valid for the three-day ride from Toronto to Vancouver (see p.32), the Maritime Rail Link ($260) from Montréal to Halifax, and the Gaspé Rail Link ($220) from Montréal to Gaspé. All prices assume ISIC or hostelling membership; without these, you'll pay slightly more.

---

night's accommodation by sleeping on the bus.

Any sizeable community will have a main **bus station**, but in smaller places a gas station or restaurant will double as the bus stop and ticket office – often inconveniently situated on the edge of town. Seats can be **reserved** but this is rarely necessary: only those services between cities in close proximity, like Montréal and Québec City, are likely to get booked out, and even then you'll have to wait only an hour or so for the next departure. Out in the less populated areas, buses are fairly scarce, sometimes only appearing once or twice a week, and here you'll need to plot your route with care. Reservations on Greyhound Canada services are not necessary: if a bus is full, another is laid on. However, an increasing number of services can make "seat selection" for a small fee which guarantees a specific seat on the first bus out (useful for window-seat sightseeing).

Measured by the kilometre, **fares** are pretty standard from company to company: as an example, Toronto to Winnipeg, a distance of 2100km, costs $167 one-way, while the Coach Canada express from Montréal to Toronto, a six-and-a-half hour ride, costs $130–150. The Ottawa to Montréal run (2hr 20min) is just $65 return. However, while standard fares are usually in line with the distance travelled, Apex fares between more distant destinations are often broadly similar: Vancouver to Montréal costs little more than Winnipeg to Montréal, despite the extra distance.

The free *Official Canadian Bus Guide*, containing all Canadian (and northern US) bus **timetables**, is produced bimonthly but is not made readily available to travellers. Consequently you'll need to rely on free individual timetables from the major bus stations or local tourist offices. Always double-check routes and times by phoning the local terminal (we've included phone numbers for most cities), or the relevant company.

Bus passes

If you're intending to explore Canada by bus,

but the **Moose Travel Network** doesn't appeal (see box), you can save a lot of money by buying a **pass** before leaving home, all of which are detailed (and buyable online) at @**www.greyhound.ca** – where you can also get a list of local sales agents and phone numbers around the world. In general, Canadian and US travellers must buy at least 14 days in advance, international travellers at least 21 days ahead. Prices quoted below (which exclude tax) are for adults; students and seniors get discounted rates.

The **Canada Pass** – for Canadians and non-Canadians – covers travel all round the country, as well as buses from New York, Detroit and Buffalo to Toronto, New York to Montréal and Seattle to Vancouver, and also VIA Rail trains between Toronto, Ottawa and Montréal. The pass is valid for 7, 10, 15, 21, 30, 45 or 60 days. Sample prices are C$255 for seven days, C$375 for fifteen days, up to C$575 for sixty days.

Other options – which all include travel in both the US and Canada, and so are more expensive – are split between passes for Canadian and US travellers, and everyone else. For the former, the best options are the **Domestic Westcoast CanAm Pass** and **Domestic Eastern CanAm Pass**. Both are available in ten-day (US$265) and 21 day (US$345) versions. The Westcoast pass covers travel in BC and Alberta as far north as Whitehorse, YK, as well as Washington State and the western US down to Tijuana. The Eastern pass is valid in Ontario, Québec and the Maritimes, as well as Maine and a chunk of the eastern US down to Florida.

For non-US and non-Canadian citizens, the equivalents are the **International Westcoast CanAm Pass** and **International Eastern CanAm Pass**, available in the same configurations as above, for the same prices. Note that you can't buy these at Greyhound stations in the US (although if you're not a US or Canadian citizen you can still you can get a domestic pass over the counter). In Canada, if you're not a US or Canadian citizen, you can buy these passes at international rates at the gateway cities of Vancouver, Calgary, Edmonton, Ottawa and Toronto.

Main bus companies

A.J. Bus Lines ☎705/838-3013, @ajbus.www2.onlink.net. Service around Elliot Lake in northern Ontario.
Acadian Lines ☎1-800/567-5151, @www.smtbus.com. Nova Scotia and New Brunswick services.
Alaska Direct Busline ☎1-800/770-6652, @www.tokalaska.com/dirctbus.shtml. Services from Whitehorse, YK, to Alaska.
Can-Ar Coach Service ☎905/738-2290, @www.can-arcoach.com. Services around Toronto and southern Ontario.
Canadian Trailways ☎403/265-9111. Montréal and Toronto to New York; also Vancouver to Seattle.
Cherrey Bus Lines ☎519/658-3882, @www.cherreybuslines.yp.ca. Services in southern Ontario.
Coach Canada ☎1-800/461-7661, @www.coachcanada.com. Express between Montréal and Toronto.
Dewdney Coach Lines ☎250/368-8117. Small carrier in BC interior.
Farr's Coach Lines ☎1-800/263-2106, @farrscoachlineeltd.supersites.ca. Runs from Hamilton to Dunnville in Ontario.
Frontier Coachlines ☎867/874-2566. Links Hay River to Yellowknife.
GO Transit ☎416/869-3200, @www.gotransit.com. Toronto suburban service.
Grey Goose Bus Lines ☎204/784-4500. Routes around Manitoba from Winnipeg.
Greyhound Canada ☎403/260-0877 or 1-800/661-8747 in Canada, ☎1-800/231-2222 in the US, or ☎0870/888 0225 in the UK, @www.greyhound.ca. Long-distance buses in Ontario and western Canada.
Intercar ☎418/627-9108 or 1-888/861-4592, @www.intercar.qc.ca. Services in Northern Québec.
Laidlaw ☎250/388-5248 or 1-800/318-0818, @www.victoriatours.com. Services on Vancouver Island.
Laidlaw Canadian Rockies ☎1-800/661-4946, @www.laidlaw.ca. Lake Louise to Banff.
McCoy Coach Lines ☎519/647-3444. Runs from Hamilton to Simcoe and Brantford in Ontario.
North Country Travel Lines ☎807/345-2194. Thunder Bay to Sioux Lookout in northern Ontario.
Northland Bus Lines ☎604/388-5248. Fort St James to Prince George in BC.
Ontario Northland ☎705/472-4500, @www.ontc.on.ca. Serves northern Ontario.

Orléans Express ☎514/395-4000, ⓦwww.orleansexpress.com. Québec services.
Penetang-Midland Coach Lines ☎705/526-0161, ⓦwww.pmcl.on.ca. Local Ontario service around Toronto and Georgian Bay.
Quick Shuttle ☎604/244-3744, ⓦwww.quickcoach.com. Vancouver to Seattle.
Red Arrow ☎403/531-0350, ⓦwww.redarrow.pwt.ca. Edmonton to Fort McMurray and Calgary in Alberta.
Saskatchewan Transportation ☎306/787-3340, ⓦwww.sfn.saskatoon.sk.ca. Services across Saskatchewan.
SMT (Eastern) ☎506/859-5100, ⓦwww.smtbus.com. Buses within New Brunswick, plus services from New Brunswick to New York and Charlottetown, PEI.
Southwestern Bus Line ☎204/534-7111. Brandon to Boissevain in Manitoba.
Trentway-Wagar ☎705/748-6411 or 1-800/461-7661, ⓦwww.trentway.com. Wide range of services within southern Ontario, plus routes into the US and Québec.
Voyageur ☎1-800/668-4438, ⓦwww.voyageur.com. Québec and Ontario routes.
Western Trailways of Canada ☎604/940-5561, ⓦwww.cantrail.com. Vancouver to Seattle.

By train

The railway may have created modern Canada but, following swingeing cuts in the 1990s, passenger trains are now few and far between. Many services on the national **VIA Rail** (☎1-888/842-7245, ⓦwww.viarail.ca) are notoriously slow and delays are common, since passenger trains must give way to freight, though the city links between Montréal and Toronto are speedy and efficient. However, rail travel can still be a very rewarding experience, especially on trains with special "vista dome" cars that allow an uninterrupted rooftop view of the countryside.

There are several flagship train routes that survived the cuts (albeit in sometimes altered form). In general, you get a choice of four kinds of ticket on these. **Comfort Class** (the renamed Economy) is the most basic, with a reclining seat and access to a public coffee lounge and dome car, but no extras. Beyond that are three levels of sleeper, known as **Silver & Blue Class**, all of which include meals in the restaurant car, access to comfortable lounges, a more exclusive dome car, and hot showers down the corridor. The "section" sleepers feature an upper berth and a more roomy lower berth, both curtained off; otherwise, you can opt for a "roomette" for one person, or a bedroom for two.

The sightseeing trains – which all feature renovated classic rolling stock – are targeted for an upgrade in the next few years to the kind of super-luxurious, ultra-modern trains plying the commuter routes between Toronto, Ottawa and Montréal. For more information, check ⓦwww.viarail.ca or the encyclopedic – and incredibly useful – train-buffs' website ⓦwww.seat61.com.

Train routes, fares and passes

One of the saddest losses of the VIA cutbacks was the legendary service which followed the old Canadian Pacific lines from Montréal to Vancouver. Today's **"Canadian"** departs three times a week from Toronto to Vancouver and uses the more northerly old Canadian National lines, through the muskeg of northern Ontario, stopping at Winnipeg, Saskatoon and Edmonton before hitting Jasper – beyond which, the scenery to Kamloops and on to Vancouver is some of the Rockies' best. The trip is scheduled to take three nights; in peak season, reckon on $617 in comfort class, $1197 in an upper berth, $1317 in a lower berth or $2534 in a bedroom.

Otherwise, the most popular sightseeing routes are the day-long **Ocean**, on a scenic coast-hugging line from Montréal to Halifax; the **Bras d'Or**, which runs twice a week year-round from Halifax to Sydney; and the **Skeena**, following the two-day "Totem Route" from Jasper to Prince Rupert for the Inside Passage. There are plenty of other scenic routes in operation, but most are difficult to book from outside Canada: in the **west**, these include services from Winnipeg to Churchill, and Victoria to Courtenay; in the **east**, there are trains linking Toronto with Windsor, Ottawa and Niagara Falls, as well as from Montréal to Québec City and Ottawa, and between Montréal and the Gaspé. To give an idea of fares, the trip from Toronto to Winnipeg costs $318 in comfort class, $621 for an upper berth, $731 for a lower berth and $1407 in a bedroom. Check closely for any discounts, and for reduced rates if you travel at off-peak times and/or if you book well ahead.

A handful of sightseeing trains are run by companies other than VIA Rail, often accessing otherwise inaccessible wilderness areas. Most spectacular is the **Rocky Mountaineer** (☎1-877/460-3200 or 604/606-7245, ⊛www.rkymtnrail.com). This operates from Vancouver to Jasper, or Vancouver to Banff and Calgary, and is run as a two-day trip in full daylight, with an overnight hotel stop in Kamloops included in the price. Trains, which are swiftly booked out, run from mid-April to mid-October only. Two classes operate: in peak season, reckon on on $1459 to Banff or Jasper, or $1579 to Calgary, in GoldLeaf class; or $779/849 in RedLeaf class. Ontario Northland's **Polar Bear Express** (mid-June to Aug Tues–Sun only; ☎1-800/268-9281 or 705/472-4500 ext 489, ⊛www.polarbearexpress.ca) takes four hours from Cochrane north to Moosonee for $58; other, local-oriented trains (including the Little Bear and the Northlander) run on the same track, as well as from Cochrane south to Toronto. The **Algoma Central Railway** (☎1-800/242-9287 or 705/946-7300, ⊛www.agawacanyontourtrain.com) runs a handful of excursions through Agawa Canyon year-round. The **White Pass & Yukon Railway** (mid-May to mid-Sept; ☎1-800/343-7373 or 907/983-2217, ⊛www.whitepassrailroad.com), linked to the Alaska Railroad, runs a bus service from Whitehorse that links up with the train route from Fraser to Skagway. The **Hull-Chelsea-Wakefield steam train** (May–Oct; ☎1-800/871-7246 or 819/778-7246, ⊛www.steamtrain.ca) operates Canada's last steam train from just near Ottawa for $39 return, slightly more in fall.

Non-North American visitors can cut fares greatly by buying a **Canrailpass** (June to mid-Oct $719; rest of year $448), which allows unlimited Comfort Class travel for twelve days within a thirty-day period. You can buy up to three extra days, at $61/39 each. Otherwise, the **Corridorpass** covers ten days' travel in southern Québec and southern Ontario only, for a year-round price of $235. The **North America Rail Pass**

(June to mid-Oct $975, rest of year $690) – buyable by anyone – allows unlimited travel on VIA trains in Canada and Amtrak trains in the US for thirty days. The fifteen-day **Northeastern North America Rail Pass** ($569/429) – buyable only by non-North Americans – covers travel in the northeastern US and eastern Canada. The Moose Travel Network (see box p.32) also has some handy rail passes for popular routes.

VIA Rail agents worldwide

Australia Asia Pacific Travel Marketing Services ☎02/9319 6624, ⊛www.aptms.com.au.
New Zealand Discover Holidays ☎09/529 4796, ⊛www.discoverholidays.com.
UK 1st Rail ☎0845/644 3553, ⊛www.1strail.com.

By air

The complexity of Canada's **domestic flights** network is immense, and throughout this book we have given indications of which services are most useful. Air Canada has the most prolific domestic service, with planes serving more than 125 destinations, linking up with numerous minor lines – such as Labrador Airways in Labrador – to reach the farthest-flung recesses of Canada. Several low-cost airlines are also worth a look for connections between Canada's main cities. However, no one could pretend that flying around Canada is, in general terms at least, a low-budget option. For special bargains, look in the travel sections of local newspapers, especially on Sundays, or splash out on one of the many varieties of airpass, each of which brings hefty discounts. If you're set on exploring the deep north, there is no alternative to air transport, as these zones are unpenetrated by rail line or road (with a few rare exceptions, such as Churchill).

A multitude of **airpasses** provide internal air travel at special rates. The passes have to be bought – from a travel agent – before you take your intercontinental flight into Canada. All the deals are broadly similar, involving the purchase of at least three coupons for around £200 or equivalent (with a maximum purchase of eight). Extra coupons cost around £30 each. Every coupon is valid for a flight of any duration within the continent. Air Canada, with the strongest domestic connections, has a good variety of passes; study the possibilities carefully before committing yourself.

Major airlines in Canada

Air Canada ☎1-888/247-2262, ⓦwww.aircanada.com. Also operates under regional brands Air Canada Jazz, and no-frills Tango (☎1-800/315-1390, ⓦwww.flytango.com).
Air North ☎1-800/661-0407, ⓦwww.flyairnorth.com. Northern Canada & Alaska.
Air Transat ☎1-800/587-2672, ⓦwww.airtransat.com. Charter airline.
Bearskin Airlines ☎1-800/465-2327, ⓦwww.bearskinairlines.com. Ontario and Manitoba.
Canadian North ☎1-800/661-1505, ⓦwww.airnorterra.ca.
Canadian Western ☎1-866/835-9292, ⓦwww.cwair.com.
Canjet Airlines ☎1-800/809-7777, ⓦwww.canjet.com. Eastern Canada low-cost carrier.
Central Mountain Air ☎1-888/865-8585, ⓦwww.flycma.com. Serves British Columbia and Alberta.
Jetsgo ☎1-866/440-0441, ⓦwww.jetsgo.net. Serves main Canadian cities, with connections to the US.
WestJet ☎1-888/WEST-JET, ⓦwww.westjet.com. Reliable low-cost operator between major cities.
Zip ☎1-866/4321-ZIP, ⓦwww.4321zip.com. Low-cost airline owned by Air Canada but independently run.

By car

Travelling by **car** is the best way to see Canada, even though a vehicle can be a bit of a liability in the big cities, with their stringent parking areas and rush-hour tailbacks. Any US, UK, Australian or New Zealand national over 21 with a full driving licence is allowed to drive in Canada, though rental companies may refuse to rent to a driver who has held a full licence for less than one year, and under-25s will probably get lumbered with a higher insurance premium. Car-rental companies will also expect you to have a credit card; if you don't have one they may refuse to rent to you.

Most of Canada's vehicles – and almost every rental car – run on **unleaded fuel**, which is sold by the litre. Gas stations are plentiful, though they thin out markedly in the more remote regions, where you should fill up where you can.

On the road

The best **roads** for covering long distances quickly are the straight and fast multi-lane highways that radiate for some distance from major population centres. These are generally four lanes – more in busy urban stretches – divided by a central causeway and are marked on maps with thick lines and shields that contain the highway number. The **Trans-Canada Highway** (**TCH**) travels from coast to coast and is marked by maple-leaf signs at regular intervals along its length. Different sections of the TCH do, however, carry different highway numbers and in some places the TCH forks to offer more than one possible routing. **Exits** on multi-lane highways are numbered by the kilometre distance from the beginning of the highway, not sequentially – thus exit 55 is 10km after exit 45. This system works fine, but gets a little confusing when junctions are close together and carry the same number supplemented by "A" and "B".

Outside populated areas, highways go down to one lane each way and, though

Ride-sharing

Ride-sharing is an established means of travel within the more heavily populated parts of Canada. Organizations coordinating ride-share travel come and go – local tourist offices will have the latest details – but Allo-Stop, with its main office in Montréal, is well established. With them, all you pay is a nominal registration fee and a share of the fuel costs: Toronto to Ottawa will set you back about $30, less if you are with other people. Rides are also routinely advertised on university and hostel notice boards.

paved, the hard shoulder is gravel: take care, since if you hit the gravel at speed you may be thrown into a spin. In the north and off the beaten track, highways may be entirely of gravel (cracked windscreens are an occupational hazard on some stretches of the Alaska Highway). Note also that after rain gravel and dirt roads are especially treacherous; if you're planning a lot of dirt-road driving, you'd be well advised to rent a four-wheel-drive. Lesser roads go by a variety of names – county roads, provincial routes, rural roads or forest roads.

Rural **road hazards** include bears, moose and other large animals trundling into the road – particularly in the summer, and at dawn and dusk, when the beasts crash through the undergrowth onto the highway to escape the flies, and in spring, when they are attracted to the salt on the roads. Warning signs are posted in the more hazardous areas. Headlights can dazzle wild animals and render them temporarily immobile.

In cities **parking meters** are commonplace, charging 25¢–$1 or more per hour. Car parks charge up to $30 a day. If you park in the wrong place (such as within 5m of a fire hydrant) your car will be towed away – if this happens, the police will tell you where your car is impounded and then charge you upwards of $150 to hand it back. A minor parking offence will set you back around $30; wheel-clamps are also routinely used in major cities, with a fine of between $100 and $150. Also, when parking, ensure you park in the same direction as the traffic flow.

If you're using your own vehicle – or borrowing a friend's – get the appropriate insurance and make sure you're covered for free **breakdown service**. Your home motoring organization will issue an appropriate insurance and breakdown policy with all the appropriate documentation.

Rules of the road

Canadians drive on the **right-hand** side of the road. In most **urban areas** streets are arranged on a grid system, with traffic lights at most intersections; at junctions without lights there will be either yellow triangular "Yield" signs or red octagonal "Stop" signs ("Arrêt" in Québec) at all four corners. In the latter case, **priority** is given to the first car to arrive, and to the car on the right if two or more cars arrive at the same time. Except in Montréal you can turn right on a red light if there is no traffic approaching from the left. Traffic in both directions must stop if a yellow school bus is stationary with its flashing lights on, as this means children are getting on or off. Roundabouts or rotaries are almost unknown.

Driving laws are made at provincial level, but the uniform **maximum speed limit** is 100kph on major highways, 80kph on rural highways and 50kph or less in built-up areas – though there has been some provincial tinkering with the maximum limit on the highways. Canadians have a justifiable paranoia about speed traps and the traffic-control planes that hover over major highways to catch offenders. **On-the-spot fines** are standard for speeding violations, for failing to carry your licence with you, and for having anyone on board who isn't wearing a seat belt. Possession of radar detectors is illegal in most of Canada – even if they aren't being used – and can result in confiscation and or a hefty fine.

Canadian law requires that any alcohol be carried unopened in the boot of the car, and it can't be stressed enough that **drunk driving** is a very serious offence. Bars in some provinces now have **designated driver schemes** whereby the driver of a group gives the keys to the head barperson and is then given free soft drinks all night; if the driver is spotted taking a sip of alcohol, he or she must pay for all the soft drinks consumed and leave their keys in the bar until the following morning. On the road, spot checks are frequently carried out, particularly at the entrances and exits to towns, and the police do not need an excuse to stop you. If you are over the limit your keys and licence will be taken away, and you may end up in jail.

Renting a car or RV

Often the least expensive way to **rent a car** is either to take a fly-drive package or book in advance with a major rental company like Avis, Budget, Hertz, Thrifty or Tilden (a Canadian outfit). Competition is fierce and, as you might expect, special deals are more commonplace in the shoulder and low seasons when there are scores of vehicles lying idle. It's a good idea, when you book your intercontinental flight ticket into Canada, to check whether your airline offers discounted car rental for its passengers.

In Canada itself, expect to pay from around $275 a week for a two-door economy saloon in low season to $450 for a four-door medium car in high season, though throughout the year special promotions are offered by the major companies, which can get rates down to as low as $200 per week. Provincial **taxes** and GST or HST (see box, p.30) are not included in the rates, but the biggest hidden surcharge is often the **drop-off charge**, levied when you intend to leave your car in a different place from where you picked it up. This is usually equivalent to a full week's or more rental, and can go as high as $500. Also be sure to check if **unlimited mileage** is offered – an important consideration in a country where towns are so widely dispersed. The usual free quota is 150–200km per day – woefully inadequate if you're contemplating some serious touring – after which an extra charge of around 20¢ per kilometre is standard. You should also check the policy for the excess applied to claims and ensure that, in general terms, it provides adequate levels of financial cover. Additionally, the **Loss Damage Waiver** (LDW), a form of insurance that isn't included in the initial rental charge, is well worth the expense. At around $15 a day, it can add substantially to the total cost, but without it you're liable for every scratch to the car – even if it wasn't your fault.

For **breakdown** problems, there'll be an emergency number attached to the dashboard or stored in the glove compartment. If you're stranded on a major highway, you could do as well to sit tight and wait for the RCMP (the police) who cruise by fairly regularly. An extra safety option is to **rent a mobile phone** from the car-rental agency – you often only have to pay a nominal amount unless you actually use it. Having a mobile can be reassuring at least, and a potential life-saver for trips into the northern wilderness.

If you take a rental car **into the US**, be sure to keep a copy of the contract with you. It should bear an endorsement stating that the vehicle is permitted entry into the US.

A "recreational vehicle" or **RV** (some variation on a motorhome) can be rented through most travel agents specializing in Canadian holidays. It's best to arrange rental before getting to Canada, as RV-rental outlets are not too common there, and travel agents at home will often give cheap rates if you book a flight through them as well. You can rent a huge variety of RVs right up to giant mobile homes with two bedrooms, showers and fully fitted kitchens. A price of around $1400 in low season, $2200 in high season, for a five-berth van for one week is fairly typical, and on top of that you have to take into account the cost of fuel (some RVs do less than 25km to the litre), drop-off charges, and the cost of spending the night at designated trailer parks, which is what you're expected to do. Canada also has strict regulations on the size of vehicle allowed; in Ontario, for example, the maximum length for a trailer is 48 feet, 75 feet for trailer plus car – so if you are coming in from the US check that your RV isn't over the limit.

Driveaways

A variation on car rental is a **driveaway**, where you deliver a car from one place to another for the owner. The same rules apply as for renting, but you should look the car over before taking it as you'll be lumbered with any repair costs and a large fuel bill if the vehicle's a gas guzzler. Most driveaway companies will want you to give a personal reference as well as a deposit of up to $500. The most common routes are along the Trans-Canada Highway and between Toronto or Montréal and Florida in the autumn and winter, although there's a fair chance you'll find something that needs shifting more or less to wherever you want to go. You needn't drive flat out, although not a lot of leeway is given – around eight days is the time allowed for driving from Toronto to Vancouver. We've included details of driveaway companies in some city listings, or check under "Automobile driveaways" in the phone directory.

Driving distances in kilometres

The figures shown on this chart represent the total distances in kilometres between selected cities in the Canada and the US. They are calculated on the shortest available route by road, rather than straight lines drawn on a map. For conversion, the figure in miles is roughly two-thirds of that given in kilometres: 8km equals 5 miles.

	Calgary	Chicago	Edmonton	Halifax	Montréal	New York	Ottawa	Regina	St John's	Seattle	Toronto	Vancouver	Whitehorse	Winnipeg	Yellowknife
Calgary	–														
Chicago	2760	–													
Edmonton	299	2750	–												
Halifax	4973	2603	5013	–											
Montréal	3743	1362	3764	1249	–										
New York	4294	1280	4315	1270	610	–									
Ottawa	3553	1220	3574	1439	190	772	–								
Regina	764	2000	785	4225	2979	3534	2789	–							
St John's	6334	3950	6767	1503	2602	2619	2792	5581	–						
Seattle	1204	3200	1352	5828	4585	4478	4334	1963	7200	–					
Toronto	3434	825	3455	1788	539	880	399	2670	3141	4050	–				
Vancouver	977	3808	1164	5970	4921	5382	4531	1742	7323	230	4412	–			
Whitehorse	2385	4854	2086	7099	5850	6427	5660	2871	8452	2796	5528	2697	–		
Winnipeg	1336	1432	1357	3456	2408	2966	2218	571	5010	2548	2099	2152	3524	–	
Yellowknife	1828	4240	1524	6537	5268	5600	5098	2309	7891	2500	4979	2620	1927	2681	–

International car rental companies

Avis UK ☎0870/606 0100, Ireland ☎021/428 1111, US ☎1-800/230-4898, Canada ☎1-800/272-5871, Australia ☎136333, New Zealand ☎0800/655111, Ⓦwww.avis.com.

Budget UK ☎0800/181181, Ireland ☎01/878 7814, US & Canada ☎1-800/527-0700, Australia ☎1300/362848, New Zealand ☎0800/652277, Ⓦwww.budget-international.com.

Hertz UK ☎0870/844 8844, Ireland ☎01/676 7476, US ☎1-800/654-3001, Canada ☎1-800/263-0600, Australia ☎1800/550067, New Zealand ☎0800/655955, Ⓦwww.hertz.com.

Thrifty UK ☎01494/751600, US & Canada ☎1-800/367-2277, Australia ☎1300/367227, New Zealand ☎09/309 0111, Ⓦwww.thrifty.com.

Motoring organizations

Australia AAA ☎02/6247 7311, Ⓦwww.aaa.asn.au.

Canada CAA ☎613/247-0117, Ⓦwww.caa.ca.

Ireland AA Ireland ☎01/617 9999, Ⓦwww.aaireland.ie.

New Zealand AA ☎0800/500444, Ⓦwww.nzaa.co.nz.

UK AA ☎0870/600 0371, Ⓦwww.theaa.com; RAC ☎0800/092 2222, Ⓦwww.rac.co.uk; Green Flag ☎0800/328 8772, Ⓦwww.greenflag.com.

US AAA ☎1-800/222-4357, Ⓦwww.aaa.com.

By bike

Cyclists are reasonably well catered for in ecofriendly Canada: most cities have cycling lanes and produce special maps for cyclists, and long-distance buses and trains will allow you to transport your bike, perhaps for a small fee. An interesting on-going project is the development of a coast-to-coat cyclepath, the Trans Canada trail (Ⓦwww.tctrail.ca), sections of which are already ready for cyclists. The Canadian Cycling Association (CCA) (☎613/748-5629, Ⓦwww.canadiancycling.com) has information on cycling throughout the country and publishes several books, including the invaluable *Complete Guide to Cycling in Canada*. Standard **bike-rental** costs are around $15 per day, plus a sizeable cash sum or a credit card as deposit; outlets are listed throughout the guide.

Accommodation

Accommodation isn't hugely expensive in Canada, but is still likely to take a good portion of your budget. The least expensive options are camping and dormitory beds in hostels, where prices start at around $15 but be aware that campgrounds and hostels in cities are heavily used. In hotels and motels, double rooms start at around $60 – less in rural areas away from the big sights. People on their own pay relatively more, but for travellers in pairs or groups motels and hotels can work out costing little more than hostels.

Canada is big and empty. If you're heading into remote parts of the country, always check the availability of accommodation before setting off. Places that look large on the map often have few facilities at all, and US visitors will find motels far scarcer than in similar regions back home.

Wherever you intend to stay, it's best to try to **book a room** well before you arrive,

particularly in summer and especially in big national parks like Banff and major cities such as Montréal, Québec, Toronto and Vancouver. Also look out for local events and festivals such as the Calgary Stampede, when accommodation is always at a premium. If you're arriving late, let the hotel know, as **reservations** are generally held only until 6pm, or even 4pm in major resorts. You can

Accommodation price codes

Throughout this book, accommodation prices have been graded with the **codes** below, corresponding to the cost of the least expensive double room in high season. However, with the exception of the budget motels and lowliest hotels, there's rarely such a thing as a set rate for a room. A basic motel in a seaside or mountain resort may double its prices according to the season, while a big-city hotel in Québec or Vancouver that charges $200 per room during the week will often slash its tariff at the weekend when all the business visitors have gone home. The high and low seasons for tourists vary widely across the country, but as a general rule **high season** refers to July and August, **shoulder season** is May, June, September and October, and **low season** refers to the rest of the year.

Local and federal **taxes** will also add around fifteen percent to quoted rates. Only where we explicitly say so do the room rates we've indicated include local taxes; everywhere else, they exclude taxes.

- ❶ up to $40
- ❷ $41–60
- ❸ $61–80
- ❹ $81–100
- ❺ $101–125
- ❻ $126–175
- ❼ $176–240
- ❽ over $241

reserve over the phone by credit card. Wherever possible take advantage of **toll-free numbers**, but note that some are accessible only in restricted areas, typically a single province, or in Canada only; you can often dial these numbers from abroad, but at standard international rates. It can also be worth confirming check-in/check-out times, particularly in busy areas, where your room may not be available until late afternoon. Check-out times are generally between 11am and 1pm. Be certain to **cancel** any bookings you can't make, otherwise the hotel or motel is within its rights to deduct a night's fee using your credit card details. Most places have a 24-hour-notice cancellation policy, but in places like Banff it can be as much as three days.

Also be prepared to pay for at least the first night **in advance**, and be ready for a fifteen percent surcharge to a room's advertised price, the result of provincial sales and federal **taxes**. Costs can be kept down if you're in a group – most places will set up a third bed in a double room for around $15 – though single travellers have a hard time of it, for single rooms are usually double rooms let out at only marginally reduced rates. Costs also come down outside high season, typically mid-May to early September (Labour Day), when the country's smartest hotels often offer especially large discounts.

Also be on the lookout for weekend rates, or last-minute deals offered by hotels trying to fill empty rooms.

Local **tourist information offices** can often help out with accommodation if you get stuck: most offer free advice and will book a place free of charge, but few are willing to commit themselves to specific recommendations. Some large resorts have a privately run central reservations agency that will find rooms for a small fee. Before going to Canada it's worth picking up the full accommodation and camping listings put out by the provinces (see p.22 for office addresses); they all give details of prices, size and facilities.

Hotels

It is consistently easy to find a plain room in all but the more remote backwoods. Drivers approaching any significant town or city are confronted by ranks of motels on prominent highways, neon signs advertising their presence, room rates and room availability. In-town **hotels** tend to fall into one of two categories: high-class five-star establishments or grim downtown places, often above a bar. Middle-ground spots are thin on the ground, their role often being filled by motels, which are basically out-of-town hotels by another name.

Top-of-the-range hotels can be very grand indeed, for instance particularly those run by Canadian Pacific in busy tourist spots like Québec City, Banff and Lake Louise. In the cities, the emphasis is on the business traveller rather more than the tourist. Top-notch hotels charge anywhere between $150 and $500, though $250 would get you a fairly luxurious double in most places. It's always worth enquiring about midweek reductions and out-of-season discounts, as these can reduce rates to as low as $100 a night. If you are going to treat yourself, consider whether you want the sort of old-style comfort and building offered by traditional hotels or the high-tech polish provided by an ultra-modern establishment; most cities and some resorts have both types.

Mid-price hotels are often part of a chain, such as *Holiday Inn* or *Best Western*, and usually offer a touch more comfort than middling motels. You should be able to find a high-season double in such places from around $90; more if you're in a well-known resort or the downtown area of a major city.

Bottom-bracket hotels – those costing anything from $35 to $55 – are mostly hangovers from the days when liquor laws made it difficult to run a bar without an adjoining restaurant or hotel. Found in most medium- and small-sized towns, they usually have the advantage of being extremely central – often they've been there since the town first sprang to life – but the disadvantage is that the money-generating bars usually come first, with the rooms mostly an afterthought. Many have strip joints or live music likely to pound until the small hours, and few pay much attention to their guests, many of whom are long-stay clients as seedy as the hotel itself. Rooms are mostly battered but clean, but probably won't have much in the way of facilities beyond a washbasin and TV. Basic meals are often on hand in the bar, though you'd usually do better to eat in a nearby café or restaurant.

Motels

Motels may be called inns, lodges, resorts or motor hotels, but they all amount to much the same thing: driver-friendly, reasonably priced and reliable places on the main highways almost always on the edge of town.

The simplest rooms start at around $45, with the **average** price nearer $60 – though in resorts and more remote areas it's not unusual to find well over $100 being charged for what are fairly basic rooms. As a rule of thumb, prices drop in the larger centres the further you move from downtown. Many offer **off-season rates**, usually between October and April, some have triple- or quadruple-bedded rooms, and most are fairly relaxed about introducing an extra bed into "doubles" for a nominal charge. Many also offer a **Family Plan**, whereby youngsters sharing their parents' room stay free. You may also be able to negotiate cheaper deals if you're staying more than one night, and especially if you're staying a week – many places advertise weekly rates.

In all but the most basic motels you can expect a remarkably good standard: a good-sized double bed, a private bathroom, TV and phone, while in smarter places there may be frills like free coffee and the use of saunas, Jacuzzis, sun beds and swimming pools. Often there's not much to be gained in paying extra for motels: you don't get a much better deal or better facilities by paying, say, $75 instead of $50. Some places, though, have rooms with **kitchenettes** for self-catering, or basic cooking facilities, either included in the room price or available for a few dollars more. More ritzy spots may also have a small restaurant, but generally you can expect nothing in the way of **food and drink** except for a soft-drinks machine and coffee-maker in the room. What they all have is good parking, often right in front of the door to your room.

B&Bs

In recent years there has been a dramatic increase in the number of **B&Bs** or **Gîtes du Passant** both in the big cities and in the towns and villages of the more popular resort areas. Standards in B&B homes or guesthouses are generally very high, and prices are around $50 and upwards per couple including breakfast. There are no real savings over cheaper hotels and motels. This said, you may wind up with a wonderful – if often over-homely – room in a heritage building in a great location, with the chance to meet Canadians on closer terms. There are, however, things to watch out for and ask about when making a booking. There's an increasing tendency to provide a light continental breakfast rather than a cooked meal with all the trimmings that'll set you up for the day. Establishments are often keen to indicate whether they have a private guest entrance, useful if you're likely to be staggering in late or simply don't particularly want to mix with your hosts. Another trend is for smaller hotels to advertise themselves as a "Bed and Breakfast Inn", or something similar, meaning simply that they're privately owned rather than in the hands of a chain. These are usually intimate but rather expensive places and not B&Bs in the accepted sense. B&B establishments have a quite rapid turnover, so to find one it's often best to visit tourist offices, many of which have bulging catalogues and photographs of what's available, or in the big cities contact one of the many private agencies who can line you up with something suitable. Take careful note of an establishment's location; in cities and larger towns they're often out in the suburbs and inconvenient for transport and downtown sights, though some hosts will pick you up from the airport or bus station on your arrival.

Hostels

Canada has about eighty Hostelling International (**HI**) hostels affiliated to what was formerly known as the International Youth Hostels Federation (IYHF), and many more nonaffiliated mini-hostels (also known as Homes or Backpackers' Hostels), which may or may not figure in HI literature. Reports suggest certain non-affiliated hostels are slipping in standard as their cheap beds are appropriated by long-stay clients rather than by genuine visitors on a budget. Some are downright unsafe. These sorts of places are also often shoestring operations and may close at short notice. Similarly, new ones appear each year. Try to check local reputations at tourist offices or by word of mouth.

HI hostels are graded in four categories – basic, simple, standard and superior. Accommodation is mostly in **single-sex dorms**, which cost $15–25 for members,

depending on category and location, though family and private **double rooms** are becoming more prevalent. In theory you're supposed to be an HI member to use hostels; in practice you can usually join the HI on the spot, or rely on most hostels making a slightly higher charge for nonmembers ($17–28). However, most hostels will generally give preference to HI members, which is an important consideration in some of the more popular locations. Most offer communal recreation areas and all have cooking facilities, plus pillows and blankets, though you're expected to provide, or rent, your own sheet sleeping bag and towels. Normal sleeping bags are generally not allowed.

Many hostels have improved beyond recognition in the past few years: premises have been renovated, hostels are open longer and later, cafeterias have been introduced, and the booking system has been partly computerized. You can now book up to six months in advance at the bigger, or gateway, hostels – notably those in the Rockies, where hostels at Banff and Calgary act as central booking agents for a number of smaller hostels around the region. Most major hostels now accept credit-card bookings online or by phone, with **reservations** strongly recommended in summer for city hostels and most of the Rockies' hostels. Most HI offices around the world stock the comprehensive Hostelling North America handbook, as do many of Canada's larger hostels.

Mini-hostels tend to be private homes or tiny commercial hotels with breakfast included. Prices are about $10–20, with a surcharge for nonmembers, and you must have your own sheet sleeping bag. A full current list is available from most larger hostels.

HI hostelling organizations

Australia ☎ 02/9261 1111, ⓦ www.yha.com.au.
Canada ☎ 1-800/663-5777, ⓦ www.hihostels.ca.
England & Wales ☎ 0870/870 8808,
ⓦ www.yha.org.uk.
Ireland ☎ 01/830 4555, ⓦ www.anoige.ie.
Northern Ireland ☎ 028/9032 4733,
ⓦ www.hini.org.uk.
New Zealand ☎ 0800/278299,
ⓦ www.yha.co.nz.

Scotland ☎0870/155 3255, ⓦwww.syha
.org.uk.
USA ☎301/495-1240, ⓦwww.hiayh.org.

Ys and student accommodation

Both the **YMCA** and **YWCA** – individually abbreviated to "the Y" – have establishments in most Canadian cities. In many cases the quality of accommodation is excellent, matching that of the cheaper hotels, and invariably exceeding that of most other hostel-type lodgings. Often the premises have cheap cafeterias open to all, and sports facilities, gymnasium and pools for the use of guests. **Prices**, however, reflect the comforts, and though you can usually find bunks in shared dorms from about $15, the trend is increasingly for single, double and family units (with or without private bathrooms), ranging between $30 and $100. This still reflects excellent value, especially in cities, where Ys are usually in central downtown locations. As Ys become more like hotels, so you need to treat them as such, with credit-card **reservations** in advance virtually essential to secure private singles and doubles in high summer. Most places keep a number of rooms and dorm bunks available each day for walk-in customers, though in places like Banff it's not unknown for queues for these to develop around the block first thing in the morning. The old demarcation of the sexes is also breaking down, though many YWCAs will only accept men if they're in a mixed-sex couple. Some YWCAs accept women with children, others only in emergencies.

In Canada's university cities it's possible to stay in **student accommodation** during vacations. Anyone can use the facilities, though priority is usually given to other students. Often the accommodation is adequate and functional, if soulless, and you'll have access to the campus's sports facilities; on the downside, most places are a good distance from city centres. Prices for single and double rooms start from about $35. Most campuses have a special office to handle such accommodation, and it's a good idea to call well ahead to be sure of a room.

Farm vacations

Farm vacations, on which you spend time as a paying guest on a working farm, give you the chance to eat well, sleep cheaply – and even work (if you want) – as well as mingle with your hosts. Ontario has a range of farm-based B&Bs with reasonably priced accommodation. In western Canada, it's possible to stay on a ranch and work as a ranch-hand. Due to the isolation of these places prices are usually for full board and include riding (from £75 per day). For further details, consult tourist offices and provincial accommodation guides. One agency in the UK offering ranch holidays is Farm Tours (ⓦwww.itiscanada.co.uk).

Camping

Few countries offer as much scope for **camping** as Canada. Many urban areas have a campsite; all national parks and the large proportion of provincial parks have outstanding government-run sites, and in most wilderness areas and in the vast domain of Canada's federally owned Crown Lands you can camp rough more or less where you please, though you should ask permission where possible and – for your own safety and the sake of the environment – adhere strictly to all rules and recommendations that apply to camping in the backcountry. If you're travelling with a tent, check a campsite's small print for the number of **unserviced** (tent) sites, as many places cater chiefly for recreational vehicles (**RVs**), providing them with full or partial hook-ups for water and electricity (or "serviced sites"). Anywhere described as an "RV Park" ought to be avoided completely (unless, of course, you have an RV).

During July and August campsites can become as busy as all other types of accommodation in cities, and particularly near mountain, lake or river resorts. Either aim to arrive early in the morning or **book ahead**; we've given phone numbers wherever this is possible. Generally reservations can only be made at private campsites, not – crucially – at national park or provincial park campsites, where access is mostly on a first-come, first-served basis. This state of affairs is, however, slowly changing, with places at a selection of provincial and national park campsites now reservable through a reservation phone number. Finally, check that your chosen site is open: many campsites only open seasonally, usually from May to October.

Campsite types

At the bottom of the pile are **municipal campsites**, usually basic affairs with few facilities, which are either free or cost only a few dollars – typically $5 per tent, $10 per RV, though many often have tent places only. **Private campsites** run the gamut: some are as basic as their municipal cousins, others are like huge outdoor pleasure domes with shops, restaurants, laundries, swimming pools, tennis courts, even saunas and Jacuzzis. As for **price**, private campsites have several ways of charging. Some charge by the vehicle, others per couple, comparatively few on a tent or per-person basis. Two people sharing a tent might pay anything between $2.50 and $25 each, though an average price would be nearer $15. You can book places in private campsites but there's often no need outside busy areas as most are obliged to keep a certain number of pitches available on a first-come, first-served basis.

Campsites in **national and provincial parks** are run by Parks Canada and individual provincial governments respectively. All are immaculately turned out and most, in theory, are open only between May and September. In practice most are available all year round, though key facilities are offered and fees collected only in the advertised period: off season you may be expected to leave fees in an "honesty box". You'll usually find at least one site serviced for **winter camping** in the bigger national parks, particularly in the Rockies. **Prices** vary from about $8.50 to $25 per tent depending on location, services and the time of year – prices may be higher during July and August. See "Outdoor pursuits", p.55, for more details.

Sites in the **major national parks**, especially close to towns, usually offer a full range of amenities for both tents and RVs, and often have separate sites for each. As a rule, though, provincial sites and more remote national park campsites tend to favour tents and offer only water, stores of firewood and pit toilets. Hot showers, in particular, are rare. But both national park and provincial sites, of course, invariably score highly on their scenic locations. Both types of park campsite fill most of their pitches on a first-come, first-served basis, but a growing number of parks are setting up reservation services.

Primitive camping

Camping rough – or **primitive camping** (or backcountry camping) as it's known in Canada – has certain rules that must be followed. Check that fires are permitted before you start one: in large parts of Canada they aren't allowed in summer because of the risk of forest fire. If they are permitted, use a fire pit (if provided), or a stove in preference to local materials. In wilderness areas, try to camp on previously used sites. Be especially aware of the precautions needed when in **bear country** (see p.686). Where there are no toilets, bury human waste at least 10cm into the ground and 30m from the nearest water supply and campsite. Canadian parks ask for all rubbish to be carried away; elsewhere burn rubbish, and what you can't burn, carry away. **Never drink** from rivers and streams, however clear and inviting they may look. If you have to drink **water** that isn't from taps, you should boil it for at least ten minutes, or cleanse it with an iodine-based purifier (such as Potable Aqua) or a Giardia-rated filter, available from camping or sports shops.

Eating and drinking

Canada's sheer number of restaurants, bars, cafés and fast-food joints is staggering, but at first sight there's little to distinguish mainstream Canadian urban cuisine from that of any American metropolis: the shopping malls, main streets and highways are lined with pan-American food chains, trying to outdo each other with their bargains and special offers.

However, it's easy to leave the chain restaurants behind for more interesting options – increasingly so, as the general standard of Canadian cooking has improved dramatically in the last few years. In the big cities there's a plethora of ethnic and speciality restaurants; on either seaboard the availability of fresh fish and shellfish enlivens many menus, and even out in the country – once the domain of unappetizing diners – there's a liberal supply of first-rate, family-run cafés and restaurants, especially in the more touristed areas. Non-smokers may also be relieved to know that almost every café and restaurant has a **no-smoking area** and increasing numbers don't allow smoking at all.

Breakfast

Breakfast is taken very seriously all over Canada, and with prices averaging between $5 and $13 it's often the best-value and most filling meal of the day. Whether you go to a café, coffee shop or hotel snack bar, the breakfast menu, on offer until around 11am, is a fairly standard fry-up: **eggs** in various guises, ham or **bacon** (streaky and fried to a crisp), or bland, skinless **sausages** (except for Nova Scotia's famous Lunenburg sausage, a hot spicy version pioneered by settlers from Europe). Whatever you order, you nearly always receive a dollop of fried potatoes, called **hash browns** or, sometimes, **home fries**. Other favourite breakfast options include English **muffins** or, in posher places, bran muffins, a glutinous fruitcake made with bran and sugar, and **waffles** or **pancakes**, swamped in butter with lashings of maple syrup. Also, because the breakfast/lunch division is never hard and fast, mountainous meaty **sandwiches** are common too.

Whatever you eat, you can wash it down with as much **coffee** as you can stomach: for the price of the first cup, the wait staff will – in most places – keep providing free refills until you beg them to stop. The coffee is either regular or decaf and is nearly always freshly ground and very tasty, though lots of the cheaper places dilute it until it tastes like dishwater. In the big cities, look out also for specialist coffee shops, where the range of offerings verges on the bewildering. As a matter of course, coffee comes with cream or **half-and-half** (half-cream, half-milk) – if you ask for skimmed milk, you're often met with looks of disbelief. **Tea**, with either lemon or milk, is also drunk at breakfast, and the swisher places emphasize the English connection by using imported brands – or at least brands that sound English.

Lunch and snacks

Between 11.30am and 2.30pm many big-city restaurants offer special **set menus** that are generally excellent value. In Chinese and Vietnamese establishments, for example, you'll frequently find rice and noodles, or dim sum feasts for $8 to $12, and many **Japanese** restaurants give you a chance to eat sushi very reasonably for under $18. **Pizza** is also widely available, from larger chains like *Pizza Hut* to family-owned restaurants and pavement stalls. Favourites with white-collar workers are **café-restaurants** featuring wholefoods and vegetarian fare, though few are nutritionally dogmatic, serving traditional meat dishes and sandwiches too; most have an excellent selection of daily lunch specials for around $12.

For quick **snacks**, many **delis** do ready-cooked food, including a staggering range of sandwiches and filled bagels. Alternatively,

Tipping

Almost everywhere you eat or drink, the service will be fast and friendly – thanks to the institution of **tipping**. Waiters and bartenders depend on tips for the bulk of their earnings and, unless the service is dreadful, you should top up your bill by fifteen percent or more. A refusal to tip is considered rude and mean in equal measure. If you're paying by credit card, there's a space on the payment slip where you can add the appropriate tip.

shopping malls sometimes have **ethnic fast-food stalls**, a healthier option (just about) than the inevitable burger chains, whose homogenized products have colonized every main street in the land. Regional snacks include **fish and chips**, especially in Newfoundland; Québec's traditional thick, yellow pea soup, smoked meat sandwiches and **poutine**, fries covered in melted mozzarella cheese or cheese curds and gravy; and the Maritimes' ubiquitous **clam chowder**, a creamy shellfish and potato soup.

Some city **bars** are used as much by diners as drinkers, who turn up in droves to gorge themselves on the free **hors d'oeuvres** laid out between 5pm and 7pm from Monday to Friday in an attempt to grab commuters. For the price of a drink you can stuff yourself with pasta and chilli. **Brunch** is another deal worth looking out for; a cross between breakfast and lunch served up in bars at the weekend from around 11am to 2pm. For a set price ($10 and up) you get a light meal and a variety of complimentary cocktails or wine.

Regional dishes

Largely swamped by the more fashionable regional-European and ethnic cuisines, traditional **Canadian cooking** relies mainly on local game and fish, with less emphasis on vegetables and salads. In terms of price, meals for two without wine average between $25 and $50.

Newfoundland's staple food is the cod, usually in the form of fish and chips, supplemented by salmon, halibut and hake and more bizarre dishes like cod tongues and cheeks, scruncheons (fried cubes of pork fat), smoked or pickled caplin and seal flipper pie. The island's restaurants are not usually permitted to sell moose or seal meat, but many islanders join in the annual licensed

shoot and, if you befriend a hunter, you may end up across the table from a hunk of either animal.

In the **Maritimes**, lobster is popular everywhere, whether it's boiled or broiled, chopped up or whole, as are oysters, clams, scallops and herrings either on their own or in a fish stew or clam chowder. **Nova Scotia** is famous for its blueberries, Solomon Gundy (marinated herring), Annapolis Valley apple pie, fat archies (a Cape Breton molasses cookie) and rappie pie (an Acadian dish of meat or fish and potatoes). **New Brunswick** is known for its fiddleheads (fern shoots) and dulse (edible seaweed).

Fish is **Ontario**'s most distinctive offering, though the pollution of the Great Lakes has badly affected the freshwater catch. Try the whitefish, lake trout, pike and smelt, but bear in mind that these are easier to come by in the north of the province than in the south. Pork forms a major part of the **Québec** diet, both as a spicy pork pâté known as *creton*, and in *tourtière*, a minced pork pie. There are also splendid thick pea and cabbage soups, beef pies (*cipâte*), and all sorts of ways to soak up maple syrup – *trempette* is bread drenched with it and topped with fresh cream. And, of course, Québec is renowned for its outstanding French-style food.

Northern **Saskatchewan and Manitoba** are the places to try fish like the goldeye, pickerel and Arctic char, as well as pemmican (a mixture of dried meat, berries and fat) and fruit pies containing the Saskatoon berry. The **Arctic** regions feature caribou steak, and Alberta is also noted for its beef steaks. **British Columbia** cuisine features Pacific fish and shellfish of many different types, from cod, haddock and salmon to king crab, oysters and shrimp. Here and there, there's also the odd **aboriginal** peoples' restaurant, most conspicuously at the Wanuskewin Heritage Park in Saskatoon, Saskatchewan, where the restaurant serves venison, buffalo and black-husked wild rice.

Although there are exceptions, like the **Ukrainian** establishments spread across central Manitoba, the bulk of Canada's ethnic restaurants are confined to the cities. Here, amongst dozens of others, **Japanese** restaurants are fashionable and fairly expensive; **Italian** food is popular and generally cheap, providing you stick to pizzas and basic pasta dishes; and there's the occasional **Indian** restaurant, mostly catering for the inexpensive end of the market. **East European** food is a good, filling standby, especially in central Canada, and cheap **Chinese** restaurants are common throughout the country. **French** food, of course, is widely available – though, except in Québec, it's nearly always expensive.

Drinking

Canadian **bars**, like their American equivalents, are mostly long and dimly lit counters with a few customers perched on stools gawping at the bartender, and the rest of the clientele occupying the surrounding tables and booths. Yet, despite the similarity of layout, bars vary enormously, from the male-dominated, rough-edged drinking holes concentrated in the blue-collar parts of the cities and the resource towns (dealing in mining and oil) of the north, to more fashionable city establishments that provide food, live entertainment and an inspiring range of cocktails. Indeed, it's often impossible to separate restaurants from bars – drinking and eating are no longer the separate activities they mostly were up until the 1960s.

The **legal drinking age** is 18 in Alberta, Manitoba, Saskatchewan, Québec, Northwest Territories and the Yukon, and 19 in the rest of the country, though it's rare for anyone to have to show ID, except at the government-run liquor stores (closed Sun), which exercise a virtual monopoly on the sale of alcoholic beverages of all kinds direct to the public; the main exception is Québec, where beer and wine are sold at retail grocery stores.

Beer, wine and spirits

By and large, Canadian **beers** are unremarkable, designed to quench your thirst rather than satisfy your palate. Everywhere they're served ice-cold, and light, fizzy beers rule the roost. The two largest Canadian brewers, **Molson** and **Labatts**, market a remarkably similar brew under all sorts of names – Molson Canadian, Molson Export, Labatts Ice, Labatts Blue – that inspire, for reasons that elude most foreigners, intense loyalty. The tastier **Great Western Beer** is made by the country's third largest brewer, based in Saskatoon, Saskatchewan, while the heavily marketed **Moosehead** beer, despite its Arctic image, is produced in St John, New Brunswick. There's also a niche market for foreign beers, although **Heineken**, the most popular, is made under licence in Canada; American beers like **Budweiser** and **Coors** are common, too. A welcome trend is the proliferation of independent small breweries, or **microbreweries**, whose products are sold in a pub on the premises, but as yet these remain pretty much confined to the bigger cities.

Drinking bottled beer in a bar works out a good deal more expensive than the draught, which is usually served by the 170ml glass; even cheaper is a pitcher, which contains six or seven glasses.

Once something of a joke, **Canadian wines** are fast developing an excellent reputation, particularly those from Ontario's Niagara-on-the-Lake region, which are subject to the stringent quality control of the Vintners Quality Alliance, the VQA (see p.130). However, if you don't want to experiment, **imported wines** from a wide range of countries are readily available and not too pricey.

Copying its giant neighbour, Canada excels with its **spirits**. Even in run-of-the-mill bars there are startling arrays of gins and vodkas, and usually a good selection of rums. In the more traditional places, the most popular liquor is **whiskey** – either Scottish and Irish imports or the domestically made Canadian Club and VO rye whiskey. In the smarter places you can experiment with all sorts of **cocktails**, costing anywhere between $4 and $13.

Communications

Post

Post office opening hours are Monday to Friday 8.30am to 5.30pm, though a few places open on Saturday between 9am and noon. Service counters are also found inside larger stores, pharmacies and the like, so look out for "Canada Post/Postes Canada" signs or check for the nearest outlet on ☎1-800/267-1177, ⊛www.canadapost.ca. Newsstands, pharmacies, hotels and souvenir shops usually sell **stamps** either individually or in a pack of around six. Letters and postcards up to 30g cost 48¢ within Canada, 65¢ to the US, and $1.25 for international mail. If you're posting letters to Canadian addresses, always include the **postal code** or your mail may never get there; all codes are six characters long, in the format *letter number letter*, space, *number letter number*.

Letters can be sent **poste restante** (general delivery) to any Canadian main post office by addressing them c/o Poste Restante. Make a pick-up date if known, or write "Hold for 15 days", the maximum period mail will usually be held. After that time the item is returned to sender, so it's a good idea to put a return address on the envelope. Take some ID when collecting. Letters will also be held by hotels; mark such mail "Guest Mail, Hold for Arrival". If you have an American Express card or travellers' cheques, you can have mail marked "Client Mail Service" sent to Amex offices throughout Canada. Others can pick up mail from Amex for a small fee.

Phones

When dialling any Canadian phone number, local or long-distance, you must include the three-digit **area code**.

Local calls cost 25¢ at **public phones**, which can be found along commercial streets and in shopping malls, hotels, restaurants and bars. However, local calls are free from private phones (not hotels, however), so you'll find that shops often don't mind you using their phone to dial locally.

When dialling a **long-distance** number (that is, one outside your local area code), you must prefix the ten-digit number with a "1". On public phones, this "1" puts you through to the operator, who will tell you how much money you need in order to get connected. Thereafter, you'll be asked to shovel quarters in at regular intervals – so you're likely to need a stack of them if you want to speak for any length of time. To confuse matters, some connections within an area code are charged at long-distance rates, and thus need the "1" prefix; a recorded message will tell you this is necessary as soon as you dial. Long-distance calls are cheapest from 11pm to 8am daily, and most expensive from 8am to 6pm Monday to Friday. Calling a Canadian (or American) mobile phone costs no more than making a call to a landline in that area code.

Commercial establishments often have **toll-free** (freephone) numbers, which begin with 1-800, 1-866, 1-877 or 1-888. Some of these can only be dialled from phones in the same province, others from anywhere within Canada, a few from anywhere in North America; the larger the organization, generally the wider its toll-free net.

If you'll be making a number of calls and don't feel like carrying around a stack of quarters, pick up a prepaid **phone card**, which are available from many outlets including newsagents and convenience stores, and in various denominations from $5 to $50. There are a variety of competing cards, but usually the format is that you dial a local or toll-free access number and a PIN printed on the card, and then make your call. Check the terms on the card: a cheap per-minute rate may be offset by a high connection charge (which makes getting an answering machine all the more annoying). AT&T and other companies also produce affinity cards whereby the cost of your call is debited directly from your credit- or debit-card

Useful numbers

Emergencies ☎911.

Operator ☎0.

Directory assistance (free from payphones):
- local ☎411.
- long-distance ☎1 + relevant area code + 555-1212.
- toll-free numbers ☎1-800/555-1212.

Canadian area codes
Full information at ⓦ www.areacode-info.com.

Alberta Southern AB, including Banff and Calgary ☎403; Northern AB, including Edmonton ☎780.

British Columbia Vancouver ☎604 and 778; remainder of BC ☎250.

Manitoba ☎204.

New Brunswick ☎506.

Newfoundland and Labrador ☎709.

Northwest Territories ☎867.

Nova Scotia ☎902.

Nunavut ☎867.

Ontario Toronto city ☎416 and 647; Toronto outskirts ☎905 and 289; southwest ON ☎519; Ottawa ☎613; central and northeast ON ☎705; northwest ON ☎807.

Prince Edward Island ☎902.

Québec Montréal ☎514 and 438; off-Montréal Island suburbs, including Laurentians and Eastern Townships ☎450; Upper Laurentians ☎819; eastern QC including Québec City ☎418.

Saskatchewan ☎306.

Yukon ☎867.

Phoning home
To the UK ☎011 + 44 + area code without the zero + number.

To Ireland ☎011 + 353 + area code without the zero + number.

To the US ☎1 + area code + number.

To Australia ☎011 + 61 + area code without the zero + number.

To New Zealand ☎011 + 64 + area code without the zero + number.

---

account. Avoid using hotel room phones – there's usually a service charge even for local and toll-free calls.

Needless to say, using pocketfuls of money is an inconvenient way of making **international calls**. However, many public phones accept credit cards, though you'll be charged at a higher rate; collect calls to elsewhere in Canada and the US can likewise be costly.

Phone charge cards

One of the most convenient ways of phoning home from Canada is via a **phone charge card** from your local phone compa-

ny. Using a PIN number, you can make calls from most hotel, public and private phones that will be charged to your account. Since most major charge cards are free to obtain, it's certainly worth getting one at least for emergencies; enquire first though whether calls from Canada are covered, and bear in mind that rates aren't necessarily cheaper than calling from a public phone. In addition to the services mentioned below, it's also worth checking out the calling cards offered along with ISIC and Hostelling International memberships.

In the **US**, AT&T, MCI, Sprint and other American long-distance companies all enable their customers to make credit-card calls from Canada, billed to your home number. Call your company's customer service line to find out what the toll-free access code is. In **the UK**, one option is from BT (☎0800/345 144, ⓦwww.chargecard.bt .com), which issues the Chargecard free to its customers. Elsewhere, charge cards such as Telstra Telecard or Optus Calling Card in **Australia**, and Telecom NZ's Calling Card in **New Zealand**, can be used to make calls abroad, which are charged back to a domestic account or credit card. Apply to Telstra (☎1800/038 000), Optus (☎1300/ 300 937) or Telecom NZ (☎04/801 9000).

Mobile phones

If you want to use your own **mobile phone** (or **cell phone**) in Canada, you'll need to check with your service provider whether it will work abroad. Unless you have a tri-band handset it's unlikely that a mobile bought for use outside North America will work in Canada.

Visitors from other parts of Canada may be able to make local calls at the same rates as in their home area code. If that's the case,

you're better off not answering an incoming call and instead phoning the caller right back; otherwise you, and possibly they as well, will pay long-distance charges. Some US phones will only work within the region designated by the area code in the phone number – check with your service provider whether this applies to your phone.

Email

An easy way to keep in touch while travelling is to sign up for a free web **email** address that can be accessed from anywhere, for example YahooMail (ⓦwww.yahoo.com) or Hotmail (ⓦwww.hotmail.com). Once you've set up an account, you can use these sites to pick up and send mail from any café, library, hotel or post office with Internet access. You'll also find Bell Internet kiosks in transport termini and shopping malls, but access ($2 for 10min) costs about twice the regular rate of Internet cafés. The site ⓦwww.kropla.com gives useful details of how to plug your laptop in when abroad, phone codes around the world, and information about electrical systems in different countries.

The media

Canada´s only truly national newspaper is the *National Post* – but it is of limited appeal to most Canadians, as is the daily *Globe and Mail*, a Toronto broadsheet (also published in a western edition) available more or less throughout the country.

More popular are the city-based quality newspapers, like the *Toronto Star*, *Calgary Herald*, *Ottawa Citizen* or *Vancouver Sun*, which also serve most of their respective provinces. In Québec, the French-language *La Presse* is the most widely read newspaper, and there's also the intellectual (and separatist) *Le Devoir*. Most of Canada´s major cities also have free weekly listings papers, often with news and features with an alternative slant. The conservative

Maclean's and *Time Canada* are the most popular **weekly** news magazines. The **monthly** *Canadian Geographic* covers the great outdoors through articles and high-quality photographs.

The Canadian Broadcasting Corporation (CBC), with national and regional **TV** broadcasts, has the largest volume of Canadian programmes. The main commercial station is the Canadian Television Corporation (CTV), a mix of Canadian, American and regional output. There are many other public-broadcasting channels and private broadcast companies, whose output makes Canada's TV very similar to mainstream American TV. Most US stations can also be picked up.

The majority of Canadian **radio** stations, too, stick to a bland commercial format. Most are on the AM band and display little originality – though they can be good sources of local nightlife and entertainment news, and road and weather reports. On FM, on the other hand, the nationally funded CBC channels provide diverse, listenable and well-informed programmes – for example *This Morning* (Mon–Fri 9am–noon), a phone-in programme that gives a good grasp of Canadian opinions and happenings. Although some of the large cities boast good specialist music stations, for most of the time you'll probably have to resort to skipping up and down the frequencies. Driving through rural areas can be frustrating, as for hundreds of kilometres you might only be able to receive one or two very dull stations.

Opening hours, public holidays and festivals

Most shops and supermarkets open from about 9am to 5.30pm Monday to Saturday, though in bigger towns and cities supermarkets and malls may open as early as 7.30am and close around 9pm.

Enforced **Sunday** closing of shops, bars and restaurants operates over much of the country, but a growing number of provinces now have limited Sunday hours, usually 10am to 5pm, particularly in touristy areas. As a general rule, there are limited Sunday opening hours between BC and Québec; and east of Québec shops will be shut on Sunday. Many retail shops open late on Thursday and Friday evenings. In cities you usually find a pharmacist open 24 hours and there's often a convenience store like Mac's or 7-11 that stays open around the clock.

The season makes a big difference to opening hours of **information centres**, **museums** and other attractions, most of which, particularly in remote areas, have shorter winter hours or close altogether from late September to mid-May. In cities, more upmarket **restaurants** usually open from around noon to 11pm, longer at weekends; many diner-type places, however, close around 8pm, and small-town restaurants tend to close early too. Opening regulations for **bars** – often part of a hotel or restaurant – vary tremendously from province to province; most open daily from 10am to 1am, but in certain areas all bars except a few hotel lounges are shut on Sunday.

Holidays

Banks, schools and government buildings all over the country close on Canada's **national holidays** and also within specific regions on the **provincial holidays** that fall on certain – often moveable – days throughout the year. Many shops, restaurants, museums and sights remain open, however. Campsites, smaller information centres, B&Bs and many resort hotels often use Victoria Day in spring, and Labour Day or Thanksgiving in fall, as markers for their open and closed seasons. University students have their holidays from May to early September (plus a one- or two-week break in March), while schoolchildren take theirs from the end of June to Labour Day.

National holidays

Jan 1 New Year's Day

Time zones

Canada has six **time zones**, but only four-and-a-half hours separate the eastern extremities from the western.

• In the far east, Newfoundland is on **Newfoundland time** (3hr 30min behind the UK and 1hr 30min ahead of the eastern US).

• The Maritimes and Labrador are on **Atlantic** (4hr behind the UK and 1hr ahead of the eastern US).

• Québec and most of Ontario are on **Eastern** (5hr behind the UK) – the same zone as New York and the eastern US.

• Manitoba, the northwest corner of Ontario, and Saskatchewan are on **Central** (6hr behind the UK; same as US Central).

• Alberta, the Northwest Territories and a slice of northeast British Columbia are on **Mountain** (7hr behind the UK – same as US Mountain).

• In the west, the Yukon and the remainder of British Columbia are on **Pacific** (8hr behind the UK and 1hr ahead of Alaska – same as US Pacific).

• Nunavut spans a number of time zones, from Mountain to Atlantic.

For **daylight saving** (used in all regions except Saskatchewan and northeast BC), clocks go forward one hour on the first Sunday of April, and back one hour on the last Sunday in October.

Note that train, bus and plane timetables are always given in **local time** – worth bearing in mind if you're making long journeys across several zones. Most printed timetables use the 24-hour clock; those that do not (notably Greyhound bus schedules), instead use light type to indicate "AM" and bold type for "PM".

Good Friday
Easter Sunday
Easter Monday
Monday before May 25 Victoria Day/Fête des Patriotes
July 1 Canada Day
First Mon in Sept Labour Day
Second Mon in Oct Thanksgiving
Nov 11 Remembrance Day (only a partial holiday; government offices and banks are closed, but most businesses are open).
Dec 25 (Christmas Day)
Dec 26 (Boxing Day)

Provincial holidays

Alberta Third Mon in Feb (Alberta Family Day); first Mon in Aug (Heritage Day).
British Columbia First Mon in Aug (British Columbia Day).
Manitoba First Mon in Aug (Civic Holiday).
New Brunswick First Mon in Aug (New Brunswick Day).
Newfoundland and Labrador March 17 (St Patrick's Day); third Mon in April (St George's Day); third Mon in June (Discovery Day); first Mon in July (Memorial Day); third Mon in July (Orangeman's Day).

Northwest Territories First Mon in Aug (Civic Holiday).
Nova Scotia First Mon in Aug (Civic Holiday).
Nunavut April 1 (Nunavut Day).
Ontario First Mon in Aug (Civic Holiday).
Québec Jan 6 (Epiphany); Ash Wednesday; Ascension (forty days after Easter); June 24 (Saint-Jean-Baptiste Day); Nov 1 (All Saint's Day); Dec 8 (Immaculate Conception).
Saskatchewan First Mon in Aug (Civic Holiday).
Yukon Third Mon in Aug (Discovery Day).

Festivals and events

For further details of the selected **festivals and events** listed below, including more precise dates, see the relevant account in the guide, or contact the local authorities direct. The provincial tourist offices listed on pp.24–25 can provide free calendars for each area.

January

Polar Bear Swim Vancouver, BC. A New Year's Day swim in the freezing waters of English Bay Beach – said to bring good luck for the year.
Banff/Lake Louise Winter Festival Banff and Lake Louise, AB. Ski races, skating parties and the

incrediible International Ice Sculpture Competition on the shores of Lake Louise.

February

Winterlude Ottawa, ON. Winter-warming activities like ice sculpting, snowshoe races, ice boating and skating for all on the canal.

Winter Carnival Québec City, QC. Eleven-day festival of winter-sports competitions, ice-sculpture contests and parades. Includes the Canadian ski marathon when skiers race between Lachute and Gatineau.

Montréal Highlights Festival Montréal, QC. Festival that, like Québec City's, tries to make the most of winter with a multitude of shows and food events.

March

Pacific Rim Whale Festival Vancouver Island, BC. Celebrating the spring migration of grey whales with lots of whale-spotting expeditions as well as music and dance events.

April

TerrifVic Jazz Party Victoria, BC. Dixieland, and other jazz bands, from around the globe.

Shaw Festival Niagara-on-the-Lake, ON. Highly regarded theatre festival featuring the work of George Bernard Shaw and his contemporaries. Performances from April to late October.

May

Apple Blossom Festival Annapolis Valley, NS. Community-oriented festival held in the small towns and villages of this apple-producing valley in Nova Scotia.

Stratford Festival Stratford, ON. The small town of Stratford is well known for its first-class Shakespeare Festival. Runs from May to early November.

Canadian Tulip Festival Ottawa, ON. Three million tulips in an orgy of colour all over the city.

June

Jazz City International Festival Edmonton, AB. Ten days of jazz concerts, free outdoor events and workshops.

Banff Festival of the Arts Banff, AB. Young-artist showcase: music, opera, dance, drama, comedy and visual arts.

International Blues Festival Halifax, NS. Big musical event showcasing the best of US and Maritime blues.

Metro International Caravan Toronto, ON. Nine-day multiethnic celebration with some fifty pavilions dotted across the city.

International Jazz Festival Montréal, QC. Some 2000 jazz acts, including the world's top names, and 75 percent of the performances are free.

July

Canada Day Ottawa, ON, and nationwide. Fireworks, parades and a day off for patriotic shenanigans.

Pow-wows Nationwide. Traditional aboriginal celebrations that take place on reserves across the country in July and August.

Calgary Stampede Calgary, AB. One of the biggest rodeos in the world: all the usual cowboy trappings, plus hot-air-balloon races, chuck-wagon rides, craft exhibitions, native dancing and a host of other happenings. Billed as the "Greatest Outdoor Show on Earth".

Klondike Days Edmonton, AB. Pioneer era in Edmonton revisited with gold panning, raft races, pancake breakfasts and gambling.

Loyalist City Festival St John, NB. Celebration of the city's loyalist heritage with parades in period costume.

Antigonish Highland Games Antigonish, NS. All sorts of traditional Scottish sports and activities recall the settlement of the area by Highlanders.

Atlantic Jazz Festival Halifax, NS. First-class jazz festival pulling in big names from round the world.

Caribana Festival Toronto, ON. Large-scale West Indian carnival with music, dance and a flamboyant parade.

Festival d'Été Québec City, QC. Arts performances, live bands and other shows on and off the sun-filled streets and parks of Québec City.

Juste Pour Rire Montréal, QC. The funniest festival in Canada. Internationally acclaimed comic get-together with comedians from around the world performing in theatres and outdoor stages.

Gay Pride Toronto, ON and Montréal, QC. Gigantic celebration of gay culture. With huge parades and street parties both attract between half and a million spectators.

August

Fringe Theatre Festival Edmonton, AB. One of North America's most prestigious alternative-theatre festivals.

Squamish Days Loggers Sports Festival Squamish, BC. The continent's biggest lumberjacks' convention with impressive logging competitions.

Acadian Festival Caraquet, NB. Celebration of Acadian culture in the northeast of New Brunswick.
Miramichi Folk Song Festival Newcastle, NB. New Brunswick's prestigious folk festival, featuring many of the finest fiddlers in the Maritimes.
Nova Scotia Gaelic Mod South Gut, St Ann's, NS. Seven-day Scottish heritage knees-up with all traditional sports, crafts and contests featured. One of the biggest and best of many similar events in Nova Scotia.
World Film Festival Montréal, QC. Eclipsed by Toronto's film festival, but still a good showcase for new movies.

September

Toronto International Film Festival Toronto, ON. Internationally acclaimed film festival spread over ten days, inundated with Hollywood stars.

October

Vancouver International Film Festival Vancouver, BC. Another of Canada's highly rated film fests.

Okanagan Wine Festival Okanagan, BC. One of the many wine events in this vine-growing region.
Oktoberfest Kitchener-Waterloo, ON. Alcohol and cultural events in honour of the twin towns' roots.
Black and Blue Montréal, QC. Major gay arts festival in Montréal.

November

Canadian Finals Rodeo Edmonton, AB. Pure Canuck rodeo.
Royal Agricultural Winter Fair Toronto, ON. The world's largest agricultural indoor fair, apparently.

December

Carol Ships Vancouver, BC. When carol singers sail around Vancouver harbour in sparkly boats.
New Year's Eve Nationwide, but celebrated in style in St John's, Newfoundland, where everyone heads from the pub to the waterfront for a raucous midnight party.

Outdoor pursuits

Canada's mountains, lakes, rivers and forests offer the opportunity to indulge in a vast range of outdoor pursuits. We've concentrated on hiking, skiing and canoeing – three of Canada's most popular activities – and on the national parks, which have been established to preserve and make accessible the best of the Canadian landscape.

Other popular activities such as whale-watching, horse riding, fishing and rafting are covered in some detail in the main text but, whatever activity interests you, be certain to send off to the **provincial tourist office** – or check their website – for information before you go. Once in Canada you can rely on finding outfitters, equipment rental, charters, tours and guides to help you in most areas; tourist offices invariably carry full details or contact numbers. Also make a point of visiting Canadian bookshops: most have a separate outdoor pursuits section with a wide variety of specialist guides.

The national parks

Canada's thirty or so **national parks** are administered by Parks Canada (ⓦ www.pc .gc.ca), a federal body, with information provided locally by **park information centres** (though the terminology may vary from park to park). Visit these to pick up special **permits** if you intend to fish or camp in the backcountry, and for information and audio-visual displays on flora, fauna and outdoor activities. Many offer talks and nature walks presented by park naturalists, as well as reports on snow, weather and recent bear sightings. **Regulations** common to all national parks include a total ban on firearms, hunting, snowmobiles or off-road vehicles, the feeding of wildlife, and the removal or damaging of any natural objects or features.

Note that most national park regulations relating to the care of the environment and campsite behaviour are usually applicable to **provincial parks**. Entry to these parks is free but you'll have to pay for fishing and hunting permits – though specifics vary from province to province. Where provincial parks provide facilities or contain a particular attraction, you can also expect to pay a modest admission fee and, naturally, you have to pay to use provincial park campsites.

National park permits and campsites

At national parks all motor vehicles, including motorbikes, require a park permit before entering, usually from a roadside booth at the point where the road crosses the park boundary. In the past people entering on foot, bicycle, boat or horseback have been exempt, as have vehicles passing straight through certain parks without stopping overnight. This is no longer the case and a permit based on a per-person usage of the park is now required. This costs around $5 to $15 per person per day with the customary concessions for the young and old. If you intend to visit a number of national parks, it's worth investing in either a regional or national pass – get details from any park information centre. As an illustration, an annual pass providing admission to the dozen or so eastern parks costs around $26, and a multi-park pass with entry to 27 national parks costs $45. For more on passes in the Rockies and surrounding parks, see p.678.

Additional permits are also required to **fish** in national parks (over and above any provincial permits; see "Fishing", p.58). These are available from park centres, wardens or park administration buildings, and cost around $20 annually, $11 weekly or $7 daily. There may well be quotas on the types and numbers of fish you can catch, which you can find out when you buy a permit; in all parks there's an extra surcharge to fish for salmon.

Most parks have large, well-run **campsites** close to the park's main settlement; some for tents or RVs only, others mixed. Fees depend on facilities, and currently run from $7 per tent or per vehicle for semi-primitive sites (with wood, water and pit toilets) up to about $30 for those with electricity, sewage, water and showers. Park permits do not cover campsite fees. Some park campsites have also introduced another fee (around $3) for use of firewood.

Most parks also have **primitive campsites**, which are basic backcountry sites providing, as a rule, just fire pits and firewood. Regulations vary enormously. Some parks, like Jasper in the Rockies, allow backcountry camping only in tightly defined sites; others, like Banff, have a special **primitive wildland** zone where you can pitch a tent within a designated distance of the nearest road or trailhead. Simply ask at park centres or tourist offices for latest details. Whether you want to use a primitive campsite or camp rough in parks, however, the one thing you must do is obtain an **overnight permit** from the park centre (either free or just a few dollars), which enables the authorities to keep a check on people's whereabouts and regulate numbers in the backcountry.

Hiking

Canada boasts some of North America's finest **hiking**, and whatever your ability or ambition you'll find a walk to suit you almost anywhere in the country. All the national and many of the provincial parks have well-marked and well-maintained trails, and a visit to any park centre or local tourist office will furnish you with adequate **maps** of local paths. Park trails are usually sufficiently well marked not to need more detailed maps for short walks and day-hikes. This applies to virtually all the hikes described in features in this guide. If you're venturing into the backcountry, though, try to obtain the appropriate 1:50,000 sheet from the Canadian Topographical Series. For key hiking areas we've given a brief summary of the best trails in the appropriate parts of the guide, though with over 1500km of paths in Banff National Park alone, recommendations can only scratch the surface of what's on offer. Park staff can advise on other good walks, and **trail guides** are widely available for most of the country's prime walking regions.

It's essential, of course, to be **properly equipped** if you're walking in high or rough country: good boots, waterproof jacket and spare warm clothing. Be prepared for sudden changes of weather and the sort of health problems associated with the Canadian backcountry (see "Health", p.27). Outdoor clothing can be bought easily in most towns, and in walking areas there's a good chance of being able to **rent** tents, specialized cold-weather gear and all manner of other minor outdoor gear.

Main hiking areas

In picking out the country's prime walking areas we've usually chosen the parks that are accessible by road, where maps are available and the trail system developed, and where you can turn up without too much planning or special wilderness training.

Best known and most developed of these are the **Rockies national parks** of Alberta and British Columbia. Thousands of kilometres of well-kept and well-tramped paths crisscross the "big four" parks – **Banff**, **Jasper**, **Yoho** and **Kootenay** – as well as the smaller enclaves of Glacier, Revelstoke and Waterton lakes. Scope for hiking of all descriptions is almost limitless.

More modest areas dotted all over British Columbia boast walking possibilities out of all proportion to their size: we pay less attention to these, but by most relative standards hiking here is still among the best in North America. All the following provincial parks offer a variety of day-hikes, short strolls and longer trails that could keep you happy for a week or more: **Wells Gray**, north of Kamloops; **Kokanee Glacier**, near Nelson; **Manning**, east of Vancouver; **Garibaldi**, north of Vancouver; and **Strathcona**, on Vancouver Island. Walking guides are available for all these regions in local bookstores: tourist offices, as ever, will also offer guidance.

In Manitoba, the **Riding Mountain National Park** offers about thirty hiking trails, but though there's plenty of upland walking to be had in the so-called prairie provinces, you have to move east to Québec's **Mauricie**, **Forillon** and **Gatineau**

parks for a taste of mountains comparable to the western provinces. In Ontario, **Lake Superior Provincial Park** and the **Algonquin Park** are the most challenging terrains. New Brunswick's **Fundy National Park** offers coastal walks, while Newfoundland's hiking centres on its two national parks: **Terra Nova** on the east coast, and the high plateau and fjords of the west coast's **Gros Morne**. For the truly bold, however, nothing can match the Arctic extremes of **Baffin Island**, whose principal trail lies over an icecap that never melts.

Long-distance footpaths

In areas with highly developed trail networks, seasoned backpackers can blaze their own **long-distance footpaths** by stringing together several longer trails. Recognized long-haul paths, however, are relatively rare, though more are being designated yearly. One of the best is the **Chilkoot Trail** from Dyea in Alaska to Bennett in British Columbia, a 53-kilometre hike that closely follows the path of prospectors en route to the Yukon during the 1898 gold rush (see p.1004). The most popular is probably Vancouver Island's demanding **West Coast Trail**, which runs for 80km along the edge of the Pacific Rim National Park (see p.870).

More far-reaching walks include the **Rideau Trail**, which follows paths and minor roads for 386km from Kingston to Ottawa; the 690-kilometre **Bruce Trail** from Queenston, on the Niagara River, to Tobermory on the Bruce Peninsula; and the **Voyageur Trail** along the north shores of lakes Superior and Huron, which is the longest and most rugged route in the province.

Before you set out on any long-distance trail, however, it is vital to seek local advice from either the nearest tourist or park office, or from a local adventure-tour operator.

Skiing

Wherever there's hiking in Canada, there's also usually **skiing**. The increasingly popular resorts of the Rockies and British Columbia are the main areas, followed by Québec, but there's also skiing in Newfoundland and the Maritimes, and even a few runs in Manitoba and Saskatchewan. We've provided special features on the country's leading resorts at **Whistler, Banff, Lake Louise** and **Jasper**. Most cities are close to excellent downhill and cross-country runs: Vancouver is a ninety-minute drive from Whistler, one of the world's top three resorts; Calgary is the same distance from the Rockies' six big centres; Ottawa lies just half an hour from Camp Fortune and Mont Cascade; and Montréal is around an hour from three hundred runs in the Laurentians and one hundred-plus slopes in L'Estrie (the Eastern Townships).

Canadian **ski packages** are available from travel agents worldwide, but it's perfectly feasible to organize your own trips, as long as you book well ahead if you're hoping to stay in some of the better-known resorts. **Costs** for food, accommodation and ski passes are still fairly modest by US and European standards: a day's pass in one of the Rockies' resorts, for example, costs around $53. Tourist offices in skiing areas are open in winter to help with practicalities, and many nearby towns have ski shops to buy or rent equipment. Companies and hotels in some cities even organize their own mini-packages to nearby resorts. Skiing provinces publish regional ski and winter-sports directories, all available from provincial tourist offices.

Fishing

Canada is **fishing** nirvana. While each region has its specialities, from the Arctic char of the Northwest Territories to the Pacific salmon of British Columbia, excellent fishing can be found in most of the country's super-abundant lakes, rivers and coastal waters. Most towns have a fishing shop for equipment, and any spot with fishing possibilities is likely to have companies running boats and charters. As with every other major type of outdoor activity, most provinces publish detailed booklets on everything that swims within the area of their jurisdiction.

Fishing is governed by a range of **regulations** that vary from province to province. These are baffling at first glance, but usually boil down to the need for a **nonresident permit** for freshwater fishing, and another for saltwater fishing. These are obtainable from most local fishing or sports shops for

about $32 and are valid for a year. Short-term (one- or six-day) licences are also available in some provinces. In a few places you may have to pay for extra licences to go after particular fish, and in national parks you need a special additional permit (see p.54). There may also be quotas or a closed season on certain fish. Shops and tourist offices always have the most current regulations.

Canoeing

Opportunities for **canoeing** are limited only by problems of access and expertise: some of the rapids and portages on the country's more challenging routes are for real pros only. The most straightforward regions to canoe are in **Ontario**, with its estimated 250,000 lakes and 35,000km of waterways, some 25,000km of which have been documented as practical canoe routes. The key areas are the Algonquin, Killarney and Quetico provincial parks, though the single most popular run is the 190-kilometre **Rideau Canal**, a tame run from Kingston to Ottawa.

The rivers of **British Columbia** offer generally more demanding white-water routes, though the lake canoeing – in the Wells Gray Provincial Park, for example – is among the country's most beautiful. One of the province's other recognized classics is the 120-kilometre trip near Barkerville on the Cariboo River and the lakes of the Bowron Lakes Provincial Park. More challenging still are the immense backcountry lakes and rivers of the **Mackenzie** system and the barren lands of the Northwest Territories, where you can find one of the continent's ultimate river challenges – the 300-kilometre stretch of the **South Nahanni River** near Fort Simpson. Growing in popularity, partly because of improved road access, are trips on and around the **Yukon River system**, particularly the South Macmillan River east of Pelly Crossing. Other areas that will test the resources of any canoeist are to be found in Manitoba and Labrador – all detailed in this guide.

Once you've decided on an area, provincial tourist offices can send you full lists of outfitters and rental agencies whose brochures provide a good idea of what you can expect in their various regions. When you arrive, **outfitters** are available in most centres to rent equipment, organize boat and plane drop-offs, and arrange provisions for longer trips. Typical **costs** are in the region of $80 for weekly canoe rental, $25 daily for a wetsuit. Most also supply maps. Specialist canoe **guides** are also widely available in Canadian bookshops, many giving extremely detailed accounts of particular river systems or regions.

Spectator sports

Canadians are sports-mad: ice hockey, baseball and Canadian football matches are all extremely popular – both professional games and intercollegiate competitions, the intensity of whose rivalries are notorious. Lacrosse is the "official" national sport but, unsurprisingly, the unofficial national obsession is ice hockey.

Ice hockey

The sport that really ignites the passions of all Canadians is **ice hockey**. With players hurtling around at nearly 50kph and the puck clocking speeds of over 160kph, this would be a high-adrenaline sport even without its relaxed attitude to combat on the rink (as an old Canadian adage has it: "I went to see a fight and an ice-hockey game broke out"). Players, especially in the minor leagues, are as adept at a right hook as they are at skating: the day when the national team waged a battle against a Soviet Union team is legendary – the fight only stopped when officials turned all the lights in the stadium off.

Teams have six players and perpetual substitutions are allowed during the game: most players rarely spend more than a few minutes on the ice at one time. There are three twenty-minute periods in a match, but the clock is frequently stopped for a variety of reasons so a game usually lasts for around three hours. Each team plays over eighty games a **season**, which lasts from October to May, and on alternate weeks will play two and then three games.

The North American National Hockey League, or **NHL** (ⓦwww.nhl.com), consists of thirty teams, of which six are from Canada: the Montréal Canadiens, Ottawa Senators, Toronto Maple Leafs, Vancouver Canucks, Calgary Flames and Edmonton Oilers. There are two "conferences" within the league – **Western** and **Eastern** – both of which are divided into two divisions. The Canadiens, Maple Leafs and the Senators meet teams from Buffalo and Boston in the Northeast division of the Eastern conference, while the Flames, Oilers and Canucks face Colorado and Minnesota in the Northwest division of the Western conference.

At the end of the season the top four teams in each division go on into the playoffs for the **Stanley Cup**, ice hockey's most prestigious title. The two most successful teams are the Montréal Canadiens, who have won the Stanley Cup 23 times, and the Toronto Maple Leafs, who have eleven victories under their belt.

Ticket prices range from around $20 for ordinary games to hundreds of dollars for a Stanley Cup final – indeed, you can basically forget about getting into such a high-prestige national event. For nearly all matches you have to buy a ticket in advance.

Other than the NHL there are also numerous **minor league** clubs composed of "**farm teams**", so called because they supply the top clubs with talent. Ontario and Québec both have their own minor leagues; the rest of the country plays in the Western League, all with play-offs for a variety of awards. For **college hockey**, the University of Toronto and York in Toronto, Concordia in Montréal, St Mary's in Halifax and the University of Alberta in Edmonton all have good teams.

NHL teams and venues

Eastern conference (Northeast Division)

Montréal Canadiens Centre Bell Molson, 1260 rue de la Gauchitière, Montréal ☎514/790-1245 or 932-2582, ⓦwww.canadiens.com.
Ottawa Senators Corel Centre, 1000 Palladium Drive, Kanata ☎1-800/444-SENS, ⓦwww.ottawasenators.com.
Toronto Maple Leafs Air Canada Centre, 40 Bay St, Toronto ☎416/815-5700, ⓦwww.torontomapleleafs.com.

Western conference (Northwest Division)

Calgary Flames Saddledome, Calgary ☎403/777-0000, ⓦwww.calgaryflames.com.
Edmonton Oilers Skyreach Centre, 7424 118th Ave, Edmonton ☎403/471-4000, ⓦwww.edmontonoilers.com.
Vancouver Canucks General Motors Place, 800 Griffiths Way, Vancouver ☎604/280-4400 or 899-GOAL, ⓦwww.canucks.com.

Canadian football

Professional **Canadian football** (akin to the American variety, not soccer) – played under the aegis of the Canadian Football League, or **CFL** (ⓦwww.cfl.ca) – is largely overshadowed by the National Football League in the US, chiefly because the best home-grown talent moves south in search of better money while NFL castoffs move north to fill the ranks. The two countries' football games vary slightly, but what differences do exist tend to make the Canadian version more exciting. In Canada the playing field is larger and there are twelve rather than eleven players on each team. There is also one fewer **"down"** in a game: after kickoff the attacking team has three, rather than four, chances to move the ball forward ten yards and score a first down en route to a **touchdown**. Different rules about the movement of players, and the limited time allowed between plays, results in a faster-paced and higher-

scoring sport, in which ties are often decided in overtime or in a dramatic final-minute surge.

Despite the sport's potential, the CFL has suffered a blight of media and fan indifference, which has caused immense financial problems, though recently the crisis seems to be easing, with high-profile celebrity investment. The **season**, played by two divisions of eight teams, lasts from June to November, each team playing a match a week – 72 matches in all. At the end of the season are the play-offs, which culminate with the hotly contested **Grey Cup** – which the Toronto Argonauts have won 21 times. Tickets are fairly easy to come by, except for important games, and vary in cost from $20 to a Grey Cup final price of over $150.

CFL teams and venues

West Division

BC Lions BC Place Stadium, 777 Pacific Blvd S, Vancouver ☎604/589-ROAR, ⓦwww.bclions.com.
Calgary Stampeders McMahon Stadium, 1817 Crowchild Trail NW, Calgary ☎403/289-0258, ⓦwww.stampeders.com.
Edmonton Eskimos Commonwealth Stadium, 11000 Stadium Rd, Edmonton ☎403/448-ESKS, ⓦwww.esks.com.
Saskatchewan Roughriders Taylor Field, 2940 10th Ave, Regina ☎1-888/4-RIDERS or 306/525-2181, ⓦwww.riders.com.
Winnipeg Blue Bombers Winnipeg Stadium, 1465 Maroons Rd, Winnipeg ☎204/784-2583, ⓦwww.bluebombers.com.

East Division

Hamilton Tiger-Cats Ivor Wynne Stadium, 75 Balsam Ave N, Hamilton ☎1-800/714-ROAR or 905/547-CATS, ⓦwww.tigercats.on.ca.
Montréal Alouettes Molson Memorial Stadium, McGill University, 475 Av des Pins Ouest, Montréal ☎514/871-2266, ⓦwww.alouettes.net.
Ottawa Renegades Frank Clair Stadium, Ottawa ☎613/231-5608, ⓦwww.ottawarenegades.net.
Toronto Argonauts SkyDome, 1 Blue Jays Way, Toronto ☎416/341-5151, ⓦwww.argonauts.on.ca.

Baseball

Baseball, with its relaxed summertime pace and byzantine rules, is generally considered an exclusively American sport – despite the first recorded game taking place in Beachville, Ontario. The **Montréal Expos** and the **Toronto Blue Jays** perform in the US's two major baseball leagues, the National and the American, respectively. In 1992 and 1993 the Toronto Blue Jays became national heroes when they won the World Series twice in a row, beating America at their own game. Historically a lowlier bunch, the Expos have been dogged by two major handicaps: a poor stadium in which to play baseball and insufficient funds to compete salary-wise with major-market teams. And it's debatable whether the team will stay at all – after promises to give them a downtown stadium were dashed, the team has, since 2003, begun to play half its "home" games in San Juan, Puerto Rico. Pretty much the only reason Montréal hasn't yet lost the franchise is that no American city that can afford them seems to want them.

Even if you don't understand the rules of play, a game can be a pleasant day out, drinking beer and eating burgers and popcorn in the sun, among a friendly, family-oriented crowd. Moreover, the home ground of each team is a vast, wondrous modern stadium – the Skydome in Toronto and, for the moment at least, the Olympic Stadium in Montréal. With six teams in each division, there are 81 home games each season, played from April to late September, with play-offs continuing through October; there is no set match day and games are either played in the afternoon or evening. Lasting for anything from two to three hours, baseball games never end in a tie: if the scores are level after nine innings, extra innings are played until one side wins.

Tickets for the Blue Jays are hard to come by and it's easier to get in for games in Montréal ($8–36, the cheapest in the league). Nothing can match the glitz of the big two, but there are other minor league **farm teams**, including the Edmonton Trappers, Calgary Cannons and Vancouver Canadians.

Baseball teams and venues

Major League teams

AMERICAN LEAGUE
Toronto Blue Jays SkyDome, 277 Front St W, Toronto ℡416/341-1234 or 1-888/OK-GO-JAY outside Toronto, ⊛www.bluejays.ca.

NATIONAL LEAGUE
Montréal Expos Olympic Stadium, Av Pierre-de-Coubertin, Montréal ℡514/790-1245 or 1-800/361-4595 outside Montréal, 1-800/678-5440 from USA, ⊛www.montrealexpos.com.

Minor League teams

PACIFIC COAST LEAGUE
Calgary Cannons Burns Stadium, 1817 Crowchild Trail NW, Calgary ℡403/284-1111, ⊛www.calgarycannons.com.
Edmonton Trappers John Ducey Park, 10233 96th Ave, Edmonton ℡780/414-4450, ⊛www.trappersbaseball.com.

INTERNATIONAL LEAGUE
Ottawa Lynx JetForm Park, 300 Coventry Rd, Ottawa ℡613/749-9947 or 1-800/663-0985, ⊛www.ottawalynx.com.

Basketball

Basketball was invented by a Canadian, Dr James A. Naismith, in 1891. After a 48-year absence two Canadian teams finally joined the now misnamed US National Basketball Association, or **NBA** (⊛www.nba.com), in 1995 – the Toronto Raptors and the Vancouver Grizzlies, who did about as well as could be expected in their first season, though the Raptors, with huge star Vince Carter, look like the team more on the upswing.

The NBA consists of 29 teams divided into two conferences, Eastern and Western, which are further divided into two divisions. Teams play an 82-game season with 41 home games in a season that lasts from November to April – tickets cost from $10 to $130. The Toronto Raptors play in the Central division of the Eastern conference, and are based at the Air Canada Centre, 40 Bay St, Toronto (℡416/366-DUNK, ⊛www.nba.com/raptors).

Crime and personal safety

There's little reason why you should ever come into contact with either the Royal Canadian Mounted Police (RCMP), who patrol most of Canada, or the fellow organizations – like the Toronto Police Service – which cover the rest. Canada is one of the safest countries in the world and although there are a few crime hotspots, these are confined to the peripheries of the country's three big cities – Toronto, Montréal and Vancouver.

Few Canadian citizens carry arms, muggings are uncommon, and even in the cities street crime is infrequent – though the usual cautions about avoiding poorly lit urban areas and so forth stand. Canadian officials are notorious for coming down hard if you're found with **drugs**, especially on non-Canadians. Stiff penalties are imposed, even when only traces of any illegal substance are found. Police are also diligent in enforcing traffic laws.

Petty crime

Almost all the problems tourists encounter in Canada are to do with **petty crime** – pick-pocketing and bag-snatching. As such, it's good to be on your guard and know where your possessions are at all times. Thieves often work in pairs and, although **theft** is far from commonplace, you should be aware of certain ploys, such as the "helpful" person pointing out "birdshit" (actually shaving cream or similar) on your coat, while someone else relieves you of your money; being invited to read a card or paper on the street to distract your attention; or someone in a café moving for your drink with one hand while the other goes for your bag. If you're in a crowd of tourists, watch out for people moving in unusually close.

Sensible **precautions** against petty theft include: carrying bags slung across your neck and not over your shoulder; not carrying anything in pockets that are easy to dip

into; and having photocopies of your passport, airline ticket and driving licence, while leaving the originals in your hotel. When you're looking for a hotel room, never leave your bags unattended and, similarly, if you have a car, don't leave anything in view when you park: vehicle theft is still a rarity, but luggage and valuables do make tempting targets.

If you are **robbed**, you'll need to go to the **police** to report it, not least because your insurance company will require a police report. Remember to make a note of the report number – or, better still, ask for a copy of the statement itself. Don't expect a great deal of concern if your loss is relatively small, and don't be surprised if the process of completing forms and formalities takes ages.

If you're **detained** by the police, the arresting officer(s) must identify him/herself. At the police station, detainees have the right to free but reasonable use of a phone and legal counsel. For certain sorts of suspected offence – primarily gun- and drug-related – the police are likely to strip-search detainees, though these searches, and the frequency of them, remain controversial.

> **Police, fire, or ambulance**
> ☏911.

Travellers with disabilities

At least in its cities and towns, Canada is one of the best places in the world to travel if you have limited mobility or other physical disabilities. All public buildings are required to be wheelchair-accessible and provide suitable toilet facilities, almost all street corners have dropped kerbs, and public phones are specially equipped for hearing-aid users. Wheelchair users may encounter problems when travelling on urban public transport, but matters are being remedied at a speed of knots. Out in the wilds, things are inevitably more problematic, but almost all the national parks have accessible visitor and information centres and many have specially designed accessible trails.

Provincial tourist offices are excellent sources of **information** on accessible hotels, motels and sights. You may also want to get in touch with Kéroul (☎514/252-3104, ⊛www.keroul.qc.ca), an organization in Montréal that specializes in travel for people with limited mobility, and publishes the bilingual guide *Accès Tourisme*. Most airlines, both transatlantic and internal, will do whatever they can to ease your journey. The larger car-rental companies, like Hertz and Avis, can provide cars with hand controls at no extra charge, though these are usually only available on their most expensive models; book one as far in advance as you can as demand can exceed supply. To obtain a parking privilege permit, drivers with disabilities must apply to a provincial authority, though the permit itself, once issued, is valid right across Canada. In the first instance, contact provincial tourist offices for further details. Typically, and amongst all sorts of other information, applicants need to specify their disability and attach a signed doctor's letter (*not* a photocopy) stating the applicant finds it difficult to walk more than 100m.

All VIA Rail **trains** can accommodate wheelchairs that are no larger than 81cm by 182cm and weigh no more than 114kg, though 24 hours' notice is required for the Québec–Windsor corridor and 48 hours on other routes. They offer an excellent service, including served meals, roomettes at no extra charge for blind people travelling with a guide dog, as well as help with boarding and disembarking. Those who require attendants can apply for a two-for-one fare certificate

under the **"Helping Hand"** scheme – further details from the contact organizations listed below. Although long-distance **buses** are obliged to carry passengers with disabilities if their wheelchairs fit in the luggage compartment, access is often difficult. More positively, nearly all bus companies accept the two-for-one "Helping Hand" certificates, and drivers are usually extremely helpful.

Larger **hotels** like *Holiday Inn* often have specially designed suites for guests with disabilities, and major motel chains like *Best Western* and *Journey's End* have full access – but it is always worth checking with the tourist offices (and the particular hotel) to confirm facilities.

Contacts for travellers with disabilities

In the UK and Ireland

Access Travel 6 The Hillock, Astley M29 7GW ☎01942/888 844, ⊛www.access-travel.co.uk. Small, personal-service tour operator that can arrange flights, transfer and accommodation.
Holiday Care 2nd floor, Imperial Building, Victoria Rd, Horley RH6 7PZ ☎0845/124 9971, minicom ☎0845/124 9976, ⊛www.holidaycare.org.uk. Provides free lists of accessible accommodation across North America.
Irish Wheelchair Association Blackheath Drive, Clontarf, Dublin 3 ☎01/818 6400, ⊛www.iwa.ie. Useful information provided about travelling abroad with a wheelchair.
Tripscope Alexandra House, Albany Rd, Brentford TW8 0NE ☎0845/758 5641, ⊛www.tripscope .org.uk. Registered charity providing free advice on international transport.

In the US and Canada

Access-Able ⓦ www.access-able.com. Online resource for travellers with disabilities.

Canadian Paraplegic Association. Their main office is at Suite 230, 1101 Prince of Wales Drive, Ottawa, ON, K2C 3W7 ☏ 613/723-1033, ⓦ www.canparaplegic.org. They also have offices in every province – details from the website or from ☏ 1-800/720-4933. Provides a wealth of information on travelling in specific provinces, and most of its regional offices produce a free guide on the most easily accessed sights.

Directions Unlimited 123 Green Lane, Bedford Hills, NY 10507 ☏ 1-800/533-5343 or 914/241-1700. Travel agency specializing in bookings for people with disabilities.

Mobility International USA 451 Broadway, Eugene, OR 97401 ☏ 541/343-1284, ⓦ www.miusa.org. Information and referral services, access guides, tours and exchange programmes.

Society for the Advancement of Travelers with Handicaps (SATH) 347 5th Ave, New York, NY 10016 ☏ 212/447-7284, ⓦ www.sath.org. Non-profit educational organization that has actively represented travellers with disabilities since 1976.

VIA Rail ☏ 1-888/842-7245, ⓦ www.viarail.com. VIA Rail operates almost all of Canada's train network. Their website has a specific section devoted to travellers with disabilities ("Special needs") and there's a speech- and/or hearing-impaired helpline on ☏ 1-800/268-9503.

Wheels Up! ☏ 1-888/38-WHEELS, ⓦ www.wheelsup.com. Provides discounted airfare, tour and cruise prices for disabled travellers, also publishes a free monthly newsletter and has a comprehensive website.

In Australia and New Zealand

ACROD (Australian Council for Rehabilitation of the Disabled) PO Box 60, Curtin ACT 2605; Suite 103, 1st floor, 1–5 Commercial Rd, Kings Grove 2208 ☏ 02/6282 4333, TTY ☏ 02/6282 4333, ⓦ www.acrod.org.au. Provides lists of travel agencies and tour operators for people with disabilities.

Disabled Persons Assembly 4/173–175 Victoria St, Wellington ☏ 04/801 9100 (also TTY), ⓦ www.dpa.org.nz. Resource centre with lists of travel agencies and tour operators for people with disabilities.

Directory

Addresses Generally speaking, roads in built-up areas in Canada are laid out on a grid system, creating "blocks" of buildings. The first one or two digits of a specific address refer to the block, which will be numbered in sequence from a central point, usually downtown. For example, 620 S Cedar Ave will be six blocks south of downtown. It is crucial, therefore, to take note of components such as "NW" or "SE" in addresses; 3620 King St SW will be a very long way indeed from 3620 King St NE. Where a number is prefixed to the street number, this indicates an apartment or suite number in a block at the same street address.

Bears Be aware of the dangers posed by bears. Most people blow a whistle while walking in bear country to warn them off. If confronted don't run, make loud noises or sudden movements, all of which are likely to provoke an attack. Leave the animal an escape route and back off slowly. If you have a backpack, leave it as a distraction. If attacked, climbing a tree or playing dead may save you from a grizzly, but not from black bears. Fighting back only increases the ferocity of an attack. For more on bears, see p.686.

Electric current Electricity in Canada is supplied at an alternating current of 110 volts and at a frequency of 60Hz, the same as in the US. Visitors from the UK will need transformers for appliances like shavers and hair dryers, and a plug converter for Canada's two-pin sockets. See ⓦ www.kropla.com for more.

Metric conversions

All figures are approximate.
1 centimetre = 0.39 inches; 1 inch = 2.5cm; 1 foot = 30cm.
1 metre (100cm) = 1.1 yards or 39 inches; 1 yard = 0.9m.
1 kilometre (1000m) = 0.6 miles; 1 mile = 1.6km; 8km = 5mi.
1 hectare (10,000sq m) = 2.5 acres; 1 acre = 0.4ha.
1 litre = 2.1 US pints; 1 US pint = 0.5 litres; 1 US quart = 0.9 litres.
1 litre = 0.3 US gallons; 1 US gallon = 3.8 litres.
1 litre = 1.8 UK pints; 1 UK pint = 0.6 litres.
1 litre = 0.2 UK gallons; 1 UK gallon = 4.5 litres.
1 kilogram or kilo (1000g) = 2.2lb; 1lb = 45g/0.45kg; 1oz = 28g.

Temperatures

°C	-10	-5	0	5	10	15	20	25	30	35
°F	14	23	32	41	50	59	68	77	86	95

Floors As with US usage, the "first floor" is what would be the ground floor in Britain; the "second floor" is one floor above ground level, and so on.

ID Should be carried at all times. Two pieces should suffice, one of which should have a photo; a passport and credit card are your best bet.

Measurements Canada officially uses the metric system, though many people still use the Imperial system. Distances are in kilometres, temperatures in degrees Celsius, and foodstuffs, petrol and drink are sold in grams, kilograms or litres.

Public toilets Rare even in cities, but bars, fast-food chains, museums and other public buildings invariably have excellent facilities.

Senior travellers For many senior citizens, retirement brings the opportunity to explore the world in a style and at a pace that is the envy of younger travellers. As well as the advantages of being free to travel during the quieter, less expensive seasons, and for longer periods, anyone over the age of 65, often 60, can enjoy the tremendous variety of discounts on offer to those who can produce suitable ID. VIA Rail and Greyhound, for example, offer (smallish) percentage reductions on fares to older passengers, while the majority of museums and similar attractions give at least fifty percent discounts for seniors.

Time zones See box, p.53.

Tipping Almost everywhere you eat or drink, the service will be fast and friendly – thanks to the institution of tipping. Waiters and bartenders depend on tips for the bulk of their earnings and, unless the service is dreadful, you should top up your bill by fifteen percent or more. A refusal to tip is considered rude and mean in equal measure. If you're paying by credit card, there's a space on the payment slip where you can add the appropriate tip.

Videos If you purchase a prerecorded video in Canada, make sure it's been recorded on the PAL system, or else it will be useless back in Europe. Blank videos can be used in either continent without any problem.

Guide

Guide

Ontario

CHAPTER 1 # Highlights

✳ Distillery District, Toronto
Chic arts centre in an old
Victorian distillery. **See p.91**

✳ AGO, Toronto Perhaps the
best art gallery in Canada, with
a great collection of Canadian
paintings. **See p.95**

✳ Toronto Islands When the city
gets hot and sultry, catch the
ferry over to these balmy
islands, where cars are
banned. **See p.104**

✳ Niagara Falls Simply one of
the most famous tourist
attractions in North America.
See p.120

✳ Niagara-on-the-Lake With its
antique clapboard houses and
immaculate gardens, this is
one of Ontario's prettiest
towns. **See p.127**

✳ Bayfield All leafy streets and
elegant homes, compact,
lakeside Bayfield is a perfect
place to unwind. **See p.141**

✳ Fathom Five Marine Park
Clear waters and shipwrecks
make for some outstanding
diving. **See p.146**

✳ Georgian Bay Islands The
region at its most beautiful –
crystal waters studded with
piney islands. **See p.156**

✳ Ottawa Amiable capital city,
with a lively eating scene plus
the outstanding national art
gallery. **See p.172**

✳ Algoma Central Railway
Arguably the best of Ontario's
train rides, from Sault Ste
Marie deep into the northern
wilds. **See p.203**

△ Yorkville Ave, Toronto

Ontario

Ontario, Canada's second-largest province, stretches all the way from the St Lawrence River and the Great Lakes to the frozen shores of Hudson Bay. Some two-thirds of this territory – all of the north and most of the centre – is occupied by the forests and rocky outcrops of the **Canadian Shield**, whose ancient Precambrian rocks were brought to the surface by the glaciers that gouged the continent during the last ice age. The glaciers produced a flattened landscape studded with thousands of lakes and it was the local Iroquois who first coined the name "Ontario", literally "glittering waters". The **Iroquois** – as well as their **Algonquin** neighbours to the north – hunted and fished the Canadian Shield, but their agricultural activities were confined to the more fertile and hospitable parts of southern Ontario, in which the vast majority of the province's ten million people are now concentrated.

With more than four million inhabitants, **Toronto** is Canada's biggest city, a financial and industrial behemoth that boasts a hatful of sights, the pick of which are its art galleries, a great restaurant scene and a vibrant nightlife. To the east and west of the city, along the north shore of **Lake Ontario**, is the so-called "Golden Horseshoe" – named for its economic clout rather than its looks – comprising sprawling suburbs and ugly industrial townships. The steel city of **Hamilton**, at the western end of the lake, has one or two interesting historic sights and is also near Canada's premier tourist spot, **Niagara Falls** – best visited on a day-trip from Toronto or from colonial **Niagara-on-the-Lake** nearby. Most of the rest of southwest Ontario, sandwiched between lakes Huron and Erie, is farming terrain that's as flat as a Dutch polder. Nevertheless, the car-producing town of **Windsor** is a lively place to spend a night, and both **Goderich** and **Bayfield** are charming little places tucked against the bluffs along the Lake Huron shoreline. For landscape, the most attractive regions of southern Ontario are the **Bruce Peninsula** and the adjacent **Georgian Bay**, whose **Severn Sound** is the location of the beautiful **Georgian Bay Islands National Park** as well as a pair of top-notch historical reconstructions, Discovery Harbour and **Sainte-Marie among the Hurons**.

Information and accommodation reservations

Ontario Travel is at ☎1-800/ONTARIO, ⊛www.ontariotravel.net. Almost all of Ontario's recommendable B&Bs are members of the **Federation of Ontario Bed and Breakfast Accommodation** (☎416/515-1293, ⊛www.fobba.com). Members' details are listed on their website and – at least for now – in the association's free handbook, available at most member B&Bs.

In **central Ontario**, inland from the coastal strip bordering Georgian Bay, are the myriad **Muskoka Lakes** – the epicentre of what Canadians call "cottage country". Every summer, the province's city folk arrive here in their thousands for a spot of fishing, boating and swimming, hunkering down in their lakeside cottages (though "cottages" is something of a misnomer as these second homes range from humble timber chalets to vast mansions). Locals swear this summer jaunt is the best time of the year, but touring the region as an outsider is mostly disappointing. For a start, and with the notable exception of several superb hotels, there is nowhere in particular to go and the main towns – primarily **Gravenhurst** and **Bracebridge** – are far from inspiring. If you get an invite to a cottage things may well seem very different, but otherwise, if you're after the great outdoors, you'd do best to keep going north to **Algonquin Provincial Park**. This consists of a vast wilderness where beavers and black bears roam and you can canoe for days without seeing a soul. Alternatively head east for the towns bordering the St Lawrence River, primarily **Kingston**, a handsome city with a clutch of fine colonial buildings. North of here, within easy striking distance, is **Ottawa**, the nation's capital, but a surprisingly small city of impeccable streets and parks, high-class museums and galleries, plus – and this may be something of a surprise if you're familiar with the city's bureaucratic image – a lively restaurant and bar scene.

Northern Ontario offers a natural environment stunning in its extremes, but the travelling can be hard and the specific sights too widely separated for comfort. Two main roads cross this sparsely inhabited region, **Hwy 11** in the north and **Hwy 17** to the south. The former links a series of mining towns and has little to offer, while the latter passes near – or cuts through – a string of parks, including the extravagantly wild **Lake Superior Provincial Park**. Hwy 17 also visits **Sault Ste Marie** – terminus of the **Agawa Canyon** train, which affords a glimpse of the otherwise impenetrable hinterland – as well as the gritty grain port of **Thunder Bay**, an ideal stopping point on the long journey west (or east). North of Hwy 11 lies a brutal country where hunters are the only regular visitors, though the passing tourist can get a taste of the terrain on board the Polar Bear Express train, which tracks across the Arctic tundra to link **Cochrane**, on Hwy-11, with **Moosonee** on the shores of James Bay.

Toronto is at the heart of Ontario's **public transport** system, with regular bus and rail services shuttling along the shore of Lake Ontario and the St Lawrence River to connect every major city between Niagara Falls, Ottawa and ultimately Montréal. Away from this urban core, however, the picture is far more sketchy. There are fairly regular bus services on the London–Windsor–Detroit route and along the Trans-Canada and Hwy 17, but connections between the province's smaller towns are few and far between: reckon on about one per day even for prominent places, though in some cases (Goderich, for instance) there are no buses at all.

A brief history of Ontario

The first **Europeans** to make regular contact with the aboriginal Iroquois and Algonquin peoples were the French explorers of the seventeenth and eighteenth centuries, most famously the intrepid Étienne Brûlé and Samuel de Champlain. However, these early visitors were preoccupied with the fur trade, and it wasn't until the end of the American War of Independence and the immigration of the **United Empire Loyalists** (see p.437) that mass settlement began. Between 1820 and 1850 a further wave of migrants, mostly English, Irish and Scots, made **Upper Canada**, as Ontario was known until Confederation, the most populous and prosperous Canadian region. This pre-eminence was reinforced towards the end of the nineteenth century by the **industrialization** of the region's larger towns, a process that was underpinned by the discovery of some of the world's richest mineral deposits: in the space of twenty years, nickel was found near Sudbury, silver at Cobalt, gold in Red Lake and iron ore at Wawa.

Nowadays, a highly mechanized timber industry, mineral mines, massive hydroelectric schemes and thousands of factories – making more than half the country's manufactured goods – keep Ontario at the top of the economic ladder. However, this industrial success has created massive **environmental problems**, most noticeable in the wounded landscapes around Sudbury and the polluted waters of lakes Erie and Ontario. Environmentally, at least, little was achieved in the 1990s when the province was firmly in the hands of the Progressive Conservative Party, whose flinty right-wing agenda owed much to Britain's Margaret Thatcher. The PCs were much taken up with privatization and tax cuts (plus endless carping about welfare scroungers), though, much to the relief of the left, the Liberals finally defeated them in 2003. If the new administration sticks to its reforming platform, it has much to do.

Toronto

The economic and cultural focus of English-speaking Canada, **TORONTO** is the country's largest metropolis. It sprawls along the northern shore of Lake Ontario, its vibrant, appealing centre encased by a jangle of satellite townships and industrial zones that cover (as "Greater Toronto") no less than 100 square kilometres. For decades, Toronto was saddled with unflattering sobriquets such as "Toronto the Good" or "Hogtown" that reflected a perhaps deserved reputation for complacent mediocrity and greed – and were enough to spur the city into years of image-building. Since the late 1950s, successive city administrations have lavished millions of dollars on glitzy architecture, slick museums, an excellent public-transport system, and the reclamation and development of the lakefront. As a result, Toronto has become one of North America's most likeable cities, an eminently liveable place whose citizens keep a wary eye on both their politicians and the developers.

Huge new shopping malls and skyrise office blocks reflect the economic successes of the last decades, a boom that has attracted **immigrants** from all over the world, transforming an overwhelmingly anglophone city into a cosmopolitan one of some sixty significant minorities. Indeed, getting the feel for Toronto's diversity is one of the city's great pleasures. Nowhere is this better experienced than in its myriad cafés and **restaurants**, where standards are high and prices are low. Toronto also boasts a pulsating **club** scene, not to mention a classy programme of **performing arts**, from dance to theatre and beyond.

Toronto's festivals

Within the space of twenty years the **Toronto International Film Festival** or TIFF (@www.e.bell.ca/filmfest) has gone from being an obscure celebration for hard-core film fans to one of the most respected festivals in the world – and the largest in North America. A ten-day affair, the festival begins on the first Thursday in September. Single, same-day **tickets** are available from the Film Festival's box offices (or as **rush tickets** immediately before screenings) for $13.75, or $24.50 for gala screenings. Lines to get in to the films can be fearsome but, once you're in, the directors and the stars introduce their pictures and make themselves available for question-and-answer periods after a film's first showing (all films screen twice). Many regular TIFF attendees plan their holidays around the festival, buying **books of tickets** in advance – a somewhat more economical method. There are a varieties of plans to choose from, and if you purchase before July 21st there is a modest discount: the least expensive of these is a book of ten tickets which can be used for all but Gala screenings. There's also the **Daytime Pass**, which gets you into 25 screenings, though only for those held between the hours of 8am and 6pm. All of these passes can be purchased from the TIFF website.

Otherwise, in late June, there's the outstanding **Downtown Jazz Festival** (@www.tojazz.com), which usually overlaps with the week-long **Gay & Lesbian Pride** (@www.pridetoronto.com), culminating in a whopping Pride Day Parade. Late July sees the **Caribana** (@www.caribana.com), a West Indian carnival with a fantastic parade plus music and dance, as well as the **Beaches Jazz Festival** (@www.beachesjazz.com). After the September film festival (see above), late October sees the sedate **International Festival of Authors**, held at the Harbourfront Centre (@www.harbourfront.on.ca).

GREATER TORONTO

THE TORONTO ISLANDS

Kingston

Barrie

Pearson Int'l Airport

Etobicoke

Niagara Falls

Lake Ontario

SCARBOROUGH

EAST YORK

YORK

Guildwood Park

Scarborough Bluffs

Ontario Science Centre

High Park

Humber Bay

Ontario Place

Toronto City Centre Airport

Inner Harbour

Outer Harbour

See Uptown Toronto map

See Downtown Toronto map

The Toronto Islands (see inset)

MACDONALD CARTIER FREEWAY

DON VALLEY PARKWAY

GARDINER EXPRESSWAY

THE BEACHES

GREEKTOWN

LITTLE INDIA

Eastern Gap

Ward's Island Beach

WARD'S ISLAND

Ward's Island Ferry

Inner Harbour

Algonquin Island

Snake Island

Olympic Island

Centre Island Ferry

Hanlan's Point Ferry

St Andrew's

CENTRE ISLAND

BAY OF THE ISLANDS

Centreville Amusement Park

Forestry Island

Mugg's Island

Toronto City Centre Airport

HANLAN'S POINT

Hanlan's Point Beach

Gibraltar Point

Gibraltar Point Lighthouse

Lake Ontario

0   500 m

0   5 km

N

Toronto also has its share of attention-grabbing sights and the majority are conveniently clustered in the city centre. The most celebrated of them is the **CN Tower**, the world's tallest free-standing structure, which stands next to the modern hump of the **SkyDome** sports stadium. The city's other prestige attractions kick off with the **Art Gallery of Ontario**, which possesses a first-rate selection of Canadian painting, and the **Royal Ontario Museum**, where pride of place goes to the Chinese collection. Yet it's the pick of Toronto's smaller, less-visited galleries that really add to the city's charm. There are superb Canadian paintings at the **Hudson's Bay Company Gallery**, a fascinating range of footwear at the **Bata Shoe Museum** and the eclectic **Gallery of Inuit Art** owned by the Toronto Dominion Bank. There are fascinating period homes too, most memorably the mock-Gothic extravagances of **Casa Loma** and the Victorian gentility of **Spadina House**, plus the replica colonial fortress of **Fort York**, where Toronto began. Spare time also for the good-looking buildings of the lively **St Lawrence** neighbourhood and the **Distillery District**, not actually a district at all but rather Toronto's brightest arts and entertainments complex, sited in a sprawling antique distillery.

Toronto's sights illustrate different facets of the city, but in no way do they crystallize its identity. The city remains opaque, too big and diverse to allow for a defining personality and this, of course, adds an enticing air of excitement and unpredictability to the place.

A brief history of Toronto

Situated on the slab of land separating Lake Ontario and Georgian Bay, **Toronto** was on one of the early portage routes into the interior, its name taken from the Huron for "place of meeting". The first European to visit the district was the French explorer Étienne Brûlé in 1615, but it wasn't until the middle of the eighteenth century that the French made a serious effort to control Lake Ontario with the development of a simple settlement and stockade, **Fort Rouillé**. The British pushed the French from the northern shore of Lake Ontario in 1759, but then chose to ignore the site for almost forty years until the arrival of hundreds of Loyalist settlers in the aftermath of the American Revolution.

In 1791 the British divided their remaining American territories into two, Upper and Lower Canada, each with its own legislative councils. The first capital of Upper Canada was Niagara-on-the-Lake, but this was too near the American border for comfort and the province's new lieutenant governor, **John Graves Simcoe**, moved his administration to the relative safety of Toronto in 1793, calling the new settlement **York**. Simcoe had grand classical visions of colonial settlement, but even he was exasperated by the conditions of frontier life – "the city's site was better calculated for a frog pond... than for the residence of human beings". Soon nicknamed "Muddy York", the capital was little more than a village when, in 1812, the Americans attacked and burnt the main buildings.

In the early nineteenth century, effective economic and political power lay in the hands of an anglophilic oligarchy christened the **Family Compact** by the radical polemicists of the day. Their most vociferous opponent was a radical Scot, **William Lyon Mackenzie**, who promulgated his views both in his newspaper, the *Colonial Advocate*, and as a member of the Legislative Assembly. Mackenzie became the first mayor of Toronto, as the town was renamed in 1834, but the radicals were defeated in the elections two years later and a frustrated Mackenzie drifted towards the idea of armed revolt. In 1837, he staged the **Upper Canadian insurrection**, a badly organized uprising of a few hundred farmers, who marched down Yonge St, fought a couple of half-hearted skirmishes and then melted away. Mackenzie fled across the border and two of the other ringleaders were executed, but the British parliament, mindful of their earlier experiences in New England, moved to liberalize Upper Canada's administration instead of taking reprisals. In 1841, they granted Canada **responsible government**, reuniting the two provinces in a loose confederation, prefiguring the final union of 1867 when Upper Canada was redesignated **Ontario**. Even Mackenzie was pardoned and allowed to return, arguably giving the lie to his portrayal of the oligarchs as hard-faced reactionaries: indeed, this same privileged group had even pushed progressive anti-slavery bills through the legislature as early as the 1830s.

By the end of the nineteenth century Toronto had become a major manufacturing centre dominated by a conservative mercantile elite, which was exceedingly loyal to the British interest and maintained a strong Protestant tradition. This elite was sustained by the working-class **Orange Lodges**, whose reactionary influence was a key feature of municipal politics – and prompted a visiting Charles Dickens to complain about the city's "rabid Toryism". Nevertheless, to be fair, these same Protestants were enthusiastic about public education, just like the Methodist-leaning middle classes, who also spearheaded social reform movements, principally Suffrage and Temperance. The trappings, however, remained far from alluring – well into the twentieth century Sunday was preserved as a "day of rest" and Eaton's store drew its curtains to prevent Sabbath window-shopping. Indeed, for all its capital status, the city was strikingly provincial by comparison with Montréal until well into the 1950s, when the opening of the **St Lawrence Seaway** gave the place something of a jolt and the first wave of non-white immigrants began to transform the city's complexion.

In the 1960s the economy exploded, and the city's appearance was transformed by the construction of a series of mighty, modernistic **skyscrapers**. This helter-skelter development was further boosted by the troubles in Québec, where the clamour for fair treatment by the Francophones prompted many of Montréal's Anglophone-dominated financial institutions and big businesses to up-sticks and transfer to Toronto. Much to the glee of Torontonians, the census of 1976 showed that Toronto had become **Canada's biggest city**, edging Montréal by just one thousand inhabitants, and since then the gap has grown much wider.

In the last twenty years, Toronto's economy has followed the cycles of boom and retrenchment common to the rest of the country, though real estate speculation was especially frenzied in the 1980s until the bottom fell out of the property market in 1988. In the mid-1990s, the **Progressive Conservatives** took control of Ontario, and their hard-nosed leader, **Mike Harris**, pushed through another governmental reorganization, combining the city of Toronto with its surrounding suburbs to create the "Mega City" of today. The change was deeply unpopular in the city of Toronto itself, but Harris still managed to get himself re-elected in 2000 with the large-scale support of small-town and suburban Ontario. A hated figure amongst the province's liberals and socialists, Harris's conservative social policies are often blamed for the dramatic increase in the number of homeless people on the city's streets. In 2002, Harris passed the premiership over to another Progressive Conservative, Ernie Eves, but he proved to be an inconsequential figure who lost the provincial election of 2003 to the Liberals, hopefully heralding a move towards more moderate, consensual politics.

Arrival, information and transport

Toronto's downtown core is sandwiched between Front St to the south, Bloor to the north, Spadina to the west and Jarvis to the east. **Yonge Street** is the main north–south artery: principal street numbers start and names change from "West" to "East" from here. (Note, therefore, that 1000 Queen St W is a long way from 1000 Queen St E.) To appreciate the transition between the different downtown neighbourhoods, it's best to **walk** around the centre: Front to Bloor is about 2km, Spadina to Jarvis 1km.

In an attempt to protect shoppers from Ontario's climate, there's also an enormous sequence of pedestrianized shopping arcades called the **PATH Walkway**, which begins beneath Union Station, twisting up to the Eaton Centre shopping mall and beyond. Access points, of which there are many, sport multicoloured signs and there are maps all over the walkway; they need to be, as PATH can be very disorienting.

By air

Arriving by **air**, you'll almost certainly land at Toronto's main airport, **Lester B. Pearson International** (code YYZ; ⓦ www.gtaa.com), about 27km northwest of the city centre. There are three terminals here and each has a full range of facilities, including money-exchange offices, ATMs and free hotel hotlines. The **Airport Express bus** service (daily every 30min 5am–1am, plus at 3am; $14.95 one-way, $25.75 round-trip valid for one year; ⓣ 905/564-6333, ⓦ www.torontoairportexpress.com) picks up passengers outside the terminals and takes forty to sixty minutes to reach downtown, though heavy traffic can make the journey longer. The bus drops passengers at the coach station (see below for details) and several of Toronto's major hotels, with connecting minibuses ($3.30/$5.50) taking passengers to most of the other downtown hotels. You can buy tickets either at the kiosks next to the bus stop outside the terminal buildings or from the driver. Much less expensive, if more time-consuming, are the several **bus services** linking the airport with the city's subway network. The two fastest – which leave from designated stops outside each of the terminal buildings – are operated by the TTC (the Toronto Transit Commission), which runs all of the city's public transport. Buy tickets from the driver. Their **Airport Rocket** (#192; daily every 20–30min 5.30am–2am; $2.25 one-way) takes about twenty minutes to reach Kipling subway station, at the west end of the subway network. From there, it takes another 20min by subway (which operates Mon–Sat 6am–1am, Sun 9am–1am) to get downtown. The Rocket is supplemented by a night bus (#300A; hourly 2am–5am), which leaves the airport to run downtown along Bloor St. The second option, TTC bus **#58A**, links the airport with Lawrence West subway station, north of downtown (daily 5am–1am; 45mins; $2.25 one-way). There's an airport **limo service** (a shared taxi system) next to each terminal's bus platform; you'll pay $40 per person to downtown. Unlike taxis, the price is fixed, an important consideration if you arrive (or leave) during rush hour; the disadvantage is that they mostly only leave when they're full. Individual **taxis** charge about the same – $40 from the airport to the city centre – but fares are metered.

The much smaller **Toronto City Centre Airport**, or "TCCA" (code YTZ; ⓦ www.torontoport.com/tcca.htm), which is on Hanlan's Point in Toronto's harbour, close to downtown, handles flights on Air Canada (ⓣ 1-888/247-2262) from Montréal, Ottawa and London (ON). From the airport, there's a **free minibus** to the *Royal York Hotel*, on the corner of Front St West and York St.

By bus, train and car

Well connected to most of the major towns of eastern Canada, Toronto's **coach station** is conveniently located downtown at 610 Bay St, metres from Dundas St West. The nearest subway station is a five-minute walk east at Yonge and Dundas. From here, PMCL (☎1-800/461-1767, ⓦwww.pmcl.on.ca) operates buses to Midland, Penetang and Owen Sound; Coach Canada

RESTAURANTS

Babur	16
Bangkok Garden	3
Bangkok Paradise	14
Barberian's	4
Bo De Duyen	10
Canoe	23
Fressen Herbacious Cuisine	11
Happy Seven	6
La Fenice	22
Lai Wah Heen	8
Le Commensal	2
Le Papillion	24
Le Select	15
Lee Garden	5
Lucky Dragon	1
Monsoon	21
Nami	20
Noce	13
Pho 88 Restaurant	9
Queen Mother Café	12
Rodney's Oyster House	19
Sushi Bistro	17
Tundra	18
Vien Dong	7

ONTARIO | Toronto: Arrival, information and transport

The Beaches ▶

ACCOMMODATION

Bond Place	B
Canadiana Backpackers Hostel	C
Delta Chelsea Inn	A
Fairmont Royal York	I
Global Village Backpackers	D
Hotel Le Germain	E
Hotel Victoria	G
Le Royal Meridian King Edward	F
Novotel Toronto Centre	J
Strathcona	H
Westin Harbour Castle Hotel	K

(☎1-800/461-7661, ⓦwww.coaccanada.com) to Niagara Falls, Montréal and Kingston; and Greyhound Canada (☎416/367-8747, ⓦwww.greyhound.ca) operates a range of long-distance buses. If you're arriving at night, note that the bus station's immediate environs are unsavoury, but it only takes a couple of minutes to reach more reassuring parts of downtown. Nonetheless, if you're travelling alone or late at night, it's probably best to take a taxi.

All incoming **trains** – including VIA Rail (☎1-888/842-7245, ⓦwww
.viarail.ca) – arrive at **Union Railway Station**, at the junction of Bay St and
Front St West. The station complex, which is the hub of the city's public transportation system, includes a subway station and also holds the main terminal for
the GO trains and buses (ⓦwww.gotransit.com) that service the city's suburbs.
Details of GO services are available at their station ticket offices, or by calling
toll-free ☎1-888/438-6646 (within Toronto ☎416/869-3200). Note also that
Ontario Northland (☎1-800/461-8558, ⓦwww.northlander.ca), which operates trains north to Cochrane and the Polar Bear Express to Moosonee (see
p.196), has an information desk in the main hall.

From Niagara Falls and points west along Lake Ontario, most **road traffic**
arrives via the QEW (Queen Elizabeth Way), which funnels into the Gardiner
Expressway, an elevated motorway that cuts across the southern side of downtown, just south of Front St. The Gardiner is notorious for delays. From the
east, most drivers opt for the equally busy **Hwy 401**, which sweeps along Lake
Ontario before veering off to slice through the city's suburbs north of downtown. Driving in from the north, take **Hwy 400**, which intersects with Hwy
401 northwest of the centre, or **Hwy 404**, which meets Hwy 401 northeast of
the centre. To relieve congestion on Hwy 401, an alternative motorway, **Hwy
407ETR**, has been built further north on the city's edge. It was North
America's first all-electronic toll highway: instead of toll booths, each vehicle is
identified by an electronic tag (a transponder), and the invoice is mailed on
later. Toll charges are fixed at 11.5¢ per kilometre and there's also a small
supplementary charge per trip for any vehicle without a transponder – these
vehicles are identified by licence plate photos. If you rent a car, be aware that
rental companies slap on an extra administration charge (of around $15) if you
take their vehicles on this road.

Information

The excellent **Ontario Tourism Travel Information Centre** (Mon–Fri
10am–9pm, Sat 9.30am–7pm, Sun noon–5pm; ☎1-800/ONTARIO, or
within Toronto ☎905/282-1721), on Level 1 of the Eaton shopping centre at
Yonge and Dundas, stocks a comprehensive range of information. Of particular interest are the free city maps, the *Ride Guide* to the city's transport system,
and accommodation and entertainment details in the monthly magazine
Where. They will also book hotel accommodation on your behalf both in
Toronto and across all of Ontario. Alternatively, the **Info T.O. visitor information centre** (daily 9am–5pm) is located in the city's Convention Centre at
255 Front St W, a couple of minutes' walk west from Union Station. Privately
run, it is more geared up for selling tour tickets than providing information,
though it has a reasonable supply of free literature on the city and its environs.
Finally, **Tourism Toronto**, the city's official visitor and convention
bureau, operates a telephone information line (☎416/203-2500 or
1-800/499-2514; Mon–Fri 8.30am–5pm, Sat 9am–5pm, Sun 10am–5pm) that
can handle most city queries and will make hotel reservations. Toronto has two
first-rate **newspapers**, the *Toronto Star* and the *Globe and Mail*, the latter sold
all over Canada.

City transport

Fast, frequent and efficient, Toronto's public transportation is operated by the
Toronto Transit Commission, or the TTC (☎416/393-4636 daily
8am–6pm, ⓦwww.ttc.ca), whose integrated network of subways, buses and

streetcars serves virtually every corner of the city. With the exception of downtown, where all the major sights are within easy walking distance of one another, your best option is to use public transport to hop between attractions – especially in the cold of winter or the sultry summertime. Much to its credit, the TTC has gone to great lengths to assure the safety of its passengers: all subway stations have **DWAs** (Designated Waiting Areas), which are well lit, have an intercom connection with TTC staff and are monitored by closed-circuit TV. In addition, TTC buses operate a **Request Stop Program**, which allows women travelling alone late at night (9pm–5am) to get off buses wherever they want, and not just at regular TTC stops. A similarly positive approach has been adopted for passengers with **disabilities**, who can use a dedicated service, Wheel-Trans (☏ 416/393-4111).

On every part of the TTC system a single journey costs $2.25. **Tickets** are available at all subway stations and from bus and streetcar drivers. Metallic **tokens** can also be used, issued at subway stations, but they're small and easy to lose. A batch of five tickets or tokens can be bought for $9.50 (ten for $17) at any station and at most convenience stores and newsstands. Each ticket or token entitles passengers to one complete journey of any length on the TTC system. If this involves more than one type of transport, it is necessary to get a paper **transfer** at your point of entry. Streetcar and bus drivers issue transfers, as do the automatic machines located at every subway station. A **day pass** costs $7.75 and provides one adult with unlimited TTC travel after 9.30am on weekdays and all day on Saturdays. On Sundays, the same pass becomes a terrific deal for families: it covers up to six people (though only two can be adults).

Toronto's **subway** is a simple, two-line system. The Bloor–Danforth line cuts east to west along Bloor St, while the Yonge–University–Spadina line forms a loop with Union Station at its head; north of Union, this subway line runs along University Ave and Yonge St. Transferring between the two lines is possible at three stations only: Spadina, St George and Bloor–Yonge. The subway operates Mon–Sat 6am–1/2am, Sun 9am–1/2am.

The system of **buses and streetcars** couldn't be simpler, as a bus and/or streetcar station adjoins every major subway stop. Hours of operation vary with the route, but are comparable with subway times; there is also a limited network of **night buses** running along key routes roughly hourly between 1am and 6am.

Taxis cruise the city and can be hailed from any street corner. Give the driver your destination and ask the approximate price before you start. **Fares** are generally reasonable, based on a fixed tariff of $2.50 for the first 235m and 25¢ for every 235m thereafter. As an example, a ride from Union Station to the far side of Cabbagetown should cost around $10. Of the multitude of cab companies to choose from, the most reliable tend to be **Co-op Cabs** (☏ 416/504-2667) or **Diamond Taxicab** (☏ 416/366-6868).

Accommodation

As Toronto's popularity as a tourist destination has increased, so the availability of **hotel** accommodation, especially in the mid-price range, has shrunk. Indeed, during peak season (late June to Aug) and throughout most of the city's big festivals, it is essential to book well in advance. Most of the city's hotels occupy modern skyscrapers and there is much stylistic uniformity in the

UPTOWN TORONTO

RESTAURANTS

Avli	5
Bar Italia	6
Café Nervosa	3
Joso's	1
Le Pecherie	2
Mövenpick	4
Nataraj	

ACCOMMODATION

Au Petit Paris B&B	I
Days Inn Downtown Toronto	P
Four Seasons	E
High Park B&B	G
Howard Johnson's Yorkville	D
Innis College, Uni. Of Toronto	K
Les Amis B&B	Q
Madison Manor Boutique Hotel	C
Massey College, Uni. of Toronto	J
The Mulberry Tree	O
Palmerston Inn	F
Park Hyatt	N
Sutton Place	A
Terrace House	L
Victoria College, Uni. of Toronto	H
Windsor Arms	B
YWCA Woodlawn Residence	

standardized fittings and furnishings. Prices reflect floor space and tend to fluctuate depending on when and for how long you stay, but, in general, a clean, centrally located hotel room starts at $80–100. **Bed-and-breakfast** accommodation tends to be slightly cheaper – even with breakfast thrown in. While most of these establishments are not as central as the city's hotels, they often take you off the beaten track and into Toronto's quainter neighbourhoods. Budget-conscious travellers might also want to consider the dreary **hostels**, but at this end of the market the best deal in town is the **summer residences** at local universities. You'll get the bare essentials here, but the rooms are much cheerier than the hostels and are available – with some variation – from the second week in May to the end of August; prices start at about $50.

The Ontario Tourism Travel Information Centre (see p.80), in the Eaton Centre shopping mall, will help in **finding a hotel room**, or you can call Tourism Toronto's hotel reservation line (see p.80). In addition, Ontario Tourism will issue you with an *Annual Visitor's Guide* that contains a comprehensive list of the city's accommodation.

Hotels and B&Bs

Bond Place 65 Dundas St E ☎416/362-6061 or 1-800/268-9390, ⓦwww.bondplacehoteltoronto.com. Popular with package-tour operators and handily located, just a couple of minutes' walk from the Eaton Centre; simple, unassuming doubles; some weekend reductions. Dundas subway. **④**

Days Inn Toronto Downtown 30 Carlton St ☎416/977-6655 or 1-800/DAYS-INN, ⓦwww.daysinn.com. Routine modern hotel with competitively priced rooms. Occupies a chunky tower block metres from College subway. **⑤**

Delta Chelsea Inn 33 Gerrard St W ☎416/595-1975, ⓦwww.deltachelsea.com. Near the Eaton Centre, this is the biggest hotel in town with excellent leisure facilities, including swimming pool, gym, sauna and childcare. The comfortable, attractively furnished rooms are a comparative bargain, with substantial weekend discounts. Dundas subway. **⑥**

Fairmont Royal York 100 Front St W ☎416/368-2511 or 1-800/441-1414, ⓦwww.fairmont.com. When it was completed in 1927, the Royal York was the largest hotel in the British Empire and it still retains much of its original grandeur, especially in the sprawling lobby, which is decked out with mosaic floors, coffered ceilings and massive chandeliers. The guest rooms aren't as pricey (or as stylish) as you might expect and there are substantial off-season and weekend discounts. Union subway. **⑥**

Four Seasons 21 Avenue Rd ☎416/964-0411 or 1-800/332-3442, ⓦwww.fourseasons.com. This well-appointed establishment, situated in the heart of the Yorkville neighbourhood, has a reputation for hosting the city's most famous guests. The hotel's restaurants and wine cellar are as stellar as the impeccable service, and while the prices here are off the charts, this is a fine place to be if you want to splurge. Subway: Bay. **⑨**

Howard Johnson Yorkville 89 Avenue Rd ☎416/964-1220 or 1-877/967-5845, ⓦwww.hojo.com. This small, budget-friendly hotel is tucked away in a busy section of Avenue Rd, just blocks from Yorkville. The helpful staff are attentive, and the large rooms are tidy, comfortable and well equipped for the business traveller. Subway: Bay **④**

Hotel Le Germain 30 Mercer St ☎416/345-9500 or 1-866/7345-9501, ⓦwww.hotelgermain.com. Spanking new from the ground up, this stylish boutique hotel offers well appointed rooms done in minimal modernist style. Streetcar: King St (#504). **⑧**

Le Royal Meridian King Edward 37 King St E ☎416/863-3131 or 1-800/543-4300, ⓦwww.lemeridien-kingedward.com. Designed by E.J. Lennox (see p.92) in 1903 and with a long list of famous guests – from Mark Twain to John and Yoko – this distinguished old hotel has recently been restored to its Beaux Arts best. Rooms range from chic minimalism to faux Edwardian. Subway: King. **⑦**

Madison Manor Boutique Hotel 20 Madison Ave ☎416/922-5579 or 1-877-561-7048, ⓦwww.madisonavenuepub.com. Located in the heart of the Annex neighbourhood, this inn has 22 comfortable, non-smoking rooms, some with fireplaces and all with en-suite bathrooms as well as the amenities (hair dryers, Internet access) that you would expect in a luxury hotel. A great find. Subway: St George. **④**

Novotel Toronto Centre 45 The Esplanade ☏416/367-8900 or 1-800/668-6835, ⊛www.novotel.com. Located in a splendidly converted old building, with an elegant arcaded facade and other Art Deco flourishes, this chain hotel offers excellent service at moderate prices. Its affordability may be linked to its noisy location – it abuts the railway – but otherwise, the location is excellent, close to the downtown core, the Harbourfront and the Distillery District. Subway: Union Station. ❺

Park Hyatt 4 Avenue Rd ☏416/924-5471 or 1-800/977-4197, ⊛www.hyatt.com. On the edge of the posh Yorkville neighbourhood, this luxury hotel boasts a rooftop cocktail bar with spectacular views of the city. The recently refurbished rooms offer the ultimate in comfort, albeit at a premium price. Subway: Museum or Bay. ❼

Strathcona 60 York St ☏416/363-3321 or 1-800/268-8304, ⊛www.toronto.com /strathconahotel. A good bet for the business traveller, with all the standard amenities. The location – about half a block from Union Station, and five minutes from the SkyDome and the CN Tower – is its most distinctive feature. Subway: Union Station. ❺

Sutton Place 955 Bay St ☏416/924-9221 or 1-800/268-3790, ⊛www.suttonplace.com. Long associated with the Toronto International Film Festival (see p.73), this classy hotel is a favourite with visiting celebrities, and the service and amenities are predictably excellent. Nicely situated for all the downtown sights, and only a five-minute walk from the Gay Village. Subway: Wellesley. ❼

Hotel Victoria 56 Yonge St ☏416/363-1666 or 1-800/363-8228, ⊛www.hotelvictoria-toronto.com. This charming hotel occupies a dignified old building in the heart of downtown. The fifty rooms are clean and crisply furnished, but a tad cramped. Complementary continental breakfast. Subway: King. ❻

Westin Harbour Castle 1 Harbour Square ☏416/869-1600 or 1-800/937-8461, ⊛www.westin.com. York Quay stop on the LRT from Union Station. This massive hotel has a prime location right on the edge of Lake Ontario. It's hardly intimate, but many of the rooms, which are decorated in extremely comfortable style, offer splendid lake views. Every amenity. ❻

Windsor Arms 18 St Thomas St ☏416/971-9666, ⊛www.windsorarmshotel.com. One of the city's most distinctive hotels, the Windsor occupies an immaculate brick-and-stone-trimmed building with neo-Gothic flourishes that is a replica of the original 1911 edifice that was burnt down in the 1990s. Open fires, columns, stained-glass windows and Georgian-style furniture characterize the interior. What's new are the condominiums on top, plus the no-expense-spared spa; top-notch service too. Subway: Bay. ❽

B&Bs

Au Petit Paris B&B 3 Selby St ☏416/928-1348, ⊛www.bbtoronto.com/aupetitparis. Attractive B&B in a meticulously renovated Victorian house. Each of the guest rooms is decorated in modern style, with hardwood floors and pastel-painted walls, and comes complete with a queen-size bed and en-suite facilities. Vegetarian breakfasts are the house speciality. Subway: Sherbourne. ❺

High Park B&B 4 High Park Blvd, High Park ☏416/531-7963. This spacious home has three rooms, two of which share a bathroom. The largest room has its own balcony, which overlooks the leafy confines of the surrounding Victorian neighbourhood. The breakfasts here are scrumptious, and the service is infinitely friendly. Subway: Dundas West. ❷

Les Amis B&B 31 Granby St ☏416/591-0635, ⊛www.bbtoronto.com. Downtown B&B, a short stroll from the Eaton Centre, holding a handful of pleasantly furnished rooms with shared facilities. Vegetarian breakfasts are a speciality – the crepes go down a treat. Air conditioned. Subway: College. ❹

The Mulberry Tree 122 Isabella St ☏416/960-5249, ⊛www.bbtoronto.com. This delightful B&B, one of Toronto's most agreeable, occupies a tastefully decorated heritage home close to the city centre. Each of the guest rooms is comfortable and relaxing – indeed the whole atmosphere of the place is just right, combining efficiency and friendliness. Breakfasts are first rate, too, home cooking at its best and eaten at one large table where guests can chat away. A short walk from Wellesley or Bloor-Yonge subway stations. Highly recommended. ❺

Palmerston Inn 322 Palmerston Blvd ☏416/920-7842, ⊛www.toronto.com/palmerstoninn. This oak-panelled mansion has eight rooms of varying degrees of comfort, with features such as fireplaces, fresh flowers and bathrobes. Bonuses include afternoon sherry and a daily room service. Streetcar: College (#506). ❺

Terrace House 52 Austin Terrace ☏416/535-1493, ⊛www.terracehouse.com. This pre-World War I, mock-Tudor house is perched high on a hill overlooking the city and close to Casa Loma and Spadina House (see p.103). There are three rooms (two with fireplaces, one with a private bath), all decked out with antiques and North African rugs. A five-minute walk from the Dupont subway station. Subway: St Clair West. ❹

Hostels and student rooms

Canadiana Backpackers Hostel 42 Widmer St ☎416/598-9090 or 1-877/215-1225, ⓦwww.canadianalodging.com. This hip, clean hostel is right in the midst of Toronto's clubs, steps away from Queen St W and within easy walking distance of downtown. Dorm bed $25; ten percent off with HI or student card. Streetcar: King St (#504).

Global Village Backpackers Hostel 460 King St W ☎416/703-8540 or 1-888/844-7875, ⓦwww.hostelworld.com. This former hotel (once famed for a free-wheeling Art Deco tap room) has four private/family rooms; everything else is dormitory-style with shared bathrooms. The above-standard facilities include laundry facilities, a kitchen and a games room. Close to the Richmond St/Queen St West action. Dorm bed $25; ten percent off with HI or student card. Streetcar: King (#504).

YWCA Woodlawn Residence 80 Woodlawn Ave E ☎416/923-8454, ⓦwww.ywcator.org. Tucked away in a cul-de-sac in the pretty Summerhill neighbourhood, this women-only residence offers dormitory, single and double rooms at daily and monthly rates, and includes a continental breakfast. Laundry facilities. Subway: Summerhill. Dorm bed $22.

Student rooms

University of Toronto – Innis College 111 St George St ☎416/978-2553, ⓦwww.utoronto.ca/innis/residence/summer. This recently built residence, with air-conditioning and daily room service, offers daily and weekly rentals for single rooms, while doubles are only available for long-term stays. Subway: St George. Single room $30.

University of Toronto – Massey College 4 Devonshire Place ☎416/978-2549, ⓦwww.utoronto.ca/massey. Apart from being the one-time stomping ground of author Robertson Davies, this beautiful college reportedly boasts the presence of at least one ghost. Singles and doubles are available with breakfast included on weekdays May–July; rates are lower in August, when breakfast is no longer served. Subway: St George. Single room May–July $50, Aug $45.

University of Toronto – Victoria College 140 Charles St W ☎416/585-4524, ⓦwww.vicu.utoronto.ca/. This huge campus site includes accommodation in Annesley Hall, Burwash Hall, Law House and Margaret Addison Hall. The daily rates for doubles and singles include a full cafeteria breakfast. Subway: Museum. Single room $47.

Downtown Toronto

Toronto evolved from a lakeside settlement, but its growth was sporadic and often unplanned, resulting in a cityscape that can strike the visitor as a random mix of the run-down and the new. This apparent disarray, combined with the city's muggy summers, means that, rather than walking the streets, most newcomers to Toronto spend their time hopping from sight to sight on the efficient public transport system. Indeed, there's no doubt that if you've only got a day or two to spare this is the way to get a grip on the city.

On the other hand, if you've the time to get below the surface, the best thing to do is stroll through **Downtown Toronto**, and the logical place to start is the **CN Tower**, from where you can take in the lie of the land for kilometres around. Nearby **Union Station**, hub of the city's public transport system, lies on the edge of the **Business District**, whose striking skyscrapers march up Yonge as far as Queen St, where they give way to the main shopping area, revolving around the enormous **Eaton Centre**. To the west of this commercial zone lie **Chinatown** and the **Art Gallery of Ontario**, while to the northwest, University Ave is the most obviously English-influenced area of town around Queen's Park. Here you'll find the imposing **Ontario Parliament** building, the University of Toronto, the **Royal Ontario Museum** and the outstanding **Gardiner Museum of Ceramic Art**. Moving on to the northern periphery of downtown Toronto, the key attractions are the fascinating Bata Shoe Museum and a pair of contrasting Victorian mansions –

Toronto's neighbourhoods

One of Toronto's most striking features is its division into distinct **neighbourhoods**, many of them based on ethnic origin, others defined by sexual preference or income. Bilingual street signs identify some of these neighbourhoods, but architecturally they are often indistinguishable from their surroundings. The following rundown will help you get the most from the city's demographic mosaic, whether you want to shop, eat or just take in the atmosphere. But bear in mind that there is a certain artificiality in the nomenclature: Chinatown, for instance, has hundreds of Vietnamese residents, Little Italy many Portuguese.

The Beaches South of Queen St East between Woodbine and Victoria Park Ave. A prosperous and particularly appealing district with chic boutiques, leafy streets and a sandy beach trimmed by a popular boardwalk. Glenn Gould (see box, p.94) was born here.

Cabbagetown East of Jarvis and roughly bounded by Gerrard St East on its south side, Wellesley to the north and the Don River to the east. Renowned for its Victorian housing. Its name comes from the district's nineteenth-century immigrants, whose tiny front gardens were filled with cabbages.

Chinatown Concentrated along Dundas between Bay and Spadina. This is one of Toronto's most distinctive neighbourhoods, with busy restaurants and stores selling anything from porcelain and jade to herbs and pickled seaweed.

The Gay and Lesbian Village Centred around Church and Wellesley, with a plethora of bars, restaurants and bookshops.

Greektown A burgeoning neighbourhood along Danforth Ave, between Pape and Woodbine. With scores of authentic restaurants, this is the place to go for Greek food.

Kensington Market Just north of Dundas between Spadina and Augusta. The most ethnically diverse part of town, combining Portuguese, West Indian and Jewish Canadians, who pack the streets with a plethora of tiny shops and open-air stalls.

Little India Along Gerrard St East, running one block west from Coxwell Ave. Visually, it's not too appealing, but the area does have a number of fine restaurants.

Little Italy The so-called Corso Italia runs along College between Bathurst and Clinton, and is one of Toronto's liveliest neighbourhoods.

Little Portugal A crowded, vital area packed with shops and neighbourhood food joints, focused on Dundas, west of Bathurst as far as Dovercourt Rd.

Queen St West Between University and Spadina. Has one of the highest retail rents in the city and is home to all things trendy and expensive. The students and punks who once hung around here have moved on to what is known as "West Queen West", between Bathurst and Ossington.

Yorkville Just above Bloor between Yonge and Avenue Rd. Was "alternative" in the 1960s, with appearances by the likes of Gordon Lightfoot and Joni Mitchell. Today, the alternative jive is long gone, and the district holds some of Toronto's most expensive clothing shops and art galleries, as well as several good bars and restaurants.

grandiose **Casa Loma** and genteel **Spadina House**. Spare time also for **Fort York** to the west of downtown and the redeveloped **Harbourfront** south of Union Station, which offers flashy shops, the **Power Plant Gallery** of modern art, as well as the jetty from where ferries make the short hop over to the bucolic **Toronto Islands**.

The CN Tower and the SkyDome

Much to the dismay of many Torontonians, the **CN Tower**, 301 Front St West (daily: Jan–April 10am–10pm; May–Dec 8am–11pm; observation deck

$18, Sky Pod $8 extra; Union Station subway), has become the city's symbol. It's touted on much of the city's promotional literature, features on thousands of postcards and holiday snaps, and has become the obligatory start to most tourist itineraries. From anywhere in the city, it's impossible to miss its slender form poking high above the skyline, reminding some of French novelist Guy de Maupassant's quip about another famous tower: "I like to lunch at the Eiffel Tower because that's the only place in Paris I can't see it."

Unlikely as it may seem, the celebrity status of the CN Tower was entirely unforeseen, its origins plain and utilitarian. In the 1960s, the Canadian Broadcasting Company (CBC) teamed up with the railway conglomerate Canadian National (CN) to propose the construction of a bigger and better transmission antenna. CBC eventually withdrew from the project, but CN, who owned the land and saw a chance for profit, forged ahead. Much to the company's surprise, they found that the undertaking stirred intense public interest – so much so that long before the tower was completed, in 1975, it was clear that its potential as a tourist sight would be huge: today, broadcasting only accounts for about twenty percent of the tower's income, with the rest provided by the two million tourists who throng here annually. Come early (especially on school holidays) to avoid the crowds.

Only die-hard critics could deny the sleek elegance of the tower, which tapers to a minaret-thin point 553m (1815ft) above the city centre. It's the **tallest structure in the world**, and details of its construction are provided in a series of photographs and touch-screen displays on the main access ramp and on the mezzanine level beyond. The background information is interesting – especially tidbits revealing that the tower is hit by lightning between sixty and eighty times a year – but the "Daredevil Thrills" film simulations (for an extra charge) of bungee jumping, tightrope walking and the like, in the neighbouring concourse, are eminently missable.

From the foot of the tower, glass-fronted elevators whisk you up the outside of the building to the indoor and outdoor **Look Out level** galleries at 346m. These circular galleries provide views over the whole of the city, which appears flattened and without much perspective – though markers help by pointing out the most conspicuous sights. This is also where you'll find *360 The Restaurant* (which slowly revolves around the tower, taking 72 minutes to make one revolution), as well as experience the vertigo shock of the reinforced **glass floor** – a thrill that goes some way to justifying the tower's pricey admittance fee. You're still 100m from the top of the tower, though; a separate set of lifts carry visitors up to the **Sky Pod**, a confined little gallery that doesn't justify the extra expense.

Next door to the CN Tower is the **SkyDome**, home to two major Toronto sports teams – the Blue Jays baseball team and the Argonauts, of Canadian football fame. The stadium seats 53,000 and is also used for special events and concerts. Opened in 1989, it was the first stadium in the world to have a fully retractable roof (it takes only twenty minutes to cover the stadium's eight acres of turf and terrace). It was an extraordinary feat of engineering and one that was much touted by the city but, unfortunately, the end result is pretty ugly: when the roof is closed it looks like a giant armadillo. **Guided tours** (call for schedule ☎416/341-2770; $12.50), worth it only if you're sticking around for a sporting event, last an hour and begin with a fifteen-minute film about the stadium's construction. The ensuing walking tour takes in the media centre, a dressing room and a stroll on the field.

The Banking District

To the east of the CN Tower, the *beaux-arts* niceties of Union Railway Station and the matching Royal York Hotel opposite mark the boundary of the **Banking District**, whose bizarre juxtapositions of old and low buildings and high-rises evidence one of Toronto's stranger ordinances. The city's buildings have a notional maximum altitude and although owners of older properties are not allowed to extend their buildings, they are permitted to sell the empty space between their roofs and this notional maximum. Thus, the builders of new structures can purchase this space and add it to their own maximum, thereby creating the skyscrapers that the ordinance would seem to forbid. The arrangement enhances neither the old nor the new, but some of the high-rises are undeniably impressive, such as the colossal twin towers of the **Royal Bank Plaza**, at Bay and Front, and the four reflective-black blocks of the **Toronto Dominion Centre**, along Wellington St West between Bay and York. Just one of these four blocks is on the south side of Wellington and here you'll find the **Toronto Dominion Gallery of Inuit Art** (Mon–Fri 8am–6pm, Sat & Sun 10am–4pm; free), which boasts an exquisite collection of Inuit sculpture. Spread over two levels, the collection is owned by the Dominion Bank, who commissioned a panel of experts to collect the best of postwar Inuit art in 1965. Their haul features some simple and forceful stone carvings by Johnny Inukpuk, whose impressionistic style – in such pieces as *Mother Feeding Child* – contrasts with the precision of the *Migration* by Joe Talirunili, in which the rowers crane forward in eagerness and anxiety.

Around the corner at 234 Bay St, the old **Toronto Stock Exchange** has been mutilated by its incorporation within a skyrise that imitates – but doesn't match – the sober black blocks of the adjacent Toronto Dominion Centre. Nevertheless, the facade has survived, its stone lintel decorated with muscular carvings of men at work, a frieze given a political twist by the top-hatted figure – the capitalist – who dips his hand into a worker's pocket, a subversive subtext by an unknown stonemason. The interior of the Stock Exchange now accommodates the temporary exhibitions of the **DX** or **Design Exchange** (Tues–Fri 9am–6pm, Sat & Sun noon–5pm; free except during some exhibitions) – whose purpose is to foster innovative design. From the DX, it's a short stroll to the old Bank of Montréal building, a solid Neoclassical edifice of 1885 that now houses the **Hockey Hall of Fame**, 30 Yonge St at Front St West (late June to Aug Mon–Sat 9.30am–6pm, Sun 10am–6pm; Sept to late June Mon–Fri 10am–5pm, Sat 9.30am–6pm, Sun 10.30am–5pm; $12). The place is stuffed with ice-hockey memorabilia, has a replica of the Montréal Canadiens' dressing room and proudly exhibits the sport's Holy Grail, the Stanley Cup.

Afterwards, you can either detour west to Fort York (see below), stroll east to visit the St Lawrence and Distillery districts (see p.90) or push on up to City Hall (see p.92).

West of Union Station: Fort York

Modern-day Toronto traces its origins to **Fort York**, an appealing reconstruction of a colonial stockade marooned in the shadow of the Gardiner Expressway a fifteen-minute stroll west from Union Station, on Garrison Rd, off Fleet St (mid-May to Aug daily 10am–5pm; Sept to late May Mon–Fri 10am–4pm, Sat & Sun 10am–5pm; $5). To get there, follow Front St West to its end, turn left along Bathurst St and, after crossing the railway bridge, take the signposted footpath on the right; this leads to the fort's rear entrance. To reach the front entrance, take either the Bathurst streetcar (#511) or streetcar

△ Henry Moore sculptures in the Art Gallery of Ontario, Toronto

#509 from Union Station, and get off on Fleet St at the foot of Garrison Rd; from here the fort is a ten-minute walk.

Built in 1793 on the shores of Lake Ontario to bolster British control of the Great Lakes, Fort York was initially a half-hearted, poorly fortified affair, partly because of a lack of funds, but mainly because it was too remote to command much attention. However, in 1811, the deterioration in Anglo-American relations put it on active duty. There was a sudden flurry of activity as the fort's ramparts and gun emplacements were strengthened – but it was still too weak to hold off the American army that marched on York in 1813. Hurriedly, the British decided to evacuate the fort and blow up the gunpowder magazine to stop its contents falling into enemy hands. Unfortunately, they completely underestimated the force of the explosion, and killed or wounded ten of their own men as well as 260 of the advancing enemy, the fatalities including the splendidly named American general Zebulon Montgomery Pike. After the war, Fort York was rebuilt and its garrison made a considerable contribution to the development of Toronto, as York was renamed in 1834.

Opened as a **museum** in 1934, Fort York is staffed by guides who provide informative, free forty-minute **tours**; or you can wander around on your own, but be sure to pick up a plan at reception. The carefully restored earthen **ramparts** are low-lying, thick and constructed in a zigzag pattern, both to mitigate against enemy artillery and to provide complementary lines of fire. They enclose a haphazard sequence of log, stone and brick buildings, notably a couple of well-preserved **blockhouses**, complete with heavy timbers and snipers' loopholes. In one of them – **building no. 5** on the plan – an introductory video outlines the history of the fort and an exhibit explores the various military crises that afflicted Canada from 1792 to 1967. Moving on, **building no. 6** started out as a magazine but ended up as a storehouse. Its ground floor now holds a modest display on the role of black soldiers and settlers in the early history of Ontario. Up above, an archaeological section displays the various bits and pieces unearthed at the fort – buckles, brooches, plates, clay pipes, tunic buttons and so forth. The most interesting piece is a "Sacred to Love" stick-pin, an example of the mourning jewellery that was popular amongst Victorians. Across the fort, **building no. 4**, the Blue Barracks, is a 1930s reconstruction of the junior officers' quarters, whilst **building no. 3** is the former Officers' Quarters and Mess. The latter boasts several period rooms and two original money vaults, hidden away in the cellar. Opposite, the stone and brick powder magazine – **building no. 8** – has two-metre-thick walls and spark-proof copper and brass fixtures.

East of Union Station: St Lawrence and beyond

The **St Lawrence District**, lying just to the east of Yonge St, between Adelaide St East, Frederick St and The Esplanade, is one of the city's oldest, enjoying its first period of rapid growth after the War of 1812. In Victorian times, St Lawrence became one of the most fashionable parts of the city, and although it hit the skids thereafter, it has recently been revamped and (partly) gentrified. The district is best approached by heading east from Yonge St along Front St East. From this direction, you'll soon reach the **South St Lawrence Market**, at Front and Jarvis (Tues–Thurs 8am–6pm, Fri 8am–7pm, Sat 5am–5pm), a capacious Neoclassical red-brick building of 1844 that holds the city's best food and drink market. Spread out across the main and lower levels, there are stalls selling everything from fish and freshly baked bread to international foodstuffs, all sorts of organic edibles and Ontario specialities: cheese, jellies, jams and fiddlehead ferns to name but four. The market is at its busiest on Saturday, which also means that you can drop by **North St Lawrence Market**, a farmers' market (Sat 5am–5pm) housed in a plain brick building just opposite the main market, on the north side of Front St.

Strolling north along Jarvis St, it only takes a couple of minutes to reach **St Lawrence Hall**, at Jarvis and King, one of the city's most attractive Victorian buildings, a palatial edifice whose columns, pilasters and pediments are surmounted by a dinky little cupola. Dating from 1850, the hall was built as the city's main meeting-place, with oodles of space for balls, public lectures and concerts. Some performances were eminently genteel, others decidedly mawkish. The bad taste award goes to the American showman and circus proprietor P.T. Barnum (1810–91), who saw the potential of the diminutive Charles Sherwood Stratton, aka Tom Thumb (1838–83), exhibiting him as a curiosity here in St Lawrence Hall as well as anywhere else that would pay. Poor old Stratton was just 60cm (2ft) tall when he first went on tour.

On the other side of King St, a couple of hundred metres from St Lawrence Hall, rises the graceful bulk of **St James Anglican Cathedral**, whose yellowish stone is fetchingly off-set by copper-green roofs and a slender spire. An excellent example of the neo-Gothic style once popular in every corner of the British Empire, the cathedral boasts scores of pointed-arch windows and acres of sturdy buttressing. Inside, the nave is supported by chunky high-arched pillars and flanked by an ambitious set of stained-glass windows that attempts to trace the path by which Christianity reached Canada from Palestine via England. It's all a little confusing but, broadly speaking, the less original windows depict Biblical scenes, whereas those that focus on English history are noticeably inventive.

Distillery District

The **Distillery District**, just fifteen minutes' walk east from St Lawrence Market, is home to Toronto's newest arts and entertainment complex, sited in the former **Gooderham and Worts distillery**, an appealing industrial "village" at 55 Mill St, just east of the foot of Parliament St (Mon–Wed 11am–7pm, Thurs–Sat 11am–9pm, Sun 11am–7pm; ☎416/866-8687, Ⓦwww.distillerytours.ca). In use as a distillery until 1990, this rambling network of over forty old brick buildings once comprised the largest distillery in the British Empire, and now lays claim to be the best-preserved Victorian industrial complex in the whole of North America. The distillery was founded in 1832, when ships could sail into its own jetty (though landfill subsequently marooned it in the lee of the railway lines and the tail end of the Gardiner Expressway). Otherwise unruffled for decades, much of the distillery's machinery has survived, as have its walkways and bottle runways, features that have been carefully integrated into the revamp. One of the architectural highlights is the **Pure Spirits building**, which features French doors and a fancy wrought-iron balcony. When the complex is complete, it will hold, amongst much else, over twenty art galleries, a visitor centre (offering guided tours), furniture designers, bakeries, shops, a microbrewery, and no fewer than three performance venues. The redevelopment of the distillery has been led by a small group of entrepreneurs, who decided (with refreshing integrity) to exclude all multinational chains. Try not to miss it.

From the distillery, it takes about 25 minutes to walk to Nathan Phillips Square.

Nathan Phillips Square and around

Nathan Phillips Square, one of the most distinctive of Toronto's landmarks, lies on Queen St, just north of the Banking District. Laid out by the Finnish architect Viljo Revell, the square is framed by an elevated walkway and focuses on a reflecting pool, which becomes a skating rink in winter. Toronto's modernist **City Hall** overlooks the square, its curved glass-and-concrete towers fronted by *The Archer*, a Henry Moore sculpture that resembles nothing so much as a giant propeller. Revell won all sorts of awards for this project, which was then considered the last word in 1960s dynamism, though today its rain-stained blocks look rather dejected. Had Revell's grand scheme been carried out fully, the city would have bulldozed the **Old City Hall**, a flamboyant pseudo-Romanesque building on the east side of the square. Completed in 1899, it was designed by Edward J. Lennox, who developed a fractious relationship with his paymasters on the city council. They had a point: the original cost of the building had been estimated at $1.77m, but Lennox spent an extra $750,000 and took all of eight years to finish the project. Nevertheless, Lennox had the last laugh, carving gargoyle-like representations of the city's fathers on the arches at the top of the front steps and placing his name on each side of the building – something the city council had expressly forbidden him to do.

The Hudson's Bay Company Gallery

Across the street from the Old City Hall, the **Hudson's Bay Company Gallery** (Tues–Sat 11am–5pm; $4; Queen subway) is located on the ninth floor of The Bay department store at Queen St and Yonge. The gallery offers an outstanding introduction to many of Canada's finest artists, especially the **Group of Seven** (see box p.96); its paintings are on loan from the newspaper tycoon Ken Thomson. One of the gallery's strengths is its modest size, providing an intimate setting for what is very much a connoisseur's collection – but unfortunately there are plans afoot to close the place down and move into the AGO (see p.95), probably in 2005.

For now, gallery highlights include an impressive selection of paintings by **Lawren Harris** (1885–1970), one of the Group of Seven's most distinctive artists. His surreal *Lake Superior* (1923) is a representative piece; it's one of several inspired by the wild, cold landscapes of the lake's north shore. Harris was also partial to city street scenes and there are three here – including two of Toronto – each painted in a careful pointillist style very different from his wilderness works. **J.E.H. MacDonald** (1873–1932), another member of the Group of Seven, also features prominently; amongst a fine sample of his canvases, look out for the superb *Rowan Berries*, painted in 1922, and the startling sweep of *October Shower Gleam*. Their colleague **Tom Thomson** (1877–1917) is well represented by over thirty preparatory sketches of lakes and canyons, waterfalls and forests, each small panel displaying the vibrant, blotchy colours that characterize his work. Larger Thomson paintings include the sticky dabs of colour of *Maple Springs*, as well as his *Autumn's Garland*, an oil on panel finished the year before he died. The talents of **A.J. Casson** are perhaps best recalled by the jumble of snow-covered roofs of his *House Tops in the Ward*, though his work is slight when compared with the vital canvases of **A.Y. Jackson** (1882–1974), the sweeping colours and forms of his *Yellowknife Country* being a case in point. A contemporary of the Group – but not a member – the gifted **Emily Carr** (1871–1945) focused on the Canadian west coast in general, and its dense forests and native villages in particular, as in her dark and haunting *Thunderbird* of 1930.

In a separate section, the gallery's assortment of paintings by early and mid-nineteenth century Canadians is less distinguished than the Group of Seven, but there are still some fascinating works. One noteworthy canvas is a curiously unflattering *Portrait of Joseph Brant* by **William Berczy** (1748–1813). A Mohawk chief, **Joseph Brant** (1742–1807), was consistently loyal to the British interest, his followers fighting alongside them during the American War of Independence. Brant's reward was a large chunk of Ontario land and a string of official portraits; this was one of them. Brant is shown in a mix of European and native gear – he carries an axe and has a Mohawk hairdo, but wears a dress coat with a sash – an apt reflection of his twin loyalties. Brant spoke English fluently, even translating parts of the Bible into Mohawk, and was a Freemason and Anglican as well, feted by high society during a visit to England in 1776. At the same time, under his Mohawk name, Thayendanega (Two Bets), Brant was a powerful figure in the Iroquois Confederacy, leading one of its four main clans in both war and peace.

Near to Brant's portrait there are also a number of winter scenes by **Cornelius Krieghoff** (see p.181). In particular, look out for his *The Portage Aux Titres*, whose autumnal colours surround a tiny figure struggling with a canoe, and the light-hearted humour of his (larger) *Toll Gate*. Equally interesting is the work of **Paul Kane** (1810–71). Born in Ireland, Kane first emigrated to Toronto in the early 1820s. In 1840 he returned to Europe, where, curiously enough, he was so impressed by a touring exhibition of paintings on the American Indian that he promptly decided to move back to Canada. In 1846 he wrangled a spot on a westward-bound fur-trading expedition, beginning an epic journey: he travelled from Thunder Bay to Edmonton by canoe, crossed the Rockies by horse, and finally returned to Toronto two years later. During his trip Kane made some seven hundred sketches, which he then painted onto canvas, paper and cardboard. Interestingly, and like many early Canadian artists, Kane's paintings often displayed a conflict in subject and style – that is, the subject was North American but the style European; indeed, it wasn't until the Group of Seven that a true Canadian aesthetic emerged. Perfect examples of this conflict are Kane's *Landscape in the Foothills with Buffalo Resting* and *At Buffalo Pound*, where bison are pictured in what looks more like a placid German valley than a North American prairie. Finally, there's *The Passing Storm* by **Homer Watson** (1855–1936), whose glossy Ontario landscapes, with their vigorous paintwork and dynamic compositions, made him a popular artist; Queen Victoria even purchased one of his paintings, and Oscar Wilde dubbed him "the Canadian Constable".

The Eaton Centre and Elgin Theatre

A second-floor walkway crosses Queen St to connect The Bay with the **Eaton Centre** (Mon–Fri 10am–9pm, Sat 9.30am–7pm, Sun noon–6pm) a mainly three-storey assortment of shops and restaurants spread out underneath a glass-and-steel arched roof. By shopping mall standards, the design is appealing and the flock of fibreglass Canada geese suspended from the ceiling adds a touch of flair. Maps of the shopping mall are displayed on every floor, but the general rule is the higher the floor, the more expensive the shop. The centre takes its name from **Timothy Eaton**, an Ulster immigrant who opened his first store here in 1869. His cash-only, fixed-price, money-back-guarantee trading revolutionized the Canadian market and made him a fortune. Soon a Canadian institution, Eaton kept a grip on the pioneer settlements in the west through his mail-order catalogue, known as the "homesteader's bible" – or the

Glenn Gould

In the 1970s, anyone passing the Eaton's department store around 9pm on any day of the year might have seen the door unlocked for a distracted-looking figure swaddled in overcoat, scarves, gloves and hat. This character, making his way to a recording studio set up for his exclusive use inside the shop, was perhaps the most famous citizen of Toronto and the most charismatic pianist in the world – **Glenn Gould**.

Not the least remarkable thing about Gould was that very few people outside the CBS recording crew would ever hear him play live. In 1964, aged just 32, he retired from the concert platform, partly out of a distaste for the accidental qualities of any live performance, partly out of hatred for the cult of the virtuoso. Yet no pianist ever provided more material for the mythologizers. He possessed a memory so prodigious that none of his acquaintances was ever able to find a piece of music he could not instantly play perfectly, but he loathed much of the standard piano repertoire, dismissing romantic composers such as Chopin, Liszt and Rachmaninoff as little more than showmen. Dauntingly cerebral in his tastes and playing style, he was nonetheless an ardent fan of Barbara Streisand – an esteem that was fully reciprocated – and once wrote an essay titled **"In Search of Petula Clark"**. He lived at night and kept in touch by phoning his friends in the small hours of the morning, talking for so long that his monthly phone bill ran into thousands of dollars. Detesting all blood sports (a category in which he placed concert performances), he would terrorize anglers on Lake Simcoe by buzzing them in his motorboat. He travelled everywhere with bags full of medicines and would never allow anyone to shake his hand, yet soaked his arms in almost scalding water before playing in order to get his circulation going. At the keyboard he sang loudly to himself, swaying back and forth on a creaky little chair made for him by his father – all other pianists sat too high, he insisted. And even in a heatwave he was always dressed as if a blizzard were imminent. To many of his colleagues, Gould's eccentricities were maddening, but what mattered was that nobody could play like Glenn Gould. As one exasperated conductor put it, "the nut's a genius".

Gould's first recording, Bach's *Goldberg Variations*, was released in 1956, and became the best-selling classical record of that year. Soon after, he became the first Western musician to play in the Soviet Union, where his reputation spread so quickly that for his final recital more than a thousand people were allowed to stand in the aisles of the Leningrad hall. On his debut in Berlin, the leading German critic described him as "a young man in a strange sort of trance" whose "technical ability borders on the fabulous". The technique always dazzled, but Gould's fiercely wayward intelligence made his interpretations controversial, as can be gauged from the fact that Leonard Bernstein, conducting Gould on one occasion, felt obliged to inform the audience that what they were about to hear was the pianist's responsibility, not his. Most notoriously of all, he had a very low opinion of Mozart's abilities – and went so far as to record the Mozart sonatas in order to demonstrate that Wolfgang Amadeus died too late rather than too soon. Gould himself died suddenly in 1982 at the age of 50 – the age at which he had said he would give up playing the piano entirely.

Gould's legacy of recordings is not confined to music. He made a trilogy of radio documentaries on the theme of solitude: *The Quiet in the Land*, about Canada's Mennonites; *The Latecomers*, about the inhabitants of Newfoundland; and *The Idea of North*, for which he taped interviews with people who, like himself, spent much of their time amid Canada's harshest landscapes. Just as Gould's Beethoven, Bach and Mozart sounded like nobody else's, these were documentaries like no others, each a complex weave of voices spliced and overlaid in compositions that are overtly musical in construction. However, Gould's eighty-odd piano recordings are the basis of his enduring popularity, and nearly all of them have been reissued on CD and DVD, spanning Western keyboard music from Orlando Gibbons to Arnold Schoenberg. One of the most poignant is his second version of the *Goldberg Variations*, the last record to be issued before his death.

"wish book" among aboriginal peoples – whilst Eaton department stores sprang up in all of Canada's big cities. In recent years, however, the company has struggled to maintain its profitability and this branch has now been taken over by Sears.

Across from the Eaton Centre at 189 Yonge St, the **Elgin Theatre and Winter Garden** (guided tours only, Thurs 5pm & Sat 11am; $7; 90min; ☏ 416/597-0965) is one of the city's most unusual attractions. The first part of the guided tour covers the Elgin, an old vaudeville theatre which has been restored after years of neglect and is now equipped with ornate furnishings and fittings, columns, engravings and gilt mirrors. The Elgin was turned into a cinema in the 1930s and, remarkably enough, its accompaniment, the top-floor **Winter Garden**, also a vaudeville theatre, was sealed off. Such double-decker theatres were introduced in the late nineteenth century in New York and soon became popular along the east coast, but only a handful have survived. Even better, when this one was unsealed, its original decor was found to be intact, the ceiling hung with thousands of preserved and painted beech leaves illuminated by coloured lanterns. In the event, much of the decor had to be replaced, but the restoration work was painstakingly thorough and the end result is simply delightful.

West to the Campbell House

Immediately to the west of Nathan Phillips Square, along Queen St, stands **Osgoode Hall**, a Neoclassical pile built for the Law Society of Upper Canada early in the nineteenth century. Looking like a cross between a Greek temple and an English country house, it's protected by a wrought-iron fence designed to keep cows and horses off the lawn. The elegant Georgian mansion on the opposite side of University Ave is **Campbell House** (Mon–Fri 9.30am–4.30pm; also Sat & Sun late May to Sept noon–4.30pm; $4.50), built on Adelaide St for Sir William Campbell, Chief Justice and Speaker of the Legislative Assembly – it was transported here in 1972. There are regular guided tours of the period interior and these provide a well-researched overview of early nineteenth-century Toronto. At the time, Campbell was a leading figure, and a progressive one too, eschewing the death penalty whenever feasible and even awarding the radical William MacKenzie damages when his printing press was wrecked by a mob of Tories in 1826.

Art Gallery of Ontario

A short walk from the Campbell House, just west of University Ave along Dundas St West, the **Art Gallery of Ontario** (Tues–Fri 11am–6pm, Wed until 8.30pm, Sat & Sun 10am–5.30pm; $12, free on Wed after 6pm; St Patrick subway; Ⓦ www.ago.net) is celebrated both for its wide-ranging collection of foreign and domestic art and its excellent temporary exhibitions. It also runs a first-rate programme of free guided tours. The gallery is, however, housed in an oddly discordant and rather confusing building, the result of several different phases of construction. There is not enough room to exhibit all of the permanent collection at any one time, which means that the exhibits are rotated, though this problem will be at least partly resolved with the opening of a new extension in 2005 or 2006. The exterior of the AGO (as it's commonly known) is a stern, modern facade decorated by a scaffold-like tower and a matching pair of Henry Moore sculptures, large and chunky bronzes uninspiringly called *Two Forms*. Inside, the AGO's **Street Level** boasts European works as well as an art shop and café, whilst the **Upper Level** is devoted to contemporary art, a superb clutch of Canadian paintings and an extensive collection of Henry Moore sculptures. Museum **maps** are issued free at reception.

Just beyond the main entrance, turn right and stroll down the corridor (S2), where a long series of cabinets display a marvellous sample of European applied art, including ivory and alabaster pieces, exquisite cameos and fine porcelain. All are on permanent loan from Ken Thomson's private collection – the same tycoon who equips the Hudson's Bay Company Gallery (see p.92). The corridor leads to the first part of S10, a rectangular room given over to selected items from the permanent collection, noteworthy sculptures by the likes of Moore and Hepworth and paintings by such luminaries as Picasso, Van Gogh, Monet and Francis Bacon, among others. Just to the left, **Walker Court** is surrounded on three sides by the main **European art galleries** (S3–S9), which cover the Italian Renaissance through to French Impressionism. Amongst the **Impressionists** there's Degas's archetypal *Woman in the Bath*, Renoir's screaming-pink *Concert* and Monet's wonderful *Vétheuil in Summer*, with its hundreds of tiny jabs of colour.

Upper Level

The Upper Level of the AGO holds the outstanding **Canadian Art to 1960** section (U8–U20), whose strongest suite is the work of the **Group of Seven** (see box) and their contemporaries, bundled together in rooms U11–U12. To provide some artistic context it's best to start with the earliest Canadian works – in U17 – and work backwards to U16 and so forth. U17 kicks off with a light scattering of early to mid-nineteenth-century paintings, including **Paul Kane**'s (see p.93) *Indian encampment on Lake Huron*, a softly hued oil on canvas dating to 1845. The adjacent U16 features several paintings by **Cornelius Krieghoff** (see p.427), characteristic winter scenes – like his *Settler's Log House* – intermingled with portraits. In this room too is **John O'Brien**'s (1832–91) *The Ocean Bride leaving Halifax Harbour*. Self-taught, O'Brien specialized in

---

The Group of Seven

In the autumn of 1912, a commercial artist by the name of **Tom Thomson** returned from an extended trip to the Mississauga country, north of Georgian Bay, with a bag full of sketches that were to add a new momentum to Canadian art. His friends, many of them fellow employees of the art firm of Grip Ltd in Toronto, saw Thomson's naturalistic approach to indigenous subject matter as a pointer away from the influence of Europe, declaring the "northland" as the true Canadian "painter's country". World War I and the death of Thomson – who drowned in 1917 – delayed these artists' ambitions, but in 1920 they formed the **Group of Seven**. Initially, the group comprised Franklin H. Carmichael, Lawren Harris, A.Y. Jackson, Arthur Lismer, J.E.H. MacDonald, F.H. Varley and Frank Johnston; later, they were joined by A.J. Casson, L.L. Fitzgerald and Edwin Holgate. Working under the unofficial leadership of **Lawren Harris**, they explored the wilds of Algoma in Northern Ontario in the late 1910s, travelling around in a converted freight car, and later foraged even further afield, from Newfoundland and Baffin Island to British Columbia.

They were immediately successful, staging forty shows in eleven years, a triumph due in large part to Harris's many influential contacts. However, there was also a genuine popular response to the intrepid frontiersman element of their aesthetic. Art was a matter of "taking to the road" and "risking all for the glory of a great adventure", as they wrote in 1922, whilst "nature was the measure of a man's stature", according to Lismer. Symbolic of struggle against the elements, the Group's favourite symbol was the lone pine set against the sky, an image whose authenticity was confirmed by reference to the "manly" poetry of Walt Whitman.

maritime scenes, turning out dozens of brightly coloured pictures of sailing ships and coastal settings. U14 and U13 concentrate on the folksy and/or romanticized country scenes and landscapes that were in vogue from the 1850s through to the early twentieth century. By and large this is pretty dull stuff, but **Homer Watson**'s (see p.93) *The Old Mill* is an especially handsome and well-composed canvas, whilst his *Death of Elaine* – inspired by a Tennyson poem – stands out as a bizarrely unsuccessful venture into ancient legend.

One of the most distinctive artists of the Group of Seven, whose works are displayed in U11–U12, was **Lawren Harris** (1885–1970), whose 1922 *Above Lake Superior* is a pivotal work – its clarity of conception, with bare birch stumps framing a dark mountain beneath Art Deco clouds, is quite exceptional. The adjacent *West Wind* by **Tom Thomson** (1877–1917) is another seminal work, an iconic rendering of the northern wilderness that is perhaps the most famous of all Canadian paintings. Thomson was the first to approach wilderness landscapes with the determination of an explorer and the sense that they could encapsulate a specifically Canadian identity. Several of his less familiar (but no less powerful) works are here as well, including the moody *A Northern Lake* and the Cubist-influenced preparatory painting, *Autumn Foliage 1915*.

J.E.H. MacDonald (1873–1932) was fond of dynamic, sweeping effects, and his panoramic *Falls, Montreal River* sets turbulent rapids beside hot-coloured hillsides. His friend **F.H. Varley** (1881–1969) dabbled in portraiture and chose soft images and subtle colours for his landscapes, as exemplified by the sticky-looking brushstrokes he used for *Moonlight after Rain*. A sample of **A.Y. Jackson**'s (1882–1974) work includes the characteristically carpet-like surface of *Algoma Rocks, Autumn*, painted in 1923, while **A.J. Casson**'s (1898–1992) bright, rather formal *Old Store at Salem* offers a break from the scenic preoccupations of the rest of the Seven. **Emily Carr** (1871–1945), represented by several works here, was a great admirer of the Seven, but she was never accepted as a member despite her obvious abilities – the deep green foliage of her *Indian Church* and *Western Forest*, both painted in 1929, are good examples of her talent.

Close by, in U8, there are two small galleries of **Inuit art**, mostly sculpture, beside and above the spiral staircase. Highlights here include **Pauta Saila**'s (born 1916) *Dancing Bear* and **Joe Talirunili**'s (1906–76) *Migration*, in which a traditional Inuit boat – an *umiak* – is crowded with Inuit seemingly bent on escaping danger. Talirunili carved a large number of migration boat scenes throughout his long career (see p.88 another), the inspiration derived from a dramatic incident in his childhood when the break-up of the pack ice caught his family unawares, forcing them to evacuate their encampment hurriedly. Look out also for the work of **John Tiktak** (1916–81), generally regarded as one of the most talented Inuit sculptors of his generation. The death of Tiktak's mother in 1962 had a profound effect on him, and his *Mother and Child* forcefully expresses this close connection, with the figure of the child carved into the larger figure of the mother. Tiktak's *Owl Man* is another fine piece, an excellent example of the metamorphic figures popular amongst the Inuit, as is **Thomas Sivuraq**'s (born 1941) *Shaman Transformation*.

Most of the rest of the Upper Level (U3–U7) is given over to the AGO's collection of **contemporary art**, showcasing works by European, British and American artists. Pieces are regularly rotated, but watch out for Warhol's *Elvis I and II*, Mark Rothko's strident *No.1 White and Red* and Claes Oldenburg's quirky if somewhat frayed *Giant Hamburger*. The contemporary art section culminates in the **Henry Moore Sculpture Centre** (U1), the world's largest collection of pieces by Moore (1898–1986), with the emphasis firmly on his plaster casts, alongside a selection of his bronzes. Given a whole gallery, the sheer size and volume of Moore's output is impressive, but actually it was something of an accident that his work ended up here at all. In the 1960s, Moore had reason to believe that London's Tate Gallery was going to build a special wing for him. When the Tate declined, Moore chose the AGO instead, persuaded to do so by the gallery's British representative, Anthony Blunt, the art expert who was famously uncovered in 1979 as a Soviet spy.

The Grange

Attached to the back of the AGO is **The Grange**, an early nineteenth-century brick mansion with Neoclassical trimmings built by the Boultons, one of the city's most powerful and reactionary families. The last of the line, William Henry – "a privileged, petted man...without principle", according to a local journalist – died in 1874, and his property passed to his widow, Harriette, who promptly married an English expatriate professor named Goldwin Smith. Goldwin enjoyed Toronto immensely, holding court and boasting of his English connections, and when he died in 1910 (after Harriette) he bequeathed the house to the fledgling Art Museum of Toronto, the predecessor of the AGO. The Grange remains part of the AGO and it has been restored to its mid-nineteenth-century appearance. Guides dressed in period costume show you around, enthusiastically explaining the ins and outs of life in nineteenth-century Toronto. Several of Harriette's paintings have survived, and while the antique furnishings and fittings are appealing, it's the beautiful wooden staircase that really catches the eye.

Chinatown and Kensington Market

The Art Gallery of Ontario is hemmed in by **Chinatown**, a bustling and immensely appealing neighbourhood cluttered with shops, restaurants and street stalls selling every and any type of Asian delicacy. The boundaries of Chinatown are somewhat blurred, but its focus, since the 1960s, when the original Chinatown was demolished to make way for the new City Hall, has been Dundas St West between Bay and Spadina. The first Chinese to migrate to Canada arrived in the mid-nineteenth century to work in British Columbia's gold fields. Subsequently, a portion of this population migrated east, and a sizeable Chinese community sprang up in Toronto in the early twentieth century. Several more waves of migration – the last influx following the handing over of Hong Kong to mainland China by the British in 1997 – have greatly increased the number of Toronto's Chinese in recent years, bringing the population to approximately 250,000 (about eight percent of the city's total).

Next door to Chinatown, just north of Dundas St West, between Spadina and Augusta, lies Toronto's most ethnically diverse neighbourhood, pocket-sized **Kensington Market**. It was here, at the beginning of the twentieth century, that Eastern European immigrants squeezed into a patchwork of modest little brick and timber houses that survive to this day. On Kensington Ave they established the **open-air street market** that has been the main feature of the neighbourhood ever since, a lively, entertaining bazaar whose stall owners stem from many different ethnic backgrounds. The lower half of the market, just off Dundas St, concentrates on secondhand clothes, while the upper half is crowded with fresh-food stalls.

Around Toronto University

Peering down University Ave, a short walk northeast of Kensington Market, the pink sandstone mass of the **Ontario Legislative Assembly Building** dates to the 1890s (late May to late Sept daily 10am–4pm; late Sept to late May Mon–Fri 10am–4pm; free, with frequent 30min guided tours; ☎ 416/325-7500; Queen's Park subway). Elegant it certainly isn't, but although the building is heavy and solid, its ponderous symmetries do have a certain appeal, with block upon block of roughly dressed stone assembled in the full flourish of the Romanesque Revival style. Seen from close up, the design is even more engaging, its intricacies a pleasant surprise: above the chunky columns of the main entrance is a sinuous filigree of carved stone, with mythological creatures and gargoyle-like faces poking out from every nook and cranny. The main facade also sports a Neoclassical frieze in which the Great Seal of Ontario is flanked by allegorical figures representing art, music, agriculture and so forth. Inside, the foyer leads to the wide, thickly carpeted Grand Staircase, whose massive timbers are supported by gilded iron pillars. Beyond, among the long corridors and arcaded galleries, is the **Legislative Chamber**, where the formal mahogany and sycamore panels are offset by a series of whimsical little carvings: look for the owl overlooking the doings of the government and the eagle overseeing the opposition benches. Under the Speaker's gallery, righteous inscriptions have been carved into the pillars – which is a bit of a hoot considering the behaviour of the building's architect, Richard Waite. Waite was chairman of the committee responsible for selecting an architect; and, as chairman, he selected himself. The provincial assembly typically sits from late September to late June, with breaks at Christmas and Easter, and although guided tours avoid the chamber when the body is in session, the **visitors' gallery** is open to the public during its deliberations Monday through Thursdays; call for further details and times.

Behind the Legislative Building, in **Queen's Park**, stands a heavyweight equestrian statue of King Edward VII in full-dress uniform. Originally plonked down in Delhi, this imperial leftover looks a bit forlorn – and you can't help but feel the Indians must have been pleased to off-load it. A couple of hundred metres to the west are the various faculties of the **University of Toronto**, opened in 1843 and the province's most prestigious academic institution. The university's older buildings, with their quadrangles, ivy-covered walls and Gothic interiors, deliberately evoke Oxbridge with **Hart House**, at the west end of Wellesley St, being the best example. Hart House is attached to the **Soldier's Tower**, a neo-Gothic memorial erected in 1924 to honour those students who had died in World War I. It adjoins an arcaded **gallery**, which is inscribed with a list of the dead and Canadian **John McCrae**'s *In Flanders Fields*, arguably the war's best-known poem. Optimistically, the builders of the memorial didn't leave any space to commemorate the dead of any further war – so the names of the university students killed in World War II had to be inscribed on the walls under the arches at the foot of the tower.

Royal Ontario Museum

From the Legislative Building it's a brief walk north to the **Royal Ontario Museum**, at 100 Queen's Park (Mon–Thurs 10am–6pm, Fri 10am–9.30pm, Sat 10am–6pm & Sun 11am–6pm; $10, but free after 4.30pm on Fri; ⓦ www.rom.on.ca; Museum subway). Known as the ROM, this is Canada's largest and most diverse museum, with ambitious collections of fine and applied art from all over the world, as well as a varied programme of temporary exhibitions. That said, the museum is currently in the middle of a major redevelopment and, until the new wing opens in late 2005, visitors have to take pot luck as to which galleries are open. The ROM makes a cheery start with a domed and vaulted **entrance hall** whose ceiling is decorated with a brilliant mosaic of imported Venetian glass. Just beyond, bolted into the stairwells, are four colossal and stunningly beautiful Native Canadian **crest poles** (commonly but erroneously referred to as totem poles). Dating from the 1880s, these west coast poles are decorated with stylized carvings representing the supernatural animals and birds that were associated with particular clans. Currently, they are the most significant Canadian artefacts on display – the rest are in storage until the construction work makes further progress. The ROM's **Canadian collection** is strong on prehistoric archaeology and late eighteenth- and early nineteenth-century trade silver, comprising an intriguing assortment of silver ornaments – brooches, earrings, crucifixes, medals and the like – which European traders swapped with natives for furs.

Beyond the crest poles, straight back from the main entrance on **Level 1** is the **Bishop White Gallery of Chinese Temple Art**, one of the ROM's most significant sections. The gallery features three Daoist and Buddhist wall paintings dating from around 1300 AD, including a matching pair of Yuan Dynasty murals depicting the lords of the Northern and Southern Dipper, each of whom leads an astrological procession of star spirits. The murals are complimented by an exquisite sample of Buddhist sculpture, temple figures dating from the twelfth to the fourteenth centuries.

Close by, the **South Asian Gallery** contain artefacts spanning six millennia, from 4500 BC to 1900 AD. Among the most important pieces is a remarkable collection of toy-sized tomb figurines – a couple of hundred ceramic pieces representing funerary processions of soldiers, musicians, carts and attendants dating from the early sixth to the late seventh century. Perhaps the most popular component of the Chinese galleries, however, is the **Ming Tomb**. The aristocracy of the Ming Dynasty (1368–1644 AD) evolved an elaborate style of monumental funerary sculpture and architecture, and this is the only example outside of China – though it is actually a composite tomb drawn from several sources rather than an intact, original whole. Central to the Ming burial conception was a Spirit Way, a central avenue with large-scale carved figures of guards, attendants and animals placed on either side. At the end of the alley was the tumulus, or burial mound – in this case the tomb-house of a seventeenth-century Chinese general by the name of Zu Dashou.

Upstairs, the focal point of **Level 2**'s Life Sciences exhibits is the **Dinosaurs Gallery**. Dioramas and simulations have made this one of the most informative parts of the museum and also one of the most popular. Among the assorted fossil-skeletons, the pick are those retrieved from the Alberta Badlands (see p.658), near Calgary. These Badlands are the richest source of dinosaur fossils in the world, having yielded over 300 complete skeletons and 35 dinosaur species – ten percent of all those known today. The ROM has a superb collection, including several **Albertosaurus**, but it's the rampant herd of **Allosaurus** – a Jurassic-period carnivore of large proportions and ferocious appearance – that commands the most attention.

Other popular sections on Level 2 are the replica **bat cave** and a large display on Canada's **insects** – and a fearsome-looking bunch they are too, including the No-see-um, which drives caribou to distraction by burrowing into their nostrils. There's also the **Discovery Gallery**, one of the best education facilities in Toronto, giving children the opportunity to handle and study museum artefacts. Expect queues when the gallery is at its busiest, Monday through Friday 10am to noon during school terms. Children under 10 must be accompanied by an adult, while 10- to 12-year-olds must have an adult supervisor on the premises.

Level 3 holds the **Samuel European Galleries**, which kick off with a beginner's exposition on the History of Style, exploring changing fashions and tastes, and continue with a string of period rooms, mostly English, from the sixteenth to the eighteenth century. There are also discrete collections of arms and armour, Art Nouveau and Art Deco, metalwork, glass and ceramics. Amongst the latter is a superb collection of Delftware and Italian majolica (see below, under the Gardiner Museum, for more on majolica). Level 3 also has a substantial section devoted to the **Mediterranean World**, with the particular highlight being the **Ancient Egypt Gallery**, where there are several finely preserved mummies, including the richly decorated sarcophagus of a certain Djedmaatesankh, a court musician who died around 850 BC. Even more unusual is the assortment of mummified animals, including a crocodile, a hawk and a weird-looking cat.

George R. Gardiner Museum of Ceramic Art

Named after its wealthy patron, the **George R. Gardiner Museum of Ceramic Art** (Mon–Fri 10am–6pm, Tues & Thurs until 8pm, Sat 10am–5pm, Sun 11am–5pm; $5; free on first Tues of every month; Museum subway), just across the street from the ROM at 111 Queen's Park, holds a superb connoisseur's collection of ceramics. Spread over two small floors, the museum's exhibits are beautifully presented, and key pieces are well labelled and explained. There is, however, insufficient room to display all the permanent collection at any one time, so some of the exhibits are regularly rotated – which means the description below should be taken with a grain of salt. An audioguide is also available.

Downstairs, the **pre-Columbian** section is especially fine, composed of over three hundred pieces from regions stretching from Mexico to Peru. One of the most comprehensive collections of its kind in North America, it provides an intriguing insight into the lifestyles and beliefs of the Mayan, Incan and Aztec peoples. The sculptures are all the more remarkable for the fact that the potter's wheel was unknown in pre-Columbian America, and thus everything on display was necessarily hand-modelled. Also downstairs is an exquisite sample of fifteenth- and sixteenth-century tin-glazed **Italian majolica**, mostly dishes, plates and jars depicting classical and Biblical themes designed by Renaissance artists. The early pieces are comparatively plain, limited to green and purple, but the later examples are brightly coloured, for in the second half of the fifteenth century Italian potters learnt how to glaze blue and yellow – and ochre was added later. The most splendid pieces are perhaps those from the city – and pottery centre – of Urbino, including two wonderful plates portraying the fall of Jericho and the exploits of Hannibal.

The upstairs level is devoted to eighteenth-century **European porcelain**, with fine examples of hard-paste wares (fired at very high temperatures) from Meissen, Germany, as well as an interesting sample of Chinese-style blue and white porcelain, long the mainstay of the European ceramic industry. On this floor also is a charming collection of Italian *commedia dell'arte* figurines, doll-sized representations of theatrical characters popular across Europe from the middle of the sixteenth to the late eighteenth century. The predecessor of pantomime, the *commedia dell'arte* featured stock characters in improvized settings, but with a consistent theme of seduction, age and beauty: the centre-piece was always an elderly, rich merchant and his beautiful young wife. Lastly, the museum **gift shop** also merits special mention, as it specializes in contemporary Canadian ceramics.

Bata Shoe Museum

Within easy walking distance of the ROM, the **Bata Shoe Museum**, 327 Bloor St West at St George St (Tues–Sat 10am–5pm, Thurs until 8pm, Sun noon–5pm; $6; St George subway), was built for Sonja Bata, of the Bata shoe manufacturing family, to house the extraordinary assortment of footwear she has spent a lifetime collecting. A leaflet issued at reception steers visitors around the museum, starting with an introductory section entitled "All About Shoes" on **Level B1**, which presents an overview on the evolution of footwear. Among the more interesting exhibits in this section are pointed shoes from medieval Europe, where different social classes were allowed different lengths of toe, and tiny Chinese silk shoes used by women whose feet had been bound. Banned by the Communists when they came to power in 1949, foot binding was common practice for over a thousand years, and the "ideal" length of a woman's foot was a hobbling three inches. A small adjoining section is devoted to specialist footwear, including French chestnut-crushing clogs from the nineteenth century, inlaid Ottoman platforms designed to keep aristocratic feet well away from the mud, and a pair of US army boots from the Vietnam War with the sole shaped to imitate the sandal prints of the Vietcong. Moving on, **Level G** features a large glass cabinet that displays all sorts of celebrity footwear. The exhibits are rotated regularly, but look out for Buddy Holly's loafers, Marilyn Monroe's stilettos, Princess Diana's red court shoes, Shaquille O'Neal's colossal Reebok trainers and Elton John's ridiculous platforms. **Level 2** and **Level 3** are used for temporary exhibitions – some of which are very good indeed – and there's also a small section explaining the museum's role in restoring and repairing old footwear.

Casa Loma and Spadina House

From Dupont subway station it's a brief walk north up the slope of Spadina Rd to the corner of Davenport Rd, where a flight of steps leads to Toronto's most bizarre attraction, **Casa Loma**, 1 Austin Terrace (daily 9.30am–5pm, last admission 4pm; $12, parking $2.30), an enormous towered and turreted mansion built for Sir Henry Pellatt between 1911 and 1914. Every inch the self-made man, Pellatt made a fortune by pioneering the use of hydroelectricity, harnessing the power of Niagara Falls to light Ontario's expanding cities. Determined to construct a house no one could ignore, Sir Henry gathered furnishings from all over the world and even imported Scottish stonemasons to build the wall around his six-acre property. He spent more than $3m fulfilling his dream, but business misfortunes and the rising cost of servants forced him to move out in 1923, earning him the nickname of "**Pellatt the Plunger**". His legacy is a strange mixture of medieval fantasy and early twentieth-century technology: secret passageways and an elevator, claustrophobic wood-panelled rooms baffled by gargantuan pipes and plumbing.

The clearly numbered route around the house goes up one side and down the other. It begins on the ground floor in the **Great Hall**, a pseudo-Gothic extravaganza with an eighteen-metre-high cross-beamed ceiling, a Wurlitzer organ and enough floor space to accommodate several hundred guests. Hung with flags, heavy-duty chandeliers and suits of armour, it's a remarkably cheerless place, but in a touch worthy of Errol Flynn, the hall is overlooked by a balcony at the end of Pellatt's second-floor bedroom: presumably Sir Henry could, like some medieval baron, welcome his guests from on high. Pushing on, the **Library** and then the walnut-panelled **Dining Room** lead to the **Conservatory**, an elegant and spacious room with a marble floor and side-panels set beneath a handsome Tiffany domed glass ceiling. Well lit, this is perhaps the mansion's most appealing room, its flowerbeds kept warm even in winter by the original network of steam pipes. The nearby **Study** was Sir Henry's favourite room, a serious affair engulfed by mahogany panelling and equipped with two secret passageways, one leading to the wine cellar, the other to his wife's rooms.

On the second floor, **Sir Henry's Suite** has oodles of walnut and mahogany panelling, which stands in odd contrast to the 1910s white-marble, high-tech bathroom, featuring an elaborate multi-nozzle shower. **Lady Pellatt's Suite** wasn't left behind in the ablutions department, either – her bathroom had a bidet, a real novelty in George V's Canada – and she had a lighter decorative touch, too, eschewing wood panelling for walls painted in her favourite colour, Wedgewood Blue, with pastel furniture to match. Up above, the third floor holds a mildly diverting display on Pellatt's one-time regiment, the **Queen's Own Rifles**, tracing their involvement in various campaigns from the suppression of the Métis rebellion in western Canada (see p.602) in 1885 through to World War I and beyond. From the third floor, wooden staircases clamber up to two of the house's **towers**, from where there are pleasing views over the house and gardens.

Back on the ground floor, stairs lead down to the Lower Level, which was where Pellatt's money ran out and his plans ground to a halt. Work never started on the bowling alleys and shooting range he had designed, and the swimming pool only got as far as the rough concrete basin that survives today – never mind that Pellatt conceived a marble pool overlooked by golden swans. Pellatt did, however, manage to complete the 250-metre-long **tunnel** that runs from the house and pool to the **carriage room** and **stables**, where his thoroughbred horses were allegedly better-treated than his servants, chomping away at their oats and hay in splendid iron and mahogany stalls.

The stables are a dead-end, so you'll have to double back along the tunnel to reach the house and the exit. Before you leave, spare time for the **terraced gardens** (May–Oct daily 9.30am–5pm; no extra charge), which tumble down the ridge at the back of the house. They are parcelled up into several different sections and easily explored along a network of footpaths, beginning on the terrace behind the Great Hall.

Spadina Historic House and Gardens

Quite what the occupants of **Spadina House** (guided tours only, May–Aug Tues–Sun noon–5pm; Sept–Dec Tues–Fri noon–4pm, Sat & Sun noon–5pm; $5; Dupont subway) must have thought when Casa Loma went up next door can only be imagined, but there must have been an awful lot of curtain-twitching. The two houses are a study in contrasts: Casa Loma a grandiose pile, Spadina an elegant Victorian property of genteel appearance dating from 1866. Spadina was built by James Austin, a wealthy banker banker of Irish extraction whose descendants lived here until 1983, when the house was bequeathed to the city. The Austins' long and uninterrupted occupation means that the house's furnishings are nearly all genuine family artefacts, and they provide an intriguing insight into their changing tastes and interests. Narrated by enthusiastic volunteers, the **guided tour** is a delight. Particular highlights include the conservatory trap door that allowed the gardeners to come and go unseen by their employers, an assortment of period chairs designed to accommodate the largest of bustles, the original gas chandeliers and a couple of canvases by Cornelius Krieghoff (for more on whom, see p.181). Pride of place, however, is the **Billiard Room**, where an inventive Art Nouveau decorative frieze dating from 1898 is complemented by several fine pieces of furniture, including a sturdy oak desk, bentwood chairs and a swivel armchair that imitated the designs of Englishman William Morris.

The waterfront and the Toronto Islands

Toronto's docks once disfigured the shoreline on the edge of the city centre, a swath of warehouses and factories that was unattractive and smelly in equal measure. Today it's another story: the port and its facilities have been concentrated further east, beyond the foot of Parliament St, while the **waterfront** west of Yonge has been redeveloped in grand style, sprouting luxury condominium blocks, jogging and cycling trails, offices, shops and marinas. The focus of all this activity is the **Harbourfront Centre**, between York and Simcoe, whose various facilities include an open-air performance area and the **Power Plant Contemporary Art Gallery** (Tues & Thurs–Sun noon–6pm, Wed noon–8pm; $4, but free on Wed after 5pm), housed in an imaginatively converted 1920s power station. The gallery presents about a dozen exhibitions of contemporary art every year and often features emerging Canadian artists. It is mostly cutting-edge stuff, indecipherable to some, exciting to others. The gallery shares the power station with the du Maurier Theatre Centre (see p.113). To reach the Harbourfront Centre by public transport, take the #509 or #510 streetcar from Union Station and get off at the Queens Quay Terminal.

The Toronto Islands

Originally a sandbar peninsula, the **Toronto Islands**, arching around the city's harbour, were cut adrift from the mainland by a violent storm in 1858. First used as a summer retreat by the Mississauga, the islands became popular in the late nineteenth century with day-tripping Torontonians, who rowed across to enjoy the cool lake breezes. The islands also held the baseball stadium where slugger Babe Ruth hit his first professional home run and once served as a World War II training base for the Norwegian Air Force. Today, the archipelago, roughly 6km long and totalling around 800 acres, is maintained by the Toronto Parks Department, which keeps the islands spotless, in part by not allowing visitors to bring their **cars**.

The city side of the archipelago is broken into a dozen tiny islets dotted with cottages, neat gardens and clumps of wild woodland. By comparison, the other (more appealing) side of the archipelago is a tad wilder and more windswept, consisting of one long sliver of land that is somewhat arbitrarily divided into three "islands". From the east, these begin with **Ward's Island**, a quiet residential area with parkland and wilderness. Next up is **Centre Island**, the busiest and most developed of the three and home to **Centreville** (mid-May to Aug daily, plus early May & Sept weekends, from 10.30am to 5pm, 6pm, 7pm or 8pm), a children's amusement park with charmingly old-fashioned rides, notably paddle boats shaped as swans. Finally, **Hanlan's Point** island, edging Toronto's tiny City Centre Airport, has the best sandy **beach**, a stretch of tawny sand which is perhaps more valued as an environmentalist's haven than a sunbathers' retreat, especially as Lake Ontario is too polluted for swimming. One way to enjoy the islands is to cycle or walk along the archipelago's south (lake) side – there is a combined footpath and cycle track between all three ferry docks. This route is also taken by a free but irregular trackless **train**. Bikes can be rented on the islands – there are several outlets – or you can bring your own over on the ferry, though restrictions may apply on busy weekends.

Three separate **ferries** depart for the Toronto Islands from the mainland **ferry terminal**, located behind the conspicuous *Westin Harbour Castle Hotel*, between the foot of Yonge and Bay streets. To get to the ferry terminal from Union Station, take the #509 or #510 streetcar and get off at the first stop – Queen's Quay (Ferry Docks). The Ward's Island and Hanlan's Point ferries run year-round, while the ferry shuttling visitors over to Centre Island only operates from spring to early fall. During peak season (May to early Sept), all the ferry lines depart every twenty minutes; at other times of the year they operate at regular intervals, either every half-hour, every forty-five minutes, or on the hour. Ferries begin running between 6.30am and 9am and end service between 9pm and 11.30pm, depending on the service and the season. For schedule details, telephone ☎416/392-8193. Regardless of the time of year, a return **fare** for adults is $6.

The suburbs

The satellite **suburbs** and industrial areas that make up most of Toronto are of little appeal, a string of formless settlements sprawling over a largely flat and dreary landscape that extends from Scarborough in the east to Mississauga in the west and north beyond Steeles Ave. That said, the region is home to several prestige attractions, notably the **Ontario Science Centre**, which comes complete with dozens of interactive science displays, the **Toronto Zoo** and the **McMichael Canadian Art Collection** of the Group of Seven's paintings.

Ontario Science Centre

Featuring over eight hundred exhibits on science and technology, the **Ontario Science Centre**, 770 Don Mills Rd (daily 10am–5pm; $13, children ages 5–12 $7; ⓦ www.ontariosciencecentre.ca), draws more than one million visitors a year with children to the fore. One of the most popular exhibits is **The Human Body**, where visitors can discern the inner workings of human biology through life-sized three-dimensional displays and various quizzes and games. There's also information on complex medical advances like bioengineering, DNA fingerprinting and immunology, all presented in an easily accessible format. Another big pull is the **OMNIMAX Theatre** (call ☎416/696-1000 for show schedules). The 320-seat theatre features a 24-metre-high wraparound screen with digital sound that creates an enveloping cinematic experience. Admissions to the Omnimax shows are either seperate from the general admission ($10 for adults) or can be combined with general admission, which costs $18 for adults, $10 for children ages 5–12, and $12 for students and seniors. To reach the Science Centre by **car** from downtown Toronto, take the Don Valley Parkway and follow the signs from the Don Mills Rd North exit. By **public transport**, take the Yonge St subway line north to Eglington station and transfer to the Eglington East bus; get off at Don Mills Rd. The trip should take about thirty minutes from the vicinity of downtown's Union Station.

Toronto Zoo

Set on the hilly edge of the Rouge Valley, **Toronto Zoo** (daily: Mar–Sept 9am–7.30pm; Oct–Feb 9.30am–5.30pm; $18, children aged 4–12 $10; ⓦ www.torontozoo.com) encompasses a 710-acre site that does its best to place animals in their own environments. To this end, seven **pavilions** representing different geographic regions are filled with indigenous plants and more than five thousand animals. Hardy species live outside in large paddocks, and an open train, the **Zoomobile** ($5), zips around the vast site for those opposed to hiking between enclosures. Some of the most popular attractions include the **Underwater Exhibits**, featuring South African fur seals, beavers and the otters, and **Edge of Night**, an extension of the Australasian Pavilion, which simulates night-time in the Australian outback. The zoo also has an extensive breeding, recovery and reintroduction programme, which has helped a variety of threatened species back into their indigenous environment. Arriving by **car**, take Hwy 401 to Scarborough (exit 389) and drive north on Meadowvale Rd, following the signs for the zoo. Via **public transport** – which takes about fifty minutes from downtown – catch the Sheppard East #85B bus from the Sheppard subway station. **Eating** at the zoo is dominated by McDonald's, but there are picnic areas.

McMichael Canadian Art Collection

Situated in the village of Kleinburg, the **McMichael Canadian Art Collection**, 10365 Islington Ave (daily May–Oct 10am–5pm; Nov–Apr Tues–Sat 10am–4pm, Sun 10am–5pm; $15; ☎905/893-1121 or 1-888/213-1121, ⓦwww.mcmichael.com), is housed in a series of handsome log and stone buildings in the wooded Humber River valley. The collection was put together by Robert and Signe McMichael, devoted followers of the Group of Seven (see box on p.96), and given to the province in 1965. On the collection's **Lower Level** a series of small galleries focuses on various aspects of the Group of Seven's work. Gallery Two, for example, begins with the artistic friends and contemporaries who influenced the Group's early style, while Gallery Three zeroes in on the Group's spiritual founder, Tom Thomson, who died in a canoeing accident three years before the Group showed as a collective. The galleries boast fine paintings here by J.E.H. MacDonald, Lawren Harris, Edwin Holgate, F.H. Varley and L.L. Fitzgerald, as well as works by their talented contemporary Emily Carr. The museum's **Upper Level** is devoted primarily to modern First Nations Art and Inuit soapstone carvings and lithographs. Rotating temporary exhibitions appear on the Upper Level as well. The variety of exhibits on this level have posed a thorny question for the Collection: namely, is the gallery's function to advance Canadian art, or is it to collect, present and conserve the works of the Group of Seven and their contemporaries? The latest round in this curatorial struggle goes to the Group, and it must be said that recent shows reinterpreting the works of their members and associates have been extraordinarily successful. When you've finished with the paintings, allow a little time to stroll the footpaths that lattice the **woods** surrounding the McMichael. Maps are provided free at reception, and as you wander around you'll bump into various pieces of sculpture, as well as Tom Thomson's old wooden shack, moved here from Rosedale in 1962. For true Group of Seven devotees, the McMichael grounds also contain the graves of five Group members. To get here by **car** from downtown, take Hwy 401 to Hwy 400 north to Major Mackenzie Drive. Turn left (west) on Major Mackenzie Drive to Islington Ave. Turn right (north) on Islington Ave to the village of Kleinburg. There's no direct public transport.

Eating and drinking

Toronto heaves with **cafés** and **restaurants**, everything from smart and expensive designer places to informal neighbourhood joints. Some of the best of the city's restaurants emphasize their use of Canadian ingredients – fish and wild animal meat, especially – but there's no real distinctive local cuisine: if there is a Toronto dish, it's hamburger, fries and salad. **Prices** range from de luxe restaurants, where a meal will set you back upwards of $60, to bargain-basement cafés and fast-food chains, where a decent-sized snack or sandwich works out at just a few dollars. The majority of places fall somewhere in between – a $25 bill per person for a two-course meal, excluding drinks, is a reasonable average. Most of the city's busier cafés and restaurants feature inexpensive daily specials from about $9 upwards and serve food till about 10pm, drinks till 1am. We've coded each of the restaurants listed below as either inexpensive (under $15–20), moderate ($20–35), expensive ($35–50), or very expensive ($50 and over) based on a three-course meal for one excluding drinks. Many restaurants are **closed on Sundays** and sometimes Mondays too: call ahead before you start a major excursion.

For **drinking**, many of Toronto's traditional **bars** are rough-and-ready places that look and feel like beer halls. Until fairly recently it was common for them to have one entrance for men accompanied by women, the other for men only, but although these old-fashioned bars remain popular with many of the city's blue-collar workers, they have largely been supplanted by the **café–bar**. The latter are much more amenable and stylish places and many offer a good line in food, rendering the traditional distinction between eating and drinking places (largely) obsolete – but also see bars, on p.110.

Cafés and café-bars

Balzac's 55 Mill St. In the midst of the Distillery District, *Balzac's* has the look and feel of an airy Parisian café, and churns out nicely presented espresso-type coffees plus matching sweets. Streetcar: King (#504); bus: Parliament St (#65A from Castle Frank Station).

Bonjour Brioche 812 Queen St E. This patisserie-café draws hordes from all over the city on account of its fruit tarts, buttery croissants, puffy brioche and delectable *pissaladiere*, a variation on pizza from Provence. The sit-down menu is a blackboard full of soups, sandwiches, omelettes and quiche. There's always a line for Sunday brunch, and almost everything is eaten by 2pm – so come early. Streetcar: Queen (#501).

Café Bernate 1024 Queen St W. The steam machine is in full swing at this neighbourhood spot, and the sunny yellow walls are hung with local artists' work. The menu offers 29 plump sandwiches for all tastes, and those drinking regular coffee get free refills. Streetcar: Queen (#501).

Insomnia Internet Bar Café Inc 502 Bloor St W. This fully licensed Internet café has six computer terminals and a kitchen that stays open until 2am, plus a large screen TV and couches on which to snuggle. Booths are available, too. Subway: Bathurst.

Java House 537 Queen St W. The exterior of this popular local hangout is painted to look like a hut from some sort of South Pacific village, while inside it is all café, steamy and busy serving up light meals and gallons of caffeinated beverages of all descriptions. Streetcar: Queen (#501).

Kensington Café 73 Kensington Ave, Downtown. The international soup-and-sandwich menu gives a nod to the Middle East. A small, cozy place to slip into if the hectic pace of Kensington Market gets to be too much. Streetcar: Spadina (#510).

Moon Bean Coffee 30 St Andrew's St. One of a dwindling number of cafés that care enough to roast their own beans, *Moon Bean* is a Kensington Market tradition. Its patio is a perfect spot to watch the daily parade go by. Streetcar: Spadina (#501).

Sugar Café 942 Queen St W. This little café on the West Queen West strip has all the usual elements – espresso coffees, sweets and light fare – but presented in a charming, light-hearted way. Streetcar: Queen (#501).

Tequila Bookworm 490 Queen St W. Part second-hand bookshop, part coffee house, this charming place has garage-sale armchairs and bare brick walls. Espresso drinks and simple desserts are served without any fuss. Streetcar: Queen (#501).

Restaurants

Asian fusion

Monsoon 100 Simcoe St ☎416/979-7172. The award-winning interior here mirrors the Asian influence on the menu. Make time to stop for a martini in the glamorous bar before proceeding to the dining room. Starters are served on delicate *rakku* dishes, and the light, assured cooking boasts imaginative combinations (seared tofu in green tea marinade, maple-ginger grouper etc). Subway: St Andrew. Expensive.

Queen Mother Café 208 Queen St W ☎416/598-4719. Neither the name nor the cosy, wood-panelled interior gives a hint about the menu: Asian specialities like pad Thai, crispy spring rolls, and lots of chicken-and-shrimp entrees. Vegetarians take heart: the house veggie burger is a local tradition. Streetcar: Queen (#501). Moderate to expensive.

Canadian

Canoe In the Toronto Dominion Tower, 66 Wellington St W ☎416/364-0054. Way up on the 54th floor of an office tower, this elegant restaurant serves up imaginative Canadian cuisine (Yukon caribou, feral greens, wild berries) alongside one of the best wine lists in the city. Subway: King or St Andrew. Very expensive.

Le Papillon 16 Church St ☎416/363-0838. Large Breton crepes served sweet or savoury with a Québecois flair are the house specialities. The menu also includes *tortier* (a Québec meat pie), and bistro standards like onion soup and steak *frites*, all in a casually trendy environment. Subway: Union Station. Moderate.

Tundra 145 Richmond St W ☎416/869-3456. As the name suggests, this sleekly turned-out dining room – with its rich woods and granite embellishments – is intended to be as Canadian as the Great White North. In this case, "Canadian" means the ingredients (Arctic char, venison tenderloin, Malpeque oysters) more than any particular cuisine. Streetcar: Queen (#501). Moderate to expensive.

Chinese

Happy Seven 358 Spadina Ave ☎416/971-9820. Predominantly Cantonese-style cooking with a few spicy Szechuan dishes, tanks of soon-to-be seafood, and large, attractively presented servings. Bright and spotless, this establishment is extremely popular. Open until 5am. Streetcar: Dundas (#505). Inexpensive.

Lai Wah Heen Metropolitan Hotel, 108 Chestnut St ☎416/977-9899. The name means "elegant meeting place", which it most certainly is. The high-end dining room atmosphere is matched by the complex menu, best described as Hong Kong *moderne*, with dishes like Lustrous Peacock (a salad of barbecued duck, chicken and jellyfish on slivered melons garnished with eggs). Very popular on Sundays for dim sum. Streetcar: Dundas (#505). Expensive.

Lee Garden 331 Spadina Ave ☎416/593-9524. Expect long lines at this beloved restaurant. Locals esteem *Lee's* for the boneless chicken with black bean sauce and the large selection of fresh fish dishes. The cuisine is mostly Cantonese with plenty of daily specials that may demand your waiter's translation. Streetcar: Dundas (#505). Inexpensive to moderate.

Lucky Dragon 418 Spadina Ave ☎416/598-7823. The extensive pan-China menu features over five hundred items from every part of China. The noodle dishes contain some delicate surprises, like a fine noodle dressed simply in green onion and ginger. Delicious and authentic. Streetcar: Spadina (#510). Inexpensive.

French

Le Select 328 Queen St W ☎416/596-6406. Gallic favourites are served in a bistro atmosphere, with embellishments like a genuine Parisian zinc bar and little baskets of bread raised and lowered at each table by an idiosyncratic pulley system. Use Sunday brunch as an excuse to sample an ultra-fluffy omelette served with the best *frites* in town. Streetcar: Queen (#506). Moderate to expensive.

Greek

Avli 401 Danforth Ave ☎416/461-9577. An authentic Greek restaurant with a strong emphasis on fancy starters, a combination of which could easily make a full meal. Classic seafood dishes, a variety of pot-pies and sublime *baklava* round out the meal. The most theatrical dish in the house is *saganaki*, a slab of a mozzarella-like cheese doused in brandy and set aflame. Subway: Chester. Moderate to expensive.

Indian

Babur 237 Queen St W ☎416/599-7720. Rich, buttery sauces, delicately spiced stews and fluffy naan and pori breads, all delivered to your linen-cloth table by helpful waiters. Streetcar: Queen (#501). Moderate.

Nataraj 394 Bloor St W ☎ 416/928-2925. Delhi-specific dishes with a tandoori twist. The tandoori oven is on view to diners through a window into the kitchen. Try the spicy stews and shrimp pakoras. Subway: Spadina. Moderate.

Italian
Bar Italia 584 College St ☎ 416/535-3621. Antipasti, risotto, pasta and panini are dished up amid the clatter of wine glasses by a solicitous staff. One of their best buys is a huge antipasti platter – you can view the daily selections in a luncheon counter near the front – that is meant to share and perfect for a light meal. Chic little patio out front too. Streetcar: College (#506). Moderate.

Café Nervosa 75 Yorkville Ave ☎ 416/961-4642. One of the few reasonably priced restaurants left in Yorkville, *Café Nervosa* is strong on salads, pastas and pizzas. In particular, don't miss the two-person, regionally named pizzas with thin, crispy crusts and an authentic variety of toppings. Subway: Bay. Moderate.

La Fenice 319 King St W ☎ 416/585-2377. The high standards of this long-time favourite are one reason its clientele keep coming back. Another is the deliberate unfashionability of the antipasti, pastas, risottos and fish dishes. Tradition reigns supreme with venison, veal and lamb featuring as the weighty mains. Streetcar: King (#504). Expensive.

Noce 875 Queen St W ☎ 416/504-3463. On the corner of Queen West and Walnut (hence the nut name), this little house has become an exceptional Italian restaurant. The pasta is rolled by hand, the beef carpaccio virtually melts on the tongue, and the meat falls right off the bone. Streetcar: Queen (#501). Moderate to expensive.

Japanese
Nami 55 Adelaide St E ☎ 416/362-7373. A very fine Japanese restaurant with a dark, elegant interior lined with discrete private booths. The sushi bar is the standard fare, but the *robata* counter (grilled seafood prepared in front of you) is the main draw. Streetcar: King (#504). Expensive.

Sushi Bistro 204 Queen St W ☎ 416/971-5315. Pick of the city's many sushi joints. Entrees come with soup, salad, tea and rice, and there is an impressive sake selection. Streetcar: Queen (#501). Moderate.

Seafood
Joso's 202 Davenport Ave ☎ 416/925-1930. This celebrated restaurant, described at length by

Margaret Atwood in her novel *Robber Bride*, is famous for two things: its squid-ink risotto and the plethora of breasts and buttocks in owner Joso Spralja's paintings and statues. Reservations essential. No public transport – take a taxi. Expensive.

La Pecherie Mövenpick 133 Yorkville Ave ☎ 416/926-9545. *La Pecherie* offers a first-rate selection of seafood, expertly prepared and in sedate surroundings. Pastas, chicken dishes and salads are also featured, as is an excellent wine list. Subway: Bay. Expensive.

Rodney's Oyster House 209 Adelaide St E ☎ 416/363-8105. Toronto's favourite oyster bar serves up tons of the slippery delicacies, plus scallops, mussels and shrimp. The only regular fish is the smoked salmon. Streetcar: King (#504). Expensive.

Steaks
Barberian's 7 Elm St ☎ 416/597-0335. *Barberian's* hasn't changed much since it opened its doors in 1959, catering to Richard Burton and Elizabeth Taylor during the first days of *Camelot*. It continues to offer no-nonsense dining geared towards carnivores in a comfy, clubby environ-ment. The wine list is excellent. Subway: Dundas. Expensive.

Thai
Bangkok Garden 18 Elm St ☎ 416/977-6748. In one of Elm Street's old brownstones, the menu of this softly lit restaurant covers a Thai take on fresh lake fish as well as a standard selection of salads, noodles and curries. Subway: Dundas. Moderate to expensive.

Bangkok Paradise 506 Queen St W ☎ 416/504-3210. Informal and usually packed, the menu of the funky *Bangkok Paradise* has all the satay, noodle and curry classics you'd expect, plus a wide range of vegetarian options. Streetcar: Queen (#501). Moderate.

Vegetarian
Bo De Duyen 254 Spadina Ave (upstairs) ☎ 416/703-1247. This popular place offers Chinese-Vietnamese cooking for vegetarians. The absence of any animal by-products means that even the strictest vegan can eat here with a clear conscience. Pages and pages of selections, includ-ing "mock" meat and seafood items. Streetcar: Spadina (#510). Moderate.

Fressen Herbacious Cuisine 478 Queen St W ☎ 416/504-5127. Ultra cool vegetarian restaurant where regulars ignore the pastas and pizzas and head straight for the entrees. A full meal can also be made of the excellent appetizers, and the juice/smoothie list is extensive. Streetcar: Queen (#501). Moderate.

Le Commensal 655 Bay St (entrance off Elm St) ☎416/596-9364. The cafeteria-style set-up of this large, airy restaurant is its only drawback. Otherwise, the variety of offerings is excellent: soups, great salads, hearty pot-pies, stews, casseroles and baked goods are clearly marked for vegans or vegetarians. A large dessert counter too plus take-out. Subway: Dundas. Moderate.

Vietnamese

Pho 88 Restaurant 270 Spadina Ave ☎416/971-8899. The speciality here is *pho*, a spicy noodle soup with beef and vegetables that can have numerous variations. Streetcar: Spadina (#510). Inexpensive.

Vien Dong 359 Spadina Ave ☎416/593-6265. Primarily a Vietnamese restaurant, with lots of Cantonese influence and a few Gallic touches (frogs' legs, for example). Also serves a variety of fresh tropical fruit shakes. Streetcar: Spadina (#510). Inexpensive.

Nightlife and entertainment

Toronto is the cultural centre of English-speaking Canada and has gone to great expense to maintain a wide-ranging programme of **performing arts**, from theatre and opera to ballet and classical music. The city's strength is its **theatre scene**, which is the third-largest in the English-speaking world (after London and New York), but **dance**, **opera** and **classical music** are also well represented. Predictably enough, **ticket prices** vary enormously, but T.O. Tix (Tues–Sat noon–7.30pm; ☎416/536-6468), located right across from the Eaton Centre on Dundas Square, sells spare dance and theatre tickets at half-price for that day's performances, though note that you have to buy the tickets in person. As for film, Toronto's mainstream **cinemas** show Hollywood releases long before they reach Europe and, as you'd expect from a university city, it has good outlets for art-house stuff. The city also hosts what is generally regarded as the world's best film festival, the renowned **Toronto International Film Festival**. In addition, the city of the Cowboy Junkies obviously has some life in its **music** scene, and though many local bands who hit the big time move to the States, the city does have its fair share of venues, especially for **jazz**. Several bars and clubs sponsor a range of modern and traditional jazz, and there are free open-air jazz concerts at various downtown locations throughout the summer. For club and live music **listings**, consult *NOW, eye* or *TRIBE*, three free weekly newspapers which are available in stores, restaurants and street newsboxes. The most comprehensive listings are in *NOW*, which puts the emphasis on live music, while *TRIBE* specializes in dance/rave/house discos, and *eye* does a bit of both.

Bars, clubs and music venues

Bovine Sex Club 542 Queen St W. Despite its evocative name, the *Bovine* doesn't proclaim its existence with a sign nor does it have anything to do with cows or sex. The exterior is encrusted with layers of industrial scrap and bicycle parts, offering no glimpse of the playground within, which is filled with kinetic sculptures built from old portable record players, and has a couple of bars and pool tables. Streetcar: Queen (#501).

The Cameron House 408 Queen St W. This old tap house has been a performance space and refuge for members of Toronto's alternative arts

scene for two decades, and includes its own vibrant cabaret. The beautiful interior is covered with trompe l'oeil skies and angels and gilt plaster while, outside, artists have been rearranging the facade for twenty years now, the only constant being the huge, red metal ants marching up the side of the building. Streetcar: Queen (#501).

C'est What? 67 Front St E. Located in the dark, low-ceilinged basement in the St Lawrence Market area, *C'est What* has over twenty micro brews on tap – including the popular house brand, hemp beer – plus an impressive selection of single malt scotches and hearty pub food. The performance space here has seen the likes of Bare Naked Ladies and Jeff Buckley, to name just two. Subway: Union Station.

Element Bar 553 Queen St W. Despite concerns that this trendy bar was simply too cool and too good to last, *Element* continues apace with its winning Retro-Mod interior and progressive DJs, drawing a youngish but sophisticated crowd. The only downside is the line to get in on Saturday night, which can be daunting. Streetcar: Queen (#501).

Clubs and music venues

Bambu by the Lake 245 Queens Quay W. When the *Bamboo* shut its doors on Queen West, many said that an era had passed. Now, the same owners, staff and chef have reopened one of Toronto's best-loved clubs as *Bambu by the Lake*, in the former Pier Museum. Like its predecessor, the space is cavernous, needing a happy, dancing crowd to warm it up. It's a good thing, then, that the bookings – mostly salsa and reggae – are usually hot, keeping the big dance floor moving. Streetcar: Harbourfront (#509).

Big Bop 651 Queen St W. This vast space is filled with urban rockers and holds several different stages, all of which cater to the live alternative rock scene. The main stage was recently decorated with sumptuous mural-sized reproductions of famous nineteenth-century paintings – making the walls the best-dressed thing in the joint. Streetcar: Queen (#501).

College St Bar 574 College St. A laid-back jazz bar that often dips into the realm of R&B. An excellent alternative to some of the over-hyped, trendier establishments in the area. Open nightly until 2am. Streetcar: College (#506).

Easy and the Fifth 225 Richmond St W. Movie stars and supermodels are fond of this expensive, well-appointed nightclub, which is also known for its very fine restaurant. Great rooftop patio. Streetcar: Queen (#501).

El Convento Rico 750 College St. Walking into this lively joint, replete with red velvet, flocked wallpaper and baroque spot welding, makes you feel like you've stumbled on the best party in town – and you may well have. The crowd ranges from earnest suburbanites to dishy Latino drag queens, and the DJs spin Latin and disco classics Mon–Sat until 4am (Sun until 10pm). Streetcar: College (#506).

El Mocambo 464 Spadina Ave. The stuff of legends insofar as live acts are concerned, having had visits from luminaries like the Rolling Stones, B.B. King, Blondie, and hometown faves like Nash

the Slash. The tables are sticky and the carpet is scary, but the bands are (usually) great. Streetcar: Carlton/College (#506) or Spadina (#510).

Guvernment Queens Quay E. Down on the shores of Lake Ontario, this huge barn of a dance club books live bands for its downstairs cavern and has a multitude of DJs spinning in the two discos upstairs. Subway: Union Station.

Horseshoe Tavern 368 Queen St W. Lots of Toronto bands got their start here, and it's still a favourite place for the now-famous to sit in for a set or stage a special one-off concert. The interior is relentlessly unglamorous, but the phenomenal bar staff is a major compensation. Streetcar: Queen (#501).

Hush 457 Adelaide St W at Spadina. *Hush*'s old, rough exterior gives way to a high-toned, mahogany-stained bar and lounge that is part Rat Pack and part *2001: A Space Odyssey*. If you've nothing else to do in this swank space, you can amuse yourself with a game of chess played on one of the upright chessboard "pods". Streetcar: King (#504).

Joker 318 Richmond St W. A stylish behemoth of a club whose weekend patrons are willing to line up around the block. The music is generally heavy-handed techno, with smatterings of hip-hop and R&B in the third-floor disco. Streetcar: Queen (#501).

Lee's Palace 529 Bloor St W. *Lee's* continued popularity has nothing to do with the decor, the food or even the draft beer. Its reputation is entirely based on the outre bands it consistently books. Patrons can also check out the DJ dance action upstairs at the aptly named Dance Cave. Subway: Bathurst.

Matador 466 Dovercourt. This noble institution has been memorialized in song by none other than Leonard Cohen in "Closing Time". When everyone else starts to shut down, the *Matador* opens. Don't think about showing up before 1.30am. A good place to star-watch and catch great bands trying out new material. Streetcar: College (#506).

Phoenix Concert Theatre 410 Sherbourne St. An imaginative renovation – and equally imaginative booking agents – makes this venue a popular place to catch a concert. Big-name acts looking for intimate venues, guitar legends and world music divas perform on the main stage space, which looks lie a cross between a Wild West saloon and an old vaudeville theatre. Streetcar: Dundas (#505).

The Rex Hotel Jazz Bar and Grill 194 Queen St W, Downtown. In arguments about which is the best jazz club in town, this one is consistently near the top of the list. A well-primped crowd lounges in the spiffed-up interior, but any reservations about pretensions evaporate once the music – which is always top-notch – begins.

This Is London 364 Richmond St. Yet another club you have to enter off an alleyway (and up a flight of stairs). When it opened, people were appreciative of its stylish interior, DJ selections of disco, soul and good old Top 40, but the real buzz was about the women's washrooms: they take up the whole top floor, and hairdressers and make-up artists are on hand for touch-ups. Streetcar: Queen (#501).

Top O' The Senator 249 Victoria St. Right near the new Yonge/Dundas Square, this upstairs bar to the *Senator* restaurant serves light entrees and snacks along with a good line in scotch and beer. Its main claim to fame, however, is the superior jazz: when the big names play a Toronto club, it's usually this one. Subway: Dundas.

Performing arts and cinema

Theatre

Hummingbird Centre 1 Front St E ☎416/872-2262, ⓦwww.hummingbirdcentre.com. With over 3000 seats, the Hummingbird is the venue of choice for family-oriented musicals. It is also the home of the Canadian Opera Company and the National Ballet (see below). Subway: Union Station

Princess of Wales Theatre 300 King St W ☎416/872-1212, ⓦwww.mirvish.com. Built in 1993 to accommodate the helicopter in *Miss Saigon*, and currently home to the blockbuster musical *The Lion King*, this addition to Toronto's more traditional playhouses has a deceptively intimate feel, despite its 2000 seats. Subway: St Andrew.

Royal Alexandra Theatre 260 Yonge St ☎416/872-1212, ⓦwww.mirvish.com. Built in 1906, the "Royal Alex" is a graceful Beaux Arts theatre that has been fully restored to its Edwardian splendour. Puts on everything from classical repertory theatre to exuberant musicals like *Mamma Mia*. Subway: St Andrew.

St Lawrence Centre for the Arts 27 Front St E ☎416/386-3100, ⓦwww.stlc.com. The St Lawrence Centre contains two stages: the Bluma Appel Theatre, which specializes in presenting new works by contemporary artists, and, upstairs, the studio-sized Jane Mallett Theatre showcasing experimental and workshop productions. Subway: Union Station.

Tarragon Theatre 30 Bridgman St ☎416/531-1827, ⓦwww.tarragontheatre.com. A renovated factory space, the Tarragon has contributed much to Toronto's thriving theatrical community, by consistently presenting challenging, innovative performances. Subway: Dupont.

Classical music

Glenn Gould Studio 250 Front St W ☎416/205-5555. Named for the great pianist and composer (see p.941), this small, boxy hall downtown in the Canadian Broadcasting Centre is so sprung for sound that enthusiastic performances leave audiences literally vibrating. The programming is first-rate, generally showcasing Canadian talent. Streetcar: King (#504).

Massey Hall 178 Victoria St ☎416/872-4255. A turn-of-the-century recital hall that boasts great acoustics, and has hosted a wide variety of performers – everyone from Maria Callas to Jarvis Cocker. The austere architecture is offset by Moorish details, like the fanciful moulding along the balconies. Subway: Dundas.

Roy Thompson Hall 60 Simcoe St ☎416/593-4828. Home to the Toronto Symphony Orchestra (☎416/593-4828, ⓦwww.tso.on.ca), this modern hall looks like an upturned soup bowl during the day, but at night the place is transformed, its glass-panelled walls glow, casting light over the reflecting ponds outside. Inside, the circular hall has excellent sightlines, and its acoustics have recently been tweaked to rave reviews. Subway: St Andrew.

Spectator sports in Toronto

Baseball The Blue Jays (☎416/341-1234, ⓦwww.bluejays.com), of the American Baseball League, play at the SkyDome.

Canadian football The Argonauts (☎905/607-5328, ⓦwww.argonauts.on.ca), of the CFL, also play at the SkyDome.

Ice hockey The Maple Leafs (☎416/815-5500, ⓦwww.torontomapleleafs.com), of the NHL, play home fixtures in the Air Canada Centre, behind Union Station.

Opera

Canadian Opera Company The Hummingbird Centre, 1 Front St E ℡416/363-6671, ⓦwww.coc.ca. Canada's national opera troupe, the COC has impressed international audiences for years with its ambitious productions, devotion to young talent and the musical erudition of its director, Richard Bradshaw. Seats are often scarce, particularly for the eagerly anticipated season premieres, so reserve as far in advance as possible – ticket prices vary widely from $35 to $165. Rush tickets are only available to seniors and students, and are not released until two hours before a performance. Union Station.

Dance

du Maurier Theatre 231 Queens Quay W ℡416/973-4000. Part of the lakeshore's Harbourfront Centre (see p.104), this modern theatre stages primarily dance recitals, but also the occasional theatrical or musical performance. LRT (from Union Station) to Queens Quay.
National Ballet Company Hummingbird Centre, 1 Front St E ℡416/345-9595, ⓦwww.national.ballet.ca. The NBC's prima ballerinas, notably Karen Kain and Veronica Tennant, are much admired, as is the company itself, performing classical ballet and contemporary dance with equal artistry. Subway: Union Station.

Film

Bloor Cinema 506 Bloor St W ℡416/532-6677. Though this cinema won't win any beauty contests, it's still a great place to view second-run films. Frequently plays host to the numerous film festivals in Toronto. Subway: Bathurst.
Canada Square 2200 Yonge St ℡416/483-9428. A sprawling thirteen-screen cineplex offering a mix of foreign, independent and mainstream films. Subway: Eglinton.

Carlton 20 Carlton St ℡416/598-2309. When Garth Drabinsky's Cineplex chain muscled in on the Toronto scene, a number of art-house cinemas closed. To compensate for this, Drabinsky set aside the Carlton to show first-run art films, and its eleven screens are still doing just that. The café and espresso bar make a nice change from standard concessions fare, although that too is available. The smaller cinemas here can feel cramped. Subway: College.
Cineforum 463 Bathurst ℡416/603-6643. An independent among independents, Cineforum is indispensible to film students and buffs who want to catch up on the history of film without resorting to cropped video and DVD versions. Streetcar/Subway: Bathurst.
Cinematheque Jackman Hall, Art Gallery of Ontario, 317 Dundas St W, ℡416/968-FILM. Cinematheque is a year-round extension of the Toronto International Film Festival; its programmer, James Quandt, is so respected that the French awarded him with a Legion d'Honneur. The quality of prints he finds are beyond compare. Streetcar: Dundas #505.
Uptown 764 Yonge St ℡416/922-6361. One of the last cinema palaces left in the city. The main theatre upstairs has a huge curved screen plus opulent gold curtains, plush red upholstery and plenty of plaster ornamentation. Its 921 seats ensure that this is where the biggest blockbusters open; during the Toronto International Film Festival it's always packed to capacity. Subway: Bloor/Yonge.
Varsity 55 Bloor St W ℡416/961-6303. A recent expansion has turned this two-screener into an eleven-cinema behemoth, replete with displays of Hollywood costumes, premium prices and full-service (drinks and snacks delivered to your seat) screening rooms. The cinemas are well appointed with deep, comfortable seats. Subway: Yonge-Bloor.

Listings

Bike rental McBride Cycle, 180 Queen's Quay W ℡416/203-5651.
Bookshops World's Biggest Bookshop, 20 Edward St, near Yonge and Dundas (℡416/977-7009), is a huge warehouse-like affair with a vast selection of titles. Canada's own Indigo (ⓦwww.indigo.ca) has several branches, including one in the Eaton Centre, another at 55 Bloor St W.
Car rental Budget, 150 Cumberland St ℡416/927-8300; Discount, 595 Bay St ℡416/597-2222, or ℡416/310-CARS for 33

other Toronto locations; Dollar, 1108 Bay St ℡416/515-8800, or 1-800/800-400 for thirteen other Toronto locations; National, Union Station, 65 Front St E ℡416/364-4191 or 1-800/227-7368; Thrifty, in the *Royal York Hotel*, 100 Front St W ℡416/947-1385 or 1-800/847-4389.
Consulates Australia, 175 Bloor St E ℡416/323-1155; Ireland, 20 Toronto St, Suite 1210 ℡416/366-9300; New Zealand, 225 MacPherson Ave, Suite 2A West ℡416/947-000; UK, 777 Bay St ℡416/593-1267; US, 360 University Ave ℡416/595-1700.

Internet access Cyber Orbits, 1 Gloucester St ☎416/920-5912; Geocity Net, 30 Eglinton Ave E ☎416/483-8288; Ground Zero Network, 211 Yonge St ☎416/328-2133; Internet Café, 370 Yonge St ☎416/408-0400; Net Space, 275 Queen St W ☎416/597-2005; and Netropolis Internet Lounge, 721 Yonge St ☎416/961-7707.

Laundry The Laundry Lounge, 531 Yonge St ☎416/975-4747; 24-hour Coin Laundry, 566 Mt Pleasant Ave ☎416/487-0233; Splish Splash Cleaning Centre, 590 College St ☎416/532-6499.

Left luggage Union Station, 65 Front St, has lockers (24-hour maximum), as do the Toronto Coach Terminal, 610 Bay St at Dundas, and the Bloor-Yonge St subway station.

Library Toronto Reference Library, 789 Yonge St (Mon–Thurs 10am–8pm, Fri & Sat 10am–5pm, Sun during winter 1.30–5pm, closed Sun during summer; ☎416/393-7131).

Pharmacies Shopper's Drug Mart, 700 Bay St ☎416/979-2424, also 722 Yonge St ☎416/920-0098. For a holistic pharmacy, including herbal and traditional treatments, try the Big Carrot Wholistic Dispensary, 348 Danforth Ave ☎416/466-8432.

Post offices Canada Post operates branches in scores of locations, mostly as a distinct part of a larger retail outlet, mainly pharmacies and stationery stores. One handy location is downtown inside the Royal Bank Plaza, 200 Bay at Front.

Weather Information ☎416/292-1010, then 3180.

Southwest Ontario

The chain of towns to the east and west of Toronto, stretching 120km along the edge of Lake Ontario from Oshawa to Hamilton, is often called the **Golden Horseshoe**, a misleadingly evocative name that refers solely to their geographic shape and economic success. This is Ontario's manufacturing heartland, a densely populated strip whose principal places of interest are in the steel-making city of **Hamilton**, the home of both the Royal Botanical Gardens and the delightful mansion of Dundurn Castle. Further round the lake are the famous **Niagara Falls**, undoubtedly Canada's most celebrated sight, though the falls adjoin the uninspiring town of the same name – and it's best to use the charming, colonial village of **Niagara-on-the-Lake** as a base for a visit. At neighbouring Queenston the **Niagara Escarpment** begins its rambling journey across the region to the Bruce Peninsula, the major interruption in a generally flat terrain. To the west of this limestone ridge the main attractions lie on the coast, most notably **Point Pelee National Park**, the vigorous town of **Windsor**, and the small-town pleasures of **Goderich** and leafy **Bayfield**. The **Bruce Peninsula** itself boasts dramatic coastal scenery and incorporates two outstanding national parks, which make for some great walking, climbing and scuba diving. To the east of the Niagara Escarpment, along the southern shore of **Severn Sound**, there's a string of lethargic ports, the most agreeable of which is **Penetanguishene**, located a few kilometres from the sturdy palisades of the replica Jesuit mission of **Sainte-Marie among the Hurons**. The northern shore of the Sound boasts the lion's share of the stunningly beautiful **Georgian Bay Islands National Park**, an elegiac land and waterscape of rocky, pine-dotted islets and crystal-blue lake. The park – and its campsites – are best approached by boat from the tourist resort of **Honey Harbour**, but you can sample the scenery on a variety of summer island cruises from Penetanguishene and **Midland** to the south and the dinky little port of **Parry Sound** further north.

There are fast and frequent **buses** and **trains** between Toronto and Niagara Falls, and a similarly efficient service between the region's other major settlements, like Windsor, London and Kitchener. But if you're visiting the smaller towns be aware that transport is much more patchy: Hamilton, Penetanguishene and Midland, for instance, have reasonably good bus connections, but not so Niagara-on-the-Lake. Worse still, there are no buses along the east shore of Lake Huron (to Goderich and Bayfield) and up the Bruce Peninsula – where Tobermory has a **car ferry** service to South Baymouth on Manitoulin Island (see p.200), a useful short cut to northern Ontario.

Kitchener, Elora and Stratford

The industrial city of **Kitchener** is southern Ontario at its most mundane, but amid the prevailing architectural gloom it does have a couple of sights that are worth an hour or so. In marked contrast, **Elora**, 30km north of Kitchener, is a pleasant little village of old stone houses and mills on the periphery of the **Elora Gorge**, a narrow limestone ravine that's a popular spot for a day's walk and picnic. Fifty kilometres west of Kitchener, **Stratford** is different again, a modest country town that hosts one of Canada's most prestigious cultural events, the **Stratford Festival**.

Kitchener

Just off Hwy 401 about 100km west of downtown Toronto, **KITCHENER** lies at the centre of an industrial belt whose economy is based on rubber, textiles, leather and furniture. The town was founded as Sand Hills in 1799 by groups of **Mennonites**, a tightly knit Protestant sect who came here from the States, where their pacifist beliefs had incurred the wrath of their neighbours during the Revolution. Soon after, German farmers began to arrive in the area, establishing a generally good-humoured trading relationship with the Mennonites. The new settlers had Sand Hills renamed Berlin in 1826, but during World War I it was thought prudent to change the name yet again and to prove their patriotism they chose "Kitchener" after the British field marshal. Today around sixty percent of Kitchener's inhabitants are descendants of German immigrants, a heritage celebrated every year during **Oktoberfest**, nine days of alcoholic stupefaction when even the most reticent of men can be seen wandering the streets in lederhosen. The Mennonites have drifted out of Kitchener itself, and are concentrated in the villages north and west of **Waterloo**, Kitchener's glum northerly neighbour.

Kitchener's centre is marked by the **Farmers' Market** – open on Saturdays from 6am to 2pm year-round and Wednesdays 8am to 2pm June to September – where you should be sure to sample the delicious German sausages. The Mennonite traders are unmistakable, with the men wearing traditional black suits and broad-brimmed hats, or deep-blue shirts and braces, the women ankle-length dresses and matching bonnets. The Ontario Mennonites are, however, far from being an homogeneous sect – over twenty different groups are affiliated to the Mennonite Central Committee (MCC). They all share certain religious beliefs reflecting their Anabaptist origins – the sole validity of adult baptism being crucial – but precise practices and dress codes vary from group to group. Members of the traditional wing of the Mennonite movement, sometimes called **Amish** or Ammanites after the seventeenth-century elder Jakob Ammann, own property communally and shun all modern machinery, travelling to the market and around the back lanes on spindly horse-drawn buggies. To explain their history and faith, the MCC runs **The Mennonite Story** (May–Oct Mon–Fri 11am–5pm, Sat 10am–5pm, Sun 1.30–5pm; Nov–April Sat 11am–4.30pm, Sun 2–4.30pm; donation), a small tourist-office-cum-interpretation-centre at 1408 King St North in the village of **ST JACOBS**. The village is located just north of Waterloo on Hwy 85 and there's a popular Mennonite craft shop here too. Back in Kitchener, the only conventional tourist sight of note is **Woodside**, boyhood home of prime minister William Lyon Mackenzie King, about 1km northeast of the centre at 528 Wellington St N (mid-May to mid-Dec daily 10am–5pm; $3.50). Set in a pretty little park, the house has been restored to its late-Victorian appearance and has an interesting display in the basement on King's life and times, though it doesn't give much away about his eccentricities. A dog lover and spiritualist, he amalgamated the two obsessions by believing his pets were mediums.

Kitchener's **bus station** is on Charles St, one block west of the main street, King, and the town centre. The **train station** is a ten-minute walk north of downtown, at Victoria and Weber. The **Kitchener–Waterloo tourism office**, downtown opposite the town hall at 185 King St W (Tues–Fri 9am–4.30pm & Sat noon-4pm; ☎519/745-3536, ⓦwww.kw-visitor.on.ca), has free maps and **accommodation** listings, including several B&Bs (❶–❷); during Oktoberfest many families offer similarly priced rooms. There's a clutch of **motels** north of the centre along Kitchener's Victoria St.

Elora

Sloping up from the craggy banks of the Grand River, **ELORA** was founded in the 1830s by settlers who harnessed the river's waters to run their mills. Some of their limestone cottages have survived, along with a large grist mill, the main landmark, which has been converted into the *Elora Mill Country Inn*, a clever adaptation of what has long been the most important building in town. Nonetheless, most visitors come here to gaze at the waterfalls beside the inn – even though they're only a few metres high – and then stroll on to viewpoints overlooking the neighbouring three-kilometre-long **Elora Gorge**, a forested ravine with limestone cliffs. To get to the gorge from the inn, walk up Price St to the top of the hill, turn left on James St and proceed as far as the park area at the end of Henderson, from where footpaths lead across to the gorge. Elora itself, just ten-minutes' walk from end to end, is most pleasantly approached from the south – along Route 21 – across a narrow bridge that leads into the main street, Metcalfe, which cuts across tiny Mill St, adjoining the falls. Elora is well equipped with **B&Bs**. One of the best is *The Old Bissell House*, 84 Mill St E (☎519/846-6695, ⓦwww.bbcanada.com/2481.html; ❹), a smart, modern, lodge-like house with river views and three pleasant guest rooms, all en suite. There's only one **hotel**, the enjoyable *Elora Mill Country Inn*, on Mill St (☎519/846-9118 or 1-866/713-5672, ⓦwww.eloramill.com; ❼), which boasts period bedrooms, log fires and beamed ceilings. The hotel also has a first-rate **restaurant**. If you're keen to see more of the gorge, the **Elora Gorge Conservation Area** (daily dawn–dusk) is a popular picnic and camping spot spread out along the Grand River 2km southwest of Elora: it's signposted from the bridge near Metcalfe.

Stratford

Surrounded by flat and fertile farmland, **STRATFORD** is a homely and like-able town of 30,000 people, which is brightened by the **Avon River** trimming the centre and by its grandiose **city hall**, a brown-brick fiesta of cupolas, towers and limestone trimmings. More importantly, the town is also the home of the **Stratford Festival** (ⓦwww.stratford-festival.on.ca), which started in 1953 and is now one of the most prestigious theatrical occasions in North America, attracting no fewer than half a million visitors from early April to mid-November. The core performances are Shakespearean, but there's much other drama too, from Racine to O'Casey and Beckett. The **Festival Box Office** at the Festival Theatre (Jan to early April Mon–Sat 9am–5pm, Sun 9am–2pm; early April to early Nov Mon–Sat 9am–8pm, Sun 9am–2pm; ☎1-800/567-1600) accepts ticket orders by letter, phone, fax, in person and by email. Tickets cost anywhere between $30 and $90 depending on the performance and which seat category you have. Many plays are sold out months in advance, but the box office does set aside a limited number of half-price rush tickets for two of the three main theatres – the Festival and the Avon, but not the Tom Patterson. These are for sale from 9am on the day of the performance, but the seats are the worst in the house. The box office also organizes a number of **discount packages** with savings upwards of ten percent for various categories of performance, plus accommodation ranging from hotels to guesthouses.

From Stratford **train and bus stations**, on Shakespeare St, it's a fifteen-minute stroll north via Downie St to the centre of town on the south bank of the River Avon. There are two tourist offices. The main one is **Tourism Stratford** at 47 Downie St (Mon–Sat 9am–5pm, but closed Sat Sept–May; ☎519/271-5140 or 1-800/561-7926, ⓦwww.city.stratford.on.ca). The second is the **Visitor Information Centre** (May–Sept Mon–Fri 9am–5pm, Sat & Sun 9am–6pm), located by the river on York St, immediately northwest of the town's main intersection, where Erie, Downie and Ontario streets all meet. Stratford has over 250 guesthouses and B&Bs plus around a dozen hotels and motels, but **accommodation** can still be hard to find during the Festival's busiest weekends in July and August. The walls of the tourist offices are plastered with pictures and descriptions of many of these establishments and standards (and prices) are high. Both will help you find somewhere to stay, but one good and convenient recommendation is *Avonview Manor B&B*, 63 Avon St (☎519/273-4603, ⓦwww.bbcanada.com/avonview; ❺), which occupies an expansive Edwardian villa overlooking the north bank of the River Avon across from the town centre. The four bedrooms here are tastefully decorated and immaculately maintained. Another excellent choice is the *Deacon House B&B Inn*, 101 Brunswick St (☎519/273-2052 or 1-877/825-6374, ⓦwww.bbcanada.com/1152.html; ❺), whose six lovely guest rooms – all en suite – are centrally located in a good-looking Edwardian villa with a wide veranda. A third very recommendable option is the *Duggan Place B&B Inn*, 151 Nile St (☎519/273-7502 or 1-888/394-1111, ⓦwww.dugganplace.com; ❻), in a well-kept Victorian villa a five-minute walk from the centre. There are four en-suite rooms here, all done out in immaculate style, and two have private balconies overlooking a splendid garden. Stratford has plenty of excellent **cafés and restaurants**, with one of the best being *Fellini's Italian Café & Grill*, 107 Ontario St, which offers a good range of fresh pizzas and pastas at reasonable prices. There are tasty snacks and light meals at *Tango*, 104 Ontario St, which also has live music on the weekend, and pastries and gourmet coffees at *Balzac's*, 149 Ontario St. *Rundles*, 9 Coburg St (☎519/271-6442; closed in winter), is arguably the classiest restaurant in town, serving up imaginatively prepared French-style cuisine at finger-burning prices. The strikingly modern surroundings help compensate too.

Hamilton

Some 70km from Toronto, **HAMILTON** lies at the extreme western end of Lake Ontario and was the focus of a district first surveyed by George Hamilton, a Niagaran storekeeper-turned-landowner who moved here in 1812 to escape the war between America and Britain. Strategically located, the town was soon established as a trading centre, but its real growth began with the development of the farm-implements industry in the 1850s. By the turn of the last century, Hamilton had become a major steel producer and today its mills churn out sixty percent of the country's output.

For a city of over 300,000 people, Hamilton is not over-endowed with attractions. The finest downtown building is **Whitehern** (mid-June to Aug Tues–Sun 11am–4pm; Sept to mid-June Tues–Sun 1–4pm; $5), a couple of minutes' walk east of Main St's prominent city hall at 41 Jackson St W. A good example of early Victorian architecture, its reworked interior holds an eccentric mix of styles, ranging from a splendid mid-nineteenth-century circular stairway to a dingy wood-panelled 1930s basement – all the garbled legacy of the McQuestern family, who lived here from 1852 until the 1960s. Also in the centre, nearby at 123 King St W, is the **Art Gallery of Hamilton** (Tues & Wed and Fri–Sun 11am–5pm, Thurs 11am–9pm; free), a brutally modern building whose two floors display a representative sample of Canadian painting drawn from the permanent collection. The gallery is in the throes of a major refurbishment, but it does possess a good selection of works by the Group of Seven (see box, p.96). Harris, Lismer, J.E.H. MacDonald and Edwin Holgate all make distinctive contributions and there's an especially fine painting by Tom Thomson, *The Birch Grove*, dated to 1917. Look out also for Alex Colville's iconic *Horse and Train* of 1954 and for several folksy paintings by Cornelius Krieghoff (see p.427). The gallery also features an imaginative programme of temporary exhibitions.

From James St N in the city centre it's a twenty-minute walk west straight down York Boulevard to the entertaining **Dundurn Castle** (late May to Aug daily 10am–4pm; Sept to late May Tues–Sun noon–4pm; $10), a handsome villa built in the 1830s for Sir Allan Napier MacNab, a soldier, lawyer and land speculator, who became one of the leading conservative politicians of the day. He was knighted for his loyalty to the Crown during the Upper Canada Rebellion of 1837, when he employed bands of armed Indians to round up supposed rebels and loot their property. Carefully renovated, Dundurn is an impressive, broadly Palladian building with an interior that easily divides into "upstairs" and "downstairs", the former filled with fine contemporaneous furnishings, the latter a warren of poorly ventilated rooms for the dozens of servants. Nearby, the gatekeeper's cottage has been turned into a small **military museum** (July–Aug daily 11am–5pm; Sept–June Tues–Sun 1–5pm; free admission with castle), detailing local involvement in the War of 1812 and in the Fenian (Irish–American) cross-border raids of the 1860s. From Dundurn Castle, York Boulevard clips over the western reaches of Hamilton harbour bound for the neighbouring city of Burlington. The **Royal Botanical Gardens** (⊕905/527-1158, ⊛www.rbg.ca) cover some 3000 acres on the far side of the harbour, their several sections spread over 15km of wooded shoreline. The flower displays here are simply gorgeous with highlights including the Hendrie Park Rose Garden (best June–Oct) and the neighbouring Laking Garden with its irises and peonies (May & June). These two gardens adjoin the main **RBG visitor centre** (daily 9am to dusk), where there's a shop, café and several inside areas featuring forced bulbs, orchids, cacti and so forth. Wilder parts of the RBG are round to the west with the 800-hectare Cootes Paradise Marsh nature sanctuary latticed with hiking trails. The outdoor garden areas are open daily from 9am to dusk and admission is $10. There are modest additional charges for some of the inside areas, which also close a little earlier – either 4pm or 5pm. As for transport, most Hamilton–Burlington **buses** stop outside the RBG centre and from here a shuttle bus (late April to Aug every 15min; free) visits every section of the gardens. At other times of the year, you'll need a car.

Hamilton **bus station** is at the corner of Hunter St and James St S, a couple of blocks south of Main St – which, together with King St, one block further to the north, forms the downtown core. The **tourist information office** is in between Main and King at 34 James St S (Mon–Sat 9am–5pm; ☎905/546-2666 or 1-800/263-8590, ⊛www.hamiltonundiscovered.com). They can supply you with brochures on the city and its surroundings, plus restaurant and hotel lists. Most of the major **hotel** chains have branches in Hamilton, with rooms starting from around $85; one of the most comfortable is the centrally located *Ramada Plaza Hotel*, 150 King St E (☎905/528-3451, ⊛www.ramadahamilton.com; ❺).

West of Hamilton: Brantford and the Bell Homestead

The modest manufacturing town of **BRANTFORD**, 40km or so to the west of Hamilton beside the Grand River, takes its name from Joseph Brant (also see p.938), who led a large group of Loyalist Iroquois here after the American War of Independence, then worked to form a confederation of Iroquois to keep the United States out of Ohio. His dream was undermined by jealousies amongst the Indian nations, whereupon he withdrew to Burlington and lived the life of an English gentleman. The town was later the birthplace of ice-hockey's greatest player, Wayne Gretzky, but no one's built a museum – yet.

The most interesting thing to see in the town itself is the **Brant Museum & Archives**, 57 Charlotte St (Wed–Fri 10am–4pm & Sat 1–4pm, plus July & Aug Sun 1–4pm; $2), where there's a reasonable collection of Iroquois artefacts. However, Brantford's main sight – the **Bell Homestead**, 94 Tutela Heights Rd (Tues–Sun 9.30am–4.30pm; $3.50) – is located about 4km south of the centre, in the low wooded hills overlooking the river. **Alexander Graham Bell** left Edinburgh for Ontario in 1870 at the age of 23, a reluctant immigrant who came only because of fears for his health after the death of two close relatives from tuberculosis. Soon after his arrival he took a job as a teacher of the deaf, motivated by his mother's loss of hearing and, in his efforts to discover a way to reproduce sounds visibly, he stumbled across the potential of transmitting sound along an electrified wire. The consequence was the first long-distance call, made in 1876 from Brantford to the neighbouring village of Paris and the rest is, as they say, history. The Bell Homestead consists of two simple, clapboard buildings. The first, moved here from Brantford in 1969, housed Canada's original Bell company office and features a series of modest displays on the history of the telephone. The second, the cosy family home, fronts a second small exhibition area devoted to Bell's life and research. There's no public transport from Brantford to the homestead.

Niagara Falls and the Niagara River

In 1860 thousands watched as Charles Blondin walked a tightrope across **Niagara Falls** for the third time. Midway, he paused to cook an omelette on a portable grill and then had a marksman shoot a hole through his hat from the *Maid of the Mist* tug boat, 50m below. As attested by Blondin and the antics of innumerable lunatics and publicity seekers – not to mention several million tourist photos – the falls simply can't be beat as a theatrical setting. Yet the stupendous first impression of the Niagara doesn't last long, especially on jaded modern palates. Consequently, to prevent the twelve million visitors who arrive each year from getting bored by the sight of a load of water crashing over

▲ Botanical Gardens & Niagara-on-the-Lake

NIAGARA FALLS

ACCOMMODATION

Brock Plaza Hotel	E
Comfort Inn-Clifton Hill	F
Comfort Inn North of the Falls	A
Eastwood Lodge B&B	D
Gretna Green B&B	C
Niagara Falls Hostel	B
Quality Inn Clifton Hill	G
Sheraton Fallsview Hotel	H

RESTAURANTS & CAFÉS

Big Anthony's	1
Golden Griddle	G
Mama Mia's	2
Skylon Revolving Dining Room	3

Niagara Glen
Nature Area

The
Whirlpool

Spanish
Aero Car

NIAGARA PARKWAY

Niagara
Helicopter
Rides

Niagara
Glen View
Camping

White Water
Boardwalk

Whirlpool Rapids

Whirlpool
Rapids
Bridge

LEADER LANE

FERGUSON STREET

BUTTREY STREET

VICTORIA AVENUE

Train
Station

Bus & Transit Station

ZIMMERMAN AVE
ERIE AVE
ONTARIO AVE

BRIDGE STREET

QUEEN STREET

CATARACT AVE

SIXTH AVE
FIFTH AVE
FOURTH AVE
THIRD AVE
SECOND AVE
FIRST AVE

MORRISON STREET

1ST LAURENT LANE
BUCKLEY STREET

SIMCOE STREET

MORDEN DRIVE
ARTHUR STREET

VALLEY WAY

JEPSON STREET

ARMOURY ST

RYERSON CRES

ORCHARD
PARKWAY
CHILTON AVE
ASHLAND AVE
ELMWOOD AVE

MCRAE STREET

STAMFORD STREET

STANLEY AVENUE

VICTORIA AVENUE

EASTWOOD CRES

PALMER AVENUE
ONTARIO AVENUE

RIVER ROAD

SPRUCE AVE
CEDAR AVE

**Ontario
Travel
Centre**

ⓘ

(420) (ROBERTS ST)

KITCHENER STREET

PINE AVE

CANADA
USA

**Niagara Falls
Visitor &
Convention
Bureau**

ⓘ

NORTH STREET

LEWIS AVENUE

BUCHANAN AVENUE

DESSON AVENUE

MCGRAIL AVENUE

ELLEN AVENUE

VICTORIA AVENUE

FALLS AVENUE

WALNUT AVE

ⓣ

?

Casino

F E

G

Rainbow
Bridge

FERRY AVENUE

MAIN STREET

NIAGARA STREET

1ST STREET

SPRING STREET

STANLEY AVENUE

FERRY STREET

ROBINSON STREET

BUCHANAN AVENUE

**Queen
Victoria
Park**

**Maid
of the
Mist**

RAINBOW BOULEVARD

**Skylon
Tower**

3

MURRAY STREET

**American
Falls**

DIXON STREET

Minolta Tower

**Table
Rock House
& Journey behind
the Falls**

ⓘ

GOAT ISLAND

DUNN STREET

ALLANTHUS AVE

PORTAGE ROAD

FALLS VIEW BOULEVARD

H

**Horseshoe
Falls**

Niagara River

USA
CANADA

0   500 m

▼ Fort Erie

◄ Toronto

◄ Lundy's Lane

ONTARIO | Niagara Falls and the Niagara River

1

121

a 52-metre cliff, the Niagarans have ensured that the falls can be seen from every angle imaginable – from boats, viewing towers, helicopters, cable cars and even tunnels in the rock face behind the cascade. The **tunnels** and the **boats** are the most exciting, with the entrance to the former right next to the falls and the latter leaving from the bottom of the cliff at the end of Clifton Hill, 1100m downriver. Both give a real sense of the extraordinary force of the waterfall, a perpetual white-crested thundering pile-up that had Mahler bawling "At last, fortissimo" over the din.

Trains and **buses** from Toronto and many of southern Ontario's larger towns serve the town of **NIAGARA FALLS**, 3km to the north of the action. The availability of discount excursion fares makes a day-trip a straightforward proposition, although, if you do decide to spend the night, quaint **Niagara-on-the-Lake**, 26km downstream beside Lake Ontario, is a much better option than the crassly commercialized town of Niagara Falls itself. The problem is that hundreds of people agree, the result being that accommodation there can get mighty tight in high season, when you'd be well advised to book up a couple of days in advance. Both the **Niagara Parkway** road and the **Niagara River Recreation Trail**, a jogging and cycle path, stretch the length of the Niagara River from Fort Erie, 32km upstream from the falls, to Niagara-on-the-Lake.

Arrival and information

Amongst a number of **bus** services, there are fast and frequent **Coach Canada** buses (☎ 1-800/461-7661, ⓦ www.coachcanada.com) to the town of Niagara Falls from Toronto, Buffalo and New York. There is also a less frequent VIA **train** service (☎ 1-888/842-7245, ⓦ www.viarail.ca) linking Niagara Falls with the same three cities two or three times daily. By train or bus, the journey time from Toronto is about two hours. From Toronto, the train is the more scenic way to travel, but delays on the return leg – on which trains usually originate in New York – can be a real pain. If you're travelling by **car**, a day is more than enough time to see the falls and squeeze in a visit to Niagara-on-the-Lake.

Trains to Niagara Falls pull in at the VIA **train station** on Bridge St, in the commercial heart of the town, 3km north of the falls themselves. The **bus station** is across the street at Bridge St and Erie Ave. Next door to the bus station is **Niagara Transit** (☎ 905/356-1179, ⓦ www.niagaratransit.com), which operates a limited range of town and suburban services. The most useful is the **Falls Shuttle** (daily: May–Oct every 30min; Nov–April hourly; single ticket $3, all-day pass $6), which runs across town, stopping – amongst many other places – at the foot of Clifton Hill and beside the Skylon Tower. The Shuttle links with the very handy Niagara Parks' **People Mover System** (mid-May to Aug Mon–Fri 11am–8pm, Sat & Sun 10am–9pm; Sept to mid-Oct daily 11am–6pm; ☎ 905/357-9340), whose buses travel 30km along the riverbank between Queenston Heights Park, downriver from the falls – a little more than halfway towards Niagara-on-the-Lake – and the Rapids' View car park just above. People Movers appear at twenty-minute intervals and an all-day pass costs $5.50. There is, however, no public transport along the river beyond either Queenston Heights Park or the Rapids' View car park; the bus shuttle that used to link Niagara Falls and Niagara-on-the-Lake is not currently in operation, though it may be revived – ask at any of the information centres. Meanwhile, a **5-0 taxi** (☎ 905/358-3232) from Niagara Falls to Niagara-on-the-Lake costs just $10 one-way, $15 return.

Car drivers should be aware that **parking** anywhere near the falls can be a real hassle. In summer, try to arrive before 9.30am when there's usually space in the convenient car park beside Table Rock House; any later and you can expect a long line.

Information – and the Great Gorge Adventure Pass

For **visitor information**, avoid the privately run tourist offices that spring up here and there, now and again, and head instead for the main **Niagara Parks information centre** (℡905/371-0254 or 1-877/642-7275, ⓦwww.niagaraparks.com) at the Table Rock complex beside the falls. Here, from mid-May to mid-October only, you can purchase the **Niagara Falls Great Gorge Adventure Pass**, a combined ticket covering all-day transportation on the People Mover and admission into four of the main attractions. These are the Journey Behind the Falls, Maid of the Mist, White Water Boardwalk and the Butterfly Conservatory. The pass can also be purchased at each of the four attractions and costs $38 for adults and $24 for children aged 6–12.

Another good place to pick up information is the official **Niagara Falls Tourism**, 5515 Stanley Ave (June–Aug daily 8am–8pm; Sept–May Mon–Fri 8am–6pm, Sat 10am–6pm, Sun 10am–4pm; ℡905/356-6061 or 1-800/563-2557, ⓦwww.discoverniagara.com). It has a full range of information on the town and the falls and will – if required – help you find a place to stay. The office is located about 100m south of Hwy 420, the main road to the falls from the QEW freeway. Close by, actually on Hwy 420 at the Stanley Ave intersection, is the provincial **Ontario Travel Centre** (mid-May to mid-June Sun–Thurs 8.30am–6pm, Fri & Sat 8am–8pm; mid-June to Aug daily 8am–8pm; Sept to early Oct Sun–Thurs 8.30am–5pm, Fri & Sat 8.30am–6pm; early Oct to mid-May daily 8.30am–5pm; ℡905/358-3221), where you'll find a wide range of free literature on the whole of Ontario.

Accommodation

Niagara Falls is billed as the "Honeymoon Capital of the World", which means that many of its **motels** and **hotels** have an odd mix of cheap, basic rooms and gaudy suites with heart-shaped bathtubs, waterbeds and the like. Quite what the connection is between water and nuptial bliss is hard to fathom – but there it is. In summer, hotel and motel rooms fill up fast, so either ring ahead or seek help from Niagara Falls Tourism (see above). Out of season it's a buyer's market, which means that haggling can often bring the price way down. For the most part, the least expensive choices are either out along **Lundy's Lane**, an extremely dispiriting motel strip that extends west of the falls for several kilometres, or in the uninteresting town centre near the bus and train stations, 3km from the falls. Neither area is much fun (especially Lundy's Lane) and you're much better off spending a little more to stay either in the **Clifton Hill area**, which has – once you've adjusted to it – a certain kitsch charm, or on leafy **River Rd**, running downriver from the foot of Clifton Hill, where there are a couple of good B&Bs and a modern inn. If you want a room with a decent view of the falls, you'll be paying premium rates. The premier hotels near the **Minolta Tower** on Fallsview Boulevard offer some of the best views but you should always check the room before you shell out: descriptions can be fairly elastic and some rooms claiming to be in sight of the falls require minor gymnastics for a glimpse.

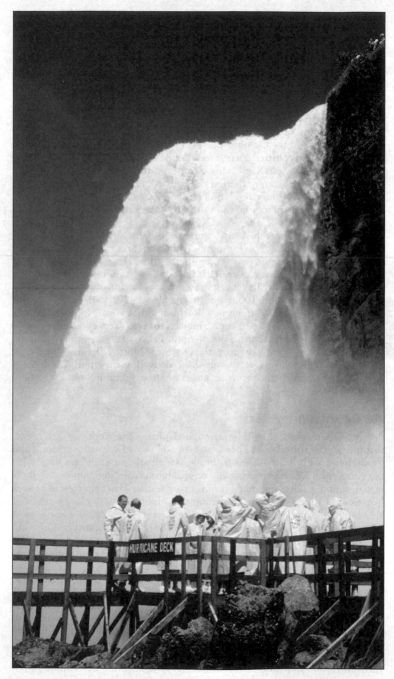

△ Niagara Falls

Hotels

Brock Plaza Hotel 5685 Falls Ave ☎ 905/374-4444 or 1-800/263-7135, ⓦ www .niagarafallshotels.com. Just metres from the foot of Clifton Hill, this is one of Niagara's older hotels, a tidy tower block whose upper storeys (and more expensive rooms) have splendid views over the American Falls. Marilyn Monroe stayed here in Room #801 while filming *Niagara*. ❻

Comfort Inn – Clifton Hill 4960 Clifton Hill ☎ 905/358-3293 or 1-800/801-8557, ⓦ www.comfortniagara.com. Nothing extraordinary, perhaps, but this chain motel has entirely adequate rooms decorated in a brisk, modern style, and is handily located near the falls. ❻

Comfort Inn North of the Falls 4009 River Rd ☎ 905/357-3366 or 1-800/503-3666, ⓦ www .niagarafallscomfortinn.com. Similar to the Comfort Inn listed above, but with a more attractive location, flanked by parkland near the Spanish Aero Car (see p.127), about 4.5km north of the falls. ❻

Quality Inn – Clifton Hill 4946 Clifton Hill ☎ 905/358-3601 or 1-800/801-8557, ⓦ www.qualityniagara.com. Comfortable, pleasantly furnished motel-style rooms in a 800-room inn on its own grounds (or rather car park) on Clifton Hill. ❺

Sheraton Fallsview Hotel 6755 Fallsview Boulevard ☎ 905/374-1077 or 1-800/267-8439, ⓦ www.fallsview.com. Big, lavish hotel and conference centre overlooking the falls. Near the Minolta Tower. One of the smartest places in town, with two tariffs: for rooms with or without views over the falls. ❻–❼

B&Bs

Eastwood Lodge B&B 5359 River Rd ☎ 905/354-8686, ⓦ www.eastwood.com. Six commodious, air-conditioned en-suite bedrooms in a rambling old villa with wide balconies and attractive garden. ❻

Gretna Green B&B 5077 River Rd ☎ 905/357-2081, ⓦ www.gretnagreenniagara.com. Pleasant and well-tended B&B in an attractive older house with four guest rooms. ❺

Hostel

Niagara Falls Hostel (HI) 4549 Cataract Ave ☎ 905/357-0770 or 1-888/749-0058, ⓔ niagara.falls@hihostels.ca. HI hostel a 5min walk from the bus and train station in the town centre, 3km from the falls. Occupies a two-storey brick building in a dreary location: Cataract Ave is a narrow side street off Bridge St as it approaches the Whirlpool Rapids Bridge over to the States. There are laundry facilities, a kitchen and a lounge. Open all year; 85 beds. Members $19, non-members $23.

Campsite

Niagara Glenview RV Resort 3950 Victoria Ave ☎ 905/358-8689. There are several campsites out along Lundy's Lane, but this site, along the river about 3.5km downriver from Clifton Hill, occupies a far more agreeable location at the corner of Victoria Ave and the Niagara Parkway. It has nearly three hundred pitches for tents and trailers. Pitches with an electrical hook-up and water cost $35, $28 without.

The falls

Though you can hear the roar of the **falls** miles away, nothing quite prepares you for your first glimpse of the deluge, a fearsome white arc shrouded in clouds of dense spray with the river boats struggling down below, mere specks against the surging cauldron. There are two actually cataracts, as tiny **Goat Island** – which must be one of the wettest and bleakest places on earth – divides the accelerating water into two channels: on the far side, across the frontier, the river slips over the precipice of the **American Falls**, 320m wide but still only half the width of the **Horseshoe Falls** on the Canadian side. The spectacle is, if anything, even more extraordinary in winter, when snow-covered trees edge a jagged armoury of freezing mist and heaped ice blocks. It looks like a scene of untrammelled nature, but it isn't. Since the 1910s, successive hydroelectric schemes have greatly reduced the water flow, and all sorts of tinkering has spread what's left of the Niagara more evenly over the crest line. As a result, the process of erosion, which has moved the falls some 11km upstream in 12,000 years, has slowed down from 1m per year to just 30cm. This obviously has advantages for the tourist industry, but the environmental consequences of harnessing the river in such a way are still unclear. At least the cardsharps and charlatans who overran the riverside in Blondin's day are long gone – the **Niagara Parks Commission**, which controls the area along the river and beside the falls, ensures that the immaculately tended tree-lined gardens and parkland remain precisely so.

Beside Horseshoe Falls, **Table Rock House** has a small, free observation platform and elevators which travel to the base of the cliff, where tunnels, grandly named the "**Journey Behind the Falls**" (daily 9am to dusk; $7.50), lead to points directly behind the waterfall. It's a stupendous sight, but for a more panoramic view you might take the pint-sized **Incline Railway** ($1) up the hill behind Table Rock House to the **Minolta Tower**, 6732 Fallsview Boulevard (daily: June–Sept 9am–midnight; Oct–May 9am–11pm; $8). The observation platforms here provide wide views over the falls, though the vistas are rather better from the Skylon tower.

From Table Rock House, a wide and crowded path leads north along the edge of the river gorge, with the manicured lawns of Queen Victoria Park to the left and views over to the American Falls to the right. After a few minutes, turn left up Murray St to visit the **Skylon** tower (daily 8am–midnight; $9.50), on Robinson St; or continue along the path to the foot of Clifton Hill, the main drag linking the riverside area with Niagara Falls town. From the jetty below Clifton Hill, **Maid of the Mist boats** edge out into the river and push up towards the falls, an exhilarating and extremely damp trip that no one should miss (daily: April to mid-June 9.45am–5.45pm; late June to July 9am–7.45pm; Aug 9am–7pm; Sept to late Oct 9.45am–5pm; boats leave every 15min in high season, otherwise every 30min; $13, $8 for children aged 6–12, including waterproofs).

Clifton Hill itself is a tawdry collection of fast-food joints and bizarre attractions, from the innocuous "House of Frankenstein" to the absurdity of the "Believe It or Not Museum", where, amongst other wonders, you can spot a dog with human teeth. Just off Clifton Hill on Falls Ave is the area's second-biggest crowd puller, the 24hr **casino** (☎1-888/266-7258), a bristlingly modern structure where – to use the old cliché – college kids can watch their parents fritter away their inheritance. The casino is near the Rainbow Bridge leading over to the States. If you're keen to avoid all this commercialization, then stick to the **riverside** where the Niagara Parks Commission keeps everything in order. There are a string of attractions further downstream, beginning with the White Water Boardwalk, 3km away (see below).

Eating and drinking

There are literally dozens of cheap chain **restaurants** and fast-food joints along and around Clifton Hill. Most of them are unremarkable, but at least the *Golden Griddle*, in the *Quality Inn – Clifton Hill*, 4946 Clifton Hill, has a good basic breakfast menu with all the standards at very reasonable prices. Other possibilities include Italian pastas at both *Mama Mia's*, 5719 Victoria Ave at Clifton Hill, and *Big Anthony's*, nearby at 5677 Victoria Ave. The latter is a family-run place owned by a well-known ex-professional wrestler, pictures of whom decorate the windows. For something more distinctive, take lunch or dinner at the Skylon tower's *Revolving Dining Room* (☎905/356-2651), a smart and fairly formal restaurant with panoramic views over the falls. At 236m, the restaurant takes an hour to complete one revolution – a gentle, almost imperceptible ride.

Downstream from the falls

The **Niagara River Recreation Trail** is a combined bicycle and walking track that travels the entire length of the Niagara River from Lake Erie down to Lake Ontario; it runs parallel to the main road, the scenic **Niagara Parkway**. Downstream from the falls, trail and parkway cut across the foot of Clifton Hill before continuing north for a further 3km to reach the **White Water Boardwalk** (May–Oct daily dawn to dusk; $6.30). This comprises an elevator and then a tunnel, which leads to a boardwalk overlooking the Whirlpool Rapids, where the river seethes and fizzes as it makes an abrupt turn to the east. From here it's a further 1km to the brightly painted **Spanish Aero Car** (mid-June to Aug daily 9am or 10am to dusk; rest of year call for times; ☎905/371-0254; $6), a cable-car ride across the gorge that's as near as you'll come to emulating Blondin's tightrope antics. Another 1.5km brings you to **Niagara Helicopter Rides**, 3731 Victoria Ave (☎905/357-5672, ⓦ www.niagarahelicopters.com), which offers a breathtaking twelve-minute excursion over the falls for $100 per person, though costs can be reduced considerably if you are in a group. You don't need to book ahead, as the helicopters whizz in and out with unnerving frequency from 9am until sunset, weather permitting.

Pushing on, it's another short hop to the **Niagara Glen Nature Area** (daily dawn to dusk; free), where paths lead down from the clifftop to the bottom of the gorge. It's a hot and sticky trek in the height of the summer, and strenuous at any time of the year, but rewarding for all that – here at least you get a sense of what the region was like before all the tourist hullabaloo. Nearby, about 800m further downstream, is the Niagara Parks Commission's pride and joy, the immensely popular **Niagara Parks Botanical Gardens** (daily dawn to dusk; free), whose immaculate flowerbeds are at their best from late May to September. The rhododendrons are, for instance, in full bloom from mid-May to June, while roses are a special highlight from mid-June to September. The gardens also contain a huge, climate-controlled **Butterfly Conservatory** (daily: May–Sept 9am–9pm; Oct–April 9am–6pm; $8.50), which houses over 2000 exotic butterflies in a tropical rainforest setting.

About 3km further on, **Queenston Heights Park** marks the original location of the falls, before the force of the water – as it adjusts to the hundred-metre differential between lakes Erie and Ontario – eroded the riverbed to its present point, 11km upstream. Soaring above the park there's a grandiloquent monument to Sir Isaac Brock, the Guernsey-born general who was killed here in the War of 1812, leading a head-on charge against the invading Americans. From beside the park, the Niagara Parkway begins a curving descent down to the little village of **QUEENSTON**, whose importance as a transit centre disappeared when the falls were bypassed by the Welland Canal, running west of the river between lakes Erie and Ontario and completed in 1829. In the village, on Partition St, the **Laura Secord Homestead** (May–Aug daily 10am–5pm; $2.50) is a reconstruction of the simple timber-frame house of Massachusetts-born Laura Ingersoll Secord (1775–1868). Secord's dedication to the imperial interest was such that she ran 30km through the woods to warn the British army of a surprise attack planned by the Americans in the War of 1812.

Niagara-on-the-Lake

One of the prettiest places in Ontario, **NIAGARA-ON-THE-LAKE**, 26km downstream from the falls, boasts lines of elegant clapboard houses trimmed by well-kept gardens, all spread along tree-lined streets. The town, much of which dates from the early nineteenth century, was originally known as Newark, and became the first capital of Upper Canada in 1792. Four years later it lost this distinction to York (Toronto) because it was considered too close to the

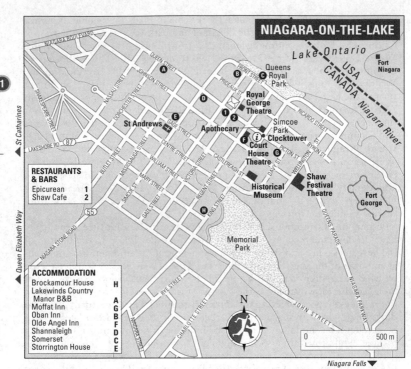

NIAGARA-ON-THE-LAKE

Lake Ontario

Fort Niagara

USA
CANADA

Niagara River

Queens Royal Park

Royal George Theatre

Simcoe Park

St Andrews   Apothecary   Clocktower

Court House Theatre

RESTAURANTS & BARS
Epicurean   1
Shaw Cafe   2

Historical Museum

Shaw Festival Theatre

Fort George

Memorial Park

ACCOMMODATION
Brockamour House   H
Lakewinds Country
  Manor B&B   A
Moffat Inn   G
Oban Inn   B
Olde Angel Inn   F
Shannaleigh   D
Somerset   C
Storrington House   E

N

0   500 m

Niagara Falls ▼

American frontier for comfort – a prudent decision given that the Americans crossed the river and destroyed it in 1813. The town was rebuilt (and renamed) immediately afterwards, and has managed to avoid all but the most sympathetic of modifications ever since. Nowadays, it attracts a few too many day-trippers for its own good, but the crowds are rarely oppressive, except on weekends in July and August. Niagara-on-the-Lake is also well known as the location of one of Canada's more acclaimed theatre festivals, the **Shaw Festival** (see box), which focuses on the works of George Bernard Shaw, and is surrounded by **wineries**, many of which encourage visitors (see box p.130).

It's the general flavour of Niagara-on-the-Lake that appeals rather than any specific sight, but **Queen St**, the short main drag, does hold a pretty **clock tower** and the **Apothecary** (mid-May to Sept daily noon–6pm; free), worth a peep for its beautifully carved walnut and butternut cabinets, crystal gasoliers and porcelain jars. Nearby, the town's finest building is the church of **St Andrews**, at Simcoe and Gage streets, a splendid illustration of the Greek Revival style dating to the 1830s. The church has a beautifully proportioned portico and the interior retains the original high pulpit and box pews. Also of some interest is the **Niagara Historical Museum**, at 43 Castlereagh St and Davy (daily: May–Oct 10am–5.30pm; Nov–April 1–5pm; $5), whose accumulated tackle tracks through the early history of the town and includes mementoes of the Laura Secord family (see p.127).

More diverting still is the British military post of **Fort George** (May–Oct daily 10am–5pm; $8), 700m southeast of town via Picton St. In the early nineteenth century, so many of its soldiers were hightailing it off to the States that

The Shaw Festival

Showcasing the second-largest repertory theatre company in Canada – after Stratford (see p.117) – Niagara-on-the-Lake's **Shaw Festival** (☎1-800/511-7429, ⓦwww.shawfest.com) is the only festival in the world devoted solely to the works of Shaw and his contemporaries. Indeed, it is mandated to produce only plays written in the playwright's lifetime (1856–1950), which the company refer to as "plays about the beginning of the modern world". **Ticket prices** are $40–75, but substantial discounts are available for previews, matinees, lunchtime and Sunday-night performances. The festival runs from April to late October.

the British had to garrison the fort with the Royal Canadian Rifle Regiment, a troop of primarily married men approaching retirement who were unlikely to forfeit their pensions by deserting. If they did try and were caught, they were branded on the chest with the letter "D" (for "Deserter"), and were either lashed or transported to a penal colony – except in wartime, when they were shot. The fort was one of a line of stockades slung across the waterways of the Great Lakes to protect Canada from the US. The original version was destroyed during the War of 1812, but the site was thoroughly excavated and the fort reconstructed in splendid style in the 1930s. The thick earth-and-stone rampart that encircles the fort is set close to the lie of the land to mitigate against artillery bombardment, while the projecting bastions once enabled the defenders to fire on attackers from a variety of angles. Inside, the central **compound** holds ten buildings, including officers' quarters and three pine blockhouses that doubled as soldiers' barracks. The difference between the quarters and the barracks is striking. The former are comparatively spacious and were once – as recorded on shipping lists – furnished with fancy knick-knacks, while the latter housed the men and some of their wives (six wives out of every hundred were allowed to join the garrison) in the meanest of conditions. The only original building to survive is the powder magazine of 1796, its interior finished in wood and copper to reduce the chances of an accidental explosion; as an added precaution, the soldiers working in here wore shoes with no metal fastenings. There are also lantern-light **ghost tours** of the fort – good fun with or without an apparition (May–June Sun at 8.30pm; July–Aug Mon, Wed, Thurs & Sun at 8.30pm; $10). Tours leave from the parking lot in front of the fort; tickets can be purchased either in advance at the fort's gift shop, or from the guide at the beginning of the tour.

Practicalities

At time of writing, there are no **public transport** links between Niagara Falls and Niagara-on-the-Lake: the shuttle bus that linked the two has been discontinued. It's possible that someone will pick up the service – Niagara Parks (ⓦwww.niagaraparks.com) for one – but in the meantime the best bet is **5-0 Taxis** (☎905/358-3232), which charges $10 for the one-way fare or $15 return. The Niagara-on-the-Lake **tourist office** is on the main drag at 26 Queen St, in the lower level of the Court House (daily: May to mid-Oct 10am–7.30pm; mid-Oct to April 10am–5pm; ☎905/468-1950, ⓦwww.niagaraonthelake.com). Staff issue town maps and operate a free room reservation service, which can be a great help in the summer when the town's hotels and B&Bs get mighty busy. It only takes a few minutes to stroll from one end of town to the other, but to venture further afield – especially to the falls – you might consider renting a **bicycle** from Zoom, 275 Mary St (☎905/468-2366).

Ontario wines

Until the 1980s **Canadian wine** was something of a joke. The industry's most popular product was a sticky, fizzy concoction called "Baby Duck", and other varieties were commonly called "block-and-tackle" wines, after a widely reported witticism of a member of the Ontario legislature: "If you drink a bottle and walk a block, you can tackle anyone." This state of affairs was, however, transformed by the **Vintners Quality Alliance** (VQA), which has, since 1989, come to exercise tight control over wine production in Ontario, which produces eighty percent of Canadian wine. The VQA's appellation system distinguishes between – and supervises the quality control of – two broad types of wine. Those bottles carrying the Provincial Designation on their labels (that is, Ontario's) must be made from 100 percent Ontario-grown wines from an approved list of European varieties of grape and selected hybrids; those bearing a Geographic Designation (ie Niagara Peninsula, Pelee Island or Lake Erie North Shore), by comparison, can only use *Vitis vinifera*, the classic European grape varieties, such as Riesling, Chardonnay and Cabernet Sauvignon. As you might expect from a developing wine area, the results are rather inconsistent, but the **Rieslings** have a refreshingly crisp, almost tart flavour with a mellow, warming aftertaste – and are perhaps the best of the present range, white or red.

More than twenty **wineries** are clustered in the vicinity of **Niagara-on-the-Lake**, and most are very willing to show visitors around. Local tourist offices carry a full list with opening times, but one of the most interesting is **Inniskillin**, Line 3 (Service Rd 66), just off the Niagara Parkway, about 5km south of Niagara-on-the-Lake (daily: May–Oct 10am–6pm; Nov–April 10am–5pm; ☎905/468-3554, ⓦwww.inniskillin.com). Here you can follow a twenty-step self-guided tour or take a free guided tour, sip away at the tasting bar and buy at the wine boutique. Inniskillin has produced a clutch of award-winning vintages and has played a leading role in the improvement of the industry. It is also one of the few Canadian wineries to produce **ice wine**, an outstanding sweet dessert wine made from grapes that are left on the vine till December or January, when they are hand-picked at night when frozen. The picking and the crushing of the frozen grapes is a time-consuming business and this is reflected in the price – about $50 per 375ml bottle.

Niagara-on-the-Lake has over a hundred **B&Bs**, with a few dotted round the leafy streets of the centre and the majority on the outskirts of town. The most distinctive occupy lovely old villas dating from the early nineteenth century, but these tend to be expensive – reckon on $100–150 for a double room per night. The town's B&Bs are also extremely popular, so advance reservations are pretty much essential throughout the summer, when you're likely to need the tourist office's free **room reservation service**. If you arrive after the tourist office has closed, look for a list of last-minute vacancies in their window. The town also possesses several quality **hotels** and **inns**. By sheer weight of numbers, the day-trippers set the gastronomic tone in town, but one or two good **cafés** and **restaurants** have survived the flood to offer tasty meals and snacks.

Hotels and B&Bs

Adam Lockhart's Storrington House 289 Simcoe St ☎905/468-8254, ⓦwww.storringtonhouse.com. Niagara-on-the-Lake boasts dozens of charming B&Bs, but this is one of the best, with each of the guest bedrooms of this 1817 house decked out in impeccable style. Breakfasts are a treat, too, and it's an easy stroll from here to the town centre. ⑥

Brockamour Manor 433 King St at Mary ☎905/468-5527, ⓦwww.brockamour.com. This elegant B&B has six en-suite guest rooms ranging from the commodious Sir Brock's Bedchamber to the two smaller rooms in the old servants' quarters. With its high gables and wide veranda, the house itself is a splendid affair dating from 1812, surrounded by an attractive wooded garden. ⑥–⑧

Lakewinds Country Manor B&B 328 Queen St at Dorchester ℡905/468-1888, ⓦwww.lakewinds.niagara.com. Expansive Victorian mansion with six air-conditioned guest rooms and suites, each of which is decorated in a particular style – the Florentine and Singapore rooms for example. The house possesses a handsome veranda and is surrounded by a well-kept garden. Two nights minimum stay on the weekend. Rates vary with the room and the season. ❻

Moffat Inn 60 Picton St ℡905/468-4116, ⓦwww.moffatinn.com. This modest hotel is located in a modernized building close to the centre of town. The rooms are pleasant but undistinguished – which means that its prices are lower than most of its rivals and there is sometimes space here when everyone else is full. ❹

Oban Inn 160 Front St ℡905/468-2165 or 1-888/669 5566, ⓦwww.vintageinns.com. A delightful and luxurious hotel across from the lake and within easy walking distance of the town centre. The original *Oban* burnt to the ground in 1992, but its replacement was built in full-flush colonial style, with an elegant wooden veranda. The gardens are beautiful and the breakfasts are first-rate. ❼

Olde Angel Inn 224 Regent St just off Queen St ℡905/468-3411, ⓦwww.angel-inn.com. Dating from the 1820s, this is the oldest inn in town. Offers a handful of simple rooms in the main building and a couple of annexe-cottages too. ❹

Shannaleigh 184 Queen St at Simcoe ℡905/468-2630, ⓦwww.shannaleigh.niagara.com. This rambling mock-Tudor mansion of 1910 has five spacious, en-suite guest rooms and splendid gardens. ❻

Somerset 111 Front St at Victoria ℡905/468-5565, ⓦwww.somersetbb.info. This flashy brick villa of modern design looks almost shocking when compared with the old wooden houses that characterize the rest of the centre, but it is one of only a couple of places actually on the lake. Great views and very comfortable, air-conditioned guest rooms. ❼

Restaurants and bars

Epicurean 84 Queen St. Inexpensive but very competent café, featuring Mediterranean dishes. Vegetarian options offered most days. Inexpensive.

Oban Inn 160 Front St ℡905/468-2165. This hotel restaurant is smart and comparatively formal and the food – steak, salmon and so forth – is reliably good.

Olde Angel Inn 224 Regent St. With its low-beamed ceilings and flagstone floors, this is the town's most atmospheric pub, serving a first-rate range of draught beers as well as quality bar food – Guinness steak-and-kidney pies and so forth – and has a smart à la carte restaurant at the back. Just off Queen St.

Shaw Café and Wine Bar 92 Queen St at Victoria. This café-restaurant caters to theatre-goers rather than day-trippers. The decor is a tad overdone, but the pastas and salads are tasty and well prepared. Closes 8pm.

Upstream from Niagara Falls to Fort Erie

Heading upstream from the falls, the **Old Scow** soon comes into view – it's the rusting barge stuck against the rocks in the middle of the river. In 1918 the barge was being towed across the Niagara River when the lines snapped and the barge – along with the two-man crew – hurtled towards the falls. There must have been an awful lot of praying going on, because – just 750m from the precipice – the barge caught against the rocks, and it's stayed there ever since.

Pressing on past the Old Scow, both the **Niagara Parkway** road and the **Niagara River Recreation Trail** stay close to the river giving pleasant views over to the US. Nonetheless, this portion of the river is much less appealing than the stretch to the north – especially so beyond dreary Chippawa, where America's Grand Island divides the river into two drowsy channels. Further upriver, just 32km from the falls, the Niagara Parkway peters out at **FORT ERIE**, a small industrial town that also marks the end of the Queen Elizabeth Way linking Toronto with the American city of Buffalo. The one noteworthy site here is **Fort Erie National Historic Site** (mid-May to Aug daily 10am–6pm; mid-April to mid-May & Sept–Oct daily 10am–4pm; $6), which overlooks Lake Erie from the mouth of the Niagara River just 2km south of town. The Americans razed the original fort in 1814, but it was painstakingly rebuilt in the 1930s as a Depression make-work scheme. The layout is similar to that of Fort George (see p.128) with a dry ditch, earth-and-stone ramparts and protruding bastions encircling a central compound, though here the outer gate is much more imposing, comprising a pair of huge double doors strengthened by iron studs. The central compound holds the usual spread of army buildings, including officers' quarters, barracks and a powder magazine, plus a modest museum that explores the fort's history.

London

The citizens of **LONDON**, 125km west of Hamilton, are justifiably proud of their clean streets, efficient transport system and neat suburbs, but to the outsider the main attractions are the leafiness of the centre and the city's two **music festivals** in late June and July – the nine-day Royal Canadian Big Band Festival (☏519/663-9467) and the three-day Home County Folk Music Festival (☏519/432-4310, ⓦwww.homecounty.ca). London owes its existence to a one-time governor of Upper Canada, **John Graves Simcoe**, who arrived in 1792 determined to develop the wilderness north of Lake Ontario. Because of its river connections to the west and south, he chose the site of London as his new colonial capital and promptly renamed its river the Thames. Unluckily,

Simcoe's headlong approach to his new job irritated his superior, Governor Dorchester, who vetoed his choice with the wry comment that access to London would have to be by hot-air balloon. When York (present-day Toronto) was chosen as the capital instead, Simcoe's chosen site lay empty until 1826, yet by the 1880s London was firmly established as the economic and administrative centre of a prosperous agricultural area. With a population of some 326,000, it remains so today.

The Town

London's **downtown core** is laid out as a grid on either side of its main east–west thoroughfares, Dundas St and, one block to the north, Queens Ave. At the west end of Dundas, close to the river, is the chunkily modernist **Museum London**, 421 Ridout St N (Tues–Sun noon–5pm; donation), designed by Raymond Moriyama of Toronto. A once fashionable architect, Moriyama favoured dramatic concrete buildings characterized by a preference for contorted curves and circles rather than straight lines, but here the end result isn't all that successful. Inside, the gallery's permanent collection features a somewhat indeterminate mix of lesser eighteenth- and nineteenth-century Canadian painters and there's a modest local history section too, but the temporary modern art exhibitions – some of which come here straight from Toronto – are usually excellent.

London's oldest residence, the **Eldon House** (Tues–Sun noon–5pm; donation) is a couple of minutes' walk north from the museum, at 481 Ridout St North. Built in the 1830s by John Harris, a retired Royal Navy captain, the house is a graceful clapboard dwelling, whose interior has been returned to its mid-nineteenth-century appearance. The British influence is also easy to pick out in the nearby **St Paul's Anglican Cathedral** – take Fullarton from the Eldon House as far as Richmond. A simple red-brick structure built in the English Gothic Revival style in 1846, it's in marked contrast to the rival **St Peter's Catholic Cathedral**, just to the north at Dufferin and Richmond, a flamboyant, high-towered, pink-stone edifice typical of the French Gothic style that was popular amongst Ontario's Catholics in the late nineteenth century.

Though not exactly required viewing, the replica **Ska-Nah-Doht Iroquoian village** (late May to early Sept daily 9am–4.30pm; early Sept to late May Mon–Fri 9am–4.30pm; donation; ☎519/264-2420), situated 32km southwest of London on Hwy 2, makes for an enjoyable jaunt. Built in 1972, the complex contains a resource centre, where you can gather background information before walking out to the village, which is enclosed by a timber palisade. Inside the palisade are storage areas, drying and stretching racks, a sweat house and three long-houses; outside are a deer run, burial area, a cultivated field and three log cabins dating from the 1850s. The arrangement of the village accurately reflects the archaeological evidence unearthed at several prehistoric settlements, one of which was close by. The village also has a lovely rural setting and – if the school groups that come here begin to wear – you can stroll out into the woods. To get here, head south from London and then go west on Hwy 402. After about 12km, come off Hwy 402 (at Exit 86) and follow Hwy 2 south for about 6km.

Practicalities

London's **train station** is centrally situated at York and Richmond, a couple of minutes' walk east of the **bus depot** at York and Talbot. The most central **tourist office** is at 267 Dundas St (Mon–Fri 8.30am–4.30pm; ☎519/661-5000, ⓦwww.londontourism.ca). As far as accommodation is concerned, the best

hotel in town is the smart and polished *Delta London Armouries Hotel*, 325 Dundas St and Waterloo (☎519/679-6111 or 1-800/668-9999, ⓦwww .deltahotels.com; ❹), part of which occupies an old Edwardian drill hall with a robust, crenellated facade. A less expensive but equally convenient option is the *Comfort Hotel – Downtown*, a standard-issue chain hotel at 374 Dundas St and Colborne (☎519/661-0233 or 1-800/228-5150, ⓦwww.choicehotels.ca; ❸). Incidentally, the cheapest hotels in town are in the vicinity of the bus station, but these are little more than flop-houses and are best avoided. London also has a handful of **B&Bs**, several of which are in fetching Victorian or Edwardian villas. The tourist office has the complete list, but one recommendation is the extremely fetching *Idlewyld Inn*, to the south of the centre at 36 Grand Ave (☎519/433-2891 or 1-877/435-3466, ⓦwww.someplacesdifferent.com; ❹). The inn occupies a rambling Victorian mansion that retains many of its original fittings and its graceful public rooms come complete with fine open fireplaces. Each of the 27 guest rooms beyond is attractively furnished and en suite.

In recent years, **eating out** in London has become much more enjoyable, with the opening of a string of café-restaurants along and around Richmond St; the majority offer a broadly Mediterranean cuisine at affordable prices. The best deli sandwiches, coffees and finger-licking cakes are sold at *Café One*, 551 Richmond St. Tempting restaurants include *Garlic's*, 481 Richmond (☎519/432-4092), where the emphasis is firmly Italian, and *Michael's on the Thames*, 1 York St (☎519/672-0111), an Italian joint serving up excellent food at affordable prices and with pleasing views over the river. For something different, *Budapest*, 348 Dundas at Waterloo (☎519/439-3431), is a family-run establishment offering first-rate Hungarian food – the goulash is a treat. London has a **music** scene too: try the *Old Chicago Speakeasy & Grill* (☎519/434-6600), 153 Carling, a short side street off Richmond just north of Dundas, where quality R&B, soul and blues bands sometimes perform.

Windsor

"I'm going to Detroit, Michigan, to work the Cadillac line," growls the old blues number, but if the singer had crossed the river from Detroit he'd have been equally at home amongst the car plants of **WINDSOR**, 190km southwest of London. The factories are American subsidiaries built as part of a complex trading agreement which, monitored by the forceful Canadian United Automobile Workers Union, has created thousands of well-paid jobs. Living opposite Detroit makes the "Windsors" feel good in another way too: they read about Detroit's problems – the crime and the crack – and the dire difficulties involved in rejuvenating that city, and shake their heads in disbelief and self-congratulation. A robustly working-class place, Windsor has a clutch of good restaurants, a lively café-bar nightlife, and is also a good base for visiting both the remains of the British **Fort Malden** in Amherstburg, 25km to the south, and **Point Pelee National Park**, some 50km away to the southeast. The main Windsor shindig is the International Freedom Festival with all sorts of folksy events spread over an eighteen-day period in late June and early July.

Windsor itself has few specific sights, but **Dieppe Gardens**, stretching along the waterfront from the foot of Ouellette Ave – and part of a longer riverside park – is a good place to view the audacious Detroit skyline. Close by, just to the east at the bottom of McDougall St, is the fantastically popular and

DOWNTOWN WINDSOR

Detroit

Detroit River

Sculpture Garden

Dieppe Gardens

RIVERSIDE

Art Gallery
of Windsor

Windsor
Community
Museum

PITT

CHATHAM

Bus Station

UNIVERSITY AVENUE

PARK

Canadian Club Distillery

Windsor
Casino
& Hotel

Bridge

CAFÉS, RESTAURANTS & BARS

Chanoso's   3
Chatham Street Grill   2
Coffee Exchange   6
Marathon Restaurant   4
Fillmore East   1
Aar'd' Vark Blues Café   5

ACCOMMODATION

Days Inn Windsor   D
Hilton Windsor   B
Quality Suites   C
Radisson Riverfront
  Hotel Windsor   A

**TUNNEL
PLAZA**

WYANDOTTE

N

0   100 m

ultra-glitzy **Casino Windsor**, which is open 24hrs a day, 365 days of the year.
The casino has played a leading role in the rejuvenation of downtown Windsor,
whose formative years are recalled at the **Windsor Community Museum**,
one block south of the riverfront at 254 Pitt St W (Tues–Sat 10am–5pm, plus
May–Sept Sun 2–5pm; free). The museum occupies a pretty brick house built
in 1812 by François Baby (pronounced *Baw-bee*), scion of a powerful French-
Canadian clan who proved consistently loyal to the British interest after the fall
of New France, an example of the money going with the power. Back on the
riverfront, the **Art Gallery of Windsor**, 401 Riverside Drive West
(Wed–Thurs noon–5pm, Fri noon–9pm, Sat & Sun 11am–5pm; $2;
Ⓦwww.artgalleryofwindsor.com), has a well-deserved reputation for the excellence of its temporary exhibitions. The permanent collection is first-rate too,
its forte being late nineteenth- and early twentieth-century Canadian paintings. In particular, look out for some good examples from the Group of Seven
(see p.96) – including Lawren Harris's skeletal *Trees and Snow* and the
dramatic perspectives of Arthur Lismer's *Incoming Tide, Cape Breton Island*. Also
on display is a splendid sample of Inuit art, with a particular highlight being
Hunters and Polar Bear, a dark and elemental soapstone carving by Juanasialuk.
There's more art at the open-air, open-access **Sculpture Garden**, a whimsical
assortment of seventeen modern sculptures dotted along the riverfront lawn
between Curry Ave and the Ambassador Bridge, about 1.2km west of
Ouellette Ave. Lastly, you might venture further afield, some 3km east of the
casino, to join a free tour of Hiram Walker & Sons' **Canadian Club
Distillery**, 2072 Riverside Drive E at Walker Rd (year-round; 1hr; times on
Ⓣ519/561-5499, Ⓦwww.canadianclubwhisky.com), on which guides explain
how whisky is manufactured. Windsor boomed during Prohibition from the
proceeds of its liquor industry, with bootleggers smuggling vast quantities of
whisky across the border into the US.

Practicalities

Well connected to London, Toronto and Niagara Falls, Windsor's **bus station** is right in the centre of town on Chatham, just east of the main street, Ouellette Ave, which runs south from the river. From the bus station, Transit Windsor (☎519/944-4111) runs a shuttle service (1–3 hourly) over to downtown Detroit via a tunnel whose entrance is bang in the middle of town at Goyeau and Park; traffic bypassing Windsor en route to Detroit uses the Ambassador Bridge, on Hwy 3. Windsor **train station** is some 3km east of the city centre, near the waterfront at 298 Walker Rd and Wyandotte; to get into the centre from here, take a taxi ($8). The Windsor **Convention and Visitors' Bureau**, Suite 103, City Centre Mall, 333 Riverside Drive W (Mon–Fri 8.30am–4.30pm; ☎519/255-6530 or 1-800/265-3633, ⓦwww .city.windsor.on.ca/cvb), is located just west of Ouellette and issues free maps and glossy local brochures. They also run a tourist information kiosk (open daily) in the casino. In addition, there's an **Ontario Travel Information Centre** just off Ouellette and beside the Detroit tunnel at 110 Park St E (mid-May to mid-June Sun–Thurs 8.30am–6pm, Fri & Sat 8am–5pm; mid-June to Aug daily 8am–8pm; Sept to mid-May daily 8.30am–5pm; ☎519/973-1338).

The city's downtown core is surprisingly compact, with most of the action focused on Ouellette from the river to Wyandotte – merely five-minutes' stroll from top to bottom. If you're staying the night, convenient options near the river include several chain **hotels** like the *Days Inn Windsor*, 675 Goyeau St (☎519/258-8411 or 1-800/329-7466, ⓦwww.daysinn.com/canada; ❹), and *Quality Suites*, 250 Dougall Ave (☎519/977-9707 or 1-800/228-5151, ⓦwww.choicehotels.ca; ❹). The best rooms in the city centre are, however, to be found in the plush tower blocks along the riverfront in view of the Detroit skyline. Options here include the splendid *Radisson Riverfront Hotel Windsor*, 333 Riverside Drive W (☎519/977-9777 or 1-800/267-9777, ⓦwww.radisson.com/windsorca; ❼), where the rooms are large and extremely comfortable; and the comparable *Hilton Windsor*, 277 Riverside Drive W (☎519/973-5555 or 1-800/445-8667, ⓦwww.hilton.com; ❻), which is graced by a string of Art Deco flourishes. Otherwise, the Convention and Visitors' Bureau has the details of a handful of **B&Bs** (❷–❸), though most of their addresses are a good way from the centre. The city's budget **motels** are strung out along Huron Church Rd (Hwy 3) just to the west of downtown on the way to the Ambassador Bridge over to the US.

Amongst a bevy of busy but affordable **café-bars** dotted on and around Ouellette, two of the best are the excellent *Chatham St Grill*, 149 Chatham St W (☎519/256-2555), which specializes in grilled meats, and the stylish *Chanoso's*, 255 Ouellette (☎519/254-8530), where you assemble your own stir fry and/or other Asian dish. Alternatively, there are snacks and cakes at the *Coffee Exchange*, 341 Ouellette, and Ethiopian cuisine at the *Marathon Restaurant*, 60 University Ave W (☎519/253-2215). Windsor has a vibrant **club** and **live music** scene. In the city centre, *Fillmore East*, 53 Pitt St E (☎519/971-0457), has jazzy live music at the back end of the week, and there's also the earthier *Aar'd'vark Blues Café*, 89 University Ave W at Pelissier (☎519/977-6422), which has R&B and blues five nights a week (Wed–Sun), often featuring the cream of the Detroit crop. That said, this is small musical beer compared with what's happening over the river. Detroit remains one of the USA's foremost musical cities, so watch out for flyers and posters in Windsor advertising what's on and where or drop by the tourist office.

Amherstburg and Fort Malden

Hwy 20 runs south from Windsor, slicing through the industrial region that edges the Detroit River, whose murky waters form the border with the US. The one-time enmity of the Americans prompted the British to build a fort here, close to the mouth of the Detroit River at **AMHERSTBURG** in 1796, but it proved difficult to supply and they were forced to abandon the stockade during the War of 1812. Reoccupied after the war, the British made half-hearted attempts to improve the fort's defences, but it probably would have been abandoned had it not been for the Upper Canada Rebellion of 1837. In a panic, the colonial powers rebuilt what was now called Fort Malden and garrisoned it with four hundred soldiers, stationed here to counter the efforts of the insurgents and their American sympathizers. The last troops left in 1859 and the fort was handed over to the province, which turned it into a lunatic asylum.

Now renovated, the early nineteenth-century ditches and corner bastions of **Fort Malden** (May–Oct daily 10am–5pm; Nov–April daily except Sat 1–5pm; $3.50) are easy to pick out. They comprise a sequence of grassy defensive lines surrounding the excavated foundations of several buildings and a single-storey brick **barracks** of 1819. The interior of the barracks, complete with British army uniforms, is deceptively neat and trim for, as the guides explain, conditions were appallingly squalid. Across from the barracks, the asylum's old laundry and bakery has been turned into an **interpretive centre** with intriguing accounts of the various episodes of the fort's history, including the War of 1812 and the Rebellion of 1837. Original artefacts are few and far between, but you'll spy the powder horn of the **Shawnee** chief and staunch British ally, **Tecumseh**, one of the most formidable and renowned of the region's leaders. Born in what is now Ohio in 1769, Tecumseh spent the better part of his life struggling to keep the American settlers from spreading west into Shawnee territory. To this end he allied himself to the British, who were, he felt, less of a territorial threat, and managed by the sheer force of his personality to hold together an aboriginal army of some size. He was killed in the War of 1812 at Moraviantown and his army promptly collapsed.

Leamington and Pelee Island

About 400km long, the largely flat and often tedious northern shoreline of **Lake Erie** is broken up by a string of provincial parks and a handful of modest port-cum-resorts, such as Port Stanley, whose popularity declined when the more beautiful landscapes around Georgian Bay became accessible. **LEAMINGTON**, 50km southeast of Windsor and with a population of 14,000, is the largest agricultural centre in this highly productive region and the nearest town to the north shore's most distinctive attraction, the elongated peninsula of Point Pelee National Park (see below). Leamington's centre is itself uninspiring, though the **tourist office** (late May to mid-Oct daily 10am–5pm; Ⓦ www.leamington.ca) always raises a smile: it's sited in a large plastic tomato, a reminder that Leamington is billed as the "tomato capital of Canada" – there's a massive Heinz factory here. Much more enticing is the revamped **dock area** just south of the centre at the foot of Erie St. It's here you'll find the town's best **restaurant**, the *Tropicana* (☎519/326-2697), where the Greek and Italian dishes are very competent, and the best **hotel** – the spick-and-span and modern *Seacliffe Inn*, at 388 Erie St S (☎519/324-9266, Ⓦ www.seacliffeinn.com; ❺). Less expensive accommodation is available back towards the town centre on Erie St in several chain **motels**: the *Comfort Inn*, at no. 279 (☎519/326-9071, ⓦwww.choicehotels.ca; ❸) is as good as any. There is a once-daily **bus** service from Toronto to Leamington, but there are no connections on to Point Pelee Park, which begins 8km to the south of town.

From the docks, **ferries** (March–July 2–3 daily; 1hr 30min; one-way: $7.50 per person, bikes $3.75, cars $16.50; ☎519/724-2115 or 1-800/661-2220, ⓦwww.bmts.com) sally out across Lake Erie to **Pelee Island**, whose quiet country roads are flanked by orchards and vineyards. Some 15km long and 6km wide, the island possesses a pair of nature reserves – Lighthouse Point and Fish Point – at its northern and southern extremities and one significant settlement, **PELEE ISLAND VILLAGE**, where the boat docks, but it's the rural atmosphere that is of most appeal. The best way to explore the island is by **bike** and these can be rented from Comfortech (☎519/724-2828; advance booking required), metres from the dock and just behind the *Westview Tavern*. Ferry sailing schedules make it easy to visit the island on a day-trip, but there are several **places to stay**. The pick is the *Blueberry Hill B&B*, in a comfortable, well-kept modern timber dwelling a short drive north from the ferry dock at 86 North Shore Rd (☎519/724-1109, ⓔblueberrypelee@canada.com; ❸). Island maps and information are available at Leamington tourist office.

Point Pelee National Park

Occupying the southernmost tip of Canada's mainland and on the same latitude as Rome and Barcelona, **Point Pelee National Park** (daily: April to mid-Oct 6am–9.30pm; mid-Oct to March 7am–6.30pm; $3.25; no camping) fills the southern half of a twenty-kilometre sandspit. The park boasts a variety of habitats rarely matched in Canada, including marshlands and open fields, but most remarkably it is one of the few places where the ancient **deciduous forest** of eastern North America has survived. One-third of the park is covered by jungle-like forest, packed with a staggering variety of trees, from hackberry, red cedar, black walnut and blue ash to vine-covered sassafras. The park's mild climate and its mix of vegetation attract thousands of **birds** on their spring and autumn migrations. In the latter season – in September – the sandspit also funnels thousands of southward-moving **monarch butterflies** across the park, their orange and black wings a splash of colour against the greens and browns of the undergrowth. From the **park entrance** it's a three-kilometre drive down behind the shore to the start of the Marsh Boardwalk nature trail, where there's a restaurant and also bike and canoe rental during the summer. It's a further 4km to the **visitor centre** (early April to late May daily 8am–5pm; late May to mid-Oct daily 10am–5pm; mid-Oct to March Sat & Sun only 10am-5pm; ☎519/322-2365), at the beginning of the Tilden's Wood and Woodland trails. From April to October propane-powered "trains" shuttle the last 3km from the visitor centre to the start of the short footpath leading to the tip of the peninsula. However, the tip itself is merely a slender wedge of coarse brown sand that can't help but seem a tad anticlimactic – unless, that is, a storm has piled the beach with driftwood.

Sarnia and around

The large chunk of farmland rolling 100km west from London to the inconsequential border town of **Sarnia** is one of the less absorbing parts of the
province. It was also one of the last parts of southern Ontario to be cleared and
settled, its heavy clay soil being difficult to plough and becoming almost
impassable in rain. The district is bisected by **Hwy 21**, which serves as a handy
short cut between Windsor and Point Pelee (see above) and the good-looking
towns of the Lake Huron shoreline, primarily Bayfield and Goderich (see
p.141). Fortunately, Hwy 21 also passes by the area's three points of interest.
These are – from south to north – **Uncle Tom's Cabin Historic Site**, where
a group of escaped US slaves found refuge in the 1830s, the **Oil Museum of
Canada**, recalling the local oil boom of the middle of the nineteenth century,
and small-town **Petrolia**, also a result of the oil rush. You'll need a car for Hwy
21: there are **no buses**.

Uncle Tom's Cabin

Highway 401 trucks east from Windsor to intersect with Hwy 21 after about
100km. Turn north onto Hwy 21 and it's a further 30km to the agricultural
town of **DRESDEN**, which is itself just 2km from **Uncle Tom's Cabin
Historic Site** (mid-May to Aug Wed–Sat 10am–5pm, Sun noon–5pm; plus
July & Aug Mon 10am–5pm, Sun noon–4pm; $6.25), comprising a handful of
old wooden buildings, most notably a plain and simple church. Here also is the
clapboard house that was once the home of the **Reverend Josiah Henson**, a
slave who fled from Maryland to Canada in 1830 by means of the
Underground Railroad (or UGRR; see box). Henson and a group of abolitionist sympathizers subsequently bought 200 acres of farmland round Dresden
and founded a vocational school for runaway slaves known as the "British
American Institute". Unable to write, Henson dictated his life experiences and
in 1849 these narrations were published as *The Life of Josiah Henson – Formerly
a Slave*. It's a powerful tract, unassuming and almost matter of fact in the way
it describes the routine savagery of slavery – and it was immediately popular.
One of its readers was **Harriet Beecher Stowe**, who met Henson and went
on to write the most influential abolitionist text of the day, *Uncle Tom's Cabin*
(1852), basing her main character on Henson's accounts. Most of the Dresden
refugees returned to the US after the Civil War, but Henson stayed on,

The Underground Railroad

The **Underground Railroad** – the UGRR – started in the 1820s as a loose and
secretive association of abolitionists dedicated to smuggling slaves from the southern states of America to Canada. By the 1840s, the UGRR had become a well-
organized network of routes and safe houses, but its real importance lay not
so much in the number of slaves rescued – the total was small – but rather in the
psychological effect it had on those involved in the smuggling. The movement of a
single runaway might involve hundreds of people, if only in the knowledge that
a neighbour was breaking the law. To the extent that white Americans could be
persuaded to accept even the most minor role in the Railroad, the inclination to
compromise with institutional slavery was undermined, though the psychology of
racism remained intact: like Beecher Stowe's Uncle Tom, the freed negroes were
supposed to be humble and grateful, simulating childlike responses to please their
white parent-protectors.

accumulating imperial honours that must have surprised him greatly. He was even presented to Queen Victoria and, in commemoration of this royal connection, a crown surmounts his tombstone, which stands outside the complex. He died in 1883. Henson's book is hard to get hold of, but copies are sold here at the **interpretive centre**, where there's also a small museum on slavery and the UGRR plus an intriguing video giving more details on Henson's life and times.

Oil Springs and Petrolia

Some 25km north of Dresden, Hwy 21 scuttles past the Oil Museum of Canada (see below) just before it reaches tiny **OIL SPRINGS**, which once formed the nucleus of a rough-and-ready frontier district whose flat fields were packed with hundreds of eager fortune-seekers and their hangers-on. The first prospectors were attracted to the area by patches of black and sticky oil that had seeped to the surface through narrow fissures in the rock. These **gum beds** had long been used by local native peoples for medicinal and ritual purposes, but it was not until Charles and Henry Tripp of Woodstock incorporated their oil company in 1854 that serious exploitation began. Four years later, James Miller Williams dug North America's **first commercial oil well**, and in 1862 a certain Hugh Shaw drilled deeper than anyone else and, at 49m, struck the first **gusher**. The shock of seeing the oil fly up into the trees prompted Shaw, a religious man, to use the words of his Bible – "And the rock poured me out rivers of oil" (Job 29:6). Shaw became rich, but his luck ran out just one year later when the gas and sulphur fumes of his own well suffocated him. At the height of the boom, the oilfields produced about 30,000 barrels of crude a day, most of it destined for Sarnia, transported by stagecoach and wagon along a specially built plank road. The **Oil Museum of Canada** (May–Oct daily 10am–5pm; Nov–April Mon–Fri 10am–5pm; $4) has been built next to the site of James Williams' original well 1km south of Oil Springs. Highlights of the open-air display area include a nineteenth-century blacksmith's shop, with some fascinating old sepia photos taken during the oil boom, and an area of gum bed. The inside of the museum has a motley collection of oil-industry artefacts and background geological information. Oil is still produced in the fields around the museum, drawn to the surface and pushed on into an underground system of pipes by some seven hundred low-lying pump jacks.

Located some 10km to the north of Oil Springs, just off Hwy 21, the grand stone-and-brick buildings of tiny **PETROLIA** speak volumes about the sudden rush of wealth that followed the discovery of the oil. This was Canada's first oil town and as the proceeds rolled in so the Victorian mansions and expansive public buildings followed. Several have survived, dotted along and around the main drag, Petrolia Line. Three prime examples are the **Municipal Offices**, at Petrolia and Greenfield, **Nemo Hall**, an impressive brick building decorated by splendid wrought-iron trimmings at 419 King and Victoria, and **St Andrew's Presbyterian church**, close by at Petrolia and Queen, which is awash with neo-Gothic gables and towers. To emphasize the town's origins, its streetlamps are cast in the shape of oil derricks, but once you've had a scout round the architecture there's no strong reason to hang round.

Sarnia

Pushing on along Hwy 21 from Petrolia, it's about 10km to **Hwy 402**, the motorway linking London, 160km to the east, and Sarnia, 25km away to the west, and a further 80km north – on Hwy 21 – to Lake Huron's Bayfield. Given these rival destinations, there's precious little reason to detour to

SARNIA, but the town does offer several places to stay and is one-way to get into Michigan without having to pass through Detroit. Established as a lumber port in 1863, Sarnia is a negligible sort of place with a workaday gridiron of streets making up its modest centre. The **train station**, with connecting services to London, Toronto, Port Huron and Chicago, is on the southern edge of town, at the end of Russell St, a $10 taxi ride from the centre. The (moveable) Greyhound **bus depot** is currently located beside Mac's Convenience Store, some 5km east of Sarnia's waterfront at 580 Murphy Rd – but long-distance services are few and far between. There's a useful **Ontario Travel Information Centre** on the northern side of Sarnia, beside the approach road to the Bluewater Bridge over to the US (mid-May to mid-June Thurs–Sun 8.30am–6pm, Fri & Sat 8am–8pm; mid-June to Aug daily 8am–8pm; Sept to mid-May daily 8.30am–5pm; ☎519/344-7403). The inforcentre has details of local **accommodation**, which includes a reasonable selection of chain **motels** strung out along London Rd, one of the main drags running south of (and parallel to) Hwy 402. There is also a handful of **B&Bs** (❷), the pick of the bunch being *Buenos Dias*, 309 N Brock St (☎519/336-3221; ❷), set on a quiet leafy street and with four pleasant but unassuming guest rooms, two of which are en suite.

Bayfield and Goderich

A popular summer resort area, the southern section of the **Lake Huron shoreline** is trimmed by sandy beaches and a steep bluff that's interrupted by the occasional river valley. The water is much less polluted than Lake Ontario, the sunsets are fabulously beautiful, and in **Bayfield** and **Goderich** the lakeshore possesses two of the most appealing places in the whole of the province. You will, however, need your own transport to get to either: there are no **buses** at all.

Bayfield

Of these two lakeshore towns, the more southerly is **BAYFIELD**, a wealthy and good-looking village whose handsome timber villas nestle amongst well-tended gardens beneath a canopy of ancient trees – all about 80km north of London. The villagers have kept modern development at arm's length – there's barely a neon sign in sight, never mind a concrete apartment block – and almost every old house has been beautifully maintained: look out for the scrolled woodwork, the fanlights and the graceful verandas. Historical plaques give the lowdown on the older buildings that line Bayfield's short **Main St**, and pint-sized **Pioneer Park** on the bluff overlooking the lake at the west end of Main St is a fine spot to take in the sunset. If you've the time, you should also venture down to the **harbour** on the north side of the village and from there ramble up along the banks of the Bayfield River where, in season, you can pick wild mushrooms and fiddleheads. The Mara St footpath down to the harbour begins just behind Pioneer Park – it's signed. In winter there's ice fishing and skating to enjoy.

The **tourist office** (May–Sept daily 10am–6pm; ☎519/565-2499 or 1-866/565-2499, ⓦwww.bayfieldchamberofcommerce.on.ca), in the booth by Hwy 21 just north of the Bayfield River bridge, has a full list of local **accommodation** and staff will help you find a room, though their assistance is only really necessary in July and August when most places – including the B&Bs –

are heavily subscribed. At other times of the year, it's easy enough to find a place yourself. The best **hotel** for miles around is the outstanding *Little Inn of Bayfield*, Main St (☎519/565-2611 or 1-800/565-1832, ⓦwww.littleinn.com; ❻), a tastefully modernized early nineteenth-century timber-and-brick building with a handsome second-floor veranda and delightfully furnished rooms, most of which have whirlpool baths. The hotel has an annexe just across the street and, once again, the rooms here are simply splendid. Incidentally, do not confuse this hotel with the *Bayfield Village Inn*, a very different proposition. Other good places to stay include the pleasant *Albion Hotel*, in another old building on Main St (☎519/565-2641, ⓦwww.thealbionhotel.com; ❺), and several charming **B&Bs**. Amongst the latter, the pick is *Clair on the Square*, beside the village green at 12 The Square (☎519/565-2135, ⓦwww.claironthesquare.ca; ❺). There's **camping** at **Pinery Provincial Park** (reservations on ☎1-888/668-7275, ⓦwww.pinerypark.on.ca), a popular chunk of forested sand dune beside Lake Huron about 40km south of Bayfield.

Bayfield has several great places to **eat**, but it's hard to beat the smart and chic restaurant of the *Little Inn of Bayfield*, which is the best place to sample fish from Lake Huron – perch, white fish, pickerel or steelhead. Footsteps away, the *Red Pump Restaurant* (☎519/565-2576) is similarly classy, whilst the *Albion Hotel* has more routine, but still appetizing bar food and meals.

Goderich

Just 20km north of Bayfield at the mouth of the Maitland River, **GODERICH** is a delightful country town of eight thousand inhabitants that's saved from postcard prettiness by its working harbour. It began life in 1825, when the British-owned Canada Company bought two and a half million acres of southern Ontario – the **Huron Tract** – from the government at the ridiculously low rate of twelve cents an acre, amid rumours of bribery and corruption. Eager to profit on their investment, the company pushed the **Huron Rd** through from Cambridge in the east to Goderich in the west, an extraordinary effort that was witnessed by a certain Mr Moffat – "The trees were so tall, the forest was eternally dark and with the constant rains it was endlessly damp… Clearing the centuries of undergrowth and tangled vines was only the beginning, the huge rotted deadfalls of hardwood had to be hauled deeper into the bush, already piled high with broken pine. Since each man was responsible for cooking his own food after a hard day's work, the men sometimes ate the fattest pork practically raw… To make up for such fare, a barrel of whiskey with a cup attached always stood at the roadside." Completed in 1828, the road attracted the settlers the company needed. Indeed, within thirty years, the Huron Tract had two flourishing towns, Stratford (see p.117) and Goderich, and was producing large surpluses of grain for export, as it continues to do today.

The wide tree-lined avenues of the geometrically planned centre of Goderich radiate from a grand octagonal **central circus** dominated by the town's white-stone courthouse. From here, the four main streets follow the points of the compass with North St leading in a couple of minutes to the compendious **Huron County Museum** (Mon–Sat 10am–4.30pm & Sun 1–4.30pm; Sept–April closed Sat; $5, $7.50 with Gaol, see below), which concentrates on the district's pioneers. Highlights include a fantastic array of farm implements, from simple hand tools to gigantic, clumsy machines like the steam-driven thresher. There's also a beautifully restored Canadian Pacific steam engine and intriguing displays on the history of Huron County and the

Canada Company, as well as exhibition areas featuring furniture, transportation and military memorabilia, plus a string of period rooms.

A ten-minute walk up to the far end of North St and right along Gloucester brings you to the high stone walls of the **Huron Historic Gaol** at 181 Victoria St (mid-May to early Sept daily 10am–4.30pm; $5, $7.50 with Huron County Museum). One of the province's most intriguing attractions, the gaol was constructed as a combined courthouse and jail between 1839 and 1842. Start on the third floor of the main block, whose claustrophobic courtroom and council chamber were originally situated next to a couple of holding cells. The design was most unpopular with local judges, who felt threatened by the proximity of those they were sentencing. The other problem was the smell: several judges refused to conduct proceedings because of the terrible odour emanating from the privies in the exercise yard below. In 1856, the administration gave way and built a new courthouse in the town centre. On the second and first floors, there are the original jailer's apartment and a string of well-preserved prison cells, reflecting various changes in design between 1841 and 1972, when the prison was finally closed. The worst is the leg-iron cell for "troublesome" prisoners, where unfortunates were chained to the wall with neither bed nor blanket. End your tour at the **Governor's House**, with its attractively restored late Victorian interior.

Back in the centre, **West St** leads the 1km through a cutting in the bluffs to the Lake Huron shoreline at the south end of the harbour and salt works. A footpath leads northeast round the harbour, passing the grain elevators on its way to the **Menesetung Bridge**, the old CPR railway bridge that now serves as a pedestrian walkway across the Maitland River. On the north side of the river you can pick up the **Maitland Trail** for the brief but enjoyable jaunt along the river's north shore. In the opposite direction – south from the harbour – some 1.5km of shoreline has been tidied up to create a picnic area, but although the sunsets are spectacular the sandy **beach**, right at the end, is unenticingly scrawny.

Practicalities

Goderich **tourist office** sits beside Hwy 21 at the intersection of Nelson and Hamilton, a couple of minutes' walk to the northeast of the central circus (mid-May to Sept daily 9am–7pm; Oct to mid-May Mon–Fri 9am–4.30pm; ☏519/524-2513 or 1-800/280-7637, ⓦwww.town.goderich.on.ca). It has details of the town's twenty-odd **B&Bs**, which average out at about $60 per double per night. One of the more appealing (and expensive) options is the *Colborne B&B*, 72 Colborne St (☏519/524-7400 or 1-800/390-4612, ⓦwww.colbornebandb.com; ❹), in a large, plain-brick building dating from the early twentieth century and located just to the west of the central circus. There are four guest rooms here, all en suite, and each is decorated in a modern version of period style. More appealing, however, is *Twin Porches B&B*, 55 Nelson St E at Victoria (☏519/524-5505, ⓦwww.bbcanada.com/3694.html; ❷; May–Oct), in a lovely and well-kept Victorian house of buff-coloured brick embellished with fine gingerbread scrollwork. Also near the central circus – and metres from both the tourist office and a petrol station – this B&B, with its antique furnishings, has three air-conditioned guest rooms with shared bathroom. The **hotel** scene is less varied, but the reasonably priced *Hotel Bedford*, right in the centre at 92 Court House Square (☏519/524-7337, ⓦwww.hotelbedford.on.ca; ❸), is certainly distinctive. Built in 1896, the *Bedford* has an enormous open stairwell fitted with a grandiose wooden staircase just like a saloon in a John Ford movie – though the modernized rooms beyond are a tad disappointing. Much better is the plush *Benmiller Inn* (📞519/524-2191 or 1-800/265-1711, 🌐www.benmiller.on.ca; ❻), which occupies a converted 1830s woollen mill in an attractive wooded dell east of Goderich. To get there, take Hwy 8 out of town and watch for the sign after about 6km. There's **camping** near Goderich, too, just 7km north along the lakeshore at **Point Farms Provincial Park** (mid-May to early Oct; 📞519/524-7124).

For **food**, you're hardly spoiled for choice, but *Big Daddy's Pizza and Grill*, 42 West St (📞519/524-7777), serves up tasty, standard dishes at reasonable prices. The more upscale *Robindale's Fine Dining*, across from the tourist office at 80 Hamilton St (📞519/524-4171), is a comparatively formal restaurant where the pork dishes are delicious. The *Park House Tavern & Eatery*, 168 West St, is the town's liveliest bar and has wide views of Lake Huron.

Bruce Peninsula and Nottawasaga Bay

Separating the main body of Lake Huron from Georgian Bay, the **Bruce Peninsula** holds two of Ontario's national parks. The more distinctive is the **Fathom Five National Marine Park**, at the northern tip of the peninsula, where extraordinary rock formations, plentiful shipwrecks and crystal-clear waters provide wonderful sport for divers. The second is the **Bruce Peninsula National Park**, comprising two slabs of forested wilderness on either side of Hwy 6, its northern portion offering magnificent coastal hiking on a small section of the Bruce Trail. There's camping at both parks and a reasonable choice of hotel and motel accommodation at lively **Tobermory**, an amiable combination of fishing village, port and resort. Spare time also for a quick zip round the interesting old port of **Owen Sound** at the base of the peninsula.

East of Owen Sound the southern curve of Georgian Bay forms **Nottawasaga Bay**, one of the province's most popular holiday areas. In summer the focus of attention is the crowded resort of **Wasaga Beach**, where a seemingly endless string of chalets and cottages fringe the several kilometres of protected sand that make up **Wasaga Beach Provincial Park**. To the west of Wasaga Beach, inland from the gritty port of **Collingwood**, is the **Blue Mountain ski area**, whose slopes utilize the Niagara Escarpment, the limestone ridge that weaves its way from near Niagara Falls to the Bruce Peninsula.

The only catch is the lack of public transport – the Bruce peninsula has no **bus** services. Note also that Tobermory is where you catch the ferry to Manitoulin Island in northern Ontario (see p.200).

Owen Sound

Just under 200km northwest of Toronto, **OWEN SOUND** occupies the ravine around the mouth of the Sydenham River, at the foot of the Bruce Peninsula. In its heyday, Owen Sound was a rough and violent port packed with brothels and bars, prompting the Americans to establish a consulate whose main function was to bail out drunk and disorderly sailors. For the majority it was an unpleasant place to live, and the violence spawned an especially active branch of the Women's Christian Temperance Organization, whose success was such that an alcohol ban was imposed in 1906 and only lifted in 1972. The town was in decline long before the return of the bars, its port facilities undercut by the railways from the 1920s, but it's managed to reinvent itself and is now an amiable sort of place well worth at least a pit stop. There are three central sights of some interest, kicking off with the **Marine-Rail Museum**, overlooking the harbour in the old railway station at 1165 1st Ave W (June–Aug Mon–Sat 9.30am–4.30pm, Sun noon–4.30pm; Sept–May Mon–Fri 9am–4pm & Sat–Sun 11am–3pm; donation). The museum has photos and scale models of old trains and ships and there is an old log tug and a caboose outside. Perhaps more diverting are the **Tom Thomson Memorial Art Gallery**, 840 1st Ave W (July & Aug Mon–Sat 10am–5pm, Sun noon–5pm; Sept–June Tues–Fri 11am–5pm, Sat & Sun noon–5pm; $2 donation), where there are temporary exhibitions by Canadian artists and a clutch of Thomson's less familiar paintings; and the **Billy Bishop Museum**, 948 3rd Ave W (July–Aug daily 10am–4pm; Sept–Dec & March–June Tues–Sun noon–4pm; Jan & Feb Tues–Fri noon–4pm; $4), concentrating on the military exploits of Canada's Victoria Cross-winning air ace.

Owen Sound **bus station** is on 3rd Ave East at 10th St East, ten-minutes' walk from the **tourist office**, which is next door to the Marine-Rail Museum at 1155 1st Ave W (Mon–Fri 9am–4.30pm; June–Aug also Sat & Sun noon–4pm; ☎519/371-9833, ⓦwww.e-owensound.com). It has a list of local accommodation, including details of a dozen **B&Bs** (❶–❷). One of the handiest is the *Brae Briar*, 980 3rd Ave W (☎519/371-0025, ⓦwww.bbcanada.com/622.html; ❷), in a pleasant but unassuming two-storey brick house with three guest rooms downtown off 10th St. The town's **motels** are strung out along highway 6/10 on the south side of town. Incidentally, orientation in Owen Sound is a tad difficult, but the main rules to remember are that *Avenues* run one way, *Streets* the other, while the river, which bisects the compact town centre, separates Avenues and Streets *East* from those marked *West*. For downtown **food**, stick to *Jazzmyns Tapas & Taps*, 261 9th St E, where they serve up excellent, inexpensive snacks – anything from tapas to pizzas and burgers.

The Bruce Peninsula National Park and Tobermory

Heading north from Owen Sound, Hwy 6 scoots up the middle of the Bruce Peninsula to reach – after about 100km – the turning for the **Bruce Peninsula National Park** at **Cyprus Lake**. The park is a mixture of limestone cliff, rocky beach, wetland and forest that's best visited in June when the wild flowers are in bloom and it's not too crowded. At Cyprus Lake are the park's headquarters and all-year **campsites**, which operate on a first-come, first-served basis in winter, by reservation from May to September on ☎519/596-2263. Four hiking trails start at the northern edge of Cyprus Lake and three of them connect with one of the most dramatic portions of the **Bruce Trail** (see box below).

Just 11km beyond the Cyprus Lake turning, Hwy 6 slips into **TOBERMORY**, a bustling fishing village and holiday resort at the northern tip of the peninsula. There are no sights as such, but it's a pleasant spot, its tiny centre focused on a slender inlet, the **Little Tub harbour**. Here, **car ferries** (May to mid-Oct 2–4 daily; $12 one-way, cars $27; ☎519/596-2510 or 1-800/265-3163, ⓦwww.bmts.com) leave for South Baymouth on Manitoulin Island (see p.200) and passenger boats shuttle out to Fathom Five National Marine Park (see below). At the back of the harbour, the **National Park office** (Mon–Fri 9am–4.30pm; ☎519/596-2233) covers both of the Bruce Peninsula's national parks, issuing maps and free brochures. The Fathom Five National Marine Park is known across Canada for the excellence of its diving; the waters are clear and they are dotted with around twenty shipwrecks. Prospective divers must register in person at the harbourfront **Registration Centre** (April–Sept daily 8am–4.30pm; ☎519/596-2503). Diving gear can be rented footsteps away at G&S Watersports (☎519/596-2200, ⓦwww.gswater-sports.com). There are a dozen or so **hotels** and **motels** in and around Tobermory, mostly brisk, modern affairs that are comfortable without being especially charming. The pick is the *Grandview Motel* (☎519/596-2220, ⓦwww.grandview-tobermory.com; ❹), with eighteen spick-and-span rooms on the east side of the harbour at the junction of Bay and Earl streets. A second good choice, also on the east side of the harbour, is the two-storey, balconied *Blue Bay Motel* (☎519/596-2392, ⓦwww.bluebay-motel.com; ❹). The *Grandview Motel* has the town's best **restaurant** with views out across the harbour and tasty, reasonably priced dishes with seafood a speciality – try the whitefish and ocean perch. There are also several lively **bars** and **cafés** beside the harbour – the *Crow's Nest* is as good as any.

Fathom Five National Marine Park

At **Fathom Five National Marine Park** nineteen uninhabited islands are enclosed within a park boundary that is drawn round the waters at the end of the peninsula, offshore from Tobermory. To protect the natural habitat, only **Flowerpot Island**, 4km from the mainland, has any amenities, with limited space for **camping** – six sites only – and a couple of short hiking trails that explore its eastern reaches. A delightful spot, Flowerpot takes its name from two pink-and-grey rock pillars that have been eroded away from its eastern shore, and are readily seen on the islet's Loop Trail. From May to mid-October, Flowerpot Island is easily reached by **boat** from Tobermory. Several operators run regular boats out to the island, either dropping passengers off and then collecting them later or pausing at Flowerpot as part of a longer excursion – just stroll along Little Tub harbour until you find the service that suits. One reliable company is Blue Heron (☎519/596-2999, ⓦwww.blueheronco.com). The return fare from Tobermory to Flowerpot is around $20, a few dollars more for the longer trips. Prospective campers need to make reservations at and get permits from the Diver Registration office (see above). Both hikers and campers need to pack food and drink.

Wasaga Beach and around

With its amusement parks and fast-food joints, there's nothing subtle about **WASAGA BEACH** on Nottawasaga Bay, but the beach is of fine golden sand, the swimming excellent and you can rent out all manner of watercraft from jet skis to canoes. There's also one historical curiosity at the **Nancy Island Historic Site** (late May to mid-June Sat & Sun 10am–6pm; mid-June to Aug daily 10am–6pm; Sept to mid-Oct Sat & Sun 10am–5pm; free, but parking charge), on the main drag – Mosley St – behind Beach Area 2. In the War of 1812 the Americans managed to polish off the few British ships stationed in the upper Great Lakes without too much difficulty, and the last Royal Navy vessel, the supply ship *Nancy*, hid out here just off the bay at the mouth of the Nottawasaga River. The Americans tracked down and sunk the *Nancy*, but silt subsequently collected round the sunken hull to create Nancy Island. In 1927, the hull was raised from the silt and today it forms the main exhibit of the island's museum, whose imaginative design resembles the sails of a schooner.

Wasaga Beach makes for a good day's swimming and sunbathing, but if you do decide to stay the night you have the choice of lots of reasonably priced **motels** as well as cottages and campsites; just drive along Mosley St until some place takes your fancy. Alternatively, the local Chamber of Commerce's year-round **information centre** at 550 River Rd W, in Beach Area 1 (Mon–Sat 9am–5pm, Sun 10am–4pm; ☎705/429-2247 or 1-866/292-7242, Ⓦwww.wasagainfo.com), will help you find accommodation. Public transport is thin on the ground, but PMCL **buses** (☎1-800/461-1767, Ⓦwww.pmcl.on.ca) do call at Collingwood and the *Blue Mountain Inn* once or twice daily (Mon–Sat) on their way between Toronto and Owen Sound.

Collingwood and the Blue Mountain ski area

The small-time port of **COLLINGWOOD**, 20km west along the bayshore from Wasaga Beach, has a clutch of fine early twentieth-century buildings dotted along its main street, **Hurontario** – red-brick facades decorated with geometric designs and roughly dressed sandstone sills. More importantly, the town is also the gateway to the **Blue Mountain**, a segment of the Niagara Escarpment whose steepish slopes are now a major winter sports area, mainly for **alpine skiing** though several cross-country trails have also been developed. To get there from Collingwood, take the Blue Mountain Rd (Route 19) which reaches – after about 10km – the **downhill ski slopes** at the *Blue Mountain Inn* (☎705/445-0231, Ⓦwww.bluemountain.ca; ❹), a large and modern lodge that is the centre of wintertime activity. This is not, however, the best place to stay: instead continue along the Blue Mountain Rd for another 400m as far as the *Blue Mountain Auberge* (☎705/445-1497; ❸), an informal and attractive lodge, built in Alpine style with a dozen rooms, sauna, kitchen and barbecue area. Tucked into the wooded slopes of the Blue Mountain, it's a great location and reservations are advised both in the winter and summer, when hikers use the *Auberge* as a jumping-off point for the Bruce Trail (see box p.145) which passes close by. The *Auberge* doesn't rent out ski gear, but this is readily available from outlets nearby. In total, the Blue Mountain has 39 downhill ski slopes of varying difficulty with a maximum vertical drop of 219m. The prime season is from mid-December to mid-March.

Severn Sound

Severn Sound, the southeastern inlet of Georgian Bay, is one of the most beautiful parts of Ontario. Its sheltered southern shore is lined with tiny ports and its deep-blue waters are studded by the outcrops of the **Georgian Bay Islands National Park**, whose glacier-smoothed rocks and wispy pines were celebrated by the Group of Seven painters. In **Discovery Harbour**, on the edge of **Penetanguishene**, and **Sainte-Marie among the Hurons**, outside

Midland, Severn Sound also possesses two of the province's finest historical reconstructions – the first a British naval base, the second a Jesuit mission. Leaving Severn Sound, there's more lovely Canadian Shield scenery on the road north to **Parry Sound**, an agreeable little port that also serves as a convenient stopping point on the long road north to Sudbury and Northern

Ontario (see p.199). Alternatively, you can head southeast from Severn Sound to **Orillia**, home of the Stephen Leacock Museum – and just 120km from Toronto on highways 11 and 400.

There's a reasonably good network of **bus** services running north from Toronto to – and along – the southern shore of Severn Sound. These services are operated by PMCL (☎1-800/461-1767, ⓦwww.pmcl.on.ca), who also link Toronto and Orillia. The Toronto to Port Severn, Parry Sound, Sudbury bus route is operated by Ontario Northland (☎1-800/461-8558, ⓦwww.webusit.com).

Penetanguishene

The most westerly town on Severn Sound, homely **PENETANGUISHENE** – "place of the rolling white sands" in Ojibwa – was the site of one of Ontario's first European settlements, a Jesuit mission founded in 1639, then abandoned in 1649 following the burning of Sainte-Marie (see p.151). Europeans returned some 150 years later to establish a trading station where local Ojibwa exchanged pelts for food and metal tools. However, the settlement remained insignificant until just after the War of 1812, when the British built a naval dockyard that attracted shopkeepers and suppliers from both French and British communities. Today Penetanguishene is one of the few places in southern Ontario that maintains a bilingual tradition.

The town's **Main St** is a pleasant place for a stroll, its shops and bars installed behind sturdy red-brick facades. It's the general atmosphere that appeals rather than any particular sight, but the **Centennial Museum**, 13 Burke St (May–Oct Mon–Sat 9am–4.30pm, Sun noon–4.30pm; $4.50), a couple of minutes' walk east of Main St along Beck Boulevard, is worth a quick visit. The museum occupies the old general store and offices of the Beck lumber company, whose yards once stretched right along the town's waterfront. The company was founded in 1865 by Charles Beck, a German immigrant who made himself immensely unpopular by paying his men half their wages in tokens that were only redeemable at his stores. The museum has several displays on the Beck lumber company, including examples of these "Beck dollars", and there's also a fascinating selection of old photographs featuring locals at work and play in the town and its forested surroundings. Doubling back, it's a short walk to the jetty at the north end of Main St, from where there are enjoyable, three-hour **cruises** of the southern stretches of Georgian Bay and its myriad islands – known collectively as the Thirty Thousand Islands (mid-June to Aug 1–2 cruises daily; May, early June, Sept & early Oct occasional sailings; $20; ☎705/549-7795 or 1-800/363-7447, ⓦwww.georgianbaycruises.com).

Discovery Harbour and Awenda

Penetanguishene's prime attraction, **Discovery Harbour** (mid-May to June Mon–Fri 10am–5pm; July & Aug daily 10am–5pm; $5.50; ⓦwww .discoveryharbour.on.ca), situated about 5km north of the town centre, is an ambitious reconstruction of the important British naval base that was established here in 1817. The principal purpose of the base was to keep an eye on American movements on the Great Lakes following the War of 1812, and between 1820 and 1834 up to twenty Royal Navy vessels were stationed here. Ships from the base also supplied the British outposts further to the west and, to make navigation safer, the Admiralty decided to chart the Great Lakes. This monumental task fell to Lieutenant Henry Bayfield, who informed his superiors of his determination "to render this work so correct that it shall not be easy to render it more so". He lived up to his word, and his charts remained in use for decades. The naval station was more short-lived. By 1834, relations with the US were sufficiently cordial for the Navy to withdraw, and the base was turned over to the Army, who maintained a small garrison here until 1856. Staffed by enthusiastic costumed guides, the sprawling site spreads along a hillside above a tranquil inlet, its green slopes scattered with accurate reconstructions of everything from a sailors' barracks to several period houses, the prettiest of which is the **Keating House**, named after the base's longest-serving adjutant, Frank Keating. Only one of the original buildings survives – the dour limestone **Officers' Quarters**, dating from the 1840s. However, pride of place goes to the working harbour-cum-dockyard, where a brace of fully rigged **sailing ships**, the HMS *Bee* and HMS *Tecumseth*, have been rebuilt to their original nineteenth-century specifications. In addition, Discovery Harbour also accommodates the **King's Wharf Theatre** (☎705/549-5555, ⓦwww.kingswharftheatre.com), which offers a season of plays as well as concerts and musicals from early June to August.

Just 11km northwest of Penetanguishene, **Awenda Provincial Park** (☎705/549-2231) is one of Ontario's larger parks, its delightful mainland portion dominated by a dense deciduous forest that spreads south from the Nipissing Bluff on the edge of Georgian Bay. The other section, Giants Tomb Island, lies offshore, but you need your own boat to get there. Awenda has a few small rock-and-pebble beaches, four good **campsites** (mid-May to early Oct), and a handful of hiking trails starting near the park office, which issues trail guides and maps. A recommended route is to take the Bruce Trail through the forest to connect with the Dune Trail, which leads to a vantage point above the bay – 5km in all.

Practicalities

With regular services from Midland and Toronto, Penetanguishene's tiny **bus depot** is at Main St and Robert. From here, it's a five- to ten-minute walk north to the harbour, where the **tourist office** (Mon–Fri 9am–5pm plus summer weekends 9am–5pm; ☎705/549-2232, ⓦwww.town.penetanguishene.on.ca) has details of local **hotels** and **B&Bs**. Amongst them, easily the pick is the delightful *No.1 Jury Drive B&B*, 1 Jury Drive (☎705/549-6851, ⓦwww.jurydrbb.huronia.com; ❹), whose five comfortable en-suite guest rooms occupy an attractive modern house built in traditional style near Discovery Harbour. The leafy suburban setting is very relaxing and the breakfasts are superb – especially the home-made carrot muffins. A second very appealing option is the *Hillside Inn B&B*, 27 Church St (☎705/549-3508 or 1-866/806-3508, ⓦwww.hillsideinn.ca; ❸), a handsome old house with a capacious veranda and cosy guest rooms. The B&B is in town and offers wide views of the bay from its hillside location. If you decide to use Penetanguishene as a base, you can zip off to other local attractions with Union Taxi (☎705/549-7666), which is next door to the bus station. Local buses are run by PMCL (☎1-800/461-1767). For **food**, the *Blue Sky Family Restaurant*, 48 Main St, is a most agreeable small-town diner offering good-quality snacks and meals at very affordable prices.

Midland

MIDLAND, just east along the bay from Penetanguishene, has suffered badly from recurrent recession, losing its engineering plants in the 1930s, its shipyards in 1957 and much of its flour-mill capacity in 1967. But it has bounced back, shrugging off these setbacks with the help of provincial and federal grants, and nowadays the town has a sprightly air, its main drag – **King St** – an amenable parade of shops and cafés with the occasional mural to brighten up the sturdy brick buildings. Efforts to cash in on the tourist industry have included the construction of a marina and the redevelopment of the harbourfront, where sightseeing **cruises** of the Thirty Thousand Islands that necklace Georgian Bay leave from mid-May to early October (1–3 daily; $19; reservations on ☎705/549-3388, ⓦwww.midlandtours.com). Sooner or later, every schoolkid in Midland gets taken to the **Huronia Museum & Huron–Ouendat Village** (daily: May–Dec 9am–5/6pm; Jan–April 9am–5pm, but phone to confirm times on ☎705/526-2844; $6), a twenty-minute walk south of the harbour along King St. Highlights of the **museum** include a large number of Huron artefacts and a series of photos tracing the pioneer settlement of Midland. The adjacent **village** is a replica of a sixteenth-century Huron settlement, its high palisade encircling storage pits, drying racks, a sweat bath, a medicine man's lodge and two long houses. These long houses are characteristic Huron constructions, their bark-covered walls of cedar poles bent to form a protective arch and containing tiers of rough wooden bunks draped with furs, whilst herbs, fish, skins and tobacco hang from the roof to dry. It's all very interesting and feels surprisingly authentic, but still lags far behind the comparable section of the nearby Sainte-Marie among the Hurons (see below).

Midland **bus station** is close to the waterfront on Bay St, metres from Central Taxi (☎705/526-2218) and a couple of minutes' walk east of the **tourist office**, at the foot of King St (June–Aug Mon–Fri 8.30am–5pm, Sat & Sun 10am–6pm; Sept–May Mon–Fri 9am–5pm; ☎705/526-7884, ⓦwww.southerngeorgianbay.on.ca). It has the details of local and regional **accommodation** – anything from cottage rental through to a handful of downtown **B&Bs** (❷). Amongst the latter, two perfectly adequate and fairly central options are the *Victorian Inn B&B*, in a good-looking Victorian house with wraparound veranda at 670 Hugel Ave and 5th St (☎705/526-4441 or 1-877/450-7660, ⓦwww.victorianinn.on.ca; ❸); and the unusual *Little Lake B&B*, 669 Yonge St at 5th St (☎705/526-2750, ⓦwww.littlelakeinn.com; ❹), where the modern front part of the house leads to an older section at the back with high-beamed ceilings and park views; Yonge St cuts across King about 600m south of the harbourfront. There are also several reasonably priced **motels** in and around town – the *Comfort Inn*, about 2km from the harbour at 980 King St and Hwy 12 (☎705/526-2090, ⓦwww.comfortinnslakelands .com; ❹), is as good as any. For **food**, the *Daily Perk*, 292 King St, serves first-class deli-style sandwiches and meals; *Midland Fish & Chips*, 311 King, does what it does rather well; and *Scully's Waterfront Grill*, by the town dock, is a popular, boisterous place with bar food.

Sainte-Marie among the Hurons

One of Ontario's most arresting historical attractions is **Sainte-Marie among the Hurons** (mid-May to mid-Oct daily 10am–5pm; $9.75), the carefully researched and beautifully maintained site of a crucial episode in Canadian history. It's located 5km east of Midland beside Hwy 12 – and although there are no buses, the taxi fare from Midland is only $7.

In 1608 **Samuel de Champlain** returned to Canada convinced that the only way to make the fur trade profitable was by developing alliances with native hunters. The Huron were the obvious choice, as they already acted as go-betweens in the exchange of corn, tobacco and hemp from the bands to the south and west of their territory, for the pelts collected to the north. In 1611, having participated in Huron attacks on the Iroqouis, Champlain cemented the alliance by a formal exchange of presents. However, his decision to champion one tribe against another – and particularly his gifts of firearms to his allies – disrupted the balance of power amongst the native societies of the St Lawrence and Great Lakes area and set the stage for the destruction of Sainte-Marie almost forty years later. Meanwhile, the **Jesuits**, who established their centre of operations at Sainte-Marie in 1639, had begun to undermine social cohesion within the Huron community itself. The priests succeeded in converting a substantial minority of the Huron – by then enfeebled by three European sicknesses, measles, smallpox and influenza – and thus divided them into two camps, Christian and non-Christian. Furthermore, in 1648 the Dutch on the Hudson River began to sell firearms to the Iroquois, who launched a full-scale invasion of Huronia in March 1649, slaughtering their enemies as they moved in on Sainte-Marie. Fearing for their lives, the Jesuits of Sainte-Marie burnt their settlement and fled. Eight thousand Hurons went with them; most starved to death on Christian Island, in Georgian Bay, but a few made it to Québec. During the campaign two Jesuit priests, fathers **Brébeuf and Lalemant**, were captured at the outpost of Saint-Louis, near present-day Victoria Harbour, where they were bound to the stake and tortured, as per standard Iroquois practice. The image of Catholic bravery and Indian cruelty lingered in the minds of French-Canadians long after the sufferings of the Hurons had been forgotten.

A visit to Sainte-Marie starts in the **reception centre** with an audiovisual show that provides some background information before the screen lifts dramatically away to reveal the painstakingly restored **mission site**. There are 25 wooden buildings here, divided into two sections: the Jesuit area with its watchtowers, chapel, forge, living quarters, well-stocked garden and farm buildings, complete with pigs, cows and hens; and the native area, including a hospital and a pair of bark-covered long houses – one for Christian converts, the other for heathens. Fairly spick-and-span today, it takes some imagination to see the long houses as they appeared to Father Lalemant, who saw "…a miniature picture of hell… on every side naked bodies, black and half-roasted, mingled pell-mell with the dogs… you will not reach the end of the cabin before you are completely befouled with soot, filth and dirt". Costumed guides act out the parts of Hurons and Europeans with great gusto, answering questions and demonstrating crafts and skills, though they show a certain reluctance to eat the staple food of the region, sagamite, a porridge of cornmeal seasoned with rotten fish. The grave in the simple wooden **church of St Joseph** between the Christian and native areas is the place where the (remaining) flesh of Brébeuf and Lalemant was interred after the Jesuits had removed the bones for future use as reliquaries.

A path leads from the site to the excellent **museum**, which traces the story of the early exploration of Canada with maps and displays on such subjects as fishing and the fur trade, seen in the context of contemporary European history. This leads into a section on the history of the missionaries in New France, with particular reference to Sainte-Marie. Information on the archaeology of the site follows: the mission's whereabouts were always known even though Victorian settlers helped themselves to every chunk of stone – from what was known locally as "the old Catholic fort" – because the Jesuits had deposited the necessary documentation in Rome. Excavations began on the site in the 1940s and work is still in progress.

The Martyrs' Shrine and Wye Marsh

The eight Jesuits who were killed in Huronia between 1642 and 1649 are commemorated by the **Martyrs' Shrine** (mid-May to mid-Oct daily 9am–9pm; $2), a twin-spired, 1920s church which overlooks Sainte-Marie from the other side of Hwy 12. Blessed by Pope John Paul II in 1984 – when he bafflingly remarked that it was "a symbol of unity of faith in a diversity of cultures" – the church, along with the assorted shrines and altars in its grounds, is massively popular with pilgrims. Inside, the transepts hold a number of saintly reliquaries, most notably the skull of Brébeuf, and a stack of crutches discarded by healed pilgrims. Back across Hwy 12 and next door to Sainte-Marie is the **Wye Marsh Wildlife Centre** (daily 9am–5pm, 6pm from late June to Aug; $6.50), whose footpaths explore a patch of wetland and the surrounding woodland.

Orillia

If you're heading south from Severn Sound towards Toronto, you might consider a brief detour to **ORILLIA**, beside Lake Couchiching, which is separated from the much larger Lake Simcoe by a short and narrow promontory; the town is also on Hwy 11, the road to Algonquin Provincial Park (see p.161). Orillia lies just to the west of the narrow channel – **The Narrows** – that connects the two lakes, a waterway that was once a centre of Huron settlement. When **Samuel de Champlain** arrived here in 1615, he promptly handed out muskets to his Huron allies, encouraging them to attack their Iroquois rivals in order to establish French control of the fur trade. This intervention was to lead to the destruction of the Jesuit outpost at Sainte-Marie in 1649 (see opposite). Two hundred years later, a second wave of Europeans cleared the district's forests, and today Orillia is a trim little town of 27,000 citizens – part lakeside resort, part farming centre.

Orillia's humdrum **town centre** spreads out on either side of the main drag, Mississaga St, which runs east from Hwy 11 to Lake Couchiching. At the foot of Mississaga, **Centennial Park** incorporates a marina, a harbour and a boardwalk that runs north to **Couchiching Beach Park**, complete with an Edwardian bandstand and a bronze statue of Champlain. However, the town's principal attraction, the **Stephen Leacock Museum** (May & Sept Mon–Fri 10am–5pm; June–Aug daily 10am–5pm; $8), is located some 3km southeast of the centre along the lakeshore – just follow the signs. Built in 1928 in the colonial style, with symmetrical pitched roofs and an ornate veranda, this was the summer home of the humorist and academic Stephen Leacock until his death in 1944. His most famous book, *Sunshine Sketches of a Little Town*, gently mocks the hypocrisies and vanities of the people of Mariposa, an imaginary town so clearly based on Orillia that it caused great local offence. Some of the rooms contain furnishings and fittings familiar to Leacock, others shed light on his career, interests and attitudes. Indeed, although the books may be engagingly whimsical, you can't help but wonder about a man who had concealed spyholes in his library so that he could watch his guests and, perhaps worse, carefully positioned his favourite living-room chair so that he could keep an eye on his servants in the pantry via the dining-room mirror. After you've explored the house, take a few minutes for the easy stroll out along the adjacent wooded headland and drop by the giftshop, which sells almost all of his works.

Orillia's **bus station** occupies the former railway station at the southern end of the town centre off Front St South. From here it's 2km south to the Leacock Museum and around 800m north along Front St South to the seasonal **tourist** office (June–Aug Mon–Fri 8.30am–5pm, Sat 10am–4pm & Sun 10am–3pm), right by the harbour. The Chamber of Commerce year-round tourist office is at 150 Front St S (Mon–Fri 9am–5pm; T705/326-4424). There's no special reason to hang around after you've done the sights, but if you do decide to stay you can get details of local accommodation from either office.

Port Severn and around

Sitting on the northern shore of Severn Sound at the mouth of the Severn River, tiny **PORT SEVERN** is the gateway to the **Trent–Severn Waterway**, a 400km canalized route that connects Georgian Bay with Lake Ontario. With a maximum depth of only 2m, it's of little commercial importance today, but until the late nineteenth century this was one of the region's principal cargo routes. It's open from the middle of May to the middle of October and takes about a week to travel from one end to the other. If you've the inclination for a serious **boating trip**, your first port of call should be the Friends of the Trent–Severn Waterway, who provide a free **cruise planning service** (T1-800/663-2628, W www.ftsw.com). In addition, two-and-a-half-hour taster **cruises** (June to mid-Oct 1 daily; $16; T1-888/833-2628, W www.mid-landtours.com) leave from Lock #45 in Port Severn, travelling as far as the **Big Chute Marine Railway**, where boats are lifted over the eighteen-metre drop between the upper and lower levels of the river. Frankly, the Big Chute is something of a yawn, but it certainly attracts its share of visitors, most of whom drive here – just follow the signs off Hwy 400 (Exit 162) north of Port Severn. There are three recommendable **hotels** in Port Severn, beginning with *Rawley Lodge* (T1-800/263-7358, W www.rawleylodge.on.ca; ❹ including meals; May–Oct), which occupies a rambling, 1920s building with a charming river-side setting. The rooms are modern and a tad spartan – both in the main lodge and the adjacent chalets – but perfectly adequate; they also rent out canoes. The second hotel is the smart and briskly modern *Inn at Christie's Mill* (T705/538-2354 or 1-800/465-9966, W www.christiesmill.com; ❻), which also has the district's best **restaurant** with views out across the river. Even better, however, is the delightful *Severn Lodge* (T705/756-2722 or 1-800/461-5817, W www.severnlodge.on.ca), which has a wonderful solitary location amongst dense forests overlooking a wide and quiet section of the Trent–Severn Waterway. The lodge has all the facilities of a mini-resort, including canoe and motorboat rental, an artificial beach, a restaurant and an outside swimming pool, and is extremely popular with families. **Rooms** are available in the main lodge and in the chalets that dot the surrounding woods. Rates vary enormously, and there's usually a minimum stay of two nights, but a lodge room for two nights including meals works out at about $300 per person in summer. To get there, leave Hwy 400 at Exit 162 (also the turning for the Big Chute Marine Railway – see above) and it's 7km along Route 34. The Ontario Northland **bus** service (T1-800/461-8558) from Toronto to Sudbury drops passengers at the fuel station on Hwy 400 on the edge of Port Severn; there are no connections on to Honey Harbour.

Honey Harbour

It's 13km northwest from Port Severn across the mouth of the river and down Route 5 to **HONEY HARBOUR**, the nearest port – with water taxis – to the Georgian Bay Islands National Park. Little more than a couple of shops, a liquor store and a few self-contained hotel resorts, the village achieved some notoriety in the 1970s when the bar of the *Delawana Inn* was the site of

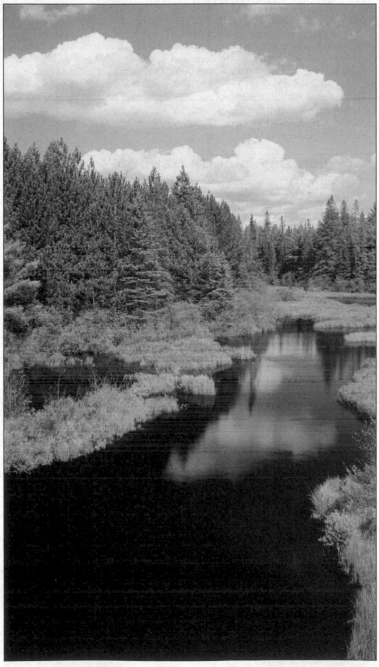

△ Algonquin Provincial Park

violent confrontations between Toronto's Hell's Angels and local Ojibwa families. The feud ended with the Angels walking home after their bikes had been dynamited. Things are much more civil today, but Honey Harbour is still a lively place in summer, with motorboats whizzing in and out as cottagers drop by to collect supplies. If you decide to stay here – eschewing the offshore campsites of the national park – the best place is the lakeside *Delawana Inn* (T705/756-2424 or 1-888/335-2926, Wwww.delawana.com; ❽ for full board in high season, with discounts on package deals; mid-May to early Sept). The inn comprises an extensive, resort complex with spacious chalet cabins dotted round its pine-forested grounds. Guests also have use of the resort's canoes, kayaks and windsurfing boards.

Georgian Bay Islands National Park

A beautiful area to cruise, the **Georgian Bay Islands National Park** consists of a scattering of about sixty islands spread between Honey Harbour and Twelve Mile Bay, about 50km to the north. The park's two distinct landscapes – the glacier-scraped rock of the Canadian Shield and the hardwood forests and thicker soils of the south – meet at the northern end of the largest and most scenic island, **Beausoleil**, a forty-minute boat ride west of Honey Harbour. Beausoleil has eleven short **hiking trails**, including two that start at the **Cedar Spring landing stage**, on the southeastern shore. These are the Treasure Trail, which heads north behind the marshes along the edge of the island, and the Christian Trail, which cuts through beech and maple stands to the balsam and hemlock groves overlooking the rocky beaches of the western shoreline. At the northern end of Beausoleil, within comfortable walking distance of several other **jetties**, are the Cambrian and Fairy trails, two delightful routes through the harsher scenery of the Canadian Shield. Nearby, just to the west, is the Dossyonshing Trail, which tracks through a mixed area of wetland, forest and bare granite in the transitional zone between the two main landscapes. The **national park office** in Honey Harbour (late June to early Sept Mon–Fri 8am–4.30pm, Sat 8am–4pm & Sun 8am–noon; T705/756-2415) provides a full range of information on walking trails and flora and fauna. In winter, a visit to the park office is essential as the wardens will advise on where it's safe to ski across the ice to the islands – ring ahead to check their availability; the wardens maintain a marked ski trail out to Beausoleil.

The park has eleven **campsites**, all on Beausoleil. The charge is $13 a night and all operate on a self-registration, first-come, first-served basis, with the exception of Cedar Spring ($17), where the visitor centre (T705/756-5909) takes reservations on half the 87 sites for an additional $10 fee. For everywhere else, ask about availability at the park office before you set out – and don't forget the insect repellent. Three Honey Harbour operators run a **water taxi** service over to three of the park's islands – Beausoleil ($35–40 one-way),

The Massasauga rattlesnake

The endangered **Massasauga rattlesnake** is the only venomous snake in eastern Canada and there is a small population of them in and around the Georgian Bay Islands National Park. Tan-coloured with dark brown blotches, an adult specimen is 50 to 70cm long with a heavy body and triangular head. In the unlikely event you stumble across one, give it a wide berth. The snake prefers marsh and mixed forest, so if you are hiking in this kind of habitat, be sure to pick up one of the advisory leaflets at the park office.

Centennial Island ($40–45) and Island 95 ($40–45). Honey Harbour Boat Club (☎705/756-2411), about 700m from the park office at the marina at the end of Route 5, is as good as any. Water taxi prices are fixed – the park office has the list – but times are negotiable; be sure to arrange an agreed pick-up time before you get dropped off. If you want to head southwest, a one-way water-taxi trip to Midland costs around $100. In addition – and much more economical – are **day-trips to Beausoleil**, giving four hours on the island, with the park's own Georgian Bay Islands Day Tripper (July to early Sept Thurs to Mon 3 daily; $20 return; ☎705/756-2415). Advance reservations are essential for both the day trip and the water taxis.

Parry Sound

A cheerful little place, **PARRY SOUND**, beside an inlet of Georgian Bay 85km north of Port Severn, was named after the Arctic explorer Sir William Edward Parry, but it earned the nickname "Parry Hoot" because the water-bound log-drivers hereabouts chose this as the place to get drunk in. Things are more genteel today and the town has become a popular stopover for boats roaming the Thirty Thousand Islands out in the bay. Parry Sound is the home port of the "Island Queen", which squeezes through these same islands in a spectacular **cruise** that has become one of the region's most popular attractions (June to mid-Oct 1–2 daily; 3hr; $25; ☎705/746-2311 or 1-800/506-2628; ⓦwww.island-queen.com). The jetty for the Island Queen is at Government Wharf, just below the centre of town at the end of Bay St. Otherwise, Parry Sound is short of specific sights, though its pocket-sized harbour is overshadowed by a splendid Edwardian railway **trestle bridge** and the few blocks that make up the commercial centre – along and around **James St** – are dotted with good-looking old brick and stone buildings. In addition, the town rustles up the well-respected **Festival of the Sound** of classical music (details on ☎705/746-2410 or 1-866/364-0061, ⓦwww.festivalofthesound.on.ca), in the second half of July and early August.

Parry Sound is on the Ontario Northland (☎1-800/461-8558) **bus** route from Toronto to Sudbury. Buses pull into Richard's Coffee House, 119 Bowes St, well to the east of the town centre. To get downtown from here, call Parry Sound Taxi (☎705/746-1221). The **tourist office** is in the former railway station at 70 Church St (May–Sept Mon–Thurs 8am–4pm, Fri 8am–6pm, Sat 10am–2pm; ☎705/746-4213 or 1-800/461-4261). From here, it's 800m south along Church St to the centre and 300m more to Government Wharf. The tourist office has details of local accommodation including several central **B&Bs**. One especially good option is the *Victoria Manor*, in a handsome old house with turrets and with a lovely garden at 43 Church St and Rosetta (☎705/746-5399, ⓦwww.solutionsforu.com/victoria; ❹). *The Comfort Inn* (☎705/746-6221, ⓦwww.choicehotels.ca; ❸) is east of the centre on the way out to Hwy 69 at 120 Bowes St. For **food**, head for *The Country Gourmet*, in the centre at 65 James St (Mon–Fri 7am–5pm & Sat 8am–4pm) – a smashing deli and bakery selling the tastiest of meals and snacks. In the evening, try the *Bay St Café* (☎705/746-2882), down by Government Wharf at 22 Bay St, where the menu runs from pizza and sandwiches to fish and chips.

Killbear Provincial Park

The wild Georgian Bay shoreline, formed by glaciers that scoured the rock and dumped mighty boulders onto its long beaches, is seen to fine advantage in **Killbear Provincial Park**, reached by driving 18km north from Parry Sound on Hwy 69 then 20km southwest on Route 559. The park occupies a tapering peninsula, with spindly cedars and black spruce clinging precariously to a shoreline of pink-granite outcrops, the classic Canadian Shield scenery that was beloved by Tom Thomson (see p.96). The rugged, rocky interior of the park is a forest of maple, beech and yellow birch. The easy 3.5km loop of the **Lookout Point Trail**, which slips through forest to reach a lookout across Parry Sound, is the best of the park's three short hiking trails; allow a couple of hours. Killbear has seven **campsites**, (mid-May to early Oct; reservations on ☎705/342-5492), some by the water, others in the forest, some with showers, others not, and all costing between $18 and $24.

Central Ontario

Lying between Lake Ontario's northern shore and the Ottawa River Valley, **central Ontario** is largely defined by the **Canadian Shield**, whose endless forests, myriad lakes and poor soils dip down from the north in a giant wedge. This hostile terrain has kept settlement down to a minimum, though latterly the very wildness of the land has attracted thousands of Canadian holiday-makers, who come here to hunker down in their lakeside cottages. The centre of all this holiday activity is the **Muskoka Lakes**, a skein of narrow lakes and rivers whose main supply towns – **Gravenhurst** and **Bracebridge** – lie on Hwy 11. Staying in a cottage or a resort is the one sure-fire way of appreciating the beauty of the area, but passing visitors are better off heading further north to the wondrous expanse of **Algonquin Provincial Park** with its abundant wildlife and extraordinarily large network of canoe routes. The implacability of the Shield breaks up as it approaches the **St Lawrence River** at the east end of Lake Ontario and it's here you'll find a string of interesting historic towns. The pick is **Kingston**, founded by United Empire Loyalists (see p.437) and renowned for its fine limestone buildings, not to mention its good restaurants and quality B&Bs. Kingston is also useful as a stepping stone on the road east to either Montréal (see p.224) or **Ottawa**, Canada's engaging capital city, which boasts some of the country's finest museums and a first-rate restaurant and bar scene.

Public transport along the St Lawrence River is excellent by bus and quite good by rail. Things get trickier in the Muskoka Lakes area, but Ontario Northland (☎1-800/461-8558, ⓦwww.webusit.com) operates two routes from Toronto, one linking Orillia, Parry Sound and Sudbury, the other Orillia, Gravenhurst, Bracebridge, Huntsville (for Algonquin Park) and North Bay.

The Muskoka Lakes

The main route from Toronto to Algonquin Provincial Park passes through the **Muskoka Lakes**, a region of more than 1500 lakes and hundreds of urbanite **cottage** retreats. Named after an Ojibwa chief, Mesqua-Ukee, who settled here with his people after aiding the British during the War of 1812, the area was opened to tourism in 1860, when two hikers made the two-day trek from Toronto to a small Ojibwa settlement at what is now Gravenhurst. By the 1890s the lakes had become the haunt of wealthy families from Southern Ontario and although things are more democratic today, this is still primarily the preserve of the well heeled. The main access towns to the Muskoka Lakes – **Gravenhurst**, **Bracebridge** and **Huntsville** – are strung out along Hwy 11. None has much to offer the passing visitor and neither, for that matter, do the lakes. Just driving round is well-nigh pointless and you're much better off either aiming for a cottage (if you're lucky enough to have been invited) or heading for one of the area's splendid hotel resorts, one of the best being the Sherwood Inn near **Port Carling**.

Public transport is limited to Hwy 11 with Ontario Northland **buses** (☎1-800/461-8558) going to all three major Muskoka towns on their way from Toronto to North Bay. Huntsville and Gravenhurst can also be reached by **rail**.

Gravenhurst

The gateway to Muskoka is humdrum **GRAVENHURST**, sited at the southern end of Lake Muskoka, some 170km north of Toronto. Cottagers whizz in and out to collect supplies and arrive in numbers for the **Muskoka Winter Carnival**, in late February, when all manner of events are held from demolition derbies to ice-sculpture competitions. Apart from carnival time, the main attraction is the **Bethune Memorial House**, 235 John St N (tours: June–Oct daily 10am–4pm; Nov–May Mon–Fri 1–4pm; $3.50), the birthplace of

The beaver

The **beaver** is the national animal of Canada: it appeared on the first postage stamp issued by the colony in 1851, and now features on the back of the 5¢ piece. There was nothing sentimental about this choice – beaver pelts kick-started the colonial economy – and only recently has the beaver been treated with restraint and protected from being indiscriminately bumped off.

Beavers are aquatic rodents, growing to around 75cm long and weighing about 35kg. Native Canadians hunted the beaver for its thick, soft **pelt**, composed of long guard hairs and a dense undercoat, to use for clothing. Thereafter, European fur traders soon realized the value of beaver pelts, particularly in the manufacture of the all-weather, all-purpose **hat** worn by every man of any substance. To keep up with demand the beaver was extensively trapped, and the *voyageurs* pushed further and further west along the lake and river systems in pursuit of the animal, thereby opening up much of the interior. The beaver was hunted to the point of extinction in much of eastern Canada, but was reprieved when the beaver hat went out of fashion in the late nineteenth century; today beavers are comparatively commonplace.

Beavers start to build their **dams**, which can be up to 700m wide, by strategically felling one tree across a stream. This catches silt and driftwood and the beaver then reinforces the barrier with sticks, stones, grass and mud, which is laboriously smoothed in as a binding element. The **lodge** is constructed simultaneously; sometimes it forms part of the dam and sometimes it is fixed to the shore or an island in the pond. It is about 2m in diameter and has two entrances – one accessible from land and one from underwater – both for its own convenience and to be able to escape its predators in any emergency. Lodges are topped with grass thatch and a good layer of mud, which freezes in winter, making them virtually impenetrable. During the autumn, the beaver stocks its **pond** with the soft-bark trees and saplings that make up its diet. It drags them below the water line and anchors them to the mud at the bottom before retiring to the lodge for the winter, only emerging to get food from the pond or repair the dam. Beaver lakes are not, however, the tree-fringed paradises portrayed by some nature-film makers; a mud-banked pond, surrounded by untidily felled trees and with a bedraggled-looking domed heap of sticks and sludge somewhere along its banks is often nearer the mark.

Norman Bethune (1890–1939), a doctor who introduced Western medicine to the Chinese in the 1930s and invented mobile blood-transfusion units. The house has been restored to its appearance in 1890 and has displays on Bethune's considerable accomplishments – he was even praised by Chairman Mao – all detailed in English, French and Chinese. Afterwards, you could hop aboard RMS *Segwun*, a 105-year-old steamship – the oldest still operating in North America – that cruises up Lake Muskoka from the town wharf (mid-June to mid-Oct daily; $12 for a 1hr cruise up to $35 for 4hr; ☎705/687-6667), giving fine views of the hills and its many mansions. In the unlikely event you decide to **stay**, aim for the *Pinedale Inn*, 200 Pinedale Lane (☎705/687-2822; ❹), a well-maintained motel on the shore of Gull Lake surrounded by pine trees and with rooms that have kitchenettes and bathrooms. For **food**, head for either the pleasant *White Pine Café*, on the main street in a tastefully converted old general store at 195 Muskoka Rd S, or *Sloan's*, 155 Muskoka Rd S, which has been here as long as Gravenhurst, and serves a divine blueberry pie.

Bracebridge and Port Carling

BRACEBRIDGE, situated 25km north of Gravenhurst, prides itself on being "Halfway to the North Pole" – and on that basis is allegedly the summer home of Santa Claus, who hangs out amongst the theme-park rides of **Santa's Village** just southwest of town (late June to Aug daily 10am–6pm; adults and children over 5 $16.95, 2–4s $11.95, under 2s and reindeer free). There's not much else, though the short main drag, **Manitoba St**, is lined with a pleasant ensemble of Victorian red-bricks, worth at least a few minutes. The **tourist office**, in the mews by the bridge at the foot of Manitoba St (April–Sept Mon–Sat 9am–5pm & Sun 10am–4pm; Oct–March Mon–Fri 9am–5pm & Sat 10am–4pm; ☎705/645-8121, ⊕www.bracebeidgechamber.com), has town maps and buckets of local information.

Driving west from Bracebridge along Hwy 118, it's about 25km to the lakeside hamlet of **PORT CARLING**, the nearest settlement to one of the region's finest hotel–resorts, the *Delta Sherwood Inn*, 1090 Sherwood Rd (☎1-800/461-4454, ⊕www.deltahotels.com; ❽ all inclusive), a handsome complex of luxurious chalet-villas set deep in the Muskoka woods – call for directions. Each of the guest rooms is kitted out in smart modern style and the food, served in the main lodge, is first-rate.

Huntsville

Workaday **HUNTSVILLE**, 35km beyond Bracebridge on Hwy 11, is as near as the buses and trains get to Algonquin Park. **Ontario Northland buses** (☎1-800/461-8558) pull into the centre at Main and Centre St, **VIA trains** pause at the station about 600m away. Hammond Transportation runs a reliable if fairly infrequent minibus service on into Algonquin Provincial Park, but if you find yourself stuck here in town, head for the inexpensive chain **motels** lined up along King William St. Reliable options here include the *Comfort Inn*, at no. 86 (☎705/789-1701 or 1-866/398-7480, ⊕www.comfortinnslakelands.com; ❹), and the *King William Inn* at no. 23 (☎705/789-9661 or 1-888/995-9169, ⊕www.kingwilliaminn.com; ❹).

Algonquin Provincial Park

Created in 1893 at the behest of logging companies keen to keep the farmers out, **Algonquin Provincial Park** is Ontario's oldest and largest provincial park and for many is the quintessential Canadian landscape. Located on the southern edge of the Canadian Shield, the park straddles a **transitional zone**, with the hilly two-thirds to the west covered in a hardwood forest of sugar maple, beech and yellow birch, whilst in the drier eastern part jack pines, white pines and red pines predominate. Throughout the park, the lakes and rocky rounded hills are interspersed with black spruce bogs, a type of vegetation typical of areas far further north. Canoeing is very popular here and with an astounding 1600km of routes there's a good chance of avoiding all contact for days on end. **Wildlife** is as varied as the flora – any trip to Algonquin is characterized by the echo of birdsong, from the loons' ghostly call to the screech of ravens. Beavers, moose, black bears and raccoons are all resident, as are white-tailed deer, whose population thrives on the young shoots that replace the trees felled by the park's loggers. Public "howling parties" – which can attract up to 2000 people – set off into the wilderness during August in search of **timber wolves**, or rather their howls: many of the rangers are so good at howling that they can get the animals to reply.

Access to the park is via either the **West Gate**, 45km from Huntsville on Hwy 60, or – if you are arriving from Ottawa and points east – the **East Gate**.

A day-pass costs $12 per vehicle. The two gates are linked by the 56km-long **Parkway Corridor** – also known as the Frank McDougall Parkway – the park's only road. Away from the corridor, walking and canoeing are the only means of transport. The well-signposted main **visitor centre** is 43km inside the park from the West Gate (late April to Oct daily 10am–5pm, July & Aug till 9pm; Nov to late April Sat & Sun 10am–5pm; ℡705/633-5572, www.algonquinpark.on.ca). Besides the usual gift shop, it holds a series of dioramas explaining the park's general and natural history. The visitor centre also has a comprehensive range of literature describing every aspect of the park, from maps and detailed hiking trail and canoeing route guides through to booklets on native folklore. The **park offices** at both the West and East gates have trail descriptions and other park information, but there's not so wide a range. Furthermore, individual trail guides are available at most trailheads. If you're heading for the backcountry, pick up **food and water** before you get here as outlets in the park are few and far between. In all cases, **backcountry camping** requires a permit. These are available at both the West and East gates and at the visitor centre ($8 per person per night).

For **all-in tours**, *Call of the Wild*, 23 Edward St in Markham (℡905/471-9453 or 1-800/776-9453, www.callofthewild.ca), runs personalized and relaxed adventure canoe trips in the park (three/four/five days: $350/450/550). Prices include all meals, permits, equipment and transport from Toronto. It's essential to book in advance. If you're reliant on **public transport**, the nearest you'll get by train or bus is Huntsville (see p.161). However, Hammond Transportation (℡705/645-5431, www.hammondtransportation.com) operates the Algonquin Park Shuttle from Huntsville to points along the Parkway Corridor in July and August (3 weekly; $20).

The Parkway Corridor

Along the Parkway Corridor, the location of trailheads and campsites is indicated by distances from the West Gate. Ten **day-hikes** begin beside the road and of these the two-kilometre **Beaver Pond Trail** (km 45) is a rugged but easy trail that takes you past huge beaver dams, while the equally short but steeper **Lookout Trail** (km 39) gives a remarkable view of the park. For a longer trail with greater chances of spotting wildlife, the eleven-kilometre **Mizzy Lake Trail** (km 15) is recommended. Spare time also for the illuminating **Algonquin Logging Museum** (mid-May to mid-Oct daily 9am–5pm; free with day-pass), just inside the East Gate at km 54.5. Here, an easy 1.3km loop trail threads past some fascinating old logging leftovers, including a tugboat, a locomotive, sawlog camp and sleighs.

Strung along the Parkway Corridor are eight park **campsites**. The less popular sites are those that prohibit motorboats – namely Canisbay Lake (km 23; mid-May to early Oct), Coon Lake (km 40; mid-June to Aug) and Kearney Lake (km 37; mid-June to Aug). Year-round camping is only available at Mew Lake (km 30). Car camping sites, holding up to six people, cost $20–28. **Reservations** are well-nigh essential and cost $9. To make an advance reservation, contact Ontario Parks (℡1-888/668-7275, www.ontarioparks.com). The rangers who roamed the park in its early years built dozens of **log cabins**, some of which have survived and are now rented out for $50–80 for two people per night. Contact the park authorities for further details.

Also lining the Parkway Corridor are several privately owned **lodges** and **mini-resorts**, ranging from the simple and unaffected to the comparatively lavish. One of the best is *Killarney Lodge* (℡705/633-5551, www .killarneylodge.com; ❽ including all meals; May to mid-Oct), whose cosy, prettily painted log cabins dot a spindly promontory that hooks out into the Lake of Two Rivers at km 32. A second good option is *Bartlett Lodge* (℡705/633-5543, 🖳www.bartlettlodge.com; ❼ including all meals), comprising a scattering of older cabins overlooking Cache Lake at km 23. The lodge can only be reached by boat – pick up the marked phone at the jetty and someone will come to pick you up.

The park interior

The park interior is best explored by **canoe**, and there are several **outfitters** dotted along the Parkway Corridor. One of the best is the Portage Store at Canoe Lake, km 14 (daily: May, Sept & early Oct 8am–7pm; June–Aug 7am–9pm; in summer ℡705/633-5622, in winter 705/789-3645, 🖳www.portagestore.com). **Rates** vary enormously depending on the sort of canoe you rent, but the simplest models cost $20 per day, $17 per day for five days and more. The Portage Store also rents out tents, life vests and all the associated canoeist's tackle and organizes guided canoe trips. Advance reservations are pretty much essential. Note also that given Algonquin's immense popularity, canoeing is best avoided at holiday weekends: horror stories abound of three-hour jams of canoeists waiting their turn to tackle the portages between some of the more accessible lakes. Incidentally, Canoe Lake was where the artist Tom Thomson (see p.96) drowned in 1917 – and there's a monument to him about forty-minutes' canoe paddle from the Portage Store.

If you don't fancy canoeing, the interior can also be experienced on either of two long-distance hiking trails. The **Western Uplands Backpacking Trail** (km 2.5) is composed of a series of loops that allow you to construct a hike of up to 71km, while the equally challenging **Highland Backpacking Trail** (km 29) has loops of up to 35km.

Kingston

Birthplace of the rock singer Bryan Adams but prouder of its handsome limestone buildings, the town of **KINGSTON**, a fast 260km east of Toronto along Hwy 401, is the largest and most enticing of the communities along the northern shore of Lake Ontario. It occupies an attractive and strategically important position where the lake narrows into the St Lawrence River, its potential first recognized by the French who built a fortified fur-trading post here in 1673. It was not a success. The commander of **Fort Frontenac**, the Comte de Frontenac, managed to argue with just about everybody, and his deputy, Denonville, pursued a risky sideline in kidnapping, inviting local Iroquois to the fort and then forcibly shipping them to France as curiosities. Nevertheless, the fort struggled on until 1758 when it fell to a combined force of British, Americans and Iroquois, a victory soon followed by an influx of United Empire Loyalists, who promptly developed Kingston – as they renamed it – into a major shipbuilding centre and naval base. The money rolled in and the future looked rosy when the completion of the Rideau Canal (see p.167), linking Kingston with Ottawa in 1832, opened up its hinterland. Indeed, Kingston became the capital of Canada in 1841 and although it lost this distinction just three years later it remained the region's most important town until the end of the nineteenth century. In recent years, Kingston – and its 110,000 inhabitants – has had as many economic downs as ups, but it does benefit from the presence of **Queen's University**, one of Canada's most prestigious academic

KINGSTON

▲ Thousand Islands Parkway, Prescott & Gananoque

◀ Ottawa & Montréal

◀ Bus Station

◀ Train Station

Cataraqui River

Navy Bay

Kingston Harbour

Lake Ontario

Fort Henry

Royal Military College

Fort Frederick Museum

Point Frederick

Thousand Islands Cruises

City Hall

Confederation Park

Marine Museum of the Great Lakes

St George

Market Square

Frontenac County Courthouse

QUEEN'S UNIVERSITY
Agnes Etherington Arts Centre

Victoria Park

City Park

Murney Tower Museum

MacDonald Park

Breakwater Park

Bellevue House

NIAGARA PARK

MAIN STREET

FORT HENRY DRIVE

PRECISION DRIVE

VALOUR DRIVE

LA SALLE CAUSEWAY

PLACE D'ARMES

WELLINGTON ST

BARRACK ST

RIDEAU STREET

CATARAQUI ST

CHARLES STREET

JAMES ST

MONTREAL STREET

JOHN STREET

BAGLAN ROAD

PATRICK STREET

SYDENHAM STREET

ORDNANCE ST

BAY STREET

QUEEN STREET

BROCK STREET

PRINCESS STREET

CLERGY STREET

WILLIAM STREET

JOHNSON STREET

EARL STREET

COURT STREET

KING STREET EAST

ONTARIO STREET

WELLINGTON ST

BAGOT STREET

KING STREET

LOWER UNION STREET

WEST STREET

COWDY STREET

PINE STREET

YORK STREET

BARRIE STREET

ARCH STREET

GEORGE ST

ADELAIDE STREET

HAMILTON STREET

ELM STREET

COLBURNE STREET

DIVISION STREET

DIVISION STREET

UNIVERSITY AVENUE

ALFRED STREET

ALFRED STREET

FRONTENAC STREET

FRONTENAC STREET

ALBERT STREET

LWR ALBERT ST

QUEEN'S CRESCENT

STUART STREET

LWR UNIVERSITY

UNION STREET

KING STREET WEST

COLLINGWOOD STREET

BEVERLEY STREET

CONCESSION STREET

VICTORIA STREET

NELSON STREET

MACK STREET

BROCK STREET

JOHNSON STREET

EARL STREET

KENSINGTON ST

EDGEHILL ST

CENTRE STREET

PARK STREET

MACDONNELL STREET

NAPIER STREET

DUNDAS STREET

WILLINGDON AVENUE

REGENT STREET

ELLERBECK STREET

LIVINGSTON AVENUE

PEMBROKE STREET

COLLEGE STREET

VICTORIA STREET

500 m

0

RESTAURANTS, CAFÉS & BARS	
Chez Piggy	7
Coffee and Co.	5
Curry Village	2
Kingston Brewing Company	11
Le Chien Noir	8
Minos Restaurant	9
Prince George Hotel	10
Second Cup	1
Sleepless Goat	3
Toucan	6
White Mountain Ice-Cream	12
Windmills Café	4

ACCOMMODATION	
Alexander Henry B&B	H
Hochelaga Inn	F
Holiday Inn Kingston Waterfront	B
Louise House	A
Summer Hostel	C
Painted Lady Inn	
Radisson Plaza Kingston	G
Rosemount B&B Inn	E
Secret Garden B&B	D

institutions, and of the **Royal Military College**, the country's answer to Sandhurst and West Point.

Central Kingston's medley of old buildings displays every architectural foible admired by the Victorians, from neo–Gothic mansions with high gables and perky dormer windows to elegant Italianate villas. Cream of the crop, however, are the city's Neoclassical limestone buildings – most notably **City Hall** and the **Cathedral of St George**. Kingston also holds the first-rate **Agnes Etherington Art Centre** gallery and **Bellevue House**, once the home of Prime Minister Sir John A. Macdonald. Add to this several delicious **B&Bs**, a cluster of good **restaurants** and scenic **boat trips** round the **Thousand Islands** just offshore, and you have a town that is well worth a couple of days.

Arrival, information and accommodation

Trains from Toronto (4–6 daily; 2hrs 40mins) terminate at the VIA Rail **station** on Hwy 2, an inconvenient 7km northwest of the city at the junction of Princess and Counter streets; Kingston Transit bus #4 (Mon–Sat only; every 30mins) connects with downtown Kingston. The terminus for long-distance Coach Canada **buses** is on the corner of Division and Counter streets, about 6km to the north of the city centre; Kingston Transit bus #2 (Mon–Sat only; hourly) runs downtown from here. Kingston Transit's **local bus** information line is ☎613/546-0000. Kingston's helpful **tourist office** is in the centre of the city, across from the waterfront at 209 Ontario St (June–Aug daily 9am–7pm; May & Sept–April daily 9am–5pm; Oct–April Mon–Fri 9am–5pm, Sat & Sun 10am–1pm; ☎613/548-4415 or 1-888/855-4555, ⓦwww .kingstoncanada.com). It has a wide range of local and regional information and operates a free room reservation service.

Kingston offers a full range of **guided tours**. Top of the list is **cruises** out amongst the Thousand Islands from the dock at the foot of Brock St. The islands, which litter the St Lawrence River as it leaves Lake Ontario, range from tiny hunks of rock to much larger islands with thick forest and lavish second homes. It's a pretty cruise at any time of the year, but especially so in autumn when the leaves turn. Several companies offer cruises, but the benchmark is set by Kingston 1000 Islands Cruises (☎613/549-5544, ⓦwww.1000islandscruises.ca), whose three-hour cruises in a replica steamboat, the *Island Queen*, are as good as any (mid-May to mid-Oct 1–2 daily; $22.50). Another enjoyable outing is the Haunted Walk of Kingston, a 90-minute narrated stroll through the older parts of town beginning in the centre outside the Prince George Hotel (early May to Oct 1–2 daily; $12; ☎613/549-6366). Before the creation of the St Lawrence Seaway in the 1950s regulated the depth of Lake Ontario and flooded its various rapids, the waters off Kingston had been extremely treacherous; the bottom of the lake is still dotted with shipwrecks. The tourist office publishes an excellent booklet explaining what is where and several companies rent out **diving** gear and organize diving trips – one is Kingsdive, 119 Princess St (☎613/542-2892).

Kingston has an excellent range of **accommodation**, much of it in or near the city centre. The best places are those **inns** and **B&Bs** that occupy grand old buildings, but there are less expensive options too, including a **hostel** and – most unusual of the lot – beds/berths in a decommissioned **coastguard ship**. At the top end of the market, advance reservations are advised in July and August.

Hotels and inns

Hochelaga Inn 24 Sydenham St ☎613/549-5534 or 1-800/267-0525, ⓦwww.someplacesdifferent.com. This twenty-room inn occupies a good-looking Victorian mansion with a playful central tower, bay windows and wraparound veranda. There are 23 guest rooms, all en suite, and although the furnishings and fittings are rather pedestrian, each is very comfortable. In a residential area within easy walking distance of the centre. ❼

Holiday Inn Kingston Waterfront 1 Princess St ☎613/549-8400 or 1-800/465-4329, ⓦwww .kingstonholidayinn.com. Not the most distinctive of the city's hotels, for sure, but the rooms are comfortable enough and it couldn't be more convenient for the centre. Most rooms have lake views. ❻

Painted Lady Inn 181 William St ☎613/545-0422, ⓦwww.paintedladyinn.on.ca. Appealing Victorian redbrick with three storeys and an inviting porch has seven well-maintained guest rooms, all en suite. Central location. ❹

Radisson Plaza Kingston Harbourfront Hotel 1 Johnson St ☎613/549-8100 or 1-888/548-6726, ⓦwww.radissonkingston.com. Smart, chain hotel with standard-issue modern furnishings and fittings, but great views out over Lake Ontario and the marina. ❼

Rosemount B&B Inn 46 Sydenham St ☎613/531-8844 or 1-888/871-8844, ⓦwww.rosemountinn.com. An eminently appealing B&B in a strikingly handsome, distinctively Italianate old limestone villa – arguably Kingston's finest. The *Rosemount* has nine guest rooms, all en suite, decorated in period style. The breakfasts are delicious. ❻

Secret Garden B&B 73 Sydenham St ☎613/531-9884 or 1-877/723-1888, ⓦwww.the-secret -garden.com. One of Kingston's most enjoyable B&Bs, there are six extremely comfortable guest rooms here, all en suite and each decorated in immaculate style. The house itself is a fetching Victorian building of timber and brick with verandas and porches and a splendid bay-windowed tower. Faces the slender limestone symmetries of Sydenham St United Church. Recommended. ❺

Ship

Alexander Henry Bed and Breakfast 55 Ontario St ☎613/542-2261, ⓦwww.marmuseum.ca. Kingston's most unusual lodgings are provided here in this former coastguard ice-breaker, moored downtown next to the Marine Museum. Berths vary from a bunk in a tiny cabin ($35 per person) to more comfortable quarters ($80–100 for a two-person cabin). The ship itself dates from the 1960s and is a sturdy affair with narrow stairways and corridors and the salty taste of the sea. Open mid-May to late Sept. ❸

Hostel

Louise House Summer Hostel (HI) 329 Johnson St at Barrie ☎613/531-8237, ⓔkingston@ hihostels.ca. This Queen's University residence is used as an HI-affiliated hostel during the summer. Sixty beds in male, female and co-ed sleeping areas, plus laundry facilities and breakfast at $20 per person per night – a few dollars more for non-HI members. Handy for the city centre. Open May to late Aug.

The City

The obvious place to start a visit is **City Hall** (guided tours late May to Oct Mon–Fri 10am–4pm, plus Sat & Sun in July & Aug 11am–3pm; 30mins; free), a copper-domed, stone extravagance which, with its imposing Neoclassical columns and portico, dominates the waterfront as was intended – a suitably grand structure for what was scheduled to be the Canadian Parliament. By the time the building was completed in 1844, however, Kingston had lost its capital status and – faced with colossal bills – the city council had to make some quick adjustments, filling the empty corridors with shops and stalls and even a saloon. Things are more sedate today, with municipal offices occupying most of the space, but the tour provides a fascinating insight into the development of the city and includes a trip up the **clock tower** via a magnificent circular stairway. Back outside, the **Market Square**, at the back of City Hall, is home to an excellent open-air **farmers' market** on Tuesdays, Thursdays and Saturdays, while on summer Sundays the square is given over to craft and antiques stalls. In front of City Hall is the site of the original French outpost and this is now marked by the waterfront **Confederation Park**, whose manicured lawns run behind the harbour with its marina and squat, nineteenth-century Martello

1

Kingston to Ottawa via the Rideau Canal

Heading on **from Kingston to Ottawa**, the obvious route is east along Hwy 401 and then north up Hwy 416, a fast journey of around 175km. With more time, however, it's worth considering taking **Hwy 15** and then, at Smiths Falls, **Hwy 43** (and ultimately hwys 2, 5, 13 and 73) inland from Kingston as these minor roads follow much of the route of the **Rideau Canal**. Completed in 1832 after a mere six years' work, the 120-mile canal – and its 27 lock stations – cuts through the chunk of coniferous and deciduous forest, bogs, limestone plains and granite ridges that separate Ottawa and Kingston. It was intended to provide safe inland transport at a time of poor Anglo-American relations, but after the political situation improved it developed as an important route for regional commerce. The canal's construction led to the development of Bytown, renamed Ottawa in 1855, but in the second half of the nineteenth century the railways made it obsolete. Today, it is plied by holiday traffic and motorists visit its **locks**. The two most interesting are **Kingston Mills** (Locks 46–49), 12km inland from Kingston and, even better, **Jones Falls** (Locks 39–42), about 50km from Kingston. At the latter, the complex includes four locks, a dam, a former blacksmith's forge and a defensible lockmaster's house.

To break the journey, aim for the pleasant little canalside town of **MERRICKVILLE** (Locks 21–23), 100km or so from Kingston. A popular tourist spot, there are several places to stay here, including *Sam Jakes Inn*, in a good-looking Victorian building with thirty guest rooms at 118 Main St E (☏613/269-3711 or 1-800/567-4667, Ⓦwww.samjakesinn.com; ❻), and the *Nicholson House B&B*, in another attractive old building with spick and span decor at 378 Heritage Rd (☏613/269-2545, Ⓦwww.bbcanada.com/2202; ❸).

Alternatively, it takes five days to get from Kingston to Ottawa **by boat** on the Rideau Canal with Kawartha Voyageur (☏1-800/561-5767, Ⓦwww.ontariowaterwayscruises .com) at a cost of $1400; there are between four and six cruises monthly from early May to late October.

tower. Here also, from the dock at the foot of Brock St, there are regular **cruises** out amongst the Thousand Islands (see p.170).

Back on dry land, it's a couple of minutes' walk from Confederation Park to Kingston's finest limestone building, the **Anglican Cathedral of St George**, at King St and Johnson (mid-April to Sept Mon–Thurs 10am–4pm, Fri 10am–7pm & Sat 10am–1pm; Oct to mid-April Mon–Fri 1–4pm; free). Dating from the 1820s, the graceful lines of the cathedral, with its Neoclassical portico and dainty domes, are deceptively uniform, for the church was remodelled on several occasions, notably after severe fire damage in 1899. The capacious interior holds some delightful Tiffany stained-glass windows and, attached to the wall of the nave, a plain **memorial** to Molly Brant (1736–97), a Mohawk leader and sister of Joseph Brant (see p.120). From the cathedral, it's a brief stroll to the main commercial drag, **Princess St**, whose assorted shops, offices and cafés stretch up from the lakeshore. Alternatively, it's a short hop back to the waterfront and the **Marine Museum of the Great Lakes** (June–Oct daily 10am–5pm; Nov–May Mon–Fri 10am–4pm; $4.25), a somewhat dowdy accumulation of maritime bygones, where the shipbuilders' gallery is of some mild interest. Moored alongside is the unusual *Alexander Henry Bed and Breakfast*.

From the corner of Princess and King streets, it's a good ten-minute stroll west to the **Murney Tower Museum**, on Barrie St (mid-May to Aug daily 10am–5pm; $2). The most impressive of four such towers built in Kingston to defend the dockyards against an anticipated US attack, during the Oregon

Crisis of 1846–47, this one holds incidental military memorabilia including old weapons, uniforms and re-created nineteenth-century living quarters. The design of the tower, built as a combined barracks, battery and storehouse, was copied from a Corsican tower (at Martello Point) which had proved particularly troublesome to the British navy. A self-contained, semi-self-sufficient defensive structure with thick walls and a protected entrance, the Martello design proved so successful that towers like this were built throughout the empire, only becoming obsolete in the 1870s with advances in artillery technology. Incidentally, on Christmas Day 1885, members of the Royal Canadian Rifles regiment left the tower equipped with their field hockey sticks and a lacrosse ball, skidding round the frozen lake and thereby inventing the sport that has become a national passion.

Striking inland up Barrie St, with City Park on the right, it's a ten-minute walk to the top of the park, where the **Frontenac County Courthouse** of 1858 is another grand limestone pile whose whopping Neoclassical portico is fronted by a fanciful water fountain and surmounted by a copper dome. Head west from here, along Union St, and you'll soon be in the midst of the **Queen's University** campus, whose various sturdy stone college buildings fan out in all directions. The place to aim for is the first-rate **Agnes Etherington Art Centre**, on the corner of University Ave and Queen's Crescent (Tues–Fri 10am–4.30pm, Sat & Sun 1–5pm; $4). The gallery has an excellent reputation for its temporary exhibitions, so paintings are regularly rotated, but the first room (Room 1) usually kicks off in dramatic style with a vivid selection of Canadian Abstract paintings (1940–60), with French-speaking artists on one side and English-speaking artists on the other. Beyond, there is a strong showing for the **Group of Seven**, including a striking *Evening Solitude* by **Lawren Harris** and the carpet-like, rolling fields of **Lismer**'s *Quebec Village*, while **Tom Thomson** weighs in with his studied *Autumn, Algonquin Park*. Other exhibits to look out for are the **Inuit** prints of Kenojuak and Pitseolak – two of the best-known Inuit artists of modern times – as well as heritage **quilts** from eastern Ontario, which date back to 1820, and an excellent collection of West African sculpture.

Out of the centre

Born in Glasgow, **Sir John A. Macdonald** (1815–91) emigrated to Canada in his youth, settling in Kingston, where he became a successful corporate lawyer, an MP – representing the town for well-nigh forty years – and ultimately prime minister (1867–73 and 1887–91). A shrewd and forceful man, Macdonald played a leading role in Canada's Confederation, with a little arm-twisting here and a little charming there, to ensure the grand plan went through. In the 1840s, Macdonald rented **Bellevue House** (daily: April–May & Sept 10am–5pm; June–Aug 9am–6pm; $3.50), a bizarrely asymmetrical, pagoda-shaped building located about 2km to the west of the city centre, beyond the university campus, at 35 Centre St. The idea was that the country air would improve the health of Macdonald's wife, Isabella, whose tuberculosis was made worse by the treatment – laudanum. Isabella never returned to good health and died after years as an invalid, leaving Macdonald alone (with the bottle). Both the house and gardens have been restored to the period of the late 1840s, when the Macdonalds lived here.

The twin headlands to the east of downtown Kingston over the Lasalle Bridge have long been used by the military. The first is home to the **Royal Military College**, the training academy for officers of all three services; the second to **Fort Henry National Historic Site** (mid-May to Sept daily

10am–5pm; $11; programme details on ☎613/542-7388), a large and imposing fortress built to keep the Americans at bay after the War of 1812. The fort's thick stone-and-earth ramparts are flush with the lie of the land to protect against artillery bombardment, but as it turned out it was all a waste of time and money. Anglo-American relations improved and the fort never saw a shot fired in anger, so when the last garrison upped sticks at the end of the nineteenth century, the fortress fell into disrepair. Restored in 1938, the fort's focus is now the large **parade ground**, where students dress up in military gear and fill the fort with the smoke of muskets and cannons and the racket of bugles, drums and fifes. Everything on offer is aimed at families, and there's masses for kids to do, from drill parades and helping with the gun salute, to participating in lessons in a Victorian schoolroom and doing the laundry. If this doesn't appeal you can explore the ramparts, with their vistas of Lake Ontario and the Thousand Islands, and examine the fort's magazines, kitchens and officers' quarters. Proto-militarists can also double their fun by visiting the Royal Military College's **Fort Frederick Museum** (July & Aug daily 10am–5pm; donation), a Martello tower stuffed with military bric-a-brac.

Eating and drinking

For a city its size, Kingston has a good supply of quality **restaurants** and a wide range of inexpensive **cafés**, many of which prosper from the large student population. The city also has several lively British- and Irish-style **pubs** and a modest live music scene: for **listings**, see the bimonthly *Key to Kingston*, available from major hotels, restaurants and the tourist office.

Cafés and restaurants

Chez Piggy 68 Princess St at King St E ☎613/549-7673. Kingston's best-known restaurant is housed in restored stables dating from 1810. The patio is packed in summer and the attractive interior has handcrafted pine and limestone walls. The wide-ranging menu features all manner of main courses, from Thai and Vietnamese through to South American and standard North American dishes. The best place in town; main courses average around $19.

Coffee & Co 53 Princess St. Standard-issue, modern coffee house, but the coffees are tangy and there's the added bonus of having Belgian *Godiva* chocolates on sale.

Curry Village 169A Princess St ☎613/542-5010. Popular, reasonably priced Indian restaurant above a shoe shop. Just north of Bagot St. Reservations recommended.

Le Chien Noir 69 Brock St ☎613/549-5635. Spirited bar-cum-bistro with smart, modern decor and a fancy – some would say over-elaborate – menu featuring some unusual combinations. Main courses average around $20.

Minos Restaurant 248 Ontario St at Brock ☎613/548-4654. All the Greek favourites at this long-established downtown restaurant. Don't be deterred by the ugliness of the building. Main courses $10–20.

Second Cup 251 Princess St. Downtown branch of this reliable coffee-house chain.

Sleepless Goat 91 Princess St at Wellington. Laid-back bakery-cum-café serving good sandwiches, delicious breads and rolls, and great desserts, all at affordable prices.

White Mountain Ice-Cream 176 Ontario St. Seriously rich home-made ice cream and waffle cones. Try the White Mountain special – vanilla dotted with chocolate, pecan and maple brittle.

Windmills Café 184 Princess St at Montréal. Good cakes and a wide-ranging menu at this agreeable café-restaurant, which serves up everything from tapas and pizzas to salads and noodles. Inexpensive.

Pubs

Kingston Brewing Company 34 Clarence St. The best pub in town, serving natural ales and lagers brewed on the premises, as well as tasty bar food. Outside patio area, too.

Prince George Hotel 200 Ontario St. Opposite the tourist office, the ground floor of this old inn is subdivided into three bars. There's *Tir Nan Óg*, an Irish pub with Irish brews, *Monte's*, which specializes in Belgian beers and cocktails, and the English-style *Old Speckled Hen*.

Toucan 76 Princess St. Student pub with excellent live music from blues to traditional Irish, and also bar food. Till 2am nightly.

The upper St Lawrence River

To the east of Kingston, Hwy 401 and the prettier Hwy 2 strip along the northern shore of the **St Lawrence River**, whose island-studded waters were tricky-going until the 1950s when the US and Canadian governments created the **St Lawrence Seaway**. An extraordinarily ambitious project, the Seaway extends 3790km inland from the Atlantic by means of lakes, rivers and locks to the west end of Lake Superior. Fifteen locks were installed on the St Lawrence, each big enough to handle massive ocean-going freighters, whilst a string of dams harnessed the river's hydroelectric potential. But it all came at a price: the Seaway necessitated the relocation of many riverside towns, a process which one local newspaper bewailed with the headline "once again another patch of Ontario is sicklied o'er with the pale cast of progress". There were long-term **environmental** costs, too, with the ships transporting species previously unknown here on their hulls and in their bilge. What's more, the Seaway has been something of a flop, its decline directly related to the move towards road and air.

Leaving Kingston, **Hwy 2** begins by cutting across rolling farmland and offering fleeting views of the region's scenic highlight, the **Thousand Islands**. Native Canadians called these tiny, lightly forested granite chunks Manitouana – the "Garden of the Great Spirit" – in the belief they were created when petals of heavenly flowers were scattered on the river; more prosaically the islands later gave their name to a salad dressing. Geologically, they form part of the Frontenac axis, a ridge of million-year-old rock that stretches down into New York State. The islands are seen to best advantage on a **cruise** and these are available at most riverside towns, including Kingston (see p.163), though those from **Gananoque** are often rated the best. In themselves, the towns that dot the river are not especially enthralling – the pick is probably low-key **Prescott** – and this is especially true as the varied charms of Ottawa (see p.172), are within easy string distance: from Kingston to Ottawa is only 175km. The most scenic part of the drive is along the **Thousand Islands Parkway**, a 40km stretch of Hwy 2 beginning just to the east of Gananoque where the road is shadowed by a combined cycle and footpath. There are fast and frequent **buses** along Hwy 401 and VIA **trains** shadow the north bank of the river too, on their way from Kingston to Montréal.

Gananoque and beyond

Some 30km east of Kingston, workaday **GANANOQUE** offers several types of Thousand Island boat **cruise**. The lead operator is Gananoque Boat Line (℡613/382-2144, Ⓦwww.ganboatline.com), which provides one-hour (May–Sept 2–5 daily; $12) and three-hour (May–Sept 3–8 daily; $18) excursions. Highlights of the cruise include a good look at Just Room Enough Island, with its single tiny home, and, at the other extreme, Millionaire's Row on Wellesley Island. In the late 1830s, the islands were the haunt of an irascible Canadian pirate, one William Johnston, whose irritation with the British prompted him and his gang to spend several years harrying British shipping and Canadian farmers until he retired (with his booty) to New York state. Thereafter, the islands became a popular retreat for the rich and famous – Irving Berlin and Jack Dempsey, to name but two – but it was George Boldt, the owner of New York's *Waldorf Astoria*, who distinguished himself by excess. In 1899, he bought one of the islands and reshaped it into a heart as a tribute to his wife – hence the name Heart Island. He then spent $2m building the huge, turreted **Boldt Castle** (mid-May to mid-Oct daily 10am–5pm; US$4.75) with material from around the world, but promptly abandoned it when his wife died, taking his new salad-dressing recipe back with him to New York. Lots of cruises pass by the castle, but few stop, two of the exceptions being cruises from Ivy Lea and Rockport (see below). Note that the castle is in US waters, so – unless you're a US citizen – you'll need to take your **passport**.

Moving on from Gananoque, it's a pleasant 15km drive east via the **Thousand Islands Parkway** to **IVY LEA**, from where Gananoque Boat Line (T 613/382-2144, W www.ganboatline.com) operates a three-hour cruise that often includes a stopoff at Boldt Castle. Pushing on, it's a further 8km or so to tiny **ROCKPORT**, the nearest Canadian dock to Boldt Castle – Heritage 1000 Island Cruises, 17 Front St (T 613/659-3151 or 1-888/229-9913, W www.1000islandcruises.com), and Rockport Boat Line, 23 Front St (T 1-800/563-8687, W www.rockportcruises.com), do the nautical honours from May to October.

From Rockport, it's another short hop to **BROCKVILLE**, a substantial little town that takes its name from the Canadian general Isaac Brock, who was killed near Niagara Falls during the War of 1812. Brockville was at its busiest in the second half of the nineteenth century, when it became a prosperous river port and holding station for thousands of immigrants, who were temporarily detained in enormous sheds on the waterfront Hospital Island. Today the town centre is somewhat careworn, but the harbourfront is pleasant enough and the main square remains suitably commanding, fanning out from an ambitious war memorial. The square is flanked by sturdy stone buildings, notably the neo-Romanesque pinkish former **post office** and, at the top, the rambling Neoclassical **County Courthouse** to either side of which are no less than three good-looking Victorian **churches**. The other Victorian building of note is **Fulford Place**, east of the centre at 287 King St E (guided tours: Sat & Sun 11am–4pm; $2.50), a vast mansion built for George Taylor Fulford, who made his fortune with a cure-all remedy that he marketed brilliantly as "Pink Pills for Pale People". Nevertheless, most visitors skip the architecture in favour of a Thousand Island **cruise** with Brockville Thousand Islands Seaway Cruises (T 613/345-7333 or 1-800/353-3157, W www.1000islandcruises.com). They provide one-hour (May–Oct 1–4 daily; $12) and three-hour (May–June & Sept–Oct 1–2 weekly; July–Aug 2–4 daily; $18) excursions, which sail west to cover pretty much the same itinerary as boats departing Gananoque.

Prescott

Pocket-sized **PRESCOTT**, which trails along the riverside some 20km east of Brockville, was rendered well-nigh obsolete by the St Lawrence Seaway, but previously it was important as a deep-water port and transhipment centre. Its busier days are recalled by the crumbling, dark-black **timbers** of the old town jetty that poke up out of the water beside the grassed-over riverbank and by the imposing bulk of **Fort Wellington** (mid-May to Sept daily 10am–5pm; $4). Both are located beside Hwy 2 on the east side of town. Work started on the fort in 1812 during the Anglo–American war, but by the time it was finished the war was over. There was another spurt of imperial activity after the Upper Canada Rebellion of 1837, when – in something of a tizz – the British strengthened the earthen ditches and ramparts surrounding the fort and plonked a set of military buildings in the middle. These included a two-storey blockhouse-cum-barracks, officers' quarters, powder magazine and a cook house. The military moved out in 1869 and, after years of neglect, the fort has now been returned to its 1830s appearance, complete with a miscellany of period furnishings and fittings. The Americans never attacked Fort Wellington, but it did serve as the muster station for the militia in the lead-up to the **Battle of the Windmill** in 1838. In the aftermath of the shambolic Upper Canada

Rebellion, hundreds of refugee rebels took off into the Ontario bush or fled to the States. One of the larger groups hunkered down in the Thousand Islands and, together with their American sympathizers, planned an attack on Canada, hoping that this would stir a general rebellion. Two hundred of them landed beside a stone windmill 2km east of Prescott, but there was no widespread uprising and the invaders ended up occupying the windmill instead. Here, they were surrounded by the militia and eventually – after a dogged fight – forced to surrender; eleven were executed and most of the rest were transported to Australia. The **windmill**, which later became a lighthouse, has survived and makes for a pleasant, albeit brief, excursion – it's signed from Hwy 2.

Prescott has one excellent **place to stay**, the *Blue Heron Inn*, just west of the handful of shops that passes for the town centre at 1648 Hwy 2 (℡613/925 0562, ⓦwww.blueheroninn.on.ca; ❸). Occupying an attractively revamped old stone house, the inn has four well appointed en-suite guest rooms decorated in attractive, unfussy style and the breakfasts are first rate. For **food**, try the *Blue Stone Café* (℡613/925-0255), just off the main drag, where they serve a simple but tasty range of pasta dishes with main courses averaging about $13. Opening times vary, especially out of season, so ring ahead to confirm.

Heading east from Prescott, it's just 5km to **JOHNSTOWN**, where there's a choice of routes: the bridge leads south over the river to the US; Hwy 416 cuts north to Ottawa and Hwy 401 ploughs on east along the riverside, passing the Upper Canada Village on its way to Montréal.

Upper Canada Village

In the 1950s, the construction of the St Lawrence Seaway raised the river level, threatening many of the old buildings that dotted the river bank. The pick were painstakingly relocated to a purpose-built complex some 40km east of Prescott and this, the **Upper Canada Village** (late May to mid-Oct daily 9.30am–5pm; $17), has become one of the region's most popular attractions. Covering a sixty-acre site, the village re-creates rural Ontario life as of 1860 and contains a wide range of buildings, from farmhouses and farm outhouses to a bakery, a parsonage, a church, a woollen factory, a saw mill and a blacksmiths. It is all very well done and the staff dress up in period gear to demonstrate traditional skills, producing cheeses, quilts, brooms, bread and cloth in exactly the same way as their pioneer ancestors. Finally, in the adjacent riverside park is the **Battlefield Monument**, which – along with a visitor centre – commemorates the Battle of Crysler Farm in 1813, when a small force of British and Canadian soldiers drove off American invaders. Crysler Farm was itself submerged by the Seawa.

The main Montréal–Toronto **bus** route passes by the village's front gate, but double check the driver will stop here before you embark. From the Village, it takes about an hour and a half to drive to Ottawa, via hwys 2 and then 31.

Ottawa

The capital of the second-biggest country on the planet, **OTTAWA** wrestles with its reputation as a bureaucratic labyrinth of little charm and character. The problem is that many Canadians who aren't federal employees – and even some who are – blame Ottawa for all the country's woes. All too aware of this, the Canadian government has spent lashings of dollars to turn Ottawa into "a city of urban grace in which all Canadians can take pride" (so the promotional literature runs) and despite the undoubted success of the policy, this very invest-ment is often resented. The innate hostility is deeply rooted, dating back as far as 1857 when Queen Victoria, inspired by some genteel watercolours, declared Ottawa the capital, leaving Montréal and Toronto smarting at their rebuff.

In truth, Ottawa is neither grandiose nor tedious, but a lively cosmopolitan city of over one million inhabitants that boasts a clutch of outstanding **national museums**, a pleasant riverside setting and superb cultural facilities like the National Arts Centre. Throw in acres of parks and gardens, miles of bicycle and jogging paths, lots of good **hotels** and **B&Bs** and a busy **café–bar** and **restaurant** scene and you have enough to keep the most diligent sightseer going for a day or three, maybe more. Here too, for once in English-speaking Ontario, Canada's bilingual laws make sense: French-speaking **Gatineau**, just across the river in Québec, is commonly lumped together with Ontario's Ottawa as the "Capital Region", and on the streets of Ottawa you'll hear as much French as English.

Ottawa's festivals

Ottawa uses every excuse in the book to put on a **festival**. Federal funding ensures that national holidays – especially Canada Day – are celebrated in style, while seasonal shindigs like the Winterlude and the Canadian Tulip Festival are as lavish as any in the country. Other than these large bashes, ethnic festivals embracing the city's diverse population are smaller but equally entertaining and there's a wide variety of musical festivals too. The list below is arranged chronologically.

Winterlude ☎613/239-5000. A ten-day snow-and-ice extravaganza held during February. Concentrated around the frozen Rideau Canal, it includes ice sculptures at Confederation Park – renamed the Crystal Garden for the duration – and snow sculptures around Dows Lake. Other events include speed skating, bed- and dog-sled races.

Canadian Tulip Festival ⓦwww.tulipfestival.ca. Held over three weeks from early May, this is the oldest of Ottawa's festivals. It began in 1945 when the Dutch sent 100,000 tulip bulbs to the city both to honour those Canadian soldiers who had lib-erated the Netherlands from the Germans and as a thank you for sheltering Queen Juliana, who had taken refuge in Ottawa during the war. The bulbs are planted around Parliament, along the canal and around Dows Lake, a gigantic splash of colour that's accompanied by concerts, parades, fireworks and a huge craft show. The major events take place in Major's Hill Park and Dows Lake – but few are free, and the festival now has a reputation for being rather touristy.

Franco-Ontarien Festival ⓦwww.ffo.ca. Held in late June, this five-day celebration of French culture features bands and street dancers; Dalhousie St is closed off to traffic for the duration.

Canada Day ☎1-800/465-1867. July 1, the country's national day, is celebrated with vim and gusto. Parades, processions and much flag waving are the hallmarks.

Bluesfest ⓦwww.ottawa-bluesfest.ca. Held over ten days in early July, this is Canada's largest festival of blues and gospel with concerts held in various venues and free shows in Confederation Park.

Ottawa International Jazz Festival ⓦwww.ottawajazzfestival.com. Mid-July. One of Ottawa's most popular festivals, showcasing more than 400 musicians. The main stage is in Confederation Park with concerts several times daily. In addition, local bands play around Byward Market and at city clubs.

Ottawa Chamber Music Festival ⓦwww.chamberfest.com. Late July to early Aug. North America's largest classical chamber music festival, with concerts in venues and churches across the city.

A brief history of Ottawa

The one-time hunting ground of the Algonkian-speaking Outaouais, **Ottawa** received its first recorded European visitor in 1613 in the shape of Samuel de Champlain. The French explorer pitched up, paused to watch his aboriginal guides make offerings of tobacco to the misty falls which he christened Chaudière (French for "cauldron") and then took off in search of more appealing pastures. Later, the **Ottawa River** became a major transportation route, but

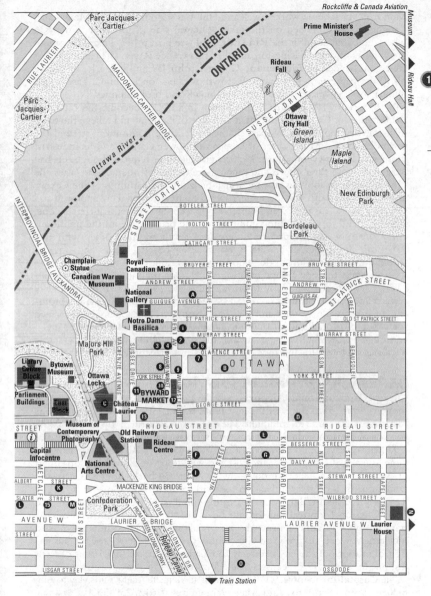

the Ottawa area remained no more than a camping spot until 1800, when **Philemon Wright** snowshoed up here along the frozen Ottawa River from Massachusetts. Wright founded a small settlement, which he called Wrightstown and subsequently **Hull** (now **Gatineau**) after his parents' birthplace in England. Aware that the British navy was desperate for timber, Wright then worked out a way of shifting the tall trees that surrounded him by squaring them off, tying them together and floating them as rafts down the river to

Montréal. His scheme worked well and Hull was soon flourishing. Meanwhile, nothing much happened on the other (Ottawa) side of the river until 1826 when the completion of the **Rideau Canal** (see box, p.167) linked the site of present-day Ottawa to Kingston and the St Lawrence River. The canal builders were commanded by **Lieutenant-Colonel John By** and it was he who gave his name to the new settlement, **Bytown**, which soon became a hard-edged lumber town characterized by drunken brawls and broken bones.

In 1855 Bytown relabelled itself **Ottawa** in a bid to become the capital of the Province of Canada, hoping that a change of name would relieve the town of its tawdry reputation. As part of their pitch, the community stressed the town's location on the border of Upper and Lower Canada and its industrial prosperity. In the event, Queen Victoria granted their request, though this had little to do with their efforts and much more to do with her artistic tastes: the Queen had been looking at some romantic landscape paintings of the Ottawa area and decided this was the perfect spot for a new capital. Few approved and Canada's politicians fumed at the inconvenience – Sir Wilfred Laurier, for one, found it "hard to say anything good" about the place. Nor did the politicians enjoy the mockery heaped on them from south of the border with one American newspaper suggesting it would never be attacked as any "invader would inevitably get lost in the woods trying to find it".

Give or take the odd federal building – including the rambling Parliament – Ottawa remained a workaday town until the late 1940s, when the Paris city planner **Jacques Greber** was commissioned to beautify the city with a profusion of parks, wide avenues and tree-lined pathways. The scheme transformed the city and defined much of its current appearance and today Greber's green and open spaces confine a city centre that is a fetching mix of neo-Gothic Victorian architecture and modern concrete-and-glass office blocks.

Arrival, information and transport

Ottawa International Airport (code YOW; ⓦwww.ottawa-airport.ca) is located about 15km south of the city. From the airport, a **Hotel Shuttle bus** (daily every 30min 5am–midnight; $12 one-way, $20 return; ⓣ613/260-2359, ⓦwww.ottawaairportshuttle.ca) runs to various downtown hotels. City bus #97 (daily every 20min 5am–2am; $2.50), operated by OC Transpo, makes the same journey at a fraction of the cost and will drop you downtown on Albert St. A taxi from the airport to downtown will set you back about $25. Ottawa's **train station** is on the southeastern outskirts off Hwy 417 Queensway at 200 Tremblay Rd, about 5km from the centre, with direct VIA Rail services to and from Kingston, Montréal and Toronto. Local bus #95 goes downtown from the train station; the same journey by taxi is about $15. Long-distance **buses**, including Voyageur Express and Greyhound (ⓣ613/238-5900), use the bus station, 3km south of the city centre at 265 Catherine St, on the corner of Kent just off the Hwy 417 Queensway. Take local bus #4 to get downtown.

The **Capital Infocentre**, 90 Wellington St at Metcalfe (daily: mid-May to Aug 8.30am–9pm; Sept to mid-May 9am–5pm; ⓣ613/239-5000, ⓦwww .canadascapital.gc.ca), is handily located right opposite the Parliament Buildings. It's a busy place, but the staff will help you find accommodation and hand you masses of free literature, including a useful *Visitor Guide* plus city and public transport maps. Owl Rafting (ⓣ1-800/461-7238, ⓦwww.owlrafting.com) offers an excellent programme of **white-water rafting** on the Ottawa River, near Pembroke, about 120km west of Ottawa. A one-day excursion costs $80–100 with rental of all the necessary tackle and a buffet lunch included.

Most of Ottawa's important attractions as well as many of its better restaurants, bars and hotels are clustered in the downtown area within comfortable walking distance of Confederation Square. If you're venturing further afield, however, you may need to use a **bus**. OC Transpo (℡613/741-4390, Ⓦwww.octranspo.com) provides a comprehensive network of bus services across Ottawa and its suburbs, while STO buses (℡819/770-3242, Ⓦwww.sto.ca) cover Gatineau and the north side of the river. The hub of the OC Transpo system is the **Central Transitway**, which runs from the Mackenzie King Bridge along Albert St (one-way west) and Slater St (one-way east). STO buses leave for Gatineau from outside the Rideau Centre at the west end of Rideau St, between Nicolas and Sussex. Key buses operate from 5am or 6am to around midnight daily. **Ticket prices** are very reasonable and start at just $1.25, but for many visitors the best deal is a **DayPass** ($5), which allows unlimited travel on the OC Transpo system for one day. Tickets can be bought at corner stores, the tourist office and many hotels, or paid for on the bus itself (exact fare only). The same applies to the DayPass. If you're travelling on an ordinary ticket and need to change buses to complete your journey, ask for a free transfer at the point of embarkation. There are **taxi** ranks outside major hotels and nightspots.

Accommodation

As the federal honeypot, Ottawa hosts dozens of business conferences and, although there are hundreds of rooms in the city, things can still get tight – with **hotel** prices rising accordingly. At other times – especially when parliament is in recess and at the weekend – it's much more of a buyer's market and even the poshest hotels offer big discounts. That said, the best bet for a reasonably priced room is in an **inn** or **B&B**, the pick of which offer prime lodgings close to the centre. If you stick to the list below you should find somewhere, but if not the tourist office (see above) will assist, though note that staff won't actually make a booking. The cheapest beds in town are at two **hostels**, both of which are open year-round and right downtown, and there are inexpensive **student rooms** too.

Hotels, inns and motels

Albert House Inn 478 Albert St at Bay ℡613/236-4479 or 1-800/267-1982, Ⓦwww.albertinn.com. Occupying a good-looking Victorian villa with a sweeping portico, this inn has seventeen en-suite guest rooms, each of which is pleasantly furnished. Full breakfast included. Light sleepers may prefer the rooms at the back, away from busy Albert St. ❺

Arc 140 Slater St ℡613/238-2888 or 1-800/699-2516, Ⓦwww.arcthehotel.com. Immaculate, medium-sized designer hotel with minimalist decor and a green-apple theme. The guest rooms are kitted out in style, too, all wood and leather with Egyptian cotton sheets. ❽

Capital Hill Hotel and Suites 88 Albert St ℡613/235-1413 or 1-800/463-7705, Ⓦwww.capitalhill.com. This smart, high-rise hotel is furnished in brisk, modern style and all its 150 rooms are spacious and comfortable. Handy down-

town location, just off Confederation Square. Very competitive prices. ❻

Days Inn Downtown 319 Rideau St ℡613/789-5555 or 1-800/329-7466, Ⓦwww.the.daysinn.com. Nothing special, perhaps, but this reliable chain motel offers good quality accommodation at reasonable prices in a downtown location. ❺

Doral Inn 486 Albert St at Bay ℡613/230-8055 or 1-800/263-6725, Ⓦwww.doralinn.com. Forty guest rooms and suites with straightforward modern furnishings in this well-maintained Victorian house. Continental breakfast and swimming pool. ❺

Fairmont Château Laurier 1 Rideau St ℡613/241-1414 or 1-800/441-1414, Ⓦwww.fairmont.com. This superb hotel, Ottawa's finest, has pretty much everything. It was opened in 1912 as a prestige railway hotel for the Grand Trunk Pacific Railway, whose president, Charles Hayes, lavished millions on its construction. A fine example of the French Renaissance – or château – style, the exterior boasts a forest of copper-clad turrets, spires and towers. Inside, the grand public areas boast marble floors, high ceilings, chandeliers and soaring columns, plus extravagantly embossed lifts. The rooms themselves are not quite as grand, but they are thoroughly comfortable and the best offer delightful views over the river. **❼**

Lord Elgin Hotel 100 Elgin St at Laurier Ave W ☎613/235-3333 or 1-800/267-4298, ⓦ www.lordelginhotel.ca. Occupying a fine château-style-meets-Art-Deco 1940s high-rise close to Confederation Square, this classy hotel has comfortable rooms decked out with crisp, modern furnishings. Reasonable prices and discounts on the weekend. **❻**

Novotel Ottawa 33 Nicholas St ☎613/230-3033 or 1-800/668-6835, ⓦ www.novotelottawa.com. This hotel doesn't win any beauty contests – it's overshadowed by a hulking brick high-rise – but the public areas are done out in sharp, modernistic style and the 280 rooms are tastefully and cheerfully decorated; the service is excellent too. Downtown location. **❻**

Quality Hotel Downtown Ottawa 290 Rideau St ☎613/789-7511 or 1-800/424-6423, ⓦ www.choicehotels.ca. Spick-and-span modern, chain hotel in a handy downtown location. **❺**

B&Bs

Australis Guest House 35 Marlborough Ave ☎613/235-8461, ⓦ www.bbcanada.com/1463.html. Straightforward Australian-run B&B with three rooms in an older house about 2km southeast of Parliament Hill. Price includes full delicious breakfast. **❸**

Gasthaus Switzerland Inn 89 Daly Ave at Cumberland ☎613/237-0335 or 1-888/663-0000, ⓦ www.gasthausswitzerlandinn.com. Twenty-two en-suite rooms in this unassuming three-storey inn. Central location, but the streets roundabout are seedy. **❹**

L'Auberge du Marché 87 Guiges Ave ☎613/241-6610 or 1-800/465-0079, ⓦ www.members.rogers.com/aubergedumarche. In the heart of Byward Market, this extremely appealing B&B occupies a modest two-storey nineteenth-century brick house, whose interior has been immaculately renovated in sympathetic style – all pastel colours and wood floors. Often full, and very popular, the B&B has four air-conditioned bedrooms and serves great breakfasts too. **❹**

Hostels

Ottawa Backpackers Inn 203 York St ☎613/241-3402, ⓦ www.ottawahostel.com. Spartan 35-room hostel in the Byward Market area. Self-catering facilities, Internet access and linen supplied. $18 per night in four- and six-bed dormitories. Doubles **❷**

Ottawa International Hostel (HI) 75 Nicholas St at Daly ☎613/235-2595, ⓦ www.hihostels.ca. Stay in cells complete with bars on the windows in Ottawa's nineteenth-century jail now converted into an HI hostel. The solitary confinement area is now a laundry, but Death Row remains the same with its 1m-by-2m cells. There are a couple of single rooms, but most of the 150 beds are in four-, five- and six-bed rooms. Members pay $20 per night, non-members $25. The hostel is handily located downtown, just south of Rideau St's Rideau Shopping Centre. Advance reservations strongly recommended. Doubles **❷**

Student rooms

University of Ottawa 100 University St ☎613/564-5400. From May to August, student rooms in the Stanton Residence, on the University of Ottawa campus off Nicolas St, are rented out to visitors. Double rooms cost $50, singles $39 ($42/28 for students). The campus has sports and laundry facilities, a pool and café and is located about 1km southeast of Parliament Hill.

The City

Ottawa's major sights are clustered on the steep, south banks of the Ottawa River to either side of the Rideau Canal. It's here you'll find the monumental Victorian architecture of **Parliament Hill**, the outstanding art collection of the **National Gallery**, the military memorabilia of the **Canadian War Museum**, the imposing **Notre Dame Basilica** and **Byward Market**, the hub of the restaurant and bar scene. Many visitors stop there, but there are a clutch of other, lesser attractions too, beginning with the **Laurier House**, packed with the possessions of the former prime minister William Lyon Mackenzie King and located 2km or so east of downtown. Northeast of the centre, on the far side of the Rideau River, is the ritzy suburb of **Rockcliffe**, home to both the governor-general's mansion, **Rideau Hall**, and the **Canada Aviation Museum**.

Parliament Hill

Perched on the limestone bluff of Parliament Hill, above the Ottawa River, Canada's handsome **Parliament Buildings** have, with their spires, pointed windows and overweening clock tower, a distinctly ecclesiastical air – though that certainly didn't overawe the original workmen, who urinated on the copper roof to speed up the oxidization process. Comprising a trio of sturdy neo-Gothic structures, the complex was begun in 1859 after the land was purchased from the British army, who had plonked a barracks here during the construction of the Rideau Canal. **Centre Block** (guided tours: mid-May to Aug Mon–Fri 9am–8pm, Sat & Sun 9am–5pm; Sept to mid-May daily 9am–4pm; free), home of the Senate and the House of Commons, dominates proceedings, though it is actually a replacement for the original building, which was destroyed by fire in 1916. This second structure was supposed to be the same as its predecessor, but it ended up about twice the size. The **Peace Tower**, rising from the middle of the facade, was added in 1927 as a memorial to Canadians who served in World War I. Highlights of the guided tour include a quick gambol round the **House of Commons**, where the Speaker's chair is made of English oak from Westminster Hall and from Nelson's ship *Victory*, and the red-carpeted **Senate** with its murals of scenes from World War I surmounted by a beautiful gilded ceiling. At the back of the Centre Block is the **Library**, the only part of the building to have survived the fire; the circular design and the richly carved wooden galleries make this the most charming part of the building. The **debates** in both the House of Commons and the Senate are open to the public, who can observe proceedings from the visitors' galleries. Passes are required and are issued by security at the main Peace Tower entrance. For information about Senate and House of Commons debates, call ☎613/239-5000, ⓦ www.parl.gc.ca. Parliament's liveliest debates are held during **Question Period**, when the Opposition interrogates the Prime Minister.

Flanking Centre Block are **West Block** (no public access) and **East Block** (July & Aug daily 10am–5pm; free), where the guided tour pops into four Confederation-era rooms: the original governor general's office, the offices of Sir John A. Macdonald and Sir George Etienne Cartier, and the Privy Council Chamber. Costumed guides provide the history. The manicured lawns surrounding the Parliament Buildings are dotted with **statues** of the great and the good with two of the more interesting occupying a tiny hillock just to the west of Centre Block. Here, **Queen Victoria** has been stuck on a plinth guarded by a lion and offered laurels from below, whilst **Lester Pearson** (Prime Minister 1963–68) lounges in an armchair, the epitome of the self-confident statesman. Round the back of Centre Block there are pleasant views across the Ottawa River to Gatineau (see p.186) and of the Library's handsome design.

Two events pull the tourist crowds onto Parliament Hill, beginning with the **Changing of the Guard** when the Governor General's Foot Guards and Grenadier Guards march onto the Hill dressed in full ceremonial uniform – bright-red tunics and bearskins (late June to late Aug daily between 10am and 10.30am). The second is a free summer-evening **sound and light show** (early July to early Sept), illustrating Canada's history with alternate French and English performances nightly. Finally, from mid-May to August a white **Infotent** goes up in front of West Block to explain what's going on and where.

Wellington Street and around

Behind West Block, in between the river and Wellington St, are more **federal buildings**, château-style monoliths with perky dormer windows and green-copper roofs culminating in the **Supreme Court of Canada building**, a sturdy 1930s Art Nouveau edifice which blends it neatly with its neighbours. Turn inland from Wellington St and you'll soon reach Sparks St, where the **Sparks St Mall** – one of the country's earliest pedestrianized shopping streets – runs from Confederation Square to Lyon St. The design can't help but look a little tired today, despite serious efforts to jazz it up, and the main reason to visit is the **Currency Museum**, 245 Sparks St (May–Aug Mon–Sat 10.30am–5pm, Sun 1–5pm; Sept–April Tues–Sat 10.30am–5pm, Sun 1–5pm; free), housed in the old HQ of the Bank of Canada. When it expanded the premises, the bank encased the original 1937 stone building within their new offices, which were themselves enclosed by two green-glass towers with an indoor jungle-like garden court. Within the garden, in front of the museum, is a huge Yap stone, a symbol of wealth in the South Pacific; such stones usually remain at the bottom of the sea, their possession simply changing hands among the islanders by agreement. Inside, the museum focuses on Canadian currencies, from the small beads and shells known as wampum through to playing cards, beaver pelts and modern banknotes.

Confederation Square and the Rideau Canal

The eastern end of the Sparks St Mall empties into the triangular **Confederation Square**, a breezy open space dominated by the magnificent **National War Memorial**, in which a soaring stone arch is surmounted by representations of liberty and peace. Down below, a swirling, finely executed bronze of 1926 depicts returning service men and women passing through the arch – from war to peace – and manages to convey both their exultation and sorrow. On the southeast side of the square is the complex of low concrete buildings that houses the **National Arts Centre** (see p.189), which clunks down to the **Rideau Canal**, a narrow sliver of water that becomes the world's longest skating rink in winter, with hot chocolate and muffin stands warming everyone up. Opposite, across the canal, rise the stirring lines of Ottawa's former **railway station**, a grand Beaux Arts edifice of 1911 that has now – rather sadly – been recycled as a conference centre.

Following the west side of the Rideau Canal north towards the river, it only takes a minute or two to reach the pretty flight of **locks** that connects canal and river with Parliament Hill rising directly above. On the west side of the locks is the **Bytown Museum** (early May to mid-Oct Sun–Fri 10am–4pm, Sat noon–4pm; $5), Ottawa's oldest building, where military supplies were stored during the construction of the canal. Here, a short video display explains the history of the waterway, while the rest of the museum features assorted Ottawan memorabilia, including some of Colonel By's belongings and temporary exhibitions. During the summer, canal **boat trips** leave from the top of the locks, river trips from the bottom. There are several operators, but Paul's Boat Lines (☎613/225-6781) is as good as any, charging $12 for an hour-long canal cruise, $15 for the river. There are departures every couple of hours or so from May to October; reservations are a good idea.

Doubling back, climb up the steps to the bridge abutting Confederation Square and it's the briefest of strolls to the splendid *Château Laurier Hotel* and the adjacent **Canadian Museum of Contemporary Photography** (May to mid-Oct daily 10am–6pm; mid-Oct to April Wed–Sun 10am–5pm, except Thurs till 8pm all year; free). The museum's collection numbers around 160,000 photographs, which are used for research as well as being displayed in changing exhibitions.

From the *Château Laurier Hotel* it's a brief walk east to **Sussex Drive**, whose southern section is one of Ottawa's oldest streets: the stone buildings between George and St Patrick hark back to Ottawa's pioneer days and now house expensive shops and galleries. Nearby **Major's Hill Park** rolls across a small hill above the Ottawa River. This was where Colonel By decided to build his house and the extant foundations bear a plaque attesting to its history. Major's Hill Park slopes down towards **Nepean Point**, a pint-sized headland that nudges out into the river bisected by the main road – and bridge – to Gatineau (see p.186). On the far side of the road a path climbs up the headland to an outside theatre and, at the tip, a statue of Champlain, from where there are wide river views. The statue is actually a foul-up: erected in 1915, Champlain holds his astrolabe – his navigational aid – aloft, but it is upside down.

National Gallery of Canada
Back on Sussex Drive, the **National Gallery of Canada** (May to mid-Oct daily 10am–6pm, Thurs till 8pm; mid-Oct to April Wed–Sun 10am–5pm, Thurs till 8pm; free; ⓦ www.national.gallery.ca) occupies a cleverly conceived building, whose acres of glass, designed by Moshe Safdie, reflect the turrets and pinnacles of Parliament Hill. The collection was founded in 1880 by the Marquis of Lorne, then the governor general, who persuaded each member of the Royal Canadian Academy to donate a painting or two. Over the next century artworks were gathered from all over the world, resulting in a permanent collection that now numbers more than 25,000 pieces – too many to be exhibited at any one time. This means that the exhibits are rotated, so although the paintings mentioned below will probably be on display, there are no guarantees. Note also that the new **Portrait Gallery of Canada** will open next to the Capital Infocentre, on Wellington St, in the next year or two and this will mean some further adjustments as to what is shown where. The National Gallery also holds world-class temporary exhibitions for which an admission fee is usually charged. The collection spreads over two levels – Level 1 and Level 2 – and **free plans** are issued at the reception desk; in addition, the gallery shop sells a useful guide for $5.

The Canadian Galleries
The **Canadian Galleries**, laid out in roughly chronological order on Level One, are the finest in the building, following the history of Canadian painting from the mid-eighteenth century to modern times. They begin (in Room A101) with religious art from Québec, including a flashy gilded high altar by Paul Jourdain, followed by a room showing the emergence of secular art in the early nineteenth century, with paintings by immigrant artists trained in Europe. The most notable of these was **Joseph Légaré**, who was not only a painter but also a politician and nationalist – his *Cholera Plague, Québec*, is a fine example of his fastidiously romantic work. For popularity, though, none could match **Cornelius Krieghoff**, who could turn his hand to anything requested by his patrons from the emerging middle classes – as illustrated by his *Winter Landscape* and *White Horse Inn by Moonlight*. Close by is the gallery's most unusual exhibit, the **Rideau St Chapel**, rebuilt piece by intricate piece after it was threatened by demolition in 1972. Designed in 1887 by the architect and priest Canon Georges Bouillon for a convent school in Ottawa, it has slender cast-iron columns supporting a fan-vaulted ceiling – one of the few examples of its kind in North America. Contained in the chapel is a modest collection of ecclesiastical silverware and mawkish wooden sculptures from Québec.

Moving on, Room A104 kicks off a small collection of early nineteenth-century paintings from the Maritimes and Ontario. John Poad Drake's *Port of Halifax* and **John O'Brien**'s dramatic depiction of a storm-tossed frigate illustrate the importance of the sea trade, while the native population make an appearance in the evocative portraits of **Paul Kane**, Canada's first artist-explorer. Also here is the unique **Croscup** room from Nova Scotia. Once the living room of a shipping family, it is covered in murals that juxtapose images from mid-nineteenth-century North America and Europe – portraits of Micmac Indians next to bagpipe-playing Scots and so forth.

The construction of the railroads made it much easier for artists to explore the wilder reaches of Canada, a development encapsulated – in Room A105 – by **Lucius O'Brien**'s *Sunrise on the Saguenay* of 1880. However, painters of this period were still in thrall to European masters – the Royal Canadian Academy of Arts sent its students to Paris to complete their training – and this state of affairs continued into the twentieth century. Illustrative of this is the impressionistic work of Newfoundland's **Maurice Cullen** and the soberly romantic rural scenes of George A. Reid and **Homer Watson**, both of whom were inspired by the Dutch and Barbizon school.

Indeed, it was only with the **Group of Seven** (see box p.96) that a purely Canadian style emerged, a style which aimed to capture the spirit and vastness of the northern landscape, rather than rendering it into a tamer European version and vision. That said, the Group was influenced by the work of contemporary Scandinavian painters, who were wrestling with similar problems of scale on the other side of the Atlantic. The two rooms devoted to the Group's works – A108 and A109 – feature the seminal paintings of **Tom Thomson**, whose startling *The Jack Pine* of 1916 was in effect the Group's clarion call – trees, often windswept or dead, are a constant symbol in the Group's paintings of Canada's wilderness. Using rapid, brash, often brutal brushstrokes, the works here are faithful less to the landscape itself than to the emotions it evoked – **Lawren Harris**'s ejaculatory *North Shore, Lake Superior*, A.Y. Jackson's *Red Maple* and J.E.H. Macdonald's *The Solemn Land* are all memorable examples.

Following Macdonald's death in 1932, the Group of Seven formed the Canadian Group of Painters, embracing all Canadian artists of the time whatever their style. Initially landscape remained the predominant genre, but the effects of the Depression forced politics to the fore – *Ontario Farm House* by **Carl Schaefer** turns a landscape into a social statement, while Jack Humphrey, Miller Brittain and Sam Borenstein depict the harsh realities of urban life.

A subsequent section focuses on **abstract** works produced in Montréal from the 1940s to the 1970s. In Canada abstraction was first explored by the Montréal Automatistes, whose emphasis on the expressive qualities of colour was rejected by the Platiciens, with whom geometrical and analytical forms were the preoccupations. Both groups are represented here, as are postwar artists from British Columbia and Ontario – look out for the aggressive abstractions of William Ronald, as in his *Monarch*.

The contemporary art and Inuit collections

Beginning with the 1960s, the **Contemporary Art Collection** is spread over Levels 1 and 2. The highlights here are almost exclusively the work of American artists, most notably Andy Warhol's *Brillo* sculpture, George Segal's life-size assemblage *The Gas Station* and a couple of distinctive pieces by Claes Oldenburg. Canadians pop up here and there, but they almost always seem to take the lead from foreigners – witness the shadow of New York's Abstract Expressionists falling over Charles Gagnon's *Cassation/Open/Ouvert*.

Also displayed on Level 1, in a separate area off the Great Hall, is the gallery's small but eclectic collection of **Inuit art and sculpture**. The kernel of the Inuit material is soapstone sculptures, but there are whale bone and ivory pieces too, as well as brightly coloured drawings. One particular sculptor to look out for is **Charlie Inukpuk**, who carved the elemental *Woman who Killed a Bear with a Mitten*.

The European galleries

Located on Level 2, the **European galleries** begin with a medley of medieval and **Renaissance** paintings and panel paintings from Northern Europe. There's a strong showing for religious works produced in Siena and Florence, though the Italian highlight is Filippino Lippi's *Triumph of Mordecai* and *Esther at the Palace Gate*, painted for chests that contained a bride's dowry. The Low Countries are well represented too, with works by Hans Memling, Bouts and Quentin Matsys, who was responsible for a *Crucifixion*, in which Jerusalem looks like a Flemish town encircled by ramparts, and an especially sorrowful *Lamentation*. The collection of works from **seventeenth-century** Europe is, however, even more impressive. There's Bernini's sculpture of his patron Pope Urban VIII, Claude Lorrain's *Landscape with a Temple of Bacchus*, an *Entombment* by Rubens, Rembrandt's sumptuous *Heroine from the Old Testament* and Van Dyck's *Suffer the Little Children to Come Unto Me*, an early, finely observed work that includes portraits thought to be of Rubens and his family. Venetian genre paintings include Canaletto's elegaic *Campo di Rialto* and Guardi's *Santa Maria Della Salute*.

From Britain in the **eighteenth century** there are portraits by Reynolds and Gainsborough, and Romney's *Joseph Brant (Thayendanega)*, a portrait of the anglophile Mohawk chief while he was on a visit to London. Also here is *The Death of General Wolfe* by **Benjamin West**, an American who became George III's official painter. West depicts Wolfe in a Christ-like pose, lying wounded and surrounded by his adjutants; the painting made Wolfe a British hero. The **nineteenth-century** selection is basically a show of minor paintings by great artists: Delacroix's romantic *Othello and Desdemona*, Corot's orderly *The Bridge at Narni*, Constable's *Salisbury Cathedral from the Bishop's Grounds* and Turner's *Mercury and Argus*, with a sunset that anticipates his future masterpieces. In stark contrast, the gritty realism of a later generation of European painters is well represented by Courbet's *The Cliffs at Étretat* and Millet's *The Pig Slaughter*, though tranquillity is soon restored by Monet's *Waterloo Bridge: The Sun through the Fog*, beautifying London's notorious fog, and two canvases by Pissarro. Van Gogh's *Iris* and Cézanne's *Forest* are the two most noteworthy Post-Impressionist works. The final European galleries push on into the twentieth century, featuring a diverse and top-quality range of paintings and sculptures from the disturbing *Hope I* by Gustav Klimt and Matisse's *Nude on a Yellow Sofa*, through to Francis Bacon's macabre *Study for Portrait No. 1* and pieces by Picasso, Léger, Epstein, Mondrian, Dali and Duchamp.

In the middle of the European galleries, Room C214 is devoted to American **Abstract Expressionists**. This is where you'll find **Barnet Newman**'s *Voice of Fire*, the very mention of which causes some Canadians to break out in a cold sweat – not because of its artistic significance but because it cost a cool $1.76m. The artist intended the 5.5-metre-high piece to give the viewer a "feeling of his own totality, of his own separateness, of his own individuality, and at the same time of his connection to others, who are also separate". Such blandishments did not, however, satisfy everyone with one Manitoba Tory MP ranting that it could have been "done in ten minutes with two cans of paint and two rollers". The same room contains lesser works by Jackson Pollock and Mark Rothko.

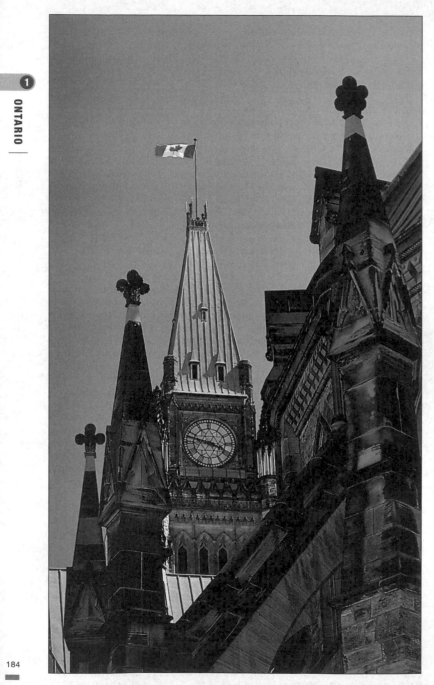

△ Parliament Buildings, Ottawa

Canadian War Museum, the Mint and Notre Dame

Next door to the National Gallery, protected by a tank and a couple of cannons, is the **Canadian War Museum** (May to early Oct daily 9.30am–5pm, Thurs till 8pm; early Oct to April Tues–Sun 9.30am–5pm, Thurs till 8pm; $4, free Thurs 4–8pm), whose three floors are jam-packed with military bits and pieces, from regimental photos through to old guns and uniforms. The museum kicks off with a display on the War of 1812 and then examines every major military conflict thereafter down to World War II and Canada's postwar peace-keeping role. It's an enjoyable collection and the accompanying text is well-researched and well-considered, but in the next year or so it will be closed down when the new and much-trumpeted Canadian War Museum opens on Lebreton Flats, a parcel of land by the river about 2km west of Confederation Square.

Metres away, further up Sussex Drive, is the castellated **Royal Canadian Mint** (May–Aug Mon–Fri 9am–8.30pm, Sat–Sun 9am–5.30pm; Sept–April daily 9am–5pm; $2), where you can view different aspects of currency production and design – though the printing and the minting is now done in Winnipeg.

Doubling back down Sussex Drive, the twin silver spires of the capital's Catholic cathedral, the **Notre Dame Basilica** (Mon 11.30am–6pm, Tues–Sat 7.30am–6pm & Sun 8am–6pm; $2), poke high into the sky across the street from the National Gallery. Completed in 1890, the cathedral is broadly neo-Gothic in style, its long and slender nave reaching a sort of ecclesiastical crescendo in a massive high altar piece, which is surrounded by dozens of pious wooden sculptures, many of which were carved by the carpenters and masons who worked on the Parliament Buildings.

The Laurier House and Rockcliffe

About 2km east of Byward Market is the **Laurier House**, 335 Laurier Ave E (April to mid-May Mon–Fri 9am–5pm; mid-May to mid-Oct Mon–Sat 9am–5pm, Sun 1–5pm; $3.75), former home of prime ministers Sir Wilfred Laurier and William Lyon Mackenzie King. Laurier, Canada's first French-speaking prime minister, served from 1896 to 1911, while Mackenzie King, his self-proclaimed "spiritual son", was Canada's longest-serving (1921–30 and 1935–48). Notoriously pragmatic, King enveloped his listeners in a fog of words through which his political intentions were barely discernible. The perfect illustration – and his most famous line – was "Not necessarily conscription, but conscription if necessary", supposedly a clarification of his plans at the onset of World War II. Even more famous than his obfuscating rhetoric, however, was his personal eccentricity. His fear that future generations would view him simply as the heir of his grandfather William Lyon Mackenzie – who led the Upper Canada rebellions of the 1830s (see p.264) – eventually led him into spiritualism. He held regular seances to tap the advice of great dead Canadians, including Laurier, who allegedly communicated to him through his pet dog.

The house is dominated by King's possessions, including his crystal ball and a portrait of his obsessively adored mother, in front of which he placed a red rose every day. Other mementoes include the programme Abraham Lincoln held the night of his assassination, a painting by Rogier van der Weyden and a guest book signed by Churchill, Roosevelt, de Gaulle, Nehru, the Dionne quintuplets (see p.193) and Shirley Temple. The house also contains a reconstruction of a study belonging to prime minister Lester B. Pearson, who was awarded the Nobel peace prize for his role in the 1956 Arab–Israeli dispute.

Pearson also had a stab at devising a new flag for his country and although it was rejected the mock-up he commissioned, with blue stripes at either end to symbolize the oceans, is on display.

Laurier Ave East eventually meets the **Rideau River**, which is escorted by walkways and bicycle paths north to the **Rideau Falls**, whose twin cataracts are separated by Green Island – the site of the Ottawa City Hall, an unattractive building built in the 1950s. The falls themselves were once enveloped in an industrial complex, but this has now been cleared away to allow excellent views across the river to Gatineau.

Northeast of the falls lies **Rockcliffe**, Ottawa's ritziest district, a leafy suburb colonized by parliamentary bigwigs and diplomats – and in the evening by local lovers, who canoodle in the pavilions on the river shore, looking across to the Gatineau Hills. The prime minister lives here too, holed up in a stately stone mansion that is barely visible through the trees on the lakeshore at 24 Sussex Drive (no public access). On the opposite side of Sussex Drive is the stately, Neoclassical **Rideau Hall** (free guided tours, call ☎613/991-4422, Ⓦ www.gg.ca for schedule), which has been the home of Canada's governors general since Confederation. The hall's gardens of maples and fountains are usually open from 9am to one hour before sunset – but call ahead if you want to be sure. At the east end of Rockcliffe Parkway, 5km from downtown, is the huge hangar of the **Canada Aviation Museum** (May–Aug daily 9am–5pm, Thurs till 9pm; Sept–April Tues–Sun 10am–5pm, Thurs till 9pm; $6). Highlights include a replica of the *Silver Dart*, which made the first powered flight in Canada in 1909; it flew for a full nine minutes, a major achievement for a contraption that seems to be made out of spare parts and old sheets. There are also bombers from both world wars and some excellent videos, including a programme to simulate a helicopter flight and a virtual reality hang-glider.

Gatineau

Though firmly incorporated within the Capital Region, **GATINEAU** (until recently named **Hull**), lying just across the river from Ottawa in Québec, remains distinctly separate and predominantly francophone. For years, it served mainly as Ottawa's nightlife spot as its bars were open two hours longer than those in the capital, but with this alcoholic advantage now gone – and its paper mills relegated to minor importance – Gatineau is attempting to re-invent itself as an appealing adjunct to its wealthier neighbour. It's an interesting ten-minute walk from Ottawa to the Musée Canadien des Civilisations, but there's also a fast and frequent **bus** service, operated by **STO buses** (☎819/770-3242, Ⓦ www.sto.ca) from outside the Rideau Shopping Centre at the west end of Rideau St. There are no buses to Gatineau Park, but Gatineau Hills Experience (☎613/276-4394, Ⓦ www.hillsidefun.com) provides a wide range of small-group, day-long excursions, including hikes, beginning in Ottawa; prices start at $75 per person.

Musée Canadien des Civilisations

Gatineau's pride and joy, standing on the far side of the Alexander Bridge from the National Gallery, is the whopping **Musée Canadien des Civilisations** (May to June & Sept to mid-Oct Mon–Wed & Fri–Sun 9am–6pm, Thurs 9am–9pm; July–Aug Mon–Wed, Sat & Sun 9am–6pm, Thurs & Fri 9am–9pm; mid Oct to April Tues–Wed & Fri–Sun 9am–5pm, Thurs 9am–9pm; $10; Ⓦ www.civilization.ca), whose curvy limestone contours are supposed to represent the rocky sweep of the Canadian Shield. Not everyone was convinced, but the architect – Douglas Cardinal, a Blackfoot from Red Deer, Alberta – certainly mounted a spirited argument and the building is certainly distinctive; the best view is from the Ottawa side of the river.

The museum spreads over four floors and the entrance, where you can pick up a **free plan**, is on Level 2. Also on **Level 2** is a mixed bag of attractions, including a Canadian Postal Museum, a Children's Museum, offering an interactive "world tour", a theatre and a giant IMAX cinema screen showing nature and adventure films (for a supplementary fee of $7–10). Upstairs, **Level 3** holds **Canada Hall**, which tracks through Canada's history from the Viking colony on Newfoundland (see p.508) to the 1970s. It's an ambitous affair, featuring life-size reconstructions of historical environments, from an Acadian settlement and a fur-trading post to a Métis camp, a frontier farm, a Maritime shipyard, an Ontarian main street circa 1900, a Canadian Pacific train station, a Union Hall and a Chinese laundry. **Level 4** holds temporary exhibitions and then it's down to **Level 1** for the **Grand Hall**, easily the largest room in the museum and perfectly designed to display a magnificent collection of around twenty Pacific Coast **totem poles** – more properly house posts. The main line of poles stands outside six native "houses" which explore Pacific Coast native culture, including displays on trade, religious beliefs, tribal gatherings and art.

Gatineau Park

The second good reason to venture north from Ottawa is the rolling forested hills and lakes of **Gatineau Park**, which extends northwest from Gatineau and is a favourite with the region's hikers and cyclists, who troop off here in their hundreds every summer weekend. From the Musée Canadien des Civilisations, it's just 3km west – follow the signs – to the park's southern entrance. The park was founded in 1934 when the government snaffled the land up to stop its deforestation for firewood during the hard years of the Depression. The park is latticed with **footpaths** and many of these are readily reached along the park's main road, the **Champlain Parkway**. This meanders its way across the southern half of the park before reaching its conclusion at the **Champlain Lookout**, 24km from the park entrance. The belvedere here provides a grand view of a distinctive landscape, where the granite outcroppings of the Canadian Shield shelve down to the rich green fields of the St Lawrence lowlands. Among the **hikes** passed by the parkway, one of the most appealing is the short and easy, one-hour hoof through the woods to **Larriault Falls and Mulvihill Lake**. Also beginning beside the Parkway is the easy 2.5km gambol to the geologically rare meromictic **Pink Lake** – named for an early settler, not its colour; meromictic lakes have high-density lower waters. Trail leaflets and park maps are available at the **Visitor Centre**, just beyond the southern park entrance on rue Scott (June–Aug daily 9am–7pm; Sept–May daily 9am–5pm; ☎819/827-2020, Ⓦ www.canadascapital.gc.ca/gatineau).

Enclosed within the park – and signed from the Parkway – is the **Mackenzie King Estate** (mid-May to mid-Oct Mon–Fri 11am–5pm; Sat & Sun 10am–6pm; $10 per car), once the summer retreat of William Lyon Mackenzie King, prime minister between 1921 and 1948. In a characteristically eccentric manner, King littered the grounds of his estate with architectural follies – chunks of the old Ottawa Parliament buildings and so forth – and his former house, **Moorside**, now offers light meals and high teas (advance reservations on ☎819/827-3405).

Eating and drinking

As you might expect of a capital city, Ottawa has a good range of **restaurants**, some geared firmly to the expense account, but the majority informal, reasonably priced affairs – surprisingly so considering the amount of political money floating around – and a main course should rarely cost you more than $25. Ethnic restaurants are commonplace – from Italian through Mexican, Chinese and Spanish – and although there is no distinctive Ottawa cuisine as such, the city's chefs borrow strongly from the French-Québecois tradition – Québec is, after all, just across the river. The trendiest joints are in the Byward Market area (see box), but there are also a number of good places in the few blocks to the south of Parliament Hill, and a small Chinatown on Somerset West and Bronson. In addition, Ottawa has sprouted dozens of **café-bars**, some offering little more than glorified bar food, but many dipping into Asian, French and Italian cuisines to provide excellent food at very affordable prices – $10–15 should see you fixed in all but the priciest of places. These café-bars have dented Ottawa's **bar and pub** scene, but there is still a reasonable range of downtown drinking places with a particular concentration in and around the Byward Market, which heaves with revellers on the weekend. Byward Market is also home to the city's best **delicatessens** and fresh produce stalls, and sprouts **fast-food** vans at night. These are something of an Ottawa institution, mainly on account of their *poutine* – fries covered in gravy and cheese curds. Another muncipal institution, albeit a recent one, is "**Beavertails**", a half-pizza, half-doughnut snack, fried and covered either in garlic butter and cheese or cinnamon and sugar, and on sale at **Hooker's All Canadian Beavertails**, a fast-food kiosk in Byward Market at the junction of George and William streets.

Ottawa was one of the first Canadian cities to apply a **no smoking** ordnance in all its cafés, restaurants, bars and clubs.

Cafés, café-bars and diners

Bagel Bagel 92 Clarence St. Nine different types of bagel with an assortment of fillings from $3. Open late every day. Byward Market.

Byward Market Café Byward Market. Straightforward café inside Byward Market (at the south end) selling a wide range of snacks and light meals – sandwiches, salads and so forth – at very reasonable prices.

Café Crepe de France 76 Murray St at Parent. Divine crepes from $10 in a distinctive French-style café. Byward Market.

Medithéo 77 Clarence St. Fashionable Byward Market hangout with stone walls, angular modern furniture and a good menu with a Mediterranean slant.

Second Cup Slater at Metcalfe St. Reliable coffee house chain with great coffee and trim modern furnishings. Ottawa has six of them. Opening hours are mostly Mon–Fri 6.30am–7pm, Sat & Sun 8.30am–6pm.

Zak's Diner 16 Byward Market. A 1950s-style time warp with chrome decor, rock'n'roll blaring from the jukebox and good all-American food. Open daily until midnight, all night Friday and Saturday.

Byward Market

Since the 1840s the **Byward Market** neighbourhood, just east of Sussex and north of Rideau St, has been a centre for the sale of farm produce, but in the last few years it has become Ottawa's hippest district. At its heart, the 1920s Byward Market building (Mon–Thurs 9.30am–6.30pm, Fri 9.30am–8pm, Sat 9am–6pm & Sun 10am–5.30pm) is home to cafés and delis, specialist food and fresh fruit and vegetables stalls and these merge with the street stalls outside. Most of Ottawa's best restaurants and bars are located here too, and at night the area buzzes till the early hours of the morning.

Restaurants

Arc 140 Slater St ☎613/238-2888. In immaculate, modernistic surroundings – see hotels, p.177 – this attractive little restaurant serves a tasty line in Asian food alongside Canadian dishes featuring local ingredients. Main courses average $25.

Coriander Thai 282 Kent St ☎613/233-2828. Arguably the best Thai in Ottawa. Amazing satays, rich green and red curries, lemongrass tea and other classic dishes at fair prices. Not far from Parliament Hill, but still off the tourist track – and none the worse for that. Main courses $10–14.

Courtyard 21 George St ☎613/241-1516. This long-established restaurant has a wide-ranging, reasonably priced menu. It's best to visit in sunny weather as the outside terrace enjoys a particularly pleasant location in an attractive cobbled courtyard. Byward Market area.

Domus Café 87 Murray St at Parent ☎613/241-6007. Part of the immaculate Domus houseware store, this chi-chi, pastel-painted restaurant serves top-quality food from an imaginative menu. Local ingredients are a feature of the menu too. Main courses hover around $25. Near Byward Market. Recommended.

Empire St Grill 47 Clarence St at Parent ☎613/241-1343. Smart and polished restaurant in the Byward Market area. First-rate steaks and an extensive wine list. The bar, chic and appealing, offers smooth background music, with jazz the particular favourite.

Havely 39 Clarence St at Sussex ☎613/241-1700. Comfortable, if fairly formal Indian restaurant offering all the classics plus a good range of vegetarian options. Byward Market area. Main courses $12–15.

Kinki 41 York St ☎613/789-9559. Smart Asian fusion restaurant with a creative menu – mango-dusted scallops for one. Main courses hover at $18.

La Pointe 55 York St ☎613/241-6221. Atmospheric Byward Market restaurant serving quality seafood at reasonable prices in informal, basement premises.

Saigon 83 Clarence St ☎613/789-7934. First-rate and inexpensive Vietnamese cuisine in the Byward Market.

Social 537 Sussex Drive ☎613/789-7355. Stylish restaurant graced by slick modern furnishings and fittings, plus a good, wide-ranging menu with a Mediterranean slant. Near Byward Market.

Suisha Gardens 208 Slater St ☎613/236-9602. Tasty sushi, tempura, sukiyaki and teriyaki. There's also a *tatami* room where you can sit on rush mats and eat Japanese-style. Good deals at lunchtime. South of Parliament Hill.

Nightlife and entertainment

Ottawa is a major port of call for big-name rock and pop acts, most of whom appear at the Corel Centre, about 15km southwest of downtown in Kanata (☎613/599-0250 or 1-800/444-7367, ⓦwww.corelcentre.com). Otherwise, things aren't too exciting, though downtown is home to a number of busy **bars** and several good **clubs**, featuring both live music and DJ sounds. For **listings**, the free *Where Ottawa* is a monthly promotional magazine that details what's coming up and where, but the reviews are cursory. It's available at the tourist office as is the *Xpress*, a weekly freebie that provides much better reviews and is a good deal hipper. The Friday edition of the *Ottawa Citizen* newspaper also provides thorough listings and perceptive reviews.

Ottawa's cultural focus is the National Arts Centre, 53 Elgin St (☎613/947-7000, ⓦwww.nac-cna.ca), which presents plays by its resident **theatre** company as well as touring groups, **concerts** by its resident orchestra, **operas** and **dance** from (among others) the National Ballet of Canada and the Royal Winnipeg Ballet. The acoustics are outstanding. Quality **theatre** is also on offer from the mainstream Great Canadian Theatre Company, 910 Gladstone Ave (ⓦwww.gctc.ca), and the Ottawa Little Theatre, 400 King Edward (ⓦwww.o-l-t.com), which presents avant-garde Canadian plays with strong social or political overtones. Ottawa has a good selection of **cinemas**. Options include the Bytowne Cinema, 325 Rideau (☎613/789-3456), the capital's most popular repertory cinema, and the Canadian Film Institute, 2 Daly Ave (☎613/232-6727), which shows art-house and mainstream films arranged by theme.

Bars

Blackthorn Café 15 Clarence St at Sussex. In the Byward Market area, this trendy spot incorporates an English-style pub and has a pleasant outside terrace.

Blue Cactus 2 Byward Market. Hectic bar with a good line in cocktails and stylish modern decor.

Centretown Pub 340 Somerset St West. Popular gay bar, ten minutes' walk south of Laurier Ave W along O'Connor St.

The Collection 56 Byward Market. Busy modern bar at the heart of the Byward Market.

Heart and Crown 121 Parent Ave. Popular Irish-style bar with large outside terrace.

The Mayflower 201 Queen St. English-style pub that gets jam-packed on the weekend.

Clubs and music venues

Babylon 317 Bank St ⓦwww.babylon-club.ca. Live bands of different persuasions play here, but the DJs are the big deal – spinning eveything from funk, punk and metal through to hop and world music.

Barrymore's Music Hall 323 Bank St ⓦwww .barrymores.on.ca. Former Vaudeville theatre converted into a huge seven-level venue with commercial, mainstream and local bands perform-ing live most nights. Showcases big names too: both U2 and Tina Turner have played here.

Mercury Lounge 56 Byward Market, ⓦwww.mercury–lounge.net. Big loft with great Martinis and vinyl couches. House, hop and techno with DJs from all over Canada along with weird and wacky live acts. Above *The Collection* bar.

Rainbow Bistro 76 Murray St, ⓦwww .soundzgood.com/rainbow. Atmospheric blues and folk club with regular jam sessions. Downtown above a crêpe restaurant.

Zaphod Beeblebrox 27 York St, ⓦwww .zaphodbeeblebrox.com. The whole spectrum of live bands from C&W to alternative plus featured DJ slots. Downtown.

Listings

Airlines Air Canada ☎1-888/247-2262; British Airways ☎1-800/247-9297; Continental ☎1-800/231-0856; Delta ☎1-800/221-1212.

Airport enquiries ☎613/248-2000, ⓦwww.ottawaairport.ca.

Bike rental Rent-A-Bike, 1 Rideau St, at the back of the Château Laurier hotel (☎613/241-4140, ⓦwww.cyberus.ca/~rentabike). Standard bikes from $28 a day, performance bikes from $40.

Bookshops Chapters, 47 Rideau St (☎613/241-0073), has a fine selection of Canadian literature and nonfiction. The Book Market, on the corner of Dalhousie and Rideau sts, buys and sells secondhand books (☎613/241-1753). A World of Map and Travel Books, 1235 Wellington St at Holland Ave (☎613/724-6776), specializes in travel books. Mother Tongue Books, 1067 Bank at Sunnyside (☎613/730-2346), are feminist, First Nation, gay and countercultural specialists.

Car rental Discount, downtown at 421 Gladstone and Kent (☎613/310-2277); Hertz, Queen at Lyon in the *Crowne Plaza Hotel* (☎613/230-7607) and at the airport (☎613/521-3332); National, 226 Queen St (☎613/232-3536) and at the airport (☎613/737-7023).

Embassies Australia, 50 O'Connor St (☎613/236-0841); Ireland, 130 Albert St (☎613/233-6281);

Netherlands, 350 Albert St (☎613/237-5030); New Zealand, 99 Bank St (☎613/238-5991); Poland, 443 Daly Ave (☎613/789-0468); UK, 80 Elgin St (☎613/237-1530); US, 490 Sussex Drive (☎613/238-5335).

Gay & lesbian life Gayline Information & Counselling ☎613/238-1717.

Ice hockey From Sept to May, the Ottawa Senators play NHL games at the 18,500-capacity Corel Centre, 1000 Palladium Drive, Kanata (☎613/599-0200, ⓦwww.ottawasenators.com), about 15km southwest of downtown.

Internet access Chapters, 47 Rideau St at Sussex (Mon–Sat 9.30am–11pm, Sun 9.30am–10pm; ☎613/241-0073).

Laundry Rideau Coinwash, 436 Rideau St (daily 8am–10pm).

Left luggage Coin-operated lockers at the train and bus stations.

Outdoor equipment The Expedition Shoppe, 43 York St (☎613/241-8397).

Pharmacy Rideau Pharmacy, 390 Rideau St (Mon–Fri 9am–9pm, Sat 9am–6pm, Sun noon–6pm).

Post office Sparks St, corner of Confederation Sq (Mon–Fri 8am–6pm).

Taxis Blue Line ☎613/238-1111; Capital Taxi ☎613/744-3333.

Weather Information ☎613/998-3439.

Northern Ontario

Stretching north from the shores of lakes Huron and Superior to the frozen reaches of Hudson Bay, **northern Ontario** is a land of sparse population and colossal distances. Give or take the odd ridge and chasm, the landscape is almost entirely flat, an endless expanse of forest pouring over the mineral-rich rocks of the **Canadian Shield** and interrupted by thousands of lakes. To the anglophile elite of the south, the region was (and still is) seen as barbarous and crude. Canadian humourist Stephen Leacock, for instance, dismissed it: "The best that anyone could say of the place was that it was a 'sportsman's paradise', which only means a good place to drink whiskey in." Such disdain always ignored the economic facts. The north once produced the furs that launched the Canada's economy and its raw materials – gold, silver, nickel, timber and so forth – paid (and pay) for Toronto's gleaming skyscrapers. The extractive nature of the northern economy and the harshness of the climate have defined the locals' attitude to their surroundings. **Hunting** and **fishing** are extremely popular – and most visitors who come here join in – but other types of appreciation have been slow to grow.

Given that the distances are so great, it's important to plan an itinerary carefully. Northern Ontario is traversed by two main highways, Hwy 11 and the much more interesting Hwy 17. **Hwy 11** begins by slicing through workaday **North Bay**, 345km north of Toronto, before pushing on to the hunting and fishing resort of **Temagami**. From here, it's a manageable hop onto **Cochrane**, uninteresting in itself but useful as the starting point for the lonely rail line that strikes north beyond the road network to **Moosonee** on the bleak and barren shores of James Bay, part of Hudson Bay. This rail line, plied by Ontario Northland's Polar Bear Express trains, makes for one of the most unusual excursions in the country and is a comfortable way of seeing something of the Arctic north, way beyond the tree line. From Cochrane, Hwy 11 leads west to a series of mining towns, but this part of the highway holds little of interest and is best avoided, even if you have to double back on yourself.

There are two obvious ways to join **Hwy 17**. The faster route comes up from Parry Sound (see p.157) to meet Hwy 17 at the mining town of **Sudbury**, or you can catch the ferry from Tobermory (see p.146) to cross rusticated **Manitoulin Island** on Hwy 6 and join Hwy 17 west of Sudbury. Whichever route you choose (and both have their scenic advantages), your first port of call on Hwy 17 should be **Sault Ste Marie**. In itself, this industrial town is only of middling interest, but it serves as the terminus for a splendid wilderness train trip on the **Algoma Central Railway**. From Sault Ste Marie, Hwy 17 begins its long haul round **Lake Superior** passing by or through a string of parks, notably **Lake Superior Provincial Park** and **Pukaskwa National Park**,

---

Train journeys in northern Ontario

Advance booking is strongly recommended for both of Northern Ontario's notable **train** rides. The **Cochrane–Moosonee** route is operated by Ontario Northland (☎1-800/461-8558, ⓦwww.northlander.ca), whilst the Algoma Canyon excursion is run by **Algoma Central Railway**, 129 Bay St, Sault Ste Marie (☎705/946-7300 or 1-800/242-9287, ⓦwww.agawacanyontourtrain.com).

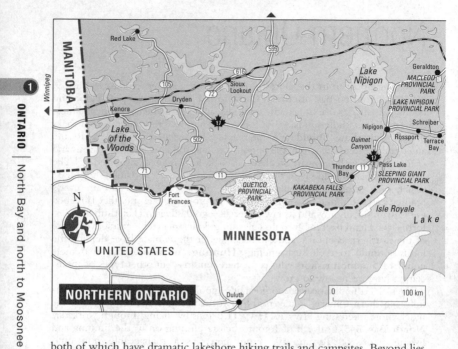

both of which have dramatic lakeshore hiking trails and campsites. Beyond lies the inland port of **Thunder Bay**, home to the replica fur trading post of Fort William and the last place of much appeal before Winnipeg (see p.534), a further 680km away to the west.

Ontario Northland **buses** (T 1-800/461-8558, W www.webusit.com) shuttle between the major towns on both Hwy 17 and Hwy 11, but all the parks and many of the smaller places require private transport. Note also that if you're heading for a particular hotel, motel or campsite, you should check to see how near you'll get by bus – bus stops are often on the edge of towns. In winter, driving on both Hwy 11 and Hwy 17 can be perilous. Remember too that in summer mosquitoes and blackfly can make life absolutely miserable, so take the necessary precautions. The best time to go hiking is either at the start of spring or in the autumn.

North Bay and north to Moosonee

Hwy 11 cuts a 1000km arc through Northern Ontario, eventually meeting up with Hwy 17 as it nears Thunder Bay. En route, it links a string of gritty resource towns, who endure a climate which, far from the moderating effects of Lake Superior, is as savage as any in the world. In winter, Hwy 11 is subject to ferocious blizzards, which make it impassable to ordinary vehicles, and at any time of the year there is – to be frank – little point in travelling much of the highway at all. Content yourself with the first stretch, the 400km trip from **North Bay**, a small lakeshore town with hotels and motels, to **Cochrane**, even smaller but the starting point for the region's star turn, the train ride to **Moosonee**, beyond the road network close to the frozen shores of James Bay.

Trains and buses connect most of the larger settlements between North Bay and Cochrane, but you really need a car to be sure of getting where you want, when you want – and you certainly don't want to be hanging around too long for a connection. The train from Cochrane to Moosonee is operated by Ontario Northland (see p.196) and should be booked in advance. Note also that food is more expensive in this region than elsewhere in Ontario; on many occasions, your best bet is to eat where you sleep.

North Bay

Once an important halting point on the canoe route to the west and now a useful place to break your journey on the long drive north, the workaday city of **NORTH BAY**, some 160km from Bracebridge (see p.160), is a relative giant hereabouts with a population of about 55,000. Glued to the shores of Lake Nipissing, it has one notable attraction, the **Dionne Quints Museum**, just where Hwy 11 hits the south side of town (daily: late May to June 9am–4pm; July–Aug 9am–7pm; Sept to mid-Oct 9am–4pm; $3). The museum is housed in the small log cabin from Corbeil, just west of North Bay, where the Dionne quintuplets were born on May 28, 1934. Kept alive with drops of whiskey, the quins were considered miracle children by the economically depressed nation, and at the age of three months the government took custody of them, removing them from their parents and five other siblings. Until they were nine years old, the quins were put on display in a glassed-in playground, to the delight of up to 6000 sightseers who turned up each day to watch them and to pay for souvenirs such as "birth-promoting" stones picked up from the North Bay area. The girls were educated in a synthetic "normal school atmosphere" provided by ten classmates, five of whom were English to help the quins with their second language. This bizarre childhood eventually caused a highly publicized estrangement between the quins and their parents, and doubtless contributed to the unhappiness of their later lives, a story dominated by illness, depression and failed marriages. Indeed, three of the quins – Yvonne, Annette and Cécile – published a shared autobiography accusing their father of sexual abuse, their mother of verbal abuse and the Ontario government of exploitation. The small museum contains dresses, toys, photographs, advertising hoardings and souvenirs of the quins' childhood, including the bed they were born in.

Ontario Northland **trains** from Cochrane and Toronto and all long-distance **buses** terminate at the Intermodal station at 100 Station Rd, to the east of – and a local bus ride from – the downtown core, which zeroes in on Main St, one block from the lakeshore. The town's **tourist office** is on the south side of town, beside Hwy 11 and next door to the Dionne Quints Museum at 1375 Seymour St (daily: mid-June to Aug 8.30am–8.30pm; Sept to mid-June 9am–5pm). Most of North Bay's **accommodation** is concentrated on Lakeshore Drive, beside Lake Nipissing. Proficient chain **motels** here include the *Comfort Inn*, 676 Lakeshore Drive (☎705/494-9444 or 1-877/449-4484, ⓦwww.comfortnorthbay.com; ❹), and the *Best Western North Bay Hotel*, 700 Lakeshore Drive (☎705/474-5800 or 1-800/461-6199, ⓦwww.bestwesternnorthbay.com; ❹). For **food**, stick to *Churchill's*, 631 Lakeshore Drive (☎705/476-7777), which has – so locals claim – the best ribs in Ontario.

Temagami and Cobalt

Surrounded by lakes and forests, the pleasant resort village of **TEMAGAMI**, 100km beyond North Bay on Hwy 11, started life as a rest stop on the long portage from Snake Lake to Lake Temagami. It has been attracting tourists since the turn of the century, when it was the site of the region's first grand hotel and introduced a steamship company and rail line to transport holiday-makers here. Nowadays, it serves as a base for extended forays into the wilderness – mostly hunters and fishermen travelling by float plane and/or canoe, but note that the terrain is much too wild for the novice: you have to be well equipped with outback experience to be safe. To get a view of this wilderness, climb the 30-metre-high **Temagami Tower** just before you hit town; you may even spot a peregrine falcon – they were was reintroduced in 1997 after previously being polished off by DDT. **Trains** and **buses** pull in at the station on Hwy 11 close to the **Welcome Centre**, at 7 Lakeshore Drive (July & Aug daily 8am–8pm; Sept–June Mon–Fri 9am–5pm; ☎705/569-3344 or 1-800/661-7609, ⓦwww.temagamiinformation.com). The centre has details on **accommodation**, most of which is geared up for hunting and fishing. There's also the rather more comfortable *Smoothwater Wilderness Lodge* (☎705/569-3539, ⓦwww.smoothwater.com), 14km north of town on Hwy 11, and **camping** (mid-May to late Sept; ☎705/569-3205 or 1-888/668-7275) at **Finlayson Point Provincial Park**, beside Lake Temagami just south of town. Of the park's hundred or so sites, a quarter have hook-ups. There is a good range of facilities – including a laundromat, a shop and swimming – and sites cost from $18.75 to $25.50, but note that prebooking is advised. For complete **canoe outfitting**, head for Smoothwater Outfitters (☎705/569-3539, ⓦwww.smoothwater.com), who can provide everything from first-aid kits to frying pans.

Local legend has it that the silver boom at **COBALT**, just off Hwy 11 some 50km north of Temagami, started when a blacksmith named Fred La Rose threw a hammer at a fox and hit a rock instead, breaking off a great hunk of

Grey Owl

Temagami was once the domain of one of Canada's most colourful characters – Wah-Sha-Quon-Asin, or **Grey Owl**. One of the world's first conservationists, he travelled Canada, Britain and the US spreading the message of respect for the flora and fauna of the wilderness, publishing articles in such magazines as *Country Life*, and turning out books that became bestsellers. In 1938, at the age of 50, Grey Owl died – and it was only then that it became known just how extraordinary his life had been.

Grey Owl was born **Archie Belaney** in Hastings, England. He emigrated at the age of 17 to escape an authoritarian aunt and, on arrival in Canada, made his way to the silver strike in Cobalt. On a sudden whim he got off the train at Temagami, where he worked as a guide in the tourist camps and became fascinated with the Ojibwa population of the reserve on Lake Temagami's Bear Island. He learned the native stories and customs, and eventually married a young Ojibwa named **Angele**, with whom he had a daughter. Prone to drinking and causing trouble, Belaney was finally run out of town after a brawl. He moved to Biscotasing and became a forest ranger, but soon his arrest warrant caught up with him and he had to leave town again – though not before making another Indian woman, **Marie Girard**, pregnant. She died of consumption shortly after giving birth to their child.

During World War I Belaney temporarily abandoned his Indian ways to fight with the army in Flanders, where he was wounded by shrapnel. During his convalescence in England, he married his nurse, thereby adding **bigamy** to his many accomplishments. The call of the Canadian wilderness proved this marriage's undoing, and Belaney returned to Biscotasing, stopping en route to see Angele for four days, during which another child was conceived.

By then Biscotasing had been taken over by the whites, who were busy cutting down the trees and scaring away the wildlife that Archie had grown to love. His determination to renounce his European roots now became even stronger, and his anarchic attitude made his persona as a "drunken Injun" the more convincing. In 1925 Belaney – by this time almost exclusively known as Grey Owl – returned to Temagami to live with Angele and their two children. He then met **Anahereo**, a 19-year-old Iroquois. Angele was duly dumped as Grey Owl eloped with Anahereo to a hut in northern Québec, where their only companions were two beavers. It was these two animals (and a third that followed) that inspired much of Grey Owl's writing and prompted him to start a beaver colony to prevent the extinction of Canada's national animal. To raise money for the project Grey Owl began writing and lecturing about his life, a publicity campaign that also secured him the post of warden of Riding Mountain National Park and later Prince Albert National Park.

Grey Owl's long absences and the days spent writing led to the collapse of his relationship with Anahereo, but it didn't take long for him to marry someone else, this time a French-Canadian who adopted the Indian name **Silver Moon**. Grey Owl made a lecture tour of Britain and the US in 1938, which included an audience with King George and the princesses Elizabeth and Margaret, but it left him so exhausted that he died later the same year. Only then did his wives, friends and family find out the truth behind his charade.

---

silver. Whatever the truth, mining began here in earnest in 1903. Subsequently, in the frantic search for silver, new mine shafts were dropped every few weeks and within a decade the haphazard collection of tents, log cabins and huts had swollen to contain seven thousand people. With output burgeoning, Cobalt merged with nearby Haileybury and New Liskeard to form the "tritowns": the miners lived in Cobalt, the managers on the Lake Temiskaming waterfront in Haileybury and the mine owners kept their distance in New Liskeard. Life in

Cobalt was perilous: typhoid, smallpox and influenza were common and many of the homes were built from wooden dynamite boxes, and so were regularly wrecked by fires. The high times ended with the Great Depression, but Cobalt struggled on until the steep decline in silver prices in the 1980s. The last mine closed in 1990 and Cobalt's future looks decidedly gloomy. Cobalt today is hardly compulsive viewing, but you might drop by Canada's oldest **Mining Museum** (June–Sept daily 9am–5pm; Oct–May daily 1–4pm; $3.50), housed in a converted newspaper office, with a vast collection of ores from the mines, including a collection of luminous stones. Up the street, an old head frame (the top of the mine shaft) protrudes from the roof of what was once the grocery store – the store used the disused shaft as a refrigerator – and opposite a small park has a large painted sign listing the 104 mines operating in 1908.

Cochrane and beyond

Some 100km north of Cobalt, Hwy 11 passes over the **Arctic Watershed**, or Height of Land, a slight elevation in the Canadian Shield that divides Ontario's water flow: to the north, all water flows to James and Hudson bays, and to the south it flows to the Great Lakes and the St Lawrence.

Beyond, it's a tedious haul on Hwy 11 to **COCHRANE**, 280km from Temagami, a modest little place that grew up as a repair and turntable station for the railroad companies serving the far north. Most of the workshops have closed down, but this is still the departure point for Ontario Northland's **Polar Bear Express train**, which ventures north beyond the road network to Moosonee, on James Bay (see below). The popularity of the train sustains several workaday **motels** in Cochrane – the *Chimo*, on Hwy 11 (☎705/272-6555; ❸), is as good as any. There's also the more comfortable *Station Inn*, by the train station at 200 Railway St (☎705/272-3500 or 1-800/265-2356; ❸).

Cochrane to Moosonee by train

A popular excursion, the **Polar Bear Express** (late June to Aug 1 daily except Mon) cuts across 300km of Arctic tundra on its way from Cochrane to Moosonee, on the Moose River as it empties into James Bay. This is as far north as anyone can easily (or reasonably) go in Ontario – but, despite the name of the train, you won't see any polar bears. It departs Cochrane at 8.30am and arrives in Moosonee at 12.50pm, departing Moosonee 6pm and arriving back in Cochrane at 10.05pm. The return fare is just $60 return and the service is operated by Ontario Northland (☎1-800/461-8558, ⓦwww.northlander.ca), which also runs the year-round **Little Bear train**, one of Canada's last remaining flagstop trains (departs Cochrane Mon, Wed & Fri 11.15am, arrives Moosonee 4.15pm; departs Moosonee Tues, Thurs & Sat 9am, arrives Cochrane 2.30pm; $95 return), taking freight and stopping along the way to pick up trappers, fishers, hunters and local Crees.

The Crees have been hunting and fishing Hudson Bay for about 10,000 years and they make up the majority of the population in **MOOSONEE**, which was founded in 1903 by a French fur-trading company, Révillon Frères – today's Revlon. The **Révillon Frères Museum** (late June to Aug daily 9am–5pm; free), in one of the original company buildings, traces the history of the settlement and its largely unsuccessful attempt to challenge the local monopoly of the **Hudson's Bay Company**. The latter had established the trading post of **Moose Factory Island**, just offshore from Moosonee, in 1673, which makes it the oldest English-speaking community in Ontario. **Water taxis** zip travellers over from Moosonee to the island, where the **Moose**

Kirkland Lake and Sir Harry Oakes

The mining community of **Kirkland Lake**, off Hwy 11 between Cobalt and Cochrane, isn't much to look at, but it does have an interesting tale to tell. To begin with, the town produces one-fifth of Canada's **gold** and the main street, Government Rd, is actually paved with gold – the construction crew used the wrong pile of rocks, gold ore instead of waste rock. The town also featured in one of the most sensational stories of Canada's recent past – the tale that Nic Roeg made into the film *Eureka* with Gene Hackman and Rutger Hauer.

In the summer of 1911, **Sir Harry Oakes** arrived in Swastika, close to Kirkland Lake, with $2.65 in his pocket. He left in 1934 with $20 million, the largest fortune ever gained through mining in Canada. Oakes began his quest for gold in 1898, his search taking him to Alaska, where his vessel was blown into the Bering Strait and then captured by Cossacks. He escaped under rifle fire and continued his explorations in Australia, West Africa, Mexico and California until, fleeing a revolution in South America, he joined the **gold rush in northern Canada**. In 1912, he founded a mine here in what was later to become Kirkland Lake and this produced $100,000-worth of gold a month. Not content, in 1928 Oakes also opened up the Lake Shore gold mine, to exploit the most lucrative ore ever discovered in Canada. Oakes, obsessed with keeping his wealth from the tax man, then emigrated to the tax-free Bahamas and it was here that he came to a sticky end.

Around midnight on July 8, 1943, Oakes was murdered in his bed in Nassau, a crime that momentarily knocked World War II off the front pages of the newspapers. Detectives immediately arrested Alfred de Marigny, a handsome playboy who had eloped with Oakes's daughter, Nancy, two years previously. The case against him was thin, resting on the presence of a single fingerprint in Oakes's bedroom and the motive of money – with Oakes dead his daughter would inherit a fortune. During the trial it became obvious that the detectives had planted the fingerprint and de Marigny was acquitted. The case was never reopened, but the murder of Sir Harry Oakes has prompted a variety of theories. Alfred de Marigny implicated Oakes's debt-ridden friend Harold Christie, who had defrauded Oakes in a property deal that was about to be exposed by the auditors. Rumours of voodoo and Mafia involvement were rife at the time, but more intriguing is a possible cover-up involving Oakes's confidant, the **Duke of Windsor**. Apparently, the Duke and Oakes were involved in a money-laundering operation with a Swedish industrialist and alleged Nazi agent. The suggestion is that the Duke, terrified that the scam would come to light in the course of a prolonged police investigation, might have wanted de Marigny's quick arrest in order to throw people off the scent.

Oakes's 1919 Frank Lloyd Wright-style chateau is now the **Museum of Northern History** (Mon–Sat 10am–4pm, Sun noon–4pm; $3), located near the west end of Kirkland Lake. The museum details his climb from rags to riches and displays antique mining equipment, ores, minerals and stuffed animals. One room also highlights the famous hockey players who have come from the town: it has produced an amazing 51 NHL stars.

Factory Centennial Museum Park (late June to early Sept; free) holds the original blacksmith's shop, graveyard, powder magazine (the island's only stone building), and a tepee where the locals sell bannock (freshly baked bread). South of here, **St Thomas Anglican Church**, built in 1860, has an altar cloth of beaded moose hide, prayer books written in Cree, and removable floor plugs to prevent the church floating away in floods. There are other nautical possibilities from Moosonee, too, beginning with the Polar Princess **cruise boat**, which sails down the Moose River to James Bay (late June to early Sept 6 weekly, 9am–3pm; $55 including lunch). Alternatively, large **freight canoes**

The Hudson's Bay Company

In 1661 two Frenchmen, **Medard Chouart des Groseilliers** and **Pierre-Esprit Radisson**, reached the southern end of Hudson Bay overland and realized it was the same inland sea described by earlier seafaring explorers. They returned to the St Lawrence laden down with furs, upon which the French governor arrested them for trapping without a licence. Understandably peeved, they turned to England, where Charles II's cousin, Prince Rupert, persuaded the king to finance and equip two ships, the *Eaglet* and the *Nonsuch*. After a mammoth voyage, the *Nonsuch* returned with a fantastic cargo of furs and this led to the incorporation of the **Hudson's Bay Company** by Charles II on May 2, 1670. The Company was granted wide powers, including exclusive trading rights to the entire Hudson Bay watershed – to be called **Rupert's Land**.

The HBC was a joint-stock company, the shareholders annually electing a governor and committee to hire men, order trade goods and arrange fur auctions and shipping. By 1760, **trading posts** had been built at the mouths of all the major rivers flowing into the bay; these were commanded by **factors**, who took their policy orders from London. The orders were often unrealistic and based on the concept of native trappers bringing furs to the posts – the direct opposite to the Montréal-based North West Company, whose mainly Francophone employees spent months in the wilderness working with the natives. Unsurprisingly, the NWC undercut the Company's trade and there was intense competition between the rival concerns right across the north of the continent, occasionally resulting in violence. In 1821 a compromise was reached and the two companies **merged**. They kept the name Hudson's Bay Company and the British parliament granted the new, larger company a commercial monopoly from Hudson Bay to the Pacific. However, the administrative structure of the Company was changed. A North American chief factor was appointed and his councils dealt increasingly with local trading concerns, though the London governor and committee continued to have the last word.

The extensive monopoly rights ceded to the new company were fiercely resented by local traders, and, in a landmark case of 1849, a local jury found a Metis trader by the name of Sayer guilty of breaking the monopoly, but simultaneously refused to punish him. Thereafter, in practice if not by law, the Company's stranglehold on the fur trade was dead and gone. Furthermore, the HBC's quasi-governmental powers seemed increasingly anachronistic and when a company official, **James Douglas**, became governor of British Columbia in 1858, the British government forced him to resign from the HBC. This marked the beginning of the end of the Company's colonial role.

In 1870 the HBC sold Rupert's Land to Canada. In return it received a cash payment, but, more importantly, retained the title to the lands on which the trading posts had been built and one-twentieth of the fertile land open to settlement. Given that the trading posts often occupied land that was the nucleus of the burgeoning western cities, this was a remarkably bad deal for Canada – and a great one for the HBC. Subsequently, the HBC became a major real-estate developer and retail chain, a position it maintains today.

visit either Moose Factory Island (late June to early Sept 1 daily; $22) or Fossil Island (late June to early Sept 6 weekly; $20), 10km upriver, where 350-million-year-old fossils have been found. All these excursions are operated by Two Bay Tours, 16 Ferguson Rd, Moosonee (☏705/336-2944, ⓦwww .twobay.com); advance reservations are strongly recommended.

Clearly, if you want to undertake any of the longer trips, the five hours allowed between the arrival and departure of the Polar Express is not enough – and with the Little Bear train you have to stay the night anyway. Moosonee

accommodation must be reserved ahead of time. There are two main choices: the *Polar Bear Lodge* (☎416/244-1495; ❹) and the *Osprey Country Inn* (☎705/336-2226; ❹). Note also that Ontario Northland offers three- to five-day packages from Cochrane to Moosonee and these can be less expensive than arranging everything yourself.

Sudbury

The economic centre of northeastern Ontario, sprawling **SUDBURY**, some 165km north of Parry Sound (see p.157), is parked on the edge of the Sudbury Basin, a pit created either by a volcano or, the preferred theory, by a giant **meteor**. Whatever did the damage, the effect was to throw one of the world's richest deposits of **nickel and copper** towards the surface. It was the nickel – used to temper steel – that made Sudbury's fortune, but its by-products caused devastation. Most of the damage was done by a smelting method known as heap roasting, used until the 1920s, which spread clouds of sulphurous fumes over forests already ravaged by lumber firms and mineral prospectors, who often started fires to reveal the traces of metal in the bare rocks. Likened to Hell or Hiroshima, the bleak landscape had only one advantage: in 1968 it enabled Buzz Aldrin and Neil Armstrong to practise their great leap for mankind in a ready-made lunar environment. Having continued to produce sulphur-laden smoke from the stacks of their nickel smelters, the mining companies were finally forced to take action when a whole community of workers from **Happy Valley**, just northeast of Sudbury (and now ringed off by a large steel fence), were evacuated in the 1970s because of the number of sulphur-induced illnesses. Since then, pollutants have been greatly reduced and the city has implemented an ambitious re-greening programme, which has been widely acclaimed by environmentalists. One result has been that large chunks of wasteland have spluttered back to life and the thirty lakes in the vicinity of Sudbury, including one in the middle of town, are no longer stagnant pools of vinegar.

Sudbury's multinational population of around 160,000 – over half of them French-speaking – are fiercely proud of their city, though it can seem that the main effect of the recent redevelopment has been an efflorescence of shopping malls. The key attractions are located to the south and west of the downtown core, which is focused on Elm St between Notre Dame Ave and Durham St. Making the most of the city's unusual geology, **Science North** (daily: mid-Jan to April 10am–4pm; May–June 9am–5pm; July–Aug 9am–6pm; ☎1-800/461-4898, ⓦwww.sciencenorth.ca), a huge snowflake-shaped structure south of the centre on Ramsey Lake Rd, is installed in a cavern blasted into the rock of the Canadian Shield. The hands-on displays enable you to simulate a miniature hurricane, gauge your fitness, lie on a bed of nails, learn to lip-read, call up amateur radio hams worldwide, tune in to weather-tracking stations and try different sensory tests, all under the guidance of students from the city's Laurentian University. The museum also has a collection of insects and animals, some of which can be handled, an **IMAX Theatre** with a 22-metre-wide screen, and various virtual-reality rides. An all-day pass covering everything in Science North costs $28, children under 13 $22.

The town's symbol, a nine-metre-high steel replica of a five-cent piece, known as the **Big Nickel**, stands by the Trans-Canada on the western approach to town. The nickel marks the entrance to **Dynamic Earth** (daily:

early March to April 10am–4pm; May–June 9am–5pm; July–Aug 9am–6pm; $13, children under 13 $10; ⓦwww.dynamicearth.ca), where an imaginative range of attractions have been located in an old nickel mine, from multimedia features on the world's cultures through to an exploration of old mine shafts and multimedia stories exploring Sudbury's bumpy history.

Practicalities

Sudbury's principal **train station** – Sudbury Junction – is about 10km northeast of the town centre on Lasalle Boulevard, with services south to Toronto and west to Winnipeg. There are no buses into town: you have to take a taxi. The Greyhound **bus** depot is at 854 Notre Dame, about 3km north of the centre. Sudbury **tourist office** is about 10km south of downtown beside Hwy 69 (ⓣ1-877/304-8222, ⓦwww.sudburytourism.ca).

As regards **accommodation**, Sudbury has a number of proficient chain motels. Options include the *Travelway Inn*, 1200 Paris St (ⓣ705/522-1122 or 1-800/461-4883, ⓦwww.travelwayinnssudbury.com; ❸) and the nearby *Travelodge*, 1401 Paris St (ⓣ705/522-1100 or 1-800/578-7878, ⓦwww.the.travelodge.com; ❸). More central is the *Days Inn Sudbury*, 117 Elm St (ⓣ705/674-7517 or 1-800/461-6717, ⓦwww.daysinn.com/canada; ❸). For **food**, *The Red Lobster*, 1600 Lasalle (ⓣ705/560-9825), does a good line in local pickerel and so does the more expensive *Teklenburg's* (ⓣ705/560-2662), just down the street at no.1893. Alternatively, there's good quality Italian food – and smashing home-made pasta – at *Pasta & Vino*, 118 Paris St (ⓣ705/674-3050).

Manitoulin Island

The Ojibwa believed that when Gitchi Manitou (the Great Spirit) created the world he reserved the best bits for himself and created **Manitoulin** (God's Island) – the world's largest freshwater island – as his own home. A continuation of the limestone Niagara Escarpment (see p.114), Manitoulin is strikingly different from the harsh grey rocks of the Canadian Shield, its white cliffs, wide lakes, gentle woodland and stretches of open, prairie-like farmland presenting an altogether more welcoming aspect. This rural idyll has long attracted hundreds of summer sailors, who ply the lakes that punctuate the island, and has proved increasingly popular with motorized city folk, who arrive here in numbers on the car ferry from Tobermory (see p.146) in southwest Ontario. Nevertheless, it's easy enough to escape the crowds, either by driving along the north shore, the prettiest part of the island, or by hunkering down in one of Manitoulin's **resorts** or **B&Bs**.

About a quarter of the island's 12,000 inhabitants are aboriginals, descendants of groups believed to have arrived here over 10,000 years ago. Archeologists have uncovered evidence of these Paleo-Indians at **Sheguiandah**, on the east coast, and the small display of artefacts at the museum here contains some of the oldest human traces found in Ontario. Much later, in 1836, the island's aboriginal peoples – primarily, Ojibwa and Odawa – reluctantly signed a treaty that turned Manitoulin into a refuge for several Georgian Bay bands who had been dispossessed by white settlers. Few of them came, which was just as well because the whites soon revised their position and wanted the island for themselves. In 1862, this pressure culminated in a second treaty that gave most of the island to the newcomers. It was all particularly shabby and, to their credit, the Ojibwa band living on the eastern tip of the island at **Wikwemikong** refused to sign. Their descendants still live on this so-called "unceded reserve" and, during the August Civic Weekend, **Wiky**, as it's always known, holds the largest **powwow** in the country.

Manitoulin can be reached either by **road** (and bridge) from Hwy 17 to the north or by **car ferry** from Tobermory in the south (May to mid-Oct 2–4 daily; $12 one-way per passenger, cars $27; reservations ☎519/596-2510 or 1-800/265-3163, ⓦwww.bmts.com). Ferries arrive on the island's south coast at South Baymouth. There are no bus or train services to or around the island.

East Manitoulin

Heading north from the South Baymouth ferry dock, Hwy 6 cuts inland before veering east to reach – after 30km – the lakeshore at the hamlet of **MANITOWANING**, where the treaty of 1836 was signed. There's nothing much to detain you here, though you could drop by the modest **Assiginack Museum** (June–Oct daily 10am–5pm; $1.50), whose pioneer bygones are mostly housed within the sturdy limestone building that once served as the local jail. Near here also is the splendid *Manitowaning Lodge and Resort* (mid-June to Sept; ☎705/859-3136, ⓦwww.manitoulin-island /manitowaninglodge; ❼), which nestles amongst the woods beside the bay. The timber cabins are plain, but decorated in the most tasteful of styles and the lodge itself, dating to the 1940s, is graced by unusual sculptures, one of which – a representation of the Great Manitou – drapes over the open fire. The food is simply wonderful too and there is a good range of sporting facilities. Rates include breakfast and dinner.

From Manitowaning, a side road runs east to the village of **WIKWEMIKONG**, 14km from Hwy 6 on Smith Bay and the focus of the eponymous Indian Reserve. Frankly, it's a dispiriting place badly scarred by poverty, but once every year, on the August Civic Weekend, Wiky is transformed by the country's largest **powwow**, which brings in the best of the continent's performers and is packed with stalls selling native foods and crafts. Amongst the programme of traditional dances and ceremonies, the local theatre group **De-Ba-Jeh-Mu-Jig** (Story Teller) relates native legends and performs contemporary plays by native playwrights – call ☎705/859-2317 for details of other performance dates and locations.

North from Manitowaning, Hwy 6 cuts a straight line across rolling farmland on its way to **Ten Mile Point Lookout**, which overlooks the waters of Georgian Bay as they funnel into the North Channel on the north side of the island. Shortly afterwards, the highway clips through the bayshore village of **SHEGUIANDAH**, where the homely **Centennial Museum of Sheguiandah** (May–Oct daily 10am–4.30pm; $3) is mainly concerned with the pioneer families who first farmed and traded here. Named photographs tell you who was who – and who was related to whom – in what was once an extremely isolated and tightly knit community, whose inhabitants were called "Haweaters" by outsiders after their liking for the scarlet fruit of the hawthorn tree. A ragbag of pioneer knick-knacks further illustrates their life and times – as does an 1870s log cabin, barn and sugar shack outside. It was in this wooded bayshore setting that archeologists found the remains of a Paleo-Indian settlement around 10,000 years old. A remarkable find, most of the artefacts were carted off to big museums elsewhere, leaving this museum with a display case of crudely fashioned quartzite tools – a weak display for something so important.

From the museum, it's another short hop to **LITTLE CURRENT**, Manitoulin's largest settlement – though that's not exactly a major claim to fame as the population is a mere 1500. It is, however, the site of the island's main **tourist office** (late April to late Oct daily 9am–5pm; ☎705/368-3021, Ⓦwww.manitoulin.ca), whose staff will help arrange accommodation, an especially useful service in July and August when vacancies can be hard to find. They are located beside the swing bridge just outside town. From Little Current, **Hwy 6** travels north to the mainland over a swing bridge and a series of inter-island causeways. It is 63km to Hwy 17 and a further 75km east to Sudbury (see p.199) or 235km to Sault Ste Marie.

North Manitoulin

Hwy 540 ducks and weaves its way right along the northern edge of Manitoulin, giving long, lingering views over the North Channel. It also accesses several popular **hiking trails**, notably the six-kilometre **Cup and Saucer Lookout Trail**, which starts near – and is signposted from – the junction of Hwy 540 and Bidwell Rd, about 22km west of Little Current. The trail reaches the highest point of the island (460m) and involves climbing ladders through natural rock chimneys.

KAGAWONG, about 45km west of Little Current, is arguably the best-looking village on the north shore, its attractive ensemble of old timber houses draped around a wide and gentle bay. It also has **Bridal Veil Falls**, the place for cool dips on hot days, and they have given their name to one of Kagawong's finer B&Bs, the *Bridal Veil B&B* (☎705/282-3300; ❸), in a century-old home in the centre of the village.

Sault Ste Marie

Strategically situated beside St Mary's River, the tortuous link between lakes Superior and Huron, industrial **SAULT STE MARIE** – more popularly **The Soo** – sits opposite the Michigan town of the same name and sees constant two-way traffic, with two sets of tourists keen to see how the other lot lives. The Soo is northern Ontario's oldest community, originally settled by Ojibwa fishing parties who gathered here beside what was then – before the river was canalized – a set of rapids. The French called these Ojibwa *Saulteux* – "people of the falls" – and the Jesuit missionaries who followed added the Christian sobriquet to give the town its present name. Initially, the Soo flourished as a gateway to the fur-rich regions inland, but it was the construction of a **lock and canal** in the nineteenth century that launched its career as a Great Lakes port and industrial centre, churning out pulp, paper and steel. Actually, the American locks were always bigger and better – and indeed the Canadian locks have only just been reopened after overcoming a catalogue of engineering difficulties.

Too industrial to be pretty, the Soo rustles up a reasonable range of attractions and motels, but its real appeal is as the starting point for a splendid wilderness train ride on the **Algoma Central Railway**.

The City

Some 2km long and three blocks wide, Soo's **downtown** runs parallel to the waterfront to either side of the main drag, Queen St East. All the principal sights are here, beginning with the enjoyable **Ermatinger Old Stone House**, right at the east end of the town centre at 831 Queen St E and Pim (mid-April to May Mon–Fri 10am–5pm; June–Sept daily 10am–5pm; Oct & Nov

The Algoma Central Railway

The 500km-long **Algoma Central Railway** (ACR) was constructed in 1901 to link the Soo's timber plants with the forests of the interior. It was first used for recreational purposes by members of the Group of Seven (see box p.96), who shunted up and down the track in a converted boxcar, stopping to paint whenever the mood took them. The ACR's timber days are long gone, but today the railway offers one of Ontario's finest excursions, with the train snaking through a wonderfully wild wilderness of deep ravines, secluded lakes and plunging gorges. To see it all, sit on the left-hand side – otherwise you'll end up looking at an awful lot of rock.

There are **three tours** to choose from and all depart from the Algoma Central Railway Terminal, in downtown Soo, at 129 Bay St and Dennis (☎705/946-7300 or 1-800/242-9287, ⊛www.agawacanyontourtrain.com). The **Agawa Canyon Tour Train** takes the whole day to cover the first 200km of track and back (mid-June to mid-Oct departs daily at 8am, returns 5pm; June to early Sept $59, early Sept to mid-Oct $78). Advance reservations are strongly advised and are pretty much essential in the autumn, when the leaves turn. A two-hour stop within the canyon's 180-metre-high walls allows for a **lunch break** and a wander around the well-marked nature trails, which include a lookout post from where the rail line appears as a thin silver thread far below. Unless you are properly equipped don't miss the train back – the canyon gets very cold at night, even during the summer, and the flies are merciless. During the winter when the lakes are frozen and the trees are bent low with ice, the **Snow Train** (mid-Jan to mid-March on Sat only; departs 8am, returns 4.30pm; $59) travels a little further north. It passes right through the canyon to the dramatic exit, where the walls are only 15m apart, before returning to the Soo. The third and longest trip is the **Tour of the Line** (early May to Oct Wed & Fri–Sun departs 9.20am, arrives Hearst 7pm; Nov to early May Fri–Sun departs 9am, arrives 6.40pm; $160 return, excluding accommodation), a return trip that takes two days with an overnight stay in Hearst, the ACR's northern terminus. This is arguably the weakest of the three excursions as the scenery north of the canyon is dreary pine forest and small-town Hearst is hardly riveting. Note also that passengers are responsible for arranging their own accommodation in Hearst – ring the Hearst Chamber of Commerce (☎1-800/655-5769) well ahead of time for details of availability; or contact the *Companion Hotel*, 930 Front St, Hearst (☎705/362-4304 or 1-888/468-9888; ❹), direct.

In addition to these well-publicized tourist jaunts, the ACR runs a regular **passenger train** from the Soo to Hearst four times weekly from early May to October, three times weekly in winter. Passengers on this train, which is commonly called the "moose meat special" on account of its popularity with hunters and trappers, get off and on at various points along the line and pay as little as $14 for a short journey up to $109 for the whole trip up to Hearst. This service enables serious hikers to step out into the great unknown comforted by that they can always flag down the next train up. Schedule details are available from the ACR, which also has information about renting **boxcars** and details of the several **outback lodges** that dot the line.

Mon–Fri 1–5pm; $2). Built in 1814, the house was originally home to the fur trader Charles Ermantinger and his Ojibwa wife Manonowe – also known as Charlotte – and their thirteen children. Since then the house has served as an hotel, the sheriff's house, a meeting hall for the YWCA and a social club. Restoration has returned its early nineteenth-century appearance and the period-costumed staff bake tasty cakes in the summer. Across the street, and entirely different, is the special-interest **Canadian Bushplane Heritage Centre** (daily: mid-May to mid-Oct 9am–6pm; mid-Oct to mid-May 10am–4pm; $7.50), whose collection of antique bushplanes is stored within a giant hangar. Bushplanes are of particular use in locating forest fires and there are several sections dealing with this aspect of their work. Models on display include a de Havilland Beaver, a Republic Seabee and a Beech 18 – and there's even a replica fire tower to climb.

The spruced-up section of The Soo's elongated **waterfront** begins just five-minutes' walk away to the west of the Heritage Centre, at the foot of East St – and a block or two from Queen St East. First up is the **Art Gallery of Algoma**, 10 East St (Mon–Sat 9am–5pm & Sun 1–4pm; $2), whose temporary exhibitions usually feature local artists. Moving on, it's a couple of minutes more to the **MS Norgoma** (guided tours daily from June to mid-Oct; $3), an old Great Lakes' passenger ferry that has ended up moored here, and the **Roberta Bondar Pavilion**, a prominent tent-like permanent structure named after Canada's first astronaut, who came from The Soo. The pavilion is used for concerts and exhibitions and locals are proud of the murals running round its exterior, which show aspects of the area painted inside wigwam shapes; subjects range from shipping and lake scenes to autumn colours and winter landscapes. From May to October on Wednesdays and Saturdays, a Farmers' Market, selling fruit and vegetables, is held here, and cruises of The Soo lock system (see below) begin from the adjacent jetty. Strolling on, you'll soon come to the **Station Mall**, a sprawling shopping centre that has sucked the commercial heart out of downtown Soo, and in front of this is the Algoma Central Railway station.

A good twenty-minute walk west of the Station Mall, Canal Drive crosses one of the river's narrow channels to reach St Mary's Island, home to the **Sault Ste Marie Canal National Historic Site** (open access). Here, you can stroll along the lock and investigate the old stone buildings that surround it with the help of a series of explanatory plaques. It's all mildly interesting – and if your nautical interest is stimulated there are two-hour **cruises** through the Soo lock system with Lock Tours Canada (late May to mid-Oct 2–4 daily; $24; ☎705/253-9850, ⓦwww.locktours.com). Cruises leave from beside the Roberta Bondar Pavilion.

Practicalities

The Soo's Greyhound **bus station** (☎705/949-4711) is handily located at 73 Brock St and Bay, in between Queen St East and the waterfront. Local and provincial information is available at the **Ontario Travel Centre**, 261 Queen St W (daily: mid-May to mid-June & Sept 8am–6pm; mid-June to Aug 8am–8pm; Oct to mid-May 8.30am–5pm; ☎705/945-6941 or 1-800/668-2746), a ten-minute walk west from the bus station along Queen St.

Amongst the town's many chain **motels** and **hotels**, two of the most convenient are the *Sleep Inn*, at the east end of downtown, close to the waterfront at 727 Bay St (☎705/253-7533 or 1-877/953-7533, ⓦwww.sleepinn.on.ca; ❹), and the *Days Inn*, plumb in the centre, steps from the ACR station at 320 Bay St and Bruce (☎705/759-8200 or 1-800/329-7466, ⓦwww.daysinnsault.com; ❹). The town's cheapest accommodation is in the **hostel**, sited in the former Algonquin Hotel, a stern-looking brick building at the east end of the centre at 864 Queen St E and Pim (☎705/253-2311 or 1-888/269-7728, ⓦwww.hihostels.ca; $20 dorm beds, doubles ❶).

For **food**, *Ernie's Coffee Shop*, 13 Queen St E at Gore (Tues–Sat 7am–7pm), is a popular and inexpensive spot serving breakfast specials for as little as $5, and jukeboxes on each table. Also great fun is *Mike's Quick Lunch*, 518 Queen St E at Spring, a classic 1960s diner with high stools, a long counter and old pictures of the Soo plastered on the walls. The best downtown **restaurant** is *A

Thymely Manner, 531 Albert St at Brock (℡705/759-3262; Tues–Sun), which is well known for its lamb from nearby St Joseph's Island and its great Caesar salad; reservations are a must. Otherwise, try well-prepared and well-presented Italian dishes at *Cesira's*, 133 Spring St at Albert (℡705/949-0600).

Lake Superior north shore

With a vast surface area of 82,000 square kilometres, **Lake Superior** is the largest freshwater lake in the world, and one of the wildest. Its northern shore between Sault Ste Marie and **Sleeping Giant Provincial Park** is a windswept rugged region formed by volcanoes, earthquakes and glaciers, its steep, forested valleys often overhung by a steely canopy of grey sky. In 1872 Reverend George Grant wrote of Superior: "It breeds storms and rain and fog, like a sea. It is cold… wild, masterful and dreaded." The native Ojibwa lived in fear of the storms that would suddenly break on the lake they knew as Gitche Gumee, the Big-Sea-Water, and white sailors were inordinately suspicious of a lake whose icy waters caused its victims to sink like stones: Lake Superior never gives up its dead. For the most part, **Hwy 17** sticks close to the shore of Lake Superior between Saulte Ste Marie and Sleeping Giant Provincial Park, but a screen of trees almost always keeps the lake out of view. This stretch of road is about 690km long so, unless you're up for a gruelling thrash or have to reach Thunder Bay (see p.209) or bust, it's much better to dawdle. Along the way are three magnificent parks, **Lake Superior Provincial Park**, **Pukaskwa National Park** and **Sleeping Giant Provincial Park**, where there's camping and hiking – though the insects can be unbearable from May to August, sometimes longer. The small towns dotted along the highway mostly fail to inspire, but low-key **Wawa**, about a third of the way along, has several good places to stay, while diminutive **Rossport**, a further 300km west, is easily the prettiest settlement hereabouts.

Greyhound **buses** regularly travel Hwy 17 between Toronto and Winnipeg, but don't expect them to drop you exactly where you want. If you are aiming for a specific motel or campsite check how far you'll have to walk.

Lake Superior Provincial Park

Heading north from Sault Ste Marie on Hwy 17, it's about 120km to the southern perimeter of **Lake Superior Provincial Park** (April–Oct), which offers ready access to Lake Superior's granite shoreline and its immediate hinterland. Autumn is the best time to visit, when the blackflies have abated and the forests of sugar maples and yellow birch flash with colour, but the scenery and wildlife are enthralling throughout the year. Moose, chipmunks and beavers are the commonest mammals, sharing their habitat with more elusive species including white-tailed deer, woodland caribou, coyote, timber wolves and black bears, as well as myriad migratory and resident birds. Hwy 17 cuts through the park for around 100km, passing three campsites, a series of trailheads and, after about 70km, the **park office** (May–Oct daily 9am–6pm; ℡705/856-2284), which sells hiking and canoe route maps as well as backcountry camping permits ($6.50), which are compulsory if you're heading off into the wilderness. The office also has information on vacancies at the park's three major **campsites**. These are the basic **Crescent Lake** (late June to late Sept) on the southern boundary, popular **Agawa Bay** (mid-May to late Sept), 8km further north and right on Lake Superior, plus **Rabbit Blanket Lake**

(May to late Oct) just north of the Park Office and ideal for forays into the interior. The last two campsites have electrical hook-ups, showers and laundry facilities. Prices are $17–28 per pitch; pay at the campsite. Day-use **parking** costs $9 per vehicle. The rangers will warn you if weather conditions look perilous, but always expect the worst – the park receives more rain and snow than any other area in Ontario. There are no park services of any kind from November to April, when service roads (but not of course Hwy 17) are barred and gated.

For thousands of years the Ojibwa used this stretch of the Lake Superior shoreline for hunting and fishing and their presence is recalled by a number of **rock carvings**. Most are inaccessible, but an exception is **Agawa Rock**, where the carvings represent a crossing of the lake by Chief Myeegn and his men, during which they were protected by Misshepexhieu, the horned lynx demigod of Lake Superior. To reach Agawa Rock, take the short, signed access road west of Hwy 17 about 16km from the southern border of the park; from here a 400-metre trail leads to a rock ledge from where the pictographs can be viewed.

The finest of the park's trails – the **Coastal Trail** – begins some 140km from Sault Ste Marie at Sinclair Cove and runs north to Chalfant Cove, a challenging route of high cliffs, sand and cobbled beaches, sheltered coves and exposed granite ledges. There are numerous designated backcountry campsites on the trail and the burnt-out fires on the beaches indicate where most people choose to pitch. The entire trek takes about five to seven days but access points enable you to do shorter sections of the trail; the southern part of the trail is not as demanding, with fewer climbs and easier going on sand rather than cobbled beach.

Wawa

The unassuming former iron-mining town of **WAWA**, just 14km north of the park, was named after the Ojibwa word for wild goose – and to hammer home the point there's a great big steel model of the bird at the entrance to town. The model has helped to make Wawa a busy stopping point on the Trans-Canada Highway (Hwy 17), which was just the idea. In the 1960s, much to the chagrin of local businessfolk, the TCH was routed a couple of kilometres to the west of town – hence the goose to pull passing motorists in. Modern **motels** line up along Wawa's main drag, Mission Rd. Amongst them, two good choices are the well-kept, two-storey *Bristol Motel*, 46 Mission Rd (☎705/856-2385, ⓦwww.bristolmotel.com; ❸), and the comparable *Sportsman's Motel*, with bright-red paint and faux stonework across the street at no. 45 (☎705/856-2272, ⓦwww.onlink.net/sportman; ❸). The latter probably has the edge if for no other reason than the stuffed fish on the foyer walls, including the rare fur-bearing trout (yes, it's a joke). **Eat** at the *Wawa Motor Inn*, at the west end of town at 100 Mission St, where *Reich's Restaurant* features Austrian specialities as well as Lake Superior trout and walleye.

White River

Beyond Wawa, the mixed deciduous–coniferous forest gives way to a boreal forest of balsam fir, white birch, trembling aspen, and white and black spruce – and you have plenty of time to observe it on the 90km haul to the next settlement of any interest, **WHITE RIVER**. There's nothing much to the place, but it does have two claims to fame. First, in 1935 the temperature here dropped to a mind-boggling -57°C (-72°F), the lowest ever recorded in the whole of Canada – and hence the whopping thermometer hanging by Hwy

17. Second, this was the original home of Winnie the Pooh, a small bear cub named Winnipeg who was exported to London Zoo in 1914. To emphasize the connection, you'll spot a fibreglass Winnie up a tree beside the highway. **Winnie's Hometown Festival** on the third weekend of August is when masses of teddy-bear enthusiasts gather here to get down and groove.

Pukaskwa National Park

Pushing on, Hwy 17 loops inland to skirt an enormous headland that harbours **Pukaskwa National Park**, a chunk of hilly boreal forest interspersed with muskeg and lake that rolls down to a stunningly beautiful coastline. The only access to the park is from the north down the 15km-long Hwy 627, which forks off from Hwy 17 just short of Marathon and 85km west of White River. Hwy 627 goes to **Hattie Cove**, where there is the park's one and only serviced **campsite**, three sandy beaches and a visitor centre (early June to Sept daily 8.30am–6.30pm; ☎807/229-0801), which sells trail guides and backcountry camping permits. From here, the **Coastal Hiking Trail** travels 60km south through the boreal forest and over the ridges and cliffs of the Canadian Shield. It is not an easy hike by any means, but it is simply magnificent and there are regular backcountry campsites on the way. In the summer boats will drop you off at various points along the trail, so you can just hike one-way back to Hattie Cove.

Rossport

Some 130km from the Pukaskwa turning, Hwy 17 passes close to **ROSSPORT**, a picture-perfect village draped around a tiny, sheltered bay. Originally a Hudson's Bay Company trading post, the settlement prospered as a fishing port until the 1960s, when a combination of overfishing and a sea-lamprey attack on the lake trout led to the industry's decline. The railway station was closed down too and today Rossport is the quietest of villages and one that makes for a perfect overnight stay on the long trek north. With more time, explore the steel-grey waters of Lake Superior with Rossport's Superior Outfitters (☎807/824-3314), who rent canoes and kayaks on a daily or weekly basis, and give tuition. As for **accommodation**, the tiny *Rossport Inn* (☎807/824-3213 or 1-877/824-4032, Ⓦ www.rossportinn.on.ca; rooms ❸, cabins ❷), whose mock-Tudor flourishes date from the 1880s, occupies a fine lakeside setting. It has seven bedrooms in the main house and ten wooden cabins, with double beds, in the garden. The inn has a good restaurant, but the place to eat is the *Serendipity Café* (☎807/824-2890; closes 7/8pm), a surprisingly sophisticated spot with feta cheese, rocket salad, smoked salmon and the like – all at reasonable prices. Lastly, there are two fine **campsites** in the woods by the lake in Rainbow Falls Provincial Park (☎807/824-2298; $19–22; late May to Aug), just 7km east of Rossport off Hwy 17.

Ouimet Canyon Provincial Park

From Rossport, it's 80km to **NIPIGON**, where Hwy 11 finishes its mammoth trek across northern Ontario to merge with Hwy 17. After a further 35km or so, Hwy 17 reaches the eleven-kilometre-long turning that leads north away from the lake to one of the region's more spectacular sights in **Ouimet Canyon Provincial Park** (mid-May to mid-Oct daily; free; day-use only; ☎807/977-2526). The canyon was formed during the last ice age, when a sheet of ice 2km thick crept southward, bulldozing a fissure 3km long, 150m wide and 150m deep. Nearly always deserted, the canyon has two lookout points that hang over the terrifyingly sheer sides looking down to the

Terry Fox

West of Nipigon, highways 17 and 11 merge to become the **Terry Fox Courage Highway,** named after Terrance Stanley Fox (1958–81), one of modern Canada's most remarkable figures. At the age of 18 Terry developed cancer and had to have his right leg amputated. Determined to advance the search for a cure, he nevertheless planned a money-raising run from coast to coast and on April 12, 1980, he set out from St John's in Newfoundland. For 143 days he ran 26 painful miles a day, covering five provinces by June and raising $34m. In September, at mile 3339, just outside Thunder Bay, lung cancer forced Terry to abandon his run; he returned home to Port Coqitlam in British Columbia, where he died the following summer. More than $85m has now been raised for cancer research in his name. In his honour, the **Terry Fox Monument,** a finely crafted bronze showing the lad running, has been placed on top of a ridge in a little park above the highway just to the east of Thunder Bay. From the monument, there are panoramic views over Lake Superior; Thunder Bay tourism also has its main office here.

permanently dark base – an anomalous frozen habitat whose perpetual snow supports some very rare arctic plants. The vistas are especially stimulating in the autumn, when the forests glint red, orange and yellow.

West to Sleeping Giant Provincial Park

Doubling back to Hwy 17 from Ouimet Canyon, it's about 25km west along the main highway to Hwy 587, which branches south to scuttle down the 42-kilometre-long **Sibley Peninsula**. Almost all of the peninsula is given over to the dramatically scenic **Sleeping Giant Provincial Park** (open year-round), so named because of the recumbent form of the four mesas that constitute its backbone. Established in 1944 to protect what the logging companies had left of the red and white pines, the park covers 243 square kilometres of high, barren rocks and lowland bogs, crisscrossed with 100km of trails. Acting as a sort of catch net for animals, the peninsula is inhabited by beaver, fox, porcupine, white-tailed deer and moose. There are also wolves in the more remote areas and on a still night you can hear them howling.

Hwy 587 enters the park about 6km beyond the village of **PASS LAKE**. Admission is $9 per vehicle. Pick up maps and hiking trail details either here or at the visitor centre (May–Aug Mon–Fri 8am–4.30pm; ☎807/977-2526), about 20km further south at the far end of Lake Marie Louise. Also at the south end of Lake Marie Louise is the park's one and only **campsite** (mid-May to early Oct; $20–25); reservations are advised in high season. Backcountry camping is possible too – pick up a permit ($6.50) at the visitor centre. Of the park's hikes, the 40km **Kaybeyun Trail** is the most spectacular and the hardest. Beginning at the southern end of Hwy 587, it runs around the tip of the peninsula via the rock formation known as the Sealion to the Chimney, at the Sleeping Giant's knees, then on to Nanabijou Lookout at the chest of the Giant, and finally to the Thunder Bay Lookout. You have to be fit – the walk to the Chimney takes about nine hours of hard graft up rugged pathways, where the boulders are the size of cars. Other less ambitious trails include the **Talus** and the **Sawyer** – which leave the Kaybeyun at Sawyer Bay on the southwest side of the peninsula – and easier still are the **Joe Creek Trail** and the **Pinewood Hill Trail**, both of which are situated in the northern end of the park near Hwy 587. The latter leads to a fine viewpoint over Joeboy Lake – a favourite spot for moose escaping the flies. The brief **Sibley**

Creek Trail, which passes a number of beaver dams, begins near Lake Louise, so you're likely to share the wilderness with a number of other hikers.

At the southern tip of Hwy 587 is the curious **Silver Islet**, not an island at all, but the ice-blasted remains of a thriving silver town, some fifty houses in all, including a customs house, a log jail, and a weathered general store, plus a population of two. Mining magnate Alexander Sibley founded Silver Islet in 1872 and his ambitious plans involved building a wall from his new town to Burnt Island just offshore to get at a silver deposit – you can still see bits of the wall today. Over the years the town exhausted the local firewood supply and had to rely on coal for fuel – and this was to be its undoing. One winter, the coal boat got stuck in the ice and, rather than freeze to death, the miners were forced to leave; they never came back.

Doubling back to the top of Hwy 587, it's 30km west on Hwy 17 to Thunder Bay.

Thunder Bay and around

The Lake Superior port of **THUNDER BAY** is much closer to Winnipeg than to any city in Ontario, and consequently its 120,000 inhabitants are prone to see themselves as westerners. Economics as well as geography define this self-image, for this was until recently a booming **grain-handling port**, and the grain, of course, is harvested in the Prairies. The grain still arrives here by rail to be stored in gigantic grain elevators and then shipped down the St Lawrence Seaway to the Atlantic, but not in the same quantities as before. In the 1990s, the economics of the grain trade changed in favour of Canada's Pacific ports and Thunder Bay suffered accordingly. As a result, many of the **grain elevators** that dominate the harbourfront are literally rotting away, while others are hanging on by the skin of their teeth. This unwarranted reversal of fortunes has encouraged Thunder Bay to reinvent itself by encouraging manufacturing and tourism. To boost the latter, the city council has created a cheerful **marina** and built a spanking new **casino**, though this proved very controversial. Such was the opposition that the casino was, in a rather bizarre compromise, called the "Charity Casino" to remind the citizenry that the profits are and will be spent on good causes.

Thunder Bay was created in 1970 when the two existing towns of Fort William and Port Arthur were brought together under one municipal roof. **Fort William** was the older of the two, established in 1789 as a fur-trading post and subsequently becoming the upcountry headquarters of the North

---

Amethysts

Amethyst, a purple-coloured variety of quartz, was first discovered near the shores of Lake Superior between the Ouimet Canyon and Thunder Bay, some 70km to the west, in the middle of the nineteenth century. It is still mined hereabouts and in addition particular deposits have been turned into well-signposted tourist attractions; Hwy 17 whizzes past a string of them. One of the best is the **Thunder Bay Agate Mine**, about 4km east of the city – 1km off Hwy 17 along Hwy 527 (mid-May to mid-Oct daily; Ⓦwww.agatemine.com). Tours of the open-pit mine are free, but you can pick up a bucket and digging tool to gather as many lumps of rock as you want, and pay a minimal amount for your booty on the way out. Amethysts can be polished with baking soda.

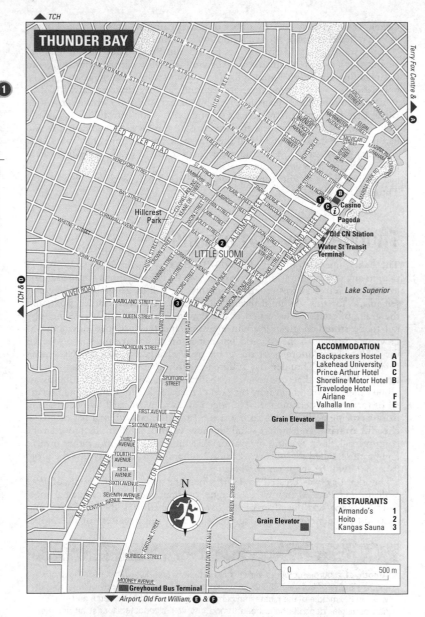

THUNDER BAY

TCH

Terry Fox Centre & ▲ A

ACCOMMODATION
Backpackers Hostel	A
Lakehead University	D
Prince Arthur Hotel	C
Shoreline Motor Hotel	B
Travelodge Hotel Airlane	F
Valhalla Inn	E

RESTAURANTS
Armando's	1
Hoito	2
Kangas Sauna	3

Casino
Pagoda
Old CN Station
Water St Transit Terminal

LITTLE SUOMI

Hillcrest Park

Lake Superior

Grain Elevator

Grain Elevator

0   500 m

N

Greyhound Bus Terminal

▼ Airport, Old Fort William, E & F

West Company. It lost its pre-eminent position when the North West and Hudson's Bay companies merged, but it remained a fur-trading post until the end of the nineteenth century. Meanwhile, in the middle of the nineteenth century, rumours of a huge **silver** lode brought prospectors to the Lake Superior shoreline just north of Fort William and here they established **Port Arthur**. But the silver didn't last and the Port Arthur, Duluth and Western railway (PD&W), which had laid the lines to the mines, was soon nicknamed "the Poverty, Distress and Welfare". The Canadian Northern Railway, which took over the abandoned PD&W lines, did much to rescue the local economy, but did not bring Fort William and Port Arthur closer together. Rudyard Kipling noted that, "The twin cities hate each other with the pure, passionate, poisonous hatred that makes cities grow. If Providence wiped out one of them, the other would pine away and die." Fortunately, the 1970 amalgamation bypassed Kipling's prediction and nowadays these parochial rivalries have all but vanished.

Scarred by industrial complexes and crisscrossed by rail lines, Thunder Bay is not immediately enticing, but it does have enough of interest to make a pleasant stopover on the long journey to or from Winnipeg. The most agreeable part of town is the few blocks stretching inland from behind the marina in **Thunder Bay North** – north of Central Ave – and here you'll also find several good cafés and restaurants. **Thunder Bay South** is much less appealing, but on its outskirts is the city's star turn, the replica fur-trading post of **Old Fort William**.

The Town

Thunder Bay's 5km-long **waterfront** is home to a string of **grain elevators**, whose striking architecture – all modernist lines and pure functionalism – can't fail to impress. In the middle of the industrial jangle is the **marina** and behind that is the old **CN railway station**, whose distinctive high-pitched gables, turrets and dormer windows were built to resemble a French chateau. The station was erected in 1906 and three years later CN dipped into their pockets again to create the **Pagoda**, a fanciful bandstand just across the street that now houses a tourist office (see p.212). At one time, the local band would strike up a tune or two to welcome any visiting bigwig – which must have been a pleasant way to forget just how long it had taken to actually get here.

Thunder Bay North's most appealing enclave is the Finnish district of **Little Suomi**, focused on the Bay and Algoma streets intersection, about ten minutes' walk southwest from the Pagoda. There are over forty ethnic groups in Thunder Bay and several of them maintain their own institutions, but no one more so than the Finns – though for most of its history the port has been a deeply divided community. Arriving in the 1870s, the first Finns to get here were left-wing refugees escaping the tender mercies of the Tsar, whereas those who arrived after 1917 were right-wing opponents (plus the odd anarchist) of the Bolsheviks. Little Suomi's architecture is resolutely suburban, but the town's most atmospheric restaurants are here (see below). Keep on going west along Bay St from Algoma and you'll soon reach **Hillcrest Park**, perched on a low ridge and with flowerbeds, offering great views out across the lake.

Thunder Bay's tour de force is the reconstructed fur-trading post of **Old Fort William** (mid-May to mid-Oct daily 10am–5pm; $12), in a loop of the Kaministiquia River about 15km southwest of the Pagoda – and 13km upriver from its original site. At the entrance is a **visitor centre**, where a first-rate film traces the history of the fort and explains its workings. From here, it's a quick stroll or bus ride to the fort, a large palisaded compound which has been restored to its appearance in 1815, when it was the inland headquarters of the North West Company and their major trans-shipment base. Impeccably researched and staffed by students dressed in period gear, the forty-odd buildings that fill out the compound illuminate the fort's original purpose with everything from simple storehouses to the capacious Great Hall. Look out also for the fur warehouse, festooned with the pelts of beaver, lynx and arctic fox, and the canoe workshop, where exquisite birch-bark canoes are made to traditional designs for museums all over Canada. There are demonstrations of contemporary trades and crafts, as well as a working kitchen, kitchen garden and a farm complete with sheep, pigs and cows.

Practicalities

Thunder Bay Airport (Ⓦwww.tbairport.on.ca) is on the southwest edge of the city, about 13km from Thunder Bay North. To get from one to the other, take local **bus #3 Airport** (every 30min) to the Brodie St bus terminal in Thunder Bay South and then either change or stay on the bus (depending on the service) for onward transportation to Thunder Bay North, where buses pull into the Water St terminal behind the marina. **Local buses** are operated by Thunder Bay Transit (Ⓣ807/684-3744, Ⓦwww.city.thunder-bay.on.ca /transit). The flat fare is $2.25; ask for a transfer if you need more than one bus to complete your journey. The long-distance Greyhound **bus station** (Ⓣ807/345-2194), about 3km south of Thunder Bay North at 815 Fort William Rd, is the terminal for buses arriving from Sault Ste Marie, Winnipeg (via Kenora) and Duluth. There are no trains. **Car rental** options at the airport include Avis (Ⓣ807/473-8572), Hertz (Ⓣ807/473-8111) and National (Ⓣ807/577-1234). For a **taxi**, call Diamond-Laceys (Ⓣ807/622-6001) or Roach's (Ⓣ807/344-8481).

There are two **tourist offices**. One is downtown in the landmark Pagoda building on Water St at the foot of Red River Rd (June–Sept daily 9am–5pm; Ⓣ1-800/667-8386, Ⓦwww.city.thunder-bay.on.ca), the other is in the Terry Fox Centre by the Terry Fox Monument (daily: June–Aug 8am–8pm; Sept–May 9am–5pm; Ⓣ1-800/667-8386), on Hwy 17 just north outside of town. Up-to-date **weather** bulletins are on Ⓣ807/345-9111. The Medical Centre Pharmacy is at 63 Algoma St N (Ⓣ807/345-1421).

Thunder Bay has a healthy supply of reasonably priced **motel** and **hotel** accommodation, as well as lodgings in **student rooms** on Lakehead University's campus and, further out, a good **hostel**. The best places to **eat** are in Little Suomi, at and around Bay and Algoma streets, where you can sample tasty Finnish food in healthy portions – but note that most places here close early. There is a cluster of blue-collar **bars** on Cumberland St, just up from the Pagoda.

Hotels and motels

Prince Arthur Hotel 17 Cumberland St N at Red River Rd Ⓣ807/345-5411 or 1-800/267-2675, Ⓦwww.princearthur.on.ca. Built by the CNR in 1908, this imposing stone-and-brick block is just up from the Pagoda. Inside, there are flashes of the original Edwardian elegance, but most of the furnishings are modern and the rooms, reached along echoing corridors, are similar, as well as being large and comfortable. ❹

Shoreline Motor Hotel 61 Cumberland St N at Camelot Ⓣ807/346-9763. Standard-issue budget motel, but handily located just a couple of blocks from the Pagoda. ❸

Travelodge Hotel Airlane 698 West Arthur St and Expressway Ⓣ807/473-1600 or 1-800/465-5003, Ⓦwww.travelodge-airlane.com. Within easy reach of Old Fort William and the airport, this bright, modern hotel has all modern conveniences and three restaurants. ❺

Valhalla Inn 1 Valhalla Inn Rd Ⓣ807/577-1121 or 1-800/964-1121, Ⓦwww.valhallainn.com. Perhaps the best-looking of the city's hotels, this brick-and-timber modern hotel offers over two hundred spacious and well-equipped rooms. ❺

Hostel

Thunder Bay International Backpackers Hostel Longhouse Village 1594 Lakeshore Drive, RR #13 Ⓣ807/983-2042, Ⓦwww .thunderbayhostel.com. This hostel has a friendly commune-like atmosphere and an attractive

wooded setting 18km northeast of Thunder Bay.
There's free use of bicycles, inexpensive Internet
access but no laundry. Nor is there any public transport here – ring ahead for advice. Rooms (no dorms)
cost $19 per person. Camping is also available in
the hostel grounds for $19 for two, $12 for one.

Student rooms

Lakehead University Lakehead University
Campus, off Oliver Rd ☎807/343-8612. With its
manicured lawns and miniature lake – students
call it Lake Inferior – the university campus is a
pleasant spot. Both single $28 and double $40
rooms are available in several student blocks
during the summer. Access to the university's
sports facilities is included. The campus is located
about 4km southwest of the Pagoda; the #2
Crosstown bus from the Water St terminal by the
marina goes past the university campus.

Cafés and restaurants

Armando's 28 Cumberland St N at Red River Rd
☎807/344-5833. Trim Italian restaurant offering
good pizzas, pastas and more. Reasonable prices.
Closed Sun.

Hoito Restaurant 314 Bay St at Algoma
☎807/345-6323. Established in 1918,
Thunder Bay's best-known Finnish café-cum-
canteen is always full and the specials on the
board should not be missed. The salt fish,
potatoes and viili (clabbered milk) is delicious.
Open Mon–Fri 7am–8pm, Sat & Sun 8am–8pm.

Kangas Sauna 379 Oliver Rd ☎807/344-6761.
Previously a small counter service for the sauna
users, now a larger café-restaurant with delicious
home-made soups, omelettes and sweet berry
pies. On the edge of Little Suomi. Open daily
7.30am–11pm.

West of Thunder Bay

Heading west from Thunder Bay on Hwy 17 towards Manitoba, it's a long,
gruelling drive of almost 500km through the interminable pine forests of the
Canadian Shield to the next town of any real interest, **Kenora**, where hundreds of fishermen gather every summer before sidling off into the vast **Lake
of the Woods**. The lake straddles the Ontario–Manitoba border and Kenora
is itself just 200km from Winnipeg (see p.534). Regular long-distance buses
ply Hwy 17.

Kenora and the Lake of the Woods

KENORA used to be known as Rat Portage until a flour company refused to
build a mill here, arguing that the word "rat" on their sacks wouldn't do much
for sales. Nowadays the permanent population of 9000 quadruples in the
summer, when droves of Americans arrive with their fishing tackle – no
wonder the town has a twelve-metre statue of a fish at its entrance. Rod or not,
Kenora is a pleasant enough spot to break the long journey west (or east), especially in summer when there's a really laid-back feel to the place. From the foot
of Main St, the MS *Kenora* **cruises** the Lake of the Woods' islands and channels for two hours (mid-May to mid-Sept Mon–Sat 4 daily, Sun 1 daily; $20;
☎807/468-9124), offering an opportunity to see **Devil's Gap Rock** at the
entrance to the town harbour. In 1884, the rock was painted to resemble a
human face and it has been regularly repainted ever since. This is not, however,
a gimmicky attraction: Devil's Gap is an Ojibwa spirit rock, to which food and
tobacco offerings were once made to propitiate Windigo, the large and threatening personification of winter. Windigo's powers could only be controlled by
powerful shamen, and when hunters disappeared in the bush they were
thought to have been eaten by him. As an introduction to the **Lake of the
Woods**, the boat trip does just fine, but the sheer vastness of the lake – and its

Remember to put your watch back one hour when you cross into the **Central
time** zone, about 60km west of Thunder Bay.

14,000 islands – is hard to grasp. One way of sampling much more is to rent a **houseboat** with Houseboat Adventures, at the Main St wharf (☎1-800/253-6672, Ⓦwww.houseboatadventures.com). Their boats have all modern conveniences – from toasters through to freezers – and the onboard fish-cleaning stations reveal the predilections of their customers, but it is still a wonderful way to experience the outback. Prices from $1700 to $4000 per week per boat for up to six people.

Kenora's **bus terminus** is at 610 Lakeview Drive (☎807/468-7172) and the **tourist office** is on Hwy 17 just east of town (☎1-800/535-4549). First choice for **accommodation** is the landmark, eleven-storey tower of the *Best Western Lakeside Inn*, 470 1st Ave S (☎807/468-5521, Ⓦwww.bestwestern.com; ❺), from where there are panoramic views. Other chain **motels**, several of which are dotted along the highway just east of town, include the Travelodge Kenora, 800 Hwy 17 (☎807/468-3155 or 1-800/465-1127, Ⓦwww.travelodge.com; ❸) and the *Days Inn – Kenora*, 920 Hwy 17 (☎807/468-2003, Ⓦwww.daysinn.com; ❸); in all cases, reservations are strongly advised in summer.

Travel details

Trains

Cochrane to: Moosonee (1–2 daily except Mon in summer, 3 weekly in winter; 5hr 15min).
Kingston to: Montréal (4–6 daily; 2hr 15min); Toronto (4–6 daily; 2hr 20min).
Ottawa to: Brockville (3–4 daily; 1hr 15min); Gananoque (1 daily; 1hr 35min); Kingston (3–4 daily; 1hr 45min–2hr 30min); Montréal (2–4 daily; 2hr 20min); Toronto (3–4 daily; 4hr 7min–4hr 12min).
Toronto to: Buffalo, NY (1 daily; 4hr); Chicago, IL (1 daily; 11hr); Cobalt (6 weekly; 7hr); Cochrane (6 weekly; 10hr); Gravenhurst (6 weekly; 2hr); Huntsville (6 weekly; 2hr 45min); Kingston (7 daily; 2hr); Kitchener (5 daily; 1hr 45min); London (7 daily; 3hr); Montréal (4–6 daily; 4hr 45min; express daily except Sat; 4hr); New York, NY (1 daily; 12hr); Niagara Falls (2 daily; 2hr); North Bay (6 weekly; 4hr 40min); Ottawa (3–4 daily; 4hr); Parry Sound (3 weekly; 4hr 15min); Sarnia (2 daily; 4hr 15min); Stratford (2 daily; 2hr 10min); Sudbury Junction (3 weekly; 7hr 15min); Temagami (6 weekly; 6hr 20min); Windsor (4 daily; 4hr); Winnipeg (3 weekly; 29hr 45min).

Buses

Kenora to: Winnipeg (5 daily; 2hr 30min).
Kingston to: Montréal (2 daily; 3hr 25min); Ottawa (4 daily; 2hr 45min).
London to: Hamilton (2 daily; 2hr); Kitchener (2 daily; 2hr); Niagara Falls (2 daily; 3hr 45min);

Owen Sound (1 daily; 3hr 45min); Stratford (2 daily; 1hr); Windsor (1 daily; 3hr).
North Bay to: Cobalt (4 daily; 1hr 50min); Cochrane (5 daily; 6hr 15min–7hr); Haileybury (2 daily; 2hr); Kirkland Lake (7 daily; 3hr 15min–4hr); Sudbury (3 daily; 2hr); Temagami (4 daily; 1hr 10min).
Ottawa to: Brockville (1 daily; 2hr 10min); Kingston (4 daily; 2hr 45min); Montréal (11 daily; 2hr 20min); North Bay (6 daily; 2hr 30min–4hr 50min); Sudbury (3 daily; 6hr 45min); Toronto (6 daily; 5hr 30min).
Sault Ste Marie to: Kenora (1–3 daily; 16hr); Nipigon (1–4 daily; 7hr 40min–8hr 30min); Terrace Bay (1–3 daily; 7hr 30min); Thunder Bay (1–4 daily; 9–10hr); Toronto (3 daily; 10hr 50min); Wawa (1–3 daily; 3hr); White River (1–4 daily; 4hr–5hr 30min); Winnipeg (1–4 daily; 18hr 30min–19hr).
Sudbury to: Montréal (3 daily; 11hr); North Bay (3 daily; 2hr); Ottawa (3 daily; 7hr 30min); Sault Ste Marie (4 daily; 4–5hr); Toronto (4 daily; 5hr 30min).
Thunder Bay to: Kenora (3 daily; 5hr); Winnipeg (3 daily; 8hr).
Toronto to: Collingwood (4 daily; 2hr 50min); Espanola (4 daily; 6hr); Gravenhurst (4 daily; 3hr); Hamilton (every 15min–hourly; 1hr); Hunstsville (3 daily; 4hr); Kingston (7 daily; 3hr); Kitchener (8 daily; 1hr 45min); London (8 daily; 2hr 20min–3hr); Midland (3 daily; 2hr 35min); Montréal (10 daily; 7hr); New York, NY (express 7 daily; 12hr); Niagara Falls (hourly; 1hr 30min–2hr); Nipigon (4 daily; 18hr 15min); North Bay (1 daily; 4hr 45min);

Ottawa (10 daily; 5–8hr); Owen Sound (3 daily; 3hr 15min); Parry Sound (6 daily; 2hr–4hr 15min); Penetanguishene (3 daily; 2hr 45min); Sault Ste Marie (4 daily; 10hr 50min); Sudbury (4 daily; 5hr); Thunder Bay (4 daily; 21hr 30min); Wasaga Beach (2–3 daily; 2hr 15min); Wawa (4 daily; 13hr 50min); White River (4 daily; 17hr); Windsor (8 daily; 4hr 30min); Winnipeg (3 daily; 30hr 30min).

Flights

Ottawa to: Banff (5–9 daily; 3hr 40min); Calgary (5–9 daily; 3hr 40min); Halifax (3–6 daily; 2hr); Montréal (7–16 daily; 30min); Québec City (6–18 daily; 1hr); Vancouver (8 daily; 5hr 20min); Winnipeg (6–7 daily; 2hr 20min).

Toronto to: Calgary (5–7 daily; 4hr 15min); Edmonton (5–7 daily; 1hr 40min); Fredericton (5–6 daily; 1hr 45min); Halifax (7–9 daily; 2hr); Montréal (15–26 daily; 1hr 15min); Ottawa (11–22 daily; 1hr); Québec City (8–19 daily; 1hr 45min); Saint John (4–5 daily; 1hr 45min); St John's (6–7 daily; 3hr); Saskatoon (2–3 daily; 3hr 30min); Thunder Bay (2–5 daily; 1hr 30min); Vancouver (6–7 daily; 5hr); Winnipeg (5 daily; 2hr 45min).

Québec

CHAPTER 2   # Highlights

* **Montréal Jazz Festival** From late June, crowds gather for free outdoor shows. **See p.228**

* **Vieux-Montréal** Wander through narrow streets lined with centuries-old buildings. **See p.234**

* **Plateau Mont-Royal** Montréal's cultural melting pot has cosy cafés, wild nightlife and restaurants for all tastes. **See p.249**

* **Cycling the P'tit Train du Nord** A 200km disused rail bed converted into a scenic bicycle trail. **See p.268**

* **Mont-Tremblant** Eastern Canada's premier ski resort is a great spot year-round for outdoor pursuits. **See p.269**

* **Québec City** Vieux-Québec, the only walled city in North America, is full of romantic nooks and crannies. **See p.284**

* **Ice Hotel** Stay in the continent's only ice hotel, hidden in the mountains north of Québec City. **See p.307**

* **Driving the Gaspé Peninsula** Hwy 132 encircles the peninsula, passing forested hills and rugged coastal scenery. **See p.315**

* **Tadoussac** A lively base for exploring the Saguenay fjord or joining a whale-watching trip. **See p.345**

* **Mingan Archipelago** Kayak around the eerie "flowerpot" islands inhabited by unique flora and fauna. **See p.364**

△ Montréal

Québec

A
s home to the only French-speaking society in North America, **Québec** is totally distinct from the rest of the continent – so distinct, in fact, that its political elite have been obsessed with the politics of secession for decades. The genesis of Québec's potential political separation from its English-speaking neighbours tracks back to France's ceding of the colony to Britain after the conquest of 1759. At first this transfer saw little change in the life of most Québecois. Permitted to maintain their language and religion, they stayed under the control of the Catholic Church, whose domination of rural society – evident in the huge churches of Québec's tiny villages – resulted in an economically and educationally deprived subclass whose main contribution was huge families. It was these huge families, though, that ensured French-speakers would continue to dominate the province demographically – a political move termed the *revanche du berceau* ("revenge of the cradle").

Québec is **Canada's largest province**, accounting for a sixth of the country's territory; its area could enclose Portugal, Spain, France, Belgium, Germany and Switzerland. Of this vast expanse, sixty percent is forest land peppered with more than a million lakes and waterways and, though some mining towns dot the interior, the majority of the population is concentrated in the rich arable lands along the southern stretches of the mighty St Lawrence.

The Gallic ancestry of most Québecois is clear in their attitude towards hedonistic pleasures: they eat and drink in a style that combines the simplicity of the first Norman settlers with the rich tastes of the contemporary French. Nowhere is this more evident than in the island metropolis of **Montréal**, premier port of the province and home to a third of all Québecois. Montréal's skyscrapers and nightlife bear witness to the economic resurgence of French-speaking Canada, whereas in **Québec City** the attraction lies more in the ancient streets and architecture. Beyond these centres, the hilly and forested **Laurentians** and **Eastern Townships** offer easily accessible outdoor activities, from cycling and hiking to downhill skiing. Further east, the **Gaspé Peninsula**, poking into the Gulf of St Lawrence, is the most appealing area with its inspiring mountain scenery and rocky coastline. Part of the peninsula, protected as parkland, provides sanctuary for a variety of wildlife, from moose

---

Information and hotel reservations

Tourisme Québec ☎1-877/266-5687, ⓦ www.bonjourquebec.com. Information and a province-wide accommodation booking facility.

Fédération des Agricotours ⓦ www.agricotours.qc.ca. An excellent service listing quality-inspected bed and breakfasts throughout Québec.

to herons. Here, a score of once-remote fishing villages have become mini-resorts, the most attractive of which is **Percé**. Some 200 miles southeast of the peninsula, in the Gulf of St Lawrence, the beach-trimmed islands of the **Îles-de-la-Madeleine**'s windswept archipelago are Québec's version of the Caribbean.

Along the north shore of the St Lawrence, the agricultural – and intermittently industrial – settlements that dot the landscape around Montréal and Québec City give way to the bleak desolation of a coastal road that stretches beyond **Havre–St–Pierre**. On the way, you'll pass through the delightful resorts of **Baie–Saint–Paul** and **Tadoussac**; the latter offers magnificent opportunities to go **whale–watching**. The contrasting landscapes of the **Saguenay fjord**, west of Tadoussac, and the northerly **Mingan Archipelago** are among Québec's most dramatic sights. Beyond the regions covered in this guide, Québec's inhospitable and largely roadless **tundra** is inhabited only by pockets of Inuit and other aboriginal peoples; it's a destination only for those travellers who can afford an expensive bush plane and the equipment needed for survival in the wilderness.

Train services within the province serve Montréal, Gaspé, Québec City and Jonquière, and there are also services to Ontario, New Brunswick and into the US – with Montréal very much the pivot. Though a little slower, the **jetfoil** makes an interesting alternative for the Montréal to Québec City run. For most destinations, though, **buses** are your best bet for getting around, with the major places connected by Orléans Express and Intercar services, supplemented by a network of smaller local lines. However, distances between communities in the outlying areas can be immense, and in order to reach more remote parks and settlements on secondary roads a **car** is pretty much essential. Around Montréal and Québec City the shores of the St Lawrence are linked by bridges, and towards the north a network of **ferries** links the Gaspé with the Côte-Nord. In the far northeast the supply ship *Nordik Express* serves the Île d'Anticosti and the roadless lower north shore as far as the Labrador border – the ultimate journey within Québec.

A brief history of Québec

Although various **First Nations** have lived in pockets of the province for millennia and there had been sporadic European contact to the east, Québec's history really begins with Jacques Cartier's 1535 voyage. He sailed up the St Lawrence stopping at Stadacona and Hochelaga, where settlements in the early seventeenth century have evolved into present-day Québec City and Montréal – see p.277 and p.224 for a detailed history of those two cities. The early days of the colony revolved around the fur trade and attempts to convert the natives to **Christianity**. The Récollets (reformed Franciscans) and Jesuit missionaries – called the "Black Robes" by the natives who suspected them of sorcery – were more often than not put to death. The priests' tasks were not made any easier by the fact that the French had aligned with the Algonquin and Huron nations to gain access to their **fur-trading networks**, while those groups' traditional enemies, the Iroquois Confederacy, had formed alliances with the Dutch and subsequently the British. Periodic bouts between the factions over control of the industry would continue over the next half-century. Louis XIV made New France a royal province in 1663 despatching troops and, subsequently, unmarried Frenchwomen, the so-called **filles du roi**, who were shipped over by the boatload. Periodic skirmishes between the French and British and their native allies continued to be a destabilizing factor, stunting the growth of the colony. Matters were resolved somewhat when 1200 colonists

Aboriginal peoples in Québec

Francophone–anglophone relations may be the principal concern of most Québecois – eighty percent of them have French as their mother tongue – but the province's population also includes eleven nations of **aboriginal** peoples, the majority of whom live on reservations "granted" them by the early French settlers. Resentment and racism are as rife here as elsewhere in Canada, but aboriginal grievances are particularly acute in Québec as most of the province's tribes are English-oriented – the **Mohawks** near Montréal even fought on the side of the British during the conquest. Still, relations are even bad between the authorities and French-speaking groups. The **Hurons** (see p.305) near Québec City, for example, battled in courts for eight years to retain their hunting rights, while around James Bay the **Cree** fought and won the right to block the expansion of Québec's hydro-electric network which, had it been completed as planned, would have covered an area the size of Germany. Begun in 1971, the project nonetheless resulted in the displacement of Cree and **Inuit**, due to flooded lands as well as the pollution of rivers that had not been safely channelled.

Aboriginal peoples have categorically voted against separation and have used mostly peaceful methods to register their land claims, which amount to 85 percent of the province's area. There was violence at the Mohawk uprising at Oka near Montréal in 1990 (see p.265), which, though condemned by most Canadians and aboriginals, drew attention to the concerns of aboriginal Canadians. This led to the creation of the Royal Commission on Aboriginal Peoples, a nationwide examination of the issues at stake. In 1996, the commission recommended a revamping of the aboriginal welfare system, greater self-government and a settlement of land-claims negotiations. Some of these have been enacted – such as the Nisga'a treaty in British Columbia – but scarcely any movement has been made on other issues. First Nations have also been asserting ownership of natural resources, especially in the eastern provinces where fishing rights are a hotly contested issue, and these have also been upheld by the Supreme Court of Canada. Each decision in favour of aboriginal land claims carries implications for Québec's aboriginal groups who have repeatedly refused to join their territories to a sovereign Québec state in the event of secession.

met with an even greater number of natives from across eastern North America at Pointe-à-Callière in Montréal to sign **La Grande Paix**, the Great Peace treaty of 1701. The signing of the Treaty of Utrecht with the British a decade later further allowed the fur trade to flourish.

It wasn't until mid-century that further serious conflict broke out, with the British and French again at odds in the **Seven Years' War** (also known as the French and Indian War). Although the early years of fighting were concentrated in the Atlantic colonies, the turning point took place in 1759 with the Battle of the Plains of Abraham (see p.294). The British consolidated their hold with the 1774 Quebec Act, allowing the Québecois to maintain their language, civil code, seigneurial system and religion, a pre-emptive move that helped resist American attempts to take over the colony. After the Americans won independence from Britain in their own land, however, a flood of **United Empire Loyalists** fled across the Canadian border, settling primarily in the Eastern Townships and present-day Ontario.

The creation of Lower and Upper Canada in 1791 emphasized the inequalities between anglophones and francophones, as the French-speaking majority in Lower Canada were ruled by the so-called **Château Clique**, an assembly of francophone priests and seigneurs who had to answer to a British governor and council appointed in London. Rebellions against this hierarchy by the mainly French *Patriotes* in 1837 led to an investigation by Lord Durham who concluded that English and French relations were akin to "two nations warring within the bosom of a single state". His prescription for peace was immersing French-Canadians in the English culture of North America, and the subsequent establishment of the Province of Canada in 1840 can be seen as a deliberate attempt to marginalize francophone opinion within an English-speaking state.

French-Canadians remained insulated from the economic mainstream until nineteenth-century **industrialization**, financed and run by the better-educated anglophones, led to a mass francophone migration to the cities. By the mid-twentieth century, a French-speaking middle class had begun to articulate the grievances of the workforce and to criticize the suffocating effect the Church was having on francophone opportunity. The shake-up of Québec society finally came about with the so-called **Quiet Revolution** in the 1960s, spurred by the provincial government under the leadership of Jean Lesage and his Liberal Party of Québec. The provincial government took control of welfare, health and education away from the Church and, under the slogan *Maîtres chez-nous* ("Masters of our own house"), established state-owned industries that reversed anglophone financial domination by encouraging the development of a francophone entrepreneurial and business class.

In order to implement these fiscal policies, Québec needed to administer its own taxes, and the provincial Liberals, despite being staunchly federalist, were constantly at loggerheads with Ottawa. Encouraged and influenced by other nationalist struggles, Québecois' desire for recognition and power reached a violent peak in 1970 with the terrorist actions of the largely unpopular **Front de Libération du Québec** (FLQ) in Montréal. The kidnapping of Cabinet Minister Pierre Laporte and British diplomat James Cross, with Laporte winding up dead in the trunk of a car, led then-Prime Minister Pierre Trudeau to enact the War Measures Act and send Canadian troops into the streets of Montréal. Six years later a massive reaction against the ruling provincial Liberals brought the separatist **Parti Québécois** (PQ) to power in Montréal. Led by René Lévesque, the PQ accelerated the process of social change with the *Charte de la langue française*, better known as **Bill 101**, which established French as the province's official language. With French dominant in the workplace and the classroom, many Québecois thought they were on the brink of cultural and social independence. In 1980, a **referendum** on sovereignty was held but, still reeling from the terrorist activities of the FLQ and scared that separatism would leave Québec economically adrift, the 6.5-million population voted 60:40 against. Prime Minister Trudeau then set about repatriating the country's **constitution**. In 1981 he called a late-night meeting on the issue and did not invite Lévesque, literally denying Québec a seat at the table. "The night of the long knives", as the event became known, wound up imposing a Constitution on the province that placed its language rights in jeopardy and removed its veto power over constitutional amendments. The provincial government refused to sign it – and still hasn't to this day.

In 1993, Québec's displeasure with federalism was evident in the election of Lucien Bouchard's Bloc Québécois to the vastly ironic status of Her Majesty's Loyal Opposition in Ottawa. The cause received added support in 1994 when the PQ was returned to provincial power after vowing to hold a province-wide **referendum** on separation from Canada. The referendum was held a year later and the vote was so close – Québec opted to remain within Canada by a margin of less than one percent – that calls immediately arose for a third referendum (prompting pundits to refer to the process as the "neverendum").

Bouchard left federal politics in 1996 to take the leadership of the PQ, determined to become the leader of a new country. After further steps at constitutional reform got nowhere, the federal Liberals enacted the **Clarity Act** in 1999 – a sharp departure from their previous kowtowing tactics: the act laid out the requirements Québec needed to meet in order to secede. Matters stumbled on until Bouchard's sudden resignation as Premier of Québec in 2001; his successor, Bernard Landry, couldn't match Bouchard's powers of oratory and charisma. Today, little hope remains of achieving the dream of a sovereign Québec in the near future – if ever.

In any event, the current political climate suggests Québecois are tired of the constitutional wrangling and would rather see a new deal that keeps them in Canada. After suffering through a long recession (due, in large part, to the political battles), Québecois have a vested interest in maintaining the momentum of economic growth the province is currently experiencing. And, for the time being, they appear more interested in maintaining political peace than encouraging old fights – an attitude that no doubt led Jean Charest and his Liberals to victory on mainly bread-and-butter issues in 2003.

Montréal

MONTRÉAL, Canada's second-largest city, is geographically as close to the European coast as to Vancouver, and in look and feel it combines some of the finest aspects of the two continents. Its North American skyline of glass and concrete rises above churches and monuments in a melange of European styles as varied as Montréal's social mix. This is also the world's third-largest French-speaking metropolis after Paris and Kinshasa, but only two-thirds of the city's three and a half million people are of French extraction, the other third being a cosmopolitan mishmash of *les autres*, including British, Eastern Europeans, Chinese, Italians, Greeks, Jews, Latin Americans and Caribbeans. The result is a truly multidimensional city, with a global variety of eateries, bars and clubs, matched by a calendar of festivals that makes this the most vibrant place in Canada.

It is also here that the two main linguistic groups – anglophones and francophones – come into greatest contact with one another. In the wake of the "francization" of Québec, English-Canadians hit Hwy 401 in droves, tipping the nation's economic supremacy from Montréal to Toronto. Though written off by Canada's English-speaking majority, the city did not sink into oblivion. Instead, it has undergone a resurgence, becoming the driving force behind the high-tech industries that are transforming Canada's economy.

Everywhere you look there are the signs of civic pride and prosperity. In the historic quarter of **Vieux-Montréal**, on the banks of the St Lawrence River, the streets and squares are flanked by well-tended buildings, from the mammoth **Basilique Notre-Dame** and steepled **Chapelle de Notre-Dame-de-Bon-Secours**, to sleek and stately commercial buildings and chic new boutique hotels. Old houses have been converted into lively restaurants and shops, abandoned warehouses into condos and the disused **Vieux-Port**

225

into a summer playground with landscaped parklands facing onto the St Lawrence. Beneath the forested rise of **Mont Royal**, the boulevards and leafy squares of **downtown** are alive from the morning rush hour right through to the wee hours, when revellers return from the clubs of **rue Ste-Catherine** and the more intimate bars and lounges of the nearby **Plateau** and **Quartier Latin** districts. Below ground are the walkways of the **Underground City** and the outstanding **Métro** system, while towards the eastern outskirts the **Stade Olympique**'s leaning tower overshadows the vast **Jardin Botanique**, second in international status only to London's Kew Gardens.

In addition, the city boasts some excellent museums. The **Centre Canadien d'Architecture** has one of the continent's most impressive specialist collections the **Musée d'Art Contemporain** is Canada's only museum devoted entirely to contemporary art and the **Musée des Beaux-Arts** is the oldest fine-arts museum in the country. Equally outstanding are the museums devoted to Montréal and Canadian history; of these, the **Musée McCord** has a mint collection of native artefacts, while the **Musée d'Archéologie et d'Histoire de Montréal** delivers a state-of-the-art presentation of archeological findings at the site of Montréal's founding in 1642.

Some history

The island of Montréal was first occupied by the St Lawrence **Iroquois**, whose small village of Hochelaga ("Place of the Beaver") was situated at the base of Mont Royal. The first European contact occurred in 1535 when Jacques-Cartier was led here while searching for a northwest route to Asia. However, a permanent presence was not instigated until 1611; the French settlement was little more than a small garrison, and it wasn't until 1642 that the colony of Ville-Marie was founded. The soldiers were on orders from Paris to "bring about the Glory of God and the salvation of the Indians", a mission that predictably enough found a frosty response from the aboriginal peoples. Bloody conflict with the Iroquois, fanned by the European fur-trade alliances with the Algonquins and Hurons, was constant until the **Great Peace treaty** of 1701 prompted the growth of Montréal into the main embarkation point for the fur and lumber trade. When Québec City fell to the British in 1759, Montréal briefly served as the capital of New France. The ensuing **British occupation** saw a flood of Irish and Scottish immigrants who soon made Montréal North America's second-largest city. It was not a harmonious expansion, however, and in 1837 the predominantly French *Patriotes* led by Louis-Joseph Papineau rebelled against the British ruling class. Their insurgency failed and was followed by hangings and exiles.

With the creation of the **Dominion of Canada** in 1867, Montréal emerged as the nation's premier port, railroad nexus, banking centre and industrial producer. Its population reached half a million in 1911 and doubled in the next two decades with an influx of émigrés from Europe. It was also during this period that Montréal acquired its reputation as Canada's "sin city". During Prohibition in the US, Québec became the main alcohol supplier to the entire continent: the Molsons and their ilk made their fortunes here, while prostitution and gambling thrived under the protection of the authorities. Only in the wake of World War II and the subsequent economic boom did a major anti-corruption operation begin, tied in with rapid architectural growth. The most glamorous episode in the city's face-lift came with **Expo '67**, the World's Fair that attracted fifty million visitors to Montréal. However, it was the city's anglophones who were benefiting from the prosperity, and beneath the smooth surface francophone frustrations were reaching dangerous levels.

The crisis peaked in 1970, with the terrorism of the **Front de Libération du Québec** (FLQ), who kidnapped a British diplomat and then a Québec cabinet minister, Pierre Laporte. As ransom, the FLQ demanded the publication of their manifesto, the transportation to Cuba of 25 FLQ prisoners and $500,000 in gold bullion. Prime Minister Pierre Trudeau responded by suspending civil liberties and putting troops on the streets of Montréal. The following day, Laporte's body was found. Although the Briton was later released, and his captors and Laporte's murderers arrested, the reverberations shook the nation.

Recognizing the need to redress social imbalances, the federal government poured money into schemes to promote French-Canadian culture. Francophone discontent was further alleviated by the provincial election of the Parti Québécois (PQ) in 1976, the year Montréal staged the **Olympic Games**. The consequent language laws, known as **Bill 101**, have made French a compulsory part of the school curriculum and banned English signs on business premises, only allowing them inside establishments – providing the signs are bilingual and the French is printed twice as large as the English. Businesses that fail to comply are at the mercy of the "language police", inspectors of the Office de la Langue Française (OLF) who can go to extraordinary lengths – such as measuring signs and checking business cards – to ensure that French is the dominant form of communication. This, for many anglophones, combined with the threat of sovereignty, prompted an exodus in their tens of thousands from Montréal, chiefly to Toronto.

A Canada-wide economic recession in the mid-1990s saw Québec lag behind the rest of the country in economic growth. But the turning point came after 1995, when a tacit truce was made on the issue of separation. The boarded-up shops that lined rue Ste-Catherine in the mid-1990s have reopened and now do good business. Derelict pockets on the edges of downtown and Vieux-Montréal were renovated to house the booming multimedia industry. And with **rising prosperity**, popular residential areas like the Plateau are being gentrified; apartment developments abound. Even the city's nightlife scene is changing, as working people opt for the weekday *cinq à sept* early-evening cocktail hour rather than partying late into the night. But perhaps the most enduring change is that the gaps left by departing anglophones have been filled by young **bilingual** francophones, who feel in charge of their own culture and economy. At the same time, many anglophones that stayed have also become bilingual, and these days it's perfectly normal to hear the two languages intermingling with one another wherever you may be.

Arrival, information and city transport

Montréal's main international **airport** is the recently renamed Aéroport International Pierre-Elliott-Trudeau de Montréal, or just **Montréal-Trudeau** for short (code YUL; ☎514/394-7377 or 1-800/465-1213, ⊛www.admtl.com), 22km southwest of the city – though it's likely to keep its old name of **Dorval** for some time. The Aérobus airport shuttle service (daily every 30min 7am–1am; takes 35–45 min; $12 one-way, ☎514/931-9002) links to the Station Centrale d'Autobus Montréal and the Gare d'Aérobus, adjacent to the train station, from where you can take the complimentary shuttle service to major downtown hotels (some hotels also have vans that pick up guests directly from the airport – ask when booking). Several local buses also connect Dorval to downtown but they take ages. A taxi downtown is $31. Montréal's second airport, **Mirabel** (same contact details; code YMX), 55km

Montréal's festivals and events

Montréal has a different festival every week throughout the summer months (pick up the quarterly *What to do in Montréal* guide at the tourist office for a comprehensive list or visit ⓦwww.tourism-montreal.org). Most event **tickets** can be purchased through Admission (☎514/790-1245 or 1-800/361-4595, ⓦwww.admission.com).

The **Festival International de Jazz de Montréal** (ⓦwww.montrealjazzfest.com) is North America's largest, with more than 400 shows in late June and early July, most of them free at huge open-air stages surrounding Place des Arts. The mid-July **Juste pour Rire** ("Just For Laughs"; ⓦwww.hahaha.com) is the world's largest comedy festival, with past headliners including Tim Allen, Rowan Atkinson, Jim Carrey, John Candy and Lily Tomlin. Just afterwards, the **Francofolies** (ⓦwww .francofolies.com) brings French musicians from around the world to various downtown stages. The most visually spectacular of the city's shindigs is the **International Fireworks Competition** (ⓦwww.lemondialsaq.com), whose participants are competing to get contracts for the July 4 celebrations in the US. Held in June and July, the music-coordinated pyrotechnics are a breathtaking sight. The action takes place at the La Ronde amusement park and tickets are around $40 (including ride pass), but across the water and on the Jacques-Cartier Bridge the spectacle is free, and the music for the displays is broadcast live on local radio. There are many food-tasting events and, in some cases, boozy ones, like the June **Mondiale de la Bière** (ⓦwww.festivalmondialbiere.qc.ca) in the Gare Windsor, which offers the opportunity to sample more than 250 brands of beer from around the world. In late January, Île Ste-Hélène hosts ice-sculpting and general carousing with the **Fête des Neiges de Montréal** (ⓦwww.fetedesneiges.com). Of the many film festivals, the most notable is the **Montréal World Film Festival** in late August (ⓦwww .ffm-montreal.org). The late-April **Vues d'Afrique** (ⓦwww.vuesdafrique.org) is gaining prominence for bringing African and Caribbean films to Montréal. Finally, the **Cirque du Soleil** (ⓦwww.cirquedusoleil.com) is a world-renowned circus company that travels all over the world; every other year it has a big-top season in its home city. Refusing to exploit animals, the circus's acrobats, trapeze artists, clowns, jugglers and contortionists present an incredible show, with original music scores, extravagant costumes and mind-blowing stunts.

northwest of the city, is used solely for charter flights and even that service will cease in late 2004. From Mirabel to the same locations downtown takes just over an hour by the shuttle bus, although the service is irregular, based on flight arrival times (☎514/931-9002; $22 one-way). The taxi fare is around $70.

Montréal's main **train station**, Gare Centrale, is below the *Queen Elizabeth Hotel* on the corner of boul René-Lévesque and rue Mansfield, and is entered at 895 rue de la Gauchetière ouest. The station is the major terminus for Canada's VIA Rail trains from Halifax, Toronto, Ottawa, Québec and the Gaspé, as well as US Amtrak trains from Washington and New York. The Underground City links it to Bonaventure Métro station and the rest of downtown. Long-distance **buses** use the Station Centrale d'Autobus Montréal, at 505 boul de Maisonneuve est (☎514/842-2281 for info on all bus lines). The Berri-UQAM Métro station is beneath it. A number of bus lines – including Orléans Express (☎1-888/999-3977, ⓦwww.orleansexpress.com), Québec's main coach company – serve various destinations.

Montréal's main information centre, **Infotouriste** (daily: June to early Sept 7am–8pm; rest of year 9am–6pm; ☎514/873-2015 or 1-877/266-5687, ⓦwww.bonjourquebec.com), is at 1001 rue du Square-Dorchester on the corner of rue Metcalfe. The nearest Métro is Peel: walk south on rue Peel past rue Ste-Catherine. In addition to masses of useful free information, it offers an accommodation service, which will make any number of free calls to find vacancies for you. The **Tourist Information Centre of Old Montréal**, on the northwest corner of Place Jacques-Cartier at 174 rue Notre-Dame est (daily: early June to early Sept 9am–7pm; rest of year 9am–5pm; ⓦwww.tourism-montreal.org) provides information on the city only.

Transport

The **public transport** system is one of the city's greatest assets, linking the 65-station **Métro** to 150 bus routes, all run by the STM (Société de transport de Montréal; ⓣ514/288-6287, ⓦwww.stm.info). The clean, speedy, reliable and cheap Métro system has four colour-coded lines; the major interconnecting stations are **Berri-UQAM** (which links the orange, green and yellow lines), **Lionel-Groulx** (green and orange), and **Snowdon** and **Jean-Talon** (blue and orange). Coloured signs indicate the direction of each line by showing the name of the end-station. A **correspondance**, available from machines beyond the turnstiles at the Métro stations, allows you to complete your journey by bus at no extra cost, but you must get one at the beginning of your journey, not as you depart the Métro. The transfer system also works in reverse, from buses to Métro: ask the driver for one as you board. Most **buses** stop running at 12.30am, shortly before the Métro, though some run all night.

A one-way **fare** on either Métro or bus is $2.50 (exact change required on buses), and a strip of six tickets costs $10. The STM **tourist pass** allows unlimited travel in a day for $7 (or $14 for three consecutive days); it's available from the information centres, Berri-UQAM and Bonaventure Métro stations and, from April to October, at all downtown Métro stations. For longer stays, the weekly CAM-Hebdo pass is a better deal at $16, but note that it is only valid from a Monday through to a Sunday.

It is rarely necessary to take a **taxi**. They cost $2.75 plus $1.30 per kilometre, and an additional fifteen percent tip is normal. You can pick one up from the ranks outside hotels and transport terminals, by flagging it down in the street, or by ordering by phone: Taxi Diamond (☎514/273-6331) and Taxi Co-op (☎514/725-9885) are two reliable services.

Accommodation

Much of Montréal's **accommodation** is geared towards expense-account travellers in the downtown hotels, although a recent growth in boutique hotels in Vieux-Montréal offers more atmospheric options. Moderately priced hotel rooms are concentrated around the livelier St-Denis area, with even cheaper options in the rundown area along rue St-Hubert east of the bus terminal. A better option is one of the growing number of **B&Bs**, which offer budget accommodation in interesting neighbourhoods like the Plateau. Rock-bottom prices are charged in the city's **hostels** and **university residences**. The **campsites**, though, are at least twenty-minutes' drive off the island, with no public transport.

Hotels and B&Bs

Abri du Voyageur 9 rue Ste-Catherine ouest ☎514/849-2922 or 1-866/302-2922, ⓦwww.abri-voyageur.ca. While the location could be better – it is smack in the middle of the red-light district – the rooms are clean, several have exposed brick walls, and it is just steps away from Chinatown and Vieux-Montréal. Métro St-Laurent. ❸

Anne ma Soeur Anne 4119 rue St-Denis ☎514/281-3187, ⓦwww.annemasoeuranne.com. On a prime stretch of rue St-Denis, this stylish seventeen-room hotel is a great find. The sunny, yellow rooms feature kitchenettes, large bathrooms and some have "Eurobeds" that tuck up into the wall. Métro Mont-Royal. ❻

Auberge Bonaparte 447 rue St-François-Xavier ☎514/844-1448, ⓦwww.bonaparte.com. A handsome upscale inn, steps from the Basilique Notre-Dame, built in 1886 and shaded by smart burgundy awnings. Inside, the quarters are decked

out with wrought-iron headboards, hardwood floors, high ceilings and French dormer windows. Breakfast included. Métro Place-d'Armes. ❻

Auberge Les Passants du Sans Soucy 171 rue St-Paul ouest ☎514/842-2634, ⓦwww.lesanssoucy.com. Brass beds and hardwood floors contribute to the romantic atmosphere at this charming inn, and some rooms have wooden beams and stone walls. Breakfast, served in a skylit nook, is included. Métro Place-d'Armes. ❻

Le Breton 1609 rue St-Hubert ☎514/524-7273 or 1-888/231-3113, ⓦwww.lebreton.ca. Near the bus station, this clean and friendly European-style hotel has smallish rooms; half have a/c, and most have private bath; Métro Berri-UQAM. ❶–❸

Castel Saint-Denis 2099 rue St-Denis ☎514/842-9719, ⓦwww.castelsaintdenis.qc.ca. One of the better small hotels in Montréal, it's right in the trendy St-Denis area, but quiet. Métro Berri-UQAM or Sherbrooke. ❸

Château de l'Argoat 524 rue Sherbrooke est ℡ 514/842-2046, ⓦ www.hotel -chateau-argoat.qc.ca. A fanciful cream-coloured fortress offering 25 spacious and attractive rooms with high ceilings, quaint chandeliers and private bath. Breakfast and parking included. Métro Sherbrooke. **❹**

Château Versailles 1659 rue Sherbrooke ouest ℡ 514/933-3611 or 1-888/933-8111, ⓦ www .versailleshotels.com. A unique, beautifully furnished hotel located in four stone buildings on the northwestern edge of downtown. Book well in advance, as it is one of the city's most popular hotels; family discounts and cheap winter weekend rates also available. Métro Guy-Concordia. **❼**

Hôtel Gault 449 rue Ste-Hélène ℡ 514/904-1616 or 1-866/904-1616, ⓦ www.hotelgault.com. Most glamorous of the recent crop of boutique hotels, the Gault is the place to stay – if you can afford it. The 30 individually designed loft-style rooms in this 1871 warehouse are a design-junkie's dream, with Arne Jacobsen fixtures, white-oak panelling and custom-made linens. Métro Square-Victoria. **❽**

Manoir des Alpes 1245 rue St-André ℡ 514/845-9803 or 1-800/465-2929, ⓦ www.hotelmanoirdesalpes.qc.ca. This Victorian building near the bus station is a three-star hotel with Swiss overtones but rates include buffet breakfast and parking. Métro Berri-UQAM. **❹**

Manoir Ambrose 3422 rue Stanley ℡ 514/288-6922, ⓦ www.manoirambrose.com. Two adjoining Victorian houses a couple of blocks from the heart of downtown. Cheap rooms, some with a/o and private bathrooms. Continental breakfast included. Métro Peel. **❹**

Hôtel de Paris 901 rue Sherbrooke est ℡ 514/522-6861 or 1-800/567-7217, ⓦ www.hotel-montreal.com. An old mansion near rue St-Denis with a balcony café to hang out in, with other rooms in two nearby properties. The cheaply furnished rooms have tiny beds but all are en suite with TVs, telephone and most have a/c. Several apartments (**❻**) with kitchenettes are available. Métro Sherbrooke. **❹**

Le Saint-Malo 1455 rue du Fort ℡ 514/931-7366, ⓦ www.hotel-saint-malo.com. Near the western edge of downtown; the 13 rooms are clean, if on the small side, and some have quaint architectural features. Métro Guy-Concordia or Atwater. **❸**

Hôtel St-Paul 355 rue McGill ℡ 514/380-2222 or 1-866/380-2202, ⓦ www.hotelstpaul.com. Housed

in a former bank, this most minimalist of Vieux-Montréal's new boutique hotels has a very trendy restaurant, Cube. Upstairs, white walls and linens contrast with the dark wood floors and elegantly simple furnishings of the rooms and suites. Métro Square-Victoria. **❼**

B&Bs

Bienvenue Bed & Breakfast 3950 av Laval ℡ 514/844-5897 or 1-800/227-5897, ⓦ www.bienvenuebb.com. Moderately priced but rather plain rooms in a Victorian house located on a tree-lined Plateau street steps away from boul St-Laurent and rue St-Denis. Métro Sherbrooke. **❹**

Boulanger Bassin B&B 4293 rue Brébeuf ℡ 514/525-0854, ⓦ www.bbassin.com. The chatty owner of this B&B north of Parc Lafontaine will tell you all about the Plateau neighbourhood over extravagant breakfasts. The three bright and colourful rooms are simple but nicely furnished and all have private bath. Kids under 12 stay free. Métro Mont-Royal. **❺**

À la Maison de Pierre et Dominique 271 Square St-Louis ℡ 514/286-0307, ⓦ www.pier-dom.qc.ca. In a lovely house facing a picturesque square, the three rooms are tastefully decorated, though none has private bathroom. Métro Sherbrooke. **❼**

La Maison du Patriote 169 rue St-Paul est ℡ 514/397-0855, ⓦ www.bbcanada.com /patriote. Surprisingly cheap given that it's around the corner from Place Jacques-Cartier, this old house feels like a student flat, a notion reinforced by the youth of the friendly owner and the fact that you can rent the entire top floor and squeeze in up to twelve people for $240. Métro Champ-de-Mars. **❸**

Petite Auberge les Bons Matins 1393 av Argyle ℡ 514/931-9167 or 1-800/588-5280, ⓦ www.bonsmatins.com. Located on a tree-lined street near downtown and busy rue Crescent, this well-appointed B&B-style inn has fifteen large rooms and six apartments (**❼**), each with special architectural features (archways, exposed brick, fireplace), large windows, and private bathroom. Métro Lucien-l'Allier. **❺**

Aux Portes de la Nuit 3496 av Laval ℡ 514/848-0833, ⓦ www.bbcanada.com/767.html. Well situated on one of the Plateau's most attractive streets, this Victorian house has five rooms, all with private bath. Métro Sherbrooke. **❹**

Hostels, student rooms and campsites

Auberge Alternative du Vieux-Montréal 358 rue St-Pierre ℡ 514/282-8069, ⓦ www

.auberge-alternative.qc.ca. Montréal's finest hostel is located in a refurbished 1875 Vieux-Montréal

Bed-and-breakfast agencies

These agencies can be big time savers if you're looking to stay at a B&B, as each represents several guesthouses across town in a range of prices – and offers booking too.

Bed & Breakfast à Montréal ☎514/738-9410 or 1-800/738-4338, ⓦwww .bbmontreal.com. Montréal's original B&B agency lists good-quality houses downtown, in the Quartier Latin and Québec City, starting at $85 for shared bath, $115 for private, for two people in high season.

Downtown B&B Network in Montréal ☎514/289-9749 or 1-800/267-5180, ⓦwww.bbmontreal.qc.ca. Almost always has a vacancy in one of their hundred or so homes downtown or in the Quartier Latin, starting at around $85 and ranging from quaint Victorian homes to modern apartments.

Fédération des Agricotours ⓦwww.agricotours.qc.ca. An excellent service listing quality-inspected B&Bs throughout Montréal and Québec – you must book directly with the B&Bs, however. The information is also published in the annual *Inns and Bed & Breakfasts in Québec* guide ($17.95), which can be ordered online or by calling ☎514/252-3138. Rates for B&Bs start at $65.

Montréal Downtown Network ☎514/287-9635 or 1-800/363-9635, ⓦwww.martha-pearson.com. A service offering placement in a number of B&Bs situated in downtown or Vieux-Montréal. They also list apartments for longer stays.

Montréal Oasis ☎514/935-2312, ⓦwww.avenetmkt.com/bb. Most B&Bs at this agency are centrally located, with the emphasis on lavish breakfasts.

---

warehouse. Rooms for six to sixteen people and some doubles. You don't need to be a member to stay here. Métro Square-Victoria. ❶–❷

Auberge Chez Jean 4136 av Henri-Julien ☎514/843-8279, ⓦwww.aubergechezjean.com. You'll either love or hate this very unofficial hostel. Guests bunk down all over the common rooms on its three floors, making it a great place to make new friends quickly, but forget about privacy unless you take one of the closed rooms or sleep in the van out back. Métro Mont-Royal. ❶

Auberge de Jeunesse Internationale de Montréal (HI) 1030 rue Mackay ☎514/843-3317 or 1-866/843-3317, ⓦwww.hostellingmontreal.com. Check-in 1pm–2am. 250 beds, air-con, showers in every room. Single, family or shared rooms. Advisable to reserve from June to September. Métro Lucien-L'Allier. ❶–❷

Gîte Plateau Mont-Royal 185 rue Sherbrooke est ☎514/284-1276 or 1-877/350-4483, ⓦwww.hostelmontreal.com. Bright six- to eight-bed dorms and private rooms (with shared bath), an extremely chill common room and great Plateau location make this one of the city's best backpacker options. The main drawback is that the kitchen is only open 5–8pm. Métro Sherbrooke. ❶–❸

Hôtel Y des Femmes (YWCA) 1355 boul René-Lévesque ouest ☎514/866-9942,

ⓦwww.ydesfemmesmtl.org. Single, double and triple rooms for men and women in this rather pricey downtown YWCA, but only women have access to the pool and gym facilities. Kitchen and laundry facilities and Internet access also available. Métro Lucien L'Allier or Guy-Concordia. ❸

Student rooms

La Maison du Prêt d'Honneur 1 boul René-Lévesque est ☎514/982-3420 ext 5501 or 5502. A college residence on the edge of Chinatown that has studios with one or two single beds as well as a few two-bedroom apartments. All have kitchenette, private bath, phone and Internet access. Summer only. Métro Place-d'Armes or St-Laurent. ❸

McGill University Residences 3935 rue University ☎514/398-6367, ⓦwww.residences.mcgill.ca/summer.html. Popular residences for visiting anglophones and consequently often full. Four of the buildings are on the slopes of Mont Royal but Royal Victoria College is on the edge of downtown. Good weekly rates. Summer only. Métro McGill. ❶–❷

Les Résidences Universitaires UQAM 303 boul René-Lévesque est ☎514/987-6669, ⓦwww .residences-uqam.qc.ca. Over a hundred clean and simply furnished studios with double bed, kitchenette and private bath, as well as apartments, in this Quartier Latin student residence. Summer only. Métro Berri-UQAM. ❷

Vacances Canada 5155 av de Gaspé ☎514/270-4459, ⑭www.vacancescanadamd.montrealplus.ca. Two hundred beds available all year, and 550 in July and August in two locations: the Collège Français residence has rooms with one to seven beds that are popular with school groups, so often booked up. Check in 9am–2pm & 5–7pm. Second location has good deals for longer stays. Métro Laurier. ❶

Campsites

Camping Alouette 3449 rue de l'Industrie, Saint-Mathieu-de-Beloeil ☎450/464-1661 or 1-888/464-7829, ⑭www.campingalouette.com. Exit 105 off Hwy 20 east. With 300 sites this is the largest of the city's campsites with a store, washing machines, hook-ups and outdoor swimming pool. Sites $23.

Camping St-Claude 415 montée St-Claude, Saint-Philippe ☎450/659-3389, ⑭www.angelfire.com/sc/stclaude. Hwy 30 west, exit 104, Hwy 104 east. Big, charmless campsite with hook-ups, playground, showers, washing machines and restaurant. Sites $17.

KOA Montréal Sud 130 boul Monette, St-Philippe-de-la Prairie ☎450/659-8626 or 1-800/562-8636, ⑭www.koa.com. About 20km south of downtown; take exit 38 off Hwy 15, turn left, and it's 3km further on. Full facilities at well-kept campsite. Sites from $22.

The City

Though the island of Montréal is a large 51km by 16km, the heart of the city is very manageable, and is divided into Vieux-Montréal along the St Lawrence River, a downtown high-rise business core on the south side of the hill of Mont Royal, and the lively Plateau and Quartier Latin neighbourhoods to the east. The main east–west arteries are Rue Sherbrooke, boulevard de Maisonneuve, rue Ste-Catherine and boulevard René-Lévesque, all divided into east (*est*) and west (*ouest*) sections by the north–south **boulevard St-Laurent**, known locally as "The Main". North–south street numbers increase as you progress north from the St Lawrence River.

You're most likely to start by sampling the old-world charm of **Vieux-Montréal**. The narrow streets, alleys and squares are perfect for strolling, and every corner reveals an architectural gem, from monumental public edifices to the city's early steep-roofed homes. Close by, the parklands of the **Vieux-Port** adjoin a child-friendly science centre and departure points for getting onto the water. To the northwest, in the compact **downtown** area, the glass frontages of the office blocks reflect Victorian terraces and the spires of numerous churches, underlain by the passages of the **Underground City**, which link hotels, shopping centres and offices with the Métro. Rising above downtown, the city's landmark, **Mont Royal** – which the residents simply call "The Mountain" – is best accessed from the easterly Plateau Mont-Royal. This is the spot where the city's pulse beats fastest, as the cafés, restaurants and bars of **The Main** and rue St-Denis throng with people day and night. Further out to the east, the enormous **Stade Olympique** complex and the vast green space of the **Jardin Botanique** are the main pull. For a breath of fresh air, the islands facing the

Museum passes

The **Carte Musées Montréal** (Montréal Museums Pass; $20) grants free admission to 25 museums in the city on any two of three consecutive days at a significant discount; buy it at tourist offices or participating museums. In addition, the Nature Package covers admission to the Botanical Garden, Insectarium and Biodôme for $17, while the Get an Eyeful package ($25) covers all three plus a trip up the Olympic Tower; none of these four is covered by the Carte Musées.

Vieux-Port that make up Parc Jean-Drapeau and the westerly Lachine Canal offer all manner of activities, many of them family-friendly.

Vieux-Montréal

Severed from downtown by the Autoroute Ville-Marie, the gracious district of **Vieux-Montréal** was left to decay until the last couple of decades, when developers stepped in with generally tasteful renovations that brought colour and vitality back to the area. North America's greatest concentration of seventeenth-, eighteenth- and nineteenth-century buildings has its fair share of tourists, but it's popular with Montrealers, too – formerly as a symbolic place to air francophone grievances; more recently as a spot to wander around, take in the sights and, increasingly, to inhabit the condos converted from the old warehouses. Place d'Armes is the most central Métro station, although Square-Victoria or Champ-de-Mars are handier for the western and eastern ends of the district.

Place d'Armes and around

The focal point of Vieux-Montréal is **Place d'Armes**, its centre occupied by a century-old statue of Maisonneuve, whose missionary zeal raised the wrath of the displaced Iroquois. The mutt among the luminaries represents the animal who warned the French of an impending attack in 1644; legend has it that the ensuing battle ended when the supposedly unarmed Maisonneuve killed the Iroquois chief on this very spot.

Despite the addition of an ugly skyscraper on its west side, the square is still dominated by the twin-towered, neo-Gothic **Basilique Notre-Dame** (daily 7am–5pm; $3, light show $10; Ⓦwww.basiliquenddm.org; Métro Place-d'Armes), the cathedral of the Catholic faithful since 1829. Its architect, the Protestant Irish-American James O'Donnell, was so inspired by his creation that he converted to Catholicism in order to be buried under the church. The western of the two towers, named Temperance, holds the ten-tonne Jean-Baptiste bell, whose booming could once be heard 25km away. The breathtaking gilt and sky-blue interior, flooded with light from three rose windows unusually set in the ceiling, and flickering with multicoloured votive candles, was designed by Montréal architect Victor Bourgeau. Most notable of the detailed furnishings are Louis-Philippe Hébert's fine wooden carvings of the prophets on the pulpit and the awe-inspiring main altar by French sculptor Bouriché. Imported from Limoges in France, the stained-glass windows depict the founding of Ville-Marie. Behind the main altar is the **Chapelle Sacré-Coeur**, destroyed by a serious fire in 1978 but rebuilt with an impressive modern bronze reredos by Charles Daudelin. Time your visit for the "And then there was light" *son et lumière* show for a history lesson and a chance to see the architectural details artfully lit up; otherwise take advantage of one of the 20-minute guided tours (half hourly; included in entry).

Behind the fieldstone walls and wrought-iron gates to the right of Notre-Dame is the low-lying, mock-medieval **Séminaire de St-Sulpice**, saved from blandness by a portal that's topped by North America's oldest public timepiece, which began chiming in 1701. Generally considered Montréal's oldest building, the seminary was founded in 1685 by the Paris-based Sulpicians, who instigated the establishment of Montréal by Maisonneuve as a religious mission. They liked the place so much that they bought the whole island, and until 1859 were in charge of religious and other affairs as the *seigneurs* of the colony. The seminary is still the Canadian headquarters of the Sulpicians (and thus not open to the public), but their duties are now limited to maintaining the basilica.

VIEUX-MONTRÉAL

▲ Quartier Latin
▲ Métro Champ-de-Mars
▲ Chinatown
▲ Downtown
▲ Square-Victoria
▲ Cité Multimédia
▲ Lachine Canal
▲ Parc des Écluses

Lieu Historique Sir-George-Étienne-Cartier

Maison du Calvet

Chapelle Notre-Dame-de-Bon-Secours

RUE ST-DENIS

RUE BONSECOURS

Marché Bonsecours

RUE ST-LOUIS

RUE GOSFORD

RUE DU CHAMP-DE-MARS

Hôtel de Ville

Château Ramezay

Champ de Mars

Quai de l'Horloge

BASSIN BONSECOURS

PLACE VAUQUELIN

Old Courthouse

RUE NOTRE-DAME EST

Édifice Ernest-Cormier

PLACE JACQUES-CARTIER

RUE ST-VINCENT

RUE ST-PAUL EST

QUAI JACQUES-CARTIER

AUTOROUTE VILLE-MARIE

RUE ST-ANTOINE EST

Palais de Justice

RUE ST-GABRIEL

VIEUX-PORT

Promenade du Vieux-Port

BOULEVARD ST-LAURENT

RUE ST-JEAN-BAPTISTE

RUE DE LA COMMUNE EST

RUE ST-DIZIER

QUAI KING-EDWARD

Place d'Armes

RUE ST-ANTOINE OUEST

Palais des Congrès

Banque de Montréal

Aldred Building

PLACE D'ARMES

Basilique Notre-Dame

RUE ST-SULPICE

RUE DE BRÉSOLES

COURS LE ROYER

Centaur Theatre

Centre des Sciences de Montréal

N

250 m

0

Banque Nationale

RUE ST-JACQUES

Séminaire de Saint-Sulpice

RUE ST-FRANÇOIS-XAVIER

RUE DE L'HÔPITAL

Old Customs House

Musée d'Archéologie et d'Histoire de Montréal

Place Royale

Quai Alexandra

Banque Royale

RUELLE DES FORTIFICATIONS

RUE ST-JACQUES

RUE DU ST-SACREMENT

RUE ST-PAUL OUEST

Centre d'Histoire de Montréal

Place de la Grande-Paix

AVENUE VIGER OUEST

Centre de Commerce Mondial de Montréal

720

RUE NOTRE-DAME OUEST

RUE ST-PIERRE

Youville Stables

Musée Marc-Aurèle Fortin

PLACE D'YOUVILLE

RUE DOLLARD

RUE DES RÉCOLLETS

RUE STE-HÉLÈNE

RUE LE MOYNE

Hôpital Général des Soeurs-Grises

RUE NORMAND

DU PORT

RUE ST-PIERRE

RUE WILLIAM

RUE MCGILL

RUE DE LONGUEUIL

RUE ST-MAURICE

RUE DES SOEURS-GRISES

RUE KING

RUE WELLINGTON

② A ② E

ACCOMMODATION

Auberge Alternative		
du Vieux-Montréal	F	
Auberge Bonaparte	C	
Auberge Les Passants		
du Sans Soucy	D	
Hôtel Gault	A	
La Maison du Patriote	B	
Hôtel St-Paul	E	

RESTAURANTS & CAFÉS

Bio Train	2
Bonaparte	C
Chez Delmo	1

BARS & CLUBS

| Aux Deux Pierrots | 3 |

QUÉBEC | Montréal: The City

❷

235

The domed shrine of Montréal's financial rulers, the **Banque de Montréal**, stands opposite. This grand, classical-revival building still houses the headquarters of Canada's oldest bank, which rose from its foundation by a few Scottish immigrants to serve the entire nation until the creation of the Bank of Canada in the 1930s. Erected in 1837, it was built to resemble the Roman Pantheon. The interior marble counters, black granite pillars and gleaming brass and bronze fittings ooze wealth and luxury. A small **numismatic museum** (Mon–Fri 10am–4pm; free) displays early account books, banknotes, coins and pictures. British names once controlled the finances of the continent from the stately limestone, griffin-capped institutions along **rue St-Jacques**, once the Wall Street of Canada, but French businesses now rule the roost. The red-sandstone building on the northeast corner of Place d'Armes and rue St-Jacques was built for the New York Life Insurance Co. in 1888 and, at eight storeys high, was the city's first skyscraper. Next door at 501 Place d'Armes, the Aldred Building is among the city's finest examples of the Art Deco style. Both are dwarfed today by the black monolith on the west side of the square that houses the Banque Nationale, built in 1967 as a symbol of new-found francophone business strength. Transformations have also occurred alongside the basilica, in the area around **rue St-Sulpice**, where the warehouses constructed in the Victorian era to cope with the growing trade of Montréal's harbour have been converted into luxurious flats and offices, as well as a couple of boutique hotels. Many of the continent's first explorers once lived here, including Pierre Gaulthier de Varennes, who charted South Dakota, the Rockies and Wyoming, and Daniel Greysolon, Sieur du Lhut, who roamed over Minnesota. Peek along rue le Royer, extending eastward, an austere courtyard lined with late-nineteenth-century warehouses that recall Montréal's past as a major shipping port and whose conversion into offices and apartments was the first development in the revival of Vieux-Montréal.

Along rue Notre-Dame

Ville-Marie's first street, **rue Notre-Dame**, was laid out in 1672 and runs east–west across Vieux-Montréal. Other than the financial buildings of rue St-Jacques, there is little of particular interest to the west of Place d'Armes; it's more rewarding to head east along Notre-Dame from the top of rue St-Sulpice, past the black glass behemoth of the **Palais de Justice** on the corner of boulevard St-Laurent. It overshadows its forerunner, the imposing **Old Courthouse**, erected by the British to impress upon the French population the importance of abiding by their laws. It went on to become the site of civil trials under the Napoleonic Code after the courts were divided in 1926, and today serves as municipal offices. Criminal trials took place across the street, at 100 rue Notre-Dame est, in the **Édifice Ernest Cormier**, which was built in 1925 and only recently returned to its calling as the appellate court; step inside to admire the impressive colonnade and unique Art Deco lamps. Further along, the 1800 Maison de La Sauvegarde at no. 160, with its rough-hewn limestone facade, high chimneys and steeply pitched roof and dormers, was among the last homes to be built in the local French vernacular. Opposite, on the eastern side of the Old Courthouse, **Place Vauquelin**, centred on a pretty fountain and statue of the naval commander Jean Vauquelin, gives views of the **Champ de Mars** to the north. Excavations to build a car park here hit rock, which turned out to be the original city walls. After a public vote, the car park scheme was abandoned, the walls were excavated and restored, and the area was transformed into a pleasant grassy space.

East of Place Vauquelin, the ornate **Hôtel de Ville** (City Hall) was built in the 1870s and is a typical example of the area's civic buildings of the time when French-speaking architects looked to the mother country for inspiration. On a visit to Expo '67, General de Gaulle chose its second-floor balcony to make his "Vive le Québec libre!" speech, which left the city's anglophones reeling at the thought that Québec was on its way to independent status and infused francophones with a political fervour that ended in the October Crisis (see p.223).

The cobbled **Place Jacques-Cartier** opposite City Hall slopes down towards the river and offers spectacular views of the Vieux-Port, but is overrun with buskers, street artists and hair-braiders throughout the summer months. The city-run **tourist office** (early June to early Sept 9am–7pm; rest of year 9am–5pm) occupies a stone building at the northwest corner. Restaurants and cafés surrounding the square hustle for business, while the narrow **rue St-Amable** to the west is choked with struggling artists selling quaint watercolours and tinted photos of Montréal scenery alongside garish caricatures of film and music stars. Your best bet for souvenirs here is the small courtyard market hidden away from the street, where jewellery stalls offer some decent artisan-crafted pieces. A few buildings on the square – Maison Vandelac, Maison del Vecchio and the Maison Cartier – show the architectural features typical of Montréal architecture in the 1800s, with pitched roofs designed to shed heavy snowfall and small dormer windows to defend against the cold. At the top of the square itself, the controversial **Nelson Monument** stands above the few stalls that serve as the only reminders that this was once Montréal's main marketplace. The city's oldest monument – the column is a third the height of its more famous London counterpart, but predates it by a few years – was funded by anglophone Montrealers delighted with Nelson's defeat of the French at Trafalgar in 1805. Québec separatists adopted it as a rallying point in the 1970s. Ironically, the anglophones never liked the monument much either, because it faced away from the water.

East of Place Jacques-Cartier, the long and low fieldstone manor of the **Château Ramezay** (June–Aug daily 10am–6pm; Sept–May Tues–Sun 10am–4.30pm; $7; @www.chateauramezay.qc.ca; Métro Champ-de-Mars) looks much as it did in 1705 when it was built for the eleventh governor of Montréal, Claude de Ramezay – it was the finest of the colony's 200 homes at the time. It then served as the North American headquarters for the Compagnie des Indes, before passing into the hands of the British after the Conquest in 1760. During the fleeting American invasion fifteen years later, Benjamin Franklin stayed here in an attempt to persuade Montrealers to join the United States, but he lost public and church support by not promising the supremacy of the French language in what would have been the fourteenth state. Nowadays, after a variety of other uses, it is an historical museum; the collection of oil paintings, domestic artefacts, tools, costumes and furniture from the eighteenth and nineteenth centuries is thorough and informative. The most impressive room is a reconstruction of the *Salle des Nantes*, complete with mahogany walls and woodwork imported from the Compagnie des Indes headquarters in France. Other rooms are furnished in the bourgeois style of New France, while in the whitewashed stone vaults below, the exhibits take on more of an educational slant, re-creating domestic scenes of the early European settlers that include a kitchen with a dog-powered roasting spit.

At the intersection of rues Notre-Dame and Berri, a five-minute walk east, the **Lieu historique national de Sir-George-Étienne-Cartier** (late May to Aug daily 10am–6pm; April to late May & Sept to late Dec Wed–Sun 10am–noon & 1–5pm; $4; @www.pc.gc.ca/cartier; Métro Champ-de-Mars) comprises two adjoining houses that were inhabited by the Cartier family from

1848 to 1871. The cocky Sir George-Étienne Cartier was one of the fathers of Confederation, persuading the French-Canadians to join the Dominion of Canada by declaring: "We are of different races, not for strife but to work together for the common welfare." Today, leaders of French-Canadian nationalism decry Cartier as a collaborator, and the displays in the east house diplomatically skirt over the issue of whether he was right or wrong and emphasize instead his role in the construction of Canada's railways. This collection is decidedly bizarre, however, with Muppet-like figures representing the founding fathers on the main floor, while eight white-painted papier-mâché models of Cartier himself sit at a round, glass-domed table upstairs. The stuffily decorated rooms in the west house are more interesting, furnished with more than a thousand original artefacts to evoke the period when Sir George lived here. Strangely, part of the display is concentrated around a dinner theme, and recordings of conversations between fictitious house staff automatically start playing once the infrared sensor catches movement in the room.

Rue St-Paul

A block south of rue Notre-Dame, **rue St-Paul**, one of Montréal's most attractive thoroughfares, is lined with nineteenth-century commercial buildings and Victorian lampposts, the buildings little changed from when Charles Dickens stayed here, although they now house restaurants, art galleries and specialist shops selling everything from Inuit crafts to kites.

Mark Twain noted that, in Montréal, "you couldn't throw a brick without hitting a church", and near rue St-Paul's eastern end is Montréal's favourite: the delicate and profusely steepled **Chapelle Notre-Dame-de-Bon-Secours** (Tues–Sun: May–Oct 10am–5.30pm; mid-March to April & Nov to mid-Jan 11am–3.30pm; free), or the Sailors' Church. The outstretched arms of the Virgin on the tower became a landmark for ships on the St Lawrence and, once safely landed, the mariners would endow the chapel with wooden votive lamps in the shape of ships, many of which are still here. The chapel dates back to the earliest days of the colony, when Maisonneuve helped cut the wood for what was Ville-Marie's first church, under the instigation of Marguerite Bourgeoys, who had been summoned to Ville-Marie to teach the settlement's children. The devout Bourgeoys also founded the nation's first religious order and was in charge of the *filles du Roi* – orphaned French girls sent to marry bachelor settlers and multiply the colony's population. She was canonized in 1982, becoming Canada's first saint. Today's chapel, postdating Bourgeoys by some seventy years, contains a small **museum** devoted to her life (same hours; $6; Ⓦ www.marguerite-bourgeoys.com; Métro Champ-de-Mars). The entry price is worth it mainly for the chance to climb the narrow stairs leading to the summit of the tower above the apse, where the "aerial chapel" affords excellent views over the port and the old town.

Opposite the chapel is the three-storey, high-chimneyed **Maison du Calvet**, built in 1725 and one of Montréal's best examples of French domestic architecture. Photographed, painted and admired more than any other house in the district, it was the home of a Huguenot draper and justice of the peace called Pierre Calvet, a notorious turncoat who changed his allegiances from the French to the British and then to the Americans. It houses a pricey inn and restaurant today.

Rue Bonsecours, which links rue St-Paul to rue Notre-Dame, is another typical Vieux-Montréal street. The grey-painted, many-dormered **Maison Papineau** at no. 440 was home to four generations of the Papineau family, including Louis-Joseph who, as Speaker of the Assembly, championed the *habitants* of the St Lawrence farmlands against the senior Catholic clergy, the British government and Montréal's business class. Calling for democratic election of the executive officers of church and government, he fuelled the rage of the *Patriotes* – the leaders of Lower Canada reform – but deserted the scene as the 1837 rebellion reached a bloody climax (see p.223). The house remains a private residence, but renovations have significantly altered its exterior facade from the days when the Papineaus lived here. The silver-domed **Marché Bonsecours** (ⓦwww.marchebonsecours.qc.ca), with its long facade of columns, extends beyond the intersection of rue Bonsecours and rue St-Paul. For years this elegant building was used for municipal offices, but for the city's 350th birthday in 1992 it was restored and transformed to house restaurants, designer boutiques, expensive artworks and special exhibitions.

Vieux-Port

The south side of the Marché Bonsecours faces onto the **Vieux-Port de Montréal**, once the import and export conduit of the continent. When the main shipyards shifted east in the 1970s they left a lot of vacant space, which has since been renovated for public use, with biking, cross-country skiing and jogging paths and exhibitions in the quayside hangars.

At the Vieux-Port's easternmost point, the **Tour de l'Horloge** on the Quai de l'Horloge rises 51m above sea level. The clock tower was built in 1922 to commemorate the men of the Merchant Fleet who died in World War I; ships were recorded as having entered the harbour as soon as they had passed it. If you can stand the walk up the 192 steps leading to the observatory, you'll be rewarded with excellent views of the harbour, the St Lawrence Seaway, Vieux-Montréal, the islands and Mont Royal. Westward, across the pedalboat-filled Bassin Bonsecours, there's a seasonal information centre (May–Sept daily 8am–8pm; ⓦwww.oldportofmontreal.com) located at the northeast corner of the **Pavillon Jacques-Cartier**, which is a good place to find out about weekend activities and performances portside. The main events of the Vieux-Port are clustered in and around the next hangar westward, the **Quai King-Edward**. There's an IMAX cinema here, with eye-popping films on the seven-storey-high screen (English screening times vary), which is part of the **Centre des Sciences de Montréal** (daily 10am–5pm; exhibit or film $10, both $17; ⓦwww.montrealsciencecentre.com; Métro Place-d'Armes), an interactive science and entertainment complex that is heavy on new technology. Divided into three exhibition halls, focusing on themes of life, information and matter,

---

Boat trips in and around Montréal

The Vieux-Port is the major departure point for various **boat trips**. The best by far is the **jet boat** run by Saute-Moutons, departing every two hours from the Quai de l'Horloge (May to mid-Oct daily 10am–6pm; $55; ☏514/284-9607, ⓦwww .jetboatingmontreal.com). Scooting through the Lachine Rapids, the trip will leave you wet, exhilarated and terrified. Meandering Bâteau Mouche **cruises** leave from the Quai Jacques-Quartier (May–Oct 4 daily; $21; ☏514/849-9952 or 1-800/361-9952, ⓦwww.bateau-mouche.com). The glass-topped boats offer lovely views of the surrounding islands and the river. Most tours last around two hours, though there are longer dinner cruises. A more unique way to see the area is the **Amphi-bus** (May–Oct 10am–midnight; $20.75; ☏514/849-5181, ⓦwww.amphitours.com), which leaves from the corner of rue de la Commune and boulevard St-Laurent, or the Centre Infotouriste downtown. In true James Bond style, this customized military landing craft sails on water and drives along the streets of Vieux-Montréal.

△ Mural in Montréal

the massive rooms contain little that will keep you occupied, but most kids will enjoy some of the hands-on exhibits, including how to design the perfect paper airplane, record a radio show and stay balanced on a tightrope. At the end of the pier itself there is a **lookout point** up a few flights of stairs, with explanatory panels showcasing a panorama of Vieux-Montréal and the islands.

Place Royale to Place d'Youville

Once the site of duels, whippings and public hangings amidst the peddlers and hawkers who sold wares from the incoming ships, **Place Royale** is dominated by the neat classical facade of the Old Customs House. After a nine-day journey from Québec City, Maisonneuve and his posse moored their boats at nearby **Pointe-à-Callière**, now landlocked after the changes in the Vieux-Port.

The **Musée d'Archéologie et d'Histoire de Montréal**, 350 Place Royale (late June to early Sept Mon–Fri 10am–6pm, Sat & Sun 11am–6pm; rest of year Tues–Fri 10am–5pm, Sat & Sun 11am–5pm; $10, $16.50 ticket for two buyable at the gift shop only; ⓦwww.pacmuseum.qc.ca; Métro Square-Victoria), occupies the striking modern Éperon building on the Pointe, visible across the parkland from the Quai King-Edward. The $27m centre, which spreads underground below Place Royale as far as the Old Customs House, focuses on the development of Montréal as a meeting and trading place, as told through the archeological remains excavated here at the oldest part of the city. The high-tech audiovisual presentation gives an excellent introduction to the museum, to archeology generally, and to that of Montréal in particular. Early remnants of the city include a cemetery from 1643, eighteenth-century water conduits and sewage systems, and walls dating from different centuries: you can see from the foundations of each subsequent building how the street level has risen three metres over the years and traces of the variety of roles Place Royale has played. The underground sections emerge into the Old Customs House, which holds a dull exhibition and a gift shop. The layout is terribly confusing: time your visit for one of the free but infrequent guided tours, or look for the interactive map downstairs near the cemetery. Be sure to leave time for the generally excellent temporary shows, all with an archeological theme, on the Eperon building's upper floors.

Directly behind the museum is **Place d'Youville**, a charming public square that includes the Founder's Obelisk, a monument to the city founders. The square's eastern portion was renamed **Place de la Grande-Paix** in 2001, to mark the tercentennial of the Great Peace of Montréal, a treaty signed here to end the conflict between the Natives and French settlers. On the south side of the square, the **Youville Stables**, with its shady courtyard, gardens, restaurants and offices, was one of the first of the area's old buildings to be gentrified. (The complex was in fact a warehouse; the stables were next door.) Dating from 1825, the courtyard layout is a throwback to a design used by the earliest Montréal inhabitants as a protection against the hostilities of the Iroquois.

Halfway along the square, a century-old red-brick fire station has been converted into the **Centre d'Histoire de Montréal** (May–Aug Tues–Sun 10am–5pm; Sept–April Wed–Sun 10am–5pm; $4.50; ⓦwww.ville.montreal.qc.ca/chm; Métro Square-Victoria). Multimedia exhibits of the city's history, from its first days of European settlement to its present expansions under and above ground, aren't terribly interesting, but are fine for a sketchy overview. The competing soundtracks of films shown in the warren of rooms upstairs (including a locker room and a kitchen circa 1950) attempt to capture daily life in Montréal. Kids will love the mock tram: enter it and images start running past the windows while a recording of a bus driver calls out stops in French and English. Temporary exhibitions, too, are usually quite stimulating. Ask for an English-language guidebook when you enter the museum. The barren car park covering the western half of Place d'Youville gives no indication that this was once a marketplace, which also served as the Parliament of United Canada from 1844 until it was torched by Tory rioters in 1849.

Square Victoria and around

To reach downtown (in a roundabout fashion), head back towards the archeology museum and detour up rue St-François-Xavier to find the **Centaur Theatre**. Located at no. 453, and housed in the former Montréal Stock Exchange – Canada's first – it is the main English-language theatre in Montréal today. Continue north to reach rue St-Jacques, where to the west you'll pass the sumptuous **Molson and Royal banks** at nos. 360 and 362. When it was built in 1866, the 23-storey Royal Bank was the tallest building in the British Empire.

At the northwestern end of Vieux-Montréal, the entire block of rue St-Jacques between rue St-Pierre and Square Victoria is taken up by the **Centre de Commerce Mondial**, an architectural gem and prominent business address. Inaugurated in 1991 with the hope of reviving the former business district, the structure incorporates the facades of the centuries-old buildings that formerly stood there. Inside, the **ruelle des Fortifications**, so named because the former alley marked the location of the city's stone walls, was transformed into a lofty interior arcade adorned with boutiques, restaurants, a soothing fountain and a statue of Amphitrite, Poseidon's wife. At its easternmost end is a chunk of the Berlin Wall.

Across the street, renovations to **Square Victoria** have made it a more welcoming space, but it's still a far cry from its heyday when it was surrounded by Second Empire and neo-Renaissance buildings and bustling with activity from the city's haymarket. The imposing skyscraper bracketing the west side of the square used to be the digs of the **Montréal Stock Exchange**, but futures are traded there now instead of shares. Also of note is the **Art Nouveau grill** adorning the Métro station entranceway – which once graced a station on the Paris Métro – donated to the city for Expo '67.

Downtown Montréal

Montréal's **downtown** lies roughly between rue Sherbrooke and rue St-Antoine to the north and south, towards rue St-Denis in the east and overlapping with the Golden Square Mile as it stretches west beyond rue Guy. Of the main streets, **rue Ste-Catherine** offers the most in the way of shopping, dining and entertainment, while **boulevard de Maisonneuve** is more business-oriented. A number of Métro stations on the green and orange lines provide easy access to downtown's attractions – most are linked to the so-called Underground City (see box p.244). Though the main sights are the high-rises and shopping complexes, the area is also dotted with old churches, museums and public squares filled with activity from buskers, artists and market vendors.

Square Dorchester and around

Formerly a Catholic cemetery, **Square Dorchester** is a leafy spot right in the centre of downtown that is as good a place as any to get your bearings – the Art Deco-inspired Dominion Square Building on the north side of the square is the site of the Infotouriste office (daily: June to early Sept 7am–8pm; rest of year 9am–6pm) and the starting point for guided bus tours. The park also hosts occasional lunchtime concerts in summer, and in good weather the wedding-cake-like Sun Life building and the office blocks around the square empty their personnel onto the park benches for a snack and a chat. The southern half of the square is partitioned off as **Place du Canada**, which commemorates the 1967 centennial. Along its west side, the area's oldest building is the Victorian **St George's Anglican Church** (Tues–Sun 8.30am–4pm, Sat from 9am; Ⓦ www.st-georges.org). Its solid Neo-Gothic exterior gives way to a lofty interior with vaulting double hammer-beam trusses that rise in a series of arches to support the gabled roof.

Dwarfed by its high-rise neighbours, the **Basilique-Cathédrale Marie-Reine-du-Monde** (daily 7am–7.30pm, except during Mass: 7.30am, 8am, 12.10pm & 5pm; Ⓦ www.cathedralecatholiquedemontreal.org; Métro Bonaventure) was commissioned by Bishop Ignace Bourget as a reminder that Catholicism still dominated the largest city in the new Dominion of Canada. Impressed by St Peter's while visiting Rome, Bourget created a scaled-down replica of the famous church. While the statues crowning St Peter's facade are of the Apostles, the thirteen statues atop its smaller cousin represent the patron saints of the parishes that donated them. The inside is not as opulent as you might expect, though the high altar of marble, onyx and ivory is surmounted by a gilded copper reproduction of Bernini's baldachin over the altar in St Peter's. To your left on entering is the Chapelle des Souvenirs, which contains various relics, including the wax-encased remains of the obscure St Zoticus.

The city's legendary ice-hockey team, the Montréal Canadiens, play in the 21,000-seat **Centre Bell**, at 1260 rue de la Gauchetière ouest. The centre is also the venue for rock concerts, classical-music performances and family entertainment. English guided tours take place daily at 11.15am and 2.45pm ($8). If you fancy a puck souvenir or a hockey jersey, head inside to the Canadiens' Souvenir Boutique (Mon–Wed 9.30am–6pm, Thurs & Fri 9.30am–9pm, Sat 9.30am–5pm).

A few blocks west of the Centre Bell, the **Centre Canadien d'Architecture** (CCA), 1920 rue Baile (June–Sept Tues–Sun 11am–6pm, Thurs until 9pm; Oct–May Wed & Fri 11am–6pm, Thurs 11am–8pm, Sat & Sun 11am–5pm; $6, free on Thurs after 5.30pm; Ⓦ www.cca.qc.ca; Métro Guy-Concordia) inhabits a wonderfully sleek building with a curiously windowless facade and vast glass doors. The Peter Rose design incorporates the beautifully restored Shaughnessy Mansion (the former residence of a president of the Canadian Pacific Railway) and its Art Nouveau conservatory, while the light-filled galleries display the museum's vast collection of prints, drawings and books in exhibitions ranging from individual masters to whole movements from all cultures and periods. Behind the museum on the south side of boulevard René-Lévesque are the whimsical **CCA Sculpture Gardens** (daily 6am–midnight; free). Designed by prominent Montréal artist and architect Melvin Charney, the sculptures are a wacky mishmash of architectural references, arranged in a way reminiscent of ancient stone circles.

Rue Ste-Catherine and around

Proceeding north for two short blocks brings you to **rue Ste-Catherine**, the city's main commercial thoroughfare since the early 1900s. The street stretches for 15km across the island of Montréal, with the part east of rue Guy serving as the main shopping artery, featuring department stores interspersed with exclusive boutiques, souvenir shops and fast-food outlets. For all its consumerist gloss the road still has its seedy bits, peepshows and strip clubs

▲ Oratoire St-Joseph

DOWNTOWN MONTRÉAL

0   300 m

ACCOMMODATION

Abri du Voyageur	F
Auberge de Jeunesse	
Internationale de Montréal	I
Château Versailles	C
La Maison du Prêt d'Honneur	G
Manoir Ambrose	B
McGill University Residences	A
Petite Auberge les Bons Matins	J
Ritz-Carlton	D
Le St-Malo	E
Hôtel Y des Femmes (YWCA)	H

enlivening the streetscape. Further along, the street passes through the Quartier Latin, forms the heart of the gay village, and extends into the working-class neighbourhoods of east Montréal.

From the intersection of rues Peel and Ste-Catherine you can see the elegant **Cours Mont-Royal**. Formerly the largest hotel in the British

---

The Underground City

Place Ville Marie marks the beginning of Montréal's famous **Underground City**, planned as a refuge from the city's weather – outrageously cold in the winter and humid in the summer. The underground network began with the construction of the cruciform Place Ville Marie in the 1960s. Montrealers flooded into the first climate-controlled shopping arcade, and the Underground City duly spread. Today its 33km of passages provide access to the Métro, major hotels, shopping malls, transport termini, thousands of offices, apartments and restaurants, and a good smattering of cinemas and theatres. Everything underground is signposted, but you're still likely to get lost on your first visit – pick up a map of the ever-expanding system from the tourist office. However, while the pamphlets make the Underground City sound somewhat exotic, it's a pretty banal place – most Montrealers just use it to get from place to place, or drop in on a number of fairly standard shopping malls. If you're on a budget, check out the inexpensive food courts on the lowest floor of any of the malls (also handy for public toilets).

Commonwealth, it now contains four floors of shops (including those of expensive designers), topped by apartments and offices. Peek inside and gawk up at the fourteen-storey-high atria and chandeliers preserved from the hotel. One of these hangs from the coffered ceiling over a permanent catwalk – a testament to the fashion aspirations of the shopping centre. Standing out amongst the skyscrapers and malls, the cross-shaped, 46-storey **Place Ville Marie** has been a Montréal landmark since the 1960s, its rooftop searchlight visible for miles around, while below ground its shopping mall was one of the main catalysts of the Underground City (see box opposite). It marks one end of **avenue McGill College**, a broad boulevard lined with skyscrapers that frame a view of McGill University and the mountain beyond.

A block or so further east, the grounds of the 1859 Anglican **Christ Church Cathedral**, 635 rue Ste-Catherine ouest (daily 8am–6pm; Ⓦ www.montreal .anglican.org/cathedral; Métro McGill) and Square Phillips, opposite, provide a break in the commercial strip. By 1927, the church's slender stone spire was threatening to crash through the wooden roof and was replaced with the peculiar aluminium replica. Inside, the soaring Gothic arches are decorated with heads of angels and the evangelists, but the most poignant feature is the Coventry Cross, made from nails salvaged from England's Coventry Cathedral, which was destroyed by bombing during World War II. With the decline in its congregation, the cathedral authorities' desperation for money led them to lease all the land around and beneath the church. For nearly a year, Christ

Church was known as "the floating church" – it was supported on concrete struts while the developers tunnelled out the glitzy Promenades de la Cathédrale, a boutique-lined part of the Underground City.

A couple of blocks east of Square Phillips, Ste-Catherine slopes down towards **Place des Arts**, Montréal's leading performing-arts centre and the site of major festivals throughout the summer. The layout tends to throw newcomers: the entrances to all the performance halls are via an underground concourse. Atop that is a large plaza, with a series of gardens and fountains. The wide steps create a seating area for use during outdoor concerts, and the walls around the fountains are a popular snoozing spot for nearby office workers during the summer. Occupying the west side of the Place des Arts plaza, the **Musée d'Art Contemporain de Montréal** (Tues–Sun 11am–6pm, Wed till 9pm; $6, free Wed evenings; ⓦ www.macm.org; Métro Place-des-Arts) is Canada's first museum devoted entirely to contemporary art. The city's fore-most showcase for work by Québecois artists, such as Paul-Émile Borduas and Jean-Paul Riopelle, the museum also has works by other Canadian and inter-national artists. One wing is devoted to the permanent collection; the other stages temporary exhibitions. There's a nice restaurant terrace, often filled with live music, and a small sculpture garden – though difficult to find, it holds a Henry Moore sculpture amidst the greenery.

Rue Sherbrooke and around

Rue Sherbrooke crosses half of the island of Montréal but, other than the Stade Olympique far out east, its most interesting part is the few blocks from McGill University to rue Guy, an elite stretch of private galleries, exclusive hotels and boutiques – the likes of Yves Saint-Laurent, Ralph Lauren and Armani. At the corner of rue Drummond is the **Ritz-Carlton Hotel**, Montréal's most ornate hotel; Elizabeth Taylor married Richard Burton here. Inside, the small **Claude Lafitte Art Gallery** (Mon–Sat 10.30am–5pm, Sun noon–5pm) has works by Picasso, Miro, Chagall and Canadian artists Riopelle, Fortin, Lemieux, Borduas and Pellan. The hotel remains a symbol of what was once known as the **Golden Square Mile**; although downtown has encroached upon its southern precincts, the area between rue Sherbrooke, chemin de la Côte-des-Neiges, the mountain and McGill University retains many of the sumptuous mansions (though many now do duty as commercial or university buildings). From the late nineteenth century to World War II, about seventy percent of Canada's wealth was owned by a few hundred people who lived here. Known as the Caesars of the Wilderness, the majority were Scottish immigrants who made their fortunes in brewing, fur trading and banking, and who financed the railways and steamships that contributed to Montréal's industrial growth.

West of the Ritz, at the corner of rue Crescent – a lively street filled with boutiques and bars – stands Canada's oldest museum, the **Musée des Beaux-Arts**, with a pavilion on either side of rue Sherbrooke at nos. 1379 and 1380 (Tues–Sun 11am–5pm, special exhibits Wed until 9pm; July & Aug also Mon 11am–5pm; free, special exhibits $10–15, half price on Wed after 5pm; ⓦ www.mbam.qc.ca; Métro Guy-Concordia). The Canadian art collection is one of the country's most impressive, covering the spectrum from the devo-tional works of New France, through paintings of the local landscape by, among others, James Wilson Morrice, Maurice Cullen and Clarence Gagnon, to the more radical canvases by the Automatistes – Paul-Émile Borduas and Jean-Paul Riopelle – who transformed Montréal's art scene in the 1940s. The Group of Seven get a showing too, but the most accomplished paintings are in the European section, where many of the canvases – by such masters as El Greco, Rembrandt and Memling – were donated by merchants during Montréal's heyday. Their contributions are supplemented by equally high-class later acquisitions by Rodin, Picasso, Henry Moore and other twentieth-century luminaries. The decorative arts collection is also substantial, notably the twentieth-century designs from the likes of Charles and Ray Eames, Arne Jacobsen and Alvar Aalto.

Just east of the museum, at the intersection of rues Sherbrooke and Redpath, is another reminder of the Scottish roots of this neighbourhood – the **Church of St Andrew and St Paul**, the regimental church of the Black Watch, the Highland Regiment of Canada. Though the Gothic Revival building is not particularly impressive, Burne-Jones' stained-glass windows are worth a quick peek. Further east still is the city's most prestigious university, entered through a Neoclassical stone gate at the top of **avenue McGill College**, a principal boulevard with wide pavements adorned with sculptures, most notably Raymond Mason's *The Illuminated Crowd*, portraying a mass of larger-than-life people – generally faced by an equally large crowd of tourists. The leafy campus of **McGill University** was founded in 1813 from the bequest of James McGill, a Glaswegian immigrant fur trader, and the university is now world-famous for its medical and engineering schools. The ornate limestone buildings and their modern extensions are perfect for relaxing or for a walk above the street level of downtown. A boulder on the campus near Sherbrooke marks the spot where the original Iroquois village of Hochelaga stood before European penetration. In the middle of the campus is the **Musée Redpath** (Mon–Fri 9am–5pm, Sun 1–5pm, closed Sat all year; late June to Aug closed Fri also; free; ⓦ www.mcgill.ca/redpath; Métro McGill), the first custom-built Canadian museum, with an eclectic anthropological collection that includes a rare fossil collection, crystals, dinosaur bones and two Egyptian mummies.

Facing the campus, in the handsome early twentieth-century McGill Union building at 690 rue Sherbrooke ouest, is the **Musée McCord d'Histoire Canadienne** (Tues–Fri 10am–6pm, Sat, Sun & Mon 10am–5pm; winter closed Mon; $9.50, free on Sat before noon; guided tours Sat 2pm; ⓦ www .mccord-museum.qc.ca; Métro McGill), an extensive museum of Canadian history. The main part of the collection was amassed by the rich and worthy Scots-Irish McCord family over an eighty-year period from the mid-nineteenth century and represents a highly personal vision of the development of Canada, which they saw as a fusion of colonial and declining native elements. The museum is particularly strong on native artefacts, textiles, costumes and photographs, and examples of these are found in the high quality temporary shows as well as in the "Simply Montréal" exhibition on the second floor. Highlights include First Nations items such as furs, ivory carvings and superb beadwork. Nearby, ornate jewellery and other memorabilia from elite Montréal families contrast with the gritty floor-to-ceiling black-and-white photographs of the city taken by William Notman at the turn of the nineteenth century.

Mont Royal and the Plateau

Boulevard St-Laurent – **The Main** – leads all the way up from Vieux-Montréal to the northern extremities of the city. North of rue Sherbrooke is the absorbing **Plateau Mont-Royal** district, where Montréal's cosmopolitan diversity is evident in distinct enclaves of immigrant neighbourhoods. Running parallel to **rue St-Denis**, the Plateau's other main artery and, at its southern end, the

MONTRÉAL: PLATEAU MONT-ROYAL

Maison de Culture

AVENUE DU MONT-ROYAL EST

Mont-Royal

Sanctuaire Très St-Sacrament

RUE MARIE-ANNE OUEST   RUE MARIE-ANNE EST

Parc du Portugal

Parc des Amériques   Église St-Jean-Baptiste

RUE RACHEL OUEST   RUE RACHEL EST

AVENUE DULUTH OUEST   AVENUE DULUTH EST

RUE BAGG   Oboro

RUE NAPOLÉON

Schwartz's   RUE ST-CUTHBERT

RUE ROY EST

AVENUE DES PINS EST

RUE CHERRIER

Agora de la Danse

Square St-Louis   Sherbrooke

RUE PRINCE-ARTHUR EST

Ex-Centris

RUE MILTON   RUE SHERBROOKE EST

0   200 m

▲ Little Italy

Parc du Mont-Royal

McGill University &

▼ Quartier Latin

ACCOMMODATION		RESTAURANTS & CAFÉS				BARS & CLUBS	
Anne ma Soeur Anne	C	Amelio's	30	Laloux	21	Angels	26
Auberge Chez Jean	B	Beauty's	1	Maestro SVP	25	Balattou	7
Bienvenue Bed & Breakfast	D	La Binerie Mont-Royal	3	Moishe's	16	Bifteck St-Laurent	22
Boulanger Bassin B&B	A	ChuChai	10	Pizzédélic	6	Bily Kun	5
Château de l'Argoat	H	Eduardo	14	Red Thai	28	Blizzarts	15
Gîte Plateau Mont-Royal	I	Café El Dorado	4	Café Santropol	13	Café Campus	27
À la Maison de Pierre		Eurodeli	24	Schwartz's	18	Else's	20
et Dominique	E	L'Express	17	Toqué!	19	Envy / Exit	29
Hôtel de Paris	G	Fonduementale	8			Living	2
Aux Portes de la Nuit	F	La Jardin de Panos	12			Sofa	9
		Laïka	11			Le Swimming	23

heart of the upbeat studenty **Quartier Latin**, this zone is where the most fun can be had in Montréal, with a huge array of ethnic food outlets and bars spilling out onto the streets. If the party atmosphere is too much, you can head for the landscaped expanse of **Mont Royal** or the reverent hush of the **Oratoire St-Joseph** on the mountain's northwest flank.

Plateau Mont-Royal and the Quartier Latin

Traditionally, **boulevard St-Laurent** divided the English in the west from the French in the east of the city. Montréal's immigrants, first Russian Jews, then Greeks, Portuguese, Italians, East Europeans and, more recently, Latin Americans, settled in the middle and, though many prospered enough to move on, the area around the Main is still a cultural mix where neither of the two official languages dominates. Delis, bars, nightclubs, hardware stores, bookshops and an increasing number of trendy boutiques provide the perfect background to a wonderful jumble of sights, sounds and smells.

Wandering north from rue Sherbrooke on the Main, you'll pass through the strip's flashiest block, filled with see-and-be-seen restaurants and clubs, before arriving at one of Montréal's few pedestrianized streets, **rue Prince-Arthur**, thronged with buskers and caricaturists in the summer. Its eastern end leads to the beautiful fountained and statued **Square St-Louis**, the city's finest public square. Designed in 1876, the square was originally the domain of bourgeois Montrealers, and the magnificent houses were subsequently occupied by artists, poets and writers. The east side of the square divides the lower and upper areas of **rue St-Denis**. The part of rue St-Denis leading south from rue Sherbrooke to rue Ste-Catherine – the **Quartier Latin** – has long had a rather grubby reputation, but has become increasingly colonized by terrace cafés and bars crammed with students from the nearby Université du Québec à Montréal (UQAM) well into the early hours. By contrast, the Plateau stretch of rue St-Denis north of the square is the stamping ground of the francophone intellectual set, where a different yet equally heady atmosphere pervades the sidewalks. Here you'll find some of the city's most upscale boutiques and restaurants.

Mont Royal

Little more than a hill to most tourists but a mountain to Montrealers, **Mont Royal** reaches just 233m but its two square kilometres of greenery are visible from almost anywhere in the city. Mont Royal holds a special place in the history of the city – it was here that the Iroquois established their settlement and that Maisonneuve declared the island to be French – but for centuries the mountain was privately owned. Then, during an especially bitter winter, one of the inhabitants cut down his trees for extra firewood. Montrealers were outraged at the desecration and in 1875 the land was bought by the city for the impressive sum of $1m. Frederick Law Olmsted, designer of New York's Central Park and San Francisco's Golden Gate Park, was hired to landscape the hill, which now provides 56km of jogging paths and 20km of skiing trails to keep city inhabitants happy year-round. The city has steadfastly refused any commercial developments on this lucrative site, the only construction being **Lac aux Castors**, built in the 1930s as a work-creation scheme for the unemployed; it now serves as a skating rink in the winter and pedal-boat playground in the summer. In the 1950s, protection of the mountain reached a puritanical extreme when a local journalist revealed that young couples were using the area for amatory pursuits and, even worse, that people were openly drinking alcohol. Consequently all of the underbrush was uprooted, which only succeeded in killing off much of the ash, birch, maple, oak and pine trees.

ACCOMMODATION		RESTAURANTS & CAFÉS		BARS & CLUBS			
Le Breton	B	Area	10	Aigle Noir (Black Eagle)	14	Jello Bar	4
Castel Saint-Denis	A	Bato Thai	22	Aria	20	Jet	11
Manoir des Alpes	C	Le Commensal	6	Bistro à Jojo	8	Magnolia	15
Résidences Univ UQAM	D	Kilo	18	Cabaret Mado	12	Le Saint-Sulpice	7
		Mikado	5	Le Cheval Blanc	1	Le Ste-Élisabeth	9
		La Paryse	3	Le Drugstore	23	Sky	19
		Le Resto du Village	24	Foufounes Électriques	17	Stereo	21
		Saloon	16	L'Île Noire	2	Unity 2	13

Within five years Mont Royal was dubbed "Bald Mountain" and a replanting campaign had to be instigated.

There are various access points for a walk up the mountain but the most popular starting point is at the **George-Étienne Cartier monument** along avenue du Parc, most easily accessed by following rue Rachel westward from boulevard St-Laurent. You can also take the Métro to Mont-Royal station, walk west along avenue du Mont-Royal and turn left on avenue du Parc, or get off the Métro at Place-des-Arts and take bus #80, disembarking halfway along the park. However you get there, the angel-topped monument is hard to miss on summer Sundays, when buskers and people of all ages congregate with "tam tam" drums until the sun goes down, in a display out of a Woodstock love-in. From here, several paths lead towards the summit and the illuminated cross that commemorates Maisonneuve placing a wooden cross here in 1642. The gentlest slope is along Chemin Olmsted, a carriage trail that winds lazily up from the monument, past the top of rue Peel (the easiest access from downtown), and along the summit. In addition to the aforementioned Lac aux Castors, Chemin Olmsted provides access to the **Maison Smith** (daily 9am–5pm; free; Ⓦ www.lemontroyal.com), which houses an information centre and exhibition on the mountain, and proceeds to the Chalet, fronted by a **lookout point** offering fine views of downtown and the St Lawrence beyond.

On the northwest side of the mountain the awesome **Oratoire St-Joseph** (daily: late June to late Aug 6.30am–9.30pm; rest of year 7am–9pm; Ⓦ www.saint-joseph.org) rises from its green surroundings near Montréal's highest point. If you don't want to walk across the summit, the nearest Métro is Côte-des-Neiges, from where the way to the oratory is signposted; buses #51, #165, #166 and #535 also stop nearby. In 1904, Brother André built a small chapel here to honour St Joseph, Canada's patron saint. Before long, André's ability to heal people had earned him the sobriquet "The Miracle Man of Montréal", and huge numbers of patients took to climbing the outside stairs on their knees to receive his grace. Satisfied clients donated so much money that in 1924 he could afford to begin work on this immense granite edifice, which was completed in 1967, thirty years after his death. It is topped by a dome second in size only to St Peter's in Rome. The interior of St Jo's (as it's known locally) does not live up to the splendour of the Italianate exterior, though the chapel in the apse is richly decorated with green marble columns and a gold-leaf ceiling. In the adjoining anteroom, thousands of votive candles burn along the walls, and proof of Brother André's curative powers hang everywhere: crutches, canes and braces are crammed into every available space. The roof terrace, above the portico, has excellent views of the city and provides access to the gardens. A small upstairs museum displays items relating to Brother André's life, including the room in which he died, which was shifted here from a local hospice. Brother André's heart is enclosed in a glass case; the devout believe it quivers occasionally. Outside, the **Way of the Cross** has some particularly beautiful sculptures in smooth, white Carrara marble and Indiana buff stone by Montréal artist Louis Parent – a tranquil site used as a setting for the Denys Arcand film *Jésus de Montréal*. You can also visit the small building a few metres away from the Oratory that contains the original chapel and Brother André's tiny room.

The Parc Olympique and Jardin Botanique

It's best to take the Métro to Pie-IX (pronounced "pee-nuhf") station in order to view Montréal's most infamous architectural construction, the **Parc Olympique**. The main attraction, the **Stade Olympique**, is known by Montrealers as the "Big O" for three reasons: its name, its circular shape and the fact that the city owes so much money for its construction. The main facilities for the 1976 Summer Olympics were designed by Roger Taillibert, who was told that money was no object. Mayor Jean Drapeau declared, "It is as unlikely that Montréal will incur a debt as for a man to bear a child." The complex ended up costing $1.4 billion (over $2 billion with subsequent interest and maintenance), of which a large chunk is *still* outstanding – and it was not even completed in time for the games. It's now one of the most heavily used stadiums in the world: in a desperate attempt to pay the debts, the ceaseless schedule features everything from monster truck races to baseball games played by the Montréal Expos. Daily **guided tours** are available ($5.50; ☎514/252-4737 or 1-877/997-0919 for schedule) but for just a few bucks more you can take it in from the cheap seats at an Expos game. The stadium's 175-metre **tower** is a major engineering feat – the highest inclined tower in the world. Its main function was to hold a retractable 65-tonne roof, but the 45-minute retraction process never really worked properly, and today sections of the roof are prone to falling in. The attraction is the **funicular** that takes you up the tower to an observation deck with sixty-kilometre views and an exhibition of historic photos of Montréal (daily: late June to early Sept 9am–7pm; mid-Feb to late June & early Sept to Dec 9am–5pm; tower $10, or tower plus stadium tour $12.50; ⓦ www.rio.gouv.qc.ca).

In the stadium's shadow is the **Biodôme** (daily 9am–5pm, summer until 7pm; $10.50; ⓦ www.biodome.qc.ca; Métro Viau), housed in a building shaped like a bicycle helmet that started life as a venue for the Olympic cycling events. Now it is a stunning environmental museum comprising four ecosystems: tropical, Laurentian forest, St Lawrence maritime and polar. You can wander freely through the different zones, which are planted with appropriate flourishing vegetation and inhabited by the relevant birds, animals and marine life. It's all highly educational and good fun, but try to avoid visiting on Sundays, when, it seems, the entire population of Québec and its children head there.

Just north of the stadium and linked by a free shuttle bus (mid-May to mid-Sept daily every 30min 11am–5pm) is the **Jardin Botanique de Montréal**, 4101 rue Sherbrooke est (daily: 9am–4pm; late June to early Sept until 6pm; mid-Sept to early Nov until 9pm; $10.50 May–Oct, $7.75 rest of year; Ⓦ www.ville.montreal.qc.ca/jardin; Métro Pie-IX). The grounds and greenhouses contain some thirty types of gardens from medicinal herbs to orchids. Highlights include a Japanese garden, its ponds of water lilies bordered by greenish sculptured stone and crossed by delicate bridges. Especially resplendent during the autumn lantern festival is the nearby Chinese garden. Other attractions include the Insectarium (same hours and ticket), a bug-shaped building containing insects of every shape and size. If you visit in November, you'll get a chance to eat some of the insects at the Insectarium's annual bug fry.

Parc Jean-Drapeau

The former Parc des Îles, renamed **Parc Jean-Drapeau** following the death of the colourful and long-time mayor, comprises Île Ste-Hélène and the artificial Île Notre-Dame, constructed from fill dredged from the river and from the construction of the Métro (whose yellow line includes the Jean-Drapeau stop, located on Île Ste-Hélène). Bus #167 links the Métro with the attractions on both islands.

Not far from the station hovers the **Biosphère** (June–Sept daily 10am–6pm; Oct–May Mon & Wed–Fri noon–5pm, Sat & Sun 10am–5pm; $8.50; joint ticket with Musée Stewart $15; Ⓦ www.biosphere.ec.gc.ca), a giant sphere of interlocking aluminum triangles designed by Buckminster Fuller for Expo '67. Today, it's an interactive museum focusing on the St Lawrence Seaway and the Great Lakes. The exhibits change yearly and there's lots to amuse children, from interactive touch-screens to skill-testing games, movies and multimedia displays. On the fourth floor, a stupendous lookout point takes in the St Lawrence River and the city, foregrounded by the giant Alexander Calder stabile, *Man* – one of many pieces of public art dotted about the island. A twenty-minute walk from the Biosphère around the winding chemin du Tour de l'Île will get you to the grounds of Montréal's only **fort**, a U-shaped building situated close to the river's edge. Built by the British between 1820 and 1824 as a defence against the threat of American invasion – which never came – it played a number of roles, including a World War II prison camp, before opening as the **Musée Stewart** (mid-May to mid-Oct daily 10am–6pm; rest of year Wed–Mon 10am–5pm; $8, joint ticket with Biosphère $15; Ⓦ www .stewart-museum.org). In the fortified arsenal commissioned by the Duke of Wellington, the museum contains a collection of weapons and assorted domestic and scientific artefacts. The fort is also the summer venue for the re-enactment of seventeenth- and eighteenth-century military manoeuvres by actors dressed as the Fraser Highlanders and Compagnie Franche de la Marine. The shrieking sounds that can be heard all over the island's eastern point, beyond the Jacques-Cartier bridge, emanate from **La Ronde** (mid- to late

May Sat & Sun 10am–8pm; early to mid-June daily 10am–8pm; mid-June to late Aug daily 10am–10.30pm; Sept Sat & Sun 10am–7pm; Oct Fri 5–9pm, Sat noon–9pm, Sun noon–8pm; rides $29.55, grounds only $22.60; ⓦwww .laronde.com). The city's amusement park is the venue for various celebrations throughout the year, including the annual Fireworks Competition from June to July.

Île Notre-Dame, with its beach, canals and gardens, seems quieter than its neighbour – unless you venture here during one of the big motorsports weekends, when cars tear their way along the Circuit Gilles-Villeneuve, which rings the island.

Eating

Montrealers conduct much of their business and their social lives in the city's **eating places**, and Montréal food is as varied as its population, ranging from the rich meat dishes of typical Québecois cuisine to bagels bursting with cream cheese: Montréal comes a close second to New York as the **bagel** capital of the world, and they are sold everywhere from grimy outlets to stylish cafés – particularly delicious when fresh, warm and crammed with cream cheese and lox (smoked salmon).

Montréal's ethnic diversity is amply displayed by the variety of **cuisines** available and Montrealers try to outdo each other by indulging in exotic fare from Japanese rotis to earthy Portuguese nosh. The city has its own **Chinatown** just north of Vieux-Montréal, a **Little Italy** around Jean-Talon Métro, a **Greek** community whose cheaper restaurants are concentrated along Prince Arthur – but for more traditional Greek cuisine head further north along avenue du Parc where a number of Greek-Canadians live. Most prominent of the ethnic eateries are the **Eastern European** establishments dotted around the city. Opened by Jewish immigrants who came to work in the garment factories, their speciality is **smoked meat**, which has become a Montréal obsession, served between huge chunks of rye bread with pickles on the side. Masses of restaurants line the area around rue Ste-Catherine downtown, though American fast-food chains seem to be taking over, while Vieux-Montréal has an ever-expanding number of places to eat, but here most are touristy and slightly overpriced. The best for food, and upbeat atmosphere, is in the more French area of the metropolis, around the Plateau and Quartier Latin. *Apportez votre vin* ("bring your own wine") establishments, of which there are many on rue Prince Arthur and av Duluth, are the cheaper restaurant alternatives serving good ethnic cuisine.

Cafés and snack outlets

Bagel Etc. 4320 boul St-Laurent; Métro Mont-Royal or bus #55. Trendy New York-type diner. Excellent bagels from the simple cream cheese to caviar and extravagant breakfasts. Daily 8am–5pm.

Beauty's 93 av du Mont-Royal ouest ⓦwww.beautys.ca; Métro Mont-Royal or bus #55. A brunch institution with wonderful 1950s decor. Be prepared to get up early on the weekend to avoid the lineup.

Ben's Delicatessen 990 boul de Maisonneuve ouest; Métro Peel. Lithuanian Ben Kravitz opened his deli in 1908 and his sons and grandsons still run this Montréal institution. Its gaudy 1930s interior still draws a few people in the wee hours for delicious smoked meat and diner fare, but the wall of fame attests to happier days.

La Binerie Mont-Royal 367 av du Mont-Royal est; Métro Mont-Royal. Four tables and a chrome counter seat the hundreds of people who visit this

well-known café daily. The menu consists of beans, beans and more beans with ketchup, vinegar or maple syrup. Also served is pork, beef, *tourtière* (a minced pork pie) and *pouding chômeur* ("unemployed pudding"), a variation on bread pudding.
Bio Train 410 rue St-Jacques; Métro Square-Victoria. Self-serve health-food restaurant with tasty soups and hearty sandwiches. The muffins – especially the tangy cranberry ones – make great snacks.
Briskets 1073 Côte du Beaver Hall; Métro Square-Victoria. Plain decor with wooden tables, popular with students. Smoked meat to eat in or take away. Closed Sat & Sun.
Café El Dorado 921 av du Mont-Royal est; Métro Mont-Royal. Coffees from all over the world, and fine desserts.
Café Santropol 3990 rue St-Urbain; ⓦ www.santropol.com; bus #55 or Métro Sherbrooke or Mont-Royal. Mostly vegetarian café on the corner of av Duluth. Spectacular during the summer when its blooming back terrace is a welcome oasis from the busy streets, *Santropol* still retains its charm in winter thanks to its cozy atrium. Huge sandwiches, quiches and salads are offered as well as various herbal teas and coffees. Killer milkshakes, too.
Chez Claudette 351 av Laurier est; Métro Laurier. Cheap family bistro, great for a big breakfast fry-up.
Euro Deli 3619 boul St-Laurent; Métro Sherbrooke or bus #55. Busy deli where you can stuff yourself for about $5 on sandwiches, calzone, pasta and veggie food.
Fairmount Bagel Bakery 74 av Fairmount ouest; Métro Laurier or bus #55. Possibly the best bagel outlet in Montréal, offering a huge variety of bagels. There is nowhere to sit, but arm yourself with a bag of bagels, a pot of cream cheese and some smoked salmon (lox), perch on

the nearest curb and you'll soon be in bagel heaven. Open daily 24hr.
Faubourg Ste-Catherine 1616 rue Ste-Catherine ouest; ⓦ www.lefaubourg.com; Métro Guy-Concordia. A gigantic restored building on the corner of rue Guy. Downstairs is a wealth of food stalls from cookies to fresh veg; upstairs a fast-food mall to surpass all others – everything from fresh salmon to crepes and cookies.
Kilo 5206 boul St-Laurent; Métro Laurier or bus #55. Creating the most divine cakes, particularly the cheesecake, this patisserie is expensive but worth every cent. Open late on weekends. There's a second location in the Village at 1495 rue Ste-Catherine (Métro Beaudry).
Laïka 4040 boul St-Laurent; bus #55 or Métro Sherbrooke or Mont-Royal. The sleek interior draws urbane hipsters from the Plateau for daily specials and *cafés au lait.*
Reuben's Deli 1116 rue Ste-Catherine ouest; Métro McGill. An excellent deli with great jars of pimentos in the window and a wealth of smoked meats. Frantic atmosphere and friendly service. A favourite with local business types, and thus packed at lunchtime. A second outlet, a couple of blocks east at no. 888, is cheaper as it's in a (cosy) basement.
Schwartz's 3895 boul St-Laurent; bus #55 or Métro Sherbrooke. A Montréal institution: a small, narrow deli serving up colossal smoked-meat sandwiches, with surly service thrown in as part of the package. Line-up out the door on weekends.
Wilensky's Light Lunch 34 av Fairmount ouest; Métro Laurier or bus #55. Used for countless film sets because the decor hasn't changed since 1932 and that includes the till, the grill and the drinks machine. The Wilensky Special includes bologna and three types of salami and costs around $3. Mon–Fri 9am–4pm only.

Restaurants

Asian

Azuma 5263 boul St-Laurent ☎ 514/271-5263; Métro Laurier or bus #55. A popular Japanese restaurant with a reasonable $20 a head menu.
Chu Chai 4088 rue St-Denis ☎ 514/843-4194, ⓦ www.chuchai.com; Métro Mont-Royal or Sherbrooke. Excellent, fresh vegetarian Thai at budget prices.
Katsura 2170 rue de la Montagne ☎ 514/849-1172; Métro Peel. Large and popular downtown Japanese restaurant. Fairly expensive but they serve cheaper bento boxes ($13) and the like for weekday lunch.

Mikado 368 av Laurier ouest ☎ 514/279-4809; Métro Laurier or bus #80. Excellent sushi in a smashing setting, but it's expensive at around $30. Also at 1731 rue St-Denis ☎ 514/844-5705; Métro Berri-UQAM.
Pho Bang New York 970 boul St-Laurent ☎ 514/954-2032; Métro Place-d'Armes. The servings of *pho* (tonkinoise) noodle soup are huge and delicious, and extremely affordable. If it's full, try the similar *Pho Bac 97* up the street at no. 1016.
Red Thai 3550 boul St-Laurent ☎ 514/289-0998; Métro Sherbrooke or St-Laurent. This resto serves

up exquisite Thai in a decor straight out of *Anna and the King*.

Ruby Rouge 1008 rue Clark ☎514/390-8828; Métro Place-d'Armes. Montréal's vast temple to dim sum, right in the heart of Chinatown. Well-priced menu but not dirt-cheap. There are often long queues so get there early.

Soto 500 rue McGill ☎514/864-5115, ⓦwww.soto.ca; Métro Square-Victoria. Also at 3527 boul St-Laurent ☎514/842-1150; Métro Sherbrooke. Simple yet sleek decor meets excellent sushi and *maki*, though prices aren't cheap.

Soy 5258 boul St-Laurent ☎514/499-9399; bus #55. Deliciously prepared light dishes from the Orient. *Soy* is especially good for lunch, when a three-course meal costs under $10.

Thai Express 3710 boul St-Laurent ☎514/287-9957; Métro Sherbrooke. The name says it all: speedy Thai at low prices – for around $8, you'll get a seriously hearty serving of rice or noodles with wonderfully aromatic spices.

French

Bonaparte 443 rue St-François-Xavier ☎514/844-4368, ⓦwww.bonaparte.ca; Métro Place d'Armes. Moderately priced, well-situated French restaurant in Vieux-Montréal. The fish is good and there are tables on the balconies.

L'Express 3927 rue St-Denis ☎514/845-5333; Métro Sherbrooke. Fashionable Parisian-style bistro, with hectic service. Pretty expensive, and reservations are essential – though you might be able to squeeze in at the bar without one.

Fonduementale 4325 rue St-Denis ☎514/499-1446, ⓦwww.fonduementale.com; Métro Mont-Royal. Set in a historic two-storey house with a warm fireplace in winter and a blooming outdoor terrace in summer. The fondue is divine and the meals are long and languid.

Laloux 250 av des Pins est ☎514/287-9127, ⓦwww.laloux.com; Métro Sherbrooke. This Parisian-style bistro serves pricey – and exquisite – *nouvelle cuisine*.

Au 917 917 rue Rachel ☎514/524-0094; Métro Mont-Royal. An inexpensive bistro with a reliable menu in a comfortable atmosphere. Bring your own wine.

Au Petit Extra 1690 rue Ontario est ☎514/527-5552, ⓦwww.aupetitextra.com; Métro Papineau. Large, lively and affordable bistro with great food and authentic French feel but it's a bit of a hike east.

Toqué! 3842 rue St-Denis ☎514/499-2084, ⓦwww.restaurant-toque.com; Métro Sherbrooke. Renowned chef Normand Laprise holds court here and the dining experience is ultra chic, high-end

and unforgettable – if you can get a seat and afford the price tag. Reservations are essential.

Mediterranean

Amelio's 201 rue Milton ☎514/845-8396; Métro Place-des-Arts or bus #24. Basic and hearty pasta and pizza in a tiny half-basement restaurant in the heart of the McGill University student ghetto. The prices are excellent and the service friendly. Bring your own wine.

Arahova Souvlaki 256 rue St-Viateur ouest ☎514/274-7828; bus #80. Superb, yet inexpensive choice for authentic Greek cuisine.

Eduardo 404 av Duluth est ☎514/843-3330; Métro Sherbrooke or Mont-Royal. Crowded cheap Italian with huge portions. Bring your own alcohol and expect a queue.

La Jardin de Panos 521 av Duluth est ☎514/521-4206, ⓦwww.lejardindepanos.com; Métro Sherbrooke or Mont-Royal. Beats out the numerous cheap Greek *brochetteries* on rue Prince Arthur in taste and has a garden to boot. Bring your own wine.

Maestro SVP 3615 boul St-Laurent ☎514/842-6447, ⓦwww.maestrosvp.com; Métro Sherbrooke or bus #55. When oysters are in season, this is the place to go to get them, served in a myriad of ways. Try one in a shooter with vodka and horseradish sauce for a quick kick.

Milos 5357 av du-Parc ☎514/272-3522; bus #80. Expensive, but the finest Greek restaurant in the city, especially notable for its fresh seafood. Early-bird and Sunday dinners are cheaper at $35.

Misto 929 av du Mont-Royal est ☎514/526-5043, ⓦwww.restomisto.com; Métro Mont-Royal. Chic design, hip bourgeois francophones, and deliciously creative pasta and thin-crust pizzas. No *fettucine alfredo* here. Reservations advised.

Pizzédélic 3467 boul St-Laurent ☎514/845-0404; Métro St-Laurent or bus #55. Modern decor and experimental pizzas.

Pizzeria Napoletana 189 rue Dante ☎514/276-8226; ⓦwww.napoletana.com; bus #55. Very cheap and authentic Little Italy pizzeria; take your own alcohol and expect to queue at the weekend.

North American

L'Anecdote 801 rue Rachel est ☎514/526-7967; Métro Mont-Royal. Small, cosy hamburger and sandwich joint.

Bar-B-Barn 1201 rue Guy ☎514/931-3811, ⓦwww.barbbarn.ca; Métro Guy-Concordia. Top chicken and ribs served amidst yeee-haa decor; a favourite with the local "cowboy" business world – hundreds of business cards are stuck in the log rafters. Just south of rue Ste-Catherine.

Chez Delmo 211 rue Notre-Dame ouest
☎514/849-4061; Métro Place-d'Armes. Popular
with anglophones and workers from the nearby
stock exchange in Vieux-Montréal, the food doesn't
come cheap. Eat in the first room with its two long
oyster bars. Fish and seafood dishes are the speciality, and the chowder is a treat. No lunch Sat,
closed Sun, no dinner Mon.
Le Commensal 1204 av McGill College
☎514/871-1480; Métro McGill. Cheap vegetarian
with hot or cold buffet paid for by weight. The St-
Denis location has the best atmosphere. Open
daily until late. Also in the Quartier Latin at 1720
rue St-Denis (☎514/854-2627; Métro Berri-
UQAM).
Laurier BBQ 381 av Laurier ouest ☎514/273-
3671; bus #80. Great hunks of Québec-style barbecued chicken and huge salads; a Montréal
favourite for half a century.

Moishe's 3961 boul St-Laurent ☎514/845-3509,
🌐www.moishes.ca; bus #55 or Métro Sherbrooke.
Favourite haunt of Montréal's business community.
Excellent (and huge) steaks, but very expensive,
with notoriously bad-tempered service.
Reservations recommended.
La Paryse 302 rue Ontario est ☎514/842-2040;
Métro Berri-UQAM. Delicious home-made hamburgers and chips in a 1950s-style diner. Highly
recommended.
Patati Patata 4177 boul St-Laurent ☎514/844-
0216; bux #55. Small place with excellent and
cheap home-made food.
Shed Café 3515 boul St-Laurent ☎514/842-
0220; Métro St-Laurent or Sherbrooke. Hamburger,
salad and sandwich joint where trendy
Montrealers come to see and be seen. Avant-
garde, wacky interior. Open until 1am (weekend
3am).

Nightlife and entertainment

Montréal's **nightlife** keeps going into the small hours of the morning, and its
bars and clubs cater for everyone – from the students of the Quartier Latin and
the punks who hang out on the corner of rue Ste-Catherine and boul
St-Laurent to the anglophone yuppies of rue Crescent. The **bars** listed here are
the best of the bunch and are open until 3am unless stated otherwise. Always
tip the bar staff: the perks constitute most of their wages. Many bars have
regular music nights, with **jazz** being especially popular. Other than the bars,
there are numerous venues in the city, with top-name touring bands playing at
the Centre Bell and other large venues. For up-to-date **information**, the
Mirror (🌐www.montrealmirror.com) and *Hour* (🌐www.hour.ca) are free
English alternative weekly newspapers with excellent listings sections. The
English-language daily *Montreal Gazette* also carries comprehensive listings; the
Friday weekend guide is particularly good.

Bars

Le Bifteck 3702 boul St-Laurent; Métro
Sherbrooke or bus #55. Studenty, cheap beer bar
with taped music from grunge to hip-hop.
Bily Kun 354 av du Mont-Royal est
🌐www.bilykun.com; Métro Mont-Royal. Packed
brasserie-pub, with stuffed ostrich heads on the
walls. Occasional live bands.
Blizzarts 3956a boul St-Laurent; bus #55.
Funked-out lounge-bar with retro furnishings,
Sputnik-lighting, and a tiny dance floor. Draws a
late-twenty-something Plateau crowd.
Le Cheval Blanc 809 rue Ontario est; Métro
Berri-UQAM. Old-style Montréal pub with the same
Art Deco decor as when it opened in the 1940s.
They brew their own beer, and it's good.
Else's 156 rue Roy est; Métro Sherbrooke. A

warm and friendly neighbourhood bar-pub with
green walls, huge windows onto the street,
newspapers and magazines for loan and plants
galore.
Hurley's Irish Pub 1225 rue Crescent
🌐www.hurleysirishpub.com; Métro Peel or Guy-
Concordia. Very popular Irish pub with smooth
Guinness on tap.
L'Île Noire 342 rue Ontario est; Métro Berri-
UQAM. Sophisticated Scottish-type bar with warming whiskeys.
Jello Bar 151 rue Ontario est; Métro St-Laurent.
Enjoy live jazz and blues at this bar furnished with
1960s and 1970s novelties. Martini cocktails are
the house speciality.
Laïka 4040 boul St-Laurent; bus #55. Café by day,
lounge by night, *Laïka*'s got it all: good food,

drinks, music and chic decor, though the service can be a bit spotty.

Sir Winston Churchill Pub 1459 rue Crescent; Métro Peel or Guy-Concordia. Known locally as *Winnie's*, this large English-style pub attracts an older crowd of local and visiting anglophone professionals. Pool tables and a small dance floor. Prime pick-up joint.

Le Ste-Élisabeth 1412 rue Ste-Élisabeth; Métro Berri-UQAM. Nice outdoor courtyard with ivy-covered walls that give the impression of drinking a quaff with good friends in your very own backyard.

Le St-Sulpice 1680 rue St-Denis Ⓦwww .lesaint-sulpice.com; Métro Berri-UQAM. A bar complex comprising paired three-storey greystone houses with a warren of often-crowded rooms in the heart of Montréal's Quartier Latin. Terrace at the back and front, perfect for people-watching.

Sofa 451 rue Rachel est Ⓦwww.sofa-bar.com; Métro Mont-Royal. A cigar-bar lounge with an extensive scotch and porto list, funky furniture to sit in, and groovy music from acid jazz to house, depending on the night. Cover charge ($4–6) usually applies after 10pm.

Le Swimming 3643 boul St-Laurent Ⓦwww.leswimming.com; Métro Sherbrooke or bus #55. In a bizarre c. 1900 building, this is a massive pool hall and happening bar with occasional live acts on the weekend.

Le Vieux-Dublin 1219 rue University; Métro McGill. The "Old Dublin" is an Irish pub with Celtic music and a massive choice of draught beers. Popular with everyone.

Whisky Café 5800 boul St-Laurent Ⓦwww.whiskycafe.ca; Métro Outremont or bus #55. Elegantly decorated bar up at the corner of rue Bernard that attracts a young wealthy clientele. The prices aren't cheap, but then, there are no blended malts on the menu here. What there is in addition, though, is a girl's urinal – the only one in Montréal.

Clubs and music venues

Altitude 737 1 Place Ville Marie; Métro McGill or Bonaventure. Popular with financial district crowd; the main selling point is the panoramic view of the city, not the meat-market atmosphere.

Angels 3604 boul St-Laurent; Métro Sherbrooke or bus #55. Young, university hangout, with the atmosphere of the average common room downstairs and hip-hop, R&B and house music upstairs.

Aria 1280 rue St-Denis Ⓦwww.arianightclub.com; Métro Berri-UQAM. From 1.30am until 10am, Montréal's club kids dance the night and morning away to house music, with occasional detours into techno and trance, led by big-name guest DJs in the main room. Fri & Sat only; $20–25.

Aux Deux Pierrots 104 rue St-Paul est; Métro Champ-de-Mars. Québecois folk singers are the mainstay of this club and everyone sings along. There's usually a good crowded atmosphere but don't expect to understand a word unless your French is excellent. Outside terrace in the summer.

Le Balattou 4372 boul St-Laurent; bus #55. Montréal's only African nightclub. Dark, smoky, crowded, hot, loud and friendly. Live acts every night; entrance $5 on weekdays, $7 at weekends (includes one drink).

Bistro à Jojo 1627 rue St-Denis Ⓦwww.bistroajojo.com; Métro Berri-UQAM. Low ceilings and stone walls give this unpretentious blues cave an intimate feel. Shows nightly from around 10pm.

Cabaret Music Hall 2111 boul St-Laurent; Métro St-Laurent. Probably the best place in town to see a live act – it's an old-school venue with a balcony and chandeliers.

Café Campus 57 rue Prince-Arthur est; Métro Sherbrooke. Great place to see live acts, the cover is always reasonable as is the price of beer.

Casa del Popolo 4873 boul St-Laurent ℡514/284-3804, Ⓦwww.casadelpopolo.com; bus #55 or Métro Laurier. "The House of the People" is a sofa-strewn, low-key Plateau spot where high-calibre spoken-word evenings and folk and other bands perform for a marginal fee. A good spot to mingle with the locals any time from noon until 3am.

Club 6/49 1112 rue Ste-Catherine ouest; Métro Peel. Long-running Latin dance club with plenty of tables to sit at if you don't have the spirit for salsa and merengue. Free lessons on Monday and Thursday nights.

Club Soda 1225 boul St-Laurent Ⓦwww .clubsoda.ca; Métro St-Laurent. One of Montréal's most popular venues. Attracts good acts, especially during the comedy and jazz festivals.

Exit 3553 boul St-Laurent Ⓦwww.exit3553.com; Métro Sherbrooke or bus #55. The hip-hop sessions (Thurs–Sat) attract a mostly under-25 crowd to this long and narrow space; older clubbers head to the top floor (open Sat only) for Christian Pronovost's popular house set. Cover $10.

Les Foufounes Électriques 87 rue Ste-Catherine est Ⓦwww.foufounes.qc.ca; Métro St-Laurent. A bizarre name ("The Electric Buttocks") for a bizarre and wonderful bar-club venue. Known as *Foufs*, it's the best place in Québec for alternative bands, attracting a young crowd from ravers to punks. Huge outside terrace perfect for summer evenings. Tickets for bands $5–15, club nights free–$8; admission to the bar is free and pitchers of beer are cheap.

Montréal has an excellent **gay** scene, with the action concentrated in the area known as **The Village** – roughly located on rue Ste-Catherine est between rue Amherst and the Papineau Métro station. There's a **tourist information centre** here, at 1260 rue Ste-Catherine est, Suite 209 (late June to early Sept Mon–Thurs 11am–6pm, Fri–Sun 10am–8pm; rest of year Mon–Fri and weekends during major events 10am–6pm; ℡514/522-1885 or 1-888/595-8110, ⓦwww.infogayvillage .com). As well, two **help lines** can provide up-to-date news on the latest events: Gay Line (daily 7–11pm; ℡514/866-5090, ⓦwww.gayline.qc.ca) is in English; Gai Écoute (℡514/866-0103) in French. Priape, 1311 rue Ste-Catherine est, is a Village-based sex shop and clothing store that also sells tickets to most events. *Fugues* (ⓦwww.fugues.com) is the city's monthly French gay and lesbian magazine (there's usually a small English section hidden among the ads and pictures). In early August, **Divers/Cité** (ⓦwww.diverscite.org), the gay and lesbian pride parade, is the event of the year; also popular are the September **image + nation** film festival (ⓦwww.image-nation.org) and the week of events leading up to the massive **Black & Blue** circuit party (ⓦwww.bbcm.org) on Thanksgiving weekend.

Cafés and restaurants

Most of the **restaurants** and hangouts in The Village cater to a lesbian, bisexual and gay crowd in the evening, but are more mixed during the day. Unless noted otherwise, Métro Beaudry is the nearest station.

Area 1429 rue Amherst ℡514/890-6691, ⓦwww.rest-area.qc.ca; Métro Beaudry. Well-designed restaurant with a stylish and airy atmosphere reflected in the exquisite French and Asian fusion dishes (and high prices). Dinner only; closed Sun & Mon.

Bato Thai 1310 rue Ste-Catherine est ℡514/524-6705. An excellent Thai restaurant, but with slow service. Cheap lunch specials during the week.

La Paryse 302 rue Ontario est; Métro Berri-UQAM. Extraordinary and exotic range of burger fillings.

Jet 1003 rue Ste-Catherine est ⓦwww .jetnightclub.com; Métro Beaudry. One of the city's top spots for danceable R&B, with a dash of old school, house and club anthems. Dress code. Fri & Sat 10pm–3am.

Living 4521 boul St-Laurent ⓦwww .livingnightclub.com; Métro Mont-Royal or bus #55. A three-floor club in a former bank frequented by under-35 yuppies and musically ruled by urban beats ranging from R&B to deep house. Wed to Sun.

Stereo 858 rue Ste-Catherine est ⓦwww .stereo-nightclub.com; Métro Beaudry. Said to have the best sound system in Montréal. The stereo in question kicks techno, house and drum'n'bass all night long, usually manned by an internationally renowned DJ. Opens at 2am and closes whenever. Fri & Sat only. $25–30.

Upstairs 1254 rue Mackay ⓦwww.upstairsjazz.com; Métro Guy-Concordia. Upstairs is actually downstairs in a cosy half-basement with fresh jazz and blues on tap nightly (Wed–Sun in summer, post-Jazz Festival) in a wonderfully attitude-free atmosphere. Cover charge of $10–20 Fri–Sun.

The performing arts and cinema

Montréal's most prestigious centre for the **performing arts** is the Place des Arts, 175 rue Ste-Catherine ouest (ⓦwww.pdarts.com), a five-hall complex with a comprehensive year-round programme of dance, music and theatre. The Théâtre de Verdure in Parc Lafontaine is an outdoor theatre with a summer-long programme of free plays, ballets and concerts. Another eclectic venue is the Théâtre St-Denis, 1594 rue St-Denis (ⓦwww.theatrestdenis.com), which presents blockbuster musicals and other shows. The Saidye Bronfman Centre for the Arts, 5170 chemin de la Côte-Ste-Catherine (ⓦwww.saidyebronfman.org),

Piccolo Diavolo 1336 rue Ste-Catherine est ☎514/526-1336, ⓦwww .piccolodiavolo.com. Hip place to eat Italian. Pizzas, pastas and meatier dishes, including good veal *osso buco*.

Le Resto du Village 1310 rue Wolfe. Just off rue Ste-Catherine, this small diner serves filling comfort food such as *pâté chinois* (shepherd's pie) and *poutine* to a largely gay crowd. Open 24hr.

Saloon 1333 rue Ste-Catherine est. Pizzas, burgers, salads and brunch. Mixed crowd of young and old, gay and straight.

Bars, clubs and discos

Aigle Noir 1315 rue Ste-Catherine est ⓦwww.aiglenoir.com. Trashy leather bar, better known among anglophones as *Black Eagle*.

Cabaret Mado 1115 rue Ste-Catherine est ⓦwww.mado.qc.ca. Local drag celebrity Mado and her cohorts camp it up for a mixed, fun-loving clientele. Also musical cabaret nights.

Le Drugstore 1366 rue Ste-Catherine est. Multilevel bar complex drawing lesbians and gay men that's busiest before 11pm. Rooftop terrace.

Magnolia 1329 rue Ste-Catherine est ⓦwww.magnolia.com. The only spot in Montréal that's primarily for lesbians. Quieter pub atmosphere early on becomes one big dance floor later ($3–5). Men allowed as guests.

Sky 1474 rue Ste-Catherine est. The upstairs lounge and dance floor are hit-and-miss but the massive ground-floor bar attracts the beautiful-people set after work. Sunday afternoon happy hour has two-for-one deals.

Unity II 1171 rue Ste-Catherine est ⓦwww.club-unity2.com. A young and outgoing crowd fill the large dance floor here, though the Bamboo Bar upstairs tends to get more packed and sweaty – head to the rooftop terrace to cool off. Wed–Sun 10pm–3am.

contains an exhibition centre and a three-hundred-seater venue for English (and Yiddish) music, dance, film and theatre.

The Orchestre Symphonique de Montréal (ⓦwww.osm.ca) and Orchestre Métropolitain (ⓦwww.orchestremetropolitain.com) stage regular **concerts** at Place des Arts and the Basilique Notre-Dame. The city also has a programme of free summer concerts in various city parks. L'Opéra de Montréal (ⓦwww.operademontreal.com) produces five bilingually surtitled productions a year at Place des Arts. The city's foremost French-language **theatre** is the Théâtre du Rideau Vert, 4664 rue St-Denis (ⓦwww.rideauvert.qc.ca), which gives prominence to Québec playwrights, while the Théâtre du Nouveau Monde, 84 rue Ste-Catherine ouest (ⓦwww.tnm.qc.ca), presents a mix of contemporary and classic plays in French. Montréal's main English-language theatre is the Centaur Theatre, 453 rue St-François-Xavier (ⓦwww .centaurtheatre.com). Montréal has more than ten excellent **dance** troupes, from Les Grands Ballets Canadiens (ⓦwww.grandsballets.qc.ca) and Les Ballets Jazz de Montréal (ⓦwww.balletsdemontreal.com) to the avant-garde La La La Human Steps and O Vertigo, who perform at various times at the Place des Arts, Théâtre de Verdure and during the festivals.

Films in English, usually the latest releases from the US, can be caught at most cinemas; the Paramount, 977 rue Ste-Catherine ouest, features armchairs and a wide screen. The main repertory cinema in English is the Cinema du Parc, 3575 av du Parc (ⓦwww.cinemaduparc.com), along with the NFB (National Film

Spectator sports in Montréal

Baseball Home ground of the Montréal Expos (ⓦwww.expos.mlb.com) is the Olympic Stadium, 4141 av Pierre-de-Coubertin (Métro Pie-IX). Tickets cost $8–36.

Canadian football The Montreal Alouettes (ⓦwww.montrealalouettes.com) represent the city in the Canadian Football League (CFL). Home games are at McGill University's Molson Stadium, 475 av des Pins ouest. Tickets cost $18–65.

Ice hockey The Montréal Canadiens, known as the Habs (ⓦwww.canadiens.com), play at the Centre Bell, 1250 rue de la Gauchetière ouest (Métro: Lucien L'Allier or Bonaventure). Tickets start at $22.

Board) Cinema, 1564 rue St-Denis (ⓦwww.nfb.ca). The Cinémathèque Québécoise, 335 boul de Maisonneuve est (ⓦwww.cinematheque.qc.ca), has excellent screening and exhibition programmes; Ex-Centris, 3536 boul, St-Laurent (ⓦwww.ex-centris.com), has a penchant for alternative French film and experimental digital works. Check online (ⓦwww.cinemamontreal.com) or in the *Montreal Gazette* or the free weeklies for show times – make sure to verify that the English film you want to see is playing in **v.o.** (*version originale*), not v.f. (*version français*); the latter means it's dubbed.

Listings

Airlines Air Canada ☏1-888/247-2262; Air Canada Tango ☏1-888/315-1390; Air France ☏1-800/667-2747; American Airlines ☏1-800/433-7300; British Airways ☏1-800/247-9297; Canjet ☏1-800/809-7777; Continental ☏1-800/231-0856; Delta ☏1-800/221-1212; Jetsgo ☏1-866/440-0441; KLM/Northwest ☏1-800/225-2525; United ☏1-800/241-6522; WestJet ☏1-888/937-8538; Zip ☏1-866/432-1947.

Airport enquiries ☏514/394-7377 or ☏1-800/465-1213, ⓦwww.admtl.com.

Bike and blade rental Cycle Pop, near Parc Lafontaine at 1000 rue Rachel est (☏514/526-2525, ⓦwww.cyclepop.ca), rents from $25 per day. In the Vieux-Port, try Vélo Aventure, on the Quai des Convoyeurs, 100m west of Quai King-Edward (☏514/847-0666, ⓦwww.veloaventure.com) or Ça Roule, 27 rue de la Commune est, facing Quai King-Edward (☏514/866-0633, ⓦwww.caroulemontreal.com); both offer lessons and guided tours. The Maison des Cyclistes, 1251 rue Rachel est (☏514/521-8356, ⓦwww.velo.qc.ca), is an excellent resource for cycling information and organized tours out of the city but does not rent bikes.

Books and maps English books can be bought from most major bookshops. Paragraphe, 2220 av McGill College, is one of the best bookstores in town. Double Hook, 1235a av Greene, specializes in English-Canadian authors. Chapters, 1171 rue Ste-Catherine ouest, is huge, as is Indigo, 1500 av McGill College; both have large travel sections. Travel books in English and French are also available at Librairie du Voyage Ulysse, 4176 rue St-Denis and 560 av du President-Kennedy. Aux Quatre Points Cardinaux, 551 rue Ontario est (ⓦwww.aqpc.com; Métro Berri-UQAM), carries 1:50,000 topographic maps of Québec.

Camping equipment You can rent or buy all you need for the outdoors at Inukshuk, 1472 rue Peel (☏514/288-8010 or 1-888/592-8010, ⓦwww.inukshukpleinair.com; Métro Peel), or Altitude Sports Plein-Air, 4140 rue St-Denis (☏514/847-1515 or 1-800/729-0322, ⓦwww.altitude-sports.com; Métro Mont-Royal).

Car rental Avis, 1225 rue Metcalfe (☏514/866-7906); Budget, 1240 rue Guy (☏514/938-1000); Discount, 607 boul de Maisonneuve ouest (☏514/286-1554); Hertz Canada, 1073 rue Drummond (☏514/938-1717); Thrifty, 845 rue Ste-Catherine est (☏514/845-5954); and Via Route, 1255 rue Mackay (☏514/871-1166), which charges a bit less than the majors.

Consulates UK, 1000 rue de la Gauchetière ouest ☏514/866-5863; US, 1155 rue St-Alexandre ☏514/398-9695. For Australia, Ireland, New Zealand and South Africa, contact the embassy in Ottawa; see p.190.

Currency exchange American Express, 1141 boul de Maisonneuve ouest (☎514/284-3300); Bureau de Change du Vieux-Montréal, 230 rue St-Jacques (☎514/284-8686); Calforex, 1250 rue Peel (☎514/392-9100); Thomas Cook, Centre Eaton, 705 rue Ste-Catherine ouest (☎514/284-7388). Most large downtown banks will change currency and travellers' cheques. You can also withdraw money at ATMs throughout the city, so long as your card is Cirrus or Plus compatible.

Internet access CyberGround, 3672 boul St-Laurent ($7/hr), open until 11pm; L'Inter-Café.net, 1455 rue Amherst ($6/hr), open until 8pm (weekends 7pm); and a number of places clustered around Concordia University, including Net 24, 2157 rue Mackay ($4/hr), which has free coffee to keep you going 24 hours a day. Larger post offices have free access but a 15min limit.

Laundry Net-Net, 310 av Duluth est ☎514/844-8511, will wash, dry and fold your clothes for you within 24 hours for 77¢ per pound; doing it yourself works out to around $4–5. Buanderie du Village, 1499 rue Amherst ☎514/526-4084, will wash your clothes in a few hours for $6/load, around $4 if you do it yourself.

Left luggage There are $2 lockers at the main bus terminal (24hr only; $5/day charge thereafter) accessible until 11pm, as well as left-luggage storage ($4–6 with hefty late charges) open 7am to 7pm. The train station has left-luggage facilities for passengers only ($2.50/24hr, $5 oversized); open until 11pm.

Medical emergencies Central English-language hospitals that are part of the McGill University Health Centre "superhospital" (☎514/934-1934) are the Montreal General Hospital, 1650 av Cedar, on the mountain's slope northwest of downtown, and Royal Victoria Hospital, 687 av des Pins ouest, up the hill from McGill University. Centre Dentaire, 3546 av Van-Horne (☎514/342-4444) is a 24hr dental clinic, and there's a walk-in dental clinic on the 3rd floor of Montreal General Hospital (Mon–Fri 8am–noon & 1–4pm, but go as early as possible; after-hour emergencies call ☎514/934-8075).

Pharmacies Most downtown outlets of Jean Coutu (www.jeancoutu.com) and Pharmaprix (www.pharmaprix.ca) are open until 11pm and midnight, respectively. The Pharmaprix near the Oratory, at 5122 chemin de la Côte-des-Neiges, is open 24hr (☎514/738-8464).

Post office 1250 rue University (Mon–Fri 8am–5.45pm).

Taxis Co-op ☎514/725-9885; Diamond ☎514/273-6331.

Weather and road conditions Environment Canada (☎514/283-3010, www .weatheroffice.ec.gc.ca) for info on weather and winter road conditions; Transports Québec (☎514/284-2363, www.mtq.gouv.qo.oa) for roadworks. Up-to-the-minute traffic reports are also on radio stations such as CJAD (800 AM). Skiers can check snow conditions at www .quebecskisurf.com.

Southwest Québec

Beyond the city limits, Montrealers are blessed with superb holiday regions, most within an hour or two of the metropolis. The lake-dotted countryside of **Southwest Québec** offers a range of recuperative pleasures for the city-dweller, from relaxing country drives and nosing about historic sites, to cycling and hiking in summer and a plethora of ski hills to choose from come winter.

Information for Southwest Québec

Outaouais ☎819/778-2222 or 1-800/265-7822, www.outaouais-tourism.ca.
Laurentides ☎450/436-8532 or 1-800/561-6673, www.laurentides.com.
Eastern Townships ☎819/820-2020 or 1-800/355-5755, www .easterntownships.cc.
Mauricie ☎819/536-3334 or 1-800/567-7603, www.icimauricie.com.

SOUTHWEST QUÉBEC

**Inset map labels:**
ME
Sherbrooke
U S A
Québec City
Trois-Rivières
Montréal
Ottawa
Lake Ontario
Toronto
NY
VT
NH

N

0 — 40 km

Québec City
Trois-Rivières
Victoriaville
Drummondville
Sherbrooke
North Hatley
Magog
Ayer's Cliff
Coaticook
Mont Orford
EASTERN TOWNSHIPS (CANTONS DE L'EST)
Abbaye St-Benoît-du-Lac
Georgeville
Owl's Head
Knowlton (Lac Brome)
Sutton
Granby
Bromont
Dunham
Cowansville
St-Hyacinthe
Mont-St-Hilaire
Chambly
St-Hubert
St-Jean-sur-Richelieu
Longueuil
Lachine
Kahnawake
Montréal
Dorval
Laval
Terrebonne
Repentigny
Joliette
LANAUDIÈRE
St-Donat
Val-David
Mont-Blanc
Ste-Agathe-des-Monts
Le Chantecler
Ste-Adèle
St-Jérôme
St-Sauveur-des-Monts
LAURENTIANS (LAURENTIDES)
St-Eustache
Oka
La Trappe
d'Oka
Hudson
Lachute
Hawkesbury
Cornwall
ONTARIO
St-Jovite
Mont-Tremblant
Gray Rocks
PARC DU MONT-TREMBLANT
Sorel
Lac St-Pierre
Rivière Richelieu
Lac Champlain
MONTÉRÉGIE
Hemmingford
Memphrémagog
CANADA
U S A   VERMONT
NEW YORK
NEW HAMPSHIRE
St Lawrence River
Ottawa River

Directional labels:
Québec City
Boston
New York & Boston
New York
Montebello
Ottawa
Toronto & Detroit

Route numbers (selection):
117, 323, 329, 125, 131, 158, 40, 37, 158, 55, 153, 155, 132, 122, 143, 20, 116, 161, 162, 165, 112, 141, 147, 55, 247, 243, 139, 10, 104, 202, 133, 223, 15, 104, 30, 25, 640, 117, 148, 158, 50, 344, 40, 20, 132, 138, 89, 87, 401, 2, 43, 34, 17, 417, 148, 55, 137

□ (compass/symbol)

Just across the river to the northwest of Montréal, along the fertile banks of the St Lawrence, the **Basses Laurentides** (Lower Laurentians) are dotted with whitewashed farm cottages and manor houses, a monastery and a provincial park that all make an easy day-trip from Montréal. Continue along to the largely wilderness stretch of the **Outaouais** region beginning around 130km west of Montréal and extending along the north side of the Rivière Outaouais (Ottawa River). Once the domain of Algonquin tribes, the region was not developed until the 1800s, when it became an important centre for the lumber industry. While the bulk of the activities in the region are of an outdoorsy nature – hiking, canoeing, snowmobiling, cycling and cross-country skiing – it's worth stopping in **Montebello** for its atmosphere and historical heritage.

Extending along the north side of the St Lawrence from the Ottawa River to the Saguenay are the **Laurentians** – one of the world's oldest ranges – where five hundred million years of erosion have moulded a rippling landscape of undulating hills and valleys. The most accessible stretch lies north of Montréal but, unlike the more historic Basses Laurentides, settlement in the upper Laurentians did not begin until the 1830s, when the construction of the P'tit Train du Nord railway tracks let in the mining and lumber industries. When the decline in both industries left the area in a depression, salvation came in the form of the recreational demands of the growing populace of Montréal. The region is now one of North America's largest ski areas, with the number of resorts increasing annually, and the train tracks have been replaced by a terrific cycling trail.

Along the US border to the east of Montréal, the charm of the **Cantons-de-l'Est** (Eastern Townships) lies in the acres of lush farmlands, vineyards, orchards, maple woods and lakeshore hamlets popular among antique collectors. Like the Laurentians, the region is also a popular getaway for city dwellers in search of active pursuits on the lakes, trails and pistes.

Along the north shore of the St Lawrence, the rather dull drive to Québec City (see p.277) provides access to a couple of worthwhile distractions. The **Mauricie** valley, home to the province's smallest national park, has a web of waterways and lakes amidst a landscape of mountainous forest. Spanning the mouths of the Rivière Mauricie, **Trois-Rivières** is a seemingly unprepossessing town unless you detour to its historic centre.

The Lower Laurentians (Les Basses Laurentides)

Once the domain of various aboriginal groups, the **Lower Laurentians** (Basses Laurentides) were granted by Ville-Marie's governors to the colony's first seigneurs, who, using a modified version of the feudal land system of the motherland, oversaw the development of the land by their tenants, or *habitants*. As the rivers were the lifeline of the colony, these tenant farms were laid out perpendicular to the water in long, narrow, rectangular seigneuries that shaped life under the long regime.

St-Eustache and Oka

The first town of note in the region is **ST-EUSTACHE**, about forty-minutes' drive through the suburbs northwest of Montréal by Hwy 13 or 15, then Hwy 640; the main tourist office is en route, just off exit 14 from Hwy 640 (daily:

The rebellion of 1837

In the early 1800s, British immigrants to Lower Canada were offered **townships** (*cantons*), while the francophones were not allowed to expand their holdings, exacerbating the resentment caused by the favouritism extended to English-speaking businesses in Montréal. The situation was worsened by high taxes on British imports and a savage economic depression in 1837. Wearing Canadian-made garments of *étoffe du pays* as a protest against British imports, the leaders of Lower Canada reform – known as **the Patriotes** – rallied francophones to rebel in Montréal. As Louis-Joseph Papineau, the Outaouais region seigneur whose speeches in the Assembly had encouraged the rebellions, fled the city, fearful that his presence would incite more rioting, the government sent military detachments to the countryside, the hotbed of the *Patriotes*. Two hundred *Patriotes* took refuge in Saint-Eustache's church, where eighty of them were killed by British troops, who went on to raze much of the town.

late June to late Aug 8.30am–6.30pm; rest of year 9am–4pm; ℡450/491-4444, ⓦwww.basseslaurentides.com). Alternatively, take bus #46 from Métro Henri-Bourassa in Montréal ($2.85; 1hr). Most of the town is a dull sprawl, except for the riverside historic centre, **Vieux St-Eustache**, where the frustrations of the *habitants* with the British occupancy met a tragic end in the 1837 Rebellion. About thirty buildings survived the battle that put down the rebellious *Patriotes* led by Louis-Joseph Papineau (see box above) and these are located along two narrow streets in Vieux St-Eustache. Most are simply marked with heritage signs, and inaccessible to the public, but the **church**, at 123 rue St-Louis, still bears a few scars and offers free guided tours (Thurs & Fri 9.30am–4.30pm). The cross street, rue St-Eustache, has two sights worth visiting, the most impressive being the wedding-cake Manoir Globensky at no. 235 (Tues–Sun 10am–5pm; $3), which doubles as the **Musée de St-Eustache et des Patriotes** and includes displays, films and temporary exhibitions on local history. Opposite, the eighteenth-century **Moulin Légaré**, at no. 232, is the oldest water-powered flour mill in continuous operation in North America; guided tours are available ($3; ℡819/974-5400 for schedules) but you can get a glimpse of the works from the bakery shop in front. *Café Bistro Coincidence*, a block back towards the church at 198 rue St-Eustache (℡819/623-8094), is a good spot for ciabatta sandwiches and salads in a house dating from 1812.

Southwest of St-Eustache, on Hwy 344, lies the small lakeside town of **OKA**. Although associated with the armed stand-off between the Mohawks and police (see box opposite), there isn't much to see in the town itself, though worth a visit is the **Abbaye Cistercienne d'Oka**, 1600 chemin d'Oka (daily 4am–8pm; ⓦwww.abbayeoka.com), one of North America's oldest monasteries. Commanding a spectacular site just outside town, its century-old bell tower rises amidst the hills. The Trappists arrived here from France in 1880, their life in Canada beginning in a miller's house that's now overshadowed by the rest of the complex and the landscaped gardens of the abbey. The nearby monastery shop (closed Sun) sells organic Trappist products, from maple syrup and chocolates to variations on the delicious Oka cheese. Between the town and monastery, the **Calvaire d'Oka** with its seven mid-eighteenth-century stone chapels is best visited on September 14, when native pilgrims hold the Feast of the Holy Cross along the banks of Lac des Deux Montagnes. The Calvaire is reached by a 5.5km trail up the Colline d'Oka, a hill that gives views of the region, and is set within the **Parc National d'Oka** (open year-round; $3.50

The Oka Mohawk stand-off

In the summer of 1990, Oka became the stage for a confrontation between **Mohawk** warriors from Kanesatake and the provincial government. The crisis began when Oka's town council decided to expand its golf course onto a sacred burial ground, a provocation to which the Mohawks responded by arming themselves and staking out the territory. Québec's public security minister sent in the provincial police to storm the barricades. In the ensuing fracas a policeman was killed – no one knows by whom, but the autopsy established it was not by a police bullet. Hostilities reached a new pitch and the two sides became ever more polarized. As sympathetic Mohawks from the Kahnawake reserve south of Montréal set up barricades across the Mercier Bridge, one of Montréal's main commuter arteries, groups of white Québecois attacked them with stones, while other groups of aboriginal people showed solidarity with the Mohawks throughout Canada and the USA. The federal government offered to buy the land for the natives on the condition that they surrender, but the stand-off continued as negotiators failed to agree on terms. The crisis lasted 78 days, until the core of fifty Mohawks was encircled by 350 Canadian army soldiers and forced to give up. The fate of the disputed land, along with hundreds of other similar claims, is still being negotiated (though there have been other improvements for the Kanesatake community). However, many believe that the natives went too far at Oka, and the existing distrust between aboriginal Canadians and other Canadians seems to have deepened. As Georges Erasmus, former national chief of the Assembly of First Nations, said: "Our demands are ignored when we kick up a fuss – but they are also ignored if we do not."

plus $5 parking; ☎450/479-8365 or 1-888/727-2652; ⓦwww.sepaq.com), a magnificent provincial park with 45km of hiking and cycling trails and a long stretch of sandy beach. Bicycles and watercraft can be rented, while in winter cross-country skis and snowshoes are available for exploring the trails. There are serviced campsites ($30.65) and more rustic spots to pitch a tent ($22); you can rent all the gear you need from $82 for a minimum of two nights (including pitch rental) – enquire at the entry kiosk.

Montebello and around

The drive from Montréal to Gatineau (see p.186) on scenic Hwy 148 takes in a few riverside villages that used to be thriving logging towns. The first stop en route, 135km west of Montréal, is **MONTEBELLO**, a picturesque village named after seigneur and Rebellion leader Louis-Joseph Papineau's estate. Today, the town is the Outaouais' star attraction thanks to a resort-like atmosphere that includes horseback riding, boating, upscale boutiques and the inimitable *Fairmont Le Château Montebello*, 392 rue Notre-Dame (☎819/423-6341 or 1-800/441-1414, ⓦwww.fairmont.com; ❼), the world's largest log building. Built by the Seigneury Club in 1930 in 90 days, the original three buildings are made up of 10,000 red-cedar logs. Today, it's a five-star hotel; even if you can't afford to stay, check out the six-hearthed fireplace in the massive hexagonal lobby and tour the photo gallery. The *Château* abuts the **Site historique national du Manoir Papineau** (mid-May to June & Sept to mid-Oct Wed–Sun 10am–5pm; July & Aug daily 10am–5pm; site free; house tour $7; ⓦwww.pc.gc.ca/papineau), Papineau's tranquil estate comprising his spectacular manor house, chapel and granary over a sizeable tract of land. The ticket office is on the main road at 500 rue Notre-Dame in an old train station shared with the tourist information centre. A ten-minute forested walk leads to the verandah-fronted **house**, which contains a ground-floor ballroom, a turreted library tower and another tower that was formerly a three-storey greenhouse, and which can only be seen on a guided tour. Along the path to the house, the **Papineau Memorial Chapel**, a modest stone building (1855) nestled among tall pines and maples, is especially remarkable for being of Anglican, not Catholic, denomination: Papineau's son converted to Anglicanism after his father was refused a Catholic burial. Papineau senior and eleven other family members are buried here, and the Patriotes' flag is on display.

Tourist information is available in an old train station at 502 rue Notre-Dame (late June to early Sept daily 10am–7pm; rest of year daily 9am–4pm). Voyageur **buses** drop passengers off twice daily down the street at no. 535. The most reasonable **accommodation** in Montebello is *Gîte des 3D Chez Dodo*, an unremarkable B&B at 493 rue Notre-Dame (✆819/423-5268; ❷). *Le Clos des Cèdres*, 227 rue St-Joseph (✆819/423-1265; ⓦwww.bbcanada.com/4148.html; ❸), has more character. Otherwise, try the attractive *Motel l'Anse de la Lanterne*, 646 rue Notre-Dame (✆819/423-5280; ❸), which has a good restaurant for dinner. Most **restaurants** are on the main drag; *Le Pot au Feu*, 489 rue Notre-Dame (✆819/423-6901), serves Italian and French for under $20; and the cheaper resto-bar *Le Zouk*, at no. 530, has a pub-bistro menu and sunny terrace.

The only other stop of interest between Montréal and Gatineau is **PLAISANCE**, 15km west of Montebello (and 30km east of Gatineau). Once the region's main lumber centre, the main draw today is the **Parc National de Plaisance** (mid-May to mid-Oct), a tiny provincial park made up of three *presqu'îles* replete with hiking and cycling trails, picnic areas and footbridges. A dull interpretation centre in the old presbytery on Hwy 148 tells the town's history (late June to early Sept daily 10am–6pm; $3); admission also allows access to see the 75m-high waterfall. **Camping** is available at the provincial park (✆819/427-5334 or 1-877/752-4726; from $21.95 for a two-person site); bikes, canoes and kayaks can be rented on-site.

If you're not planning to head any further west, you can follow **Hwy 323** northeast from Montebello to Mont-Tremblant (see p.269) and return to Montréal via the Laurentians. It's a pleasant trip – a flat valley laced with rivers gives way to rising terrain where the road twists through forested hills – and there's a lake with a sandy beach half-way along.

The Laurentians (Les Laurentides)

The slopes of the **Laurentians**, a vast sweep of coniferous forest dotted with hundreds of tranquil lakes and scored with rivers, was once Montréal's "wilderness back yard". Nowadays, winter sports have done away with the region's former tranquillity as thousands of Québecois take to the slopes at more than 25 ski resorts, causing mind-numbing traffic jams. Still, much of the land has remained relatively untouched – like the **Parc National du Mont Tremblant** – and the area is a must when autumn colours take over. The Laurentians really cater to families on a week's sporty vacation, and much of the **accommodation** is pricey, as it includes gyms, tennis courts, golf courses and the like. However, a smattering of B&Bs and numerous motels offer an alternative to those on a tight budget, as do the hostels in Val-David and Mont-Tremblant itself.

Two **roads** lead from Montréal to this area of the Laurentians: the Autoroute des Laurentides (Hwy 15) and the slower Hwy 117, which is the one to choose if you want to go antique-hunting, as there are a number of large shops around Piedmont. Limocar Laurentides (☎514/842-2281 or 1-866/700-8899, ⓦwww.limocar.ca) offers a regular **bus** service from the Station Centrale d'Autobus de Montréal to most of the towns. Other than Tremblant – which costs a small fortune – rates for **ski passes** are around $30 a day in the decent areas, a few dollars more at weekends.

Saint-Sauveur-des-Monts

The ski resorts start 60km from Montréal and can be visited easily as day-trips. The first is **SAINT-SAUVEUR-DES-MONTS**, with 46 pistes in the immediate vicinity and an ever-increasing number of apartment complexes. Its resident population of seven thousand is boosted to a peak-season maximum of thirty thousand, and the main drag, rue Principale, reflects the influx by boasting every type of restaurant imaginable, as well as designer boutiques and craft shops. Come nightfall, skiers take to the numerous glitzy clubs and discos.

Information on shopping and skiing is available from the Bureau Touristique, 605 chemin des Frênes near exit 60 from Hwy 15 (Mon–Fri 9am–5pm, late May to early Sept until 9pm; ☎450/227-3417 or 1-800/898-2127, ⓦwww.saint-sauveur.net or ⓦwww.tourismepdh.org); there's also a kiosk near the church on rue Principale in the warmer months. For those with money, Saint-Sauveur is the top place to be seen, and **hotel** prices reflect the fact: the excellent *Le Relais St-Denis*, 61 rue St-Denis (☎450/227-4766 or 1-888/997-4766, ⓦwww.relaisst-denis.com; ❻), leads the way for class with a pool and beautifully decorated rooms. For home comforts, there are **B&Bs** like *Les Bonheurs de Sophie*, at no. 342 (☎819/227-6116 or 1-877/227-6116, ⓦwww.lesbonheursdesophie.com; ❹), and the pricier *Le Bonnet d'Or*, 405 rue Principale (☎450/227-9669 or 1-877/277-9669, ⓦwww.bbcanada.com /bonnetdor; ❺). For **eating** on a budget you'll be pretty well limited to the food (and excellent coffee) at *Brûlerie des Monts*, 197 rue Principale, or branches of Montréal outfits like *Pizzédélic*, 16 rue de la Gare, or *Mexicali Rosa's* average Mexican fare at no. 61. Mid-price local spots are a better bet: try *La Bohème*, 251 rue Principale (☎450/227-6644, ⓦwww.restoboheme.com), which serves French specialities like frog's legs and bœuf bourguignon, or the lively Italian restaurant *Papa Luigi*, 155 rue Principale (☎450/227-5311, ⓦwww .papa-luigi.com).

Val-David

Further north along Hwy 117, **VAL-DAVID** is the bohemian resort of the Laurentians, favoured by artists and craftspeople; the main street, rue de l'Église, has galleries and shops run by the artisans themselves. The town also has some non-ski-related activities come summertime, with plenty of hiking trails and rock climbing faces in the area and the P'tit Train du Nord bicycle path (see box). On a wholly different note, the tackiest attraction in the Laurentians, the **Village du Père Noel**, 987 rue Morin (early June to early Sept daily 10am–6pm; $8.50), is a Santa's village that features games and animals. Save your money.

The **tourist office** is at 2501 rue de l'Eglise (mid-April to mid-Oct Sun–Thurs 9am–5pm, Fri & Sat 9am–6pm; mid-Nov to mid-March daily 9.30am–5pm; other times Wed–Sun 9.30am–5pm; ☎819/322-3104 or 1-888/322-7030 ext 235, ⓦwww.valdavid.com). Val-David's excellent but noisy **hostel**, *Le Chalet Beaumont*, 1451 rue Beaumont (☎819/322-1972, ⓦwww.chaletbeaumont.com; ❷; dorms $20), is a massive chalet with roaring fires in the winter and great views all year. A twenty-minute walk from the bus station, the hostel offers a pick-up service. Other **accommodation** is fairly expensive: the most affordable options are **B&Bs** – at *La Maison de Bavière*, 1470 chemin de la Rivière (☎819/322-3528, ⓦwww.maisondebaviere.com; ❸), you can watch the river rapids from the fireplace-warmed sitting room after an extravagant breakfast. At the other end of the scale, the swishest ski lodge, *La Sapinière*, by Mont Alta at 1244 chemin de la Sapinière (☎819/322-2020 or 1-800/567-6635, ⓦwww.sapiniere.com; ❽), is built of logs. At the one **campsite** along Hwy 117, *Camping Laurentien* (☎819/322-2281, ⓦwww.campinglaurentien.com), pitches start at $22. Rue de l'Église has decent, well-priced **restaurants**, including the friendly *Le Grand Pa*, at no. 2481 (☎819/322-3104), which serves simple French food and has live music at the weekend; and *L'Express* (8am–4pm, weekends until 6pm), a café-bistro at rue de l'Eglise and de la Sapinière that's great for breakfast, as well as specials like *tourtière*. Vegetarians are well catered for at the co-operative restaurant *Aux Vivres d'en Haut*, 2360 rue de l'Eglise, where they serve fair-trade coffee and organic vegan dishes in a ramshackle house.

The P'tit Train du Nord bicycle trail

The bed of **Le P'tit Train du Nord**, a disused railway line that once ferried Montrealers to the Laurentians' resorts, now sees brisk business as a major **bicycle trail** as thousands of cyclists pedal their way among the mountains throughout the summer. The former stations have been renovated as well, now often housing tourist information centres, some with facilities such as showers and snack bars for cyclists taking a break. Access to the 200km trail, which runs north from St-Jérôme to Mont-Laurier, costs $5/day, or $10 for the whole month May to October season. In winter, the snow-covered route is equally in demand by **cross-country skiers** ($7/day), who can explore numerous side-trails branching off into the hills between St-Jérôme and Val-David, and to **snowmobilers** – the Ste-Agathe to Mont-Laurier stretch is part of the network of thousands of kilometres of trails that crisscross the province. **Information**, as well as a guide with maps and list of services (including cycle repair, baggage transport and accommodation) along the route, is available from the Association Touristique des Laurentides (see p.261).

Les Excursions Rivière du Nord (☎450/229-1889 or 1-866/342-2668, ⓦwww .riviere-du-nord.ca) gives you the chance to **canoe or raft** downriver for a couple of hours from Mont Rolland station (near Ste-Adèle) to Piedmont (just east of St-Sauveur) and then cycle the 7km back north, starting at $64 per couple. Similar trips are available for the 4-hour return trip between Val-David and Mont Rolland from Pause Plein Air, 1381 chemin de la Sapinière, Val-David (☎819/322-6880 or 1-877/422-6880, ⓦwww.pause-plein-air.com); they also rent bikes for $6/hr or $18/day (including trail permit) and canoes and kayaks starting at $15.

Ste-Agathe-des-Monts

On the shores of Lac des Sables is **STE-AGATHE-DES-MONTS**, a luxurious resort since the 1850s and the largest town in the Laurentians. Situated 97km from Montréal and almost entirely quashed by commercialism, it's a good base for exploring the less developed towns and the wildlife reserves further north; there is little to do here.

For **information** and facilities for cyclists on the P'tit Train du Nord (see box), go to the old train station at 24 rue St-Paul est (late June to early Sept daily 8am–9pm; early Sept to late June 9am–5pm), across the street from the **bus** stop. The least expensive **accommodation** is the clean if unexciting *Motel Clair-Mont*, out along Hwy 117 at 1591 rue Principale (☎819/326-1444 or 1-800/520-1444, ⓦwww.motelclair-mont.com; ❷). Of the five **B&Bs**, the charming *Gîte Aux Jardins d'Hillside*, 16 rue Hillside (☎819/326-2476 or 1-866/326-2476, ⓦwww.bbcanada.com/auxjardinshillside; ❸) is the most affordable; there are big breakfasts, a swimming pool and a friendly dog to welcome you. The pricier *Auberge de la Tour-du-Lac*, nearby at 173 chemin Tour du Lac (☎819/326-4202 or 1-800/622-1735, ⓦwww.aubergedelatourdelac .com; ❹), is one of the town's most beautiful historic homes with its pointed roof and wraparound veranda. The nearest **campsite** is *Parc des Campeurs* (☎819/324-0482 or 1-800/561-7360, ⓦwww.parcdescampeurs.com; from $25), 1.5km south of town (take exit 83 off Hwy 15 and follow signs), an enormous place with a beach on Lac des Sables and cross-country skiing in winter. Most of Ste-Agathe's **restaurants and bars** are near the lakefront, the most attractive part of town: *Del Popolo*, at 1 rue Principale est (☎819/326-4422), serves Italian, and *Chez Girard*, at 18 rue Principale ouest (☎819/326-0922), has reasonably priced, delicious *cuisine du terroir* (regional market cuisine). *La Sauvagine*, 1592 Hwy 329 nord (☎819/326-7673 or 1-800/787-7172, ⓦwww.lasauvagine.com), is a chapel converted into a gastronomic Belgian restaurant with comfy **rooms** upstairs (❸–❹).

Mont-Tremblant

Situated some 130km north of Montréal, **MONT-TREMBLANT** is the Laurentians' oldest and most renowned ski area, focused on the range's highest peak, **Mont Tremblant** (960m), so called because the native population believed it was the home of spirits that could move the mountain. In 1997, the company that developed British Columbia's ski resort of Whistler (see p.902) pumped some $50m into Tremblant, and the resulting European-style ski village has made it a premier ski destination. The 92 runs are for all levels, with a maximum vertical drop of more than 640m and the longest ski run in Québec. One-day **ski passes** cost $53.

Mont-Tremblant comprises the resort itself plus the merged town of **St-Jovite**, the area's commercial centre, and tiny **Mont-Tremblant Village**, 10km north. The main **tourist information** office is just off Hwy 117 as you enter St-Jovite, at 48 chemin de Brébeuf (June–Sept Sun–Thurs 9am–7pm, Fri & Sat 9am–8pm; Oct–May daily 9am–5pm; ☎819/425-3300 or 1-800/322-2932, ⓦwww.tourismemonttremblant.com); a second tourist office is located further north at 5080 montée Ryan (☎819/425-2434). Mont-Tremblant Village has only the most basic services but some cheap accommodation, including a **hostel** – the *Auberge de Jeunesse International du Mont-Tremblant*, 2313 chemin du Village (☎819/425-6008, ⓦwww.hostellingtremblant.com), with dorms for $20, double rooms (❷–❸) and plenty of organized activities. Throughout the area are a variety of **lodges**, though two of the most glamorous in the Laurentians are both slope-side: *Fairmont Tremblant*, by Lac

Tremblant facing the base of the mountain (℡819/681-7653 or 1-877/441-1414, ⓦwww.fairmont.com; ❽), and *Auberge Gray Rocks*, at the smaller resort midway to St-Jovite (℡819/425-2771 or 1-800/567-6767, ⓦwww.grayrocks.com; ❽). Less pricey **rooms** are available at *Hôtel Mont Tremblant*, 1900 chemin du Village (℡819/425-3232 or 1-888/887-1111, ⓦwww.hotelmonttremblant.com; ❹ including breakfast), right where the P'tit Train du Nord bike path (see box p.268) passes Lac Mercier. On the lakeshore facing the hotel, *Tremblant Onwego*, 112 chemin Plouffe (℡819/429-5522 or 1-866/429-5522, ⓦwww.tremblantonwego.com; ❹), a friendly spot well equipped for active visitors, is one of a dozen **B&B**s in the area.

For **eating**, there are plenty of options at Tremblant resort itself in all price brackets. In the St-Jovite sector, there's a cheap pub-style restaurant, *Bagatelle Saloon*, at 852 rue de St-Jovite, and a decent-priced café-bar, *Le Bistro Brunch Café*, at no. 814, in the same complex as La Crémerie du Hameau, a candy store. For dinner, *Chez Roger*, 444 rue St-Georges (℡819/429-6991), offers rich French cuisine at slightly elevated prices – the three-course *table d'hôte* starts at $30. The best **party scene** is at the resort's *après-ski* spots; elsewhere, you can kick things off at *Le Saint Georges*, a relaxed pub with a terrace at 890 rue de St-Jovite.

The **Parc National du Mont Tremblant**, a large wilderness area spreading northwards from the villages, is a favourite with Québecois. Skiing, snowmobiling and snowshoeing are favoured winter sports; in summer the park attracts campers, canoeists, hunters and hikers – in remote areas you may see bears (see box on p.686), deer and moose. The park's three lakeside **campsites** must be reserved in advance (℡819/688-2281 or 1-877/688-2289, ⓦwww.sepaq.com; $16.50 and up). There's no public transport.

The Eastern Townships (Cantons-de-l'Est)

Beginning about 80km east of Montréal and extending to the US border, the **Eastern Townships** were once Québec's best-kept secret, but the nineteenth-century villages are fast becoming no more than shopping arcades fringed with vacation complexes for Montréal weekenders. A growing ski industry – concentrated around Mont Sutton, just north of the Vermont border – is making its mark on the land, too. However, the region's agricultural roots are still evident, especially in spring, when the maple trees are tapped for syrup. At this time of year, remote *cabanes à sucre* offer sleigh rides and Québecois fare such as maple taffy – strips of maple syrup frozen in the snow.

The land, once the domain of scattered groups of aboriginal peoples, was later settled by United Empire Loyalists hounded out of the US after the American Revolution. Their loyalty to the crown resulted in freehold land grants from the British, and townships with very English names like **Sherbrooke** and **Granby** were founded. In the mid-nineteenth century the townships opened up to industry, which attracted an influx of French-Canadians seeking work: today, nearly 95 percent of the 400,000 population are francophone. For the most part, relations between the linguistic groups have been amicable, though pockets like the towns and villages around **Knowlton** and **North Hatley** remain staunchly tied to their anglophone heritage, and the English-language cultural scene is much stronger than the size of the population would suggest.

You can reach the region from Montréal by the Autoroute des Cantons-de-l'Est (Hwy 10), which has a useful **information centre** for the whole region at exit 68, southwest of Granby (daily: June–Sept 10am–6pm; Oct–May 9am–5pm; ☎819/820-2020 or 1-800/355-5755, ⓦwww.easterntownships .cc). Slower Hwy 112 wends through small villages and past forests and lakes; if you've got plenty of time, detour south onto the secondary roads nearer the US border that pass rustic barns, duck under covered bridges and wind through the province's fledgling vineyards. A dozen or so Limocar **buses** a day from Montréal (☎514/842-2281 or 1-866/700-8899, ⓦwww.limocar.ca) stop in Magog and Sherbrooke; less often in Granby (4/day) and Bromont (2/day).

Granby and Bromont

Approached from Montréal, the Cantons-de-l'Est begins at the unappealing city of **GRANBY**. The **Zoo de Granby** (ⓦwww.zoodegranby.com) is Québec's best-known zoo, but it is truly awful. Most of the animals are kept in terrible conditions, without a blade of grass in sight; they look almost suicidal. An on-site water park accounts for a lot of the place's popularity. Granby redeems itself with the **Centre d'interprétation de la Nature du Lac Boivin**, 700 Drummond (daily 8.30am–4.30pm; free) where observation towers allow a terrific vantage point for watching birds peck and preen on the marsh. Granby's **information centre** is at 650 rue Principale (daily: June to early Sept 8am–6pm; rest of year 9am–5pm; ☎450/372-7273 or 1-800/567-7273).

Just south of Granby, **BROMONT** is much more pleasant, focused on the 405m ski and snowboarding hill at its centre, **Ski Bromont** (☎450/534-2200 or 1-866/276-6668, ⓦwww.skibromont.com; $44). In summer, the hill metamorphoses into a hiking and mountain biking centre and watery playground thanks to the slides and pools of the **Bromont Aquatic Park** (early to late June daily 10am–4pm; late June to late Aug daily 10am–6.30pm; Sept to late Oct Sat & Sun 10am–4pm; $27). Less energetic options include the large **flea market** alongside Hwy 10 (May–Oct Sun 9am–5pm) and the tiny **Musée du Chocolat**, 679 rue Shefford (Mon–Fri 10am–6pm, Sat & Sun 9am–5.30pm; free), where you can learn about chocolate-making while nibbling on some fine specimens from the attached candy store. Cross the street to the 1889 **Église St-Francois-Xavier**, with a delicate tin-clad tiered steeple and a vault decorated in minty pastels.

The least expensive **B&B** is *La Maison aux Pignons Verts*, at 129 rue Adamsville in the village of Adamsville, 10km southwest of Bromont (☎450/260-1129, ⓦwww.lamaisonauxpignonsverts.com; ❸). *Auberge Nuits de St-Georges*, 792 rue Shefford (☎450/534-0705 or 1-888/534-0708, ⓦwww .aubergenuitsdestgeorges.com; ❺), is a handsome red-brick house with six suites; though pricier, it includes a five-course breakfast. Otherwise, try the *du Badouillard*, 871 rue Shefford (☎450/534-2502, ⓦwww.aubergedubadouillard .ca; ❹ including breakfast) for more traditional hotel accommodation. For **eating**, *L'Âme du Pain*, 702 rue Shefford, is a bakery serving good sandwiches and salads on a shady terrace; pizza and more substantial dishes are available later on. *Auberge Le Madrigal*, 46 boul de Bromont (☎450/534-3588, ⓦwww.lemadrigal.ca), serves expensive regional cuisine.

Magog and around

The summer resort town of **MAGOG**, about 40km east of Bromont, gets its name from a corruption of an aboriginal word meaning "great expanse of water" – the expanse of which is one of the township's largest lakes, **Lac Memphrémagog**, on which it borders. A strange beast known as Memphré supposedly lurks in its waters (the subject of various fishy tales since 1798). A cruise boat plies the lake (summer daily; Sept & Oct Sat & Sun only; 1hr 45min tour; $15). You can also opt for a day-long cruise south over the border to Newport, Vermont ($55; ☎819/843-8068 or 1-888/842-8068, ⓦwww.croisiere-memphremagog.com; passport needed). Magog is a lively spot fairly teeming with bars and restaurants along its main street, rue Principale. One quirky diversion is at the **Labyrinthe Memphrémagog** on the westernmost of the beaches fronting the lake – you can navigate a maze on blades or on foot (May to mid-Oct daily 10am–dusk; $7, $4 extra to rent blades). Explore the area on numerous well-kept bike trails; Ski-Vélo Vincent Renaud, set back from the main drag at 395 rue Principale ouest (☎819/843-4277, ⓦwww.skivelo.com), rents bicycles for $15 per half-day.

The **bus** stops on rue Sherbrooke, near its intersection with rue Principale. The **information centre**, midway between the town and the labyrinth at 55 rue Cabana, is accessed by Hwy 112 (June to mid-Oct daily 8.30am–8pm; mid-Oct to May daily 9am–5pm, Fri until 7pm; ☎1-800/267-2744, ⓦwww.tourisme-memphremagog.com). There are many places to stay. Among the **B&Bs** are a few century-old houses clustered together: *Ô Bois Dormant*, 205 rue Abbot (☎819/843-0450, ⓦwww.oboisdormant.qc.ca; ❹), comes with a veranda and pool; *Au Coeur de Magog*, 120 rue Merry Nord (☎819/868-2511, ⓦwww.aucoeurdemagog.com; ❸), is a fine old house; *La Belle Victorienne*, 142 rue Merry Nord (☎819/847-0476 or 1-888/440-0476, ⓦwww.bellevic.com; ❹), has beautiful gardens and comfy rooms. **Hotels** are expensive: *Le Manoir St-Christophe*, 2316 Hwy 112 (☎819/843-3355 or 1-877/447-3355, ⓦwww.manoirsaintchristophe.ca; ❻), is a modern country inn with ten rooms just west of town. *L'Auberge du Grand Lac*, 40 rue Merry Sud (☎819/847-4039 or 1-800/267-4039, ⓦwww.grandlac.com; ❹–❺), is nearer the centre of things, with a rooftop terrace for sunsets, full facilities and a continental breakfast. Several **bars** and **restaurants** are clustered along rue Principale ouest: *Le Panier à Pain*, at no. 382, serves up healthy sandwiches, soups and home-made ice cream, while *Le Martimbeault*, at no. 341 (☎819/843-3182), is a good dinner option that charges about $30 for a meal of rich French food. Alternatively, get a veggie fix at *La Petite Place* at 108 Place du Commerce, opposite the bistro-bar *La Grosse Pomme* at 276 rue Principale. A better bet for drinking and eating is *La Memphré*, 12 rue Merry Sud, a pleasant bar with views of the lake from the veranda where they serve quality pub food and a tasty local beer.

Abbaye Saint-Benoît-du-Lac

About 25km southwest of Magog via Hwy 245 along the lakeshore is the **Abbaye Saint-Benoît-du-Lac**, its presence signalled by white-granite turrets. Occupied by some sixty Benedictine monks renowned for their Gregorian chants (daily 7.30 & 11am; also Mon–Wed & Fri–Sun 5pm, Thurs 7pm) and their Ermite blue cheese (shop Mon–Sat 9am–4.30pm), it often serves as a refuge for flustered politicians and prominent figures who need time for contemplation. The abbey's doors are open to anyone who wants to stay, but you'll need to reserve months in advance. Food and **accommodation** are free, though a donation of $35 is expected (☎819/843-4080 men or 843-2340 women; appropriate clothing required; ⓦwww.st-benoit-du-lac.com). There is no public transport to the abbey; a taxi costs about $25 from Magog.

Mont Orford

A mature sugar maple forest blankets three-quarters of the small **Parc National du Mont-Orford**, 10km north of Magog via Hwy 141. Ski on Mont Orford (859m) in winter (passes $44) or hike in the summer: the chair-lift operates year-round. There's not much to see in the tiny town of **ORFORD** itself, but the summertime **hostel** on Hwy 141, *Auberge du Centre d'Arts Orford*, 3165 chemin du Parc (☎819/843-8595 or 1-800/567-6155; ❶; May–Oct), is a great base for exploring the park and Magog. You can also **camp** at one of the park's sites or off in the woods (☎819/843-9855 or 1-877/843-9855, ⓦwww.sepaq.com; $18–32). The only other accommodation options are more upscale in price and service: *Auberge de la Tour*, 1837 Alfred-Desrochers (☎819/868-0763, ⓦwww.auberge-de-la-tour.com; ❹), is a charming country inn, while the *Auberge Au Lion d'Or*, 2240 chemin du Parc (☎819/843-6000 or 1-877/843-6000, ⓦwww.auliondor.com; ❹), has a health spa and a heated outdoor pool. For **dining**, *Tonnerre de Brest*, 2197 chemin du Parc (☎819/847-1234), serves up crêpes, mussels and fries, and *La Mérise*, at no. 2329 (☎819/843-6288), has regional cuisine, crêpes and, in winter, fondue.

North Hatley

The region east of Magog holds its Loyalist connections dear, and this is one of the few areas in Québec where you'll encounter vestiges of the snobbish anglophone attitudes that once pervaded the whole province. **NORTH HATLEY**, a thirty-minute drive east from Magog along Hwy 108, is an anglophone bastion, with boutiques selling Lipton teas, Liberty products, tweeds and Aran jumpers; the resident population steadfastly refuses to change the town's name to "Hatley Nord". Otherwise the village is home to Québec's longest-running English-language **theatre**, The Piggery (☎819/842-2431, ⓦwww.piggery.com), which puts on several quality productions throughout the summer, and there are several art galleries and antique shops clustered along the waterfront.

North Hatley boasts two of Québec's classiest **inns**: the romantic *Manoir Hovey* (☎842-2421 or 1-800/661-2421, ⓦwww.hoveymanor.com; ❻), nestled along the lake with its private beach and boats; and *Auberge Hatley* 325 rue Virgin (☎819/842-2451 or 1-800/336-2451, ⓦwww.northhatley.com; ❽), set on the wooded hillside overlooking the lake and town. Cheaper and in the village itself, *Serendipity Bed & Breakfast*, 340 chemin de la Rivière (☎819/842-2970, ⓦwww.bbcanada.com/1441.html; ❹), is a century-old house; the owner runs fly-fishing trips on the lake. Decent **food** can be had at either the English-style gastro-pub *Le Pilsen*, 55 rue Principale, with its locally brewed Massiwippi ales, or *Café de Lafontaine*, which serves standard salads, burgers and the like next door at no. 35. The expensive but exquisite *Café Massawippi*, 3050 chemin Capelton (☎819/842-4528), serves original variations on international classics but is open in the evenings only.

Sherbrooke

The 100,000-strong university town of **SHERBROOKE**, 147km east of Montréal, revels in the title "Queen of the Eastern Townships", a strange accolade for a town that's no great shakes and has just a few minor attractions, clustered in Vieux-Sherbrooke around the 1.5km gorge carved by the Rivière Magog, which is lined by walkways and lookouts. The city's two main museums are modest in scope. The **Musée des Beaux Arts de Sherbrooke**, 241 rue Dufferin (late June to early Sept Tues–Sun 11am–5pm, Wed until 9pm; rest of year Tues–Sun 1–5pm, Wed until 9pm; $6; Ⓦmba.ville.sherbrooke.qc.ca), the better of the two, displays nineteenth- and twentieth-century pieces by Québecois artists – including a couple by naive painters – and visiting collections of good quality. The hands-on exhibits at the **Musée de la Nature et des Sciences**, 225 rue Frontenac (late June to early Sept daily 10am–5pm; rest of year Tues–Sun 10am–5pm; $7.50; Ⓦwww.mnes.qc.ca), will keep kids occupied for a couple of hours. The largest section explores the flora and fauna of Québec's forests throughout the seasons, with both live and stuffed animals, videos and bird calls kids can activate. There's also an interactive theatre for an educational look into the brain and how the senses work. The **Centre d'interprétation de l'histoire de Sherbrooke**, 275 rue Dufferin (July & Aug Tues–Fri 9am–5pm, Sat & Sun 10am–5pm; Sept–June Tues–Fri 9am–noon & 1–5pm, Sat & Sun 1–5pm; $5; Ⓦshs.ville.sherbrooke.qc.ca), focuses on the history of Sherbooke and on various historical subjects; ask for an English text at the desk. They also rent audio tapes for two-hour walking or driving tours of the city ($10, or just the map for $2.50) and organize tours of normally inaccessible religious buildings (call to reserve on ☎819/821-5406).

Rue King ouest is like one big, long strip mall, and divides the town into nord and sud; rue Wellington splits it into ouest and est. The **bus** station, with connections to and from Montréal, Québec City and local towns, is downtown at 20 rue King ouest; the **information centre** is on the same street, but at the west end of town 5km away at no. 2964 (mid-June to mid-Aug daily 9am–7pm; rest of year Mon–Sat 9am–5pm, Sun 9am–3pm; ☎819/821-1919 or 1-800/561-8331). Sherbrooke's **accommodation** lacks charm; the few inexpensive options include the student residence at 2500 boul de l'Université (☎819/821-8000, ext 2851; summer only; ❷). Otherwise, you could try one of the numerous modern motels along rue King ouest: the three-star *L'Ermitage* at no. 1888 (☎819/569-5551 or 1-888/569-5551; ❸) or *Hôtellerie Jardins de Ville* at no. 4235 (☎819/566-6464 or 1-800/265-7119, Ⓦwww.hotelleriejardinsdeville.com; ❸). The *Delta Sherbrooke*, 2685 rue King ouest (☎819/822-1989 or 1-800/268-1133, Ⓦwww.deltahotels.com; ❺), is the plushest hotel in town, while the *Marquis de Montcalm* (☎819/823-7773, Ⓦwww.marquisdemontcalm.com; ❹) is an atmospheric B&B near the gorge. For **restaurants**, *Café Bla-Bla*, 2 rue Wellington sud, has a good selection of imported beers in addition to its well-priced bistro fare. Well to the east, *Délia Egg-xtra*, 661 rue King est, has more than a hundred breakfast options, while *Au Four à Bois*, opposite the tourist office at 3025 rue King ouest, is a sound pizza joint. For dining downtown, *Le Petit Parisien*, 243 rue Alexandre (☎819/822-4678), is an ambient bring-your-own-wine resto; regional produce is the focus of the French cuisine at *La Falaise St-Michel* at 100 rue Webster (☎819/346-6339).

Montréal to Québec City

Two **autoroutes** (expressways) cover the 270km between Montréal and Québec City, though plenty of VIA Rail **trains** and Voyageur **buses** also trawl the route: the boring Hwy 20 cuts along the south shore of the St Lawrence, and the even more banal Hwy 40 takes to the north side with very few rest-stops en route, so fill up before leaving Montréal. Hwy 138, the old Chemin du Roi (King's Highway), also meanders along the north shore but gives a closer look at rural Québec and farms left over from the seigneurial regime, like the **Seigneurie de**

By jetfoil from Montréal to Québec City

The long journey from Montréal to Québec City is best experienced from the **jetfoil** – a unique way to experience the St Lawrence River with a bit of commentary thrown in. From late May to mid-October, Les Dauphins du St-Laurent (☎1-877/648-4499 or 514/288-4499, @www.dauphins.ca) runs daily trips, with a stop in Trois-Rivières en route, for $109 (July & Aug $149, when there are two sailings a day).

Terrebonne (late June to Aug Wed–Sat 10.30am–8.30pm, Sun 10am–5.30pm; free, guided tours $5; @www.ile-des-moulins.qc.ca), on the Île des Moulins about thirty minutes northeast of downtown Montréal via Hwy 25 (exit 22 est). A seigneury from 1673 to 1883, the restored nineteenth-century buildings – including the manor house of the area's last seigneur and Canada's first francophone millionaire, Joseph Masson – powerfully evoke life under the old regime.

Trois-Rivières

The major town between Montréal and Québec City is **TROIS-RIVIÈRES**, located midway between the two, at the point where the Rivière St-Maurice splits into three channels – hence the name "Three Rivers" – before meeting the St Lawrence. The European settlement dates from 1634, when the town established itself as an embarkation point for the French explorers of the continent and as an iron-ore centre. Lumber followed, and today Trois-Rivières is one of the world's largest producers of paper, the delta chock-full of logs to be pulped. It's often dismissed as an industrial city and little else, but its shady streets of historic buildings – neither as twee as Québec City, nor as monumental as Vieux-Montréal – are well worth a wander, and the town is a good starting point for exploring the Mauricie Valley.

Trois-Rivières' compact downtown core branches off from the small square of **Parc du Champlain** and extends south down to the waterfront. Facing the park to the east, at 363 rue Bonaventure, the **Cathédrale de l'Assomption** (Mon–Fri 7–11.30am & 1.30–5.45pm, Sat 7am–8pm, Sun 9.30am–noon & 2–5.45pm; free), is notable for its stained-glass windows by Guido Nincheri and massive Gothic Revival style reminiscent of Westminster Abbey. Head south, past the pretty **Manoir de Niverville** at no. 168, one of the town's oldest buildings and the home of the local seigneur, until the water is in sight. Take a left turn to reach the narrow and ancient rue des Ursulines, the city's most attractive thoroughfare; two art galleries, at nos. 802 and 864, are especially worth a visit for contemporary printmaking during the Biennale Internationale d'Estampe Contemporain (odd-numbered years, mid-June to Aug). Further along is the **Musée des Ursulines**, whose slender, silver dome dominates the street. A former convent established by a small group of Ursuline nuns who arrived from Québec City in 1697, it includes a chapel with attractive frescoes and gilt sculptures. The nunnery's treasures are displayed in a little museum in the old hospital quarters (May–Nov Tues–Fri 9am–5pm, Sat & Sun 1–5pm; March & April Wed–Sun 1.30–5pm; Nov–Feb by appointment only; $3 including chapel visit; @www.musée-ursulines.qc.ca). Just east of the cathedral, the **Musée Québécois de Culture Populaire**, 200 rue Laviolette (June to early Sept daily 9.30am–6.30pm; rest of year Tues–Sun 10am–5pm; museum or prison $6.50, both $9; @www.culturepop.qc.ca or www.enprison.ca) has entertaining folk and pop culture exhibitions – such as one on food and society (until 2005) – but the real highlight is the old **prison** that adjoins it. Dating from 1822, the stone structure housed up to eighty inmates at a time until 1980, and while the decades of graffiti tell a story, it's nothing compared to the tales of the guides – they all once served time here.

You may want to make a pilgrimage across the river east of downtown to the **Sanctuaire Notre-Dame-de-Cap**, 626 rue Notre-Dame (free; ⓦwww .sanctuaire-ndc.ca; bus #2), in the merged town of Cap-de-la-Madeleine, accessible from Hwy 40 (exit 205); a few of the Québec–Montréal buses also stop here. Adjacent to a pleasant park marked by the Stations of the Cross is the 1720 Petit Sanctuaire; the fieldstone chapel is "the oldest church in Canada to retain its primitive state" (ignoring the jarring modern addition, presumably). It's overshadowed, though, by the massive octagonal basilica, a mid-twentieth-century concrete structure with a vertigo-inducing 38m-high vault best experienced when the 75-stop Casavant organ reverberates throughout the space. Finally, the ruins of **Les Forges du Saint-Maurice**, 10,000 boul des Forges (mid-May to Oct daily 9am–5pm; $4; ⓦwww.pc.gc .ca/forges), which put the town on the map as a supplier to the farmers and arsenals of Québec and Europe, is now a national historic site. Its pretty riverside grounds are 12km north of Vieux Trois-Rivières, linked to downtown by bus #4 – get on at the bus terminal on rue Badeaux – and Hwy 55 (exit 191).

Practicalities

The **information centre** at 1457 rue Notre Dame (late June to early Sept daily 8am–8pm; rest of year Mon–Fri 9am–5pm; ☏819/375-1122 or 1-800/313-1123, ⓦwww.v3r.net) gives out maps and has an accommodation service. For a place **to stay**, the cheapest option is the clean and comfortable **hostel**, *La Flottille*, in the heart of downtown at 497 rue Radisson (☏819/378-8010; ❶–❷). A number of attractive **B&Bs** are situated in heritage homes in Vieux Trois-Rivières: *La Campanule*, 634 rue des Ursulines, offers three rooms and access to a garden with whirlpool hot tub (☏819/373-1133; ❷); *Le Fleurvil*, across the street at no. 635, has five rooms in a low-lying house (☏819/372-5195, ⓦwww.fleurvil.qc.ca; ❸); and the gorgeous *Manoir DeBlois*, 197 rue Bonaventure, an 1828 stone house with original wood floors and an antique-strewn salon (☏819/373-1090 or 1-800/397-5184, ⓦwww .multimania.com/manoirdeblois; ❹). Centrally located, modern **hotels** include the high-rise *Delta*, 1620 rue Notre-Dame (☏819/376-1991 or 1-877/814-7706, ⓦwww.deltahotels.com; ❻), and *Hôtel Gouverneur*, 975 Hart (☏819/379-4550 or 1-888/910-1110, ⓦwww.gouverneur.com; ❻).

Most of the city's **restaurants** are located in the downtown core, their terraces lining rue des Forges between the waterfront and rue Royale. *Le Bolvert*, 1556 rue Royale, is a hearty, affordable breakfast option and *Angeline*, 313 rue des Forges, has imaginative pasta and pizza choices for under $10. The nearby *Gaspard* at no. 475 offers steak, fish and chicken, plus some cheaper lunch specials. *Le Zenob*, 171 rue Bonaventure, is a chilled **bar** with two leafy terraces that also sells sandwiches; for coffee and a snack, head to *Café Morgane*, at 100 rue des Forges, a sleek coffee shop with three other outlets around town. For **nightlife**, the multistorey *Le Temple*, 300 rue des Forge, caters to all types.

Parc National de la Mauricie

Some 60km north of Trois-Rivières lies the mountainous area of the Saint-Maurice valley – known as the **Mauricie** – where the best of the landscape is demarcated by the **Parc National du Canada de la Mauricie** (May to mid-Oct & mid-Dec to March; $5; ☏819/533-7272, ⓦwww.pc.gc.ca/mauricie).

Situated on the southernmost part of the Canadian Shield, the park comprises soft-contoured hills, lakes and rivers, waterfalls and sheer rock faces. The one drawback is the lack of public transport; to get there, take Hwy 55 north of Trois-Rivières to exit 226 and follow the signs to the St-Jean-des-Piles entrance.

The park offers numerous hiking trails of various lengths and abilities, ranging from the Cache Trail, a mere 1km walk leading to the Lac du Fou where a raised platform has a telescope for marine and wildlife watching, to the Laurentian Trail, a 75km trek which takes five to eight days to complete (reservation required; camping permit $39 for four nights). Information centres at the park's entrances have excellent maps and booklets about the park's well-maintained trails, canoe routes and bike paths, and also provide canoe rentals (for $18/day). The park has hundreds of **camping** places ($13–23 a pitch, plus $7 reservation fee) allocated on a first-come, first-served basis, and they're rarely filled to capacity. If you'd rather sleep under a roof, there are also two **lodges** located 3.5km from the nearest parking lot: the *Wabenaki's* two dormitories sleep up to 24 people and *Andrew's* four rooms each sleep four (℡819/537-4555 for both lodges; weekdays $24 per person, weekends $50–54 per person). Both open again in winter (mid-Dec to March) to accommodate cross-country skiers who use the park (trail permit $8).

Québec City

Spread over Cap Diamant and the banks of the St Lawrence, **QUÉBEC CITY** (sometimes referred to just as "Québec") is Canada's most beautifully located and most historic city. Vieux-Québec, surrounded by solid fortifications, is the only walled city in North America, and a UNESCO World Heritage Site. In both parts of the Old City – Haute- and Basse-Ville (Upper and Lower Town) – the winding cobbled streets are flanked by seventeenth- and eighteenth-century stone houses and churches, graceful parks and squares, and countless monuments. Although some districts have been painstakingly restored to give tourists as seductive an introduction to Québec as possible, this is nevertheless an authentically and profoundly French-Canadian city: 95 percent of its 600,000 population are French-speaking, and it is often difficult to remember which continent you are in as you tuck in to a croissant and a steaming bowl of *café au lait* in a Parisian-style café. Moreover, despite the fact that the city's symbol is a hotel, the **Château Frontenac**, the government remains the main employer, not tourism, and some of the more impressive buildings are government-run and thus off-limits.

Arriving from Montréal you're immediately struck by the differences between the two cities. Whilst Montréal is international, dynamic and forward-thinking, Québec City is more than a shade provincial, often seeming too bound up with its religious and military past – a residue of the days when the city was the bastion of the Catholic Church in Canada. On the other hand, the Church can claim much of the credit for the creation and preservation of the finest buildings, from the quaint **Église Notre-Dame-des-Victoires** to

QUÉBEC CITY

Rivière St-Charles

500 m

See Vieux-Québec map

Bassin Louise

Marché du Vieux-Port

Gare du Palais & Bus Terminal

AUTOROUTE DUFFERIN

ST-ROCH

RUE DU ROI

RUE ST-FRANÇOIS EST

RUE DES GLACIS

RUE ST-VALLIER EST

CÔTE D'ABRAHAM

RUE DORCHESTER

Martello Tower 4

FAUBOURG ST-JEAN-BAPTISTE

Église St-Jean-Baptiste

Le Grand Théâtre de Québec

MONTCALM

RUE SHERBROOKE

Musée National des Beaux-Arts du Québec

Martello Tower 2

GRANDE-ALLÉE EST

Parc de Champs de Bataille (Plaines d'Abraham)

Martello Tower 1

RUE CHAMPLAIN

BOULEVARD CHAMPLAIN

Hôtel-Dieu

VIEUX-QUÉBEC (HAUTE VILLE)

Musée des Ursulines

Ursuline Convent

Séminaire

Château Frontenac

BASSE VILLE

Musée de la Civilisation

VIEUX-PORT

Cruise ship terminal

St Lawrence River

Lévis

Observatoire de la Capitole

Parc de l'Amérique Française

Parc de l'Esplanade

Hôtel du Parlement

Place George V

Discovery Pavilion

Parc Jeanne d'Arc

Citadelle

CÔTE DE LA CITADELLE

BOULEVARD CHAMPLAIN

N

BARS & CLUBS	
L'Amour Sorcier	2
Dagobert	12
Le Drague	5
Maurice	4
Pub Java	9
Sacrilège	3

RESTAURANTS & CAFÉS	
Le Café du Monde	11
Café Krieghoff	8
Le Cochon Dingue	6
Cosmos Café	13
Jaune Tomate	7
Kookening	14
L'Orange Bleue	1
Pizzédélic	10

the **Basilique-Cathédrale Notre-Dame de Québec** and the vast **Séminaire**. In contrast, the austere defensive structures, dominated by the massive **Citadelle**, reveal the military pedigree of a city dubbed by Churchill as the "Gibraltar of North America", while the battlefield of the **Plains of Abraham** is now a national historic park. Of the city's rash of museums, two are essential visits: the modern **Musée de la Civilisation**, in Basse-Ville, expertly presenting all aspects of French-Canadian society, and the **Musée National des Beaux-Arts du Québec**, in Haute-Ville, west of the walls, which has the finest art collection in the province.

Outside the city limits, the town of **Lévis** and the Huron reservation, **Wendake**, make worthwhile excursions, whilst the churches and farmland of the **Côte-de-Beaupré** and the **Île d'Orléans** hark back to the days of the seigneurs and *habitants*. The gigantic **Basilique de Ste-Anne-de-Beaupré**, attracting millions of pilgrims annually, is one of the most impressive sights in Québec, and for equally absorbing natural sights there are the spectacular waterfalls at **Montmorency** and in the **Canyon Ste-Anne**, and the wildlife reserve in the **Laurentian mountains** where they arc north of the city.

Some history

For centuries the clifftop site of what is now Québec City was occupied by the **Iroquois** village of Stadacona, and although Cartier visited in the sixteenth century, permanent **European settlement** did not begin until 1608, when Samuel de Champlain established a fur-trading post here. To protect what was rapidly developing into a major inland trade gateway, the settlement shifted to the clifftop in 1620 when Fort St-Louis was built on the present-day site of the Château Frontenac. Québec's steady expansion was noted in London, and in 1629 Champlain was starved out of the fort by the **British**, an occupation that lasted just three years.

Missionaries began arriving in 1615, and by the time Bishop Laval arrived in 1659 Québec City and the surrounding province were in the grip of **Catholicism**. In the city's earliest days, however, the merchants of the fur trade wielded the most power and frequently came into conflict with the priests, who wanted a share in the profits in order to spread their message amongst the aboriginal peoples. The wrangles were resolved by **Louis XIV**, who assumed power in France in 1661 and was advised to take more interest in his kingdom's mercantile projects. By 1663, New France had become a royal province, administered by a council appointed directly by the crown and answerable to the king's council in France. Three figures dominated the proceedings: the governor, responsible for defence and external relations; the intendant, administering justice and overseeing the economy; and, inevitably, the bishop. Before the century was out, the long-brewing European struggles between England and France spilled over into the colony, with French attacks on the English in New York and New England in 1689 and a foiled naval attack by Sir William Phipps, governor of Massachusetts, in the following year. It was at this time that the **Comte de Frontenac**, known as the "fighting governor", replaced Champlain's Fort St-Louis with the sturdier Château St-Louis, and began work on the now-famous fortifications that ring Vieux-Québec.

In 1759, during the Seven Years' War (also known as the French and Indian War), the most significant battle in Canada's history took place here, between the British under General **James Wolfe** and the French commander Louis Joseph, **Marquis de Montcalm**. The city had already been under siege from the opposite shore for three months and Montcalm had carefully protected the city from any approach by water. Finally, Wolfe and his four thousand troops heard of an unguarded track, scaled the cliff of Cap Diamant and crept up on the unprepared French regiment from behind. The twenty-minute battle on the Plains of Abraham left both leaders mortally wounded and the city of Québec in the hands of the English, a state of affairs ultimately confirmed by the Treaty of Paris in 1763. Madame de Pompadour commented: "It makes little difference; Canada is useful only to provide me with furs."

In 1775 – the year after the Québec Act, which allowed French-Canadians to retain their Catholic religion, language and culture – the town was attacked again, this time by the Americans, who had already captured Montréal. The battle was won by the British and for the next century the city quietly earned its livelihood as the centre of a **timber-trade** and **ship-building** industry. By the time it was declared the provincial capital of Lower Canada in 1840, though, the accessible supplies of timber had run out. The final blow came with the appearance of steamships that could travel as far as Montréal (earlier sailing ships had found it difficult to proceed beyond Québec City). Ceasing to be a busy seaport, the city declined into a centre of small industry and local government, its way of life still largely determined by the Catholic Church.

With the Quiet Revolution in the 1960s and the rise of Québec **national-ism**, Québec City became a symbol of the glory of the French heritage: the motto *Je me souviens* ("I remember"), for instance, placed above the doors of its parliament buildings, was transferred to the licence plates of Québec cars, to sweep the message across Canada. Though the city played little active part in the changes, it has grown with the upsurge in the francophone economy, developing a suburbia of shopping malls and convention centres as slick as any in the country.

Arrival, information and accommodation

Québec City's **Aéroport Jean-Lesage** (ⓦwww.aeroportdequebec.com), 20km west, caters almost exclusively for domestic flights; most international flights arrive at Montréal. The twenty-minute trip to Vieux-Québec by taxi is a fixed rate of $24.50. VIA Rail **trains** from Montréal arrive at the central Gare du Palais in Basse-Ville, whereas services from the Atlantic provinces stop at Charny, across the St Lawrence, occasionally at inconvenient times; a shuttle is available to Gare du Palais but reservations must be made in advance. The long-distance **bus terminal** is at 320 rue Abraham-Martin (ⓣ418/525-3000), adjoining the Gare du Palais. Other options include **ridesharing** (see p.304) and the **jetfoil** (see p.275), which docks at the Vieux-Port. **Parking** downtown can be a real pain: it's best to leave your vehicle outside the walls, near the tourist office off Grande-Allée or in the Vieux-Port area (for parking details, see "Listings" on p.304).

For **information**, the main tourist office is beside the Voltigeurs de Québec armoury, off Place Georges V at 835 av Wilfrid-Laurier (late June to early Sept daily 8.30am–7.30pm; early Sept to mid-Oct daily 8.30am–6.30pm; mid-Oct to late June Mon–Sat 9am–5pm, Fri until 6pm, Sun 10am–4pm; ⓣ418/641-6290, ⓦwww.quebecregion.com), in the same building as the Discovery Pavilion of the Plains of Abraham. Information on the whole province (as well as Québec City) is available at the **Centre Infotouriste** on the other side of Place d'Armes from the Château Frontenac, at 12 rue Ste-Anne (daily: late June to early Sept 8.30am–7.30pm; rest of year 9am–5pm; ⓣ1-877/266-5687,

Québec City festivals

Québec City is renowned for its large annual **festivals**. The eleven-day **Carnaval de Québec** (ⓦwww.carnaval.qc.ca) is in freezing early February, when large quantities of the warming Caribou – a lethal mix of red wine, spirits and spices – are consumed amid parades and ice-sculpture competitions, all presided over by the mascot snowman called Bonhomme Carnaval. In early July, the ten-day **Festival d'Été** (ⓦwww.infofestival.com) is an equally cheery affair, especially as the provincial law prohibiting drink on the streets is temporarily revoked. The largest festival of francophone culture in North America attracts hundreds of artists, and everyone is roped in to the celebration, with restaurants offering discounts and all of Québec's major performers pitching up to dance, make music and lead the party from massive open-air stages all over town. A month later, the **Fêtes de la Nouvelle France** (ⓦwww.nouvellefrance.qc.ca) returns Basse-Ville to the seventeenth and eighteenth centuries. It's great fun if you're in the mood: thousands of Québecois from around the province dress up in period costume, often ones they've sewn themselves. It's also worth being in the city on **St-Jean Baptiste Day** (June 24), the provincial holiday, when an outpouring of Québecois pride spills onto the streets in a massive celebration, with the entire city decked with thousands of fleur-de-lis flags.

ⓦwww.bonjourquebec.com). Both centres offer an accommodation service and provide a free booklet, *Greater Québec Area*, which has a good map.

Québec City's sights and hotels are packed into a small area, so **walking** is the best way to get around. Motorcycles are banned from Vieux-Québec. For sights further out, like the Musée National des Beaux-Arts du Québec, RTC **local buses** (☏418/627-2511, ⓦwww.rtcquebec.ca) are efficient and run from around 6am to 1am (certain routes until 3am Fri & Sat). Fares are a standard $1.95 per journey by prepaid ticket, available at newsstands, grocery stores and supermarkets across town, as are one-day passes ($5.25; valid for two people Sat & Sun); the cash fare per journey is $2.35, exact fare only. If you need more than one bus to complete your journey, pick up a **transfer** (*une correspondance*) from the driver, which enables you to take the second bus for no extra charge. The main bus stop in Vieux-Québec is on its west side at Place d'Youville, near Porte St-Jean. The main transfer points for RTC buses are here and at Place Jacques-Cartier; many buses stop at both locations. Even if it means a longer walk, the frequency of the RTC's Métrobus services (#800, etc) makes them the best option.

Accommodation

The **accommodation** in Québec City is perfect for budget travellers. In Vieux-Québec there are two **hostels**, and the budget **hotels** are as well located as those at the top end. As the city is one of Canada's most frequented tourist destinations, try to reserve in advance, particularly during the summer months and the Carnaval in February. Even at those times, though, you're not likely to find the city completely full, as there are plenty of standard chain hotels outside the walls and the suburbs have masses of motels and B&Bs, all of them just a local bus ride away. All of Québec City's **campsites** are around 20km from the old town, convenient only for those with their own transport; we've listed the closest.

The hotels in Vieux-Québec are usually renovated town houses with the rooms fitted to provide a variety of accommodation. For cheaper rooms in the $40–80 range, head for the area around rue Ste-Ursule; the posher places are around the Jardin des Gouverneurs, in the shadow of the prestigious Château Frontenac. With such a variety of characterful places to stay in the old parts of town, we've focused on accommodation within the walls and a couple of special places in the old part of Basse-Ville.

Hotels

Basse-Ville

Auberge St-Antoine 10 rue St-Antoine ☎418/692-2211 or 1-888/692-2211, ⓦwww.saint-antoine.com. Cosy hotel divided into two buildings next to the Musée de la Civilisation. Some rooms have views of the river and all are tastefully decorated. ❽

Hôtel Belley 249 rue St-Paul ☎418/692-1694 or 1-888/692-1694, ⓦwww.oricom.ca/belley. Eight-bedroom, slickly designed hotel near the Gare du Palais. Three-star rooms, with off-season price reductions. ❸

Hôtel Dominion 1912 126 rue St-Pierre ☎418/692-2224 or 1-888/833-5253, ⓦwww.hoteldominion.com. Fabulous boutique hotel with all the touches – feather pillows and duvets, subdued lighting, stylish modern decor and cool frosted-glass sinks lit from below. Some rooms have river views. ❼

Hôtel Le Priori 15 rue du Sault-au-Matelot ☎418/692-3992 or 1-800/351-3992, ⓦwww.hotellepriori.com. Tastefully modernized old house with a large courtyard for breakfast; an excellent place to stay. ❻

Jardin des Gouverneurs area

B&B des Grisons 1 rue des Grisons ☎418/694-1461, ⓦwww.bbcanada.com/2608.html. A late-nineteenth century home with high ceilings, wood-strip floors and antiques from various epochs. The larger of the five rooms have sofa-beds and all have shared bath. ❹

Hôtel Cap-Diamant 39 av Ste-Geneviève ☎418/694-0313, ⓦwww.hcapdiamant.qc.ca. Nine-bedroom guesthouse with Victorian furnishings and a courtyard for breakfast. All rooms are en suite, and have air-conditioning, minifridges and TVs. ❺

Hôtel Château Bellevue 16 rue de la Porte ☎418/692-2573 or 1-800/463-2617, ⓦwww.vieux-quebec.com/bellevue. Quality modern hotel lurking behind the facades of a row of town houses facing the Jardin. Free parking. ❻

Le Château Frontenac 1 rue des Carrières ☎418/692-3861 or 1-800/441-1414, ⓦwww.fairmont.com. This opulent Victorian "castle", built for William Van Horne, president of

CP Railways, opened in 1893, and has accommodated such dignitaries as Churchill, Roosevelt, Madame Chiang Kai-shek and Queen Elizabeth II. It's the most expensive place in town, with splendid rooms, and even offers its own guided tours (see p.284). ❽

Hôtel Château de Léry 8 rue de la Porte ☎418/692-2692 or 1-800/363-0036, ⓦwww.quebecweb.com/chateaudelery. Bright rooms with hardwood floors; simply but nicely furnished. Includes breakfast. ❺

Le Château de Pierre 17 av Ste-Geneviève ☎418/694-0429, ⓦwww.quebecweb.com/chateaudepierre. An 1853 mansion with fifteen plush rooms; all are en suite and those without a/c have balconies. ❺

Au Jardin du Gouverneur 16 rue Mont-Carmel ☎418/692-1704 or 1-877/692-1704, ⓦwww.quebecweb.com/hjg. On the corner of the Jardin. Seventeen decent-sized rooms with modern furnishings and adjoining bathrooms. ❸

Hôtel Manoir Ste-Geneviève 13 av Ste-Geneviève ☎418/694-1666 or 1-877/694-1666, ⓦwww.quebecweb.com/msg. This charming two-star hotel dating from 1820 has nine beautiful Victorian rooms and a few very cheap basement rooms. ❷–❹

Hôtel Manoir sur le Cap 9 av Ste-Geneviève ☎418/694-1987 or 1-866/694-1987, ⓦwww.manoir-sur-le-cap.com. Fourteen bright rooms with exposed beams or stone walls. All have private bath and TVs; a few have kitchenettes. ❺

La Marquise de Bassano 15 rue des Grisons ☎418/692-0316 or 1-877/692-0316, ⓦwww.marquisedebassano.com. An 1888 house with a friendly young owner, comfy living room and five tastefully decorated bedrooms – the more expensive have private bath and perks like four-poster beds or a roof terrace. ❹–❻

Hôtel Terrasse-Dufferin 6 place Terrasse-Dufferin ☎418/694-9472, ⓦwww.terrasse-dufferin.com. The better rooms (❻) in this 1830 private mansion have the best views in town, overlooking the St Lawrence – book months ahead. ❹

Rue Ste-Ursule area

Auberge St-Louis 48 rue St-Louis ☎418/692-2424 or 1-888/692-4105, ⓦwww

.aubergestlouis.ca. A simple inn comprising two three-storey houses dating from the 1830s. Muted olive-coloured rooms feature IKEA-style furnishings but are comfy nonetheless. ❹–❺

Hôtel Le Clos St-Louis 69 rue St-Louis ☏418/694-1311 or 1-800/461-1311, ⓦwww.clossaintlouis.com. Elegant hotel in two interconnected 1840s houses with Victorian decor – four-poster beds in some of the rooms, gilt mirrors and lots of antiques. Hot breakfast. ❼

Hôtel Acadia 43 rue Ste-Ursule ☏418/694-0280 or 1-800/463-0280, ⓦwww.hotelacadia.com. Three ancestral dwellings with cosy rooms. A few with shared bathrooms. ❹–❺

Hôtel La Maison Demers 68 rue Ste-Ursule ☏418/692-2487 or 1-800/692-2487. Parking and breakfast included in the price of this family-run old house. A few of the rooms have balconies. ❸–❹

Hôtel La Maison Ste-Ursule 40 rue Ste-Ursule ☏418/694-9794, ⓦwww.quebecweb.com/maisonsteursule. Built in 1759, with green shutters and tiny doors, this is a clean hotel with bare-bones furnishing. There's also a small courtyard with picnic tables. ❷–❹

Maison Historique James Thompson 47 rue Ste-Ursule ☏418/694-9042, ⓦwww.bedandbreakfastquebec.com. B&B in historic 1793 house with sleigh beds, antiques throughout and a lovely sitting room. ❸–❹

Hôtel Manoir d'Auteuil 49 rue d'Auteuil ☏418/694-1173, ⓦwww.quebecweb.com /dauteuil. Lavish 1835 town house by the city walls, with Art Deco rooms. Free breakfast and a cheery owner. ❹

Hôtel Manoir La Salle 18 rue Ste-Ursule ☏418/692-9953. Small century-old red-brick hotel. Only two of the eleven rooms are en suite, one of which has a kitchenette. ❷–❸

Au Petit Hôtel 3 ruelle des Ursulines ☏418/694-0965, ⓦwww3.sympatico.ca/aupetithotel. Situated in a peaceful cul-de-sac just off rue

Ste-Ursule. Beds and rooms are a bit small but all are en suite. ❸

Rue Ste-Anne

Auberge de la Place d'Armes 24 rue Ste-Anne ☏418/694-9485, ⓦwww.quebecweb.com/placedarme. Perfectly situated opposite the Anglican Cathedral, on the pedestrianized part of rue Ste-Anne. Upper floor a bit stuffy in summer; others have a/c. All rooms have shower but some shared WCs. ❹–❺

Auberge du Trésor 20 rue Ste-Anne ☏418/694-1876 or 1-800/566-1876, ⓦwww.quebecweb.com/aubergedutresor. Decent modern rooms with private bathrooms in a house built in 1679. ❺

Hôtel Clarendon 57 rue Ste-Anne ☏418/692-2480 or 1-888/554-6001, ⓦwww.hotelclarendon.com. Québec City's oldest hotel, dating from 1870. Renovated in the 1930s, it has a classic Art Deco reception area. ❻

Hôtel Jardin Ste-Anne 109 rue Ste-Anne ☏418/694-1720 or 1-866/694-1720, ⓦwww.jardinsteanne.com. Century-old house with 18 small but characterful air-conditioned rooms and a courtyard. ❺

Elsewhere in Vieux-Québec

Hôtel Manoir des Remparts 3 1/2 rue des Remparts ☏418/692-2056, ⓦwww.manoirdesremparts.com. At the north end of Vieux-Québec on the ramparts, with views of the St Lawrence from the third-floor terrace. Simple hotel with bland mostly en-suite rooms; others have dorm-type showers. ❷–❹

Hôtel Manoir Victoria 44 Côte du Palais ☏418/692-1030 or 1-800/463-6283, ⓦwww.manoir-victoria.com. A four-star hotel, off rue St-Jean. Rambling manor with pool, sauna, gym and modern rooms. ❻

Motels, hostels, student rooms and campsites

Motels

Auberge Michel Doyon 1215 chemin Ste-Foy ☏418/527-4408 or 1-888/433-6966, ⓦwww.aubergemicheldoyon.com. One of the cheapest motels around, in the suburb of Ste-Foy. Basic but clean, with free parking. 10min bus ride to Vieux-Québec. ❷–❸

Hostels

Auberge de la Paix 31 rue Couillard ☏418/694-0735. Situated just off rue St-Jean,

this is by far the better of the city's two hostels. Large courtyard to hang out in; rate includes breakfast. ❶

Centre International de Séjour de Québec (HI) 19 rue Ste-Ursule ☏418/694-0755 or 1-800/461-8585, ⓦwww.cisq.org. The 300-bed HI hostel, in a former hospice run by nuns, is often full and can be impersonal, though it offers laundry facilities, Internet access ($1 for 15min), luggage lockers, kitchens and a bar. No curfew, but you need to be buzzed in after 11pm. ❶

QUÉBEC | Québec City: Arrival, information and accommodation

YWCA 855 av Holland ☎418/683-2155, ⓦwww.ywcaquebec.qc.ca. Men are accepted as well as women here, though there are no double beds. Just off chemin Ste-Foy, about a 15min bus ride from the Old Town. ❷

Student rooms

Services des Résidences de l'Université Laval Pavillon Alphonse-Marie-Parent, Room 1618, Cité Universitaire, Ste-Foy ☎418/656-5632, ⓦwww.ulaval.ca/sres. Single and double rooms are available in the student residences, a fifteen-minute bus ride from Vieux-Québec. Cheap breakfast in cafeteria, but it's best avoided. Early May to mid-Aug. Check in after 2pm. ❶–❷

Campsites

Camping Aéroport 2050 rte de l'Aéroport ☎418/871-1574 or 1-800/294-1574, ⓦwww.geocities.com/vacance.geo. Take exit 305 nord off Hwy 440 onto rte de l'Aeroport – the campsite is around 5km north of the airport itself. Sites from $20 ($24 for four adults).
Camping Municipal de Beauport 95 rue Sérénité, Beauport, off boul Rochette ☎418/641-6112, ⓦwww.campingquebec.com/beauport. Take exit 322 off Hwy 40. Bus #800 to Beauport, then #50 or #55. Mid-June to early Sept. $22 for four adults.

The City

Québec City spreads from its historic heart into a bland suburbia but the high-lights lie beside the St Lawrence, with main attractions being evenly distributed between the upper and lower portions of what is known as **Vieux-Québec** (Old Québec). On the Cap Diamant, **Haute-Ville** (Upper Town) continues along the St Lawrence from the old city walls and the furthest you need to wander from here is to the Musée National des Beaux-Arts du Québec, set in the extensive parkland of the Plains of Abraham that unfurls west of the magnificent Citadelle. The Terrasse Dufferin is also worth a stroll to watch street entertainers, unproductive students or the views over the river, but it gets overcrowded in the evening. It overlooks the second part of the old city, **Basse-Ville** (Lower Town), connected to Haute-Ville by funicular and several winding streets and stairs. One of the main pleasures of the area, besides the wonderful old houses and small museums, is the Musée de la Civilisation.

This itinerary begins at Vieux-Québec's Place d'Armes and then explores the upper part of Vieux-Québec and the rest of Haute-Ville as far west as the Musée National des Beaux-Arts du Québec. To finish the tour, you can explore Vieux-Québec's compact Basse-Ville, which can be reached directly from Place d'Armes. Strapped between the cliffs and the St Lawrence, this district is of considerable interest and is a pleasant area to wander around; if you're only in Québec City for a short while, head here straight from Place d'Armes and then return to the upper town for the remainder of the sights as time permits.

Place d'Armes and around

The ten square kilometres of Vieux-Québec's Haute-Ville, encircled by the city walls, form the Québec City of the tourist brochures. Its centre of gravity is the main square, the **Place d'Armes**, with benches around the central fountain serving in the summer as a resting place for weary sightseers. It was here that Champlain established his first fort in 1620, on the site now occupied by the gigantic **Château Frontenac**, probably Canada's most photographed building. New York architect Bruce Price drew upon the French-Canadian style of the surroundings to produce a pseudo-medieval red-brick pile crowned with a copper roof. Although the hotel he designed was inaugurated by the Canadian Pacific Railway in 1893, its distinctive main tower was only added in the early 1920s – during which time the hotel never closed –

VIEUX-QUÉBEC

RESTAURANTS & CAFÉS

Aux Anciens Canadeins	16
Buffet de l'Antiquaire	2
Casse-Crêpe Breton	7
Chez Temporel	4
Conti Caffe	15
L'Échaudé	3
Le Cochon Dingue	18
La Crémaillère	8
Les Frères de la Côte	6
La Maison de Serge Bruyère	5
Le Marie Clarisse	13
Le Petit Coin Latin	12
Le St-Amour	17

BARS & CLUBS

Chez Son Père	10
L'Emprise	E
L'Inox	1
Le Pape Georges	14
Le Pub St-Alexandre	9
Bar Ste-Angèle	11
Bar St-Laurent	0

ACCOMMODATION

Auberge de la Paix	D
Auberge de la Place d'Armes	H
Auberge du Trésor	J
Auberge St-Antoine	G
Auberge St-Louis	R
Au Jardin du Gouverneur	S
Au Manoir Site-Geneviève	aa
Au Petit Hôtel	Q
B&B des Grisons	W
Hôtel Belley	A
Hôtel Cap-Diamant	cc
Centre International de Séjour de Québec	K
Hôtel Château Bellevue	V
Hôtel Château de Léry	X
Le Château Frontenac	O
Le Château de Pierre	bb
Hôtel Clarendon	I
Hôtel Le Clos St-Louis	U
Hôtel la Maison Demers	T
Hôtel La Maison Ste-Ursule	M
Hôtel Dominion 1912	B
Hôtel Manoir La Salle	L
Hôtel Manoir Victoria	E
Hôtel Manoir des Remparts	C
Maison historique James Thompson	P
Hôtel Manoir d'Auteuil	N
La Marquise de Bassano	Y
Hôtel Le Priori	F
Hôtel Terrasse-Dufferin	Z

0 — 250 m

285

resulting in an over-the-top design that makes the most of the stupendous location atop Cap Diamant. Numerous celebrities, including Queen Elizabeth II, have stayed here, and the hotel has hosted one pair or more of newlyweds every night since it opened. The hotel has fifty-minute guided tours departing on the hour from the lower level (May to mid-Oct daily 10am–6pm; mid-Oct to April Sat & Sun noon–5pm, call for weekday times; $7; reservations preferable ☎418/691-2166).

Beside the Château Frontenac, where rue St-Louis enters the square, is the **Maison Maillou**, which houses the Québec chamber of commerce. Dating from 1736, this grey-limestone house, with metal shutters for insulation and a steeply slanting roof, displays the chief elements of the climate-adapted architecture brought over by the Norman settlers. On the west side of the square, on the spot where the Récollet missionaries built their first church and convent, stands the former **Palais de Justice**, a Renaissance-style courthouse designed in 1877 by Eugène-Étienne Taché, architect of the province's Parliament Buildings.

On the northeast corner of Place d'Armes, where rue Ste-Anne intersects with rue du Fort, is the **Musée du Fort** (April–Oct daily 10am–5pm, by reservation at other times; $7.50), whose sole exhibit is a 37-square-metre model of Québec City circa 1750. You can only see it as part of the quaint thirty-minute sound and light show, when the city's six major battles, including the battle of the Plains of Abraham and the American invasion of 1775, are re-enacted – a fairly pricey, if engaging, history lesson.

Parallel to rue du Fort is the narrow alley of **rue du Trésor** where French settlers paid their taxes to the Royal Treasury; nowadays it is a touristy artists' market. You're better to visit the row of stalls manned by local artisans in the churchyard that runs alongside the portraitists on the pedestrianized stretch of rue Ste-Anne. Nearby, the Centre Infotouriste occupies the former Union Hotel at 12 rue Ste-Anne, while at no. 22 the impressive 1732 Maison Vallée houses a missable waxworks museum. Production values are a bit higher at the **Québec Expérience** show back around the corner at 8 rue du Trésor (mid-May to mid-Oct 10am–10pm, rest of year 10am–5pm; 30min; $7.50; ⓦ www.quebecexperience.com), where a 3D multimedia extravaganza, complete with holographic characters and animatronics, gives a potted history of Québec.

Terrasse Dufferin and the ramparts

Fronting the Château Frontenac the wide clifftop boardwalk of the **Terrasse Dufferin** overlooks the narrowing of the river that was known to the aboriginal peoples as the *kebec* – the source of the province's name. Underlying part of the boardwalk are the foundations of Frontenac's Château St-Louis, which served as the governor's residence for two centuries until a fire destroyed it in 1834. The leafy park running alongside the boardwalk was the château's garden – hence its name, the **Jardin des Gouverneurs** (see p.291). To the south, a long flight of stairs leads up to the Promenade des Gouverneurs, a narrow boardwalk perched precariously on the cliff face below the Citadelle that leads to the Plaines d'Abraham (see p.294).

At the north end of the terrace – which offers charming views of the river – stands a romantic statue of **Champlain** and, beside it, a modern sculpture symbolizing Québec City's status as a UNESCO World Heritage Site. From here a **funicular** descends to Vieux-Québec's Basse-Ville (see p.296); save that for the weary walk back up and instead take the stairs down at the north end of the terrace to the **Porte Prescott**, one of the city's four rebuilt gates.

Rather than descending to street level, you can continue across the top of the gate to **Parc Montmorency**; tucked between the upper and lower parts of the old city, its monuments recall the historic figures of the area. This land was granted by Champlain to Canada's first agricultural settler and seigneur, Louis Hébert, and was later the meeting place of Québec's first legislature in 1694. The park gives wonderful views of Québec's port and its massive grain elevators, as does the flanking rue Port Dauphin, which becomes **rue des Remparts**, where the cannons that once protected the city still point across to Lévis.

The ten-minute walk along rue des Remparts circles around the north side of the Séminaire past nineteenth-century homes to the **Hôtel-Dieu du Précieux Sang**, the oldest hospital north of Mexico. At the end of rue Remparts, turn left onto Côte du Palais; from here, you can turn right on rue McMahon to reach Artillery Park, or left on rue St-Jean and continue up the hill to the basilica.

Basilique-Cathédrale Notre-Dame de Québec

From Place d'Armes, you can follow rue du Trésor directly north towards the impressive bulk of the **Basilique-Cathédrale Notre-Dame de Québec** (Mon–Fri 9am–2pm, Sat & Sun 9am–5pm, and between shows; free; Ⓦwww.patrimoine-religieux.com/ndq). The oldest parish north of Mexico, the church was burnt to the ground in 1922 – one of many fires it has suffered – and was rebuilt to the original plans of its seventeenth-century forebear. Absolute silence within the cathedral heightens the impressiveness of the Rococo-inspired interior, culminating in a ceiling of blue sky and billowy clouds. The altar, a gilded replica of St Peter's, is surmounted by an elaborate baldachin uncharacteristically supported by angelic caryatids rather than columns due to the narrow space, and is topped by a statue of Jesus standing on a gilded sphere. The pewter sanctuary lamp, to the right of the main altar, was a gift from Louis XIV and is one of the few treasures to survive the fire. In the crypt more than nine hundred bodies, including three governors and most of Québec's bishops, are interred. Champlain is also rumoured to be buried here, though archeologists are still trying to work out which body is his. Unfortunately, the only part of the crypt you can see on the informative **guided tours** (daily every 30min 8.30am–3.30pm) is a mundane modern corridor – skip it and the tour is free; otherwise it's a dollar.

In the afternoons, access to the cathedral is limited to half an hour at a time unless you pay for the half-hour Heavenly Lights **sound and light show** (May to mid-Oct Mon–Fri 6 shows daily from 3.30pm, Sat & Sun 3 shows daily from 6.30pm; $7.50). Architectural details are illuminated and isolated in the darkness to give you a sense of the volumes that make up the church's interior.

Séminaire de Québec

Next door to the cathedral and sprawling to the north is the old **Séminaire de Québec**, founded by the aggressive and autocratic Monseigneur François de Laval-Montmorency in 1663. In the three decades of his incumbency, Laval secured more power than the governor and intendant put together, and any officer dispatched from France found himself on the next boat home if Laval did not care for him. Laval retired early due to ill health, brought on by a religious fervour that denied him blankets and proper food. Death finally came in 1708 after his feet froze on the stone floor of the chapel during his morning prayer session.

At its construction, the seminary was the finest collection of buildings the city had seen, leaving Governor Frontenac muttering that the bishop was now housed better than him. Primarily a college for priests, the seminary was also open to young men who wanted to follow other professions, and in 1852 it became Laval University, the country's first francophone Catholic university. Today, only the school of architecture remains; most of the other departments were moved to the western suburb of Ste-Foy.

Public access is limited mainly to the ever-expanding **Musée de l'Amérique Française** (June–Sept daily 9.30am–5pm; Oct–May Tues–Sun 10am–5pm, Ⓦ www.mcq.org; $4; Sept–June free on Tues), whose four sections occupy a small part of the old Séminaire. The entrance – and departure point for one-hour guided tours of the seminary – is in the Welcome Pavilion in the Maison du Coin, next to the basilica. It has a small exhibition on the early colonists upstairs and adjoins the Roman-style **chapel**, whose Second Empire interior houses Canada's largest collection of relics – bones, ashes and locks of hair, a few of which are on display. Laval's memorial chapel contains his ornate marble tomb, but not his remains, which were moved to the basilica when the chapel was deconsecrated in 1993. The whole interior is a bit of a sham, though: fed up with rebuilding after the chapel burnt down yet again in 1888, the church authorities decided to construct the pillars and coffered ceilings out of tin and paint over them; the stained-glass windows have been painted on single panes of glass and even the tapestries are the result of some deft brushwork.

The wrought-iron gates between the Welcome Pavilion and the basilica lead into a vast courtyard flanked by austere white buildings with handsome mansard roofs, through which you can pass to visit the rest of the museum. Alternatively, take the underground corridor directly from the chapel; a photo exhibit fills in the history of the Séminaire's buildings. Either way, you end up at the museum's **Pavillon Jérôme-Demers**, which displays mostly well-presented, historical exhibitions. A tiny sample of the eclectic items gathered by Québec's bishops and the academics at Laval – scientific instruments, an Egyptian mummy (with a remarkably well-preserved penis) – as well as ecclesiastical silverware and some of Laval's personal belongings are on display. The museum's name derives from the exhibition on the second floor, **The Settling of French America**, which illustrates the history of the emigration and settlement of the more than nineteen million North Americans of French stock.

Around the Hôtel de Ville

The edifices of the colony's once-powerful Church face the home of democratic power in the city today – the **Hôtel de Ville** (City Hall), which dates from 1883 and is surrounded by the park space of the Jardins de l'Hôtel de Ville, scene of numerous live shows in the summer. To the north, the shops on Côte de la Fabrique extend down the hill to the lively restaurants and bars of rue St-Jean; while to the south, the Hôtel de Ville is overlooked by the far more impressive Art Deco buildings of the **Hôtel Clarendon** and the **Édifice Price** (the city's first skyscraper), at nos. 57 and 65 rue Ste-Anne, respectively.

By the corner of rue Ste-Anne and rue des Jardins stands the first Anglican cathedral built outside the British Isles, the **Cathedral of the Holy Trinity** (daily: May to late June 10am–6pm; late June to Aug 9am–8pm; Sept–Nov

10am–6pm; free guided tours; ⓦwww.quebec.cathedral.ca). The king of France gave the site to the Récollet Fathers but their church burnt down in the late eighteenth century. Its replacement, constructed in 1800–04 on orders from George III, followed the lines of London's church of St Martin-in-the-Fields. The simple interior houses the 1845 bishops' throne, reputedly made from the wood of the elm tree under whose branches Samuel de Champlain conferred with the Iroquois. Many of the church's features came from London, including the silverware from George III and Victorian stained glass, shipped in vats of molasses for protection. The brass bars on the balcony denote the seats for the exclusive use of British sovereigns (or their representatives); humbler parishioners had wooden doors on the box pews to keep the winter cold out. In the courtyard are Les Artisans de la Cathédrale, Québec-based artisans whose small crafts and clothes stalls avoid tourist tack.

Couvent des Ursulines and around

Heading south along rue des Jardins brings you to the narrow rue Donnacona, where a sculptured hand holding a quill – a monument to the women who, since 1639, have dedicated their lives to teaching young Québecois – rests on a pedestal. It seems to point the way to the **Couvent des Ursulines**, built by a tiny group of Ursuline nuns who arrived in Québec in 1639 calling themselves "the Amazons of God in Canada". Their task was to bring religion to the natives and later to the daughters of the settlers, a mission carried out in the classrooms of North America's first girls' school – the buildings still house a private school. They also cared for the *filles du roi*, marriageable orphans and peasant girls imported from France to swell the population. These girls were kept in separate rooms in the convent for surveillance by the local bachelors, who were urged to select a wife within fifteen days of the ship's arrival – a fine of three hundred livres was levied on any man who failed to take his pick within the period. Fat girls were the most desirable, as it was believed they were more inclined to stay at home and be better able to resist the winter cold.

The Ursulines' first mother superior, Marie Guyart de l'Incarnation, was widowed at age 19 and left her son with family when she entered the Ursulines de Tours monastery twelve years later. Her letters to him once she finally made it to Québec give some sharp insights into the early days of the city: "It would be hard to live here an hour without having the hands protected and without being well covered. Although the beds are covered well with quilts or blankets, scarcely can one keep warm when lying on them." Her likeness can be seen in a posthumous portrait attributed to Pommier in the interesting little **museum** (May–Sept Tues–Sat 10am–noon & 1–5pm, Sun 1–5pm; Oct–Nov & Feb–April Tues–Sun 1–4.30pm; $5), housed in the former home of one of the first nuns. A painting by Frère Luc, though executed in France, pictures a Canadian version of the Holy Family: Joseph is shown presenting a Huron girl to Mary, while through the window one can glimpse Cap Diamant and the St Lawrence flowing past. Other paintings, documents and household items testify to the harshness of life in the early days of the colony, but lace-work and embroidery are the highlights, particularly the splendid liturgical ornaments and vestments produced by the early Ursulines and shot through with gold and silver thread.

Marie de l'Incarnation's remains are entombed in the oratory adjoining the **chapel** (May–Oct Tues–Sat 10–11.30am & 1.30–4.30pm, Sun 1.30–4.30pm; free), rebuilt in 1902 but retaining the sumptuous early eighteenth-century altar and sculptures by Pierre-Noël Levasseur. A plaque indicates General

△ Alley in Québec City

Montcalm's former resting place below the chapel (only his skull was found there during renovations, and this has subsequently been re-interred in a suburban military cemetery). The collection of seventeenth and eighteenth-century paintings were acquired from post-Revolution France in the 1820s. Next to the museum, the **Centre Marie-de-l'Incarnation** (Feb–Nov same hours as chapel; free) sells religious and historical books, and displays a few of Marie's personal effects.

Musée d'Art Inuit Brousseau

On the corner of rue des Jardins and rue St-Louis – a touristy restaurant strip – stands **Maison Jacquet**, occupied by the restaurant *Aux Anciens Canadiens*. The name comes from Québec's first novel, whose author, Philippe Aubert de Gaspé, lived here for a while in the middle of the nineteenth century. Dating from 1677, the house is another good example of seventeenth-century New France architecture, as is the blue and white **Maison Kent** at no. 25 on the other side of rue St-Louis, which was built in 1649. Once home of Queen Victoria's father, the Duke of Kent, it's best known as the place where the capitulation of Québec was signed in 1759 and now ironically houses the French consulate.

Between the two historic houses the delightful **Musée d'Art Inuit Brousseau**, 39 rue St-Louis (daily 9.30am–5.30pm; $6; W www.inuitart.ca), traces the development of Inuit art from the naive works of the mid-twentieth century to the highly narrative and intricately carved sculptures by contemporary artists. The few ancient items include simple ivory works from the nomadic Dorset and Thulé cultures. Stone sculpture really began in the 1940s, replacing the declining fur and hunting industries as a source of income – the Inuit artists used aspects of everyday life such as animals and hunting for inspiration, but would also carve an ashtray if they thought they could sell it to a traveller passing through. One such man, James Houston, became convinced that these sculptures needed a wider audience and organized sales of their work in the south – the nucleus of the Brousseau's collection came from these sales, one sculpture per year. A video shows the surprisingly coarse tools used to make the graceful objects.

Jardin des Gouverneurs and around

Rue Haldimand, around the corner from the Musée d'Art Inuit, leads to the **Jardin des Gouverneurs**, whose wonderful prospect of the St Lawrence was once the exclusive privilege of the colonial governors who inhabited the Château St-Louis, upon whose foundations the Terrasse Dufferin was built. The garden's Wolfe–Montcalm obelisk monument, erected in 1828, is rare in paying tribute to the victor and the vanquished. Converted merchants' houses border this grandiose area, and the nearby streets are some of the most impressive in Vieux-Québec – check out rue de la Porte and the parallel rue des Grisons on the park's west side, which boasts some fine eighteenth-century homes.

To escape the tourist hordes for a bit, follow rue Mont-Carmel, on the northern side of the square, to the almost unnoticed **Parc du Cavalier du Moulin**, a quiet little park that's perfect for a picnic. The remnant of a defensive bastion built atop Mont Carmel hill, this was part of the seventeenth-century French fortifications that protected the city's western side. You can't really see the walls from this angle, but you can see the rear facades of the houses on rue St-Louis.

From the Jardin des Gouverneurs, av Ste-Geneviève runs west past handsome nineteenth-century houses towards Porte St-Louis. En route, turn right onto rue Ste-Ursule for the **Chalmers-Wesley United Church** at no. 78 (July & Aug Mon–Fri 10am–5pm; free), built in 1852 and one of the most beautiful in the city. Its slender, Gothic Revivalist spires are a conspicuous element of the skyline and, inside, the stained-glass windows are worth a look. Opposite, the 1910 **Sanctuaire de Notre-Dame du Sacré-Coeur** (daily 7am–8pm; free) also has impressive stained-glass windows.

The fortifications and Artillery Park

A left turn onto rue St-Louis leads to the Porte St-Louis, one of the four gates in the city wall. It's surrounded by **Parc de l'Esplanade**, the main site for the Carnaval de Québec, and departure point for the city's smart horse-drawn calèches. The park's **Centre d'interprétation des Fortifications-de-Québec**, 100 rue St-Louis (mid-May to mid-Oct daily 10am–5pm; $3.50; Ⓦ www.pc.gc.ca/fortifications), includes a powder house constructed in 1815 and a dull exhibition on the fortifications. Most visitors start their 4.5-kilometre stroll around the city wall from here. You can also take a ninety-minute tour focusing on the fortifications' military history with a costumed guide for $10 (under-16s free).

The entrance to the Citadelle (see below) lies south of here along the Côte de la Citadelle. Alternatively, head north on rue d'Auteuil as it descends alongside the fortifications to Porte Kent, next to the **Chapelle des Jésuites**, 20 rue Dauphine (late June to Aug Mon–Fri 10am–12.30pm; free). Framed by the rose and powder-blue vault, the church's delicately carved altar and ecclesiastical sculptures are by **Pierre-Noël Levasseur**, one of the most illustrious artists to work on the early Québec parish churches.

Immediately north of the **Porte St-Jean** lie the defensive structures of **Artillery Park**, raised in the early 1700s by the French in expectation of a British attack from the St Charles River, and subsequently a barracks for the Royal Artillery Regiment for more than a century. In 1882 it became a munitions factory, providing the Canadian army with ammunition in both world wars. The foundry, added in 1902, now houses an interpretation centre (April to early May Wed–Sun 10am–5pm; early May to mid-Oct daily 10am–5pm; $4; Ⓦ www.pc.gc.ca/artillery), which has displays on the military pedigree of the city, including a vivid model of Québec City in 1808. It's also the starting point for one-hour guided tours ($4 extra) and visits of the site's four buildings, including the Officers' Quarters furnished as it was in 1830 and the massive Dauphine Redoubt. The latter typifies the changes of fortune here: used by the French as the barracks for their garrison, it became the officers' mess under the British and then the residence of the superintendent of the Canadian Arsenal.

The Citadelle

Dominating the southern section of Vieux-Québec, the massive star-shaped **Citadelle** can only be visited on one of the worthwhile **guided tours** (every 30min: July & Aug 9am–6pm; every hour: April 10am–4pm, May & June 9am–5pm, Sept 9am–4pm, Oct 10am–3pm; once daily: Nov–March Mon–Fri 1pm; $8; Ⓦ www.lacitadelle.qc.ca). The *tour de force* of Québec City's fortifications, the Citadelle occupies the highest point of Cap Diamant, 100m above the St Lawrence. This strategic site was first built on by the French, but most of the buildings were constructed by the British under orders from the Duke of Wellington, who was anxious about American attack after the War of 1812.

Faubourg St-Jean-Baptiste

If you want to take a break from the tourist sights, head through the Porte St-Jean and across Place D'Youville to where rue St-Jean picks up again in the former *faubourg* – the name given to the settlements that once stood undefended outside the city walls – of **St-Jean-Baptiste**. The quarter's studenty atmosphere is more laid-back than the rest of Québec, with cheaper restaurants and great nightlife spots. A five-minute walk will bring you to the **Protestant Burying Ground** (May to mid-Nov daily 7am–11pm), Québec City's first Protestant cemetery and now the oldest one remaining in the province. Many historical figures were buried here between 1772 and 1860, including Lt Col James Turnbull, Queen Victoria's presumed half-brother. Further along on the same side of the street, **Maison Jean-Alfred Moisan** has been in the grocery trade since 1871, making it the oldest grocery store in North America. The tin ceilings and wooden furnishings provide a backdrop for fine foods and baked goods. The district's namesake, the **Église St-Jean-Baptiste**, 410 rue St-Jean (late June to mid-Sept Mon–Fri & Sun 11am–4pm, Sat 9am–4pm), dominates the *faubourg*, its spire rising to 73m. When reconstruction began after a fire destroyed the original church in 1881, local architect Joseph Ferdinand Peachy looked to France for inspiration – the facade is a close reproduction of the Église de la Trinité in Paris.

The complex of 25 buildings covers forty acres and is the largest North American fort still occupied by troops – it's home to the Royal 22nd Regiment, Canada's only French-speaking regiment. Around the parade ground are ranged various monuments to the campaigns of the celebrated "Van-Doos" (*vingt-deux*), as well as the summer residence of Canada's governor general and two buildings dating back to the French period: the Cap Diamant Redoubt, built in 1693 and thus one of the oldest parts of the Citadelle, and the 1750 powder magazine, now a mundane museum of weaponry and military artefacts.

In addition to the mandatory but entertaining hour-long guided tours, the admission price includes the colourful Changing of the Guard (late June to early Sept daily 10am), which you can catch at the end of a 9am tour (otherwise arrive by 9.45am), and the Beating of the Retreat tattoo (July & Aug Fri–Sun 7pm, at the end of the 6pm tour).

Grande-Allée and the Parliament Buildings

Sweeping out from Porte St-Louis and flanked by grand Victorian mansions, the tree-lined boulevard of **Grande-Allée** is proclaimed the city's equivalent of the Champs-Élysées, with its bustling restaurants, hotels and bars. Adjacent to the *Loews Le Concorde* hotel, Place Montcalm has a monument to Montcalm and a more recent statue of Charles de Gaulle, the French president who declared "Vive le Québec libre" in the 1960s, much to the separatists' delight. This area is now known as Parliament Hill, a new name that caused a lot of controversy, as Canada's Parliament area in Ottawa has the same title and anglophones thought it presumptuous of Québec City to label itself like a capital city.

However, there is indeed a hill here, and upon it, at the eastern end of Grande-Allée, stand the stately buildings of the **Hôtel du Parlement** (late June to early Sept Mon–Fri 9am–4.30pm, Sat & Sun 10am–4.30pm; early Sept to late June Mon–Fri 9am–4.30pm; ☎418/643-7239 or 1-866/337-8837, ⓦwww.assnat.qc.ca), designed by Eugène-Étienne Taché in 1877 in the

Second Empire style using the Louvre for inspiration. The ornate facade includes niches for twelve bronze statues by Québecois sculptor Louis-Philippe Hébert of Canada's and Québec's major statesmen, while finely chiselled and gilded walnut panels in the entrance hall depict important moments in Québec's history, coats of arms and other heraldic features. From here the corridor of the President's Gallery, lined with portraits of all the Legislative Assembly's speakers and presidents, leads to the Chamber of the National Assembly, where the 125 provincial representatives meet for debate. You can't see much, though, unless you take one of the free half-hour guided tours – call ahead as the schedule changes daily.

Among the government buildings clustered to the west of here, the Édifice Marie-Guyart, 1037 rue de la Chevrotière, is the tallest structure in the city. On its 31st floor, the **Observatoire de la Capitole** (late June to mid-Oct daily 10am–5pm; mid-Oct to late June Tues–Sun 10am–5pm; $4; Ⓦ www.observatoirecapitale.org) offers a 360-degree panoramic view over Vieux-Québec, the Citadelle and beyond, with panels usefully providing background info on what you can see.

Battlefields Park

Westward of the Citadelle are the rolling grasslands of the **Battlefields Park** (Parc des Champs-de-Bataille), a sizeable chunk of land stretching along the cliffs above the St Lawrence. The park encompasses the historic **Plains of Abraham**, which were named after Abraham Martin, the first pilot of the St Lawrence River in 1620. The Plains were to become the site on which Canada's history was rewritten. In June 1759 a large British force led by **General Wolfe** sailed up the St Lawrence to besiege **General Montcalm** in Québec City. From the end of July until early September the British forces shuttled up and down the south side of the river, raking the city with cannon fire. Montcalm and the governor, Vaudreuil, became convinced that Wolfe planned a direct assault on the citadel from Anse de Foulon (Wolf's Cove), the only handy break in the cliff face – opinion confirmed when lookouts observed a British detachment surveying Cap Diamant from across the river in Lévis. Montcalm thus strengthened the defences above Anse de Foulon, but made the mistake of withdrawing the regiment stationed on the Plains themselves. The following night the British performed the extraordinary feat, which even Wolfe had considered "a desperate plan", of scaling the cliff below the Plains via Anse de Foulon, and on the morning of September 16 Montcalm awoke to find the British drawn up a couple of kilometres from the city's gate. The hastily assembled French battalions, flanked by aboriginal warriors, were badly organized and rushed headlong at the British, whose volleys of gunfire mortally wounded Montcalm. On his deathbed Montcalm wrote a chivalrous note of congratulations to Wolfe, not knowing that he was dead. Québec City surrendered four days later. The park's **Discovery Pavilion**, below the tourist office at 835 av Wilfrid-Laurier est (daily 8.30am–5pm, mid-June to mid-Oct until 5.30pm; Ⓦ www .ccbn-nbc.gc.ca), has maps, information panels and a short film. It offers a multimedia history show (10am–4pm; $6.50), which does a reasonable job of covering the after-effects of the Conquest, marred by irksome 3D-enhanced "interviews" with Wolfe, Montcalm and other historical personages.

The dead of 1759 are commemorated by a statue of Joan of Arc in a beautifully maintained sunken **garden** just off av Wilfrid-Laurier at Place Montcalm by the Ministry of Justice. More conspicuous, standing out amid the wooded parklands, scenic drives, jogging paths and landscaped gardens, are two Martello towers, built between 1805 and 1812 for protection against the Americans. Martello Tower 2, on the corner of Wilfrid-Laurier and Taché, is only open to school groups, whilst **Martello Tower 1** (June to mid-Oct Sat & Sun 10am–5.30pm, except mid-June to Aug daily 10am–5.30pm; $4), further south in the park, has superb views of the St Lawrence from its rooftop lookout. The views are almost as good from the base of the tower, and you don't have to pay for an unmemorable exhibition in order to reach the top; children get to dress up in costumes for the optional tour, though. Further west, outside the Musée National des Beaux-Arts du Québec, there's a monument to General Wolfe, whose body was shipped back to England for burial, pickled in a barrel of rum. Beyond the park's western peripheries, cannons ring the perimeter of a large playing field and there's another lookout point above where Côte Gilmour winds down the cliffs at Anse de Foulon.

Musée National des Beaux-Arts du Québec

Canadian art had its quiet beginnings in Québec City and the full panoply of this output can be found on the western edge of the Parc des Champs-de-Bataille in the **Musée National des Beaux-Arts du Québec** (daily 10am–6pm, Wed until 9pm; permanent collection free, special exhibitions $10; ☎418/643-2150 or 1-866/220-2150, ⊛www.mnba.qc.ca; bus #11). The Grand Hall, with its cruciform skylight, connects the museum's two buildings (its original home, the Pavillon Gérard-Morisset, and a renovated Victorian prison renamed the Pavillon Charles-Baillairgé) and also serves as the main entrance.

For a chronological tour, start with Gallery 7 on the second floor of the **Pavillon Gérard-Morisset**, which provides a good survey of Québecois art from the early seventeenth to late nineteenth centuries. As Québec churches were the primary art commissioners at the time, most of the earliest works are **religious art**, including the output of **Frère Luc**, represented here by *The Guardian Angel*. The most notable contributions to the collection are by two dynasties: the works of brothers **Pierre-Noël** and **François-Noël Levasseur** from the mid-1700s and the three generations of **Baillairgés** who succeeded them, their copious output including the architecture of churches as well as their interior decoration. Under the British, the subject matter broadened to include portraiture, seen here in **Antoine Plamondon**'s poised *Madame Tourangeau*, and Canadian landscapes by Québec-born **Joseph Légaré** and, more famously, Amsterdam-born **Cornelius Krieghoff**, noted for his romanticized landscapes of landmarks in the region.

Gallery 8, opposite, covers the period from 1860 to 1945, from the late-nineteenth-century **salons** to the development of **modernist art**. In the first room, paintings fight for space on the walls; one that grabs your attention as you enter is **Horatio Walker**'s *Ploughing, the First Gleam at Dawn*, a romantic vision of the lives of the French-Canadian *habitants* who so engrossed him that he repudiated his Ontario roots. The tug-of-war of styles in Europe is played out in many of the subsequent works, including **Maurice Cullen**'s Impressionist-influenced view onto Basse-Ville, *Wolfe's Cove*, and the evocative scene of a horse-drawn carriage in a snowstorm, *Craig Street, Montréal*. Urban life is also admirably recorded by **Adrien Hébert**'s *Rue St-Denis*, which wonderfully captures the spirit of Montréal in the 1920s.

Downstairs, in gallery 2, the impact of **Alfred Pellan**, who returned from Paris in 1940 to teach at Montréal's École des Beaux-Arts, plays out in the development of post-war **figurative** and **abstract art**. His comparative radicalism, evident in his Cubist-influenced still life, *Flowers and Dominoes*, was the catalyst for a generation of Québecois artists to pick up on the avant-garde movements of the time. The move to non-figurative representation can be seen in **Jean Dallaire**'s softly muted abstract figures in his 1957 *Julie*, which contrasts with his surreally colourful and strident *Coq Licorne* (Unicorn Rooster) painted five years earlier. The process reaches its apogee with the Neo-Plasticism represented by **Fernand Leduc**'s boldly coloured geometric abstract *The Mountain Climber*.

At the same time, two of Québec's best-known artists were developing their signature styles. **Paul-Émile Borduas** applied the automatic writing technique of the surrealists to painting – his *Cabalistic Signs* is almost a doodle in oils. His progression to the increasingly spare canvases that have rooms devoted to them in Montréal's museums (see p.246 and p.246) can also be noted here. Gallery 3, across the hall, is devoted solely to the work of **Jean-Paul Riopelle**. The gallery's highlight is his *L'Hommage à Rosa Luxemburg* (1992), a 40-metre-long triptych in thirty segments, with ghostly spray-painted outlines of birds and man-made objects.

In the **Pavillon Charles-Baillairgé**, the red brick interior walls of the former jail have been spruced up, creating a warm atmosphere surprisingly conducive to displaying art. Vaillancourt's *Tree on rue Durocher* sweeps up into the atrium, which then leads visitors into the galleries and a few of the old prison cells. These lie en route to gallery 10, where "Je me souviens" portrays the personages and events in Québec's history through paintings and sculptures by some of the province's leading artists, and includes the studies for public works by sculptors Louis-Philippe Hébert and Alfred Laliberté. In the prison's tower, Montréal sculptor David Moore has created a unique two-storey sculpture of bodies scaling walls – just what you might expect in an old prison.

Gallery 12 on the third floor is devoted to Québec-born painter Jean-Paul Lemieux. His style varies wildly, from landscapes inspired by the Group of Seven such as the Charlevoix-set *Afternoon Sunlight*, through a phase of folk-art-style painting (including a fun look at the Corpus Christi parade winding down côte de la Montagne), to end with a series of uncluttered Expressionist portraits.

Basse-Ville

The birthplace of Québec City, **Basse-Ville** (Lower Town), can be reached from Terrasse Dufferin either by the steep **escalier casse-cou** (Breakneck Stairs) or by the **funicular** alongside (daily 7.30am–11pm, until midnight in summer; $1.50). The Basse-Ville station of the funicular is the 1683 **Maison Louis-Jolliet**, 16 rue du Petit-Champlain, built for the retired discoverer of the Mississippi, Louis Jolliet; it now houses a second-rate souvenir shop.

Dating back to 1685, the narrow, cobbled **rue du Petit-Champlain** is the city's oldest street, and the surrounding area – known as **Quartier du Petit-Champlain** – is the oldest shopping area in North America. The boutiques and art shops in the quaint seventeenth- and eighteenth-century houses are not too overpriced and offer an array of excellent crafts, from Inuit carvings to the products of the glass-blowing workshop and gallery, **Verrerie La Mailloche** (Ⓦwww.lamailloche.com), at the base of the escalier casse-cou. Older artefacts can be seen closer to the river, on the corner of rue du Marché Champlain and rue Notre-Dame, in the 1752 **Maison Chevalier** (May to late June & early Sept to Oct Tues–Sun 10am–5pm; late June to early Sept daily 9.30am–5pm;

Nov–April Sat & Sun 10am–5pm; free), a grand town house and one-time London Coffee House, where merchants would meet throughout the nineteenth century. Its rooms excellently depict interior scenes comprising period furniture, costumes and domestic objects – compare the plush drawing room of a nineteenth-century bourgeois family with the all-in-one common room a tradesman and his family might have occupied a century earlier. Take a peek, too, into the vaulted cellars, where local artisans today sell traditional works.

Place Royale and around

From here it's a short walk along rue Notre-Dame to **Place Royale**, where Champlain built New France's first permanent settlement in 1608, to begin trading fur with the aboriginal peoples. The square – known as Place du Marché until the bust of Louis XIV was erected here in 1686 – remained the focal point of Canadian commerce until 1759, and after the fall of Québec the British continued using the area as a lumber market, vital for shipbuilding during the Napoleonic Wars. After 1860 Place Royale was left to fall into disrepair, a situation reversed as recently as the 1970s, when the scruffy area was renovated. Its pristine stone houses, most of which date from around 1685, are undeniably photogenic, with their steep metal roofs, numerous chimneys and pastel-coloured shutters, but it's a Legoland townscape, devoid of the scars of history. Fortunately, the atmosphere is enlivened in summer by entertainment from classical orchestras to juggling clowns, and by the Fêtes de la Nouvelle-France (see box, p.281), when everyone dresses in period costume and it once again becomes a chaotic marketplace.

In Maison Hazeur, a merchant's house dating in part to 1684, the **interpretation centre** at 27 rue Notre-Dame (late June to Aug daily 10am–5pm; Sept to late June Tues–Sun 10am–5pm; $3, free Nov–March and Tues except in summer), outlines the stormy past of Place Royale, the mercantile aspects and the changes in the look of the square from the days when it was inhabited by the Iroquois to its recent renovation – search out the tucked away exhibit on level one rather than sitting through the hokey multimedia show. Domestic objects and arrowheads are on the upper floors, from where you can see Gille's Girard's *À rebrousse-temps*, an enigmatic three-storey sculpture that plays with the idea of determining an artefact's original purpose. The vaulted cellars have modern-looking displays of 1800s domestic scenes for kids to try on period costumes and act out a role.

The **Église Notre-Dame-des-Victoires** (daily 9am–4.30pm), on the west side of the square, nearly always has a wedding in progress during the summer. It was instigated by Laval in 1688 but has been completely restored twice – after being destroyed by shellfire in 1759 and after a fire in 1969. Inside, the fortress-shaped altar alludes to the two French victories over the British navy that gave the church its name: the destruction of Admiral Phipps' fleet by Frontenac in 1690 and the sinking of Sir Hovenden Walker's fleet in 1711. Paintings depicting these events hang above the altar, while the aisles are lined with copies of religious paintings by Van Dyck, Van Loo and Rubens, gifts from early settlers to give thanks for a safe passage. The large model ship suspended in the nave has a similar origin.

Place Royale exits to the east past rue St-Pierre – the heart of the old financial district – onto **Place de Paris**, where a white cubic sculpture called *Dialogue with History* marks the disembarkation place of the first settlers from France. Visible to the south (but accessible only from rue St-Pierre), the **Batterie Royal**, a crenellated rampart trimly restored in the 1970s, was used to defend the city during the siege of 1759. The **ferry to Lévis** (6.30am–2am; June–Sept

$2.50 one-way, Oct–May $2; ☎418/644-3704, ⓦwww.traversiers.gouv.qc.ca; see p.308) leaves from the waterfront just to the southeast.

Musée de la Civilisation

A walk north along rue Dalhousie from Place de Paris brings you to one of Québec City's most impressive museums, the **Musée de la Civilisation**, 85 rue Dalhousie (late June to early Sept daily 9.30am–6.30pm; otherwise Tues–Sun 10am–5pm; $7; Sept–June free on Tues; ⓦwww.mcq.org). Designed by prominent Canadian architect Moshe Safdie, the museum references the steep-pitched roofs of the early settlers in a structure that incorporates a rooftop terrace with great views and three historic buildings – be sure to check out the vaulted cellars in the 1751 **Maison Estèbe**, which survived the British bombardment to eventually become the museum's gift shop (ask for the leaflet detailing the house's history). In the main foyer, a 1730s barque discovered on the site is displayed between a stone wall (the edge of the quay built a couple of decades later) and Astri Reusch's *La Débâcle*, a sculpture that symbolizes the break-up of the ice in the spring thaw.

Concentrating primarily on Canadian subjects but also diversifying into a worldwide perspective, the museum presents engaging temporary exhibitions that have ranged from whimsical pop culture interests to serious looks at earlier historical periods. The first of the two permanent exhibitions upstairs, **Memories**, expertly displays life in Québec from the early days of the settlers to the present (pick up an English-language text at the entrance). Cross the atrium for the **Encounter with the First Nations** exhibition, set up in consultation with all eleven of the First Nations of Québec. It presents the history and culture of these earlier residents using artefacts and videotaped oral histories; the larger items – including a *rabaska*, an enormous birch-bark canoe – were crafted in recent years.

Vieux-Port and around

To the east and north, near the confluence of the St Charles and the St Lawrence rivers, lies the **Vieux-Port de Québec**, the busiest harbour in the province until its eclipse by Montréal. Much of the harbour has been renovated as a recreational area, with theatres, yuppie flats, sheltered walkways, restaurants and a marina packed with pleasure boats and yachts. A remodelled cement plant bordering the Bassin Louise at 100 rue St-André now hosts an **interpretation centre** for the Vieux-Port (daily: early May to Aug 10am–5pm; Sept to mid-Oct 1–5pm; rest of year by reservation: ☎418/648-3300, ⓦwww.pc.gc.ca/vieuxport; $3.50), housing a display on the lumber trade and shipbuilding in the nineteenth century. Nearby, along the basin, the **Marché du Vieux-Port** (March–Nov daily from 8am) is a throwback to how the port used to be – its busy market stalls selling cheap, fresh produce from the local area.

Also on the south side of the Bassin Louise, the next street down from St-André is rue St-Paul, heart of Québec's **antiques district**. Numerous cluttered antique shops, art galleries, cafés and restaurants now occupy warehouses and offices abandoned after the demise of the port. From rue St-Paul the steep Côte du Colonel Dambourgès leads to rue des Remparts on the northern borders of Haute-Ville (see p.287).

Cartier-Brébeuf National Historic Site

Northwest of Vieux-Québec, on the banks of the St-Charles River (bus #3, #4 or #801), the **Cartier-Brébeuf National Historic Site**, 175 de l'Espinay (daily: early May to Aug 10am–5pm; Sept to early Oct 1–4pm; $3.50; @www.pc.gc.ca/brebeuf) has a double claim to fame. It marks the spot where Jacques Cartier spent the winter of 1535–36 in friendly contact with the people of the surrounding Iroquoian villages – a cordial start to a relationship that Cartier later soured by taking a local chief and nine of his men hostage. It is also where Jean de Brébeuf, with his Jesuit friends, built his first Canadian residence in 1625: Brébeuf is best known for his martyrdom near today's Midland in Ontario (see p.151). The **interpretation centre** features an excellent account of Cartier's voyages and of the hardship he and his crew endured during the winter and a backgrounder on the Jesuits' role in New France. The guided tour of the site (included in the entrance fee) leads to a mock-up of an Iroquoian longhouse and sweat lodge set within a palisade, where costumed guides demonstrate daily tasks, mostly to the benefit of the kids. Keep an eye out for the resident muskrat.

Eating

It is when you start **eating** in Québec City that the French ancestry of the Québecois hits all the senses: the city's eateries present an array of culinary delights adopted from the mother country, from beautifully presented gourmet dishes to humble baguettes. Whether you are on a tight budget or not, the lively **cafés** are probably where you will want to spend your time, washing down bowls of soup and *croûtons* (toasted baguettes dripping with cheese) with plenty of coffee.

As you might expect, Vieux-Québec (both upper and lower) is home to most of the gourmet **restaurants** and cafés; within Haute-Ville's walls you'll generally find better value along rue St-Jean than rue St-Louis. Other areas have their fair share of eating spots as well – notably along rue St-Jean (quirky and cheaper) and, just outside the walls, Grande-Allée (generally touristy and expensive). Your best bet for good-value mid-price restaurants is to head for the numerous terrace-fronted establishments on avenue Cartier, near the Musée National des Beaux-Arts du Québec. Although prices tend to be rather high, even the poshest restaurants have cheaper lunch-time and table d'hôte menus. For a change of taste, the dishes of other countries are also represented, including Italian, Greek and Thai. Strangely though, typical French-Canadian cooking – game with sweet sauces followed by simple desserts with lashings of maple syrup – is available at very few places in town, although the many *cabanes à sucre* on Île d'Orléans (see p.308) offer typical meals to tourists.

Cafés and snack outlets

A.L. Van Houtte 995 Place D'Youville. Reliable chain with sandwiches and salads until late evening. Internet access $6/hr.
Brûlerie Tatum Café 1084 rue St-Jean. All-day omelettes and light snacks. Exposed brick walls and roasting coffee beans provide ambience. Open 8am–11pm.
Buffet de l'Antiquaire 95 rue St-Paul. An old-school diner popular with locals for breakfast (from 6am) and home-cooked comfort food like *poutine* and *pâté chinois* (shepherd's pie).

Café Buade 31 rue Buade. In a central location, with good light breakfasts and passable bistro-ish fare throughout the day. It's nicer upstairs. Open from 7am.
Café Dépot 36 Côte de la Fabrique. Basic wraps, filled baguettes and pastries at the front of a convenience store. Open 24hr.
Le Casse-Cou 90 rue du Petit-Champlain. Cute little spot at the end of pedestrianized rue du Petit-Champlain for $5 breakfast fry-ups and decent light meals until 9pm.

Chez Temporel 25 rue Couillard. Bowls of steaming *café au lait*, croissants and *chocolatines* make this café, a few doors from the *Auberge de la Paix* hostel, a perfect place for breakfast. Soups and sandwiches are also available until 1.30am.

Kookening 565 rue St-Jean ☎418/521-2800. Chilled-out café-bar with bright walls and board games. Mainly Tex-Mex menu with some eclectic choices like *Mole de canard confit* (duck with Aztec chocolate sauce) and kaiser rolls filled with tandoori chicken. Daily from 4pm.

L'Omelette 66 rue St-Louis. Adequate tourist joint with omelette specialities; breakfast from 7am.

L'Orange Bleue 526 rue St-Jean. A tiny cooperative vegetarian café with changing art displays and music acts on various nights. Closed Mon; no lunch weekends.

Tutto Gelato 716 rue St-Jean. Fantastic Italian ice cream (with a few soya varieties thrown in) five minutes west of the walls. There's another at 1190 av Cartier.

Restaurants

Haute-Ville
(within the walls)

L'Apsara 71 rue d'Auteuil ☎418/694-0232. Cambodian, Vietnamese and Thai food in a muted dining room near the Porte St-Louis. Three-course lunch is around $10, dinners in the $25 region.

Aux Anciens Canadiens 34 rue St-Louis ☎418/692-1627, ⓦwww.auxancienscanadiens.qc.ca. This overly expensive and touristy restaurant (table d'hôte around $35) is in one of the oldest homes in Québec City. It serves refined Québecois specialities like *tourtière* (meat pie) and *pattes de cochon* (pigs' trotters) and house inventions such as duck glazed with maple syrup and caribou in blueberry-wine sauce.

Café de la Paix 44 rue des Jardins ☎418/692-1430. The desserts in the front window taste as good as they look, and the rest of the menu – pricey French classics and game – is equally delicious. Closed Sun.

Casse-Crêpe Breton 1136 rue St-Jean ☎418/692-0438. Diner-style restaurant where crepes are made in front of you with two or three fillings, costing around $5. There's often a queue, but it moves quickly. 7am to around 11pm.

Charles Baillairgé At *Hôtel Clarendon*, 57 rue Ste-Anne ☎418/692-2480. Opened in 1870, this is supposedly Canada's oldest restaurant and serves classic French cuisine. Expensive, and dress is formal.

Conti Caffe 32 rue St-Louis ☎418/692-4191. Moderate–expensive. Sharing the kitchen of *Le Continental* next door, this casual Italian eatery is the best choice on a street swamped with mediocre, touristy restaurants. Veal is a speciality – the medallions in porcini mushroom sauce are rich and succulent. Recommended.

Le Continental 26 rue St-Louis ☎418/694-9995. Old-fashioned place down the street from the *Château Frontenac*. Seafood, veal and flambéed dishes appear on the three-course table d'hôte for $34–41.

La Crémaillère 21 rue St-Stanislas ☎418/692-2216. Superior French and Italian cuisine in a romantic, stone-walled 1829 residence that feels miles away from busy rue St-Jean just beyond the windows.

Les Frères de la Côte 1190 rue St-Jean ☎418/692-5445. A friendly and crowded bistro that draws locals as well as tourists for steaks, smoked salmon and great mussels and pizzas, as well as an excellent steak tartare. Make sure to check the daily specials on the blackboard. Recommended.

Gambrinus 15 rue du Fort ☎418/692-5144. Good Italian and French food on the corner of Place d'Armes, with seafood specialities. Musicians nightly.

La Maison de Serge Bruyère 1200 rue St-Jean ☎418/694-0618. Three restaurants under one roof: the *Restaurant la Grande Table* is one of the best in the city, serving fresh produce, beautifully prepared and presented. The eight-course *ménu découverte* ($85 per person, $145 with wine) is a French nouvelle cuisine extravaganza. Closed Sun & Mon. The adjacent *Bistro Livernois* is more affordable and the streetfront café even cheaper.

Au Petit Coin Breton 1029 rue St-Jean ☎418/694-0758. A pretty good and reasonably priced specialist creperie, where servers wear traditional Breton costume – it may put you in the mood.

Le Petit Coin Latin 8.5 rue Ste-Ursule ☎418/692-2022. Cosy café-bistro with a secluded courtyard. Raclette is a speciality, but they also serve steaks and a caribou *tourtière* (meat pie) for heartier appetites. Breakfast (7.30–11.30am, until 4pm weekends) ranges from straightforward fry-ups to eggs Benedict.

Le Rétro 1129 rue St-Jean ☎418/694-9218. Well-priced if touristy café-restaurant; serves everything from spaghetti to *filet mignon*.

Le St-Amour 48 rue Ste-Ursule ☎ 418/694-0667, ⊛ www.saint-amour.com. Romantic French restaurant with a glass-roofed winter garden. Excellent food at around $85 for two – the foie gras is exquisite.

Haute-Ville
(outside the walls)

L'Astral 1225 Place Montcalm ☎ 418/647-2222. Rotating restaurant on the top floor of the *Hôtel Loews Le Concorde*. The international menu is generally expensive but the views can't be beaten. The all-you-can-eat Buffet Royal costs $40, half that at lunch.

Café Krieghoff 1089 av Cartier ☎ 418/522-3711, ⊛ www.cafekrieghoff.qc.ca. A typical French bistro *à la Québécois* that serves up some of the city's best coffee, big breakfasts and light meals including traditional *croûtons* (a baguette topped with garlic butter and melted cheese). Good spot to sit and read or write in the day, especially on the terrace.

Le Cochon Dingue 46 boul René-Lévesque ouest ☎ 418/523-2013, ⊛ www.cochondingue.com. Close to av Cartier, this branch draws locals rather than tourists, as in Basse-Ville (see below).

Le Commensal 860 rue St-Jean ☎ 418/647-3733. Great spot for vegetarians five minutes from Vieux-Québec's gates. Buffet where the food is sold by weight.

Cosmos Café 575 Grande-Allée est ☎ 418/640-0606, ⊛ www.lecosmos.com. By far the best spot on the Grande-Allée – cool decor, great breakfasts and imaginative menu. Crowded and lively at lunch and for the *cinq à sept* cocktail hour.

Garam Massala 1114 av Cartier ☎ 418/522-4979. Indian restaurant in a cosy basement specializing in tandoori chicken. Dinner for two is around $38, lunch for $10 or less a head.

Le Graffiti 1191 av Cartier ☎ 418/529-4949. Chic French-Italian restaurant with decent lunch specials that also does a good Sunday brunch (10am–3pm).

Le Hobbit 700 rue St-Jean ☎ 418/647-2677. A popular local spot where a mixed studenty crowd who come for the great vegetarian options, as well as burgers, pasta and bistro dishes like steak and trout filet.

Jaune Tomate 120 boul René-Lévesque ouest ☎ 418/523-8777, ⊛ www.jaunetomate.com. Terrace-fronted house with tasty and reasonably priced Italian dishes like *osso bucco, linguini del mare* and a range of pizzas. The two-course lunch is a good filler-upper at around $10.

Piazzetta 707 rue St-Jean ☎ 418/529-7489. Trendy pizzeria with funky furnishings – the pizzas

come close to perfection and are quite cheap. Pasta and focaccia sandwiches, too. There's another in Basse-Ville at 63 rue St-Paul (☎ 418/529-7489).

Pizzédélic 1145 av Cartier ☎ 418/525-5981. Trendy spot with creative pizzas and pastas and a large, packed terrace.

Basse-Ville

Aviatic Club Gare du Palais ☎ 418/522-3555. Surprisingly good international cuisine from sushi and Thai to Tex-Mex in the train station with a large patio alongside.

Le Café du Monde 84 rue Dalhousie ☎ 418/692-4455, ⊛ www.lecafedumonde.com. This large and sleek Parisian-style bistro may be in the cruise ship terminal, but it's a hit with locals for its brash atmosphere and fantastic terrace overlooking the St Lawrence. And the food – mussels, veal sweetbreads, *confit de canard*, steak tartare and the like – is quite good, too.

Le Cochon Dingue 46 boul Champlain ☎ 418/692-2013, ⊛ www.cochondingue.com. Fun and reasonably priced bistro serving the likes of brochettes, pasta, mussels, *bavette* (flank steak) and *steak-frites*.

Le Délice du Roy 33 rue St-Pierre ☎ 418/694-9161. Around the corner from Place Royale, this place dishes up hearty if plain traditional Québecols food at reasonable prices.

L'Échaudé 72 rue du Sault-au-Matelot ☎ 418/692-1299, ⊛ www.echaude.com. Upscale but unpretentious bistro with a terrace on the pedestrian portion of the street. A good selection of wines accompanies bistro classics like *confit de canard*, steak tartare and stuffed quail, as well as daily fish specials.

Initiale 54 rue St-Pierre ☎ 418/694-1818, ⊛ www.restaurantinitiale.com. One of Québec City's best restaurants, and priced accordingly ($49 table d'hôte). A chic place with a lighter take on fine French classics.

Le Lapin Sauté 52 rue du Petit-Champlain ☎ 418/692-5325, ⊛ www.lapinsaute.com. Very popular, informal bistro specializing in rabbit – even the breakfast menu includes a rabbit dish. Great terrace, too.

Laurie Raphael 117 rue Dalhousie ☎ 418/692-4555, ⊛ www.laurieraphael.com. Warm but formal atmosphere in a restaurant focusing on *cuisine du marché* (market cuisine). Specialities include fish, sweetbreads, Québec venison and scallops from the Mingan Islands.

Le Marie Clarisse 12 rue du Petit-Champlain ☎ 418/692-0857, ⊛ www.marieclarisse.qc.ca. Fine fish and market-fresh seafood in a tiny stone-walled restaurant at the foot of the *escalier casse-cou*. A four-course meal goes for $40–45; advance booking advised. A good spot for people-watching.

Poisson d'Avril 115 quai St-André ☎418/692-1010, ☜www.poissondavril.net. Seafood and grilled steaks in the $25–30 range near the Vieux-Port.

Bars and nightlife

Nightlife in Québec City is far more relaxed than in Montréal: an evening spent in an intimate bar or a jazz or blues soiree is more popular than a big gig or disco, except among the younger set. Few major bands tour here, except during the Festival d'Été in July, when everyone lets their hair down. Québec City's main bar and nightclub strip is around rue St-Jean; the stretch outside the city walls in the Faubourg St-Jean-Baptiste has studenty bars and gay nightspots. Places on Grande-Allée tend to cater to tourists, but there are a few decent clubs at either end of the strip. For up-to-date **information** check the local media (see "Performing arts" p.303).

Bars and music venues

L'Amour Sorcier 789 Côte Ste-Geneviève. Popular, intimate lesbian bar with cheap beers, soft music (which gets louder and more danceable later on) and a great roof terrace.

Chez Son Père 24 rue St-Stanislas ☜www.barchezsonpere.qc.ca. Overlooking rue St-Jean in Vieux-Québec. Québecois folk singers create a great thigh-slapping atmosphere. Free admission and drink specials.

Le Drague 815 rue St-Augustin ☜www.ledrague.com. A gay bar, café and night-club, with cheap imported beers. Sunday night drag shows are great fun.

L'Emprise *Hôtel Clarendon*, 57 rue Ste-Anne. Art Deco surroundings attract a sophisticated touristy crowd to evenings of smooth jazz and blues (nightly 9.30pm, weekends only in winter; free).

L'Étrange 275 rue St-Jean ☜www.etrange.qc.ca. Relaxed upstairs bar with regular two-for-one specials and a mix of rock tunes from the speakers. Twenty-something crowd.

Le Fou Bar 525 rue St-Jean. Packed studenty hangout with table football and cheap beer.

L'Inox 37 quai St-André. The city's original brew-pub, serving artisanal cheeses and European sausages to go with the fine ales.

Jules et Jim 1060 av Cartier. Long-time local hangout, it's a small, quiet place amidst all the restaurants on av Cartier.

Le Pape-Georges 8 rue Cul-de-Sac ☜www.papegeorges.com. Tiny cellar of a bar near Place Royale with acoustic acts (Wed–Sun) and pavement terrace.

Pub Java 1112 av Cartier. Good selection of imported and draught beers and you can even come back for breakfast. The Irish pub *Salon*

Galway upstairs has large armchairs by the fire-place.

Le Pub St-Alexandre 1087 rue St-Jean ☜www.pubstalexandre.com. More than 200 beers and 40 single malts in this yuppie English-style pub.

Sacrilège 447 rue St-Jean. Friendly and cheap watering hole with a popular terrace in back. In the Faubourg St-Jean-Baptiste.

Bar Ste-Angèle 26 rue Ste-Angèle. A dark and smoky neighbourhood bar with a beamed ceiling and cozy nook that hasn't noticed it's in the middle of tourist central. Open from 8pm.

Bar St-Laurent 1 rue des Carrières ☎418/692-3861. The Château Frontenac address may be a bit stuffy and alcohol pricey at the polished octag-onal bar, but you don't need to dress to the nines and the view from the terrace is stupendous.

Les Yeux Bleus 1117 rue St-Jean. Despite the name, there's no blues at this *boîte à chansons* tucked down an alleyway. You can catch acoustic acts in the dark and smoky interior or hang out on the crowded and lively terrace.

Clubs and discos

Casablanca 1169 rue St-Jean Weekend dance club playing reggae, African and Arabic beats hidden away down a passageway off rue St-Jean. Only gets going around 11pm (Fri & Sat only). No cover.

Dagobert 600 Grande-Allée est ☜www.dagobert.ca. This sprawling old house has been one of the city's most raucous nightspots for decades. Young dressed-up-for-it clubbers head upstairs for the large Eighties-ish dance floor. Downstairs a slightly older crowd sit at tiered tables to catch cover bands from 10.30pm. There's rarely a cover charge.

Kashmir 1018 rue St-Jean. Loud and packed full some nights, dead others, depending on the DJ or the band playing. Very young crowd, usually.

Maurice 575 Grande-Allée est ⓦwww .mauricenightclub.com. Happening club with a rotating crew of DJs that attracts a stylish 20s to mid-30s crowd for R&B and house nights (Wed–Sun only in winter). Dress up to get by the selective door policy. The $3 cover ($4 on weekends) includes the more laid-back *Charlotte*

upstairs, with couches for chilling out or smoking a cigar, though on the funk and latino nights it can be just as hopping.

Sonar 1147 av Cartier. Swish basement club-lounge that grooves to R&B on Thursdays and house on the weekend after the tapas plates have been cleared away. Mid-20s to mid-30s crowd.

Zazou 811 rue St-Jean. Mixed gay club with a mezzanine-encircled dance floor and a chilled bar and packed terrace off to the side.

Performing arts and cinema

Québec City is not especially renowned for its high culture, but from May to September there are dance, theatre and music events at various outdoor venues, and throughout the year performances can be caught at the city's theatres. The liveliest periods are in February and July, when the entire city is animated by its two principal **festivals**: the excellent Carnaval and the equally frenzied Festival d'Été (see box p.281). **Tickets** for most events can be purchased through the Admission agency (☏1-800/361-4595, ⓦwww.admission.com) and Réseau Billetech (ⓦwww.billetech.com). For up-to-date **information** on the city's goings-on, check out the listings section in the French daily newspapers *Le Soleil* and *Journal de Québec* and the free weekly newspaper *Voir* (ⓦwww.voir.ca). The quarterly bilingual magazine for tourists *Voilà Québec* also carries information, as does the English *Québec Chronicle Telegraph* (ⓦwww.qctonline.com), published every Wednesday.

Québec City has a fair smattering of **theatres**, all producing plays in French only. The city's main theatre for the performing arts is the Grand Théâtre de Québec, 269 boul René-Lévesque est (ⓦwww.grandtheatre.qc.ca), which has a sound programme of drama, as well as opera, dance shows and classical music concerts. For small-scale dramatic productions, check out the Théâtre de la Bordée, 315 rue St-Joseph est (ⓦwww.bordee.qc.ca), while Théâtre Le Capitole, 972 rue St-Jean (ⓦwww.lecapitole.com), hosts dinner theatre, cabaret and flashy musicals. Canada's oldest symphony **orchestra**, L'Orchestre Symphonique de Québec (ⓦwww.osq.org), performs at the Grand Théâtre, as does the Opéra de Québec (ⓦwww.operadequebec.qc.ca) and the chamber ensemble Les Violons du Roy (ⓦwww.violonsduroy.com). Other **classical concerts** can be caught at the Bibliothèque Gabrielle-Roy, 350 rue St-Joseph est. Seventeenth- and eighteenth-century music is performed at the chapel in the Séminaire in summer. In summer, **open-air venues** are particularly popular in Québec. The largest is the Agora, in the Vieux-Port at 120 rue Dalhousie, a huge amphitheatre used for a range of productions from comedies to classical music. A summer-long programme of activities is also enacted on open stages in the Jardins de l'Hôtel de Ville; at the Parc de la Francophonie beside Grande-Allée, just beyond the Parliament Buildings; and in the Place D'Youville. In Place Royale and at the Kiosque Edwin-Bélanger bandstand on

Spectator sports in Québec City

Ice hockey Les Remparts de Québec (ⓦwww.remparts.qc.ca), who are not in the NHL, play at the Colisée Pepsi, 250 boul Wilfred-Hamel (tickets ☏418/691-7211 or 1-800/900-SHOW). Season is mid-Sept to April.

the Plains of Abraham, there are various free classical music concerts in the summer.

Most **cinemas** are out in the suburbs – the most convenient are the multiplexes in Ste-Foy's shopping malls, which occasionally have some undubbed English films. Films are often listed under their English titles, but make sure that it says "**v.o.a.**" (original English version) or "**s-t.f.**" (in the original language but with French subtitles); ask if you're not sure. The city's rep cinema, Cinéma le Clap, also in Ste-Foy at no. 2360 chemin Ste-Foy (Ⓦwww.clap.qc.ca; bus; #7), has the odd English film, too – pick up their monthly programme at cafés and bookstores.

Listings

Airlines Air Canada Ⓣ1-888/247-2262; Air Canada Tango Ⓣ1-888/315-1390; Continental Airlines Ⓣ1-800/231-0856; Jetsgo Ⓣ1-866/440-0441; Northwest Ⓣ1-800/225-2525.

Airport enquiries Ⓣ418/640-2700, Ⓦwww.aeroportdequebec.com.

Banks and currency exchange American Express, Place Laurier, 2700 boul Laurier, Ste-Foy (Ⓣ418/658-8820); Banque Royale, 700 Place d'Youville and 140 Grande-Allée est. Caisse Populaire Desjardins du Vieux-Québec, 19 rue des Jardins (summer daily 9am–6pm; winter Mon–Fri 10am–3pm, Thurs until 6pm) has exchange facilities and a 24hr cashpoint (ATM) in Vieux-Québec; as does Banque Nationale, 1199 rue St-Jean (summer: Mon–Fri 9am–8pm, Sat & Sun 9.30am–8pm (May, June, Sept & Oct daily until 6pm only); winter: Mon–Thurs 9am–5pm, Fri 9am–4.30pm).

Bike and blade rental Vélo Passe-Sport Plein Air, 22 Côte du Palais (Ⓣ418/692-3643) is conveniently situated, but Cyclo Services, in the Marché du Vieux-Port, 160 quai St-André (Ⓣ418/692-4052), is cheaper and is next to the bike trail. Information on cycle trails from Promo-Vélo (Ⓣ418/522-0087).

Bookshops The two main English bookshops are in the suburb of Ste-Foy: Librairie Smith, Place Laurier, 2700 boul Laurier; and La Maison Anglaise, Place de la Cité, 2600 boul Laurier. In Vieux-Québec there's a small selection at Pantoute, 1100 rue St-Jean, and a counter selling travel books inside the tourist office on Place d'Armes.

Car rental Avis, *Hôtel Hilton*, 900 boul René-Lévesque est Ⓣ418/523-1075, and at the airport Ⓣ418/872-2861; Budget, 380 boul Wilfred-Hamel ouest Ⓣ418/687-4220, 29 Côte du Palais Ⓣ418/692-3660, and at the airport Ⓣ418/872-9885; Discount, 12 rue Ste-Anne Ⓣ418/692-1244; Hertz, airport Ⓣ418/871-1571, 44 Côte du Palais Ⓣ418/694-1224, and 580 Grande-Allée est

Ⓣ418/647-4949; Thrifty, near the airport at 6375 boul Wilfred-Hamel Ⓣ418/877-2870.

Consulate US, 2 Place Terrasse-Dufferin Ⓣ418/692-2095.

Gay and lesbian life Gai Écoute and Gay Line (Ⓣ1-888/505-1010; in English 7–11pm only).

Laundry Lavoir la Lavandière, 625 rue St-Jean (Mon–Sat 8am–9pm, Sun 9am–6pm); Lavoir Ste-Ursule, 17B av Ste-Ursule (daily 8am–9pm).

Left luggage $2 lockers in the bus station.

Medical emergencies 24hr medical advice and referral service Ⓣ418/648-2626. Hôtel-Dieu Hospital, 11 Côte du Palais (Ⓣ418/691-5042), is in Vieux-Québec; Jeffrey Hale Hospital, 1250 chemin Ste-Foy (Ⓣ418/683-4471), is better for English-speakers. Dental emergencies Ⓣ418/653-5412 (Mon 8am–8pm, Tues 8am–7pm, Wed & Thurs 8am–5pm, Fri 8am–4pm) or Ⓣ418/656-6060 (Sat 10am–3pm, Sun 10am–1pm; emergencies only).

Parking In Vieux-Québec off rue Pierre-Olivier Chauveau (below the Hôtel de Ville); rue Haldimand (near the Jardin des Gouverneurs). Outside the walls at av Wilfrid-Laurier outside Porte St-Louis; near Place D'Youville; rue Dalhousie in the Vieux-Port. Long-term parking is opposite the bus terminal.

Pharmacy The only late-closing pharmacy is Pharmacie Brunet, Les Galeries Charlesbourg, 4250 av 1ère, in the northwesterly suburb of Charlesbourg (daily 8am–midnight; Ⓣ418/623-1571).

Post office 300 rue St-Paul, 5 rue du Fort and 59 rue Dalhousie. All are open Mon–Fri 8am–5.45pm and have a free internet station (max 15min).

Ridesharing Allo-Stop, 665 rue St-Jean (Ⓣ418/522-0056, Ⓦwww.allostop.com).

Taxis Taxi Coop Ⓣ418/525-5191; Taxi Québec Ⓣ418/525-8123.

Weather and road conditions Environment Canada (Ⓣ418/648-7766,

ⓦwww.weatheroffice.ec.gc.ca) for recorded
weather forecast; Transports Québec (☎1-
888/355-0511, ⓦwww.mtq.gouv.qc.ca) for road-

works and winter road conditions. Skiers can
check snow conditions at
ⓦwww.quebecskisurf.com.

Around Québec City

Options for day-trips on the fringes of the city include **Wendake**, to see the past and present crafts of Canada's only surviving Huron community and **Lévis**, on the opposite shore of the St Lawrence – less inundated by visitors than Québec City and with great views of its more illustrious neighbour. Also in easy striking distance of the city is tranquil, charming **Île d'Orléans** where the agricultural landscape is dotted with gîtes and auberges, and the homes of the well heeled. The island is just offshore of the **Côte-de-Beaupré** further to the northeast, which, though something of a city annexe, boasts the spectacular waterfalls of **Chute Montmorency** and the **Canyon Ste-Anne**. For those in search of a longer jaunt into the great outdoors, the **Réserve Faunique des Laurentides** is within easy reach and there are a number of **ski hills** in the area.

City **buses** and bicycle paths run to Chute Montmorency and Wendake, and a quick **ferry** trip lands you in Lévis. A few Intercar buses go daily to **Ste-Anne-de-Beaupré**, but the most practical and highly recommended local transport service is the Sherpa Plein Aire (☎418/640-7437, ⓦwww .sherpaleinaire.com) shuttle bus, which heads to all major attractions in the area – including all those listed below except Lévis. They offer straight fares for transport as well as packages that include entry prices where applicable, will transport your bike for free and can even rent you out a bike; rental bike and shuttle packages start at $29.

Wendake

Just to the northwest of Québec City lies **WENDAKE**, the only **Huron reserve** in Canada. Its name derives from the Hurons' own name for their people – *Wendat*, meaning "people of the island". In 1650, French Jesuit missionaries led three hundred Huron from Ontario's Georgian Bay to the shores of the St Lawrence around today's Vieux-Québec, thereby saving the smallpox-weakened population from extermination at the hands of the Iroquois. As more French settlers arrived, so the Hurons were successively relocated, ending up here beside the St-Charles River in 1697. Today, with a population of 1600, the central village core of the reserve retains typical Québecois wooden houses with sloping and gabled roofs, but is rather dilapidated – the main activities for visitors are at Onhoüa Chetek8e (see below), though there is also a pretty waterfall.

In nice weather, the best way to get here is by bike – a 25km round trip along the bike path (La Route Vert 6) from the Vieux-Port; all the climbing is on the way there, making the journey back to town an easy cycle. The STCUQ #801 bus runs from Place D'Youville to its terminus at Charlesbourg, from where the #72 goes to Wendake; get a transfer (*une correspondance*) and the 45-minute or so journey will set you back $2.25. The bus arrives at the 1730 church of **Notre Dame-de-Lorette** on boul Bastien. Canada's only Huron church, you'll find snowshoes on the altar and a small museum displaying old manuscripts and religious objects. To visit the church, you must first visit the **Maison Aroüanne** opposite (late June to late Aug daily 10am–5pm; free), an early wooden house

As you'd expect for a region that spends half its life under several feet of snow, winter activities are well developed around Québec City. You'll find good opportunities to just about every imaginable winter sport, particularly **cross-country skiing** and **ice-climbing**, but the most popular activites are **skiing** and **snowboarding** at three varied and challenging ski resorts – Stoneham, Mont-Sainte-Anne and Le Massif, which all lie within easy striking distance of Québec City. All are superbly equipped for intermediate skiers, while beginners will also find many good runs and excellent-value lesson, rental and lift ticket packages. Some experts in search of big bowls and deep powder snow might find the terrain a little limited, but for most, the fine steep mogul fields, tricky glades, well thought-out terrain parks and extensive night-skiing more than compensate. The resorts all get plenty of good snow. Le Massif and Mont-Sainte-Anne in particular are on the front line for storms travelling up the Saint-Lawrence Seaway laden with heavy Atlantic clouds. Yet at all three the combination of wind and busy weekend traffic – all the resorts are primarily day use areas – can polish many runs to an icy glaze.

The resorts

Nearest to town, only 6km beyond the city limits off Rte 73, is the pleasantly casual **Stoneham** (late Nov to early April Mon–Fri 9am–10pm, Sat 8.30am–10pm, Sun 8.30am–9pm; ☎418/848-2415 or 1-800/463-6888, ⒲www.ski-stoneham.com; day pass $36), a locals' mountain with limited expert terrain, but loved for its closeness to the city as well as its position in a wind-protected horseshoe valley – a good place to shelter from cold temperatures and the harsh winds of the region's more brutally cold winter days. Despite a minimal vertical drop of 1,380ft and a modest 322 acres of terrain, the resort has been sculpted into an impressive ski area, thanks in part to its huge night skiing operation, which keeps around two-thirds of the resort open after dark, and attracts crowds from Québec City particularly at weekends, when the après ski can get wild.

The largest of Québec City's major ski areas is **Mont-Sainte-Anne** (mid-Nov to early May Mon–Fri 9am–4pm, Sat 8.30am–4pm, Sun 8.30am–4pm; ☎418/827-4561 or 1-888/827-4579, ⒲www.mont-sainte-anne.com; day pass $47) – 40km away via Rte 440, which becomes Rte 138, northeast out of town. It offers a well-balanced mix of terrain and comprehensive base area facilities. Centred on single peak and covering a mere 428 acres, it's easily navigable yet still provides a remarkably varied high-density trail system. The presence of novice runs extending from summit to base on both sides of the mountain is particularly pleasing, while first-timers can benefit from free access to bunny slopes conveniently adjoining the base area. The resort's greatest strength, however, is its wealth of intermediate-level pistes which make up almost half the ski zone. Most start from the resort's rapid gondola to follow a consistently smooth and steep grade back to the minimal lift queues at its base. The resort's smoothly efficient night-skiing operation even keeps fifteen of these runs open until 10pm. Those hunting for steeps, moguls, trees and high-speed carving will quickly find their niche among a cluster of black diamonds on the south side of the trail map. Here steep terrain ensures empty pistes, even though the fall-line is beautifully even.

The third main mountain in the area is **Le Massif** (late Nov to late April Mon–Fri 9am–4pm, Sat & Sun 8.30am–4pm; Dec and Jan lifts close at 3pm; ☎418/632-5876

displaying a collection of Huron cultural objects, including ceremonial attire beaded with pearls and porcupine quills, drums of moose hide and feathered headdresses used for festive occasions. The waters of the **Chute Kabir–Kouba** tumble into a 42m-deep canyon visible from the bridge just west of the church.

or 1-877/536-2774, ⓦ www.lemassif.com; day pass $42), around an hour's drive from Québec City, 73km along Rte 138. Towering above the majestic ice floes that speckle the vast expanse of the St Lawrence Seaway to the horizon, Le Massif has some of the most spectacular views of any resort in the world, so stunning that it can be distracting as you make your way down the resort's more taxing slopes. In spite of the presence of a couple of narrow, tricky and busy beginner runs, Le Massif is best at providing wonderful intermediate-level carving slopes. In addition, the mountain's painstaking grooming regime puts several black diamond runs well within the capacity of intermediates. But to ski Le Massif's moguls, or its pride, the terrifying triple-diamond La Charlevoix, you'll need plenty of talent and you'll find yourself rubbing shoulders with international athletes on this hugely steep racecourse.

Many **other sports** are also possible: tubing, ice-skating and an indoor climbing wall at Stoneham; and ice-skating, snowshoeing, dog-sledding, paragliding, sleigh riding and snowmobiling at Mont-Sainte-Anne. From mid-December to mid-April the **Mont-Sainte-Anne Nordic Center**, 7km east of the ski area base, is a splendid local resource – the largest of its kind in Canada. It boasts over 223km of trails, of which over half are set up for skating. There are plenty of trails through hardwoods and evergreens, also expert possibilities to ascend and ski down some double-black diamond rated terrain. Day tickets to the network cost $15, rentals another $15, and lessons are also available. For more of a wilderness experience cross-country skiers should also explore the rolling hills around Camp Mercier (see p.314) which are suitable for every level of skier. Back down the highway, and just on the fringes of Québec City at Montmorency Falls (see p.311), is the world's largest **ice-climbing** school, L'Ascensation Ecole d'escalade (☎1-800/762-4967, ⓦ www.rocgyms.com), which charges from around $60 per day to tutor novices.

Practicalities

Both Mont-Sainte-Anne and Stoneham have slopeside **accommodation** with this and ski packages available through their websites, or you can conveniently stay in one of Beaupré's motels (see p.311) most of which also offer ski packages. If you have your own transport and fancy a novel splurge on your accommodation, consider staying in the **Ice Hotel** (☎418/875-4522 or 1-877/505-0423, ⓦ www .icehotel-canada.com; ❼; Jan to early April) in Sainte-Catherine-de-la-Jacques-Cartier, beyond Wendake on Rte 367. Carved afresh each winter from ice and snow, its interior temperatures hover around -5°C, making the deer pelt mattresses and thick sleeping bags all the cosier. Far more convenient are hotels in Québec City (see p.282), which are linked to the resorts via a top-notch **ski shuttle**, the Hiver Express (☎418/525-5191 ⓦ www.taxicoop-quebec.com; round trips $23). Services run the duration of the ski season from sixteen downtown hotels and the tourist information office to both Stoneham and Mont-Sainte-Anne. Le Massif runs a complimentary shuttle designed to link with the Hiver Express service, which departs from Mont-Sainte-Anne's shuttle parking area. Alternatively Hiver Express also takes private bookings for **taxi services**, to the resorts priced at $60 each way per cab. You don't need your own gear, with all three resorts offering stock **equipment for rent** at reasonable prices: skis for around $22/day, snowboards $31. For a better selection of higher end gear and lower prices – allowing significant savings if you're renting for several days – check the stores scattered along the highway in Beaupré.

For a closer look, take the path, which starts at the end of the car park directly opposite the church and leads to the slippery rocks below.

From Maison Aroüanne head along boul Valcartier and past the bike path Vert 6 (there's parking here) to follow signs to the **Onhoüa Chetek8e** site, 575 rue

Stanislas Kosca (daily 9am–5pm; $9; Ⓦ www.huron-wendat.qc.ca), a thirty-minute walk north. This replica of a seventeenth-century Huron village constructed for the benefit of tourists consists of wooden long houses, with Hurons in traditional garb and delicious native foods such as bison, caribou, trout and sunflower soup at the *Nek8arre* restaurant (May–Oct noon–3pm). These are available in six different table d'hôte combinations ($13-20). You're greeted by a traditional welcome dance; participatory activities such as shooting arrows cost extra. The few souvenirs – mini totem poles, suede bags, moccasins and the like – in the shop not made by Huron artisans come from other First Nations reserves.

Lévis

It's hard to think of any commuters who have as pleasant a morning trip as those who cross the St Lawrence from **LÉVIS** to Québec City. Lévis itself is an attractive Victorian town, but the views of Québec make the visit a treat. The regular ferry leaves day and night (until 2am) from near Québec City's Place Royale, and costs $2 ($2.50 June–Sept) for the fifteen-minute crossing – double that if you go back (whether or not you disembark). Most tourists stay on the ferry for the return trip, but those dauntless enough to scale the staircase (five-minutes' walk, to the right as you exit the ferry terminal) to the **Terrasse** on the heights of Lévis are rewarded with an even greater panorama. That vantage point is also accessible via the half-hour bus tour ($1) available at the tourist office in the Lévis terminal.

The Terrasse and its landscaped park lie at the northwestern end of the old quarter, **Vieux-Lévis**, whose main drag, avenue Bégin, has a small-town feel with low-rise modernized buildings. For a quick pastry, sandwich or salad, stop at the café and fine-foods grocery, *Aux P'tits Oignons*, 45 avenue Bégin, or at the patrician house opposite, where you can purchase home-made chocolates and ice cream. The streets between here and the river are wider than those in Québec City, lined with large single-family homes – on rues Notre-Dame, Wolfe and Guénette, look out for examples of elaborate brickwork and ornate roof lines that are as fine as those across the water. The **Maison Alphonse-Desjardins**, 6 rue du Mont-Marie (Mon–Fri 10am–noon & 1–4.30pm; free), is a particular delight with its cake-frosting-like façade facing onto a leafy park whose centrepiece is a statue of Father Joseph David Déziel, founder of Lévis. Inside, a permanent exhibition explains the evolution of the *caisse populaire* (cooperative credit union) in Québec, and the early twentieth-century interior furnishings convey the family lifestyle of the period. From here you can walk east a couple of blocks to rue St-Jean, where a second staircase leads back to the ferry terminal.

Île d'Orléans

From just northeast of Québec City to a short distance beyond Ste-Anne-de-Beaupré, the St Lawrence is bottlenecked by the **ÎLE D'ORLÉANS**, a fertile islet whose bucolic atmosphere and handy location have made it a popular spot for holiday-making Québecois. More than most places on the mainland, Île d'Orléans, with its old stone churches, little cottages and seigneurial manors, has kept a flavour of eighteenth-century French Canada. This is largely because it was cut off from the mainland until 1935, when a suspension bridge was constructed from Hwy 440, about 10km out of the city, connecting it to the west end of the island.

To its first inhabitants, the **Algonquins**, the island was known as Minigo, which means "enchanting place". Jacques Cartier christened it Île de Bacchus because the wild grapes he saw here were "such as we had seen nowhere else in the world". (He was soon to change the name to Île d'Orléans in honour of the king's son.) Tourism and agriculture are the mainstays for the population of seven thousand: roadside stalls heave under the weight of fresh fruit and vegetables, jams, dairy products, home-made bread and maple syrup, and the island's restaurants and B&Bs are some of the best in the province, thanks to the supplies from local farms.

Around the island

Encircling the island, the 67-kilometre Hwy 368 – called the Chemin Royal for most of its length – dips and climbs over gentle slopes and terraces past acres of neat farmland and orchards, passing through the six villages with their churches evenly spaced around the island's periphery.

Following a counter-clockwise route around the island, the first village you come to is **STE-PÉTRONILLE**, the island's oldest and most beautifully situated settlement and a district still characterized by the grand homes of the merchants who made their fortunes trading farm produce with Québec City. Wolfe observed the city from this spot before his bombardment. The white **Maison Gourdeau-de-Beaulieu** at no. 137 chemin Royal was the island's first permanent dwelling, built in 1648 and still the private residence of the Beaulieu family. Some of the best views can be had from rue Horatio Walker, named after the landscape painter who had his home and studio here. Known unofficially as the grand seigneur of Ste-Pétronille, **Horatio Walker** lived here from 1904 until his death in 1938. He despised his English heritage, continually emphasizing a French branch in his ancestry and refusing to speak English. His subject matter was almost entirely based on the Île d'Orléans, which he viewed as a "sacred temple of the muses and a gift of the gods". Many of his paintings now grace Canada's larger galleries. Until the 1950s the south shore of the island was the domain of sailors and navigators, with the village of **ST-LAURENT** being the island's supplier of *chaloupes*, the long rowing boats that were the islanders' only means of getting to the mainland before the bridge was built. At the **Parc maritime de St-Laurent interpretation centre**, 120 chemin de la Chalouperie (May to mid-June & early Sept to mid-Oct Sat & Sun 10am–5pm; mid-June to early Sept daily 10am–5pm; $2), you can get details of attractions like **La Forge à Pique-Assaut**, 2200 ave Royale (June to mid-Oct daily 9am–5pm; rest of year Mon–Fri 9am–noon & 1.30–5pm; free), which features a blacksmith's shop and an eighteenth-century bellows and sells forged metal crafts.

ST-JEAN, on the east side of the island, was similarly nautical; the cemetery of its red-roofed local church contains gravestones of numerous mariners. In the prettiest village on the island, most of the mid-eighteenth-century mariners' homes have dormer windows and wide porches, with Victorian-inspired filigree. St-Jean's museum of antique furniture and domestic objects, housed in the stately 1734 **Manoir Mauvide-Genest**, 1451 Royal ($5). At this one-time home of Louis XV's surgeon, the metre-thick walls withstood the impact from Wolfe's bombardment – you can still see dents in the wall. From St-Jean, the road continues to the island's easterly tip and the village of **ST-FRANÇOIS**, where a precarious observation tower offers a view of both shores of the St Lawrence. The village church was rebuilt in the early 1990s after a suicidal driver wrecked the 1734 church; the wall in front was added to avoid a repeat. Among the French-Regime stone buildings in **STE-FAMILLE**, the **Maison Canac-Marquis**, 4466 chemin Royal, is a particularly fine example, but only the 1675 **Maison Drouin**, at no. 4700 (late

June to early Sept daily 10am–6pm; early Sept to Oct daily 10am–6pm; $2), with its exhibits on the architecture of these early houses, is open to the public. The richly decorated **church**, built in 1743, includes a painting of the Holy Family by Québec's foremost early painter, Frère Luc. **ST-PIERRE**, to the west of Ste-Famille, is notable for its **church**, the oldest in rural Québec; constructed in 1718, it has pews with special hot-brick holders for keeping bottoms warm on seats. The town, by far the largest on the island, is however best know as the long-time home and final resting place of Félix Leclerc (1914-88), the poet and singer–songwriter who penned "P'tit Bonheur" and the first musician to bring Québecois music international acclaim. The **Espace Félix Leclerc**, 682 Chemin Royal (mid-Feb to mid-Dec Tues–Sun 9am–6pm; $3) covers a site that not only pays homage to the life and work of Leclerc, but also has several hiking trails and picnic tables.

Practicalities

The island's **information office**, 490 côte du Pont (☎418/828-9411, Ⓦ www.iledorleans.qc.ca), is on the right at the top of the hill after the bridge from the mainland. It's well set up for finding a B&B; it has descriptions with photos and prices and a free phone for bookings. Properties have numbers corresponding to roadside plaques that are marked on an adequate map in the *l'Île d'Orléans Tourist Guide* ($1), which also lists other stops of interest. The centre also has self-guided driving tours (cassette or CD; English available) for $10. Budget travellers wanting to stay on the island should head straight for *Auberge Le P'tit Bonheur*, 183–186 Côte Lafleur (☎418/829-2588), a **hostel** in an old stone manor with dorm beds ($18) and bike and cross-country ski rental. For others the choice is more bewildering, but of good **B&Bs** try *Le Vieux Presbytère*, 1247 ave Monseigneur D'esgly (☎418/828-9723 or 1-888/828-9723, Ⓦ www.presbytere.com; ❸), in St-Pierre – a charming inn with low ceilings, beams and antiques in an old presbytery just behind the village church. It has terrific river views and rents bicycles ($6/hr, $25/day). In Ste-Pétronille try to get a room in the often-full *Gîte le 91 du Bout de l'Île*, 91 chemin du Bout de l'Île (☎418/828-2678; ❸), a clean and cosy spot with a view of the Chute Montmorency from the garden. To **camp** head to St-François, to the lovely and convenient *Camping Orléans*, 357 chemin Royal (☎418/829-2953; $25 unserviced, $38 for hookup; mid-May to early Oct), near the village jetty, which has a small onsite pool.

The island is replete with **restaurants** serving fine French cuisine, but particularly good bets are *La Goéliche*, 22 chemin du Quai (☎418/828-2248; ❺), in Ste-Pétronille, where table d'hôte starts at $25 and always includes great views. In St-Laurent, *Canard Huppé*, 2198 Chem Royal (☎418/828-2292) is a gourmand's treat with local duck, trout and maple on the menu. *Le Vieux Presbytère* (see above) in St-Pierre also has a good restaurant that serves game dishes. *Le Bistro de bout de l'Île*, 148 du Bout de l'Île opposite rue Horatio Walker in Ste-Pétronille, serves salads, pizza and *croque monsieur* (all around $10). The *Chocolaterie* in the basement has exquisite chocolates and ice creams – a good accompaniment to a stroll along the rocky waterfront here. In St-Laurent, beside the Parc Maritime interpretation centre, the open-air seafood restaurant *Les Honerdises de l'Île* is on the waterfront; the table d'hôte menu is $11. On the opposite side of the island in Ste-Famille the local *boulangerie*, G.H. Blouin, 3967 chemin Royal, is one of the island's oldest and best, with mouthwatering bread and pastries. Next door, *Café de mon Village* (May–Oct) serves cheap snacks and a pricier table d'hôte on a terrace overlooking the river.

Côte-de-Beaupré

Dubbed the "coast of fine meadows" by Jacques Cartier, the **Côte-de-Beaupré** stretches along the St Lawrence past the **Basilique de Ste-Anne-de-Beaupré**, 40km northeast of Québec City, as far as the migratory bird sanctuary on Cap Tourmente, where you can see the greater snow goose in spring and autumn. There are two roads along the coast: the speedy Autoroute Dufferin-Montmorency (Hwy 440, then Hwy 138) and the slower Avenue Royale (Hwy 360), which is served by local buses. The latter gives a far better introduction to the province's rural life, passing through little villages with ancient farmhouses and churches lining the way. Beyond Ste-Anne-de-Beaupré, Hwy 360 leads to one of the best ski resorts in the province – **Mont Ste-Anne** (see box p.306), which has everything from golf to world-championship mountain biking in summer.

Chute Montmorency

Some 9km northeast of Québec City the waters of the Montmorency River cascade 83m down from the Laurentians into the St Lawrence, which makes the **Chute Montmorency** one and a half times the height of Niagara, though the volume of water is considerably less. The falls, named by Champlain in honour of the governor of New France, were the site of Wolfe's first attempt on the colony. However, Wolfe and his men were driven off by Montcalm's superior forces. In those days – before a hydroelectric dam cut off much of the flow – the falls were far more impressive, but the cascade remains an awesome spectacle, especially in winter, when the water and spray become a gigantic cone of ice, known locally as the "sugar loaf". Inevitably, the falls attract droves of tourists, especially now that the site has been thoroughly developed. From the main car park ($7.50), a **cable car** (Feb to mid-April Sat & Sun 9am–4pm; mid-April to Oct daily 8.15am–7pm except mid-June to Aug until 9pm; closed Nov–Jan; $5.50 one-way, $7.50 return) shoots up to the **interpretation centre** (daily 9am–8pm; June–Aug until 10pm; ⓦ www.chutemontmorency .qc.ca; free), in the Manoir Montmorency, which also has a bar and restaurant with a terrace. You can also walk up to the centre, but be warned this involves 487 steps. From the centre, a cliffside walkway leads to the bridge over the falls (wooded trails follow the river upstream) and onto the zigzag path down the other side. Local STCUQ bus #53 stops at the bottom of the falls, #50 at the top; both buses leave from Place Jacques-Cartier in Québec and take around fifty minutes, each costing $2.25. You can also cycle here – 25km round-trip from the Vieux-Port, and the path passes the **Domaine Maizerets** park, where you can have a pleasant break.

Ste-Anne-de-Beaupré

Québec's equivalent of Lourdes, the **Basilique de Ste-Anne-de-Beaupré**, 39km northeast of Québec City (25min by Intercar coach from Gare Centrale; 3 daily; $6), dominates the immediate area, its twin spires soaring proudly above the St Lawrence shore. The church began in 1658 as a small wooden chapel devoted to St Anne (the Virgin Mary's mother). During its construction a crippled peasant was cured. The legend of St Anne's intercession really got going, though, when some Breton sailors were caught in a storm on the St Lawrence in 1661 and vowed to build a chapel to St Anne if she saved them. The ship capsized at nearby Cap Tourmente but the sailors survived. Word of this miracle spread, and from then on everyone caught in the St Lawrence's frequent storms prayed to St Anne and donated *ex votos* to the shrine. In 1876, the same year that St Anne was declared patron saint of Québec, the church was distinguished as a basilica (or pilgrimage church), to which the devout came on their knees from the beach or walked shoeless from Québec City; now, one and a half million pilgrims flock to the site every year in comfortable coachloads.

The neo-Romanesque granite cathedral with lofty symmetrical spires is the fifth church to stand here, fires and floods having destroyed the first four. The statue of St Anne between the steeples miraculously survived the 1922 destruction of the fourth church, even though the roof and both steeples fell in the blaze. The basilica seats 1500, though on St Anne's feast day (July 26) up to 5000 pilgrims crowd inside. Most of its decoration – countless stained-glass windows and massive murals – depict the miraculous powers of St Anne, though the wooden pews bear delightful animal carvings. Behind the ornate golden statue of St Anne, depicted holding her daughter Mary, is a chapel said to contain a portion of Anne's forearm, donated by the pope in 1960. Those who have been cured by her intervention have left a vast collection of crutches and wooden limbs hanging on the basilica's pillars near the entrance. The **information centre** in front of the basilica (daily: 8.30am–4.30pm; Ⓦwww.ssadb.qc.ca) runs pious, free, guided tours daily at 1pm from the basilica entrance. The hours of the basilica itself vary, but it is open 8am–4.30pm at a minimum, and 6am–10pm at the height of the mid-summer pilgrimage. The church is open to all even during Mass although photos are prohibited at that time. The information centre has a schedule of Masses conducted in English.

Several little chapels cringe in the basilica's shadow. The simple **Chapelle Souvenir** (early May to mid-Sept daily 8am–7pm), across the street behind the basilica, contains some of the stones from the second chapel and was built in the nineteenth century on the foundations of the transept of the third church (1676–1877), hence its north–south orientation. Nearby, the small white chapel of the **Scala Santa** (same hours) contains stairs that replicate those climbed by Christ on his meeting with Pontius Pilate. Glass boxes, embedded in each stair, contain lumps of earth from various holy places, and the devout accomplish the ascent on their knees. Another obligatory part of the penitential route is the nearby **Way of the Cross**, which curves steeply up the hillside. There are two daytime processions, and on some summer evenings torch-lit processions wend their way through each station. Less athletic visitors can pay their respects to the basilica's collection of *ex votos* and treasures in the **Musée de Ste-Anne** (mid-April to mid-Oct daily 10am–5pm; $2), which contains displays on the early churches and some of the surviving furnishings.

The vaguely Middle Eastern building at the other end of the car park contains the **Cyclorama de Jerusalem** (daily: late April to June & Sept–Oct 9am–6pm; July–Aug 9am–8pm; Ⓦwww.cyclorama.com; $6), an enormous 360-degree painting set at the time of Christ's crucifixion. It has been there longer than the present basilica, though the 3D cutouts were added in the 1950s in a misguided attempt to make it more realistic.

Practicalities

There's a glut of inexpensive **motels** sprawling along Rte 138 in Ste-Anne-de-Beaupré, with prices and standards fairly uniform between them. *Motel St Löis,* 9657 Boulevard Ste-Anne (Ⓣ418/827-4298 or 1-800/736-4298, Ⓦmotelstlouis.com; ❸), is a basic and scrupulously clean motel with ugly 1970s furnishings. Alternatives to motels include random **camping** opposite the basilica itself and several pleasant **B&Bs**, including *Auberge Baker,* 8790 av

Royale (☎418/824-4478 or 1-866/824-4478, ⓦwww.auberge-baker.qc.ca; ❹), a wonderfully atmospheric B&B occupying a 150-year-old farmhouse set well back from the busy Rte 138. Rooms have rough-hewn beams and gloriously mismatched antique furnishings; guests have use of a communal kitchen. More central in Ste-Anne-de-Beaupré, *Auberge La Camarine*, 10947 boul Ste-Anne (☎418/827-5703 or 1-800/567-3939, ⓦwww.camarine.com; ❸), offers pleasant hotel units, stylishly decorated with surreal art, in a large wooden lodge beside Rte 138. Many are equipped with wood-burning fires. The inn's **restaurant** (☎418/827-1958; 6–8.30pm only) is the best in the area, serving an eclectic variety of French, Italian and Asian dishes, often fused and off a frequently changing menu. The food is of the highest standard, so expect a meal to cost $45–70 per head, excluding drinks. Reservations are essential. For more modest prices but almost as satisfying a meal try *Auberge Baker* (see above), a classy but relaxed restaurant serving hearty traditional items: *Migneron de bai St Paul* ($6.50), a local cheese in filo pastry with maple syrup sauce, earthy yellow pea soup ($4) and entrees that include meat pies, pork meatball stew, duck or salmon (around $16). The $27 table d'hôte keeps tabs on spending.

Mont-Sainte-Anne and around

On the fringes of Beaupré, the **MONT STE-ANNE** ski resort (see box p.306) has successfully marketed itself as an off-season destination and it's now the longest-standing venue on the **mountain bike** world-cup circuit. In summer you can explore the extensive cross-country mountain bike trails ($8), either staying around the base area to test your trials skills on the North-Shore-style wooden obstacles ($13), or using the gondola ($24 per day) to explore one of the hardest downhill mountain bike courses in the world – though there are easier routes down the mountain too. Bikes can be rented at the base area by the hour with front-suspension mountain bikes going for $35 for two hours; full-suspension for $45. The gondola up the mountain is also open to and hikers wanting to enjoy the remarkable views over the St Lawrence and Québec City as well as several marked trails. But one of the best hiking trails leaves out of the car park at the base area – head down the hill and over the bridge – to the **Chutes Jean-Larouse**, a twenty-minute walk. The trail leads to a series of dramatic waterfalls, though the latticework stairway that's been constructed alongside is just as dizzying and almost more impressive. The resort also operates a respectable golf course, and has a pleasant campsite (☎418/827-5281 or 1-800/463-1568; $24). At the resort, *Au Café Suisse*, 1805 boul Les Neiges (☎418/826-2184), is a twee place with fondues (from $20), raclettes ($24) and some more unusual items like Japanese-style steak with noodles and a curry broth.

For even grander waterfalls head some 6km east of Ste-Anne-de-Beaupré along Hwy 138 to **Canyon Ste-Anne** (daily: May to late June & early Sept to Oct 9am–5.30pm; late June to early Sept 8.30am–6.30pm; $7; ⓦwww .canyonste-anne.qc.ca) about a thirty-minute drive from Québec City. Here, the river has carved a gorge where the water tumbles 74m in a waterfall flanked by a chasm fringed with woodlands and short nature trails. A bridge crosses just before the precipice, giving views down the canyon, while in front of the falls a precarious suspension bridge allows for splendid and terrifying views. With your own transport you can head 2km from the canyon towards the coast via Saint-Joachim to the **Cap-Tourmente National Wildlife Area** ($5). It's a favourite with snow geese, who stop to gather strength on its sandbars during their spring and autumn migrations. Another 250 species of bird also inhabit the park and naturalists are on hand to answer questions.

Réserve Faunique des Laurentides

The zone of the Laurentians 40km to the north of Québec City – via Hwy 73 and 175 – is considerably wilder than the mountains near Montréal, thanks to the creation of the **Réserve Faunique des Laurentides**. The vast wooded terrain, with summits of more than 1000m towards the east, was once a hunting ground of the Montagnais, until the Hurons, armed by the French, drove the small population further north. The wildlife reserve became a protected area in 1895 to conserve the caribou herds, an intervention that was not a great success – very few exist today. However, though it allows controlled moose-hunting, the reserve's main function is still to preserve native animals such as the beaver, moose, lynx, black bear and deer, all of which you may see in remote areas. Intercar (☎418/525-3000 or 1-888/861-4592) runs a **bus** service through the park from Québec City's bus station to Alma (3 daily; 2hr 45min) and Chicoutimi (4–5 daily; 2hr 30min).

In 1981, the southernmost portion of the reserve was set off as the **Parc de la Jacques–Cartier** ($3.50). A visitor centre (mid-May to late Oct), 10km from Hwy 175, serves as the gateway to the Jacques–Cartier river valley, enclosed by 550m-high forested slopes. The park is ideal for canoeing, although the river runs beside the road for most of the way, detracting from the wilderness experience. Rent canoes, kayaks, inflatable rafts and bicycles from Les Excursions Jacques–Cartier (☎418/848-7272), who also manage the park's **campsites**. Pitches are available from $16.50, both near the visitor centre and in more peaceful spots further into the park.

The reserve proper ($3.50) begins further north along Hwy 175 where **Camp Mercier** (daily 8.30am–4pm; ☎418/848-2422 or 1-800/665-6527, ⓦwww.sepaq.com) near its southern perimeter gives out **information**. The heavy snowfall makes the park an excellent place for cross-country skiing on a 192km network ($6/day). Hwy 175 traverses the reserve; halfway through is **L'Étape**, the only spot to fill your tank (or yourself) until just before Chicoutimi or Alma. Nearby there's **camping** beside Lac Jacques–Cartier at the *La Loutre* campsite (☎418/846-2201; $18), and chalets available ($80 for two).

Northern Québec

Northern Québec stretches out as two separated entities on either side of the St Lawrence, connected by a series of ferries over the immense estuary; this means you can explore one shore then plot a varied return trip on the other. The southern shore is the less remote, with the agricultural **Bas Saint-Laurent** (Lower St Lawrence) the gateway to the rugged and lightly populated **Gaspé Peninsula**. East of here, stuck out in the middle of the Gulf of St Lawrence, the **Îles-de-la-Madeleine** are most easily reached by ferry from Prince Edward Island (see p.451). This windswept archipelago has majestic, treeless landscapes, fringed by fine beaches and crazily eroded sandstone cliffs, and appeals particularly to cyclists, walkers and people who just want to lie on a beach in complete solitude.

Tourist information in northern Québec

The areas to the north of Québec City and the offshore islands are divided into the following regional tourist associations, each providing an excellent free guide including basic maps of the region. All the main offices in each region will usually have a stock of guides for other regions. For general information, contact Tourisme Québec ☎514/873-2015 or 1-877/266-5687, ⊛www.bonjourquebec.com.

Bas Saint-Laurent ☎418/867-3015 or 1-800/563-5268, ⊛www.tourismebas-st-laurent.com.

Charlevoix ☎418/665-4454 or 1-800/667-2276, ⊛www.tourisme-charlevoix.com.

Cote Nord ⊛www.tourismecote-nord.com, Manicouagan ☎418/294-2876 or 1-888/463-5319, Duplessis ☎418/962-0808 or 1-888/463-0808.

Gaspésie ☎418/775-2223 or 1-800/463-0323, ⊛www.tourisme-gaspesie.com.

Îles-de-la-Madeleine ☎418/986-2245 or 1-877/624-4437, ⊛www.tourismeilesdelamadeleine.com.

Saguenay–Lac-Saint-Jean ☎418/543-9778 or 1-877/253-8387, ⊛www.tourismesaguenaylacsaintjean.qc.ca.

The rest of the region spreads out north of the St Lawrence. Québec's **north** is a mighty, inhospitable tundra inhabited only by mining communities, groups of Inuit and the hardy characters who staff the hydroelectric installations with which so many of the rivers are dammed. The only readily accessible region, along the north shore of the St Lawrence and its main tributary, the **Saguenay**, covers an area that changes from trim farmland to a vast forest bordering the barren seashore. Immediately northeast of Québec City is the beautiful **Charlevoix** region of peaceful villages and towns that bear the marks of Québec's rural beginnings – both in the architecture of the seigneurial regime and in the layout of the land. Often the winding highways and back roads pass through a virtually continuous village, where the only interruptions in the chain of low-slung houses are the tin-roofed churches. The beguiling hills and valleys give way to dramatic ravaged rock just beyond the Charlevoix borders, where the **Saguenay River** crashes into the immense fjord that opens into the St Lawrence at the resort of **Tadoussac**. Protected as a marine park these waters are popular for whale-watching, the adjacent cliffs superb for hiking. Inland, **Lac Saint-Jean** – source of the Saguenay – is an oasis of fertile land in a predominantly rocky region, and its peripheral villages offer glimpses of native as well as Québecois life. Adventurous types following the St Lawrence can head beyond Tadoussac along the **Côte Nord** through a desolate, sparsely populated region where the original livelihoods of fishing and lumber have largely given way to ambitious mining and hydroelectric projects. The remoteness of Gulf of St Lawrence islands such as the **Île d'Anticosti** and the sculptured terrain of the **Mingan archipelago** – a national park, well served by boats from Havre-St-Pierre – is matched by the isolation of the fishing communities along the **Lower North Shore**, where no roads penetrate and visits are possible only by supply ship, plane or snowmobile.

Bas Saint-Laurent and Gaspé Peninsula

Heading east from Québec City along the southern shore of the **St Lawrence**, the most scenic route is Hwy 132, which sticks close to the

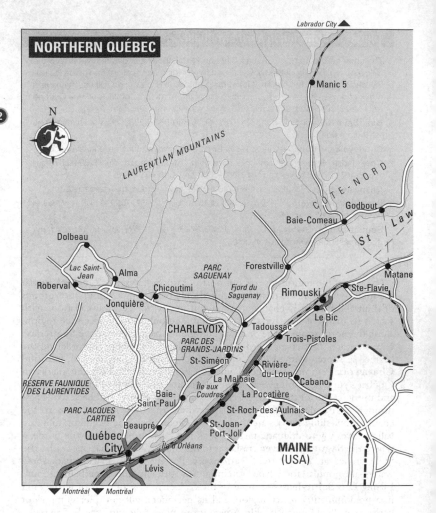

NORTHERN QUÉBEC

shoreline showcasing the highlights of a region of fertile lands with farming and forestry covering gently rolling hills. The landscape is an agricultural one and dominated by long, narrow fields that are remnants of the old seigneurial system (see box, p.319), and the road passes through a string of quiet villages overshadowed by their oversized Catholic churches. The three stops worth making on the 180-kilometre trip to Rivière-Du-Loup are at the woodcarving centre of **St-Jean-Port-Joli**, the seigneurial **St-Roche-des-Aulnaies** and the architecturally quaint **Kamouraska**.

Running parallel to Hwy 132, the Trans-Canada (Hwy 20) is a much faster route to the attractive town of **Rivière-du-Loup**, effectively the start of the **Gaspé Peninsula**. Bounded by the Gulf of St Lawrence to the north and west, and by the Baie des Chaleurs to the south and east, the Gaspé Peninsula is roughly 550km long, with a chain of mountains and rolling highlands dominating the interior and the northern shore. It has always been sparsely inhabited and poor, its remote communities eking out an existence from the

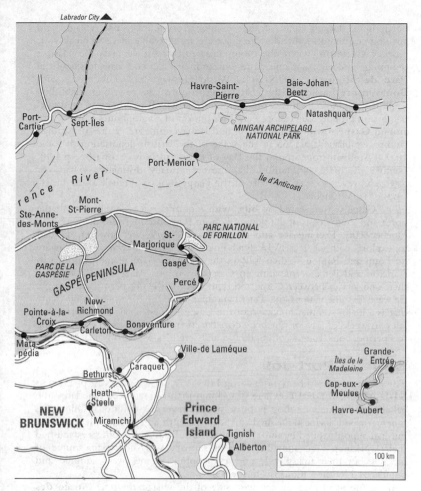

turbulent seas and the rocky soil. But the landscape provides some wonderful scenery. Forested hills cut with deep ravines and vistas of craggy mountains tumble to a jagged coastline fronted by the St Lawrence where the winding coastal drive along Hwy 132 is a delight. The principal towns strung along this shore – **Rimouski**, **Matane** and **Gaspé** – are less appealing than its many smaller villages or the peninsula's two outstanding parks: the extravagantly mountainous **Parc de la Gaspésie**, inland from **Ste-Anne-des-Monts**, and the **Parc National de Forillon**, at the tip of the peninsula, with its mountain and coastal hikes and wonderfully rich wildlife. Just to the south of the Forillon park, the village of **Percé** is famous for the offshore **Rocher Percé**, an extraordinary limestone monolith that has been a magnet for travellers for more than a hundred years.

The **south coast** of the peninsula runs along the **Baie des Chaleurs**, a long wedge of sheltered ocean with relatively warm waters that separates the Gaspé from New Brunswick. For the most part, it's flatter and duller than the north here, though some of the seaside resorts-cum-fishing villages and farming communities that dot the coast are an agreeable place to break your journey. **Carleton**, where the mountains return to tower over the coast, is tempting, especially as it's near the extraordinary fish and plant fossils of the **Parc de Miguasha**, a UNESCO World Heritage Site. This, along with **Bonaventure** further up the coast, is also one of the few long-established English-speaking settlements on the peninsula which is otherwise predominantly and proudly Québecois – another pocket of Anglophones exists in and around **Gaspé** town. Both Carleton and Bonaventure are centres of Acadian culture, established in 1755 in the wake of the British deportation of some 10,000 Acadians from around the Bay of Fundy in Nova Scotia (see p.408). Neither of these communities has created visually distinctive villages or towns, however, so even this part of the Gaspé looks as French as the heartlands of rural Québec.

The Gaspé is well served by **bus**, with regular services travelling both the north and south coasts of the peninsula from Rimouski, Rivière-du-Loup and Québec City. The interior and the peninsula's parks are, however, difficult to explore without a car. VIA Rail links Montréal by **train** with Rivière du Loup and Rimouski, then follows the southern coast of the peninsula to Carleton and Percé, terminating in Gaspé town after more than 17 hours – there's no service between Gaspé and Rimouski on the northern coast, though. Be warned: some stations (like Percé) are miles from the towns they serve. Note that as a major summer holiday spot the Gaspé gets especially busy during the last two weeks of July for Québec's **construction holiday**; if you travel during this period, book your accommodation and activities well in advance.

St-Jean-Port-Joli

The first settlement of any note along Hwy 132, some 80km east of Lévis, is **ST-JEAN-PORT-JOLI**, where the long main street accommodates the galleries of the region's most popular **woodcarvers**. A traditional Québecois folk art, woodcarving flourished in the eighteenth and nineteenth centuries, but had almost expired by the 1930s, when the Bourgault brothers established their workshop here. Initially, religious statuary was their main source of income, but their folksy style and Francophile themes were adopted and popularized by the nationalists in the 1960s.

Along the main road, on the west side of the village, the ugly **Musée des Anciens Canadiens**, 332 ave de Gaspé ouest (May–June & Sept–Oct daily 9am–5.30pm; July & Aug 8.30am–9pm; $5), has an interesting collection of woodcarvings cut in white pine and walnut, many of which are the work of the Bourgaults. The most impressive piece is the giant *Les Patriotes*, a tribute to the Québecois rebels of 1837 who, under the leadership of Louis-Joseph Papineau, tried to drive out the British (see p.264). The studied romance of the woodcarving bears little relation to the actual rebellion, though, which was badly organized and easily suppressed. A few doors down the same road at no. 322, the **Maison Médard-Bourgault** (mid-June to early Sept daily 10am–6pm; $4) concentrates on the life and work of Médard Bourgault. He was the most talented of the brothers – he even carved the walls and furniture. The delicate and ornate interior of the village church, **Église St-Jean Baptiste** at no. 2, celebrates the work of an earlier generation of Québecois woodcarvers from the 1770s, the Baillairgé brothers. Any of the dozen or so galleries along the main road sell woodcarvings; the shop adjoining the museum is one of the best.

There are some pleasant **B&B**s, of which *La Maison de L'Ermitage*, 56 rue de l'Ermitage (☎418/598-7553; ❹), has a lovely, turreted, red and white roof – if you're feeling particularly flush you can stay in one of the turrets (❺). Numerous motels line Hwy 132, but one of the cheapest options is the **campsite** *De La Demi-Lieue*, on the grounds of a former seigneury farther down the road at no. 589 Hwy 132 est (☎418/598-6108 or 1-800/463-9558; $19–23; May–Oct). For **food** try the inexpensive *La Boustifaille*, 547 Ave de Gaspé ouest, for gigantic portions of Québecois fare, or the pricier *Café la Coureuse des Greves*, 300 Hwy 204, where tables are arranged on a lushly flowered outdoor terrace and good breakfasts served. For upscale regional dining with views of the river, try the *Auberge du Faubourg*, 280 Hwy 132 ouest.

St-Roch-des-Aulnaies and beyond

About 14km east of St-Jean-Port-Joli is the village of **ST-ROCH-DES-AULNAIES**, where a gorgeous water mill and manor house have survived on a nineteenth-century seigneurial estate formerly the home of a rich merchant. Offering a fascinating glimpse into that era, **La Seigneurie des Aulnaies** (late May to early Sept daily 9am–6pm; $6), is named after the alder trees that grow along the banks of the Ferrée River. The river powered Québec's largest bucket wheel in the estate's three-storey communal grist mill. Now refurbished and in full working order, the mill has frequent flour-grinding displays and mouth-watering muffins and pancakes in the café. Just upstream from the mill, the veranda-wrapped manor house has period rooms, guides in costume and diverting interactive displays on the seigneurial system. A few minutes' drive from St-Roch, agricultural **LA POCATIÈRE** sits on a ridge above the coastal plain, bereft of charm. It's worth stopping if you want information on the Bas Saint-Laurent region that stretches from here to Rimouski. The **information centre** is at exit 439 from Hwy 20 (daily; late June to early Sept 9am–8pm; mid-May to late June & early Sept to mid-Oct 9am–5pm), and signposted from Hwy 132.

The seigneurial system

In the seventeenth century the agricultural settlement of New France – now Québec – was conceived as an extension of European-style feudalism with the granting of **seigneuries** to religious orders, nobleman, merchants and, in a break from tradition, others of humble birth. The average seigneury covered around fifty square kilometres and part of the land was owned by the seigneurs, the rest rented by **habitants**, who were secure in their tenancy (they could sell the land and pass it on to their children) provided they met certain obligations. They had to pay a yearly tithe for the upkeep of the parish church, pay rent in kind (usually grain, as the seigneurs had a monopoly on milling), work on the roads and make themselves available for the militia.

In the early days the waterways provided the easiest form of transportation and so each *habitant's* farm had a river frontage of around a couple of hundred metres in length, with the rest of his land extending back in a narrow strip. One result of this was that *habitants* lived near their neighbours and, content with this decentralized way of life, long resisted the development of nuclear settlements. You can still see these ribbon farms and villages, which are very much in evidence along the St Lawrence today.

The seigneurial system was **abolished** in 1854 by legislation that passed land-ownership rights to the *habitants*.

Some 40km further east along Hwy 132 is **KAMOURASKA**, a pretty village where well-heeled citizens of Québec City once congregated to take the air. While they no longer visit to the same degree, it's not for lack of good air, which still has its way with the town's current residents, many of whom live to more than 100 years of age. The village boasts many examples of the Bas-St-Laurent region's most distinctive architectural feature, the Kamouraska roof. Extended to keep the rainwater off the walls, the arched and rounded eaves project from the houses in a design borrowed from the shipyards. One of the best examples is the **Villa St-Louis**, at 125 ave Morel, a private residence that was once the home of Adolphe Basile-Routhier, the man who scripted the words to Canada's national anthem. You may also spot several nets attached to wooden stakes emerging out of the river – these ensnare eels, traditionally the village's economic mainstay. Learn something about the industry at the slightly bizarre **Site d'interprétation de l'anguille**, 205 ave Morel (June to mid-Oct daily 9am–6pm; $5); aside from a barn filled with nets, there's not much to see here except the taxidermy collection of various non-eel animals ensnared in the nets, which is particularly morbid. The enormous **Palais de Justice**, 111 ave Morel (June–Oct daily 9am–noon & 1–5pm; $3), at the centre of town, once served as the region's superior court, but today merely displays early registries, maps and various pictures of the village. A better collection of arte-facts – crockery, farming tools and the like – is at the **Musée de Kamouraska**, 69 ave Morel (June to mid-Oct daily 9am–5pm; mid-Oct to mid-Dec hours vary; $4), housed in a former convent. Kamouraska has a host of charming **B&Bs**. *Gîte Chez Nicole et Jean*, at 81 ave Morel (☎418/492-2921; ❹), is one of the best, with cheerful rooms and a bountiful breakfast of regional and organic food. For views of the river, try the simple *Motel Cap Blanc*, 300 ave Morel (☎418/492-2919; ❸). A fine **bakery** is at no. 82 ave Morel, and there's a **café** at no. 88, while *Au Relais de Kamouraska* at no. 253 (☎418/492-6246) is a family-orientated restaurant and a good place to sample the local eel.

Rivière-du-Loup

A prosperous-looking place, whose hilly centre is complete with broad streets and handsome Victorian villas, **RIVIÈRE-DU-LOUP** owes its development to the timber industry and the coming of the railway in 1859. This established Rivière-du-Loup as a crossroads for traffic between the Maritimes, the Gaspé peninsula and the rest of Québec. Its significance as an administrative and commercial centre has grown accordingly and today it has a population of around 18,000.

Boat trips from Rivière-du-Loup

Rivière-du-Loup is a good place for **boat trips** on the St Lawrence River. Beginning at around $40 per person, these excursions are not cheap, but they are well organ-ized and you may see beluga, minke and finback whales throughout the summer. All the companies are located by the marina at 200 rue Hayward; Croisières AML (☎418/867-3361 or 1-800/563-4643) specializes in three-hour **whale-watching** trips on large boats, while Exceptionelle Aventure (☎418/862-7775) takes in the river's aquatic life in twelve-person zodiacs – inflatable raft-type boats that get you very close to the whales. Alternatively, La Société Duvetnor (☎418/867-1660, ⓦwww.duvetnor.com; June–Oct) has daily cruises to various midstream sea-bird and mammal sanctuaries, with overnight stops offered ($20–185 per person; reservations required).

The river that gives the place its name crashes down a thirty-metre drop close to the centre, at the top of rue Frontenac, near **Parc de la Croix Lumineuse**, which offers a panoramic view of the mountains on the north shore. The town's **waterfall** is disappointing, however: although it generates a lot of noise and spray, even the specially built platform that crosses it fails to make the view enthralling. Similarly modest are the town's three museums. The central **Musée du Bas-St-Laurent**, 300 rue St-Pierre (June–Sept daily 10am–6pm; Oct–May Mon & Wed 6–9pm, Tues & Thurs–Sun 1–5pm; $5), combines ethnological displays of the region with historical exhibits and works of modern art by local artists. On the eastern edge of town the **Musée des Carillons**, 393 rue Témiscouata (late June to early Sept daily 9am–8pm; Sept & Oct daily 9am–5pm; $5), is a unique collection of 250 bells of all types from around the world. The **Musée de bateaux miniatures et légendes du Bas-St-Laurent**, 80 boul Cartier (late June to early Sept daily 8.30am–10pm; May, June & early Sept to Oct daily 10am–8.30pm; $4), houses an interesting collection of model boats built by local craftspeople. If you're interested in the architectural heritage pick up the interpretation booklet ($1) from the **tourist office**, at 189 boul de l'Hôtel-de-Ville, and stroll round the centre: although there's nothing special, it's a pleasant way to pass an hour. The most intriguing historical site in town is **Le Manoir Fraser**, 32 rue Fraser (late June to mid-Oct daily 10am–5pm; $4), the home of Seigneur Fraser; instead of costumed guides, a computer-animated seigneur introduces you to his life and times. The red-brick manor house also has a fancy tearoom and garden.

Highway 132 runs through the centre of Rivière-du-Loup. The town's **bus station** is on boul Cartier, beside the junction of Hwys 132 and 20, about ten minutes' walk northeast of the centre. The **train** station (☎1-888/842-7245) is on Rue La-fontaine and Rue Fraserville and only open when VIA Rail trains arrive here from destinations including Montréal, Gaspé and Halifax. A **car ferry** (Jan & mid-April to Dec 2–5 trips daily; 65min; ☎418/862-5094, ⊛www.travrdlstsim.com; $11.30, cars $29) provides service to and from the marina to St-Siméon on the north shore (see p.343). The **tourist office**, 189 blvd de l'Hôtel-de-Ville (late June to early Sept daily 8.30am–8.30pm; rest of year Mon–Fri 8.30am–noon & 1.30–5pm; ☎418/862-1981 or 1-888/825-1981), provides accommodation listings. The **hostel** (☎418/862-7566 or 1-800/461-8585; ❷), on the same street at no. 46, occupies an attractive wooden building. Dorm beds are $20. An equally convenient option is the *CÉGEP*, 325 rue St-Pierre (☎418/862-6903 ext 282; ❶), a college residence offering a hundred spartan rooms throughout the summer. **Motels** and **hotels** include the *Auberge de la Pointe*, 10 boul Cartier (☎418/862-3514 or 1-800/463-1222; ❹), with comfortable rooms and its own health spa. Two magnificent **B&Bs** are virtually across from each other on a gorgeous tree-lined stretch of Hwy 132 west of town: *Auberge La Sabline*, 343 rue Fraser (☎418/867-4890; ❸), and the summer residence of Canada's first prime minister, Sir John A. MacDonald, *Les Rochers*, at no. 336 (☎418/868-1435; ❹). The municipal **campsite**, exit 507 from Hwy 20 (☎418/862-4281; $15-27; mid-May to late Sept), is off Hwy 132, near the harbour.

Pricey **restaurants** abound in the centre of town – *Le St-Patrice*, 169 rue Fraser (☎418/862-9895), is among the best, devoted to serving regional produce. A walk down rue Lafontaine, near the river, reveals less expensive alternatives – the best value is *La Gourmande* at no. 120 (☎418/862-4270), where salads and vegetarian meals average about $11, though things get more pricey in the evenings. For breakfast head to *Les Sucreries de Jojo* at no. 340. *L'Estaminet*, 299 rue Lafontaine, is a bar with 150 types of beer and good pub food, including mussels with fries (from $7). Later on, let your hair down in the cellar nightclub *Le Jet*, 409 rue Lafontaine, and *Le Kojak* next door.

Cabano and Lac Témiscouata

The area southeast of Rivière-du-Loup, along the Trans-Canada Highway towards Edmundston, New Brunswick (see p.447) – just beyond which is the US border – is saved from mediocrity by the graceful sweep of **Lac Témiscouata**, where a combination of lake, river, woods and hills is adorned by a dazzling display of wild flowers in spring. The Trans-Canada Highway offers glimpses of the lake, but it's Hwy 232 that tracks along the prettiest stretches, leaving the main road at the sprawling lakeside village of **CABANO**. Aside from **Fort Ingall** (June–Sept daily 9.30am–6pm; $6.50), a restored British fortification dating from 1839, there's little to do here except hang out by the lake. Built during a border dispute with the Americans, the fort was part of a series of schemes that strengthened the land link between the St Lawrence and the Bay of Fundy, protecting the area's timber resources. Abandoned in 1842, having seen no action, Ingall has been painstakingly reconstructed, its high stockade surrounding a squat wooden barracks, blockhouse and officers' quarters. Inside the officers' quarters are enjoyable displays on the background to the fort's construction, contemporary army life and local archeological finds. There's also a section on Archie Belaney, aka **Grey Owl**, the British conservationist turned native, who settled in the area in the 1920s (see p.195). From Cabano, Hwy 232 follows the shore of the lake before snaking back to the St Lawrence at Rimouski – or you can take the more direct Hwy 293 from the lake's northern extremity to Trois-Pistoles.

There are several **campsites** along the shores of Lac Témiscouata, the nearest to Cabano being the *Témilac*, 33 rue de la Plage, near the junction of Highway 232 and the TCH (☏418/854-7660; $14; mid-May to Sept). For more comfortable **accommodation** the unpretentious *Hébergement Témilac* (same number; ❹). Alternatively, you could try the *Motel Royal*, 19 rue St-Louis (☏418/854-2307; ❷), a decent and inexpensive place to stay. For **food**, *Le Quai des Brumes*, 140 rue Commercial (☏418/854-1888), is a cheerful place with a terrace; *Auberge de la Gare*, 5 rue de la Gare, specializes in crêpes and pasta and offers **B&B** accommodation upstairs (☏418/845-9315 or 1-888/463-4273; ❷).

Trois-Pistoles and beyond

Heading northeast from Rivière-du-Loup along Hwy 132, with the far bank of the St Lawrence clearly visible, the coastal highway passes through a succession of farming and fishing villages on its way to **TROIS-PISTOLES**, said to be named after a silver goblet worth three *pistoles* (gold coins) that a French sailor dropped into the river while trying to fill it with water in 1621. The town is dominated by the enormous church of **Notre Dame-des-Neiges-de-Trois-Pistoles** (late June to early Sept daily 9am–4.30pm), built between 1882 and 1887. From a distance the church looks like something out of Disneyland, as the roof, surmounted by four pinnacles, is painted silver. Inside,

---

Edmundston, New Brunswick (see p.447) – just beyond Cabano – is on **Atlantic time**, one hour ahead of Québec's **Eastern time**. However, note that if you carry on over the bridge at Edmundston, which marks the border with the US state of Maine, you have to switch back to Eastern.

the vaulted Italianate ceiling is supported by massive trompe-l'oeil marble columns with ornate gilded capitals, while the walls are dotted with nineteenth-century devotional paintings. The most interesting museum in town is the **Parc de l'Aventure Basque en Amérique**, 66 Rue du Parc (daily: late June to early Sept 9am–6pm; early June & early Sept to mid-Oct noon–4pm; $6). Built on the site of the first Basque village in Québec, the informative displays examine their early history in the region. An accompanying English-language booklet is available for the museum. The first weekend of July sees the centre host a Basque festival, during which the traditional stick-and-ball game of pelote is played. The town's other main museum is the **Musée St-Laurent**, 552 rue Notre Dame ouest (late June to mid-Sept daily 9am–5pm; $4), which has a great ensemble of cars, with vehicles from the 1930s to the 1970s and an eclectic collection ranging from old packs of cigarettes to harpoons. **Whale-watching** excursions are handled by Les Écumeurs (℡418/851-9955 or 1-888/817-9999; $35–55; trip times vary up to 5hr) and you can **sea-kayak** with Dayak de Mer des Îles, 60 ave du Parc (mid-May to mid–Sept; ℡418/851-4MER; $30).

The town's **information centre** is on Hwy 132 with a miniature windmill and lighthouse outside (late June to early Sept daily 9am–7pm; ℡418/851-4949). A **car ferry** crosses to Les Escoumins (mid-May to mid-Oct 2–3 daily; 90min; ℡418/851-4676; $11.50, cars $29) on the Côte-Nord (see p.358). Should you want to break your journey here, try *Motel Trois-Pistoles*, 64 Hwy 132 ouest (℡418/851-2563; ❷), which has 32 comfortable rooms, some with views of the river. There's not much in the way of **B&Bs** in the downtown area, with the exception of *Le Pistolois*, 15 rue Rousseau (℡418/851-4481; ❷). *Aux Terroir des Basques* at 65 rang 2 est (℡418/851-2001; ❸; summer only) is worth a try. *L'Ensoleillé*, at 138 rue Notre Dame ouest (℡418/851-2889), serves up vegetarian and fish dishes on an outdoor terrace.

Parc du Bic and Le Bic

Heading east from Trois-Pistoles, Hwy 132 crosses a comparatively tedious landscape of fertile agricultural land, until it reaches the rocky wooded hummocks of the shoreline's **Parc du Bic**. At this naturalists' paradise, whose headlands push up tight against the river, it's possible to see herds of grey seals, especially at dusk. The park (entry $3.50) has three short hiking trails, a beach and a visitors' centre (mid-June to Sept daily 10am–5pm; ℡418/869-3333) – from which shuttle buses head up to the highest peak, Pic Champlain ($5 return trip), and around the park (2hr; $14). You can also view the park from a **bicycle** (rental $18/day) or a **sea kayak** from Rivi-Air Aventure (℡418/736-5252, ⓦwww.rivi-air.qc.ca; $30–60 per person). The **campsite** (℡418/736-4711; $21; early June to early Sept) is pleasant, but highway noise is a problem.

Just beyond the park along Hwy 132, the elongated village of **LE BIC**, perched on a low ridge above its snout-shaped harbour, is a handsome medley of old and modern architectures. Samuel de Champlain named the place "Pic" (for peak), but the name morphed. The *Auberge du Mange Grenouille*, 148 rue Ste-Cécile (℡418/736-5656; ❸; May to mid-Oct), has a superb **restaurant** (reservations advised) and attractively furnished double **rooms**. *Aux Cormorants* (℡418/736-8113; ❷) is a serene waterside **B&B** nestled along Pointe des Anglais. The **bakery**, *Folles Farines*, at 113 rue St-Jean Baptiste, has a wicked selection of tasty breads, croissants and thin-crust pizzas. Up the hill and facing the handsome church, *Chez Saint-Pierre*, 129 du Mon St-Louis (℡418/736-5051), is a sunny bistro with an imaginative menu and a terrace overlooking the town's rooftops.

Rimouski

Some 20km northeast of Bic, **RIMOUSKI** – "Riki" to its residents – appears quite unattractive from Hwy 132 thanks to a major fire that destroyed one-third of the buildings from the river to midtown in 1950, forcing the city to rebuild in 1960s strip-mall style. But forge past the highway and into the town, the administrative capital of eastern Québec, and you'll find a youthful city – thanks to the number of educational institutions here – and the interesting **Musée régional de Rimouski**, at 35 rue St-Germain (mid-June to mid-Sept daily 10am–6pm, Wed–Sat until 9pm; rest of year Wed–Sun noon–5pm, Thurs until 9pm; $4). It's housed in the oldest church in eastern Québec whose exterior has stayed intact, while the three floors inside have been renovated and now focus on rotating exhibits on local history and contemporary art.

The Orléans Express **bus** station is at 90 ave Léonidas (☎418/723-4923), the **train** station at 57 de l'Évêché est (☎418/722-4737 or 1-800/361-5390) and the rideshare outfit Allô-Stop at 106 rue St-Germain est (☎418/723-5248, ⓦwww.allo-stop.com). There's a **car ferry** to Forestville on the Côte-Nord (☎418/725-2725 or 1-800/973-2725; late April to early Oct 2–4 trips daily; 55min; $14, cars $34), which only holds thirty cars so reservations are essential. The Relais Nordick departs Rimouski every week.

Rimouski's **tourist office**, 50 rue St-Germain ouest (mid-June to early Sept daily 9am–8pm; early June & early Sept to early Oct daily 9am–4.30pm; early Oct to mid-June Mon–Fri 9am–4.30pm; ☎418/723-2322 or 1-800/746-6875), is in the centre of town, on the waterfront. It has **accommodation** listings, including the college rooms available during the summer vacation at *CÉGEP Residences*, 320 rue St-Louis (☎418/723-4636 or 1-800/463-0617; ❶), where single rooms cost as little as $12. For **B&B** accommodation, *Chez Charles et Marguerite*, 686 boul St-Germain ouest (☎418/723-3938; ❸), has cheery rooms looking out onto fields that lead down to the St Lawrence. The town's cheapest motel is the *Motel St-Laurent*, 740 boul St-Germain ouest (☎418/723-9217 or 1-888/440-9241; ❷). For **camping**, *Le Bocage*, 124 Hwy 132 (☎418/739-3125; $20), is 13km east of Rimouski in Sainte-Luce, a quiet village that's become a lively beach resort. Rimouski has a number of affordable places to **eat**, not least the *Central Café*, 31 rue de l'Évêché ouest (☎418/722-4011), a bistro with great salads and pizza in a home decorated with birdcages. The *Maison du Spaghetti* at 35 boul St-Germain est (☎418/723-6010) serves up hearty pasta; and if you're into kitsch, plump for *Retro 50* across the street at no. 38 (☎418/723-4858), a themed 1950s diner.

A few kilometres east from Rimouski along Hwy 132, the small town of **POINTE-AU-PÈRE** holds not much more than the **Maison Lamontagne**, 707 boul du Rivage (mid-May to mid-Oct daily 9am–6pm; $3), the oldest house in eastern Québec; though there's not much inside that's worth your time or money, the gardens are free and quite educational. Further down the road, the **Musée de la Mer** (daily: late June to late Aug 9am–7pm; June & late Aug to mid-Oct 10am–5pm; $6) is housed in a modern building that resembles a tilting ship. The exhibit includes a 3D film on the *Empress of Ireland*, a luxury liner that sank offshore here in 1914, a disaster second only to the *Titanic*, with more than a thousand lives lost.

Sainte-Flavie and Matane

From Rimouski to Matane a few places are worth a stop. The first is **SAINTE-FLAVIE**, a small coastal town that's home to Gaspésie's **regional tourist office**, 357 rue de la Mer (daily: mid-June to mid-Sept 8am–8pm;

rest of year 8.30am–4.30pm; ☎418/775-2223). Nearby at no. 564, the **Centre d'art Marcel Gagnon** (daily: May–Sept 8am–11pm; Oct–April 8am–9pm; ☎418/775-2829, ⓦwww.centredart.net; free) offers a unique sight. The artist's outdoor work, *Le Grand Rassemblement* (The Great Gathering), groups more than eighty life-size statues and seven rafts, starting on a strip of land and then leading into the water. The works are especially remarkable at high tide, as the statues emerge out of the river, and the rafts seem to float. Another visual feast lies 9km further east down Hwy 132. Here the **Jardins de Métis** (June–Oct daily 8.30am–6.30pm; ⓦwww.redfordgardens.com; $12) is a gigantic aristocratic mansion and garden complex with over 100,000 introduced species of plants neatly presented among forty acres of features such as miniature bridges and tumbling brooks. Whatever your tastes, it's an impressive horticultural feat.

MATANE, 98km from Rimouski, appears to be dominated by oil refineries and cement works, but in fact fishing and forestry have long been the mainstays of the local economy. The Matane River, which bisects the town, is spanned by a pair of bridges – one beside the harbour (part of Hwy 132), the other a shorter affair a few hundred metres north, next to the fish ladder, which was built to help salmon head upstream to spawn. The **Festival de la Crevette**, during the last week in June, takes its name from the prawn harvest but celebrates the entire range of local seafood; all the town's restaurants and bars participate. At the **Barrage Mathieu-d'Amours**, the dam's observation area allows visitors to watch salmon battling to get upstream. Matane's **tourist office** (late June to mid-Sept daily 8.30am–8.30pm; rest of year Mon–Fri 8.30am–5pm; ☎418/562-1065 or 1-877/762-8263) is beside Hwy 132, just west of the centre, in the lighthouse at 968 ave du Phare ouest. Simple institutional **accommodation** can be rented at *CÉGEP de Matane*, 616 ave St-Rédempteur (☎418/562-1240; ❶), while *Auberge la Seigneurie*, at 621 ave St-Jérôme (☎418/562-0021 or 1-877/783-4466, ⓦwww.aubergelaseigneurie.com; ❷), is a good B&B. Most of Matane's **hotels** and **motels** are pricey: *Motel Le Beach*, 1441 rue Matane-sur-Mer (☎418/562-1350; ❷), is the least expensive and has sea views but is nothing special. There's a huge **campsite** at 150 rte Louis-Félix-Dionne (☎418/562-3414; $13–19; mid-June to Aug) southwest of the centre of town – follow the river past the industrial park – where sites are pleasant and amid trees. A casual **restaurant** decorated by local artists, *Le Vieux Rafiot*, 1415 ave du Phare Ouest (☎418/562-8080), alongside Hwy 132, is the best bet for shrimp, while *Bistro de l'Estuaire*, 50 rue d'Amours (☎418/562-2939), is the place to go for mussels. *Italia Pizzeria*, 101 St-Pierre, serves great, moderately priced pizza.

From Matane, **car ferries** (☎418/562-2500 or 1-877/562-6560) cross to the Côte-Nord (see p.358) on two routes: to Godbout (April–Dec 1–3 trips daily; Jan–March Mon–Sat 1 daily; 2hr 10min; $13, cars $30); and to Baie-Comeau (April–Dec 1–2 trips daily; Jan–March 4 weekly; 2hr 20min; same fares).

Sainte-Anne-des-Monts and around

East of Matane the highway hugs the shoreline, passing through increasingly rugged scenery where the forested hills of the interior push up against the fretted, rocky coast. A string of skimpy fishing villages breaks up this empty landscape – places like Capucins, with its fine headland setting, and **Cap Chat**, whose 76 towering wind turbines are visible for miles around. Of these, the 110m-tall **Éole de Cap-Chat** (mid-June to Oct daily 9am–5pm; $5) is the tallest and most powerful vertical-axis wind tower in the world.

Just 16km beyond Cap-Chat, unenticing **SAINTE-ANNE-DES-MONTS** sprawls along the coastline, its untidy appearance only offset by its relaxed atmosphere and its convenience – it's an easy place to break your journey before heading on to the cape, or inland to the Parc de la Gaspésie. The lone sight is the **Explorama** at 1 rue du Quai (June & mid-Aug to mid-Oct daily 9am–6pm; late June to mid-Aug daily 9am–8pm; mid-Oct to May Mon–Fri 9am–5pm, Sat & Sun 1–5pm; $8; ⓦwww.explorama.org), a marine and birdlife discovery centre on two floors. Head to the aquarium downstairs, where you can handle starfish, sea cucumbers and scallops. The **hostel** *Auberge internationale l'Échouerie*, 295 1ère Ave est (☎418/763-1555; dorm beds $19), has great views over the river and offers bike rental and transportation to Parc de la Gaspésie, while the *Motel Manoir sur Mer*, 475 1ère Ave ouest (☎418/763-7844; ❷), has rooms backing onto the beach. For **B&B** accomodation, try *La Villa des Roses*, 500 1ère Ave ouest (☎418/763-3529; ❷).

Parc de la Gaspésie

As you travel south from Ste-Anne-des-Monts on Hwy 299, the snowcapped **Chic-Choc Mountains** – which make up most of the **Parc de la Gaspésie** – can be spotted in the distance, a stark and forbidding backdrop to the coastal plain. The Chic-Chocs are the most northerly protrusions of the Appalachian Ridge, which extends deep into the US, and the serpentine road reveals the full splendour of their alpine interior. The sequence of valleys framed by thickly wooded slopes culminates in the staggering ravine that lies at the foot of the towering **Mont Albert**. In this ravine, 40km from Sainte-Anne-des-Monts, the park's extremely helpful reception and interpretation centre (early June to early Sept daily 8am–8pm; call for hours at other times; ☎418/763-5435 or 1-866/727-2427, ⓦwww.sepaq.com; park admission $3.50) rents out hiking equipment and has details and maps of half a dozen well-signposted **hiking trails**; most are about a day's duration, though a couple around the base are shorter. Prospective hikers should come equipped with warm clothes, food and water, and log their intended route at the centre. The trails ascend to the summits of the area's three highest mountains – Mont Jacques-Cartier, Mont Richardson and Mont Albert – and are remarkable in that they climb through three distinctive habitats. Herds of Virginia deer thrive in the rich vegetation of the lowest zone, while moose live in the boreal forest, and caribou in the tundra near the peaks. This is the only place in Québec where the three species exist in close proximity. The park is linked by **shuttle bus** to Ste-Anne-des-Monts (late June to Sept daily 8am; $6 roundtrip) with buses travelling between the town's tourist office and the interpretation centre.

The park has four **campsites**, one of which, *Camping Mont Albert* (☎418/763-1333; $23), is conveniently near the interpretation centre, though *Camping Lac Cascapédia*, around 20km back towards Ste-Anne-des-Monts, is smaller, with an exceptionally beautiful setting. Close by is the smart, modern *Gîte du Mont-Albert* (☎418/763-2288 or 1-888/270-4483; ❻), which offers the only fixed **lodgings** in the park; room prices rocket during the summer and skiing seasons, but you couldn't wish for a handier location. The *Gîte* includes excellent pricey restaurant and also controls a number of **chalets** (❸) around the park, offering simple but reliable facilities.

Mont-Saint-Pierre

Heading east from Sainte-Anne-des-Monts towards the tip of the Gaspé Peninsula, the road often squeezes between the ocean and the sheer rock faces of the mountains, its twists and turns passing tumbling scree and picturesque coves.

The view as you approach **MONT-SAINT-PIERRE** is particularly majestic, the curving seashore and the swelling mountains together framing this little community set at the mouth of a wide river valley. This low-key resort is dedicated to bathing and sea fishing, except during the ten-day **hang-gliding festival** at the end of July. During the rest of the summer you can fly in tandem for $100 with Carrefour Aventure (T418/797-5033 or 1-800/463-2210, W www.carrefouraventure.com) who also rent out sea kayaks ($10/hr) and mountain bikes. There are several inexpensive **motels** along rue Prudent-Cloutier: try *Chalets Auberge Bernatchez* at no. 12 (T418/797-2733; ❶) or *Motel Restaurant au Délice* at no. 100 (T418/797-2850 or 1-888/797-2955, W www.audelice.com; ❸). *Auberge les Vagues*, at no. 84 (T418/797-2851; ❷), is a motel that doubles as a hostel (dorm beds $15). For **camping**, there's *Du Pont* on Hwy 132 (T418/797-2951; $14.50; June–Sept) and a larger **municipal campsite** at 103 rue Pierre-Godfroie-Coulombe (T418/797-2250; $16; June–Sept). There are a couple of good places to **eat**: *Le Croissant d'Art*, on the main thoroughfare, is an inexpensive artsy café ideal for light lunches, while *Les Joyeux Naufragés*, 7 rte Pierre-Mercier, offers more substantial fare at equally affordable prices.

Parc National de Forillon

At the very tip of the peninsula, the **PARC NATIONAL DE FORILLON** is the scenic culmination of the Gaspé, encompassing thick forest and mountains, crossed by hiking trails and fringed by stark cliffs along a deeply indented coastline. The splendour of the landscape is complemented by the **wildlife**: black bears, moose, beavers, porcupines and foxes are all common to the area. To chance sighting them, you're best to arrive early in the morning or at dusk. More than two hundred species of birds have also been seen, ranging from sea birds like gannets, cormorants and guillemots, to songbirds such as the skylark and chaffinch. From the coastal paths around Cap Gaspé itself, **whales and porpoises** can also be spotted (May–Oct). As Thomas Anburey, a British soldier, observed in the 1770s, "They cause most beautiful fireworks in the water: for being in such abundance, and darting with amazing velocity, a continued stream of light glides through the water, and as they cross each other, the appearance is so picturesque that no description can reach it." Roughly triangular in shape, the park is sandwiched between the Gulf of St Lawrence and the Baie de Gaspé and encircled by Hwys 197 and 132, the former crossing the interior to delineate the park's western limits, the latter mostly keeping to the seashore and threading through Anse-au-Griffon and Cap-des-Rosiers – tiny coastal villages with views onto the river and Forillon's wooded parkland. Make the time to take this route as the views are spectacular. You can also stop for a cup of tea at the **Manoir Le Boutillier**, a restored 1850s house at 578 boul Griffon, in Anse-au-Griffon (June to mid-Oct daily 9am–5pm; $4; guided tours only). Closer to the park, the **lighthouse** at Cap-des-Rosiers is the tallest in Canada.

Parc Forillon has numerous hiking trails, the best of which takes you to the tip of **Cap Gaspé**, otherwise known as "land's end". The ninety-minute return trip starts a few kilometres south of the **interpretation centre** (see below). The trail extends from the end of the paved road beyond Grande-Grave, a restored fishing village founded by immigrants from Jersey – the inhabitants were relocated as recently as 1970, when the park was established. Their historical presence is enshrined in two sites situated along the trail that follows the southern coast of the cape. The first, **Hyman & Son's General Store and Warehouse** (mid-June to mid-Oct 10am–5pm; free with park entry) is a marvellous restoration of a 1920s general store; nearby **Anse-Blanchette** (mid-June to mid-Sept 10am–5pm; free with park entry), a fisherman's house dating from the same era, has also been painstakingly restored; the onsite barn frequently does duty as a stage for storytelling and musical acts. You'll also note unfinished buildings down near the edge of the cliff: these are the remnants of the set for the popular Québec television series *L'Ombre de l'Épervier*. After these, the path rises and falls until it makes the final steep ascent to the **lighthouse**, which is set on a 150m cliff with the ocean on three sides.

Park practicalities

Admission to Parc Forillon costs $3.75. The park's **interpretation centre** (daily: early June 1–4pm; mid-June to early Sept 9am–6pm; early Sept to mid-Oct 9am–4pm; ☎418/892-5572, ⓦwww.pc.gc.ca/forillon) is close to the lighthouse, near the village of Cap-des-Rosiers on the park's north side. Here, you can get an imaginative overview of the natural and human history of the area and a wealth of suggestions as to how to spend your time. There are also two **visitors' centres** off Hwy 132 – one at Anse-au-Griffon (daily: early June to Aug 8.30am–9.30pm; Sept to mid-Oct 9am–4pm; ☎418/368-5505 or 1-800/463-6769), the other on the south coast at Penouille (same hours; ☎418/892-5661). Leisurely pursuits include two-hour **boat trips** along the northern shore to see seals and a bird sanctuary, from the quay near the interpretation centre (mid-June to mid-Sept every 2hr from 9am; 2hr; $20), and **whale-watching** excursions departing from Grande-Grave (May–Oct 10am; ☎418/892-5500, ⓦwww.baleines-forillon.com; $33).

The park's half-dozen **campsites** (all ☎418/368-6050; $16.50–20) are pleasantly situated and well maintained; *Camping Cap Bon-Ami* ($17; early June to early Sept) has a particularly delightful setting just south of the interpretation centre. The visitors' centres and interpretation centre have details on all sites and can also arrange accommodation in **chalets** (❸) around the park, which are cheaper if booked by the week. Alternatively, the villages edging the park offer plain accommodation that includes Anse-au-Griffon's *Motel le Noroît*, 589 boul Griffon (☎418/892-5531; ❷), and Cap-aux-Os's **hostel**, 2095 boul Grande-Grève (☎418/892-5153; $16; May–Nov), with a café, laundry facilities and a **mountain-bike rental** shop.

Gaspé

The town of **GASPÉ**, straddling the hilly estuary of the York River – its name derived from *Gespeg*, "the end of the land" in the Micmac language – is a disappointment after the scenic drama of the national park, a humdrum settlement of about 17,000 people whose hard-pressed economy is reliant on its deep-water port. This is the spot where the French navigator and explorer **Jacques Cartier** landed in July 1534, on the first of his three trips up the St Lawrence. He stayed here for just eleven days, time enough to erect a wooden cross engraved with the escutcheon of Francis I, staking out the king's – and Christianity's – claim to this new territory. Cartier's first aim was to find a sea route to the Orient, but he also had more extensive ambitions – to acquire land for himself and his men, exploit the Indians as fur gatherers and discover precious metals to rival the loot the Spaniards had taken from the Aztecs. Naturally, Cartier had to disguise his real intentions on the first trip and his initial contacts with the Iroquois were cordial. Then, in the spring of 1536, he betrayed their trust by taking two of the local chief's sons back with him to Francis I. They were never returned, and when Cartier made his third trip in 1541 the Iroquois were so suspicious that he was unable to establish the colony he had been instructed to found. Desperate to salvage his reputation, Cartier sailed back to France with what he thought was a cargo of gold and diamonds. His cargo turned out to be iron pyrite and quartz crystals.

Just to the east of the town centre, at 80 boul Gaspé, the **Jacques Cartier monument** looks out over the bay from the grounds of the town museum. It consists of six striking bronze dolmens carved in relief that record Cartier's visit and treatment of the natives in ambivalent terms, along with anodyne homilies on the nature and unity of humankind. The **museum** itself, 80 boul Gaspé (late June to mid Oct daily 9am–5pm; mid-Oct to mid–Dec & mid-Jan to mid-June Tues–Fri 9am–5pm, Sat & Sun 1–5pm; $4), illuminates the social issues that have confronted the inhabitants of the peninsula to the present – isolation from the centres of power, depopulation and, more recently, unemployment. Temporary displays concentrate mostly on local subjects, like the peninsula's artists and musicians. A good ten-minutes' walk west, near the top of rue Jacques-Cartier, stands the **Gaspé Cathedral**. Built in 1970, it's the only wooden cathedral in North America and its barn-like exterior has an extraordinarily dour and industrial appearance. The interior is completely different: the nave – all straight lines and symmetrical simplicity – is bathed in warm, softly coloured light that pours in through an enormous stained-glass window in the style of Mondrian.

Just outside town, the white **Sanctuaire Notre Dame-des-Douleurs** is a popular pilgrimage site due to the healing powers it's said to have, supported by the collection of crutches, braces and canes found in the chapel entombing Father Watier, the sanctuary's founder. Up a slight incline behind the church, the replica of the Lourdes Grotto (replete with outdoor altar) and the Garden of Mary's Sorrows are both attractive gardens with remarkable religious sculptures. Next door, the **Site Historique Micmac de Gespeg**, 783 boul Pointe Navarre (June to mid-Oct daily 9am–5pm; guided tours only; $5), is a replica of the aboriginal village that stood here in 1675, when aboriginal trading with Europeans was in full swing. The site offers interesting insight into how to build tepees and animal traps and carve utensils, but the visit is overlong at two hours.

Practicalities

Buses to Gaspé stop on the main street, rue Jacques-Cartier, at the *Motel Adams*. The **tourist office** (daily 8am–8pm; ☎418/368-6335) is on the far side of the river from the town centre along Hwy 132; it has accommodation listings and maps of the town. **College rooms** are available during the summer at the *CÉGEP de la Gaspésie et des Îles*, 94 rue Jacques-Cartier (☎418/368-2749, ⓦwww.cgaspesie.qc.ca; ❶; mid-June to mid-Sept). Most of the town's **B&B** accommodation is of high quality, but *Les Petits Matins*, 129 rue de la Reine (☎418/368-1370, ⓦwww.bbcanada.com/petitsmatins; ❷), is the best, located in an old bank building and with excellent breakfasts. Bargain-basement **motel** accommodation is available at *Motel Plante*, 137 rue Jacques-Cartier (☎418/368-2254 or 1-888/368-2254, ⓦwww.motelplante.com; ❷).

Le Bourlingueur, next to the Jacques-Cartier mall opposite the main bridge at 207 de la Reine, is recommended for **breakfast** (around $4), though the Chinese and Canadian dishes on the evening menu are rather pricey, with main courses costing $13. *Brise-Bise*, 2 Côte Carter (☎418/368-1456), is a great bistro and a swinging bar at night. If you can afford to splurge, do it at the *Café des Artistes*, 249 boul Gaspé (☎418/368-2255) – it's one of the best restaurants on the peninsula for French cuisine. The upstairs cigar room nestled under the eaves is worth a visit whether you eat or not.

Percé and around

Once a humble fishing community, **PERCÉ** is a prime holiday spot, thanks to the tourist potential of the gargantuan limestone rock that rears up from the sea here facing the reddish cliffs of the shore. One of Canada's most celebrated natural phenomena, the **Rocher Percé** – so named for the hole at the western end – is nearly 500m long and 90m high, and is a surreal sight at dawn, when it appears bathed in an eerie golden iridescence. The town is now replete with tacky gift shops and mediocre restaurants and bars; off-season, when much of the resort closes down, Percé maintains a delightfully relaxed and sleepy feel. At low tide it's possible, if you hurry, to walk around most of the rock – ideally wearing waterproof shoes with good treads – starting from the lookout beyond the red-roofed houses at the end of rue Mont-Joli. Access to the rock now costs $1 – allegedly for upkeep of the belvedere and stairway leading to the stone beach – tide times are posted at the top. One of the most spectacular longer-range views of the monolith is from the top of **Mont Sainte-Anne**, which rises directly behind Percé town; the path is signposted from behind the church on avenue de l'Église, and the walk takes about an hour each way. A separate trail leads to the **Grotto**, a lovely spot with waterfalls and statues of the Virgin Mary nestled into the mountain's crevasses.

Apart from the rock, there's precious little to see in Percé, though the **Centre d'Interprétation du Parc de l'Île-Bonaventure-et-du-Rocher-Percé** (early June to mid-Oct daily 9am–5pm; free), some 2km to the south of the centre (exit Hwy 132 at route des Failles and turn left along route d'Irlande), has some enjoyable displays on the area's flora and fauna. In the middle of town, in the old Charles Robin Company building formerly used for processing and storing fish, the **Musée la Chafaud**, 145 Hwy 132 (daily: June to early Sept 10am–10pm; early Sept to early Oct 10am–8pm; $5), displays traditional and contemporary art and occasionally gets high-calibre exhibitions. A small room downstairs has some old pictures of Percé. A few kilometres west of

Boat trips from Percé

From the wharf in the centre of Percé, frequent **boat trips**, operated by Les Traversiers de l'Île (1hr 30min to 3hr; ☎418/782-2750; $20–30), go around the nearby **Île Bonaventure** bird reserve (daily: June & Sept to mid-Oct 8.15am–4pm; July & Aug 8.15am–5pm; $3.50), whose precipitous cliffs are favoured by gannets in particular, as well as kittiwakes, razorbills, guillemots, gulls, cormorants and puffins. You can also arrange to disembark at the island's tiny jetty, where all of the lengthy walking trails lead to the clifftops above the gannet colonies, and one includes a visit to **Le Boutillier**, a restored nineteenth-century fisherman's home.

The wharf is also the departure point for **whale-watching** excursions – between May and October the blue and humpback whales are often in the area, and you may also see porpoises, seals and the rarer white-sided dolphins. Zodiacs speed out with Observation Littoral Percé (☎418/782-5359; $40), but as they fill up quickly, you may have to opt for a larger glassed-in boat with Les Croisières Julien Cloutier (☎418/782-5606 or 1-877/782-2161; $20). Trips last two or three hours and should be reserved in advance at the various ticket kiosks lining the main drag.

Percé, **La Vieille Usine de l'Anse-à-Beaufils** (daily 10am–10pm; Ⓦ www.levieilleusine.qc.ca) showcases a wide range of local art in a renovated fish-packing plant that fronts a decent beach. Otherwise, Percé makes a useful base for visiting several natural attractions, including the **Grande Crevasse**, a volcanically formed split in a rocky outcrop that's just a few millimetres wide but several hundred metres deep. The clearly marked path takes about an hour to walk in each direction and begins behind the *Auberge de Gargantua*, a first-class restaurant on route des Failles.

Highway 132 bisects Percé and passes just to the north of the main wharf, close to the **tourist office** (late May to late-Oct daily 9am–7pm; Ⓣ 418/782-5448), which operates a free room-reservation service and keeps boat and tide timetables. Arriving from Carleton or Gaspé, **buses** drop passengers in the centre of Percé at the Petro-Canada service station, but the VIA Rail **train** station is 10km south of town on Hwy 132. Most of Percé's **accommodation** is open during the summer months only, when advance booking is advised; in the off-season, you'll likely have to stay in Gaspé. Some of the cheapest **rooms** in town are at the seasonal *Maison Avenue House* guesthouse, 38 ave de l'Église (Ⓣ 418/782-2954; $35). **Motels** dot Hwy 132 – including *Le Macareux*, no. 262 (Ⓣ 418/782-2414; ❷), and *Le Mirage*, no. 288 (Ⓣ 418/782-5151 or 1-800/463-9011; ❸). Rather more upmarket, the *Hôtel la Normandie*, 221 Hwy 132 ouest (Ⓣ 418/782-2112 or 1-800/463-0820, Ⓦ www.normandieperce.com; ❹), has a clutch of bright, modern bedrooms with superb views along the coast. Also on Hwy 132 is the town's dynamic **hostel** *La Maison Rouge*, 125 Rte 132 (Ⓣ 418/782-2227; ❸; dorm beds $20), which has kayaks for rent. *Camping Gargantua*, 222 rte des Failles (Ⓣ 418/782-2852; $20–25), is one of five nearby campgrounds and has great views of the rock.

La Maison du Pêcheur, 155 Place du Quai (Ⓣ 418/782-5331) just up from the wharf, has fine **seafood** dishes, with mains priced $14–22; while more mid-priced *Le Matelot*, 7 rue de l'Église (Ⓣ 418/782-2569), serves candlelit lobster with live entertainment. Substantial **snacks**, coffees and vegetarian dishes are best in the faintly bohemian atmosphere of *Les Fous de Bassan*, 162 Rte 132 (Ⓣ 418/782-2266), also on the main street. For very fine food, dine at *Auberge Gargantua*, 222 rte des Failles (Ⓣ 418/782-2852), with gourmet French cuisine and great panoramas over town, or *La Normandia*, 221 Hwy 132 (Ⓣ 418/782-2112), for such delights as lobster baked in champagne.

Chandler and Bonaventure

Along the coastal road to the southwest of Percé, the dramatic mountains that dominate the north and east of the peninsula are replaced by a gently undulating landscape of wooded hills and farmland. **CHANDLER**, the first town of any size on this route, is an ugly lumber port notable solely for the wreck of the Peruvian freighter *Unisol* in the mouth of the harbour. It ran aground in a gale in 1983, allegedly because its captain, unable to negotiate entry into the port for his cement-laden vessel, got drunk and allowed the vessel to run onto the sandbank where it remains today. The most easterly resort on the bay is **BONAVENTURE**, whose tiny centre, beside Hwy 132, edges the marshy delta and man-made lagoon of the river that sports its name. The town is, uniquely, a centre for the production of fish-leather products such as purses and wallets, but it's usually visited for its salmon fishing and sandy beach. A wildlife observation centre, **Bioparc de la Gaspésie**, 123 rue des Vieux Ponts (daily: June & Sept to mid-Oct 9am–5pm; July & Aug 9am–6pm; Ⓦ www.bioparc.ca; $10), showcases the region's animals – caribou, lynx, otters and mountain lions included – in their respective ecosystems. But Bonaventure is really known for being a stronghold of **Acadian** culture. Their traditions and heritage are celebrated at the **Musée Acadien du Québec**, 95 ave Port-Royal (late June to early Sept daily 9am–6pm; early Sept to mid-Oct daily 9am–5pm; mid-Oct to late June Mon–Fri 9am–noon & 1–5pm, Sat & Sun 1–5pm; Ⓦwww .museeacadien.com; $5), set in an imposing blue and white wooden building, once the church hall, in the town centre. Highlights of the collection include some delightful handmade furniture dating from the eighteenth century and a range of intriguing photographs that encapsulate something of the hardships of Acadian rural life.

Next door, Bonaventure's **tourist office**, 91 ave Port-Royal (mid-June to Aug daily 9am–6pm; ☎418/534-4014), has background information on the town and **accommodation** lists. The latter includes *Motel Grand Pré*, 118 ave Grand-Pré (☎418/534-2053 or 1-800/463-2053; ❹), and more reasonable **B&Bs** like the bohemian *Au Foin Fou*, 204 rte de la Rivière (☎418/534-4413; ❷), and *Auberge du Café Acadien*, 168 ave Beaubassin (☎418/534-4276; ❸) – above the excellent *Café Acadien*, which serves imaginative French-Canadian **food**. *Cime Aventure*, 200 chemin Arsenault (☎418/534-2333 or 1-800/790-2463, Ⓦwww.cimeaventure.com), has tepees ($40) to sleep in alongside the Bonaventure river and runs adventure trips into the local area (3hr to 6 days; prices vary). *Camping Plage Beaubassin*, 154 ave Beaubassin (☎418/534-3246; $16–25; early June to Aug), is a municipal **campsite** on the spit of land between the lagoon and the bay.

New Richmond and around

NEW RICHMOND, 30km from Bonaventure, has only one worthy attraction, the **Centre d'Héritage Britannique de la Gaspésie**, beside the bay towards the west end of town, 7km from the highway, at 351 boul Perron ouest (daily: June to late Sept 9am–5pm; last admission 4pm; $8). Set in wooded parkland around the old lighthouse at Duthie's Point, near the mouth of the Rivière Cascapédia, it's a kind of Loyalist theme park-cum-ghost town made up of a collection of wooden buildings assembled from the surrounding region. Although they were all restored to their nineteenth- or early twentieth-century appearance, many are ill-kept and falling into disrepair today. Even so, the centre is spacious enough for a pleasant stroll along the shore. It even has its own tiny beach.

Carleton and the Miguasha Peninsula

Just west of New Richmond, Hwy 299 runs north along the banks of the Cascapédia towards the Parc de la Gaspésie (see p.326), while the coastal Hwy 132 continues on to the popular bayside resort of **CARLETON**, where the mountains of the interior return to dominate the landscape. Founded in 1756 by Acadian refugees, Carleton is an unassuming little place that stands back from the sea behind a broad lagoon, linked to the narrow coastal strip by a couple of long causeways. The town has a bird sanctuary – a favourite haunt of wading species like the sandpiper and plover – and several accessible bathing beaches where you can rent kayaks (☎418/364-7802). But what makes the place special is the contrast between the coastal flatlands and the backdrop of wooded hills that rise up behind the town. At 582m, **Mont Saint-Joseph** is the highest of these and is presided over by the **Oratoire Notre Dame-du-Mont-Saint-Joseph** (daily: mid-June to early Sept 8am–8pm; early Sept to early Oct 8am–5pm; $4), a disappointing church that incorporates the walls of a stone chapel built on the site in 1935. A 3km maze of steep footpaths slip past streams and waterfalls before they reach the summit. You can also take the less adventurous option and drive up to see the splendid panoramic views over the bay and across to New Brunswick.

Carleton is a good place to stay overnight and, while you're here, the hilly **Miguasha Peninsula**, some 20km to the west off Hwy 132, makes a pleasant excursion. Famous for its fossils, this tiny peninsula is home to the **Parc de Miguasha**, where the cream of the fossil crop is displayed at the combined **research centre and museum** (daily: June to Aug 9am–6pm; Sept to mid-Oct 9am–5pm; free). Frequent and free guided tours take in the museum, the research area and a walk along the beach and cliffs. About 800m from the museum is the jetty for the little **car ferry** (late June to early Sept hourly 7.30am–7.30pm; 20min; ☎506/684-5107; $12 one-way for driver and car, $1 per additional passenger), a two-minute ride to Dalhousie in New Brunswick, a short cut that avoids the tip of the Baie des Chaleurs.

Carleton's many **motels** line the main street, boul Perron: *Manoir Belle Plage*, no. 474 (☎418/364-3388 or 1-800/463-0780, ⓦwww.manoirbelleplage.com; ❸) has a touch of class. A **B&B**, *Les Leblanc*, is at no. 346 (☎418/364-7601; ❷). The town has a well-situated **campsite**, *Camping Carleton*, on the causeway, Banc de Larocque (mid-June to Aug ☎418/364-3992; from $19). *Le Bleu Marine*, 203 rte du Quai, offers affordable lunchtime menus overlooking the beach, while more substantial seafood **meals** are available at *Restaurant le Héron*, at no. 561 (where the **bus** stops), and the expensive but superb *La Maison Monti*, at 840 boul Perron (☎418/364-6181). If you're heading off to the Parc de Miguasha, pack up a picnic lunch at the bakery *La Mie Véritable*, 578 boul Perron.

Pointe-à-la-Croix and around

Some 50km west of Carleton, humdrum **POINTE-À-LA-CROIX** is the site of the inter-provincial bridge over to Campbellton, New Brunswick. During the summer, a **tourist booth** in the tiny wooden house by the turn-off for the bridge on Hwy 132 (daily 8am–8pm) offers a full range of information on the Gaspé Peninsula.

Just before the bridge, a right turn leads to the little waterside community of **LISTUGUJ** (Restigouche), the heart of a Micmac Indian reservation that functions on New Brunswick time because the children go to school in Campbellton. The village is home to the Micmacs, an Algonquian-speaking people who spread across the Atlantic seaboard from Nova Scotia through to the Gaspé and east Newfoundland. Their history is a familiarly sad one: trading furs for European knives, hatchets and pots, the Micmacs quarrelled with other aboriginal groups over hunting grounds until there was a state of perpetual warfare. In later years, the Micmacs proved loyal allies to the French military cause, but, as with all other aboriginal groups, their numbers were decimated by European diseases and they remain a neglected minority. However, the reserve is self-governing and one of the five richest in Canada (of 800-odd reserves). On your right as you enter the reserve, the locals have reconstructed **Fort Listuguj** (June to mid-Oct daily 10am–7pm; $6), based on a 1760 Acadian fort where the last battle for New France took place. Built entirely of cedar with a tepee circle in the centre, the fort is staffed by costumed guides and the atmosphere is entertaining and laid-back with traditional

New Brunswick is on **Atlantic time**, one hour ahead of Québec.

singing, drumming, storytelling, craft-making and incredible food – try the local bread (*lusgnign*), baked in the outside ovens, or the Acadian-style smoked fish. It's possible to **stay** in the tepees on a bed of fir boughs (❶) and in the bunks of the soldiers' cabins (❶) – warm bedding is provided. Opposite the fort's entrance, the **Listuguj Arts and Cultural Centre** (May–Sept daily 9am–5pm; $5) offers a small display of traditional crafts and buildings from before European contact. The clothing, canoes and porcupine quill boxes are all made locally to rekindle interest in Micmac culture and traditional skills.

A couple of kilometres west of the bridge, back along Hwy 132, **La Bataille-de-la-Restigouche**, a national historic site, commemorates the crucial naval engagement of 1760, which effectively extinguished French hopes of relieving their stronghold in Montréal, the year after the fall of Québec City. The French fleet, which had already taken casualties in evading the blockade of Bordeaux, was forced to take refuge in the mouth of the Rivière Restigouche and then, despite assistance from local Micmacs and Acadians, was overpowered by superior British forces. The site's excellent **interpretation centre** (daily: June to early Oct 9am–5pm; ⓦwww.pc.gc.ca; $4) contains relics of the French fleet, especially the frigate *Le Machault*, which has been partly reconstructed. An audiovisual display provides a graphic account of the battle and of its strategic significance.

There's no need to stay in Pointe-à-la-Croix, but if you're marooned here, try an unusually regal **hostel**, *Auberge du Château Bahia* (☎418/788-2048; ❷; dorms $18), in **POINTE-À-LA-GARDE**, some 6km east of Listuguj and signposted off Hwy 132. It's in an eccentric Renaissance-style wooden castle built by the owner and his father – and the food is excellent. Rates include breakfast, and banquet-style dinners are served ($12).

Matapédia

At the western tip of the Baie des Chaleurs, at the confluence of the Restigouche and Matapédia rivers, the tiny village of **MATAPÉDIA**, a Micmac term meaning "there where the two rivers meet", is surrounded by steep green hills and lies at the centre of an excellent salmon-fishing region. Not a lot else happens here aside from canoe trips down the river, and the **restaurants** leave much to be desired: *La Vieille Gare*, at 50 boul Perron ouest, (☎418/865-2007) has somewhat pricey seafood fare and, close by, the *Motel Restigouche*, at no. 5 (☎418/865-2155; ❸), is the place to **stay** if you're into fishing and hunting. From Matapédia, Hwy 132 cuts north across the interior of the peninsula through Amqui, a dreary little town that serves as a ski resort in the winter, before heading back up to Ste-Flavie (see p.324).

Îles-de-la-Madeleine

The archipelago of the **Îles-de-la-Madeleine** (Magdalen Islands), in the middle of the Gulf of St Lawrence some 200km southeast (and one hour ahead) of the Gaspé Peninsula and 100km east of Prince Edward Island (see p.451), consists of twelve main islands, seven of which are inhabited. Six of these are connected by narrow sand spits and crossed by paved and gravel roads, while the last is only accessible by boat. Together these dozen islands form a crescent-shaped series of dunes, lagoons and low rocky outcrops that measures about 80km from end to end, with the main village and ferry port roughly in the middle at **Cap-aux-Meules**. The islands lie in the Gulf Stream, which makes the winters warmer than those of mainland Québec, but they are subject to almost constant winds, which have eroded the red-sandstone cliffs along parts of the shoreline into an extraordinary array of arches, caves and tunnels. These rock formations, the archipelago's most distinctive attraction, are at their best on the central **Île du Cap-aux-Meules** and the adjacent **Île du Havre-aux-Maisons**.

In 1534, **Jacques Cartier** stumbled across the Îles-de-la-Madeleine on his way west to the St Lawrence River. Cartier, always keen to impress his sponsors with the value of his discoveries, wrote with characteristic exaggeration, "The islands are full of beautiful trees, prairies, fields of wild wheat, and flowering pea plants as beautiful as I've ever seen in Brittany." Despite Cartier's eulogy, the islands attracted hardly any settlers until the Deportations of 1755, when a few Acadian families escaped here to establish a mixed farming and fishing community. Remote and isolated, the **Madelinots**, as the islanders came to be known, were unable to control their own economic fortunes, selling their fish at absurdly low prices to a series of powerful merchants who, in turn, sold them tackle and equipment at exorbitant rates. The most notorious of these men was **Isaac Coffin**, who was granted the land in 1798 by the British Crown in return for services rendered during the American Civil War. Coffin developed a classically colonial form of oppression by forcing most of the islanders to pay him rent for their lands. Only in 1895 did a provincial statute allow the Madelinots to buy them back, and Québec purchased the islands outright in 1958.

Today the 15,000 inhabitants are largely dependent on **fishing** in general, and the lobster catch in particular. Herring, mackerel, scallops and halibut are also mainstays, and most people work at local companies that freeze, can, smoke, ship or market the catch. Until recently, when international pressure brought it to an end, the annual seal hunt supported many islanders (in March, the seals can be easily spotted on the ice floes). Other sectors of the fishery are now suffering because of fish-stock depletion, and the community's future livelihood revolves around tourism. Many residents worry about preserving their way of life and the fragile ecology of their beautiful islands. Tourists come to the archipelago for its wide-open landscapes and sense of isolation – it's easy to find a dune-laden beach where you can be alone with the sea. Bear in mind, though, that throughout the islands powerful currents and changeable weather conditions can make sea bathing dangerous, and the waters are occasionally home to stinging jellyfish.

Île du Cap-aux-Meules

The ferry from Souris, PEI (see p.463), docks in the middle of the archipelago, at **Île du Cap-aux-Meules**, which boasts the islands' largest community – **CAP-AUX-MEULES**, on the eastern shore. A useful base for exploring the neighbouring islands, the town is the islands' administrative and business centre and their least attractive enclave. However, just a couple of kilometres west of the village, there are fine views of the entire island chain from the **Butte du Vent**, the area's highest hill. Further west, on the other end of the island near the fishing port of **ÉTANG-DU-NORD**, you'll find some extravagant coastal rock formations and a port where kayaking tours take off. In the opposite direction, the main road skirts the southern tip of the islands' longest lagoon before heading on across the Île du Havre-aux-Maisons.

Reasonable **accommodation** options include the *Motel Bellevue*, 40 chemin Principal (℡418/986-4477; ❹), and the *Auberge du Village*, 205 chemin Principal (℡418/986-3312; ❺). Alternatively, the large *Château Madelinot*, 323

Time zone
The Îles-de-la-Madeleine and Prince Edward Island are on **Atlantic time**, one hour ahead of Québec's **Eastern time**.

Getting there
Every month except February and March a CTMA **ferry** goes to Cap-aux-Meules **from Souris** on Prince Edward Island (Souris ☏902/687-2181; Cap-aux-Meules ☏418/986-6600; Montréal ☏514/937-7656; Ⓦwww.ilesdelamadeleine.com/cmta) – the number of weekly departures varies from five to ten depending on the season (takes 5hr). A return trip costs $295 for a car with two passengers. Reservations are mandatory in July and August and need to be made several months in advance. The *Voyageur*, a cargo and fifteen-passenger ship, also operated by CTMA, departs **from Montréal** for the islands every Friday (takes 48hr; around $550 one-way including meals; plus $250 for a car).

Daily scheduled **flights** on Air Canada leave Gaspé town, Québec City, Montréal (around $600 roundtrip) and Halifax, NS. Book two weeks in advance, and include a Saturday overnight stay for discount flights. The only alternative airline is Pascan Aviation (☏418/877-8777 or 1-888/313-8777, Ⓦwww.pascan.com) which flies from Montréal and Québec City.

Arrival and information
The islands' **airport** is inconveniently situated at the north end of Île du Havre-aux-Maisons, some 20km from Cap-aux-Meules. Some flights have connecting buses to Cap-aux-Meules, but otherwise you'll have to take a **taxi** (about $35), or **rent a car** from National (☏418/969-4209) or Thrifty (☏418/969-9006) at the airport; book in advance in the summer. The **ferry terminal** at Cap-aux-Meules is near the **tourist office**, 128 chemin Principal (late June to Aug daily 7am–9pm; Sept to mid-Oct daily 9am–9pm; mid-Oct to late June Mon–Fri 9am–5pm; ☏418/986-2245 or

Hwy 199 (☏418/986-3695 or 1-800/661-4537;Ⓞ), offers fine sea views, great food and comfortable rooms. There are several **campsites**: try the peaceful *Le Barachois*, chemin du Rivage, Fatima (☏418/986-6065; $20 for two; May–Oct), or *Hostel and Camping Gros Cap*, 74 chemin du Camping, Étang du Nord (☏418/9886-4505 or 1-800/986-4505, Ⓦwww.leradar.qc.ca /parcdesgroscap.htm; dorms $24, camping site $18 for two; May–Sept).

For outstanding but pricey **food**, try the seafood at *La Table des Roy*, 1188 Hwy 199 (☏418/986-3004; closed Mon) in La Vernière just west of Cap-aux-Meules; dinner will set you back over $50. Better everyday choices are the *Petit Café* (☏418/986-2130) in the Château Madelinot, 323 Hwy 199, open all year, with a menu that ranges from hamburgers to lobsters (evening specials cost about $25), and *La Factrie*, 521 chemin Gros Cap ☏418/986-2710), a fun and inexpensive cafeteria-style lobster restaurant attached to a lobster-processing plant.

Île du Havre-aux-Maisons
Île du Havre-aux-Maisons' smooth green landscapes contrast with the red cliffs of its southern shore. Crisscrossed by narrow country roads and littered with tiny straggling villages, this island is best known for a unique oral tradition. The Acadians that settled here post-deportation were so irate with their treatment they decided never to utter the word "king" (*roi* in French) again; over the years, they wound up dropping the letter "r" altogether from their language. The weird shapes of the coastal rocks around **Dune-du-Sud** are well

1-877/624-4437, ⓦwww.tourismeilesdelamadeleine.com). They have masses of free leaflets and operate a free room-reservation service with a special emphasis on B&Bs. With few **inns**, **motels** and **hotels** on the islands, it's a good idea to book a bed before you arrive. The tourist office also has details of cottage and apartment rentals, starting at roughly $250 per week. The cheapest way to stay is either at the **hostel** – where you can also camp – or one of the other half-dozen commercial **campsites** on the islands.

Transport, boat trips and water sports

The best way to tour the principal islands is by a **bike**, which may be rented at Le Pédalier, 365 chemin Principal, Cap-aux-Meules (☎418/986-2965). **Mopeds** can be rented from Cap-aux-Meules Honda, Hwy 199 at La Vernière, southwest of Cap-aux-Meules (☎418/986-4085).

Departures for **boat** and **fishing trips** are near the ferry terminal throughout the summer by Aventure en zodiac (☎418/986-4745, ⓦwww.excursiosenmer.com) and Explorivage (☎418/986-3255, ⓦwww.ilesdelamadeleine.com/explorivage).

In the past many of the visitors to these out-of-the-way islands have been hippies and drifters looking for a break from the mainstream and the mainland, and some elements of this still exist among the some of the islands' artsy newer inhabitants. But recently the bigger attraction for many adventurous visitors has been the strong winds that blow here. Between late August and late October conditions for **wind-surfing** and **kite-surfing** are exemplary and the Canadian Professional and Amateur Windsurf Championship heads here every year. Aerosport Carrefour d'Aventures 1390 route 199 (☎418/986-6677) in Etang-du-Nord can be contacted for advice and rentals for all things kite. Winds have also played their part in leaving so many ships to founder around the coast – leaving behind some superb **wreck-diving** for scuba fans. For information and trips contact Le Repère du Plonger, 18 Allée Léo Leblanc (☎418/986-3962).

worth a visit, as is the **Fumoir d'Antan**, 27 chemin du Quai (daily 9am–5pm; free tour), the last remaining traditional herring smokehouse on the islands. Down by the lagoon, the hodgepodge collection of artefacts at the **Centre d'interprétation de Havre-aux-Maisons** (June to mid-Sept daily 9am–9pm) is on loan from local families and offers an excellent introduction to the local lore. Next door, **Les Excursions de la Lagune** takes off three times daily for a two-hour tour of the lagoon on a glass-bottom boat (☎418/969-2088; $20) that's both highly entertaining and educational. Deserted twin beaches edge the hamlet islet of **Pointe-aux-Loups** north of here, across the sand spit and along Hwy 199.

Should you want to **stay**, the *Auberge la P'tite Baie*, 187 Hwy 199 (☎418/969-4073, ⓦwww3.sympatico.ca/auberge.petitebaie; ❸), with its lovely rooms and sea vistas, is your best bet. Or **camp** by the beach on the east side of the island at *Camping Les Sillons* (May to mid-Oct; ☎418/969-2134; $22 for two). For great **seafood**, try the restored convent *Au Vieux Couvent*, 292 Hwy 199 (☎418/969-2233), which also has a lively basement **bar** with regular live music acts – even without, the place gets packed nightly until 11pm.

Grosse-Île and Île de la Grande-Entrée

At the far end of the archipelago, the twin islets of anglophone **Grosse-Île** and francophone **Île de la Grande-Entrée** border the wildlife reserve of the **Pointe-de-l'Est**, whose entrance is beside the main road. On its south side, the reserve is edged by the enormous sandy expanse of La Grande Échouerie **beach**, whose southern end is framed by yet more splendid rock formations at Old Harry's Point. This is where Europeans first came to the islands in order to slaughter walruses, depleting the stock by 1800. Nowadays, the 10km walk down the beach offers a good chance to spot seals, and there have been renewed – albeit very rare – walrus sightings. A kilometre past the rustic wharf at **Old Harry**, a pretty white church with beautifully sculptured doors uses the islands as backdrop for biblical tales. A little further, the old red schoolhouse is home to the Council for Anglophone Magdalen Islanders and a **museum** (July & Aug Mon–Fri 9am–4pm, Sat & Sun 1–4pm; Sept–June by appointment; ☏418/985-2116; free) tells the history of the anglophone population, most of whom are of Scottish descent. To learn more about seals head to the **Centre d'interprétation du Phoque**, 377 Hwy 199 (mid-June to late Aug daily 10am–6.30pm; rest of year by appointment; ☏418/985-2833 or 1-888/537-4537, ⓦwww.ilesdelamadeleine.com/cip; $5.50).

The lobster port of **Île de la Grande-Entrée**, the last island to be inhabited, has a couple of **accommodation** options: *Domaine de la Grenouille sur Mer*, 83 chemin des Pealey (☏418/985-2365 or 514/645-9855; ❸), and *Club Vacances "Les Îles"*, 377 Hwy 199 (☏418/985-2833 or 1-888/537-4537, ⓦwww.clubiles.qc.ca; ❸), which is open all year and has camping space as well as rooms and a great cafeteria. The **food** is expensive but you can save money by opting to pay for full board; it's also open to non-guests. The club also offers various activities, like trips to the caves on offshore Île Boudreau and seal-spotting excursions in the summer.

Île du Havre-Aubert

To the south of Île du Cap-aux-Meules, **Île du Havre-Aubert** has one significant community, **HAVRE-AUBERT**, that's edged by round, sloping hills. It's the most attractive of the islands' communities, and its picturesque location and undoubtable charm attract a lot of visitors. It is situated around **La Grave**, a pebbly beach flanked by a boardwalk and wooden buildings once used by sailors and fishermen and now transformed into bars, cafés, restaurants, souvenir shops and an art gallery for the island's new trade in tourists; for the best spot to buy things, from lampshades and fish-heads to household decorations made of sand, try Les Artisans du Sable. On the beach the **Aquarium** (early June to mid-Aug daily 10am–6pm; mid-Aug to mid-Oct 10am–5pm; ⓦwww.ilesdelamadeleine.com/aquarium; $5.50) displays fish and crustaceans found in the waters around the island, and there's a small seal tidal pool out back. Overlooking La Grave, the **Musée de la Mer** (June–Aug daily 9am–6pm; Sept–May Mon–Fri 9am–5pm, Sat & Sun 1–5pm; $4) has a series of displays on local fishing techniques and the history of the islands. Especially interesting is the exhibit focused on the more than 400 shipwrecks that have occurred just offshore.

Set apart from Havre-Aubert, in the community of Bassin, the **Site d'Autrefois** (daily: June–Aug 9am–6pm; Sept 10am–4pm; $6) is a fanciful spot that tells the story of Madelinot life through life-sized mannequins of fishermen, boats and model houses. La Chevauché des Iles (☏418/937-2368 or 937-5453; $25–40) also in Bassin, offers **horseback riding** tours of the island while Centre Nautique de l'Istorlet, 100 chemin de l'Isorlet (☏418/937-5266 or 1-888/937-8166, ⓦwww.istorlet.qc.ca), rents out **sea and surf kayaks**, a fun way to explore the cliffs and caves of the coast, and also rents out **rooms** (❶).

You can **stay** on La Grave at *Chez Charles Painchaud*, 930 Hwy 199 (☏418/937-2227; ❸), or *Le Berceau des Îles*, 701 chemin principal in

Havre-Aubert (☎418/937-5614; ❸) which has some more luxurious rooms. Both are **B&Bs** and can arrange for pick-ups from the airport or ferry as well as organize winter and summer activities – they even rent cars. *Auberge Chez Denis à François*, 404 chemin d'en Haut (☎418/937-2371, ⓦwww .ilesdelamadeleine.com/auberge; ❸), offers fine views of the strip. **Restaurants** are of good quality in Havre-Aubert: even if you don't stay at *Auberge Chez Denis à François*, you should definitely try the seafood – they even have seal on the menu. *La Saline*, 1009 Hwy 199 (☎418/937-2230) in La Grave, is open for delicious evening fare – there's also live music in the adjoining bar. The much more expensive *La Marée Haute*, 25 chemin des Fumoirs (☎418/937-2492), is also only open at night and serves up some of Canada's finest seafood, including sea urchins and smoked seal. For chunky sandwiches and clam chowder served in bread, head for the atmospheric *Café de la Grave* (☎418/937-5244) in the old general store. *Le Petit Mondrain* on chemin de La Grave is popular with locals, and its seafood is among the islands' cheapest.

Île d'Entrée

To the southeast, tiny anglophone **Île d'Entrée** is the only inhabited island not linked by land to the rest of the archipelago. Home to 175 people, this grassy hillock is encircled by footpaths and makes a pleasant day out, providing the sea is calm on the **ferry** trip from Cap-aux-Meules (Mon–Sat 2 daily; ☎418/986-8452 or 986-5705; $16 return). Horses and cows roam freely on the slopes of the Îles-de-la-Madeleine's highest point, **Big Hill** (174m), accessible from the port by taking chemin Main and then chemin Post Office, and following the path across the fields to the top for a view of the whole archipelago. On your way towards the path, a tiny **museum** (June–Sept hours vary ☎418/986-6622; free) displays island artefacts and historical household items. The only official lodging is the basic **B&B** *Chez McLean* (☎418/986-4541; ❷). Otherwise, you'll probably end up in someone's home. For **food**, there's a bar-restaurant and a grocery store near the port.

Charlevoix

Stretching along the **north shore** of the St Lawrence east of Québec City, from the Beaupré coast to the Saguenay Fjord, the area of **Charlevoix**, named after the Jesuit historian Francois Xavier de Charlevoix, is a UNESCO World Biosphere Reserve. Species like the arctic caribou and great wolf, not usually associated with such southerly latitudes, can be seen in the more remote areas, and because the Ice Age that shaped the rest of eastern Canada missed this breathtaking portion of the Canadian Shield, numerous pre-glacial plants still thrive here. It consists of gently sloping hills, sheer cliffs and vast valleys veined with rivers, brooks and waterfalls, a landscape that Québec's better known artists – Clarence Gagnon, Marc-Aurèle Fortin and Jean-Paul Lemieux – chose for inspiration. Though Charlevoix has been a tourist destination for years and especially popular with people from Québec City on weekend breaks, the land has been carefully preserved, and quaint villages and tin-roofed churches still nestle in an unspoiled countryside. The tourist office produces a brochure, *La Route des Saveurs de Charlevoix*, which is useful on a gastronomic trip: it lists agricultural producers and the restaurants that use local products in regional cuisine.

Hwy 138, the main route through Charlevoix, travels 225km from Québec City to Baie-Ste-Catherine on the Saguenay. The main towns along this highway are served by Intercar **buses** from Québec City, but many of the quintessential Charlevoix villages – in particular those along the coastal Hwy 362 – are not served by public transport. Be prepared to rent a car or bike; the expense is well worth it.

Baie-Saint-Paul and around

One of Charlevoix's earliest settlements and longtime gathering place for Québec's landscape painters, the picture-perfect **BAIE-SAINT-PAUL** is tucked into the Gouffré valley at the foot of the highest range of the Laurentian mountains. Dominated by the twin spires of the church, the streets wind from the centre of town flanked by houses that are more than two hundred years old – and just wandering around Baie-Saint-Paul is the main attraction. For an overview of the works of art produced in Charlevoix, visit the **Centre d'Art de Baie-Saint-Paul**, behind the church at 4 rue Ambroise-Fafard (April to late June, Sept & Oct daily 10am–6pm; Nov to April Wed–Sun 10am–5pm; $3), which has excellent exhibitions of paintings and sculptures mostly inspired by the surrounding countryside; the Centre's boutique also sells local crafts. Opposite, at no. 23, the plush **Centre d'Exposition** (daily: late June to Sept 10am–7pm; rest of year 10am–5pm; $3) has established an international reputation for the excellence of its temporary exhibitions of Québecois and international art. Also every August to early September, at a symposium, the public can watch young Canadian and European artists at work in the nearby arena. From beside the church, the rue St-Jean-Baptiste slips through the commercial heart of the town edged by numerous quaint cottages characteristic of Québec's earliest houses, with curving roofs and wide verandas, many converted into commercial galleries. At 58 rue St-Jean-Baptiste, the **Maison de René Richard** (daily 10am–6pm; $2.50) offers an insight into the works of René Richard, an associate of the Group of Seven. The 1852 house has been left exactly the same since Richard died in 1982; bilingual guided tours take you around his studio and living quarters, a rare glimpse at the Charlevoix of the 1940s when some of Québec's finest painters hung out here.

The **information centre** for Baie-Saint-Paul and the whole Charlevoix area is at the Belvédère Baie-Saint-Paul off Hwy 138 before you descend into town from the west (daily: mid-June to early Sept 9am–7pm; rest of year 9am–4.30pm; ☎418/435-4160 or 1-800/667-2276, ⓦwww.baiestpaul.com), where there's a free museum detailing the geography of the area. There is also a seasonal office in the Centre d'Art, 4 rue Ambroise-Fafard (late June to late Sept daily 10am–7pm; ☎418/435-5795). The Intercar **bus** stops at *Restaurant La Grignote*, 2 rte de l'Equerre (☎418/435-6569), in the shopping centre by Hwy 138, twenty minutes' walk from downtown.

Baie-Saint-Paul has an excellent variety of **accommodation**. The best hotels are the 1840 *Auberge la Maison Otis*, 23 rue St-Jean-Baptiste (☎418/435-2255 or 1-800/267-2254, ⓦwww.maisonotis.com; ❺), and the *Auberge La Pignoronde*, 750 boul Mgr-de-Laval (☎418/435-5505 or 1-888/554-6004, ⓦwww.aubergelapignoronde.com; ❸). Next door to each other on the waterfront, the *Domaine Belle-Plage*, 192 rue Ste-Anne (☎418/435-3321, ⓦwww.cormoranbelleplage.com; ❸), and the *Auberge le Cormoran* at no. 196 (☎418/435-6030; ❸), both have comfortable doubles, while in the centre of town is the *Auberge La Muse*, 39 rue St-Jean-Baptiste (☎418/435-6839 or 1-800/841-6839, ⓦwww.lamuse.com; ❹). Further up the street is *Gîte la Tourterelle*, 77 rue St-Jean-Baptiste (☎418/435-2441; ❸), one of the town's numerous **B&Bs**. The town's best bargain is the **hostel** and **campsite** Le Balcon Vert (☎418/435-5587, ⓦwww.balconvert.charlevoix.net; mid-May to early Oct) up a gravel road about 3km out on Hwy 362 to Malbaie, with four-berth cabins ($45), camping ($20 for a four-person site) and dorm beds ($20). The views are tremendous from here and the on-site bar and restaurant (there are no guest kitchens) ensure a sociable vibe. Summer **camping** is also available at the heavily wooded riverside *Camping du Gouffre*, 439 chemin St-Laurent (☎418/435-2143; $16–23), or the larger *Camping le Genévrier*, 1175 boul Mgr-de-Laval (☎418/435-6520 or 1-877/435-6520, ⓦwww.genevrier .com; $19–29).

Food is plentiful within a block or two of the church: *Café d'Artistes*, 25 rue St-Jean-Baptiste, has desserts, coffees and thin-crust pizzas, while *Les Deux Soeurs* is an excellent patisserie-café across the street at no. 48. *Le Mouton Noir*, 43 rue Ste-Anne (☎418/240-3030), serves hearty country cooking, like smoked sausages with maple syrup. The restaurant of the *Belle-Plage* also serves traditional Québecois cuisine, with a buffet for around $15. Two good spots combine eating and **drinking**: *Le Saint-Pub*, 2 rue Racine (corner of St-Jean-Baptiste), a terrific brewpub with delicious bistro fare, and *Cuore di Lupo*, 29 rue Ambroise-Fafard, which has a terrace and reasonably priced pizza and pasta.

Around Baie-Saint-Paul

At 41 rue St-Jean-Baptiste in Baie-Saint-Paul, Randonnées Nature-Charlevoix (☎418/435-6275) runs excellent **bike tours** of the environs (2hr; $6; or $4 if you rent a bike for $20/day), as well as hiking tours in the Parc des Grands-Jardins and tours around the **Charlevoix Crater** – one of the planet's largest craters, made by a meteorite – by bus (late June to early Sept; 1 daily; 2hr; $15). Down at the marina, L'Air du Large, 210 rue Ste Anne (☎418/435-2066, ⓦwww.quebecweb.com/airdularge) rent bicycles, kayaks, canoes and paraglid-ers and offer courses in kayaking and paragliding. They also run boat trips to explore nearby islands.

Some of the province's most dramatic **skiing** can be found at **Le Massif** perched over the St Lawrence to the west of town. Baie-Saint-Paul also makes a good base to explore the **Parc des Grands-Jardins** (daily: June–Aug 8am–8pm; Sept–May 9am–5pm; ⓦwww.sepaq.com; $3.50), 42km away on Hwy 381 but with no public transport. Within the forests and lakes of the park, the 900m Mont du Lac des Cygnes gives the best of all Charlevoix panoramas; it's a four-hour climb there and back from the trailhead just beyond the **Thomas–Fortin reception centre** at the park entrance on Hwy 381. (Hwy 381 continues to Chicoutimi on the Rivière Saguenay; see p.353.) You can rent canoes ($28/day) here and **chalets** (❹), huts (❶) and campsites ($19) are also available but must be reserved in advance (☎1-800/665-6527).

Attracting hikers, mountain bikers and cross-country skiers, the long-distance **Traversée de Charlevoix** (☎418/639-2284, ⓦwww.charlevoix.net/traverse) begins near the park on Hwy 381, crossing 100km of mountainous terrain including the Parc des Hautes-Gorges-de-la-Rivière-Malbaie before ending at Mont Grand-Fonds near La Malbaie. Accommodation in cabins or cottages starts at $122 for the six nights needed to complete the hike.

Les Éboulements and around

From Baie-Saint-Paul the main route onwards is Hwy 138, but if you have your own transport you should opt for the coast-hugging detour of Hwy 362, which twists and turns through a succession of cliff-top villages along the shore of the St Lawrence.

The first settlement on this route is **LES ÉBOULEMENTS**, which means "landslides" – named after the massive earthquake of 1663, one of many that shaped this region. Just west of the village at no. 157 rue Principale is the eighteenth-century **Moulin Banal** (late June to early Sept daily 10am–5pm; $3), an operating flour mill atop a pretty waterfall on the well-kept grounds of the **Manoir de Sales-Laterrière**. The manor and mill are among the few intact structures left from the seigneurial regime of New France. The manor (a school) is not actually open to the public but a path leads up from the mill, with interpretation panels on the grounds. At the entrance to the grounds is a charming chapel (1840) built of wood and relocated here from St-Nicholas, a village on the St Lawrence. Further down the road, in the village itself, the **Centre d'interprétation de la Forge Tremblay**, 214 rue Principale (Nov to mid-May; free but reservations required), dating from 1888, is still used by blacksmiths.

From Les Éboulements, a steep secondary road leads to the pretty coastal village of **SAINT-JOSEPH-DE-LA-RIVE**, once a shipyard; some heritage can be seen in the **Exposition Maritime**, 304 rue Félix-Antoine-Savard (mid-May to late June & early Sept to early Oct Mon–Fri 9am–4pm, Sat & Sun 11am–4pm; late June to early Sept daily 9am–5pm; $3), a museum with a few nautical displays, a workshop and boat-building yards. Pop into the local **church** (June–Oct daily 9am–8pm; free) on chemin de l'Église, where anchors prop up the altar and the font is a huge seashell from Florida. *Le Loup-Phoque*, 188 rue Félix-Antoine-Savard, a funky spot good for **food** and views, has occasional live music.

Île aux Coudres

The 16km-long island of **Île aux Coudres** is said to have been formed when an earthquake shook it from the escarpment at Les Éboulements. Cartier celebrated Canada's first Mass here in 1535 and named the island after its numerous hazelnut trees. Missionaries were the first permanent settlers, arriving in 1748, and the growing population came to depend on shipbuilding and beluga-whale hunting for their livelihoods. Ship- and canoe-building still takes place here, but the main industry of its 1600 inhabitants is harvesting peat moss from the bogs in the centre of the island.

Access is on a free **car ferry** (8–24 trips daily 7am–11.30pm; takes 15min; ☎418/438-2743) from Saint-Joseph-de-la-Rive. The island's stone manors and cottages nowadays attract huge numbers of visitors, who drive and **cycle** around the 26km peripheral road that connects – in a clockwise direction – the three villages of **ST-BERNARD, LA BALEINE** and **ST-LOUIS**. Of the incidental attractions along the way, the only real diversions are the restored wind and adjacent water mills – **Les Moulins de l'Isle-aux-Coudres** (mid-May to late June & mid-Aug to mid-Oct daily 10am–5pm; late June to mid-Aug daily 9am–6.30pm; $2.75) – in the southwest corner of the island, both of which are in full working order. There is an **information centre** (mid-June to Aug daily 10am–7pm) near the ferry dock in St-Bernard, with maps of the island. **Bikes** can be rented from Gérard Desgagnés, near the jetty at 34 rue du Port (☎418/438-2332), or Vél 'O'-Coudres, 743 chemin des Coudriers in La Baleine (☎418/438-2118), which has a wider selection but is 5km from the dock, linked by free hourly shuttle. Rent **kayaks** for $29 per half-day at Kayak de Mer, down the road at no. 783 (☎418/438-4388); they also offer guided trips for $25–70.

Places **to stay** are unexciting, but many have reasonable restaurants. In La Baleine the best deals are the *Motel la Baleine*, 138 rue Principale (☎418/438-2453; ❷), and *Motel Écumé*, 808 chemin des Coudriers (☎418/438-2733; ❷), a bizarre place with deliberately tilted windows and mismatched furniture in very basic rooms. The best bargain is the *Motel l'Islet*, 10 chemin de l'Islet (☎418/438-2423, ⓦwww.quebecweb.com/lislet; ❷; May to mid-Oct), in an isolated spot near St-Louis, on the west tip of the island. The posh hotel *Cap-aux-Pierres*, 246 rue Principale in La Baleine (☎438/2711 or 1-888/554-6003; ❻), provides half-board accommodation and has a good restaurant. **Campsites** include *Camping Leclerc*, 183 rue Principale, La Baleine (☎418/438-2217; $16–22) and *Camping Sylvie*, 191 rue Royale ouest, St-Bernard (☎418/438-2420; tents $12–18, chalets $40), where you can rent canoes. For good local **meals** head to *La Mer Veille*, 160 des Coudriers in St-Louis; the lunch menu is $10.

La Malbaie

Highways 362 and 138 converge about 50km from Baie-Saint-Paul at **LA MALBAIE** ("Bad Bay"), so called because Champlain ran aground here in 1608. Situated at the mouth of the Malbaie River, the town – an amalgamation of five villages – sprawls along the riverfront with little to detain you, though it's a good base for a day trip to the Hautes-Gorges; and the ritzy resort area **POINTE-AU-PIC** – back along Hwy 362 – is worth a quick look for its late nineteenth-century tourist-château. Originally built in 1899 for the Richelieu and Ontario Navigation Company, who ferried tourists here from New York and Montréal, the hotel was rebuilt after a fire in the 1920s, and has been recently renovated. It makes for a delightful overnight stay – and you can wager the rest of your travel budget at the *Casino de Charlevoix* next door.

Descente Malbaie (☎418/439-2265), who are based just north of St Aimé des Lacs halfway to the Hautes-Gorges, run white-water **rafting** in summer (around $50 for 2hr); overnight trips are also available. In winter the Rac du Mont Grand Fords has **downhill skiing** and **snowboarding** (☎418/664-0095 or 1-877/667-0095; day pass $28) on fourteen trails or **cross-country skiing** at the Centre de Plein Aire Les Sources Joyeuses (☎418/665-4858; $8) where 82km of trails – and 5km of ice-skating trails – are maintained. Instruction and equipment rental is available at both ski centres.

The **tourist office**, beside the main road at 630 boul de Comporté (mid-June to Sept daily 8.30am–9pm; rest of year Mon–Fri 8.30am–4.30pm, Sat & Sun 9am–5pm; ☎418/665-4454), has a full range of regional tourist info. **Buses** arrive nearby at Dépanneur Otis, 46 rue Ste-Catherine (☎418/665-2264). The nearest **car ferry** service across the St Lawrence leaves from the hillside village of **Saint-Siméon** 25km northeast on Hwy 138 towards Rivière du Loup (see p.320). Much of the classiest **accommodation** is in Pointe-Au-Pic, home to the luxurious château-like *Le Manoir Richelieu*, 181 rue Richelieu (☎418/665-3703 or 1-800/441-1414, ⓦwww.fairmont.com; ❼) and many manor houses that have been converted into charming country inns. The *Auberge des 3 Canards*, 115 Côte Bellevue (☎418/665-3761 or 1-800/461-3761, ⓦwww.aubergedes3canards.com; ❻), is an inn with one of the finest restaurants in Québec, and prices to match. The Victorian **B&B** *Gîte Harrop's*, 400 rue Richelieu (☎418/665-4120, ⓦwww.harrops.com; ❸), has gardens overlooking the St Lawrence. In the main part of La Malbaie is *Motel Murray Bay*, 40 rue Laure-Conan (☎418/665-2441; ❷), and *Gîte E.T. Harvey* (☎418/665-2779; ❷) on the same street at no. 19. Cap-à-l'Aigle, an agricultural village to the east, has an excellent B&B, *Claire Villeneuve*, 215 rue St-Raphaël (☎418/665-2288; ❷), a great example of Québecois rural architecture. If you have transport, head for Charlevoix's oldest and most beautifully situated **campsite**, *Camping Chutes Fraser*, 500 chemin de la Vallée (☎418/665-2151; $17–27, chalets $40; mid-May to mid-Oct), by the falls of the same name about 3km north of La Malbaie. For **food** try the *Manoir Richelieu's Winston* bar and restaurant for inexpensive breakfasts. At the La Malbaie marina *Café de la Gare*, 100 chemin du Havre (☎418/665-4272), has a limited menu of items like paninis, mussels and nachos (mains $9–16). For pub food head to *Club des Monts*, 110 Ruisseau des Frênes (☎418/439-3711), a busy bar with frequent live music.

The Hautes-Gorges

One sight not be missed in the Charlevoix region is the **Parc des Hautes-Gorges-de-la-Rivière-Malbaie**, a network of valleys that slice through a maze of lofty peaks 45km west of La Malbaie. To get there take Hwy 138 to **SAINT-AIMÉ-DES-LACS**, a small town 13km northwest of La Malbaie from where the way to the park is well marked. Admission to the park is $3.50 and the park's **information centre**, Chalet l'Écluse (daily mid-May to early Oct 7am–9pm; ☎418/439-1227 or 1-800/665-6527), is located beside the Malbaie River just off rue Principale. You must leave your car here and rent a bike ($23/day) or take the frequent, free shuttle bus into the park as far as the l'Écluse dam.

As you enter the park, cliff faces on all sides rise up to more than 700m, making it Canada's deepest canyon east of the Rockies, formed by a slip in the earth's crust 800 million years ago. Its uniqueness lies not just in this astounding geology but also in the fact that all of Québec's forest species grow in this one comparatively small area. From the Chalet l'Écluse a tiring but rewarding five-kilometre hike on the **Mont des Érables trail** leads to the canyon's highest point, passing through a Laurentian maple grove on the way to the arctic–alpine tundra of the 800m summit; reckon on six hours for the roundtrip. Other shorter trails from the **l'Écluse dam** offer less strenuous alternatives. From here you can take a leisurely ninety-minute river cruise ($26) or rent **canoes or kayaks** ($10/hr; $32/day) for the six-kilometre paddle along the calm "Eaux Mortes" of the river. All these must be paid for first at the park information centre where you can also reserve sites at the park's one **campsite**, *Camping du Pin Blanc* ($19–24; June–Aug), and get permits for wild camping – some of which is only accessible by canoe.

The Saguenay and Lac Saint-Jean

Quebec's most schizophrenic region, the **Saguenay** encompasses some of the province's most spectacular scenery, tremendous marine life and also the dreariest of industrial towns. Fortunately, the two extremes are kept nicely separate along the Saguenay River, so that you can explore the rich landscapes along its fjord and source – **Lac Saint-Jean** – in peace. Best known for its **whale-watching** opportunities, the region is also exceptional for canoeing, backcountry hiking and cycle touring.

The main tourist centre of the region is **Tadoussac**, 78km north of La Malbaie and 227km from Québec City via Hwy 138. It lies at a pretty spot at the neck of the Saguenay Fjord, and its confluence with the St Lawrence. Many just come here to catch a boat to head out to the whales, but it's a pretty town in its own right, from which you can often see the whales, and it also makes a great base to explore a number of other outdoor attractions in the vicinity. Many of these are centered on the national parks along the **Fjord du Saguenay** where both the land and sea are protected (as the Parc du Saguenay and Parc Marin du Saguenay–St-Laurent; ☎418/235-4703 or 1-800/463-6769, ⓦwww.sepaq.com). The marine park contains six different ecosystems and supports hundreds of marine species, but as part of the hydrographic basin of the Great Lakes and the St Lawrence – once the most polluted waterway in Canada thanks to toxic waste discharges – it had its work cut out protecting the area. Since the creation of the park, government initiatives have eliminated ninety percent of the pollutants from industrial plants in the immediate vicinity. The damage has already been done, though: pollutants remain in the sediment and the number of St Lawrence **beluga whales** is down from five thousand a century ago to one thousand today, placing them on Canada's list of endangered species. That said, the area continues to attract the whales because the mingling of the cold Labrador Sea waters with the highly oxygenated freshwater of the Saguenay produces a uniquely rich crop of krill and plankton. The white St Lawrence beluga lives in the area all year round, and from May to October it is joined by six species of migratory whales including the minke, finback and gigantic **blue whale**, the largest animal on earth.

If you have the time, continue west to the **Upper Saguenay** past the industrial centres of **Chicoutimi** and **Jonquière** and make a circuit of the flat farming country of **Lac Saint-Jean**. It's an ideal location to cycle, and the recently completed **Véloroute des Bleuets** allows you to travel the 256km around the lake without trucks forcing you off the road.

Tadoussac and around

One of Canada's oldest villages, **TADOUSSAC** is beautifully situated beneath the rounded hills that gave the place its name; the Algonquian word *tatoushak* means "breasts". Basque whalers were the first Europeans to live here and by the time Samuel de Champlain arrived in 1603 Tadoussac was a thriving trading post. The mid-nineteenth century saw Tadoussac evolve into a popular summer resort for the anglophone bourgeoisie: the first hotel opened in 1846 and by the 1860s steamer-loads of rich anglophones were arriving every summer to escape the heat of the city. Nowadays it's the best place in Québec, along with Bergeronnes and Les Escoumins just north along the coast, for **whale-watching** (see box, p.348). Late June is a good time to be here, when traditional Québecois folk singers, jazz pianists and rock guitarists all play a part in the popular **Festival de la Chanson**.

The waterfront rue de Bord-de-l'Eau is dominated by the red roof and green lawns of the *Hôtel Tadoussac*, a landmark since 1864 and the focus of the historic quarter. Across the road is the oldest wooden church in Canada, the tiny **Chapelle de Tadoussac** (late June to early Oct daily 9am–9pm; $2), built in 1747; visits are possible out of season by reservation (☎418/235-4324). Tucked on the other side of the hotel, the steep-roofed wooden **Poste de Traite Chauvin** (daily: late May to mid-June & early Sept to mid-Oct 10am–6pm; mid-June to mid-Sept 9am–8.30pm; $3) exactly replicates – right down to the handmade nails – the first trading post on the north shore of the St Lawrence as described in Champlain's 1603 diary. It houses a small museum of beaver pelts and bits and pieces pertaining to the fur trade, but a peek in from the doorway will suffice. Following the waterfront towards the harbour

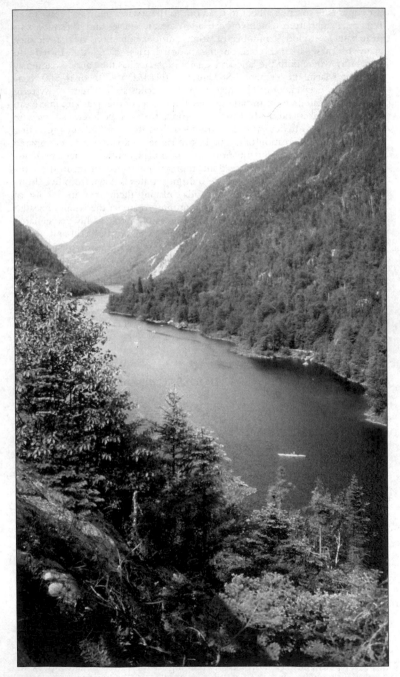

△ Hautes-Gorges

brings you to the modern **Centre d'Interprétation des Mammifères Marins**, 108 rue de la Cale-Sèche (daily: mid-May to mid-June & late Sept to late Oct noon–5pm; mid-June to late Sept 9am–8pm; Ⓦ www.gremm.org; $5.50), run by the nonprofit Group for Research and Education on Marine Mammals (GREMM). This is a must if you intend to go whale-watching, as its excellent documentary films and displays explain the life cycles of the whales in the St Lawrence and the efforts being made to save their ever-diminishing numbers. The small but informative **Musée Maritime de Tadoussac**, back near the ferry terminal at 145 rue du Bateau-Passeur (late June to Aug daily 10am–4pm; $2.50), has exhibits on the history of shipbuilding and navigation in the area.

The Tadoussac sector of the Parc du Saguenay offers some easy **hikes** around the village and a 42km trek to Baie-Ste-Marguerite further along the fjord; an **information office** (mid-June to Sept daily 9am–5pm) in the car park just after the ferry terminal supplies maps of the trails. From near the Chapelle there is a two-hour walk along the beach; check what time the tide rolls in as you'll have to clamber over rocks at high tide. It ends northeast of Tadoussac at the long terraced **sand dunes** on the Baie du Moulin-Baude, known locally as *le désert*. To reach the 112m-high dunes, you can also follow chemin du Moulin-Baude for 5km to the interpretation centre, the Maison des Dunes (early June to mid-Oct daily 9am–5pm; ☎418/272-1556 or 1-877/272-5229; $3.50).

Practicalities

Traffic crosses the neck of the fjord by a free **car ferry** from Baie-Ste-Catherine to Tadoussac, but you may have to wait as long as an hour or two to board in midsummer. The nearest ferries across the St Lawrence depart and arrive from Les Escoumins in the north (see p.350) and Saint-Siméon in the south (see p.343). Tadoussac's **bus** terminus is at 443 rue du Bâteau-Passeur on Hwy 138 by the campsite (☎418/235-4653). The excellent **information** centre for the entire Côte-Nord is in the smart red-brick manor at 197 rue des Pionniers (daily: late June to early Sept 8am–9pm; early Sept to late June 9am–noon & 1–5pm; ☎418/235-4744 or 1-866/235-4744). They have a load of leaflets, an accommodation service and next door you can watch videos of the area.

The pick of Tadoussac's wealth of **accommodation** is the *Hôtel Tadoussac*, 165 rue du Bord de l'Eau (☎418/235-4421 or 1-800/561-0718, Ⓦ www.hoteltadoussac.com; ❺), with surcharged riverview rooms. Cheaper is the *Motel de l'Anse-à-l'Eau*, 173 rue des Pionniers (☎418/235-4313; ❸), which does a fine breakfast. A number of the town's **B&Bs** are ranged along rue des Pionniers, including *Maison Clauphi* at no. 188 (☎418/235-4303; ❸), a B&B-cum-motel. *Maison Hovington*, at no. 285 (☎418/235-4466; ❸; mid-May to Oct), is a century-old B&B with five beautifully decorated rooms; the bilingual owners will pick you up from the bus station. *La Maison Boularch*, near the harbour at 118 rue de la Cale Sèche (☎418/235-2000; ❷), is another friendly bilingual place, with comfy beds in mostly tiny rooms. The beatnik **hostel** *Maison Majorique*, 158 rue du Bateau-Passeur (☎418/235-4372, Ⓦ www.fjord-best.com/ajt; dorms $19), is one of the best in Québec and – thanks to its own bar – determinedly lively and sociable. Canoes, cross-country skis, skidoos and snowshoes are all available for rent; various activities such as guided hikes, snowshoe excursions and dog-sleigh trips are organized in their relative seasons. All-you-can-eat breakfasts for $3.50 are optional, and camping ($6) is available in the hostel grounds. Family-style **camping** away from the hostel is

QUÉBEC | The Saguenay and Lac Saint-Jean

Whale-watching from the Tadoussac area

Every season more companies appear offering **whale-watching trips** from Tadoussac and the surrounding communities (mid-May to mid-Oct). Prices for two- to three-hour trips from Tadoussac are around $45 in a large, sturdy and comfortable boat, and $52 in a zodiac, which provides a more exciting ride. The price drops the more northerly the starting-point: similar excursions from Bergeronnes and Les Escoumins cost around $35 in a zodiac. Pop into **La Croisière**, 231 rue des Pionniers in Tadoussac, who have full information and sell tickets (at the same price as the companies) for all the available trips; you can also compare directly down at the quay. Officially, boats are not allowed to stray within 400m of the protected belugas, but the whales don't know that and often come thrillingly close to the craft.

If you can't afford a boat trip, or would rather leave the whales in peace, take the short **hike** around the Pointe de l'Islet from the marina in Tadoussac, which has lookout points for beluga-spotting where you may be lucky to see whales. Or improve your chances by heading to even better lookout points along the shore: the two best are at **Baie-Ste-Marguerite** west of Tadoussac (see p.345) and **Cap-de-Bon-Désir** just past Bergeronnes (see p.349). A bewildering array of interpretation centres supplement the whale-watching adventures, but don't miss the excellent Centre d'Interprétation des Mammifères Marins in Tadoussac (see p.347).

Aviation du Fjord, 231 rue des Pionniers in Tadoussac (☎418/235-4640), can take you up in a **seaplane** (mid-July to mid-Oct; $55 for 20min) to view whales, the fjord and backcountry from the air.

From south of Tadoussac

Croisières Famille-Dufour (☎418/692-0222 or 1-800/463-5250, ⓦwww .familledufour.com) offers a ten-hour trip from **Québec City** for $169, with pick-ups and drop-offs in **Ste-Anne-de-Beaupré**, **Île aux Coudres** and **Pointe-au-Pic**. A coach trip and cruise package is the other option from Québec City: Croisières AML (☎418/692-1159 or 1-800/563-4643, ⓦwww.croisieresaml.com) charges $75. They also run a boat from **Rivière-du-Loup** on the south shore of the St Lawrence (☎418/867-3361; 3 daily; 3hr 30min; $42).

available in summer at *Camping Tadoussac*, 428 rue du Bateau-Passeur (☎418/235-4501; $21), 2km from the ferry terminal on Hwy 138 – arrive early in summer for a spot.

For a unique stay, opt for the keeper's house at the **lighthouse** on Île Rouge in the middle of the St Lawrence (☎418/237-5050). The rooms are more luxurious than what the keeper would have been used to, and it's reflected in the price – an expensive $530 for two people ($299 if you go solo), that includes transport by zodiac (including an hour whale-watching), breakfast, a five-course dinner and tour of the island. Day-trips (2 daily; 2hr 30min; $23) will suffice for most people.

Eating possibilities include: the *Hôtel Tadoussac*, which has a vast dining room and a reasonably priced set menu; *Chez Georges*, 135 rue du Bateau-Passeur, which is in Tadoussac's oldest house and has seafood and steaks on the table d'hôte for $21; *La Bolée*, 164 rue Morin (☎418/235-4750), which is a pricey place with crêpes, salads and a takeaway deli underneath with delicious breads; and *Le Bâteau*, 246 rue des Forgerons, a popular place that churns out an all-you-can-eat buffet of Québecois food for $17, but has the atmosphere of a school cafeteria. Cheaper food and great evenings of **drinking** can be had at *Le Gibard*, 135 rue Bord de l'Eau, which stays open until 3am, and at *Café du Fjord*, 154 rue du Bateau-Passeur (☎418/235-4626) near the hostel, a young

2

348

From Tadoussac

If you're worried about missing a reservation in **Tadoussac** because of the ferry queue, it's worth asking if you can board at the quay in **Baie-Ste-Catherine** instead – many of the companies fill up their boats on both shores of the mouth of the Saguenay before heading off to see the whales. Some firms also run cruises up the Saguenay fjord, as well as combined whale/fjord packages. Load up with brochures at the tourist office and compare what's on offer.

For trips in zodiacs contact Les Croisières Express, 161 rue des Pionniers (☎418/235-4770 or 1-888/235-6842); Compagnie de la Baie de Tadoussac, 145 rue du Bord de l'Eau (☎418/235-4548 or ☎1-800/757-4548); or Otis Excursions, 431 rue Bateau-Passeur (☎418/235-4197). Croisières AML (☎418/237-4274 or 1-800/563-4643) gives you the option of a large boat or 24-person zodiac, and the other big outfit, Croisières Famille-Dufour at the *Hôtel Tadoussac*, 165 rue du Bord de l'Eau (☎418/235-4421 or 1-800/561-0718), offers whale safaris aboard a catamaran, a 48-person zodiac or a more sedate 1922 schooner. *Tayout*, 148 rue du bord de L'Eau (☎418/235-1056, ⓦ www.tayout.com), offers whale-watching trips in sea kayaks.

From north of Tadoussac

Although you'll spend less time on the water with the following companies, their points of departure on the Côte-Nord are closer to where the whales are most likely to be, so you get about the same amount of contact time for less money. Heading north on Hwy 138, there's a turn-off on the right just after the overpass at **Bergeronnes**, where Les Croisières Neptune has a ticket office at 507 rue du Boisé (☎418/232-6716) for trips in zodiacs only. The Montagnais company Croisière Essipit, 498 rue de la Mer (☎418/232-6778 or 1-888/868-6666, ⓦ www.essipit.com), uses the quay in Bergeronnes as well and has a wider variety of craft. Les Pionniers des Baleines, 41 rue des Pilotes (☎418/233-3274), is the least expensive in the area and launches its zodiacs from Les Escoumins, at the northern limit of the marine park.

hangout with good music; they also have food, including a good $16 dinner buffet. The best spot is *Le Père Coquart Café*, 115 rue Coupe de L'Islet (☎418/235-1170; early June to Oct), with its large terrace, around the corner from *Le Gibard*. They serve light meals until 9pm when the place morphs into an intimate place to hear Québecois and other music.

North of Tadoussac

The landscape **north of Tadoussac** takes in lakes surrounded by granite outcroppings and boreal forest, interspersed with stretches of sandy beaches and salt marshes. The craggy terrain is the chief attraction here with lookout points and short trails in many of the villages, as well as interpretation centres for just about everything. The area is particularly known for cheaper and more convenient whale-watching, spectacular diving and first-rate birding, particularly during the migratory seasons.

As accommodation fills up in Tadoussac in high season, you may wind up having to stay in the community of **BERGERONNES**, 22km along the road. Otherwise if you're here its generally for the good lookout post by a popular whale-feeding ground beside the Cap de Bon Désir lighthouse which now serves as the **Centre d'Interprétation et d'Observation de Cap-de-Bon-Désir**, 13 chemin du Cap-Bon-Désir (mid-June to mid-Oct daily 8am–8pm;

$5), which has displays on whales. Also in town is the Archéo Topo, 498 rue de la Mer (mid-May to mid-Oct daily 9am–5pm; $4), a worthwhile research and exhibition centre devoted to archeology along the Côte-Nord, where finds date back eight thousand years. **Accommodation** is available at *Le Bergeronnette*, 65 rue Principale (May–Oct ☎418/232-6642 or 1-877/232-6605, ⓦwww.bergeronnette.com; ❷), which has simple rooms and a reasonable restaurant – and there's a **campsite**, off the highway east of town, whose beautiful site has views over the St Lawrence: *Camping Bon Désir* (☎418/232-6297; $17–26), which charges more for a pitch with a view.

Though whale-watching is also popular at **LES ESCOUMINS**, the big deal here is the diving, especially at night when the phosphorescence creates an eerie underwater landscape. **Le Centre des Loisirs Marins**, 41 rue des Pilotes (interpretation centre: 9.30–11am & 1.30–3.30pm; $5), is only worthwhile if you intend to dive (diving card required). The dive shop downstairs, Centre de plongée Atlan (☎418/233-4242), rents out a complete set of gear for $55 a day. The only other reason to visit is for the excellent **birding**: the Promenade du Moulin brings you to a rugged shoreline with hundreds of birds. The town's **hostel**, *Auberge de la plongée*, 118 rue St-Marcelin (☎418/233-3289 or 1-800/375-3465, ⓦwww.escoumins.com; dorms $18), is a bit shabby. If you want to **eat**, try the excellent burgers at *Auberge Manoir Bellevue*, 27 rue de l'Église (☎418/233-3325 or 1-888/233-3325; ❹), which also does a pricey table d'hôte for dinner and has comfortable rooms.

About 152km north of Les Escoumins on Hwy 138 – and 20km short of Baie-Comeau – is the tip of a broad peninsula where the **Parc Nature de Pointe-aux-Outardes** (daily: June to early Sept 8am–6pm; early Sept to mid-Oct 8am–5pm; ⓦwww.virtuel.net/prpao; $5), is worth the admission price when migratory birds flock here around May and mid-September. Easy trails take in a variety of ecosystems including salt marshes and sand dunes, and ninety-minute guided tours of the plant- and birdlife are included in midsummer. **Camping** is available ($16–22). If you want to visit the beach (where the water is warm enough for swimming after a few hot sunny days), there's access at the Quai municipale on rue Labrie.

From Les Escoumins there's a **ferry** to Trois-Pistoles (see p.322), while the seasonal **ferry** to Rimouski (see p.324 for details) leaves 59km along the coast from Forestville. While waiting in Forestville you can picnic next to the river or hang out on a pleasant beach, where camping is permitted.

Fjord du Saguenay

One of the world's longest, the **Fjord du Saguenay** cuts through the Canadian Shield before merging with the St Lawrence. A stupendous expanse of rocky outcrops, sheer cliffs and thick vegetation, the land flanking the fjord on both sides is protected as the provincial Parc du Saguenay. The walls of the fjord extend to a depth of 270m in places, almost as much as the height of the cliffs above the waterline. Wedged between the two halves of the Parc du Saguenay are some of the most attractive parts of the Parc Marin du Saguenay–St-Laurent. But since **no bridges** cross the Saguenay for the 126km between Tadoussac and Chicoutimi, you may need to backtrack to explore both shores. For a taste of both the terrestrial and marine parks, drive as far as **Rivière-Éternité** on the south shore, and then double back. From Tadoussac, Hwy 172 runs parallel to the north side of the fjord past the turn-offs to Baie Ste-Marguerite and the pretty waterside village of **Ste-Rose-du-Nord** before reaching the bridge to **Chicoutimi**.

The southern shore

Coming from Charlevoix, the best approach to the Parc du Saguenay is to drive along the wriggling Hwy 170 from Saint-Siméon, a road that strikes the **southern shore** of the Saguenay fjord after about 50km, close to L'Anse-St-Jean. Both this town and Rivière-Éternité, 33km further west, are easy entry points to the park and arguably the most attractive places on the fjord to take a boat trip.

The only village on the Saguenay when it was founded in 1838, **L'ANSE-ST-JEAN** is famous for its Pont du Faubourg, the covered bridge that was featured on the back of the now-retired $1000 note and which managed to survive the flood of 1996, though the rest of the village was badly affected. The town's other claim to fame is that, on January 21, 1997, it became a monarchy following a local referendum. The new ruler, King Denys I, an artist and professor, also known as "l'Illustre Inconnu" (the Illustrious Unknown), didn't reign for long, though. In the face of local political wrangling he lost much of his popularity and consequently abdicated in 2000. Though clearly difficult to rule, at least this kingdom has a terrific view of the Saguenay fjord and surrounding hills from the marina, and makes a good base to explore the park. L'Anse-St-Jean also boasts a particularly fine view of the Saguenay from the **L'Anse-de-Tabatière lookout**; the 500m trail begins at the lookout's car park. From the quay in L'Anse-St-Jean you can take a two- or four-hour **cruise** (June–Sept 2 daily; from $25) or join Fjord en kayak, 4 rue du Faubourg (℡418/272-3024, ⓦwww.fjord-en-kayak.qc.ca) – three-hour trips are $39, two- to five-day excursions start at $230. Alternatively, ride along the fjord on **horseback**: the Centre équestre des Plateaux, 31 chemin des Plateaux (℡418/272-3231, ⓦwww.aei.ca/~cep), offers three-hour rides for $45, as well as multiday excursions. Inland from L'Anse-St-Jean, **Mont-Edouard** (℡418/272-2927, ⓦwww.montedouard.com), with a 450m vertical and 28 trails, attracts skiers in the winter. L'Anse-St-Jean's cheapest **accommodation** is a medicinal plant farm doubling as a hostel – the laid-back *Auberge Chez Monika*, 12 chemin des Plateaux (℡418/272-3115; dorms $10), at the top of a steep hill. The village has a few **B&Bs** – *Le Nid de l'Anse*, the last house on rue St-Jean-Baptiste (℡418/272-2273; ❷; June–Sept), overlooks the fjord and is close to the quay and walking trails. Other options are the clifftop cottages and condos at *Gîtes du Fjord*, 344 rue St-Jean-Baptiste (℡418/272-3430 or 1-800/561-8060; ❹), as well as a couple of **campsites** – *Camping de l'Anse* (℡418/272-2554; $18-25) is in a good position close to the fjord and has excellent facilities. For moderately priced **seafood** try *Le Maringoinfre*, 212 rue St Jean Baptiste (℡418/272-2385).

Continuing along the fjord, scrappy **RIVIÈRE-ÉTERNITÉ**, 83km from Saint-Siméon on Hwy 138 and 61km east of Chicoutimi, is the main gateway to the Parc du Saguenay (admission $3.50). The park's **information centre** (daily: mid-May to mid-Oct 9am–5pm; late June to early Sept 9am–9pm; ℡418/272-3008 or 1-877/272-5229, ⓦwww.parcsquebec.com), 8km from the village, has maps of hiking trails ($3) and kayak routes ($4) – kayak rental from here is $27 per day – and expert naturalists on hand. A smaller information post lies 1.5km from the village, on the park's border. Halfway between the two is the park's main **campsite** (sites $18-25); reservations are available from the information centre. Beware: blackflies love this area, though the worst is over by late July. From the main information centre, a couple of short **hikes** and a long one are laid out through this sector of the park. The best short hike is the Statue Hike, a four-hour round trip up the massive bluff of Cap Trinité, which flanks the deep-blue water of the Baie Éternité. The summit is topped by a huge statue known as *Our Lady of the Saguenay*, erected in 1881 by Charles-Napoléon Robitaille after he was saved from drowning in the river. The long-distance hike (25km) follows the bay of the Éternité River back to L'Anse-St-Jean via massive plateaus, ravines, waterfalls and stunning views. It takes about three days and there are wilderness campsites and a couple of refuges along the way; registration with the information centre is a must. A number of companies offer **water-taxi** services for backpackers, enabling you to hike as far as Tadoussac (it takes a week) – and you can even have your vehicle sent on to your destination by boat. Ninety-minute **cruises** of the Cap Trinité, one of the prettiest spots on the fjord, are offered by Croisières du Cap Trinité (May–Sept 2–3 daily; $20; ☎418/272-2591); boats leave from near the information centre. Guided **kayak** trips are available from next to the information centre at *Explo-Fjord* (☎418/545-3737 or 1-877/272-5229; 3 daily; 2–3hr; $29–39), which also runs zodiac cruises (same prices and times).

The northern shore

Running parallel to the Saguenay fjord, Hwy 172 is a dramatic route along the less-frequented **northern shore** of the Saguenay that gives occasional panoramas over the water and provides access to a couple of pretty towns en route, where cruises are available or kayaks can be rented. The daily (except Sat) Intercar **bus** from Tadoussac follows the highway, terminating at Chicoutimi.

A 42km hiking trail from Tadoussac ends at **BAIE-STE-MARGUERITE**, where the main interpretation centre (early June to mid-Oct daily 9am–5pm; ☎418/236-1162 or 1-877/272-5229, ⓦwww.sepaq.com) for the northern part of the Parc du Saguenay ($3.50) is located. To get here by car, you need to travel 3km down a dusty gravel road that exits the highway just after tiny Rivière-Ste-Marguerite, itself worth a quick stop for its covered bridge. The main draw here is **belugas**, and the interpretation centre has displays that cover all facets of them as well as the fjord in general; ask at the desk for an English-language guidebook. An easy three-kilometre trail leads through the woods to an observation platform where the belugas can frequently be spotted. Despite its appearances, the centre's cafeteria serves up good, hearty grub for hungry hikers from 7am in summer.

About 80km from Tadoussac is the turn-off for **STE-ROSE-DU-NORD**, a tiny village of white houses crammed beneath the precipitous walls of the fjord, 3km from the main road. The seasonal **tourist office**, 213 rue du Quai (late June to mid-Sept 9.30am–7.30pm), has free maps of **hiking trails**, including the Plate-Forme trail that leads to a fabulous panoramic viewpoint above the town. The **Musée de la Nature**, 199 rue de la Montagne (daily 9am–9pm; $4.50), is a small but surprisingly informative museum housing an eclectic range of exhibits from stuffed animals to knotty roots from the local region. The church of **Ste-Rose-de-Lima** (daily 8am–8pm), with its interior of wood, birch bark, branches and roots, is also worth a peek. Explo-Fjord (☎418/545-3737) offers boat excursions on zodiacs and Croisière Marjolaine runs three-hour **cruises** of the fjord's most stunning stretch (late June to early Oct 10.15am & 1.15pm; $32; ☎418/543-7630 or 1-800/363-7248, ⓦwww.croiseremarjolaine.com). The boat then travels on to Chicoutimi from Ste-Rose-du-Nord in the late afternoon (2hr; $18), useful if you intend to visit Lac Saint-Jean. Sometimes there's a boat connection with Tadoussac as well; enquire at the information centre for details. Should you want to **stay** over, you could try the award-winning *Auberge le Presbytère*, 136 rue du Quai (☎418/675-1362 or 1-866/303-1326, ⓦwww.aupresbytere.com; ❸), which has an outstanding **restaurant**, with full menus at around $21. Rooms are also available above the Musée de la Nature (℡418/675-2348; ❷), while *Camping la Descente des Femmes* (℡418/675-2581; June to mid-Oct) has sites for $12–17 and incredible views.

The Upper Saguenay and Lac Saint-Jean

The Saguenay fjord's source – the vast **Lac Saint-Jean** – sits 210km inland, linked by the Rivière Saguenay. Along this stretch, a glut of aluminium and paper plants using the river as a power source has resulted in the growth of characterless industrial towns, the largest of which is **Chicoutimi**. Further west, beyond **Jonquière**, the lake's farmland periphery is still relatively untouched and offers the opportunity to stay on the Montagnais reserve at **Mashteuiatsh** near Roberval, a unique zoo at **Saint-Félicien** and the strange sight of **Val-Jalbert**, Québec's most accessible ghost town. A bike route connects the lake's towns and is an increasingly popular option for travellers from Montréal or Québec who pop their bike on the train or bus for a three- to five-day tour of the lake. In 1996, the Saguenay–Lac-Saint-Jean region was devastated by one of the biggest catastrophes in Canada's recent past – a flood that wiped out homes and businesses in several towns. As the flood was an "act of God" no one received insurance, but those who lost their homes were helped out by donations from across the country.

From the Lac Saint-Jean's southern shore it's about five hours to Montréal on Hwy 155 (via Trois-Rivières); from the southeast, you can take the moose-infested Hwy 169 until it joins up with Hwy 175 on its way to Québec City.

Chicoutimi

Since its founding by a Scottish immigrant in 1842, the regional capital of **CHICOUTIMI** has grown from a small sawmill centre into one of the province's largest towns. It's not a particularly enticing place, though the pedestrianized port area is pleasant enough. The town is, however, host to one of Québec's best **festivals** – the mid-February ten-day **Carnaval Souvenir** when what seems like the entire population dresses in costumes from circa 1900; lumber camps, can-can clubs, operetta shows and period-authentic heavy drinking augment the pioneer atmosphere. Outside this time, the main local attraction is **La Pulperie de Chicoutimi**, 300 Dubuc (June & Sept to mid-Oct Wed–Sun 10am–4pm; Aug & Sept daily 9am–6pm; mid-Oct to May Wed–Sun 10am–4pm; ⓦwww.pulperie.com; $12), five austere brick buildings built along the rapids by the Chicoutimi Pulp Company, which was founded in 1896 and quickly became Canada's largest producer of paper pulp. Left to rot in 1930, these gigantic ghosts of Chicoutimi's industrial past had been restored to prime condition but the flood of 1996 caused $1m damage and the site lost its restaurant and summer theatre. Exhibits explain the mill's history and include the strange **Maison du Peintre Arthur Villeneuve** which was relocated here in 1994. The former home of naive painter Arthur Villeneuve, the house is in effect one big painting, with murals covering inside and out. The subject matter is unadventurous, but the artist's work is bright and cheery, while scenes of 1950s Chicoutimi – when Villeneuve started his project after retiring as a barber – are intriguing.

Chicoutimi's **bus station**, 55 rue Racine est (℡418/543-1403), is on the corner of Tessier and Racine, right in the centre of town. Buses from Montréal, Québec City, Lac Saint-Jean and Tadoussac all connect here. The CITS local bus (℡418/545-2487) links with Jonquière's **train station** (arrival point for trains from Montréal), running at least hourly from 7.15am to 9.45pm. There's a municipal **tourist office** at 295 Racine est (Mon–Fri 8am–noon & 1.30pm–4.30pm; ☏418/698-3167 or 1-800/463-6565). **Accommodation** is readily available as the town hosts business conferences all year round. Budget rooms can be obtained through the college *CÉGEP de Chicoutimi*, 534 rue Jacques-Cartier est (☏418/549-9520 ext 258 or 257; ❶). *Auberge Centre-Ville*, 104 rue Jacques-Cartier est (☏418/543-0253; ❸), is a small, central **hotel**, while *Le Montagnais*, 1080 boul Talbot (☏418/543-1521 or 1-800/463-9160, ⓦwww.lemontagnais.qc.ca; ❹), is a modern hotel further out. There are numerous small **restaurants** on rue Racine, east of the tourist office. Recommended is *La Cuisine Café-Resto* at no. 387, which has French food in the $10–20 range, though for a better class of meal try the elegant *La Bourgresse*, 260 rue Riverin (☏418/543-3178), where French cuisine is $20–40. Most **nightlife** is also on rue Racine, in lively bars.

If you're using Chicoutimi as a gateway to the Saguenay Fjord, you might be tempted by a **cruise** with Croisière Marjolaine (☏418/543-7630 or 1-800/363-7248; $37; late June to Aug) as far as Cap Trinité, stopping both ways at Ste-Rose-du-Nord (see p.352), where they provide a coach back to Chicoutimi on the morning run (in the afternoon, the first Chicoutimi–Ste-Rose-du-Nord leg is by coach).

Jonquière

Some 15km west of Chicoutimi, **JONQUIÈRE** thrives due to its Alcan aluminium smelter, one of the largest in the world, and its two paper mills. The smelter brought many Eastern European immigrants to the area when it was first opened in 1925, and the industry overtook the Price sons and their wood empire as the largest employer. A modern town with wide avenues and the world's only large-scale aluminium bridge (across the Saguenay), it can make a good stop for budget travellers because of an Allo-Stop office and train connections with Montréal; it also has a better nightlife than Chicoutimi.

The **tourist office** is at 2665 boul du Royaume in the Centre des Congrès (Mon–Fri 8am–noon & 1.30pm–4.30pm; ☏418/548-4004 or 1-800/561-9196, ⓦville.jonquiere.qc.ca). **Buses** terminate at 2249 rue St-Hubert (☏418/547-2167) and **trains** arrive at the VIA Rail station (☏1-800/361-5390, ⓦwww.viarail.ca). To **stay**, try *CÉGEP*, 2505 rue St Hubert (☏418/542-2643; ❶), which has good, clean, college rooms. The *Auberge des Deux Tours*, 2522 rue Saint-Dominique (☏418/695-2022 or 1-888/454-2022, ⓦwww.aubergedeuxtours.qc.ca; ❸), is reasonable, or there's the *Holiday Inn Saguenay*, 2675 boul du Royaume (☏418/548-3124 or 1-800/363-3124; ❹). You can **eat** at the stately 1911 *Auberge Villa Pachon*, 1904 rue Perron (☏418/542-3568 or 1-888/922-3568), whose very expensive restaurant is excellent. Another pricey option is *L'Amandier*, 5219 chemin St-Andre (☏418/542-5395), out of town but worth the trip for the bizarre dining room of carved plaster and wood. For an everyday meal head to the Rue St-Dominique: *Le Puzzle*, no. 2497, is a fun place with cool decor; *Les Pâtes Amato*, 2655 boul de Royaume, has coffees, pasta and Italian desserts to die for. The tawdry nightclubs and gritty **bars** along the same road are a good laugh.

Lac Saint-Jean

To the west of Chicoutimi, around **Lac Saint-Jean**, stretches a relatively untouched area whose tranquil lakeshore villages are linked by the circular route of Hwy 169. Named after Father Jean Duquen, the first European to visit the region in 1647, the huge glacial lake is fed by most of the rivers of north-eastern Québec and – unusually for an area of the rocky Canadian Shield – is bordered by sandy beaches and a lush, green terrain that has been farmed for over a century. The local cuisine, especially the delicious coarse meat pie called a *tourtière* and the thick blueberry pie, is renowned throughout the province.

A relatively flat 256km **bike route** – the **Véloroute des Bleuets** (Ⓦ www.veloroute-bleuets.qc.ca) – encircles the whole lake, mostly as a wide paved shoulder, but a total of 60km of the route is completely free of cars. The path passes close to most of the major attractions and through many of the villages around Lac Saint-Jean and there are beaches all along the lakeshore where you can cool off after a hard day's ride. It's well set up for getting there: the **train** from Montréal to Jonquière stops at Chambord on the south shore near Val-Jalbert and there's a **bus** from Québec City to Alma. A growing number of **B&Bs** and other services are popping up to serve the two-wheeled visitors, and even the locals are laying out a warm welcome – some have even set up garden chairs to rest on near the bike path. A minivan service, Gilles Girard (Ⓣ 418/342-6651) can even help take the strain by transporting your luggage around the lake for $20 per trip. An annual **bike marathon** is held for three days in early June.

Alma and west around the lake

The dull aluminium-producing city of **ALMA**, 50km west of Jonquière, is useful for its **buses** – to Chicoutimi and Québec City and various points around Lac St-Jean – and is a practical starting point for the cycle ride around Lac St-Jean. Liberté à Vélo (Ⓣ 418/668-8430 1-877/668-8430, www .liberteavelo.ca) provides guided **tours** along the cycle route – a service which includes luggage transport. Should you need to **rent** a bicycle try Vélo Jeunesse, 1691 ave du Pont Alma (Ⓣ 418/662-9785; $20/day). The **information centre** is at 1682 av du Pont Nord (Mon–Fri 8am–noon & 1.30pm–4.30pm; Ⓣ 418/668-3611 or 1-877/668-3611). A number of motels along avenue du Pont Sud provide predictable **accommodation**, including *Motel Rustik* at no. 1350 (Ⓣ 418/668-2373; ❷).

In a clockwise direction beyond Alma, the cycle path follows along shoreline inaccessible by highway, joining up with Hwy 170 beyond **SAINT-GÉDÉON**, a popular beach town. To treat yourself, head for the lakefront *Auberge des Îles*, 250 rang des Îles (Ⓣ 418/345-2589 or 1-800/680-2589, Ⓦ www.aubergedesiles.com; ❸), a lovely inn just north of St-Gédéon with a four-course menu of game and local flavours for $35.

One of the main attractions of the region, the historical village of **VAL-JALBERT** (daily: mid-May to mid-June & late Aug to late Oct 9am–5pm; mid-June to late Aug 9am–7pm; Ⓣ 418/275-3132 or 1-888/675-3132, Ⓦ www.sepaq.com; $12) is 52km beyond Alma along the cycle route and 92km west of Chicoutimi along Hwy 170 and 169. The 72m-high Ouiatchouan waterfall, which dominates the town, led to the establishment of a pulp mill here a century ago, and by 1926 the village had around 950 inhabitants. In the following year, the introduction of chemical-based pulping made the mill redundant, and the village was closed down. Val-Jalbert was left to rot until 1985, when the government decided to renovate it as a tourist attraction. From the site entrance a bus (with on-board French commentary) runs around the main sights of the village, ending at the mill at the base of the falls. You can then wander around whatever catches your eye along the way – the abandoned wooden houses, a former convent (now a museum) or the general store (now a souvenir shop). From the mill, itself converted into an excellent crafts market and cafeteria, a **cable car** leads to the top of the falls, from where there are stunning views of the village and Lac Saint-Jean beyond. It is possible to stay in Val-Jalbert's renovated **hotel** above the general store (**❹**), in apartments in the converted houses on St George St ($72–112 for one to six people), or in the **campsite** ($20–26) just outside the village. From late October to April, when the site is officially closed, you can still gain access for free – it is a beautifully tranquil place to spend some time.

Mashteuiatsh

Some 10km west of Val-Jalbert, at **Roberval**, a turn-off leads to the Montagnais reserve of **MASHTEUIATSH**, also known as **Pointe-Bleue**. Before European contact the Montagnais ("Ilnu" in the local language) were a migratory people who split into small family groups for summer hunting. When the Europeans arrived they found the Montagnais in bitter conflict with the Iroquois, an enmity that Champlain intensified by allying himself with the Montagnais for trade. By the late seventeenth century their population had been greatly weakened by warfare, European diseases, depletion of game and displacement from their lands. This reserve was created in 1856, and today around 1800 of eastern Québec's 14,000 Montagnais live here. Like many Canadian reserves, Mashteuiatsh is dry, in an attempt to reduce alcoholism and its attendant problems, yet the Montagnais suffer a great deal of prejudice from the surrounding white communities – so much so that there's no bus service, because Québecois bus drivers refuse to go there.

The village is situated right on the lake, and has an **information centre** on the main street at 1427 Ouiatchouan (mid-June to Sept daily 8am–8pm). At the end of July a **powwow** is held on the waterfront by the four concrete tepee sculptures that represent the seasons. Up the hill, at 1787 rue Amishk, is the recently renovated **Musée Amérindien** (mid-May to mid-Oct daily 10am–6pm; rest of year Mon–Thurs 9am–noon & 1–4pm, Fri 9am–noon & 1–3pm; $7), where you start with a twenty-minute film showing traditional Montagnais life, much of it revolving around hunting and fishing. The permanent exhibition Pekuakami Ilnuatsh, which translates as "the Lac St-Jean Montagnais", continues the theme with artefacts and interpretation panels that also describe domestic life and the impact of European contact; temporary exhibitions highlight the works of aboriginal artists.

From August to September, Ashuapmushuaniussi, at 1562 Ouiatchouan (☎418/275-2473), organizes **adventure trips** into the bush where you are immersed in the traditional way of life, relying on the resources of the surrounding woodlands and rivers to build shelters, make fires and prepare food (from $150 per person per day).

Saint-Prime and Saint-Félicien

In the village of **SAINT-PRIME**, 13km west of Roberval, is a surprising little museum, the **Musée du fromage cheddar**, 148 ave Albert-Perron (daily: June & Sept 10.15am–5.30pm; late June to Aug 9.15am–5.30pm; $6.95), where four generations of cheese-makers have worked their craft since 1895. The one-hour guided tour covers the whole process of producing cheddar here – almost all of which was shipped to England. The unexpected part of the tour is upstairs, where the Perron family residence appears as it would have in 1922 and a very convincing "Marie Perron" tells about her life, how the best piece of furniture was reserved for the priest who visited but once a year, and why kitchen counters used to be so low – so the children could make themselves useful. You also get to try a bit of the cheese produced by the modern cheese factory.

Situated on the western extremity of the lake on the Ashuapmushuan River, **SAINT-FÉLICIEN** is the site of Québec's best zoo, the **Zoo Sauvage de**

Saint-Félicien (daily: June–Aug 9am–6pm; Sept to mid-Oct 9am–5pm; Nov–May by appointment; ☎418/679-0543 or 1-800/667-5687, Ⓦwww.zoosauvage.qc.ca; $21.73), located on Chamouchouane Island. Don't let the giant car park put you off: the first part of the zoo is in a beautiful riverside setting. The rest mimics a number of ecosystems where around eighty, mainly Canadian, species roam free all over the site. It is the humans who are the ones in cages, hauled around on the back of a mini-train (provisions are made for disabled travellers). The Arctic environment for the polar bears allows you to see the magnificent beasts swim underwater; they put on their best show at feeding time. The zoo also has an historical angle, with mock-ups of an Indian village, trading post, loggers' camp and settlers' farm, staffed by costumed guides performing everyday tasks to match the setting. An English guidebook is available at the entrance. Saint-Félicien's **information office** is at 1209 boul Sacré-Coeur (late June to early Sept Mon–Fri 8.30am–8pm, Sat & Sun 9am–8pm; rest of year Mon–Fri 8.30am–noon & 1–4.30pm; ☎418/679-9888). For **accommodation**, try *Hôtel Bellevue*, 1055 boul Sacré-Coeur (☎418/679-0162; ❷), or one of the ten **B&Bs** (❶–❷) in the town and surrounding farmland.

East around the lakeshore to Alma

From Saint-Félicien the highway and bike path separate, rejoining 15km inland at **NORMADIN**, where **Les Grands Jardins de Normandin**, 1515 ave du Rocher (daily: late June to early Sept 9am–6pm; Ⓦ www.cigp.com/jardin.html; $10) is an overpriced and over-hyped formal garden. More worthwhile is one of the local **B&Bs**: at *Les Gîtes Makadan*, 3km off the highway at 1728 rue St-Cyrille (☎418/274-2867 or 1-877/625-2326, Ⓦwww.gitemakadan.cjb .net; ❷), where the owners serve up huge portions of local country dishes, much of which is fresh produce from their farm down the road; you need to tell them ahead of time that you want dinner ($15).

Continuing clockwise around the lake brings you to **DOLBEAU-MISTASSINI**, 28km further on. Dolbeau, the western half of town, is at its best during mid-July's ten-day **Western Festival**, with rodeos and people wandering around in stetsons and spurs. Mistassini, the region's blueberry capital, outdoes its neighbour in early August, with the **Festival du Bleuet** – one big blowout on blueberries dipped in chocolate, blueberry pie, blueberry cheesecake and a potent blueberry wine. Over the Mistassini River 7km up the road to St Eugéne d'Argentenay the **Monastère des Pères Trappistes** sells its own organic produce; a large quantity of the berries are on offer in season along with their home-made chocolates (the chocolate-covered blueberry bar is regionally famous). Another worthwhile trip out of town is south in the direction of Ste-Marguerite-Marie, following route de Vauvert to its end where you'll find the 7km **beach** at the Centre Touistique Vauvert (☎418/374-2746). Here, there's a restaurant and a few free places to pitch a tent; discreet no-trace camping on the beach is also tolerated. Of **accommodation** in Dolbeau-Mistassini the *Hôtel du Boulevard*, 1610 boul Wallberg (☎418/276-8207 or 1-800/268-1061; ❸), is passable, but the *Auberge La Diligence*, 414 ave de la Friche (☎418/276-6544 or 1-800/361-6162; ❺), is nicer. *Gîte Bonjour, Bienvenue*, 1824 boul Wallberg (☎418/276-1291; ❷), is a good, inexpensive **B&B**.

Another 20km round the shore, a short walk just west of the village of **SAINTE-MONIQUE**, is a **hostel** and **campsite** on it's own little island: the *Auberge de l'Île du Repos de Péribonka* (☎418/347-5649; ❷; dorms $19, camping from $17). Its location is useful for an excursion to **Parc de la**

Pointe-Taillon (☎418/347-5371, ⓦwww.sepaq.com; free, parking $5), which also has rustic camping available 2–4km from the car park ($19 for a six-person site); they'll give you a lift if you need one. Occupying a finger of land that juts into Lac Saint-Jean, the park is bordered by long and often deserted beaches, and there are 45km of cycle trails, a portion of which coincides with the Véloroute des Bleuets.

From Sainte-Monique, it's 29km round to Alma.

The Côte-Nord

The St Lawrence River was the lifeline of the wilderness beyond Tadoussac until the 1960s, when **Hwy 138** was constructed along the **Côte-Nord** to Havre-St-Pierre, 625km away. In 1996, the road was extended to Natashquan, a further 145km. The road sweeps from high vistas down to the rugged shoreline through the vast regions of Manicouagan and Duplessis, the few distractions offered in the villages and towns en route being supplemented by panoramas of spruce-covered mountains, the vast sky and the mighty river. **Bears** and **moose** often lumber out of the stunted forest onto the highway, and in the summer you can frequently spot the shiny backs of **whales** arching out of the water.

Basque whalers were the first Europeans to penetrate this chilly shore in the sixteenth century, but later, when they began to trade fur with the aboriginal Montagnais, Naskapi and Inuit, they were ousted by French merchants. After the British conquest the fur trade continued but fishing remained the main industry until the twentieth century, when mining, lumber and hydroelectric projects led to the growth of a few settlements into fair-sized towns. Despite this, the region has a population density of just five people per square mile, and the distances between communities become longer and longer the further you travel.

The Intercar **bus** from Québec City to Tadoussac serves the Côte-Nord as far as Baie-Comeau, from where another travels to Sept-Îles, where you have no choice but to spend the night before continuing on to Havre-St-Pierre. At the time of writing there is no public transport to Natashquan, but a bus service is expected – ask at tourist information for details. At Natashquan the highway gives out altogether and the only onward transport is by snowmobile, plane or the supply **ship** from Rimouski, which serves the wildlife haven of Île d'Anticosti and undertakes a breathtaking journey along the inlets of the windswept coastline of the Basse Côte-Nord (Lower North Shore).

Manicouagan

The Manicouagan refers largely of a string of settlements along the side of the St Lawrence. The stretch between the two major industrial conurbations, **Baie-Comeau** and **Sept-Îles**, is rugged and desolate, the road twisting over passes and down to the occasional pretty fishing village like **Godbout**, but attractions are thin on the ground and most travellers here are just passing through on their way to the Mingan Coast (see p.363) or Labrador City (see p.523) via the Hwy 389 from Baie-Comeau or the railway from Sept-Îles. If you are on your way through, stop for a quick look at the gigantic **Manic dams** and pause at Sept-Îles to explore some first-rate **Innu** museums and events – they will help to make more sense of the indigenous culture, which becomes more evident as you travel north.

Baie-Comeau

The road into the western sector of **BAIE-COMEAU** may be a fairly drab landscape of strip malls, but it's nothing compared to the eastern sector, where a monstrous newsprint mill plant churns out poisonous emissions 24 hours a day. It was established in 1936 by Colonel Robert R. McCormick, the publisher of the *Chicago Tribune*, and Baie-Comeau has done nothing but boom ever since: with a population of 26,000, it dwarfs the communities around it. There's no reason to hang around here, but while waiting for a northward bus or a ferry to Gaspé's Matane you might stroll through the quartier Sainte-Amélie in the eastern Marquette sector, where the streets are lined by grand houses dating from the 1930s. The **Église Sainte-Amélie**, 37 ave Marquette (daily: June to mid-Sept 9am–6pm; rest of year 10am–5pm; free), is worth a peek for its frescoes and stained-glass windows, designed by the Italian artist Guido Nincheri.

There's a seasonal **tourist information** office on the western edge of town at 3503 boul Laflèche (June–Aug daily 8am–8pm; ☎418/589-3610). **Buses** terminate at 212 boul Lasalle (☎418/296-6921); the departure point for the **car ferry** to Matane (see p.325) is beyond the eastern end of boul Lasalle on rue Cartier. **Accommodation** is available at the rambling stone hotel *Le Manoir*, 8 Cabot (☎418/296-3391 or 1-800/463-8567; ❸), which overlooks the St Lawrence. Less expensive **motels** are along boul Lasalle; try the modern *Hôtel-Motel La Caravelle*, at no. 202 (☎418/296-4986 or 1-800/463-4986; ❷). The cheapest place in town is *Motel du Rosier*, 228 boul Lasalle (☎418/296-6696; ❷), but for a few dollars more there are a few **B&Bs**, like *Gîte Le Champlain*, 67 rue Champlain (☎418/296-3814; ❸). For **camping**, *Camping Manic 2* at km24 on Hwy 389 (☎418/296-3951 or 2810) near the dam has six-person sites for $15–19. The hotel *Le Manoir* is pricey for **eating** but excellent. For down-to-earth eats, *try Brasserie Le Boucannier*, 720 boul Laflèche in the western sector, for surf-and-turf and pizza.

The Manic Dams

One of the few roads to penetrate the bleak terrain north of the St Lawrence is the partly paved Hwy 389 (Manic Road), which runs 215km into the forest from the east sector of Baie-Comeau. The road was built as a supply route for the hydroelectric company that built the colossal **dam system** on the Rivière Manicouagan, the only artificial site to rival the landscape in these parts. The first dam in the system, **Manic 2**, is 22km from Baie-Comeau, a journey that takes in great views of the rocky Canadian Shield. A free guided tour takes you inside the massive wall (late June to early Sept daily 9am, 11am, 1.30pm & 3.30pm), but an even more stupendous structure awaits two and a half hours' drive further north at the end of the paved stretch of the road – the awesome **Manic 5**, or Daniel Johnson Dam, 214km north of Baie-Comeau. Constructed in 1968, it is named after the premier of Québec who died here on the morning of the opening ceremony. With a length of 1314m and a central arch of 214m, this is the world's largest multiple-arch structure, and apparently contains enough concrete to build a pavement from pole to pole. Free guided tours (same hours as Manic 2) take visitors to the foot of the dam and across the top, giving panoramic views of the Manicouagan valley and the huge reservoir. The 90km-wide donut-shaped depression was created by a massive meteor impact more than 200 million years ago, but the water level only became high enough to fill in the entire depression after the dam was constructed. You can **fly** here with Air Satellite (☎418/589-8923) from Baie-Comeau for around $150 round-trip, which is great for the overhead views of the dam. There's **accommodation** 2km before Manic 5 at the *Motel de L'Énergie* (☎418/584-2301 or 1-800/760-2301; ❸).

Beyond Manic 5, it's another 385km along a gravel highway to Labrador City (see p.523), a six-hour journey through the wilderness with very little in the way of services. For road and weather conditions call ☎418/589-6911.

Godbout and beyond

The attractive village of **GODBOUT**, situated on a crescent-shaped bay 54km from Baie-Comeau, is not just the most pleasant place hereabouts and excellent for salmon fishing, it also has an excellent **Musée Amérindien et Inuit**, 134 rue Pascal-Comeau (June–Oct daily 9am–10pm; $3). The museum was founded by Claude Grenier, who spent ten years in the frozen north in the 1970s on a government scheme to boost the Inuit economy by promoting aboriginal culture. Consequent commercialism has diluted the output since then, but the private collection of Grenier features nothing but genuine pieces, from the characteristic soapstone carvings to domestic artefacts. Just down the road, the old general store houses a seasonal **tourist office** (mid-June to early Sept Mon–Fri 8am–6pm, Sat & Sun 9am–6pm; ☎418/568-7647) with a few relics from its former life on display. The village is linked to Matane on the south shore by **car ferry** (see p.325). For **accommodation**, you can get a simple room above a convenience store Dépanneur Proprio, 156 rue Pascal Comeau (☎418/568-7535; ❶), where fishing licences are sold. Or, try one of the **B&Bs** facing the water, like the pretty, century-old *La Maison du Vieux Quai*, 142 rue Pascal-Comeau (☎418/568-7453; ❷). There's **camping** at *Camping de la Traverse*, 180 rue Pascal-Comeau (☎418/568-7816; $12–20).

Situated where the St Lawrence River merges into the Gulf of St Lawrence, scenic **POINTE-DES-MONTS**, 28km from Godbout (and a further 11km off the highway), has changed little since the nineteenth century. Mind you, there's not a lot to change – all that stands on this rocky outcrop is Canada's oldest **lighthouse** dating from 1830 and a small missionary **chapel** built in 1898. The lighthouse now contains a small **museum** (mid-June to mid-Sept daily 9am–7pm; ⓦwww.pointe-des-monts.com; $5), whose nautical displays and history of the lighthouse-keeper and his family provide adequate distraction as you make your way to the top. The adjacent house contains a fairly expensive seafood **restaurant** and a **B&B**, while nearby chalets handle the overflow of this popular spot (☎418/939-2242; ❷; June–Oct). **Camping** is available at *Domaine de l'Astérie* (☎418/939-2327; mid-June to Sept; $16), 2km before the lighthouse. You can camp for free on the public beach at **POINTE-AUX-ANGLAIS** 40km northeast along Hwy 138; there are no facilities, but the nearby restaurant will let you shower for $5.

From Pointe-aux-Anglais it's another 63km to the lumber and iron-ore centre of **PORT-CARTIER**. The town is the entrance to the **Réserve Faunique de Port-Cartier-Sept-Îles** (admission $3.50), a wildlife reserve with more than a thousand lakes, popular for its hunting and salmon and trout fishing. Information, permits and reservations are available from the administration offices, 24 boul des Îles in Port-Cartier (☎418/766-2524, ⓦwww.sepaq.com). It's a bumpy 27km drive to the **reception post** (May–Sept 7am–7pm; ☎418/766-4743) at the southern tip of Lac Walker, where **campsites** ($18–23) and **chalets** (❺) are available, as well as canoe rentals ($15/day) and hiking trails.

Sept-Îles

The largest ore-exporting port in eastern Canada, **SEPT-ÎLES** is a good base for trips further north, owing to its **rail** links with Labrador. The town itself

Innu Nikamu festival

One of the more offbeat Canadian music chart successes of recent years was the local aboriginal group Kashtin, the only nationally known band to perform in a native tongue. Although Claude McKenzie and Florent Vollant have gone on to solo careers, they still appear occasionally at the excellent **Innu Nikamu Festival** of song and music (information ☎418/927-2985), held in early August, 14km east of Sept-Îles in the Montagnais reserve of **Maliotenam**. Inspired by Kashtin's success, numerous other groups travel to the four-day festival to produce some of the best of Canada's contemporary and traditional native music. As well as the music, the festival includes native food and craft stalls; despite the reserve's alcohol ban, there is always a good buzz. There is no public transport to the reserve: by car, take Hwy 138 towards Havre-St-Pierre and turn right at the Moisie intersection for the Maliotenam entrance. Tickets, available at the gate, cost around $10.

has as much character as a pile of iron ore, but it's pleasantly situated on the St Lawrence shore and you could spend an enjoyable day here thanks to two fantastic museums that explore native culture and, in August, the presence of one of Québec's foremost native-music festivals nearby. A trip to Île Grande Basque is also a worthwhile, easy adventure.

The town is best appreciated along the waterfront. A 27km bike path leads from **Parc Rivière des Rapides**, with a three-kilometre walking trail and ice-fishing in winter, to the beaches east of town. The road down to the third beach, **Plage Routhier**, offers the best view of the seven islands that gave Sept-Îles its name. Along the way, the path passes through the Jardins de l'Anse – a good spot for bird-watching – and along the riverfront promenade in the **Parc du Vieux Quai**, where evening concerts of Québecois music are held under the yellow tent (late June to Aug Thurs–Sun; free). Rent **bikes** from Rioux Vélo Plein Air, 391 ave Gamache (☎418/968-8356). An interesting overview of local history is offered by **Le Vieux-Poste**, on boulevard des Montagnais, west of the centre (late June to mid-Aug daily 9am–5pm; $2). Prior to the British conquest, when the Hudson's Bay Company took over the trade here, Sept-Îles was leased by the French crown to merchant traders. Settlements like these opened up Québec for the Europeans but practically destroyed the lives of the native Montagnais. Converted to Christianity and overwhelmed by their desire for and subsequent need of European goods – particularly firearms, which aided them in their battles against the feared Iroquois – the Montagnais were forced by market pressure to hunt more and more fur-bearing animals. The resulting depletion of game was worsened so much by the later lumber and mining industries that the Montagnais were obliged to live on official reserves in order to become eligible for state hand-outs. The reconstructed Vieux-Poste, with its small chapel, store and postmaster's house, presents an absorbing portrayal of the Montagnais culture and is staffed by local Montagnais who produce crafts and food, which are sold at a decently priced handicrafts store.

The excellent **Musée Shaputuan**, 290 boul des Montagnais (late June to early Sept daily 8am–5pm; rest of year Mon–Fri 8am–4.30pm; ⓦ www .museeshaputuan.org; $3), presents the traditional life of the Innu (Montagnais) people as it is shaped by the seasons. Unlike most descriptive museums, the exhibits speak to the viewer – often literally. Trilingual interpretation panels and audio and video recordings continue the tradition of oral history, with the stories of hunting, fishing, food preparation and scapulomancy (predicting the movement of caribou herds by "reading" the scorch marks left on a bone placed in the fire) told by specific individuals. Artefacts on display supplement the histories, and sculptures illustrate the myths and folk tales of the Innu. Temporary exhibitions in summer feature works by aboriginal artists, while in winter they are more educational, focusing on a single aspect of life such as trapping. The round hall is used for symposia, primarily for Innu people who want to learn more about their own culture.

Just offshore, the largest island in the archipelago, **Île Grande Basque**, has 12km of easy walking trails and picnic spots; you can buy camping permits for $7 at the kiosk in Parc du Vieux Quai. From June to September, the quay is the departure point for regular **passenger ferries** (10 daily 15min; $15) and **cruises** offered by Les Excursions La Petite Sirène (T418/968-2173; 1–3 daily; 2–4hr) and Croisière Petit Pingouin (T418/968-9558; June–Sept 1–3 daily; 20min–3hr). Whales and a sea-bird sanctuary are the main attractions, but fishing trips are also available; you can also catch herring right from the quay in early summer. **Kayak tours** are another possibility: Vêtements des Îles, 637 ave Brochu (T418/962-7223 or 1-800/470-7223, Wwww.vetementsdesiles.com), offers rentals for $39 per day and two-day guided tours for $150.

Practicalities

Sept-Îles has a seasonal **tourist office**, 516 rue Arnaud (mid-June to Aug daily 9am–6pm; T418/968-1818), down by the waterfront in the Parc du Vieux-Quai, and another on the outskirts of town at 1401 boul Laure (daily: mid-June & late Sept daily 8am–9pm; late June to mid-Sept 7.30am–10pm; rest of year 8.30am–5pm; T418/968-0022, Wwww .ville.sept-iles.qc.ca/tourisme). The **bus** station, 126 rue Monseigneur-Blanche (T418/962-2126), has buses east to Havre-St-Pierre, while the QNS&L **train** station, with 2–3 trains a week to Labrador City and Schefferville (see p.523), is on rue Retty at the east end of town. The *Nordik Express* supply **ship** (see box p.367) from Rimouski leaves Sept-Îles every Wednesday morning at 6am, arriving at Port-Menier on the Île d'Anticosti ($48) that afternoon and Havre-St-Pierre ($68) in the evening, before continuing along the Basse Côte-Nord to Blanc-Sablon near the Labrador border. It does not stop in Sept-Îles on the return trip.

The *Le Tangon* **hostel**, 555 rue Cartier (T418/962-8180 or 1-800/461-8585; June–Sept; dorms $19), is a cheap, cramped, family-run place with breakfast for $3.50; you can camp in the grounds for $10. Alternatively, try the luxurious *Hôtel Gouverneur Sept-Îles*, 666 boul Laure (T418/962-7071 or 1-888/910-1111, Wwww.gouveneur.com; **④**), or the *Hotel Sept-Îles*, 451 ave Arnaud (T418/962-2581 or 1-800/463-1753; **②**), on the waterfront. The town's **B&Bs** are more attractive than the motels along the highway: *Gîte Les Tournesols*, 388 rue Évangéline (T418/968-1910; **③**), is nearest the quay. Two **campsites** lie 27km to the east, off Hwy 138 next to the salmon-filled Rivière Moisie: *Camping Laurent-Val* (T418/927-2899; $16–25; mid-May to mid-Oct) and *Camping de la rivière Moisie* (T418/927-2021; $16–28; mid-May to early Sept).

For **eating**, Sept-Îles has great seafood restaurants such as the rather expensive *Chez Omer*, 372 ave Brochu (T418/962-7777). Get cheaper seafood, pizza and pasta (as well as a few rounds of **drinks**) at nearby *Café du Port* at no. 495 (T418/962-9311), while further down the road *Pub St-Marc*, 588 ave Brochu (T418/962-7770), is a surprisingly stylish bar serving microbrews, with a more expensive restaurant upstairs where there's great pasta and a vast selection of salads. Montagnais specialities are pricey but well prepared at *Chez Jonathan*, in the Musée Shaputuan at the west end of town.

The Mingan coast

There is little of specific interest along the stretch of shore east of Sept-Îles, known as the **Mingan coast** – blackfly-ridden from May to June – until you reach **Longue-Pointe-de-Mingan**, but the scenery changes constantly with sand dunes followed by granite outcroppings of the Canadian Shield, then eerie landscapes of rounded grey boulders surrounded by scrubby vegetation. Most visitors make the journey for the stunning islands of the **Mingan Archipelago**, a unique environment of sculptured rock formations and profuse wildlife lying off the coast between Longue-Pointe-de-Mingan and **Havre-St-Pierre**, the region's largest town and a good base for visiting the archipelago. As the tourist season is short here, accommodation can be at a premium – it's a good idea to book ahead.

If you want to break up the journey, park your car at the small tourist office 86km east of Sept-Îles (just after the marker for km61 – distances are measured from the Rivière Moisie) and visit the **Chutes Manitou**. Cross the river via the highway bridge and walk five minutes on the marked trail along the river to a viewing point beside the rocky cascades. A more substantial waterfall is ten minutes further down the trail, with secluded pebble beaches along the way. It's dangerous to swim here, though; a couple of drownings have occurred.

Longue-Pointe-de-Mingan

Although Havre-St-Pierre is the more popular departure point for cruises of the Mingan Archipelago, it is worth stopping in **LONGUE-POINTE-DE-MINGAN** for the Centre de Recherche et d'Interprétation de la Minganie, or CRIM, 625 rue du Centre (mid-June to mid-Sept daily 8.30am–6pm; $4.75), a joint venture between Parks Canada and the Mingan Island Cetacean Study. In addition to a film and displays on whales and other marine life, the centre provides information on excursions to the islands, issues camping permits and, for the more adventurous, offers a day with one of the **whale researchers** (☎418/949-2845; June–Oct; $80). The latter are not cruises – you are with a marine biologist in a small boat from dawn until whenever their work is finished – but they are a unique experience. Less taxing cruises are offered by Excursions du Phare, 126 rue de la Mer (☎418/949-2302, ⓦ www.minganie.info), who lead trips to the westernmost islands – an important consideration if you want to see **puffins**, as most of the cruises from Havre-St-Pierre only visit the islands in the centre sector.

Longue-Pointe-de-Mingan has little accommodation and isn't much of a gourmet hot spot, but adequate **accommodation** and **seafood** is available at the restaurant of the basic *Hôtel-Motel de la Minganie*, 860 chemin du Roi (☎418/949-2992; ❷). Alternatively you can camp at several campsites dotted along rue de la Mer, all a few steps from the wooden seafront promenade.

Havre-St-Pierre

The community of **HAVRE-ST-PIERRE** would have remained a tiny fishing village founded in 1857 by fleeing Acadaians but for the discovery in the 1940s of a huge deposit of ilmenite, the chief source of titanium. The quarries are 45km north of the town itself, where fishing and tourism provide employment for the non-miners, the latter industry having received a major boost when the forty islands of the **Mingan Archipelago** were made into a national park in 1983. Before setting off to the park, check out the **interpretation centre**, 975 de l'Escale (mid-June to Aug hours vary; ☎418/538-5264; free), with a film and photographic displays and information on the flora, fauna and geology of the islands. It opens around 8.30am if the weather is too poor for the tour boats to depart. At a smaller kiosk on the wharf, part of a row of kiosks, you can book cruises to the archipelago.

Havre-St-Pierre's **information centre** shares the old general store at 957 rue de la Berge (daily: mid-June to mid-Sept 9am–9pm; mid-Aug to early Sept 11am–9pm) with a *centre d'interprétation* that depicts the local history (same hours; $2). The **bus station** is at 843 rue de l'Escale (☎418/538-2033). The wharf is the departure point for the *Nordik Express* (see box p.367). The *Auberge de la Minganie* **hostel** (☎418/538-1538; dorms $15, camping $8; May–Nov) is inconveniently situated 17km west of town, but the bus from the west will let you off nearby, leaving you to walk the remaining 700m. An old fishing camp on a pretty bay with minimum renovations and lots of bugs, the hostel doesn't serve breakfast, but does have kitchen facilities and canoes for rent. In town, you could try the *Hôtel-Motel du Havre*, 970 rue de l'Escale (☎418/538-2800 or 1-888/797-2800; ❸), or *Camping Municipal* (☎418/538-2415; $17) at the east end of ave Boréal. The tourist office can provide a list of **B&Bs** which includes the *Gîte 4 Saisons*, 1264 rue Boréale (☎418/538-1329; ❷). For good seafood and smoked-salmon pizza, try the **restaurant** *Chez Julie*, 1023 Dulcinée (☎418/538-3070). *Resto-Bar Les Moutons Blancs*, 1121 ave Boréale, has occasional live music and also serves seafood.

The Mingan Archipelago

Immediately offshore from Havre-St-Pierre, the **Mingan Archipelago National Park Reserve** (Ⓦwww.pc.gc.ca) offers some of the most beautiful landscapes in Québec. Standing on the islands' white-sand shorelines are innumerable eight-metre-high **rocks** like ancient totem poles, with bright orange lichen colouring their mottled surfaces and bonsai-sized trees clinging to their crevices. These formations originated as underwater sediment near the equator. The sediment was thrust above sea level more than 250 million years ago and then covered in an icecap several kilometres thick. As the drifting ice melted, the islands emerged again, seven thousand years ago, at their present location. The sea and wind gave the final touch by chipping away at the soft limestone to create the majestic monoliths of today. But bizarre geology isn't the archipelago's only remarkable feature. The **flora** constitutes a unique insular garden of 452 arctic and rare alpine species, which survive here at their southerly limit due to the limestone soil, long harsh winters and cold Gulf of Labrador current. As for **wildlife**, other than the Gulf's whale populations, the permanent inhabitants of the national park include puffins, who build nests in the scant soil of three of the islands from early May to late August, and 199 other species of birds.

Information is available from two visitor centres: 625 rue du Centre in Longue-Pointe-de-Mingan and 975 rue de l'Escale in Havre-St-Pierre (☎418/538-5264). There's also an info kiosk (☎418/538-3285) on the wharf at 1010 Promenade des Anciens in Havre-St-Pierre. Biologists on some islands meet passengers from the cruise boats (mid-June to Aug) to explain aspects of the geology and flora.

One of the best ways to see the islands is by **sea kayak**. The friendly folks at Expédition Agaguk, 1062 ave Boréale in Havre-St-Pierre (☎418/538-1588, Ⓦwww.expedition-agaguk.com), organize one- to six-day excursions (May–Sept) for $79 a day, $129 a day if you want them to supply camping equipment and local cuisine. Even if you have your own gear, this is an excellent place for tips on currents and other conditions. On prior request, they will also organize backcountry trips to the lakes and rivers to the north.

Boat tours (June–Sept) around portions of the archipelago are available from the wharf at Havre-St-Pierre, but they must be booked in advance; *La Relève II* operates from kiosk no. 3 (3 daily; $33; ℡418/538-2865), while Tournée des Îles at kiosk no. 2 (℡418/538-2547) runs the *Perroquet de Mer* (3 daily; $33) and *Le Calculot* (2 daily; $33), a small boat whose captain's unrelenting commentary may spoil your trip. Tours in zodiacs offered by Pneumatique Transport (℡418/538-1222) from kiosk no. 4 cover the central area (1–2 daily; $39) and eastern area (2 daily; $51) where puffins cavort on Île à Calculot. Cruises to see the puffins in the western sector of the park depart from Longue-Pointe-de-Mingan (see p.363).

Camping is allowed on Île Quarry ($9) and five other islands ($6) but the only transport besides a sea kayak is the *Bateau-Mouche* sea bus (℡418/538-3427; $17–34 depending on destination). Obtain permits from the interpretation centre in Longue-Pointe or the wharfside kiosk in Havre-St-Pierre.

Île d'Anticosti

In the Gulf of St Lawrence between the Jacques Cartier and Honguedo straits, the remote 220km-long **Île d'Anticosti** was once known as the "Graveyard of the Gulf", as more than four hundred ships have been wrecked on its shores, including Admiral Phipp's fleet, retreating from Québec City in 1690. The island's vast expanse is made up of windswept sea cliffs and forests of twisted pine, crisscrossed by turbulent rivers and sheer ravines. Known as Notiskuan – "the land where we hunt bears" – by the natives, and a walrus- and whale-fishing ground for the Basques, Île d'Anticosti became the private domain of Henri Menier, a French chocolate millionaire, in 1873. He imported white-tailed Virginia deer, red fox, silver fox, beaver and moose to his domain in order to gun them down at his leisure. Nowadays a less exclusive horde of hunters and fishers comes here to blast the deer from the back of their four-wheel-drives and to hoist the salmon from the rivers, which now fall under the jurisdiction of the province. For other travellers it presents an opportunity to explore an area that's untamed and still practically deserted, with a population of just 340.

Menier established the tiny village of Baie Ste-Claire on the western tip in 1873; fewer than thirty years later the settlers moved to **PORT-MENIER** on the south side of this tip, and Baie-Ste-Claire's homes were left to the ravages of the salt air. The human population is now concentrated in the blue-roofed houses of Port-Menier, where the *Nordik Express* comes in once a week each from Havre-St-Pierre and from Sept-Îles (see box p.367).

Port-Menier edges the westerly portion of the **Parc national d'Anticosti** (℡418/535-0156, Ⓦwww.sepaq.com; $3.50) whose protected landscapes are continued further east in the reserve's two other sectors – one deep in the interior, the other covering the island's eastern tip. The twisting gravel road that crosses the island, jokingly called the "Trans-Anticostian", provides access to the central and eastern portions of the reserve. Driving is the only way to get there: a four-wheel-drive is necessary, and it's not uncommon to get a few dents or a flat tyre. You can rent a car in Port-Menier at Location Pelletier (℡418/535-0204). En route, a rough track leads from the "main" road to Québec's largest cave. Discovered in 1982, the glacial **Caverne de la Rivière à la Patate**, 120km east of Port-Menier, has a modest opening that leads into a cathedral-like chamber and a warren of 500-metre-long passages. Some 10km further on you can glimpse the impossible canyon of the **Rivière Observation**, whose bleak walls rise to over 50m. The reserve's scenery is equally impressive and a good basis for its attempt to encourage **adventure tourism** during the summer months. SÉPAQ Anticosti, the government body responsible for the Réserve Faunique, runs a variety of ecologically sound packages which, although pricey (around $550 a week per person, based on two people flying from Sept-Îles; ☎418/535-0156), include transport to the island, meals, accommodation and four-wheel-drive vehicles. Other outfits offer similar fly-in packages starting around $250 for a 24-hour excursion from Sept-Îles. Safari Anticosti has 24-hour packages starting at $219 from Havre-St-Pierre (☎418/538-1414, ⓦwww.safarianticosti.com), and $259 from the Îles-de-la-Madeleine.

The *Nordik Express* **supply ship** from Havre-St-Pierre costs $38 one-way, from Sept-Îles $49. You can also stop off for two hours en route. There is no boat from Port-Menier to Sept-Îles – it goes straight on to Rimouski instead. A number of local **airlines** serve the island from Gaspé, Baie-Comeau, Sept-Îles and Havre-St-Pierre. **Accommodation** is available in Port-Menier at *Auberge Port-Menier* (☎418/535-0122; ❹) or at the two **hostels**: *Auberge Au Vieux Menier*, 26 chemin de la Faune (☎418/535-0111; ❶; mid-June to mid-Oct), which also has camping for $10, and will pick you up from the airport and wharf and organize excursions; or *Auberge Pointe-Ouest*, 20km west of Port-Menier (☎418/535-0155; ❶), which also has camping ($10/day).

Basse Côte-Nord

Until 1996, Hwy 138 terminated at Havre-St-Pierre, leaving the dozen or so villages along the rugged **Basse Côte-Nord** (Lower North Shore) cut off from the rest of Québec, as they had been for centuries – to such an extent that many inhabitants speak only English. Now a section of Hwy 138 links Havre-St-Pierre with **Natashquan** and three other villages on the 145-kilometre stretch. If you make the lonely journey by car – as yet there is no bus – you will receive a welcome unique to a people that have only recently been connected by road to the rest of Canada.

The original inhabitants of the area were Montagnais, Naskapi and Inuits, who were invaded by Vikings in the year 1000. Cartier saw the coast in 1534 but did not register it as a discovery because it was already seasonally occupied by Basque, Spanish and Portuguese fishermen, and fishing is still the only industry on this desolate coast. The current 7500 inhabitants are descendants of fishermen from the Channel Islands and Newfoundland.

The first settlement, 65km east of Havre-St-Pierre, is the 100-strong village of **BAIE-JOHAN-BEETZ**, named after the painter and sculptor whose extraordinary and enormous house is open to the public (late June to early Sept daily 10am–5pm; reservations recommended ☎418/539-0137, ⓦwww.baiejohanbeetz.com; $5); you can also sleep in one of its seven historic bedrooms (❸).

Beyond, you pass through the tiny hamlets of **Aguanish** and **Île-à-Michon**. At the end of the 780km road from Tadoussac, a small church, wooden houses and the old fishing huts are about all there is to see in **NATASHQUAN**, the one-time home of highly revered Québecois poet Gilles Vigneault. The century-old general store has been reborn as yet another **centre d'interprétation** that focuses on local history (late June to Aug daily 9am–5pm; $3.50) and is less impressive than the town's long sandy beach. **Accommodation** is available in the ten rooms of *Auberge la Cache*, 183 chemin d'en Haut (☎418/726-3347 or 1-888/726-3347; ❸), whose seafood restaurant is open from June to August.

The Nordik Express

When the road peters out at Natashquan, access further up the Basse Côte-Nord is by snowmobile in winter, floatplane, or boat. The **Nordik Express supply ship** (April to Jan; ℡418/723-8787 or 1-800/463-0680) makes a weekly journey here on a trip that affords stunning views of a rocky, subarctic landscape, which is so cold that icebergs occasionally float past the ship even in the height of summer. The boat is evenly split between its role as a freighter and passenger ship; the majority of its passengers are locals skipping between settlements or heading for a longer jaunt to Québec's bigger towns. Its voyage begins in **Rimouski** on Tuesdays, stopping in **Sept-Îles**, **Port-Menier** on Île d'Anticosti, **Havre-St-Pierre** and **Natashquan**, before calling in at the roadless communities along the Basse Côte-Nord, reaching **Blanc-Sablon** (see p.516), Québec's most easterly village on the Labrador border, on Fridays. The same route is then followed in reverse – though the boat does not stop in Sept-Îles on the way back – to arrive back in Rimouski on Monday.

The journey up this stretch of the St Lawrence is far more impressive than the destinations. During the day, whales, dolphins and seals along with a wealth of sea birds are a common sight; while at night the northern lights often present an unforgettable display. At some stops the village inhabitants surround the boat, as its twice-weekly arrival is about all that happens hereabouts. With careful planning you can arrange to spend a couple of days in one community and catch the boat on the return voyage. Plan ahead, though: although each village receives at least one daytime visit, either the upstream or downstream stop may be in the middle of the night. But the vast majority of travellers just hop off at each port of call for the couple of hours that the boat needs to load and unload freight. A rented bicycle is particularly handy if you want to see much.

Chief stops include the village of **Kegaska**, whose roads are made from crushed seashells, and **La Romaine**, a scrappy Innu town further on. Beyond here the land becomes increasingly rocky and picturesque, the coastline cut with many intriguing inlets and leading to **Harrington Harbour**, a pretty village and easily the sightseeing highlight of the trip: it's set on an island whose topography of large rounded rocks made it necessary to make the pavements out of wood. Harrington Harbour is best seen on the upstream journey, when the boat arrives in the daytime rather than at midnight. **Accommodation** is available at *Amy's Bed & Breakfast* (℡418/795-3376; ⑤), which includes three meals a day; they also have a shop selling local handicrafts. At some villages – particularly those some distance from the boat – a shuttle bus and tour of the local village is offered, but in all cases this doesn't really add much to the experience. And the bus tour of Blanc Sablon ($20) in particular is a bare-faced, if good-humoured, money-making exercise: the bus spends most of its time at the driver's souvenir shop. The website of the local residents' group, the Coasters Association (ⓦwww.htmlweb.com/LNS), has a comprehensive listing of what you can do in each village.

Fares on the ship are reasonable and it's possible either to travel all-inclusive (with three surprisingly good daily meals and a cabin berth) or to bed down on the aircraft-style seats and picnic on the deck or in the cafeteria. You can start and finish your journey from any of the stops along the coast, but the basic fare to travel the entire length of the route on a return trip to Rimouski is $397. This with a spot in the most basic four-berth cabin is $762, while you pay $1256 to do the trip in a two-berth cabin with porthole and shower. Food is extra: breakfast $7, lunch $15, dinner $18. As another example, a round trip to Blanc-Sablon from Havre-St-Pierre costs $228, or from Natashquan $189 ($447 and $363 respectively for a basic cabin). You can also bring your car, although it is inaccessible during the voyage; fares are based on distance and the weight of the car. A one-way journey from Natashquan to Blanc-Sablon – useful if you are continuing or returning from Newfoundland and Labrador – costs at least $221 for the car. A bike adds a flat rate of $20 to the fare.

Travel details

Trains

Montréal to: Bonaventure (3 weekly; 13hr 10min); Carleton (3 weekly; 12hr); Cornwall (4–5 daily; 1hr 5min); Gaspé (3 weekly; 17hr 30min); Jonquière (3 weekly; 8hr 55min); Kingston (4–5 daily; 2hr 30min); Matapédia (6 weekly; 10hr 10min); New York (1 daily; 9hr 40min); Ottawa (4–6 daily; 2hr 10min); Percé (3 weekly; 16hr 5min); Québec City (4–5 daily; 3hr); Rimouski (6 weekly; 7hr 40min); Rivière-du-Loup (6 weekly; 5hr 55min); Toronto (4–5 daily; 4hr 30min–5hr 30min; express daily except Sat; 4hr; sleeper daily except Sat; 8hr 50min); Washington, DC (1 daily; 16hr 10min including bus to St Alban's, Vermont).
Sept-Îles to: Labrador City (2–3 weekly; 8hr 30min–10hr 30min); Schefferville (1 weekly; 11hr 15min).

Buses

Baie-Comeau to: Baie-St-Paul (2 daily; 5hr 30min); Godbout (1 daily; 50min); Port-Cartier (1 daily; 2hr 15min); Sept-Îles (1 daily; 3hr 30min).
Chicoutimi to: Alma (2 daily; 1hr); Dolbeau (2–3 daily; 3hr 30min); Jonquière (9 daily; 25min); St-Félicien (2 daily; 2hr 55min); Val-Jalbert (2 daily; 2hr 15min).
Dolbeau to: Alma (1 weekly; 1hr 15min); Péribonka (1 weekly; 30min).
Montréal to: Bromont (2 daily; 2hr); Chicoutimi (4 weekly; 4hr 55min); Chicoutimi via Québec City (5–6 daily; 6hr 30min); Granby (4–8 daily; 1hr 30min); Jonquière (4 weekly; 5hr 25min); Jonquière via Québec City (3–5 daily; 6hr 15min); Kingston (7 daily; 3hr); Magog (7–11 daily; 1hr 30min); Mont-Tremblant (3 daily; 2hr 40min); New York (8 daily; 8hr 30min); North Bay (2 daily; 7hr 40min); Orford (3 daily; 3hr); Ottawa (hourly; 2hr 20min); Québec City (hourly; 3hr); Rimouski (3 daily; 7hr); Rivière-du-Loup (4 daily; 5hr 30min); Ste-Adèle (6 daily; 1hr 25min); Ste-Agathe (6 daily; 1hr 45min); St-Jovite (5 daily; 2hr 15min); St-Sauveur (6 daily; 1hr); Sherbrooke (7–11 daily; 2hr 5min); Tadoussac (2 daily; 7hr 30min); Toronto (8 daily; 6hr 45min); Trois-Rivières (6–8 daily; 2hr); Val-David (6 daily; 1hr 30min).
Québec City to: Alma (3 daily; 2hr 45min); Baie-Comeau (2 daily; 6hr 5min); Baie St-Catherine (2 daily; 3hr 20min); Baie-St-Paul (3 daily; 1hr 15min); Chicoutimi (5-6 daily; 2hr 30min); Dolbeau (2 daily; 5hr 25min); Forestville (2 daily; 4hr 45min); Jonquière (3–5 daily; 3hr); La Malbaie (3

daily; 1hr 50min); Les Escoumins (2 daily; 4hr 10min); Rimouski (5 daily; 3hr 55min); Rivière-du-Loup (4 daily; 2hr 20min); St-Félicien (2 daily; 4hr 25min); St-Siméon (2 daily; 2hr 20min); Sherbrooke (2 daily; 3hr 30min); Tadoussac (2 daily; 4hr); Val-Jalbert (2 daily; 3hr 45min).
Rimouski to: Bonaventure (2 daily; 6hr); Cap-aux-Os (summer 1 daily; 6hr 50min); Carleton (2 daily; 4hr 15min); Gaspé via Carleton (2 daily; 9hr 10min); Gaspé via Matane (2 daily; 6hr 50min); Matane (2–3 daily; 1hr 50min); Matapédia (2 daily; 2hr 50min); Mont St-Pierre (2 daily; 4hr 20min); New Richmond (2 daily; 5hr 30min); Percé (2 daily; 8hr 20min); Ste-Anne-des-Monts (2–3 daily; 2hr 50min); Ste-Flavie (2–3 daily; 30min).
Rivière-du-Loup to: Edmundston, NB (3 daily; 3hr).
Sept-Îles to: Baie-Comeau (1 daily; 3hr 30min); Havre-St-Pierre (1 daily; 2hr 30min).
Sherbrooke to: Trois-Rivières (4 weekly; 2hr 10min).
Tadoussac to: Chicoutimi (1 daily; 1hr 40min); Rivière Ste-Marguerite (6 weekly; 30min); Ste-Rose-du-Nord (6 weekly; 55min).
Trois-Rivières to: Grand-Mère (3 daily; 1hr).

Ferries

Baie-Ste-Catherine to: Tadoussac (1–3 hourly; 10min).
Blanc-Sablon to: St Barbe, NL (May–Dec 1–3 daily; 1hr 30min).
Matane to: Baie-Comeau (4 weekly–2 daily; 2hr 20min); Godbout (1–3 daily; 2hr 10min).
Québec City to: Lévis (1–3 hourly; 15min).
Rimouski to: Forestville (April–Oct 2–4 daily; 55min).
Rivière-du-Loup to: St-Siméon (April–Dec 2–5 daily; 1hr 15min).
St-Joseph-de-la-Rive to: Île-aux-Coudres (8 daily–2 hourly; 15min).
Trois-Pistoles to: Les Escoumins (May–Oct 2–3 daily; 1hr 15min).

Nordik Express

Continuous voyage (see p.367). Broken down into segments here for clarity.

Havre-St-Pierre to: Natashquan (1 weekly; 6hr 15min); Kegaska (1 weekly; 11hr 30min); La Romaine (1 weekly; 16hr); Harrington Harbour (1 weekly; 24hr 45min); Tête-à-la-Baleine (1 weekly; 29hr 15min); La Tabatière (1 weekly; 32hr 45min); St-Augustin (1 weekly; 37hr 15min); Blanc-Sablon (1 weekly; 43hr 45min).

Rimouski to: Blanc-Sablon (1 weekly; 78hr 30min); Sept-Îles (downstream only; 1 weekly; 11hr 30min).
Sept-Îles to: Havre St-Pierre (1 weekly; 15hr 15min); Port-Menier (1 weekly; 7hr 45min).

Flights

Montréal to: Baie-Comeau (3–4 daily; 1hr 30min); Bathurst (2–3 daily; 1hr 45min); Calgary (3–4 daily; 4hr 30min); Chicoutimi (5 daily; 1hr 5min); Fredericton (3–4 daily; 1hr 30min); Gaspé (2–3 daily; 2hr 40min); Halifax (10–12 daily; 1hr 25min); Îles-de-la-Madeleine (1–3 daily; 3hr 50min); Moncton (3–4 daily; 1hr 20min); Mont Joli (3–4 daily; 1hr 25min); Ottawa (9–11 daily; 40min); Québec City (13–20 daily; 50min); Saint John, NB (3–5 daily; 1hr 35min); St John's, NL (1–2 daily; 2hr 35min); Sept-Îles (3–6 daily; 2hr 45min); Toronto (19–40 daily; 1hr 15min); Vancouver (4–6 daily; 5hr 20min); Wabush (2 daily; 4hr 5min); Winnipeg (2–3 daily; 2hr 55min).
Québec City to: Baie-Comeau (1–3 daily; 1hr 35min); Gaspé (1–2 daily; 2hr 10min); Halifax (1 daily; 1hr 40min); Îles-de-la-Madeleine (1–2 daily; 3hr 20min); Ottawa (2–7 daily; 1hr 10min); Sept-Îles (2–3 daily; 1hr 30min); Toronto (6 daily; 1hr 30min); Wabush (1–2 daily; 2hr 50min).

The Maritime Provinces

CHAPTER 3 # Highlights

❋ **Halifax** The British lost the US, but they intended to hold on to Canada – as the imposing Citadel shows. **See p.384**

❋ **Lunenburg** This handsome fishing port is small-town Nova Scotia at its best, dotted with frilly Victorian mansions. **See p.394**

❋ **Annapolis Royal** The perfect place to unwind, with some great B&Bs, public gardens and a postcard-pretty coastal location. **See p.404**

❋ **Cape Breton Highlands National Park** Rearing coastal headlands and plunging forested valleys provide some fine hiking. **See p.416**

❋ **Bay of Fundy** Swirling waters, whale-watching and world-beating tides – nowhere more so than in Fundy National Park. **See p.441**

❋ **Fredericton** The Beaverbrook Art Gallery has an outstanding collection of Canadian paintings. **See p.427**

❋ **Fort Beauséjour** The grassy ditches and mounds that remain from this old British fort offer superlative views over the Bay of Fundy. **See p.445**

❋ **Charlottetown** The leafy, urbane capital of PEI makes a perfect hideaway. **See p.454**

❋ **Prince Edward Island National Park** A splendid beach of pristine, red-hued sand set against the deep blue of the ocean. **See p.459**

△ Harbour, Blue Rocks, NS

The Maritime Provinces

he Maritime Provinces – **Nova Scotia**, **New Brunswick** and **Prince Edward Island** – are Canada's three smallest provinces, and their combined population of around two million has been largely confined to the coasts and river valleys by the thin soils of their forested interiors. Even today, the bulk of the region remains intractable – 84 percent of New Brunswick, for example, is covered by pine, maple and birch forests – and this rough and ready **wilderness** combines with a ruggedly beautiful **coastline** to form one of Canada's most scenic regions. Of some appeal too are the chunks of fertile **farmland** that punctuate the forests, principally in the undulating fields of Prince Edward Island (PEI) and the lowlands around New Brunswick's Grand Falls, both of which produce massive crops of potatoes, and in Nova Scotia's Annapolis Valley, a major fruit-producing area.

Most visitors to the Maritimes come for the coastal scenery and the slow pace of the "unspoilt" fishing villages, but the Maritimes were not always as sleepy as they appear today. When the three provinces joined the Dominion in the middle of the nineteenth century, their economies were prospering from the export of fish and timber and the success of their shipyards. But, as opponents of the confederation had argued, the Maritimers were unable to prevent the passage of protectionist measures favouring the burgeoning industries of Ontario and Québec. This discrimination, combined with the collapse of the shipbuilding industry as steel steamers replaced wooden ships, precipitated a savage and long-lasting recession. Within the space of thirty years, the economic collapse transformed most of the Maritimes from a prosperous, semi-industrialized region to a pastoral backwater dependent on the sale of its raw materials – chiefly wood and fish. In recent years, tourism has helped to keep the region's economy afloat and the tourist industry hereabouts is extremely well organized, though out of season –

Toll-free information numbers and websites

Nova Scotia Department of Tourism ☏ 1-800/565-0000, ⓦ www.novascotia.com.
Tourism New Brunswick ☏ 1-800/561-0123, ⓦ www.tourismnewbrunswick.ca.
PEI Department of Tourism ☏ 1-888/734-7529, ⓦ www.peiplay.com. PEI also operates a specialist accommodation line during the summer on ☏ 1-888/268-6667.

before mid-May and after mid-October – many attractions and B&Bs are closed.

Bypassed economically, many of the region's villages still retain their nineteenth-century appearance, with pastel-shaded clapboard houses set around rocky coves and bays. However, the Maritimes offer much more variety than this bucolic image suggests. In **Nova Scotia**, the southwest coast does

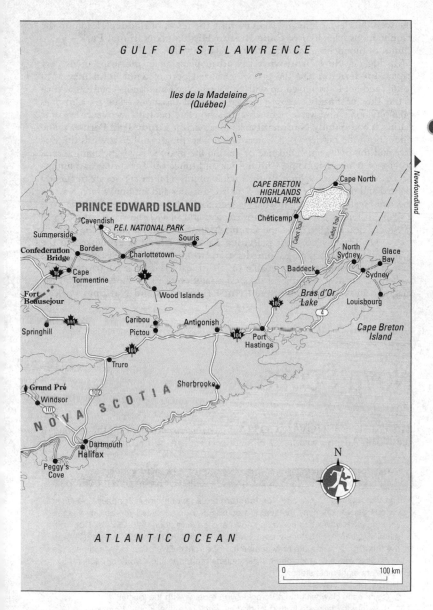

GULF OF ST LAWRENCE

Iles de la Madeleine
(Québec)

CAPE BRETON
HIGHLANDS
NATIONAL PARK

Cape North

Chéticamp

PRINCE EDWARD ISLAND

Cavendish
P.E.I. NATIONAL PARK

Summerside

Souris

North
Sydney

Glace
Bay

Confederation
Bridge

Borden

Charlottetown

Baddeck

Sydney

Cape
Tormentine

Bras d'Or
Lake

Louisbourg

Fort
Beausejour

Wood Islands

Cape Breton
Island

Springhill

Caribou
Pictou

Antigonish

Port
Hastings

Truro

Sherbrooke

Grand Pré
Windsor

N O V A   S C O T I A

N

Dartmouth
Halifax

Peggy's
Cove

ATLANTIC OCEAN

0   100 km

indeed have a clutch of quaint fishing ports, but it also harbours the busy
provincial capital of **Halifax**, whilst **Annapolis Royal**, with its genteel mansions, is only a few kilometres from **Port Royal** and its reconstruction of the
fort Samuel de Champlain built in 1605. Further east, **Cape Breton Island**,
connected to the mainland by a causeway, is divided into two by **Bras d'Or
Lake**: the forested plateau flanking industrial **Sydney** is unremarkable, but in

375

the west the elegiac hills and lakes framing the resort of **Baddeck** lead into the mountainous splendour of **Cape Breton Highlands National Park** – a rare chunk of mountain in a region that is relatively flat.

Moving on, **New Brunswick** has urban pleasures in the shape of its cosy capital **Fredericton** and the gritty, revitalized port of **Saint John** (never "St John", and not to be mixed up with St John's, Newfoundland) – but its star turn is the **Bay of Fundy**, whose taper creates tidal variations of up to 12m. This phenomenon is observable right along the shoreline, but has a spectacularly scenic setting at both **Fundy National Park** and along the **Fundy Trail Parkway**. The tides churn the nutrient-rich waters down near the ocean bed towards the surface and this draws an abundance of marine life into the bay – including several species of **whale**, beginning with finback and minkes in late spring, and humpbacks from mid- to late June. By the middle of July all three species are frequently sighted and they usually stay around till late summer and autumn, which is when the rare North Atlantic right whale is seen too. Whale-watching trips leave from a string of Fundy ports in both Nova Scotia and New Brunswick – those from Westport, near **Digby**, Alma and **Grand Manan Island** are among the best.

Last but certainly not least is **Prince Edward Island** (**PEI**), linked to the mainland by the whopping Confederation Bridge in 1997. The island possesses one of the region's most amenable towns in leafy, laid-back **Charlottetown**, well worth at least a couple of days especially as it's just a short hop from the magnificent sandy beaches of the **Prince Edward Island National Park**.

Nova Scotia

The character of **NOVA SCOTIA** has been conditioned by the whims of the North Atlantic weather, a climate so harsh in wintertime that the Nova

Eating a lobster

Throughout Nova Scotia and PEI, **lobsters** are a favourite dish and they appear, in various guises, on many restaurant menus. For whole lobster, you pay by weight, with the smaller lobsters averaging 450g and costing about $20–25. Also, look out for all-you-can-eat lobster suppers, rural community events held in village halls and the like, though these are now something of a rarity. Given that the Maritimers are so familiar with eating lobster, it's particularly embarrassing if you don't know how. There are eight main steps:

1. Twist off the claws.
2. Crack each claw with the nutcracker you receive with the lobster.
3. Separate the tailpiece from the body by arching the back until it breaks.
4. Bend back and break off the flippers from the tailpiece.
5. Insert a fork where the flippers broke off and push.
6. Unhinge the back from the body – the meat in the back, the tomalley, is considered by many to be the choicest part of a lobster.
7. Open the remaining part of the body by cracking it apart sideways.
8. Suck out the meat from the small claws.

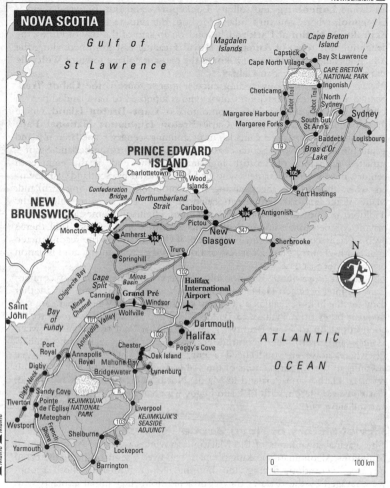

Scotian colonists of the eighteenth century earned the soubriquet **"Bluenoses"** for their ability to stand the cold. The descendants of these hardened sailors do not, however, typify the whole province. The farmers of the Annapolis Valley and their Acadian neighbours were quite distinct from the mariners of the Atlantic coast, and different again were the mixed bag of emigrants who came to work the coal mines and steel mills of central Nova Scotia and Cape Breton Island from the 1880s – differences that remain noticeable today.

To get the full sense of Nova Scotia you have to do a tour, and the logical place to start is the capital, **Halifax**, which sits beside a splendid harbour on the south coast. With its excellent restaurants, lively nightlife and handful of historic attractions, the city can easily fill a couple of days. To continue, it's best to take in the beguiling fishing villages of the southwest shore, amongst which handsome **Lunenburg** and solitary **Lockeport** stand out. Between them is **Liverpool**, where you turn inland for both the remote forests and lakes of **Kejimkujik National Park** and, beyond, on an arm of the Bay of Fundy, the delightful little town of **Annapolis Royal**. Heading east from here along the Annapolis Valley, it's a further 110km to the pleasant college town of **Wolfville** and another 90km back to Halifax.

Nova Scotia's other outstanding circular tourist route is the **Cabot Trail**. Named after the explorer John Cabot, who is supposed to have landed here in 1497, it encircles the northern promontory of **Cape Breton Island**, where the mountainous landscapes of **Cape Breton Highlands National Park** constitute some of eastern Canada's most stunning scenery. Cape Breton Island – and the strip of Nova Scotia coast bordering the Northumberland Strait – attracted thousands of Scottish highlanders at the end of the eighteenth century, mostly tenant farmers who had been evicted by Scotland's landowners when they found sheep-raising more profitable than renting farmland. Many of the region's settlements celebrate their Scots ancestry and Gaelic traditions in one way or another – museums, Highland Games and bagpipe-playing competitions – and in **South Gut St Ann's**, on the Cabot Trail, there's even a Gaelic college. The final attraction of Cape Breton is the reconstructed eighteenth-century French fortress of **Louisbourg**, stuck in splendid isolation on the southeast coast.

Southwest Nova Scotia is reasonably well served by **bus**, with daily connections running between Halifax and Yarmouth via the south shore and another daily service linking Halifax and Digby via the Annapolis Valley. There are also frequent buses from Halifax to Baddeck and Sydney as well as to Truro, for connections on to New Brunswick and PEI. VIA Rail **trains** run between Halifax and Truro, then continue on to New Brunswick and Québec. Elsewhere, however, you'll need a **car**, particularly if you're keen to see anything of the wilder sections of the Cabot Trail. **Car ferries** link Yarmouth with Bar Harbor and Portland in Maine; North Sydney with Newfoundland; Caribou, near Pictou, with PEI; and Digby with Saint John, which often makes a useful short cut.

A brief history of Nova Scotia

The original inhabitants of the Maritime Provinces were the **Micmacs** and **Malecites**, Algonquian-speaking peoples who lived a semi-nomadic life based on crop cultivation, fishing and hunting. Never numerous, both groups were ravaged by the diseases they contracted from their initial contacts with Basque and Breton fishermen in the late sixteenth century. Consequently, they were too weak to contest European colonization, although the Micmacs were later employed by the French to put the frighteners on the colonists of northern Maine.

Founded by the French in 1605, **Port Royal**, on the south shore of the Bay of Fundy, was Nova Scotia's first European settlement, but in 1613 it was razed by Virginian raiders and abandoned the following year. In 1621, James I, King of England and Scotland, granted "**Nova Scotia**" – as New Scotland was termed in the inaugural charter – to William Alexander, whose colony near Port Royal lasted just three years. The French returned in the mid-1630s, establishing themselves on the site of today's Annapolis Royal and this time designating the region as the French colony of **Acadie**. These competing claims were partly resolved by the **Treaty of Utrecht** in 1713 – when Britain took control of all the Maritimes except Cape Breton Island and today's PEI – and finally determined after the fall of New France in 1759. The British victory was subsequently tarnished by the cruel expulsion of the Acadians from their farms along the Bay of Fundy.

With France defeated and the British keen to encourage **immigration** there was a flood of settlers from Ireland, England and Scotland as well as United Empire Loyalists escaping New England during and after the American War of Independence. This increase in the population precipitated an administrative reorganization, with the creation of Prince Edward Island in 1769 and New Brunswick in 1784. The new, streamlined Nova Scotia prospered from the development of its agriculture and the expansion of its fishing fleet. Further profits were reaped from shipbuilding, British-sanctioned privateering and the growth of Halifax as the Royal Navy's principal North Atlantic base. In 1867 Nova Scotia became part of the Dominion of Canada confident of its economic future. However, the province was too reliant on shipbuilding and, when this industry collapsed, Nova Scotia experienced a dreadful recession, whose effects were only partly mitigated by the mining of the province's coalfields and the industrialization of Cape Breton's **Sydney**, which became a major steel producer. Most of the pits and steel mills were closed in the 1950s, and the province is now largely dependent on farming, logging, fishing and tourism, though there is a new kid on the economic block – **oil and gas**. The first oil and gas reserves were discovered off the Nova Scotian coast in the 1970s, but production did not commence until the early 1990s. Reserves are substantial and promise a massive injection into the provincial economy.

Halifax

HALIFAX, set on a steep and spatulate promontory beside one of the world's finest harbours, has become the focal point of the Maritimes, the region's financial, educational and transportation centre, whose metropolitan population of over 500,000 makes it seven times the size of its nearest rival, New Brunswick's Saint John. This pre-eminence has been achieved since World War II, but long before then Halifax was a naval town *par excellence*, its harbour defining the character and economy of a city which rarely seemed to look inland.

The British were the first to develop Halifax, founding a base here in 1749 to counter the French fortress of Louisbourg (see p.421) on Cape Breton Island. When New France was captured shortly afterwards, the town became a heavily fortified guarantor of the Royal Navy's domination of the North Atlantic, a role reinforced when the British lost control of New England. The needs of the garrison called the tune throughout the nineteenth century: the waterfront was lined with brothels; martial law was in force till the 1850s; and most Haligonians, as the local citizenry are known, were at least partly employed in a service capacity.

In the twentieth century Halifax acted as a key supply and convoy harbour in both world wars, but since then its military importance has declined, even though the ships of the Canadian navy still dock here. Workaday office blocks reflect the city's new commercial successes, but interrupt the sweep of the town as it tumbles down to the harbour from the **Citadel**, the old British fortress that is the town's most significant sight. Nevertheless, Halifax retains a compact, bustling centre whose appealing and relaxing air is a far cry from the tense industriousness of many a metropolis.

THE MARITIME PROVINCES

3

Dartmouth

Ferry Terminal

Historic Properties

Maritime Museum

Art Gallery

BEDFORD ROW

GEORGE

Province House

GRANVILLE STREET

UPPER WATER STREET

DUKE STREET

SCOTIA SQUARE

Grand Parade

St Pauls Church

ARGYLE ST.

CARMICHAEL ST.

PRINCE S.

GRAFTON ST.

MARKET STREET

MARKET ST

COGSWELL STREET

BRUNSWICK STREET

Clock Tower

SACKVILLE STREET

Police Station

GOTTINGEN STREET

RAINNIE DRIVE

Citadel

J

AHERN AVENUE

BELL ROAD

TROLLOPE STREET

Nova Scotia Museum of Natural History

SUMMER STREET

ACCOMMODATION
Casino Nova Scotia Hotel **A**
Dalhousie University
 Residences **H & N**
Delta Barrington **D**
Delta Halifax **G**
Halifax Heritage
 House Hostel **E**
YWCA **F**
Halifax's Waverley Inn **I**
Halliburton House Inn **C**
Lord Nelson Hotel **K**
St Mary's University **L**
Virginia Kinfolks B&B **M**
Westin Nova Scotian **B**
YMCA **J**

380

M

MARGINAL ROAD

LOWER WATER STREET

HOLLIS STREET

TERMINAL RD.

Train and Bus
Station

B

Cornwallis
Park

C

BARRINGTON STREET

BISHOP STREET

BLOWERS ST.

Old Burying
Ground

9 **E** **F**

H **I** **10**

12 **14**

16

MORRIS STREET

HARVEY ST.

SOUTH STREET

KENT STREET

CHURCH ST.

20

21

QUEEN STREET

SPRING GARDEN ROAD

27

BIRMINGHAM STREET

23

FENWICK STREET

DRESDEN ROW

N

BRENTON STREET

26

27

K **28**

SOUTH PARK STREET

Public
Gardens

TOWER ROAD

L ▲ Point Pleasant Park

TOWER ROAD

RESTAURANTS, CAFÉS & BARS

Baan Thai	24	Marquee Club	25
Bearly's House of Blues	9	Mediterraneo	8
Birmingham Bar & Grill	26	Midtown Tavern and Grill	17
Bitter End	12	New Palace Cabaret	19
Bluenose	4	Old Triangle	3
Daily Grind Café	27	Peddlers' Pub	6
Dharma Sushi	13	Reflections Cabaret	7
Economy Shoe Shop	11	Salty's	1
Five Fishermen	15	Satisfaction Feast	16
Granite Brewery	10	Split Crow	5
Il Mercato	23	Steve-o-Reno's	20
Italian Gourmet	21	Timothy's World of Coffee	22
La Cave	14	Velvet Olive	18
Lower Deck	2	Your Father's Moustache	28

0   200 m

Arrival, information and transport

Halifax International Airport is located 35km northeast of the city centre and has its own smart, large and extremely efficient provincial tourist information office (daily 9am–9pm). Airbus runs a **bus shuttle** service from the airport to the classier downtown hotels (daily 6am–11pm, every 30min/1hr; takes 40min–1hr 15min depending on traffic; $12 one-way, $20 return). If you're not staying at one of these hotels, ask the driver how near to your destination he will let you off; for downtown in general get off at the *Delta Barrington Hotel*, which is on Barrington Street at Duke, right in the centre. The **taxi** fare from the airport to the centre is around $40.

Buses to Halifax with Acadian Lines (from Digby, Truro and New Brunswick) and DRL Coachlines (from Yarmouth) pull into the **bus terminal**, 1161 Hollis Street at Cornwallis Park. Sharing the same premises is the VIA Rail station, which handles just six **trains** a week, connecting Halifax with Truro, New Brunswick, the Gaspé and Montréal. From the train station it's a fifteen-minute walk into the centre, or else catch bus #7 or #9 along Barrington Street (Mon–Fri every 15min, Sat & Sun hourly).

Both of Halifax's main **tourist offices** cover the city and province, and are centrally situated. The **International Visitor Centre**, at 1595 Barrington St and Sackville (June–Aug daily 8.30am–8pm; May & Sept to mid-Oct daily 9am–6pm; mid-Oct to April Mon–Fri 8.30am–4.30pm; ☎902/490-5946, ⓦwww.halifaxinfo.com), will provide you with armfuls of maps, brochures and leaflets, including the comprehensive *Halifax Visitor Guide*. They will also advise on guided tours and fix you up with accommodation in any part of the province for free. Five-minutes' walk away, at the foot of Sackville Street, the **Waterfront Visitor Information Centre** (May–Oct daily 9am–7pm; Nov–April Wed–Sun 9am–4.30pm; ☎902/424-4248) offers a similar service.

The best way to see downtown Halifax is **on foot**, but for outlying attractions and accommodation **buses** operated by Metro Transit (☎902/490-4000) are reliable and efficient, though they are sharply curtailed in the evenings and on weekends. There's a flat fare of $1.75 in the Halifax area (exact fare only). If you need to change buses on the same journey, ask for a free transfer ticket at the outset. The **ferries** that cross Halifax harbour from the downtown terminal to Dartmouth and Woodside (see p.389) are part of the Transit system and apply the same tariff. Free Metro Transit route maps and schedules are available from the International Visitor Information Centre.

Accommodation

Finding **accommodation** in Halifax is rarely a problem and the International Visitor Centre is especially helpful in emergencies. To get a flavour of the city your best bet is to stay in – or at least close to – downtown. Here you'll find a number of modern sky-rise **hotels**, ranging from the comfortable to the luxurious, as well as several more distinctive offerings. These include a couple of stylish hotels with Art Deco flourishes, two **inns** occupying tastefully converted old town houses and the occasional **B&B**, though most of the city's B&Bs are way out from the city centre. Halifax's **motels** are stuck out on the peripheries of town too, inconveniently concentrated about 10km northwest of the centre along Bedford Highway (Hwy 2), beside Bedford Basin bay. The main budget alternatives are the **student rooms** offered by several city universities between mid-May and mid-August, and the pleasant, centrally located **hostel**. There is no city-centre campsite.

Hotels and inns

Casino Nova Scotia Hotel 1919 Upper Water St ☎902/421-1700 or 1-866/425-4329, ⓦwww.casinonovascotiahotel.com. One of the city's largest hotels, a spankingly modern affair built in a broadly retro style to blend in with the adjacent Historic Properties. Overlooks the waterfront and has all mod cons – saunas, swimming pool and whirlpool plus casino. ⑤

Delta Barrington 1875 Barrington St ☎902/429-7410 or 1-800/268-1133, ⓦwww.deltahotels.com. Modern luxury, bang in the middle of downtown, with weekend discounts of up to thirty percent. Attached to one of the city's larger shopping malls. ⑥

Delta Halifax 1990 Barrington St ☎902/425-6700 or 1-800/268-1133, ⓦwww.deltahotels.com. Large, modern downtown hotel occupying a concrete-and-glass tower block with attractive, spacious rooms that are discounted at weekends. ⑥.

Halifax's Waverley Inn 1266 Barrington St ☎902/423-9346 or 1-800/565-9346, ⓦwww.waverleyinn.com. Elegant Victorian mansion, with thirty rooms, that's been sympathetically refurbished with splendid period furnishings. Oscar Wilde stayed here on a North American lecture tour, apparently turning up in green velvet pantaloons – outlandish gear which only seems to have added to his popularity amongst the locals. The inn is situated about a 5min walk from the train station; reservations advised. All rooms are en suite. Rates include breakfast. Highly recommended. ⑨

Halliburton House Inn 5184 Morris St ☎902/420-0658, ⓦwww.halliburton.ns.ca. Near the railway station off Barrington St, this long-established thirty-room inn occupies three adjacent buildings. The oldest, the original inn, has a Victorian period look to its public rooms, but the bedrooms beyond are firmly modern. The nicer – and larger – bedrooms, many of which have balconies, are in the other two buildings. ⑥

Lord Nelson Hotel 1515 South Park St ☎902/423-6331 or 1-800/565-2020, ⓦwww.lordnelsonhotel.com. Opposite the Public Gardens at the corner of Spring Garden Rd. The lobby of this popular brown-brick hotel is spacious and elegant, with Art Deco details dating from its 1920s construction. The 200-odd rooms do not quite live up to the lobby, but they are comfortable and furnished in smart modern style – and certainly compare well with those of their rivals. ⑥

Westin Nova Scotian 1181 Hollis St ☎902/421-1000 or 1-877/993-7846, ⓦwww.westin.ns.ca. Massive, luxurious hotel in the upgraded premises of the old railway hotel, which – with its Art Deco touches – is next door to the train station. A 15min stroll along Barrington or Hollis streets from the city centre. ⑤

B&Bs and hostels

Halifax Heritage House Hostel (HI) 1253 Barrington St ☎902/422-3863, ⓔhalifax @hihostels.ca. Only 500m from the train station, this clean and agreeable HI hostel with family rooms (doubles $40) and dorm beds ($24) has a laundry, kitchen, patio and parking.

Virginia Kinfolks B&B 1722 Robie St at Jubilee ☎902/423-6687 or 1-800/668-7829. Situated beside a busy main road about 1.5km west of downtown – opposite the Halifax Infirmary – this well-kept B&B occupies a suburban house with front and rear sun decks. Four spacious en-suite rooms and gourmet breakfast. Discounts for stays of more than three days. ⑥

YMCA 1565 South Park St at Sackville ☎902/423-9622, ⓦwww.ymcahrm.ns.ca. Opposite the Public Gardens, this YMCA, for men and women, has fifty single rooms, none of which are en suite but there's a gym. $35.

YWCA 1239 Barrington St ☎902/423-6162, ⓦwww.ywcahalifax.com. Near the train station, this women-only hostel has facilities that include kitchen, gym, pool, laundry and sauna. Twenty-seven rooms, mostly shared bathrooms. Singles $45, doubles $60.

Student accommodation

Dalhousie University Conference Services Room 407, Student Union Building, 6136 University Ave ☎902/494-8840, ⓦloc.housing.dal.ca. Halifax's premier academic institution, Dalhousie University is geared up for conferences during the summer recess, and also offers rooms to tourists from mid-May to late August. There are several locations, beginning at the west end of University Ave – 2km southwest of the centre – with facilities that include swimming pool and sports halls. Also at the university's DalTech, O'Brien Hall, 5217 Morris St (off Barrington St), a 10min walk south of the centre. Single and double rooms available, usually with shared bathrooms, but breakfast is included. Singles $37, doubles $58.

St Mary's University 923 Robie St ☎902/420-5485 or 1-888/347-5555. About 2km southwest of the centre, on the way to Point Pleasant Park; singles and doubles available; shared bathrooms. Open mid-May to mid-August. Singles $30, doubles $45.

The City

With its shopping malls and brusque tower blocks, the commercial and social heart of modern Halifax clambers up the steep hillside from the harbourfront, its narrow streets dotted with scores of bustling bars and restaurants. The city's main attractions – most notably the **Art Gallery**, with its eclectic collection of modern Canadian paintings, the **Maritime Museum** and the Georgian **Province House** – all huddle close together in the lower part of town beneath Halifax's star turn, the Vaubanesque **Citadel**. On a sunny day a pleasant diversion is a trip to see a couple of the **outer fortifications** built to defend Halifax harbour, and you can also catch the ferry over to neighbouring **Dartmouth**, home of the old **Quaker House**.

The Citadel

The distinctively bright-white Georgian **Clock Tower**, a solitary landmark sitting at the top of George Street beside the path up to the Citadel, looks somewhat confused, its dainty balustraded tower set on top of the dreariest of rectangular shacks. Completed in 1803, the tower is a tribute to the architectural tastes of its sponsor, Edward, Duke of Kent and father of Queen Victoria, who was sent here as military commandant in 1794. The Duke insisted on having a clock on each of the tower's four faces so none of the garrison had an excuse for being late, a preoccupation typical of this unforgiving martinet.

Up above the Clock Tower, the present fortifications of the **Citadel National Historic Site** (daily: July & Aug 9am–6pm; rest of year 9am–5pm; $9 June to mid-Sept, $5.75 in shoulder season, otherwise free) are Victorian, the fourth in a series dating from Edward Cornwallis's stockade of 1749. It's a star-shaped fortress, constructed flush with the crest of the hill to protect it from artillery fire, a design that makes it seem insignificant until you reach the massive double stone and earth walls which flank the deep encircling ditch. Close up, it's a forbidding approach to one of Britain's most important imperial strongholds, but despite their apparent strength, the walls, faced with granite and ironstone, were a source of worry to a succession of British engineers. The sunken design simply didn't suit the climate – in winter the earth in the ramparts and the water in the mortar froze and the spring melt came with regular collapses.

A slender footbridge spans the ditch and leads into the fort, whose expansive **parade ground** is flanked by stone walls and dominated by the three-storey general **barracks**, whose long, columned galleries now mostly hold offices, though one particular barrack room has been returned to its appearance as of 1869. Here also is an **Army Museum**, which adopts an earthy soldier's outlook in the labelling of its wide collection of small arms. Ancient and sometimes rare photos track the Canadian army through its various imperial entanglements – from the Boer War onwards – and there's an interesting section tracing Canadian involvement with the Anglo-French attack on Bolshevik Russia after World War I. The walls themselves contain a string of **storehouses** stuffed with military bric-a-brac. Here you'll find a couple of reconstructed powder magazines, the former garrison school room and several exhibits exploring the Citadel's history, including a small theatre where a fifty-minute-long film, *The Tides of History*, details the development of Halifax. Also of interest is the **Communications Exhibit**, which explains the niceties of the Admiralty's signalling system – a complicated affair with, for instance, different flags for different types of ship and whether they had been sighted or had actually arrived.

Free and entertaining half-hour **guided tours** (May to late Oct) of the Citadel depart from the information office in the barracks building every hour or so. Throughout the summer bagpipe bands and marching "soldiers" perform on the parade ground in period uniform and one of the cannons is ceremoniously fired every day at noon. If militarism leaves you cold, the Citadel is still worth a visit for the grand view from its ramparts over the city and harbour.

Downtown

Retracing your steps down past the Clock Tower, keep straight along George Street to reach the tree-lined, elongated square known as the **Grand Parade**, the social centre of the nineteenth-century town. For the officer corps, this was the place to be seen walking on a Sunday, when, as one obsequious observer wrote, "their society generally [was] sought, frequently courted, and themselves esteemed" – a judgement rather different from that of the radical journalist Joseph Howe, who hated their "habits of idleness, dissipation and expense". The southern edge of the Grand Parade borders the handsome **St Paul's Church** (Mon–Fri 9am–4.30pm; free), whose chunky cupola and simple timber frame date from 1750, making it both the oldest building in town and the first Protestant church in Canada. Inside, the church's simple symmetry – with balcony and sturdy pillars – is engaging, an unpretentious garrison church enlisting God to the British interest; look out, too, for the piece of wood embedded in the plaster above the inner entrance doors, a remnant of the 1917 Halifax Explosion (see box, p.387). Following the disaster the vestry was used as an emergency hospital and the bodies of hundreds of victims were laid in tiers around the walls.

Charles Dickens, visiting in 1842, described the graceful sandstone **Province House**, a couple of minutes' walk from Grand Parade down George Street on Hollis (July & Aug Mon–Fri 9am–5pm, Sat & Sun 10am–4pm; rest of year Mon–Fri 9am–4pm; free), as "a gem of Georgian architecture" whose proceedings were "like looking at Westminster through the wrong end of a telescope". Highlights of the free **guided tour** include a peek into the old upper chamber, with its ornate plasterwork and matching portraits of Queen Caroline and her father-in-law, George I. She should have been pictured with her husband, George II, rather than her father-in-law, but no one ever bothered to rectify this costly decorative error. The present legislature meets in the Assembly Room, a cosy chamber that partly resembles a Georgian bedroom rather than Nova Scotia's seat of government.

Art Gallery of Nova Scotia

Across the road from the Province House, the **Art Gallery of Nova Scotia**, 1741 Hollis St (daily 10am–5pm, Thurs till 9pm; $10, free on Thurs after 5pm), occupies two adjacent buildings – one a stern Art Deco structure, the other an embellished Victorian edifice that has previously served as a courthouse, police headquarters and post office. The gallery is attractively laid out and although there is some rotation of the exhibits most of the pieces described here should be on view. Pick up a free gallery plan at the entrance in the more southerly of the two buildings, Gallery South.

The ground floor – Floor 1 – of **Gallery South** contains a delightful section devoted to the Nova Scotian artist **Maud Lewis** (1903–70). The daughter of a Yarmouth harness maker, Lewis overcame several disabilities, including rheumatoid arthritis, to become a painter of some regional renown, creating naive, brightly coloured works of local scenes. Lewis's tiny cabin – awash with her bright paintwork – has been moved here intact from the outskirts of Digby.

An underground passageway connects Gallery South with **Gallery North**, where the bottom floor – the Lower Level – holds temporary exhibitions of modern sculpture and painting. Upstairs, Level 1 has further temporary displays plus – concentrated in Room 7 – an enjoyable selection of **Canadian historical paintings** with the Maritimes to the fore. The earlier canvases are distinguished by four intriguing views of Halifax in the 1760s produced by Dominique Serres in the minutely observed Dutch land- and seascape tradition. Surprisingly, Serres never actually visited Canada, but painted Halifax while in Europe, from drawings produced by a camera obscura. In the same gallery, there's also Joshua Reynolds' flattering *Portrait of George Montagu Dunk, 2nd Earl of Halifax*. As the man responsible for colonial trade, Dunk permitted his recently acquired title to be used in the naming of Halifax – what would have happened but for his timely ennoblement is anyone's guess (perhaps "Dunktown"). Close by, Room 4 holds several canvases by Cornelius Krieghoff (see p.427) and a small sample of the work of the **Group of Seven** (see p.96). In particular, look out for Lawren Harris's haunting *Algoma* landscape and A.Y. Jackson's diminutive *Houses of Prospect*, typical of Jackson's later (post-Group) style of softly coloured landscapes. Moving on, Room 6 features a small selection of modern Canadian paintings drawn from the permanent collection: the egg tempera on masonite *Island in the Ice* by the Nova Scotian artist Tom Forrestall is perhaps the most striking painting here, its sharp, deep-hued colours and threatening ice- and seascape enhanced by a tight control of space.

Level 2 focuses on modern Atlantic Canadian painters. Tom Forrestall makes another appearance here, but it's his mentor, **Alex Colville**, who takes pride of place, with several characteristically disconcerting works, a sort of Magic Realism of passive, precisely juxtaposed figures caught, cinema-like, in mid-shot. Look out also for the precise draughtsmanship and appealing clarities of **Donald Cameron Mackay** and more paintings by members of the Group of Seven. The final two floors – Level 3 and 4 – are used for temporary displays of mostly modern and contemporary European artists.

The Waterfront

One block south of the east end of George Street stands the **Maritime Museum of the Atlantic**, 1675 Lower Water St (May–Oct Mon–Sat 9.30am–5.30pm, Tues until 8pm, Sun 1–5.30pm; Nov–April Tues 9.30am–8pm, Wed–Sat 9.30am–5pm, Sun 1–5pm; $8), which contains a fascinating exhibition covering all aspects of Nova Scotian seafaring from colonial times to the present day. By the entrance there's a reconstruction of a nineteenth-century chandlery, stocked with everything from chains, ropes, couplings and barrels of tar through to ships' biscuits and bully beef. Other displays include a collection of small boats and cutaway scale models illustrating the changing technology of shipbuilding, a feature on the history of the schooner *Bluenose* (see below) and a number of gaudy **ships' figureheads**; look out for the turbaned Turk once attached to the British barque *Saladin*. In 1844, the *Saladin*'s crew mutinied in mid-Atlantic, killed the captain and ran the boat aground near Halifax, where they were subsequently tried and hanged. There's also a feature on the Halifax Explosion, illustrated by a first-rate video, *One Moment in Time*, and don't miss the section on the **Titanic**, which sank east of Halifax in 1912. Several pieces of fancy woodwork found floating in the ocean after the sinking have ended up in the museum, a pathetic epitaph to the liner's grand Edwardian furnishings and fittings. Docked outside the museum are an early twentieth-century steamship, the CSS *Acadia*, and a World War II corvette,

The Halifax Explosion

Nothing in the history of the Maritimes stands out like the 1917 **Halifax Explosion**, the greatest man-made cataclysm of the pre-atomic age. It occurred during World War I when Halifax was the departure point for convoys transporting troops and armaments to Europe. Shortly after dawn on December 6, a Norwegian ship called the *Imo*, a vessel carrying relief supplies to Belgium, and a French munitions carrier called the *Mont Blanc* were manoeuvring in Halifax harbour. The Norwegian ship was steaming for the open sea, while the *Mont Blanc*, a small, decrepit vessel, was heading for the harbour stuffed with explosives and ammunition, including half a million pounds of TNT – though it flew no flags to indicate the hazardous nature of the cargo. As the ships approached each other, the *Imo* was forced to steer into the wrong channel by a poorly positioned tugboat. With neither ship clear about the other's intentions and each attempting to take evasive action, they collided, and the resulting sparks caused the ignition of the drums of flammable liquid stored on the *Mont Blanc*'s deck. A fire took hold, and the crew abandoned their vessel, which drifted under the force of the impact towards the Halifax shore.

A large crowd had gathered on the waterfront to witness the spectacle when the TNT exploded. The blast killed 2000 people instantly and flattened over 300 acres of north Halifax, with fire engulfing much of the rest. Windows were broken in Truro over 90km away and the shock wave was felt in Cape Breton. Nothing remained of the *Mont Blanc*, and part of its anchor, a piece of metal weighing over half a ton, was later found more than 4km away. To make matters worse, a blizzard deposited 40cm of snow on Halifax during the day, hampering rescue attempts. The bodies of many victims were not recovered until the spring.

It's hard to appreciate today the vision of Armageddon that haunted Halifax after the explosion, but haunt the city it did, as the poignant newspaper cuttings in the Maritime Museum show.

HMCS *Sackville*. The first is part of the museum, the second is a (free) attraction in its own right; both can only be boarded in the summer.

The much-vaunted **Historic Properties** comprise an area of refurbished wharves, warehouses and merchants' quarters situated below Upper Water Street, 400m or so north of the Maritime Museum – and just beyond the Dartmouth and Woodside ferry terminal. The ensemble has a certain urbane charm – all bars, boutiques and bistros – and the narrow lanes and alleys still maintain the shape of the harbourfront during the days of sail, but there's not much to see unless the schooner **Bluenose II** is moored here, as it often is during the summer. The original *Bluenose*, whose picture is on the 10¢ coin, was famed throughout Canada as the fastest vessel of its kind in the 1920s, although she ended her days ingloriously as a freighter, foundering off Haiti in 1946. The replica has spent several years as a floating standard-bearer for Nova Scotia, but it's now on its last sea legs and its future is uncertain. Pressure groups are campaigning to have it berthed permanently here at Halifax or at its home port of Lunenburg (see p.394).

The Old Burying Ground and the Nova Scotia Museum

Mysterious and spooky at dawn and dusk, the **Old Burying Ground** is a five-minute walk south of Grand Parade at Barrington Street and Spring Garden Road. The cemetery manages to look something like the opening shot of David Lean's *Great Expectations* despite the best efforts of the over-blown memorial by the gates in honour of a brace of Canadian officers killed in the Crimean War. Many of the tombstones are badly weathered, but enough inscriptions survive to give an insight into the lives (and early deaths) of the colonists and their offspring. The oldest tomb is that of a certain John Connor, who ran the first ferry service over to Dartmouth and died in 1754.

Walking west up Spring Garden Road from the Burying Ground, it's about 800m to South Park Street, where a set of handsome iron gates serve as the main entrance into the city's **Public Gardens** (dawn–dusk; free). First planted in the 1870s, the gardens cover sixteen acres of meticulously maintained exotic shrubs, flowerbeds and trees set around ornamental statues, water fountains, ponds and a brightly painted bandstand. All together, the gardens are a pleasant interlude on the way to the **Nova Scotia Museum of Natural History**, 1747 Summer St – to the rear of the old grassy commonland that trails back from the Citadel (June to mid-Oct Mon–Sat 9.30am–5.30pm, Wed till 8pm, Sun 1–5.30pm; mid-Oct to May Tues–Sat 9.30am–5pm, Wed till 8pm, Sun 1–5pm; $3). The museum is compact, but still manages to touch all its bases, from an acrylic honeybee hive through to illuminating sections on whales and the province's land-based wildlife. There's also a modest display of Micmac (or, more properly, Mi'kmaq) archaeological finds.

The outer fortifications

In the eighteenth century the British navy protected the seven-kilometre-long sea passage into **Halifax harbour**, and the Bedford Basin behind it, with coastal batteries strung along the shore between the city and the Atlantic. Two of these are worth a visit, though more for their commanding views than the ragbag of military remains. There's one at **Point Pleasant**, at the tip of the Halifax peninsula about 3km south of the city, whilst the other is on **McNab's Island**, sitting in the middle of the main seaway, 4km south of the city.

At the end of South Park Street and its continuation, Young Avenue, **Point Pleasant Park** (bus #9 from Barrington St) incorporates the remains of four gun batteries and the squat **Prince of Wales Martello Tower** (July & Aug daily 10am–6pm; free), which was built at the end of the eighteenth century as a combined barracks, battery and storehouse. One of the first of its type, the design was copied from a Corsican tower (at Martello Point) which had proved particularly troublesome to the British. The self-contained, semi-self-sufficient defensive fortification with its thick walls and protected entrance proved so successful that Martello towers were built throughout the empire, only becoming obsolete in the 1870s with advances in artillery technology. Path and trails crisscross the surrounding park, 200 acres of wooded hills and shoreline that were unlucky enough to be badly mauled by a hurricane in 2003. Incidentally, this is one of the few places in North America where heather grows, supposedly originating from seeds shaken from the bedding of Scots regiments stationed here.

McNab's Island, 5km long and 2km wide, contains the remnants of five different fortifications, the earliest dating from the middle of the eighteenth century, the last being Fort McNab, which was built in 1890. The island, half of which is parkland, is laced with hiking trails and dotted with picnic spots, making it a relaxing retreat from the city, though again many of the island's trees were ripped up by "Hurricane Juan" in 2003. There are several informal **ferry** services over to the island, the most convenient being the summer excursions running from downtown Halifax (June to mid-Sept 2 daily; $14 return) – times and further details from the tourist office.

Dartmouth

Humdrum **DARTMOUTH**, across the harbour from Halifax, is often ignored by visitors as it lacks the more obvious appeal of its neighbour. Nevertheless, it is the province's second largest town, with 70,000 inhabitants, and although it's primarily an industrial centre the ferry ride over there does provide wide views of the harbour and downtown Halifax – and there are a couple of minor attractions to further justify a sortie. The Dartmouth **ferry** leaves the Halifax waterfront from beside the Historic Properties at the foot of George Street (Mon–Sat 6.45am–11.30pm every 15–30min; June–Sept also Sun noon–5.30pm; $1.75). The journey takes about ten minutes. The twin cities are also connected by two road bridges: the MacDonald, running just to the north of both city centres, and the Mackay, part of the outer ring road. Metro Transit bus #1 uses the MacDonald.

Turn left outside Dartmouth ferry terminal and then take the first right for the five-minute stroll to the **Quaker House**, 57 Ochterloney St (June–Aug Tues–Sun 10am–1pm & 2–5pm; $2), a small, grey-clapboard residence sitting three blocks up the hill from the dock near King Street. After the American War of Independence, several Quaker whaling families emigrated from Nantucket Island, off Cape Cod, to Dartmouth, but this is the only one of their houses to survive. The interior has been painstakingly restored to its late eighteenth-century appearance, its spartan fittings reflecting Quaker values. Among the exhibits are a two-hundred-year-old pair of shoes found under the floorboards during renovations in 1991, and the eye of a Greenland whale preserved in formalin – though the staff won't show you this if they think you're squeamish. From here, it's another five-minute walk along – and left at the end of – King Street to a very short stretch of the **Shubenacadie Canal**, which once connected the Bay of Fundy to Dartmouth, a distance of 90km. Begun in 1826, this monumental feat of engineering, linking a dozen existing lakes with new watercourses and locks, was completed in 1860, but the canal only made a profit for ten years before it was superseded by the railways – and then left to rot.

To return to the Dartmouth ferry terminal, double back across the end of King Street and keep straight until you reach the **park** that leads round the harbourfront – in all, a five- to ten-minute walk.

Eating

It's easy to **eat** well and inexpensively in Halifax. There's a wide selection of **downtown** cafés, diners, café-bars and restaurants within easy walking distance of Grand Parade with particular concentrations along Spring Garden Road from Queen Street to South Park, Argyle Street, and Granville Street north of Duke. All three of these areas largely cater to locals, whereas the more touristy spots are clustered down on the waterfront in the Historic Properties. At the majority of restaurants, a substantial meal will only set you back about $15–20, excluding drinks. **Seafood** is the leading local speciality, with **lobster** being a particular favourite – expect to pay about $30 for a medium-sized specimen. Bear in mind also that most kitchens start to finish up at around 9.30–10pm and that many restaurants close on Sunday, sometimes Monday too.

For something a bit different, Freak Lunchbox, 1723 Barrington St, boasts a phenomenal range of **sweets** and **candy** – from the traditional to the kitsch via the bizarre.

Cafés, café-bars, grills and diners

The Bluenose 1824 Hollis at Duke St. Something of an institution, this long-established diner serves filling and fairly tasty meals until 10pm. Lobster, in various guises, is the speciality.

Daily Grind Café 5684 Spring Garden Rd at South Park. Easy-going, amenable coffee house where you can browse a vast selection of newspapers and glossy magazines.

Economy Shoe Shop Café 1663 Argyle St. Everything here is imaginative – from the name and the off-beat decor through to the menu, offering tapas to Italian. One of a cluster of fashionable café-bars on Argyle.

The Italian Gourmet 5431 Doyle St. A wide selection of good quality Italian meals, snacks, salads and cakes at this large and relaxed deli-café.

Mediterraneo 1571 Barrington St, between Sackville and Blowers. Inexpensive downtown café serving tasty Lebanese dishes. Popular spot with a youthful clientele.

Midtown Tavern and Grill At Prince and Grafton. One of the most enjoyable places in town, this blue-collar favourite serves up tasty steaks at amazingly reasonable prices. It's a far cry from the tourist-industry niceties down on the waterfront, and none the worse for it. Closed Sun.

Steve-o-Reno's Brunswick St, just off Spring Garden Rd. Fashionable café-bar with pastel decor and angular, modern furnishings. The breakfasts are tip-top, with a bewildering range of coffees.

Timothy's World Coffee 5475 Spring Garden Rd at Queen. This competent coffee house sells great coffees and delicious pastries – the cheesecake is especially lip-smacking. Also a branch at 1791 Barrington St.

Restaurants

Baan Thai 1569 Dresden Row ☎902/446-4301. There's often a queue here to sample the city's best Thai food, but it's well worth the wait. Hidden away upstairs. Inexpensive.

Dharma Sushi 1576 Argyle St ☎902/425-7785. First-rate Japanese restaurant serving all the favourites. Faded decor, but very easy on the pocket with main courses from around $12.

Five Fishermen 1740 Argyle St at Carmichael ☎902/422-4421. One of Halifax's best restaurants, where the all-you-can-eat mussel bar is a popular (at no extra charge) adjunct to the restaurant, whose speciality is seafood. The cosy interior is decked out in antique nautical style. Fairly expensive with main courses $15–25, but well worth it. Reservations required. A popular spot.

Il Mercato 5475 Spring Garden Rd at Dresden ☎902/422-2866. Laid-back, tastefully decorated restaurant featuring well-prepared, very tasty Northern Italian dishes. Main courses for around $15.

La Cave 5244 Blowers at Grafton ☎902/429-3551. Tiny bistro serving French and Italian cuisine and great desserts at affordable prices – their cheesecake is famous hereabouts. Tucked away in a basement.

Salty's Historic Properties ☎902/423-6818. On the waterfront, this busy restaurant with its large patio area heaves with tourists, who feast on the lobster – generally thought to be as well prepared as anywhere.

Satisfaction Feast 1581 Grafton St at Blowers ☎902/422-3540. Vegetarian restaurant with an imaginative menu. Vegan options available. Main courses around $10. Open daily 11am–10pm.

Nightlife and entertainment

They say Halifax has more **bars** per head than anywhere in Canada except St John's, Newfoundland, and although cafés and café-bars have made substantial inroads, there are still plenty of good bars, many of which offer pub food (of variable quality). Incidentally, bars and restaurants sometimes occupy different floors of the same premises and this can be a little confusing.

If you want to go out and groove, Halifax has a vibrant **live music scene** with around forty of its café-bars and bars offering everything from blues and jazz through to indie and techno. Many of these places have live music on just a couple of nights a week, and detailed entertainment listings, along with reviews, are given in a free weekly newssheet, *The Coast*, which is available at record shops, bars and the tourist office. The local newspaper *The Chronicle-Herald* carries reviews and listings on Thursdays, and *Where*, a free monthly magazine supplied by the tourist office, has a section describing the city's most popular bars and giving some opening hours. The venues listed below are places where you can expect to see live music on most nights of the week. The main **musical event** is the eight-day Atlantic Jazz Festival, held in mid-July and featuring many of the biggest international names. Halifax, as the provincial capital, also attracts major live acts in key **classical** and theatrical performances and has a well-regarded **theatre** scene.

Bars

The Bitter End 1570 Argyle St. Well known for their martinis, this polished cocktail bar provides a quietly cool beginning to – or end of – a night on the tiles.

Granite Brewery 1222 Barrington St at South. In the style of a British pub, this charmingly intimate bar occupies a nineteenth-century stone building not far from the train station. Most of the ale is brewed on the premises – try the "Peculiar", a fair approximation of the sultry grandeur of the legendary British ale Theakstons.

Old Triangle 5136 Prince St at Hollis. An Irish-style pub with a whole network of cosy snugs and a warm and welcoming atmosphere. Live Gaelic music on the weekend.

Peddlers' Pub Granville St at Duke. Occupying part of an old commercial block at the pedestrianized northern end of Granville St, this pub has a pleasant outside area and a big and breezy bar.

Split Crow 1855 Granville St at Duke. Another supposedly English pub. Very central, often featuring live Maritime fiddle music.

Your Father's Moustache 5686 Spring Garden Rd at South Park. Good range of ales with frequent live acts – blues a speciality. Seasonal rooftop patio.

Live music and clubs

Bearly's House of Blues 1269 Barrington St ☎902/423-2526. Near the HI hostel, this low-key bar has regular acts with the emphasis – you guessed it – on blues. Thurs–Sun.

Birmingham Bar and Grill 5657 Spring Garden Rd at South Park St ☎902/420-9622. Wide range of wine and beers with nightly jazz.

Lower Deck In the Privateer's Warehouse, one of the Historic Properties down on the waterfront ☎902/425-1501. Traditional Maritime folk music most nights of the week.

Marquee Club 2037 Gottingen St ☎902/429-3020, ⊛www.themarqueeclub.ca. Upstairs, rock bands play to an energetic and enthusiastic audi-

ence. Downstairs, it's laid-back acoustic jazz and blues. Ten minutes' walk from the centre off Cogswell St.

New Palace Cabaret 1721 Brunswick St ☎902/420-0015, ⊛www.thenewpalace.com. Massive, brash and noisy nightclub where Halifax's young more than get acquainted. Open nightly until 3.30am.

Reflections Cabaret 5184 Sackville St ☎902/422-2957, ⊛www.reflectionscabaret.com. Halifax's main gay and lesbian bar and nightclub. House music predominates.

Velvet Olive 1770 Market St at Carmicheal ☎902/492-2233, ⊛www.velvetolive.com. The classiest joint in town where the dudded-up come to live it up to the sound of top-ranking DJs and up-and-coming bands. There's an achingly hip art gallery and restaurant here too.

Classical music

Symphony Nova Scotia Box office at the Dalhousie Arts Centre, 6101 University Ave ☎902/494-3820, ⊛www.symphonynovascotia.ca. Professional orchestra that usually performs at the university's Rebecca Cohn Auditorium (University Ave and Marchant St). Concert season from September to April. Everything from Beethoven to Piaf.

Film

Empire Bayers Lake 190 Chain Lake Drive ☎902/876-4801. Mainstream multiscreen near Hwy 102, about 6km west of downtown.

Famous Players 5657 Spring Garden Rd ☎902/423-4598. Mainstream cinema in the Park Lane Mall.

Drama

Neptune Theatre 1593 Argyle St ☎902/429-7070, ⊛www.neptunetheatre.com. The doyen of Halifax's live theatres, offering a wide range of mainstream dramatic productions; closes for three months in summer.

Listings

Airlines Air Canada ☎1-888/247-2262; Air St-Pierre ☎902/873-3566.
Banks Amongst many downtown branches, there's a Bank of Novia Scotia at Scotia Square, Barrington St and Duke; a CIBC at 1809 Barrington

St; and a Royal Bank at the corner of Spring Garden Rd and Queen St.
Bike rental Bike and Sea, 1781 Lower Water St ☎902/423-1185.
Bookshops There are several good bookshops on

and around Barrington St, both new and second-hand. The Book Room, 1546 Barrington at Blowers (☎902/423-8271; closed Sun), originated in 1839 (Canada's oldest) and has a good selection of new books, with its Maritimes section especially noteworthy. JWD Books, 1684 Barrington at Blowers (☎902/429-1652; closed Sun), specializes in antiquarian and secondhand books. The chain Smithbooks (☎902/423-6438), with an outlet at Scotia Square, is more mainstream.

Buses Acadian Bus Lines ☎1-800/567-5151, ⓦwww.acadianbus.com (to Sydney and Truro, for NB and PEI); DRL Coachlines ☎902/450-1987 or 1-877/450-1987, ⓦwww.drlgroup.com/coachlines (to Yarmouth via the south shore); Halifax Metro Transit ☎902/490-4000.

Car rental Budget, 1588 Hollis ☎902/492-7500, and at the airport (same number); Discount, 1240

Hollis ☎902/468-7171; Dollar, 1589 Lower Water St ☎902/422-4455, and at the airport ☎902/573-3527.

Consulate US, Cogswell Tower ☎902/429-2480.

Internet access Ceilidh Connections, 1672 Barrington St at Prince ☎902/422-9800, ⓦwww.ceilidhconnect.ns.ca.

Laundry Bluenose Laundromat, 2198 Windsor at Duncan (daily 7.30am–9pm) does self-service and service washes, with dry-cleaning too.

Post office 1680 Bedford Row and Prince (Mon–Fri 7.30am–5.15pm).

Taxis Yellow Cab ☎902/422-1551, Casino Cabs ☎902/425-6666.

Trains VIA Rail ☎1-888/842-7245, ⓦwww.viarail.ca.

Weather Up-to-date bulletin on ☎902/426-9090.

Southwest Nova Scotia

The jagged coastline running southwest of Halifax to **Yarmouth**, a distance of 300km, boasts dozens of tiny fishing villages glued tight against the shore by the vast forest that pours over the interior. Most were founded by Loyalists, whose dedication to the British interest both during and after the American War of Independence obliged them to hotfoot it out of the US, often as penniless refugees. Today, the most beguiling of these villages are **Peggy's Cove**, an incredibly picturesque smattering of higgledy-piggledy clapboard houses dotted along a wild shore, and lesser-known **Lockeport**, with its old-fashioned air and fine sandy beaches. Equally diverting are the towns of **Lunenburg**, with its stunning Victorian architecture, and ritzy, leafy **Chester**, both of which derived their former prosperity, like their coastal neighbours, from the now-defunct shipbuilding business and from privateering.

Travelling the shoreline is the **Lighthouse Route**, a tourist trail that details everything of any possible interest, but you're better off sticking to the main road, Hwy 103, and dropping down to the coast for the highlights. At workaday **Liverpool**, there's a choice of routes: you can cut across the peninsula to Annapolis Royal (see p.404) on Hwy 8, past the wilderness splendours of **Kejimkujik National Park**, or – with more time – you can press on along the coast, sampling the fine coastal scenery of the clumsily named **Seaside Adjunct of Kejimkujik National Park** before arriving at Lockeport and ultimately **Yarmouth**. Beyond Yarmouth, a second tourist route, the **Evangeline Route**, pushes up the **French Shore** to Annapolis Royal. The coast is popular with tourists, but not oppressively so, and almost every settlement has at least a couple of fine old Victorian mansions that have been converted into **inns** or **B&Bs**. These provide first-rate accommodation at reasonable prices and reservations are only essential in the height of the season and on holiday weekends. In terms of **restaurants**, seafood is the big deal around here – usually simply prepared and quite delicious.

For **public transport**, DRL Coachlines (☎1-877/450-1987, ⓦwww .drlgroup.com/coachlines), based at the Halifax bus station, operates a once-daily service between Halifax and Yarmouth along the southern shore; and

Acadian Lines (☎1-800/567-5151, ⓦwww.acadianbus.com) connects Halifax with Digby daily via the Annapolis Valley.

Peggy's Cove

Highway 333 leaves Hwy 103 a few kilometres west of Halifax to make its slow progress through the forested hinterland that so successfully confined the region's early settlers to the coast. Once at the shoreline, the road slips through ribbon fishing villages, past glacial boulders and round rocky bays to reach tiny **PEGGY'S COVE**, 45km from Halifax. Founded in 1811, the hamlet, with a resident population of just sixty souls, surrounds a rocky slit of a harbour, with a spiky timber church, a smattering of clapboard houses and wooden jetties on stilts. It's a beautiful spot, the solitary lighthouse set against the sea-smoothed granite of the shore, and it attracts swarms of tourists; try to visit at sunrise or sunset, when the coach parties leave the village to the locals. Behind the lighthouse, *The Sou'wester* dispenses mundane meals, while the three-roomed *Peggy's Cove B&B*, overlooking the harbour from the end of Church Road (☎902/423-1102 or 1-800/725-8732, ⓦwww.nsinns.com; ❹), provides simple but perfectly adequate accommodation – advance reservations are advised.

Beyond Peggy's Cove Hwy 333 sticks closely to the coastline, meandering through a magnificently desolate landscape of stunted firs and cumbersome seashore boulders. Pull in at any of several places for a stroll along the shore or press on north through the gentler scenery that leads back to Hwy 103.

Chester

It's a thirty-minute drive north from Peggy's Cove to Hwy 103 and a further 40km west to **CHESTER**, a handsome and prosperous-looking town tumbling over a chubby little peninsula. Founded by New Englanders in 1759, the town, with its fine old trees and elegant frame houses, has long been the favoured resort of yachting enthusiasts whose principal shindig is the **Race Week** regatta held in mid-August. Chester is also home to the first-rate **Chester Playhouse**, right in the centre on Pleasant St, which offers a lively programme of concerts and plays from mid-March to mid-December (☎902/275-3933 or 1-800/363-7529, ⓦwww.chesterplayhouse.ns.ca; tickets around $20), with a crescendo of activity in July and August during a festival of contemporary music and Canadian-oriented drama. Finally, a **passenger ferry** (Mon–Fri 4 daily, Sat & Sun 2 daily; 45min; $5 return) sallies out from Chester bound for the offshore islet of **Big Tancook**, whose quiet country roads and benign scenery are popular with walkers, who pop across for a day's ramble. There's somewhere to eat here too – *Carolyn's Café & Crafts* (June–Oct), opposite the jetty, which also supplies island maps.

Chester **tourist office** (July & Aug Mon–Sat 9am–7pm, Sun 10am–5pm; June, Sept & Oct Mon–Sat 10am–5pm, Sun noon–5pm; ☎902/275-4616) is located in the old train station on the northern edge of town, beside Hwy 3. They issue free town maps, which are very useful as Chester's lay-out is a tad confusing, and Tancook Island ferry timetables. They will also arrange **accommodation**, though the options are limited and you'll be extremely lucky to find a vacant room during the festival. There are only a couple of **B&Bs** in and around town, the better of which is the ultra-expensive *Haddon Hall Inn* (☎902/275-3577, ⓦwww.haddonhallinn.com; ❽; May–Oct), just to the northwest of the centre, off Highway 3 on Haddon Hill Road. The inn occupies an immaculately modernized villa dating from 1905 and offers wide views over the bay from the top of a hill. It has an outside pool and a long verandah and the guest rooms and suites are kitted out in a smart rendition of period style. Much more affordable, if a good deal more modest, is the *Mecklenburgh Inn*, whose four guest rooms – two with shared facilities – are in a pleasant Victorian house in the centre at 78 Queen St (☎902/275-4638, ⓦwww .bbcanada.com/298.html; ❹; May–Dec). For delicious **seafood** head for the *Rope Loft* (☎902/275-3430) down by the jetty, where main courses average around $15, half that for fish and chips.

Mahone Bay

In 1813, the wide waters of **Mahone Bay** witnessed the destruction of the splendidly named American privateer the *Young Teaser*, which had been hounded into the bay by a British frigate. On board was a British deserter who knew what to expect if he was captured, so he blew his own ship up instead – a tribute to the floggers of the Royal Navy. Legend has it that the ghost of the blazing vessel reappears each year and this is not the only strange story attached to the area. In 1795, three boys discovered the top of an underground shaft on tiny **Oak Island**, a low-lying, offshore islet a few kilometres west of Chester. The shaft, or "Money Pit", soon attracted the attentions of treasure hunters, who were convinced that this was where a vast horde of booty had been interred. At first the betting was on Drake, Kidd or Morgan, but present favourites include the Templars and even the Rosicrucians. No treasure has ever been found, but the diggings became so dangerous that the island's owners have closed it to the public. If you go – the 1.3km turning is clearly signed on Hwy 3 – you can only get to the chain at the start of the causeway over to the island.

The village of **MAHONE BAY** spreads along the seashore just 25km west of Chester, its elongated waterfront dominated by three adjacent **church towers**, which combine to create one of the region's most famous vistas. There's not much else to the place, though you might drop by the **Settlers' Museum**, 578 Main St (June–Sept Tues–Sat 10am–5pm, Sun 1–5pm; free), to examine its hotchpotch of period furniture and early nineteenth-century ceramics. The village also possesses one of the best delis-cum-**cafés** in the area, *Jo-Ann's Deli & Bakeshop*, beside the main crossroads and selling a superb selection of filled rolls and baguettes. Another good option is the *Ocean Grill Restaurant*, a five- to ten-minute walk south from the crossroads at 662 Main St, where they serve up delicious lunches in attractive waterfront surroundings. Nearby, the well-tended *Heart's Desire B&B*, 686 Main St (☎902/624-8470, ⓦwww.heartsdesirebb.com; ❸), occupies an attractive older building with pleasant views out across the bay.

Lunenburg

Comely **LUNENBURG**, 10km south of Mahone Bay village, perches on a narrow, bumpy peninsula, its older central gridiron of streets clambering up from the main harbourfront flanked by brightly painted wooden houses. Dating from the late nineteenth century, the most flamboyant of these mansions display an arresting variety of **architectural features** varying from Gothic towers and classical pillars to elegant verandas, high gables and peaked windows, all embellished with intricate scrollwork. Amidst the virtuousity, a distinctive municipal style is noticeable in the so-called "**Lunenburg Bump**", where overhanging window dormers are surmounted by triple-bell cast roofs – giving the town a vaguely European appearance appropriate to its original

LUNENBURG

ACCOMMODATION

1775 Solomon House B & B	B
Bluenose Lodge	F
Daniel Rudolf House B & B	C
Kaulbach House Inn	E
Lunenburg Campground	A
Mariner King Inn	D

RESTAURANTS & CAFÉS

Laughing Whale Café	1
Magnolia's Grill	2
Old Fish Factory Restaurant	4
Rum Runner	3

HIGHWAY 332

KISSING BRIDGE ROAD

BLOCKHOUSE HILL ROAD

HILL STREET

KEMPT STREET

HOPSON STREET

PRINCE STREET

KING STREET

DUKE STREET

CORNWALLIS STREET

KAULBACH STREET

CREIGHTON STREET

YORK STREET

KING STREET

LAWRENCE STREET

FOX STREET

TOWNSEND STREET

CUMBERLAND STREET

LINCOLN STREET

PELHAM STREET

MONTAGUE STREET

BLUENOSE DRIVE

LOWER STREET

LINDEN AVENUE

STARR STREET

DUFFERIN STREET

LORNE STREET

MEDWAY STREET

YOUNG STREET

FALKLAND STREET

Lunenburg Academy

Lutheran Church

St John's Anglican Church

Zwicker House

Dory Shop

Fisheries Museum

Theresa E. Connor

Bluenose II

Boat & Whale-watching trips

Lunenburg Harbour

Bus Stops

0   100 m

395

settlement. Lunenburg was founded in 1753 by German and Swiss Protestants, who of necessity soon learned to mix the farming of their homeland with fishing and shipbuilding. They created a prosperous community with its own fleet of trawlers and scallop-draggers, although nowadays the town earns as much from the tourist industry as from fishing.

Arrival, information and accommodation

DRL **buses** from Halifax and Yarmouth pull in at the Bluenose Mini-Mart, a five- to ten-minute walk from the main harbourfront at 35 Lincoln St. The town's **visitor centre** (daily: May–Sept 9am–8pm, Oct 9am–6pm; ☎902/634-8100) occupies an imitation blockhouse on Blockhouse Hill Road, a stiff 700m walk up from the harbourfront. They operate a free room-reservation service, which is especially useful in the height of the season, and supply a somewhat stodgy (but free) leaflet detailing the town's architectural high points. As regards **accommodation**, visitors are spoilt for choice with many of the town's historic houses turned into first-class **inns** and **B&Bs**.

Inns and B&Bs

1775 Solomon House B&B 69 Townsend St ☎902/634-3477, ⓦwww.bbcanada.com/5511.html. Clad in cedar shingles, this Georgian house has many of its original features from its double entrance stairway outside to the plank floors within. Three attractive guest rooms. ❹

Bluenose Lodge Corner of Falkland Ave & Dufferin St ☎902/634-8851 or 1-800/565-8851, ⓦwww.bluenoselodge.ca. A couple of minutes' walk from the central gridiron, this splendidly well-preserved 1860s mansion has nine well-appointed guest rooms kitted out in a pleasing version of period style. May–Oct. ❸

Daniel Rudolf House B&B 325 Lincoln St ☎902/634-8668 or 1-877/858-1883, ⓦwww.rudolfhouse.ns.ca. Handy downtown location for this immaculate B&B in a handsome olive and maroon, bay-windowed Victorian villa, Four capacious, well-appointed guest rooms and tasty, filling breakfasts. ❸

Kaulbach House Historic Inn 75 Pelham St ☎902/634-8818 or 1-800/568-8818, ⓦwww.kaulbachhouse.com. One of the best preserved of Lunenburg's Victorian mansions, this comfortable inn, with its salmon-pink exterior, has seven comfortable guest rooms, most with sea views and all decorated in an attractive version of period style. Creative European breakfasts too. Open mid-March to Oct. ❸

Mariner King Inn 15 King St ☎902/634-8509 or 1-800/565-8509, ⓦwww.marinerking.com. Bang in the centre of town, this delightful inn has been sympathetically – but not lavishly – restored with acres of stripped wood and crisply modern furnishings and fittings. ❸

Campsite

Lunenburg Board of Trade Campground Blockhouse Hill Rd ☎902/634-8100. Plain, unadorned campground with fifty pitches next door to the visitor centre at the top of the town. Great views – and big winds. May–Oct.

The Town

Lunenburg's pride and joy is its **Fisheries Museum of the Atlantic** (May to late Oct daily 9.30am–5.30pm; late Oct to April Mon–Fri 8.30am–4.30pm; $9), housed in an old fish-processing plant down by the quayside. The museum has an excellent aquarium, a room devoted to whales and whaling, and displays on fishing and boat-building techniques. Another section features the locally built 1920s schooner *Bluenose* and its replica *Bluenose II* (see p.387), whilst the August Gales display has wondrous tales of mountainous seas and helmsmen tied to the mast to stop being swept overboard. Moored by the jetty, there's a trawler and a scalloper, but the real high spot here is the *Theresa E. Connor*, a saltbank fishing **schooner** launched in 1938. Superbly restored, the schooner was one of the last boats of its type to be built, a two-masted vessel constructed to a design that had changed little since the early eighteenth century; if you read *Treasure Island* as a child and were confused by the layout of the boat, all is revealed. The main change in schooner design came with the installation of engines in the early 1900s: the helmsman no longer needed to keep an eagle-eye on the sails and so he could be moved aft. Further protection was provided by a wheelhouse, though there were teething problems with these and initially an alarming number were lost at sea. With or without engines, fishing schooners worked in the same way: each carried several **dories**, small row boats that were launched at the fishing grounds. The men rowed the dories away from the schooner, fanning out to trail long hand-lines with baited hooks over the ocean – line-fishing. At the end of the day, the catch would be brought back to the schooner. Dory fishing was a dangerous business – the transfer of the catch was especially risky and there was always the chance of being caught in the dory by a sudden squall. Not surprisingly, therefore, local fishermen didn't need much persuading to abandon their schooners and dories for the larger **trawlers** that replaced them in the 1950s. The *Theresa E. Connor* soldiered on, but her last voyage was an ignominious failure: in 1963 she sailed out of Lunenburg bound for Newfoundland to raise the rest of her 25-man crew. No one turned up and the schooner had to return home empty-handed.

There's more of maritime interest down along the harbourfront at the **Dory Shop**, where they make wooden boats in traditional style and hire out sail and row boats. If you haven't the confidence/experience to sail out on your own, regular boat trips leave the jetty near the museum throughout the summer. There are also two- to three-hour **whale-watching** trips operated four times daily from May to October by Lunenburg Whale Watching Tours (T 902/527-7175, W www.whalewatchingnovascotia.com; $42).

The rest of the centre

Take King Street from the harbourfront and it's a couple of blocks to one of the finest of Lunenburg's mansions, the **Zwicker House** – now the Mariner Inn (see below) – at no.15. The house was built in the 1820s, but its exterior, including a fine illustration of the Lunenburg bump, was added later, probably in the 1870s. From here, it's a couple of minutes walk to the **Kaulback Inn**, at 75 Pelham St (also see below), which has changed little since its construction for one of the town's premier families in 1890. At heart, the house is a simple clapboard frame, but perky dormer windows have been tacked on as has the triple-bell cast roof of the "bump". From the inn, it's another short stroll to Lunenburg's fanciest building, **St John's Anglican Church**, whose original oak frame was imported lock, stock and barrel from Boston in 1754. This first church was plain and simple and by the early nineteenth century this just didn't match the expectations of the town's increasingly prosperous burghers, so they had it remodelled, once in the 1840s and again fifty years later. The end result is a superb illustration of decorative Gothic, its frilly wooden scrollwork punctuated by slender pinnacles that poke up from every one of its façades. All this Anglican brouhaha stimulated the Lutherans, who, in 1890, erected a **Lutheran Church** in grand Victorian Gothic style, from its pointed windows through to its soaring spire, nearby at Cornwallis and Fox St. Round the corner from the Lutheran church, on Gallows Hill at the far end of Kaulback St, is **Lunenburg Academy**, a whopping maroon, black and white timber school building of 1895. Three storeys high, with towers and a mansard roof, the construction costs were enormous, partly because the interior was finished in ash and birch – a clear indication of the importance the townsfolk attached to education. From the academy, it takes about five minutes to walk back to the harbourfront.

Eating and drinking

Lunenburg has a goodly supply of restaurants and cafés, though standards do vary considerably, partly because of the number of summer day-trippers. While you're here, look out for two local culinary delights, the **Lunenburg sausage**, traditionally served at breakfast, which is made of lean pork and beef, flavoured with coriander and allspice, and the **Solomon Gundy**, marinated herring with sour cream or occasionally mustard.

Easily the best **café** in town is the *Laughing Whale*, at the corner of King and Lincoln, a large, modern place with contemporary paintings on the walls and offering tasty snacks and zippy coffees. For **restaurants**, the prime spot has long been considered the *Old Fish Factory Restaurant* (℡902/634-3333; May–Oct), on the waterfront next to the Fisheries Museum, but although it still serves a splendid range of seafood, it's become a tad canteen-like. Instead, you're much better off heading for the moderately priced *Magnolia's Grill*, just off the waterfront at 128 Montague St (℡902/634-3287; closed Sun). This cosy little place, with its diner-like booths, has a wide and inventive menu, featuring everything from burgers through to lobster, mussels and fish cakes. A second first-rate choice is the *Rum Runner* (℡902/634-9200), opposite the Fisheries Museum: the modern decor is a bit naff, but the food is well prepared and served, fish being its forte; main courses here average $15.

Liverpool and around

Like its British namesake, **LIVERPOOL**, 140km from Halifax along Hwy 103, skirts the mouth of a Mersey River and has a strong seafaring tradition, but there the similarities end. Nova Scotia's Liverpool was founded in 1759 by Cape Cod emigrants, who established a fearsome reputation for privateering during both the American Revolution and the War of 1812, when their most famous ship, the *Liverpool Packet,* claimed no less than a hundred American prizes. These piratical endeavours were cheekily celebrated in a local broadsheet as upholding "the best tradition of the British Navy". Nowadays, Liverpool is a minor fish-processing and paper-making town, a desultory sort of settlement only cheered by the fine old houses grouped around the eastern end of Main Street. One of these, the **Perkins House** (June to mid-Oct Mon–Sat 9.30am–5.30pm, Sun 1–5.30pm), has been restored to its late eighteenth-century condition, when it was the home of Simeon Perkins, who moved here from New England in 1762. A local bigwig, Perkins was a shipowner, a merchant, a colonel in the militia and a justice of the court, but he still had time to keep a detailed diary from 1766 until his death in 1812. The diaries provide an insight into the life and times of colonial Nova Scotia and they show Perkins as a remarkably unflappable man: in 1780 Liverpool was attacked by Americans, who Perkins outwitted and drove off, describing the dangerous emergency as just a "dubious and difficult affair". Copies of the four-volume diary are on display at the house, whilst the adjacent **Queens County Museum** (June to mid-Oct Mon–Sat 9.30am–5.30pm, Sun 1–5.30pm; mid-Oct to May Mon–Sat 9am–5pm; free) sometimes sells excerpts ($2) – and also possesses a diverting collection of early local photographs.

Liverpool has one recommendable **place to stay**, *Lane's Privateer Inn & B&B*, just across the bridge from the centre of town at 27 Bristol Ave (℡902/354-3456 or 1-800/794-3332, ⓦwww.lanesprivateerinn.com; ❹). The inn occupies a spick and span, modern, two-storey, motel-like structure and the B&B is an annex. The inn is also the **place to eat**, either in the restaurant, where well-prepared steak and seafood dishes average $17, or in the adjoining café, which

serves a good line in coffees, teas and gourmet treats, including hand-made
Belgian chocolates.

Kejimkujik National Park
There's no better way to experience the solitude and scenery of the southwest
Nova Scotian hinterland than to head northwest 70km from Liverpool along
Hwy 8 to Maitland Bridge and the entrance to the **Kejimkujik National
Park**. This magnificent tract of rolling wilderness has a rich variety of forest
habitats – both hardwood and softwood – interrupted by rivers and brooks
linking about a dozen lakes. In the spring and autumn the park is alive with
wild flowers, whose brilliant colours provide cover for an abundance of porcupines, white-tailed deer and beavers, as well as three sorts of turtle. There the
Painted and Snapping turtle and, rarest of all, the Blanding's turtle, a green and
yellow amphibian that grows to around 25cm.

Hiking trails crisscross Kejimkujik, but the easiest way to explore the park
and its flat-water rivers and lakes is by **canoe**. These can be rented for $25 a
day – plus deposit – from **Jakes Landing** (☎902/682-5253; reservations
recommended), roughly 10km by road from the entrance to the park. A couple
of clearly defined, day-long **canoe trips** begin here, the delightful paddle
amongst the islets of Kejimkujik Lake and an excursion up the Mersey River
beneath a canopy of red maples. For overnight trips, the park has around fifty
primitive **campsites** dotted along both canoe routes and hiking trails, which
are a better bet than the large year-round campsite (reservations ☎1-800/414-
6765) at **Jeremys Bay**, also 10km by road from the main entrance. A park
entrance fee of $4.50 per adult per day is levied from mid-May to mid-
October. For backcountry camping, you must register at the **information
centre** (late June to Aug daily 8.30am–9pm; Sept to late June Mon-Fri
8.30am–4.30pm; ☎902/682-2772), near the entrance, where you can also pick
up detailed maps and trail advice. The best time to visit is in the early spring
and autumn, when the insects aren't too troublesome: the blackfly peak
between mid-May and late June. The nearest **beds** are at the eight-room
Whitman Inn (☎902/682-2226 or 1-800/830-3855, ⊛www.whitman.ns.ca;
❸), in an attractive, two-storey, white and yellow timber house, set in its own
grounds 2km south of the park entrance on Hwy 8. The nearest town is
Annapolis Royal (see p.404), 50km to the north.

Kejimkujik's "Seaside Adjunct"
Back on Hwy 103, heading southwest from Liverpool, it's about 25km to the
6km-long turning for the **Seaside Adjunct of Kejimkujik National Park**,
a parcel of pristine coastline that provides an ideal half-day's hike. The Adjunct
straddles the tip of a beautiful but inhospitable peninsula where the mixed
forests and squelchy bogs of the interior back onto the tidal flats, lagoons, headlands and beaches of the coast. If you're lucky, you'll catch sight of the rare
piping plover, which nests here between May and early August. From the parking lot, the **Harbour Rocks Trail** follows the route of an old cart track
straight down to the seashore, a fairly straightforward if often wet and squelchy
3km hike. At the coast, this trail meets a longer trail, which weaves its way along
most of the park's coastline, taking in Macleods Cove and Port Joli Head.
Access to the Adjunct is free, but there are no facilities, so be sure to carry in
food and water.

Lockeport
Well off the beaten track, 65km southwest of Liverpool, the sleepy fishing

village of **LOCKEPORT** sits on a tiny island that's reached across a 1.5-kilometre-long causeway, fringed by the white sands of **Crescent Beach**. The beach is never crowded, the sea is deep and clear, and the village features a row of five contrasting houses built by the prosperous Locke family over a forty-year period in the nineteenth century. It's a lovely, relaxing spot, where nothing much seems to happen except for the comings and goings of the odd fishing smack. It also boasts several **B&Bs**, including the *Beach Side B&B*, a comfortable modern place at 196 Locke St (T 902/656-2983; ❷). If it's full, the seasonal tourist office (T 902/656-3123), in the brash building at the end of the causeway, has details of a few other local B&Bs and beachside cottages. Lockeport has a good restaurant too, in *Locke's Island Dining*, 18 North St.

Shelburne and around

SHELBURNE, 70km southwest of Liverpool on Hwy 103, took heart when it was chosen as the backdrop for the 1994 cinematic version of Nathaniel Hawthorne's classic *The Scarlet Letter*, but the film was such a dodo that it did the town no favours at all. Indeed, despite the well-kept shingle and clapboard houses that string down from Water Street, the main drag, to Dock Street and the waterfront, Shelburne manages a vaguely disconsolate air. It does, however, boast the third largest harbour in the world, after Halifax and Sydney – easily big enough, so the plan went, to accommodate the British fleet if Hitler managed to launch a successful invasion of Great Britain. The British would have been welcome: Shelburne has been intensely anglophile ever since thousands of Loyalists fled here in the 1780s – including two hundred free blacks, ancestors of the town's present black community.

Shelburne is home to the **Nova Scotia Museum Complex**, centred on Dock Street, which has three distinct elements. The **Shelburne County Museum** (June to mid-Oct daily 9.30am–5.30pm; mid-Oct to May Tues–Sat 2–5pm; $3) provides a broad overview of the town's history and its maritime heritage; the adjacent **Ross-Thomson House** (June to mid-Oct daily 9.30am–5.30pm; $3) is a Loyalist merchant's store and home, pleasingly restored to its appearance circa 1800; and the nearby **Dory Shop** (June to mid-Sept daily 9.30am–5.30pm; $3) comprises a waterfront boat factory/museum. Rarely more than 5m long and built to ride the heaviest of swells, the flat-bottomed **dory** was an integral part of the fishing fleet during the days of sail. Each schooner carried about six of them; manned by a crew of two, they were launched from the deck when the fishing began, fanning out to maximize the catch. The Dory Shop produces three a year, but only for private use for hand-fishing – the few dories used today in the offshore fishery are steel-hulled. Allow about an hour to visit the three sites, a little more if you throw in the **Muir-Cox Shipbuilding Interpretive Centre** (June to mid-Oct daily 9.30am–5.30pm; $3; joint ticket $8). While you're here, you may as well take a peek at the handful of heavyweight shingle buildings left over from the film set, just off Dock Street.

There's no special reason to stay in Shelburne, but the **tourist office** (summer daily 9am–7pm; T 902/875-4547), at the north end of Dock Street, does operate a free room-reservation service. The most agreeable **hotel** in town is the *Cooper's Inn*, which occupies a lavishly refurbished old shingle house at 36 Dock St (T 902/875-4656 or 1-800/688-2011, ⓦ www3.ns .sympatico.ca/coopers; ❹; April–Oct). Wooded, lakeside **camping** is available 5km west round the bay at the *Islands Provincial Park* (T 902/875-4304; $18; mid-May to Aug). There's inexpensive and unpretentious **food** at *Claudia's*

❸

Diner, 149 Water St; wholesome meals at *Charlotte Lane Café*, down an alley – Charlotte Lane – off Water Street; and first-rate cuisine at the *Cooper's Inn* restaurant – try the steaks.

Barrington

There's not much to delay you on the 100-kilometre journey west from Shelburne to Yarmouth, but you should make a brief stop at minuscule **BARRINGTON**, where the **Old Meeting House** (June–Sept Mon–Sat 9.30am–5.30pm, Sun 1–5.30pm; donation), with its simple wooden pews and severe pulpit, reflects the intellectual rigour of the Nonconformist settlers who migrated here from New England in the mid-eighteenth century. In its simplicity, it's a beautiful building, which is more than can be said for the adjacent **Lighthouse Museum** (same hours; free), where a smattering of light-keepers' memorabilia is housed in a replica of the lighthouse that once stood on remote Seal Island – though this version stands on a hillside apropos of nothing in particular.

Yarmouth and the French Shore

Arriving by ferry from Maine, many American visitors get their first taste of Canada in **YARMOUTH**, and most of them leave immediately. And indeed this is a mundanely modern place, though gallant efforts have been made to freshen up the waterfront and the town's deep, tidal bay provides a modicum of scenic interest. It's also a good place for tourist information with the **Nova Scotia Visitor Centre**, just uphill from the ferry terminal (daily: July & Aug 8am–7pm; May, June, Sept & Oct 9am–5pm; ℡902/742-5033), issuing bucketloads of free leaflets and brochures. There's a comfortable **B&B** right opposite the visitors' centre, the *Murray Manor*, 225 Main St (℡902/742-9625 or 1-877/742-9625, ⊛www.murraymanor.com; ❹). Alternatively, the *Midtown Motel*, 13 Parade St (℡902/742-5333 or 1-877/742-5600; ❼), offers simple but adequate rooms a ten-minute walk north along Main Street from the ferry terminal.

North from Yarmouth, Hwy 101 and the much slower Hwy 1 slip across the flat littoral of the 100-kilometre **French Shore**, whose straggling villages house the largest concentration of Acadians in the province (see p.408 for more on the Acadians). Their gold-starred red, white and blue flags are everywhere, but there's nothing worth stopping for – **METEGHAN**, the main town, is noticeably ugly – until you reach **POINTE DE L'EGLISE** (Church Point). Here, right next to the sea, is the massive church of **St Mary's** (July to mid-Oct daily 9am–5pm; free), whose stolid tower and steeple, finished in 1905, reach a giddy 56m. Unfortunately, the fastidiously clean interior holds some of the worst religious paintings imaginable, nineteenth-century dross with none of the medievalism suggested by the reliquaries beside the altar, amongst which

---

Ferries from Yarmouth to Maine

From Yarmouth, Bay Ferries (℡902/742-6800 or 1-888/249-7245, ⊛www.catferry .com) operates high-speed, car-carrying **catamarans** to Bar Harbor, Maine (mid-May to mid-Oct 1–2 daily; 3hr; passengers $60–70, vehicles $110–125). In addition, Scotia Prince (℡1-866/229-2597, ⊛www.scotiaprince.com) runs **car ferries** to Portland, Maine (May to mid-Oct 1 daily; 11hr; passengers $70–90, cars $90–110, cabins $25–140; up to forty percent discounts for returns and on some midweek sailings).

are wooden shards purportedly from the Holy Cross. Some 10km further north is the church of **St Bernard** (June–Sept daily 9.30am–5pm; free), a cumbersome granite pile that took 32 years to complete (1910–42) – and is, if nothing else, certainly a tribute to the profound Catholicism of the local Acadians.

Digby and Digby Neck

It's around 30km from St Bernard to the fishing port of **DIGBY**, whose workaday centre spreads over a hilly headland that pokes out into the Annapolis Basin. The latter is connected to the Bay of Fundy by a narrow channel known as the Digby Gut, thereby subjecting Digby **harbour** to the swirling effects of the Fundy tides – and it's the pocket-sized harbour, with its rickety wooden piers, which is the most appealing part of town. Otherwise, Digby is notable for two things: its **smoked herrings** or "Digby chicks" – chewy, dark and salty delicacies on sale beside the north end of the harbour at the Royal Fundy Seafood Market; and its delicious, world-beating **scallops**, which you can sample at the popular *Fundy Restaurant*, 34 Water St (☎902/245-7500), the pick of several restaurants lining the harbourfront's Water Street and its continuation, Montague Row.

Acadian Lines **buses** to Digby stop at the Irving fuel station, 77 Montague Row. From here, it's a couple of minutes walk north along the waterfront to the **tourist office** (☎902/245-5714), which operates a room-reservation service and gives information on Digby Neck whale-watching trips. Digby has several pleasant **places to stay**, beginning with the agreeable *Thistle Down Inn*, an old two-storey house with a motel-style annexe at 98 Montague Row (☎902/245-4490 or 1-800/565-8081, ⓦwww.thistledown.ns.ca/theinn; ❸; May–Oct). There's also the *Bayside Inn*, 115 Montague Row (☎902/245-2247 or 1-888/754-0555, ⓦwww3.ns.sympatico.ca/bayside; ❸), which occupies an old timber house, has eleven rooms – seven en suite – and is equipped with an airy patio.

Digby's **ferry port** is located 5km north of town; from here Bay Ferries (☎1-888/249-7245, ⓦwww.nfl-bay.com) runs regular **car ferries** (1–3 daily; 3hr; passengers $20–35 one-way, cars $70–75, bicycles $10) across the Bay of Fundy to Saint John in New Brunswick (see p.433), thereby saving a long drive.

Digby Neck

Heading west from Digby, the 70km-long **Digby Neck** comprises a narrow finger of land that gingerly nudges out into the Bay of Fundy, sheltering the French Shore from the full effects of the ocean. The Neck's far reaches are broken into two little islands – **Long Island** and, at the tip, **Brier Island** – and a pair of **car ferries** shuttle across the narrow channels between them, running every hour, 24 hours a day and charging $3 each for the return trip. Ferry times are coordinated, so it takes about two hours to reach Brier Island from Digby (ferry timetables are available at Digby tourist office). For the most part, the road along the Neck travels inland and is fairly monotonous, but then most people only venture down here to join a **whale-watching trip** (see box opposite).

From either Digby or (even better) Annapolis Royal (see p.404), it's easy enough to complete both the drive along the Neck and the whale-watching cruise in a day, but if you do decide to stay the night, there are two good options. The first is in **TIVERTON**, a quiet sprawl of wooden houses dotted

Digby Neck whale-watching

The nutrient-rich waters of the **Bay of Fundy** attract dozens of whales and several local companies organize daily **whale-watching excursions** from June to early October. They are heavily subscribed, so advance reservations are highly recommended; if the weather is poor, check to see if a sailing has been cancelled before you set out. Trips usually last about three hours and cost in the region of $40. To state the obvious, no one can guarantee you'll spy a whale, but there's every chance, beginning with finback and minkes in late spring, and humpbacks from mid-to late June. By the middle of July all three species are sighted and usually hang around the Bay of Fundy till late summer and autumn, which is when the rare North Atlantic right whale is seen too – see p.1080 for more.

Amongst several Digby Neck whale-watching companies, one of the more proficient is **Ocean Explorations Whale Cruises** (☎902/839-2417, ⓦwww .oceanexplorations.ca), which uses zodiac boats and is based in tiny Tiverton on Long Island. In addition, there are several whale-watching companies in the forlorn little fishing village of Westport, on Brier Island. These include **Brier Island Whale & Seabird Cruises** (☎902/839-2995 or 1-800/656-3660, ⓦwww .brierislandwhalewatch.com) and **Mariner Cruises** (☎902/839-2346 or 1-800/239-2189, ⓦwww.marinercruises.ns.ca).

round a forested bay on the first of the Neck's two islands, Long Island. Here you'll find the appealing *Seacliff B&B* (☎902/839-2241; ❸; mid-June to late Sept), in a pretty Victorian house overlooking the harbour and with two guestrooms – and shared bath. The second is the *Olde Village Inn* (☎902/834-2202 or 1-800/834-2206, ⓦwww.oldevillageinn.com; ❹; June to mid-Oct), a cosy nineteenth-century inn set among the densely wooded coastal hills of **SANDY COVE**, a picturesque little place of old white-painted houses about 30km along the Neck from Digby. The inn has six rooms in the old building and seven more in the annexe.

The Annapolis Valley

The **Annapolis Valley**, stretching 110km northeast from Annapolis Royal to Wolfville, is sheltered from the winds and fog that afflict much of the central part of the province by a narrow band of coastal hills. This factor, combined with the fertility of the soil, makes the valley and the coast as far as Windsor – another 25km to the east – ideal for fruit growing. As a consequence, the brief weeks of apple-blossom time, from late May to early June, are the subject of much sentimental and commercial exploitation – as well as the communal knees-up of the **Apple-Blossom Festival**. The string of little towns that dot the valley were settled by Loyalists from New England after the expulsion of the Acadians, but although several of them are pretty places where old wooden houses are sheltered by mature trees only two stand out. These are delightful **Annapolis Royal**, with its handsome Victorian mansions and proximity to the historic site of **Port Royal**, and **Wolfville**, an amiable university town of some charm. Wolfville is also within easy striking distance of **Grand Pré National Historic Site** and the harsh scenery of **capes Blomidon** and **Split**. Further east, **Windsor** is no great shakes, but it is the site of the Haliburton House Museum, the former home of the nineteenth-century humorist Thomas Haliburton.

Annapolis Royal and Wolfville – but not Windsor – are both reachable on the daily Acadian Lines **bus** service between Halifax and Digby.

Annapolis Royal

With a population of just seven hundred the township of **ANNAPOLIS ROYAL**, 40km northeast of Digby and 120km northwest of Liverpool, spreads across a podgy promontory that lies tucked in between the Annapolis River and its tributary, the Allain River. The long main drag, **St George Street**, part of Hwy 8, sweeps through the leafy southern outskirts to reach the end of the promontory, where it turns right to run parallel to the waterfront through the commercial heart of town. Here, restaurants and shops have replaced the merchants and shipwrights of yesteryear and there's a tourist-oriented boardwalk near the jetty, but it's all very low-key and the town maintains a relaxed and retiring air that's hard to resist.

Edging St George Street just before it swings right are the substantial remains of **Fort Anne** (open access), whose grass-covered ramparts surround the old parade ground. A few military remains are encased within the ramparts – namely a couple of powder magazines and a sally port – but the most significant survivor is the old **officers' quarters** right in the middle of the compound. The British built these quarters during the Napoleonic Wars and, surmounted by three outsize chimney stacks, they now house a small **museum** (mid-May to mid-Oct daily 9am–6pm; $3.50) comprising a ragbag of military memorabilia, a reconstruction of an Acadian domestic interior and an outline of the fort's development. There's also a contemporaneous copy of the original charter by which James I incorporated "Nova Scotia" in 1621, and a cheerful community tapestry tracing the town's history. The view downriver from Fort Anne is simply delightful and it's a lovely peaceful spot, but it wasn't always so. Both colonial powers, France and England, neglected the fort and its garrison, and when a new military governor arrived at the fort in 1708 he told his superiors in Paris that the officers stationed here were "more in need of a madhouse than a barracks". If you want more of the flavour of early Annapolis Royal, ask at the museum (or your B&B) for details of the candlelight tours of the **old graveyard** (June to mid-Oct 3 weekly) next to the fort – good fun, and a snip at $5.

Five-minutes' walk from the fort – back along St George Street – lie the ten-acre **Annapolis Royal Historic Gardens** (mid-May to mid-Oct daily 8am–dusk; $6). These feature a string of enjoyable "theme gardens", from the formality of a Victorian garden to an extensive rose collection in which the different varieties are arranged broadly in chronological order. The whole site slopes gently down towards the Allain River, with a dykewalk offering views of mud flats and salt marshes and also twisting through elephant grass, a reed imported by the Acadians to thatch their cottages.

Practicalities

In each direction, one **bus** a day on the Acadian Lines route between Halifax and Digby stops at the Annapolis Royal Inn on Hwy 1, an inconvenient 1.3km west of St George Street and the town centre. The **tourist office** is on the other side of town, inside the generating station on the Hwy 1 bridge about 1.4km north of the centre (daily: July & Aug 8am–8pm; late May to June & Sept to mid-Oct 10am–5pm; ☎902/532-5454). They can arrange accommodation. Best are the **B&Bs**, several of which are in immaculately maintained heritage properties. The *Hillsdale House Inn*, 519 St George St (☎902/532-

2345 or 1-877/839-2821, Ⓦwww.hillsdalehouse.ns.ca; ❸), and the *Queen Anne Inn*, opposite at no. 494 (☎902/532-7850 or 1-877/536-0403, Ⓦwww.queenanneinn.ns.ca; ❹; mid-April to Oct), are the finest choices: the former occupies an elegant villa of 1849, the latter a grand turreted and towered extravagance of the 1860s. Alternatively, try *At the Turret*, 372 St George St (☎902/532-5770, Ⓦwww.attheturret.20m.com; ❹), in another old but rather more modest house, or the well-tended *Bread and Roses Inn*, a spiky late Victorian mansion at 82 Victoria St (☎902/532-5727 or 1-888/899-0551, Ⓦwww.breadandroses.ns.ca; ❹). The well-equipped *Dunromin* **campsite** (☎902/532-2808; May to mid-Oct), 1km beyond the tourist office on the far side of the Annapolis River, occupies a wooded position by the riverside.

Eating well and in style is easy here, and prices are reasonable. Right in the centre, *Newman's*, 218 St George St (☎902/532-5502), has a brisk and pleasant atmosphere and offers delicious meals featuring local ingredients – beef stew, scallops and the like – with main courses averaging $15. Next door, *Leo's Café* (closes 5.30pm) serves first-rate snacks and lighter meals, while the inexpensive *Fort Anne Café*, opposite the entrance to the fort, sells tasty and substantial meals from a traditional Canadian menu – don't be put off by the downbeat decor. *Ye Olde Towne Pub* at 9 Church St – just down the street from Newman's and across from the boatyard – serves good draught **beer**. The King's Theatre, 209 St George St (☎902/532-5466 or 1-800/818-8587), showcases everything from films and drama through to folk music, storytellers, comedians and mime artists.

Port Royal

Port Royal National Historic Site (mid-May to mid-Oct daily 9am–6pm; $3.50), 12km west of Annapolis Royal on the opposite side of the Annapolis River, was where Samuel de Champlain and Pierre Sieur de Monts first set up camp in 1605 after their dreadful winter on the Île Saint-Croix. Scared of English attack, the scurvy-ridden party hastily constructed an *habitation* similar in design to the fortified farms of France, where a square of rough-hewn, black-painted timber buildings presented a stern, partly stockaded face to any enemy. The stronghold dominated the estuary from a low bluff, as does today's **replica**, a painstaking reconstruction relying solely on the building techniques of the early seventeenth century. The *habitation* was captured by roving Virginians in 1613 and passed over to the British, who, led by Sir William Alexander, settled the district in 1629. This venture was enthusiastically supported by King James I, who wished to found a New Scotland – "Nova Scotia" in the Latin of the deeds – near Port Royal, but after three years of hardship and starvation, the Scots settlers were forced to withdraw, like their French predecessors.

For both French and Scot settlers alike, the problem of survival was compounded by acute boredom during the months of winter isolation. To pass the time Champlain constituted the **Order of Good Cheer**, whose "entertainment's programme" starred the poet Marc Lescarbot – though the role hardly filled him with colonial zeal, to judge from a poem he wrote for a gang of departing buddies:

> *We among the savages are lost*
> *And dwell bewildered on this clammy coast*
> *Deprived of due content and pleasures bright*
> *Which you at once enjoy when France you sight.*

There are **no buses** from Annapolis Royal to the *habitation*.

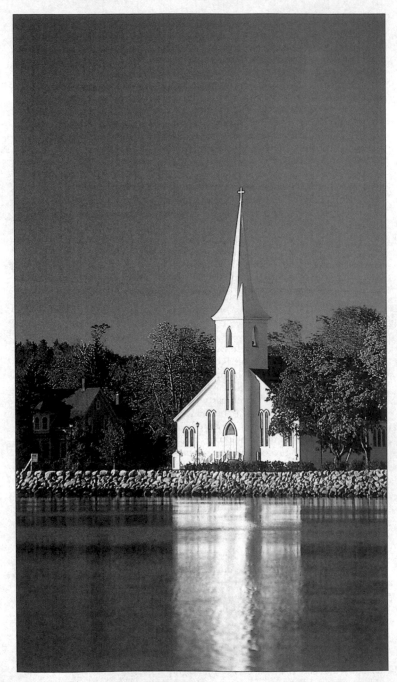

△ Church at Mahone Bay, NS

Wolfville and around

The orderly, well-heeled university town of **WOLFVILLE**, 110km northeast from Annapolis Royal, was originally called Mud Creek until the daughter of a local dignitary, Justice DeWolf, expressed her embarrassment at the hick-sounding name. He modestly had the place renamed after himself, but the mud flats around the little **harbour** – now a park located just off Main Street along Harbourside Drive – remain the town's most distinctive feature. They are the creation of the **Fundy tides**, which rush up the Cornwallis River from the Minas Basin to dump the expanse of silt that's become home to hundreds of herons and waders, with thousands of sandpipers arriving in early August on their annual migration from Arctic breeding grounds. From Wolfville harbour, two short and easy loop **walking trails** lead out along the causeway that encircles a portion of the wetland and its enclosing dykes. The more westerly route, the Wolfville Dyke Trail – running from the harbour to Cherry Lane – is the one to take as it also provides pleasing views of Wolfville, its skyline punctured by the sedate lines of **Acadia University**, whose three thousand students double the resident population. Wolfville's other curiosity is the **Robie Tufts Nature Centre**, down Elm Avenue from Main Street, which is best visited an hour before sunset on a summer's evening – usually from the second or third week in May till late August – to see the **chimney swifts**. These brown-grey birds give an amazing performance. After a long day hunting for insects, an enormous flock of them fly in ever-decreasing circles above the centre, which is no more than a wooden shelter built around an old chimney, before suddenly swooping en masse into the chimney to roost for the night.

Wolfville is on the Acadian Lines **bus** route connecting Halifax and Digby. Buses stop – inconveniently – on the Acadia University campus, a good ten-minute walk west of the tiny town centre, which consists of a few blocks of Main Street and several subsidiary side streets. The **tourist office** is located on the east side of the town centre, just off Main Street in Willow Park on Willow Avenue (daily: July & Aug 9am–7pm; May, June & Sept to mid-Oct 9am–5pm; ☏902/542-7000). They have information on the whole of the Annapolis Valley as well as local accommodation lists and – a necessary preparation – details of the hike along Cape Split (see p.409). The town has several splendid **inns and B&Bs**, the pick of the bunch in attractively renovated old mansions. Tempting choices lead off with *Victoria's Historic Inn & Carriage House*, an immaculately maintained grand mansion with fancy gingerbread scrollwork just 800m or so west of the centre at 600 Main St (☏902/542-5744 or 1-800/556-5744, ⓦ www.victoriahistoricinn.com; ❺). There are sixteen guest rooms here, both in the inn and the adjacent carriage house, and each is decorated in a plush version of period style. A second choice is the *Blomidon Inn*, a five-minute walk east of downtown at 195 Main St (☏902/542-2291 or 1-800/565-2291, ⓦ www.blomidoninn.com; ❹). This inn occupies an ornate sea captain's mansion of 1882, but although the house is splendidly Victorian with public rooms to match, not all the 21 guest rooms live up to their setting, especially those in the modern annexe at the back. A less expensive option is the three-roomed *Garden House B&B*, 220 Main St (☏902/542-1703, ⓦ www.gardenhouse.ca; ❸), in a humbler, plainer old property also just east of downtown.

For **food**, there are good snacks and great coffee at *Just Us! Café*, in the front of the old Art Deco Acadia Cinema at 448 Main St; everything from pizzas through to burgers at inexpensive *Jo's Food Emporium* just along the street; and delicious salads, meats and seafood at the smart *Acton's Grill & Café*, 406 Main St (☏902/542-7525); main courses here hover around $18.

Acadia – *Acadie* in French – has at different times included all or part of Maine, New Brunswick and Nova Scotia. The etymology of the name is as vague as the geographical definition, derived from either the local Micmac word *akade*, meaning "abundance", or a corruption of *Arcadia*, an area of Greece that was a byword for rural simplicity when transient French fishermen first arrived here in the early 1500s. Whatever the truth, the origins of Acadian settlement date to 1604, when a French expedition led by Pierre Sieur de Monts and Samuel de Champlain built a stockade on the islet of **Saint-Croix**, on the west side of the Bay of Fundy. It was a disaster: with the onset of winter, the churning ice floes separated the colonists from the fresh food and water of the mainland, and many died of malnutrition. The following spring the survivors straggled over to the sheltered southern shore of the bay, where they founded **Port Royal**, considered Canada's first successful European settlement.

However, Champlain and Sieur de Monts soon despaired of Port Royal's fur-trading potential and transferred to the banks of the St Lawrence, which soon became the main conduit of French colonization, leaving Acadia a remote and neglected backwater. Port Royal was **abandoned** in 1614 and, although it was refounded on the site of present-day Annapolis Royal in 1635, there were few immigrants. Indeed, the bulk of today's Acadians are the descendants of just forty French peasant families who arrived in the 1630s. Slowly spreading along the **Annapolis Valley**, the Acadians lived a semi-autonomous existence in which trading with their English-speaking neighbours was more important than grand notions of loyalty to the French Empire. Consequently, when the British secured control of Port Royal under the Treaty of Utrecht in 1713, the Acadians made no protest.

But then, in the 1750s, the tense stand-off between the colonial powers highlighted the issue of Acadian loyalty. In **1755**, at the start of the Seven Years War, British government officials attempted to make the Acadians swear **an oath of allegiance** to the Crown. They refused, so Governor Lawrence decided – without consultation with London – to **deport** them en masse to other colonies. The process of uprooting and removing a community of around 13,000 was achieved with remarkable ruthlessness. As Lawrence wrote to a subordinate, "You must proceed with the most vigorous measures possible not only in compelling them to embark, but in depriving those who should escape of all means of shelter or support, by burning their houses and destroying everything that may afford them the means of subsistence in the country."

By the end of the year over half the Acadians had arrived on the American east coast, where they faced a cold reception – the Virginians even rerouted their allocation to England. Most of the rest spread out along the North Atlantic seaboard, establishing communities along New Brunswick's Miramichi Valley, on Prince Edward Island and in St-Pierre et Miquelon. Many subsequently returned to the Bay of Fundy in the 1770s and 1780s, but their farms had been given to British and New England colonists and they were forced to settle the less hospitable lands of the **French Shore**, further west. For other deportees, the expulsion was the start of wider wanderings. Some went to Louisiana, where they were joined in 1785 by over 1500 former Acadian refugees who had ended up in France – these were the ancestors of the **Cajuns**, whose name is a corruption of "Acadian".

The Acadian communities of the Maritime Provinces continued to face discrimination from the English-speaking majority and today they remain firmly planted at the bottom of the economic pile. Nevertheless, the Acadians have resisted the pressures of assimilation and have recently begun to assert their cultural independence, most notably in New Brunswick, where Moncton University has become their academic and cultural centre.

Grand Pré

In 1847, Henry Wadsworth Longfellow chose **GRAND PRÉ**, 5km east of Wolfville along Hwy 1, as the setting for his epic poem *Evangeline – A Tale of Acadie*, which dramatized the Acadian deportations through the star-crossed love of Evangeline for her Gabriel. Horribly sentimental and extremely popular, the poem turned the destruction of this particular community into a symbol of Acadian suffering and British callousness. However, the **Grand Pré National Historic Site** (May–Oct daily 9am–6pm; $5.75), located amidst the dykelands of the Minas Basin, is a strangely antiseptic tribute. The visitor centre explains the history and describes Acadian culture very competently, but the rest of the site, with its trim lawns, planted trees and statues of Longfellow and Evangeline, only plods along and the main building, the chapel, which stands on the site of the original church, is uninspiring.

Cape Blomidon and Cape Split

The rugged, hook-shaped peninsula north of Wolfville encompasses the dramatic scenery of **Cape Blomidon**, which, local legend has it, takes its name from the sailors' phrase "Blow me down", and of wilder and bleaker **Cape Split**. To reach the peninsula from Wolfville, begin by taking Hwy 1 west for a couple of kilometres and then turn north along Hwy 358 for the 10km drive to the township of **CANNING**. Just after Canning, there's a choice of routes. Stay on Hwy 358 for Cape Split (see below) or take the signed 13km-long turning leading down to **Blomidon Provincial Park**, a narrow slice of seashore where steep sea cliffs back onto a lush, coastal forest of maple, birch, fir and beech. It's a lovely spot with around 14km of footpath and the park has a popular, shaded **campsite** (℡902/582-7319; mid-Mid to Aug).

Beyond the Blomidon turning, Hwy 358 clambers the 3km up to the peninsula's highest point, the **Look-off**, from where the views over the Annapolis Valley and the Minas Basin are truly spectacular. There's a café here as well as the *Look-off Camping Park* (℡902/582-3022; mid-May to mid-Oct), one of the best-sited in the province. From the Look-off, it's a further 17km to **Scots Bay**, a scattered farming village that straggles along the edge of a wide and muddy bay. The road ends abruptly just beyond the village at the start of one of the region's most popular and not-too-difficult hiking trails that leads the 7km to the tip of **Cape Split**. Reckon on two hours each way and be sure to pick up trail information and maps at Wolfville tourist office before you set out. The trail begins by threading up through thick forest beneath towering cliffs and passes heavily eroded rock formations before emerging onto a small open area, from where there are wondrous views across the Bay of Fundy.

Windsor

Pint-sized **WINDSOR**, sloping along the shore of an inlet of the Minas Basin 25km from Wolfville, was originally settled by Acadians and it was here in 1750 that the British built a fort to overawe them. The stockade was subsequently used to hold Acadians during the deportations, but all that remains today is a sorry-looking timber blockhouse conserved as the **Fort Edward National Historic Site** (mid-June to Aug Tues–Sat 10am–6pm, Sun & Mon noon–6pm; free). The blockhouse, complete with musket loopholes and cannon portholes, perches on a grassy, treeless hill at the east end of town, overlooking Hwy 101 and the tidal mud flats that stretch out towards the basin. On the other side of town, set in its own leafy grounds on a hillside 1km west of the centre, is the **Haliburton House Museum** (June to mid-Oct Mon–Sat 9.30am–5.30pm, Sun 1–5.30pm; $3), one-time home of

Thomas Chandler Haliburton, a mid-nineteenth-century judge and humorist. The house has been returned to something akin to its appearance when Haliburton lived here, writing the short stories that made him famous – cuttingly sarcastic tales whose protagonist, the itinerant Yankee clock pedlar Sam Slick of Slickville, travels Nova Scotia meanly defrauding its gullible, unenterprising inhabitants. Immensely popular at the time, the stories are interesting as literary history, but leave a nasty High-Tory taste, although it was through Slick that Haliburton coined a bucketload of epigrams that remain in use: "six of one and half a dozen of the other"; "facts are stranger than fiction"; "raining cats and dogs"; "the early bird gets the worm"; and "as quick as a wink" – and many more – all came from his pen. Most of Haliburton's work is out of print, but the museum has a small supply and, if you're keen to sample his stories, begin with *The Clockmaker*.

Central Nova Scotia

Most visitors hurry through **central Nova Scotia**, the chunk of forested land north and east of Halifax, on their way to Cape Breton Island, PEI or New Brunswick. By and large they're right to do so, but there is the odd pleasant diversion en route, and a couple of places make for a convenient overnight stay. One place it's difficult to avoid is humdrum **Truro**, the region's largest town and major crossroads, situated at the east end of the Minas Basin and so subject to the Bay of Fundy tides. The most appealing parts of the bay are well to the west in New Brunswick (see p.440), but if time is tight view the **tidal bore** here at Truro – the downtown tourist office, right in the centre beside Prince St (☎902/893-2922), has tide tables and will provide directions.

Heading northwest from Truro, the Trans-Canada Highway heads off to New Brunswick's Fort Beauséjour (see p.445), scooting past the old coal-mining centre of **Springhill**, home to the Anne Murray Centre detailing the life and times of the town's most famous daughter. Beyond Springhill on the north Fundy Coast – though there's absolutely no need to actually go there – is **Spencer's Island**, not an island at all, but a former shipbuilding centre and home port of the *Mary Celeste*. This vessel posed one of the most celebrated mysteries of Victorian times when she was discovered in mid-Atlantic without a crew – and with the table set for dinner – and although all sorts of theories have been promulgated, no one has ever really worked out what happened. In the opposite direction from Truro, the Trans-Canada travels just inland from the northeast shore, whose gently rolling countryside was a centre of Scottish settlement from the end of the eighteenth century. The Scots first landed in **Pictou**, and this is the pick of the fishing, lumber and agricultural communities hereabouts – especially as it's both conveniently close to the PEI ferry terminal and midway between Halifax and Cape Breton.

An alternative route between Halifax and Cape Breton is along the **southeast shore**, an isolated region of skinny bays and the tiniest of fishing villages connected by a tortuous 320-kilometre road. The coastal scenery is often quite delightful, but the villages don't deserve their redolent names – Spanish Ship Bay, Ecum Secum, Mushaboom – and the only place worthy of attention is **Sherbrooke**, where around thirty old buildings have been preserved to create an enjoyable village museum. Sherbrooke lies some 200km east of the capital on the coastal road, but is more rapidly reached from the Trans-Canada Highway from outside either New Glasgow or Antigonish.

Acadian Lines **buses** run four times daily from Halifax to Truro, with three buses daily continuing either northeast to New Glasgow and Cape Breton Island, or northwest to New Brunswick's Moncton. VIA Rail's Halifax–Montréal **trains** pass through Truro en route to Moncton. There's no public transport to either Pictou or Sherbrooke.

Springhill

Just off the Trans-Canada, 200km from Halifax and 30km from the New Brunswick border, **SPRINGHILL** is an Appalachian lookalike, its tangle of modern buildings set amidst a vast forest that rolls over the surrounding hills. A coal mine was first sunk here in 1872 and it was coal that dominated the local economy until the last mine closed in the 1970s, leaving the town's population – which now numbers about 4000 – pretty much high and dry. Of all the coalfields in Canada, Springhill's was the most disaster-prone, with three major tragedies grabbing national headlines: 125 miners perished in an underground explosion in 1891, 39 died in a gas explosion in 1956 and in 1958 a tunnel collapse – or "bump" as it is known locally – accounted for 75 more. As if this wasn't enough, in 1957 and 1975 fires wiped out the town's commercial district. A **memorial** in the centre of town – beside the junction of highways 142 and 2 – remembers the dead miners and there are contemporary photographs of the sites of the two later disasters at the **Tour a Mine, Springhill Miners' Museum**, on Black River Road, 2.5km south of town just off Hwy 2 (mid-May to mid-Oct daily 9am–5pm; $4.50). The museum's outdoors section contains several wooden shacks looking exactly as they did when the pit closed in the 1970s. One is the lamp room and another the wash house, outside of which is what the miners themselves called the Liars' Bench – after, no doubt, a certain tendency to exaggerate coal-cutting feats. What you won't see is winding gear: Springhill's coal seams were fairly near the surface and the miners walked down to the coalface – as visitors can do today in the company of a guide. Coalface or not, it's the **Anne Murray Centre**, 36 Main St (mid-May to mid-Oct daily 9am–5pm; $5.50), which pulls the crowds to Springhill – an exercise in organized sycophancy that tracks through the extraordinarily successful career of the Springhill-born balladeer. Murray shot to fame with her sugary song *Snowbird* in 1970 and her latest releases keep up the easy listening. Naturally enough, if you're a fan you'll love it – and you can feel good that all the centre's proceeds go to the local community.

Pictou

Signs proclaim **PICTOU**, 170km from Halifax, as the "Birthplace of New Scotland" on the basis of the arrival in 1773 of the ship *Hector*, loaded with settlers from Ross-shire, the advance guard of the subsequent Scots migrations. To maintain the connection, the town has its own middle-of-August **Hector Festival**, a five-day affair featuring Scottish traditional dancing and the playing of the bagpipes – and very good it is too. Pictou has also spent years building itself a replica of the *Hector*, an expensive and time-consuming project because

Ferries from Caribou to PEI

Some 8km north of Pictou is **Caribou**, from where there are frequent **car ferries** over to Wood Islands on Prince Edward Island (May to late Dec 4–9 daily; 1hr 15min; $12 return, $50 for car and passengers; ☏1-888/249-7245, ⓦwww.nfl-bay.com).

they stuck to the original shipbuilding techniques. The boat was finally launched in 2000 and now either bobs around the harbour or sallies forth along the Nova Scotian coast. The dock where the boat was built forms part of the **Hector Heritage Quay Interpretative Centre** (mid-May to mid-Oct Mon–Sat 9am–5pm, Sun noon–5pm, except June–Aug Sun 10am–5pm; $5), which gives the historical lowdown on the original voyage, complete with nautical sound effects. It's all excellently done and spruces up Pictou's unassuming centre, where the narrow streets slope up from the harbour dotted with stone buildings of Scottish demeanour. A second sight is the **Northumberland Fisheries Museum** (mid-May to mid-Oct Mon–Sat 10am–6pm, Sun noon–5pm; $4), currently in the old train station at 71 Front St, but scheduled to be moved to new and larger premises shortly.

Pictou is a convenient place to spend the night and there are several quality **inns and hotels** to choose from. One of the best is the *Consulate Inn*, 157 Water St (☎902/485-4554 or 1-800/424-8283, ⓦwww.consulateinn.com; ❸), housed in an elegant early nineteenth-century mansion that once served as a US consulate and with ten comfortable suites and guest rooms. There's also the *Customs House Inn*, 38 Depot St (☎902/485-4546, ⓦwww.customshouseinn .ca; ❺), which has eight spacious rooms with exposed brick walls and hardwood floors, all in a stately redbrick down on the waterfront. A third recommendable option is the *Auberge Walker Inn*, 34 Coleraine St (☎902/485-1433 or 1-800/370-5553, ⓦwww.townofpictou.com/walkerinn; ❸), a pleasantly renovated Victorian house with neat and trim guest rooms metres from the Hector Quay.

The best of Pictou's **restaurants** is *Fougere's*, 91 Water St (☎902/485-1575), where both the seafood and the steaks are delicious. Alternatively, and amongst several rather average town-centre **cafés**, try the filling snacks of the *Stone House Café*, just up from the Hector Quay at 11 Water St. The town also possesses a **performing arts** centre, the deCoste Entertainment Centre on Water St (☎902/485-8848 or 1-800/353-5338, ⓦwww.decostecentre.ca), where much of the summer season is taken up by ceilidhs, pipe bands and Highland dancing.

Sherbrooke

Developed as a timber town in the early nineteenth century, **SHERBROOKE** boomed when gold was found near here in 1861, the start of a short-lived gold rush that fizzled out within the space of twenty years, though a handful of mines struggled on until the 1940s. Most of the population checked out after the gold rush, and Sherbrooke returned to the lumber trade but without much success: the decline of the industry gradually whittled the population down to the 400 of today. One result has been the creation of the open-air museum of **Sherbrooke Village** (June to mid-Oct daily 9.30am–5.30pm; $9), which encompasses those late nineteenth- and early twentieth-century buildings that are, for the most part, now surplus to requirements. It's a large site, several streets situated beside St Mary's River just beyond the modern part of the village, and costumed "interpreters" preside. Amongst the thirty-odd buildings highlights include the Neoclassical lines of the surprisingly grand 1850s Court House and the Victorian luxury of the high-gabled Greenwood Cottage nearby. Also of special note are the assorted baubles and throne-like chairs of the Masonic Lodge, which still meets on the second floor of the Masonic Hall, the Temperance Hall of 1892, and the good-looking Cummings Bros General Store. Take a peek too at the jail, where jailer and prisoner lived cheek by jowl right up until the 1960s, and the replica nineteenth-century water-powered sawmill, built about 600m outside the village. Allow two to three hours to do the place justice.

There are three main ways to reach Sherbrooke: from the west along Nova Scotia's southeast shore and from the north by turning off Hwy 104 (the Trans-Canada) either along Hwy 347 just east of New Glasgow or down Hwy 7 about 50km further east near Antigonish. The most agreeable of the three **places to stay** in Sherbrooke is *Daysago B&B*, 15 Cameron Rd (☎902/522-2811 or 1-866/522-2811, ⓦ www.bbcanada.com/daysago; ❷; May–Oct), in a 1920s house with lovely river views and four homely rooms. The tiny *St Mary's Riverside Campground* (☎902/522-2913; mid-May to Oct) is near the sawmill. There's not much choice about where to eat, but fortunately the central *Bright House* is an excellent **restaurant** – be sure to try the seafood casserole. The *Main Street Café* sells competent snacks and pizzas.

Cape Breton Island

"I have travelled the globe. I have seen the Canadian and American Rockies, the Andes and the Alps and the Highlands of Scotland, but for simple beauty Cape Breton outrivals them all." With these words Alexander Graham Bell summed up a part of Nova Scotia whose scenery continues to attract its share of hyperbole. From the lakes, hills and valleys of the southwest to the ripe, forested mountains of the north, **CAPE BRETON ISLAND** – or at least its more westerly half – offers the most exquisite of landscapes, reaching its melodramatic conclusion along the fretted, rocky coast of the **Cape Breton Highlands National Park**. Encircling the park and some of the adjacent shore is the **Cabot Trail**, a 300-kilometre loop that is reckoned to be one of the most beguiling drives on the continent – best approached in a clockwise direction.

By contrast, the more easterly half of Cape Breton – east, that is, of **Bras d'Or Lake** and its subsidiary channels – was once a busy coal-mining and steel-milling region, centred on the town of **Sydney**. It was here in the early 1920s that the struggles of the miners against the pit companies grabbed national headlines. The worst of several disputes began when the owners, the British Empire Steel Corporation (BESCO), decided to cut the men's wages by a third. The miners went on strike and the dispute escalated until BESCO persuaded prime minister King to send in the militia – and the colliers were driven back to work. Today the area's industries have largely collapsed and a deindustrialized sprawl blotches the landscape, only relieved by the splendid reconstruction of the French fortress town of **Louisbourg**, stranded out on the east coast.

The scenic delights of Cape Breton attract thousands of summer tourists and, consequently, although there's a liberal sprinkling of **accommodation** across the island – especially in the west – it's still a good idea to make a reservation a day or two beforehand. Failing that, all the island's tourist offices offer a free room-reservation service. Most visitors stay in the tiny ribbon villages that dot the island, but two of the more enjoyable spots are undoubtedly the busy resort of **Baddeck** and the quieter coastal community of **Chéticamp**.

Without your own transport, getting around much of Cape Breton is a struggle, but Acadian Lines **buses** (3 daily; ☎1-800/567-5151, ⓦ www.acadianbus .com) from Halifax and Truro (for Fredericton and Moncton) bomb along

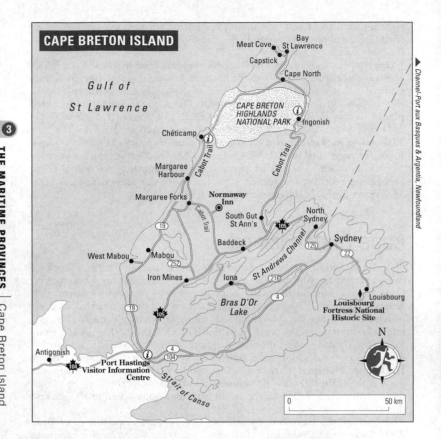

Hwy 105 en route to Sydney. On the way, they shoot through Baddeck and **North Sydney**, the departure port for ferries to Newfoundland. To get onto Cape Breton, all traffic has to cross the **Strait of Canso causeway**. There are no buses to either Louisbourg or the Cape Breton Highlands National Park, though a local company does run minibus excursions to the park from Baddeck, starting from around \$35.

Finally, note that Cape Breton's **weather** is notoriously unpredictable, even in summer. The Cabot Trail is pretty miserable in mist and rain, so if possible you should build a bit of flexibility into your itinerary.

The Cabot Trail

Just up the hill from the Canso causeway is the **Port Hastings Visitor Information Centre** (daily: July & Aug 8.30am–8.30pm; late March to June & Sept to early Dec 9am–5pm; ☎902/625-4201), where you can get your bearings and make advance room reservations on all of Cape Breton Island. From here it's about 45km on Hwy 105 (the Trans-Canada) through low, forested hills to the hamlet of **IRON MINES**, overlooking a small inlet at the western limit of Bras d'Or Lake – a pleasant foretaste of the splendours beyond. From Iron Mines, it's a further 30km to the **Cabot Trail**, which begins at Hwy

Music on Cape Breton Island

Cape Breton is not just about scenery and sights: the Scottish Highlanders who settled much of the island in the late eighteenth and early nineteenth centuries brought with them strong cultural traditions and today these are best recalled by the island's **musicians**, especially the fiddle players. Names to watch out for include Buddy MacMaster, Ashley MacIsaac, Natalie MacMaster and the Rankin family, not to mention Glenn Graham, Rodney MacDonald and Jackie Dunn – though it's impossible to pick out the "best" as each fiddler has their own particular style. Local tourist offices will gladly advise you on **gigs**, whether it be a ceilidh, concert or square dance, and listings are given in the weekly *Inverness Oran*, a local newspaper available at tourist offices and convenience stores. During the summer there's something happening almost every day – the Saturday night **Family Square Dance** at West Mabou Hall is especially well regarded. The largest festival is **Celtic Colours** (☎902/562-6700 or 1-877/285-2321, ⊛www.celtic-colours.com), with performances all across Cape Breton held over ten days in early to mid–October.

105 (Exit 7) by weaving its way northwest over the hills before slipping along the **Margaree River Valley**, whose soft, green landscapes are framed by bulging hills. The road veers north at the hamlet of Margaree Forks and then pushes on to the coast at **MARGAREE HARBOUR**, 50km from the Trans-Canada. This is handsome scenery indeed – all rolling fields and wooded hills – and there's a great place to stay too – the *Normaway Inn* (☎902/248-2987 or 1-800/565-9463, ⊛www.normaway.com; mid-June to late Oct), 4km off the Cabot Trail along Egypt Road, about 28km from Hwy 105. Deep in the countryside, the inn occupies a tastefully maintained 1920s farmhouse and stands in its own estate. There are nine rooms (❹) in the main lodge and nineteen one- and two-bedroomed cabins (❺), mostly with wood stoves. The inn has contacts with local ghillies, so you can try your hand at fishing, and it also hosts folk-music concerts and serves a delicious evening meal by prior reservation.

Chéticamp

North from Margaree Harbour, the Cabot Trail offers lovely views of land and sea as it slices across the wide grassy littoral with a range of forested hills looming inland. The scattered dwellings hereabouts are home to an **Acadian** community whose earliest members hid out in the woods during the troubles of 1755 (see p.408). As news filtered through of their survival, returning deportees joined them and – in a dramatic change of policy – the British formally ceded the land to them in 1790. After 35km, the road slips into the district's main village, **CHÉTICAMP**, where the towering Catholic church of **St–Pierre**, with its soaring silver steeple, was built in 1893 of stones lugged across the ice from the Île-de-Chéticamp, just offshore. Inside, the lines of the cavernous nave are interrupted by two long galleries and oceans of elaborate wood and plasterwork. The striking frescoes were added later – in the 1950s – and, even though they're awfully sanctimonious, they do have a certain cheery charm. Below the church – 200m back down the road – is the **Co-operative Artisanale** (daily: mid-June to Sept 8am–9pm; mid-May to mid-June & Oct 9am–6pm; ☎902/224-2170), where a tiny Musée Acadien features a selection of the crudely patterned hooked rugs that are a characteristic craft of the area. The display is hardly spellbinding, but the co-operative's simple café-style **restaurant** *Acadien* is excellent and great value. In particular, the *poulet fricot* (chicken stew) is mouthwatering, and so are the fruit pies and pea soup. There's a much better exhibition of Acadian crafts at the north end of the village in **Les Trois Pignons** (daily: mid-May to June & Sept to mid-Oct 9am–5pm; July & Aug 8am-7pm; $3.50), a cultural centre that proudly displays the hooked mats of Elizabeth LeFort, an artist of some local renown. LeFort's hooked mats often depict religious and historical scenes, mostly large-scale, multicoloured affairs that took as long as a year to complete, but her portraits are perhaps more unusual, pushing the limits of mat-making with admittedly mixed results – though her *Jackie Onassis* of 1962 is quite delightful.

Chéticamp straggles along the main road for about 5km. In between the church – at the south end of the village – and Les Trois Pignons is a seashore **tourist kiosk** (July–Sept), where they have the latest details on a variety of boat trips, several of which leave from the adjacent jetty. Options here include **deep-sea fishing** on board the *Danny Lynn* (mid-May to mid-Oct 1–3 daily; 3–4hr; ☎902/224-3606 or 1-800/813-3376) and **whale-watching** with the highly reputable Whale Cruisers (mid-May to mid-Oct 2–3 daily; 3hr; ☎902/224-3376 or 1-800/813-3376). Summer whale-watching cruises are big business in these parts and they are available at almost every significant settlement – usually three-hour trips for about $40.

There are around twenty **motels** and **B&Bs** in and around Chéticamp. A good choice is the *Ocean View Chalets & Motel* (☎902/224-2313 or 1-877/743-4404, ⊛www.oceanviewchalets.com; ❹; May–Oct), whose well-maintained, shingle-clad chalets sit right by the seashore on the main road opposite Les Trois Pignons. Another option is *L'Auberge Doucet Inn* (☎902/224-3438 or 1-800/646-8668, ⊛www.aubergedoucetinn.com; ❸; May to late Oct), above the main road on the south side of the village, which has eleven straightforward, modern rooms. More distinctive is *Chéticamp Outfitters Inn B&B* (☎902/224-2776, ⊛www.cheticampns.com; ❷; April to mid-Dec), perched on a hilltop just off the main road about 4km south of the village and with splendid views over the surrounding shoreline. The rooms are plain and simple, but the breakfasts (and views) are good and the Acadian family who run the place offer bike rental. A third choice, the *Parkview Motel* (☎902/224-3232, ⊛www.parkviewresort.com; ❸; mid-May to late Oct), occupies a pair of well-kept but routine motel blocks on the main road about 8km north of Chéticamp – in a pretty wooded dell across the Chéticamp River from the national park.

For **food**, stick to the *Restaurant Acadien* (see above); a reserve option is the *L'Auberge Doucet Inn* (also see above), where the crab dinners are well known hereabouts.

Cape Breton Highlands National Park

The extensive **Cape Breton Highlands National Park**, beginning 9km north of Chéticamp, offers some of the most gorgeous scenery anywhere in the Maritimes – a mix of deep wooded valleys, rocky coastal headlands, soft green hills and boggy upland. Although visitors get a sniff of the park travelling by car – 120km of highway trimming all but its southern edge – the essence of the place is only revealed on foot: thirty **hiking trails** are signposted from the road, some of them the easiest of woodland strolls, others striking deep into the interior to the small lakes and wetlands of the central plateau. One of the most popular is the 7km-long **Skyline loop trail** which clambers up the coastal mountains north of Corney Brook, a few kilometres up the coast from Chéticamp. Another good trail is the 7km **Franey loop trail**, a steep walk up through the mountains and lakes north of Ingonish Beach. Most of the wildlife inhabits the inner reaches of the park: garter snakes, red-backed salamanders, snowshoe hares and moose are common, while bald eagles, black bear and lynx are rarer. The only artificial sight is the **Lone Sheiling**, a somewhat battered replica of the stone shelters once built by Highlanders beside their mountain pastures. The hut is on the northern perimeter of the park in a valley that was settled by Scots in the early 1800s; it is accessible along a short and easy footpath from the road.

The park has two **information kiosks** – one at the west-coast entrance just beyond Chéticamp (daily: mid-June to Aug 8am–8pm; mid-May to mid-June & Sept to mid-Oct 9am–5pm; ☎902/224-2306), the other at the east-coast entrance near Ingonish Beach (same details). There's also a **visitor centre** (same details) at the west-coast entrance with displays on local flora and fauna and a well-stocked bookshop. Both the visitor centre and the east-coast kiosk sell 1:50,000 maps, have details of the park's hiking trails, which are in peak condition from July to September, and issue backcountry camping permits ($18). There is a park entrance fee of $4.50 per adult per day. The park has six serviced **campsites** ($18–24), all within easy reach of the road, and one **wilderness campsite** – Fishing Cove – along one of the more arduous trails. Campsite services are only available from mid-May to mid-October, but you can camp in the park at any time of the year. Reservations are not required.

Cape North

Beyond the northern perimeter of the national park is **Cape North**, a forested hunk of hill and valley that juts out into the sea where the Gulf of St Lawrence meets the Atlantic Ocean. The Cabot Trail threads its way across the base of the cape, passing through the tiny village of **CAPE NORTH**, no more than a few lonely buildings straggling along the road. There are, however, several **places to stay** round here, beginning with the handy *Macdonald's Motel & Cabins* (☎902/383-2054; ❸; mid-May to Oct), a modern affair at the village crossroads. Much more enticing, however, is *Oakwood Manor B&B* (☎902/383-2317, ⓦwww.capebretonisland.com/oakwood; ❸; May–Oct), whose en-suite guestrooms are in a charming 1930s timber farmhouse. The 200-acre farm occupies a gentle valley and is dotted with shingle-clad barns and outbuildings. To get there, take the Bay St Lawrence road north from Cape North village and, after about 1.3km, turn left at the sign, down the 1.2km-long gravel road leading to the farm. The best place to **eat** is *Morrison's Restaurant*, a casual café serving tasty seafood at the village crossroads.

There aren't many reasons to push on up the North Cape, away from the Cabot Trail, but one of them is to join a **whale-watching trip** at tiny **BAY ST LAWRENCE**, 17km from Cape North village. Several operators line up beside the harbour; one of the most dependable is Captain Cox, whose cruises depart from here throughout the summer (mid-June to mid-Sept 2–3 daily; 2–3hr; $25; ☎902/383-2981 or 1-888/346-5556, ⓦwww .whalewatching-novascotia.com). Just before you reach Bay St Lawrence, there's a 5km-long turning to the hamlet of **CAPSTICK**, where a string of houses spreads out along a wide bay with wooded hills pressing in from behind. Beyond, at the end of a bumpy, occasionally hairy 8km-long gravel road, lies **MEAT COVE**, which passing sailors once raided for moose and caribou – hence the name. The small **campsite** here (☎902/383-2379; June–Oct; sites $18) is full of the roar of the ocean.

Ingonish and the Gaelic Coast

Beyond Cape North village, the main road skirts the national park, cutting east across the interior before veering south along the coast to reach the series of roadside resorts that make up **INGONISH**. Amongst several **places to stay** here, the *Glenghorm Beach Resort* (☎902/285-2049 or 1-800/565-5660, ⓦwww.glenghormbeachresort.com; mid-May to late Oct) is as good as any – and better than most – its neat and trim motel rooms (❹) and cabins (❺) spreading out along a pleasant slice of seashore. The attractions of Ingonish, however, pale in comparison with *Keltic Lodge* (☎902/285-2880 or 1-800/565-0444, ⓦwww.signatureresorts.com), one of the province's finest hotel complexes, perched high above the cliffs amidst immaculate gardens on a rocky promontory some 40km from Cape North village – and close to the national park's east entrance. The lodge has a comprehensive range of facilities, from beaches, restaurants and tennis courts through to hiking trails that explore the locale's scenic nooks and crannies. You can stay in the main lodge (❽), a handsome Edwardian mansion with high gables and brick chimneys, or the modern *Keltic Inn* (❽), but the cottages (❻) are perhaps more enjoyable, the best of them prettily located amongst the woods that cover much of the promontory.

Leaving the national park, the Cabot Trail threads its way down the 80km-long **Gaelic Coast** – named after the Scottish Highlanders who first settled here – passing through **SOUTH GUT ST ANN'S**, the location of the **Gaelic College** of Celtic Arts and Crafts. Standing on its own campus in the hills, the college offers courses in the Gaelic language and all manner of Highland activities – bagpiping, tartan-weaving, dancing and Scots folklore. The main focus of a visit here is the **Great Hall of the Clans** (mid-June to Sept daily 8.30am–6pm; $2.50), which provides potted clan descriptions alongside wax models dressed in the appropriate tartan.

From the college, it is a few hundred metres to the Trans-Canada for either Baddeck to the southwest or Sydney (see p.419) to the east.

Baddeck

The amenable resort and yachting town of **BADDECK**, some 90km east of the Canso causeway along Hwy 105, enjoys an attractive lakeside setting on St Patrick's Channel, an inlet of the Bras d'Or Lake. It is also home to the fascinating **Alexander Graham Bell Museum** (daily: July & Aug 8.30am–6pm; June, Sept & early Oct 9am–6pm; mid-Oct to May 9am–5pm; $5.75), which overlooks the waterfront from a tiny park and whose excellent exhibits do full justice to the fertility of the great man's mind. The museum is a mine of general biographical information about Bell (1847–1922) and gives detailed explanations of all his inventions – both successful and unsuccessful. Most famous for the invention of the **telephone**, Bell also made extraordinary advances in techniques for teaching hearing-impaired children, a lifelong interest inspired by the deafness of his mother, and undertook pioneering experiments in animal husbandry. He also worked on aircraft and boats, and his nautical adventures culminated in 1919 with the launch of the world's first hydrofoil, the HD-4 (of which there's a full-scale replica in the museum), which reached a speed of 70mph on the lake right in front of town. Bell spent his last 37 years in Baddeck, working away at **Beinn Bhreagh** (no public access), the family mansion that still stands amongst the trees just across the bay from town. The museum is Baddeck's only significant sight, but the town's waterfront makes for an enjoyable stroll and in July and August the local Lion's Club runs a free shuttle-boat service from the municipal jetty to **Kidston Island**, a couple of hundred metres offshore, where you can take a walk in the woods.

Baddeck is on the Acadian Lines **bus** route between Halifax and Sydney, with one or two buses daily in each direction stopping at the Irving fuel station

3.5km west of town on Hwy 105 (Exit 8). The **tourist office** (June–Oct daily 9am–7pm; ☎902/295-1911) has lots of useful local information and sits by the side of the resort's main intersection – at Shore Road and the top of the short main drag, Chebucto Street. Baddeck is a popular holiday spot, so there's a wide range of **accommodation**, but it fills up fast in the height of the season. Downtown **B&Bs** include the delightful *Duffus House Inn* (☎902/295-2172; ❹; June to mid-Oct), with seven en-suite rooms occupying two attractively renovated Victorian town houses by the lake at 108 Water Street; and *Heidi's B&B* (☎902/295-1301; ❷; June–Nov), in a pleasant old timber building with a terrace about 400m from the tourist office at 64 Old Margaree Rd, with six rooms, three en-suite.

In addition, several smart **resort-hotels** line up along Shore Road, west of the town centre. These include the *Silver Dart Lodge* (☎902/295-2340 or 1-888/662-7484, ⓦwww.maritimeinns.com; ❹; mid-May to mid-Oct), whose spacious chalets spread over a hillside in view of the lake, and *Auberge Gisele's Inn* (☎902/295-2849 or 1-800/304-0466, ⓦwww.giseles.com; ❻; May–Oct), where the seventy commodious bedrooms are decked out in modern style. Best of the lot is the *Inverary Resort* (☎902/295-3500 or 1-800/565-5660, ⓦwww.inveraryresort.com), an extensive and immaculately maintained complex that spreads down from Shore Road to the bay. The *Inverary* offers rooms in the main lodge (❺) and in several different types of cottage (from ❻). If your budget doesn't stretch that far, the *Restawyle B&B* (☎902/295-3253; ❷; mid-May to mid-Oct), also on Shore Road, occupies a good-looking Edwardian house set in its own grounds. This B&B has four comfortable guest rooms, two with shared bath. The nearest **campsite** is the *Bras d'Or Lakes* (☎902/295-2329; mid-June to Sept), about 6km west on Hwy 105.

Most visitors **eat** where they sleep: Baddeck is surprisingly short on cafés and restaurants. The best café in town is the *High Wheeler*, on Chebucto Street, which serves up a reasonable range of wholefood snacks and cakes, whilst the *Bell Buoy*, further down Chebucto Street, is OK for steaks and seafood.

For those without their own transport, Bannockburn Tours (☎902/295-3310 or 1-888/577-4747) runs day-long **excursions** in summer along the Cabot Trail through the Cape Breton Highlands National Park, at $65 per person. **Car rental** is available in Baddeck with Macaulay's, 404 Shore Rd (☎902/295-2500).

Sydney

Poor old **SYDNEY**, sprawling along the east bank of the Sydney River 430km from Halifax and 80km from Baddeck, was once the industrial dynamo of eastern Canada. From the late nineteenth century to the 1950s, its steel mills processed Newfoundland iron ore with Nova Scotian coke, but as gas and oil came on stream this arrangement became uneconomic and the subsequent decline has been severe and long-lasting: the city has regularly recorded an unemployment rate twice the national average. It's hardly surprising, therefore, that the town lacks charm, though brave efforts have been made to reinvigorate the **North End** waterfront, along and around the **Esplanade**, downtown between Prince and Amelia streets. This is the district to head for and it's here you'll find Sydney's oldest buildings, including the early nineteenth-century **St Patrick's Church**, 87 Esplanade, a broadly Gothic structure that now holds a local history museum (June–Aug Mon–Sat 9.30am–5.30pm, Sun 1–5.30pm; donation). Nearby, the **Cossit House**, 75 Charlotte St (June to mid–Oct same hours), was built for the town's first Anglican minister in 1787.

Ferries from North Sydney to Newfoundland

From **North Sydney**, 21km west of Sydney along Hwy 125, Marine Atlantic
(☎1-800/341-7981, ⓦwww.marine-atlantic.ca) operates two **car ferry** routes over
to Newfoundland. The first is **to Channel-Port aux Basques** (see p.511; 2–4 daily;
5–6hr, or 6–8hr at night; $25 one-way, $72 for a car up to 20 feet). Cabins, which
should be reserved in advance, cost $40–50 on day ferries, $75–90 at night; there
are also dormitory bunks for $15. The second car ferry connects North Sydney **to
Argentia**, 130km southwest of St John's (see p.491; late June to mid-Sept 3 weekly,
late Sept 1 weekly; 14–15hr; $70 one-way; $146 for a car up to 20 feet). Vehicles
must be booked in advance as must cabins, which cost $125; there are also dormi-
tory bunks for $25.

North Sydney is itself unremarkable, but if for some reason you get stuck here,
the *Best Western North Star Inn*, on the hill next to the ferry terminal at 39 Forrest
St (☎902/794-8581 or 1-800/561-8585, ⓦwww.bestwestern.com; ❹) is a comfortable chain hotel. Acadian Lines **buses** on their way to and from Sydney – which
usually run to meet sailing times – drop off and pick up passengers at the *Best
Western North Star Inn*. Inside the ferry terminal building is a **Newfoundland
tourist office**, which operates a room-reservation service for that province and has
armfuls of free literature.

Arriving from Halifax and Baddeck, Acadian Lines buses pull into the **bus
station** at 99 Terminal Rd off Prince Street. From here, it's a good fifteen-minute
walk west to the Esplanade. Sydney **tourist office** (☎902/539-9876) is on the
southern edge of town beside Hwy 125 (Exit 6). Staff have details of all the town's
accommodation and can also advise on local minibus services to Louisbourg
fortress (see p.421). There are several **hotels** along the Esplanade; two good
options are the *Delta Sydney* (☎902/562-7500 or 1-800/268-1133,
ⓦwww.deltasydney.com; ❺), a large and well-equipped chain hotel at no. 300,
and *Pauls Hotel* (☎902/562-5747 or 1-866/562-5747; ❷), on the Esplanade at the
corner of Pitt Street. The latter has twelve pleasant guest rooms and five suites, all
en suite. Sydney **airport** offers the shortest and least expensive flights (1–3
weekly; $169 one-way, $305 return) from the mainland to St-Pierre et Miquelon
(see p.493) with Air St-Pierre (☎902/562-3140, ⓦwww.airsaintpierre.com).

Louisbourg and beyond

Beginning work in 1719, the French constructed the coastal fortress of
LOUISBOURG, 37km southeast of Sydney, to guard the Atlantic approaches
to New France and salvage their imperial honour after the humiliation of the
Treaty of Utrecht. The result was a staggeringly ostentatious stronghold covering a hundred acres and encircled by ten-metre-high stone walls; it took so
long to build and was so expensive that Louis XV said he was expecting its
towers to rise over the Paris horizon. However, Louisbourg was wildly ill-
conceived: the humid weather stopped the mortar from drying, the fort was
overlooked by a score of hillocks, and developments in gunnery had already
made high stone walls an ineffective means of defence. As Charles Lawrence,
the British governor, confirmed, "the general design of the fortifications is
exceedingly bad and the workmanship worse executed and so disadvanta-
geously situated that…it will never answer the charge or trouble." And so it
proved: Louisbourg was only attacked twice, but it was captured on both occasions, the second time by the celebrated British commander, James Wolfe, on
his way to Québec in 1758.

A visit to the **Fortress of Louisbourg National Historic Site** (daily: July & Aug 9am–6pm; May, June & Sept to mid-Oct 9.30am–5pm; $13.50) begins just 2km beyond the modern village at the Reception Centre, where there's a good account of the fort's history and its reconstruction in the 1960s. From here, a free shuttle bus runs to the fort, whose stone walls rise from the sea to enclose more than four dozen restored buildings, a mid-eighteenth-century fortress town set beneath a soaring church spire. There are powder magazines, forges, guardhouses, warehouses, barracks and, last but not least, the chilly abodes of the soldiers, all accompanied by costumed guides to provide extra atmosphere. It's an extraordinary reconstruction in a lovely coastal setting and particular care has been taken with the **governor's apartments**, which have been splendidly furnished according to the inventory taken after the death of Governor Duquesnel here in 1744. It's amazing the man hadn't died before: already minus a leg from early in his military career, Duquesnel's body was buried under the chapel floor and when it was exhumed in the 1960s the remains showed him to have been suffering from a bewildering variety of ailments from arthritis and arteriosclerosis through to dental abscesses. Allow at least a couple of hours to look round the fortress and sample the authentic refreshments that are available at the taverns and eating houses; the most sustaining food of all is the soldiers' bread (wheat and rye wholemeal), sold by the loaf at the bakery.

Stringing along the seashore down the bay from the fortress, the modern village of Louisbourg has a cheerful setting and several good **places to stay**. Choices include the *Stacey House B&B*, 7438 Main St (✆902/733-2317 or 1-866/924-2242; ❷; June to mid-Oct), an attractive, high-gabled old home with just four guest rooms; the fiercely pink *Cranberry Cove Inn*, 12 Wolfe St (✆902/733-2171 or 1-800/929-0222, ⓦwww.louisbourg.com /cranberrycove; ❹; May–Oct), a lavishly refurbished old home on the edge of the village on the way to the fort; and the *Louisbourg Manse B&B*, 10 Strathcona St (✆902/733-3155 or 1-866/733-3155; ❸), which occupies a pleasant Victorian house down an alley just off Main Street. There's a no-frills **campsite**, the *Louisbourg Motorhome Park* (✆902/733-3631 or 1-866/733-3631; mid-May to Oct), down by the harbour in the centre of the village. The **tourist office**, on Main Street (June & Sept Mon–Fri 9am–5pm; July & Aug daily 8am–8pm), has the complete lodgings list. Amongst several **cafés** and **restaurants**, the *Grubstake*, 7499 Main St (✆902/733-2308; mid-June to early Oct), is recommended for its fish platters and home-baked pastries. Both the breakfast and dinner at the *Cranberry Cove Inn* are excellent.

From Louisbourg to the Canso causeway via Iona

From Louisbourg, it's a dreary 220km thrash north then west along highways 22 and 4 back to the Canso causeway. Instead, if you have the time, leave Hwy 4 west of Sydney and take Hwy 216 over the hills and along a tapering arm of Bras d'Or Lake to **IONA**, a remote hamlet where some of the inhabitants still speak Gaelic. Iona is home to the **Highland Village Museum** (daily: mid-May to mid-Oct 9am–6pm; $7), a modest collection of old pioneer buildings brought here from all over Cape Breton. The views from the museum, over the lake, are, however, quite delightful – as they are from the nearby *Highland Heights Inn* (✆902/725-2360 or 1-800/565-5660, ⓦwww.highlandheightsinn .com; ❸; mid-May to late Oct), a smart modern place with thirty well-appointed, motel-style rooms.

Iona is 13km – and a five-minute ferry ride – from the Trans-Canada Hwy 105 (Exit 6) between Baddeck and the Canso causeway.

New Brunswick

The province of **NEW BRUNSWICK**, roughly 320km long and 260km wide, attracts less tourist attention than its Maritime neighbours, and it's hard to understand quite why. It's true that the forested upland that makes up the bulk of the province is a trifle repetitious, but the long river valleys that furrow the landscape compensate and the funnel-shaped **Bay of Fundy**, with its dramatic tides and delightful coastline, is outstanding. Equally, in **Fredericton**, the capital, the province has one of the region's most appealing towns, a laid-back sort of place which, besides offering the bonus of the Beaverbrook Art Gallery, also possesses strings of fine old villas and a good-looking cathedral. Handsome scenery is within easy reach of the capital too – it's a short journey south to scenic **Passamaquoddy Bay**, an island-studded inlet of the Bay of Fundy that's home to the likeable resort of **St Andrews**. Southeast of Fredericton, the Saint John River snakes a tortuous route to the Bay of Fundy at the busy port of **Saint John**. Along with most of the settlements of southern New Brunswick, Saint John was founded by **United Empire Loyalists**, whose descendants, mingled with those of British colonists, account for around sixty percent of the province's 725,000 inhabitants. Some 130,000 people live here in Saint John, making this the province's big city – it's much larger than Fredericton – and although hard times have left the place frayed at the edges the city boasts a splendid sample of Victorian architecture. Also, although industry has scarred the Fundy coast hereabouts, there's still no denying the rugged charms of Saint John's setting, and not far away are the more pristine land- and seascapes of both the coastal **Fundy Trail Parkway** and **Fundy National Park**.

The remaining third of New Brunswick's population are **French-speakers**, the descendants of those Acadians who settled in the region after the deportations of 1755. To avoid further persecution, these refugees clustered in the remote northern parts of the province, though since the 1960s they have become more assertive, following the example set by their Québecois cousins. As a result, they have made **Moncton**, in southeast New Brunswick, the effective capital of modern Acadia, with a French-speaking university as their cultural centre. Moncton is, however, of limited interest to the passing visitor – it's a modern, brassy, breezy sort of place – and is chiefly of use as a stepping stone either west to Fundy National Park or east to the beautifully remote remains of **Fort Beauséjour**.

As for the other Acadian districts, they are best visited on the way to Québec. Two main roads link Fredericton with its northern neighbour. The first – which is both more scenically diverting and more direct – slices up the western edge of the province along the Saint John River Valley to French-speaking **Edmundston**, en route to Rivière-du-Loup (see p.320). The second cuts northeast for the long haul up the **Miramichi River Valley** to the cluster of small towns that are known collectively as **Miramichi City**. Near here are the untamed coastal marshes of the **Kouchibouguac National Park** and, in the northeast corner of the province, the **Acadian Peninsula**, whose pride and joy is the re-created **Village Historique Acadien**, near the fishing village of **Caraquet**.

Acadian Lines **buses** (☎1-800/567-5151, ⓦwww.acadianbus.com) provides a reasonable but far from exhaustive range of services across the province. There

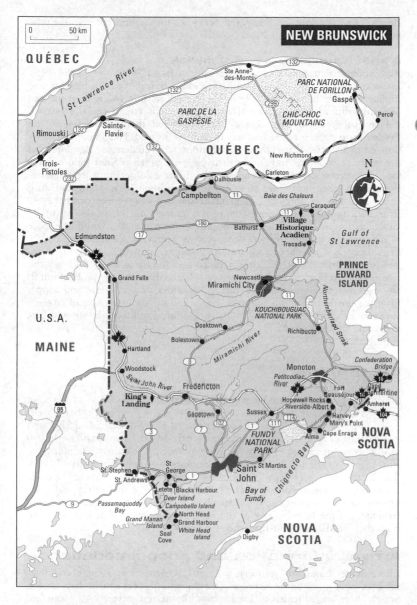

are daily connections between the three main towns – Moncton, Saint John and Fredericton – and services along the Miramichi valley from Fredericton, up the coast from Moncton to Campbellton and in the west from Fredericton to Edmunston. Beyond Edmunston and Campbellton, buses continue on to Montréal, Ottawa and Toronto. There are also regular buses from Fredericton, Saint John and Moncton over to Charlottetown on PEI, via the Confederation

Bridge. The Saint-John-to-Digby **car ferry** is a useful short cut if you're travelling to or from southwest Nova Scotia.

A brief history of New Brunswick

Administered as part of the British colony of Nova Scotia until 1784, New Brunswick was created to cope with the sudden arrival of thousands of united Empire Loyalists in the early 1780s. The New Englanders were concentrated in **Saint John**, which they expected to be the new provincial capital. However, the governor's aristocratic claque outmanoeuvred them, managing to get **Fredericton** chosen as the seat of government instead. This unpopular decision led to an unusual separation of functions, with Fredericton developing as the province's political and administrative capital, whereas Saint John became the commercial centre. Throughout the nineteenth century conservative Fredericton stagnated whilst liberal Saint John boomed as a **shipbuilding** centre, its massive shipyards, dependent on the vast forests of the New Brunswick interior, becoming some of the most productive in the world. By 1890, the province was Canada's most prosperous region, but within the space of twenty years its economy had collapsed as wooden ships were replaced by steel steamers. The **recession** was long-lasting, ultimately reflecting New Brunswick's inability to develop a diversified industrial economy, and this remains the problem today. The province splutters along on the profits from its raw materials, principally timber, fish and potatoes, plus zinc, lead and copper from the northeast around Bathurst, but – like its Maritime neighbours – it exercises no control over price-setting mechanisms, and sharp boom-and-bust economic cycles continue.

Fredericton

Situated 80km or so inland from the Bay of Fundy on the banks of the Saint John River, **FREDERICTON**, the capital of New Brunswick, has a well-padded air, the streets of its tiny centre graced by well-established elms and genteel villas. There's scarcely any industry here and the population of 46,000 mostly work for the government or the university, at least partly fulfilling the aims of one of the town's aristocratic sponsors, who announced in 1784: "it shall be the most gentlemanlike place on earth". Fredericton has few specific sights, but the **Beaverbrook Art Gallery**, the gift of that crusty old reactionary Lord Beaverbrook, is outstanding and there are several intriguing reminders of the British army in the handful of buildings that have survived from the old **Military Compound**.

Arrival, information and accommodation

The Acadian Lines **bus** terminal is at 101 Regent St at King, about five-minutes' walk south of the river and one block south of the main drag, Queen Street. There are no **trains** to Fredericton: the nearest service is to Moncton. Air Canada provides a wide range of domestic and a few international flights into Fredericton **airport**, 16km southeast of town; the taxi fare into the centre will cost you around $25.

Fredericton's main **Visitors Information Centre** is downtown in City Hall on the corner of Queen and York streets (mid-May to mid-June & Sept to mid-Oct daily 8am–5pm; mid-June to Aug daily 8am–8pm; late Oct to mid-May Mon–Fri 8.15am–4.15pm; ☎506/460-2129, ⓦwww.fredericton.ca).

DOWNTOWN FREDERICTON

CAFÉS, RESTAURANTS & BARS			
Brewbakers	9	Dolan's Pub	5
Bruno's Café	3	Lobster Hut	10
Coffee & Co.	7	Lunar Rogue Pub	8
Cosmo Bar	9	M&T Deli	2
Dimitri's Souvlaki		Molly's Coffee House	1
Restaurant	4	Snooty Fox	6

ACCOMMODATION	
Carriage House Inn	F
Colonel's In B&B	C
Elmcroft Place B&B	D
Fredericton	
International Hostel	H
Lord Beaverbrook Hotel	A
Sheraton Fredericton	
Hotel	B
The very best, A	
Victorian B&B	E
UNB Residences	G

They will call ahead to reserve accommodation for free and have all manner of leaflets on the city and its surroundings.

Finding a **place to stay** is rarely a problem, though you should try to avoid the humdrum motels on the outskirts in favour of the downtown area, where there are a couple of tip-top **hotels** as well as an increasing number of **B&Bs**, the best of which occupy grand old timber houses. For those strapped for cash, the university rents out **student rooms** in the summer and there's a downtown HI **hostel**. There are several **campsites** out of town along the Saint John River Valley.

Hotels, B&Bs and inns

Carriage House Inn B&B 230 University Ave at George ☎506/452-9924 or 1-800/267-6068, ⓦwww.bbcanada.com. This eleven-room inn, on the east side of the city centre, occupies a grand Victorian house in one of the older residential areas. Comes complete with antique furnishings, ballroom, and capacious veranda. Rate includes delicious breakfast. ❹

The Colonel's In B&B 843 Union St ☎506/452-2802 or 1-877/455-3003, ⓦwww.bbcanada.com/1749.html. On the north side of the Saint John River, this enjoyable B&B has three en-suite guest rooms decorated in appealing pastel shades. The house itself, dating from the early twentieth century, offers splendid views back across to Fredericton's downtown.

Great breakfasts too. A 15min-walk from the centre via the old railway bridge. ❹

Elmcroft Place B&B 9 Elmcroft Place ☎506/452-1700 or 1-888/354-4588, ⓦwww.bbcanada.com. Fredericton has several Georgian mansions and one of them has been turned into this B&B, whose four guest rooms are large and comfortable and decorated in appropriate period style. Situated about 2km east of downtown, in its own grounds and close to the south bank of the river. ❹

Lord Beaverbrook Hotel 659 Queen St ☎506/455-3371 or 1-866/444-1946, ⓦwww.lordbeaverbrook.com. Polished downtown hotel with Art Deco flourishes; overlooks the river. Facilities include an indoor pool. ❺

Sheraton 225 Woodstock Rd ☎506/457-7000 or 1-800/325-3535, ⓦwww.sheraton.com. Modern high-rise hotel in an attractive retro style with dormer windows and stone finishings. Luxurious suites and posh doubles with views of the river; located a few blocks west of the centre. ❺

The Very Best – A Victorian B&B 806 George St at Church ☎506/451-1499, ⓦwww.bbcanada.com/2330.html. This pleasant B&B, in a rambling old house within easy walking distance of the centre, offers three tastefully renovated, en-suite guest rooms as well as an outside pool and sauna. "The very best" is a common aphorism in Miramichi, which is where one of the owners comes from. ❺

Hostel

Fredericton International Hostel (HI) 621 Churchill Row ☎506/450-4417, ⓦwww .hihostels.ca. Friendly HI hostel in a sparse, but well-kept older building about 500m south of downtown at the corner of Regent St. Kitchen

facilities and study areas. Dorm beds for $20 (non-members $25). Also doubles. ❷

Student rooms

UNB Residence Accommodation Residence Administration Building, University of New Brunswick, 20 Bailey Drive ☎506/458-7549, ⓦwww.unbf.ca/housing. Over a thousand single ($31) and double ($46) rooms for rent, on the university campus, at the south end of University Ave just beyond Beaverbrook St, about 2km south of the river. June to mid-Aug.

Campsite

Mactaquac Provincial Park Campground 1256 Route 105, Mactaquac ☎506/363-4747. Large, popular and well-equipped campsite some 20km west of Fredericton, on the north side of the Saint John River off Hwy 105. Sites $24. May–Oct.

The City

The **Saint John River**, running from northern Maine to the Bay of Fundy, was long the fastest way to reach **Fredericton**, whose early streets, bounded by Brunswick Street to the south and York Street to the west, were laid out close to a curve of the river bank. Here the provincial administration set up shop and the garrison, stationed to counter the threat of American attack, paraded on the **Officers' Square**, at the foot of Regent Street. Mostly grassed over, the square still has space for the Changing of the Guard, a re-enactment of British drill that takes place during the summer (July & Aug Tues–Sat 11am & 7pm). If you miss it, the sentry changes every hour on the hour, a brief march between the square and City Hall just along the street.

The square formed the eastern perimeter of the **Military Compound**, which once stretched over to York Street between Queen Street and the river. It was a large garrison for such a small place and, once Canada–US relations were on a secure footing, the attitude of the local citizenry towards the antics of the military hardened. They could put up with the grog shops and brothels discreetly located on the other side of the river, but they were infuriated by a huge brawl between soldiers and sailors that swept right across town and when the British regulars finally departed in 1869 many were relieved. One reminder of the British presence is the elegant three-storey **Officers' Quarters**, on the square's west side, whose symmetrical columns and stone arches follow a design much used by Queen Victoria's Royal Engineers. Inside, the **York-Sunbury Historical Museum** (May & early June Tues–Sat 1–4pm; mid-June to Aug daily 10am–5pm; Sept to mid-Dec Tues–Sat noon–5pm; $3) possesses an intriguing assortment of local bygones, which fills every nook and cranny of this warren-like building. The ground floor kicks off with displays on Fredericton under the British and up above – on the second floor – are military uniforms, armaments and a reconstruction of a World War I trench. Moving on, the third floor holds a couple of Native Canadian rooms, with a ragbag of archeological finds, plus the stuffed remains of the twenty-kilo "Coleman Frog", a giant-sized amphibian of dubious origins. It's not known whether the creature is real or not, but the local innkeeper, who produced it in the 1880s, claimed to have fed it on beer and buttermilk.

A few metres west along Queen, at the foot of Carleton Street, is the **Guard House** (June–Aug daily 10am–6pm; free), where guides in period British uniforms show you round a restored orderly room, a guardroom and detention cells that create a fearsome picture of military life in the middle of the nineteenth century. The guardroom is not, actually, too different from the airless cells where villains were locked up waiting to be flogged, branded or transported. Directly opposite, with its back to Queen Street, is the **Soldiers' Barracks** (same times) a sturdy three-storey block that at one time accommodated more than two hundred squaddies. Most of the building has been turned into offices and its street-level arcades house arts and craft stalls, but one room has been restored to its appearance in the early 1800s.

Beaverbrook Art Gallery

Lord Beaverbrook (1879–1964), the newspaper tycoon and champion of the British Empire, was raised in New Brunswick's Newcastle, and although he moved to England in 1910 – becoming a close friend of Churchill and a key member of his war cabinet – he sustained a sentimental attachment to his homeland. In Fredericton his largesse was extended to the university, the Playhouse Theatre, and the **Beaverbrook Art Gallery**, by the river at the foot of St John Street (June–Sept Mon–Fri 9am–6pm, Sat & Sun 10am–5pm; Oct–May Tues–Fri 9am–5pm, Sat 10am–5pm, Sun noon–5pm; $5). It's a first-rate gallery, where an eclectic and regularly rotated collection of mostly British and Canadian art is squeezed into a dozen or so rooms, sharing valuable space with an imaginative programme of temporary exhibitions; free plans are issued at reception. The entrance is dominated by a permanent fixture, Salvador Dali's monumental *Santiago el Grande* depicting St James being borne up towards a vaulted firmament on a white charger. After Dali's blitzkrieg, it takes time to adjust to the subtler works beyond, where the Brits are represented by Hogarth, Reynolds, Gainsborough, Constable, Turner, Landseer, Augustus John, Francis Bacon and Lowry. There's also a small sample of medieval paintings and a haunting *Lady Macbeth Sleep-Walking* by Delacroix.

The extensive **Canadian collection** features well-known artists like Paul Kane (see p.93), the Group of Seven (see p.96) and Emily Carr, as well as lesser figures like the early nineteenth-century artist George Chambers, whose *"The Terror" Iced-in off Cape Comfort* is a wonderfully melodramatic canvas, the creaking ship crushed by the ice underneath a dark and forbidding sky. Dominique Serres (1722–93), a favourite of George III, never visited Canada, but he saw sketches made by returning naval officers, sufficient for him to produce *The Bishop's House with Ruined Town of Québec* and *The Intendant's Palace, Québec*, townscapes in the soft-hued Italian style. There's also a good selection of the works of the prolific **Cornelius Krieghoff** (1815–72), who made a living churning out souvenir pictures of Indians and French Canadians from the time of his arrival in Canada in 1840. Krieghoff had a roller-coaster life. Born to a German father and Dutch mother, he emigrated to New York in 1836 and promptly joined the US army, serving in the Second Seminole War down in Florida. Discharged in 1840, Krieghoff immediately re-enlisted, claimed three months' advance pay and deserted, hotfooting it to Montréal with the French-Canadian woman he had met and married in New York. Montréal was a disaster – no one would buy his paintings – but when he moved to Québec City he found a ready market for his work amongst the British officers of the large garrison and their well-heeled friends. This was

Krieghoff's most productive period and the finely detailed, carefully composed anecdotal scenes of French-Canadian life he painted during these years are his best. Two of the finest, *Merrymaking* and *Coming Storm at the Portage*, can be seen here amongst no fewer than 27 of his paintings.

Legislative Assembly Building and around

The **Legislative Assembly Building** (guided tours: June–Aug daily 9am–7pm; Sept–May Mon–Fri 9am–4pm; free), the home of New Brunswick's parliament, stands opposite the art gallery, its robust and imposing exterior topped by a ponderous tower and cupola. The interior holds a sumptuously decorated Assembly Chamber, adorned with portraits of George III and Queen Charlotte by Joshua Reynolds, as well as a splendid oak and cherry spiral staircase leading to the chamber's visitors' gallery. The Reynolds were rescued from the previous parliament building, which burnt down in 1880.

The Legislature occupies the grandest building in Fredericton, but the nearby **Christ Church Cathedral**, King Street and Church (mid-June to Aug Mon–Fri 9am–6pm, Sat 10am–5pm, Sun 1–5pm; Sept to mid-June Mon–Fri 9am–4pm; free guided tours from mid-June to Aug), comes a close second. A mid-Victorian copy of the fifteenth-century parish church of Snettisham, in Norfolk, England, it's distinguished by the elegance of its tapering spire and the intricate grace of its red-pine hammerbeam ceiling. The church also marks the beginning of the smartest part of town, whose leafy streets, lined by handsome Victorian mansions complete with gingerbread scrollwork and expansive verandas, stretch south towards tiny **Queen Square Park**. Near here too – at the east end of Brunswick Street – the old **railway bridge** has been pedestrianized and is easily the nicest way to cross the Saint John River. The bridge is actually part of a system of hiking trails that loops through and around Fredericton focused on the river. There are several jetties dotted along the trails and in the summertime **passenger boats** ($2 per trip, $3 return) link them several times daily, except in bad weather. Maps of the hiking trails and boat timetables are available from the tourist office.

Eating and drinking

Downtown Fredericton offers a reasonable range of informal **cafés** and **restaurants** and there are enough **bars** to entertain for a night or two. In the summer there's also free outdoor theatre and live music down on Officers' Square. The Playhouse (☎506/458-8344, ⓦwww.theplayhouse.nb.ca), beside the Legislative Assembly Building, puts on a good variety of shows and is home to the province's only professional English-speaking **theatre** company, Theatre New Brunswick (Sept–April season). The tourist office has the details of all up-and-coming events.

Cafés and restaurants

Brewbakers 546 King St between Regent and Carleton ☎506/459-0067. First-rate wood-fired pizzas at affordable prices, plus steaks and seafood. Jam-packed at the weekend.

Bruno's Café At the *Sheraton*, 225 Woodstock Rd ☎506/451-7935. One of the most popular spots in town, this café-restaurant is noted for its lavish help-yourself buffets where the emphasis is on pasta and seafood. Eat either inside the hotel or outside on the large riverside patio and watch the sunset.

Coffee & Co 415 King St at York. Great coffees – probably the best range in town – plus tasty cakes and sandwiches. Inexpensive.

Dimitri's Souvlaki Restaurant Pipers Lane, 349 King St ☎506/452-8882. Good, standard-issue Greek restaurant amongst the café-bars crowding Pipers Lane, in between King and Queen sts, just west of York. Closed Sun.

The Lobster Hut In the *City Motel*, 1216 Regent St ☎506/455-4413. Nautical decor and lobsters galore, kept fresh in a whopping water tank.

Prices fluctuate with the season. Closed Sun & Mon.

M&T Deli 602 Queen at Regent St. Arguably Fredericton's best deli, specializing in New York-style bagels and Montréal smoked meat. Mon–Fri 7.30am–4.30pm.

Molly's Coffee House 554 Queen St. Fine coffee and tasty snacks in this pocket-sized, touch-of-New-Age café. Opposite Officers' Square.

Bars

Cosmo Bar 546 King St. Above *Brewbakers* (see above), this fashionable bar, with its dark wood

and stained glass, is an enjoyable spot to savour an accomplished drinks list.

Dolan's Pub Pipers Lane, 349 King St ☏506/454-7474. Bustling bar with imported and domestic beers on draught. Some live folk music.

Lunar Rogue Pub 625 King St ☏506/450-2065. Busy bar serving British and Maritime ales as well as filling bar food. Live music on most weekends. Summer patio.

Snooty Fox 66 Regent St at Queen ☏506/474-1199. Filling bar food as well as a range of 24 draught beers, both domestic and imported, at this bustling downtown bar.

Gagetown

When it comes to **moving on from Fredericton**, you're spoiled for choice: you could head northwest up the Saint John River Valley to Edmundston (see p.447) and Québec, northeast along the Miramichi River Valley to Miramichi City and the Acadian Peninsula (see p.450), or southwest a short way to Passamaquoddy Bay (see below).

A fourth option is to head **southeast** to Saint John (see p.433), either on the fast and direct Hwy 7 or, more leisurely, along **Hwy 102**, which weaves its way along the rusticated banks of the Saint John River. If you choose Hwy 102, be sure to spend an hour or two in **GAGETOWN**, a pretty little village whose graceful old houses are sprinkled along the riverside about 60km from Fredericton and 100km from Saint John. There are several enjoyable craft and pottery shops here, including **Grimross Crafts**, where thirty artists exhibit under one roof, as well as gentle riverside walks, a prim and proper Anglican church, and a grand old courthouse, now home to a modest local museum. *Beamsley's Coffee House*, 44 Front St, offers tasty snacks and sandwiches and, there are several **places to stay**. Two recommendations are the *Steamers Stop Inn* (☏506/488-2903 or 1-877/991-9922; ●; May–Dec), in a good-looking nineteenth-century building down by the river, and the well-kept, if somewhat plainer, 1880s *Step-Aside B&B* (☏506/488-1808; ●; May–Dec), also down by the river.

Passamaquoddy Bay

In the southwest corner of New Brunswick, abutting the US state of Maine, lies **Passamaquoddy Bay**, a deeply indented inlet of the Bay of Fundy whose sparsely populated shoreline is a bony, bumpy affair of forest, rock and swamp. Easily the prettiest of the region's coastal villages is **St Andrews**, a Loyalist settlement turned seaside resort, 135km south of Fredericton and equipped with a battery of great inns and B&Bs. The other main attraction is the **Fundy Islands** archipelago at the mouth of Passamaquoddy Bay. Here, accessible from the US by road and from mainland New Brunswick by ferry (via **Deer Island**), lies **Campobello Island**, the site of Franklin Roosevelt's immaculately maintained country home. Finally, stuck out in the bay two hours by ferry from the Canadian mainland, the far larger **Grand Manan Island** is a much wilder and remoter spot, noted for its imposing sea cliffs and variety of birdlife.

St Andrews

ST ANDREWS was once a busy fishing port and trading centre but is now a leafy resort with a laid-back air that makes for a restful place to spend a night. The town is at its prettiest amongst the antique clapboard houses flanking King Street – which leads up the hill from the busy little pier – while **Water Street**, the main drag, tracks along the waterfront lined with cafés and craft shops. The only sights as such are the **Horticultural Garden** (May–Oct daily 9am-6pm; $8) on the crest of King Street and the squat, minuscule **St Andrews blockhouse**, a replica of the original wooden fort built in 1813 to protect the area from the Americans. It's at the west end of Water Street, and at low tide you can scramble around the reefs and rock pools just below. The pier is packed with boat-tour companies. Amongst several, Quoddy Link Marine (☎506/529-2600 or 1-877/688-2600, ⓦwww.quoddylinkmarine.com) operates first-class **whale-watching** cruises (late May to Sept; 3hr; $50), each of which has a naturalist on board; and Seascape runs regular **kayak** trips from $60 per half-day (same months ☎506/747-1844 or 1-866/747-1884, ⓦwww.seascapekayaktours.com). Of particular interest also are the guided tours of **Minister's Island** (June to mid-Oct 1–2 daily; 2hr; $5; ☎506/529-5081), whose undulating farmland is reached by car along a tidal causeway. The island was once the property of William Van Horne, a Victorian railway baron, who built a grand stone mansion here alongside a clutter of farm buildings. Highlights of the two-hour tour include a romp round the dilapidated mansion and inspection of the windmill, with its kerosene-powered reserve engines. You also get to check out the tidal bathhouse down on the seashore and the magnificent, state-of-the-art livestock barn, where Horne pampered his horses and cattle – treating them, according to local legend, rather better than he did his workforce.

St Andrews is accessible by Acadian Lines **bus** from Saint John (1 daily; 1hr 15min or 40min) and passengers are dropped on Water Street, a couple of blocks east of the pier. The **tourist office** is on Hwy 127 as you enter the town (May to late Oct daily 9am–8pm; ☎506/529-3556, ⓦwww.town.standrews.nb.ca). They issue free tide tables and town maps, supply information on local bike rental, have the schedule for visits to Minister's Island, and will happily help you with accommodation, though advance bookings are a good idea during the height of the season. Most illustrious of the **hotels** is the *Kingsbrae Arms*, 219 King St (☎506/529-1897, ⓦwww.kingsbrae.com; ➑), a sumptuous, immaculately maintained mansion overlooking the botanical gardens. There are just eight guest rooms here, six of them suites with balconies offering wide views of the gardens and the bay, and each is decorated in lavish modern style. An excellent second choice is *The Windsor House*, on the seafront at 132 Water St (☎506/529-3330 or 1-888/890-9463, ⓦwww.windsorhouseinn.com; ➑; April–Dec), a beautifully restored eighteenth-century inn with antiques in the public rooms and six opulent guest rooms beyond. The largest hotel in town is the *Fairmont Algonquin* (☎506/529-8823 or 1-866/540-4405, ⓦwww.fairmont.com; ➑), a sprawling and well-equipped resort complex whose turrets and gables, dating from 1915, dominate the northwest of town, about 1.5km from the waterfront on Prince of Wales Street.

More affordable are the **B&Bs**, beginning with the *Maplehurst B&B*, 134 Carleton St (☎506/529-9100, ⓦwww.bbcanada.com/maplehurstbb; ➎; June–Oct), which occupies an elegant Georgian house near the botanical gardens. Set in its own grounds, this B&B has just two comfortable, en-suite guest rooms decorated in soft pastel hues. Other reasonably priced B&Bs

within a few minutes' walk of the pier include the *Harris Hatch Inn*, 142 Queen St (☎506/529-4713, ⓦwww.bbcanada.com/1439.html; ❹; May–Oct), in an elegant, broadly Georgian mansion with shutters, fanlight and Neoclassical columns; and the *Garden Gate*, whose wide Edwardian verandas and lovely garden are in a quiet part of town at 364 Montague St (☎506/529-4453, ⓦwww.bbgardengate.com; ❺; June–Oct). Very different is *Salty Towers*, 340 Water St (☎506/529-4585; ❷). A far cry from the cutesy character of many a B&B, guests are encouraged to treat this charmingly ramshackle old house as their own in what can only be described as a cross between a 1960s commune and a 1940s guesthouse; it is unique and great fun. Finally, the popular *Passamaquoddy Park Campground* (☎506/529-3439; May–Oct) has a great seaside location just over 1km east of the town centre along Water Street.

St Andrews has an excellent range of **cafés** and the occasional good **restaurant**. The inexpensive *Gables Restaurant Bar & Patio*, 143 Water St (☎506/529-3440), is a funky little place, serving tasty food from its bayshore location, while the *Lobster Bay Eatery*, just along the street at no. 113 (☎506/529-4840), is a family-oriented restaurant offering up delicious lobsters. For a special meal in fairly formal surroundings, head for the outstanding restaurant of *The Windsor House*, at 132 Water St (☎506/529-3330).

Deer Island and Campobello Island

Deer Island, a pint-sized member of the Fundy archipelago, is uninspiring – its handful of ribbon villages straggling amongst low forested hills – but you do have to cross it to reach Campobello Island from the rest of New Brunswick. **Ferries** to Deer Island (summer: Mon–Sat every 30min 7am–7pm, then hourly till 10pm, Sun same hours, hourly; less frequent in winter; 25min; free; first-come first-served) leave from Letete on the southeast shore of Passamaquoddy Bay, 14km south of Hwy 1 (and the village of St George). They dock at the island's northern shore, from where it's 16km south to the **Deer Island–Campobello ferry** (late June to mid-Sept hourly 8.30am–6.30pm; 35min; car & driver $18, foot passenger $2; ☎506/747-2159; first-come first-served). Ferries also sail from this jetty to Eastport in Maine (late June to mid-Sept hourly 9am–7pm; 20min; car & driver $15). Metres from the jetty, at the southern tip of the island, is **Deer Island Point Park**, which overlooks a narrow sound where it's sometimes possible to hear the whirlpool known as the Old Sow; it's caused by the Fundy tides as they sweep round the island and is at its peak three hours before high tide. There's a well-appointed seashore campsite in the park (☎506/747-2423; June–Sept).

Franklin D. Roosevelt loved **Campobello Island**, 16km long by 5km wide, for its quiet wooded coves, rocky headlands and excellent fishing. Those sleepy days are long gone, but although the island is now sprinkled with second homes and busy with day-trippers – who come here by ferry from Deer Island or over the bridge from Lubec in Maine – the southern half is protected as the **Roosevelt Campobello International Park**. Here, mixed forests, marshes, tidal flats, beaches and gullies are explored by 24km of gravel road, which give access to a variety of gentle hiking trails. Several of these – including the enjoyable, 1.5-kilometre-long walk over to Friar's Head – begin beside the island's star turn, the red and green **Roosevelt**

Remember that Maine is on **Eastern time**, one hour behind New Brunswick's **Atlantic time**.

Cottage (late May to mid-Oct daily 10am–6pm; free), set amongst the woods by the seashore about 3km south of the ferry dock. One look at the place and you'll see that "cottage" is an understatement – it's a 35-room mansion built in a Dutch colonial style and packed with memorabilia, from the great man's childhood potty to the Christmas list he made when he was knee-high and the megaphone with which the children were summoned to dinner. It was at the cottage in 1921 that Roosevelt contracted polio and, poignantly, the stretcher on display was the one used to carry him off the island. Campobello is easily seen in a day, but if you decide **to stay** head for *Lupine Lodge* (☎506/752-2555 or 1-888/912-8880, ⓦwww.lupinelodge .com; ❸; late May to mid–Oct), whose delightful log cabins, with their Art Deco lines, occupy a clearing in the woods, in sight of the sea about 500m north of Roosevelt Cottage. The lodge itself dates from 1915 and holds a first-class and reasonably priced **restaurant** featuring local ingredients – Fundy haddock, Maine shrimp and so forth.

Grand Manan Island

At the mouth of the Bay of Fundy is **Grand Manan Island**, a rugged nature hotspot some 30km from tip to toe. The unique geology, wildlife and atmosphere of the place make it a popular destination for day-trippers as well as holiday-makers, with ornithologists and geologists leading the way. A geological fault essentially splits the island in two: the west side of the island is dominated by dark, imposing craggy cliffs of volcanic origin, the east by reddish sedimentary rock, whose crumblings have created some beautiful sandy – and occasionally magnetic – beaches. The ferry docks at the north end of the island at the tiny settlement of **NORTH HEAD**, home to the **Whale and Seabird Research Centre** (June–Oct daily 9am–5pm; donation), which runs several research and release programmes for porpoises and the endangered right whale. The centre provides an excellent introduction to the several sorts of whale that haunt the waters hereabouts – Grand Manan is a popular place to come whale-watching (see below). North Head also has a **tourist office** inside the Grand Manan Business Centre on the main coastal road, Hwy 776 (May–Sept Mon–Fri 8am–7pm, Sat & Sun 9am–5.30pm; ☎506/662-3442 or 1-888-525-1655, ⓦwww.grandmanannb.com). They provide an invaluable booklet of trails and footpaths and will also help with booking accommodation, although it's advisable to book in advance before you catch the ferry in high season. The rocky coast to the north of North Head provides some of the island's best **hiking**, Swallows Tail Lighthouse and Hole in the Wall rock formation both being just over a kilometre from the ferry. Alternatively, you can hire a **sea kayak** or **bike** from Adventure High (☎506/662-8144 or 1-800/732-5492, ⓦwww.adventurehigh.com).

From North Head, the main road hugs the coast southwards to **GRAND HARBOUR**, the main settlement, where the **Grand Manan Museum** (June & Sept Mon–Sat 10am–4pm; July & Aug Mon–Fri 10am–4.30pm, Sun 1–5pm; $5) houses an exceptional collection of stuffed birds, including many of the 300 plus species that congregate on the island throughout the year. The naturalist and painter James John Audubon first documented the island's assembly of puffins, gannets, guillemots, stormy petrels and kittiwakes during his visit in 1831. The best bird-watching times are in the spring migratory period (early April to early June), the summer nesting season and the autumn migration (late Aug through Sept).

Pushing on south from Grand Harbour, it's 3.5km to **Ingalls Head**, from where a toll-free **ferry** (4–10 daily; 25min) scuttles over to **White Head Island**, a tiny islet whose delightfully quiet beach makes for a pleasant day trip. Back on Grand Manan, it's a brief drive south to **SEAL COVE**, a fishing village that still bears the signs of the once-thriving smoked herring industry. Restored smokehouses and rickety wharves crowd the small harbour, where the prize catch now is lobster. The village is also home to the very dependable Sea Watch Tours (☎506/662-8552, ⓦwww.seawatchtours.com), run **whale-watching** trips from mid-July to mid-Sept; also offer **bird-watching** tours from mid-June to August; both cost around $50 per person.

Practicalities

To get to Grand Manan, catch the **car ferry** from **Blacks Harbour**, located 10km from Hwy 1 between St Andrews and Saint John (June–Sept 6–7 daily; Oct–May 3–4 daily; 1hr 30min–2hr; cars $28.75, passengers $9.60; ☎506/662-3724). Spaces are allocated on a first-come, first-served basis so it is advisable to arrive at least an hour before the departure time, and be prepared to queue, especially in July and August.

There's a healthy supply of **accommodation** on Grand Manan – nothing pretentious and all pleasantly low-key. A good choice is *The Inn at Whale Cove*, 26 Whale Cove Cottage Road (☎506/662-3181; ❺), which holds three cosy, shaker-furnished en-suite rooms in a peaceful seashore location. To get there, turn off the main road in North Head and head 700m up Whistle Road. Also in North Head, just up from the post office, is the unassuming *Marathon Inn,* 19 Marathon Lane (☎506/662-8488, ⓦwww.angelfire.com/biz2/marathon; ❹), a wing of which was won in a poker game at the turn of the twentieth century and then promptly transported here 1km along the road. There are 28 rooms, with basic comforts and many have sea views. A third choice is Seal Cove's *McLaughlin's Wharf Inn* (☎506/662-8760; ❸; June–Sept), which occupies an old post office that overhangs the harbour with a large deck where great home-cooked meals are served. As regards **camping**, the *Hole-in-the-Wall Campground* (☎506/662-3152 or 1-866/662-4489, ⓦwww.grandmanancamping.com; May–Oct) offers some breathtaking cliff-top pitches, but they are popular, so arrive early or book ahead.

The island has a fair crop of **cafés** and **restaurants**, but the dining room of *The Inn at Whale Cove* (June–Sept) is the best. They do excellent lunches and evening meals with an abundance of fresh produce and they also run a gourmet take-away lunch shop. Not far away, the *North Head Bakery,* 199 Hwy 776, bakes French artisan bread and pastries and is a great place to stock up for a picnic. Don't forget to sample some of Grand Manan's pride and joy: **dulse** (edible seaweed). It grows on the western shore, in the shade of the cliffs, and is sold all over the island – just look for the signs.

Saint John

At first sight **SAINT JOHN** (never "St John", and not to be mixed up with St John's, Newfoundland) seems a confusing hotchpotch of industrial and residential zones spread over the bluffs, valleys and plateaus where the Saint John River twists and turns its way into the Bay of Fundy, 100km southeast of Fredericton. In fact, the downtown area is squeezed onto a chubby peninsula immediately east of the river mouth – a surprisingly compact centre for a city

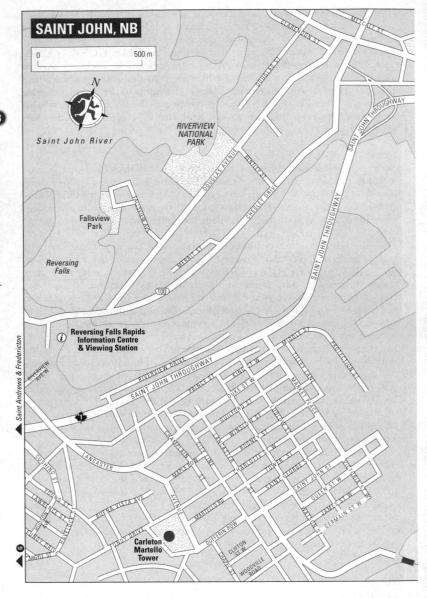

SAINT JOHN, NB

0 ——————————— 500 m

N

Saint John River

RIVERVIEW NATIONAL PARK

PLACE JOHN ST
METCALF ST
DOUGLAS STREET
SAINT JOHN THROUGHWAY

Fallsview Park

Reversing Falls

DOUGLAS AVENUE
BENTLEY ST
CHESLEY DRIVE
SAINT JOHN THROUGHWAY

FALLSVIEW AVE
MERRITT ST
100

(i) **Reversing Falls Rapids Information Centre & Viewing Station**

RIVERVIEW DRIVE
SAINT JOHN THROUGHWAY
MITCHELL ST
TILLEY LANE
PROTECTION ST

RIVERVIEW AVE W
PRINCE ST
KING ST W
DUKE ST W
GUILFORD ST
WINSLOW ST
RODNEY
MARKET PLACE

LANCASTER
CHAMPLAIN
CITY LINE
ALBERT ST
CHARLOTTE
WATSON
SAINT GEORGE
SAINT JOHN ST

CUSHING ST
YOUNG ST
MAPLE ROW
TOWER ST
QUEEN ST W
KING ST W
LAWRENCE ST
BUENA VISTA AVE
AVENUE
MARTELLO RD
JAMES ST W
GERMAIN ST W
ST

ARGYLE ST
TILTON DRIVE
DUFFERIN ROW
CLIFTON ST W
WOODVILLE ROAD

● **Carleton Martello Tower**

of 130,000 people with the focus firmly on the short main drag, **King Street**. In 1877, a fire wiped out most of the town, but as a major shipbuilding centre Saint John was sufficiently wealthy to withstand the costs of immediate reconstruction. Consequently, almost all the city's older buildings – at their most resplendent along and around **Prince William Street** – are late Victorian. Most of the shipyards have now gone and the place survives as a modest

**CAFÉS, RESTAURANTS
AND BARS**

Beatty and the Beastro	10
Billy's Seafood Company	5
D'Amico	8
Grannan's Seafood Restaurant	4
Incredible's	11
O'Leary's	12
Reggie's	3
Taco Pico	9
Tapps Brewpub	7
Three Mile Pub	1
Vito's Restaurant	2
Wild Carrot Café	6

ACCOMMODATION

Delta Brunswick Hotel	D
Earle of Leinster B&B	E
Garden House B&B	B
Inn on the Cove	G
Mahogany Manor B&B	F
Rockwood Park Camping	A
Saint John Hilton Hotel	C

seaport and manufacturing town – hence the belching chimneys – with a good range of restaurants. Apart from its diverting Victorian architecture, Saint John's leading attractions are the **New Brunswick Museum** and the **Reversing Falls Rapids**; the latter is a good place to see the effects of the Fundy tides. The town's most famous son is Donald Sutherland; its most celebrated product, Moosehead beer.

Arrival, information and accommodation

Saint John **bus station**, 300 Union St at Carmarthen, ten-minutes' walk east of Market Slip, is where Acadian Lines buses arrive from – and depart to – all of New Brunswick's major settlements. There are no **rail** services; the nearest you'll get is Moncton. Saint John's **ferry terminal**, 5km west of the centre across the mouth of the Saint John River, is served by Bay Ferries (℡1-888/249-7245, Ⓦwww.nfl-bay.com), which has services across the Bay of Fundy to Digby, Nova Scotia (1–3 daily; 3hr; passengers $20–35 single, cars $70–75, bicycles $10). There are no buses direct to the centre from the terminal – take a waiting cab or call Diamond Taxi (℡506/648-8888). **Driving** into downtown Saint John can be a baffling experience; the easiest route is to keep on Hwy 1 and follow the signs from Exit 122.

The main **tourist office** is right in the centre of town in the Market Square mall, beside Market Slip at the foot of King Street (daily: early June to Sept 9am–8pm; rest of year 9am–6pm; ℡506/658-2855 or 1-866/463-8639, Ⓦwww.tourismsaintjohn.com). They will help with accommodation and have a wide range of local and provincial information. This is also the best place to get the latest details of local **boat trips**; the two most appealing are jetboat rides up the Reversing Falls Rapids (see p.438) and Bay of Fundy whale-watching excursions. Of particular note, too, is the tourist office's excellent (and free) walking-tour leaflet on the city's architectural heritage. As for **city transport**, Saint John Transit (℡506/658-4700) operates a reasonable range of bus services; most start and finish downtown at King's Square. The East–West bus (#1, #2, #3 or #4), running from King's Square to the Reversing Falls Rapids, is the one you're most likely to use.

There's no shortage of **accommodation**. Budget motels line up along the main routes into the city, but for something more interesting – and often no more expensive – you're much better off staying in a downtown hotel or B&B, or just west of the city, beside the Bay of Fundy.

Hotels and inns

Delta Brunswick Hotel 39 King St ℡506/648-1981 or 1-800/268-1133, Ⓦwww.deltahotels.com. Right in the thick of downtown, this efficient, modern hotel has 250 high-rise rooms decorated in a crisp, chain style. Fitness facilities and a pool. ❻

Inn on the Cove 1371 Sand Cove Rd ℡506/672-7799 or 1-877/257-8080, Ⓦwww.innonthecove.com. This is a fabulous place to stay. The mainly modern inn, with its five ornately furnished bedrooms, overlooks the Bay of Fundy from the top of a bluff. You can survey the whole of the seashore from the splendid breakfast-cum-dining room. The food is as inventive as it is mouthwatering, with the emphasis on the freshest of local ingredients. Needless to say, reservations are pretty much essential and anyway you won't get dinner unless you've booked at least 24hr in advance. It takes about 10min to drive there from downtown: take Hwy 1 west to exit 119A, where you turn off to travel south along Bleury, watching for Sand Cove Rd, a turning on the right. ❹

Saint John Hilton Hotel One Market Square ℡506/693-8484 or 1-800/561-8282, Ⓦwww.hilton.com. Most rooms have waterfront views at this plush, modern tower block right beside Market Slip. Check at the Market Square tourist office for Hilton special offers. ❼

B&Bs

Earle of Leinster B&B 96 Leinster St at Wentworth ℡506/652-3275, Ⓔleinster@nbnet.nb.ca. Seven en-suite guest rooms in a rather solemn Victorian house, in a frayed area, about 15min walk east of the Market Slip. The hosts/owners couldn't be more helpful. ❸

Garden House B&B 28 Garden St ℡506/646-9093, Ⓔghouse@nbnet.nb.ca. Comfortable, downtown B&B with just four guest rooms occupying a Victorian timber house. To get there, walk east along King, turn left at Charlotte and keep straight on to Coburg, which you follow round; Garden St is on the left. ❸

Mahogany Manor B&B 220 Germain St at Queen ℡506/636-8000 or 1-800/796-7755,

@ www.sjnow.com/mm. This is the pick of the town's B&Bs, just five en-suite guest rooms in an elegant Victorian villa with high gables and wraparound veranda. Located in a quiet, leafy part of town about 10min walk southeast of Market Slip. ❹

Campsite

Rockwood Park Campground Lake Drive South ☎ 506/652-4050. Popular campsite located near the southern entrance of Rockwood Park about 2km east of the city centre. Take Exit 125 off Hwy 1. From $23 per tent site with electricity. May–Sept.

The city and beyond

The tiny rectangular harbour at the foot of King Street, known as the **Market Slip**, witnessed one of the more dramatic Loyalist migrations, when three thousand refugees disembarked here in 1783. They were not overly impressed by their new country; one recorded that it was "the roughest land I ever saw… such a feeling of loneliness came over me that I sat down on the damp moss with my baby in my lap and cried." The Slip no longer functions as a port, but it's still at the heart of Saint John and is next to its most entertaining "shop" (really a museum), **Barbour's General Store** (June–Sept 9am–6pm), a refurbished emporium stuffed with Victorian paraphernalia from formidable-looking sweets to an old barber's chair. The opposite side of the Slip has been gentrified, the old brick wharf warehouses converted into wine bars, restaurants and boutiques that front the modern Market Square shopping mall behind. Inside the mall, the **New Brunswick Museum** (mid-May to Oct Mon–Fri 9am–9pm, Sat 10am–6pm, Sun noon–5pm; Nov to mid-May

The Loyalists

The forty thousand **United Empire Loyalists** who streamed north to British Canada in the aftermath of the American War of Independence accounted for a sizeable chunk of the New England population. Many had been subjected to reprisals by their revolutionary neighbours and most arrived virtually penniless. All but eight thousand settled in the Maritime Provinces, where they and their descendants formed the kernel of powerful commercial and political cliques. As a result, the Loyalists have frequently – and not altogether unfairly – been pilloried as arch-conservatives, but in fact they were far from docile subjects: indeed shortly after their arrival in Canada they were pressing the British for their own elective assemblies. Crucially, they were also to instil in their new country an abiding dislike for the American version of republican democracy – and this has remained a key sentiment threading through Canadian history.

Before their enforced exile, the Loyalists conducted a fierce debate with their more radical compatriots, but whereas almost everyone today knows the names of the revolutionary leaders, the Loyalists are forgotten. The Loyalist argument had several strands: loyalty to Britain, fear of war, the righteousness or otherwise of civil obedience and, rather more subliminally, the traditional English Tory belief that men live most freely in a hierarchical society where roles are clearly understood. One of their most articulate spokesmen was **Daniel Leonard**, who during his epistolary debate with John Adams wrote: "A very considerable part of the men of property in this province are at this day firmly attached to the cause of government… [and will,] if they fight at all, fight under the banners of loyalty… And now, in God's name, what is it that has brought us to this brink of destruction? Has not the government of Great Britain… been a nursing mother to us? Has she not been indulgent almost to a fault?… Will not posterity be amazed, when they are told that the present destruction took its rise from a threepenny duty on tea, and call it a more unaccountable frenzy… than that of the witchcraft?"

Tues–Fri 9am–5pm, Thurs until 9pm, Sun noon–5pm; $6) is devoted to the province's human, natural and artistic life and has a particularly revealing section on the Age of Sail as well as a fine collection of Chinese decorative and applied art. In addition, there's much on the region's marine life, including the skeleton of a rare North Atlantic Right whale in the "Hall of Great Whales" and a thirteen-metre-high tidal tube constructed to illustrate the rise and fall of the Bay of Fundy tides.

From Market Slip, it's a five-minute walk east on King Street and left along Germain to the white wooden **Loyalist House**, at 120 Union St (May & June Mon–Fri 10am–5pm; July & Aug daily 10am–5pm; $3). Built in 1810 for merchant David Merritt – whose descendants lived here for six generations – the house boasts an attractive interior kitted out with early nineteenth-century furnishings and fittings, most notably a fine, sweeping staircase, cleverly worked curved doors and hand-carved mouldings. Costumed guides give the lowdown on Loyalist life. Just down the hill, back along Germain, is the entrance to the lively **City Market** (Mon–Thurs 7.30am–6pm, Fri 7.30am–7pm, Sat 7.30am–5pm), heaped with the characteristic foods of New Brunswick – **fiddleheads**, a succulent fern tip that tastes rather like asparagus, and **dulse**, a dried seaweed that enlivens the chowders hereabouts. Behind the market are the Union Jack paths and fanciful Edwardian bandstand of **King's Square**.

Prince William Street

After the fire of 1877, the city's merchant class funded a rebuilding programme that would, they believed, properly reflect Saint John's status as a major seaport and shipbuilding centre. Blissfully unaware of the hard years ahead, they competed with each other in the construction of grand offices and banks, brimmingly self-confident structures that line up along **Prince William Street**, south of the Market Slip. There's an extraordinary attention to detail here, the careful symmetries of each red brick facade patterned with individualistic designs – everything from angular stone trimmings and dog-tooth window ledges through to hieroglyphic insets and elaborately carved window arches. Amongst the predominate red-brick are the grandiose Neoclassical and Second Empire facades of the Old Post Office at no. 115, the Old City Hall at no. 116, and the Nova Scotia Bank's Palatine Building at no. 124. These finely worked stone extravagances, with their columns, pediments and arcades, were built as institutional confirmation of the city's excellent prospects. To the middle class of the time this was all in good taste, but there were limits. The Chubb building, 111 Prince William St at the corner of Princess, was – and still is – decorated by a singular series of mini-gargoyles: "We trust no more of our buildings will be adorned by such buffoonery," thundered the local newspaper.

The outskirts

Like just about every other place along the shores of the Bay of Fundy, Saint John is proud of its tides. What you have here are the **Reversing Falls Rapids**, created by a sharp bend in the Saint John River about 3km west of the centre. At low tide, the river – still some 60m deep – flows quite normally, but the incoming tide forces it into reverse, causing a brief period of equilibrium when the surface of the water is totally calm, before a churning, often tumultuous, surge upstream. You need to stick around for a couple of hours to see the complete process, and there's a **viewing station** (mid-May to mid-Oct daily 8am–7pm; free) high above the river at the far end of the bridge on Hwy 100. To get there by public transport, take the East–West transit bus (#1, #2, #3 or #4) from King's Square. The attached **information centre** shows a film telescoping a day's tidal flow into fifteen minutes. There are also a couple of **mini-parks** beneath the bridge where you can view the phenomenon from near the river bank: one upstream in eyeshot of a noxious paper mill, the other downstream and reached via a short, steep path from the car park. Better still, Reversing Falls Jet Boat operates **boat trips** through the Reversing Falls during the summer from their jetty near the bridge (June to mid-Oct; 30min; $32; ☎506/634-8987 or 1-888/634-8987, ⓦwww.jetboatrides.com).

When you've finished with the river, it's another short drive west via Hwy 100 to the **Carleton Martello Tower** on Fundy Drive (June to early Oct daily 10am–6pm; $3): beyond the viewing station, take the first left along Lancaster Avenue and follow the signs. This stone tower was raised as part of a projected series to protect the Fundy coast from American attack, its squat design – and that of several hundred others dotted across the empire – copied from a Corsican tower that had previously proved especially troublesome to the British navy. Completed in 1815, too late to be of much use in the struggle against the States, the tower was soon abandoned, though it was eventually recycled as a detention centre for deserters in World War I. Later still, in World War II, it became the focal point of the coastal defence system protecting Saint John harbour – hence the ungainly concrete structure plonked on top. Inside, there's a reconstruction of a nineteenth-century barrack room and displays on World War II – plus splendid views over town and bay.

The tower is perched on the same headland as the ferry port beyond which – just 1km out in the bay – you'll spy **Partridge Island**, the first quarantine station in North America. A lighthouse was built on this 24-acre islet in 1791, but by the middle of the nineteenth century no fewer than thirteen hospitals had been placed here as well, with teams of doctors separating the healthy from the sick. The busiest period was during the Irish famine and a Celtic cross commemorates the many Irish who died on the island. After a hundred years, the station was closed in 1938. The island bristles with World War II ruins and holds six cemeteries, where over one thousand unfortunate would-be immigrants are buried. It's uninhabited now and usually inaccessible, but sometimes there are boat trips out to the island – check with the tourist office.

Eating, drinking and nightlife

Saint John is a boisterous, lively place to **eat and drink**. A good place to start is *Reggie's*, a well-lived-in diner near the city market at 26 Germain St, which serves up superb chowders, all sorts of sandwiches, and whopping breakfasts. Alternatively, inside the market, the *Wild Carrot Café* provides wholesome snacks, and *Billy's Seafood Company* serves up fine fresh seafood and has an oyster bar. Down by the Market Slip, amongst a string of bars and cafés, the pick is *Grannan's Seafood Restaurant* (☎506/634-1555), where the catch of the day is a treat. For something a little spicier, try *Taco Pica*, a Mexican-Guatemalan restaurant at 96 Germain St (☎506/633-8492). Nearby is *Incredible's*, 42 Princess St at Canterbury (☎506/633-7554), which has a wide-ranging menu specializing in simply prepared and thoughtfully presented seafood and vegetarian dishes. *Vito's Restaurant*, at 1 Hazen Ave at Union (☎506/634-3900), specializes in Greek and Italian food and *Beatty and the Beastro*, 60 Charlotte St (☎506/652-3888), is a café-restaurant offering crepes, pasta and seafood through to delicious New Brunswick lamb. Best of the lot, however, is *D'Amico*, 33 Canterbury St and Church (☎506/648-2377), where they serve delicious, reasonably priced pizzas and pastas in an imaginatively converted old warehouse with high ceilings and oceans of wood.

After dark, the rollicking *Three Mile Pub,* 1 Golden Grove Rd (℡506/657-8325), northeast of the centre off Hwy 100 (Rothesay Ave) – exit onto McAllister Drive and it's the first on the left – puts on all sorts of live shows and dances but is best for live C&W **music**. More convenient is *O'Leary's,* 46 Princess St (℡506/634-7135), which has draught imported and domestic beers and features live music towards the end of the week – mostly folk, Irish or Maritime. *Tapps Brewpub,* 78 King St (℡506/634-1957), the city's first microbrew pub, offers several especially tasty light ales as well as regular live music. For **performance arts**, the city's leading venue is the Imperial Theatre, a refurbished Edwardian theatre at 24 King's Square (℡506/674-4100 or 1-800/323-7469, ⓦwww.imperialtheatre.nb.ca).

The Fundy Coast east of Saint John

About 40km east of Saint John along Hwy 111, one of the most beautiful portions of New Brunswick's coastline has been opened up by the **Fundy Trail Parkway**, a newly created, 13km-long scenic highway that drifts along a dramatic stretch of seashore. It begins at the attractive seaside village of **St Martins**, which boasts two covered bridges and where there are several first-rate places to stay. Even more beautiful and a good deal wilder – but much further east – is **Fundy National Park**, whose rugged sea cliffs, bays and coves are patterned with superb hiking trails. Highway 114 cuts a diagonal through the park, branching off the Trans-Canada about 100km east of Saint John to access its trails and campsites, before finally emerging at the seaside hamlet of **Alma**, the only sizeable settlement hereabouts and a handy spot to break your journey. If you're after visiting both the parkway and the park, allow at least a couple of days especially as the drive between the two is a time-consuming, wearying business – though there are long-term plans to build a coastal road between St Martins and Alma.

East of Alma, a lovely coastal drive passes by turnings for tide-battered **Cape Enrage**, the bird sanctuary of **Mary's Point**, and the curiously shaped **Hopewell Rocks** on the way to workaday **Moncton**, the province's third city. Beyond Moncton, the isthmus linking New Brunswick with Nova Scotia lies beside Chignecto Bay, at the east end of the Bay of Fundy. Of brief strategic significance after the Treaty of Utrecht, with the British in control of Nova Scotia and the French in Québec, the isthmus has long been a sleepy backwater of tiny fishing and marshland farming villages, with past imperial disputes recalled by the splendid windswept remains of **Fort Beauséjour**.

The Fundy coast is a popular holiday spot, so it's a good idea to book **accommodation** ahead of time. Also, pick up a tide table at any local tourist office – the tides rise and fall by about nine metres, making a spectacular difference to the shoreline – and be prepared for patches of pea-soup fog: the Bay of Fundy is notoriously prone to them.

There is **no public transport** to either St Martins or the national park.

St Martins and the Fundy Trail Parkway

The fishing village of **ST MARTINS** drizzles along the Bay of Fundy shoreline to the east of Saint John. To get there from downtown Saint John take Hwy 100 and exit at Loch Lomond Road (Hwy 111). First impressions of St Martins aren't especially favourable, but things improve when you finally (after 3km) reach the harbour, a compact affair of lobster pots and skiffs set within a ring of hills. A matching pair of covered bridges flanks the harbour and you drive through one of them for the journey 8km east to the **Fundy Trail Parkway** ($5 per car), one of the province's most recent tourist initiatives. It works very well. The 13km-drive is a pleasurable jaunt along the seashore, threading past craggy headlands, and the road is shadowed by a multi-use trail that offers fine and comparatively easy hiking as well as access to several beaches. The Parkway ends at the **Salmon River Interpretive Centre** (mid-May to mid-Oct daily 9am–5pm; $4; ☎506/529-1384), whose exhibits provide lots of details about the Parkway and give the historical low-down on the lumber town of Big Salmon River, whose inhabitants packed up shop in the 1940s; the centre is actually built on the site of an old bunkhouse. From the centre, you can stroll down the hillside and cross the suspension bridge to the river below or negotiate the steep ninety-minute hike up into the hills to the hunting and fishing **lodge** built here by the Hearsts – of newspaper fame – in the 1960s. The Interpretive Centre will advise on routes and conditions.

Exploring the Parkway takes time (a day is about long enough), which means you'll need to overnight in St Martins. **Accommodation** here includes several good options, most notably the first-rate *St Martins Country Inn* (☎506/833-4534 or 1-800/565-5257, Ⓦwww.stmartinscountryinn.com; ❺; April–Dec), whose high Victorian gables and fancy gingerbread scrollwork overlook Hwy 111 (but not the shore). A good, second bet – and it's less expensive – is the *Village B&B*, also in a Victorian house and with four comfortable guestrooms (☎506/833-1893 or 1-877/833-1893, Ⓦwww.bbcanada.com; ❷; May–Oct).

Moving on from St Martins involves a long, looping drive inland along Hwy 111, though the provincial government does have plans to bulldoze a link along the coast east from St Martins to Fundy National Park.

Fundy National Park

Bisected by Hwy 114, **Fundy National Park** encompasses a short stretch of the Bay of Fundy shoreline, all jagged cliffs and tidal mud flats, and the forested hills, lakes and river valleys of the central plateau behind. This varied scenery is crossed by more than 100km of **hiking trails**, mostly short and easy walks taking no more than three hours to complete – though the 45km Fundy Circuit links several of the interior trails and takes between three and five days. The pick of the hiking trails are, however, along the Fundy shore and it's here you'll find the spectacular Point Wolfe Beach trail, a moderately steep, 300-metre hike down from the wooded highlands above the bay to the beach below. Of equal appeal is the 4.5km loop of the Coppermine trail, which meanders through the forests with breathtaking views out along the seashore.

All the park's trails are described in a free booklet issued on arrival at either of the two Hwy 114 **entrance kiosks** (mid-May to mid-Oct $5 entry; free at other times). One is at the west entrance near Lake Wolfe, about 20km south of the Trans-Canada (mid-May to mid-Oct daily 8am–6pm), the other is about 20km to the east, on the coast next door to Alma (same details). In addition, there is a **visitor centre** (daily: mid-May to mid-June & Sept to early Oct 8am–4.30pm; mid-June to Aug 8am–10pm; ☎506/887-6000) on Hwy 114 near the east entrance. The visitor centre features displays on local flora and fauna, organizes guided walks, issues backcountry permits and sells hiking maps and trail descriptions. The park is well equipped for **camping**, with two serviced ($14–20) and two unserviced ($10–14) campsites as well as a string of backcountry sites ($4). Both serviced campsites – *Chignecto North* (mid-May to mid-Oct) and *Headquarters* (June–Aug) – are located near the east entrance (close to Alma) along with most of the park's tourist facilities. They largely operate on a first-come, first-served basis, though reservations are taken for a minority of pitches on ☎1-800/414-6765. **Backcountry** sites require reservations with the visitor centre. You can either take pot luck and register on arrival or ring ahead, which is certainly the better option in July and August. For a greater degree of isolation, take the 10km-long byroad southwest from the visitor centre to **Point Wolfe**, where a medium-sized, unserviced campsite (late June to Aug) is tucked in amongst the wooded hills above the coast – and near the starting point of the Point Wolfe Beach and Coppermine trails.

If you're after a roof over your head, there are a couple of modern **chalet** complexes just inside the park near the visitor centre. These are *Fundy Park Chalets* (☎506/887-2808, Ⓦwww.fundyparkchalets.com; ❸; May–Oct) and the marginally more comfortable, air-conditioned *Fundy Highlands Inn & Chalets* (☎506/887-2930 or 1-888/883-8639, Ⓦwww.fundyhighlandchalets .com; ❹; May–Oct). In both, the rooms come with kitchenettes. Note that there's more accommodation close by in Alma (see below).

East to Alma, Cape Enrage and beyond

Across the Salmon River from the east entrance to the national park is **ALMA**, a pleasant little village whose 300 inhabitants make a tidy living from fishing, farming and tourism. All Alma's facilities are clustered on a short stretch of its Main Street including several **motels** and **hotels**. The pick is the trim *Captain's Inn B&B* (☎506/887-2017, Ⓦwww.captainsinn.ca; ❸) with nine cosy rooms. There is also the spick-and-span, bayshore *Alpine Motor Inn* (☎506/887-2052, Ⓦwww.alpinemotorinn.ca; ❸; May–Sept) and the two-storey, motel-like *Parkland Village Inn* (☎506/887-2313, Ⓦwww.parklandvillageinn.com; ❸; April–Oct). **Food** is a bit of a problem, but the *Parkland* has a (just about) competent restaurant – stick to the simpler dishes. *Kelly's Bake Shop* is well known for its enormous, delicious sticky buns.

On the east edge of Alma, **Hwy 915** branches off Hwy 114 to stick close to the coast, threading over the hills and along the valley past isolated farmsteads sheltering behind rugged sea-cliffs. Here and there the coast comes into view – wide vistas of beach and cliff – but the most dramatic scenery is at **Cape Enrage**, 6km down a side road off Hwy 915, where the lighthouse is glued to a great shank of rock soaring high above the sea. It's remarkable that you can drive down to the cape at all. When the lighthouse was automated in 1988, the keepers moved away, abandoning their old house to the elements. Offended by the neglect, a Moncton schoolteacher initiated an ambitious plan to protect and develop the site with the enthusiastic help of his students. In the last decade, they've transformed the place. There's now a wooden walkway up to the foot of the lighthouse and the old keepers' house has been converted into a pleasant café (try the fish chowder). The students staff the cape in the summer and help run a programme of adventurous pursuits, principally sea-kayaking (May–Oct; 4hr; half-day $60) and rappelling (May–Oct; 2–3hr; $55); book on ☎506/887-2273, Ⓦwww.capenrage.com.

Mary's Point bird reserve, Harvey and Riverside-Albert

Doubling back to Hwy 915, it's a short drive east to the two country lanes that lead to **Mary's Point bird reserve** – though only the second turning is currently signposted; the two lanes connect to form a (partly gravel) 6km-long loop off Hwy 915. Mary's Point is the prettiest of headlands, a varied terrain of forest, beach, marsh and mud flat that attracts thousands of migrating shorebirds on their way south from the Arctic in the late summer. The migration begins in July and continues until early October, depending on the age of the particular bird and the species. Of all the birds, it's the **semi-palmated sandpiper** that attracts most attention, a small grey and white creature with black bill and legs. They appear in late July and peak in the first two weeks of August, tearing round in formation, the greyish white of their undersides flashing in the sun. They can't swim, so the best time to see them – and it is an extraordinary sight – is a couple of hours either side of high tide when they fly closest to the shore. The reserve's **information office** (T506/882-2544) will advise on what birds are around and when is best to see them. Even if the birds are gone, Mary's Point makes for some delightful walking with a network of **footpaths** running down from the information office to explore its nooks and crannies.

If you're after **accommodation**, head for the minuscule hamlet of **HARVEY** at the junction of Hwy 915 and the second lane to Mary's Point as you approach from the west. Here you'll find two good options, leading off with the *Sandpiper's Rest B&B* (T506/882-2744, Wwww.sandpipersrest.nb.ca; ❸; May–Oct), in an appealing nineteenth-century cottage and with three guest rooms, one en suite. The other recommendation is the *Florentine Manor* (T506/882-2271 or 1-800/665-2271; ❹; closed March), a large Victorian house set in its own grounds and with period furnishings. The manor has nine guest rooms, all en suite.

Some 3km north of Harvey, Hwy 915 rejoins Hwy 114. At the crossroads is the local **tourist office** (T506/882-2015), distinctively housed in the old bank building, a Victorian extravagance that comes complete with its original vault and wickets. The tourist office marks the start of **RIVERSIDE-ALBERT**, an elongated village that trails along the bayshore for several kilometres. There's a good place to stay here too – the *Cailswick Babbling Brook B&B* (T506/882-2079, Wwww.bay-of-fundy.com/cailswick; ❸), in an older house set in its own grounds beside Hwy 114.

The Hopewell Rocks

Beyond Riverside-Albert, Hwy 114 travels east passing through farmland and offering attractive views of headlands and tidal flats on its way to Hopewell Cape, where the Petitcodiac River flows into the bay. The cape is the site of the red-sandstone **Hopewell Rocks** (daily: mid-May to mid-June & Sept to mid-Oct 9am–5pm; mid-June to Aug 8am–7pm; $6), gnarled pinnacles rising up to 15m above the beach and snared within a coastal park – formally an Ocean Tidal Exploration Site – that attracts too many visitors for its own good. The interpretive centre explains the cape's geological wherewithal and the marine complexities of the Bay of Fundy, but you'll soon be wandering down the footpath – past several vantage points – to the rocks. The rocks were pushed away from the cliff face by glacial pressure during the Ice Age, and the Bay of Fundy tides have defined their present, eccentric shape. At high tide they resemble stark little islands covered in fir trees, but at low tide look like enormous termite hills. Steps lead down to the beach and you can safely walk round the rocks two to three hours either side of low tide, or you can paddle round them at high tide by hiring a kayak for a nominal fee.

From the Hopewell Rocks, it's 50km along the west bank of the Petitcodiac River to Moncton.

Moncton

MONCTON, 80km from Alma, was named after Colonel Robert Monckton [sic], though the Acadians had originally called the place *Le Coude* ("the elbow"), which at least hinted at its setting on a sharp bend of the Petitcodiac River. Indeed, the river provides Moncton with its most singular attraction, the tidal bore, which sweeps up from the Bay of Fundy, 35km downstream. Otherwise, Moncton is a minor commercial centre and major transport junction surrounded by marshy flatlands. This may sound unpromising, but the downtown area has recently been spruced up and there are now enough good restaurants, bars and hotels to make an overnight stay enjoyable, and the town is a convenient stop on the journey between Fundy National Park and PEI via the Confederation Bridge. Moncton's rejuvenation partly reflects the increasing confidence of local Acadians: the town hosts the province's only French-speaking university and is proud of its bilingualism – the result of Acadian ex-deportees settling here in the 1790s.

Moncton's **tidal bore** is a wave that varies from a few centimetres to a metre in height, depending on weather conditions and the phase of the moon. At low tide you'll be in no doubt as to why the locals called the Petitcodiac the "chocolate river" – but the mud flats disappear after the bore arrives and the river level rises by up to 8m. Tiny **Tidal Bore Park**, downtown at Main and King streets, has information plaques on the tide times and a small grandstand so you can watch the phenomenon in comfort. The town's other oddity is **Magnetic Hill** (mid-May to mid-Sept daily 8am–8pm, $5, otherwise free), an extraordinarily popular motorized attraction where your car appears to travel uphill when it is in neutral along an otherwise ordinary bit of road. Local farmers first observed this optical illusion in the nineteenth century, when they noticed their horses were straining to go uphill just as they felt they were going down. The idea today is that you drive to what appears to be the bottom of the hill, put your vehicle in neutral and then coast backwards, apparently uphill – which is really rather weird. Magnetic Hill is located just off the Trans-Canada Highway (Exit 488) about 9km northwest of downtown.

Practicalities

Moncton's **bus station** is about 1km west of Tidal Bore Park, at 961 Main Street. Acadian Lines buses arrive here from most major settlements in New Brunswick and twice or three times daily from PEI's Charlottetown; there are also buses to and from Halifax in Nova Scotia. Moncton's **train station** is nearby – behind the Eaton Centre, a couple of blocks further west along Main Street – with services running to Halifax and Montréal. Moncton's main **tourist office** is in Tidal Bore Park (daily: May & Sept 8.30am–4.30pm, June–Aug 9am–8pm; ☎506/853-3590, ⓦwww.gomoncton.com). They'll book accommodation for free, provide free city maps and give information on forthcoming events.

Moncton has a healthy supply of convenient **accommodation**. Amongst several downtown **hotels**, the *Delta Beauséjour*, at 750 Main St (☎506/854-4344 or 1-800/268-1133, ⓦwww.deltahotels.com; ❺), is the most lavish, a big modern high-rise bang in the middle of town. However, the motel-style rooms of the much more modest *Rodd Parkhouse Inn*, beside Tidal Bore Park at 434 Main St (☎506/382-1664 or 1-800/565-7633, ⓦwww.rodd-hotels.ca; ❸), are much less expensive and perfectly adequate if rather routine. Alternatively, several pleasant **B&Bs** are dotted amongst the leafy residential avenues to the north of Main Street. The pick of the bunch is the *Bonaccord House B&B*, 250 Bonaccord St (℡506/388-1535; ❷), north of the bus station in an attractive Victorian villa with picket fence and portico. A good reserve is the *Archibald B&B*, 194 Archibald St (℡506/382-0123 or 1-877/389-0123, ⓦwww.archibaldbed-breakfast.com; ❸), which offers six comfortable guest rooms in a wide-verandahed house on a quiet leafy street just to the north of Main Street.

For **food**, *Le Château à Pape*, 2 Steadman St (℡506/855-7273), serves the finest of Acadian cuisine from its premises in a big old house a couple of minutes' walk west along the river bank from Tidal Bore Park. Less expensive places include *Rye's Deli & Pub*, 785 Main St, where the bagels and daily specials are excellent, and *Jean's Diner*, 369 St George St, about three blocks north of Main Street, which is worth a trip for its clams not to mention its 1950s booths. Another good bet is *Graffiti*, 897 Main St (℡506/382-4299), which specializes in moderately priced Greek food. **Bars** throng the centre – try the popular *Pump House Brewpub*, at 7 Orange Lane, just off Main Street a few metres east of the gleaming modern City Hall, or *Doc Dylan's*, 841 Main St (℡506/382-3627), which has a large selection of Scotches and live music several times a week. Moncton's biggest **club** is *Club Cosmopolitan*, 700 Main St (℡506/857-9117, ⓦwww.clubcosmo.com), where hip hop and dance rule the musical roost. At the adjoining *Kramer's Corner* (℡506/857-9118), a combined restaurant and bar, things are more laid-back with jazz on Fridays and a massive outdoor patio. With regard to the **performing arts**, Moncton's Capitol Theatre, 811 Main St (℡506/856-4379 or 1-800/567-1922, ⓦwww.capitol.nb.ca) has been impressively restored to its original 1920s vaudeville glory, all gold leaf and plush velvet, and now plays host to both Theatre New Brunswick and the provincial symphony orchestra.

Fort Beauséjour

Providing gorgeous views over the broad sweep of Chignecto Bay, **Fort Beauséjour National Historic Site** (June to mid-Oct daily 9am–5pm; $3.50) is stuck on a grassy, treeless hill about 50km south of Moncton and just 2km from the junction of Trans-Canada highways 2 and 16. The fort stands on the isthmus connecting New Brunswick and Nova Scotia and its strategic value was first recognized by the French, who fortified the site in 1751. Four years later, the British captured the fort and promptly strengthened it with a beady eye fixed firmly on the local Acadians, who they thought might rebel against them. In the event, the Acadians did no such thing, but they were deported anyway and the British garrison stayed on until 1835 as a defence against the Americans.

Flush with the brow of the hill, the **remains** of the star-shaped fort include much of the original earthwork, the concentric ditches and mounds typical of the period, as well as a sally port and a couple of deeply recessed casements, used for general storage. The site also has a delightful **museum** with excellent displays on the history of the fort and of the Acadian farmers who settled the region in the 1670s. Some of the most interesting exhibits, like ancient clogs and farm tools, were recovered when the fort was repaired and restored in the 1960s. The Acadians enclosed and drained the marshes below the fort to produce hay, grain crops and vegetables – and the lines of their dykes and ditches are still visible from the hill.

The Saint John River Valley

The **Saint John River Valley** between Fredericton and **Edmundston**, a distance of 275km, is not consistently beautiful but it does have its moments, especially when it slips through maple and pine forests or, to the north, where its low-lying hills and farmland are replaced by more mountainous, heavily forested terrain. The valley towns, dotted along the Trans-Canada, are not particularly memorable, but the restored pioneer village of **King's Landing** is first-rate and well worth at least a couple of hours, as is the waterfall at **Grand Falls**.

Acadian Lines operates a twice-daily **bus** between Fredericton and Edmundston, with services continuing on to Rivière-du-Loup, Québec City, Montréal, Ottawa and Toronto.

King's Landing and beyond

Some 25km west of Fredericton on Hwy 102 lies the **Mactaquac dam**, part of a hydroelectric project whose reservoir stretches 75km up the valley. **King's Landing Historical Settlement** (June to mid-Oct daily 10am–5pm; $14), 10km west of the dam, exists because of the project. Making a virtue of necessity, several nineteenth-century buildings were carefully relocated here to form the nucleus of an open-air museum of rural life as of about 1850. Since then, further judicious purchases have added to the housing stock and, supplemented by a handful of replicas, there are now no fewer than thirty buildings spread out amidst delightful waterside woods and fields. Like similar reconstructions, King's Landing aims to provide a total experience to its visitors, with its "inhabitants" engaged in bread-making, horseshoeing, logging, milling, weaving, cattle-driving, and so on. Themed villages are not to everyone's taste, but this one works very well and several of the buildings are fascinating in their own right – particularly the Jones House, a stone dwelling built into the hillside in a manner typical of this area; the Ingraham House, once the property of a well-to-do farmer; and the fully operational sawmill.

Surrounded by forest, **HARTLAND**, some 90km from King's Landing, advertises itself exclusively on the size of its **wooden bridge**, which at 391m is by far the longest covered bridge in the world. It was completed in 1901, the idea being to protect the timbers of the bridge from the elements by means of a long shed-like affair built in the manner of a barn. It's not graceful – but it is long.

North of Hartland, the scenery changes as the maples give way to a great undulating belt of potato fields. A surprise lies in store at **GRAND FALLS**, 105km from Hartland. Here, right in the centre of an otherwise nondescript town, a spectacular weight of water squeezes through hydroelectric barriers to crash down a 23-metre pitch. Even if the diversion of water through nearby turbines has deprived the falls of their earlier vigour, they're still impressive, as is the two-kilometre gorge they've carved downstream, a steep-sided ravine encircling half the town. A 253-step **stairway** (daily: mid–May to June & Sept to mid-Oct 9am-6pm; July & Aug 9am-9pm; $3) leads down into the gorge; it begins just across the bridge from the conspicuous **Visitor Centre** (☎506/475-7788), which perches on the bridge above the falls. There's nothing else to see in Grand Falls, but there's straightforward **accommodation** right by the gorge and its waterfall at the *Hill Top Motel*, 131 Madawaska Rd (☎506/473-2684 or 1-800/496-1244, ⓦwww.sn2000.nb.ca/hilltop; ❸), should you need it.

Québec (just north of Edmundston) and Maine (just south, across the bridge) both run on **Eastern time**, one hour back from New Brunswick's **Atlantic time**.

Edmundston

Lying at the confluence of the Saint John and Madawaska rivers, wood-pulping **EDMUNDSTON** is the largest town in the north of New Brunswick, with a population of nearly twelve thousand. It's a brash, modern place, where a profusion of flashing neon signs proclaim the proximity of the USA, which lies just over the biggest of the town's three bridges. Edmundston is mainly French-speaking and, curiously, regards itself as the capital of an enclave known as the **Republic of Madawaska**, the snout-shaped tract of Canadian territory jutting out into the state of Maine. While the idea of an independent state here is preposterous, the "Republic" is more than a publicity stunt: it signifies the frustration of a population over whom the British and Americans haggled for thirty years until 1842, and who still feel ignored by Fredericton. Yet the town also packages the Republic frivolously, with Ruritanian touches such as a coat of arms, a flag, honorary knights and a president (otherwise the mayor).

Acadian Lines **buses** pull in at 169 Victoria St, just off Boulevard Hébert before the Fournier Bridge over the Madawaska River into the town centre. There's a seasonal **tourist office** (☎506/739-4636) just off the Trans-Canada (Exit 18) near the top of Boulevard Hébert, which runs downtown. For downtown **accommodation**, head for the standard-issue comforts of the *Howard Johnson Plaza Hotel*, 100 Rice St (☎506/739-7321 or 1-800/576-4656, ⓦ www.hojo.com; ❺). A second, less expensive option is the simple *Praga Hotel*, near the marina at 127 Victoria St (☎506/735-5567; ❷).

The Miramichi Valley

Running northeast from Fredericton, Hwy 8 traverses the **Miramichi River Valley**, passing endless stands of timber en route to the **City of Miramichi**, an amalgamation of the six tiny logging ports that flank the mouth of the river – and amongst which **Newcastle** is easily the most diverting. The 180-kilometre trip takes three to four hours, longer if you pause at the one sight of any real interest, the Woodmen's Museum in **Boiestown**. The river valley is, however, much more famous for its **salmon fishing**, which draws anglers from all over the world. The season begins anywhere between April and July, depending on the waters to be fished, and every angler has to buy a licence, with non-residents charged between $40 and $120. A veritable raft of regulations controls the sport but any local tourist office will have the details. The other big deal hereabouts is the **Miramichi Folksong Festival** (☎506/623-2150, ⓦ www.miramichifolksongfestival.com), held over five days in early August in Miramichi City and generally reckoned to be one of the best of its kind, with fiddle music its forte. Miramichi City is also within easy striking distance of **Kouchibouguac National Park**, a slab of protected coastline noted for its superb sandy beach.

Acadian Lines **buses** ply Hwy 8 once daily, passing through Miramichi City bound for Campbelltown, Québec City, Montréal and Ottawa. At Miramichi

City there are also connecting bus services south along the coast past the Kouchibouguac National Park to Moncton.

Boiestown and Doaktown

Some 70km north of Fredericton, **BOIESTOWN** was once a rowdy loggers' settlement whose drunken "goings-on" inspired the region's balladeers – "If you're longing for fun and enjoyment, or inclined to go out on a spree, come along with me to Boiestown, on the banks of the Miramichi." The **Woodmen's Museum**, beside Hwy 8 (May–Sept daily 9am–5pm; $5), recalls these rougher days beginning with a pair of large huts jam-packed with loggers' artefacts, from all sorts of strange-looking tools to fascinating photographs of the men floating the logs downstream. There are more intimate exhibits too: the loggers collected resin from spruce trees, chewed it until it was smooth and sweet and then placed it in "gumbooks", a couple of which are on display, to give to their kids back home. After the huts, it only takes a few minutes to wander the rest of the site, where there's an incidental assortment of old lumber-industry buildings, including a sawmill, pitsaw, an earthy bunkhouse and cookhouse, and a fire tower. For some obscure reason, an old and well-built fur-trapper's cabin has ended up here as well, and a small train, the *Whooper*, runs round the edge of the museum.

DOAKTOWN, 20km further down the valley, is a favourite spot for fishermen, who congregate here to catch the **Atlantic salmon** as it struggles up the Miramichi on the last leg of its complex life cycle (see box). Doaktown's **Atlantic Salmon Museum** (daily: early June to Sept 9am–5pm; $5; ☎506/365-7787), beside Hwy 8, illustrates the salmon's arduous life cycle, has a small aquarium, and looks at different fishing techniques – but you're much better off having a go at fishing yourself: there are lots of outfitters and guides in and around town; ask for information at the museum.

Atlantic salmon

The life cycle of the **Atlantic salmon** is a complicated affair, which culminates in the battle upriver to spawn; the Miramichi is one of the salmon's major spawning rivers, a fact taken advantage of by fishermen in Doaktown.

Early each spring, thousands of tiny fish emerge from pea-sized orange eggs deposited in the riverbed the previous autumn. These young fish – or **fry** – soon acquire dark markings and are then known as **parr**. The parr remain in the river for two to six years (determined by water temperature and the availability of insects and other aquatic food) before a springtime transformation when their internal systems adapt for saltwater life and they turn silver, becoming **smolt**. It seems that the odours of the smolt's native river are imprinted in its memory before it heads out to sea, to be recalled when it returns to spawn. Some fish, the **grilse**, return to spawn after a year, but the majority, the salmon, swim back after two years or more, entering the Miramichi between April and November and weighing anywhere between 4kg and 20kg. Once they're back in the fresh water, the salmon stop feeding and their bodies deteriorate in favour of egg or sperm production, with the male developing a hooked lower jaw or kype. After they spawn in late autumn, the adults (by then known as **kelt**, or black salmon) return to the ocean to begin the cycle again – unlike their Pacific cousins, all of whom die after their first and only spawning. It's an unfortunate fact that the kelt are nowhere near as tasty as the smolt.

Miramichi City: Newcastle and Nelson

Now incorporated within sprawling **MIRAMICHI CITY**, the old shipbuilding centre of **NEWCASTLE** sits on the north bank of the Miramichi River as
it nears the sea. Its compact centre is cheered by a pleasant little park at **Ritchie
Wharf** and by the trim town square which, with its Italian gazebo and English
garden seats, was spruced up at the whim of local-lad-made-good Max Aitken,
otherwise Lord Beaverbrook, whose bust sits in the square too. There's nothing
much else to the place, but it is a convenient stopping point on the long drive
north to Québec's Gaspé Peninsula (see p.315) and there are a handful of
reasonable **places to stay**. These include the modern, motel-like *Wharf Inn*,
near the bridge at 1 Jane St (T506/622-0302 or 1-800/563-2489, Wwww
.cityhotels.ca; ❸), and the *Comfort Inn*, 201 Edward St (T506/622-1215 or
1-800/228-5150, Wwww.choicehotels.ca; ❹). Alternatively, across the river
from Newcastle in **NELSON**, the *Governor's Mansion B&B*, at 62 St Patrick's
Drive (T506/622-3036 or 1-877/647-2642, Wwww.governorsmansion.ca; ❸),
occupies a handsome Victorian villa that was once the Lieutenant-Governor's
residence. The mansion is graced by antique furnishings and holds eight
guest rooms on the two upper floors.

The *Wharf Inn*'s **restaurant** offers a reasonable range of seafood and meat
dishes. If you're in town for the Miramichi Folksong Festival (see p.447), go to
the **visitor centre**, in the Lighthouse on Ritchie Wharf (mid-May to early
Sept daily 9am–6pm; T506/623-2152), which has gig details.

Kouchibouguac National Park

From Chatham on the eastern edge of Miramichi City, Hwy 11 slices southeast
across the interior for the 50km trip to the coastal forests, bogs, salt marshes,
lagoons and sandy beaches of the **Kouchibouguac** ("Koo-she-boo-gwack")
National Park. Near the park's main **entrance** (mid-May to early Oct $4, free
at other times) is the **visitor centre** (daily: early June to Aug 8am–8pm; early
May to early June & Sept to mid-Oct 9am–5pm; T506/876-2443), where
displays explore the area's complex ecology and the habits of some of its rarer
inhabitants. From here, it's a few kilometres' drive, past the trailheads of several
woodland walks, to the turning down to the sandy expanse of **Kellys beach** –
the park's main attraction. The sea water here is, you're assured, the warmest
north of Virginia, with temperatures between 18°C and 24°C. Further on, past
the turning, there's a restaurant as well as bike, kayak and canoe rental at seasonal
Ryans Rental Centre, on the south bank of the Kouchibouguac River. Just
upriver is the trailhead of the longest trail, the 13km-long **Kouchibouguac
River Trail**, which wriggles west along the river bank passing one of the park's
few wilderness campsites. Hikers have to use the same trail in both directions
and the whole excursion takes at least six hours, but check trail conditions at
the visitor centre before you set out – superactive beavers have closed the trail
on several recent occasions. Another and much shorter option is the 800m
Cedar Trail loop, which offers wide views over salt marshes, lagoons and dunes.
Hikers should on no account forget the insect repellent.

The park has two serviced and three wilderness **campsites**. One of the latter
is open all year, the rest are seasonal. Easily the biggest serviced campsite is the
South Kouchibouguac (mid-May to mid-Oct; $13–22), near Ryans Rental
Centre. The park fills up fast, so either arrive early in the day or take advantage
of the reservation system (T506/876-1277). If you're not camping, the park is
easily visited on a day-trip from Newcastle, or you can stay in one of the

settlements nearby. The modern and rather conventional *Habitant Restaurant and Motel,* 9600 Main St (℡506/523-4421 or 1-888/442-7222, Ⓦwww .habitant.nb.ca; ❸), is located in **RICHIBUCTO**, a short drive south of the park entrance on Hwy 134 – take Exit 64 off Hwy 11.

The Acadian Peninsula

The **Acadian Peninsula**, which protrudes some 130km into the Gulf of St Lawrence in the northeast corner of New Brunswick, is promoted as a part of the province where the twentieth century has yet to gain a foothold. For the Acadians who fled here to avoid the deportations (see p.408), this isolation was a life-saver, and more than anywhere else in the Maritimes this is where they have maintained their traditional way of life. Many locals are still reliant on fishing and marshland farming, though frankly there's precious little actually to see: the countryside is uniformly dull and the ribbon villages are hardly enticing. The mundane port of **Caraquet**, on the north shore, serves as the peninsula's cultural focus and is the best base for a visit to the replica **Village Historique Acadien**, the one sight of any note.

There are **no buses** along the peninsula.

Caraquet

Heading east from the mining town of Bathurst, Hwy 11 bobs along the Acadian Peninsula's northern shore, trimming the edge of the rolling countryside before reaching, after about 60km, the district's pride and joy, the **Village Historique Acadien** (daily: June to early Sept 10am–6pm; $14). This holds around forty old Acadian buildings relocated from other parts of New Brunswick – only the church was built specifically for the village. Costumed "inhabitants" emphasize the struggles of the early settlers and demonstrate traditional agricultural techniques as well as old methods of spinning, cooking and so on – all in a rustic setting. Another section focuses on the early years of the twentieth century with a hotel and train station amongst a modest assortment of urban buildings. From the historic village, it's a further 11km east on Hwy 11 to **CARAQUET**, a fishing port that was founded by Acadian fugitives in 1758 and now straggles along the seafront for some 13km. It may not be much to look at, but Caraquet does have one or two sights, beginning with **Le Musée Acadien de Caraquet**, at 15 Blvd St-Pierre East/Hwy 145 (June to mid-Sept Mon–Sat 10am–6pm, Sun 1–6pm; $3), which chronicles the life and times of the early settlers and has a small gallery devoted to the work of local artists. At the west end of town, there's also the shrine of **Ste-Anne-de-Bocage** built to commemorate the founding families' trials and tribulations. Finally, Caraquet is also the setting for the region's most important **Acadian Festival** (℡506/727-2787, Ⓦwww.festivalacadiencaraquet .com), a two-week programme of music and theatre held in early August, which begins with the blessing of the fishing fleet by a local bishop.

Amongst a bevy of Caraquet **motels**, **inns** and **B&Bs**, the pick is the *Hotel Paulin,* 143 Blvd St-Pierre West (℡506/727-9981 or 1-866/727-9981, Ⓦwww.hotelpaulin.com; ❺), a smart and comfortable, family-operated inn with eight guest rooms in an attractive older building graced by an expansive verandah. The restaurant here is first-rate, too, featuring traditional Acadian cuisine – the pea soup is a real treat. Less expensive rooms are on offer at *Le Pignon Rouge,* a B&B in a sympathetically renovated old house at 338 Blvd St-Pierre East (℡506/727-5983; ❹).

Prince Edward Island

The freckly face and pert pigtails of Anne of Green Gables are emblazoned on much of **PRINCE EDWARD ISLAND**'s publicity material, and her creator, local-born novelist Lucy Maud Montgomery, was the island's most gushing propagandist, depicting the place floating "on the waves of the blue gulf, a green seclusion and haunt of ancient peace… invested with a kind of fairy grace and charm". Radical William Cobbett, who soldiered here in the 1780s, was not so dewy-eyed, and saw instead "a rascally heap of sand, rock and swamp… a lump of worthlessness [that] bears nothing but potatoes". Each had a point. The economy may not be quite as uniform as Cobbett suggested, but PEI does remain thoroughly agricultural: Million-Acre Farm, as it's sometimes called. On the other hand, Canada's smallest province – a crescent-shaped slice of land separated from Nova Scotia and New Brunswick by the Northumberland Strait – can be beguiling. The island's long and complicated shoreline is banded by sandy **beaches** in the north and serrated by dozens of bays and estuaries, where the ruddy soils and grassy tones of the rolling countryside are set beautifully against the blue of the sea.

Charlottetown, the capital and only significant settlement, sits on the south coast beside one of these inlets, the tree-lined streets of the older part of town occupying a chunky headland that juts out into a wide and sheltered harbour. With its graceful air, wide range of accommodation and good restaurants, this is easily the best base for exploring the island, especially as almost all of PEI's

---

Transport to PEI

There are regular domestic **flights** to Charlottetown airport from most cities in eastern Canada, but the majority of visitors arrive via the 13km-long **Confederation Bridge** spanning the Northumberland Strait between New Brunswick's Cape Tormentine and Borden, 60km west of Charlottetown. There's a toll of $38.50 per vehicle for using the bridge, collected as you leave the island. Cycling is a popular pastime on PEI, but cyclists still aren't allowed on the bridge; instead, they are transported across in a free shuttle bus within two hours of arrival – advance reservations are not accepted. The bridge is used by the twice- or three times daily Acadian Lines **bus** service (☎1-800/567-5151, ⓦwww.acadianbus.com) connecting Fredericton or Saint John, NB with Charlottetown via Moncton.

You can also reach the island by **ferry**: Northumberland Ferries take 75 minutes to cross from **Caribou**, NS to **Wood Islands**, 61km east of Charlottetown ($49.50 return for car and passengers; ☎902/566-3838 or 1-888/249-7245, ⓦwww .nfl-bay.com). Again, fares are collected when you leave the island. Ferries run roughly every one and a half hours from July to September and every three hours in May, June, October, November and early December. There's no ferry from late December to April. Ferries operate on a first-come, first-served basis and queues are common in high season, when you should arrive about an hour and a half before departure to be safe.

A second ferry (☎418/986-3278 or 1-888/986-3278, ⓦwww.ilesdelamadeleine .com/ctma) does the five-hour hop between **Cap-aux-Meules** on the Magdalen Islands (Îles-de-la-Madeleine) and **Souris**, 81km northeast of Charlottetown (summer & autumn 6–10 weekly; winter 3–5 weekly; Feb & March no ferries). A one-way adult fare is $39 ($26 in winter), plus $73 ($51) per car .

PRINCE EDWARD ISLAND

▲ Îles-de-la-Madeleine

20 km

0

Basin Head

East Point

16

16

Souris

North Cape

Cascumpec Bay

Mimenegash

2

14

14

142

West Cape

West Point

CEDAR DUNES PARK

14

Gulf of St Lawrence

GREEN PARK MUSEUM & PARK

2

Tyne Valley

PRINCE

Wellington

Miscouche

Mont-Carmel

Summerside

Cap Egmont

Malpeque Bay

Springbrook

Woodleigh

20

New London

Kensington

2

Borden

Confederation Bridge

▼ New Brunswick

Cavendish

6

Saint Ann's

New Glasgow

Hunter River

13

North Rustico

Robinson's Island

South Rustico

PRINCE EDWARD ISLAND NATIONAL PARK

Stanhope

Dalvay

Tracadie Bay

15

Victoria

2

13

3

QUEENS

Milton

Cornwall

Charlottetown

Fort Amherst

Hillsborough River

2

Northumberland Strait

3

Macphail Homestead

Orwell Corner Historic Village

210

Montague

KINGS

313

Cardigan

4

St Peters

313

Greenwich

St Peter's Bay

Wood Islands

▼ Nova Scotia

villages are formless affairs whose dwellings ribbon the island's roads. One exception is **Victoria**, a tiny old seaport southwest of Charlottetown, which makes a peaceful overnight stay. Otherwise, **Orwell Corner Historic Village**, just to the east of the capital, is an agreeable attempt to re-create an island village as of 1890; **Cavendish**, on the north coast, boasts the house that Montgomery used as the setting for her books; and, close by, **Prince Edward Island National Park**, the island's busiest tourist attraction, has kilometres of magnificent sandy beach. Further east is the careworn township of **Souris**, ferry port for the Îles-de-la-Madeleine (Magdalen Islands, see p.334) and located just down the coast from the intriguing beach and fishery museum of **Basin Head**. In the west, the chief interest is social: descendants of PEI's **Acadian** settlers – once the majority of the population – today constitute some fifteen percent of the island's inhabitants and many of them live on the wedge of land that runs down from the village of Wellington to Cap-Egmont.

PEI is a major holiday spot, so there's plenty of **accommodation** to choose from with B&Bs, inns, cottages and campsites liberally sprinkled across the whole of the island – though it's still a good idea to make advance reservations during July and August. Note, also, that although it's easy to reach Charlottetown by Acadian Lines **bus** the rest of PEI has hardly any public transport. On a culinary note, PEI has a reputation for the excellence of its **lobsters**, which are trapped on the west side of the island during August and September and in the east from June to July. A number of restaurants specialize in lobster dishes, but keep a look out for local posters advertising lobster suppers, inexpensive buffet meals served in several church and community halls during the summer.

A brief history of Prince Edward Island

Jacques Cartier claimed Prince Edward Island for France on the first of his voyages across the Atlantic, naming it the **Île-St-Jean** in 1534. However, the French and the Acadian farmers he brought with him from the Bay of Fundy made little impact on the island until they were reinforced in 1720 by three hundred French colonists, who founded a tiny capital at **Port La Joye**, near the site of present-day Charlottetown. In 1754 there were about three thousand settlers, but their numbers doubled the following year with the arrival of refugees from the deportations (see p.408), a sudden influx with which the island was unable to cope. After the capture of Louisbourg in 1758, the British army turned its attention to Île-St-Jean and its starving, dispirited population. Lord Rollo, the local British commander, rounded up and shipped out all but three hundred of the Acadians and the colony was subsequently renamed the Island of St John in 1763, and **Prince Edward Island** in 1799.

After the expulsion of the Acadians, the island was parcelled out to wealthy Englishmen on condition that they organized settlement, but few did. Consequently, when the island's population climbed from around seven thousand to eighty thousand in the first half of the nineteenth century, the majority of the colonists were tenant farmers or squatters, victims of an absentee landowning system that was patently unjust and inefficient. Although most of these immigrants were drawn from the poor of the Scottish Highlands and Ireland, the new citizens had come here in the hope of owning land. Their ceaseless petitioning eventually resulted in the compulsory **Land Purchase Act** of 1875, and within a decade PEI became a land of freeholders.

With the agricultural, fishing, shipbuilding and logging industries buoyant, the late 1870s marked the high point of the island's fortunes, but this prosperity was short-lived. The Canadian government's protectionist **National Policy** discriminated in favour of the manufactured goods of Ontario and Québec and the result was a long-lasting recession that helped precipitate a large-scale emigration with PEI now a forgotten backwater, derisively nicknamed **Spud Island**. Depopulation remains a problem to this day, though the successful exploitation of the island's tourist potential has brought much relief, as has the modernization of its agriculture and fishery. Many islanders also argued that the construction of a bridge between PEI and the mainland would provide a further economic boost, though their opponents asserted that the island would be swamped by outsiders, its farms bought up as second homes and its closely knit communities overwhelmed. Those in favour of the bridge won the day (if not the argument) and the **Confederation Bridge** was completed in 1997. It is still too early to assess the long-term consequences, but the bridge has undoubtedly been a fillip to the tourist industry.

Charlottetown

Tiny **CHARLOTTETOWN**, the administrative and business centre of PEI, is the most urbane spot on the island, its comfortable main streets – Grafton and Kent – hemmed in by leafy avenues of clapboard villas, the most opulent of which spread west of the centre towards **Victoria Park**. Yet although these well-disposed streets give the place a prosperous and sedate appearance, this is not the whole truth: Charlottetown has a relatively high rate of unemployment and this is reflected in some of the bargain-basement department stores – in contrast to the upmarket tourist shops on the snazzily developed harbourfront. That said, Charlottetown is an exceptionally pleasant place to spend a couple of days and it also has, in small-island terms, a reasonable **nightlife**, with a handful of excellent restaurants and a clutch of good bars.

Arrival, information and accommodation

Connected with all of Canada's major cities, Charlottetown **airport** is located 8km north of the town centre. There's no public transport from here to town, but the **taxi** fare costs just $10. Incoming **buses** all arrive at the Acadian Lines depot, 156 Belvedere Ave, about 3km north of downtown out along University avenue.

Inside the airport, a seasonal **tourist information desk** has buckets of information and provides a free room-reservation service – as does PEI's main **Visitor Information Centre**, on the harbourfront, a couple of minutes' walk from the town centre at the foot of Hillsborough Street (June daily 8am–8pm; July & Aug 8am–10pm; Sept–May Mon–Fri 9am–4.30pm; ☎902/368-4444, ⓦ www.peiplay.com). Both have copies of the comprehensive *Visitors' Guide,* but the larger office has much more on the island's B&Bs, national park and farm-holiday spots as well as free Charlottetown maps. The main local daily **newspaper**, *The Guardian* ("covers PEI like the dew"), makes an enjoyable read.

Charlottetown has no shortage of **places to stay** and only in the height of the season (July & Aug) is there any difficulty in finding somewhere reasonably convenient. To get the flavour of the place, you're much better staying in the oldest part of town – between Fitzroy Street and the waterfront. Options here include several reasonably priced **inns** and **B&Bs**, the best of which occupy grand late nineteenth-century houses, as well as a smattering of **hotels**, mostly expensive places that are either smart, modern high-rises or well-conceived conversions of some of the town's oldest properties. At the other end of the market are a handful of small **guesthouses** – only some of which accept credit cards – and, to the north of town, **student rooms**, available in the summer at the university.

Hotels, inns and B&Bs

Delta Prince Edward Hotel 18 Queen St ☎902/566-2222 or 1-800/268-1133, ⓦ www.deltaprinceedward.pe.ca. Charlottetown's plushest hotel, in a high-rise overlooking the harbour; luxurious rooms with superb facilities including pool and health centre. **⑦**

Fairholm National Historic Inn 230 Prince St ☎902/892-5022 or 1-888/573-5022, ⓦ www.fairholm.pe.ca. A fine example of mid-nineteenth century "Picturesque" architecture, this inn, with its elegant redbrick exterior, is a designated National Historic Site. The interior is matchingly plush with seven capacious guest rooms, mostly equipped with Jacuzzis and all with open fireplaces. **⑥**

Fitzroy Hall 45 Fitzroy St at Pownal ☎902/368-2077, ⓦ www.peisland.com/fitzroyhall. This lavishly restored Victorian mansion with pillars, portico, dormer windows and wrought ironwork has eight well-appointed, en-suite guest rooms, one of which has a Jacuzzi. Excellent place to stay. Breakfast included. **⑤**

Hillhurst Inn 181 Fitzroy St at Hillsborough ☎902/894-8004, ⓦ www.hillhurst.com. Classily renovated Georgian Revival mansion with finely carved interior. Nine large, en-suite guest rooms, each with ornate antique furnishings. It is open year-round, but by advance reservation only from late November to March. Breakfast included. **⑤**

The Inns on Great George Great George St ☎902/892-0606 or 1-800/361-1118, ⓦ www.innsongreatgeorge.com. Bang in the centre of town, opposite St Dunstan's, a row of old timber houses has been carefully renovated to hold this immaculate and atmospheric hotel. All the rooms are comfortable and tastefully decorated – the most appealing overlook the Basilica. Continental breakfast included. Highly recommended. **⑥**

Rodd Charlottetown Kent at Pownal ☎902/894-7371 or 1-800/565-7633, ⊛www.rodd-hotels.ca. Imposing 1930s hotel (part of a chain) with appealing Art Deco flourishes, though the rooms lack a certain intimacy. ⑥
Shipwright B&B Inn 51 Fitzroy St ☎902/368-1905 or 1-888/306-9966, ⊛www.shipwrightinn.com. Crammed with antiques, this rambling nineteenth-century mansion has nine well-appointed and individually decorated guest rooms. Very appealing – especially with its thoughtful additions (fresh popcorn to mention one) and its superlative breakfasts. ⑥

Guesthouses
Aloha Tourist Home 234 Sydney St at Hillsborough ☎902/892-9944 or 1-866/892-9944, ⊛www.alohaamigo.com. This well-kept, unpreten-

tious guesthouse occupies a 1930s home in the town centre facing a little park. Three guest rooms with shared bathroom. ❷
Ambrose Tourist Home 17 Passmore St, off University Ave ☎902/566-5853 or 1-800/665-6072. Six unassuming but neat and trim guest rooms here in a duplex on a quiet street. Ten minutes' walk from downtown. ❷

Student rooms
University of Prince Edward Island 550 University Ave. May–Aug: ☎902/566-0442; Sept–April: ☎902/566-0568; ⊛www.upei.ca/conference. Single ($35–45) and double ($50) rooms on the university campus, 3km north of town. Rooms available May to late Aug. Advance reservations required; breakfast included.

The Town

The island's most famous historical attraction, the **Province House** (June & Sept daily 9am–5pm; July & Aug daily 9am–6pm; Oct–May Mon–Fri 9am–5pm; free) is right in the heart of Charlottetown, at the foot of University Avenue. This squat brownstone structure, dominated by its overlarge portico, hosted the first meeting of the **Fathers of Confederation** in 1864, when representatives of Nova Scotia, New Brunswick, Ontario, Québec and PEI met to discuss a union of the British colonies in North America. Today it's used by the island's legislature, but some of its rooms are open to visitors. On the ground floor, a fifteen-minute film provides a melodramatic account of that original meeting and explains its historical context, whilst the Confederation Chamber up above looks pretty much like it did in 1864, though frankly it's not exactly riveting – just a large table and some heavy-duty chairs.

Next door, the **Confederation Centre of the Arts** (daily 9am–5pm, June–Aug till 8pm; free) is housed in a glass and concrete monstrosity built in 1964 to commemorate the centenary of the epochal meeting. Each of Canada's provinces paid fifteen cents for each of its residents to cover its construction and they continue to contribute towards its upkeep. The centre contains the island's main library, a couple of theatres, and a museum and **art gallery** (mid-June to mid-Oct daily 9am–5pm; mid-Oct to mid-June Wed–Sat 11am–5pm, Sun 1–5pm; $5), whose changing exhibitions are often first-rate and always have a Canadian emphasis. Items from the permanent collection are also regularly displayed, and although much is fairly average look out for the manuscripts, papers and scrapbooks of Lucy Maud Montgomery and the portraits of Robert Harris, who painted most of PEI's business elite in the 1880s. Harris also painted the iconic *Fathers of Confederation*, a picture of bewhiskered representatives in debate that has been reproduced for everything from postage stamps to postcards, though the original was actually lost in a fire in 1916.

Metres away, fringed by the pretty terraced houses of Great George Street, rise the twin spires and imposing facade of **St Dunstan's Basilica** (daily 8am–5pm; free). Finished in 1897 and ten years in the making, the church has all the neo-Gothic trimmings, from blind arcaded galleries and lancet windows through to heavy-duty columns and a mighty vaulted ceiling. There were, however, some economies – tap the marble inside and you'll find it's mostly

456

wood painted like marble. The basilica marks the centre of the oldest part of Charlottetown and the surrounding side streets are lined with rows of simple wood and brick buildings, mostly dating from the middle of the nineteenth century. Some of the best ensembles are concentrated on and around **King Street** to either side of Great George Street, whilst pedestrianized **Victoria Row**, also near the church, has the city's finest example of commercial architecture, a long and impressive facade that now holds a series of restaurants and bars.

Below Water Street, the sequence of jetties that make up the **harbourfront** has been neatly refurbished with ice-cream parlours and restaurants, a yacht club, the lavish *Delta Prince Edward Hotel* and the souvenir shops of Peake's Wharf. Big cruise liners are often moored here too, disgorging hundreds of day-trippers. Here also, on the waterfront at 6 Prince St, is a new interactive museum, **Founders' Hall** (mid-May to June, Sept & Oct Mon–Sat 9am–5pm, Sun 9am–4pm; July & Aug Mon–Sat 9am–8pm, Sun 9am–4pm; $4.50), with yet more on the founding fathers. From the harbourfront, it's a pleasant ten-minute stroll west to **Victoria Park**, on the edge of which is the grandiose lieutenant-governor's residence. Inside the park are the scant remains of the gun battery built to overlook the harbour in 1805.

Eating, drinking and nightlife

Charlottetown has a reasonable range of **restaurants** – quite enough to keep you going for a day or two, and several are excellent. The best are downtown, with particular concentrations along Victoria Row, beside the Confederation Centre and on Sydney Street at Queen. The best **cafés** and **bars** are here too, nothing amazingly exciting, but still amenable, easygoing places to enjoy a drink. Note also that in several cases restaurants share their premises with bars: food below, booze up above. *Cows*, something of an island institution, makes delicious **Ice cream**; there are outlets down on the harbourfront and on the corner of Grafton and Queen, opposite the Confederation Centre.

As for the **performing arts**, the programme of events at the Confederation Centre of the Arts (☎902/566-4648 or 1-800/565-0278, ⓦwww.confederationcentre.com) encompasses an extensive variety of acts, from rock and jazz through to comedians, magicians, theatre, opera and ballet. The centre is also the home of the main show of the annual **Charlottetown Festival** (June to mid-Oct; ⓦwww.confederationcentre.com/festival.asp), which – surprise, surprise – is a musical adaptation of *Anne of Green Gables* (tickets $25–58). The musical has been running for years, though modifications are made every year to freshen it up. During festival time in particular, Charlottetown also offers all sorts of comedy revues and shows both indoors and out. *The Buzz*, a free monthly newssheet available all over town and at the tourist office, carries comprehensive listings and reviews.

Cafés and restaurants

Beanz 38 University Ave and Grafton. Great coffee and a range of tasty sandwiches and snacks from around $8 at this agreeable little café. Popular at lunch times with the town's office workers.

Cedar's Eatery 81 University Ave and Kent ☎902/892-7377. Cosy and intimate café-cum-restaurant serving Lebanese specialities at bargain prices.

Claddagh Room Restaurant 131 Sydney at Queen ☎902/892-9661. Pleasant, fairly traditional restaurant offering a good selection of reasonably priced seafood – including lobster – and beef dishes. Closed Mon eve. It's beneath the *Olde Dublin Pub* (see below).

Meeko's Victoria Row, 146 Richmond St at Queen ☎902/892-9800. For something a little different, try this cheerfully decorated Mediterranean café and grill.

Off-Broadway Restaurant 125 Sydney St at Queen ☎ 902/566-4620. Almost certainly the best restaurant in town, Off-Broadway features a creative menu of traditional and modern dishes – but not always lobster! The house specialities are exotic crêpes and home-made desserts. Prices are reasonable: a salmon main course costs about $20.
Sirenella 83 Water St ☎ 902/628-2271. Quality north Italian cuisine featuring the usual suspects from pastas and grilled meats through to seafood. Inexpensive.
Water Prince Corner Shop 141 Water St ☎ 902/365-3212. It may look like a corner shop, but locals swear by the seafood here. The lobster dinners and chowders are, many feel, the best on the island, but then the scallop burger is a real groove too. Booking is essential. Moderately priced.

Bars

D'Arcy McGee's 185 Kent St at Prince ☎ 902/894-3627. They do serve food here, but it's perhaps as a neighbourhood bar that the place has most appeal. Occupies an old but extensively remodelled clapboard house and has an outside terrace.
42nd Street Lounge 125 Sydney St at Queen ☎ 902/566-4620. Laid-back lounge bar above the *Off-Broadway Restaurant*. Good range of brews.
Myron's 151 Kent at University ☎ 902/892-4375. Long a popular spot, *Myron's* puts on a wide range of live music and club nights.
Olde Dublin Pub 131 Sydney ☎ 902/892-6992. Intimate and justifiably popular spot with imported and domestic ales. Live folk music – mostly Irish – nightly from May to September.

Listings

Airlines Air Canada ☎ 1-888/247-2262.
Bike rental Smooth Cycle, 172 Prince St at Kent ☎ 902/566-5530 or 1-800/310-6550; MacQueen's, 430 Queen St ☎ 902/368-2453 or 1-800/969-2822.
Bus companies The Shuttle ☎ 902/566-3243 connects Charlottetown with Cavendish. Long-distance services to New Brunswick and Nova Scotia are provided by Acadian Lines, 156 Belvedere Ave ☎ 902/628-6432 or 1-800/567-5151. PEI Express Shuttle ☎ 902/462-8177 operates a minibus service between Charlottetown and Halifax (4hr; $50); advance reservations are essential.
Car rental Avis, at the airport ☎ 902/892-3706; Budget, 215 University Ave ☎ 902/566-5525;

Hertz, at the airport ☎ 902/566-5566; National, at the airport ☎ 902/368-2228. All these companies do good deals on short-term rentals.
Internet access Café Diem, 128 Richmond St, opposite the Confederation Centre (daily 9am–9pm; ☎ 902/892-0494). Free access at The Confederation Public Library, Queen St (Tues–Thurs 10am–9pm, Fri & Sat 10am–5pm).
Laundry Midtown Laundromat and Café, 238 University Ave at Bishop ☎ 902/628-2329.
Pharmacy Shoppers Drug Mart, 128 Kent St ☎ 902/566-1200 and 390 University Ave ☎ 902/892-2273.
Post office 135 Kent St (Mon–Fri 8am–5.15pm).
Taxis City Cab, 168 Prince St ☎ 902/892-6567; Co-op Taxi, 91 Euston St ☎ 902/628-8200.

The rest of PEI

Prince Edward Island is divided into three counties. In the middle is **Queens County**, which incorporates the province's most popular tourist attractions and has some of its prettiest scenery. It also boasts the island's finest **beaches**, stretching along the northern shore and protected within the **Prince Edward Island National Park**. To the east of Queens lies **Kings County**, comprising two broad geographical areas, with the tree-dotted farmland and estuary townships of the south preceding the wilder scenery further north. To the west of Queens is **Prince County**, which makes up the flattest part of PEI, its broad-brimmed, sparsely populated landscapes curving round a handful of deep bays. The provincial government has worked out three **scenic drives** covering each of the counties: Lady Slipper Drive (287km) to the west, Blue Heron Drive (191km) in the centre, and the Kings Byway Drive (367km) to the east. However, although these drives visit everything of interest, they are frequently dreary, so unless you really love driving it's better to be more selective.

PEI's **public transport** system is rudimentary, but from early June to September there is a **shuttle** (2–4 daily; $18 return; ☎902/566-3243) linking Charlottetown's visitors centre with Cavendish visitor centre, at the junction of Hwy 6 and Hwy 13. Alternatively, several Charlottetown companies operate **sightseeing tours**; the busiest is Abegweit, 157 Nassau St (☎902/894-9966, ⓦwww.peisland.com/abegweit/tours.htm), which offers tours of the southern and northern shores ($55 each) as well as Charlottetown ($9). The island is also good for all manner of outdoor sports, with specialist companies offering everything from diving and deep-sea fishing to canoeing and sailing. PEI is also strong on **cycling**. There are several **cycle-tour operators**, though it's a good deal less expensive (and entirely straightforward) to plan your own route: in Charlottetown, both Smooth Cycle, 172 Prince St at Kent (☎902/566-5530 or 1-800/310-6550), and MacQueen's, 430 Queen St (☎902/368-2453 or 1-800/969-2822), rent out all the necessary gear and will advise on routes. The most popular is the **Confederation Trail**, a combined hiking and cycling trail that weaves its way right across the island, partly following the route of PEI's old railway, which was closed in the 1980s.

Queens County

Drawing thousands of visitors every summer, **Queens County**'s main attraction is the **Prince Edward Island National Park**, whose gorgeous sandy beaches, extending along the north shore for some 40km, are ideal for swimming and sunbathing. Rarely more than one or two hundred metres wide, the park incorporates both the beaches and the sliver of low red cliff and marram-covered sand dune that runs behind – a barrier which is occasionally interrupted by slender inlets connecting the ocean with a quartet of chubby little bays. A narrow road runs behind the shoreline for most of the length of the park, spanning several of these inlets, but forced into a detour at the widest, the main channel into Rustico Bay, which effectively divides the park into two. The smaller, more **westerly portion** runs from Cavendish – the site of Green Gables House – to North Rustico Harbour; the **easterly section**, which is much more enjoyable, goes from Robinson's Island to Dalvay and Tracadie Bay. In either section, it's easy enough to drive along the shore road behind a goodly proportion of the beach until you find a place to your liking.

There's a seasonal **visitor centre** or **information kiosk** at every entrance to the park and from mid-June to August they levy an entrance fee of $5 per adult per day. On arrival, you're issued with a free and comprehensive guide and out of season this is available at Charlottetown's Visitor Information Centre (see p.455). The park has eight short **hiking trails**, easy strolls that take in different aspects of the coast from its tidal marshes and farmland through to its woodlands. The most strenuous is the 5km–long Woodlands Trail, up through a red-pine plantation near Dalvay. It doesn't take long to cycle to the park from Charlottetown, but **bike rental** is also available amongst the many tourist facilities on the park's peripheries.

The park has three **campsites**. The largest is the well-equipped *Cavendish* (early June to Aug), where there's a supervised sandy beach that's great for swimming. The *Stanhope* (mid-June to late Sept), a short walk from the beach in the eastern section, is similarly well equipped and appointed, while *Robinson's Island* (late June to late Aug) occupies a quieter location, in a lovely spot amongst the wooded dunes beside Rustico Bay. A few sites are allocated on a first-come, first-served basis, but most can be reserved (☎1-800/414-6765). Pitches cost $19–23.

PEI National Park (east section)

The fastest route from Charlottetown to the eastern section of the park is the half-hour, 22-kilometre thump along **Hwy 15**, which branches off Hwy 2 on the north side of town. This takes you past long ranks of chalet-style second homes and, as you near the park, the delightful *Dunes Studio Gallery and Café*, located just 600m beyond the Hwy 6 and Hwy 15 junction. The *Dunes* is a combined **café** (June–Sept only), pottery shop and art gallery (daily: May, June, Sept & Oct 9am–6pm, July & Aug 9am–10pm; ☎902/672-2586), which serves mouthwatering and reasonably priced snacks and meals from an imaginative menu of seafood and vegetarian dishes; it's one of the best places to eat on the island. Close by, another 1km or so north on Hwy 15, is the pick of the resort and cottage complexes hereabouts, the charmingly rustic *Shaw's Hotel and Cottages* (☎902/672-2022, ⊛www.shawshotel.ca; full board ❼), whose hotel rooms (June–Sept) and all-year chalets and cottages occupy extensive grounds and farmland about ten-minutes' walk from the beach; *Shaw's* also does **canoe**, **kayak** and **bike rental** for guests and non-guests alike.

Inside the park, at the end of Hwy 15, you turn left along the coast for the causeway over to wooded **Robinson's Island** (and its campsite) and right for the 5km trip to **STANHOPE**, the setting for a string of perfectly placed beachside cottage complexes. These include the little red and white *Del-Mar Cottages* (☎902/672-2582 or 1-800/699-2582; ❹ sleeps up to 4 people; June–Sept) and *Surf Cottages* (☎902/651-3300, ⊛www.peisland.com/surfcottages; ❹ sleeps up to 6 people; June to mid-Sept). Just 6km further east, at the end of the beach road, is pocket-sized **DALVAY**, whose most conspicuous asset is the *Dalvay-by-the-Sea Inn* (☎902/672-2048, ⊛www.dalvaybythesea .com; half board ❽; early June to early Oct). By any standard, the inn is an especially grand affair, a Victorian mansion that comes complete with high gables, rough-hewn stonework, a magnificent wraparound veranda, a yawning wood-panelled and balconied foyer, and even a croquet lawn. The inn holds just 26 tastefully decorated rooms and has an ideal location inside the park just a couple of hundred metres from the beach. Advance reservations are well-nigh essential.

Along the coast to the east of Dalvay, there are two more segments of the national park, the first being the slender sandspit that shelters much of **Tracadie Bay** from the ocean. There are no roads to this part of the park – just hiking trails – and a similar caution applies to the second segment, the spatulate, partly wooded headland at the mouth of **St Peter's Bay**. In this case, Hwy 313 travels west from Hwy 2 along the north shore of the bay, slipping through **GREENWICH** before grinding to a halt at the car park. From here, hiking trails head across the headland, exploring its beaches, dunes and wetlands.

Cavendish and PEI National Park (west section)

The 40km-journey from Charlottetown to Cavendish and the western portion of the National Park covers some of PEI's prettiest scenery – take Hwy 2 west from the capital and, after about 23km, turn north along Hwy 13 at Hunter River. This country road wends over hill and dale and then threads through the tiny settlement of **NEW GLASGOW**, whose matching pair of black and white clapboard churches sit on opposite sides of an arm of Rustico Bay. In the centre of the village, the Prince Edward Island Preserve Company (☎902/964-4300; June–Oct) is a great place to buy local jams, mustards and maple syrups, and the attached **café** serves first-rate breakfasts, lunches and – in the summer – evening meals: try the Atlantic salmon. There are **lobster suppers** available in the village too, at *New Glasgow Lobster Suppers*, on Hwy 258 (June to early Oct daily 4–8.30pm; reservations ☎902/964-2870), though those at the church of **SAINT ANN**, a neighbouring hamlet about 5km west of New Glasgow along Hwy 224 – follow the signs – are generally considered better (June–Oct Mon–Sat 4–9pm; reservations ☎902/621-0635). At both, reckon a 500g (1lb) lobster in its shell will set you back about $30.

Northwest from New Glasgow, clumped around the junction of Hwy 6 and Hwy 13, is **CAVENDISH**, an inconsequential village little more than a stone's throw from the park's long sandy beaches. However, the busloads of visitors who descend on the place are mostly headed for **Green Gables House** (daily: May to late June, late Aug to Oct 9am–5pm; late June to late Aug 9am–8pm; $5.75), situated in a dell just 500m west of the crossroads. Part of a tourist complex, with a gift shop and visitor centre, the two-storey timber Green Gables House was once occupied by the cousins of Lucy Maud Montgomery, one of Canada's best-selling authors. In 1876, when Montgomery was just two years old, her mother died and her father migrated to Saskatchewan, leaving her in the care of her grandparents in Cavendish. Here she developed a deep love for her native island and its people and, although she spent the last half of her life in Ontario, PEI remained the main inspiration for her work. Completed in 1905 and published three years later, *Anne of Green Gables* was her most popular book, a tear-jerking tale of a red-haired, pigtailed orphan girl that Mark Twain dubbed "the sweetest creation of child life ever written". As for the house itself, the mildly diverting period bedrooms and living rooms – supposedly the setting for *Anne* – are worth a quick look, though you may think twice when you see the crowded car park. Surprisingly, many of the tourists are Japanese: the book has been on school curricula there since the 1950s and remains extremely popular. If you decide **to stay** in Cavendish, go for *Shining Waters Country Inn & Cottages* (☎902/963-2251 or 1-877/963-2251, ⓦ www.peisland.com/shiningwaters; ❸; May–Oct), 200m north of the crossroads on the way to the park. They have rooms in the old inn, a pleasant, homely structure with a wide veranda, as well as in a motel-style annexe and a string of modern chalets. The petrol station at the crossroads rents out **bikes**.

The Cavendish crossroads is about 600m from the national park's **Cavendish beach** and **campsite**. From here, the park's coastal byroad travels east, sticking close to the beach and its swelling dunes on the way to the scrawny fishing port of **NORTH RUSTICO**, the home of the *Fisherman's Wharf Restaurant* (☎902/963-2669; mid-May to mid-Oct), another good place to sample the island's lobsters. Beyond the port, Hwy 6 leaves the park, slipping round the peaceful waters of Rustico Bay on its way to meet – after 15km – Hwy 15 from Charlottetown (see p.454).

West of Cavendish

West of Cavendish, Hwy 6 passes through the most commercialized part of the island, an unappealing tourist strip stretching as far as **New London**. Here, Hwy 20 branches north along the coast and you'll soon see signs to PEI's most bizarre sight, the large-scale reproductions of famous British buildings that make up **Woodleigh** (daily: June & Sept to mid-Oct 9am–5pm; July & Aug 9am–7pm; $10). Built by a certain Colonel Johnston, who developed an obsessional interest in his ancestral home in Scotland, it features models of such edifices as the Tower of London, York Minster and Anne Hathaway's cottage. Some of the structures are even big enough to enter and their interiors have been painstakingly re-created, right down to the Crown Jewels in the Tower.

The deep inlet of Charlottetown harbour splits the southern reaches of Queens County into west and east. In the west, the **Confederation Bridge** has become a major attraction in its own right and the tourist facilities of the adjoining Gateway Village take a stab at introducing visitors to the island. Elsewhere, **Port-La-Joye/Fort Amherst National Historic Site** (mid-June to Aug daily 9am–5pm; $2.50), perched on an isolated promontory across the bay from Charlottetown, marks the spot where the Acadians established their island headquarters, Port-La-Joye, in 1720. The British subsequently built Fort Amherst here, but all that survives today is a scattering of grass-covered earthworks. Much more diverting is the old seaport of **VICTORIA**, overlooking the Northumberland Strait about 30km west of Charlottetown. There's nothing remarkable among its gridiron of nineteenth-century timber houses, but it's a pretty spot and a relaxing place to while away a couple of hours. Victoria also has an attractive old **hotel**, the *Orient* (☎902/658-2503 or 1-800/565-6743, Ⓦwww.theorienthotel.com; ❹; June–Sept), and is home to the Victoria Playhouse (☎902/658-2025 or 1-800/925-2025, Ⓦwww.victoriaplayhouse .com), where a good range of modern **plays** and musical evenings are performed from July through to September. There are several places to **eat**, the pick of the bunch being the *Landmark Café,* near the playhouse in the centre of the village, where they serve excellent and moderately priced home-made meals.

Some 30km east of Charlottetown just off the Trans-Canada Highway lies the delightfully rustic **Orwell Corner Historic Village** (late May to June Mon–Fri 9am–5pm; late June to Aug daily 9am–5pm; Sept to early Oct Tues–Sun 9am–5pm; early to mid-Oct Mon-Fri 10am-3pm; $5), which was originally settled by Scottish and Irish pioneers in the early nineteenth century. At first, the village prospered as an agricultural centre, but by the 1890s it was undermined by the expansion of Charlottetown and mass emigrations to the mainland. Orwell was finally abandoned in the 1950s, but the historic graveyard and a handful of buildings remained, principally the main farmhouse-cum-post-office-cum-general-store, the schoolhouse and the church. In recent years, these have been restored and supplemented by replicas of some of the early buildings, like the blacksmith's shop, barns and shingle mill. What's more, the interiors give a particularly authentic flavour of Orwell's rusticated past, from the farmhouse's darkened, cluttered living rooms and the austerity of the Presbyterian church to the cheeky graffiti carved into the schoolhouse desks. In addition, the gardens are splendidly maintained in period style, farm animals root around purposefully, and the village hosts a wide variety of special events – ploughing contests, ceilidhs and so forth.

Close by – just 1.4km further up the same side road as the village – is the **Sir Andrew MacPhail Homestead** (daily: late June & Sept 10am–5pm; July & Aug 10am–8pm; donation). This features MacPhail's farmhouse, a comfortable nineteenth-century building whose period furnishings and fittings have a real sense of Victorian gentility, albeit in what was then the backcountry. It was from here that MacPhail (1864–1938) ran his farm, dabbled in medical research, and wrote as a journalist, banging on about the decline of the hierarchical, rural society he (as a Tory) loved. The veranda accommodates a pleasant **tearoom** (☎902/651-2789), where they serve dinner in the evenings from June to September, except on Saturdays; advance reservations are recommended. Bordered by the Orwell River, the homestead's woods and meadows offer several nature trails; details at the farmhouse.

Kings County

Just 600m beyond the Orwell/MacPhail turning, **Hwy 210** branches off the Trans-Canada to snake its way east across the rich farmland bordering the Montague River en route to the little town of Montague. From here, Hwy 4 – **Kings County**'s principal north–south road – leads the 40km or so to PEI's northeast corner, where **SOURIS**, curving round the shore of Colville Bay, has a busy fishing port and harbour with a regular ferry service to the Magdalens (Îles-de-la-Madeleine; see p.334). The docks are a few hundred metres north of the scrabble of older houses that passes for the centre, and the stretch of shoreline between the two is the most elegant part of town. Here you'll find a sequence of Victorian mansions that includes the excellent *Matthew House Inn B&B*, 15 Breakwater Street (☎902/687-3461, ⓦwww.matthewhouseinn.com; ❻; mid-June to mid-Sept), which has six attractive guest rooms. Alternatively, the nearby *Dockside B&B* (☎902/687-2829 or 1-877/687-2829, ⓦwww.bbcanada.com/4010.html; ❷; mid-June to mid-Oct) is a more economical option, occupying a 1960s house of expansive, open design with views out across the ferry terminal and ocean; there are four guest rooms here, two en suite.

The **Basin Head Fisheries Museum** (mid- to late June & most of Sept Mon–Fri 10am–3pm; July & Aug daily 10am–6pm; $4), a 13km drive up the coast from Souris, has a lovely setting, lodged on a headland overlooking a wedge of sandy beach which is, in turn, trapped between the sea, the dunes and a narrow stream that drains an elongated lagoon. Too isolated and barren for any settlement, Basin Head was never more than a fishermen's outpost, and the museum details the lives of these men with displays of equipment, photographs of boats and miniature dioramas showing the fishing techniques they employed. However, it's the setting that really appeals and several timber huts have been built here to provide shelter, picnic and changing facilities, erected alongside the original timber cannery building.

From here, it's possible to drive right round the island's northeast corner along Hwy 16 but, with the possible exception of the mid-nineteenth-century lighthouse at **East Point**, there's nothing much to see.

Prince County

Some 50km west of Charlottetown, Hwy 2 crosses the **Prince County** boundary, from where it's another 10km to **SUMMERSIDE**, PEI's second largest settlement, a sprawling and uninspiring bayside city of fifteen thousand people that was once the island's main port. If you're in town, pop into the curious **International Fox Museum and Hall of Fame**, a couple of blocks from the harbourfront at 286 Fitzroy St (June–Sept Mon–Sat 9am–6pm; donation). This traces the history of the island's fox-ranching industry from its beginnings in 1894 to its heyday in the 1920s, when fox-fur collars reached the height of their popularity in the cities of Europe and the US. There are potted biographies of the leading fox-ranchers, some of whom grew extremely rich from the furs of the silver fox, a rare variety of the common red fox, whose pelts reached astronomical values – up to $35,000 each. At one time, indeed, fox pelts became PEI's leading export.

Heading west from Summerside, it's a few minutes' drive along Hwy 2 to **MISCOUCHE**, where the **Acadian Museum** (July & Aug daily 9.30am–7pm; rest of year Mon–Fri 9.30am–5pm, Sun 1–4pm; $3) is devoted to the island's French-speaking community. Miscouche was the site of the second Acadian Convention in 1884, when the assembled representatives boldly chose their own flag – the French tricolour with a gold star, the *Stella Marae* ("Star of Mary"), inserted onto the blue stripe. The museum's exhibits are, however, rather paltry, no more than a series of modest displays outlining Acadian history from pioneer days and deportation through to today, though the interesting 15-minute video partly saves the day. There are around 17,000 Acadians on PEI, of whom only 7000 speak French as their first language, a state of linguistic affairs that has made Acadian community leaders apprehensive of the future. The museum aims to support the Acadian identity and houses an Acadian Research Centre, complete with a library and extensive archives.

Continuing west, the headland south of the village of **WELLINGTON** is a centre of Acadian settlement, but it doesn't look any different from the surrounding districts until you reach **MONT-CARMEL**. This tiny coastal village is dominated by the hulking red-brick mass and mighty spires of the **Église Notre-Dame**, whose fantastically ugly appearance is made bizarre by a series of peculiarly sentimental statues and statuettes dotted around the entrance.

Malpeque Bay to West Point

After the church, there's nothing else of any real interest around here, and it's a time-consuming drive north before you leave the flattened farmland of this part of Prince County for the slightly hillier scenery along the west shore of **Malpeque Bay**. The bay's reedy waters were once fringed by tiny shipbuilding yards and the scant remains of one of them have been conserved as part of the **Green Park Shipbuilding Museum** (June–Sept daily 9am–5pm; $5). The museum also incorporates an interpretive centre, focusing on PEI's shipbuilding industry, and the **James Yeo house**. The most successful of the island's shipbuilders, the Yeos, the descendants of Cornish immigrants, maintained close contacts with their Cornish relatives and the two branches of the family combined to develop a prosperous transatlantic shipping business. Some of the proceeds were spent on the Yeo House, whose slender gables and mini-tower date from the 1860s. The interior, with its fetching Victorian furnishings and fittings, is a real delight: look out for the beautiful wax fruit in the parlour.

There's no strong reason to hang around once you've visited the museum, but there is a bayshore **campsite** in the Green Park Provincial Park next door (☏902/831-7912; June to late Sept). Furthermore, the minuscule village of **TYNE VALLEY**, 4km away, is home to the pleasant *Doctor's Inn B&B* (☏902/831-3057, ⓦ www.peisland.com/doctorsinn; ❸), which occupies a big old house and has just a couple of guest rooms. The owners run the adjoining two-acre organic garden, whose produce is well known hereabouts, and you can have dinner at the inn providing you make an advance booking.

It's about 70km from Green Park to the southwest corner of the island – via highways 2 and 14 – where the remote and windswept **West Point Lighthouse** (early June to late Sept daily 8am–8pm) holds a small collection of photographs and memorabilia portraying the lives of the lighthouse keepers. One room in the lighthouse and eight more in the adjoining building, all en suite and decorated in cheery modern style, comprise the *West Point Lighthouse Inn* (☏902/859-3605 or 1-800/764-6854, ⓦ www .westpointlighthouse.com; ❹; late May to Sept), which makes the most of a great seaside location, overlooking a long sandy beach. The lighthouse is surrounded by the **Cedar Dunes Provincial Park**, which has a **campsite** about 500m down the coast (☏902/859-8785; mid-June to early Sept).

Travel details

Trains

*Information from VIA Rail ☎ 1-888/VIA-RAIL,
🌐 www.viarail.ca.*
Halifax to: Moncton (1–2 daily except Tues; 4hr
20min); Montréal (1–2 daily except Tues; 19hr);
Truro (1–2 daily except Tues; 1hr 30min).
Moncton to: Halifax (1–2 daily except Tues; 4hr
20min); Montréal (1–2 daily except Tues; 14hr).

Buses

*The bus services listed below are all provided by
Acadian Lines (☎ 1-800/567-5151, 🌐 www
.acadianbus.com) with the exception of the bus
from Halifax to Yarmouth along the southwest
shore, which is operated by DRL Coachlines
(☎ 1-877/450-1987, 🌐 www.drlgroup.com
/coachlines). Not all the services listed here are
direct, some involve changing.*
Charlottetown to: Fredericton (2 daily; 6hr); Halifax
(2 daily; 7hr); Moncton (2–3 daily; 3hr); Saint John
(2–3 daily; 5hr 30min); Sydney (1 daily; 19hr).
Edmundston to: Fredericton (3 daily; 3hr 30min);
Québec City (3 daily; 4hr); Rivière-du-Loup,
Québec (3 daily; 1hr).
Fredericton to: Charlottetown (2 daily; 6hr);
Edmundston (3 daily; 3hr 30min); Halifax (2 daily;
7hr); Moncton (2 daily; 2hr); Montréal (2 daily;
12hr); Newcastle, Miramichi City (1 daily; 2hr
20min); Saint John (2 daily; 1hr 30min).
Halifax to: Annapolis Royal (1 daily; 3hr 30min);
Charlottetown (2 daily; 7hr); Fredericton (2 daily;
7hr); Liverpool (1 daily; 3hr); Lunenburg (1 daily;
1hr 30min); Moncton (3 daily; 3hr 30min);
Montréal (2 daily; 18hr); Sydney (2 daily; 7hr);
Truro (4 daily; 1hr 30min); Yarmouth via the southwest shore (1 daily; 5hr 30min).
Moncton to: Charlottetown (2–3 daily; 3hr);
Fredericton (2 daily; 2hr); Halifax (3 daily; 3hr
30min); Miramichi City (1 daily; 2hr 20min); St
Andrews (1 daily; 3hr or 5hr); Saint John
(2 daily; 2hr).
Sydney to: Halifax (2 daily; 7hr); North Sydney
(2 daily; 40min); Truro, for New Brunswick and PEI
(2 daily; 5hr 30min).
Yarmouth to: Chester (1 daily; 4hr 30min);
Halifax via the southwest shore (1 daily; 5hr
30min); Liverpool (1 daily; 2hr 45min); Lunenburg
(1 daily; 4hr).

Boats

Ferries

Caribou, NS: to Wood Islands, PEI (May to late
December 4–9 daily; 1hr 15min) with Bay Ferries
☎ 1-888/249-7245, 🌐 www.nfl-bay.com.
Digby, NS to: Saint John, NB (1–3 daily; 3hr)
with Bay Ferries ☎ 1-888/249-7245,
🌐 www.nfl-bay.com.
North Sydney, NS to: Channel-Port aux
Basques, NF (2–4 daily; 5–6hr or 6–8hr) and
Argentia, NF (late June to mid-Sept 3 weekly,
late Sept 1 weekly; 14–15hr) with Marine
Atlantic ☎ 1-800/341-7981; 🌐 www
.marine-atlantic.ca.
Saint John, NB to: Digby, NS (1–3 daily; 3hr)
with Bay Ferries ☎ 1-888/249-7245, 🌐 www
.nfl-bay.com.
Souris, PEI to: Cap-aux-Meules, on the Magdalen
Islands, in Québec (Feb & March no ferries;
summer & autumn 6–10 weekly; winter 3–5
weekly; 5hr) with CTMA ☎ 1-888/986-3278,
🌐 www.ilesdelamadeleine.com/ctma.
Wood Islands, PEI to: Caribou, NS (May
to late December 4–9 daily; 1hr 15min) with
Bay Ferries ☎ 1-888/249-7245, 🌐 www
.nfl-bay.com.
Yarmouth, NS to: Portland, Maine (May to mid-Oct
1 daily; 11hr) with Scotia Prince ☎ 1-866/229-
2597, 🌐 www.scotiaprince.com.

Catamarans

Yarmouth, NS to: Bar Harbor, Maine (mid-May to
mid-Oct 1–2 daily; 3hr) with Bay Ferries
☎ 1-888/249-7245, 🌐 www.catferry.com.

Flights

Charlottetown to: Halifax (8 daily; 35min);
Montréal (5 daily; 1hr 40min); St John's, NF (5
daily; 3hr 30min); Toronto (4 daily; 2hr).
Fredericton to: Halifax (3 daily; 1hr 20min);
Montréal (2 daily; 45min); St John's, NF (3 daily;
3hr 30min); Toronto (4 daily; 2hr).
Halifax to: Charlottetown (8 daily; 35min);
Fredericton (3 daily; 1hr 20min); Montréal (3 daily;
1hr 40min); St John's, NF (5 daily; 2hr); Toronto
(7 daily; 2hr 20min).
Sydney to: St-Pierre (1–3 weekly; 45min).

Newfoundland and Labrador

CHAPTER 4 # Highlights

* **St John's** This lively port, with its fine coastal setting and bustling nightlife, provides the best introduction to Newfoundland life. **See p.475**

* **Witless Bay sea-bird reserve** Puffins galore as well as thousands of other sea birds gather here from May to October. **See p.489**

* **Trinity** The best-looking village in Newfoundland, its handsome clapboard houses and white picket fences sitting pretty by the bay. **See p.498**

* **Gros Morne National Park** Some of the wildest scenery in eastern Canada, a wonderful mix of plunging fjords and rearing mountains. **See p.505**

* **L'Anse aux Meadows** The Vikings reached North America long before Columbus and the archeological evidence is here to prove it. **See p.508**

* **Red Bay** Once the world's largest whaling port, now a historic highlight of the southern Labrador coast. **See p.517**

* **The Northern Ranger** Summer-only steamship dodging icebergs on a route up the north Labrador coast, offering superb whale-watching. **See p.522**

△ Trinity, NL

Newfoundland and Labrador

I n 1840 an American clergyman named Robert Lowell described **Newfoundland** as "A monstrous mass of rock and gravel, almost without soil, like a strange thing from the bottom of the deep, lifted up, suddenly, into sunshine and storm", an apt evocation of this fearsomely beautiful island, which is still referred to – by Newfoundlanders and mainlanders alike – as "The Rock". The island's distant position between the Atlantic Ocean and the Gulf of St Lawrence has fostered a distinctive culture, distinguished by a close sense of community and a remarkable **dialect**, in essence an eclectic and versatile mix of old Irish and English. The dialect developed because the outports – the ancient fishing settlements that were home to the first Europeans – could originally be reached only by boat; today almost all are connected to the skein of side roads that plug into the principal highway, the Trans-Canada. This sweeps 900km from the southwest corner of the island to the Avalon Peninsula, where St John's, the capital of the province (officially entitled "Newfoundland and Labrador") and its largest settlement, sits on the northeast shore.

Ferries from North Sydney in Nova Scotia plough across the turbulent waters of the Atlantic, bound for Channel-Port aux Basques in the southwest and Argentia much further to the east on the Avalon Peninsula, but most visitors fly straight to **St John's**, which provides the best introduction to island life, not least for its museums, good restaurants, bars and flourishing folk music scene. The city is also within easy striking distance of the **Witless Bay seabird reserve**, the twin lighthouses of **Cape Spear** and the **East Coast Trail**, which runs for several hundred kilometres from Topsail to Trepassey, providing opportunities for everything from a short ramble to a full-scale expedition.

Information and time zones

Newfoundland and Labrador Tourism ☎1-800/563-6353, ⊛www.gov.nl .ca/tourism. All of Newfoundland, as well as the Labrador coastal communities south of Cartwright (from L'Anse au Claire to Batteau Harbour), is on **Newfoundland time**. However, most of Labrador (Cartwright itself, plus Happy Valley-Goose Bay, Labrador City and elsewhere), as well as the Maritime Provinces, is on **Atlantic time**, half-an-hour behind Newfoundland time.

4

0   300 km

N

Ungava Bay

Torngat Mts

Hebron

ATLANTIC OCEAN

George River

NEWFOUNDLAND

Labrador Sea

Nain

Hopedale

Cape Harrison

Schefferville

Rigolet

LABRADOR

Cartwright

& LABRADOR

Happy Valley-Goose Bay

MEALY MOUNTAINS

▲ *Baie-Comeau, Québec*

Labrador City

Churchill Falls

500

Churchill River

389

Red Bay

L'Anse aux Meadows

Petit Mecatina

Blanc-Sablon

Strait of Belle Isle

St Anthony

Moisie

QUÉBEC

▲ *Baie-Comeau, Québec*

La Romaine

Havre-St-Pierre

Natashquan

GROS MORNE NATIONAL PARK

Sept-Îles

Aby Island

Île d'Anticosti

Deer Lake

Gander

Bonavista Peninsula

▲ *Baie-Comeau, Québec*

St Lawrence River

Corner Brook

Trinity

St John's

Gaspé Peninsula

Gulf of St Lawrence

Newfoundland

Argentia

Avalon Peninsula

Channel-Port aux Basques

Grand Bank

St-Pierre et Miquelon (France)

Burin Peninsula

Îles-de-la-Madeleine

▼ *North Sydney*

Neither do Newfoundland's attractions end on the Avalon – far from it. Tiny **Trinity**, on the Bonavista Peninsula, is perhaps the most beguiling of the outports, though **Twillingate** comes a close second, while **Gros Morne National Park**, in the west, features wondrous mountains and glacier-gouged lakes. At the far end of the Northern Peninsula are the scant but evocative remains of an eleventh-century Norse colony at **L'Anse aux Meadows**, the only such site in North America, as well as a remarkable hotel in the old light-house on **Quirpon** island. From the southern shore of Newfoundland, it's also a quick ferry ride over to French-speaking **St-Pierre et Miquelon**, a tiny archipelago with a light scattering of fishing villages that is – as an imperial oddity – a *département* of France.

Iron ore mines and hydroelectric schemes drive the **Labrador** economy, but these industrial blemishes are mere pinpricks in the barely explored **wilderness** that defines this part of the province. Unimaginably vast, Labrador boasts some of Canada's highest mountains, wonderful fjords, crashing rivers, a spectacular shoreline with minuscule coastal settlements and a forested hinterland teeming with wildlife. A trip is not something to be undertaken lightly, but its intimidating landscapes match anything in Canada's far north – recommendation indeed. The biggest hydro scheme in Labrador is at **Churchill Falls**, completed in the 1970s despite being the subject of a bitter dispute between Newfoundland and Québec. Neither side could agree on the allocation of the profits, forcing some surprisingly bellicose exchanges. In one, a Newfoundland senator, a certain Alexander Baird, was roused to declare, "We Newfoundland-Canadians don't want to fight, but, by jingo, if we have to, then I say we have the ships, the money and the men", to which Québecois senator Maurice Bourget added sneeringly – "and the fish".

Newfoundland

The first European settlers on **Newfoundland** – mostly English and Irish – were kept glued to the coast by the inhospitality of the interior and the fertility of the ocean when they founded scores of tiny **outports** in the sixteenth and seventeenth centuries. These remote fishing villages were only linked to each other by boat and were named, in the manner of the times, after geographical features, notable events and even emotional responses – from Tickle Harbour and Cape Race to Heart's Content, Witless Bay and Chance Cove. The new settlers were largely reliant on the codfish of the **Grand Banks**, whose shallow waters, concentrated to the south and east of the island, constituted the richest fishing grounds in the world, though in winter they did hunt **seals** on the pack ice for meat, oil and fur. It was a singularly harsh life, prey to vicious storms, dense fogs and the whims of the barter system operated by the island's merchants, who exercised total control of the trade price of fish until as late as the 1940s in some areas. The arrival of several thousand servicemen in World War II did much to break down Newfoundland's long-standing isolation, but this was small beer compared with the development of a **road network** in the years that followed. Finally the outports could be reached with ease, providing their inhabitants with opportunities their ancestors could barely have imagined.

Distances within Newfoundland are considerable, so it's worth weighing up itineraries carefully. The weather is also notoriously unreliable, so try not to be too ambitious; the last thing you want to be doing is thrashing across the island through dense fog or blinding rain. The obvious place to start a visit is **St John's**, whose varied attractions could easily fill out two or three days. St John's is also a good base for day-tripping out into the **Avalon Peninsula**, the most populated part of Newfoundland. Pick of the Avalon day trips are **Cape Spear** and **Bay Bulls**, from where there are regular whale-watching boat trips, though the attractive little outport of **Brigus** runs a close third. Here as elsewhere it is, however, the rocky, craggy coast that makes the most lasting impression: the **East Coast Trail**, beginning in St John's, offers endless hiking opportunities. Further afield, but still within a half-day's drive from the capital, is the **Bonavista Peninsula**, where the prime objective is the picture-postcard prettiness of **Trinity**, and the stirring fjords of **Terra Nova National Park**.

QUÉBEC

LABRADOR
Red Bay
Cape
Onion
L' Anse aux Meadows
Strait of Belle Isle
Quirpon
St Anthony
Blanc-
Sablon
St Barbe
St Anthony
Airport

N

Port au Choix

ATLANTIC

OCEAN

GULF OF ST LAWRENCE

430

Northern Peninsula

Western Brooke
Pond
Rocky
Harbour
GROS
MORNE
NATIONAL PARK
Notre
Dame
Bay
Twillingate
Little
Harbour

Norris
Point
Deer
Lake
Lewisporte
Lumsden

Woody
Point

Port au Port
Peninsula
Corner
Brook
Buchans
Grand
Falls-Windsor
Gander
Gambo
Bonavista
Peninsula
Bonavista
Bay

Bonavista

Stephenville

480

TERRA NOVA
NATIONAL PARK
Trinity
Port Rexton

360
New Bonaventure
Trinity Bay

Rose
Blanche
Grand
Bruit
Burgeo
Hermitage
-Sandyville
Terrenceville
Clarenville
Heart's
Content

Harbour
Grace
Conception Bay
St
John's

Channel-Port
aux Basques
South Coast Ferry
François
Harbour Breton

Brigus
Topsail
Cape
Spear
Bay Bulls
EAST COAST
TRAIL

Ramea

Fortune Bay
Marystown
Argentia

Grande
Miquelon
Fortune
Grand Bank
St
Bride's
Placentia
Ferryland
Avalon
Peninsula
Witless
Bay

Langlade

St-Pierre
Burin
Peninsula
Placentia Bay
Cape
St Mary's
Trepassey Cape Race
Cappahayden

ISLAND OF NEWFOUNDLAND

0   100 km

◀ North Sydney, Nova Scotia

▼ North Sydney, Nova Scotia

Thereafter, distances between the island's highlights get much longer. From Clarenville, on the Trans-Canada at the foot of the Bonavista Peninsula, it's 230km south to Fortune and the ferry to the **St-Pierre et Miquelon**; or 250km to the handsomely craggy coastline surrounding **Twillingate**; or 500km to the spectacular scenery of **Gros Morne National Park**; or a whopping 900km to the former Viking colony of **L'Anse aux Meadows** at the tip of the Northern Peninsula.

To get anything like the best from the island you pretty much have to have a **car** as public transport is extremely thin on the ground. There are no trains and only one daily long-distance **bus**, a DRL Coachlines service running the length of the Trans-Canada from Channel-Port aux Basques to St John's. Otherwise, a number of **minibus** companies provide a limited service across much – but certainly not all – of the island (see p.474 for further details).

A brief history of Newfoundland

The Vikings may have settled the island before him, but it was **John Cabot**, sailing in 1497 from the English port of Bristol for Henry VII, who stirred a general interest in Newfoundland when he reported back that "the sea is swarming with fish, which can be taken not only with the net, but in baskets let down with a stone". This was the effective start of the **migratory ship fishery**, with boats sailing out from France and England in the spring and returning in the autumn, an industry that was soon dominated by the merchants of the English West Country, who grew fat on the profits. In the early 1700s the English fishery began to change its modus operandi, moving towards an **offshore bank fishery** based in the harbours of the eastern coast. This encouraged greater permanent settlement, with the British concentrated in St John's and the French around Placentia, their main fishing station since the 1660s. Mirroring the wars of Europe, these rival nationalities fought a series of desultory skirmishes until the **Treaty of Utrecht** finalized matters in 1713. Under its terms, France gave up her claims to the island in return for the right to catch, land and dry fish on the northwest coast, the so-called **French Shore** – an arrangement that lasted until 1904. In 1763 the French also swapped Labrador for St-Pierre et Miquelon.

Meanwhile, in 1729 the British government had introduced a bizarre system whereby the commanders of the naval convoy accompanying the fishing fleet became the temporary **governors** of Newfoundland, even though they returned home in the autumn. Largely left to their own devices, the English and Irish settlers, who numbered about thirty thousand by 1790, spread out along the coasts, massacring the native **Beothuks** who were completely wiped out by the end of the 1820s. A permanent governor was eventually appointed in 1817; the island was recognized as a colony in 1824; and representative, ultimately responsible government followed shortly after.

Struggling through a period of sectarian violence, Protestant English against Catholic Irish, Newfoundlanders decided not to join newly formed Canada in the 1860s, opting instead for self-governing **dominion** status. However, by the 1910s class conflict had replaced religious tension as the dominant theme of island life, reflecting the centralization of the economy in the hands of the bourgeoisie of St John's – a process that impoverished the outports and fuelled the growth of the trade unions. The biggest of these, the **Fishermen's Protective Union**, launched a string of hard-fought campaigns that greatly improved the working conditions of the deep-sea fishermen and sealers. These were steps in the right direction, but Newfoundland's export-oriented economy collapsed during the Great Depression of the 1930s, and the bankrupt dominion turned to Great Britain for help. The British suspended the legislative chamber and replaced it with a London-appointed commission, though in the event the economy was revived not so much by their efforts as by the boom created by World War II when a strategically important Newfoundland was garrisoned by 16,000 American and Canadian servicemen.

After the war, a narrow majority voted in favour of **confederation** with the rest of Canada in a referendum of 1948. It was a close-run thing and the result might well have been different had it not been for the tireless campaigning of **Joe Smallwood** (1900–92), who became Newfoundland's first provincial premier. Smallwood remained in office until 1972, dominating the political landscape, though he was an extremely controversial figure. The root of his popularity was in the outports, where he was seen – with much justification – as the champion of the working man and woman against the merchant middle class of St John's. In this regard, it's certainly true that he tried hard to diversify the island's economy and save his fellow islanders from their over-reliance on the fishery, but the results were very mixed. Some of Smallwood's efforts to attract industry proved successful, but most did not. There were ill-considered social initiatives too, most notoriously a **resettlement programme** in which the government persuaded 28,000 Newfoundlanders to move to designated

Air Canada (☎1-888/247-2262, ⓦwww.aircanada.ca) has flights to St John's from a variety of foreign and domestic destinations, including London (UK) and Halifax, Nova Scotia. **Canjet** (☎1-800/809-7777, ⓦwww.canjet.com) has services to St John's from Halifax, Moncton, Montréal, Ottawa and Toronto, as well as flights to Deer Lake from all of those bar Moncton. Regional carriers include **Air Labrador** (☎709/753-5593, ⓦwww.airlabrador.com), which flies between St John's, St Anthony and Deer Lake and also links St John's with coastal Labrador; **Air St-Pierre** (☎709/726-9700, ⓦwww.airsaintpierre.com), with flights from St John's to St-Pierre, from where there are flights on to Moncton, Halifax, Sydney and Montréal; and **Provincial Airlines** (inside Newfoundland ☎1-800/563-2800, elsewhere ☎709/576-1666, ⓦwww.provair.com), flying from St John's to St Anthony and Labrador destinations including Goose Bay, Blanc Sablon and Churchill Falls.

Marine Atlantic (☎1-800/341-7981, ⓦwww.marine-atlantic.ca) operates two **car ferry** routes to Newfoundland from North Sydney, Nova Scotia (see p.420). The first, **to Channel-Port aux Basques** (2–4 daily), takes between five and six hours (six to eight hours at night). One-way tickets cost $25 for passengers and $72 for a car up to 20 feet. Cabins, which should be reserved in advance, cost $40–50 ($75–90 at night); there are also dormitory bunks for $15. The second car ferry connects North Sydney **to Argentia**, 130km southwest of St John's (late June to mid-Sept 3 weekly, late Sept 1 weekly; 14–15hr). One-way tickets cost $70 for passengers and $146 for a car up to 20 feet. Vehicles must be booked in advance as must cabins, which cost $125; there are also dormitory bunks for $25. Newhook's Transportation (see below) runs minibuses from Argentia to downtown St John's for $25, but be sure to confirm minibus departure details before you set out. Labrador Marine (☎1-866/535-2567, ⓦwww.gov.nl.ca/ferryservices) runs a car ferry from Québec's **Blanc Sablon to St Barbe**, on Newfoundland's Northern Peninsula (May–Nov 1–3 daily; 1hr 30min; $9 one-way, car $18.50).

The only long-distance **bus** on Newfoundland is operated by DRL Coachlines (☎709/738-8088, ⓦwww.drlgroup.com/coachlines), a once-daily service running from Channel-Port aux Basques 900km east to St John's, via the Trans-Canada Highway, stopping at points en route. The one-way fare costs $100 and the whole trip takes 14 hours; be sure to confirm bus tickets and departure details before you set out. Otherwise, a patchy public transport network is provided by a string of **minibus** companies, most of whom are based in St John's. Amongst them, Bonavista Taxi (☎709/536-3044) links St John's with the Bonavista Peninsula; Foote's Taxi (☎1-800/866-1181) connects St John's with Fortune and the St-Pierre ferry; and Newhook's Transportation (☎709/682-4877) goes from the capital to Argentia for the Nova Scotia ferry.

One final word about the **moose**: Newfoundland has thousands of them and they present a real danger to the motorist at dawn and dusk and to a lesser extent at night – so much so that many locals prefer not to drive at these times. The problem is that this large and powerful animal is both drawn to and almost hypnotized by vehicle headlights, but in the event of a collision cars typically knock the moose's legs away – leaving the animal's body to come barrelling through the windscreen directly at you.

"growth centres", thereby abandoning over 300 of the smaller outports. The scheme began in 1954 and finally fizzled out in 1975, leaving behind a sorry tale of community dislocation.

In 1977, the Canadian government extended the country's territorial waters to two hundred nautical miles, partly to restrict access to its fishing grounds and partly as a prelude to large-scale investment in eastern Canada's **offshore**

fishery. At first, it worked a treat – catches increased and so did the number of Newfoundlanders involved in the fishery – but within a decade fish stocks were down and there were dire warnings about the future of the entire cod fishery. The crisis came to a head in 1992 when a **moratorium** on most cod fishing was imposed; it remains in place today, and was widened in scope as recently as 2003. Newfoundland was hit terribly hard and there were bitter recriminations. Some thought the demise of the cod was brought about by foreign deep-sea trawlers, others blamed the burgeoning seal population, some scientists put it down to a change in sea temperature and some islanders denied there was a problem at all, pointing out that cod had always been prone to appear and disappear. Whatever the truth – and Mark Kurlansky's book *Cod* convincingly points the finger of blame at the development of Canada's off-shore fishery after 1977 – the moratorium put 30,000 Newfoundlanders out of work. The federal government dispensed $26 billion in aid over the ensuing decade, but many islanders decided to **emigrate**: in the years from 1994 to 2001, Newfoundland's population dropped by sixty thousand (to 512,000).

Given these problems, many Newfoundlanders regarded Ottawa's preoccupation with Québec's claims to distinct status – the dominant political theme of the 1990s – with a mix of contempt and incredulity. There was, however, some good news: **oil** and **gas** had been discovered in significant quantities southeast of Newfoundland and began to be shipped ashore in 1997. The first half of 2003 saw production of 62 million barrels of oil. The profits seem set to revive the island's economy. And, after the demise of the cod, many of the inshore fishermen have diversified, fishing other species, most profitably snow crab, shrimp and scallops. Newfoundland's future looks rosier now than it has for years and there were smiles all round when it was revealed that between 2001 and 2003 the population had started to increase.

St John's

For centuries life in **ST JOHN'S** has focused on its harbour, a dramatic jaw-shaped inlet approached through the 200-metre-wide channel of **The Narrows**. In its salad days, the port was packed with sailing ships from a score of nations and still today, although traffic is not as brisk, it draws a mixed maritime bag of trawlers, container ships and oil construction barges. St John's is not, however, the tempestuous seaport of yesteryear. It still possesses a boisterous nightlife, no mistake, but the rough houses of the waterfront have been replaced by shops and offices and its inhabitants – of whom there are about 170,000 – are less likely to be seafarers than white-collar workers. These squirrel away in a string of downtown skyscrapers and in the Confederation Building, the huge government complex on the western outskirts, far – in Newfoundland terms – from the swell of the sea. Yet although the city's gravity has moved inland, the waterfront remains the social hub, sprinkled with good **restaurants** and lively **bars** that feature the pick of Newfoundland **folk music** – one good reason for visiting in itself.

Devastating fires in the nineteenth century and developers in the twentieth have taken their toll on the fine old buildings of St John's, but much has survived, most notably the grand Catholic **Basilica of St John the Baptist**, the handsomely proportioned **Colonial Building** and the imposing **Courthouse**. Nonetheless, it's the overall appearance of the centre that pleases most, its higgledy-piggledy mix of the old and new clambering up the hillside

Quidi Vidi ▲ ⓚ , Signal Hill & Johnson ▲ Geo Channel

▲ A, B, C. A. Pippy Park & Memorial University (MUN) ▲ Airport

▶ The Narrows

St John's Harbour

ST JOHN'S

Government House

Commissariat House

St Thomas

Colonial Building

Bannerman Park

Basilica of St John the Baptist

Masonic Temple

St John the Baptist Cathedral

Tête de Pommes

War Memorial

Fred's

LSPU Hall

Former City Museum

Court House

O'Brien's Music Store

City Hall

Newhook's Transportation

Boat Trips

Harbourside Park

CAVENDISH SQUARE

ACCOMMODATION

At Wit's Inn	K	Oh What a View	H
Banberry House B&B	B	Pippy Park Campground	D
Bonne Esperance House	E	Prescott Inn B&B	G
Delta St John's Hotel	J	Harbourview	L
Fairmont Newfoundland Hotel	F	The Roses B&B	I
MUN Student Rooms	C	Winterholm Heritage Inn	A

RESTAURANTS, BARS & CAFÉS

Aqua Restaurant	14
Auntie Crae's Food Shop	12
Chucky's Fish n' Ships	3
Classic Café	5
Crooked Crab Café	4
Duck Street Bistro	2
Duke of Duckworth Pub	7
Erin's Pub	8
Fat Cat Blues Bar	13
Gypsy Tea Room	16
Hava Java	11
Hungry Fisherman	17
Leo's Restaurant & Take-Out	1
O'Reilly's	15
Rose & Thistle	9
The Ship	6
Zone 216	10

0 ___ 250 m

to the brightly painted clapboard houses that are the hallmark of the older residential districts with **Gower Street** being a prime example. Beside the basilica are **The Rooms**, the brand new and lavish home for the province's excellent art and historical collections, and no visit to the city would be complete without a jaunt up **Signal Hill**, overlooking The Narrows and offering fabulous views over city and ocean. St John's is also the starting point of the **East Coast Trail**, a hiker's trail that threads its way along the rugged coastline of the Avalon Peninsula for 220km – with more to follow – and a short drive from the bare and windswept **Cape Spear**, the continent's most easterly point. The other obvious excursion from the capital is to **Bay Bulls**, from where boat trips sail out to inspect the sea-bird colonies of the offshore **Witless Bay Ecological Reserve**.

Arrival, information and transport

St John's **airport** is about 6km northwest of the city centre. There's a handy **tourist information desk** (open year round) inside the terminal building – in Arrivals – and this is a good place to pick up the comprehensive, annually updated and free *Newfoundland & Labrador Travel Guide* which covers all the leading attractions, festivals, outdoor pursuits and accommodation. The desk also provides a free provincial road **map**, which is good enough for most purposes, though if you're intending to do a lot of driving it's useful to have a second source. Rand McNally currently publishes the best provincial road map (1:895,000) on the market, whilst MapArt do the clearest map of St John's – as an inset in their 1:1,000,000 Newfoundland map; both, however, can be hard to find in the city – gas stations are the most likely stockists. There's no public transport from the airport to the city centre, but the **taxi** fare is only around $17.

St John's has no train service and, rather surprisingly, no **bus station**: Newhook's Transportation minibuses, arriving from the Argentia ferry (see p.474), pull in outside their downtown office at 13 Queen Street. Arriving on the DRL Coachlines bus from Channel-Port aux Basques and points along the Trans-Canada Highway is a pain: their buses don't stop in the city centre and the nearest you'll get is the Student Centre on the Memorial University of Newfoundland (MUN) campus, about 3km west of downtown. To get to the city centre from there, either take a taxi or local Metrobus #3 (every 20min; 15min).

The **city tourist office** (Mon–Fri 9am–4.30pm; ☎709/576-8106, ⓦwww.stjohns.ca) is in the City Hall annex, on the east side of New Gower Street. Amongst all sorts of material, they issue free city and provincial maps as well as the official *Newfoundland & Labrador Travel Guide* mentioned above.

The best way to explore St John's is on **foot**, but for the more outlying attractions you might want to catch a bus. These are operated by **Metrobus** (☎709/722-9400, ⓦwww.metrobus.com), which has a dozen or so routes serving most parts of the city. Services are frequent Monday through Saturday, infrequent on Sundays. A standard single **fare** costs $1.75, a ten-ride pass $15.75; tickets are from the driver, exact fare only. Bus timetables can be picked up from the foyer of City Hall, on New Gower Street.

Tours

St John's does a good line in **guided tours**, everything from a quick gambol round the city's principal sights by bus through to organized walks and sea cruises. Amongst the many land-based options, one of the most enjoyable is the gossipy one- to one-and-a-half-hour tour of downtown offered by **Heritage Walking Tours** (July & Aug 3 weekly; $10; ℡709/726-7056). Another excellent choice is **St John's Haunted Hike** (5 weekly; $5; ℡709/685-3444, ⓦ www.hauntedhike.com), who arrange intriguingly spooky walking tours delving into the city's dishevelled past. Alternatively, **Legend Tours** (reservations ℡709/753-1497, information ℡709/753-1498) provides two-hour bus trips round the city centre, Signal Hill and Quidi Vidi for $32 and a three-hour tour covering pretty much the same ground plus Cape Spear for $42; they operate all year, weather permitting.

Summer produces a whole fleet of **boat trips** promising whales, icebergs, sea birds and dramatic coastal scenery – or different permutations of these depending on the month. The boats line up along the harbourfront to either side of the foot of Beck's Cove with two- to three-hour excursions costing in the region of $30. **Scademia Adventure Tours** (℡709/726-5000, ⓦ www.nfld.com/scademia) are slightly more expensive, but they sail out to Cape Spear on the *Scademia*, a refurbished two-masted schooner.

Accommodation

As you might expect of a provincial capital, St John's has a healthy supply of downtown **hotels**, but – with one or two notable exceptions – its **B&Bs** are rather more distinctive, the pick of them occupying fine Victorian houses. For those on a tighter budget, there are several chain **motels** (❷–❸) along Kenmount Road, one of the main approach roads running south into the city from the Trans-Canada, and a **campsite** within easy striking distance of the centre, though camping is something of an acquired taste, given the climate.

Hotels and inns

Delta St John's Hotel & Conference Centre 120 New Gower St ℡709/739-6404 or 1-800/268-1133 ⓦ www.deltahotels.com. St John's does not have many tower blocks, but this is one, built to house a smart chain hotel with nearly 300 rooms and first-rate facilities. Expense-account sort of place. ❽

Fairmont Newfoundland Hotel 115 Cavendish Square ℡709/726-4980 ⓦ www.fairmont.com. The exterior of this chain hotel is all modern clunkiness, but the interior has a real sense of itself as befits the city's most famous hotel, whose earliest incarnation dates back to 1926. All the rooms are kitted out in top-whack chain style and most have great views over the harbour in general and The Narrows in particular. Indoor pool, fitness facilities and free 24hr Internet access. Convenient location at the northern end of Duckworth St. Weekend and off-season discounts of up to thirty percent. ❼

Quality Hotel Harbourview 2 Hill O'Chips ℡709/754-7788 or 1-800/228-5151, ⓦ www.choicehotels.ca. Great address and great location – right by the waterfront – but otherwise no surprises at this standard-issue, modern chain. ❺

Winterholme Heritage Inn 79 Rennie's Mill Rd ℡709/739-7979 or 1-800/599-7829,

ⓦ www.winterholmeheritageinn.com. Eleven splendidly luxurious rooms with all mod cons in a sympathetically renovated and especially handsome Queen Anne revival mansion of 1905. Set in its own grounds facing Bannerman Park and within comfortable walking distance of the centre. ❻

B&Bs

At Wit's Inn 3 Gower St ℡709/739-7420 or 1-877/739-7420 ⓦ www.atwitsinn.ca. Renovated Victorian row house with a handy central location. Four pleasant en-suite guest rooms turned out in attractive, uncluttered style; Internet access too. ❹

Banberry House B&B 116 Military Rd ℡709/579-8006 or 1-877/579-8226 ⓦ www .banberryhouse.com. Four en-suite guest rooms here in this delightful Victorian house of 1892. Each room is attractively decorated, comfortable without being fussy, and the owners have got the atmosphere just right – a perfect mix of friendliness and efficiency. Tasty breakfasts taken either at the main table or, for the more bashful, at a table for two. Highly recommended. ❺

Bonne Esperance House 20 Gower St ℡709/726-3835 or 1-888/726-3835 ⓦ www.wordplay.com/bonne_esperance. Central

B&B in an attractive Victorian terrace. The interior is decked out with antiques and each of the guest rooms, all en suite, is well appointed; good breakfasts as well. ❹

Oh What a View 184 Signal Hill Rd ☏ 709/576-7063. Four unassuming rooms, both en suite and shared facilities, in a modern home, but with views over the city and harbour that fully justify the name. A steep 700m up from the Fairmont Newfoundland Hotel. Open mid-May to mid-Oct only. ❸

Prescott Inn B&B 21 Military Rd ☏ 709/753-7733 or 1-888/263-3786, ⓦ www.prescottinn.nf.ca. Recently refurbished, long-established B&B in a good-looking, double-bayed clapboard house. Has two well-tended double rooms decorated in smart modern style plus four suites. Convenient central location, at the north end of Military Road. ❸

The Roses B&B 9 Military Rd ☏ 709/726-3336 or 1-877/767-3722 ⓦ www.wordplay.com/the_roses. Pleasing conversion of an old house into a four-bedroom B&B. Breakfast is served in the balconied rooftop kitchen, which has harbour views. Downtown location. ❸

Student rooms

Memorial University of Newfoundland (MUN) Off Prince Philip Drive ☏ 709/737-7657, ⓦ www.mun.ca. Student rooms on the MUN campus at Paton College, some 3km west of the centre, are available from May to late August. Paton College is just beyond the main sports field. The rates are $33 per single per night (students $25), doubles $54 ($39).

Campsite

Pippy Park Trailer Park and Campground Nagle's Place, Pippy Park ☏ 709/737-3655, ⓦ www.pippypark.com. Almost 200 sites, both serviced and unserviced, located about 4km west of the city centre, near the Confederation Building. To get there, proceed west along Allandale Rd and Nagle's Place is on the left, just beyond Prince Philip Drive. Clean, accessible washrooms. Convenience store. Open May–Sept.

The City

Running the length of the city centre, **Water Street** has long been the commercial hub of St John's, though the chandlers and tanners, ship suppliers and fish merchants that once clustered here are gone, replaced by an engaging mix of shops, restaurants and bars. Along with neighbouring George Street, this is the centre of the city's nightlife and there's one outstanding building, too – the grand and domineering **Courthouse**. Nearby stand several other imposing old structures, but St John's finest buildings string along **Military Road**, culminating in the gargantuan **Basilica of St John the Baptist** and the catch-all new museum of **The Rooms**. Further afield, the prime objective is **Signal Hill**, not so much for the conspicuous Cabot Tower perched on top but for the panoramic views. With the exception of Signal Hill, which is a fair old hoof out from the centre, all the main downtown attractions are within easy walking distance of each other. Incidentally, the appellation "cove", which is commonplace in the city centre, means a short side street.

Harbourside Park and the War Memorial

Tiny **Harbourside Park**, on Water Street, is the logical place to start a visit to the city for it was here – or at least hereabouts – that Sir Humphry Gilbert landed in 1583 to claim the island for England, thereby kickstarting the British Empire. Quite what the itinerant fishermen who had already been harvesting the Grand Banks for several decades made of the claim and the simple ceremony that accompanied it is unknown, as is the reaction of the Beothuks, if any were unwise enough to be hanging around. Both may have been surprised by some of the things Gilbert packed in his bags – hobby horses and Morris dancing bells "to delight the savage people, whom we intend to winne by all faire means possible". A series of historical plaques in the park gives all the background; behind are two bronze dogs, a Newfoundland and a Labrador. The early settlers were very reliant on their dogs and the Newfoundland breed,

Sealing

The Newfoundland seal hunt has always been dependent on the **harp seal**, a gregarious animal that spends the summer feeding around the shores of Greenland, Baffin Island and northern Hudson Bay. In the autumn they gather in a gigantic herd that surges south ahead of the arctic ice pack, passing the coast of eastern Labrador before dividing into two. One group pushes down the Strait of Belle Isle into the Gulf of St Lawrence to form the **Gulf herd**, the other continues south as far as Newfoundland's northeast coast, where they congregate as the **Front herd**. From the end of February to early March, the seals of the Front herd start to breed, littering the ice with thousands of helpless baby seals or **whitecoats**, as they're known. It's just two or three weeks before the pups begin to moult and their coats turn a shabby white and grey.

From early days, the Front herd provided the people of northeast Newfoundland with fresh meat during the winter, but it was the value of the whitecoats' fur that spawned a clutch of hunting centres – primarily Bonavista, Trinity and Twillingate – and thousands of jobs. In 1853, the seal fleet consisted of 4000 ships manned by 15,000 sailors, who combined to kill no fewer than 685,000 harps. However, in the 1860s **steamers** made the old sailing ships obsolete and provoked a drastic restructuring of the industry. The new vessels were too expensive for the shipowners of the smaller ports and control of the fleet fell into the hands of the wealthy merchants of St John's. By 1870, the bulk of the fleet was based in the capital and hundreds of Newfoundlanders were obliged to travel here for work every winter.

For those "lucky" enough to get a berth, conditions on board were appalling: as a government report noted, a captain could "take as many men as he could squeeze onto his ship... When the seal pelts began to come aboard, the crew had to make way until, by the end of a successful voyage, the men would be sleeping all over the deck, or amongst the skins piled on the deck, even in the most savage weather conditions." All this hardship was endured on a basic diet of "hardtack", hard bread or ship's biscuit, and "switchel", black unsweetened tea, enlivened by the odd plate of "duff", a boiled-up mixture of old flour and water. "Small wonder," as one of the sealers – or **swilers** – recalled, "that most of us learned to eat raw seal meat. The heart, when it was cut out and still warm, was as good as steak to we fellows." There

with its double-layered waterproof coat and webbed feet, was perfect for their requirements, though the Labrador – a cross between a Newfoundland and a Pointer – proved better for hunting.

Across Water Street from the park a short flight of granite steps climbs up to the **War Memorial**, which was unveiled in 1924 in front of a crowd of thousands. The island suffered grievous losses in World War I, especially during the battle of the Somme, but nevertheless the imperial-minded authorities placed the figure of Victory on top and invited Field Marshal Haig to unveil it, the very man whose ineptitude many soldiers blamed for the slaughter. Before the battle Haig wrote "I feel that every step in my plan has been taken with the Divine help" – a monstrous hoot considering the imperial army sustained nearly 60,000 casualties on the first day.

From the Courthouse to Gower Street

From the War Memorial, it's a five- to ten-minute walk south along Water Street to the **Courthouse**, the city's most impressive structure, a monumental Romanesque Revival building of 1901 made of granite and equipped with rounded turrets, a tumble of different gables and a clock tower. Take the steps were two compensations: money and status – as it left for the Front herd the seal fleet was cheered on its way and the men of the first ship back, the **highliner**, dispensed seal flippers, an island delicacy, and got free drinks all round.

In the early 1900s, the wooden-walled steamships were, in their turn, replaced by **steel steamers**. Once again, the traders of St John's invested heavily, but the shrinking seal population reduced their profit margins. Increasingly, they began to cut corners, which threatened the safety of the swilers. The inevitable result was a string of disasters that culminated in 1914 in the loss of the *Southern Cross* with all 173 hands. Shortly afterwards, a further 78 men from the *Newfoundland* died on the ice as a consequence of the reckless greed of one of the captains. These twin catastrophes destroyed the hunt's communal popularity, and a decade later the economics of the industry collapsed during the Great Depression. By 1935 most of the sealing firms of St John's had gone broke.

After World War II sealing was dominated by the ships of Norway and Nova Scotia, with the Newfoundlanders largely confining their activities to an inshore cull of between 20,000 and 40,000 whitecoats per year – enough work for about four thousand people. Thus, sealing remained an important part of the island's bedraggled economy up until the 1960s, when various conservationist groups, spearheaded by **Greenpeace**, started a campaign to have it stopped. Slowly but surely the pressure built up on the Canadian government until it banned all the larger sealing ships and closely restricted the number of juvenile and adult (but not whitecoat) seals the islanders were allowed to kill. This remains the position today.

The **conservationists** have always objected to the cruelty of the cull, and it's certainly true that the killing of a hapless seal is a brutal act. Yet the furore has much to do with the doleful eyes and cuddly body of the baby seal, an anthropomorphism that doesn't wash with an island people whose way of life has been built on the hunting of animals. To add grist to the mill, many islanders are convinced that the decline in fish stocks has everything to do with the increasing number of seals and there are frequent attempts to get the hunting restrictions removed or at least lessened. As a consequence of all this, nothing angers many Newfoundlanders more than the very mention of Greenpeace, whose supporters are caricatured as well-heeled, urban outsiders who have no right to meddle in traditional hunting practices.

that run up beside the Courthouse and at the top, on Duckworth Street, turn right and it's a few metres to the **old city museum**. The main body of the building is sullen red brick, but the facade boasts a coat of arms and three finely cast panels – one each for the island's miners, loggers and fishermen. Opposite, Cathedral Street scuttles up to the **Masonic Temple**, whose cliff-face of a facade looks challengingly across to the bluestone **Anglican Cathedral of St John the Baptist** (mid-June to Sept Mon–Fri 10am–2pm, Sat 11am–noon & Sun 11am–3pm; free) designed in Gothic Revival style by the English architect Sir George Gilbert Scott. Begun in 1847, much of the church burnt down in 1892 but Scott's son rebuilt it to the original plans, though the work was never fully completed. Inside, the stone walls are capped by a handsome vaulted timber ceiling and the stained glass is of exceptionally high quality.

Immediately below the Masonic Temple, wooden stairs climb up to a huddle of old clapboard houses set around a tiny **courtyard** that marks the end of Willcott's Lane. The city once possessed dozens of these little hideaway courtyards and this is one of the very few to have survived. Willcott's Lane leads to **Gower Street**, one of the city's prettiest residential streets, its long line of brightly painted clapboard (or vinyl imitation) houses festooned by a quaint cobweb of power and telephone cables. Some of the houses are the simplest of structures, no more than wooden rectangles with doors set right on the street, but others have bay windows, outside stairways (once a real status symbol) and fancy gingerbread scrollwork – altogether a pleasing variety that leads north to Military Road.

Military Road

From the north end of Gower Street it's a couple of minutes' walk west to the perky dormer windows and pastel-painted clapboard of the **Commissariat House Provincial Historic Site**, on Kings Bridge Road (mid-June to mid-Oct daily 10am–5.30pm; $3). Dating from the early nineteenth century, this comprises the home and offices of the assistant commissary general, who was responsible for keeping the British garrison paid, fed, watered and clothed. The most intriguing rooms are the clerk's office, into which the soldiers entered by a side door to collect their wages, and the small sewing room upstairs, where there are two tiny paintings by Turner. The coach house out at the back completes the ensemble. The British garrison left St John's once and for all in 1871 and the Commissariat House then became the rectory for the adjacent Anglican **Church of St Thomas** (late June to Aug daily 9.30am–5.30pm; free), a wooden structure of 1836 whose sturdy tower and main entrance face onto Military Road. The church's unusual shape – the nave seems unnaturally long with outhouse-like structures tacked onto the side – is no accident: in 1846 a gale moved the whole church six inches and, in a panic, the commander of the garrison had his men add what amounted to stabilizing tail fins.

From the church it's the briefest of walks along **Military Road** to the elegant red sandstone symmetries of **Government House**, which was completed at great expense in 1831 to serve as the residence of the Governor-General the Queen's representative on the island. Initially, the Governor-General had extensive powers, but by the time Newfoundland joined Canada in 1949 the position had become almost entirely ceremonial. Just along the street stands the limestone **Colonial Building**, a perfectly proportioned Neoclassical edifice fronted by a stirringly grand portico. It was here that the island's legislature met in session from 1850 until the 1950s, but despite the serenity of the architecture things could get mighty rough: in 1932 the disgruntled citizenry attacked the place and made a determined if unsuccessful effort to lynch the Prime Minister, one Richard Squires.

Continuing along Military Road, it's only a few minutes to the grandest of the city's churches, the **Catholic Basilica of St John the Baptist** (Mon–Fri 9am–4.30pm, Sat 9am–1.30pm, Sun 9am–noon; free), whose twin-towered limestone and granite mass overlooks the harbour from the crest of a hill. The church was completed in 1855, but there was no ecumenical rejoicing: the church's prominent position irritated the Protestants no end. The facade of the basilica makes a competent attempt to mimic the Romanesque churches of Italy, but the interior is rather better, the stained-glass windows illuminating a delightfully ornate and embossed gold, maroon and deep-green ceiling. Look out also for the ceremonial arch in front of the church, an over-egging of the architectural pudding where the statue of St John the Baptist is blessed with strangely lopsided buttocks.

The Rooms

Across from the basilica, on Bonaventure Avenue, **The Rooms** (mid-June to mid-Oct daily 9am–9pm; mid-Oct to mid-June Tues–Sat 9am–4.45pm, Wed until 9.45pm, Sun noon–4.45pm; ⓦ www.therooms.ca) occupy lavish new

The Beothuks

The Algonquian-speaking **Beothuks**, who reached Newfoundland in about 200 AD, were semi-nomadic, spending the summer on the coast catching fish, seals and sea birds, and moving inland during the winter to hunt caribou, beaver and otter. They were also the first North American natives to be contacted by British explorers, who came to describe them as **"Red Indians"** from their habit of covering themselves with red ochre, perhaps as some sort of fertility ritual or simply to keep the flies off. Initial contacts between the two cultures were quite cordial, but the British soon began to encroach on the Beothuks' ancient hunting grounds, pushing them inland, a process that the Beothuks were unable to resist, partly because they had been stricken by the diseases the Europeans had brought with them.

In the late eighteenth century, British attitudes hardened and the Beothuks were casually slaughtered in a manner summarized by a contemporary observer named Joseph Banks: "The English fire at the Indians whenever they meet them, and if they happen to find their houses or wigwams, they plunder them immediately." With the Beothuks fast disappearing, some white settlers organized expeditions into the interior to catch one or two alive – John Peyton of Twillingate being a case in point (see p.503) – but the last of the tribe, a young woman by the name of **Shanawdithit**, died of tuberculosis aged 29 in 1829. She spent the last years of her life in the protective custody of the attorney general in St John's, and it was here that she built a small model of a Beothuk canoe and made ten simple drawings of her people and their customs. Copies of the drawings will no doubt be on display in The Rooms as a modest memorial to a much-abused people.

premises built to exhibit in one setting the various historical, ethnographic and fine art collections that were previously distributed across the city. The Rooms is scheduled to open in the summer of 2004 and outside in the grounds archeological work is proceeding on the British fort that originally occupied the site. At time of writing, the final layout of the complex has not been decided, but there is bound to be a substantial section on the prehistoric peoples of Newfoundland and Labrador, beginning with the Maritime Archaic Peoples and their successors, the Dorset Inuit and the Beothuks. Inevitably, substantial space will also be allocated to the province's fishermen and the fishery, plus logging and mining. One of the museums being subsumed into The Rooms had a fascinating exhibition on life in the outports at the turn of the twentieth century and this is likely to reappear – in one form or another – too. Many of the outports remained beyond the cash economy right up until the 1940s, and consequently much of their furniture was made from packing cases and driftwood. The old museum had a diverting sample of this furniture, from the brightly painted pieces placed in the average outport kitchen through to the dark-brown stained furniture, sometimes with imitation draws, that were installed in the parlour.

Signal Hill

Rearing up above The Narrows, **Signal Hill National Historic Site** (open access) is a protuberant, grass-covered, lake-studded chunk of rock with views that are dramatic enough to warrant the strenuous half-hour (2km) walk up from the northern end of Duckworth Street – there's no city bus. Originally known as The Lookout, Signal Hill took its present name in the middle of the eighteenth century, when it became common practice for flags to be hoisted here to notify the city of impending arrivals. The signallers would also indicate whose ship or ships were approaching, thereby giving the city's merchants a couple of hours to prepare docking and supplies. The hill was also an obvious line of defence for the garrison of St John's, and the simple fortifications that were first established during the Napoleonic Wars were embellished every time there was a military emergency, right up until World War II.

Signal Hill is bare and treeless, but the road to the top is dotted with a string of attractions, beginning with the flashy **Johnson Geo Centre** (June to mid-Oct Mon–Sat 9.30am–5pm, Sun 1–5pm; mid-Oct to May Tues–Sat 9.30am–5pm, Sun 1–5pm; $6), which is devoted to earth sciences. An introductory film illustrates various natural phenomena and then there's a floor each on the Earth, Newfoundland and Labrador's geology, the Earth's peoples, and the future, including a so-called Stellarium, examining the stars. In addition, side exhibits focus on geothermal heating, the *Titanic* and icebergs, and on oil and gas (the last funded by ExxonMobil).

Moving on, you soon reach Parks Canada's **Signal Hill Visitor Centre** (daily: mid-June to early Sept 8.30am–8pm; mid-Sept to Dec and May to mid-June 8.30am–4.30pm; $3.50 for exhibit), whose well-chosen displays explore the history of the city and the island. Beside the centre is **Gibbet Hill**, where the bodies of hanged criminals were once left to rot as a grisly warning to sailors passing through The Narrows, and just above, further up the road, the antiquated guns of the **Queen's Battery** peer over the entrance to the harbour. The plot of ground beside the battery is used for period military tattoos from the middle of July to the middle of August (call for times ℡709/772-5367) and down below, by the water, is **Chain Rock**, from where a chain used to be dragged across The Narrows in times of danger.

Plonked on top of Signal Hill is **Cabot Tower** (daily: June–Aug 8.30am–9pm; Sept to mid-Oct 9am–7pm; rest of year 9am–5pm; free), a short and stout stone structure built at the end of the nineteenth century to commemorate both John Cabot's landing of 1497 and Queen Victoria's Diamond Jubilee. The tower holds a small display on electronic signalling, and outside in the car park there's a **plaque** honouring Guglielmo Marconi, who confirmed the reception of the first transatlantic radio signal here in December 1901. The views back over the city and out to sea are nothing short of fabulous and a trio of **hiking trails** is outlined on a notice board beside the car park. The shortest is the comfortable 500m stroll back down Signal Hill to the Queen's Battery, another is the wild and windswept trek down the headland to The Narrows and onto Outer Battery Road, by means of which you can return to the city centre.

Quidi Vidi village

Tiny **Quidi Vidi** ("kiddy-viddy"), a couple of kilometres north of the city centre, is a well-known beauty spot, where a handful of old fishing shacks are backdropped by sharp-edged cliffs and set beside the deep-blue waters of a slender inlet. A spate of new construction has robbed the village of much of its charm, but it is home to both **Mallard Cottage Antiques** (May–Oct daily 9am–5pm; March, April & Nov Wed–Sun 9.30am–5pm), in an attractive old building dating from the 1750s, and **Quidi Vidi Brewery**, which occupies the old fish plant. The brewery offers tours and tastings year-round, Monday through Saturday (times and bookings on ℡709/738-4040); look out for their well-regarded "1892 Traditional Ale". From the centre of the village it's a short walk to **Quidi Vidi battery** (mid-June to mid-Oct daily 10am–5.30pm; $3), which overlooks the inlet and the narrow channel that connects it to the sea from the side of a hill. The gun battery has been restored to its 1812 appearance, when it was readied against potential attack from the US.

To get to Quidi Vidi from the city centre, take Forest Road from behind the *Fairmont Newfoundland Hotel* and keep going – or take bus #15 from beside the same hotel. En route, you'll travel the length of **Quidi Vidi Lake**, the site of the annual Royal St John's Regatta, held every August. This is one of the oldest continuing sporting events in North America, featuring fixed-seat rowing races and a huge garden party.

C.A. Pippy Park: the Botanical Gardens and the Fluvarium

C.A. Pippy Park occupies a large chunk of land behind the Memorial University of Newfoundland (MUN), about 3km west of the city centre. It's geared up for a variety of leisure activities with walking trails, picnic areas and playgrounds and it's here you'll also find the **MUN Botanical Gardens** (May–Nov daily 10am–5pm; $2), comprising over a hundred acres of natural habitat and gardens, all set beside Mount Scio Road. The park's other leading attraction is the **Fluvarium** in the ultra-modern Freshwater Resource Centre on Nagle's Place, towards the east end of the park off Allandale Road (April to mid-June Mon–Fri 9am–5pm, Sat & Sun noon–5pm; mid-June to Sept Mon–Fri 9am–5pm, Sat & Sun 10am–5pm; Oct–March Mon–Fri 9am–4.30pm; $5). There are displays here on freshwater ecosystems and the marine life within them, but the star turn is the glass-sided gallery that allows visitors a cross-sectional view of the brook that flows outside the building. Three distinct parts of the stream are clearly visible – a shallow pool, fast-flowing water and a deep pool – and an assortment of eels, trout and salmon swim by. The best time to visit is at **feeding time** at 4pm, the worst after rain, which can make the water murky.

Eating, drinking and entertainment

St John's **café** and **restaurant** scene is very much on the up, with a string of good places dotted round the city centre and a particular concentration down on Water Street. Seafood remains the key ingredient on many menus, but with the exception of fish and chips traditional Newfoundland dishes – most notably cods' tongues (throats), toutons (fried bread dough with molasses) and seal-flipper pie – can be hard to track down.

The city has dozens of **bars** and **pubs** – indeed it's said to have more drinking places per square kilometre than any other city in the country. Most of the more popular joints are on Water and adjoining George streets and they can get mighty crowded (and boisterous) on the weekend. The vast majority are small with no-frills decor, and the pick offer regular live **folk music**, anything from C&W with an idiosyncratic nautical twist to traditional unaccompanied ballads, though Celtic music is very much in vogue at present. If you're content to take pot luck, follow the crowds along George Street, but otherwise either watch for flyers or ask at O'Brien's Music Store, 278 Water St (☏709/753-8135), where you can get a comprehensive list of up-and-coming gigs. Another good contact is the St John's Folk Arts Council, 155 Water St (☏709/576-8508), which organizes regular folk-music concerts and folk dances. The best of the island's dozen folk festivals, the **Newfoundland and Labrador Folk Festival** (☏709/576-8508, ⓌÝwww.sjfac.nf.net), is held in Bannerman Park in St John's on the first weekend in August. Finally, the LSPU Hall, in the centre on Victoria St (☏709/753-4531, Ⓦwww.rca.nf.ca), offers an inventive programme of **theatre** and **cinema**.

Newfoundland folk music

The English and Irish settlers who first colonized Newfoundland brought their music with them: party nights would typically begin with step dances and square sets performed to the accompaniment of the **fiddle** and the **button accordion**, followed by the unaccompanied **singing** of locally composed and "old country" songs. The music was never written down, so as it passed from one generation to the next a distinctive Newfoundland style evolved, whose rhymes and rhythms varied from village to village – though its Irish and English roots always remained pronounced.

Newfoundland's traditional music was in fine fettle until the advent of radio and thousands of soldiers in World War II began to modify and influence many of the island's musicians. Country & western was the key catalyst with, for example, an old story or ballad given a C&W melody and rhythm, the accordion supported by lead and bass guitar and drum. Nonetheless, the traditional style of folk music lingered on, as exemplified by the island's most famous fiddlers, **Rufus Guinchard** and **Émile Benoit**. The two died in the 1980s, but their approach was adopted, albeit in modified form, by younger artists like singer-songwriters Jim Payne and Ron Hynes, musician-producer Kelly Russell and groups such as **Figgy Duff**. At present, Celtic music – mainly Irish – is the big deal in the bars of St John's, but local musicians regularly perform in a more traditional idiom. In particular, look out for **Dermot O'Reilly**, **Phyllis Morrissey** and **Anita Best**, not to mention two of the most popular bands, **Great Big Sea** and the **Irish Descendants**.

St John's has two good specialist record shops – **O'Brien's Music Store**, 278 Water St (☎709/753-8135, ⓦwww.obriens.nf.ca), and **Fred's**, 198 Duckworth St (☎709/753-9191, ⓦwww.freds.nf.ca). **Pigeon Inlet Productions** (☎1-877/738-3435, ⓦwww.tidespoint.com/music) is the label to look for; their website has a detailed catalogue.

Cafés and restaurants

Aqua Restaurant 310 Water St ☎709/576-2782. One of the new breed of restaurants to appear on the island with cool decor and an ambitious menu featuring the likes of chicken with mangoes and a raspberry vinaigrette. Main courses hover around $15.

Auntie Crae's Food Shop 272 Water St. It's worth popping in here for the premises alone – a good old-fashioned general store that has been updated with a minimum of fuss. Selling food is the main event, but there is a small and simple café and they do soups and salads, croissants and muffins plus filled sandwiches to order. Daily 8am–7pm.

Chucky's Fish 'n' Ships 10 King's Rd ☎709/579-7888. Great place serving freshly caught snow crab, as well as mussels, scallops, salmon, caribou and moose to a background of Newfoundland sea shanties. Delicious fish and chips for just $7, most main courses around $15. Be sure to look at the map on the wall pinpointing all the shipwrecks from the 1830s to the present. Highly recommended, but closed Sun.

Classic Café 364 Duckworth St ☎709/726-4444. An atmospheric 24hr diner-cum-café serving traditional Newfoundland main courses and desserts

from $9. The opposite of quiet and romantic late at night.

Crooked Crab Café and Savage Lobster Restaurant 98 Duckworth St ☎709/738-8900. Cosy bistro-restaurant offering a well-considered menu that is strong on seafood. Main courses average $14.

Duck Street Bistro 250 Duckworth St ☎709/753-0400. Smashing little bistro that has long been popular with locals for its well-judged and inventive menu featuring seafood through to meat. Main courses $11–15.

Gypsy Tea Room 195 Water St ☎709/739-4766. Not a tea room at all, but perhaps the best restaurant in town, a lively informal place with a groovy sound track and an amazingly creative menu with a dozen or so specials every day – seafood and grilled meats often Greek in inspiration.

Hava Java 216 Water St. The best coffee in town, plus sandwiches at lunchtimes. A fashionable spot, so the flyers here are likely to give good ideas about what's on and where.

The Hungry Fisherman In the Murray Premises, off Water St ☎709/726-5791. Smart and well-established restaurant that excels in the range of its fish dishes with herring, cod and halibut main courses averaging $19. The Newfoundland

Screech pie – a chocolate mousse cake on a dark crumble crust filled with rum (Screech) – is a highlight.
Leo's Restaurant and Take-Out 27 Freshwater Rd ⊕709/726-2658. Good spot to try some of the local specialities like cods' tongues and, in season, seal-flipper pie, as well as first-rate fish and chips. Closed Sun.

Music bars, pubs and clubs

Duke of Duckworth Pub 325 Duckworth St. Popular bar just down the steps from Duckworth towards Water Street. Serves a wide range of Newfoundland ales and lagers, but its speciality is English pints.
Erin's Pub 186 Water St ⊕709/722-1916. Popular and well-established bar, showcasing the best of folk acts several nights a week.

Fat Cat Blues Bar 5 George St ⊕709/739-5554. Lively spot with live R&B and jazz through to folk on most nights. Good range of beers on draught.
O'Reilly's 15 George St ⊕709/722-3735. Irish pub with Irish booze and a mixed bag of live entertainment including an open mike night once a week.
Rose & Thistle 208 Water St ⊕709/579-6662. Small and long-established pub that pulls in the punters and live bands with folk at the fore.
The Ship Solomon's Lane, at 265 Duckworth St ⊕709/753-3870. Down the steps from Duckworth, this dark, earthy pub showcases an eclectic mix of live music that attracts everyone from grizzled old-timers to arty, black-clad students.
Zone 216 216 Water St. St John's liveliest gay bar. Dark, cramped and sweaty. Thursday through Saturday only. Above *Hava Java* (see above)

Listings

Bike rental Canary Cycles, 294 Water St ⊕709/579-5972.
Bookshops Wordplay, 221 Duckworth St ⊕709/726-9193, has a large range of Newfoundland titles, both new and used. If the island dialect intrigues you, St John's is the place to pick up the substantial *Newfoundland Dictionary* edited by Story, Kirwin and Widdowson – available at any good bookshop.
Buses DRL Coachlines (⊕709/738-8088, ⓦwww.drlgroup.com/coachlines) operates a once daily bus from Channel-Port aux Basques to St John's along the Trans-Canada Highway, with calls at over twenty places on the way. Note that there is currently no DRL downtown bus stop – the nearest is outside the Student Centre on the Memorial University (MUN) campus. Otherwise, an assortment of minibus companies combine to connect St John's with all of the island's larger settlements – see p.474 for more details. One of the larger minibus companies, Newhook's Transportation (⊕709/682-4877), has an office at 13 Queen St.
Camping equipment Outfitters' Adventure Gear, 220 Water St ⊕709/579-4453, ⓦwww.theoutfitters.nf.ca.

Car rental Budget, at the airport ⊕709/747-1234; Discount, 350 Kenmount Rd ⊕709/722-6699; Hertz, at the airport ⊕709/722-4333; National, at the airport ⊕709/722-4307.
Consulates UK ⊕709/579-2002.
Laundry Mighty White's, 152 Duckworth St ⊕709/753-7947, near the *Fairmont Newfoundland Hotel.*
Pharmacy Downtown Pharmacy, 736 Water St ⊕709/576-3004.
Police ⊕709/729-8333.
Post office 354 Water St and Queen (Mon–Fri 8am–5pm).
Shopping Good places to purchase Newfoundland handicrafts, knitwear and jewellery include The Cod Jigger, 245 Duckworth St; Devon House Craft Shop and Gallery, 59 Duckworth St; the Newfoundland Heritage Gift Shop, Murray Premises, Harbour Drive; the Newfoundland Weavery, 177 Water St; and Nonia, 286 Water St.
Taxis Bugden's ⊕709/726-4400; Jiffy Cabs ⊕709/722-2222. There's a rank outside the *Fairmont Newfoundland Hotel.*
Weather Up-to-date bulletins ⊕709/772-5534.

Around St John's

By car, St John's is within easy striking distance of three enjoyable attractions, each of which can occupy half a day. The nearest is **Cape Spear**, where a Victorian lighthouse guards the island's easternmost point, followed by **Bay Bulls**, the starting point for boat trips out to **Witless Bay Ecological Reserve**. From Bay Bulls, it's another short haul to **Ferryland**, where

The East Coast Trail

Negotiating much of the length of the Avalon Peninsula, the **East Coast Trail** has brought together backcountry routes and hunting paths to create a long-distance hiking trail that passes through fishing communities, provincial parks, national historic sites and a couple of ecological reserves. At present, the 220km stretch from St John's to Cappahayden has been completed – along with nearly forty trailheads – but construction is under way to extend the trail to Topsail, on Conception Bay in the north, and Trepassey in the south. It's an extraordinarily ambitious enterprise and one that is largely reliant on volunteer labour – in itself a real tribute to the Newfoundlanders. To assist hikers, the **East Coast Trail Association** (℡709/738-4453, ⓦwww.eastcoasttrail.com) is in the process of preparing five guide books ($23 each) covering different sections of the trail and including first-rate 1:25,000 topographical maps. The first one – from St John's to Petty Harbour – has already been published and is superb, beautifully illustrated and with all sorts of advice and information on everything from flora and fauna through to historical anecdotes and biographical snippets.

The East Coast Trail is linear, which means that if you're after a day's hiking you really need two cars and at least two people, but there are places to stay along the trail and it is possible to arrange to be picked up (and/or taken out) by taxi. The Association is always glad to help and advise and also organizes a programme of group hikes for free. As for particular recommendations, the 3.7km hike from the former fishing village of **Blackhead to Cape Spear** is one of the easier and more accessible portions of the trail and it covers a handsomely rugged stretch of coastline; allow one and a half to two hours.

archeologists are exploring the site of the seventeenth-century English colony of **Avalon**, from which the whole peninsula received its name. St John's is also where the **East Coast Trail** begins (see box).

Cape Spear

It's a 15km-drive along Route 11 from St John's – take the signposted turning off Water Street south of the centre – to **Cape Spear National Historic Site** (open access), a rocky, windswept headland which is a popular day-trip mainly because it's nearer Europe than any other part of mainland North America. To cater for tourists, the cape is crisscrossed by boardwalks, the most obvious of which leads up from the car park past the heritage shop and the modern lighthouse to the squat and rectangular **Lighthouse** (mid-May to mid-Oct daily 10am–6pm; $3.50), at the cape's highest point. Built in the 1830s, the lighthouse's interior has been pleasantly decked out in period style, down to imitation barrels of sperm oil and the neatly made bed, though there's surprisingly little on the lighthouse-keepers themselves. The other specific attraction is the substantial remains of the World War II **gun emplacement** at the tip of the cape, but the views are really the main event, right along the coast and up to The Narrows of St John's. In spring and early summer, the waters off the cape are a great place to spy the blue-tinged icebergs that have floated south from the Arctic pack ice and there's a reasonable chance of spotting a whale too. If you're really lucky, you'll see entire pods of whales in pursuit of the capelin (smelt), which roll onto the Avalon Peninsula's sandier coves to spawn in their millions from about the middle of June to mid-July. This can be a truly remarkable sight, but there's no way of knowing which cove and when, and the capelin don't appear as frequently as they used to; the rangers may be able to point you in the right direction.

Bay Bulls and the Witless Bay Ecological Reserve

Doubling back from Cape Spear, turn left along the road to Petty Harbour and, after about 18km, you'll reach Route 10 just 16km short of **BAY BULLS**. Joe Smallwood (see p.501) had Bay Bulls designated a town, but really it's only a village, which straggles around the head of a deep and pointed bay. It was here that one of the last active German U-boats surrendered in 1945 – much to the amazement of the locals – and today the town makes much of its living from boat tours around the four tiny offshore islets that comprise the **Witless Bay Ecological Reserve**. The best time to visit is between mid-June and mid-July, when over 800,000 birds gather here – the reserve has the largest puffin colony in eastern Canada and there are also thousands of storm petrels, common murres, kittiwakes, razorbills, guillemots, cormorants and herring gulls. In addition, the area is home to the largest population of **humpback whales** in the world, and finback and minke whales are often spotted between June and August.

Several companies offer daily **boat trips** to the waters surrounding the reserve. These include O'Brien's Whale & Bird Tours (May–Oct; ☎709/753-4850 or 1-877/639-4253, ⓦ www.obriensboattours.com); Mullowney's Puffin and Whale Tours (mid-May to Sept; ☎709/334-3666 or 1-877/783-3467, ⓦ www.puffinswhales.com); and Gatheralls Puffin and Whale Watch (May–Oct; ☎709/334-2887 or 1-800/419-4253, ⓦ www.newfoundland-whales .com). All three companies run two-hour sea trips ($30–40) and reservations are advised. They will also provide transport to and from major hotels in St John's for roughly $25 return, though this has to be arranged ahead of time. Another option is to go **sea kayaking** in the (relatively) sheltered waters of Bay Bulls harbour with Bay Bulls Sea Kayaking Tours (☎709/334-3394, ⓦ www.netfx.ca/kayak).

From Bay Bulls, it's 30km straight back to St John's or you can press on south the 40km to Ferryland.

Ferryland

George Calvert (1580–1632), the first Baron Baltimore, was a favourite of King James I of England, who gave him a slab of land in Newfoundland to settle as a colony. Calvert obligingly sailed out to what is now **FERRY-LAND** in 1620 and took a shine to the place, naming it **Avalon** and dispatching a band of prospective colonists the following year. The settlers sent him such wonderful reports that he decided to move there himself a few years later, but he only lasted one winter. Everything that could go wrong did, as Calvert penned to a friend back home: "I have sent [my family] home after much sufferance in this woful country, where with one intolerable wynter were wee almost undone. It is not to be expressed with my pen what wee have endured."

Archeologists have set about unearthing the remains of Calvert's colony, which lies at the base of a narrow and low-lying headland that hooks out into the ocean opposite today's Ferryland. They have discovered a surprising amount, including the foundations of several buildings, part of the original sea wall, a well and – a real surprise – a small strip of cobblestone street. The whole site has been attractively landscaped and afterwards you can follow the track that leads along the headland to the lighthouse. There's also a **Visitor Centre** (daily: June to Aug 9am–7pm; Sept to mid-Oct 9am–5pm; $6), at the base of the headland some 400m from the actual site, which gives the historical background.

The Avalon Peninsula

St John's sits on the northeast corner of the **Avalon Peninsula**, a jagged, roughly rectangular slab of land connected to the rest of Newfoundland by a narrow, tapering isthmus. Almost invariably, the Avalon's towns and villages stick resolutely to the coast and there's a particular concentration around populous **Conception Bay**, whose eastern shore lies just 15km west of the capital. Setting aside Cape Spear, Bay Bulls and Ferryland (see above), the peninsula has half a dozen places that are well worth a visit, a varied bunch including **Brigus**, home to the delightful Hawthorne Cottage; **Heart's Content**, with its antique cable station; **Castle Hill**, from where there are panoramic views over Placentia Bay; and the sea-bird colonies of **Cape St Mary's**. With the exception of the cape, which is a tad too far away for comfort, all make good day-tripping destinations from St John's.

Brigus

Captain Robert Bartlett (1875–1946) was no ordinary seaman, but a much sought-after ice navigator and Arctic explorer who helped get Peary to his base camp prior to his dash to the North Pole in 1909. Captain Bob was also a Newfoundlander and his old home in **BRIGUS**, on the south shore of Conception Bay, about 80km from St John's, has become the **Hawthorne Cottage National Historic Site** (mid-May to mid-June and Sept to mid-Oct 10am–6pm; mid-June to Aug 10am–8pm; $3). The house is littered with his keepsakes, but just as interesting is the architecture. Bartlett was a man of substance and style and the family home, built in 1830, eschewed the clapboard of the traditional Newfoundland house for a decorative Regency style, complete with an elevated wrought-iron, wraparound balcony. The Cottage is in the old part of Brigus, a pint-sized pocket of good-looking Victorian houses that backs onto the bay.

Harbour Grace

HARBOUR GRACE, one of Conception Bay's prettiest settlements, sits on the bay's western shore, tucked in against Route 70, 30km or so from Brigus. The village stretches out along Water Street, which is at its most attractive near the northern end, where a handful of elegant clapboard houses flank a slender inlet and are overseen by two **churches**, a handsome silver and green-spired Catholic effort and the pretty stonework of the Anglicans. The old red-brick Customs House has been turned into a mildly entertaining **museum** (June–Sept Mon–Fri 10am–5pm; free), featuring sepias of the village and its Victorian inhabitants, and an outdoor plaque commemorates Peter Easton, the so-called "Pirate Admiral". Easton, who was based here at the beginning of the seventeenth century, ran a phenomenally successful fleet, which was manned by five thousand sailors, who made their leader rich enough to retire to a life of luxury in the south of France. Next door, the tiny park has another plaque, this one in honour of the early aviators who flew across the Atlantic from the Harbour Grace area, including **Amelia Earhart**, the first woman to complete the journey solo in 1932.

Heart's Content

In the middle of the nineteenth century, **HEART'S CONTENT**, 30km northwest of Harbour Grace on the shores of Trinity Bay, was packed with engineers attempting to connect North America with Britain by **telegraph cable**. The project had begun when the USS *Niagara* had hauled the first transatlantic line ashore here in 1858, but after Queen Victoria and the American president James Buchanan had swapped inaugural jokes the cable broke. It was eight years before an improved version, running from Valentia in Ireland, could be installed and thereafter Heart's Content became an important relay station to New York, a role it performed until technological changes made it obsolete in the 1960s. Tight against the waterfront, in the centre of the village, the **Cable Station Provincial Historic Site** (mid-June to early Oct daily 10am–5.30pm; $2.50) contains an intriguing old cable operating room that has been preserved in pristine condition. It also houses a series of displays on the history of telecommunications, including a replica of the original Victorian cable office and details of the problems encountered during the laying of the first telegraph lines.

From Heart's Content, it's a pleasant 60km south along the eastern shore of Trinity Bay to the Trans-Canada Highway just near the turning for Castle Hill National Historic Site.

Castle Hill National Historic Site

The thumb-shaped promontory filling out the southwest corner of the Avalon Peninsula is a foggy wilderness of marsh and rock, whose westerly shoreline is negotiated by **Route 100**, branching off the Trans-Canada some 80km from St John's. Route 100 begins by whistling across the interior for the 50km dash to the ferry terminal of **ARGENTIA**, and most people drive straight past the turning for the tiny **Castle Hill National Historic Site**, just 5km short of the port (open access; free). This is a pity, because Castle Hill is magnificently located overlooking the watery web of channel and estuary that edges **Placentia Harbour**, one of Newfoundland's finest anchorages. The harbour's sheltered waters first attracted the French, who established "Plaisance", their regional headquarters, here in 1662, with Fort Royale (now Castle Hill) up above as the key defensive position. As the fortunes of war seesawed, so harbour and fort were successively occupied and re-fortified by the British and the French, a turbulent history skillfully explored at the **visitor centre** (mid-May to mid-Oct daily 10am–6pm; $3.50). Little remains of these works today – just a few stone walls and ditches – but make the trip for the views and maybe have a look at one of the historical re-enactments that take place in the summer – ring ☎709/772-5367 for programme details.

St Bride's and Cape St Mary's

Viewed from Castle Hill, the village of **Placentia** way down below looks a pretty affair, a ribbon of buildings sandwiched between the green of the hills and the blue of the bay. However, on closer inspection, the village doesn't live up to its setting and you'll soon be continuing along on Route 100 as it sets out on its 50km journey to the quiet outport of **ST BRIDE'S** (see below). From here, it's a further 20km to **Cape St Mary's Ecological Reserve**, which is best visited between early May and early August, when thousands of sea birds, principally gannets, kittiwakes, razorbills and murres, congregate on its rocky sea cliffs and stumpy sea stacks. A **visitor centre** (daily: May & Oct 9am–5pm; June–Sept 8am–7pm; ☎709/277-1666) close to the parking lot provides all the background information and from here a clearly marked footpath cuts across the cape. The best vantage point is generally considered to be at Bird Rock Cove, a twenty-minute walk away, though note a few cautions: wear good walking shoes, carry or wear warm clothing and stick to the footpath as the cape can be engulfed by fog as quick as a wink.

Cape St Mary's is just over 200km from St John's, which makes it rather too far away for a day-trip, but there are three **places to stay** in St Bride's. These are the dramatically sited and well-equipped *Bird Island Resort* (℡709/337-2450 or 1-888/337-2450, ⓦwww.birdislandresort.com; ❸); the *Atlantica Inn* (℡709/337-2860 or 1-888/999-2860; ❷), which has just three guest rooms; and the *Cape Way Motel* (℡709/337-2163 or 1-866/337-2163; ❷), which has seven unassuming en-suite rooms.

The Burin Peninsula

The bony mass of the **Burin Peninsula** pokes out into the Atlantic from the north end of the isthmus connecting the Avalon Peninsula with the rest of Newfoundland. Much of its length is crossed by **Route 210**, which forks off the Trans-Canada about 160km from St John's. Route 210 starts promisingly with the handsome scenery of the **Piper's Hole River estuary**, but thereafter it's a singularly lonely journey across boggy plateaux and on down to the ship-yard town of **Marystown**, easily the biggest settlement hereabouts and 150km from the Trans-Canada. From here, it's a further 50km to the peninsula's most interesting spot, the fishing village of **Grand Bank**, and a couple more to **Fortune**, the departure point for **passenger ferries** over to St-Pierre et Miquelon (see p.495).

Foote's Taxi, on Queen Street in St John's (℡709/832-0491 or 1-800/866-1181), operates a once-daily service to Grand Bank and Fortune; the fare is $35 and the journey takes six hours. Given the length of the journey and the scarcity of accommodation on the Burin, both car drivers and bus passengers should book their overnight stay before they go out. Note that Foote's schedule does not coincide with the times of the ferry over to St Pierre.

Grand Bank and Fortune

Looking firmly out to sea, the older streets of **GRAND BANK** incorporate a charming assortment of late nineteenth-century timber houses, a few of which are equipped with the so-called "widow's walks", rooftop galleries from where the women watched for their returning menfolk. Some of these houses are splendid, reflecting a time when the village's proximity to the Grand Banks fishing grounds brought tremendous profits to the shipowners, if not to the actual fishermen. Nowadays the Grand Banks fishery is in an acute state of decline, much to the frustration of local people, who apportion blame amongst a number of old enemies: foreigners who overfish, big marketing corporations who are indifferent to local interests, greedy seals and a government that imposes unrealistic quotas. What makes it particularly hard to bear is the affinity many locals have for the fishing – as one of their representatives declared: "Without fish there is no soul, no pride, no nothing."

To see something of this tradition, visit the **Seamen's Museum** (May to late Oct daily 9am–4.45pm; $2.50), situated on Marine Drive in a modern building shaped like the sails of a schooner. It has all sorts of models, paintings and photographs of different types of fishing boat, and a relief model of Newfoundland and the surrounding ocean that shows exactly where the illustrious "Banks" are. The Banks comprise a great belt of shallow ocean lying to the southeast of Newfoundland. It's here that the cold waters from Labrador bump into the much warmer Gulf Stream, creating pea-soup fogs and, more importantly, a density of plankton that attracts fishes by the million. For four and a half centuries, the Banks teemed with cod but trawling – as distinct from line fishing – eventually took care of that, though admittedly there are lots of competing theories as to quite why the cod has declined; the results in places like the Burin are not, however, in dispute.

Grand Bank has one **B&B**, the *Thorndyke*, a stately and well-maintained old sea captain's house at 33 Water St (T709/832-0820 or 1-866/882-0820; ❸; May–Sept). There's also a recently renovated **motel**, *Granny's Motor Inn*, on Grandview Boulevard (T709/832-2180 or 1-888/275-1098; ❸). The motel is where you should **eat**.

From Grand Bank, it's a couple of kilometres to **FORTUNE**, a slightly smaller village and the departure point for ferries over to St-Pierre et Miquelon (see below). These are passenger ferries only and there's a fenced-off and patrolled **car park** near the ferry terminal.

St-Pierre et Miquelon

The tiny archipelago of **St-Pierre et Miquelon**, 25km off the coast of the Burin Peninsula, became a fully fledged *département* of mainland France in 1976 and a *collectivité territoriale* in 1985, justifying the billing of the islands as "a little bit of France at your doorstep". The tag certainly pulls in several thousand visitors each year and manages to put a gloss on the lack of actual attractions and the wetness of the climate, though the islands are still worth a day or two. The main appeal is the francophone atmosphere of the main settlement, the town of **St-Pierre**, whose good restaurants and simple guesthouses have a genuinely European flavour. All but 700 of the 6500 islanders live here, with the remainder – mainly of Acadian and Basque descent – marooned on **Grande Miquelon** to the north. The third and middle island, **Langlade**, or **Petite Miquelon**, has just a scattering of houses and is only inhabited in summer.

A brief history of St-Pierre et Miquelon

The Portuguese stumbled across the archipelago in 1520, but it was **Jacques Cartier** who claimed it for the French king in 1536. Subsequently settled by fishermen from the Basque provinces, Normandy and Brittany, the islands were alternately occupied by Britain and France until the British gave them to the French as a commercial sop after the loss of the rest of their North American colonies in 1763. St-Pierre et Miquelon soon became a vital supply base and safe harbour for the French fishing fleet, and provided France with a yearly harvest of salted cod.

After World War I, the French colonial authorities wanted to expand the local fishing industry, but their efforts became irrelevant with **Prohibition** in 1920. Quite suddenly, St-Pierre was transformed from a maritime backwater into a giant transit centre for booze smuggling: even the main fish-processing plant was stacked high with thousands of cases of whisky destined for Boston and

Since St-Pierre is a part of France, local currency is the **euro** (€), made up of 100 cents. Canadian dollars are also widely accepted, but you'll usually get change in euros. Approximate **exchange rates** at the time of writing are €1=C$1.60 or C$1=€0.63. For up-to-date rates, check ⓦwww.oanda.com.

To clear St-Pierre et Miquelon's **customs control**, Canadians need only present an official photo identity, but EU and US nationals need a passport.

Long Island. It was an immensely lucrative business, but when Prohibition ended thirteen years later the St-Pierre economy dropped through the floor. Those were desperate days, but more misery followed during World War II, when the islands' governor remained controversially loyal to the collaborationist **Vichy** regime. Both the Canadians and the Americans considered invading, but it was a **Free French** naval squadron that got there first, crossing over from their base in Halifax and occupying the islands in late 1941 without a shot being fired.

There was further trouble in 1965 when a **stevedores' strike** forced the administration to resign. **De Gaulle** promptly dispatched the navy, who occupied the islands for no fewer than nine years. Perhaps surprisingly, the St-Pierrais remained largely loyal to France, and they certainly needed the support of Paris when the Canadians extended the limit of their territorial waters to 200 nautical miles in 1977. The ensuing wrangle between Canada and France over the islands' claim to a similar exclusion zone was finally resolved in 1994, although the tightening of controls on foreign vessels has largely ended St-Pierre's role as a supply centre.

The town of St-Pierre

The tidy streets of the town of **ST-PIERRE** nudge back from the harbour, altogether a pleasant ensemble of plain stone and brightly painted timber buildings with a quintessentially French demeanour. The central area makes for an enjoyable stroll, though there's nothing special to aim for, with the possible exception of the early twentieth-century **cathédrale**, which does at least attempt to look imposing with its large stone bell tower. Nearby, on rue Gloanec, a **fronton** (a court on which the game of *pelote*, or *jai alai*, is played) proclaims the island's Basque heritage and behind it – almost as a rival – is a (French) *pétanque* field. The town **musée** (museum; June–Aug Tues–Sun 10am–noon & 2–5.30pm; rest of year daily 2–5.30pm; €3), perched on a slope above the harbour to the west of the centre, is housed in a striking building whose upswept roof emulates the curves of a ship's hull. The displays focus on the islands' history and there's a particularly good section on local architecture. To the rear of the building is the flamboyant **Le Monument aux Morts** (War Memorial), raised in honour of the dead of the two world wars, and below it, at the foot of the hill, is the airy concrete and glass-walled French language teaching centre, the **Francoforum**. From the town centre it's easy to walk out into the surrounding countryside, passing bare hillocks and marshy ponds to reach the rugged cliffs of the northern shore, just 8km away.

Across the harbour from the town quayside lies the minuscule **Île aux Marins**, where the rocks were once strewn with thousands of drying cod fish. After centuries of use, the islet was abandoned in 1964, its assorted buildings pretty much left to their own weather-beaten devices. **Guided tours** (May to Sept 2 daily; €16 including 10min boat trip; ☏508/41 23 84) take in the lighthouse, the old town hall, school (incorporating a museum), wash-house, and a garish Stations of the Cross that leads to a small cemetery perched on the windiest of promontories. Across the cove from the cemetery is the rusted hulk of the German ship *Transpacific*, which was wrecked there in 1971. The islet's most intriguing building is **Notre Dame des Marins**, a large and good-looking church whose original furnishings, dating from 1874, have survived, including a large black-wrapped catafalque, used for carrying coffins.

Arrival and information

Air St-Pierre (☎508/41 00 00, ⓦwww.airsaintpierre.com) **flies** to St-Pierre et Miquelon from Montréal, Halifax and Sydney, NS, Moncton, NB, and St John's, Newfoundland. The least expensive flights are from St John's (2–5 daily; 45min), where the company has a desk at the airport (☎709/726-9700); in summer a return flight costs in the region of €170. The St-Pierre et Miquelon **airport**, with its startlingly pink terminal, is located just south of the town of St-Pierre; taxis run into the centre.

SPM Express (St-Pierre ☎508/41 24 26, Fortune ☎709/832-0429) operates **passenger ferries** (May–Sept 1 daily, Oct to early Dec 2 weekly; 1hr 20min; $52 one-way, $78 return) from Fortune in Newfoundland to the town of St-Pierre, but be aware that the crossing can get mighty rough. The ferry schedule means that you almost always have to spend the night on St-Pierre – book your accommodation ahead. To sample St-Pierre on a **day-trip** from Fortune, contact St Pierre Tours (☎1-800/563-2006, ⓦwww.stpierretours .com), who organize nine-hour ferry and bus excursions (July & Aug Mon–Sat 1 daily) for about $80. They also offer a shuttle service from St John's to the Fortune ferry.

The St-Pierre et Miquelon **tourist office** is in the town of St-Pierre, metres from the ferry dock on Place du Général de Gaulle (July & Aug daily 8.30am–6pm; May, June & Sept Mon–Sat 8.30am–noon & 1–6pm, Sun 8.30–11.30am & 1–6pm; ☎1-800/565-5118, ⓦwww.st-pierre-et-miquelon .com). They supply all sorts of information about the archipelago and also have the timetables of the **local passenger ferry** from St-Pierre town to Miquelon village (1–2 daily, on 3 days a week; 1hr; €20 return). It is, however, much easier to join a guided tour if you're after venturing beyond St-Pierre and there are several excellent bus and boat **day-trips** on offer. One particular recommendation is the bus and boat excursion to Miquelon village and the Grand Barachois lagoon (mid-June to mid-Sept daily; June & Sept not Thurs; 11hr; €33).

Accommodation and restaurants

The town of St-Pierre has a good selection of **accommodation**, though reservations are strongly recommended from July to early September. Smarter **hotels** include the *Hôtel Île de France*, 6 rue Maître Georges-Lèfvre (☎508/41 03 50, ⓦwww.domtomfr.com; doubles €90), and the *Hôtel/Motel Robert*, 10–12 rue du 11 Novembre (☎508/41 24 19; doubles €103), which was where Al Capone stayed during Prohibition; a small museum off the foyer has one of his straw hats and other memorabilia. For **pensions**, which charge a fixed rate per double including breakfast, try the comfortable *Chez Hélène*, 15 rue Beaussant (☎508/41 31 08; €42; April–Dec) or *Chez Roland Vigneau*, 12 rue des Basques (☎508/41 38 67; €40; April–Sept).

St-Pierre's **restaurants** are splendid, combining the best of French cuisine with local delicacies such as *tiaude*, a highly seasoned cod stew. Prices are fairly high – reckon on about €20 for a main course – but it really is worth splashing out. One excellent spot is *Le Cabestan*, 2 rue Marcel-Bonin (☎508/41 21 00), which features *nouvelle cuisine* at its best, whereas *Le Caveau*, 2 rue Maître Georges-Lefèvre, specializes in Basque-style seafood and lamb. If you're on a tight budget go to *Le Maringouin'fre*, 22 rue Général-Leclerc, which serves delicious crêpes as well as steaks and burgers.

Grande Miquelon and Langlade

At the north end of the archipelago, the stubby little island of **Grande Miquelon** comprises peat bog, marsh and a couple of hills which slope away from the only village – **MIQUELON**. The village has two sights of some interest, beginning with **L'Eglise** (church) of 1865, whose sombre exterior hides a folksy interior filled with faux-marble columns and containing a good copy of a Murillo *Virgin* donated by Napoléon III – it's above the altar. Just down the street from the church is the cramped **musée** (museum), which displays all manner of items salvaged from local shipwrecks, plus a curious reconstruction of a 1913–14 photography laboratory set up by a local doctor. Otherwise, the **tourist office** (call ☎1-800/565-5118 for hours) can provide you with details of local walks or you can rent a *rosalie* (bicycle) from them and cycle off towards Grand Barachois (see below). Of the handful of **places to stay** in Miquelon village, the unassuming *Maxotel*, 42 rue Sourdeval (☎508/41 64 57; €58) has the advantage of a seashore location.

The archipelago's most unusual feature is the **Dune of Langlade**, a sweeping ten-kilometre sandy isthmus that links Grande Miquelon with **LANGLADE**, otherwise **PETITE MIQUELON**. The isthmus began to surface above the ocean two hundred years ago as a result of sand collecting around a shipwreck and is now anything up to 2500m wide. There's a road along the length of the Dune, but note that heavy seas can swamp parts of it, so be sure to stick to the guided tours. These stop at the **Grand Barachois**, a large saltwater pool at the northern end of the isthmus that's a favourite haunt of breeding seals. Langlade itself has a more varied landscape than the other islands – high hills, deciduous forests and rushing brooks – and is at its liveliest in summer, when the St-Pierrois arrive in droves to open up their summer homes.

The Bonavista Peninsula

Crossed by Route 230, which leaves the Trans-Canada 220km west of St John's near Clarenville, the thickly wooded **Bonavista Peninsula** pokes out into the ocean for some 120km, its shredded shoreline confettied with bays, coves and islands. The English settled here in numbers during the seventeenth century, establishing dozens of tiny outports and one administrative centre, **Trinity**, whose handsome headland setting and medley of fine old buildings make it the most beguiling of all Newfoundland's towns. Trinity is also the ideal base for exploring the rest of the peninsula: it's close to several first-rate hiking trails and is within comfortable striking distance of the wild and windswept **Cape Bonavista**, right at the tip of the peninsula. Trinity also offers **whale-watching tours** and possesses a clutch of **B&Bs**, though the best accommodation is in neighbouring **Port Rexton** – another of the twelve settlements that are collectively known as **Trinity Bight**. If you're intent on **hiking**, look out for the *Hiking on The Discovery Trail* booklet ($6), which describes a dozen or so trails supported by photos, potted descriptions of the peninsula's ouports, flora and fauna plus some (pretty rudimentary) maps. The problem is getting hold of a copy – try the district's shops and museums or your B&B.

As regards public transport, Bonavista Taxis (☎709/536-3044) provides a thrice-weekly **minibus** service from St John's to the peninsula with the journey to Trinity costing $25. However, before you catch the minibus check to see exactly where you'll be dropped off, otherwise you might be facing an awful long hike to the nearest settlement.

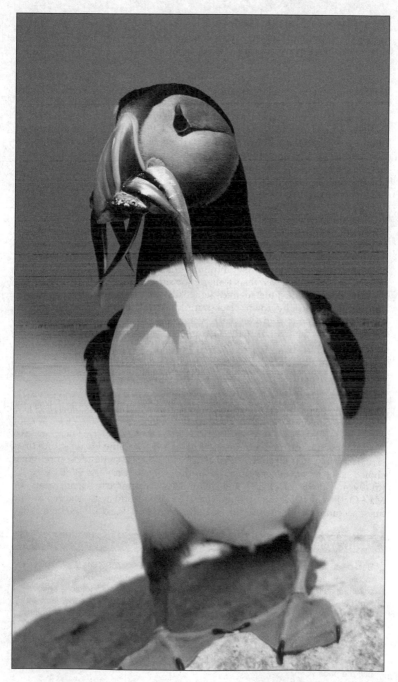

△ Puffin at Witless Bay

Trinity and around

Situated about 70km from the Trans-Canada, just off Route 230, the narrow lanes of tiny **TRINITY** are edged by a delightful ensemble of white and pastel-painted clapboard houses, all set between a ring of hills and the deep and intricate Trinity Bay. The architectural high point is **St Paul's Anglican Church** of 1892, whose exterior is perfectly proportioned, its height balanced by elaborate scrollwork. Inside, the graceful and dignified nave is divided into three, the side aisles entered through arches carved to resemble whale bones and the ceiling up above fashioned in the shape of an upturned boat. A series of **memorial plaques** tacked to the walls witnesses both the dedication of the islanders to the British imperial interest, with many a young man killed on a foreign battle field, and the dangers of the sea, drownings and shipwrecks being all too commonplace. Opposite the church, there's the modest but entertaining **Trinity Historical Museum** (mid-June to mid-Sept daily 10am–1pm & 2–5.30pm; $2), which crowds together an eccentric collection of bygones, such as an old shoemaker's kit, sealing gear, an early cooperage and a fire engine of 1811.

From the church, it's a few paces to both the cream and green **Hiscock House** (June to mid-Oct daily 10am–5.30pm; $3), where guides in period costume explain the intricacies of early twentieth-century life in this old merchant's house, and the uncommonly grand **Parish Hall**. Beyond, West Street chalks up no fewer than four minor sites, beginning with the **Green Family Forge** (mid-June to mid-Sept daily 10am–1pm & 2–5.30pm; $2), which focuses on the town blacksmith, and the **Trinity Interpretation Centre** (mid-June to mid-Oct daily 10am–5.30pm; free), where the emphasis is on local history. Next up are the **Lester-Garland House** (mid-June to mid-Sept daily 10am–1pm & 2–5.30pm; $2.50), a reconstructed three-storey Georgian brick house with period rooms, and the **Ryan general store** (same hours), returned to something like its appearance circa 1910.

Practicalities

Trinity has several appealing **B&Bs**, foremost of which is the *Campbell House*, in a good-looking Victorian building on High St (☎709/464-3377 or 1-877/464-7700, ⓦwww.trinityvacations.com; ➎; May–Oct). There are two guest double rooms and two suites here, all en suite, and the breakfasts are first-class, featuring such local delicacies as partridge-berry crepes. A second good choice, also in an older property, is the *Eriksen Premises B&B*, West St (☎709/464-3698 or 1-877/464-3698, ⓦwww.trinityexperience.com; ➍; May–Oct), which has six en-suite guest rooms, mostly with sea views. The finest accommodation hereabouts is, however, in Port Rexton (see below).

Trinity whale-watching

Based at the *Village Inn* in Trinity, Ocean Contact (☎709/464-3269, ⓦwww.oceancontact.com) runs an extensive programme of **whale-watching** excursions, or rather, as they insist, whale "contact" trips designed to encourage close encounters between whales and humans. They can't, of course, guarantee contact, but there is an excellent chance of sighting minke, finbacks and humpbacks, particularly between mid-June and early August. Expertly run, these excursions take place daily during the whale season from June to October, and prices begin at $55 for a half-day trip with an introductory talk thrown in. If the sea is too rough for a boat trip, Ocean Contact provides escorted whale-watching walks along the nearby cliffs at half the price.

The best **restaurant** in town is on the first floor of the *Eriksen Premises*, on West Street, with seafood the forte. Another good bet is the *Dock Marina Restaurant* (☎709/464-2133), on the water's edge near the Parish Hall, where both the seafood and the meat are well prepared and they do a good line in traditional Newfoundland cuisine. Afterwards, you can stroll up to *Rocky's Place* for a drink.

In summer, Trinity plays host to a professional **theatre** company, Rising Tide Theatre (☎709/464-3847, ⓦ www.risingtidetheatre.com), which puts on an excellent programme of Canadian plays in the **Summer in the Bight festival** running from June to October. They are also involved in the **Trinity Pageant** (☎709/464-3232), a sort of community street theatre performed on various days from late June to August with costumed actors strolling the town relating and enacting scenes from yesteryear.

South of Trinity: New Bonaventure

Interrupted by four spindly headlands, **Trinity Bay** is a particularly pretty slice of coastline, its rough, bulging hills decorated with woods and brightened by the odd patch of farmland, bright green after the grass has been mown. Trinity sits on one of these headlands and you have to double back a kilometre or so to the west to pick up **Route 239**, which weaves its way south, passing through a string of lonely outports. Eventually, after about 15km, the road slips into **NEW BONAVENTURE**, a haphazard assortment of clapboard houses edging a rocky bay. On a rainy day it seems like the end of the world, but a side road pushes on even further – fork right over the hill as you descend into the village and continue for another 500m until you reach the church at the end of the road. The **church** seems surprisingly large considering the size of New Bonaventure, even larger when you realise the locals had to roam far and wide to collect the wood for its construction in the 1920s.

Beginning at the church, a 600m-long gravel road leads down to the **Cape Random Passage film set** (June to mid-Oct daily 9.30am–7.30pm; free), which consists of a replica early-1800s outport with fishing stages, shacks, a church and a school. Built in 2000, the set was used for filming *Random Passage* and *Waiting for Time*, two romantic novels written by Newfoundland's Bernice Morgan (b.1935) and telling the tale of the Andrews family who settled here in the 1820s. Beyond the film set, a **hiking trail** proceeds to the abandoned outport of **Kerley's Harbour**, a charming and fairly straightforward coastal walk of 2km (40min each way) along the old cart road.

East of Trinity: Port Rexton and Trinity East

From Trinity, it's about 8km round Trinity Bay – via Route 230 – to **PORT REXTON**, which actually consists of two pocket-sized outports (Robin Hood and Ship Cove) on either side of a headland. These twin communities once flourished on the back of the Labrador fishery, but things are very quiet today with a haphazard jigsaw of houses rambling across the foreshore. Overlooking Ship Cove from the side of a hill is *Fishers' Loft Inn* (☎1-877/464-3240, ⓦ www.fishersloft.com; ❺; May–Nov), whose five separate houses – and 21 en-suite guest rooms – are of recent construction, though they are built in various versions of traditional Newfoundland style. It's an extraordinarily successful ensemble and the interiors are simply superb, a well-conceived balance of the intimate and the smart from the wooden floors through to the handmade furniture and the large and comfortable beds. The views over Ship Cove and out across Trinity Bay are similarly delightful and breakfasts, which feature local ingredients, are tasty and filling, but note that **dinners** ($40) are by prior arrangement only.

The signposted side road that leads from Route 230 past the turning to the Fishers' Loft Inn carries on for another 2km to reach the hamlet of **TRINITY EAST**, the starting point of the popular **Skerwink Trail**, a 5.4km loop trail that negotiates the jutting headland that lies beyond. It's a lovely two-hour walk offering handsome coastal views and lots of wildlife.

Cape Bonavista and Bonavista

Some 40km north of Trinity, **Cape Bonavista** is violently beautiful, a desolate headland of dark-grey rock and pounding sea inhabited by hundreds of puffins. This is supposed to be the spot where the English-sponsored Genoese explorer **John Cabot** first clapped eyes on the Americas in 1497, exclaiming – so it's claimed – "O buona vista!" ("O, happy sight") and, true or not, a statue has been erected in his honour. The cape has always been hazardous to shipping and it's overseen by a red-and-white-striped **lighthouse** (June–Oct daily 10am–5.30pm), which has been attractively restored to its appearance in 1870 when it was occupied by an 80-year-old lighthouse keeper, Jeremiah White, and his family; costumed guides give the background.

The cape is 5km from the expansive fishing village of **BONAVISTA**, which spreads out across the flattish headlands surrounding its double harbour. Settled by the English in the seventeenth century, Bonavista was long a successful trading centre and fishing station, a history explored at the **Ryan Premises National Historic Site** (mid-May to mid-Oct daily 10am–6pm; $3.50), sited in the old fish-processing complex. There's more nautical stuff nearby at the docks in the form of a replica of **Cabot's ship**, the *Matthew* (mid-June to Sept daily 10am–6pm; $3), with tours above and below deck and an attached interpretation centre. Bonavista's other noteworthy sight is the plain white clapboard **Mockbeggar Property** on Roper Street (June–Oct daily 10am–5.30pm; $3), once the home of F. Gordon Bradley, one of the island's first representatives in the Canadian Senate. The house has been returned to its appearance in the 1930s and comes complete with a full set of heavy-duty, English-made Victorian and Edwardian furniture.

Bonavista has a handful of **B&Bs** with one of the better options being *Butler's by the Sea*, whose two en-suite guest rooms overlook the sea at 15 Butler Crescent (⊤709/468-2445 or 1-877/968-2445, ⓦwww.bbcanada.com/1412.html; ❸). Another good bet is *White's Bed & Breakfast*, 21 Windlass Drive (⊤709/468-7018 or 1-866/468-7018, ⓦwww.bbcanada.com/3821.html; ❷), which also overlooks the coast and has three en-suite guest rooms. They also rent out bikes and from here it's an easy 3km to the lighthouse. **Restaurants** are thin on the ground – try the *Baie-Vista*, on John Cabot Drive, right in the centre.

Terra Nova National Park to Deer Lake

The **Trans-Canada Highway** cuts a long and lonely course across central Newfoundland on its way west from Clarenville to Deer Lake, a distance of 450km. Of the towns it encounters, **Grand Falls–Windsor** has an intriguing museum and **Deer Lake**, with its airport and car rental outlets, is a handy starting point for the journey up the Northern Peninsula (see p.504). The highway also threads through **Terra Nova National Park**, with its handsome coastal scenery. The most obvious detour is the 100km dash north to the old fishing port and trading centre of **Twillingate**, set amidst a craggy broken coastline that attracts icebergs by the score from May to August.

Terra Nova National Park

Heading north from Clarenville along the Trans-Canada – past the turnings for the Bonavista Peninsula (see p.496) – it's about 40km to the southern edge of **Terra Nova National Park** (mid-May to early Oct; admission $3.25), whose coniferous forests, ponds and marshes border a deeply indented slice of rugged coastline. The Trans-Canada slices right through the park, giving clearly signed access to its various facilities, most of which are concentrated about 40km into the park at the head of **Newman Sound** – though technically it's not a sound at all, but a channel linking the ocean with an estuary. The Sound is the best place to start a visit to the park as it's here you'll find the **Salton's Marine Interpretation Centre** (daily: July & Aug 9am–8pm; mid-May to June & Sept to early Oct 10am–5pm; no extra charge; ☎709/533-2801), whose excellent displays explain and illustrate the park's flora and fauna. The Centre also supplies oodles of information about guided walks, boat trips, safe swimming areas, canoeing and sea kayaking. The **boat trips** are operated by Ocean Watch Tours (mid-May to Oct 2–4 cruises daily; ☎709/533-6024, ⓦwww3.nf .sympatico.ca/oceanwatch), which runs a varied programme from cruises around the Sound to trips out into the Atlantic and along the coast; trips cost $30 or more per person. The Centre also has the details of over a dozen **hiking trails**, from short strolls to full-scale expeditions, including the strenuous **Outport Loop Trail**, a 55km endurance test that takes eighteen hours to complete. En route are several primitive **campsites** ($8), permits for which must be arranged at the interpretation centre before you set out. The most stunning part of the Outport Trail is the first 18km (5hr), with the trail snaking its way along the south shore of Newman Sound to **South Broad Cove**, where Ocean Watch **water taxis** will pick you up or drop you off – details at the Interpretation Centre.

The national park also has several serviced **campsites**, the largest being the *Newman Sound Campground* (reservations advised on ☎1-888/533-3186; $12–18), reached along a side road off the Trans-Canada just to the south of the Salton's Marine turning. If camping seems too daunting a prospect, then aim for the village of **CHARLOTTETOWN**, about 15km south of Newman Sound, where there's a **motel**, the *Clode Sound* (☎709/664-3146, ⓦwww.clodesound.com; May–Oct; ❸), with a reasonably priced **restaurant** known for its apple pies and apple crisps.

Gambo and Gander

The Trans-Canada Highway leaves Terra Nova National Park to reach, after 32km, the logging and former railway town of **GAMBO**, where the **Smallwood Interpretation Centre** (daily 11am–7pm; $3) celebrates the life and times of its most famous son, Joe Smallwood (1900–92). Smallwood, the larger-than-life Newfoundland premier who dominated the political scene from 1949 to 1972, was a controversial figure, whose various grand designs had very mixed consequences. Most islanders would now agree that his main contribution was in squeezing through the vote for Confederation in the referendum of 1948, but his attempts to diversify the economy by attracting industry were too often ill-considered and very costly. Even worse, his resettlement programme, in which the inhabitants of dozens of the remoter outports were pushed into so-called "growth centres", was well-nigh disastrous – though Smallwood was so formidable a party boss that few would have said so to his face.

From Gambo it's just 40km to **GANDER**, an inconsequential town built around an airport, whose site was chosen carefully by the British in the 1930s

– it was far enough inland to escape Newfoundland's coastal fogs, but still near enough to Europe to facilitate the introduction of regular transatlantic flights. During World War II, the airport was a major staging point for American planes on their way to England and later, in the 1960s and 1970s, it became a major re-fuelling stop for incoming flights from Europe. It lost this role years ago and has developed into an important air-traffic control centre for much of the northwest Atlantic instead, though its past was reprised when over twenty jets were diverted here after the attack on the World Trade Center in New York on September 11, 2001.

Twillingate

Heading north from Gander, away from the Trans-Canada, **Route 330** slips across the inhospitable wastes of the interior before slipping down to the coast at the mouth of the River Gander. From here, Route 331 shuttles north through a string of outports before meeting **Route 340**, which cuts an improbable course, its causeways and bridges negotiating the jigsaw of islets, headlands and inlets that distinguish this part of the coast. Eventually, 100km from Gander, the road meanders into **TWILLINGATE**, where a scattering of bright-white houses strings along the seashore. One of Newfoundland's oldest settlements, Twillingate was settled by the English in the early eighteenth century after several decades of use by itinerant French fishermen, who gave the place its original name, "Toulinguet", from an island back home in Brittany. By the 1780s Twillingate had become the most important cod fishing station on the north coast and a flourishing seaport on account of its fine, sheltered harbour. As elsewhere on Newfoundland, the merchants kept an economic stranglehold on the fishermen, who could only barter their catch in return for food, provisions and equipment – at a rate set by the merchant. The merchants also brought a compulsion for respectability and, by the 1820s, there were churches, masonic lodges and schools. Yet what really

---

Twillingate iceberg-spotting

Every year, from May to August, the myriad headlands and inlets of the coast near Twillingate ensnare dozens of **icebergs** as they float down from the Arctic. Tinted in shades of blue and white by reflections from the sea and sun, they can be wondrously beautiful and, if you're particularly lucky, you might witness the moment when one of them rolls over and breaks apart, accompanied by a tremendous grating and wheezing and then an ear-ringing bang. Several local companies offer **iceberg-watching boat tours**; one of the best known is Twillingate Adventure Tours, on Path End (mid-May to mid-Sept 3 daily; 2hr; $30; ☎709/884-5999 or 1-888/447-8687, ⊛www.daybreaktours.com). Another recommended operator is Twillingate Island Boat Tours, 50 Main St (May–Sept 3 daily; 2hr; $30; ☎709/884-2242 or 1-800/611-2374, ⊛www.icebergtours.ca). Twillingate Island Boat Tours also operates the **Iceberg Shop**, an arts and crafts shop and iceberg interpretive centre in an old barn in **DURRELL**, a couple of kilometres north of Twillingate. With both companies, boat tours should be booked ahead of time.

Landlubbers still stand a good chance of spotting an iceberg from the **Long Point Lighthouse**, which occupies a commanding position on a high rocky cliff at the north end of Main Street – incidentally the approach is rocky and often slippery, so you'll need appropriate footwear. The **Long Point Interpretive Centre**, across the street from the lighthouse (daily: May to mid-Oct 10am–9pm; free), has a tearoom, crafts shop and a small display on local culture and natural history.

excited the majority was the "**Great Haul**" of 1862, when ice floes carrying thousands of seals drifted into the shore close to Twillingate harbour. This provided a bonanza of seal meat, skins and cash – seals were beyond the barter system and the town's fishermen and women could sell what they could kill. In the 1880s the switch from sail to steam did the town no favours, but it remained a busy fishing port until the demise of the cod fishery in the 1990s. The best time to be in Twillingate is during the four-day **Fish, Fun and Folk Festival** (ⓦ www.fishfunfolkfestival.com), held over the last full weekend of July and attracting folk musicians from all over the province.

There are about ten **B&Bs** in and around Twillingate as well as a couple of inns. One of the better options is the *Hillside*, 5 Young's Lane (ⓣ 709/884-5761; ❸; June–Sept), whose three en-suite guest rooms are in a pleasant old house dating from the 1870s. The *Toulinguet Inn*, down on the waterfront at 56 Main St (ⓣ 709/884-2080 or 1-877/684-2080, ⓦ www.toulinguetinn.ca; ❸; May–Sept), also has three en-suite guest rooms, though in a 1920s building. Finally, there's the delightful *Beach Rock B&B* (ⓣ 709/884-2292, ⓦ www .bbcanada.com/beachrock; ❷; April–Oct), which occupies a charmingly renovated, two-storey timber house of 1904. There are three guest rooms here, all en suite and breakfasts feature home-made bread and muffins. The *Beach Rock* is located on the seashore about 5km south of Twillingate, just off Route 340 in the hamlet of Little Harbour. For **food**, book an evening meal ahead of time at the *Beach Rock*.

Grand Falls-Windsor

GRAND FALLS, 96km west of Gander along the Trans-Canada, sits amongst some of the island's best stands of timber, an expanse of **forest** that's been intensively exploited ever since Alfred Harmsworth, later Lord Northcliffe, had a paper mill built here in 1905. Harmsworth, the founder of Britain's *Daily Mirror* and *Daily Mail* newspapers, funded the project to secure a reliable supply of newsprint well away from Europe, which he believed was heading towards war. It was an immensely profitable venture, which also established the first Newfoundland community sited, as one contemporary put it, "out of sight and sound of the sea". For many of Northcliffe's employees, recruited from the outports, it was the first time they had ever received a cash wage, though this particular pleasure was countered by some bitter disputes between management and unions. The worst was in 1959, when the Mounties broke a well-supported strike with appalling barbarity, at the behest of Newfoundland's premier Joe Smallwood.

Grand Falls remains a timber town, an unprepossessing place built around the hulking mass of the paper mill that towers over the Exploits River. Nevertheless, there is one pleasant surprise, the **Mary March Regional Museum**, 16 St Catherine St (May to mid-Oct daily 9.30am–4.45pm; $2.50), just to the south of the Trans-Canada – come off at Cromer Avenue, where the highway separates Grand Falls from the adjacent (and unremarkable) township of **WINDSOR**. The museum has a good section on the history of the town and an intriguing series of displays on the **Beothuks** (see p.483). The focus is on one of the last of the tribe, Mary March or Demasduit, who was captured near here in March 1819. The story makes depressing reading. An Englishman by the name of John Peyton settled in Twillingate in 1812 and, over the next few years, became increasingly irritated with the Beothuks, who he thought were damaging his traps and stealing his fish. Peyton wanted to teach the Beothuks a lesson and he set about organizing an expedition into the interior.

The end result was the capture of Mary March – named after the month of her seizure – and thereafter Peyton carted the hapless woman around the island, first to St John's and then to Twillingate, where she was deposited for safe-keeping with the local minister; she died of tuberculosis shortly afterwards. Next door to the museum there's a replica **Beothuk village** (mid-June to early Sept daily 9am–5pm; $2).

Deer Lake

More than anything else, **DEER LAKE**, 210km west of Grand Falls, is a convenient pitstop on either the long road west to Channel-Port aux Basques – and the Nova Scotia ferry – or the journey north to Gros Morne National Park (see p.505) and ultimately L'Anse aux Meadows (see p.508). It has the added advantage of having an **airport**, with Air Labrador (☎709/896-6777, ⓦwww.airlabrador.com) providing regular services to St John's and St Anthony: a flight in or out is one way of reducing the driving considerably. In addition, Canjet (☎1-800/809-7777, ⓦwww.canjet.com) links Deer Lake with Halifax, Montréal, Ottawa and Toronto. There is a clutch of **car-rental** offices inside the terminal building, including Budget (☎709/747-1234), Hertz (☎709/722-4333) and National (☎709/722-4307).

DRL Coachlines **buses** from St John's and points on the Trans-Canada pull into Deer Lake's Irving Big Stop gas station on the highway just outside town – you'll need a taxi to move on. The **tourist office** (daily: June–Aug 8.30am–9pm; Sept & Oct 10am–7pm) is also beside the Trans-Canada and supplies free town maps. As regards **accommodation**, Deer Lake has half a dozen places, one of the more convenient being the recently renovated *Deer Lake Motel* (☎709/635-2108 or 1-800/563-2144, ⓦwww.deerlakemotel.com; ❹), on the Trans-Canada just 2km from the airport. Alternatively, there are several B&Bs in the centre of town amongst the grid of streets that stretch east from the Trans-Canada as it sweeps round the edge of Deer Lake. Options here include the *Lakeview B&B*, 1 Young's Ave (☎709/635-8104; ❷), which has eight en-suite guest rooms, and the less expensive *Watkins House B&B*, 17 Phillip Drive (☎709/635-3723 or 1-877/935-3723; ❷), which has two guest rooms with shared facilities. Perhaps the smartest B&B is *Humberview*, located out of the centre on the north side of the Trans-Canada at 11 Humberview Drive (☎709/635-4818 or 1-888/635-4818, ⓦwww.thehumberview.com; ❸). Both the *Lakeview* and the *Humberview* do **evening meals** by prior arrangement.

The Northern Peninsula

Stretching out between Deer Lake and the township of St Anthony, a distance of about 450km, the **Northern Peninsula** is a rugged, sparsely populated finger of land that separates the Gulf of St Lawrence from the Atlantic. Its interior is dominated by the spectacular **Long Range Mountains**, a chain of flat-topped peaks that are some of the oldest on earth, punctuated by the starkest of glacier-gouged gorges above the bluest of lakes – or "ponds" as the locals incongruously call them. Most of the region remains inaccessible to all except the most experienced of mountaineers, but **Route 430** trails along the length of the western part of the peninsula, connecting the small fishing villages of the narrow coastal plain. The highway also connects with the minor roads that lead to the region's most remarkable sight, the remains of the Norse colony at

L'Anse aux Meadows, at the tip of the peninsula some 50km beyond St Anthony.

Travelling around the peninsula by **minibus** is just too difficult to contemplate for all but the most energetic (or foolhardy), but Viking Express (☎709/634-4710) has a service from Deer Lake to St Anthony, and Pittman's (same number) connects Deer Lake and Rocky Harbour. The nearest **car rental** is at Deer Lake airport (see p.504).

Gros Morne National Park

Beginning about 30km from Deer Lake, the southern section of the Long Range Mountains has been set aside as the **Gros Morne National Park**, a UNESCO World Heritage Site that incorporates a large slice of the peninsula's finest and most approachable scenery. Indeed, the imposing beauty of the park can be almost overpowering, its bays, scrawny beaches, straggling villages and wizened sea stacks backclothed by bare-topped, fjord-cut mountains, whose forested lower slopes are home to moose, woodland caribou and snowshoe hare. It's possible – weather permitting – to drive into the park at any time, but from mid-May to mid-October there's an entry charge of $7.50 per car.

The best place to start a tour is the main **visitor information centre** (daily: late June to Aug 9am–9pm; mid-May to late June and Sept to mid-Oct 9am–5pm; ☎709/458-2066, ⓦwww.parkscanada.gc.ca/grosmorne), situated beside Route 430 as it approaches Rocky Harbour just 70km from Deer Lake. The centre has a series of excellent displays on the geology, botany, biology and human history of the park, and also issues free maps, brochures on the park's key hiking trails and details of local boat excursions; it also runs a programme of guided walks. If you intend to use one of the park's **primitive campsites** ($8 per person), which are dotted along the longer trails, then you have to register here first. If all this sounds too much like hard work consider Gros Morne Adventures (☎709/458-2722 or 1-800/685-4624, ⓦwww.grosmorneadventures.com) which offers a wide-ranging programme of guided hikes, cycling, sea kayaking and winter sports.

Rocky Harbour

It's a couple of minutes' drive from the visitor centre to **ROCKY HARBOUR**, the park's largest and prettiest village, which curves around a long and sweeping bay with the mountains lurking in the background. Although there's nothing special to do or see here, the long walk round to the **Lobster Cove Head Lighthouse** is a pleasant way to spend an afternoon. Rocky Harbour is also near several of Gros Morne's **hiking trails**, notably the lung-bursting, 16km Gros Morne Mountain Trail. The trail – for experienced hikers only – begins beside Route 430, just 7km east of the village, and climbs to the top of Gros Morne Mountain where, at 806m above sea level, the views are stupendous. There's a primitive **campsite** on the way down from the summit (July–Oct) should you decide to stay on the mountain overnight.

Rocky Harbour is the best place to stay in the park, not least because it's relatively compact and has a reasonable range of tourist facilities. **Accommodation** includes the comfortable *Ocean View Motel*, beside the waterfront on Main St (☎709/458-2730 or 1-800/563-9887, ⓦwww.oceanviewmotel.com; ❹), and *Bottom Brook Cottages* (☎709/458-2236; ❹), also on Main Street and consisting of six fully equipped chalets. In both cases advance booking is recommended in July and August. Of the **campsites** hereabouts, the pick is *Berry Hill* (no phone; $15.25 per night; June to mid-Oct), whose 150 unserviced sites are located 4km north of Rocky Harbour along Route 430. For **food**, stick to the restaurant of the *Ocean View Motel*, where they serve very good seafood dishes for around $14.

Bonne Bay and Woody Point

From Rocky Harbour, it's just 11km south to **NORRIS POINT** on the north shore of **Bonne Bay** at the point where this deep and mountainous fjord divides into two inlets – East Arm and South Arm. The best way to see the bay is by **boat** with Bontours (mid-June to early Sept daily 10am & 2pm; 2hr; $25; ℡709/458-2730 or 1-800/563-9887, ⓦwww.oceanviewmotel .com), departing from Government Wharf in Norris Point. The same company also operates a **water taxi** (foot passengers only) across Bonne Bay from Norris Point to minuscule **WOODY POINT**, thereby saving a circuitous 70km-long drive. On the edge of Woody Point – some 3km west along Route 431 – is a brand new **Discovery Centre** (daily: mid-May to late June and Sept to mid-Oct 9am–5pm; late June to Aug 9am–6pm; free), operated by the national park and examining the area's geology, plant and animal life. The Centre is also close to the trail head for the **Tablelands Hiking Trail**, a four-kilometre circular track that cuts across a forbidding landscape of bare and barren rock. Another 8km along Route 431 leads to the sixteen-kilometre loop of the **Green Gardens Trail**, which twists its way to some secluded coves, caves and sea stacks and is equipped with three primitive campsites. Continuing down Route 431, it's a further 4km to **Trout River Pond**, sandwiched by the yellowed bareness of the Tablelands and the massive cliffs bordering the Gregory Plateau. Here, in dramatic profile, you can see the extraordinary force of the uplift created by the collision of the North American and European continents 450 million years ago. The views are splendid, but the best way to see the lake is on the **Trout River Pond Boat Tour** (mid-June to Sept 3 daily; 2hr 30min; $30; ℡709/451-3236).

Western Brook Pond

The remote **Western Brook Pond**, reached by just one access point, 25km north of Rocky Harbour beside Route 430, is one of eastern Canada's finest landscapes, 16km of deep, dark-blue water framed by mighty mountains and huge waterfalls. From the access-point car park it's a forty-minute walk on a well-maintained trail through forest and over bog to the edge of the lake's gorge along the **Western Brook Pond Trail**, which crosses the narrow coastal plain. When you get to the end, don't skimp on the **boat trip** operated by Bontours, the same company which runs trips on Bonne Bay (reservations required; July & Aug 3 daily; June & Sept 1 daily; 2hr 30min; $30; weather permitting). The boat inches its way between the cliffs right to the extreme eastern end of the lake, past several huge rockslides, dramatic hanging valleys and former sea caves now marooned high above the water. If you're without a car, Pittman's Taxis (℡709/634-4710) will take you from Rocky Harbour to the pond's access point for about $35.

Port au Choix

The tiny fishing village of **PORT AU CHOIX** sits on a bleak headland about 160km from Rocky Harbour. Its main claim to fame is the **Port au Choix National Historic Site** (daily: mid-June to Aug 9am–8pm; early June & Sept to mid-Oct 9am–5pm; $5.75), established where a mass of prehistoric bones, tools and weapons were accidentally discovered in the 1960s. The ensuing archeological dig unearthed three ancient cemeteries, confirming the area as a centre of settlement for the **Maritime Archaic Peoples**, hunter-gatherers who lived here around 2000 BC. Begin at the visitor centre, which details what is known of these peoples by means of an assortment of artefacts and touch-screen presentations. It also examines two later groups of settlers, the **Groswater** and **Dorset Eskimo**, whose scant remains, dating from between two and three thousand years ago, have also been unearthed near here at what is their most southerly known place of settlement. Afterwards, you can walk over to **Philip's Garden** to take a look at the exposed remains of a Dorset settlement; a dig is in progress.

Port au Choix has several unassuming **places to stay**, beginning with *Jeannie's Sunrise B&B* (℡709/861-2254 or 1-877/639 2789, ⓦwww.bbcanada.com/3032.html; ❷), in the centre on Fisher Street and with views out to sea. The obvious alternative is the *Sea Echo Motel*, also on Fisher Street (℡709/861-3777 or 1-800/861-3777, ⓦwww.seaechomotel.com; ❹). For **food**, the choices are limited, the pick of the bunch being the *Anchor Café*, beside the burial ground, where for $12 or so you'll get a plate heaped with fresh cod, salmon or the local speciality, shrimp.

St Barbe and St Anthony

Pressing on from Port au Choix, it's about 100km to the hamlet of **ST BARBE**, from where Labrador Marine (℡1-866/535-2567, ⓦwww.gov.nl.ca/ferryservices) runs a **car ferry** (May–Nov 1–3 daily; 1hr 30min; $9 one-way, vehicle $18.50) across the Strait of Belle Isle to Blanc Sablon (see p.516) on the Québec–Labrador border. Ferry tickets can be purchased at the *Dockside Motel and Cabins* just up the road from the terminal (℡709/877-2444, ⓦwww.docksidemotel.nf.ca). While waiting for the ferry the only place to eat is in the motel dining room.

Beyond St Barbe, Route 430 slips through a handful of fishing villages and then cuts east across the peninsula, passing the byroad to L'Anse aux Meadows (see below) before thumping on to the fishing and supply centre of **ST ANTHONY**. With a population of around four thousand, this is the area's largest settlement, but it's not much more than a humdrum port stretched out around the wide sweep of its harbour. It does, however, possess one worthwhile attraction, the **Grenfell House Museum** (daily: late May to mid-June & Sept 9am–5pm; mid-June to Aug 9am–8pm; $3), tucked behind the Charles S. Curtis Hospital. The house, a dark-green shingled structure in New England cottage style, is the restored home of the pioneering missionary doctor, Sir Wilfred Grenfell, an Englishman who first came here on behalf of the Royal National Mission to Deep Sea Fishermen in 1892. He never moved back home and, during his forty-year stay, he established the region's first proper hospitals, nursing stations, schools and cooperative stores. Behind the house, there's a pleasant woodland path that leads – in twenty minutes – to the top of Tea House Hill, where Grenfell and his wife were buried. Back down the hill, beyond the hospital, the **Grenfell Interpretation Centre** (same hours; $6 including museum) expands upon its subject with two floors on Grenfell's life and times and a shop that sells local handicrafts.

Practicalities

Air Labrador (℡709/753-5593, ⓦwww.airlabrador.com) and Provincial Airlines (inside Newfoundland ℡1-800/563-2800, elsewhere ℡709/576-1666, ⓦwww.provair.com) combine to provide regular **flights** to St Anthony

from St John's. **St Anthony airport** is near Seal Bay, a rather distant 55km
west of town on Hwy 430, and 60km from L'Anse aux Meadows. Onward
transport is by taxi only; reckon on $50–60 to either. Note that St Anthony is
50km from L'Anse aux Meadows and once again it's a taxi or car ride. Bargain
short-term **car-rental** deals are available at St Anthony airport – try National
(☎709/454-8522).

For **accommodation** in St Anthony, the best bet is *Lynn's Bed & Breakfast*,
340 West St (☎709/454-2677 or 1-877/510-2287; ❷), a pleasant place with
two guest rooms surrounded by flowerbeds and with views of the harbour.
Alternatives include the *Spruce Inn B&B*, 1 Spruce Lane, off East St
(☎709/454-3402 or 1-877/454-3402; ❷; May–Nov), and the *Haven Inn*, 14
Goose Cove Rd (☎709/454-9100 or 1-877/428-3646, Ⓦwww.haveninn.ca;
❸). As regards **food**, the *Lightkeeper's Café* (☎877/454 4900), on Fishing Point,
at the end of West Street, serves a tasty line in seafood.

L'Anse aux Meadows

L'Anse aux Meadows National Historic Site (daily: mid-June to Aug
9am–8pm; early June & Sept to mid-Oct 9am–5pm; $7) is a UNESCO World
Heritage Site comprising the scant remains of the earliest verified European
settlement in the Americas. It's also a tribute to the obsessive drive of **Helge
Ingstad**, a Norwegian writer and explorer who from 1960 onwards hunted
high and low to find Norse settlements on the North Atlantic seaboard. His
efforts were inspired by two medieval Icelandic sagas, which detailed the
establishment of the colony of **Vinland** somewhere along this coast in about
1000 AD.

Vinland and the Vikings

The first **Viking** voyages, in the eighth century, had no wider purpose than the
plunder of their neighbours, but by the start of the ninth century overpopulation
at home had pushed the Vikings towards migration and colonization. By 870 they
had settled on the shores of Iceland, and by the start of the eleventh century
there were about three thousand Norse colonists established in Greenland. As
good farmland became scarce, so it was inevitable that there would be another
push west.

The two **Vinland sagas** – the *Graenlendinga* and *Eirik's Saga* – give us the only
extant account of these further explorations, recounting the exploits of Leif Eiriksson
the Lucky and Thorfinn Karlsefni, his merchant brother-in-law, who founded a colony
they called **Vinland** in North America around 1000 AD. Crucially, the Norse settlers
failed to establish reasonable relations with their native neighbours – whom they
called *skraelings*, literally "wretches" – and the perennial skirmishing that ensued
eventually drove them out of Vinland, though they did return to secure raw materials for the next few decades; it seems likely that **L'Anse aux Meadows** is the result
of one of these foragings.

The Norse carried on collecting timber from Labrador up until the fourteenth
century, when a dramatic deterioration in the climate made the trip from
Greenland too dangerous. Attacks from the Inuit and the difficulties of maintaining trading links with Scandinavia then took their toll on the main Greenland
colonies. All contact between Greenland and the outside world was lost around
1410 and the last of the half-starved, disease-ridden survivors died out towards
the end of the fifteenth century – just as Christopher Columbus was eyeing up his
"New World".

At L'Anse aux Meadows, a local took Ingstad to a group of grassed-over bumps and ridges beside Epaves Bay. It was an unremarkable location, beside a peat bog, but in the event the bumps contained the remnants of the only **Norse village** ever to have been discovered in North America. These comprised the foundations of eight turf and timber buildings and a ragbag of archeological finds, including a cloak pin, a stone anvil, nails, pieces of bog iron, an oil lamp and a small spindle whorl. Ingstad concluded that these were left behind by a group of about one hundred sailors, carpenters and blacksmiths who probably remained at the site for only one or two years, using it as a base for further explorations.

The site was thoroughly excavated between 1961 and 1968 and there followed an acrimonious academic debate about whether it was actually "Vinland". The geographical clues provided in the sagas are extremely vague, so the argument is essentially linguistic. They hinge on the various possible interpretations of the old Icelandic word "Vinland": one side insists it means "Wine-land" and therefore cannot refer to anywhere in Newfoundland, the other suggests the word means "fertile land" and therefore could.

Whatever the truth, hundreds of tourists come here every summer and begin at the **visitor centre**, where the Norse artefacts appear alongside changing exhibitions on Viking life and culture, all beefed up by an excellent (if somewhat melodramatic) thirty-minute film entitled *The Vinland Mystery*. From here it's a few minutes' walk to the cluster of gentle mounds that make up what's left of the original village, and another short stroll to a group of full-scale replicas of a **long house**, storage shed, workshop and a *faering*, a small boat used in coastal waters.

Practicalities

L'Anse aux Meadows is not easy to reach. One sensible solution is to **fly** from Deer Lake, at the foot of the Northern Peninsula 450km from Clarenville, to St Anthony and then work your way back **by car** – or the other way round; it's also possible to fly from St John's to St Anthony. As a sample fare, Air Labrador flights from Deer Lake to St Anthony cost around $300 one-way and the car rental drop-off charge for picking up in St Anthony and leaving in Deer Lake is $150.

The tourists visiting L'Anse aux Meadows have fuelled a mini-boom in local **B&Bs** and **inns**. There are two star turns, kicking off with the *Tickle Inn* (℡709/452-4321, off-season 739-5503, Ⓦwww.tickleinn.net; ❷; June–Sept), whose four guest rooms share an attractive 1890s house in a superb location on the shores of a secluded cove at remote **Cape Onion**. Reservations are essential and evening meals – as well as boat trips along the rugged coast nearby – need to be booked in advance. The Cape is about 45km from L'Anse aux Meadows – backtrack along Route 436, turn down Route 437 and keep going.

Perhaps even better, and certainly closer to L'Anse aux Meadows, is the *Quirpon Lighthouse Inn* (℡709/634-2285 or 1-877/254-6586, Ⓦwww .linkumtours.com; ❸; May–Oct), where ten rooms in the old lighthouse keeper's house have been intelligently upgraded. The inn boasts a spectacular location, standing on its own islet next to the lighthouse with the cliffs jagging down below. A double room costs $250 per night, but this does include the boat trip over and all meals; the islet is 8km from L'Anse aux Meadows along a short gravel turning off Route 436.

One other possibility is the all-year *Viking Nest B&B* (℡709/623-2238 or 1-877/858-2238, Ⓦwww.bbcanada.com/vikingnest; ❶), in Hay Cove, 1km from L'Anse aux Meadows.

Channel-Port aux Basques and the southwest coast

From Deer Lake (see p.504), it's a long-winded 270km along the Trans-Canada to **Channel-Port aux Basques**, from where Marine Atlantic car ferries (see p.474) sail to North Sydney in Nova Scotia. En route, nowhere special commands attention, though you might pause at industrial **Corner Brook**, Newfoundland's second-largest city. Neither is Channel-Port aux Basques particularly riveting, but it is a short drive from the handsomely appointed outport of **Rose Blanche**, which is itself the starting point for ferries to the remote outports of the **southwest coast**, most of which are still beyond the road network. The submerged rocks and jutting headlands of this southwest coast have witnessed the shipwreck of hundreds of vessels as they attempted to steer round Newfoundland into the Gulf of St Lawrence, some running aground in a fog bank, others driven ashore by tremendous gales. Such was the frequency of these disasters that many locals came to rely on washed-up timber for firewood and building materials, a bonus for communities all too dependent on the trade price of fish. The flotsam and jetsam days are long gone, but if you're after a slice of traditional outport life, then this is the nearest you'll come, though pre-planning is crucial.

In many outports – though not the ones mentioned below – the Newfoundland tourist office has no listed accommodation and instead you'll have to hunt down the details of the simple **guesthouses** (usually in price category ❷, including all meals) that almost every outport possesses. Unfortunately, there's no central agency with lists of which families in which outports take guests, but you might consider checking the phone book for each community to see if there's a chamber of commerce – or at least a town office – and give them a call. If you do express interest in a particular outport, you shouldn't have any problem finding accommodation: the locals will be pleased you're coming and will set you up for a couple of days or a week.

With regard to public transport, DRL Coachlines **buses** link Deer Lake and the ferry terminal at Channel-Port aux Basques once daily, though buses do arrive late in the evening (at 9pm). On the southwest coast, **ferry schedules** (℡709/292-3402, ⓦwww.gov.nl.ca/ferryservices) require careful attention. In theory it's still possible to travel by boat from **Rose Blanche to Hermitage-Sandyville**, about 180km to the east, but this is – in terms of time – a mammoth commitment involving several changes of ferry and several overnight stays of two or three days, as boats run to irregular timetables. Consequently, it's best to limit your ambitions and aim for **Ramea**, arguably the most dramatic of the coast's outports and just 83 nautical miles from Channel-Port aux Basques. Ramea lies just offshore from **Burgeo**, from where Route 480 makes the heroic 150km journey north across the interior to the Trans-Canada; Stew's Bus Line (℡709/886-2955) links Burgeo with Corner Brook.

Corner Brook

CORNER BROOK, 50km south of Deer Lake, is magnificently sited, surrounded by steep wooded hills dropping down to the blue waters of the Humber Arm, which funnels into the Bay of Islands. The city is Newfoundland's second biggest, a workaday pulp-and-paper town supplying newsprint to much of the world, and with the mill to prove it. The coast hereabouts was charted by Captain Cook, who now accounts for the city's most enjoyable attraction, the **Cook Monument**, to the west of the centre in a small park at the top of Crow Hill Road. Otherwise aim for **Main Street**, about 500m long and lined by several of the city's better-looking old buildings. Main Street intersects with West Street, where *13 West*, at no. 13, is an excellent bistro serving reasonably priced food from a creative, international menu.

DRL Coachlines pause at Pike's Irving gas station on the Trans-Canada; you'll need a taxi to travel the 3km on into the centre.

Channel-Port aux Basques and beyond

An important port and ferry terminal, **CHANNEL-PORT AUX BASQUES** divides into two distinct sections, an older part stuck on a bare and bumpy headland about 1.5km seaward from the ferry dock and a newer section spread out along Grand Bay Road about 3km to the west. Most people drive straight through the town, but it does have a **tourist information office**, on the outskirts beside the Trans-Canada, and a substantial supply of affordable **accommodation**. In the newer part of the port, two options are the *Caribou Bed and Breakfast*, 42 Grand Bay Rd (☎709/695-3408, ⓦ www.home.thezone.net/~gibbons; ❷; May to mid-Oct), with five en-suite guest rooms; and the *Hotel Port aux Basques*, 2 Grand Bay Rd (☎709/695-2171 or 1-877/695-2171; ❸).

From Channel-Port aux Basques, it's a 45km drive east to end-of-the-road **ROSE BLANCHE**, a postcard-pretty village of steep lanes, brightly coloured houses and a fine old lighthouse (May–Oct daily 9am–9pm; $3), set high above the seething sea. Next to the lighthouse is a B&B, the *Hook, Line & Sinker* (☎709/956-2767; ❷; May–Oct).

From Rose Blanche, **ferries** (4 weekly; 2hr 30min) head east to **GRAND BRUIT**, where there is one listed lodging, the *Blue Mountain Cabins* (☎709/492-2753, ⓦ www.holidayjunction.com; ❸; June–Oct). Here at Grand Bruit, you change for the ferry (1 weekly; 3hr) to **BURGEO**, a much larger community with a road link with the Trans-Canada. There are frequent ferries from Burgeo (mid-May to mid-Oct Sun–Fri 1–3 daily; rest of year 1–3 daily; 1hr 20min) to **RAMEA**, which perches on a tiny rugged island; there's one B&B here, too, the *Four Winds* (☎709/625-2002 or 1-877/625-2003; ❷).

Labrador

Labrador, a huge swathe of sub-arctic wilderness on the northeastern edge of the Canadian Shield, is a place so desolate that it provoked Jacques Cartier to remark, "I am rather inclined to believe that this is the land God gave to Cain." It's a land full of rocky expanses with little vegetation but soaring mountains and cool, clean rivers that seem to run forever. Much of it is an unspoiled, barely accessible wilderness where caribou roam, well outnumbering the people of Labrador thirty to one, with the largest herd being around 800,000 head.

The region divides into two zones. Half the population of 29,000 live along the **coast** – the traditional preserve of fisherman and whalers since the sixteenth century. Most are scattered along the more accessible south coast, while the communities dotted along the northern coast are small and remote, and for a large part made up of native peoples. The other half of the population live in the towns of the interior: **Happy Valley-Goose Bay**; **Churchill Falls**; and **Labrador City-Wabush**. These settlements have emerged since the 1960s (the products respectively of military bases, immense dam projects and vast mining operations) and are populated chiefly by white southerners with a very different outlook on the use of natural resources from that of the indigenous population. The original owners of this land, the **Naskapi**, **Innu** and **Inuit**, who collectively number around five thousand people, were more or less left alone – excepting the work of Moravian missionaries between the 1770s and 1950s and the devastating 1918–19 influenza epidemic which killed around one-third of them. But in the last few decades the recognition of the enormous economic potential of Labrador has led to dams and mines that disrupt the local ecology. The Labrador Trough, in the west, has the highest concentration of **iron ore** in North America, and in 1997 Inuit and Innu set up blockades in an attempt to disrupt the construction of a **nickel mine** and mill at Voisey Bay, in northern Labrador.

This barren terrain was also long a bone of contention between Québec and Newfoundland, whose current **common border** was fixed in the 1920s, although these days the disputes (concerning Newfoundland's jurisdiction over

Labrador, and then again over hydroelectric potential) have been patched up and more or less consigned to history.

The Labrador coast

According to local lore, God built the world in six days and on the seventh he pelted Labrador with rocks, leaving a wind-cracked and ice-chiselled **coast** that is inhospitable to say the least, with barely a twig in sight along its jagged length.

Inhabited for over nine thousand years, this coast was first used by caribou-hunters and then by Basque whalers, but permanent settlements did not evolve until the turn of the eighteenth century, when fishermen from Newfoundland began summer migrations to these well-stocked waters. Those who chose to live here all year – often of English West Country origin – were known as "livyers" (literally "we live 'ere"); they generally married "Esquimaux" women, and led terribly harsh lives under the control of the English merchants' corrupt truck system and the supplies of alcohol that kept them in a constant state of debt. Their standard of living was greatly improved by Wilfred Grenfell, the superintendent of the Mission to Deep Sea Fishermen from 1892, who established hospitals, orphanages and nursing stations all along the coast, and succeeded in bringing the truck system to an end. The livyers, incidentally, were the first to train **Labrador retriever dogs** to catch any fish that fell off the hook.

But the subsistence farming and fishing, once common here, has today pretty much disappeared, thanks to overfishing and consequent government moratoriums. Hunting and trapping still play a role, giving shape to the annual calendar of many communities, but unemployment along the coast is high, and government funds underpin many local economies. The character of local people, the majority an ethnic mix of European and Native American, is generally marked by dogged determination and resilience. They're a friendly bunch, who still use phrases like "heaken!" and "dout the lights", and have developed a distinct vocabulary, referring to the multitude of narrow inlets along the coast as "tickles" and dolphins as "jumpers".

The history of the area is at its most evocative in some of the old settlements along the **Labrador Straits**, the most temptingly accessible portion of the region. This is particularly so at **Red Bay**, unquestionably the historic highlight along the coast, though the newly rebuilt fishing centre of **Battle Harbour** further up the southern coast, runs a close second. But despite recent progress in road-building in the south, the **northern coast** is still only accessible by plane and a passenger ferry (see box p.514) which makes for remarkable trip, particularly as besides the whales, seals, auk and other wildlife, you're certain to see **icebergs**. Around three thousand bergs drift over from Greenland every year, taking two years to reach Labrador, and they make for a stunning, if ghostly, sight – but have also sounded the death knell for many boats along the coast here, including the *Caron* – once the passenger ferry here before it sank in 1977 – and more famously, the *Titanic*, which also foundered on Labrador ice.

The Labrador Straits and southern coast

The most accessible portion of Labrador, the **Labrador Straits** is a short ferry ride from St Barbe in Newfoundland (see box p.507) across the 18km-wide Strait of Belle Isle to Blanc-Sablon. The trip is an experience in itself, with the

Labrador practicalities

The harsh **climate** and **remoteness** make Labrador one of Canada's most forbidding areas for travellers. January temperatures in Happy Valley-Goose Bay average -16°C (3°F) and the annual snowfall is around five metres – with much of it covering the ground for half the year. Further inland and up north the climate is even colder. Most major roads are unpaved and can close for days in snowy or rainy conditions. Tourist facilities are generally scarce and costly, though most major towns have formal accommodation of some sort. In many smaller towns you'll have to ask around to find a room for rent in someone's home and the same goes for local boat trips. Any trip needs a fair amount of organization – especially if you are heading for the hinterland.

Most visitors to Labrador are **adventure** seekers who come to trek, paddle the coastline, or hunt and snowmobile in the interior. Be warned that unless you have expensive backcountry experience it's best to join an organized **tour** (see p.515), which make the exploration of Labrador's wilds as safe and trouble-free as possible. With good camping equipment, an adventurous spirit and a healthy budget, there are few landscapes that match the untouched, rugged beauty of the area. This is particularly so under the **Aurora borealis** (northern lights; see also p.974), visible in Labrador on average 243 nights per year. The location of magnetic north here makes it the best place in Canada to experience the lights – though at the height of summer the long daylight hours can make it difficult to see the show. Wherever you go, and whenever you go, make sure to take the strongest insect repellent you can find and heavy winter clothing, as even in the height of summer fierce snowstorms can occur.

Getting to Labrador

Labrador is connected to the rest of the world by **flights** from Newfoundland, Nova Scotia and Québec. The major carrier is Air Canada (T 1-888/247-2262, W www .aircanada.ca), which flies to Goose Bay from Halifax and to Wabush from Montréal, Québec City and Sept-Îles. Air Labrador (T 709/753-5593 or 1-800/563-3042, W www.airlabrador.com) flies from St John's, Deer Lake, Stephenville and St Anthony in Newfoundland to their hub at Goose Bay; and Provincial Airlines (T 709-576-3091 or 1-800/563-2800, W www.provincialairlines.ca) flies from these and from Halifax to Goose Bay and Blanc Sablon. Expect to pay around $600–700 for the longer flights from Montréal, Québec City and Halifax; around half that for shorter hops from Newfoundland.

Labrador has **ferry** links from St Barbe, about 80km north of Port au Choix, to Blanc-Sablon (May–Dec 1–3 daily; 1hr 30min; T 1-866-535-2567; $9, car $19); reservations are generally advised. Bear in mind that Blanc-Sablon is on Atlantic time – half an hour behind the neighbouring southern Labrador coastal communities and Newfoundland. There are also the less frequent sailings of the *Nordik Express* (see p.367), which takes several days to find its way here from Rimouski via numerous communities on the north shore of the St Lawrence.

Trains run by the Québec North Shore and Labrador Railway (QNS&L; T 709/944-8205 or 418/968-7805) follow the 416km line from Sept-Îles on Quebec's North Shore to Labrador City and Schefferville. It's primarily an industrial link, but there is limited space for passengers and the journey is an exhilarating ride over high bridges, through dense forest and tundra, past 70m waterfalls, deep gorges and rocky mountains; a special dome car allows passengers to appreciate the awesome views. Trains leave Sept-Îles for Labrador City (Tues 7pm & Thurs 9am; 8hr; $115 return) and for Schefferville (Thurs 9am only; 11hr; $156 return); return trips are from Labrador City (Tues, Wed & Fri noon).

It's also possible to **drive** to Labrador from Québec, via the 580-kilometre Route 389 from Baie-Comeau to Labrador City and Wabush; the road is partly paved and partly gravel and has fuel, food and accommodation services along much of its length.

Specialist tour companies

BreakAway Adventures ☎709/896-9343, ✉lbradley@cancom.net. Guided or unguided wilderness river trips in a kayak, at $40–60 per day with instruction available. Also offered are 5–14 day all-inclusive hiking expeditions priced $1500–3000. April–Oct.

Experience Labrador ☎709/938-7444 or 1-877/938-7444, ⓦwww .experiencelabrador.com. Outdoor adventure company operating out of Cartwright, offering local kayak and walking tours. July & Aug.

Flowers River Lodge ☎709/754-8663 or 1-877/725-6664, ⓦwww.flowersriver .com. Float plane-accessible lodge in northern Labrador with ideal hunting fishing, canoeing and hiking. The outfit also offers float plane charters to anywhere in Labrador. June–Oct.

Labrador Scenic Limited ☎709/497-8326. Wilderness tours lasting up to two weeks, from around $180 per day. Also canoe and kayak rentals. March–Oct. Winter snowmobile tours (half-day $90, full day $180).

Nature Trek Canada ☎250/653-4265, ⓦwww.naturetrek.ca/Labrador. Offers a 17-day hiking expedition in the Torngat Mountains of Northern Labrador ($4750), a coastal tour and an inland wilderness tour that trys to catch the Caribou on their summer migration. May–Oct.

Information and local transport

Advance **information**, maps and timetables are available in advance from the Department of Tourism, Culture and Recreation in St John's, Newfoundland (☎709/729-2830 or 1-800/563-6353, ⓦwww.gov.nl.ca/tourism). The government site also contains a section run by the Department of Works Services and Transportation (☎709/896-7840, ⓦwww.gov.nl.ca), which has up-to-date information on road conditions and ferry schedules. An even better bet for advance information and a comprehensive collection of links is ⓦwww.explorelabrador.nf.ca. For information on the snowmobiling trail system contact Labrador Winter Trails (☎709/896-8750 or 1-877/884-7669, ✉labtrail@cablelab.net).

With the exception of the **rail** line between Labrador City and Schefferville, there is no land-based public transport in Labrador and **driving** on the region's unpaved roads can be difficult, particularly in harsh conditions. But some roads have improved dramatically in recent years and it is now possible to drive around the southern coast and across the interior with regular vehicles. A coastal **ferry** service, run by Coastal Labrador Marine (☎1-866/535-2567), connects the two sections of the road network between Cartwright and Happy Valley-Goose Bay with a car ferry, the *Sir Robert Bond* (mid-June to mid-Nov 2–3 weekly; 12hr; $40 one-way, car $65, 2-berth cabin $43). The passenger-only *Northern Ranger* steamship, also operated by Coastal Labrador Marine, sails weekly from Cartwright and is the main lifeline for the northern coast, providing a bare-bones transport link between coastal communities in the north (see p.522). But if you want to reach the distant outposts quickly, the only choice is by **internal flights** with Air Labrador or Provincial Airlines (see above). Between them they serve 14 coastal communities, most with daily flights; reckon on paying around $450 to fly from Happy Valley-Goose Bay to Nain and back.

vessel dwarfed by icebergs floating down the strait from Greenland, and minke and humpback whales a common sight. From Blanc-Sablon Hwy 510 joins coastal villages for 81km to Red Bay, before turning into a gravel road and heading inland and then along the **Southern Coast** a further 350km to Cartwright.

If you don't have your own transport, the only way to get around is to **rent a car** from National in Blanc-Sablon (☎418/461-2955 or 1-800/227-7368). Exploring the coast is easily done in a couple of days and some visitors even head back to Newfoundland the same day.

Blanc-Sablon and around

Just across the border in Québec, **BLANC-SABLON** is the main transport hub between Newfoundland and Labrador. The town sprawls, beginning 2km west of the ferry terminal along Hwy 501. This road continues further west into Québec, with several explanatory boards illuminating aspects of the area's whaling history alongside it, for a total of 74km to link the three villages of Middle Bay, St Paul and Vieux Fort. It's a scenic drive, the route passing the Brador River and waterfall around 19km from Blanc-Sablon, the first of a number of falls along the way. The highlight on this stretch of road are the impressive views over the St Paul river, but the villages themselves have only the most basic services.

Most travellers head **east** out of Blanc-Sablon into Labrador, along Hwy 510, a road which connects villages that are mostly descendants of the fishing camps and still huddle against the coastal cliffs. The first community along the way is **L'ANSE AU CLAIRE** 8km east of the ferry terminal, which has the main visitor centre (see Practicalities below) and a relatively good range of hotels and restaurants. Another 13km along is **FORTEAU**, the largest community along this stretch of coast, at its liveliest during the annual three-day Bakeapple Festival in mid-August that celebrates the locally abundant cloudberries. A couple of worthwhile short hikes out of Forteau include the 4km long Overfall Brook Trail, which leads to a 30m-high waterfall, and the Schooner Cove Trail, a 3km hike from Hwy 510 east of town to a cove used by prehistoric tribes. Also east of town, the **Labrador Straits Museum** (July to mid-Sept daily 10am–6pm; $2) traces the area's history, with particular emphasis on the important contributions made by Labrador women.

The most significant sights in the area are the 7500-year-old **burial mound** of a 12-year-old Indian boy at **L'ANSE-AMOUR** – the oldest-known funeral monument in North America – and the 36m-high **Point Amour lighthouse** (June–Oct daily 10am–5.30pm; $2.50) further along the same side road. This mid-nineteenth-century lighthouse is Canada's second largest, has spectacular views from the top of its 127-step climb and some informative displays about the area's maritime past in a museum that's staffed by costumed guides.

Further up the coast, **L'ANSE AU LOUP** has all basic services (including fuel) and a 2km marked hiking trail through a stunted tuckamore forest to the summit of the Battery for views over the sea. Beyond the village, and 10km short of Red Bay, the **Pinware River Provincial Park** (☎709/927-5516 or 1-800/563-6353, ⓦwww.gov.nl.ca/parks&reserves) is one of the

The town of Blanc-Sablon is in a part of Québec that uses **Atlantic time** – half an hour behind its neighbouring southern Labrador coastal communities (from L'Anse au Claire to Mary's Harbour), which are on Newfoundland time.

most scenic stretches in the Labrador Straits, with the rushing, white-water Pinware its centrepiece. It's a great place to pick blueberries and bake apples in August.

Practicalities

For **information** head to the "Gateway to the Straits" Visitor Centre (mid-June to Sept Mon–Sat 9am–5pm, Sun 9am–1pm; ☎709/931-2360, ⓦwww.labradorstraits.net), housed in a 1909 church at L'Anse au Claire.

Most of the **places to stay** on this coast are either basic hotels or B&Bs; most offer dinner at an additional charge (to which non-guests are welcome). In Blanc-Sablon *Pension Quatre Saisons*, 2 Beaudoin St (☎428/461-2024; ❸) has motel rooms. But there's a greater selection at L'Anse au Claire: at the inexpensive *Beachside Hospitality Home*, 9 Lodge Rd (☎709/931-2053 or 1-877/663-8999; ❷), three rooms share two bathrooms, a whirlpool tub and guest kitchen; while the *Northern Light Inn* (☎709/931-2332 or 1-800/536-3188, ⓦnli.labradorstraits.net; ❹) is a modern motel with a restaurant.

In Forteau, the *Grenfell Louie A Hall B&B*, 3 Willow Ave (☎709/931-2916 or 1-877/931-2916, ⓦwww3.nf.sympatico.ca/peggy.hancock; ❷), has pleasant rooms, a common room and occupies a 1946 nursing home; and the *Seaview Restaurant and Cabins*, 33 Main St (☎709/931-2840 or 1-866-931-2840; ❸), has basic motel rooms and a good restaurant known for its seafood. Further northeast, the *Lighthouse Cove B&B* (☎709/927-5690; ❷) in L'Anse Amour and *Barney's Bed & Breakfast* (☎709/927-5634; ❷) in L'Anse-au-Loup are both excellent value, with ocean views and excellent home cooking.

In West St Modeste, a few kilometres north of L'Anse-au-Loup overlooking Pinware Bay, the *Oceanview Resort* (☎709/927-5288 or 927-5787, ⓦoceanview .labradorstraits.net; ❺) has four cottages, ten pleasant hotel rooms and several serviced RV sites. You can **camp** ($9) up the valley in the *Pinware River Provincial Park* (☎709/729-2424).

Red Bay to Cartwright

The world's largest whaling port in the late sixteenth century, **RED BAY** is now the most worthwhile place to visit on Labrador's southern coast. Archeological digs here are ongoing; new objects are constantly being discovered and can be viewed at the **Red Bay National Historic Site Visitor Centre** (daily: July–Sept daily 9am–8pm; late June & early Oct 9am–5.30pm; ☎709/920-2051, ⓦwww.parkscanada.gc.ca/parks/newfoundland_bay; $5). The most impressive find is one of the Basque whaling vessels that had foundered in the bay and been beautifully preserved in its ice-cold waters. The story of its discovery and excavation is told in an hour-long documentary film. If you're feeling adventurous, take a **boat trip** to Saddle Island (Mon–Sat 3 daily 9am–4pm; $2), where you can roam around the whaler's cemetery on a self-guided tour of the archeological sites. If you are lucky you may also spot a few whales in the distance.

From Red Bay the road switches from asphalt to well-maintained gravel and heads inland to re-emerge 80km later at the coast by **MARY'S HARBOUR**, a settlement which dates back only to 1955 and was built when fire wiped out Battle Harbour. A short boat-trip from Mary's Harbour – contact Jones Charters and Tours (May–Oct; ☎709/921-6249 or 921-6948; $40 round-trip) – Battle Harbour was early nineteenth-century Labrador's most significant settlement and has now been rebuilt as a historic village (June–Sept; ⓦwww .battleharbour.com). At its height, the cod and seal fishery centre of Battle

Basque whalers at Red Bay

At its peak in the late sixteenth century, over two thousand men lived in Red Bay during the **whaling** season, producing half a million gallons of whale oil to be shipped back on a month-long voyage to Europe. Whale oil was used for light, lubrication and as an additive to drugs, soap and pitch, and one 55-gallon barrel could fetch a price equal to $10,000 today – so for the **Basques** the discovery of Labrador's right-whale stocks was equivalent to striking gold. However, as well as the treacherous journey from Spain to what they knew as Terranova, the Basques withstood terrible hardships to claim their rich booty. Once in Labrador, they rowed fragile wooden craft called *chalupas* into these rough seas and then attached drogues to the whales to slow them down. It was then a matter of following their prey for hours until the whale surfaced and could be lanced to death. Three factors brought the whale boom to an end: first, the Basques were so successful that within thirty years they had killed off more than 15,000 whales; second, the industry became more hazardous with early freeze-ups in the 1570s; and, finally, the Basque ships and men were absorbed into the ill-fated Spanish Armada of 1588.

Serious study of this fascinating area began in 1977, when marine archeologists discovered the remains of three Basque **galleons** and several *chalupas*. Most notable of these vessels was the *San Juan* galleon, which was split in half by an iceberg in 1565, with the loss of one black rat – its bones were found in a wicker basket with a scattering of codfish bones, which showed that the heading and splitting techniques were identical to those used by the Labrador fishermen today. On land, excavations uncovered try-works (where the whale blubber was boiled down into oil), personal artefacts and, in 1982, a cemetery on Saddle Island where the remains of 160 young men were found. Many were lying in groups, indicating that they died as crew members when chasing the whales, but some had not been buried – which suggests that the community had died of starvation when an early freeze dashed their chances of getting home.

Harbour was so busy that you could cross the decks of the schooners tied side by side in its harbour to get from Battle Harbour Island to the mainland. Today there's a visitor centre here, several walking trails have been laid out and you can stay in some of the old houses.

CARTWRIGHT, the northern terminus of Hwy 510, around 270km from Mary's Harbour, is named after Captain George Cartwright. He was one of the first Europeans to survive and coexist with the natives, even taking several people back to England in 1772 to visit the king and Dr Johnson – though smallpox claimed all except Cartwright, and none returned to tell the tale. In recent years Cartwright has become a relatively busy port, with **ferries** from here to Goose Bay and along the coast, but it's still best known for the amazing 56km-long sandy beach **Porcupine Strand** nearby – originally called Wonderstrands.

Practicalities

For **accommodation**, Red Bay's *Whaling Station Cabins*, 61 East Harbour Drive (℡709/920-2156; ❸), offers en-suite rooms with cable TV, and has the best restaurant in the area, while the *Basinview Bed & Breakfast*, 145 Main Hwy (℡709/920-2002; ❷), is more basic but run by friendly owners with a good knowledge of the town's Basque whaling history.

At Mary's Harbour you can stay and eat at the *Riverview Hotel* (℡709/921-6948, ✉riverviewlodgehotel@yahoo.ca; ❹; June–Oct), but it's more pleasant, if less convenient, to stay in Battle Harbour itself (℡709/921-6325 or

921-6216, ⓦ www.battleharbour.com), where the options include a two-storey restored fishing house – the *Battle Harbour Inn* (❺) – and a hostel-style fisherman's bunkhouse (❸). At both, daily rates include all meals. Alternatively, several old self-catering cottages around the village are available (❺).

In Cartwright the *Cartwright Hotel* (Ⓣ 709/938-7414, ⓦwww .cartwrightlabrador.com; ❹) is a friendly place near the airport that also serves good local cuisine.

Happy Valley–Goose Bay and around

Located on the westernmost tip of the huge Hamilton Inlet – also called Lake Melville – the adjacent towns of **HAPPY VALLEY-GOOSE BAY** are the principal transport and service hub for the entire Labrador Coast. There's not much to tempt you here, but a couple of museums, here and up the road in **North West River**, together with some short hikes in the surrounding spruce forest that's interspersed with sparkling lakes and rivers, make it easy to pass a pleasant day or two. One of the liveliest times to visit is in late July or early August during the **Labrador Canoe Regatta**, the area's most important festival. The hectic, carnival-like event is held over a weekend and features canoe races, musical performances and pavilions serving traditional food.

The former trapping community of Happy Valley is where most of the shops and restaurants are located and it's a fairly quiet, laid-back place, with sandy paths instead of sidewalks, which peter out into dirt and gravel tracks at the edges of town. It lives to service Goose Bay, which, since World War II, has been a military air-base for NATO forces. They train here, with particular emphasis on low-level sorties, so that the roar of **low-flying military aircraft**, a thunderous noise swelling up when you least expect it, and lasting for about ten seconds at a time, frequently punctuates the stillness.

The town's two museums largely focus on its military heritage: the **Northern Lights Military Museum**, 170 Hamilton River Rd (Mon–Sat 9am–5.30pm, Thurs & Fri until 9pm; free), has an eclectic collection of military memorabilia, stuffed wildlife displays and model trains; and the **Labrador Military Museum**, in a large hangar on C Street on the base (June–Aug Mon–Fri 10am–5pm, Sat & Sun 2–4pm; rest of year by appointment; Ⓣ709/896-6900 ext 2177), documents the history of the British, American, Dutch and German – as well as Canadian – military presence with displays of flags, insignia and radar apparatus. Particularly poignant are the references to the all-too-frequent fatal air crashes that have occurred here in the past decades.

To experience the countryside around Happy Valley-Goose Bay at its most awe-inspiring, make a trip to **Muskrat Falls**, a thunderous falls on the Churchill River. To get there, drive out of Happy Valley on the Trans-Labrador Route 500. After about 40km, watch for a small sign on the left indicating a narrow dirt road, down which you drive about 10km. From here it's a twenty-minute hike on a rough unmarked trail down to the bank of the river, where

Travelling north from Mary's Harbour to Cartwright, put your watch back half-an-hour, from Newfoundland time to **Atlantic time**, which operates in northern and western Labrador (including Cartwright, Happy Valley-Goose Bay, Labrador City and elsewhere). Note that areas of Québec west of Labrador City are on **Eastern time**, one hour behind Atlantic.

you can view the falls from a spray-covered rocky outcrop. Be sure to take good walking shoes, plenty of drinking water and insect repellent. Both Labrador Scenic Limited and Breakaway Adventures (see box p.515) offer tours here.

Practicalities

The tiny **airport** is located on the military base, a couple of kilometres north of town. As there's no shuttle bus or public transport, you'll have to rely on **taxis** – about $7.50 to Goose Bay, $10 to Happy Valley – or renting a car. National and Budget have booths at the airport and charge about $40 per day, with the first 100km per day free. To get to town, take C Street and Loring Drive and turn right at the traffic lights (the only ones in town) onto Hamilton River Road. The chain-link fence marks the line between the base and civilian territory. The helpful staff at the Labrador Lake Melville Tourism Association **Visitor Centre**, 365 Hamilton River Rd (June–Aug daily 9am–9pm; rest of year Mon–Fri 9am–5pm; ☎709/896-8787, ⓦwww .tourismlabrador.com), can provide brochures and help you plan trips out of town. Some of the staff will even act as your tour guide. If you'd like to strike out on your own you can also get tips and gear from **Labrador Aquatic Rentals**, 1 Hamilton River Rd (☎709/896-2766 or 896-0875), which not only specializes in boat charters, but also rents out various boats, canoes, bicycles and ATVs; in winter snowmobiles are available.

Happy Valley-Goose Bay has a reasonable range of **accommodation**. The least expensive options are the B&Bs in town, particularly *TMT B&B*, 451 Hamilton River Road (☎709/896-4404; ❷), located close to the ferry terminal or the more central *Davis' B&B*, 14 Cabot Crescent (☎709/896-5077; ❸). The *Royal Inn*, 3 Royal Ave (☎709/896-2456 or 1-888/440-2456; ❸), is an average hotel where continental breakfasts are included. The impersonal Old-English-style *Labrador Inn*, 382 Hamilton River Rd (☎709/896-3351 or 1-800/563-2763, ⓦwww.labradorinn.nf.ca; ❺), is the town's fanciest lodging choice.

The best places to **eat** are *Tricia Dee's*, 96 Hamilton River Rd, specializing in steaks and ribs, and the *Midway Gardens Restaurant*, 350 Hamilton River Rd. At *Trappers Cabin Bar and Grill*, 1 Aspen Rd, you cook your steak yourself on their grill. Happy Valley-Goose Bay is a hard **drinking** town: the liveliest bars are *Mulligan's Pub*, 368 Hamilton River Rd, and *Maxwell's II/Bentley's*, 97 Hamilton River Rd, the main nightspot.

North West River and Sheshatsheits

From Happy Valley-Goose Bay a paved road heads north 30km to **North West River** and **Sheshatsheits**, passing the turn-off for the Cartwright ferry and then a large ski hill. Be sure to stop to see **Simeon Falls**, a forest waterfall in the middle of a dense, moss-covered thicket. It's easy to miss: watch for a sign on the road that says "Waterfall 600ft" and then walk along a short winding trail over a tangle of tree roots. In winter cross-country skiers should head to the 30km of trails groomed by the Birch Brook Nordic Ski Club (☎709/896-5573, ⓦwww.birchbrook.com), 13km from Happy Valley-Goose Bay on Northwest River Road.

NORTH WEST RIVER itself is a small, former fur-trading community picturesquely sited on a broad isthmus between two vast bodies of water: Grand Lake, a deep freshwater lake to the west, and Lake Melville, an inland sea with tides and long sandy beaches to the east. For a panoramic **view**, drive the 2km up to **Sunday Hill** on a rather rough, potholed road; you'll be rewarded with sweeping vistas of both lakes and the Mealy and Mokami ranges in the distance. In the village the main attraction is the home and **studio of John Goudie**, on River Road (Mon–Fri 8am–5pm, Sat & Sun 10am–5pm), a local artist who makes furniture and jewellery out of Labradorite, a lustrous crystallized stone. He'll show you his studio where he and his assistants craft the stone and then take you into his house to see the furniture he's made, as well as a huge Labradorite-studded fireplace. The **Labrador Heritage Museum** on Portage Road (Wed–Fri 8.30am–4.30pm; ⓦ www3.nf.simpatico.ca/lab.heritage; $2) off Hwy 520 on the north side of town incorporates the 1923 Hudson Bay store and a trapper's cabin with history of the area, furs and minerals on which much of Labrador's economy is based. The museum also has an intriguing account of the ill-fated 1903 Wallace-Hubbard expedition into Labrador's interior. Leonidas Hubbard, his friend Dillon Wallace and guide George Elson hoped to cross from Lake Melville to Ungava Bay on the northern fringe of Québec. But misunderstanding directions from the natives, they travelled up the wrong river valley. Eventually running out of food, Hubbard died in the wilderness, but his wife Mina – who never forgave Wallace for abandoning him – completed the spectacular trek two years later. She documented the trip in the book *A Woman's Way Through Unknown Labrador*, a 1983 edition of which is still in print. If the museum whets your appetite for more information on Labrador's history try to pick up a copy of the widely sold *Them Days, Them Days*, a quarterly publication published in Happy Valley-Goose Bay that presents an oral history largely through interviews with old-timers. The **Labrador Interpretion Centre** on Portage Road (most days 1–4pm, but hours vary; ☎709/497-8566; $3), has displays of Innu and Inuit crafts, quilts and sculpture, as well as ancient artefacts found in nearby graves. Directions to the centre are poor: take the road sharp left immediately after crossing the bridge and continue driving up the hill to the end of the road.

The Innu village of **SHESHATSHEITS** (pronounced "shesh-ah-shee"), across the small harbour, is worth a stroll as long as you don't linger too long: it's a traditional village and doesn't really encourage tourists.

The northern Labrador coast

The **north** is the most untouched area of Labrador and few visitors venture this far: the coastal boat from Happy Valley-Goose Bay (see box p.522) takes three days to reach **Nain** – and a sudden storm can leave you stranded for days in one of the tinier midway settlements. But the desolate, rocky coast and floating icebergs are spectacular and the mixed native-white communities and their history is intriguing. To some extent traditional patterns of life have been preserved here. There are no cars in most of the settlements, arctic char are still hung in the street to dry, and activities change according to what is in season to hunt or trap – but also conspicuous is the unemployment and alcoholism. For better or worse, life is likely to change soon along this coast as a gigantic mining development is set to take place at **Voiseys Bay** at the northern, and scenically most spectacular, end of the coast. North of here the Torngat Mountains beckon the adventurous – an area which appears destined to become a national park.

Happy Valley-Goose Bay to Nain and beyond

Most of the coastal villages beyond Happy Valley-Goose Bay began as fur-trading posts in the nineteenth century, though some date back to the eighteenth-century establishment of missions by the **Moravian Brethren**, a small German

The Northern Ranger

Northern Labrador is the region at its most remote, yet the coast is fairly easy to explore, thanks to the weekly, summer-only **ferry service** of the *Northern Ranger*, which is becoming popular as a budget cruise. The foot-passenger only steamship, run by Coastal Labrador Marine (℡1-866-535-2567), leaves once-weekly from Cartwright on a route that takes it to Nain via Happy Valley-Goose Bay, with stops at every larger community along the way. In most cases the hour or so the ferry spends at every stop is plenty to have a look around. Should you decide to stop for longer, you'll have to stay for several days until the ferry docks in again, and will have to ask around for somewhere to stay; it's generally not too hard to find accommodation. The ferries run from early July to around mid-October; soon after this, the Arctic ice pack closes in to seal up the area for the rest of year. The late-season schedule is notoriously unreliable since storms can delay sailings, sometimes for days. It's late in the season that the sea can also be at it's roughest; the naturalist Sir Joseph Banks noted that his 1766 voyage down the coast was "one continual puke".

Fares are very reasonable, based on the number of nautical miles travelled, with supplements for cabin space which you should reserve well in advance, otherwise it's likely you'll have no option but to make yourself as comfortable as possible on the aircraft-style seats). A round-trip from Happy Valley-Goose Bay to Nain costs around $350 return in an economy two-berth cabin. Prices at the **onboard restaurant** are slightly elevated and though there's a reasonable range of choice, it's worth stocking up on provisions beforehand.

missionary sect active along the Labrador coast from the late 1700s to the 1950s. The Moravians were originally invited to settle in 1762 by the government in London, who considered the people of the area to be some of the world's most savage. The evangelical group did its best to undermine traditional spirituality and culture, while helping the local population make better sense of their contacts with the outside world. The prim old white Moravian mission – consisting of a 1782 church, residence, store, storehouse and small huts to house visiting native peoples – still stands at **HOPEDALE**, 150km south of Nain (June–Sept by appointment; $5; ℡709/933-3777), its hymn-books printed in Inuktitut. In town the *Amaguk Inn* (℡709/933-3750; ❺) provides comfortable motel-quality rooms and food.

NAIN, despite its hugely picturesque setting in a deep fjord, is sometimes dubbed "Viet-Nain" by Labradorians for its social problems. Fishing is the main industry and centuries-old hunting and trapping traditions continue, but the small town of 1000 people is gearing up to service the gigantic cobalt and copper mine that is being developed just north at Voiseys Bay. The Moravian mission here had been converted into a museum called Piulimatsivik (Inuit for "place where we keep the old things") but burnt down in 1999. Some artefacts were rescued, however – ask around to find where they are currently displayed. You can stay in town at the *Atsanik Lodge*, Sand Banks Rd (℡709/922-2910; ❺; April–Oct).

From Nain you can travel onwards to the treeless tundra of the flat-topped **Torngat Mountains**, the highest range east of the Rockies. The region is best visited with experienced guides like Torngat Mountain Labrador Tours in Nain (℡709/896-4292 or 579-0995, ✉winstonw@roadrunner.nf.net), which offers canoeing, kayaking, walking and camping trips year-round – in igloos in the winter. At Nain you can also charter a boat to sail up the coast with Webb Services (℡709/922-2865; July–Nov), who will show you the deserted misson at Hebron and take you to the **Nachvak Fjord**, near Labrador's northernmost extremity, where the razorback mountains soar out of the sea at an angle of nearly eighty degrees to a height of 915m. En route you're likely to spot grey seals, whales, peregrine falcons and golden eagles.

Western Labrador

Developed entirely in the last fifty years, **western Labrador**, a vast expanse of low, rolling, forested mountains and tracts of tundra, is punctuated by towns that live to serve the remarkable mining and engineering projects here. Unless you have a deep interest in exploring some of the world's largest mines and hydroelectric projects, it's hard to find a reason to come here – although for some the spectacular **rail** journey to Labrador City from Sept-Îles in Québec (see p.360) is reason enough. You can also **drive** here from Québec via Hwy 389, from Baie-Comeau (see p.359) – a route which has services at Manic 5 and Gagnon. The other road into the region is the Trans-Labrador Highway (Hwy 500) which is of poorer quality: the unpaved 526-kilometre road links Happy Valley-Goose Bay to **Labrador City-Wabush** via **Churchill Falls**. This is one of the least frequented stretches of major road in eastern Canada and before driving it you should make enquires about its current condition at the Department of Works Services and Transportation. On average it takes nine hours to traverse and, as there are no services along the route, you'll need to take all necessary supplies (including fuel) with you.

Churchill Falls

Rising from a spring high on the Labrador plateau, the **Churchill River** plunges 75m into McLean Canyon as **Churchill Falls**, located about 300km west of Happy Valley-Goose Bay. In order to exploit the massive power of this tumult, 6700 square kilometres – an area three and a half times the size of Lake Ontario – was dammed for the incredible Churchill Falls hydroelectric development, a project conceived by the premier, Joey Smallwood, in 1952 as part of a drive to save Newfoundland's economy. Wrangling with possible US backers, and then with the Québec government, delayed its construction until 1967, when a workforce of thirty thousand finally began the largest civil engineering project in North America. The Churchill Falls Hydro-Electricity Facility (Mon–Fri 8am–5pm; Ⓦ www.k12.nf.ca/eglambert; free, but book in advance) now offers two-and-a-half-hour **tours** of the resulting 550 megawatt plant which provides enough power for most of New England. The town of **CHURCHILL FALLS** – simply an outgrowth of the power plant – contains two **accommodation** options: the *Black Spruce Chalet* (℡709/925-3233; ❸) which has a common area and kitchen, and the smarter *Churchill Falls Inn* (℡709/925-3211 or 1-800/229-3269; ❹) which also serves **food**.

Labrador City-Wabush

Some 260km west of Churchill Falls it's a shock to come across **LABRADOR CITY** and neighbouring **WABUSH**, two planned mining communities of wide streets and a couple of malls in the middle of nowhere. Both were

Note that Québec west of Labrador City is on **Eastern time**, one hour behind Atlantic.

established in the 1950s and, with a population of 12,000, make up the largest concentration of people in Labrador. Half of Canada's iron ore output is produced here from vast open pit mines that are serviced by oversized 20m-long dump trucks adorned with giant 3m tires. The mines can be toured (July–Sept Wed & Sun 1.30pm) by appointment with Labrador West Tourism (℡709/944-7631, Ⓦwww.exploringlabrador.com).

Given the relatively sizeable population, a few recreation facilities have been developed in the vicinity of the towns. **Duley Lake Park** (late June to early Sept; $4), 10km from town, has excellent facilities for swimming and boating, while the **Menihek Interpretive Trails** (Ⓦwww .labrador-west.com/menihektrails) make an appealing place to hike in summer and snowshoe or cross-country ski in winter, with 34km of trails groomed for all ability levels by the Menihek Nordic Ski Club (Nov–April ℡709/944-2154, Ⓦwww.crrstv.net/~menihek). There's more skiing, though of the downhill variety, at **Smokey Mountain** in the Wapusakatto Mountains 5km from town. The ski hill offers nineteen runs with a 300m vertical drop and some night-skiing. But the most popular local winter activity is **snowmobiling**, which can conveniently be done from the Northern Lights Lodge (℡709/944-7475, Ⓦwww.northernlightsfishhunt.com) which lies beside a network of trails and offers rentals and guided tours and custom packages.

The helpful Destination Labrador **information office**, 118 Humphrey Rd (℡709/944-7788 or 1-800/563-6353), can point you in the right direction for all of these attractions and provides a full list of in-town **accommodation**. For a cheap room try the *Tamarack B&B*, 835 Tamarack Dr (℡709/944-6003; ❷), where three rooms share a bathroom, or head to the *Two Seasons Inn*, Avalon Drive (℡709/944-2661 or 1-800/670-7667, Ⓦwww.twoseasonsinn.nf.ca; ❹), a solid, good-value hotel. To **camp** head to the Duley Lake Park (see above), where sites cost $8.

Good choices for **eating** are the *Two Seasons Inn*, and *Jed's Pub* (℡709/282-5522) on Grenfell Drive, for good pub food and, occasionally, caribou.

Schefferville

Journey's end for the railway from Sept-Îles is **SCHEFFERVILLE**, 190km north of Labrador City. When the IOC mining operation opened the first Labrador iron-ore mine here in the 1950s they recruited a band of migratory Naskapi as cheap labour, so beginning a particularly woeful episode in the history of Canada's native peoples. In 1978 the natives signed an agreement, finally giving them compensation for their lost land and exclusive hunting and fishing rights, but by that time the majority were so debilitated by alcohol that a return to their former existence was impossible. When the mine closed in the late 1980s, the Naskapi were left to fend for themselves, while the white workers moved on to employment in other mines. Schefferville is now a run-down, blackfly-ridden reserve, where houses can be bought for less than $10. Lying just over the border in Québec, the town is essentially a dead-end spot and only worth visiting as the terminus of the spectacular train journey; there's no vehicular road access. The only **accommodation** is the *Hotel-Motel Royal*, 182 Rue Montagnais (℡709/585-2605; ❹).

Travel details

Trains

Labrador City to: Sept-Îles (3 weekly; 8hr).
Schefferville to: Sept-Îles (1 weekly; 11hr).

Buses

St John's to: Channel-Port aux Basques (1 daily; 12hr 35min); Clarenville (1 daily; 3hr); Corner Brook (1 daily; 10hr 25min); Grand Falls (1 daily; 6hr 45min); Lewisporte (1 daily; 5hr 55min).

Ferries

Argentia to: North Sydney, NS (mid-June to Aug 3 weekly; early Sept to mid-Sept 2 weekly; 14hr).
Channel-Port aux Basques to: North Sydney, NS (early Jan to mid-Jan Wed–Sun 1–2 daily; mid-Jan to mid-June & mid-Sept to Dec 1–2 daily; mid-June to mid-Sept 1–3 daily; 5–7hr).
Cartwright to: Happy Valley-Goose Bay (4–6 weekly; 12hr); Nain (1 weekly; 84hr).
St Barbe to: Blanc-Sablon (May–Dec 1–3 daily; 1hr 30min).

Flights

Happy Valley-Goose Bay to: Charlottetown (2 daily; 3hr 45min); Churchill Falls (3 weekly; 45min); Deer Lake (3 daily; 1hr 20min); Halifax (3 daily; 3hr 10min); St John's (4 daily; 2hr–2hr 20min); Wabush (1 daily; 1hr 15min).
Labrador City-Wabush to: Deer Lake (7 weekly; 1hr 55min–2hr 15min); Happy Valley-Goose Bay (1–2 daily; 1hr 5min); Montréal (2–3 daily; 3hr 10min); Québec City (2–3 daily; 2hr 20min); St John's (2 daily; 3hr 15min); Sept-Îles (6 weekly; 55min).
St John's to: Charlottetown (4–6 daily; 2hr 50min); Churchill Falls (3 weekly; 4hr 20min); Corner Brook (2–4 daily; 1hr 10min); Deer Lake (2–4 daily; 50min); Gander (3–6 daily; 40min); Halifax (4–6 daily; 1hr 10min); Happy Valley-Goose Bay (4 daily; 2hr–2hr 20min); Montréal (3–6 daily; 2hr 55min); Ottawa (4–5 daily; 3hr 35min); Québec City, no direct flights (3–5 daily; 4hr 40min); St Anthony (1–2 daily except Sat; 1hr 15min); St Pierre (3 weekly; 1hr 15min); Toronto (5–7 daily; 3hr 25min); Wabash (1–2 daily; 3hr 15min).

5

Manitoba and Saskatchewan

CHAPTER 5

Highlights

* **Winnipeg** The region's biggest city, with an array of museums and some excellent restaurants. **See p.534.**

* **Small-town rodeos** Alberta's Calgary Stampede aside, there are hundreds of rodeos across the prairies with a more authentic vibe – the biggest is at Morris, near Winnipeg. **See p.559**

* **Regina** A small prairie town trying to be big. **See p.565.**

* **Moose Jaw** Pluck up your courage for a tour of the tunnels, once the haunt of Chicago gangsters. **See p.575**

* **Grasslands** Strike out off the beaten track to this beautiful but under-visited national park. **See p.579**

* **Little Manitou Lake** Experience near-weightlessness while floating in the salty lake waters, or at adjacent spas. **See p.592**

* **Canoeing** Easily organized canoe adventures get you into the deep wilderness; aside from Whiteshell and Riding Mountain, the Prince Albert National Park is a top draw. **See p.593**

* **Saskatoon** Surprisingly hip and cultured city, with summer festivals, a lively atmosphere and some great berry pie. **See p.595.**

* **Churchill** Make a once-in-a-lifetime trip north to watch polar bears in the wild. **See p.613**

△ Pick-your-own Saskatoon berries

5

Manitoba and Saskatchewan

The provinces of **Manitoba** and **Saskatchewan** (and eastern Alberta) together form a vast tract bounded by the Ontario border to the east and the Rocky Mountains to the west. Although commonly known as "**the prairies**", this area in fact has flat treeless plains only in its southernmost part, and even then they are broken up by the occasional river valley and range of low-lying hills, which gradually raise the elevation from sea level at Hudson Bay to nearly 1200m near the Rockies. Furthermore, the plains themselves are divided into two broad geographical areas: the semi-arid short **grasslands** that border the United States in Alberta and Saskatchewan, and the **wheat-growing belt**, a crescent-shaped expanse to the north. In turn, this wheat belt borders the low hills, mixed farms and sporadic forests of the **aspen parkland**, a transitional zone between the plains and the **boreal forest**, whose trees, rocky outcrops, rivers and myriad lakes cover well over half of the entire central region, stretching to the Northwest Territories and as far as the treeless **tundra** beside Hudson Bay.

The prairie provinces are certainly not one of Canada's glamour areas, the main cities caricatured as dull, the scenery as monotonous. To some extent, these prejudices stem from the route of the Trans-Canada Highway, which treks through a desultory prairie landscape, avoiding nearly everything of interest: many Canadians prefer to do the long and boring drive to Calgary at night when, so it's said, the views are better. Yet, in truth, this image is grossly unfair. Busy **Winnipeg** – the largest city in central Canada – is well worth a visit for its museums, restaurants and nightlife. And many of Manitoba's most significant

Information and time zones

Travel Manitoba is on ☎1-800/665-0040, ⊛www.travelmanitoba.com. **Tourism Saskatchewan** is on ☎1-877/237-2273, ⊛www.sasktourism.com.

Manitoba and Saskatchewan are both on **Central time**. In winter, both provinces run one hour behind Ontario and one hour ahead of Alberta. However, in summer, Manitoba adopts daylight saving but Saskatchewan does not: this means that between April and October Saskatchewan runs on the same time as Alberta and is one hour behind Manitoba.

NORTHWEST TERRITORIES

WOOD BUFFALO
NATIONAL PARK

Lake
Athabasca

N

SASKATCHEWAN

La
Loche

Churchill River

La
Ronge

Athabasca River

ALBERTA

MEADOW LAKES
PROVINCIAL PARK

North Saskatchewan River

PRINCE ALBERT
NATIONAL PARK

Edmonton

16

Prince Albert

Lloyd-
minster

Battleford

Duck
Lake

Batoche

11

Saskatoon

2

Drumheller

Watrous

7

South Saskatchewan River

4

11

Calgary

Moose Jaw

2

GREAT
SAND HILLS

Regina

Medicine Hat

Swift
Current

Lethbridge

Maple
Creek

3

CYPRESS HILLS
INTERPROVINCIAL
PARK

GRASSLANDS
NATIONAL PARK

Coronach

Hudson Bay

Churchill

York Factory

Reindeer Lake

Nelson River

MANITOBA

GRASS RIVER PROVINCIAL PARK

Flin Flon

CLEARWATER LAKE PROVINCIAL PARK

Cranberry Portage

The Pas

Lake Winnipeg

ONTARIO

Lake Winnipegosis

AIKAKI PROVINCIAL PARK

DUCK MOUNTAIN PROVINCIAL PARK

Lake Manitoba

HECLA PROVINCIAL PARK

NOPIMIMG PROVINCIAL PARK

YELLOWHEAD TRAIL 16

Yorkton

Dauphin

RIDING MOUNTAIN NATIONAL PARK

Gimli

Selkirk

Victoria Beach

WHITESHELL PROVINCIAL PARK

Fort Qu'Appelle

Wasagaming

Neepawa

Winnipeg

Thunder Bay

MOOSE MOUNTAIN PROVINCIAL PARK

Minnedosa

Brandon

Assiniboine River

Portage la Prairie

Morris

Steinbach

Cannington Manor

Souris

TURTLE MOUNTAIN PROVINCIAL PARK

SPRUCE WOODS PROVINCIAL PARK

Winkler

UNITED STATES

0   200 km

attractions lie within easy striking distance, along the **Red River Corridor** to **Lake Winnipeg**, whose lakeside marshes and forests of Hecla Park are great for bird-watching. East of here in the Canadian Shield three excellent provincial parks – **Whiteshell**, **Nopiming** and **Atikaki** – are replete with canoeing routes amid dramatic landscapes.

Heading west from Winnipeg the **Trans-Canada Highway** passes several provincial parks on its way to sprawling and easygoing **Regina** and the rapidly rejuvenating town of **Moose Jaw**, well north of the the coulees and buttes of the **Grasslands National Park**, before arriving at the Alberta border alongside **Cypress Hills** Interprovincial Park, which includes the restored Mountie outpost of **Fort Walsh**.

An alternative route west from Winnipeg is the **Yellowhead Route** (Hwy 16) – a far more agreeable journey. You'll pass through more attractive prairie towns before arriving at **Saskatoon**, Saskatchewan's largest city, which has an attractive riverside setting, good restaurants and several interesting sites, including **Batoche** National Historic Park. This route is also the natural gateway to central Canada's two outstanding parks, **Riding Mountain National Park** in Manitoba and **Prince Albert National Park** in Saskatchewan, where the aspen parkland of the south meets the boreal forests and lakes of the north. Both parks are renowned for their lakes, forest hiking and canoeing.

In the **northern** reaches of both Manitoba and Saskatchewan much of the boreal forest is inaccessible except by private float plane, but all the major tourist offices have lists of tour operators and suppliers who run or equip a whole variety of trips into these more remote regions – from white-water rafting and canoeing through to hunting, fishing and bird-watching. But the north's big draw is the remote and desolate settlement of **Churchill**, on the southern shore of Hudson Bay. One of the world's best places to see **beluga whales** and **polar bears**, in season it's overrun by visitors and documentary film crews.

Reasonably regular **bus** services link Manitoba's main settlements, and most of the village bus stops are within walking distance of at least one hotel. However, nearly all of Manitoba's parks are difficult to reach and impossible to tour by bus, with the exception of Riding Mountain Park, where the service from Winnipeg stops right in the centre of Wasagaming; Whiteshell Park, where a bus passes through on the Trans-Canada on its way east; and Spruce Woods Park, close to the bus routes from Carberry and Brandon. Saskatchewan's public bus services are even more limited, but there are regular connections between most of the major towns, and a useful once-daily summertime bus from the town of Prince Albert to Waskesiu Lake (in Prince Albert Park) and La Ronge. VIA Rail operates just two **train** services in the region, each running three times weekly: the main east–west line connects Toronto with Vancouver via Winnipeg, Saskatoon and Jasper, while a northern line runs from Winnipeg to Churchill, well beyond the reach of the road.

A brief history of the prairie provinces

If you're in the prairie provinces in the winter, when the temperature can fall to between -30°C and -40°C, and the wind rips down from the Arctic, it's hard to imagine how the European pioneers managed to survive, huddled together in remote log cabins or even sod huts. Yet survive they did, and they went on to cultivate, between about 1895 and 1914, the great swath of land that makes up the wheat belt and the aspen parkland, turning it into one of the most productive wheat-producing areas in the world. By any standards, the development of this farmland was a remarkable achievement, but the price was high: the nomadic culture of the **Plains Indians** was almost entirely destroyed and the disease-ravaged, half-starved survivors were dumped in a string of meagre reservations. Similarly, the **Métis** – descendants of white fur traders and native women – who for more than two centuries had acted as intermediaries between the two cultures, found themselves overwhelmed, their desperate attempts to maintain their independence leading to a brace of futile rebellions under the leadership of Louis Riel in 1869–70 and 1885.

With the Métis and the Indians out of the way, thousands of European immigrants concentrated on their wheat yields, but they were the victims of a one-crop economy, their prosperity dependent on the market price of grain and the freight charges imposed by the railroad. Throughout the twentieth century, the region's farmers experienced alarming changes in their fortunes as bust alternated with boom, and this situation continues to dominate the prairie economies. Saskatchewan in particular remains as dependent on agriculture as it was when the province was established in 1905, today producing 42 percent of Canada's wheat, 39 percent of its canola, 35 percent of its rye and 20 percent of its barley. Saskatchewan's farmers often struggle to make ends meet when international prices fall, and consequently they have formed various **Wheat Pools**, which attempt to control freight charges and sell the grain at the best possible time. The political spin-off has been the evolution of a strong socialist tradition, built on the farmers' mistrust of the market. For many years Saskatchewan was a stronghold of the **Cooperative Commonwealth Federation (CCF)**, the forerunner of the New Democratic Party (NDP), and in 1944 the CCF formed the country's first leftist provincial government, pushing through bills to set up state-run medical and social security schemes.

Provincial parks

Manitoba and to a lesser extent Saskatchewan are distinguished principally by their **parks**: thousands of acres of wilderness, lake, river and forest that boast wonderful scenery, great hikes and hundreds of kilometres of canoe routes.

Entry to any of **Manitoba's** provincial parks is $5 per car (good for 3 days); entry by foot or bike is free. Campsites and RV sites in Manitoba's provincial parks can be reserved from April to September by calling the Parks Reservation Service (☎204/948-3333 or 1-888/482-2267). There is a charge of $6.75 for each reservation. For detailed information and to obtain complimentary **maps** contact or visit Manitoba Conservation, 200 Saulteaux Crescent in Winnipeg (Mon–Fri 8am–4.30pm; ☎204/945-6784 or 1-800/214-6497, ⊛www.manitobaparks.com). They are the people to turn to for specialist advice on anything from weather conditions to outfitters and guides. Those planning a backcountry hike, wilderness canoeing, rafting or kayaking can get topographic, angling and illustrated maps and aerial photographs of thirteen major canoe routes from Manitoba Conservation, Land Information Centre, 1007 Century St in Winnipeg (☎204/945-6666 or 1-877/627-7226, ⊛www.canadamapsales.com).

Entry to any of **Saskatchewan's** provincial parks is $7 for a day, $17 for three days, $25 weekly, $42 annual. Information is on ☎306/787-2700 in Regina or 1-800/205-7070, ⊛www.saskparks.net. Camping fees are $11–24 depending on the services provided. Between late June and mid-August you can reserve a site in advance at six of the parks for a $5 fee: Cypress Hills ☎306/662-5484; Duck Mountain ☎306/542-5513; Greenwater Lake ☎306/278-3532; Lac La Ronge ☎306/425-4234 or 1-800/772-4064; Meadow Lake ☎306/236-7690; and Moose Mountain ☎306/577-2611. A good walking guide is *Saskatchewan Trails – A Guide to Nature Walks and Easy Hikes* by Robin and Arlene Karpan, which outlines over a hundred hikes in the province.

Winnipeg

With 667,000 inhabitants, **WINNIPEG** accounts for roughly two-thirds of the population of Manitoba, and lies at the geographic centre of the country, sandwiched between the US frontier to the south and the infertile Canadian Shield to the north and east. The city has been the gateway to the prairies since 1873, and became the transit point for much of the country's transcontinental traffic when the railroad arrived twelve years later. From the very beginning, Winnipeg was described as the city where "the West began", and its polyglot population, drawn from almost every country in Europe, was attracted by the promise of the fertile soils to the west. But this was no classless pioneer town: as early as the 1880s the city had developed a clear pattern of residential segregation, with leafy prosperous suburbs to the south along the **Assiniboine River**, and "Shanty Town" to the north. The long-term effects of this division have proved hard to erase, and today the dispossessed still gather round the cheap dorms just to the north of the business district, a sad rather than dangerous corner near the main intersection at Portage Ave and Main St.

ACCOMMODATION

Carlton Inn	C
Best Western Charter House	E
Delta Winnipeg	D
Hotel Fort Garry	F
Ivey House International Youth Hostel	G
Radisson Hotel Winnipeg Downtown	A
St Regis	B

RESTAURANTS

Amici	5
Le Beaujolais	3
Chocolate Shop	2
The Forks Market	4
Pasquale's	6
Tre Visi	1

DOWNTOWN WINNIPEG

Lower Fort Garry & Hwy 9

Little Italy ▼   Riel House and ▼ Fort Whyte   Whiteshell Park ▼

Winnipeg's skid row is only a tiny part of the downtown area, but its reputation has hampered recent attempts to reinvigorate the city centre as a whole: successive administrations have refurbished warehouses and built walkways along the **Red River** and Assiniboine River, but the new downtown apartment blocks remain hard to sell, and most people stick resolutely to the suburbs.

That apart, Winnipeg makes for an enjoyable stopover, and all of the main attractions are within easy walking distance of each other. The **Manitoba Museum of Man and Nature** has excellent displays on the history of the province and its various geographic areas; the **Exchange District**, recently declared a National Historic Site, features some good examples of Canada's early twentieth-century architecture; the Winnipeg **Art Gallery** has the world's largest collection of Inuit art; and, just across the Red River, the suburb of **St Boniface** has a delightful museum situated in the house and chapel of the Grey Nuns, who arrived here by canoe from Montréal in 1844. Winnipeg is also noted for the excellence and diversity of its restaurants, while its flourishing performing-arts scene features everything from ballet and classical music through to C&W and jazz.

The city also makes a useful base for exploring the area's attractions (see p.551), the most popular of which – chiefly **Lower Fort Garry** – are on the banks of the Red River as it twists its way north to **Lake Winnipeg**, 60km away. On the lake itself, **Grand Beach Park** has the province's finest stretches of sandy beach, just two hours' drive from the city centre.

A brief history of Winnipeg

Named after the **Cree** word for murky water ("win-nipuy"), Winnipeg owes much of its history to the Red and Assiniboine rivers, which meet just south of today's city centre at the confluence called **The Forks**. The first European to reach the area was **Pierre Gaultier**, Sieur de la Vérendrye, an enterprising explorer who founded Fort Rouge near the convergence of the two rivers in 1738. This settlement was part of a chain of fur-trading posts he built to extend French influence into the west. Prospering from good connections north along the Red River to Lake Winnipeg and Hudson Bay, and west along the Assiniboine across the plains, the fort became one of the region's most important outposts within twenty years.

After the defeat of New France in 1763, local trading activity was absorbed by the Montréal-based **North West Company**, which came to dominate the fur trade at the expense of its rival, the Hudson's Bay Company. The latter continued to operate from fortified coastal factories staffed by British personnel, expecting their Indian trading partners to bring their pelts to them – unlike their rivals, who were prepared to live and travel among the natives. This inflexible policy looked like the ruination of the company until it was rescued by Thomas Douglas, the **Earl of Selkirk**, who bought a controlling interest in 1809.

In the three years Lord Selkirk took to turn the business round, he resettled many of his own impoverished Scottish crofters around The Forks, buying from his own company a huge tract of farmland, which he named the Red River Colony, or Assiniboia. The arrival of these colonists infuriated the Nor'Westers, who saw the Scottish settlement as a direct threat to their trade routes. They encouraged their **Métis** allies and employees to harry the Scots and for several years there was continuous skirmishing, which reached tragic proportions in 1816, when 21 settlers were killed by the Métis in the Seven Oaks Massacre.

Just five years later the two rival fur-trading firms amalgamated under the "Hudson's Bay Company" trade name, bringing peace and a degree of prosperity to the area. Yet the colony remained a rough-and-ready place, as a chaplain called John West lamented: "Almost every inhabitant we passed bore a gun upon his shoulder and all appeared in a wild and hunter-like state." For the next thirty years, the colony sustained an economic structure that suited both the farmers and the Métis hunters, and trade routes were established along the Red River with Minnesota, south of the border. But in the 1860s this balance of interests collapsed with the decline of the buffalo herds, and the Métis faced extreme hardship just at the time when the Hudson's Bay Company had itself lost effective administrative control of its territories.

At this time of internal crisis, the politicians of eastern Canada agreed the **federal union** of 1867, opening the way for the transfer of the Red River Colony from British to Canadian control. The Métis majority – roughly 6000 compared to some 1000 whites – were fearful of the consequences and their resistance took shape round **Louis Riel**, under whose dexterous leadership they captured the Hudson's Bay Company's Upper Fort Garry and created a provisional government without challenging the sovereignty of the crown. A delegation went to Ottawa to negotiate the terms of their admission into the Dominion, but their efforts were handicapped by the **execution** by Métis of an English settler from Ontario, Thomas Scott. The subsequent furore pushed prime minister John A. Macdonald into dispatching a military force to restore "law and order"; nevertheless, the Manitoba Act of 1870, which brought the Red River into the Dominion, did accede to many of the demands of the Métis, at the price of Riel's exile, and guaranteed the preservation of the French culture and language in the new province – although in practice this was not effectively carried out.

The eclipse of the Métis and the security of Winnipeg – as it became in 1870 – were both assured when the **Canadian Pacific Railway** routed its transcontinental line through The Forks in 1885. With the town's commodity markets handling the expanding grain trade and its industries supplying the vast rural hinterland, its population was swelled by thousands of **immigrants**, particularly from the Ukraine, Germany and Poland; in 1901 it had risen to 42,000. By World War I Winnipeg had become the third-largest city in Canada and the largest grain-producing centre in North America, and by 1921 the population had reached 192,000. More recently, the development of other prairie cities, such as Regina and Saskatoon, has undermined something of Winnipeg's pre-eminence, but the city is still the economic focus and transport hub of central Canada.

Arrival, information and transport

Winnipeg **airport** (Ⓦ www.waa.ca) is some 7km west of the city centre. There's a tourist **information** desk inside the airport concourse, which has a good range of leaflets on the city and its principal attractions along with accommodation listings. Close by, there's a complimentary hotel-booking phone and display board. From outside the terminal building, Winnipeg Transit bus #15 (daily every 20–30min 6.15am–12.45am; $1.65) runs downtown, dropping passengers at or near most of the larger hotels; buy tickets from the driver. Taxis charge around $20; limos cost $20–30 per person. The Mall Centre **bus station** is on the west side of the downtown area at Portage Ave and

Tours in and around Winnipeg

Boat tours of the city leave from the dock beside Provencher Bridge at The Forks (see p.543), from where city tours on a **double-decker bus** also depart (June–Sept; 9am; 3hr; basic tour $20). There are **walking tours** of the Exchange District from Old Market Square (May–Aug Tues–Sun hourly 10am–3pm; 1hr 30min; $5; ℡204/942-6716, ⓦwww.exchangedistrict.org); around local art galleries from Winnipeg Art Gallery (July & Aug Wed, Thurs & Sat; $4.95; ℡204/786-6641); and of Selkirk Ave in the North End (June–Aug Tues–Sat 10am & 2pm; free; 1hr; ℡204/586-3445 or 586-2720). **Horse-drawn carriages** are available to take you around St Boniface, the French quarter (June–Aug; ℡204/235-8343 or 1-866/808-8338, ⓦwww.tourismeriel.com).

Out of Winnipeg
Akeesha Dove ℡204/339-1154. A visit to the Spirit Sands "desert". May–Oct.

Anishinabe Camp and Cultural Tours ℡204/925-2030. To Riding Mountain National Park, for aboriginal culture, sleeping in tepees and participating in traditional ceremonies and powwow dancing. May–Sept.

Aurora Canada Tours ℡204/942-8140. One-day to two-week tours observing bird and plant life and viewing the Northern Lights. Nov–April.

B&B Scuba ℡204/257-3696 or 1-888/257-3696, ⓦwww.bbscuba.com. Week-long scuba-diving tours that include snorkelling with beluga whales. Year-round.

Canadian Trails Adventure Tours ℡1-800/668-2453, ⓦwww.canadiantrails.com. Bicycle tours. Year-round.

The Great Gray Owl Wilderness Adventure Camp ℡204/237-5253 or 1-800/565-2595, ⓦwww.greatgrayowl.com. Ecologically sound trips to Atikaki Wilderness Provincial Park. Year-round.

Memorial Boulevard (daily 6.30am–midnight). Bus companies include Beaver, 339 Archibald St (℡204/989-7007); Greyhound, 487 Portage Ave (℡204/783-8857); and Grey Goose, 487 Portage Ave (℡204/783-4537). Union Station, the city's **train station**, is on Main St, just south of Portage, and has connecting trains to Churchill, Toronto and Saskatoon for Vancouver. Arrival and departure information is on ℡1-800/835-3037, while VIA Rail fares and reservations are on ℡1-800/561-8630. For details of left luggage facilities, see "Listings" on p.550.

Tourism Winnipeg has an information office at 279 Portage (Mon–Fri 8.30am–4.30pm; ℡204/943-1970 or 1-800/665-0204, ⓦwww.tourism .winnipeg.mb.ca), as well as at the airport. A comprehensive range of leaflets on both the city and province is also available at the **Explore Manitoba** Centre (daily 10am–6pm; ℡204/945-3777 or 1-800/665-0040, ⓦwww .travelmanitoba.com), adjacent to the Johnston Terminal at the Forks, where travel counsellors can also help plan your itinerary. All outlets provide free city maps, a Winnipeg Transit bus plan, accommodation listings, a restaurant guide, an historic and architectural guide to the downtown area and free listings of activities and attractions.

Although you can stroll across the downtown core in twenty minutes, the suburbs and more outlying attractions are easy to reach by bus. **Winnipeg Transit** (Mon–Sat 6am–10pm, Sun 6.30am–10pm; ℡204/986-5700, ⓦwww.winnipegtransit.com) has an excellent range of citywide services (flat fare $1.65 per journey), with tickets and transfers for trips involving more than one bus available from the driver (exact fare only). For details of bike rental, car rental and taxis, see "Listings", p.550.

Accommodation

Most of Winnipeg's **hotels** are within walking distance of the bus and train stations, and there's rarely any difficulty in finding somewhere to stay. The modern hotels are standard-issue skyscrapers that concentrate on the business clientele; some offer weekend discounts and up to twenty percent reductions if you stay for three or four nights. At a lower budget, avoid the "flophouses", the cheap dorms calling themselves "hotels" on Main St, just north of Portage Ave. Breakfast is extra almost everywhere. The major approach roads are dotted with **motels** (from ❶ up to ❹), of which the largest concentrations are along the Pembina Highway, which runs south from the city centre as Donald St and Route 42, and along Portage, which runs west forming part of the Trans-Canada Highway (Route 1).

Tourism Winnipeg (☎1-800/665-0040) will help arrange hotel and B&B accommodation and has details of some thirty **B&B** addresses (mostly ❷), with breakfasts that vary from frugal continental to a complete meal. Most of these are affiliated to Bed and Breakfast of Manitoba (☎204/661-0300 or ☎1-877/304-0300, ⓦwww.bedandbreakfast.mb.ca), an agency that makes reservations upon payment of a deposit equivalent to one night's stay. Most of their B&Bs are far from central, but some of the more convenient locations are given below. The **hostel**, within easy walking distance of the bus station, is supplemented in summer by less conveniently located rooms at the University of Manitoba.

Hotels and motels

Balmoral Motor Hotel 621 Balmoral St at Notre Dame Ave ☎204/943-1544. In the northwest corner of downtown, with a laundry room, a coffee shop and the opportunity to get a tan on their sunbeds. ❶

Best Western Charter House 330 York Ave at Hargrave St ☎204/942-0101 or 1-800/782-0175. A good location and reasonable rates make up for the absence of character. ❸

Carlton Inn 220 Carlton St ☎204/942-0881 or 1-877/717-2885, ⓦwww.carltoninn.mb.ca. One of the more agreeable budget hotels, centrally located opposite the city's Convention Centre, with motel-style rooms, restaurant and pool. ❸

Comfort Inn South by Journey's End 3109 Pembina Highway ☎204/269-7390 or 1-800/228-5150. No-frills motel with a restaurant and free local calls. ❹

Delta 350 St Mary Ave at Hargrave St ☎204/942-0551 or 1-800/268-1133, ⓦwww.deltahotels.com. Stay in tasteful, opulent rooms adjoining the Convention Centre, with restaurants and pools. ❹

Fort Garry 222 Broadway ☎204/942-8251 or 1-800/665-8088, ⓦwww.fortgarryhotel.com. Built in Neo-Gothic style between 1911 and 1914 near the train station and lavishly refurbished, with an elegant, balconied foyer leading to 250 rooms. Rates include a breakfast buffet. ❹

Gordon Downtowner 330 Kennedy St at Ellice Ave ☎204/943-5581, ⓦwww.downtowner.mb.ca. Probably Winnipeg's most comfortable budget hotel, with restaurant and bar and in a central location. ❷

Mariaggi's Theme Suite Hotel 231 McDermot Ave ☎204/947-9447, ⓦwww.mariaggis.com. Pay through the nose but reap the rewards of Hawaiian, Mexican, Moroccan or African themed suites or a tropical penthouse. Couples only. ❼

Osborne Village Motor Inn 160 Osborne St ☎204/452-9824, ⓦwww.osbournevillage.com. Basic but decent choice in the heart of lively Osborne Village. Bands often play downstairs and the rooms (none are non-smoking) are not soundproofed. ❶

Radisson Hotel Winnipeg Downtown 288 Portage Ave at Smith St ☎204/956-0410 or 1-800/333-3333, ⓦwww.radissonhotel.com. One of the city's largest and most recently renovated hotels, with fine views from the top floors, as well as a gym, saunas, whirlpool, swimming pool, plus baby-sitting services. Offers big discounts at weekends. ❹

Red Lion Inn 3252 Portage Ave ☎ & ⓕ204/837-5871. Small drive-up hotel on the Trans-Canada Highway. ❷

St Regis 285 Smith St ☎204/942-0171 or 1-800/663-7344, ⓦwww.stregishotel.net. An historic hotel (dating from around 1900) in the downtown area. Tastefully furnished with dining room and coffee shop. The honeymoon suites have hot tubs. Under-18s stay free. ❷

B&Bs

Bob & Margaret's 950 Palmerston Ave ☎204/774-0767. A 15min ride on bus #10 from downtown, this riverside B&B has one bedroom suite only, with TV room and private bathroom. Bikes and canoes can be rented. ❷

Cowan's Castle 39 Eastgate ☎204/786-4848, ⓦ www.cowanscastle.tripod.com. A 1907 four-bed heritage home on the Assiniboine River, twenty minutes' walk to downtown. Serves delicious home-cooked breakfasts. ❷

Gîte de la Cathédrale 581 rue Langevin, St Boniface ☎204/233-7792. Run by French Manitobans, this B&B in the heart of St Boniface offers Québecois breakfasts of pancakes and maple syrup, omelettes and French toast, with service in French. Five flowery bedrooms with shared bathroom. ❷

Mary Jane's Place 144 Yale Ave ☎204/453-8104. A gracious Georgian-style home with oak panelling and stained-glass windows, ten minutes by bus #29 from Portage Ave. ❷

West Gate Manor 71 West Gate ☎204/772-9788. Pleasant rooms with Victorian period furnishings in Armstrong Point, within walking distance of downtown. ❷

Hostels

Guest House International Hostel 168 Maryland St ☎204/772-1272 or 1-800/743-4423. A restored Victorian house with six comfortable dorms (beds $16), four private bedrooms (doubles $38) and walls decorated with art by aboriginal children. Bus #29 from the train station, or a nine-block walk from the bus station. The area, though residential, can be a bit dodgy at night. Facilities include a laundry, kitchen, game room and Internet access. Reservations recommended in summer. April–Nov. ❶

Ivey House International Youth Hostel 210 Maryland St at Broadway ☎204/772-3022. A friendly, forty-room hostel, clean and well run with dorm beds ($16) and some private rooms sleeping 2–4. There's also a lounge, a big kitchen, sun deck, lockers and bike rental. Bus #17 from Vaughan St near the bus station, or #29 from the train station. Often full in the summer. Check-in: June–Nov daily 8am–midnight, rest of year daily 8–10am & 4pm–midnight. ❶

Student rooms

University of Manitoba Fort Garry campus ☎204/474-9942. Double rooms ($20 per person) available from mid-May to mid-August in basic student digs. An inconvenient 10km south of the city centre, but low monthly rates (around $300) make this a good long-stay option. ❶

Campsites

Conestoga Campground 1341 St Anne's Rd at Perimeter Hwy ☎204/257-7363. Located 13km southeast of town; most sites have electricity and water. Mid-May to mid-Oct. $12–18.

Jones Campground 588 Trans-Canada Hwy, St François Xavier ☎ & ⓕ204/864-2721. In a small town on the Assiniboine River, 15km west of Winnipeg, this campsite has 44 unreserved sites, most with water and electricity as well as toilets, showers and a BBQ area. May–Sept. $10–15.

Traveller's RV Resort Murdock Rd ☎204/256-2186. Just off the Trans-Canada, some 14km southeast of the centre, with over fifty unreserved sites and facilities that include mini-golf and a swimming pool. May–Sept. $16–25.

The City

Winnipeg's main north–south artery is **Main Street**, which runs roughly parallel to the adjacent Red River. The principal east–west drag is **Portage Avenue**, which begins at its junction with Main. The downtown core falls on either side of Portage, beginning at Main and ending at Memorial Boulevard; it's bounded by Broadway to the south and Logan Ave to the north. A twenty-minute stroll takes you from end to end.

The traditional centre of Winnipeg is the intersection of Portage and Main just north of **The Forks**, close to the Red River at the start of what was once the main Métis cart track (the Portage Trail) west across the prairies to the Hudson's Bay Company posts, and the principal trail north to Lake Winnipeg linking the riverside farm lots and Lower and Upper Fort Garry. Main St was, in fact, called the Garry Road until the mid-1870s. Despite its historic associations, in 1979 the city council closed most of the junction to pedestrians in return for the construction of an underground shopping concourse, Winnipeg Square. While you're here, have a look at the grand Neoclassical **Bank of Montréal** on the southeast side of the intersection, its fussily carved capitals in stark contrast to the sharp, clean lines of its skyscraper neighbours. The intersection is also known as the **windiest** of any town in Canada.

The Exchange District

Just north of the Portage and Main intersection, the **Exchange District National Historic Site** is a rough rectangle of old warehouses, former commodity exchanges and commercial buildings that are the best-preserved group of any city in Canada. Many of them were converted, from the late 1970s onwards, into art galleries, boutiques, antique shops and restaurants. The district is also one of the city's principal cultural centres, home to such buildings as the Manitoba Museum of Man and Nature, the Ukrainian Cultural and Educational Centre and the artist-run Artspace.

The effective centre of the district is the **Old Market Square** at King and Albert streets and Bannatyne Ave, with its weekend produce market, flea markets and buskers. This part of town was built during Winnipeg's boom, a period of frenzied real-estate speculation and construction that peaked in 1882, but lasted only until the outbreak of World War I. The standard architectural design, used for most of the office buildings and nearly all the warehouses, was simple and symmetrical, the plain brick walls topped off by decorative stone cornices. However, one or two companies financed extravagant variations, notably the Electric Railway Chambers Building at 213 Notre Dame Ave, an imaginative blend of Italian Renaissance and early twentieth-century motifs, its terracotta facade lined with some six thousand electric lights. Possibly the most gracious building in the Exchange District is the former Winnipeg Grain Exchange, opposite the *Lombard Hotel* on Lombard Ave. It was built between 1906 and 1928 and was the largest building of its type in Canada; grain offices still occupy some of the floors. Other imposing buildings are the ten-storey Confederation Life Building, 457 Main St, which has a curved facade of white terracotta, and the massive Royal Bank Building at the corner of Main St and William Ave.

The Manitoba Museum

In the heart of the Exchange District, at 190 Rupert Ave, the **Centennial Centre** incorporates the **Manitoba Museum** (late May to early Sept daily 10am–6pm; rest of year Tues–Fri 10am–4pm, Sat & Sun 10am–5pm; ⓦ www.manitobamuseum.mb.ca; $6.50), an excellent introduction to the province's geographical regions and the history of its peoples.

Highlights of the **natural history** galleries include an imposing polar bear diorama, a well-illustrated explanation of the Northern Lights and the evocative Boreal Forest gallery, where you'll find a waterfall, a family of moose, and a diorama of Cree gathering food and painting sacred designs on rocks. There's also a disconcerting section devoted to the more malicious insects of Manitoba – starring the "no-see-um", a deer fly that specializes in burrowing into the nostrils of caribou. The **Grasslands Gallery** has a small display of Assiniboine Indian artefacts, along with a reconstruction of a tepee and a copy of a pioneer log cabin. There's also an example of the sod houses that the pioneers were forced to build in many parts of the treeless southern plains, and a replica of the odd-looking Red River cart, the Métis's favourite

The history of the railway in Canada

Even before Confederation in 1867, Sir John A. Macdonald, Canada's first prime minister, grasped the need to physically link the disparate provinces of the new nation. Each area needed lines of communication to the east and west to counteract the natural tug of the neighbouring parts of the USA to the south. Both the Maritime Provinces and British Columbia joined the Confederation on the condition that **rail** links would be built to transport their goods throughout the land. Railway construction of this scale was a huge undertaking for such a young country and outside finance was the only answer.

From 1855, lines were constructed in eastern Ontario and Québec, culminating in the completion in 1876 of the **Intercolonial Railway**, which linked central Canada with the Maritime Provinces. Progress of the transcontinental line to the Pacific, however, was impeded by the Riel rebellion at the Red River in 1869–70, and in 1871 the Parliamentary Opposition labelled the entire scheme "an act of insane recklessness". Two years later Macdonald's Conservative government fell after implication in scandals involving the use of party funds in railway contracts, and Alexander Mackenzie's subsequent Liberal ministry proceeded so slowly with the railway plans that British Columbia openly spoke of secession if construction was not speeded up. The eventual completion of the **Canadian Pacific Railway (CPR)** in 1885 finally made Canada "more than a geographical expression", and by the early twentieth century another coast-to-coast line had been completed.

Passage across the hitherto virtually impenetrable Canadian Shield was now feasible and the full agricultural potential of the prairies to the west could be realized. Between 1896 and 1913 more than one million people arrived by train to settle in the prairies, and wheat production rose from 20 million to more than 200 million bushels a year. Additionally, some of the first major mineral finds in northern Ontario were brought to light during the construction of the railway. The years following World War I were a period of economic consolidation, which culminated in the union of various smaller lines into a nationwide system: the **Canadian National Railways (CNR)**, a government-controlled organization.

What has been called "the bizarre project" of the **Hudson Bay Railway** stemmed from the prairie farmers' desire to create an outlet for trade with the rest of the world that was not dependent on the bankers back east. A first attempt in 1886 foundered when the promoters ran out of money after the first 65km. After many delays this major engineering feat was accomplished in 1929, just in time for the Great Depression.

The impact of the Depression on Canadian railways was particularly severe, leading to stringent economies and pooling of competing lines. World War II saw a rise in profits, but over the subsequent decades the story has been one of gradual decline, with freight increasingly travelling by road and air, and passenger services pruned almost to extinction on some lines. By 1992, passengers could no longer cross Canada on the CPR, and one of the world's great train rides was gone for ever. Grain and minerals are still moved by train, however, and the privately owned CPR is now exclusively a freight line. **VIA Rail**, the passenger branch of CNR, operates virtually all of Canada's passenger services, including the Hudson Bay line in roadless northern Manitoba – probably the only rail route in North America still to exist primarily as a passenger service.

form of land transportation, with massive wheels that could tackle the prairie mud and mire.

The museum's most popular exhibit, moored in a massive display area that reproduces a seventeenth-century River Thames dockside, is an impressive full-scale working replica of **the Nonsuch**, the ship whose fur-collecting voyage to Hudson Bay in 1668 led to the creation of the Hudson's Bay Company. The new Hudson's Bay Company Gallery comprises more than 10,000 artefacts and documents amassed by the Company and which form a record of its links with Manitoba and its impact on Canada as a whole. A reconstructed trading post showcases goods that were exchanged for furs – everything from beads and guns to canned foods. There's also the last surviving York boat used for river and lake travel from the 1800s to the early 1900s, including relics from the ill-fated Franklin Expedition's search for the Northwest Passage and beautiful artworks and crafts produced by the First Nations, Métis and Inuit, among them carved ivory and immaculate beadwork that can't fail to impress. At the end of the gallery a reconstruction of the Hudson's Bay Company's boardroom in London includes a huge ram's head used, unbelievably, as a snuff holder and passed around at dinner parties. The last section of the museum is the **Urban Gallery**, which re-creates the Winnipeg of the early 1920s, a street complete with pharmacy, barber shop, dentist, promenade and cinema showing period films. The **Parklands Gallery** houses displays and dioramas on the province's largest region.

Also in the Centennial Centre are the **Planetarium** (May to early Sept daily; schedule varies; call ☎204/943-3139 for hours; $5) and the "Touch the Universe" **Science Gallery** (same hours as museum; $5), where more than sixty interactive exhibits focus on the way the universe is perceived by the five senses. A Value Pass for the museum, planetarium and science centre costs $15, and allows 3-day all-inclusive admission.

Next door is the **Centennial Concert Hall**, where performances of the Manitoba Opera, Winnipeg Symphony Orchestra and Royal Winnipeg Ballet are held (see p.549). Just across the street from the Concert Hall is the modern **City Hall**.

The Ukrainian Centre, Artspace and Chinatown

Two blocks north of the Centennial Centre, the **Ukrainian Cultural and Educational Centre** (Oseredok), 184 Alexander Ave East at Main St (Mon–Sat 10am–4pm; July & Aug also Sun 1–5pm; $2), occupies a 1930s office building on the edge of the Exchange District. The second largest ethnic group in Manitoba, the Ukrainians arrived here around 1900, a peasant people united by language and custom, but divided by religion and politics – Orthodox against Catholic, nationalist against socialist. By 1940, the various factions managed to amalgamate to create the Ukrainian Canadian Committee, a loose coalition committed to the country's institutions and the promotion of Ukrainian interests. Their collection of folk art in the fifth-floor museum of the complex is an excellent introduction to their strongly maintained traditions, with delightful examples of embroidery, weaving, woodcarving and the exquisite designs of *pysanky*, Easter egg painting. There's also an art gallery, library and gift shop.

Artspace, in a warehouse building at the corner of Arthur St and Bannatyne Ave, is the largest artist-run centre in Canada and houses a cinema (see p.550), several galleries and offices for art groups. To see the best of contemporary local and Canadian art, check out the SITE Gallery, 2nd floor, 55 Arthur St (Tues–Sun 11am–4pm), while the Floating Gallery, 100 Arthur St (Tues–Sun 11am–5pm), focuses on photography. A few blocks away, Plug-In, 286 McDermot Ave (Tues & Wed 11am–6pm, Thurs 11am–7.30pm, Fri 11am–5.30pm, Sat 10.30am–4.30pm), is housed in a former warehouse and promotes new art in all media, which entails some wacky multimedia installations.

Adjacent to the Exchange District, north of Rupert St and west of Main St, is **Chinatown**, originally settled in the 1920s by immigrants brought to Manitoba to help build the railway into the west. The area has many good restaurants and groceries, as well as shops selling silk fabrics and exotic herbs and spices – though, other than that, not much in the way of sights.

The Forks

South of Portage Ave along Main St (take bus #38 or #99 from Portage Ave) rises the ponderous dome of the Beaux Arts-style Union Station, designed by the same architects as Grand Central Station in New York; it has an indoor market and the **Winnipeg Railway Museum** upstairs (June–Aug Thurs–Sun 11am–5pm; rest of year Sat & Sun noon–4pm; donation). Immediately south of the station is the present headquarters of the Hudson's Bay Company. Across the street, in a small park, is the stone gate that's the sole remnant of Upper Fort Garry, a Hudson's Bay Company fort from 1837 to 1870 and thereafter the residence of Manitoba's lieutenant governors until 1883, when the fort was dismantled. The pointed dormers and turrets behind it belong to the *Hotel Fort Garry*, a château-like structure built for the Grand Trunk Railroad.

Behind the station, the chunk of land bordering the Red River as it curves round to **The Forks** (🌐www.theforks.com) was, until recently, one of the country's largest railway yards – you can still see CNR freight cars and cabooses dotted around the grounds. Subsequent redevelopment has turned The Forks into Winnipeg's most visited sight due to its **Explore Manitoba Centre** (see p.537), half tourist information point, half museum, with six reasonably interesting themed displays covering the province's tourist areas. It's worth a quick visit, if only to pick the brains of the very helpful staff and admire the magnificent stuffed polar bear from Churchill, a persistent and dangerous marauder of the town's dump who came to a sticky end. Just east along the river from here is The **Forks National Historic Site**, bearing plaques to celebrate the role of the fur traders and pioneers who first settled here. An archeological excavation site welcomes volunteer diggers from July to October (advance registration required; for further information, call ☎204/983-6757 or 1-888/748-2928).

Nearby, the 1889 rail maintenance shed houses the **Manitoba Children's Museum** (June–Aug Sun–Wed 9.30am–4.30pm, Thurs–Sat 9.30am–8pm; rest

---

Boat tours around Winnipeg

On the banks of the Red River there's a quay beside Provencher Bridge where you can take **boat trips** (May–Oct daily 1pm; 2hr; $12.75; sunset dinner cruise daily 7pm; 3hr; $13.75; moonlight cruise Fri & Sat 10pm; 3hr; $13.75; ☎204/942-4500, 🌐www.paddlewheelcruises.com). These run parallel to the attractive riverwalk path, back along the Assiniboine River as far as the Legislative Building on Broadway and in the opposite direction up the Red River. The **Historic Fort Cruise** (July & Aug Wed–Fri 9am–4.30pm; $20) takes you to Lower Fort Garry (see p.552) and back. One of the boats is a replica paddlewheel vessel. **Water taxis** also leave every fifteen minutes from a quay closer to the market (daily 11am–sunset; 30min; ☎204/783-6633, 🌐www.icenter.net/~gordcart; $6) and run along the same route. You can **rent canoes** (daily 11am–10pm, weather permitting; $7.50/hr; ☎204/783-6633) at the Johnston Terminal. Alternatively check the river out for an hour aboard a 26-foot replica of a **birch-bark canoe** paddled by a guide in *voyageur* garb; tickets cost $30 and are available from the Explore Manitoba Centre or from Wild-Wise Wilderness Adventures on ☎204/788-1070.

year Mon–Wed 9.30am–5pm, Thurs & Fri 9.30am–8pm, Sat 10am–8pm, Sun 10am–5pm; Ⓦwww.childrensmuseum.com; $4.50), a hands-on, state-of-the-art enterprise that appeals equally to adults. Five different sections cover aspects of history, science, nature and technology. A vintage steam-engine with a couple of Pullman carriages and a mail office is equipped with tickets, luggage, uniforms and mail; close by, bear, lynx and raccoon costumes are on hand for kids to don while they explore a huge model of an oak tree and its ecosystem. Visitors to the museum can be filmed and have their activities shown simultaneously on two huge video screens, with added optical effects. For older kids, the highlight is probably the fully functioning TV studio where they can experiment with lights and cameras; at certain times, staff conduct interviews with them on their views of current events, which are relayed by one of the local stations.

A couple of minutes' walk away, **The Forks Market** (July & Aug Mon–Sat 9.30am–9pm, Sun 9.30am–6pm; rest of year daily 9.30am–6.30pm Fri until 9pm) and the Johnston Terminal, both old railway buildings, house shops, food stalls, bars and restaurants. Paths from the two buildings lead down to the **Assiniboine River** via an outdoor amphitheatre, where buskers entertain the gathered crowds with anything from hard rock to bagpipe music. Nearby is The Wall Through Time, a curving brick barricade covered with plaques and inscriptions recording the historic events of the area.

Downtown

Lined by department stores and offices, **downtown Portage Avenue** is the city's main shopping street, with a web of underground passageways and glass-enclosed overhead walkways linking the various malls and large stores and providing welcome relief from the summer heat and winter cold. The largest complex is the ugly mall **Portage Place** (Mon–Sat 10am–6pm, Thurs & Fri until 9pm, Sun noon–5pm), on the north side of the avenue. There are over 160 shops and services here, plus a giant-screen IMAX cinema on the third level (information ℡204/956-IMAX, tickets ℡204/780-SEAT). Among the many modern buildings that line Portage are some earlier ones that are architecturally attractive: the Paris Building at no.259, with a splendid piered facade and delicate cornice, and the Boyd Building at no.388, with cream and bronze terracotta decoration.

The uncompromisingly modern **Winnipeg Art Gallery** (WAG), a wedge-shaped building at 300 Memorial Blvd and Portage Ave (Tues–Sun 11am–5pm, Wed until 9pm; $6, free on Sat; Ⓦwww.wag.mb.ca), is the home of the largest public collection of Inuit art in the world, a decent selection of Gothic and Renaissance paintings and a reasonable assortment of modern European art, including works by Miró, Chagall and Henry Moore. The problem is that little of these collections is on display at any one time: much of the available space is taken up by offices while the main display area, on the third floor, is given over to temporary (and often dire) exhibitions of modern Canadian art. The mezzanine level, and often the third floor galleries, are devoted to the Inuits, each temporary display developing a particular theme – from the symbolic significance of different animals to the role of women sculptors in the isolated communities. The gallery also has an open-air sculpture court and a rooftop restaurant.

Legislative Building, Osborne Village and Dalnavert
A few minutes' walk south of the Art Gallery, along Memorial Boulevard, is the **Manitoba Legislative Building** (July–Sept hourly tours 9am–6pm; rest of

year Mon–Fri by appointment; ☎204/945-5813; free), built between 1913 and 1919 and surrounded by trim lawns and flower borders. The building, made of local Tyndall stone embedded with fossils, has a central pediment decorated with splendidly pompous sculptures representing the ideals of Canadian nationhood. A half-kneeling figure, symbolizing progress, beckons his lazy neighbour to come to the land of promise, whilst a muscular male figure, with a team of powerful horses, idealizes the pioneer spirit. High above, a central square tower rises to a copper-green dome that's topped by the **Golden Boy**, a four-metre-high gold-plated bronze figure that's supposed to embody the spirit of enterprise and eternal youth. Inside, the marble columns and balconies of the foyer house two magnificent life-size buffalo bronzes by the French sculptor Charles Gardet, framing a staircase of brown-veined Carrara marble. The mural over the entrance to the legislative chamber depicting World War I scenes is by the English artist Frank Brangwyn.

Just behind the Legislative Building, across the Assiniboine, lies **Osborne Village**, the bohemian part of town, whose inexpensive bars, restaurants and music joints – strung along Osborne St – are favourites with the city's students. West off Osborne St is Corydon Ave, whose several blocks and side streets comprise **Little Italy**, known for its cappuccino bars and restaurants.

A couple of blocks east of the Legislative Building, **Dalnavert**, 61 Carlton St (Jan & Feb Sat & Sun noon–4pm; March–May & Sept–Dec Tues–Thurs, Sat & Sun noon–4.30pm; June–Aug Tues–Thurs, Sat & Sun 10am–4.30pm; guided tours every 30min; ⓦwww.mhs.mb.ca; $4), was the home of Hugh John Macdonald, the son of Canada's first prime minister and, briefly, premier of Manitoba. Built in 1895 in Queen Anne Revival style, the house has been painstakingly restored, its simple red-brick exterior engulfed by a fanciful wooden veranda, the interior all heavy, dark-stained woods and strong deep colours. Macdonald's conservatism, reflected in the decor, was mellowed by a philanthropic disposition – he even reserved part of his basement for some of the city's destitute.

St Boniface

The suburb of **St Boniface**, a ten-minute walk east of the downtown area just across the Red River (or by bus #10 or #56 from Portage Ave), was a centre of early French-Canadian and Métis settlement. Founded by two French-Canadian Catholic priests in 1818, it retains something of its distinctive character and even today, decades after its incorporation into the city of Winnipeg, roughly 25 percent of its population speaks French as a first language. Walking tours of St Boniface, run from June to August (Mon–Fri 10am, 1pm & 3pm; 1hr; free; ☎204/235-1406 or 945-1715).

St Boniface's principal historic sights are situated beside the river, along **avenue Taché**. Walking south from the Provencher Bridge, the massive white-stone facade on the left is all that remains of St Boniface Cathedral, a huge neo-Romanesque structure built in 1908 and largely destroyed by fire in 1968. Its replacement, just behind, was designed with an interior in the style of a giant tepee. The large silver-domed building immediately to the east is the **Collège Universitaire** de Saint-Boniface, formerly a Jesuit college and now the French-speaking campus of the University of Manitoba. Here you'll see a controversial modern statue of Louis Riel that portrays him as naked and deformed. Its original location was on the grounds of the Legislative Building, but it caused such a storm of protest that it was moved here in 1994. In front of the cathedral is the cemetery containing Riel's grave, whose modest tombstone gives little indication of the furore surrounding his execution in Regina on November 16, 1885. Only after three weeks did the authorities feel safe enough to move the body, which was then sent secretly by rail to St Boniface. The casket lay overnight in Riel's family home in the suburb of St Vital (see below) before its transfer to the cathedral, where a Requiem Mass was attended by most of the Métis population. That same evening, across the river, Riel's enemies burnt his effigy on a street corner, a symptom of a bitter divide that was to last well into the twentieth century.

The **Musée de Saint-Boniface** (May–Sept Mon–Fri 9am–5pm, Sat 10am–5pm, Sun 10am–8pm; Oct Mon–Fri 9am–5pm, Sat & Sun 10am–4pm; Nov–April daily noon–4pm; $2; guided tours available by reservation on ☎204/237-4500) is housed in an attractive whitewashed building across from the cathedral. The oldest building in Winnipeg and the largest squared-oak log building in North America, it was built between 1846 and 1851 as a convent for the Grey Nuns, a missionary order whose four-woman advance party had arrived by canoe from Montréal in 1844. Subsequently, the building was adapted for use as a hospital, a school and an orphanage. Inside, a series of cosy rooms are devoted to the Red River Colony, notably an intriguing collection of Métis memorabilia that includes colourful sashes – the most distinctive feature of Métis dress. You can also see the battered wooden casket used to transport Riel's body from Regina to St Boniface. There's also a lovely little chapel, whose papier-mâché Virgin was made from an old newspaper that one of the original Grey Nuns found outside Upper Fort Garry when she walked across the frozen river to buy food.

Out of the centre

The **Riel House National Historic Site**, 330 River Rd (mid-May to Aug daily 10am–6pm; donation; ☎204/257-1783 or 1-888/748-2928; bus #16 from the Portage Place Mall), in the suburb of **ST VITAL**, about 10km south of the city centre, is just about worth the trip. The main feature of the site is a tiny clapboard house that was built by the Riels in 1880–81 and stayed in their possession until 1968. Louis Riel never actually lived here, but this was where his body was brought after his execution in 1885, and the house has been restored to its appearance at that time, complete with black-bordered photographs and a few artefacts left by his wife, Marguerite. Other period furnishings and fittings give a good idea of the life of a prosperous Métis family in the 1880s. The railway had reached St Boniface in 1877, a time when the simple products of the Red River could be supplemented by manufactured goods from the east with relative ease: the iron stove, the most obvious import, improved the quality of the Riels' life immeasurably. Costumed guides provide an enjoyable twenty-minute tour of the house and garden, the sole remnant of the once sizeable Riel landholdings.

Across the Red River from St Vital, at the city's southern limits, is the **Fort Whyte Centre**, 1961 McCreary Rd (Mon–Fri 9am–5pm, Sat & Sun 10am–5pm; ⓦwww.fortwhyte.org; $5), an environmental education centre dealing with the diversity of plants and animals of the prairie ecosystem. It's a real outdoors experience, with a wildlife observation tower, herd of bison, deer enclosure and a maze of self-guiding trails through woodlands and marsh, plus an interpretive centre. There's no public transport to Fort Whyte.

Assiniboine Park and the Living Prairie Museum

Some 8km west of the city centre, to the south of Portage Ave, a great chunk of land has been set aside as **Assiniboine Park** (daily 9am–sunset; free; bus

#66 from Broadway at Smith St), whose wooded lawns, gardens, cycling paths, playing fields and zoo attract hundreds of visitors every summer weekend. The park's English gardens of daisies, marigolds, roses and begonias bloom beneath columns of spruce trees and blend into the excellent **Leo Mol Sculpture Garden**, which contains the works of Ukrainian artist Leo Mol, who moved to Winnipeg in 1949. Dozens of his graceful sculptures – deer, bears, nude bathers and other whimsical figures – are featured here reflecting in the pond. More can be seen in the nearby glass-walled **gallery** (June to late Sept Tue–Sun 10am–8pm; free). Mol's studio, just behind the gallery, is also on view. The park's best-known feature is a large, half-timbered pavilion in mock-Tudor style – a favourite meeting place for Winnipeggers at the weekend and home to the **Pavilion Gallery Museum** (Tues–Sun 11am–5pm; free) with a permanent collection of three local artists: Ivan Eyre, Walter J. Phillips and Clarence Tillenius. By the pavilion, completed in 1999, the similarly Tudoresque bandshell of the **Lyric Theatre** has free performances by the Royal Winnipeg Ballet and the Winnipeg Symphony Orchestra, and hosts jazz, folk and drama festivals (☎204/885-5466, ext 5). The **zoo** (daily 9am–sunset; $3) has over 1300 animals and a giant tropical conservatory with a foyer displaying local artwork, a steamy Palm House, floral displays and a restaurant. A statue of Winnie the Pooh on the zoo grounds is a reminder that the fictitious bear was named after a real bear called Winnipeg. Adjoining the park to the south, the 700-acre nature reserve of Assiniboine Forest (sunrise–sunset; free), the largest in Canada, is home to deer, ruffled grouse and waterfowl.

A couple of kilometres further west, the **Living Prairie Museum**, 2795 Ness Ave (April–June Sun 10am–5pm; July & Aug daily 10am–5pm; free; guided tours $2.25; bus #24 along Portage), is worth a brief visit, its thirty acres of land forming the largest area of unploughed tall-grass prairie in Manitoba. A small visitor centre provides a wealth of background information on the indigenous plants, whose deep-root systems enable them to withstand both the extreme climate and prairie fires. There's a daily programme of half-hour guided walks, or you can pick up a brochure and stroll alone. Come prepared with insect repellent: the native bugs that thrive among the grass and wild flowers are particularly vicious.

Eating, drinking and entertainment

Winnipeg boasts literally dozens of good, inexpensive places **to eat**, though many of them in truth emphasize quantity over finesse. The wide variety of ethnic restaurants are the exception, ranging from de luxe establishments serving fine French and Italian delicacies through to Ukrainian and French-Canadian restaurant-bars that cater mainly for their own communities. In the more expensive places it's possible to pay upwards of $50 per person for a full dinner, but $25 per head is a reasonable average elsewhere. Many of Winnipeg's more staid restaurants and restaurant-bars are concentrated in and around the downtown shopping malls, but there's a cluster of more interesting ones in Osborne Village and the Exchange District, and several other good places dotted around the edges of the centre, notably the Jewish delis and Ukrainian restaurants in the North End, around Selkirk Ave. For **drinking**, many of the city's bars are cheerless places, so it's best to stick to the restaurant-bars.

Restaurants and restaurant-bars

Alycia's 559 Cathedral Ave at McGregor St ☎204/582-8789. A long-established Ukrainian restaurant, 4km north of the centre, which also serves as an informal social centre with cheap, filling food, including borscht and *holubchi* (stuffed cabbage rolls); dishes for $5–8. Closed Sun.

Amici 326 Broadway ☎204/943-4997. Expensive but superb and elegant restaurant with Italian food – the desserts are sensational. Dishes for $15–36.

Baked Expectations 161 Osborne St ☎204/452-517. Delicious burgers and salads, but especially known for its cheesecakes. Dishes for $3–8.

Bistro Bohemia 159 Osborne St ☎204/453-1944. Czech restaurant with great herring. Dishes for $8–14.

Carlos & Murphy's 129 Osborne St ☎204/284-3510. Huge portions of Mexican food are $5–10; eat out on the pleasant patio or inside adjacent to the raucous and dingy bar.

The Chocolate Shop 268 Portage Ave ☎204/942-4855. Winnipeg's oldest restaurant, dating its roots to 1918, where you can have your tea leaves and tarot read from 1 to 9pm. Diner-style establishment with great desserts. Popular karaoke night on Tues.

Forks Market The Forks. A converted railway shed incorporating some cheap, pleasant bars selling a variety of fast food from Caribbean to Greek; try *Yudyta's* for Ukrainian and *Tavola Calda* for Italian food, both of which are dirt cheap.

Green Gates 6495 Robin Blvd ☎204/897-0990. A converted farmhouse, thirty-minutes' drive from downtown but worth the trip for the delicious salads, posh food like grilled pork with scalloped potatoes and salmon with a fresh fruit salsa. Beautiful surroundings and very expensive, with dishes $10–20.

Kelekis 1100 Main St, between Aberdeen and Redwood aves. Another true Winnipeg institution, dishing out greasy fries, hotdogs and enormous hamburgers to people from all walks of life –

including Pierre Trudeau – since 1931. Dishes $3–9. Closes 9.45pm.

Le Beaujolais 131 Blvd Provencher, St Boniface ☎204/237-6276. Winnipeg's premier French restaurant, with prices to match; reservations recommended. Dishes for $19–26.

Le Café Jardin Centre Culturel Franco-Manitobain, 340 Blvd Provencher at rue des Meurons, St Boniface. A large cultural complex housing an attractive open-air restaurant featuring traditional French-Canadian food – try the meat pies (*tourtière*) and the bread pudding. Open Mon–Fri 11.30am–2pm. A full meal costs around $15.

Pasquale's 109 Marion St, St Boniface. Delightful, busy little place with well-prepared Italian dishes from $6.

Pembina Village 333 Pembina Hwy. A local favourite serving excellent Greek food: big feta salads, gyro sandwiches, great roast potatoes and retsina to wash it all down. It's cheap too: dishes around $5.

Rogue's Gallery 432 Assiniboine Ave ☎204/947-0652. Hip coffee house serving light meals like falafels and burgers, and decorated with local art.

Sofia's Caffè 635 Corydon Ave ☎204/452-3037. In the heart of Little Italy, this restaurant, with outdoor patio, serves large portions of veal, pasta and the like from $7.

Tavern in the Park The Pavilion in Assiniboine Park. Perfectly situated in a glass atrium on the back of the fake Tudor Pavilion, and a favourite with Winnipeggers. Expensive, with a lavish buffet on Sundays. Dishes for $16–24.

Tre Visi 173 McDermot Ave ☎204/949-9032. Tiny, extremely popular Italian restaurant with good atmosphere and food. Reservations essential. Dishes for $7.50–18.

Wasabi 105–121 Osborne St ☎204/474-2332. Buzzing, trendy sushi bar in Osborne Village. Sushi from 95¢, $18.95 for a combo platter.

Nightlife and entertainment

Winnipeg tries hard to be the cultural centre of the prairies, and generous **arts** sponsorship arrangements support a good range of theatre, ballet, opera and orchestral music. The city also has some lively **nightlife**, featuring the best of local and national rock and jazz talent. For listings, consult the Thursday edition of the *Winnipeg Sun* (🌐www.fyiwinnipeg.com), the *Winnipeg Free Press* newspaper or the free news sheet *Uptown* (🌐www.uptownmag.com), available from self-serve kiosks all over the city and issued every Thursday. The free magazine *Where*, available from tourist offices, also has listings, but its reports are never critical.

Spectator sports in Winnipeg

Baseball The Winnipeg Goldeyes (☎204/982-2273, ⊛www.goldeyes.com) play Northern League games (mid-May to early Sept) at the Can West Global Park adjacent to The Forks. Tickets cost $5–13.

Basketball The Winnipeg Cyclone (☎204/925-HOOP, ⊛www.cyclone.mb.ca) play seventeen home games a season (Dec–March) at the Wind Tunnel, Winnipeg Convention Centre, 375 York Ave.

Canadian football The Winnipeg Blue Bombers (☎204/784-2583, 1-888/780-7328, ⊛www.bluebombers.com), ten-time winners of the Grey Cup, play at the Canad Inns Stadium, 1430 Maroons Rd (June–Nov).

Ice hockey The Manitoba Moose (☎204/780-7328, ⊛www.moosehockey.com) play American Hockey League games at Winnipeg Arena (Oct–April).

Major performances by the **Winnipeg Symphony Orchestra** (Sept–May; $13–41; ⊛www.wso.nb.ca) as well as the **Manitoba Opera** ($16–66; ⊛www.manitobaopera.mb.ca) take place at the Centennial Concert Hall, 555 Main St (☎204/956-1360) in the Exchange District. The **Royal Winnipeg Ballet** (⊛www.rwb.org) – Canada's finest dance company – also performs at the Concert Hall and has an extensive programme of traditional and contemporary ballets; tickets are $11–50, with student and senior-citizen discounts of up to twenty percent.

Winnipeg has an ambitious summer programme of open-air concerts, notably the nine-day **Jazz Winnipeg Festival** (tickets free to $35; ⊛www.jazzwinnipeg.com) towards the end of June, and the **Winnipeg Folk Festival** ($40 per day, $110 for 4-day pass; ⊛www.winnipegfolkfestival.ca), a three-day extravaganza featuring over a hundred concerts, held in early July at Birds Hill Provincial Park, 25km northeast of the city. Apart from the music festivals, the biggest festival in Manitoba is **Folklorama** ($3; ⊛www.folklorama.ca), held during the first two weeks in August to celebrate Winnipeg's multiethnic population. The festival has over forty pavilions spread out over town, each devoted to a particular country or region. The **Winnipeg Fringe Festival** (tickets free to $10; ⊛www.mtc.mb.ca) is a ten-day event of theatrical productions, held in mid-July in the Exchange District. St Boniface's French-Canadian heritage is honoured annually in the **Festival du Voyageur** (⊛www.festivalvoyageur.mb.ca) – ten days of February fun, whose events lead up to a torchlit procession and the Governor's Ball, where everyone dresses up in period costume.

Music venues and clubs

Centre Culturel Franco-Manitobain 340 Blvd Provencher, St Boniface ☎204/233-8972, ⊛www.ccfm.mb.ca. Hosts free weekly concerts (Fri) by French-Canadian musicians. Also jazz sessions (Tues 9pm).

Club 200 190 Garry St. A popular gay and lesbian club.

The Empire 436 Main St ☎204/943-3979. Roman-themed upscale dance club in an old bank building. Has a non-smoking lounge.

Gio's Club & Bar 272 Sherbrooke St ☎204/786-1236. One of Winnipeg's better-known gay and lesbian bars, with regular pool tournaments, karaoke, women's night and strippers.

Jazz on the Rooftop Winnipeg Art Gallery, 300 Memorial Blvd ☎204/786-6641 ext 232. Showcases frequent performances by some of Canada's best-known jazz musicians.

Kokonuts 114 Market Ave ☎204/944-1117. Live music venue with a huge aquarium.

Mezzo 291 Bannatyne Ave ☎204/987-3399. Ultra-swank, high-tech club with catwalks and fashionably offhand patrons.

Ms Purdy's 226 Main St ☎204/989-2344. Long-running women-only lesbian bar.

Palomino Club 1133 Portage Ave ☎204/722-0454. Best place for a good boot-scoot if you're looking for line dancing.

Times Change Cafe Main and St Mary ☎204/957-0982. Rough-and-ready jazz and blues

place. Live entertainment Thurs–Sun.

Toad in the Hole 112 Osborne St. Osborne Village's busy pub with British beer and dance floor upstairs.

The Zoo 160 Osborne St ☎204/452-9824. Alternative/rock bar in *Osborne Village Inn* with live heavy-rock acts.

Cinema and theatre

Winnipeg's largest mainstream **cinema** is the Cineplex-Odeon, 234 Donald St, while Cinema 3, 585 Ellice Ave at Sherbrook St, shows foreign and second-run films. Cinémathèque, 100 Arthur St (☎204/925-3457), in the Artspace building, concentrates on Canadian releases. In summer there's also the Cineplex Odeon Drive-In on Portage St West (☎204/837-4979). Winnipeg plays host to **Film Exchange**, the world's only all-Canadian film festival, organized by the National Screen Institute Canada (🌐www.nsi-canada.com) in late February.

The city has several professional **theatre** groups: principally the Prairie Theatre Exchange, Portage Place (🌐www.pte.mb.ca; $30–32), which performs traditional and avant-garde comedy and drama. The Manitoba Theatre Centre, 174 Market Ave (🌐www.mtc.mb.ca; $11–59), and the Warehouse Theatre, 140 Rupert Ave (mid-Oct to mid-May; 🌐www.mtc.mb.ca; $12–41), feature local talent, though Winnipeg's main theatrical events are performed by international touring companies in the Centennial Concert Hall.

Listings

Airlines Air Canada ☎1-888/247-2262; Bearskin ☎204/774-2327; British Airways ☎1-800/247-9297; Calm Air ☎1-800/839-2256; Canada 3000 ☎204/784-0500 or 777-3000; Westjet ☎204/984-9207.

Bike rental Corydon Cycle Sports, 753 Corydon Ave at Cockburn St ☎204/452-6531 ($17/day); Olympia Cycle and Ski, 242 Henderson Hwy ☎204/669-5590 ($12–27/day); Portage Cycle & Sports, 1841 Portage Ave ☎204/837-6785 ($15/day).

Bookshops Mary Scorer, 389 Graham St at Edmonton St, is the city's best bookshop, with an excellent range of titles on the Canadian West. The Global Village, 167 Lilac St, is a map and travel shop with a comprehensive selection of specialized maps. Heaven Art and Book Café, 659 Corydon Ave, has a good selection of titles by Manitoban writers and also hosts readings. Dominion News, 263 Portage Ave, has a wide variety of international newspapers.

Car rental Avis, 234 York Ave (☎204/989-7521) and at the airport (☎204/956-2847); Budget, 593 Ellice Ave & 1355 Regent Ave (☎204/989-8505), and at the airport (☎204/989-8510); Discount, at the airport (☎204/775-2282); Hertz, 276 Colony St (☎204/925-6600), 1577 Erin St

(☎204/925-6600) and at the airport (☎204/925-6625); National, five in-town locations (☎204/925-3531) and at the airport; Rent-a-wreck, at the airport (☎204/779-0777 or 1-800/327-0116); and Thrifty, 112 Garry St (☎204/949-7620) and at the airport (☎204/949-7608).

Consulates UK, 229 Athlone Drive ☎204/896-1380.

Disabled visitors There's a Handi-Transit door-to-door minibus facility for disabled visitors (Mon–Fri 6.30am–midnight, Sat 7.30am–midnight, Sun 8.30am–10pm; information on ☎204/986-5722).

Gay and lesbian life Rainbow Resource Centre, 1-222 Osborne St (Wed–Fri 1–4.30pm, ☎204/474-0212; recorded information Mon–Sat 7.30–10pm ☎204/284-5208). Pride Week is held in mid-June.

Internet access Centennial Library, 251 Donald St ☎204/986-6450. Osborne Cyber Café, 118 Osborne St (daily until midnight).

Laundries Shop N Wash, 189 Isabel St at Portage Ave; Zip-Kleen, 110 Sherbrook St at Westminster Ave.

Left luggage 24hr coin-operated lockers at the

train and bus stations.
Lost property VIA baggage information on
☏ 204/949-7481; Winnipeg Transit, at the Portage
and Main office ☏ 204/986-5054.
Medical emergencies Health Sciences Centre,
820 Sherbrook St ☏ 204/787-3167. For dental
emergencies, Broadway Dental Centre, 640
Broadway ☏ 204/772-3523.

Pharmacy Shoppers Drug Mart, 471 River Ave
and Osborne St (open 24hr).
Post office 266 Graham Ave at Smith St
☏ 1-800/267-1177 (Mon–Fri 8am–5.30pm).
Taxis Duffy's ☏ 204/772-2451; Unicity
☏ 204/925-3131. Charges are $2.95 flat rate
and then 10¢ every 8 seconds thereafter.
Weather information ☏ 204/983-2050.

Around Winnipeg

The trip along the **Red River** is easily the best day out from Winnipeg, a pleasing diversion along the gentle hills that frame the wide and sluggish river. The sixty-kilometre stretch from the city to Lake Winnipeg was once a tiny part of the supply route that connected the Red River Colony to Hudson Bay, and nowadays it harbours the region's most absorbing tourist attractions, notably a couple of elegant nineteenth-century houses and the refurbished **Lower Fort Garry**. In season the area is also outstanding for **birding** in two marsh areas, one of which fills the mouth of the Red River as it opens into **Lake Winnipeg**. The eastern shores of the lake have some exceptional dunes which serve as fine sandy beaches, while the west harbours the Icelandic community of Gimli, which is close to the Narcisse Wildlife Area – which protects thousands of garter snakes – and the woods and marshes of **Hecla Provincial Park**.

From Lake Winnipeg, the edge of the Canadian Shield begins and spreads east encompassing the **Whiteshell**, **Nopiming** and **Atikaki Provincial Parks**. Whiteshell is by far the most popular and accessible, and gets busy on summer weekends – but all have an excellent network of canoe routes which link multiple backcountry campsites.

If you've only a day to spare and an interest in seeing some typical prairie scenery and the something of the local Mennonite culture, head **south** to the small towns scattered between Winnipeg and the US border.

The Red River corridor and Lake Winnipeg

As Winnipeg's dreary suburbs fade into the seamless prairie landscape, the only major interruption is provided by the course of the **Red River** to the north. Driving out from the city on Main St, which becomes Hwy 9, it's about 10km to the turning for the River Road Heritage Parkway (Provincial Road 238), a rough, twisting gravel track that leads to some of the Corridor's lesser attractions. Alternatively, you can keep on Hwy 9 for **Lower Fort Garry** and **Selkirk**, the only major settlement in the area. Ornithologists should head to **Netley Marsh** and the **Oak Hammock Marsh Wildlife Area**: the latter is home to thousands of migrating birds, particularly snow and Canada geese, between April and September.

To the north lies **Lake Winnipeg**, a giant finger of water some 400km long that connects the Red River with the Nelson River and subsequently Hudson Bay. It's a shallow lake, subject to violent squalls and, aboriginal reservations aside, the only settlement has been around its southern rim. Here, on the east shore, Winnipeg's wealthy have built their cottages in and around **Victoria Beach** and **Hillside Beach**, but **Grand Beach Provincial Park** still has the lake's finest bathing and long lines of sand dune stretching as far as the eye can see. The beaches of the west shore are poor by comparison, and the old fishing and farming villages that trail up the coast are not of major interest. But **Gimli**, on the west side of Lake Winnipeg, has a pleasant museum tracing the history of its Icelandic settlement and nearby the **Narcisse Wildlife Management Area** is a must-see attraction in April and May when thousands of red-sided garter snakes gather to mate. Further north, scattered on islands in the centre of Lake Winnipeg, **Hecla Provincial Park** is more agreeable for the squeamish; the developed facilities of Gull Harbour Resort supplemented by unspoilt marsh and forest.

Beaver (☎204/989-7007) runs a regular **bus** service from the bus station at 339 Archibald St in Winnipeg to Lower Fort Garry (or you can catch the boat, see p.543) and Selkirk, but there's no public transport along the Parkway and the road is too rough to cycle easily. From Winnipeg, there's a Grey Goose bus service to Grand Beach on Thursdays and Fridays, and one Grey Goose bus daily (not Sat) to **Gimli**, on Hecla Island in Hecla Park.

The Heritage Parkway to Lower Fort Garry

Turning off the main road, down the River Road Heritage Parkway, it's a few minutes' drive to Twin Oaks, built in the 1850s as part of a girls' school for the daughters of Hudson's Bay Company employees, before curving round to **St Andrew's Rectory National Historic Site** (mid-May to early Sept daily 10am–6pm; free), where you'll find exhibits on the Anglican Church's role in helping to settle the prairies and on its early occupants – stern-looking Victorians determined to save the Métis from themselves. Just opposite, the tidy mid-Victorian St Andrew's Church has a number of benches still partly covered by buffalo hide, and stained-glass windows brought here from England packed in barrels of molasses.

A couple of minutes' drive further north, the pretty **Captain Kennedy Tea House and Museum** (mid-May to Sept Mon–Sat 11am–4.30pm, Sun 11am–6pm; free) was once the home of Captain William Kennedy, an English-speaking Métis who resigned his Hudson's Bay Company commission because of its increasing involvement with the liquor trade. The house's three main-floor rooms are furnished in 1870s style, and the twee little glassed-in tearoom overlooks the delightful gardens whose terraces, planted with a variety of heritage plant species rare in Canadian public gardens, border the Red River.

A few minutes' drive north of the teahouse, on Hwy 9, 32km from Winnipeg near Selkirk, stands **Lower Fort Garry National Historic Site** (grounds open daily until sunset; visitor centre: mid-May to Aug daily 9am–5pm; $5.50), built as the new headquarters of the Hudson's Bay Company between 1830 and 1847. It was the brainchild of George Simpson, governor of the company's northern department, an area bounded by the Arctic and Pacific oceans, Hudson Bay and the Missouri River Valley. Nicknamed the "Little Emperor" for his autocratic style, Simpson selected the site because it was downriver from the treacherous waters of the St Andrew's Rapids and was not prone to flooding, as Upper Fort Garry had been. However, the settlers round The Forks were reluctant to cart their produce down to the new camp and when the governors of Assiniboia refused to move here his scheme collapsed. Sandwiched between Hwy 9 and the Red River, Lower Fort Garry begins at the visitor reception centre, where there's a comprehensive account of the development of the fort and its role in the fur trade. A couple of minutes' walk away, the low, thick limestone walls of the fort protect reconstructions of several company buildings, including the retail store, where a small museum is devoted to Inuit and Indian crafts. Several of the exhibits here are exquisite, particularly the decorated skin pouches and an extraordinary necklace fringed by thin strips of metal cut from a sardine can. Next door, the combined sales shop and clerk's quarters has a fur loft packed with pelts, while the middle of the compound is dominated by the Big House with its low sloping roof, built for Governor Simpson in 1832. People in 1850s period costume stroll the grounds, ensuring the right atmosphere. The **restaurant** sells good *tortière* – a Québecois meat pie – and bannock (freshly baked bread).

Selkirk

About 8km north of the fort, along Hwy 9A, the township of **SELKIRK** was originally chosen as the point where the proposed transcontinental railway was to cross the Red River. Realizing the importance of the railway, the business leaders of Winnipeg – Selkirk's great trade rival – launched a campaign to have the route changed. Their efforts were successful, not least because one of the leading lights of the CPR syndicate, Donald Smith, was a key shareholder in the Hudson's Bay Company, which owned five hundred acres of land around The Forks. Bypassed by the trains, Selkirk slipped into relative obscurity, though it did achieve a degree of prosperity through its shipyards, and retains the dubious title of "Catfish Capital of the World".

Selkirk's only real attraction is the **Marine Museum of Manitoba** (mid-May to Aug Mon–Fri 9am–5pm, Sat & Sun 10am–6pm; $3.50), situated on the edge of Selkirk Park at Eveline and Queen streets. The museum consists of seven passenger and freight ships, dragged out of the water and parked on a lawn, as well as a lighthouse, plus a mildly interesting video on the history of Lake Winnipeg's shipping and fishing industries. In **Selkirk Park** there's a bird sanctuary and a 6.5-metre-high oxcart, said to be the world's largest. If you're in Selkirk in early July, you could take in the **Manitoba Highland Gathering**, a Scottish festival honouring the original settlers.

Places to stay include the *Selkirk Motor Hotel*, 219 Manitoba Ave (℡204/482-1900; ❷), and the *Evergreen Gate B&B*, 1138 River Rd (℡204/482-6248 or 1-877/901-0553, ⓦwww.evergreengate.ca; ❷). You can camp at the *Willow Springs Campground*, 13km north of Selkirk on Hwy 320 (℡204/482-1344; $12–14; May–Oct). For **food**, try *Barney Gargles*, 185 Main St, which has delicious main courses from $6, or *The Garden on Eaton*, 205 Eaton Ave (closed Sun), for its fresh home-cooked food.

Netley Marsh and Oak Hammock Marsh

From Selkirk, Provincial Road 320 heads north 16km to the edge of **Netley Marsh**, a huge swampy delta formed by the Red River as it seeps into Lake Winnipeg. At the end of the road, there's a small recreation park with a snack bar, an observation tower and a series of plaques that detail the way of life of the area's native peoples. The marsh is an impenetrable maze for the inexperienced, but you can hire a boat and guide at the park for about $110 a day. On the lake side of the delta, the Bird Refuge is one of North America's largest waterfowl nesting areas and there are lots of good fishing spots; the pickerel, or wall-eye, are delicious. The *Tree House Bed and Breakfast* (℡204/941-0920; ❷), on the edge of the marsh near the village of Matlock, is a relaxing place to stay and absorb the tranquil charms of the wetlands area. Go north on Hwy 9 and turn onto the gravel Route 202.

The **Oak Hammock Marsh Wildlife Management Area** (daily: May–Aug 10am–8pm; Sept & Oct 8.30am to dusk; Nov–April 10am–4.30pm; ℡204/467-3300, ⓦwww.ducks.ca/ohmic; $4) is all that remains of the wetlands that once stretched from St Andrews, near the Red River, up to the village of Teulon, and to the west of Netley Creek. Most of this wetland was drained and farmed around the beginning of the twentieth century, but in the 1960s some of the area was restored to its original state and protected by a series of retaining dykes. In addition, a number of islands were built to provide marshland birds a safe place to nest. To get there from Winnipeg take Hwy 7 or Hwy 8 north for 10km, turn east along Hwy 67; from Selkirk take Hwy 67 west, from just south of town. In both cases, follow the signs to the Main Mound Area, where an excellent interpretive centre has hands-on displays about the local environment and wildlife, a picnic site and a couple of observation decks, all connected by a system of dykes and boardwalk trails. The best time to come is in spring or autumn, when the grebes, coots and other residents are joined by thousands of migrating birds, including Canada geese. Another part of the Wildlife Area has been returned to tall-grass prairie, carpeted from mid-June to August with the blooms of wild flowers such as the purple Blazing Star and the speckled red Prairie Lily.

Grand Beach Provincial Park

Approached along Hwy 59, the southeast shore of Lake Winnipeg has one major attraction, **Grand Beach Provincial Park**, whose long stretch of powdery white sand, high grass-crowned dunes and shallow bathing water make it the region's most popular day-trip. The beach, a favourite swimming spot with Winnipeggers since the 1920s, is divided into two distinct parts, separated by a narrow channel that drains out of a knobbly lagoon, set just behind the lakeshore. The channel is spanned by a tiny footbridge: on the beach to the west are privately owned cottages, sports facilities, motor- and rowboat rental, grocery stores and a restaurant; the eastern section of the beach is less developed, although it does have the large *Grand Beach Campground* (T 1-888/482-2267; $12–14; May–Sept) tucked away amongst the dunes. Both parts of the beach get very crowded on summer weekends. By the campsite office, the **Ancient Beach Trail** follows the line of the prehistoric lake that dominated southern Manitoba in the last Ice Age; allow about an hour for the walk. At **GRAND MARAIS**, just outside the park, you'll find an array of motels, beachside cottages and cabins (❷–❹; most May–Sept).

Roughly 20km north of Grand Beach Provincial Park, the twin townships of **HILLSIDE BEACH** and prettier **VICTORIA BEACH** have good sandy beaches, but their well-heeled inhabitants avoid catering for outsiders. There are no campsites and the only **motel** is the *Birchwood* (T 204/754-2596; ❷) on the highway, 6km south of Victoria Beach at Traverse Bay; the motel's star facility is the huge patio overlooking the bay.

Gimli and the Interlake

In 1875, some two hundred Icelanders moved to the southwestern shore of Lake Winnipeg, where they had secured exclusive rights to a block of land that stretched from today's Winnipeg Beach to Hecla Island, named after a volcano in their homeland. The next year the colonists were struck by a smallpox epidemic, yet they managed to survive and founded the **Republic of New Iceland**, a large self-governing and self-sufficient settlement with its own Icelandic-language school, churches and newspaper. Their independence lasted just twenty years, for in 1897 they acquiesced in the federal government's decision to open their new homeland to other ethnic groups. An identifiable Icelandic community had ceased to exist by the 1920s, but this part of Manitoba still has the largest number of people of Icelandic descent outside Iceland. The residents celebrate their heritage during the Islendingadagurinn

(Icelanders' Day) festival, on the first weekend in August, when they dress up in Viking helmets and organize beauty pageants, concerts and firework displays. This rather commercial festival – not to everyone's taste – is held in the largest township, **GIMLI** (literally "paradise"). There's little else to attract visitors to this part of the lake, though Gimli's harbourside, with a fibreglass Viking statue and a massive wharf, is modestly attractive. The **New Iceland Heritage Museum**, at 62 2nd Ave (Mon–Fri 9am–5pm, Sat & Sun 10am–4pm; ☏204/642-4001, ⓦcollection.ic.gc.ca/iceland; $4), chronicles the history of New Iceland. The **tourist office** is located downtown on 7th Ave (May–Aug daily 10am–8pm; ☏204/642-7974). Gimli doesn't have a lot of **places to stay**, but the best of the lot is the *Lakeview Resort*, 10 Centre St (☏204/642-8565; ❹–❺), which has comfortable suites and rooms, each of which has a balcony overlooking either Gimli or the lake. More affordable is the B&B accommodation at *Sunny Side Up B&B*, which has an indoor pool (☏204/642-8191, ⓦwww.sunnysideup.mb.ca; ❷). There's also a campsite near the beach, 8km south of town, *Idle-Wheels Trailer Park* (☏204/642-5676; $14–17; mid-May to Oct). *Seagull's*, 10 Centre St (☏204/642-4145), serves Icelandic **food** like gyro and deep-fried fish, which you can wash down with potent schnapps; eat in the large dining room or on the beachside patio.

Known as the **Interlake**, the marginal farmland that lies between Lake Winnipeg to the east and lakes Manitoba and Winnipegosis to the west is as flat as a pancake and one of the most boring parts of the prairies. The only significant attraction is at the **Narcisse Wildlife Management Area**, 25km west of Gimli on Hwy 231 or 90km north of Winnipeg on Hwy 17, where thousands of red-sided garter snakes gather to mate in late April and early May, writhing around the bottom of a series of shallow pits in slithering heaps. It's not for the squeamish.

Roughly 100km north of Gimli, **Hecla Provincial Park** consists of several islands and a slender peninsula that jut out into Lake Winnipeg, almost touching the eastern shore. The park is approached along Hwy 8, which runs across a narrow causeway to the largest of the islands, **Hecla**, where the tourist township of **GULL HARBOUR** has a comprehensive range of facilities. Nearby, on the east side of the island, the original **Hecla Village** (☏204/279-2056 or 378-2261 for hours) has a number of old houses, a church and a school dating from the early years of Icelandic settlement; a short heritage trail covers the highlights (guided tours available in summer), or you can strike out on one of the island's hiking trails through forest and marsh. For **accommodation**, there's the luxurious *Gull Harbour Resort* at Riverton (☏204/279-2041 or 1-800/267-6700, ⓦwww.gullharbourresort.com; ❺), the B&B *Solmundson Gesta Hus*, in Hecla Village (☏204/279-2088, ⓦwww .heclatourism.mb.ca; ❸), with home-cooked dinners, and a medium-size **Gull Harbour Campground** (☏204/948-3333 or 1-888/482-2267; $12–14; May–Sept) on the neck of land between Gull Harbour and the lake.

East of Lake Winnipeg

The great slice of Manitoban wilderness that extends north from the Trans-Canada Highway between Lake Winnipeg and the Ontario border is set on the rock of the Canadian Shield, an inhospitable and sparsely inhabited region of lake, river and forest that's home to three of the province's largest parks. The most southerly, **Whiteshell Park**, is the oldest and most developed, with a rel-atively extensive road system, fifteen campsites and one-quarter of Manitoba's holiday and fishing lodges. Just north of Whiteshell Park, **Nopiming Park** is more isolated, with a handful of lakeside campsites that can be reached along two bumpy gravel roads. North of here, the **Atikaki Wilderness Park** is the most remote of the three, accessible only by canoe or float plane. The Atikaki's mile upon mile of rugged forest and granite outcrop are connected to the east shore of Lake Winnipeg by the Bloodvein and Leyond rivers, two of Manitoba's wildest white-water canoe routes.

From Winnipeg, there's a twice-weekly Greyhound **bus** service (Tues & Wed) to Rennie and West Hawk Lake in the Whiteshell, and one Grey Goose bus a day to Lac du Bonnet, the nearest point to Nopiming Park.

Whiteshell Provincial Park

Whiteshell Provincial Park takes its name from the small, white seashell, the *megis*, that was sacred to the Ojibwa, who believed the Creator blew through the shell to breathe life into the first human being. These shells, left by the prehistoric lake that covered the entire region, were concentrated along the park's two main rivers, the Whiteshell to the south and the Winnipeg to the north, the latter an important part of the canoe route followed by the *voyageurs* of the North West Company on their way from Montréal to the Red River.

Most of the park's visitors head for **FALCON LAKE** and **WEST HAWK LAKE**, two well-developed tourist townships situated on either side of the Trans-Canada Highway, near the Ontario border. Crowded throughout the summer, neither has much to recommend it, though each has a full range of facilities from serviced campsites ($12–17), resort hotels – try the *Penguin Resort* at Falcon Lake (☏204/349-2218; **②**–**⑤**) – fuel stations, grocery stores and miniature golf through to boat and water-sports equipment rental. The best places to **eat** are in West Hawk Lake: the *Nite Hawk Café*, for home-made burgers, and the *Landing Steak House*, which serves juicy steaks and prime rib.

West Hawk Lake, which was formed by a meteorite, is the deepest lake in Manitoba and particularly good for scuba diving. On its south side the sixteen-kilometre loop of the **Hunt Lake Hiking Trail** passes through cedar and white-pine forests, across sticky, aromatic bogs and over rocky outcrops, all in the space of about eight hours. There's a primitive campsite on the trail at Little Indian Bay, but be sure to register at the West Hawk Lake **park office** (May–Sept daily 8.30am–4.30pm; Oct–April Mon–Fri same hours; ☏204/349-2245) if you're planning to stay overnight.

From West Hawk Lake, Route 44 cuts north towards **CADDY LAKE** (with campsites and two holiday lodges), the starting point for one of the area's most beautiful **canoe routes**, the 160-kilometre journey along the Whiteshell River to Lone Island Lake, in the centre of the park. Experienced walkers could tackle the sixty-kilometre loop of the **Mantario Hiking Trail** just to the east of Caddy Lake, along Provincial Road 312. For beginners, there are the **Bear Lake trail** (8km) and **McGillivray trail** (4km), clearly signposted from Hwy 44 to the west of Caddy Lake; they reveal a good sample of the topography of the park – dry ridges dominated by jack pine, bogs crammed with black spruce, and two shallow lakes brown from algae and humic acid. Opposite the start of the Bear Lake Trail, the **Frances Lake** canoe route makes for a pleasant overnight excursion, a twenty-kilometre trip south to the Frances Lake campsite, with three portages past the rapids, and twelve hauls round beaver dams.

Further west, 32km from West Hawk, the village of **RENNIE** is home to the **park headquarters** (Mon–Fri 8.30am–4.30pm; July & Aug also Sat & Sun 9am–4.30pm; ☏204/369-5426), which has a comprehensive range of information on local trails and canoe routes. The nearby **Alf Hole Goose**

Wilderness trips

The **Manitoba Naturalists Society** runs an excellent programme of Whiteshell Wilderness Adventures during July and August. The trips last for five days, cost $395, and are based at a cabin on secluded Lake Mantario. All equipment is provided, as are the services of fully experienced guides, who organize classes in canoeing and survival skills. Reservations are essential: check ⓦwww .manitobanature.ca for details.

Sanctuary (late May to mid–Oct Mon–Fri 10am–5pm, also Sat & Sun until early Sept 10.30am–6pm; free) is best visited in spring or autumn, when the Canada geese pass through on their migration. If you need to **stay** in Rennie as a base for excursions into the park, your choices are the rather primitive *Rennie Hotel* (☏204/369-5536; ❷) or the *Rocky Ridge Campground* (☏204/369-5507; $12–15; May–Sept). From Rennie, the eighty-kilometre stretch of Route 307 passes most of the park's other campsites, lodges, trails and canoe routes.

Nopiming Provincial Park

Separated from the Whiteshell by the Winnipeg River, **Nopiming Provincial Park** is a remote rocky area whose granite shoreline cliffs spread out above black-spruce bogs and tiny sandy beaches; the name is Ojibwa for "entrance to the wilderness". The park's four campsites (all May–Sept; ☏1-888/482-2267 or 204/948-3333 for camping reservations; ☏1-800/214-6497 for park information; $7–10) lie close to its two gravel roads; Route 314, which meanders across the 80km of its western edge, and the shorter Route 315, a thirty-kilometre track that cuts east below Bird Lake to the Ontario border. Nopiming Park is crossed by the Oiseau and Manigotagan waterways, whose creeks and rivers trickle or rush from lake to lake, forming no less than 1200km of possible canoe route. Towards the south of the park, **BIRD LAKE** is a useful base, with a main settlement on the south shore that's equipped with a campsite ($7), a grocery store and the cabins of the *Nopiming Lodge* (☏204/884-2281, ⓕ204/884-2402; ❸–❹; year-round). There's also motorboat rental, as well as canoe and guide rental for excursions to Snowshoe Lake, around falls and over rapids (55km). Near **Bissett**, in the north of the park, there are several abandoned gold-mining shafts from the 1930s.

Atikaki Provincial Wilderness Park

Accessible by float plane from Winnipeg and Lac du Bonnet, the **Atikaki Provincial Wilderness Park** has half a dozen holiday cottages and fishing lodges dotted across some of the finest Canadian Shield scenery in the province. There are no campsites or roads through the park, but the rough gravel track that makes up most of Route 304 does reach Wallace Lake, at the park's southern tip, via the east shore of Lake Winnipeg or Nopiming Park's Route 314. The Atikaki is crisscrossed by canoe routes that give glimpses of the region's ancient pictograph sites, but they all include difficult white-water stretches that should only be attempted by experienced canoeists.

The park's more popular canoe routes include the dramatic journey down the **Bloodvein River** to Lake Winnipeg, its rapids, falls and wild twistings balanced by peaceful drifts past quiet lakes and wild-rice marshes, and the **Kautunigan Route**, a 500-kilometre excursion that starts at Wallace Lake and threads its way to the mouth of the Berens River on Lake Winnipeg, well to the north of the park. Both routes pass stands of white birch, black spruce, jack pine, elm, oak and maple, and you may catch sight of moose, timber wolves, coyotes and black bears.

To obtain **information** on canoe routes, call the Manitoba Recreational Canoeing Association (☏204/925-5078). **Maps** are available from Manitoba Conservation (☏204/945-6666 or 1-877/627-7226), and you should file trip plans with the Lac du Bonnet Natural Resource Office (☏204/345-1454). Alternatively, several of the outfitters in Winnipeg and Lac du Bonnet organize **guided excursions**: Wilderness Odysseys, based in Virginia, USA (☏703/922-0823 or 1-800/443-6199), offers three-, five- and ten-day canoeing and white-water rafting excursions in the park, and details of other operators are on the Travel Manitoba website (ⓌWwww.travelmanitoba.com).

South of Winnipeg

A pleasant day's outing from Winnipeg can be had by driving a loop through the towns and villages **south** of the city. It's here that you'll encounter the quintessential prairie town: squat false-gabled buildings lining a wide main street, parked half-ton trucks filled with bales of hay, sacks of horsefeed, a sleeping dog or two, and quiet side streets bordered by tall Manitoba oaks or trembling aspen. The drive takes you along part of the Red River and across vast golden wheatfields punctuated only by **grain elevators**, huge storage silos situated at the edge of almost every town, usually with the town's name painted high up in large white letters – though most of these will soon disappear to be replaced by massive concrete terminals (see box below). Grey Goose **bus** lines depart from their terminal at 487 Portage Ave, in Winnipeg, out to a number of these spots.

A good first stop is the sprawling town of **STEINBACH**, about 60km southeast of Winnipeg (2 buses daily), where the **Mennonite Heritage Village** (July & Aug Mon–Sat 10am–6pm, Sun noon–6pm; May, June & Sept closes 5pm; Ⓦwww.mennoniteheritagevillage.com; $8), on the north edge of

Grain elevators

Canada hasn't exactly set the world afire with its contributions to the field of architecture; in fact, it's most distinctive form of building may be the ubiquitous **grain elevators** found throughout the prairies, warehouses built to store wheat before it was shipped off by the railroad. Most are wooden, while the more modern ones are made of steel – but both have the same simple, functional lines rising above the flat prairie land that have earned them the nickname "prairie sentinels".

The first grain elevators were built in the 1880s. By 1938 there were 5800 dotted across the region emblazoned with the names of the small towns they mark. However, as transportation of grain switched from rail to road their numbers dwindled to the present seven hundred. In 2000, the Canadian Wheat Board decided to build massive central concrete terminals at main transit points, a move that will make the old-style elevator redundant and no doubt dramatically alter the rural prairie-scape. Grain will now travel by trucks from the new terminals, much to the detriment of the region's already abysmal roads.

In **Inglis**, a tiny town on the west side of Riding Mountain National Park, about 20km east of the Saskatchewan border, a row of 1920s elevators beside an abandoned railway line has been declared a National Historic Site. With very little local concern to preserve the grain elevators, these may be the only "castles of the New World" to survive.

town off Hwy 12, is worth a peek for its good reconstruction of a nine-teenth-century pioneer settlement. This includes a church, a windmill and a couple of stores and farmhouses, but it's the general flavour of the place that appeals rather than any particular structure. The **Mennonites**, a Protestant sect, were founded in the Netherlands under the leadership of Menno Symons in the early sixteenth century. Subsequently the movement divided into two broad factions, with one group refusing to have anything to do with the secular state and sustaining a hostile attitude to private property, and the more "liberal" clans being inclined to compromise. Many of the former – the Ammanites – moved to the United States and then Ontario, settling in and around Kitchener-Waterloo, while the more liberal Untere migrated to Russia and then Manitoba in the 1870s. There are about 100,000 Mennonites in Canada today. Few of the Manitoba Mennonites, who congregated in and around Steinbach, wear the traditional black and white clothes or live on communal farms, but like all Mennonite communities they maintain a strong pacifist tradition. Costumed guides at the Heritage Village provide an intriguing account of their history, augmented by displays in the tiny museum and the interpretive centre. For a Mennonite **meal**, eat at the cafeteria-style *Livery Barn* in the Heritage Village, with borscht, stone-ground bread, smoked sausages and other delights priced inexpensively. For a more formal meal try the *Dutch Connection*, 88 Brandt St (T204/326-2018), one of the province's better places serving Dutch and Indonesian food at reason-able prices; a **motel** (❷) has sprung up around this successful restaurant. To camp try the RV-orientated *Steinbach Campground* just west of Hwy 12 on Park Road (T204/326-6892).

The pleasant small town of **MORRIS**, 59km west of Steinbach via hwys 52, 29 and 23, is home to the annual **Manitoba Stampede** and Exhibition, one of Canada's largest, which takes place during the third week of July in and around a huge recreational complex dominating the town. The area where the Morris River joins the Red River is great for catching wall-eye and catfish, and a Catfish Derby is held here in August. Following Hwy 75 a bit further south, **ST JEAN BAPTISTE** is an attractive French-speaking community known for producing the type of pea that's used in French-Canadian pea soup. **EMERSON**, 30km south, right on the border with Minnesota and North Dakota, has some interesting architectural titbits, like the log customs house, Fort Dufferin (the original site of the North West Mounted Police), and the 1917–18 town hall and courthouse, at the corner of Church St and Winnipeg Ave (Mon–Fri 9am–4pm; free) done in the Neoclassical Prairie style. For lunch or afternoon tea, the place to visit is *Aunt Maud's Tea Room*, 57 4th St (closed Mon–Wed). **GRETNA**, 25km west of Emerson, is another Mennonite community, as is **WINKLER**, to the northwest, which has several arts and crafts shops, a farmers' market (July–Sept Fri eve), and the August Harvest Festival. It's also a great place to sample genuine Mennonite food, served in almost all the cafés and restaurants; be sure to try *platz*, a rhubarb dessert.

West of Winkler is the large town of **MORDEN**, site of the annual Corn and Apple Festival in August, and **DARLINGFORD**, 20km farther west, where a large granite boulder marks the route taken by the eighteenth-century French explorer Sieur de la Vérendrye on his way west in search of a reputed vast "western sea". The land to the south and west of Darlingford begins to descend into the Pembina River Valley, which offers magnificent, sweeping views of the prairies. Kaleida, a tiny village about 15km southwest of Darlingford, has a charming pioneer stone church and an attractive cemetery.

Trans-Canada Highway

Slicing east–west across both Manitoba and Saskatchewan, the **Trans-Canada Highway** (Hwy 1), rushes past brilliant yellow canola (rapeseed) fields, for around 1000km before hitting the Alberta border. Dotted with campsites and fast-food joints, it follows the route of the original transcontinental railroad, pushing past a series of charmless towns that are at the heart of the province's most fertile farming region. Driving across, the novelty of the big skies and vast spaces quickly begins to wear off and the journey can easily become dull. But this needn't be so if you're prepared to leave the highway for breaks along the way. Several **Provincial Parks** offer the chance to stretch your legs and put the monotonous asphalt out of mind and a few attractions such as **Cannington Manor** and the **Tunnels of Moose Jaw** are genuinely entertaining. Surrounding the latter, **Moose Jaw** is a pleasant small town for an overnight break, as is **Regina** – the largest town en route. However, the only sight for which it's genuinely worth travelling in from afar is the pristine and wonderfully empty **Grasslands National Park**.

West of Winnipeg

West of Winnipeg, the Trans-Canada soon hits the workaday agricultural town **Portage La Prairie**, located roughly halfway en route to **Brandon**, the province's second largest city, which has a handful of Victorian mansions and a lively arts centre. Between them, **Spruce Woods** Provincial Park, contains the exceptional dune landscape of Manitoba's only desert, while other easy day-trips from Brandon include the pleasant little prairie town of **Souris** and **Turtle Mountain** Provincial Park on the US border. Over the provincial border in the southeast corner of Saskatchewan, the lakes, hillocks and aspen, birch and poplar forests of **Moose Mountain** Provincial Park come complete with campsites, nature trails and a resort village and are close to the delightful **Cannington Manor** Provincial Historic Park.

Portage La Prairie

The first major settlement west of Winnipeg is the food-processing centre of **PORTAGE LA PRAIRIE**, Manitoba's third largest city, located in the richest agricultural land in the province. East of the town is the mildly interesting **Fort la Reine Museum and Pioneer Village** (mid-May to mid-Sept daily 9am–6pm; $5), located at the junction of hwys 1A and 26, which remembers an original fort that served as the headquarters of Pierre Gaultier, Sieur de la Vérendrye, during his explorations in the 1740s. The present complex re-creates nineteenth-century life through a trading post, a log homestead, a trapper's cabin, a schoolhouse and a railway caboose. In the city centre, the limestone **city hall**, on the main drag, Saskatchewan Ave, is the most attractive building; it was built in the 1890s by the same architect who designed the Parliament Buildings in Ottawa. On the same street is the **Portage Arts Centre and Gallery** (Tues–Sat 11am–5pm; free), featuring frequent exhibitions. Just south of the centre, the large **Island Park** is worth a stroll. It's almost completely surrounded by Crescent Lake, an oxbow of the Assiniboine River, formed when a river cuts across the narrow end of a loop in its course and creates an isolated crescent of water.

You'll find the **tourist bureau** (Mon–Fri 8.30am–5pm; ☎204/857-7778) in the Glesby Centre at 11 2nd St NE. The library next door also keeps a stock of tourist pamphlets and has public Internet access. For **accommodation**, your best bet is the 61-room *Westward Village Inn*, 2401 Saskatchewan Ave W (☎204/857-9745 or 1-800/817-7855, ⓦwww.westwardvillageinn.com; ❹), with a pool and hot tub, or the recently renovated *Westgate Inn Motel*, 1010 Saskatchewan Ave E (☎204/239-5200, ⓦwww.westgateinn.com; ❷). The well-equipped *Portage Campground* (☎204/267-2191 or 1-866/887-330; $17–23; mid-April to Sept) is 16km east of the city on the Trans-Canada, with a playground, store and hiking trails. The range of good **restaurants** in Portage is limited; try *Bill's Sticky Fingers*, a local rib joint at 210 Saskatchewan Ave E, or *Essence Tea House*, 818 Saskatchewan Ave E, for great cheesecake.

Around Portage La Prairie

Delta Marsh, 25km north of the city on Provincial Road 240, is a wetland extending for some 40km along the southern shore of Lake Manitoba, and is one of the largest waterfowl marshes in North America. From May to mid-September, Delta Marsh Canoe Trips (☎204/243-2009) arranges guided tours.

West of town, near **Austin**, 3km south of the Trans-Canada on Hwy 34, the **Manitoba Agricultural Museum** (mid-May to Sept daily 9am–5pm; ⓦwww.ag-museum.mb.ca; $5) has an exhaustive collection of early twentieth-century farm machinery, from gigantic steam tractors through to threshing machines and balers. The site also includes a homesteaders' village, which simulates village life of the late nineteenth century and has the province's largest collection of pioneer household articles. The immensely popular **Manitoba Threshermen's Reunion and Stampede** is held here every year in mid-July, featuring all things "Western" – four days of rodeo riding, threshing displays, ploughing competitions, square dancing, jigging and Central Canada's Fiddle Festival. You can camp in the grounds of the museum ($12–15; mid-May to Oct); otherwise, B&B **accommodation** is available next door at *The Oak Tree* (☎204/637-2029, ⓦwww.bedandbreakfast.mb.ca; ❷).

Spruce Woods Provincial Park

Between Austin and Brandon, about 15km south of the Trans-Canada along Hwy 5, **Spruce Woods Provincial Park** falls on either side of the Assiniboine River, whose confused loops twist slowly south and west. The park has several walking trails that begin beside or near the road. To the north, the **Epinette Creek Trails** run through woodland and marsh, the longest being the 25km Newfoundland Trail. There are a number of unserviced campsites along the various paths.

Roughly 5km south of the Epinette Creek Trails, the **Spirit Sands Trails** cross an area of mixed-grass prairie before entering the shifting sand dunes and pots of quicksand that constitute Manitoba's only **desert**. These "Spirit Sands" were of great religious significance to the Ojibwa who, according to one of the earliest fur traders, Alexander Henry, told "of the strange noises heard in its bowels, and its nightly apparitions". Hire a guide or, if it's too hot to walk, try one of the horse-drawn **wagon tours** that leave from the start of the trail throughout the summer (May–Sept; 1hr 30min; for times call ☎204/827-2800, or off-season 379-2007; $8). The park is filled with strange, bluish-green ponds formed by the action of underground streams, and has some rare animals, notably the hognose snake and the prairie skink (a lizard); there's also a lot of poison ivy about, so take care. About 1km south of the start of the Spirit Sands, there's a **visitor centre** (mid-May to early Sept daily; summer ☏204/827-8850, rest of year ☏204/834-8800) and a full range of tourist facilities at **KICHE MANITOU LAKE**, including a large campsite (☏204/948-3333 or 1-888/482-2267; $14–16; mid-May to Sept), a caravan park, grocery stores, restaurants, a beach and canoe rental.

CARBERRY is the nearest community of any size to Spruce Woods, and you can use it as a base to explore the park. Other than the **Seton Centre**, 116 Main St (June–Aug Mon–Sat 9am–5pm; $2), displaying the artwork and memorabilia of the naturalist Ernest Thompson Seton, and the local history **Carberry Plains Museum** (July & Aug daily 1–6pm; June & Sept by appointment ☏204/834-2284; free), there's not much to see. You can **stay** at the no-frills *4-Way Motel* (☏204/834-2878; ❷) or the more comfortable *Carberry Motor Inn* (☏204/834-2197; ❷).

Brandon

In 1881, when the CPR decided to route the transcontinental railroad through Winnipeg, it was clear that they would need a refuelling depot in the western part of the province. The ideal location was on the east bank of the Assiniboine River, opposite today's **BRANDON**, 160km from Winnipeg, but a certain Dugald McVicar was already established here. The sudden arrival of all sorts of speculators encouraged McVicar to overreach himself, and he attempted to sell his farm and sod hut to the CPR for around $60,000, prompting a railway negotiator to exclaim, "I'll be damned if a town of any kind is built here." It wasn't, and Brandon was founded 4km to the west. Nowadays, the city is a major agricultural centre, home to several research institutions, Manitoba's largest livestock show – the Royal Manitoba Winter Fair – in late March, the huge First Nations Winter Celebration in January, rodeo finals in November and the Brandon Film Festival in February.

If you want to know what's going on in Brandon and the surrounding region, visit the swish **Riverbank Discovery Centre** (May–Sept Mon–Fri 8.30am–8.30pm, Sat & Sun 10.30am–8.30pm; Oct–April Mon–Fri 8.30am–5pm; ☏204/729-2141 or 1-888/799-1111, ⊛www.brandon.com) a short drive south of the Trans-Canada Highway along 18th St N. The bureau is also the starting point of several trails along the Assiniboine River and can provide leaflets on self-guided tours, including the one downtown that highlights historic buildings. Some of these are on the south side of Rosser Ave where a terrace in the Romanesque Revival style includes the former Mutter Brothers Grocery Store, whose interior has been removed to the **Daly House Museum**, 122 18th St (Tues–Sun 10am–noon & 1–5pm; $3), the restored home of Brandon's first mayor. The highlight of the house is an illuminated four-storey doll's house in one of the upstairs bedrooms, complete with minuscule mice and mousetraps. Other imposing late nineteenth-century residences are located on the stretch of Louise Ave as you walk west to **Brandon University**. The university itself has a small campus dotted with a mix of old and new buildings, most impressive of which is the original college building, with its ragged silhouette facing you to the right as you approach from Louise Ave. The former **courthouse** topped by an octagonal cupola, at 11th St and Princess Ave, is Brandon's grandest building. The **Art Gallery of Southwestern Manitoba**, 710 Rosser Ave (Mon, Tues & Fri–Sun

10am–6pm, Thurs 10am–9pm; Ⓦ www.agsm.ca; free), has changing exhibitions concentrating on the work of Manitoba artists and craftspeople.

Brandon's **bus terminal**, at 141 6th St (☎204/727-0643 or 1-800/661-8747), handles Greyhound buses running to Winnipeg, Regina and Saskatoon, as well as smaller places in southwest Manitoba, and also Grey Goose Lines, which runs buses south on Hwy 10. VIA Rail **trains** on the thrice-weekly Winnipeg to Vancouver run stop north of Brandon along Hwy 10, from where it's a twenty-minute taxi ride into town ($15).

Brandon has lots of good places to **stay**. Just off the Trans-Canada is the eccentric *Barney's Motel*, 105 Middleton Ave (☎204/725-1540 Ⓦ www.barneysmotel.com; ❷), where every dead fly brought reduces your bill by 10 cents. Some rooms have kitchenettes. The *Super 8 Motel*, 1570 Highland Ave, just off the Trans-Canada (☎204/729-8024 or 1-800/800-8000, Ⓦ www.super8.com; ❹), is good value, with a free continental breakfast, plus a pool and hot tub. Other recommended places are the *Royal Oak Inn*, 3130 Victoria Ave (☎204/728-5775; ❹), the city's most reputable accommodation, with a 1930s theme restaurant. There are two **campsites** just outside town: *Curran Park Campground* (☎204/729-2486; $15–25; May–Sept), beside the Assiboine River 2km west of the visitor centre on Grand Valley Road, and smaller *Meadowlark Campground* (☎204/728-7205 or 1-800/363-6434; $20–21), just off the Trans-Canada Highway west of *Barney's Motel*. The city's selection of **restaurants** is poor. The best are along Rosser Ave and include *Oliver's Bistro and Steakhouse* at no. 935 (☎204/727-3333) where chandeliers hang among red drapes and classical melodies, but meat entrees start at a reasonable $12 – veggie options are a bit cheaper still. More expensive but excellent *Jerry's Bistro* (☎204/727-7781), at no. 926, serves up such exotic fare as emu and ostrich. Also on Rosser is the favourite meeting place of Brandon's sophisticates, the *Casteleyn*, at no. 908, where you can sip cappuccinos in minimalist splendour; they also sell beautiful chocolates. Around the corner at 139 110th St, *Timothy Beans* has Internet access as well as coffees and great sandwiches. The bland *Double Decker Tavern & Restaurant*, 943 Rosser Ave, regularly has live music.

Souris and beyond

An easy 43km drive southwest of Brandon, **SOURIS** is a pretty tree-shaded town on the steep banks of the Souris River and easily reached by Greyhound. Its main attraction is the vertigo-inducing cable **suspension bridge**, which is the longest in Canada. Beside the bridge is the charming local history **Hillcrest Museum**, 26 Crescent Ave (May & June Sun 2–5pm; July & Aug daily 10am–6pm; $3). You can prospect for agates, jaspers and other semi-precious stones at the pits outside town. The Rock Shop, 8 1st St South (May–Sept Mon–Fri 9.30am–6pm, Sat 10am–6pm, Sun noon–5pm; Oct–April Mon–Fri 10am–5pm, Sat 11am–5pm), sells some of the stones as well as the permit ($10.70), and can direct you to the pits. You can take away as much as you can carry.

Turtle Mountain Provincial Park

Further south, 97km south of Brandon along Hwy 10, you come to **Turtle Mountain Provincial Park**, a mixed area of marsh, rolling hills and deciduous forest, whose four hundred shallow lakes form an ideal habitat for the western painted turtle, after which the park takes its name. There's also a substantial moose population, most visible in late September. Turtle

Mountain's main facilities are beside the main road at **ADAM LAKE**, where there's the large *Adam Lake Campsite* (☎1-888/482-2267 or 204/948-3333; $13–15; mid-May to mid-Sept), a beach, a store, a **park office** (Mon–Thurs 10am–noon & 1–6pm, Fri & Sat 10am–10pm, Sun 1–4pm; ☎204/534-2578) and a number of walking and cross-country skiing trails. There's a smaller, prettier campsite at **MAX LAKE** ($10; May–Sept), south of Hwy 3 on Provincial Road 446. This campsite gives easy access to the **Oskar Lake Canoe Route**, a nineteen-kilometre paddle and portage excursion across ten of the park's lakes. Best in the spring or autumn, the route should be tackled in an anticlockwise direction to eliminate the need to climb steep hills, and can be completed in one or two days. There's an overnight cabin at James Lake – register at the district office of the Manitoba Department of Natural Resources in **Boissevain**, 40km north (☎204/534-7204) if you intend to use it. Oddly, there are no canoe-rental facilities in the park.

On the southeastern edge of Turtle Mountain Park, and straddling the US border, is the landscaped shrub and formal flower garden of the **International Peace Garden** (☎204/534-2510). The dubious attractions on offer here include a Peace Chapel (built right on the border), the starkly modern Peace Tower and a large, floral clock. You can also take one of three self-guided **walking tours**. The garden costs $10 per vehicle (useful if you want to drive around the outlying trails) or $5 per pedestrian.

Moose Mountain and Cannington Manor

Moose Mountain Provincial Park in southeastern Saskatchewan – 60km south of the Trans-Canada on Route 9 – is a rough rectangle of wooded hill and lake whose main resort, **KENOSEE LAKE**, is packed with holiday-makers throughout the season. There's a full range of amenities here, including a **parks office** (Mon–Fri 8am–5pm; ☎306/577-2600), restaurants, bars, sports facilities, waterslides and canoe and paddleboat rental, but it's still easy enough to escape the crowds and wander off into the surrounding poplar and birch groves. For **accommodation**, *Kenosee Condos and Gardens* (☎306/577-2331 or 584-1028), in the resort village, has luxurious two-bedroom units (❺), and there are also a number of **campsites** spread out around the lake. Hotel rooms and cabin rentals are also available through the *Kenosee Inn* (☎306/577-2099, ⓦwww.kenoseeinn.com; ❸–❹), which is near two golf courses, tennis courts and waterslides. The *Fish Creek* and *Lynwood* **campsites** (☎306/577-2611 or 577-2600; $15–20; mid-May to early Sept) have the advantage of being right on the western edge of the developed area, a good 2km from the busiest part of the park. For **food**, try the *Moose Head Dining Room*, on the lake, which serves pizza, pasta, steaks and Saskatoon berry pie.

A short-lived experiment in transplanting English social customs to the prairies is the subject of the **Cannington Manor Provincial Historic Park** (mid-May to Aug Mon & Wed–Sun 10am–5pm; $2), a partly reconstructed Victorian village about 30km east of Kenosee Lake. Founded in 1882 by Edward Pierce, the would-be squire, the village attracted a number of British middle-class families determined to live as "gentlemen farmers", running small agricultural businesses, organizing tea and croquet evenings and even importing a pack of hounds to stage their own hunts. Their efforts failed when the branch rail line was routed well to the south of Cannington Manor, and by 1900 the settlement was abandoned.

Regina

REGINA, 575km west of Winnipeg, is the capital city of Saskatchewan, its commercial and administrative services anchoring a vast network of agricultural villages and towns. Yet despite its status, its brash shopping malls and 200,000-plus population, Regina acts and feels like a small prairie town. It's a comfortable, if unremarkable, place to spend a couple of days, with the offbeat attraction of the Royal Canadian Mounted Police Training Academy and Museum, and more hours of sunshine than any other major city in Canada.

In 1881 the Indian Commissioner **Edward Dewdney** became lieutenant-governor of the Northwest Territories, a vast tract of land that spread west from Ontario as far as the Arctic and Pacific oceans. Almost immediately, he decided to move his capital south from the established community of Battleford to **Pile o'Bones**, an inconsequential dot on the map that took its name from the heaps of bleached buffalo bones left along its creek by generations of native hunters. The reason for Dewdney's decision was the routing of the Canadian Pacific transcontinental railroad across the southern plains: the city was renamed Regina (Latin for "queen") after Queen Victoria, and Dewdney petitioned for it to be expanded on land to the north of the creek, a plot coincidentally owned by him. The site was terrible: the sluggish creek provided a poor water supply, the clay soil was muddy in wet weather and dusty in the summer, and there was no timber for building. Accordingly, the railway board refused to oblige, and the end result was farcical: Government House and the Mounted Police barracks were built where Dewdney wanted them, but the train station was a three-kilometre trek to the south.

In 1905 Regina became the capital of the newly created province of **Saskatchewan**, and settlers flocked here from the United States and central

Europe. At the heart of an expanding wheat-growing district, the city tripled its population during its first fifteen years. It also overcame its natural disadvantages with an ambitious programme of tree-planting, which provided shade and controlled the dust, and by damming the creek to provide a better source of water. However, the city's success was based on the fragile prosperity of a one-crop economy, and throughout the twentieth century boom alternated with bust.

Arrival, information and accommodation

Regina's **airport** (☏306/761-7555, ⓦwww.yqr.ca) is about 5km west of the city centre. The taxi trip downtown costs roughly $10, or you can take the Hobo Express Shuttle bus (☏306/949-2121 or 1-877/828-4626) to Regina's downtown hotels or locations in Moose Jaw ($25). A ten-minute walk east of the airport brings you to the junction of Regina Ave and Pasqua St, from where Regina Transit's **buses** #11 and #13 head for the city centre (Mon–Sat every 25min 6am–12.30am, Sun hourly 11am–6pm). The **bus station** is downtown at 2041 Hamilton St, just south of Victoria Ave, with services from Greyhound and the provincial carrier, the Saskatchewan Transportation Company (☏306/787-0101 or 1-800/663-7181).

Tourism Regina operates a tourist bureau east of town on Hwy 1, really only accessible by car (mid-May to early Sept Mon–Fri 8am–7pm, Sat & Sun 10am–6pm; rest of year Mon–Fri 8am–5pm; ☏306/789-5099 or 1-800/661-5099, ⓦwww.tourismregina.com). The **Tourism Saskatchewan** office, in the Leaderpost building at 1922 Park St (Mon–Fri 8am–5pm; ☏306/787-2300 or 1-877/237-2273, ⓦwww.sasktourism.com), has a comprehensive range of leaflets and booklets and can help with specific info on Regina.

The best way to see the centre is on **foot**, though the area around McIntyre St and Saskatchewan Drive, and sections of Osler St, six blocks east, are rundown neighbourhoods that are best avoided. Similarly accessible is the **Wascana Centre**, a large multipurpose park and recreational area, whose northern boundary is a few minutes' stroll south of the centre. **Regina Transit** runs bus services; a standard one-way fare is $1.60 (exact fare payable to driver), day-pass $4.50, and a book of ten tickets $14, available at the Tourism Saskatchewan Office or the transit information centre, 2124 11th Ave (Mon–Fri 7am–9pm, Sat 9am–4pm; ☏306/777-7433, ⓦwww .reginatransit.com).

Central Regina has a reasonable range of moderately priced and convenient **hotels**, as well as an excellent **hostel**. There's rarely any difficulty in finding a room, but most of the very cheapest places listed by the Tourism Saskatchewan office are grim and cheerless establishments. There's a cluster of reasonably

Tours in and around Regina

Great Western Adventure Tours, 41 Wesley Rd (☏306/584-3555), runs **tours** of the city (4hr 30min; $15), as well as to Moose Jaw (6hr; $22) and the Qu'Appelle Valley (7hr; $32 including lunch). Heritage Regina Tours (☏306/585-4214) has free guided walking tours of the city (July to mid-Sept Sundays). RC Tours (☏306/545-0555) has minibus tours of the city's highlights including the Legislative Building, Royal Canadian Mounted Police Museum and Government House (10am & 1pm, pick-up from downtown hotels; 3hr 30min; $22). The Saskatchewan History & Folklore Society, 1860 Lorne St (☏306/780-9204 or 1-800/919-9437), organizes one- to four-day tours of the province's historic sites.

priced, standard **motels** east of the centre along Hwy 1, which doubles as Victoria Ave East, and another group of motels south of the centre, along Albert St.

Hotels and motels

Coachman Inn 835 Victoria Ave ☎306/522-8525. An excellent budget choice close to Wascana Centre Park, major shopping and sights. ❷

Delta Regina Hotel 1919 Saskatchewan Drive at Hamilton St ☎306/525-5255 or 1-800/209-5255, ⓦwww.deltahotels.com. One of Regina's most luxurious hotels, but located in a slightly offputting part of town. Facilities include cable and satellite TV, and a pool with a three-storey waterslide. ❺

Hotel Saskatchewan Radisson Plaza 2125 Victoria Ave at Scarth St ☎306/522-7691 or 1-800/333-3333, ⓦwww.hotelsask.com. This large, luxurious hotel, overlooking Victoria Park, provides a full range of facilities, including a fitness centre with whirlpool. Complimentary pick-up at airport. ❹

Quality Hotel 1717 Victoria Ave at Broad St ☎306/569-4656 or 1-800/228-5151. A good downtown bargain, with comfortable rooms. Ask about the occasional weekend discounts. ❸

Ramada Hotel & Convention Centre 1818 Victoria Ave at Broad St ☎306/569-1666 or 1-800/667-6500, ⓦwww.ramada.ca. One of the most attractive and well equipped of Regina's hotels, including comfortable, spacious singles, doubles and en suites, and a large recreation complex. ❹

Regina Inn Hotel 1975 Broad St ☎306/525-6767 or 1-800/667-8162, ⓦwww.reginainn.com. Top-quality high-rise hotel in the centre of downtown. The majority of rooms are nonsmoking and there are one-bedroom and Jacuzzi suites available. Rates halve at weekends. ❹

Regina Travelodge Hotel 4177 Albert St S ☎306/586-3443 or 1-800/578-7878, ⓦwww.travelodgeregina.com. Large hotel offering a wide range of facilities, including free coffee in rooms and free local calls. There's also a restaurant, pub and gift shop on the premises. ❹

West Harvest Inn 4025 Albert St ☎306/586-6755 or 1-800/853-1181, ⓦwww .westharvestinn.com. One of the best bargains in the Regina area. Singles, doubles and en suites all

come with free in-room coffee and local calls. The inn also has a health spa and gym. ❹

B&Bs

Daybreak B&B 316 Habkirk Drive ☎306/586-0211. In the south of the city, east of Albert St, near the Trans-Canada. Two rooms with a nice old-fashioned feel and the owners offer free pick-up and delivery to airport or bus station. ❶

Morning Glory Manor Broad St & College Ave ☎306/525-2945 ⓦwww.morningglorymanor.ca. Charming 1920s home, minutes from downtown and Wascana Centre Park. Off-street parking. ❷

Hostels

Turgeon International Hostel (HI) 2310 McIntyre St ☎306/791-8165 or 1-800/467-8357, ⓦwww.hihostels.ca. Extremely clean HI hostel in a restored heritage house, immediately south of the downtown core, with cooking and laundry facilities and a small library. Dorm beds $17.

YMCA 2400 13th Ave ☎306/757-9622. Small budget rooms with weekly rates available. Facilities include a pool and cafeteria. Men only. Singles $24.

YWCA 1940 McIntyre St ☎306/525-2141. Budget rooms available, including weekly rates, but about twice as much as at the YMCA. Women only. Singles $36.

Campsites

Buffalo Lookout Campground South of Hwy 1 E ☎306/525-1448. Located 5km east of downtown and includes a store, shower house, phones and indoor recreation facilities, as well as a 24hr on-site manager. $15. May to mid-Sept.

Kings' Acres Campground Hwy 1 E ☎306/522-1619. Located on a spacious property 1km east of town, behind the Tourism Regina Bureau. With a full range of serviced and unserviced sites, with store, phone, pool, and TV and games room. $19–21. March–Oct.

The City

Fifteen minutes' walk from end to end, Regina's downtown business and shopping core is known as the **Market Square**, a simple gridiron bounded by Saskatchewan Drive and 13th Ave to the north and south, Osler and Albert streets to the east and west. The rather mundane **Regina Plains Museum** (Mon–Fri 10am–4pm; free; ⓦwww.reginaplainsmuseum.com) is within

Market Square, on the fourth floor of the mall at 1801 Scarth St and 11th Ave – its modest displays on the city's history are less diverting than the stories of the elderly volunteers who staff the museum. Exhibitions of innovative, and often controversial, contemporary art can be seen at the **Dunlop Art Gallery**, in the Public Library, west of the museum at 2311 12th Ave (Mon–Thurs 9.30am–9pm, Fri 9.30am–6pm, Sat 9.30am–5pm, Sun 1.30–5pm; free; ⓦwww.dunlopartgallery.org). If the museum and gallery has whetted your appetite you should visit the **Antique Mall**, the largest in western Canada, located beyond the railway tracks north of Market Square, at 1175 Rose St (Mon–Sat 10am–6pm, Wed & Thurs until 9.30pm, Sun 1.30–5pm; free).

Immediately to the west of the Market Square district, across Albert St, is **Cathedral Village**, with 13th Ave as its heart. It's an old area with an eclectic mix of boutiques, coffee shops, craft shops and classy restaurants.

Wascana Centre Park

Roughly eight times the size of the Market Square, Regina's most distinctive feature is **Wascana Centre Park** (ⓦwww.wascana.sk.ca), which begins three blocks south of 13th Ave and extends southeast to the city limits, following the curves of **Wascana Lake**, which was created as part of a work project for the unemployed in the 1930s. The city's main recreation area, the park is equipped with a bandstand (performances Sun 2–4pm), barbecue pits, snack bars, boating facilities and waterfowl ponds, but for the most part it's a cheerless combination of reed-filled water and bare lawn.

In the northwest corner of the park, near College Ave and Albert St, the **Royal Saskatchewan Museum** (daily: May–Aug 9am–5.30pm; Sept–April 9am–4.30pm; donation $2; ⓦwww.royalsaskmuseum.ca) is devoted to the province's geology and wildlife, starring a giant animated dinosaur called Megamunch. Informative dioramas portray aspects of aboriginal life in the First Nations Gallery, including storytelling, shown in the scene of a grizzled grandfather recounting stories to a couple of rapt youths. In the new Life Sciences Gallery the relationships between habitat, plants and animals are explored with a multitude of skilfully stuffed animals and plastic flora set against backdrops that evoke the diverse eco-regions of Saskatchewan. A couple of minutes' walk to the east is the ferry boat to **Willow Island** (mid-May to Aug Mon–Fri noon–4pm; $2), a favourite picnic spot. **Boat tours** are available, departing from the observation deck, near the swimming pool (mid-June to Aug Sun 1–5pm; 20min; $2).

Further east, reached by the winding Wascana Drive, is perhaps Regina's main tourist attraction, the **Saskatchewan Science Centre** (May to early Sept Mon–Thurs 9am–6pm, Fri 9am–8.30pm, Sat & Sun 11am–6pm; rest of year Tues–Fri 9am–5pm, Sat & Sun noon–6pm; variable hours, call ⓣ306/522-4629 or 1-800/667-6300, ⓦwww.sciencecentre.sk.ca; $6.50). The open, airy building houses more than a hundred interactive scientific exhibits, live stage shows and demonstrations; of particular interest is a display on uranium mining and a room which has a direct video link to NASA headquarters in Houston, enabling you to watch the live proceedings when a mission is under way. Another gallery is devoted to the soils and weather of Saskatchewan, and here you can learn about what's involved in running a farm. Also on the premises is an IMAX cinema ($7, or joint ticket with centre $12).

On the other side of the lake, accessible from Albert St, is the grand **Legislative Building** (daily: late May to Sept 8am–9pm; rest of year 8am–5pm; free tours every 30min; 2hr), a self-confident cross-shaped structure of Manitoba limestone with an impressive domed tower at its centre. Guided tours take in the oak-and-marble-panelled Legislative Chamber and six small art galleries, the best of which houses Edmund Morris's portraits of local Indian leaders, presented to the province in 1911. A neighbouring corridor is occupied by the paintings of the **Native Heritage Foundation**, some thirty canvases featuring the work of contemporary Métis and native artists, notably Allen Sapp from North Battleford, who has won some international acclaim for his softly coloured studies of life on Saskatchewan's Indian reserves as he remembers them from the 1930s. A few minutes' walk south of the Legislative Building, just off Albert St at 23rd Ave, the **MacKenzie Art Gallery** (daily 11am–6pm, Wed & Thurs until 10pm; free) has several spacious modern galleries devoted to temporary exhibitions by modern Canadian artists, plus a good permanent collection. It's also the stage for the city's principal theatrical event, **The Trial of Louis Riel** (mid-July to Aug Wed–Fri; $12), whose text is based on the transcripts of the trial in Regina in September 1885. No other single event in Canada's past has aroused such controversy: at the time, most of English-speaking Canada was determined he should hang as a rebel, whereas his French-Canadian defenders saw him as a patriot and champion of a just cause. Though Riel was subject to visions and delusions, the court rejected the defence of insanity on the grounds that he knew what he was doing. As he exclaimed: "No one can say that the North-West was not suffering last year... but what I have done, and risked, rested certainly on the conviction [that I was] called upon to do something for my country." The jury found him guilty, but the execution was delayed while prime minister John A. Macdonald weighed the consequences; in the end, he decided against clemency.

The **Diefenbaker Homestead** (mid-May to Aug daily 10am–8pm; free), about 1km east of the gallery but still within the park, was the boyhood home of John Diefenbaker, Conservative prime minister of Canada from 1957 to 1963. Moved from the township of Borden, SK in 1967, the tiny wooden house has been decked out with original and contemporary furnishings and memorabilia reflecting both Diefenbaker's homespun philosophies and the immense self-confidence that earned him the nickname "Dief the Chief". In the extreme southeast corner of the park, reached by buses #10 or #12 or by car along Arcola Ave East and Prince of Wales Drive from the city centre, is the **Wascana Waterfowl Park** (May–Nov daily 9am–9pm; free; guided tours Mon–Fri 9am–4pm), a group of ponds that's a habitat for ducks, pelicans and Canada geese.

Royal Canadian Mounted Police Training Academy

All Mounties do their basic training at the **Royal Canadian Mounted Police Training Academy**, 4km west of the city centre at Dewdney Ave West, accessible by bus #8 from 11th Ave at Cornwall St. Beside the main parade ground of Sleigh Square – site of the closely choreographed Sergeant Major's parade (late May to Aug Mon–Fri 12.50pm) and Sunset Retreat Ceremony (July to mid-Aug Tues 6.45pm) – is the RCMP **Centennial Museum** (daily: mid-June to Aug 8am–6.45pm; rest of year 10am–4.45pm; free tours Mon–Fri 9am (summer only), 10am, 11am, 1.30pm, 2.30pm & 3.30pm; ⓦ www.rcmpmuseum.com; free). This traces the history of the force, from early contacts with the Plains Indians and Métis through to its present role as an intelligence-gathering organization.

Inside the museum, a series of contemporary quotations illustrates the **Long March** that first brought the Mounties to the west from Ontario in 1874. Their destination was Fort Whoop-up, near present-day Lethbridge, AB where they intended to expel the American whiskey traders. However, by the time

The Mounties

The heroes of a hundred adventure stories, from *Boys' Own* yarns to more eccentric epics such as the movie *Canadian Mounties versus the Atomic Invaders*, the **Mounties** have been the continent's most charismatic good guys ever since Inspector James Morrow Walsh rode into Chief Sitting Bull's Canadian encampment to lay down the law. Coming straight after the Sioux's victory at the battle of the Little Bighorn in 1876, this was an act of extraordinary daring, and it secured the future of the Mounties. The **North West Mounted Police**, as the Mounties were originally called, had been created in Ottawa during the autumn of 1873, simply in order to restore law and order to the "Whoop-up Country" of southern Saskatchewan and Alberta in the aftermath of the Cypress Hills Massacre (see box p.583). There was no long-term strategy: the force's areas of responsibility were undecided, and even their uniforms had been slung together from a surplus supply of British army tunics that happened to be handy. However, they did a brilliant job of controlling the whiskey traders who had created pandemonium through the unscrupulous sale of liquor to the Plains Indians, and it was soon clear – after Walsh's dealings with Sitting Bull – that they were to become a permanent institution.

The Mounties came to perform a vital role in administering the west on behalf of the federal government, acting both as law enforcement officers and as justices of the peace. From the 1880s their patrols diligently crisscrossed the territory, their influence reinforced by a knowledge of local conditions that was accumulated in the exercise of a great range of duties – from delivering the mail to providing crop reports. Despite this level of autonomy, the Mounties saw themselves as an integral, if remote, part of the **British Empire**, their actions and decisions sanctioned by the weight of its authority. In this sense, they despised the individualism of the American sheriff and marshal, for the Mounties expected obedience because of the dignity of their office, not because of their speed with a firearm.

The officer corps, most of whom were recruited from the social elite of the eastern provinces, became respected for an even-handedness that extended, remarkably for the period, to their dealings with the Plains Indians. **Crowfoot**, the Blackfoot leader, was even moved to remark, "If the police had not come to the country, where would we all be now? They have protected us as the feathers of a bird protect it from the frosts of winter." Yet the officers' class prejudices had a less positive influence on their approach to law and order: socially disruptive crimes of violence were their main priority, whereas prostitution and drunkenness were regarded as predictable and inevitable nuisances that were confined to the "lower orders". They had a cohesive view of the society they wanted to create, a WASP-ish patriarchy where everyone knew their place.

After 1920, when the force lost its exclusively western mandate to become the **Royal Canadian Mounted Police**, this conservative undertow became more problematic. Time and again the RCMP supported reactionary politicians who used them to break strikes – like prime ministers Bennett in Saskatchewan in 1933 and 1934, and Joey Smallwood in Newfoundland during 1959 – and they have often been accused of bias in their dealings with the Québecois. That said, although the Mounties are seen by some as a bastion of reaction at odds with multicultural definitions of Canada, for the most part they remain a potent symbol of nationality.

they arrived they were in a state of complete exhaustion, and it was fortunate that the Americans had already decamped. Another small section deals with **Sitting Bull**, who crossed into Canada after his victory at the Battle of the Little Bighorn in 1876. Fearing reprisals from the furious American army, Sitting Bull spent four years in and around the Cypress Hills, where he developed a friendship with Police Inspector James Walsh. A picture of the chief and his braves, taken at Fort Walsh in 1877, shows an audience of curious Mounties in their pith helmets. To reinforce the romantic Hollywood image of the Mounties, an onsite cinema has continuous free runnings of such glorified interpretations as *Rose Marie* (1936), starring Nelson Eddy and Jeanette MacDonald.

On the **tour** of the grounds you're shown the various buildings, including mock-ups of houses where recruits practise family arrests, search warrants and surveillance techniques; the drill hall where new recruits are put through their paces; and the 1883 chapel – Regina's oldest building – a splendid structure furnished in dark, polished oak where you can escape the intense training activity outside.

Government House

Government House, a couple of kilometres west of the city centre at 4607 Dewdney Ave and Lewvan Drive (Tues–Sun 10am–4pm; tours every 30min; free; bus #1, #11 or #13), was the residence of the lieutenant-governors of the Northwest Territories and subsequently Saskatchewan from 1891 to 1945. A stolid yellow-brick building, it has been delightfully restored to its appearance at the end of the nineteenth century, with offices and reception areas downstairs and a splendid, balconied staircase leading up to the bedrooms. The men's billiards room is decorated with an enormous bison head and a lemon-water stand, where the governor and his cronies would dip their fingers to hide the smell of the cigars. There are also a couple of mementos of one of the more eccentric governors, Amédée Forget, whose specially designed "salesman's chair", beside the entrance, was meant to be uncomfortable, with protruding gargoyles sticking into the visitor's spine, legs shorter at the front than the back and a flesh-pinching crack cut across the middle of the seat. The rocking horse in the office was for Forget's pet monkey. High tea, complete with finger sandwiches and fragile china cups, is served in the ballroom one weekend each month between 1.30pm and 4pm.

Eating, drinking and entertainment

Regina has a clutch of good downtown **restaurants**, lively places whose prices are usually very reasonable. However, many of them close early and don't open at all on Sundays; in emergencies try the big hotels whose standard-issue snack bars are nearly always open daily to 9.30pm.

The city's **nightlife** is hardly inspiring, but the university's students provide a little stimulation for the couple of downtown clubs, whilst local roustabouts and government workers alike tend to stick to C&W. As a general rule, avoid the downtown **bars**, which are really not very pleasant, and try one of Regina's **brewpubs**, though most are a bit far from the centre. A couple are on the city's main strip of – fairly unexciting – clubs on Dewdney Ave, which is just north of downtown in Regina's Old Warehouse District.

For **theatre**, the Regina Performing Arts Centre, 1077 Angus St (☎306/779-2277, ⓦnonprofits.accesscomm.ca/reginaperformingartscentre), stages work by the Saskatchewan Community Theatre and the Regina Little Theatre. The Regina Symphony Orchestra (ⓦwww.reginasymphonyorchestra.sk.ca) performs at the Saskatchewan Centre of the Arts, 200 Lakeshore Drive (☎306/525-9999 or 1-800/667-8497). The *Prairie Dog* is Regina's free weekly entertainment newspaper and useful for listings; pick it up at roadside dispensers or in cafés and bars. **Buffalo Days** is a week-long festival (end July & early Aug) of craft and livestock exhibitions and music shows, ending with a fireworks display. The **Kinsmen Rock in the Valley**, held in Craven, a 20min drive north of town, is a four-day contemporary and classic rock festival in mid-July. The mid-June **Folk Festival** is held in Victoria Park; and the **Mosaic Multicultural Festival**, held in early June at various locations throughout the city, is a multiethnic celebration featuring folk dancing and pavilions serving food and drink. On the first weekend of September, Chinese dragon boats rowed by large teams race each other in Wascana Park.

Cafés and restaurants

Alfredo's Fresh Pasta and Bistro 1801 Scarth St ☎306/522-3366. Specializes in home-made pasta dishes and combines a tasty and imaginative menu with good-value main courses from $8. Closed Sun.

Brass Lantern 2317 Albert St ☎306/584-0345. Reasonable diner-quality restaurant on the same block as the hostel on the south side of town. Lunches around $7; dinners $15.

Cathedral Village Free House 3062 Albert St at 13th ☎306/359-1661. Busy bar and restaurant with locally brewed beers and a good line in wood-fired pizzas, sandwiches and burritos or try something a bit fancier like the excellent Freehouse Bouillabaisse which combines halibut, salmon, scallops, shrimp, walleye and tiger prawns.

Classic Buffet Co. 100 Albert St ☎306/545-6955. Help yourself to the table laid out with pizza, roast beef and fifteen other hot dishes. Early closing.

The Copper Kettle 1953 Scarth St ☎306/525-3545. Central Greek–Canadian place overlooking Market Square; pick the fabulous spinach and feta pizza over the very average pasta ($9).

Da Lat by Night 1312 Broad St ☎306/757-7291. Popular place for huge helpings of Vietnamese or Chinese food. Filling set meals run from $15 for two people. Take out and delivery available.

Golf's Steak House 1945 Victoria Ave ☎306/525-5808. Special-occasion steakhouse with top-notch prime rib and charbroiled steaks.

Heliotrope 2204 McIntyre St ☎306/569-3373. A wholefood vegetarian restaurant with a pleasant patio on a quiet side street south of downtown. The emphasis is on Asian and Middle Eastern food: rice bowls, Thai curries and falafel.

The Keg 4371 Albert St ☎306/585-1717. Popular chain specializing in steak but also with chicken and seafood dishes from $12.

La Bodega 2228 Albert St ☎306/546-3660. Hip restaurant with great patio where movies are screened on a neighbouring wall and which hosts a drum night (Tues). Food is equally adventurous, with Thai mango and palm salads available and a confusing array of tapas and so-called tappetizers which include odd bedfellows like sushi and bannok brushetta. But execution is excellent and prices consequently fairly steep.

Neo Japonica 2167 Hamilton St ☎306/359-7669. Among the best Japanese restaurants in Canada; excellent tempura and sushi.

Nicky's Café & Bake Shop 1005 8th Ave. Good Canadian menu at reasonable prices, especially their breakfasts, Saskatoon berry pie and bread. Fresh turkey served daily. Closed Sun.

Sage Gourmet Café 2330 Albert St 13th Ave and Ketallack St ☎306/569-9726. Modest café with a small fine-dining menu (mains $18–25) and lots of lighter snacks: salads, bagels and excellent gamey sandwiches with ostrich, buffalo or venison put in a pita with grilled veggies for $5.

Soup Nutsy 1950 Hamilton St ☎306/596-7687. Seinfeld inspired soup takeaway, with eight excellent daily soups like Ukrainian hotpot or Dukhobor Borscht (from $4).

Bars and clubs

Bonzinni's 4634 Albert St ☎306/586-3553. Sociable South Regina brewpub with big screen TV, games room and good Italian food.

Brewster's 1832 Victoria Ave E. One of a chain of three brewpubs known for their extensive range of beer; branches also on 480 North McCarthy Blvd and 4180 Albert St.

The Bushwakker 2206 Dewdney Ave ☎306/359-7276. Successful chain brewpub with twelve types of beer and a large selection of single-malt scotches.

Gabbo's 2338 Dewdney Ave. One of several fairly basic nightclubs in a row of old warehouses; choose between them by following the crowds. Small cover Sat & Sun.

Good Time Charlie's In *Plains Hotel*, 1965 Albert St. Biker bar – the best blues club in Regina. Jam sessions Thurs, Sat & Sun nights, plus Sat afternoons. $3–5 cover charge.

Manhattan Club 2300 Dewdney Ave. Disco with a chaotic combo of Top 40 and dance mix. Small cover charge on Sat. Closed Sun & Mon.

McNally's Tavern 2226 Dewdney Ave ☎306/522-4774. Large brewpub on the strip with 24 beers on tap, decent food and frequent live music to liven things up later on.

OUTside Bar 2070 Broad St. Popular gay venue.
The Owl University of Regina. Busy college bar that heaves with masses on Fri.
The Pump 641 Victoria Ave E. C&W venue with a huge dance floor. Closed Sun.

The State 1326a Hamilton St. Alternative rap, pop, 1980s hits – all on a jammed multi-level dance floor. Great live bands most nights. $7 cover charge on Fri. Closed Sun.

Listings

Airlines Air Canada ☎1-888/247-2262; Air Sask ☎1-800/665-7275; Athabaska Airways ☎1-800/667-9356; Northwest Airlines ☎1-800/447-4747; WestJet ☎1-877/952-4638.
Bike rental Joe's Cycle, 2255 Albert St ☎306/347-7711; Western Cycle, 1745 Hamilton St ☎306/522-5678. Both charge about $23/day.
Bookshops Book and Brier Patch, 4065 Albert St, has the biggest selection of books in the province; Canada Book, 1861 Scarth St, off 11th Ave, has a good range of titles.
Car rental Avis, 655 Broad St ☎306/757-1653, and at the airport ☎306/757-5460; Budget, at the airport ☎306/791-6810, and 601 Albert St ☎306/791-9136 or 1-800/267-6810; Hertz, 2755 Caribou St ☎306/791-9130, and at the airport ☎306/791-9131; Thrifty, 1975 Broad St and at the airport ☎306/525-1000.
Gay and lesbian life Gay-Lesbian Community, 1422 Scarth St ☎306/522-7343, information line 525-6046. Pride Week is in the middle of June.
Internet access Café Ultimate, 1852 Scarth St, also with delicious cakes and refreshments. Located in the pedestrianized section of Scarth.
Laundries Cathedral Laundromat, 2911 13th Ave ☎306/525-2665; Cheap Charlie's Laundry, 515 Broad St ☎306/545-1070.

Left luggage Coin-operated lockers at the bus station.
Lost property ☎306/777-7433.
Medical emergencies Regina General Hospital, 1440 14th Ave ☎306/766-4444. Cathedral Dental Clinic, 3032 13th Ave ☎306/352-9966.
Pharmacy Shopper's Drug Mart, 4602 Albert St. Open 24hr.
Police ☎306/569-3333.
Post office 2200 Saskatchewan Drive, opposite the Cornwall Centre.
Shopping Cowtown Western Wear, at Western Feed Mills, 745 Park St, for western clothing, boots, hats and accessories; Gourmet Pantry, upper level, Scotia Centre Galleria, 1783 Hamilton St, for Saskatchewan foods, such as Saskatoon berry products; Painted Buffalo, 2741 Dewdney Ave, for aboriginal arts and crafts; The Prairie Peddlar, 2206 Dewdney Ave, and Keepsakes Gallery, 2227 14th Ave, for local handicrafts; Fresh Air Experience, 532 Victoria Ave, for most outdoor supplies; Great Northern Rod & Reel, 1121 11th Ave, for fishing gear; Surplus Plus, 2415 11th Ave, for backpacking, canoeing and camping supplies.
Taxis Capital Cab ☎306/791-2219; Co-op Taxi ☎306/525-2727; Regina Cab ☎306/543-3333. Minimum $2.55, then 10¢ per 89m.
Weather line ☎306/780-5744.

The Qu'Appelle River Valley

The slow-moving **Qu'Appelle River** flows 350km from Lake Diefenbaker – 160km west of Regina – to the border with Manitoba, its lush, deep and wide valley filled with a series of lakes coming as a welcome break from the prairies. You can leave the Trans-Canada at its junction with Hwy 9 to explore the pleasantly quiet Round and Crooked lakes (both have several good campsites) or head on to the river's main township, the pleasant **Fort Qu'appelle**, which sits sandwiched between Hwy 10 and the grooved escarpments of the neighbouring lakes, an hour's drive northeast of Regina.

Roughly ten minutes' walk from end to end, **FORT QU'APPELLE** has leafy gridiron streets that fall on either side of Broadway St, the main drag, whose attractively restored red-brick **Hudson's Bay Company store**, on the corner of Company Ave, dates from 1897 – the oldest original Hudson's Bay store in Canada. Nearby, at the top end of Bay Ave, the **museum** (June–Aug daily 10am–noon & 1–5pm; other times by appointment; ☎306/332-4319; $2.50) has a small display on the area's European pioneers and the North West Mounted Police and is joined to the Hudson's Bay

Company trading post of 1864. Three blocks to the south, the stone **obelisk** at Fifth St and Company Ave commemorates the signing of Treaty Number 4 between the Ojibwa, Cree and Assiniboine of the southern prairies and Lieutenant-Governor Morris in 1874. It was a fractious process. The Ojibwa insisted that the Hudson's Bay Company had stolen "the earth, trees, grass, stones, all that we see with our eyes", hectoring Morris to the point where he finally snapped. He confined the more militant Indian leaders to their tents, an authoritarian manoeuvre that undermined the unity of the Indians, who then signed the treaty in return for various land grants, pensions and equipment. **Buses** make the seventy-kilometre journey from Regina to Fort Qu'Appelle two or three times daily. The **tourist information centre** is in the old CNR station at the junction of Boundary Ave and Hwy 10 (June–Aug daily 9am–7pm; ☎306/332-4426). One of the town's three **motels**, the *Country Squire Inn* (☎306/332-5603, ⓦwww.fortquappelle.com; ❷), is beside Hwy 10 at the bottom end of Bay St. There's also an attractive **B&B** in the town: *Company House*, 172 Company Ave (☎306/332-6333 or 332-7393; ❷), which serves up hearty home-cooked breakfasts and is near beaches and fishing, hiking and canoeing areas. On the north side of town, beside Echo Lake and near the golf course, is the *Fort* **campsite** (☎306/332-4614; $11–15; mid-May to mid-Sept). There are several **restaurants** on Broadway St, including the Chinese *Jade Palace* at no. 215, and *Bubba's* next door. For more imaginative food, head for the *Off Broadway Bistro*, 12 Boundary Ave, where you can dine on turkey lasagne or *tourtière*.

Near Fort Qu'Appelle, the river bulges into a chain of eight little lakes known collectively as the **Fishing Lakes**. It's possible to drive alongside all of them, but the pick of the bunch is the nearest, **Echo Lake**, which affords pleasant views over the river valley. Between this lake and Pasqua Lake is the scenic **Echo Valley Provincial Park** (year-round; visitor centre and Parks office mid-May to Aug ☎306/332-3215; $7 entry fee, camping $13–20), while **Katepwa Point Provincial Park**, an even tinier park (mid-May to Sept; free), sits at the southernmost point of the chain of lakes.

About 35km east of Fort Qu'Appelle, just off Hwy 22 south of the village of Abernethy, is the **Motherwell Homestead National Historic Site** (late May to Sept daily 9am–5pm; ☎306/333-2116; $4). This large, square house, with its odd assortment of multicoloured fieldstones embedded in the exterior walls, and lacy wrought-iron "widow's walk" on the roof, was built in 1898 for W.R. Motherwell, a local farmer and politician who moved to Saskatchewan from Ontario in 1882. He brought with him his knowledge of domestic architecture, for the six-bedroom building is similar to the gracious stone farmhouses of southern Ontario and looks a bit incongruous in its prairie surroundings. Just behind the house, which is restored to its 1912–14 appearance, there's a large red 1907 barn, with farm equipment and roaming farm animals to complete the rustic setting.

Southern Saskatchewan

From Regina the 400km drive west across **southern Saskatchewan** on the Trans-Canada Highway is monotonous, and the only town worth a stopover is **Moose Jaw**, once a Prohibition hangout of American gangsters. Otherwise the rest of southern Saskatchewan is mostly undulating farmland, broken up by a handful of lakes and rivers, stretches of arid semi-desert and the odd range of wooded hills. South of Moose Jaw near the US border are the **Big Muddy Badlands**, weathered buttes and conical hills that can easily be explored on the tours that leave the tiny town of Coronach throughout the summer. Directly west of here, the **Grasslands National Park** is still being developed and extended, two separate slices of prairie punctuated by coulees and buttes that add a rare touch of drama to the landscape.

Back along the Trans-Canada, beyond the small city of Swift Current and just north of the quintessential cowboy town of Maple Creek – the market town for several Hutterite colonies – are the **Great Sand Hills**, a starkly beautiful desert landscape. Finally, straddling the Alberta border, **Cypress Hills Interprovincial Park** is also well worth a visit, its heavily forested hills and ridges harbouring a restored Mountie outpost, **Fort Walsh**.

Apart from the daily bus services along the Trans-Canada, the region's **public transport** system is abysmal; to see the parks, you'll need a car.

Moose Jaw

MOOSE JAW, 70km west of Regina, was founded as a railway depot in 1882 and is now Saskatchewan's fourth largest city, with 35,000 inhabitants – a number that has remained almost static since the 1940s. Its name may have come from a local word for "warm breezes", or the jaw-like turn that the river takes just outside town, or even the repairs made to a cartwheel by an early pioneer with the assistance of a moose's jawbone.

Moose Jaw achieved some notoriety during Prohibition in the 1920s, when liquor was smuggled south by car or by train along the Soo Line, which ran from here to Chicago. For most locals this period of bootleggers, gangsters, gamblers and "boozoriums" (liquor warehouses) was not a happy one, and for years various schemes to attract tourists by developing the "Roaring Twenties"

The tunnels of Moose Jaw

A network of **tunnels** in Moose Jaw runs underneath River St from the basements of the old buildings. No one knows who built the tunnels, or why. What is known is that they were extended and used in the early 1900s by Chinese railway workers and their families hoping to escape the $500 "head tax", a measure designed to force them to return to famine-stricken China after the completion of their work on the railway. Later, during Prohibition, Chicago gangsters used the tunnels to negotiate their deals for Canada's liquor supplies and to hide out when things got too "hot" in Chicago.

The city runs two entertaining 45-minute **Tunnels of Moose Jaw tours** (hours vary every month: roughly summer Mon–Fri 10am–7pm, Sat & Sun 10am–9pm; Oct–May daily noon–5.30pm; tours every 20min; ☏306/693-5261, ⓦwww.tunnelsofmoosejaw .com; one tour $12, two tours $19). These are entitled the **Chicago Connection**, a light-hearted look at the capers of Al Capone's men in the tunnels, complete with a speakeasy, a police bust and an actor playing the particularly slimy Chief of Police; and the more serious **Passage to Fortune**, which tells the horrific story of the Chinese immigrants, with re-creations of a Chinese laundry, sweatshops, a herbalist and an opium den. Costumed guides ham it up through the network of narrow tunnels beneath Main St, helped by old movies and state-of-the-art animatronics: moving, talking mannequins.

Tours begin at **Tunnel Central**, 16 Main St North, in a reception area with a beautiful copper ceiling and walls adorned with local photos from the early decades of the twentieth century.

theme met with considerable opposition from the substantial portion of the population that actually experienced them. Those suffering from aches and pains, however, welcomed the 1995 opening of the wonderful **Temple Gardens Mineral Spa**, 24 Fairford St E (Sun–Thurs 9am–11pm, Fri & Sat 9am–midnight; $13) where you can soak in pools of mineral-rich hot waters piped from an underground spring 1km away. For a treat, take a dip in the outdoor pool when it's snowing or at sunset.

The **downtown** area is bisected by Main St, running from north to south, and Manitoba St, the east–west axis, which is adjacent to the railway line and the Moose Jaw river. The central area is dispiriting, though a string of **murals** of early pioneer days, concentrated along 1st Ave NW between Manitoba and Hochelaga streets, do their best to cheer things up. That apart, some of the streets look as if they haven't changed much since the 1920s, the wide treeless avenues framed by solemn brick warehouses and hotels and porticoed banks. One block north of Manitoba, the best example is **River St**, whose rough-and-ready *Royal* and *Brunswick* hotels were once favourite haunts of the gangsters; the street is earmarked for redevelopment as a cobbled, partly pedestrian street with an amphitheatre for shows.

Next door to "Tunnel Central" (see box p.575), Joyner's General Store, 30 Main St N, is worth a quick look for the complicated **cash carrier system** used by department stores, before the invention of the till, that carried shoppers' cash by cable to the accountants upstairs. It's one of only two in the world still operating and was kept in Moose Jaw despite Euro-Disney's attempts to purchase it.

A replica of one of Moose Jaw's original electric trams, the **Moose Jaw Trolley**, travels the local sights with a guide who dwells on the town's shady past (May–Sept 3 daily; Oct–Dec Thurs–Sat 2 daily; 1hr 15min; $8); it leaves from opposite Temple Gardens and from the *Heritage Inn* on Main St. You can also ride the trolley without a guide (May–Dec Thurs–Sat 11am–3pm; $2) to Moose Jaw's branch of the **Western Development Museum** (Jan–March Tues–Sun 9am–6pm; April–Dec daily 9am–5pm; ⓦwww.wdmuseum.sk.ca; $6), about 2km from the centre, beside the Trans-Canada as it loops around the northern edge of town. Divided into sections covering air, land, water and rail transport, the museum exhibits include a replica of a steamship, several Canadian Pacific railway coaches, a number of fragile old planes, and a 1934 Buick car converted to carry the chief superintendent up and down the rail line.

Practicalities

Moose Jaw's **bus station**, 63 High St E (☎306/692-2345), is a couple of minutes' walk from Main St and two blocks north of Manitoba St, served by four to six buses daily from Regina. There are no trains. The **Tourism Moose Jaw** bureau (July & Aug daily 9am–5pm; rest of year Mon–Fri 9am–5pm; ☎306/693-8097 or 1-866/693-8097, ⓦwww.citymoosejaw.com/tourism) is on the east side of town alongside the Trans-Canada. Out-of-province visitors get **free parking** at any of the town's meters.

The town has several reasonably priced, central **hotels** and **motels**, including the renovated, good-value *Capone's Hideaway*, 1 Main St N opposite the defunct train station (☎306/692-6422 or 1-877/443-3003; ❷), where the rooms have been given a 1920s feel; alternatively the *Midtown Hideaway Hotel* is also centrally located at 134 Athabasca St E (☎306/692-0601; ❷). Further out there's a *Comfort Inn*, 155 Thatcher Drive W (☎306/693-2100 or 1-800/228-5150; ❹), and nearby the *Super 8 Motel*,

1706 Main St N (☎306/692-8888 or 1-800/800-8000; ❸). Book well in advance for the four-star *Temple Gardens Mineral Spa*, 24 Fairford St East (☎306/694-5055 or 1-800/718-7727, ⓦwww.templeparkgardens.sk.ca; ❹–❼), which has luxurious rooms (each with its own Jacuzzi) and spa suites, geothermal pools and facilities for massage, facials, reflexology and hydrotherapy treatments; guests receive a free rubber duck, too. The *Redland Cottage* **B&B** in a tree-lined residential area at 1122 Redland Ave (☎306/694-5563 or 1-866/292-4640, ⓦwww.bbcanada.com/3418.html; ❷–❹) has comfortable bedrooms and full breakfasts. The *River Park Campground* (☎306/692-5474; $13–18; mid-April to mid-Oct) is 2km southeast of the centre at 300 River Drive.

There are a few worthwhile **places to eat**. The *Copper Café*, part of the Yvette Moore Gallery in the 1910 Land Titles building at 76 Fairford St W, has wonderful daily specials, and the adjacent gallery (Jan–April Mon–Sat 10am–5pm; May–Dec Mon–Sat 10am–5pm, Sun 1–4pm; free) features work by Yvette Moore and her prairie contemporaries. *Houston Pizza and Steak House*, 117 Main St North, has Italian dishes from $6; the *National Café*, 20 Main St, has a good-value daily smorgasbord; the *Prairie Oasis Restaurant*, junction of Hwy 1 E and Thatcher Drive, specializes in freshly baked pies; and the *Hopkins Dining Parlour*, 65 Athabasca St W, located in a pleasant Victorian house, is a more formal affair with a wide-ranging menu and main courses from $18. For something more exotic, try the very good *Nit's Thai Food*, 124 Main St N, which has main courses from $6.

Moose Jaw is home to the precision-flying team The Snowbirds, who zoom across the huge prairie skies at the **Saskatchewan Airshow** in July ($10).

The Big Muddy Badlands

At the end of the last Ice Age, torrents of meltwater produced a massive gash in the landscape to the south of the site of Moose Jaw, near the US border. Edged by rounded hills and flat-topped buttes that rise up to 200m above the valley floor, the **Big Muddy Valley** can best be explored with organized tours from dreary **CORONACH**, about 200km from Regina (July & Aug Sat & Sun; at other times June–Sept, tours by appointment; $25 by minibus, $10 in your own car with a guide; ☎306/267-3312 or 267-2150). The tours include visits to Indian burial cairns, the dramatic **Castle Butte**, a sandstone formation rising above the plains that resembles the backdrop for a Western movie (without a guide you'll find it by turning west off Hwy 34 in the Big Muddy Valley along the only road), the small prairie town of **BIG BEAVER** where Aust's general store ("If we don't have it you don't need it") is the social centre, and a couple of outlaw caves, the refuge of American rustlers and robbers like Butch Cassidy and Dutch Henry. Cassidy and his Wild Bunch gang established an outlaw trail that connected the Big Muddy with Mexico via a series of safe houses; their antics were curtailed by the arrival of a detachment of Mounties in 1904 led by a certain Corporal Bird, known ruefully as the "man who never sleeps". The **tourist information** centre on the highway (mid-June to Aug 9am–7pm; ☎306/267-3312) can provide information on the history and geography of the area. **Accommodation** in Coronach includes the *Country Boy Motel* at the junction of hwys 18 and 36, opposite the Pioneer Grain elevator (☎306/267-3267; ❶–❸), with complimentary coffee and fridges in each of its 21 rooms, and the very basic but clean and friendly four-room *Coronach Hotel* on Main St (☎306/267-2063; ❶). The trailer-based *Schwab B&B* is outside Big Beaver, north along Hwy 34

(☎306/267-4554; ❶). The only place worth **eating** at is the coffee shop in the small Coronach Mall, 111 Centre St.

Swift Current

Driving west from Moose Jaw along the Trans-Canada Highway, it's about 180km to **SWIFT CURRENT**, a small industrial city and farm-research centre that's a convenient stopoff on the long journey between Regina and Calgary. It has limited attractions, but if you decide to stay here drop in to the helpful **tourist office**, at the junction of hwys 1 and 4 (May–Sept daily 9am–7pm; Oct–April Mon–Fri 9am–noon & 1–5pm; ☎306/773-7268). The **bus** station is at 143 4th Ave NW, serviced by three buses daily from Regina and one from Saskatoon.

In Kinetic Park, at 17th Ave and South Railway St East, is a **Mennonite Heritage Village** (June–Sept Fri–Sun 2–8pm; other times by appointment ☎306/773-7685 or 773-6068; free), consisting of a long, rectangular house and adjoining barn built in 1911–15, and six buildings comprising **Doc's Town** (July & Aug Fri–Sun 2–6pm; other times by appointment ☎306/773-2944; $2), a replica of an early twentieth-century prairie village – highlights are a fully functioning windmill, a one-room prairie school-house and an old dancehall (now a tearoom), transported here from a rural Saskatchewan town. The only other worthwhile stopoff is the **Art Gallery of Swift Current**, 411 Herbert St E (Mon–Thurs 2–5pm & 7–9pm, Fri–Sun 1–5pm; July & Aug closed Sun; free), where you'll see exhibitions of paintings, sculpture and ceramics by artists from Saskatchewan and elsewhere in Canada.

Reached by Hwy 4, around 40km north of Swift Current is the pretty little **Saskatchewan Landing Provincial Park**, situated on both banks of the South Saskatchewan River, where it emerges from razorback hills and opens out into the large, finger-like artificial **Lake Diefenbaker**. The park area was once an important river crossing for Native Canadians and early white settlers, and the staff at the park's **Goodwin House** Visitors' Centre (June–Sept Mon–Fri 8am–4pm, Sat & Sun 10am–6pm; Oct–May Mon–Fri 8am–4pm), a beautiful century-old stone house built by a retired member of the North West Mounted Police, can organize nature-trail hikes through coulees and explain the significance of the crossing – once one of the most difficult river crossings in western Canada. There are remains of several ancient tepee encampments in the area. You can **camp** in the north of the park at the *Bear Paw Campground* (☎306/375-5525 or 375-5527; $15–20; mid-May to Oct) and rent kayaks at the small marina ($6/hr).

Strung out along the Trans-Canada as it skirts the north of the city, and along Hwy 4 south towards the US border, are several comfortable **motels**, the best of which are the de luxe *Best Western Inn*, 105 George St (☎306/773-4660 or 1-800/773-8818, ⓦ www.bestwestern.sk.ca; ❸–❻), just off the Trans-Canada; the enormous *Imperial 400*, 1150 Begg St E (☎306/773-2033 or 1-800/781-2268; ❷–❸), also near the Trans-Canada, which has waterslides; and the *Super 8 Motel*, 405 North Service Rd E (☎306/778-6088 or 1-800/800-8000; ❸–❹), which has a pool and whose rates include a small breakfast. Just north of the Trans-Canada is a small but convenient **campsite**, *Trail Campground* (☎306/773-8088; $12–15; May to mid-Oct). For **restaurants**, try *Carol's Diner*, 914 Central Ave N, specializing in Belgian waffles, or *Humpty's*, at the junction of hwys 1 and 4 East, which does a low-priced all-day breakfast. *Gramma Bep's* on the east side of town on Hwy 1 does berry pies and coffee, while a shop inside also sells jams, soups and sauces made to traditional Saskatchewan recipes.

Grasslands National Park

Directly west of the Big Muddy, accessible along Hwy 18, the **Grasslands National Park** is predominantly mixed-grass prairie, a flat, bare badlands landscape broken up by splendid coulees, buttes and river valleys – notably the wide ravine edging the Frenchman River in the western block. Far from the moderating influence of the oceans, the area has a savage climate, with an average low in January of -22°C and temperatures that soar to 40°C in summer. Even so, this terrain is inhabited by many species that are adapted to cope with the shortage of water, from flora such as prairie grasses, greasewood, rabbit brush, sagebrush and different types of cacti, to fauna like the graceful pronghorn antelope, the rattlesnake and Canada's only colonies of black-tailed prairie dog.

At present, Grasslands National Park consists of east and west sections separated by private ranches and farms, which the federal government eventually intends to buy, creating a single park stretching from Hwy 4 in the west to Hwys 2 and 18 in the east. The **west** section is both more scenic and accessible, its limited system of gravel tracks and roads cutting in from hwys 18 and 4, south and east of **VAL MARIE**. This tiny township houses the **Grasslands National Park Reception Centre**, at the junction of Hwy 4 and Centre St (late May to Aug daily 8am–5pm; rest of year Mon–Fri 8am–noon & 1–4.30pm; ☎306/298-2257, Ⓦ www.parkscanada.gc.ca/grasslands), whose rangers provide advice on weather and road conditions, hand out maps, arrange for guided or self-guided eco-tours, issue camping permits and give tips on animal-spotting and hiking. The few places to **stay** in town include the *Val Marie Hotel*, 221 Centre St (☎306/298-2007 or 298-2003; ❶), with seven basic rooms, and the far more attractive *Convent B&B*, 4515 Hwy 4 (☎306/289-4515; ❷), a converted convent with lots of character that is also the best place to eat in town. Opposite is a well-worn **campsite** (☎306/298-2022; $7–10; May–Oct). There are no campsites within the park, but camping is allowed within 1km of its roads; take a good supply of water, a stout pair of walking shoes and a stick to sweep in front of you in tall grass or brush as a warning to **rattlesnakes**. Animal activity is at its height at dawn and dusk and during spring and autumn; whatever the season, you'll need a pair of binoculars.

One of the best **hikes** is the one to the 70 Mile Butte, a massive flat-topped promontory that is the highest point of land in the region, rising 100m above the valley floor with wonderful views of the waving prairie grasslands all around. To get there, drive south of Val Marie on Hwy 4 and turn east at Butte Rd and continue to the end of the road. While there is no marked trail, the way becomes obvious as you begin walking over the hills from the end of the road. Even just a couple of hours' walk will take you through exceptional country.

Eastend

In 1994, one of only thirteen Tyrannosaurus Rex skeletons in the world was discovered 40km south of the 695-strong town of **EASTEND**, 150km west of the park. The T-Rex was named Scotty, after the bottle of scotch its discoverers consumed in celebration, and there is now a swish **T-Rex Interpretive Centre** (May–Sept daily 9am–6pm; for Oct–April hours, call ☎306/295-4009, Ⓦ www.dinocountry.com; $3) on the gravel Grid Road no. 614, about 1km north of town – worth hitting if you're travelling with children. After seeing a

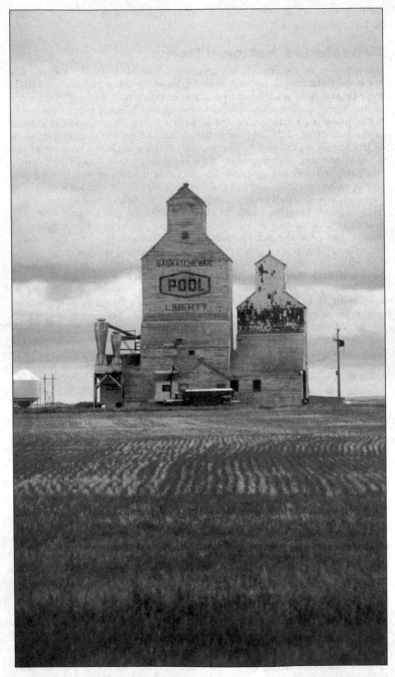

△ Grain elevator on prairies

film on the difficulties involved in excavating Scotty, there's a small hands-on museum in which to view replica bones of various dinosaurs. If you're keen on the prehistory of the area, you may want to join one of the **Dinocountry tours** (July & Aug daily 9am & 1pm; 3hr; $25), which depart from the centre to visit a fossil quarry where you can watch paleontologists unearthing fossils. For a more hands-on experience there's an archeological site for dinosaur bones near Eastend, where you can dig yourself (July & Aug daily 8.30am; $50). In the town itself is a **museum and cultural centre** with a small information centre, located in the old theatre on Red Coat Drive (July & Aug daily 10am–8pm; mid-May to June by appointment ☎306/295-3375; $2), featuring paleontological exhibits and a pioneer log house from a century ago.

If you want to base yourself in Eastend for a more thorough exploration of the Grasslands park and the Frenchman River Valley, you could **stay** at the *Riverside Motel*, just west of town on Hwy 13 (☎306/295-3630 or 295-3773; ❷–❸), which also has **camping** on its grounds for $15, or at the basic but comfortable *Cypress Hotel*, 343 Red Coat Drive (☎306/295-3505; ❶), in the middle of town. For **food**, *Alleykatz*, 115 Fir Ave, offers up coffees and bagels and has a gift shop that sells pottery made from the local white clay. For more substantial meals head to *Jack's Café* on Red Coat Drive.

Maple Creek and the Great Sand Hills

From Swift Current it's another 130km along the Trans-Canada to **MAPLE CREEK**, situated 8km south of the highway. Nicknamed "old cow town", Maple Creek lies at the heart of ranching country, and its streets are full of pickup trucks, cowboy boots and stetsons, reaching wild heights in early September for the **Cowboy Poetry Gathering**, a literary celebration of the wrangler that draws cowboys from across North America. Some of the late nineteenth-century brick storefronts have survived, and the trim and tidy **Old Timers' Museum**, 218 Jasper St (May–Sept Tues–Sat 9am–5.30pm, Sun & Mon 1–5pm; $3), has good displays on pioneer life and the Mounties. The place is also the market town for a number of **Hutterite colonies**, whose women stand out with their floral dresses and headscarves (see box).

The Hutterites

The **Hutterites**, the only prairie community to have maintained a utopian communal ideal, are members of an Anabaptist sect that takes its name from their first leader, Jacob Hutter. Originating in central Europe (in the Tyrol and Moravia) in the sixteenth century, they gradually moved east, ending up in Russia, which they abandoned for South Dakota in the 1870s. It was fifty years before they felt obliged to move again, their pacifism recoiling from the bellicosity that gripped their American neighbours during World War I. They moved north between 1918 and 1922, and established a series of **colonies** where they were allowed to educate their own children, speak their own language and avoid military service. In these largely self-sufficient communities tasks are still divided according to ability and skill, property is owned communally, and social life is organized around a common dining room and dormitories. Economically prosperous, they continue to multiply, a new branch community being founded whenever the old one reaches a secure population of between one hundred and two hundred. Apart from the occasional skirmish with the outside world when they buy new land, the Hutterites have been left in peace and have resisted the pressures of assimilation more staunchly than their kindred spirits, the Mennonites and the Doukhobors (see box p.943).

Perhaps the best reason for stopping at Maple Creek is its proximity to the Cypress Hills (see below) and the **Great Sand Hills**. The latter incorporate a large area of giant sand dunes, home to hordes of kangaroo rats as well as mule deer and antelope. The best place to view the dunes is east off Hwy 21. From the village of **LIEBENTHAL** follow the road east in the direction of Fitters Ranch for 17.6km before turning off north for the final 2km to the dunes parking lot. You can also get here from **SCEPTRE**, 18.4km to the north of the dunes where the small **Great Sandhills Museum** on Hwy 32 (June–Sept Mon–Sat 9am–noon & 1–4pm, Sun 1–5pm; $3) has displays on the ecology of the hills and can provide printed directions.

The Cypress Hills

South of the Trans-Canada Highway, between Maple Creek and Irvine, AB, the wooded ridges of the **Cypress Hills** rise above the plains in a 130-kilometre-long plateau that in places reaches a height of 1400m – the highest point in Canada between Labrador and the Rockies. Because of its elevation, this area was untouched by glaciers as they moved south during the Ice Age, scouring the land bare of vegetation, and the Cypress Hills are an anomaly in the landscape of the prairies, having a wetter and milder climate than the treeless plains that surround them, creating a rich variety of woodland, wetland and grassland. In turn, this comparatively lush vegetation supports a wealth of wildlife, from the relatively rare elk, lynx, bobcat and coyote through to the more common gopher and raccoon, plus about two hundred species of bird, over half of whom breed in the hills. (Watch out for the colonies of long-necked wild turkeys, as well as the sage grouse, whose bizarre courting rituals involve the male swelling out his chest and discharging air with a sound akin to a gunshot.) One surprise – considering the name – is the absence of cypress trees: the early French *voyageurs* seem to have confused the area's predominant lodgepole pines with the jack pines of Québec, a species they called *cyprès*. Literal-minded translation did the rest.

There are a variety of guided **tours** of both the Centre and West blocks of the Cypress Hills Interprovincial Park that will help you to better appreciate the rugged beauty of the area and the high-altitude flora and fauna – much of which is found nowhere else in western Canada except the Rocky Mountains. A tour of the **Centre Block** (2hr $65) includes trips to Lookout Point and Bald Butte on the edge of the park, where there are panoramic views north down into the valleys and plains. The more rugged **West Block** can be experienced on longer tours (4hr $140; 6hr $180) that take you over the bone-rattling Gap Road to points of interest such as Fort Walsh and the Conglomerate Cliffs. All tours are led by trained local guides; to book, call ☎306/662-5411 (Mon–Fri 8am–5pm).

Cypress Hills Interprovincial Park

In amongst the cattle ranches two separate sections of the Hills have been set aside to form the **Cypress Hills Interprovincial Park**: Saskatchewan's Centre Block lies to the south of Maple Creek along Hwy 21, and the larger West Block spans the Saskatchewan–Alberta border, accessible from Maple Creek along Hwy 271 in the east and via Alberta's Hwy 41 in the west. The Saskatchewan part of the West Block is also attached to Fort Walsh National Historic Park, incorporating a partly refurbished Mountie station and a replica of one of the Battle Creek trading posts. The three north–south access

The Cypress Hills massacre

From the mid-eighteenth century, the Cypress Hills lay in a sort of neutral zone between the **Blackfoot** and the **Cree**, whose intermittent skirmishing was small-scale until the 1860s, when the depletion of the Crees' traditional hunting grounds forced them to move west. Some three thousand Cree reached the Cypress Hills in 1865 and the violence began just four years later with the murder of the Cree peace-maker, Maskepetoon. The ensuing war was overshadowed by the Red River rising of 1869–70 in Manitoba, but casualties were high and its effects were compounded by two smallpox epidemics. In 1871 the Cree sued for peace, but both sides were exhausted, their morale, health and social structures further undermined by the whiskey traders who had moved into the region.

These **whiskey traders**, who were mostly American, brought their liquor north in the autumn, returning south in late spring laden with furs and buffalo robes. Though it was illegal to supply the Indians with booze, the traders spread out across the southern plains, aptly nicknamed **Whoop-up Country**, establishing dozens of trading posts whose occupants were protected from their disorderly customers by log stockades. (They needed to be, as the stuff they sold was adul-terated with such substances as red ink, gunpowder and strychnine.) In the spring of 1873, there were two such outposts beside **Battle Creek**, deep in the Cypress Hills, owned by a certain Abel Farwell and his rival Moses Solomon. For reasons that remain obscure, though the prevailing drunkenness played a part, this was the scene of a violent confrontation between a group of white wolf-hunters, whiskey traders and a band of Assiniboine. Equipped with the latest fast-action rifles, the hunters riddled an Assiniboine camp with bullets, killing up to seventy (according to some sources) before returning to the trading posts to celebrate. News of the incident, known as the **Cypress Hills Massacre**, filtered back to Ottawa, and this speeded up the recruitment of the newly formed **North West Mounted Police**, who in the autumn received their first posting west as a detach-ment to Fort MacLeod, near today's Lethbridge, Alberta. They reached it in early 1874, where they set about suppressing the whiskey trade and establishing law and order.

To consolidate their control of the area, the Mounties built **Fort Walsh**, near Battle Creek, the following year. An unpopular posting, the fort was considered "unhealthy, isolated and indefensible", but it could not be abandoned until 1883, when the last of the restless Indian bands were moved to reservations further north. It was during this period that the fort's first inspector, **James Morrow Walsh**, was faced with an extremely delicate situation. In 1876, **Chief Sitting Bull's** Sioux had exterminated General Custer's army at the battle of the Little Bighorn. Fearing reprisals, five thousand Sioux moved north, establishing their camp at Wood Mountain, 350km east of Fort Walsh. Aware of the danger, Walsh rode into the Sioux encampment with just four other constables to insist that they obey Canadian law. This act of bravery established a rough rapport between the two leaders, and by his tactful dealings with the Sioux Walsh enhanced the reputation of the Mounties, whose efficiency ensured there were no more massacres in the Canadian west.

highways present no problems, but it's difficult to drive across the park from east to west as the paved road, known as the Gap Road, is interrupted by two long stretches of gravel and clay track suitable only for high clearance four-wheel drive vehicles in dry weather.

Just 30km south of Maple Creek, on Hwy 21, a paved side road heads into the park's **Centre Block** (entry fee $5), a rough rectangle of hilly land domi-nated by a forest of lodgepole pines. At the centre, a pleasant tourist resort surrounds tiny **Loch Leven**, complete with canoe- and bike-rental facilities, shops and a petrol station. There's also a modest nature centre adjoining the park's **administration office** (Mon–Thurs 8am–8pm, Fri–Sun 8am–10pm; ☎306/662-5411 or 1-800/205-7070, ⓦwww.cypresshills.com), which has useful maps and trail brochures. The resort is a popular holiday destination, but it's easy to escape the crowds along the half-dozen hiking trails. There's one **hotel**, the modern *Cypress Park Resort Inn* (☎306/662-4477), with rooms and cabins (both ❷–❸) and apartments (❸–❻). Close by, there are several busy summer **campsites** (all $13–22), which have to be booked at the campsite office on Pine Ave, west of the centre (mid-May to Aug daily 8.30am–10pm; ☎306/662-4459).

The eastern side of the park's **West Block** has alternating areas of thick forest and open grassland broken up by steep hills and deep, sheltered ravines. Hwy 271 enters this section from the east and becomes increasingly bumpy as it twists south towards the **Fort Walsh National Historic Park** and Visitors Information Centre (mid-May to Aug daily 9.30am–5.30pm; ☎306/662-3590, off-season 662-2645; $7), which has excellent displays on the Plains Indians, the history of the fort and the development of the RCMP. A five-minute walk behind the information centre, Fort Walsh sits in a wide, low-lying valley, its trim stockade framed by pine forests. Built in 1875, the fort was abandoned in favour of Maple Creek just eight years later; in 1942 the RCMP acquired the land, and most of the present buildings date from that decade. Guides in period costumes enliven a tour of whitewashed log buildings, the whole site having returned to its original appearance. Close to the fort is a cemetery containing the tombstones of several North West Mounted Police officers. Every 45 minutes a minibus makes the trip from the information centre over the hills to Battle Creek, where Abel Farwell's whiskey trading post has been reconstructed to commemorate the 1873 Cypress Hills Massacre (see box p.583). Guides will also take you to the actual site of the Massacre. The main **accommodation** in this part of the park is the *West Block Campground* (☎306/662-5489 or 1-800/205-7070; $13; May–Sept), 5km north of Fort Walsh, in a dense stand of lodgepole pines and with a brook running through it. It's in an isolated spot, so take your own food and drink. From the campsite you can make an expedition to the **Conglomerate Cliffs**, a few kilometres to the northeast near Adams Lake. These are strange-looking walls of rock, some 150m high, composed of multicoloured cobblestones.

The lodgepole forests and deep coulees of the Alberta section of the park's West Block are centred on the tourist resort of **ELKWATER**, 34km south of the Trans-Canada on Hwy 41. Curving round the southern shore of Elkwater Lake, the village has a comprehensive range of facilities, from boat and bike rental through to a sandy beach and sauna baths. There's also a **park office** (Mon–Fri 8.15am–noon & 1–4.30pm; ☎403/893-3777) and a **visitors' centre** (mid-May to early Sept Mon–Fri 10am–6pm; ☎403/893-3833), which has maps and hiking brochures and runs guided walks throughout the summer. For **accommodation**, there's the *Green Tree Motel* (☎403/893-3811; ❷–❸), which also has self-contained cabins, while the *Elkwater Campground* is relatively luxurious, with both simple and hooked-up sites. Southwest of Elkwater a paved road leads to Horseshoe Canyon and **Head of the Mountain**, where there are striking views over the hills towards Montana; other roads lead east to Reesor Lake and Spruce Coulee Reservoir. Beside the roads there are twelve other campsites, bookable through the visitors centre.

Yellowhead Route (Hwy 16)

Highway 16, one of central Canada's most appealing long-distance drives, is better known as **the Yellowhead Route** – taking its name from a light-haired Iroquois explorer and guide who was called *Tête Jaune* ("yellow head") by the *voyageurs*, the French-speaking boatmen who plied the waterways transporting people, furs and supplies. It's a good alternative to the Trans-Canada Highway, with more interesting sights along the way – including several towns, like **Dauphin**, where some of the culture of original groups has been preserved – and also more varied scenery. This not only includes vast tracts of prairie, but also some of the aspen parklands and boreal forest to the north. And if you have the time you can easily make a foray into the enticingly wild **Prince Albert National Park**. The Yellowhead route also runs through **Saskatoon**, 781km from Winnipeg, which makes a good point at which to break a journey and has several important historic sites in the vicinity that help bring alive the region's history.

Winnipeg to Saskatoon

The Yellowhead Route follows the Trans-Canada highway west out of Winnipeg as far as Portage la Prairie (see p.560), from where it cuts northwest from the Trans-Canada to form a more attractive route across the prairies, passing through the pretty little villages of **Neepawa** and **Minnedosa** before running south of **Riding Mountain** National Park which protects attractive areas of deciduous and boreal forest, lake and grassland. Just north of the park is the strongly Ukrainian town of **Dauphin** which can form a base for exploring **Duck Mountain** Provincial Park, noted for its fishing canoe routes. This park continues over the border in Saskatchewan and is close to the intriguing Doukhobor settlement of **Veregin** and the dreary prairie hub of **Yorkton**. From here the Yellowhead embarks on one of its dullest stretches across the prairies and if you've a few days to spare you should try to veer off the highway to head due north to the lakes and wooded hills of the **Prince Albert** National Park, with innumerable canoe and hiking routes into the wilderness.

Neepawa and around

About 90km along the road from Portage la Prairie lies one of Manitoba's more pleasant townships, tiny **NEEPAWA**, whose streets are lined with elms and cottonwoods. The oldest buildings are spread along and around the principal drag, Mountain Ave – notably the cosy neo-Romanesque Knox Presbyterian Church at Mill St and 1st Ave, with an unusual thick, turreted bell tower, and the tidy, late-Victorian County Court House, close to Mountain Ave and Hamilton St. Also in the centre, in the old CNR station at the west end of Hamilton St, the **Beautiful Plains Museum** (mid-May to Aug Mon–Fri 9am–5pm; July & Aug also Sat & Sun 1–5pm; other times by appointment; $1; ☏204/476-3896 or 476-5292 off-season) has diverting displays on the life of the district's pioneers. Margaret Laurence (1926–87), one of Canada's best-known writers, lived in Neepawa in her early years and used the town (renamed Manawaka) as a setting for many of her novels, which portray strong women struggling against small town life, beginning with the highly acclaimed *The Stone Angel* (1964) and ending with *The Diviners* (1974).You can visit her home, now the **Margaret Laurence Museum**, at 312 1st Ave N (mid-May to Aug Mon–Fri 10am–6pm, Sat & Sun noon–6pm; July & Aug daily 10am–6pm; other times by appointment; T204/476-3612; $2). Laurence is buried in the Riverside Cemetery, in the north of town.

The Yellowhead Hwy doubles as Neepawa's Main St, marking the southern perimeter of the town centre.The **tourist office** (June–Aug daily 11am–7pm, Tues & Wed closes 5pm; T204/476-5292) is on the Yellowhead just east of town, beside the Whitemud River. The **bus station** is attached to the Petro Canada fuel station at 52 Main St. For accommodation, there's a central riverside **campsite** on Hamilton St, the *Lions Riverbend Park* (T204/476-7607; $9–12; May–Sept) with fishing, a playground and a pool. The down-at-heel *Hamilton* **hotel** is convenient at Mountain Ave and Mill St (T204/476-2368; ❶), with bars beneath, but you'd do better at the three **motels**, all west of town on Hwy 16, particularly the spotlessly clean *Westway Inn* (T204/476-2355; ❷ including breakfast). Or try the *Garden Path B&B*, 536 2nd Ave at Main St (T204/476-3184; ❸), in a beautiful 1903 former lumber merchant's home. The **restaurants** downtown are unappealing but the best of the bunch on Hwy 16 (Main St) is the busy *Mr Ribs*, which offers dinners from $6. Better to head out to the *Prairie Orchard Tea House* (T204/368-2486), 13.6km east on Hwy 16, which serves locally grown organic food.

More varieties of lilies grow in the area around Neepawa than any other part of the world. To see the flowers in bloom, visit the **Lily Nook** (July to mid-Aug daily 9am–6pm; donation), 4km south of town on Hwy 5.There's also a **Lily Festival** in Neepawa in the third week of July.

Minnedosa

The approach to **MINNEDOSA**, 28km west of Neepawa, is stunning, as the attractive town sits on the flat of a long valley that slowly rises up at each end. The relaxing small-town atmosphere of the place is most appealing and, as it's about halfway between Winnipeg and the Saskatchewan border, it can make for a convenient stopoff. It's also only thirty minutes from Riding Mountain National Park (see p.587). There's not much to see here except for a **bison compound** near the Little Saskatchewan River (March–Oct; free), reached by crossing the swinging bridge over the river or turn off Main St onto 2nd Ave SE, and then drive five minutes along Beach Rd; you can view the bison from a platform in a public car park. You can also reach the compound and Minnedosa's pleasant **public beach** by following the two-kilometre **Heritage Village Walk** from a 1920s CPR caboose and diesel engine, located beside the boulder-strewn river at the bridge on Main St.The walk takes you on a pretty amble along the riverbank, past a salmon ladder to a small collection of heritage buildings, none of which are particularly inspiring.

Minnedosa's **tourist information** centre (daily 11am–7pm; T204/867-2741, W www.minnedosa.com/chamber) is west of town at a rest stop where Hwy 10 meets Hwy 16. In town there's a handful of acceptable **motels**, including the *Minnedosa Inn*, 138 Main St (T204/867-2777; ❷). One of the more attractive **B&Bs** in western Manitoba, *The Castle*, is at 149 2nd Ave SW (T204/867-2830; ❸), a Queen Anne-style house on the banks of the Little Saskatchewan River. Delicious German and French food is available at *Brede's*, 121 Main St S (Wed–Sun dinner); otherwise the choice is limited to nondescript places along Main St.

Riding Mountain National Park

One of the region's best parks is **Riding Mountain National Park** ($5 per person per day; multi-day and $25 annual passes also available), 250km northwest of Winnipeg and bisected by Hwy 10 on its way from Hwy 16 to Dauphin. The park derives its name from the fur trappers who changed from canoe to horseback to travel across its wooded highlands and it's still a vast expanse of wilderness, roughly 50km long and 100km wide, providing some of Manitoba's finest hiking and biking trails and most beautiful scenery. Its **eastern perimeter** is formed by a 400-metre-high ridge studded with a dense evergreen forest of spruce, pine, balsam fir and tamarack. This soon gives way to a **highland plateau** whose mixed forests and lakes form the central, and most scenic, part of the park, bordered to the west by an area of aspen woodland, meadow and open grassland – the habitat of moose, elk and a carefully tended herd of buffalo, best viewed in the morning or evening, near Lake Audy (45min drive northwest of Wasagaming on a gravel road; no public transport; open year-round; free).

Wasagaming

For Riding Mountain National Park, the tourist village of **WASAGAMING** is the only settlement of any significance and so a useful base. Located beside the main highway on the southern edge of the park, beside Clear Lake, it has a campsite, motels and restaurants, grocery stores, petrol stations, a 1930s log theatre, and boat and canoe rental. But its narrow, scrawny **beach** is desperately overcrowded in July and August, while the lake, though spring-fed, is infested with a parasitic flatworm that can cause the painful skin irritation "Swimmer's Itch".

Beside the beach, the park **visitor information centre** (late May to early Sept daily 9am–8pm; ☎204/848-7275 or 1-800/707-8480; ⓦwww.parkscanada.gc.ca/ridingmountain) has a collection of stuffed animals and environmental displays, and publishes *The Bugle*, a free broadsheet guide to the park's amenities. The staff organize a programme of summer events, featuring free day-long **walks** and **hikes**. The centre also issues fishing permits ($7) and backcountry permits ($8), which are compulsory for overnight stays in the bush. From mid-October to mid-May, when the centre is closed, the **administration office** opposite (Mon–Fri 8am–4pm; ☎204/848-7208) provides a similar service.

Most of the trails that begin in or near Wasagaming are short and easy, the longest being the newly completed Clear Lake Trail around Clear Lake's shore (24km). The best of the park's trails is the eight-kilometre **Grey Owl Trail** to Beaver Lodge Lake from Hwy 19, where Grey Owl (see p.195) lived for six months in 1931. This trail connects with the nearest of the overnight routes, the **Cowan Lake Trail**, which branches off to pass through a region of dense forest, small lakes and meadows. All the overnight trails have primitive campsites. To get deep into the rugged beauty of the park, contact Riding Mountain Nature Tours (☎204/636-2968, ⓦwww.churchillnaturetours.com), which offers a variety of longer **tours**, including horseback riding, hiking, birdwatching and wildlife safaris. To learn more about the history of the park – including Grey Owl's stay here – visit the **Pinewood Museum** at 154 Wasagaming Drive (July & Aug daily 2–4pm; free).

Served by daily buses from Winnipeg, Brandon and Dauphin, Wasagaming's main **bus stop** is on the corner of Wasagaming Drive and Mooswa Drive. For **accommodation**, the *Mooswa Resort*, Mooswa Drive (☎204/848-2533; ❷), has modern chalets, motel rooms and bungalows, but the basic bungalows and log cabins at *Johnson Cabins*, 109 Ta-Wa-Pit Drive (☏204/848-2524 or 1-888/848-2524, ⓦwww.johnsoncabins.com; ❷), are a bit cheaper. *Clear Lake Lodge*, at Ta-Wa-Pit Drive and Columbine St (☏204/848-2345, ⓦwww .clearlakelodge.com; ❸), is a comfortable, nonsmoking hotel, but to save money head for the *Manigaming Resort*, 137 Ta-Wa-Pit Drive (☏204/848-2459, ⓦwww.manigaming.com; ❷), or the *Southgate Motor Hotel* in Onanole, 5km south of the park (☏204/848-2158; ❷). Most accommodation in the park is open from May to September or October only; one of the few year-round possibilities is the *New Chalet*, 116 Wasagaming Drive (☏204/848-2892; ❸), with its kitchenette units. There's only one **campsite**, *Wasagaming Campground*, (☏204/848-7275 or 1-800/707-8480; $12–20; May to mid-Oct; reservations advised) in the village just beyond the main park gate.

Wasagaming's **restaurants** are poor, with the notable exception of *TR McKoys* in the same log building as the Park Theatre on Wasagaming Drive – it has lunch and dinner menus with pasta dishes from $10 and delicious sandwiches from $7. You can also try the *Mooswa*, where a delicious fresh fish meal will set you back about $20. The best of the cheaper establishments is the *Whitehouse*, also on Wasagaming Drive with burgers, sandwiches and other fast food. The Tempo fuel station opposite rents out **bikes** (☏1-800/816-2524; $12/hr, $50/day), while **canoe** and **powerboat** rentals ($17/hr) are available from the jetty on Clear Lake. **Horseback riding** is available at the riding stables at Triangle Ranch ($17/hr; ☏204/848-4583).

Dauphin and around

Despite the diverse backgrounds of the European immigrants who cleared and settled Manitoba in the late nineteenth century, there is little evidence of this in most of the province's virtually indistinguishable settlements – except for clues left in place names. Most cultures were rapidly and almost entirely assimilated, but at least the onion domes of the Ukrainians' Orthodox churches in and around **DAUPHIN** are still a reminder of their ancestry. Dauphin was founded as a fur-trading post by the French in 1739 and is now a pleasant town that straggles across the flat prairie landscape just to the east of the Vermilion River. Its long Main St features some good examples of early twentieth-century Canadian architecture, but there's only one real attraction, the **Fort Dauphin Museum** (May, June & Sept Mon–Fri 9am–5pm; July & Aug daily 9am–5pm; Oct–April by appointment ☏204/638-6630; $3). This tidy wooden replica of a North West Company trading outpost, located by the river at the end of 4th Ave SW, fifteen-minutes' walk from Main St, holds the stockade where there are reconstructions of several sorts of pioneer building, including a trapper's cabin. If you have time to kill, nose around the huge CNR **railway station** on 1st Ave NW and the modest **arts centre** and gallery at 104 1st Ave NW (Mon–Fri noon–5pm; free), in a striking Romanesque Revival building. At the corner of 1st St SW and 11th Ave SW is the Ukrainian **Church of the Resurrection**, with its distinctive clustered domes (call for hours ☏204/638-5511 or 638-4196).

The fertile river valley that runs west of Dauphin towards Roblin was a centre of Ukrainian settlement between 1896 and 1925, and its village skylines are still dominated by onion-domed church spires. There's a modest collection of Ukrainian pioneer artefacts and traditional handicrafts in Dauphin at the **Selo Ukraina Office**, 119 Main St S (call for hours ☏204/638-9401; free), but their main task is to organize the **National Ukrainian Festival**, which takes place on the first weekend of August at a purpose-built complex 12km south of Dauphin, just off Hwy 10 on the edge of Riding Mountain Park. The complex has a tiny heritage village dedicated to the early Ukrainian settlers (call for hours ☎204/638-9401; free) and a splendid amphitheatre built into a hillside, ideal for the festival's music and dance performances.

If you want to absorb still more Ukrainian ambience, visit the **Wasyl Negrych Pioneer Farmstead**, near the village of Gilbert Plains, 30km west of Dauphin. Here you'll find Canada's best-preserved and most complete Ukrainian homestead (June–Aug daily 1–5pm; rest of year by appointment; ☎204/548-2477 or 548-2689; $2). Wasyl and Anna Negrych arrived here in 1897 with their seven children from the Carpathian Mountains. Over the next few years they built the farmstead, which now has ten buildings: an 1899 home that replaced their first log house after it burnt down, three granaries, barns, a chicken coop, pigsty, garages and a bunkhouse with a fully preserved, working peech (the log and clay cookstove that was once the heart of every Ukrainian household). Amazingly, two of Wasyl and Anna's children ran the farmstead according to traditional practices until their deaths in the 1980s, never introducing electricity, sewers or phone lines.

Practicalities

Dauphin's **bus station**, 404 Main St N (☎204/622-9500), is a couple of minutes' walk from the town centre. The **Chamber of Commerce**, 21 3rd Ave NE (Mon–Fri 8.30am–4.30pm; ☎204/638-4838), provides tourist information. There's also a **tourist bureau** (mid-May to Aug Mon–Thurs 10am–6pm, Fri–Sun 9am–7pm; ☎204/638-5295), 2km away on the southern edge of town on Hwy 10, beside the airport.

For **accommodation**, the *Boulevard Motor Hotel*, 28 Memorial Blvd (☎204/638-4410 or 1-877/999-2228; ❷), and the *Dauphin Community Inn*, 104 Main St N (☎204/638-4311; ❶), are both fairly seedy downtown **hotels**; you may opt instead for either the *Canway Inn Motel and Suites* (☎204/638-5102 or 1-888/325-3335, ⓦ www.canwayinn.com; ❷–❺), about 4km south of town near the junction of hwys 5 and 10, with a pool, a sauna and more appealing rooms – four of them have Jacuzzis en suite. The *Touch of Africa B&B* (☎204/638-7936; ❷), on Hwy 10, south of Dauphin opposite the tourist information centre, keeps ostrichs on its grounds. The *Vermillion Trailer Park & Campground*, 21 2nd Ave NW (☎204/638-3740 or 622-3109; $12–17; May–Oct), is ten minutes' walk north of Main St. You can **eat** at *Irving's Steak House & Lounge*, 26 1st Ave NW, which has a real honky-tonk feel, or *Zamrykut's Ukrainian Family Restaurant*, 119 Main St N, a plain establishment that serves delicious home-made food, from borscht through to pierogies and kielbossa (sausage).

Duck Mountain Provincial Park

Straddling the Manitoba–Saskatchewan border, **Duck Mountain Provincial Park** is a large slice of the Manitoba Escarpment run as two separate and strikingly different entities by the park authorities of each province.

In Manitoba

On the **Manitoba side** the park is huge and wild, comprising several thousand acres of thickly wooded rolling hills punctuated by meadows, bogs, streams and hundreds of tiny lakes. Most of the park is boreal forest, a mixture of white spruce, jack pine, balsam fir, aspen and birch, but many of its eastern slopes are covered by maple, burr oak and elm, which are usually found further south. Portions of this are regularly harvested for lumber, but care is taken not to disturb the black bears, moose, white-tailed deer and lynx that inhabit the park; it's not unusual to hear the cries of coyotes and wolves at night or the unmistakeable bugling of a bull elk amongst the dense woodland. The park is noted for its fishing, with pickerel, pike and trout in most of its lakes, and the delicious arctic char to the north.

Access, some 100km northwest of Dauphin, is along two partly paved roads: the east–west Route 367, which branches off Hwy 10 just north of Garland and cuts across the middle of the park to Hwy 83, a distance of 80km; and the south–north Route 366, connecting the town of Grandview, on Hwy 5 just 45km west of Dauphin, with the village of Minitonas, 130km away. Approached along Route 366, the park's best section is in the southeast corner, where **Baldy Mountain** (831m) is the highest point in Manitoba, complete with an observation tower which provides views over the forest. A few kilometres to the north, the twin **West** and **East Blue Lakes** are among the park's finest – curving strips of clear water fed by underground springs. Between the lakes is the *Blue Lakes Campground* (☎1-888/482-2267; May to mid-Sept), close to both the **Blue Lakes Trail**, a six-kilometre cross-country hike, and the **Shining Stone Trail**, a short path along the peninsula that juts out into West Blue Lake. The campsite has a beach, a grocery store and fuel station; the camp office advises on boat rental and fishing. There are only unserviced sites here ($10). For serviced sites, try *Childs Lake Campground* (☎204/546-2463; $12–14; May to mid-Sept), with similar facilities; it's on Route 367 on the west edge of the park. Great West Trails (☎204/734-2321) organizes **horseback riding** excursions through the park that include camping and fishing. High Mountain Outfitters (☎204/967-2077), based in Kelwood on the east edge of the park, can also arrange a variety of one- to seven-day camping trips.

In Saskatchewan

By contrast, the **Saskatchewan side** of the Duck Mountain park is a highly regulated environment with much better, but far more crowded, facilities. It has toll booths at park entrances, a more extensive system of walking trails – including one trail that is wheelchair-accessible – and is open year-round. In winter, it has some of the best snowmobiling and cross-country skiing in the province.

Located some 100km northeast of Yorkton on hwys 9 and 5, Saskatchewan's part of the park centres on the roughly circular **Madge Lake**, ringed with aspens, where you'll find a beach, several stores, canteens, recreational and picnic areas, and places that rent canoes, paddleboats and ski equipment. The **parks office** is near the lake (year-round; ☎306/542-3482) and has full information on dates and times of the various activities. Some of the most popular attractions are the various **horseback-riding** excursions organized by Coyote Creek Stables, located on Lakeshore Drive, just inside the park's main entrance ($16/hr; ☎306/542-3439). The chalet-style *Duck Mountain Lodge*, overlooking the lake (☎306/542-3466; ❷–❹), is a relaxing place to stay; you can sleep in the large lodge, the two-bedroom town-house units with fireplaces, or the woodland cabins nearby. There's also a campsite at Pickerel Point, 4km east of the main Saskatchewan entrance (☎306/542-3479; $9–17; mid-May to Aug).

KAMSACK, a small Saskatchewan town about 10km west of Duck Mountain, is the best place to **stay** if you want to explore the park but not camp in it. The *Woodlander Inn*, corner of Railway Ave and 3rd St (☎306/542-

2125 or 542-2105; ❶), and the *Duck Mountain Motel and Campground*, 335 Queen Elizabeth Blvd E (☎306/542-2656; ❷), are the only two options in town and are fairly basic. A better bet is the *Border Mountain Country Bed & Breakfast* (☎306/542-3072, ⓦwww.bbcanada.com/bordermountaincountry; ❷), 15km southeast of Kamsack.

Yorkton

Heading west along Hwy 16 into Saskatchewan, **YORKTON** is the first town of any note – and the last sizeable place before you come to Saskatoon 333km away. It was founded as an agricultural community in the 1880s by farmers from Ontario, although – as with so many other places hereabouts – it's the Ukrainian community that features most strongly in the town and the surrounding area. The silver-painted dome and barrel roof of the nave of the white-brick **St Mary's Ukrainian Catholic Church**, at 155 Catherine St, is the town's most distinctive feature. Inside, there's a large illusionistic painting of the Coronation of the Virgin (1939–41) on the surface of the dome – about as close as you'll get in western Canada to the Baroque painted domes in Italian

Veregin and the Doukhobors

An hour's drive northeast of Yorkton, and 12km west of Kamsack, the tiny town of Veregin is named after **Peter Veregin**, the leader of the pacifist Doukhobor sect whose seven thousand members migrated to Saskatchewan at the end of the nineteenth century. The town is home to the **National Doukhobor Heritage Village** (mid-May to mid-Sept daily 10am–6pm; rest of year by appointment; ☎306/542-4441 or 542-4370; $3).

The first **Doukhobors** developed their dissenting beliefs within the Russian Orthodox Church during the eighteenth century, rejecting both the concept of a mediatory priesthood and the church's formal hierarchy. Later they established an independent sect, but their pacifist and protocommunist views made them unpopular with the tsars, who subjected them to periodic persecution. In the late 1890s they fled Russia for Saskatchewan under the leadership of **Peter Veregin**, a keen advocate of communal labour and the collective ownership of property. Veregin maintained his authority until 1907, when the Canadian government insisted that all Doukhobor homesteads be registered as private property. The colonists were divided, with over one-third accepting the government's proposals despite the bitter opposition of the collectivists, who showed their contempt for worldly possessions by destroying their belongings; some even burnt their clothes and organized Canada's first nude demonstrations. Irretrievably divided, Veregin and his supporters left for British Columbia, but the rest stayed behind to create a prosperous, pacifist and Russian-speaking community, which remained separate and distinct until the 1940s.

A modest museum in the **Heritage Village** traces the history of the sect and a large, square, refurbished two-storey prayer home contains the living quarters of their leader, complete with many original furnishings. The building, with its encircling veranda and wrought-iron adornment on both levels, dominates a large green lawn and faces the other buildings of the village, most of which were moved here from Doukhobor colonies in other parts of the province. Lined up in a neat row are a farmhouse, blacksmith's shop, granary, bakery, and bathhouse equipped with dried oak leaves that were used to cleanse the skin and make it fragrant. Another smaller prayer home features a Russian library and a display on Tolstoy, whose financial support helped the Doukhobor to migrate. On the grounds is an imposing bronze statue of the writer, donated by the Soviet Union.

and German churches. The Ukrainian community features strongly in Yorkton's branch of the **Western Development Museum** (May–Aug daily 9am–6pm; Ⓦ www.wdm.ca; $6), devoted to the various ethnic groups who have settled in the region. You'll also find a replica of the interior of a 1902 Catholic church and a superb collection of early twentieth-century Fords and Buicks. However, the most startling sights are the bright-red, huge-wheeled early fire trucks, looking entirely too fragile for their function. If you want to see farmworkers and their fierce-looking machines in action, you could attend the **Threshermen's Show**, held in the grounds of the museum in early August. Also in the city, at the corner of Smith St and 3rd Ave, is the **Godfrey Dean Cultural Centre** (Mon–Fri 1–5pm, Sat & Sun 2–5pm; free), which has a small but striking permanent collection of the work of Saskatchewan artists, plus several galleries which display temporary exhibitions; the **Sports Hall of Fame** (10am–noon & 1–4pm; free), located in the older part of the building is also part of the centre. After the long winter, the town is ready to host the **Yorkton Short Film and Video Festival** (Ⓦ www.yorktonshortfilm.org) in May, the oldest festival of its kind in North America, started in 1947.

Just south of the city, on the Yellowhead Hwy near Rokeby, is the **Parkland Heritage Centre** (mid-May to Sept Mon–Fri 1–8pm, Sat 1–5pm; $2.50), a modest but interesting group of nineteenth-century pioneer buildings brought here from other parts of Saskatchewan. Much further out, 48km northwest of Yorkton off the Yellowhead Hwy, **Good Spirit Lake** Provincial Park is an attractive area noted for its ecologically fragile sand dunes and the warm, shallow lake itself, which has exceptionally clear water. Here you'll find fine sandy beaches on the south shore, a fuel station, miniature golf course, tennis courts, riding stables, dining and snacking facilities, plus a **campsite** (Ⓣ306/792-4750 or 786-1463; $15–20; mid-May to Sept).

Practicalities

Yorkton's **bus station**, served by three buses daily from Saskatoon, is located downtown on 1st Ave. The smart **Visitors' Information Centre** is located at the junction of hwys 9 and 16 (June–Aug Mon–Fri 8am–6pm, Sat & Sun 9am–5pm; Sept–May Mon–Fri 9am–5pm; Ⓣ306/783-8707 or 1-877/250-6454, Ⓦ www.tourismyorkton.com) and can supply a good range of information and maps. There are several reasonably priced central **hotels**, including the *Holiday Inn*, 100 Broadway St E (Ⓣ306/783-9781 or 1-800/667-1585, Ⓦ www.holidayinn-yorkton.com; ❸–❺); and the *Imperial 400 Motel*, 207 Broadway St E (Ⓣ306/783-6581 or 1-800/781-2268; ❸), both of which serve great Ukrainian food; and the basic *City Limits Inn*, off Broadway St at 8 Betts Ave (Ⓣ306/782-2435; ❶). A pleasant **B&B** is *Lazy Maples*, 111 Darlington St W (Ⓣ306/783-7078; ❷); the owner is an excellent cook and can serve you Ukrainian pierogies for breakfast. You can **camp** in town at the well-shaded *City of Yorkton Campground* (Ⓣ306/786-1757 or 786-1750; $15–20; mid-May to mid-Oct), on Hwy 16A near the Western Development Museum. Yorkton's dining scene is drab, with several predictable places along Broadway.

Little Manitou Lake

Some 260km west of Yorkton and 120km east of Saskatoon on the Yellowhead Hwy is **Little Manitou Lake**. Set in a rather arid landscape, it looks just like any other lake, until you submerge yourself in its murky waters – or try to, for it has a saline content three times saltier than ocean water and denser than that of the famous Dead Sea in the Middle East. You couldn't sink if you tried, and you'll inevitably find yourself floating on the surface, feet up. The lake has long been known for its healing properties, even by the Indians in the eighteenth and nineteenth centuries, who camped on its shores and called it "lake of the healing waters".

Today, most people head to the tiny, rather ramshackle resort town of **Manitou Beach** on the lake's south shore to bathe in heated indoor mineral pools. Here you can experience near-weightlessness and sooth any rheumatic or arthritic pains in the heated comfort of *Manitou Springs Mineral Spa* (daily 9am–10pm; ☎306/946-2233; $9), one of the largest and oldest mineral **spas** in Canada. You can also stay and eat in their **hotel**, whose rates (❷–❹) include a swim in the spa.

Prince Albert

Founded as a Presbyterian mission in 1866, **PRINCE ALBERT**, 141km north of the Yellowhead route along Hwy 9, has a thriving timber industry, is a major transport centre and is the province's oldest and third-largest city. But it's a dull spot, its long main drag, **Central Avenue** (Hwy 2), lined with fast-food joints, fuel stations and shopping malls. Apart from the Northern Lights Casino (ⓦwww.siga.sk.ca), which brings thousands of visitors to town, the only conceivable attractions are the **Historical Museum** at River St and Central Ave (mid-May to Aug Mon–Sat 10am–6pm, Sun 10am–8pm; $1), given over chiefly to the area's first farmers and loggers, and **Diefenbaker's House**, 246 19th St W (May–Sept Mon–Sat 10am–6pm, Sun 10am–8pm; free), where the politician John Diefenbaker lived from 1947 until he donated it to the city in 1975.

The appeal of the town is that it has the only **bus** to Prince Albert National Park (see below) and La Ronge (see p.610), a daily service leaving from the station at 99 15th St E (☎306/953-3700). A daily bus also arrives here from Saskatoon. The **tourist office** (June–Aug Mon–Fri 8.30am–8pm, Sat & Sun 10am–8pm; Sept–May Mon–Fri 8.30am–6pm; ☎306/953-4386), in the south of town beside a police museum at 3700 2nd Ave W, provides free town maps and brochures.

There's no reason **to stay**; the town's central hotels are either grim or – thanks to the casino – noisy. At the south end of Hwy 2 is the comfortable *South Hill Inn*, 3245 2nd Ave W (☎306/922-1333 or 1-800/363-4466; ❸), which also has some outlandish Jacuzzi suites (❻) and a popular bar downstairs. For **campers**, the *Mary Nisbit Campground* (☎306/953-4880; $13–16; mid-May to Sept) is about 2km north of town, across the river beside Hwy 2. There's not much choice for good **eating** places, but the most expensive and renowned place is *Amy's on Second*, 2990 2nd Ave W, with three-course lunches from $30, and local fish such as pickerel. There's also *Diggers Road House*, 2901 2nd Ave W, with inexpensive specials, and *WK Kitchen*, 2840 2nd Ave W, which dishes up big Chinese buffets at reasonable prices.

Prince Albert National Park

Some 56km north of Prince Albert (and 230km north of Saskatoon) **Prince Albert National Park** is a great tract of wilderness where the aspen parkland of the south meets the boreal forest of the north, a transitional landscape that incorporates a host of rivers and creeks, dozens of deep lakes, pockets of pasture and areas of spruce bog. The shift in vegetation is mirrored by the wildlife, with prairie species such as coyote and wild bison giving way to black bear, moose, wolf, caribou, osprey and eagle further north. There's an entry fee of $4 to the park, with reductions for groups and longer stays.

The tourist village of **WASKESIU**, approached from the south by Hwy 263 and from the east by hwys 2 and 264, is the only settlement in the park. Spread out along the southern shore of Waskesiu Lake, it has all the usual facilities, a narrow sandy beach that gets ridiculously overcrowded in summer, and the park's **nature centre**, on Lakeview Drive (mid-May to Sept generally daily noon–4pm; ☎306/663-4522 or 1-877/255-7267), which has a hands-on display on the southern boreal forest and its inhabitants. In the centre of Waskesiu, at the junction of Lakeview Drive and Waskesiu Drive, the park's main **information office** (mid-May to Aug daily 8am–10pm; Sept to mid-Oct daily 8am–5pm; mid-Oct to mid-May Mon–Sat 8am–4pm; ☎306/663-4522 or 1-877/255-7267, ⓦwww.parkscanada.gc.ca/albert) gives advice on wildlife and the condition of the hiking trails, along with weather forecasts. The information office also runs a programme of **guided walks** in July and August and issues backcountry camping permits ($3), which allow visitors to use the primitive, seasonal **campsites** dotted along most of the more substantial trails. Shearwater Boat Cruises runs **boat** trips on the lake (July to mid-Sept daily 1pm, 3pm, 5pm & 7pm; 1hr; $15; ☎306/982-4478 or 1-888/747-7572). Whatever you do in the park, remember to take insect repellent.

Several of the park's easier **hiking trails** begin in or near Waskesiu, most notably the thirteen-kilometre Kingfisher Trail, which loops through the forest just to the west of the resort. However, the best trails and **canoe routes** begin roughly 15km further north at the bottom end of Kingsmere Lake, accessible by boat or car from Waskesiu. They include a delightful week-long canoe trip that skirts the west shore of Kingsmere Lake before heading through a series of remote lakes amidst dense boreal forest. There's also a twenty-kilometre hike or canoe paddle to the idyllic spot of **Grey Owl's Cabin** (May–Sept), situated beside tiny Ajawaan Lake, near the northern shore of Kingsmere Lake. Grey Owl (see p.195) lived in this cabin from 1931 until 1937, the year before his death, and it was here that he wrote one of his better books, *Pilgrims of the Wild*, and where he, his wife Anahereo and daughter Shirley Dawn are buried. For further information on the trip to the cabin, and on other canoe routes in the park, call the park information office.

Park practicalities

Connected by bus to La Ronge to the north (see p.610) and Prince Albert to the south, Waskesiu's **bus stop** is right in the centre, beside a **tourist kiosk** (mid-May to Aug daily 8am–10pm; Sept–Dec & April to mid-May Mon–Fri 8am–4pm; Jan–March daily 8am–4pm; ☎306/663-5410), which provides free maps of the town. Waskesiu's stores sell a full range of outback **equipment**, but no one rents out camping gear. **Canoe** and **kayak rentals** (☎306/663-5994) are available at three marinas within the park.

Waskesiu's main street, Waskesiu Drive, runs roughly parallel to and just south of the lake, its western section curving round behind Lakeview Drive. Almost all the **hotels** and **motels** are on or near these two streets, including the *Lakeview Hotel*, Lakeview Drive (☎306/663-5311; ❸), and the more luxurious *All Season Waskesiu Lake Lodge*, Lakeview Drive (☎306/663-6161 ⓦwww.waskesiulakelodge.com; ❺; May to mid-Oct), with one- and two-bedroom apartments that include lakeside decks and barbecues. **Bungalow** and **cabin** accommodation tends to be block-booked from May to mid-October, but you could try the *Armstrong Hillcrest Cabins*, corner of Lakeview Drive and Willow St (☎306/663-5481 or 922-2599; ❷–❺; May to mid-Oct), or *Kapasiwin Bungalows* (☎306/663-5225 or 1-877/963-5225, ⓦwww.kapasiwin .com;❹; May to mid-Oct), 2km round the lake to the east of the resort, which has cabins that form a quiet mini-resort with its own private beach.

Waskesiu has two **campsites**: the centrally situated *Trailer Park* (☎306/663-4522 or 1-877/255-7267; $20; mid-May to Sept) on the north end of Waskesiu Drive near *Waskesiu Lodge*, and the nearby *Beaver Glen Campground* (☎306/663-4522 or 1-877/255-7267; $14–18; mid-May to Sept), near Waskesiu Lake. The basic, unserviced *Kingsmere Lake Campgrounds* (☎306/663-4522 or 1-877/255-7267; $3 backcountry permit from park office; year-round) is near Grey Owl's Cabin. For reservations at all other Prince Albert campsites, call ☎1-800/333-7267.

There are several low-priced **restaurants** and **snack bars** in the centre, while on the beachfront, *The Beach House* is good for cappuccinos, wraps, desserts and sunsets. For more expensive dining, try the Mackenzie's Dining Room at the *Hawood Inn*, 851 Lakeview Drive, where main courses start at around $15, and include good cuts of local beef.

Saskatoon

Set on the wide South Saskatchewan River at the heart of a vast wheat-growing area, **SASKATOON**, 781km west of Winnipeg, is a commercial, manufacturing and distribution centre with a population of around 236,000 – making it Saskatchewan's largest city and, in the opinion of many of its inhabitants, a better claimant to the title of provincial capital than Regina. Ontario Methodists founded the town as a temperance colony in 1883 and named it after the purple berry that grows in the region, but in spite of their enthusiasm the new settlement made an extremely slow start, partly because the semi-arid farming conditions were unfamiliar to them and partly because the Northwest Rebellion of 1885 raised fears of Indian hostility. Although the railroad reached Saskatoon in 1890, there were still only 113 inhabitants at the beginning of the twentieth century. In the next decade, however, there was a sudden influx of European and American settlers and, as the agricultural economy of the prairies expanded, so the city came to be dominated by a group of entrepreneurs nicknamed **boomers**, under whose management Saskatoon became the economic focus of the region. This success was underpinned by the development of a particularly sharp form of municipal loyalty: people who dared criticize any aspect of the city, from the poor quality of the water to tyrannical labour practices, were dubbed **knockers**, and their opinions were rubbished by the press. The boomers established a city where community solidarity overwhelmed differences in income and occupation, a set of attitudes that palpably still prevails, making this a pleasant, well-groomed place, albeit one with just a trio of principal tourist attractions – the **Mendel Art Gallery**, a branch of the **Western Development Museum** and, on the outskirts, **Wanuskewin**, a complex dedicated to the Plains Indians.

Arrival, information and accommodation

Saskatoon **airport** (☎306/975-8900, ⓦwww.yxe.ca), 5km northwest of the city centre, is connected to downtown by taxi (roughly $15); otherwise, the nearest bus service is the half-hourly #21, which leaves from the junction of

DOWNTOWN SASKATOON

Airport

Wanuskewin Heritage Park

ACCOMMODATION
Delta Bessborough Hotel   E
Park Town Motor Hotel   C
Patricia Hotel   A
Radisson Hotel Saskatoon   F
Hotel Senator   D
YWCA   B

RESTAURANTS
Amigos Cantina   7
Calories   6
Earl's   1
Fude Bistro   4
Grainfields   9
John's Prime Rib   5
The Keg   10
Saigon Rose   3
Saskatoon
  Station Place   2
Taj Mahal   8

Mendel
Art Gallery

University of
Saskatchewan

Diefenbaker
Canada Centre

Bus Station

Ukrainian
Museum

South Saskatchewan River

Boat Cruise

Meewasin Valley
Trail Centre

Western Development Museum

0   1 km

Airport Drive and 45th St, a five-minute walk from the terminal building. The
train station (☎1-800/835-3037) is 7km west of the centre, on Chappell
Drive, a five-minute walk from the route of bus #3 on Dieppe St; a taxi to the
downtown core costs about $15. Far more convenient is the city's **bus station**,
in the centre at 23rd St East and Pacific Ave, served by Greyhound and the
Saskatchewan Transportation Company (both ☎306/933-8000).

The main office of **Tourism Saskatoon** (mid-May to Aug Mon–Fri 9am–5pm; rest of year Mon–Fri 9am–5pm; ☏306/242-1206 or 1-800/567-2444, Ⓦwww.tourismsaskatoon.com) is in the old CP train station at 6-305 Idylwyld Drive North. In addition to maps and brochures, it has copies of *The Broadway Theatre*, a free bimonthly news sheet that carries details of cultural events. There's also an information centre at the corner of Ave C North and 47th St (mid-May to Aug daily 10am–7pm; ☏306/242-1206).

Saskatoon's compact city centre is best explored **on foot**, though it takes a little time to work out the street plan. Streets run east–west, avenues north–south. Edged to the south and east by the river and the adjacent strip of city park, the **downtown core** is bounded by 25th St East to the north and 1st Ave to the west. Numbered sequentially, these central streets are all suffixed "East", with their western extensions starting at either 1st Ave or Idylwyld Drive. However, the avenues change from "South" to "North" right in the centre at 22nd St East. For the suburbs, Saskatoon Transit (☏306/975-3100) operates an efficient and fairly comprehensive **bus** system, with a standard adult fare of $1.60 (pay on board). **Cruises** along the South Saskatchewan River, with its weir, sand bars and fast-flowing currents, are organized by Shearwater Boat Cruises on its ship, the *Saskatoon Lady* (May–Sept daily; for times call ☏306/549-2452 or 1-888/747-7572, Ⓦwww.shearwatertours.com; $10); the boat departs for the one-hour trip from the wharf at the Mendel Art Gallery.

Saskatoon has a good choice of downtown **hotels**. Convenient alternatives include a YWCA and summer **hostel** for women, and a **campsite**. There are also lots of reasonably priced **motels** on Hwy 11 south of town and Hwy 16 going east, with standard facilities (❷–❹).

Hotels and motels

Colonial Square Motel 1301 8th St E ☏306/343-1676 or 1-800/667-3939, Ⓦwww.colonialsquaremotel.com. Eighty simple singles and doubles, all with cable TV. Close to the Broadway Ave area. ❸

Delta Bessborough Hotel 601 Spadina Crescent & 21st St E ☏306/244-5521 or 1-800/268-1133, Ⓦwww.deltahotels.com. Built for the CNR in 1931, the Bessborough is an enormous turreted and gabled affair that has been tastefully refurbished in a French château style that makes it the city's most striking building. Set in Kiwanis Memorial Park, beside the river. ❹–❼

Hotel Senator 243 21st St E at 3rd Ave ☏306/244-6141. One of the cheapest places in town, but with primitive rooms. ❸

Park Town Motor Hotel 924 Spadina Crescent & 25th St E ☏306/244-5564 or 1-800/667-3999, Ⓦwww.parkhotel.com. Large hotel with standard rooms and river views. Better weekend rates. ❹

Radisson Hotel Saskatoon 405 20th St E ☏306/665-3322 or 1-800/333-3333, Ⓦwww

Saskatoon's festivals

Saskatoon's biggest and best shindig is the **Saskatchewan Jazz Festival** (Ⓦwww.saskjazz.com) in the last week of June or first week of July; over five hundred musicians perform jazz, gospel and blues across the city, mostly for free. The **Shakespeare on the Saskatchewan Festival** (Ⓦwww.shakespeareonthe saskatchewan.com), where the bard's plays are performed in tents on the riverbank by the Mendel Art Gallery, is held on various days from early July to mid-August. The **Saskatoon International Fringe Festival** (Ⓦwww.saskatoonfringe.org), a week of alternative performances held at the end of July and the beginning of August, features some fifty theatre groups from all over the world performing on stages dotted along Broadway Ave. **Folkfest** (Ⓦwww.folkfest.sk.ca), a large ethnic festival held in mid-August at various venues, rounds out the summer's activities.

.radisson.com. Tower block with luxurious rooms. Fourteen en suites. Good weekend rates. ❺

B&Bs

Brighton House 1308 5th Ave N ☎306/664-3278, ⓦwww.bbcanada.com/567.html. Nonsmoking clapboard house with a pretty garden and equally flowery bedrooms furnished with antiques. One suite has a private bathroom and sun patio whilst upstairs a family suite is large enough for kids to play in. There's also a hot tub and the use of bikes and a croquet set. ❸
College Drive Lodge 1020 College Drive ☎306/665-9111. Budget air-conditioned rooms; laundry, kitchen, complimentary coffee and tea; free parking. Close to the university. ❶
Ninth St Bed & Breakfast 227 9th St E ☎306/224-3754, ⓦwww.bbcanada.com/949.html. Three attractive suites with shared bath, great gourmet breakfasts and bike rental. In the historic Nutana district and near the Broadway Ave area. ❷
Savelia's Guesthouse 330 6th Ave N ☎306/653-4646, ⓦwww.brama.ca/savelia. A cottage-style white, wooden house, with an old-world atmosphere and attractively decorated, nonsmoking rooms. Near Mendel Art Gallery and Ukrainian Museum. ❷

Hostels

Patricia Hotel 345 2nd Ave N at 25th St E ☎306/242-8861. Low-budget downtown hotel

above a noisy nightclub with basic dorms ($14), singles and doubles ($40–50). Free parking but no other facilities and no showers for those staying in dorm rooms.
YWCA Residence 510 25th St E at 5th Ave N ☎306/244-0944. Accommodation for single women; long- and short-term stays possible, with good weekly and monthly rates. Women only. ❶

Student rooms

University of Saskatchewan 91 Campus Drive ☎306/966-8600. Dorm accommodation – private rooms with shared washrooms – in student residences available to those who call at least a day in advance. May–Oct. ❶

Campsites

Gordon Howe Campsite Ave P South, off 11th St ☎306/975-3328 or 975-3331. Most comfortable and central of the three city campsites, located near the South Saskatchewan River, 4km south of the centre. Over 130 serviced sites, with barbecue, picnic area, laundry and on-site manager. Mid-April to Sept. $12–19.
Saskatoon 16 West RV Park Hwy 16, 1.5km northwest of the city ☎306/931-8905 or 1-800/478-7833. Twenty-five pull-through sites, plus fifty serviced sites with electric and water hook-ups. Convenience shop on grounds selling Saskatchewan crafts. April–Oct. $17–24.

The City

Most of Saskatoon's principal sights are on or near the **Meewasin Valley Trail**, a circular, nineteen-kilometre walking and cycle route that follows the narrow strip of park along both banks of the river between the Idylwyld Drive and Circle Drive bridges. At the start of the trail, the **Meewasin Valley Centre**, 402 3rd Ave South at 19th St East (daily 9am–5pm; free; ⓦwww .meewasin.com), provides a useful introduction to the region's history and geography with the aid of maps, old photographs and a video film; a tourist information office is part of the centre. A few minutes' walk from the Valley Centre, along the west bank, the **Ukrainian Museum of Canada**, 910 Spadina Crescent E at 24th St East (Tues–Sat 10am–5pm, Sun 1–5pm; ⓦwww.umc.sk.ca; $3), is the more interesting of the city's two Ukrainian museums, representing the Orthodox as distinct from the Catholic tradition. Displays cover the history of Ukrainian migration, traditional textile design, festivals and Easter-egg painting. The **Mendel Art Gallery**, overlooking the river from Spadina Crescent, just north of 25th St East (daily 9am–9pm; free), features temporary shows of modern Canadian and international art. The gallery is named after local magnate Fred Mendel, whose personal collection includes paintings by many of the country's renowned artists – Emily Carr, Lawren Harris and David Milne – and a good selection of Inuit sculpture, a small sample of which is always on display. The building also has a delightful conservatory full of plants, a snack bar and an excellent gift shop.

Across the river from the Mendel Art Gallery, over University Bridge, the campus of the **University of Saskatchewan** (Ⓦwww.usask.ca), with a number of dignified grey-stone buildings in Gothic Revival style, occupies a prime riverbank site just to the north of College Drive. Departmental collections include a **Museum of Antiquities** (May–Aug Mon–Fri 9am–4pm; rest of year Mon–Fri 9am–noon; closed mid-Dec to mid-Jan; free), in the Murray Building and the small **Kenderdine Gallery** (Mon–Fri 11.30am–4.30pm, Sun 12.30–5pm; free). Neither of these draws as many visitors as the **Diefenbaker Canada Centre** (Mon–Fri 9.30am–4.30pm, Sat & Sun noon–4.30pm; $2), a museum, archive and research centre at the west end of the campus, beside the river. Prime minister from 1957 to 1963, John Diefenbaker was a caricaturist's dream with his large flat face, protruding teeth and wavy white hair, and the museum's high point is its assortment of newspaper cartoons. He was buried just outside the centre in 1979. One of the finest **views** of the city, across the river, is from the grounds of the centre.

On the south side of the river, 8km from the centre, is the Saskatoon branch of the **Western Development Museum**, 2610 Lorne Ave S (Jan–March Tue–Sun 9am–5pm; April–Dec daily 9am–5pm; Ⓦwww.wdm.ca; $6), a few minutes' walk from the route of bus #1 from 2nd Ave in downtown. The principal exhibit here is Boomtown, an ambitious reconstruction of a typical Saskatchewan small-town main street circa 1910, complete with boardwalk sidewalks and parked vehicles. More like a film set than a museum, its mixture of replica and original buildings includes a school, a general store, a church, a theatre, a train station and a combined pool hall and barbershop. There's a shop with a range of unusual gifts, and the Boomtown Café serves delicious home-cooked meals with a pioneer flavour.

Wanuskewin Heritage Park

Wanuskewin Heritage Park (April to late-May & Sept daily 9am–5pm; late-May to Aug daily 9am–9pm; Oct–March Wed–Sun 9am–5pm; Ⓦwww.wanuskewin.com; $6.50), twenty minutes' drive north of the city centre – along Hwy 10 then Warman and Wanuskewin roads – is designed to be Saskatoon's principal tourist attraction, a lavish tribute to the culture of the Northern Plains Indians. It's well worth the trip out here, as the commercial aspect is played down in favour of a sensitive interpretation of the Indians' spiritual relationship to the land and to living creatures. Bordering the South Saskatchewan River in the attractive wooded Opamihaw Valley, the park embraces a string of marshy creeks and wooded ridges that have been used by native peoples for more than six thousand years. All along the trails are ecologically fragile plants and flowers that must not be picked. The nineteen sites are connected by trails and walkways to a visitor centre that features reconstructions of tepees, a buffalo pound and a buffalo jump as well as displays on traditional skills as diverse as tool-making and storytelling. The park can also arrange for overnight camping in tepees with breakfast, dinner cooked on the fire and interpretive programmes including storytelling and bannock-making (mid-May to Sept; reservation essential), plus longer sessions of two or three nights. The attached **restaurant** specializes in indigenous foodstuffs such as buffalo meat and bannock bread, and a gift shop has a full range of authentic arts and crafts by native people. Wanuskewin has been developed with the cooperation of local native peoples, who provide most of the interpretive staff. There is no public transport; a **taxi** from downtown costs around $20.

Eating, drinking and nightlife

Saskatoon has a useful assortment of **restaurants** clustered in and around the downtown core and along the first couple of blocks of Broadway Ave,

Saskatoon berry pie

The thing to try while in town is **Saskatoon berry pie**, made with berries grown on the outskirts of the city. Arguably the best place for this is the *Berry Barn*, 830 Valley Rd (May–Sept daily 10am–9pm; Oct–Dec Mon–Thurs 10am–5pm, Fri–Sun 10am–9pm; ☏306/978-9797), located 11km southwest of town off Hwy 11. It's one of a number of places along this road that allows you to pick your own fruit, and also has a good restaurant serving hearty home-made food.

which lies just across the river via the bridge at 4th Ave South and 19th St East. Broadway is the nearest thing the city has to a "cultural centre", the home of the Broadway Theatre and a handful of vaguely alternative shops and cafés. **Nightlife** is a little slow, but there are a few pubs and clubs which can reward the determined, with a concentration in the old warehouse district around corner of 24th St and Pacific Ave. The local newspaper, *The Star Phoenix*, has bland reviews and nightlife listings at the weekend. While you're in town try a bottle of Great Western Beer (especially the Brewhouse brand), the product of a local factory whose future was threatened by the merger of two of Canada's giant brewing companies, Molson and Carling O'Keefe. The workers bought the factory themselves and can now barely keep up with demand.

The Broadway Theatre, 715 Broadway Ave (☏306/652-6556), has the best of foreign and domestic **films**. For **theatre**, the Persephone, 2802 Rusholme Rd (☏306/384-7727, ⊕www.persephonetheatre.org; tickets $14–25), is the best known of the city's professional companies; their season runs from October to May. The Twenty-Fifth Street Theatre, 816 Spadina Crescent E (☏306/664-2239), concentrates on local work. Visiting ballet, theatre and opera stars appear at the Saskatoon Centennial Auditorium, 35 22nd St E (☏306/975-7777 or 1-800/970-7328, ⊕www.saskcent.com).

Restaurants

Amigos Cantina 632 10th St E ☏306/652-4912. Mexican specialities, with live background music. Closed Sun.

Calories Bakery & Restaurant 721 Broadway Ave ☏306/655-7991. An atmospheric French-style bistro, with main courses around $8.

Earl's 610 2nd Ave N & Queen St ☏306/664-4060. Trendy chain with an imaginative menu; vegetarian and other dishes between $5 and $15.

Fude Bistro 119 Ave B ☏306/652-2028. Expensive but stylish place for classy regional cooking; mains (like the grilled beef tenderloin with cardamom spiced pumpkin, Saskatoon berry relish and roast potatoes) average $20.

Grainfields Pancake and Waffle House Grosvenor Park Centre, 2105 8th St E ☏306/955-1989. Huge, mouthwatering selections of pancakes and waffles with a multitude of toppings.

John's Prime Rib and Steakhouse 401 21st St E ☏306/244-6384. Probably the best steaks in town, done any way you want. Closed Sun.

The Keg Steakhouse & Bar 1110 Grosvenor Ave ☏306/653-3633. Popular chain serving standard steak and seafood dishes for $10–20.

Saigon Rose 69 24th St E ☏306/242-1351. Simple place with plastic tablecloths and fantastic cheap and filling Vietnamese and Chinese food; most dishes are $7–10.

Samurai 601 Spadina Crescent ☏306/683-6926. Good but pricey Japanese sushi restaurant inside the *Delta Bessborough Hotel*.

Saskatoon Station Place Corner of Idylwyld Drive and 23rd St. Eat in Pullman cars in a converted train station. Great Sunday brunches.

Taj Mahal 1013 Broadway Ave ☏306/978-2227. Outstanding Indian restaurant, arguably the best in Canada. The most delicious dishes are those made with coconut (naryal); the menu has a large vegetarian section. The chutneys are home-made as is the mango ice cream, whilst the lassis are made with buttermilk. A meal for two will cost around $40. Closed Mon.

Bars and clubs

Amigos Cantina 632 10th St E ⓦwww.amigoscantina.com. Mexican restaurant that becomes a club at night with local bands often playing.

The Bassment 245 3rd Ave S ⓣ306/683-2277, ⓦwww.jazzbassment.com. Great jazz venue attracting international performers (live jazz mid-Sept to mid-June Sat nights).

Black Duck Freehouse 154 2nd Ave S. Comfortably familiar pub, with the biggest selection of scotch and beer in Saskatchewan.

Buds 817 Broadway Ave. Rough-and-ready bar with nightly R&B acts, plus jam sessions Saturday afternoon. $3–5 cover charge.

Cheers Brew Pub 2105 8th St E. Beer brewed on the premises and large portions of ribs and Cajun food for about $10.

Jax Nite Club 302 Pacific Ave. One of several middling dance clubs in the warehouse area; follow the crowds.

Odeon 241 2nd Ave, ⓦwww.odeonclub.com. Saskatoon's hippest club, attracting the city's chic crowd. Occasional live music but mostly dance and techno.

The Pat 345 2nd Ave N. Vast middle-of-the road nightclub catering to just about everybody, though the college crowd dominates. Mostly Top 40.

Stovin's Lounge 601 Spadina Crescent E. The *Bessborough Hotel's* quiet and comfortable lounge: ideal for chatting and unwinding if all the other options sound like too much effort.

Yard and Flagon Pub 718 Broadway Ave. Broadway bar with a lively rooftop that pulls in the college crowd.

Listings

Airlines Air Canada ⓣ1-888/247-2262; Air Sask ⓣ1-800/665-7275; Athabaska Airways ⓣ1-800/667-9356; Northwest ⓣ1-800/225-2525; Westjet ⓣ1-800/538-5696.

Bike rental Bike Doctor, 623 Main St ⓣ306/664-8555; also from the Ramada and Bessborough hotels.

Car rental Avis, at the airport ⓣ306/652-3434 or 1-800/879-2847; Budget, 2215 Ave C N, 234 1st Ave S, 2508 8th St E & at the airport ⓣ306/664-1692; Discount, 1550 8th St E ⓣ306/242-6556; Enterprise, 718D Circle Drive E ⓣ306/652-9119 or 1-800/736-8222 & 215 Idylwyld Drive N ⓣ306/244-6900; Thrifty, 2130 Airport Drive ⓣ306/244-8000.

Gay and lesbian life G&L info ⓣ306/665-1224.

Pride Week is at the end of June.

Hospitals Saskatoon City Hospital, 701 Queen St ⓣ306/655-8000; St Paul's, 1702 20th St W ⓣ306/665-5000.

Laundries Off-Broadway Laundromat, 835b Broadway Ave at Main St (daily 8am–9pm); Wash 'n' Slosh is a laundrette-bar, 834B Broadway Ave (daily 8am–9pm).

Left luggage Coin-operated machines at the bus station.

Police 130 4th Ave N ⓣ306/975-8300.

Post office 202 4th Ave N.

Taxis Radio Cabs ⓣ306/242-1221; United Cabs ⓣ306/652-2222.

Weather line ⓣ306/975-4266.

Around Saskatoon

North of Saskatoon, Hwy 11 cuts across the narrow slice of prairie that separates the final stretches of the North and South Saskatchewan rivers, before they flow together further to the northeast. There's nothing to see on the road itself, but on the way the briefest of detours will take you to one of the province's more interesting attractions, **Batoche National Historic Site**, where the Métis rebellion of 1885 reached its disastrous climax. Setting out early and with your own transport, this can be visited as part of an exceptional day-trip that also includes Wanuskewin (see p.599) on the north side of town, a museum at **Duck Lake** and the reconstructed **Fort Carlton** where you can camp overnight.

Batoche National Historic Site

The site of the Métis's last stand – and the last place where Canadians fought against Canadians – **Batoche National Historic Site** (May–Sept daily

The Northwest Rebellion

The 1869–70 Red River rebellion in Manitoba, led by **Louis Riel**, won significant concessions from the Canadian government but failed to protect the Métis's way of life in subsequent years against the effects of increasing white settlement. Many Métis moved west to farm the banks of the **South Saskatchewan River**, where the men worked as freighters, traders, horse breeders and translators, acting as intermediaries between the Indians and the Europeans. In itself, the development of these homesteads was a recognition by the Métis that the day of the itinerant buffalo hunter was over. However, when the government surveyors arrived here in 1878, the Métis realized, as they had on the Red River twenty years before, that their claim to the land they farmed was far from secure.

Beginning with the Métis, a general sense of instability spread across the region in the early 1880s, fuelled by Big Bear's and Poundmaker's increasingly restless and hungry **Cree** and by the discontent of the white settlers at the high freight charges levied on their produce. The leaders of the Métis decided to act in June 1884, when they sent a delegation to Montana, where Riel was in exile. Convinced that the Métis were God's chosen instrument to purify the human race, and he their Messiah, Riel was easily persuaded to return to Canada, where he spent the winter unsuccessfully petitioning the Ottawa government for confirmation of Métis rights.

In March 1885, Riel and his supporters declared a provisional government at **Batoche** and demanded the surrender of the nearest Mountie outpost, **Fort Carlton**, just 35km to their west on the North Saskatchewan River. The police superintendent refused, and the force he dispatched to re-establish order was badly mauled at **Duck Lake**. When news of the uprising reached Big Bear's Cree, some 300km away, they attacked the local Hudson's Bay Company store and killed its nine occupants in the so-called **Frog Lake Massacre**. Within a couple of weeks, no fewer than three columns of militia were converging on Big Bear's Cree and the meagre Métis forces at Batoche. The total number of casualties – about fifty altogether – does not indicate the full significance of the engagement, which for the Métis marked the end of their independence and influence. Riel's execution in Regina on November 16, 1885, was bitterly denounced in Québec and remains a potent symbol of the deep divide between English- and French-speaking Canada. In Ontario there was a mood of unrepentant triumphalism, the military success – however paltry – stirring a deep patriotic fervour that excluded Métis and Indian alike.

9am–5pm; $6) occupies a splendid site beside the east bank of the South Saskatchewan River, 90km from Saskatoon, just off Provincial Hwy 225. At the entrance to the park, a **visitor reception centre** (T306/423-6227) has displays on the culture of the Métis and provides a detailed account of the rebellion, supplemented by a glossy brochure and an exceptional 45-minute audiovisual presentation combining clips of re-enactments, spoken narration, music and tableaux of realistic mannequins. This is great for an insight into the Métis way of life and a blow-by-blow account of the battle, but rather glosses over the cause of the actual conflict; the displays are perhaps too sympathetic to the Métis, instead of appreciating the government's concern to avoid Canada being split in half – the west was still very much an open territory at the time.

Behind the centre, the main footpath leads to a refurbished Catholic church and adjacent rectory, all that's left of the original village. A few minutes' walk away, in the cemetery perched above the river bank, memorials inscribed with the hoary commendation "a credit to his race" contrast with the rough chunk of rock that commemorates Riel's commander in chief **Gabriel Dumont**. A stern and ferocious man, Dumont insisted that he be buried standing up, so that he could enjoy a good view of the river.

The church and cemetery are at the centre of the park's **walking trails**, which extend along the river bank in both directions. Roughly 1km to the south, there's a military graveyard, a Métis farmhouse and the remains of some rifle pits; about the same distance to the north, there's the site of the old ferry crossing, more rifle pits and the foundations of several Métis buildings. With a knowledge of the history, the park becomes an extremely evocative spot.

Duck Lake and Fort Carlton

Back on Hwy 11, on the west side of the South Saskatchewan, the tiny farming community of **DUCK LAKE** – many of whose buildings have outdoor murals depicting local history – is home to a **Regional Interpretive Centre**, 5 Anderson Ave (mid-May to early Sept daily 10am–5.30pm; ⓦwww .dlric.com; $4), with displays on Indian, Métis and pioneer society from 1870 to 1905. Prize exhibits include some elaborate Cree costumes; an outfit that belonged to the Sioux chief Little Fox, an adviser to Sitting Bull; and Gabriel Dumont's gold watch, presented to him in New York where he was appearing in Buffalo Bill's Wild West Show. The buildings huge tower gives views a long way over the prairies.

Continuing 26km west along Hwy 212, you'll reach **Fort Carlton Provincial Historic Park** (mid-May to Aug daily 10am–6pm; ⓦwww .saskparks.net; $2.50), a reconstruction of a Hudson's Bay Company trading post circa 1860. Founded in 1810, the riverbank station was fortified in successive decades and became an important centre of the fur and pemmican trade, until the demise of the buffalo brought an end to its success. Reduced to a warehouse facility in the early 1880s, the fort was garrisoned by the Mounties during the Northwest Rebellion (see box), but it was finally burnt down and abandoned in 1885. The **visitors' centre** provides an historical introduction to the fort, whose stockade shelters replicas of the clerk's quarters, a sail and harness shop, a fur and provisions store with piles of colourfully striped Hudson's Bay Company blankets and bottles of bright Indian trading beads, and a trading shop, where the merchandise included gunpowder – which meant the clerks were forbidden to light a stove here, no matter what the temperature. Just outside the walls of the stockade are three tepees, neatly aligned along a path. The centre, also offers guided **trail walks**, which allow you to see the remains of rutted wagon trails made by carts carrying supplies to and from the fort. There's also an on-site **campsite** (☎306/467-5205 or 933-7937; $9; mid-May to early Sept). Take care when hiking or camping as the wooded gullies of the North Saskatchewan River are home to a number of **black bears**.

West of Saskatoon

From Saskatoon it's only another 275km to the Alberta border, where sits the dull town of **Lloydminster**. But **Redberry Lake** is a must for keen birders, and the **Battlefords** make another good short stop if you want to see a refurbished Mountie stockade.

Redberry Lake

The **Redberry Lake** World Biosphere Reserve (ⓦwww.redberrylake.com; free), about 100km northwest of Saskatoon via hwys 16, 340 and 40, is one of the province's best areas to view over two hundred species of birds. The north shore of Redberry Lake is home to several rare species, including piping plovers and white pelicans. There are trails around the lakeshore, as well as the Stuart Houston Ecology Centre (mid-May to mid-Sept daily 9am–5pm), an interpretive centre with videos and dioramas on the lake's fragile ecosystem. Shearwater Boat Cruises (June to mid-Sept; ☎1-888/747-7572, ⓦwww .shearwatertours.com; 1hr; $25), offers boat tours, while you can also book guided walking tours ($3 per person) and get information on a driving tour of the region at the centre. Within the reserve, the **Redberry Lake Regional Park** (May–Sept; $5) has **camping** ($10–14).

The Battlefords

Following the Yellowhead Hwy towards Edmonton, you'll come to the **Battlefords**, roughly 150km from Saskatoon. These twin townships consist of grimy and impoverished **North Battleford** and, facing it from the opposite bank of the North Saskatchewan River, sedate little **Battleford** with its trim riverside streets and refurbished Mountie stockade.

From the middle of the eighteenth century, this stretch of the North Saskatchewan River formed a natural boundary between the **Blackfeet** to the south and the **Cree** to the north. These two groups were temporary trading partners, the Cree and their Ojibwa allies controlling the flow of European goods, the Blackfeet providing the horses. However, with the arrival of **white traders** at the start of the nineteenth century, the Blackfeet developed a flourishing trade direct with the Europeans, and by 1870 the Cree and Blackfeet were waging war across the entire length of their frontier, from the Missouri River to Fort Edmonton. In the 1870s, apprehensive after the Cypress Hills Massacre and the arrival of Sitting Bull and his warriors (see box p.583), the government speeded its policy of containment and control, determined to push the Plains Indians into reservations and thereby open the area for

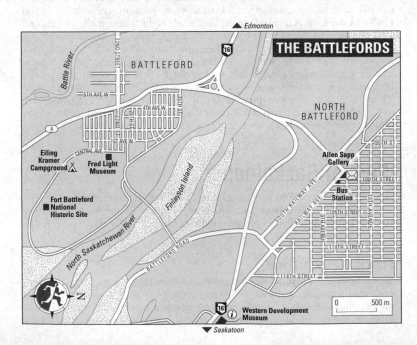

European settlers. Their chosen instrument was the North West Mounted Police, who in 1876 established a post at Battleford, which then became the regional capital.

With the virtual **extinction of the buffalo** herds in the late 1870s, the Plains Indians began to starve and Lieutenant Governor Dewdney used his control of emergency rations to force recalcitrant Indians onto the reservations. Several bands of Cree resisted the process, fighting a series of skirmishes at the same time as the Métis rebellion in Batoche, but by the mid-1880s their independence was over. Meanwhile, Battleford had lost its pre-eminence when the Canadian Pacific Railway routed its transcontinental line through Regina, which became the new capital in 1883. Twenty years later, its prospects were further damaged by the Canadian Northern Railway, which laid its tracks on the other side of the river, creating the rival town of North Battleford. Since then, Battleford has stagnated and shrunk, while its rival has become a moderately successful industrial and distribution centre, with a population of around fourteen thousand.

The townships

Situated on the east side of the river valley, North Battleford's downtown core is arranged into streets running north–south and avenues running west–east, forming a central gridiron that intersects with Railway Ave, which runs southeast to northwest. Across the river, some 5km away, Battleford sprawls next to Hwy 4, its streets running from west to east and avenues from north to south. There are two roads between the two: a modern flyover that's part of Hwy 16, and the shorter old Route 16A.

On the Yellowhead Hwy, just east of **NORTH BATTLEFORD**, this town's branch of the **Western Development Museum** (May–Sept daily 9am–5pm; ⓦ www.wdm.ca; $6) deals with the farming history of Saskatchewan. Inside, vintage vehicles and a "Jolly Life of the Farmer's Wife" exhibit of old ranges and laundry equipment recall older, and harder, times, while outside is the Heritage Farm and Village, which contains 36 buildings, saved from around the province, including tiny churches and homesteads, banks, a general store, creaky barns and a grain elevator from 1928. The museum is an excellent way to acquaint yourself with prairie history and realize the harshness and the changes in farming life over the last century. Try to visit on the second weekend in August when the "ghost" village comes alive in the "Those Were the Days" event, which features costumed locals bread-baking and craft-making.

The old municipal library in the centre of North Battleford, 1091 100th St at 11th Ave, now houses the **Allen Sapp Gallery** (June–Sept daily 10.30am–5.30pm; Oct–May Wed–Sun 1–5pm; ⓦ www.allensapp.com; free), showcase for the work of Allen Sapp, a local Cree. Perhaps the best known of Canada's contemporary native artists, Sapp trawls his childhood recollections of life on the Red Pheasant reserve in the 1930s for most of his material. His simply drawn figures are characteristically cast in the wide spaces of the prairies, whose delicately blended colours hint at a nostalgic regard for a time when his people had a greater sense of community.

In **BATTLEFORD**, the **Fred Light Museum**, 11 20th St E at Central Ave (mid-May to Aug daily 9am–8pm; free), has a substantial collection of early firearms and military uniforms and a replica of an old general store, but is thoroughly upstaged by **Fort Battleford National Historic Site** (mid-May to early Sept daily 9am–5pm; ⓦ www.parkscanada.gc.ca/battleford; $5), overlooking the river valley from the top of a steep bluff just down the road, accessed from Central Ave. At the entrance to the park, the visitors' information centre provides a general introduction to the fort and, next door, the restored barracks contains a display explaining its history, assisted by well-informed, costumed guides. Within the replica stockade stand four original buildings, including the **Sick Horse Stable**, where the delicate constitutions of the Mounties' horses – most of which came from Ontario – were coaxed into accepting the unfamiliar prairie grasses. Centrepiece of the park is the **Commanding Officer's Residence**, which has been returned to its appearance in the 1880s. Broadly Gothic Revival in style, the hewn-log house contains an enormous carved bedhead and a couple of magnificent black and chrome oven ranges, which must have been a nightmare to transport this far west. However, the house was not as comfortable as it seems today, principally because the high ceilings made the rooms almost impossible to heat. As the first commanding officer, James Walker, moaned in 1879, "This morning with the thermometer 37 degrees below, water was frozen on the top of the stove in my bedroom."

Practicalities

All long-distance and local bus services use **North Battleford bus station**, located on the edge of the town centre at 75 E Railway Ave; there's a daily service from Saskatoon at 5.15pm (4.30pm on Sat). The **tourist information centre** (June–Aug daily 8am–8pm; ☎306/445-6226 or 1-800/243-0394) is in the outskirts 2km away, at the junction of hwys 16 and 40 East, and there's also one in the Fred Light Museum in Battleford, at the junction of hwys 4 and 40 (mid-May to Aug daily 9am–8pm; ☎306/937-7111). City buses connect the two towns, and there's also one **taxi** firm, Crown Cab (☎306/445-8155), which charges about $12 for the trip from the bus station to Fort Battleford.

Most of **North Battleford**'s central **hotels** are the dispiriting haunts of the drunk and the dispossessed. Better alternatives include the *Best Canadian Motor Inn*, 11th Ave and 100th St (☎306/445-8115 or 1-888/700-2264, Ⓦwww.bestcdn.com; ❷), with reasonably comfortable rooms, and the pleasant *Tropical Inn*, on Hwy 16 (☎306/446-4700 or 1-800/219-5244, Ⓦwww .tropicalinns.com; ❸–❻), about 1km east along the Yellowhead Hwy from the bus station. North Battleford is short on good **restaurants**, but several cheap, central places have filling menus. Try *Dragon Palace*, 1292 101st St at 13th Ave, for simple Chinese dishes; or *O'Grady's*, 2491 99th St, for standard steak-and-rib fare. *Smitty's Family Restaurant*, 1001 Hwy 16, just outside the centre in the *Tropical Inn*, has good, basic dishes from $9, and *Da Vinci's*, also in the *Tropical Inn*, features some Saskatchewan specialities on its menu.

In **Battleford**, the popular **hotel** *Five Star*, 322 22nd St W (☎306/937-2651; ❶–❸), has simple, clean, air-conditioned rooms, plus large family units with kitchenettes. The town also has the splendid *Eiling Kramer* **campsite** (☎306/937-6212; $12–15; May–Sept), overlooking the river valley from beside Fort Battleford. For **food**, *Pennydale Junction*, in a converted 1908 CNR train station at 92 22nd St and Main St, has great seafood, pizzas and steaks from $12. The **Saskatchewan Handcraft Festival**, held in the town each mid-July, is one of the largest and best for crafts in the province.

Lloydminster

Some 140km northwest of the Battlefords you hit the Saskatchewan–Alberta border, and the drab city of **LLOYDMINSTER**, which was founded in 1903 by a group of two thousand British pioneers known as the Barr colonists. Top draw is the underwhelming **Barr Colony Heritage Cultural Centre** (late May to early Sept daily 9am–8pm; rest of year Wed–Fri noon–5pm, Sat & Sun

1–5pm; $4), located in Weaver Park beside the Yellowhead Hwy at 44th St and 45th Ave, featuring a small display on the founders, together with a couple of art galleries and a wildlife exhibition. Perhaps the most interesting aspect of the city is its geographical location: the 4th Meridian runs right down 50th Ave, the main street. Thirty-metre-high metal border markers, shaped like the survey stakes used by the original surveyors when they laid out the border between the two provinces, line Hwy 16 on the north and south sides, and smaller markers line the main street.

Yet Lloydminster is a popular town for a break in the journey, and has a **tourist office** at 5001 50th Ave (Mon–Fri 8am–5pm; ☎306/825-6180 or 1-800/825-6180). Both Tourism Saskatchewan and Alberta Tourism run seasonal **visitor reception centres** on either side of the border. The **bus station**, served by four buses daily from Saskatoon, is on the Alberta side at 50th St. Lots of **hotels** and **motels** line its two main streets, 44th St (the Yellowhead) and 50th Ave (Hwy 17). The pick of these are the *Best Canadian Motor Inn*, 4320 44th St (☎306/825-4400 or 1-888/700-2264, ⓦwww.bestcdn.com; ❸) with an indoor pool and cable TV; and the *Best Western Wayside Inn* (☎780/875-4404 or 1-800/658-4404; ❸), a sprawling complex just west of the city on Hwy 16 on the Alberta side. For **camping**, *Weaver Park Campground* (☎306/825-3726; May to mid-Oct; $15–20), next door to the heritage centre, has a full range of facilities, including showers and a playground. Options for **eating out** are limited: try *David's Steak House*, 5501 44th St, or one of the pizza chains around town.

Northern Manitoba and Saskatchewan

Stretching from the edges of Lake Winnipeg and Prince Albert National Park all the way to the Northwest Territories and Nunavut, **northern Manitoba and Saskatchewan** is an inhospitable and sparsely inhabited expanse that accounts for roughly half of each province.

The region divides into two slightly different areas, the marginally richer flora and fauna of the **Interior Plains** lying south of the more spartan landscapes of the **Canadian Shield**, which stretches north of a rough curve drawn between La Loche, La Ronge and Flin Flon, whose shallow soils support a gigantic coniferous forest broken up by a complex pattern of lakes and rivers. It's a hostile environment, the deep, cold winter alternating with a brief, bright summer, when the first few centimetres of topsoil thaw out above the permafrost to create millions of stagnant pools of water, ideal conditions for mosquitoes and blackflies. There are compensations: out in the bush or along the shores of Hudson Bay you'll find a sense of desolate **wilderness** that's hard to find elsewhere, and a native wildlife that includes caribou, polar bear and all sorts of migratory birds.

Most of the region is inaccessible and the bulk of its limited highway system was built to service the resource towns just to the north of lakes Winnipeg and Winnipegosis. One of these, the paper-and-pulp complex at **The Pas**, in Manitoba, is served by buses from Dauphin and Winnipeg, and provides a convenient base for the region's two main parks, **Clearwater Lake** and **Grass River**. Similarly, in northern Saskatchewan the tourist-resort-cum-mining-centre **La Ronge** is also a good hub for exploring the outdoors, much of which is best seen along superb and wildly varied canoe routes in several provincial parks.

The key tourist centre in the region is **Churchill**, a remote and windswept township in northern Manitoba, far beyond the reach of the highway network on the southern shore of Hudson Bay (but accessible by train), where the main attractions are the **polar bears** that congregate along the shore from late June to early November.

One word of warning: the boreal forests of the north swarm with voracious insects such as **blackflies** and **mosquitoes**, so don't forget your insect repellent.

The Pas and around

Situated 400km north of Dauphin on Hwy 10, on the southern bank of the Saskatchewan River, **THE PAS** – a former fur-trading and missionary centre founded in 1750 – is a town with no specific sights. However, it does host the annual **Northern Manitoba Trappers' Festival** in the third week of February, four days of revelling that include competitions in a number of traditional pioneer skills like tree-felling, trap-setting, ice-fishing and muskrat-skinning, with the highlight being the World Championship Sled Dog Races and its 50km mushes. If you're in town in mid-August, you can join in the aboriginal celebrations honouring the Cree people during **Opasquiak Indian Days**.

The town's **bus** and **train stations** are right in the centre, a few minutes' walk from the Municipal Offices, 324 Ross Ave (Mon–Fri 9am–1pm; ☎204/623-7256), where you can get basic tourist information. There's also a summer **tourist booth** (June–Aug daily 9am–5pm) at the foot of Edwards Ave, beside the tiny *Devon Park and Kinsmen Campground* (☎204/623-2233 or 1-866/627-1134; $11–18; mid-May to early Oct) and close to **accommodation** on Gordon Ave: the *Golden Arrow* at no. 1313 (☎204/623-5451; ❶), the *Rupert House Hotel* (☎204/623-3201; ❶) and the three-star *Kikiwak Inn* (☎204/623-1800 or 1-888/545-4925, ⓦwww.kikiwakinn.com; ❸–❺). Back in the centre, near the train station, the comfortable *Wescana Inn*, 439 Fischer Ave (☎204/623-5446; ⓦwww.wescanainn.com; ❸), is also a good **place to eat**.

Clearwater Lake Provincial Park

Just 19km north of The Pas, the square-shaped lake and adjoining strip of conif-erous forest that constitute **Clearwater Lake Park** are a favourite haunt of the region's anglers, who come here to catch northern pike, whitefish and highly prized lake trout. The park's amenities are concentrated along Route 287, a turning off Hwy 10, which runs along the lake's southern shore past The Pas airport. Beside the road there are two summer **campsites** (☎204/482-2267 or 1-888/482-2267; mid-May to mid-Sept; $14), and the *New Vickery lodge* (☎204/624-5429 or 1-888/624-5429; ❹–❺; May–Oct). For a **wilderness**

excursion, Clearwater Canoe Outfitters (☎204/624–5606 or 624–5467) rents out a full range of equipment and organizes canoe trips from $25 a day.

Grass River Provincial Park

A further thirty minutes' drive north on Hwy 10 brings you to **Grass River Provincial Park**: several thousand square kilometres of evergreen forest, lake and river interspersed by the granite outcrops of the Canadian Shield. Its channels and lakes were first charted in the 1770s by Samuel Hearne, an intrepid employee of the Hudson's Bay Company, and are still noted as excellent **canoe routes**. Hearne, who became the first European to reach the Arctic Ocean by land, witnessed both the development of the Grass River's fur trade and the cataclysmic effects of the smallpox epidemic that followed. He estimated that about ninety percent of the local Chipewyan population was wiped out in the space of a decade, an indication of the scale of a tragedy whose results were compounded by other European diseases, particularly whooping cough and measles. On this and other matters Hearne was an acute observer of Indian culture and customs. His *Journey to the Northern Ocean* records, for example, the comments of his Chipewyan guide concerning the importance of women:

" 'Women', added he, 'were made for labour; one of them can carry, or haul, as much as two men can do. They also pitch our tents, make and mend our clothing, keep us warm at night; and, in fact, there is no such thing as travelling any considerable distance in this country without their assistance.' "

The most popular canoe route in the park runs 180km from the **Cranberry Lakes**, on the park's western perimeter, to its eastern boundary, where the southern tip of **Tramping Lake** is located near Hwy 39. It's an excursion of about ten days – all of the route's portages are short and fairly easy and there are lots of basic campsites on the way. The start of the canoe route, on the first of the three Cranberry Lakes, is situated close to **CRANBERRY PORTAGE**, a straggling township on Hwy 10, which runs along the western edge of the park. The settlement has its own park **information kiosk**; the small *Cranberry Portage Park* **campsite** (☎204/472–3219; $18; mid-May to Sept), 1km west of Hwy 10 with its own beach; a couple of **hotels**, including the *Northern Inn*, 112 Portage Rd (☎204/472–3231; ❶); and a handful of holiday **lodges** (mid-May to early Oct) along its lakeshore, such as the *Viking Lodge* (☎204/472–3337; ❹). Most of the lodges have boat and canoe rentals, and can arrange guided trips and flights to the remoter lakes. There are other access points to Grass River Park along Hwy 39, which runs along its southern boundary. This road passes three small summer **campsites** (all $10) – *Gyles* (24km east of Hwy 10), *Iskwasum* (40km) and *Reed Lake* (56km) – where park entry points lead to circular canoe trips that can be accomplished within one day.

A worthwhile side-trip can be made from the park to **Wekusko Falls**, about 35km beyond the east boundary of the park along Hwy 39 and then south along a short stretch of gravel road (Hwy 596). Here the Mitishto River drops dramatically in a series of falls and rapids. You can view the spectacle from two suspension footbridges or along the walking trails below.

Flin Flon

At the northern end of Hwy 10, about 60km from Cranberry Portage, the mining township of **FLIN FLON**, on the Manitoba–Saskatchewan border, gouges copper, gold, lead and zinc from a massive seam that was discovered in

1914. A stark, rough-looking town, full of precipitously steep streets, where the houses are built on sheer rock in a barren landscape, Flin Flon takes its unusual name from the hero of an obscure dime-novel entitled *The Sunless City*, which one of the first prospectors was reading at the time of the discovery. In the book, Josiah Flintabbatey Flonatin builds a submarine and enters the bowels of the earth, where he discovers that everything is made of gold. The nearest you'll come to his trip here is on the free guided tours of the town's **Hudson Bay Mining and Smelting Plant** (by appointment ☎204/687-2050; over-16s only). Surprisingly, you'll see greenhouses in the depths of the mine, where warm and humid conditions are perfect for growing flowers such as orchids. The mine was due to shut down in 2004, a move that would have meant the end of Flin Flon, but in the summer of 2000 some $400 million from mining companies (the biggest industrial investment in Manitoba) ensured the mine's and the town's future. There's not much else to see, except in July, when the town hosts the **Trout Festival**, with a parade, a Queen Mermaid Pageant, the Great Northern Duck Race – and the tantalizing smell of frying fish.

Flin Flon's **bus station** is right in the centre at 63 3rd Ave. About 1km to the east, along Hwy 10A, the **tourist office** (May–Sept daily 8am–8pm; ☎204/681-7502) runs the main **campsite** ($13–15; May–Sept) opposite a large statue of the intrepid Flintabbatey Flonatin. Otherwise try the central **hotel** *Royal*, 93 Main St (☎204/687-3437 or 1-800/308-2224; ❶–❸), or, for dorm accommodation, the *Flin Flon Friendship Centre Hostel*, 57 Church St (☎204/687-3900; ❶). For a basic **meal**, try *Mugsy's*, on Main St, or the *Victoria Inn's* restaurant, 160 Hwy 10.

Northern Saskatchewan

The shallow soils of **northern Saskatchewan** are unable to support any form of agriculture, and its native peoples, the **Woodland Cree**, have traditionally survived by hunting, trapping and fishing. In recent times, this precarious and nomadic existence has been replaced by a more settled and restricted life on the reservations which are concentrated around **Lake Athabasca** in the extreme northwest corner of the province. Nearly all the other settlements in the north are mining towns, the result of the discovery of uranium in the 1950s. Of these, **La Ronge**, situated on the edge of the lakes and forests is one of the few that is appealing to visit, thanks to the nearby presence of both **Lac La Ronge** Provincial Park and a section of the **Churchill River**, whose remote waters boast some of the north's longest and most varied canoe routes. Further northwest, near the Alberta border, **Clearwater River** Provincial Park provides some of the region's most challenging white-water canoeing, while at the northernmost limit of the province the **Athabasca Sand Dunes** Provincial Wilderness Park provides a unique getaway for the well heeled with a taste for wilderness.

Although Northern Saskatchewan attracts hundreds of hunters, anglers and canoeists throughout the summer, it has an extremely poor public transport system. There's just one really useful **bus**, a daily service connecting Saskatoon, Prince Albert, Waskesiu (mid-May to mid-Sept only) and La Ronge.

La Ronge and around

Some 350km west of Flin Flon and 242km north of Prince Albert along Hwy 2, the scrawny, straggling resort of **LA RONGE** is sandwiched between the

Wilderness canoeing in northern Saskatchewan

Northern Saskatchewan has an abundance of **canoe routes** sprinkled across its thousands of lakes. It's important, though, that prospective canoeists come fully prepared both in terms of equipment and knowledge of the proposed route. For independent and experienced wilderness travellers, Saskatchewan Environment (⊛**www.se.gov.sk.ca**) issues a comprehensive range of free material that includes route descriptions, lists of outfitters, details of campsites and information on climate, wildlife and potential hazards. Some park offices also sell detailed local maps. The department has offices in a number of towns, but its headquarters are at 3211 Albert St, Regina (Mon–Fri 8am–5pm; ☎306/787-2700). This office operates a **toll-free advice line** in summer on ☎1-800/667-2757. You can also get information on canoe routes from Horizons Unlimited/Churchill River Canoe Outfitters (☎1-877/511-2726, ⊛www.churchillrivercanoe.com) and on other canoe outfitters from the Saskatchewan Outfitters Association (☎306/763-5434, ⊛www.soa.ca). Saskatchewan has a host of **tour operators** running hunting, fishing and canoe excursions into the north of the province from the middle of May to September. A full list of hunting and fishing outfitters is provided in the *Saskatchewan Fishing and Hunting Guide*, while the *Saskatchewan Vacation Guide* lists operators offering canoeing, bird-watching and wildlife-viewing excursions throughout the province. Both books are available through Tourism Saskatchewan (☎306/787-2300 or 1-877/237-2273) and at most tourist offices. For a complete range of topographic maps and canoe-route charts and booklets, plus secondary road maps, contact SaskGeomatics, 2151 Scarth St, Regina (☎306/787-2799, ⊛www.geomatics.isc-online.ca/saskgeo.htm).

road and the western edge of Lac La Ronge. It was home to an isolated Cree community until the road reached here in 1948. Since then, gold mines and forestry operations have started just to the north of town and the area's lakes and rivers have proved popular with visiting canoeists and anglers.

Falling either side of Boardman St, the town is fronted by La Ronge Ave, which runs parallel to the waterfront, the location of the **bus depot**. A few minutes' walk away, in Mistasinihk Place, is the office of the **Saskatchewan Parks Department** (Mon–Fri 8am–noon & 1–5pm; ☎306/425-4245 or 1-800/772-4064) and an interpretive centre (same days and hours) with exhibits on northern lifestyles, crafts and history. The nearest **visitor reception centre** (mid-May to mid-Sept Mon–Fri 8am–9pm, Sat & Sun 10am–8pm; ☎306/425-5311) is 2km south of town beside Hwy 2.

A good base for exploring the region, La Ronge has several reasonably priced and central **hotels** and **motels**. These include the *Drifters Motel*, at the entrance to town, beside Hwy 2 (☎306/425-2224; ❸) and the *La Ronge Motor Hotel*, 1120 La Ronge Ave (☎306/425-2190 or 1-800/332-6735; ❸). There's a series of **campsites** strung along Hwy 102 north of town, the nearest of which is *Nut Point* (☎306/425-4234 or 1-800/772-4064; $13–18; mid-May to Aug), 1km north via La Ronge Ave. One of the few places to **eat** that isn't run-of-the-mill is the vaguely Greek *Kostas II*, 707 La Ronge Ave.

La Ronge is on the western edge of **Lac La Ronge Provincial Park**, which incorporates Lac La Ronge itself and extends north to encompass a number of smaller lakes and a tiny section of the **Churchill River**, once the main route into the northwest for the voyageurs. The Churchill swerves across the width of the province, from west to east, before heading on into Manitoba, its waterways providing some of the region's longest canoe routes. The parks department in La Ronge (☎306/425-4245 or 1-800/772-4064) provides a detailed description of the river and its history in the booklet *Saskatchewan's Voyageur Highway: A Canoe Trip*. The park is one of the few areas in the province where you can hike the Canadian Shield. The 15km **Nut Point Hiking Trail** leaves the campsite and runs along a narrow peninsula that juts into Lac La Ronge, crossing rock ridges through forests and over high, open ridges where you can view the enormous island-studded lake. Less strenuously, these waters are also good for fishing – the walleye, pike and lake trout are delicious. A number of La Ronge **tour operators** and **outfitters** run and equip fishing and canoeing trips into the park, most of them using its web of lakeside holiday **lodges** and **cabins**; the parks department office has the details. There are also several **campsites** along Hwy 102 including the *Missinipe* (☎306/425-4234 or 1-800/772-4064; $9–22; mid-May to Aug) on Otter Lake, where the highway crosses the Churchill River.

North of La Ronge, Hwy 102 deteriorates long before it reaches **MISSINIPE**, 80km away, the home of Horizons Unlimited/Churchill River Canoe Outfitters (☎1-877/511-2726, ⓦwww.churchillrivercanoe.com), a highly recommended wilderness-holiday company. Beyond here, the road joins Route 905, a bumpy 300-kilometre track that leads to the uranium mines around Wollaston Lake.

Clearwater River Provincial Park

Apart from Hwy 2/102, the only other paved road running into the heart of northern Saskatchewan is Hwy 155, which extends as far as the tiny town of **LA LOCHE**, near the Alberta border. From here, a rough, gravel track, Route 955 (the Semchuk Trail), passes through **Clearwater River Provincial Park** before continuing on to the uranium mines of Cluff Lake. The park's main feature is the rugged **Clearwater River Valley**, whose turbulent waters are recommended only to the experienced white-water canoeist – you have to navigate 28 sets of rapids. There's a small and simple free **campsite** (☎306/822-1700; May to mid-Nov) where the river meets the road, but otherwise the nearest accommodation is back in La Loche, 60km to the south. The town has one **motel**, the *Pines Motel* (☎306/822-2600; ❷), located beside the highway, and a parks department office (Mon–Fri 8am–5pm; ☎306/822-1700). Clearwater Raft Tours (☎306/665-7238 or 1-800/661-7275) offers an exciting five-day white-water rafting adventure, including transportation by float plane, services of a guide, tenting accommodation, fishing and all meals.

Lake Athabasca

A particular favourite of the hook-and-bullet brigade – and, in recent years, ecotourists – wild and remote **Lake Athabasca**, close to the 60th parallel, can be reached only by private float plane. This is the region's largest lake, and much of its southern shore is protected as the **Athabasca Sand Dunes** Provincial Wilderness Park, the most northerly sand dunes in the world. Several companies organize excursions to the area that include flights, food, accommodation and boat rental; if you can afford $3000–4000 for a six-day trip, try Athabasca Camps in Saskatoon (☎306/653-5490 or 1-800/667-5490, ⓦwww.athabascalake.com), or TourQuest in Regina (☎306/731-2377). If you want to take an **ecotour** of this remote northern region, Athabasca Eco Expeditions in Saskatoon (☎306/653-5490 or 1-800/667-5490, ⓦwww.athabascalake.com) does one- or two-week summer tours led by aboriginal guides who know the area well.

Churchill

Sitting on the east bank of the Churchill River where it empties into Hudson Bay, **CHURCHILL** has the neglected appearance of many of the settlements of the far north, its unkempt open spaces dotted with the houses of its mixed Inuit, Cree and white population. These grim buildings are heavily fortified against the biting cold of winter and the insects of the summer: ample justification for a local T-shirt featuring a giant mosquito above the inscription "I gave blood in Churchill". That said, the town has long attracted a rough-edged assortment of people with a taste for the wilderness, and nowadays tourists flock here for the wildlife, particularly the polar bears – a lifeline, now that Churchill's grain-handling facilities are underused.

In 1682, the Hudson's Bay Company established a fur-trading post at **York Factory** (see p.616), a marshy peninsula some 240km southeast of today's Churchill. The move was dictated by the fact that the direct sea route here from England was roughly 1500km shorter than the old route via the St Lawrence River, while the Hayes and Nelson rivers gave access to the region's greatest waterways. Within a few years, a regular cycle of trade had been established, with the company's Cree and Assiniboine go-betweens heading south in the autumn to **hunt and trade** for skins, and returning in the spring laden with

Churchill's flora and fauna

Churchill occupies a transitional zone where the stunted trees of the taiga (subarctic coniferous forest) meet the mosses of the tundra. Blanketed with snow in the winter and covered by thousands of bogs and lakes in the summer, this terrain is completely flat until it reaches the sloping banks of the Churchill River and the ridge around Hudson Bay, whose grey-quartzite boulders have been rubbed smooth by the action of the ice, wind and water.

This environment harbours splendid **wildlife**, including Churchill's premier attraction, the **polar bears**, who start to come ashore when the ice melts on the bay in late June. They must then wait for the ice to form again to support their weight before they can start their seal hunt; a polar bear can detect scent from 32km away and can pick up the presence of seals under a metre of snow and ice. The best months to spot bears are September, October and early November, just before the ice re-forms completely.

In mid-June, as the ice breaks on the Churchill River, the spreading patch of open water attracts schools of white **beluga whales**. As many as three thousand of these intelligent, inquisitive and vocal mammals spend July and August around the mouth of the river, joining the **seals**, who arrive in late March for five months. The area around the town is also on one of the major migration routes for **birds** heading north from April to June and returning south in August or early September. Nesting and hatching take place from early June until early July. A couple of hundred species are involved, including gulls, terns, loons, Lapland longspurs, ducks and geese. The star visitor is the rare Ross's Gull, a native of Siberia, which has nested in Churchill for some years now. The *Birder's Guide to Churchill* ($7) by Bonnie Chartier lists them all and is available in the town and at the Eskimo Museum.

Churchill is also a great place to see the **aurora borealis** (Northern Lights), whose swirling curtains of blue, green and white are common in the skies between late August and April; occasionally it's seen all year round, and is at its best from January to March. Finally, in spring and autumn the tundra is a colourful sheet of moss, lichens, flowers and miniature shrubs and trees that include dwarf birch, spruce and cranberry.

pelts they could exchange for the company's manufactured goods. Throughout the eighteenth century, before the English assumed control of all facets of the trade and laid off their native intermediaries, both sides seem to have benefited economically, and the reports of the company's traders are sprinkled with bursts of irritation at the bargains forced on them by the natives. The company was always keen to increase its trade, and it soon expanded its operations to Churchill, building the first of a series of forts here in 1717.

In the nineteenth century the development of faster trade routes through Minneapolis brought decline, and by the 1870s both York Factory and Churchill had become remote and unimportant. Then the development of agriculture on the prairies brought a reprieve. Many of the politicians and grain farmers of this new west were determined to break the trading monopoly of Sault Ste Marie in northern Ontario and campaigned for the construction of a new port facility on Hudson Bay, connected **by rail** to the south through Winnipeg. In the 1920s the Canadian National Railway agreed to build the line, and it finally reached Churchill in 1929. Unfortunately, despite all the efforts of the railway workers in the teeth of the ferocious climate, the port has never been very successful, largely because the bay is ice-free for only about three months a year.

The Town

On the northern side of town, the unprepossessing Bayport Plaza is a good place to start a visit, as it incorporates the **Parks Canada Visitor Reception Centre** (see "Practicalities"), where displays on the history of the fur trade and the Hudson's Bay Company are jazzed up by films dealing with arctic wildlife,

Churchill tour operators

Local wildlife **tour operators** have proliferated in Churchill over the past few years, offering everything from diving with the whales to viewing the polar bears from helicopters.

One of the best value is **Churchill Wilderness Encounter** (☎204/675-2248 or 1-800/265-9458), whose bus meets the train at the station in Churchill. It offers beluga-whale boat trips (July & Aug; $45); a six-day bird-watching adventure ($1895); afternoon nature tours (July–Sept; $45), involving a drive through the taiga, a walk in the Akudlik Marsh and a trip into the boreal forest region; and bird-watching tours (late May to July; $95).

Based in the Bayport Plaza, **North Star Tours** (☎204/675-2356 or 1-800/665-0690) organizes excursions like snorkelling with whales and iceberg-viewing trips in the middle of June from around $70. **Sea North Tours**, 39 Franklin St (mid-June to late Aug; ☎204/675-2195 or 1-888/348-7591), visits the Prince of Wales Fort and listens in on whales using stereo hydrophones (tours 3hr; $75). **Kayaks & Belugas** (May to mid-Sept; ☎204/675-2534) guides paddlers to the whales and icebergs (3hr; $55); no experience necessary. **Tundra Buggy Tours** (July–Nov; ☎204/675-2121 or 1-800/593-8881) has a range of excursions in vehicles specially designed to avoid damaging the tundra (starting from $65 for a half-day tour) – some trips offer overnight lodge accommodation in the heart of the wilderness wildlife area. **Midwest Helicopters** (☎204/675-2576) operates helicopter sightseeing tours ($470 for 30min for up to 4 people) with guaranteed polar-bear sightings. **Northern Expedition Tours** (same phone as Tundra Buggy Tours) is a specialist aurora borealis operator that offers a chance to see the Northern Lights away from the bright lights of Churchill, while **B&B Scuba** (☎204/257-3696) will take you diving amongst the whales for up to a week at a time if you're part of a group (July & Aug only).

Prince of Wales' Fort and the construction of the railway. Opposite the plaza, the Town Centre Complex offers a good view over Hudson Bay and has recreational facilities, including a curling rink, hockey rink, swimming pool, bowling alley and a cinema.

Just down the road, the **Eskimo Museum**, 242 La Vérendrye Ave (June–Aug Mon 1–5pm, Tues–Sat 9am–noon & 1–5pm; Sept–May Mon & Sat 1–4.30pm; donation), houses the Inuit collection of the Oblate Fathers of Mary Immaculate, whose missionary work began around here around 1900. The museum's one large room is dominated by two animal-hide canoes and several stuffed Arctic animals, with Inuit art arranged in cases round the walls. It's a fine range of material, from caribou-antler pictographs and highly stylized soapstone figurines through to walrus-tooth scrimshaws and detailed ivory and stone carvings. The sculptures fall into two distinct periods. Up until the 1940s, the artistic work of the local Inuit was essentially limited to the carving of figurines in walrus ivory, modelled on traditional designs. However, in 1949 a Canadian painter, James Houston, travelled the east coast of Hudson Bay in Québec, encouraging the Inuit to vary their designs and experiment with different materials – which led, in particular, to the development of larger and more naturalistic sculptures carved in soapstone. One corner of the museum functions as a **gift shop** selling a wide range of prints and carvings, plus a good collection of books on the north. Northern Images, a five-minute walk south on Kelsey Boulevard, sells similar work at higher prices – but its profits go back to the producers.

A couple of minutes' walk from the town centre, Churchill's grain elevators and silos stand at the base of a narrow peninsula that sticks out into the mouth of the Churchill River. At the tip, approached along a gravel track, **Cape Merry National Historic Site** (guided tours June Tues, Thurs & Sat 10am–2pm; July & Aug Sat 10am–2pm; free) has the remains of an eighteenth-century gun emplacement and a cairn commemorating the Danish explorer Jens Munck, who led an expedition that was forced to winter here in 1619; most of the crew died from cold and hunger.

On the other side of the estuary, **Prince of Wales' Fort National Historic Site** (free tours daily July & Aug, times dependent on tides and weather conditions – ask at the visitors' centre) is a partly restored eighteenth-century stone fortress that was built to protect the trading interests of the Hudson's Bay Company from the French. Finished in 1771, this massive structure took forty years to complete, but even then it proved far from impregnable. When a squadron of the French fleet appeared in the bay in 1782 the fort's governor, Samuel Hearne, was forced to surrender without firing a shot because he didn't have enough men to form a garrison. The French spiked the cannon and undermined the walls, and after this fiasco the Company never bothered to repair the damage. The Fort is only accessible as part of a guided tour of the Churchill River organized by Sea North Tours (see box opposite).

East of town, a road runs behind the shoreline past a series of rather eccentric attractions. Near the airport, the **polar bear "prison"** is a large hangar-like compound where dangerous bears are kept until they can be released safely. The problem is that some of the beasts wander into town in search of food and, although most can be scared off quite easily, a handful return. These more persistent specimens are shot with tranquillizers and transported to the compound. It's a necessary precaution, as polar bears can run and swim faster than humans and there are occasional horror stories, such as the owner of a fire-damaged house returning to empty his freezer, only to be trapped and killed by a bear. Repeat bear offenders are given three chances, after which they are humanely destroyed.

Practicalities

Churchill is well beyond the reach of Manitoba's highways, but it is connected to Winnipeg and The Pas **by train** along one of the longest railway lines in the world. VIA Rail (☎1-800/561-8630, ⓦwww.viarail.ca) runs a service from Winnipeg (summer five weekly; rest of year three weekly; from $274 return; takes 34hr). There are also regular excursion **flights** from Winnipeg. Churchill's **airport** is 7km from the centre, and each flight attracts the minibuses of the main tour operators, who will provide onward transport for about $10. Alternatively, Churchill Taxi, 31 Thompson St (☎204/675-2345), charges about $12 for the same service. The **train station** is right in the town centre, a few metres from the **Visitor Information Bureau** on Kelsey Boulevard (July & Aug Tues–Fri 8am–1.30pm, Sat 8am–3.30pm; ☎204/675-2022 or 1-888/389-2327) and a five-minute walk from the Bayport Plaza, where there's a **Parks Canada Visitor Reception Centre** (June–Nov daily 1–5pm & 6–9pm; Dec–May Mon–Fri 8am–4.30pm; ☎204/675-8863).

There are no campsites or hostels in Churchill, so visitors are dependent on the town's **hotels**, which are so uniformly drab it's hard to see why they vary in price. All are within easy walking distance of the train station, and all should be booked in advance. The best of the bunch are the *Northern Nights Lodge*, 101 Kelsey Blvd (☎204/675-2403; ❸; June–Nov), with an adjacent restaurant, and the *Polar Inn*, 15 Franklin St (☎204/675-8878; ❻), with mountain bikes for rent. The hotels can get booked up by tour groups so you may prefer to stay at the friendly **B&Bs** run by Vera Gould and her family: Vera's is at 87 Hearne St (☎204/675-2544; ❸); and her son Donald runs the *Polar Bear Bed & Breakfast*, 26 Hearne St (☎204/675-2819; ❸), lending out bikes to guests for free.

Churchill's handful of **restaurants** leave a lot to be desired, with the exception of the expensive *Trader's Table*, 141 Kelsey Blvd, where you can sample caribou burgers, or try the local speciality, arctic char, for around $18. The best snack bar is in the Town Centre Complex, which has burgers from $5; all the hotels also have their own restaurants.

York Factory

The remote **York Factory National Historic Site** (June to mid-Sept daily 8am–5pm, depending on river conditions) lies 240km southeast of Churchill,

---

Canoeing the Seal River

The wild rivers that drain into Hudson Bay constitute some of the most challenging **canoe routes** in Canada, their long stretches of white water demanding considerable planning, experience and skill. One of the more popular is the **Seal River**, whose principal canoe route begins at the tiny Chipewyan village of Tadoule, and then passes through regions of boreal forest and tundra before emptying into Hudson Bay, just 45km west of Churchill. In the summer the estuary is a gathering place for several thousand beluga whales, an amazing sight to witness. There's float-plane transportation to the start of the canoe route and from the mouth of the river at the end, which can take between two and four weeks to reach. For details, contact Dymond Air Services, 23 Selkirk St, Churchill (☎204/675-8875). For something a bit shorter, you can stay at the *Seal River Heritage Lodge* (☎204/675-8875 or 1-888/326-7325) on a three-day ($1450) or six-day package ($2300) including all meals, services of a guide, whale-watching expeditions, canoeing trips and wildlife tours.

at the mouth of the Hayes and Nelson rivers. This was the central storehouse of the northwestern fur trade throughout the eighteenth century, its wooden palisades the temporary home of soldiers and explorers, travellers and traders, and settlers bound for the Red River Colony at present-day Winnipeg. With the amalgamation of the North West and Hudson's Bay companies in 1821, it was here that the new governor **George Simpson** set about the delicate task of reconciling the feuds stirred by a generation of inter-company rivalry. In October he arranged his first formal joint banquet, 73 traders facing each other across two long and narrow tables. It was, according to a contemporary, "dollars to doughnuts [whether it would be] a feed or fight", but Simpson's diplomatic skills triumphed, leading to a successful reorganization of trading operations. In its heyday, there were some fifty buildings within the stockade, including a guesthouse, fur stores, trading rooms, living quarters and shops, but they were all destroyed in the 1930s, with the exception of the **main warehouse** (1832), a sturdy wooden building that serves as a reminder of the fort's earlier significance. Wandering around the desolate site today, it's hard to imagine that it was once the largest community in western Canada. Guided tours of the site are available (June to mid-Sept daily 8am–5pm; contact the Parks Canada Visitor Reception Centre in Churchill ☎204/675-8863; $5).

This remote spot can only be reached by **charter flight** – weather permitting – from Thompson, Churchill or Gillam, a hydroelectric centre on the rail line between Winnipeg and Churchill. Or you can get there by **canoe** along the Hayes River from Norway House on the north shore of Lake Winnipeg – an arduous journey of 600km, which should not be undertaken without advice from the Manitoba Parks Department in Winnipeg (☎204/945-6784 or 1-800/214-6497, ⓦwww.gov.mb.ca). Because of the disturbance to polar bears in the area, camping is not allowed at York Factory. The only **place to stay** is the *Silver Goose Lodge*, and this must be arranged in advance with the owners (☎204/652-2776; ❹). There are no services, and all supplies must be brought in.

Travel details

Trains

Winnipeg to: Brandon North (3 weekly; 2hr 25min); Churchill (summer 5 weekly, rest of year 3 weekly; 34hr); Dauphin (3 weekly; 3hr 55min); Edmonton (3 weekly; 14hr 30min); Jasper (3 weekly; 21hr 15min); Portage La Prairie (3 weekly; 1hr); Saskatoon (3 weekly; 8hr 20min); Sioux Lookout (3 weekly; 6hr 20min); Sudbury (3 weekly; 24hr 40min); The Pas (3 weekly; 11hr 20min); Toronto (3 weekly; 31hr 40min); Vancouver (3 weekly; 38hr 35min).

Buses

Prince Albert to: La Ronge (1 daily; 3hr 15min); Waskesiu (mid-May to mid-Sept 1 daily; 1hr 10min). **Regina** to: Calgary (4 daily; 10hr 15min); Coronach (1 daily; 4hr 40min); Medicine Hat (4 daily; 6hr 15min); Moose Jaw (4 daily; 1hr); Prince Albert (1–2 daily; 6hr 50min); Saskatoon (3–5 daily; 3hr 5min); Swift Current (3 daily; 4hr 15min); Yorkton (3 daily; 2hr 35min–4hr 55min).
Saskatoon to: Calgary (2 daily; 8hr 30min); Edmonton (4 daily; 6hr 30min); Lloydminster (3 daily; 3hr 15min); North Battleford (2–4 daily; 1hr 40min); Prince Albert (1 daily; 1hr 50min); Swift Current (1 daily; 3hr 30min); Yorkton (1 daily; 5hr 5min).
Swift Current to: Eastend (1 daily; 2hr).
Winnipeg to: Brandon (1 daily; 4hr 15min); Dauphin (1–3 daily; 4hr 50min); Gimli (1 daily; 1hr 45min); Grand Beach Provincial Park (1 daily; 1hr 40min); Kenora (5 daily; 2hr 30min); Lac du Bonnet (Mon, Wed, Thurs & Sun 3 daily; 2hr); Neepawa (1–3 daily; 2hr 40min); Portage La Prairie (1–3 daily; 1hr 10min); Regina (4 daily; 8hr); Rennie (1 daily; 2hr); Riding Mountain (1–3 daily; 3hr 30min); Saskatoon

(1–3 daily; 12hr); Sault Ste Marie (3 daily; 16hr);
Sudbury (3 daily; 25hr); Thunder Bay (3 daily; 10hr
35min); Toronto (3 daily; 31hr); West Hawk Lake (1
daily; 2hr 30min); Yorkton (1–3 daily; 6hr 25min).

Flights

Regina to: Calgary (7 daily; 1hr 20min); Saskatoon
(9 daily; 40min); Toronto (5 daily; 3hr); Vancouver
(3 daily; 2hr 30min).

Saskatoon to: Calgary (3 daily; 1hr); Regina (8
daily; 40min); Toronto (5 daily; 4hr); Vancouver
(4 daily; 2hr 10min).
Winnipeg to: Calgary (3 daily; 2hr 20min);
Churchill (Mon–Fri 2 daily; 3hr 40min); Flin
Flon (Mon–Fri 1 daily; 2hr 25min); Regina
(4 daily; 1hr 10min); Saskatoon (4 daily;
1hr 20min); The Pas (Mon–Fri 2 daily; 1hr
30min); Toronto (8 daily; 2hr 20min);
Vancouver (3 daily; 4hr).

6

Alberta
and the Rockies

CHAPTER 6

Highlights

* **Calgary** Let your inner cowboy or cowgirl shine at the annual Stampede in this likeable plains city. **See p.642**

* **Waterton Lakes** Superb hiking and stunning scenery at this small park on the US border. **See p.666**

* **Kananaskis Country** As the crowds stream past to Banff, get out and draw breath. **See p.678**

* **Banff** Hugely popular region at the heart of the Rockies, with sublime scenery and tons of activities. **See p.687**

* **Lake Louise** Magnificent landscapes within easy reach of Banff. **See p.709**

* **Rafting** Get up close and personal with the mountains, out on the water. **See p.724**

* **Jasper** Head north on the legendary Icefields Parkway for some memorable back-country walks. **See p.733**

* **Mount Robson** Explore west of Jasper for breathtaking vistas over the Rockies' highest peak. **See p.742**

* **Yoho** Awesome grandeur and outstanding hikes in a compact setting. **See p.744**

* **Glacier and Revelstoke** Thrilling mountain scenery and award-winning trails west of Yoho. **See p.755**

△ Emperor Falls, Mt Robson Provincial Park

6

Alberta and the Rockies

lberta is Canada at its best. For many people the **Canadian Rockies**, which rise with overwhelming majesty from the prairies, are one of the main reasons for coming to Canada. Few North American landscapes come this loaded with expectation, so it's a relief to find that superlatives are scarcely able to do credit to the beauty or immensity of the forests, lakes, rivers and snowcapped mountains here. Joined to their smaller cousins in the US, the Canadian Rockies extend from the border north for almost 1500km, where they merge with ranges in the Yukon and Alaska, forming the vast watershed of the Continental Divide that separates rivers flowing to the Pacific, Arctic and Atlantic oceans. But the main focus for most visitors is the half-dozen national and provincial parks that lie at the heart of the range, all of them managed with remarkable efficiency and integrity and easily accessible from nearby cities.

If you're approaching the Rockies from the east or the US, you have little choice but to spend time in either Edmonton or Calgary, the transport hubs for northern and southern Alberta respectively. Poles apart in feel and appearance, the two cities are locked in an intense rivalry, in which **Calgary** comes out top in almost every respect. Situated on the Trans-Canada Highway, less than ninety minutes from Banff National Park, it is more convenient than Edmonton whether you plan to take in Yoho, Kootenay, Glacier or Revelstoke, or push on to southern British Columbia and the west coast. It also has far more going for it in its own right: the weather is kinder, the Calgary Stampede is one of the country's rowdiest festivals, and the vast revenues from oil and natural gas have been spent to good effect on its civic infrastructure.

Edmonton is a bleaker city, on the edge of an immense expanse of boreal forest and low hills that stretches to the border of the Northwest Territories and beyond. Bypassed by the Canadian Pacific Railway, which brought Calgary its early boom, Edmonton's main importance to travellers is as a gateway to the

Information and hotel reservations

Alberta Accommodation ⓦ www.alberta-accommodation.com.
Travel Alberta ☎ 1-800/661-8888, ⓦ www.travelalberta.com.

▲ Saskatoon

▲ Regina

CYPRESS HILLS
PROVINCIAL PARK

Lloydminster

Medicine Hat

DINOSAUR
PROVINCIAL PARK

Drumheller

Brooks

Lethbridge

Edmonton

Red Deer

Fort
Macleod

Calgary

High River

Pincher
Creek

Rocky
Mountain
House

Airdrie

WATERTON
LAKES-GLACIER
NATIONAL PARK

Whitecourt

BANFF
NATIONAL
PARK

Canmore

Kananaskis
Country

Elkford

Sparwood

Edson

Banff

KOOTENAY

Crowsnest
Pass

Fernie

Hinton

JASPER
NATIONAL PARK

Lake
Louise

NATIONAL
PARK

Windermere

Kimberley

Cranbrook

Mt. Columbia
3747m

YOHO
NATIONAL
PARK

Radium
Hot Springs

Invermere

Grande Cache

Jasper

Yellowhead
Pass

ICEFIELDS PARKWAY

CANADIAN

Golden

Nelson

GLACIER
NATIONAL
PARK

Revelstoke

ROCKIES

Nakusp

Creston

Mt. Robson
3954m

MOUNT ROBSON
PROVINCIAL PARK

Castlegar

Trail

Valemount

Blue
River

REVELSTOKE
NATIONAL
PARK

Salmon
Arm

Greenwood

WELLS GRAY
PROVINCIAL PARK

Clearwater

Kelowna

100 km

Kamloops

0

U.S.A.

▼ Prince George

▼ Vancouver & Fraser Canyon

▼ Vancouver

Alaska Highway and the Arctic extremities of the Yukon, as well as to northern British Columbia. The **Yellowhead Highway** and Canada's last transcontinental **railway** link Edmonton to the town and park of Jasper in about four hours.

West of the two cities lies an almost unbroken north–south chain of national and provincial parks. At the southern end of the range and coupled with Glacier National Park in the US is small but impressive **Waterton Lakes** National Park. North of here lie a series of less restrictively managed provincial parks, collectively known as **Kananaskis Country**. These exist partly to take the pressure off the adjacent **Banff** National Park, the region's best known park. Further north the range is protected by the much less busy **Jasper** National Park, by far the largest park in the region. The western boundary of both Banff and Jasper parks is also the provincial border, so that adjacent lands are protected in a separate set of parks managed by British Columbia: **Mount Robson Provincial Park**, just west of Jasper – which protects the highest and most dramatic peak in the Canadian Rockies – and **Yoho** and **Kootenay** west of Banff. Two smaller parks, **Glacier** and **Mount Revelstoke**, lie separate and firmly in BC.

Alberta and the Rockies in winter

With a reliable cover of snow, terrific terrain, low prices and generally uncrowded pistes above world-class resorts the Rockies are phenomenally tempting for a **ski or snowboard** vacation. The area is also ideal for a host of other **winter sports** like cross-country skiing, snowshoeing, dog sledding and snowmobiling (though the latter is not allowed in national parks). Opportunities for ice climbing, skating, canyon crawling and ice fishing are also plentiful. The season at most resorts runs from mid-December until the end of May, with the best conditions usually in March, when the days are getting warmer and longer, the snow is deepest and resort accommodation – hard to come by during Christmas week, the mid-February school holidays and at Easter – easy to find.

Best known and invariably the busiest and most expensive resorts are those in **Banff National Park**. All within easy reach of Banff, these are the small, steep and taxing **Mount Norquay**; the well-rounded intermediate-friendly **Sunshine Village**; and the vast, varied and hugely challenging **Lake Louise**. The three promote themselves with a common lift-ticket system. Locals make up a sizeable chunk of the business: weekends and holidays are peak times, leaving working weekdays particularly quiet. Smaller-scale alternatives within striking distance of Banff are in Kananaskis Country. Here **Nakiska** is one of the most user-friendly resorts on the continent, with state-of-the-art facilities and plenty of fine cross-country skiing. **Fortress Mountain**, 15km south, is a much smaller area, where you're likely to share the slopes with school groups and families. A glorious three-hour drive north of Banff into **Jasper National Park** through craggy montane scenery along the Icefields Parkway lies **Marmot Basin**. A far more modest affair than the ski areas surrounding Banff, it nevertheless has the advantage of being both quieter and less expensive. The town of Jasper, centre of the skiing area, is less commercial than Banff, and its surroundings remain more conspicuously wild, with almost limitless cross-country skiing possibilities.

Aside from these big names the region also contains many other equally worthy, though less accessible resorts, further west in the British Columbia Rockies. Blessed with much the same light snow that's made the whole region famous – with the added advantage of much milder temperatures – this area has the extra benefit of being located outside strictly regulated national park lands.

The result has been not only the emergence of the world's highest concentration of heli-skiing operations, but also both heavy investment in the industry and an ongoing programme of rapid expansion at resorts here. The newest and closest to Banff is **Kicking Horse**. Though still in its infant stages of growth, given the fabulous quality of its expert terrain, it is tipped by many to steal much of Banff's business. South along the western fringe of the Rockies, **Panorama** is a fantastic mountain for cruising and carving, with a superlative setting for its quiet resort village. Another couple of hours' drive south is the cheerful family-orientated ski hill **Kimberley**, where the quantity of spacious ideal beginner and intermediate terrain almost distracts from the presence of a few incredible bump runs. Multi-day tickets here are interchangeable with those at **Fernie**, with its bountiful mountain bowls and ridges, becoming Banff's greatest regional competitor for the international ski trade.

Edmonton and northern Alberta

Unless transport connections oblige you to pass through **Edmonton**, there's no substantial reason, apart from the Folk Music Festival, to visit the more downbeat of Alberta's pair of pivotal cities. It is, though, a starting point from which you can either head west into the Rockies and Jasper National Park, or aim for the unimaginable vastness of the far northern interior. **Northern Alberta** contains the only all-weather road link to Yellowknife, capital of the Northwest Territories, but other than **Wood Buffalo National Park** – the largest protected area in Canada – and a surfeit of fishing possibilities, the region has almost nothing to waylay most casual visitors.

Edmonton

Alberta's provincial capital, **EDMONTON** is among Canada's most northerly cities, and at times – notably in the teeth of its bitter winters – it can seem a little too far north for comfort. Situated above the waters of the North

Edmonton addresses

Addresses in Edmonton can look complicated. Avenues run east–west, with numbers increasing as you travel further north, while streets run north–south, the numbers increasing as you move westwards. This is easy enough, but note that building numbers tend to be tacked onto the end of street numbers: for instance, 10021-104th Ave is building number 21 on 100th St, at the intersection with 104th Ave.

Saskatchewan River, whose park-filled valley winds below the high-rises of downtown, the city tries hard with its festivals, parks, restaurants and urban-renewal projects. With a downtown area that still has the somewhat unfinished feel of a frontier town, however, it's perhaps appropriate that the premier attraction for the vast majority of visitors is a shopping centre, the infamous **West Edmonton Mall**. This certainly has curiosity value, but not enough to merit a special journey here. Downtown has a handful of modest sights, though most enjoyment in the city is to be had in **Old Strathcona**, a rejuvenated "historic" district south of the North Saskatchewan River filled with heritage buildings, modest museums and plenty of eating and drinking venues. Edmonton lacks the big set-piece museums of Calgary and Vancouver, but its **Space and Science Centre** is a sight within a whisker of the first rank.

Some history

Edmonton's site attracted aboriginal peoples for thousands of years before the arrival of white settlers, thanks to the abundance of local **quartzite**, used to make sharp-edged stone weapons and tools. **Fur traders** arrived in the eighteenth century, attracted by river and forest habitats that provided some of Canada's richest fur-producing territory. Better still, the area lay at the meeting point of the territory patrolled by the Blackfoot to the south and the Cree, Dene and Assiniboine to the north. Normally these aboriginal peoples would have been implacable enemies, but around Edmonton's future site they were able to coexist when trading with intermediaries like the North West Company, which built Fort Augustus on Edmonton's present site in 1795. The fort was joined later the same year by **Fort Edmonton**, a redoubtable log stockade built by William Tomison for the Hudson's Bay Company (and named in fine sycophantic fashion after an estate owned by Sir James Winter Lake, the Hudson's Bay Company's deputy governor).

Though the area soon became a major trading district, **settlers** arrived in force only after 1870, when the HBC sold its governing right to the Dominion of Canada. The decline of the fur trade in around 1880 made little impact, as the settlement continued to operate as a staging point for travellers heading north. Worldwide demand for grain also attracted settlers to the region, now able to produce crops despite the poor climate thanks to advances in agricultural technology. Crucially, though, the first trans-Canada railway was pushed through Calgary at Edmonton's expense, and when a spur was built by the Edmonton Railway Company in 1891 it finished south of the town at Strathcona, where a new settlement developed. The city only became firmly established with the Yukon gold rush of 1897, and only then through a scam of tragic duplicity. Prompted by the city's outfitters, newspapers lured prospectors with the promise of an "All Canadian Route" to the gold fields that avoided Alaska and the dreaded Chilkoot Trail (see p.1004). In the event, this turned out to be a largely phantom trail across 3000km of intense wilderness. Hundreds of men perished as they pushed north; many of those who survived, or who never set off, ended up settling in Edmonton. World War II saw the city's role reinforced by its strategic position relative to Alaska, while its post-war growth was guaranteed by the **Leduc oil strike** in 1947. By 1956 some three thousand wells were in production within 100km of the city. If Edmonton has achieved any fame since, it has been in the field of **sports**, as the home of Wayne Gretzky, the greatest player in ice-hockey history. Oil money continues to bankroll all sorts of civic improvements, though never quite manages to disguise the city's rather rough-and-ready pioneer roots.

Arrival, information and transport

Edmonton is one of the easiest places to reach in western Canada. Its road and rail links are excellent, and the international **airport** (code YEG; ⓦ www.edmontonairports.com), 29km south of downtown off Hwy 2 (Calgary Trail), is served by many airlines. There's a small **visitor information desk** (Mon–Fri 7.30am–11.30pm, Sat & Sun 10am–11.30pm; ☎780/890-8382 or 1-800/268-7134) in the arrivals area; **foreign exchange** facilities (daily 5am–11pm) are upstairs in departures. (Note that the city centre airport north of downtown, code YXD, still occasionally mentioned in tourist material, closed to almost all commercial traffic in 1996.) A shuttle **bus**, the Sky Shuttle (daily every 20–30mins 4.30am–12.15am; $11 one-way; ☎780/465-8515 or 1-888/438-2342), runs to downtown hotels on three different routes – two serving the university district and one west of the city; the bus leaves from outside arrivals, and you buy tickets from the driver. A taxi costs around $35. The airport shuttle's "West End" route will take you directly to the West Edmonton Mall (see p.633); this bus runs every 45 minutes on weekdays and every hour on weekends. The Jasper Express service links Edmonton airport directly with Jasper (☎1-800/661-4946).

The VIA Rail **station** is some 3km northwest of downtown at 12360-121st St (ticket office usually daily 8am–3.30pm, longer hours when trains are due; ticket office ☎780/422-6032; VIA Rail ☎1-800/561-8630, ⓦ www .viarail.ca). The Greyhound **bus terminal** (daily 5.30am–midnight; depot ☎780/413-8747, Greyhound ☎1-800/661-8747, ⓦ www.greyhound.ca) is also central at 10324-103rd St, within easy walking distance of central downtown. **Red Arrow** buses serving Calgary (four daily; ☎780/424-3339 or 1-800/232-1958, ⓦ www.redarrow.pwt.ca) use their terminal at the *Howard Johnson Plaza* hotel at 10010-104th St.

Tourist information centres can be found at the airport in arrivals and dotted around the city, but the most central is on the Pedway Level (one level down from the street and pretty well hidden – follow signs for "Economic Development Edmonton") in the Shaw Conference Centre, 9797 Jasper Ave NW (Mon–Fri 8.30am–4pm; ☎780/496-8400 or 1-800/463-4667, ⓦ www.tourism.ede.org). All have all the usual maps and pamphlets and can also help with accommodation. There's another big information centre south of the city at 2404 Calgary Trail Northbound SW, site of the Imperial Leduc 1 Oil Derrick and Interpretive Centre (June to early Sept daily 8am–9pm; rest of year Mon–Fri 8.30am–4.30pm, Sat & Sun 9am–5pm). For **tours** Out an' About Travel (☎780/909-8687) has tours in and around the city; Edmonton Discovery (☎780/482-5991) runs nature tours; and Nite Tours (☎780/453-2134) has after-dark excursions on London double-decker buses.

The downtown area is easily negotiated **on foot**. Longer journeys can be made using Edmonton Transit, an integrated **bus and light-rail** (LRT) system. Interchangeable tickets for bus and LRT cost $1.65; day-passes cost $5. You can buy tickets on buses or from machines in the ten LRT stations. Transfers are available from drivers on boarding for use on other services for ninety minutes. The LRT is free between Grandin and Churchill stations (Mon–Fri 9am–3pm, Sat 9am–6pm only). Call ☎780/496-1611 for route and timetable **information** or visit the Customer Services Outlet at Church LRT Station, 99th St (Mon–Fri 8.30am–4.30pm).

Accommodation

Edmonton has no shortage of **hotels**, due to its importance among business travellers. As the city sees fewer tourists than Calgary, its budget **accommodation** is more available but also less salubrious than that of its southern neighbour. However, there are plenty of reasonably priced beds in the big middle-ranking hotels, especially out of season. **Motels** can be found in the

Edmonton's festivals

Hardly any area of entertainment goes uncelebrated by a festival at some time of the year in Edmonton, the self-proclaimed "Festival City". There's almost always something good on. One of the best events – and one of the few to merit a special pilgrimage here – is the **Edmonton Folk Music Festival** (☎780/429-1899), rated the best in North America by *Rolling Stone*; it's held at Gallagher Park (near the Muttart Conservatory) at the end of the first week in August. Also well regarded are the **International Street Performers Festival** (☎780/425-5162), which attracts over 1000 street performers in early July; the **International Jazz City Festival** (☎780/432-7166) at the end of June; and the increasingly popular August **Fringe Festival**, or Fringe Theatre Event (☎780/448-9000), a ten-day theatrical jamboree that's turned into one of the largest festivals of its kind in North America. The more contrived and commercial **Klondike Days** (☎780/471-7210 or 423-2822) is less compelling, a blowout that claims to be the continent's largest "outdoor entertainment" but has rather too obviously been cobbled together to steal some of Calgary's Stampede thunder. Held for ten days during July, this popular outing revolves around a re-creation of the 1890s gold-rush era, with plenty for kids, and a panoply of events: one of the best is "A Taste of Edmonton", where 40-odd local restaurants set up stalls and let you taste tidbits from their menus.

unlovely outskirts of the city, the main concentrations being along Stony Plain Rd (northwest of downtown) and on the Calgary Trail (south).

For a free **accommodation reservation** service, contact Alberta Express Reservations (☎780/464-3515 or 1-800/884-8803, ⊛www.hotelforyou.com). For details of **B&B** lodgings, contact the visitor centre or Alberta Central Bed & Breakfast Association (☎780/437-2568, ⊛www.bbcanada.com/albertacentral); however, hotel beds in the city are generally not expensive, so you won't necessarily make much of a saving by opting for a B&B.

Hotels and motels

Alberta Place Suite Hotel 10049-103rd St ☎780/423-1565 or 1-800/661-3982, ⊛www.albertaplace.com. Large, well-equipped suites with kitchens and extra facilities; weekly rates available. **❹**

Coast Edmonton Plaza Hotel 10155-105th St ☎780/423-4811 or 1-800/663-1144, ⊛www.coasthotels.com. Edmonton's top-of-the-pile 299-room hotel is worth considering if you want modern facilities rather than the *Macdonald*'s old-world charm (see below). **❻**

Days Inn Downtown 10041-106th St ☎780/423-1925 or 1-800/267-2191, ⊛www.daysinn.com. Mid-sized and renovated central motel with parking just off Jasper Ave. **❹**

Econo Lodge Downtown 10209-100th Ave ☎780/428-6442 or 1-800/613-7043. Reliable downtown motel with covered parking, TV, phone and usual facilities. **❹**

Edmonton House Suite Hotel 10205-100th Ave ☎780/420-4000 or 1-800/661-6562, ⊛www.edmontonhouse.com. Bigger (300 suites) and more expensive than the *Alberta Place*, but rooms have balconies and views; also an indoor pool and a free shuttle to the West Edmonton Mall. **❺**

Grand Hotel 10266-103rd St ☎780/422-6365 or 1-888/422-6365. Handily located near the bus terminal, this hotel is anything but grand: its 65 rooms, only some with private bath, are used mainly by long-stay residents. **❷**

Inn on Seventh 10001-107th St ☎780/429-2861 or 1-800/661-7327, ⊛www.innon7th.com. Modern, quiet and civilized high-rise, with variously priced rooms; probably the best of the middle-range hotels and close to two good restaurants – the *Portico* and *Café Select*. **❹**

Hotel Macdonald 10065-100th St ☎780/424-5181 or 1-800/441-1414, ⊛www.fairmont.com. One of the big historic "railway" hotels run by Canadian Pacific, and undoubtedly the first choice if you want to stay in Edmonton in traditional style. Some rooms are a little small for the price, but there are lots of facilities including pool and health club. **❼**

Hostels

Hostelling International Edmonton (HI) 10647-81st Ave ☎780/988-6836 or 1-877/467-8336, ⊛www.hihostels.ca. This 104-bed HI hostel in a former convent in the Old Strathcona district is not so convenient for downtown, though the airport shuttle will drop you close by if you ask. Plenty of smart facilities, including laundry, library, bike rental and roomy kitchen. Check-in after 11am; open 24hr with no curfew. Dorm beds $18–20, plus some private rooms. **❶**

St Joseph's College 114th St & 89th Ave ☎780/492-7681. Small, cheap and popular student rooms; reservations required in summer. Out of the centre but well served by buses, including the #43. **❶**

YMCA 10030-102A Ave ☎780/421-9622. Men and women are welcome in this clean, refurbished building in an excellent downtown location. Simple three-bunk dorms ($20; 2 nights maximum), small private singles and doubles (from $55) are available. Weekly and monthly rates. **❷**

Campsites

Androssan Campground Located 18km east of downtown on Hwy 16; 24 free sites, but no water or facilities other than fire pits.

Half Moon Lake Resort 21524 Township Rd 520, Sherwood Park ☎780/922-3045, ⊛www.halfmoonlakeresort.com. A large 229-site private campsite with extensive facilities and outdoor activities, 29km east of town on 23rd Ave/Hwy 520 and then 4km down a signposted side road. May to early Oct. $19.

Rainbow Valley Campground 13204-45th Ave ☎780/434-5531. The only site within the city limits: 85 sites off the Whitemud Freeway at 119th St and 45th Ave, in Whitemud Park. It's full by afternoon in summer, so arrive early or be sure to book. Mid-April to mid-Oct. $15.

Shakers Acres Tent and Trailer Park 21530-103rd Ave ☎780/447-3564. A rather exposed 170-site ground northwest of the city north of Stony Plain Rd; exit Hwy 16 at Winterburn Rd. April–Oct. $14.

The City

Edmonton feels oddly dispersed, even in the six-block **downtown** area around Sir Winston Churchill Square and along the main east–west drag, **Jasper Ave** (101st Ave). Bounded to the south by the North Saskatchewan River, this grid holds a few assorted points of interest, though much of the younger and more cosmopolitan Edmonton resides south of the river in **Old Strathcona** (see also "Eating and drinking"). For the **West Edmonton Mall**, the **Space and Science Centre**, and the **Provincial Museum**, you'll need to take transport west from downtown. To stretch your legs, wander up and down the big string of attractive parks that protects the river, or cross the Low Level Bridge to the **Muttart Conservatory**, another worthwhile sight consisting of four space-age glass pyramids filled with flora and natural-history displays.

Downtown

Downtown Edmonton only really comes alive as a place to wander on sunny days when office workers pour out for lunch; otherwise it's really not much of a place to linger unless you're in town for one of the city's many festivals. However, with time to kill the following low-key sites would keep you occupied. The **Edmonton Art Gallery** (Mon–Wed 10.30am–5pm, Thurs & Fri 10.30am–8pm, Sat, Sun & holidays 11am–5pm; $4, free Thurs 4–8pm), part of the Civic Centre on 99th St and 102nd Ave on the north edge of Sir Winston Churchill Square, deals mainly in modern Canadian artists, though it also hosts many visiting exhibitions. To get here, if you're not already downtown, take the #2 bus or LRT to Churchill station. More satisfyingly offbeat is the **Edmonton Police Museum and Archives** on the third floor of the central police station at 9620-103A Ave (Mon–Sat 9am–3pm, closed public holidays; free), which traces the long arm of Albertan law enforcement from the formation of what would become the RCMP (Royal Canadian Mounted Police) in 1873 to the city's current flatfoots. Marvel at handcuffs, old jail cells and a stuffed rat that served time as an RCMP mascot.

Walk across the Low Level Bridge to the distinctive glass pyramids of the **Muttart Conservatory** (Mon–Fri 9am–6pm, Sat & Sun 11am–6pm; $4.75), just south of downtown and the river at 9626-96A St. Three high-tech greenhouses reproduce tropical, temperate and arid climates, complete with the trees and plants (and occasional exotic birds) which flourish in them; a fourth houses a potpourri of experimental botanical projects and temporary exhibitions. If you don't want to walk, take **bus** #51 (Capilano) travelling south on 100th St just south of Jasper Ave as far as 98th Ave and 97A St, then walk one block south. Finally, you might stop by for a free guided tour of the domed sandstone **Alberta Legislature Building** (March to late May & early Sept to Feb Mon–Fri 9am–4.30pm, Sat & Sun noon–5pm; late May to early Sept Mon–Fri 8.30am–5pm, Sat & Sun 9am–5pm) south of Jasper Ave on 97th Ave and 107th St (the nearest LRT station is Grandin). Set in the manner of a medieval cathedral over an ancient shrine, it was built in 1912 on the original site of Fort Edmonton. Topped by a vaulted dome, it's a big city landmark, its interior reflecting the grandiose self-importance of the province's early rulers, who imported wood for their headquarters from as far afield as Belize: the marble came from Québec, Pennsylvania and Italy, the granite from rival British Columbia. Just to the north, amidst parkland that flanks the building, stands the **Alberta Legislative Assembly Interpretive Centre**, where you can learn more than you probably want to know about Alberta's political history and the building in which much of it took place (same hours; ☎780/427-7362 for tour information and booking).

Old Strathcona

The **Strathcona** district south of the North Saskatchewan River grew up at the end of the nineteenth century, thanks to a decision by the Calgary and Edmonton Railway Company (C&E) to avoid the expense of a bridge across the North Saskatchewan River by concluding a rail spur from Calgary south of the river and Edmonton proper. In 1912, when its population had reached about 7500, the new town was incorporated into the city. Today the streets and many of the older buildings have been spruced up in a manner typical of urban-renewal projects – lots of new pavements and fake period street furniture. This said, it's still the city's best-preserved old quarter, and the nicest to wander around on a sunny day. Plenty of buses run here from downtown, or you can walk across the river via the Walterdale or High Level bridges. The best approach is to take the LRT to University station and board buses #8, #43 or #46 to 104th St and 82nd Ave.

The area centres on **Whyte Avenue** (82nd Ave) to the south, 109th St to the west, and 103rd to the east. Most of the cafés, restaurants and shops are on or just off Whyte or 103rd, which makes the **Old Strathcona Foundation** office (summer Mon–Fri 8.30am–4.30pm; rest of year Tues & Wed 8.30am–4.30pm), at 401-10324 Whyte Ave, on the corner of these two thoroughfares, a sensible first port of call. Here you can pick up pamphlets detailing walks and drives that take in the area's historic buildings. Just to the north, on 83rd Ave, is the **Old Strathcona Farmers' Market** (July & Aug Sat 8am–3pm, Tues & Thurs noon–4pm; rest of year Sat 8am–3pm; free), a happy hunting ground for picnic supplies and craft goods. If you tire of wandering or sitting in cafés, you can give a little structure to your exploration by heading for one or both of the area's two small museums. Rail buffs should check out the **C&E Railway Museum**, 10447-86th Ave (June to Aug Tues–Sat 10am–4pm; winter by appointment; $2; ☎780/433-9739), a collection of railway memorabilia, costumes and photos housed in a replica of Strathcona's original 1891 station. Nostalgia buffs might make for the **Telephone Historical Information Centre**, 10437-83rd Ave (Tues–Fri 10am–4pm, Sat noon–4pm; $3), a collection of exhibits and displays housed in Strathcona's original 1912 telephone exchange.

Provincial Museum of Alberta

Housed in a drab building well out in the western suburbs – a ten-minute drive from downtown – at 12845-102nd Ave, the **Provincial Museum of Alberta** (daily 9am–5pm; $6.50) makes a reasonable introduction to the history, culture, flora and fauna of western Canada, worthwhile if Edmonton is your first stop in the region. To reach it by **bus**, take the #1, #14, #100, #111, #113, #114 or #120 buses heading west to "Jasper Place" on Jasper Ave. **Natural history** exhibits include painted dioramas and stuffed animals, taxidermy being the stock in trade of virtually all western Canada's museums; by far the best section concerns the region's bison herds and their virtual extinction. Other displays include a humdrum collection of domestic appliances, a couple of beautiful chrome stoves and vintage jukeboxes and a rundown of the **native peoples** of the province. This last collection includes a series of state-of-the-art multimedia displays that do justice to the history and culture of the Blackfoot and other aboriginal cultures with displays of art, artefacts and other exhibits. Other engaging parts of the museum are the Bug, a showcase of live and often exotic insects, and "Earth's Changing Face", a geological display of gems, minerals, rocks and dinosaur exhibits. The museum also comes into its own when hosting temporary and travelling exhibitions from collections and museums around the world – ask at the visitor centre for details of the latest exhibitions.

Fort Edmonton Park and the Space Centre

Located southwest of the city on a deep-cut bend of the North Saskatchewan River at the southwest end of Quesnell Bridge and Fox Drive, the 158-acre **Fort Edmonton Park** (daily late May to late June Mon–Fri 10am–4pm, Sat & Sun 10am–6pm; late June to early Sept daily 10am–6pm; rest of Sept Mon–Sat 11am–3pm, Sun & holidays 11am–6pm; $7.25 late June to early Sept, otherwise $5.50) undertakes to re-create the history of white settlement in Edmonton during the nineteenth century. Everything has been built from scratch and, while you can't fault the attention to detail, the pristine woodwork of the supposedly old buildings hardly evokes period authenticity (though the carpentry methods are apparently those used around 1846). To get here take the LRT to University station and there pick up buses #4, #30, #32 or #106 to Fox Drive, Whitemud Drive and Keillor Rd, about ten-minutes' walk from the site, which is off the Whitemud Freeway near the Quesnell Bridge. The heart of the complex is a facsimile of **Fort Edmonton**, a fur-trading post dominated by the Big House, former home of the Chief Factor, John Rowland, head of the (then) ill-defined Saskatchewan District between 1828 and 1854. Arranged around the house are the quarters of the 130 or so people who called the fort home and who are now represented by appropriately dressed guides pretending to be blacksmiths, shopkeepers and schoolteachers from the era. Edmonton's later, pre-railway age is represented by a rendition of Jasper Ave as it appeared in 1885, while two other streets simulate 1905 and 1920, complete with working steam engines and trams, which you can ride at no additional cost, to bolster the period effect.

The splendid **Edmonton Space and Science Centre**, in Coronation Park, 11211-142nd St, is one of the city's principal attractions (Tues–Sun 10am–8.30pm; $6.95, Combo Pack $11.95 includes Zeidler Star Theatre Shows, exhibits and scientific demonstrations or one IMAX film presentation; ⓦwww.edmontonscience.com). The complex has two main attractions: the **Margaret Zeidler Star Theatre** (daily 11am–7pm) houses Canada's largest planetarium dome and several galleries, and presents different laser and star shows hourly; and the **IMAX Theatre**, housed with a café and shop in the so-called Lower Gallery, is a large-screen cinema with special-format films and laser shows (prices and times vary according to shows). Elsewhere, the Middle Gallery features a range of temporary exhibitions on scientific and technological themes, while the Upper Gallery contains the **Challenger Centre** and its "Astronaut Missions", designed to allow you to make simulated space missions. There are also assorted displays on advanced communications technology, and a selection of the various science demonstrations you can expect to see around the centre throughout the day. Computers are dealt with in the Dow Computer Lab, while budding astronomers can check in to the centre's **Observatory** (weather allowing Fri 8pm–midnight, Sat & Sun 1–5pm & 8pm–midnight). To get here on public transport take a #5 (Westmount) bus travelling west on 102nd Ave and then north on 124th St – ask the driver to tell you when you're close.

West Edmonton Mall

"Your Adventure Awaits" announces the brochure to **West Edmonton Mall** (ⓦ www.westedmall.com), preparing you for a place that gets eleven mentions in the *Guinness Book of World Records*, including its main claim to fame as the largest shopping mall in the world. Built at a total cost of $1.1 billion, the complex extends over the equivalent of 115 American football fields (or 48 city blocks) and boasts more than 800 shops – of which some 110 are restaurants – plus nineteen cinemas, and eleven department stores. There's almost a queue of superlatives. Its car park is the world's largest, with room for 20,000 cars; it has the world's largest water park (fifty million litres of water); it uses enough power to run a town of 50,000 people. The mall's effect on Edmonton has been double-edged: it employs 15,000 people but has captured thirty percent of the city's retail business, thus crippling the downtown shopping area, though it has also succeeded, to everyone's surprise, in attracting twenty million visitors a year (that's 55,000 a day).

Funnily enough, many of the shops are rather downmarket (retail hours are Mon–Fri 10am–9pm, Sat 10am–6pm, Sun noon–6pm), though the sheer size of the place is enough to keep you browsing all day. But its size aside it's the clutch of extra attractions that make the mall unique. Among these are the world's only **indoor bungee jump** (about $60 and up) and the world's largest indoor lake (122m long). The latter is part of a cluster of attractions known as **Deep Sea Adventure** (Mon–Thurs 11pm–4.30pm, Fri & Sat 11am–7.30pm, Sun 11am–5.30pm; $13), containing a full-sized replica of Columbus's *Santa Maria*, and four working submarines – more than are owned by the Canadian navy – offering an underwater trip past some 200 different species of marine life. Other distractions here include dolphin shows ($2), canoe rentals, scuba diving and an underwater aquarium ($3 on its own) laced with the inevitable sharks.

Then there's the world's largest indoor **amusement park**, the Galaxyland (Mon–Thurs noon–8pm, Fri & Sat 10am–10pm, Sun 11am–7pm; day-pass $24.95), which features such attractions as the *Drop of Doom*, a thirteen-storey "free-fall experience", and the fourteen-storey *Mindbender* triple-loop roller coaster. The latter, it comes as no surprise to learn, is the world's largest indoor roller coaster. The **World Waterpark**, by contrast, is a superb collection of vast swimming pools, immense water slides and wave pools (Mon–Thurs noon–7pm, Fri & Sat 10am–8pm, Sun 11am–6pm; day-pass $29.95, cheaper after 5pm). If you've still any energy, you can also ice-skate on a National Hockey League-size skating rink ($4.50 a session, skate rental $3). You could round off the day or indulge yourself further in one of the mall's many **cinemas** (including IMAX), the Ice Palace, Dolphin Presentations, Sea Life Caverns, Professor Wem's Golf Adventure, or a variety of clubs.

If you want to go the whole hog, then spend the night in the 354-room **Fantasyland Hotel** (ⓣ 780/444-3000 or 1-800/661-6454; ❼) where 118 of the rooms are intricately equipped and decorated to fulfil various assorted fantasies: Roman, Hollywood, Arabian, Victorian Coach, African, Igloo, Canadian Rail and, most intriguing of all, Truck. Cheaper rooms are available without Jacuzzis and mirrored ceilings. There are over a hundred places to **eat** – the best of which are listed below, some lined up on two "theme" streets: Europa Boulevard and a New Orleans-style Bourbon St.

Bus services to the mall heading west out of downtown include #100, #109, #111 and #113. The monster's location, so far as it has an address (it has five different postal codes and 58 entrances – remember which one you parked by if you've come by car), is 170th St and 87th Ave. Maps are available throughout the main building at information booths, where you can also get

information and any number of facts and figures. To save tired feet, you can rent a scooter from about $6 an hour.

Eating, drinking and nightlife

Edmonton has 2000-odd **restaurants**, some of them very good. There's plenty in or near downtown, but if you want a bit of nocturnal zip to go with your meal you'd do best to head out to **Old Strathcona**, a vibrant district of café culture, nightlife and alternative arts located principally along 82nd (Whyte) Ave between 102nd and 105th streets – any bus marked "University Transit Centre" from 100th St will get you there. Ethnic options – notably restaurants serving Edmonton's populations of Ukrainian and Eastern European origin – complement the standard Italian-influenced cuisine or steak-and-salmon offerings. Otherwise, the stalls in the downtown mall and streetfront snack bars are lively at lunch time, and all the usual fast-food, snack and breakfast options are available. **Beer** drinkers should be sure to try the local real ale, Big Rock.

Edmonton's enthusiastic self-promotion as Canada's "Festival City" may have something to do with its relative shortage of indigenous **nightlife**. There are any number of small-time nightspots, especially in Old Strathcona, putting on live music, but larger clubs capable of attracting big names are thin on the ground. Such big-name acts as do appear – as well as theatre companies, **Alberta Ballet** and **Edmonton Opera** – tend to use the University of Alberta's Jubilee Auditorium, 87th Ave and 114th St (Ⓦ www.jubileeauditorium.com), and the Citadel Theatre, 9828–101A Ave (Ⓦ www.citadeltheatre.com). Some companies, plus the **Edmonton Symphony Orchestra** (Ⓦ www.edmontonsymphony .com), use the excellent Francis Winspear Centre for Music, 4 Sir Winston Churchill Square (Ⓦ www.winspearcentre.com). The season for most of the city's dozen or more theatre companies runs from May to September. For revivals, foreign films and art-house **cinema**, try the old Princess Theatre, 10337–82nd Ave (Ⓣ 780/433-0728). The best **listings** source is the free weekly *Vue* (published Thurs; from stores, hotels and kiosks), as well as the entertainment sections of the city's main newspapers, the *Edmonton Journal* and the *Sun*. **Tickets** for most classical music, dance, opera, theatre and other events – including big-name concerts and Edmonton Oilers **ice-hockey** games, which are played in the Skyreach Centre (formerly the Edmonton Coliseum), 118th Ave and 74th St – are available from Ticketmaster outlets (Ⓣ 780/451-8000) around the city.

Cafés and restaurants

Bistro Praha 10168-100A St Ⓣ 780/424-4218. A good opportunity to sample Eastern European cuisine, Edmonton style, in the city's oldest European-style restaurant. Slightly highbrow and expensive, though – better for lunch or late at night.

Café Select 10018-106th St Ⓣ 780/423-0419. An excellent, intimate place, trendy without being intimidating. Serving fine, simple bistro-type food, it's one of downtown's best choices for a late-night treat; book ahead. Moderate.

Earl's 11830 Jasper Ave Ⓣ 780/448-6582. This invariably excellent chain of relaxed and popular mid-range restaurants has no fewer than eight Edmonton outlets serving modern North American cuisine. This branch, known as the *Tin Palace*, is the most central.

Grabbajabba Coffee 82nd Ave and 104th St. Coffee, cake and the works at this very popular nonsmoking café in the heart of Old Strathcona; other outlets around the city.

Hardware Grill 9698 Jasper Ave Ⓣ 780/423-0969. The seasonally inspired Canadian cuisine in the best restaurant in Edmonton is served in a chic modern environment with dark hardwood floors, simple lines and elegant linen. Be sure to book. Expensive.

Il Portico 10012-107th St Ⓣ 780/424-0707. A tasteful and innovative Italian restaurant opposite the *Inn on 7th* hotel with lovely outdoor terrace for dining in good weather. Moderate.

Jack's Grill 5842-111th St Ⓣ 780/434-1113. Probably a tad too south of the city centre unless you have a car, but this is one of the top-rated places in Edmonton for modern, innovative Pacific Rim cuisine. Moderate.

The King and I 8208-107th St ☎ 780/433-2222. If you want a change from steaks, salmon and the Italian-based cuisine of many Edmonton restaurants, then you can't do better than this superlative Thai restaurant. Moderate.

La Ronde 10111 Bellamy Hill ☎ 780/428-6611. Stunning views of Edmonton from the city's only revolving dining room (atop the *Crowne Plaza Château Lacombe*). The Albertan cooking – steaks, bison, berries – is good too. Dancing nightly, live entertainment Fri–Sun. Expensive.

Mandarin 11044-82nd Ave ☎ 780/433-8494. Edmonton's best Chinese restaurant is located on the western side of the Old Strathcona district. Inexpensive.

Packrat Louie 10335-83rd Ave ☎ 780/433-0123. Bright, young and welcoming bistro in Old Strathcona with generous portions of steaks, salads, chicken and other more sophisticated international dishes. Closed Sun & Mon. Inexpensive to moderate.

Silk Hat 10251 Jasper Ave ☎ 780/425-1920. A fine place to knock back a Molson from the brewery up the road, this local institution's dim interior hasn't altered in forty years. Best known for the 1950s jukeboxes at each booth, but the inexpensive, basic food is as good as the ambience.

Sorrentino's 10162-100th St ☎ 780/424-7500. Downtown branch of an enormously successful local chain of family-run Italian restaurants with great atmosphere and service serving good affordable food in a pleasant, stylish setting.

Zenari's Kitchen 10180-101 St NW ☎ 780/423-5409. Great Italian deli/houseware shop with a tremendous lunch counter for soups, salads, sandwiches, pasta, pizza and other Italian staples.

Clubs and music venues

Blues on Whyte At the *Commercial Hotel*, 10329-82nd Ave ☎ 780/439-3981. One of the city's better live music clubs; bands most nights; jam sessions Sat.

Cook County Saloon 8010-103rd St ☎ 780/432-2665. Deservedly popular old Strathcona C&W venue, cited many times as Canada's best country nightclub. Free dance lessons Thurs 7.30pm to 9pm.

O'Byrne's Irish Pub 10616-82nd Ave ☎ 780/414-6766. Old Strathcona's popular verion of an Irish pub has good food, live music, drink and reasonably authentic atmosphere.

Yardbird Suite 10203-86th Ave ☎ 780/432-0428. Live groups nightly (10pm–2am) in the city's top jazz venue; admission is lower for the Tuesday night jam session. Nonsmoking rule enforced on Friday.

Yuk Yuk's Bourbon St, Entrance 6, West Edmonton Mall ☎ 780/481-9857. Assorted comedy acts every night, featuring well-known US and Canadian names. Wednesday is amateur night; Tuesday, hypnotist night.

Listings

Airlines Air Canada and Air BC (☎ 780/423-1222 or 1-888/247-2262); American (☎ 1-800/433-7300); Canada 3000 (☎ 780/890-4592); Delta (☎ 780/426-5990, 890-4410 or 1-800/221-1212); Northwest Airlines (☎ 780/1-800/225-2525); NWT Air (☎ 1-800/267-1247).

Airport information ☎ 780/890-8382.

Bike rental River Valley Cycle & Snowboards, 9124-82nd St ☎ 780/465-3863.

Bookshops Old Strathcona is renowned for its many stores selling new and secondhand books: Greenwood's (☎ 780/439-2005), on 82nd Ave between 103rd and 104th, is one of the city's best; Athabasca Books (☎ 780/431-1776), on 105th St north of 82nd Ave, is a quality secondhand outlet. Or try big modern outlets such as Chapters, 9952-170th St (☎ 780/487-6500). For maps and guides, go to Map Town, 10344-105th St (Mon–Fri 9am–6pm, Sat 10am–2pm; ☎ 780/429-2600).

Car rental Avis (☎ 780/890-7596 or 423-2847); Budget (☎ 780/448-2000, 448-2060 or 1-800/661-7027); Discount (☎ 780/448-3888 or 1-800/263-2355); Hertz (☎ 780/450-9610 or 1-800/263-0600); National (☎ 1-800/227-7368); Rent-a-Wreck (☎ 780/986-3335 or 1-800/223-3033); Thrifty (☎ 780/428-8555); Tilden (☎ 1-800/227-7368).

Exchange Thomas Cook, ManuLife Place, 10165-102nd St (Mon–Fri 9.30am–5.30pm, Sat 11am–4pm; ☎ 780/448-3660).

Hospitals Edmonton General, 1111 Jasper Ave (☎ 780/482-8111), has no emergency service. Emergency departments at Royal Alexandra Hospital, 10240 Kingsway (☎ 780/477-4111); Misericordia Community Hospital & Health Centre, 16940-87th Ave (☎ 780/930-5611); and University of Alberta Hospital, 8440-112th St (☎ 780/407-8822). For dentists, contact the Alberta Dental Association (☎ 780/432-1012).

Laundry Jasper Place Coin Laundry, 11122-153rd St (daily 7.30am–8pm).

Left luggage Lockers ($2) at the Greyhound station.

Library Centennial Library, 7 Sir Winston Churchill Square (Mon–Fri 9am–9pm, Sat 9am–6pm, Sun 1–5pm).
Outdoor equipment Mountain Equipment Co-op, 12328-102nd Ave (☎780/488-6614); Totem, 7430-99th St (☎780/432-1223).
Police ☎780/423-4567, 421-3333 or 945-5330.

Post office 9808-103A Ave ☎780/944-3271 or 1-800/565-3271.
Road conditions ☎780/471-6056.
Taxis Alberta Co-op (☎780/425-2525); Barrel (☎780/489-777); Checker Cabs (☎780/484-8888); Skyline (☎780/468-4646); Yellow Cabs (☎780/462-3456).
Weather Information ☎780/468-4940.

Northern Alberta

North of Edmonton stretches an all but uninhabited landscape of rippling hills, rivers, lakes, lonely farms, open prairie and the unending mantle of the northern forests. Compared with the spectacular mountain scenery to the west, northern Alberta is more akin to the monotony of the central plains of Saskatchewan and Manitoba. Unless you're fishing or boating, or just into sheer untrammelled wilderness, little here is worth detouring for, with the possible exception of the huge **Wood Buffalo National Park** on the border with the Northwest Territories.

The two great north-flowing waterways – the **Peace River** and **Athabasca River** – were the area's traditional arteries, but they have now been superseded by three main roads. The most travelled is **Hwy 16** (the Yellowhead Hwy), which runs due west from Edmonton to Jasper and onwards through the Rockies to Prince George and Prince Rupert (both in BC); **Hwy 43–Hwy 2** heads to Grande Prairie and Dawson Creek (BC) – Mile Zero of the Alaska Highway; and **Hwy 43–Hwy 35** (the Mackenzie Hwy) bisects northern Alberta and provides its only road link to the Northwest Territories.

Direct long-haul Greyhound **buses** run on all these routes from Edmonton, supplemented by the VIA Rail **train** service from Edmonton to Jasper (with connections on to Vancouver or Prince Rupert). Few roads merit travelling for their own sake, particularly for trips to Wood Buffalo National Park or Hay River (NWT). **Flying** can be a valuable time-saving option, but is likely to be very expensive unless you've organized internal flights before coming to Canada.

Hwy 16 towards Jasper

Hwy 16, or the Yellowhead Highway, is, as Edmonton's Chamber of Commerce likes to call it, "the other Trans-Canada Highway", the second and less-travelled transcontinental route and – by comparison with the Calgary–Banff route – a longer way of making for the Rocky Mountain national parks. For the first three hours or so it's dull going, but the scenery picks up considerably for the last hour through the eastern margins of the Jasper National Park (see p.726). Jasper town lies 357km west of Edmonton on the highway, an easy journey by car, **bus** (4–5 daily; $50) or **train**, whose tracks run parallel to the highway for much of the route (Mon, Thurs & Sat; $125).

Numerous **campsites** and **motels** service the road at regular intervals, the main concentrations being at **EDSON**, halfway to Jasper, and **HINTON**. Edson's ten or so motels are all much of a muchness, the cheapest of those you'd want to stay in being the *Summit Motel*, 4818-4th Ave (☎780/723-6199; ❷). Two nearby sites provide camping: the *Lions Club Campground* (☎780/723-3169; $15; May–Sept) on the east side of town, and the *Willmore Recreation Park*

(℡780/723-4401; $10; May–Oct), 6km south on 63rd St. The **tourist office** is in RCMP Centennial Park, 5433 3rd Ave (summer daily 8am–6pm; rest of year Mon–Fri 9am–5pm; ℡780/723-3339). For **food**, try *Ernie O's*, 4320 2nd Ave, good for breakfast, or the smarter *Mountain Pizza & Steakhouse*, 5102 4th Ave.

Hwy 43–Hwy 2 towards Dawson Creek

Hwy 43 out of Edmonton to Grande Prairie, and **Hwy 2** thereafter, ambles through terminally unexceptional towns, hills and prairie scenery on its way west to Dawson Creek, BC (see p.997). It's a mind-numbing day's journey by car or **bus** (2 daily): bus connections run via Grande Prairie (2–4 daily), 463km from Edmonton, where you may wash up if you're forced to break your journey.

Failing dismally to live up to its evocative name, **GRANDE PRAIRIE**'s unfocused sprawl is a legacy of having the luxury of unlimited space in which to build (the centre is a little nicer). The **infocentre** (daily June to early Sept 8.30am–8.30pm; ℡780/539-7688, ⓦwww.city.grand-prairie.ab.ca) is by Bear Creek Reservoir, off the main highway, which bypasses the main part of town to the west (it's staffed by volunteers, so hours may vary). The **bus** depot is at 9918-121st St (℡780/539-1111). Most of Grande Prairie's many **motels** are on the strip known as Richmond Ave (100th Ave), which links the southern part of the highway bypass to downtown. All are vast affairs with bargain prices – the top-of-the-line is the *Golden Inn Hotel*, 11201-100th Ave (℡780/539-6000 or 1-800/661-7954; ❺), and one of the cheapest is the *Lodge Motor Inn*, 10909-100th Ave (℡780/539-4700 or 1-800/661-7874; ❸). For **food**, head for the *Trax Dining Room*, 11001-100th Ave, open early until late for breakfast, lunch and dinner.

One of Canada's ultimate **cowboy bars**, incidentally, has to be *Kelly's Bar* in the *Sutherland Inn* at **CLAIRMONT**, immediately north of Grande Prairie. Owned by a Calgary Stampede chuck-wagon champion, it's the sort of place that has saddles for bar stools and serves up shooters in bull-semen collection tubes.

North on Hwy 35: Peace River country

Alberta's northern reaches are accessible only from **Hwy 35**, still a route for the adventurous and one which, according to Albertans, shows the real side of the province: a world of redneck homesteads, buffalo burgers and the sort of genuine C&W bars where strangers on a Friday night meet silent stares but wind up being invited to the hoedown anyway. You'll find such spots more or less everywhere along the route, but very little in the way of motels, garages or campsites, so come prepared. The road itself is well kept and straight, allowing healthier progress than on the more serpentine Alaska Highway to the west. Two Greyhound **buses** run daily from Edmonton to Peace River, and one all the way to Hay River (NWT), where you can make connections for Yellowknife and Fort Smith.

If you're travelling under your own steam you'll probably have to stay overnight in **PEACE RIVER**, 486km from Edmonton and the starting point of Hwy 35. The largest town in the region, it has a handful of standard **motels**: the *Peace Valley Inn,* 9609-101st St (℡780/624-2020 or 1-800/661-5897; ❹), alongside a 24-hour *Smitty's Restaurant*; the central *Best Canadian Motor Inn*, 9810-98th St (℡780/624-2586 or 1-800/461-9782; ❷); and – probably the best choice – the large *Traveller's Motor Hotel*, on the northern edge of downtown at 9510-100th St (℡780/624-3621 or 1-888/700-2264; ❸). There's also the 84-site *Peace River Lion's Club* **campsite** with showers (℡780/624-2120; $13; May–Oct) at Lion's Club Park on the west side of the river. The

Greyhound bus depot is downtown at 9801-97th Ave (☎780/624-1777) while the **tourist office** operates out of the old station building at 9309-100th St (summer daily 10am–6pm; ☎780/624-2044) on the northern edge of the downtown core; the *Peace Valley Inn* and *Traveller's Motor Hotel* are both close by.

Modern **MANNING**, 50km north of Peace River, is the last sizeable community and services centre for another 200km, making its pair of **motels** vital and often very busy as a result. The sixteen-unit *Garden Court* (☎780/836-3399; ❹) has kitchenettes and is smaller and a shade more expensive than the 42-unit *Manning Motor Inn* (☎780/836-2801; ❸). For the tiny nine-site municipal **campsite** (☎780/836-3606; $10; May–Sept) on the Notikewin River, turn east at the summer-only **infocentre** (summer daily 9am–5pm; ☎780/836-3875) on the highway. Camping (25 sites) is also sometimes available on the Condy Meadows golf course (☎780/836-2176), north of town on Hwy 35 – look for signs ($10).

North of Manning, only a couple of basic campsites and the odd wind-blown store disturb the peace, though if you're camping it's as well to know you can expect the unwelcome nocturnal attention of bears in these parts. Official tenting spots are *Notikewin Provincial* (☎780/554-1348; $9; May–Oct), 30km east of Hwy 35 on Hwy 692 – look for the junction 37km north of Manning, and the 49-site *Twin Lakes Provincial Recreation Area* (☎780/554-1348; $9; May–Sept), a total of 65km north of Manning on Hwy 35.

You're only going to stop in **HIGH LEVEL**, 199km north of Manning, if you want a place to bed down. Room rates begin to creep up the further north you go, and most of the town's six **motels** charge around $60. Book ahead, as rooms are often filled with away-from-home workers. The ritziest are the 75-unit *Four Winds Hotel* (☎780/926-3736, ⓦwww.4windshotel.com; ❷) and the *Our Place Apartment Hotel* (☎780/926-2556; ❸), which has twenty two-bedroom suites with kitchenettes. Then comes the *Stardust Motor Inn* (☎780/926-4222; ❷). The best option for **campers** is to splash out for the private facilities of the forty site *Aspen Ridge Campground* (☎780/926-4540; $15; April–Oct), 3km south of the centre on the main road (Hwy 35). The **tourist office** (summer daily 9am–5pm; rest of year Mon–Fri 9am–5pm; ☎780/926-4811) is at the southern end of town in the same building as the town's small museum.

North of High Level to the NWT border (191km) and beyond to Hay River, a string of campsites provides the only **accommodation**, and three aboriginal hamlets – Meander River, Steen River and Indian Cabins – offer only food and fuel.

Wood Buffalo National Park

Straddling the border between Alberta and the Northwest Territories, **WOOD BUFFALO NATIONAL PARK** covers an area larger than Switzerland, making it Canada's largest national park and the world's second-largest protected environment (the largest is in Greenland). Though wild and vast in its extent, the park is limited to low hills, lakes, grasslands, boreal forest, salt plains and marsh; these drain into the Peace and Athabasca rivers and then into Lake Claire, forming one of the world's largest freshwater deltas in the process. To the casual visitor the landscape is likely to be a disappointment – there are no real "sights" or scenic set pieces to compare with the Rockies – but for dedicated naturalists, or those who are prepared to spend time (and money) letting the landscapes get under their skin, the park holds much of interest, embracing North America's finest karst (limestone) scenery, classic swaths of boreal forest and rare salt-plain habitats in the park's topography.

Buffalo kill

Clean-living Canada rarely causes international environmental outrage, but since 1990 the federal government has been at the heart of a long-simmering row with conservationists. Wood Buffalo's herd of **wood buffalo** (a unique subspecies of the plains buffalo) is partially infected with tuberculosis and brucellosis, and government scientists on the Environmental Advisory Board claim the only way to prevent the spread of the diseases (which they claim are highly infectious) to Alberta's valuable beef herds is to kill the buffalo off. Scientists opposed to the government plan point out that the herd has been infected for years (since they were brought here 75 years ago in fact), has kept the disease to itself, and has survived by internal regulation and natural balance; animals show no outward signs of the diseases or of suffering. Furthermore there has never been an instance of disease transferring itself to humans. Most locals, who are largely opposed to the cull, argue that killing or inoculating every animal would be a daunting task, given the immensity of the animals' range, and that, if even a few were missed, the whole cull would be fruitless as disease would presumably erupt afresh when the herd regenerated. The last partial cull occurred in 1967, following on from a large-scale slaughter in the 1950s.

The restocking issue has opened another can of worms, for at last count there were just eighteen pure-bred, disease-free wood buffalo kept in captivity, and it is from these that the government intends to restart the herd. Most experts argue that the resultant weak, inbred group would compare badly with the large and long-evolved gene pool of the present herd. Other scientists take a completely different line, maintaining that wood buffalo aren't genetically different from their plains cousins and so it wouldn't matter if they were wiped out. The dispute quickly became extremely messy, reflecting fundamental changes in Canadian attitudes towards the rival claims of business and the environment in a tough financial climate. Some see the hand of Canada's powerful beef lobby guiding the government's actions, while others view it as part of a move to relax the powerful injunctions protecting Canada's national parks and open the way for economic growth in what are, almost by definition, regions of depression and high unemployment. This has already started, with Alberta's government taking plains buffalo off the protected list and putting it onto restaurant menus by promoting buffalo farming to boost its northern economy.

In the saga's most ironic twist, tuberculosis and brucellosis have turned up in farmed game animals (mainly elk), and a huge increase in game farming has led to an explosion in the very diseases a cull of the wild herds would seek to eradicate. Animals bred in captivity are more susceptible to such diseases, and escaping farmed elk are spreading them to areas far beyond the range of Wood Buffalo's supposed culprits. The federal government appointed a committee of interested parties to review the affair. No action was taken, and in 1995 a five-year Research and Containment programme was instigated to review long-term management; as the results are reviewed, the park's buffalo – now around 2500 in all – still nibble contentedly.

In addition to the park's 46 species of mammals, including black and grizzly bear and lynx, the Peace–Athabasca river delta in the park's southeast corner boasts 227 species of wildfowl – no fewer than four major migration routes overfly the area. The park is the world's only river rookery of rare white pelicans and the last refuge of the critically endangered **whooping crane** – first discovered in a remote part of the park as late as 1954. Though there were only 21 of the majestic birds when they were first discovered, there are over 130 today – about half the total world population (most of the others being in captivity) – each boasting a 2.4-metre wingspan and nesting far from any human contamination on the park's northern fringes.

The first refuge here was created in 1922 to protect a rather different species – an estimated 1500 **wood buffalo**, the longer-legged, darker and more robust relative of the plains buffalo. At the time they were being hunted to the edge of extinction, much in the manner of the plains bison in the preceding century. Six years later the federal government moved some 6000 plains buffalo to the park from the now nonexistent Buffalo National Park near Wainright, Alberta, when their grazing lands were appropriated for a firing range. Most of the present herd, now down to some 2500 members, is probably a hybrid strain, and has become the subject of considerable controversy (see box p.639). At present you'll still see plenty at the roadsides, more often than not wallowing in dust to escape the region's ferocious mosquitoes. The presence of the bisons, not to mention that of the cranes and the various rare and unspoiled habitats, saw the park declared a UNESCO World Heritage Site in 1983.

Fort Smith

Located just over Alberta's northern border in the Northwest Territories, **FORT SMITH** (pop. around 2500) is the only conceivable base for exploring Wood Buffalo National Park. Virtually the only settlement for several hundred kilometres east and north, the town developed along one of the major water routes to the north. Its site was particularly influenced by the need to avoid a violent set of rapids, an interruption to waterborne transport that required a 25-kilometre portage (a stretch of water where canoes had to be carried on land). The Dene natives' name for the area, not surprisingly, was Thebacha, meaning "along the rapids". In 1872 the Hudson's Bay Company built a post, Fort Fitzgerald, at the rapids' southern end. Two years later Fort Smith was established at their northern limit. In time the settlement became the administrative capital of the NWT (despite being only a kilometre from Alberta), a function it fulfilled until the federal government promoted Yellowknife to the role in 1967.

The disappearance of government jobs has left its mark on the town, as has the opening of the all-weather road between Hay River and Yellowknife, which captured a lot of the freight that used to pass through the region by boat. Nonetheless it's a reasonable enough base, with a handful of things to see around town before visiting the park or pressing on towards Yellowknife. The **Northern Life Museum**, 110 King St (mid-June to early Sept daily 1–5pm), is worth look to enjoy an excellent collection of traditional artefacts, crafts, fur-trading memorabilia and archive photographs. You might also want to glance at the old **Fort Smith Mission Historic Park**, on the corner of Mercredi Ave and Breynat St, former home to the region's bishop, who for years took on many of Fort Smith's bureaucratic responsibilities. For a chance of seeing the area's famous white pelicans, head for the **Slave River Lookout** on Marine Drive, where there's a telescope trained on their nesting site.

Practicalities

The easiest access to Fort Smith and the park is **by plane**, but isn't cheap; scheduled flights arrive from Edmonton, Hay River, Yellowknife and Vancouver, as well as any number of charters. Fort Smith airport is 5km west of town on McDougal Rd. If you need a taxi from the airport or around town call Portage Cabs (℡867/872-3333), and for **car rental** contact J&M Enterprises, on Portage Ave (Mon–Sat 8am–6pm; ℡867/872-2221). Getting to the park **by road** can be a slow business, and is possible only via Hwy 5 from Hay River (NWT) – a 280km haul to Fort Smith, the last 150km of which are within the park boundaries (this is the park's only all-weather road). Frontier Coachlines, 16-102 St, Hay River (☎867/874-2566), runs **buses** from Hay River (3 weekly on Tues, Thurs & Sat; $49 one-way), with services timed to connect with the daily Greyhound from Edmonton. Buses also arrive from Yellowknife.

Fort Smith's summer-only **infocentre** on Portage Rd near the corner with McDougal Rd (June–Sept daily 10am–10pm; ☎867/872-2512) supplies information on the town and Wood Buffalo National Park. The **park visitor centre** and headquarters is a short distance west in the Federal Building at 126 McDougal Rd (summer Mon–Fri 8.30am–5pm, Sat & Sun 10am–5pm; rest of year Mon–Fri 8.30am–5pm; ☎867/872-7900 or 872-2349). Excellent **maps and guides** can be had from North of 60 Books (☎867/872-2606), just opposite the town infocentre.

It's essential to prebook **accommodation** in summer. The cheapest of the town's three hotels is the 24-room *Pinecrest Hotel*, 163 McDougal Rd (☎867/872-2320; ❹), but it's worth paying a bit more to stay in the *Pelican Rapids Inn* almost across the road at 152 McDougal Rd (☎867/872-2789; ❺), a 31-room hotel built in 1997. The *Portage Inn*, 72 Portage Rd (☎867/872-2276, ✉portageinn@auroranet.nt.ca; ❺), has two doubles, five singles and a suite. Lower prices can be found in one of a handful of **B&Bs**: try the three-roomed *Whispering Pines Cottage Tourist Home* (☎867/872-2628; ❹) or the similarly priced *Thebacha B&B River Trails North* (☎867/872-2060; ❹), which has two doubles and two singles (no smoking and no alcohol). There's a public **campsite** alongside the Slave River on the northern edge of town and the *Queen Elizabeth* site ($12) 4km east towards the airport. Most of Fort Smith's stores and its few **restaurants** are clustered in a tiny two-block area of downtown. Many locals make for the *Old Skillet Restaurant* in the *Pinecrest Hotel*; for snacks and light meals, try the *J-Bell Bakery* almost opposite the park information office on the corner of McDougal Rd and Portage Ave.

Exploring the park

Aside from scenic Hwy 5 into Fort Smith from Hay River, there's a 298-kilometre summer-only **loop road** branching off Hwy 5 at a point 8km south of Fort Smith, through the park's southeast corner; some stretches of this are impassable after heavy rain, so check conditions with the park centre in Fort Smith. The west leg of the loop leads to three developed **trails** – Salt River (after 15km), Rainbow Lakes (after 20km) and Pine Lake (after 65km), the last with a nearby **campsite**. Backwoods camping is allowed anywhere as long as it's at least 1500m from Pine Lake or any road or trail. **Canoeing** is wide open: the Athabasca and Peace river system was once the main route for trade from the south, and still offers limitless paddling options.

The park's most-visited backcountry destination is the meadowland and delta habitat at **Sweetgrass Station**, 12km south of the Peace River. Built in 1954 to cull and vaccinate diseased bison (see box p.639), the area is a prime spot from which to watch bison and admire the wildlife of the Lake Claire region. You can stay in the cabin (bunks) here free of charge, but must first register with the park visitor centre in Fort Smith. Drinking water comes from the river and needs to be boiled and treated. To get here you'll need to canoe or pay heftily for a flight. Northwestern Air also runs sightseeing flights over the region (around $70 per person).

For most people the best way to see the park and its wildlife is to sign up for a **tour**. Fort Smith has plenty of operators: one of the longest-established is Subarctic Wildlife Adventures (☎867/872-2467 or 872-2126, ☯www

.subarcticwildlife.nt.ca), who offer nine-day "Wildlife Explorer" tours in the park and Peace–Athabasca delta region, and twelve- or fourteen-day tours in Wood Buffalo and the Slave River Rapids area before continuing to the *Bathurst Inlet Lodge* for tundra scenery, musk ox, caribou, birds, wildlife and Inuit culture. They also offer six-hour **rafting** trips on the Slave River and day bus trips into the park. River Trails North (☎867/872-2060) and Res Delta Tours (☎867/394-3141) in the town of **Fort Resolution**, east of Hay River, specialize in fishing and two- to seven-day river tours on the Slave River delta, as well as a three-day trip from Fort Resolution to Fort Smith.

Calgary and southern Alberta

Located an easy hour's drive from where the prairies buckle into the Rockies, **Calgary** is the obvious focus of **southern Alberta**, and is the best point from which to strike out west into the mountains. Yet, with some of the continent's most magnificent scenery practically on its doorstep, it takes some self-restraint to give the city the couple of days it deserves. Within day-tripping distance lie two unexpected gems: the dinosaur exhibits of the **Royal Tyrrell Museum**, near Drumheller in the strange **Badlands** country to the east; and the **Head-Smashed-In Buffalo Jump**, an aboriginal site in the heart of Alberta's cowboy country to the south. The latter is most easily visited if you're following the southern route of Hwy 3 across the province en route to Waterton Lakes National Park.

Calgary

A likeable and booming place, whose downtown skyscrapers soared almost overnight on the back of an oil bonanza in the 1970s, **CALGARY**'s tight high-rise core is good for wandering, and holds the prestigious **Glenbow Museum**. The wooden houses of the far-flung suburbs, meanwhile, recall the city's pioneering frontier origins, which are further celebrated in the annual **Calgary Stampede**, a hugely popular cowboy carnival in which the whole town – and hordes of tourists – revel in a boots-and-stetson image that's still very much a way of life in the surrounding cattle country. Year-round you can dip into the city's lesser museums and historic sites, or take time out in its scattering of attractive city parks.

Some history

Modern Calgary is one of the West's largest and youngest cities, its close to 850,000-strong population having grown from almost nothing in barely 125 years. Long before the coming of outsiders, however, the area was the

CALGARY

RESTAURANTS
Barley Mill	3
Caesar's Steakhouse	6
Ceil's	7
Divinos	10
Galaxie Diner	12
Hys	5
James Joyce	8
Joey Tomato's	3
Nellie's Kitchen	11
River Café	1
Roasterie	2
Silver Dragon	4
Teatro	9

ACCOMMODATION
Calgary International Youth Hostel	F
Calgary Marriott	I
Cecil	B
Delta Calgary Airport	A
Holiday Inn	K
Lord Nelson Inn	G
Palliser	J
Ramada	H
Regis Plaza	E
Sandman	D
YWCA	C

St Patrick's Island, St George's Island & Calgary Zoo

Airport & A

Bow Trail & Trans-Canada Highway (Canada Olympic Park)

Olympic Saddledome

Stampede Park

Heritage Park

Fort Calgary

City Hall

Glenbow Museum

Olympic Plaza

The Bay

Calgary Tower

Chinese Cultural Centre

Eau Claire Market

YMCA

Prince's Island

Bow River

Elbow River

Devonian Gardens

Eaton's

Toronto Dominion Square

Energeum

C-Train

Calgary Mountain Equipment Co-op

Louise Bridge

Centre St. Bridge

Bus Terminal

500 m

The Calgary Stampede

An orgy of all things cowboy and cowgirl, the annual **Calgary Stampede** brings around a quarter of a million spectators and participants to the city for ten days during the middle of July. This is far more than a carefully engineered gift to Calgary's tourist industry, however, for the event is one of the world's biggest rodeos and comes close to living up to its billing as "The Greatest Outdoor Show on Earth". During "The Week", as it's known by all and sundry, the city loses its collective head; just about everyone turns out in white stetsons, bolo ties, blue jeans and hand-tooled boots, addressing one another in a bastardized cowboy C&W slang.

But for all its heavily worked visitor appeal, the competition end of things is taken very seriously. Most of the cowboys are for real, as are the injuries – the rodeo is said to be North America's roughest – and the combined prize money is a very serious $500,000. Even the first show in 1912, masterminded by entrepreneur Guy Weadick, put up $100,000 (raised from four Calgary businessmen) and attracted 60,000 people to the opening parade, a line-up that included 2000 aboriginal people in full ceremonial rig and Pancho Villa's bandits in a show erroneously billed as a swan song for the cowboy of the American West ("The Last and Best Great West Frontier Days"). Around 40,000 daily attended the rodeo events (today's figure is 100,000), not bad considering Calgary's population at the time was only 65,000.

Stampede events

Nowadays things kick off on Thursday evening at Stampede Park with a show previewing the next ten days' events. Next day there's the traditional **parade**, timed to begin at 9am, though most spectators are in place by 6am along the parade route (which is west along 6th Ave from 2nd St SE, south on 10th St SW and east along 9th Ave). The march takes two hours, and involves around 150 entries, 4000 participants and some 700 horses. For the rest of the Stampede the **Olympic Plaza** in downtown (known as Rope Square for the duration) offers free pancake breakfasts daily (8.30–11.30am) and entertainment every morning. Typical events include bands, mock gunfights, square dances, native dancing and country bands. Square dancing also fills parts of Stephen Ave Mall at 10am every morning. **Nightlife** is a world unto itself, with Stampede locations giving way to music, dancing and mega-cabarets, which involve casts of literally thousands. There's also lots of drinking, gambling, fireworks and general partying into the small hours. Barbecues are the norm, and even breakfast is roped into the free-for-all – outdoor bacon, pancake and flapjack feasts being the traditional way to start the day. "White hatter stew" and baked beans are other inevitable staples.

Stampede's real action, though – the rodeo and allied events – takes place in **Stampede Park**, southeast of downtown and best reached by C-Train (every 10min) to Victoria Park–Stampede Station. This vast open area contains an amusement park, concert and show venues, bars and restaurants and a huge range of stalls and

domain of the **Blackfoot**, who ranged over the site of present-day Calgary for several thousand years. About 300 years ago, they were joined by **Sarcee**, forced south by war from their northern heartlands, and the **Stoney**, who migrated north with Sitting Bull into southern Saskatchewan and then Alberta. Traces of old campsites, buffalo kills and pictographs from all three peoples lie across the region, though these days local aboriginal lands are confined to a few reserves.

Whites first began to gather around the confluence of the Bow and Elbow rivers at the end of the eighteenth century. Explorer **David Thompson** wintered here during his travels, while the Palliser expedition spent time nearby en route for the Rockies. Settlers started arriving in force around 1860, shows that take the best part of a day to see. Entrance is $8, which allows you to see all the **entertainments** except the rodeo and chuck-wagon races. Things to see include the aboriginal village at the far end of the park, where members of the Five Nations peoples (Blackfoot, Blood, Sarcee, Stoney and Piegan) set up a tepee village (tours available); the John Deere Show Ring, scene of the World Blacksmith Competition; the Centennial Fair, which hosts events for children; the Agricultural Building, home to displays of cattle and other livestock; the outdoor Coca-Cola Stage, used for late-night Country shows; and the Nashville North, an indoor Country venue with bar and dancing until 2am.

If you want to see the daily **rodeo** competition – bronco riding, bull riding, native-buffalo riding, branding, calf-roping, steer-wrestling, cow-tackling, wild-cow milking and the rest – you need another ticket ($8 on the day), though unless you've bought these in advance (see below) it's hardly worth it: you'll probably be in poor seats miles from the action and hardly see a thing. Rodeo heats are held each afternoon from 1.30pm for the first eight days, culminating in winner-takes-all finals on Saturday and Sunday (prize money for the top honcho is $50,000). If you want to watch the other big event, the ludicrously dangerous but hugely exciting **chuck-wagon** races (the "World Championship"), you need yet another ticket ($8 on the day, though again you need to buy these in advance to secure anything approaching decent seats. The nine contests are held once-nightly at 8pm, the four top drivers going through to the last-night final, where another $50,000 awaits the winner.

Stampede practicalities

It's worth planning ahead if you're coming to Calgary for Stampede. **Accommodation** is greatly stretched – be certain to book ahead – and prices for most things are hiked for the duration. **Tickets** for the rodeo and chuck-wagon races go on sale anything up to a year in advance. They're sold for the Stampede Park grandstand, which is divided into sections. "A" is best and sells out first; "B" and "C" go next. Then comes the smarter Clubhouse Level (D–E are seats; F–G are Clubhouse Restaurant seats, with tickets sold in pairs only). This is enclosed and air-conditioned, but still offers good views and the bonus of bars, lounge area and restaurants. The top of the stand, or Balcony (J–K) is open, and provides a good vantage point for the chuck-wagon races as you follow their progress around the length of the course. Rodeo tickets range from about $17 to $35, chuck-wagon races from $17 to $40; tickets for the finals of both events are a few dollars more in all seats.

For ticket order forms, **advance sales** and general information, check ⓦwww .calgarystampede.com, or call in person at Stampede Headquarters, 1410 Olympic Way SE, or the visitor centre. Tickets are also available from Ticketmaster outlets (ⓣ403/270-6700).

when hunters moved into the region from the United States, where their prey, the buffalo, had been hunted to the edge of extinction. Herds still roamed the Alberta grasslands, attracting not only hunters but also **whiskey traders**, who plied their dubious wares among whites and aboriginal peoples alike. Trouble inevitably followed, leading to the creation of the West's first North West Mounted Police stockade at Fort Macleod (see p.663). Soon after, in 1875, a second fort was built further north to curb the lawlessness of the whiskey traders. A year later it was christened **Fort Calgary**, taking its name from the Scottish birthplace of its assistant commissioner. The word *calgary* is Gaelic for "clear running water", and it was felt that the ice-clear waters of the Bow and Elbow rivers were reminiscent of the "old country".

By 1883 a station had been built close to the fort, part of the new trans-Canadian **railway**. The township laid out nearby quickly attracted **ranchers** and British gentlemen farmers to its low, hilly bluffs – which are indeed strongly reminiscent of Scottish moors and lowlands – and cemented an enduring Anglo-Saxon cultural bias. Ranchers from the US – where pasture was heavily overgrazed – were further encouraged by an "open grazing" policy across the Alberta grasslands. Despite Calgary's modern-day cowboy life – most notably its famous annual **Stampede** – the Alberta cattle country has been described as more "mild West" than Wild West. Research suggests that there were just three recorded gunfights in the nineteenth century, and poorly executed ones at that.

By 1886 fires had wiped out most of the town's temporary wooded and tented buildings, leading to an edict declaring that all new buildings should be constructed in sandstone (for a while Calgary was known as "Sandstone City"). The fires proved no more than a minor historical hiccup and within just nine years of the railway's arrival Calgary achieved official city status, something it had taken rival Edmonton over a hundred years to achieve. Edmonton was to have its revenge in 1910, when it was made Alberta's provincial capital.

Cattle and the coming of the railway generated exceptional growth, though the city's rise was to be nothing compared with the prosperity that followed the discovery of **oil**. The first strike, the famous Dingman's No. 1 Well, took place in 1914 in the nearby Turner Valley. An oil refinery opened in 1923 and since then Calgary has rarely looked back. In the 25 years after 1950 its population doubled. When oil prices soared during the oil crisis of the 1970s, the city exploded, becoming a world energy and financial centre – headquarters for some four hundred oil and related businesses – with more American inhabitants than any other Canadian city.

Falling commodity prices subsequently punctured the city's ballooning economy, but not before the city centre had been virtually rebuilt and acquired improved and oil-financed cultural, civic and other facilities. Today only Toronto is home to the headquarters of more major Canadian corporations, though the city's optimism is tempered, as elsewhere in Canada, by the notion of **federal disintegration**. Much of the West, which still harbours a sense of a new frontier, is increasingly impatient with the "old East", and happy – if election results are anything to go by – to become increasingly self-sufficient.

Arrival, information and transport

Approaching Calgary **by air** you're rewarded (in the right weather) with a magnificent view of the Rockies stretching across the western horizon. **Calgary International Airport** (code YYC; Ⓦ www.calgaryairport.com), a modern, often half-deserted strip, is within the city limits about 10km northeast of downtown. There's a small **information centre** disguised as a stagecoach (daily 10am–10pm) in Arrivals and another in Departures (6am–midnight). The Arrivals level also offers courtesy phones to hotels and car-rental agencies, though most of the hotels are well away from the centre. A taxi downtown costs $30. The widely advertised free hotel coaches tend to be elusive, but the reliable Airporter Bus (Ⓣ 403/531-3909) shuttles into the city every thirty minutes and drops at nine downtown hotels: the *Delta Bow, International, Westin, Sheraton Suites, Prince Royal, Ramada, Sandman, Palliser* and *Marriott* (first bus 6.30am, last bus 11.30pm; $8.50 one-way, $15 return). If you're heading for the city bus terminal, the nearest drop-off is the *Sandman*: from here, walk south a block to 9th Ave and turn right (west) and the

Calgary addresses

For all its rapid expansion, Calgary is a well-planned and straightforward city engineered around an inevitable grid. Streets run north–south, avenues east–west, with numbers increasing as you move out from the centre. The Trans-Canada (Hwy 1) passes through the city to the north of downtown. During its spell in the city limits it becomes 16th Ave. The major north to south road through the city, Hwy 2, is rechristened the Deerfoot Trail, while the main route south from the US and Waterton Lakes is known as the Macleod Trail, much of which is a fairly grim strip of malls, motels and fast-food joints. The metropolitan area is divided into **quadrants** (NW, NE, SE and SW) with the Bow River separating north from south, Centre St–Macleod Trail east from west. Downtown – and virtually everything there is to see and do – is in a small area in or close to the SW quadrant. As with Edmonton, the last digits of the first number refer to the house number: 237-8th Ave SE is on 2nd St at no. 37, close to the intersection with 8th Ave. It's easy to overlook the quadrant, so check addresses carefully.

terminal's a fifteen-minute walk. Buy Airporter tickets from one of a bank of bus-ticket desks lined up in Arrivals (Level 1) by the exit doors: buses depart from Bay 3 immediately outside the terminal.

Direct **buses** from the airport **to Banff** and Lake Louise mean you can be in Banff National Park a couple of hours after collecting your baggage. Services include those run by Laidlaw (1 daily May–Nov, 2 daily Dec–April; $30 to Banff, $38 to Lake Louise; ☎403/762-9102 or 1-800/661-4946, ⓦwww .laidlawbanff.com); Banff Airporter (8 daily; $36 to Banff; ☎403/762-3330 or 1-888/449-2901, ⓦwww.banffairporter.com); Brewster Transportation (3 daily to Banff and Lake Louise, 1 daily to Jasper in summer; $36 to Banff, $41 to Lake Louise, $71 to Jasper; ☎403/762-6767 in Banff, ☎403/221-8242 in Calgary, ☎780/852-3332 in Jasper). **Tickets** are available from separate desks adjacent to the Airporter desk in Arrivals. Services leave from Bay 4 or (close by) outside the Arrivals terminal.

Calgary's Greyhound **bus terminal** (☎403/265-9111 or 1-800/661-8747, ⓦwww.greyhound.ca) is comfortable but not convenient. It's located west of downtown at 8th Ave SW and 850-16th St, an uninspiring thirty-minute walk to the city centre. Fortunately free transit buses operate to the C-Train at 7th Ave SW and 10th St, the key to the city's central transport system (free from this point through the downtown area). The shuttles leave from Gate 4 within 20 minutes of every bus arrival to the terminal and are announced over the tannoy: keep your ears open. Shuttles return from the same point more or less hourly on the half-hour. Alternatively, taxis for the short run to downtown ($6) are plentiful outside the terminal.

The main **Visitor Information Services** is rather pitiful and located downtown in the front of the Riley & McComick Western Store, 220 8th Ave SW (daily: June–Aug 8am–8pm; rest of year 8am–5pm; ☎403/263-8510 or 1-800/661-1678, ⓦwww.tourismcalgary.com).

City transport

Almost everything in Calgary, barring Stampede locations and a few minor diversions, is a comfortable walk away – except in winter, when low temperatures can make any excursion an ordeal. The city's much-vaunted **Plus 15 Walking System**, a labyrinthine network of enclosed walkways 4.5m above ground, is designed to beat the freeze. It enables you to walk through downtown without setting foot outside, but is too confusing to bother with when the weather's fine.

Calgary's **public transport** system is cheap, clean and efficient, comprising an integrated network of buses and the **C-Train** (every 15 to 30min; no late-night service), the latter a cross between a bus and a train, which is free for its downtown stretch along the length of 7th Ave SW between 10th St and City Hall at 3rd St SE. An on-board announcement tells you when the free section is coming to an end. For route information, call ☎403/276-7801. **Tickets**, valid for both buses and C-Train, are available from machines on C-Train stations, shops with a Calgary Transit sticker, and from the main Information and Downtown Sales Centre, also known as the **Calgary Transit Customer Service Centre**, 240-7th Ave SW (Mon–Fri 8.30am–5pm), which also has free schedules and route planners. The one-way fare is $1.60, a day-pass $5. You can pay on the bus if you have the exact change. Request a transfer from the driver (valid for 90min) if you're changing buses. The sales centre also provides timetables and an invaluable **information line** (Mon–Fri 6am–11pm, Sat & Sun 8am–9.30pm; ☎403/262-1000): tell them where you are and where you want to go, and they'll give you the necessary details.

You can easily get a **taxi** from outside the bus terminal, or see "Listings" (p.658) for numbers of cab companies.

Accommodation

Budget **accommodation** in Calgary is not plentiful, but the little that exists is rarely at a premium except during Stampede (mid-July) when prepaid reservations, in central locations at least, are essential months in advance. Remember that even smart hotels are likely to offer vastly reduced rates on Friday nights and over the weekend, when their business custom drops away. In addition to the recommendations given below, motels abound, mostly well away from the centre along Macleod Trail heading south and on the Trans-Canada Highway heading west. "Motel Village" is a cluster of a dozen or so motels in the $60–70 a night bracket, grouped together at the intersection of 16th Ave NW and Crowchild Trail; a taxi ride out here costs about $10.

If you run into difficulties consult the Alberta Hotel Association's ubiquitous *Accommodation Guide*. **B&B agencies** to try include the Bed & Breakfast Agency of Alberta (☎403/543-3901 or 1-800/425-8160, @altabba@home.com); Canada-West (☎403/604/990-6730, @www.b-b.com); Bed and Breakfast Association of Calgary (☎403/277-0023, @www.bbcalgary.com); or the Alberta Bed & Breakfast Association (☎403/282-2728, @www.bbalberta.com).

Hotels and motels

Calgary Marriott 110-9th Ave SE ☎403/266-7331 or 1-800/228-9290, @www.marriott.com. Not the most expensive of Calgary's smart hotels, but probably the best outside the *Palliser* if you want to stay in some style. ❼

Cecil Corner of 4th Ave and 3rd St SE ☎403/266-2982. Clean and cheap, but a grim place – to say the least – on a busy junction (the airport road); its bar has a rough reputation. No phones, TV or private baths. Rock-bottom budgets and emergencies only. ❷

Delta Calgary Airport Hotel 2001 Airport Rd ☎403/291-2600 or 1-800/441-1414,

@www.deltahotels.com. Soundproofed hotel right at the airport – ideal if you arrive late or have an early flight out – but it's not cheap. ❻

Holiday Inn Calgary Downtown 119-12th Ave SW ☎403/266-4611 or 1-800/661-9378, @www.holidayinn-calgary.com. An amenity-loaded hotel, but a few blocks off the centre of town. ❼

Lord Nelson Inn 1020-8th Ave SW ☎403/269-8262 or 1-800/661-6017, @wilklord@shaw.ca. A ten-storey modern but slightly faded block with 56 rooms close to the more expensive *Sandman*, to which it is inferior. Just a block from the free C-Train. ❹

Palliser 133-9th Ave SW ☎403/262-1234 or 1-800/441-1414, ⓦwww.fairmont.com. Built in 1914, this is the hotel royalty chooses when it comes to Calgary, and is as smart as you can find in the city if you want traditional style and service (though avoid the back rooms overlooking the rail tracks). ❻

Ramada Hotel Downtown 708-8th Ave SW ☎403/263-7600 or 1-800/661-8684, ⓦwww.ramadacalgary.com. A large, comfortable hotel with 200 predictably good rooms and a swimming pool at the heart of downtown. ❺

Regis Plaza Hotel 124-7th Ave SE ☎403/262-4641, ⓦwww.regisplazahotel.com. An old and unappealing hotel for those who are desperate or almost broke, but just two blocks from the Calgary Tower. Bathroom facilities are shared in ten of the forty rooms: other rooms only have washbasins; beware the rough bar. ❸

Sandman Hotel Downtown Calgary 888-7th Ave SW ☎403/237-8626 or 1-800/726-3626, ⓦwww.sandmanhotels.com. An excellent and first-choice mid-range hotel, with 300 totally dependable clean, modern rooms with private bathrooms in a high-rise block: extremely handy for the free C-Train. ❺

Travelodge 2760 Sunridge Blvd NE ☎403/291-1260 or 1-800/578-7878; 2304-16th Ave ☎403/289-0211 or 1-888/294-6444; and 7012 Macleod Trail ☎403/253-7070 or 1-888/314-1444. Inexpensive out-of-town chain motels; the first is convenient to the airport; the second north of town along the Trans-Canada Highway; the third south along the arterial Macleod Trail. ❸

Hostels

Calgary International Youth Hostel (HI) 520-7th Ave SE ☎403/269-8239, ⓦwww.hihostels.ca. Sociable hostel in seedy area close to downtown; two blocks east of City Hall and the free section of the C-Train. Laundry, six- and eight-bed dorms (120 beds in total), four double/family rooms, cooking facilities, bike storage, snack bar. Members $16–18, nonmembers $20–22; family rooms/doubles add $5 per person. The hostel organizes lots of evening activies. ❶

Calgary YWCA 320-5th Ave SE ☎403/263-1550. Hotel comfort for women and children only in quiet, safe area; food service, pool, gym, health club and squash courts; book in summer. Singles available from about $40 for singles ($50 double) without bath, $60 with. ❷

Student rooms

University of Calgary 3330-24th Ave NW ☎403/220-3202. Way out in the suburbs, but cheap with a huge number of dorm ($20) and private rooms (around $30) and apartments ($50–100) from early May to late August. Take the C-Train or bus #9. The 24hr room-rental office (call first) is in the Kananaskis Building on campus; 33 percent discount for student ID holders. ❷

Campsites

Calaway Park 245033 Range Rd 33 ☎403/249-7372, ⓦwww.calawaypark.com. About 10km west of the city on the Trans-Canada Hwy to Banff and the Rockies. It's also within walking distance of the Calaway Park amusement park – Canada's largest. Full facilities, including showers. Mid-May to early Oct. $15.

KOA Calgary West 221-101 St SW ☎403/288-0411 or 1-800/562-0842, ⓦwww.koa.com. Off the south side of Hwy 1 at the western end of the city, close to Canada Olympic Park: 400 sites, laundry, store and outdoor pool. Shuttle services to downtown. Mid-April to mid-Oct. $24.

Mountain View Farm Campground ☎403/293-6640, ⓦwww.calgarycamping.com. A 202-site full service campsite situated on a farm 3km east of the city on the Trans-Canada (Hwy 1). April to Oct. $18.

The City

Downtown Calgary lies in a self-evident cluster of mirrored glass and polished granite facades bounded by the Bow River to the north, 9th Ave to the south, Centre St to the east and 8th St to the west. A monument to oil money, the area is about as sleek as an urban centre can be: virtually everything is brand-new, and the modern architecture is easy on the eye. The **city centre**, so far as it has one, is traditionally 8th Ave between 1st St SE and 3rd St SW, a largely pedestrianized area known as **Stephen Ave Mall**.

Any city tour, though, should start with a trip to the **Glenbow Museum**, while a jaunt up the **Calgary Tower**, across the street, gives a literal overview of the Calgarian hinterland. Thereafter a good deal of the city lends itself to wandering on foot, whether around the mall-laden main streets or to **Prince's**

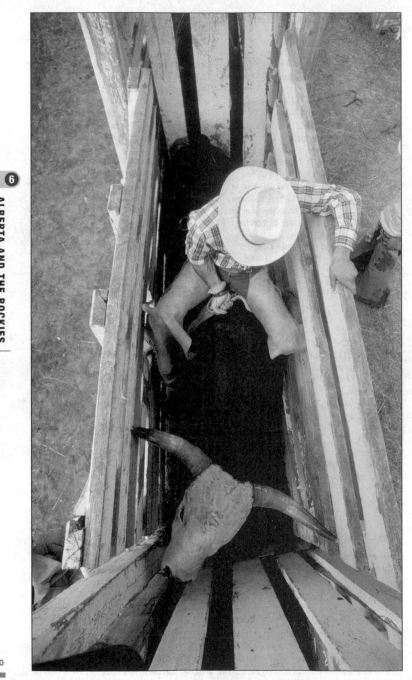

△The Calgary Stampede

Island, the nearest of many parks, and gentrified **Kensington**, a busy shopping and café district. The appeal of attractions further afield – **Fort Calgary**, **Heritage Park** and the **Calgary Zoo** – will depend on your historical and natural-history inclinations. These sights, together with a crop of special interest **museums**, can be easily reached by bus or C-Train.

Glenbow Museum

The excellent and eclectic collection of the **Glenbow Museum** (Tues–Sat 9am–5pm, Sat noon–5pm; $8; Ⓦ www.glenbow.org) is, the Stampede apart, the only sight for which you'd make a special journey to Calgary. Although it's opposite the Calgary Tower at 130-9th Ave SE, the main entrance is hidden alongside the Skyline Plaza complex a short way east down the street (there's another entrance from the Stephen Ave Mall). Built in 1966, the no-expense-spared museum is a testament to sound civic priorities and the cultural benefits of booming oil revenues. Its three floors of displays make a fine introduction to the heritage of the Canadian west.

The permanent collection embraces the eclectic approach, starting with a section devoted to ritual and **sacred art** from around the world and an **art gallery** tracing the development of western Canadian indigenous art. Better still is the European art depicting the culture of aboriginal peoples. Two outlooks prevail – the romantic nineteenth-century image of the Indian as "noble savage", and the more forward-looking analysis of artists from the same period such as Paul Kane, a painter determined to make accurate representations of aboriginal peoples and cultures before their assimilation by white expansion. The second floor runs the gamut of western Canadian history and heritage, including an outstanding exhibit on First Nations or **aboriginal peoples**. In the treaties section, hidden in a corner almost as if in shame, the museum text skates over the injustices with a glossary of simple facts. On display are the original documents that many chiefs were confused into signing, believing they were peace treaties, when in fact the contracts gave away all land rights to those who drafted them in deliberately incomprehensible legalese. All facets of **native crafts** are explored on this floor, as well, with stunning displays of carving, costumes and jewellery; whilst their emphasis is on the original inhabitants of Alberta – with a special new display on the Blackfoot – the collection also forays into the Inuit and the Métis – the latter being the offspring of native women and white fur traders, and the most marginalized group of all. Following a historical chronology, the floor moves on to exhibits associated with the fur trade, Northwest Rebellion, the Canadian Pacific, pioneer life, ranching, cowboys, oil and wheat – each era illustrated by interesting and appropriate artefacts of the time – adding up to a glut of period paraphernalia that includes a terrifying exhibit of frontier dentistry, an absurdly comprehensive display of washing machines, and a solitary 1938 bra. The eccentric top floor kicks off with a pointless display of Calgary Stampede merchandising, before moving on to a huge collection of **military paraphernalia** and a dazzling display of **gems and minerals**, said to be among the world's best. These exhibits are mainly for genre enthusiasts, though the gems are worth a look if only to see some of the extraordinary and beautiful things that come out of the drab mines that fuel so much of western Canada's economy.

Other downtown sights

The **Calgary Tower** (daily: May–Sept 7.30am–midnight; Oct–April 8am–11pm; Ⓦ www.calgarytower.com; $6.15), the city's favourite folly, is a good deal shorter and less imposing than the tourist material would have you believe. An obligatory tourist traipse, the 190m-tall salt cellar (762 steps if you don't take the lift) stands in a relatively dingy area at the corner of Centre St–9th Ave SW, somewhat overshadowed by downtown's more recent buildings. As a long-term landmark, however, it makes a good starting point for any tour of the city, the Observation Terrace offering outstanding views, especially on clear days, when the snowcapped Rockies fill the western horizon, with the ski-jump towers of the 1988 Canada Olympic Park in the middle distance. Up on the observation platform after your one-minute elevator ride you'll find a snack bar (good value and excellent food), cocktail bar and revolving restaurant (expensive).

Any number of shopping malls lurk behind the soaring high-rises, most notably Toronto Dominion Square (8th Ave SW between 2nd and 3rd streets), the city's main shopping focus and the unlikely site of **Devonian Gardens** (daily 9am–9pm; free). Like something out of an idyllic urban Utopia, the three-acre indoor gardens support a lush sanctuary of streams, waterfalls and full-sized trees, no mean feat given that it's located on the fourth floor of a glass and concrete glitter palace (access by elevator). Around 20,000 plants round off the picture, comprising some 138 local and tropical species. Benches beside the garden's paths are perfect for picnicking on food bought in the takeaways below, while impromptu concerts are held on the small stages dotted around.

Calgary pays homage to its oil industry in the small but oddly interesting **Energeum** plonked in the main lobby of the Energy Resources Building between 5th St and 6th St SW at 640-5th Ave SW (June–Aug Mon–Fri & Sun 10.30am–4.30pm; Sept–May Mon–Fri same hours; free). Its audiovisual and presentational tricks take you through the formation, discovery and drilling for coal and oil. Alberta's peculiar and problematic oil sands are explained – granite-hard in winter, mud-soft in summer – and there are dollops of the stuff on hand for some infantile slopping around.

The **Calgary Science Centre** is located one block west of the 10th St SW C-Train at 701-11th St and 7th Ave SW (mid-May to June Tues–Thurs 10am–4pm, Fri–Sun 10am–5pm; call for winter hours; $11; ⓦwww .calgaryscience.ca). Here you can look through the telescopes of its small

Chinooks

Winters in Calgary are occasionally moderated by **chinooks**, sudden warming winds that periodically sweep down the eastern flanks of the Rockies. Often heralded by a steely cloud band spreading from the mountains over the city, a chinook can raise the temperature by as much as 10°C in a couple of hours and evaporate a foot of snow in a day. Chinooks are the result of a phenomenon that occurs on leeward slopes of mountains all over the world, but nowhere more dramatically than in the plains of southwestern Alberta. The effect has to do with the way prevailing westerly winds are forced to rise over the Rockies, expanding and cooling on the way up and compressing and warming up again on the way back down. On the way up the cooling air, laden with Pacific moisture, becomes saturated (ie clouds form) and drops rain and snow on the windward (western) side of the mountains. All this condensation releases latent heat, causing the rising air to cool more slowly than usual; but on the leeward descent the air, now relieved of much of its moisture, warms up at the normal rate. By the time it reaches Calgary it's both drier and warmer than it was to start with. The name comes from the people that traditionally inhabited the area around the mouth of the Columbia River in Washington and Oregon, from where the winds seem to originate; the Chinook people also lent their name to the largest species of Pacific salmon.

observatory, which are trained nightly on the moon, planets and stars (weather permitting). Other daytime highlights here include the interactive exhibits of the Discovery Hall (these change regularly) and the **Discovery Dome**, a multimedia theatre complete with cinema picture images, computer graphics, slide-projected images and a vast speaker system. The on-site **Pleiades Theatre** offers a series of "mystery and murder plays" throughout the year. For details of current shows and exhibitions, call ☏403/221-3700. To get here, take the C-Train along 7th Ave SW and walk the last block.

Prince's Island, the Bow River and Kensington

Five minutes' walk north of downtown via a footbridge, **Prince's Island** is a popular but peaceful retreat offering plenty of trees, flowers, an outstanding restaurant, the *River Café* (see p.656), kids' playground and enough space to escape the incessant stream of joggers pounding the walkways. Between the island and downtown, at the north end of 3rd St SW (six blocks north of the free C-Train), the wonderful **Eau Claire Market** (Mon–Wed & Sat 10am–6pm, Thurs & Fri 10am–8pm, Sun and holidays noon–5pm – though shops and restaurants have varying hours; ⊛www.eauclairemarket.com) is a bright and deliberately brash warehouse mix of food and craft market, cinemas (including a 300-seat IMAX large-screen complex), buskers, restaurants, walkways and panoramic terraces. All in all it brings some heart to the concrete and glass of downtown – the large communal eating area, in particular, is a good place to people-watch and pick up bargain takeaway Chinese, Japanese, wholefood and burger snacks. Note that the tremendous **YMCA** opposite the market at 101-3rd St SW has no rooms, though the superb swimming pool, Jacuzzi, sauna, squash courts, running track and weights room are open to all (Mon–Fri 5.30am–10.30pm, Sat & Sun 7am–7.30pm; $8; increased admission Mon–Fri 11am–1.30pm and daily 4–6.30pm). Swimmers might be tempted by the broad, fast-flowing **Bow River** nearby, but it's for passive recreation only – the water is just two hours (were you travelling by car) from its icy source in the Rockies – its dangers underlined by lurid signs on the banks. The river is the focus for Calgary's civilized and excellent 210-kilometre system of recreational **walkways**, asphalt paths (also available to cyclists) that generally parallel the main waterways: maps are available from the visitor centre. Just east of the market and five blocks north of the C-Train at 197-1st St SW lies the **Calgary Chinese Cultural Centre** (daily: centre 9am–9pm, museum 11am–5pm; $2), its big central dome modelled on the Temple of Heaven in Beijing and it claims to be one of the largest Chinese centres in Canada. It forms the focus for Calgary's modest Chinatown and large Chinese-Canadian population, most of whom are descendants of immigrants who came to work on the railways in the 1880s. It contains a small museum and gallery, and a gift shop and restaurant.

A twenty-minute jaunt along the walkway system from Prince's Island in the other direction from the market, **Kensington** is a gentrified café district on 10th St NW and Kensington Rd. Shops here sell healing crystals and advertise yoga and personal-growth seminars, though the older cafés, bookshops and wholefood stores are beginning to give way to trinket shops. As an eating area, though, Kensington has been superseded by the increasingly trendy section of 4th St SW, beyond 17th Ave.

Fort Calgary

Fort Calgary, the city's historical nexus, stands at 750-9th Ave SE (daily May–Oct 9am–5pm; ⊛www.fortcalgary.ab.ca; $6.50), a manageable eight-block walk east of downtown; you could also take bus #1 to Forest Lawn, bus #14 (East Calgary) from 7th Ave, or the C-Train free to City Hall and walk the remaining five blocks. Built in under six weeks by the North West Mounted Police in 1875, the fort was the germ of the present city, and remained operative as a police post until 1914, when it was sold – inevitably – to the Canadian Pacific Railway. The whole area remained buried under railway tracks and derelict warehouses until comparatively recently. Period photographs in the adjoining interpretive centre provide a taste of how wild Calgary still was in 1876. Even more remarkable was the ground that men in the fort were expected to cover: the log stockade was a base for operations between Fort Macleod, 160km to the south, and the similar post at Edmonton, almost 400km to the north. It's not as if they had nothing to do: Crowfoot, most prominent of the great Blackfoot chiefs of the time, commented, "If the Police had not come to the country, where would we all be now? Bad men and whiskey were killing us so fast that very few of us indeed would have been left. The Police have protected us as the feathers of a bird protect it from the winter." Only a few forlorn stumps of the original building remain, much having been torn down by the developers, and what survives is its site, now a pleasant forty-acre park contained in the angled crook of the Bow and Elbow rivers. Moves have recently been made to begin construction of an exact replica of the original log stockade. The interpretive centre traces Calgary's development with the aid of artefacts, audiovisual displays and "interpretive walks" along the river. Among the more kitsch activities on offer is the opportunity to dress up as a Mountie.

Across the river to the east is **Hunt House**, built in 1876 for a Hudson's Bay official and believed to be Calgary's oldest building on its original site. Close by, at 750-9th Ave SE, on the same side of the Elbow River, is the renovated **Deane House Historic Site and Restaurant** (☎403/269-7747), built in 1906 by Mountie supremo Superintendent Richard Deane (free tours daily 11am–2pm). It subsequently served time as the home of an artists' co-operative, a boarding house and a stationmaster's house. Today it's a teahouse and restaurant.

St George's Island

St George's Island is home to Calgary's most popular attractions, the **Calgary Zoo**, **Botanical Gardens and Prehistoric Park**, all at 1300 Zoo Rd (daily 9am–5pm; $12–15; ⊛www.calgaryzoo.ab.ca). It can be reached from downtown and Fort Calgary by riverside path, by C-Train northeast towards Whitehorn, or by car (take Memorial Drive E to just west of Deerfoot Trail). Founded in 1920, this is now Canada's largest zoo (and one of North America's best), with 850,000 annual visitors and some 1200 animals, 400 species and innovative and exciting displays in which the animals are left as far as possible in their "natural" habitats. There are underwater viewing areas for polar bears and sea creatures, darkened rooms for nocturnal animals, a special Australian section, greenhouses for myriad tropical birds, and any number of pens for the big draws like gorillas, tigers, giraffes and African warthogs. Check out the extended North American and Canadian Wilds, Aspen Woodlands and Rocky Mountains sections for a taste of a variety of fauna. Also worth a look are the Tropical, Arid and Butterfly gardens in the conservatory. A fast-food concession and picnic areas can help you make a day of it. The **Botanical Gardens** are dotted throughout the zoo, while the **Prehistoric Park** annexe – a "re-created Mesozoic landscape" – is accessible by suspension bridge across the Bow River (June–Sept daily; free with general admission). Its nineteen life-size dinosaur models, none too convincing in their incongruous settings, are a poor substitute for the superb museum at Drumheller (see p.658), and only the fossils in two adjoining buildings are of more than fleeting interest.

Natural-history enthusiasts might also want to visit the **Inglewood Bird Sanctuary** (dawn–dusk; free), on the Bow River's forested flats at 9th Ave and 20A St SE, 3km downstream of the zoo and east of downtown. Some 230 species are present year-round – more during migratory cycles, around 266 species having been recorded across the sanctuary, a portion of land once owned by Colonel James Walker, one of Calgary's original North West Mounted Police. Some of the birds you might see include bald eagles, Swainson's hawks, ring-necked pheasants, warblers, grey partridges and great horned owls. Numerous duck, geese and other waterfowl are also present, and you may also catch sight of muskrats, beavers, white-tailed and mule deer, foxes and long-tailed weasels. A visitor centre (May–Sept daily 9am–5pm) offers information, details of the year-round walking trails, and occasional natural history courses to guide nonexperts. To get here, follow 9th Ave SE to Sanctuary Rd and follow signs to the parking area on the river's south bank. On weekdays the #14 bus (East) turns off 9th Ave at 17th St SE, leaving you just a short walk from the Sanctuary.

Heritage Park Historical Village

A sixty-acre theme park centred on a reconstructed frontier village 16km southwest of downtown, **Heritage Park** (mid-May to Aug daily 9am–5pm; Sept to mid-Oct partial weekdays, Sat & Sun 9am–5pm; $29 admission with rides, $15 without rides; free pancake breakfast with admission 9–10am; Ⓦ www.heritagepark.ab.ca) replicates life in the Canadian West before 1914 and panders relentlessly to the myth of the "Wild West". Full of family-oriented presentations and original costumes, this "heritage" offering – the largest of its type in Canada – is thorough enough for you never to feel obliged to see another. The living, working museum comprises more than 150 **restored buildings**, all transported from other small-town locations. Each has been assigned to one of several communities – fur post, native village, home-stead, farm and c.1900 – and most fulfil their original function. Thus you can see a working blacksmith, buy fresh bread, buy a local paper, go to church, even get married. Transport, too, is appropriate to the period, including steam trains, trams, horse-drawn bus and stagecoaches. If you're here for the day you can pick up cakes and snacks from the traditional Alberta Bakery, or sit down to a full meal in the old-style *Wainwright Hotel*. To get there by car, take either Elbow Drive or Macleod Trail south and turn right on Heritage Drive (the turn-off is marked by a huge, maroon steam engine); **bus** #53 makes the journey from downtown, or you can take the C-Train to Heritage Station and then bus #20 to Northmount.

Eating, drinking and nightlife

Alberta claims, with some justification, to have some of the best **steaks** in the world; Calgary's cuisine can be heavily meat-oriented. With its particular immigration history the city lacks the Ukrainian influences that grace cooking to the north, and often prefers instead to follow the fusion and Pacific Rim trends that have been adopted by most of western Canada's more ambitious restaurants. Most bars and even the live-music venues double up as restaurants and invariably serve perfectly good food. The Toronto Dominion Square and Stephen Ave malls, on 8th Ave SW between 1st and 3rd, are riddled with ethnic takeaways and café-style restaurants – hugely popular and perfect for lunch or snacks on the hoof. The nicest thing to do is buy food and eat it either in the superb Eau Claire Market, which is packed with food stalls and restaurants, or amid the greenery of Devonian Gardens. Elsewhere, the city has an impressive range of middle- to upper-bracket restaurants, where prices are low by most standards.

Calgary is rarely a party town, except during Stampede and a brief fling in summer when the weather allows barbecues and night-time streetlife. Nonetheless, its **bars, cafés and clubs** are all you'd expect of a city of this size, the vast majority of them found in five distinct areas: **Kensington**, with its varied cafés; **"Electric Avenue"**, as 11th Ave SW between 5th and 6th streets is called, which has lost most of its brash and mostly trashy bars, night-time action having moved more to **17th Ave SW**, a more varied collection of pubs, bars, high-quality restaurants, speciality shops and ethnic eating, and **4th St SW**, a similarly more refined restaurant area. **Downtown** cafés and pubs are fine during the day but fairly desolate in the evening. In the specialist clubs the quality of **live music** is good – especially in jazz, blues and the genre closest to cowtown Calgary's heart, country. The Country Music Association has details of local gigs (T 403/233–8809). Major **festivals** include an annual jazz festival (third week in June) and a folk festival at the end of July on Prince's Island. Tickets for virtually all events are available on T 403/270–6700, and through several Marlin Travel offices around the city. You'll find events listings in the *ffwd* (W www.ffwdweekly.com) or *Calgary Straight* listings tabloids (both free from stores, hotels, cafés, bars and so on) and Calgary's main dailies, the *Herald* and the *Sun*.

Cafés and restaurants

Bistro Jo Jo 917-17th Ave SW T 403/245-2382. If you want to eat good French food, but balk at the typically high prices, try the exceptional cuisine in this marble-tiled and red-banquette-filled restaurant. Moderate to expensive.

Caesar's Steakhouse 512-4th Ave SW and 10816 Macleod Trail S T 403/264-1222 or 278-3930. Best place for a huge, perfect steak in the sort of wonderfully cheesy steakhouse – think dimly lit "Roman" decor – that's been around for decades.

Chianti Café and Restaurant 1438-17th Ave SW T 403/229-1600. A favourite local spot for years: dark, noisy, well priced and extremely popular (try to book), with no-nonsense pasta basics and the odd fancy dish. Patio for summer dining outdoors. Recommended.

Divino's 1st St and 9th Ave SW. Café and wine bar opposite the *Palliser* hotel with rather faux mahogany-Tiffany chandelier interior, but good Italian food and particularly noteworthy desserts.

Earl's 2401-4th St SW T 403/228-4141, and five other outlets around Calgary. Ever-reliable mid-range chain, serving North American food.

Galaxie Diner 1413-11th St SW T 403/228-0001. Very popular place with authentic diner decor, great breakfasts and fine open grill served at moderate prices. Daily 8am–4pm.

Hy's 316-4th Ave SW T 403/263-2222. This deep red-carpeted institution has been serving prime Albertan beef in vast quantities since 1955. Moderately expensive.

Joey Tomato's Eau Claire Market T 403/263-6336. This inexpensive Mediterranean-style grill is part of a small chain, but no worse for that, and is a lively, informal place for a good meal among the plethora of choices in and around the Eau Claire market.

Nellie's Kitchen 17th Ave and 7th St SW. Laid-back, popular café and informal, and especially busy at breakfast – which they do superbly. Open for breakfast and lunch only.

River Café Prince Island Park T 403/261-7670, W www.river-cafe.com. With *Teatro* (see below), this is the best of Calgary's restaurants: innnovative Canadian "Northwestern" cuisine and an informal atmosphere on Prince's Island Park, across the bridge from the Eau Claire Market. Be sure to book. Entrees average $17.

Silver Dragon 106-3rd Ave SE T 403/264-5326. The first choice in town for a Chinese meal: this place has been around for over 30 years and uses a team of 15 Hong Kong-trained chefs to conjure up a menu of some 200 dishes.

Teatro 200-8th Ave SE T 403/290-1012, W www.teatro-rest.com. This is the place to come if you want to dress up a little and drop a little money: the fine Italian-influenced food is on a par with that of the less formal *River Café*. Booking is essential.

The Roasterie 314-10th St NW near Kensington Rd. Nice café and hangout attracting an artsy crowd – no meals, but newspapers, notice board and twenty kinds of coffee and snacks.

Bars

Barley Mill Eatery & Pub 201 Barclay Parade, Eau Claire Market. Busy neighbourhood pub that looks and feels the part in Eau Claire Market with an outside patio and a 100-year-old bar imported from Scotland inside; 24 draught beers, 40 bottled brews and lots of whiskies.

Ceili's 513 8th Ave SW. Large and generally lively "Irish" pub.

James Joyce 114-8th Ave SW. All the usual clutter, antique bar and drinks associated with faux Irish pubs; popular, and a little calmer and more intimate than its rival, *Ceili's*.

Ship and Anchor 17th Ave SW on the corner of 5th St. Long-established neighbourhood pub – friendly and laid-back but jumping, with darts, fine music and excellent pub food. Recommended.

Clubs and music venues

Cowboys Dance Hall 826-5th St SW. Holds over 1000 people on two levels with nightly live ents.

Crazy Horse 1311-1st St SW. Popular dance venue with live music on Thursday nights. Small dance floor.

Desperados 1088 Olympic Way. This huge sports and "cowboy" bar, a Calgary institution and supposedly with room for 3500 people.

Kaos Jazz and Blues Bistro 718-17th Ave. Best location in the city for jazz, with blues, acoustic and soul also on offer.

The King Edward Hotel 438-9th Ave SE. Much-loved, down-at-heel location, with consistently good C&W and R&B bands. The Saturday jam session – the blues event of the city – is invariably packed.

Piq Niq Café 811-1st St SW. This place isn't bad as a café, but it really comes into its own Thursday to Saturday with good live jazz acts.

Ranchman's Steak House 9615 Macleod Trail S. A classic honky-tonk and restaurant, known throughout Canada for the live, happening C&W. Free dance lessons at 7.30pm Monday to Thursday. Free admission before 8pm on Thursday. Closed Sunday. Packed with cowboys during the Stampede.

Performing arts and cinema

Calgary might come on as a redneck cow town, but it has ten or more professional theatre companies, a ballet company, an opera company and a full-blown symphony orchestra. Much of the city's highbrow cultural life focuses on the **Calgary Centre for the Performing Arts**, a dazzling modern downtown complex with five performance spaces close to the Glenbow Museum, at 205-8th Ave SE (T403/294-7455). It's also an occasional venue for the acclaimed Calgary Philharmonic Orchestra (Sept–June; W www.cpo-live.com), Theatre Calgary (T403/294-7440) and the well-known Alberta Theatre Projects (T403/294-7475), which usually produces five fairly avant-garde plays annually. More modest classical concerts include the Music at Noon offerings in the Central Library (Sept–April), and the sessions – planned and impromptu – on the small stages in Devonian Gardens. The long-running **Lunchbox Theatre**, 2nd Floor, Bow Valley Square, 205-5th Ave SW (T403/265-4292), offers a popular and wildly varied programme aimed at downtown shoppers and passers-by; performances run from September to May and are somewhat irregular, but tend to start daily at noon (except Sun) in the Bow Valley Square on the corner of 6th Ave and 1st St SW. Calgary's **ballet** world is dominated by the excellent Alberta Ballet Company (T403/245-4222), who perform at various locations around the city. **Opera** is the preserve of Calgary Opera (T403/262-7286), whose home base is the Jubilee Auditorium at 1415-14th Ave NW. The season runs from October to April. For repertory, art-house, classic and foreign **films**, try the restored Uptown Stage & Screen, 612-8th Ave (T403/265-0120) or Plaza Theatre at 1113 Kensington Rd NW; the National Film Board Theatre, 222-1st St SE, puts on free lunchtime shows. The **Museum of Movie Art** at the University of Calgary, 9-3600-21st St NE (Tues–Sat 9.30am–5.30pm), is home to some 4000 cinema posters, some dating back to 1920.

Listings

Airlines Air BC (☎403/265-9555); Air Canada (☎403/265-9555 or 1-800/372-9500); Alaska Airlines (☎1-800/426-0333); American (☎403/254-6331 or 1-800/433-7300); British Airways (☎1-800/247-9297); Canada 3000 (☎403/266-8095); Cathay Pacific (☎1-800/268-6868); Delta (☎1-800/221-1212); Northwest (☎1-800/225-2525); United (☎1-800/241-6522); West Jet (☎403/444-2630 or 1-800/538-5696).

Airport enquiries ☎403/292-8400 or 735-1372.

American Express 421-7th Ave SW (☎403/261-5982 or 1-800/221-7282).

Bookshops Canterbury's Bookshop, 513-8th Ave SW, is the best general bookshop. For maps and travel books, check out Mountain Equipment Co-op, 830-10th Ave SW (☎403/269-2420), or Map Town, 640-6th Ave SW (☎403/266-2241).

Car rental Avis, 211-6th Ave SW (☎403/269-6166 or 1-800/879-2847); Budget, 140-6th Ave SE (☎403/226-1550 or 1-800/267-0505); Hertz (☎403/221-1681 or 1-800/263-0600); Thrifty, 123-5th Ave SE (☎403/262-4400; airport 221-1806; also 1-800/367-2277).

Consulates US, 1000-615 Macleod Trail SE ☎403/266-8962.

Exchange Currencies International, Calgary Tower, 304-8th Ave SW ☎403/290-0330.

Hospital Foothills Hospital, 1403-29th Ave ☎403/670-1110.

Left luggage Facilities at the bus terminal, 850-16th St SW; $2 per 24hr.

Library Central Library, 616 Macleod Trail SE (Mon–Thurs 10am–9pm, Fri–Sat 10am–5pm).

Lost property ☎403/268-1600.

Outdoor gear Mountain Equipment Co-op, 830-10th Ave SW (☎403/269-2420) is Calgary's largest camping and outdoor store.

Pharmacy ☎403/253-2605 (24hr).

Police 316-7th Ave SE (☎403/266-1234); RCMP (☎403/230-6483).

Post office 220-4th Ave SE (☎403/292-5434).

Taxis Associated Cabs ☎403/299-1111; Calgary Cab Co ☎403/777-2222; Checker ☎403/299-9999; Yellow Cab ☎403/974-1111.

Travellers with disabilities Information on wheelchair-accessible transport services ☎403/262-1000; Calgary Handi-Bus ☎403/276-8028.

Weather Information ☎403/263-3333.

The Alberta Badlands

Formed by the meltwaters of the last Ice Age, the valley of the Red Deer River cuts a deep gash through the prairie about 140km east of Calgary, creating a surreal landscape of bare, sunbaked hills and eerie lunar flats dotted with sagebrush and scrubby, tufted grass. On their own, the **Alberta Badlands** – strangely anomalous in the midst of lush grasslands – would repay a visit, but what makes them an essential detour is the presence of the **Royal Tyrrell Museum of Paleontology**, amongst the greatest museums of natural history in North America. The museum is located 8km outside the old coal-mining town of **Drumheller**, a dreary but obvious base if you're unable to fit the museum into a day-trip from Calgary. Drumheller is also the main focus of the **Dinosaur Trail**, a road loop that explores the Red Deer Valley and surrounding badlands; you'll need your own transport for this circuit, and for the trip to the **Dinosaur Provincial Park**, home to the Tyrrell Museum Field Station and the source of many of its fossils.

Drumheller

A downbeat town in an extraordinary setting, **DRUMHELLER** is roughly ninety minutes' drive northeast of Calgary. As you approach it from the west, the town is hidden until you come to a virulent-red water tower and the road suddenly drops into a dark, hidden canyon. The otherworldliness of the gloomy, blasted landscape is spookily heightened by its contrast to the vivid colours of the earlier wheat and grasslands. Drumheller sits at the base of the canyon, surrounded by the detritus and spoil heaps of its mining past, the Red

The Dinosaur Trail from Drumheller

The **Dinosaur Trail** is a catch-all circular road route of 51km from Drumheller embracing some of the viewpoints and lesser historic sights of the badlands and the Red Deer Valley area. The comprehensive *Drumheller Valley Visitor's Choice* (free from the Drumheller infocentre) lists thirty separate stopoffs, mostly on the plain above the valley, of which the key ones are: the **Little Church** (6km west of Drumheller), the "Biggest Little Church in the World" (capacity six); **Horsethief Canyon** (17.6km west of the museum) and **Horseshoe Canyon** (19km southwest of the museum on Hwy 9), two spectacular viewpoints of the wildly eroded valley, the latter with good trails to and along the canyon floor; the **Hoodoos**, slender columns of wind-sculpted sandstone, topped with mushroom-like caps (17km southeast of Drumheller on Hwy 10); the still largely undeveloped **Midland Provincial Park**, site of the area's first mines and crisscrossed by badland trails, now home to an interpretive centre (daily 9am–6pm; free); and the **Atlas Coal Mine** (guided tours mid-May to mid-Oct daily 9am–6pm; $4, or $6 for guided tour; ☎403/822-2220), dominated by the teetering wooden "tipple", once used to sort ore and now a beautiful and rather wistful piece of industrial archeology.

Deer River having exposed not only dinosaur fossils but also (now exhausted) coal seams. The coal attracted the likes of Samuel Drumheller, an early mining pioneer after whom the town is named. The first mine opened in 1911, production reaching a peak after the opening of a rail link to Calgary two years later. In less than fifty years it was all over, coal's declining importance in the face of gas and oil sounding the industry's death knell. These days Drumheller is sustained by agriculture, oil – there are some 3000 wells dotted around the surrounding farmland – and tourism, the Tyrrell Museum of Paleontology ranking as one of Alberta's biggest draws.

The town is best reached by taking Hwy 2 north towards Edmonton and branching east on Hwy 72 and Hwy 9. It's an easy day-trip with your own transport, and most people make straight for the Tyrrell Museum, signposted from Drumheller on Hwy 838. Using one of the two **Greyhound buses** daily from Calgary to Drumheller (around $20 one-way) makes a day-trip more of a squeeze. The depot (☎403/823-7566) is some way out of the town centre at the Suncity Mall on Hwy 9. It's definitely too far to walk from here or the town centre to the museum, particularly on a hot day, but Badlands Taxis (☎403/823-6552) or Jack's Taxi (☎403/823-2220) will run you there from the bus depot for about $10.

There's not much to do in the town, despite the best efforts of its **infocentre** at the corner of Riverside Drive and 2nd St West (June–Aug daily 9am–9pm; rest of year Mon–Fri 8.30am–4.30pm; ☎403/823-1331). For all its half million visitors a year, Drumheller has just 350 or so beds; you don't really want to spend a night here. If you have no choice, be sure to book well in advance. The best of the downtown **hotels** is the overpriced *Lodge at Drumheller* (☎403/823-3322; ❸). Other central options include the *Rockhound Motor Inn*, South Railway Drive (☎403/823-5302; ❹); *Drumheller Inn* (☎403/823-8400; ❺), a modern motel on a bluff at 100 S Railway Ave (Hwy 9) off the Hwy 56 approach from the west; and the tasteful log cabins of the pleasanter *Badlands Motel* (☎403/823-5155; ❺), 1km out of town on Hwy 838. For **camping**, head to the *Dinosaur Trailer Park* (☎403/823-3291; $15; April–Oct), across the river north of downtown at the junction of Hwy 56 and Hwy 838. The visitor infocentre has lists of the many other private and provincial campsites up and down the valley (*Little Fish Lake Provincial Park*, 50km southeast of Drumheller on Hwy 573, is the best). For cheap eating, the *Diana* on Main St is half-diner, half-Chinese restaurant, and the *Bridge Greek Restaurant*, 71 Bridge St N, has a relaxed ambience and good food. Better-quality **restaurants** have a reputation of going broke once the tourists have gone home, but currently the two best places to eat are *Jack's Bistro*, 70 Railway Ave (T403/823-8422), serving hearty Canadian fare, and the reasonably priced and little-known *Sizzling House*, 160 Centre St (T403/823-8098), reckoned to be one of Alberta's best Chinese restaurants. The cafeteria at the museum also makes a reasonable eating option.

Royal Tyrrell Museum of Paleontology

Packed with high-tech displays, housed in a sleek building and blended skilfully into its desolate surroundings, the **Royal Tyrrell Museum of Paleontology**, 6km outside Drumheller, (mid-May to Aug daily 9am–9pm; Sept to mid-Oct daily 10am–5pm; mid-Oct to late May Tues–Sun 10am–5pm; $10; W www.tyrrellmuseum.com) is an object lesson in museum design. It attracts half a million-plus visitors a year, and its wide-ranging exhibits are likely to appeal to anyone with even a hint of scientific or natural curiosity. Although it claims the world's largest collection of complete dinosaur skeletons (fifty full-size animals and 80,000 miscellaneous specimens), the museum is far more than a load of old bones, and as well as tracing the earth's history from the year dot to the present day it's also a leading centre of study and academic research. Its name comes from Joseph Tyrrell, who in 1884 discovered the Albertosaurus, first of the dinosaur remains to be pulled from the Albertan badlands.

Laid out on different levels to suggest layers of geological time, the open-plan exhibit guides you effortlessly through a chronological progression, culminating in a huge central hall of over two hundred dinosaur specimens. If there's a fault, it's that the hall is visible early on and tempts you to skip the lower-level displays, which place the dinosaurs in context by skilfully linking geology, fossils, plate tectonics, evolution and the like with Drumheller's own landscape. You also get a chance to peer into the preparation lab and watch scientists working on fossils in one of the world's best-equipped paleontology centres.

By far the most impressive exhibits are the **dinosaurs** themselves. Whole skeletons are immaculately displayed against three-dimensional backgrounds that persuasively depict the swamps of sixty million years ago. Some are paired with full-size plastic dinosaurs, which appear less macabre and menacing than the freestanding skeletons. Sheer size is not the only fascination: Xiphactinus, for example, a four-metre specimen, is striking more for its delicate and beautiful tracery of bones. Elsewhere the emphasis is on the creatures' diversity or on their staggeringly small brains, sometimes no larger than their eyes. The museum naturally also tackles the problem of the dinosaurs' extinction, pointing out that around ninety percent of all plant and animal species that have ever inhabited the earth have become extinct. Leave a few minutes for the wonderful **paleoconservatory** off the dinosaur hall, a collection of living prehistoric plants, some unchanged in 180 million years, selected from fossil records to give an idea of the vegetation that would have typified Alberta in the dinosaur age.

Dinosaur Provincial Park

Drivers can feasibly fit in a trip to **Dinosaur Provincial Park**, 174km from Drumheller, on the same day as the Tyrrell Museum, and still be able to head back to Calgary on the Trans-Canada Highway, which runs just south of the park. The nearest town is **BROOKS**, 48km west of the **Royal Tyrrell**

Museum Field Station, the park's obvious hub (late May to early Oct daily 8.30am–9pm; rest of year Mon–Fri 9am–4pm; $2; ☎403/378-4344). The excellent Dinosaur Provincial Park **campsite** in the park beside Little Sandhill Creek is open year-round, but only serviced from May to September ($13) – book on ☎403/378-3700.

Nestled among some of the baddest of the badlands, the region's landscape is not only one of the most other-worldly in Canada, but also one of the world's richest fossil beds, a superb medley of prairie habitats and ecosystems and a UN World Heritage Site. Over 300 complete skeletons have been found and dispatched to museums across the world, representing 35 (or ten percent) of all known dinosaur species. The field station has five self-guided **trails**, the Badlands Trail and Cottonwood Flats Trail being the most worthwhile, and giving a good taste of this extraordinary region. The centre also has a small museum that goes over the same ground as its parent in Drumheller, leaving the real meat of the visit to the **Badlands Bus Tour**, an excellent ninety-minute guided tour of the otherwise out-of-bounds dinosaur dig near the centre of the park (May–Sept Mon–Fri tours 3 or more daily, Sat & Sun 7 times daily; $4.50). A few exposed skeletons have been left *in situ*, with panels giving background information. The station also organizes two-hour guided **hikes**, most notably the Centrosaurus Bone Bed Hike (Tues, Thurs, Sat & Sun 9.15am; $4.50), which visits a restricted area where some 300 centrosaurus skeletons have been uncovered. All tours fill up quickly, so it's worth trying to book ahead.

Hwy 3: Medicine Hat to Crowsnest Pass

The most travelled route across southern Alberta is the Trans-Canada Highway, direct to Calgary; **Hwy 3**, branching off at **Medicine Hat**, takes a more southerly course across the plains before finally breaching the Rockies at Crowsnest Pass. This quieter and less spectacular route into the mountains holds a couple of worthwhile diversions: the new **Carriage Centre** near Cardston and **Head-Smashed-In Buffalo Jump** heritage site.

Medicine Hat

Though **MEDICINE HAT** is barely a hundred years old, the origin of its wonderful name has already been confused. The most likely story has to do with a Cree medicine man who lost his headdress while fleeing a battle with the Blackfoot; his followers lost heart at the omen, surrendered, and were promptly massacred. These days you rarely see the town mentioned without the adage that it "has all hell for a basement", a quotation from Rudyard Kipling coined in response to the huge reserves of natural gas that lurk below the town. Discovered by railway engineers drilling for water in 1883, the gas fields now feed a flourishing petrochemical industry which blots the otherwise park-studded downtown area on the banks of the South Saskatchewan River. Medicine Hat may claim that its 1440 hours of summer sunshine make it Canada's sunniest city, but its main function is as a major staging post on the Trans-Canada Highway. The world's **tallest tepee** (twenty storeys tall and actually made of metal), on the highway close to the visitor centre, and the nightmare **Riverside Waterslide** at Hwy 1 and Powerhouse Rd (mid–May to early Sept daily 10am–8pm; $12.50; ☎403/529-6218) are the only attractions of note.

The best place for coffee and snacks is *Café Mundo*, 579 3rd St SE; for lunch try *Caroline's*, 101 4th Ave SE (☎403/529-5300); and for a novelty "Wild West" setting the place to go is the historic *Rustler's*, 901 8th St SW (☎403/526-8004), one of the town's oldest restaurants. The least expensive of the many **motels** is the *Bel-Aire*, 633 14th St (☎403/527-4421; ❶), conveniently situated at the junction of the Trans-Canada and Hwy 3, though the *Best Western Inn*, on the Trans-Canada at 722 Redcliff Drive (☎403/527-3700 or 1-800/527-6633, ⓦwww.bestwestern.com; ❺), is more appealing if around three times the price. The best place around is the smart and comfortable *Medicine Hat Lodge*, 1051 Ross Glen Drive (☎403/529-2222 or 1-800/661-8095, ⓦwww.medhatlodge.com; ❺). The main downtown accommodation is the *Medicine Hat Inn Downtown*, 530 4th St SE (☎403/526-1313 or 1-800/730-3887; ❸).

Lethbridge

Alberta's third city, **LETHBRIDGE** is booming on the back of oil, gas and some of the province's most productive agricultural land; none of which is of much consequence to people passing through, whom the city attempts to side-track with the **Nikka Yuko Centennial Gardens** (mid-May to June & Sept daily 9am–5pm; July & Aug daily 9am–9pm; $4) in its southeastern corner at 7th Ave and Mayor Macgrath Drive in Henderson Lake Park. Built in 1967 as a symbol of Japanese and Canadian amity, the gardens were a somewhat belated apology for the treatment of Japanese-Canadians during World War II, when 22,000 were interned, 6000 of them in Lethbridge. Four tranquil Japanese horticultural landscapes make up the gardens, along with a pavilion of cypress wood handcrafted in Japan perpetually laid out for a tea ceremony. Far removed from the gardens' decorum is **Fort Whoop-Up** (June–Aug Mon–Sat 10am–6pm, Sun noon–5pm; rest of year Tues–Fri 10am–4pm, Sun 1–4pm; $2.50) at Indian Battle Park (Scenic Drive at 3rd Ave), a reconstruction of the wild whiskey-trading post set up in 1869 by American desperadoes from Fort Benton, Montana (the first of several in the region). It became the largest and most lucrative of the many similar forts which sprang up illegally all over the Canadian prairies, and led directly to the arrival of the North West Mounted Police in 1874. Aboriginal peoples came from miles around to trade anything – including the clothes off their backs – for the lethal hooch, which was fortified by grain alcohol and supplemented by ingredients such as red peppers, dye and chewing tobacco. The fort was also the scene of the last armed battle in North America between aboriginal peoples (fought between the Cree and Blackfoot nations in 1870). Lethbridge's third significant sight is the **Sir Alexander Galt Museum** (daily 10am–4.30pm; donation) at the western end of 5th Ave South off Scenic Drive, one of Canada's better small-town muse-ums. It's named after a Canadian high commissioner who in 1882 financed a mine that led to the foundation of Lethbridge. Revamped at vast expense in 1985, the museum offers an overview of the city's history, with displays that cover coal mining, irrigation, immigration and the shameful internment episodes during the 1940s. There are also a couple of galleries devoted to art and other temporary exhibitions.

Four Greyhound **buses** operate daily from Calgary; the Lethbridge bus terminal is at 411-5th St S (☎403/327-1551). Two buses run daily to Fort Macleod, and two to Medicine Hat and the US border for connections to Great Falls and Helena in Montana. The **tourist office** is at 2805 Scenic Drive at the corner of Hwy 4 and Hwy 5 (summer daily 9am–8pm; winter Mon–Sat

9am–5pm; ☎403/320-1222 or 1-800/661-1222). Most of the city's **motels** are on a single strip, Mayor Macgrath Drive, including the top-of-the-pile *Sandman Hotel Lethbridge*, at no. 421 (☎403/328-1111 or 1-800/726-3626; ❹). Downtown the best value is the *Days Inn*, 100 3rd Ave S (☎403/327-6000 or 1-800/661-8085; ❸). The *Henderson Lake Campgrounds* (☎403/328-5452; $14; May–Oct) are near Henderson Lake on 7th Ave S alongside the Nikka Yuko gardens. The best downtown **eating** is to be found in the *Lethbridge Lodge Hotel*, 320 Scenic Drive (☎403/328-1123 or 1-800/661-1232), which boasts *Anton's*, an upmarket restaurant with modern American food, and the cheaper but pleasant and popular *Garden Café*. For downtown coffee and snacks, make for *The Penny Coffee House*, 331 5th St S.

Fort Macleod and around

FORT MACLEOD catches traffic coming north from the US and south from Calgary on Hwy 2, which eases around the town centre via the largely rebuilt wooden palisade of the **Fort Museum**, 219 25th St (May, June & Sept to mid-Oct daily 9am–5pm; July & Aug daily 9am–8pm; mid-Oct to Dec, March & April Mon–Fri 9am–5pm; $5). One for die-hard Mountie fans, this was the first fort established in Canada's Wild West by the North West Mounted Police, who got lost after being dispatched to raid Fort Whoop-Up in Lethbridge, allowing the whiskey traders to flee; finding Whoop-Up empty, they continued west under Colonel James Macleod to establish a permanent barracks here on Oldman Island on the river in 1874. The RCMP "musical ride", a display of precision riding, is performed four times daily in July and August by students in replica dress. Two daily **buses** serve the town from Lethbridge and between three and five from Calgary, the latter continuing west to Cranbrook, Nelson and eventually to Vancouver in British Columbia. The depot is at 2302 2nd Ave (☎403/553-3383). The **tourist office** is at the east end of town on 24th St (mid-May to Aug daily 9am–8pm; ☎403/553-4955). The town has nine similarly priced **motels**, the most central being the *Fort Motel* on Main St (☎403/553-3606; ❷). Top choice is the *Sunset Motel* (☎403/553-4448 or 1-888/554-2784; ❹), located on Hwy 3 at the western entrance to town. All fill up quickly in summer.

Head-Smashed-In Buffalo Jump

The image of Indians trailing a lone buffalo with bow and arrow may be Hollywood's idea of how aboriginal peoples foraged for food, but the truth, while less romantic, was often far more effective and spectacular. Over a period of 10,000 years, Blackfoot hunters perfected a technique of luring buffalo herds into a shallow basin and stampeding them to their deaths over a broad cliff, where they were then butchered for meat (dried to make pemmican, a cake of pounded meat, berries and lard), bone (for tools) and hide (for clothes and shelter). Such "jumps" existed all over North America, but the **Head-Smashed-In Buffalo Jump**, in the Porcupine Hills 18km northwest of Fort Macleod on Hwy 785, is the best preserved (daily: mid-May to early Sept 9am–6pm; rest of year 10am–5pm). Its name is a literal description of how a nineteenth-century Blackfoot met his end after deciding the best spot to watch the jump was at the base of the cliff, apparently unaware he was about to be visited by some five hundred plummeting buffalo. The modern **interpretive centre**, a seven-storeyed architectural tour de force, is built into the ten-metre-high and 305-metre-wide cliff near the original jump. Below it, a ten-metre-deep bed of ash and bones accumulated over millennia is protected by the threat of a

$50,000 fine for anyone foolish enough to rummage for souvenirs. All manner of artefacts and objects have been discovered amidst the debris, among them knives, scrapers and sharpened stones used to skin the bison. Metal arrowheads in the topmost layers, traded with white settlers, suggest the jump was used until comparatively recently. The multilevel facility delves deep into the history of the jump and native culture in general, its highlight being a film, *In Search of the Buffalo*, which attempts to re-create the thunderous death plunge using a herd of buffalo, which were slaughtered, frozen and then somehow made to look like live animals hurtling to their deaths (shown half-hourly on Level Four). Around the centre the jump is surrounded by a couple of kilometres of **trails**, the starting point for tours conducted by Blackfoot native guides. No public transport serves the site; taxis from Fort Macleod cost about $20.

Remington-Alberta Carriage Centre

The **Remington Carriage Centre**, 623 Main St (daily: mid-May to early Sept 9am–6pm; rest of year 10am–5pm; ⓦ www.remingtoncentre.com; $6.50), lies immediately south of **CARDSTON** (across the river from the town centre), just off Hwy 2 about 50km south of Fort Macleod. Although brilliantly executed, the museum's appeal is more limited, centring on horse-drawn vehicles and evoking the atmosphere of their nineteenth-century heyday. The main hall boasts around sixty working carriages – the core of a private collection begun by Don Remington in the 1950s – and around 140 in passive display, the exhibits cleverly integrated with 25 "stories" that place the carriages in their social and cultural context. Additionally there's the chance to ride the carriages (usually for free), see working stables and admire the magnificent Quarters and Clydesdales that make up the centre's horse herd. Guides are often in period dress, and you can watch craftspeople in the process of building and renovating various carriages. Free guided tours run regularly around the site.

The road to Crowsnest Pass

Crowsnest Pass (1382m) is the most southerly of the three major routes into the Rockies and British Columbia from Alberta, and far less attractive than the Calgary and Edmonton approaches. As Hwy 3 pushes west out of Fort Macleod across glorious windblown prairie, it augurs well: the settlements are bleaker and more backwoods in appearance, and the vast unbroken views to the mountain-filled horizon appear much as they must have to the first pioneers. As the road climbs towards the pass, however, the grime and dereliction of the area's mining heritage make themselves increasingly felt. Hopes a century ago that Crowsnest's vast coal deposits might make it the "Pittsburgh of Canada" were dashed by disasters, poor-quality coal, complicated seams, cheaper coal from British Columbia and rapid obsolescence. Today much of the area has been declared an Historic District and turned into Alberta's only "ecomuseum", a desperate attempt to bring life and tourist cash back to economically blighted communities (many people commute to work in British Columbia's mines over the Pass or have left altogether). To a limited extent they've succeeded. If mines and disaster sites don't appeal, the Crowsnest route west is of most use as a direct route if you're hurrying to Vancouver or aim to explore the Kootenays in southern British Columbia. After breasting the pass, Hwy 3 drops into BC passing through Fernie (see p.961) and following the often spectacular Elk River Valley to join Hwy 95 at Cranbrook (see p.960).

Bellevue and the Frank Slide

Sleepy **BELLEVUE** is the first village worthy of the name west of Fort Macleod, an oddball and close-knit spot with an old-world feel unusual in these parts. It's distinguished by a church the size of a dog kennel and a wooden tepee painted lemon yellow, as well as the claim to have "the best drinking water in Alberta". Nonetheless, it supports a small summer-only **infocentre** by the campsite and provides visitors with the opportunity to explore – complete with hard hat and miner's lamp – a wonderfully dark and dank 100m or so of the old **Bellevue Mine** (30min tours every half-hour mid-May to early Sept daily 10am–5.30pm; $6). The only mine open to the public locally, it ceased production in 1962, but remains infamous for an explosion in 1910 that destroyed the ventilator fan. Thirty men died in the disaster, though not from the blast, but by breathing so-called "afterdamp", a lethal mixture of carbon dioxide and carbon monoxide left after fire has burnt oxygen from the atmosphere. As if this wasn't enough, Canada's worst mining disaster ever had occurred five years earlier at **HILLCREST**, a village immediately south of Bellevue (signed from Hwy 3), when 189 men were killed by an explosion and the effects of "afterdamp". All were buried together a few centimetres apart in mass graves, now the Hillcrest Cemetery on 8th Ave.

Bellevue has a quaint **campsite**, the *Bellecrest Community Association Campground* (☎403/564-4696; donation), located just off the highway just east of the village: it's open May to October and has 22 "random" sites, toilets, tap water and an on-site ten-seat church with recorded sermons. The site is also handy for the **Leitch Collieries Provincial Historic Site** (mid-May to mid-Sept daily 10am–4pm; winter site unstaffed; $2), just off the main road to the north before the campsite. This was once the region's largest mining and coking concern; it was also the first to close (in 1915). Today there's little to see in the way of old buildings, but displays and boardwalk interpretive trails past "listening posts" fill you in on mining techniques. The overgrown site is also enthusiastically described by interpretive staff.

The Crowsnest Pass trail of destruction, death and disaster continues beyond Bellevue. Dominating the skyline behind the village are the crags and vast rock fall of the **Frank Slide**, an enormous landslide that has altered the contours of Turtle Mountain, once riddled with the galleries of local mines. On April 29, 1903 an estimated 100 million tonnes of rock on a front stretching for over 1km and 700m high trundled down the mountain, burying 68 people and their houses in less than two minutes. Amazingly none of the miners working locally were killed – they dug themselves out after fourteen hours of toil. The morbidly interesting **Frank Slide Interpretive Centre** (daily: mid-May to mid-Sept 9am–6pm; rest of year 10am–5pm; ⓦwww.frankslide.com; $6.50), situated 1.5km off the highway about 1km north of the village, highlights European settlement in the area, the coming of the Canadian Pacific Railway to Alberta and the technology, attitudes and lives of local miners. It's well worth wandering around the site and slide area – there's a 1.5-kilometre trail or you can walk up the ridge above the car park for good views and an idea of the vast scale of the earth movement: no one to this day quite understands the science of how boulders travelled so far from the main slide (several kilometres in many cases). "Air lubrication" is the best theory, a device by which the cascading rock compressed the air in front of it, creating a hovercraft-like cushion of trapped air on which it "rode" across the surface.

Blairmore, Coleman and Crowsnest Pass

BLAIRMORE, 2km beyond the slide, is a scrappy settlement redeemed for the casual visitor only by the walks and four winter and night ski runs on Pass Powder

Keg Ski Hill (☎403/562-8334) above it. Largest of the Crowsnest towns (pop. around 1800), it has a handful of "historic" buildings, notably the *Cosmopolitan Hotel* – built in 1912 – at 13001-20th Ave (☎403/562-7321; ❷), but neither town or hotel are places to linger. **COLEMAN** is the place to spend the night if you absolutely have to; the town, battered and bruised by mine closures, amounts to little – the small Crowsnest Museum has interesting mining exhibits in the old schoolhouse at 7701-18th Ave (mid-May to Oct daily 9am–6pm; Nov to mid-May Mon–Fri 10am–noon & 1–4pm; $2), a single road, a dilapidated strip of houses, three garages and a battered **motel**, the 24-unit *Stop Inn* (☎403/562-7381; ❷). More appealing is the dubiously named ten-unit *Kozy Knest Kabins Triple K Motel* (☎403/563-5155; ❷), open from May to October and more scenically situated 12km west of Coleman on Hwy 3 beside Crowsnest Lake.

Beyond Coleman the road climbs towards **Crowsnest Pass** itself and, after a rash of sawmills, the natural scenery finally takes centre stage in a reassuring mix of lakes, mountains and trees protected by **Crowsnest Provincial Park**. A rustic provincial **campsite** overlooks the lake at Crowsnest Creek, about 15km west of Coleman ($5).

Waterton Lakes National Park

Located in an isolated position well to the south of the other Canadian Rockies parks, **WATERTON LAKES NATIONAL PARK** appears at first glance to be simply an addendum to the much larger Glacier National Park, which joins it across the US border. Despite its modest size, however, it contains scenery – and trails – as stupendous as any of the bigger Canadian Rockies parks. In particular this is a great place to come for day-hikes, most of which – unlike equivalent walks in Banff and Jasper – can be easily accessed from the park's principal focus, **Waterton Townsite** (or just Waterton).

Founded in 1895, the park was relaunched in 1932 as an "International Peace Park" to symbolize the understated relationship between Canada and its neighbour. The two parks remain separate, but Canadian and US citizens who are backpacking can cross the border without formalities. However, if you're not a national of either country you're limited to using trails that begin and end in the same park unless you have secured visas in advance. To drive from one to the other, everyone has to exit the park and pass through immigration controls, which are as stringent as anywhere else. A **park permit** is required between April and the end of September for all who enter the park: a day-pass is $4 (yearly $28), and group passes (2–10 people) cost $12 daily (see box p.678 for more details concerning park entry fees).

A history of the park

These days Waterton is on the road pretty much to nowhere. It was a different story in the past, for the region provided a happy hunting ground for **Ktunaxa** (Kootenay) First Peoples, whose home base was across the Continental Divide in the Kootenay region of present-day British Columbia. Around 200 archeological sites betraying their presence have been found in the park. Anything up to 9000 years ago aboriginal peoples crossed the mountains to fish and hunt bison on the prairie grasslands fringing the Waterton region, foodstuffs denied to them in their own aboriginal heartlands. By about 1700 the diffusion of the horse across North America (introduced by the Spanish) allowed rival peoples, namely the Blackfoot, to extend their sphere of influence from central Alberta into the

WATERTON LAKES NATIONAL PARK

▲ Cardston & Lethbridge

N

0 ___ 5 km

▲ Pincher Creek

Belly River

Crooked Creek

Waterton River

Kesler Lakes

CHIEF MOUNTAIN INTERNATIONAL HIGHWAY

Maskinonge Lake

Buffalo Paddocks

Park Entrance

ENTRANCE ROAD

Lower Waterton

Sofa Creek

Sofa (2515m) ▲

Crypt Lake

Belly River Campground

North Belly River

Customs

CANADA

USA

▲ Glacier National Park & Great Falls (MT)

Dungarvan (2560m) ▲

Galwey (2348m) ▲

Coppermine Creek

Bellevue (2112m) ▲

RED ROCK CANYON PARKWAY

Crandell Campground

Crandell (2378m) ▲

Middle Waterton

Vimy Trail

Vimy (2379m) ▲

Crypt Lake Trail

Hell Roaring Falls

Boswell (2439m) ▲

Goat Haunt Ranger Station ▶

Glendowan (2653m) ▲

Newman (2515m) ▲

Goat Lake

Goat Lake Trail

Red Rock Canyon

Blakiston Falls

Blakiston (2904m) ▲

Crandell Lake

AKAMINA PARKWAY

Waterton Lakes Townsite

Upper Waterton

Bertha Falls

Richards (2416m) ▲

MONTANA

Anderson (2698m) ▲

Bauerman Creek

Lone Creek

Lineham Lakes

Rowe Lake Trail

Rowe Lakes

Carthew Summit (2630m) ▲

Carthew Lakes

Summit Lake

Bertha Lake

Anderson Lake

Cameron Lake

ALBERTA

Lost Lakes

Wall Lake Trail

Twin Lakes

South Kootenay Pass

Tamarack Trail

Forum Lake

CONTINENTAL DIVIDE

Wall Lake

BRITISH COLUMBIA

KISHINENA FORESTRY RD

The natural environment of Waterton Lakes NP

The Waterton area's unique **geological history** becomes clear when you compare its scenery with the strikingly different landscapes of Banff and Jasper national parks to the north. Rock and mountains in Waterton moved eastward during the formation of the Rockies (see box p.677), but unlike the ruptured strata elsewhere it travelled as a single vast mass known as the Lewis Thrust. Some 6km thick, this monolith moved over 70km along a 300-kilometre front, the result being that rocks over 1.5 billion years old from the Rockies' "sedimentary basement" – now the oldest surface rocks in the range – finally came to rest undisturbed on *top* of the prairies' far more recent 60-million-year-old shales. Scarcely any zone of transition exists between the two, which is why the park is often known as the place where the "peaks meet the prairies", and its landscapes as "upside-down mountains". The effect was to produce not only slightly lower peaks than to the north, but also mountains whose summits are irregular in shape and whose sedimentary formations are horizontal (very different from the steeply tilted strata and distinctive sawtooth ridges of Banff National Park).

The classic glacial U-shaped Waterton Valley and Upper Waterton Lake (at 150m, the Rockies' deepest lake) are more recent phenomena, gouged out 1.9 million years ago by Ice Age **glaciers** as they carved their way northwards through the present Waterton valley before expiring on the prairies. Upper Waterton Lake and the other two Waterton lakes are residual depressions left after the ice's final retreat 11,000 years ago. Cameron Lake, by contrast, was created when a glacial moraine (debris created by a glacier) dammed the waters of Cameron Creek. The flat townsite area has different origins again, consisting of deposits of silt, mud and gravel washed down from the mountains over the millennia and deposited as an alluvial "fan" across Upper Waterton Lake.

Flora and fauna

The huge variety of altitude, habitats and climate within the park – a combination of prairie, montane and alpine – mean that plants and wildlife from prairie habitats co-mingle with the species of the purely montane, subalpine and alpine regions found elsewhere. The result is the greatest diversity of **flora and fauna** of any of the western national parks: 1200 plant species – well over half of all those grown in Alberta – and 250 species of birds. The variety is immediately noticeable. As you approach the park on Hwy 5 from the north, a route almost as scenic as the park, you pass through dry prairie **grassland**. This is home to native grasses such as

area around Waterton. Their presence and increased mobility made it increasingly difficult for the Ktunaxa to make their habitual incursions, though Blackfoot supremacy in turn was to be cut short by the arrival of pioneer guns and white homesteads. By the mid-nineteenth century the Blackfoot had retreated eastwards, leaving the Waterton area virtually uninhabited. The region was named by Lieutenant Thomas Blakiston, a member of the famous Palliser expedition, in honour of the eighteenth-century British naturalist Charles Waterton.

The area's first permanent white resident, **John George Brown** – or "Kootenai Brown" – was a character straight out of a Wild West fantasy. Born in England and allegedly educated at Oxford, he spent time with the British Army in India, decamped to San Francisco, chanced his arm in the gold fields of British Columbia and worked for a time as a pony express rider with the US Army. Moving to the Waterton region he was attacked by Blackfoot natives, supposedly wrenching an arrow from his back with his own hands. He was then captured by Chief Sitting Bull and tied naked to a stake, but managed to escape at dead of night to join the rival Ktunaxa natives, with whom he grama and rough fescue, local species now rapidly disappearing, displaced over the years by cultivated crops. Here, too, you should see the prickly wild rose, Alberta's floral emblem, sagebrush, buckbrush (yellow rose) and pincushion cactus. Entering the park you pass the **wetlands** of Maskinonge Lake on your left, while in the Blakison Valley and around *Belly River Campsite* you are in the realms of **aspen parkland**, a transitional zone between prairie and forest habitats dominated by aspen, willow, white spruce, balsam poplar and flowers such as prairie crocus, snowberry and lily of the valley. Higher up you encounter **montane forest** and subalpine zones, fecund zones rich in plant and animal life easily explored on hikes such as the Bertha Lake and Carthew Lakes trails (see p.672). On the eastern slopes above Cameron Lake are copses of 400-year-old subalpine trees (lodgepole pine, larch, fir, whitebark pine and Engelmann spruce), the oldest forest growth in the park. Here, too, you'll see vast spreads of so-called bear grass, a bright flower-topped grass which can grow up to a metre in height. Trees largely give out in the **alpine zone**, an area of which the park's Crypt Lake is a good example. It is the preserve of heathers, hardy lichens, flower-strewn meadows and rarer high-altitude alpine plants. See Contexts p.1074 for more on these various habitats.

If you want to see **fauna**, enquire at the park centre for likely locations and times – autumn days at dawn and dusk are usually best. **Birds** are best seen on Maskinonge and Lower Waterton lakes, Linnet Lake, Cameron Lake and along the easy 45-minute Wishbone Trail off Chief Mountain Highway. The best time to look is during the migratory season between September and November, as the park lies under two major migration routes. Ospreys also nest close to Waterton Townsite. Maskinonge Lake is the place to sit in the hope of seeing mink and muskrats. As for **mammals**, beavers can be seen on the Belly River, and golden-mantled ground squirrels around Cameron Lake and on the Bear's Hump above town; Columbian ground squirrels are ubiquitous. The park has about fifty black bears, but you'll be lucky to see them: your best bet is to scan the slopes of Blakison Valley in July and August as they forage for berries in readiness for hibernation. Grizzlies, moose and cougars are also prevalent, but rarely seen. White-tailed deer nibble up and down the Red Rock Canyon Parkway, while elk and mule deer often wander in and around Waterton town itself. Mountain goats are shy and elusive, but you may glimpse one or two in the rocky high ground above Bertha, Crypt and Goat lakes. Bighorn sheep congregate above the Visitor Centre and the northern flanks of the Blakison Valley.

spent years hunting and trapping, until their virtual retreat from the prairies. Marriage in 1869 calmed him down, and encouraged him to build a cabin (the region's first) alongside Waterton Lake. In time he was joined by other settlers, one of whom, Frederick Godsal, a rancher and close personal friend, took up Brown's campaign to turn the region into a **federal reserve**. In 1895 a reserve was duly established, with Brown as its first warden. In 1910 the area was made a "Dominion Park"; a year later it was designated a **national park**, the fourth in Canada's burgeoning park system. Brown, then aged 71, was made its super-intendent, but died four years later, still lobbying hard to extend the park's borders. His grave lies alongside the main road into Waterton Townsite.

For all Brown's environmental zeal it was he, ironically, who first noticed globules of **oil** on Cameron Creek, a local river, a discovery that would bring oil and other mineral entrepreneurs to ravage the region. Brown himself actually skimmed oil from the river, bottled it, and sold it in nearby settlements. In 1901 a forest road was ploughed into Cameron Creek Valley. In September of the same year the Rocky Mountain Development Company struck oil, leading to western Canada's first producing oil well (and only the second in the entire country). The oil soon dried up, a monument on the Akamina Parkway (see below) now marking the well's original location. Tourists meanwhile were giving the park a conspicuously wide berth, thanks mainly to the fact that it had no railway (unlike Banff and Jasper), a situation that changed when the Great Northern Railway introduced a bus link here from its Montana to Jasper railway. Visitors began to arrive, the *Prince of Wales* hotel was built, and the park's future was assured. In 1995, some time after the other big parks, UNESCO declared Waterton a World Heritage Site. Today, the park is becoming ever more popular, with the same tell-tale proliferation of souvenir shops on Waterton Ave, Waterton Townsite's main street, as you find in Banff.

Waterton Townsite

WATERTON TOWNSITE, the park's only base, accommodation source and services centre, is beautifully set on Upper Waterton Lake, but offers little by way of cultural distraction. Most people are here to walk (see box p.672), windsurf, horse ride or take boat trips on the lake (see p.675). There are also a handful of town trails, and a trio of great hikes – Bertha Lake, Crypt Lake and the Upper Waterton Lakeshore – which start from the townsite (see box p.672). Having long been a poor relation to the "big four" national parks in the Rockies, Waterton is now so popular that it's essential to book accommodation well in advance for much of July and August.

Two wonderfully scenic access roads from Waterton probe west into the park interior and provide picnic spots, viewpoints and the starting point for most other trails: the **Akamina Parkway** follows the Cameron Creek valley for 20km to Cameron Lake, a large subalpine lake where you can follow easy trails or rent canoes, rowing boats and paddleboats. The **Red Rock Canyon Parkway** weaves up Blakiston Creek for about 15km to the mouth of the water-gouged Red Rock Canyon, so called because of the oxidation of local argillite, a rock with a high iron content that turns rust-red on exposure to the elements. The road is one of the best places to see wildlife in the park without too much effort and, like the Akamina Parkway, has the usual pleasant panoply of picnic sites, trailheads and interpretive notice boards. If you're without transport for these roads see below for details of hiker shuttle services and car and bike rentals. The third named road in the park, the **Chief Mountain International Highway** (25km), runs east from the park entrance at Maskinonge Lake along the park's eastern border. After 7km it reaches a fine **viewpoint** over the mountain-backed Waterton Valley and then passes the park-run *Belly River Campground* (see p.674) before reaching the US–Canadian **border crossing** (open June to late Sept 7am–10pm). When this crossing's closed, depending on your direction of travel, you have to use the crossings on Alberta's Hwy 2 south of Cardston or Hwy 89 north of St Mary in Montana.

Arrival and information

Canadian **access** to Waterton by road is from Fort Macleod via either Hwy 3 west and Hwy 6 south (via Pincher Creek) or on Hwy 2 south to Cardston and then west on Hwy 5. Calgary is 264km and three hours' drive away; Lethbridge (which has the nearest airport), 130km (75min); and St Mary, Montana, 60km (45min). More than other Rockies' parks this is somewhere you really need your own transport to reach. A small taxi-bus service, the Shuttleton Services (usually three times daily, but call for services; ☎403/627-2157), runs between Waterton and the nearest Greyhound depot at Pincher

Park Entrance, Pincher Creek, Cardston ▲ & Red Rock Canyon Parkway

WATERTON TOWNSITE

0 ——— 200 m

N

Cameron Lake (16 km) ▲

Trail to Alderson & Carthew Lakes ▲

ACCOMMODATION

Aspen Village Inn	E
Bayshore Inn	D
Crandell Mountain Lodge	C
Kilmorey Lodge	B
Northland Lodge	H
Prince of Wales Hotel	A
Stanley Hotel	F
Waterton Lakes Lodge	G

RESTAURANTS

New Frank's	3
Pearl's	4
Pizza of Waterton	2
Windsor Lounge	1

Emerald Bay

Marina

Water Shuttle Service

Administration Office

Tamarack Mall

Pat's Convenience Store

Heritage Centre

RCMP (Police)

ENTRANCE RD

AKAMINA PARKWAY

EVERGREEN AVENUE

FIR GROVE ST

FOUNTAIN AVENUE

FERN ST

MOUNT VIEW ROAD

WINDFLOWER AVENUE

CLEMATIS AVE

CAMERON FALLS DRIVE

CLEMATIS AVENUE

HARWELL ROAD

WINDFLOWER AVENUE

WATERTON AVENUE

TOWNSITE LOOP

Cameron Falls

Cameron Creek

EVERGREEN AVENUE

VIMY AVENUE

Townsite Trailer Court & Campground

▼ *Trail to Bertha Lake*

6

ALBERTA AND THE ROCKIES | Waterton Lakes National Park

Creek 50km away ($15 one-way, $25 return); a cab from Crystal Taxi (☎403/627-4262) will cost around $60 for the same run, otherwise there's no public transport to the town or within the park.

Waterton Townsite has all the accommodation (bar the campsites) and the national park **visitor centre**, on Entrance Rd at the road junction just to the north (daily: May & early Sept 9am–5pm; June–Aug 8am–9pm; ☎403/859-2445 or 859-2224, ⓦwww.watertoninfo.ab.ca). Further information is available from the Chamber of Commerce (☎403/859-2303) and, outside the visitor centre's summer hours, at the park's administration office at 215 Mount View Rd (Mon–Fri 8am–4pm; ☎403/859-2477). The free weekly *Waterton-Glacier Views* newspaper also contains visitor information. Be sure to buy the Canadian Parks Service 1:50,000 **map** *Waterton Lakes National Park* ($9.50), if you're going to do any serious walking. It's usually available from the visitor centre and the **Waterton Heritage Centre** in the old firehall at 117 Waterton Ave (May–Oct 1–5pm, July & Aug longer hours; admission to museum by donation; ☎403/859-2267), a combined art gallery, small natural-history museum and bookshop.

671

Waterton Lakes' 255km of trails are among the best constructed in the Canadian Rockies, and also some of the most easily graded, well marked and scenically routed. Like Moraine Lake in Banff National Park – and unlike Banff and Jasper – you can also access superb walks easily without a car. Bar one or two outlying hikes, three key areas contain trails and trailheads: the **townsite** itself, which has two magnificent short walks; the **Akamina Parkway**; and the **Red Rock Canyon Parkway**. Most walks are day-hikes, climaxing at small alpine lakes cradled in spectacular hanging valleys. Options for backpacking are necessarily limited by the park's size, though the 36-kilometre **Tamarack Trail**, following the ridges of the Continental Divide between the Akamina Parkway (trailhead as for Rowe Lakes – see opposite) and Red Rock Canyon, is rated as one of the Rockies' greatest high-line treks (maximum elevation 2560m); the twenty-kilometre Carthew–Alderson Trail from Cameron Lake to Waterton (maximum elevation 2311m), a popular day's outing, can be turned into a two-day trip by overnighting at the Alderson Lake campsite. To do it in a day, take advantage of the hiker shuttle service to the trailhead offered by Park Transport (☎403/859-2378) based in the Tamarack Mall on Mount View Rd.

In summary, this is a great park in which to base yourself for a few days' hiking: details of hikes are given below, but as a general guide to do the cream of the hikes you'd first stroll the **Bear's Hump** for views of Waterton town and the lakes; then walk all or part of the **Bertha Lake Trail** (day or half-day) from the townsite. Next day take a boat to Goat Haunt and walk back on the **Waterton Lakeshore Trail**. Then try the **Crypt Lake Trail** from the townsite and/or the **Rowe Lake–Lineham Ridge Trail**, both ranked among the best day-walks in the Rockies. Finally gird your loins for the longer **Carthew–Alderson Trail**, possible in a day.

Walks from Waterton Townsite

In and around the town there are various short loops: stroll to Cameron Falls, try the Prince of Wales from the Visitor Centre (2km; 45min) or climb the more demanding **Bear's Hump**, also from the centre (1.2km; 200m vertical; 40min one-way); the latter is one of the park's most popular short walks, switchbacking up the slopes to a rocky outcrop with great views of the Waterton Valley. More surprisingly good views can be had from the easily reached viewpoint near the Bison Paddock. Another obvious, and very simple, walk from the town is the Waterton Lakeshore Trail (13km one-way; 100m ascent; 4hr), which follows Upper Waterton Lake's west shore across the US border to Goat Haunt; regular lake ferries sail back to the townsite, completing a lovely round trip (ferry details from the marina or call ☎403/859-2362; see p.675). Alternatively, catch an early boat and walk back so as not to worry about making a boat connection.

The single most popular half-day or day's walk from the townsite is the classic **Bertha Lake Trail** from Waterton, 5.8km each way with an ascent of 460m (allow 3–4hr for the round trip). It's a short, steep hike beginning on Evergreen Drive to a busy but remarkably unsullied mountain-ringed lake and there's an easy trail that runs right round the lakeshore (adding about another 5km to the trip). If you're not up to this, you can just do the first part of the trail and break off at Lower Bertha Falls (2.9km from the townsite; 150m ascent; 1hr); this deservedly popular section corresponds to the route of the *Bertha Falls Self-Guiding Nature Trail* pamphlet available from the Visitor Centre.

Another excellent, if challenging, walk out of Waterton is the unique **Crypt Lake Trail**, often touted as one of the best in Canada. The 8.7-kilometre hike (one-way;

Accommodation and eating

Waterton has a range of **hotel** accommodation. In addition to the private campsites – and three Canadian Parks Service park-run campsites, which are

675m ascent) involves a boat trip ($9 round trip) across Upper Waterton Lake to the trailhead on the east side of the lake, a (perfectly safe) climb up a ladder, a crawl through a rock tunnel and a section along a rocky ledge with cable for support. The rewards are the crashing waterfalls and the great glacial amphitheatre containing Crypt Lake (1955m); rock walls tower 600m on three sides, casting a chill shadow that preserves small icebergs on the lake's surface throughout the summer. Allow time to catch the last boat back to Waterton (again, ferry details are on ☏403/859-2362), and note that it's a good idea to make reservations in summer. Campers should be aware that the site here is one of the most heavily used in the park's back-country.

Trails from the Akamina Parkway

Most of the trails accessed by the Akamina Parkway leave from the road's end near Cameron Lake. To stretch your legs after the drive up, or if you just want a stroll, try either the Akamina Lake (0.5km; 15min) or Cameron Lakeshore (1.6km; 30min) trails. The best of the longer walks is to Carthew Summit (7.9km one-way; 660m ascent), a superb trail that switchbacks through forest to Summit Lake (4km), a good target in itself, before opening out into subalpine meadow and a final climb to a craggy summit (2310m) and astounding viewpoint. The trail can be followed all the way back to Waterton Townsite (another 12km) – it's then the **Carthew–Alderson Trail** (see opposite), most of whose hard work you've done in getting up to Carthew Summit; from the summit it's largely steeply downhill via Carthew and Alderson lakes (1875m) to Cameron Falls and the townsite (1295m).

Another highly rated trail from the Akamina Parkway is equally appealing – the **Rowe Lakes Trail** (5.2km one-way; 555m ascent), which is accessed off the Parkway about 5km before Cameron Lake (it is also the first leg of the Tamarack Trail – see opposite). Most people make their way to the Rowe Basin (where there's a backcountry campsite) and then, rather than pushing on towards the Upper Rowe Lakes (1.2km beyond), either camp, turn around or – for stronger walkers – take the trail that branches right from the Upper Rowe path to walk to Lineham Ridge (another 3.4km and 540m ascent). This **Rowe Lake–Lineham Ridge** combination has been cited as some as one of the top five day-hikes in the Rockies. The stiffish walk is rewarded by Lineham Lake, sapphire blue in the valley far below, and a vast sea of mountains stretching to the horizon. Only come up here in good weather, as it's particularly hazardous when visibility's poor and the winds are up.

Trails from the Red Rock Canyon Parkway

Most trails on the Red Rock Canyon Parkway, such as the short Red Rock Canyon Trail (700m loop) and Blackiston Falls (1km; 30min), leave from Red Rock Canyon at the end of the road. The most exhilarating option from the head of the road, how-ever, is the **Goat Lake Trail** (6.7km; 550m ascent), which follows Bauerman Creek on an old fire road (flat and easy, but a little dull) before peeling off right at the 4.3-kilometre mark for the climb to tranquil Goat Lake and ever-improving views (there's a backcountry campsite at the lake). If you ignore the lake turn-off and follow the fire road for another 4km, you come to a junction: one trail leads north to Lost Lake (2km), the other south to the spectacular Twin Lakes area (3.2km). This latter option will bring you to the long-distance Tamarack Trail (see opposite). Walk south on this from Twin Lakes (3.1km) and you can pick up the **Blackiston Creek Trail**, which will take you back to the head of the Red Rock Canyon Parkway.

first-come, first-served, and fill quickly in summer – that are detailed below, the national park has provided thirteen designated **backcountry campsites**, where you'll find dry toilets and a surface-water supply; a few of them also have shelters and cooking facilities. To use any, you need a backcountry camping permit, also issued on a first-come, first-served basis by the Visitor Centre or Administration Office. A quota system is operated to prevent overcrowding. For information on these and other park campsites call ☎403/859-2224. Unrestricted camping within the park is usually permitted only at Lineham Lakes, reached by a 4.2-kilometre trail off the north side of the Akamina Parkway 9.5km from Waterton. Note that at park sites you can pay an optional $3 to use the firewood provided.

Hotels and motels

Aspen Village Inn Windflower Ave ☎403/859-2255 or 1-888/859-8669. Quiet spot with mountain views opposite the municipal pool; 35 motel rooms and 16 "cottage" rooms, some with kitchenettes. April to mid-Oct. **6**

Bayshore Inn 111 Waterton Ave ☎403/859-2211 or 1-888/527-9555, ⓦ www.bayshoreinn.com. Just south of the marina; very comfortable hotel, with 49 of its seventy units on the lakefront; two-unit and de luxe suites available. Mid-April to mid-Oct. **6**

Crandell Mountain Lodge 102 Mount View Rd, corner of Evergreen Ave ☎403/859-2288, ⓦ www.crandellmountainlodge.com. Just seventeen nicely finished nonsmoking rooms (two with special wheelchair access) in a pretty lodge; more intimate than some of the town's hotels, with kitchenette and fireplace units available. Easter–Oct. **6**

Kilmorey Lodge 117 Evergreen Ave ☎403/859-2334 or 1-888/859-8669, ⓔ kilmorey @telusplanet.net. At the northern entrance to town on Emerald Bay; 23 antique-decorated rooms with a lakefront setting and historic old-fashioned feel. Some rooms are small for the price, while others score by virtue of their views (book in advance for these); there's also an excellent restaurant (the *Lamp Post*) and nice *Gazebo Café on the Bay* with outdoor waterfront deck for snacks and light meals. Open all year. **5**

The Lodge At Waterton Lakes Cameron Falls Drive and Windflower Ave ☎403/859-2151 or 1-888/985-6343, ⓦ www.watertonresort.com. Smart 80-room resort hotel; health spa with indoor pool, recreational centre with 18m pool and lots of extra facilities such as kitchenettes in certain de luxe rooms. **7**

Northland Lodge Evergreen Ave ☎403/859-2353, ⓦ www.northlandlodge.ab.ca. Nine non-smoking and cosy rooms, seven with private bathroom, east of the town site in the lee of the mountains one block south of Cameron Falls; some with kitchenettes. Mid-May to mid-Oct. **3**

Prince of Wales Hotel Waterton Lake ☎403/859-2231. Famous and popular old hotel – the best in town – whose 1927 Gothic outline is in almost every picture of Waterton; worth it if you can afford it. Lakeside rooms with views are pricier, but some are rather small, so check what you're getting for your $245. Mid-May to mid-Sept. **7**

Stanley Hotel 112b Waterton Ave ☎403/859-2345. Old-fashioned and often full nine-roomed hotel. Mid-May to Sept. **3**

Campsites

Belly River Campground 29km from the town-site, 1km off Chief Mountain Parkway on Hwy 6 ☎403/859-2224. Smallest (24 sites) and simplest of the park-operated campsites. Self-registration; tap water; kitchen shelters; fireplaces; chemical and pit toilets. Mid-May to Sept. $10.

Crandell Mountain Campground 8km west of Waterton on the Red Rock Canyon Parkway off Hwy 5 ☎403/859-2224. Semi-serviced park-run campsite with 129 sites. Tap water, fireplaces, no showers. Mid-May to late Sept. $13.

Crooked Creek 5.6km east of Waterton Park Gateway on Hwy 5 ☎403/653-1100. Has 46 sites, seven of which have full service for RVs. Mid-May to early Sept. $11.

Homestead Campground 3km north of Waterton Park Gateway on Hwy 6 ☎403/859-2247. Large private 276-site campsite with services, showers, store, video games, laundry, heated outdoor pool, dance floor and many other distractions. May to mid-Sept. $16.

Riverside Campground 5km east of Waterton Park Gateway ☎403/653-2888. Private; seventy sites with showers, services, breakfasts and live entertainment and barbecue suppers every Saturday. Mid-May to mid-Sept. $12.

Waterton Townsite Campground Off Vimy Ave ☎403/859-2224. 238-site serviced park-run campsite in town. First-come, first-served basis, and fills up by mid-afternoon in summer. Showers, no open fires; wheelchair-accessible. Open May to Thanksgiving (second Mon in Oct) but self-registration after Labour Day (in early Sept). $16.

Restaurants

Lakeside Kootenai Brown Dining Room Waterton Ave at the *Bayshore Inn* ☎403/859-2211.

One of the better and more elegant spots in town to treat yourself; the dining room overlooks the lake. Open all day for breakfast, lunch and dinner. Moderate.

Lamp Post Dining Room 117 Evergreen Ave at the *Kilmorey Lodge* ☎403/859-2334. Old-world appeal and tempting good food without the stuffiness of *Windsor Lounge*; the moderate prices are lower too (7.30am–10pm). The hotel's *Gazebo* café on the waterfront is also good for snacks (10am–10pm).

New Frank's Restaurant 106 Waterton Ave ☎403/859-2240. This restaurant serves cheap, odd combinations of breakfasts, burgers, a Chinese buffet plus lunch and six-course buffet specials.

Pearl's 305 Windflower Ave ☎403/859-2284. Fresh baking; great first choice for cheap breakfast, lunch, coffee, deli meats, picnic provisions and hikers' takeaway lunches. Indoor and outdoor tables.

Pizza of Waterton 103 Fountain Ave ☎403/859-2660. Dough made daily on the premises; good, cheap pizzas to eat in or take away. Open daily 4.30–10pm.

Windsor Lounge At *Prince of Wales Hotel* ☎403/859-2231. One of several lounges, bars and dining rooms in this posh hotel open for non-patrons to enjoy afternoon tea, a good breakfast or a refined hour with a drink and great lake views. Dress well, as the place is fairly smart. The *Garden Court* is the most elegant restaurant in the hotel (reservations required).

Listings

Bike and scooter rental Pat's Rentals & Convenience Store, a fuel station and camping store on the corner of Mount View Rd and Waterton Ave (☎403/859-2266), rents out bikes and scooters by the hour or day and also sells bikes and spares. There's also an ATM here.

Exchange Royal Bank in Tamarack Mall on Waterton Ave, or the Alberta Treasury Branch Agency upstairs at Caribou Clothing on Waterton Ave (☎403/859-2604). Pat's Rentals has an ATM.

Hospitals The nearest are in Cardston (☎403/653-4411) and Pincher Creek (☎403/627-3333).

Laundry Itussististukiopi Coin-Op, 301 Windflower Ave (mid-June to mid-Sept daily 8am–10pm).

Outdoor equipment Waterton Sports and Leisure in Tamarack Mall stocks maps, fishing licences and camping, walking, fishing and mountain-biking equipment and accessories.

Police ☎403/859-2244. In life-threatening emergencies, use the 24-hour park emergency number ☎403/859-2636.

Post office Alongside the fire station on Fountain Ave.

Park activities

If you want to **cruise the lakes**, the most popular summer activity round these parts, contact Waterton Shoreline Cruises at the marina (☎403/859-2362). It runs scenic two-hour cruises (June–Aug 5 daily, fewer in May & Sept; $21 or $13 one-way) up and down the lake across the US–Canadian border to Goat Haunt in Montana, little more than a quayside and park ranger station, where there is a scheduled thirty-minute stop before the return to Waterton (note that after the ranger station closes in mid-Sept boats no longer stop at Goat Haunt). No immigration procedures are required, but if you wish to camp overnight in the backcountry you need to register with the ranger station. You can take an early boat to Goat Haunt and then return on foot to Waterton on the **Waterton Lakeshore Trail**, an easy four-hour walk (13km one-way). The same company runs a ferry to various trails around the lake, most notably a passage ($11 return) to the trailhead of the famed Crypt Lake walk (see box p.672) and the myriad longer hikes from Goat Haunt in the US. Park Transport in Tamarack Mall on Mount View Rd (☎403/859-2378) organizes two-hour tours round the park ($25), but will also lay on a **taxi** shuttle (from $7.50) to trails on the area's two Parkways; the most popular drop-off is the beginning of the Carthew–Alderson trail (see box p.673).

Windsurfing is also surprisingly popular locally, thanks to the powerful winds – anything up to 70kph – which often roar across the lakes (Waterton is wetter, windier and snowier than much of Alberta). Winds generally gust south to north, making the beach at Cameron Bay on Upper Waterton Lake a favourite spot for surfers to catch the breeze. The water's cold and deep, though, so you'll need a wet suit. If you want to **swim**, head for the cheap outdoor heated pool on Cameron Falls Drive. **Fishing** is good on the lakes, but remember to pick up the compulsory national park permit ($6 a week, $13 annual) from the visitor centre or park administration office. Off the water, **horse riding** is available from the Alpine Stables (☎403/859-2462), located just east off the highway about 1km north of the Visitor Centre. On offer are one-hour outings (hourly on the hour; from $17) and two-hour (3 daily; $31), daily and overnight treks. Canadian Wilderness Adventures (☎403/859-2334) offers a range of guided walks and tours long and short. Four kilometres north of town on the main highway is the beautiful eighteen-hole **Waterton Lakes Golf Course** (☎403/859-2383 or 859-2114); green fees are around $30 (cheaper after 5pm) and club rental from about $8.

The Canadian Rockies

Few North American landscapes come as loaded with expectation as the **Canadian Rockies**, so it's a relief to find that the superlatives are scarcely able to do credit to the region's immensity of forests, lakes, rivers and snowcapped mountains. Although most visitors confine themselves to visiting just a handful of **national parks**, the range spans almost 1500km as far as the Yukon border, forming the vast watershed of the Continental Divide, which separates rivers flowing to the Pacific, Arctic and Atlantic oceans. Landscapes on such a scale make a nonsense of artificial borderlines, and the major parks are national creations that span both Alberta and British Columbia. Four of the parks – Banff, Jasper, Yoho and Kootenay – share common boundaries, and receive the attention of most of the millions of annual visitors to the Rockies.

There's not a great deal to choose between the parks in terms of scenery – they're all fairly sensational – and planning an itinerary that allows you to fit them all in comfortably is just about impossible. It also rather unnecessary, since to really experience the Rockies you're best off homing in on just one or two parks and then heading into the backcountry. Most visitors start with **Banff** National Park, then follow the otherworldly **Icefields Parkway** north to the larger and much less busy **Jasper** National Park. From there it makes sense to continue west to **Mount Robson** Provincial Park, which protects the highest and most dramatic peak in the Canadian Rockies. Thereafter you're committed to leaving the Rockies unless you double back from Jasper to Banff – no hardship, given the scenery – to pick up the Trans-Canada Highway through the smaller **Yoho**, **Glacier** and **Revelstoke** national parks. Finally, **Kootenay** National Park is more easily explored than its neighbours, though you'll have to backtrack towards Banff or loop down from Yoho to pick up the road that provides its only access. Our account of the more peripheral, but no less impressive Waterton Lakes National Park, hugging the US border, begins on p.666.

The creation of the Canadian Rockies

About 600 million years ago the vast granite mountains of the Canadian Shield covered North America from Greenland to Guatemala (today the Shield's eroded remnants are restricted largely to northeast Canada). For the next 400 million years, eroded debris from the Shield – mud, sand and gravel – was washed westward by streams and rivers and deposited on the offshore "continental slope" (westward because the Shield had a very slight tilt). Heavier elements such as gravel accumulated close to the shore; lighter deposits like sand and mud were swept out to sea or left in lagoons. The enormous weight and pressure of the sediment, which built up to a depth of 20km, converted mud to shale, sand to sandstone and the natural debris of the reefs and sea bed – rich in lime-producing algae – into limestone. Two further stages were necessary before these deposits – now the strata so familar in the profile of the Rockies – could be lifted from the sea bed and left several thousand metres above sea level to produce the mountains we see today.

The mountain-building stage of the **Rockies** took just 100 million years, with the collision of the North American and Pacific continental plates (gigantic 50-kilometre-thick floating platforms of the earth's crust). About 200 million years ago, two separate strings of volcanic Pacific islands, each half the size of British Columbia, began to move eastward on the Pacific Plate towards the North American coast. When the first string arrived off the coast, the heavier Pacific Plate slid beneath the edge of the North American Plate and into the earth's molten interior. The lighter, more buoyant rock of the islands stayed "afloat", detaching itself from the plate before crashing into the continent with spectacular effect. The thick, orderly deposits on the continental slope were crumpled and uplifted, their layers breaking up and riding over each other to produce the coast's present-day interior and Columbia Mountains. Over the next 75 million years the aftershock of the collision moved inland, bulldozing the ancient sedimentary layers still further to create the Rockies' Western Main Ranges (roughly the mountain edge of Yoho and Kootenay national parks), and then moving further east, where some 4km of uplift created the Eastern Main Ranges (the mountains roughly on a line with Lake Louise). Finally the detached islands "bonded" and mingled with the new mainland mountains (their "exotic" rocks can be found in geological tangles as far east as Salmon Arm in BC).

Behind the first string of islands the second archipelago had also now crashed into the continent, striking the debris of the earlier collision. The result was geological chaos, with more folding, rupturing and uplifting of the earlier ranges. About 60 million years ago, the aftershock from this encounter created the Rockies' easternmost Front Ranges (the distinct line of mountains that rears up so dramatically from the prairies), together with the foothills that spill around Kananaskis and Waterton lakes. The third stage of the Rockies' formation, erosion and glaciation, was relatively short-lived, at least three Ice Ages over the last 240,000 years turning the mountains into a region resembling present-day Antarctica. While only mountain summits peeked out from ice many kilometres thick, however, glaciers and the like were applying the final touches, carving sharp profiles and dumping further debris.

Though you can get to all the parks by **bus**, travelling by **car** or **bike** is the obvious way to get the most out of the region. Once there, you'd be foolish not to tackle some of the 3000km of trails that crisscross the mountains, the vast majority of which are well worn and well signed. We've highlighted the best short walks and day-hikes in each area, and you can get more details from the excellent **park visitor centres**, which sell 1:50,000 topographical maps and usually offer small reference libraries of trail books; *The Canadian Rockies Trail Guide*, by Brian Patton and Bart Robinson, is invaluable for serious hiking or backpacking. Other activities – fishing, skiing, canoeing, white-water

Admission fees to the Rockies national parks

Anyone entering any of the Rockies national parks – Banff, Jasper, Yoho and Kootenay – must buy a permit. The cost of a **Day Pass** valid for all four is $5. Or you may buy a **Great Western Annual Pass** for $35, valid for unlimited entry to all eleven national parks in western Canada for a year. "Group" day-passes are available for anything between two and ten people at a flat rate: $10 daily, $70 annual. Thus four people in a car, for example, are charged just $10. If you come in by bus you'll not be charged at your point of entry – it's up to you to be honest and buy a pass.

Passes can bought at the road entrances to all parks, park information centres, some park campsites and (in summer) at automated pass machines within parks. They are also sold at some Husky fuel stations and at the Mountain Equipment Co-op shops in Calgary and Vancouver. If you buy a couple of day passes and decide you want to stay on, then you can redeem their cost against a year's pass at park centres, on presentation of receipts. There's no fee to enter provincial parks.

A separate **backcountry Wilderness Pass** ($6 per person per night, or $42 for an annual pass), valid in Banff, Jasper, Yoho and Kootenay and available from any park visitor centre or infocentre, is required for all overnight backcountry use. Note that all backcountry areas in all parks have a quota and that it's vital to make bookings well in advance (up to three months) if you wish to walk – and camp on – some of the most popular trails requiring overnight stops. We've indicated the most popular trails throughout this section. Reservations can made by phone or in person at some of the more backcountry campsites, but not for the major park-run campsites. There is a $10 nonrefundable booking fee.

rafting, cycling, horse riding, climbing and so on – are comprehensively dealt with in visitor centres, and you can easily **rent equipment** or sign up for organized tours in the bigger towns.

The Rockies harbour several major **winter sports** resorts – in Kananaskis Country, and around Banff, Lake Louise and Jasper. Along with Whistler in British Columbia, these are some of the best, the most popular and the fastest-growing areas in Canada – and not only for downhill and cross-country skiing but also for dog-sledding, ice climbing, skating, snowshoeing, canyon crawling and ice fishing (snowmobiling is not allowed in the parks). At most resorts, the season runs from mid-December until the end of May; conditions are usually at their best in March, when the days are getting warmer and longer, and the snow is deepest. Resort accommodation is hardest to come by during Christmas week, the mid-February school holidays and at Easter.

A word of warning: don't underestimate the Rockies. Despite the impression created by the summer throngs in centres like Banff and Lake Louise, excellent roads and sleek park facilities, the vast proportion of parkland is wilderness and should be respected and treated as such. See Basics p.53, for more.

Kananaskis Country

Most first-time visitors race straight from Calgary to Banff, ignoring **Kananaskis Country**, a dramatic foothill area that sprawls along the eastern boundary of Banff National Park. Created out of existing provincial parks to take pressure off Banff, Kananaskis remains almost the exclusive preserve of locals, who come to ski in the winter and to hike, bike and camp in the summer. The mountain scenery rivals that of parks and the possibilities for outdoor pursuits even better, thanks to more liberal protection policies. **Canmore** is the region's natural focus, much as Banff is in the neighbouring national park – though in many other ways the towns are dissimilar. The scope and variety of facilities and services are far more limited at Canmore, but then so are the levels of crowds and commercialism, and accommodation is cheaper and easier to find. Plenty of excursions are possible on foot from the town itself, but to get deep into adjacent **provincial parks** you'll need your own transport.

Canmore

Long considered a gateway to the parks, youthful and outdoorsy **CANMORE** has begun to compete with Banff, 28km away, for visitors, and it's a decent alternative if you'd rather stay in a less touristy place and can live without Banff's huge selection of restaurants and shops. Canmore began life in 1883 as a supply point for the CPR railroad, before booming as a mining centre after the company were delighted to discover coal in surrounding hills. It quickly became a boom town and lived off mining for almost a century until 1979 when the last mine closed. Things looked bleak, but not for long as it was soon decided that the town would host all the Nordic skiing events for the 1988 Calgary Olympics, which gave the town its impressive **Canmore Nordic Centre**. On the back of this and thanks to the town's splendid location between rows of towering mountains and outside the tight restrictions of the national parks, the town grew. Over the last twenty years its population has tripled to 11,000 and its expected to double again in the next twenty. Occasional references to it as the "Aspen of Alberta" overstate the case, but certainly many young adventurous types and artists are relocating here to escape cities. It's a good place to visit as well as live, with good hiking, climbing, biking, skiing and fishing on the fringes of town – and opportunities for many more activites, including caving and rafting, not much further away.

Arrival, information and accommodation

Most shuttles between Calgary Airport and Banff (see p.687) make a stop at Canmore, with fares around $45 one-way. You can also take the Greyhound here from Calgary and Banff, with services arriving at the **bus station**, 801 8th St (T 403/678-4465). From here it's a long walk to the town's information centre, part of the **Travel Alberta Visitor Information Centre**, 2801 Bow Valley Trail (June–Aug 8am–8pm; Sept–May 9am–6pm; T 403/678-5277 or 1-800/661-8888, W www.discoveralberta.com) just off the Trans-Canada. The centre is an excellent place to pick up information about the whole Rocky Mountain region as well as Canmore.

Downtown Canmore can easily be explored **on foot**, though a bike is useful on the extensive trail network in and around town. Gear Up, 1302 Bow Valley Trail (T 403/678-1636), is one of several places that **rents bikes**. The only car rental outlet in town is Hertz (T 403/678-1630) in the *Radisson Hotel*, 511 Bow Valley Trail. For a taxi call Apex (T 403/609-0030).

The bulk of Canmore's **accommodation** is in new hotels and motels squatting beside the Trans-Canada Highway and the parallel road the Bow Valley Trail. In summer prices are a little steep for what's offered, though levels are much saner than in Banff. In winter rates are typically cut by at least a third. For a less anonymous experience you can stay in one of around fifty B&Bs in and around town which are brought together by the Canmore Valley Bed and Breakfast Association (T 403/609-7224, W www.bbcanmore.com).

Hotels and motels

Akai Motel 1717 Mountain Ave T 403/678-4664 or 1-877/900-2524. Small basic motel on the northern edge of town with some of the cheapest rooms around. **4**

Bear and Bison 705 Benchlands Trail T 403/678-2058, W www.bearandbison.com. Elegant idyllic timber-and-stone B&B with gourmet breakfasts, pleasant gardens, library and hot tub. **8**

Best Western Green Gables Inn 1602 2nd Ave T 403/678-5488 or 1-800/661-2133, W www.bestwestern.com. Reliable mid-range chain hotel where many rooms have a whirlpool. **6**

Bow Valley Motel 610 8th St T 403/678-5085 or 1-800/665-8189, W www.bowvalleymotel.com.

Average motel, but with a location – downtown and an easy walk from the restaurants and bars – that sets it apart from the rest. **3**

Canmore Hotel 738 8th St T 403/678-5181. Dowdy central hotel above the bar of the same name, with excellent location and prices but shabby rooms. **2**

Lady Macdonald Country Inn 1201 Bow Valley Trail T 403/678-3665 or 1-800/567-3919, W www.ladymacdonald.com. Highly recommended friendly twelve-room B&B, with hot tub and great breakfasts. **6**

Quality Inn Chateau Canmore 1720 Bow Valley Trail T 403/678-6699 or 1-800/424-5151, W www.chateaucanmore.com. Chain hotel with

big, well-equipped rooms with kitchenettes, fitness facilities and pool. **❼**
Riverview and Main 918 8th St ☎403/678-9777, ⓦ www.riverviewandmain.com. One of Canmore's many small B&Bs with reasonable rates and breakfasts. **❹**

Hostel
Canmore Clubhouse Indian Flats Rd ☎403/678-3200, ⓦ www.alpineclubofcanada.ca. Run by the Alpine Club of Canada, this hostel at the base of Grotto Mountain, 5km south east of downtown, has a wonderful mountaineering feel, exceptional

valley views and the usual facilities – with the library and sauna definite plus points. Members $17, non-members $21.

Campsites
Bow River Campground ☎403/673-2163, ⓦ www.bowvalleycampgrounds.com. A good option at the Three Sisters Overpass 3km east of Canmore. Sites $17.
Restwell Trailer Park ☎403/678-5111, ⓦ www.restwelltrailerpark.com. A regimented and unattractive place, an easy walk from downtown. Sites $24–37.

The town and around

Canmore straddles the Trans-Canada Highway, though its downtown area is entirely south of the road, and centred on laid-back Main St (8th St). The **Canmore Centennial Museum and Geoscience Centre**, 907 7th Ave (Mon–Fri 9am–5pm, Sat & Sun noon–4pm; free), is a good wet-weather option, doing a fine job of rooting around the town's past from its geological and First Nation origins to its Olympic glory days. At the far end of Main St is a spur of the extensive network of local **bike paths**, which leads down to and alongside the Bow River. Parts of it are reasonable for **fishing** for bull trout, brown trout and whitefish; the Green Drake Fly Shop, 102–512 Bow Valley Trail (☎403/678-9522), can provide tackle and advice. The other main form of recreation in town is **golf**. The most modest of the three courses is run by the Canmore Golf and Curling Club (☎403/678-4785), on the north side of town; green fees are around $50. Far more impressive is the Silver Tip course (☎403/678-1600, ⓦ www.silvertipresort.com), which offers a unique and challenging course just east of town; green fees here are $90–130.

West of downtown and the Bow River the land begins to rise and the town starts to thin out, so that by the time Spray Lakes Rd has climbed to **Canmore Nordic Centre** (☎403/678-2400), you're only left with views of the urban area. This state-of-the-art former Olympic facility is as popular in summer as in winter, since 70km of the total 300km cross-country network is maintained for mountain biking and suitable for every level of rider. Free trail maps are available, as are bike rentals ($30/day). Beyond the Nordic Centre Spray Lakes Rd soon loses its asphalt cover and begins to climb in earnest, but just before it does there's a small turn-off to a parking lot beside a reservoir. This is the trailhead for an easy 2km hike up to **Grassi Lakes**, a series of small picture-book lakes high above town on a route that affords exceptional views over the valley. The trail up is rough and steep, though there's also the option of descending back down a rough access road, which is much easier going. On reaching the upper lake, be sure to take an easy scramble up the scree slope to four **pictographs** of human figures painted onto the first large boulder of the gorge. The surrounding cliffs are invariably busy with rock climbers testing their skill; along with Heart Creek, Cougar Creek and Grotto Canyon this is one of the best local areas for the sport. For a local guiding service, contact the Yamnuska Mountain School (☎403/678-4164, ⓦ www.yamnuska.com), which also offers novice rock-climbing courses for $220.

High above Grassi Lakes, Spray Lakes Rd climbs out of view of Canmore to enter **Spray Valley Provincial Park**, the most accessible part of high-mountain Kananaskis Country. The main feature of the park is its 16km-long

Spray Lakes Reservoir, which is used to generate electricity. Despite its industrial use the lake is a tranquil spot and surrounded by huge, impressively contorted mountains. A campground (late May to early Sept; no reservations; $14) is strung out along the western shore and is an exceptionally attractive spot to pitch a tent, though facilities are basic and you need to bring all your own supplies except firewood ($6 per bundle). An added bonus is the great hiking trail that heads out from the campground to the small **Jakeroy Glacier**, perched high up in the goat range. The trail (4km; 4hr round-trip) begins opposite campsite no. 17 and is fairly well marked – at the only river crossing be sure to head straight on up the scree slope rather than right up to the waterfall – and climbs steeply through pine, willow, spruce and larch forests to a narrow hanging valley.

The east side of Canmore is also good for shorter hikes: an easy informal trail with good views follows the course of **Cougar Creek**. It's possible to follow this all the way to the boundary of Banff National Park. An even better trail starts from Grotto Pond, 12km east of Canmore on Hwy 1. It starts fairly unpromisingly, following a powerline road, but soon cuts into the woods to **Grotto Canyon**. There's no formal trail but the way up the canyon is clear enough; look for pictographs around 300m into the canyon. Further into the canyon, about 2km in, is an impressive little waterfall and beyond this the valley opens up, passing a cave and some hoodoos. If these strange landforms whet your appetite, be sure to tour **Canmore Caverns** (☎403/678-8819, Ⓦwww.canadianrockies.net /wildcavetours) in the base of Grotto Mountain. Groups are shuttled to the limestone caves here from Canmore, with easy half-day tours costing $85 per person. Even more fun is the full day tour ($110) which involves some rapelling through the extensive cave network; dress warmly and expect to get dirty.

Eating, drinking and nightlife

Recently, several smarter **restaurants** serving imaginative regional food have opened up in Canmore, alongside a number of long-standing dependable downtown **pubs** for bar food. Though there is one very average nightclub in town – *Hooligan's*, 103 Bow Valley Trail – the most popular form of **nightlife** is the deliberately cheesy theatrical performance *Oh Canada Eh!* (☎403/609-0004 or 1-800/773-0004). A musical dinner show, it's a slapstick celebration of Canada using costumed performers, staged nightly at 125 Kananaskis Way; the food served alongside is hearty local fare.

Craigs' Way Station 1727 Mountain Ave ☎403/678-2656. Cheerful family-orientated place amid the motels on the north side of town. Good full breakfasts and inexpensive diner food.
Drake Inn 909 Railway Ave. Locals' pub with outdoor patio, non-smoking section, pool and occasional live music.
Grizzly Paw 622 Main St. The Rockies' only microbrewery, with decent pub grub and reasonable beers; the Grumpy Bear Honey Wheat Ale is the most refreshing after a day in the outdoors.
Rocky Mountain Bagel Company 830 Main St. One of several decent cafés on Main St that's

ideal for a simple breakfast, light lunch or just hanging out.
Sherwood House 838 Main St ☎403/678-5211. Log cabin that's a long-standing local favourite with lots of Rocky Mountain charm. The huge patio-cum-beer-garden catches the sun until late and there lots of game served – including a great buffalo stew – along with decent pizza.
Zona's 710 9th St ☎.403/609-2000. Chic bistro with earthtone decor and highly inventive meals like the Moroccan molasses lamb curry or the Thai vegetable lasagne. Main courses $12–18.

The Kananaskis Valley

The **Kananaskis Valley** is the mainstay of Kananaskis Country. Hwy 40, which intersects with the Trans-Canada Highway 30km east of Canmore,

Nakiska and Fortress Mountain ski areas

Generally written off in favour of the local headline acts Sunshine Village and Lake Louise, **Nakiska** and **Fortress Mountain** are two ski areas in Kananaskis Country Provincial Park which, in good conditions (the snowphone for both is ☎403/244-6665), have skiing and riding of a quality that justifies a trip from even Banff. Lift passes at the two are interchangeable.

Developed specifically for the 1988 Winter Olympics, **Nakiska** (☎403/591-7777, ⓦwww.skinakiska.com) lies 25km south of the Trans-Canada Highway, around an hour's drive from either Calgary or Banff, and beside Kananaskis Village. Designed from scratch, the ski area has vertical drop of 735m (2412ft), is one of the most user-friendly on the continent, and includes all the usual rental, instruction and childcare facilities. Intended for downhill racers to fly down, the runs here are mostly smooth and steep, making it a great intermediate mountain for cruising – seventy percent of the runs are blue – and a useful schoolroom for beginner boarders. The lack of snow at the ski area – only 250cm (98 inches) annually – is rarely a problem, since snowmaking covers 85 percent of the mountain, and though conditions can be a little crusty, the ski area's grooming helps with this. The area also maintains two competition-standard half-pipes and a terrain park.

Located 15km south of Nakiska on Hwy 40, **Fortress Mountain** (☎403/591-7108, ⓦwww.skifortress.com) is a very different ski area. In place of smart regimented runs is largely untamed terrain, huddled beneath several vast, craggy rock outcrops. Particularly renowned for its tree-skiing, gullies and many natural obstacles as well as its well-maintained half pipe, Fortress Mountain offers a vertical drop of 280m (918ft) and spreads over 328 acres, the majority of its 47 trails are intermediate. In contrast with Nakiska, the snowfall at Fortress is a reassuring 630cm (23 feet) which, coupled with a sixty-percent snowmaking capacity, means decent conditions are virtually guaranteed.

travels south along its length, bisecting the high-mountain country, linking all the most significant provincial parks, and providing a ribbon to which most of the trails, campsites and scattered service centres cling. About 3km down the highway is the **Barrier Lake Information Centre** (daily: June to mid-Sept 9am–6pm; rest of year 9am–4pm; ☎403/673-3985), where you can get a full breakdown on outdoor activities.

Kananaskis Village

The only real settlement around is **KANANASKIS VILLAGE**, a resort based around a golf course and ski area (see box) which can be used as a useful base. A number of hiking and biking trails radiate from here. Peregrine Sports (☎403/591-7453) offers rentals of mountain bikes, fishing rods and canoes and can advise on local conditions for these pursuits. Of the hiking trails, the 9km hike to **Ribbon Falls** is deservedly popular and arrives at the eponymous campsite, which in common with all Kananaskis backcountry campsites costs $3 per person; buy permits from the Barrier Lake Information centre or on ☎403/678-3136. From here you can either head back, or with basic rock climbing skills head on and complete a loop by following the Galetea Creek trail below the hulking Mt Kidd. If you're fit and want to bag a peak, **Mount Allan**, just north of Kananaskis Village beckons: it's one of the few maintained trails in the Rockies that leads to a summit at 2990m. Other than excellent **golf** (☎403/591-7272 or 1-877/591-2525, ⓦwww.kananaskisgolf.com), the other organized pursuit in the area is **white-water rafting**, run by the Canmore-based Mirage Adventure Tours (☎403/678-4919, ⓦwww.miragetours.com).

The **accommodation** choices in Kananaskis Village itself are between the *Delta Lodge* (℡403/591-771 or 1-800/268-1133, ⓦwww.deltahotels.com; ❼) or smaller *Kananaskis Mountain Lodge* (℡403/591-7500 or 1-888/591-7501, ⓦwww.kananaskismountainlodge.com; ❼). The *Kananaskis Wilderness Hostel* (℡403/521-8421 or 1-866/762-4122, ⓦwww.hihostels.ca; ❷; dorms $18) is beside Ribbon Creek just off the Village access road. There are two good **campsites**: *Sundance Lodges* (℡403/591-7122, ⓦwww.sundancelodges.com; mid-May to Sept), which has regular sites ($19) hidden in the trees as well as cheerful hand-painted furnished tepees (❷); and the impressive *Mount Kidd RV Park* (℡403/591-7700, ⓦwww.mountkiddrv.com; sites $20–32), which boasts hot tubs, saunas and tennis courts.

Peter Loughead Provincial Park

Around 40km south of Kananaskis Village on Hwy 40, a short spur leads to Upper Kananaskis Lake, the head of the valley the main focus of **Peter Loughead Provincial Park** and probably the biggest concentration of accessible boating, fishing, camping and hiking possibilities in the region. Around 4km off Hwy 40 en route to the lake is the excellent Peter Loughead Park **Information Centre** (daily: mid-May to Aug 9am–7pm; rest of year 9am–5pm; ℡403/591-6322), whose staff are only too happy to give you information on the plentiful camping and hiking. Top trails include the rewarding half-day jaunt to Rawson Lake and the magnificent multi-day backpacking adventure over Burstall Pass to Banff, easily one of the best in the region. This hike is well detailed, along with many others in the Kananaskis area, in the definitive *Where Locals Hike in the Canadian Rockies* by Kathy and Craig Copeland, which is widely available.

Banff National Park

BANFF NATIONAL PARK is the most famous of the Canadian Rockies' parks and Canada's leading tourist attraction – so be prepared for the crowds that throng its key centres, **Banff** and **Lake Louise**, as well as the best part of its 1500km of trails, most of which suffer a continual pounding during the summer months. That said, it's worth putting up with every commercial indignity to enjoy the sublime scenery – and if you're camping or are prepared to walk, the worst of the park's excesses are fairly easily left behind. The best plan of attack if you're coming from Calgary or the US is to make straight for Banff, a busy and commercial town where you can pause for a couple of days to soak up the action and handful of sights, or stock up on supplies and make for somewhere quieter as quickly as possible. Then head for nearby Lake Louise, a much smaller but almost equally busy centre with some unmissable landscapes plus readily accessible short trails and day-hikes if you just want a quick taste of the scenery. Two popular highways within the park offer magnificent vistas: the **Bow Valley Parkway** from Banff to Lake Louise is a far preferable route to the parallel Hwy 1 (Trans-Canada), and the much longer **Icefields Parkway** leads from Lake Louise to Jasper. Both are lined with trails long and short, waterfalls, lakes, canyons, viewpoints, pull-offs and a seemingly unending procession of majestic mountain, river, glacier and forest scenery.

A history of the park

The modern road routes in the park provide transport links that have superseded the railway that first brought the park into being. The arrival of the **Canadian**

Below the map, the following labels appear:

Map labels:

▲ Jasper   ▲ Red Deer & Edmonton

BANFF NATIONAL PARK

Wilcox Creek
Sunwapta Pass
Cirrus Mountain
Hilda Creek Hostel
DAVID THOMPSON HIGHWAY
Columbia Icefield
Rampert Creek Hostel
Castleguard Meadows
Glacier Lake
Saskatchewan River Crossing
North Saskatchewan River
11
ALBERTA
Waterfowl Lake
ICEFIELDS PARKWAY
93
Peyto Lake
Bow Lake
Mosquito Creek Hostel
Hector Lake
BANFF NATIONAL PARK
Whiskey Jack Hostel
Skoki Valley
Emerald Lake
Lake Louise
YOHO NATIONAL PARK
Field
Corral Creek Hostel
Castle Mountain Hostel
Lake Minnewanka
Golden
Lake O'Hara
Moraine Lake
BOW VALLEY PARKWAY
Banff
Banff Hostel
▲ Glacier National Park & Revelstoke
95
BRITISH COLUMBIA
KOOTENAY NATIONAL PARK
93
MT. ASSINIBOINE PROVINCIAL PARK
Sunshine Village
Canmore
40
Calgary ►
KANANASKIS COUNTRY
N
0   50 km
Radium Hot Springs
▼ Invermere & Cranbrook

6

ALBERTA AND THE ROCKIES | Banff National Park

Pacific Railway at the end of the nineteenth century brought to an end some 10,000 years of exclusive aboriginal presence in the region, an epoch which previously had been disturbed only by trappers and the prodigious exploits of explorers like Mackenzie, Thompson and Fraser, who had sought to breach the Rockies with the help of native guides earlier in the century. Banff itself sprang to life in 1883 after three railway workers stumbled on the present town's Cave and Basin hot springs, its name coined in honour of Banffshire, the Scottish birthplace of two of the Canadian Pacific's early financiers and directors. Within two years the government had set aside the Hot Springs Reserve as a protected area, and in 1887 enlarged it to form the **Rocky Mountains Park**, Canada's first national park. However, the purpose was not entirely philanthropic, for the new government-sponsored railway was in desperate need of passengers and profit, and spectacular scenery backed up by luxurious hotels was seen – rightly – as the best way to lure the punters. Cars were banned from the park until 1916.

Today the park is not quite at crisis point, but some hard decisions are having to be made. Around four million visitors come to Banff every year and another four million pass through. Together they pump a staggering $750m or more annually into the local economy. Such numbers, despite the best efforts and

685

Two types of **bears** roam the Rockies – black bears and grizzlies – and you don't want to meet either. They're not terribly common in these parts (sightings are all monitored and posted at park centres) and risks are pretty low on heavily tramped trails, but if you're camping or walking it's still essential to be vigilant, obey basic rules, know the difference between a black bear and a grizzly (the latter are bigger and have a humped neck), know how to avoid dangerous encounters, and understand what to do if confronted or attacked. Popular misconceptions about bears abound – that they can't climb trees, for example (they can, and very quickly) – so it's worth picking up the parks service's pamphlet *You are in Bear Country*, which cuts through the confusion and lays out some occasionally eye-opening procedures. Be prepared, and if you don't want to be attacked, follow the cardinal rules: store food and garbage properly, make sure bears know you're there, don't approach or feed them, and, if you find yourself approached by one, don't scream and don't run.

When hiking, walk in a group – bears rarely attack more than four in a group – and make noise, lots of it, as you traverse the wilderness; bears are most threatened if surprised, so warning of your approach will give them time to leave the area. Many people shout, rattle cans with stones in or carry a whistle; be warned, the widely touted hand-held, tinkling bells are not loud enough. Be especially alert and noisy when close to streams, in tall vegetation, crossing avalanche slopes or when travelling into the wind, as your scent won't carry to warn bears of your approach: move straight away from dead animals and berry patches, which are important food sources. Watch for bear signs – get out quick if you see fresh tracks, diggings and droppings – and keep in the open as much as possible.

Camp away from rushing water, paths and animal trails, and keep the site scrupulously clean, leaving nothing hanging around in the open. Lock food and rubbish in a car, or hang it well away from a tent between two trees at least 4m above ground (many campsites have bear poles or steel food boxes). Take all rubbish away – don't bury it (bears'll just dig it up) and certainly don't store it in or near the tent. Avoid smelly foods, all fresh, dried or tinned meat and fish, and never store food, cook or eat in or near the tent – lingering smells may invite unwanted nocturnal visits. Aim to cook at least 50m downwind of the tent: freeze-dried meals and plastic-bag-sealed food is best. Likewise, keep food off clothes and sleeping bags, and sleep in clean clothes at night. Bears have an acute sense of smell, so avoid *anything* strongly scented – cosmetics, deodorant, shampoo, gel, lip balm, insect repellents, toothpaste, sun screen. Bears can be attracted to women during menstruation, so dispose of tampons in an airtight container; they're also attracted

intentions of the park authorities, inevitably have an effect on the environment. Scientists believe, for example, that the black and grizzly bear populations are dying out (combined numbers of both types of bear here are probably just 100 to 130), while numbers of wolves are declining at only a slightly lower rate than in areas where they have no protection at all (the park has just 35 or 40). Conversely, elk numbers have exploded beyond internally sustainable limits to about 3200, almost entirely because they've realized the town offers food (tasty surburban grass) and total safety from their natural predators. In the past, there have been about sixty usually provoked elk attacks on humans in Banff every year. The sight of elk nibbling on verges in downtown Banff will soon be a thing of the past, however, for around 120 of the beasts have been removed and relocated elsewhere, and there are plans to remove the remainder.

These are just a handful of symptoms of a greater ecological malaise. In response, a ceiling of 10,000 has been put on Banff's human population (it's by the smell of sex, so watch what you do in your tent if you don't want a rather drastic coitus interruptus.

Bears are unpredictable, and experts simply can't agree on best tactics: there's no guaranteed life-saving way of coping with an aggressive bear. Calm behaviour, however, has proved to be the most successful strategy in preventing an attack after an encounter. Bears don't actually want to attack; they simply want to know you're not a threat. Mothers with cubs are particularly dangerous and prone to suspicion. A bear moving towards you can be considered to have it in for you, other signs being whoofing noises, snapping jaws, and the head down and ears back. A bear raised on its hind legs and sniffing is trying to identify you: if it does it frequently, though, it's getting agitated; ideally, on first encounter you want first to stand stock still, never engage in direct eye contact (perceived as aggressive by the bear) and – absurd as it sounds – start speaking to it in low tones. Whatever you do, don't run, which simply sets off an almost inevitable predator–prey response in the bear (a bear can manage 61kph – that's easily faster than a racehorse or the fastest Olympic sprinter); instead, back away quietly and slowly at the first encounter, speaking gently all the while to the bear. If the backing off seems to be working, then make a wide detour, leave the area or wait for the bear to do so – and always leave it an escape route. If things still look ominous, set your pack gently on the ground as a distraction as you continue to back away.

If you're attacked, things are truly grim, and quack tactics are unlikely to help you. With grizzlies, playing dead – curling up in a ball, protecting face, neck and abdomen – may be effective. Fighting back will only increase the ferocity of a grizzly attack, and there's no way you're going to win. Keep your elbows in to prevent the bear rolling you over, and be prepared to keep the position for a long time until the bear gets bored. You may get one good cuff and a few minutes' attention and that's it – injuries may still be severe but you'll probably live. With a black bear the playing dead routine won't wash, though they're not as aggressive as grizzlies, and a good bop to the nose or sufficient frenzy on your part will sometimes send a black bear running: it's worth a try. Don't play dead with either species if the bear stalks or attacks while you're sleeping: this is more dangerous, as bears are often after food. Instead, try and get away or intimidate – people who have survived such attacks have often had a brave companion who has attacked the bear in return with something big and heavy.

Chemical repellents are available, but of unproven efficacy, and in a breeze you're likely to miss or catch the spray yourself. If this all sounds too scary to make you even contemplate walking or camping, remember that attacks are very rare.

currently around 7600), building is strictly controlled and areas are being closed to the public: even the famous Bow Valley Parkway is closed to traffic for parts of the year. The airport, too, is now all but closed, for it – like much of Banff town and the Bow River Valley – lies right in the path of major wildlife routeways. Many of the big mammals require large areas to survive, larger even than the park. Experts suggest that Banff's ecosystem is on a knife edge: it may be saved and previous damage restored only if action is taken. There's much more work to be done.

Banff

BANFF is the unquestioned capital of the Canadian Rockies, and with its intense summer buzz it can be a fun, bustling and likeable base – but if you've come to commune with nature, you'll want to leave as soon as possible.

Cascade Ponds, Lake Minnewanka, Two Jack Lake & Bankhead ▲

BANFF TOWNSITE

RCM Police

Bus Depot

Infocentre ℹ

WOLF

OTTER

MUSKRAT

CARIBOU

GRIZZLY

BEAVER

② ③ ④
⑤
⑥ ⑨
⑦ ⑧

LYNX

BOW AVE

Ⓙ

Ⓝ Ⓛ ⑩ Ⓚ

⑪
⑫

Ⓜ

Ⓞ

Whyte Museum
of the Rockies

⑬

Post Office/
Weather Office

Public
Library

BUFFALO

Banff Park Museum

▲ Park Entrance, Cannmore & Calgary

◀ Bow Valley (1A) Parkway Junction & Lake Louise

⑥

ALBERTA AND THE ROCKIES | Banff National Park

▼ Mt Norquay

MT. NORQUAY RD.

TRANS-CANADA HIGHWAY

40 Mile Creek

MT. NORQUAY RD.

Tunnel Mtn
Campgrounds △

Village I

Village II

HAWK

CRES

MARMOT

ANTELOPE

DEER

TUNNEL MOUNTAIN ROAD

Ⓕ

Trailer
Court

① Ⓐ
Ⓑ

Ⓓ

Ⓔ

COUGAR

AVENUE

Train
Station

RABBIT

SQUIRREL

BIRCHAM

ELK

MARTEN

MOOSE

Ⓖ
Ⓗ

Fenland

Echo Creek

RAILWAY

GOPHER

RCM Police
Bus Depott

See inset for detail

LYNX

BOW AVE.

WOLF

BEAVER

OTTER

MUSKRAT

CARIBOU

GRIZZLY

WOLVERINE

ST. JULIEN ROAD

Tunnel
Mountain ▲

TUNNEL MOUNTAIN DRIVE

Bow River-hoodoos Trail

1st
Vermilion
Lake

2nd
Vermilion
Lake

VERMILION LAKES DRIVE

Post Office/
Weather Office

BUFFALO

Public
Library

BIRCH

Luxton
Museum

CAVE AVENUE

MARSH LOOP

SUNDANCE

Ⓟ

JASPER

GLACIER

PARK AVENUE

ANTON

NAHANNI

MORAINE

KOOTENAY

GLEN

SPRAY

RUNDLE

AVENUE

Bow River

Bow
Falls

GOLF COURSE LOOP ROAD

Cave & Basin
Centennial Centre

MIDDLE SPRINGS

N

MOUNTAIN AVENUE

Spray River

Ⓠ

Upper Hot
Springs

Ⓡ

Sulphur
Mountain
Gondola

Sanson
Peak ▲

Sulphur
Mountain

◀

0   1 km

ACCOMMODATION

Banff International Hostel	C
Banff Park Lodge	J
Banff Springs Hotel	Q
Banff Voyager Inn	B
Banff Squrrel's Nest	I
Blue Mountain Lodge	K
Bumper's Inn	A
Dynasty Inn	E
High Country Inn	H
King Edward Hotel	N
Mount Royal Hotel	L
Mountain Country B&B	F
Mountain Home B&B	O
Red Carpet Inn	G
Rimrock Resort	R
Spruce Grove Motel	D
Tan-y-Bryn	M
Y Mountain Lodge	P

RESTAURANTS

Aardvark	8
Balkan Village	10
Barbary Coast	12
Bistro	3
Bumper's	1
Coyote's Grill	9
Evelyn's	11
Joe Btfsplk's Diner	4
Le Beaujolais	13
Melissa's	5
Rose & Crown	7
Saltlik	2
St James Gate	4
Sukiyaki House	11
Sunfood Café	6

Although the town is quite small, it handles an immense amount of tourist traffic, much of it of the RV and coach-tour variety. Anything up to 50,000 visitors arrive daily in high season, making this the largest and busiest urban focus of any national park anywhere in the world. Backpackers are abundant in summer, and an East Asian presence is also marked, with a huge number of Japanese signs and menus in shops and restaurants. Around a third of the town's accommodation is Japanese-owned, including two of the largest hotels; this investment is an ongoing bone of contention among some townspeople who would prefer local money.

What's rather odd, given all the people, however, is that there's next to nothing to do or see in Banff, save a couple of small museums, a cable-car ride and the chance to gawp at the crowds on **Banff Ave**, a thoroughfare lined with probably more souvenir stores and upmarket outdoor clothing and equipment shops than anywhere in North America. Whether or not your main aim is to avoid the crowds, however, some contact with the town is inevitable, as it contains essential shops and services almost impossible to come by elsewhere in the park. Many of the more rewarding **walks** locally are some way from the town – you'll need a car or have to rent a bike to explore properly – but some surprisingly good strolls start just minutes from the main street.

Arrival and information

Banff is a ninety-minute **drive** from Calgary along the Trans-Canada Highway (Hwy 1). Several operators offer efficient shuttle services **from Calgary Airport** including Laidlaw (☎403/762-9102 or 1-800/661-4946, ⓦwww.laidlawbanff.com); Banff Airporter (☎403/762-3330 or 1-888/449-2901, ⓦwww.banffairporter.com); Brewster Transportation (☎403/762-6767) and Sky Shuttle (☎403/762-1010 or 1-888/220-7433, ⓦwww.banffskyshuttle.com). The various companies' ticket desks are in the Arrivals area of Calgary Airport and all charge around $36 one-way to Banff. Daily **Greyhound buses** (☎403/762-1092 or 1-800/661-8747, ⓦwww.greyhound.ca) also ply the route from the centre of Calgary (5 daily; 1hr 40min; $20 one-way), arriving in Banff's bus terminal at 100 Gopher St (7.30am–10.45pm; ☎403/762-6767 or 1-800/661-1152). Buses also arrive from Vancouver (4 daily; 13hr; $100).

Once in Banff it's easy to get around **on foot**, though a frequent town **bus** service, operated by Banff Transit ($1; ☎403/760-8294), provides transport to outlying areas, including the campgrounds on Tunnel Mountain Rd and the *Banff Springs Hotel*.

The showpiece **Banff Information Centre** is an excellent joint venture by the park and Banff and Lake Louise Tourism, located at 224 Banff Ave (daily: mid-May to mid-June and during Sept 8am–6pm; mid-June to early Sept 8am–8pm; Oct to mid-May 9am–5pm; ☎403/762-8421, ⓦwww.banfflakelouise.com; park information ☎403/762-1550, ⓦwww.pc.gc.ca/banff). The centre is also the place to pick up a **park permit** if you haven't already done so (see box p.678). Among the many free handouts, make a point of asking for the *Banff and Vicinity Drives and Walks* and *The Icefields Parkway* for maps of park facilities, the *Backcountry Visitors' Guide* for an invaluable overview of backpacking trails and campsites, and *Trail Bicycling in the National Parks* for conditions and a full list of mountain-bike trails. In the centre is a selection of maps and guides you can consult free; you can also buy excellent topographical maps from the "Friends of Banff National Park" shop (☎403/762-8918) on the left, but many of the shorter and more popular trails are signed and well trodden, so you won't really need detailed maps unless you're venturing into the backcountry. You can also pick up details or book a place on the various

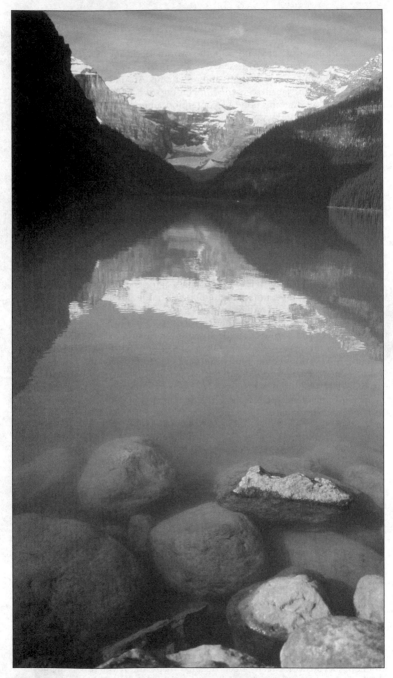

△ Lake Louise, Banff National Park

events offered by the "Friends", which in past years have included free guided walks daily in the summer to Vermilion Lakes (10am; 2hr 30min), a Discovery Tour of the Cave and Basin Hot Springs (45min) and a Park Museum Wildlife Tour (45min).

Accommodation

It's almost impossible to turn up after midday in Banff during July and August and find reasonably priced **accommodation**: preplanning is essential. Anything that can be booked has usually been snapped up – and Banff has over 3500 beds at its disposal nightly – and many visitors are forced to accept top-price places ($150 plus) or backtrack as far as Canmore or even Calgary to find space. The Tourism Bureau maintains a constantly updated vacancies board (though staff aren't allowed to make specific recommendations) and a free courtesy phone. There are also several fee-based alternatives (see box below).

The Bed & Breakfast and Private Home accommodation list at the infocentre lists forty-plus places with **private rooms** and **B&Bs**, but don't expect too much – they're usually cheapish by Banff standards (typically around $90–125) but among the first places to go each day. Note, too, that "breakfast" usually means just toast, coffee and cereal. The majority are also nonsmoking. Most of the town's **motels** are on the busy strip-cum-spur from the Trans-Canada into town, and charge uncommonly high rates for basic lodgings – typically around $150 and up for doubles. Off season (Oct–May), rates are usually considerably lower. Note that some of the best-value, least-known and most conveniently located double rooms are offered by the excellent *Y Mountain Lodge* (see under "Hostels"). **Campsites** are not quite as bad (the town offers over a thousand pitches), but even these generally fill up by 2pm or 3pm in summer – especially the excellent government campsites, which do not take reservations except for group bookings. In addition to the places we've listed, remember that there are lovely and less-developed park-run sites available along both the Bow and Icefields parkways to the north.

Hotels and motels

Banff Park Lodge 222 Lynx St ☎ 403/762-4433 or 1-800/661-9266, ⓦ www.banffparklodge.com. Quietly sophisticated, low slung cedar and oak hotel, a block from the town centre and offering the best downtown deal. Scandinavian-style rooms are simple and airy; some have whirlpools and fireplaces. Hotel facilities include hot tub, steam room, indoor pool, laundry and dry cleaning service. ❽

Banff Springs Hotel Spray Ave ☎ 403/762-2211 or 1-800/441-1414, ⓦ www.fairmont.com. One of

Room and ski package operators

Banff Accommodation (rooms and ski packages) ☎ 403/762-0260 or 1-877/226-3348, ⓦ www.banffaccommodations.com.

Banff Accommodation Reservations ☎ 403/762-0260 or 1-8777/226-3348, ⓦ www.banffinfo.com.

Banff Central Reservations (rooms and ski packages) ☎ 403/705-4020 or 1-877/542-2633, ⓦ www.banffreservations.com.

Canadian Rocky Reservation Centre (rooms) ☎ 403/609-3665 or 1-877/609-3665.

Good Earth Travel (ski packages) ☎ 403/678-9358 or 1-888/979-9797.

Resorts of the Canadian Rockies (ski packages) ☎ 403/256-8476 or 1-800/256-7669.

Ski Banff–Lake Louise (ski packages) ☎ 403/762-4561 or 1-800/754-7080, www.skibig3.com.

the continent's most famous hotels – built in Scots Baronial style with turrets and cornices towering above its thick nine-storey granite walls – offering luxurious service that borders on pageantry. The glut of facilities, which include a world-class fitness and spa complex, several stores and restaurants, make the hotel almost entirely self-contained. Rates are extravagant but the winter season offers a chance to stay here for around half price. ❽

Banff Voyager Inn 555 Banff Ave ☎ 403/762-3301 or 1-800/879-1991. Predictably comfortable motel; one of the last of a number that line the road from the town centre. With chilly outdoor pool, hot tub, sauna and the cheapest bar in town. ❺

Bumper's Inn Banff Ave and Marmot Crescent ☎ 403/762-3386 or 1-800/661-3518. Small, well-priced, 1970s motel on the northeastern fringe of town but only 50m from the nearest ski shuttle stop. Facilities are limited to the basics, though some units have kitchenettes. ❻

Douglas Fir Resort Tunnel Mountain Rd ☎ 403/762-5591 or 1-800/661-9267, ⓦ www.douglasfir.com. Collection of low-rise wood-clad condo blocks in secluded wooded area on Tunnel Mountain, a fifteen-minute walk from the town centre. Ideally equipped for families or groups, units have a kitchen and lounge with fireplace as well as access to a host of leisure facilities, including squash courts and pool with waterslides. Laundromat and small convenience store on-site. ❹

Dynasty Inn 501 Banff Ave ☎ 403/762-8844 or 1-800/667-1464. Fancy-looking 99-unit motel, a five-minute walk from town, whose gables, loft window, stucco and stone-clad walls make it stand out from neighbouring complexes. The smart and spacious rooms are much more run-of-the-mill, though some have fireplaces and Jacuzzi tubs. Other amenities include a steam room, hot tub and underground parking. ❻

High Country Inn 419 Banff Ave ☎ 403/762-2236 or 1-800/661-1244, ⓦ www.banffhigh countryinn.com. Mid-range 1980s motel with some luxury suites in a great central location. Facilities include two hot tubs and an indoor pool – rare in Banff. ❻

King Edward Hotel 137 Banff Ave ☎ 403/762-2202 or 1-800/344-4232, ⓦ www.banffking edwardhotel.com. Century-old building in the centre of town with 21 basic, but suitably well-priced rooms, most overlooking Banff Ave. ❻

Mount Royal Hotel 138 Banff Ave ☎ 403/762-3331 or 1-800/267-3035, ⓦ www.mountroyal hotel.com. Bland, three-storey building amid

downtown shops at the centre of town. Most guests in the newly renovated rooms have mountain views; all have access to a large health club with whirlpool and exercise equipment. ❼

Red Carpet Inn 425 Banff Ave ☎ 403/762-4184 or 1-800/563-4609. Pastel shaded inside and out, this no-frills 1970s motel is a clean, central and decent value option for those looking for no more than very soft mattresses and the most basic in-room facilities. ❻

Rimrock Resort Mountain Ave ☎ 403/762-3356 or 1-800/661-1587, ⓦ www.rimrockresort.com. Elegant and richly furnished hotel in imposing, ten-storey angular building that nestles alone among thick stands of trees on the lower slopes of Sulphur Mountain, 3km south of town. The smart, modern rooms come with views of Bow Valley. Excellent and extensive fitness facilities are offered, as is a free shuttle into town. ❽

Spruce Grove Motel 545 Banff Ave ☎ 403/762-2112. The least expensive motel in town is an aging one and the last of a generation designed for guests to pull right up to the door of their unit; some sleep four and include kitchenette facilities. ❸

B&Bs

Banff Squirrel's Nest 332 Squirrel St ☎ 403/762-4432. Pleasant rooms in quiet residential side street an easy walk from downtown. Rooms have queen beds and own bathroom. Continental buffet breakfast included. ❹

Blue Mountain Lodge 137 Muskrat St ☎ 403/762-5134, ⓦ www.bluemtnlodge.com. Friendly budget place in centre with ten small rooms all equipped with private bathrooms and spectacular mountain views. Common amenities include a guest kitchen and lounge, and laundry facilities. ❹

Eleanor's House 125 Kootenay Ave ☎ 403/760-2457, ⓦ www.bbeleanor.com. One of the better but more expensive ($135) B&Bs in town: location-wise it's not perfect – across the river in a quiet side street. Both rooms (twin and double) are en suite and there's a library for idle browsing on rainy days. Open Feb to mid-Oct. ❻

Mountain Country Bed & Breakfast 427 Marten St ☎ 403/762-3288, ⓦ www.banffmountain country.com. Large barn-shaped house close to downtown Banff and a block from the ski shuttle route. The large, dark-wood furnished rooms are equipped with private Jacuzzi tubs, queen-size beds and duvets. Light continental breakfast. ❸

Mountain Home Bed & Breakfast 129 Muskrat St ☎ 403/762-3889, ⓦ www.mountain homebb.com. Elegant 1940s tourist lodge converted into a B&B a couple of minutes' walk to downtown Banff. Spacious, antique-furnished en-suite guest rooms have down comforters on king-size beds. Delicious cooked breakfasts with daily menu. **5**

Tan-y-Bryn 118 Otter St ☎403/762-3696. Eight simple and extremely reasonable B&B rooms (and one cheap "emergency" room) with private or shared bathrooms and in-room continental breakfast. Quiet residential district three blocks from downtown. No credit cards. **2**

Hostels

Banff International Youth Hostel (HI) Tunnel Mountain Rd ☎403/762-4122, ☜www.hihostels.ca. Friendly modern 216-bed hostel in great setting, but 3km from downtown and a $6 cab ride from the bus depot. Great facilities include large kitchen, laundry, lounge with fireplace, ski workshop and an adjoining inexpensive restaurant that can save trips downtown. Dorm beds are $21; private doubles also available. Ski packages cost $192 per person for three nights. No curfew. Several other hostels in Banff national park – including Castle Mountain, Hilda Creek, Mosquito Creek, Rampart Creek, Ribbon Creek and Whiskey Jack – can be also be reserved through this hostel. **2**

Global Village Backpackers 449 Banff Ave ☎403/762-5521 or 1-888/844-7875, ☜www.globalbackpackers.com. A 100-bed hostel on the strip just north of town, with a hot tub and sauna and all the more usual hostel facilities. Dorm beds cost $25, doubles available. **4**

Y Mountain Lodge 102 Spray Ave ☎403/762-3560 or 1-800/813-4138, ☜www .ywca-banff.ab.ca. Clinically clean, but reasonably relaxed, hostel a short walk from downtown. You can use your own sleeping bag in the dorm bunks ($21) or rent blankets and pillows ($5). Alternatively stay inexpensively in the large spartan singles, doubles and triples (some with private

bathroom). In addition to a huge living room with gigantic stone fireplace, the hostel also has a café with reasonable food as well as a kitchen, laundry facilities and showers ($2.50 for nonresidents). **3**

Campsites

Bow Valley Parkway There are three park campsites on or just off the Bow Valley Parkway road between Banff and Lake Louise, all within easy reach of Banff if you have transport (less than 30-minutes' drive): Johnston Canyon, Castle Mountain and Protection Mountain. See p.707 for full details.

Tunnel Mountain Village I 4.3km from town and 1km beyond the hostel on Tunnel Mountain Rd. Huge 622-pitch government-run campsite ($17 plus optional $4 for firewood and fire permit), the nearest to downtown, on the Banff Transit bus from Banff Ave. Arrive early – like all frontcountry park campsites, it's first-come, first-served. Electricity and hot showers. The nearby 322-site *Tunnel Mountain Trailer Court* ($24) is only for RVs. Early May to late Sept.

Tunnel Mountain Village II 2.4km from town and close to *Village I* site. In the summer, available for group camping and commercial tenting only. However, after *Tunnel I* shuts (in late Sept) this government-run 189-pitch site becomes available for general walk-in winter camping ($21 plus optional $4 fire permit). Electricity and hot showers. The two sites are set amid trees, with lovely views, plenty of space and short trails close at hand. Bighorn sheep, elk and even the odd bear may drop in. Year-round.

Two Jack Lakeside 12km northeast of town on the Lake Minnewanka Rd. Fully serviced eighty-site park-run campsite ($17 plus optional $4 fire permit) with showers. Open mid-May to mid-Sept.

Two Jack Main 13km northeast of town on Lake Minnewanka Rd. Semi-serviced 381-site park campsite ($13 plus optional $4 fire permit); no showers. Open mid-June to mid-Sept.

In and around Banff

With some of the world's most spectacular mountains on your doorstep, sight-seeing in Banff might seem an absurd undertaking, yet it's good to have some rainy-day options. The **Banff Heritage Passport** ($7) gives entry to the Banff Park Museum, the Whyte Museum and the Cave & Basin National Historic Site.

The downtown **Banff Park Museum** at 93 Banff Ave (June–Sept daily 10am–6pm; Oct–May Mon–Fri 1–5pm, Sat & Sun 10am–6pm; $2.50), near the Bow River bridge, bulges with two floors of stuffed animals, many of which are indigenous to the park. In many ways the museum chronicles the changes of attitudes to wildlife in the park over the years. Many Victorians wanted to see the park's animals without the tiresome business of having to venture into the backcountry – so they killed and stuffed the beasts for permanent display. The hunting of game animals was eventually banned in the park in 1890, but not before populations of moose, elk, sheep, goats and grizzlies had been severely depleted. Game wardens only arrived to enforce the injunction in 1913, and even then they didn't protect the "bad" animals – wolves, coyotes, foxes, cougars, lynx, eagles, owls and hawks – which were hunted until the 1930s as part of the park's "predator-control program". Many of the stuffed victims in the museum date from this period. Sixty years ago a hapless polar bear was even displayed in the park behind the museum, one of sixty species of animals kept in the Banff Zoo and Aviary between 1904 and 1937. Until as recently as the 1970s hotels were organizing trips to the town's rubbish dumps to view foraging bears. Oddly enough, the museum – a fine building whatever your views on what's inside it – might have gone the same way as the animals. In the 1950s, changing attitudes saw the exhibits condemned as dated, and plans were mooted for the museum's demolition. In the event, it survived as a fine piece of frontier Edwardiana, distinguished, in particular, by its preponderance of skylights, essential features at a time when Banff was still without electricity. The lovely wood-panelled **reading room** – a snug retreat, full of magazines and books on nature and wildlife – makes a perfect spot to while away a cold afternoon. In summer, by contrast, the beautiful **riverside park** behind the museum is ideal for a snooze or picnic.

Nearby, the excellent **Whyte Museum of the Canadian Rockies** (mid-May to mid-Oct daily 10am–6pm; rest of year Tues–Sun 1–5pm, Thurs till 9pm; $6; ⓦ www.whyte.org), next to the library at 111 Bear St, contents itself, among other things, with a look at the Rockies' emergence as a tourist destination through paintings and photographs, and at the early expeditions to explore and conquer the interior peaks. Pictures of bears foraging in Banff rubbish bins and of park rangers grinning over a magnificent lynx they've just shot give some idea of how times have changed. The museum, which opened in 1968, forms part of the Whyte Foundation, created in the 1950s by artists Peter and Catherine Whyte to collate and preserve as great a range of material as possible relating to the Rockies. The gleaming complex is also home to the 2075-volume Alpine Club of Canada library and the 4000-volume Archives of the Canadian Rockies – the largest collection of artistic and historical material relating to the mountains. The museum also hosts temporary exhibitions by local, national and international artists, as well as presenting lectures and walking, nature and gallery tours.

The **Natural History Museum**, upstairs in the Clock Tower Mall at 112 Banff Ave (daily noon–5pm; free), is a rather throwaway venture that concentrates on the Rockies' geological history, with a sketchy account of its forests, flowers and minerals. Across the river, dated displays of native history, birds and animals fill the **Luxton Museum**, an aboriginal peoples-run enterprise attractively housed in a huge wooden stockade at 1 Birch Ave (mid-May to mid-Oct daily 9am–7pm; rest of year Wed–Sun 1–5pm; $6). The museum takes its name from Norman Luxton, a local who ran a trading post here and forged a close relationship with Banff's Stoney native population over the course of sixty years. The exhibits aren't exciting, but the museum shop has some good craft and other items if you're in spending mode.

The Banff Springs Hotel

At around $900 a night for some suites – $1600-plus for the presidential ensemble and its personal glass-sided elevators – plus $20 for any pets, the **Banff Springs Hotel** may be way out of your league, but you can't spend much time in town without coming across at least one mention of the place, and it's hard to miss its landmark, Gothic superstructure. Initiated in 1888, it got off to a bad start when the architect arrived to find the place being built 180 degrees out of kilter: while the kitchens enjoyed magnificent views over the river the guestrooms looked blankly into thick forest. When it finally opened, with 250 rooms and a rotunda to improve the views, it was the world's largest hotel. The thinking behind the project was summed up by William Cornelius Van Horne, the larger-than-life vice-president of the Canadian Pacific Railway, who said of the Rockies, "if we can't export the scenery we'll import the tourists". One of the best ways to make the railway pay, he decided, was to sell people the idea of superb scenery and provide a series of jumbo hotels from which to enjoy it: the *Banff Springs* was the result, soon followed by similar railway-backed accommodation at Lake Louise and Yoho's Emerald Lake. Horne was also the man who, when he discovered the *Banff Springs* was being built back to front, pulled out a piece of paper and quickly sketched a veranda affair, which he decided would put things to rights: he was no architect, but such was his overbearing managerial style that his ad hoc creation was built anyway.

Today the 828-room luxury pile, largely rebuilt between 1911 and 1928, costs around $90,000 a day just to run, but boasts an extraordinary hundred percent occupancy – or over 1700 guests nightly – for half of the year. The influx has prompted further rebuilding, including a spa centre talked of as one of North America's best and a ballroom for 1600 people. Don't bother with the hotel's guided tours: a voyeuristic hour or so can be spent looking around the hotel's first three floors on your own (pick up a map in reception) or taking a coffee, beer or afternoon tea in the second-floor café and Sunroom off the main reception; prices for anything else in most of the sixteen various eating places are ludicrous. It's also worth walking out onto the terrace beyond the Sunroom for some truly spectacular views.

If you have the time and money try and visit the hotel's vast **spa complex,** The Solace (T403/762-2211), which competes with the Upper Hot Springs (see p.699). It centres on a circular mineral pool beneath a high-topped glass ceiling and offers outdoor saltwater hot tubs, steam rooms, lounges, fireplaces, and complimentary drinks and snacks, with an extensive array of therapeutic services on offer. Rates for using the facility are steep at $50 per day, but this fee is waived if you buy a service – say a half-hour massage for $80.

You can get out to the hotel either by walking along the south bank of the Bow River (taking in Bow Falls) or picking up the Banff Transit bus from downtown ($1). Walking up or down Spray Ave is very dull.

Sulphur Mountain Gondola

Banff is rightly proud of the **Sulphur Mountain Gondola** on Mountain Ave (daily: mid-May to late June & mid-Aug to early Sept 8.30am–8pm; late June to mid-Aug 7am–9pm; early Sept to early Oct 8am–6.30pm; early Oct to mid-Dec 8am–4.30pm; $21.50; Wwww.banffgondola.com), some 5km south of town. High-price tickets buy you crowds, great views and a commercialized summit (2255m), but also the chance to do some high-level hiking without the slog of an early morning climb – a glimpse of the remote high country if you're short of time or unable to walk the trails. The best times to take a ride are early morning or evening, when wildlife sightings are more likely, and when the play of light gives an added dimension to the views.

The gondola trundles 700m skywards at a stomach-churning 51 degrees to immense panoramas from two observation terraces. It takes just eight minutes

The information centre carries extensive lists and contact information for guides and outfitters for all manner of **outdoor activities**; the box on p.700 details some of the best **walks** in and around Banff, while for all kinds of **winter sports** turn to p.704.

For general **bus tours**, contact Brewster Transportation (☎403/762-8400), who've been running trips for decades. There's **golf** at the stunning Banff Springs Golf Course (☎403/762-6801; from \$35 for nine holes, \$125 for eighteen holes, club rental from \$35 for steel, \$50 for graphite). You'll need to book well in advance. Free shuttles run to the clubhouse from the *Banff Springs Hotel*. **Bird-watching** with Halfway to Heaven Birdwatching (☎403/673-2542) costs \$30 for a half-day, \$65 for a day, with snack or lunch included.

Indoor climbing and swimming

Indoors, some of the best **fitness facilities** in town are in the Banff Recreation Centre, St Julien Rd (daily 6.30am–11pm; \$10 admission, \$4 swim only), and in the less expensive Community Fitness Centre (3–10pm) which also has a six-metre **climbing wall**. Climbers should additionally investigate the free climbing and bouldering walls at Mountain Magic, 224 Bear St, where instruction and gear rental are also offered. Another large pool complex is at the Douglas Fir Resort Tunnel Mountain Drive (Mon–Fri 4–9.30pm, Sat & Sun 10am–9.30pm; \$8), which also has two massive indoor **waterslides**. Note that the only swimmable lake in the park is Johnson Lake northeast of town off Lake Minnewanka Rd: the others are usually glacier-fed and thus too cold.

Biking and skating

Mountain biking is big, with plenty of rental places around town (see "Listings" on p.703). One of the cheapest, Bactrax Bike Rentals, 225 Bear St, has easy bike tours from one to four hours (\$15/hr, including bike) on paved routes around Sundance Canyon and Vermilion Lakes. More ambitious rides on the Icefields and Bow Valley parkways or around Moraine Lake can be arranged in Lake Louise at the *Chateau Lake Louise* hotel (see p.711) through Cycling the Rockies (☎403/522-2211; groups of six or more; \$69 per person half-day, \$109 full day). If you're exploring on a bike under your own steam, pick up the *Trail Bicycling Guide* from the infocentre, which outlines some of the dedicated cycling trails: the best known are Sundance (3.7km one-way); Rundle Riverside (8km one-way); Cascade Trail (9km one-way); and the Spray River Loop (4.3km). The paved Sundance Canyon Trail near the Cave and Basin centre is a popular **inline skate** run.

Boating and fishing

Boat trips can be taken on Lake Minnewanka (see p.699), as can **fishing** trips, which can be arranged through Lake Minnewanka Boat Tours (☎403/762-3473). Monod Sports, 129 Banff Ave (☎403/762-4571), has all-day drift-boat fishing trips on the Bow River and Nakoda Lake for cutthroat and bull trout plus brown and brook trout (both are catch and release, meaning you have to put any caught fish back into the water) at \$375 for two people, and walk and wade trips (\$110 per person); trips include guide, instruction, tackle, wader, drinks and food. Beginner fly-fishers can

for the glass-enclosed four-passenger cars to reach the high point, where there's an ugly but surprisingly good-value summit restaurant, Canada's highest. (Far too much of its food ends up being eaten by bighorn sheep which gather here for handouts; don't encourage them – feeding wildlife is against park regulations and can land you with a stiff fine.) From the restaurant a one-kilometre path, the **Summit Ridge Trail**, has been blazed to take you a bit higher, while take an instructional tour with the company. Banff Fishing Unlimited (☎403/762-4936) has Bow River float trips and walk and wade trips (from $100 per person) and half-day fishing cruises on Lake Minnewanka ($80 per person in a group of six). Similar trips are also offered by Adventures Unlimited (☎403/762-4554). Tackle can be rented from Performance Ski and Sports, 208 Bear St (☎403/762-8222). Remember you need a national park licence to fish, available for $6 a week, $13 a year, from tackle shops, most of the above companies or the infocentre. If you want to **rent canoes** for paddling on the Vermilion Lakes or quiet stretches of the Bow River, contact Bow River Canoe Docks ($16/hr, $40/day; ☎403/762-3632); the dock is on the river at Wolf St. Or learn to **kayak** with Alpine Adventures (☎403/678-8357; six-hour course $99).

Horse riding

Horse riding is easy to organize, with anything from one-hour treks to two-week backcountry expeditions available. The leading in-town outfitters are Holiday on Horseback, 132 Banff Ave (☎403/762-4551). One-, two- and three-hour rides start at about $25, while a six-hour trip up the Spray River Valley costs about $115. You can also take overnight trips to the *Sundance Lodge* from around $300 including all meals. Martin Stables, off Cave Ave across the river from downtown, has hourly to full-day rides ($25–115) and rents out horses by the hour from $25. The Corral (☎403/762-4551) at the *Banff Springs Hotel* lets them out for $29 and offers a three-hour ride from the hotel to Spray River, Sulphur Mountain and Mount Rundle ($64).

White-water rafting

Best among adrenaline-rush activities is **white-water rafting** on the Kicking Horse River, located a few kilometres up the road in Yoho but accessed by some eight companies in Banff and Lake Louise, most of them providing all necessary gear and transportation. Other gentler "float" trip options with the same companies are available on the Kananaskis, Kootenay and Bow rivers. Long-established Hydra River Guides, 209 Bear St (☎403/762-4554 or 1-800/644-8888, ⓦwww.raftbanff.com), has two daily six- and seven-hour trips ($85) in paddle or oar rafts on the Kicking Horse. Wet 'n' Wild Adventures (☎403/344-6546 or 1-800/668-9119) has full ($78) and half-day ($55) trips in the Kicking Horse Canyon, a half-day trip ($55) in the wilder lower part of the canyon for more advanced rafters, two-day trips and raft and horse-riding combination trips. Wild Water Adventures from Lake Louise (☎403/522-2211 or 1-888/647-6444) has a half-day trip in the canyon ($69) plus rafting in the canyon for those seeking a gentler look at the Kicking Horse ($59). Rocky Mountain Raft Tours (☎403/762-3632) offers more sedate one- and three-hour rides (3 daily; $24) down the Bow River from the canoe docks at Bow Ave and Wolf St. For half-day trips ($54) on the Kootenay River, contact Kootenay River Runner (☎403/762-5385 or 1-800/664-4399), which also has three-day ventures and is one of only three companies to offer trips on the wilder, lower section of the Kicking Horse canyon (day-trips at $79 on the Kicking Horse River or $105 in the lower canyon). For gentle float trips on the Bow or Kananaskis rivers, contact Canadian Rockies Rafting (☎403/678-6535 or 1-877/226-7625): $39 for the Bow, $45 for Kananaskis.

the short **Vista Trail** leads to the restored weather station and viewpoint on Sanson Peak. Norman Betheune "N.B." Sanson was first curator of the Banff Park Museum, and between 1903 and 1931 made around a thousand ascents of the mountain – that's before the gondola was built – to take his weather readings. Note that if, like him, you slog the 5.5km up from the car park you can ride the gondola down for free.

If you're without transport note that the only options for getting to the base station are to walk (dull and tiring) or take a taxi from downtown. In summer Brewster Transportation (℡403/762-6700) runs a short **tour shuttle** from the town centre (mid-May to mid-Aug daily on the hour 9am–4pm; mid-Aug to early Oct until 6pm); the price ($25) includes the cost of the gondola ticket and return bus shuttle, which leaves the base station hourly on the half-hour.

Cave & Basin Hot Springs

Banff boasts eight **hot springs**, and the next stop after the gondola ride on the standard itinerary is to plunge into the only one of these that's currently commercialized. Today's immersions are usually for pleasure, but in their early days these springs were vital to Banff's rise and popularity, their reputedly therapeutic effects being of great appeal to Canada's ailing Victorian gentry. Dr R.G. Brett, chief medical officer to the Canadian Pacific Railway, used his position to secure an immensely lucrative virtual monopoly on the best springs. In 1886 he constructed the Grandview Villa, a money-spinning sanatorium promising miracle cures and wonders such as "ice-cold temperance drinks". Its handrails were reinforced by crutches abandoned by "cured" patients, though the good doctor reputedly issued crutches to all comers whether they needed them or not.

There may be quieter places in western Canada to take the waters, but hot springs always make for a mildly diverting experience, and even if the crowds are a pain the prices are reasonable. On the face of it, the springs at the recently renovated **Cave & Basin National Historic Site** (mid-June to Aug daily 10am–6pm; rest of year Mon–Thurs 11am–4pm, Fri–Sun 9.30am–5pm; $2.50, or $7 with the Banff Heritage Passport, see p.693; guided tours free with admission summer daily 11am), southwest of downtown at the end of Cave Ave, are the best place to indulge. The original cave and spring here are what gave birth to the national park, discovered on November 8, 1883 by three railway navvies prospecting for gold on their day off. Having crossed the Bow River by raft they discovered a warm-watered stream, which they proceeded to follow to a small eddy of sulphurous and undergrowth-clogged water. Close by lay a small hole, the water's apparent source, which on further exploration turned out to be the entrance to an underground cave and warm mineral pool. The government quickly bought the three out, promoting travel to the springs as a means of contributing to the cost of the railway's construction. A small reserve was established in 1885, from which the present park eventually evolved. The first bathhouse was built in 1887, but over the years succumbed to the corrosive effects of chlorine and the pool's natural minerals. The pools finally closed in 1975, were restored (at a cost of $12m), opened in 1985 and closed again in 1993 – again because of corrosion and low visitor numbers.

Today the pools are still shut to bathers, leaving a popular **interpretive centre** to delve into their history and geology. You can walk here in a few minutes from town. From the foyer, where the faint whiff of sulphur is unmistakable, a short tunnel leads to the original cave, where the stench becomes all but overpowering. Smell aside, it's still a rather magical spot, with daylight shining in from a little hole in the roof and the limpid water inviting but tantalizingly out of bounds. Back down the tunnel and up the stairs brings you to a few rooms of displays, with a film show, some illuminating old photographs and several pertinent quotations, among which is the acid comment of an early travel writer, Douglas Sladen: "Though it consists of but a single street," he grumbled about Banff in 1895, "it is horribly overcivilized." Down the stairs from the displays at the rear brings you to the "basin", a small outdoor hot spring that's separate from the cave-spring system, but no less inviting. Alongside is a wooden hut theatre with a half-hour film show.

Immediately outside the centre, the short Discovery Trail (15min) heads up the hill for a view over the site, together with the nearby start of the excellent **Sundance Canyon** surfaced path (see box p.700). Just below the centre is the **Marsh Loop Trail** (2km; 25min), a treat for bird-watching enthusiasts in particular. The area's low-elevation wetlands teem with waterfowl during the winter and spring migrations, with the chance to see – among others – Barrow's goldeneye and all three species of teal: cinnamon, blue-winged and green-winged. The warm microclimate produced here by the springs' warm waters supports mallards over the winter, as well as attracting seasonal rarities such as killdeer, common snipe and rusty blackbird. During the summer you might see belted kingfisher, common yellowthroat, willow flycatcher and red-winged blackbird. Just across the river from here on Vermilion Lakes is the single most important area for bird-watching in the entire park, accessed via trails and the Vermilion Lakes Road. Ospreys and bald eagles both nest here, and other highlights include tundra swan, hooded merganser and northern shoveler.

Upper Hot Springs

Unlike the Cave & Basin, there's no problem with swimming in the **Upper Hot Springs**, 4.5km from Banff town centre on Mountain Ave (mid-May to mid-Sept daily 9am–11pm; rest of year Mon–Thurs & Sun 10am–10pm, Fri & Sat 10am–11pm; $7 mid-May to mid-Oct, $5.50 at other times; rental of lockers, towel and swimming costumes (1920-style or modern) is extra; ✆403/762-1515 or 762-2500 for spa bookings). Originally developed in 1901, the springs have since undergone several renovations and now offer soaking at 38°C in a large outdoor pool, use of a steam room and cold plunge, with the possibility of signing up for relaxing therapeutic massages ($45) or aromatherapy wraps ($32). There's a good poolside restaurant with outside terrace, fresh juice bar and hot and cold snacks.

Lake Minnewanka

Lake Minnewanka lies a few kilometres north of Banff town centre and is easily accessed by bike or car from the Trans-Canada and the northern end of Banff Ave on Lake Minnewanka Road. The largest area of water in the national park, its name means "Lake of the Water Spirit", and with the peaks of the Fairholme Range as backdrop it provides a suitably scenic antidote to the bustle of downtown. Various dams augmented the lake to provide Banff with hydroelectric power, though they've done little to spoil the views, most of which are best enjoyed from the various **boat trips** run by Lake Minnewanka Boat Tours (mid-May to Aug daily 8.30am–9pm; Sept to early Oct 8.30am–7pm; $26; ⓦ www.minnewankaboattours.com) that depart regularly from the quay in summer – this lake is the only one in the national park where public motorboats are allowed. Fishing trips can be arranged through the same company. Brewster Transportation offers an inclusive bus tour and cruise from Banff for around $41 (mid-May to early Oct 4–5 daily). You should confirm current sailing times and arrive a good half hour before sailing to pick up tickets.

Eating and drinking

Banff's hundred-plus **restaurants** – more per head of population than anywhere else in Canada – run the gamut from Japanese and other ethnic cuisines

Walks from Banff downtown

Banff Townsite is one of two obvious bases for walks in the park (the other is Lake Louise), and trails around the town cater to all levels of fitness. The best short stroll from downtown – at least for flora and fauna – is the **Fenland Trail**, a 1.5-kilometre loop west through the montane wetlands near the First Vermilion Lake (there are three Vermilion lakes, fragments of a huge lake that once probably covered the whole Bow Valley at this point; all can be accessed off Vermilion Lakes Drive). Marsh here is slowly turning to forest, creating habitats whose rushes and grasses provide a haven for wildlife, birds in particular. Ospreys and bald eagles nest around the lake, together with a wide range of other birds and waterfowl, and you may also see beaver, muskrat, perhaps even coyote, elk and other deer. You can walk this and other easy local trails in the company of the "Friends of Banff" – see p.689 for more.

For a shorter walk, and a burst of spectacular white water, stroll the level and very easy Bow Falls Trail (1km) from beneath the bridge on the south side of the river, which follows the river bank east to a powerful set of waterfalls and rapids just below the *Banff Springs Hotel*. The Hoodoos Trail on the other side of the river (starting at the eastern end of Buffalo St) offers similar views with fewer people, linking eventually to Tunnel Mountain Rd if you walk it all the way, which make this a good way to walk into town for the hostel and campsites.

The **Marsh Loop Trail** (2km) from Cave Ave leads along a boardwalk through a marshy habitat renowned for its flora and birds (see p.699): warm waters from the Cave and Basin hot springs immediately above have created a small, anomalous area of lush vegetation. In winter Banff's own wolf pack has been known to hunt within sight of this trail. The **Sundance Canyon Trail** (3.7km), an easy and deservedly popular stroll along a paved path (also popular with cyclists and rollerbladers – be warned) to the picnic area at the canyon mouth, also starts from close to the springs; you can extend your walk along the 2.1-kilometre loop path up through the canyon, past waterfalls and back down a peaceful wooded trail. Finally, the most strenuous walk near town is to the summit of Tunnel Mountain. It's approached on a windy track (300m ascent) from the southwest from Tunnel Mountain Drive, culminating in great views over the townsite, Bow River and flanking mountains.

Day-hikes near Banff

Day-hikes from the town centre are limited – you need transport and usually have to head a few kilometres along the Trans-Canada to reach trailheads that leave the flat valley floor for the heart of the mountains. Only a couple of longish ones strike out directly from town: the **Spray River Circuit**, a flat, thirteen-kilometre round trip past the *Banff Springs Hotel* up the Spray River; and the Sulphur Mountain Trail, a 5.5-kilometre switchback that climbs 655m up to the Sulphur Mountain gondola terminal at 2255m (you're better off simply taking the gondola).

to nouvelle-frontier grub. For cheap eats you're best sticking to hostel cafés, though Banff Ave is lined with good little spots for coffee and snacks, many with pleasant outdoor tables; some of the bars in town are also decent value. For **groceries** try the big Safeway supermarket at 318 Marten St and Elk (daily 9am–10pm), and the less hectic Kellers, 122 Bear St (daily 7am–midnight).

Cafés and restaurants

Aardvark Pizza and Sub 304a Caribou St. Tiny takeaway place with subs, wings, tacos, nachos, poutine and fantastic thick-crust pizzas. There's virtually nowhere to sit but with the best takeout food in town, and open until 4am, popularity's assured.

Park wardens at the infocentre seem unanimous in rating the **Cory Pass Trail** (5.8km; 915m ascent), combined with the Edith Pass Trail to make a return loop, as the best day-hike close to Banff. The trailhead is signed 6km west of the town off the Bow Valley Parkway, 500m after the junction with the Trans-Canada. The stiff climbing involved, and a couple of scree passages, mean that it's not for the inexperienced or faint-hearted. The rewards are fantastic, with varied walking, a high-mountain environment and spine-tingling views. From the pass itself at 2350m you can return on the Edith Pass Trail (whose start you'll have passed 1km into the Cory Pass walk), to make a total loop of a demanding 13km.

Another popular local day-hike, the trail to **Cascade Amphitheatre** (2195m), starts at Mount Norquay Ski Area, 6km north of the Trans-Canada Mount Norquay Rd. This offers a medley of landscapes, ranging from alpine meadows to deep, ice-scoured valleys and a close view of the knife-edge mountains that loom so tantalizingly above town. Allow about three hours for the walk (7.7km; 610m ascent). For the same amount of effort you could tackle **Elk Lake** (2165m) from the ski area, though at 13.5km each way it's a long day's hike; some people turn it into an overnight hike by using the campsite 2.5km short of Elk Lake. Shorter, but harder on the lungs, is the third of Banff's popular local walks, **C Level Cirque** (1920m), reached by a four-kilometre trail from the Upper Bankhead Picnic Area on the Lake Minnewanka road east of Banff. Elsewhere, the Sunshine Meadows area has five high trails of between 8km and 20km, all possible as day-hikes and approached either from the Sunshine Gondola (if running) or its parking area, 18km southwest of Banff. There are also some good short trails off the Bow Valley Parkway, most notably the **Johnston Canyon** path (see box p.708).

The best **backpacking** options lie in the Egypt Lake area west of Banff Townsite, with longer trails radiating from the lake's campsite. Once you're in the backcountry around Banff, however, the combination of trails is virtually limitless. The keenest hikers tend to march the routes that lead from Banff to Lake Louise – the Sawback Trail and Bow Valley Highline, or the tracks in the Upper Spray and Bryant Creek Valley south of the townsite.

If you're planning long walks and overnight trips in backcountry you must have a **Wilderness Pass** ($6 a night from park centres). You should also book backcountry campsites (contact Parks Canada at Lake Louise or Banff visitor centres; ☏403/762-1556) and walks well in advance ($10 nonrefundable booking fee), as **quotas** operate for all backcountry areas – if the quotas fill, you won't be able to walk or camp or may have to make do with a second-choice hike. The most popular of the fifty-odd campsites are Marvel Lake, Egypt Lake, Luellen Lake, Aylmer Pass, Mystic Meadow, Fish Lakes, Paradise Valley, Hidden Lake, Baker Lake, Merlin Meadows, Red Deer Lakes and Mount Rundle. Be sure to pick up or send for the Parks Canada *Backcountry Visitors' Guide* pamphlet for further details of the system and of recommended routes.

Baker Creek Bistro Baker Creek Chalets, Bow Valley Parkway ☏403/522-2182. Romantic dining in softly lit log cabin outfitted with deer-antler chandeliers midway between Banff and Lake Louise on the Bow Valley Parkway. The menu has innovative steaks and pastas, and good game dishes; apple cake is the house speciality.
Balkan Village 120 Banff Ave ☏403/762-3454. Cheerful blue and white decorated Greek place, best known for frantic belly dancing on Tuesdays and large portions of decent, if rather curious,

Greek-style food: chose from the likes of Greek ribs (pork ribs in a lemon sauce) $16; Greek chow mein, Greek spaghetti; or better, stick to the traditional favourites like souvlakia ($13) or if you're ravenous the two-person Greek platter ($39) which includes beef souvlaki, ribs, moussaka, lamb chops and salad.
Banff Springs Hotel 405 Spray Ave ☏403/762-6860. With around fifteen dining options under one roof, the *Banff Springs* has plenty of variety; all are open to non-guests. The Bow Valley Grill is the

largest restaurant, its menu focused around reliably popular seafood and rotisserie-grilled meats. The Sunday brunch ($25) here is legendary for its variety and value, while some of the other buffets offered include a tour of the hotel. Other places to eat range from the 24-hour deli serving pizza, to the super-luxurious Banffshire Club, which stipulates formal attire and includes Castello Ristorante for top-class Italian foods and the Samurai, which serves excellent sushi. For light snacks try Grapes Wine Bar which has good salads, a fine selection of pâtés and cheese and a highly esteemed fondue.

Barbary Coast Upstairs at 119 Banff Ave ☎ 403/762-4616. Excellent, if obvious, food – pizza, steaks, burgers and salads – at good prices: the restaurant is full of sporting memorabilia, and the separate popular bar at the front, open till 2am, also does food (with occasional live music).

Bistro Corner of Wolf and Bear next to the Lux Cinema ☎ 403/762-8900. A cheaper sister restaurant of *Le Beaujolais*, this is a pleasantly calm place a block or so off Banff Ave where you can enjoy first-rate food in intimate surroundings.

Bumper's 603 Banff Ave ☎ 403/762-2622. Busy, good-value steakhouse with adjoining laid-back bar located a little outside downtown. Entrée prices start at around $18 and vegetarians can console themselves with a decent salad bar.

Cilantro Mountain Café At *Buffalo Mountain Lodge*, Tunnel Mountain Rd ☎ 403/762-2400. A good café-restaurant, with the usual North American fare, that's ideal if you're staying at the hostel or campsite and want a modest treat; has a nice outside terrace for the summer. Inexpensive.

Coyotes Grill 206 Caribou St. Small simple café just off the main drag, serving top-notch breakfasts. One of the best is the cream-cheese-filled French Toast with fruit ($9). But the hungry should try the huge Mountain Man Breakfast ($9.50) which includes two eggs, two pancakes bacon or sausage and roasted potatoes. Evenings see fine renditions of pizza, pasta and Southwestern Tex-Mex entrees ($15–25).

Evelyn's 201 Banff Ave ☎ 403/762-0352. A superb range of coffees wash down pastries and muffins here in a café that's popular enough to justify a second outlet, Evelyn's Too, at 229 Bear Ave. Both are open 7am–11pm, and put together deli sandwiches (around $5) that make ideal picnic food.

Joe Btfsplk's [sic] Diner 221 Banff Ave ☎ 403/762-5529. Red vinyl seats and black and white tiles help make this 1950s-style diner feel authentic, as do the giant portions of dependable, if slightly overpriced, classic foods like meatloaf. And yes, the name is *Joe Btfsplk's*.

Le Beaujolais 212 Banff Ave at Buffalo St ☎ 403/762-2712. Longstanding gourmet restaurant whose reputation for fine French renditions of regional cuisine extends all over western Canada. Pick from a choice of three set-price menus between $55 and $90, which help keep tabs on spending and range from two to six courses – though only the six course meal includes drinks from the lavish wine list.

Melissa's 218 Lynx St ☎ 403/762-5511. Probably Banff's most popular daytime destination, set in an old log cabin: big breakfasts, superb mignon steaks, salads and burgers, plus a good upstairs bar, *Mel's*, for a leisurely drink, and a summer patio for food and beer in the sun. Recommended, particularly for lunch. Moderate.

Saltlik 221 Bear St ☎ 403/762-2467. Swanky second-floor restaurant with wacky lamps and loud art in an otherwise understated but stylized interior. A nouvelle-steakhouse, it does Alberta proud with its almost finicky preparation of the 10oz prime sirloin ($20). But most entrees, including rotisserie chicken, smoked Alaskan black cod and sea bass, are under the $20 mark – but the price doesn't include the interesting sides (mushrooms, spinach, corn, shrimp) that you use to assemble your own meal. The wide selection of wines suffer little markup and the trendy first-floor bar is a good place for a drink before or after dinner – or with dinner as it has the best bar menu in town; don't miss the crisp, seasoned shoestring fries.

Sukiyaki House 211 Banff Ave ☎ 403/762-2002. Sit low among Japanese visitors at the squat tables of this chic Japanese restaurant. With a broad menu, it's hard to choose, but almost impossible to go wrong; the easy option is to pick the Love Boat ($35), a well-priced and varied selection for two people.

Sunfood Café 215 Banff Ave ☎ 403/760-3933. Vaguely bohemian vegetarian eatery tucked away in a mall. Great for light meals, salads, sandwiches and wraps; most well under $10. Hot meals include items like teriyaki tofu steak ($12) and mushroom stroganoff ($15).

Drinking and entertainment

Given Banff's huge number of summer travellers and a large young seasonal workforce, there are plenty of people around looking for **nightlife** (winter is rarely as busy) and the town has no shortage of **bars** – most within a short walk of one another – and several late-night clubs to stagger to afterwards. Among the less boozy entertainments are **billiards** upstairs at the *King Edward Hotel*, 137 Banff Ave ($12/hr), ten-pin **bowling** at the *Banff Springs Hotel* ($3.75 a game, $1.10 shoe rental) and new-release **films** at the Lux Cinema, 229 Bear St (☎403/762-8595).

Aurora 110 Banff Ave. Loud, pricey and popular bar and nightclub in the Clock Tower Village Mall. This pick-up joint usually gets going around midnight when a young crowd gather to dance until 2am nightly, generally to live music on Friday and Saturday evenings.
Banff Springs Hotel ☎403/762-6892. The giant hotel has a selection of bars, including the neighborhood-style *Waldhaus Pub*, the cigar-friendly *Ramsay Lounge*, the *Rundle Balcony* with its own pianist, and wine bar *Grapes*.
Barbary Coast 119 Banff Ave. Popular, chaotic and occasionally rowdy bar, bulging with pool tables and sporting memorabilia. There's also great-value bar food – daily dinner specials for $7 – and a long happy hour (4.30–7.30pm). Open until 2am.
Outa Bounds 137 Banff Ave. Soulless basement bar – the main competition for Banff's other major nightclub, the *Aurora* – that nevertheless draws in crowds of 20-somethings for average food, pool, dancing and occasional live music.
Rose and Crown 202 Banff Ave. Victorian-style pub with family-oriented restaurant serving decent bar food, which include fantastic hot wings. There's pool here too and occasionally live music,

particularly blues and funk, making it a cornerstone of town nightlife.
St James Gate 205 Wolf St. Genuinely dingy dark-wood pub, originally built in Ireland then reassembled here to become hugely popular with locals and visitors alike. The thirty beers on tap include good Guinness, as do many of the dishes on the satisfying bar menu; Guinness, crab and asparagus soup ($6), or Guinness, steak and mushroom pie ($11). Other menu items are equally earthy like the tasty kilpatrik's cabbage and sausage soup ($6) and the juicy halibut fish and chips ($11) and decent meatloaf $12. Occasional live Celtic music.
Voyager Inn 555 Banff Ave. Workaday bar adjoining eponymous motel on the edge of town. Locals who appreciate the cheapest drinks in town – along with nightly specials – converge here.
Wild Bill's Legendary Saloon 203 Banff Ave. Lively country-and-western bar with live bands (country Wed–Sat; rock & blues Sun–Thurs) and weekly line-dancing lessons (Wed 8.30pm). There's also a pool hall and games room here, and before 8pm good Tex-Mex and vegetarian food is served in a more family-oriented atmosphere.

Listings

American Express 130 Banff Ave ☎403/762-3207.
Bike and inline skate rental Bactrax, 225 Bear St (☎403/762-8177); Banff Adventures Unlimited, 211 Bear St (☎403/762-4554); Inns of Banff, 600 Banff Ave (☎403/762-4581); Mountain Magic, 224 Bear St (☎403/762-2591); Performance Ski and Sport, 2nd Floor, 208 Bear St (☎403/762-8222); Ski Stop outlets at 203a Bear St and *Banff Springs Hotel* (☎403/760-1650 or 762-5333).
Bookshop Banff Book & Art Den, Clock Tower Mall, 94 Banff Ave (daily: summer 10am–9pm; winter 10am–7pm; ☎403/762-3919) is excellent for general books and local guides.
Car rental Book well in advance. Avis, Cascade Plaza, Wolf St (☎403/762-3222 or 1-800/879-2847); Banff Rent-a-Car, 230 Lynx St (☎403/762-3352), for low-priced older vehicles; Budget, 208 Caribou St (☎403/762-4546 or 1-800/268-8900); Hertz, at the *Banff Springs Hotel* (☎403/762-2027

or 1-800/263-0600); National, corner of Caribou and Lynx (☎403/762-2688 or 1-800/387-4747).
Exchange CTM Currency Exchange at 108 Banff Ave, Clock Tower Mall (☎403/762-4698 or 762-9353), 317 Banff Ave (Cascade Plaza) and the *Banff Springs Hotel*. Visa advances at CIBC, 98 Banff Ave (☎403/762-4417); MasterCard advances at Bank of Montréal, 107 Banff Ave.
Internet access Public library, 101 Bear St (Mon–Sat 11am–6pm, Tues & Thurs until 9pm, Sun 1–5pm; ☎403/762-2661), has free access but requires prior booking.
Laundries Cascade Plaza Coin Laundry, Lower Level, Cascade Plaza, 317 Banff Ave (☎403/762-2245); Johnny O's Emporium, 223 Bear St (Mon–Sat 8am–midnight, Sun 9am–midnight; last wash 10.30pm).
Lost property ☎403/762-1218.
Medical emergencies Mineral Springs Hospital, 301 Lynx St ☎403/762-2222. A dentist is at 210

As enticing in winter as it is the rest of the year, Banff National Park is a virtual paradise if you're a skier or snowboarder. The terrain here is some of the best and most varied in North America and three world-class resorts lie in the park: two close to Banff – **Mount Norquay** and **Sunshine Village** – and one in **Lake Louise** (see p.718). On top of great snow and pristine runs, you get crisp air, monumental mountains, sky-high forests, and prices and space that make a mockery of Europe's crowded and exorbitant winter playgrounds. You're also pretty certain of snow, sensational views, plenty of nightlife and comfortable hotels – much cheaper than in summer and connected to the ski hills via frequent shuttle buses. On top of this the park also offers the full gamut of **winter activities**, embracing everything from skating, ice-fishing and toboggan trips to dog-sledding, snowshoeing and sleigh rides. However, what the brochures don't tell you is that here – as in Lake Louise – it can be bitterly cold for much of the skiing season.

Mount Norquay

Mount Norquay (☎403/762-4421, ⓦwww.banffnorquay.com) is the closest resort to Banff, just 6km and ten minutes' drive from downtown. Skiing started on the mountain's steep eastern slopes in the 1920s. In 1948 it gained Canada's first-ever chairlift, immediately gaining a reputation as an experts-only resort thanks largely to horrors like the double-black diamond Lone Pine run. This reputation has only recently disappeared, the result of a complete revamp and the opening of a new network of lifts on and around Mystic Ridge to provide access to intermediate terrain and 31 runs suitable for all levels of skiers and boarders alike.

As a result Norquay is now equally renowned for its uncrowded beginners' slopes as for its expert runs, the terrain breaking down as follows: Novice (20 percent), Intermediate (36 percent) and Expert (44 percent). The average snowfall is 300cm, and there's snow-making on ninety percent of the terrain. The season runs from December to mid-April. The highest elevation is 2133m, giving a vertical drop of 503m to the resort's base elevation at 1636m. Amenities include a visitor centre, ski school, rental shop, day-care and – on Fridays – the promise of night skiing. Lift tickets are around $47 a day.

Sunshine Village

Sunshine Village (☎403/762-6500, ⓦwww.skibanff.com) is a stunning resort, situated way up in the mountains at 2160m, 18km southwest of Banff. If anything the scenery's better than at Norquay – you're higher – and you have the plus of the national park's only on-hill accommodation. There's also an incredible 10m of snow a year – so there's no need for snow-making machines – with superb soft, light powder that *Snow Country* magazine has repeatedly voted "The Best Snow in Canada". Skiing started here in 1929 when two locals got lost on Citadel Pass and came back with tales of fantastic open bowls and dream slopes just made for skiing. In 1938 the Canadian National Ski Championships were held here, and by 1942 a portable lift had been installed on site. The biggest change in the area's fortunes came in 1980, when a gondola (cable car) was built to carry skiers (and occasionally summer walkers) the 6km from the Healy Creek parking area to the self-contained Sunshine Village resort.

Today some 103 uncrowded runs can be accessed on the gondola, three high-speed detachable quads, a triple chair, four double chairs, two T-bars and two beginner rope tows. There's as much here for the advanced skier as at Norquay, as well as plenty for the beginner and competent intermediate. Terrain breaks downs as follows: Novice (22 percent), Intermediate (31 percent) and Expert (47 percent). The top elevation is an incredible 2730m at Lookout Mountain and there's 3168 acres of terrain to chose from. Lift tickets are around $63 a day. Amenities include a day-lodge, day-care, outdoor hot pool, ski school, rental shop and overnight rooms in the Village at the 85-room *Sunshine Inn*, the Rockies' only on-slope accommodation (℡403/762-6555; ❽). Ski packages are available here, with three nights' skiing and lodging around $270 per person. Shuttle buses run round the hotels and cost $18 for the round trip.

Other winter activities

If you really want to see the park, head out on either **cross-country skis** or **snowshoes** on the myriad summer walking trails groomed for these purposes. Details of the full network are given in the *Nordic Trails in Banff National Park* pamphlet available from the town's visitor centre ($1). Popular areas include Johnston Lake, Golf Course Rd, Spray River and Sundance Canyon, along with several areas around Lake Louise (see p.718). An additional 300km of cross-country trails crisscross the Kananaskis region, many developed for Olympic competitions, radiating from Canmore Nordic Centre (see p.680). But if these networks aren't enough and you're interested in ski tours of Banff's backcountry, it's best to have the company of an experienced guide; Banff Alpine Guides (℡403/678-6091) is a reliable local company. Good local sources of rentals, repairs, accessories and advice are Trail Sports (℡403/678-6764) and Mountain Magic (℡403/762-2591). Both stores also rent out snowshoes and can help with suggestions for local hikes.

One of the best **winter walks** in the area is the hike through the fairytale scenery of Johnston Canyon, on boardwalks suspended from its limestone walls to impressive pillars of glassy ice. Though icy, the boardwalks are navigable in winter with the right gear and knowledge, so that White Mountain Adventures (℡403/678-4099, ⓦwww.canadiannatureguides.com) can offer a 3.5hr trip down the canyon. Similar packages, down the less spectacular Grotto Canyon, are offered by Discover Banff tours (℡403/760-1299 or 1-877/565-9372), which only take an hour. One of the highlights of this trip is to watch the ice-climbers in this canyon, as this is one of the area's most popular intermediate pitches. Other popular sites in the area include Goat Mountain, past Yamnuska, a fairly moderate area, and Cougar Canyon, a more intermediate challenge. Beginners should head to Canmore Junkyards, past Nordic Center turn-off in Canmore, while death-defying experts might like to explore the internationally notorious Terminator just outside the Banff National Park boundary. For detailed **ice climbing** information visit the National Park desk in Banff's Information Center (℡403/762-1550) where climbers should also register.

Of the large selection of local commercial tours one of the best is **dog-sledding**. Thrilling trips are offered for a rather steep fee (around $100/hr) by Howling Dog Tours (℡403/678-9588) or Snowy Owl Sled Dog Tours (℡403/678-4369), while Mountain Mushers (℡403/762-3647) will take you for a shorter spin around the town's golf course. For less adrenaline-filled **sleigh rides** on the frozen Bow River, contact Holiday on Horseback (℡403/762-4551), while those who seek the positively calming experience of **ice-fishing** on surrounding lakes should contact Banff Fishing Unlimited (℡403/762-4936).

For a session of **ice-skating** or **tobogganing**, head to the *Banff Springs Hotel* where the outdoor rink is made particularly appealing by a fire beside it. Ice skates can be rented from The Ski Shop (℡403/762-5333) in the hotel for $5/hr; you can also rent sleds here ($4/hr) for use on the unofficial run beside the rink. Many other hotels in town also provide sleds for toboggan runs, of which there are several unofficial examples around town and an alternative venue for ice-skating is the rinks of Banff High School, on the Bow River (off Bow St).

Bear St ☎ 403/762-3144. Two doctors are Dr Ian MacDonald, 216 Banff Ave ☎ 403/762-3155, and Dr Elizabeth J. Hall-Findlay, 317 Banff Ave ☎ 403/762-2055.

Outdoor equipment Tents, outdoor gear and ski equipment to rent from Performance Ski and Sport, 208 Bear St (☎ 403/762-8222).

Pharmacy Cascade Plaza Drug, Lower Level, Cascade Plaza, 317 Banff Ave; Gourlay's, 229 Bear St (Wolf and Bear Mall).

Police ☎ 403/762-2226.

Post office 204 Buffalo St at the corner of Bear St (Mon–Fri 9am–5.30pm). Stamps and other basic postal services also at Cascade Plaza Drug, Lower Level, Cascade Plaza, 317 Banff Ave; Mailboxes Etc, 226 Bear St; and Goro Canyon Gifts, Banff Park Lodge.

Road conditions ☎ 403/762-1450.

Taxis Alpine (☎ 403/762-3727); Banff Limousine (☎ 403/762-5466); Banff Taxi (☎ 403/762-4444); Legion (☎ 403/762-3353); Mountain (☎ 403/762-3351). All charge a $2.60 flagfall and around $1.35/km – from the bus terminal to the hostel or the *Banff Springs Hotel* should cost around $7.

Trail conditions ☎ 403/762-1550 or 760-1305.

Weather ☎ 403/762-4707 or 762-2088 (24hr recording).

Hwy 1 and the Bow Valley Parkway

Two roads run parallel through the Bow Valley from Banff to Lake Louise (58km): the faster **Hwy 1** (the Trans-Canada); and the quieter **Bow Valley Parkway**, on the north side of the river, opened in 1989 as a special scenic route. After Banff, there's only one link between the two roads, at Castle Junction, 30km from Lake Louise. Both routes are staggeringly beautiful as the mountains start to creep closer to the road. For the entire run, the mighty Bow River, broad and emerald green, crashes through rocks and forest. Despite the tarmac and heavy summer traffic, the surroundings are pristine and suggest the immensity of the wilderness to come. Sightings of elk and deer are common, particularly around dawn and sundown, and occasionally you'll spot moose.

Both roads offer some good **trails**: if you want to tackle one of the most highly rated day-walks in Banff National Park, make for the Bourgeau Lake Trail off Hwy 1 (see box p.708); for a shorter walk, make for the Johnston Canyon on the Parkway.

Hwy 1

Most people tend either to cruise **Hwy 1**'s rapid stretch of the Trans-Canada without stopping – knowing that the road north of Lake Louise is more spectacular still – or leap out at every trail and rest stop, overcome with the grandeur of it all. On Greyhound or Brewster **buses** you're whisked through to Lake Louise in about forty minutes; if you're driving, try for the sake of wildlife to stick to the 90kph speed limit. The vast fences that march for kilometre after kilometre along this section of the road are designed to protect animals, not only from traffic but from the brainless visitors who clamber out of their cars to get close to the bears occasionally glimpsed on the road. You won't have to be in the Rockies long during the summer before you're caught in a **bear jam**, when people – contrary to all park laws, never mind common sense – abandon their cars helter-skelter on the road to pursue hapless animals with cameras and camcorders.

Note that the 17km of the Bow Valley Parkway between Johnston Canyon and the east entrance off the Trans-Canada (that is, the entrance closest to Banff) is **closed** every day from March 1 to June 25 between 6pm and 9am. This lets animals forced down to look for food at lower altitudes by late snow to graze. Access at these times to the Johnston Canyon trails and campsite is from Hwy 1 only.

Sunshine Meadows

A beautiful and unusually large tract of alpine grassland, **Sunshine Meadows**, 18km southwest of Banff off Hwy 1, is cradled by Sunshine Village ski resort and straddles the continental divide. The area may be better known for its winter sports, but for the short summer season the valley is replete with hundreds of wild flowers and ideal for high-mountain hiking. Access to the valley is on foot on an arduous 6km access trail from the resort's parking lot, but a much better option is to take a shuttle bus. A service is run by White Mountain Adventures (☎403/678-4099 or 1-800/408-005, ⓦwww.canadiannatureguides.com; $35 round-trip), departing from both Banff and the Sunshine Village parking lot. Once you're in Sunshine Meadows two connecting gravel trails can be followed. The **Rock Isle Trail** loop starts at the Sunshine Meadows Nature Centre. After 1km, branch right to pass Rock Isle Lake on the left (take the left fork and you'd eventually come to Lake Assiniboine). Around 600m after the branch right you come to a fork: turn left and you loop around the Garden Path Trail (3.8km) past Larix Lake, the Simpson Viewpoint and Grizzly Lake back to the fork. From here it's 500m to a 1.2-kilometre detour to the right to Standish Viewpoint (a dead end). Otherwise head straight on and after 2.8km you come to a junction and the Monarch Viewpoint, where a 1.6-kilometre walk takes you back to the Nature Centre (11.5km total with all loops and detours). Ask for a sketch map of this area from the information centre.

The Bow Valley Parkway

If anything, the **Bow Valley Parkway** boasts more scenic grandeur than Hwy 1 – which is saying something – and offers more distractions if you're taking your time: several trails, campsites, plus plenty of accommodation choices and one excellent eating option. The largest concentration of sightseers is likely to be found at the Merrent turn-off, enjoying fantastic views of the Bow Valley and the railway winding through the mountains.

If you have the time, therefore, the Parkway is the preferable route, and you should budget some time to walk one of the **trails** en route, in particular the easy but impressive Johnston Canyon Trail (see box p.708). En route, some of the various viewpoints and signed pull-offs deserve more attention than others. Around 8km down the highway, look out for the **Backswamp Viewpoint**, where views one way extend to the mountains and the other across a river swamp area where you might see beaver, muskrat, ospreys and other birds, as well as the common butterwort, a purple-flowered carnivorous plant whose diet consists largely of marsh insects. In winter Backswamp Viewpoint is also known locally as one of the most likely areas to spot wolves; at other times of the year you might also see bighorn sheep or mountain goats on the mountain slopes above. About 3km further on you come to **Muleshoe Picnic Area**, also noted for its birds and wildfowl. Some of the area around shows signs of having been burnt in forest fires, though these areas were deliberately torched by the park authorities to encourage fresh undergrowth and the return of wildlife excluded from more mature forests. Some 11km on, a 400m trail takes you to a lovely little lake once known as Lizard Lake after the long-toed salamanders that thrived here. These were eaten when the lake was stocked with trout, and the name's now been changed to Pilot Lake. About 3km beyond is the trailhead for the **Johnston Canyon Trail** deservedly the most popular in the area; 3km beyond that is **Moose Meadows**, where – name notwithstanding – you'll be mighty lucky to see any moose: habitat changes have forced them out.

Of interest to **bird-watchers**, Johnston Canyon is one of only two known breeding sites in Alberta of the black swift – you may see the birds flitting back to their nests at dusk – and is also a breeding place for American dippers, buxom grey birds that have the ability to walk along stream beds underwater and habitually nest below waterfalls. Elsewhere on the Parkway the various turn-offs give you the opportunity to spot species associated with montane forest and meadow zones, notably at the Muleshoe Picnic Area, 21km southeast of Castle Junction, where you might spot western tanagers, pileated woodpeckers and orange-crowned warblers. At various points on the Bow River along the entire run from Banff to Lake Louise you may spot harlequin ducks on the river's islands and gravel bars, as well as spotted sandpipers and common mergansers.

Practicalities

The road's **accommodation** possibilities make a more rural alternative to Banff and Lake Louise, and are close enough to both to serve as a base if you have transport; as ever, you should book rooms well in advance. Four **lodges** are spaced more or less equally en route and, though expensive, they may have room when Lake Louise's hotels are stretched. First is the *Johnston Canyon Resort*, 26km west of Banff and close to the trail that leads to the canyon (☎403/762-2971, ⓦwww.johnstoncanyon.com; ❺; mid–May to late Sept), which consists of rustic cabins (some with fireplaces and some with kitchenettes), a shop, garage, tennis court and basic groceries. Next come the chalets, laundry and grocery store of *Castle Mountain Chalets*, 32km west of Banff near Castle Junction (☎403/762-3868, ⓦwww.castlemountain.com; ❼; year-round); the log chalets for four with kitchenettes and fireplaces are more expensive, but the best options of all here are the delightful de luxe cabins for

Bow Valley Trails

Five major trails branch off the Bow Valley Parkway. The best short walk is the **Johnston Canyon Trail** (2.7km each way), 25km from Banff, an incredibly engineered path to a series of spray-veiled waterfalls. The Lower Falls are 1.1km, the Upper Falls 2.7km from the trailhead on the Parkway. From the upper falls you can continue on to the seven cold-water springs of the Ink Pots, which emerge in pretty open meadows, to make a total distance of 5.8km (215m ascent). Another short possibility is the **Castle Crags Trail** (3.7km each way; 520m ascent) from the signed turn-off 5km west of Castle Junction. Short but steep, and above the tree-line, this walk offers superb views across the Bow Valley and the mountains beyond. Allow ninety minutes one-way to take account of the stiff climb.

The best day-hike is to **Rockbound Lake** (8.4km each way), a steepish climb to 2210m with wild lakeland scenery at the end; allow at least two and a half hours one-way, due to the 760m ascent. Another fifteen-minutes' walk beyond Rockbound and Tower lakes at the end of the trail lies the beautiful Silverton waterfall. The other Parkway trails – **Baker Creek** (20.3km) and **Pulsatilla Pass** (17.1km) – serve to link backpackers with the dense network of paths in the Slate Range northeast of Lake Louise.

The two outstanding trails along Hwy 1 are the trek to **Bourgeau Lake** (7.5km one-way), considered by many among the top five day-hikes in Banff: it starts from a parking area 10km west of Banff – allow two and a half to three hours for the 725-metre ascent – and the long day-hike to **Shadow Lake** (14.3km each way), where the lakeside campsite (at 1840m), in one of the Rockies' more impressive subalpine basins, gives access to assorted onward trails. The main trail starts from the **Redearth Creek** parking area 20km west of Banff (440m ascent; allow 4hr).

four, five or six people (complete with full kitchens, dishwashers and Jacuzzis). Some 5km south of Hwy 1 on Hwy 93 to Radium (27km from Banff) is *Storm Mountain Lodge* (☎403/762-4155; ❻; late May to late Sept), with highly appealing log cabins. Finally there's *Baker Creek Guest Lodge & Bistro*, 12km east of Lake Louise (☎403/522-3761, ⓦwww.bakercreek.com; ❻; year-round), with 25 one- and two-room log cabins and lodge rooms for between one and six people; there's also an excellent **restaurant** here that comes with local recommendations and an annexe with eight smart motel-type rooms. By far the least expensive possibility is the Parkway's charming HI **hostel**, *Castle Mountain Hostel*, 1.5km east of Castle Junction (☎403/762-2367 or 762-4122, ⓦwww.hihostels.ca; dorms $13; ❶; year-round but closed Wed).

Three national park **campsites** provide excellent camping retreats. In order of distance from Banff these are the very popular 140-pitch *Johnston Canyon* ($17; mid-May to mid-Sept), 25km from Banff – the best equipped, with full facilities including showers and wheelchair access; the 40-pitch *Castle Mountain*, 32km from Banff near Castle Junction ($13; late June to early Sept), with no facilities beyond water and flush toilets; and the similarly simple 89-pitch *Protection Mountain*, 5km north of Castle Junction (same details). An additional $4 fee is payable at all three if you wish to use firewood.

Lake Louise

The Banff National Park's other main centre, **LAKE LOUISE**, is very different from Banff – less a town than two distinct artificial resorts. The first is a small mall of shops and hotels just off the Trans-Canada known as **Lake Louise Village**. The second is **the lake** itself, 4.5km from the village (and 200m higher) on the winding Lake Louise Drive, the self-proclaimed "gem of the Rockies" and – despite its crowds and monster hotel – a sight you have to see. You can walk between the two, the uphill hike from the townsite to the lake totalling 2.7km on the Louise Creek Trail or 4.5km along the Tramline Trail. But, really, you're better off saving the walking for around the lake and taking a taxi (☎403/522-2020; around $10) from the village (if anything, save the two linking trails for coming down from the lake). A third area, **Moraine Lake**, 13km south of the village, has almost equally staggering scenery and several magnificent and easily accessed trails. All three areas are desperately busy in summer while in winter things slow down a little, though crowds still turn up for some of Canada's best powder **skiing** at the nearby resort (see box p.718).

Nonetheless, the mountains around offer almost unparalleled **hiking country** and the park's most popular day-use area. You'll have to weigh awesome scenery against the sheer numbers, for these are some of the most heavily used trails on the continent – 50,000-plus people in summer – though longer backpacking routes lead quickly away to the quieter spots. If you do intend to hike – and the trails are all a little more accessible and manageable than at Banff – then in an ideal world you'd have two or three days here: one to walk the loop around above Lake Louise (Lake Agnes–Big Beehive–Plain of the Six Glaciers–Lake Louise Shoreline) or the more demanding Saddleback (at a push you could do both in a day if you were fit and keen). Then you'd bike, taxi or drive to Moraine Lake (if you're not staying there), where in a day you could easily walk to Consolation Lake, return to Moraine Lake and then tackle the Moraine Lake–Larch Valley–Sentinel Pass or Moraine Lake–Larch Valley–Eiffel Lake trail. A third day could be spent in Paradise Valley between Lake Louise and Moraine Lake.

If, on the other hand, you merely want to take in the scenery and enjoy **modest strolls** in the course of a day, then cruise up to Lake Louise, walk up

LAKE LOUISE VICINITY

0   2 km

Icefields Parkway & Jasper

Field

Trail to Lake O'Hara

BRITISH COLUMBIA

Ross Lake

Lake Louise Gondola

Lake Louise Hostel

Lake Louise Village

Skoki Valley

Teahouse

Chateau Lake Louise

Lake Agnes

Mt Whyte

Lake Louise 'Tenting' Campground

Lake Louise 1731m

Bow River

Teahouse

Fairview Mtn 2744m

Saddleback

MORAINE LAKE ROAD

Banff & Calgary

Plain-of-the-Six Glaciers

Mt Aberdeen 3152m

ALBERTA

Victoria Glacier

Mt Victoria 3564m

Paradise Valley

Lake Annette

Moraine Creek

Abbot Pass

Mt Lefroy

Trail to Lake O'Hara

Lake Oesa

Mt Temple

Yukness Mtn

Sentinel Pass

Pinnacle Mtn 3067m

Larch Valley

Moraine Lake Lodge

Panorama Ridge

Eiffel Peak

Mt Biddle

Eiffel Lake

Moraine Lake 1887m

2824m

Wenkchemna Pass 2605m

Valley of the Ten Peaks

Consolation Lakes

YOHO NATIONAL PARK

KOOTENAY NATIONAL PARK

Mt Allen 3301m

Mt Fay 3235m

and down the shore, then drive the twenty minutes or so to Moraine Lake and do the same.

Arrival and information

Four Greyhound **buses** a day ($8) link Banff and Lake Louise (50min) and stop in the Samson Mall car park at the little office known as The Depot

(☎403/522-2080); three continue to Vancouver and the west. Four buses a day return from Lake Louise to Banff and Calgary. Laidlaw (☎403/762-9102 or 1-800/661-4946) runs one bus daily ($8) and Brewster Transportation (☎403/762-6700) three buses a day from Banff ($11), and also continue to the *Chateau Lake Louise* (a good way to get up here if you're without transport – you can walk back down to the village). There are also direct Brewster and other connections to and from Lake Louise and Calgary airport; see p.689 for details. Brewster also runs one daily service to Jasper from Lake Louise village and lake ($44; departs Samson Mall at 4.15pm) as well as bus tours on the Icefields Parkway (8hr; $82 one-way, $112 return excluding accommodation in Jasper). If you need a taxi to ferry you to the lakes, call Lake Louise Taxi & Tours (☎403/522-2020). The only **car rental** agency is National at The Depot (☎403/522-3870), but you're better off renting in Banff or elsewhere as their cars go quickly.

The impressive **Lake Louise Information Centre**, a few steps from the car park, offers not only information but also high-tech natural-history exhibits (daily: mid-June to early Sept 8am–8pm; early Sept to late Sept & early to mid-June 8am–6pm; Oct–May 9am–4pm; ☎403/522-3833). Almost as useful is the excellent Woodruff and Blum bookshop (☎403/522-3842) in the mall, which has a full range of maps, guides and background reading. A couple of doors down, Wilson Mountain Sports (☎403/522-3636) is good for **bike rental** ($8–12/hr, $29–45/day), inline skate rental ($5–8/hr), fishing tackle for sale or rent (fly rod $11, spin rod $7 and waders $10) and **equipment rental** (stoves $7, pack $9 and tent $19). Staff will also fill you in on the possiblity of **canoe rentals** for trips downstream on the Bow River to Banff.

The Samson Mall takes care of most practical considerations including a **post office** (daily 6.30am–7pm). Behind The Depot, which doubles up as a bag storage and booking office for coach tours and river-rafting trips, are a laundrette and public washrooms with showers. The general store is good and can change money. There's also exchange at the *Chateau Lake Louise* hotel (see below). For the **police**, call ☎403/522-3811. The nearest hospital is in Banff.

Accommodation

Hotel **accommodation** in or near Lake Louise Village is pricey all year round and almost certain to be full in summer. Bookings are virtually essential everywhere (make them direct or through Banff's **reservation services**; see p.691). At the excellent hostel, reservations six months in advance are not unusual. The various options on the Bow Valley Parkway, covered on p.707, are all within easy driving or cycling distance.

Hotels

Château Lake Louise Lake Louise Drive ☎403/522-3511 or 1-800/441-1414, ⓦwww.fairmont.com. Imposing landmark hotel, a five-minute drive from the townsite, with commanding views over Lake Louise from its 511 grand rooms and suites. The hotel is worth a look alone for the bizarre appeal of its fusion of alpine and neocolonial of furnishings. Rooms and suites cost up to $579, but rates are savagely cut in the off-season (Oct–Dec), some rooms occasionally going for around $100, when good value ski packages are also offered. The hotel's battery of five-star facilities includes an exercise room, pool, and several bars and restaurants. ⓼

Deer Lodge Lake Louise Drive ☎403/522-3747 or 1-800/661-1595, ⓦwww.crmr.com. Labyrinthine lodgings in a 1920s log teahouse. Contrasting with the pomp of its neighbour, Château Lake Louise, a short walk away, it's far more laid back and few of the modest rooms here have phones or TV. The rooftop hot tub has fantastic views and there's a sauna too. ⓺

Lake Louise Inn 210 Village Rd ☎403/522-3791 or 1-800/661-9237, ⓦwww.lakelouiseinn.com. The least expensive of the village hotels, with a variety of rooms, some with self-catering facilities. ⓻

LAKE LOUISE VILLAGE
(NOT TO SCALE)

ACCOMMODATION	
Baker Creek Chalets	G
Castle Mountain Hostel	H
Chateau Lake Louise	E
Deer Lodge	D
International Youth Hostel	A
Lake Louise Inn	B
Moraine Lake Lodge	I
Paradise Lodge & Bungalows	F
Post Hotel	C

Moraine Lake Lodge Moraine Lake ☏ 403/522-3733, ⓦ www.morainelake.com. One of the most enticing and magnificently executed hotels in the entire Rockies: perfect if you're on honeymoon, or just want to splash out. Accommodation consists of a nicely landscaped collection of high-quality cabins and lodge rooms designed by eminent architect Arthur Erickson (also responsible for Vancouver's UBC Museum of Anthropology and the Canadian Embassy in Washington DC). Their open fires probably make the cabins best. The friendly staff and great privacy here gives it an edge over the more lacklustre hotels in the village and near Lake Louise. May–Oct. ❽

Paradise Lodge and Bungalows Lake Louise Drive ☏ 403/522-3595, ⓦ www.paradiselodge.com. A short walk from Lake Louise, this is the pricier of the near-lake options, but with reasonable off-season rates for its 21 self-contained bungalows and 24 one- and two-bedroom suites (some with kitchens). Mid-May to mid-Oct. ❻

Post Hotel Village Rd ☏ 403/522-3989 or 1-800/661-1586, ⓦ www.posthotel.com. Grand log chalet-hotel that is the top hotel in the village, with a noted restaurant and bar but expect to pay $300-plus for a room here in summer. ❽

Hostels

Castle Mountain Youth Hostel (HI) 1.5km east of Castle Junction on Hwy 93 S ☏ 403/762-4122, ⓦ www.hihostels.ca. Well situated for the Bow Valley Parkway and its trails. Sleeps just 36, with bookings possible through the Banff hostel. Dorm beds $13. ❷

Lake Louise International Hostel (HI) Village Rd ☏ 403/522-2200, ⓦ www.hihostels.ca. Standard-setting, mountain chalet-style 150-bed hostel just north of the village mall, offering dorm beds ($23) and private rooms. Clean, superior-quality facilities include communal kitchen, laundry, Internet access, a mountaineering library and a handy restaurant. Reservations are virtually essential (up to six months in advance) for summer and winter ski weekends. ❸

Campsites

Lake Louise Campground Lovely park-run site with 220 pitches close to the village – follow the signs off Fairview Rd up to the lake. Gets busy in summer. It's open between mid-May and early October, is partially serviced (it has showers) and

sites cost $17; no fires. Sites are close together, though the trees offer some privacy and, with the railway close by, it can be noisy.

Lake Louise Trailer Site Near to the above, but for RVs only. Year-round. $23.

Lake Louise Village

Lake Louise Village doesn't amount to much, but it's an essential supply stop, with more or less everything you need in terms of food, shelter (at a price), information and equipment rental. Most of it centres round the Samson Mall and car park, with a smart hostel and a few outlying motels dotted along the service road to the north.

A short way from the village, the **Lake Louise Gondola** (the "Friendly Giant"; daily: June & Sept 8.30am–6pm; July & Aug 8am–6pm; $13.95) takes thirteen minutes to get to 2042m, partway up Mount Whitehorn (2669m). To reach it, pick up the free shuttle which operates from some village hotels or return to and cross over the Trans-Canada, and follow the road towards the ski area; the gondola is signed left after about 1km. You can choose between enclosed gondola cars, open chairs, or chairs with bubble domes. At the top are the usual sensational views – rated some of the best in the Rockies – a self-service

Lake Louise activities

As for **activities**, most operators – especially rafting companies – are based in Banff or elsewhere (see p.696), though many offer pick-ups in Lake Louise, typically with a $10 add-on to their listed Banff prices; a handful operate trips directly out of Lake Louise itself. Companies actually based in or near the village include Wild Water Adventures (℡403/678-5058, 522-2211 or 1-888/771-9453) who run half- or full-day white-water rafting trips on the Kicking Horse River in nearby Yoho National Park (half-day trips at 8.30am and 1.30pm, from $69). If you don't want to hike alone, or wish to know more about what you're walking past, the national park and Friends of Banff run **guided walks** three or four times a week in July and August: the Lake Louise Lakeshore Stroll (Mon & Fri 10am; 2hr) and the Plain of the Six Glaciers (Tues, Thurs & Sun 9am; 6hr; $12). Drop by the visitor centre's Friends of Banff store to confirm latest timings and to reserve a place (do so in good time – the walks are popular) or call ℡403/522-3833. Cyclists can rent bikes from Wilson Mountain Sports in the mall (see p.711), or sign up for **cycling tours** (from $55 for half a day, $85 full day) and transfers that'll take you up to Bow Summit on the Icefields Parkway so you can pedal down hill or freewheel all the way back to Lake Louise. Serious canoeists can rent canoes from Wilson for trips on the Bow River, while more sedate paddlers can **rent canoes** and kayaks (daily in summer 10am–7pm; $30 per hour) at *Chateau Lake Louise* to dabble on Lake Louise itself (℡403/522-3511).

Good **trout fishing** is possible on the Bow River between Lake Louise and Banff, with support and advice available at the *Castle Mountain Chalets* on the Bow Valley Parkway (see p.707). Rental equipment is again on offer at Wilson Mountain Sports. Compulsory fishing permits ($6 weekly) are available from the visitor centre. If you fancy **horse riding**, contact Brewster Lake Louise Stables at the *Chateau Lake Louise* hotel (℡403/522-3511 ext 1210, or 762-5454) and enquire about their ninety-minute trips along the shores of Lake Louise ($45), half-day tours ($60) to the Lake Agnes or Plain of the Six Glaciers (see box p.716) or full-day treks to Paradise Valley and Horseshoe Glacier ($120 including lunch). Timberline Tours (℡403/522-3743) runs similar if slightly cheaper treks from the Lake Louise Corral behind the *Deer Lodge* hotel; all-day trips to the Skoki Valley east of Lake Louise; and one- and three-hour trips at Bow Lake on the Icefields Parkway from the *Num-Ti-Jah Lodge* (see p.721).

restaurant, sun decks, picnic areas, souvenir shops and several trailheads through the woods and meadows. One takes you to the summit of Mount Whitehorn.

Lake Louise

Before you see **Lake Louise** you see the hotel: *Chateau Lake Louise*, a grandiose monstrosity that would surely never get planning permission today. Yet even so intrusive an eyesore fades into insignificance beside the immense beauty of its surroundings. The lake is brilliant turquoise, the mountains sheer, the glaciers vast; the whole ensemble is perfection. Outfitter Tom Wilson, the first white Canadian to see Lake Louise when he was led here by a local native in 1882, wrote: "I never, in all my explorations of these five chains of mountains throughout western Canada, saw such a matchless scene… I felt puny in body, but glorified in spirit and soul."

You can't help wishing you could have been Tom Wilson, and seen the spot unsullied by the hotel and before the arrival of the tourists and general clutter. Around 10,000 people daily in peak season come here to gawp (car parks often fill by noon), while noticeboards on the waterfront seem obsessed with the profoundly dull account of how the lake came by its name – it was named in honour of the fourth daughter of Queen Victoria. The native name translates as the "Lake of the Little Fishes". Wilson, showing precious little wit, originally called it Emerald Lake. More interesting is the account of Hollywood's discovery of the lake in the 1920s, when it was used to suggest exotic European locations. After Wilson's "discovery" all access was by rail or trail – the station, then known as Laggan, was 6km away. The first hotel appeared in 1890, a simple two-bedroom affair which replaced a tumbledown cabin on the shore. Numerous fires, false starts and additions followed until the present structure made its unwelcome appearance; the final wings were added as recently as 1988. The first road was built in 1926. Be sure to walk here, despite the paths' popularity (see box p.716). Alternatively, escape the throng by renting an old-style canoe from the office to the left as you face the lake (June–Sept daily 10am–8pm; $30/hr; maximum of three adults per boat). Don't think about swimming: the water's deep and cold – highest temperature in summer is a numbing 4°C.

Moraine Lake

Not quite so many people as visit Lake Louise make the road journey 13km to **Moraine Lake**, which is smaller than its neighbour although in many ways its scenic superior. If you're without your own transport, you'll have to rely on a bike or taxi ($35) to get here or the park-run "Vista" bus shuttle (daily every 30min from outside the hostel and Lake Louise campsite; free on production of park pass). The last has been introduced because of the sheer number of visitors in cars and RVs trying to cram into the tiny car park and clogging the approach road. No wonder they come, for this is one of the great landscapes of the region, has some cracking trails (see box) and the splendid yet discreet *Moraine Lake Lodge*, which is one of the best places to stay in the region (see p.712). Bar the *Lodge*, with its good little café and top-notch restaurant, nothing disturbs the lake and its matchless surroundings. Until comparatively recently the scene graced the back of Canadian $20 bills, though the illustration did little justice to the shimmering water and the jagged, snow-covered peaks on the eastern shore that inspired the nickname "Valley of the Ten Peaks". The peaks are now officially christened the Wenkchemna, after the Stoney native word for "ten".

The lake itself, half the size of Lake Louise, is the most vivid turquoise imaginable. Like Lake Louise and other big Rockies lakes (notably Peyto on the Icefields Parkway), the peacock blue is caused by fine particles of glacial silt, or till, known as rock flour. Meltwater in June and July washes this powdered rock into the lake, the minute but uniform particles of flour absorbing all colours of incoming light except those in the blue–green spectrum. When the lakes have just melted in May and June – and are still empty of silt – their colour is a more normal sky-blue. You can admire the lake by walking along the east shore, from above by clambering over the great glacial moraine dam near the lodge (though the lake was probably created by a rock fall rather than glaciation), or from one of the **canoes for rent** on the right just beyond the *Lodge* and car park. For the best overall perspective, tackle the switchback trail through the forest on the east shore (see box p.716), but check with the visitor centre at Lake Louise for the latest on bear activity – a young grizzly has made the Moraine Lake region its home, and areas are sometimes closed to avoid its coming into contact with humans.

Eating and drinking

Excellent basic **food** – snacks and coffee – can be had in Lake Louise Village at the always busy *Laggan's Mountain Bakery* (daily 6am–7pm) on the corner of the mall opposite the general store. For something more substantial than snacks, wander to the relaxed and reasonably priced *Bill Peyto's Café* for full and

All the Lake Louise **hiking trails** are busy in summer, but they're good for a short taste of the scenery. They're also well worn and well marked, so you don't need to be a seasoned hiker or skilled map-reader. The two most popular finish up at teahouses – mountain chalets selling welcome, but rather pricey, snacks.

The signed **Lake Agnes Trail** (3.4km), said to be the most-walked path in the Rockies (but don't let that put you off), strikes off from the right (north) shore of the lake immediately past the hotel. It's a gradual, 400m climb, relieved by ever more magnificent views and a teahouse beautifully situated beside mountain-cradled Lake Agnes (2135m); allow one to two hours. Beyond the teahouse, if you want more of a walk things quieten down considerably. You can continue on the right side of the lake and curve left around its head to climb to an easily reached pass. Here a 200-metre stroll to the left brings you to **Big Beehive** (2255m), an incredible eyrie, 1km from the teahouse. Almost as rewarding is the trail, also 1km from the teahouse, to **Little Beehive**, a mite lower, but still privy to full-blown panoramas over the broad sweep of the Bow Valley.

Keener walkers can return to the pass from Big Beehive and turn left to follow the steep trail down to intersect another trail; turning right leads west through rugged and increasingly barren scenery to the second teahouse at the **Plain of the Six Glaciers** (2100m). Alternatively, the more monotonous Six Glaciers Trail (leaving out the whole Lake Agnes–Big Beehive section) leads from the hotel along the lakeshore to the same point (5.3km to the teahouse; 365m ascent). However, a better option is to follow the Lake Agnes and Big Beehive route to the Plain, then use the Six Glaciers Trail for the return to *Chateau Lake Louise*, which neatly ends the day's loop with a downhill stroll and an easy but glorious finale along the shore of Lake Louise (see our map to make sense of what is a pretty straightforward and very well-worn loop).

The main appeal of the less-used **Saddleback Trail** (3.7km one-way) is that it provides access to the superlative viewpoint of Fairview Mountain. Allow from one to two hours to Saddleback itself (2330m; 595m ascent); the trail to the summit of Fairview (2745m) strikes off right from here. Even if you don't make the last push, the Saddleback views – across to the 1200m wall of Mount Temple (3544m) – are staggering. Despite the people, this is one of the park's top short walks.

Skoki Valley

The **Skoki Valley** region east of Lake Louise offers fewer day-hikes; to enjoy it you'll need a tent to overnight at any of the six campsites. The main access trail initially follows a gravel road forking off to the right of the Lake Louise Ski Area, off Hwy 1. Many people hike as far as Boulder Pass (2345m), an 8.6-kilometre trek and 640-metre ascent from the parking area, as a day-trip, and return the same way instead of pushing on to the *Lodge*, 8km beyond. Various well-signposted long and short trails from the *Lodge* or the campsites are documented in the *Canadian Rockies Trail Guide*.

Moraine Lake

Each of the four basic routes in the **Moraine Lake** area is easily accomplished in a day or less, two with sting-in-the-tail additions if you want added exertion; all start from the lake, which lies 13km from Lake Louise Village at the end of Moraine Lake Rd. Before hiking, check with the visitor centre in Lake Louise on the latest restrictions imposed to protect both the bears known to have made the area part of their territory as well as the tourists who hope to catch a glimpse of them. At the time of writing, walks in the Larch Valley and around were restricted. You must walk in groups of at least six people (there are often people waiting to join a group, so you should have no trouble making up the numbers).

The easiest walk is the one-kilometre amble along the lakeshore – hardly a walk at all – followed by the three-kilometre stroll to **Consolation Lake**, an hour's trip that may be busy but can provide some respite from the frenzy at Moraine Lake itself. This almost level walk ends with lovely views of a small mountain-circled lake, its name coined by an early explorer who thought it a reward and "consolation" for the desolation of the valley which led up to it. If you're tenting, fairly fit, or can arrange a pick-up, the highline **Panorama Ridge Trail** (2255m) branches off the trail (signed "Taylor Lake") to run 22km to the Banff–Radium highway 7km west of Castle Junction.

The most popular walk (start as early as possible) is the Moraine Lake–**Larch Valley–Sentinel Pass Trail**, one of the Rockies' premier hikes, which sets off from the lake's north shore 100m beyond the lodge. A stiffish hairpin climb through forest on a broad track, with breathtaking views of the lake through the trees, brings you to a trail junction after 2.4km and some 300m of ascent. Most hikers branch right, where the track levels off to emerge into Larch Valley, broad alpine upland with stands of larch (glorious in late summer and autumn) and majestic views of the encircling peaks. If you have the energy, push on to Sentinel Pass ahead, in all some two hours' walk and 720m above Moraine Lake. At 2605m, this, along with the Wenkchemna Pass, is the highest point reached by a major trail in the Canadian Rockies. You can see what you're in for from the meadows – but not the airy views over Paradise Valley from the crest of the pass itself. You could even continue down into Paradise Valley, a tough, scree-filled descent, and complete an exceptional day's walk by picking up the valley loop (see below) back to the Moraine Lake Rd. Otherwise return to the 2.4-kilometre junction and, if legs are still willing – you'll have done most of the hard climbing work already – think about tagging on the last part of the third Moraine Lake option.

This third option, the less-walked Moraine Lake–**Eiffel Lake–Wenkchemna Pass Trail**, follows the climb from the lake as for the Larch Valley path before branching off left instead of right at the 2.4-kilometre junction. It's equally sound, virtually level and if anything has the better scenery (if only because less barren than Sentinel Pass) in the stark, glaciated grandeur to be found at the head of the Valley of the Ten Peaks. It's also much quieter once you're beyond the trail junction. At 2255m, Eiffel Lake is a 5.6-kilometre hike and 370-metre climb in total (allow 2–3hr) from Moraine Lake, and you don't need to go much further than the rock pile and clump of trees beyond the lake to get the best out of the walk. Ahead of you, however, a slightly rougher track continues through bleak terrain to Wenkchemna Pass (2605m), clearly visible 4km beyond. Having got this far, it's tempting to push on; the extra 350-metre climb is just about worth it, if lungs and weather are holding out, for the still broader views back down the Valley of the Ten Peaks. The views beyond the pass itself, however, over the Great Divide into Yoho and Kootenay parks, are relatively disappointing.

Paradise Valley

In 1894, the mountaineer Walter Wilcox deemed **Paradise Valley** an appropriate name for "a valley of surpassing beauty, wide and beautiful, with alternating open meadows and rich forests". North of Moraine Lake, it's accessed via Moraine Lake Rd about 3km from its junction with Lake Louise Drive. The walk here is a fairly straightforward hike up one side of the valley and down the other, a loop of 18km with a modest 385m of vertical gain. Most people take in the Lake Annette diversion for its unmatched view of Mount Temple's 1200-metre north face (unclimbed until 1966), and many overnight at the campsite at the head of the valley (9km from the parking area), though this is one of the busiest sites in the park. Others toughen the walk by throwing in the climb up to Sentinel Pass on the ridge south of the valley, which gives the option of continuing down the other side to connect with the Moraine Lake trails.

Winter sports in and around Lake Louise

In a region already renowned for its **skiing** Lake Louise stands out, regarded by many as among the finest winter resorts in North America. In addition to skiing and snowboarding there are hundreds of kilometres of cross-country trails, numerous other winter activities, and landscape that's earned the area the title of "North America's Most Scenic Ski Area" from *Snow Country* magazine. It's also Canada's largest ski area, with over forty square kilometres of trails, plenty of mogul fields, lots of challenging chutes, vast open bowls and some of the best "powder" on the continent. Skiing started here in the 1920s. The first chalet was built in 1930, the first lift in 1954. The resort's real birth can be dated to 1958, when a rich Englishman, Norman Watson – universally known as the "Barmy Baronet" – ploughed a large part of his inheritance into building a gondola on Mount Whitehorn. Further lifts and other developments followed. More would have materialized had it not been for environmental lobbying. Further protests forestalled a bid for the 1968 Winter Olympics and put an end to a plan for a 6500-bed megaresort in 1972. Even so, the resort has grown, and now regularly hosts World Cup skiing events. The only drawback is the phenomenally low temperatures during January and February.

Ski areas

Naturally dividing into three distinct zones, the core of the Lake Louise ski area is the **Front Side** (sometimes called the South Face). Climbing from the base area, this is particularly attractive to beginners and intermediates, who will find all the best groomed green and blue runs here. Tucked behind the Front Side, the **Back Bowls** are a very different proposition; flecked with above-tree-line black diamonds that offer wide-open runs particularly rewarding for those prepared to hike. From the Back Bowls a long, fairly flat, run-out leads to the base of the **Ptarmigan** and **Larch** area, and some of the mountain's best glade runs. Slopes here face in several directions allowing you to follow the sun, and trees can give shelter from winds, a combination that makes this the best area to zero in on when conditions are harsh. The 4200 acre terrain divides as follows: Novice (25 percent), Intermediate (45 percent) and Expert (30 percent) and sees an average annual snowfall (early Nov to mid-May) of 360cm. The top elevation is 2637m, giving a 1000m drop to the base elevation at 1645m. Lift tickets are around $61 a day, but bear in mind that you can

varied meals (daily 7am–9pm; ☏403/522-2200), within the hostel but open to all; in summer the nice outdoor eating area is a good place to meet people. The unique *Lake Louise Station Restaurant* (☏403/522-2600) is housed in the restored 1909 station building; choose between hearty Canadian fare in the informal station building (garden dining in summer) and the more formal and expensive restored railway-dining carriages. Some of the best (and pricier) meals can be found in the *Post Hotel* (daily 7am–2pm & 5–9.30pm; ☏403/522-3989) – reservations are essential in the evening. The best local's hangout is the hotel's *Outpost Pub* (☏403/522-3989), a snug **bar** that serves light meals from late afternoon. Other good drinking spots include the *Lake Louise Bar and Grill* (☏403/522-3879) upstairs in the mall, and the lively *Explorers Lounge* (☏403/522-3791) in the *Lake Louise Inn*, 210 Village Rd.

The Icefields Parkway

The splendour of the **Icefields Parkway** (Hwy 93) can hardly be overstated: a road 230km from Lake Louise to Jasper through the heart of the Rockies, it invest in the Ski Banff/Lake Louise **Tri-Area Pass**, which you can buy for a minimum of three days ($175) skiing in Lake Louise, Mount Norquay and Sunshine Village (see p.704). **Facilities** in the ski area include three day-lodges, each of which has a restaurant and bar, a ski school, ski shop, rental shop, day-care, nursery and lockers. Free shuttles run from Lake Louise, while transfers from Banff cost around $15 return: however, these transfers are included free if you buy the Tri-Area Pass. Free tours of the mountain are also available three times daily. For further **information** and **reservations**, contact Skiing Louise (℡403/522-3555 or 1-800/258-7669, Ⓦwww.skilouise.com).

Cross-country skiing in Lake Louise is also phenomenal, with plenty of options around the lake itself, on Moraine Lake Rd and in the Skoki Valley area north of the village. For **heli-skiing**, contact RK Heli-Ski (℡403/342-3889) who have a desk in the *Chateau Lake Louise* hotel (winter daily 4–9pm); one of their shuttle buses leaves from the hotel daily for the two-hour drive to the Purcell Mountains in BC (the nearest heli-skiing).

Other activities

The Chateau is also the hub for other winter activities, particularly **ice-skating** and **sleigh rides**, while several tour operations also offer pickups here for **dog sled** or **snowmobiling** tours. Brewster Lake Louise Sleighrides (℡403/762-5454 or ℡403/522-3511 ext 1210 in *Chateau Lake Louise*; Ⓦwww.brewsteradventures.com) offer sleigh rides from outside the Chateau, hourly departures from 1pm to 4pm and night rides Monday to Saturday, and morning rides at 10am and 11am on weekend days. The hour-long ride costs $22 per person and reservations are necessary. The hotel is also the place to hire skates (at Monod Sports in the chateau ℡403/522-3837; $10 per day) for **ice-skating** on the floodlit lake, probably one of the most inspirational spots imaginable for the activity.

For more exciting adventures you need to look further afield. Kingmik Expeditions (℡250/344-5298 or 1-877/919-7779) runs **dog sled tours** – from 35 minute romps ($90) to multi-day adventures (around $250/day) – while Wet 'n' Wild adventures in Golden (℡250/344-6546 or 1-800/668-9119) offers an all-inclusive full day of **snowmobiling** for $180 per person.

ranks as one of the world's best drives. Its unending succession of huge peaks, immense glaciers, iridescent lakes, wild-flower meadows, wildlife and forests – capped by the stark grandeur of the Columbia Icefield – is absolutely overwhelming. Fur traders and natives who used the route as far back as 1800 reputedly christened it the "Wonder Trail", though in practice they tended to prefer the Pipestone River Valley to the east, a route that avoided the swamps and other hazards of the Bow Valley. Jim Brewster made the first recorded complete trek along the road's future route in 1904. The present highway was only completed in 1939 and opened in 1940 as part of a Depression-era public-works programme. Although about a million people a year make the journey to experience what the park blurb calls a "window on the wilderness", for the most part you can go your own way in relative serenity.

After 122km, at about its midway point, the Icefields Parkway crosses from Banff into Jasper National Park (about a 2hr drive); you might turn back here, but the divide is almost completely arbitrary, and most people treat the Parkway as a self-contained journey, as we do here. Distances in brackets are from Lake Louise, which is virtually the only way to locate places on the road, though everything mentioned is clearly marked off the highway by distinctive brown-green national park signs. Pick up the Parks Canada *In the Shadow of the*

Great Divide pamphlet from visitor centres for a detailed map and summary of all the sights and trailheads.

You could drive the whole highway in about four hours, but to do so would be to miss out on the panoply of short (and long) trails, viewpoints and the chance just to soak up the incredible scenery.

Access, transport and accommodation

Tourist literature often misleadingly gives the impression that the Icefields Parkway is highly developed. In fact, the wilderness is extreme, with snow often closing the road from October onwards, and there are only two points for **services**, at Saskatchewan Crossing (the one place campers can stock up with groceries, 77km from Lake Louise), where the David Thompson Highway (Hwy 11) branches off for Red Deer, and at the Columbia Icefield (127km).

Brewster Transportation (T403/762-6767) runs several tours and a single scheduled bus daily in both directions between Banff or Lake Louise and Jasper from late May to mid-October ($51 one-way from Banff, $44 from Lake Louise), though services at either end of the season are often weather-affected. A word with the driver will usually get you dropped off at hostels and trailheads en route. If you're **cycling** – an increasingly popular way to tackle the journey – note that the grades are far more favourable if you travel from Jasper to Banff (Jasper's 500m higher than Banff).

Five **hostels** (four open year-round) and twelve excellent park **campsites** (two year-round) are spaced along the Parkway at regular intervals; we've given details of each in the account below. It's essential to book the hostels, either direct if they have contact details, through the hostel at Banff or online at Ⓦwww.hihostels.ca. As ever, the frontcountry park campsites are available on a first-come, first-served basis. If you want more comfort, you'll have to overnight at Banff, Lake Louise or Jasper, as the only other accommodation – invariably booked solid – is hotels at Bow Lake, Saskatchewan Crossing, the Columbia Icefield and Sunwapta Falls. The **Summer Hostel Shuttle** (early June to Sept) runs an extremely useful shuttle service, connecting twelve hostels between (and including) Calgary, Banff and Jasper, as well as all the places on the Icefields Parkway and beyond. Shuttles currently depart daily Calgary–Lake Louise–Calgary (leaves Calgary 8.30am, leaves Lake Louise 1pm for Banff, Calgary and Calgary Airport); Sat only Jasper–Lake Louise–Jasper (leaves Jasper 8.30am, leaves Lake Louise 1.30pm); Mon, Wed and Fri at 1pm Lake Louise–Jasper; and Sun, Tues and Thurs at 8.30am Jasper–Lake Louise. Typical fares are $90 for Calgary to Maligne Canyon (Jasper), the longest possible journey, and $25 for the trip between Lake Louise and *Hilda Creek* hostel near the Columbia Icefield. Banff to Lake Louise is $12, Banff to *Jasper International Hostel* $57, and Lake Louise to Jasper $45. Extra fees are payable for bikes (Calgary to Banff costs $10), canoes and other cargo. For hostels book no later than 6pm the day before your desired departure with full details of your journey. Once the hostel has confirmed your booking, buy a ticket from any participating Alberta hostel, confirming the shuttle's departure time at the time of purchase. Stand-by tickets may be bought from the van driver at departure, subject to availability. All passengers must have reservations at their destination hostel.

North from Lake Louise

One of the biggest problems in the Rockies is knowing what to see and where to walk among the dozens of possible trails and viewpoints. The Parkway is no exception. We've picked out the must-sees and must-dos along the 122-kilometre stretch of the Parkway from Lake Louise to the Columbia Icefield: the best view is at Peyto Lake; the best lake walk is at Bow Lake; the best waterfalls are the Panther–Bridal Falls; the best quick stroll is at Mistaya Canyon; the best short walk is at Parker Ridge; and the best walk if you do no other is Wilcox Pass.

The first **hostel** north of Lake Louise is *Mosquito Creek* (28km; no phone, reservations ☎403/762-4122; $13; year-round, but closure dates may apply; check-in 5–11pm), four log cabins which sleep 38 and have basic food supplies, a kitchen, large common room and a wood-fired sauna. Slightly beyond is the first park **campsite**, *Mosquito Creek* ($10; mid-June to mid-Sept; 32 sites; water and dry toilets, but no other facilities) and one of the Parkway's two winter campsites (free after mid-Sept; 32 walk-in sites only). You're near the Bow River flats here, and the mosquitoes, as the campsite name suggests, can be a torment. Two hikes start from close to the site: **Molar Pass** (9.8km; 535m ascent; 3hr), a manageable day-trip with good views, and **Upper Fish Lake** (14.8km; 760m ascent; 5hr), which follows the Molar Pass trail for 7km before branching off and crossing the superb alpine meadows of North Molar Pass (2590m).

On the *Num-Ti-Jah Lodge* access road just beyond (37km), a great short trail sets off from beside the lodge to **Bow Lake** and **Bow Glacier Falls** (4.3km; 155m ascent; 1–2hr), taking in the flats around Bow Lake – one of the Rockies' most beautiful – and climbing to some immense cliffs and several huge waterfalls beyond (the trail proper ends at the edge of the moraine after 3.4km, but it's possible to pick your way through the boulders to reach the foot of the falls 900m beyond). If you don't want to walk, take a break instead at the picnic area on the waterfront at the southeast end of the lake. The *Num-Ti-Jah Lodge* itself, just off the road, is one of the most famous old-fashioned lodges in the Rockies, built in 1920 by legendary guide and outfitter Jimmy Simpson (who lived here until 1972). It's the only privately owned freehold in the park – all other land and property is federally owned and leased; be sure to book well in advance to have any chance of securing a room (☎403/522-2167; ❻; May–Sept). There's a **coffee shop** here if you need a break, or want to admire the *Lodge's* strange octagonal structure, forced on Jimmy because he wanted a large building but only had access locally to short timbers. You aren't allowed in the lodge (so guests can enjoy their privacy), but you can take dinner here, or sign up for **horse riding** with Timberline Tours (☎403/522-3743), available to residents and nonresidents alike; rides include a one-hour trip to Bow Lake, a three-hour ride to Peyto Lake (see below) and a full-day excursion to Helen Lake.

Peyto Lake and beyond

Another 3km up the Parkway comes the pass at Bow Summit, source of the Bow River, the waterway that flows through Banff, Lake Louise and Calgary. (At 2069m this is the highest point crossed by any Canadian highway.) Just beyond is the unmissable twenty-minute stroll to **Peyto Lake Lookout** (1.4km; elevation loss 100m), one of the finest vistas in the Rockies (signed from the road). The beautiful panorama only unfolds in the last few seconds, giving a breathtaking view of the vivid emerald lake far below; mountains and forest stretch away as far as you can see. Another 3km along the Parkway lies a viewpoint for the Peyto Glacier, part of the much larger Wapta Icefield.

After 57km you reach the *Waterfowl Lakes* **campsite** (116 sites; $13; mid-June to mid-Sept) and the **Chephren Lake Trail** (3.5km; 80m ascent; 1hr), which leads to quietly spectacular scenery with a minimum of effort. The next pause, 14km further on, is the **Mistaya Canyon Trail**, a short but interesting 300m breather of a stroll along a river-gouged "slot" canyon. *Mistaya* is a Cree word meaning "grizzly bear".

Saskatchewan Crossing and beyond

SASKATCHEWAN CROSSING (77km) is the lowest point on the road before the icefields; the 700m descent from Bow Summit brings you from the high subalpine ecoregion into a montane environment with its own vegetation and wildlife. Largely free of snow, the area is a favourite winter range for mountain goats, bighorn sheep and members of the deer family. The bleak settlement itself offers expensive food (restaurant and cafeteria), petrol, a spectacularly tacky gift shop and a 66-room **hotel-restaurant**, *Crossing*, that is surprisingly comfortable (☎403/761-7000; ❺; early March to mid-Nov).

Some 12km north is the *Rampart Creek* **hostel** (☎403/439-3139; $13; June–Oct open daily all day, check-in 5–11pm; Nov–May Sat & Sun only with reservation), with thirty beds, two cabins, the "best sauna in the Rockies", a basic food store and a fifty-pitch park-run **campsite** ($10; late June to early Sept). Apparently this area is one of the best black bear habitats close to the road anywhere in the park. The last of the Banff National Park campsites is the tiny sixteen-pitch *Cirrus Mountain* site at the 103km mark ($10; late June to early Sept), but its position is precarious, so check it's open before planning a stay (☎403/762-1550).

Shortly before the spectacular **Panther Falls** (113.5km) the road makes a huge hairpin climb (the so-called "Big Hill"), to open up yet more panoramic angles on the vast mountain spine stretching back towards Lake Louise. The unmarked and often slippery one-kilometre trail to the falls starts from the lower end of the second of two car parks on the right. Beyond it (117km) is the trailhead to **Parker Ridge** (2.4km one-way; elevation gain 210m; allow 1hr one-way, less for the return), which, at 2130m, commands fantastic views from the summit ridge of the Saskatchewan Glacier (at 9km, the Rockies' longest). If you're only going to do one walk after the Peyto Lake Lookout, make it this one: it gets cold and windy up here, so bring extra clothing. Ideally placed for this area and the Columbia Icefield 9km north is the busy *Hilda Creek* **hostel** (☎403/439-3139 or 762-4122; $12; check-in 5–11pm) 1km beyond. The setting is stunning, and accommodation (for 21) is in cosy log cabins.

Nearby **Sunwapta Pass** (2023m) marks the border between Banff and Jasper national parks and the watershed of the North Saskatchewan and Sunwapta rivers: the former flows into the Atlantic, the latter into the Arctic Ocean. From here it's another 108km to Jasper.

The Columbia Icefield

Just beyond, covering an area of 325 square kilometres, the **Columbia Icefield** is the largest collection of ice and snow in the entire Rockies, and the largest glacial area in the northern hemisphere outside the Arctic Circle. It's also the most accessible of some seventeen glacial areas along the Parkway. Meltwater flows from it into the Arctic, Atlantic and Pacific oceans, forming a so-called "hydrological apex" – the only other one in the world is in Siberia. This is fed by six major glaciers, three of which – the Athabasca, Dome and Stutfield – are partially visible from the highway. The ugly and extremely busy **Icefield Centre** (daily: May to early June & Sept to mid-Oct 9am–5pm; early

June to Aug 9am–6pm) provides an eerie viewpoint for the most prominent of these, the Athabasca Glacier, as well as offering the Parks Canada Exhibit Hall and information and slide shows on the glaciers and Canada's most extensive cave system – the Castleguard Caves, which honeycomb the ice but are inaccessible to the public. This is not a place to linger, however, thanks to the legions of people and dozens of tour buses.

You can walk up to the toe of the **Athabasca Glacier** from the parking area at Sunwapta Lake, noting en route the date-markers, which illustrate just how far the glacier has retreated (1.5km in the last 100 years). You can also walk onto the glacier, but shouldn't, as it's riddled with dangerous crevasses. People are killed and injured every year on the glacier: even a slip can rip off great slivers of skin. Full-scale expeditions are the preserve of experts but you can join an **organized trip**. Brewster's special "Snocoaches" run ninety-minute, five-kilometre rides over the glacier with a chance to get out and walk safely on the ice (daily every 15min: early May to Sept 9am–5pm; Oct 10am–4pm depending on weather; $25.95; book tickets at the Centre or call ☎1-877/ICE RIDE). They're heavily subscribed, so aim to avoid the peak midday rush by taking a tour before 10.30am or after 3pm. More dedicated types can sign up for the Athabasca Glacier ice walks (3hr walks mid-June to early Sept daily at 11.30pm, $31; 5hr walks Thurs & Sun 11.30am, $37), led by licensed guides. Sign up on the spot at the front desk of the Icefields Centre – be sure to bring warm clothes, boots and provisions.

The 32-room *Columbia Icefields Chalet* (☎780/852-6550; ❺–❼) provides excellent but much-sought-after **accommodation** in the Icefields Centre between May and mid-October (note that lower rates apply in May and October). Brewster bus services between Jasper and Banff stop here: it's possible to take a Banff-bound Brewster bus out of Jasper at lunchtime (arrives at the Icefields at 3pm), see the Icefield, and pick up the evening Jasper-bound bus (leaves Icefield at 6.30pm) later the same day.

Two unserviced but very popular **campsites** lie 2km and 3km south of the Icefield Centre respectively: the tent-only 33-site *Columbia Icefield* ($10; mid-May to mid-Oct, or until the first snow) and the 46-site *Wilcox Creek*, which takes tents and RVs ($10; early June to mid-Sept). This latter is also the trailhead for one of the very finest **hikes** in the national park, never mind the highway: the **Wilcox Pass Trail** (4km one-way; 335m ascent; allow 2hr round trip), highly recommended by the park centres and just about every trail guide going. The path takes you steeply through thick spruce and alpine fir forest before emerging suddenly onto a ridge that offers vast views over the Parkway and the high peaks of the icefield (including Mount Athabasca). Beyond, the trail enters a beautiful spread of meadows, tarns and creeks, an area many people choose to halt at or wander all day without bothering to reach the pass itself. You could extend the walk to 11km by dropping from the pass to Tangle Creek further along the parkway.

Beyond the Columbia Icefield

If there's a change **beyond the Columbia Icefield**, it's a barely quantifiable lapse in the scenery's awe-inspiring intensity over the 108-kilometre stretch towards Jasper. As the road begins a gradual descent the peaks retreat slightly, taking on more alpine and less dramatic profiles in the process. Yet the scenery is still magnificent, though by this point you're likely to be in the advanced stages of landscape fatigue. It's worth holding on, though, for two good, short trails at Sunwapta and Athabasca falls. About 17km beyond the icefield is the

If lazing around Maligne Lake in Jasper, or walking the odd trail elsewhere in the Rockies, sounds a bit tame, think about **white-water rafting** – currently all the rage in the national parks, and Jasper in particular. Many operators, notably in Jasper, Golden (near Yoho National Park) and in Banff, cater to an ever-growing demand. Not all trips are white-knuckle affairs. Depending on the river and trip you choose, some rafting tours are just that – gentle rafting down placid stretches of river. Others require that you be fit and a strong swimmer. Trips last anything from a couple of hours to a couple of days.

While no previous experience is required for most tours, one or two things are worth knowing; the most important is how rivers are **graded**. White water is ranked in six classes: Class 1 is gentle and Class 6 is basically a waterfall. The **season** generally runs from May to mid-September, with the "biggest" water in June and July, when glacial meltwater is coursing down rivers. Operators are licensed by the park authorities and invariably supply you with everything you need, from the basics of helmet and life jacket to wet suits, wool sweaters and spray jackets depending on the likely severity of the trip. They also provide shuttle services from main centres to the rivers themselves, and many on longer trips include lunch, snack or barbecue in the tour price. Bigger operators may also have on-site shower and changing facilities if you're on a run where you're likely to get seriously wet. On any trip it's probably a good idea to have a change of clothes handy for when you finish, wear training shoes or something you don't mind getting wet, and have a towel and bag for any valuables. Many people sport swimming costumes beneath clothing. Often you can choose between trips – gentle or severe – where you sit back and hang on while others do the work in oared boats, or you join a trip where everyone gets a paddle who wants one.

At Banff the **Bow River** has no major rapids, so gentle one-hour float trips are offered through pretty scenery by several operators. Most companies in Banff or Lake Louise offer trips on one of two rivers to the west of the park. The **Kootenay River** in Kootenay National Park, two hours from Banff, is a Class 2–3 river. The **Kicking Horse River**, a premier destination just an hour from Banff, is a much more serious affair. In and just outside Yoho National Park, it has Class 4 sections (Cable Car, Man Eater Hole, Goat Rapid, Twin Towers and the Roller Coaster) in its upper sections and stretches in the Lower Kicking Horse Canyon which give even seasoned rafters pause for thought.

Jasper has perhaps the most possibilities on its doorstep. The Class 2 **Athabasca River** (from Athabasca Falls, 35km south of the town) is scenic and provides gentle rafting for families or those who just want a quiet river trip from May to October, but it also has one or two harmless white-water sections. The **Sunwapta River** nearby, 55km south of Jasper, is a Class 3 river with some

24-berth, two-cabin *Beauty Creek* **hostel** (reservations ☎780/852-3215; $10; May–Sept; hostel open all day, check-in 5–11pm; partial closure possible Oct–April). Some 9km further is the unserviced 25-site *Jonas Creek* **campsite** ($10; mid-May to first snowfall).

A one-kilometre gravel spur leads off the highway to **Sunwapta Falls** (175km from Banff, 55km from Jasper), fifteen minutes' walk through the woods from the road: they're not terribly dramatic unless in spate, but are interesting for the deep canyon they've cut through the surrounding valley. A short trail along the river bank leads to more rapids and small falls downstream. The 35-pitch *Honeymoon Lake* **campsite** with kitchen shelter, swimming and dry toilets is 4km further along the Parkway ($10; mid-June to first snowfall).

thrilling stretches of water, magnificent scenery and good chances to spot wildlife. The **Maligne River**, 45km from town, is Class 2–3+, offering a wide variety of trips between July and September for the many operators who use this river (including a lively 1.6-kilometre stretch of rapids). Yet the most riotous local river is the **Fraser**, accessed an hour west of Jasper in Mount Robson Provincial Park. This is Class 4 in places, but also has some gentle sections where the chance to watch salmon spawning at close quarters from mid-August to September provides an added attraction.

Operators in Jasper include Maligne River Adventures, 627 Patricia St (℗780/852-3370), who run some of the wildest trips in the park: the four-hour "Sunwapta Challenge" uses six-passenger paddle-assisted rafts to ride parts of the Sunwapta – which means "turbulent river" in the local Stoney language. All equipment is supplied as are changing rooms and hot showers. They also offer two-hour "Mile 5 Run" (3 daily; $40) raft trips on the Athabasca River on small but lively rapids and three-hour "Heritage Run" trips (small paddle raft $55, larger passenger oar raft $40) on the same river suitable for families and children, as well as a three-day wilderness trip to the Kakwa and Smoky rivers. Jasper Raft Tours at Jasper Adventure Centre, 604 Connaught Drive (℗780/852-2665 or 1-888/553-5628) offer good trips for first-timers: two- to three-hour jaunts twice daily in summer on the Athabasca River in comfortable oar rafts. Tickets include shuttle to and from the river, with possible pick-ups from your hotel by prior arrangement; tickets are also available from the Brewster office in the train station. Another long-established company offers similar trips at similar prices to suit all ages and courage levels on several rivers: White Water Rafting (Jasper) Ltd (℗780/852-7238 or 1-800/557-7238, ℗www.whitewaterjasper.com), with advance reservations from Freewheel Cycles, 618 Patricia St, and Alpine Petro Canada, 711 Connaught Drive – they claim to run trips in all weathers and make special provisions for visitors with disabilities.

If you want the real **rough stuff** on the Fraser contact Sekani Mountain Tours, Work World Store, 618 Patricia St (℗780/852-5211), for twenty Class 3 and 4 rapids along the fourteen-kilometre "Rearguard Run" (6hr 30min). If you're experienced you can join the 16km of continuous Class 4 and 4+ rapids on the "Canoe River" (8hr) or put these together with the Rearguard in a two-day camping trip. At the other extreme, the same company runs quiet punt-like trips to admire Mount Robson and see the salmon on the Fraser (10km; 5hr 30min), as do Mount Robson Adventure Holidays (2hr; ℗1-800/882-9921), whose twice-daily raft departures are complemented by an evening run during August. They also offer three-hour guided trips by canoe to Moose Marsh to spot birds and wildlife, with no experience necessary for this or their rafting trips.

The last main stop before you're in striking distance of Jasper Townsite, **Athabasca Falls** (30km from Jasper) are impressive enough, but the platforms and paths show the strain caused by thousands of tramping feet, making it hard to feel you're any longer in wilderness. One kilometre away, however, is the excellent *Athabasca Falls* **hostel** (℗780/852-5959; $11; hostel open all day, but check-in 5–11pm), with forty beds in three cabins. About 3km back down the road is the 42-site *Mount Kerkeslin* **campsite**, with swimming, kitchen shelter and dry toilets, spread over a tranquil riverside site ($10; mid-June to early Sept).

Highway 93A, the route of the old Parkway, branches off the Icefields Parkway at Athabasca Falls and runs parallel to it for 30km. This alternative route has less dramatic views than the Parkway, as dense trees line the road, but the chances of spotting wildlife are higher.

Jasper National Park

Although traditionally viewed as the second-ranking of the Rockies' big-four parks after Banff, **JASPER NATIONAL PARK** covers an area greater than Banff, Yoho and Kootenay combined, and looks and feels far wilder and less commercialized than its southern counterparts. Its backcountry is more extensive and less travelled, and **Jasper Townsite** (or Jasper), the only settlement, is more relaxed and far less of a resort than Banff and has just half Banff's population. Most pursuits centre on Jasper and the **Maligne Lake** area about 50km southeast of the townsite. Other key zones are **Maligne Canyon**, on the way to the lake; the Icefields Parkway (covered on p.718); and the **Miette Hot Springs** region, an area well to the east of Jasper and visited for its springs and trails.

The park's **backcountry** is a vast hinterland scattered with countless rough campsites and a thousand-kilometre trail system considered among the best in the world for backpackers. Opportunities for day and half-day-hikes are more limited and scattered than in other parks. Most of the shorter strolls from the townsite are just low-level walks to forest-circled lakes; the best of the more exciting day-hikes start from more remote points off the Maligne Lake road, Icefields Parkway (Hwy 93) and Yellowhead Highway (Hwy 16).

A history of the park

Permanent settlement first came to the Jasper area in the winter of 1810–11. The great explorer and trader David Thomson left **William Henry** at Old Fire Point (just outside the present townsite), while he and his companions pushed on up the valley to blaze a trail over the Athabasca Pass that would be used for more than fifty years by traders crossing the Rockies. In the meantime, Henry established **Henry House**, the first permanent European habitation in the Rockies (though its exact location has been lost). Two years later the North West Company established Jasper House at the eastern edge of the park's present boundary. Named after Jasper Hawes, a long-time company clerk there, it moved closer to Jasper Lake in 1829, when the North West and Hudson's Bay companies were amalgamated. By 1880, and the collapse of the fur trade, the post had closed. By 1900, the entire region boasted just seven homesteads.

Like other parks and their townsites, Jasper traces its real origins to the coming of the railway in the late nineteenth century. The Canadian Pacific had brought boom to Banff and Yoho in 1885 when it spurned a route through the Jasper region in favour of a more southerly route. The **Grand Trunk Pacific Railway** hoped for similar successes in attracting visitors when it started to push its own route west in 1902, and the Jasper Forest Park was duly created in 1908. The government bought up all land locally except for the homestead of Lewis Swift, which remained in stubborn private hands until 1962: the town is now "run" by Parks Canada. By 1911 a tent city known as **Fitzhugh**, named after the company's vice president, had grown up on Jasper's present site, and the name "Jasper" was adopted when the site was officially surveyed. Incredibly, a second railway, the **Canadian Northern Railway** (CNR), was completed almost parallel to the Grand Trunk line in 1913, the tracks at some points running no more than a few metres apart. Within just three years, the line's redundancy became obvious and consolidation took place west of Edmonton, with the most favourably graded portions of the two routes being adopted. The ripped-up rails were then shipped to Europe and used in World War I, and Jasper became a centre of operations for the lines in 1924, greatly boosting its importance and population. The first tourist accommodation here was ten tents on the shores of Lac Beauvert, replaced in 1921 by the first *Jasper Lake Lodge*, forerunner of the present hotel. The first road link from Edmonton was completed in 1928. Official national-park designation came in 1930. Today Jasper's still a rail town, with around a third of the population employed by the CNR.

Arrival and information

Where Banff's strength is its convenience from Calgary, Jasper's is its ease of access from Edmonton, with plenty of **transport** options and approaches, as well as a wide range of onward destinations. Driving time from Edmonton (362km) or Banff (287km) is around four hours; from Kamloops (443km) and Calgary (414km) it's five or six hours; from Vancouver nine or ten hours (863km). Greyhound (☎780/852-3926 or 1-800/661-8747, ⓦwww .greyhound.ca) runs four **buses** daily from Edmonton (4hr 45min; $50 one-way) along the Yellowhead Highway (Hwy 16), plus onward services (4 daily) to Kamloops (5hr; $57) and Vancouver (11hr 30min; $99) via scenic Hwy 5, and Prince George (2 daily; $49). Brewster Transportation (☎780/852-3332 or 1-800/661-1152, ⓦwww.brewster.ca) operates services to Banff (4hr 30min; $62) via Lake Louise (3hr; $53) and continuing to Calgary and Calgary Airport (1 daily; $71), and also runs day-trip tours to Banff, taking in sights on the Icefields Parkway; note, however, that weather can play havoc with Brewster's schedules in October and April. Both companies share the

The range of hiking trails on offer in and around Jasper is vast – far more than we could possibly outline here. We've sketched out some ideas in this box; at a glance, the best walks in Jasper are:

- Best stroll: Maligne Canyon
- Best short walk: Wilcox Pass
- Best day-hike (easy): Cavell Meadows
- Best day-hike (moderate): Opal Hills
- Best day-hike (strenuous): Sulphur Skyline
- Best backpacking trail: Skyline Trail

Day-hikes

If you haven't travelled to Jasper on the Icefields Parkway (see p.718), remember that several of the national park's top trails can be accessed from this road: the **Wilcox Pass Trail** in particular is one of the finest half-day-hikes anywhere in the Rockies. If you just want a simple stroll closer to town, then think about walking the **Old Fort Point Loop** (see p.736), the **Maligne Canyon** (see p.736) and the easy path on the eastern shore of **Maligne Lake** (see p.736). If you're at Maligne Lake and want a longer walk, one of Jasper's best day-hikes, the **Opal Hills Circuit** (8.2km round trip; 460m vertical ascent), starts from the picnic area to the left of the uppermost Maligne Lake car park, 48km east of Jasper. After a heart-pumping haul up the first steep slopes, the trail negotiates alpine meadows and offers sweeping views of the lake before reaching an elevation of 2160m; the trip takes about four hours, but you could easily spend all day loafing around the meadows. The **Bald Hills Trail** (5.2km one-way; 480m ascent) starts with a monotonous plod along a fire road from the same car park, but ends with what Mary Schaffer, one of the area's first white explorers, described as "the finest view any of us had ever beheld in the Rockies"; allow four hours for the round trip, which goes as high as 2170m.

To get to the trailhead for another outstanding day-hike, **Cavell Meadows** (3.8km one-way; 370m ascent) – which is named after a British nurse who was executed for helping the Allies during World War I – drive, cycle or taxi 7.5km south on the Icefields Parkway, then 5km along Hwy 93A and finally 14km up Mount Edith Cavell Rd; there's a daily shuttle bus from Jasper and it takes bikes so you can ride back down. Note that if you're driving, an alternating one-way system has been instigated to reduce traffic flow up Mount Edith Cavell Rd every day from 10am to 9.30pm between mid-June and mid-October: contact the park information centre for latest timings. The walk's scenery is mixed and magnificent – but the hike is popular, so don't expect solitude. As well as Cavell's alpine meadows, there are views of Angel

same **bus terminal** (daily 6am–8pm; outside regular hours, the terminal opens briefly a few minutes before bus departures), located in the train station building at 314 Connaught Drive. There are also left-luggage lockers here and **car rental** offices for Hertz (☎780/852-3886) and National (☎780/852-1117). Be sure to have booked cars in advance if you're hoping to pick up vehicles at these outlets: all cars go very quickly, especially on days when trains come in from Vancouver and Edmonton. Other car-rental agencies in town are Avis at the Petro-Canada Service, 300 Connaught Drive (☎780/852-3970) and Budget, Jasper Shell Service, 638 Connaught Drive (☎780/852-3222).

VIA Rail **trains** operate to Jasper from Winnipeg and Edmonton and continue to Vancouver (via Kamloops) or Prince Rupert (via Prince George). As this is the only scheduled rail route through the Rockies, summer places are

Glacier and the dizzying north wall of Mount Edith Cavell. Allow two hours for the round trip; the maximum elevation reached is a breathless 2135m.

Further afield – you'll need transport – another superlative short, sharp walk starts from Miette Hot Springs, 58km northeast of Jasper. The **Sulphur Skyline** (4km one-way; 700m ascent) offers exceptional views of knife-edged ridges, deep gorges, crags and remote valleys. Be sure to take water with you, and allow two hours each way for the steep climb to 2070m. The trailhead is signed from the Miette Hot Springs complex, reached from Jasper by heading 41km east on Hwy 16 and then 17km south; in the past the shuttles have made the trip in summer – check latest timetables. More soothing, and a good way to round off a day, are the **springs** themselves, the hottest in the Rockies – so hot in fact they have to be cooled for swimming; there's one pool for soaking, another for swimming, with massages by appointment and not included in pass price (mid-June to early Sept daily 8.30am–10.30pm, $5.50 or $7.75 day-pass; mid-May to mid-June and early Sept to mid-Oct daily 10.30am–9pm, $4.50 or $7 day-pass; ☎780/866-3939 or 1-800/767-1611, ⓦwww.pc.gc.ca). You can rent bathing suits, towels and lockers for an extra $3–5. Other trails from the springs make for the **Fiddle River** (4.3km one-way; 275m ascent) and **Mystery Lake** (10.5km one-way; 475m ascent).

Backpacking trails

Jasper's system of **backpacking trails** and 111 backcountry campsites makes it one of the leading areas for backcountry hiking in North America. To stay overnight in the backcountry, pick up a Wilderness Permit ($6) within 24 hours of your departure, from the park information centre in Jasper Townsite or at the Columbia Icefield. All trails and campsites operate quota systems; contact the park information office for details and book yourself a backcountry campsite(s) – and thus trail place – as soon as you can. Reservations cost $10 (nonrefundable). Trails remain busy even into September; the busiest are Skyline, Maligne Lake, Brazeau and Tonquin Valley.

The office staff offer invaluable advice, and issue excellent low-price strip maps of several trails. Overnight hikes are beyond the scope of this book – talk to staff or get hold of a copy of *The Canadian Rockies Trail Guide* – but by general consent the finest long-distance trails are the **Skyline** (44km; 820m ascent) and **Jonas Pass** (19km; 555m ascent), with the latter often combined with the **Nigel** and **Poboktan** passes (total 36km; 750m ascent) to make a truly outstanding walk. Not far behind come two hikes in the Tonquin Valley – **Astoria River** (19km; 445m ascent) and **Maccarib Pass** (21km; 730m ascent) – and the **Fryat Valley** (3–4 days). Others to consider are Maligne Pass and the long-distance North and South Boundary trails (the latter both over 160km).

hard to come by, but at other times there's little need to book a seat. Fares are considerably more than those of equivalent buses, and journey times considerably longer. The **ticket office** is open on train days only (☎780/852-4102 or 1-888/VIA-RAIL, ⓦwww.viarail.ca).

Jasper's superb national park **visitor centre** is at 500 Connaught Drive, 50m east of the station, back from the road on the left in the open grassy area (mid-May to mid-June daily 8am–5pm; mid-June to early Sept daily 8am–7pm; early Sept to mid-May Mon–Fri 9am–5pm, Sat & Sun 8am–5pm; ☎780/852-6176, ⓦwww.pc.gc.ca). This is for park-related and campsite information only, and sells compulsory **national park permits** ($5 daily, $35 annual; see box above) and backcountry wilderness permits ($6), and lets you register for backpacking trails. For weather reports, call Environment Canada (☎780/852-3185). The centre also has a shop (good for **maps**) run by the Friends of Jasper

JASPER TOWNSITE

Patricia & Pyramid Lakes (7km) ▲

Edmonton, Maligne Lake & Ⓐ ▲

RESTAURANTS

Andy's Bistro	7
Coco's Café	5
Earl's	4
Fiddle River Seafood Restaurant	6
Jasper Pizza Place	1
Mountain Foods & Café	3
Papa George's	2
Soft Rock Internet Café	8
Villa Caruso	9

HOTELS & MOTELS

Amethyst Motor Lodge	F
Astoria Hotel	G
Athabasca Hotel	H
Bear Hill Lodge	E
Jasper Park Lodge	D
Lobstick Lodge	C
Marmot Lodge	B
Sawridge Hotel	J
Tekarra Lodge	I
Whistlers Inn	I

Aquatic Centre

Jasper-Yellowhead Museum

Jasper Activity Centre

Park Information Centre

Rocky Mountain Unlimited

Chamber of Commerce

Bus Terminal

Train Station

Library

RCMP Police Station

Hospital

Laundry

Freewheels Cycles

Maligne Tours

N

0   200 m

Mount Robson & Kamloops ▼▼ Hostel, Campgrounds & Icefields Parkway

Athanaska River

Old Fort Point ▶

Icefields Parkway, Campgrounds & Hostel

Miette River

(☏780/852-4767), who offer a couple of **guided walks** which delve into the history of the town and some of the legends and stories of the region. You should register at the centre for both; payment is by donation. Other popular Friends' activities include performances at the Whistler's Campground Theatre (July–Sept daily) and wildlife talks at the Wabasso Campground Campfire Circle (July–Sept).

ALBERTA AND THE ROCKIES | Jasper National Park

6

Taxis and shuttle services

One of the problems you're likely to have in Jasper if you're without transport is getting to some of the more outlying sights, strolls and trailheads. One option is to rent a bike (see p.738). Another is take advantage of a variety of small-scale **shuttle services** that run to various sights. These tend to come and go year by year, but there's always someone prepared to start up a service. Currently services include the **Tramway Shuttle** (☎780/852-4056 or 852-8255), which runs nine times daily in summer from outside the VIA Rail-bus depot to the Jasper Tramway (cable car) at a cost of $24, including Tramway ticket; more importantly, it also takes in the *Jasper International* (or *Whistlers*) *Hostel* for $4. The **Trailhead Shuttle** (☎780/852-3898 or 852-8389) leaves from Freewheel Cycles, 618 Patricia St, and runs once or twice daily to a variety of trailheads, including the Valley of the Five Lakes, Maligne Canyon and Overlander (all $10) and Marmot Basin Rd ($15). Finally, there's the long-established **Maligne Lake Shuttle**, run by Maligne Tours, 627 Patricia St (☎780/852-3370; 6 departures daily late June to late Sept, 3 daily mid-May to late June and last week of Sept), which will run you all the way to Maligne Lake ($12 or $24 round trip) to coincide with the company's boat cruises on the lake (see p.737), or drop off at Maligne Canyon ($8), *Maligne Canyon Hostel* ($8) and other points on the Maligne Lake Rd such as the Skyline trailheads (north $8, south $12).

For a **taxi**, call Heritage Cab (☎780/852-5558), Michael Angelo (☎780/852-7277) or Jasper Taxi (☎780/852-3600).

For information on the town of Jasper, and accommodation in particular, contact the Jasper Chamber of Commerce **infocentre** behind the park office about 100m east on Patricia St at no. 409 (June to early Sept daily 9am–7pm; rest of year Mon–Fri 9am–5pm; ☎780/852-3858, ⊛www.jaspercanadianrockies.com).

Accommodation

Beds in Jasper are not as expensive or elusive as in Banff, but hotel rooms are still almost unobtainable in late July and August. The Chamber of Commerce will help with accommodation, but does not offer a booking service. If you're desperate, try Jasper Adventure Centre, which offers an accommodation service (☎780/852-5595 or 1-800/565-7547, ⊛www.jasperadventurecentre.com), as does the Jasper Travel Agency, 623 Patricia St (☎780/852-4400 or 1-800/672-1127, ✉jtravel@telusplanet.net), and Rocky Mountain Unlimited, 414 Connaught Drive (☎780/852-4056, ⊛www.sundogtours.com). You could also ask the Chamber of Commerce for the *Private Home Accommodation List* published by the Jasper Home Accommodation Association (⊛www.stayinjasper.com) – Jasper has rooms in around sixty **private homes**, which are virtually all priced between $55 and $70 a double (up to a maximum of around $100 for the most expensive), sometimes with a continental breakfast thrown in. Virtually all are nonsmoking. Most **motels** are spaced out along Connaught Drive on the eastern edge of town – there's relatively little right in the middle of town; prices drop sharply off-season. An often cheaper and in many ways more pleasant option is to plump for motels made up of collections of **cabins**; most are within a few kilometres of town. The four park-run **campsites** close to the townsite and the three local hostels all fill up promptly in summer – and it's first-come, first-served – but don't forget the hostels and campsites strung along the Icefields Parkway.

6

ALBERTA AND THE ROCKIES | Jasper National Park

Hotels, motels and chalets

Alpine Village 2.5km south of town on Hwy 93A
☎ 780/852-3285, ⓦ www.alpinevillagejasper.com.
An assortment of 41 serene one- and two-room
cabins, including twelve de luxe cabins and lodge
suites, most with great mountain views; big outdoor tub. May to mid-Oct. ❻

Amethyst Motor Lodge 200 Connaught Drive
☎ 780/852-3394 or 1-888/852-7737,
ⓦ www.mtn-park-lodges.com. Workaday 100-
room motel, devoid of alpine pretensions, within
easy walking distance of downtown and with an
outdoor hot tub. ❼

Astoria Hotel 404 Connaught Drive ☎ 780/852-
3351 or 1-800/661-7343,
ⓦ www.astoriahotel.com. Downtown Alpine-look
hotel, family owned and run since 1920s, with
fridges in all its fairly basic rooms. Under-18s stay
free. ❻

Athabasca Hotel 510 Patricia St
☎ 780/852-3386 or 1-800/563-9859,
ⓦ www.athabascahotel.com. Despite the grand
lobby dotted with the disembodied heads of wild
animals, rooms (some without private bathroom)
are very plain, functional and cramped – but the
downtown location fantastic. Try to get a room
higher up in the building, if the din of the hotel's
lounge bar is likely to disturb. ❻

Bear Hill Lodge 100 Bonhomme St ☎ 780/852-
3209, ⓦ www.bearhilllodge.com. Thirty-seven
simple-looking but comfortable bungalows,
suites, chalet and lodge units in the townsite but
in a pleasant wooded setting. Mid-April to late
Oct. ❺

Becker's Chalets 5km south of Jasper on Hwy
93 and Athabasca River ☎ 780/852-3779,
ⓦ www.beckerschalets.com. Ninety-six of the best
local one-, two-, three- and four-bedroom log
cabins, most with wood-burning stoves and kitchenettes. May to mid-Oct. ❹

Jasper Park Lodge Lac Beauvert ☎ 780/852-
3301 or 1-800/441-1414, ⓦ www.jasperpark
lodge.com. Reminiscent of a summer camp, this
collection of luxurious log cabins blends in well
with its surroundings on the secluded shores Lac
Beauvert 6km northeast of Jasper. The vast main
lodge is replete with large lounges, several restaurants and an underground mall. ❽

Lobstick Lodge 94 Geikie St ☎ 780/852-4431 or
1-888/852-7737, ⓦ www.mtn-park-lodges.com.
Arguably the pick of the east end motels, with
large, simply furnished and clean rooms – though
the dingy basement ones are worth avoiding.
Some rooms have kitchens; indoor pool, outdoor
hot tub. ❻

Marmot Lodge 92 Connaught Drive
☎ 780/852-4471 or 1-888/852-7737,
ⓦ www.mtn-park-lodges.com. Cheapest motel in
town and one of the biggest; spreading over three
separate buildings. Rooms, all decorated with
Native American items, range dramatically in size,
and some units have kitchens, fireplaces and fine
mountain views. Communal amenities include a
hot tub and sauna. ❻

Patricia Lake Bungalows 5km northwest of
downtown ☎ 780/852-3560 or 1-888/499-6848,
ⓦ www.patricialakebungalows.com. Quiet motel or
cabin out-of-town base; 35 units on Pyramid Lake
Rd, some with fine views over Patricia Lake; fishing and rentals of boats, canoes and paddle boats
available. May to mid-Oct. ❸

Pine Bungalows 2km east of Jasper on the
Athabasca River ☎ 780/852-3491,
ⓦ www.jasperadventures.com. Around eighty
good-looking wooden cabins in forest setting,
half with wood-burning stoves and most with
kitchenettes. Grocery shop on site. Three-day
minimum stay from mid-June to mid-Sept. Open
May to mid-Oct. ❸

Sawridge Hotel Jasper 82 Connaught Drive
☎ 780/852-5111 or 1-800/661-6427,
ⓦ www.sawridge.com/jasper. Plush and expensive
154-room hotel on the eastern edge of town. ❽

Tekarra Lodge ☎ 780/852-3058 or 1-888/404-
4540, ⓦ www.tekarralodge.com. Forty-two quiet,
nicely kitsch wood cabins with wood-burning
stoves, located 1km south of town on the
Athabasca River off Hwy 93A. Open May–Oct. ❻

Whistlers Inn 105 Miette Ave ☎ 780/852-3361 or
1-800/282-9919, ⓦ www.whistlersinn.com.
Central but unexciting 41-room motel, opposite the
station. ❼

B&Bs

A-1 Tourist Rooms 804 Connaught Drive
☎ 780/852-3325, ⓔ lwhitema@telusplanet.net.
Two rooms with shared bathroom on Main St close
to bus and train. Two-night minimum stay for
advance reservations. ❷

Aspen Lodge 8 Aspen Crescent ☎ 780/852-5908,
ⓔ aspnlodg@telusplanet.net. Two clean, comfortable rooms with private bathrooms on a quiet
street 10min walk from downtown. ❸

B&G Accommodation 204 Colin Crescent
☎ 780/852-4345, ⓔ wgunrau@telusplanet.net.
Three well-priced rooms with shared bathroom
three blocks from downtown. ❷

Creekside Accommodation 1232 Patricia
Crescent ☎ 780/852-3530, ⓔ rushacom
@telusplanet.net. Two bright, clean rooms (shared
bath) near Cabin Creek and trails. ❷

6

Kennedy's Mountain Holiday Rooms 1115 Patricia Crescent ☎780/852-3438. Pair of rooms that share bath, patio, living room and great views. ❷

Rooney's Accommodation 1114 Patrica St ☎780/852-4101, ℮ mismaeil@telusplanet.com. Just out of the town centre comprising two nice rooms with and without private baths. ❷

TassonInn 706 Patricia St ☎780/852-3427, ℮ tassinn@incentre.net. Two bright and newly renovated rooms with shared bathroom less than a block from the town centre. ❷

Hostels

Jasper International Hostel (HI) Whistlers Mountain Rd ☎780/852-3215, Ⓦwww.hihostels.ca. Large, sterile and highly institutional hostel, the biggest of three in the vicinity of Jasper, and located 7km south of town via the Icefields Parkway (Hwy 93). The 4km uphill walk from Hwy 93 is a killer, but shuttles run from downtown, as do taxis (about $15). Check-in operates from noon to midnight when HI members are charged $18 for dorm beds. It has all the usual hostel facilities and no curfew. The eighty beds fill up quickly in summer, so arrive early or book.

Maligne Canyon Hostel (HI) ☎780/852-3215, Ⓦwww.hihostels.ca. Two cabins in lovely setting with beds for 24 in six-bed rooms 11km east of town near Maligne Canyon; the Maligne Lake Shuttle from downtown or Alberta Hostel Shuttle drop off here daily in summer. Dorms $11. Open all day, year-round but check-in 5–11pm and may have closures in winter. ❶

Mount Edith Cavell Hostel (HI) Edith Cavell Rd, 13km off Hwy 93A, 26km south of Jasper ☎780/852-3215, Ⓦwww.hihostels.ca. Check-in 5–11pm. Cosier than the *Jasper International*, close to trails and with great views of the Angel Glacier. Sleeps 32 in two cabins; outdoor wood-burning sauna. Dorms $11. Mid-June to Oct. Occasionally opens up with key system for skiers in winter. ❶

Campsites

Pocahontas 45km east of Jasper and 1km off Hwy 16 on Miette Rd. One of two to the northeast of Jasper on this road; 130 pitches, hot and cold water and flush toilets but no showers. Mid-May to mid-Oct. $13 plus $4 for use of firewood.

Snaring River 16km east of Jasper on Hwy 16. Simple 66-site park-run facility. The other simple park campsite east of Jasper; tap water, kitchen shelter, dry toilets only and no showers. Mid-May to early Sept. $10 plus $4 for use of firewood.

Wabasso 16km south of Jasper on Hwy 93A. A 228-pitch riverside park-run site with flush toilets, hot water but no showers. Wheelchair-accessible. Mid-June to early Sept. $13 plus $4 for use of firewood.

Wapiti 4km south of the townsite and 1km south of *Whistlers* campsite (see below) on Hwy 93. Big 362-pitch park-run place with flush toilets and coin showers that accepts tents but also caters for up to forty RVs. Wheelchair-accessible. Some ninety sites remain open for winter camping from October – the park's only year-round serviced campsite. Summer $15–18 plus $4 for use of firewood; winter, when there are no showers or other services save water and flush toilets, $13–15 plus $4 for use of firewood.

Whistlers 3km south of Jasper just west off Hwy 93. Jasper's main 781-site park-run campsite is the largest in the Rockies, with three sections, and prices depending on facilities included. Wheelchair-accessible. If you're coming from Banff, watch for the sign; Brewster buses also usually stop here if you ask the driver. Taxis and shuttles run from Jasper. Early May to early Oct. $15–24 plus $4 for use of firewood.

Jasper Townsite and around

JASPER's small-town feel comes as a relief after the razzmatazz of Banff: its streets still have the windswept, open look of a frontier town and, though the mountains don't ring with quite the same majesty as Banff, you'll probably feel the town better suits its wild surroundings. Situated at the confluence of the Miette and Athabasca rivers, its core centres around just two streets: **Connaught Drive**, which contains the bus and train terminal, restaurants, motels and park information centre, and – a block to the west – the parallel **Patricia St**, lined with more shops, restaurants and the odd hotel. The rest of the central grid consists of cosy little houses and the fixtures of small-town life: the post office, library, school and public swimming pool. Apart from the **Yellowhead Museum & Archives** at 400 Pyramid Rd, with its fur trade and railroad displays (mid-May to early Sept daily 10am–9pm; early Sept to Oct daily

AROUND JASPER TOWNSITE

Edmonton & Miette Hot Springs ▲

Athabasca River

Maligne River

MALIGNE ROAD

Hostel
Maligne Canyon

Maligne Lake ▶

Pyramid Lake

Pyramid Overlook ▲

Lake Edith

Patricia Lake

Lake Annette

Patricia Lake Bungalows ◉

Riley Lake

Pine Bungalows ◉

Trefoil Lakes

See 'Jasper Townsite' map

Mina Lake

Jasper Park Lodge ◉

Lac Beauvert

Jasper

16

Cabin Lake

Old Fort Point ▲

93A

Tekarra Lodge ▲

Marjoire Lake

Miette River

93

YELLOWHEAD HWY

Jasper Tramway

Jasper International Hostel ◉

Whistlers Campground 🏕

Athabasca River

Wapiti Campground 🏕

N

0   2 km

ICEFIELDS PARKWAY

Mount Robson & Prince George ◀

Valley of the Five Lakes ▶

▲ The Whistlers

Lake Louise & Banff ▼

6

ALBERTA AND THE ROCKIES | Jasper National Park

10am–5pm; Nov to mid-May Thurs–Sun 10am–5pm; $3 or donation) and a cable car (see below), nothing here even pretends to be a tourist attraction; this is a place to sleep, eat and stock up. If you're interested in getting to know a little more about the town or park from the locals, contact the Friends of Jasper National Park (☎780/852-4767), who offer guided walks between July and August, or pick up *Jasper: A Walk in the Past* from local bookshops. A lot of people head 58km northeast of town for a dip in Miette Hot Springs (see box p.738).

With little on offer in town you need to use a bike, car or the shuttle services to get anything out of the area. The obvious trip is on Canada's longest and highest cable car, the **Jasper Tramway**, 7km south of town on Whistlers Mountain

Behind every triumph of military ingenuity in World War II there were probably dozens of spectacular and deliberately obfuscated failures. Few have been as bizarre as the one witnessed by Jasper's Patricia Lake. By 1942, Allied shipping losses in the North Atlantic had become so disastrous that almost anything was considered that might staunch the flow. One Geoffrey Pike, institutionalized in a London mental hospital, managed to put forward the idea of a vast aircraft carrier made of ice, a ship that would be naturally impervious to fire when torpedoed, and not melt in the icy waters of the North Atlantic.

Times were so hard that the innovative scheme, despite its odd source, was given serious consideration. Louis Mountbatten, one of the Allied Chiefs of Staff, went so far as to demonstrate the theories with ice cubes in the bath in front of Winston Churchill at 10 Downing St. It was decided to build a thousand-tonne model somewhere very cold – Canada was ideal – and **Operation Habbakuk** was launched. Pike was released from his hospital on special dispensation and dispatched to the chilly waters of Patricia Lake near Jasper. Here a substance known as pikewood was invented, a mixture of ice and wood chips (spruce chips were discovered to add more buoyancy than pine). It soon became clear, however, that the 650m-long and twenty-storey-high boat stood little chance of ever being seaworthy (never mind what the addition of 2000 crew and 26 aircraft would do for its buoyancy). Pike suggested filling the ice with air to help things along. Further complications arose when the labourers on the project, mostly pacifist Doukhobors (see p.943), became aware of the boat's proposed purpose and refused to carry on working. Spring thaws brought the project to a halt. The following season, with $75m budgeted for it, the scheme was moved to Newfoundland, where it died a quiet death.

Rd, off the Icefields Parkway (daily: April to mid-May and Oct 9.30am–4.30pm; mid-May to early Sept 8.30am–10pm; Sept 9.30am–9pm; $18 return). In peak season you may well have a long wait in line for the 2.5-kilometre cable-car ride, whose two thirty-person cars take seven minutes to make the 1000m ascent (often with running commentary from the conductor). It leaves you at an interpretive centre, expensive restaurant, and an excellent viewpoint (2285m) where you can take your bearings on much of the park. A steep trail ploughs upwards and onwards to the Whistlers summit (2470m), an hour's walk that requires warm clothes year-round and reveals even more stunning views. A tough but rather redundant ten-kilometre trail follows the route of the tramway from *Jasper International Hostel*; if you walk up, you can ride back down for next to nothing.

Also near the town, a winding road wends north to **Patricia** and **Pyramid lakes**, pretty moraine-dammed lakes about 5km from Jasper and full of rental facilities for riding, boating, canoeing, windsurfing and sailing. Food and drink is available locally, but if you're thinking about staying here as a more rural alternative to the townsite the two lakefront lodges are usually heavily booked (the one at Pyramid Lake is open year-round). Short trails, generally accessible from the approach road, include the Patricia Lake Circle, a 4.8-kilometre loop by the Cottonwood slough and creek offering good opportunities for seeing birds and beavers during early morning and late evening. The island on Pyramid Lake, connected by a bridge to the shore, is an especially popular destination for a day out: continue on the lake road to the end of the lake and you'll find everything a little quieter. Slightly closer to town on the east side of the Athabasca River, **Lake Edith** and **Lake Annette** are the remains of a larger lake that once extended across the valley floor. Both are similarly busy day-use areas. Their waters are the warmest in the park, thanks to the lakes' shallow depth. In summer you can lie out on sandy beaches or grassy areas. A clutch of picnic sites are the only development, and the wheelchair-accessible Lee Foundation Trail meanders around Lake Annette (2.4km).

Few other hikes from town are spectacular, but the best of the bunch, the **Old Fort Point Loop** (6.5km round trip), is recommended. Despite being just thirty minutes out of town, it's remarkably scenic, with panoramic views and lots of quiet corners. To reach the trailhead (1.6km from town) use the Old Fort Exit, following Hwy 93A across the railway and Hwy 16 until you come to the Old Fort Point–Lac Beauvert turn-off, then turn left and follow the road to the car park beyond the bridge. The Valley of the Five Lakes Trail (4.6km) is also good, but the path starts 10km south of town off the Icefields Parkway. For full details of all park walks, ask at the information centre for the free *Day-hiker's Guide to Jasper*.

Maligne Lake Road

Bumper to bumper with cars, campers and tour buses in the summer, the **Maligne Lake Road** runs east from Jasper for 48km, taking in a number of beautiful but rather busy and overdeveloped sights before reaching the sublime Maligne Lake (pronounced *ma-leen*), the Rockies' largest glacier-fed lake. If you have time to spare, and the transport, you could set aside a day for the trip, white-water raft the Maligne River, or walk one of the trails above Maligne Lake itself. Maligne Tours, 627 Patricia St (☎780/852-3370, ⓦwww.malignelake.com), books boat tours on the lake (advance booking is highly recommended) and rents out any equipment you may need for canoeing, fishing and so forth (rental reservations are also essential in summer). The company also runs a **bus**, the Maligne Lake Shuttle, to the lake eight times daily ($12 one-way), with drop-offs (if booked) at *Maligne Canyon* hostel ($8) and the northern ($8) and southern ends ($8/$12) of the Skyline Trail, one of the park's three top backpacking trails (see box p.728). Joint tickets are offered for the shuttle and other activities organized by the company, notably the cruises, raft trips and horse rides on and around Maligne Lake.

The often rather crowded **Maligne Canyon** is a mere 11km out of Jasper, with an oversized car park and a tacky café/souvenir shop. This heavily sold excursion promises one of the Rockies' most spectacular gorges: in fact the canyon is deep (50m), but almost narrow enough to jump across – many people have tried and most have died in the attempt. In the end the geology is more interesting than the scenery; the violent erosive forces that created the canyon are explained on the main trail loop, an easy twenty-minute amble that can be extended to 45 minutes (few people do this, so the latter part of the trail is often quiet), or even turned into a hike back to Jasper. In winter, licensed guides lead tours (more like crawls) through the frozen canyon.

Next stop is picture-perfect **Medicine Lake**, 32km from Jasper, which experiences intriguing fluctuations in level. Its waters have no surface outlet; instead the lake fills and empties through lake-bed sink holes into the world's largest system of limestone caves. They re-emerge some 17km away towards Jasper (and may also feed some of the lakes around Jasper Townsite). When the springs freeze in winter, the lake drains and sometimes disappears altogether, only to be replenished in the spring. The lake's strange behaviour captivated local natives, who believed spirits were responsible, hence the name. Few people spend much time at the lake, preferring to press on to Maligne Lake, so it makes a quietish spot to escape the headlong rush down the road.

At the end of the road, 48km from Jasper, is the stunning **Maligne Lake**, 22km long and 92m deep, and surrounded by snow-covered mountains. The largest lake in the Rockies, its name comes from the French for "wicked", and was coined in 1846 by a Jesuit missionary, Father de Smet, in memory of the difficulty he had crossing the **Maligne River** downstream. The road peters out at a warden station, three car parks and a restaurant flanked by a picnic area and the start of the short, self-explanatory Lake Trail along the lake's east side to the Schäffer Viewpoint (3.2km loop; begin from Car Park 2). A small waterfront area is equipped with berths for glass-enclosed boats that run ninety-minute narrated **cruises** on the lake to Spirit Island: the views are sensational (daily hourly on the hour: mid-May to late June 10am–4pm; late June to early Sept 10am–5pm; early Sept to late Sept 10am–3pm; $32). The boats are small, however, and reservations are vital during peak times, especially as tour companies often block-book entire sailings; again, contact Maligne Tours (see opposite). Riding, fishing, rafting and guided hiking tours are also available, as are fishing tackle, rowing boat and canoe rentals ($10/day and $45/day) and sea kayaks ($60/day). There are no accommodation or camping facilities here, but two backcountry campsites on the lakeshore can be reached by canoe; get details from Jasper's information centre.

Eating and drinking

Though a far cry from the selection in Banff, Jasper has just about enough **restaurants** to ensure variety and a reasonable choice for a week-long vacation, though hearty North American food dominates local menus.

Wholly unpretentious, generally gritty and regularly raucous, **nightlife** in Jasper's limited number of **bars** tends to make up in enthusiasm what it lacks in style. And with the presence of plenty of friendly local folk to share a beer with, a good night out is easy to come by. Yet many of the hostels and campsites are too far out of town for people to get in, so the fun there is generally of the make-your-own variety. For alternative evening entertainment, consult the town's summer or winter guide available from the tourist office or contact Arts Jasper (℡780/852-3964) for information on local theatre, music, dance performances and movies. Every second year (even years) the town hosts the **Jasper Heritage Folk Festival** with performers from across North America playing in Centennial Park. The town's biggest **cinema** is the Chaba Movie Theatre, 604 Connaught Dr (℡780/852-4749).

Restaurants

Andy's Bistro 606 Patricia St ℡780/852-4559. Staid but popular and unpretentiously upscale place serving good Swiss food and some interesting gamey options (entrees $18–30). Arrive early for a seat on Wednesdays or Fridays, when a three-course set meal is offered for $25. At other times, finding space is usually easy, thanks to the big *Stammtisch*, a sociable communal table seating up to ten where people come and go independently.

Coco's Café 608 Patricia St ℡780/852-4550. Tiny, earthy and fun café with a glut of fabulous home-made items including tasty eggy (free range) breakfasts, wraps, sandwiches, cakes and smoothies. Most items are available to take away and great for picnic lunches.

Earl's 600 Patricia St ℡780/852-2393. Branch of Canada-wide chain with cheerful staff and a dependable, mid-priced and generally North American menu, though the burgers, a huge rib platter and perfectly broiled salmon steaks are offset by the presence of some eclectic options like sushi and Thai stir-fry. There's also a cocktail bar here.

Fiddle River Seafood Restaurant 620 Connaught Drive ℡780/852-3032. Stylish restaurant with dried flower and oil lamp decor, mountain panoramas and excellent fresh seafood at prices that reflect its distance from the sea; expect to pay $35–40 per person for three courses. Entrees range from basic beer-battered cod fish and chips to more exotic seafood jambalaya and green curry grilled swordfish.

Jasper Park Lodge Lac Beauvert ℡780/852-3301, 🖰 www.jasperparklodge.com. The area's most prestigious lodging address has several restaurants to chose from, all under one roof. Choices include fresh sushi at the small basic *Oka Sushi*, a large bar menu at the *Tent City*

The presence of the Athabasca and other rivers around Jasper makes the town a focus of white-water and other **rafting** trips (see box p.724). If the idea of water appeals, but in a much gentler context, the town's Aquatic Centre at 401 Pyramid Lake Rd (☎780/852-3663) is popular, and provides a large **swimming pool**, whirlpool, wading pool, steam room and showers. You can rent towels and costumes. For other forms of indoor exercise try the **Activity Centre**, 303 Pyramid Ave (☎780/852-3381), where facilities include racquetball and squash courts, weight room, climbing wall, curling lanes and indoor ice rink (for skating and regular minor-league hockey games).

Tours and excursions

Other tours and activities can be accessed through several operators around town, amongst whom the most wide-ranging is **Rocky Mountain Unlimited**, 414 Connaught Drive (☎780/852-4056, ⓦwww.sundogtours.com), who run their own tours but also act as a one-stop booking agent for a huge range of tours, including seeing the park by **helicopter** ($149), a five-hour bus and hiking tour of the Maligne Valley ($169) or white-water rafting ($79 and up). The town's other big operator is **Maligne Tours**, 627 Patricia St (☎780/852-3370, ⓦwww.malignelake.com) – though note that nowhere on the shopfront at this address does it actually say the company's name. Among other things, the company runs boat cruises on Maligne Lake, guided hiking and fishing trips, canoe rentals and rafting excursions.

All manner of short or strenuous and generally cheap guided hiking or wildlife tours are widely available: contact the Chamber of Commerce for details of the other operators. For the free walking tours run by the Friends of Jasper National Park in the summer, contact the park visitor centre. If you need to **rent outdoor equipment**, the best bet is On-Line Sport & Tackle, 600 Patricia St (☎780/852-3630), or the Totem Ski Shop, 406 Patricia St (☎780/852-3078).

Bikes and skates

You can **rent bikes** in town from On-Line Sport & Tackle ($6/hr, $18/day) or from Freewheel Cycles, 618 Patricia St (same rates; ☎780/852-3898, ⓦwww .freewheeljasper.com). The latter is a good place for all things connected with bikes, including repairs and spares. Drop in and ask for their *Mountain Biking Trail Guide*, a summary of trails to suit all types of riders. On-Line offers a one-way rental with all necessary kit from Jasper to Banff, should you be up to riding the length of the Icefields Parkway. Out of town you can rent bikes at the *Jasper International Hostel*; at Beauvert Boat & Cycles, which is at the *Jasper Park Lodge* on the shore of Lac Beauvert ($8/hr, $20 for 4hr, $30/day; ☎780/852-5708); and at Patricia Lake Bungalows, 4.8km northwest of town on Pyramid Lake Rd (from $6/hr, $18 per half-day, $24/day). For **in-line skate rental**, make for Source for Sports, 406 Patricia St (from $4/hr, $12/day; ☎780/852-3654).

Fishing, golf and horse riding

If you want **fishing** tours, tackle for rent or just free advice if you're fishing alone, On-Line Sport & Tackle (see above) is again the operator to go for: it has trips to Maligne Lake and Talbot Lake for trout and various other lake and river-fishing destinations. A full day's (8hr) fishing costs $289, $189 if there are two of you; a half-day costs $249/$149. It'll rent you tackle, too – boots and waders from $30 a day, spin rod and reel ($15), fly-rod and reel ($25) and nets ($5). The company also organizes rafting and horse-riding tours, rents rowboats ($40 daily, $25 for a half-day after 3pm) and canoes (same rates), and sells and rents a wide range of camping gear. Currie's Guiding, 414 Connaught Drive (☎780/852-5650, ⓦwww.curriesguiding.com), offers similar trips on the rivers and over twenty lakes, with fly-fishing lessons also available.

Golf on a highly rated eighteen-hole course – "Number one in Canada" according to *Score Magazine* – is available at the *Jasper Park Lodge* (green fees $44–95, cheaper twilight fees available; ☏780/852-6090). You can rent clubs and carts. **Horse-riding** enthusiasts should contact Pyramid Stables, 4km from Jasper on Pyramid Lake Rd (☏780/852-3562), who run day-treks and one-, two- and three-hour trips (from $25/43/65; full-day rides $125) around Patrician and Pyramid lakes. Ridgeline Riders at Maligne Tours (see above) offers a ride above the tree line at Maligne Lake to the Bald Hills Fire Lookout at 2134m with great views of the lake (3hr 30min; $55). Skyline Trail Rides (☏780/852-4215) at *Jasper Park Lodge* have a more varied programme which includes a one-hour ride to Lake Annette ($25), ninety-minute rides along the Athabasca River ($33), two-hour "Valley View" treks ($35) and four-hour rides to Maligne Canyon ($70). They can also organize overnight trips and anything up to 21-day expeditions using a variety of backcountry lodges.

Winter sports

Jasper's **winter sports** tend to be overshadowed by the world-class ski resorts in nearby Banff and Lake Louise. This said, the park has plenty of winter activities and a first-rate ski area in **Marmot Basin** (early Dec to late April; ☏780/852-3816, ⓦwww.skimarmot.com), a twenty-minute drive from the townsite, and a resort that has the advantages of cheaper skiing and far less crowded runs than its southern rivals. Scenically it's every bit as spectacular, and the quality of the snow is superb. Yet the limited amount of expert terrain makes it best for intermediate skiers and riders. Skiing in the region began in the 1920s, though the first lift was only introduced in 1961, just a few years after the first road. Today there are a total of eight lifts serving 1500 acres of terrain with a vertical drop of 700m and a choice of 75 trails. Lift passes cost around $52 per day and equipment rental is available at the resort. To get here, jump aboard one of the three daily buses ($5 one-way, $9 return) from downtown hotels, whose rates, incidentally, tumble dramatically during the winter. For local taxis call Jasper Taxi ☏780/852-3600 or Heritage Cabs ☏780/852-5558.

Where Jasper rates as highly, if not more so, than Banff National Park is in the range and quality of its **cross-country skiing**, for its summer backcountry trails lend themselves superbly to winter grooming. Pick up the *Cross-Country Skiing* leaflet from the park information centre: the key areas are around the Whistlers campsite, Maligne Lake, around Athabasca Falls and along Pyramid Lake Rd. To buy or rent cross-country skis try Totem Ski Rentals, 408 Connaught Drive (☏780/852-3078), and for a guiding service contact Beyond the Beaten Path (☏780/852-5650). You can **ice-skate** on parts of Pyramid Lake and Lac Beauvert that are cleared for the purpose. The Sports Shop, 406 Patricia St (☏780/852-3654), does skate rentals.

Jasper also has some good winter **hiking** and snowshoeing, and particularly outstanding are the ice formations within Maligne Canyon. From late December the torrential river here freezes into spiny contortions within the narrow canyon, creating frozen waterfalls and ice caves, all shining with magically translucent colours. The hike in is only a mile, but made difficult but icy conditions and the clambering and squeezing required, so that it's best to go on a tour. One of several companies offering trips is Rocky Mountain Unlimited, 414 Connaught Drive (☏780/852-4056, ⓦwww.sundog-tours .com), whose three-hour tours set out three times per day (with one at night, led by the light of headlamps) and cost $35 per person. The company runs dog sledding, snowmobiling, and heli-skiing trips and will also take you down to Banff to go skiing. Brewster (☏780/852-3332, ⓦwww.brewster.ca), too drops in for a quick look at Maligne Canyon on its 3hr daily winter sightseeing tour ($35) of the Jasper area.

You can also indulge in activities that disturb the peace a little more and are banned in the park: Valemount, a major **snowmobiling** centre, is 116km west in British Columbia.

Sports Lounge and the 500-seater be*auvert Dining Room*, an everyday choice, particularly recommended for its buffet breakfast and Sunday brunch ($20). A notch above these, the Moose's Nook serves local mountain fare, which generally includes the excellent whiskey-soaked salmon and, occasionally, musk ox (entrées around $27). But the lodge's best restaurant – and the only one really worth the trek out here if you are based in town – is the *Edith Cavell Room*, a fine dining establishment with white glove service, where you can expect to part with around $70 for five courses from an expertly crafted menu that's basically French with some Canadian accents.

Jasper Pizza Place 402 Connaught Drive ☎780/852-3225. Despite the open kitchen and everyday bar furnishings that make for a chain-restaurant ambience, the wood-fired pizzas (from $10.50) here are little short of unique. The choice of zany toppings include DIjon mustard, escargot, smoked oysters and palm hearts. The small salads like the spinach, mushroom and citrus and honey ($5.25) combination are less exciting but still. Other options include a gargantuan lasagne ($9), burgers and pita-pizzas that are ideal for a quick snack. Pool tables in the basement invite you to hang out after your meal.

Mountain Foods and Café 606 Connaught Drive ☎780/852-4050. Reasonable place opposite the station for a basic budget meal in no-nonsense surroundings though quality has become variable. Still, the menu is cheap and varied (including vegetarian courses), the staff friendly, and it's a good place to meet people.

Papa George's 406 Connaught Drive ☎780/852-3351. Though it looks plain and dowdy this locals' favourite is one of the town's oldest restaurants (opened in 1924); it has excellent very varied food and gargantuan portions.

Soft Rock Internet Café 622 Connaught Dr ☎780/852-5850. Good breakfast choice with encyclopedic selection of coffee and mouth-watering waffles heaped with fresh fruit and cream and satisfying all-day breakfasts. The best place in town to both browse the web and pick up fantastic, massive cinnamon buns.

Villa Caruso 640 Connaught Drive ☎780/852-3920. Upmarket steakhouse with subdued lighting, wood accents and orange hues the backdrop for meat feasts, largely focused on flame-grilling Alberta's best cuts, though seafood, pasta and pizzas (most entrées around $23) are also available. Execution of dishes is unexciting but the pleasant ambience compensates; the adjoining fireside lounge is particularly tempting for a drink before or after your meal.

Bars

Atha-B At *Athabasca Hotel*, 510 Patricia St. Uninspired, but large and occasionally rowdy, this is Jasper's most reliably busy venue, with nightly dancing – mostly to mainstream chart hits – and regular live music. Small cover.

Bonhomme Lounge At *Château Jasper*, 96 Geikie St. With a harpist most nights, ideal if you want a smoochy evening.

De'd Dog Bar and Grill 404 Connaught Drive. Regularly unruly sports bar that's almost inevitably full of extrovert, 30-something locals. Other diversions here include pool, darts, big-screen sports and a bar menu with great burgers. The generous happy hour runs 5–7pm.

Downstream Grill 620 Connaught Drive. Funky, spacious, airy and non-smoking bar with several laid-back sofas, below the *Fiddle River Seafood Restaurant* (see p.737). Good bar food at reasonable prices.

Pete's Bar 614 Patricia St. Big bustling young bar with big screens – frequently for snowboarding videos – pool, darts and, on weekend nights, live music, varying from blues to Irish; locals jam here on Tuesdays.

Villa Caruso 640 Connaught Drive. Elegantly laid-back fireside martini and cocktail bar (adjoining a restaurant – see above) with piped jazz and blues; as relaxing and stylish a place as you'll find to sip a drink in town.

Listings

Bookshop Jasper Camera and Gift, 412 Connaught Drive ☎780/852-3165, has a small selection.
Hospital Seton General, 518 Robson St ☎780/852-3344.
Internet access Soft Rock Internet Café, 633 Connaught Drive (☎780/852-5850).
Laundry Coin Clean, 607 Patricia St ☎780/852-3852.

Library Elm Ave (Mon–Thurs 2–5pm & 7–9pm, Fri 2–5pm, Sat 10am–3pm). Has a huge number of books on the park.
Pharmacy Cavell Drugs, 602 Patricia St ☎780-852-4441.
Police ☎780/852-4848.
Post office 502 Patricia St ☎780/852-3041.

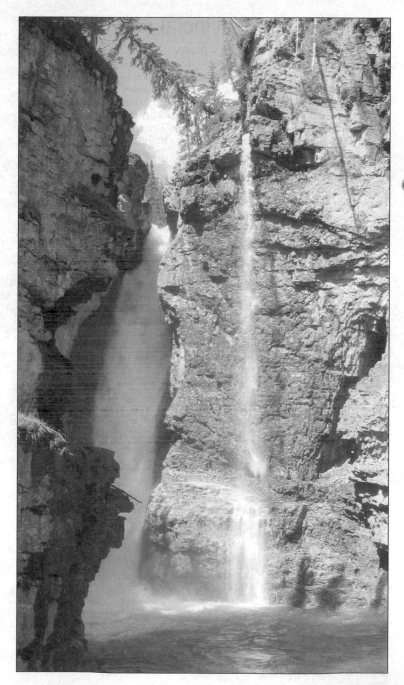

△ Johnston Canyon

Mount Robson Provincial Park

The extensive **MOUNT ROBSON PROVINCIAL PARK** borders Jasper National Park to the west and protects Mount Robson, at 3954m the highest peak in the Canadian Rockies. Its scenery equals anything anywhere else in the Rockies, and Mount Robson itself is one of the most staggering mountains you'll ever encounter. Facilities are thin on the ground, so stock up on food and fuel before entering the park. Around 16km beyond the park's western boundary Hwy 16 comes the Tête Jaune Cache, where you can pick up one of two immensely scenic roads: the continuation of Hwy 16 north to Prince George (for routes to Prince Rupert, northern BC and the Yukon), or Hwy 5, which heads south past Wells Gray Provincial Park to Kamloops and a whole range of onward destinations; the latter route is covered on p.922.

Both road and rail links to the park from Jasper climb through **Yellowhead Pass** (1131m), 20km west of Jasper Townsite, long one of the most important native and fur-trading routes across the Rockies. This stretch of road is less dramatic than the Icefields Parkway, but then most roads are, given over to mixed woodland – birch interspersed with firs – and mountains that sit back from the road with less scenic effect. The railway meanders alongside the road most of the way, occasionally occupied by epic freight trains hundreds of wagons long – alien intrusions in the usual beguiling wilderness of rocks, river and forest. Just down from the pass, **Yellowhead Lake** is the park's first landmark. Look for moose around dawn and dusk at aptly named **Moose Lake**, another 20km farther west.

Even if the first taste of the park seems relatively tame, the first sight of **Mount Robson** itself is among the most breathtaking in the Rockies. The preceding ridges creep up in height hiding the massive peak itself from view until the last moment. The British explorer W.B. Cheadle described the mountain in 1863: "On every side the mighty heads of snowy hills crowded round, whilst, immediately behind us, a giant among giants, and immeasurably supreme, rose Robson's peak... We saw its upper portion dimmed by a necklace of light, feathery clouds, beyond which its pointed apex of ice, glittering in the morning sun, shot up far into the blue heaven above." The overall impression is of immense size, thanks mainly to the colossal scale of Robson's south face – a sheer rise of 3100m – and to the view from the road, which frames the mountain as a single mass isolated from other peaks. A spectacular glacier system, concealed on the mountain's north side, is visible if you make the popular backpacking hike to the Berg Lake area (see box opposite). The source of the mountain's name has never been agreed on, but could be a corruption of Robertson, a Hudson's Bay employee who was trapped in the region in the 1820s. Local natives called the peak Yuh-hai-has-hun (the "Mountain of the Spiral Road"), an allusion to the clearly visible layers of rock that resemble a road winding to the summit. Not surprisingly, this monolith was one of the last major peaks in the Rockies to be conquered: it was first climbed in 1913, and is still considered a dangerous challenge.

Yellowhead Pass marks the boundary between the Jasper park, which is in Alberta (on **Mountain time**), and the Mount Robson park, which is in British Columbia (on **Pacific time**, one hour behind).

Starting 2km north of the park visitor centre, the **Berg Lake Trail** (22km one-way; 795m ascent) is perhaps the most popular short backpacking trip in the Rockies, and the only trail that gets anywhere near Mount Robson. You can do the first third or so as a comfortable and highly rewarding day-walk, passing through forest to lovely glacier-fed Kinney Lake (6.7km; campsite at the lake's northeast corner). Many rank this among the Rockies best day-hikes and it's particularly good for naturalists. Trek the whole thing, however, and you traverse the stupendous Valley of a Thousand Waterfalls – the most notable being sixty-metre Emperor Falls (14.3km; campsites 500m north and 2km south) – and eventually enjoy the phenomenal area around Berg Lake itself (17.4km to its nearest, western shore). Mount Robson rises an almost sheer 2400m from the lakeshore, its huge cliffs cradling two creaking rivers of ice, Mist Glacier and Berg Glacier – the latter, one of the Rockies' few "living" or advancing glaciers, is 1800m long by 800m wide and the source of the great icebergs that give the lake its name. Beyond the lake you can pursue the trail 2km further to Robson Pass (21.9km; 1652m ascent; campsite) and another 1km to Adolphus Lake in Jasper National Park. The most popular campsites are the *Berg Lake* (19.6km) and *Rearguard* (20.1km) campsites on Berg Lake itself; but if you've got a Jasper backcountry permit you could press on to Adolphus where there's a less-frequented site with more in the way of solitude.

Once you're camped at Berg Lake, a popular day-trip is to Toboggan Falls, which starts from the southerly *Berg Lake* campsite and climbs the northeast (left) side of Toboggan Creek past a series of cascades and meadows to eventual views over the lake's entire hinterland. The trail peters out after 2km, but you can easily walk on and upward through open meadows for still better views. The second trail in the immediate vicinity is Robson Glacier (2km), a level walk that peels off south from the main trail 1km west of Robson Pass near the park ranger's cabin. It runs across an outwash plain to culminate in a small lake at the foot of the glacier; a rougher track then follows the lateral moraine on the glacier's east side, branching east after 3km to follow a small stream to the summit of Snowbird Pass (9km total from the ranger's cabin).

Two more hikes start from Yellowhead Lake, at the other (eastern) end of the park. To get to the trailhead for **Yellowhead Mountain** (4.5km one-way; 715m ascent), an excellent day-hike, follow Hwy 16 for 9km down from the pass and then take a gravel road 1km on an isthmus across the lake. After a steep two-hour climb through forest, the trail levels out in open country at 1830m, offering sweeping views of the Yellowhead Pass area. The **Mount Fitzwilliam Trail** (13km one-way; 945m ascent), which leaves Hwy 16 about 1km east of the Yellowhead Mountain Trail (but on the other side of the highway), is a more demanding walk, especially over its last half, but if you don't want to backpack to the endpoint – a truly spectacular basin of lakes and peaks – you could easily walk through the forest to the campsite at Rockingham Creek (6km).

Practicalities

Trains don't stop anywhere in the park, but if you're travelling by bus you can ask to be let off at Yellowhead Pass or the **Mount Robson Information Centre** (June to early Sept daily 9am–7pm; ☎250/566-4325 or 1-800/689-9025), located at the Mount Robson viewpoint near the western entrance to the park. Most of the park's few other facilities are found near the infocentre: a **café/garage** (May–Sept) and two fully serviced commercial **campsites** – *Emperor Ridge* (☎250/566-8438; $18; mid-May to early Oct), 300m north of Hwy 16 on Kinney Lake Rd, and *Robson Shadows Campground* (☎250/566-9190 or 1-888/566-4821; $14.50; mid-May to early Oct), 25 nice sites on the

Fraser River side of Hwy 16, 5km west of the park boundary. The 144-site *Mount Robson Provincial Park Campground* (☏250/566-4325; $17.50; mid-May to early Oct) comprises two closely adjacent campsites – *Robson River* and *Robson Meadows* – and is situated further afield on Hwy 16, 22km north of Valemount. It offers hot showers and flush toilets; reservations can be made in advance (see box above). Another park campsite with the same name and the tag "Lucerne" (which has no reservations, dry toilets only and no showers; $12; May–Sept) is situated 10km west of the Alberta border on Hwy 16, just west of the eastern boundary of the Mount Robson Provincial Park.

The only other beds in or near the park are *Mountain River Lodge* (☏250/566-9899 or 1-888/566-9899, ⓦwww.mtrobson.com; ❹), a B&B with five different rooms; the eighteen log-sided riverfront units (some with kitchens for $5 extra) at the *Mount Robson Lodge* (☏250/566-4821 or 1-888/566-4821, ⓦwww.mountrobsonlodge.com; ❹; May–Oct), which also organizes meals, river rafting, helicopter tours and horse riding; and the cabins belonging to Mount Robson Adventure Holidays (☏250/566-4351; ❸; June–Sept), 16km east of the infocentre (towards Jasper), though preference for these may go to people signed up for the company's **canoeing** and **hiking** day-trips. **Backcountry camping** in the park is only permitted at seven wilderness campsites dotted along the Berg Lake Trail (see box p.743); to use these you have to register and pay an overnight fee at the infocentre.

Yoho National Park

Wholly in British Columbia on the western side of the Continental Divide from Lake Louise, **YOHO NATIONAL PARK**'s name derives from a Cree word meaning "wonder" – a fitting testament to the awesome grandeur of the region's mountains, lakes and waterfalls. At the same time it's a small park, whose intimate scale makes it perhaps the finest of the four parks and the one favoured by Rockies' connoisseurs. The Trans-Canada divides Yoho neatly in half, climbing from Lake Louise over the **Kicking Horse Pass** to share the broad, glaciated valley bottom of the Kicking Horse River with the old Canadian Pacific Railway. The only village, **Field**, has the park centre, services

Although in BC, Yoho runs on **Mountain time**.

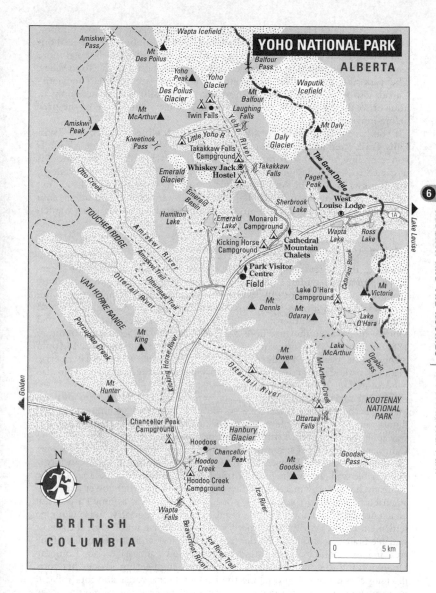

and limited accommodation (the nearest full-service towns are Lake Louise, 28km east, and **Golden**, 54km west). Other expensive accommodation is available at the central hubs, **Lake O'Hara**, the **Yoho Valley** and **Emerald Lake**, from which radiate most of the park's stunning and well-maintained trails – **hiking** in Yoho is magnificent – and a couple of lodges just off the Trans-Canada. Thus these areas – not Field – are the focal points of the park, and get very busy in summer. Side roads lead to Emerald Lake and the Yoho Valley, so if you choose you can drive in, do a hike and then move on at night.

Access to Lake O'Hara is far more difficult, being reserved for those on foot, or those with lodge or campsite reservations, who must book for a special bus (full details are on p.752). The other five park-run campsites are all much more readily accessible, and there's a single road-accessible hostel in the Yoho Valley. The park also operates six backcountry campsites (see p.748). The Trans-Canada also gives direct access to short but scenic trails; as these take only an hour or so, they're the best choice if you only want a quick taste of the park before moving on.

If you have time for one day walk, make it the **Iceline–Whaleback–Twin Falls Trail**, rated among the top five day-hikes in the Rockies (see p.750). If you're cycling, note that **mountain biking** – very popular in the park – is restricted to several designated trails only: these are Kicking Horse (19.5km); the Amiskwi Trail to the Amiskwi River crossing (24km); the Otterhead Trail to Toche Ridge junction (8km); Ice River to Lower Ice Ridge warden cabin (17.5km); the Talley-Ho Trail (3km); and the Ottertail Trail as far as the warden cabin (14.7km).

Field

No more than a few wooden houses backed by an amphitheatre of sheer-dropped mountains, **FIELD** looks like an old-world pioneer settlement, little changed from its 1884 origins as a railroad-construction camp (named after Cyrus Field, sponsor of the first transatlantic communication cable, who visited Yoho that year). As in other national parks, it was the railway that first spawned tourism in the area: the first hotel in Field was built by Canadian Pacific in 1886, and within a few months sixteen square kilometres at the foot of Mount Stephen (the peak to Field's east) had been set aside as a special reserve. National park status arrived in 1911, making Yoho the second of Canada's national parks.

Passenger services (other than private excursions) no longer come through Field, but the **railway** is still one of the park "sights", and among the first things you see whether you enter the park from east or west. That it came this way at all was the result of desperate political and economic horse trading. The Canadian Pacific's chief surveyor, Sandford Fleming, wrote of his journey over the proposed Kicking Horse Pass route in 1883: "I do not think I can forget that terrible walk; it was the greatest trial I ever experienced." Like many in the company he was convinced the railway should take the much lower and more amenable Yellowhead route to the north. The railway was as much a political as a transportational tool, and designed to unite the country and encourage settlement of the prairies. A northerly route would have ignored great tracts of valuable prairie near the US border (around Calgary), and allowed much of the area and its resources (later found to include oil and gas) to slip from the Dominion into the hands of the US. Against all engineering advice, therefore, the railway was cajoled into taking the Kicking Horse route, and thus obliged to negotiate four-percent grades, the greatest of any commercial railway of the time.

The result was the infamous **Spiral Tunnels**, two vast figure-of-eight galleries within the mountains; from a popular viewpoint about 7km east of Field on Hwy 1, you can watch the front of goods trains emerge from the tunnels before the rear wagons have even entered. Still more notorious was the **Big Hill**, where the line drops 330m in just 6km from Wapta Lake to the flats east of Field (the 4.5% grade was the steepest in North America). The very first construction train to attempt the descent plunged into the canyon, killing three railway workers. Runaways became so common that four blasts on a whistle became the standard warning for trains careering out of control (the rusted wreck of an engine can still be seen near the main *Kicking Horse Park Campground*). Lady Agnes MacDonald, wife of the Canadian prime minister, rode down the Big Hill on the front cowcatcher (a metal frame in front of the locomotive to scoop off animals) in 1886, remarking that it presented a "delightful opportunity for a new sensation". She'd already travelled around 1000km on her unusual perch; her lily-livered husband, with whom she was meant to be sharing the symbolic trans-Canada journey to commemorate the opening of the railway, managed just 40km on the cowcatcher. Trains climbing the hill required four locomotives to pull a mere fifteen coaches; the ascent took over an hour, and exploding boilers (and resulting deaths) were recurrent.

The Burgess Shales

Yoho today ranks as highly among geologists as it does among hikers and railway buffs, thanks to the world-renowned **Burgess Shales**, an almost unique geological formation situated close to Field village. The shales – layers of sedimentary rock – lie on the upper slopes of Mount Field and consist of the fossils of some 120 types of soft-bodied marine creatures from the Middle Cambrian period (515–530 million years ago), one of only three places in the world where the remains of these unusual creatures are found. Soft-bodied creatures usually proved ill-suited to the fossilization process, but in the Burgess Shales the fossils are so well preserved and detailed that in some cases scientists can identify what the creatures were eating before they died. Plans are in hand to open a major new museum in Field devoted to the shales, but in the meantime access is restricted to protect the fossils, and fossil-hunting, needless to say, is strictly prohibited. The area can only be seen on two **guided hikes** to Walcott's Quarry (760m ascent; 20km round-trip; departs 8am Fri–Mon; $59) and the trilobite beds on Mount Stephen (780m ascent; 6km round-trip; departs 10am Sat & Sun; $26.75). The walks – note the considerable ascents involved – are led by qualified guides, limited to fifteen people and run between late June and October. For details and reservations, contact the Yoho Burgess Shale Foundation (T 1-800/343-3006, W www.burgess-shale.bc.ca). Phone reservations can be made only Mon–Fri 10am–3.30pm.

Practicalities

Yoho's **park information centre**, marked by a distinctive blue roof about 1km east of Field (daily: mid-May to late June & Sept 9am–5pm; late June to Aug 9am–7pm; Oct to mid-May 9am–4pm; T 250/343-6783, W www.pc.gc.ca), sells park permits ($7), makes backcountry registrations, takes bookings for Lake O'Hara (see p.749), has displays, lectures and slide shows (notably on the famous Burgess Shales), and advises on trail and climbing conditions. It also gives out a useful *Backcountry Guide* with full details of all trails and sells 1:50,000 **maps** of the park. Backcountry camping requires a permit, and if you intend to camp at Lake O'Hara it's essential to make **reservations** at the information centre. The Park Administration Building in Field offers similar help and services in and out of season (Mon–Fri 8am–4.30pm; T 250/343-6100). Enquire at the park centre for details of activities arranged by the "Friends of Yoho" (T 250/343-6393; information also available on Parks Canada website) and the two free guided walks: "Emerald Lakeshore Stroll" (July to late Aug Sat 10am; 2hr 30min; 5km; meet at Emerald Lake Trailhead) and "Walk into the Past" (July & Aug Mon & Thurs 7pm; 1hr 30min; meet at the Old Bake oven at *Kicking Horse Campground*). Other park-run activities include Kicking Horse Campground Theatre (July & Aug Sat, Sun & Tues at 9pm, 8pm last ten days of Aug) and wildlife and other talks at the Hoodoo Creek Campfire Circle (July & Aug Mon & Fri 9pm, 8pm last ten days of Aug).

Whatever other literature may say, there are now no VIA Rail passenger **trains** to Field. The village is, however, a flag stop for Greyhound **buses** (5 daily in each direction) – wave them down from the Petro-Canada just east of the turn-off from the highway to the village, though most stop anyway to drop packages.

Accommodation

Yoho's popularity and accessibility mean there is huge pressure on **accommodation** in late July and August: if you're really stuck, you can always make for one of the motels in Golden (see p.754). The only officially listed **rooms** in Field itself, a fine base if you have transport, are at the excellent *Kicking Horse Lodge*, 100 Centre St (☎250/343-6303 or 1-800/659-4944, ⓦwww .kickinghorselodge.net; ❺), though you can also try one of the recent spate of fully furnished suites in private homes – of which there were twelve dotted around the village at last count. These are all similarly priced – either $95 or $125 for a double – and of a similar arrangement: a private entrance, usually only one or two rooms; non-smoking; some cooking provisions; and all within a few minutes' walk of each other in Field's small grid of streets. They are: *Alpenglow Guesthouse* 306 Kickinghorse Ave (☎250/343-6356, ⓔalpenglow@redshift.bc.ca; ❹); *Bear's Den Guesthouse*, 414 1st St W (☎250/343-6439, ⓔzirke@rockies.net); *Canadian Rockies Guesthouse*, 308 Stephen Ave (☎250/343-6046; ❺); *Coyote's Den Guesthouse*, 213 2nd Ave (☎250/343-6034; ❹); *Lynx Lair*, 412 1st Ave (☎250/343-6421; ❹); *Mount Burgess Inn*, 314 Kickinghorse Ave (☎250/343-6480, ⓔmtburgess@telus .net; ❹); *Mount Stephen Guesthouse*, 343 Kickinghorse Ave (☎250/343-6441, ⓔsuncity@rockies.net; ❹); *Old Church Inn*, 308 Kickinghorse Ave (☎250/343-6345, ⓔnikki@rockies.net; ❹); *Spiral Tunnels Guesthouse*, 306 1st Ave (☎250/343-6067 or 1-877/FIELD-BC, ⓔspirals@rockies.net; ❺); *Sunset Guesthouse*, 416 1st Ave (☎250/343-6333, ⓔsunsetgh@rockies.net; ❹); *Wildflower Guesthouse*, 303 Kickinghorse Ave (☎250/343-6707; ❹); and *Yoho Accommodation*, 310A 1st Ave (☎250/343-6444 or 343-6445; ❹). All are easily found in the tiny village, most lying on the central 1st Ave or parallel Kicking Horse Ave.

Away from the village, but on or just off the Trans-Canada (Hwy 1), are the 21 units of *Cathedral Mountain Chalets* (☎250/343-6442, ⓦwww.cathedralmountain .com; ❼; June to mid-Oct), 4km east of Field and fifteen minutes' drive from Lake Louise (leave the highway at the Takakkaw Falls turn-off), and the bigger and less expensive fifty-room *West Louise Lodge* (☎250/343-6311, 1-888/682-2212 or 1-800/258-7669, ⓔwestlouiselodge@skilouise.com; ❺) just inside the park boundary, 11km west of Lake Louise (with café, restaurant and indoor pool). There's also the **hostel** in the Yoho Valley (see p.753), perfectly situated for many superb walks, and an expensive lodge at Emerald Lake.

The most central of the five park-run **campsites**, the 92-site *Kicking Horse* ($22; late June to Sept), lies 3km east of Field just off the Trans-Canada (Hwy 1) near the junction with Yoho Valley Rd for Takakkaw Falls. It's fully serviced (coin showers) and pleasingly forested, though it echoes somewhat with goods trains rumbling through day and night. In summer a separate overflow site is often opened (no showers), but even this fills up and you should aim to arrive extremely early. Remember: all park campsites are first-come, first-served. A short distance east up Yoho Valley Rd is the second of the park's major campsites, the 46-site *Monarch* ($14; mid–May to early Sept); the third, the 35-site *Takakkaw Falls* ($14; late June to first snow), lies at the end of the same road (17km from Field and 300m from the falls' day-use car park) by the eponymous falls (great views from many pitches) and is the best-placed for local hikes (see box overleaf). The remaining site is close to the park's western border, lying just north of the Trans-Canada: the 106-site *Hoodoo Creek* (no showers; $14; late June to early Sept. An additional fee of $5 is charged at all campsites for use of firewood.

The six **backcountry campsites** are *McArthur Creek* (ten sites); *Float Creek* (four sites); *Yoho Lake* (eight sites); *Laughing Falls* (eight sites); *Twin Falls* (eight sites); and *Little Yoho* (ten sites). The only facilities are privies (except *Float Creek*) and bear poles. All of these campsites are popular, but unlike the front country campsites (where it's first-come, first-served) between one and three sites at each campsite can be reserved ($12 fee) up to 21 days in advance through the park centre at Field. **Random camping** is allowed in the Amiskwi, Otterhead, Lower Ice River and Porcupine valleys, but check current closures: you must be at least 3km from any road, 100m from water, 50m from a trail and purchase the usual $8 backcountry pass.

Lake O'Hara

Backed up against the Continental Divide at the eastern edge of the park, **Lake O'Hara** is one of the Rockies' finest all-round enclaves – with staggering scenery, numerous lakes, and an immense diversity of alpine and subalpine terrain. It's a great base for concentrated hiking: you could easily spend a fortnight exploring the well-constructed trails that strike out from the central lodge and campsite. The setting is matchless, the lake framed by two of the peaks that also overlook Lake Louise across the ridge – mounts Lefroy (3423m) and Victoria

6

Hikes from Lake O'Hara

For walking purposes the **Lake O'Hara region** divides into five basic zones, each of which deserves a full day of exploration: Lake Oesa, the Opabin Plateau (this area and others are often closed to protect their grizzlies), Lake McArthur, the Odaray Plateau and the Duchesnay Basin.

If you have time to do only one day-hike, the classic (if not the most walked) trails are the **Wiwaxy Gap** (12km; 495m ascent), rated by some among the top five day-walks in the Canadian Rockies, or the **Opabin Plateau Trail** (3.2km one-way; 250m ascent), from the *Lake O'Hara Lodge* to Opabin Lake. Despite the latter's brevity, you could spend hours wandering the plateau's tiny lakes and alpine meadows on the secondary trails that crisscross the area. Most people return to O'Hara via the **East Circuit Trail**, but a still more exhilarating hike – and a good day's outing – is to walk the **Yukness Ledge**, a section of the Alpine Circuit (see below) that cuts up from the East Circuit just 400m after leaving Opabin Lake. This spectacular high-level route leads to the beautiful Lake Oesa, from where it's just 3.2km down to Lake O'Hara. Oesa is one of many beautiful lakes in the region, and the **Lake Oesa Trail** (3.2km one-way; 240m ascent) from Lake O'Hara is the single most walked path in the O'Hara area. Close behind comes the **Lake McArthur Trail** (3.5km one-way; 310m ascent) which leads to the largest and most photographed of the lakes in the Lake O'Hara area. The **Odaray Plateau Trail** (2.6km one-way; 280m ascent) is another highly rated, but rather overpopular hike.

The longest and least-walked path is the **Linda Lake–Cathedral Basin** trip, past several lakes to a great viewpoint at Cathedral Platform Prospect (7.4km one-way; 305m ascent). The most challenging hike is the high-level **Alpine Circuit** (11.8km), taking in Oesa, Opabin and Schaffer lakes. This is straightforward in fine weather, and when all the snow has melted; very fit and experienced walkers should have little trouble, though there's considerable exposure, and some scrambling is required. At other times it's best left to climbers, or left alone completely.

Yoho Valley and Emerald Lake hikes

Most trails in the **Yoho Valley area** start from the Takakkaw Falls campsite and car park at the end of the Yoho Valley Rd. Many of the area's trails connect, and some run over the ridge to the Emerald Lake region, offering numerous permutations. We've tried to highlight the very best. If you want a stroll from the main trailhead at the campsite after a drive or cycle, then walk to **Point Lace Falls** (1.9km one-way; minimum ascent) or **Laughing Falls** (3.8km one-way; 60m gain). Another shortish, extremely popular walk from the same car park is the **Yoho Pass** (10.9km; 310m ascent, 510m height loss), which links to Emerald Lake and its eponymous lodge (though you'll need transport arranged at the lake). A southern branch from this hike will take you over the Burgess Pass and down into Field, another manageable day-trip with fine overviews of the entire area.

If you want to follow the most tramped path in the Yoho Valley, however, take the **Twin Falls Trail** (8.5km one-way; 290m ascent) from the Takakkaw Falls car park. This easy six-hour return journey passes the Laughing Falls and has the reward of the Twin Falls cataract at the end, plus fine scenery and other lesser waterfalls en route. Stronger walkers could continue over the highly recommended **Whaleback Trail** (4.5km one-way; 1hr 30min) to give some quite incredible views of the glaciers at the valley head. A complete circuit returning to Takakkaw Falls with the Whaleback is 20.1km.

If you're allowing yourself just one big walk in Yoho it's going to be a hard choice between the Takakkaw Falls–Twin Falls–Whaleback Trail just described or the **Iceline–Little Yoho Valley–(Whaleback)–Twin Falls** combination. The latter is often cited as one of the top five day-walks in the Rockies, and on balance might be the one to go for, though both options duplicate parts of one another's route. The Iceline (695m vertical gain), specially built in 1987, also starts close to the Takakkaw Falls car park at the *Whiskey Jack* hostel, climbing west through a large avalanche path onto a level bench with jaw-dropping views of the Emerald Glacier above and the Daly Glacier across the valley. It contours above Lake Celeste (a trail drops to this lake, making a shorter 17km circuit in all back to the car park) and then drops to the Little Yoho Valley and back to Takakkaw Falls for a 19.8-kilometre circuit. If you're very fit (or can camp overnight to break the trip), tagging on the Whaleback before returning to Takakkaw Falls makes a sensational 27-kilometre walk with 1000m of ascent. Most people will want to do this as a backpacking option (there are four backcountry sites up here) – and they don't come much better – though the Iceline–Little Yoho walk coupled with the trek west to the **Kiwetinok Pass** (30km; 1070m) is also in many people's list of top-five day/backpacking Rocky Mountain walks. Juggling further with the permutations brings the Whaleback into this last combination to make one of the best backpacking routes in the Rockies: Iceline–Little Yoho Valley–Kiwetinok Pass–Whaleback (35.5km; 1375m ascent), a route up there with the Rockwall Trail in Kootenay, Skyline in Jasper and Berg Lake in Mount Robson Provincial Park.

From Emerald Lake, if you just want a stroll, then follow the self-guided and wheelchair-accessible **nature trail** (4.6km circuit; minimal ascent) around the lake from the parking area to the bridge at the back of the lake. Even shorter is the trail from the entrance to the parking area to **Hamilton Falls** (1.6km return; minimal ascent). The best day-trip is the comparatively underused but interesting **Hamilton Lake Trail** (5.5km one-way; 850m vertical; 2–3hr), again leaving from the parking area at the end of Emerald Lake Rd. It's demanding and steep in places, and confined to forest for the first hour or so – thereafter it's magnificent, culminating in a classic alpine lake. The more modest climb to **Emerald Basin**, which you could manage in half a day (4.3km one-way; 300m vertical; 1–2hr), also gives relative peace and quiet, following the lakeshore before climbing through a forest of yew and hemlock, and ending in a small, rocky amphitheatre of hanging glaciers and avalanche paths.

Hikes from the Trans-Canada

Five short walks can be accessed off the **Trans-Canada Highway** as it passes through Yoho. From east to west these are: **Ross Lake** (1.3km), a stunning little walk given the loveliness of the lake and the ease with which you reach it (accessed 1km south of the Great Divide picnic area); **Sherbrooke Lake** (3.1km), a peaceful subalpine lake accessible from the Wapta Lake picnic area (5km west of the Great Divide), where stronger walkers can peel off after 1.4km to Paget Lookout for huge views of the Kicking Horse Valley (3.5km; 520m ascent); **Mount Stephen Fossil Beds** (2.7km), a short but very steep trail, for fossil lovers only, from 1st St East in Field; **Hoodoo Creek** (3.1km), on the western edge of the park (22km west of Field), accessed from the 600-metre gravel road from the *Hoodoo Creek* campsite (the steep path leads to the weirdly eroded hoodoos themselves, pillars of glacial debris topped by protective capping stones); and finally **Wapta Falls** (2.4km), an excellent and almost level forty-minute walk on a good trail to Yoho's largest waterfalls (by volume of water), accessed via a 1.6-kilometre dirt road 25km west of Field.

(3464m). The one problem is **access**, which is severely restricted to safeguard the mountain flora and fauna.

To get there, turn off the Trans-Canada onto Hwy 1A (3.2km west of the Continental Divide), cross the railway and turn right onto the gravel road leading to the parking area (1km). This fire road continues all the way up to the lake (13km), but it's not open to general traffic (or bikes: **no bikes** are allowed on the road or anywhere else in the Lake O'Hara region). Getting up here, therefore, is quite a performance, but worth it if you want to hike some of the continent's most stunning scenery. Anybody can walk the 13km up the road, or the more picturesque **Cataract Brook Trail** (12.9km), which runs roughly parallel to the road, but a quota system applies for the bus up here and the campsite at the end; and, after 13km, of course, you'd need to be superfit to get in any meaningful walking in the area where it matters. Aim instead for the special **bus** from the car park up to the lake, but note that priority is given to those with reservations or those with reservations for the lodge, campsite or Alpine Club huts. Reservations for bus and campsite can be made three months in advance by phone only (mid-March to April Mon–Thurs 8am–noon & 1–4pm; May Mon–Fri 8am–noon & 1–4pm; mid-June to Aug daily 8am–4pm; Sept reduced hours; ☎250/343-6433). If you're going **for the day**, your only feasible buses leave at 8.30am and 10.30am (there are also 3.30pm and 5.30pm departures, with returns at 9.30am, 11.30am, 2.30pm, 4.30pm and 6.30pm from mid-June to early Oct; and outbound at 10am and 3pm and returns at 11am and 4pm for the rest of Oct), and the maximum number in a party is six. If you want to use the campsite you have to have dates ready (up to a maximum of four nights), state the number of people, the number of sites required (maximum of two per party, one tent per site) and your preferred bus time (first and second choices from 8.30am, 10.30am, 4.30pm or 7.30pm). The reservation fee for bus (day-use or camp) is $12 and the return bus fare $15, payable by credit card over the phone. Cancellation must be made to an answering machine (☎250/343-6344); you forfeit your booking fee, and you can't just cancel the first day of several you booked to camp and expect to come later. Cancellations made less than three days in advance mean you lose the booking fee, half the bus fare and, if you're camping, the first night's campsite fee ($8 per person per night). Cancel after 4pm on the day before your trip and you lose everything.

If all this sounds horribly complicated, remember the park does merit attention, but if you don't manage to plan in advance there are arrangements for **stand-bys**: six day-use places are available daily and three to five sites are kept available each night. You must reserve at the Field park information centre in person the day *before* you wish to take the bus and/or camp; these places are *not* available over the phone, and you'll have to get to the centre early. To stay in one of the 23 rooms at *Lake O'Hara Lodge* (☎250/343-6418, Ⓦwww.lakeoharalodge.com; ❾; mid-June to late Sept & Feb to mid-April), you need to reserve weeks in advance and be prepared to part with a large amount of money. Out of season you can book on ☎250/678-4110.

The Yoho Valley and Emerald Lake

Less compact an area than Lake O'Hara, the **Yoho Valley** and nearby **Emerald Lake** are far more accessible for casual visitors, and offer some great sights – the Takakkaw Falls in particular – and a variety of top-rated trails. Both areas were formerly used by the Cree to hide their women and children while the men crossed the mountains into Alberta to trade and hunt buffalo. The

Mont Des Poilus 3161m

Yoho Glacier

Yoho Peak

Waterfall Valley

Mt Balfour 3246m

ALBERTA

Des Poilus Glacier

BRITISH COLUMBIA

Waputik Icefield

Mt Pollinge

Twin Falls

Little Yoho River

Kiwetinok Pass

Duchesnay Lake

Lake Celeste

Emerald Glacier

Daly Glacier

Mt Niles

The President 3139m

Takakkaw Falls Campground

Takakkaw Falls

Whiskey Jack Hostel

Mt Carnarvon 3042m

Emerald Basin

Yoho Pass

Kiwetinok River

Yoho River

Mt Ogden 2684m

Emerald Peak 2545m

Yoho Lake

Wapta Mtn 2788m

Sherbrooke Lake

Hamilton Lake

Emerald Lake

Mt Field 2638m

Monarch Campground

Amiskwi River

Hamilton Falls

Emerald Lake Lodge

Burgess Pass

Kicking Horse Campground

N

Emerald River

Mt Burgess 2583m

Lake Louise & Banff

Kicking Horse River

0   5 km

Field

Mt Stephen

Cathedral Mtn

Golden

eradication of the buffalo herds, and the arrival of the railway in 1884, put paid to such ways. The lake was "discovered" by Tom Wilson, the same Canadian Pacific employee who first saw Lake Louise. He named it Emerald Lake after its colour. Now the lake and valley combine to form one of the Rockies' most important backpacking zones. Though popular and easily reached – access roads head north from the Trans-Canada to both the Emerald and Yoho valleys – the region is not, however, quite as crowded as its counterpart to the south. The scenery is equally mesmerizing, and if fewer of the trails are designed for day-hikes, many of them interlock so that you can tailor walks to suit your schedule or fitness (see box on p.750).

Most trails start from the end of the Yoho Valley Rd at the **Takakkaw Falls** parking area; the road leaves the Trans-Canada about 5km east of Field (signed from the *Kicking Horse* campsite), a narrow and switchbacking route unsuitable for trailers and RVs and open in the summer only. It's 14km from the Trans-Canada to the parking area. The cascades' total 254-metre drop makes them among the most spectacular road-accessible falls in the mountains: *takakkaw* is a Cree word roughly meaning "it is wonderful". The *Whiskey Jack* HI **hostel**,

ideally placed just beyond the end of the Yoho Valley Rd, 500m south of Takakkaw Falls, has room for 27 in three dorms (℡250/670-7580 or 1-888/762-4122, ⓦwww.hihostels.ca; ❶; dorms $19; mid-June to mid-Oct). Close by is the park-run *Takakkaw Falls* **campsite** with 35 unserviced sites ($14; mid-June to mid-Sept). Trails to the north (see box p.750) lead to four further backcountry campsites, while the Alpine Club of Canada operates a members-only trail hut 8.5km north of Takakkaw Falls ($15); reservations are required on ℡250/762-4481.

The Emerald Lake Rd leaves the Trans-Canada about 2km west of Field and ends, 8km on, at the *Emerald Lake Lodge* (℡250/343-6321 or 1-800/663-6336, ⓦwww.crmr.com; ❽), which has a **restaurant** where walking boots are certainly not in order, and a less formal **bar** for drinks and snacks. If you want to stay, advance reservations are essential and prices are steep – between $300 and $400 in high season, less outside summer. Like the Yoho Valley Rd, this road offers access to easy strolls and a couple of good day- or half-day hikes (see box p.750).

Golden

GOLDEN, 54km west of Field and midway between Yoho and Glacier national parks, is the nearest town to either. Despite its name and mountain backdrop, the part of Golden most people see is little more than an ugly ribbon of motels and garages at the junction of Hwy 1 and Hwy 95. The town proper occupies a semi-scenic site down by the Columbia River, way below the highway strip, but only if you use the municipal campsite, use one of the enormous number of motels, or book one of the many rafting and other **tours** based here will you do anything but look down on it from above. Note that finding places in Golden can be difficult if you don't know that all the "South" streets are on one side of the river, all the "North" streets on the other.

Much is likely to change here in the next few years, however, following approval of plans to develop **Kicking Horse** (℡1-888/706-1117, ⓦwww.kickinghorseresort.com), the most significant new BC **ski resort** in decades since the creation of Blackcomb at Whistler. The resort is still expanding, but there is already enough here to suggest that it will one day be in the same league as Lake Louise or Whistler, but without – at least for a while – the crowds. The resort is 13km from Golden itself, with a state-of-the-art eight-person gondola (12 minutes to a pair of fine alpine bowls) and a vertical rise of 1245m. On-hill accommodation is planned.

Golden has a small **museum** at 1302-11th St (July & Aug daily 9am–5pm; $3). The main **infocentre** is at 500-10th Ave N (year-round; ℡250/344-7125 or 1-800/622-4635, ⓦwww.goldenchamber.bc.ca), but a small infocentre also usually opens in summer at the strip's southern end (June–Sept). Some 200m north is the **bus terminal**, next to the Chinese-Canadian *Golden Palace Restaurant* – open 24 hours a day, like several of the local joints. All the **motels** on the strip, like the *Selkirk Inn*, Hwy 1 (℡250/344-6315 or 344-5153, ⓦwww.selkirkinn.com; ❸), look over the road or onto the backs of garages opposite. None has anything you could call a view of the mountains, but at least the big *Sportsman*, 1200-12th St N (℡250/344-2915 or 1-888/477-6783, ⓦwww.sportsmanmotel.net; ❸), is off the road. Around 16km northwest of Golden, the *Blaeberry Mountain Lodge*, on Moberly School Rd (℡250/344-5296, ⓦwww.blaeberrymountainlodge.bc.ca; ❹), is first-rate and beautifully situated; accommodation consists of simple but comfortable log cabins and a lodge. There are also plenty of outdoor activities and the owners will often pick

you up in Golden if you're travelling without your own transport. Down in the town proper, a good place to **eat** standard Canadian fare like salads, chicken, pasta and seafood is the *Turning Point*, 902 11th Ave S.

Campsites have prettier settings, particularly the *Whispering Spruce* (☎250/344–6680, Ⓦwww.whisperingspruce.net; $14–17; mid-April to mid-Oct) at 1430 Golden View Rd on Hwy 1 2km east of the Hwy 95 intersection. The town's own site, the *Golden Municipal Campground* (☎250/344-5412, Ⓔesutter @redshift.bc.ca; $14–17; mid-May to mid-Oct), is on the banks of the river at 1407 9th St, three blocks east of the main street. It has flush toilets, hot showers, wash houses, firewood and is adjacent to a swimming pool and tennis courts.

Glacier National Park

Strictly speaking, **GLACIER NATIONAL PARK** is part of the Selkirk and Columbia Mountains rather than the Rockies, but on the ground little sets it apart from the magnificence of the other national parks, and all the park agencies include it on an equal footing with its larger neighbours. It is, however, to a great extent the domain of ice, rain and snow; the weather is so atrocious that locals like to say that it rains or snows four days out of every three, and in truth you can expect a soaking three days out of five. As the name suggests, **glaciers** – 422 of them – form its dominant landscape, with fourteen percent of the park permanently blanketed with ice or snow. Scientists have identified 68 new glaciers forming on the sites of previously melted ice sheets in the park – a highly uncommon phenomenon. The main ice sheet, the still-growing **Illecillewaet Neve**, is easily seen from the Trans-Canada Highway or from the park visitor centre.

The Columbia range's peaks are every bit as imposing as those of the Rockies – Glacier's highest point, **Mount Dawson**, is 3390m tall – and historically they've presented as much of a barrier as their neighbours. Aboriginal peoples and then railwaymen shunned the icefields and the rugged interior for centuries until the discovery of **Rogers Pass** (1321m) in 1881 by Major A.B. Rogers, the chief engineer of the Canadian Pacific. Suffering incredible hardships, navvies drove the railway over the pass by 1885, paving the way for trains that, until 1916, helped to open the region both to settlers and tourists. Despite the railway's best efforts the pounding of repeated avalanches eventually forced the company to bore a tunnel under the pass, and the flow of visitors fell to almost nothing. In the 1950s the pass was chosen as the route for the Trans-Canada Highway, whose completion in 1962 once again made the area accessible. This time huge snowsheds were built, backed up by the world's largest **avalanche-control system**. Experts monitor the slopes year-round, and at dangerous times they call in the army, who blast howitzers into the mountains to dislodge potential slips.

Glacier is easy enough to get to, but it doesn't tie in well with a circuit of the other parks; many people end up traversing it at some point simply because the main route west passes this way, but comparatively few stop, preferring to admire the scenery from the road. The visitor centre is a flag stop for Greyhound **buses**, which zip through up to seven times a day in each direction.

The Glacier and Revelstoke parks, like most of the rest of BC, run on **Pacific time**, one hour behind Yoho NP and Alberta.

GLACIER NATIONAL PARK

Golden

Heather

N

Nordic

Mountain Creek

Park Gate

☩ Picnic area

Interpretive trail

Glacier

Alpine area

Rogers Hermit

Bear Creek
Falls

Grizzly Creek

Sifton Tupper

Ursus
Minor Grizzly

Connaught Creek

Ursus Creek

Casualty Creek

Macdonald

Beaver River

Cookenham Creek Trail

Ursus
Major Rogers Pass
Visitor Centre

Avalanche
Crest

McGill

Cheops

Illecillewaet
Campground

Cougar

Illecillewaet R.

Uto

Sir Donald

Bostock Creek Trail

Illecillewaet River

Loop Brook
Campground

Loop Brook

Beaver River Trail

Fidelity

Abbot's
Ridge

Flat Creek

Flat Creek Trail

Bonney

Illecillewaet
Neve

Smart

Jupiter Youngs

Macoun

Slick

Fox

Fortitude

Incomappleux River

Dawson

Deville
Neve

Wheeler

0   5 km

Purity

Virtue   Charity

Grand

Revelstoke National Park

Practicalities

The **Rogers Pass visitor centre** (daily: April to mid-June & mid-Sept to Oct 9am–5pm; mid-June to mid-Sept 8/9am–8/9pm; Nov Thurs–Mon 9am–5pm; Dec–March 7am–5pm; ☎250/837-6274 or 837-7500, ⓦwww.pc.gc.ca), 1km west of Rogers Pass, is a draw in itself, attracting some 160,000 visitors annually. It sells park permits ($7) and houses a variety of high-tech audiovisual aids, including a fun video on avalanche control called *Snow Wars*. In summer (July

Hiking in Glacier National Park

Glacier's primary renown is among serious climbers, but **day-hikers** and **backpackers** have plenty of options. Some of the park's 21 trails (140km of walking in all) push close to glaciers for casual views of the ice – though only two spots are now safe at the toe of the Illecillewaet – and the backcountry is noticeably less busy than in the Big Four parks to the east.

The easiest short strolls off the road are the **Abandoned Rails Trail** (1.2km one-way; 30min), along old rail beds to abandoned snowsheds betweeen the Rogers Pass centre and the Summit Monument (suitable for wheelchairs); the **Loop Trail** (1.6km) from the viewpoint just east of the Loop Brook campsite, full of viewpoints and features relating to the building of the railway; the **Hemlock Grove Boardwalk** (400m), a stroll through old-growth stands of western hemlock trees, some more than 350 years old (wheelchair-accessible; trailhead midway between *Loop Brook* campsite and the park's western boundary); and the **Meeting of the Water Trail** (30min) from the *Illecillewaet* campsite, the hub of Glacier's trail network. Six manageable day-hikes from the campsite give superb views onto the glaciers, particularly the Great Glacier, Avalanche Crest and Abbott's Ridge trails. Other hikes, not centred on the campsite, include **Bostock Creek** (9km) and **Flat Creek** (9km), a pair of paths on the park's western edge heading north and south respectively from the same point on the Trans-Canada.

Among the backpacking routes, the longest is the **Beaver River Trail** (30km-plus), which peels off from the highway at the Mount Shaughnessy picnic area on the eastern edge (also a favourite mountain-bike route). The single best long-haul trail, however, is the **Copperstain Creek Trail** (16km), which leaves the Beaver River path after 3km, and climbs to meadows and bleak alpine tundra from where camping and onward walking options are almost endless.

& Aug), book here for **guided walks** (1–6hr) featuring flowers, wildlife and glaciers, some of them fairly strenuous. Walks start at the Illecillewaet Campground Welcome Station. Also ask about trips to the **Nakimu Caves**, some of the largest in Canada; they were opened to the public (in the company of experienced guides only) in 1995. If you're heading for the backcountry, pick up *Footloose in the Columbias*, a hiker's guide to Glacier and Revelstoke national parks; you can also buy good walking **maps**. Next to the visitor centre, a **garage** and a **shop** are the only services on the Trans-Canada between Golden and Revelstoke, an hour's drive east and west respectively.

Accommodation is best sought in Golden (see p.754). The sole in-park **hotels** are the excellent fifty-room *Best Western Glacier Park Lodge* (☎250/837-2126 or 1-800/528-1234; ❻), located just east of the visitor centre, and the 24-unit *Heather Mountain Lodge* (☎250/344-7490; closed Nov), 20km east of the Pass; both tend to be full in season. The latter has a useful 24-hour service and cafeteria. Other places close to Glacier's borders are the ten-unit *Purcell Lodge* (☎250/344-2639; ❻; mid-June to mid-Oct & mid-Dec to April; two-night minumum stay), a remote lodge at 2180m on the eastern border accessible only by hiking trail, scheduled helicopter flights or winter ski trails; the *Canyon Hot Springs Resort Campground*, 35km east of Revelstoke (☎250/837-2420; cabins ❼, tent sites $19–25; May–Sept), which has mineral hot and warm springs, secluded sites, café, firewood and twelve cabins with B&B deals available; *Hillside Lodge*, 1740 Seward Front Rd (☎250/344-7281; ❹), nine cosy cabins set in sixty acres 13km west of Golden at Blaeberry River with breakfast included; and *Big Lake Resort*, Kinbasket Lake (no phone; rooms ❷, tents $12; May–Oct), 25km west of Golden off Hwy 1 at Donald Station.

6

ALBERTA AND THE ROCKIES | Glacier National Park

The park-run **campsites** are the 57-site *Illecillewaet* ($14; mid-June to early Oct; also winter camping), 3.4km west of the visitor centre just off the Trans-Canada (and the trailhead for eight walks), and the twenty-site *Loop Brook*, 2km farther west ($14; mid-June to mid-Oct; self-serve check-in), which provides the luxuries of wood ($6), water and flush toilets only on a first-come, first-served basis. If you don't manage to get into these, or want more facilities, there are three commercial campsites west of the park on the Trans-Canada towards Revelstoke. Wilderness camping is allowed anywhere if you register with the visitor centre, pay for a nightly backcountry camping permit ($8) and pitch more than 5km from the road.

⑥ Mount Revelstoke National Park

The smallest national park in the region, **MOUNT REVELSTOKE NATIONAL PARK** is a somewhat arbitrary creation, put together at the request of local people in 1914 to protect the Clachnacudainn Range of the Columbia Mountains. The lines on the map mean little, for the thrilling scenery in the 16km of no-man's-land between Glacier and Revelstoke is largely the same as that within the parks. The mountains here are especially steep, their slopes often scythed clear of trees by avalanches. The views from the Trans-Canada, as it peeks out of countless tunnels, are of forests and snow-capped peaks aplenty and, far below, the railway and the Illecillewaet River crashing through a twisting, steep-sided gorge.

The main access to the park interior is the very busy **Summit Road**, or **Summit Parkway** (generally open June or mid-July to Oct), which strikes north from the Trans-Canada at the town of Revelstoke and winds 26km almost to the top of Mount Revelstoke (1938m) through forest and alpine meadows noted for glorious displays of wild flowers (best during July and

Aug).You can also walk this stretch on the **Summit Trail** (10km one-way; 4hr) from the car park at the base of Summit Rd. Damage to the delicate ecosystem has prompted park authorities to rethink, and often the last 2km of the road is closed to cars, leaving the choice of a walk or regular shuttle bus to the summit from a car park at Balsam Lake.There is a park "**welcome station kiosk**" at the start of the road for park information (daily mid-June to Aug long weekend 9am–10pm; Aug long weekend to Oct 9am–6/7pm; information the rest of the year from the small office in Revelstoke post office at 300-3rd St West; year-round Mon–Fri 8.30am–noon & 1–4.30pm).The Summit Parkway itself is open limited hours (mid-June to Aug 9am–10pm; the rest of Aug 7am–8pm; early June, Sept and early Oct 9am–5pm).

Many of the longer of the park's ten official **trails** start from the top of Summit Rd; serious backpackers prefer to head to **Eagle Lake**, off Summit Rd, rather than take the more popular **Miller Lake Trail** (6km one-way).The award-winning **Giant Cedars Trail** is a wooded one-kilometre jaunt with ten interpretive exhibits off the road on the park's eastern edge, its boardwalks negotiating a tract of ancient forest crammed with 800-year-old western red cedars and rough-barked western hemlock (the trailhead begins at the Giant Cedars Picnic Area). You could also try the **Skunk Cabbage Boardwalk** (1.2km), an easy trail through temperate forest and wetland inhabited by muskrat, beaver, numerous birds and the eponymous skunk cabbage. **Meadows in the Sky Trail**, by contrast, is a quick one-kilometre paved loop through alpine meadows at the top of Summit Rd. Look out for the so-called Icebox, a shaded rock cleft that contains what is reputedly the world's smallest glacier. The *Footloose in the Columbias* booklet, available from Glacier's Rogers Pass visitor centre, has further trail information.

Revelstoke

REVELSTOKE, the only community within striking range of the park, sits just outside the western boundary, but in its promotional pitch chooses to ignore its scenic appeal in favour of a somewhat unimpressive claim to be "Home of the World's Largest Sculpted Grizzly Bears" (they stand at Mackenzie Ave at the entrance to downtown). Like many mountain towns, it's divided between a motel-and-garage strip along the Trans-Canada and a dispersed, frontier-type collection of houses some distance away.The river and rugged scenery round about redeem it, and the downtown area also has a nice feel, having been spruced up as a placatory measure following the disaster at the dam site (see p.761). If you're without your own vehicle, note that it's a good twenty-minute walk from the strip. In downtown, you might dip into the small but polished **Revelstoke Railway Museum** (May, June, Sept daily 9am–5pm; July & Aug daily 9am–8pm; April & Oct Mon–Sat 1pm–5pm; Nov Mon–Fri 9am–5pm; Dec–March Mon–Fri 1–5pm; $6), which has a steam engine, snowploughs and assorted memorabilia relating to the building of the stretch of the CPR between Field and Kamloops. If you want to relax close to town, try warm-watered **Williamson Lake**, a favourite swimming spot for locals with mini-golf and campsite 4km south of town east of Airport Way.

Seven daily Greyhound **buses** stop at the town of Revelstoke between Kamloops and Calgary; the terminal is at the west end of the strip, just after the big blue Columbia River bridge (☎250/837-5874).The **infocentre** is 200m beyond on the left at 204 Campbell Ave (daily: May & June 10am–6pm; July & Aug 8am–8pm; ☎250/837-5345, fax 837-4223). Between May and September there's a small additional office where the Trans-Canada and Hwy

23N meet (☎250/837-3522; same hours). Get park information at these offices, or visit the **Park Administration Office** on 3rd St in the **post office** building (park office: Mon–Fri 8.30am–noon & 1–4.30pm; ☎250/837-7500) or the Rogers Pass visitor centre. The park office also has a store for the Friends of Mount Revelstoke National Park (☎250/837-2010) that is useful for **maps** and guides. **Eating** possibilities include the *Frontier Restaurant* on the Trans-Canada, part of the eponymous motel near the infocentre, which serves up superior steak-and-salad meals at reasonable prices, with friendly service and a genuine cowpoke atmosphere. In town, the *One-Twelve Restaurant* in the Regent Inn at 112 Victoria Rd (☎250/837-2107) is a favourite, with good food, a lively pub and dance floor.

A far more amenable place to stay than Golden, the town of Revelstoke has plenty of **accommodation** – fifteen-plus motels and half a dozen campsites. Backcountry camping in the park is free, with tent-pads, outhouses and food-storage poles provided at Eva and Jade lakes, but no camping is allowed in the Miller Lake area or anywhere within 5km of the Trans-Canada and Summit Rd. Registration at the Park Administration Office is obligatory. The park is so small, however, that you might be better off at some of the area's more developed private campsites.

Hotels and motels

Best Western Wayside Inn 1901 Laforme Blvd ☎250/837-6161 or 1-800-528-1234, ⓦwww.bestwestern.com. The priciest and best of the town's hotels. ❺

Columbia Motel 301 Wright St–2nd St W ☎250/837-2191 or 1-800/663-5303, ⓦwww.columbia.revelstoke.com. With 54 rooms, one of the larger places in town; air-conditioned and heated pool in season as an extra draw. ❷

Daniel's Hostel Guesthouse 313 1st St ☎250/837-5530. Choice of dorm beds at $15 or private singles and doubles ($30) in a three-storey, 100-year-old house; shared bathrooms and communal kitchen; smoking outside only. ❶

Frontier Motel and Restaurant 122 N Nakusp Hwy ☎250/837-5119 or 1-800/382-7763, Ⓔwelcome@revelstoke.net. On the main Trans-Canada near the junction with Hwy 23 away from the town centre; good motel and first-rate food. ❷

Nelles Ranch Bed and Breakfast Hwy 23 S ☎250/837-3800 or 1-888/567-4177, Ⓔnellesranch@revelstoke.net. Just six units on a working horse and cattle ranch 2km off the Trans-Canada Hwy. ❸

Peaks Lodge 5km west of Revelstoke off Hwy 1 ☎250/837-2176 or 1-800/668-0330, Ⓔpeaks@revelstoke.net. Nice small place (15 units) in a reasonably rustic setting convenient for hikes, bird-watching and the like. Open mid-May to mid-Oct & mid-Nov to mid-April. ❸

'R' Motel 1500 1st St ☎250/837-2164, Ⓔrmotel@revelstoke.net. One of the cheapest motels in town, but some rooms still have kitchenettes and air-conditioning. ❷

Samesun Budget Lodge 400 2nd St W ☎250/837-4050, ⓦwww.samesun.com. Cheap private, semi-private and dorm beds convenient for local restaurants and supermarkets. Well run and offers Internet access, bike rentals and kitchen facilities. ❶

Sandman Inn 1821 Fraser St ☎250/837-5271 or 1-800/726-3626, ⓦwww.sandmanhotels.ca. Part of a usually reliable mid-range hotel chain. Has 83 comfortable, modern rooms, so a good chance of finding space. ❹

Campsites

KOA Revelstoke 5km east of Revelstoke ☎250/837-2085 or 1-800/562-3905, ⓦwww.revelstokekoa.com. The best of the area's campsites. Free showers, plus shop and swimming pool. May–Oct. $18.50–28.

Lamplighter Campground ☎250/837-3385. Off Hwy 1 before the Columbia River bridge; take Hwy 23 south towards Nakusp and turn into Nixon Rd (first left). A peaceful, fully serviced tent and RV site within walking distance of downtown. Fifty fully serviced sites. Mid-April to mid-Oct. $17–24.

Williamson Lake Campground 1818 Williamson Lake Rd ☎250/837-5512 or 1-888/676-2267, ⓦwww.williamsonlakecampground.com. Nice 41-site lakeside campsite 4km south of the town centre. Free hot showers, canoe and rowboat rentals, flush toilets and beach. Mid-April to Oct. $15.

Revelstoke Dam

A trip to Canada's largest dam may sound dull, but the **Revelstoke Dam** (daily: mid-March to mid-June & early Sept to late Oct 9am–5pm; mid-June to early Sept 8am–8pm; free) makes an interesting outing. Located 4km north of the town on Hwy 23, the 175m-tall barrier holds back the waters of the Columbia River, around 500km from its source. Its sleek, space-age **visitor centre** offers a two-hour self-guided tour, which omits to tell you that insufficient mapping during the construction caused a landslide that threatened to swamp Revelstoke: millions had to be spent or it would have been curtains for the town. The boring bits of the tour can be skipped in favour of a lift to the top for a great view of the dam and surrounding valley.

Kootenay National Park

KOOTENAY NATIONAL PARK, lying across the Continental Divide from Banff in British Columbia, is the least known of the four contiguous parks of the Rockies, and the easiest to miss out – many people prefer to follow the Trans-Canada through Yoho rather than commit themselves to the less enthralling westward journey on Hwy 3 imposed by Kootenay. The park's scenery, however, is as impressive as that of its neighbours – it draws three million visitors a year – and if you're not determined to head west you could drive a neat loop from Banff through Kootenay on Hwy 93 to **Radium Hot Springs** (the only town in this area), north on Hwy 95, and back on the Trans-Canada through Yoho to Lake Louise and Banff. You could drive this in a day and still have time for a few short walks and a dip in Radium's hot springs to boot.

In many ways the park's mountains seem closer at hand and more spectacular than on the Icefields Parkway, partly because the road climbs higher over the Continental Divide, and partly because the park's origins guaranteed it an intimate link with the highway. In 1910 Randolph Bruce, a local businessman, persuaded the Canadian government and Canadian Pacific to push a road from Banff through the Rockies to connect the prairies with western seaports (prompted by the hope of promoting a fruit-growing industry in the Columbia Valley). Previously the area had been the reserve of the Kootenai or Ktunaxa peoples (*Kootenay* is an aboriginal word meaning "people from beyond the hills") and had been explored by David Thompson, but otherwise it was an all but inviolate mountain fastness. The project began in 1911 and produced 22km of road before the money ran out. To wangle more cash British Columbia was forced to cede 8km of land on each side of the highway to the government and, in 1920, 1406 square kilometres of land were established as a national park.

Kootenay lends itself to admiration from a car, bus or bike, mainly because it's little more than a sixteen-kilometre-wide ribbon of land running either side of Hwy 93 for around 100km (the highway here is known as the **Kootenay** or **Banff–Windermere Parkway**). All its numerous easy **short walks** start immediately off the highway, though the scenery, of course, doesn't simply stop at the park boundary. Options for **day-hikes** are more limited, though the best of the longer walks are as good as anything in the Rockies and can be extended into outstanding two-day (or more) backpacking options. If you want no more than a stroll from a car or bike follow the **Marble Canyon** and **Paint Pots** trails; for something longer but not too long go for the **Stanley Glacier** walk;

KOOTENAY NATIONAL PARK

Lake Louise

Castle Junction

Bow Valley Parkway

Bow River

Johnson Canyon

Banff

ALBERTA

Vermilion Pass

Storm Mtn

Stanley Glacier

Stanley Cr

Mt Ball

Goodsir Pass

Ottertail Pass

Helmet Creek

Marble Canyon

Marble Canyon Campground

Stanley Peak

Paint Pots

Tumbling Cr

Numa Cr

Kootenay Park Lodge

Vermilion Crossing

Numa Peak

Honeymoon Pass

The Monarch

Floe Lake

Floe Creek

See 'Kootenay Hikes' map

BRITISH

COLUMBIA

Mt Verendrye

Vermilion Crossing

Vermilion River

Mt Shanks

Wardle Creek Picnic Area

Mt Shanks Lookout

Mt Wardle

Simpson River

Hector Gorge Viewpoint

Golden

93

Mt Selkirk

Kootenay Crossing

Kootenay River

Dolly Varden Picnic Area
Winter Campground

Dog Lake

Kindersley Creek

Columbia River

95

McLeod Meadows

Campground

Kootenay River Picnic Area

Mt Kindersley

Kootenay Valley Viewpoint

Kindersley Pass

Sinclair Pass

Kimpton Cr

Sinclair Canyon

West Gate Infocentre

Aquacourt

Sinclair Cr

Redstreak Cr

Radium Hot Springs

Redstreak Campground

N

0   10 km

Invermere

ALBERTA AND THE ROCKIES | Kootenay National Park

6

762

if you're after the best day-hike the choice is the **Kindersley Pass Trail**, though it's a close-run thing with the Floe Lake Trail to Floe Lake and its possible continuation northwest over the Numa Pass and down Numa Creek back to the highway. If you have time do both of these two day-hikes – if you do, you'll have done two of the top ten or so walks in the Rockies. If you have more time, the Rockwall Trail (Floe Lake–Numa Pass–Rockwell Pass–Helmet

Falls) is widely considered among the Rockies' top three or four backpacking routes. See the box on p.764 and our maps to make sense of these routes.

Practicalities

The only practicable access to Kootenay is on Hwy 93, a good road that leaves the Trans-Canada at Castle Junction (in Banff National Park), traverses Kootenay from north to south, and joins Hwy 95 at Radium Hot Springs at the southern entrance. Radium offers the only practical accommodation options, bar a trio of park-run campsites and handful of rooms at Vermilion Crossing, a summer-only huddle of shop, cabins and petrol station midway through the park. The two daily Greyhound **buses** east and west on the southern British Columbia route between Cranbrook, Banff and Calgary stop at Vermilion Crossing and Radium. **Park permits** are required for entry unless you already have a valid permit from Banff, Jasper or Kootenay: $7 per person per day, or $45 for an annual pass valid for eleven parks in western Canada: group passes for two to ten people cost $14 (see box on p.678 for more on passes).

If you come from the east you'll hit the *Marble Canyon* campsite about 15km from Castle Junction, where occasionally in summer there's a simple information kiosk (mid-June to early Sept Mon & Fri–Sun 8.30am–8pm, Tues–Thurs 8.30am–4.30pm; no phone); coming the other way, the main **park visitor centre** is at the corner of Main St East and Redstreak Rd at 7556 Main St in the town of Radium Hot Springs (daily mid-May to mid-Oct 9am–5pm; ☏ 250/347-9505, ⓦ www.pc.gc.ca). Main St East is a turn south off Hwy 93 close to its junction with Hwy 95. The park entrance, however, is on Hwy 93 itself farther east close to the Radium Hot Springs Pools (see p.767). The centre provides a free *Backcountry Guide to Kootenay National Park*, all you need walk-wise if you're not planning anything too ambitious. There is a season visitor centre at the Kootenay Park Lodge (see below), 68km north of Radium on Hwy 93 (no phone; mid-April to mid-May Fri–Sun 11am–6pm, mid-May to Sept daily 11am–7pm).

Kootenay, like the other major Rockies parks, has a "Friends" organization (☏ 250/347-6525), which helps run **guided walks** and other activities: walks should be booked at the visitor centre. In Kootenay, there are three good walks: Stanley Glacier (July & Aug; 5hr; 10km; meet at Stanley Glacier trailhead on Hwy 93) and two walks in Sinclair Canyon – "Walk of the Two Lions" (July; 2hr) and "Into the Secret Canyon" (Aug Fri 10am; 1hr 30min) meet for both walks at the front entrance of the Radium Hot Springs Pools – call for latest days and start times.

Park staff are also usually on hand at the park's only two roadside serviced **campsites**: the 98-site *McLeod Meadows*, 25km north of Radium ($17; mid-May to mid-Sept; no showers), and the 61-site *Marble Canyon*, near the Information Centre ($17; mid-June to early Sept; no showers). If you want more comforts (including hot showers) and easier access use the big 242-site *Redstreak* campsite, Kootenay's major park tent and RV campsite. It's located 3km north of Radium Hot Springs ($22–30, firewood $6; May–Sept; ☏ 250/347-9567); the turn-off for the site is Redstreak Rd. To reach it, carry on along Main St East from the park visitor centre until Main St becomes Redstreak Rd. If you're staying at the campsite, incidentally, note that the Redstreak Campground Trail (2.2km) takes you from the northwest corner of the site to the Radium Hot Springs Pools. The Valleyview Trail (1.4km) takes you from the campsite entrance into Radium village, avoiding Redstreak Rd. A dozen or more **backcountry sites** with pit toilets and firewood are

If you have time and energy for only one long walk in Kootenay, make it the **Kindersley Pass Trail**, a strenuous 9.8-kilometre trail that climbs to **Kindersley Pass** and then cuts northeast for the steep final push to Kindersley Summit (2210m). Here you can enjoy the sublime prospect of an endless succession of peaks fading to the horizon away to the northeast. Rather than double back down through the open tundra, many people push on another 2km (trail vague) and contour around the head of the Sinclair Creek valley before dropping off the ridge (the Kindersley–Sinclair Col) to follow the well-defined **Sinclair Creek Trail** (6.4km) down to meet the highway 1km from the starting point (be sure to do the hike this way round – the Sinclair Creek Trail is a long, dull climb).

Most of Kootenay's other longish day-walks are in the park's northern half, accessed on the west side of the highway from the Marble Canyon, Paint Pots, Numa Creek and Floe Lake parking areas. The **Rockwall Trail**, an incredible thirty-kilometre (54km including approach trails; 1450m ascent), backpacking high-level trail, follows the line of the mountains on the west side of the highway, and can be joined using four of the six trails described below. You could walk it in two days, but could easily spend longer, particularly as there are five backcountry campsites en route.

From north to south on the highway, the trails start with the **Kaufmann Lake Trail** (15km one-way; 570m ascent; allow 4–6hr one-way), which climbs to one of the park's loveliest high-mountain lakes (there's also a campsite here). A trail from the Paint Pots runs for 2km before dividing to provide three onward options: the first to the dull **Ottertail Pass**, the second up **Tumbling Creek** (10.3km; 440m ascent to the intersection with the Rockwall Trail), and the third and best option the **Helmet Creek Trail** (14.3km; 310m ascent), a long day-hike to the amazing 365-metre **Helmet Waterfalls** (another intersection with the Rockwall Trail). The best of the day-hikes after Kindersley Pass is the easier **Floe Lake Trail** (10.5km; 715m ascent), up to a spellbinding lake edged by a 1000m sheer escarpment and a small glacier. There are campsites on the route, and another tie-in to the Rockwall Trail. The **Numa Creek Trail** (6.4km; 115m ascent) to the north is less enthralling – though you could use it as a downhill leg to add to the Floe Lake Trail – as are the series of fire-road walks advertised in the park: unless you're mountain biking, therefore, ignore the Simpson River, West Kootenay, Honeymoon Pass and East Kootenay trails.

scattered within easy backpacking range of the highway, for which you need a **permit** from the infocentres ($8). The small seven-site *Dolly Varden* park camp-site just north of McLeod Meadows opens for **winter camping** (Sept–May; flush toilets only; free).

The only indoor **accommodation** in the heart of the park is ten rustic cottages of the *Kootenay Park Lodge* at Vermilion Crossing (℡250/762-9196, ⓦwww.kootenayparklodge.com; ❹; mid-May to Sept). You'll need to book these well in advance.

Vermilion Pass

Vermilion Pass (1637m) marks the northern entrance to the park, the Continental Divide's watershed and the border between Alberta and British Columbia. Little fanfare, however, accompanies the transition – only the barren legacy of a huge forest fire (started by a single lightning bolt) that ravaged the area for four days in 1968, leaving a 24-square-kilometre blanket of stark, blackened trunks. Take the short **Fireweed Trail** (1km) through the desolation from the car park at the pass to see how nature deals with such disasters, indeed how it seems to invite lightning fires to promote phoenix-like regeneration.

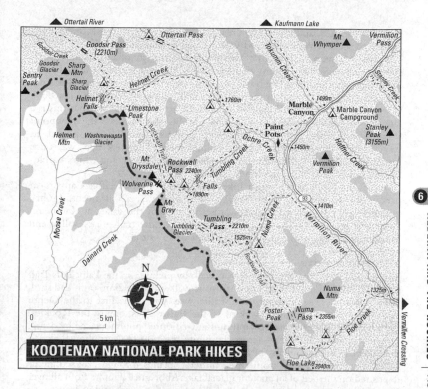

Ottertail River

Kaufmann Lake

Ottertail Pass

Goodsir Creek
Goodsir Pass
(2210m)

Mt
Whymper

Vermilion
Pass

Goodsir
Glacier
Sharp
Mtn

Sentry
Peak

Helmet Creek

Sharp
Glacier

Tokumm Creek

Stanley Creek

Helmet
Falls

Limestone
Peak

1760m

Marble
Canyon

1490m

Marble Canyon
Campground

Rockwall Trail

Paint
Pots

Stanley
Peak
(3155m)

Helmet
Mtn

Washmawapta
Glacier

Ochre Creek

1450m

Mt
Drysdale

Rockwall
Pass 2240m

Tumbling Creek

Vermilion
Peak

Haffner Creek

Wolverine
Pass

Falls
1890m

93

1410m

Moose Creek

Mt
Gray

Tumbling
Glacier

Tumbling
Pass

2210m

1525m

Numa Creek

Vermilion River

Dainard Creek

Rockwall Trail

N

Numa
Mtn

1325m

Vermilion Crossing

Foster
Peak

Numa
Pass

2355m

Floe Creek

0   5 km

KOOTENAY NATIONAL PARK HIKES

Floe Lake 2040m

6

ALBERTA AND THE ROCKIES | Kootenay National Park

The ubiquitous lodgepole pine, for example, specifically requires the heat of a forest fire to crack open its resin-sealed cones and release its seeds. Strange as it seems, forests are intended to burn, at least if a healthy forest is to be preserved: in montane regions the natural "fire return cycles" are a mere 42–46 years; in lower subalpine habitats, 77–130 years; and in upper subalpine areas, 180 years. Forests any older are actually in decline, providing few species and poor wildlife habitats. Ironically, as a result of the national parks' success in preventing forest fires over the last fifty years, many woods are now over-mature and the need for controlled burning is increasingly being addressed. At Vermilion Pass a broad carpet of lodgepole pines have taken root among the blasted remnants of the earlier forest, while young plants and shrubs ("doghair forest") are pushing up into the new clearings. Birds, small mammals and deer, elk and moose are being attracted to new food sources and, more significantly, black and grizzly bears are returning to the area. Burning takes place in the park, and some trails may be closed as a result: latest details are posted at the park centre or the Parks Canada website.

Stanley Glacier and Marble Canyon

About 3km south of Vermilion Pass, the small, well-defined **Stanley Glacier Trail** (4.2km; 365m ascent; 1hr 30min) strikes off up Stanley Creek from a parking area on the eastern side of the highway. In its first 2km the trail provides you with a hike through the Vermilion Pass Burn (see above), but more to the point pushes into the beautiful hanging valley below Stanley Peak. Here you can enjoy close-up views of the Stanley Glacier and its surrounding recently glaciated landscapes. The area is also known for its fossils, and for the chance to see marmots, pikas and white-tailed ptarmigan.

Marble Canyon, 8km south of Vermilion Pass, the site of a park-run **campsite**, has an easy trail (800m) that's probably the most heavily trafficked of Kootenay's shorter hikes. The track crosses a series of log bridges over Tokumm Creek, which has carved through a fault in the limestone over the last 8000 years to produce a 600m-long and 37m-deep gorge. In cold weather this is a fantastic medley of ice and snow, but in summer the climax is the viewpoint from the top of the path onto a thundering waterfall as the creek pounds its way through the narrowest section of the gorge. The rock here was once mistakenly identified as marble – hence the canyon's name; the white marble-like rock is actually dolomite limestone.

One of the park's better longer hikes also starts from the Marble Canyon car park – the **Kaufmann Lake Trail** (15km one-way; 570m ascent; 4–6hr), which follows Tokumm Creek towards the head of the valley at Kaufmann Lake (see box p.764). The first few kilometres of the trail – easy valley and meadow walking – make an appealing hour or so's stroll.

The Paint Pots

You could extend the Marble Canyon walk by picking up the Paint Pots Trail south, which puts another 2.7km onto your walk, or drive 2km south and stroll 1km to reach the same destination. Either way you come first to the Ochre Beds (after 800m) and then (1.5km) to the **Paint Pots**, one of the Rockies' more magical spots: red, orange and mustard-coloured pools prefaced by damp, moss-clung forest and views across the white water of the Vermilion River to the snowcapped mountains beyond. The pools' colours are created by iron-laden water bubbling up from three mineral springs through clay sediments deposited on the bed of an ancient glacial lake. Aboriginal peoples from all over North America collected the coloured clays from the ponds and ochre beds to make into small cakes, which they baked in embers. The fired clay was then ground into powder – **ochre** – and added to animal fat or fish oil to use in rock, tepee or ceremonial body painting. Ochre has always had spiritual significance for North American natives, in this case the Stoney and Ktunaxa, who saw these oxide-stained pools and their yellow-edged surroundings as inhabited by animal and thunder spirits. Standing in the quiet, rather gloomy glade, particularly on overcast days, it's easy to see why – not that the atmosphere or sanctity of the place stopped European speculators in the 1920s from mining the ochre to manufacture paint in Calgary.

The car park is the trailhead for three longer (day or backpack) trails, all of which kick off along the Ochre Creek Valley: Tumbling Creek Trail, Ottertail Pass Trail and the Helmet Creek–Helmet Waterfalls Trail (see box, p.764).

Vermilion Crossing and Kootenay Crossing

VERMILION CROSSING, 20km south of the Paint Pots Trail, is gone in a flash, but it's the only place, in summer at least, to find lodgings, petrol and food in the park. It also has a new visitor centre, built on the site of a 1920 CPR railway camp. You can also stop to walk the **Verendyre Creek Trail** (2.1km), accessed west off the highway, an easy stroll, but forest-enclosed, and with only limited views of Mount Verendrye as a reward. One of the Rockies' tougher walks heads east from the Crossing, up over Honeymoon Pass and Redearth Pass to Egypt Lake and the Trans-Canada Highway in Banff National Park, while to the south equally demanding trails provide the only westside access into the wilderness of **Mount Assiniboine Provincial Park**. Sandwiched between Kootenay and Banff, this wilderness park was created in honour of Mount Assiniboine (3618m), a sabre-tooth-shaped mountain with one of the most dramatic profiles imaginable, whose native Stoney name means "those who cook by placing hot rocks in water". The **Simpson Road Trail** (8.2km) leads to the park boundary, and then divides into two paths (20km and 32km) to Lake Magog in the heart of Assiniboine. Some 8.5km beyond the Crossing look out for the Animal Lick, a spot where animals come down to lick nutrients from a natural mineral source: with luck you may see elk, mule deer and even moose here. Over the next few kilometres, for similar reasons, you might also see mountain goats by banks at the side of the road.

Kootenay Crossing is no more than a ceremonial spot – it was where the ribbon was cut to open Hwy 93 in 1923 – though a clutch of short trails fan out from its park warden station, and the nearby *Dolly Varden* campsite (see p.764) is the park's only specific site for winter camping. **Wardle Creek** nearby is a good place to unpack a picnic if you're determined to stick to the road.

Around 11km south of the Kootenay Crossing is the **McLeod Meadows** campsite (see p.763), and immediately behind it to the east the easy **Dog Lake Trail** (2.7km), much tramped as an after-dinner leg-stretcher by campers (the trail can also be accessed from the highway at the picnic area 500m south). The path offers glimpses of the Kootenay Valley through the trees, and ends in a marsh-edged lake whose temperate microclimate makes it ideal for nature study. You may see deer, elk and coyotes, and – if you're lucky – bears and moose. Several types of orchid also bloom here in early summer (June & July), including white bog, round-leafed, calypso and sparrow's egg. About 11km further on, the **Kootenay Valley Viewpoint** offers one of the broadest views on the highway, with great vistas of the Mitchell and Vermilion mountain ranges, and with them the inevitable hordes in search of a photo opportunity.

Sinclair Pass

For its final run down out of the park, the highway doglegs west through the **Sinclair Pass**, a red-cliffed gorge filled with the falling waters of Sinclair Creek and the start of the **Kindersley Pass Trail**, possibly the most scenic day-hike in the park (see box on p.764). If this seems too much of a slog, Sinclair Pass offers three far easier short trails, all marked off the highway to the west. The best is the **Juniper Trail** (3.2km), accessed just 300m inside the park's West Gate. The trail drops to Sinclair Creek and over the next couple of kilometres touches dry canyon, arid forest slopes of juniper and Douglas fir, and thick woods of western red cedar, before emerging at the hot springs, or Aquacourt, 1.4km up the road from the start. The **Redstreak Creek Trail** (2.7km), 4.5km east of the West Gate, starts off as a good forest walk, but tails off into dullness subsequently, as does the **Kimpton Creek Trail** (4.8km), also on the south side of the road and canyon, accessed 7.5km east of the West Gate.

Radium Hot Springs

RADIUM HOT SPRINGS is far less attractive than its evocative name suggests but, as the service centre for Kootenay, its tacky motels and garages are likely to claim your attention and money. The town spreads across the flats of the Columbia Valley, 3km from the southern/western entrance at the junction of Hwy 93 and Hwy 95. For **information** visit the park centre, which has a Chamber of Commerce desk (Tues–Sat 10am–4pm; ☏250/347-9331 or 1-800/347-9704, ⓦwww.radiumhotsprings.com).

The **hot springs** (or Aquacourt) themselves – plus park visitor centre – are nicely away from the settlement, 2km north of town off the Banff–Windermere Parkway (Hwy 93) and are administered by the park authorities. There is a hot pool and cool pool with a single admission ($6.50, unlimited day use $9.75) but slightly different opening times: hot pool (daily: mid-May to mid-Oct 9am–11pm; mid-Oct to mid-May Sun–Thurs noon–9pm, Fri & Sat noon–10pm); cool pool (daily: mid-May to late June & early Sept to mid-Oct noon–9pm; late June to early Sept 9am–11pm; mid-Oct to mid-May Fri 6–9m, Sat & Sun noon–9pm; ☎250/347-9485). Aboriginal peoples used the springs for centuries, and commercial white development started as early as 1890 when Roland Stuart bought the area for $160. Traces of supposedly therapeutic radium found in the water turned Stuart's investment into a recreational gold mine. When the government appropriated the springs for inclusion in the national park, it paid him $40,000 – a small fortune, but considerably less than what they were worth, which at the time was estimated to be $500,000. The pools today are outdoors, but serviced by a large, modern centre. In summer, 4000 people per day take the plunge into the odourless 45°C waters, enough to discourage any idea of a quiet swim, though in late evening or off-season (when the hot pool steams invitingly) you can escape the bedlam and pretend more easily that the water is having some sort of soothing effect. The radium traces sound a bit worrying, but 300,000 visitors a year don't seem to mind.

If you have the choice, aim **to stay** in Invermere (see p.966) or one of the newer **motels** creeping up the Sinclair Valley around the hot springs area away from downtown: they're more expensive, but far more attractively sited than the thirty-odd mirror-image motels in town (where there are any number of rooms in the $50–70 bracket). Try the big 120-room *Radium Resort* for something of a treat, 1km south of the springs at 8100 Golf Course Rd (☎250/347-9311 or 1-800/667-6444, ⊛www.radiumresort.com; ⑥), for all the trimmings (including swimming pool and massage therapist); or *Addison's Bungalows*, 4920 Dorney Rd (☎250/347-9545 or 1-800/794-5024, ⊛www.addisonsbungalows.com; ❹; April–Oct), a mix of thirty motel and cabin rooms nearby with units offering anything up to five bedrooms and kitchenettes. Almost alongside the park entrance are the fourteen-room *Alpen Motel* (☎250/347-9823 or 1-888/788-3891, ⊛www.alpenmotel.com; ❸), sixteen-room *Kootenay* (☎250/347-9490 or 1-877/908-2020; ❸) and nine-room *Crescent* (☎250/347-9570; ❸) motels. The *Radium International Hostel*, located at the Misty River Lodge at the edge of the park (☎250/347-9912; ❶), has a kitchen, common room, bicycle storage and rental and two dorms with five or six beds ($15–20 a head) and one private room (❷).

Travel details

Trains

Calgary to: Vancouver with private Rocky Mountaineer Railtours (see Basics, p.33).
Edmonton to: Prince Rupert via Jasper and Prince George (3 weekly; 30hr); Vancouver (3 weekly; 24hr); Winnipeg via Saskatoon (3 weekly; 24hr).
Jasper to: Edmonton (3 weekly; 5hr 30min); Prince Rupert via Prince George (3 weekly; 20hr); Vancouver (3 weekly).

Buses

Calgary to: Banff (6 daily; 1hr 40min); Coutts in the US (connections for Las Vegas and Los Angeles) via Fort Macleod and Lethbridge (1 daily; 4hr 30min); Creston via Banff, Radium Hot Springs and Cranbrook (1 daily; 7hr 30min); Dawson Creek (2 daily; 7hr 15min); Drumheller (2 daily; 1hr 50min); Edmonton (14 daily; 3hr 30min); Fort St John (2 daily; 9hr 15min); Lake Louise (6 daily; 2hr 35min); Prince George (2 daily; 14hr); Saskatoon (2 daily; 9hr); Vancouver via Fort Macleod, Cranbrook, Nelson, Osoyoos and Hope (2 daily; 24hr); Vancouver via Kamloops (7 daily; 13hr); Vancouver via Vernon, Kelowna and Penticton (3 daily; 16hr); Winnipeg via Lethbridge, Medicine Hat and Regina (2 daily; 24hr).
Edmonton to: Calgary (14 daily; 3hr 30min); Drumheller (1 daily; 4hr 45min); Grande Prairie (4 daily; 6hr); Hay River via Peace River (1 daily; 17hr); Jasper (6 daily; 4hr 30min); Peace River (3 daily; 6hr 30min); Saskatoon (4 daily; 5hr); Vancouver (6 daily; 14hr); Whitehorse (mid-May to mid-Oct 1 daily; rest of year 3 weekly; 28hr); Winnipeg (2 daily; 21hr).

Flights

Calgary to: Edmonton (every 30min; 50min); Montréal (12 daily; 5hr); Toronto (14 daily; 4hr); Vancouver (every 30min; 1hr 20min).
Edmonton to: Calgary (every 30min; 50min); Montréal (9 daily; 5hr); Toronto (10 daily; 4hr 10min); Vancouver (every 30min; 1hr 25min).

Southern
British Columbia

CHAPTER 7 — # Highlights

* **Vancouver** Ocean, mountains and a glittering skyline make this one of the world's most visually stunning cities. **See p.777**

* **Royal British Columbia Museum** Victoria's cultural highlight is regularly rated among North America's top ten museums. **See p.839**

* **Pacific Rim National Park** The scenic highlight of beautiful Vancouver Island. **See p.870**

* **The Inside Passage** Take this day-long ferry ride to enjoy the best of British Columbia's magnificent coastline. **See p.894**

* **Whistler** Come here for superlative outdoor activities in summer or winter. **See p.902**

* **Wells Gray Provincial Park** This vast tract of wilderness has scenery that is the equal of the Canadian Rockies. **See p.924**

* **The Kootenays** A pristine region of lakes, mountains, forests, hot springs and charming old-world villages. **See p.945**

* **Nelson** British Columbia's most compelling town, thanks to over 350 glorious historic buildings. **See p.955**

△ Vancouver skyline

Southern British Columbia

The pristine scenery of **British Columbia** more than lives up to most people's image of the wilds of Canada. What may come as a surprise, however, is the region's sheer natural diversity: between the expected extremes of the mountainous, forested interior and the fjord-cut mountains of the coast lies a jigsaw of landscapes, including genteel farmland, ranching country, immense lakes and even a patch of genuine desert. British Columbia contains both Canada's wettest and its driest climates, and more species of flora and fauna than the rest of the country put together. The range of recreational possibilities is equally impressive: the country's biggest ski area, its warmest lakes and some of its best beaches are all here, not to mention hot springs and hiking, sailing and canoeing galore, as well as some of the best salmon fishing in the world. Interior towns may not always be terribly interesting – **Nelson** is a notable exception – but from almost anywhere in the region you can be sure that secluded and peaceful countryside and myriad outdoor pursuits lie just a few kilometres away.

Culturally and logistically, southern British Columbia stands apart from the northern half of the province, containing most of the roads, towns and accessible sights. Ninety-five percent of the population lives in the south, mainly in **Vancouver**, Canada's third largest city. A cosmopolitan, sophisticated and famously hedonistic place, Vancouver gives the lie to the stereotype of the Canadian west as an introverted, cultural wasteland, its combination of glittering skyline and generous open spaces standing as a model of urban planning. The province's modest capital is **Victoria**, a considerably smaller city on the southern tip of Vancouver Island, which affects a somewhat English ambience to lure more tourists than it probably deserves.

If you're making a circuit of the interior, or even just cutting across it as part of a transcontinental route, you'll want to set aside time for the mountain-hemmed

Information and hotel reservations

Tourism British Columbia ☎1-800/HELLO-BC (435-5622) toll-free in North America, or ☎604/435-5622, ⓦwww.HelloBC.com.
Tourism Vancouver ☎604/683-2000, ⓦwww.tourismvancouver.com.

773

lakes and tidy mining towns of the **Kootenays**, or – if you're into wine tasting or rowdy lakeside resorts – the **Okanagan**. For big wilderness and waterfalls, **Wells Gray Provincial Park** stands out, though exhilarating hikes and camping are possible in dozens of other parks. And if you're looking to ski or snowboard, **Whistler** is one of the world's top resorts. Variety is also the byword for **Vancouver Island**, by far the largest of an archipelago of islets off BC's coast, where in a short time you can move from wild seascapes and rainforest to jagged, glaciated peaks. Vancouver Island can also be used as a springboard for the ferry up the famed **Inside Passage** to Prince Rupert and beyond, or the new Discovery Coast Passage to Bella Coola; inland, roads and rail lines converge to follow a single route north through the endless expanse of the **Cariboo** region of the interior plateau.

A history of British Columbia

Long before the coming of Europeans, British Columbia's coastal region supported five key **First Peoples** – the Kwakiutl, Bella Coola, Nuu-chah-nulth, Haida and Tlingit – all of whom lived largely off the sea and developed a culture in many ways more sophisticated than that of the nomadic and hunting-oriented tribes of the interior. Although it's rare these days to come across aboriginal faces in interior southern BC, aboriginal villages still exist on parts of Vancouver Island, and you can find examples of their totemic art in the excellent museum displays of Victoria and Vancouver.

The British explorer **Francis Drake** probably made the first sighting of the mainland by a European, during his round-the-world voyage of 1579. Spanish explorers sailing from California and Russians from Alaska explored the coast almost two centuries later, though it was another Briton, **Captain Cook**, who made the first recorded landing in 1778. Captain George Vancouver first mapped the area in 1792–94, hard on the heels of the Nuu-chah-nulth Convention of 1790 – a neat piece of colonial bluster in which the British wrested from the Spanish all rights on the mainland as far as Alaska.

Exploration of the interior came about during the search for an easier way to export furs westwards to the Pacific (instead of the arduous haul eastwards across the continent). **Alexander Mackenzie** of the North West Company made the first crossing of North America north of Mexico in 1793, followed by two further adventurers, **Simon Fraser** and **David Thompson**, whose names also resonate as sobriquets for rivers, shops, motels and streets across the region. For the first half of the nineteenth century most of western Canada was ruled as a virtual fiefdom by the **Hudson's Bay Company**, a monopoly that antagonized the Americans, which in turn persuaded the British to formalize its claims to the region to forestall American expansion. The 49th Parallel was agreed as the national boundary, though Vancouver Island, which lies partly south of the line, remained wholly British and was officially designated a crown colony in 1849. The "Bay" still reigned in all but name, however, and took no particular interest in promoting immigration; as late as 1855 the island's white population numbered only 774 and the mainland remained almost unknown except to trappers and the odd prospector.

The discovery of **gold** on the Fraser River in 1858, and in the Cariboo region three years later, changed everything, attracting some 25,000 people to the gold fields and creating a forward base on the mainland that was to become Vancouver. It also led to the building of the **Cariboo Road** (the present Hwy 97) and the **Dewdney Trail** (Hwy 3), which opened up the interior and helped attract the so-called **Overlanders** – a huge straggle of pioneers that tramped from Ontario and Québec in the summer of 1862. Britain declared mainland British Columbia a crown colony in 1858 to impose imperial authority on the region and, more importantly, to lay firm claim to the huge mineral wealth that was rightly believed to lie within it. When Canada's eastern colonies formed the Dominion in 1867, though, British Columbia dithered over joining until it received the promise of a **railway** to link it to the east in 1871 – though the Canadian Pacific didn't actually arrive for another fifteen years.

While British Columbia no longer dithers over its destiny, it still tends to look to itself and the Northwest – and increasingly to the Pacific Rim – rather than to the rest of Canada. The francophone concerns of the east are virtually nonexistent here: for years, for example, there was just one French school in the entire province. For the most part British Columbians are well off, both

Reserving provincial campsites

Tent and RV pitches at certain **campsites** in British Columbia's provincial parks (ⓦwlapwww.gov.bc.ca/bcparks) can be reserved in advance. Not all parks accept reservations and some parks have more than one campsite. To make **reservations**, call Discover Camping (☎1-800/689-9025 or 604/689-9025 in greater Vancouver; March to mid-Sept Mon–Fri 7am–7pm, Sat & Sun 9am–5pm) or go to ⓦwww .discovercamping.ca. Reservations can be made from three months to 48 hours in advance. A non-refundable **booking fee** of $6.42 per night (to a maximum of $19.26 for three or more nights) is charged (rates include tax). Payment in advance is by Visa or MasterCard only; payment for extra nights once you're at a campsite is in cash only. You can stay in up to a maximum of fourteen days in any single BC provincial park.

financially and in terms of quality of life, and demographically the province is one of the region's youngest. If there are flies in the ointment, they're the **environmental pressures** thrown up by an economy which relies on primary resources for its dynamism: British Columbia supplies 25 percent of North America's commercial timber and exports significant amounts of hydroelectric power, fish, zinc, silver, oil, coal and gypsum. Few of these can be exploited without exacting a toll on the province's natural beauty; British Columbians may be well off, but they're increasingly aware of the environmental price being paid for their prosperity.

Vancouver

Cradled between the ocean and snowcapped mountains, **VANCOUVER** has a dazzling downtown district that fills a narrow peninsula bounded by Burrard Inlet to the north, English Bay to the west and False Creek to the south. Greater Vancouver sprawls south to the Fraser River. Edged around its idyllic waterfront are fine beaches, a dynamic port and a magnificent swath of parkland, not to mention the mirror-fronted ranks of skyscrapers that look across Burrard Inlet and its bustling harbour to the residential districts of North and West Vancouver. Beyond these comfortable suburbs, the Coast Mountains rise in steep, forested slopes to form a dramatic counterpoint to the downtown skyline and the most stunning of the city's many outdoor playgrounds. Small wonder, given Vancouver's surroundings, that Greenpeace was founded in the city.

Vancouver's 1.9 million residents exploit their spectacular natural setting to the hilt, and when they tire of the immediate region can travel a short distance to the unimaginably vast wilderness of the BC interior. Whether it's sailing, swimming, fishing, hiking, skiing, golf or tennis, locals barely have to move to indulge in a plethora of **recreational whims**. Summer and winter the city oozes hedonism and healthy living – it comes as no surprise to find that you can lounge on beaches downtown – typically West Coast obsessions that spill over into its sophisticated **arts and culture**. Vancouver claims a world–class

GREATER VANCOUVER

N

0 ——— 4km

Hope ▲

Hope ▲

Squamish & Whistler ▲

Horseshoe Bay

BC Ferries Terminal ◆

CYPRESS PROVINCIAL PARK

WEST VANCOUVER

Lighthouse Park

MARINE DRIVE

Lions Gate Bridge

Grouse Mountain ▲

Capilano Lake

Capilano River Regional Park

LYNN HEADWATERS REGIONAL PARK

LYNN VALLEY RD

MONASHEE DRIVE

DOLLARTON HWY

NORTH VANCOUVER

Lonsdale Quay

Stanley Park

See Central Vancouver map

Burrard Inlet

English Bay

False Creek

KITSILANO

NW MARINE DRIVE

SW MARINE DRIVE

University of British Columbia

PACIFIC SPIRIT REGIONAL PARK

MOUNT SEYMOUR PROVINCIAL PARK

Indian Arm

INDIAN ARM PROVINCIAL PARK

BELCARRA REGIONAL PARK

PORT MOODY

7A

COQUITLAM

COMO LAKE AVE

AUSTIN AVE

BARNET HWY

Second Narrows Bridge

7A

HASTINGS ST

BOUNDARY ROAD

LOUGHEED HIGHWAY

BURNABY

CANADA WAY

Fraser River

COLUMBIA ST

NEW WESTMINSTER

104 AVE

Skytrain

MARINE DRIVE

KINGSWAY

BROADWAY

33RD AVE

49 AVE

GRANVILLE STREET

Queen Elizabeth Park

41ST AVE

99

Vancouver International Airport ✈

Tsawwassen Ferry Terminal ▶

museum and symphony orchestra, as well as opera, theatre and dance companies at the cutting edge of contemporary arts. Festivals proliferate throughout its mild, if occasionally rain-soaked, summer while numerous music venues provide a hotbed for up-and-coming rock bands and a burgeoning jazz scene.

Business growth continues apace in Canada's third-largest city, much of its prosperity stemming from a **port** so laden with the raw materials of the Canadian interior – lumber, wheat and minerals – that it ranks as one of North America's largest, handling more dry tonnage than the West Coast ports of Seattle, Tacoma, Portland, San Francisco and San Diego put together. The port in turn owes its prominence to Vancouver's much-trumpeted position as a gateway to East Asia, and its increasingly pivotal role in the new global market of the **Pacific Rim**. This lucrative realignment is strengthened by a two-way flow in traffic: in the past decade Vancouver has been inundated with Hong Kong Chinese (the so-called "yacht people"), an influx which has pushed up property prices and slightly strained the city's reputation as an ethnically integrated metropolis.

Much of the city's earlier immigration focused on Vancouver's extraordinary **Chinatown**, just one of a number of ethnic enclaves – Italian, Greek, Indian and Japanese in particular – which lend the city a refreshingly gritty quality that belies its sleek, modern reputation. So too do the city's semi-derelict eastern districts, whose worldly lowlife characters, addicts and hustlers are shockingly at odds with the glitzy lifestyles pursued in the lush residential neighbourhoods. Low rents and Vancouver's cosmopolitan young have also nurtured an unexpected **counterculture**, distinguished by varied restaurants, secondhand shops, avant-garde galleries, clubs and bars – spots where you'll probably have more fun than in many a Canadian city. And at the top of the scale there are **restaurants** as good – and as varied – as any in North America.

These days Vancouver is more dynamic than ever, its growth and energy almost palpable as you walk the streets. The downtown population, currently just over half a million, is the fastest-growing on the continent. In response the downtown area is spreading to the older and previously run-down districts southeast of the old city core. Development over the last decade is symbolized by a superb library and performing-arts complex which constitutes the most expensive capital project ever undertaken in the city. Real estate here is now more expensive than in Toronto, and in the 1990s the city became North America's largest **film and TV** production centre after Los Angeles and New York: *The X Files* is just the most famous of the many movies and programmes that have been, or are being, made here (see p.829 for details of *X Files* tours). Yet, in the peculiar way that seems second nature to Canadians, the changes are being handled in a manner that's enhancing rather than compromising the city's beguiling combination of pleasure, culture, business and natural beauty.

A brief history of Vancouver

Vancouver in the modern sense has existed for a little under 120 years. Over the course of the previous nine millennia the Fraser Valley was home to the Tsawwassen, Musqueam and another twenty or so native tribes, who made up the **Stó:lo Nation**, or "people of the river". The fish, particularly salmon, of this river were the Stó:lo lifeblood. Over the millennia these people ventured relatively little into the mountainous interior, something that remains true to this day. One of the things that makes modern Vancouver so remarkable is how wild and empty British Columbia remains beyond the Fraser's narrow corridor. The Stó:lo inhabited about ten villages on the shores of Vancouver's

Burrard Inlet before the coming of the Europeans. A highly developed culture, the Stó:lo were skilled carpenters, canoe-makers and artists, though little in the present city – outside its museums – pays anything but lip service to their existence. Vancouver Island is the nearest best bet if you're in search of latter-day tokens of aboriginal culture.

Europeans appeared on the scene in notable numbers during the **eighteenth century**, when Spanish explorers charted the waters along what is now southwestern British Columbia. In 1778 **Captain James Cook** reached nearby Nootka Sound while searching for the Northwest Passage, sparking off immediate British interest in the area. In 1791 José Maria Narvaez, a Spanish pilot and surveyor, glimpsed the mouth of the Fraser from his ship, the *Santa Saturnia*. This led to wrangles between the British and Spanish, disputes quickly settled in Britain's favour when Spain became domestically embroiled in the aftermath of the French Revolution. **Captain George Vancouver** officially claimed the land for Britain in 1792, but studying the Fraser from a small boat decided that it seemed too shallow to be of practical use. Instead he rounded a headland to the north, sailing into a deep natural port – the future site of Vancouver – which he named "Burrard" after one of his companions. He then traded briefly with several Squamish tribespeople at X'ay'xi, a village on the inlet's forested headland (the future Stanley Park). Afterwards the Squamish named the spot Whul-whul-Lay-ton, or "place of the white man". Vancouver sailed on, having spent just a day in the region – scant homage to an area that was to be named after him a century later.

Vancouver's error over the Fraser was uncovered in 1808, when Scottish-born **Simon Fraser** made an epic 1368-kilometre journey down the river from the Rockies to the sea. In 1827 the Hudson's Bay Company set up a fur-trading post at **Fort Langley**, 48km east of the present city, bartering not only furs but also salmon from the Stó:lo, the latter being salted and then packed off to company forts across Canada. The fort was kept free of homesteaders, despite being the area's first major white settlement, their presence deemed detrimental to the fur trade. Major colonization of the area only came after the Fraser River and Cariboo gold rushes in 1858, when **New Westminster** bustled with the arrival of as many as 25,000 hopefuls, many of whom were refugees from the 1849 Californian rush. Many also drifted in from the US, underlining the fragility of the national border and the precarious nature of British claims to the region. These claims were consolidated when British Columbia was declared a crown colony, with New Westminster as its capital. Both were superseded by Fort Victoria in 1868, by which time the gold rush had dwindled almost to nothing.

In 1862, meanwhile, three British prospectors, unable to find gold in the interior, bought a strip of land on the southern shore of Burrard Inlet and – shortsightedly, given the amount of lumber around – started a brickworks. This soon gave way to the Hastings Sawmill and a shantytown of bars that by 1867 had taken the name of **Gastown**, after "Gassy" – as in loquacious – Jack Leighton, proprietor of the site's first saloon. Two years later Gastown became incorporated as the town of **Granville** and prospered on the back of its timber and small coal deposits. The birth of the present city dates to 1884, when the **Canadian Pacific Railway** decided to make it the terminus of its transcontinental railway. In 1886, on a whim of the CPR president, Granville was renamed Vancouver, only to be destroyed on June 13 that year when fire razed all but half a dozen buildings. The setback proved short-lived, and since the arrival of the first train from Montréal in 1887 the city has never looked back.

Arrival

Vancouver International Airport (☎604/207-7077, ⓦwww.yvr.ca) is situated on Sea Island, 13km south of the city centre. Its often-used coded abbreviation is YVR. International flights arrive at the majestic main terminal; domestic flights at the smaller and linked old Main Terminal. If you're an international passenger, you'll find a **tourist information** desk (daily 7am–midnight; ☎604/688-5515) as you exit customs and immigration and before entering the terminal's public spaces. On the left just before this are desks for direct bus services from the airport to Victoria (Pacific Coach Lines) and Whistler. There are also services for Bellingham Airport (Seattle) and Sea-Tac Airport in the US available outside Arrivals; see below. There are also plenty of **foreign exchange** and other facilities, along with complimentary phones to several upmarket hotels in the area. Domestic passengers also have a tourist information desk (same hours as above) just before the terminal exit.

The best way to get into Vancouver is on the private **Airporter bus** (6.45am–1.10am; $12 single, $18 return; ☎604/946-8866 or 1-800/668-3141, ⓦwww.yvrairporter.com), which leaves every 15 minutes from a bay to the left immediately outside the main door of the international arrivals; from domestic arrivals you can walk here if you need Airporter information or wait at the domestic arrivals pick-up outside the terminal. You can buy **tickets** from the driver or at the bus stop by international arrivals. Resourceful staff and a pamphlet with a useful map help you figure out which drop-offs on the shuttle's three routes are most useful. Note that if you're headed straight for the bus depot (see below) on route #3 you need to transfer to another Airporter service closer to downtown: the driver will tell you all you need to know. Returning to the airport, buses run round the same pick-up points, including the bus depot.

Taxis into town cost about $25–30, limos $42. **Public transport** is cheaper but slower and involves a change of bus – from the domestic terminal, take the BC Metro Transit bus #100 (roughly every 30min) to the corner of 70th Street and Granville, then change to the #20 or #21 which drops off downtown on Granville Street. Tickets cost $3 during rush hour, $2 off-peak (Mon–Fri after 6.30pm, Sat & Sun all day), and exact change is required to buy tickets on board: make sure you get a transfer if the driver doesn't automatically give you one (see "City transport", p.784, for more on peak and off-peak hours and transfers).

It's also useful to know that Pacific Coach Lines (☎604/662-7575 or 1-800/661-1725, ⓦwww.pacificcoach.com) runs direct buses from the airport **to Victoria** (1–3 daily year-round; mid-May to June, Sept & Oct 2–4 daily; late June to early Sept 7 daily; $36 single, $71 return). Ask for details at the bus desk in international arrivals, or go straight to the hotel shuttle bus stop outside the international terminal. Other **bus services from the airport** are run by Perimeter (☎604/266-5386 or 905-0041, ⓦwww.perimeterbus.com) for services **to Whistler**; Quick Shuttle (☎604/940-4428 or 1-800/665-2122, ⓦwww.quickcoach.com) to **Bellingham** Airport, downtown **Seattle** and SeaTac Airport; and Malaspina Coach Lines (☎604/885-2217 or 1-877/227-8287, ⓦwww.roughlife.com) to the **Sunshine Coast**, Powell River, Whistler, Pemberton and **Nanaimo** on Vancouver Island.

By bus

Vancouver's main **bus terminal** is used by **Pacific Coach Lines** (☎604/662-7575 or 1-800/661-1725, ⓦwww.pacificcoach.com; for Victoria, Vancouver

Vancouver is at the hub of transport links to many parts of western Canada. Deciding where to move **onward from the city** – and how to go – presents a wealth of possibilities. We've listed the basic alternatives, together with cross-references to more detailed accounts of the various options.

Note that all passengers departing from Vancouver International Airport must pay a **departure tax**, or Airport Improvement Fee: $5 if travelling within BC, $10 within North America (including Mexico and Hawaii), $15 elsewhere. The tax is levied as you pass through to the gates and must be paid on the spot with cash or credit. Save time by prepaying at the automatic machines dotted around the various check-in areas in the national, international and US departures zones.

The Yukon and Alaska

You can **fly** to **Whitehorse** (see p.1002) in the Yukon directly from Vancouver, but there are no nonstop flights to Alaska from the city: all go via Seattle in the US. Flying to Seattle or taking a bus to Sea-Tac Airport takes around three hours from Vancouver Airport or various downtown hotels and other locations (see p.781 for bus details). You can **drive** to Alaska through southern British Columbia to **Dawson Creek**, where you can pick up the **Alaska Hwy** (see p.997), which runs through the Yukon to Fairbanks. Allow at least three days. Alternatively drive to Prince George, head west towards Prince Rupert and then strike north up the more adventurous **Cassiar Hwy** (see p.992) to connect with the Alaska Hwy in the Yukon. Using **public transport** you could take a Greyhound bus to Prince George (one day), connecting with another Greyhound to Dawson Creek and Whitehorse (two days). Buses link Whitehorse with other Yukon and Alaskan destinations. To travel to Alaska **by boat** from Vancouver you need to go via Bellingham (in the US), Prince Rupert, or Port Hardy on Vancouver Island (see p.895).

BC, Calgary and the Canadian Rockies

Two main **road** routes strike east from Vancouver towards Alberta and the

Island), **Malaspina Coach Lines** (☎604/885-2217 or 1-877/227-8287, ⓦwww.roughlife.com; for the Sunshine Coast) and all **Greyhound** services (☎604/482-8747 or 1-800/661-8747, ⓦwww.greyhound.ca; for BC, Alberta, Yukon and long-haul destinations including Seattle and the US). It is in a slightly dismal area alongside the VIA Rail Pacific Central train station at 1150 Station St; ticket offices for all companies are inside on the right as you enter. There are **left-luggage** facilities here and a useful **hotel board**, whose freephone line connects to some of the city's genuine cheapies (but check their locations) – some of whom will deduct the taxi fare from the terminal from your first night's bill.

It's too far to walk to downtown from the bus terminal, so bear left from the station through a small park to the Science World–Main St SkyTrain station, from where it's a couple of stops to downtown (take the train marked "Waterfront"); tickets ($2) are available from platform machines. Alternatively, you could take a taxi downtown from the station for about $6–8.

By train

Skeletal **VIA Rail** services operate out of Pacific Central Station (☎1-888/VIA-RAIL, ⓦwww.viarail.ca); they run to and from Jasper (3 weekly; see p.727), where there are connections (also 3 weekly) for Prince George and Prince Rupert, and on to Edmonton and the east. There is one service run by **VIA–Amtrak** (☎253/931-8917 or 1-800/872-7245, ⓦwww.amtrak.com)

Canadian Rockies – the **Trans-Canada Highway** and **Hwy 3**, both served by regular Greyhound buses. Both give access to **the Okanagan** (see p.930), known for its warm-watered lakes and summer resorts, and to the beautiful mountain and lakes enclave of the **Kootenays** (see p.945). VIA trains run three times weekly through the region via Kamloops to **Jasper** (for the Rockies) and **Edmonton**. Buses also serve the **Cariboo** region, the duller central part of the province (see p.911). Several mouthwatering itineraries can be put together by combining car or public transport journeys in the **BC interior** with BC Ferries' connections from Port Hardy on Vancouver Island to either Bella Coola or Prince Rupert.

It takes between ten and twelve hours to drive to **Calgary** on the Trans-Canada Hwy, and about ninety minutes less to reach the heart of the Canadian Rockies, **Banff**. Special express-service Greyhound buses operate over the same route. There is no longer a VIA Rail passenger service to Calgary. Very frequent one-hour flights connect Vancouver and Calgary, and charter operators and no-frills airlines offer highly competitive rates on this route (though cheap flights often leave very early or very late in the day).

Vancouver Island

Numerous **ferries** ply between Vancouver and three points on **Vancouver Island** – Swartz Bay (for Victoria), Nanaimo and Comox. Most leave from Tsawwassen and Horseshoe Bay, terminals about thirty minutes' drive south and west of downtown respectively. As a foot passenger you can buy inclusive bus and ferry tickets from Vancouver to Victoria or Nanaimo. Car drivers should make reservations well in advance for all summer crossings (see p.834 for full details of getting to Vancouver Island). **Public transport** connects to the Pacific Rim National Park, the island's highlight, and to Port Hardy on the island's northern tip for ferry connections to Prince Rupert and Bella Coola.

between Vancouver and Seattle (departs both stations daily 6pm; arrives Vancouver 9.30pm, arrives Seattle 9.55pm).

A second train station, belonging to the provincial **BC Rail**, at 1311 W 1st St, in North Vancouver (☎604/984-5246 or 1-800/339-8752 in BC, 1-800/663-8238 in the rest of North America, ⓦ www.bcrail.com), once provided passenger services to and from Whistler, Lillooet and Prince George via 100 Mile House, Williams Lake and Quesnel. This service, however, has been suspended indefinitely, as have their popular excursion trips to Squamish aboard the *Royal Hudson* steam train.

Information and city transport

The excellent Vancouver visitor centre – most commonly called the "**Touristinfo Centre**" – is almost opposite Canada Place (see p.795) at the foot of Burrard Street in the Waterfront Centre, 200 Burrard St at the corner of Canada Place Way (mid-May to Sept daily 8am–6pm; rest of year Mon–Sat 8.30am–5pm; ☎604/683-2000 or 1-800/663-6000 or 1-800/435-5622, ⓦ www.tourismvancouver.com). Besides information on the city and much of southeastern British Columbia, the office provides **foreign exchange** facilities, BC TransLink (transit or **public transport**) tickets and information, and tickets to sports and entertainment events through a separate Ticketmaster booth. Same-day tickets for events are often available at a discount. It also has one of the most comprehensive **accommodation services** imaginable, backed up by bulging photo albums of hotel rooms and B&Bs: the booking service is free.

Smaller **information kiosks** open in the summer (July & Aug daily 9.30am–5.30pm, Thurs & Fri till 9pm) in a variety of locations, usually including Stanley Park and close to the Vancouver Art Gallery on the corner of Georgia and Granville.

City transport

Vancouver's **public transport** system is an efficient, integrated network of bus, light rail (known as SkyTrain), SeaBus and ferry services that are operated by TransLink, formerly – and occasionally still – known as BC Transit (daily 6.30am–11.30pm; ☎604/953-3333, ⓦ www.translink.bc.ca).

Tickets are valid across the system for bus, SkyTrain and SeaBus. Generally they cost $2 for journeys in the large, central Zone 1, and $3 or $4 for longer two- and three-zone journeys – though you're unlikely to go out of Zone 1 unless you're travelling to the airport from downtown, which involves crossing from Zone 1 to 2. These regular fares apply in **peak hours**: Monday to Friday from start of service until 6.30pm. In **off-peak hours** – after 6.30pm and all day Saturday, Sunday and public holidays – a flat $2 fare applies across all three zones. Tickets are valid for **transfers** throughout the system for ninety minutes from the time of issue; on buses you should ask for a transfer ticket if the driver doesn't automatically give you one. Otherwise, you can buy tickets individually (or in books of ten for $18 for Zone 1) at station offices or machines, 7-Eleven, Safeway and London Drugs stores, or any other shop or newsstand displaying a blue TransLink sticker (so-called "FareDealer" outlets). You must carry tickets with you as proof of payment.

Probably the simplest and cheapest deal if you're going to be making three or more journeys in a day is to buy a **DayPass** ($8), valid all day across all three zones; Zone 1 monthly passes are $63 (weekly passes are not available). If you buy these over the counter at stores or elsewhere (not in machines) they're "Scratch & Ride" – you scratch out the day and month before travel.

See "Listings" on p.828 for details of **car and bicycle rental** and **taxis**.

Buses

The useful *Transit Route Map & Guide* ($1.95) is available from the Touristinfo Centre and FareDealer shops, while free **bus** timetables can be found at the Touristinfo Centre, 7-Eleven stores and the central library. You can buy tickets on the bus, but make sure you have the right change (they don't carry any) to shovel into the box by the driver; ask specially if you want a transfer ticket. If you have a pass or transfer, simply show the driver. Normal buses stop running around midnight, when a rather patchy "Night Owl" service comes into effect on major routes until about 4am. Note that blue **West Van buses** (☎604/985-7777) also operate in the city (usually to North and West Vancouver destinations, including the BC Ferries terminal at Horseshoe Bay) – TransLink tickets are valid on these buses as well.

SeaBuses

The **SeaBuses** ply between downtown and Lonsdale Quay in North Vancouver, and they're a ride definitely worth taking for its own sake: the views of the mountains across Burrard Inlet, the port and the downtown skyline are

Some of the more important Vancouver **bus routes** are:

#1 Gastown–English Bay loop.

#3 and #8 Gastown–Downtown (Robson at Granville)–Marine Drive at Main.

#4 UBC and #10 UBC Granville Street–University of BC–Museum of Anthropology.

#17 and #20 Downtown–Marine Drive; transfer at Granville and 70th Street to #100 (for the airport).

#19 Pender Street (Downtown)–Stanley Park (Stanley Park Loop).

#23, #35, #123 and #135 Downtown (Pender and Burrard)–Stanley Park.

#50 Gastown–False Creek–Broadway.

#51 SeaBus Terminal–Downtown–Granville Island.

#236 Lonsdale Quay terminal (North Vancouver)–Capilano Suspension Bridge–Grouse Mountain.

Some scenic routes

These are some **scenic bus routes**, worth travelling for their own sakes:

#52 "Around the Park" service takes 30min through Stanley Park (April–Oct Sat & Sun only); board at Stanley Park Loop (connections from #23, #35 or #135) or Denman Street (connections from #1, #3 or #8).

#210 Pender Street–Phibbs Exchange; change there for the #211 (mountain route) or #212 (ocean views) to Deep Cove.

#250 Georgia Street (Downtown)–North Vancouver–West Vancouver–Horseshoe Bay,

#351 Howe Street–White Rock–Crescent Beach (1hr each way).

superb. The downtown terminal is Waterfront Station in the old Canadian Pacific station buildings at the foot of Granville Street. There is no ticket office, only a ticket machine, but you can get a **ticket** (same price as bus tickets) from the small newsagent immediately on your left as you face the long gallery that takes you to the boats. Two 400-seat catamarans make the thirteen-minute crossing every fifteen to thirty minutes (6.30am–12.30am). Arrival in North Vancouver is at Lonsdale Quay, where immediately to the left is a bus terminal for connections to Grouse Mountain and other North Vancouver destinations. Bicycles can be carried on board.

Ferries

The city also has a variety of small **ferries** – glorified bathtubs – run over similar routes by two rival companies: Aquabus (☎604/689-5858, Ⓦwww.aquabus.bc.ca) and False Creek Ferries (☎604/684-7781, Ⓦwww.granvilleislandferries.bc.ca). These provide a useful, very frequent and fun service (daily 7am–10.30pm, winter until 8.30pm). Aquabus runs boats in a continuous circular shuttle from the foot of Hornby Street to the Fish Docks on the seawalk to Vanier Park and the museums ($2), to Granville Island ($2), and to the Yaletown dock by the road loop at the east foot of Davie Street ($3). False Creek Ferries also runs to Granville Island ($2) and to Vanier Park ($3 from Granville Island, $2 from the Aquatic Centre) just below the Maritime Museum – this is a good way of getting to the park and its museums (see p.807). You buy **tickets** on board with both companies. Both companies also offer what amount to **mini-cruises** up False Creek, with connections from Granville Island to Science World and the Plaza of Nations. You can pick up the Aquabus boat at the Arts Club Theatre on Granville Island, the foot of Hornby Street downtown or – with False Creek Ferries – below the Aquatic Centre at the foot of Thurlow and northern end of Burrard Bridge, on Granville Island, or below the spit and small harbour near the Maritime Museum in Vanier Park.

SkyTrain

Vancouver's single light-rail line – **SkyTrain** – is a model of its type: driverless, completely computerized and magnetically propelled, half underground and half on raised track. It covers 28km between the downtown Waterfront Station (housed in the CPR building with the SeaBus terminal) and the southeastern suburb of New Westminster. Only the first three or four stations – Waterfront, Burrard, Granville and Stadium – are of any practical use to the casual visitor, but the 39-minute trip along the twenty-station line is worth taking if only to see how the Canadians do these things: with spotless interiors and Teutonic punctuality.

Accommodation

Vancouver has a surprisingly large number of inexpensive **hotels**, but some – mainly in the area east of downtown – are of a dinginess at odds with the city's highly polished image. If you're on a low budget, you're better off in the **hostels** or the excellent **YWCA**. Mid-range hotels are still reasonable, but Vancouver is a tourist city and space can get tight in summer: you'll need to **book ahead**. A lot of the nicer options (including the *Sylvia*) are in the West End, a quiet residential area bordering Vancouver's wonderful Stanley Park, only five or ten minutes' walk from downtown. Another option, if you're here to explore the parks on the city's fringe, is to take advantage of the hotels and **B&Bs** on the North Shore. Vancouver is not a camper's city: the majority of the in-city **campsites** are for RVs only and will turn you away if you've only got a tent.

Hotels

Gastown, Chinatown and the area between them hold central Vancouver's cheaper **hotels**, often located on top of a bar where live bands and late-night drinking will keep you awake till the small hours. These areas are not safe for women at night, and everyone needs to avoid the backstreets. If you really need

B&Bs

B&B accommodation can be booked through agencies, but most of them operate as a phone service only and require two days' notice – it's better to try the Touristinfo Centre's accommodation service first (see p.783). Though seldom central or cheap – reckon on $80-plus for a double – B&Bs are likely to be relaxed and friendly, and if you choose well you can have beaches, gardens, barbecues and as little or as much privacy as you want. The following **B&B agencies** have accommodation throughout the city, in Victoria (see pp.831–847), the Gulf Islands and beyond: Best Canadian Bed & Breakfast Network (☎604/738-7207, ⓦ wwwbestcanadianbb.com), Emerald Park (☎604/878-1328, ⓦ www.travelsuites.com) and Western Canada Bed and Breakfast Innkeepers' Association (☎604/952-0982, ⓦ www.wcbbia.com).

to stick to the rock-bottom price bracket, and don't fancy the hostels or YWCA, as a last resort go for one of the invariably dodgy hotels north of the Granville Street Bridge, a tame but tacky red-light area. Further up the scale, you should book in advance for the best and most popular places such as the *Sylvia* and *Kingston*.

The **North Shore** embraces North Vancouver – the area across the Burrard Inlet opposite the downtown peninsula – and West Vancouver, the mix of residential and open country along Marine Drive and the Trans-Canada Highway (Hwy 1) towards Lighthouse Park and Horseshoe Bay. The main reasons you may want to stay here are to access the BC Ferries terminal at Horseshoe Bay easily (see p.898) or to be more handily placed for the hikes and other outdoor activities afforded by Grouse Mountain and the Capilano River, Mount Seymour and Lyon Canyon parks. If this is your intention, there are some delightful **B&B** options close to the parks. However, there's no point staying here if you want to get to grips with downtown, even if you have a car, as traffic across the Lions Gate Bridge – the only vehicular access – is often bad. Despite this, there are several reasonably priced **motels** in the area, mostly just over the Lions Gate Bridge on or close to the junction of Capilano Road and Marine Drive. If you're relying on public transport, then you'll need to use buses or the SeaCat. The city's reservation services (see p.784) can help out with North Shore lodging, but North Vancouver also has its own **visitor centre** at 102–124 West 1st St (☎604/987-4488, ⓦ www.nvchamber.bc.ca) with information on the area's accommodation.

Out of season, hotels in all categories offer reductions, and you can reckon on thirty percent discounts on high-season prices. Even the smartest hotels will introduce an extra bed into a double room at very little extra cost if there are three of you.

Central Vancouver

Barclay Hotel 1348 Robson St between Jervis and Broughton sts ☎604/688-8850, ⓦ www .barclayhotel.com. A good bargain, the *Barclay* is one of the nicer of several hotels at the north end of Robson St, with ninety rooms and a chintzy French rustic ambience. **⑤**

Buchan Hotel 1906 Haro St between Chilco and Gilford sts ☎604/685-5354 or 1-800/668-6654, ⓦ www.buchanhotel.com. Some smallish rooms, past their prime, but still a genuine bargain given the peaceful residential location, only a block from Stanley Park and English Bay Beach. **❸–❻**

Burrard Motor Inn 1100 Burrard St near Helmcken St ☎604/681-2331 or 1-800/663-0366, ⓦ www.vancouver-bc.com/burrardmotorinn. A fairly central and pleasantly dated motel with standard fittings: some rooms look onto a charming garden courtyard, and some have kitchens. **⑤**

Comfort Inn Downtown 654 Nelson St ☎604/605-4333 or 1-888/605-5333, ⓦ www.comfortinndowntown.com. There have been lodgings of sorts in this heritage building for years – the last was the *Hotel Dakota* – but after a 1950s retro-inspired refit, complete with lots of black and white photographs and period neon, this

82-room boutique hotel now has a hip and stylish look. Rooms all come with high-speed Internet access, voicemail, dataports and air-conditioning. The location isn't the best but is convenient for the restaurant and clubs of both Yaletown and the lower end of Granville St. **⑤**

Days Inn Vancouver Downtown 921 W Pender St at Burrard St ☎604/681-4335 or 1-877/681-4335, ⓦ www.daysinnvancouver.com. A city institution, this old seventy-room, seven-storey block in the central financial district has more character than most and lots of original Art Deco touches. While it looks tatty from the outside, the interior was renovated in 1999 and the rooms are clean and comfortable; streetfront rooms are likely to be noisy. **❼**

Dominion Hotel 210 Abbott St at Water St ☎604/681-6666 or 1-877/681-1666, ⓦ www.dominionhotel.bc.ca. A nice, refurbished old hotel on the edge of Gastown let down by its thunderous live music: it's almost impossible to find a room where you're not kept awake, but at least try to ask for one of the newer rooms with private bathroom as far away as possible from the live bands that play in the bar downstairs. **❸**

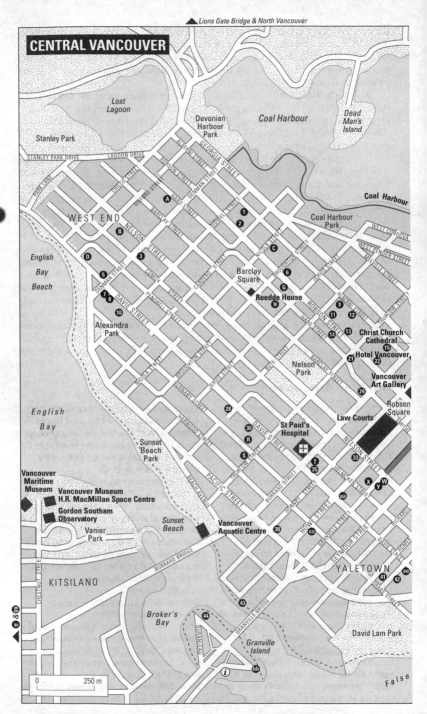

7

CENTRAL VANCOUVER

Lions Gate Bridge & North Vancouver

Coal Harbour

Dead Man's Island

Lost Lagoon

Devonian Harbour Park

Coal Harbour

Stanley Park

STANLEY PARK DRIVE   LAGOON DRIVE

PARK LANE

WEST END

Coal Harbour Park

WEST CORDOVA

WEST PENDER STREET

MELVILLE STREET

English Bay Beach

Barclay Square

Roedde House

Christ Church Cathedral

Hotel Vancouver

Vancouver Art Gallery

English Bay

Alexandra Park

Nelson Park

Law Courts

Robson Square

St Paul's Hospital

Sunset Beach Park

Vancouver Maritime Museum

Vancouver Museum
H.R. MacMillan Space Centre

Gordon Southam Observatory

Vanier Park

PACIFIC STREET

BEACH AVENUE

Sunset Beach

Vancouver Aquatic Centre

BURRARD BRIDGE

KITSILANO

YALETOWN

David Lam Park

Broker's Bay

Granville Island

GRANVILLE BRIDGE

False

0   250 m

EATING AND DRINKING

Allegro Café	33	Ezogiku Noodle Café	6	Milestone's	7&13
Bavaria	19	Floata Seafood	31	Old Spaghetti Factory	18
Bin 941	35	Gallery Café	26	The Only Café	27
Blake's	20	Hamburger Mary's	28	Phnom-Penh	34
Blue Water Café	39	The Hermitage	22	Piccolo Mondo	21
Boulangerie la Parisienne	40	Hon's Wun-Tun House	32	Pink Pearl	25
Bread Garden	3	Il Giardino di Umberto	38	Raincity Grill	5
C Restaurant	43	Imperial Chinese Seafood	4	Shanghai Chinese Bistro	12
Capers	2	Kirin Mandarin	9	Simply Thai	41
Chartwell	0	La Luna Café	17	Stepho's	30
Chiyoda	15	Le Crocodile	24	Terra Breads	44
CinCin	14	Le Gavroche	1	Villa del Lupo	37
Cioppino's	42	Liliget Feast House	8	Water St Café	16
Diva at the Met	23	Lucy Mae Brown	36	Wild Rice	29
Earl's	11	Mescalero's	10		

Burrard Inlet

Seawall

Canada Place

Centennial Pier

Seaplane Terminal

Marine Building

Waterfront Centre

Bentall Centre

Granville Square

SeaBus Terminal

Helijet Terminal

Sinclair Centre

Burrard.

Waterfront

CP Railway Station

DOWNTOWN

American Express

Harbour Centre Tower

Mapletree Square

Granville

WATER STREET

POWELL STREET

Hong Kong Bank

Pacific Mall

WEST PENDER STREET

WEST HASTINGS STREET

GASTOWN

EAST CORDOVA ST

EAST HASTINGS ST

Vancouver Police Museum

Deals

Queen Elizabeth Theatre

CHINATOWN

EAST PENDER ST

Library Square

Stadium

Dr Sun Yat-Sen Garden

KEEFER STREET

Orpheum Theatre

Vancouver Public Library

GM Place

DUNSMUIR VIADUCT

EXPO BOULEVARD

EAST GEORGIA STREET

The Centre in Vancouver for the Performing Arts

ROBSON STREET

GEORGIA VIADUCT

BC Place Stadium

PACIFIC BOULEVARD

PRIOR STREET

SkyTrain

Pacific Central Station

The Roundhouse

Plaza of Nations

Science World

Creek

ACCOMMODATION

Barclay Hotel	G	Dufferin Hotel	U	Sandman Hotel	V
Buchan Hotel	B	Fairmont Hotel	L	Shato Inn Hotel	B
Burrard Motor Inn	T	Fairmont Waterfront	F	Sunset Inn & Suites	R
Cambie Int'l Hostel Gastown	J	Four Seasons	O	Sylvia Hotel	D
Cambie Int'l Hostel Seymour	K	Global Village Backpackers	Y	Travelodge Vancouver Centre	cc
Central Station Hostel	dd	Granville Island Hotel	hh	Vancouver Central Hostel	X
Comfort Inn	W	Holiday Inn Downtown	aa	Vancouver Downtown Hostel	S
C&N Backpackers	bb	Kingston Hotel	Q	Vancouver Jericho Beach Hostel	ff
Days Inn	H	Opus Hotel	ee	Vanier Hostel	gg
Dominion Hotel	M	Pan Pacific	E	Victorian Hotel	P
		Patricia Budget Inn	N	West End Guest House	I
		Riviera Hotel	C	YWCA	Z

7

SOUTHERN BRITISH COLUMBIA

Dufferin Hotel 900 Seymour St ☎604/683-4251 or 1-877/683-5522, ⊚www.dufferinhotel.com. This 72-room hotel is not far from the preferable *Kingston* (see below), and tends to pick up its overflow. It's not as calm, cheap or pleasant as its near rival, but does offer free parking, dining room and a choice of family rooms and rooms with and without private bathrooms. Noise and late-night bustle can be an issue here, as there is a (predominantly gay, but straight-friendly) pub on the premises. ❹

Fairmont Hotel Vancouver 900 W Georgia St at Burrard St ☎604/684-3131 or 1-800/441-1414, ⊚www.fairmont.com. This traditional old hotel, given a multimillion-dollar face-lift in 1996, is the city's most famous and prestigious. It's the place to stay if money's no object and you want old-world style and downtown location. Whether you stay here or not, the ground floor *900 West* restaurant and bar is good, as are the various other restaurants, including *Griffins* on the same floor. Doubles among the 550 rooms range from $269 to $589, but low-season rates around $190 are available. ❽

Fairmont Waterfront 900 Canada Place Way ☎604/691-1991 or 1-800/441-1414, ⊚www.fairmont.com. Another prestigious *Canadian Pacific* hotel, this time a fabulous multistorey affair on the dazzling downtown waterfront. ❽

Four Seasons Hotel Vancouver 791 Georgia St at Howe ☎604/689-9333 or 1-800/332-3442, ⊚www.fourseasons.com. A Four Seasons hotel rarely disappoints, and Vancouver's is no exception. The location is central, a block from Robson and the Vancouver Art Gallery, and the 385 rooms occupy a 28-storey high-rise building above the Pacific Centre mall. Rooms are enormous, the service immaculate, and the common parts stunning. If you're staying or not, you should definitely think about taking the buffet breakfast which is served on the Garden Terrace – it's one of the best in the city (from $13). Similarly, the hotel's main restaurant, the *Chartwell*, is widely considered among the city's elite, and is open to non-patrons – see p.818) Doubles range from $400 to $570 for an executive suite. ❽

Granville Island Hotel 1253 Johnson St ☎604/683-7373 or 1-800/663-1840, ⊚www.granvilleislandhotel.com. You're away from central downtown, but on the other hand you're in the heart of one of the city's trendiest and most enjoyable little enclaves. You pay a premium for this and for the spectacular waterfront setting. ❼

Holiday Inn Hotel & Suites Downtown 1110 Howe St between Helmcken and Davie sts

☎604/684-2151 or 1-800/663-9151 in Canada and the US (also 1-800/HOLIDAY), ⊚www.hivancouverdowntown.com. Reasonably central, large and – unlike the dingier hotels nearby – you'll know what to expect, though at this price there's plenty of alternative choice around town. Lots of facilities, including sauna, pool and kids' activity centre, plus rooms with kitchenettes for self-catering. ❼

Kingston Hotel 757 Richards St at Robson St ☎604/684-9024 or 1-888/713-3304, ⊚www.kingstonhotelvancouver.com. This popular bargain is handily sited for downtown and its clean and nicely decorated interior affects the spirit of a "European-style" hotel. Rooms are available with or without private bathroom and there's a modest but free breakfast to start the day. Along with the *Sylvia*, it's by far the best hotel at its price in the city, so book well ahead. Long-stay terms available. ❸

Opus Hotel 322 Davie St ☎604/642-6787 or 1-866/642-6787, ⊚www.opushotel.com. It was only a matter of time before Yaletown aquired a hypertrendy hotel, and in the *Opus*, opened in 2002, it has a stylish, contemporary place to stay that lives up to its location's hip reputation. Outside it's just another seven-storey former warehouse, but inside is a bold palette of decorative colours and materials (mosaic, marble, expensive fabrics). The 97 rooms are equally fetching – expensive linens, firm beds, CD players, big windows and great bathrooms. The cool *Opus Bar* and *Elixir* French brasserie mean you need never leave the hotel precincts for food, drink and evening relaxation – though with the temptations of Yaletown just seconds away, this would be a mistake. Rooms start from $290, with suites coming in at $479, but off-season rates are far more manageable. ❽

Pan Pacific 300–999 Canada Place ☎604/662-8111 or 1-800/663-1515 in Canada, 1-800/937-1515 in the US, ⊚www.panpacific.com. If you walk around Canada Place and wonder what happens in the magnificent white high-rise that rises above the complex's famous "sails" then wonder no more, for it's occupied by the *Pan Pacific*, the most expensive and spectacularly situated of Vancouver's modern luxury hotels. An eight-storey atrium and lobby set the tone, with vast 12m picture windows that look out over the harbour. All 504 rooms enjoy great views (the hotel rooms start on the building's eighth floor), and if you can snaffle rooms 10 and 20 on each floor, then your bathroom will also have a sweeping panorama. Service and facilities are impeccable, and the heated outdoor pool and health centre are both state of the art. Rooms start at around $490. ❽

Patricia Budget Inn Hotel 403 E Hastings St near Gore St ☎604/255-4301, ⓦwww.budgetpathotel.bc.ca. A well-known and widely advertised budget choice with 92 rooms, but far from downtown in the heart of Chinatown (too far to walk comfortably): an exciting or grim location, depending on your point of view, though some women have reported feeling distinctly unsafe in the area. Generally clean and reasonably renovated, it's the best of the many in this district. ❸

Riviera Hotel 1431 Robson St between Nicola and Broughton sts ☎604/685-1301 or 1-888/699-5222, ⓦwww.rivieraonrobson.com. Reasonably priced central motels such as this place, around midway between Stanley Park and the Vancouver Art Gallery, are rare; the one- and two-room suites have kitchenettes. ❻

Sandman Hotel Downtown 180 W Georgia St at Beatty St ☎604/681-2211 or 1-800/726-3626, ⓦwww.sandmanhotels.com. Flagship of a mid-price chain with hotels all over western Canada and well placed at the eastern edge of downtown. Rooms are bland but fine and spacious as far as chain hotels go, which makes this first choice if you want something one up from the *Kingston*. ❶

Shato Inn Hotel at Stanley Park 1825 Comox St between Gilford and Denman sts ☎604/681-8920. A small, quiet, family-run place two blocks from the park and the beach. Some of the rooms have balconies and/or kitchen units. ❺

Sunset Inn & Suites 1111 Burnaby between Davie and Thurlow sts ☎604/688-2474 or 1-800/786-1997, ⓦwww.sunsetinn.com. One of the best West End "apartment" hotels and a good spot for a longer stay – spacious studio, double or triple rooms (all with kitchens and balconies) with on-site laundry and many nearby shops. Ten minutes' walk to downtown. ❺

Sylvia Hotel 1154 Gilford St ☎604/681-9321, ⓦwww.sylviahotel.com. A local landmark located in a "heritage" building, this is a popular place with a high reputation, making reservations essen-

tial. It's by the beach two blocks from Stanley Park, and its snug bar, quiet, old-world charm and sea views make it one of Vancouver's best. Rooms are available at different prices depending on size, view and facilities. ❹–❼

Travelodge Vancouver Centre 1304 Howe St ☎604/682-2767 or 1-800/578-7878, ⓦwww.travelodge.com. This 66-room chain hotel has seen better days, and at $129 upwards, the rates are rather high, but like many other hotels in the area – a block off Granville and a block up from the Granville Street Bridge – extensive restoration work is putting a new gloss on the place and making the prices rather better value. Ask for a refurbished room, and you'll get clean and comfortable interiors, air-conditioning, TV, free local phone calls, free parking and access to a restaurant and heated outdoor pool. Despite the "Centre" in the name, it's not terribly central, but is convenient for the Granville Island ferry jetty. ❻

Victorian Hotel 514 Homer St on the corner of Pender ☎604/681-6369 or 1-877/681-6369, ⓦwww.victorianhotel.com. The family-run *Victorian* is situated about as far east as you'd want to be, but remains within easy walking distance of Gastown and the rest of downtown. It was built in 1898 as one of the city's first guesthouses, and has been carefully restored, so that many of its 26 rooms have a period feel, with high ceilings, hardwood floors, elegant bathrooms and old features such as original fireplaces and mouldings. Prices vary by up to $60 between double rooms, depending on whether they have private bathrooms and/or kitchenettes. All rooms have phones and small TVs, and a continental breakfast is included in the room rate. ❹

West End Guest House 1362 Haro St at Jervis St ☎604/681-2889, ⓦwww.westendguesthouse.com. A wonderful small guesthouse with an old-time parlour and bright rooms, each with private bathroom; book well in advance. Full breakfast included. No smoking. ❻

The North Shore

A Cottage Garden B&B 2810 Wembley Drive ☎604/980-9255 or 1-877/787-3813, ⓦwww.bedandbreakfasts.bc.ca. Two rooms in Lyon Canyon park with forest views. To get here follow Hwy 1 and take exit 19 or 21. Private entrance and shared bathroom and living room/kitchen. ❸

Best Western Capilano Inn & Suites 1634 Capilano Rd ☎604/987-8185 or 1-800/644-4227, ⓦwww.bestwesterncapilano.com. Virtually on the junction of Marine Drive and Capilano Road, this

74-room is one of several chain motels just east of the Lions Gate Bridge. Standard rooms or rooms with kitchenettes for an additional $20, as well as laundry, restaurant and outdoor summer pool. ❹

Holiday Inn Express Vancouver-North Shore 1800 Capilano Rd ☎604/987-4461 or 1-800/663-4055 in Canada and the US (also 1-800/HOLIDAY), ⓦwww.hiexpressnv.com. One block north of the Capilano Rd and Marine Drive intersection. Rates include continental breakfast, and some rooms have kitchens and/or microwaves and fridges. ❺

Lonsdale Quay Hotel 123 Carrie Cates Court ☎604/986-6111 or 1-800/836-6111, ⓦwww.lonsdalequayhotel. Tastefully appointed rooms and a location right on the Lonsdale Quay waterfront (with fabulous harbour views) and above the quay's superb market (see p.810): escalators from the market itself lead you to the hotel reception on the third floor. Posted room rates are as low as $80 off season, but you far more likely to pay anything up to $225. ❼
Lynn Canyon B&B 3333 Robinson Rd ☎604/986-4741, ⓦwww.vancouverinn.com. A Tudor-style home with two guest rooms in 13km from downtown in lovely gardens and wooded setting close to the eponymous 250-hectare park and its hiking trails. ❹
Mountainside Manor 5909 Nancy Greene Way ☎604/990-9772 or 1-800/967-1319, ⓦwww.mtnsideaccom.com. Situated off the road to Grouse Mountain (exit Hwy 1 at Capilano Rd exit north and follow the Grouse Mountain signs for about 2.5km), this ultramodern contemporary home offers four bright and airy B&B rooms. Best rooms are the Panorama Room (with Jacuzzi and views of the city, mountains and the ocean as far as Vancouver Island) and the City Room (with four-poster and view of the city skyline). ❺
Park Royal Hotel 540 Clyde Avenue ☎604/926-5511 or 1-800/877-926-5511, ⓦwww.parkroyalhotel.com. This "Tudor-style inn" is close to the junction of Marine Drive and Taylor Way virtually across the road from the vast Park Royal

Shopping Centre. It sits on the river (you can fish for salmon from the grounds should you wish) and is shielded from the outside world by gardens. The fact that there are only thirty rooms makes it more intimate than the motels close by, and there's an aimiable English-style pub and Tudor Room restaurant for eating and drinking. ❼
The Grouse Inn 1633 Capilano Drive ☎604/988-7101 or 1-800/779-7888, ⓦwww.grouseinn.com. Close to downtown road links – one block east of the Lions Gate Bridge and one block south of Hwy 1 at Exit 14. Choose between 80 regular or superior rooms and one or two-bedroom kitchen suites (the kitchens cost an extra $29). ❺
Thistledown House B&B 3910 Capilano Rd ☎604/986-7173 or 1-888/633-7173, ⓦwww.thistle-down.com. A 1920 heritage building immediately east of the Capilano River park (just north of Edgemont Boulevard) and en route for Grouse Mountain, offering easy access to trails; en-suite rooms are tastefully restored and furnished with antiques; there are lovely gardens; and the room rate includes a full breakfast and afternoon tea. ❻
Travelodge Vancouver Lions Gate 2060 Marine Drive ☎604/985-5311 or 1-800/578-7878, ⓦwww.lionsgatetravelodge.com. Noise can be a problem at this 61-room chain motel, given its busy (but convenient) position between the Lions Gate Bridge and Capilano Road. In its favour is the fact that it was refurbished in 2002, the rooms are air-conditioned, there's an outdoor pool, and rates are reasonable. ❸

Hostels

Vancouver has three good Hostelling International (HI) **hostels**, plus a handful of other reasonable privately run hostels. Be warned, though, that there are a rash of dirty, badly run and occasionally dangerous "hotels", "hostels" and "rooming houses", particularly on Hastings Street a few blocks either side of Main Street: don't be tempted into these. In addition to the hostels, relatively low-price accommodation is available in summer at the *Vanier Hostel* of the **University of British Columbia**, though this is a long way from downtown.

Cambie International Hostel Gastown 300 Cambie St at Cordova ☎604/684-6466 or 1-888/395-5335, ⓦwww.cambiehostels.com. A private hostel located in Vancouver's oldest hotel and pub (built in 1897) just off Gastown's main streets, and so with a much nicer and more central position than many of the city's hostels. Beds are arranged in two-, four- or six-bed bunk rooms and there are laundry, luggage-storage and bike-storage (but no cooking) facilities. There's a deservedly popular and inexpensive bar-grill with good patio (the *Cambie Saloon & Grill*) downstairs, so aim for beds away from this area if you want a

relatively peaceful night's sleep. Also check out the linked and good-value *General Store & Bakery* nearby at 312 Cambie. No curfew. $20 per person in a dorm room (Oct–April $17.50); private double or quad rooms $22.50 person (off season $20). Weekly rates available.
Cambie International Hostel Seymour 515 Seymour St at W Pender ☎604/684-7757 or 1-888/395-5335, ⓦwww.cambiehostels.com. This is the second, newer, calmer and more central of the *Cambie*'s stable of hostels (there's a third on Vancouver Island). Like the Gastown hostel (see above), the management has made an effort to

ensure that rooms in this heritage building are pleasant, secure and well kept, and provide laundry, storage, Internet and food and drink in the shape of *The Big Dog Delic/Café* and *Malone's Bar & Grill* next door. No curfew. Pricing is slightly different to the Gastown hostel. Doubles in a bunk room cost $22.50 per person (Oct–April $20) and $27.50 per person for a double bed ($22.50 off season).

Central Station Hostel 1038 Main St ☎604/681-9118 or 682-2441 or 1-800/434-6060, ⍟www.centralstationhostel.com. This hostel opened near the main railway station in 2001 in the former *Ivanhoe Hotel*, a location that can be most kindly be described as "edgy". Each of the 104 rooms (renovated when the hostel opened) comes with sink, fridge and TV, and there's Internet access and an inexpensive restaurant and bar (with pool and darts) on site. Beds in six-bed dorm $16 ($90 weekly), singles $20, private doubles from $32.

C&N Backpackers Hostel 927 Main St ☎604/682-2441 or 1-888/434-6060, ⍟www.cnnbackpackers.com. A well-known backpackers' retreat that has been renovated, renamed – previously it was known as *Vincent's* – and considerably improved under new management. Still, it's not exactly dazzling and its location on the eastern edge of downtown is hardly the best and so far from anything but the Pacific Central Station and bus depot – which is 150m away – that it's hard to see why anyone should want to stay here unless you'd just got in on a late bus. This said, it's convenient for the SkyTrain station, and buses #3 or #8 from downtown run along Main St. Book or arrive early (office open 8am–midnight). No curfew. Beds at $14, $35 and $35 for a bunk (maximum of three- or four-bed dorms), single and double respectively. Weekly rates available.

Global Village Backpackers 1018 Granville St at Nelson ☎604/682-8226 or 1-888/844-7875, ⍟www.globalbackpackers.com. *Global Village* has followed up the success of a popular hostel in Toronto with a zippy, bright hostel in Vancouver, although their chosen location on Granville St – while central and away from the worst of this street's tawdriness – is not the quietest in the city. The hostel has 250 beds in two- and four-bed rooms, and offers a free shuttle from the bus/train station, secure lockers, modern kitchen and common area, games room and Internet access. No curfew. From $21 per person, doubles from $59.

Vancouver Central Hostel (HI) 1025 Granville St ☎604/685-5335 or 1-888/203-8333,

⍟www.hihostels.ca. Vancouver's newest and smartest HI hostel on busy Granville St is a far cry from the humble days of hostelling. It offers 226 beds in private double rooms with TV and en-suite bathrooms, four-bed dorms and air-conditioning in most rooms. Family rooms are also available. Facilities include a kitchen, pub, reading lounge and shuttle runs to the other city HI hostels and the Pacific Central Station. Check-in is at noon and check-out 11am. Dorm beds start at $20 for members and $24 for non-members. Private doubles start at $57.

Vancouver Downtown Hostel (HI) 1114 Burnaby St at the corner of Thurlow ☎604/684-4565 or 1-888/203-4302, ⍟www.hihostels.ca. Located in a former nunnery and health-care centre in the city's West End. There are 223 beds split up between shared and private rooms (maximum of four per room). Bike rental and storage as well as laundry, kitchen, Internet access and storage lockers are available. A free shuttle (look for the blue HI logo) operates between this hostel, the Jericho Beach hostel (see below) and the Pacific Central railway and bus terminal; if there's no bus, call the hostel to find when the next one is due. No curfew. Check-in 24 hours a day; check out by 11am. Reservations are essential. Beds cost $20 for members ($24 for non-members), private doubles $55 for members, $64 for non-members.

Vancouver Jericho Beach Hostel (HI) 1515 Discovery St off NW Marine Drive ☎604/224-3208 or 1-888/203-4852, ⍟www.hihostels.ca. Canada's biggest HI hostel has a superb and safe position surrounded by lawns by Jericho Beach south of the city. The 286-bed hostel – a former barracks – fills up quickly, occasionally leading to a three-day limit in summer. There are dorm beds and ten private rooms (sleeping up to six) which go quickly, with reductions for members and free bunks occasionally offered in return for a couple of hours' work. Family rooms are available. Facilities include kitchen, licensed café (April–Oct), bike rental and storage, storage lockers, Internet access and an excellent cafeteria. There is no curfew, but a "quiet time" is encouraged between 11pm and 7am. Check-in 24 hours a day. Dorm beds cost $18 for members, $22 for non-members. Doubles are $51 for members, $61 for non-members.

Vanier Hostel University of British Columbia (UBC), 5961 Student Union Blvd ☎604/822-1000, ⍟www.conferences.ubc.ca. This "hostel" is on the UBC campus, which means it's a long way from downtown (see p.784 for transport details), but close to the Museum of Anthropology and trails and sights such as Wreck Beach (see p.805). You get clean, safe accommodation (bed linen included), TV lounge, laundry, an Internet kiosk in the lobby, affordable campus food outlets and pubs and access to the university's fitness facilities, tennis courts and indoor and outdoor pools. No curfew. Additional discounts are available for HI and ISIC cardholders on the room rates which start at around $25 single, $50 double. Open early May to late Aug only.

The YWCA

YWCA Hotel-Residence 733 Beatty St between Georgia and Robson ☎604/895-5830 or 1-800/663-1424, ⓦwww.ywcahotel.com. Vancouver's main "Y" – open to men, women, couples and families – is an excellent place, offering the best inexpensive accommodation in the city. It was purpose-built in 1995 in a handy east downtown location close to the stunning central library. The nearest SkyTrain station is Stadium, a five-minute walk. Top-value rooms (especially for small groups) are spread over eleven floors with a choice of private, shared or hall bathrooms. There are no dorm beds. Most rooms have TVs, plus there are sports and cooking facilities, Internet access, lounges, air-conditioning, laundry rooms as well as a cheap cafeteria and rooms with mini-kitchens. Check-in is 3pm, check-out by 11am. Rates for the various configurations of rooms come in three bands: A (from mid-Oct to April), B (May) and C (June to mid-Oct). Singles cost $49/51/57 in the three bands; doubles $56/64/69 with shared bathroom or $75/98/113 with private bathroom; triples with shared bathroom $73/92/99. Four-person rooms (two double beds) are also available from $84/113/132, plus $5 for each additional adult.

Campsites

In a city famed for its natural beauty and opportunities for outdoor activities it's something of a disappointment – and a municipal failing – that not only are there no public or private **campsites** in or near the city centre, but also none of the handful of sites that do exist could be described as memorable. To pitch a tent or hook up an RV you'll have to head to North Vancouver or the suburbs of Richmond and Burnaby, neither of which are places you'd choose to camp.

Burnaby Cariboo RV Park 8765 Cariboo Place, Burnaby ☎604/420-1722, ⓦwww.bcrvpark.com. This 237-pitch site about 16km east of the city centre has luxurious facilities (indoor pool, Jacuzzi, laundry, free showers and convenience store) and a separate tenting area away from the RVs (for which there are full hook-up facilities). Take the Gaglardi Way exit (#37) from Hwy 1, turn right at the traffic light, then immediately left. The next right is Cariboo Place. Open year-round. $25–39.50 per site.

Capilano RV Park 295 Tomahawk Ave, North Vancouver ☎604/987-4722, ⓦwww.capilanorvpark.com. This is a pretty unattractive place – think car park rather than verdant pastures – but it is the city's most central site for trailers and tents, located beneath the north foot of the Lion's Gate Bridge and a short walk from the Park Royal Shopping Centre: exit Capilano Rd S or Hwy 99 exit off Lion's Gate Bridge. There are full RV facilities and hookups, plus swimming pool, free showers, washrooms and laundry, ice and water. Reservations (with deposit) essential June to August. $29.68–40.28 per site.

Park Canada Recreational Vehicles Inn 4799 Hwy 17, Delta ☎604/943-5811 or 1-877/943-0685, ⓦwww.parkcanada.com. Convenient for the Tsawwassen ferry terminal to the southwest, this 145-pitch site has partial and three-way hookups for RVs and – despite the name – some separate tent sites. There free showers, washrooms, laundry, heated pool, grocery store and, if this is your thing, the site's right next to a waterslide and golf course. Tent sites $18.50, RV sites $21–27.50.

Peace Arch RV Park 14601-40 Ave, Surrey ☎604/594-7009, ⓦwww.peacearchrvpark.com. Calling this a city campsite is a bit of a stretch as it's about 30km southeast of downtown near the junctions of Hwy 99 and the King George Highway. However, it's a good place to pause before hitting Vancouver if you've driven up from the US. There are 250 tent and RV sites with full hookups, a games room and a swimming pool. $18.50–27.50 per site.

Richmond RV Park and Campground 6200 River Rd at Hollybridge and River Rd, Richmond ☎604/270-7878, ⓦwww.richmondrvpark.com. Best of the RV outfits in terms of location, with the usual facilities (including free showers), but there are also tent sites. Located 14km from downtown; take Hwy 99 N to the Westminster Hwy exit (#36) and follow the signs. April–Oct. $17–27 per site.

The City

Vancouver is not a city that offers or requires lots of relentless sightseeing. Its breathtaking physical beauty makes it a place where often it's enough just to wander and watch the world go by – "the sort of town", wrote Jan Morris, "nearly everyone would want to live in". In summer you'll probably end up doing what the locals do, if not actually sailing, hiking, skiing, fishing or whatever, then certainly going to the beach, lounging in one of the parks or spending time in waterfront cafés.

In addition to the myriad leisure activities, however, there is a handful of sights that make worthwhile viewing by any standards. You'll inevitably spend a good deal of time in the **downtown** area and its Victorian-era equivalent, **Gastown**, now a renovated and less than convincing pastiche of its past. **Chinatown**, too, could easily absorb a morning, and contains more than its share of interesting shops, restaurants and rumbustiously busy streets. For a taste of the city's sensuous side, hit **Stanley Park**, a huge area of semi-wild parkland and beaches that crowns the northern tip of the downtown peninsula. Take a walk or a bike ride here and follow it up with a stroll to the **beach**. Be certain to spend a morning on **Granville Island**, by far the city's most tempting spot for wandering and people-watching. If you prefer a cultural slant on things, hit the formidable **Museum of Anthropology** or the museums of the Vanier Park complex, the latter easily accessible from Granville Island.

At a push, you could cram the city's essentials into a couple of days. If you're here for a longer stay, though, you'll want to venture further out from downtown: trips across Burrard Inlet to **North Vancouver**, worth making for the views from the SeaBus ferry alone, lend a different panoramic perspective of the city, and lead into the mountains and forests that give Vancouver its tremendous setting. The most popular trips here are to the Capilano Suspension Bridge, something of a triumph of PR over substance, and to the more worthwhile cable-car trip up **Grouse Mountain** for some staggering views of the city.

Downtown

You soon get the hang of Vancouver's **downtown** district, an arena of streets and shopping malls centred on **Robson Street**. On hot summer evenings it's like a latter-day vision of *La Dolce Vita* – a dynamic meeting place crammed with bars, restaurants, late-night stores, and bronzed youths preening in bars or cafés, or ostentatiously cruising in open-topped cars. At other times a more sedate class hangs out on the steps of the Vancouver Art Gallery or glides in and out of the two big department stores, Sears and The Bay. Downtown's other principal thoroughfares are **Burrard Street** – all smart shops, hotels and offices – and **Granville Street**, partly pedestrianized with plenty of shops and cinemas, but curiously seedy in places, especially at its southern end near the Granville Street Bridge. New development, however, is taking downtown's reach farther east, and at some point in your stay you should try to catch the **public library**, opened in 1995, at 350 W Georgia, a focus of this growth and a striking piece of modern architecture to boot.

For the best possible introduction to Vancouver, though, you should walk down to the waterfront and **Canada Place** (walkways open daily 24 hours, information ☎604/775-7200, ⊛www.canadaplace.ca; free), the Canadian pavilion for Expo 86, the huge world exhibition held in the city in 1986, and another architectural tour de force that houses a luxury hotel, cruise-ship terminal and two glitzy convention centres. For all its excess, however, it makes a superb viewpoint, with stunning vistas of the port, mountains, sea and buzzing boats, helicopters and float planes. The port activity, especially, is mesmerizing. One of North America's busiest **ports** began by exporting timber in 1864 in the shape of fence pickets to Australia. Today it handles seventy million tonnes of cargo annually, turns over $40 billion in trade and processes 3000 ships a year from almost a hundred countries. Canada Place's design, and the manner in which it juts into the port, is meant to suggest a ship, and you can walk the building's perimeter as if "on deck", stopping to read the boards that describe the immediate cityscape and the appropriate pages of its history. Inside are expensive shops, an unexceptional restaurant and an IMAX cinema ($9–16; ☏604/682-IMAX or 1-800/582-4629, ⓦ www.imax.com/vancouver).

An alternative to Canada Place's vantage point, the nearby **Harbour Centre Building** at 555 W Hastings, is one of the city's tallest structures, and is known by locals either as the "urinal" or, more affectionately, the "hamburger", after its bulging upper storeys. On a fine day it's definitely worth paying to ride the stomach-churning, all-glass SkyLift elevators that run up the side of the tower – 167m in a minute – to the fortieth-storey observation deck, known as "The Lookout!", with its staggering 360-degree views (daily: May–Sept 8.30am–10.30pm; Oct–April 9am–9pm; $10; ☏604/299-9000 ext 2626, ⓦ www.vancouverlookout.com). Admission is valid all day so you can return and look out over the bright lights of Vancouver at night.

Much of the **Expo site** here and at other points to the south and east has been levelled or is undergoing rigorous redevelopment, and to see its remaining sights requires a long walk from central downtown (take the SkyTrain or ferries from Granville Island instead). The geodesic dome is the main survivor, and has become a striking city landmark – but the museum it now houses, **Science World** at Québec St–Terminal Avenue, near the Science World–Main St SkyTrain station – is something of a disappointment (Mon–Fri 10am–5pm, Sat & Sun 10am–6pm; Science World $12.75, Omnimax $11.25 for a single feature; joint ticket for Science World entry and one Omnimax film $17.75; ☏604/443-7440 or 24-hour recorded line ☏604/443-7443, ⓦ www .scienceworld.bc.ca). Probably only children, at whom the place seems largely aimed, will be satisfied by the various high-tech, hands-on displays, which include the opportunity to make thunderous amounts of noise on electronic instruments and drum machines. Galleries deal with all manner of science-related themes, but probably the best things here if you're an adult are the building itself and the vast screen of the Omnimax Cinema at the top of the dome – though as with the similar screen at Canada Place, only a limited range of quality movies have been produced to suit the format.

Another remnant of the Expo is the 60,000-seat **BC Place Stadium**, 1 Robson St (tours mid-June to early Sept once weekly; $6; ☏604/661-7362, ⓦ www.bcplacestadium.com), the world's largest air-inflated dome. Unless you're there for a sporting event such as a BC Lions Canadian football game, the "mushroom" or "marshmallow in bondage", in popular parlance, isn't worth the bother, other than to visit the Hall of Fame, which pays homage to BC's leading sports stars (enter at Gate A). If you're heading to a game, take the SkyTrain to Stadium station or bus #15 east on Robson or #17 on Burrard.

The Vancouver Art Gallery

Centrally located in the imposing old city courthouse is the rather exorbitant **Vancouver Art Gallery**, located at the corner of Howe and Robson streets (mid-April to mid-Oct daily 10am–5.30pm, Thurs until 9pm; rest of year

Tues–Sun same hours; $12.50; ☎604/662-4700, ⓦwww.vanartgallery.bc.ca). The permanent collection has over 8000 works and is valued at over $100 million – but there's a problem: the only part of the collection you can be sure of seeing is the Emily Carr portion on the top floor. The other three floors are given over to (admittedly excellent) touring shows and a rotating display of parts of the permanent collection: you can never be sure quite what you will see.

The permanent collection features a rather sparse international assortment, with some of the lesser works of Warhol and Lichtenstein, and Italian, Flemish and British paintings spanning the sixteenth to twentieth centuries. In recent years, though, the gallery has made a determined effort to concentrate on contemporary works – videos, sculptures, installations and, in particular, photo-based and photoconceptual art. In the last area the gallery boasts the largest such collection in North America, including wonderful pieces by Cindy Sherman (notably her "self" portraits), Jeff Wall, Rachel Whiteread, Jenny Holzer and the magnificent monumental photographs by Andreas Gursky.

But, of course, you can't be sure you'll see these, although the fact that there are three or four temporary shows means there's often something of interest. The steep admission fee means casual visitors are taking a rather expensive chance unless you know you want to see a particular exhibition. What ulti-mately redeems the place are the powerful and almost surreal works of **Emily Carr** (see box p.798), who was born on Vancouver Island in 1871 and whose paintings – characterized by deep greens and blues – evoke something of the scale and intensity of the West Coast and its native peoples. The **gallery café** is also excellent, with a sun-trap of a terrace if you want to sit outside.

Gastown

An easy walk east of downtown – five minutes from Canada Place and concentrated largely on Water Street – **Gastown** is a determined piece of city rejuvenation aimed fair and square at the tourist, distinguished by new cobbles, fake gas lamps, *Ye Olde English Tea Room*-type cafés and a generally over-polished patina. The name derives from "Gassy" (as in loquacious) Jack Leighton, a retired sailor turned publican and self-proclaimed "mayor", who arrived on site by canoe with his native wife and a mangy yellow dog in 1867, quickly opening a bar to service the nearby lumber mills, whose bosses banned drinking on or near the yards. Leighton's statue stands in **Maple Tree Square**, Gastown's heart, focus of its main streets and reputed site of this first tavern. Trade was brisk, and a second bar opened, soon followed by a village of sorts – "Gassy's Town" – which, though swept away by fire in 1886, formed in effect the birthplace of modern Vancouver. Over the years, the downtown focus moved west and something of Gastown's boozy beginnings returned to haunt it, as its cheap hotels and warehouses turned into a skid row for junkies and alcoholics. By the 1970s the area was declared a historic site – the buildings are the city's oldest – and an enthusiastic beautification programme was set in motion.

The end product never quite became the dynamic, city-integrated spot the planners had hoped, and was slated for years by locals as something of a tourist trap, though recent signs suggest that interesting cafés, clubs and restaurants are slowly beginning to make themselves felt. It's certainly worth a stroll for its buskers, Sunday crowds and occasional points of interest. These do not include the hype-laden two-tonne **steam-powered clock**, the world's first (and hopefully last), at the west end of Water Street. It's invariably surrounded by

Emily Carr is western Canada's most celebrated painter. Born into a prosperous Victoria family in 1871, she led an almost caricatured artistic life – one that was eccentric, thwarted, ridiculed, bohemian and impoverished by turn, but also one that was ultimately successful and triumphant.

Things got off to a bad start. Having been orphaned at an early age, her remaining family tried to persuade her against an artistic career, a way of life that was then deemed unsuitable for a woman. Ignoring their advice, she made her own way to San Francisco's California School of Art in 1890, aged just 19. Here, unable to make ends meet, she was forced to teach for a living, an activity she continued on her return to Victoria in 1893.

The event that sparked her creative life came in 1899, when she travelled to Ucluelet on the west coast of Vancouver Island. Here she came into contact with the aboriginal art and culture of the indigenous Nuu-chah-nulth, an experience that would influence and feature in Carr's own work for the rest of her life. She quickly realized she needed formal instruction in landscape painting, and used her teaching to finance a trip to London and further training at art schools in Westminster and Cornwall. Her sojourn in England, however, was marked by illness, and was a less than happy time. She returned to Victoria in 1904.

By now her lifestyle was what in later decades would be called artistic, but which in the provincial and largely hidebound world of early twentieth-century British Columbia was viewed as wildly eccentric or worse. Carr often travelled with either a dog or parrot for company, and in time acquired a menagerie that included cats, cockatoos, a white rat named Susie and a Capuchin monkey known as Woo. Carr made pinafores for her charges to wear on walks in the park with their owner. In 1906, after travelling in Europe and Canada, she moved to a studio in Vancouver at 570 Granville St. A year later she travelled with her sister to Alaska, and for the first time encountered the aboriginal cultures and northern landscapes that would change the focus of her art. Four years later, still feeling her work lacked power and technique, she travelled to Paris where she absorbed the lessons of the new art

visitors armed with cocked cameras, all awaiting the miniature Big Ben's toots and whistles every fifteen minutes, and bellowing performances on the hour that seem to presage imminent explosion. The steam comes from an underground system that also heats surrounding buildings.

Probably the most surprising aspect of Gastown, however, is the contrast between its manicured pavements and the down-at-heel streets immediately to the south and east. The area between Gastown and Chinatown is both a thoroughly unpleasant skid row and, nearer Gastown, a haven for secondhand clothes shops, bookshops, galleries, new designers and cheap five-and-dimes. In places, however, this area recalls Gastown's bad old days: unpleasantly seedy, pocked with the dingiest of dingy bars and hotels, and inhabited by characters to match.

The Police Centennial Museum

One sight that is worth hunting out in the area between Gastown and Chinatown is Vancouver's **Police Centennial Museum** at 240 E Cordova St (May–Aug Mon–Sat 10am–3pm; rest of year Mon–Fri 9am–3pm; $6; ☎604/665-3346, ⓦ www.city.vancouver.bc.ca/police/museum), a bizarre and fascinating little museum that is easily seen and leaves you well placed for a short two-block walk south to the centre of Chinatown. It's housed in the city's old Coroner's Court Building and takes its name from the fact that it movements sweeping the city. Chief of these was the Fauve ("wild beast") school of painters, so called for the frenzied distortions, patterns and bright, almost violently coloured nature of its exponents' works. This was one of the most fertile artistic periods of the century, and in one of Europe's most febrile cities, but Carr, unable to speak French and with a dislike of big cities, seems not to have met the likes of Picasso and the other ground-breaking artists of the time.

Returning to Vancouver in 1911, Carr exhibited work from her French sojourn. The show – and another in 1913 – was panned, and her work rejected as impenetrable or offensive by British Columbia's staid critics. Ridiculed and outcast at 42, Carr retired to land inherited from her family, where she built a home, bred sheepdogs, and became a landlady to pay her bills. She also began making pottery, digging her own clay and wheeling it home in a dilapidated pram-cum-shopping trolley.

It would be almost another twenty years, in the late 1920s, before Carr's work began to find fame. Her change of fortune followed a meeting with the Group of Seven painters, a celebrated assembly of eastern Canadian artists who, like Carr, looked to the Canadian landscape for much of their inspiration. Working with renewed confidence, and gaining a degree of international recognition in the process – but little financial gain – she made repeated visits to aboriginal villages and settings. Over the next ten years she completed some of her most accomplished work, often working in the wilderness from a ramshackle caravan equipped with improvised shelters for her pets. With her health failing – she would suffer four heart attacks – she began to write during a period of convalescence. Her first book, *Klee Wyck*, was published when she was 70, taking its name – "the laughing one" – from the name given to her by the Kwakiutl people of the Pacific coast. The book dealt with her travels and life among aboriginal people, and won the Canadian Governor General's medal for literature. Three other books followed – *The Book of Small* (a chronicle of her Victoria childhood), *The House of All Sorts* (about her career as a landlady), and *Growing Pains* (her autobiography). Carr died in 1945, secure in her status as Canada's first major female artist.

was established in 1986 to celebrate the centennial of the Vancouver police force.

The building has its own place in Vancouver folklore, not least for the fact that it was here that the actor **Errol Flynn** was brought after he died in Vancouver in 1959. Flynn arrived in the city in October 1959 with his best acting days well behind him. With him was his "personal assistant", a 17-year-old blonde girl not known for her secretarial skills. Within two days Flynn had dropped dead in his rented West End apartment. The body was brought to the Coroner's Court, where the pathologist conducting the autopsy is said to have removed a piece of Flynn's penis and placed it in formaldehyde to keep as a souvenir. The horrified chief coroner Glen McDonald, a rather more fastidious operator, is said to have pulled rank and reattached the missing piece of member to the corpse with sticky tape. The body was then dispatched to Los Angeles for burial. This was not the end of the story, for it emerged that somewhere between the West End and the morgue, a key to a Swiss safety-deposit box that Flynn wore round his neck had disappeared. When Flynn's lawyers opened the box three years later, the stock certificates and half a million dollars in cash they had expected to find were nowhere to be seen.

The **autopsy room** is still there, together with a suitably macabre selection of mangled and preserved body parts arranged around the walls. Check out the **morgue**'s cooler, penultimate resting place of many over the years. Other rooms include a **forensics lab**, a simulated autopsy room, police cell and radio room, while a variety of themed displays include sections on notorious local criminals, weapons seized from criminals (some pretty unusual), crime-scene reconstructions, gambling, uniforms, counterfeit money and a sizeable collection of firearms. More light-hearted exhibits include a collection of model police cars from around the world. Finally, the museum's **"Cop Shoppe"** has an interesting line in police-related gifts and souvenirs.

To get here by public transport, take buses #10, #16, #20, #23, #35 or #150 along Hastings St to Main then walk one block north to E Cordova.

Chinatown

Vancouver's vibrant **Chinatown** – clustered mainly on Pender Street from Carrall to Gore and on Keefer Street from Main to Gore (buses #22 or #19 east from Pender, or #22 north from Burrard) – is a city apart. Vancouver's 100,000 or more Chinese make up one of North America's largest Chinatowns and are the city's oldest and largest ethnic group after the British-descended majority. Many crossed the Pacific in 1858 to join the Fraser Valley gold rush; others followed under contract to help build the Canadian Pacific Railway. Most stayed, only to find themselves being treated appallingly. Denied citizenship and legal rights until as late as 1947, the Chinese community sought safety and familiarity in a ghetto of their own, where clan associations and societies provided for new arrivals and the local poor – and helped build the distinctive houses of recessed balconies and ornamental roofs that have made the area a protected historic site.

Unlike Gastown's gimmickry, Chinatown is all genuine: shops, hotels, markets, tiny restaurants and dim alleys vie for attention amidst an incessant hustle of jammed pavements and the buzz of Chinese conversation. Virtually every building replicates an Eastern model without a trace of self-consciousness, and written Chinese characters feature everywhere in preference to English. Striking and unexpected after downtown's high-rise glitz, the district brings you face to face with Vancouver's oft-touted multiculturalism, and helps explain why Hong Kong immigrants continue to be attracted to the city. It is, however, a district with a distinct edge, and visitors should avoid the area's dingier streets at night and parts of East Hastings near Main Street just about any time.

Apart from the obvious culinary temptations (see "Eating and drinking", beginning on p.814), Chinatown's main points of reference are its **shops**. Some of the best boast fearsome butchery displays and such edibles as live eels, flattened ducks, hundred-year-old eggs and other stuff you'll be happy not to identify. Check out the open-air **night market** at Main and Keefer streets (summer 6pm–midnight), a wonderful medley of sights. Keefer Street is **bakery** row, with lots of tempting stickies on offer like moon cakes and *bao*, steamed buns with a meat or sweet-bean filling. On the corner of Keefer and Main is the Ten Ren Tea and Ginseng Company, with free tastings of a vast range of teas, many of which promise cures for a variety of ailments. In a similar vein, it's worth dropping in to one of the local **herbalists** to browse amongst their panaceas: snakeskins, reindeer antlers, buffalo tongues, dried sea horses and bears' testicles are all available if you're feeling under the weather. Ming Wo, 23 E Pender, is a fantastic cookware shop, with probably every utensil ever devised, while China West, 41 E Pender, is packed with slippers, jackets, pens, cheap toys and the like. Most people also flock dutifully to the 1913 **Sam Kee Building**, at the corner of Carrall and Pender; at just 1.8m across, it's officially the world's narrowest building.

Chinatown's chief cultural attraction is the small **Dr Sun Yat-Sen Garden**, at 578 Carrall St near Pender Street, a 2.5-acre park billed as the first authentic, full-scale classical Chinese garden ever built outside China (May to mid-June & Sept daily 10am–6pm; mid-June to Aug daily 9.30am–7pm; Oct daily 10am–4.30pm; Nov–April Tues–Sun 10am–4.30pm; $8.25; Ⓦwww .vancouverchinesegarden.com). Named after the founder of the first Chinese Republic, who was a frequent visitor to Vancouver, the park was created for Expo 86. The whole thing is based on classical gardens developed in the city of Suzhou during the Ming dynasty (1368–1644) to achieve a subtle balance of Yin and Yang: small and large, soft and hard, flowing and immovable, light and dark. Every stone, pine and flower was carefully placed and has symbolic meaning. Hourly free guided tours on the half-hour explain the Taoist philosophy behind the carefully placed elements. After a time the chances are you'll find the garden working its calm and peaceful spell.

Alongside the entrance to the gardens, the **Chinese Cultural Centre Museum & Archives** (Tues–Sun 11am–5pm; $3), Chinatown's community focus and a sponsor of New Year festivities, offers classes and hosts changing exhibitions. It also has a museum – the first of its kind dedicated to Chinese-Canadian history – which focuses on early Chinese pioneers and Chinese veterans who served Canada in the two world wars. Next to the gardens and centre is a small and slightly threadbare Dr Sun Yat-Sen Park (free), which, though less worked than the main garden, is still a pleasant place to take time out. Hours are the same as for the garden, and there's an alternative entrance on Columbia Street and Keefer.

Stanley Park

One of the world's great urban spaces, **Stanley Park** is Vancouver's green heart, helping lend the city its particular character. At nearly 1000 acres, it's the largest urban park in North America – a semi-wilderness of dense rainforest, marshland and beaches. Ocean surrounds it on three sides, with a road and parallel cycleway/pedestrian promenade following the sea wall all the way round the peninsula for a total of 10.5km (see p.804 for the park practicalities). From here, views of the city and across the water to the mountains are particularly worthwhile. Away from the coastal trail network and main draw – the aquarium – the interior is nearly impenetrable scrub and forest, with few paths and few people. At the same time there are plenty of open, wooded or flower-decorated spaces to picnic, snooze or watch the world go by.

The peninsula was partially logged in the 1860s, but in 1886 the newly formed city council – showing typical Canadian foresight and an admirable sense of priorities – moved to make what had become a military reserve into a permanent park. Thus its remaining first-growth forest of cedar, hemlock and Douglas fir, and the swamp now known as Lost Lagoon, were saved for posterity in the name of Lord Stanley, Canada's governor general from 1888 to 1893.

In the park

Taking time in the park, especially on a busy Sunday, gives a good taste of what it means to live in Vancouver. The first thing you see is the **Lost Lagoon**, a fair-sized lake that started life as a tidal inlet, and got its name because its water all but disappeared at low tide. Dozens of waterfowl species inhabit its shoreline. Just east are the pretty Rose Garden and Vancouver Rowing Club, before which stands a statue of Scottish poet Robbie Burns. From here you can follow the sea-wall path all the way, or make a more modest loop past the **totem poles** and round Brockton Point.

Walking all the way round the **sea-wall path** takes about two hours at a brisk lick. Moving around anticlockwise, odd little sights dot the promenade, all signed and explained, the most famous being the *Girl in a Wetsuit* statue, a rather lascivious update of Copenhagen's *Little Mermaid*. If you want a more focused walk, the **Cathedral Trail**, northwest of the Lost Lagoon, takes you past some big first-growth cedars. **Beaver Lake**, carpeted green with water lilies, is a peaceful spot for a sleep or a stroll. **Lumberman's Arch**, near the aquarium (see below) was raised in 1952 to honour those in the lumber industry, an odd memorial given that the industry in question would probably give its eyeteeth to fell the trees in Stanley Park. Its meadow surroundings are a favourite for families and those looking for a good napping spot. **Prospect Point**, on the park's northern tip, is a busy spot but worth braving for its beautiful view of the city and the mountains rising behind West Vancouver across the water. There's a café-restaurant here, popular for its outdoor deck and sweeping views. West of here lies **Siwash Rock**, an outcrop which has defied the weather for centuries, attracting numerous native legends in the process, and which is distinguished by its solitary tree (not visible from the road, but quickly reached by path). Further around the wall there are various places to eat and drink, the best being the *Teahouse Restaurant* at Ferguson Point, about a kilometre beyond Siwash Rock.

Though people do swim in the sea at beaches around the park's western fringes, most bathers prefer the **swimming pool** next to Second Beach (see box on p.804). Facilities of all sorts – cafés, playgrounds, golf, outdoor dancing – proliferate near the downtown margins. Guided **nature walks** are also occasionally offered around the park; ask at the Touristinfo Centre for details.

Vancouver Aquarium Marine Science Centre

Stanley Park Zoo, home to some all too obviously distressed animals, has now thankfully closed, leaving the **Vancouver Aquarium Marine Science Centre** as the park's most popular destination (daily: July to early Sept 9.30am–7pm; rest of year 10am–5.30pm; $15.95; ⓦ www.vanaqua.org). At its entrance at 845 Avison Way stands a vast killer whale in bronze, the work of celebrated Haida artist Bill Reid, whose famous *Raven and the Beast* sculpture forms the centrepiece of the Museum of Anthropology (see p.808). The aquarium is ranked among North America's best, and with over a million visitors a year claims to be the most-visited sight in Canada west of Toronto's CN Tower. It contains over 8000 living exhibits representing some 600 different species, though in truth this is a relatively modest summation of the eighty percent of the world's creatures that live in water. Like the zoo before it, the complex has been targeted by animal-rights campaigners for its treatment of performing beluga and killer whales, not to mention cooped-up seals and otters. Given the aquarium's reputation as a tourist attraction, however, as well as its claims as a research centre, the campaigners have a long, uphill battle. The whales in particular are huge draws, but you can't help but feel they should really be in the sea, for all the hoopla surrounding their $14m marine-mammal area.

There are several key areas to see in the aquarium. The **Arctic Canada** section concerns itself with the surprisingly fragile world of the Canadian north, with a chance to see whales face to face through glass and hear the sounds of whales, walruses, seals and other creatures in this icy domain. The **Amazon Gallery** displays the vegetation, fishes, iguanas, sloths and other creatures of the rainforest in a climate-controlled environment, while the **Pacific Northwest Habitat** performs a similar role for otters, beavers and other creatures of the waters of BC. The **BC Waters Gallery** and **Ducks Unlimited Wetlands** displays are fairly self-explanatory.

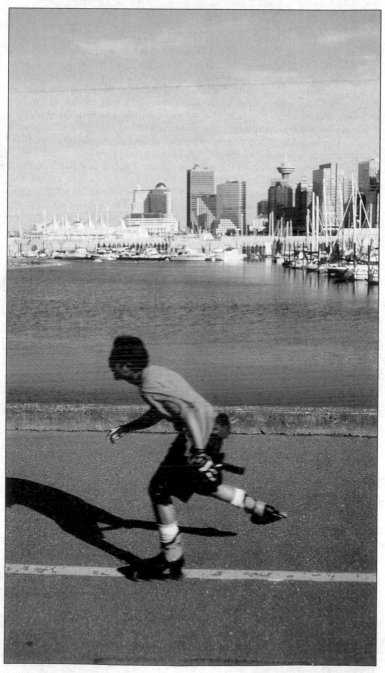

△ Skater on Vancouver waterfront

Park practicalities

The park is a simple though rather dull **walk** from most of downtown: Beach
Avenue to the south and Georgia to the north are the best approaches if you're
on foot, leading to either end of the sea wall. Alternatively, grab a Stanley Park
bus #23, #35 or #135 from the corner of Burrard and Pender streets downtown, which drop you near the so-called Stanley Park Loop just inside the park
by Lost Lagoon – and in summer continue deeper into the park to the Stanley
Park Loop. Other buses that will take you close to the park are the #1 (Beach)
to Davie and Beach Avenue and the #3 (Robson) to Denman Street. A neat
itinerary would be to stroll or cycle all or part of the sea wall and then walk
back to Denman Street, where you can pause at one of several cafés (the *Bread
Garden* midway down on the left at 1040 Denman and Comox is good) before
heading on down Denman to the grass or sand at English Bay Beach.

The corner of Denman and Georgia streets has a cluster of **bike rental** outlets. Spokes, 1798 W Georgia (℡604/688-5141, Ⓦwww.vancouverbikerentals
.com), is a big, busy place established in 1938 (from $3.75/hr for a wide vari-
ety of bikes, including children's bikes and tandems with child trailers). You
need to leave ID, and a cash or credit-card deposit. Helmets, which are
compulsory in BC, and locks are included in the rental. A few metres up the
street, Bikes 'n' Blades (℡604/602-9899) is smaller, less busy and rents **blades**

Vancouver's beaches

Vancouver, it's rather surprising to find, has **beaches** – even if much of the sand
comes from Japan in container ships. All are clean and well kept; the clarity of the
water is remarkable given the size of the city's port and the majority have lifeguards
during the summer months.

English Bay Beach and north

The best face each other across False Creek and English Bay, starting with Stanley
Park's three adjacent beaches: **English Bay Beach**, ranged along Beach Avenue is
the most readily accessible, and easily visited after seeing Stanley Park; **Second
Beach**, to the north, which also features a shallow onshore swimming pool (mid-May
to mid-June Mon–Fri noon–8.45pm, Sat & Sun 10am–8.45pm; mid-June to mid-Sept
daily 10am–8.45pm; $4); and **Third Beach**, further north still, least crowded of the
three and the one with the best views of West Vancouver and the mountains.

Kitsilano Beach

Across the water to the south and west of the Burrard Bridge, **Kitsilano Beach**, or
"Kits", is named – like the district behind it – after Chief Khahtsahlano, a Squamish
chieftain of a band who once owned the area. Walk here from Vanier Park and the
museums on the coast path (30min) or, from downtown, take **bus #22** southbound
on Burrard Street. Kits is the busiest and most self-conscious of the beaches. It's
especially popular with the university, volleyball and rippling torso crowds. Families
also come here to take advantage of the warm and safe swimming area, while sunbathers can take up a position on the grass to the rear. Vancouver's largest and most
popular outdoor heated pool is the **lido** at Yew and Cornwall (mid-May to mid-June
Mon–Fri noon–8.45pm, Sat & Sun 10am–8.45pm; mid-June to mid-Sept Mon–Fri
7am–8.45pm, Sat & Sun 10am–8.45pm; $4), while the **shoreline path** is a lovely
place for an evening stroll, cycle or time out on a bench to watch the street life.
Follow the path all the way east and it takes you to Granville Island by way of Vanier
Park and the museums. A former hippie and alternative-lifestyle hangout, Kits still
betrays shades of its past and, with nearby bars and restaurants to fuel the party
spirit, there's always plenty going on.

as well. Directly opposite at 745 Denman St is Bayshore Bicycle & Rollerblade Rentals (℡604/688-2453, ⓦwww.bayshorebike.ca). From Denman it's just a minute's pedalling to the park, but watch the traffic.

A special TransLink "Stanley Park Shuttle" **bus**, which makes fourteen stops around the park, runs on a fifteen-minute schedule in summer (June–Aug/early Sept daily 9/10am–6.30pm; ℡604/257-8400).You can transfer to the service from the #1 and #5 buses on Denman or the #23, #35 and #135 at Stanley Park Loop: both Denman and the Loop are a few moments' walk from the shuttle's stops at Stanley Park Entrance, Pipeline Road or the Rowing Club. The service is free, though fees may be introduced. Don't bother taking a **car** into the park, especially at weekends, when parking is just about impossible.

Granville Island

Granville Island, huddled under the Granville Street Bridge south of downtown, is the city's most enticing "people's place" – the title it likes for itself – and pretty much lives up to its claim to be the "heart of Vancouver". Friendly, easy-going and popular, its shops, markets, galleries, marina and open spaces are juxtaposed with a light-industrial setting whose faint whiff of warehouse

Jericho Beach and west

Jericho Beach, west of Kits and handy for the hostel, is a touch quieter and serves as a hangout for the windsurfing crowd. Still further west, Jericho blurs into **Locarno Beach** and **Spanish Banks**, progressively less crowded, and the start of a fringe of sand and parkland that continues round to the University of British Columbia (UBC) campus. Locals rate Spanish Banks the most relaxed of the city's beaches, while Locarno is one of its most spectacular, especially at low tide, when the sand seems to stretch for ever. Bikers and walkers use the dirt track at the top of Locarno, beyond which a broad sward of grass with picnic tables and benches runs to the road. You can **rent canoes** from Ecomarine Ocean Kayak, 1668 Duranleau St (℡604/689-7575 or 1-888/425-2925, ⓦwww.ecomarine.com). It also has an office at the Jericho Sailing Centre at 1300 Discovery St on Jericho Beach itself. At low tide the more athletically inclined could walk all the way round to UBC (otherwise take the bus as for the Museum of Anthropology; see p.808), where the famous clothing-optional **Wreck Beach** lies just off the campus area below NW Marine Drive – ask any student to point you towards the half-hidden access paths. It's inevitably aroused a fair bit of prudish criticism in the past, but attitudes seem more relaxed now. The atmosphere is generally laid-back – though women have been known to complain of voyeurs – and nude hawkers are often on hand to sell you anything from pizza and illegal smokeables to (bona fide) massage and hair-braiding. The beach's reputation shouldn't hide the fact that it's also a very beautiful and broad strand, edged by the ocean on one side (with many shallow and often warm pools) and bordered by lofty trees on three other flanks. It's also well looked after, thanks to the Wreck Beach Preservation Society (ⓦwww.wreckbeach.org). The best of the Wreck Beach sand is below trail #6, the trailhead for which you'll find just beyond the Nitobe garden heading away from the Museum of Anthropology.

North Vancouver

Finally, **Ambleside**, west of the Park Royal Mall along Marine Drive (turn south at 13th St W), is the most accessible beach if you're in North or West Vancouver.

squalor saves the area from accusations of pretentiousness. The island was reclaimed from swampland in 1917 as an ironworks and shipbuilding centre, but by the 1960s the yards were derelict and the place had become a rat-infested dumping ground for the city's rubbish. In 1972 the federal government agreed to bankroll a programme of residential, commercial and industrial redevelopment that retained the old false-fronted buildings, tin-shack homes, sea wall and rail sidings. The best part of the job had been finished by 1979 – and was immediately successful – but work continues unobtrusively today, the various building projects only adding to the area's sense of change and dynamism. Most people come here during the day, but there are some good restaurants, bars and the Arts Club Theatre, which are all enough to keep the place buzzing at night.

Virtually the first building you see on the island walking from the bus stop augurs well: the **Granville Island Brewery**, 1441 Cartwright St (tours only: June–Sept Mon–Fri on the hour noon–5pm, Sat & Sun on the half-hour 11.30am–5pm; $7; call for latest hours ☎604/687-2739), a small but interesting concern which offers guided tours that include tastings of its additive-free beers. Dominant amongst the maze of shops, galleries and businesses, the **Granville Island Public Market** (daily 9am–6pm; closed Mon in winter) is the undisputed highlight of the area. On summer weekends it's where people go to see and be seen and it throngs with arts-and-crafts types, and a phalanx of dreadful buskers. The quality and variety of **food** is staggering, with dozens of kiosks and cafés selling ready-made titbits and potential picnic ingredients. Parks, patios and walkways nearby provide lively areas to eat and take everything in. Other spots to look out for include Blackberry Books, the Water Park and Kids Only Market (a kids-only playground with hoses to repel intruders) and the bright-yellow *Bridges* pub/restaurant/wine bar, which has a nice outdoor drinking and eating area. You can also **rent canoes** for straightforward paddling in False Creek and English Bay, from Ecomarine Ocean Kayak on the island at 1688 Duranleau St (☎604/689-7575).

The island also has a trio of small, linked **museums** almost opposite the brewery at 1502 Duranleau St (all daily 10am–5.30pm; $6.50 for all three; ⓦwww.modeltrainsmuseum.bc.ca): these are the self-explanatory Granville Island Model Trains Museum, Model Ships Museum and Sport Fishing museum – all of limited appeal. The Model Trains Museum claims to contain the largest collection of toy trains in the world on public display.

Island practicalities

The most direct approach to Granville Island is to take **bus** #50 from Gastown or Granville Street. The walk down Granville Street and across the bridge is deceptively long, not terribly salubrious, and so probably only worthwhile on a fine day when you need the exercise. Alternatively, and more fun, private **ferries** ($2, pay on board) ply back and forth almost continuously between the island and little quays at the foot of Hornby Street or the Aquatic Centre at the foot of Thurlow Street. They also connect from Granville Island to Science World (hourly) and, more significantly, to Vanier Park (half-hourly). A logical and satisfying day's **itinerary** from downtown, therefore, would take you to Granville Island, to the museums and back by ferry. You might also choose to **walk** from the island along the False Creek sea wall (east) or west to Vanier Park and Kitsilano Beach.

There's a good **infocentre** at the heart of the island for Island-related information only (☎604/666-5784, ⓦwww.granvilleisland.bc.ca), with a **foreign exchange** facility in the same building and ATM machines on the wall outside. Stamps are available from the LottoCentre inside the Public Market Building. Note that many of the island's shops and businesses close on Mondays, and that if you want a **bus back** to downtown you should *not* take the #51 from the stop opposite the infocentre (it will take you in the wrong direction): walk out of the island complex's only road entrance, and at the junction the #50 stop is immediately on your right.

Vanier Park museum complex

A little to the west of Granville Island, **Vanier Park** conveniently collects most of the city's main museums: the **Vancouver Museum**, the **Maritime Museum** and the **H.R. MacMillan Space Centre** (the last combines the old planetarium and observatory). The complex sits on the waterfront at the west end of the Burrard Bridge, near Kitsilano Beach and the residential-entertainment centres of Kitsilano and West 4th Avenue; Vanier Park itself is a fine spot to while away a summer afternoon. You could easily incorporate a visit to the museums with a trip to Granville Island using the **ferry**, which docks just below the Maritime Museum. Coming from downtown, take the #22 Macdonald **bus** south from anywhere on Burrard or West Pender – get off at the first stop after the bridge and walk down Chester Street to the park. The park is pleasant but open – there's little shade – and has a few nice patches of sandy beach on its fringes.

The Vancouver Museum

The **Vancouver Museum**, 1100 Chestnut St (daily 10am–5pm, Thurs until 9pm; $10; ⓦ www.vanmuseum.bc.ca), traces the history of the city and the lower British Columbian mainland, and invokes the area's past in its very form: the flying-saucer shape is a nod to the conical cedar-bark hats of the Northwest Coast natives, former inhabitants of the area. The fountain outside, looking like a crab on a bidet, recalls the animal of native legend that guards the port entrance.

Though it's the main focus of interest at Vanier Park, the museum is not as captivating as you might expect. It claims 300,000 exhibits, but it's hard to know where they all are, and a visit needn't take more than an hour or so. A patchy collection of baskets, tools, clothes and miscellaneous artefacts of aboriginal peoples – including a huge whaling canoe, the only example in a museum – homes in on the 8000 years before the coming of white settlers. After that, the main collection, weaving in and out of Vancouver's history up to World War I, is full of offbeat and occasionally memorable insights if you have the patience to read the material – notably the accounts of early explorers' often extraordinary exploits, the immigration section (which re-creates what it felt like to travel steerage) and the forestry displays. The twentieth-century section is a disappointment, much of it looking more like an antique shop than a museum.

The H.R. MacMillan Space Centre

The **H.R. MacMillan Space Centre**, also sometimes known as the Pacific Space Centre (daily 10am–5pm; Sept–June closed Mon; evening laser shows at varying times Thurs–Sun; Space Centre $13.50, additional Virtual Voyage rides $6, evening laser shows $9.35; ⓣ 604/738-7827, ⓦ www .hrmacmillanspacecentre.com), incorporates the MacMillan Planetarium and a range of space-related displays and shows. Like the Vancouver Museum – which is nearby – it lies in Vanier Park and can be accessed at 1100

Crescent St or from the small ferry landing in the park. Its main draws are its 40-minute star shows – the standard planetarium fare, held several times daily – and very loud, very brash evening laser and music extravaganzas (staged Thurs–Sun at varying times; $9.35), which are very popular: arrive in good time or make reservations.

Many of the centre's exhibits are high-tech and hands-on, especially in the so-called Cosmic Courtyard, where interactive displays allow you to battle an alien, design a spaceship, guide a lunar robot or plan a voyage to Mars. Many displays also involve lots of impressive computer and other audiovisual effects, notably the Virtual Voyages Simulator, a flight simulator complete with the "motion" you might encounter during space travel and other journeys. The "rides" on the simulator last about five minutes (entrance is included with admission) and experiences range from collisions with a comet to trips on a roller coaster and simulated space flights to the planets. The GroundStation Canada Theatre shows 20-minute films on aspects of space roughly hourly from mid-morning. The **Gordon Southam Observatory**, the small domed building close to the Space Centre, has a telescope that is usually available for public stargazing on clear weekend nights (usually Fri & Sat 7–11pm, but call Space Centre or ☎604/736-2655 for hours); astronomers are on hand to show you the ropes and help you position your camera for a "Shoot the Moon" photography session of the heavens ($10).

The Maritime Museum

The **Maritime Museum**, 1905 Ogden Ave (May–Sept daily 10am–5pm; Oct–April Tues–Sat 10am–5pm, Sun noon–5pm; $8; ⓦwww.vmm.bc.ca), is a short 150-metre walk from the Vancouver Museum and features lovely early photographs evoking turn-of-the-century Vancouver, though the rest of the presentation doesn't quite do justice to the status of the city as one of the world's leading ports. The less arresting displays, however, are redeemed by the renovated *St Roch*, a two-masted schooner that was the first vessel to navigate the famed Northwest Passage in a single season; it now sits impressively in its own wing of the museum, where it can be viewed by guided tour only. Special summer shows spice things up a little, as do the recent Pirates' Cove and Children's Maritime Discovery Centre, both aimed at making the museum more attractive to children. Outside, just below the museum on **Heritage Harbour** (quay for ferries to and from Granville Island), you can admire, free of charge, more restored old-fashioned vessels.

The Museum of Anthropology and around

Located well out of downtown on the University of British Columbia campus, the **Museum of Anthropology**, 6393 NW Marine Drive, is far and away Vancouver's most important museum (mid-May to early Sept daily 10am–5pm, Tues until 9pm; rest of year Tues 11am–9pm, Wed–Sun 11am–5pm; $9, free on Tues 5–9pm; ⓦwww.moa.ubc.ca). Emphasizing the art and culture of the natives of the region, and the Haida in particular, its collection of carvings, totem poles and artefacts is unequalled in North America.

Much is made of the museum's award-winning layout, a cool and spacious collection of halls designed by Arthur Erickson, the eminent architect also responsible for converting the Vancouver Art Gallery. Particularly outstanding is the huge **Great Hall**, inspired by native cedar houses, which makes as perfect an artificial setting for its thirty-odd **totem poles** as you could ask for. Huge windows look out to more poles and Haida houses, which you're free to wander around, backed by views of Burrard Inlet and the distant mountains. Most of the poles and monolithic carvings, indoors and out, are taken from the coastal tribes of the Haida, Salish, Tsimshian and Kwakiutl, all of which share cultural elements. The suspicion – though it's never confessed – is that scholars really don't know terribly much of the arcane mythology behind the carvings, but the best guess as to their meaning is that the various animals correspond to different clans or the creatures after which the clans were named. To delve deeper into the complexities, it's worth joining an hour-long, all-year **guided walk**.

One of the museum's great virtues is that none of its displays is hidden away in basements or back rooms; instead they're jammed in overwhelming numbers into drawers and cases in the galleries to the right of the Great Hall. Most of the permanent collection revolves around **Canadian Pacific** cultures, but the **Inuit** and **Far North** exhibits are also outstanding. So, too, are the jewellery, masks and baskets of Northwest native tribes, all markedly delicate after the blunt-nosed carvings of the Great Hall. Look out especially for the argillite sculptures, made from a jet-black slate found only on BC's Haida Gwaii or Queen Charlotte Islands. The **African** and **Asian** collections are also pretty comprehensive, if smaller, but appear as something of an afterthought alongside the indigenous artefacts. A small, technical archeological section rounds off the smaller galleries, along with a new three-gallery wing designed to house the Koerner Collection, an assortment of six hundred European ceramics dating from the fifteenth century onwards.

The museum saves its best for last. Housed in a separate rotunda, **The Raven and the Beast**, a modern sculpture designed by Haida artist Bill Reid, is the museum's pride and joy and has achieved almost iconographic status in the city. Carved from a 4.5-tonne block of cedar and requiring the attention of five people over three years, it describes the Haida legend of human evolution with stunning virtuosity, depicting terrified figures squirming from a half-open clam shell, overseen by an enormous and stern-faced raven. However, beautiful as the work is, its rotunda setting makes it seem oddly out of place – almost like a corporate piece of art.

To get to the museum, catch **bus** #10 or #4 bus south from Granville Street and stay on until the end of the line. The campus is huge and disorienting: to find the museum, turn right from the bus stop, walk along the tree-lined East Mall to the very bottom (10min), then turn left on NW Marine Drive and walk till you see the museum on the right (another 5min). In the foyer pick up a free mini-guide or the cheap larger booklet – a worthwhile investment, given the exhibits' almost total lack of labelling, but still pretty thin.

Around the museum

There are any number of odds and ends dotted around the museum, but they amount to little of real interest. For the exception, turn right out the front entrance and a five-minute walk leads to the **Nitobe Memorial Garden**, a small Japanese garden that is good for a few minutes of peace and quiet (daily: mid-March to mid-May & Sept to mid-Oct 10am–5pm; mid-May to Aug 10am–6pm; mid-Oct to mid-March Mon–Fri 10am–2.30pm; $3, joint ticket with Botanical Garden $6, free from mid-Oct to mid-March; ⓦ www .nitobe.org). This is considered the world's most authentic Japanese garden outside Japan (despite its use of many non-Japanese species), and is full of gently curving paths, trickling streams and waterfalls, as well as numerous rocks, trees and shrubs placed with Oriental precision.

Beyond the garden lies the greater seventy-acre area of the university's **Botanical Garden**, 16th Avenue and SW Marine Drive (daily 10am–6pm; mid-Oct to mid-March closes 3pm; $4.50, joint ticket with Nitobe Garden $6; Ⓦ www.ubcbotanicalgarden.org), established in 1916, making it Canada's oldest such garden. Non-gardeners will probably be interested only in the macabre poisonous plants of the Physick Garden, a re-created sixteenth-century monastic herb garden – though most plants here are actually medicinal rather than lethal – and the swaths of shrubs and huge trees in the Asian Garden. Dip in, as well, to the BC Native Garden, the Alpine Garden and the Food Garden.

While you're out at the university, you might also take advantage of the **University Endowment Lands**, on the opposite, west side of the museum. A huge tract of wild parkland – as large as Stanley Park, but used by a fraction of the number of people – the endowment lands boast 48km of trails and abundant wildlife (including blacktail deer, otters, foxes and bald eagles). Best of all, there are few human touches – no benches or snack bars, and only the occasional signpost.

North Vancouver

Perhaps the most compelling reason to visit **North Vancouver** (known colloquially as North Van) is the trip itself – preferably by SeaBus – which provides views of not only the downtown skyline but also the teeming port area, a side of the city that's otherwise easily missed. Most of North Van itself is residential, as is neighbouring **West Vancouver**, whose cosseted citizens boast the highest per capita income in Canada. You'll probably cross to the north shore less for these leafy suburbs than to sample the outstanding areas of natural beauty here: **Lynn Canyon**, **Grouse Mountain**, **Capilano Gorge** (the most popular excursion), **Mount Seymour** and **Lighthouse Park**. All are found in the mountains that rear up dramatically almost from the West Van waterfront, the proximity of Vancouver's residential areas to genuine wilderness being one of the city's most remarkable aspects. Your best bet if you wish to hike, and want the wildest scenery close to downtown, is Mount Seymour.

Most of North Vancouver is within a single bus ride of **Lonsdale Quay**, the north shore's SeaBus terminal. **Buses** to all points leave from two parallel bays immediately in front of you as you leave the boat; blue West Van buses are run by an independent company but accept TransLink tickets. If you've bought a ticket to come over on the SeaBus, remember you have ninety minutes of transfer time to ride buses from the time of purchase, which should be long enough to get you to most of the destinations below.

The **Lonsdale Quay Market**, 123 Carrie Cates Court (Sat–Thurs 9.30am–6.30pm, Fri 9am–9pm; Nov–March Fri closes 8pm; restaurants remain open later; Ⓦ www.lonsdalequay.com), to the right of the buses, is worth making the crossing for whether or not you intend to explore further. While not as vibrant as Granville Island Market, it's still an appealing place, with great food stalls and takeaways, plus walkways looking out over the port, tugs and moored fishing boats.

Grouse Mountain

The trip to **Grouse Mountain**, named by hikers in 1894 who stumbled across a blue grouse, is a popular one. This is mainly due to the Swiss-built **cable cars** – North America's largest – which run from the 290-metre base station at 6400 Nancy Greene Way to the mountain's 1250-metre summit (daily 9am–10pm; $24.95; Ⓦ www.grousemountain.com). A favourite among people learning to ski or **snowboard** after work, the mountain's brightly illuminated slopes and dozen or so runs are a North Vancouver landmark on winter evenings. A day-pass costs $39; for more information call ☎604/984-0661 or visit the website. In summer, it's possible to walk up on the aptly named Grouse Grind Trail from the base station, but it's not a great hike, so you'd do better to settle instead into the inevitable queue for the cable-car ticket office (get here early if you can). After two stomach-churning lurches over the cables' twin towers you reach the summit, which, with its restaurants and allied tourist paraphernalia, is anything but wild. The views, though, are stunning, sometimes stretching as far as the San Juan Islands 160km away in Washington State. Have a quick look at the interpretive centre off to the right when you leave the cable car. A 3-D film is shown in the theatre downstairs (admission covered by your cable-car ticket). Of the two cafés, *Altitudes Bistro* has panoramic views, but fills up quickly. The smarter restaurant *The Observatory* (☎604/998-4403) serves dinner accompanied by a fine prospect of the sunset and city lights below. Rides up on the cable car are free with a restaurant booking. Ask at the centre, or small information desk just beyond the centre, about easy **guided walks** (summer daily 11am–5pm); the "Tribute to the Forest" (30min) leaves on the hour, the "Walk in the Woods" on the half-hour (35min).

Walk up the paved paths away from the centre for about five minutes and you pass a cabin office offering guided "gravity assisted" (read downhill) **bike tours** from the summit (May–Oct 3 daily; 20km trips cost from around $85, 30km $95, including cable-car fee); behind the office you can sign up for expensive helicopter tours. On the left up the path lies the scene of the "Logging Sports" shows (twice daily; free); involving various crowd-pleasing sawing and wood-chopping displays. Just beyond this is the **Peak Chairlift** (also included in your ticket), which judders upwards for another eight minutes to the mountain's summit; views of the city and Fraser delta are even better. Check with the office at the lower cable-car base station for details of long **hikes** – many are down below rather than up at the summit proper. The best easy stroll is to **Blue Grouse Lake** (15min); the Goat Ridge Trail is for experienced hikers. More rugged paths lead into the mountains of the West Coast Range, but for these you'll need maps.

The latest attractions on the mountain are four **grizzly bears**, which were found as orphaned cubs (their mother had probably been shot by hunters). In an ideal world the bears would not need to have been taken in, but they would not have survived long in the wild and, once habituated to humans, return to the wild is in any case almost impossible. Today most locals seem rather pleased to know the bears are there, even those initially sceptical about the rights and wrongs; the animals also have a generous amount of space to live in – ringed around by a big electric fence.

To get directly to the base station of the cable car from Lonsdale Quay, take the special #236 Grouse Mountain **bus** from Bay 8 to the left of the SeaBus terminal. You can also take a #246 Highland bus from Bay 7 and change to the #232 Grouse Mountain at Edgemount Village.

Lynn Canyon Park

Among the easiest targets for a quick taste of backwoods Vancouver is **Lynn Canyon Park** (open all year dawn to dusk), a quiet, forested area with a modest ravine and suspension bridge which, unlike the more popular Capilano Suspension Bridge (see below), you don't have to pay to cross. Several walks of up to ninety minutes take you through fine scenery – cliffs, rapids, waterfalls and, naturally, the eighty-metre-high bridge over Lynn Creek – all just twenty minutes from Lonsdale Quay. Take bus #228 from the quay to its penultimate stop at Peters Street, from where it's a ten-minute walk to the gorge; alternatively, take the less-frequent #229 Westlynn bus from Lonsdale Quay, which drops you about five minutes closer. Before entering the gorge, it's worth popping into the **Ecology Centre**, 3663 Park Rd, off Peters Road (June–Aug daily 10am–5pm; Oct–Feb Mon–Fri 10am–5pm, Sat & Sun noon–4pm; donation; ⓦ www.dnv.org), a friendly and informative place where you can pick up maps and pamphlets on park trails and wildlife.

Capilano River Regional Park

Lying just off the approach road to Grouse Mountain, **Capilano River Park**'s most publicized attraction is the inexplicably popular seventy-metre-high and 137-metre-long **suspension bridge** – the world's longest pedestrian suspension bridge – over the vertiginous Capilano Gorge (daily: mid-March to mid-April & late Oct 9am–6pm; late April 9am–6.30pm; early May & Sept to mid-Oct 9am–7.30pm; mid-May to Aug 8.30am–8pm; Nov to mid-March 9am–5pm; admission May–Oct $14.95, Nov–April $10.25; ⓦ www .capbridge.com). The first bridge here was built in 1889, making this Vancouver's oldest "attraction", though the present structure dates from 1956. Although part of the park, the footbridge is privately run as a money-making venture. Elsewhere in the park stick to the paths – and avoid the pedestrian toll, which buys you miscellaneous tours, forestry exhibits, trails and a visit to a native carving centre, which frankly don't amount to much. More interesting is the **salmon hatchery** just upstream (daily June–Aug 8am–8pm; May & Sept 8am–7pm; April & Oct 8am–6pm; Nov–March 8am–6pm; free; ⓦ www-heb.pac.dfo-mpo.gc.ca), a provincial operation dating from 1977 designed to help salmon spawn and thus combat declining stocks. The building is well designed and the information plaques interesting, but it's a prime stop on city coach tours, so the place can often be packed.

Capilano is probably best visited on the way back from Grouse Mountain: from the cable-car station it's an easy downhill **walk** (1km) to the north end of the park, below the Cleveland Reservoir, source of Vancouver's often disconcertingly brown drinking water. From there, marked trails – notably the **Capilano Pacific Trail** – follow the eastern side of the gorge to the hatchery (2km). The area below the hatchery is worth exploring, especially the Dog's Leg Pool (1km), which is along a swirling reach of the Capilano River, and if you really want to stretch your legs you could follow the river the full 7km to its mouth on the Burrard Inlet. Alternatively, you could ride the #236 Grouse Mountain bus to the Cleveland Dam or the main park entrance – the hatchery is quickly reached via a side road (or the Pipeline Trail) from the signed main entrance left off Nancy Greene Way. This comes not far after the busy roadside entrance to the Capilano Suspension Bridge (on the bus, ring the bell for the stop after the bridge).

Mount Seymour Provincial Park

At 8668 acres, **Mount Seymour Provincial Park** is the biggest of the North Vancouver parks, the most easterly and the one that comes closest to the flavour of high-mountain scenery. It's 16km north of Vancouver and named after the short-serving BC provincial governor, Frederick Seymour (1864–69). Four major **trails** here are manageable in a day, but you should be aware that conditions can change rapidly and snow lingers as late as June. The easiest hikes go out to Goldie Lake, a half-hour stroll, and to Dog Mountain, an hour from the parking area (one-way), with great views of the city below. Still better views, requiring more effort, can be had on the trails to First and Second Pump. The wildest and most demanding hike by-passes Mount Seymour's summit and runs by way of an intermittently marked trail to the forest- and mountain-circled Elsay Lake.

Adjacent to the park to the northwest is the **Lower Seymour Conservation Reserve**, still occasionally known by its old name, the **Seymour Demonstration Forest** (Ⓦ www.gvrd.bc.ca/lscr), a 14,000-acre area of mostly temperate rainforest, nestled in the lower part of a glacier-carved valley. It's situated at the northern end of Lillooet Road and, if going by public transport, you need to take the #229 Lynn Valley bus to Dempsey Road and Lynn Valley Road. From here it's a ten-minute walk over Lynn Creek via the bridge on Rice Lake Road. You're far better off coming up here on a bike, for the 40km of trails in the area offer some of the best **mountain biking** close to downtown. Forestry education is the area's chief concern, as the area's name suggests, and you can follow various sixty- and ninety-minute marked **hiking trails** that will top up your general knowledge about local trees, soils, fish and wildlife.

For **information** on the park, call ☎604/924-2200, visit Ⓦ www.gov .bc.ca/bcparks, or ask at the city Touristinfo Centre for the blue *BC Parks* pamphlet. To get here by **bus**, take the #239 from Lonsdale Quay to Phibbs Exchange and then the #215 to the Mount Seymour Parkway (1hr) – from there you'll have to walk or cycle up the thirteen-kilometre road to the heart of the park. The road climbs to over 1000m and ends at a car park where boards spell out clearly the trails and mountaineering options available. Views are superb on good days, particularly from the popular **Vancouver Lookout** on the parkway approach road, where a map identifies the city landmarks below. There's also a café, toilets and a small infocentre (summer only). In winter this is the most popular family and learners' **ski area** near Vancouver (☎604/986-2261, Ⓦ www.mountseymour.com; a day pass is $33).

Cypress Provincial Park

Cypress Provincial Park, most westerly of the big parks that part-cover the dramatic mountains and forest visible from Vancouver's downtown, is among BC's most visited day-use parks and probably the most popular of the north shore's protected areas. It takes its name from the huge old red and yellow cedars that proliferate here. Something of a hit with locals who prefer their wilderness just slightly tamed, its trails can be rugged and muddy, but they're always well marked, and even just a few minutes from the parking area you can feel in the depths of the great outdoors. There are several good trails, including the three-kilometre **Yew Lake Trail** – wheelchair-accessible – and the main park trail, which climbs through forest and undergrowth, occasionally opening up to reveal views. The trail also shadows part of Cypress Creek, a torrent that has cut a deep and narrow canyon. For more **information**, ask for the relevant *BC Parks* pamphlet at the Touristinfo Centre, call ☎604/926-6007 or visit Ⓦ www.gov.bc.ca/bcparks. To get here, take the #253 Caulfield/Park Royal **bus**. The park also has two closely linked **ski** and snowboard areas: the Alpine skiing area at Cypress Bowl (☎604/926-5612, Ⓦ www .cypressmountain.com) and the Nordic ski area (☎604/922-0825) at Hollyburn just to the southwest. Day passes cost $42.

Lighthouse Park

Lighthouse Park, just west of Cypress, offers a seascape semi-wilderness at the extreme western tip of the north shore, 8km from the Lion's Gate Bridge.

Smooth granite rocks and low cliffs line the shore, backed by huge Douglas firs up to 1500 years old, some of the best virgin forest in southern BC. The rocks make fine sun beds, though the water out here is colder than around the city beaches. A map at the car park shows the two trails to the 1912 Point Atkinson **lighthouse** itself – you can take one out and the other back, a return trip of about 5km which involves about two hours' walking. Although the park has its secluded corners (no camping allowed), it can be disconcertingly busy during summer weekends. For more **information**, contact the Touristinfo Centre or call ☎604/925-7200 or 925-7000. The West Van #250 **bus** makes the journey all the way from Georgia Street in downtown.

Eating and drinking

Vancouver's **restaurants** are some of Canada's finest, and span the price spectrum from budget to blowout. If you want to eat well, you'll be spoilt for choice – and you won't have to spend a fortune to do so. As you'd expect, the city offers a wide range of ethnic eateries. **Chinese** and **Japanese** cuisines have the highest profile (though the latter tend to be expensive), followed by **Italian**, **Greek** and other European imports. **Vietnamese** and **Thai** are more recent arrivals and can often provide the best starting points if you're on a tight budget. Specialist **seafood** restaurants are surprisingly thin on the ground, but those that exist are of high quality and often remarkably cheap. In any case, seafood does crop up on most menus and salmon is heavily featured. **Vegetarians** are well served by a number of specialist places.

Countless **cafés** are found mainly around the beaches, in parks, along downtown streets, and especially on Granville Island. Many sell light meals as well as coffee and snack staples. The city also has a commendable assortment of **bars**, many a cut above the functional dives and sham pubs found elsewhere in BC.

Note that the definitions of bar, café, restaurant and nightclub can be considerably blurred: food in some form – usually substantial – is available in most places, while daytime cafés and restaurants also operate happily as nighttime bars. In this section we've highlighted places whose main emphasis is food and drink; entertainment venues are listed under "Nightlife". Note, too, that Vancouver has a handful of places that stay open all night or until the small hours; a selection of these is given below.

Cafés and snack outlets

Little Italy, the area around Commercial Drive (between Venables and Broadway), is good for cheap, cheerful and downright trendy cafés, though as new waves of immigrants fill the area Little Italy is increasingly becoming "Little Vietnam" and "Little Nicaragua". The heavily residential **West End**, notably around Denman and Davie streets – Vancouver's "gay village" – is also booming, having gained a selection of interesting shops and eateries.

Bavaria 203 Carrall St. A simple, no-frills Gastown place with a couple of tables outside on Maple Tree Square almost in front of Gassy Jack's statue. Particularly recommended for its inexpensive all-day breakfast: if you want something a touch more upmarket, then head for the fine *Pistol Burnes* café on the corner to the right (with lots more outside seating) or *Blake's* (see below) and *The Irish Heather* (see p.820), both just a few doors away.

Blake's 221 Carrall St near Water St. One of several cosy and relaxed places on this short Gastown stretch of Carrall St for a coffee, sandwich or snack; a good place to while away an hour writing a postcard or reading the newspaper.

Boulangerie la Parisienne 1076 Mainland St near Helmcken. A Yaletown café and bakery with striking and very pretty all-blue interior that – true to its name – opens up French-style on to the pavement in summer.

Bread Garden 1040 Denman St at Comox ☎604/685-2996. Also in Kitsilano at 1880 W 1st at Cypress; and at 812 Bute, downtown, off Robson. Locals love to moan about the slow service, but food in these hypertrendy deli-cafés is some of the best – and best looking – in the city. Great for people-watching. There are now twelve branches in the Vancouver area. Recommended.

Capers 1675 Robson, and outlets. Capers is a three-branch chain of pristine supermarkets selling natural and organic foods, many of which can be bought as sandwiches and snacks in the onsite cafés. There is a branch in West Vancouver (too far from downtown to be useful to most casual visitors) and at 2285 West 4th Ave.

Flying Wedge 3499 Cambie ☎604/874-8284. If you want pizza this is the place; cheap, thin-crust pizza by the slice (but no alcohol) at five outlets, including Library Square (lunch only), Cornwall Ave (for Kits beach) and just south of the Burrard St Bridge.

Gallery Café Vancouver Art Gallery, 750 Hornby St. Relaxed, stylish and pleasantly arty place at the heart of downtown for coffee, good lunches and healthy, high-quality food (especially desserts); also has a popular summer patio. Recommended.

Hamburger Mary's 1202 Davie St between Bute and Jervis sts ☎604/687-1293. These may well be the best burgers in the city, though there are

plenty of other things on the menu. Lots of people end the evening for a snack at this former West End diner. Outside tables when the weather is fine. Open very late (usually until 3am). Recommended.

La Luna Café 117 Water St between Cambie and Abbot sts. One of only a couple of places on Gastown's main street that has the character to raise it above the usual tourist-oriented cafés in this part of the city.

The Only Café 20 E Hastings and Carrall St. One of Vancouver's most famous institutions, founded in 1912, and worth the trip to the less than salubrious part of town to sample the food and old-world atmosphere. This counter-seating greasy spoon has little more than seafood (perhaps the best in town) and potatoes on its menu. No toilets, no credit cards, no licence and no messing with the service. Mon–Sat 11am–8pm.

Sophie's Cosmic Café 2095 W 4th Ave at Arbutus St ☎604/732-6810. This excellent 1950s-style diner is a Kits institution and is packed out for weekend breakfasts and weekday lunch; renowned for its vast, spicy burgers, milkshakes and whopping breakfasts.

Terra Breads Granville Island Public Market and branches. Tremendous rustic, grainy and fresh-baked breads are the speciality here, with black olive, rosemary, focaccia, cheese, onion, rye, raisin, grape, pine nut and other variations also available. You can also pick up the odd accompaniment and sandwich to combine with a drink from elsewhere.

Restaurants

Restaurants are spread around the city – check locations carefully if you don't want to travel too far from downtown – though are naturally thinner on the ground in North and West Vancouver. Places in Gastown are generally tourist-oriented, with some notable exceptions, in marked contrast to Chinatown's bewildering plethora of authentic and reasonably priced options. Downtown also offers plenty of chains and huge choice, particularly with top-dollar places and fast-food fare: the local *White Spot* chain was founded in 1928 and has some thirty locations in Vancouver, offering good and glorified fast food if time and money are tight – the branch at 1616 W Georgia St between Seymour and Granville is the most central downtown outlet. Superior chains like *Earl's* and *Milestones* are highly commendable, and provide a reliable choice for downtown eating right on Robson (see "West Coast" restaurants, p.817). The old warehouse district of **Yaletown**, part of downtown's new southeasterly spread, is also a key – and still developing – eating and nightlife area. Similar places line 4th Avenue in Kitsilano and neighbouring West Broadway, though these require something of a special journey if you're based in or around downtown: perhaps try them for lunch if you're at the beach or visiting the nearby Vanier Park museums.

Chinese

Floata Seafood Restaurant 400-180 Keefer St ☎604/602-0368, Ⓦwww.floata.com. Canada's largest Chinese restaurant, and one of the city's most popular places for dim sum. Despite its size – the main dining area is nearly the length of a city block – it is not easy to find: it's on the third floor of a mall close to the Dr Sun Yat-Sen Garden. Dim sum is popular – and cheap – at lunch (choose from the carts being wheeled around by countless waitresses), but in the evening menu items become more adventurous and more expensive (shark-fin and bird's-nest soups, Peking duck and so forth).

Hon's Wun-Tun House 108-268 Keefer at Gore St ☎604/688-0871. Started life as a cheap, basic and popular place known for the house specialities, "potstickers" – fried meat-filled dumplings – and ninety-odd soups (including fish ball and pig's feet). Success has spawned other branches and a slight smartening-up, but the encouraging queues, good food and low prices are mercifully unchanged. No alcohol or credit cards.

Imperial Chinese Seafood Restaurant 355 Burrard St near Pender St ☎604/688-8191, Ⓦwww.imperialrest.com. A grand and opulent spot in the old Marine Building with good views and busy atmosphere, serving fine, but pricey, food.

Kirin Mandarin 1166 Alberni near Bute St ☎604/682-8833, Ⓦwww.kirinrestaurant.com. Among the first of the city's smart Chinese arrivals with an elegant decor that's a world away from old-fashioned Chinatown. The superior food is at top-dollar prices but you're repaid with great views of the mountains.

Pink Pearl 1132 E Hastings near Glen St ☎604/253-4316, Ⓦwww.pinkpearl.com. Big, bustling and old-fashioned with a highly authentic feel but in a dingy part of town. The moderately priced food has a Cantonese slant, strong on seafood and great for dim sum. It frequently emerges as the city's top Chinese restaurant in dining polls. Recommended.

Shanghai Chinese Bistro 1128 Alberni St and Thurlow St ☎604/683-8222. A modern-looking but less ostentatious and more reasonably priced alternative to the *Imperial,* if you want to eat Chinese downtown. The handmade noodles are a must. Open very late (until 2–3am).

Wild Rice 117 West Pender St ☎604/642-2882, Ⓦwww.wildricevancouver.com. A western take on Chinese food from a former chef at Bin 941 (see p.818), with dishes and ingredients from across China refined and reworked for Canadian consumption. Go for bite-size tasters or platters to share and don't worry too much about cost – this is high quality food at reasonable prices. Dishes might include wild boar with jasmine rice and plantain, rabbit wontons, winter melon salad, crispy fried duck and warm rice pudding with chocolate and ginger. Good, short wine list and a choice of teas and martinis.

Italian

Allegro Café 1G-888 Nelson St ☎604/683-8485. The location on the ground floor of an office building opposite the Law Courts may not be promising, but the recently revamped interior is warm and romantic, while the Italian and Mediterranean food is excellent and good value for downtown. Camp at the bar for a drink and people-watching session – this is a popular drop-in for lawyers and the smart urban young – or try the great soups (roast garlic a standout), exotic pastas (cappelli with scallops, leeks and Roma tomaotoes) or ambitious mains (pan-seared halibut medallions in apple fennel butter sauce with celery-root chips).

CinCin 1154 Robson St at Bute St ☎604/688-7338, Ⓦwww.cincin.net. An excellent downtown option, with stylish, buzzy setting (try to book an outside table in summer), food that merits the highish prices and includes top-grade home-made pastas and desserts. Check the wine list – it's one of the best in the city.

Il Giardino di Umberto 1382 Hornby St at Pacific St ☎604/669-2422, Ⓦwww.umberto.com. Sublime and expensive food with a bias towards pasta and game served to a trendy and casually smart thirty-something clientele. Weekend reservations are essential, especially for the nice vine-trailed outside terrace.

The Old Spaghetti Factory 55 Water St at Abbot St ☎604/684-1288. Part of an inexpensive chain and hardly *alta cucina*, but a standby if you're in Gastown and better than the tourist trap it appears from the outside, with its spacious 1920s Tiffany interior.

Piccolo Mondo 850 Thurlow St at Smithe St ☎604/688-1633, Ⓦwww.piccolomondoristorante .com. Pricey but excellent food and an award-winning selection of Italian wines. A nicely restrained dining room, just off Robson St, that's not as formal as it first appears. The clientele are expense accounts at lunch and smoochy couples in the evenings. Recommended.

Villa del Lupo 869 Hamilton St near Smithe St ☎604/688-7436, ⓦwww .villadellupo.com. Authentic and expensive, high-quality food in a renovated country house –

French

Cioppino's Mediterranean Grill 1133 Hamilton St ☎604/688-7466, ⓦwww.cioppinosyaletown.com. It's hard to categorize this inviting Yaletown restaurant with warm, cherrywood interior – the name comes from San Francisco's *cioppino* fish stew, but some food is French-influenced, other Italian. It's an attractive and convenient place if you are in this part of town. If the food seems too expensive, make instead for the *Cioppino* wine bar next door for a drink.

The Hermitage 115-1025 Robson near Thurlow St ☎604/689-3237, ⓦwww.thehermitage vancouver.com. Warm brick walls, a big fireplace, crisp linen, French-speaking waiters and a court-yard setting give this central and very highly rated restaurant a cosy, almost European feel. The chef here once cooked for King Leopold of Belgium, so he knows his way around food – the onion soup is unbeatable.

Le Crocodile 100-909 Burrard St, entrance on Smithe St ☎604/669-4298, ⓦwww .lecrocodilerestaurant.com. Plush French-Alsace upmarket bistro establishment that pushes *Bishop's* (see below) close for the title of the city's best restaurant and, unlike its rival, it's located downtown. The menu has something for tradition-alists and the more adventurous alike. A memo-rable meal is guaranteed – but check your credit limit first.

"West Coast"

Bishop's 2183 W 4th near Yew St, Kitsilano ☎604/738-2025. Consistently ranked one of Vancouver's best restaurants, though it's some way from downtown. Although there's a frequent film-star and VIP presence, the welcome is as warm for everyone. The light and refined "contemporary home cooking" – Italy meets the Pacific Rim – com-mands high prices but is worth it. First choice for the big, one-off splurge, but booking is essential.

Blue Water Café 1095 Hamilton St ☎604/688-8078, ⓦwww.bluewatercafe.net. This big restau-rant has quickly become one of Yaletown's most popular fixtures, thanks to the sushi, fish and seafood, and to the attractive terrace and long inte-rior, the last a dark, comfortable space of exposed beams and brick originally used as ballast in ships

unfussy and elegant – on the eastern edge of downtown midway between the library and Yaletown: there's not a better *osso bucco* in Vancouver.

Le Gavroche 1616 Alberni St at Cardero St ☎604/685-3924. The similarly priced *Le Crocodile* may just take the culinary plaudits, but this other top French restaurant (with a West Coast twist) is not far behind. A formal but amiable place and rated as one of the most romantic places in the city.

Lucy Mae Brown 862 Richards St ☎604/899-9199. This intimate, moderately priced restaurant is currently one of the most popular in the city, and takes its name from the owner of a former brothel and boarding house on the site. The appealing decor is a rhapsody of blues, offset by stone and wood floors and high ceilings. Food changes regu-larly with the seasons, but is always lusty (lamb shanks, ahi tuna with capers) without forgetting its sophisticated French and West Coast inspiration. Downstairs is a secret, club-like little bar that opens late and has a simplified menu. Dinner only Mon–Sat.

Lumière 2551 W Broadway near Trafalgar St, Kitsilano ☎604/739-8185, ⓦwww .lumiererestaurant.ca. Local food critics have named this Vancouver's best restaurant twice in recent years. Cooking here is "contemporary French", and a touch lighter than *Le Crocodile*, though prices are equally elevated. Visitors based in downtown will need to take a cab here; you'll also need to book, for the simple, tasteful dining room accommodates just fifty diners.

that sailed to Vancouver in the 1890s. There's an open kitchen for the fish and seafood staples (great halibut dishes, BC sablefish or salmon with pumpkin seed gnocchi), plus Eastern and Western bars (for sushi or ceviche, caviar and other treats repec-tively), and an Ice Bar, where you can indulge in chilled vodkas and freshly squeezed fruit juices. Service is amiable and unstuffy and quality is excel-lent, as you'd expect from a place run by James Walt, who has had stints at two other superb BC restaurants – *Sooke Harbour House* on Vancouver Island (see p.855) and *Araxi* in Whistler (see p.907).

Bridges 1696 Duranleau, Granville Island ☎604/687-4400. Unmissable big, yellow restau-rant upstairs, pub and informal bistro (the best option) downstairs, with a large outdoor deck. A reliable and very popular choice for a drink or meal on Granville Island.

C Restaurant 2-1600 Howe St near Pacific Blvd ⌾604/681-1164. The *Fish House at Stanley Park* (see p.818) is *C*'s only serious rival for the title of best fish and seafood restaurant. The lengthy menu, which contains Southeast Asian influences, might include a choice from the "raw bar" – say a trio of scallop, wasabi salmon and smoked chilli tuna – and unusual fish such as Alaskan arctic char. Views from the dining room are good, too.

Chartwell At *Four Seasons Hotel*, 791 W Georgia St ⌾604/844-6715. Don't let the fact that this is a hotel dining room put you off: the gracious, almost gentleman's club-like ambience is good if you want to dress up or have an indulgent lunch, and fine service, great wine list and progressive Pacific Rim-influenced food makes this one of the top-ten restaurants in Vancouver.

Diva at the Met At *Metropolitan Hotel*, 645 Howe St ⌾604/602-7788, ⓦ www.metropolitan.com. Like the *Chartwell* (see above), *Diva* has carved out a character completely separate to the hotel in which it's lodged. This is among Vancouver's leading restaurants, thanks to the punchy, imaginative food and the modern, clean-lined dining room. Starters might include smoked salmon with Québec foie gras, followed by a main course of halibut cheeks with black-olive tapinade. Expensive, but a great pace for a treat or full-on brunch.

Earl's On Top 1185 Robson St near Bute St ⌾604/669-0020. Come here first if you don't want to mess around scouring downtown for somewhere to eat. The mid-priced, and often innovative, high-quality food is served in a big, open and casual dining area, with outside terrace in the summer. Recommended.

Ferguson Point Teahouse Ferguson Point, Stanley Park ⌾604/669-3281. A very pretty and romantic spot – ocean view, outside dining – and the best place for a lunch or brunch during a walk or ride round Stanley Park. Be sure to book ahead.

The Fish House at Stanley Park 2099 Beach Ave and Stanley Park Drive, at the north end of Beach Ave ⌾604/681-7275. The leafy setting in the southwest corner of Stanley Park is almost that of a country estate, and the seafood arguably the city's best. Indulge at the oyster bar, order any available fish baked, broiled, steamed or grilled, and check out the daily specials. Excellent wine list. Expensive but worth it.

Isadora's 1540 Old Bridge St, Granville Island ⌾604/681-8816. Popular Granville Island choice for a beer or a meal, though *Bridges* is probably a shade better. Fine breakfasts, weekend brunches and light meals with plenty of good veggie/wholefood options. Lots of outdoor seating, but expect queues and slower service at weekends, particularly Sunday brunch. Moderately priced.

Liliget Feast House 1724 Davie St at Bidwill St ⌾604/681-7044. This West End aboriginal restaurant – the only one in Vancouver – serves types of food you'll get nowhere else in the city: seaweed, steamed ferns, roast caribou and barbecued juniper duck. However, the cedar tables and benches, designed to resemble a Coast Salish long house, making the dining room a mite austere. Moderately priced.

Milestone's 1145 Robson St between Bute and Thurlow sts ⌾604/682-4477, also at 1210 Denman St ⌾604/662-3431 and 1109 Hamilton on the corner of Helmcken ⌾604/684-9112. Popular mid-market chain restaurants with cheap drinks and food (especially good breakfasts) in very generous portions. Located at the heart of downtown (fast and noisy), the English Bay Beach end of Denman St (more laid-back) and in Yaletown (popular, with outdoor terrace).

Raincity Grill 1193 Denman St ⌾604/685-7337, ⓦ www.raincitygrill.com. The candles and a position in the West End near Davie St overlooking English Bay make for a romantic dining experience, but it is the food and wine, both of which make the most of BC and Pacific Northwest ingredients (more than 100 varieties of Northwest and Californian wines by the glass are available) which are the main attraction – as you'd expect from a place which has connections with the outstanding *C Restaurant* (see p.818). The moderately priced regional menu changes regularly, but you can always be sure to find salmon, seafood and other locally sourced food (much of it organic) and at least four vegetarian options. Each dish comes with a suggestion for wine. Dinner daily; brunch Sat & Sun.

Water Street Café 300 Water St at Cambie St ⌾604/689-2832. The café-restaurant of choice if you wind up in Gastown (located close to the famous steam clock). An airy and casual atmosphere that offers a short but well-chosen menu; consider booking an outside table if you're going to be here for lunch.

Other cuisines

Bin 941 941 Davie St, West End ⌾604/683-1246, ⓦ www.bin941.com. Also at 1521 W Broadway ⌾604/734-9421. It's not surprising that no one seems to have a bad word for *Bin 941*. Both outlets are tiny, on the slightly crazy side of funky, and packed long and late with people drawn by the up-tempo bars (the West Broadway location is marginally more subdued) and some of the city's best – and best-value – bite-size food. The menu's "tapatizers" include great fries ($3 for a mountain of hand-cut Yukon Gold potato fries), jumbo scallops, tiger-prawn tournedos, crabcakes, charred bok choy and many more. Open for dinner daily until 2am.

Greek

Orestes 3116 W Broadway between Trutch and Balaclava sts, Kitsilano ℡604/738-1941. Good, basic food in one of the city's oldest Greek restaurants. Belly dancers shake their stuff Thursday to Saturday and there's live music on Sunday.

Ouzeri 3189 W Broadway at Trutch St, Kitsilano ℡604/739-9995. A friendly and fairly priced restaurant that is the first port of call if you're at the hostel or beach in Kitsilano.

Stepho's 1124 Davie St between Thurlow and Bute sts ℡604/683-2555. This West End restaurant has simple interior, fine food, efficient service and is very popular. Recommended.

Indian

Vij's 1480 W 11th Ave near Granville St, Fairview ℡604/736-6664. The Indian cooking here has won just about every award going in Vancouver for Best Ethnic Cuisine. The inexpensive menus change regularly; some excellent vegetarian options.

Japanese

Chiyoda 1050 Alberni St at Burrard St ℡604/688-5050. Everything here, down to the beer glasses, was designed in Japan. A chic but convivial place – the emphasis is on grilled food (*robata*) rather than sushi – that draws in Japanese visitors and business people at lunch and the fashionable in the evenings for moderately priced dinners.

Ezogiku Noodle Café 1329 Robson St at Jervis St ℡604/685-8608. This tiny Japanese noodle house is a perfect place for quick food downtown. The queues are prohibitive, but the turnover's speedy.

Tojo's 777 W Broadway at Willow St, Fairview ℡604/872-8050. Quite simply the best Japanese food (sushi and more – try the tuna or shrimp dumplings with hot mustard sauce) in the city. Very expensive.

Mexican

Mescalero's 1215 Bidwell between Burnaby and Davie sts ℡604/669-2399. Very popular Mexican-Latin restaurant in the West End with appropriately rustic atmosphere and fit young punters. Moderately priced.

Topanga Café 2904 W 4th Ave near Macdonald St, Kitsilano ℡604/733-3713. A small but extremely popular and moderate Mexican restaurant; a Vancouver institution.

Southeast Asian

Phnom-Penh 244 E Georgia near Gore St ℡604/682-5777; also at 955 W Broadway near Oak St ℡604/734-8988. Excellent, cheap Vietnamese and Cambodian cuisine, especially seafood, in a friendly, family-oriented restaurant. Recommended.

Pho Hoang 3610 Main at 20th ℡604/874-0810; also at 238 E Georgia near Gore St ℡604/682-5666. The first and perhaps friendliest of the many Vietnamese *pho* (beef soup) restaurants now springing up all over the city. Choose from thirty soup varieties with herbs, chillies and lime at plate-side as added seasoning. Open for breakfast, lunch and dinner. The new Chinatown branch is right by the *Phnom-Penh* (see above).

Simply Thai 1211 Hamilton St, corner of Davie St ℡604/642-0123. This plain, modern but inviting Yaletown restaurant is packed at lunch (11.30am–3pm) and dinner, thanks to the keen prices and good, authentic food – the chefs are all from Bangkok. Another place, *Thai Urban Bistro*, just up the street at 1119 Hamilton (℡604/408-7788) is almost as good.

Vegetarian

The Naam 2724 W 4th Ave near Stephens St, Kitsilano ℡604/738-7151. The oldest and most popular health-food and vegetarian restaurant in the city. Comfortable and friendly ambience with live folk and other music and outside eating some evenings. Open 24hr. Inexpensive and recommended.

Pubs and bars

Alibi Room 157 Alexander St between Columbia and Main ℡604/623-3383, ⓦwww.alibiroom .com. Various movie-makers and shakers put money into this unashamedly hip bar-restaurant –

and the result is a crowd that is trendy, but not so trendy that it spoils what is a good place for drinks and – perhaps – dinner. Excellent and eclectic food is served upstairs, with a short, modern menu at surprisingly reasonable prices; downstairs you can drink and venture onto the small dance floor.

Arts Club 1585 Johnston on Granville Island ⑦604/687-1354. The *Arts Club*'s popular *Backstage Lounge*, part of the theatre complex, has a waterfront view, easy-going atmosphere, decent food and puts on blues, jazz and other live music Friday and Saturday evenings. Recommended.

Bar None 1222 Hamilton St ⑦604/689-7000. Busy, reasonably smart and hip New York-style Yaletown bar and club where you can eat, drink, watch TV, smoke cigars (walk-in humidor), play backgammon or shoot pool and listen to live music.

Blarney Stone 216 Carrall near Water St ⑦604/687-4322. A lively Irish pub and restaurant in Gastown, complete with live Irish music and dance floor. Closed Sun.

Bridges 1696 Duranleau St on Granville Island ⑦604/687-4400. You can eat here, but when the sun's shining it's a close-run thing between the busy patio here and the *Dockside Brewing Company* as to which is the nicest place to have a waterside drink on Granville Island: *Bridges* is more central and thus more convenient.

The Cambie 300 Cambie St ⑦604/684-6466. An obvious place to drink if you're staying at the linked hostel (see p.792), but the roomy (and invariably crowded) outdoor area and cheap pitchers of beer bring in a fair number of locals and other passing trade. Inside, it's all smoke, pool tables and down-to-earth drinking.

Cardero's Marine Pub 1583 Coal Harbour Quay on Cardero St ⑦604/669-7666. The location of this pub-restaurant is neither one thing nor the other, around midway between Stanley Park and Burrard, but the waterfront location and patio (heated on cooler evenings) at the northern end of Cardero St offers great views of the park, moored boats, Burrard Inlet and the North Shore.

Cloud Nine At *Empire Landmark Hotel*, 1400 Robson St at Nicola St ⑦604/687-0511. Vancouver has several bars with a view – notably the lounge in the *Sylvia* and *Bridges* on Granville Island – but none can match the panorama from this super-sleek lounge bar on the 42nd floor of the *Empire Landmark Hotel*. The bar rotates, so your view changes by six degrees every sixty seconds. There's a modest cover charge for entry on Fri and Sat, but it's worth paying for the panorama.

Darby D. Dawes 2001 Macdonald St and 4th Ave ⑦604/731-0617. A pub handy for Kits Beach and the hostel. People often start the evening here, meals are served 11.30am–7pm, snacks till 10pm, and then move on to the *Fairview* for live blues (see p.822). Live music is only played on Friday and Saturday evenings with jam sessions on Saturday afternoons.

Dockside Brewing Company 1253 Johnston St, Granville Island ⑦604/685-7070. Beer buffs may want to try this stylish lounge in the *Granville Island Hotel* to sample some of the establishment's on-site microbrewery's ales. The atmosphere is relaxed and the generally well-heeled crowd thirty-something. Things tend to be more lively early in the evening, and in summer there's a fine outdoor patio.

Gerard's 845 Burrard at Robson St ⑦604/682-5511. The smooth wood-panelled lounge and piano bar with leather chairs and tapestries, all make this very elegant downtown drinking. Also, the place to spot the stars currently filming in town.

The Irish Heather 217 Carrall St near Water St ⑦604/688-9779. A definite cut above the usual mock-Irish pub, with an intimate bar, live Irish music some nights, excellent food, good Guinness (apparently it sells the second largest number of pints of the stuff in Canada); and an unexpectedly pretty outdoor area in the back.

La Bodega 1277 Howe near Davie St ⑦604/684-8815. One of the city's best and most popular places, with tapas and excellent main courses, but chiefly dedicated to lively drinking. It's packed later on, so try to arrive before 8pm. Recommended. Closed Sun.

Shark Bar & Grill At *Sandman Hotel*, 180 W Georgia ⑦604/687-4275. The best and busiest of several sports bars in the city. There are 30 screens, a 180-seat oak bar, 22 beers on tap, Italian food from the kitchen, and lots of testosterone.

Sylvia Hotel 1154 Gilford and Beach ⑦604/688-8865. This nondescript but easy-going hotel bar is popular for quiet drinks and superlative waterfront views, and pleasant after a stroll on English Bay Beach.

Yaletown Brewing Company 1111 Mainland St ⑦604/681-2739. An extremely large and unmissable bar and restaurant with their own six-beer on-site brewery. Currently very popular, and leading the way in the funky Yaletown revival.

Nightlife and entertainment

Vancouver gives you plenty to do come sunset, laying on a varied and cosmopolitan blend of **live music**. **Clubs** are more adventurous than in many a

Canadian city, particularly the fly-by-night alternative dives on and around Main Street and Commercial Drive, and in the backstreets off Gastown, Chinatown. There's also a choice of smarter and more conventional clubs, a handful of discos and a selection of **gay** and **lesbian** clubs and bars. Summer nightlife often takes to the streets in West Coast fashion, with outdoor bars and (to a certain extent) beaches becoming venues in their own right. Fine weather also allows the city to host a range of **festivals**, from jazz to theatre, and the **performing arts** are as widely available as you'd expect in a city as culturally self-conscious as Vancouver.

The most comprehensive **listings** guide to all the goings-on is *Georgia Straight* (Ⓦ www.straight.com), a free weekly published on Thursday and available in larger stores and street boxes around the city. Many other free magazines devoted to different musical genres and activities are available at the same points, but they come and go quickly. Selected club listings can also be found at Ⓦ www.clubvibes.com, while Ⓦ www.vancouverjazz.com/directory offers a list of jazz venues, but no critical commentary.

Tickets for many major events are sold through Ticketmaster, based at 1304 Hornby St, which has forty outlets throughout the city (Ⓣ 604/280-4444 for concerts, 280-4400 for sporting events and 280-3311 for the performing arts; Ⓦ www.ticketmaster.ca); they'll sometimes unload discounted tickets for mid-week and matinee performances. Half-price and last-minute same-day tickets are available via "Tickets Tonight" (Ⓦ www.ticketstonight.ca) at participating venues, or through the outlet at the main TouristInfo visitor centre at 200 Burrard St (see p.783).

Live music and clubs

Vancouver's live-music venues showcase a variety of musical styles, but mainstream **rock** groups are the most common bill of fare; the city is also a fertile breeding ground for **punk** bands, with particularly vocal audiences. **Jazz** is generally hot news in Vancouver, with a dozen spots specializing in the genre (ring the Jazz Hot Line at Ⓣ 604/682-0706 for current and upcoming events). And, while Vancouver isn't as cowpoke as, say, Calgary, it does have several clubs dedicated to **country music**, though many are in the outer suburbs. Many venues also double as **clubs** and discos, and as in any city with a healthy alternative scene there are also plenty of fun, one-off clubs that have an irritating habit of cropping up and disappearing at speed. Cover charges are usually nominal, and tickets are often available (sometimes free) at record shops. At the other end of the spectrum, the 60,000-seat Pacific Coliseum is on the touring itinerary of many international acts.

Rock

The Cave Plaza of Nations, 750 Pacific Blvd and Cambie St Ⓣ 604/603-8597, Ⓔ cavenightclub@shaw.ca. A loud and young, progressive dance and live-music club (for a long time known as *The Rage*) with a big 1000-plus capacity. It's blessed with five bars, staggeringly loud sound system and a huge and invariably packed dance floor – think warehouse or aircraft hangar.

Commodore Ballroom 870 Granville St at Smithe St Ⓣ 604/681-7838, Ⓦ www.commodoreballroom.com. Still fresh from a $1 million face-lift –

which retained its renowned 1929 dance floor – the *Commodore* is the city's best mid-sized venue. There is an adventurous music policy and both local and national DJs frequently spin.

Piccadilly Pub 620 W Pender near Granville Ⓣ 604/682-3221. The "Pic" is a long-established pub with a guarantee of raucous music of some description (garage, rock, punk, rockabilly) most nights, usually Thursday to Saturday. It's a laid-back, non-posey sort of place aimed at those who simply want beer, music and a good time.

Railway Club 579 Dunsmuir St at Seymour St Ⓣ 604/681-1625. Long-established favourite with excellent bookings, wide range of music (folk, blues, jazz) and a casual atmosphere. Has a separate "conversation" lounge, so it's ideal for a drink (and weekday lunches). Arrive before 10pm at weekends – the place is tiny.

Roxy 932 Granville St at Nelson St ☎604/684-7699, ⓦ www.roxyvan.com. Nightly live bands with emphasis on retro 1950s to 1970s music. Casual and fun place for college crowd and people in from the burbs.

Sonar 66 Water St at Abbott St ☎604/683-6695, ⓦ www.sonar.bc.ca. Central Vancouver's best-known music venue, with live bands nightly. Convenient mid-Gastown location attracts a varied clientele – it's also known as something of a pick-up spot. Bar food and piano lounge until 9pm, when the band strikes up.

Jazz and blues

Arts Club Theatre Backstage Lounge 1585 Johnston, Granville Island ☎604/687-1354. The lounge is a nice spot to hear R&B, jazz and blues, or watch the boats and sunset on False Creek.

Capone's 1141 Hamilton St ☎604/684-7900. This Yaletown spot is primarily a restaurant, but has a stage for live jazz renditions while you eat.

Cellar Restaurant & Jazz Club 3611 W Broadway ☎604/738-1959, ⓦ www.cellarjazz.com. Kitsilano has only recently acquired clubs, and this tiny 70-seat red-walled basement with black booths and low tables is one of the most popular, frequently offering the best live jazz in the city four or more nights a week (generally Wed–Sat). Join the enthusiastic crowd for top local outfits or big international names.

Fairview 898 W Broadway at the *Ramada Inn* ☎604/872-1262. Good local blues and 1950s rock in a pub atmosphere with only a small dance floor. Snacks are served during the day and good-value meals in the evening. Closed Sun.

Purple Onion 15 Water St near Abbot St ☎604/602-9442, ⓦ www.purpleonion.com. Casual club right in the heart of Gastown: top-notch jazz and live Latin music upstairs, dance floor, cigars, oysters and cabaret downstairs. Currently a very popular choice, so expect to wait in line on Friday and Saturday.

Yale 1300 Granville St at Drake St ☎604/681-9253. An outstanding venue: the top place in the city to hear hardcore blues and R&B. Relaxed air, big dance floor and occasional outstanding international names. Often jam sessions with up to fifty players at once, on Sat (3–8pm) and Sun (3pm–midnight). Recommended. Closed Mon & Tues.

Country

Boone County Cabaret 801 Brunette Ave, Coquitlam ☎604/523-3144. Just off the Trans-Canada (take bus #151) this is suburbia's favourite country music club and it shows – it's typically raucous and crowded. There's no cover Mon–Thurs, and free dance lessons Mon, Tues & Thurs 8pm. Closed Sun.

Clubs and discos

Au Bar 674 Seymour St ☎604/648-2227. Downtown club for suits and miniskirts, with martinis the (expensive) drink of choice. Strict dress code and vetting on the door (you'll spot the Seymour St queues from afar), but the exclusive air is what attracts punters. If you get in, people-watching may prove the most entertaining part of your evening. Three bars and small dance floor with safe Top 40, hiphop and R&B.

Big Bam Boo 1236 W Broadway near Oak St ☎604/733-2220. Sports on TV, pool and sushi upstairs; dancing downstairs to safe Top 40 stuff and 1980s throwbacks. Smart place with a strict dress code and generally queues on Thurs–Sat. Wed & Sat are two of the best "Ladies" nights in the city.

Plaza Club 881 Granville St ☎604/646-0064, ⓦ www.plazaclub.net. A popular, no-nonsense dance club with great sound and lighting in a former cinema in central Granville St location. Music has a strong British bias, but there are also theme nights. Saturday is very popular, so expect to queue.

Richard's on Richards 1036 Richards St at Nelson St ☎604/687-6794. A well-known club and disco, but pretentious and aimed at the BMW set. Long waits and dress code. Open Thurs–Sat.

Shine 363 Water St ☎604/408-4321. Conveniently located and happening Gastown club which attracts some of the city's top DJs, notably Dicky Doo. Understated decor, with comfortable retro 1960s couches and all-white colour scheme provide a sophisticated setting for house, reggae, soul, R&B, hiphop and other sounds. Dress up a bit.

Urban Well 888 Nelson St at Hornby ☎604/638-6070, ⓦ www.urbanwell.com. The combination of club-like bar and restaurant, with nightly DJs and comedy and other event nights, has proved so successful that there are two Urban Wells in town – the one here in downtown just two blocks from Robson and the other in Kitsilano at 1516 Yew St (☎604/737-7770). You'll probably have to queue for both at busy times.

Voda At *Westin Grand Hotel*, 783 Homer St ☎604/684-3003, ⓦ www.voda.com. Arrive early in this very roomy hotel lounge near the central library and chances are it'll be empty. Come later and you'll find it heaving, for this is one of the newer and most popular of the city's clubs. The sleek look and and fittings – wood panelling, back-lit bar, lots of candles, waterfalls, rocks, angled beams – are offset by the generally very elegant and fashion-conscious clientele. Don't wear your jeans, Music for the smallish dance floor covers most bases, from R&B and funk to electro and old-school house. Closed Sun & Mon.

Comedy

Yuk Yuk's Plaza of Nations, 750 Pacific Blvd at Cambie St ☎604/687-LAFF. Top US and Canadian stand-up acts and the usual scary amateur night (Wed). Shows at 9pm, plus Sat & Sun 11.30pm. Closed Mon & Tues.

Performing arts

Vancouver serves up enough highbrow culture to suit the whole spectrum of its cosmopolitan population, with plenty of unusual and avant-garde perform-ances to spice up the more mainstream fare you'd expect of a major North American city. The main focus for the city's performing arts is the **Queen Elizabeth Theatre**, 600 Hamilton St at Georgia (☎604/299-9000, Ⓦwww.city.vancouver.bc.ca/theatres), which plays host to visiting theatre, opera and dance troupes and even the occasional big rock band, along with the **Centre in Vancouver for the Performing Arts** opposite the central library at 777 Homer St (☎604/602-0616, Ⓦwww.centreinvancouver.com). The refurbished **Orpheum Theatre**, 884 Granville at Smithe (☎604/665-3050, Ⓦwww.city.vancouver.bc.ca/theatres), is Vancouver's oldest theatre and head-quarters of the Vancouver Symphony Orchestra. Farther afield, the **Chan Centre for the Performing Arts**, 6265 Crescent Rd at the University of British Columbia (☎604/822-2697, Ⓦwww.chancentre.com), has the 1400-seat Chan Shun Concert Hall, the main space of the three-hall UBC performance complex. It has the best acoustics in the city, and hosts shows by outside and university music, drama and other groups, as well as fashion shows, world-music and other events, The UBC has a smaller Recital Hall at Gate 4, 6361 Memorial Rd. **Tickets** can be obtained from individual box offices or through the Ticketmaster agency (see p.821).

Classical music

Early Music Vancouver ☎604/732-1610, Ⓦwww.earlymusic.bc.ca. Early music with original instruments where possible; concerts all over the city, and at the UBC during the Early Music Festival in July & Aug.

Festival Concert Society ☎604/736-3737. Often organizes cheap Sunday morning concerts (jazz, folk or classical) at the Queen Elizabeth Playhouse.

Music-in-the-Morning Concert Society 1270 Chestnut, Vanier Park ☎604/873-4612, Ⓦwww.musicinthemorning.org. This began mod-estly in someone's front room over a decade ago but now organizes innovative and respected con-certs of old and new music with local and visiting musicians.

University of British Columbia School of Music Recital Hall, Gate 4, 6361 Memorial Rd ☎604/822-5574, Ⓦwww.music.ubc.ca. The UBC presents around eight major and many smaller performances during Jan & Feb and also Sept–Nov. Many are free.

Vancouver Bach Choir ☎604/921-8012, Ⓦwww.vancouverbachchoir.com. The city's top non-professional choir performs three major con-certs yearly at the Orpheum Theatre.

Vancouver Cantata Singers 5115 Keith Rd ☎604/921-8588, Ⓦwww.cantata.org. Various locations are used by this 40-strong, semi-profes-sional choir for performances of traditional and contemporary choral music.

Vancouver Chamber Choir ☎604/738-6822, Ⓦwww.vancouverchamberchoir.com. One of two professional, internationally renowned choirs in the city. They perform at the Orpheum and on some Sunday afternoons at the *Hotel Vancouver*.

Vancouver New Music Society ☎604/663-0861, Ⓦwww.newmusic.org. Responsible for several annual concerts of cutting-edge twentieth-century music, usually at the East Cultural Centre (see "Drama" below).

Vancouver Opera ☎604/638-0222, Ⓦwww.vanopera.bc.ca. Four operas are produced annually

Vancouver is a tolerant and welcoming city for **gays and lesbians**. It may not have the profile or élan of San Francisco, but it enjoys the same laid-back West Coast attitudes. There is a large, vibrant and unabashed gay and lesbian community, much of which is culturally and politically active and aware. There's also a lively and diverse scene when it comes to entertainment and nightlife, with plenty of clubs – theme nights are a popular phenomenon – drag shows and up-to-the-minute bars and discos. **Davie Village**, which runs from Burrard along Davie to Denman, is where you will find the highest concentration of long-established gay clubs, pubs and stores, though there are plenty of other venues throughout the city, while lesbians have traditionally hung out on **Commercial Drive** ("The Drive"). Most clubs are late-night opening, usually until 4am, a relatively new freedom following the relaxation of licensing laws.

For detailed information on **gay and lesbian** events, check out *X-tra* (ⓣ604/684-XTRA, ⓦwww.xtra.ca) a regular free magazine available at clubs, bookshops and many of the *Georgia Straight* distribution points. Also useful is the monthly *Outlooks* (ⓦwww.outlooks.ca) and the **Gay & Lesbian Centre Help Line** (ⓣ604/684-6869). *Little Sister's Book and Art Emporium* at 1238 Davie St (ⓣ604/669-1753) sells everything from dildos to greetings cards, and also has a comprehensive noticeboard. It also sells tickets for various events, as does *GayMart* at 1148 Davie (ⓣ604/681-3262).

Bars, pubs and restaurants

Café Luxy 1235 Davie St ⓣ604/669-5899. Davie Village and the West End have no shortage of gay-friendly places to eat and drink, but this stands out by virtue of its fresh, home-made pastas and jazz-groove DJ nights, currently every Tuesday.

Dufferin 900 Seymour St and Smithe St ⓣ604/683-4251, ⓦwww.dufferinhotel.com. This is one of the city's key places for gay men to shake their stuff on the dance floor, but it also hosts a lot of drag-nights – the Buff at the Duff drag shows (Mon–Thurs) are an institution – as well as providing strippers, go-go boys (Fri and Sun) and karaoke.

Fountainhead Pub 1025 Davie ⓣ604/687-2222, ⓦwww.thefountainheadpub.com. A popular and pleasantly buzzing place at the heart of Davie Village for good food, drink (including microbrewed beers) and a large, heated patio from which to spy on all the street action. Also has a pool table, darts and multiple TV screens. Tends to attract a slightly older, more mellow crowd.

Global Beat 1249 Howe St ⓣ604/689-2444. A gay-owned restaurant and lounge with billiard tables that makes a good place for an inexpensive meal (fine Italian-influenced food) or a drink – there's no heavy cruising – to start the evening, especially if you're heading to *Odyssey*, a club which stands right next door (see opposite).

Oasis 1240 Thurlow ⓣ604/685-1724, ⓦwww.theoasispub.com. Vancouver's only gay piano bar. Comfortable upstairs place for people who want to be heard above the music. Long list of martinis and a tapas menu, with daily specials and a roof-top patio. Daily 9pm until late.

Pump Jack Pub 1167 Davie ⓣ604/685-3417, ⓦwww.pumpjackpub.com. A spacious spot and Vancouver's leather bar of choice: it's favoured by Western Canada Leather Pride and the BC Bears, a gay affiliation for those with a penchant for the hirsute. Arrive early to guarantee a cruisey window-side bar stool to watch the men go by. There are pool tables and uniform nights. Expect queues at the weekends.

Sugar Daddy's 1262 Davie St ⓣ604/632-1646. Another West End gay rendezvous of some standing, thanks to video sports, big-screen TVs, and good burgers, beer and margheritas. Open for lunch and dinner daily.

Clubs

Club 23 23 West Cordova ☎604/662-3277. A cool, dark split-level club, perfect for the various theme nights held here, such as the naked parties held by the Pacific Canadian Association of Nudists, "Lesbians on the loose" and "Sin City" fetish nights.

Heritage House Hotel 455 Abbott St ☎604/685-7777. The three bars here host a number of gay and lesbian nights: *Charlie's Bar and Grill* on the main floor fills up with women only on Sat and *Chuck's Pub* has "Guys in Disguise" on Fri and men-only on Sat; call for latest details. The *Lotus Sound Lounge* downstairs has a women-only dance club (Fri) and a lesbian hangout every Wed to Sat at the Lick Bar. There are some mixed nights and occasional fetish and other theme nights. Call before you go for latest permutations and times.

Lava Lounge 1180 Granville St ☎604/605-6136. This is a gay and lesbian club with different theme nights several times a week: "Sexy Friday" has go-go boys, while "Soirée la Femme" is a girls-only night every third Sun of the month.

Numbers 1042 Davie St and Burrard St ☎604/685-4077. This is a cruisy multi-level venue which has been in business for over twenty years, with a gay disco, kitsch mirrored dance floor, movies and pool tables upstairs, men and women downstairs – but with very few women. Tends to attract a slightly more mature crowd. As with virtually all other clubs listed here, there are a wide variety of theme nights.

Octane 1188 Davie ☎604/688-0677. A hip club and bar with DJs and a happening, youngish crowd. Best of the spinning is at the late-night event on Sun. There's currently live jazz on Sat.

Odyssey 1251 Howe St near Davie St ☎604/689-5256, ⓦwww.theodyssey nightclub.com. A young gay and bisexual club with house and techno disco and theme shows on most nights. Expect to queue on Fri & Sat as it currently has the reputation as the hippest and wildest place in town.

Sublime 816 Granville St Ⓔsublimenightclub@hotmail.com. A good place to wind up in the small hours if you're still raring to go at the weekend: the after-hours dance club runs Fri & Sat night 1–6am.

Events and festivals

While there are no vast **events** or **festivals** in the manner of Sydney's Mardi Gras, there are plenty of one-off and occasional events that have become, or are becoming, permanent fixtures. The main draw in Vancouver's gay calendar is **Pride** (☎604/687-0955 or 737-7433, ⓦwww.vanpride.bc.ca), which celebrated 25 years in 2003. It usually takes place over three days during the first long weekend in August. Special events are held in clubs across the city, while the traditional parade along Denman and Beach has, by general consent, become bigger and better each year, with ever-more exuberant floats. Over the years, the parade has spawned stalls and stages at Sunset Beach up to Davie Street, with lots of beer gardens and live performances. Special **club events** can be found in the *Georgia Straight* or *Xtra West* (see p.824) free magazines in the week or so preceding Pride. The **Queer Film and Video Festival** (ⓦwww.outonscreen.com) takes over the city's movie theatres shortly after Pride in August. It marked its 15th anniversary in 2003. Other noteworthy events include **Gay Ski Week** (ⓦwww.outontheslopes.com), which has attracted thousands every year since its inception in 1991. Event organizers also now have a summer event, with riding, biking and rafting among warmer-weather activities.

at the Queen Elizabeth Theatre and productions currently enjoy an excellent reputation.

Vancouver Recital Society ☎604/736-0363, ⓦ www.vanrecital.com. Hosts two of the best and most popular cycles in the city: the summer Chamber Music Festival (at St George's School) and the main Vancouver Playhouse recitals (Sept–April). Catches up-and-coming performers plus a few major international names each year.

Vancouver Symphony Orchestra ☎604/876-3434, ⓦ www.vancouversymphony.ca. Presents most concerts at the Orpheum or Chan Shun Hall on Crescent Rd off NW Marine Drive, but also sometimes gives free recitals in the summer at beaches and parks, culminating in a concert on the summit of Whistler Mountain.

Drama

Arts Club Theatre ☎604/687-1644, ⓦ www.artsclub.com. A leading light in the city's drama scene, performing at three venues: the main stage, at 1585 Johnston St on Granville Island, offers mainstream drama, comedies and musicals; the next-door bar presents small-scale revues and cabarets; and a third stage, at 1181 Seymour and Davie streets, focuses on avant-garde plays and Canadian dramatists – a launching pad for the likes of Michael J. Fox. The theatre has cult status for its "theatre sports", in which teams of actors compete for applause with improvization. Beware, as audience participation features highly.

Firehall Arts Centre 280 E Cordova at Gore St ☎604/689-0926, ⓦ www.firehall.org. The leader of Vancouver's community and avant-garde pack, presenting mime, music, video and visual arts.

Theatre Under the Stars (TUTS) Malkin Bowl, Stanley Park ☎604/687-0174 or 257-0366, ⓦ www.tuts.bc.ca. Summer productions here are fun and lightweight, but can suffer from being staged in one of Canada's rainiest cities.

Vancouver East Cultural Centre 1895 Venables St at Victoria St ☎604/251-1363, ⓦ www.vecc.bc.ca. Renowned performance space housed in an old church, used by a highly eclectic mix of drama, dance, mime and musical groups.

Vancouver Playhouse Theatre Company Hamilton St at Dunsmuir St ☎604/665-3050. One of western Canada's biggest companies. It usually presents six top-quality shows with some of the region's premier performers and designers during its Oct–May season.

Waterfront Theatre 1411 Cartwright St, Granville Island ☎604/685-6217. Home to three resident companies that also hold workshops and readings.

Dance

Anna Wyman Dance Theatre ☎604/685-5699, ⓦ www.annawyman.com. Although their repertoire is wide, this group specializes in contemporary dance. As well as standard shows, they occasionally put on free outdoor performances at Granville Island and at Robson Square near the Art Gallery.

Ballet British Columbia ☎604/732-5003, ⓦ www.ballet.bc. The province's top company performs – along with major visiting companies – at the Queen Elizabeth Theatre.

EDAM ☎604/876-9559, ⓦ www.edamdance.org. Experimental Dance and Music present modern mixes of dance, film, music and art.

Karen Jamieson Dance Company ☎604/893-8807. Award-winning company and choreographer that often use Canadian composers and artists, and incorporates native cultural themes.

Scotiabank Dance Centre 677 Davie St ☎604/689-0926. This new dance centre in a former bank building was converted by Arthur Erickson, architect of the Museum of Anthropology and other Vancouver buildings. It provides studio and rehearsal space for around 30 companies, and is open to the public for workshops, classes, exhibitions and other events. It also houses the Vancouver Dance Centre, a major source of information on dance in Vancouver and beyond (☎604/606-6400, ⓦ www.thedancecentre.ca). Contact it for details of the major Dancing on the Edge Festival in July.

Film

The western capital of Canada's **film** industry, Vancouver is increasingly favoured by Hollywood studios in their pursuit of cheaper locations and production deals. It's therefore no surprise that the spread of cinemas is good. Home-produced and Hollywood first-run films play in the downtown cinemas on "Theatre Row" – the two blocks of Granville between Robson and Nelson streets – and other big complexes, and there's no shortage of cinemas for more esoteric productions.

Capitol 6 820 Granville Mall ☎604/669-6000. This complex is one of the biggest first-run venues in the centre of the city, and – as it's bang in the middle of downtown and shows all the new releases – the main 1000-seat screen makes a good first choice if you want to see the movies of the moment. Screens in the upstairs theatres are much smaller.

Cinemark Tinseltown 88 Pender St at Abbott ☎604/806-0799. Just two blocks south of Water St and the heart of Gastown, this multi-screen in the International Village complex has the most modern and high-tech of the city centre's first-run cinemas, with big screens, underground parking and good seating.

Denman Cinema 1737 Comox St at Denman ☎604/683-2201. A good choice in the West End if you need a break after Stanley Park or want to catch a movie before or after hitting the cafés and bars on Denman Street. Expect second-run or near first-run films at good prices.

Fifth Avenue Cinemas 2110 Burrard St at W 5th Ave ☎604/734-7469. Fiveplex cinema in south Vancouver run by the founder of the Vancouver Film Festival. It is one of the better in the city for art-house or more arty first-run films.

Hollywood 3123 W Broadway between Tutch and Barclay sts ☎604/738-3211, ⊛www .hollywoodtheatre.ca. A Kitsilano repertory cinema which can also always be relied on for good (and good-value) double bills and second-run (or just over first-run) movies.

Pacific Cinémathèque 1131 Howe St near Helmcken St ☎604/688-3456, ⊛www.cine matheque.bc.ca. The non-profit film society that runs this screen is devoted to furthering the understanding of cinema and contemporary visual arts. As part of its brief, it shows a good range of arthouse, overseas and experimental films. All of which makes it the best non-mainstream cinema in the city. The programmes can be hit or miss, but any film buff will find something to tempt them.

Raja Cinema 639 Commercial Drive at Georgia ☎604/253-0402. The place to come when only Bollywood will do.

Ridge Theatre 3131 Arbutus St at W 15th Ave ☎604/738-6311, ⊛www.ridgetheatre.com. A little too far south to catch its target Kits audience, but still a great neighbourhood place for second-run, classic and other films. Look out for its provocatively paired double bills and late-lunch (1.30pm) "Movies for Mommies" screenings. Built in 1950, it's virtually unchanged – there's even an enclosed "crying room" for parents with boisterous children or howling infants.

The Blinding Light! 36 Powell St ☎604/684-8288, ⊛www.blindinglight.com. A great 100-seat Gastown venue for diehard film buffs who can expect to see all manner of offbeat, experimental and plain crazy films, as well as home movies, crazed animation, and lunacies such as industrial and training films from the 1950s and 1960s. It helps host the Vancouver Underground Film Festival and presents theme nights such as "bring-your-own-movie" sessions.

Festivals

Warm summers, outdoor venues and a culture-hungry population combine to make Vancouver an important **festival** city. To learn more about events and shows, contact Tourism Vancouver (☎604/683-2000, ⊛www .tourismvancouver.com), or pick up *The Vancouver Book*, an annually updated listing of festivals and general information available free from the Touristinfo Centre (see p.783). Other listings can be found by visiting ⊛www.foundlocally .com/vancouver and ⊛www.bcpassport.com/festivals.

Among the major festivals is the annual **Du Maurier International Jazz Festival** (late June to early July), organized by the Coastal Jazz and Blues Society (☎604/872-5200, ⊛www.coastaljazz.ca). Past line-ups have featured such luminaries as Wynton Marsalis, Youssou N'Dour, Ornette Coleman, Carla Bley and John Zorn. Some 800 international musicians congregate annually, many offering workshops and free concerts in addition to paid-admission events. The **Vancouver International Folk Music Festival** (☎604/602-9798 or 1-800/985-8363, ⊛www.thefestival.bc.ca) hosts a bevy of international acts centred on Jericho Park and the Centennial Theatre for several days during the third week of July. Vancouver loses its collective head over the July **Sea Festival** (☎604/684-3378) – nautical fun, parades and excellent fireworks around English Bay. Farther afield in Whistler (see p.902), there's a **Country & Bluegrass Festival** in mid-July.

Theatre festivals come thick and fast, particularly in the summer. The chief event is the **Fringe Festival** (℡604/257-0350, ⓦ www.vancouverfringe .com), modelled on the Edinburgh equivalent. It currently runs to more than 550 shows, staged by some ninety companies at ten venues. There's also an annual **Bard on the Beach Shakespeare Festival** (℡604/739-0559, ⓦ www.bardonthebeach.org; June–Aug) in Vanier Park and an **International Comedy Festival** (℡604/683-0883, ⓦ www.comedyfest.com) in early August on Granville Island. Many of the city's art-house cinemas join forces to host the **Vancouver International Film Festival** (℡604/685-0260, ⓦ www.viff.org), an annual showcase for more than 150 films running from late September to mid-October.

Listings

Airlines Air Canada ℡604/688-5515 or 1-888/247-2262 or 1-800/661-3936, ⓦ www .aircanada.ca; American Airlines ℡604/222-2532 or 1-800/433-7300, ⓦ www.aa.com; Baxter: float-plane services to Victoria's Inner Harbour ℡604/688-5136, ⓦ www.baxterair.com; British Airways ℡604/270-8131 or 1-800/247-9297, ⓦ www.ba.com; Continental ℡1-800/525-0280, ⓦ www.continental.com; Delta ℡1-800/241-4141, ⓦ www.delta.com; Harbour Air Seaplanes: services to Victoria Inner Harbour ℡604/274-1277 or 1-800/665-0212, ⓦ www.harbour-air.com; Helijet Airways: helicopter service to Victoria ℡604/273-1414 or 1-800/665-4354, ⓦ www.helijet.com; KLM ℡604/303-3666; United ℡1-800/241-6522, ⓦ www.united.com; West Coast Air: seaplane services to Victoria and Gulf Islands ℡604/688-9115 or 606-6888 or 1-800/347-2222, ⓦ www.westcoastair.com; Whistler Air: direct flights to Whistler from Vancouver Harbour Air Terminal by the *Pan Pacific Hotel* ℡604/932-6615 or 1-888/806-2299.

American Express Park Place Building, 666 Burrard St, enter at Hornby and Dunsmuir ℡604/669-2813 or 1-800/772-4473; Mon–Fri 8.30am–5.30pm, Sat 10am–4pm.

BC Ferries ℡1-888/223-3779 in BC, or 250/386-3431 elsewhere in Canada, ⓦ www.bcferries.com. Runs services to Vancouver Island, the Gulf Islands, the Sunshine Coast, Prince Rupert, the Inside Passage, Bella Coola and the Haida Gwaii–Queen Charlotte Islands.

Bike rental Bayshore Bicycles & Rollerblade Rentals, 745 Denman St ℡604/688-2453, ⓦ www.bayshorebike.ca; Harbour Air, Harbour Air Terminal at the waterfront one block west of Canada Place and the foot of Burrard St ℡604/688-1277 – also rents blades and motorcycles; Spokes, 1798 Georgia at Denman ℡604/688-5141, ⓦ www.vancouverbikerentals.com.

Books and maps Chapters, 788 Robson St ℡604/682-4066, ⓦ www.chapters.ca. International Travel Maps, 552 Seymour St ℡604/687-3320, ⓦ www.itm.com. The Geological Survey of Canada, 101-605 Robson near Richards (℡604/666-0529; Mon–Fri 8.30am–4.30pm) is a superb source of official survey maps, including all 1:50,000 maps of BC and Yukon.

Car rental Budget: airport, 501 W Georgia St & 1705 Burrard St ℡604/668-7000 or 1-800/268-8900 in Canada, 1-800/527-0700 in US, ⓦ www.bc.budget.com; Hertz: 1128 Seymour St ℡604/688-2411 or 1-800/263-0600, ⓦ www.hertz.com; Lo-Cost: 1835 Marine Drive ℡604/986-1266, ⓦ www.locost.com; National: airport & 1130 W Georgia at Thurlow ℡1-800/227-7368, ⓦ www.nationalcar.com; Rent-a-Wreck: 1349 Hornby St ℡604/688-0001, ⓦ www.rentawreckvancouver.com.

Consulates Australia, 1225-Suite 888 Dunsmuir St ℡604/684-1177; Ireland, 1400-100 W Pender St ℡604/683-8440; New Zealand, 1200-Suite 888 Dunsmuir St ℡604/684-7388; UK, 800-1111 Melville St ℡604/683-4421; US, 1095 W Pender ℡604/685-4311.

Exchange Custom House Currency, Unit 60-200 Granville St ℡604/608-1763, ⓦ www .customhouse.com; International Securities Exchange, 1169 Robson St near Thurlow ℡604/683-9666; QuickEx, 300-609 W Hastings ℡604/683-6789, ⓦ www.quickex.ca; Travelex-Thomas Cook, Suite 130, 999 Canada Place

Tⓣ604/641-1229; Vancouver Bullion & Currency Exchange, 402 Hornby St ⓣ604/685-1008, ⓦwww.vbc.ca.

Laundry Davie Laundromat, 1061 Davie St ⓣ604/682-2717; Scotty's One Hour Cleaners, 834 Thurlow near Robson ⓣ604/685-7732.

Left luggage At the bus station ($2 per 24hr).

Lost property For items lost on the TransLink transport system, go to the office at the SkyTrain Stadium Station (Mon–Fri 8.30am–5pm; ⓣ604/682-7887, or 985-7777 for items left on West Van buses). Otherwise: police ⓣ604/665-2232; airport ⓣ604/276-6104.

Medical facilities St Paul's Hospital is the closest to downtown at 1081 Burrard St near Davie St ⓣ604/682-2344. The city hospital is Vancouver General at 855 W 12th near Oak, south of Broadway ⓣ604/875-4111. The College of Physicians can provide names of three doctors near you (ⓣ604/733-7758). Drop-in service at Bentall Centre Rexall Drugstore, Suite 400, Bental 4, 1055 Dunsmuir and Burrard ⓣ604/684-8204, ⓦwww.rexall.ca; Ultima Vancouver Airport Medical Clinic, Vancouver International Airport, Domestic Terminal ⓣ604/207-6900, ⓦwww.ultimamedical.ca; Vancouver Mediclinics is also in the Bentall Centre (ⓣ604/683-8138, ⓦwww.medicentre.ca; Mon–Fri 8am–4.30pm), as is the drop-in dentist Dentacare (ⓣ604/669-6700; Mon–Fri 8am–5pm only), Shopper's Drug

Mart is a 24-hour pharmacy at 1125 Davie and Thurlow ⓣ604/669-2424.

Optician Opticana Eyewear, 455 Granville St (ⓣ604/685-1031, ⓦwww.opticana.ca).

Parking Main downtown garages are at The Bay (entrance on Richards near Dunsmuir), Robson Square (on Smithe and Howe), and the Pacific Centre (on Howe and Dunsmuir) – all are expensive and fill up quickly. A better idea might be to leave your car at the free Park'n'Ride in New Westminster (off Hwy 1).

Police Non-emergency 24hr ⓣ604/717-3321. RCMP ⓣ604/264-3111; Vancouver City Police ⓣ604/665-3535.

Post office Main office at 349 W Georgia and Homer (Mon–Fri 8am–5.30pm; ⓣ604/662-5722). Post office information at ⓣ1-800/267-1177.

Taxis Black Top ⓣ604/731-1111 or 681-2181; Vancouver Taxi ⓣ604/255-5111 or 874-5111; Yellow Cab ⓣ604/681-3311 or 681-1111.

Weather ⓣ604/664-9010.

X-Files tours X-tour.com (ⓣ604/609-2770, ⓦwww.x-tour.com) runs three basic tours of locations used in the TV show *The X Files*, which is filmed in Vancouver: Agent Scully Apartment X-Tour on foot ($29), Quik X-Tour ($145) and North Star X-Tour ($188). The last two are by limousine with a guide and last around 3hr 30min. Per person prices are lower if there are more than two people, up to a maximum of six.

Vancouver Island

The proximity of **VANCOUVER ISLAND** to Vancouver makes it one of western Canada's premier tourist destinations, though its popularity is slightly out of proportion to what is, in most cases, a pale shadow of the scenery on offer on the region's mainland. The largest of North America's west-coast islands, it stretches almost 500km from north to south, but has a population of around only 500,000, mostly concentrated around **Victoria**, whose small-town feel belies its role as British Columbia's second metropolis and provincial capital. Victoria is also the most British of Canadian cities in feel and appearance, something it shamelessly plays up to attract its two million – largely American – visitors annually. While Victoria makes a convenient base for touring the island – and, thanks to a superlative museum, merits a couple of days in its own right – little else here, or in any of the island's other sizeable towns, is enough to justify an overnight stop.

For most visitors Vancouver Island's main attraction is the great outdoors and, increasingly, **whale-watching**, an activity which can be pursued from Victoria, **Tofino**, **Ucluelet** and several other places up and down the island. The scenery is a mosaic of landscapes, principally defined by a central spine of snowcapped

⑦

SOUTHERN BRITISH COLUMBIA | Vancouver Island

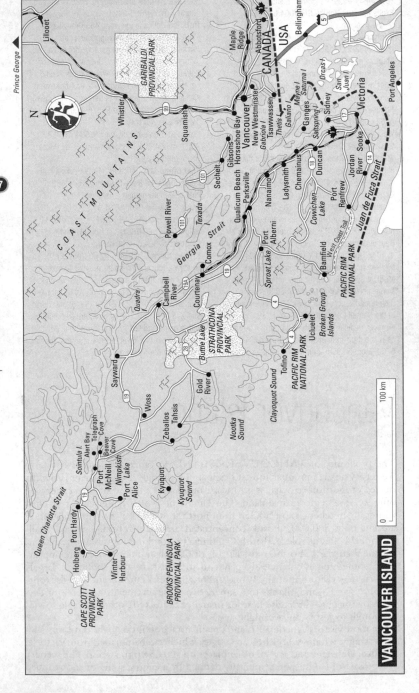

Seattle

Prince George

Lillooet

GARIBALDI
PROVINCIAL PARK

Maple
Ridge

Abbotsford

Bellingham

CANADA

USA

5

Port
Angeles

Orcas I

San
Juan I

N

Whistler

99

Squamish

C O A S T   M O U N T A I N S

Gibsons

Horseshoe Bay

Vancouver

New Westminster

Tsawwassen

Gabriola I

Galiano I

Mayne I

Saturna I

Ganges

Saltspring I

Thetis I

Sidney

Victoria

17

Sechelt

101

Qualicum Beach

Parksville

Nanaimo

Ladysmith

Chemainus

18

Duncan

Cowichan
Lake

Port
Renfrew

Jordan
River

14

Sooke

Powell River

101

Texada I

Georgia   Strait

Comox

Courtenay

19

Port
Alberni

Sproat Lake

4

Bamfield

Broken Group
Islands

West Coast Trail

Juan de Fuca Strait

PACIFIC RIM
NATIONAL PARK

Campbell
River

19A

Quadra I

Buttle Lake

STRATHCONA
PROVINCIAL
PARK

28

Gold
River

Nootka
Sound

Ucluelet

4

PACIFIC RIM
NATIONAL PARK

Tofino

Clayoquot Sound

Sayward

19

Woss

Zeballos

Tahsis

Sointula I

Alert Bay

Telegraph
Cove

Beaver
Cove

Port
McNeill

Nimpkish

Port
Lake

Alice

Kyuquot

Kyuquot
Sound

Queen Charlotte Strait

19

Port Hardy

Holberg

Winter
Harbour

CAPE SCOTT
PROVINCIAL
PARK

BROOKS PENINSULA
PROVINCIAL PARK

VANCOUVER ISLAND

0   100 km

mountains that divide it decisively between the rugged and sparsely populated wilderness of the west coast and the more sheltered lowlands of the east. Rippling hills characterize the northern and southern tips, and few areas are free of the lush forest mantle that supports one of BC's most lucrative logging industries. Apart from three minor east–west roads (and some rough logging and gravel roads), all the urban centres are linked by a good highway running along almost the entire length of the east coast.

Once beyond the main towns of **Duncan** and **Nanaimo**, the northern two-thirds of the island is distinctly underpopulated. Locals and tourists alike are lured by the beaches at **Parksville** and **Qualicum**, while the stunning seascapes of the unmissable **Pacific Rim National Park**, protecting the central portion of the island's west coast, and **Strathcona Provincial Park**, which embraces the heart of the island's mountain fastness, are the main destinations for most visitors. Both of these parks offer the usual panoply of outdoor activities, with hikers being particularly well served by the national park's **West Coast Trail**, which is a tough and increasingly popular long-distance path. A newer, but less dramatic (and less busy) trail, the **Juan de Fuca Trail** runs to the south of the park. Shuttle buses and once-daily scheduled bus services from Victoria to points in the park, together with a wonderful approach by **boat** from Port Alberni, offer a choice of beguiling alternative itineraries for exploring the region. Another **boat trip** on a smaller working vessel from the tiny settlements of Tahsis and Gold River to the north is also becoming deservedly popular.

For a large number of travellers, however, the island is little more than a necessary pilgrimage on a longer journey north. Thousands annually make the trip to **Port Hardy**, linked by bus to Victoria, at the northern tip, to pick up the ferry that follows the so-called **Inside Passage**, a breathtaking trip up the British Columbia coast to Prince Rupert. More are likely to pick up on the newer scenic ferry service, the **Discovery Coast Passage**, from Port Hardy to Bella Coola, south of Prince Rupert. You'll probably meet more backpackers plying these routes than anywhere else in the region, many of them en route to the far north, taking the ferries that continue on from Prince Rupert to Skagway and Alaska.

Victoria

VICTORIA is British Columbia's provincial capital and the region's second city after Vancouver. It's a popular excursion from Vancouver, and though it's possible to come here for the day – especially if you take a seaplane from Vancouver's harbour – you'd be better advised to stay overnight and give the city the two or so days it deserves.

This said, Victoria has a lot to live up to. Leading US travel magazine *Condé Nast Traveler* has voted it one of the world's top ten cities to visit, and world number one for ambience and environment. It's not named after a queen and an era for nothing. Much of the waterfront area has an undeniably quaint and likeable English feel – "Brighton Pavilion with the Himalayas for a backdrop," said the writer Rudyard Kipling – and Victoria has more British-born residents than anywhere in Canada. However, its tourist potential is exploited chiefly for American visitors, served up with lashings of fake Victoriana and chintzy commercialism, and ersatz echoes of empire at every turn. Despite the seasonal influx, and the sometimes atrociously tacky attractions designed to part tourists

VICTORIA

0   100 m

CHINATOWN

HERALD STREET ❶ ❷

SWIFT STREET

FISGARD STREET ❸

FISGARD STREET

McPherson
Theatre

City Hall ❹

CORMORANT STREET

Ⓐ

Upper
Harbour

Train
Station

PANDORA   AVENUE ❺

MARKET
SQUARE

PANDORA AVENUE

Ⓑ & Esquimalt

JOHNSON ST BRIDGE

JOHNSON STREET

JOHNSON STREET

Ⓒ
❼

❻

YATES STREET Ⓓ

❽

❾

Bastion Square

Maritime Museum

❿

YATES STREET

VIEW STREET

TROUNCE ALLEY

The Bay Centre ⓫

VIEW STREET

⓬

FORT STREET

N

Inner
Harbour

⓭ Ⓔ & Craigdarroch Castle

⓮

BROUGHTON STREET

Harbour
Square
Mall

COURTNEY STREET

Greater Victoria
Public Library

COURTNEY STREET

Royal
Theatre

Infocentre ⓘ
⓯

HUMBOLDT STREET

Windsor
Court

Ⓕ

Empress
Hotel

BURDETT AVENUE

Ⓖ

RUPERT TERRACE

Ⓗ

Royal London
Wax Museum

Pacific
Undersea
Gardens

BELLEVILLE   STREET

Convention
Centre

Bus Terminal

Crystal
Garden

FAIRFIELD ROAD

⓳

QUEBEC STREET

Parliament
Buildings

Helmcken House ❶

KINGSTON STREET

Royal
British
Columbia
Museum

St. Anne's
Schoolhouse

ELLIOT ST

ACADEMY CLOSE

Ⓙ

SUPERIOR STREET

Ⓚ

SUPERIOR STREET

Beacon
Hill Park

SOUTHGATE STREET

Ⓛ   Ⓜ & Ⓝ

ACCOMMODATION

Abigail's Hotel	G	Rosewood Inn	N
Cherry Bank Hotel	H	Ryan's	J
Crystal Court Motel	I	Selkirk Guest House	B
Heathergate House	L	Shamrock Suites	
James Bay Inn	M	on the Park	K
Ocean Island		Strathcona Hotel	F
Backpacker's Inn	C	Turtle Refuge Hostel	A
Prior House	E	Victoria Youth Hostel	D

EATING AND DRINKING

Barb's Fish and Chips	16	Milestone's	15
Blethering Place	6	Murchie's	11
Da Tandoor	13	Pagliacci's	14
Demitasse Coffee Bar	7	Re-Bar	10
Dutch Bakery &		Sally's	
Coffee Shop	12	Süze	8
Earl's	3	Swans Brewpub	5
Herald Street Café	1	Taj Mahal	2
Il Terrazzo	9		

from their money, it's a small, relaxed and pleasantly sophisticated place, worth lingering in if only for its inspirational museum. It also provides plenty of pubs, restaurants (and the odd club) and serves as a base for a range of outdoor activities and slightly more far-flung attractions. Chief of these is **whale-watching**, with a plethora of companies on hand to take you out to the teeming waters around the city. And as a final lure the weather here – though often damp – is extremely mild; Victoria's meteorological station has the distinction of being the only one in Canada to record a winter in which the temperature never fell below freezing.

A brief history of Victoria

Victoria's site was originally inhabited by **Salish natives**, and in particular by the Lekwammen, who had a string of some ten villages in the area. Here they cultivated camas bulbs – vital to their diet and trade – and applied their advanced salmon-fishing methods to the shoals of migrating salmon in net-strung reefs offshore. At the time the region must have been a virtual paradise. Captain George Vancouver, who was mapping the North American coast apparently ignorant of the aboriginal presence, described his feelings on first glimpsing this part of Vancouver Island: "The serenity of the climate, the innumerable pleasing landscapes, and the abundant fertility that nature puts forth, require only to be enriched by the industry of man with villages, mansions, cottages and other buildings, to render it the most lovely country that can be imagined."

The first step in this process began in 1842 when Victoria received some of its earliest **white visitors**, notably Hudson's Bay Company representative James Douglas, who disembarked at present-day Clover Point during a search for a new local headquarters for the company. One look at the natural harbour and its surroundings was enough; this, he declared, was a "perfect Eden", a feeling only reinforced by the friendliness of the indigenous population, who helped him build **Fort Camouson**, named after an important aboriginal landmark (the name was later changed to **Fort Victoria** to honour the British queen). The aboriginal peoples from up and down the island settled near the fort, attracted by the new trading opportunities it offered. Soon they were joined by British pioneers, brought in to settle the land by a Bay subsidiary, the Puget Sound Agricultural Company, which quickly built several large company farms to accommodate settlers. In time, the harbour became the busiest West Coast port north of San Francisco and a major base for the British navy's Pacific fleet, a role it now fulfills for the bulk of Canada's modern **navy**.

Boom time came in the 1850s following the mainland gold strikes, when Victoria's port became an essential stopoff and supplies depot for prospectors heading across the water and into the interior. Military and bureaucratic personnel moved in to ensure order, bringing morals and manners of Victorian England with them. Alongside there grew a rumbustious shantytown of shops, bars and brothels, with one bar run by "Gassy" Jack Leighton, unwittingly soon to become one of Vancouver's founders.

Though the gold-rush bubble soon burst, Victoria carried on as a military, economic and political centre, becoming the capital of the newly created British Columbia in 1866 – years before the founding of Vancouver. British values were cemented in stone by the **Canadian Pacific Railway**, which built the *Empress Hotel* in 1908 in place of a proposed railway link that never came into being. Victoria's planned role as Canada's western rail terminus was surrendered to Vancouver, and with it any chance of realistic growth or industrial development. These days the town survives quite well almost entirely on

There are three ways to reach Victoria – by **bus and ferry**, by **car and ferry**, or by **air**. Most people travelling under their own steam from Vancouver use the first, which is a simple matter of buying an all-inclusive through-ticket from Vancouver's bus terminal (see p.781) to Victoria's bus depot. By far the quickest approach, however, is to take a seaplane from Vancouver's port: this takes just 25 minutes – as opposed to 3hr 30min by bus and ferry – and drops you right in Victoria's Inner Harbour; however, it works out around three times as expensive.

By bus and ferry from Vancouver

If you're without your own transport, the most painless way to Victoria from Vancouver is to buy a ticket on **Pacific Coach Lines** (T604/662-8074 or 1-800/661-1725, @www.pacificcoach.com) at the Vancouver bus terminal at 1150 Station St, which takes you, inclusive of the ferry crossing and journeys to and from ferry terminals at both ends, to Victoria's central bus station at 700 Douglas St. Buses leave hourly in the summer, every two hours in the winter; total journey time is about 3hr 30min and a single ticket costs $29 ($56 return). No bookings are necessary: overflow passengers are simply put on another coach. Be sure to keep your ticket stub for reboarding the bus after the crossing. You can save yourself about $15 by using public transport at each end and buying a ferry ticket separately, but for the extra hassle and time involved it hardly seems worth it.

A similar all-inclusive bus/ferry arrangement also operates from Vancouver **to Nanaimo** on Vancouver Island via the Horseshoe Bay Terminal, located about fifteen minutes north of West Vancouver on Hwy 1. You can reach the Horseshoe Bay Terminal by taking bus #250 or #257 from Georgia Street. The ferry charges are the same for foot passengers.

You can also reach Victoria directly **from Vancouver Airport** by inclusive coach and ferry arrangements: ask for details at the bus desk in international arrivals of Pacific Coach Lines bus services (7 daily; $36 single, $71 return). Journey time is about 3hr 30min. However, if you intend to visit Victoria before Vancouver, and are flying, then it usually only costs a little more to fly direct to the city from farther afield: it's not usually worth flying to Vancouver and then taking the bus-ferry option to save money.

By car from Tsawwassen, Horseshoe Bay and Powell River

BC Ferries operates four routes to Vancouver Island across the Georgia Strait from mainland British Columbia (information on T1-888/223-3779 in BC, otherwise T250/386-3431, @www.bcferries.com). Reservations (on T1-888/724-5223 in BC, otherwise T604/444-2890) are essential in summer to avoid long waits. The route used by most Vancouver–Victoria drivers is the **Tsawwassen–Swartz Bay** connection, also the route used by Pacific Coach Lines' buses. Ferries ply the route almost continuously from 7am to 10pm (sixteen sailings daily in summer, minimum of eight daily in winter). Car tickets in high season (from late June to early Sept) cost $34.75 at weekends (noon Fri to last sailing on Sun) or $32.75 on weekdays; in shoulder season (from mid-March to mid-June and early Sept to Oct) fares are $31.50/29.75. Bicycles cost $2.50 year-round. You need to add on per-person fares, which are $10 daily in peak season and $9.50 daily in the shoulder season.

The Mid-Island Express **Tsawwassen–Nanaimo** (Duke Point terminal), midway up the island, has eight or so departures daily on the two-hour crossing. More boats

the backs of tourists (four million a year), the civil-service bureaucracy and – shades of the home country – retirees in search of a mild-weathered retreat. Its population today is around 350,000, almost exactly double what it was just thirty years ago.

SOUTHERN BRITISH COLUMBIA | Victoria

7

cover the **Horseshoe Bay–Nanaimo** (Departure Bay terminal) route, a 95-minute journey from a terminal about fifteen minutes' drive from West Vancouver. Fares for both these routes are the same as for Tsawwassen to Swartz Bay. The fourth route is **Powell River–Comox**, Powell River being some 160km northwest of Vancouver on the Sunshine Coast.

By air from Vancouver

Flying into Victoria **from Vancouver** Airport is an expensive option. Open return fares typically run to around $150, excursion fares (with restrictions) around $100. It's more fun and more direct to fly from Vancouver harbour to Victoria harbour **by helicopter** or float plane: Harbour Air (☎250/384-2215 or 1-800/665-0212, ⓦwww.harbour-air.com) and West Coast Air (☎250/388-4521 or 1-800/347-2222, ⓦwww.westcoastair.com) fly in 35min from the Tradewinds Marina just west of Canada Place in Vancouver (see p.795 for details) for a one-way price of $99. Helijet Airways (☎604/273-1414, ⓦwww.helijet.com) flies either from the helipad east of Canada Place or from Vancouver Airport for $140 one-way, less if you book in advance.

By ferry from the US

Washington State Ferries, at 2499 Ocean Ave, Sidney (in Victoria ☎250/381-1551; in Sidney ☎250/656-1531; in Seattle ☎206/464-6400; in Washington State ☎1-888/808-7977; ⓦwww.wsdot.wa.gov/ferries) runs ferries from **Anacortes**, ninety minutes north of Seattle, to Sidney, thirty minutes (and 30km) north of Victoria (summer 2 daily in each direction, winter 1 daily; 3hr–3hr 30min). One of the two summer departures goes via Orcas Island and Friday Harbor on the San Juan Islands. Passenger fares for the full trip are around US$13.10 (a little less in winter), a car and driver US$44.25. Car reservations are required from Orcas and Friday Harbor and can be made by calling at least a day in advance (☎360/378-4777 in Friday Harbor).

    Black Ball Transport, 430 Belleville St, Victoria (in BC ☎250/386-2202 or 1/800-972-6509; in WA ☎360/457-4491 or 1-800/833-6388; ⓦwww.cohoferry.com) operates a ferry across the Juan de Fuca Strait from **Port Angeles** right to Victoria's Inner Harbour (1–4 daily; 95min). Passenger fares are US$8.50, plus US$32.50 for a car. Reservations are not accepted. Car drivers should call ahead in summer to have some idea of how long they'll have to wait. For foot passengers, and day-trippers in particular, a speedier option is **Victoria Express**'s service from Port Angeles to Victoria's Inner Harbour (late June to Aug 3 daily; late May to late June & Sept to mid-Oct 2 daily; 55min; in Canada ☎250/361-9144; in the US ☎360/452-8088 or ☎1-800/633-1589; ⓦwww.victoriaexpress.com). The fare is US$12.50 one-way, US$25 return; bicycles cost $3 one-way or return.

    The 300-passenger-only **Victoria Clipper** catamaran travels between Pier 69 in downtown **Seattle** and Victoria's Inner Harbour in 3hr (mid-May to mid-Sept 4 daily; early May and late Sept 2 daily; rest of year 1 daily) – or 2hr if you take the quicker "Turbojet" departures (250 Bellevue St, Victoria; in Victoria ☎250/382-8100; in Seattle ☎206/448-5000; elsewhere in North America ☎1-800/888-2535; ⓦwww.victoriaclipper.com). Ticket prices in summer are US$68 single and US$113 return for three-hour crossings, or US$77/129 for the Turbojet; and in the off-season US$62/103.

Arrival, information and transport

Victoria International Airport (☎250/953-7500, ⓦwww.victoriaairport .com) is 26km north of downtown on Hwy 17 near the Sidney ferry terminal. Hwy 17 runs south and takes you to the city outskirts where it becomes Douglas St, which runs to the heart of downtown. The Akal Airporter shuttle bus heads downtown (where it stops at major hotels) every half-hour between about 4.30am and 1am; a single fare for the 45-minute journey is $13 (☎250/386-2525 or 1-877/386-2525, ⓦwww.akalairporter.travel.bc.ca). They can also arrange pick-ups to the airport.

The **bus terminal** is downtown at 700 Douglas St and Belleville Street, close to the Royal British Columbia Museum. Pacific Coach Lines' buses (☎250/385-4411, ⓦwww.pacificcoach.com) from Vancouver or Vancouver airport drop you here, and it is the base for Greyhound (☎250/388-5248 or 1-800/663-8390, ⓦwww.greyhound.com) as well as onward connections on Vancouver Island provided by Laidlaw Coach Lines (☎250/385-4411 or 1-800/318-0818, ⓦwww.grayline.ca/victoria). Victoria's **train station**, at the northern end of Wharf St, is useful only if you are taking the one daily service on Via Rail (☎1-888/842-7245, ⓦwww.viarail.ca) to or from Nanaimo and points north (journey time to Nanaimo is 2hr 25min; $23.50 one way).

Victoria's busy **infocentre** is at 812 Wharf St, in front of the *Empress Hotel* on the harbour (daily: May–Sept 8.30am–6.30pm; Oct–April 9am–5pm; ☎250/953-2033, ⓦwww.tourismvictoria.com). The staff can help you book whale-watching and other tours (see box p.841), and provide a huge range of general information.

The most enjoyable means of transport are the tiny Inner Harbour **ferries** that run around the harbour. Stops include Fisherman's Wharf, Ocean Pointe Resort and West Bay Marina, but they're worth taking just for the ride: try an evening mini-cruise around the harbour (buy tickets on ferries in the Inner Harbour or book at the infocentre). You're unlikely to need to take a local **bus** if you stick to the downtown area, but if you do venture out, most services run from the corner of Douglas and Yates streets. The fare within the large central zone is $1.75 – tickets and the DayPass ($5.50) are sold at the infocentre, 7-Eleven stores and other marked outlets, or you can pay on board if you have the exact fare. For 24-hour recorded information on city transport, call the Busline (☎250/382-6161, lost property 995-5637, ⓦwww.bctransit.com).

Accommodation

Victoria fills up quickly in the summer, and most of its budget **accommodation** is well known and heavily patronized. Top-price hotels cluster around the Inner Harbour area; **hostels** and more downmarket alternatives are scattered all over, though the largest concentration of cheap **hotels** and **motels** is around the Gorge Road and Douglas Street areas northwest of downtown. Reservations are virtually obligatory in all categories, though the infocentre's accommodation service (☎1-800/663-3883) will root out a room if you're stuck. They are more than likely to offer you **B&B** accommodation, of which the town has a vast selection; prices for many are surprisingly elevated, though owners of many of the more far-flung places will pick you up from downtown. Victoria's commercial **campsites** are full to bursting in summer, with most space given over to RVs. Few of these are convenient for downtown – given that you'll have to travel, you might as well head for one of the more scenic provincial park sites. Most are on the Trans-Canada Highway to the north, or on Hwy 14 east of Victoria.

Hotels, motels and B&Bs

Abigail's Hotel 960 McClure St ☎250/388-5363 or 1-800-561-6565, ⓦwww.abigailshotel.com. A | very classy, small hotel in a fine building with log fires, voluminous duvets, Jacuzzis and a good breakfast. If you want to treat yourself, this is the place. All rooms are non-smoking. Situated on the corner of Quadra St, a block east of Blanshard St and within easy walking distance of the city centre. ❽

Cherry Bank Hotel 825 Burdett Ave ☎250/385-5380 or 1-800/998-6688, ⓦwww.bctravel.com/cherrybankhotel.html. Reservations are essential at this deservedly popular and pleasantly eccentric 26-room budget hotel (note the rotating mermaid on the roof), which has excellent rooms and breakfast included. First choice at this price. ❸

Crystal Court Motel 701 Belleville St ☎250/384-0551, ⓦwww.crystalcourtmotel.supersites.ca. This is a large, functional and fairly priced motel well located just one block from the Inner Harbour, though it fronts a fairly busy road. ❹

James Bay Inn 270 Government St at Toronto St ☎250/384-7151 or 1-800/836-2649, ⓦwww.jamesbayinn.bc.ca. This 45-room hotel vies with the *Cherry Bank* as Victoria's best reasonably priced option, though rates have climbed in the last couple of years. The Edwardian building was the home of painter Emily Carr. Simple rooms at varying prices, with a restaurant and pub in the basement. Two blocks south of the Parliament Buildings. ❻

Rosewood Inn 595 Michigan St near Government St ☎250/384-6644 or 1-866/986-2222, ⓦwww.rosewoodvictoria.com. A comfortable and smart, small hotel located a couple of blocks south of the Royal BC Museum. ❺–❼

Shamrock Suites on the Park 675 Superior St at the corner of Douglas ☎250/385-8768 or 1-800/294-5544, ☏385-1837. The *Shamrock* lies a block from the Royal BC Museums close to Beacon Hill Park. It has just sixteen units, upgraded from simple motel status to "suites" following a renovation in 2002. Prices have gone up, but the studios and one-bedroom suites are roomy and come with kitchenettes at no extra cost: some rooms have park views. A continental breakfast is included in the rates between July and September. ❺

Strathcona Hotel 919 Douglas St ☎250/383-7137 or 1-800/663-7476, ⓦwww.strathconahotel.com. Large, modern hotel where rooms include baths and TVs. There's a British-style pub and restaurant downstairs with booming live and DJ music which may not be to all tastes. ❹

B&Bs

Heathergate House 122 Simcoe St ☎250/383-0068 or 1-888/683-0068, ⓦwww.heathergatebb.com. This small B&B offers three rooms plus a separate two-bed cottage within walking distance of the Inner Harbour and the sights. All rooms are en suite. There's a private floor for guests with a lounge and TV room. ❺

Prior House 620 St Charles St ☎250/592-8847 or 1-877/924-3300, ⓦwww.priorhouse.com. A very smart five-room B&B; once the home of Victoria's lieutenant governor – ask for his suite, complete with bathroom with chandelier. About 2.5km east of downtown in the smart Rockland area, so it's better if you have transport. ❼

Ryan's 224 Superior St ☎250/389-0012 or 1-877/389-0012, ⓦwww.ryansbb.com. A very pretty 1892 heritage building south of the Royal BC Museum and a five-minute walk to downtown; all seven rooms are nicely decorated and have private bathrooms. ❼

Selkirk Guest House 934 Selkirk Ave ☎250/389-1213 or 1-800/974-6638, ⓦwww.selkirkguesthouse.com. Fine historic waterfront home dating from 1909 northwest of the Inner Harbour: take bus #14 from Douglas St (to within two blocks) or cross the Johnston Bridge and follow the water past Bay St and Banfield Park: then take Arcadia, a right turn from Craigflower Rd to Selkirk Ave. It's well placed for bike and walking trails (it's on the Galloping Goose Trail) and you can rent boats and canoes. Dorm places cost $20 and there's a choice of four other good double rooms $75–90 with breakfast at $5. ❹

University residences, hostels and campsites

Ocean Island Backpacker's Inn 791 Pandora Ave at Blanshard St ☎250/385-1788 or 1-888/888-4180, ⓦwww.oceanisland.com. A good, reasonably central location in the northeast corner of downtown. Facilities include private and shared rooms, Internet access, a music room with instruments, no curfew, free morning coffee, laundry room, free bike storage, linen and towels provided and limited parking at $4 a day. The restored 1893 heritage building has a wide variety of dorms and rooms (singles and doubles with and without bathroom) on a sliding scale depending on the time of year, the day of the week (more on Fri and Sat) and whether you have a HI card. The following prices are Fri and Sat rates and assume you do not have card (subtract $1–3 if you do): dorm beds cost $17.75 from mid-Oct to mid-March up to $23 in July and Aug. Private doubles cost from $40 to $55. Weekly and monthly rates are available on dorms and rooms.

Turtle Refuge Hostel 1608 Quadra St at corner of Pandora ☎ 250/386-4471, ✉ turtlerefuge @hotmail.com. Central residential home (also known as the *Backpackers' Lodge*) with 25 dorm beds, two doubles and two four-bed family rooms. There's a communal kitchen, laundry, no curfew, parking, luggage storage and free morning coffee. Dorm beds cost $13 (Nov–April $12), doubles $40 ($30) plus $10 for each extra person.

University of Victoria Corner of Sinclair and Finnerty Rd ☎ 250/721-8395, ⓦ www.hfcs.uvic.ca. Good, if plain rooms (single or double) on the university campus are available May–Sept when not required for students or conferences. Shared bathroom, laundry and kitchen facilities. Good-value four-room suites with bathroom, kitchen and living room are also available. For a small extra fee guests have access to the university pool and other sports facilities. It is a half-hour car or bus (#4 or 14) ride to downtown. Singles $44 (with breakfast), doubles $55.

Victoria Youth Hostel (HI) 516 Yates and Wharf sts ☎ 250/385-4511 or 1-888/883-0099, ⓦ www.hihostels.ca. Large, modern, welcoming and extremely well-run place just a few blocks north of the Inner Harbour. The bunk rooms, though, can be noisy: the reception, rather ominously, sells earplugs. The notice boards are packed with useful information on the city. Members $16–20, nonmembers $17–24. A hand-

ful of private doubles are available at $38 for members, $48 for nonmembers. Open Mon–Thurs 7.30am to midnight, Fri–Sun 7am–2am.

Campsites

Fort Victoria RV and Park Campground 340 Island Hwy 1A ☎ 250/479-8112, ⓦ www .fortvicrv.com. Closest site to downtown, located 6km north of Victoria off the Trans-Canada Hwy. Take bus #14 (for Craigflower) from the city centre; it stops right by the gate. Large 300-pitch site mainly for RVs but with a few tent sites; free hot showers. $29 for two persons.

Goldstream Provincial Park 2930 Trans-Canada Hwy ☎ 604/689-9025 or 1-800-689-9025, ⓦ www.discovercamping.ca. Bus #50 from Douglas St downtown. Although 20km north of the city of Hwy 1, this site is set in old-growth forests of cedar and Douglas fir and is Victoria's best camping option. Flush toilets and free hot showers, with plenty of hiking, swimming and fishing opportunities. $22 per site.

Thetis Lake Trans-Canada Hwy at 1938 West Park Lane ☎ 250/478-3845, ✉ thetislake@shaw.ca. Runs a close second to Goldstream Provincial Park's campsites for the pleasantness of its setting, and is only 10km north of downtown. Family-oriented, with 147 sites, as well as laundry and coin-operated showers. $16 per two persons.

The City

The Victoria that's worth bothering with is very small: almost everything worth seeing, as well as the best shops and restaurants, is within walking distance of the **Inner Harbour** area and the Old Town district behind it. On summer evenings this area is alive with strollers and buskers, and a pleasure to wander as the sun drops over the water. Foremost among the daytime diversions are the **Royal British Columbia Museum** and the **Empress Hotel**. Most of the other trumpeted attractions are dreadful, and many charge entry fees out of all proportion to what's on show. If you're tempted by the Royal London Wax Museum, the Pacific Undersea Gardens, Miniature World, English Village, Anne Hathaway's Thatched Cottage or any of Victoria's other dubious commercial propositions, details are available from the infocentre. Otherwise you might drop by the modest **Maritime Museum** and think about a trip to the celebrated **Butchart Gardens**, some way out of town, but easily accessed by public transport or regular all-inclusive tours from the bus terminal. If you're around for a couple of days you should also find time to walk around **Beacon Hill Park**, a few minutes' walk from downtown to the south.

The best of the area's beaches are well out of town, around three or four miles on Hwy 14 and Hwy 1, but for idling by the sea drop down to the pebble shore along the southern edge of Beacon Hill Park. For some local swimming, the best option by far is **Willows Beach** on the Esplanade in Oak Bay, 2km east of Victoria; take bus #1 to Beach and Dalhousie Road. Other good stretches of sand can be found on Dallas Road and at Island View Beach.

Festivals in Victoria

Summer brings out the buskers and **free entertainment** in Victoria's people-places – James Bay, Market Square and Beacon Hill Park in particular. Annual highlights include:

TerrifVic Jazz Party April. A showcase for about a dozen top international bands held over four days.

Jazz Fest June. More than 100 assorted lesser-known bands perform in Market Square.

Canada Day July 1. Celebration of Canada's national day on concentrated in and around the Inner Harbour and include fireworks, food, music and other cultrual events.

Victoria International Festival July & Aug. Victoria's largest general arts jamboree.

Folk Fest Last week of July. Multicultural arts extravaganza.

First People's Festival Early Aug. Celebration of the cultures of Canada's aboriginal peoples.

Canadian International Dragon Boat Festival Mid-Aug. Over 100 international teams take part in dragon-boat races on the Inner Harbour.

Classic Boat Festival Aug 30–Sept 1. Dozens of wooden antique boats on display.

Royal Victoria Marathon Early Oct. Marathon and half-marathon around the city streets and surroundings held on the Canadian Thanksgiving weekend.

Fringe Festival Sept. Avant-garde performances of all kinds.

Great Canadian Beer Festival Second week of Nov. Selections of beer from some of the province's best micro-breweries can tasted at the Victoria Conference Centre, 720 Douglas St.

Merrython Fun Run Mid-Dec. A 10-kilometre run through downtown Victoria.

The Royal British Columbia Museum

The **Royal British Columbia Museum** (daily 9am–5pm, National Geographic IMAX Theatre daily 9am–8pm; museum $9.75, IMAX Theatre $9.75, combined ticket $20.75, IMAX double feature $15; ⓦ www.rbcm .gov.bc.ca) is a short stroll along the waterfront from the infocentre at 675 Belleville St. Founded in 1886, it is arguably the **best museum in Canada**, and regularly rated, by visitors and travel-magazine polls, as one of North America's top ten. All conceivable aspects of the province are examined, but the aboriginal peoples section is probably the definitive collection of a much-covered genre, while the natural-history sections – huge re-creations of natural habitats, complete with sights, sounds and smells – are mind-boggling in scope and imagination. Allow at least two trips to take it all in.

From the first thing you see – a huge stuffed mammoth – you can tell that thought, wit and a lot of money have gone into the museum. Much of the cash must have been sunk into its most popular display, the **Open Ocean**, a self-contained, in-depth look at the sea and the deep-level ocean. Groups of ten are admitted into a series of tunnels, dark rooms, lifts and mock-ups of submarines at thirty-minute intervals. You take a time-coded ticket and wait your turn, so either arrive early or reckon on seeing the rest of the museum first. Though rather heavy-handed in its "we're-all-part-of-the-cosmic-soup" message, it's still an object lesson in presentation and state-of-the-art museum dynamics. It's also designed to be dark and enclosed, and signs wisely warn you to stay out if you suffer even a twinge of claustrophobia.

The **first floor** contains dioramas, full-scale reconstructions of some of the many natural habitats found in British Columbia. The idea of re-creating shorelines, coastal rainforests and Fraser Delta landscapes may sound far-fetched, yet all are incredibly realistic, down to dripping water and cool, dank atmospheres. Audiovisual displays and a tumult of information accompany the exhibits (the beaver film is worth hunting down), most of which focus attention on the province's 25,600km of coastline, a side of British Columbia usually overlooked in favour of its interior forests and mountains.

Upstairs on the **second floor** is the mother of all the tiny museums of bric-a-brac and pioneer memorabilia in BC. Arranged eccentrically from the present day backwards, it explores every aspect of the province's social history over two centuries in nitpicking detail. Prominently featured are part of an early twentieth-century town, complete with cinema and silent films, plus comprehensive displays on logging, mining, the gold rush, farming, fishing and lesser domestic details; all the artefacts and accompanying information are presented with impeccable finesse.

Up on the mezzanine **third floor** is a superb collection of **aboriginal peoples' art, culture and history**. It's presented in gloomy light against muted wood walls and brown carpet, which creates a solemn atmosphere in keeping with the tragic nature of many of the displays. The collection divides into two epochs – before and after the coming of Europeans – tellingly linked by a single aboriginal carving of a white man, starkly and brilliantly capturing the initial wonder and weirdness of the new arrivals. The whole collection takes a thoughtful and oblique approach, taking you to the point where smallpox virtually wiped out in one year a culture that was eight millennia in the making. A section on land and reservations is left for last – the issues are contentious even today – and even if you're succumbing to museum fatigue, the arrogance and duplicity of the documents on display will shock you. The highlights in this section are many, but try to make a point of seeing the short film *In the Land of the War Canoes* (1914), the **Bighouse** (a facsimile of a meeting hall) and its chants, and the audiovisual display on aboriginal myths and superstition.

The **National Geographic Theatre** in the museum plays host to a huge IMAX screen and a changing programme of special-format films. Outside the museum, there's also **Thunderbird Park**, a strip of grass with a handful of totem poles.

Helmcken House and around

Helmcken House (May–Oct daily 10am–5pm; rest of year Mon & Thurs–Sun 11am–4pm; $5) stands strangely isolated off Belleville St, directly adjacent to the museum. The oldest house in BC still on its original site, built in 1852, it is a predictable heritage offering that showcases the home, furnishings and embroidery talents of the Helmcken family. Dr John Helmcken was Fort Victoria's doctor and local political bigwig, and his house is a typical monument to stolid Victoria values. Upstairs it contains various attic treasures and some fearsome-looking medical tools. It's probably only of interest, however, if you've so far managed to avoid any of Canada's many thousands of similar houses. If you do visit, pick up the free guided tapes and hear "voices from history" (those of actors and actresses) that give a more personalized slant on the building.

Just behind the house there's another old white-wood building, the **St Anne's Pioneer Schoolhouse**, originally purchased by a Bishop Demers for four sisters of the Order of St Ann, who in 1858 took it upon themselves to

Whale-watching from Victoria

The waters around Victoria are not as **whale**-rich as those around Tofino on the west coast of Vancouver Island, but there's still a very good chance of spotting the creatures. Three pods of orcas (**killer whales**) live in the seas around southern Vancouver Island, around a hundred animals in all, so you may see these, though **minke** are the most common whale spotted, with occasional **greys** and **humpbacks** also present. Few outfits offer guaranteed sightings, and many cover themselves by preparing you for the fact that if you don't see whales you stand a good chance of seeing Dall's **porpoises**, harbour or elephant **seals** and California and Steller **sea lions**.

While there are many outfits to choose from, they offer almost identical trips at the same prices, typically around $60 to $90 for a three-hour outing. There's usually a naturalist, or at least a knowledgeable crew member, to fill you in on what you're seeing (or not). The only real variables are the **boats** used, so you need to decide whether you want a rigid-hull cruiser (covered or uncovered), which is comfortable and sedate (and usually the most expensive at around $90), a catamaran ($75–90), or a high-speed aluminium-hull inflatable known as a "zodiac" ($60–90), which is infinitely more exhilarating, but can offer a sometimes bumpy ride and lacks toilets on board. The two companies below have been around longer than most; the info-centre (p.836) has details on others.

Seacoast Expeditions Located across the Inner Harbour at the Boardwalk Level, Ocean Pointe Resort, 45 Songhees Rd (℗250/383-2254 or 1-800-386-1525, ⓦwww.seacoastexpeditions.com) – a ten-minute walk across the Johnson Street bridge or a three-minute harbour ferry crossing (it also has a shuttle-bus pick-up from downtown hotels). Victoria's founding whale-watching company, Seacoast has been in the business over a decade and offers one trip daily in April and October, four three-hour trips daily in May, June and September, and five daily in July and August ($79). It also offers a guaranteed sighting deal (May–Aug only) whereby you carry a pager that tells you to turn up at the office for a tour only when whales have been spotted. All trips are in one of the company's three zodiacs.

Five Star Charters 706 Douglas St (℗250/388-7223 or 1-800-634-9617, ⓦwww .5starwhales.com). Has been in business since 1985 and in the past claimed the highest percentage of whale sightings out of all the tour operators (thanks to spotter boats and a good network of contacts). It runs three daily three-hour trips from mid-April through September ($79) and two daily two-hour trips from October to mid-April ($60). Trips are in 12-passenger open cruiser or 40-person "Supercat" boats.

---

leave their Québec home to come and teach in Victoria. Built between 1843 and 1858, it's believed to be the oldest building in Victoria still in use.

The Parliament Buildings

The huge Victorian pile of the **Parliament Buildings** (daily 9am–5pm; Sept–May closes 4pm; free; Oct–April guided tours every 20–30min; rest of year booked tours only Mon–Fri hourly 9am–3pm, plus one public tour at 4pm; ℗250/387-3046 or 1-800-663-7867 in BC), one block west of the museum at 501 Belleville St, is old and imposing in the manner of a large and particularly grand British town hall. Beautifully lit at night by some three hundred tiny bulbs (though locals grumble about the cost), the domed building is fronted by the sea and well-kept gardens – a pleasant enough ensemble, though it doesn't really warrant the manic enthusiasm visited on it by hordes of summer tourists. You're more likely to find yourself taking

SOUTHERN BRITISH COLUMBIA | Victoria

time out on the front lawns, distinguished by a perky statue of Queen Victoria and a giant sequoia, a gift from the state of California. Designed by the 25-year-old Francis Rattenbury, who was also responsible for the nearby *Empress Hotel*, the building was completed in 1897, at a cost of $923,000, in time for Queen Victoria's jubilee. Figures from Victoria's grey bureaucratic past are duly celebrated, the main door guarded by statues of Sir James Douglas, who chose the site of the city, and Sir Matthew Baillie Begbie (aka the "Hanging Judge"), responsible for law and order during the heady days of gold fever. Sir George Vancouver keeps an eye on proceedings from the top of the dome. Free tours start to the right of the main steps and are led by guides who are chirpy and full of anecdotes. Look out for the dagger that killed Captain Cook, and the gold-plated dome, painted with scenes from Canadian history.

Beacon Hill Park

The best park within walking distance of the town centre is **Beacon Hill Park**, south of the Inner Harbour and a few minutes' walk up the road behind the museum. Victoria is sometimes known as the "City of Gardens", and at the right times of the year this park shows why. Victoria's biggest green space, it has lots of paths, ponds, big trees and quiet corners, and plenty of views over the **Juan de Fuca Strait** to the distant Olympic Mountains of Washington State (especially on the park's southern side). These pretty straits, incidentally, are the focus of some rather bad feeling between Victoria and the US for the city has a dark secret: it dumps raw sewage into the strait, excusing itself by claiming it's quickly broken up by the sea's strong currents. Washington State isn't so sure, and there have been plenty of arguments over the matter and, more to the point for city elders, economically damaging convention boycotts by American companies. Either way, it's pretty bad PR for Victoria and totally at odds with the city's image.

The gardens in the park are by turns well tended and wonderfully wild and unkempt, a far cry from its earliest days, when it was known by the local Salish as *Meeacan*, their word for a belly, as the hill was thought to resemble the stomach of large man lying on his back. The park was a favoured retreat of celebrated Victorian artist Emily Carr. They also claim the **world's tallest totem pole**, as well as the "Mile Zero" marker of the Trans-Canada Hwy and – that ultimate emblem of Englishness – a cricket pitch. Some of the trees are massive old-growth timbers that you'd normally only see on the island's unlogged west coast. Come here in spring and you'll catch swaths of daffodils and blue camas flowers, the latter a floral monument to Victoria's earliest aboriginal inhabitants, who cultivated the flower for its edible bulb. Some 30,000 other flowers are planted in the gardens annually.

Crystal Garden

The heavily advertised **Crystal Garden** (daily: mid-June to mid-Sept 9am–8pm; mid-March to mid-June & mid-Sept to Oct 9am–6pm; Nov to mid-March 10am–4.30pm; $9; ⓦwww.bcpcc.com/crystal), behind the bus terminal at 713 Douglas St, was modelled after London's Crystal Palace and on opening in 1925 was billed as housing the "Largest Saltwater Swimming Pool in the British Empire". Now much restored, the greenhouse – filled with flora and fauna – makes for an unaccountably popular tourist spot; only the exterior has any claims to architectural sophistication, and much of its effect is spoilt by the souvenir and other shops on its ground-floor arcade. Once the meeting place of the town's tea-sipping elite, it still plays host to events such as the "Jive

The Butchart Gardens

If you're into things horticultural you'll want to make a trek out to the celebrated **Butchart Gardens**, 22km north of Victoria at 800 Benvenuto Ave, Brentwood Bay on Hwy 17 towards the Swartz Bay ferry terminal (daily: mid-June to Aug 9am–10.30pm; first two weeks of Sept & Dec 9am–9pm; rest of year 9am–sunset; admission $10.50 in early Jan, then on a sliding scale through the year up to $20 between mid-June and Sept; ⓦwww.butchartgardens.com). The gardens were started in 1904 by Jenny Butchart, wife of a mine-owner and pioneer of Portland Cement in Canada and the US. Her initial aim was to landscape one of her husband's quarries; the garden now covers fifty breathtaking acres, comprising rose, Japanese and Italian gardens and lots of decorative details. About half a million visitors a year tramp through the foliage, which includes over a million plants and seven hundred different species. At the same time, the amount of space actually given over to gardens may strike you as slightly disproportionate to the space alloted to the car park, gift shop and restaurant. The gardens are renowned for the stunning **firework displays** that usually take place each Saturday evening in July and August. There is also a restaurant and various other commercial enterprises, with musical entertainments well to the fore. The gardens are illuminated during the late-evening opening hours between mid-June and the end of September.

To get here by public transport take bus #75 for "Central Saanich" from downtown. Otherwise, there are regular summer **shuttles** (May–Oct daily, hourly in the morning, half-hourly in the afternoon; ⓣ250/388-5248) from the main bus terminal, where tickets ($4) are obtainable not from the main ticket office but a separate Gray Lines desk.

and Ballroom Dance Club" and the "People Meeting People Dance". The daytime draws are the conservatory-type tearoom and tropical gardens. Inhumanely enclosed birds, butterflies and monkeys, though, are liable to put you off your scones.

The Empress Hotel

A town is usually desperate when one of its key attractions is a hotel, but in the case of Victoria the **Empress Hotel** is so physically overbearing and plays such a part in the town's tourist appeal that it demands some sort of attention. You may be unlikely to be staying here – rooms are expensive – but it's worth wandering through the huge lobbies and palatial dining areas for a glimpse of well-restored colonial splendour. In a couple of lounges there's a fairly limp "Smart Casual" dress code – no dirty jeans, running shoes, short shorts or backpacks – but elsewhere you can wander freely. If you want to **take tea**, which is why most casual visitors come, enter the Tea Lounge by the hotel's side entrance (the right, or south side); there you can enjoy scones, biscuits, cakes and, of course, tea over six courses but you have to abide by the dress code and be prepared for an enormous outlay. In other lounges like the *Bengal* (see below) you can ask for just tea and scones.

The hotel's **Crystal Lounge** and its lovely Tiffany-glass dome form the most opulent area on view, but the marginally less ornate entrance lounge is the top place for the charade of afternoon tea, and indulging can be a bit of a laugh. There's also a reasonably priced bar and restaurant downstairs, **Kipling's**, and the attractive **Bengal Lounge**, complete with tiger-skin over the fireplace, where you can have a curry and all the trimmings for about $15. For a bigger treat, take dinner amidst the Edwardian splendour of *the Empress Dining Room*.

The old town

The oldest part of Victoria focuses on **Bastion Square**, original site of Fort Victoria, from which it's a short walk to Market Square, a nice piece of old-town rejuvenation, and the main downtown shopping streets. Bastion Square's former saloons, brothels and warehouses have been spruced up and turned into offices, cafés and galleries. The modest **Maritime Museum** at 28 Bastion Square (daily 9.30am–4.30pm; $6; ⓦ www.mmbc.bc.ca) is of interest mainly for the lovely chocolate and vanilla coloured building in which it's housed, the former provincial courthouse. Displays embrace old charts, uniforms, ships' bells, old photographs, lots of models and a BC Ferries section on the second floor. On the top floor is the restored vice-admiralty courtroom, once the main seat of justice for the entire province. Note the old open elevator built to reach it, commissioned by Chief Justice Davie in 1901, supposedly because he was too fat to manage the stairs.

Two blocks away to the north of the square lies the attractive **Market Square**, the old heart of Victoria but now a collection of some 65 speciality shops and cafés around a central courtyard (bounded by Store, Pandora and Johnson streets). This area boomed in 1858 following the gold rush, providing houses, saloons, opium dens, stores and various salacious entertainments for thousands of chancers and would-be immigrants. On the Pandora Avenue side of the area was a ravine, marked by the current sunken courtyard, beyond which lay **Chinatown** (now centred slightly further north on Fisgard St), the oldest on North America's west coast. Here, among other things, 23 factories processed 90,000 pounds of opium a year for what was then a legitimate trade and – until the twentieth century – one of BC's biggest industries.

As for the **shopping streets**, it's worth looking out for E.A. Morris, a wonderful old cigar and tobacco shop next to Murchie's coffee shop at 1110 Government St, and Roger's Chocolates, 913 Government St, whose whopping Victoria creams (among other things), are regularly dispatched to Buckingham Palace for royal consumption.

Other attractions

Outside the Inner Harbour, Victoria has a scattering of **minor attractions** that don't fit into any logical tour of the city – and at any rate are only quick-stop diversions – the most compelling of which is Craigdarroch Castle.

Craigdarroch Castle and the Art Gallery of Greater Victoria

Craigdarroch Castle (daily: mid-June to early Sept 9am–7pm; rest of year 10am–4.30pm; $10; ⓦ www.craigdarrochcastle.com) is perched on a hilltop at 1050 Joan Crescent in Rockland, one of Victoria's more prestigious neighbourhoods. It was built by Robert Dunsmuir, a caricature of a Victorian politician, strike-breaker, robber baron and coal tycoon, who was forced to put up this gaunt Gothic pastiche to lure his wife away from Scotland. Only the best was good enough, from the marble, granite and sandstone of the superstructure to the intricately handworked panels of the ceilings over the main hall and staircase. The dastardly Dunsmuir never enjoyed his creation: he died in 1889, two years after the castle was begun and a year before it was finished. Among the 39 rooms there's the usual clutter of Victoriana and period detail, in particular some impressive woodwork and stained and leaded glass. To get here by **bus** take the #11-University or #14-University from downtown to the foot of Joan Crescent, two minutes' walk from the castle. If you decide to walk the whole way, allow 45 minutes from the Inner Harbour.

The **Art Gallery of Greater Victoria** (Mon–Sat 10am–5pm, Thurs till 9pm, Sun 1–5pm; $5; ⓦ www.aggv.bc.ca) is near Craigdarroch Castle at 1040 Moss St, just off Fort St. It's of little interest unless you're partial to contemporary Canadian paintings and the country's best collection of Japanese art; the building, housed in the 1890 Spencer Mansion, boasts the only complete Shinto shrine outside Japan. It does, however, have a small permanent collection of Emily Carr's work (see p.798) as well as a temporary exhibition, usually interesting, that changes every six weeks. To get here by **bus**, take the #10-Haultain, #11-Uplands/Beacon Hill or #14-University from downtown.

The Emily Carr House, Point Ellice and Craigflower Manor

Ten rooms are open to the public at **Emily Carr House** (daily 10am–5pm; $5.35), two blocks from the Inner Harbour at 207 Government St. This was the early home of British Columbia's best-known artist (see p.798), born here during a blizzard in 1871 in the old wooden bed still visible in what would become her bedroom. The building was constructed in 1864, and has been painstakingly restored to its former state. Fans of the artist may want to pay homage, but the works on the walls are copies.

The 1861 Victorian-Italianate **Point Ellice House and Gardens** (guided tours mid-May to mid-Sept daily noon–5pm; $5.35; ⓣ 250/387-4697) at 2616 Pleasant St is magnificently re-created but less enticing than Craigdarroch Castle because of its slightly shabby surroundings. These can be overlooked, however, if you make a point of arriving by sea, taking one of the little Harbour Ferry services to the house (10min) from the Inner Harbour. The restored Victorian-style gardens here are a delight on a summer afternoon. The interior – one of the best of its kind in western Canada – retains its largely Victorian appearance thanks partly to the reduced circumstances of the O'Reilly family, whose genteel slide into relative poverty over several generations (they lived here from 1861 to 1974) meant that many furnishings were simply not replaced. Tea is served on the lawns in the summer; it's a good idea to book ahead. Bus #14-University will get you here from downtown if you don't fancy the approach by water.

In its day, **Craigflower Manor and Farmhouse** (May–Oct daily 10am–5pm; $5; ⓣ 250/387-4697) on Admiral's Rd about 9km and fifteen minutes' drive from downtown, was among the earliest of Victoria's farming homesteads, marking the town's transition from trading post to permanent community. It was built in a mock-Georgian style in 1856, apparently from timbers salvaged from the first four farmhouses built in the region. Its owner was Kenneth McKenzie, a Hudson's Bay Company bailiff, who recruited fellow Scottish settlers to form a farming community on Portage Inlet. The house was to remind him of Scotland, and soon became the foremost social centre in the fledgling village – mainly visited by officers because McKenzie's daughters were virtually the only white women on the island. As with Point Ellice House, reservations for tea are recommended. Take **bus** #14-Craigflower from downtown.

Eating, drinking and nightlife

Although clearly in Vancouver's culinary shadow, Victoria still has many **restaurants**, some extremely good, offering greater variety – and higher prices – than you'll find in most other BC towns. **Pubs** tend to be plastic imitations of British equivalents, with one or two worthy exceptions, as do the numerous **cafés** that pander to Victoria's self-conscious afternoon-tea ritual. Good snacks and pastry shops abound, while at the other extreme there are budget-busting establishments if you want a one-off treat or a change from the standard Canadian menus that await you on much of the rest of the island.

Nocturnal diversions are for the most part tame: highbrow tastes, though, are surprisingly well catered for, and there's a smattering of **bars**, as well as **live music** venues and **clubs** to keep you happy for the limited time you're likely to spend in the city. **Jazz** is particularly popular; for information, contact the Victoria Jazz Society, 250-727 Johnson St (T250/388-4423, Wwww.vicjazz .bc.ca). **Listings** appear in the main daily newspaper, the *Times-Colonist,* and in a variety of free magazines distributed to shops, cafés and hotels, including the excellent *Monday* magazine (Wwww.mondaymag.com), published every Thursday. **Tickets** for most offerings are available from the city's main performance space, the McPherson Playhouse, 3 Centennial Square, Pandora and Government streets (T250/386-6121 or 1-888-717-6121, Wwww .rmts.bc.ca).

Cafés, tea and snacks

Barb's Fish and Chips 310 St Lawrence St, Fisherman's Wharf, off Kingston St T250/384-6515. A much-loved floating shack that offers classic home-cut chips, fish straight off the boat and oyster burgers and chowder to boot; the small bathtub-size ferries from the Inner Harbour drop you close by.

Blethering Place 2250 Oak Bay Ave T250/598-1413 or 1-888-598-1413. Along with the *Empress Hotel,* this is known as a place to indulge in the tea-taking custom. Scones, cakes and dainty sandwiches are served up against the background of hundreds of toby jugs and royal-family memorabilia – perhaps a tad overrated.

Demitasse Coffee Bar 320 Blanshard St near Pandora Ave. A popular, elegantly laid-back hole-in-the-wall café with excellent coffee, salads, bagels, lunch-time snacks and an open fire in season. Recommended.

Dutch Bakery & Coffee Shop 718 Fort St. A Victoria institution serving pastries and chocolate to take away. You can also eat in the popular if plain coffee shop at the back.

Empress Hotel 721 Government St T250/348-8111. Try tea in the lobby, with tourists and locals alike on their best behaviour amidst the chintz and potted plants. A strict dress code allows no dirty jeans, anoraks or sportswear.

Murchie's 1110 Government St. The best place for basic tea, coffee and cakes in the centre of Victoria's shopping streets.

Re-Bar 50 Bastion Square at Langley St. A great place that serves teas, coffees (charcoal-filtered water) and health food at lunch (usually organically grown), but most remarkable for its extraordinary range of fresh-squeezed juices in strange combinations, smoothies, "power tonics" and frighteningly healthy wheatgrass drinks ("Astro Turf": a blend of carrot, beet, garlic and wheatgrass).

Sally's 714 Cormorant St near Douglas St. Funky little café that's very popular with locals and local office workers despite its location on the northern edge of downtown. Drop by if you're up this way, but don't come specially.

Restaurants

Da Tandoor 1010 Fort St T250/384-6333. Tandoori specialist that is, with the *Taj Mahal,* the best of Victoria's half-dozen or so Indian restaurants offering good food and an over-the-top interior.

Earl's 1703 Blanshard St and Fisgard St T250/386-4323. You'll find an *Earl's* in many Canadian towns, but the restaurants are none the worse for being part of a chain: good – not fast – food, with a lively, pleasant interior and friendly service.

Herald Street Café 546 Herald St T250/381-1441. An excellent and stylish old favourite for Italian food with a Northwest twist. Pricey, but good value, along with a relaxed atmosphere and lots of art on the walls. Well worth the walk from the Inner Harbour.

Il Terrazzo 555 Johnson St, Waddington Alley T250/361-0028. Smooth, laid-back ambience with lots of red brick and plants and a summer patio that provides the setting for good North American versions of Italian food. With *Pagliacci's* (see below), this is the best place in town for Italian food.

Milestone's 812 Wharf St T250/381-2244. Popular mid-priced place for burgers, pastas, steaks and the like, slap-bang on the Inner Harbour beneath the infocentre, so expect lots of bustle, passing trade and good views.

Pagliacci's 1011 Broad St between Fort and Broughton T250/386-1662. The best restaurant in Victoria if you want a fast, furious atmosphere, live music, good Italian food and excellent desserts. A rowdy throng begins to queue almost from the moment the doors are open.

Süze 515 Yates St ☎ 250/383-2829. This is a great place for an early or late-evening drink, thanks to its snug, informal and vaguely exotic feel, and to its wonderful broad bar. Its eclectic menu ranges from Asian cuisine to steak, pasta, chicken and seafood, which you can take either at tables up on the tiny mezzanine or in the cosy dining room through the velvet curtains to the right.

Taj Mahal 679 Herald St ☎ 250/383-4662. Housed in a mini Taj Mahal and a bit of a walk from the centre, this restaurant serves good Indian food with chicken, lamb and tandoori specialities.

Bars and pubs

Bartholomew's Bar and Rockefeller Grill At *Executive House Hotel*, 777 Douglas St. This is an upbeat pub with a steady diet of local bands. For the same sort of place, try *Steamers*, 570 Yates St, where you'll catch enthusiastic local bands most nights, and most types of music from reggae to Celtic.

Big Bad John's 919 Douglas St. Next to the *Strathcona Hotel* this is Victoria's most atmospheric bar by far with bare boards, a fog of smoke, and authentic old banknotes and IOUs pasted to the walls. It also hosts occasional live bands and singers, usually of a country-music persuasion.

D'Arcy McGee's 1127 Wharf St. It was only a matter of time before Victoria acquired an "Irish pub". This one has a prime site on the edge of Bastion Square, offers predictable food and beer, and has excellent occasional live Irish music.

Spinnakers BrewPub 308 Catherine St near Esquimalt Rd. Thirty-eight beers, including several

home-brewed options, a restaurant, live music, occasional tours of the brewery and good harbour views draw a mixed and relaxed clientele. Bus #23 to Esquimalt Rd.

Swans Brewpub 506 Pandora Ave at Store St. This pretty and highly popular hotel-café-brewery, housed in a 1913 warehouse, is the place to watch Victoria's young professionals at play. Several foreign and six home-brewed beers on tap, with the *Neptune Soundbar* nightclub in the basement (see below).

Clubs and live music

Esquimalt Inn 856 Esquimalt Rd. A long-established venue with country bands most nights and occasional jam sessions. Take bus #23.

Evolution 502 Discovery St. One of Victoria's more interesting clubs and discos, thanks to plenty of techno, rave and alternative sounds.

Hermann's Jazz Club 753 View St. Dimly lit club thick with 1950s atmosphere that specializes in Dixieland but has occasional excursions into fusion and blues.

Legends 919 Douglas St. The biggest, best and noisiest of the live-music venues, this club occupies the garish, neon-lit basement of the *Strathcona Hotel*. Varied live bands, including the occasional big name, and dancing nightly.

Neptune Soundbar 1605 Store St at Pandora Ave. You may well have to queue to join the thirty-something crew who frequent the basement disco of *Swans Brewpub*. 1960s and 1970s classics generally rule as well as current Top 40 fodder, but there's also a sprinkling of hip-hop and more modern offerings.

Listings

American Express 1213 Douglas St (Mon–Fri 8.30–5pm, Sat 10am–4pm; ☎ 250/385-8731).

Bike and boat rental Cycle Victoria Rentals, 950 Wharf St (☎ 250/885-2453 or 1-877/869-0039, ⓦ www.cyclevictoriarentals.com); Harbour Rentals, 811 Wharf St (☎ 250/995-1661 or 1-877-733-6722), rent a big range of bikes (from $6/hr, $19/day) plus five types of scooter (from $12/hr, $45/day), also kayaks, rowing boats, motor boats and motor bikes.

Car rental Avis, 62B-1001 Douglas St (☎ 250/386-8468 or 1-800/879-2847) and Victoria Airport (☎ 250/656-6033); Budget, 757 Douglas St (☎ 250/953-5300 or 1-800/268-8900); National, 767 Douglas St (☎ 250/386-1213 or 1-800/227-7368).

Equipment rental Sports Rent, 1950 Government St at Discovery (☎ 250/385-7368, ⓦ www

.sportsrentbc.com) rents a colossal range of equipment, including bikes, rollerblades, all camping, hiking, climbing and diving gear.

Medical facilities Victoria General Hospital, 35 Helmcken Rd (☎ 250/727-4212). Most hotels have a doctor or dentist on call; otherwise contact Cresta Dental Centre in the Tillicum Street Mall at 3170 Tillicum Rd, Burnside St (☎ 250/384-7711). The Tillicum Mall Medical Clinic at the same address (☎ 250/381-8112) accepts walk-in patients.

Post office Main office, 714 Yates St at Douglas (☎ 250/953-1352 or 1-800/267-1177 in Canada; Mon–Fri 8.30am–5pm).

Taxis Blue Bird Cabs (☎ 250/382-4235); Empress Cabs (☎ 250/381-2222); Victoria Taxi (☎ 250/383-7111).

Weatherline ☎ 250/656-3978.

The Southern Gulf Islands

Scattered between Vancouver Island and the mainland lie several hundred tiny islands, most no more than lumps of rock, a few large enough to hold permanent populations and warrant a regular ferry service. Two main clusters are accessible from Victoria: the **Southern Gulf Islands** and the San Juan Islands, both part of the same archipelago, except that the San Juan group is in the United States.

You get a good look at the Southern Gulf Islands on the seaplanes from Vancouver (see p.828) or on the ferry from Tsawwassen – twisting and threading through their coves and channels, the ride sometimes seems even a little too close for comfort. The coastline makes for superb **sailing**, and an armada of small boats crisscrosses between the islands for most of the year. Hikers and campers are also well served, and **fishing**, too, is good, with some of the world's biggest salmon having met their doom in the surrounding waters. The climate is mild, though hardly "Mediterranean" as claimed in the tourist blurbs, and the vegetation is particularly lush. There's also an abundance of marine wildlife (sea lions, orcas, seals, bald eagles, herons, cormorants). All this has made the Gulf Islands the dream idyll of many people from Washington State and BC, whether they're artists, writers, pensioners or dropouts from the mainstream. For full details of what they're all up to, grab a copy of the local listings, the *Gulf Islander*, distributed on the islands and the ferries.

Planning a visit

BC Ferries (☎250/386-3431 or 1-888/223-3779, ⓦwww.bcferries.com) sails to five of the Southern Gulf Islands – **Saltspring**, **Pender**, **Saturna**, **Mayne** and **Galiano** – from Swartz Bay, 33km north of Victoria on Hwy 17. (A few other North Gulf Islands, notably Gabriola, can be reached from Chemainus and Nanaimo; see p.860 and p.861.) Reckon on at least two crossings to each daily, but be prepared for all boats to be jammed solid during the summer. Visit the website or pick up the company's *Southern Gulf Islands* timetable, widely available on boats and in the mainland infocentres, which is invaluable if you aim to exploit the many inter-island connections. All the ferries take cars, bikes and motorbikes, though with a car you'll need to make a **reservation**. Bear in mind that there's next to no public transport on the islands, so what few taxis there are can charge more or less what they wish. It costs only around $2 to take bikes on board, and **cycling** can be a great way to see the islands: most are small (if hilly), with few roads.

For the San Juans you'll have to pass through US and Canadian immigration, but you can get good stopover deals on ferries between Sidney on Vancouver Island and Anacortes on the Washington mainland. Foot passengers travel free between the four main San Juan islands.

Fares on BC Ferries

BC Ferries charges a wide range of **fares** for the numerous connections from Vancouver Island and the mainland to the Gulf Islands (many of which have more than one ferry terminal). Rates are generally lower **off season**, which most years means early September to late June. One or two routes also have cheaper fares midweek. In the following accounts we've given high-season and low-season fares for foot passengers and cars, separated by slashes, as in "foot passengers $6.25/$6 return, cars $20/$17.25". Note that larger vehicles incur higher fares.

SOUTHERN BRITISH COLUMBIA | The Southern Gulf Islands

Aim to have your **accommodation** worked out well in advance in summer. **Campers** should have few problems finding sites, most of which are located in the islands' provincial parks, though at peak times you'll want to arrive before noon to ensure a pitch – there are reservations in some parks (see p.777 for details of booking places). For help with B&Bs, use the *BC Accommodations* guide and the BC tourism website (see p.773), or contact the Victoria infocentre or **specialist agencies** such as the Canadian Gulf Islands B&B Reservation Service (☎1-888/539-2930, ⓦwww.gulfislands reservations.com).

Salt Spring Island

SALT SPRING (pop. 9500), sometimes Saltspring, is the biggest, most populated and most visited of the islands – its population triples in summer – though if you're without transport think twice about coming here on a day-trip as getting around is pretty tough. It's served by Harbour Air seaplanes from Vancouver (see p.828) and has three ferry terminals: **Fulford Harbour** in the south, with sailings from Victoria's Swartz Bay (ten daily, more in summer; 35min; foot passengers $6.25/$6 return, cars $20/$17.25); **Vesuvius Bay** in the northwest, with sailings from Crofton, near Duncan, on Vancouver Island (13 daily; 20min; same fares); and **Long Harbour**, midway down the east coast, which connects to points on the BC mainland, notably Tsawwassen, usually via other islands.

Long Harbour is also the main terminal for inter-island travel. In the past the Saltspring Island Bus service has connected the ferry terminals with **GANGES**, the island's main village, on the east coast 5km from Long Harbour, but check with the Victoria or local infocentre (see below) for the latest.

Most enjoyment on Salt Spring, as with the other Gulf Islands, is to be had from sinking back into its laid-back approach to life: grabbing a coffee at a café overlooking the water, browsing galleries, cycling the backroads, hiking the odd easy trail, and so on. If you're here to slum it on a **beach**, the best strips are on the island's more sheltered east side – Beddis Beach in particular, off the Fulford to Ganges road – as well as at Vesuvius Bay in the northwest and at Drummond Park near Fulford in the south. Beddis can be seen en route to one of the best parks in the Gulf Islands, the **Ruckle Provincial Park**, a swath of lovely forest, field and maritime scenery tucked in the island's southeast corner 10km east of Fulford Harbour. It has 15km of trails, most leaving from trailheads at Beaver Point, the rocky headland that marks the end of the access road – the best path marches north from here along the coast of tiny coves and rocky headlands to Yeo Point. The park also has an outstanding campsite at the end of the access road (see below). **Mount Maxwell Provincial Park** lies midway up the west coast; the eponymous mountain provides a tremendous 588-metre viewpoint. The park is accessed on Cranberry Rd, which strikes west midway down the island off the main Ganges to Fulford road.

Between April and October, head for the **Saturday Market** (Sat 8.30am–3pm; ⓦwww.saltspringmarket.com), in Ganges' Centennial Park, for food and crafts. Community spirit reaches a climax during the annual **Artcraft** crafts fair (late June to mid-Sept), held in Ganges' Mahon Hall, that displays the talents of the island's many dab-handed creatives. The other main focus for cultural events is the **ArtSpring** centre, 100 Jackson in Ganges (ⓦwww.artspring.ca), which hosts a summer performing arts festival (July & Aug).

The **Gulf Islands Water Taxi** (℡250/537-2510, ⓦwww.saltspring.com/watertaxi) has been a feature of island life since 1978, complementing the BC Ferries service and carrying visitors, schoolchildren, fishermen and others on two scheduled routes from the Visitors' Dock below the Oystercatcher Bar in Ganges. The **first route** runs Salt Spring (Ganges Harbour) to Galiano (Sturdies Bay) and on to Mayne Island (Miners Bay); currently Sept–June 2 daily 6.45am & 3.45pm from Salt Spring; $20 round trip between any two points, $15 one-way, no extra charge for bicycles. Prices and departure details are the same on the **second route**: from Salt Spring (Ganges Harbour) to Saturna (Lyall Harbour) to Horton Bay and on to Pender (Port Washington). An "Island Hopping" **third route** operates in summer (Wed & Sat 9am & 3pm from Ganges) calling at Galiano and Mayne. **Reservations** are recommended for all services, which are timetabled so that you can realistically make short day or sightseeing trips to other islands from Salt Spring.

7

SOUTHERN BRITISH COLUMBIA | The Southern Gulf Islands

Practicalities

Ganges, close to Long Harbour on the east coast, is armed with a small **info-centre** at 121 Lower Ganges Rd (daily 10am–4pm; ℡250/537-5252, ⓦwww.saltspringtoday.com) and a rapidly proliferating assortment of galleries, tourist shops and holiday homes.

For journeying around the island, call up Silver Shadow **taxi** (℡250/537-3030) or consider **renting a bike** from Salt Spring Kayaking & Cycling, 2923 Fulford-Ganges Rd, Fulford Harbour (℡250/653-4222, ⓦwww.saltspring.com/sskayak). Rates start at $5 hourly, $25 for 24hrs and $35 for two days. Kayak rentals are $12 hourly ($20 for a double kayak) and $45 daily ($80). The company can deliver bikes or kayaks to where you're staying on the island for $15. You can also rent a scooter, kayak or car from Saltspring Island Marina (℡1-800/334-6629, ⓦwww.mobyspub.com), one of several rental places near *Moby's Marine Pub*, 124 Upper Ganges Rd (℡250/537-5559), a very popular local hangout in Ganges for drinks, meals and occasional live music.

Ganges' infocentre is the place to check out the island's relatively plentiful **accommodation**. A lot of independent travellers are lured here by the prospect of the lovely *Salt Spring Island* **HI hostel**, set amidst ten peaceful acres on the eastern side of the island, 5km south of Ganges and just over 1km from Beddis Beach, at 640 Cusheon Lake Rd (℡250/537-4149; ❶–❸; mid-March to Oct; check-in 5–8pm). To get there from Victoria under your own steam, take the #70 Pat Bay Hwy bus ($2.50) to the Swartz Bay ferry terminal, catch the ferry to Fulford Harbour ($6.25 return) and try hitching a ride from car drivers disembarking the ferry. You can choose between dorm rooms in a cedar lodge ($17), three tepees, two adult and family tree houses (be sure to book these and be prepared to pay around $65) and private family room ($40–70) – there are 35 beds in all. There's no camping, but you can rent bikes and scooters.

Otherwise you can choose from the hundred or more, often rather expensive, **B&B** options (whose owners can arrange to pick you up from the ferry), or one of the so-called "resorts" – usually a handful of houses with camping, a few rooms to rent and little else. Each of the ferry terminals also has a range of mid-price **motels**. Some of the more reasonable include the twelve-unit *Beachcomber Motel* at 770 Vesuvius Bay Rd at Vesuvius Bay (℡250/537-5415 or 1-866/537-5415, ⓕ250/537-1753; ❹); the *Harbour House Hotel*, 121 Upper Ganges Rd, Ganges (℡250/537-5571 or 1-888/799-5571, ⓔharbourhouse@saltspring.com; ❹); and the 28-unit *Seabreeze Inn* in a park-like setting above Ganges Harbour at 101 Bittancourt Rd (T250/537-4145 or 1-800/434-4112, Wwww.seabreezeinns.com; ❺). The island's best **campsite** is in Ruckle Provincial Park – a magnificent, waterfront, 78-pitch site ($14 in summer, $9 in winter; day-use parking $3) at Beaver Point, reached by following Beaver Point Road from the Fulford Harbour ferry terminal (10km). Note that there are no reservations; it is first-come, first-served.

One of the island's better-known places to **eat** is *The Vesuvius Inn* (T250/537-2312), alongside the ferry at 805 Vesuvius Bay Rd, blessed with live music nightly and a great **bar** deck overlooking the harbour where you can enjoy expensive seafood and the usual range of pastas, chickens and salads. In Ganges, there are numerous cafés and coffee shops for high-quality sandwiches: for something more ambitious, try the appealing *Treehouse Café-Restaurant*, 106 Purvis Lane (T250/537-5379), which serves breakfast, lunch and dinner and has places to sit outside and low-key live (often acoustic) music most nights of the week. For a treat, the place to go is *House Piccolo*, 108 Hereford Ave, Ganges (T250/537-1844, dinner only), which serves high-quality European and Scandinavian food and has won *Wine Spectator* magazine awards.

Galiano Island

Long and finger-shaped, **Galiano** (pop. 1040) is just 27km from north to south and barely five kilometres wide, but it remains one of the more promising islands to visit if you want variety and a realistic chance of finding somewhere to stay. There are two ferry terminals: **Sturdies Bay** in the southeast, which takes boats from the mainland (foot passengers $10, cars $36.50), and **Montague Harbour** on the west coast, which handles the Vancouver Island crossings from Swartz Bay (foot passengers $6.50/$6.25, cars $22.25/$19.50). You can also get here with the Gulf Islands Water Taxi and there are inter-island BC Ferries connections (1–4 daily) from Salt Spring via Pender and Mayne. Go Galiano Island Shuttle (T250/539-0202) provides a taxi service.

If you're **canoeing**, stick to the calmer waters, cliffs and coves off the west coast. **Hikers** can walk almost the entire length of the east coast, or climb Mount Sutil (323m) or Mount Galiano (342m) for views of the mainland mountains. To reach the trailhead for the latter, take Burrill south from the ferry at Sturdies Bay and along Bluff Rd through the forest of Bluffs Park. A left fork, Active Pass Drive, takes you to the trailhead (total 5km from the ferry). The locals' favourite **beach** is at Coon Bay at the island's northern tip, but there are excellent marine landscapes and beaches elsewhere, notably at **Montague Harbour Provincial Marine Park**, 10km from the Sturdies Bay ferry terminal on the west side of the island. The park has stretches of shell and pebble foreshore, a café, shop, three-kilometre waterfront trail to Gray Peninsula (though you can easily do your own foreshore walks) and, more to the point, a glorious provincial **campsite** ($17 in summer, $9 in winter; 15 walk-in reservable tent sites, and 25 drive-in sites, of which eight are reservable). Booking is essential in summer; see box on p.777 for details.

The **infocentre** is a booth at Sturdies Bay at 2590 Sturdies Bay Rd (July & Aug daily 9am–5/6pm; T250/539-2233 or 1-866/539-2233, off season T250/539-2507, Wwww.galianoisland.com). Galiano Bicycle Rental is at 36 Burrill Rd in Sturdies Bay (T250/539-9906; $23 for 4hr, $28/day). You can **rent kayaks** or join guided kayak tours at Galiano Island Kayaking at the marina at Montague Harbour (T250/539-2442, Wwww.seakayak.ca). For a comfortable **stay** in peaceful and elegant surroundings (close to Montague Harbour Provincial

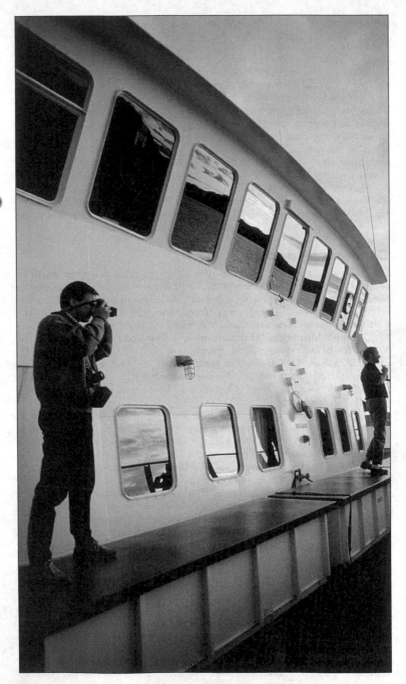

⑦

△ Ferry on the Inside Passage

Marine Park), try the excellent twelve-room *Woodstone Country Inn* (☎250/539-2022 or 1-888/339-2022, ✉woodstone@gulfislands.com; ❺) on Georgeson Bay Road, 4km from the ferry; breakfast and afternoon tea are included in the price. Right at Studies Bay is the very pleasant ten-room *Galiano Inn*, 134 Madronna Drive (☎250/539-3388, ✇www.galianoinn.com; ❼); rates include gourmet breakfast. For a romantic stay, head for one of the three rooms at the *Bellhouse Inn*, 29 Farmhouse Rd (☎1-800/970-7464, ✇www.bellhouseinn.com; ❻), an historic waterfront farmhouse set in beautiful grounds with sandy beach and great ocean views; breakfast is included. A good choice on the island's quieter northern end are the seven log cabins of the *Bodega Resort*, 120 Monastee Rd off Porlier Pass Drive and Cook Drive (☎250/539-2677, ✇www.cedarplace.com/bodega; ❸), set in acres of woods and meadows with sea views and complete with kitchens and wood-burning stoves. For **food and drink** – and to meet locals – the island's main pub, the *Hummingbird Inn* (☎250/539-5472) is about 2km from Sturdies Bay at 47 Sturdies Bay Road. Food is reasonable at the *Hummingbird*, likewise at *La Bérengerie* (☎250/539-5392; ❸), a genteel restaurant about the same distance from Montague Harbour on the corner of Montague and Clanton roads that usually rents three B&B rooms upstairs.

North and South Pender

The somnolent bridge-linked islands of **North** and **South Pender** muster about a two thousand people between them, many of whom will try to entice you into their studios to buy local arts and crafts. Otherwise you can swim, snooze or walk on one of the many tiny **beaches** – there's public ocean access at some twenty points around the island. Two of the best are Hamilton Beach near Browning Beach on the east coast of North Pender and Mortimer Spit just south of the bridge that links the two islands. The latter is also the place to pick up trails to Mount Norman and Beaumont Provincial Marine Park.

Ferries come to North Pender from Swartz Bay (up to 7 daily; 40min direct or 2hr via Galiano and/or Mayne; foot passengers $6.50/$6.25, cars $22.25/$19.50) and Tsawwassen (foot-passengers $10/$9.75 one-way, less off peak; cars $36.50/$31.50). The **infocentre** booth is just up the hill from the ferry terminal in **Otter Bay** on North Pender's west coast at 2332 Otter Bay Rd (mid-May to early Sept daily 9am–6pm; ☎250/629-6541), home to the Otter Bay Marina, where you can rent **bikes** and buy maps for a tour of the islands' rolling, hilly interior. There's a handful of **B&Bs**, and a small wooded **campsite** at Prior Centennial Provincial Park, 6km south of the Otter Bay ferry terminal (March–Sept; $14). For the only **hotel**-type rooms, try the twelve-room *Inn on Pender Island*, prettily situated in 7.5 acres of wooded country near Prior Park at 4709 Canal Rd, North Pender (☎250/629-3353 or 1-800/550-0172, ✇www.innonpender.com; ❹), or the newly refurbished *Poets Cove at Bedwell Harbour*, a plush resort at 9801 Spalding Rd, South Pender (☎250/629-3212 or 1-888/512-7638, ✇www.poetscove.com; ❼), which has a pool, marina, bistro-pub, restaurant, store, tennis, harbour views, canoe, boat and bike rentals, and a choice of rooms or cabins. Alternatively, try the three fully equipped self-catering cottages 500m sharp left from the ferry at *Arcadia by the Sea*, 1325 MacKinnon Rd, North Pender (☎250/629-3221 or 1-877/470-8439, ✇www.arcadiabythesea.com; ❺; mid-April to Oct), with tennis court, outdoor pool and private decks.

Mayne Island

Mayne is the first island to your left (Galiano is on your right) if you're crossing from Tsawwassen to Swartz Bay – which is perhaps as close as you'll get, since it's the quietest and most difficult to reach of the islands served by ferries. One-way tickets from Tsawwassen (via Galiano/Montague Harbour) in high season cost foot passengers $10, cars $36.50. It also has few places to stay, which may be as good a reason as any for heading out here – particularly if you have a bike to explore the quiet country roads which snake over the island. Best of several **beaches** is Bennett Bay, a sheltered strip with warm water and good sand. It's reached by heading east from the island's principal community at Miner's Bay (5min from the ferry terminal at Village Bay on the west coast) to the end of Fernhill Road and then turning left onto Wilks Road. If you want a **walk**, try the 45-minute climb up Mount Parke in the eponymous regional park; it starts near the Fernhill Centre on Montrose Rd.

Village Bay – don't be fooled by the name: there's no village – has a summer-only **infocentre** booth (daily 9am–6pm; no phone, ⓦ www.mayneislandchamber .ca) that should be able to fill you in on the limited but expanding number of **B&B** possibilities (currently seven). Try the *Blue Vista Cottages*, eight fully equipped cabins overlooking Bennett Bay at 563 Arbutus Drive, 6km from the ferry (☏ 250/539-2463 or 1-877/535-2424, ⓦ www.bluevistaresort.com; ❸), with ferry pick-up, sandy beach, park-like setting and bike, canoe and kayak rental. The *Tinkerer's B&B* on Miner's Bay at 417 Sunset Place off Georgina Point Road (☏ 250/539-2280; ❹; April–Oct), 2.4km from the ferry, is nicely offbeat: it rents bikes, provides hammocks and offers "demonstrations of medicinal herb and flower gardens". The best **food** around is at the waterfront *Oceanwood Country Inn*, 2km south of the ferry at 630 Dinner Bay Rd (☏ 250/539-5074, ⓦ www .oceanwood.com; ❼; March–Nov), which also has twelve smart rooms, sauna, oceanfront hot tub and a superb, quiet garden setting.

Saturna Island

Saturna, to the south, has daily **ferries** from Swartz Bay on Vancouver Island (2–3 daily; foot passengers $6.25 return, vehicles $21.50) and from Tsawwassen but only via Mayne. The island boasts some good **beaches**, the best being at Russell Reef and Winter Cove Marine Park (no campsite) on its northwest tip. There's walking, wildlife and good views to the mainland from Mount Warburton Pike (497m) and on Brown Bridge in the southwest of the island. Saturna is another **B&B** hideaway: try the three-room waterfront *Lyall Harbour B&B* (☏ 250/539-5577 or 1-877/473-9343; ❺), 500m from the ferry at 121 East Point Rd in Saturna Point, home to a shop and modest **infocentre** (May–Sept daily 8am–6pm; no phone, ⓦ www.saturnatourism.bc.ca). A relatively large place to stay is the *East Point Resort*, East Point Road (☏ 250/539-2975; ❺; no credit cards), situated in a park-like setting near a gradually sloping sandy beach; the six cabins are fully equipped and you can choose between one- and two-bedroom units – note that in July and August there's generally a minimum stay of a week. There are no campgrounds and only one or two **places to eat**, notably the pub-restaurant at the modern, waterfront *Saturna Lodge,* 130 Payne Rd (☏ 250/539-2254, ⓦ www.saturna-island.bc.ca; ❻; May–Oct), which also has seven rooms to rent; rates include breakfast.

Highway 14: Victoria to Port Renfrew

Highway 14 runs west from **Victoria** to **Port Renfrew** and is lined with numerous beaches and provincial parks, most – especially those close to the city

– heavily populated during the summer months. The 107km route is covered in summer by the West Coast Trail Bus (see box below), a private service originally for hikers walking the West Coast Trail and Juan de Fuca Trail (see p.856) but also popular for the ride alone.

Victoria city buses go as far as **SOOKE** (38km; take #50 to Western Exchange and transfer to #61), and you can also cycle here on the Galloping Goose cycle trail. Sooke is the last place of any size, so stock up on supplies if you're continuing west. It's best known for its excellent art galleries, a clutch of good restaurants and **All Sooke Day** in mid-July, when lumberjacks from all over the island compete in various tests of forestry expertise. Check out the small **Sooke Regional Museum** (daily 9am–5pm, July & Aug until 6pm; donation), across the Sooke River Bridge at 2070 Phillips and Sooke streets, to bone up on the largely logging-dominated local history. The **infocentre** lies in the same building (daily 9/10am–6pm; T250/642-6351, W www.sooke .museum.bc.ca). Sooke has a surfeit of **accommodation**, with a bias towards comfortable B&Bs. Quite a few people make the trip here just for the **food** at *Sooke Harbour House*, 1528 Whiffen Spit (T250/642-3421, W www .sookeharbourhouse.com; ❻), one of the finest restaurants on the West Coast; it's expensive, but has a surprisingly casual atmosphere. It also has 28 top-notch **rooms**, with prices ranging from a prohibitive $299 to $555 (lower off season). A far less expensive place to eat in the village centre is the cosy *Mom's*, 2036 Shields Rd.

The mostly empty beaches beyond Sooke are largely grey pebble and driftwood, but none the worse for that. The first key stop, 20km beyond Sooke, is **French Beach Provincial Park** (day-use parking $3). An info-board here fills in the natural history background of the foreshore and rich Douglas fir and Sitka forest, and there are maps of trails and the highlights on the road farther west. There's good walking on the fairly wild and windswept beach, and a 69-pitch provincial park campsite (summer $14, winter $10) on the grass immediately away from the shore. About 3km beyond, the 25 log cabins of *Point No Point*, 1505 West Coast Rd (T250/646-2020, W www.pointnopointresort.com, ❻), make a tremendous place to overnight near the water.

West Coast Trail Bus

The **West Coast Trail Bus**, or West Coast Trail Express (T250/477-8700 or 1-888/999-2288, W www.trailbus.com), provides an invaluable complement to Laidlaw's relatively limited scheduled bus services on Vancouver Island. **Reservations** are highly recommended for all services.

It offers a shuttle service (May–Sept only; days vary; call for details) from Victoria to **Gordon River** ($35), **Port Renfrew** ($35), **Pachena Bay** ($55) and **Bamfield** ($55), thus providing access to the trailheads of the West Coast Trail and to points in the Pacific Rim National Park such as Bamfield that would otherwise be difficult to reach without your own transport. It also provides **inter-town shuttles** between most combinations of these destinations – and others such as **Nanaimo** (connections to Pachena Bay and Bamfield; $55) and **Port Alberni** (to Pachena Bay and Bamfield; $35). **Departure points** are as follows: Victoria (700 Douglas St); Nanaimo (Departure Bay ferry terminal); Port Alberni (7-Eleven store on 3rd St); Pachena Bay (trailhead car park); Bamfield (Trails Motel); Gordon River (trailhead office); Port Renfrew (Parkinson Rd).

Another service runs from Victoria to Port Renfrew ($35) **along Hwy 14** with stops at Sooke, French Beach ($25), Jordan River ($30), China Beach ($30), Sombrio Beach ($30) and Parkinson Creek ($30).

Sandy, signposted trails lead off the road to beaches over the next 9km, including **Jordan River**, a one-shop, one-hamburger-stall (*Shakies*) logging community known for its good surf, which you can admire from the waterfront *Breakers* cafe. Just beyond is the best of the beaches on this coast, part of **China Beach Provincial Park** (no camping), reached after a fifteen-minute walk from the road through rainforest. The West Coast Trail Bus (see box, p.855) makes stops at all these parks and beaches on request.

Port Renfrew

The road is partly gravel from China Beach on – past Mystic and Sombrio beaches to **PORT RENFREW**, a logging community that's gained from being the western starting point of the **West Coast Trail** (see p.884). A second trail, the **Juan de Fuca Marine Trail**, also starts from near Port Renfrew, running east towards Victoria for about 50km. This does not have the complicated booking procedure of the West Coast Trail, but the scenery is also less striking and the going far easier for the less experienced or more safety conscious walker. Car parks and highway access points are also dotted along its length, allowing you to enjoy strolls or day-hikes. Beyond China Beach is the start of the **Juan de Fuca Provincial Park**, designed to protect the beaches and coastal rainforest strip explored by the trail (day-use parking $5, front-country camping $14, backcountry camping $5).

Accommodation in town is still pretty limited: try the four cottages on the San Juan River at *Gallaugher's West Coast Fish Camp* off Beach Road at 5222 Heritage Drive (☎250/647-5535, ✉gallaughers@shaw.ca; ❹; May–Oct); the five beachfront rooms of the *Arbutus Beach Lodge*, 5 Queesto Drive (☎250/647-5458, ✉arbutus@sookenet.com; ❸–❹); the *West Coast Trail Motel*, Parkinson Road (☎250/647-5565, ⓦwww.westcoasttrailmotel.com; ❸); and the *Trailhead Resort* on Parkinson Road (☎250/647-5468, ⓦwww .trailhead-resort.com; ❹), which has six rooms. South of the village on a logging road (6km) is the Juan de Fuca trailhead at **Botanical Beach**, a sandstone shelf and tidal-pool area that reveals a wealth of marine life at low tide.

If you're driving and don't want to retrace your steps, think about taking the gravel logging roads from the village on the north side of the San Juan River to either Shawnigan Lake or the Cowichan Valley. They're marked on most maps, but it's worth picking up the **detailed map** of local roads put out by the Sooke Combined Fire Organization (ask at the Victoria infocentre). Heed all warnings about logging trucks.

Highway 1: Victoria to Nanaimo

If you leave Victoria with high hopes of Vancouver Island's lauded scenery, **Hwy 1** – the final, western leg of the Trans-Canada – will come as a disappointing introduction to what you can expect along most of the island's southeast coast. After a lengthy sprawl of suburbs, blighted by more billboards than you'd see in supposedly less scenic cities, the landscape becomes suddenly wooded and immensely lush; unfortunately the beauty is constantly interrupted by bursts of dismal motels and other highway junk.

Buses operated by Laidlaw make the trip between Victoria and Nanaimo (up to 6 daily). One **train** a day (more in summer) also covers this route – and beyond to Courtenay – but it's a usually a single-carriage job and gets booked solid in summer. It also stops at every stump.

Goldstream Provincial Park

Thetis Lake Regional Park, appearing on the right 11km out of Victoria, is good for swimming, with forested trails and sandy beaches on two lakes backed by high cliffs; there's a busy beach near the car park, which is quieter round the shore, or beyond at the bottom of the hill at Prior Lake. Prettier still is **Goldstream Provincial Park**, 5km beyond Langford and 20km from Victoria city centre, where you'll find an ancient forest of Douglas fir and western red cedar and a large provincial park **campsite** with good facilities and a visitor centre (day-use parking $3, summer frontcountry camping $22, winter $9). There's also a network of marked **trails** to hilltops and waterfalls designed for anything between five minutes and an hour's walking. Try the paths towards Mount Finlayson (3hr hard walk if you go all the way to the summit) for views of the ocean – views you also get if you carry on up the highway, which soon meets Saanich Inlet, a bay with a lovely panorama of wooded ridges across the water. Look out for the Malahat Summit (31km from Victoria) and Gulf Islands (33km) viewpoints. To **stay**, the small *Malahat Oceanview Motel* (☎250/478-9231, ⓔoceanview@coastnet.com; ➌), 35km north of Victoria, is best sited to catch the sea and island vistas.

A scenic diversion off the main road takes you 7km to **Shawnigan Lake**, fringed by a couple of provincial parks; West Shawnigan Park on the lake's northwest side has a safe beach and swimming possibilities. If you're biking or are prepared to tackle pretty rough roads, note the logging road that links the north end of the lake to Port Renfrew on the west coast (check access restrictions at the Victoria infocentre).

Duncan

DUNCAN, 60km north of Victoria, begins inauspiciously, with a particularly scrappy section of highway spoiling what would otherwise be an exquisitely pastoral patch of country. Still, the town's aboriginal centre – the Quw'utsun Cultural Centre – merits a brief stop, unlike the Glass Castle, a messy affair made from glass bottles off the road to the south, and the even sillier "World's Largest Hockey Stick", arranged as a triumphal arch into the town centre.

Duncan's **infocentre** is at 381A Trans-Canada Hwy opposite the supermarket on the main road (mid-April to mid-Oct Mon–Fri 8.30am–5pm, longer hours in July & Aug; ☎250/746-4636, ⓦwww.duncancc.bc.ca), close to the **bus station**, which has up to six daily connections to and from Victoria (1hr 10min). Duncan is not a place you want to consider staying in – though there are plenty of motels and campsites – but for **meals** you could try the excellent *Arbutus Café*, 195 Kenneth St, at Jubilee (☎250/746-5443), which is much frequented by locals keen for the usual Italian- and Pacific Rim-influenced food. Just east of town, the *Quamichan Inn*, 1478 Maple Bay Rd (☎250/746-7028), serves up a similar menu and also has its devotees. You could also visit the local vineyards; one of the best is the **Vigneti Zenatta Winery**, 5039 Marshall Rd, Glenora (call for tour details on ☎250/748-2338), which has been in business for over forty years; as well as their wine, you can buy meals at the lovely (but expensive) restaurant. Some 3km south of town on Hwy 1, the *Pioneer House Restaurant*, 4675 Trans-Canada Hwy (☎250/746-5848 or 1-877/553-5848), has a rustic log-cabin feel helped by a genuine saloon bar transplanted from a period building in Montana.

Quw'utsun Cultural Centre

Out of Victoria, the first real reason to pull over is Duncan's **Quw'utsun Cultural Centre**, 200 Cowichan Way (May to early Sept Mon–Fri

Old-growth forests: going, going, gone...

While Vancouver Island isn't the only place in North America where environmentalists and the forestry industry are at loggerheads, some of the most bitter and high-profile confrontations have taken place here. The island's wet climate is particularly favourable to the growth of thick **temperate rainforest**, part of a belt that once stretched from Alaska to northern California. The most productive ecosystem on the planet, **old-growth** virgin Pacific rainforest contains up to ten times more biomass per acre than its more famous tropical counterpart – and, though it covers a much smaller area, it is being felled at a greater rate and with considerably less media outrage. Environmentalists estimate that British Columbia's portion of the Pacific rainforest has already been reduced by two-thirds; all significant areas will have been felled, they predict, within about ten or fifteen years. The powerful logging industry claims two-thirds survive, but even the Canadian government – largely in thrall to and supportive of the industry – concedes that only a small percentage of the BC rainforest is currently protected.

What is clear is that the government wants a very firm lid kept on the whole affair. In 1990 it commissioned a report into **UK public opinion** on the issue; the UK takes half of all British Columbia's plywood exports, three-quarters of all its lumber shipments to Europe, and a third of all Canada's paper pulp output. It observed that "UK public opinion appears to be highly uncritical of Canadian forestry, largely because awareness of the subject is low... [there is] a reassuringly romantic and simplistic image of Canadian forestry based on a lumberjack in a checked shirt, felling a single tree." The report concluded that "media attention and coverage of Canadian forestry management issues should not be sought". It's hard to see that opinions will have changed much since.

No such apathy exists in British Columbia, however. The controversy over logging often pits neighbour against neighbour, for some 250,000 in the province depend directly or indirectly on the industry, and big multinationals dominate the scene. **Employment** is a major rallying cry here, and the prospect of job losses through industry regulation is usually enough to override objections. The trend towards **automation** only adds fuel to the argument: by volume of wood cut, the BC forestry industry provides only half as many jobs as in the rest of Canada, which means, in effect, that twice as many trees have to be cut down in BC to provide the same number of jobs.

In the meantime, however, ninety percent of timber is still lifted from the rainforest instead of from managed stands, clear-cutting of old-growth timber is blithely described by the vast McMillan company as "a form of harvesting", and independent audits suggest that companies are failing to observe either their cutting or replanting quotas. The provincial government has pledged to improve forestry practices, but only a tiny percentage of the province lies within reserves with a degree of environmental protection.

9am–6pm, Sat & Sun 9am–9pm; rest of year closes 5/6pm daily; $11; Ⓦ www .quwutsun.ca), on your left off the highway in the unmissable wooden buildings next to Malaspina College. Duncan has long been the self-proclaimed "City of Totems", reference to a rather paltry collection of poles – arranged mostly alongside the main road – that belong to the local Cowichan tribes, historically British Columbia's largest aboriginal group. The tribes, about 3000 strong locally, still preserve certain traditions, and it's been their energy – along with cash from the civic authorities, attuned as ever to potentially lucrative tourist attractions – that has put up the poles and pulled the project together. Much of the heavily worked commercial emphasis is on shifting aboriginal crafts, especially the ubiquitous lumpy jumpers for which the area is famous, but there is a good twenty-minute film and tour of the centre (included in the price) and you can usually expect to find historical displays and demonstrations of dancing, knitting, carving, weaving and even native cooking.

British Columbia Forestry Discovery Centre

Vancouver Island is one of the most heavily logged areas in Canada, and the **BC Forest Discovery Centre**, 1km north of Duncan on Hwy 1 (early May to Sept daily 10am–6pm; $8), is run to preserve artefacts from its lumbering heritage; but with industry bigwigs as museum trustees, you can't help feeling it's designed to be something of a palliative in the increasingly ferocious controversy between loggers and environmentalists. Nonetheless, it does a thorough job on trees, and if the forestry displays in Victoria's museum have whetted your appetite, you'll have a good couple of hours rounding off your arboreal education. The entrance is marked by a small black steam engine and a massive piece of yellow logging machinery. Ranged over a hundred-acre site next to a scenic lake, the well-presented displays tell everything you want to know about trees and how to cut them down. The narrow-gauge **steam train** round the park is a bit gimmicky (ends 5.30pm), but a good way of getting around; check out the forest dioramas and the artefacts and archive material in the **Log Museum** in particular. There's also the usual array of working blacksmiths, sawmills, a farmstead, an old logging camp, and a few as-yet-underforested patches where you can take time out. The centre forms part of the **Cowichan and Chemainus Valleys Ecomuseum**, a vaguely defined park that takes in much of the surrounding area intended to preserve the logging heritage of the area – a curiously ill-defined concept that appears to be largely a PR exercise on the part of the logging companies. Ask for details of tours and maps from the Duncan infocentre.

The Cowichan Valley

Striking west into the hills from Hwy 1 north of Duncan, Hwy 18 enters the **Cowichan Valley** and fetches up at the 32-kilometre long Lake Cowichan, the largest freshwater lake on the island. Rather than drive, however, the nicest way up the valley is to walk the **Cowichan Valley Footpath**, following the river 18km from Glenora (a hamlet southwest of Duncan at the end of Robertson Rd) to Lake Cowichan Village on the lake's eastern shore. You could do the trip in a day, camp en route, or turn around at Skutz Falls and climb up to the Riverbottom Road to return to Duncan, which would be a half-day walk.

A road, rough in parts, circles **Lake Cowichan** (it's 75km round the lake by road – allow 2hr) and offers access to a gamut of outdoor pursuits, most notably fishing; the area is touted, with typical smalltown hyperbole, as the "Fly-Fishing Capital of the World". The water gets warm enough for summer swimming (the aboriginal name for the area, *Kaatza*, means the "land warmed by the sun"), and there's also ample hiking in the wilder country above. At Youbou on the north shore you can visit the **Heritage Mill**, a working sawmill (tours May–Sept); this area boasts some of the most "productive" forest in Canada, thanks to the lake's mild microclimate, and lumber is the obvious mainstay of the local economy. On the road up to the lake from Duncan you pass the **Valley Demonstration Forest**, another link in the industry's public-relations weaponry, with signs and scenic lookouts explaining the intricacies of forest management.

For details of the area's many tours, trails and outfitters contact the **infocentre** at Lake Cowichan village, 125 South Shore Rd (Mon–Sat 9am–4pm, Sun 1–4pm; ☎250/749-3244, ⓦwww.cowichanlakecc.ca). Good, cheap **campsites** line the shore, which despite minimal facilities can be quite busy in summer – don't expect to have the place to yourself. There's a municipal site, Lakeview Park, 3km west of the village at 885 Lakeview Rd (☎250/749-6681, ⓦwww.town.lakecowichan.bc.ca; $17; May–Sept), but the biggest and best is at Gordon Bay Provincial Park (day-use parking $3, summer camping $22, winter $9) on the south shore 14km from Lake Cowichan Village on South Shore Rd, a popular family place but with a quiet atmosphere and a good sandy **beach**. There are also plenty of hotels, motels and the like in all the lakeside settlements.

Chemainus

CHEMAINUS is the "Little Town That Did", as the billboards for miles around never stop telling you. Its mysterious achievement was the creation of its own tourist attraction, realized when the closure of the local antiquated sawmill in 1982 – it employed 400 and was once amongst the world's largest – threatened the place with almost overnight extinction, despite the opening of a modern, more efficient mill which employed just 150. In 1983 the town's worthies commissioned an artist to paint a huge **mural**, *Steam Donkey at Work*, recording the area's local history. This proved so successful that some 35 panels quickly followed, drawing some 350,000 (and rising) visitors annually to admire the artwork and tempting them to spend money in local businesses as they did. As murals go, these are surprisingly good, and if you're driving it's worth the short, well-signed diversion off Hwy 1. You might also want to drop in on the **Chemainus Valley Museum**, 9799 Waterwheel Crescent (March–May & Nov–Dec Wed–Sun 10am–3pm; June–Oct daily 10am–6pm; donation), a community-run museum of local history with displays on logging, mills and pioneer life. Ironically enough, the opening of the modern sawmill has done nothing to deter the welcome influx of resident painters and craftspeople attracted by the murals, a knock-on effect that has done much to enliven the village's pleasant – if occasionally over-twee – community feel.

Buses detour here on the run to Nanaimo, and the **train** drops you slap-bang next to a mural. Chemainus Tours (☎250/381-5109 in Victoria or 246-5055 in Chemainus) will bring you to the town for the day from Victoria for $53.

There's a **infocentre** in town at 9796 Willow St (June–Aug daily 9am–5pm; rest of year Mon–Fri 10am–4pm; ☎250/246-3944, ⓦwww.chemainus.bc.ca). If you fancy **staying** – the village's cosy waterside setting is nicer than either Duncan or Nanaimo – it's worth booking ahead, as increasing popularity means the local **hotel** and half-a-dozen or so B&Bs are in heavy demand in summer. For motel accommodation, try the *Fuller Lake Chemainus Motel*, 9300 Trans-Canada Hwy (☎250/246-3282 or 1-888/246-3255, ⓦwww.chemainus-fullerlakemotel.com; ❸). The best **B&B** is the pretty and whimsically decorated *Bird Song & Castlebury Cottage*, 9909 Maple St (☎250/246-9910, ⓔbirdsong@island.net; ❺). The choice of **campsites** is between the *Chemainus Gardens RV Park*, 3042 River Rd, 1km east of Hwy 1, set in 37 acres of natural forest with separate tenting area, laundry and showers (☎250/246-3569; $18–25), or the larger *Country Maples RV Resort*, 9010 Trans-Canada Hwy (☎250/246-2078, ⓦwww.holidaytrailsresorts.com; $26–33; April–Oct) in sixty acres of open and wooded parkland 16km north of Duncan above the

Chemainus River, with showers, laundry and pool. About 5km south of the village on the river is the quiet *Bald Eagle Campground*, 8705 Chemainus Rd (☎250/246-9457 or 1-800/246-9457; $16–22). All manner of little cafés, shops and tearooms have sprung up across the village: for **food**, try the *Willow Street Café*, 9749 Willow St, in the newer part of town, with cheap, varied snacks, or the *Waterford* for full meals five minutes north of the village centre at 9875 Maple St (☎250/246-1046).

You can pick up a **ferry** from Chemainus to the small islands of **Kuper** and **Thetis** (both $5 for foot passengers, $12.75 for cars).

Ladysmith

LADYSMITH's claim to fame is based solely on an accident of geography, as it straddles the 49th Parallel, the latitude that divides mainland Canada and the US. Canada held on to Vancouver Island only after some hard bargaining in the buildup to the 1846 Oregon Treaty, even though the boundary's logic ought to put much of it in the States. Ladysmith was originally named Oyster Bay, but was rechristened by Robert Dunsmuir (see below) at the time of the Boer War battle for Ladysmith (many streets bear the name of Boer War generals). There's little to the place other than the usual motels and garages, though a recent attempt to spruce up the older buildings – built as a dormitory town for Nanaimo's miners – won it a Western Canada Award of Excellence. Ladysmith's scenic profile, it has to be said, would be considerably higher were it not for a huge sawmill and a waterfront that is usually hopelessly jammed with lumber. The **infocentre** is a booth at 26 Gatacre St (July & Aug Mon & Tues 9am–4pm, Wed–Fri 9am–5pm, Sat & Sun 10am–5pm; rest of year Mon–Fri 9am–4pm; ☎250/245-2112, ⓦwww.ladysmithcofc.com) and has walking maps of the village's "heritage centre". The **Black Nugget Museum**, 12 Gatacre St (July & Aug Mon & Tues 9am–3pm, Wed–Fri 9am–4.30pm, Sat & Sun 10am–4.30pm; rest of year closed; $2), is a restored 1881 hotel stuffed with predictable memorabilia of coal mining and pioneers. If you stop off, check out **Transfer Beach Park** on the harbour, where the water's said to be the warmest in the Pacific north of San Francisco.

For **accommodation**, make for the fourteen-unit *Holiday House Motel*, 540 Esplanade St (☎250/245-2231, Ⓔhhmotel@island.net; ❷), overlooking Ladysmith's waterfront; the *Seaview Marine Resort*, 1111 Chemainus Rd (☎250/245-3768 or 1-800/891-8832, ⓦwww.chemainus.com; ❸), just off the highway 6km south of town (and 8km north of Chemainus) with five fully equipped self-catering one- and two-bedroom cottages on the ocean. The best **food** option is the oldest "English-style pub" in BC, the *Crow and Gate* off the main road 19km north of the town on Yellow Point Road.

Nanaimo

With a population of about 75,000, **NANAIMO**, 113km from Victoria, is Vancouver Island's second biggest city, the terminal for **ferries** from Horseshoe Bay and Tsawwassen on the mainland, and a watershed between the island's populated southeastern tip and its wilder, more sparsely peopled countryside to the north and west. In BC, only Vancouver and Kelowna are expanding faster. This said, the town is unexceptional, though the setting, as ever in BC, is eye-catching – particularly around the harbour, which bobs with yachts and rusty fishing boats and, if you've come from Victoria, allows the first views across to the big mountains on the mainland. If you are going to stop here, more than likely it'll be for **Petroglyph Park** or the town's increasingly famous **bungee-jumping** zone. If not, the Nanaimo Parkway provides a 21-kilometre bypass around the town.

Coal first brought white settlers to the region, many of whom made their fortunes here, including the Victorian magnate **Robert Dunsmuir**, who was given £750,000 and almost half the island in return for building the Victoria–Nanaimo railway – an indication of the benefits that could accrue from the British government to those with the pioneering spirit. Five bands of Salish natives originally lived on the site, which they called *Sney-ne-mous*, or "meeting place", from which the present name derives. It was they who innocently showed the local black rock to Hudson's Bay agents in 1852. The old mines are now closed, and the town's pockets are padded today by forestry, deep-sea fishing, tourism and – most notably – by six deep-water docks and a booming port.

Nanaimo, like any self-respecting BC town, lays on a fair few festivals, best known of which is the annual **Bathtub Race** or **Silly Boat Race**, in which bathtubs are raced (and sunk, mostly) across the 55km to Vancouver. The winner, the first to reach Vancouver, receives the silver Plunger Trophy from the Loyal Nanaimo Bathtub Society. It's all part of the four-day Marine Festival held over the third weekend of July. More highbrow is the late May to early June **Nanaimo Festival**, a cultural jamboree that takes place in and around Malaspina College, 900 Fifth St. The town's other minor claim to fame is the **Nanaimo bar**, a glutinous chocolate confection made to varying recipes and on sale everywhere.

The town and parks

In downtown Nanaimo itself, only two sights warrant the considerable amount of energy used to promote them. The **Nanaimo District Museum**, just off the main harbour area at 100 Cameron St by the Harbour Park Mall (May to early Sept daily 10am–5pm; Oct–April Tues–Sat 10am–5pm; closed Jan; $2), houses a collection that runs the usual historical gamut of pioneer, logging, mining, native peoples and natural history displays. The best features are the reconstructed coal mine and the interesting insights into the town's cosmopolitan population – a mix of Polish, Chinese, aboriginal peoples and British citizens – who all see themselves today as some of the island's "friendliest folk". The **Bastion**, two blocks north at the corner of Bastion and Front streets, is a wood-planked tower built by the Hudson's Bay Company in 1853 as a store and a stronghold against native attack, though it was never used during such an attack. It's the oldest (perhaps the only) such building in the west. These days it houses a small **museum** of Hudson's Bay memorabilia (summer only Wed–Sun 10am–4pm; $1); its silly tourist stunt, without which no BC town would be complete, is "the only ceremonial cannon firing west of Ontario" (summer only, daily at noon). This is marginally more impressive than the town's claim to have the most retail shopping space per capita in the country.

Nanaimo's outskirts are not pretty, nor, if you keep to the road through town, is the main strip of malls and billboards on and around downtown. Big efforts are being made to spruce the place up, however, not least in the town's 25 or so gardens and small parks. Many of these hug the shore, perfectly aligned for a seafront breath of air. The **Harbourfront Walkway** allows you to stroll 3km along the seafront. Also popular is the Swyalana Lagoon, an artificial tidal lagoon built on a renovated stretch of the downtown harbour in Maffeo Sutton Park. It's become a popular swimming, snoozing and picnic area. Farther afield, **Piper's Lagoon Park** offers a windblown, grassy spit, with lots of trails, flowers, rocky bluffs and good sea views; it's off Hammond Bay Road north of the city centre. For beaches you could head for **Departure Bay**, again north of the centre off Stewart Avenue. Plenty of local shops rent out a range of marine gear, as well as bikes and boats.

For the wildest of the local parks, head due west of town to **Westwood Lake Park**, good for a couple of hours' lonely hiking and some fine swimming. Tongue-twisting **Petroglyph Provincial Park**, off Hwy 1 3km south of downtown, showcases aboriginal peoples' carvings of the sort found all over BC (particularly along coastal waterways), many of them thousands of years old. Often their meaning is vague, but they appear to record important rituals and events. There are plenty of figures – real and mythological – carved into the local sandstone here, though their potential to inspire wonder is somewhat spoilt by more recent graffiti, traffic noise and the first thin edge of Nanaimo's urban sprawl.

Nanaimo's other major claim to fame is as home of North America's first legal public bungee-jumping site. The **Bungy Zone Adrenalin Centre** is 13km south of the town at 35 Nanaimo River Rd (daily 11.30am–6/8pm; ℡250/753-5867 or 1-888/668-7874, ⓦwww.bungyzone.com; jumps from $95): look out for the signed turn off Hwy 1. It's become so popular that variations have been added to the standard 42-metre plunge off the bridge, all slightly less terrifying than the bungee jump. The "Flying Fox" is a line to which you are fixed extending in a deep arc along the canyon – expect to hit speeds of 100kph; "Rap Jumping" involves a rapid mountaineering rappel straight down from the bridge; while the "Ultimate Swing" lets you jump off the bridge and swing in a big arc at speeds of up to 140kph. There's provision for **camping** here (with showers, laundry and tents for rent), and if you call in advance you should be able to book free shuttles to the site from Victoria and Nanaimo.

Practicalities

The Nanaimo-Collishaw **airport** is 15km south of downtown on Hwy 19 and is connected by regular shuttle buses to the town centre. Seaplane connections to Vancouver with Harbour Air and Baxter Aviation (see p.828) land close to downtown below Front St on the harbourfront.

Nanaimo's **bus terminal** (℡250/753-4371) is some way from the harbour on the corner of Comox and Terminal, with six daily Laidlaw buses to Victoria, two to Port Hardy and three or four to Port Alberni, for connections to Tofino and Ucluelet. **BC Ferries** (℡250/386-3431 or 1-888/223-3779, ⓦwww.bcferries.bc.ca) sail from **Departure Bay** (℡250/753-1261), 2km north of downtown, to Horseshoe Bay on the mainland (summer hourly 7am–9pm, off-season every 2hr; foot passengers $10 one-way, cars $34.75; cheaper in low season and midweek). To reach downtown from Departure Bay take the Seaporter shuttle (℡250/753-2118; $14.98) or Hammond Bay bus #2 to the north end of Stewart Ave. A newer and more convenient terminal, **Duke Point** (℡250/722-0181), just south of town, handles ferries from Tsawwassen. Nanaimo lies on the Victoria–Courtenay **train** line and sees two trains daily, northbound around 11am, southbound at 3pm; the **train station** is a little west of downtown, off Selby and near the corner of Fitzwilliam. From the station, turn left and take the latter (and Bastion).

You'll find a typically overstocked **infocentre** north of the centre off the main highway in Beban Park at at Beban House, 2290 Bowen Rd (May–Sept daily 8am–8pm; Oct–April Mon–Fri 9am–5pm; ℡250/756-0106 or 1-800/663-7337, ⓦwww.tourism.nanaimo.com). They'll phone around and help with accommodation referrals, and shower you with pamphlets. There are also details of the many **boat rides** and **tours** you can make to local sawmills, canneries, nature reserves and fishing research stations. There is a smaller downtown office at 82 Commercial St (☎250/754-8531), but it keeps unreliable hours.

Accommodation
Nanaimo's cheapest beds are at the central, private **mini-hostel**, the *Nicol Street Hostel*, 65 Nicol St (☎250/753-1188, ⓦwww.nanaimohostel.com; ❶; dorm beds from $19), located seven blocks south of the bus terminal and one block south of the Harbour Park Shopping Centre off Hwy 1. A handful of camping spots ($9) on the lawn (with ocean views) are also available, plus bike rental, laundry, kitchen and Internet access. More recent and a touch more expensive is the downtown *Cambie International Hostel*, 63 Victoria Crescent (☎250/754-5323; ❶; dorm beds $22.50), with fifty beds in small dorm rooms, and some doubles. The hostel also has a very cheap cafe, bakery and bar.

Numerous **motels** are clustered on the city limits and near the ferry terminals, among them the *Buccaneer Inn*, three blocks south of the Departure Bay ferry terminal at 1577 Stewart Ave (☎250/753-1246 or 1-877/282-6337, ⓦwww.thebuccaneerinn.com; ❸–❻). For more central lodgings, try the big *Howard Johnson Harbourside Hotel*, 1 Terminal Ave (☎250/753-2241 or 1-800/663-7322, ⓦwww.hojonanaimo.com; ❹), convenient for the bus terminal, or, for out-of-town comfort, the *Fairwinds Schooner Cove Resort Hotel and Marina*, 3521 Dolphin Drive (☎250/468-7691 or 1-800/663-7060, ⓦwww.fairwinds.ca; ❺), 26km north of town near Nanoose Bay.

If you're **camping**, by far the best choice is Newcastle Island Provincial Park (see opposite: $14 in summer, $9 in winter), which has the only pitches (18 in all, so arrive early) within walking distance of town, apart from the *Nicol Street Hostel* (see above). Other sites are spread along the main road to the north and south. The best of these – a rural, watery retreat – is *Brannan Lake Campsites*, 6km north of the Departure Bay ferry terminal off Hwy 19 (take exit 19 to Jinglepot Rd) on a 150-acre working farm at 4228 Biggs Rd (☎250/756-0404, ⓦwww.brannenlakecampsite.com; $18).

Eating and drinking
Where **eating** is concerned, get your obligatory Nanaimo bar, or other cheap edibles, at the food stands in the **Public Market**, which is near the ferry terminal on Stewart Avenue (daily 9am–9pm). The big Overwaitea supermarket is 2km north of town on Hwy 19. For meals try *Gina's*, a left turn off the north end of Front St at 47 Skinner St (☎250/753-5411) – it's an unmissable Mexican outfit perched on the edge of a cliff and painted bright pink with an electric blue roof. The town's best **seafood** choice is the *Bluenose Chowder House*, 1340 Stewart Ave (☎250/754-6611; closed Mon), also party to a nice outside terrace. Front Street has a choice of places, most with the benefit of terraces or patios looking out to sea: at the plaza at 90 Front St is *Javawocky* (☎250/753-1688), a good little café, while for fuller snacks or steaks and seafood you should try the *Globe Bar & Grille*, 25 Front St (☎250/754-4910).

Newcastle and Gabriola islands
Barely a stone's throw offshore from Nanaimo lies **Newcastle Island**, and beyond it the larger bulk of Gabriola Island, both incongruously graced with palm trees: they're beneficiaries of what is supposedly Canada's mildest climate. Ferries (☎250/391-2300, ⓦwww.scenicferries.com) make the ten-minute crossing to the former hourly (10am–7pm; foot passengers $5 one-way) from Maffeo Sutton Park (the wharf behind the Civic Arena) to **Newcastle Island**

Provincial Park, which has a fine stretch of sand, tame wildlife, no cars, and lots of walking (18km of trails in all) and picnic possibilities. It'll take a couple of hours to walk the 7.5-kilometre trail that encircles the island.

There are about fifteen daily crossings to **Gabriola Island** (6km, 20min; foot passengers $5.50/$5.25, cars $14/$12.50), a much quieter place that's home to about 2000 people, many of them artists and writers. Author Malcolm Lowry, he of *Under the Volcano* fame, immortalized the island in a story entitled *October Ferry to Gabriola Island*. Gabriola also offers several **beaches** – the best are Gabriola Sands' Twin Beaches at the island's northwest end and Drumbeg Provincial Park – and lots of scope for scuba diving, bird-watching (eagles and sea birds), beachcombing and easy walking, plus the added curiosity of the **Malaspina Galleries**, a series of caves and bluffs near Gabriola Sands sculpted by wind, frost and surf.

Both islands have numerous **B&Bs** and several **campsites**, though if you're thinking of staying the night it's as well to check first with the Nanaimo info-centre or Gabriola's own office at 575 North Rd (July & Aug daily 9am–6pm; mid-May to June & Sept to mid-Oct Sat & Sun 9am–5pm; rest of year closed; ☎250/247-9332, ⊛www.gabriolaisland.org). You can buy snacks on Newcastle from various concessions, notably the newly restored 1931 Pavilion building, but if you're camping take supplies with you.

From Nanaimo to Port Alberni

North of Nanaimo Hwy 1 is replaced by **Hwy 19**, a messy stretch of road spotted with billboards and a rash of motels, marinas and clapboard houses. Almost every last centimetre of the coast is privately owned, this being the chosen site of what appears to be every British Columbian's dream holiday home. Don't expect, therefore, to be able to weave through the houses, wooden huts and boat launches to reach the tempting beaches that flash past below the highway. For sea and sand you have to hang on for **Parksville**, 37km north of Nanaimo, and its quieter near-neighbour **Qualicum Beach**.

Parksville marks a major parting of the ways: while Hwy 19 continues up the eastern coast to Port Hardy, **Hwy 4**, the principal trans-island route, pushes west to **Port Alberni** and on through the tremendously scenic Mackenzie Mountains to the Pacific Rim National Park (see p.870). Laidlaw runs up to three **buses** daily from Nanaimo to Port Alberni, where there are connecting services for Ucluelet and Tofino in the national park.

Parksville

The approach to **PARKSVILLE** from the south is promising, taking you through lovely wooded dunes, with lanes striking off eastwards to hidden beaches and a half-dozen secluded **campsites**. Four kilometres on is the best of the beaches, stretched along 2km of **Rathtrevor Beach Provincial Park** (the tide goes out a kilometre here to reveal vast swathes of sand). In summer this area is madness – there's more beach action here than just about anywhere in the country – and if you want to lay claim to some of the park's **camping** space (summer $22, winter $9; day-use parking $5) expect to start queuing first thing in the morning or take advantage of the provincial park reservations service (see box, p.777). The public sand here stretches for 2km and sports all the usual civilized facilities of Canada's tamed outdoors: cooking shelters, picnic spots and walking trails.

The dross starts beyond the bridge into Parksville, and its eight blocks of motels and garages. The worst of the development has been kept off the promenade, however, which fronts **Parksville Beach**, whose annual **Sandfest** draws 30,000 visitors a day in July to watch the World Sandcastle Competition. The beach offers lovely views across to the mainland and boasts Canada's warmest sea water – up to 21°C (70°F) in summer. Though busy, it's as immaculately kept as the rest of the town – a tidiness that bears witness to the reactionary civic pride of Parksville's largely retired permanent population. You'll see some of these worthy burghers at play during August, when the town hosts the World Croquet Championships.

For local **information**, Parksville's Chamber of Commerce is clearly signed off the highway in downtown at 1275 E Island Hwy (June to early Sept daily 8am–8pm; rest of year Mon–Fri 9am–5pm; ℡250/248-3613, ⓦwww .chamber.parksville.bc.ca). Ask for details of the many **hiking** areas and other nearby refuges from the beaches' summer maelstrom, and **fishing**, which is naturally another of the region's big draws.

If you must **stay**, camping offers the best locations. There are a multitude of cheapish generic **motels** in town and "resort complexes" out along the beaches, though summer vacancies are few and far between. South of Rathtrevor Beach Provincial Park, try a pair of cottage resorts that look onto the sea: the big *Tigh-Na-Mara Resort Hotel*, 1095 E Island Hwy (℡250/248-2072 or 1-800/663-7373, ⓦwww.tigh-na-mara.com; ⓺), with log cottages and oceanfront apartments, forest setting, beach, indoor pool and self-catering units; or the smaller and slightly cheaper *Gray Crest Seaside Resort*, 1115 E Island Hwy (℡250/248-6513 or 1-800/663-2636, ⓦwww.graycrest.com; ⓺), which has considerably lower rates off-season. More upmarket still is the *Beach Acres Resort*, 1015 E Island Hwy (℡250/248-3424 or 1-800/663-7309, ⓦwww.beachacresresort.com; ⓻), set in 57 acres of woodland with its own pool, sandy beach, and forest or ocean-view cabins. Much cheaper is the *Sea Edge Motel*, 209 W Island Hwy (℡250/248-8377 or 1-800/667-3382, ⓦwww.seaedge.com; ⓹), with its own stretch of beach. One of the cheapest motels is the *Skylite*, 459 E Island Hwy (℡250/248-4271 or 1-800/667-1886, ⓦwww.parksvillemotel.com; ⓷).

Qualicum Beach

QUALICUM BEACH, claims its Chamber of Commerce, "is to the artist of today what Stratford-on-Avon was to the era of Shakespeare" – a bohemian enclave of West Coast artists and writers that has also been dubbed the "Carmel of the North" after the town in California. Both estimations obviously pitch things ridiculously high, but compared with Parksville the area has more greenery and charm, and it's infinitely less commercialized, though it probably has just as many summer visitors. More a collection of dispersed houses than a town, at least near the water, Qualicum's seafront is correspondingly wilder and more picturesque, skirted by the road and interrupted only by an **infocentre** at 2711 W Island Hwy, the obvious white building midway on the strand (daily 9am–6pm; longer hours in summer; ℡250/752-9532, ⓦwww.qualicum .bc.ca), and a couple of well-sited **hotels**: the *Sand Pebbles Inn* (℡250/752-6974 or 1-877/556-2326, ⓦwww.spebbles.com; ⓸) and the small *Captain's Inn* (℡250/752-6743, ⓦwww.captains-inn.com; ⓷). A cluster of **motels** also sits at its northern end, where the road swings inland. There's plenty of other local accommodation: contact the infocentre for details. Keep heading north and the road becomes quieter and edged with occasional **campsites**.

Highway 4 to Port Alberni

If you've not yet ventured off the coastal road from Victoria, the short stretch of **Hwy 4** to Port Alberni offers the first real taste of the island's beauty. The first worthwhile stop is **Englishman River Falls Provincial Park**, 3km west of Parksville (exit at Errington Rd) and then another 8km south off the highway. Named after an early immigrant who drowned here, the park wraps around the Englishman River, which tumbles over two main sets of waterfalls. A thirty-minute trail takes in both falls, with plenty of swimming and fishing pools en route. The popular year-round provincial park campsite (summer $17, winter $9; day-use parking $3) is on the left off the approach road before the river, secreted amongst cedars, dogwoods – BC's official tree – and lush ferns.

Back on the main highway, another 8km brings you to the **Little Qualicum Hatchery**, given over to chum, trout and chinook salmon, and just beyond it turn right for the **Little Qualicum Falls Provincial Park**, on the north side of Hwy 4, 19km west of Parksville, which is claimed by some to be the island's loveliest small park. A magnificent forest trail follows the river as it drops several hundred metres through a series of gorges and foaming waterfalls. A half-hour stroll gives you views of the main falls, but for a longer hike try the five-hour Wesley Ridge Trail. There's a sheltered provincial park campsite (summer $17, winter $9; day-use parking $3) by the river and a recognized swimming area on the river at its southern end.

Midway to Port Alberni, the road passes **Cameron Lake** and then an imperious belt of old-growth forest. At the lake's western end, it's well worth walking ten minutes into **McMillan Provincial Park** (no campsite) to reach the famous **Cathedral Grove**, a beautiful group of huge Douglas firs, some of them reaching 70m tall, 2m thick; they are up to a thousand years old. The park is the gift of the large McMillan timber concern, whose agents have been responsible for felling similar trees with no compunction over the years. Wandering the grove will take only a few minutes but, just to the east, at the Cameron Lake picnic site, is the start of the area's main **hike**. The well-maintained trail was marked out by railway crews in 1908 and climbs to the summit of **Mount Arrowsmith** (1817m), a long, gentle twenty-kilometre pull through alpine meadows that takes between six and nine hours. The mountain is also one of the island's newer and fast-developing ski areas. To stay locally, head for the *Cameron Lake Resort* (☎250/752-6707, Ⓦ www.cameronlakeresort.com; ❹; April–Oct), based in a park-like setting on the lake at 1313 Chalet Rd: it has a cottage and a campsite ($19–25).

Port Alberni

Self-proclaimed "Gateway to the Pacific" and – along with half of Vancouver Island – "Salmon Capital of the World", **PORT ALBERNI** is a dispersed town more or less dominated by the sights and smells of its huge lumber mills. Despite its relative ugliness, it's also an increasingly popular site for exploring the centre and west coast of the island, and a busy fishing port, situated at the end of the impressive fjord-like Alberni Inlet, Vancouver Island's longest inlet. Various logging and pulp-mill tours are available, but the town's main interest to travellers is as a forward base for the Pacific Rim National Park. If you've ever wanted to hook a salmon, though, this is probably one of the easier places to do so and there are any number of boats and guides ready to help out.

The only conventional sight is the **Alberni Valley Museum**, 4255 Wallace St and 10th Avenue (summer Tues–Sat 10am–5pm, Thurs until 8pm;

Boats from Port Alberni

The thing you'll probably most want to do in Port Alberni is to leave it, preferably on the **MV Lady Rose**, a small, fifty-year-old Scottish-built freighter that plies between Port Alberni, Kildonan, Bamfield, Ucluelet and the Broken Group Islands (see p.880). Primarily a conduit for freight and mail, it also takes up to a hundred passengers, many of whom use it as a drop-off for canoe trips or the West Coast Trail at Bamfield. You could easily ride it simply for the exceptional scenery – huge cliffs and tree-covered mountains – and for the abundant wildlife (sea lions, whales, eagles, depending on the time of year). Passengers started as something of a sideline for the company that runs the boat, but such has been the boat's popularity that another boat has been added to the "fleet" – the 200-passenger **MV Frances Barkley** – and reservations for trips are now virtually essential. Remember to take a sweater and jacket and wear sensible shoes, for these are still primarily working boats, and creature comforts are few.

The basic year-round **schedule** is as follows: the boat leaves from the Argyle Pier, 5425 Argyle St at the Alberni Harbour Quay, Port Alberni (Tues, Thurs & Sat 8am). After a stop at **Kildonan** ($12 one-way, $24 return), it arrives in **Bamfield** ($23/$45) at 12.30pm. It starts its return journey at 1.30pm, reaching Port Alberni at 5.30pm. From October to May the boat stops on advance request at the Broken Group Islands.

From June to mid-September, there are additional sailings to the **Broken Group Islands** (Mon, Wed & Fri, departs Port Alberni 8am). At 11am, the boat docks at Sechart ($23/$45), site of the *Sechart Whaling Station Lodge* (℡250/723-8313, ⓦwww.ladyrosemarine.com), the only place to stay on the archipelago if you're not wilderness camping. Cost per night is $100 per person, $155 for two people, including meals; slightly less if you stay two or more days. The boat continues to **Ucluelet**, arriving at 12.30pm. The return journey starts from Ucluelet at 2pm, calling at Sechart (3.30pm) before arriving back at Port Alberni at 7pm.

From July 6 to August 31 there is an additional sailing (Sun only) on the route from Port Alberni (8am) to Bamfield (1.30pm) and back, with an outbound stop at Sechart at 11am.

For information and **reservations**, contact Lady Rose Marine Services, 5425 Argyle St, Port Alberni (year-round ℡250/723-8313 or April–Sept ℡1-800/663-7192, ⓦwww.ladyrosemarine.com). It also offers canoe and kayak **rentals** ($35/day, double kayak $50/day, includes lifejackets, paddles, pumps and spray skirts) as well as transportation of the same to the Broken Group Islands. Smaller boats running more irregular services to the same destinations can occasionally be picked up from Tofino and Ucluelet.

donation; ℡250/723-2181), home to a predictable but above-average logging and aboriginal peoples collection, a water wheel and small steam engine. For hot-weather swimming, locals head out to **Sproat Lake Provincial Park**, 8km north of town on Hwy 4. It's a hectic scene in summer, thanks to a fine beach, picnic area and a pair of good campsites ($15; April–Oct), one on the lake, the other north of the highway about 1km away. Of peripheral interest, you can take a guided tour of the world's largest fire-fighting planes or follow the short trails that lead to a few ancient petroglyphs on the park's eastern tip.

Sproat Lake marks the start of the superb scenery that unfolds over the 100km of Hwy 4 west of the town. Only heavily logged areas detract from the grandeur of the Mackenzie Range and the majestic interplay of trees and water. Go prepared, however, as there's no fuel or shops for about two hours of driving.

Practicalities

Laidlaw (see p.863) runs five **buses** daily from Nanaimo to Port Alberni; the terminal is on Victoria Quay at 5065 Southgate (though the bus company is based at 4541 Margaret St). Jump off at the 7-Eleven, one stop earlier, to be nearer the centre of town. Laidlaw runs connections from here on to Ucluelet and Tofino. Western Bus Lines (℡250/723-3341) runs two services weekly to Bamfield (Mon & Fri; $17 one-way), as does the Pacheenaht First Nation Bus Service (℡250/647-5521). Several other companies from Victoria (see p.831) make connections to Bamfield for the West Coast Trail (see p.884).

For help and information on fishing charters, hiking options, minor summer events, or tours of the two local pulp mills, call in at the **infocentre**, unmissable as you come into town at 2533 Redford St, RR2, Site 215 Comp 10 (July & Aug Mon–Fri 8am–6pm, Sat & Sun 9am–5pm; rest of year Mon-Fri 9am–5pm, Sat & Sun 10am–2/4pm; ℡250/724-6535, Ⓦwww.avcoc.com), off Hwy 4 east of town – look out for the big yellow mural. Alternatively, check out the industry-backed **Forestry Visitor Centre** (summer daily 9.30am–5.30pm, rest of year Fri–Sun 11am–4pm; ℡250/720-2108) on the colourful harbour quay where in summer a small steam train runs from the old train station at the corner of Kingsway and Argyle for about half an hour along the waterfront to the **McLean Mill National Historic Site** (site open daily year-round; mill building and steam train mid-June to early Sept Wed & Thurs 10am–5pm; site donation; mill $6.50; train $22 round-trip, includes mill admission; Ⓦwww.alberniheritage.com), an old steam-operated mill at 5633 Smith Rd, which you might also reach by bike or on foot on the twenty-kilometre Log Trail from the infocentre.

Given the 8am departure of the MV *Lady Rose* (see box opposite), there's a good chance you may have to stay overnight in Port Alberni. For **accommodation** there are the usual motel choices – the closest to the quay is the *Bluebird*, 3755 3rd Ave (℡250/723-1153, Ⓦwww.bluebirdmotel.net; ❹), but it only has fifteen rooms, so be sure to book. For a more memorable central hotel you'll be better off with the *Coast Hospitality Inn*, 3835 Redford St (℡250/723-8111 or 1-800/663-1144, Ⓦwww.coasthotels.com; ❻) – not cheap, but probably the town's best bet. *The Best Western Barclay*, 4277 Stamp Ave (℡250/724-7171 or 1-800/563-6590, Ⓦwww.bestwesternbarclay.com; ❻), with outdoor pool, and the smaller *Somass Motel & RV*, 5279 River Rd (℡250/724-3236 or 1-800/927-2217, Ⓦwww.somass-motel.ca; ❸), are reliable choices. The infocentre has a list of the constantly changing **B&B** outlets: an excellent first choice is the *Edelweiss B&B*, 2610-12th Ave (℡250/723-5940; ❸), which is not particularly central, but does have very welcoming hosts. For **camping**, best bets are on Sproat Lake (see above). Farther afield is the bigger 250-site *China Creek Marina and Campground*, 2011 Bamfield Road (May–Sept; ℡250/723-2657; $16–25), 15km south of town on Alberni Inlet, which has a wooded, waterside location and sandy, log-strewn beach.

Eating possibilities are numerous. For coffee, good breakfasts and snacks down by the dock, try the *Blue Door Café* at 5415 Argyle St, an old-fashioned place much-patronized by locals. For lunch, make for the *Swale Rock Café*, 5328 Argyle St (℡250/723-0777), and for **seafood** check out the waterfront *Clockworks*, Harbour Quay (℡250/723-8862). The *Canal*, 5093 Johnson St (℡250/724-6555), serves good Greek food, and for cheap lunches there's the *Paradise Café*, 4505 Gertrude St (℡250/724-5050), and several deli-bakeries.

Pacific Rim National Park

The **Pacific Rim National Park** – the single best reason to visit Vancouver Island – is a stunning amalgam of mountains, coastal rainforest, wild beaches and unkempt marine landscapes that stretches intermittently for 130km between the towns of Tofino in the north and Port Renfrew to the south. It divides into three distinct areas: **Long Beach**, which is the most popular; the **Broken Group Islands**, hundreds of islets only really accessible to sailors and canoeists; and the **West Coast Trail**, a tough but increasingly popular long-distance footpath. The whole area has also become a magnet for surfing and **whale-watching** enthusiasts, and dozens of small companies run charters out from the main centres to view the migrating mammals. By taking the MV *Lady Rose* from Port Alberni (see box p.868) to Bamfield or Ucluelet or back, and combining this with shuttle buses or Laidlaw buses from Victoria, Port Alberni and Nanaimo, a wonderfully varied combination of itineraries is possible around the region.

Lying at the north end of Long Beach, **Tofino**, once essentially a fishing village, is now changing in the face of tourism, but with its natural charm, scenic position and plentiful accommodation, it still makes the best base for general exploration. **Ucluelet** to the south is comparatively less attractive, but almost equally geared to providing tours and accommodating the park's 800,000 or so annual visitors. **Bamfield**, a tiny and picturesque community with a limited amount of in-demand accommodation, lies still farther south and is known mainly as the northern trailhead of the West Coast Trail and a fishing, marine research and whale-watching centre. Unless you fly in, you'll enter the park on Hwy 4 from Port Alberni, which means the first part you'll see is **Long Beach** (shadowed along its length to Tofino by Hwy 4), so if you're dashing in by car for a day-trip, cut straight to the section dealing with this area on p.876. Long

Whales

The Pacific Rim National Park is amongst the world's best areas for **whale-watching**, thanks to its location on the main migration routes, food-rich waters and numerous sheltered bays. People come from all over the world for the spectacle, and it's easy to find a boat going out from Tofino, Ucluelet or Bamfield, most charging around $60–80 a head for the trip depending on duration (usually 2–3hr). Regulations prohibit approaching within 100m of an animal but, though few locals will admit it, there's no doubt that the recent huge upsurge in boat tours has begun to disrupt the **migrations**. The whales' 8000-kilometre journey – the longest known migration of any mammal – takes them from their breeding and calving lagoons in Baja, Mexico, to summer feeding grounds in the Bering and Chukchi seas off Siberia. The northbound migration takes from February to May, with the peak period of passage between March and April. A few dozen animals occasionally abort their trip and stop off the Canadian coast for summer feeding (notably at Maquinna Marine Park, 20min by boat from Tofino). The return journey starts in August, hitting Tofino and Ucluelet in late September and early October. **Mating** takes place in Mexico during December, after which the males turn immediately northwards, to be followed by females and their young in February. Even if you don't take a boat trip, you stand a faint chance of seeing whales from the coast as they dive, when you can locate their tails, or during fluking, when the animals surface and "blow" three or four times before making another five-minute dive. There are telescopes at various points along Long Beach, the best known viewpoints being Schooner Cove, Radar Hill, Quistis Point and Combers Beach near Sea Lion Rocks.

Beach is also the site of the park's main information centre and the nearby Wickaninnish Centre, an interpretive centre. Remember that a **park fee** – $8 per vehicle per day – is payable at the park entrance.

Weather is an important consideration: it has a well-deserved reputation for being appallingly wet, cold and windy – and that's the good days. An average of 300cm of rain falls annually, and in some places it buckets down almost 700cm, well over ten times Victoria's rainfall. So don't count on doing much swimming or sunbathing (though **surfing**'s a possibility): think more in terms of spending your time admiring crashing Pacific breakers, hiking the back-country and maybe doing a spot of beachcombing. Better still, time your visit to coincide with the worst of the weather off-season – **storm-watching** is an increasingly popular park pastime.

Tofino

TOFINO, most travellers' target base in the park, is showing the adverse effects of its ever-increasing tourist influx, but locals are keeping development to a minimum, clearly realizing they have a vested interest in preserving the salty, waterfront charm that brought them – and visitors – here in the first place. Crowning a narrow spit, the fishing village has a superb situation, bounded on three sides by tree-covered islands and water, a location that graces it with magnificent views and plenty of what the tourist literature refers to as "aqua-culture". As a service centre it fulfils most functions, offering food, accommodation and a wide variety of boat and sea-plane tours, most of which have a **whale-watching**, surfing (Canada's best surf is close at hand) and fishing angle or provide a means to travel out to **islands and hot springs** close by. Sleepy in off-season, the place erupts into a commercial frenzy during the summer, hippies, surfer types and easy-going family groups being the most visible visitors – though there's little to do in town other than walk its few streets, enjoy the views and soak up the casual atmosphere.

You might drop in to the small **Whale Centre** at 411 Campbell St (March–Oct daily 9am–8pm; free; ☎250/725-2132), one of many places to book whale-watching tours, but also home to exhibits and artefacts devoted to local seafaring and trading history, whales and aboriginal peoples' culture. Another notable place around town is the **Eagle Aerie Gallery**, 350 Campbell St at the corner of Second St (Ⓦwww.royhenryvickers.com), a gallery belonging to the noted Tsimshian artist Roy Henry Vickers and housed in a traditional long-house-style building with a beautiful cedar interior. Two blocks east is the **Rainforest Interpretive Centre**, at 451 Main St at the corner of Fourth St (free), which offers background on the ecosystems of the Pacific temperate rainforest.

Two fine beaches lie within walking distance to the southeast of the town: **Mackenzie Beach** and **Chesterman's Beach** (for access to the latter take Lynn Rd right just beyond the Dolphin Motel as you leave town), the former one of the warmer spots locally, the latter home to a fair number of out-of-town accommodation possibilities (see p.872). Beyond Chesterman lies Frank Island, a tempting proposition at low tide, but sadly private property. The quietest beach around these parts, though, is **Templar**, a miniature strip of sand: ask at the infocentre for directions.

Arrival and information

Tofino is easily reached by Laidlaw **bus** (☎250/385-4411 or 1-800/318-0818) from Port Alberni (2 daily; 3hr) and Nanaimo (1 daily; 4hr 30min), with a

SOUTHERN BRITISH COLUMBIA | Pacific Rim National Park

single early-morning connection from Victoria, changing at Nanaimo (6hr 30min). The bus depot is on 1st Street near the junction with Neil Street. There is also a daily mini-bus shuttle, the Tofino Bus, 564 Campbell St (℡250/725-2871 or 1-866/986-3466, ⓦ www.tofinobus.com), from Victoria or Nanaimo (connecting with the ferry from Horseshoe Bay). The smaller Pacific Rim 5-Star shuttle (℡250/954-8702 or 1-800/697-1114, ⓦ www.prshuttle.ca) runs daily to Nanaimo or Comox ($85) and Victoria ($170) from Tofino and Ucluelet.

Many small **airlines** have added Tofino to their schedules. Best is the excellent North Vancouver Air (℡604/278-1608 or 1-800/228-6608, ⓦ www.northvanair.com), which flies in once or twice daily from Vancouver ($175 one-way, $75 standby; 1hr) and Victoria ($200 one-way; 45min). Baxter Aviation (℡250/754-1066 or 604/683-6525 in Vancouver or 1-800/661-5599, ⓦ www.baxterair.com) also runs connecting flights to Tofino and Ucluelet from Vancouver harbour, Victoria, Seattle and many other smaller centres.

Tofino's **infocentre** at 121 Third St at the corner of Campbell St (April–Sept daily 9am–8/9pm; Oct–March Mon–Fri 9am–4pm; ℡250/725-3414, ⓦ www.tofinobc.org) can give you the exhaustive lowdown on all the logistics of boat and plane tours.

Accommodation

The infocentre may be able to get you into one of the village's ever-expanding roster of **hotels**, **motels** and **B&B**, should you be unwise enough to turn up in Tofino without reservations in high summer. There are two main concentrations of accommodation options: in Tofino itself or a couple of kilometres east of town on or near Lynn Road, which overlooks Chesterman Beach. Out of town across the water (accessed by water taxi) there are also the desirable but expensive self-contained units at the *Hot Springs Lodge* (℡250/724-8570; ⑥), the main accommodation at Hot Springs Cove (see p.876); book early. Otherwise you can try one of the near-town **campsites** (don't forget that there is a park campsite at Long Beach; see p.876) or the **private hostels** that now seem to spring up overnight and disappear just as quickly, though local reports suggest some of these places can be pretty unsalubrious. The infocentre website ⓦ www.tofinobc.org has a full listing of B&Bs.

Hotels and motels

Cable Cove Inn 201 Main St ℡250/725-4236 or 1-800/663-6449, ⓦ www.cablecoveinn.com. Stay in high style in one of six smart rooms at the westernmost edge of town that come complete with Jacuzzis, fireplaces and four-poster beds. ⑦

Dolphin Motel 1190 Pacific Rim Hwy ℡250/725-3377, ⓦ www.dolphinmotel.ca. Rooms with coffee-maker and fridge or self-catering units 3km south of town; 5min walk to Chesterman Beach. ⑧

Duffin Cove and Resort 215 Campbell St ℡250/725-3448 or 1-888/629-2903, ⓦ www.duffin-cove-resort.com. Thirteen nice cabins and suites (for one to eight people) with kitchens and seaview balconies just south of the *Cable Cove Inn* at the western edge of town overlooking the Clayoquot Sound. ⑥

Maquinna Lodge 120 1st St ℡250/725-3261 or 1-800/665-3199, ⓕ250/725-3433. Central town location at the corner of Main and 1st St, containing 32 renovated rooms, some overlooking Tofino Harbour and Meares Island. ⑤

Middle Beach Lodge 400 Mackenzie Beach ℡250/725-2900, ⓦ www.middlebeach.com. Extremely nice, secluded place south of town and west of Chesterman Beach with big stone fireplace, deep old chairs and the gentle splash of waves on tiny Templar Beach to lull you to sleep. ⑤

Ocean Village Beach Resort 555 Hellesen Drive ℡250/725-3755, ⓦ www.oceanvillageresort.com. A resort just north of Long Beach, 2km from town on the main road, with good accommodation, ocean views, kitchen units and indoor pool. ⑥

Schooner Motel 311 Campbell St ℡250/725-3478, ⓦ www.schoonermotel.net. Overlooking

Tofino Inlet and Meares Island in the town centre, this motel has some rooms complete with kitchen. **⑥**

Tofino Motel 542 Campbell St ☎250/725-2055, ⓦwww.tofinomotel.com. A small motel on the eastern edge of town including rooms with balconies offering views of the sea and neighbouring islands. **⑥**

Tofino Swell Lodge 341 Olsen Rd ☎250/725-3274, ⓕ725-3346. On the eastern edge of town near Crab Dock, this excellent lodge on the waterfront looking out to Meares Island has kitchen or plain sleeping units. **④**

Wickaninnish Inn Osprey Lane at Chesterman Beach ☎250/725-3100 or 1-800/333-4604, ⓦwww.wickinn.com. If you're feeling like a splurge (rooms start at $380, less off season), shell out for this superb $8.5-million 45-room inn, situated on a rocky promontory at the western end of Chesterman Beach. All rooms are large and have ocean views, fireplaces and baths big enough for two. As well as the obvious local attractions, storm-watching here is a growing wintertime activity. **⑧**

B&Bs

Brimar 1375 Thornberg Crescent ☎250/725-3410 or 1-800/714-9373, ⓦwww.brimarbb.com. At the south end of Chesterman Beach, off Lynn Rd, these three rooms have good Pacific Ocean views and come with a full breakfast. **⑥**

Crab Dock Guest House 310 Olsen Rd ☎250/725-2911, ⓦwww.crabdock.com. Situated a little east of the town at Crab Dock, these three recently built rooms all have private bathroom. A full breakfast is offered but you can also use the guest kitchen, as well as the living room. **④**

Gull Cottage 1254 Lynn Rd ☎250/725-3177, ⓦwww.gullcottagetofino.com. A few minutes' walk to the beach, at the west end of Lynn Rd, this Victorian-era home has three rooms (private bathrooms) and a hot tub in the woods. **⑤**

Paddler's Inn 320 Main St ☎250/725-4222. A recommended spot on the waterfront right in the middle of town; nonsmoking. **④**

Penny's Place 565 Campbell St ☎250/725-3457. A choice of rooms on the east edge of the small downtown with and without private bathrooms, offering a full breakfast. Nonsmoking. **⑤**

The Tide's Inn B&B 160 Arnet Rd ☎250/725-3765, ⓦwww.tidesinntofino.com. An easy walk south of town (walk down 1st Ave and turn right) on the waterfront with good views of Clayoquot Sound. **⑥**

Tofino by the Beach 1277 Lynn Rd ☎250/725-2441, ⓦwww.tofinobythebeach.com. Away from

the centre of Tofino on Chesterman Beach at its northern end. Rooms have private bathrooms; continental breakfast. **⑥**

Village Gallery B&B 321 Main St ☎250/725-4229, ⓕ725-3473. Quiet upper room and living room in a heritage building in the centre of town with good ocean view and full breakfast. **⑤**

West Beach Manor 1314 Lynn Rd ☎250/725-2779. Self-contained suites close to Chesterman Beach with kitchens and separate bedrooms with space for up to four people. Minimum two-night stay in high season. **⑥**

Wilp Gybuu (Wolf House) 311 Leighton Way ☎250/725-2330, ⓦwww.tofinobedandbreakfast.com. Three rooms in a walkable location south of town close to *The Tide's Inn*. Sea views, good breakfast and private en-suite bathroom. **⑤**

Hostels

Hummingbird International Hostel At Ahousaht on Flores Island ☎250/670-6979, ⓦwww.hummingbird-hostel.com. As well as the hummingbirds you stand a good chance here of seeing whales, bald eagles and sea otters, with the opportunity to hike trails and bathe in natural sulphur springs. Dorm beds cost from $20, private doubles from $70. Add on the cost of a 35-minute water-taxi or boat connection (from $14 each way; departures from First St dock at 10.30am & 4pm, returning 8.30am & 1pm). **③**

Whalers on the Point Guesthouse (HI) 81 West St ☎250/725-3443, ⓦwww.tofinohostel.com. Best hostel in town, HI-affiliated, near the west end of Main Street with fabulous ocean views. Including tax, beds are $25 per person in high season (May–Sept), $2 less the rest of the year. Private doubles cost $76–86, or $46–51 in low season. Add on $2 for one-night stays from mid-June to mid-Sept. Facilities include kitchen, games room, sauna, bike rental and storage, surf and wet-suit lockers, and a shuttle service to Long Beach. Reservations are essential. Check-in 8am–2pm & 4–10pm. **③**

WindRider Retreat for Women 231 Main St ☎250/725-3240 or 1-877/725-3240, ⓦwww.windrider.org. Women-only, non-profit-making institution, centrally located. A bed in a shared room (2–3 beds) is $25, private double/twin $60/$65. **③**

Campsites

Bella Pacifica Campground Pacific Rim Hwy ☎250/725-3400, ⓦwww.bellapacifica.com. Sites with hot showers, flush toilets and laundry 2km south of town, with wilderness and oceanfront

Tofino activities

Whale-watching

Ucluelet to the south may claim to be "whale-watching capital of the world", but **whales** – the main reason a lot of people are here – are just as easily seen from Tofino. As in Victoria, there are plenty of operators, most costing about the same and offering similar **excursions**: all you have to do is decide what sort of boat you want to go out on – Zodiacs (inflatables), which are bouncier, more thrilling and potentially wetter, or rigid-hull cruisers (covered or uncovered), which are more sedate. See the box on p.870 for more whale-watching tips. Remember that if you take tours to Meares Islands, Hot Springs Cove and elsewhere, especially in spring or autumn, you stand a good chance of seeing whales en route anyway – some operators try to combine whale-watching and excursions. Reckon on spending from around $65 for two- or three-hour trip in a Zodiac and $85 on a rigid-hull.

Operators to try in Tofino include: Cypre Prince Tours midway down the main street at 430 Campbell St (☏250/725-2202 or 1-800/787-2202, ⓦwww .tofinooutdoors.com); Chinook Charters, 450 Campbell St (☏250/725-3431 or 1-800/665-3646), which offers trips (2hr 30min) on rigid or zodiac boats; and Jamie's Whaling Station, 606 Campbell St (☏250/725-3919 or 1-800/667-9913, ⓦwww.jamies.com), the longest-running such venture in Tofino, which also offers a choice of zodiac boats or the twenty-metre *Lady Selkirk*, which comes with heated cabin. If you don't see whales, Jamie's offers vouchers which can used on another trip. See p.870 for more general information.

Fishing, surfing, kayaking and more

Many of the above companies double up as **fishing** charters, though for more a long-established specialist operator contact Bruce's Smiley Seas Charters, 210 Campbell St (May–Sept; ☏250/725-2557), which is quite happy to have novices aboard. Tofino is quickly becoming the **surfing** capital of Canada, thanks to some enormous Pacific waves, though floating driftwood and big lumps of lumber caught up in the waves can be a hazard. For information, board rental and all other equipment, contact Live to Surf, well east of the town centre at 1180 Tofino Hwy (☏250/725-4464, ⓦwww.livetosurf.com). It rents boards from $25 and many other items, as well as offering lessons (from $45 for 2hr). If you want to go out in a **kayak** (no experience required) contact Tofino Sea Kayaking, 320 Main St (☏250/725-4222 or 1-800/863-4664, ⓦwww.tofino-kayaking.com), which offers day-trips or longer **tours** with lodge accommodation or wilderness camping. Nine holes of **golf** are available at the local course near the airport (☏250/725-3332), while **guided hikes** and easy nature rambles in the forest and along the seashore are offered by several companies; contact the infocentre for details.

sites, private nature trails to Templar Beach and walk-on access to Mackenzie Beach. Reservations recommended. March–Oct. $28–40.
Crystal Cove Beach Resort Mackenzie Beach ☏250/725-4213, ⓦwww.crystalcove.cc. Sites with flush toilets, laundry and showers and some cabins; 3km south of town in a pretty secluded cove and also 1km from Mackenzie Beach with one- and two-bedroom smart log cabins with

kitchens and ocean views. Reservations recommended. $30–50. Cabins ⑥
Mackenzie Beach Resort 1101 Pacific Rim Hwy ☏250/725-3439, ⓦwww .mackenziebeach.com. Located on a fine sandy beach 2km south of Tofino and 10min walk from Long Beach; indoor pool, Jacuzzi, hot showers and kayak rentals. Some walk-in beachfront tent sites. $35–45.

Eating and drinking

For **food**, just about everyone in town clusters around the heaving tables of the *Common Loaf Bake Shop* behind the bank at 180 1st St, deservedly the most popular choice for coffee and snacks. In the evening the home-made dough is turned into pizzas instead of bread and rolls. In a similar vein is the *Alley Way Café* also behind the bank at 305 Campbell and First St, a friendly, locals' type of place. Coming into town on the main highway (which becomes Campbell St), the *Café Pamplona* in the Tofino Botanical Gardens, 1084 Pacific Hwy, is also a good spot for coffee and snacks. For reasonable steak and pizza, visit the central *Surfside Steak and Pizza*, 121 First and Main (☎250/725-2882).

One of the best views in town is available at the *Sea Shanty*, 300 Main St (☎250/725-2902), a restaurant that offers **outdoor dining** overlooking the harbour and the chance of some tremendous sunsets on fine evenings. Excellent Pacific Rim fusion food is available at the intimate and sleek *RainCoast Café*, 101-120 Fourth St (☎250/725-2215; dinner only). Equally elevated (mainly fish and seafood) cuisine can be found at breakfast, lunch and dinner at the award-winning *Schooner*, 331 Campbell St (☎250/725-3444), a romantic place set in pretty gardens with tremendous views of the Tofino Inlet. For a even bigger treat, head out of town to *The Pointe Restaurant* at the *Wickaninnish Inn* (☎250/725-3100; see hotel listings on p.873), which is the area's best upmarket restaurant, on account of both its food and its views – but you'll drop over $150 for a full gourmet nine-course special with wine.

Best place for a **beer** and **dancing** is the pub downstairs at the *Maquinna Lodge*, 120 First St, the place to be on Friday and Saturday nights.

Trips from Tofino: Clayoquot Sound

After wandering Tofino's handful of streets, most people head south to explore Long Beach, or put themselves at the mercy of the many boat and plane operators serving the stretch of ocean and landscapes around Tofino known as **Clayoquot Sound**. The name has gained tremendous resonance over the last few years, largely because it has been the focus for some of the most bitterly fought battles against loggers by environmentalists and aboriginal campaigners. It stretches for some 65km from Kennedy Lake to the south of Tofino to the Hesquiat Peninsula 40km to the north, embracing three major islands – Meares, Vargas and Flores – and numerous smaller islets and coastal inlets. More importantly, it is the largest surviving area of low-altitude temperate **rainforest** in North America. Quite incredibly the BC government gave permission to logging companies in 1993 to fell two-thirds of this irreplaceable and age-old forest. The result was the largest outbreak of **civil disobedience** in Canadian history, resulting in eight hundred arrests, as vast numbers congregated at a peace camp in the area and made daily attempts to stop the logging trucks. The stand-off resulted in partial victory, with the designation of new protected areas and limited recognition of the Nuu-chah-nulth tribe's moral and literal rights to the land. The region remains in a precarious position, however, and if it's happened once you can be pretty sure that, where forestry interests are concerned, it'll happen again.

There are five main destinations in this region for boat and float-plane trips. The nearest is **Meares Island**, easily visible to the east of Tofino and just fifteen minutes away by boat. A beautiful island swathed in lush temperate rainforest, this was one of the areas earmarked for the lumberjack's chainsaw, despite its designation as a Nuu-chah-nulth tribal park in 1985. At present its ancient cedars and hemlock are safe, and visible on the Meares Island Big Cedar Trail (3km), which meanders among some of the biggest trees you'll ever see, many of them more than a thousand years old and up to 6m across – big enough to put a tunnel through. **Vargas Island**, the next nearest target, lies just 5km from Tofino to the north, and is visited for its beauty, beaches, kayaking and swimming possibilities. **Flores Island**, 20km to the northwest, is accessed by boat or plane and, like Vargas Island, is partly protected by partial provincial park status. At the aboriginal peoples' community of Ahousaht you can pick up the Ahousaht Wild Side Heritage Trail ($20 fee unless staying at the Hummingbird hostel on the island; see "Accommodation" p.873), which runs for 16km through idyllic beach and forest scenery to the Mount Flores viewpoint (886m). This is also a chance to encounter aboriginal culture and people at first hand, with **tours** accompanied by local guides available: see the Tofino infocentre or call ☎250/725-3309 for details and information on trail conditions.

Perhaps the best, and certainly one of the most popular trips from Tofino, is the 37-kilometre boat or plane ride to **Hot Springs Cove**, site of one of only a handful of hot springs on Vancouver Island. This takes an hour by water-taxi (☎250/726-8631; from $65) or 15 minutes by float plane with Tofino Air (☎250/725-4454, ⓦwww.tofinoair.ca; from $85), though the most cost-effective way of seeing the island is to take a day tour with one of Tofino's many operators, who throw in whale-watching en route (from $85). A thirty-minute trek from the landing stage brings you to the springs, which emerge at a piping 43°C and run, as a creek, to the sea via a small waterfall and four pools, becoming progressively cooler. Be prepared for something of a crowd in summer when swimming costumes can be optional. An expensive hotel, the *Hot Springs Lodge* – a way to beat other punters by getting in an early morning or late-night dip – sits on the cove near the landing stage (see "Accommodation" p.872).

Finally, a forty-kilometre trip north takes you to **Hesquiat Peninsula**, where you land at or near Refuge Cove, site of a Hesquiat aboriginal village. Locals offer tours here and some lodgings: ask for the latest details at the Tofino infocentre.

Tofino's infocentre is also the place to pick up information on **tours**; otherwise, contact Seaside Adventures, 300 Main St (☎250/725-2292 or 1-888/332-4252) Chinook Charters, 450 Campbell St (☎250/725-3431 or 1-800/665-3646) or the whale-watching companies listed under "Activities" on p.874, most of whom also offer boat tours to the above destinations.

Long Beach

The most accessible of the park's components, **Long Beach** is just what it says: a long tract of wild, windswept sand and rocky points stretching for about 30km from Tofino to Ucluelet. Around 19km can be hiked unbroken from Schooner Bay in the west to Half Moon Bay in the east. The snow-covered peaks of the Mackenzie Range rise up over 1200m, providing a scenic backdrop, and behind the beach grows a thick, lush canopy of coastal rainforest. The white-packed sand itself is the sort of primal seascape that is all but extinct in much of the world, scattered with beautiful, sea-sculpted driftwood, smashed by surf, broken by crags, and dotted with islets and rock pools oozing with marine life. It's worth realizing that Long Beach, while a distinct beach in itself, also rather loosely refers to several other beaches to either side, the relative merits of which are outlined below. If you haven't done so already, driving or biking Hwy 4 along the beach area is the best time to call in at the Pacific Rim National Park **Information Centre** (daily mid-March to mid-June 10.30am–6pm; mid-June to Aug 8am–8pm; Sept to mid-Oct 10am–6pm; ☎250/726-4212, ⓦwww.parkscanada.gc.ca), located right off Hwy 4 3km northwest of the Ucluelet–Tofino–Port Alberni road junction. Remember that you need to pay a **park fee** of $10 per vehicle.

7

Long Beach walks

With an eye on the weather and tide, you can **walk** more or less anywhere on and around Long Beach. Various trails and roads drop to the beach from the main Hwy 4 road to Tofino. At the same time there are nine official trails, most of them short and very easy, so you could tackle a few in the course of a leisurely drive or cycle along the road. All the paths are clearly marked from Hwy 4, but it's still worth picking up a *Hiker's Guide* from the infocentre. From east to west you can choose from the following. The linked trails **1** and **2**, the **Willowbrae Trail** (2.8km round trip), are accessed by turning left at the main Hwy 4 junction and driving or biking 2km towards Ucluelet. A level wooded trail then leads from the trailhead towards the beach, following the steps of early pioneers who used this route before the building of roads between Tofino and Ucluelet. Just before the sea it divides, dropping steeply via steps and ramps, to either the tiny Half Moon Bay or the larger, neighbouring Florencia Bay to the north.

All other walks are accessed off Hwy 4 to Tofino, turning right (north) at the main Hwy 4 junction. The gentle **3 Gold Mine Trail** (3km round trip), signed left off the road, leads along Lost Shoe Creek, a former gold-mining area (look out for debris), to Florencia Beach. For walks **4**, **5** and **6**, take the turn left off the highway for the Wickaninnish Centre. The **4 South Beach Trail** (1.5km round trip) leaves from behind the centre, leading above forest-fringed shores and coves before climbing to the headlands for a view of the coast and a chance to climb down to South Beach, famous for its big rock-crashing breakers and the sound of the water ripping noisily through the beach pebbles. The **5 Wickaninnish Trail** (5km) follows the South Beach Trail for a while and then at the top of the first hill is signed left, passing through rainforest – once again this is the route of the old pioneer trail – before ending at the parking area above Florencia Beach to the east. The **6 Shorepine Bog Trail** (800m) is a wheelchair-accessible boardwalk trail (accessed on the left on the access road to the centre) that wends through the fascinating stunted bog vegetation; trees which are just a metre or so tall here can be hundreds of years old.

Moving farther west towards Tofino along Hwy 4, the **7 Rain Forest Trails** are two small loops (1km each round trip), one on each side of the road, that follow a boardwalk through virgin temperate rainforest: each has interpretive boards detailing forest life cycle and forest "inhabitants" respectively. Farther down the road on the right at the Combers Beach parking area, a road gives access to the gentle **8 Spruce Fringe Trail** (1.5km loop). This graphically illustrates the effects of the elements on spruce forest, following a log-strewn beach fringe-edged with bent and bowed trees before entering more robust forest farther from the effects of wind and salt spray. It also crosses willow and crab-apple swamp to a glacial terrace, the site of a former shoreline, past the airport turn-off. The final walk, the **9 Schooner Beach Trail** (1km one-way), leads left off the road through superb tranches of rainforest to an extremely scenic beach at Schooner Cove. This might be the end of the official trails, but don't fail to climb to the viewpoint on **Radar Hill** off to the right as you get closer to Tofino.

Scenery aside, Long Beach is noted for its **wildlife**, the BC coastline reputedly having more marine species than any other temperate area in the world. As well as the smaller stuff in tidal pools – starfish, anemones, snails, sponges and suchlike – there are large mammals like whales and sea lions, as well as thousands of migrating birds (especially in Oct & Nov), notably pintails, mallards, black brants and Canada geese. Better weather brings out lots of beachcombers (Japanese glass fishing floats are highly coveted), clam diggers, anglers, surfers, canoeists, windsurfers and divers, though the water is usually too cold to venture in without a wet suit, and rip currents and rogue lumps of driftwood crashed around by the waves can make swimming dangerous. Surf guards patrol the Long Beach day-use area in July and August. And finally, try to resist the temptation to pick up shells as souvenirs – it's against park regulations.

Beaches near Long Beach

As this is a national park, some of Long Beach and its flanking stretches of coastline have been very slightly tamed for human consumption, but in a most discreet and tasteful manner. The best way to get a taste of the area is to walk the beaches or forested shorelines themselves – there are plenty of hidden coves – or to follow any of nine very easy and well-maintained **hiking trails** (see box, above). If you're driving or biking along Hwy 4, which backs the beaches all the way, there are distinct areas to look out for. Moving west, the first of these is the five-kilometre **Florencia Beach** (1.5km from the Hwy; access by trails 1, 2, 3 and 5; see p.877), also known as Wreck Beach and formerly the home of hippie beach dwellers in driftwood shacks before the park's formation. This is something of a local favourite, with relatively few people and good rock pools.

Farther along Hwy 4 you come to a turn-off (Long Beach Rd) for the **Wickaninnish Centre** (mid-March to mid-Oct daily 10.30am–6pm; ☏250/726-4701) on a headland at the start of Long Beach, not to be confused with the similarly named well-known hotel and restaurant closer to Tofino (confusingly, the centre also has a restaurant). Wickaninnish was a noted nineteenth-century aboriginal chief, and arbitrator between Europeans and native fur traders. His name left no doubt as to his number-one status, as it means "having no one in front of him in the canoe". The centre is the departure point for several trails (see box p.877), has telescopes for whale-spotting and a variety of films, displays and exhibits relating to the park and ocean. Around 8km beyond the Long Beach Road turn-off is the entrance to the Green Point park **campsite** and farther access to Long Beach, while 4km beyond that lies the turn-off on the right to Tofino's small airstrip. Around here the peninsula narrows, with **Grice Bay** coming close to the road on the right (north side), a shallow inlet known in winter for its countless wildfowl. Beyond the airstrip turn-off comes a trail to Schooner Cove (see box p.877) and 3.5km beyond that a 1.5-kilometre turn-off to Kap'yong, or **Radar Hill** (96m), the panoramic site of a wartime radar station. By now Tofino is getting close, and 4.5km farther on (and a couple of kilometres outside the park boundary) you come to **Cox Bay Beach**, **Chesterman Beach** and **Mackenzie Beach**, all accessed from Hwy 4. Cox and Chesterman are known for their breakers; Mackenzie for its relative warmth if you want to chance a dip.

Practicalities

Long Beach's **Pacific Rim National Park Information Centre** is just off Hwy 4, 3km north of the T-junction for Tofino and Ucluelet. It provides a wealth of material on all aspects of the park, and in summer staff offer guided walks and interpretive programmes (daily mid-March to mid-June 10.30am–6pm; mid-June–Aug 8am–8pm; Sept to mid-Oct 10am–6pm; ☏250/726-4212, ⓦwww.parkscanada.gc.ca). For year-round information, call the Park Administration Office (☏250/726-7721). For more Long Beach information, viewing decks with telescopes and lots of well-presented displays, head for the **Wickaninnish Centre**, Long Beach Road (mid-March to early Oct daily 10.30am–6pm; ☏250/726-4701).

There is one park **campsite**, the *Green Point*, set on a lovely bluff overlooking the beach ($20 for the 94 drive-in sites; washrooms but no showers; 20

primitive walk-in sites $14). However, it's likely to be full every day in July and August, and it's first-come, first-served for the walk-in sites (reservations are taken up to three months in advance for the drive-in sites), so you may have to turn up for several days before getting a spot. There's usually a waiting-list system, however, whereby you're given a number and instructions as to when you should be able to return. The nearest commercial sites and conventional accommodation are in Tofino and Ucluelet.

Ucluelet

UCLUELET, 8km south of the main Hwy 4 Port Alberni junction, means "People of the Sheltered Bay", from the aboriginal word *ucluth* – "wind blowing in from the bay". It was named by the Nuu-chah-nulth, who lived here for centuries before the arrival of whites who came to exploit some of the world's richest fishing grounds immediately offshore. Today the port is still the third largest in BC by volume of fish landed, a trade that gives the town a slightly dispersed appearance and an industrial fringe – mainly lumber and canning concerns – and makes it a less appealing, if nonetheless popular base for anglers, whale-watchers, water-sports enthusiasts and tourists headed for Long Beach to the north.

If you want a breath of air in town, the nearest trails are at **Terrace Beach**, just east of the town off Peninsula Road before the lighthouse. A longer and more coherent trail, the **Wild Pacific Trail**, opened in 1999, though then it consisted of just 2.7km of path. However, the track is planned in seven phases, more of which are being completed annually. Currently, phases three and four have been accomplished, running along the rugged cliffs and shoreline northwest of the town. When the track is finished it will stretch 14km and link with Halfmoon Bay near Florencia Bay and Long Beach in the national park. The trail starts at the end of Coast Guard Rd, passing the nearby Amphirite Point Lighthouse (great views of the ocean and perfect for storm-watching) and the He-Tin-Kis Park, where a boardwalk enables you to complete this first section as a loop. Other completed phases have pushed the track from Big Beach Park to the bike path just outside Ucluelet itself.

Buses and **boats** call at Ucluelet from Port Alberni and Tofino – a local transit bus generally makes the road trip twice a day en route to and from Tofino and/or Port Alberni, with one Laidlaw connection daily from Port Alberni to Nanaimo and Victoria. Boats from Port Alberni usually dock here three days a week (see p.868). There's plenty of accommodation (though less than Tofino), much of it spread on or just off Peninsula Road, the main approach to and through town from Hwy 4 (see below). A car or bike is useful here, as there's relatively little in the small central area, though location isn't vital unless you want to be near the sea. For full details, plus information on the many whale-watching, fishing and other tours, visit the **infocentre** at the main junction of Hwy 4 (mid-May to early Sept daily 10am–6pm; ☎250/726-7289, ⓦ www.ucluinfo.com).

Practicalities

The most unusual **hotel** in town is the popular *Canadian Princess Resort* (☎250/726-7771 or 1-800/663-7090, ⓦ www.canadianprincess.com; ❺–❽; March–Sept) at 1943 Peninsula Road just west of the centre, a hotel with on-shore rooms or good-value one- to six-berth cabins (the smallest rooms share bathrooms) in a 175-metre 932 west-coast steamer moored in the harbour. You can also book upmarket whale-watching and fishing trips here in big, comfortable cabin cruisers and it has a restaurant and bar open to nonresidents. The two key inexpensive central choices are the *Pacific Rim Motel*, 1755 Peninsula Rd (☎250/726-7728, @dcorlazz@island.net; ❹), a place between the harbour and small centre near the corner of Bay Street, and the *Peninsula Motor Inn*, a short way east across the road at 1648 Peninsula Rd (☎250/726-7751 or 1-888/368-5593; ❹). Also convenient is the *Island West Fishing Resort* overlooking the boat basin and marina at 160 Hemlock St (☎250/726-4624, @www.islandwestresort.com; ❹); it has a pub on site for drinks and food and also organizes fishing charters and tours. Moving east away from the centre to prettier outskirts try the *Little Beach Resort*, 1187 Peninsula Rd (☎250/726-4202, @littlebeachresort@telus.net; ❸–❻), with quiet self-contained one- and two-bedroom suites with kitchenettes and just a few steps from Little Beach with great views to the south. Right at the end of Peninsula Road up by the lighthouse are two good **B&B** options: *Spring Cove B&B*, 963 Peninsula Rd (☎250/726-2955, @www.springbeach.com; ❹–❼), a quiet oceanfront place with three rooms at varying prices (shared bathroom), and *Ocean's Edge B&B*, 855 Barkley Crescent (☎250/726-7099, @www.oceansedge.bc.ca; ❺), a three-room place in old-growth forest with views and private entrance and bathroom.

The **public campsite** (☎250/726-4355, @www.islandwestresort.com; $18–30; April–Oct) overlooks the harbour at 260 Seaplane Base Rd (first right off Peninsula Rd after the *Canadian Princess*) to the west of the centre and has washroom and shower facilities. The central *Island West Fishing Resort* (see above) also has an RV campsite. It is also the base for a wide range of tour and charter operators.

Seafood here is as fresh as it comes, and is best sampled at *Smiley's* just a little west from the *Canadian Princess* at 1992 Peninsula Rd (☎250/726-4213): a no-frills, no-decor diner popular with locals (eat in or take out), and to work off the meal there's five-pin bowling and billiards here as well. For coffee and snacks head for *Blueberries Café* (☎250/726-7707) on the strip in town at 1627 Peninsula Rd. It also serves breakfast, lunch and dinner, is licensed, and has an outdoor patio with sea views. Other popular spots are the pub-restaurant at the *Canadian Princess* and the *Peninsula Restaurant* (☎250/726-7751) by the *Peninsula Motor Inn* (see above) for inexpensive Chinese and Canadian food.

Many companies are on hand to offer whale-watching, fishing and sightseeing **tours**. The longest-established outfit in the region is here, Subtidal Adventures, 1950 Peninsula Rd at the corner of Norah Road (☎250/726-7336). It runs all the usual boat trips in zodiacs or a ten-metre former coastguard rescue vessel, and do a nature tour to the Broken Group Islands with a beach stop.

The Broken Group Islands

The only way for the ordinary traveller to approach these hundred or so islands, speckled across Barkley Sound between Ucluelet and Bamfield, is by sea plane, chartered boat or boat tours from Port Alberni or Ucluelet (see p.879 and below); boats dock at Sechart, where you can stay at the former whaling station (see p.881). Immensely wild and beautiful, the islands have the reputation for tremendous wildlife (seals, sea lions and whales especially), the best **canoeing** in North America, and some of the continent's finest **scuba diving**. You can hire canoes and gear – contact the *Lady Rose* office in Port Alberni or Sea Kayaking at 320 Main St, Tofino (☎250/725-4222), and then take them on board the *Lady Rose* to be dropped off en route (check current arrangements). You need to know what you're doing, however, as there's plenty of

Nuu-chah-nulth whale hunts

All the peoples of the Northwest coast are famed for their skilfully constructed canoes, but only the **Nuu-chah-nulth** – whose name translates roughly as "all along the mountains" – used these fragile cedar crafts to pursue whales, an activity that was accompanied by elaborate ritual. Before embarking on a whaling expedition the whalers not only to be trained in the art of capturing these mighty animals but also to be purified through a rigorous programme of fasting, sexual abstinence and bathing. Whalers also visited forest shrines made up of a whale image surrounded by human skulls or corpses and carved wooden representations of deceased whalers – the dead were thought to aid the novice in his task and to bring about the beaching of dead whales near the village.

When the whaler was on the chase, his wife would lie motionless in her bed; it was thought that the whale would become equally docile. His crew propelled the canoe in total silence until the moment of the harpooning, whereupon they frantically back-paddled to escape the animal's violent death throes as it attempted to dive, only to be thwarted by a long line of floats made from inflated sea-lion skins. After exhausting itself, the floating whale was finally killed and boated back to the village, where its meat would be eaten and its blubber processed for its highly prized oil.

---

dangerous water and you should pick up the relevant marine chart (*Canadian Hydrographic Service Chart: Broken Group* 3670), available locally or from the CHS in Sidney (☎250/363-6358). Divers can choose from among fifty shipwrecks claimed by the reefs, rough waters and heavy fogs that beset the aptly named islands. Note that the sheer number of people now visiting the islands, and the state in which they leave some of the campsites, official and otherwise, means that measures are being considered to introduce a quota system: contact the park information centre for latest details.

The *Sechart Whaling Station Lodge* (book by calling ☎250/723-8313 or 1-800/663-7192; ❺) is a potentially magical base for exploring and the only place to **stay** if you're not wilderness camping on the archipelago. Access is via the MV *Lady Rose*, which docks nearby (see p.868 for detailed schedule to the islands). Seven rough **campsites** also serve the group, but water is hard to come by; pick up the park leaflet on camping and freshwater locations.

Bamfield

BAMFIELD (pop. 256) is a quaint spot, half-raised above the ocean on a wooden boardwalk, accessible by unpaved road from Port Alberni 102km to the north, by boat – the MV *Lady Rose* – or gravel road from Lake Cowichan 113km to the east. Shuttle **buses** run along the Port Alberni road route if you're without transport and don't want to take the boat: for details, see the "West Coast Trail" box, p.884 and the box feature on p.885. The village is best known as the northern starting point of this trail (the trailhead is 5km away at Pachena Bay), but its population jumps to well over 2000 in the summer with the arrival of divers, canoeists, kayakers and fishermen, the last attracted by its suitability as a base for salmon fishing in the waters of Alberni Inlet and Barkley Sound. Plenty of services have sprung up in the more downbeat part of the village away from the boardwalk to meet visitors' demands, with lots of tours, fishing charters, stores and galleries, but only relatively limited accommodation (see p.882).

Bamfield began life, like so many communities in Canada, as a fur-trading and fishing settlement. The Pacific Cable Board then chose it as the eastern

7

SOUTHERN BRITISH COLUMBIA | Pacific Rim National Park

terminus for its trans-Pacific cable, one of the great communication break-throughs of the late 19th century. The Bamfield cable station opened in 1902, the year in which a 6000-kilometre cable was laid to Fanning Island, a tiny atoll in the mid-Pacific, which was linked in turn to Fiji, New Zealand and Australia.

Despite the influx the village retains its charm, with the boardwalk accessing one side of Bamfield Inlet (the open sea, the other), so that the bay below the boardwalk is a constant hum of activity as boats ply across the water. Trails lead down from the boardwalk to a series of nice small beaches. The village is a good place to join in the activities, bird-watch, walk, beachcomb, sit in cafés or simply relax in a quiet corner with a book. For a short stroll, wander to **Brady's Beach** or the Cape Beale Lighthouse and Keeha and Tapaltos beaches some way beyond. And if you just want to tackle the stage to the trailhead of the West Coast Trail and return to Bamfield in a day, you can walk the 10km (round trip) to the **Pachena Lighthouse**, starting from the Ross Bible Camp on the Ohiaht First Nation campsite at Pachena Beach. After that, the route becomes the real thing.

Information and accommodation

Bamfield's **infocentre** booth is in Centennial Park (℡250/728-3006, ⓦwww.bamfieldcommunity.com & ⓦwww.bamfieldchamber.com), but is open daily (9am–7/8pm) only in July and August. The village has only limited and mainly expensive **accommodation**. If you think you'll need a bed, definitely make reservations, especially at the small *Seabeam Fishing Resort and Campground* overlooking Grappler Inlet, which runs as a campsite and a small hostel-like hotel with eight rooms (℡250/728-3286; ❶, tent and RV sites $18–20; May–Oct) and phone for directions or for a taxi pick-up. The setting is tranquil, and the resort has a small kitchen, common room with open fire and sixteen beds arranged as one-, two- or three-bed dorms. Price is $30 per person. Caravans for rent nightly are also available from $40.

Otherwise try the *Bamfield Inn*, Customs House Lane, a **lodge** built in 1923 overlooking Bamfield Harbour, Barkley Sound and the islands (℡250/728-3354; ❻; Feb–Oct): annex rooms are available at a slightly lower price. The modest *McKay Bay Lodge* (℡250/728-3323; ❹; May–Oct) also overlooks the harbour and is good for families and fishing enthusiasts. The biggest place locally is the *Bamfield Trails Motel* overlooking Bamfield Inlet at Frigate Road (℡250/728-3231 or 728-3215; ❺). Another option is the excellent *Woods End Landing Cottages*, 168 Wild Duck Rd, which has six secluded and high-quality self-contained log cottages sleeping up to four people on a two-acre waterfront site with great opportunities for outdoor activities, bird-watching, scuba diving and kayaking (℡250/728-3383; ❼). Similar but more expensive are the central and waterfront *Mills Landing Cottages*, 295 Boardwalk (℡250/728-2300, ⓦwww.woodsend.travel.bc.ca; ❼) with one- and two-bed cottages. Less expensive is the five-room *Imperial Eagle Lodge*, 168 Wild Duck Rd (℡250/728-3430, ⓦwww.imperialeaglelodge.com; ❺), which has a spectacular garden setting and fine harbour views plus hiking, fishing and other outdoor activities; breakfast is included in the room price.

B&B options open and close each year – currently there are four: first choices for location and pretty setting are *Marie's*, 468 Pachena Rd (℡250/728-3091 or 728-2000; ❹; no credit cards), just a stroll from the centre, and *West Coast Magic*, 286 Brady's Beach Trail (℡250/728-3132, ⓦwww.westcoastmagic.com; ❺), a 15-minute walk from the village in the rainforest on a bluff overlooking the ocean and Brady's Beach.

If you're **camping**, try the Ohiaht First Nation Pachena Bay campsite (℡250/728-1287, ℮pachena@island.net; call for reservations, which are essential, and for latest prices) at Pachena Beach. You can also camp at Centennial Park (℡250/728-3006) and at the *Seabeam Fishing Resort* (℡250/728-3286, ℮seabeamcanada@hotmail.com; $18–20; May–Sept), just on the edge of Bamfield on Tower Rd.

Northern Vancouver Island

It's a moot point where the **north of Vancouver Island** starts, but if you're travelling on Hwy 19 the landscape's sudden lurch into more unspoilt wilderness after Qualicum Beach makes as good a watershed as any. The scenery north of Qualicum Beach is uneventful but restful on the eye, and graced with ever-improving views of the mainland. Along Hwy 19 is the hamlet of Buckley Bay, which consists of little more than a ferry terminal to **Denman** and **Hornby islands** (16 sailings daily; 10min; foot passengers $5/$4.75 return; a car $12.25/$10.50 return).

Few of the towns along Hwy 19 amount to much, and you could bus, drive or hitch the length of Vancouver Island to Port Hardy and take the **Inside Passage** ferry up to Prince Rupert – the obvious and most tantalizing itinerary – without missing a lot. Alternatively, you could follow the main highway only as far as **Courtenay**, and from there catch a ferry across to the mainland. If you have the means, however, try to get into the wild, central interior, much of it contained within **Strathcona Provincial Park**.

Denman and Hornby islands

Denman and **Hornby Islands** are two outposts that have been described, with some justification, as the "undiscovered Gulf Islands". Big-name celebrities have recently bought property here, complementing a population made up of artists, craftspeople and a laid-back (if wary) mishmash of alternative types. Ferries drop you on Denman on the west coast a few moments' walk from Denman Village: to get to Hornby you need to head 11km across Denman on Denman Rd to another terminal at Gravelly Bay, where a fifteen-minute crossing (foot passengers $5/$4.75 return; a car $12.25/$10.50 return) drops you at Hornby's Shingle Spit dock. Most of what happens on Hornby, however, happens at **Tribune Bay** on the far side of the island, 10km away – try hitching a lift from a car coming off the ferry if you're without transport. There's no public transport on either island, so you'll need a car or bike to explore.

Highlights on Denman, the less retrogressive of the islands, are the beaches of the Sandy Island Provincial Marine Park, an island off the northwest tip (take Northwest Rd from the village), and the 800-metre loop trail of Boyle Point Park at the southernmost tip (just beyond the Gravelly Bay ferry terminal) to the Chrome Island Lighthouse. A left turn off Denman Rd about 4km, or a third of the way to the terminal, brings you to Fillongley Provincial Park, where there's a provincial campsite (see below), forest trails and a pretty stretch of coastline.

On sleepy Hornby you want to be looking at the **Helliwell Bay Provincial Park** at the island's southern tip (take Helliwell Rd from Tribune Bay) and its trails, the best a six-kilometre (1hr–1hr 30min) loop to Helliwell Bluffs, offering plenty of opportunities to see eagles, herons, spring wild flowers and lots of aquatic wildlife. Whaling Station Bay and Tribune Bay Provincial Park have

The West Coast Trail

One of North America's classic walks, the **West Coast Trail** starts 5km south of Bamfield (see p.881) and traverses exceptional coastal scenery for 77km to Port Renfrew. It's no stroll, and though becoming very popular – quotas operate to restrict numbers – it still requires experience of longer walks, proper equipment and a fair degree of fitness. Many people, however, do the first easy stage as a day-trip from Bamfield. Reckon on five to eight days for the full trip; carry all your own food, camp where you can, and be prepared for rain, treacherous stretches, thick soaking forest, and almost utter isolation.

As originally conceived, the trail had nothing to do with promoting the great outdoors. Mariners long ago dubbed this area of coastline the "graveyard of the Pacific", and when the SS *Valencia* went down with all hands here in 1906 the government was persuaded that constructing a trail would at least give stranded sailors a chance to walk to safety along the coast (trying to penetrate the interior's rainforest was out of the question). The path followed a basic telegraph route that linked Victoria with outlying towns and lighthouses, and was kept open by linesmen and lighthouse keepers until the 1960s, when it fell into disrepair. Early backpackers reblazed the old trail; many thousands now make the trip annually, and the numbers, so far as quotas allow, are rising (see below). The trail passes through the land of the Pacheenaht First Nation near Port Renfrew, passing through Ditidaht First Nation country before ending at Bamfield in the traditional territory of the Ohiaht First Nation. Wardens from each of these tribes work in association with Parks Canada to oversee the trail's management and the care of traditional native villages and fishing areas.

Weather is a key factor in planning any trip; the trail is really only passable between June and September (July is the driest month), which is also the only period when it's patrolled by wardens and the only time locals are on hand to ferry you (for a fee) across some of the wider rivers en route. However, you should be prepared for dreadful weather and poor trail conditions at all times. Take cash with you to pay for ferries and nominal fees for camping on native land.

Practicalities

Pre-planning is essential if you wish to walk the trail, as Parks Canada has a **quota system** and reservation–registration–orientation procedure to protect the environment. Numbers are limited to around 8000 a year while the path is open (mid-April/May to end-Sept). A total of sixty people are allowed onto the trail each day: 26 starting at Port Renfrew centre (trailhead is 5km north of the town; trailhead infocentre ☎250/647-5434; daily in season 9am–6pm), 26 at Bamfield-Pachena Bay (trail starts 5km south of Bamfield; infocentre ☎250/728-3234, daily in season 9am–6pm) and eight from Nitinat Village. These are the *only* allowed entrance and exit points from the trail, except in exceptional circumstances.

Note that the quota system does not apply in the shoulder season (May to mid-June & last 2 weeks of Sept), as Parks Canada found the quotas were not being taken up. However, it still makes sense to reserve the necessary West Coast Trail (WTC) Overnight Use Permit – effectively your passport to the trail its ferry crossings – in these periods.

Reservations can be made from April of the year you wish to walk for June departures, May 1 for July departures, June 1 for August departures and July 1 for September walks. The phones start ringing on the first of the month, so move fast. To make bookings, call ☎250/387-1642 or 1-800/435-5622 (Mon–Fri 7am–9pm). Be ready to nominate the location from which you wish to start, the date of departure, two alternative start dates, credit card details and the number in your party. July and August are the most popular months.

It **costs** $25 to make a reservation (payment by Visa or MasterCard). This is non-refundable, though you may change your date of departure if spaces are available on another day. Another $90 per person is payable as a user fee, paid in person at the beginning of the trail. Allow another $14 to pay for each of the two ferry crossings (at Gordon River and Nitinat narrows) along the route (paid at the WCT centres at the orientation sesssion – see below: the WTC Overnight Permit is your receipt for these crossings). The total is $143. Standby hikers pay the same rates minus the booking fee, a total of $118. You must then register in person at the park centre at Bamfield or Port Renfrew between 9am and 12.30pm on the day you have booked to start your walk. (You may want to arrive the night before – if so, be sure to book accommodation in Bamfield if you're starting there.) If you miss this deadline your place is forfeited and will be given to someone on the **waiting list**.

Of the 52 places available each day at Pachena Bay and Gordon river, a minimum of ten (five at each departure point) are available on a first-come, first-served basis. Unless you're very lucky this still doesn't mean you can just turn up and expect to start walking. You must first register in person at either the Port Renfrew or Bamfield centre. Here you'll be given a waiting-list number and told when to come back, which could be in anything between two and ten days.

Finally you must attend compulsory 90-minute **orientation** sessions at the trail-head infocentre, where you will receive your permit and a briefing on conditions, safety issues and so forth. Gordon river sessions are at 9.30am, noon, 1.30pm and 3.30pm; at Pachena Bay they take place at 9.30am, 1.30pm and 3.30pm. Reservations are not required.

Further **information** regarding the trail, path conditions and preplanning can be obtained from the Parks Canada offices near Port Renfrew at the trailhead (☎250/647-5434), or from the infocentres in Tofino, Ucluelet, Long Beach or Port Alberni. Updated details are also given at ⓦ www.parkscanada.gc.ca. An increasing amount of literature and **route guides** are appearing on the trail every year, available directly or by mail order from most BC bookshops (see "Listings" for Vancouver p.828, and Victoria p.847). Two of the best are *The West Coast Trail* by Tim Leaden (Douglas and McIntyre; $12.95) and the more irreverent *Blisters and Bliss: A Trekker's Guide to the West Coast Trail* by Foster, Aiteken and Dewey (B&B Publishing Victoria; $10.95). The recommended **trail map** is the 1:50,000 *West Coast Trail, Port Renfrew–Bamfield*, complete with useful hints for walking the trail, available locally or direct from the Ministry of the Environment, 553 Superior St, Victoria (☎250/387-1441).

Access to and from the trailheads is also an important consideration. Several small shuttle-bus companies have sprung up to run people to the trailheads, mostly from Victoria to Bamfield via Nanaimo, not all of which are likely to survive (see box feature on p.855 or consult the Victoria infocentre for latest updates). For the northern trailhead at Bamfield, the most exhilarating and reliable access is via the MV *Lady Rose* or other boats from Port Alberni (see p.868 for full details). Otherwise the West Coast Trail Express, 3954 Bow Rd, Victoria (May to early Oct; ☎250/477-8700) runs a daily shuttle bus in each direction between Victoria and Pachena Bay/Bamfield via Duncan, Nanaimo; to Port Renfrew and back from Victoria; and between Bamfield and Port Renfrew (see p.855 for prices and more details). Pick-ups are possible from these points, but reservations are essential to secure a seat from any departure point. It also has a daily service to Port Renfrew. Western Bus Lines, 4521 10th Ave, Port Alberni (☎250/723-3341), also runs a service on Monday and Friday along the 100-kilometre gravel road from Port Alberni to Bamfield.

SOUTHERN BRITISH COLUMBIA | Northern Vancouver Island

very good beaches (and there's a nudist beach at Little Tribune Bay just to the south of the latter), with a campsite (see below) at Tribune Bay.

Practicalities

Accommodation is in short supply on both islands, and it's virtually essential in summer to have prebooked rooms. On Denman the main options are the *Sea Canary Bed & Breakfast*, 3305 Kirk Rd (☎250/335-2949; ❺), close to the ferry terminal (turn left on Northwest Rd then left again on Kirk) with three **guestrooms**, and the *Hawthorn House Bed and Breakfast*, 3375 Kirk Rd (☎250/335-0905; ❹), a restored 1904 heritage building also with three rooms. There's a small (ten-site), rural provincial park **campsite** at Fillongley Provincial Park, close to old-growth forest and pebbly beach 4km across the island from the ferry on the east shore facing the Lambert Channel (summer $17, winter $9). Other B&Bs come and go: try ⓦwww.denmanisland.com for new arrivals.

Hornby has more **rooms** and **campsites**: *Sea Breeze Lodge*, Big Tree 3–2, Fowler Rd (☎250/335-2321, ⓦwww.seabreezelodge.com; ❺), with fifteen waterfront cottages with sea views; *Hornby Island Resort*, Shingle Spit Road (☎250/335-0136; ❸; tents $19), with four waterfront cabins and nine camp sites, tennis court, boat rental, pub, waterfront restaurant – a good place to **eat** – and sandy beach; *Days Gone By* at Bradsdadsland Campsite, 1980 Shingle Spit Rd (☎250/335-0757, ⓦwww.daysgoneby.org; tents $23–36; May–Oct), 3.3km from the ferry terminal; *Ford's Cove Marina* at Ford's Cove, 12km from the ferry at Government Wharf (☎250/335-2169; cottages generally let weekly, tents $18–24), with six fully equipped cottages, grocery store and camp and RV sites; and the big *Tribune Bay Campsite*, Shields Road (☎250/335-2359, ⓦwww.tribunebay.com; $18–25; April–Oct), a wooded site close to a sandy beach and with hot showers, restaurant and bike rental.

Eating places on Denman are concentrated near the ferry, the best being the *Denman Island Store and Café*. At the ferry dock on Hornby is *The Thatch*, a tourist-oriented restaurant, pub and deli with great views. Across at Tribune Bay the Co-op (no street address) is the hub of island life, with virtually everything you'll need in the way of food and supplies (☎250/335-1121). There's a café, *Jan's*, and a bike-rental outlet here, the Off-Road Bike Shop, which rents bikes in summer. For further **information** on Hornby, including accommodation, call ☎250/335-0506 or visit ⓦwww.hornbyisland.com.

Courtenay

Back along Hwy 19 beyond Buckley Bay is a short stretch of wild, pebbly beach, and then the Comox Valley, open rural country that's not as captivating as the brochures might lead you to expect. Of three settlements here – Comox, Cumberland and **COURTENAY** – only the last is of real interest for all but the most committed Vancouver Island devotee, and only then for its quaint (but tiny) downtown area and as a ferry link to Powell River on the mainland. The terminal is a good twenty minutes' drive from the town down back roads – hitching is almost impossible, so you have to take a taxi or hold out for the #11 bus from 4th Ave and Cliffe. Courtenay is connected to Nanaimo and Victoria by **bus** (4 daily), and is the terminus for **trains** from Victoria (1 daily). If you get stranded in town, there are plenty of **motels** along the strip on the southern approach, close to the black steam engine and **infocentre** at 2040 Cliffe Ave (daily 9am–5pm, longer hours in summer; ☎250/334-3234 or 1-888/357-4471, ⓦwww.comoxvalleychamber.com).

The best **camping** is 20km north of Courtenay at Miracle Beach Provincial Park – a vast, but very popular, tract of sand ($22 in summer, $9 in winter; day-use parking $5).

The **Comox Valley** scores higher inland, on the eastern fringes of Strathcona Provincial Park (see p.889) and the **skiing** areas of Forbidden Plateau and Mount Washington, 25km northwest of Comox. There's plenty of **hiking and mountain biking** in summer, when the Forbidden Plateau lifts operate at weekends. A great day-hike on Mount Washington is the five-hour walk on well-marked trails from the ski area across Paradise Meadows to Moat Lake or Circlet Lake. For details of tougher walks (Battleship Lake, Lady Lake), ask at the infocentre. Access to the trailheads is by minor road from Courtenay.

Campbell River

Of the hundred or so Canadian towns that claim to be "Salmon Capital of the World", **CAMPBELL RIVER**, 46km north of Courtenay, is probably the one that comes closest to justifying the boast. Fish and fishing dominate the place to a ludicrous degree, and you'll soon be heartily sick of pictures of grinning anglers holding impossibly huge chinook salmon. Massive shoals of these monsters are forced into the three-kilometre channel between the town and the mainland, making the job of catching them little more than a formality. The town grew to accommodate fishermen from the outset, centred on a hotel built in 1904 after word spread of the colossal fish that local Cape Mudge natives were able to pluck from the sea. Today about sixty percent of all visitors come to dangle a line in the water. Others come for the scuba diving, while for the casual visitor the place serves as the main road access to the wilds of Strathcona Provincial Park or an overnight stop en route for the morning departures of the MV *Uchuck III* from Gold River (see p.890).

If you want to **fish**, hundreds of shops and guides are on hand to help out and hire equipment. It'll cost about $25 a day for the full kit, and about $60 and upwards for a morning's guidance. Huge numbers of people, however, fish ($2 plus licence) from the 182-metre **Discovery Pier**, Canada's first saltwater fishing pier. If you merely want to know something about salmon before they end up on a plate, drop in on the **Quinsam Salmon Hatchery**, 5km west of town on the road to Gold River (daily 8am–4pm).

Campbell River's well-stocked **infocentre** is at 1235 Shopper's Row (daily 9am–6pm; ☎250/287-4636, ⓦwww.campbellriverchamber.ca). Four Laidlaw **buses** run daily to Victoria, but there's only one, occasionally two, a day north to Port Hardy and towns en route. Airlines big and small also **fly** here (see Vancouver "Listings" on p.828 for details). The **bus terminal** is on the corner of Cedar and 13th near the Royal Bank (☎250/287-7151). **Accommodation** is no problem, with numerous motels, Campbell River being a resort first and foremost: try the *Super 8 Motel*, 340 S Island Hwy, on the main road south of town (☎250/286-6622 or 1-800/800-8000, ⓦwww.super8.com; ❹), or the carving-stuffed *Campbell River Lodge and Fishing Resort,* a kilometre north of the town centre at 1760 N Island Hwy (☎250/287-7446 or 1-800/663-7212, ⓦwww.campbellriverinns.com; ❹). You won't be able to escape the fishing clutter common to all hotels unless you head for a **B&B**. Contact the infocentre for listings, or try *Pier House B&B*, 670 Island Hwy (☎250/287-2943, ⓔpierhse@island.net; ❹), a three-room 1920s antique-filled heritage home in downtown right by the fishing pier. The place to **camp** locally lies 5km west of town at the *Parkside Campground*, 6301 Gold River Hwy (☎250/830-1428; $16–22; May–Oct).

Cheap **places to eat** abound, mainly of the fast-food variety, and in the pricier restaurants there's no prize for spotting the main culinary emphasis.

Quadra Island

Quadra Island and its fine beaches and museum are fifteen minutes away from Campbell River and make a nice respite from the fish, though the famous fishing lodge here has been host to such big-name fisherfolk over the years as John Wayne, Kevin Costner and Julie Andrews. Ferries run roughly hourly from the well-signed terminal out of town ($4.50 return for foot passengers, $11.25 return for a car). The main excuse for the crossing is the **Kwagiulth Museum and Cultural Centre**, in Cape Mudge Village south of the terminal near the island's southern tip (take Cape Mudge Rd). The island's other, and main community, Heriot Bay, is on the east coast. The centre is home to one of the country's most noted collections of aboriginal regalia (closed for renovation, due for reopening in 2004; ☎250/285-3733). As elsewhere in Canada, the masks, costumes and ritual objects were confiscated by the government in 1922 in an attempt to stamp out one of the natives' most potent ceremonies, and only came back in the 1980s on condition they would be locked up in a museum. The museum has around three hundred articles, and you should also ask directions to the petroglyphs in the small park across the road.

While on the island you could also laze on its beaches, walk its **trails** – Mortle Lake (5km loop) and Newton Lake from Granite Bay (8km round-trip) – or climb Chinese Mountain (3km round-trip) in its rugged northern reaches for some cracking views. There's swimming in a warm, sheltered bay off a rocky beach at **Rebecca Spit Provincial Park**, a 1.5-kilometre spit near Drew Harbour 8km east of the ferry terminal, but the water's warmer still and a trifle sandier at the more distant **Village Bay Park**. Pick up trail **maps**, information and **bike rentals** at *Island Cycle* (☎250/285-3627, Ⓦwww .kayak-adventures.com) in Heriot Bay at 651 Taku Rd, part of the main centre for tours, hikes, kayaking and other outdoor activities on the island.

Around seven places offer **accommodation**, including the *Heriot Bay Inn & Marina* on Heriot Bay Road (☎250/285-3322, Ⓦwww.heriotbayinn.com; ❹–❻, camping $14–20), which has cottages, camping and RV sites, and the superb *Tsa-Kwa-Luten Lodge*, 1 Lighthouse Rd (☎250/285-2042 or 1-800/665-7745, Ⓦwww.capemudgeresort.bc.ca; ❺), a waterfront lodge by the Cape Mudge Lighthouse. Based on a long house, and with a predominantly aboriginal decorative scheme and design, it was built by local aboriginal people amid forest on high bluffs overlooking Discovery Passage. There is a restaurant, cottage and lodge units, and many facilities including sauna, Jacuzzi, laundry and access to numerous tours and outdoor activities. The island's only official **campsite** is at the *Heriot Bay Inn* (see above).

Cortes Island

If you've taken the trouble to see Quadra Island, then you should push on to the still quieter **Cortes Island** (Ⓦwww.cortesisland.com), 45 minutes from Quadra on a second ferry (5 daily; foot passenger $6/$5.75 return, car $15/$13.25), an island with a deeply indented coastline at the neck of Desolation Sound, among North America's finest sailing and kayaking areas. Life here is very relaxed indeed, with the main community at **Manson's Landing**, 15km from the ferry terminal at Whaletown.

Boating aside, the islands is known for its superlative clams and oysters, exported worldwide, and for one of Canada's leading holistic centres, the Hollyhock Retreat Centre on Highland Road (☎1-800/933-6339,

@www.hollyhock.bc.ca), where you can sign up for all manner of body- and soul-refreshing courses and stay in anything from a tent, dorm or private cottage. Other **accommodation** includes *The Blue Heron B&B* (T250/935-6584; ❸), while you should aim to eat at the *Old Floathouse* (T250/935-6631) at the *Gorge Harbour Marina Resort* (T250/935-6433) on Hunt Road, 5km from the ferry, where you can also stay (❻), camp ($14) and rent boats and scooters. For something less expensive, join the locals on the nice terrace at the *Cortes Café* in Manson's Landing. Cortes Connection (T250/935-6911) offers **taxi** transport Mon–Sat around the island and connections to the bus terminal in Campbell River.

Places to make for around the island include the small **Smelt Bay Provincial Park**, 25km south of the ferry, which has a provincial campsite (summer $14, winter $9) and opportunities to swim, fish, canoe and walk, and the nearly adjacent **Manson's Landing Provincial Park** (good beaches) and **Hague Lake Provincial Park**, signed from Manson's Landing, with several looped trails such as Sutil Point accessible from different points on the road. If you're in a canoe or boat then you can also make for a couple of marine parks (Von Donop and Mansons Landing) and any number of delightful small bays, lagoons and beaches.

Strathcona Provincial Park

Vancouver Island's largest protected area, and the oldest park in British Columbia, **Strathcona Provincial Park** (established in 1911) is one of the few places on the island where the scenery approaches the grandeur of the mainland mountains. The island's highest point, Golden Hinde (2220m) is here, and it's also a place where there's a good chance of seeing rare indigenous wildlife (the Roosevelt elk, marmot and black-tailed deer are the most notable

Hiking in Strathcona

Hiking, it hardly needs saying, is superb in Strathcona, with a jaw-dropping scenic combination of jagged mountains – including Golden Hinde (2220m), the island's highest point – lakes, rivers, waterfalls and all the trees you could possibly want. Seven marked **trails** fan out from the Buttle Lake area, together with six shorter nature walks, most less than 2km long, amongst which the Lady Falls and Lupin Falls trails stand out for their waterfall and forest views (see main text). All the longer trails can be tramped in a day, though the most popular, the **Elk River Trail** (10km), which starts from Drum Lake on Hwy 28, lends itself to an overnight stop. Popular with backpackers because of its gentle grade, the path ends up at Landslide Lake, an idyllic camping spot. The other highly regarded trail is the **Flower Ridge** walk, a steep 14-kilometre round-trip (extendable by 10km) which starts at the southern end of Buttle Lake and involves a very stiff 1250-metre elevation gain. The same lung-busting ascent is called for on the **Crest Mountain Trail** (10km round trip), a trail into high mountain country accessed from Hwy 28 at the park's western edge.

In the Forbidden Plateau area, named after a native legend that claimed evil spirits lay in wait to devour women and children who entered its precincts, the most popular trip is the **Forbidden Plateau Skyride** to the summit of Wood Mountain where there's a two-kilometre trail to a viewpoint over Boston Canyon. Backcountry camping is allowed throughout the park, and the backpacking is great once you've hauled up onto the summit ridges above the tree line. For serious exploration, buy the relevant topographic maps (1:50,000 -92F/11 *Forbidden Plateau* and -92F/12 *Buttle Lake* at MAPS BC, Ministry of Environment and Parks, Parliament Buildings, Victoria.

examples). Only two areas have any sort of facilities for the visitor – **Forbidden Plateau** on the park's eastern side, approached from Courtenay, and the more popular **Buttle Lake** region, accessible from Campbell River via Hwy 28. The rest of the park is unsullied wilderness, but fully open to back-packers and hardier walkers. Be sure to pick up the blue *BC Parks* pamphlet (available from the infocentre at Campbell River and elsewhere): it has a good general map and gives lots of information, such as the comforting fact that there are no grizzly bears in the park.

You'll see numerous pictures of **Della Falls**, around Campbell River, which (at 440m) are Canada's highest (and amongst the world's highest), though unfortunately it'll take a two-day trek and a canoe passage if you're going to see them.

The approach to the park along Hwy 28 is worth taking for the scenery alone; numerous short trails and nature walks are signposted from rest stops, most no more than twenty-minutes' stroll from the car. **Elk Falls Provincial Park**, noted for its gorge and waterfall, is the first stop, ten minutes out of Campbell River. It also has a large provincial park **campsite** (summer $14, winter $9; backcountry camping $5). On the access road and lakeshore proper, good **shorter trails** include the 500-metre stroll to Lupin Falls, an impressive cataract; the Karst Creek Trail (2km loop), which runs through a strange lime-stone landscape of sinkholes and vanishing streams; Bedwell Lake at the lake's southern end, a steep (600-metre ascent) ten-kilometre round-trip trail to the eponymous lake and high meadows (allow 2hr each way); and Upper Myra Falls (3km each way), which climbs from near the end of the road to a view-point over the Myra waterfall.

Fifteen **information** shelters around the lake provide some trail and wildlife information. Buttle Lake has two provincial **campsites** with basic facilities – one alongside the park centre at Buttle Lake, the other at Ralph River (both summer $14, winter $9) on the extreme southern end of Buttle Lake, accessed by the road along the lake's eastern shore. Both have good **swimming** areas nearby. Backcountry camping costs $5. The park's only commercial **accommodation** is provided by the *Strathcona Park Lodge* (☎250/286-3122, ⓦwww.strathcona.bc.ca; ❹–❼), just outside the Buttle Lake entrance, a mix-ture of hotel and outdoor-pursuits centre. You can **rent canoes**, **bikes** and other outdoor equipment, and sign up for any number of organized tours and activities.

Gold River and Tahsis

There's not a lot happening at **GOLD RIVER**, a tiny logging community 89km west of Campbell River – founded in 1965 in the middle of nowhere to service a big pulp mill 12km away at Muchalat Inlet (it closed in 1998). The place only has one hotel and a couple of shops – but the ride over on Hwy 28 is superb, and there's the chance to explore the sublime coastline by boat, the main reason for the settlement's increasing number of visitors. Year-round, the **MV Uchuck III**, a converted World War II US minesweeper, takes mail, cargo and passengers to logging camps and settlements up and down the surround-ing coast on a variety of routes. Like the MV *Lady Rose* out of Port Alberni, what started as a sideline has become far more of a commercial enterprise, with glossy pamphlets and extra summer sailings, though it's none the worse for that – you just have to book ahead to make sure of a place. For information and **reservations**, contact Nootka Sound Service Ltd (☎250/283-2515, ⓦwww.mvuchuck.com).

There are **three basic routes**, all of them offering wonderful windows onto the wilderness and wildlife (whales, bears, bald eagles and more) of the region's inlets, islands and forested mountains. The dock is at the end of Hwy 28, about 15km southwest of Gold River. The **Tahsis Day Trip** ($45) departs at 9am every Tuesday year-round for Tahsis (arriving at 1pm), returning after a one-hour stopover to Gold River at 6pm. The shorter **Nootka Sound Day Trip** ($40) leaves Gold River every Wednesday at 10am July to mid-September only (returning at 4.30pm), with longer stops at Resolution Sound and Kyuquot (the native word for "Friendly Cove"), the latter involving a $9 landing fee, proceeds from which go to the Mowachaht Band for the redevelopment of the aboriginal site. During the ninety-minute halt aboriginal guides offer guided tours around their ancestral home. The previous stop, at Friendly Cove, is equally historic, for it was here that Captain Cook made his first-known landing on the west coast in 1778, from which, among other things, was to spring the important sea-otter fur trade. Whites named the area and people here "Nootka", though locals today say *nootka* was merely a word of warning to Cook and his crew, meaning "circle around" to avoid hitting offshore rocks. If you're equipped with provisions and wish to stay over, there are **cabins** and a **campsite** here, but call first to confirm arrangements (℡250/283-2054). The third trip, the **Kyuquot Adventure** ($195 single, $310 double), is a two-day overnight cruise, departing every Thursday year-round (April–Oct 7am; Nov–March 6am). It takes you much farther north up the coast, returning to Gold River at 4 or 5pm on Friday afternoon; accommodation is included, as is breakfast – though you make it yourself from food supplied – and you can buy Thursday's evening meal on board or onshore at Kyuquot. A 25 percent deposit is required for these trips, refundable in full up until two weeks before departure. People on all trips should bring warm and waterproof clothing. There's a coffee shop on board for drinks and hot snacks. **Kayakers** should note that they can be deposited by lift into the sea at most points en route by prior arrangement.

Boat aside, one of the area's two minor attractions is **Quatsino Cave**, the deepest vertical cave in North America, parts of which are open to the public – for details ask at the infocentre; the other is the **Big Drop**, a stretch of Gold River white water known to kayakers worldwide. The local **infocentre** is at the corner of Hwy 28 and Scout Lake Rd (mid-May to mid-Sept daily 9.30am–4/5pm; ℡250/283-2418 or 283-7500, ⓦwww.village.goldriver.bc .ca). **Accommodation** is in short supply: the only large place is the *Ridgeview Motor Inn,* located in a panoramic spot above the village at 395 Donner Court (℡250/283-2277 or 1-800/989-3393, ⓦwww.ridgeview-inn.com; ④) – but the *Peppercorn Trail Motel and Campground* on Mill Road (℡250/283-2443, ⓦwww.peppercorn.bc.ca) also has ten rooms, as well as a 75-pitch **campsite** ($18–25). There is one **B&B**, the three-room *Shadowlands*, 580 Dogwood Drive (℡250/283-2513, ⓔgravesite@telus.net; ③).

Note that there are also two beautiful roads north from Gold River, both rough, but worth the jolts for the scenery. One provides an alternative approach to **TAHSIS**, another logging community 70km northwest of Gold River, which has one basic **motel** with a restaurant and pub if you need to break your journey; advance summer reservations are needed at the twelve-room *Tahsis Motel*, Head Bay Road (℡250/934-6318, ⓦwww.tahsismotel.com; ③); or try the pair of one-room B&Bs: *Fern's Place B&B*, 379 N Maquinna (℡250/934-7851, ⓔeastcott@cancon.net ③) or the *Mariner Guest House*, 876 S Maquinna (℡250/934-5527, ⓔbajoree@telus.net; ③; May–Oct), a studio cabin with kitchen overlooking Tahsis Inlet. For more background on a lovely part of the coast, with plenty of fishing, boating and hiking opportunities, contact the **infocentre**, a booth on Rugged Mountain Road (late June to early Sept Mon–Sat 10am–4.30pm; ☎250/934-6667) or the Village Office (Mon–Fri 9am–noon & 1–5pm; ☎250/934-6622).

North to Port McNeill and beyond

The main highway north of Campbell River cuts inland and climbs through increasingly rugged and deserted country, particularly after Sayward, the one main community en route. Near Sayward is the marvellously oddball **Valley of a Thousand Faces**: 1400 famous faces painted onto cedar logs, the work of a Dutch artist, and more interesting than it sounds (May–Aug daily 10am–4pm; donation). With a car, you could strike off south from here to **Schoen Lake Provincial Park**, located 12km off Hwy 19 on a rough road south of Woss village and featuring a couple of forest trails and a small, ten-pitch, well-kept campsite ($10). Sayward has one **motel**, the *Fisherboy Park*, 400m off Hwy 19 at 1546 Sayward Rd (☎250/282-3204, ⓦwww.fisherboy-park.com; ❸). **PORT McNEILL**, 180km north of Campbell River and the first real town along Hwy 19, is little more than a motel and logging centre and not somewhere to spend longer than necessary. If you get stuck here, the infocentre's at 351 Shelley Crescent (July–Aug 9am–5pm; rest of year hours variable; ☎250/956-3131, ⓦwww.portmcneill.net).

Telegraph Cove

By contrast, tiny **TELEGRAPH COVE**, 8km south of Port McNeill and reached by a rough side road, is an likeable place, though not quite the best of BC's so-called "boardwalk villages", as its growing popularity, and the fact that it is now pretty much owned by a single company, has given it a slightly artificial and commercialized air that is not evident in somewhere like Bamfield (see p.881). The whole community is raised on wooden stilts over the water, a sight that's made it rather too popular with tourists for its own good. This is not to take away from its role as one of the island's premier **whale-watching** spots, the main attraction here being the pods of orcas (killer whales) that calve locally. Some nineteen of these families live or visit Robson Bight, 20km down the Johnstone Strait, which was established as an ecological reserve in 1982 (the whales like the gravel beaches, where they come to rub). This is the world's most accessible and predictable spot to see the creatures – around a ninety percent chance in season. The best outfit for a trip to see them is founding whale company here, Stubbs Island Charters at the dock at the end of the boardwalk through the old village (☎250/928-3185, 928-3117 or 1-800/665-3066, ⓦwww.stubbs-island.com). The first whale-watching company in BC, it runs up to five three- or five-hour trips daily (June–Oct; from $65), but they're very popular, so call well in advance to be sure of a place.

In summer you can buy food at a café, boardwalk pub and resort (see below), but otherwise the only provision for visitors is an incongruous modern building with shop, ice-cream counter and coffee bar. The only **accommodation** is the large wooded *Telegraph Cove Resorts* (☎250/928-3131 or 1-800/200-4665, ⓦwww.telegraphcoveresort.com; ❻, camping $19–24; May–Oct), a short walk from the village; reservations are essential in summer. It has seventeen rooms and 121 RV/tent sites with showers, laundry, restaurant, boat rentals and access to guides, charters and whale-watching tours. The *Hidden Cove Lodge* (☎250/956-3916, ⓦwww.hiddencovelodge.com; ❺–❼) at Lewis Point, a secluded cove on Johnstone Strait 7km from Telegraph Cove, has eight superb lodge units, but they go very quickly. The big *Alder Bay Campsite* 6km off Hwy 19 en route for Telegraph Cove from Port McNeill provides grassy tent sites with ocean views (℡250/956-4117, ⓦwww.alderbayresort.com; reservations recommended; $17–26; May–Sept).

Alert Bay

The breezy fishing village of **ALERT BAY**, on Cormorant Island, is reached by numerous daily ferries from Port McNeill just 8km away (foot passenger $5.50 return, car $13.75). The fifty-minute crossing in the migrating season provides a good chance of seeing whales en route. Despite the predominance of the non-indigenous industries (mainly fish processing), half the population of the island are aboriginal 'Namgis, and a visit here offers the opportunity to get to grips with something of their history and to meet those who are keeping something of the old traditions alive. Be sure to have prebooked accommodation (see below) before heading here in high season. The **infocentre** (late June–Aug daily 9am–6pm; rest of year Mon–Fri 9am–5pm; ℡250/974-5024, ⓦwwww.alertbay .bc.ca) is at 116 Fir St to your right as you come off the ferry opposite the unmissable purple building. Also off to the right from the terminal are the totems of a 'Namgis Burial Ground; you're asked to view from a respectful distance.

Bear left from the terminal out of the main part of the village to reach the excellent **U'Mista Cultural Centre** on Front Street (mid-May to early Sept daily 9am–5pm; Oct to mid-May Mon–Fri 9am–5pm; $5.35; ℡250/974-5403), a modern building based on old models, which houses a collection of potlatch items and artefacts. It also shows a couple of award-winning films, and you might also come across local kids being taught native languages, songs and dances. More local artefacts are on show in the library and small museum, open most summer afternoons, at 199 Fir St. For years the village also claimed the world's tallest fully carved **totem pole** (other contenders, say knowing villagers, are all pole and no carving), though much to local chagrin Victoria raised a pole in 1994 that the *Guinness Book of Records* has recognized as 2.1m taller. Also worth a look is the wildlife and weird swamp habitat at **Gator Gardens** behind the bay, accessible via several trails and boardwalks.

Most people come over for the day, but **accommodation** options include: the six-room *Orca Inn*, 291 Fir St, ten-minutes' walk from the ferry terminal (℡250/974-5322 or 1-877/974-5322; ❷), with steak and seafood restaurant and café overlooking Broughton Strait and the sea; the *Ocean View Cabins*, 390 Poplar St, 1km from the ferry terminal overlooking Mitchell Bay (℡250/974-5457; ❸); and the 23-site *Alert Bay Camping and Trailer Park* on Alder Road (℡250/974-5213, ⓦwww.alertbay.com; $10–15).

Sointula

SOINTULA village is a wonderful aberration. It's located on Malcolm Island, accessible by ferry en route from Port McNeill to Alert Bay (25min; foot passenger $6/$5.75 return, car $15/$13.25) and directly from Alert Bay (35min; foot passenger $3.50 one-way, car $5.50). The fishing village would be a good place to wander at any time, thanks to its briny maritime appeal, but what gives added lustre is the fact that it contains a tiny fossil Finnish settlement. An early cult community, it was founded with Finnish pioneers as a model co-operative settlement in 1901 by Matti Kurrika, a curious mixture of guru, dramatist and philosopher. In 1905 the experiment collapsed, but 100 Finns from the original settlement stayed on. Their descendants survive to this day, and you'll still hear Finnish being spoken on the streets. You can wander local beaches, explore the island interior by logging road, or spend a few minutes in the **Sointula Finnish Museum**, which is located on 1st Street just to the left after disembarking the ferry; you'll probably need to call someone (℡250/973-6353 or 973-6764) to come and open up and show you around. There are three **B&Bs**: *430-2nd St Bed & Brekky*, 430-2nd St (℡250/973-6345, ℮frhoward@island.net; ❹) – with inevitable Finnish sauna; *Ocean Bliss*, First and Rupert (℡250/973-6121, ⓦwww.oceanbliss.com; ❷); and *Sea 4 Miles*, 2km from the ferry at 145 Kaleva Rd (℡250/973-6486; ❹).

The Inside Passage

One of Canada's great trips, the **Inside Passage** aboard BC Ferries' *Queen of the North*, between Port Hardy and Prince Rupert on the British Columbia mainland, is a cheap way of getting what people on the big cruise ships are getting: 274 nautical miles of mountains, islands, waterfalls, glaciers, sea lions, whales, eagles and some of the grandest coastal scenery on the continent. By linking up with the Greyhound bus network or the VIA Rail terminal at Prince Rupert, it also makes a good leg in any number of convenient itineraries around British Columbia. Some travellers will have come from Washington State, others will want to press on from Prince Rupert to Skagway by boat and then head north into Alaska and the Yukon (see p.981 for details on the Alaska Marine ferries). A lot of people simply treat it as a cruise, and sail north one day and return south to Port Hardy the next. If nothing else, the trip's a good way of meeting fellow travellers and taking a break from the interminable trees of the BC interior.

The boat carries 750 passengers and 160 cars and runs every two days, departing at 7.30am on **odd-numbered days** in August, **even-numbered days** in June, July, September and the first half of October. The journey takes around fifteen hours, arriving in Prince Rupert about 10.30pm, sometimes with a stop at Bella Bella. Be aware that from about October 15 to May 25 the sailings are less frequent in both directions and are predominantly at night (they leave Port Hardy in the late afternoon), which rather defeats the sightseeing object of the trip. On board there are cafeterias, restaurants and a shop (among other services); at the last, pick up the cheap and interesting *BC Ferries Guide to the Inside Passage* for more on the trip.

The cost from mid-June to mid-September (peak) is $106 single for a foot passenger (May & Oct $85/75; Nov–April $56), $218 for a car (May & Oct $154; Nov–April $114); reservations are **essential** throughout the summer season if you're taking a car or want a cabin. Bookings can be made by phone (℡1-888/223-3779 toll-free in BC, ℡250/386-3431 from elsewhere, ⓦwww.bcferries.com), or by post to BC Ferry Corporation, 1112 Fort St, Victoria, BC, V8V 4V2. Include name and address; number in party; length, height and type of car; choice of day-room or cabin; and preferred date of departure and alternatives. Full payment is required up front. **Day cabins** can be reserved by foot passengers, and range from around $24 for two berths with basin, to $45 on the Promenade with two berths, basin and toilet. If you are making the return trip only you can rent **cabins overnight**, saving the hassle of finding accommodation in Port Hardy, but if you do you are obliged to take the cabin for the following day's return trip as well: cabins are not available as an alternative to rooms in town, so don't think you can rent a cabin overnight and then disappear next morning at Prince Rupert. Two-berth overnight cabins range from about $51 with basin only to $120 for shower, basin and toilet. Reports suggest BC Ferries are not happy for passengers to roll out sleeping bags in the lounge area. If you're making a return trip and want to leave your car behind, there are several supervised lock-ups in Port Hardy. You can leave vehicles at the ferry terminal, but there have been incidents of vandalism in recent years so neither BC Ferries nor the Port Hardy infocentre recommend this. Note, again, that it is vital to book accom-

Port Hardy

Dominated by big-time copper mining, a large fishing fleet and the usual logging concerns, **PORT HARDY**, a total of 485km from Victoria and 230km from Campbell River, is best known among travellers as the departure point for ships plying one of the more spectacular stretches of the famous **Inside Passage** to Prince Rupert (and thence to Alaska) and the more

modation at your final destination before starting your trip; both Port Hardy and Prince Rupert hotels are very busy on days when the boat arrives.

The Discovery Coast Passage

The huge success of the Inside Passage sailing amongst visitors led BC Ferries to introduce the **Discovery Coast Passage**, a trip it candidly admits will only pay as a result of tourists. The route offers many of the scenic rewards of the Inside Passage, but over a shorter and more circuitous route between Port Hardy and **Bella Coola**, where you pick up the occasionally steep and tortuous road (Hwy 20) through the Coast Mountains to Williams Lake (see p.911) – it goes nowhere else. En route, the boat, the *Queen of Chilliwack*, stops at Namu, McLoughlin Bay, Shearwater, Klemtu and Ocean Falls (Namu is a request stop and must be booked in advance). If the route takes off as BC Ferries hope, you can expect visitor facilities to mushroom at these places – you can disembark at all of them – but at present the only places to stay overnight are campsites at McLoughlin Bay and a resort, hotels, cabins and B&B at Shearwater. Bella Coola is better equipped, and will probably become more so as the route becomes better known. BC Ferries is offering inclusive ferry and accommodation **packages** – even renting fishing tackle so you can fish over the side – and these too may mature as the service finds its feet.

There are **departures** roughly every couple of days between late May and the end of September, currently leaving at 9.30am on Tues and Thurs and 9.30pm on Sat, Sun and Mon. There's a slight catch, however, for while the early morning departures offer you plenty of scenery, some arrive at McLoughlin Bay at 7.30pm and Bella Coola at 6.30am in the morning, meaning that the very best bit of the trip – along the inlet to Bella Coola – is in the middle of the night. The 9.30am departures are quicker (they only stop once, at Ocean Falls) and make Bella Coola the same day, arriving at 11pm, so the problem is lessened. Alternatively take the 9.30pm departures and wake at McLoughlin Bay at 7.30am with a further daylight trip towards Bella Coola, arriving at 7.30am the next morning – read the timetables carefully. Making the trip southbound from Bella Coola gets round the problem, though there are similar staggered departure and arrival times (services currently leave Mon, Wed and Fri at 7.30 or 8am, arriving Port Hardy 9.30pm on the Mon departure, 7.45am on Wed sailing and 9am on the Fri boat), with overnight and same-day journeys and a variety of stopping points depending on the day you travel. Unlike the Inside Passage, there are **no cabins**: you sleep in aircraft-style reclining seats and – for the time being – sleeping bags seem OK on the floor: check for the latest on freestanding tents on the decks.

Reservations can be made through BC Ferries (see Inside Passage, opposite, for details). **Prices** for a foot passenger are $110 one-way to Bella Coola, $55 to Namu and $70 to all other destinations. If you want to camp or stop over and hop on and off, the boat fares between any two of McLoughlin Bay, Ocean Falls, Klemtu and Namu are $22 and $40 from any of these to Bella Coola. Cars cost $220 from Port Hardy to Bella Coola, $140 to all other destinations ($45 and $80 respectively for the single-leg options). To take a **canoe** or **kayak** costs $40.75 stowage from Port Hardy to Bella Coola, $30.75 to points en route.

recently introduced **Discovery Coast Passage** (see box p.895). If you have time to kill waiting for boats, which leave from Bear Cove 10km away from the town centre, you could drop into the modest and occasionally open **town museum** at 7110 Market St (donation) or visit the **Quatse River Salmon Hatchery** (Mon–Fri 8/9am–4.30pm) on Hardy Bay Road, just off Hwy 19 almost opposite the *Pioneer Inn*.

If possible, though, time your arrival to coincide with one of the Inside Passage **sailings** (see box p.894) that leave every other day in summer and once or twice weekly in low season. **Bus** services aren't really scheduled to do this for you, with a Laidlaw bus generally timetabled to meet each *incoming* sailing from Prince Rupert. A Laidlaw bus (℡250/949-7532 in Port Hardy, ℡250/385-4411 or 388-5248 in Victoria) also leaves Victoria daily (currently 11.45am), sometimes with a change in Nanaimo, arriving at the Port Hardy ferry terminal in the evening (currently 9.50pm) to connect with the ferry next morning; in summer an extra service departs from Victoria on the morning before ferry sailings. You can **fly** from Vancouver International Airport to Port Hardy (the airport is 12km south of the town) with Pacific Coastal Airlines (℡250/273-8666, ⓦwww.pacific-coastal.com) from $148 one-way.

The Port Hardy **ferry terminal** is visible from town but is actually 10km away at Bear Cove, where buses stop before carrying on to terminate opposite the **infocentre**, 7250 Market St (year-round Mon–Fri 9am–5pm; early June to late Sept 8am–8pm; ℡250/949-7622, ⓔchamber@capescott.bc.ca). The infocentre can give you all the details about Port Hardy's tiny but free **museum** (see above) and the immense wilderness of **Cape Scott Provincial Park**, whose interior is accessible only by foot and which is supposed to have some of the most consistently bad weather in the world (and some of the most voracious biting insects). As a short taster you could follow the forty-minute hike from the small campsite and trailhead at San Josef River to some sandy beaches. Increasingly popular, but demanding (allow eight hours plus), is the historic **Cape Scott Trail**, part of a complex web of trails hacked from the forest by early Danish pioneers. Around 28km has been reclaimed from the forest, opening a trail to the cape itself.

If you stay in town overnight, leave plenty of time to reach the ferry terminal – sailings in summer are usually around 7.30am. North Island Transportation provides a shuttle service between the ferry and the town's airport, main hotels and the **bus station** at 7210 Market Street just south of Hastings St and the infocentre, whence it departs ninety minutes before each sailing (℡250/949-6300 for information or to arrange a pick-up from hotel or campsite); otherwise call a **taxi** (℡250/949-8000).

Accommodation and eating

Many travellers to Port Hardy are in RVs, but there's still a huge amount of pressure on hotel **accommodation** in summer, and it's absolutely vital to call ahead if you're not camping or haven't worked your arrival to coincide with one of the ferry sailings. Note that the ferry from Prince Rupert docks around 10.30pm, so you don't want to be hunting out rooms late at night with dozens of others. There are **rooms** out of town at the *Airport Inn*, 4030 Byng Rd (℡250/949-9424 or 1-888-218-2224, ⓦwww.airportinn-porthardy.com; ❺), but you'd be better off in one of the slightly more upmarket central choices like the *North Shore Inn*, 7370 Market St (℡250/949-8500 or 1-877-949-8516; ❹), at the end of Hwy 19, where all units have ocean views, or the *Thunderbird Inn*, 7050 Rupert St and Granville (℡250/949-7767 or 1-877-682-0222, ⓦwww.thunderbirdinn.com❹). The former has nice views of the harbour but sometimes has noisy live music. Five minutes south of town at 4965 Byng Rd, in a park-like setting near the river, is the *Pioneer Inn* (℡250/949-7271 or 1-800/663-8744, ℮pioneer@island.net; ❺), which has rooms and RV sites ($17). Other hotels are the *Glen Lyon Inn* by the marina at 6435 Hardy Bay Rd (℡250/949-7115, ⓦwww.glenlyoninn.com; ❹) and the large forty-room *Quarterdeck Inn*, 6555 Hardy Bay Rd (℡250/902-0455 or 1-877/902-0459, ⓦwww.quarterdeckresort.net), the town's most comfortable hotel; otherwise contact the infocentre for details of the town's five or so B&B options. The *Wildwoods* **campsite** (℡250/949-6753; $7; May–Oct) is a good option, being signed and within walking distance (3km) of the ferry, though it's not too comfy for tenting – or try the *Quatse River Campground* at 5050 Hardy Rd (℡250/949-2395, ℮quatse@island.net; $14–18), with 62 spruce-shaded sites amost opposite the *Pioneer Inn*, 5km from the ferry dock. Or go for the larger 80-site *Sunny Sanctuary Campground* 1km north of Ferry Junction and Hwy 19 by the river and ocean at 8080 Goodspeed Rd (℡250/949-8111, ℮sunnycam @capescott.net; $16–21).

Food here is nothing special, but there's a bevy of budget outlets, so you should be able to fill up for well under $10. Granville and Market streets have the main restaurant concentrations: try the pub-restaurants of the *Glen Lyon* and *Quarterdeck* (see above), both popular, or *Snuggles*, next to the *Pioneer Inn*, which aims at a cosy English pub atmosphere with live music, theatre (Friday nights) and steaks, salads and salmon grilled over an open fire. The cafeteria-coffee shop in the *Pioneer* does filling breakfasts and other snacks.

The Sunshine Coast, Whistler and the Cariboo

Apart from Victoria and the Gulf Islands, two other major excursions from Vancouver are possible, each of which can easily be extended to embrace longer itineraries out of the city. The first, and less enticing, is the 150-kilometre **Sunshine Coast**, the only stretch of accessible coastline on mainland British Columbia, and a possible springboard to Vancouver Island. Ferries depart from Powell River, the coast's largest town, to Comox on Vancouver Island. From here you might explore the north of Vancouver Island, or head west to enjoy the sublime seascapes of the Pacific Rim National Park. Most people on short trips, however, make the run to Powell River and then turn tail for Vancouver – there is no alternative route back to the city and no onward road route after the village of Lund and the end of Hwy 101 beyond Powell River.

The second, and far more tempting, trip is the inland route to **Garibaldi Provincial Park**, which contains by far the best scenery and hiking country within striking distance of Vancouver, and the famous world-class ski resort of **Whistler**. The latter is well worth visiting at any time of the year, with winter an obviously busy time and summer almost equally popular, thanks to the area's many outdoor activities. En route to Whistler you'll pass through **Squamish**, nothing to rave over scenically, but rapidly emerging as one of North America's premier destinations for windsurfing, climbing and – in season – eagle-watching.

Beyond Whistler, roads lead into the **Cariboo** region, a vast and generally uninspiring tract of lakes, pastures and endless forest.

The Sunshine Coast

A mild-weathered stretch of sandy beaches, rugged headlands and quiet lagoons running northwest of Vancouver, the **Sunshine Coast** receives heavy promotion – and heavy tourist traffic as a result – though in truth its reputation is considerably overstated and the scenic rewards are slim compared with the grandeur of the BC interior. Even as a taste of the province's mountain scenery it leaves much to be desired, and the best that can be said of the region is that in summer it offers some of western Canada's best diving, boating and fishing. If you are just coming out for the day, the best parts of the trip are the various **ferry crossings** en route: the first is from Horseshoe Bay at the western extreme of West Vancouver to Langdale and Gibson's Landing, where you pick up Highway 101 for the 79-kilometre run along the coast to Earl's Cove and the beautiful (and slightly longer) crossing to Saltery Bay, where the boat provides views of some fine maritime landscapes. The road then continues 35km to Powell River before coming to an abrupt conclusion 23km later at the village of Lund.

Highway 101

Highway 101 runs almost the length of the coast from Gibsons Landing, often known simply as Gibsons, which is just 5km from the ferry terminal at Langdale for boats coming from **Horseshoe Bay** at the wend of Marine Drive and western edge of West Vancouver. You can reach the ferry terminal here from the city by taking bus #250 or the #257 express westbound from points on West Georgia St downtown. Given that the coast is hardly worth full-scale exploration by car, and that the two ferry crossings provide two of the trip's highlights, you might consider saving the price of a rental and go by **bus**; it's perfectly feasible to get to **Powell River** in a day. Malaspina Coachlines (☎604/485-5030 or 1-888-227-8287) runs two buses daily to Powell River, currently at 8.30am and 6.30pm (5hr; $37.50 one way). Returns leave at 8.30am and 2.30pm. Bus tickets include the price of the ferry crossings en route.

Along Highway 101

Soon reached and well signposted from North Vancouver, **Horseshoe Bay** is the departure point for the first of the Hwy 101 **ferry** crossings, a half-hour to forty-minute passage through the islands of fjord-like Howe Sound. There are regular sailings year-round, and tickets cost $8.25 for adults and $28.75 for cars: bikes cost $2.50; all tickets cost a little less outside the peak late-June to early September peak period. Note that each ticket is valid for one of Horseshoe Bay–Langdale (return), Earl's Cove–Saltery Bay (return) or single journeys on both the Horseshoe Bay–Langdale and Earl's Cove–Saltery Bay crossings. Ferries also ply from here to Nanaimo on Vancouver Island, with hourly sailings in summer and every other hour off-season. Tickets cost $10 per adult and $34.75 for cars (less off season and less for cars year-round outside weekends). For information on either of these services, contact BC Ferries in Vancouver (☎604/669-1211, 250/386-3431 or 1-888-223-3779, ⓦwww .bcferries.com), or pick up a timetable from the Vancouver infocentre.

Gibsons, the terminal on the other side of Howe Sound, is a scrappy place spread widely over a wooded hillside – the nicest area is around the busy marina and public wharf, a better bet if you're pausing than Upper Gibsons a little farther down the highway, which is little more than a busy strip. If you have time to kill, check out the town's two modest museums: the **Sunshine Coast Maritime Museum** (June–Aug Tue–Sat 10.30am–4pm; free) on Molly's Lane and the **Elphinstone Pioneer Museum** (May–Sept Thur–Sat 10.30am–4.30pm; free) at 716 Winn Rd, which contain predictable displays of maritime and frontier memorabilia. For more on the town and details of local trails, beaches and swimming areas, visit the **infocentre** at 1177 Stewart Rd (daily 9am–6pm; ☎604/886-2325, ⓦwww.gibsonschamber.com).

Further west on Hwy 101 is Pender Harbour, a string of small coastal communities of which **Madeira Park** is the most substantial; whales occasionally pass this section of coast – which, sadly, is the source of many of the whales in the world's aquariums – but the main draws are fishing and boating. **Earl's Cove** is nothing but the departure ramp of the second ferry hop – a longer crossing (45min) that again offers fantastic views, including an immense waterfall that drops off a "Lost World"-type plateau into the sea.

From Jervis Bay, the opposite landing stage, it's a couple of kilometres up the road to the best of all the provincial parks in this region, **Saltery Bay Provincial Park**. Everything here is discreetly hidden in the trees between the road and the coast, and the campsite ($12) – beautifully situated – is connected by short trails to a couple of swimming beaches. Further along on the main road, various **campsites** give onto the sea, notably the big *Oceanside Resort Motel* site which also has eleven cabins, 7km short of Powell River, which sits on a superb piece of shoreline (☎604/485-2435 or 1-888/889-2435, ⓦwww.oceansidepark.com; sites $16 per two persons; ❸).

Powell River and beyond

Given its seafront location, **Powell River** has its scenic side, but like many a BC town its unfocused sprawl and nearby sawmill slightly dampen the overall appeal. If you're catching the **ferry** to Courtenay on Vancouver Island (4 daily; 75min), you might not see the town site, as the terminal is 2km to the east at Westview, and some of the **buses** from Vancouver are timed to coincide with the boats; if your bus doesn't connect, you can either walk from the town centre or bus terminal or call a taxi (☎604/483-3666). The local **infocentre** (daily 9am–5pm; ☎604/485-4701 or 1-877/817-8669, ⓦwww .discoverpowellriver.com), which is immediately at the end of the wooden ferry pier at 4690 Marine Ave, can supply a visitors' map showing the many trails leading inland from the coast hereabouts; staff can also advise on boat trips on Powell Lake, immediately inland, and tours to Desolation Sound farther up the coast. The most central of several **campsites** is the 81-site *Willingdon Beach Municipal Campground* on the seafront off Marine Avenue at 6910 Duncan St (☎604/485-2242; $15–20).

The northern end-point of Hwy 101 – which, incidentally, starts in Mexico City, making it one of North America's longest continuous routes – is the hamlet of **Lund**, 28km up the coast from Powell River. **Desolation Sound Marine Provincial Park**, about 10km north of Lund, offers some of Canada's best boating and scuba diving, plus fishing, canoeing and kayaking. There's no road access to the park, but a number of outfitters in Powell River run tours to it and can hire all the equipment you could possibly need – try Westview Live Bait Ltd, 4527 Marine Ave, for **canoes**; Coulter's Diving, 4557 Willingdon Ave, for **scuba gear**; and Spokes, 4710 Marine Drive, for **bicycles**. The more modest **Okeover Provincial Park**, immediately north of Lund, has an unserviced campsite ($14).

The Sea to Sky Highway

A fancy name for Hwy 99 between North Vancouver and Whistler, the **Sea to Sky Highway** has a slightly better reputation than it deserves, mainly because Vancouver's weekend hordes need to reassure themselves of the grandeur of the scenery at their doorstep. It undoubtedly scores in its early coastal stretch, where the road clings perilously to an almost sheer cliff and mountains come dramatically into view on both sides of Howe Sound. Views here are better than along the Sunshine Coast, though plenty of campsites, motels and minor roadside distractions fill the route until the mountains of the Coast Range rear up beyond **Squamish** for the rest of the way to Whistler.

If you've a **car** you're better off driving the highway only as far as **Garibaldi Provincial Park** – the section between Pemberton and Lillooet, the Duffy Lake Road, is very slow-going and often impassable in winter, though the drive is a stunner with wonderful views of lakes and glaciers. Regular buses (see "Perimeter bus" details on p.903) connect Vancouver and Whistler (some continue to Pemberton), which you can easily manage as a day-trip (it's 2hr 30min one-way to Whistler from Vancouver by bus).

Britannia Beach

Road and rail lines meet with some squalor at tiny **Britannia Beach**, 53km from Vancouver, whose **BC Museum of Mining** is the first reason to take time out from admiring the views (early May to early Sept daily 9am–4.30pm; $12.95; ☏604/688-8735, ⓦwww.bcmuseumofmining.org). Centring around what was, in the 1930s, the largest producer of copper in the British Empire – 56 million tons of ore were extracted here before the mine closed in 1974 – the museum is housed in a huge, derelict-looking building on the hillside and is chock-full of hands-on displays, original working machinery, a 235-ton monster mine truck and archive photographs. You can also take guided underground tours (every 30min) around about 350m of the mine's galleries on small electric trains. And if parts of the complex look familiar it's because the mine has been used as a location in *The X-Files* and numerous other films and TV programmes.

Beyond Britannia Beach lie several small coastal reserves, the most striking of which is **Shannon Falls Provincial Park**, 7km beyond Britannia Beach, signed right off the road and worth a stop for its spectacular 335-metre **waterfall**. Six times the height of Niagara, you can see it from the road, but it's only five minutes' walk to the viewing area at the base, where the proximity of the road, plus a campsite and diner, detract a touch.

Squamish

The sea views and coastal drama end 11km beyond Britannia Beach at **SQUAMISH**, whose houses spread out over a flat plain amidst warehouses, logging waste and old machinery. However, if you want to climb, windsurf or mountain bike, there's almost nowhere better in Canada to do so. At a glance, all the town has by way of fame is the vast granite rock overshadowing it, "The Stawamus Chief", which looms into view to the east just beyond Shannon Falls and is claimed to be the world's "second-biggest free-standing rock" (after Gibraltar, apparently). The town rates as one of Canada's top – if not *the* top – spot for **rock climbing**, and the area recently earned provincial park status. Around 200,000 climbers from around the world come here annually, swarming over more than four hundred routes over the 625-metre monolith; the University Wall and its culmination, the Dance Platform, is rated Canada's toughest climb.

The rock is sacred to the local Squamish, whose ancient tribal name – which means "place where the wind blows" – gives a clue as to the town's second big activity: **windsurfing**. There are strong, consistent winds to suit all abilities, but the water is cold, so a wet suit's a good idea (there are rental outlets around town). Most people head for the artificial **Squamish Spit**, a dyke separating the waters of the Howe Sound from the Squamish River, a park area run by the Squamish Windsurfing Society (T604/926-WIND or 892-2235). It's around 3km from town and a small fee is payable to the Society to cover rescue boats, insurance and washroom facilities.

Rounding out Squamish's outdoor activities is the tremendous **mountain-biking** terrain – there are 63 trails in the area ranging from gnarly single-track trails to readily accessible deactivated forestry roads – and the growing trend of **bouldering**, which involves clambering (very slowly and without ropes) over large boulders.

The town has one more unexpected treat, for the Squamish River, and the tiny hamlet of Brackendale in particular (10km to the north on Hwy 99), is – literally – the world's **bald-eagle** capital. In winter around 2000 eagles congregate here, attracted by the migrating salmon. The best place to see them is the so-called Eagle Run just south of the centre of Brackendale, and on the river in the 550-hectare Brackendale Eagles Provincial Park. For more information, and for another good viewing spot, visit the Brackendale Art Gallery on Government Rd north of Depot Rd (T604/898-3333, Wwww.brackendaleartgallery.com), which has become a focus for eagle-watching locally.

For **accommodation** and **rafting trips**, contact the Sunwolf Outdoor Centre (T604/898-1537, Wwww.sunwolf.net). It is signposted off Hwy 99 – take a left onto Squamish Valley Road at the Alice Lake junction 2km past Brackendale, continue for 4km and the centre is on the right. It has ten great three-person **cabins** on the shore of the Cheakamus River for $90; some have kitchens for an extra $10. To see the eagles from a raft costs $89 per person, including light lunch; a raft trip plus cabin accommodation costs $124 per person, assuming two people sharing a cabin.

Practicalities

Most of the relevant parts of the town are concentrated on Cleveland Avenue, off Hwy 99, including the **Greyhound** bus drop and pick-up (6 buses daily to and from Vancouver, 4 to and from Pemberton), **infocentre** (May–Sept daily 9am–5pm; Oct–April Mon–Fri 9am–5pm, Sat & Sun 10am–2pm; T604/892-9244, Wwww.squamishchamber.bc.ca), a big supermarket and the most central **accommodation** if you're not at the hostel (see below): the *August Jack Motor Inn* opposite the infocentre (T604/892-3504; ❸) or cheap thirty-room *Garibaldi Budget Inn*, 38012 3rd Ave (T604/892-5204 or 1-888/313-9299, Emotorinn@shaw.ca; ❷). The superlative *Squamish Hostel* on Buckley Avenue (T604/892-9240 or 1-800/449-8614, Wwww.hostels.com/squamish; ❶) is clean and friendly, with a kitchen, common room and 18 beds including two private rooms. To get here, turn left off Hwy 99 (heading north) onto Cleveland Ave (look for the *McDonald's*) and then right on Buckley at the first set of lights: the hostel is on the right just past Carson St and the high school. Beds are $15 a night (three nights cost $40) and private rooms are $30. In 2004, the owners are set to open a larger sixty-bed hostel nearby at Mamquam Blind Channel on Hwy 99. The best **hotel** accommodation is the *Howe Sound Inn & Brewing Company*, 37801 Cleveland Ave (☎604/892-2603, ⓦwww .howesound.com; ❺), in the centre off Hwy 99 at the end of Cleveland Ave. It has a pub, restaurants, climbing wall, sauna and twenty spacious rooms.

If you're looking into **renting equipment**, Vertical Reality Sports Centre at 38154 2nd Ave (☎604/892-8248) rents climbing shoes ($10 a day) and mountain bikes ($15–40 a day), whilst Slipstream Rock & Ice (☎604/898-4891 or 1-800/616-1325, ⓦwww.slipstreamadventures.com) offers rock- and ice-climbing guiding and instruction. Most of their tours are for two days and start from about $160 and they teach all abilities. For **mountain bike rental**, contact *Tantalus* (☎604/898-2588), by the Greyhound depot at 40446 Government Rd, or *Corsa Cycles* (☎604/892-3331, ⓦwww.corsacycles.com) at Hunter Place; rates for both sart at about $20 for a half-day hire. If you are here to climb, there are several **guides**, available from bookstores in Vancouver (see p.828) as well as the climbing shops in Squamish: Kevin McLane is the author of several books, including *The Climbers' Guide to Squamish* (Elaho, $34.95).

Garibaldi Provincial Park

After about 5km the road north of Squamish enters the classic river, mountain and forest country of the BC interior. The journey thereafter up to Whistler is a joy, with only the march of electricity pylons to take the edge off an idyllic drive.

Unless you're skiing, **Garibaldi Provincial Park** is the main incentive for heading this way. It's a huge and unspoilt area that combines all the usual breathtaking ingredients of lakes, rivers, forests, glaciers and the peaks of the Coast Mountains (Wedge Mountain, at 2891m, is the park's highest point). Four rough roads access the park from points along the highway between Squamish and Whistler, but you'll need transport to reach the trailheads at the end of them. Other than camping, the only accommodation close to the park is at Whistler.

There are five main areas with trails, of which the **Black Tusk/Garibaldi Lake** region is the most popular and probably most beautiful. Further trails fan out from Garibaldi Lake, including one to the huge basalt outcrop of **Black Tusk** (2316m), a rare opportunity to reach an alpine summit without any rock climbing. The other hiking areas from south to north are **Diamond Head**, **Cheakamus Lake**, **Singing Pass** and **Wedgemount Lake**. Outside these small and defined areas, however, the park is untrammelled wilderness. For more **information**, including good advice on trails, visit ⓦwww.garibaldipark .com or pick the dedicated BC Parks pamphlet from infocentres in Vancouver and elsewhere, whose information can also be accessed at ⓦwww.gov.bc .ca/bcparks.

Whistler

WHISTLER, 56km beyond Squamish, is Canada's finest four-season resort, and frequently ranks among most people's world top-five winter ski resorts. It will also be a major venue at the 2010 Winter Olympics. Skiing and snow-boarding are clearly the main activities, but all manner of other winter sports are possible and in summer the lifts keep running to provide supreme highline hiking and other outdoor activities (not to mention North America's finest summer skiing). It is a busy place, be warned – over two million lift tickets are sold here every winter, more than any other North American resort. Fortunately it also has one of the continent's largest ski areas, so the crowds are spread thinly over the resort's 200-plus trails and 12 Alpine bowls.

The resort consists of two adjacent but separate mountains – **Whistler** (2182m) and **Blackcomb** (2284m) – each with their own extensive lift and chair systems, and each covered in a multitude of runs. Both are run by the same company, Intrawest (☎604/932-3434 or 1-800/766-0449), whose excellent website contains full details of virtually all you need to know (⊛www.whistler-blackcomb.com). Both mountains are accessed from a total of five bases, including lift systems to both mountains from the resort's heart, the purpose-built and largely pedestrianized **Whistler Village**, the tight-clustered focus of many hotels, shops, restaurants and aprés-ski activity. Around this core are two other "village" complexes: **Upper Village Blackcomb** about 1km to the northeast and the recently completed Village North about 700m to the north. Around 6km to the south of Whistler Village is **Whistler Creekside** (also with a gondola and lift base), which has typically been a cheaper alternative but is now undergoing a $50 million redevelop-ment that will see its accommodation and local services duplicating those of its famous neighbour.

Arrival, information and accommodation

There are several ways of getting to Whistler. If you're **driving**, allow about two and a bit hours for the 125-kilometre run on the highway – the road was only completed as recently as 1965; before that the area was little visited. Perimeter (☎604/266-5386 or 1-877-317-7788, ⊛www.perimeterbus.com) runs a shut-tle **bus** from Vancouver airport and various Vancouver hotels to Whistler. Reservations are required for the service, with prepayment by credit card and cancellations allowed up to noon one day prior to travel (May–Nov 7 daily, 3 of which are express services and do not stop at Vancouver hotels – there are 8 southbound departures including 3 express runs; Dec–April 11 daily, including 5 express services; 2hr 30min–3hr; $58 plus tax one-way). Note that winter sched-ules can be affected by bad weather on the Sea to Sky highway. Maverick/**Greyhound** (☎604/662-8051 in Vancouver, ☎604/932-5031 in Whistler, or 1-800/661-TRIP from anywhere in North America, ⊛www .greyhound.ca) runs six daily bus services from Vancouver's bus depot (see p.781) to the Village (2hr 30min; $21.50 one-way) via Britannia Beach, Whistler Creek and other stops. In winter (Dec–April) Greyhound's ski express leaves Vancouver at 6.30am and goes nonstop to Whistler arriving at 8.30am. If you are in a hurry, a **helicopter** with Helijet (☎604/273-1414, ⊛www.helijet.com) costs $147 one-way from Vancouver Airport (2 daily; 45min) or the terminal at Coal Harbour in downtown Vancouver (2 daily; 30min).

For **information** on all aspect of Whistler and Blackcomb mountains, including skiing, boarding, ski passes, lift schedules and summer activities, call ☎1-800/766-0449 toll-free in North America or 604/932-3434, or visit the official resort website ⊛www.whistler-blackcomb.com.

WHISTLER

ACCOMMODATION
Fairmont Chateau .... F
Fireside Lodge C
Pan Pacific .... D
Shoestring Lodge .... B
Westin Resort .... E
Whistler HI Hostel .... A

RESTAURANTS & CAFÉS
Amsterdam Café 3
Araxi's 3
Black's 4
Boot Pub 1
Longhorn Saloon 4
Rim Rock Café 2
Trattoria di Umberto 4

Pemberton

Green Lake

Nicklaus N. BLVD

Nicklaus North
Golf Course

Chateau
Whistler
Golf Club

Lost
Lake

Riverside
RV Resort
& Campground

99

MONS RD

GH

FITZSIMMONS RD. N

WESTER RD.

LOST LAKE RD.

EMBASSADOR GREENE RD

S. AMBASSADOR RD.

CHRIS

99

Valley Trail

BALSAM
WAY

EAST ST.

BALSAM WAY

CRABAPPLE DR.

N. ANDREWS ST.

NORTH RANCH RD.

BLACKCOMB WAY

Village North

Greyhound
Bus/Taxi Rank

EAGLE DR.

PAINTED CLIFF RD

Wizard Express

Upper
Village

Magic
Chair

PARK DRIVE

BLACKCOMB WAY

Excalibur
Gondola

BLACKCOMB
MOUNTAIN

GLACIER LN.

BLUEBERRY DRIVE

Whistler
Golf Club

Whistler Village Gondola

Fitzsimmons Express

PANORAMA RIDGE

ST. ANTON WAY

Whistler
Village

WHISTLER MOUNTAIN

99

HILLCREST DR.

LASSERRE DR.

A l t a
L a k e

ALTA LAKE ROAD

Nordic
Estates

NORDIC DRIVE

G

2

IN-LAKE RD.

WHISTLER RD.

Nita
Lake

Train
Station

ALTA LAKE ROAD

i

Creekside Gondola

Whistler
Creekside

GONDOLA WAY

LAKE ROAD

Alpha
Lake

N

0   1 km

Vancouver

If you're staying in or near the Village, then you won't need really transport, but Whistler's **local bus** company, WAVE (℡ 604/932-4040), runs a free shuttle service around Whistler Village, Village North and Upper Village as well as buses to Whistler Creek and other destinations ($1.50 flat fare, five-day pass $5). Buses have racks for skis and bikes. If you need **taxis** to get around locally, try Sea-to-Sky Taxi (℡ 604/932-3333), Whistler Taxi (℡ 604/938-3333) or Airport Limousine Service (℡ 1-800-278-8742 or 604/273-1331).

For recorded **information** on Whistler-Blackcomb call ℡ 1-800/766-0449 (℡ 604/664-5614 from Vancouver or ℡ 604/932-3434 from Whistler, Ⓦ www.whistler-blackcomb.com). Tourism Whistler (℡ 604/932-3928) is another source of information, though it caters towards the top end of the market; it also runs the Whistler Activity and Information Centre, in the green-roofed Conference Centre near the Village Square (daily 9am–5pm; ℡ 604/932-2394 or 1-800/WHISTLER, Ⓦ www.tourismwhistler.com). Whistler Creek is home to the more down-to-earth and friendly **Chamber of Commerce**, 2097 Lake Placid Rd (daily 9am–5pm, longer hours in summer; ℡ 604/932-5528, Ⓦ www.whistlerchamberofcommerce.com). This office can assist with general information, tickets for events and last-minute accommodation. **Information kiosks** open daily 9am to 5pm between May and early September at several points, including the main bus stop and the Village Gate Boulevard at the entrance to Whistler Village.

Accommodation

If you're here in summer and not on a package tour, all local **accommodation** can be booked through Whistler Central Reservations (℡ 604/664-5625 or 1-800/944-7853, Ⓦ www.tourismwhistler.com or Ⓦ www.mywhistler .com). If you're booking for winter, note that reservations should be made well in advance as many hotels have a thirty-day cancellation window and may insist on a minimum of three-days' stay; prices are highest at this time, too.

If you're going to do Whistler in style, the top resort **hotel** is the $75-million *Fairmont Chateau Whistler* on Blackcomb Way (℡ 604/938-8000, Ⓦ www .fairmont.com; ❽). In the same league is the spanking all-suite *Westin Resort & Spa* (℡ 604/905-5000 or 1-888/634-5577, Ⓦ www.westinwhistler.com; ❽) with ski-in, ski-out facilities and the *Pan Pacific Lodge* (℡ 604/905-2999 or 1-888/905-9995, Ⓦ www.panpacific.com; ❽).

At the other end of the scale is the 32-bed **hostel** 7km from the Village right on the shores of Alta Lake at 5678 Alta Lake Rd, one of the nicest hostels in BC (℡ 604/932-5492, Ⓦ www.hihostels.ca; beds for members $19.50, non-members $23.50), a signposted fifty-minute walk from Whistler Creek or ten-minute drive to the village centre; local buses (℡ 604/932-4020) leave the gondola base in the Village four times a day for the hostel (15min; $1.50). As it's popular year-round, reserve ahead. Check-in is between 4 and 10pm.

The *Shoestring Lodge*, with an often-rowdy adjacent pub, is an equally popular alternative. It has private rooms with small bathrooms – aim to be as far from the bar as possible – as well as dorms and is a ten-minute walk north of Whistler Village on Nancy Greene Drive (℡ 604/932-3338). Another reasonable choice is the *Fireside Lodge*, 2117 Nordic Drive (℡ 604/932-4545; ❷) at Nordic Estates, 3km south of the village.

Best of the **campsites** is the *Riverside RV Resort and Campground* (℡ 604/905-5533 or 1-877/905-5533, Ⓦ www.whistlercamping.com), 1.8km north of Whistler Village at 8018 Mons Rd, which has 14 five-person log cabins for $125–205 and 107 RV/tent sites for $25 per two persons in winter, $30 in summer.

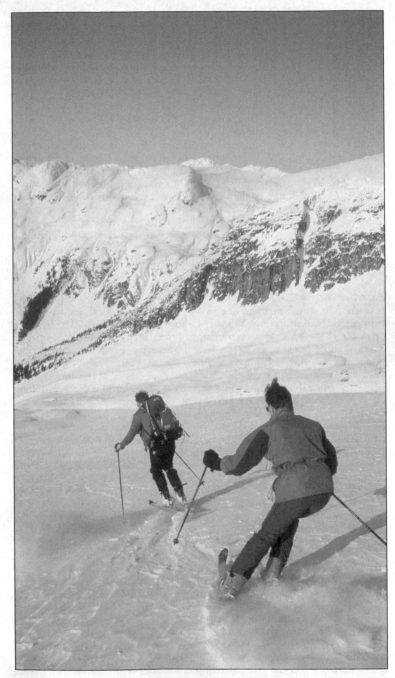

△ Skiers at Whistler

In and around Whistler

WHISTLER VILLAGE is the key to the resort, a newish and rather characterless and pastel-shaded conglomeration of hotels, restaurants, mountain-gear shops and more loud people in fluorescent clothes than are healthy in one place at the same time. Its name is said to derive either from the distinctive shriek of the marmot (a small and rather chubby mammal), or else the sound of the wind whistling through Singing Pass up in the mountains. Whatever its origins, huge amounts of money have been invested in the area since the resort opened in 1980, and the investments have paid off well; the resort's services, lifts and general overall polish are almost faultless, and those of its nearby satellites are not far behind. The resort area averages more than two million visitors a year, and Whistler's challenge is now turning towards being able to rein in development before it spoils the scenery, killing the goose that lay the golden egg.

Winter-sports enthusiasts can argue long and late over the relative merits of **WHISTLER MOUNTAIN** and its rival, Blackcomb Mountain, both accessed from Whistler Village's lifts. Both are great mountains, and both offer top-notch skiing and boarding, as evidenced by world-class events like the Snowboard FIS World Cup in December and the World Ski and Snowboard Festival in April – both held on Whistler. Each mountain has a distinctive character, however, at least for the time being, for major injections of money are on the way to upgrade Whistler Mountain's already impressive facilities. Traditionally Whistler has been seen as the more intimate and homely of the two mountains, somewhere you can ski or board for days on end and never have to retrace your steps. There are over a hundred marked **trails** and seven major bowls. **Lifts** include two high-speed gondolas, six high-speed quads, two triple and one double chair lift, and five surface lifts. Snowboarders are blessed with a half-pipe and park. The total vertical drop is 1530m and the longest run is 11km.

BLACKCOMB MOUNTAIN, the "Mile-High Mountain", is a ski area laden with superlatives: the most modern resort in Canada, North America's finest summer skiing (on Horstman Glacier), the continent's longest unbroken fall-line skiing and the longest *and* second longest lift-serviced vertical falls in North America (1609m and 1530m). Blackcomb is slightly smaller than Whistler, at 3341 acres, but has a similar breakdown of **terrain** (fifteen percent beginner, 55 percent intermediate and thirty percent expert). **Lifts** are one high-speed gondola, six express quads, three triple chair lifts, and seven surface lifts. There are over a hundred marked trails, two glaciers and five bowls along with two half-pipes and a park for snowboarders. Even if you're not skiing, come up here (summer or winter) on the ski lifts to walk, enjoy the **view** from the top of the mountain, or to eat in the restaurants like *Rendezvous* or *Glacier Creek*. If you want some **cross-country skiing** locally, the best spots are 22km of groomed trails around Lost Lake and the *Chateau Whistler* golf course, all easily accessible from Whistler Village.

Eating, drinking and nightlife

When it comes to **food and drink**, Whistler Village and its satellites are loaded with cafés and around a hundred restaurants (none really has an address). These can come and go at an alarming rate, but one top-rated restaurant of long standing is *Araxi's Restaurant and Antipasto Bar* in Village Square (☎604/932-4540), which serves up expensive West Coast-style food and inventive pasta dishes – try the amazing mussels in chilli, vermouth and lemon grass followed

The **skiing and snowboarding season** for Whistler and Blackcomb begins in late November, weather permitting. While the amount of snow varies from year to year, the yearly average is a whopping ten metres of snowfall. Blackcomb closes at the end of April, while Whistler stays open until early June. Then the mountains switch places, as Whistler closes and Blackcomb reopens in early June for glacier skiing and snowboarding (lift passes for summer skiing cost $42 a day for adults), staying open until late July. The lifts are open daily 8.30am–3pm, and until 4pm after January.

Lift tickets give you full use of both Whistler and Blackcomb mountains, and it will take days for even the most advanced skiier or snowboarder to cover all the terrain. Tickets are available from the lift base in Whistler Village, but the queues can be horrendous. Instead, plan ahead and purchase your tickets online from ⓦwww .whistler.net. Your hotel can often set you up with tickets if you pre-book far enough in advance. **Prices** increase in peak season – over Christmas and New Year and from mid-February to mid-March – and lift tickets are subject to a seven-percent tax. Regular/peak season tickets: $65/69 adults. You can save money by purchasing your lift pass before the end of September or, if you plan to ski regularly at Whistler, by purchasing an **Express Card**. These cost $79 for adults, $67 for youths and $39 for seniors, and are valid all season – scan it each time you ski and it automatically charges your credit card. Your first day skiing is free and then you pay a discounted rate of $35–53 depending on the season; call ☎1-800/766-0449 for more details.

Intermediate and expert skiers can join the **free tours** of the mountains that leave at 10.30am and 1pm daily. The Whistler All-Mountain tour departs from the Guest Satisfaction Centre at the top of the Whistler Village gondola. The Blackcomb All-Mountain tour meets at the Mountain Tour Centre, top of the Solar Coaster Express, or at the *Glacier Creek Lodge*. To explore Blackcomb's glaciers join the tour at the *Glacier Creek Lodge*, weather permitting.

For **snow conditions** call ☎604/932-4211 in Whistler or ☎604/687-7507 from Vancouver.

Other activities

Outdoor activities aside, there's not a lot else to do in Whistler save sit in the cafés and watch the world go by. In summer, though, chances are you'll be here to walk or mountain bike. If you're **walking**, remember you can ride the ski lifts up onto both mountains for tremendous views and easy access to high-altitude trails (July to early Sept daily 10am–8pm; early Sept to late Sept daily 10am–5pm; late Sept to mid-Oct Sat & Sun 10am–5pm; adults $23, youth and seniors $19). **Mountain bikers** can also take bikes up and ride down, for an additional $4 charge for the bike. You must have a helmet and the bike undergoes a safety inspection.

If you're going it alone, pick up the duplicated sheet of biking and hiking trails from the infocentres (see p.905), or better yet buy the 1:50,000 *Whistler and Garibaldi Region* map. The two most popular shorter walks are the **Rainbow Falls** and the six-hour **Singing Pass** trails. Other good choices are the four-kilometre trail to Cheakamus Lake or any of the high-alpine hikes accessed from the Upper Gondola station (1837m) on Whistler Mountain or the Seventh Heaven lift on Blackcomb: you can, of course, come here simply for the view. Among the eight walks from Whistler

by a perfect crème brulée for dessert. Equally fine, the *Rim Rock Café & Oyster Bar* at 2117 Whistler Rd (☎604/932-5565) is excellent for seafood. Other more down-to-earth places to try are *Trattoria di Umberto* (☎604/932-5858) in the *Mountainside Lodge*, beside the *Pan Pacific*, for a cosy Italian meal; *Black's Dining Room* (☎604/932-6408) in Mountain Square for pizza and pasta and a snug bar, *Black's Pub*, upstairs; the simple *Amsterdam Café* (☎604/932-8334) for

Mountain gondola station, consider the **Glacier Trail** (2.5km round trip; 85m ascent; 1hr) for views of the snow and ice in Glacier Bowl. Or go for the slightly more challenging **Little Whistler Trail** (3.8km round trip; 265m ascent; 1hr 30min–2hr), which takes you to the summit of Little Whistler Peak (2115m) and gives grand views of Black Tusk in Garibaldi Provincial Park. Remember to time your hike to get back to the gondola station for the last ride down (times vary according to season).

Snowshoe rental and tours are available to get you across some of the safer snow fields in summer. For **snowshoe tours** for novices contact Outdoor Adventures (T 604/932-0647, W www.adventureswhistler.com; from $39 for 90 minutes) or Whistler Cross Country Ski & Hike (T 604/932-7711 or 1-888/771-2382, W www.whistlerhikingcentre.com).

If the high-level hiking seems too daunting (it shouldn't be – the trails are good and lss than 4km, save the Musical Bumps trail at 19km) – then there are plenty of trails (some surfaced) for bikers, walkers and in-line skating around the Village. The **Valley Trail** system starts on the west side of Hwy 99 by the Whistler Park Gold Course and takes you through parks, golf courses and peaceful residential areas; the 30km of trails on and around **Lost Lake**, entered by the northern end of the Day Skier car park at Blackcomb Mountain, wend through cedar forest and past lakes and creeks. The eponymous lake is just over a kilometre from the main trailhead.

There are also numerous operators offering guided walks and bike rides to suit all abilities, as well as **rental outlets** for bikes, blades and other equipment around the Village. **All-Terrain Vehicles (ATVs)** can be rented from Canadian All Terrain Adventures (T 1-877/938-1616, W www.cdn-snowmobile.com) for guided tours that include splurges through mud-pits. If you want to go **riding**, contact Edgewater Outdoor Centre (T 604/932-3389), The Adventure Ranch (T 604/932-5078) or Cougar Mountain (T 604/932-4086).

Between May and September, Whistler River Adventures (T 604/932-3532, W www.whistlerriver.com; from $75 for one-hour cruise to $135 for six-hour trip) has **jet boating** on the Green River to below the Nairn Falls, with a good chance of spotting wildlife such as moose and bears. It also has rafting trips from $65 for two-hour trips and $140 for full-day tours; beginners are taken to the Green River, while experts can plump for the Class-IV thrills of the Elaho or Squamish River rapids.

You can play tennis at several public courts, or ask at the visitor centre for details of hotels which allow drop-in players to use their courts and provide raquet rental (from $10 an hour); or play squash or **swim** at the Meadow Park Sports Centre (T 604/938-7275).

The area has four great **golf** courses, including one designed by Jack Nicklaus. Despite a recent upgrade, the Whistler Golf Club course remains the cheapest course to play at between about $70 and $150 (T 1-800/376-1777 or 604/932-4544), while the others, including Nicklaus North (T 604/938-9898), all cost from about $125 at low season to $205 at peak season in July and August. After any of these activities there are umpteen **spas** for massage, mud baths and treatments that soothe all aches and pains – try Whistler Body Wrap (T 604/932-4710) at next to The Keg in the Village at 210 St Andrew's House or for utter luxury the top-of-the-range spa at the Fairmont Chateau Whistler (T 604/938-2086).

reliable pub food; and *Citta's Bistro* (T 604/932-4177), a modern American-style bistro. At the foot of the Whistler Village Gondola, the *Garibaldi Lift Co Bar & Grill* (T 604/905-2220) has a deck and terrace that's popular with people just off the slopes, and with others who come later for dinner.

Winter or summer Whistler enjoys a lot of **nightlife** and après-ski activity, with visitors being bolstered by the large seasonal workforce – among which a vocal antipodean presence figures large. If you want relative peace and quiet, the key spot is one of the smartish bars in the *Fairmont Chateau Whistler* hotel. If you're just off Whistler Mountain, the après-ski haunt is the sports-crazy *Longhorn Saloon and Grill* (☎604/932-5999) in the Village at the base of the gondolas with the lively beer-heavy *Merlin's* (☎604/938-7700) in the *Blackcomb Lodge* performing the same function for Blackcomb. As evening draws on, make for the *Dubh Linn Gate* Irish pub (☎604/905-4047) at 4320 Sundial Crescent or *Buffalo Bill's Bar & Grill* (☎604/932-6613) across from the Whistler gondola at the *Timberline Lodge*, a 30-something bar-club with comedy nights, hypnosis shows, video screens, a huge dance floor and live music.

A younger set, snowboarding hipsters among them, make for **clubs** in both the Village and North Village. These include *Tommy Africa's*, aka *Tommy's* (☎604/932-6090); the musically adventurous *Maxx Fish* (☎604/932-1904), home to hip-hop and house DJs; and the lively *Moe Joe's* (☎604/935-1152), where locals hang out to catch DJs and live music. Locals tend to make for the *Boot Pub*, away from the centre of things at the *Shoestring Lodge* on Nancy Greene Way; the beer's cheap and there's occasional live music. In Village North, the *Brewhouse Pub & Restaurant* near Blackcomb Way is the drinking and people-watching bar of choice.

North to Lillooet

Hwy 99 funnels down to two slow lanes at **PEMBERTON**, known primarily for its potatoes, of all things, where apartments are now mushrooming in the wake of Whistler's popularity – all the skiing here is via helicopter or hiking. Beyond, you're treated to some wonderfully wild country in which Vancouver and even Whistler seem a long way away. Patches of forest poke through rugged mountainsides and scree slopes, and a succession of glorious lakes culminate in Sefton Lake, whose hydroelectric schemes feed power into the grid as far south as Arizona, accounting for the pylons south of Whistler.

At the lumber town of **LILLOOET**, founded as Mile 0 of the 1858 Cariboo Wagon Road to the goldfields to the north (see below), the railway meets the Fraser River, which marks a turning point in the scenery as denuded crags and hillsides increasingly hint at the *High Noon*-type ranching country to come. In July and August, the rocky banks and bars of the sluggish, mud-coloured river immediately north of town are dotted with vivid orange and blue tarpaulins. These belong to aboriginal Canadians who still come to catch and dry salmon as the fish make their way upriver to spawn. It's one of the few places where this tradition is continued and it is well worth a stop to watch. The town's name, changed from Cayoosh Flat in the 1860s, is a misrendering of Leel-wat, one of the aboriginal peoples who lived to the north. The town boasts a handful of central **hotels and motels** if you need to stay: the best are the *Mile 0 Motel*, 616 Main St (☎604/256-7511 or 1-888/766-4530, ⓦwww.mileo motel.com; ❷), downtown, overlooking the river and mountains (kitchenettes available in some units for self-catering); and the *4 Pines Motel* on the corner of 8th Avenue and Russell Street at 108 8th Ave, also with kitchenettes (☎604/256-4247 or 1-800/753-2576, ⓦwww.4pinesmotel.com; ❺). The **infocentre/museum** is in the old church at 790 Main St (mid-May to June Mon–Sat 11am–34pm; July & Aug daily 9am–5pm; Sept Tues–Sat noon–3pm; Oct Wed–Sat 12.30–2.30pm; ☎604/256-4308, ⓔlillmuseum@lillonet.ca), with displays of local life past and present. The nearest **campsite** is the river-side *Cayoosh Creek* on Hwy 99 within walking distance of downtown

(☎604/256-4180 or 1-877/748-2628, ⓦwww.cayooshcampground.com; $16–21; mid-April to mid-Oct). To **eat**, make for the *Lillooet Inn Restaurant*, 687 Main St (☎604/256-0028).

From Lillooet, Hwy 99 heads east for 50km to Hwy 97; you can then either turn south towards Cache Creek (see p.920), or snake your way up north to the gold fields of the Cariboo.

The Cariboo

The Cariboo is the name given to the broad, rolling ranching country and immense forests of British Columbia's interior plateau, which extend north of Lillooet between the Coast Mountains to the west and Cariboo Mountains to the east. The region contains by far the dullest scenery in the province, and what little interest it offers – aside from fishing and boating on thousands of remote lakes – comes from its **gold-mining** heritage. Initially exploited by fur traders to a small degree, the region was fully opened up following the discovery of gold in 1858 in the lower Fraser Valley. The building of the **Cariboo Wagon Road**, a stagecoach route north out of Lillooet, spread gold fever right up the Fraser watershed as men leapfrogged from creek to creek, culminating in the big finds at Williams Creek in 1861 and Barkerville a year later.

Much of the old Wagon Road is today retraced by lonely **Hwy 97** (the Cariboo Hwy), which runs through hour after hour of straggling pine forests and past the occasional ranch and small, marsh-edged lake – scenery that strikes you as pristine and pastoral for a while but which soon leaves you in a tree-weary stupor. If you're forced to stop over, there are innumerable lodges, ranches and motels on or just off the highway, and you can pick up copious material on the region at the Vancouver tourist office or infocentres en route.

Clinton and Williams Lake

A compact little village surrounded by green pastures and tree-covered hills, **CLINTON** – originally 47 Mile House but renamed after a British duke – marks the beginning of the heart of Cariboo country. The town has a couple of **bed and breakfasts**, a **campsite**, *Clinton Pines Campground*, 1204 Caribbo Ave (☎250/459-0030, ⓔclintonpines@goldcountry.bc.ca; $14–24; May–Sept) and a **motel** – the *Nomad* (☎250/459-2214 or 1-888/776-6623, ⓔnomad @wkpowrerlink.com; ❷). The three tiny settlements beyond Clinton at 70, 100 and 150 Mile House are echoes of the old roadhouses built by men who were paid by the mile to blaze the Cariboo Wagon Road – which is doubtless why 100 Mile House is well short of one hundred miles from the start of the road. 100 Mile House has a year-round **infocentre** at 422 Cariboo Hwy 97 S (May–Sept daily 9am–6pm; Oct–April Mon–Fri 9am–4pm; ☎250/395-5353 or 1-877/511-5353, ⓔvisitors@100milehouse.com) for details of the fishing, riding and other local outdoor pursuits. The main place to **stay** is the big log building (it's actually one of BC's largest log structures) on the main street, the *Cariboo Lodge* (☎250/459-7992 or 1-877/459-7992, ⓦwww.caribool odge.bc.com; ❹). There are also a handful of **motels** in or a few kilometres away from town, the biggest in-town choice being the *Red Coach Inn*, 170 Hwy 97 N (☎250/395-2266 or 1-800/663-8422, ⓔredcoachinn@btinternet.net; ❹). The central *Imperial* is smaller and cheaper (☎250/395-2471; ❷).

WILLIAMS LAKE, 14km north of 150 Mile House and still 238km south of Prince George, is a busy and drab transport centre that huddles in the lee of a vast crag on terraces above the lake of the same name. It has plenty of motels, B&Bs, boat launches and swimming spots south of the town – but it's hardly a place you'd want to spend any time, unless you're dead-beat after driving or around on the first weekend in July for its famous **rodeo**. The year-round **infocentre** is at 1148 Broadway S (May–Sept daily 9am–5pm; Oct–April Mon–Fri 9am–4pm; ℡250/392-5025, ⓦwww.bcadventure.com/wlcc).

Bella Coola

Highway 20 branches west from Williams Lake, a part-paved, part-gravel road that runs 456km to **BELLA COOLA**, a wilderness-enveloped village in a superb setting likely to gain an ever-greater tourist profile in the wake of the recent visitor-oriented ferry service from Port Hardy on Vancouver Island (see p.895). Most of the road ploughs through the interminable forest or opening rancing country of the Cariboo Plateau, but there are services, campsites and the odd hotel at regular intervals and the last very worthwhile 100km or so traverses the high and stunningly spectacular peaks of the Coast Mountains and **Tweedsmuir Provincial Park**. Just outside the park – which at a million hectares is BC's largest – you encounter the notorious "Hill", a hugely winding and precipitous stretch of highway barely tamed by the various upgradings over the years. Until 1953 there was no road link here at all. Instead there was a sixty-kilometre gap in the mountain stretch, a missing link the state refused to bridge. In response the locals of Bella Coola took it upon themselves to build the road on their own, completing their so-called Freedom Road in three years. One of the park's chief sights are the **Hunlen Falls**, 260m of plunging water, though it's struggle to see them – you need to leave the road near Atnarko River (midway through the park) and take the rough road the 13km to the tailhead for the falls and Turner Lake. From here it's another 16km of walking, with an elevation gain of 2000m. This typical of a trail system that is still relatively undeveloped, and there are few day-hikes or easy trails from the highway; an exception is the 8km round trip to a series of pretty lakes from a trailhead 16km west of the Atnarko River campsites (see below).

Bella Coola itself was formerly the domain of the Bella Coola, or Nuxalk, an aboriginal people who prospered thanks to the surfeit of salmon in local rivers and were visited by Alexander Mackenzie as early as 1793. Indeed, Mackenzie's arrival here on July 22 marked the conclusion of his successful attempt to become the first man to cross North America. White visitors nicknamed the settlement the "Friendly Village" after the welcome they received from its inhabitants. In 1869 the Hudson's Bay Company opened a trading post, though permanent while settlement only began in 1894. One house belonging to a company clerk is now all that remains of the post. Besides the small **Bella Coola Museum** in the old schoolhouse and surveyor's cabin (June–Sept Mon–Sat 10am–5pm; $2) and glorious scenery, Bella Coola is hardly stacked with sights. Norwegian settlers, however, perhaps drawn by the fjord-like scenery nearby, were notable early pioneers, and half of today's non-aboriginal inhabitants trace their ancestry to 120 Norwegians led here from Minnesota in 1894 by a pastor determined to found a Utopian society (visit ⓦwww.nordic-folks.com for more background to the story).

Language, heritage and buildings here – notably the square-logged barns – all show a Scandinavian touch. **Hagensborg**, a village with accommodation 18km east of Bella Coola, preserves a particularly strong Nordic flavour. About 10km from the village, roughly midway to Bella Coola, are the **Thorsen Creek Petroglyphs**, a hundred or so rock drawings; the infocentre should be able to fix you up with a guide to explore the site.

Practicalities

No buses serve Bella Coola, and beyond the village there is no onward road route: unless you fly out, you'll have to either head back the way you came or pick up the **Discovery Coast Passage** boats to Port Hardy that stop off at the port. Boats leave three times a week at 7.30am on Wednesdays and 8am on Mondays and Fridays (June to early Sept), arriving in Port Hardy at 9pm that evening on Mondays and or 7.45am or 9am the following morning the other days depending on the number of stops en route (fares are $106.25 per person or $212.50 per car; see box p.895 for full details of the service). If you want to indulge in a plane in or out of town, contact Bella Coola Air (☎250/982-2957) or Pacific Coastal Air (☎250/982-2225) for daily flights to Vancouver and Port Hardy on the northern tip of Vancouver Island. The airport is at Hagensborg.

Bella Coola's **infocentre** is on the Mackenzie Hwy near town (Mon–Fri daily 9.30am–4.30pm; ☎250/799-5638). The ferry service will probably result in the more hotels and restaurants opening: currently **accommodation** is provided by the *Bella Coola Valley Inn* (☎250/799-5316 or 1-888/799-5316, ⓦwww.bellacoolavalleyinn.com; ❸), closest hotel to the ferry terminal, and the *Bella Coola Motel* (☎250/799-5323, ⓔmotel@bellacoolavalley.com; ❸) at the corner of Burke and Clayton – both places are downtown. In Hagensborg there's also the *Bay Motor Hotel* on Hwy 20, 14km east of Bella Coola and 1km from the airport (☎250/982-2212 or 1-888/982-2212, ⓔbellacoolan@aol.com; ❸). For another $10 you can also stay here at *Brockton Place* on Hwy 20 16km east of Bella Coola (☎250/982-2298, ⓔleskoroluk@hotmail.com; ❸) or camp in the heart of the village at *Gnome's Home Campground & RV Park* (☎250/982-2504, ⓦwww.gnomeshome.ca; $15–18); Bella Coola itself currently has no campsite. In Tweedsmuir park there is just one option: the *Tweedsmuir Lodge* (☎250/982-2402, ⓦwww.tweedsmiurlodge.com; ❸), 60km east of Bella Coola on the Atnarko River. It has 17 lodge rooms and chalets, two with kitchenettes. There are also two simple BC provincial **campgrounds** on the north side of the river (May–Oct; $14).

Along Hwy 97: north of Williams Lake

North of Williams Lake on Hwy 97, the **Fraser River** re-enters the scenic picture and, after a dramatic stretch of canyon, reinstates more compelling hills and snatches of river meadows. This also marks the start, however, of some of the most concerted **logging operations** in all British Columbia, presaged by increasing numbers of crude pepper-pot kilns used to burn off waste wood. By **QUESNEL**, home of the "world's largest plywood plant", you're greeted with scenes out of an environmentalist's nightmare: whole mountainsides cleared of trees, hill-sized piles of sawdust, and unbelievably large lumber mills surrounded by stacks of logs and finished timber that stretch literally as far as the eye can see. If you're stuck for accommodation (there are a dozen or so hotels) or tempted by any of the many mill tours, contact the **infocentre** in Le Bourdais Park at 703 Carson Ave (May–Oct daily 8am–6pm; Oct–April Tues–Sat 9am–4pm; ☎250/992-8716 or 1-800/992-4922, ⓦwww.northcariboo.com).

If you're continuing from Quesnel north to Prince George and beyond, turn to Chapter 8, "The North", beginning on p.969.

Barkerville

Most people who take the trouble to drive Hwy 97 detour from Quesnel to **Barkerville Provincial Historic Park**, 90km to the east in the heart of the Cariboo Mountains, the site of the Cariboo's biggest gold strike and an invigorating spot in its own right, providing a much-needed jolt to the senses after the sleepy scenery to the south (June–Sept daily 8am–8pm; $8 entry only, $23.50 for entry, theatre and stagecoach ride). In 1862 a Cornishman named Billy Barker idly staked a claim here and after digging down a metre or so was about to pack up and head north. Urged on by his mates, however, he dug another couple of spadefuls and turned up a cluster of nuggets worth $600,000. Within months Barkerville, as it was later dubbed, had become the largest city in the region, and rode the boom for a decade until the gold finally ran out. Today 125 buildings have been restored and are filled with costumed staff, and the main administrative building has displays on mining methods and the gold rush, together with propaganda on their importance to the province.

If you want to **stay** under cover up here, there are two options: the *St George Hotel* (℡250/994-0008 or 1-888-246-7690, ⓦwww.stgeorgehotel.bc.ca; ❻), a restored 1890s heritage building on the site, or *Kelly House B & B* (℡250/994-3328, ⓔbville@goldcity.net; ❹), also at the heart of Barkerville. In **WELLS**, 8km west of the park, are the *Hubs Motel* (℡250/994-3313; ❷); the *Wells Hotel*, 2341 Pooley St (℡250/994-3427 or 1-800/860-2299, ⓦwww.wellshotel.com; ❹), a restored 1933 heritage country inn with licensed café and breakfast included; and the *White Cap Motor Inn* (℡250/994-3489 or 1-800/377-2028, ⓦwww.whitecapinn.bc.ca; ❸) – the last also has RV and camping spaces for $15. Failing this you can **camp** at the linked 168-pitch *Government Hill*, *Forest Rose* and *Lowhee* campsites at Barkerville Provincial Park adjacent to the old town (reservations possible, see p.777; $14–17; June–Sept). Wells has an **infocentre** 4120 Pooley Street, part of a small museum (daily mid-May–Sept 9am–6/7pm; ℡250/994-3237 or 1-877/451-WELLS, ⓦwww.wellsbc.com).

The BC interior

It says something about the magnificence of British Columbia's **interior** that you can enter it from Vancouver or the Rockies and find a clutch of landscapes every bit as spectacular as those you've just left. Some people will travel inland from Vancouver, others across country from the Rockies or the US. Unfortunately, whatever your approach, both major routes through the region confine you to some of its least interesting areas. The most obvious and quickest line east or west, the **Trans-Canada Hwy**, isn't worth considering in its entirety unless you're keen to cross the region in a hurry: little west of Revelstoke compares to what you might find further north or south. Nor does **Hwy 3**, rumbling along just north of the US border, offer a convincing reason for sticking to it religiously.

The best option would be to take a meandering course towards the outstanding **Kootenay** region in the province's southeastern corner – an idyllic assortment of mountains and lakes and several towns that are fun to stay in – perhaps by way of **the Okanagan**, an almost Californian enclave of orchards, vineyards, warm lakes and resort towns, whose beaches and scorching summers suck in hordes of holidaymakers from all over Canada and the western US. From here you could push north to **Kamloops**, a far from exciting town but transport hub for the region and a jumping-off point for the magnificent **Wells Gray Provincial Park** or the Yukon. The other major option would be to head south to take in the better parts of Hwy 3 west of Osoyoos, also reasonably easily reached directly from Vancouver, and which includes a corner of **desert** and the spectacular ridges of the **Cascades** and **Coast Mountains**.

Vancouver to Kamloops

Two major routes connect **Vancouver and Kamloops**, the latter an unexceptional town in an extraordinary landscape but almost unavoidable as the junction of major routes in the region. These days anyone in any sort of hurry takes the **Coquihalla Highway** (Hwy 5). The scenery is unexceptional in the early part, but things look up considerably in the climb to the Coquihalla Pass (1244m), when forests, mountains and crashing rivers make a dramatic reappearance – compromised somewhat by old mines, clear-cuts (hillsides completely cleared of trees) and recent road-building scars. There's only a single exit, at the supremely missable town of Merritt, and literally no services for the entire 182km from **Hope** to Kamloops. Come stocked up with fuel and food, and be prepared to pay a toll at the top of the pass – a wind- and snow-whipped spot that must offer some of the loneliest employment opportunities in the province.

The older, slower and more scenic route from Vancouver is on the **Trans-Canada Highway** or by VIA Rail, both of which follow a more meandering course along the Thompson River and then the lower reaches of the Fraser River. For the first stretch you might also take the less busy but not exactly scintillating Hwy 7, which follows the north shore of the Fraser River from Vancouver and passes **Harrison Hot Springs** en route to Hope.

Hwy 7 to Hope

Flanked by dreary malls at first, the 150km drive on Hwy 7 from Vancouver to Hope cheers up considerably as the countryside opens up after the small town of **MISSION**, 30km into the journey. If you have the time, you might want to make a quick stop at **Xá:ytem**, BC's oldest dwelling site (late June to Sept daily 10am–4pm; rest of the year by appointment; ☎604/820-9725), located by the highway just before the east side of Mission. People have lived here for as long as nine thousand years, and an ongoing archeological dig has uncovered numerous lithic (stone) artefacts including arrowheads and stones used for cutting and chopping – some were made from obsidian from Oregon, an indication of early trade routes. A Stó:lo long house serves as the site's interpretation centre, and inside you can learn more about the excavations. Be sure to read up on the large boulder, known as Hatzic Rock, that rests on the grounds; it's a sacred spot to the aboriginal community, believed to be three si:yams (respected leaders) who had defied the wishes of the Creator and were turned to stone.

After Mission, the highway snakes through pretty farmland to **HARRISON HOT SPRINGS**, 129km from Vancouver and located on the southern edge of Harrison Lake. While aboriginal peoples who believed in the healing properties of the springs came here centuries ago, the springs were not popularized until they were "discovered" by gold prospectors in 1858; soon after the town became BC's first resort. Today, tourism remains Harrison Hot Spring's main industry, as you'll see from the number of modern apartment buildings and motels lining the lake. This said, it remains a scenic spot, thanks to the beautiful mountain views, mercifully free of too much neon and tat. The lake itself is 60km long – making it one of the province's largest lakes – and its waters are very clean, but also very cold. The only swimming option is in the artificial lagoon on the lake's shore, but if you want to play in the lake, boats, windsurfers and jet-skis can be hired from the deck in front of the upmarket but rather ugly *Harrison Hot Springs Resort*. If you're here the weekend after Labour Day, make a point of seeing the incredible sand sculptures on the beach that are created for the **World Championship Sand Sculpture** competition. To reach the **springs** themselves, it's a short walk along the shore and past the *Harrison Hot Springs Resort* – but they are a scalding hot 73°C at the source. In order to make the spring water suitable for soaking, the waters are cooled and redirected to the **Harrison Hot Springs Public Pool** (Mon–Thurs 9am–9pm, Fri 9am–10pm, Sat 8am–10pm, Sun 8am–9pm; $9) back in town on the intersection of Hot Springs Road and the Esplanade.

The **infocentre** (☎604/796-3425, ⓦwww.harrison.ca) is located in an old logging-camp bunkhouse on Hot Springs Road. For **accommodation** the cheapest **motel** is the *Bungalow*, 511 Lillooet Ave (☎ & Ⓕ604/796-3536; ❷), with self-contained lakeside cabins or the *Spa*, 140 Esplanade (☎604/796-2828 or 1-800/592-8828; ❷), also by the lake, with in-house massages. *Harrison Heritage House and Kottage* at 312 Lillooet Ave (☎604/796-9552 or 1-800/331-8099, ⓦwww.bbharrison.com; ❹) is a pricey but beautiful **B&B** in one of the village's few heritage buildings. The *Harrison Hot Springs Resort & Spa* (☎604/796-2244 or 1-800/663-2266, ⓦwww.harrisonresort.com; ❻), a favourite of Clark Gable's in the 1950s, is a friendly place with indoor and outside pools piped from the springs. There are also ten cabins which are cheaper than the rooms, but these need to be booked well in advance. For **camping** there are several private campsites around but it's best to head for nearby *Sasquatch Provincial Park* (reservations possible, see p.777, $14, day-use parking $5). **Eating** options are mostly along the Esplanade by the lake and you can settle for a variety of cuisines, including the Teutonic slant of the *Black Forest Steak and Schnitzel House* at no. 180 (☎604/796-9343). For French food and a treat, indulge yourself at the excellent but expensive La Côte d'Azur, 310 Hot Springs Rd.

Hope

Reputedly christened by pioneers with a grounding in Dante, **HOPE** – as in "Abandon all hope..." – is a pleasant mountain-ringed town 158km east of Vancouver that achieved a certain fame as the place wasted in spectacular fashion by Sylvester Stallone at the end of *First Blood*, the first Rambo movie. Despite the number of roads that converge here – the Trans-Canada, Hwy 3 and the Coquihalla – it remains a remarkably unspoilt stopover. In the past it was rivers, not roads, that accounted for the town's growth: the Fraser (Simon Fraser himself passed through in 1808) and two of its major tributaries, the Skagit and Coquihalla, meet at the townsite. The aboriginal villages here were forced to move when a Hudson's Bay post was established in 1848, the status quo being further disturbed when the gold rush hit in 1858. The bust that followed boom in neighbouring places was averted in Hope, largely because its situation made it an important station stop on the Canadian Pacific. Today the town's pretty location, which catches visitors slightly unaware, is turning it into something of a sight in its own right.

The **infocentre** (daily: summer 8am–8pm; rest of year 9am–5pm; T604/869-2021, Wwww.hopechamber.bc.ca) is the building next to the artfully dumped pile of antique farm machinery at 919 Water Ave. The town **museum** (May–Sept daily 9am–5pm; donation) is in the same building, and offers the usual hand-me-downs of Hope's erstwhile old-timers. Across the road, the lovely view over the Fraser as it funnels out of the mountains is one of the town's best moments. Time permitting, drop by **Memorial Park** downtown, where trees ravaged by rot have been given a new lease of life by a local chainsaw sculptor Pete Ryan; there were around thirty at last count. Nearby, the **Christ Church National Historic Site**, built in 1861, is one of BC's oldest churches still on its original site. Another one-off novelty is the "H" tree at the corner of 5th Street and Hudson's Bay Street, two trees cleverly entwined as saplings to grow together in the form of an "H" for Hope.

Hiking, fishing, canoeing, and even gold-panning are all popular time-wasters around the hundreds of local lakes and rivers, details of which are available from the infocentre. Of the hikes, the **Rotary Trail** (3km) to the confluence of the Fraser and Coquihalla rivers is popular, as is the more demanding clamber over gravel paths to the top of **Thacker Mountain** (5km). Another popular walking expedition worth pursuing is the dark jaunt through the five colossal **Othello-Quinette Tunnels** (closed Nov–April) of the Vancouver–Nelson Kettle Valley Railway, built in 1916 but abandoned in 1959 after countless avalanches, mudslides and rock falls. The tunnels are reached by a short trail from the **Coquihalla Canyon Provincial Park** parking area, 6km northeast of town off Coquihalla Hwy. This was one of the backcountry locations used during the filming of *First Blood*, and offers spectacular views over the cliffs and huge sand bars of the Coquihalla Gorge. **Kawkawa Lake Provincial Park**, 3km northeast of Hope off Hwy 3, is another popular mountain retreat, endowed with plenty of hiking, relaxing and swimming opportunities.

Practicalities

Most of what happens in Hope happens on Hwy 1, here known as Water Avenue. The Greyhound **bus terminal** (on Water Ave) is a critical juncture for bus travellers heading west to Vancouver, north to Kamloops or east to Penticton and the Okanagan. Cheap **motels** proliferate along Hwy 3 leaving town heading east. Closer in on the same road, the *Best Western Heritage Inn*, 570 Old Hope-Princeton Way (T604/869-7166 or 1-800/528-1234; **❸**), a lovely grey-wood building smothered in flowers, is also excellent. In town, the *Best Continental Motel*, 860 Fraser Ave (T604/869-9726, Ebcmhope @hotmail.com; **❸**), lies a block back from the main highway and is handy for the bus depot; or try the *Windsor Motel* overlooking the park at 778 3rd Ave (T604/869-9944 or 1-888/588-9944, Wwww.bcwindsormotel.com; **❷**). **Campsites**, too, are numerous, but most are some way from downtown. The town site is at *Coquihalla Campground* (T604/869-7119 or 1-888/869-7118, Ehopecamp@uniserve.com; $18–25; April–Oct), in a park setting off Hwy 3 and reached via 7th Avenue. The top of the pile is the *Hope Valley Campground*, 5km west of town on Flood Hope Road (T604/869-9857 or 1-866/869-6660; $20; March–Oct).

Food facilities and late-night entertainment are limited in what is, despite Vancouver's proximity, still a small-time Canadian town. For snacks, try the

Simon Fraser

The Fraser river is named after **Simon Fraser** (1776–1862), one of North America's most remarkable early explorers, who as an employee of the North West Company established western Canada's first white settlements: Fort McCleod (1805), Fort St James (1806), Fort Fraser (1806) and Fort George (1807). Having traced the route taken by fellow explorer Alexander Mackenzie across the continent, he set out in 1808 to establish a route to the Pacific and secure it for Britain against the rival claims of the US. Instead he travelled the entire 1300-kilometre length of a river – the Fraser – under the mistaken impression he was following the Columbia. "We had to pass where no man should venture," he wrote, making most of the journey on foot guided by local natives, pushing forward using ladders, ropes and improvised platforms to bypass rapids too treacherous to breach by boat. Some 35 days were needed to traverse the canyon alone. Reaching the river's mouth, where he would have glimpsed the site of present-day Vancouver, he realized his error and deemed the venture a commercial failure, despite the fact he had successfully navigated one of the continent's greatest rivers for the first time. Few people, needless to say, felt the need to follow Fraser's example until the discovery of **gold** near Yale in 1858; prospectors promptly waded in and panned every tributary of the lower Fraser until new strikes tempted them north to the Cariboo.

Hope Deli or *Sharon's Lunchbox and Deli* on Wallace Street, or the rock-bottom café in the Greyhound station. For more ambitious fare, try the *Home Restaurant*, 665 Old Hope-Princeton Way (☎869-5558).

The Fraser Canyon

Veering north from Hope, the Trans-Canada runs up the Fraser River valley, squeezed here by the high ridges of the Cascade and Coast ranges into one of British Columbia's grandest waterways. Though it's now a transport corridor – the Canadian Pacific Railway also passes this way – the **Fraser Canyon** was long regarded as impassable; to negotiate it, the Trans-Canada is forced to push through tunnels, hug the Fraser's banks, and at times cling perilously to rock ledges hundreds of metres above the swirling waters.

YALE, about 25km north of Hope, opens the canyon with a ring of plunging cliffs. Sitting at the river's navigable limit, it was once a significant site for Canada's aboriginal peoples, providing an important point of departure for the canoes of the Stó:lo ("People of the River"). Tribespeople would come from as far afield as Vancouver Island to plunder the rich salmon waters just above the present townsite. A Hudson's Bay Company post, The Falls, appeared here in the 1840s, later renamed in honour of James Murray Yale, commander of the HBC post at Fort Langley, then one of the predominant white outposts on the BC mainland. Within a decade it became the largest city in North America west of Chicago and north of San Francisco; during the 1858 gold rush, when it marked the beginning of the infamous Cariboo Wagon Road, Yale's population mushroomed to over 20,000, a growth only tempered by the end of the boom and the completion of the Canadian Pacific.

Today Yale is a small lumber town of about 200, though a visit to the **Historic Yale Museum** (June–Sept daily 9am–6pm; donation) on Hwy 1, known here as Douglas Street, offers an exhaustive account of the town's golden age. The monument in front of the building is dedicated to the countless Chinese workers who helped build the Canadian Pacific, one of only a handful of such memorials. You might also want to pay homage at **Lady Franklin Rock**, the vast river boulder which blocked the passage of steamers beyond Yale – all goods heading north to the goldfields had to transfer at this point to wagon trains bound for the Cariboo Wagon Road. The rock takes its name from Lady Franklin, wife of Sir John Franklin, the Arctic explorer who vanished on a voyage to the Arctic in July 1845. Numerous expeditions set out to find him (with no luck), and it is said that Lady Franklin, on her own personal odyssey, came as far as Yale and its big boulder. Ask locals for directions. If you fancy a longer walk, take Hwy 1 a kilometre south out of the village for the trailhead of the Spirit Cave Trail, a one-hour walk with fine views of the mountains. For **rooms**, you can't do much better than the *Fort Yale Motel* (☎604/863-2216; ❷) at the entrance to the Canyon. Some 11km north of Yale on Hwy 1, the *Colonial Inn* (☎604/863-2277; ❷) has cabins and pitches ($12). If you're **camping**, though, you might want to backtrack 10km towards Hope on Hwy 1 to the *Emory Creek Provincial Park*, a large, peaceful wooded site with river walks and camping sites from April to October ($14).

Hell's Gate and Boston Bar

Around 10km north of Yale on Hwy 1 is the famous **HELL'S GATE**, where – in a gorge almost 180m deep – the huge swell of the Fraser is squeezed into a 38-metre channel of foaming water that crashes through the rocks with awe-inspiring ferocity. The water here is up to 60m deep and as fast-flowing as any you're likely to see. For a good view of the canyon, travel 2km north of Yale on Hwy 1 to the **Alexander Bridge Provincial Park**, where an old section of the highway drops to the Alexander Bridge for some startling panoramas. Eight kilometres further there's a certain amount of resort-like commercialism to negotiate to get down to the river and an "Air-Tram" (cable car) to pay for (daily: April & late Sept to Oct 10am–4pm; May to mid-June & Sept 9am–5pm; mid-June to Aug 9am–6pm; closed Nov–March; $10; ⓦwww.hellsgate.bc.ca). Close by there are also displays on the various provisions made to help migrating **salmon** complete their journeys, which have been interrupted over the years by the coming of the road and railway beside the Fraser. The river is one of the key runs for Pacific salmon, and every summer and autumn they fill the river as they head for tributaries and upstream lakes to spawn (see p.927). The biggest obstacle to their passage came in 1913, when a landslide occurred during the construction of the Canadian Pacific Railway, yet it wasn't until 1945 that ladders were completed to bypass the fall. The numbers of salmon have never fully recovered.

BOSTON BAR, 42km north of Yale, is also the main centre for **whitewater** rafting trips down the Fraser as far as Yale. Various companies run several trips a week from May to August; contact Frontier River Adventure for details (☎604/867-9244). The village's name, apparently, was coined by locals in villages nearby amazed at the number of American prospectors who seemed to hail from Boston. A "bar", by contrast, was the name given to places where miners stopped to make camp en route for the goldfields. To **stay** locally, make for the *Blue Lake Resort* (☎604/867-9246 or 1-877/867-9246, ⓔbluelake@universe.com; ❷), located a kilometre east on Blue Lake Road off the highway 15km north of Boston Bar. As well as rooms, it also has 75 RV and tent sites ($15). The only other local **campsite**, the *Canyon Alpine RV Park & Campground* (☎604/867-9734 or 1-800/644-7275; $18–22), 5km north of Boston Bar, also has a restaurant.

Cache Creek

CACHE CREEK, 337km from Vancouver and 84km west of Kamloops, has a reputation as a hitchhiker's black hole and indeed is the sort of sleepy place you could get stuck in for days. Locals also say it didn't help that an infamous child murderer, Charles Olsen, was captured nearby in 1985 – since then they've been understandably wary of picking up strangers. The town's name is accounted for by a variety of legends, the most romantic version concerning a couple of prospectors who buried a hoard of gold and never returned to pick it up. Sadly, it's likelier to derive from early trappers' more prosaic habit of leaving a cache of supplies at points on a trail to be used later.

Cache Creek is known as the "Arizona of Canada" for its extraordinary rocky landscapes and baking summer climate, which settles a heat-wasted somnolence on its dusty streets. The parched, windswept mountains roundabout are anomalous volcanic intrusions in the regional geology, producing a legacy of hard rock and semi-precious stones – including jade – that attract climbers and rock hounds. There's not much else to do here; you can watch semi-precious stones being worked at several places, or check out **Hat Creek Ranch** (T 604/457-9722; mid-May to Sept daily 9am–6pm, W www.hatcreekranch .com; $7), a collection of original buildings including a log stopping house, the last remaining of its type, and a reconstruction of a Shuswap village. It's located ten minutes north of Cache Creek by the junction of highways 97 and 99 (the original Cariboo Wagon Rd). If you're stranded, try one of eight **motels**, such as the *Bonaparte* on Hwy 97 North (T 604/457-9693 or 1-888/922-1333; ❸), with large heated pool, and the central *Sage Hills Motel*, 1390 Hwy 97 N (T & F 604/457-6451; ❷), also with pool. The nearest **campsite**, complete with laundry, hot showers and heated outdoor pool, is the *Brookside* (T 604/457-6633, W www.brooksidecampsite.com; $15; April–Oct), located 1km east of town on the main highway.

Kamloops

Almost any trip in southern British Columbia brings you sooner or later to **KAMLOOPS**, a sprawling town 355km northeast of Vancouver and 110km west of Salmon Arm which has been a transport centre from time immemorial – its name derives from the Shuswap word for "meeting of the rivers" – and which today marks the meeting point of the Trans-Canada and Yellowhead (South) highways, the region's principal transcontinental roads, as well as the junction of the Canadian Pacific and Canadian National railways. One of the larger towns in interior southern British Columbia (pop. 77,000), it's a bland and unobjectionable place, except when the wind blows from the uptown sawmills, bringing in a putrid smell that hangs heavy in the air. If you're on public transport, there's no particular need to spend any time here; if you're camping or driving, however, it makes a convenient provisions stop, especially for those heading north on Hwy 5 or south on the Coquihalla Hwy, neither of which has much in the way of facilities.

Kamloops is determinedly functional and not a place to spend a happy day wandering, but its downtown does have a modern 1000-work **Art Gallery**, the largest in BC's interior – not that it has much competition. Located in the heart of downtown at 465 Victoria St at 5th (May–Sept Mon, Fri & Sat 10am–5pm, Tues–Thurs 10am–9pm, Sun noon–4pm; Oct–April Mon–Wed, Fri & Sat 10am–5pm, Thurs 10am–9pm, Sun

10am–4pm; @www.bcgalleries.bc.ca/kamloops; $5), the gallery showcases Canadian artists, in particular those from the West and British Columbia.

The **Kamloops Museum**, 207 Seymour St (Tues–Sat 9.30am–4.30pm; donation) is one of the more interesting provincial offerings, with illuminating archive photographs (especially the one of the railway running down the centre of the main street), artefacts, period set-pieces and a particularly well-done section on the Shuswap. The stuffed-animal display, without which no BC museum is complete, has a fascinating little piece on the life cycle of the tick presented without any noticeable irony. For a more complete picture of local aboriginal history and traditions, call at the **Secwepemec Museum & Heritage Park**, just over the bridge on Hwy 5 (summer daily 9am–5pm; winter Mon–Fri 8.30am–4.30pm; ☎250/828-9801; $6) or attend the **Kamloops Pow Wow**, held every third weekend in August ($7 a day).

Perhaps the most interesting thing about Kamloops is its surroundings, dominated by strange, bare-earthed brown hills that locals like to say represent the northernmost point of the Mojave Desert. There's no doubting the almost surreal touches of near-desert, which are particularly marked in the bare rock and clay outcrops above the bilious waters of the Thompson River and in the bleached scrub and failing stands of pines that spot the barren hills. A good way to see the river and the scenery is to take a **cruise** on the Wanda Sue, a reno-vated sternwheeler (☎250/374-7447, @www.wandasue.bc.ca; departures: mid-June to end June Mon–Fri 6.30pm, Sat 1.30pm; Sun 1.30pm, 3.30pm & 6.30pm; July to early Sept also Mon–Fri 1.30pm; $12.50). The two-hour trips depart from the Old Yacht Club Public Wharf on River St. Most scenic diver-sions lie a short drive out of town, and the infocentre has full details of every last local bolt hole, with a special bias towards the two hundred or so trout-stuffed lakes that dot the hinterland. The nearest and most popular on a hot summer's day is the 402-hectare **Paul Lake Provincial Park**, northeast of town on a good paved road (take Hwy 5 north for 5km and then Paul Lake Rd east for 17km), with swimming and a provincial campsite ($14).

Practicalities

The **infocentre**, 1290 W Trans-Canada Hwy (mid-May to mid-Oct Mon–Fri 8am–6pm, Sat & Sun 9am–6pm; mid-Oct to mid-May Mon–Fri 9am–5pm; ☎250/374-3377 or 1-800/662-1994, @www.adventurekamloops.com), is a good 6km west of downtown, close to the Aberdeen Mall. It has full accom-modation and recreational details for the town and much of the province, and various useful hiking and other guidebooks by local authors.

The **Greyhound terminal** (☎250/374-1212), on Notre Dame Avenue off Hwy 1, across from the infocentre, is a crucial interchange for buses to all parts of the province; to head into town, jump on the #3 "Crosstown" bus that leaves from outside the station. Kamloops also boasts a key regional **airport**, located 6km northwest of the centre on Tranquille Rd. It is connected to downtown by BC Transit bus #1 (Tranquille) or the Airport Shuttle ($10). The town is also served by three weekly **trains** in each direction from Edmonton, via Jasper. The VIA Rail office is at 95 3rd Ave, behind Landsdowne Street, but is open only on days trains are running (☎250/372-5858 or 1-800/561-8630, @www.viarail.ca).

Kamloops's huge volume of accommodation is aimed fair and square at the motorist and consists of thick clusters of **motels**, most of which blanket the town's eastern margins on Hwy 1 or out on Columbia Street West. The *Thriftlodge*, 2459 Trans-Canada (☎250/374-2488 or 1-800/661-7769, @www.thriftlodge.kamloops.com; ❷), is probably the cheapest of all, but it's about the last building on eastbound Hwy 1 out of town. You pay a slight premium for central beds, most of which are on Columbia Street; here the *Casa Marquis Motor Inn*, 530 Columbia St (℡250/372-7761 or 1-800/533-9233, ⓦwww.casamarquis.kamloops.com; ❷), is reasonably priced, or you can try the reliable *Sandman*, 550 Columbia St (℡250/374-1218 or 1-800/726-3626, ⓦwww.sandmanhotels.ca; ❷), part of a chain. If you want top-of-the-range comfort after a long journey, make for the central *Executive Inn*, 540 Victoria St (℡250/372-2281 or 1-800/663-2837, ⓦwww.kamloops.com/executive; ❹). A HI **hostel**, the *Kamloops Old Courthouse Hostel,* is housed downtown in a restored courthouse building at 7 W Seymour St (℡250/828-7991 or 1-866/782-9526,ⓦwww.hihostels.ca; ❶) just west off 1st Ave and south of Riverside Park; it has 75 dorm beds (members $16, non-members $20) and a few private rooms. There's also a clutch of motels around the bus terminal, in case you arrive late and have no need to drop into town. The nearest **campsite** is the *Silver Sage Tent and Trailer Park* at 771 Athabasca St E (℡250/828-2077; $20–25), but if you've got a car aim for the far more scenic facilities at Paul Lake Provincial Park (see above).

Snack **food** is cheap and served in generous portions at the popular *Swiss Pastries & Café*, 359 Victoria St, which really is run by Swiss people and does good muesli, cappuccino, sticky buns and excellent bread. The best coffee in town is found at *The Grind*, 476 Victoria St – beans are roasted daily – while for a culinary treat you should head for *Chapters Viewpoint* at the *Panorama Inn*, 610 Columbia St (℡250/374-3224), which locals have voted the town's best restaurant for several years, and which serves good steaks, salads and seafood against a panoramic backdrop (outside seating is available). Also good is *Ric's Grill*, 227 Victoria St (℡250/372-7771; closed Sun at lunch; no smoking), which is primarily a steakhouse but also offers good fish and chicken dishes. For supermarket stock-ups there's a Safeway on the corner of Seymour and 5th Avenue.

Highway 5 north of Kamloops

Northbound **Hwy 5** (here known as the Yellowhead S Hwy) heads upstream along the broad North Thompson River as it courses through high hills and rolling pasture between Kamloops and **Clearwater** and beyond. It is one of the most scenically astounding road routes in this part of the world, and follows the river as it carves through the Monashee Mountains from its source near **Valemount**, to the final meeting with the main Yellowhead Hwy (Hwy 16) at Tête Jaune Cache, a total distance of 338km. The entire latter half of the journey is spent sidestepping the immense **Wells Gray Provincial Park**, one of the finest protected areas in British Columbia.

Greyhound **buses** cover the route on their run between Kamloops and Prince George via Clearwater (3 daily in each direction), as do VIA **trains**, which connect Kamloops with Jasper via Clearwater (3 weekly). To get into Wells Gray without your own transport, however, you'd have to hitch from Clearwater up the 63-kilometre main access road – a feasible proposition at the height of summer, but highly unlikely at any other time. This access road will be enough for most casual visitors to get a taste of the park – you could run up and down it and see the sights in a day – but note that there are some less-travelled gravel roads into other sectors of the park from **Blue River**, 112km

7

north of Clearwater on Hwy 5, and from the village of **100 Mile House**, on Hwy 97 west of the park.

Clearwater

CLEARWATER is a dispersed farming community 125km north of Kamloops that's invisible from Hwy 5, and unless you need a place to stay or arrive by rail there's no need to drop down to it at all. Everything you need apart from the odd shop is on or just off the junction between the highway and the slip road to the village, including the **Greyhound bus stop** and the excellent **infocentre** (daily: June–Aug 8am–8pm; Sept–May 9am–5pm; ☎250/674-2646, ⓦwww.ntvalley.com/clearwaterchamber), a model of the genre that has immensely useful information on all aspects of Wells Gray Provincial Park. If you're planning on staying locally or doing any walking or canoeing, take time to flick through its reference books devoted to accommodation, trails and paddling routes.

Camping aside, Clearwater is the most realistic place **to stay** along Hwy 5 if you're planning on doing Wells Gray. By far the best prospect, thanks to its lovely views over Dutch Lake, is the *Jasper Way Inn Motel*, 57 E Old North Thompson Hwy, two blocks off Hwy 5 (☎250/674-3345, ⓔjwaymotl@wellsgray.net; ❸), 1km off the highway to the west and well signed from the infocentre; some rooms have cooking facilities. If it's full, try the big *Wells Gray Inn* (☎250/674-2214 or 1-800/567-4088; ❶), close by on the main road; the doubles here are more comfortable, but lack the view. The latter is virtually the only place to **eat** locally. As the park becomes more popular, so more places are opening on its fringes: the big *Clearwater RV Park & Cabins*, 373 Clearwater Valley Rd (☎250/674-3909), on the corner of the Yellowhead Hwy and the Wells Grey Park Road, is one such, a combination of cabins (❷), chalets (❷) and camping and RV sites ($18–25; March–Oct). If you've come for wilderness you probably won't want to be in such a place, but it does also have three restaurants, endless facilities and a host of equipment-rental possibilities and organized tours. Grander and larger is the 64-room *Clearwater Lodge* (☎250/674-3080 or 1-888/383-2388, ⓦwww .clearwaterlodge.bcresorts.com; ❹) near the Hwy 5 turn-off for the park.

Three other **campsites** lie more or less within walking distance of the infocentre: the best – again, on the lake – is the *Dutch Lake Resort and RV Park* (☎250/674-3351 or 1-888/884-4424; cabins ❸, pitch $19–27; ⓦwww .dutchlake.com; mid-April to mid-Oct;). Don't forget, though, that there are four simple provincial park campsites within the park (see p.924). If you want to be slightly away from Clearwater, stop at the *Birch Island Campground* (☎250/674-3991, 674-4054 or 1-877/674-3991; $15–21; mid-April to Oct), a treed seventy-acre area with tent sites and B&B units (❷) overlooking the Thompson River 8km north of the village on Hwy 5.

Blue River and Valemount

Clearwater is by far the best base locally, but you may find the **accommodation** options at Blue River and Valemount useful, though the latter is a whopping 225km north of Clearwater on Hwy 5. **BLUE RIVER**, a slip of a place 100km north of Clearwater, has far fewer possibilities, with its cheapest option being the *Blue River Motel* with one- and two-bedroom units two blocks off the highway on Spruce Street (☎250/673-8387, ⓔtab@mercuryspeed.com; ❷). Or try the Glacier Mountain Lodge (☎250/673-2393 or 1-877/452-2686, ⓔglacier@mercuryspeed.com; ❹) at 869 Shell Rd. The only **campsites** for miles are the *Eleanor Lake Campsite & Trailer Park* on Herb Bilton Way (℡250/673-8316 or 1-800/661-9170, Ⓦwww.wiegle.com; $12–21; May to mid-Oct), with free showers, store and canoe rentals, and the *Blue River Campground and RV Park*, Myrtle Lake Road and Cedar Street (℡250/673-8203, Ⓦwww.bluerivercampground.ca; $14–18; May to mid-Oct), with showers, canoe rentals and a variety of fishing, canoeing and horse-riding tours.

In **VALEMOUNT** there's a seasonal infocentre at 99 Gorse St on Hwy 5 (mid-May to mid-Sept daily 9am–5pm; ℡250/566-9893 or 566-4846, Ⓦwww.valemount.org) and around ten motels and a campsite. One block off the highway on 5th Avenue are a bunch of **motels**, of which the cheapest is the *Yellowhead* (℡250/566-4411, Ⓦwww.yellowheadmotel.com/; May–Oct; ❸); the rest have more facilities, but all are pretty soulless, including the *Canadian Lodge* (℡250/566-8222; ❺) at 5th Ave and Hwy 5 with a Jacuzzi and kitchenettes; the *Canoe Mountain Lodge* (℡250/566-9171 or 1-888/214-6611, Ⓦwww.canoemountainlodge.com; ❺); and the *Chalet Continental*, 1450 5th Ave (℡250/566-9787 or 1-877/566-7799, Ⓦwww.chaletcon.com; ❹), with an indoor pool. At 360 Loseth Road, 1km north of Valemount, is the modern *Irvins Park and Campground* (℡250/566-4781; $23–32; April–Oct), mainly aimed at RVs, with activities including riding and ATV tours. For **camping**, head 500m north of Valemount to *Wilderness Creek Camping* (℡250/566-4098; $14).

From the Yellowhead Hwy junction north of Valemount it's 270km on to Prince George (see p.976) and 77km east to the BC–Alberta border.

Wells Gray Provincial Park

WELLS GRAY PROVINCIAL PARK is the equal of any of the Rocky Mountain national parks to the east: if anything, its wilderness is probably more extreme – so untamed, in fact, that many of its peaks remain unclimbed and unnamed. Wildlife sightings are common – especially if you tramp some of the wilder trails, where encounters with black bears, grizzlies and mountain goats are a possibility, not to mention glimpses of smaller mammals such as timber wolves, coyotes, weasels, martens, minks, wolverines and beavers. Seeing the park is straightforward, at least if you have transport and only want a superficial – but still rewarding – glimpse of the interior. A 63-kilometre **access road** strikes into the park from Hwy 5 at Clearwater, culminating in Clearwater Lake – there's no further wheeled access. Various trails long and short, together with campsites, viewpoints and easily seen waterfalls, are dotted along the route, allowing you to see just about all the obvious scenic landmarks with a car in a day.

Accommodation in or near the park includes the log cabins at *Wells Gray Ranch* (℡250/674-2792 or 1-866/GO-RIDING, Ⓦwww.wellsgrayranch .com; ❺; mid-May to mid-Oct) just before the park entrance (26km from Hwy 5) on Wells Gray Park Road, or the slightly larger but equally lonely *Helmcken Falls Lodge* (℡250/674-3657, Ⓦwww.helmckenfalls.com; ❺; Jan–March & May–Oct) at the entrance itself (35km from Hwy 5), which offers similar facilities at slightly higher prices. Farther afield, there are three comfortable rooms at the *Blue Grouse Country Inn* (℡250/674-0200 or 1-866-8747, Ⓦwww.bluegrousecountryinn.com; ❺), 30km north of Clearwater and 24km off Hwy 5.

You'll be lucky to find vacancies locally in summer, so book months in advance if coming in June, July or August. Both the lodge and ranch above have tent pitches ($14–26.50), but there's far better roadside **camping** along the

Activities in the Wells Gray park

With some 250km of maintained trails and dozens of other lesser routes, the park is magnificent for **hiking**. We've outlined short walks and day-hikes from the park's access road, but serious backpackers can easily spend a week or more tramping the backcountry hikes, most of which are in the southern third of the park and link together for days of wild hiking and wilderness camping. The longest one-way trail links Clearwater Lake to Kostal Lake trail (26km) and begins on the main Wells Gray park road, just across from *Clearwater Lake* campsite. Steep switchbacks, muddy conditions, thick brush and large deadfall as well as tramping across sharp lava flow and loose rock make the going slow on many of the park's remoter trails. For all the backcountry hikes you need a map and a compass, your own food and water supplies and plenty of insect repellent. Make sure you pick up a free BC Parks map-pamphlet at the Clearwater infocentre, and if you're thinking of doing any backcountry exploration you'll want to invest in their more detailed maps and guides. **Cross-country skiing** is also possible, but there are only a few groomed routes in the park; again, details are available at the infocentre.

Another of the park's big attractions is **canoeing** on Clearwater and Azure lakes, the former at the end of the access road, which can be linked with a short portage to make a 100-plus-kilometre dream trip for paddlers; you can rent canoes for long- or short-haul trips from *Clearwater Lake Tours* situated on the south end of Clearwater Lake, 71km from Hwy 5 in Clearwater (℡250/674-3052 or 674-2971 off-season/evening). **White-water rafting** down the Clearwater River is also extremely popular and recommended, and half-day to full-week tours can be arranged through the Clearwater infocentre or at the two accommodation options below. Several local operators run shorter commercial boat trips around Clearwater Lake, as well as full-scale **tours** featuring horse riding, camping, trekking, fishing, boating and even float-plane excursions around the park – the Clearwater infocentre has the inside story on all of these.

park access road at the park's four provincial campsites: *Spahats Campground*, a small, forested site only 10km from Hwy 5 at Clearwater Lake on Clearwater Valley Road; the *Dawson Falls*, 5km from the park entrance; *Falls Creek*, 30km from the entrance; and *Clearwater Lake*, 31km from the entrance (all $14; May–Sept). All fill up promptly on summer weekends, but can be reserved (see p.777). Many backpackers' campsites ($5) dot the shores of the park's major lakes and with no services offered it's not necessary to book; *Clearwater Lake Tours* operates a water-taxi service, which can drop you off at any site on Clearwater Lake and pick you up at a prearranged time.

Sights and hikes along the access road

Even if you're not geared up for the backcountry, the **access road** to the park from Clearwater opens up a medley of waterfalls, walks and viewpoints that make a detour extremely worthwhile. The road's paved for the first 30km to the park boundary, but the remaining 33km to Clearwater Lake is gravel. Most of the sights are well signed.

About 8km north of Clearwater, a short walk from the car park at **Spahats Campground** brings you to the 61-metre Spahats Falls, the first of several mighty cascades along this route. You can watch the waters crashing down through layers of pinky-red volcanic rock from a pair of observation platforms, which also provide an impressive and unexpected view of the Clearwater Valley way down below. A few hundred metres further up the road, a fifteen-kilometre gravel lane peels off into the **Wells Gray Recreation Area**; a single trail from the end of the road strikes off into alpine meadows, feeding four shorter day-trails into an area particularly known for its bears. This is also the site of a juvenile correction centre, which must rank as possibly the most beautiful but godforsaken spot to do time in North America. About 15km further up the main access road, a second four-wheel-drive track branches east to reach the trailhead for **Battle Mountain** (19km), with the option of several shorter hikes like the Mount Philip Trail (5km) en route.

Green Mountain Lookout, reached by a rough, winding road to the left just after the park entrance, offers one of the most enormous roadside panoramas in British Columbia, and it's a sight that will help you grasp the sheer extent of the Canadian wilderness: as far as you can see, there's nothing but an almighty emptiness of primal forest and mountains. Various landscape features are picked out on plaques, and the immediate area is a likely place to spot moose.

The next essential stop is **Dawson Falls**, a broad, powerful cascade (91m wide and 18m high) just five-minutes' walk from the road – signed "Viewpoint". Beyond, the road crosses an ugly iron bridge and shortly after meets the start of the **Murtle River Trail** (14km one-way), a particularly good walk if you want more spectacular waterfalls.

Immediately afterwards, a dead-end side road is signed to **Helmcken Falls**, the park's undisputed highlight. The site is heavily visited, and it's not unknown for wedding parties to come up here to get dramatic matrimonial photos backed by the luminous arc of water plunging into a black, carved bowl fringed with vivid carpets of lichen and splintered trees, the whole ensemble framed by huge plumes of spray wafting up on all sides. At 137m, the falls are two and a half times the height of Niagara – or, in the infoboard's incongruous comparison, approximately the same height as the Vancouver skyline.

Continuing north, the park access road rejoins the jade-green Clearwater River, passing tastefully engineered picnic spots and short trails that wend down to the bank for close-up views of one of the province's best white-water-rafting stretches. The last sight before the end of the road is **Ray Farm**, home to John Bunyon Ray, who in 1912 was the first homesteader in this area. Though it's not much to look at, the farm offers a sobering insight into the pioneer mentality – Ray's struggle to scrape a living and raise a family in this harsh environment beggars belief – and the picturesquely ruined, wooden shacks are scattered in a lovely, lush clearing. The park road ends at **Clearwater Lake**, where there are a couple of boat launches, a provincial campsite and a series of short trails clearly marked from the trailhead.

Salmon Arm and the Shuswap

Given the variety of routes across southern BC there's no knowing when you might find yourself in **SALMON ARM**, 108km east of Kamloops, though that's not something that need concern you in planning an itinerary, because the town – the largest of the somewhat bland resorts spread along **Shuswap Lake**'s 1000km of navigable waterways – has relatively little to recommend it. This said, if you fancy fishing, swimming, water-skiing or houseboating, you could do worse than relax for a couple of days in one of the area's 32 provincial parks or small lakeside villages – Chase, Sorrento, Eagle Bay and others. Such sights as there are can be found in the **R.J. Haney Heritage Park** (June–Sept daily 10am–5pm; $5), 2km east of Salmon Arm on Hwy 97B. It's home to the Salmon Arm Museum, a predictable pioneer and heritage affair,

Spawn to be wild

At times it seems impossible to escape the **salmon** in British Columbia. Whether it's on restaurant menus, in rivers or in the photographs of grinning fishermen clutching their catch, the fish is almost as much a symbol of the region as its mountains and forests. Five different species inhabit the rivers and lakes of western Canada: **pink**, **coho**, **chum**, **chinook** and, most important of all, the **sockeye**.

Though they start and finish their lives in fresh water, salmon spend about four years in the open sea between times. Mature fish make their epic migrations from the Pacific to **spawn** in the BC rivers of their birth between June and November, swimming about 30km a day; some chinook travel more than 1400km up the Fraser beyond Prince George, which means almost fifty days' continuous swimming upstream. Though the female lays as many as four thousand eggs, only about six percent of the offspring survive; on the Adams River near Salmon Arm, for example, it's estimated that of four billion sockeye eggs laid in a typical year, one billion survive to become fry (hatched fish about 2cm long), of which 75 percent are eaten by predators before becoming smolts (year-old fish), and only five percent of these then make it to the ocean. In effect each pair of spawners produces about ten mature fish; of these, eight are caught by commercial fisheries and only two return to reproduce.

These are returns that clearly put the salmon's survival and British Columbia's lucrative **fishing industry** on a knife edge. Caught, canned and exported, salmon accounts for two-thirds of BC's $1 billion annual revenues from fishing – the largest of any Canadian province, and its third-ranking money-earner after forestry and energy products. Commercial fishing suffered its first setback in British Columbia as long ago as 1913, when large rockslides at Hell's Gate in the Fraser Canyon disrupted many of the spawning runs. Although fish runs were painstakingly constructed to bypass the slides, new pressures have subsequently been heaped on the salmon by mining, logging, urban and agricultural development, and the dumping of industrial and municipal wastes. An increasingly important line of defence, **hatcheries** have been built on rivers on the mainland and Vancouver Island to increase the percentage of eggs and fry that successfully mature. Meanwhile, overfishing, as the above figures suggest, remains a major concern, particularly as the **drift nets** of Japanese and Korean fleets, designed for neon squid, have over the past decade taken numerous non-target species, including BC and Yukon salmon. Under intense lobbying from Canada and the US, both nations agreed to a moratorium on large-scale drift nets as from June 1992. Since then, various measures have been implemented by the Canadian and BC governments including the closure of the Fraser and Thompson rivers to all salmon fishing in 1999. However, Greenpeace estimates that 764 stocks of salmon in BC and Yukon are either extinct or at risk of becoming extinct.

and Haney House, an early twentieth-century farmhouse, one of a handful of "historic" buildings (fire hall, blacksmith's and petrol station) in the park.

Depending on the season, you can also watch one of Canada's most famous **salmon-spawning runs** near Salmon Arm, or indulge in a little **bird-watching**, for the bay here is one of the world's last nesting areas of the western grebe. As ever in Canada, Salmon Arm and its satellites are much smaller places than their bold label on most maps would suggest. Many of the settlements are oddly dispersed and a touch scrappy and haphazard in appearance, but if you're driving they make a natural break along one of the Trans-Canada's more monotonous stretches. To get anything out of Salmon Arm proper, you'll have to pull off the main drag, which is formed by the Trans-Canada itself, and head to the village a little to the south.

The lake and the surrounding region take their name from the Shuswap natives, the northernmost of the great Salishan family and the largest single tribe in British Columbia. The name of the town harks back to a time when it was possible to spear salmon straight from the lake, and fish were so plentiful that they were shovelled onto the land as fertilizer. Shuswap Lake still provides an important sanctuary for hatched salmon fry before they make their long journey down the Thompson and Fraser rivers to the sea – the abundance of such lakes, together with ideal water temperatures, free-flowing, well-oxygenated and silt-free tributaries, and plenty of sand and gravel beds for egg-laying, make the Fraser River system the continent's greatest salmon habitat. Therefore, one of the few reasons you might make a special journey to the Salmon Arm area is to watch the huge migrations of **spawning salmon** that take place around October. Up to two million fish brave the run from the Pacific up to their birthplace in the Adams River – one of the most famous spawning grounds in the province. During the spawning time, humans also make their way here in droves; around 250,000 visitors come during the peak week alone. The spectacle takes place yearly, but is most marked on four-yearly cycles (2006 is the next "big" year). This short stretch of river is protected by **Roderick Haig-Brown Provincial Park**, reached from Salmon Arm by driving 46km west on the Trans-Canada to Squilax and then 5km north on a side road where the park is signposted. If you're thinking of dangling a line, pick up the *Fishing in Shuswap* leaflet from the infocentre in Salmon Arm, and don't forget to get a licence at the same time.

Practicalities

Greyhound **buses** serve Salmon Arm from Vancouver (7 daily), Calgary (4 daily) and Kelowna, Vernon and Penticton (4 daily). The bus terminal is at the West Village Mall on Hwy 1, and the **infocentre** (Mon–Sat 8.30am–5.30pm; ☎250/832-2230 or 1-877/725-6667) is at 751 Marine Park Drive. You might also contact Tourism Shuswap (☎250/832-5200 or 1-800/661-4800, ⓦ www.shuswap.bc.ca) for information on the whole region.

One of the most convenient of Salmon Arm's many **motels** is the *Village Motel* (☎250/832-3955; ❷) at 620 Trans-Canada Hwy. More upmarket, and still close to the highway, is the *Best Western Villager West Motor Inn*, 61 10th St SW (☎250/832-9793 or 1-877-778-6777; ❹). There is also an HI-affiliated **hostel**, the *Squilax General Store and Caboose Hostel* (☎250/675-2977; ❶) in Chase on the waterfront just off the Trans-Canada. The hostel building is the old General Store, while the 24 dorm beds (members $16, non-members $20) are housed in old railway carriages. If you are coming by Greyhound bus, the driver will usually drop you on request at the hostel. Of several **campsites**, the obvious first choice is the *Salmon Arm KOA*, 3km east of town in a big wooded site, whose excellent facilities include a heated swimming pool (☎250/832-6489 or 1-800/562-9389; $30; May–Oct). For beds or tent space, the *Salmon River Motel and RV Park*, 1km west of downtown at 910 40th St SW (☎250/832-3065; motel ❷, campsite $20–25), is also good. For **food** and drink, make for the *Hideaway Pub & Bistro*, not far from the Greyhound depot at 995 Lakeshore Drive (☎250/832-9447).

For a decidedly alternative form of accommodation, head east along the Trans-Canada to **SICAMOUS**, a pleasant but very busy waterfront village which, though crammed with motels and campsites, is better known for its many upmarket **houseboats**. A few rent by the night, but most tend to be let weekly by about half-a-dozen local agencies on the marina and scattered around the village. Agencies you might try include *Bluewater Houseboats*

(☎250/836-2255 or 1-800/663-4024, ⓦwww.shuswap.bc.ca/bluewater; $1595–5995 a week; April–Oct), one of the larger agencies, with forty boats; *Sicamous Creek Marina & Admiral Houseboats* (☎250/836-4611 or 1-866/704-4611, ⓦwww.admiralhouseboats.com; $1750–3055 a week; April–Oct); or the *Twin Anchors Houseboat Association* (☎250/836-2450 or 1-800/663-4026, ⓦwww.twinanchors.com; $4700–7300 a week; April–Oct), with 48 boats. Prices might look terrifying, but boats accommodate up to 22 people.

The village is also the place to pick up a boat for a sightseeing **cruise** on the lake, one of the best ways of enjoying a scenic slice of the region; contact the Shuswap Ferry Lake Service for details of daily summer sailings (☎250/836-2200). For **information** there's an infocentre at 110 Finlayson St by the Government Dock (Mon–Fri 10am–5pm; June Sat also 10am–3pm; July daily 9am–6pm; ☎250/836-3313, ⓦwww.sicamouschamber.bc.ca). To **eat and drink** locally, head for the *Moose Mulligan's Marine Pub* at 1120 Riverside Ave in the *Super 8 Motel* (☎250/836-4988; ❹).

Highway 97 east of Kamloops

Passing through landscapes of Eden-like clarity and beauty, **Hwy 97** is a far better entrance to (or exit from) the Okanagan than the dreary road to Salmon Arm (see p.926). The grass-green meadows, grazing cattle and low wooded hills here are the sort of scenery pioneers must have dreamed of; most of the little hamlets en route make charming spots to stay, and if you have time and transport any number of minor roads lead off to small lakes, each with modest recreational facilities.

The highway peels off the Trans-Canada 26km east of Kamloops, its first good stops being **MONTE LAKE**, served by the excellent *Heritage Campsite & RV Park* (☎250/375-2434; $14–17; April–Nov) and the equally well-tended and unspoiled public campsite at **Monte Lake Provincial Park**. Both places make good spots to overnight. **Westwold**, 5km beyond, is a dispersed ranching community of clean, old wooden houses and large pastures that present a picture of almost idyllic rural life. **FALKLAND**, 13km beyond, is an unassuming place whose **motel** blends easily into its rustic village atmosphere. The central *Highland Motel* (☎250/379-2249; ❷) is at 2968 Adelphi Street. There are also a couple of well-signposted, quiet **campsites** ($12–15). Country lanes lead north and east from here to **Bolean Lake** (10km) at 1437m, served by a lodge and campsite: *Bolean Lake Lodge*, Bolean Lake Road (☎250/558-9008; rooms ❶, tents $15; May–Oct); to **Pillar Lake** (13km) and the *Pillar Lake Resort* (☎250/379-2623; ❶; May–Oct), which provides cabins and campsite from $12; and to **Pinaus Lake** (10km) and its adjacent cabins and campsite, *Pinaus Lake Camp* (☎250/542-0624; cabins ❷, sites $15; April–Oct).

The O'Keefe Ranch

Some 12km short of Vernon, near the junction with the west-side Okanagan Lake road, stands the **Historic O'Keefe Ranch**, a collection of early pioneer buildings and a tidy little museum that's well worth a half-hour's pause (daily: May, June & Sept to mid-Oct 9am–5pm; July & Aug 9am–7pm; $6). In addition to a proficient summary of nineteenth-century frontier life, the museum contains an interesting section on the role of aboriginal peoples in the two world wars. Some 25 percent of eligible men immediately volunteered for service – a tour of duty that did little to resolve their national dilemma, which the museum sums up pithily with the observation that they belong to that "unhappy group who lost the old but are unable to obtain the new". Outside, a complete period street includes a detailed general store where you can buy oddments from staff in old-time dress – an excessively cute conceit, but one that fails to take the edge off the place's surprisingly successful evocation of an era. You feel the past most strongly in the church and graveyard, where the lovely building and its poignant handful of graves – three generations of O'Keefes, who first settled here in 1867 – capture the isolation and close-knit hardship of pioneer life.

The Okanagan

The vine- and orchard-covered hills and warm-water lakes of the **Okanagan**, located in south-central British Columbia, are in marked contrast to the rugged beauty of the region's more mountainous interior, and have made the region not only one of Canada's most favoured fruit-growing areas but also one of its most popular summer-holiday destinations. However, unless you want (occasionally) rowdy beach life or specifically enjoy mixing with families on their annual holiday, you'll probably want to ignore the area altogether in summer, despite its high word-of-mouth reputation. Three main centres – **Vernon**, **Kelowna** and **Penticton**, ranging from north to south along the hundred-kilometre-long **Okanagan Lake** – together contain the lion's share of the province's interior population, and all lay on an array of accommodation and mostly tacky attractions for the summer hordes. As ever in BC, however, things improve immeasurably if you can slip away from the towns and head for the hills or quieter stretches of lakeshore.

On the plus side, the almost year-round Californian lushness that makes this "the land of beaches, peaches, sunshine and wine" means that, in the relative peace of **off season**, you can begin to experience the region's considerable charms: fruit trees in blossom, quiet lakeside villages and free wine tastings in local vineyards. Plus, you can also expect room rates to be up to fifty percent less in the off season. Kelowna is the biggest and probably best overall base at any time of the year, but local **buses** link all the towns and Greyhounds ply Hwy 97 on their way between Osoyoos and Kamloops or Salmon Arm.

The legend of Okanagan Lake

When travelling through the Okanagan Valley, you'll find it hard to avoid **Ogopogo**, the famed lake monster of Okanagan Lake, whose smiling dragon-like face appears on all manner of postcards, billboards and bumper stickers. Its name comes from a 1920s music-hall song – "his mother was an earwig, his father a whale; a little bit of head and hardly any tail; and Ogopogo was his name" – but the myth is much older. The aboriginal Salish peoples believed in such a creature, and referred to it as **N'ha-a-itk**, meaning "Lake Demon" or "Devil of the Lake". Legend has it that the Salish people warned early white settlers of the lake monster, who apparently was a demon-possessed man punished by the gods for murdering a tribal brother. To appease him, the Salish would sacrifice animals whenever crossing near **Rattlesnake Island**, around which the monster supposedly lurked. The early white settlers feared the reptile as well, setting up armed patrols along the shores in case of an attack. Nowadays, holiday-makers would be thrilled to spot BC's version of the Loch Ness monster, demon or not, and numerous sightings are claimed every year.

Vernon

The beach scene is less frenetic in **VERNON** (pop. 35,000) than elsewhere in the Okanagan. Located at the junction of Hwys 6 and 97 near the northern edge of Okanagan Lake, the town attracts fewer of the bucket-and-spade brigade, though the emphasis on fruit and the great outdoors is as strong as ever, and the main highway through town is bumper-to-bumper with motels, fast-food joints and ever-more garish neon signs. On the whole it's easier to find a place to stay here than in Kelowna (see p.932) – but there are also fewer reasons for wanting to do so.

Downtown Vernon centres on 32nd Avenue (Hwy 97) and leaves a far more gracious impression than the town's outskirts by virtue of its elegant tree-lined streets and five hundred listed buildings. The locals are an amenable and cosmopolitan bunch made up of Britons, Germans, Chinese and Salish natives, plus an abnormally large number of Jehovah's Witnesses, whose churches seem to have a virtual monopoly on religious observance in the town. The local **museum**, the Greater Vernon Museum and Archive, by the clock tower at 3009 32nd Ave, does the usual job on local history (Mon–Sat 10am–5pm; closed Mon in winter; donation). At the southern entrance to town, **Polson Park** makes a green sanctuary from the crowds, but for beaches you should head 8km south of Vernon to **Kalamalka Provincial Park**, which sits on a stunning blue-green lake. The best beach on Kalamalka Lake is Kal Beach, fringed by trees, convenient parking just across the railway, and with a large bar with terrace at its eastern end. **Kin Beach** on Okanagan Lake west on Okanagan Landing Road is another good spot.

Other outdoor recreation (but not camping) is on hand at **Silver Star Recreation Area**, a steep 22-kilometre drive to the northeast on 48th Avenue off Hwy 97, where in summer a **ski lift** (late June to mid-Oct daily 10am–5pm; $7.50) trundles to the top of Silver Star Mountain (1915m) for wide views and meadow-walking opportunities; the most-used trail wends from the summit back to the base area. This is also a popular mountain-biking route – Monashee Adventure Tours (☏1-888/762-9253) rents out mountain bikes from the hostel (see below) and offers guided tours all over the Okanagan. If you want an eagle's-eye view of the area call Paraglide Canada (☏250/308-0387, ⓦwww.paraglidecanada.com; from $100 per person) for a tandem ride from the top of the mountains.

Heading **south from Vernon**, be sure to take the minor road, known as Okanagan Lake Road, on the western shore of Okanagan Lake – a quiet detour that offers something of the beauty for which the area is frequently praised, but which can be somewhat obscured by the commercialism of towns to the south. From the road, weaving through woods and small bays, the lake looks enchanting. The shore is often steep and there are few places to get down to the water – though at a push you might squeeze a tent between the trees for some unofficial camping.

Practicalities

Vernon's **infocentre** is south of the centre at 701 Hwy 97 (June–Aug daily 8am–6pm; Sept–May Mon–Fri 9am–5pm; ☏250/542-1415 or 1-800/665-0795 for reservations only, ⓦwww.vernontourism.com), along with a seasonal office south of town on the main highway. The **Greyhound station** is on the corner of 30th Street and 31st Avenue (☏250/545-0527) with connections to Calgary and Vancouver.

A superb **hostel**, *Lodged Inn*, 3201 Pleasant Valley Rd (☏250/549-3742 or 1-888/737-9427, ⓦwww.windsrivers.bc.ca; ❶), has dormitory accommodation and private rooms in a beautiful 1894 house – from the bus station, head east four blocks on 32nd Avenue, take a right and then the fourth left onto Pleasant Valley Drive. The 32 beds cost $16 for members, $20 for nonmembers. The most pleasant place to stay if money isn't too much of an issue is the *Best Western Vernon Lodge*, 3914-32nd St (☏250/545-3385 or 1-800/663-4422, ⓦwww.rpbhotels.com; ❺), nine blocks from Main St on Hwy 97 and with 127 air-conditioned rooms. There are also plenty of **motels** in town; a sound if bland choice is the *Sandman Inn* at 4201 32nd St (☏250/542-4325 or 1-800/726-3626, ⓦwww.sandmanhotels.ca; ❸). The *Polson Park Motel* (☏250/549-2231 or 1-800/480-2231, ⓦwww .polsonparkmotel.com; ❷), opposite the eponymous park on 24th Avenue, is one of the cheapest options. The *Schell Motel*, 2810 35th St (☏250/545-1351 or 1-888/772-4355; ❷), tempts clients with a pool and sauna. **Campsites** near town all get busy during the high season, and you may have to trek along the lakeshore for some way to strike lucky; try *Dutch's Tent and Trailer Court* (☏250/545-1023; $19–25; year-round) at 15408 Kalamalka Rd, 3km south of Vernon near Kalamalka Beach. Much more rural is *Ellison Provincial Park*, 16km off to the southwest on Okanagan Lake (reservations possible, see p.777; $17; March–Nov).

There are plenty of **eating** choices, especially amongst the many cafés and sandwich places. Downtown, try the *Bean to Cup* on 39th Avenue and 3903 27th Street (ⓦwww.beantocup.com) for soups, good coffee and sandwiches; or locals' favourite, *Intermezzo*, 3206 34th Ave (☏250/542-3853); dinner only 5–10pm) for good pastas. *The Italian Kitchen*, 3006 30th Ave (☏250/558-7899), serves up food true to its name. At 3127 30th Ave, *KT's* has saltwater aquariums alongside its tables and serves pizza, pasta, sandwiches and burgers. *Sir Winston's*, 2705 32nd St, is the downtown **pub** of choice.

Kelowna

If you want a summer suntan, big crowds and cheek-by-jowl nightlife – none of which you'd readily associate with the British Columbian interior – then **KELOWNA** ("grizzly bear" in the Salish dialect) – is the place to come. People had such a good time here in the summer of 1988 that the annual **Kelowna Regatta** turned into a full-blown and very un-Canadian alcohol-fuelled **riot** in which the police were forced to wade in with truncheons and tear gas; the main event has since been cancelled in its original format (it's now strictly a family affair), but the beach and downtown bars remain as busy as ever. That this modest city should have fostered such an urban-style melee isn't all that surprising. Compared with other interior towns, Kelowna (pop. 96,288) ranks as a sprawling metropolis, and to the unsuspecting visitor its approaches come as a very unpleasant surprise – particularly the appalling conglomeration of motels, garages and fast-food outlets on Hwy 97 at the north end of town.

That said, the lakefront and beaches, though heavily developed, aren't too bad, and off-season Kelowna's undeniably pretty **downtown** can make a good couple of days' respite from mountains and forests. Its attractions are increasingly well known across BC and remarkable jumps in population have taken place over the last few years: 37,000 people, many of them retirees, have moved here since 1990, creating something of a development nightmare for local planners.

Arrival, information and accommodation

Kelowna has a major regional **airport** 12km north of the town on Hwy 97 with regular shuttles and local buses to the centre. The **bus terminal** is at the east end of town in the Orchard Park Mall 5km from the centre at 2366 Leckie Rd on the corner of Harvey (Hwy 97), and sees off two buses daily to Calgary, Banff, Cache Creek and Kamloops respectively (☎250/860-3835). Buses #3, #7 and #19 run to downtown. The **infocentre** (June–Aug daily 8am–8pm; Sept–May Mon–Fri 8am–5pm, Sat & Sun 10am–5pm; ☎250/861-1515 or 1-800/663-4345, ⓦwww.kelownachamber.org), five blocks back from the lake at 544 Harvey, has all the information you could possibly need. To **rent a bike**, try Sports Rent at 3000 Pandosy St.

There's a staggering number of motels and campsites in and around town. However, **accommodation** can still be a major headache in the height of summer unless you can get to one of the **motels** on northbound Hwy 97 early in the morning, but it's a neon- and traffic-infested area well away from downtown and the lake (prices drop the further out you go). The HI-affiliated **hostel**, the *SameSun International Motel-Hostel*, is at 245 Harvey St just east of Abbott St (☎250/763-9814 or 1-877/562-2783, ⓦwww.samesun.com; ❶) – from the bus station take bus #10 to Queensway. Built in 2001, it has thrity private rooms and one hundred dorm beds at $15 in downtown just across from the beach. There's also an unofficial hostel south of downtown, the *Kelowna International Hostel*, 2343 Pandosy St near Guisachan Rd and the hospital (☎250/763-6024, ⓦwww.kelowna-hostel.bc.ca; ❶), where beds cost $13–15; both hostels fill quickly in summer, in which case you may go for the *Okanagan University College*, 3180 College Way (☎250/762-5445; ❷), which lets out their campus rooms from May through August.

The most affordable central downtown **hotel** is the perfectly placed but rough-edged *Willow Inn* at 235 Queensway (☎250/762-2122 or 1-800/268-1055; ❸) – ring or book very early for summer vacancies, and don't be deterred by the adjoining bar/strip-joint, which appears to be the headquarters of the Kelowna chapter of the Hell's Angels. Another slightly more expensive option is the *Royal-Anne* at 348 Bernard Ave (☎250/763-2277 or 1-888/811-3400, ⓦwww.royalannehotel.com; ❺). As ever, the chain hotels also come up trumps: the reasonably central *Sandman Hotel*, 2130 Harvey Ave (☎250/860-6409 or 1-800/726-3626, ⓦwww.sandmanhotels.ca; ❸), is a good mid-range bet. If money is tight, the strips in and out of town are crammed with standard-issue **motels**. At the other extreme, the money-no-object top choice in town is the *Grand Okanagan Lakeside Resort*, 1310 Water St (☎250/763-4500 or 1-800/465-4651, ⓦwww.grandokanagan.com; ❼).

If you're **camping**, all sites are pretty expensive, and in high season some places may only accept reservations for three days or more; mosquitoes can also be a problem. If you want to stay reasonably close to the action, two campsites conveniently back onto Lakeshore Road: the *Willow Creek Family Campground*, 3316 Lakeshore Rd (☎250/762-6302, ✉willowcreekcampground@shaw.ca; $22–35; year-round), which has free showers and a grassy tenting area flanking a sandy beach; and the *Hiawatha RV Park*, 3787 Lakeshore Rd, with separate tenting area, laundry, heated pool and free hot showers (☎250/861-4837 or 1-888/784-7275, ⓦwww.hiawatharvpark.com; $34–44; March–Oct). To be sure of camping space, try the *Bear Creek Provincial Park*, 9km west of town on Westside Road off Hwy 97 on the west side of the lake (showers and most facilities; $22; March–Nov), or the *Fintry Provincial Park*, once a working orchard, 34km north of town with similar facilities ($22; April–Oct) – reservations are accepted for both (see box on p.777). Most of the other campsites are on the other side of the lake at Westbank, a left turn off Hwy 97 on Boucherie Road just over the pontoon bridge (but really only accessible by car).

The town and around

The main attractions in downtown Kelowna are the public beach off **City Park**, a lovely green space that fronts downtown, and the strips along Lakeshore Road south of Kelowna's famed pontoon bridge, which tend to attract a younger, trendier crowd – **Rotary Beach** here is a windsurfers' hangout, and **Boyce Gyro Park**, just north, is where the town's teenagers practise their preening. Across the bridge and 2km and 14km respectively up the lake's west bank, **Bear Creek** and **Fintry Provincial Parks** are lovely spots with great beaches and campsites, but they are also horrendously popular (reservations possible at both, see p.777).

Kelowna owes its prosperity primarily to one man, Father Pandosy, a French priest who founded a mission here in 1859 and planted a couple of apple trees two years later. Much of Canada's **fruit** is now grown in the area – including virtually all the apricots, half the pears and plums, and a third of the country's apples. The infocentre can point you to dozens of juice, fruit, food and forestry tours, but if you feel like sampling the more hedonistic fruits of Father Pandosy's labours, consider visiting one of the local **vineyards**, all of them known for their open-handed generosity with free samples after a tour of the premises. You can choose from a variety of whites and reds as the valley's microclimates and soil types allow neighbouring vineyards to produce completely different wines. At one time most were crisp, fruity German-style white wines and dessert wines, but now successful red wines and drier whites are emerging. There's even organic champagne at **Summerhill Estate Winery**, 4870 Chute Lake Rd (tours generally daily on the hour 11am–2pm, but call for latest times; ☎250/764-8000 or 1-800/667-3538), in a beautiful spot near some hot springs, or try **Calona Wines**, Canada's second-biggest commercial winery and the Okanagan's oldest (founded 1932), just six blocks off Hwy 97 at 1125 Richter Ave (daily: May–Sept 11am–5pm, tours every 2 hours; Oct–April tour at 2pm; ☎250/762-9144). The infocentre can provide a full rundown of smaller, more far-flung estates. All of the wineries join together in May and late September to lay on the region's annual spring and autumn **wine festivals** (☎250/861-6654, ⓦwww.owfs.com) when free wine tastings, gourmet dinners, grape stomps and vineyard picnics take place to lure the connoisseur and beginner alike. More background can be found at the **Wine Museum**, 1304 Ellis St (Mon–Sat 10am–5pm, Sun noon–5pm), which is basically a glorified shop with a few exhibits, including a 3000-year-old clay drinking horn from Iran.

Getting away from Kelowna's crowds isn't easy, but the closest you'll come to shaking them off is by climbing **Knox Mountain**, the high knoll that overlooks the city to the north, just five minutes' drive (or a 30min walk) from downtown. It offers lovely views over the lake and town, particularly at sunset, and there's a wooden observation tower to make the most of the panorama. RVs are kept out of the area by a barrier dropped at dusk, but if you take a sleeping bag up – though perhaps not a tent – you might get away with an undisturbed night.

Eating, drinking and nightlife

Most **eating** places are crammed into the small downtown area. The variety is large, and a short walk should offer something to suit most tastes and budgets. Many travellers and young locals head for *Kelly O'Brian's* on Bernard Street, opposite the cinema, which has an "Irish" bar atmosphere and reasonable food. For a light lunch and snacks, *The Lunch Box*, 509 Bernard Ave at Ellis St, has good salads, soups and celebrated sandwiches at fair prices; you can sit outside in good weather. Despite its rather slick cocktail-lounge ambience, *Earl's Hollywood on Top*, 211 Bernard Ave near the waterfront and the junction with Queensway (☎250/763-3121) at the corner of Abbott, is good for ribs, seafood and steaks; go early to get a table on the upstairs patio. For pasta, *Joey Tomato's Kitchen* (☎250/860-8999) in the shopping mall at the junction of hwys 97 and 33 is a fun and inexpensive option.

At the top of the food tree you could splurge at *De Montreuil*, 368 Bernard Ave (☎250/860-5508) just east of Water St, widely considered the best restaurant in the Okanagan and serving local produce beef from Alberta and Pacific salmon. A three-course meal costs around $35. Also excellent in the top range is the *Williams Inn*, 526 Laurence Ave (☎250/763-5136; closed for lunch Sat & Sun), with an early evening set menu of salads and soups for $12.95 available 5–6.30pm and later an à la carte menu that includes Pacific salmon, Weiner schnitzel, venison, quail and sometimes caribou and bison. Dinner for two, with drinks, will set you back about $75. For about the same price, have a complete blow-out of West Coast food at the more recently opened *Fresco*, 1560 Water St (☎250/868-2285; dinner only; closed Mon all year; Oct to mid-May closed Sun & Mon).

If you're in town to party, or just want to catch a band and sink a beer, *O'Flaherty's* in the *Royal Anne Hotel* at 348 Bernard Ave is an unpretentious **pub** with live music. For dancing, head for *Flashbacks*, 1268 Ellis St (Fri & Sat only).

Penticton

PENTICTON is a corruption of the Salish phrase *pen tak tin* – "a place to stay forever" – but these days this is not a sobriquet the most southerly of the Okanagan's big towns even remotely deserves. Its summer daily average of ten hours of sunshine ranks it higher than Honolulu, making tourism its biggest industry after fruit (this is "Peach City"). That, along with Penticton's proximity to Vancouver and the US, keeps prices high and ensures that the town and beaches are swarming with water-sports jocks, cross-country travellers, RV skippers and lots of happy families. Off the beaches there's some festival or other playing virtually every day of the year to keep the punters entertained, the key ones being the **Wine Festival** in May and the **Peach Festival** in August.

Most leisure pastimes in Penticton – water-oriented ones in particular – take place on or near Okanagan Lake, just ten blocks from the town centre. **Okanagan Beach** is the closest sand to downtown and is usually covered in oiled bodies for most of its one-kilometre stretch; **Skaha Beach**, 4km south of town on Skaha Lake, is a touch quieter and trendier – both close at midnight, and sleeping on them is out of the question.

If you're determined to sightsee, the **museum** at 785 Main St has a panoply of predictable Canadiana (Mon–Fri 10am–5pm; donation) and you can take tours around the SS *Sicamous* (May–Sept daily 9am–7/9pm; Oct–April daily 9am–5pm; $4), a beached **paddlesteamer** off Lakeshore Drive on the Kelowna side of town (take in the lovely rose gardens alongside the boat while you're here). Just off Main Street there's the **Art Gallery of South Okanagan**, 199 Front St, which often carries high-quality shows (Tues–Fri 10am–5pm, Sat & Sun 1–5pm; $2). More tempting perhaps, and an ideal part of a day's stopover, is a trip to the **Tin Whistle Brewery**, 954 W Eckhardt Ave (drop-in tours and tastings year-round), which offers three English-type ales and a celebrated Peaches and Cream beer (summer only). If your taste is for wine rather than beer, head for the **Hillside Estate Winery**, 1350 Naramata Rd (℡250/493-4424), **Lake Breeze Vineyard**, Sammet Road (℡250/496-5659), or **Casobello Wines Vineyard**, 2km south of town off Hwy 97 on Skaha Lake Road, all of which offer tours and tastings. Otherwise, Penticton's main diversions are the curse of many Canadian tourist towns – the water slides.

Practicalities

Arriving by Greyhound, you'll pull in to the **bus depot** just off Main Street between Robinson and Ellis streets (℡250/493-4101); Penticton is a major intersection of routes, with buses bound for Vancouver (6–7 daily), Kamloops (2 daily), Nelson and points east (2 daily). The downtown area is small and easy to negotiate, particularly after a visit to the big **infocentre** at 888 Westminster Ave W (May, June & Sept Mon–Fri 9am–5pm, Sat & Sun 10am–4pm; July & Aug daily 8am–8pm; Oct–April Mon–Fri 9am–5pm, Sat & Sun 11am–4pm; ℡250/493-4055 or 1-800/663-5052, ⓦwww.penticton.org) on the north side of town – it has an adjacent BC Wine Information Centre, where bottles cost the same as they do at the vineyards. There is also a smaller summer information office south of town on Hwy 97. Both infocentres concentrate on recreational pursuits, and dozens of specialist shops around town rent out equipment for every conceivable activity. For **bike rental**, try *The Bike Barn*, 300 Westminster Ave West. For used books, **guides and maps**, visit *The Bookshop*, 238–242 Main St.

Although Penticton boasts a brimful of **accommodation**, it doesn't make finding a room in summer any easier. In high season it's best to head straight for the infocentre and ask for help, and if this fails there are so many **motels** you can easily walk from one to the next in the hope of striking lucky; most of the cheaper fall-backs line the messy southern approach to the town along Hwy 97. Three of the best and more central choices are the luxurious *Penticton Lakeside Resort & Casino*, 21 Lakeshore Drive W (℡250/493-8221 or 1-800/663-9400, ⓦwww.rpbhotels.com; ❻); *Tiki Shores Condominium Beach Resort* on the lake at 914 Lakeshore Drive (℡250/492-8769, ⓦwww.tikshores.com; ❹); and the big *Executive Inn*, 333 Martin St (℡250/492-3600 or 1-800/665-2221, ⓦwww.penticton-inn.com; ❺). Dropping down to mid-range places there's the *Sandman Hotel*, opposite the Convention Centre at 939 Burnaby Ave (℡250/493-7151 or 1-800/726-3626, ⓦwww.sandmanhotels.ca; ❸). If you're after somewhere cheap and location doesn't matter too much, try the *Plaza Motel*, 1485 Main St (℡250/492-8631; ❸), halfway between the town's two lakes; the *Waterfront Inn*, 3688 Parkview St (℡250/492-8228 or 1-800/563-6006, ⓦwww.waterfrontinn.net; ❸; May to mid-Oct); or the *Valley Star Motel*, 3455 Skaha Lake Rd (℡250/492-7205 or 1-888/309-0033, ⓦwww.valleystarpenticton.com; ❸), a couple of blocks from Skaha Lake. The HI-affiliated **hostel** is at 464 Ellis St (℡250/492-3992 or 1-866/782-9736, ⓦwww.hihostels.ca; ❶), in an old bunkhouse downtown which has 47 beds in dorms (members $17, non-members $21.50) and private rooms. To get here, walk one block south from the bus station and the hostel is on the left.

Most **campsites** have their "Full Up" signs out continuously in summer, and you may well have trouble if you arrive without a reservation. The best and therefore busiest sites are along the lake, and the bulk of the second-rank spots are near the highway on the southern approaches. Recommended are the

South Beach Gardens, 3815 Skaha Lake Rd (☎250/492-0628; $25–35; April–Sept), or *Wright's Beach Camp*, south of town on Hwy 97 on Lake Skaha (☎250/492-7120; $20–30; May–Sept). If you want to camp away from town, make for the *Camp-Along Tent and Trailer Park*, 6km south of the town off Hwy 97 in an apricot orchard overlooking Skaha Lake (☎250/497-5584 or 1-800/968-5267, Ⓦwww.campalong.com; $20–32).

Budget **eating** choices don't extend much beyond the fast-food joints and cafés bunched largely around Main Street: try the funky *Green Beanz Cafe*, 218 Martin St, for wraps and organic coffee, or head for the *Elite*, 340 Main St, the best overall downtown for basic burgers, soup and salads. *Theo's* at 687 Main St (☎250/492-4019) is a friendly, crowded and highly rated Greek place that does big portions. For something different and more upmarket, search out *Salty's Beach House*, 988 Lakeshore Drive (☎250/493-5001), a restaurant that's very popular but eccentric, with a South Seas setting of palm trees and fishing nets and a spicy menu of Caribbean, Thai, Indonesian and Malaysian food. For **drinks**, make for the perennially popular *Barking Parrot Lounge* in the *Penticton Lakeside Resort*.

Highway 3: the border towns

Unless you're crossing the US–Canada border locally, British Columbia's slightly tawdry necklace of border towns between Hope (see p.916) and the Alberta border along **Hwy 3** is as good a reason as any for taking a more northerly route across the the province. Few of the towns amount to much; if you have to break the journey, aim to do it in **Salmo** or **Castlegar**, towns on which some of the Kootenays' charm has rubbed off. Things are more interesting around **Osoyoos** and **Keremeos**, where the road enters a parched desert landscape after climbing from Hope through the gripping mountain scenery of the Coastal Ranges, passing en route through **Manning Provincial Park**.

If you're crossing over **the border** hereabouts, incidentally, don't be lulled by the remote customs posts into expecting an easy passage: if you don't hold a Canadian or US passport you can expect the sort of grilling you'd get at major entry points.

Manning Provincial Park

One of the few parks in the Coast and Cascade ranges, **Manning Provincial Park** parcels up a typical assortment of mountain, lake and forest scenery about 60km south of Princeton and is conveniently bisected by Hwy 3. Even if you're just passing through it's time well spent walking at least one of the short **trails** off the road, the best of which is the flower-festooned Rhododendron Flats path, located 3km east of the park's west portal. The most popular drive within the park is the fifteen-kilometre side road to **Cascade Lookout**, a viewpoint over the Similkameen Valley and its amphitheatre of mountains; a gravel road carries on another 6km from here to **Blackwall Peak**, the starting point for the **Heather Trail** (10km one-way), renowned for its swaths of summer wild flowers. Other manageable day-hikes leave the south side of the main highway, the majority accessed from a rough road to Lightning Lake just west of the park visitor centre.

The **park visitor centre**, 1km east of the resort (May–Sept daily 9am–8pm), is good for trail leaflets and has history and natural history exhibitions. **Accommodation** at the *Manning Park Resort* (☎604/840-8822 or

1-800/330-3321, ⓦwww.manningparkresort.com; ❹), on Hwy 3 almost exactly midway between Princeton and Hope (64km), is made up of 73 cabins and chalets, but all these go quickly in summer. The only other accommodation are the three rooms of the *Sunshine Valley B & B* (☎604/869-2143, ⓔsunshinevlybnb@uniserve.com; ❸), 3km west of the park's West Gate at 71660 Branch Bend. There are also four provincial **campsites** ($12–17; reservations possible, see p.777) on and off the highway, the best close to the road being *Hampton* and *Mule Deer*, 4km and 8km east of the visitor centre, respectively. A third, *Lightning Lake*, has free hot showers.

Highway 3 from Princeton

Lacklustre low hills ripple around **PRINCETON**'s dispersed collection of mostly drab houses. The **motels** – of which there are plenty – group around a large and grim lumber mill on the east side of town, but you're better off hanging on for Keremeos. However, if circumstances dump you in town overnight, head for the *Riverside Motel* (☎250/295-6232; ❶) at 307 Thomas Ave, three blocks north of the town centre, with fifteen nice individual log cabins. *Global Netrider* on Bridge Street is a laid-back coffee/sandwich place with Internet access. The **bus depot** is at the west end of town by the cheap-and-cheerful eatery *Billie's*, not far from the *Apple Tree Restaurant* (also a good food stop) on Vermilion Ave and the **infocentre** (daily 9am–5pm; ☎250/295-3103, ⓦwww.town.princeton.bc.ca), housed in an old Canadian Pacific rail wagon at 195 Bridge St.

HEDLEY, about 20km further on, is an old gold-mining hamlet that today is little more than a single street with great scenery and a couple of motels. The **infocentre** is part of a small but interesting **museum** with archive photos and mining memorabilia at 712 Daly St (☎250/292-8422, ⓔhedleymuseum@img .net; mid-May to Aug daily 9am–5pm; rest of year Thurs–Mon 9am–4/5pm; donation). Pick up details of the self-guided walking tour around the village's period buildings. To **stay**, try the *Colonial Inn Bed & Breakfast* (☎250/292-8131, ⓦwww.colonialinnbb.ca; ❺), an historic 1930s house built by the Kelowna Exploration Gold Mining Company to wine and dine potential investors; it has just five rooms and 16 RV sites ($20), so booking ahead is often necessary. The *Gold House B & B* 200m off Hwy at 644 Colonial Rd (☎250/292-8418 or 1-866/676-4653, ⓦwww.thegoldhouse.com; ❹) is equally historic, having been the 1904 Gold Assay Office. If these are full, make for the inexpensive *River Haven RV Park & Motel* on Hwy 3 by the river (☎250/292-8221; ❸, RVs $15–20), but note that there are no tent sites. Eat and drink in *The Gold Dust Pub* just off the highway east of the village.

Beyond Hedley and 21km east of Princeton, off the highway, lies **Bromley Rock Provincial Park**, a lovely picnic stop looking down on the white water of the Similkameen River. Also west of the village is the *Stemwinder Provincial Park* **campsite** ($14; April–Oct), a small, pine-tree dotted site with 27 pitches. Further on, on the way to Keremeos, Hwy 3 retraces the historic **Dewdney Trail**, a 468-kilometre mule track used in the 1860s to link Hope (p.916) with the Kootenay goldfields. Another of British Columbia's extremely picturesque patches of road, for much of the way it follows the ever-narrowing Similkameen Valley, backed by ranks of pines and white-topped mountains. To explore some of the backcountry off the highway, take the 21-kilometre gravel road (signed just west of Keremeos) south into the heart of **Cathedral Provincial Park**, a spectacular upland enclave with an unserviced campsite and 32km of marked trails.

Keremeos

Highway 3 meanders eventually to pretty little **KEREMEOS**, whose aboriginal name supposedly means "where the three winds meet" – a reference to the stiff breezes that are channelled through the hills hereabouts. The local landscape lurches suddenly into a far more beautiful rural mode, thanks mainly to a climate that blesses the region with the longest growing season in the country – hence the tag "Fruit Stand Capital of Canada". Keremeos, whose attractive situation rivals Nelson's (see p.955), spreads over a dried-up lake bed, with hills and mountains rising from the narrow plain on all sides. Lush, irrigated orchards surround the town, offset in spring by huge swaths of flowers across the valley floor, and depending on the season you can pick up fruit and vegetables from stands dotted more or less everywhere: cherries, apricots, peaches, pears, apples, plums and grapes all grow in abundance. If you're not tempted by the food, however, you may be by the **wine tastings** at the organic **St Laszlo Vineyards** (☎250/499-2856), 1km east of town on Hwy 3.

Keremeos itself is a rustic, two-street affair that's almost unspoilt by neon or other urban clutter. A few shopfronts are oldish, and several make a stab at being heritage houses – the wonderful *Pasta Trading Post* on Main Street, for example (see below) – and though there's little to see or do (bar the inevitable small-town museum), it's a pleasant spot to spend the night. About 1km east of town on Upper Bench Road is the **Grist Mill and Gardens** (May–Oct daily 9.30am–5pm; $5.50), a working flour mill dating from 1877 and surrounded by wheat fields and gardens. Restored to its original glory – the lovely general store still flaunts wallpaper from 1894 – it's a pleasant place to while away a half hour and if you're hungry there's a tearoom with soups, sandwiches and goods baked with the mill's flour.

The *Pasta Trading Post* on Main St at 629 7th Ave (☎250/499-2933) is a wonderful place to **eat** locally grown organic produce and home-made pasta sauces. They also have comfortable **rooms** upstairs (❸); rates include breakfast and the use of a hot tub. There are a couple of **motels** locally: the cheaper is the *Similkameen* (☎250/499-5984; ❷), 1km west of the centre in open country surrounded by lawns and orchards, with a few tent pitches ($10–15) in summer only; but the nicer is *The Elk* (☎250/499-2043 or 1-888/499-7773, ❼www.keremeos.com/elk; ❷), also with landscaped gardens.

Osoyoos

Beyond Keremeos the road climbs 46km, eventually unfolding a dramatic view, far below, of **OSOYOOS** – meaning "gathered together" – and a sizeable lake surrounded by bare, ochre hills. Descending, you enter one of Canada's strangest landscapes – a bona fide desert of half-bare, scrub-covered hills, sand, lizards, cactus, snakes (23 types of invertebrate here are found nowhere else in the world) and Canada's lowest average rainfall (around 25cm per year). Temperatures are regularly 10°C higher than in Nelson, less than a morning's drive away, enabling exotic fruit like bananas and pomegranates to be grown and prompting Osoyoos to declare itself the "Spanish Capital of Canada". The

Moving on from Osoyoos involves a major decision if you're travelling by car or bike: continue east on Hwy 3, or strike north on Hwy 97 through the Okanagan to the Trans-Canada Hwy. If you're on a Greyhound, the bus heads north and the decision can be deferred until Penticton, the major parting of the ways for services in this part of BC.

houses are supposed to have been restyled to give the place an Iberian flavour to match its climate, but on the ground it's almost impossible to find any trace of the conversion.

The town is otherwise distinguished by its position beside **Lake Osoyoos** (Canada's warmest freshwater lake, at 24°C) in the Okanagan Valley; Hwy 97, which passes through the town as an ugly strip, is the main route into the Okanagan region. In summer the place comes alive with swimmers and boaters, drawn to some of the warmest waters of any lake in Canada, and with streams of American RVs slow-tailing their way northwards to where the real action is.

A visit to the **Desert Centre** (mid-April to mid-Oct daily 10am–4.30pm, 1hr 30min tours every half-hour; ☎250/1-877/899-0897; $6), on Hwy 97 just north of town, is a good way to learn a little more about the region's oddball environment. There are tours over a 1.5km boardwalk through a small area of desert and it's a fascinating ecosystem of some 100 rare plants, including tiny cacti and sage, as well as 300 animals from rattlesnakes to pocket gophers that are now all under serious threat. Once irrigated this land becomes very fertile and only nine percent of the desert survives undisturbed, with a full sixty percent vanished altogether.

The relative lack of crowds (summer excepted) and strange scenery might persuade you to do your beach-bumming in Osoyoos, though you may be pushed to find space in any of the town's twenty or so **hotels** and **motels** during high season; a cheap choice is the *Avalon*, 9106 Main St (☎250/495-6334 or 1-800/264-5999, ⓦwww.avaloninn.ca; ❸), while at the other financial extreme is the *Best Western Sunrise Inn*, 5506 Main St (☎250/495-4000 or 1-877/878-2200, ⓦwww.bestwesternosoyoos.com; ❻), with an indoor pool and restaurant. Most of the motels are across the causeway on the southeastern shore of the lake, alongside the **Greyhound stop** at 6015 Lakeshore Drive. For more choice and help, contact the **infocentre** at the junction of Hwys 3 and 97 (☎250/495-7142 or 1-888/676-9667, ⓦwww.destinationosoyoos.com). You're more likely to get a place in one of the half-dozen local **campsites** – try the *Cabana Beach*, 2231 Lakeshore Drive (☎250/495-7705, ⓦwww.cabanabeach.com; $20–32; May–Sept), or the *Inkameep Campground and RV Park* on 45th Street 1km from Hwy 3 East (☎250/495-7279; $19–31), which also organizes local hikes and night tours of the desert. Local **eateries** are almost entirely fast food, but *Beans Desert Bistro*, 8323 Main St (☎250/495-7742), has good coffee and food, as well as Internet access, or there's *Finny's*, 8311 78th St, for a lengthier menu of salads, steaks and burgers.

Midway, Greenwood and Grand Forks

At **MIDWAY**, some 65km east of Osoyoos on Hwy 3, something of the desert atmosphere lingers, the hills strange, broad whalebacks cut by open valleys and covered in coarse scrub and brown-baked grass. The hamlet's handful of scattered homes are like a windblown and wistful ghost town, making an evocative backdrop for the overgrown train tracks and tiny **railway museum** housed alongside a rusted minuscule steam engine. It's a fascinating little spot. The Kettle River Museum (mid-May to mid-Sept daily 10am–4pm; $2) in the 1900 CPR station 3km out of the village tells the town's story. To **stay**, check-in to the *Mile Zero Motel*, 622 Palmerston St (☎250/449-2231; ❷), or put up a tent at the *Riverfront Park Campground* four blocks south of Hwy 3 on 5th Avenue, which has water, showers and toilets ($10).

East of Midway, the scenery along Hwy 3 begins to change from a flatter, drier landscape of bleached grass and sagebrush to rather more bland

7

meandering hills. At **GREENWOOD**, however, the pines reappear, heralding a wild, battered brute of a village, which has suffered from the closure of its mines and can't muster much more than a handful of old buildings and some abandoned workings. Some life is beginning to flow into the village, however, in the shape of antique and other specialist shops, while efforts are being made to spruce up some of the heritage buildings, details of which you can pick up from the **infocentre**, housed on the main road at 214 S Copper St (May–Oct daily 10am–4/5pm; ℡250/445-6355, ⓦwww.greenwoodmuseum.com). You might also want to grab a **drink** at the atmospheric *Windsor Hotel*, which claims to have the oldest saloon in BC. You're pretty sure of a welcome in any of the three **motels**, cheapest of which is the *Evening Star*, 798 N Government St (℡250/445-6733; ❷), at the eastern entrance to town. For **camping** there are a couple of small provincial park sites: *Jewel Lake* ($14; June–Sept), 1km east of Greenwood and then 12km off Hwy 3; and *Boundary Creek* ($14; April–Oct), 2km west of town off Hwy 3.

GRAND FORKS is not grand at all – it's very small and very dull and little more than a perfunctory transit settlement built on a river flat. Several Greyhound **buses** drop in daily, probably the biggest thing to happen to the place. The small **Boundary Museum** (Sept–June Mon–Fri 9am–4.30pm; July–Aug Mon–Fri 9am–4.30pm, Sat & Sun 10am–4pm; $2) by the traffic lights is the standard small-town model and can be seen in about the time it takes for the lights to change. The **infocentre** is next door (Sept–May Mon–Fri 8.30am–4.30pm; June–Aug Mon–Fri 8.30am–4.30pm, Sat & Sun 9am–5pm; ℡250/442-2833, ⓦwww.grandforkschamber.com). The history of Doukhobor settlers (see box p.943) is charted at the small **Mountainview Doukhobor Museum** (June–Aug daily 9am–6pm; $2) on Hardy Mountain Rd. About 25km north of town, 19-km long **Christina Lake** – which claims some of BC's warmest water – is a modestly unspoilt summer resort with lots of swimming, boating and camping opportunities (two other BC lakes make similar claims for their waters). A dozen or so motels and campsites sprout along its shore, mostly at the lake's southern end, with about the same number in and around the town itself, but it's doubtful that you'd want to use them except in an emergency.

Rossland

Trail is home to the world's largest lead and zinc smelter, a vast industrial complex whose chimneys cast a dismal shadow over the village's few houses. There's no reason to stop here and you'll probably want to ignore it in favour of the far more picturesque **ROSSLAND**, 11km away, which also relies on Trail's smelter for employment and has a mining foundation – gold this time, some $125 million-worth of which was gouged from the surrounding hills around the year 1900 (that's $2 billion-worth at today's prices). If you're into mining heritage, a tour of the **Le Roi Gold Mine** – once one of the world's largest, with 100km of tunnels – and the adjoining **Rossland Historical Museum** will entertain you with fascinating technical and geological background (mid-May to mid-Sept daily 9am–5pm; mine tours May, June & Sept every 1hr 30min, July & Aug every 30min; museum & mine $8, museum only $4).

The **infocentre** (mid-May to Oct daily 9am–5pm; ℡250/362-7722 or 1-888/448-7444, ⓦwww.rossland.com), in the museum at the junction of the town's two main roads (Hwy 3b and Hwy 22), offers an interesting mine tour and is useful for details of the **Nancy Greene Provincial Park** which has a ten-pitch campsite (no showers; $10; May–Sept) northwest of town. Though the park and recreation area is best known for its world-class skiing – the **Red Mountain Ski Area** (information: ☎250/362-7669, ⓦwww.ski-red.com) is a training ground for the Canadian national team – it's also excellent for hiking, an outdoor commodity that isn't easy to come by in these parts, and for mountain biking, a very popular local activity (there are over 100km of trails). **Rent bikes** and pick up information at *The Sacred Ride*, 2133 Columbia Ave (☎250/362-5688). There's a **hostel**, the rather indifferent *Mountain Shadow Hostel* at 2125 Columbia Ave (☎250/362-7160; dorm beds $17–20), and several resort hotels; or try the upmarket twelve-unit *Ram's Head Inn*, 3km west of Rossland on Hwy 3B (☎250/362-9577 or 1-877/267-4323, ⓦwww .ramshead.bc.ca; ❸), with hot tubs and bike rental.

Rossland has a few nice places to **eat**: the locals' choice is the *Sunshine Café* (breakfast & lunch only; closes 3pm) on Columbia, the main street or there is the excellent *Mountain Gypsy Café* at 2167 Washington St (☎250/362-3342), a funky place that's good for light lunches, tasty dinners and microbrewed beers. It's popular and laid back, so be sure to book for the evening. The key place to **drink** is the busy *Powder Keg* in the big 67-room *Uplander Hotel*, 1919 Columbia Ave (☎250/362-7275, ⓦwww.uplanderhotel.com; ❸), which also has a lounge for snacks and a more expensive restaurant.

Castlegar

Some 27km north of Trail on Hwy 22, **CASTLEGAR** is a strange diffuse place with no obvious centre, probably because roads and rivers – this is where the Kootenay meets the Columbia – make it more a transport hub than a community. In its time it was famous for its immigrant **Doukhobor** or "Spirit Wrestler" population (see box opposite). Much of the community's heritage has been collected in the **Doukhobor Village Museum** (May–Sept daily 9/10am–5/6pm; $4), just off the main road on the right after you cross the big suspension bridge over the Kootenay River. A Doukhobor descendant is on hand to take you through the museum, which houses a winsome display of farm machinery, handmade tools, superb archive photographs and traditional Russian clothing that's intriguing as much for its alien context as for its content. For a further taste of Doukhobor culture, visit the evocative **Zuckerburg Island Heritage Park** off 7th Avenue, named after a local teacher of Doukhobors who built a log Russian Orthodox Chapel House and other buildings and memorials here after coming to the town in 1931; it was bought and restored by the town in 1981, and is reached by a ninety-metre pedestrian suspension bridge.

Castlegar's **infocentre** (July & Aug daily 8am–7pm; rest of year Mon–Fri 9am–5pm; ☎250/365-6313, ⓦwww.castlegar.com) is at 1995 6th Ave off the main road as you come into town from Grand Forks. Most people arrive in town by bus or car, but the town is also the major regional **airport** for the Kootenays region; the landing strip is alongside Hwy 3a. There are some half-dozen places to stay in and around town: the best **motel** – small, and with a nice view – is the *Cozy Pines* on Hwy 3 on the western edge of town at 2100 Crestview Crescent (☎250/365-5613, ⓦwww.cozypines.com; ❷). Closer in, the modern and attractive *Best Western Fireside Motor Inn*, 1810 8th Ave at the junction of Hwys 3 and 22 (☎250/365-2128 or 1-800/499-6399, ⓦwww.bestwestern.com; ❸), is a touch more expensive. About 3km west of town on Hwy 3 is the *Castlegar RV Park and Campground*, 1725 Mannix Rd (☎250/365-2337, ⓦwww.castelgarrvpark.com; $16–23; April–Oct), with rural setting, separate tenting area, free hot showers, laundry and restaurant. There are

The Doukhobors

The **Doukhobors** were members of a southern Russian sect who fled their home country in 1899 after being persecuted for their religious and political views. The so-called "Spirit Wrestlers" – the name was coined by a Russian Orthodox archbiship who argued that they were in conflict with the Holy Spirit – were fiercely pacifist, rejected secular government and ignored the liturgy and procedures of the organized church, believing that God resided in each individual, rather than in a building or institution.

The flight from Russia was aided by the Quakers, whose pacifist and other ideals closely tallied with those of the Doukhobors, and by the novelist Leo Tolstoy, whose beliefs also chimed with those of the sect. Around 7500 left in the first wave, bringing their pacifist-agrarian lifestyle to western Canada, and to Saskatchewan in particular. Initially the authorities were sympathetic to their beliefs, and granted religious, educational and housing concessions. In 1905, however, sect members refused to swear an oath of allegiance, and followed their leader, Peter Verigin, to southern BC.

By the 1920s the province had around ninety Doukhobor settlements, each with a co-operative, communal population of around sixty. They arrived in Castlegar in 1908, establishing at least 24 villages in the area, each with Russian names meaning things like "the beautiful", "the blessed" or "consolation". Accomplished farmers, they laboured under the motto "Toil and a Peaceful Life", creating highly successful orchards, farms, sawmills and packing plants. Although their way of life waned after the death of Verigin in 1924, killed by a bomb planted in his railway carriage, the Doukhobors' considerable industry and agricultural expertise transformed the Castlegar area; many locals still practise the old beliefs – Doukhobor numbers are around 15,000 across the region (though those with Doukhobor roots total about 30,000) – and Russian is still spoken. These days there's also a breakaway radical sect, the Freedomites, or Sons of Freedom, infamous for their eye-catching demonstrations – of which fires and nude parades are just two – against materialism and other morally dubious values.

also regional and a provincial park **campsites** in the vicinity: *Pass Creek Regional Park*, which has a nice, sandy beach (☎250/365-3386; $12; May–Sept), 2km west off Hwy 3a at the Kootenay River Bridge; and the *Syringa Provincial Park* (reservations possible, see p.777; $17; mid-May to mid-Sept), 19km north of Hwy 3 at Castlegar on the east side of Lower Arrow Lake. For cheap **eating**, *Café Friends* back in town at 1102 3rd St has good home-cooked basics; or try *Gabes* at 1432 Columbia Ave for light meals (☎250/365-6028).

Salmo

Despite the large volume of traffic converging on it along Hwy 3 and Hwy 6, tiny **SALMO**, 43km east of Castlegar, somehow manages to retain a pioneer feel and most of its tidy wooden buildings are fronted by verandas, decked with baskets of flowers in summer. The Chamber of Commerce (Mon–Fri 9am–5pm, plus Sat & Sun same hours July & Aug; ☎250/365-6313) is at 1995 6th Ave. There's also a **museum** (May–Sept Mon–Fri 1pm–5pm; $2) at 4th Street and Railway Avenue that charts the vicissitudes of pioneer life and hosts the odd travelling exhibition. In winter there's **skiing** at the Salmo ski area, 2km east of town.

Buses usually pull in here for a long rest stop at the terminal by the Petro-Canada garage on the north side of the village. If you need to overnight, use either of the two central motels: the *Reno*, 123 Railway Ave (☎250/357-9937, ℮renohotel@telus.net; ❷), one block east of the bus terminal, or the slightly more expensive *Salcrest*, 110 Motel Ave (☎250/357-9557; ❷), at the junction of Hwys 3 and 6. The nearest **campsite** is the *Selkirk Motel and RV Sites* (☎250/357-2346 or 1-888/368-6336; $12–16; units ❶; May–Oct), 4km west of town at 307 2nd Relief Rd. For **food**, try *Charlie's Pizza and Spaghetti House*, an old-style diner on 4th Street. Just up the road, the *Silver Dollar Pub* is the town's favourite **bar**, with pool tables, a jukebox and lots of good ol' boys in an atmospheric wooden interior. Salmo Foods, opposite the bar, is the best **supermarket** for stocking up.

A classic stretch of scenic road, Hwy 3 climbs from Salmo to the fruit-growing plains around Creston via **Kootenay Pass** (1774m) – though the views are less of spectacular mountains than of a pretty tracery of creeks and rivers crashing down through forest on all sides. This is one of the highest main roads in the country – it's frequently closed by bad weather – and, beyond about 13km out of Salmo, it has no services until Creston, so check your petrol before setting out. If you're cycling, brace yourself for a fifty-kilometre uphill slog, but the reward is an unexpected and stunning lake at the pass, where there's a pull-off picnic area and views of high peaks in the far distance.

Creston

Don't stop in prosperous little **CRESTON**, 83km east of Salmo near the broad mountain-flanked floodplain of the Kootenay River, unless you're a bird-watcher or feel like hunting down such sightseeing frippery as "Canada's best mural" (the original, in McDowell's department store, had spawned another dozen or so pictures around town at last count). If you're passing through, you might want to pause for the **Stone House Museum**, 219 Devon St (May–Sept daily 10am–3.30pm, by appointment the rest of the year; ☎250/428-9262; $2), known for its replica Kuntenai (Ktunaxa) canoe. Similar canoes, with their down-pointed ends, are only found elsewhere in the world in parts of eastern Russia, underlining the fact that millennia ago migrations took place across the Bering Straits into North America. If you're not driving, another temptation is the **Columbia Brewery**, 1220 Erickson St (☎250/428-9344; tours in summer usually at 9.30am, 11.30am, 1pm & 2pm; but call to confirm current hours), whose Kokanee beers you'll find in most of the region's bars and restaurants.

The **infocentre** is in a log cabin (one of the town's few buildings of interest) on the east side of town at 711 Canyon St (Mon 9am–5pm, Tues–Sat 9am–6pm; ☎250/428-4342): use it if by mischance you need **accommodation**, though with twenty or so motels and campsites to choose from you probably won't be fighting for a bed. The cheapest and most central spot is the *Creston Hotel & Suites*, 1418 Canyon St (☎250/428-2225, ⓦwww.crestonhotel.com; ❷); motels on the town's fringes offer more salubrious, if slightly costlier alternatives. For **campers**, there's the pleasant *Little Joe's Campground* (☎250/428-2954 or 428-5372 off season, ℮faye@kootenay.com; April–Oct; $14–16), wooded site near a creek 5km east of town at 4020 Hwy 3E. If you want coffee, snacks or picnic provisions, good places to **eat** are the *Creston Valley Bakery*, 113 10th Ave, and *Annette's Delicatessen*, 1127 Canyon St. For dinner, including good vegetarian options, try *Cafe Morego*, 129 10th Ave (☎250/428-7252; closed Sun).

Probably the best reason to spend time locally is the 7000-hectare **Creston Valley Wildlife Management Area** (☎250/428-3259), located 10km northwest of town off Hwy 3. Creston overlooks a broad section of valley and lowlands – relatively rare commodities in BC, home to the idly meandering Kootenay River. Over the years the river has repeatedly burst its banks, creating a rich alluvial plain beloved by farmers, and producing the lush medley of orchards and verdant fields that fringe Creston. Much of the flood plain and its wetlands, however – the so-called "Valley of the Swans" – have been preserved in their original state, creating a haven for birds and waterfowl. This area has one of the world's largest nesting osprey populations, while a total of 250 species have been recorded in the confines of the Creston Management Area (not to mention otters, moose and other animals). Birds can be seen from several points, including rarities such as Western grebe and forester's tern, but for full details of the area visit the sanctuary's Wildlife Centre (May–Aug daily 8am–6pm, April & Oct Wed–Sun 9am–4pm; $3), which provides telescopes and lookouts, a library and theatre, and a wide range of guided walks and canoe trips (from $5) through the area's forest, marsh and grassland habitats.

For details of the trip east of Creston, see p.960.

The Kootenays

The Kootenays is one of the most attractive and unvisited parts of British Columbia, and one of the most loosely defined. It consists essentially of two major north–south valleys – the Kootenay and the Columbia, which are largely taken up by **Kootenay Lake** and **Upper** and **Lower Arrow Lakes** – and three intervening mountain ranges – the Purcells, Selkirks and Monashees, whose once-rich mineral deposits formed the kernel of the province's early mining industry. **Nelson** is the key town, slightly peripheral to the Kootenays' rugged core, but a lovely place, and one of the few provincial towns that offers real attractions in its own right. Scattered lakeside hamlets, notably **Kaslo** and **Nakusp**, make excellent bases for excursions into mountain scenery which has a pristine quality rarely found elsewhere. Water-based activities – canoeing and fishing in particular – are excellent, and you can also explore the ramshackle mining heritage of near-ghost towns like **Sandon** and **New Denver**. Many of these towns and villages also have more than their fair share of artists, painters, writers, healers and New Age enthusiasts, lending the region considerable cultural and alternative-lifestyle lustre.

Getting around the region is tricky without **private transport**, for there are next to no public services, which is a shame because the roads here are amongst the most scenic in a province noted for its scenery. Even with your own car, there's no way to do the Kootenays justice without retracing your steps at times. You can dip in and out of the region from the Trans-Canada Hwy (to the north) or Hwy 3 (to the south), but any trans-Kootenay route is more attractive than either of these main highways; the most **scenic routes** – and these are some of the loveliest drives in the province – are Hwy 31A from Kaslo to New Denver, Hwy 6 south of New Denver in the Slocan Valley and Hwy 6 from New Denver to Vernon. Given no time constraints, your best strategy would be to enter from Creston and exit via Vernon, which sets you up for the Okanagan.

Highway 3A to Kootenay Bay

Starting from just north of Creston, **Hwy 3A** picks a slow, twisting course up the eastern shore of **Kootenay Lake** to the car ferry at Kootenay Bay. Apart from the ample scenic rewards of the lake and the mountains beyond it, the highway is almost completely empty for all of its 79km, and none of the villages marked on maps amount to anything more than scattered houses hidden in the woods. The only noteworthy sight is the **Glass House** (May, June, Sept & Oct daily 9am–5pm; July & Aug 8am–8pm; $6), midway up the lake 7km south of **BOSWELL**, which ranks highly on the list of Canada's more bizarre offerings. Constructed entirely from embalming bottles, the house was built by a Mr David Brown in 1952 after 35 years in the funeral business – "to indulge", so the wonderfully po-faced pamphlet tells you, "a whim of a peculiar nature". The retired mortician travelled widely, visiting friends in the funeral profession until he'd collected 600,000 bottles – that's 250 tonnes' worth – to build his lakeside retirement home. The family continued to live here until curious tourists took the upper hand. Nearby **accommodation** is provided by the four-unit *Heidelburg Inn*, 12866 Hwy 3A (☎250/223-8263, ✉heidelburg@kootenay.com; ❷; April–Oct), overlooking the lake between the Kokanee Spring and Creston golf courses; the seven-unit *Kootenay Lake Lodge Resort*, 12622 Hwy 3A (☎250/223-8181, ⓦwww .kootenaylakelodge.com; ❺), a rustic log lodge with private beach and wood-fired cedar baths; and the lakeside *Mountain Shores Resort and Marina* (☎250/223-8258; ❸; April–Sept), a combination of twelve motel-type rooms, cottages and **campsite** ($19–25) with store, hot showers and heated outdoor pool. There's another smaller campsite, *Kootenay Kampsites* (☎250/223-8488 or 223-8559; $16–20; May–Oct), 39km north of Creston and 2km south of the Glass House with rustic, well-treed sites, laundry and hot showers.

At **GRAY CREEK**, a few kilometres onward, check out the superb **Gray Creek Store**, which boasts the once-in-a-lifetime address of 1979 Chainsaw Avenue and claims, with some justification, to be "The Most Interesting Store You've Ever Seen". The shop basically *is* Gray Creek – it's the sort of place you go to get your chainsaw fixed and where real lumberjacks come for their red-checked shirts. There is one lakeside **campsite** nearby: the small *Lockhart Beach* provincial park campsite ($14; May–Sept) with RV and tent sites 13km south of Gray Creek and 20km south of Kootenay Bay (see below). A bit more exotic, *Tipi Camp* (☎250/227-9555 or 1-866/800-2267, ⓦwww.tipicamp.bc .ca; June–Sept) is situated on Pilot Peninsula, reached by a twice a day 20min boat taxi from Gray Creek. To stay in a tepee you need your own bedding, and it costs $80 a night including water taxi and three meals; day-trips, including transportation, lunch and dinner, are also available. From Gray Greek, the Gray Greek Forest service road (July–Oct) leads 85km east to Kimberley (see p.963), not a short cut by any means, but scenic and adventurous driving nonetheless. Be sure to be stocked up on supplies before setting off.

CRAWFORD BAY and **KOOTENAY BAY** are names on the map that refer in the flesh to the most fleeting of settlements, the latter also being the **ferry terminal** for boats to Balfour on the west shore. Crawford Bay, 3.5km from the terminal, boasts the Kootenay Forge, an old-world forge, where in summer you can often watch blacksmiths working and a number of other artisan shops from traditional broom-makers to weavers. The area has also long been famous for the **Yasodhara Ashram**, 527 Walkers Landing Rd (☎250/227-9224 or 1-800/661-8711, ⓦwww.yasodhara.org; ❻), a spiritual retreat established over thirty years ago. It has 13 rooms for like-minded guests at $80 per person, including meals. As a place to stay, this side of the ferry crossing is a touch brighter, and there's an **infocentre** (June–Sept daily 9am–5pm; ☎250/227-9267) just off the road at Crawford Bay, which can help you find some of the nicer accommodation tucked away in the woods nearby. The

Wedgewood Manor Country Inn (☎250/227-9233 or 1-800/862-0022, ⓔwedgewood@netidea.com; ❹; April to mid-Oct), a 1910 heritage building set amidst fifty acres of gardens and estate, is an upmarket and extremely pleasant place to **stay**, but you'll have to book well in advance. The local **campsite** is the nicely wooded *Kokanee Chalets, Motel, Campground & RV Park* on Hwy 3A (☎250/227-9292 or 1-800/448-9292, ⓦwww.kokaneechalets.com; mid-April to mid-Oct); as well as tent and RV sites ($20–29) it also has motel and chalet rooms around seven minutes' walk from the beach (❸). Note, however, that there's also a choice of three reasonable campsites across the water in Balfour.

The nine-kilometre, forty-minute **ferry crossing** is beautiful. Boats leave every fifty minutes from June to September, and every two hours the rest of the year, but it's a first-come, first-served affair, and in high summer unless you're a pedestrian or bike passenger it may be a couple of sailings before your turn comes round.

Balfour and Ainsworth Hot Springs

Not quite the fishing village it's billed as, **BALFOUR** is a fairly shoddy and dispersed collection of motels, garages and cafés – albeit in verdant surroundings – designed to catch the traffic rolling on and off the Kootenay Lake ferry. RV **campsites** line the road south to Nelson for about 2km, the quietest being those farthest from the terminal, but a much better option is the campsite at Kokanee Creek (reservations possible, see p.777, $17.50; May–Sept), about 10km beyond Balfour with a sandy beach. The handiest **motel** for the ferry is the *Balfour Beach Inn and Motel*, 8406 Bush (☎250/229-4235, ⓦwww .balfourbeachinn.com; ❷), with heated indoor pool but convenient also for the small pebbly beach just north of the terminal.

About 16km north of Balfour on Hwy 31, **AINSWORTH HOT SPRINGS** is home to some one hundred residents, making it a town by local standards. The tasteful *Ainsworth Hot Springs Resort* (☎250/229-4212 or 1-800/668-1171, ⓦwww.hotnaturally.com; ❺) is ideal if you want to stay over while taking in the scalding water of the **mineral springs** (daily 10am–9.30pm; day-pass $12, single visit $7.50), though the chalets are expensive and, despite the lovely views and the health-giving properties of the waters, local opinion rates the Nakusp Hot Springs (see p.953) rather more highly. Note that you don't need to stay in the resort to sample the springs. The nicest local **motel** is the cheaper and smaller eight-room *Mermaid Lodge and Motel* (☎250/229-4969 or 1-888/229-4963, ⓦwww.themermaidlodge-motel .com; ❷) alongside the springs and pools. Cave enthusiasts might want to take a guided tour of **Cody Caves Provincial Park**, 12km up a rough, well-signposted gravel side road off Hwy 3 3km north of town. From the end of the road it's a twenty-minute walk to the caves, whose kilometre or more of galleries can be seen by tour only: contact Hiadventure Corporation (☎250/353-7425; $12).

A touch further up the increasingly beautiful Hwy 31 comes the self-contained **Woodbury Resort & Marina** (☎250/353-7177, ⓦwww .woodburyresort.com; ❷), a collection of motel, cottages, campsite ($18–25), restaurant, pub, store, heated pool, boat rentals and water-sport facilities all pitched on the lakeshore with lovely views and a small beach; it makes an attractive long-term accommodation prospect if you're tenting. Directly opposite is the **Woodbury Mining Museum** (July–Sept daily 9am–6pm; $4; ☎250/354-4470), a quaint pioneer building crammed with mining regalia and the entrance to a thirty-minute underground tour of the old lead, zinc and silver workings.

Kaslo and around

KASLO, 70km north of Nelson and 25km north of Ainsworth Hot Springs, must rate as one of British Columbia's most attractive and friendliest little villages. Huddled at the edge of Kootenay Lake and dwarfed by towering mountains, its half-dozen streets are lined with picture-perfect wooden homes and flower-filled gardens. It started life as a sawmill in 1889 and turned into a boom town – there were 27 bars, compared with two today – with the discovery of silver in 1893; diversification, and the steamers that plied the lakes, saved it from the cycle of boom and bust that ripped the heart out of so many similar towns. Today Kaslo remains an urbane and civilized community whose thousand or so citizens work hard at keeping it that way, supporting a cultural centre, art galleries, rummage sales – even a concert society.

The **town hall**, a distinctive green-and-white wooden building dating from 1898, is an architectural gem by any standards, as is the 1893 Anglican church of St Andrew's opposite. Yet Kaslo's main attraction is the SS *Moyie* at 324 Front St, the oldest surviving **paddle steamer** in North America (℡250/353-7323; tours May to mid-Sept daily 9am–5pm; $5), which ferried men, ore and supplies along the mining routes from 1898 until the relatively recent advent of reliable roads. Similar steamers were the key to the Kootenays' early prosperity, their shallow draught and featherweight construction allowing them to nose into the lakes' shallowest waters and unload close to the shore. They were, in local parlance, "able to float on dew". Canada claims just six of the 24 paddle steamers left in North America, but in the *Moyie* it has the oldest, launched in 1898 and only mothballed in 1957. Inside is a collection of antiques, artefacts and photographs from the steamer's heyday. Look for the small hut alongside it, the "world's smallest post office" (closed since 1970), and drop in on Kaslo's thriving **arts centre**, the Langham Cultural Society, on A Avenue opposite the post office (℡250/353-2661), for theatrical performances and art exhibitions. The building, which dates from 1893, began life as a hotel-cum-brothel for miners. If you're around in August, the **Kaslo Jazz Fest** (℡250/353-7538) has some top-notch acts; sometimes actors perform on a floating stage on Kootenay Lake.

Kaslo makes an ideal base for tackling two of the region's major parks – Kokanee Glacier Provincial Park and the Purcell Wilderness Conservancy – and for pottering around some of the charming lakeshore communities. People at the arts centre can advise on getting to **Argenta** (pop. 150), 35km north, a refugee settlement of Quakers who in 1952 came from California, alienated by growing militarism, to start a new life; it's also the western trailhead for the difficult sixty-kilometre **Earl Grey Pass Trail** over the Purcell Mountains to Invermere (p.966). It's a beautiful area, but has no services and only the occasional B&B if you want to stay; ask at the Kaslo infocentre for latest details. This area, incidentally, offers a good chance of seeing **ospreys**: the Kootenays' hundred or so breeding pairs represent the largest concentration of the species in North America.

Practicalities

Getting to Kaslo without your transport is difficult; in past years shuttle buses have made occasional runs to Nelson, but these are not reliable year on year. Finding your way round Kaslo, however, is no problem, nor is getting information – everyone is disarmingly helpful – and there's also an infocentre and **Chamber of Commerce** (early May to early Oct daily 9am–5pm; ☎250/353-2525, ⓦwww.klhs.bc.ca) at 324 Front St. More or less opposite, Discovery Canada (☎1-888/300-4453, ⓦwww.discoverycanada.ca) can guide you on local wilderness adventures by foot, mountain bike or kayak.

The best and virtually only central **accommodation** is the *Kaslo Motel*, 330 D Ave (☎250/353-2431 or 1-877/353-2431, ⓦwww.kaslomotel.com; ❶). Or there is a **hostel**, the *Kootenay Lake Backpackers' Hostel*, 232 B Ave (☎250/353-7427, ⓔklhostel@pop.kin.bc.ca; ❶), with dorm beds for $15 and four private rooms. There's a kitchen, sauna, bike, canoe and kayak rental, and Internet access. For most other alternatives head towards the marina just north of the centre where en route you'll find, amongst others, the *Sunny Bluffs Cabins & Camp*, 434 N Marine Drive (☎250/353-2277; ❷), offering cabins and camping sites ($12–14) overlooking Kaslo Bay Park. For **B&B** try the *Morningside*, 670 Arena Ave off Hwy 31 at West Kootenay Power Office (☎250/353-7681; ❷; no credit cards), or the three-room *On the Cliff B&B*, 5km south of Kaslo at 5814 Morgan Drive, Mirror Lake (☎250/353-7647, ⓔoncliff@uniserve.com; ❸).

Several more interesting accommodation possibilities are available farther up and down the lake, many with private lakeside beaches and lovely settings. The most notable are the combined hotel and campsite *Lakewood Inn* (☎250/353-2395, ⓦwww.lakewoodinn.com; ❹, tent and RV sites $15–25; April to mid-Nov), lakeside log cabins with fully equipped kitchens and camping sites with private beach and boat rentals; it's 6km north of Kaslo on Kohle Road. There are also the seven *Wing Creek Cabins* (☎250/353-2475, ⓦwww.wingcreekcabins.com; ❹), 7km north at 9114 Hwy 31, and a B&B at Argenta – *Earl Grey Pass* (☎250/366-4472; ❶).

Kaslo has a municipal **campsite** ($13–15) on the flat ground by the lake at the end of Front Street, past the SS *Moyie* on the right, *Mirror Lake Campground* (☎250/353-7102; $16; mid-April to mid-Oct), beautifully situated 2km south of town on the main road to Ainsworth, has 100 sites and more facilities. North of the village on the lake are combined campsite and motel or cabin lodgings (see above), as well as the *Kootenay Lake Provincial Park* campsite (April–Oct), two small campsites with 14 pitches each – Lost Ledge ($14) and Davis Creek ($10) – 25km north of the village on Hwy 31 with access to sandy beaches.

For **food** and **drink** in Kaslo try the rightly renowned and reasonable *Rosewood Café* (☎250/353-7673) at # 213 at the end of Front Street for glorious salads and steaks. Another option is the town's social hub, the *Treehouse Restaurant*, further down on Front Street, where you can eat superbly and easily strike up conversations. The nearby *Mariner Inn and Hotel* has a pretty unattractive beer hall, and is more of a downmarket hangout. *The Fisherman's Tale* with deck and good views on the marina at 551 Rainbow Drive is far more appealing. For less expesnive eats, *Meteor Pizza & Café* on 4th Street at Front Street serves up home-made pizzas and wraps, with a good deck for a drink. Another place for coffee and snacks is the *Silver Spoon Bakery* at 310 Front St.

Kokanee Glacier Provincial Park

Kaslo is one of several possible jumping-off points for the tremendous **Kokanee Glacier Provincial Park**, straddling the Slocan Range of the Selkirk Mountains to the southwest, and the access road from here – signed off Hwy 31A 6km northwest of town – offers the best views and choice of trails. However, the 24-kilometre drive up Keen Creek that follows from the turn-off degenerates in poor weather from compacted gravel to a severely rutted dirt road; this really only makes it suitable for four-wheel-drive vehicles. If you do make it, the road cuts to the heart of the park, reaching the Joker Millsite parking area set amidst spectacular glacier-ringed high country. Of the eleven fine trails in the area, the most obvious **hike** from the car park runs up to Helen Deane and Kaslo lakes (8km round-trip), an easy morning amble. If you're staying overnight you can choose from the usual undeveloped campsites ($5) and three basic **cabins** (summer $15; winter $35) – the main one, *Slocan Chief*, is past Helen Deane Lake alongside a park ranger office (5km by trail in total from Joker Millsite). Another 5km trail froms from the parking area to Joker Lakes, two superb peak-ringed lakes in a glacial cirque (elevation gain 450m).

An easier approach to the park is to drive south of Kaslo on Hwy 3A for around 40km and then follow the road up Kokanee Creek for 16km to park at Lake Gibson (circled by a 2.5km trail). Though farther from Kaslo it usually gets you into the park quicker. A trail from the lake leads 4km uphill to the lovely Kokanee Lake, where the trail levels out and continues 3km to Kaslo Lake and then 2km to backcountry campsites and Slocan Chief cabin (see above). Total elevation gain for the walk is 600m. Other approaches to the park are from Hwy 31 6.4km north of Ainsworth, driving 13km up Woodbury Creek into the park; from Hwy 6 some 14km north of Slocan, where you drive 13km up Enterprise Creek; and from Hwy 6 14km south of Slocan, where you follow a road up Lemon Creek for 16km. For more **information** on the park, call ☎250/825-4421 or pick up the blue *BC Parks* pamphlet from local infocentres.

Highway 31A and the Slocan Valley

After Kaslo you can either rattle north along a mostly gravel road to link with the Trans-Canada Hwy at Revelstoke, a wild and glorious 150-kilometre drive with a free ferry crossing at **GALENA BAY**, 50km south of Revelstoke, or you can stay in the Kootenays and shuffle west on the fabulously scenic **Hwy 31A** through the Selkirk Mountains to the **Slocan Valley**. The latter road ascends from Kaslo alongside the Kaslo River, a crashing torrent choked with branches and fallen trees and hemmed in by high mountains and cliffs of dark rock, whose metallic sheen suggests the mineral potential that fired the early growth of so many of the settlements in the region. Near its high point the road passes a series of massively picturesque lakes: **Fish Lake** is deep green and has a nice picnic spot at one end; **Bear Lake** is equally pretty; and **Beaver Pond** is an amazing testament to the beaver's energy and ingenuity.

Sandon

The ghost town of **SANDON**, one of five in the region, is located 13km south of Hwy 31A, up a signed gravel side road that climbs through scenery of the utmost grandeur. Unfortunately, nowadays Sandon is a little too much ghost and not enough town to suggest how it might have looked in its silver-mining heyday, when it had 24 hotels, 23 saloons, an opera house, thriving red-light district and 5000 inhabitants (it even had electric light, well before Victoria or Vancouver). It's slightly dilapidated, rather than evocative, state is due mainly to a flood, which swept away the earlier boardwalk settlement in 1955, leaving a partly inhabited rump that clutters along Carpenter Creek. Pop into the old City Hall, built in 1900, for a walking tour pamphlet ($1) from the **infocentre** (May–Oct daily 10am–6pm), then head for the new **museum** (May–Oct

Walks from Sandon

The side-trip to Sandon is enhanced if you manage a couple of local **hikes**. Idaho Peak (2,280m) is a must, being one of the most accessible and spectacular walks in the area. A twelve-kilometre gravel access road leads into alpine pastures and a car park (check on access – the road is usually only passable to normal vehicles in summer); from there it's a steep three-kilometre round trip to the summit of Mount Idaho and back, with emerging views all the way to the breathtaking panorama at the Forest Service lookout point. Or follow all or part of the **KNS Historic Trail** (14km one way) from the site to New Denver; the trail follows the course of the 1895 Kaslo–New Denver–Slocan ore-carrying railway, past old mine works and eventually to fine views of the New Denver Glacier across the Slocan Valley to the west. Coupled with leaflets from the infocentre, the walk vividly documents the area's Wild West mining history, harking back to an era when the district – known as "Silvery Slocan" – produced the lion's share of Canada's silver. "Silver, lead, and hell are raised in the Slocan," wrote one local newspaper in 1891, "and unless you can take a hand in producing these articles, your services are not required." The immense vein of silver-rich galena that started the boom was discovered by accident in 1891 by two colourful prospectors, Eli Carpenter and Jack Seaton, when they got lost on the ridges returning to Ainsworth from Slocan Lake. Back in the bar they fell out over the find, and each raced out with his own team to stake the claim. Seaton won, and was to become a vastly wealthy silver baron who travelled in his own train carriage across Canada, condemning Carpenter to return to his earlier profession as a tightrope walker and to an ultimately penurious death.

Wed–Sun 9.30am–5.30pm; $2) in Sandon's only brick building, the old general store with photos and domestic and commercial artefacts from the town's heyday.

New Denver

After the Sandon turn-off Hwy 31A drops into the **Slocan Valley**, a minor but still spectacular lake-bottomed tributary between the main Kootenay and Columbia watersheds, and meets Hwy 6 at **NEW DENVER** (pop 538), formerly known as Eldorado after its mineral riches. Born of the same silver-mining boom as Kaslo, and with a similarly pretty lakeside setting and genuine pioneer feel, New Denver is, if anything, quieter than its neighbour. The clapboard houses are in peeling, pastel-painted wood, and the tree-lined streets are mercifully free of neon, fast food and most evidence of tourist passage. In town, the **Silvery Slocan Museum**, housed in the old wooden Bank of Montréal building at the corner of 6th Avenue and Bellevue (July & Aug 9.30am–4.30pm; $2), is good for twenty minutes on the background and artefacts of the area's mining heritage.

Well signposted from the highway, the moving **Nikkei Internment Memorial Centre** at 306 Josephine St (May–Sept daily 9.30am–5pm; rest of year by appointment; $5) is the only museum in Canada dedicated to the 22,000 Nikkei (Canadians of Japanese ancestry) who, in 1942, were forcibly relocated from the coast to remote internment camps in the interior after Pearl Harbour. Beautiful Japanese gardens now surround the wooden shacks and outhouses that the Nikkei were forced to build themselves. Although the majority of Nikkei were Canadian citizens, they were all labelled "enemy aliens" and stripped of their possessions, homes and businesses. It wasn't until 1988 that former prime minister Brian Mulroney finally apologized to Japanese–Canadians and awarded them token monetary compensation. Inside the cultural centre an exhibition tells the story through photos, paintings and artefacts.

The **infocentre** in New Denver is at 202-6th Ave (late June to Aug daily 9am–5/6pm; ☎250/358-2719 or 358-2228, ⓦwww.slocanlake.com). As a stopover it's appealing but not quite as enticing as Kaslo; its **accommodation** possibilities include the Glacier View Cabins, 426 8th Ave (☎250/358-7277, ⓦwww.glaciercabins.com; ❸), five individual cabins just off Hwy 6 in town; a single beach-hut-type motel with pub and restaurant, the *Valhalla Inn*, 509 Slocan Ave (☎250/358-2228, ⓦwww.inn-valhalla.com; ❸); the lakeview *Sweet Dreams Guest House* (☎250/358-2415, ⓦwww.newdenverbc.com; ❸), a restored heritage home on Slocan Lake at 720 Eldorado Ave; and the *New Denver Municipal Campground* (☎250/358-2316; $13–16; May–Sept), unexceptional despite a waterfront location on the south side of the village. Four kilometres north of town on Hwy 6 is the *Rosebery Provincial Park* campsite ($14; April–Oct) on the banks of Wilson Creek, a lightly forested site with lake and mountain views. For **food** in the village try 6th Avenue, where at #210 you'll find the relaxed *Apple Tree Sandwich Shop* and the bistro *Panini* at #306. There's more accommodation and a campsite at Silverton, another tiny former mining village just 4.5km south of New Denver on Hwy 6.

Slocan and the Slocan Valley

Southbound out of New Denver, Hwy 6 follows the tight confines of the **Slocan Valley** for another 100km of ineffable mountain and lake landscapes. Be certain to stop at the **Slocan Lake Viewpoint**, 6km out of New Denver, where a short path up a small cliff provides stupendous views. The 125,000-acre **Valhalla Provincial Park** (☎250/825-3500) wraps up the best of the landscapes on the eastern side of Slocan Lake; a wilderness area with very few developed facilities, most of it is out of reach unless you boat across the water, though there are two trails that penetrate it from the hamlet of **SLOCAN**, another former mining village at the south end of the lake. For a taste of the local outdoors, the canter around the lake (8km) from Slocan to the west shore and the walk up the old railway bed from Slocan are popular short hikes, and there's more fresh air and good picnicking spots at the nearby Mulvey Basin and Cove Creek **beaches**. The best longer trails within the park are Gwillim Lakes (11.6km; elevation gain 701m) and Mulvey Basin (9.7km; 765m elevation gain), but both require access drives on forestry roads of 20km of more: pick up detailed directions at the New Denver or other local infocentres. Or contact the Valhalla Wilderness Society, 307-6th Ave, New Denver (☎250/358-2333), a local pressure group who campaigned hard for the establishment of the park and has gone on to to do the same for other protected areas in the province. Note that gravel roads lead up from Hwy 6 to the more accessible heights of **Kokanee Glacier Provincial Park** to the east (p.949). For more on the area, notably tours into the Valhalla park, contact Slocan's **infocentre**, 1020 Griffin Rd (daily 9am–5/6pm July–Aug; ☎250/355-2277 or 355-2666, Ⓔsolcan@telus.net).

As elsewhere in the Kootenays, getting around is difficult without your own transport, but in previous years **minibus** shuttles have run between Nelson and Slocan; call ☎250/352-8201 for latest details. If you need **accommodation** en route south there are about half-a-dozen options, most in rustic settings with mountain or lake views. Try either *Lemon Creek Lodge* (☎250/355-2403, ⓦwww.lemoncreeklodge.com; cabins ❸, campsite $12–19), 7km south of Slocan on Kennedy Road – it has great **food** as well as rooms – or the *Slocan Motel* (☎250/355-2344; ❷), at 801 Harold St in Slocan itself off Hwy 6. In addition to provincial **campsites** at Mulvey Basin and Cove Creek ($9.50; both May–Oct), there's the unserviced *Silverton Municipal Campground* (free; May–Oct), just south of New Denver. More exciting, the *Valhalla Lodge and Tipi Retreat* (T250/365-3226; ❹; May–Sept) offers an opportunity to stay in the Valhalla Provincial Park either in tepees or waterfront cabins, and use of a hot tub and sauna.

Highway 6: New Denver to Vernon

Hwy 6 may not be the most direct east–west route through British Columbia, but it's certainly one of the most dramatic, and the one to think about if you're heading towards Revelstoke to the north or the Okanagan to the west. From New Denver it initially strikes north and after 30km passes **Summit Lake**, a perfect jewel of water, mountain and forest that's served by the new *Summit Lake Provincial Park* **campsite** ($15; mid-May to mid-Sept). A rough road ("Take at Your Own Risk") runs south from here into the mountains and a small winter ski area.

Nakusp

Some 16km beyond Summit Lake and 47km north of New Denver, lakefront **NAKUSP** is, like Kaslo and Nelson, a rare thing in British Columbia: a town with enough charisma to make it worth visiting for its own sake. The setting is par for the course in the Kootenays, with a big lake – **Upper Arrow Lake**, part of the Columbia River system – and the snowcapped Selkirk Mountains to the east providing the majestic backdrop. The nearby hot springs are the main attraction, but you could happily wander around the town for an hour or so, or boat or swim off the public **beach**. The only actual sight in town is the **Nakusp Museum** in the village hall at 6th Avenue and 1st Street, full of the usual archive material, logging displays and Victorian bric-a-brac (May–Sept Tues–Thurs 12.30–4.30pm, Mon & Fri–Sun 11am–5pm; $1). The helpful **infocentre**, based in the fake paddle-steamer building next door at 92 West St and 6th Avenue just off the main street (summer daily 9am–5pm; winter Mon–Fri 10am–4pm; T250/265-4234 or 1-800/909-8819; Wwww .nakusphotsprings.com), can provide details on local fishing, boating and hiking possibilities, and – for those driving onwards – timings for the Galena Bay and Fauquier ferries. Also ask about the possibility of renting houseboats on the lake if you're staying for a few days. *Nakusp Transit* provides **buses** to and from Nelson, but only a couple of times a week (call T250/265-3674 for

---

Hot springs near Nakusp

There are some undeveloped hot springs within striking distance of Nakusp if you have a car. To reach **St Leon Hot Springs**, take Hwy 23 north out of Nakusp for 24km and then turn down the logging road after the second bridge for 10km to the trailhead; the piping-hot springs are 100m away down a steep trail to the river. If you stay on Hwy 23 for about another 10km, you'll reach the delightful **Halcyon Hot Springs** (daily 8/9am–9/10pm; $6, day-pass $9), which was first commercialized in 1888, its waters bottled and sent to England. Today, there are four pools here of varying temperatures, all of which face Upper Arrow Lake and the mountain peaks beyond. Camping is also available for $20. The resort here, the Halycon Springs Resort (T250/265-3554 or 1-888/689-4699, Wwww.halcyon-hotsprings.com; ❼), is one of the region's best – but its eleven chalets and cabins are expensive. However, there are tent and RV sites for $15–28.

latest details), and *Arrow Lakes Bus Lines* (℡250/358-7109) in the past has run to Vernon on an almost equally restricted schedule.

If you're only going to try the hot springs experience once, **Nakusp Hot Springs**, a well-signposted complex 13km northeast of town, is the place to do it (daily: June–Sept 9.30am–10pm; Oct–May 11am–9.30pm; $6, day-pass $9; ℡250/265-4528); it's not unusual for late-night informal parties to develop around the two outdoor pools. Unlike many similar enterprises, the natural pools are cleaned each night and are backed up by nice changing facilities, but bear in mind they're very popular in the summer. There is a co-owned **campsite** nearby (see below).

For a **place to stay** in or near Nakusp, Hwy 6 west along the lake is dotted with cabins, resorts and campsites. In downtown itself try the *Selkirk Inn*, 210 6th Ave W (℡250/265-3666 or 1-800/661-8007, ⓦwww.selkirkin-nakusp .com; ❷), or *Kuskanax/Tenderfoot Lodge*, 515 Broadway (℡250/265-3618 or 1-800/663-0100; ❷), which is equally central but a bit more upmarket and has a recommended Canadian-fare **restaurant** and lounge. For breakfast and snacks, head for the *Broadway Deli Bistro*, 408 Broadway, and join the locals for inexpensive food to go at *The Hut Drive Inn* or *What's Brewing* for coffee, muffins and more, both also on Broadway. Campers would do best to aim for the lovely *Nakusp Hot Springs* **campsite**, near the hot springs at 1701 Canyon Rd (℡250/265-4528 or 1-800/909-8819; $10–15; mid-May to mid-Oct); noncampers could try the adjoining seven-unit *Cedar Chalets* (℡250/265-4505; ❷), but reservations are essential in summer. Another out-of-town campsite is the *McDonald Creek Provincial Park* site ($14; April–Oct), 10km south of Nakusp on Hwy 6, and complete with lakeside beaches. Or make for the *Summit Lake Provincial Park* site ($17), 13km southeast on Hwy 6 at the crest of land between Slocan Lake and Upper Arrow Lake.

From Nakusp, you can either continue along Hwy 6 or branch off up **Hwy 23**, which heads 100km north to Revelstoke (see p.759), a lonely and spectacular journey involving a free ferry crossing halfway at **Galena Bay** (hourly sailings each way).

Fauquier to Vernon

Highway 6 doglegs south from Nakusp for 57 delightful kilometres to the ferry crossing at **FAUQUIER**. This hamlet consists of a handful of buildings including a garage, a store and the only **motel** (with a restaurant) for kilometres – the *Arrow Lake Motel* (℡250/269-7622; ❷), bang on the lakeside near the ferry at 101 Oak St. There's a **campsite** off Hwy 6 at the northern entrance ot the hamlet, the *Tukaluk* (℡250/269-7616), with twenty sites for $15.

The **free ferry** across Lower Arrow Lake to Needles takes about five minutes (departs half-hourly 5.15am–9.45pm; intermittent shuttle throughout the night). **NEEDLES** amounts to no more than a ramp off the ferry on the other side. There's an unofficial **campsite** at Whatshan Lake, 3km off the highway just after Needles, but otherwise Hwy 6 is a gloriously empty ribbon as it burrows through the staggering Monashee Mountains – though some of the time it's too hemmed in by forest for you to catch anything but trees. After cresting Monashee Pass (1198m), the highway begins the long descent through the **Coldstream Valley** towards the Okanagan. Snow dusts the mountains here almost year-round, crags loom above the meadows that increasingly break the forest cover, and beautiful flower-filled valleys wind down to the highway. The first sign of life in over 100km is the *Gold Panner* **campsite** (℡250/547-2025; $14–16; April–Oct), 55km east of Vernon and a good spot to overnight or to explore the utter wilderness of **Monashee Provincial Park** to the north. The park is reached by rough road from **CHERRYVILLE**, a hamlet 10km further west, which despite its cartographic prominence is just three houses, a garage and Frank's General Store.

LUMBY, another 22km beyond, is scarcely more substantial, although **rooms** at the *Twin Creeks Motel* (T250/547-9221; ❷) might be worth considering if it's late, given that the Okanagan lodgings ahead could well be packed. The village also boasts a simple riverside **campsite** at 2215 Shield Ave run by the local Lions Club (T250/547-2005 or 547-6346 off season; $15; May–Oct) and there's a seasonal **infocentre** on the highway at 1882 Vernon St (July & Aug; T250/547-2300, Wwww.monasheetourism.com). Beyond the village, the road glides through lovely pastoral country, with orchards, verdant meadows, low, tree-covered hills, and fine wooden barns that look like inverted longboats. Vernon (see p.931) is a short drive away.

Nelson

NELSON – reachable on Hwy 6 south of Slocan (see p.952) and Hwy 3A 34km west of Balfour (see p.947) – is one of British Columbia's best towns, and one of the few interior settlements in which you could happily spend two or three days; longer, if you use it as a base for touring the Kootenays by car. The elegant town is home to more than its share of baby-boomers, the dreadlocked, and refugees from the 1960s and later mainstream, a hangover that's nurtured a friendly, civilized and close-knit community, a healthy cultural scene and a liveliness – manifest in alternative cafés, nightlife and secondhand-clothes shops – that you'll be hard pushed to find elsewhere in the province outside Vancouver. There are, apparently, more artists and craftspeople here per head of the nine thousand population than any other town in Canada – and this is without the many similar types who live in the dozens of smaller outlying villages and isolated homesteads for which Nelson provides a natural focus. At the same time it's a young place permeated with immense civic pride, which was given a further boost by the filming here of *Roxanne*, Steve Martin's spoof version of *Cyrano de Bergerac*. Producers chose the town for its idyllic lakeside setting and 350-plus homes from the late nineteenth to the early twentieth-century, factors which for once live up to the Canadian talent for hyperbole – in this case a claim to be "Queen of the Kootenays" and "Heritage Capital of Western Canada".

Arrival and information

Nelson is served by Greyhound **buses** (T250/352-3939, Wwww.greyhound.ca) that run west to Penticton (for connections to Vancouver, the Okanagan and Kamloops) and east to Cranbrook (connections to Calgary via Banff or Fort Macleod). There are infrequent minibus services to Kaslo (T250/353-2492 for details) and Nakusp (T250/265-3674), but check with the infocentre before building a trip around these. The Greyhound depot is on the lakeshore, just below the town proper in the Chahko-Mika Mall at 1112 Lakeside Drive. To reach downtown from here, follow Lakeshore Drive west and turn left at Hall St, on which you'll find the infocentre (see above) on the left beyond Front St.

If you need **car rental**, Rent-a-Wreck has an outlet in town (T250/352-5122), as do Thrifty (T250/352-2811) and local company Whitewater Motors (T250/352-7202). For **bike rental**, visit Gerick Cycle and Sports, 702 Baker St (T250/354-4622), which also has trail maps and information on the many **mountain-biking** routes carved out by enthusiasts locally; The Sacred Ride at 213 Baker St is another good source of mountain-biking information. Note that the wild country on Nelson's doorstep, and the many old mining and logging trails, have made this a major biking centre.

The **infocentre** is on the northeast edge of the downtown grid at 225 Hall St at the corner of Lake St (June–Aug daily 8am–8pm; Sept–May Mon–Fri 8.30am–5pm; ☎250/352-3433 or 1-877/663-5706, ⓦwww .nelsonchamber.bc.ca).

Accommodation

Nelson has a reasonable spread of **accommodation**, but comparatively little in the downtown area; among the central choices are three **hostels**, notably the 43-bed *Dancing Bear Inn* between Kootenay St and Hwy 3A at 171 Baker St (☎250/352-7573, ⓦwww.dancingbearinn.com; ❶), a nicely renovated HI-affiliated place that HI voted Canada's best hostel in 2000. Bunk beds (maxiumum of six to a room) are $17 for HI members, $20 for non-members. Family rooms, some doubles (from $40) and a single are available; check-in is 4–10pm. There are two other non-affiliated downtown hostels: the *Flying Squirrel Hostel*, at the corner of Falls St at 198 Baker St (☎250/352-7285, ⓦwww.flyingsquirrelhostel.com; ❶), which has more of a hostel feel with dorm beds at $17; and the *New Grand Hotel and Hostel*, 616 Vernon St (☎250/352-7211 or 1-888/722-2258, ⓦwww.newgrandhotel.ca; dorm beds $18, hotel rooms ❸), with dorm beds and 34 hotel rooms.

Also central, and the best mid-range **hotel** choice, is the characterful 1898 four-storey *Heritage Inn*, 422 Vernon St (☎250/352-5331 or 1-877/568-0888, ⓦwww.heritageinn.org; ❸), with cosy, old-world rooms (some with views) and complimentary breakfast in the downstairs restaurant. At the top of the range, the most luxurious hotel in town is the *Prestige Lakeside Resort*, just west of the Greyhound depot (see above) at 701 Lakeshore Drive (☎250/352-7222 or 1-877/737-8443, ⓦwww.prestigeinn.com; ❻), part of Nelson's rather crass ongoing lakefront redevelopment; it has a spa, gym, marina, shops and all the other resort trimmings.

Nelson's main accommodation choice comes with its range of **B&B** options, with a dozen or so at last count and rising. The more central places include the four-room *Emory House*, 811 Vernon St (☎250/352-7007; ❸); the highly regarded seven-room *Inn the Garden*, a restored Victorian home one block south of Baker Street at 408 Victoria St (☎250/352-3226 or 1-800/596-2337, ⓦwww.innthegarden.com; ❸); and *Baker Street B&B*, a 1910 Edwardian home with two rooms at 816 Baker St (☎250/354-1852 or 1-866/354-1852, ⓔmar-stone@telus.net; ❹).

Most of the **motels** are on Hwy 31A at the north end of town or over the miniature Forth Road bridge on the north side of the lake. Here you can try the Viking Lakeview Motel, the town side of the bridge at 1301 Front St (☎250/352-3595 or 1-800/663-0102, ⓦwww.vikinglakeviewmotel.com; ❸); the *Villa Motel*, over the bridge at 655 Hwy 3A (☎250/352-5515 or 1-888/352-5515, ⓦwww.thevillamotel.com; ❷), with the use of an indoor pool; or the virtually adjacent *North Shore Inn*, 687 Hwy 3A (☎250/352-6606 or 1-800/593-6636, ⓦwww.nshoreinn.com; ❸), where rates include a coffee and muffin breakfast.

The nearest **campsite** is the *City Tourist Park*, on the corner of High Street and Willow (☎250/352-9031; $15–22; mid-May to early Oct), though it's small, pitches are relatively close together, and despite some trees, it has the definite feel of an urban site. It's about 800m east of downtown, reached by following Front St east across Hall and Cedar streets and past Cherry St on your right. Then there is *Shannon's RV Park* (☎250/825-9648; $16–24;

CITY HALL

△ "Kootenay" City Hall, Nelson

mid-May to Sept), 7km from town on the north shore of the lake at 1940 Hwy 3A. Better, but 20km northeast of town on Hwy 3A, is the *Kokanee Creek Provincial Park* campsite ($22), with 168 pitches on a forested site with visitor centre, access to sandy beaches and nature trails.

The Town

Nelson forms a 24-odd block tree-shaded grid of streets laid over the hilly slopes that edge down to the westernmost shores of Kootenay Lake. Most homes are immaculately kept and vividly painted, and even the commercial **buildings** along the parallel main east–west streets – Baker and Vernon – owe more to the vintage architecture of Seattle and San Francisco than to the drab Victoriana and worse of much of eastern Canada. If you want to add purpose to your wanderings, pick up the *Heritage Walking Tour* or the *Heritage Motoring Tour* pamphlets from the infocentre, which takes you around the sort of houses (26 in all on the walking tour) that many Canadians dream of retiring to, and only occasionally oversells a place – notably when it lands you in front of the old jam factory and the electricity substation. Better bets are the courthouse on Ward St and city hall (at the corner of Ward and Vernon), both designed by F.M. Rattenbury, also responsible for Victoria's *Empress Hotel* and Parliament Buildings. Also check out the old railway station and the *Heritage Inn*, the latter also a good place to stay. Free tours with a costumed guide are available from the infocentre in summer.

If walking tours aren't your thing, perhaps the town's **shops** may be, particularly those of its artists and craftspeople, who in summer club together to present **Artwalk**, a crawl round about a hundred of the town's artists and little galleries (call ☎250/352-2402 or visit the infocentre for more details). Most have regular openings and wine-gorging receptions, usually on the last Friday of the month, making for numerous free-for-all parties. If you don't want to walk in town, take the restored **Streetcar 23** (daily May–Sept; $2), a tram that runs the length of the lakeshore waterfront from a point about 200m north of the infocentre on Hall St. Particularly good galleries include the *Craft Connnection*, a co-operative owned by about twenty local craftspeople at 441 Baker St (☎250/352-3006), *Figments* at 458 Ward St (☎250/354-4418) for textiles, metalwork and other crafts, and the *Hummingbird Gallery*, 515B Vernon St (352-2083) for fine art, notably oils and watercolours. *Oliver's Books* at 398 Baker Street is excellent for maps, guides and general reading, with a bias towards the sort of New Age topics that find a ready market here. For second-hand books and CDs – and a great little café-restaurant – make for *Packrat Annie's* at 411 Kootenay St. Another shop worth a stop is *Hempland*, 557 Ward St, the province's first hemp store, where even snowboards and chainsaw oil are made from hemp.

For the most part the area owes its development to the discovery of copper and silver ore on nearby Toad Mountain at the end of the nineteenth century. Even though the mines declined fairly quickly, Nelson's diversification into gold and lumber, and its roads, railway and waterways, saved it from mining's usual downside. Today mining is back on the agenda as old claims are re-explored, and even if the idea of the town's **Museum of Mines** (daily 9/10am–4/5pm; free), next to the infocentre, leaves you cold, it's worth meeting the curator, an old prospector who talks at length – and interestingly – on the quest for silver, copper and gold, past and present.

It's probably less worthwhile to trek over to the **Nelson Museum**, 420 Anderson St, about twenty minutes' walk east from the centre (take Front St from downtown and follow its continuation, Anderson St, to just beyond the corner of Nelson Ave), which offers a rather haphazard display that appears to be the work of enthusiastic amateurs (summer daily 1–6pm; winter Mon–Sat

1–4.30pm; $2.50). There are, however, odd points of interest, notably a chronicle of the original 1886 Silver King Mine that brought the town to life, as well as tantalizingly scant details on the Doukhobor, a Russian religious sect whose members still live in self-contained communities around the Kootenays (see p.945). Better instead to walk to **Lakeside Park** near the Nelson Bridge, where there are surprisingly good sandy **beaches** and picnic areas, boat rentals and waterfront paths. If you're here between May and mid-October, make it a point to stop by the Saturday **Farmers and Artisans Market**, known as The Tree of Life Market, near the old railway station in Cottonwood Falls Park (9.30am–3pm). Organic fruits, vegetables, delicious breads and local arts and crafts are all for sale.

Eating, drinking and nightlife

Nelson's choice of **restaurants** is broad, and you can't go far wrong wandering around and choosing something that looks tempting. First choice for one of the Kootenays' best dining experiences is the top-flight *All Seasons Café*, in a restored heritage home at The Alley, 620 Herridge Lane (☎250/352-0101; daily for dinner from 5pm). It serves superb West Coast (or what it calls "left-coast") food and boasts a wine list with a good choice of BC wines, among others, that has won a prestigious *Wine Spectator* Award of Excellence. At the other end of the financial scale, the best place for coffees and snacks is the invariably crowded *Oso Negro* at 522 Victoria, a block up from Baker, which roasts its own beans and provides great people-watching opportunities. Much the same can be said of the café at *Packrat Annie's* bookshop (see above) at 411 Kootenay St. For good mid-range lunch or evening meals, downtown residents head to the *Main Street Diner*, 616 Baker St (☎250/354-4848; closed Sun), or the long-standing *Stanley's on Baker*, 401 Baker St (☎250/354-4458), where they also do a good breakfast and where the service is rarely less than charming. You'll also get a good breakfast in the *General Store Restaurant* (☎250/352-5331) of the *Heritage Inn*, 422 Vernon St (see "Accommodation"), while for novelty value you could do worse than spoil your breath at the *Outer Clove*, 353 Stanley St (☎250/354-1667; closed Sun), where virtually everything from decor to dessert features garlic (it's better than it sounds). At 301 Baker St, *The Rice Bowl* (☎250/354-4129), a local favourite with floor-to-ceiling windows on the main street, uses mainly organic ingredients to serve up fine and inexpensive seafood, sushi and vegan meals in a buzzing environment – note that it closes early, normally by 8pm. If you want a simple **pizza**, the thin-crust choice comes from the wood-fired oven at *Max & Irma's Kitchen*, 515 Kootenay St (☎250/352-2332).

If you're shopping for your own meals, the big **supermarkets** are in or near the mall alongside the bus depot, whilst the excellent Kootenay Co-Op in town at 295 Baker St can satisfy all your organic and wholefood needs – it's also a focus for the town's alternative types, making for excellent people-meeting and people-watching opportunities. Its organic bakery turns out a supreme loaf of bread, but has been challenged in this area by the Rising Sun Artisan Bakery at 281 Herridge Lane.

For **drinking**, join the locals and make for three-level *Mike's Bar* round the side of the *Heritage Inn*, 422 Vernon St, a usually packed spot which sells the full range of Nelson Brewing Company beers (the brewery was founded in 1893); top tipple is the flagship Old Brewery Ale (OBA). There's usually dancing from 10pm (Wed–Sat). The *Inn's* more elegant second bar, *The Library*, as its name suggests, offers a quieter drinking experience. Younger locals head the *Civic* pub, 705 Vernon St, for **dancing**, while for **live music** from good local and regional bands, the choice is the *Royal Blues Pub*, 330 Baker St.

Highway 95: north to Radium Hot Springs

Heading north from Creston and the Kootenays, Hwy 95 travels through scenery as spectacular as anything in the big Rockies parks to the north. The route follows the broad valley bottom of the **Columbia River**, bordered on the east by the Rockies and on the west by the marginally less breathtaking **Purcell Mountains**, though for the most part access to the wilderness here is limited and you'll have to be content with enjoying it from the highway. It's a fast run if you're driving, except where the road hugs the river's dramatic bluffs and sweeping meanders. Hwys 93 and 95 meet near **Cranbrook**, where you can make for either of two US border crossings, double back eastwards on Hwy 3 to Crowsnest Pass and Alberta, or head north for Radium Hot Springs and the entrance to Kootenay National Park (see p.761). Greyhound **buses** ply all these routes, with most connections at Cranbrook.

East of Creston

Some 42km east of Creston (see p.944), buses drop off at the small Shell garage in unspoilt **YAHK**, no more than a few houses nestled amidst the trees; there are two motels here for good, quiet stop-over here: the *Cozy Quilt Motel*, 8849 Hwy 3 & 95 (℡250/424-5558 or 1-877/717-5558, ⓦwww.cozyquilt.com; ❷), and the cheaper *Yahk Motel & Campground*, 8769 Hwy 3 & 95 (℡250/424-5554, ⓔyahkmotel@telus.net; tent sites $10–12; ❷), or you can camp at *Yahk Provincial Park* ($14; May to mid-Sept) east of town or private *Riverside Campground* (℡250/424-5454; April to mid-Oct; $12) south of Yahk on the Moyie River; it has a store for groceries and other basics. Hwy 95 branches off from Hwy 3 here and heads south for the US border (11km). Incidentally, the highway crosses a **time zone** between Yahk and Moyie – clocks go forward one hour.

Following Hwy 3/95 northbound you reach the tiny community of **MOYIE** – a pub, general store, 1904 church and handful of homes – on the edge of lovely **Moyie Lake**, which provides a welcome visual relief after the unending tree-covered slopes hereabouts. There's no listed accommodation here, but you may find the odd B&B advertised locally. There are, however, local **campsites**, including the excellent one at **Moyie Lake Provincial Park** (reservations possible, see p.777; $22; May–Sept), with short trails and sandy swimming beach – reach it by taking Munro Lake Road west off Hwy 3/95 for a kilometre from the northernmost point of Moyie Lake.

Cranbrook

The regional service and ex-forestry town of **CRANBROOK**, 30km north of Moyie Lake and 106km east of Creston, despite a location that marks it out as a transport hub, is one of the most dismal in the province, its dreariness hardly redeemed by the spectacular views of the surrounding mountains. A strip of motels and marshalling yards dominates a hard-hit downtown area which despite strenuous remedial efforts and "heritage walks" (pamphlets from the infocentre or railway museum, see below) still has precious little to recommend it. Local lifeblood, such as it is, flows from the motels, this being an obvious place to eat, sleep and drive away from almost immediately the next morning. The Greyhound **bus terminal** (℡250/426-3331) is hidden behind *McDonald's* opposite the Mohawk petrol station at 1229 Cranbrook St. Bus services run east to Fernie, Sparwood and southern Alberta (2 daily); west to Nelson, Castlegar and Vancouver (3 daily); north to Kimberley, Radium, Banff and Calgary (1 daily); and south to Spokane in the US (1 daily).

The only sight to speak of is the worthwhile **Canadian Museum of Rail Travel** (daily Easter to mid-Oct 8am–6pm; rest of year Tues–Sat noon–5pm; variety of tours $5.25–$11.95; Ⓦ www.trainsdeluxe.com), which once centred on the restored carriages of an old trans-Canada luxury train ("The Millionaires' Train") but has been considerably expanded in recent years to include other old rolling stock, pieces of rail memorabilia and a model railway display. Bigger exhibits are mostly outdoors on 300m of old CPR sidings along Van Horne St in downtown.

The period buildings pushed by the **infocentre**, 2279 Cranbrook St (year-round 9am–5pm; Ⓣ250/426-5914, 489-5261 or 1-800/222-6174, Ⓦ www.cranbrookchamber.com), aren't interesting enough to justify the trawl round the streets, especially if you've come from the far more genuinely appealing streets of the Kootenays' towns and villages. The infocentre was burned down by animal-rights activists in 1999 because of its stuffed-animal display, but not to be defeated they have reopened on the same spot with a new **Wildlife Museum** (same hours) filled with stuffed road-kills and other creatures from the surrounding area.

You may have to stay in Cranbrook, as there's little in the way of **accommodation** on the roads north and south; there are a dozen or so motels that fit the bill. The top of the range in town is the *Heritage Inn* at 803 Cranbrook (Ⓣ250/489-4301 or 1-800/663-2708, Ⓦ www.heritageinn.net; ❹), a large, modern motel on the main road. Cheaper and more intimate is the recommended *Heritage Estate Motel* (Ⓣ250/426-3862 or 1-800/670-1001, Ⓔheritage@cyberlink.bc.ca; ❷), near the southern edge of town at 362 Van Horne St SW and therefore removed from some of the bleaker corners. The same can be said of a nice **B&B**, the *Singing Pines*, 5180 Kennedy Rd (Ⓣ250/426-5959 or 1-800/863-4969, Ⓔsingingpinesbb@shaw.ca; ❹), situated off Hwy 95A 3km north of town in a quiet location with mountain views. The town's *Mount Baker RV Park*, at Baker Park on 14th Avenue and 1st Street (Ⓣ1-877/501-2288; $18–24; April–Oct), is the closest **campsite**, though it's a good deal less appealing than the *Jimsmith Provincial Park*, 4km southwest of town, but which has no showers ($14; May–Oct). The strip offers plenty of cheap **eating** options; for something more welcoming make for the Apollo at 1012 Cranbrook St N (Ⓣ250/426-3721) for good Italian, seafood, steaks and salads.

Highway 3 east of Cranbrook

Highway 93 leaves Hwy 95 between Fort Steele (see p.964) and Cranbrook, following Hwy 3 as far as Elko before branching off south for the United States border (91km). An unsullied hamlet of around half a dozen homes, **ELKO**, 65km east of Cranbrook, is gone in a flash, but you might want to stop and eat at *Wendy's Place*, a cosy backwoods spot, or to camp at the excellent *Kikomun Creek Provincial Park* **campsite** (reservations possible, see p.777; $22; May–Oct), on the eastern shore of the artificial Lake Koocanusa and signed off Hwy 93 3km west of town. The only other local **accommodation** is the *West Crow Motel and RV Park* at the entrance to the Elk Valley (Ⓣ250/529-7349; ❷; tents and RVs $12–15; year-round), with a secluded tenting area. Hwy 3 offers colossal **views** of the Rockies and the fast-flowing, ice-clear Elk River.

FERNIE, 32km north of Elko, is a pleasant place of tree-lined streets, a few motels and small wooden houses, surrounded by a ring of knife-edged mountains. This said, the recent expansion and increased popularity of the ski resort locally has led to a certain amount of not entirely pleasing development among the highway. The *Cedar Lodge*, 1101-7th Ave (℡250/423-4622, ⓦ www.cedarlodge.bc.ca; ❸), is the place to stay here or, failing that, one of two good **hostels**: either the basic HI-affiliated official **hostel**, the ninety-bed *Raging Elk International Hostel*, a converted motel one block south of Hwy 3 between 8th and 9th streets at 892 6th Ave (℡250/423-6811, ⓦ www.ragingelk.com; ❶); or the excellent *SameSun Budget Lodge* on Hwy 3 (℡250/423-4492 or 1-877/562-2783, ⓦ www.samesun.com; ❷), which has hotels dorm beds and lots of private rooms (members $18, non-members $22). The **infocentre** (daily 9am–5pm; ℡250/423-6868, ⓦ www.ferniechamber.com) stands alongside a reconstructed wooden oil derrick 2km north of town on Hwy 3 at 102 Commerce Road. Pick up details of the heritage walking tour of downtown, whose best buildings cluster around 6th St and 4th Ave, monuments to the rebuilding which followed a fire that ravaged the town in 1908. **Mount Fernie Provincial Park** has plenty of hiking trails, picnic areas and a pleasant forty-pitch campsite 2km west of town off Hwy 3 on Park Rd (reservations possible, see p.777; $14; mid-May to mid-Sept). **Fernie Alpine Resort** (℡250/423-4655, ⓦ www.skifernie.com), 5km west of town and 2km off the main highway, boasts what is reputedly the longest ski season in the BC Rockies (Nov–May); it also has an ever-growing variety of accommodation possibilities.

Hwy 3 leaves the Elk Valley at **SPARWOOD**, 29km beyond Fernie, where signs of the area's coal-mining legacy begin to appear. Close to the town – but barely visible – is Canada's largest open-cast **coal mine**, capable of disgorging up to 18,000 tonnes of coal daily. Tours of the mine (July & Aug Mon–Fri 1.30pm) leave from the local **infocentre** (daily 9am–6pm; ℡250/425-2423 or 1-877/485-8185, ⓦ www.sparwoodchamber.bc.ca), at the junction of Hwy 3 and Aspen Drive – look for the big miner's statue and the monster truck (it is apparently the world's biggest). The town itself is surprisingly neat and clean, and the obvious *Black Nugget Motor Inn*, Hwy 3 at Red Cedar Drive (℡250/425-2236 or 1-800/663-2706; ❸), makes a convenient place to stay. There is a **campsite**, the sixty-site *Mountain Shadows Campground* (mid-May to mid-Oct; ℡250/425-7815; $15) on Hwy 3 at the southern entrance to the town.

Elkford

The remainder of Hwy 3 in British Columbia is largely despoiled by mining; the road crests the Continental Divide 19km east of Sparwood at **Crowsnest Pass** (see p.664). Far more scenic is the drive north from Sparwood on Hwy 43, which heads upstream beside the Elk River for 35km to **ELKFORD**. Nestled against a wall of mountains to the east and more gentle hills to the west, the village claims to be the "wilderness capital of British Columbia" – a high-pitched punt, but close to the mark if you're prepared to carry on up either of two rough gravel roads to the north. The more easterly road follows the Elk a further 80km to **Elk Lakes Provincial Park** close to the Continental Divide, one of the wildest road-accessible spots in the province (camping costs $5 at the simple campsite at the main trailhead at the end of the road). The slightly better route to the west heads 55km into the heart of unbeatable scenery below 2792-metre **Mount Armstrong**. Both areas offer excellent chances of spotting wildlife like cougars, deer, moose, elk or members of North America's largest population of bighorn sheep.

Before entering either area, however, it's essential to pick up maps and information at the Elkford **infocentre** (year-round Mon–Fri 8am–5pm; ℡1-877/355-9453, ⓦ www.chamber.elkford.bc.ca), located at 4A Fronte St at the junction of Hwy 43 and Michel Road. It can also give directions to nearby **Josephine Falls**, a few minutes' walk from the parking area on Fording Mine Road. Whether you're staying here or pushing on north, a tent is helpful: the only accommodation options are the *Elkford Motor Inn*, 808 Michel Rd, next to the shopping centre (☎250/865-2211 or 1-800/203-7723, Ⓔelkfordmi@elkvalley.net; ❷) or the more expensive *Hi Rock Inn*, 2 Chauncey St (☎250/865-2226 or 1-866/865-2226, Ⓦwww.hirockinn.com; ❸). **Camping** can be had at Elkford's municipal campsite (☎250/865-2650; $12; May–Oct) and at the wilderness campsites around Elk Lakes ($5; June–Sept).

Kimberley

KIMBERLEY, a few kilometres north of Cranbrook on Hwy 95A, is Canada's highest city (1117m), and in many ways one of its silliest, thanks to a tourist-tempting ruse to transform itself into a Bavarian village after the imminent closure of the local lead and zinc mine in the 1970s threatened it with economic oblivion. The result is a masterpiece of kitsch that's almost irresistible: buildings have been given a plywood-thin veneer of authenticity, piped Bavarian music dribbles from shops with names like The Yodelling Woodcarver, and even the fire hydrants have been painted to look like miniature replicas of Happy Hans, Kimberley's lederhosened mascot. The ploy might seem absurd, but there's no doubting the energy and enthusiasm that has gone into it, nor the economic rewards that have accrued from the influx of tourists and European immigrants – Germans included – who've provided an authentic range of cafés and restaurants and a variety of family-oriented summer and winter activities.

Most of the Teutonic gloss is around the **Bavarian Platzl** on Spokane Street in the small downtown area, whose fake houses compare poorly with the authentic wooden buildings and more alpine surroundings on the outskirts. If nothing else, you can leave Kimberley safe in the knowledge that you have seen "**Canada's Biggest Cuckoo Clock**", a fraudulent affair which amounts to little more than a large wooden box that twitters inane and incessant music. The dreaded contraption performs on being fed small change, and people oblige often enough so that Happy Hans (rather than a cuckoo) makes his noisy appearance almost continuously; when he doesn't, the council often employs some unfortunate to play the accordion morning, noon and night to keep up the musical interludes.

Apart from the clock, and a small **museum** upstairs in the library down the road, the other main local sight is the **Sullivan Mine**, pre-Bavarian Kimberley's main employer and one of the world's biggest lead and zinc mines. The mine, which closed in 2001, is due to be remembered in an **interpretive**

Kimberley activities

If you're around from early December through April, and feel the need to escape Kimberley's kitsch for **skiing** and other winter activities, head for the **Kimberley Alpine Resort** (☎250/427-4881 or 1-800/258-7669 for accommodation packages, Ⓦwww.skikimberley.com), 4km west of town. Owned by Charles Locke, the owner of numerous ski resorts throughout Canada, the resort boasts eight lifts and 67 runs, the longest of which covers more than 6km. Passes cost $45 for the day, $35 for the afternoon and $15 for a night-skiing session.

Kimberley also boasts one of Canada's most popular **golf** courses, Trickle Creek on Jerry Sorenson Way (☎250/427-3878; $69 for eighteen holes, $28 for a cart), but you'll have to book ahead if you want to play here.

centre which will tell the mine's story and include a trip to the original portal – due to high insurance demands the underground mine itself cannot be opened to the public. You can also explore the local history on the **Bavarian City Mining Railway**, a seven-kilometre narrated ride on a train salvaged from a local mine. En route the train travels along steep inclines and switch-backs through the valley, highlighting Kimberley's past mining activities and its future developments now that the lifeblood has run dry. It leaves from the downtown station, a block from the Platz, on Jerry Sorenson Way (℡250/427-2929; six times daily June–Sept noon–6.30pm; $7). At the station you can also view a mini 1920s mining camp complete with a schoolhouse.

Practicalities

If you need **accommodation**, try the central *Quality Inn of the Rockies*, 300 Wallinger Ave (℡250/427-2266 or 1-800/661-7559, Ⓦwww .qualityinnkootenays.com; ❸), or the smaller *North Star Motel* (℡250/427-5633 or 1-800/663-5508; ❷) at the northern edge of town; for an extra few dollars you can have access to a kitchen. *Same Sun Budget Lodge* is a hotel connected to the *Ozone Pub* (pub food and live entertainment most nights) on the Platzl with **hostel beds** ($20) at 275 Spokane St (℡250/427-7191 or 1-877/562-2783, Ⓦwww.samsun.com; ❷). The nearest **campsite**, the inevitably named *Happy Hans Riverside Resort* (℡250/427-2929, Ⓦwww .happyhans.com; $12–24; May–Oct), is 7km south of the town centre then 3km west on St Mary's River Road and has modern facilities. Drop in to the twee but excellent *Chef Bernard* café and **restaurant** opposite the clock at 170 Spokane St (℡250/427-4820), where the owner – heartily sick of Bavaria – often plays Irish fiddle music as a mark of defiance. He's also one of the best local chefs, and people come from miles for his fondue evenings. He often has **rooms** available upstairs (℡250/427-2433; ❷). A favourite cheap place for lunch and breakfast is *Our Place*, 290 Spokane St, just down from the post office on the main crossroads, though the centre has lots of cafés and mostly Teutonic-biased places to eat cheaply. Farther afield is the *Old Bauernhaus*, about fifteen-minutes' walk or a short drive from the town centre towards the ski area off Dewdney Rd at 280 Norton Ave (℡250/427-5133; dinner only, closed Tues). The Bavarian food is good, but the draw here is the location, a 350-year-old post-and-beam building dismantled and brought from its original site in southern Bavaria. For full details of Kimberley's many summer events, call in on the **infocentre** (daily: June–Sept 9am–7pm; Oct–May 9am–5pm; ℡250/427-3666, Ⓔkimbchamber@cyberlink.bc.ca) at 115 Gerry Sorensen Way. The key draw is **Julyfest**, which includes a one-week beer festival and – almost inevitably – an international accordion championship.

Fort Steele Heritage Town

If you stick to Hwy 93/95 out of Cranbrook rather than detouring to Kimberley, you'll come to **FORT STEELE HERITAGE TOWN** (℡250/417-6000, Ⓦwww.fortsteel.bc.ca; daily: May to early June & mid-Sept to early Oct 9.30am–5.30pm; early June to mid-Sept 9.30am–8pm; $9), an impressively reconstructed c.1900 village of some 55 buildings in a superb mountain-ringed setting. It suffers somewhat by comparison with the similar reconstruction at Barkerville (125 buildings), but that's far farther from civilization deep in Cariboo country (see p.911). The Fort Steele settlement started life in the 1860s as a provisions stop and river crossing for gold prospectors heading east to Wildhorse Creek, 6km beyond. By the late 1890s, thanks both to the local discovery of silver, lead and zinc, and the mistaken assumption that the railway would push through here, the population reached four thousand. But by 1910, after the mining frenzy had settled and the Canadian Pacific Railway chose to ride through Cranbrook instead, the population had shrunk to no more than 150.

Though the site was never completely abandoned, there was still much to do when restoration began in 1961. Staffed by volunteers in period dress, the town now consists of numerous buildings, some replicas, some original (1860s), some from the period of Steele's tenure, others brought from elsewhere and rebuilt. Among them are an old-time music hall, a blacksmiths', bakery, printers', general store and many more, with the added novelty of being able to watch people shoe horses, bake bread, make quilts and so forth. More spookily, there's also a restored Masonic Lodge, where volunteers let you in on various selected "secrets" of masonic life. You can also enjoy a ride on a steam engine or take a turn on a wagon pulled by the massive Clydesdale horses that are reared in the village. Proceedings are all under the auspices of the provincial government, so generally lack the commercial frenzy that often characterizes such places. At 8pm most summer evenings the village reopens for an old-time variety show and cabaret.

A couple of ranches and B&Bs aside, there's little accommodation in the immediate vicinity, though there are two **campsites**: the *Fort Steele Resort and RV Park* across from the village (☏250/489-4268; ⓦwww.fortsteele.com; $20–37), which has all the usual facilities, and the smaller *Fort Steele Original Campground* (☏250/426-5117; $16–21; June–Sept), on Kelly Road 2km south of the village and with similar facilities. Just east of Fort Steele there's also the *Norbury Lake Provincial Park* campsite ($14; mid-May to mid-Sept) with tent and RV sites.

Hwy 95 north to Fairmont Hot Springs

Back on Hwy 93/95, the Columbia Valley's scenery picks up as the Rockies begin to encroach and the blanket of trees opens up into pastoral river meadows. First stop is **Wasa**, 30km north of Kimberley, whose lake, protected by the *Wasa Lake Provincial Park*, is warm enough for summer swimming. The lake also has a sizeable provincial park **campsite** (reservations possible, see p.777; $17; May–Sept). **Skookumchuck** ("strong water"), marked as a town on most maps, is in fact little more than a pulp mill whose chimneys belch out unpleasantness that spreads for kilometres downwind. After a few kilometres the road curves around the **Dutch Creek Hoodoos**, fantastically eroded river bluffs that were created, according to Ktunaxa legend, when a vast wounded fish crawling up the valley expired at this point; as its flesh rotted, the bones fell apart to create the hoodoos. Close by is **Columbia Lake** – not one of the area's most picturesque patches of water, though the *Mountain Village*, a fine wooden **restaurant** crammed with hundreds of old bottles, makes a good meal stop and is just short of a colossal lumber yard that blights **Canal Flats** at the head of the lake.

Just to the south of the Canal Flats mill and 28km north of Skookumchuck is the Whiteswan Lake Road turn-off for **Whiteswan Lake Provincial Park**, a handkerchief-sized piece of unbeatable scenery at the end of a twenty-kilometre gravel logging road; the park has five **campsites** ($14; May–Sept) but few trails, as its main emphasis is on boating and trout fishing. Three of the campsites are at Whiteswan Lake itself, the other two at Alces Lake; also keep an eye open for the undeveloped Lussier Hot Springs at the entrance of the park (17.5km from the main road), reached by a steep downhill trail. The same access road, called the Lussier River Road after it passes the park, continues another 30km from Alces Lake to **Top of the**

William Adolph Baillie-Grohman

The little area around Canal Flats resonates to the history of the wonderful **William Adolph Baillie-Grohman**, a man whose life was littered with eccentric catastrophes. Here, in the 1880s, he planned to build a canal to link the Columbia and Kootenay rivers, also intending to drain virtually all of the Kootenay into the Columbia to prevent flooding (residents up and down the Columbia, not to mention the Canadian Pacific Railway, quickly prevented the latter plan). The canal, however, was completed in 1889, but proved so tortuous and perilous that only two boats ever made it all the way through (in 1894 and 1902). Even then the second boat only made it by demolishing virtually all of the locks en route. Still, Baille-Grohman had the last laugh, for completing the canal – useless as it was – earned him a provincial land grant of some 30,000 acres. Head to **Canal Flats Provincial Park** (day-use only; April–Oct), 3km north of Canal Flats, if you want to view the remnants of the doomed project.

World Provincial Park, a far wilder and very beautiful alpine region where you need to be completely self-sufficient – the five walk-in campsites ($5; June–Sept), reached by an easy six-kilometre trail (200m elevation gain) from the parking area at the end of the road, offer water and firewood and spaces for twenty in the Fish Lake cabin ($15; June–Sept). Hiking in the park is good, an obvious jaunt being the trail from the parking area along the Lussier River to Fish Lake (7km one-way; 2hr), where there's an unserviced campsite and a cabin (summer only). Mount Morro (3002m), the peak that looms over the region, is believed to have had great spiritual significance for the Ktunaxa, who came here to mine chert, a hard flinty quartz used to make tools and weapons.

FAIRMONT HOT SPRINGS spills over the Columbia's flat flood plain, less a settlement than an ugly modern upmarket resort that feeds off the appeal of the hot springs themselves. The pools were commandeered from the Ktunaxa (Kootenay) in 1922 for exploitation as a tourist resource; the calcium springs (daily 8am–10pm; $7) were particularly prized by the whites because they lack the sulphurous stench of many BC hot dips. However, the locals have now got their own back by opening some cheaper, makeshift pools above the resort, which are proving very popular with tourists. If you don't fancy coughing up around $169–209 to stay in a room at the swish resort, you could try its big **campsite** (☎250/345-6311 or 1-800/663-4979, ⊛www.fairmonthotsprings .com; $25–41), one minute from the pools but only if you're in an RV – they don't want tents – or the *Spruce Grove Resort* (☎250/345-6561, ⊛www .sprucegroveresort.com; ❹, tents $20; May–Oct), near the river 2km south of Fairmont with rooms and a lovely riverside campsite with outdoor pool.

Invermere

Windermere, 15km north of Fairmont Hot Springs, is little more than a supermarket, petrol station and campsite immediately off the highway, and hardly hints at the presence of **INVERMERE**, about 1km beyond on the western shore of Windermere Lake. White settlement of the region can almost

If you're continuing north of Invermere into the **Kootenay National Park** and the Rockies, see p.761. From Invermere, if you're crossing the Crowsnest Pass into southern Alberta for **Waterton Lakes National Park**, see p.666.

be said to have begun here, for explorer David Thompson passed this way in 1807 as he travelled up the Columbia River. With his aboriginal wife, several children and eight companions, he built Kootenay House, the area's first trading post. Its site is marked by a cairn on Westside Road. A feel-good summer resort with the usual range of aquatic temptations, Invermere today makes a nicer accommodation prospect than Radium and other places on the highway hereabouts. However, droves of anglers, boaters and beach bums mean summer vacancies may be in short supply, in which case call the central **infocentre** near the junction of Hwy 93 and Hwy 95 (late July to early Sept daily 8am–8pm; ℡250/342-6316, ⓦwww.columbiavalleychamber.com) for B&B possibilities, or head for one of the town's handful of **motels** – the *Lee-Jay*, 1015 13th St (℡250/342-9227, ⓦwww.leejaymotel.com; ❸), is the most reasonable and the *Best Western Invermere Inn* at the heart of downtown at 1310 7th Ave is the smartest (℡250/342-9246 or 1-800/661-8911, ⓦwww.invermereinn.com; ❹). There's also a private **hostel** here, the *Wandering Rogue Hostel*, 1010 12th St (℡250/342-3445; ❶), with mostly dorm beds at $20. The nearest provincial **campsite**, with vehicle and tent sites, is 7km north at Dry Gulch Provincial Park ($17; May to mid-Sept), but the private *Coldstream Lakeside Campground* (℡250/342-6793; $28–30 per vehicle; May–Sept) is on the lake and has a sandy beach. For **food**, try the popular *Myrtle's on Main* at 1321 7th Avenue (℡250/342-0281) or the *Blue Dog Café* on 7th Avenue (℡250/342-3814), the latter being particularly good for vegetarians and wholefood aficionados. For highly regarded local cuisine make for *Strand's Old House*, 818 12th St (℡250/342-6344). If you want a break from eating, drinking or lazing on beaches, spend a few minutes with the mining, railway and other displays in the **Windermere Valley Museum**, 622 3rd St (June–Sept Tues–Sun 9.30am–4pm; $2; ℡250/342-9769), housed in a heritage building at the top of the hill and to the right on entering the village.

From Invermere the minor Toby Creek Road climbs west into the mountains to the burgeoning **Panorama ski resort** (18km), or Panorama Mountain Village (central reservations ℡1-800/663-2929, ⓦwww.panamaresort.com), whose slick facilities include the highly rated Greywolf golf course and a range of accommodation. At over 1000m, the big 250-room *Panorama Resort* (℡250/342-6941 or 1-800/663-2929; ❷–❻) is also open in summer for tennis, riding, white-water rafting and fishing. In summer the chief appeal of the area is hiking, particularly if you continue up the road toward the less tainted **Purcell Wilderness Conservancy** Provincial Park (the road stops 9km short of the park), one of the few easily accessible parts of the Purcell Mountains. If you have a tent and robust hiking inclinations, you could tackle the 61-kilometre **trail** through the area to Argenta (see p.948) on the northern end of Kootenay Lake, an excellent cross-country route that largely follows undemanding valleys except when crossing the Purcell watershed at Earl Grey Pass (2256m).

Radium Hot Springs (see p.767) is a little way north of Invermere.

Travel details

Trains

Kamloops to: Boston Bar (3 weekly; 4hr); Edmonton (3 weekly; 13hr 15min); Hope (3 weekly; 5hr 15min); Vancouver (3 weekly; 9hr).

Vancouver to: Edmonton via Kamloops (3 weekly; 25hr); Jasper (June–Sept daily except Wed; Oct–May 3 weekly; 19hr); Lillooet (mid-June to Oct 1 daily; rest of year 4 weekly; 5hr 30min); Prince George (mid-June to Oct 1 daily;

rest of year 3 weekly; 13hr 30min); Whistler (1 daily; 3hr).
Victoria to: Courtenay via Nanaimo (1 round trip daily; 4hr 35min).

Buses

Kamloops to: Kelowna (3 daily; 3hr 40min); Vernon (5 daily; 1hr 50min).
Kelowna to: Castlegar (2 daily; 4hr 45min); Cranbrook (2 daily; 11hr); Nelson (2 daily; 5hr 25min); Penticton (6 daily; 1hr 10min); Vancouver (6 daily; 5hr 30min).
Nanaimo to: Port Alberni (4 daily; 1hr 20min); Port Hardy (1 daily; 6hr 50min); Tofino (1–2 daily; 4hr 30min); Ucluelet (1–2 daily; 3hr 10min); Victoria (7 daily; 2hr 20min).
Port Alberni to: Nanaimo (4 daily; 1hr 20min); Tofino via Ucluelet (1–2 daily; 3hr).
Prince George to: Cache Creek (3 daily; 6hr 30min); Dawson Creek (2 daily; 6hr 30min).
Squamish to: Whistler (7 daily; 1hr 10min).
Vancouver to: Banff (4 daily; 14hr 5min); Bellingham (8–10 daily; 1hr 45min); Cache Creek (2 daily; 5hr 40min); Calgary (4 daily; 16hr); Calgary via Kamloops (6 daily; 13hr); Calgary via Penticton, Nelson and Cranbrook (2 daily; 24hr); Calgary via Princeton and Kelowna (2 daily; 18hr); Chilliwack, for Harrison Hot Springs (10 daily; 1hr 45min); Edmonton via Jasper (3 daily; 16hr 30min); Kamloops (8 daily; 5hr); Kelowna (6 daily; 5hr 30min); Nanaimo (8 daily; 5hr); Pemberton (3 daily; 3hr 10min); Penticton (3 daily; 5hr 20min); Powell River (2 daily; 5hr 10min); Prince George via Cache Creek and Williams Lake (2 daily; 13hr); Salmon Arm (6 daily; 7hr 5min); Seattle, US (8–10 daily; 3hr 15min); Sea-Tac Airport, US (8–10 daily; 4hr 10min); Squamish (6 daily; 1hr 15min); Vernon (6 daily; 6hr); Victoria (8 daily; 5hr); Whistler (6 daily; 2hr 30min).
Victoria to: Bamfield (1–3 daily; 6–8hr); Campbell River (5 daily; 5hr); Nanaimo (7 daily; 2hr 20min); Port Hardy (1 daily; 9hr 45min); Port Renfrew (2 daily; 2hr 30min); Vancouver (8–10 daily; 4hr); Vancouver Airport direct (3 daily; 3hr 30min).

Ferries

Chemainus to: Thetis Island and Kuper Island (minimum of 10 round trips daily; 35min).
Courtenay to: Powell River (4 daily; 1hr 15min).

Nanaimo to: Gabriola Island (17 daily; 20min); Vancouver/Horseshoe Bay Terminal (8 daily; 1hr 35min); Vancouver/Tsawwassen Terminal (8 daily; 2hr).
Northern Gulf Islands Denman Island to Hornby Island (minimum 12 round trips daily; 10min); Quadra Island to Cortes Island (Mon–Sat 6 daily, Sun 5 daily; 45min); Vancouver Island (Buckley Bay) to Denman Island (18 round trips daily; 10min); Vancouver Island (Campbell River) to Quadra Island (17 round trips daily; 10min).
Port Hardy to: Bella Coola (1 every two days; 15hr 30min–22hr); Prince Rupert (1 every two days; 15hr).
Powell River to: Courtenay-Comox (4 round trips daily; 1hr 15min); Texada Island (10 round trips daily; 35min).
Southern Gulf Islands Vancouver Island (Crofton) to Saltspring Island/Vesuvius Bay (14 round trips daily; 20min); Vancouver Island (Swartz Bay) to Saltspring Island/Fulford Harbour (10 round trips daily; 35min).
Sunshine Coast Horseshoe Bay–Snug Cove (15 round trips daily; 20 minutes); Horseshoe Bay–Langdale (8 round trips daily; 40min); Jervis Inlet/Earls Cove–Saltery Bay (8–9 round trips daily; 50min).
Vancouver to: Nanaimo from Horseshoe Bay Terminal (8 daily; 1hr 35min); from Tsawwassen Terminal (8 daily; 2hr); Victoria (Swartz Bay Terminal) from Tsawwassen (hourly summer 7am–9pm; rest of the year minimum 8 daily 7am–9pm; 1hr 35min).
Victoria to: Anacortes and San Juan Islands, US, from Victoria's Inner Harbour (1–2 daily; 2hr 30min); Seattle, US, from Inner Harbour (1–2 daily; 2hr 30min); Vancouver (Tsawwassen) from Swartz Bay (hourly summer 7am–10pm; rest of the year minimum 8 daily; 1hr 35min).

Flights

Vancouver to: Calgary (20 daily; 1hr 15min); Castlegar (1–2 daily; 1hr 20min); Cranbrook (1–2 daily; 2hr 30min); Edmonton (14 daily; 1hr 30min); Kamloops (4–5 daily; 1hr); Kelowna (7–9 daily; 1hr); Montréal (8 daily; 5hr 35min); Ottawa (10 daily; 4hr 40min); Penticton (3–5 daily; 50min); Prince George (5–8 daily; 1hr 10min); Toronto (15 daily; 4hr 55min); Victoria (14 daily; 25min); Winnipeg (8 daily; 2hr 40min).
Victoria to: Calgary (4 daily; 1hr 40min); Vancouver (14 daily; 25min).

8

The North

CHAPTER 8

Highlights

* **The Skeena Valley** Glorious wildlife-rich river and estuary flanked by soaring mountains. **See p.978**

* **Haida Gwaii** A superb archipelago of wild islands whose natural profusion has earned them the title of the Canadian Galapagos. **See p.983**

* **Alaska Highway** Some 2500km of stunning wilderness make this one of North America's great drives. **See p.997**

* **Dawson City** The focus of the Klondike Gold Rush is western Canada's most atmospheric and compelling historic town. **See p.1017**

* **Dempster Highway** The only public road in North America to cross the Arctic Circle offers a fascinating insight into the tundra and other landscapes of the far north. **See p.1026**

* **Nahanni National Park** Magnificent gorges, waterfalls and mountain scenery are the chief attractions in one of Canada's finest national parks. **See p.1036**

* **Auyuittuq National Park** Arctic scenery and culture are always compelling, but nowhere more so than in this largely glacial redoubt on Baffin Island. **See p.1050**

△ Gold store, Dawson City

8

The North

Although much of Canada still has the flavour of the "last frontier", it's only when you embark on the mainland push north to the Yukon that you know for certain you're leaving the mainstream of North American life behind. In the popular imagination, **the north** figures as a perpetually frozen wasteland blasted by ferocious gloomy winters, inhabited – if at all – by hardened characters beyond the reach of civilization. In truth, it's a region where months of summer sunshine offer almost limitless opportunities for outdoor activities and an incredible profusion of flora and fauna; a country within a country, the character of whose settlements has often been forged by the mingling of white settlers and **aboriginal peoples**. The indigenous hunters of the north are as varied as in the south, but two groups predominate: the **Dene**, people of the northern forests who traditionally occupied the Mackenzie River region from the Alberta border to the river's delta at the Beaufort Sea; and the Arctic **Inuit** (literally "the people"), once known as the Eskimos or "fish eaters", a Dene term picked up by early European settlers and now discouraged.

The north is as much a state of mind as a place. People "north of 60" – the 60th Parallel – claim the right to be called **northerners**, and maintain a kinship with Alaskans, but those north of the **Arctic Circle** – the 66th Parallel – look with light-hearted disdain on these "southerners". All mock the inhabitants of the northernmost corners of Alberta and such areas of the so-called Northwest, who, after all, live with the luxury of being able to get around their backcountry by road. To any outsider, however, in terms of landscape and overall spirit the north begins well south of the 60th Parallel. Accordingly, this chapter includes not just the territories of the "true north" – **Yukon**, **Nunavut** and parts of the western Arctic and **Northwest Territories** – but also northern **British Columbia**, a region more stark and extreme than BC's southern reaches.

Information numbers and websites

Tourism British Columbia ☎1-800/663-6000, ⓦ www.hellobc.com.
Northern BC ☎1-800/663-8843, ⓦ www.nbctourism.bc.ca.
Tourism Yukon ☎867/667-5340, ⓦ www.touryukon.com.
NWT Arctic Tourism ☎1-800/661-0788, ⓦ www.nwttravel.nt.ca.
Nunavut Tourism ☎867/979-6551 or 1-866/686-2888, ⓦ www.nunavuttourism.com.

Introduction to northern British Columbia

The two roads into the Yukon strike through northern British Columbia: the **Alaska Highway**, connecting **Dawson Creek** to Fairbanks in Alaska, and the adventurous **Cassiar Highway**, from near **Prince Rupert** to **Watson Lake**, on the Yukon border. Though the Cassiar's passage through the Coast Mountains offers perhaps the better landscapes, it's the Alaska Highway –

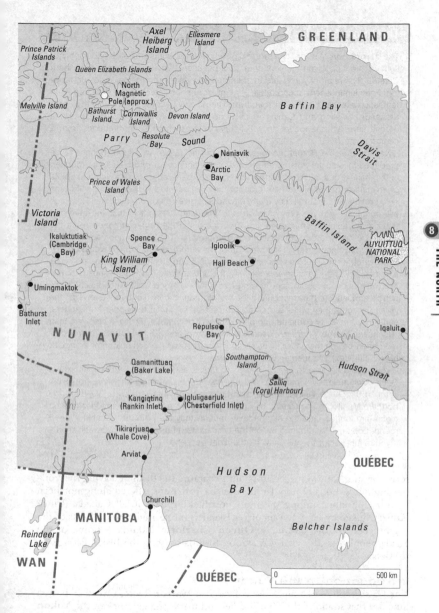

serviced by daily Greyhound **buses** and plentiful motels and campsites – that is more travelled, starting in the rolling wheatlands of the Peace River country before curving into the spruce forests and sawtooth ridges of the northern Rockies. While the scenery is superb, most towns on both roads are battered and perfunctory places built around lumber mills, oil and gas plants and mining camps, though increasingly they are spawning motels and restaurants to

The aurora borealis

The **aurora borealis**, or **"Northern Lights"**, is a beautiful and ethereal display of light in the upper atmosphere that can be seen over large areas of northern Canada. The night sky appears to shimmer with dancing curtains of colour, ranging from luminescent monotones – most commonly green or a dark red – to fantastic veils that run the full spectrum. The display becomes more animated as it proceeds, twisting and turning in patterns called "rayed bands". As a finale, a corona sometimes appears, in which rays seem to flare in all directions from a central point.

Named after the Roman goddess of dawn, the aurora was long thought to be produced by sunlight reflected from polar snow and ice, or refracted light produced in the manner of a rainbow. Certain Inuit peoples believed the lights were the spirits of animals or ancestors; others thought they represented wicked forces. Old-time gold prospectors thought they might be vapours given off by ore deposits. Research still continues into the phenomenon, but the latest thought is that the aurora is caused by radiation emitted as light from atoms in the upper atmosphere as the atoms are hit by fast-moving electrons and protons. The earth's geomagnetic field certainly plays some part in the creation of the aurora, but its source would appear to lie with the sun – auroras become more distinct and are seen spread over a larger area two days after intense solar activity, the time it takes the "solar wind" to arrive. This wind is composed of fast-moving electrically charged ions. When these hit the earth's atmosphere they respond to the earth's magnetic field and move towards the poles. En route they strike atoms and molecules of gas in the upper atmosphere, causing them to become temporarily charged or ionized. These molecules then release the charge, or energy, usually in the form of light. Different colours are emitted depending on the gases involved: oxygen produces a green colour (or orange at higher altitudes), nitrogen an occasionally violet colour.

You should be able to see the Northern Lights as far south as Prince George in British Columbia, over parts of northern Alberta (where on average they're visible some 160 nights a year) and over much of the Northwest Territories, Nunavut and northern Manitoba. They are at their most dazzling **from December to March**, when nights are longest and the sky darkest, though they are potentially visible all year round. Look out for a faint glow on the northeastern horizon after dusk, and then – if you're lucky – for the full show as the night deepens.

serve the surge of summer visitors out to capture the thrill of driving the frontier highways. Equally popular are the **sea journeys** offered along northern British Columbia, among the most breathtaking trips in all Canada. Prince Rupert, linked by ferry to Vancouver Island, is the springboard for boats to the magnificent **Haida Gwaii**, or **Queen Charlotte Islands** – home of the Haida people – and a vital way station for boats plying the Inside Passage up to Alaska.

Introduction to the Yukon

The Cassiar and Alaska highways converge at **Watson Lake**, a weather-beaten junction that straddles the 60th Parallel and marks the entrance to the **Yukon Territory** (YT), perhaps the most exhilarating and varied destination in this part of the world. Taking its name from a Dene word meaning "great", it boasts the highest mountains in Canada, wild sweeps of forest and tundra, and the fascinating nineteenth-century relic **Dawson City**. The focus of the Klondike gold rush, Dawson was also the territory's capital until that role shifted south to **Whitehorse**, a town doing well on tourism, federal jobs and the ever-increasing exploitation of the Yukon's vast mineral resources.

Provincial campsites in British Columbia

Tent and RV sites at certain campsites in British Columbia's provincial parks can be reserved in advance. To make **reservations**, call Discover Camping (☏1-800/689-9025 or 250/689-9025 in greater Vancouver; March to mid-Sept Mon–Fri 7am–7pm, Sat & Sun 9am–5pm) or visit ⓦ**www.discovercamping.ca**, where reservations can be made and confirmed online. Reservations can be made from up to three months in advance and no later than 48 hours before the first day of arrival. A nonrefundable booking fee of $6.42 per night, to a maximum of $19.26 for three or more nights, is charged (rates include tax). Payment in advance is by Visa or MasterCard only (payment for extra nights once at a campsite is by cash only). You can stay in BC provincial parks up to a maximum of fourteen days in any single park. Information on all aspects of BC's provincial parks is available by visiting ⓦwww.elp.gov.bc.ca/bcparks.

Road access is easier than you might think. In addition to the Alaska Highway, which runs through the Yukon's southern reaches, the **Klondike Highway** strikes north to link Whitehorse with Dawson City. North of Dawson the **Dempster Highway** is the only road in Canada to cross the Arctic Circle, offering an unparalleled direct approach to the northern tundra and to several remote communities in the Northwest Territories. The Yukon's other major road is the short spur linking the Alaskan port of Skagway to Whitehorse, which shadows the **Chilkoot Trail**, a treacherous track taken by the poorest of the 1898 prospectors that is now a popular long-distance footpath.

Combining coastal ferries with the Chilkoot Trail makes an especially fine itinerary. Following the old gold-rush trail, the route begins at Skagway – reached by ferry from Prince Rupert – then follows the Chilkoot to Whitehorse, before heading north to Dawson City. From there you could continue up the Dempster Highway, or travel on the equally majestic **Top of the World** road into the heart of Alaska. However, many people coming up from Skagway or plying the mainland routes from British Columbia head to Alaska directly on the Alaska Highway, to enjoy views of the extraordinary and largely inaccessible mountain vastness of **Kluane National Park**, which contains Canada's highest peaks and most extensive glacial wilderness.

Introduction to Nunavut and the Northwest Territories

If the Yukon is the far north at its most accessible, the **Northwest Territories** (NWT) is the region at its most uncompromising. Just three roads nibble at the edges of this almost unimaginably vast area, which occupies a third of Canada's landmass – about the size of India – but contains only 60,000 people, almost half of whom live in or around **Yellowknife**, the territories' peculiarly overblown capital. Unless you're taking the adventurous and rewarding **Dempster Highway** from Dawson City across the tundra to **Inuvik**, Yellowknife will probably feature on any trip to the NWT, as it's the hub of the (rather expensive) flight network servicing the area's widely dispersed communities.

Otherwise most visitors are here to fish or canoe, to hunt or watch wildlife, or to experience the Inuit aboriginal cultures and ethereal landscapes. More for convenience than any political or geographical reasons, the NWT was formally divided into eight regions. From 1999 a new two-way division has applied, the eastern portion of the NWT having been renamed **Nunavut**, a separate entity administered by and on behalf of the region's aboriginal peoples. One effect has been the **renaming** of most settlements with Inuit names, though in many cases the old English-language names appear in much literature. Nunavut and the "old" western NWT issue their own tourist material, and you should obtain a copy of their respective *Arctic Nunavut Travel Planner* and *Explorers' Guide* brochures. These summarize accommodation options, airline connections, many of the available tours – costing anything from $50 to $5000 or more – and the plethora of outfitters who provide the equipment and backup essential for any but the most superficial trip to the region.

Prince George

Lying some 780km north of Vancouver, and 380km northwest of Jasper, rough-edged **PRINCE GEORGE**, carved from the forest to become British Columbia's sixth largest city (pop. 78,000), is the general area's services and transport centre: you're likely to become acquainted with its dispersed and often half-deserted downtown streets. Forestry, in the form of pulp mills, kilns, planers, plywood plants and allied chemical works, is at the core of its industrial landscape – if you ever wanted the inside story on the lumber business, this is where to find it.

The town is a disorienting open-plan network of roads and sporadic houses between Hwy 97 and a sprawling downtown area at the junction of the Fraser and Nechako rivers. Simon Fraser established a North West Trading Company post in 1805, and named it Fort George in honour of the reigning George III. As a commercial nexus it quickly altered the lives of the local **Carrier Sekani** people, who abandoned their semi-nomadic migration from winter to summer villages in favour of a permanent settlement alongside the fort. Little changed until 1914 when the arrival of the Grand Trunk Railway – later the Canadian National – spawned an influx of pioneers and loggers. The town was connected by road to Dawson Creek and the north as late as 1951, and saw the arrival of the Pacific Great Eastern Railway in 1958, two developments that give some idea of how recent the opening up of the far north has been.

Transport to and from Prince George

Air Canada Jazz (☏1-888/247-2262, ⓦ www.flyjazz.ca) serves Prince George **by air**; the airport is 18km east of downtown and linked by regular shuttles. The town is linked three times weekly by VIA Rail **trains** (☏1-800/561-8630, ⓦ www.viarail.ca) to Jasper, Edmonton and beyond eastbound (a highly scenic journey), and Prince Rupert westbound (for the Haida Gwaii/Prince Charlotte Islands and Inside Passage ferries). The train station is downtown at 1300 1st Ave (☏250/564-5223 or 1-800/561-8630, ⓦ www.viarail.ca); if you're heading for motels or the bus terminal use a taxi from either Prince George Taxi (☏250/564-4444); or Emerald Taxi Ltd (☏250/563-3333).

Prince George is also a staging post for **Greyhound** routes to the north, and integral to the main road routes to Dawson Creek (for the Alaska Hwy) and Prince Rupert (for the Cassiar Hwy). The Greyhound **bus terminal**, well south of downtown at 1566 12th Ave (☏250/564-5454 or 1-800/661-8747, ⓦ www.greyhound.ca), is close to a handful of the town's many hotels and motels. There's one bus daily to Whitehorse in the Yukon (via Dawson Creek), two daily to Vancouver, and two daily to Prince Rupert.

As far as **sightseeing** is concerned, you might as well stick to what Prince George does best and take the surprisingly popular free **tours** around some of its big mills and processing plants; to reserve a place, contact Tourism Prince George opposite the bus terminal at 1198 Victoria St and 15th Avenue (Mon–Sat 9am–4/6pm; ☎250/562-3700 or 1-800/668-7646, ⓦwww .tourismpg.bc.ca). Company buses generally pick up from the Tourism Prince George offices and deliver you to one of several firms, the biggest currently being Northwood Pulp and Timber, where you are shown thousands of seedlings being grown in controlled conditions, the sawmills, and one of the continent's largest pulp mills. Outside, in a graphic illustration of the scale of forestry in the region, logs, planks and piles of sawdust the size of small hills stretch almost as far as the eye can see.

The best **motel** on the Hwy 97 strip is the big *Spruceland Inn* (☎563-0102 or 1-800/663-3295; ❸), at 1391 Central St at the junction of Hwy 97 and 15th Ave. At the nearby *Esther's Inn* (☎562-4131 or 1-800/663-6844, ⓦwww.esthersinn.com; ❸), one block off the highway at 1151 Commercial Drive (10th Ave), the price includes a swimming pool and Jacuzzi. Closer to downtown is the comfortable 200-room *Ramada Hotel Downtown Prince George*, 444 George St (☎250/563-0055 or 1-800/830-8833, ⓦwww .ramadaprincegeorge.com; ❺). All the campsites are some way out, the best being the big *Blue Spruce RV & Campground* about 5km west at Kimball Road on Hwy 16 (☎250/964-7272 or 964-4060, ⓔbluespruncervpark@shaw.ca; $16.50–22.50; April to mid-Oct), which includes a heated outdoor pool. With **food**, don't expect much in the way of culinary sophistication and stick to good chains like *Earl's*, 1440 E Central St, or *White Spot*, 820 Victoria St; otherwise treat yourself to Italian and other mid-priced dishes at *Da Moreno*, 1493 3rd Ave (☎250/564-7922), probably the best restaurant in town.

For the route from Prince George north and east to Dawson Creek, and the Alaska Highway, see p.997.

Prince George to Prince Rupert

To make the 735-kilometre journey west from Prince George to **Prince Rupert**, you can use either Hwy 16 or the parallel VIA Rail railway; neither are terribly scenic by BC standards until you reach the glorious river and mountain landscapes of the **Skeena Valley** 150km before Prince Rupert. Most people make this trip as a link in a much longer journey, either to to pick up **ferries** north to Alaska or south to Port Hardy on Vancouver Island, or to pick up the start of the Cassiar Hwy, a rough wilderness road that cuts north from the Skeena Valley to meet the Alaska Hwy at Watson Lake over the Yukon border. Unless you fly, it's also the only way to reach the Haida Gwaii/Queen Charlotte Islands, accessible by ferry or plane from Prince Rupert. The best place to pause during the journey is near **Hazelton**, where you can visit a little cluster of aboriginal villages.

West of Prince George: Vanderhoof and beyond

Riding out of Prince George you're confronted quickly with the relentless monotony of the Interior Plateau's rolling forests, an arboreal grind broken only by the occasional lake and the grey silhouettes of distant low-hilled horizons. At **VANDERHOOF**, 98km down the highway, gentler patches of pasture begin to poke through the tree cover, but these do little to soften the impact of the town itself. An abrupt grid of garages and motels, it's best known for its July airshow and the more graceful aerial dynamics of thousands of Canadian geese at the nearby **Nechako Bird Sanctuary**. Before pushing on, grab a coffee at the *OK Café*, part of a fine collection of half-timbered heritage houses at the town's western end. If you get stuck, or would prefer to stay in the village rather than Prince George, there are cheap **motels**: the largest of them is the *Grand Trunk Inn*, 2351 Church Ave (℡250/567-3188 or 1-877/567-3188; ❷); or you could try the slightly more expensive *Siesta Inn* downtown on Hwy 16 (℡250/567-2365 or 1-800/914-3388, ⓔsiesta @hwy16.com; ❸). For **camping**, there's the *Riverside Park Campground*, overlooking the bird sanctuary at 3100 Burrard Ave (℡250/567-4710; $15; May–Sept). The **infocentre** is at 2353 Burrard Ave (year-round; ℡250/567-2124 or 1-800/752-4094, ⓦwww.hwy16.com/chamber).

Beyond here the ride becomes more verdant towards **FORT FRASER**, 50km on a more attractive spot than Vanderhoof itself. If you're **camping**, hold out for the provincial site at Beaumont Provincial Park (℡250/565-6340; $14), 3.5km to the west, whose meadow site falls away gently to Fraser Lake.

Beyond Burn's Lake the scenery picks up still more, as if preparing for the mountains in the distance, though the run of villages continues to offer little but places to fill either the tank or the stomach. If you're going as far as to **stay** in this region, aim for the *Douglas Motel* (℡250/846-5679, ⓦwww .monday.com/douglasmotel; ❹), on the banks of the Bulkley River, just 150m out of the unspoiled hamlet of **TELKWA**, 10km east of Smithers. If you do stay, be sure to take a few minutes to stroll up the riverfront street of heritage buildings and its handsome brown-and-white, wood-planked **pioneer museum**.

SMITHERS, the largest place after Prince George (370km to the east), is focused on a single main crossroads on Hwy 16, with an **infocentre** nearby at 1411 Court St (year-round; mid-May–Aug daily 9am–5pm; Sept–mid-May Mon–Fri 9am–5pm; ℡250/847-5072 or 1-800/542-6673, ⓦwww .tourismsmithers.com) and a big Super-Valu **supermarket** for supplies on the junction itself. If you're overnighting here – and there's plenty of **accommodation** – ignore the brace of motels on the road and settle for the big white-timbered *Hudson Bay Lodge* (℡250/847-4581 or 1-800/663-5040, ⓦwww.hblodge.com; ❹) outside the village as you enter from the east. If this is out of your budget, try the *Florence Motel* (℡250/847-2678; ❷) on the west side of town – it's half the price – or the *Sandman Inn Smithers* on Hwy 16, a block from Main Street, part of an invariably trustworthy chain (℡250/847-2637 or 1-800/726-3626, ⓦwww.sandmanhotels.ca; ❸).

The Skeena Valley

Just beyond Smithers, the **Skeena River** (the "River of the Mists") carves a beautiful valley through the Coast Mountains, an important trade route for aboriginal peoples and stern-wheelers before the coming of the railway in 1912. For a couple of hours the road and railway run past a huge backdrop of snowcapped peaks half-reflected in the mist-wraithed estuary. Out on the water there's a good chance of seeing the ripples of beavers and sea otters, not to mention bald eagles perched on the river's immense log jams. Dark valleys peel off the main river's majestic course, suggestive of a deep, untrodden wilderness, and delicate threads of waterfalls are repeatedly visible though the trees.

Shortly after Hwy 16 meets the river crashing down from the north near Hazelton and New Hazelton, a couple of minor roads strike off to four nearby

Gitxsan aboriginal villages, places where something of the culture of the area's indigenous Gitxsan peoples has been preserved, along with new examples of totem carving and other crafts. 'Ksan and Kispiox, home to the best totems and long houses, are a few kilometres off Hwy 16 on the minor High Level Road (Hwy 62) out of New Hazelton; just north of 'Ksan a road links west to Gitwangak and Gitanyow (formerly Kitwancool), or they can be reached by continuing west on Hwy 16 a few kilometres and heading north on Hwy 37 (the Cassiar Hwy).

The most easterly of the west coast aboriginal peoples, the Gitxsan – "people of the river of the mists" – traditionally lived off fish and game rather than agriculture, and were consummate artists and carvers. Many of their traditions were eroded by the coming of whites, and by missionaries in particular, but in the 1950s the people's elders made a determined decision to resurrect as much of their dying culture as possible, re-creating an entire 1870 settlement at **'Ksan**. Although there's a good deal of commercialism, this is the village to concentrate on – aboriginal women act as guides around several long houses, giving a commentary on the carvings, clothes, buildings and masks on show, as well as offering accounts of local history (tours daily mid-April to Sept 9am–5pm; museum same summer hours plus daily Oct–mid-April 9.30am–4.30pm; tours $10, museum $2; ☎250/842-5544 or 1-877/842-5518, ⓦwww.ksan.org).

Kispiox, 13km north of Hazelton, is the ancient Gitxsan home of the Frog, Wolf and Fireweed clans, and was given its name by the old Department for Indian Affairs. It means "place of loud talkers" but locals not surprisingly prefer the traditional name, which is Anspayaxw, meaning "the hidden place". The highlights here are fifteen riverside totems. **Gitwangak** to the west, just 500m north of the Hwy 16 and Hwy 37 junction, means "the place of rabbits", and was the traditional village home of the Eagle, Wolf and Frog. It, too, has some impressive totems, as does **Gitanyow** – "people of a small village" – 21km north on Hwy 37, whose eighteen poles include the 140-year-old "Hole in the Ice" or "Hole in the Sky" totem. You can sometimes watch poles being repaired at one of two carving sheds around the village.

The nearest **infocentre** for the villages is near New Hazelton at the junction of Hwys 16 and 62 (mid-May to mid-Sept daily 9am–5pm; ☎250/842-6071 or 842-6571 year-round, ⓔnhazel@uniserve.com), but you should also spend a few minutes looking round the evocative old Victorian streets of old **Hazelton** 6km to the northwest on Hwy 62. **Accommodation** is limited to a couple of motels in New Hazelton, the cheapest being the *Bulkley Valley Motel*, 4444 Hwy 16 (☎250/842-6817; ❷). Kispiox also has a few rooms and campsite: the *Sportsman's Kispiox Lodge* (☎250/842-6455 or 1-800/KISPIOX, ⓦwww.kispiox.com/lodge; ❹) and the eight cabins at the *Kispiox River Resort and Campground* (☎250/842-6182, ⓔkispiox@mohaveaz.com; ❷; camping $14–22; June–Oct).

Prince Rupert

There's a bracing tang of salt and fish on the air in **PRINCE RUPERT**, a distinctive port that comes as an invigorating relief after the run out of Prince George. A good-looking place, similar in appearance to a Scottish fishing town, it looks out over an archipelago of islands and is ringed by mountains that tumble to the sea along a beautiful fjord-cut coastline. A crowd of cars, backpackers and RVs washes daily through its streets off the **Alaska**, **Queen Charlotte** and **Port Hardy ferries**, complementing the seafront's vibrant activity, and adding to the coffers of a town that's quite clearly on the up and

Ferries from Prince Rupert

Ferry terminals for both BC Ferries (for Port Hardy and the Queen Charlotte Islands) and the Alaska Marine Highway (for Skagway and Alaska Panhandle ports) are at **Fairview Dock**, 2km southwest of town at the end of Hwy 16. Walk-on tickets for foot passengers are rarely a problem at either terminal, but advance reservations are essential if you're taking a car or want a cabin for any summer crossing. A town bus passes the terminal every two or three hours for incoming sailings, but for outbound sailings it's probably best to grab a **taxi** from downtown. You can arrange a pick-up from the ferry by calling Seashore Charters (☎250/624-5645). Alternatively walk a kilometre to the corner of Pillsbury and Kootenay, where the local #52 bus passes roughly every half an hour (Mon–Sat 7.30am–5.30pm).

To the Queen Charlotte Islands
BC Ferries operates the MV *Queen of Prince Rupert* **to Skidegate** on the Queen Charlotte Islands (June to mid-Sept: Mon 9pm arriving 6am, Wed 1pm arriving 7.30pm, Thurs–Sun 11am arriving 5.30pm; rest of year: Sun & Mon 11pm, Thurs 1.30pm). The crossing takes between 6hr 30min and 8hr depending on weather, and costs $23.50 one-way for foot passengers ($19.75 low season: late Sept to early June), plus $86.50/$73.25 for cars and $6 for bikes. Two-berth cabins cost $45 year-round. Return ferries from Skidegate operate, in high season, Mon & Tues 11am arriving 6pm, Wed–Sat 11pm, arriving 7.30am, although on some summer Fridays and Saturdays the boat docks earlier to provide a connection with the Inside Passage boat to Port Hardy on Vancouver Island (see below). In winter there are three services weekly (Mon & Tues 11am, Thurs 11pm). For **reservations** or timetable information, contact Prince Rupert's infocentre or BC Ferries direct on ☎250/386-3431 or 1-888/223-3779 anywhere in BC, ⊛www.bcferries.com).

To Port Hardy
Ferries **to Port Hardy** leave every other day in summer at 7.30am (odd-numbered

up. Outdoor activities aside, there's nothing much to do, but if you're waiting for a boat it's an amiable enough spot and you'll probably bump into more fellow travellers here than almost anywhere else in northern BC.

Arrival and information
The **Greyhound station** is in the centre of town at 822 3rd Ave and 8th Street (daily 8.30am–8.30pm; ☎250/624-5090, ⊛www.greyhound.ca) and handles two buses daily (morning and evening) for the twelve-hour ride to Prince George ($85 one-way). The VIA Rail **train station** is on the waterfront at 1st Avenue and the foot of 2nd Street (open 2hr either side of departures and arrivals; ☎250/627-7589, 627-7304 or 1-800/561-8630, ⊛www.viarail.ca). Trains to Prince George for connections to Edmonton via Jasper currently leave on Wednesday, Friday and Sunday at 8am, arriving in Prince George at 8.10pm. If you're thinking of taking the train right through, note that you have to stay overnight in Prince George, as there are no through-trains to Jasper or Edmonton. The local **airport** is on Digby Island just across the harbour, with ferry connections to the BC and Alaska Marine ferry terminals (see box) and shuttle bus connections to downtown. Check-in with your airline at least two hours before flight departure for the combined shuttle-ferry service to the airport, which is on an island – so you must leave enough time for the transfer. Air Canada Jazz (☎1-888/247-2262) flies to Vancouver, as does Hawkair (☎1-866-429-5247). Air Canada Jazz shuttle buses to and from the airport drop and

days in June, July, Sept and sometimes the first half of Oct, even-numbered days in Aug and second half of May) and once every two weeks (currently Fri) in winter for a stunning fifteen-hour cruise. One-way fares are: in peak season (mid-June to mid-Sept) $102.50 for drivers or walk-on passengers, $241.50 for a car, $6.50 for a bicycle; in "peak special" (mid-May to mid-June and mid- to end-Sept) $82/$193/$5.20; in the shoulder season (Oct to early Nov and mid-Dec to early Jan) $72.50/$170.50/$6.50; and in low season (early Nov to mid-Dec) $54.25/$128/$6.50. To take on a car you'll need to have booked at least two months in advance (see also Port Hardy, p.895).

To Alaska

Ferries run by **Alaska Marine Highway** (℡250/627-1744 or 1-800/642-0066) run **to Skagway** in Alaska, via some or all of Ketchikan, Wrangell, Petersburg, Sitka, Hyder, Stewart, Juneau, Haines and Hollis and other minor halts. Frequency is almost daily in July and August, four times a week for the rest of the summer and in spring and autumn, and twice a week in winter. Schedules and fares are complicated, given the many possible permutations of route and port, but can be sourced from the excellent webpage at ⓦwww.dot.state.ak.us/amhs or by calling the central reservations number in Juneau (℡1-800/642-0066) or the Anchorage office (℡907/272-7116). Two- or four-berth cabins can also be booked: reckon on two-berth cabin from Prince Rupert costing about US$150 to and from Bellingham and just over US$100 to and from Haines or Skagway. Boats stop frequently en route, with the chance to go ashore for a short time, though longer stopovers must be arranged when buying a through-ticket. For all Alaskan sailings turn up at least an hour before departure to go through US customs and immigration procedures if you're a foot passenger, and three hours if you have a car, and note that though the journey takes two days there are various restrictions on the fresh food you can take on board.

pick up by the infocentre; Hawkair shuttles drop and pick up at the *Highliner Inn*. Local firms Inland Air (℡250/627-1351 or 1-888/624-2577) and Harbour Air (℡250/627-1341 or 1-800/689-4234) both run flights to Sandspit on the Haida Gwaii/Queen Charlotte Islands (see p.983). Many people reach Prince Rupert by **ferry**. For details of how to reach downtown from the **ferry terminal**, which is 2km from town, see the box. For **car rentals**, contact National (℡250/624-5318) in the Rupert Mall on 2nd Ave West.

Prince Rupert's **infocentre** is not in the main downtown area, but at Suite 100, Cow Bay Rd (℡250/624-5637 or 1-800/667-1994, ⓦwww .tourismprincerupert.com), a little to the north in an older part of the town known as Cow Bay, a small waterfront enclave that also boasts one or two accommodation options and some attractive cafés and restaurants. The centre will help with finding accommodation, which shouldn't present problems outside July and August, when places fill up quickly on days when the ferries come in: book ahead to be on the safe side. If there's nothing in town, you can always backtrack along Hwy 16 to the villages beyond the Skeena Valley.

Accommodation

The town's only decent budget **accommodation** option, with basic hostel-type rooms (dorm beds $16, private doubles $43) and shared bathrooms, is the quickly filled *Pioneer Hostel*, around the corner from the museum and infocentre at 167 3rd Ave (℡250/624-2334; ❷). The nearest motel to the ferry terminals is the *Totem Lodge Motel*, 1335 Park Ave (☎250/624-6761 or 1-800/550-0178; ❸); Park Avenue is a continuation of 2nd Avenue which runs south to the terminals from downtown. Perhaps the best all-round central choice, especially if you can secure a room with a sea view, is the *Inn on the Harbour*, 720 1st Ave (☎250/624-9107 or 1-800/663-8155; ❸), while most reasonable of the many mid-range establishments is the *Aleeda*, 900 3rd Ave (☎250/627-1367; ❸). *Pacific Inn*, 909 3rd Ave W (☎250/627-1711 or 1-888/663-1999, ✉pacific@citytel.net; ❸), is a big and good-value motel, but if you want to go top-of-the-range try the large *Crest Hotel*, 222 1st Ave (☎250/624-6771 or 1-800/663-8150, ⓦwww.cresthotel.bc.ca; ❻), or the more reasonable mini-skyscraper *Howard Johnson Highliner Plaza Hotel*, 815 1st Ave W (☎250/624-9060 or 1-800/668-3115, ⓦwww.hojoprincerupert.com; ❹). Farther afield, the *Parkside Resort*, 101 11th Ave (☎250/624-9131 or 1-888/575-2288, ⓦwww.parksideresortmotel.com; ❷), is a smart-looking hotel with good rates about a kilometre out of town and more likely to have room when downtown places are full.

The only big local **campsite** is the rather unattractive *Park Avenue Campground*, 1750 Park Ave (☎250/624-5861; $12–24; year-round), 1km west of town and 1km from the ferry terminals; it has tent sites but is usually full of RVs. Otherwise the *Parkside Resort* (see above) has some sites ($10–18) that few people know about, and there's also the rural *Prudhomme Lake* provincial campsite (☎250/798-2277; $14; April–Nov), with forested lakeside sites, 16km east of town on Hwy 16.

The Town

Although you wouldn't know to look at it, Prince Rupert's port is one of the world's largest deep-water terminals, and handles a huge volume of trade (grain, coal and fish in particular). In the past the region was the focal point of trade between aboriginal peoples to the north and south, one reason why the Hudson's Bay Company built a post at Fort Simpson, 30km north of the present townsite. It was also the reason why the old Hudson's Bay post was chosen as the terminus of Canada's second **transcontinental rail link**. Work began in 1906, but as time went by it was decided there was a better harbour to the south, a national competition being launched to decide on a name for the new railhead: $250 was paid for "Prince Rupert", named after the company's royal founding member, a label that was duly grafted onto the ramshackle collection of tents that constituted the settlement in 1909. A year later the first town lot was sold for around $500; within twelve months it was worth $17,000. The Grand Trunk Railway chairman, Charles M. Hays, hoped to turn Prince Rupert into a port to rival Vancouver. In 1912 he set off for Britain to raise stock for the venture, but unfortunately booked a passage on the *Titanic*. Although he went down, the railway was finished two years later – too late, in the event, to steal a march on Vancouver. By 1919 the Grand Trunk was bankrupt, though its restructuring as the Canadian National in 1923 and the magnificence of the port has allowed the town to prosper to this day. For more on the railway and its history, visit the **Kwinitsa Station Railway Museum** housed in the old 1911 station just across from the VIA Rail station near the waterfront (early June to early Sept daily 9am–6pm; donation).

Prince Rupert's excellent **Museum of Northern British Columbia** (June–Aug Mon–Sat 9am–8pm, Sun 9am–5pm; Sept–May Mon–Sat 9am–5pm; $5) is on 1st Avenue and McBride Street at the northern end of the town's tight downtown zone. It's housed in an impressive reproduction First Nation cedar longhouse and is particularly strong on the culture and history of the local Tsimshian. The museum also boasts a clutch of wonderful silent archive films on topics ranging from fishing to the building of the railway – ideal ways to whittle away a wet afternoon, of which storm-lashed Prince Rupert ("City of Rainbows") has plenty. There's also a well-stocked book and gift shop and a carving shed outside where you can sometimes see totems being crafted.

While you're here, check on some of the local **tours** or **boat trips**, many of which are inexpensive and provide a good way to see the offshore islands and wildlife. The museum runs tours to sites of archeological interest (mid-June to early Sept daily). Otherwise Seashore Charters (☎250/624-5645) is a good outfit, with two-hour harbour tours, among others, starting at around $50. For an inexpensive look at the harbour you could jump aboard the Rupert Water Taxi, which leaves for several destinations from the dock at the bottom of McBride Street (check times at the infocentre; departures vary according to school runs; from $3.50). A very popular trip locally is to **Khuzeymateen Provincial Park** (contact BC Parks on ☎250/847-7320 for information on two- to ten-day tours), a remote coastal valley 45km north of Prince Rupert created in 1994 to protect BC's largest-known coastal population of **grizzly bears**. This is the first park of its kind in the world, but there will certainly be more, especially in BC, where the damage done to declining grizzly habitats by logging, mining, hunting and other concerns – notably the slaughter of the animals for body parts in dubious Asian remedies – is rapidly becoming one of the keenest environmental issues in the province.

A little out of town, beyond the museum, the gondola ride to **Mount Hays** once gave a bird's-eye view of the harbour and the chance to spot bald eagles. It was also the most popular attraction in town, which makes you wonder why it had to close; check with the infocentre to see if there's news of it reopening. To reach it, or the steep track that currently provides the only route to the top, take the Wantage Road turn-off on Hwy 16 just out of town. It's three hours to the top but you get fairly good views after clambering just a short way up the track. Details of less energetic **walks** can be obtained from the infocentre.

Eating and drinking

Fresh fish is the obvious thing to **eat** locally, preferably at a town institution, the *Green Apple*, a shack that serves a mean halibut and chips for a few dollars; it's at 301 McBride St (☎250/627-1666) just before Hwy 16 turns into town. For something a touch more upmarket, locals flock to the *Smile's Seafood Café*, at 113 George Hills Way (☎250/624-3072), which has been doing a roaring trade on the waterfront since 1934. Also here – just across the road – is *Cowpuccinos*, a good café that's the centre of Prince Rupert's alternative scene. The *Breakers* pub just across the bridge at 117 George Hills Way (☎250/624-5990) is a popular and inexpensive place to drink and also serves decent food. Also close by, the *Cow Bay Café*, 205 Cow Bay (☎250/627-1212; closed Mon), pushes *Smile's* close for the best seafood and other meals in town. The **bar** under the *Coast Prince Rupert* high-rise hotel at 118 2nd Ave, between 6th and 7th streets, also does decent if standard Canadian food, and is one of the few places open for breakfast.

Haida Gwaii – the Queen Charlotte Islands

Ranged in a gentle arc some 150km off the Prince Rupert coast, the **Haida Gwaii**, until recently better known as the **Queen Charlotte Islands**,

The Haida

The **Haida** are widely considered to have the most highly developed culture and sophisticated art tradition of British Columbia's aboriginal peoples. Extending from the Haida Gwaii (Queen Charlotte Islands) to south Alaska, their lands included major stands of red cedar, the raw material for their huge dugout **canoes**, intricate **carvings** and refined **architecture**. Haida trade links were built on the reputation of their skill – other BC peoples considering the ownership of a Haida canoe, for example, as a major status symbol. Renowned as traders and artists, the Haida were also feared **warriors**, paddling into rival villages and returning with canoes laden with goods, slaves and the severed heads of anyone who had tried to resist. Their skill on the open sea has seen them labelled the "Vikings" of northern America. This success at warfare was due, in part, to their use of wooden slat armour, which included a protective face visor and helmets topped with terrifying images.

Socially the Haida divided themselves into two main groups, the **Eagles** and the **Ravens**, which were further divided into hereditary kin groups named after their original village location. Marriage within each major group – or *moiety* – was considered incestuous, so Eagles would always seek Raven mates and vice versa. Furthermore, descent was traced through the **female line**, which meant that a chief could not pass his property on to his sons because they would belong to a different *moiety* – instead his inheritance passed to his sister's sons. Equally, young men might have to leave their childhood village to claim their inheritance from their maternal uncles.

Haida **villages** were an impressive sight, their vast cedar-plank houses dominated by fifteen-metre totem poles displaying the kin group's unique animal crest or other mythical creatures, all carved in elegantly fluid lines. Entrance to each house was through the gaping mouth of a massive carved figure; inside, supporting posts were carved into the forms of the crest animals and most household objects were similarly decorative. Equal elaboration attended the many Haida ceremonies, one of the most important of which was the **mortuary potlatch**, serving as a memorial service to a dead chief and the validation of the heir's right to succession. The dead individual was laid out at the top of a carved pole near the village entrance, past which the visiting chiefs would walk wearing robes of finely woven and patterned mountain-goat wool and immense headdresses fringed with long sea-lion whiskers and ermine skins. A hollow at the top of each headdress was filled with eagle feathers, which floated down onto the witnesses as the chiefs sedately danced.

After **European contact** the Haida population was devastated by smallpox and other epidemics. In 1787, there were around 8000 Haida scattered across the archipelago. Their numbers were then reduced from around 6000 in 1835 to 588 by 1915. Consequently they were forced to abandon their traditional villages and today gather largely at two sites, Old Masset (pop. 650) and Skidegate (Haida pop. 550). At other locations the homes and totems fell into disrepair, and only at **Sgan Gwaii**, a remote village at the southern tip of the Queen Charlottes, has an attempt been made to preserve an original Haida settlement; it has now been declared a World Heritage Site by UNESCO.

These days the Haida number around 2000, and are highly regarded in the North American art world; Bill Reid, Freda Diesing and Robert Davidson are amongst the best-known figures, and scores of other Haida craftspeople produce a mass of carvings and jewellery for the tourist market. They also play a powerful role in the islands' social, political and cultural life, having been vocal in the formation of sites such as the Gwaii Haanas National Park Reserve (p.991), South Moresby's Haida Heritage Site and Duu Guusd Tribal Park (p.989), the last established to protect old aboriginal villages on Graham Island's northwest coast.

consist of a triangular-shaped archipelago of two major islands – **Graham** and **Moresby** – and two hundred islets that make an enticing diversion from the heavily travelled sea route up through BC. The islands are something of a cult amongst travellers and environmentalists, partly for their scenery, flora and fauna and almost legendary remoteness from the mainstream, but also because they've achieved a high profile in the battle between the forestry industry and ecology activists. At the forefront of the battle are the **Haida**, widely acknowledged as one of the region's most advanced aboriginal groups, who have made the islands their home for over 10,000 years (see box, opposite). Their culture, and in particular the chance to visit their many **deserted villages**, forms an increasing part of the islands' attraction, but many people also come here to sample the immensely rich **flora and fauna**, a natural profusion that's earned them the title of the "Canadian Galapagos".

The Haida Gwaii were one of only two areas in western Canada to escape the last Ice Age, which elsewhere altered the evolutionary progress, and which has resulted in the survival of many so-called **relic species**. Species unique to the islands include a fine yellow daisy, the world's largest **black bears**, and subspecies of pine marten, deer mouse, hairy woodpecker, saw-whet owl and Stellar's jay. There are also more **eagles** here than anywhere else in the region, as well as the world's largest population of Peale's peregrine falcons and the elusive **black-footed albatross** – whose wingspan exceeds that of the largest eagles. Fish, too, are immensely plentiful, and there's a good chance of spotting whales, otters, sea lions and other aquatic mammals.

Haida Gwaii practicalities

The islands can be accessed either by air or ferry from Prince Rupert. Ferries from Prince Rupert (see box p.980 for details) dock at tiny Skidegate near Queen Charlotte City on **Graham Island**, the northern of the group's two main collections of islands. Most of the archipelago's six thousand inhabitants live either in Queen Charlotte City or at Masset to the north, leaving the southern cluster of islands across Skidegate Channel – known for convenience as **Moresby Island** – a virtually deserted primal wilderness but for the small community at Sandspit (see p.990). Regular twenty-minute ferry crossings connect Moresby Island to Skidegate (twelve daily, year-round; $5, cars $12.50).

You can also **fly** to the islands from Prince Rupert, landing at Sandspit, which has the islands' only airstrip (float planes can land elsewhere). Air Canada Jazz (☎1-888/247-2262, ⓦwww.flyjazz.ca) flies here daily from Vancouver, but you might get better deals from carriers with offices in Prince Rupert such as Harbour Air (☎250/627-1341 or 1-800/665-0212), which flies to Sandspit once daily from Prince Rupert (currently Tues, Thur & Sat 10.30am; $330 return) and to Masset on the north of Graham Island (daily 2.30pm, also Mon–Fri 8.30am; $260). It also has other flights around the islands, as does South Moresby Air Charters (☎250/559-4222 or 1-888/551-4222, ⓦwww.smair.com) in Queen Charlotte City, who'll take you out to the deepest of the backwoods.

Car rental rates here are expensive, and unless you have a car, bike or canoe it's as well to know that you could be in for a long and expensive trip that shows you very little of what you came for. Budget (☎250/637-5688 or 1-800/557-3228) has offices in Queen Charlotte City, Masset and Sandspit airport, but in summer you'll need to have booked in advance to secure a car. Thrifty (☎250/637-2299) has an office at Sandspit airport. Rates at Rustic

Rentals (☎250/559-4641), out of Charlotte Island Tire in Queen Charlotte City, are a touch lower than the main companies. To see the **Haida villages**, in any case, virtually all of which are on inaccessible parts of Moresby, you'll need to take a boat, and more probably a pricey tour by float plane. Noncamping **accommodation** is available only at Sandspit (on Moresby) and Queen Charlotte City, Tl'ell, Masset and Port Clements (on Graham) and should always be prebooked.

Graham Island

Most casual visitors stick to **Graham Island**, where the bulk of the island's roads and accommodation are concentrated along the eastern side of the island, between **Queen Charlotte City** in the south and **Masset** some 108km to the north. These settlements and the villages in between – Skidegate, Tl'ell and Port Clements – lie along Hwy 16, the principal road, and shelter in the lee of the islands, away from a mountainous and indented rocky west coast that boasts the highest combined seismic, wind and tidal energy of any North American coastline (producing treacherous seas and a tidal range of 8m). Much of the east coast consists of beautiful half-moon, driftwood-strewn beaches and a string of provincial parks where you can appreciate the milder climes produced by the Pacific's Japanese Current, a warming stream that contributes to the island's lush canopy of thousand-year-old spruce and cedar rainforests. On the downside, though, it drenches both sides of the island with endless rainstorms, even in summer. Make sure you pack a raincoat.

Queen Charlotte City

It would be hard to imagine anywhere less like a city than the island's second-largest settlement, **QUEEN CHARLOTTE CITY** (pop. 924), a picturesque fishing village and frontier administrative centre about 5km west of the Skidegate ferry terminal. The village takes its name from the ship of Captain George Dixon, the British explorer who sailed to the Haida Gwaii in 1787, thirteen years after first European contact was probably made by the Spaniard Juan Perez. Most of its residents squeeze a living from the timber companies, whose felling exploits have cleared most of the hills around the port, and which control access to many of the island's 2000km of backcountry logging roads. For a fine overview of the place, try the stroll to the top of **Sleeping Beauty Mountain**, which is reached by a rough track from Crown Forest Road near Honna Road. The village **dump** south of the houses rates as another sight for the black bears and bald and golden eagles that often gather there at dusk. Farther afield you may be able to watch salmon and other wildlife at the **Skidegate Band Salmon Project** on the Honna Forest Service Road 3km west of town; contact the Band Council for information (☎250/559-4496). Farther away still, you can drive to **Rennell Sound**, a west-coast inlet with shingle beaches accessed by a logging road: take the main logging road north from the town for 22km and then turn left and follow the steep gravel road for 14km, but contact the infocentre before setting out (see below). At the Sound, the **Rennell Sound Recreation Site** offers paths through stands of primal rainforest to isolated sandy beaches and a couple of campsites with a total of ten beachfront wilderness pitches (free).

Otherwise the town is the major place to sign up for any number of outdoor activities; contact the **infocentre**, 3220 Wharf St (daily: mid-May to early Sept 10am–7pm; early May & late Sept 10am–2pm; closed Oct–April; ☎250/559-8316, ⓦwww.qcinfo.com). The staff are incredibly knowledgeable, and there's a good selection of detailed guides and maps to the area: be sure to pick up the invaluable *Guide to the Queen Charlotte Islands*. The centre is also the place to pick up brochures and organize **tours** of the island, some forty or more fishing, sailing, sightseeing, canoeing and other operators being based in Queen Charlotte City. It is also the place to sign up for tours of the national park reserve (see p.991). There's also a **Canadian Parks Service** office for information on Moresby Island's Gwaii Haanas National Park Reserve and Haida Heritage Site (see p.991), west of town along Hwy 33 (Mon–Fri 8am–noon & 1–4.30pm; ☎250/559-8818). The **Ministry of Forests**, in the obvious blue building on 3rd Avenue (☎250/559-8447), has information on the free primitive campsites run by the Forest Service on Graham and Moresby islands. If you're planning to drive logging roads, you must call **the logging companies** (☎250/557-6810 or 559-4224) – which control most of these roads on Graham Island – for latest access details. Enquire, too, about their regular forestry tours (they depart Port Clements museum: inquire at the infocentre or call the above numbers for latest details).

Practicalities

Accommodation is scarce and demand is high in summer, so definitely call ahead to make bookings. The cheapest option is *The Bunkhouse*, 924 3rd Ave (☎250/559-8383 or 1-888/559-8383, ✉smc@haidagwaii.net; ➊), a central **hostel** with twelve dorm beds at $10 and twelve tent sites at $5 per person. The first-choice hotel is probably the twelve-room *Premier Creek Lodging*, 3101 3rd Ave (☎250/559-8451 or 1-888/322-3388, ⓦwww.qcislands.net /premier; ➍), a splendidly restored 1910 heritage building overlooking the harbour and Bearskin Bay. Then there's the unique five-room *Gracie's Place*, 3113 3rd Ave (☎250/559-4262 or 1-888/244-4262, ⓦwww.graciesplace.ca; ➌), with characterful landlady, oceanview rooms, antique furniture and rustic decor, or intimate *Dorothy & Mike's Guest House*, 3125 2nd Ave (☎250/559-8439, ✉dormike@qcislands.net; ➍), with central rooms and full cooking facilities in a no-smoking environment. A touch closer to the ferry terminal, overlooking Bearskin Bay, is the *Sea Raven Motel & Restaurant*, 3301 3rd Ave (☎250/559-4423 or 1-800/665-9606, ⓦwww.searaven.com; ➌). If you're **camping**, try the unserviced *Haydn Turner Park* (free) in the community park at the western end of town, or the *Kagan Bay Forest Service Campground*, a handful of lovely beachfront pitches on Honna Forest Service Road 5km west of the town.

For **food**, locals make for the *Sea Raven Restaurant* (☎250/559-8583) located straight up the main road from the dock by the *Sea Raven Motel*. There are also *Margaret's Café*, 3223 Wharf St, on the east side of town, or *Hanging by a Thread* at 3207 Wharf close to the infocentre, a fine place whose produce comes from organic farms on the island.

Skidegate

There's not much doing at **SKIDEGATE** (pop. 550), other than the ferries docking at Skidegate Landing 2km away to the south and the chance to browse through the more accessible aspects of Haida culture at the **Haida Gwaii Museum**, located near Second Beach at Qay'llnagaay around 500m east of the ferry terminal (May–Sept Mon–Fri 9am–5pm, Sat 1–5pm; June–Aug also Sun 1–5pm; Oct–April Mon & Wed–Fri 10am–noon & 1–5pm, Sat 1–5pm; $5). Among other things, the museum contains the world's largest collection of the Haida's treasured argillite carvings (such carvings are also on display in Vancouver's UBC Museum of Anthropology). Argillite is a form of black slate-like rock found only on the Haida Gwaii, and only in one site whose location is kept a closely guarded secret. Also check out the platform here for viewing grey whales during their migrations (April, May, Sept & early Oct). After doing so, stop by the long-house office alongside the museum to have a chat with the **Haida Gwaii Watchmen**. Bands of Haida "watchmen" were formed in the 1970s to protect aboriginal sites from vandalism and theft, and survive to this day. Ask at the office about seeing the famous *Loo Taas* ("Wave Eater") canoe, which is generally on show here on weekdays. When it's not out on hire – for a mere $1500, or thereabouts – you're very occasionally able to take a six-hour tour in the huge vessel. It was made for the '86 Expo in Vancouver and was the first Haida canoe carved since 1909. You can obtain a permit to visit some of the five hundred or more abandoned aboriginal villages and sites on the southern islands from the long house, or alternatively from the nearby **Skidegate Mission** or Band Council Office (☎250/559-8225) close to Skidegate proper – a Haida village 2.5km from the ferry terminal. There's also a carving long house here, where you may be able to watch craftspeople at work. In July and August, the Mission usually hosts a weekly **seafood feast**, open to all-comers for around $25 (check latest details at the Queen Charlotte City infocentre).

For a boat across the channel to Moresby Island and Sandspit, the MV *Kwuna* **ferry** runs twelve times daily year-round (7.30am–10.30pm; 20min; $5 foot passengers, $12.50 cars, bicycles free).

Tl'ell and Port Clements

If you blink you'll miss the ranching community of **TL'ELL** (pop. 138), 36km north of Skidegate, first settled by outsiders in 1904 and home to the Richardson Ranch, the island's oldest working ranch. Stop here and walk down to the sea, where you can stroll for hours on deserted wind-sculpted dunes. It's a community favoured by craftspeople and alternative types – pop into the little café or gallery – and in the past there's been a **hostel** here, the intermittently open *Bellis Lodge* (☎250/557-4434; ❶) – check before turning up. Nearby is the *Tl'ell River House*, off Hwy 16 overlooking Tl'ell River and Hecate Strait, offering rooms with kitchenettes and a licensed lounge and **restaurant** (☎250/557-4211 or 1-800/667-8906; ❹). Or try the pleasantly rustic *Cacilia's B&B* just north of Richardson Ranch on the main road (☎250/557-4664; ❸; no credit cards), a renovated log house set behind the dunes on Hecate Strait 2km from the Naikoon Park (see below). **Bikes** and **kayaks** are usually available for rent here.

As the road cuts inland for **PORT CLEMENTS** (pop. 577), 21km north-west of Tl'ell, it forms the southern border of the **Naikoon Provincial Park**, an enclave that extends from Graham Island's northeast corner and designed to protect fine beach, dune and dwarf-woodland habitats. **Campers** should head for the *Misty Meadows Campground* ($9.50; May–Oct), just south of the Tl'ell River Bridge and 500m north of the **park headquarters** (☎250/557-4390) to the north of Tl'ell (backcountry camping is allowed throughout the park). About 8km beyond, look out for the picnic site and trails at the southern tip of **Mayer Lake**, one of the nicer spots to pull over. Port Clements in the past was most famous for the world's only **Golden Spruce** tree, a 300-year-old bleached albino tree – sacred to the Haida – which puzzled foresters by refusing to produce anything but ordinary green-leafed saplings; in 1997 a vandal chopped it down. A rare genetic mutation allowed the tree's needles to be bleached by sunlight and geneticists and foresters are currently trying to produce another tree.

Port Clements' little **infocentre** booth (July to early Sept daily 9am–6pm) is just out of the village, and there's a small **museum** of forestry and pioneer-related offerings at 45 Bayview Drive on the main road into the town (June–Sept Tues–Sun 2–5pm; winter hours according to availability of volunteers; donation). The one official **motel** is the twelve-room *Golden Spruce*, 2 Grouse St (℡250/557-4325 or 1-877/801-4653, ⓦwww.qcislands.net/golden; ❷), but it's worth asking around for B&B possibilities. For **food and drink**, the main option is the good *Yakoun River Inn* on Bayview Drive.

About 20km north of town on the road for Masset, look out for the signed **Pure Lake Provincial Park**, where on summer days the waters of Pure Lake should be warm enough for swimming.

Masset

MASSET, 40km north of Port Clements, is the biggest place on the islands, a scattered, rather ugly town – it is a former military base – of some 1500 people, most of whom are employed in fishing and crab-canning. Many visitors are here to bird-watch at the **Delkatla Wildlife Sanctuary**, a saltwater marsh north of the village – contact Delkatla Bay Birding Tours (℡250/626-5015) for guided visits – which supports 113 bird species, or to walk the trails around Tow Hill 26km to the east (see below). Others come to wander the neighbouring village of **Haida**, or "Old Massett" – with an extra "t" – 2km to the west, the administrative centre for the Council of the Haida First Nation and where some six hundred aboriginal people still live and work. Visitors should show respect when visiting totem sites, craft houses and community homes. Many locals are involved in producing crafts for tourists, or organizing wilderness tours, but some are restoring and adding to the few totems still standing locally (it's possible to visit various canoe and carving sheds) and there's a small museum giving some context. For more **information** on where to see carving and on the village in general, visit the Old Massett Council office on Eagle Road (Mon–Fri 9am–5pm; ℡250/626-3337), where you should also enquire about permission to visit the **Duu Guusd Tribal Park**, established by the Haida to protect villages on the coast to the northwest. Two villages here are still active, and the park is used as a base for the Haida Gwaii Rediscovery Centre, which offers courses to children on Haida culture and history.

The Masset **info booth**, at 1455 Old Beach Rd (July & Aug daily 9am–5pm; ℡250/626-3982, ⓦwww.massetbc.com), has full details of wildlife and bird-watching possibilities. The Masset Village Office on Main Street (℡250/626-3955 or 1-888/352-9292) can also provide invaluable background. Sadly they can't do much about the village's limited **accommodation** prospects, other than point you to the *Harbourview Lodging*, overlooking the harbour at 1608 Delkatla Rd (℡250/626-5109 or 1-800/661-3314, ⓔlholland@island.net; ❸), *Naden Lodge*, 1496 Delkatla St corner of Harrison (℡250/626-3322 or 1-800/771-8933, ⓦwww.nadenlodge.bc.ca; ❻), or to a handful of intermittently open B&Bs. Outside town, there's accommodation near South Beach with ocean views at the *Alaska View Lodge*, Tow Hill Rd (℡250/626-3333, ⓦwww.alaskaviewlodge.com; ❸), 10.5km from Masset airport and midway between Masset village and Tow Hill. The only nearby **campsite** is the *Village of Masset RV Site and Campground* ($9–17; no reservations) on Tow Hill Road, 2km north of town alongside the wildlife sanctuary. Farther afield there's the *Agate Beach* ($14; May–Sept) in Naikoon Provincial Park, a park site near trails and sandy beaches located 26km northeast of Masset off the secondary road towards Tow Hill (see below). To get around, call Vern's Taxi (℡250/626-3535) or Jerry's Taxi Service in Old Massett (℡250/626-5017), or **rent a car** from

Tilden, 1504 Old Beach Rd (☎250/626-3318). There are a couple of pizza and takeaway places to **eat** – try the *Café Gallery* on Collision Avenue – and a handful of **bars** on Collision Avenue and Main Street, with live music some nights.

Heading away from the village, follow Tow Hill Road to **Tow Hill**, 26km east, where you can pick up trails into the Naikoon Park; three begin by the Heillen River at the foot of Tow Hill itself. The easiest is the one-kilometre **Blow Hole Trail**, which drops down to striking rock formations and basalt cliffs by the sea. From here you can follow another path to the top of Tow Hill (109m) for superb views of deserted sandy beaches stretching into the hazy distance. The third track, the **Cape Fife Trail**, is a longer (10km) hike to the east side of the island. Naikoon means "point", a reference to Rose Spit, the twelve-kilometre spit that extends from the park and Graham Island's north-easterly tip. Today it's an ecological and wildlife reserve of beaches, dunes, marsh and stunted forest, but it's also a sacred Haida site, for it was here, according to legend, that the Haida's Raven clan were first tempted from a giant clamshell by a solitary raven.

Moresby Island

Moresby Island is all but free from human contact except for deserted Haida villages, one of which contains the world's largest stand of totems, forestry roads and the small logging community of **Sandspit** (pop. 202). The last lies 15km from the **Alliford Bay** terminal for the inter-island ferry link with Skidegate on Graham Island (12 daily; 20min crossing; $5, cars $12.50). Local airlines fly from Prince Rupert to a small airstrip near the village. Budget (☎250/637-5688 or 1-800/557-3228) and Thrifty (☎250/637-2299) have **car rental** offices at the airport; for a **taxi** for connections to the ferry, call Bruce's Taxi (☎250/637-5655).

Most locals here and on Graham Island work in Moresby's forests, and the **forestry** issue has divided the community for years between the Haida and environmentalists and the lumber workers. At stake are the islands' temperate rainforests and the traditional sites of the Haida, themselves politically shrewd media manipulators who've sent representatives to Brazil to advise local aboriginal peoples there on their own rainforest programmes. They've also occasionally provided the muscle to halt logging on the islands, and to prove a point in the past they've blocked access to **Hot Spring Island**, whose thermal pools are a favourite tourist target. On the other hand the forests provide jobs and some of the world's most lucrative timber: a single good sitka trunk can be worth up to $60,000. Currently a compromise has been reached and most of Moresby has National Park Reserve status (established in 1987), though stiff lobbying from the logging companies leaves its position perilous. If you're intending to drive any of the logging roads, however – and most of the handful of roads here *are* logging roads – note that generally they're open to the public at weekends and after 6pm on weekdays; otherwise check for latest details with the local infocentres.

Sandspit's only listed **accommodation**, apart from a couple of intermittently open B&Bs, is the *Moresby Island Guest House*, 385 Alliford Bay Rd overlooking the ocean at Shingle Bay, 1km south of the airport (☎250/637-5300, ⓦwww.moresbyisland-bnb.com; ❸); an airport pick-up is included. Many people choose to sleep on the spit's beaches: Gray Bay, 21km southeast of Sandspit, has primitive and peaceful **campsites** near gravel and sand beaches (for more details, contact the TimberWest forestry offices on Beach Rd; ☎250/637-5436). For **car rental**, Budget have offices at the airport and in

Sandspit at Beach and Blaine Shaw roads (℡250/637-5688). If you fancy going into the **interior by plane**, contact South Moresby Air Charters (℡250/559-4222 or 1-888/551-4222) for details of charter flights.

Gwaii Haanas National Park Reserve

If you're determined enough you can canoe, mountain bike or backpack the interior of northern Moresby Island, but you need to know what you're doing – the seas here are especially treacherous for canoeists – and be prepared to lug plenty of supplies. You must, however, join a tour or follow a strict procedure (see below) if you want to visit the **Gwaii Haanas National Park Reserve**, a 90km archipelago that embraces 138 islands, some 500 Haida archeological sites, five deserted Haida villages and some 1500km of coastline across the south of the island group. Treaties signed with the federal government in Ottawa in 1990 gave the Haida joint control of this region, and afforded protection to their ancient villages, but many land claims to the region remain unresolved. You need money, time and effort to see the park. There are no roads, and access is by boat or chartered planes only.

Visits to a variety of **Haida sites** and their totems, ruined dwellings and so forth are described here in order of distance (and therefore time and expense) from Sandspit. Closest are **Hlkenul** (Cumshewa) and **K'una** (Skedans) just outside the park, both accessible on day-trips by boat from Moresby Camp on the Cumshewa Inlet, 46km south of Sandspit (access to the Camp is by logging road). Farther afield, and in the park proper, are T'aanuu, Hlk'waah – one of the main battlegrounds in the fight to protect the region in the 1980s – and **Gandla K'In** (Hot Spring Island), whose hot springs make it one of the most popular destinations. The finest site of all is the one that's furthest away: **Sgan Gwaii** (Ninstints) lies close to the southern tip of the archipelago, and was abandoned by the Haida around 1880 in the wake of smallpox epidemics. Today, it contains the most striking of the ruined Haida villages, its long houses and many totems declared a UNESCO World Heritage Site in 1981.

Park practicalities

The easiest way into the park is with a **tour**; contact the Queen Charlotte City infocentre for full details. Or make direct contact with companies such as South Moresby Air Charters (℡250/559-4221 or 1-888/551-4222) or GwaiiEco Tours (℡250/559-8333 or 1-877/559-8333, ⓦwww.gwaiiecotours .com); prices start from about $135 for one-day trips. Sandspit's **infocentre** in the airport terminal building (June–Sept daily 9am–6pm; ℡250/637-5362) also has details of the many tours to the park and the limited facilities on the whole southern half of the archipelago.

To visit the reserve as an **independent traveller**, you must make an advance reservation or obtain a stand-by space. Reservations can be made by calling ℡1-800/HELLOBC (within Canada or the United States) or ℡250/387-1642 (outside North America). There is a $15 per person reservation fee (maximum of four people per reservation). If you choose not to make a reservation, then six stand-by places daily are available, on a first-come, first-served basis (starting at the 8am orientation session at the Queen Charlotte infocentre). There are also **fees** to visit the park: day-trips cost $10 per person plus $10 for each night thereafter, but trips of 6 to 14 nights are payable at a flat fee of $60; stays over 14 nights cost $80.

An **orientation session** is mandatory for all visitors entering Gwaii Haanas, Skedans or T'aanuu. Sessions take around ninety minutes and cover topics such as public safety, no-trace camping, natural and cultural heritage and the Haida

8

THE NORTH | Haida Gwaii – the Queen Charlotte Islands

Gwaii Watchmen Programme. These sessions take place at the Queen Charlotte infocentre or the Gwaii Haanas office on Airport Road, opposite the *Sandspit Inn* (☎250/559-8818). Before May 15 and after September 15, book sessions through the park office in Queen Charlotte City (see p.986); from mid-May to the end of June, sessions run twice daily – once in the QCC infocentre at 8am and once in the Sandspit Mall office at 11am. From July 1 to mid-September, there are two QCC sessions (8am & 7.30pm) and one in Sandspit (11am). If you're travelling with a tour company, companies check that you've done the orientation and some offer it as part of their package.

Apart from some restricted areas, which you are informed of during orientation sessions, you can **camp** where you wish in the reserve except in or near restricted cultural sites; fees for camping are included in the general fee you pay to enter the park. There are no hotels, hostels or other forms of **accommodation** in the restricted areas, but 10km from the Nan Sdins UNESCO site is the *Gwaii Haanas Guest and Kayaks* (☎250/559-8638, ⊛www.gwaiihaanas .com; ❸), three rooms in a family homestead (boat or float-place access only) in ancient rainforest with ocean views, organic food, sea kayak rentals and hiking, bird-watching and other outdoor activity possibilities.

The Cassiar Highway

The 733km of the **Cassiar Highway** (Hwy 37) – from the Skeena Valley east of Prince Rupert to Watson Lake just inside the Yukon – are some of the wildest and most beautiful on any British Columbian road. Though less famous than the Alaska Hwy, the road is increasingly travelled by those who want to capture some of the adventure that was found on the wilder reaches of its better-known neighbour in the 1950s and 1960s.

Some stretches are still gravel, and the petrol and repair facilities, let alone food and lodgings, are extremely patchy: don't contemplate the journey unless your vehicle's in top condition, with two spare tyres and spare fuel containers – fill up wherever possible. The road also provides a shorter route from Prince George to the Yukon than the Alaska Hwy. British Columbia's North by Northwest Tourist Association puts out complete lists of facilities, which are vital accompaniments to any journey and are available from the infocentres in Prince Rupert and Terrace.

If you're ready to drive the distances involved, you'll also probably be prepared to explore the highway's two main side roads to **Stewart** and **Telegraph Creek**, and possibly the rough roads and trails that lead into two wilderness parks midway up the highway – the **Mount Edziza Provincial Park** and the **Spatsizi Plateau Wilderness Park**. If you can't face the highway's entire length, take the side-trip to Stewart, which offers exceptional sea and mountain **scenery**, as well as the chance to cross into Alaska at **Hyder** to indulge in its vaunted alcoholic border initiation.

In summer Stewart is added to the itinerary of certain sailings of the Alaska Marine Highway **ferry** service (see box p.980) – albeit infrequently – so with careful planning you could travel overland to Stewart, or ride a boat to Ketchikan and thence to either Skagway or Prince Rupert.

Stewart and Hyder

The Cassiar Hwy starts near Kitwanga, one of several aboriginal villages off Hwy 16 (see p.977), and a crossroads of the old "grease trail", named after the

Stewart and The Thing

Stewart's history, together with that of nearby Hyder, might have marked it out as a regional player were it not quite so remote and apparently doomed to ultimate disappointment in every venture ever tried in the town. In the distant past it was an important **trading point**, marking the meeting point of territories belonging to the Nisga'a and Gitxsan interior aboriginal peoples to the south, the Thaltan to the north, and the Tsesaut and the Tlingit to the east. Captain **George Vancouver**, searching for the Northwest Passage in 1793, spoke for many who came after him when, having spent an eternity working his way inland up the Portland Canal, he declared himself "mortified with having devoted so much time to so little purpose". Almost exactly a century later the area welcomed its first settlers: in 1896 **Captain Gilliard** of the US Army Corps built four storehouses here in Hyder – Alaska's first stone buildings – and Stewart itself was named after two of its earliest settlers (Robert and John Stewart). For a time it looked as if the terminus of the trans-Canadian railway might materialize in Stewart, a hope that brought in 10,000 fortune-seeking pioneers. The railway never came, and Stewart's local line was abandoned after a few kilometres. As slump set in, **gold** was discovered – almost inevitably – and until 1948, when it closed, the Premier Gold and Silver Mine was North America's largest gold mine. Then came a **copper** mine, its eighteen-kilometre gallery apparently the longest tunnel ever built by boring from just one end. This closed in 1984, but not before 27 men were killed in a mine accident in 1965. All manner of new mining ventures have since been promised. None has materialized, leaving Stewart's scenery its main money-spinner: visitors and B-movie location scouts alike have been lured by the region's cliffs, mountains and glaciers – the *Iceman* and *The Thing* are two of the **movies** to have used the local landscape as a backdrop.

candlefish oil which was once traded between Coast and Interior peoples. Some hint of the sense of adventure required comes when you hit a section (47km beyond **Cranberry Junction**), where the road doubles up as an airstrip – planes have right of way. Another 27km on, there's another stretch used as an airstrip in emergencies. Almost immediately after you leave Hwy 16, though, the road pitches into the mesmerizing high scenery of the Coast Ranges, a medley of mountain, lake and forest that reaches a crescendo after 156km around **Meziadin Junction**, where Hwy 37A branches off; near here is the first formal place to **stay** – the 62-pitch *Meziadin Lake Provincial Park* **campsite** ($14) near 67km east of Stewart and 156km north of Kitwanga.

Some 67km west of Meziadin Junction lies **STEWART**, Canada's most northerly ice-free port. Here a series of immense glaciers culminates in the dramatic appearance of the unmissable **Bear Glacier**, a vast sky-blue mass of ice that comes down virtually to the highway and has the strange ability to glow in the dark. Stewart itself, 37km west of the glacier, is a shrivelled mining centre (pop. 2200) that sits at the end of the Portland Canal, the world's fourth longest fjord, a natural boundary between British Columbia and Alaska that lends the town a superb peak-ringed location (the ferry ride in from Prince Rupert through some of the west coast's wildest scenery is sensational). Dominating its rocky amphitheatre is **Mount Rainey**, whose cliffs represent one of the greatest vertical rises from sea level in the world. Scenery aside, the main thing to see in town is the **Stewart Historical Museum** housed in the former fire hall at Columbia and 6th Avenue (late June or early July to Aug or early Sept Wed–Sun 11am–6pm; $5). A fine little provincial museum, its exhibits are devoted largely to stuffed wildlife and the town's logging and mining heritage. You might also want to journey out 5km beyond Hyder in

Alaska to Fish Creek, where from the special viewing platform above the artificial spawning channel you may be lucky enough to see **black bears** catching some of the world's largest chum salmon. Around town there is also a handful of enticing trails, some along old mining roads: for details, contact the infocentre or visit the British Columbia Forest Service (☎250/636-2663) office at 8th and Brightwell.

The town's **infocentre** is housed at 222 5th Ave near Victoria (mid-May to mid-Sept daily 9am–8pm; ☎250/636-9224 or 1-888/366-5999, ⓦwww .stewartandhyder.homestead.com). There are three **hotels**: the *King Edward Hotel*, 5th and Columbia (☎250/636-2244 or 1-800/663-3126, ⓦwww.kingedwardhotel.com; ❹), and the *King Edward Motel*, Columbia Avenue (same details); the latter has basic housekeeping units and is $10 more expensive. The third option is the *Ripley Creek Inn* on the estuary at 306 5th Ave (☎250/636-2344 or 636-2701, ⓦwww.ripleycreekinn.homestead .com; ❹), with eleven rooms in the main lodge building and other rooms in linked buildings, including a former 1928 brothel. The nearest **campsite** is the *Rainey Creek Campground* on the edge of town on 8th Avenue (☎250/636-2537 or 1-888-366-5999; $16–20; May–Sept), and the tenting area (as opposed to RVs) is located across Rainey Creek, a pleasant little stream. Ask at the campsite office about the area's nature trails and glacier tours on offer. One of the easiest local trails, the **Rainey Creek Nature Walk**, shadowing the creek for 2.5km to the northern end of town (return to the centre on Railway St), starts here. The *King Edward Hotel* is the town's main **pub**, **restaurant** and **coffee shop** – it's where the locals eat – while visitors tend to prefer the pleasantly polished *Bitter Creek Café* (part of the *Ripley Creek Inn* complex a block west of the *King Edward*), which offers an eclectic mix of food and an outside deck on warm days. For bread and baked snacks, duck into the bakery and deli next door to the *Bitter Creek*. There's also a late-opening Chinese restaurant, *Fong's Garden*, at 5th and Conway.

Most people come to **HYDER** (pop. 70), Stewart's oddball twin, simply to drink in one or both of its two bars. It's a ramshackle place, barely a settlement at all, just 3km from Stewart across the border in Alaska – with none of the usual border formalities, there being nothing beyond the end of the road but 800km of wilderness. People use Canadian currency, the police are of the Mountie variety and the phone system (and ☎250 area code) are also Canadian. At the *Glacier Inn* the tradition is to pin a dollar to the wall in case you return broke and need a drink, and then toss back a shot of hard liquor in one go and receive an "I've Been Hyderized" card. The result is many thousands of tacked dollars: "the world's most expensive wallpaper". It sounds a bit of a tourist carry-on, but if you arrive out of season there's a genuine amiability about the place that warrants its claims to be the "The Friendliest Ghost Town in Alaska". The town's two bars are often open 23 hours a day and a couple of **motels** are on hand if you literally can't stand any more: the *Sealaska Inn*, Premier Avenue (☎250/636-9003; ❸) – which has one of the two bars in question – and the preferable *Grand View Inn* (☎250/636-9174; ❸). They're both cheaper than their Stewart equivalents, and as you're in Alaska there's no room tax to pay. If you want something to soak up the alcohol, make for the *Sealaska Inn Restaurant* (☎250/636-2486) for no-nonsense food. The community's little **infocentre** is on the right as you come into town (June to early Sept daily except Wed 9am–1pm).

Iskut and Dease Lake

For several hundred kilometres beyond the Stewart junction there's nothing along the Cassiar other than the odd garage, rest area, campsite, trailhead and patches of burnt or clear-cut forest etched into the Cassiar and Skeena mountains. In places, though, you can still see traces of the incredible 3060km Dominion Telegraph line that used to link the Dawson City gold fields with Vancouver, and glimpses of a proposed railway extension out of Prince George that was abandoned as late as 1977. At **BELL II**, 95km north of Meziadin Junction, is the *Bell II Lodge* (☎250/881-8530 or 1-877-617-2288, ⓦwww.bell2lodge.com; ❺), 22 chalet rooms in a mountain-hemmed river valley. They offer a lounge, coffee shop, petrol station, sauna and hot tub.

Next up comes **ISKUT**, an aboriginal village 130km north offering tours into the adjacent wilderness parks, which are also accessible by float plane from Dease Lake itself. For information, contact the Iskut Band Office (☎250/234-3331) or local stores and garages. Local **accommodation** amounts to the six-room *Red Goat Lodge* (☎250/234-3261 or 1-888/733-4628, ⓔredgoat-lodge@aol.com; ❹, tents $13; late May to mid-Sept) with a 26-pitch campground 3km south of the village; the four-room *Bike, Hike & Paddle Touring Co*, 6km south of Iskut on Eddontenajon Lake (☎250/234-3456, ⓦwww.bikehikepaddle.com), which has activity and accommodation packages from $150 (July–Oct only); and *Todagin Guest Ranch* (radio contact only; ❷), 30km south of Iskut, with three cabins and numerous outdoor activities.

DEASE LAKE, 65km north of Iskut, has two **motels**, the 46-room *Northway Motor Inn* on Boulder Avenue (☎250/771-5341 or 1-866/888-2588, ⓔnorthwaymotorinn@stikine.net; ❸) and cheaper eight-room *Arctic Divide Inn & Motel* on the highway (☎250/771-3119, ⓔarcticdivide@stikine.net; ❸), still 246km from the junction with the Alaska Hwy to the north. You can **camp** at the Boya Lake Provincial Park, a lovely 45-site lakeside campground 150km north of Dease Lake and 16km of Good Hope Lake ($14).

The road from Dease Lake is wild and beautiful, the 240km to the Yukon border from here passing through some of the most miraculous scenery of what is already a superb journey. Some 84km north of Dease Lake is the *Moose Meadows Resort* (radio contact only; ❶, tents $10; May to mid-Oct), which has cabins, tent and RV sites, a convenience store and canoe rentals. Much of this area was swamped with gold-hungry pioneers during the **Cassiar Gold Rush** of 1872–80, when the region got its name – possibly from a white prospector's corruption of *kaskamet*, the dried beaver meat eaten by local Kaska. In 1877 Alfred Freedman plucked one of the world's largest pure gold nuggets – a 72-ounce monster – from a creek east of present-day **CASSIAR** (133km from the junction with the Alaska Hwy to the north), though these days the mining has a less romantic allure, being concentrated in an open-pit **asbestos mine** 5km from the village. Most of the world's high-grade asbestos once came from here, and poisonous-looking piles of green chrysotile asbestos tailings are scattered for kilometres around. The mine closed in 1992, transforming the community into a virtual ghost town at a stroke. Equipment has been sold and sites cleared, and the area is off-limits to the public until reclamation is complete.

Telegraph Creek

For a taste of what is possibly a more remarkable landscape than you see on the Cassiar, it's worth driving the potentially treacherous 113-kilometre side road from Dease Lake to **TELEGRAPH CREEK** (allow 2hr in good conditions). It's a delightful river-bank town whose look and feel can scarcely have changed since the beginning of the twentieth century, when it was a major telegraph station and trading post for the gold-rush towns to the north. The road from the Cassiar navigates some incredible gradients and bends, twisting past canyons, old lava beds and touching on several **aboriginal villages**, notably at Tahltan River, where salmon are caught and cured in traditional smokehouses and sold to passing tourists. If you're lucky you might see a Tahltan bear dog, a species now virtually extinct; only ankle high, and weighing less than fifteen pounds, these tiny animals were able to keep a bear cornered by barking and darting around until a hunter came to finish it off. Telegraph Creek itself is an object lesson in how latter-day pioneers live on the north's last frontiers: it's home to a friendly mixture of city exiles, hunters, trappers and ranchers, but also a cloistered bunch of **religious fundamentalists** who have eschewed the decadent mainstream for wilderness purity. Such groups are growing in outback British Columbia, an as-yet undocumented phenomenon that's creating friction with the easygoing types who first settled the backwoods. Gold has recently been discovered locally, attracting mining companies, so ways of life may be about to change here for all concerned.

Much of the village and village life revolves around the General Delivery – a combined café (the *Riversong*), grocery and garage – and small adjoining **motel**, the *Stikine River Song* Lodge (☎250/235-3196, Ⓦwww.stikineriversong.com; ❸), whose rooms include kitchenettes. No one here, except perhaps the Bible brigade, minds if you pitch a tent – but ask around first. Also enquire at the café for details of rafting and other local trips into the backcountry.

The John Hart Hwy: Prince George to Dawson Creek

Dawson Creek is the launching pad for the Alaska Hwy. While it may not be somewhere you'd otherwise stop, it's almost impossible to avoid a night here whether you're approaching from Edmonton and the east or from Prince George on the scenically more uplifting **John Hart Hwy** (Hwy 97). Named after a former BC premier, this seemingly innocuous road is one of the north's most vital highways. Completed in 1952, it linked at a stroke the road network of the Pacific Coast with that of the northern interior, cutting 800km off the journey from Seattle to Alaska, for example, a trip that previously had to take in a vast inland loop to Calgary. The route leads you out of British Columbia's upland interior to the so-called Peace River country, a region of slightly ridged land that belongs in look and spirit to the Albertan prairies. There's some 409km of driving, and two daily Greyhound **buses** make the journey.

Out of Prince George the road bends through mildly dipping hills and mixed woodland, passing small lakes and offering views to the Rockies, whose distant jagged skyline keeps up the spirits as you drive through an otherwise unbroken tunnel of conifers. About 70km on, **Bear Lake** and the **Crooked River Provincial Park** are just off the road, and it's well worth taking the small lane west of the park entrance to reach an idyllic patch of water fringed on its far shore by a fine sickle of sand. There's a provincial park **campsite** ($14) at the park.

Both Mackenzie Junction, 152km from Prince George, and Mackenzie, 29km off the highway, are scrappy, unpleasant places, easily avoided and soon

If you're continuing north on the Cassiar Hwy to **Watson Lake** and the Alaska Hwy junction, turn to p.1001.

forgotten as the road climbs to **Pine Pass** (933m), one of the lower road routes over the Rockies, but spectacular all the same. The **Bijoux Falls Provincial Park**, just before it, is good for a picnic near the eponymous falls, and if you want to **camp** plump for the *Pine Valley Park Lodge* ($11; May–Oct), an immensely scenic lakeside spot that looks up to crags of massively stratified and contorted rock just below the pass. Thereafter the road drops steeply through Chetwynd (three motels and a campsite) to the increasingly flatter country that heralds Dawson Creek.

Dawson Creek

Arrive late in **DAWSON CREEK** (pop. 10,754) and leave early: except for a small museum next to the town's eye-catching red grain hopper, and the obligatory photograph of the cairn marking Mile Zero of the Alaska Hwy, there's almost nothing to do. Contact the **infocentre** at the museum, 900 Alaska Ave (daily 9am–6pm, longer hours in summer; ☎250/782-9595 or 1-866/645-3022, ⓦwww.tourismdawsoncreek.com), for details of the eight or so **motels**, most of which are concentrated on the Alaska Hwy northeast of town. One of the nicer places is the *Ramada Limited Dawson Creek*, 1748 Alaska Ave (☎250/782-8595 or 1-800/663-2749, ⓦwww.ramada.ca; ❸), with views of countryside rather than the highway. None of the local **campsites** and RV parks are places you'd want to linger in but the most attractive is the *Mile 0 RV Park and Campground* (☎250/782-2590, ⓔmile0campground@aol.com; $12–17; May to mid-Sept), about 1km west of the town centre at the junction of Hwy 97 North and Hwy 97 South opposite 20th Street on the Alaska Hwy. For something to **eat**, call at the excellent *Alaska Café* on 10th Street, an attractive old wooden building completely at odds with the rest of the town. The food and ambience are good – though prices aren't the cheapest – and the bar's not bad either.

The Alaska Hwy: Dawson Creek to Whitehorse

The best part of the **Alaska Hwy** – a distance of about 1500km – winds through northern British Columbia from Dawson Creek to Whitehorse, the capital of the Yukon; only 320km of the highway is actually in Alaska. Don't be fooled by the string of villages emblazoned across the area's maps, for there are only two towns worthy of the name en route, **Fort St John** and **Fort Nelson** – the rest are no more than a garage, a store and perhaps a motel. **Watson Lake**, on the Yukon border, is the largest of these lesser spots, and also marks the junction of the Alaska and Cassiar highways. All the way down the road, though, it's vital to book accommodation during July and August.

   Driving the Alaska Hwy is no longer the adventure of days past – that's now provided by the Cassiar and Dempster highways. Food, fuel and lodgings are found at between forty- and eighty-kilometre intervals, though cars still need to be in good shape. You should drive with headlights on at all times, and take care when passing or being passed by heavy trucks. It also goes without saying that wilderness – anything up to 800km of it each side – begins at the edge of the highway and unless you're very experienced you shouldn't contemplate any off-road exploration. Any number of guides and pamphlets are available to take you through to Fairbanks, but *The Milepost*, the road's bible, is, for all its mind-numbing detail, the only one you need buy.

The **Alaska Hwy** runs northeast from Mile Zero at Dawson Creek through the Yukon to Mile 1520 in Fairbanks, Alaska. Built as a military road, it's now an all-weather highway travelled by bus services and thousands of tourists out to recapture the thrill of the days when it was known as the "junkyard of the American automobile". It's no longer a driver's Calvary, but the scenery and the sense of pushing through wilderness on one of the continent's last frontiers remain as alluring as ever: around 360,000 people a year make the journey.

As recently as 1940 there was no direct land route to the Yukon or Alaska other than trails passable only by experienced trappers. When the Japanese invaded the Aleutian Islands during World War II, however, they both threatened the traditional sea routes to the north and seemed ready for an attack on mainland Alaska – the signal for the building of the joint US–Canadian road to the north. A proposed coastal route from Hazelton in British Columbia was deemed too susceptible to enemy attack (it's since been built as the Cassiar Hwy), while an inland route bypassing Whitehorse and following the Rockies would have taken five years to build. This left the so-called **Prairie Route**, which had the advantage of following a line of air bases through Canada into Alaska – a chain known as the **Northwest Staging Route**. In the course of the war, some 8000 planes were ferried along this route from Montana to Edmonton and then to Fairbanks, where they were picked up by Soviet pilots and flown into action on the Siberian front.

Construction of the highway began on **March 9, 1942**, the start of months of misery for the 20,000 mainly US soldiers shanghaied to ram a road through mountains, mud, mosquito-ridden bogs, icy rivers and forest during some of the harshest extremes of weather. Incredibly, crews working on the eastern and western sections met at Contact Creek, British Columbia, in September 1942, and completed the last leg to Fairbanks in October – an engineering triumph that had taken less than a year but cost around $140 million. The first full convoy of trucks to make Fairbanks managed an average 25kph during one of the worst winters in memory.

By 1943 the highway already needed virtual rebuilding, and for seven years workers widened the road, raised bridges, reduced gradients, bypassed swampy ground and started to remove some of the vast bends that are still being ironed out – the reason why it's now only **1488 miles** (2394km) to the old Mile 1520 post in Fairbanks. All sorts of ideas have been put forward to explain the numerous curves: that they were to stop Japanese planes using the road as a landing strip, that they simply went where bulldozers could go at the time, or even at one point that they followed the trail of a rutting moose. Probably the chief reason is that the surveying often amounted to no more than a pointed finger aimed at the next horizon. Canada took over control of the road in 1946, but civilian traffic was barred until 1948. Within months of its opening so much traffic had broken down and failed to make the trip that it was closed for a year.

Although the road is now widely celebrated, there are sides to the story that are still glossed over. Many of its toughest sections, for example, were given to African-American GIs, few of whom have received credit for their part in building the highway – you'll look in vain for African-American faces amongst the white officers in the archive photos of ribbon-cutting ceremonies. Another often overlooked fact is the road's effect on aboriginal peoples on the route, scores of whom died from epidemics brought in by the workers. Yet another was the building of the controversial "Canadian Oil" or **Canol pipeline** in conjunction with the road, together with huge dumps of poisonous waste and construction junk. Wildlife en route was also devastated by trigger-happy GIs taking recreational pot shots as they worked; the virtual eradication of several species was part of the reason for the creation of the Kluane Game Sanctuary, the forerunner of the Yukon's Kluane National Park.

From 1201 Alaska Ave in Dawson Creek, a **Greyhound bus** heads out in the morning and plies the road all the way to Whitehorse; it currently runs daily (except Sun) from mid-May to mid-October, and on Tuesday, Thursday and Saturday the rest of the year. The twenty-hour trip finishes at around 5am, with only occasional half-hour meal stops, but covers the road's best scenery in daylight.

Dawson Creek to Prophet River

You need to adapt to a different notion of distance on a 2500-kilometre drive: on the Alaska Hwy points of interest are a long way apart, and pleasure comes in broad changes in scenery, in the sighting of a solitary moose, or in the passing excitement of a lonely bar. Thus it's forty minutes before the benign ridged prairies around Dawson Creek prompt attention by dropping suddenly into the broad, flat-bottomed valley of the Peace River, a canyon whose walls are scalloped with creeks, gulches and deep muddy scars. Just across the river is **FORT ST JOHN**; until the coming of the highway (when it was the field headquarters of the road's eastern construction gangs) it was a trading post for local Sikanni and Beaver peoples, and had remained little changed since its predecessor sank into the mud of the Peace River (there have been a total of six "Fort St Johns" in various incarnations in the area). The shantytown received a boost when the province's largest oil field was discovered nearby in 1955, and it's now a functional settlement with all the services you need – though at just 75km into the highway it's unlikely you'll be ready to stop. If you are, there's a small museum at 93rd and 100th Street and a handful of **motels**: solid choices are the big *Ramada*, 10103 98th Ave (℡250/787-0779 or 1-888/346-7711, ⓦwww.ramada.ca; ❹), and the cheaper *Cedar Lodge Motor Inn*, 9824 99th Ave (℡250/785-8107 or 1-800/661-2210, Ⓔcedarlodge @mail.pris.bc.ca; ❷). The **infocentre** is at 9923 96th Ave (℡250/785-3033 or 785-6037, ⓦwww.fortstjohnchamber.com).

The next stop is the tiny hamlet of **WONOWON** (pop. 84), a military checkpoint in World War II, and at 161km from Dawson typical of the bleak settlements all the way up the road. **PINK MOUNTAIN** (pop. 19), 226km on from Dawson, is much the same, with *Mae's Kitchen* (℡250/772-3215) the only real place to eat (other places open and close here regularly). Thereafter the road offers immense **views** of utter wilderness in all directions, the trees as dense as ever, but noticeably more stunted than farther south and nearing the limit of commercial viability. Look out for the bright "New Forest Planted" signs, more often than not a token riposte from the loggers to the ecology lobby, as they are invariably backed by a graveyard of sickly looking trees. If you're **camping**, look out for two provincial sanctuaries over the remaining 236km to Fort Nelson. Around 60km north of Pink Mountain is the Buckinghorse River Provincial Park campsite ($14); another 69km farther is the Prophet River Provincial Recreation Area, with a campsite ($9) overlooking the river. This is good bird-watching country, but it's also good bear country, so be careful.

Fort Nelson and beyond

One of the highway's key stopoffs, **FORT NELSON** (pop. 4188), 381km north of Fort St John, was once noteworthy for the large welcoming poster that proclaimed "Jail is only the beginning – don't drink and drive", a sobering sign that hints at the sort of extremes to which people hereabouts might go to relieve the tedium of winter's long semi-twilight. Everything in town, except a small **museum** devoted to the highway's construction, speaks of a frontier supplies depot, the latest in a long line of trading posts attracted to a site that is fed by four major rivers and stands in the lee of the Rockies. Dour buildings stand in a battered sprawl around a windswept grid, only a single rung up civilization's ladder from the time in the late 1950s when this was still a community without power, phones, running water or doctors. Life's clearly too tough here to be geared to anything but pragmatic survival and exploitation of its huge natural-gas deposits – the town has the world's second-largest gas-processing plant and the huge storage tanks to prove it. Aboriginal and white trappers live as they have for centuries, hunting beaver, wolf, wolverine, fox, lynx and mink, as well as the ubiquitous moose, which is still an important food source for many aboriginal people.

The town does, however, have an extraordinary claim to fame, namely that it's home to the **world's largest chopstick factory**, located south of the town off the highway behind the weigh scales at Industrial Park Chopstick Road (℡250/774-4448 for details of tours). This has nothing to do with gargantuan demand for Chinese food in Fort Nelson – at last count there were only three Chinese restaurants in town – but more to do with the region's high-quality aspen, a wood apparently perfectly suited to producing the dream chopstick. The Canadian Chopstick Manufacturing Company produces an incredible 7.5 million pairs of chopsticks a day, or almost 2 billion pairs a year.

The town's three **motels** are all much the same and you'll be paying the inflated rates – about $80 for doubles worth much less – which characterize the north. On the town's southern approaches the *Bluebell Inn*, 3907 50th Ave S (℡250/774-6961 or 1-800/663-5267, ✉bluebell@pris.bc.ca; ❹), is better looking than many of the run-of-the-mill places. To **camp**, make for the *Westend Campground* (℡250/774-2340; April–Nov; $17–23) on the highway next to the museum. It has grassy tent sites, pay showers, laundry and store. The **infocentre** is at 5500 50th Ave (℡250/774-2956, ⓦwww.northernrockies .org; daily mid-May to Aug Mon–Sat 8/9am–7/8pm).

Fort Nelson to Liard Hot Springs

This stretch is the Alaska Hwy at its best. Landscapes divide markedly around Fort Nelson, where the highway arches west from the flatter hills of the Peace River country to meet the northern Rockies above the plains and plateau of the Liard River. Within a short time, once the road has picked up the river's headwaters, you're in some of the most grandiose scenery in British Columbia. The area either side of the road is some of the world's wildest – twenty million acres of nothing – and experts say that only parts of Africa surpass the region for the variety of mammals present and the pristine state of its ecosystems. Services and motels become scarcer, but those that exist – though often beaten-up looking places – make atmospheric and often unforgettable stops.

The first worthwhile stopoff, a kilometre off the highway on a gravel road, is **Tetsa River Provincial Park**, about 77km west of Fort Nelson, which has a nice and secluded campsite ($14; May–Oct) and appealing short hikes through the trees and along the river. Next up is **Stone Mountain Provincial Park**, 139km west of Fort Nelson, with a campsite ($14; May–Oct) which gives access to a short trail (10min) to two hoodoos (rock columns) claimed by myth to be the heads of two devils; a longer trail, the Flower Springs Lake Trail (6km), leads to a delightful upland mountain lake. Other accommodation and services include the *Rocky Mountain Lodge* (℡250/232-5000; ❷), 165km on from Fort Nelson with lovely views of the mountains and an adjacent **campsite** ($10).

Toad River, 195km from Fort Nelson, has perhaps the best motel of all on this lonely stretch, the *Toad River Lodge* (℡250/232-5401; ❷), with rooms and cabins offering superlative views of thickly forested and deeply cleft mountains on all sides. Note that it also has a grocery, petrol station and sites for tents and RVs ($15 for tenting). About 3km to its north is the *Poplars Campground & Café*, with four log cabins and fully serviced tent and RV sites (☎250/232-5465; ❷, tent sites $13; May to late Sept); it's an equally attractive spot despite its disconcerting claim to be "Home of the Foot-Long Hot Dog". Turn right off the highway 9km north of Toad River and you come to the Stone Mountain Safaris Lodge (☎250/232-5469, ⓔstonemountainsafaris@direcway.com; ❺), with four rooms and riding and hiking possibilities.

Muncho Lake, 260km from Fort Nelson, is the next big natural feature, and sits at the heart of a large provincial park whose ranks of bare mountains provide a foretaste of the barren tundra of the far north. There's a small motel and campsite at the lake's southern end, but it's worth hanging on for the popular *Muncho Lake Provincial Park Campground* ($14, free Oct; May–Oct), midway up the lake on its eastern side, or the fine *Northern Rockies Lodge-Highland Glen Lodge and Campground* (☎250/776-3481 or 1-800/663-5269, ⓦwww.northern-rockies-lodge.com; ❺) for a choice of log cabins or camping sites ($20–27). You can also stay at the *J & H Wilderness* Motel & RV Park (☎250/776-3453; ❷), just over a kilometre beyond the lodge; it has a store, café and petrol. Two kilometres north of the Muncho Lake settlement there is the small *McDonald Provincial Campground* ($12).

About 70km beyond the lake is the excellent *Lower Liard River Lodge* (☎250/776-7341; ❸; April–Oct), a wonderfully cosy and friendly spot for food and rooms. ("Liard" comes from the French for poplar or cottonwood tree, a ubiquitous presence in these parts.) It also has RV and tent sites ($10) and lies close to one of the most popular spots on the entire Alaska Hwy, the very obvious **Liard Hot Springs**, whose **two thermal pools** (Alpha and Beta) are amongst the best and hottest in BC. Road crews loved these during the construction of the highway, or rather the men did: women in the teams were allowed a soak just once a week. They're reached by a short wooden boardwalk across steaming marsh, and are otherwise unspoilt apart from a wooden changing room and the big high-season crowds (aim to be here early in the day for a dip ahead of the rush). As the marsh never freezes, it attracts moose and grizzlies down to drink and graze, and some 250 plant species grow in the mild microhabitat nearby, including fourteen species of orchid, as well as lobelias, ostrich ferns and other rare boreal forest plants. The nearby *Liard River Hotsprings Provincial Park* **campsite** is one of the region's most popular, and fills up early in July and August; bookings are possible through the provincial park central reservation line (May–Aug $17; Sept–April $10); see box on p.975.

Watson Lake and beyond

Beyond the Liard Hot Springs the Alaska Hwy follows the Liard River, settling into about 135km of unexceptional scenery before **WATSON LAKE**, just over the Yukon border (though the road trips back and forth across the border seven times before hitting the town). Created by the coming of the highway and air base, it's neither attractive nor terribly big, but shops, motels and garages have sprung up here to service the traffic congregating off the Cassiar and Campbell highways to the north and south. In the past the region was the preserve of the Kaska, a people whose centuries-old way of life was altered in the 1870s by the Cassiar gold rush. Another gold rush, the Klondike, gave the settlement its present name, when Frank Watson, an English prospector, gave up on his attempts to reach the northern gold fields and stopped here instead.

Even if you're just passing through it's well worth pulling off to look at the **Alaska Highway Interpretive Centre** (May–Sept daily 8am–8pm), which as well as providing information on the Yukon also describes the highway's construction through archive photos and audiovisual displays. It's situated on the highway next to the Chevron garage, close to the famous **Sign Post Forest**. This last bit of gimmickry was started by homesick GI Carl K. Lindley in 1942, who erected a sign pointing the way and stating the mileage to his home in Danville, Illinois. Since then the signs have just kept on coming, and at last count numbered around thirty thousand. You might also want to dip briefly into the **Northern Lights Centre** (June–Aug daily 2–10pm; $6–12; ⓦwww.yukon.net/northernlights), a planetarium and science centre that explores the myths, folklore and science behind phenomena such as the aurora borealis (see box p.974).

It's still 441km from Watson Lake to Whitehorse and, after the long haul on the Alaska Hwy (or Cassiar Hwy), a lot of people wisely stop overnight here to recuperate. If you're camping there are no problems, for countless small Yukon-government-run **campsites** are dotted along the length of the highway beyond the village; the closest is a rustic site 4km west of the Sign Forest ($12; May–Oct). If you decide to **stay in town** the cheapest options are the *Gateway Motor Inn* (ⓣ867/536-7744; ❸), open 24 hours a day, and the *Cedar Lodge Motel* (ⓣ867/536-7406, ⓦwww.cedarlodge.yk.net; ❸). If these are full you may have to plump for one of the smarter hotels, all of which have rooms for around $95 – the best is the *Belvedere Hotel* (ⓣ867/536-7712; ❺), followed by the *Watson Lake Hotel* (ⓣ867/536-7781; ❺). Both have dining rooms and the *Watson Lake Hotel* and *Gateway Motor Inn* has some rooms with kitchenettes.

West of Watson Lake

West of Watson Lake the road picks up more fine mountain scenery, running for hour after hour past apparently identical combinations of snowcapped peaks and thick forest. About 10km before unlovely **TESLIN**, 263km west of Watson, look out for the *Dawson Peaks Northern Resort* (ⓣ867/390-2310; ❸), which not only has cabins and a campsite, but also boasts one of the highway's better **restaurants**; fishing and boat rentals are also available. Teslin itself was founded as a trading post in 1903 and now has one of the region's largest aboriginal populations, many of whom still live by hunting and fishing. The **George Johnston Museum** (mid-May to Sept daily 9am–7pm; $3) is on the right on the way into the village and has a good collection of local Tlingit arte-facts as well as the photos of Johnston, a Tlingit who recorded his culture on film between 1910 and 1940.

Whitehorse

WHITEHORSE is the likeable capital of the Yukon, home to almost 23,000 of the region's 31,000 inhabitants, the centre of its mining and forestry indus-tries, and a busy, welcoming stop for thousands of summer visitors. Roads bring in today's business, but the town owes its existence to the **Yukon River**, a 3000-kilometre artery that rises in BC's Coast Mountains and flows through the heart of the Yukon and Alaska to the Bering Sea. The river's flood plain and strange escarpment above the present town were long a resting point for Dene peoples, but the spot burgeoned into a full-blown city with the arrival of

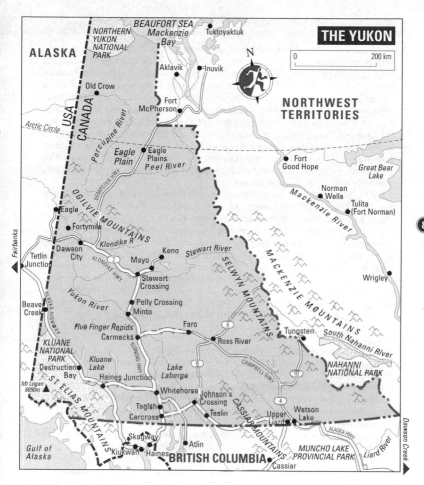

thousands of stampeders in the spring of 1898. Having braved the Chilkoot Pass (see box p.1004) to meet the Yukon's upper reaches, men and supplies then had to pause on the shores of Lineman or Bennett Lake before navigating the **Miles Canyon** and White Horse rapids southeast of the present town. After the first few boats through had been reduced to matchwood, the Mounties laid down rules allowing only experienced boatmen to take craft through – the writer Jack London, one such boatman, made $3000 in the summer of 1898, when more than seven thousand boats left the lakes. After a period the prospectors constructed an eight-kilometre wooden tramway around the rapids, and in time raised a shantytown settlement at the canyon and tramway's northern head to catch their breath before the river journey to Dawson City.

The completion of the **White Pass and Yukon Railway** (WP&YR) to Whitehorse (newly named after the rapids) put this tentative settlement on a firmer footing – almost at the same time as the gold rush petered out. In the early years of the twentieth century the town's population dwindled quickly

No single image better conjures the human drama of the 1898 gold rush than the lines of prospectors struggling over the **Chilkoot Trail**, a 53-kilometre path over the Coast Mountains between **Dyea**, north of Skagway in Alaska, and **Bennett Lake** on the BC border south of Whitehorse. Before the rush, Dyea was a small village of Chilkat Tlingit, who made annual trade runs over the trail to barter fish oil, clamshells and dried fish with the Tutchone, Tagish and other interior Dene peoples in exchange for animal hides, skin clothing and copper. The Chilkat jealously guarded access to the **Chilkoot Pass** (1122m), the key to the trail and one of only three glacier-free routes through the Coast Mountains west of Juneau. Sheer numbers and a show of force from a US gunboat, however, opened the trail to stampeders, who used it as a link between the ferries at the Pacific Coast ports and the Yukon River, which they then rode to the gold fields at Dawson City.

For much of 1897 the pass and border were disputed by the US and Canada until the Canadian NWMP (Northwest Mounted Police) established a storm-battered shack at the summit and enforced the fateful "ton of goods" entry requirement. Introduced because of chronic shortages in the gold fields, this obliged every man entering the Yukon to carry a ton of provisions – and, though it probably saved many lives in the long run, the rule laid enormous hardship on the back of the stampeders. Weather conditions and the trail's fifty-degree slopes proved too severe even for horses or mules, so that men had to carry supplies on their backs over as many as fifty journeys to move their "ton of goods". Many died in avalanches or lost everything during a winter when temperatures dropped to -51°C and 25m of snow fell. Even so, the lure of gold was enough to drag some 22,000 prospectors over the pass.

Preparation

These days most people off the ferries from Prince Rupert and the Alaska Panhandle make the fantastic journey across the mountains by car or Gray Line bus on Hwy 2 **from Skagway to Whitehorse**. This route parallels that taken by the restored White Pass & Yukon Route **railway** (WP&YR; mid-May to mid-Sept 1 daily; train from Skagway to White Pass, then connecting bus to Whitehorse; $95; ☎907/983-2217 or 1-800-343-7373, ⓦwww.whitepassrailroad.com), originally built to supersede the Chilkoot Trail.

Increasing numbers, however, are **walking** the old trail, which has been laid out and preserved by the Canadian Parks Service as a long-distance hikers' route. Its great appeal lies not only in the scenery and natural habitats – which embrace coastal rainforest, tundra and subalpine boreal woodland – but also in the numerous artefacts like old huts, rotting boots, mugs and broken bottles still scattered where they were left by the prospectors. The trail is well marked, regularly patrolled and generally fit to walk between about June and September, though throughout June you can expect snow on the trail. Most people hike the trail in **three or four days** and if you're moderately fit it shouldn't be a problem, but there are dangers from bears, avalanches, drastic changes of weather and exhaustion – there's one twelve-kilometre stretch, for example, for which you're advised to allow twelve hours. Almost everyone hikes from south to north. Although there are three warming huts on the trail, these aren't designed for sleeping in, and you'll be making use of the nine approved **campsites** spaced at intervals along the trail: no rough camping is allowed.

from about 10,000 to about 400; for forty years the place slumbered, barely sustained by copper mining and the paddle-wheelers that plied the river carrying freight and the occasional tourist. The town's second boom arrived with the construction of the Alaska Hwy, a kick-start that swelled the town's population from 800 to 40,000 almost overnight, and has stood it in good stead ever since.

Reservations and permits

An advance **information pack** ($5) can be ordered by calling the **reservation system** (℡867/667-3910 or 1-800/661-0486 between 8.30am and 4pm), or by visiting the government offices in central Whitehorse – it's the large and distinctive Elijah Smith Building at 300 Main St, and the office you want (suite 205; open Mon–Fri 8am–noon & 1–4.30pm) is on the second floor; take the stairs at the rear of the large foyer. There is no facility for booking online. Throughout the hiking season, the number of hikers crossing the Chilkoot Pass into Canada is limited to fifty per day, of which 42 places can be booked in advance ($11) by calling the reservation system. The remaining eight places are offered on a first-come, first-served basis after 1pm on the day before you plan to start the trail; to register, aim for the **Skagway Trail Center**, on Broadway at 1st Avenue (late May to early Sept daily 8am–4pm). The busy season is July and the first two weeks of August; outside this time you probably don't need to make a reservation.

Whichever way you secure a place on the trail, all hikers need to go to the Skagway Trail Center to buy a **permit** ($50), sign a register (for customs purposes) and consult the weather forecast. You'll need to carry **identification**, which means a birth certificate for North Americans (a driver's licence is not acceptable) and a passport for everyone else. You may be required to deal with Canadian customs at the Chilkoot Pass ranger station but more likely you'll do it after your hike at the Alaska–Canada border post at Fraser or in Whitehorse.

If you've made an advance reservation, you'll already have the Canadian Parks Service's *Chilkoot Trail* **map** (otherwise $2 from the Trail Center or the Canadian Parks Service office at the SS *Klondike* in Whitehorse), which is about the best available.

Transport and supplies

Dyea Dave (℡907/983-2731) runs a shuttle bus (US$10) from Skagway to **Dyea**, the start of the trail some nine miles northwest of Skagway. The trail finishes at **Bennett**, where you can get Tutshi Charters (℡867/821-4905) to take you across Lake Bennett to Caross (C$65) in order to meet the Whitehorse-bound Gray Line bus. Alternatively you can walk the eight miles to the highway at Log Cabin (there's a short cut off the trail which avoids Bennett) and meet up with Dyea Dave, who also makes pick-ups at the end of the trail (call to confirm; $25 for a combined drop-off and pick-up); or return to Skagway on the **WP&YR railroad**. In June, July and August the railroad offers the Chilkoot Trail Hikers Service (departs 1pm Alaska time; $25 one-way to Fraser, $65 to Skagway), which comprises either a railcar or one carriage of the Lake Bennett Excursion that's specially designated for smelly hikers. Remember to buy your tickets before you set off on the trail or you'll have a $15 fee added to the ticket price for the convenience of buying your ticket on the train; and note that for customs reasons the train doesn't stop at Log Cabin.

Remember to take wet-weather gear, matches, some method of water treatment, sunscreen, sunglasses, a flashlight and **thirty feet of rope** so that you can sling your food, toothpaste and any scented items over the bear poles at each campsite. Early in the season when there's plenty of snow about, consider **gaiters**, which can be rented in Skagway.

Arrival, information and tours

Whitehorse's **airport** is on the bluff above the town, 5km west of downtown; taxis (℡867/667-4111 or 393-6543) are around $10 to the centre, and the Whitehorse Transit Hillcrest bus ($1.25) runs downtown hourly during the day. If you're taking the bus to the airport, pick it up at the Qwanlin Mall at the northern end of 3rd Ave. The Greyhound **bus terminal** is at 3211 3rd Ave (T867/667-2223 or 1-800/661-8747, W www.greyhound.ca) at the extreme eastern end of downtown, ten minutes' walk from Main Street – you turn left out of the terminal for the town centre, something it's as well to know if you stagger off the six-times-weekly Greyhound from Dawson Creek, which arrives around 5am. Buses to and from other destinations, notably those in Alaska, arrive and leave from a variety of destinations. See the box on p.1012 for full details of all transport links to and from the town.

Whitehorse's large and very helpful downtown **Yukon Visitor Reception Centre** is on 2nd Ave and Hanson St (mid-May to Sept daily 8am–8pm; rest of year Mon–Fri 9am–noon & 1–4.30pm; T867/667-3084, W www.touryukon.com or W www.visitwhitehorse.com). Visiting drivers should note that they can pick up a three-day complimentary parking **pass** here. Note that the "reception centre" up on the Alaska Hwy still mentioned in some literature is now the Beringia Centre. For information on the Yukon's aboriginal cultures, stop by the office of the **Yukon First Nations Tourism Association** in the old White Pass railway station at 1109 1st Ave (Mon–Fri 8am–5pm; T867/667-7698, W www.yfnta.org) and pick up a copy of the *Yukon's First Nations Guide*. Almost as useful as these is Mac's Fireweed, 203 Main St (daily: summer 9am–9pm/midnight; winter 8am–9pm; T867/668-2434, W www.yukonbooks.com), which has a full range of Yukon books, guides, maps, nautical charts and pamphlets you probably won't find elsewhere. For **exchange**, plus reservations for ferries and **tickets** for local events, contact Thomas Cook, 2101A 2nd Ave (mid-May to early Sept daily 8am–8pm; rest of year Mon–Fri 8.30am–5.30pm, Sat 10am–5pm; T867/668-2867).

There's a **downtown walking tour** offered by the Whitehorse Heritage Buildings Walking Tours (June–Aug Mon–Sat 9am, 11am, 1pm & 3pm), which departs from Donnenworth House, 3126 3rd Ave (T867/667-4704; $2). Or you could try the variety of free summer strolls organized by the Yukon Conservation Society, 302 Hawkins St (July & Aug daily; T867/668-5678), two- to six-hour walks that delve into local and natural history, and the Yukon's geology, flora and fauna. Of the several self-guided walks in and around town, you could walk all the way round Schwatka Lake from Whitehorse, beginning from the bridge by the SS *Klondike*. Pick up details of this and other self-guiding trail booklets from the visitor reception centre.

Transport, equipment and rentals

Car rental agencies have desks or courtesy phones at the airport and occasionally a downtown office: Budget, 4178 4th Ave (T867/667-6200 or 1-800/268-8900, W www.budgetyukon.com), and National-Norcan, 213 Range Rd (T867/668-2137, 1-800/661-0445 or 1-800/227-7368, W www.norcan.yk.ca), are companies to try, but remember they may have restrictions on taking cars on gravel roads if you're thinking of heading north on the Dempster Hwy.

For **bike rental**, visit Riverdale Cycle, 310 Wood St (T867/668-7505, W www.riverdalecycles.com), which also sells new bikes, parts and accessories. **Canoes**, paddles and life-jackets plus bikes can be rented from the Kanoe People, on the river across the tram line at Strickland St and 1st Ave (T867/668-4899, www.kanoe.yk.net), who can also set you up with everything you need for a variety of guided or non-guided trips of anything from two hours to twenty days, including the paddle to Dawson (700km, but lots of people do it); they also organize guided day-trips (from $60). Bike rentals start at $15 a half day, $25 for a full day and $125 weekly. Canoe and kayaks start from $25 daily and $150 weekly. About 75m away, back across the tracks, at 103 Strickland St, you'll get similar rates on bikes and canoes, plus lots of fishing, camping and other equipment rentals from Up North Adventures (☎867/667–7035, ⓦwww.upnorth.yk.ca), which also offers lots of summer and winter tours and activities.

Should you need to buy **outdoor equipment**, the town is full of dedicated stores; the largest is *Coast Mountain Sports*, 208A Main St (☎867/667–4074).

Accommodation

Whitehorse has a surprising amount of **accommodation**, but in high summer much of it is booked up well in advance. If you arrive without a reservation, contact the visitor centre or try the string of hotels on Main Street between 1st and 5th avenues. For **B&Bs**, try the information centre's B&B list, contact the recommendations below, or visit ⓦwww.yukonbandb.com, but note that places open and close with some frequency. Note, also, that prices in B&Bs vary considerably from high to low season. In addition to the town's two good private **hostels**, at the time of writing a new summer-only hostel (under the same management as the excellent Dawson City River Hostel) was due to open opposite the visitor reception centre: call ☎867/993–6823 or visit ⓦwww.yukonhostels.com for latest details.

Hotels and B&Bs

Airline Inn 16 Burns Rd ☎867/668-4400, ⓕ867/668-2641. If you arrive late at the airport, or need an early getaway, this is the airstrip's nearest hotel – directly opposite the airport itself and serviceable enough for its purposes.

Capital Hotel 103 Main St ☎867/667-2565, ⓕ867/668-4651. This is the place to stay if you want one of the town's more lively, historic and boisterous hotels, complete with passable rooms, local beer on tap and the prospect of live music nightly. ❷

Edgewater Hotel 101 Main St ☎867/667-2572 or 1-877/484-3334, ⓦwww.edgewaterhotel.yk.ca. Good, middle-priced hotel in downtown area, but note that prices for rooms vary widely according to season. ❹

High Country Inn 4051 4th Ave ☎867/667-4471, ⓦwww.highcountryinn.yk.ca. A pleasant and easygoing hotel at the far western end of 4th Ave, a 10min walk from downtown, with a wide variety of excellent room deals and weekly rates. Also has a popular bar-patio. ❹

98 Hotel 10 Wood St ☎867/667-2641 or 867/667-2656. Cheap, fairly grim and occasionally with live bands to serenade you through the small hours. You would be better off in the hostels. ❷

Roadhouse Inn 2163 2nd Ave ☎867/667-2594, ⓕ867/668-7291. Of a similar standard to but marginally better than, the *98 Hotel* and near the bus terminal. It has thirty rooms from $45 and hostel rooms (with kitchen and laundry) from $21.40 per person without linen, $26.40 with. ❷

Stratford Motel 401 Jarvis St ☎867/667-4243 or 1-800/661-0539, ⓕ867/668-7432. Spotlessly clean, renovated rooms (some with kitchenettes) and with friendly staff. Three blocks from downtown. Weekly rates available. ❹

Town & Mountain Hotel 401 Main St ☎867/668-7644, ⓦwww.yukon.com/tm.htm. Another good and renovated middle-priced place. ❹

Westmark Klondike Inn 2288 2nd Ave ☎867/668-4747 or 1-800/544-0970, ⓦwww.westmarkhotels.com. One of two top-of-the-range, comfortable hotels belonging to the northern Westmark chain. ❻

Westmark Whitehorse Hotel 201 Wood St ☎867/393-9700 or 1-800/544-0970, ⓦwww.westmarkhotels.com. If you want to see Whitehorse in style, come to the smartest and most expensive hotel in town. Its 181 rooms underwent a $3-million refit in 2001. Prices can be high, but deals are often available off season. ❻

B&Bs

Birch Street 1501 Birch St ☎867/633-5625. On a bus route to downtown but amidst a quiet setting overlooking the Yukon River Valley close to hiking trails. Full breakfast. Some rooms have private bathrooms. ❸

Casey's 608 Wood St, between 6th and 7th Ave
☎867/668-7481, ⓦwww.caseybandb.com.
Downtown location with good breakfasts and
evening snacks; kitchen and laundry facilities are
available. ❻
Hawkins House 303 Hawkins St ☎867/668-
7638, ⓦwww.hawkinshouse.yk.ca. Old and luxurious Victorian home in downtown; laundry and
private bathrooms available. Four en-suite
rooms; full breakfast included in the price. No
smoking. ❺
Historical Guest House B&B 505 Wood St,
corner of 5th Ave ☎867/668-3907,
ⓦwww.yukongold.com. This two-storey log home

two blocks east of Main St was built in 1907 for
Sam McGee and his family, the protagonist of a
Robert Service poem (see p.1090). Modern facilities have been added in a new wing; two double
rooms with private bathrooms. Price includes continental breakfast. ❹
Midnight Sun Bed & Breakfast 6188 6th
Ave, at the corner of Cook St ☎867/667-2255,
ⓦwww.midnightsunbandbyukon
.com. On the northern edge of downtown, this
new, large home has a large guest lounge, free
email internet access and four comfortable en-
suite rooms. A full breakfast is included in the
price. ❹

Hostels and campsites

Beez Kneez Bakpakers Hostel [sic] 408 Hoge St
☎867/456-2333, ⓦwww.bzkneez.com. Cosy
place at the western end of downtown (near the
junction with 4th Ave and Robert Service Way),
with a kitchen, laundry, Internet access, free bicycle use and dorm-style and private rooms from
$20 per person. ❶
Hide on Jeckell Hostel 410 Jeckell St, near the
junction with 4th Ave ☎867/633-4933,
ⓦwww.hide-on-jeckell.com. One block farther
west than its rival, and marginally the better
choice, with the same facilities and same prices:
four dorm rooms and two private doubles. ❶

Campsites
Robert Service campsite ☎867/668-3721.
About 2km and twenty minutes' walk down South
Access Road, past the SS *Klondike* on the river
path. It's set on the banks of the Yukon River and

is specifically for tents and backpackers ($14 plus
$2 for firewood). It becomes very busy in summer;
if it's full try the woods above the lake down past
the dam beyond the campsite or along the bluff
above town by the airport. Open mid-May to mid-
Sept.
Trail of 98 RV Park 117 Jasper Rd ☎867/668-
3768 or 1-800/377-2142. The nearest to downtown of eight RV sites within striking distance
(most of them pretty utilitarian places on the
Alaska Hwy). Located off Industrial Rd, which is
off the north side of Two Mile Hill, the road
that links northern downtown to the Alaska Hwy.
$15.
Wolf Creek campsite The nearest Yukon government campsite ($12), located off the Alaska Hwy
16km south of town. It has just 11 tents sites (and
40 RV sites) and there are no services, but wood
and water are available.

The town and around

Although greater Whitehorse spills along the Alaska Hwy for several kilometres, the old **downtown** core is a forty-block grid centred on Main Street and
mostly sandwiched between 2nd and 4th avenues. Though now graced only
with a handful of pioneer buildings, the place still retains the dour integrity and
appealing energy of a frontier town, and at night the baying of timber wolves
and coyotes is a reminder of the wilderness immediately beyond the city limits.
Nonetheless, the tourist influx provides a fair amount of action in the bars and
cafés, and the streets are more appealing and lively than in many northern
towns.

The main thing to see is the **SS Klondike** (May–Sept daily, tours every half-
hour 9am–6pm, last tour 5.30pm; $5), one of only two surviving paddle steam-
ers in the Yukon, now rather sadly beached at the western end of 2nd Ave at
300 Main St, though it has been beautifully restored to the glory of its 1930s
heyday. More than 250 stern-wheelers once plied the river, taking 36 hours to
make the 700-kilometre journey to Dawson City, and five days to make the

River tours in Miles Canyon

Several **river tours** shoot the **Miles Canyon** 9km south of Whitehorse, otherwise reached off the Alaska Hwy, or from the South Access Road, which hugs the river edge beyond the SS *Klondike*. Whitehorse Transit buses ($1.25) run along the South Access Road from town every hour (Mon–Sat only). The building of a hydro-electric dam has tamed the rapids' violence and replaced them with **Schwatka Lake**, but the two-hour narrated trip on the MV *Schwatka* (May–Sept daily 2pm; mid-June to mid-Aug also 7pm; $25, or $31 with transfers from *Westmark Whitehorse* hotel; ☎867/668-4716, ⓦwww.yukonrivercruises.com) gives a better view of the river's potential ferocity and the canyon's sheer walls than the view-points off the road. Board at the dock above the dam about 3km down Canyon Road. A Taste of '98 Yukon River Tours (☎867/633-4767) runs similar three-hour sightseeing tours, as well as extended four- to 21-day guided or fully equipped tours to Dawson City and elsewhere. Contact the visitor reception centre for details of many other river and air tours locally. You could also **walk** from the main Miles Canyon car park some of the 11km to Canyon City, the all-but-vanished site of the initial stage of the stampeders' tramway at the southern end of the old rapids.

return trip against the current. The SS *Klondike* was built in 1929, sank in 1936, and was rebuilt in 1937 using the original remnants. The largest of all the river's steamers, it then battled against the river until 1955, ferrying 300 tonnes of cargo a trip and making some fifteen round trips a season. Bridges built on the improved road to Dawson increasingly hampered river traffic, though the SS *Klondike*'s end came when an inexperienced pilot ran her aground and condemned her to museum status. Beached at Whitehorse in 1960, the boat can be visited on a 25-minute guided tour only. Before or after a tour, take in the twenty-minute documentary film on the riverboat story in the white tent alongside.

Elsewhere in town you could pop in to the **MacBride Museum**, housed in a sod-roofed log cabin at 1st Ave and Wood St (May to mid-Aug Mon–Fri 10am–9pm, Sat & Sun 10am–7pm; call for winter hours; $5; ☎867/667-2709, ⓦwww.macbridemuseum.com), for the usual zoo of stuffed animals, an old WP&YR engine, pioneer and gold-rush memorabilia, as well as hundreds of marvellous archive photos and a display on the Asiatic peoples who crossed the Bering Straits to inhabit the Americas. Another in-town sight is the **Old Log Church Museum**, 3rd Avenue and Elliott Street (mid-May–early Sept daily 10am–6pm; $2.50), a modest museum devoted to the pre-contact life of the region's aboriginal peoples, whaling, missionaries, children's toys and music, the gold rush and early exploration. For free beer, there are tours and tastings at the **Yukon Brewing Co brewery** in the industrial area at 96-102A Copper Rd (Mon–Sat in summer at 11am & 4pm; free). You may find it easier to resist the widely touted Frantic Follies **stage shows** at the *Westmark Whitehorse Hotel*, however (mid-May to mid-Sept; $19; ☎867/668-2042, ⓦwww.franticfollies.com), – expensive vaudeville acts of the banjo-plucking and frilly-knickered-dancing variety that have been play-ing in town for close to thirty years; call or check the website for details of "music, mirth and magic, gay Nineties songs, cancan dances and humorous renditions".

Outside downtown, two of the most tempting attractions are up on the bluff above the town on the Alaska Hwy close to the airport. One is the excellent

Yukon Transportation Museum (mid-May to mid-Sept daily 10am–6pm; $6, or joint ticket with Beringia Interpretive Centre $9; Ⓦwww .yukontransportmuseum.homestead.com), one of the region's best museums. Devoted to the area's transportation history, its displays, murals, superb histori-cal videos, memorabilia and vehicles embrace everything from dog-sledding, early aviation and the construction of the Alaska Hwy to the Canol pipeline, the gold rush and the White Pass and Yukon Railway. Among the things on show are old army jeeps, bicycles, bulldozers, a stagecoach and – suspended from the ceiling – the *Queen of the Yukon*, the territory's first commercial plane. Right next door is the dynamic **Yukon Beringia Interpretive Centre** (mid-May to mid-Sept daily 8.30am–7pm; $6, or joint ticket with Transportation Museum $9; Ⓦwww.beringia.com), Beringia being the vast subcontinent that existed some 24,000 years ago when the Yukon and Alaska were joined by a land bridge across the Bering Sea to Arctic Russia. The centre's interactive exhibits, film shows and other displays explore the aboriginal history of the time, the people who crossed this land bridge having ultimately colonized the most distant reaches of present-day North and South America. It also looks at the flora, fauna and geology of the time with the help of paleontological and archeological exhibits, among which the skeletal remains of a 12,000-year-old mammoth figure large.

On a different tack, if you fancy total relaxation make for the topnotch **Takhini Hot Springs** (June to early Sept daily 8am–10pm; rest of year usually Fri–Sun only – call for precise hours; $7; ☎867/633-2706, Ⓦwww.takhinihotsprings.yk.ca), located 31km from Whitehorse off the Klondike Highway north to Dawson. The water in the large pool is a piping-hot 36°C, there's no sulphurous aftersmell and the pool is emptied daily. You can camp here ($8) and if you resent paying for the privilege of a hot soak use the public pool at the outflow point in the stream below, which the locals have built.

Eating and drinking

Of several friendly laid-back **eating** places, the best inexpensive option over-all is the *Talisman Café*, 2112 2nd Ave (Mon–Sat 6am–11pm), which serves a range of full meals, and is also a spot to while away time over a cup of coffee. Virtually next door is the almost equally informal *Klondike Rib and Salmon BBQ*, 2nd & Steele St (☎867/667-7554) for good fish and chips and north-ern specialities such as caribou, bison and musk ox. The *Chocolate Claim*, 305 Strickland, is a good, welcoming café for coffee, cakes and great chocolate. The *No Pop Sandwich Shop*, 312 Steele St at 4th Ave, is altogether less cosy, but it's popular all the same and the food's fine. For a **drink**, try the popular and lively pub-eatery, the *Yukon Brewing Company* at the *High Country Inn* hotel, 4051 4th Ave (☎867/667-4471), which has locally brewed Chilkoot Brewing Company beers and barbecue food on the outdoor deck in summer.

For slightly more refined dining, make for the pretty little *Cranberry Bistro* next to the Yukon Theatre at 302 Wood St (☎867/456-4898), for healthy, multiethnic food with some good vegetarian options. If you're feeling flush, try one of the town's better restaurants: *The Cellar*, in the *Edgewater Hotel* at 101 Main St (☎867/667-2572) for solid staples such as ribs, steaks, salmon, Arctic char and lobster (the *Gallery Restaurant & Lounge* in the same hotel has similar food but is less formal); or *Giorgio's Cucina*, next to the *Two-0-Two Motor Inn* at 206 Jarvis St and 2nd Ave (☎867/668-4050, Ⓦwww.giorgioscucinca.com), which has Italian dishes (including pizzas) served in a setting with ancient Roman decorative flourishes.

△ Dawson during the Klondike Gold Rush

Transport in the Yukon

Whitehorse provides the main **transport** links not only to most other points in the Yukon, but also to Alaska and the Northwest Territories. Public transport will get you to surprisingly remote places, so in an area this size of this remoteness, knowing the various bus and air options is essential. Times and schedules can change, so ask at the infocentre or call numbers directly for latest information. We have arranged the information below alphabetically by destination from Whitehorse, unless stated. Note that may of the longer bus routes (such as Whitehorse to Inuvik) are also plied by local airlines, but prices are invariably very high.

Distances from Whitehorse

Anchorage 1165km
Beaver Creek 457km
Burwash Landing 285km
Carcross 74km
Dawson City 1471km
Edmonton 2054km
Fairbanks 980km
Fort Nelson 988km

Haines 415km
Haines Junction 158km
Inuvik 1226km
Prince George 1880km
Seattle 2831km
Tok 639km
Vancouver 2702km
Watson Lake 455km

options from Whitehorse

Alaska Highway For westbound journeys, Alaska Direct Bus Lines (☎867/668-4833 or 1-800/770-6652) runs services from Whitehorse (Tues, Thurs & Sat 8am) to reach Haines Junction (arrives 11am; US$40), Beaver Creek (arrives 3pm; US$70) and points in between such as Burwash Landing (US$45). See Vancouver (below) for details of Greyhound buses to Teslin, Watson Lake and points east on the Alaska Highway.

Anchorage, Alaska Alaska Direct Bus Lines (☎867/668-4833 or 1-800/770-6652) runs to Tok (see below) on Tues, Thurs & Sat, continuing to Anchorage on Wed, Fri & Sun. Cost from Whitehorse is US$165.

Atlin (via Tagish and Carcross). The Atlin Express (☎250/651-7617 or 867/668-4444) leaves on Mon, Wed & Fri at 12.15pm from the Greyhound bus terminal, arriving at 3.30pm at the Atlin Inn. Cost is $28 one-way, $42 return. An overnight stay will be required in Atlin if you wish to return to Whitehorse.

Carcross See Atlin and Skagway.

Carmucks See Dawson City.

Dawson City The Dawson City Taxi and Courier (☎867/393-3334 or 867/993-6688) leaves at 2pm (not Sat) from opposite the Yukon Inn at the Yukon Plaza on 4th Ave, arriving at Carmucks at 4pm ($31.19) and Dawson City at 9.15pm (one-way $95.29, return $171.52).

Fairbanks from Dawson City The Parks Highway Express (☎1-888/600-6001, ⊛www.alaskashuttle.com) leaves the Dawson visitor reception centre at 8am on Sun, Wed and Fri, arriving at 6.15pm. Cost is US$155.

Fairbanks from Whitehorse Alaska Direct Bus Lines (☎867/668-4833 or 1-800/770-6652) leaves Tok (connections from Whitehorse – see below) on Sun, Wed and Fri at 2.30pm, arriving 7.30pm at Days Inn, 321 East 5th Ave, and the hostel. Cost from Whitehorse is US$140.

Haines Junction Bernie's Deliveries (☎867/668-4833) runs any day when available for $35 ($70 return; no same-day return, so overnight stay required). Call for availability and departure details. You can also use the Alaska Bus Direct Service (☎867-668-4833) service to Tok (see below), which departs at 8am from 509 Main St on Tues, Thur and Sat, arriving at 11am. Cost is US$40 one-way.

Inuvik MGM Services (☏867/777-4295, 777-1013 or 777-6444) runs services from Whitehorse via Dawson, when available, from the Yukon Inn at the Yukon Plaza on 4th Ave at 6am, arriving in Dawson at 10pm/midnight, and in Inuvik 12 to 14 hours later. Cost from Whitehorse is $225 ($375 return) and $165 from Dawson. Call for departures and availability.

Inuvik from Dawson City Dawson City Taxi and Courier (☏867/393-3334 or 867/993-6688) leaves from behind the Dawson visitor reception centre Mon & Fri at 7am (returning from Inuvik on Wed & Sun). Tickets must be booked two days in advance and the journey (with stops for lunch, sightseeing and photos) takes between 12 and 14 hours. Cost is $261 ($523).

Mayo Mayo Taxi (☏867/996-2240) runs to Mayo on demand, but you must call at least a day in advance to arrange connections with the Dawson City Taxi and Courier service (see above). Cost is $65 for two people ($130 return) and $80 ($160 return) for three or more people.

Skagway The best way to reach Skagway, and points in between, is to take a Yukon Alaska Tourist Tour (mid-May to early Sept daily 8am; ☏867/633-5710 or 1-866/626-7383 in Whitehorse, 907/983-2115 in Skagway, ⊛www.yukonalaskatouristtours .com), which depart from the old White Pass railway building. Tours call at Carcross Corner (US$5), Carcross (9.15am at the Matthew Watson Trading Post; US$20; ☏867/821-3501), Log Cabin (10.30am; US$25), Fraser (10.45am; US$25), and arrive in Skagway at 12.10pm at Sgt Preston's Trading Post (US$30). The return tours leave Skagway at 4.20pm (Yukon time), arriving back in Whitehorse at 7.20pm. Once a week, Alaska Direct Bus Lines (☏867/668-4833 or 1-800/770-6652) leaves 509 Main St at noon (Yukon time) on Mon, arriving in Skagway at 2pm (Alaska time). Cost is US$50.

Tok Alaska Direct Bus Lines (☏867/668-4833 or 1-800/770-6652) leaves 509 Main St, Whitehorse, on Tues, Thurs and Sat at 8am, arriving in Tok at 5.30pm. Cost is US$90. Connections the following days to Anchorage and Fairbanks (see above).

Vancouver via Alaska Hwy, Watson Lake and Dawson Creek. Greyhound buses (☏867/667-2223 or 1-800/661-8747, ⊛www.greyhound.ca) leave the Whitehorse Greyhound bus depot Mon–Sat at 1.30pm for Watson Lake (5–6 hours; $62.76) and Dawson Creek, where you can pick up connections for Edmonton (total journey time 28hr from Whitehorse; $267.34) and Vancouver (29hr; $347.43).

Watson Lake See Vancouver.

Airlines in the Yukon

The Yukon has several **airlines** that operate scheduled services, and several more that offer tours and charter flights only. The idea of chartering a small plane may sound expensive and far-fetched, but often the prices are not prohibitive – at least by the standards of land transportation costs in the region – especially if you can get a group of people together.

Air Canada Arrivals & departures ☏867/668-4466, reservations and schedules 1-888/247-2262, ⊛www.aircanada.ca. Flies three times daily between Vancouver and Whitehorse.

Air North ☏867/668-2228, ⊛www.flyairnorth.com. From Whitehorse: to Vancouver, Dawson City & Old Crow (Sun–Fri); to Calgary (3 weekly); to Edmonton & Inuvik (3 weekly); to Juneau (2 weekly); to Fairbanks (1 weekly). Also from Dawson City: to Inuvik & Fairbanks (3 weekly); to Whitehorse & Old Crow (Sun–Fri). Also from Inuvik to Old Crow (1 weekly). All routes also operate in reverse.

Charter airlines Alkan Air ☏867/668-2107, ⊛www.alkanair.com; Alpine Aviation ☏867/668-7725; Atlin Air Charters ☏250/651-0025 or 651-7828; Tutchone Air ☏867/667-2488, ⊛www.tutchoneair.com.

Kluane Country

Kluane Country is the pocket of southwest Yukon on and around a scenically stunning 491-kilometre stretch of the Alaska Hwy from Whitehorse to **Beaver Creek** at the border with Alaska. *Kluane* comes from a Southern Tutchone aboriginal word meaning a "place of many fish" after the area's teeming waters, and of **Kluane Lake** in particular, the Yukon's highest and largest stretch of water. These days, though, the name is associated more with the all-but-impenetrable wilderness of Canada's largest mountain park, the **Kluane National Park** – a region that contains the country's highest mountains, the most extensive non-polar ice fields in the world, and the greatest diversity of plant and animal species in the far north. The park's main centre is **Haines Junction** at the intersection of the Alaska Hwy and the Haines Road. Although motels and campsites regularly dot the Alaska Hwy, the only other settlements of any size are **Destruction Bay** and **Burwash Landing** on Kluane Lake. Gray Line's **Alaskon Express** and **Alaska Direct** buses (see box p.1012) ply the length of the Alaska Hwy, which is also very popular with hitchhikers.

Haines Junction

A blunt and ugly modern place 160km from Whitehorse, with a fine mountain-circled setting, **HAINES JUNCTION** (pop. 796) mushroomed into life in 1942 during the building of the Alaska Hwy as a base for the US Army Corps of Engineers during construction of the Haines Road – a highway that connects with Skagway's sister port at Haines, 174km to the southeast (this is one of the region's most spectacularly scenic roads, should you have the time for a detour). Today it's the biggest service centre between Whitehorse and Tok in Alaska, boasting plenty of shops, a handful of accommodation possibilities (contact the visitor centre for B&B details) and lots of tour and rental companies for river-rafting, canoeing, fishing, cycling, horse riding and glacier flights in the Kluane National Park. It's the national park's eastern headquarters – the park covers a vast tract west of the Alaska Hwy well to the north and south of the village. The combined **Parks Canada** and Yukon government **Visitor Reception Centre** is in the Kluane National Park Reserve Building on Logan Street just off the north side of the Alaska Hwy (mid-May to mid-Sept daily 8am–8pm; call for winter hours, ☎867/634-2345 or 634-7207, ⓦwww.parkscanada.gc.ca). The village also has its own information line and website (☎867/634-2519, ⓦwww .kluane.com).

The newest **motel** in town is the *Alcan Motor Inn* (open 24hr; ☎867/634-2371, ⓔalcan@yknet.yk.ca; ❸) on the junction of Haines Road and the Alaska Hwy; it has rooms with kitchenettes, laundry and café and a few serviced **sites** to the rear. Or try the *Kluane Park Inn* (open 24hr; ☎867/634-2261; ❷), or the more expensive, nonsmoking *Raven Hotel & Gourmet Dining* (☎867/634-2500, ⓔkluanerv@yknet.yk.ca; ❺), a central place with a decent restaurant that includes breakfast in its room rate. Foodies will love its elegant evening meals, rated some of the Yukon's best, but you're looking at around $80 a head. The *Cozy Corner Motel & Restaurant* (☎867/634-2511; ❸) lies just down the Alaska Hwy on the corner of Bates Road. The simple *Pine Lake* **campsite** ($12; May–Oct) is 7km east of the village signed off the Alaska Hwy, or there's the bigger and more central *Kluane RV Kampground* in town (☎867/634-2709, ⓦwww.kluanerv.com; $14; May–Sept), which has wooded RV and tent sites, laundry and a grocery store. The best general place **to eat** is the popular *Village

Bakery & Deli (daily 7.30am–9pm) on Logan St across from the Visitor Reception Centre.

Kluane National Park

Created in 1972 using land from the earlier Kluane Game Sanctuary, the **KLUANE NATIONAL PARK** contains some of the Yukon's greatest but most inaccessible scenery, and for the most part you must be resigned to seeing and walking its easterly margins from points along the Alaska Hwy (no road runs into the park). Together with the neighbouring Wrangell-St Elias National Park in Alaska the park protects the **St Elias Mountains**, though from the highway the peaks you see rearing up to the south are part of the subsidiary Kluane Range. Beyond them, and largely invisible from the road, are St Elias's monumental **Icefield Ranges**, which contain Mount St Elias (5488m), **Mount Logan** (5950m) – Canada's highest point – and Mount McKinley (6193m) in Alaska, the highest point in North America. These form the world's second highest coastal range (after the Andes). Below them, and covering half the park, is a huge base of mile-deep glaciers and ice fields, the world's largest nonpolar ice field and just one permanent resident, the legendary ice worm. Unless you're prepared for full-scale expeditions, this interior is off limits, though from as little as $100 you can take plane and helicopter **tours** over the area – information on these and other guided tours is available from the Whitehorse and Haines Junction visitor reception centres.

On the drier, warmer ranges at the edge of the ice fields a green belt of meadow, marsh, forest and fen provides sanctuary for a huge variety of **wildlife** such as grizzlies, moose, mountain goats and a 4000-strong herd of white **Dall sheep**, the last being the animals the park originally set out to protect. These margins also support the widest spectrum of **birds** in the far north, some 150 species in all, including easily seen raptors such as peregrine falcons, bald eagles and golden eagles, together with smaller birds like arctic terns, mountain blue-birds, tattlers and hawk owls.

Limited **trails** (see box) offer the chance to see some of these creatures, but the only **campsite** within the park is at the *Kathleen Lake*, on the Haines Road 16km southeast of Haines Junction ($12) – though there is hotel and camping accommodation along the Alaska Hwy.

Walking in Kluane National Park

Kluane's **trail system** is still in its infancy, though experienced walkers will enjoy wilderness routes totalling about 250km, most of which follow old mining roads or creek beds and require overnight rough camping. A few more manageable walks start from seven distinct trailheads, each signed from the highways and mapped on pamphlets available from Haines' Reception Centre, where enthusiastic staff also organize popular guided day-walks during the summer.

Three trails start from points along a twenty-kilometre stretch of Haines Road immediately south of Haines Junction. The path nearest to the town, and the most popular walk, is the nineteen-kilometre round trip **Auriol Trail**; nearby, the **Rock Glacier Trail** is a twenty-minute jaunt to St Elias Lake; the third and longest trek is the **Mush Lake Road** route (21.6km one-way). North of Haines Junction, most people walk all or part of two paths that strike out from the Sheep Mountain infor-mation kiosk on Kluane Lake – either the **Sheep Mountain Ridge** (11.5km), with good chances of seeing the area's Dall sheep, or the longer **Slim's River West Trail** (28.4km one-way), which offers a relatively easy way to see the edges of the park's ice field interior.

Kluane Lake

The Kluane region might keep its greatest mountains out of sight, but it makes amends by laying on the stunning **Kluane Lake** along some 60km of the Alaska Hwy. About 75km northwest of Haines Junction, and hot on the heels of some magnificent views of the St Elias Mountains, the huge lake (some 400 square kilometres in area) is framed on all sides by snow-covered peaks whose sinister glaciers feed its ice-blue waters. It's not part of the national park, but there's still a second park kiosk at its southern tip, the **Sheep Mountain Information Kiosk** (mid-May to early Sept daily 9am–5pm; no phone). About 5km before the kiosk is the *Kluane Bed & Breakfast* (no phone; ❸), with six cabins on the lakeshore.

If you want to boat or fish try one of the rental facilities at the two main settlements along the shores, Destruction Bay and Burwash Landing, each of which also has a small selection of accommodation to supplement the odd lodges and campsites along the Alaska Hwy. In the smaller **DESTRUCTION BAY** (pop. 44), named when a previous road construction camp was destroyed by a storm in 1942, bed down at the *Talbot Arm Motel* with restaurant, café, store and Chevron garage (☎867/841-4461; ❸). The best overall **campsite** locally is the lovely Yukon government-run *Congdon Creek* ($12) site off the Alaska Hwy, 12km south of Destruction Bay, which also offers the start of hiking trails. At **BURWASH LANDING**, 15km beyond, there's a tiny 1944 Oblate mission church and museum, Our Lady of the Holy Rosary, and the *Burwash Landing Resort* (☎867/841-4441; ❸), with restaurant, store, glacier flights, fishing trips, gold-panning and a big, unserviced campsite (free; May–Oct). Five kilometres farther south the *Cottonwood Park Campground*, a private outfit, offers rather more facilities (no phone; $12; mid-May to mid-Oct).

Moving on from Burwash, there are just two more major indoor **accommodation** possibilities before Beaver Creek: 85km east of Burwash is the *Pine Valley Bakery & Lodge* (☎867/862-7407; ❸) and, 36km beyond that, the *White River Lodge Motor Inn & RV Park* (☎867/862-7408, ⓦwww.netship.yk.ca; ❸), with café and petrol. Ten kilometres west of the *Pine Valley Bakery & Lodge* are the Yukon government campsites at Lake Creek; additional campsites are situated eleven kilometres farther at Pickhandle Lake (both $12).

Beaver Creek and the US border

BEAVER CREEK, Canada's westernmost settlement (pop. 145), is the last stop before Alaska. Following concerted lobbying from its inhabitants, however, it no longer houses the customs post – this has been moved a couple of kilometres up the road in response to complaints from the locals about the flashing lights and sirens that used to erupt whenever a tourist forgot to stop. The border is open 24 hours a day, but be warned that if US Customs staff take against you, they can insist on seeing at least $400 or so in cash, and won't be swayed by any number of credit cards. For full details on crossing the border, and what to expect on the other side, visit the **Yukon Visitor Information Centre** (mid-May to early Sept daily 8am–8pm; ☎867/862-7321).

You may wish to stay at Beaver Creek, either at the expensive *Westmark Inn* (☎867/862-7501 or 1-800/544-0970, ⓦwww.westmarkhotels.com; ❺; May–Sept), or the eccentric twenty-room *Ida's Motel and Restaurant* (☎867/862-3227; ❹; summer 6am–2am; winter 8am–10pm), a distinctive building across the highway. Failing that, try the downbeat *1202 Motor Inn* (☎867/862-7600; ❸). The *Westmark* has a large, serviced **campsite** ($20), though they're happier to see RVs than backpackers (try free camping in the woods). There's a good but small Yukon-government-run site located 10km south at the *Snag Junction* ($12; May–Oct).

Those not pushing deeper into Alaska but looping to Dawson City have a great journey in prospect: just before Tok, the **Taylor Hwy** (Hwy 5) bears northeast off the Alaska Hwy back towards the Yukon border, passing through relatively unexceptional scenery until it hits the US–Canadian border at Little Gold Creek (open daily 9am–9pm). From here, the 105km road to Dawson on the **Top of the World Hwy** offers sensational views (see p.1026).

Dawson City

Few episodes in Canadian history have captured the imagination like the **Klondike gold rush**, and few places have remained as evocative of their past as **DAWSON CITY** (pop. 1,953), the stampede's tumultuous capital. For a few months in 1898 this former patch of moose pasture became one of the wealthiest and most famous places on earth, as something like 100,000 people struggled across huge tracts of wilderness to seek their fortunes in the richest gold field of all time.

These days, most people approach the town on the Klondike Hwy from Whitehorse, a wonderful road running through almost utter wilderness; knowing the background to the place it's hard not to near the road's end without high expectations. Little at first, however, distinguishes its surroundings. Some 536km from Whitehorse the road wanders through low but steeply sided hills covered in spruce, aspen and dwarf firs, and then picks up a small, ice-clear river – the **Klondike** itself. Gradually the first small spoil heaps appear on the hills to the south, and then suddenly the entire valley bottom turns into a devastated landscape of vast boulders and abandoned workings. The desolate tailings continue for several kilometres until the Klondike flows into the much broader **Yukon River** and the town of Dawson City, previously hidden by hills, comes suddenly into view.

An ever-increasing number of tourists and backpackers come up here, many drawn by the boardwalks, rutted dirt streets and dozens of false-fronted wooden houses, others to canoe the Yukon or travel down the Dempster or Top of the World highways into Alaska and the Northwest Territories. After decades of decline Parks Canada is restoring the town, now deservedly a **National Historic Site**, a process that is bringing about increased commercialism, increased population, new hotels and a sense that some of the town's character is gradually being lost. That said, in a spot where permafrost buckles buildings, snow falls in August, and temperatures touch -60°C during winters of almost perpetual gloom, there's little real chance of Dawson losing the gritty, weather-battered feel of a true frontier town. More to the point, small-time prospecting still goes on, and there are one or two rough-and-ready bars whose hardened locals take a dim view of sharing their beers, let alone their gold, with coachloads of tourists.

You could easily spend a couple of days or more here: one exploring the town, the other touring the old Klondike creeks to the east. If at all possible prime yourself beforehand with the background to one of the most colourful chapters in Canada's history: Pierre Berton's widely available bestseller *Klondike – The Last Great Gold Rush 1896–1899* is a superbly written introduction both to the period and to the place.

Gold rushes in North America during the nineteenth century were nothing new, but none generated quite the delirium of the **Klondike gold rush** in 1898. Over a million people are estimated to have left home for the Yukon gold fields, the largest single one-year mass movement of people in the century. Of these, about 100,000 made it to the Yukon, about 20,000 panned the creeks, 4000 found something and a couple of dozen made – and invariably lost – huge fortunes.

The discovery of gold in 1896 on the Klondike, a tributary of the Yukon River, was the culmination of twenty years of prospecting in the Yukon and Alaska. A Hudson's Bay fur trader first noticed gold in 1842, and the first substantial report was made by an English missionary in 1863, but as the exploitation of gold was deemed bad for trade in both furs and religion neither report was followed up. The first mining on any scale took place in 1883 and gradually small camps sprang up along almost 3200km of river at places like Forty Mile, Sixty Mile and Circle City. All were established before the Klondike strike, but were home to only a few hundred men, hardened types reared on the earlier Californian and British Columbian gold rushes.

The discovery of the gold that started the stampede is inevitably shrouded in myth and countermyth. The first man to prospect near the Klondike River was **Robert Henderson**, a dour Nova Scotian and the very embodiment of the lone pioneer. In early 1896 he found 8¢ worth of gold in a pan scooped from a creek in the hills above present-day Dawson City. This was considered an excellent return at the time, and a sign to Henderson that the creek would make worthwhile yields. He panned out about $750 with four companions and then returned downriver to pick up supplies.

Henderson then set about finding a route up the Klondike to meet the creek he'd prospected, and at the mouth of the Klondike met **George Washington Carmack** and a couple of his aboriginal friends, known as **Skookum Jim** and **Tagish Charley**. Henderson told Carmack of his hopes for the area, and then – with a glance at the aboriginal pair – uttered the phrase that probably cost him a fortune, "There's a chance for you George, but I don't want any damn Siwashes [aboriginal people] staking on that creek." Henderson wandered off into the hills, leaving Carmack, rankled by the remark, to prospect a different set of creeks – the right ones, as it turned out. On the eve of August 16, Skookum Jim found $4 of gold in a pan on **Bonanza Creek**, a virtually unprecedented amount at the time. Next day Carmack staked the first claim, and rushed off to register the find leaving Henderson prospecting almost barren ground on the other side of the hills.

By the end of August all of Bonanza had been staked by a hundred or so old-timers from camps up and down the Yukon. Almost all the real fortunes had been secured by the winter of 1896, when the snows and frozen river effectively sealed the region from the outside world. The second phase occurred after the thaw when a thousand or so miners from the West Coast arrived drawn by vague rumours emanating from the north of a big find. The headlong rush that was to make the Klondike unique, however, followed the docking in July 1897 of the *Excelsior* in **San**

Arrival, information and accommodation

Dawson City's **airport**, 19km southeast of the town on the Klondike Hwy, is used by charter Alkan Air services to Inuvik (NWT), Old Crow, Mayo and Whitehorse, and by Air North services to Fairbanks, Whitehorse, Watson Lake and Juneau. Buses and shuttles to Inuvik, Whitehorse and points in Alaska generally arrive and depart from behind the visitor centre. See the box on p.1012 for full details of these and other **transport links** to and from Dawson. Tickets for all air services, Alaska and BC ferries, sightseeing **tours** of the gold

Francisco and the *Portland* in **Seattle**. Few sights could have been so stirring a proof of the riches up for grabs as the battered Yukon miners who came down the gangplanks dragging bags, boxes and sacks literally bursting with gold. The press were waiting for the *Portland*, which docked with two tons of gold on board, all taken by hand from the Klondike creeks by just a few miners. The rush was now on in earnest.

Whipped up by the media and the outfitters of Seattle and San Francisco, thousands embarked on trips that were to claim hundreds of lives. The most common route – the "poor man's route" – was to take a boat from a West Coast port to **Skagway**, climb the dreaded **Chilkoot Pass** to pick up the Yukon River at Whitehorse and then boat the last 500 miles to **Dawson City**. The easiest and most expensive route lay by boat upstream from the mouth of the Yukon in western Alaska. The most dangerous and most bogus were the "All Canadian Route" from **Edmonton** and the overland trails through the northern wilderness.

The largest single influx came with the melting of the ice on the Yukon in **May 1898** – 21 months after the first claim – when a vast makeshift armada drifted down the river. When they docked at Dawson City, the boats nestled six deep along a two-mile stretch of the waterfront. For most it was to have been a fruitless journey, every inch of the creeks having long been staked – yet in most accounts of the stampede it is clear that this was a rite of passage as much as a quest for wealth. Pierre Berton observed that "there were large numbers who spent only a few days in Dawson and did not even bother to visit the hypnotic creeks that had tugged at them all winter long. They turned their faces home again, their adventure over... It was as if they had, without quite knowing it, completed the job they had set out to do and had come to understand that it was not the gold they were seeking after all."

As for the gold, it's the smaller details that hint at the scale of the Klondike gold rush: the miner's wife, for example, who could wander the creek by her cabin picking nuggets from the stream bed as she waited for her husband to come home; or the destitutes during the Great Depression who could pan $40 a day from the dirt under Dawson's boardwalks; or the $1000 panned during rebuilding of the Orpheum Theatre in the 1940s, all taken in a morning from under the floorboards where it had drifted from miners' pockets half a century before; or the $200 worth of dust panned nightly from the beer mats of a Dawson saloon during 1897.

By about 1899 the rush was over, not because the gold had run out, but because the most easily accessible gold had been taken from the creeks. It had been the making of Alaska; the cities of Tacoma, Portland, Victoria and San Francisco all felt its impact; Edmonton sprang from almost nothing; and Vancouver's population doubled in a year. It was also the first of a string of mineral discoveries in the Yukon and the far north, a region whose vast and untapped natural resources are increasingly the subject of attention from multinational corporations as rapacious and determined as their grizzled predecessors.

fields, and popular four-wheel-drive vehicle tours can be arranged at the excellent Gold City Tours on Front Street opposite the SS *Keno* (☎867/993-5175 or 993-6424, ⓦwww.goldcitytours.com). For further details of tours and general information, contact the impressive Tourism Yukon–Parks Canada **Visitor Reception Centre** (mid-May to mid-Sept daily 8am–8pm; ☎867/993-5566 or 993-7200, ⓦwww.dawsoncity.com) on Front St, at the junction with King St. Loaded with a huge amount of material, the place also has a Parks Canada desk (☎1-888/773-8888, ⓦwww.parkscanada.gc.ca) and shows good introductory archive and contemporary films throughout the day,

Distances from Dawson City

Anchorage 828km	**Haines Junction** 671km
Beaver Creek 415km	**Inuvik** 766km
Burwash Landing 587km	**Keno** 285km
Carcross 610km	**Prince George** 2416km
Dawson Creek 2007km	**Skagway** 716km
Destruction Bay 798km	**Tok** 300km
Fairbanks 631km	**Vancouver** 3191km
Fort Nelson 1524km	**Watson Lake** 991km
Haines 927km	**Whitehorse** 536km

as well as letting you leave your bag or pack ($1) while you explore. It also organizes **walking tours** (June to mid-Sept several daily; $5) of the waterfront and SS *Keno* paddle steamer and the town's heritage buildings. Information is also available from the **public library** on 5th and Queen (Tues, Wed & Fri noon–7pm, Thurs noon–8pm, Sat 11am–5pm).

Another way of exploring the surroundings of Dawson is to take a Gray Line **cruise** on the 110-passenger catamaran *Yukon Queen*, which in summer runs daily on the Yukon River to Eagle, Alaska, offering a day-long round trip of 105 miles for around $210. Stand-by, round trip and one-way tickets are available from Yukon Queen River Cruise on Front Street (℡867/668-3225, ℻867/667-4494). Shorter and cheaper ($47) two-hour river trips (with salmon barbecue) are available on the *Yukon Lou* **paddle steamer** from the aboriginal-run and owned River of Culture based on the dock behind the Little Birch Cabin ticket office close to the SS *Keno* (℡867/993-5482). Trans North Helicopters (℡867/993-5494, ⓦwww.tntaheli.com) runs **helicopter trips** over the gold fields, the Klondike Valley and Midnight Dome.

Accommodation

More and more **accommodation** is opening in Dawson, but while the increased competition keeps prices steady it isn't bringing them down. In July and August it's pretty much essential to book lodging in advance. The two **hostels** are likely to be heavily oversubscribed, as are the B&B options, though calls to the latter a couple of days in advance should secure a room. Rates are high in the half-dozen or so mid-range places, most of which look the part of old-fashioned wood- and false-fronted hotels. If you arrive without a room, check with the visitor centre, which keeps an updated record of accommodation availability and will work hard to find you a bed: hotels often offer cheap last-minute deals to fill empty rooms and prices in all places drop considerably outside the high summer period. Note, though, that many places close their doors between September and mid-May.

Hotels and B&Bs

Bombay Peggy's 2nd & Princess ℡867/993-6969, ⓦwww.bombaypeggys.com. One of the nicest places in town; ten very comfortable rooms in a central, heritage house of former ill-repute. Open year-round. ❻

Bonanza House B&B Near the museum on 7th Ave & Grant ℡867/993-6789, Ⓔbonanza-house@hotmail.com. Offers a two- or three-bed-room suite with shared sitting rooms and TV. ❸

Dawson City B&B 451 Craig St ℡867/993-5649, ⓦwww.dawsonbb.com. Located near the junction of the Yukon and Klondike rivers. Arranges pick-ups from the airport or even offers car rentals. ❹

Downtown Hotel 2nd & Queen ℡867/993-5346 or 1-800/764-0514 in BC and YK, ⓦwww.downtown.yk.net. One of the town's plusher wooden-fronted hotels, and – unlike some – open year-round. Rooms are recently renovated. ❺

Eldorado 3rd & Princess ☎867/993-5451 or 1-800/661-0518, ⓦwww.eldoradohotel.ca. Much the same as the *Downtown*, with 52 central rooms (some kitchenettes), and also open 24hr year-round. ❻

Fifth Ave B&B On 5th Ave near the museum ☎867/993-5941 or 1-866/631-5237, ⓦwww.5thavebandb.com. A spacious house with shared kitchen near the museum; optional en suites. Air-conditioned rooms and full all-you-can-eat breakfast. Look out for the unmissable electric-blue exterior. ❻

Klondike Kate's Cabins & Rooms 3rd & King ☎867/993-6527, ⓦwww.klondikekates.com. Renovated, pretty and popular cabins, clean and warm; also some of the cheaper and nicer rooms in town as well as cabins. May–Sept. ❺

Triple J Hotel 5th & Queen ☎867/993-5323 or 1-800/764-3555, ⓦwww.triplejhotel.com. Has 47 rooms or cabins with kitchenettes in old-fashioned-style hotel next to *Diamond Tooth Gertie's*. Coin laundry and airport shuttle service. May–Oct. ❻

Westmark Inn Dawson 5th & Harper ☎867/993-5542 or 1-800/544-0970, ⓦwww.westmarkhotels.com. Part of an upmarket northern chain, and the town's swishest hotel; look out for out-price promotions to fill empty rooms. ❻

White Ram Manor B&B 7th & Harper ☎867/993-5772, ⓦwww.bbcanada.com/whiterammanor. A distinctive pink house that has a hot tub and outside deck. Pick-up from bus on request. ❹

Whitehouse Motel Front St ☎867/993-5576, ⓦwww.whitehousecabins.com. Six cabins with kitchenettes on the waterfront at the northern end of the street beyond the *George Black* ferry. Open year-round. ❸

Hostels

Dawson City Bunkhouse Near the corner of Front and Princess ☎867/993-6164, ⓦwww.bunkhouse.ca. A good, if noisy, hostel-type place (often known just as "The Bunkhouse") with a choice between rooms with shared bathrooms or private facilities. ❹

Dawson City River Hostel (HI) ☎867/993-6823, ⓦwww.yukonhostels.com. Across the river from downtown; first left after you jump the free ferry. An HI-affiliated collection of bunks in smart log cabins with a good view of Dawson and the river. There are bunk rooms (two to six people; $15 for HI members, $19 for non-members), rather unattractive tent sites ($12 for individuals, $8.50 per person for multiple-occupancy tents), family and private double rooms (from $39), a sweat lodge and canoe and bike rentals available. No electricity. Cash only. Open May to mid-Sept. ❶

Campsites

Gold Rush Campground At 5th and York in town ☎867/993-5247. A bleak, fully serviced but busy place designed for RVs ($20; May–Sept).

Klondike River Campground A Yukon government site ($12) on the Klondike Hwy 15km east of town. While it's a bit quieter than the *Yukon River Campground* site, it's not as pleasant.

Yukon River Campground The main town campsite for tents, government-run ($12). Located on the west bank of the Yukon on the right about 500m after the fun and free *George Black* seven-minute ferry crossing (see p.1026) from the top of Front Street near the corner of Albert. (Black, incidentally, made one of the first journeys to Dawson by car from Whitehorse in 1912 in the then record-breaking time of 33hr.) On the same bank of the river nearby is the "Informal" *West Dawson Tent City*, a chaotic pitch-where-you-can affair. The *Yukon River Campground* has no showers – the most central in town are the tight-fit bathrooms at the laundry behind the Chief Isaac Hale building alongside the visitor centre. There are also showers at the municipal swimming pool by the museum.

The Town

You should start any wander on **Front Street**, the leading edge of a street grid that runs parallel to the Yukon River. The town has a wealth of **heritage buildings** – there are 35 National Historic Sites in town, seven of which you can enter, usually as part of a tour ($5 each, $10 for three, $15 for four or $25 for all seven). The buildings are easily seen on your own, however, as are the cabins that belonged to two chroniclers of the gold rush, poet **Robert Service** and the better-known **Jack London**. The local **museum** is also good for an hour, and you might want to dabble in the casino – though it's the atmospheric streets of Dawson that are most compelling.

Opposite the Visitor Reception Centre is the **Western Arctic Information Centre**, an essential port of call if you are heading north on the Dempster

Hwy (see p.1026 for more on the centre and the highway) and, next to that, the new dramatic-looking **Dänojà Zho**, or "Long Time Ago House", also known as Tr'ondëk Hwëch'in Cultural Centre (daily June–Aug 10am–8pm; by appointment in winter; $5; ☎867/993-6768 or 867/633-6519, ⓦwww .trondek.com), which uses exhibits, guides, videos and live demonstrations to explore the traditional and present-day culture of the Tr'ondëk Hwëch'in, the region's original aboriginal inhabitants.

The heritage buildings

Fuelled by limitless avarice, between 1898 and 1900 Dawson exploded into a full-blown metropolis of 30,000 people – the largest city in the Canadian West and the equal of places like Seattle and San Francisco in its opportunities for vice, decadence and good living. There were opera houses, theatres, cinemas (at a time when motion-picture houses were just three years old), steam heating, three hospitals, restaurants with French chefs, and bars, brothels and dance halls which generated phenomenal business: one Charlie Kimball took $300,000 in a month from his club, and spent the lot within days. Showgirls charged miners $5 – payable in gold – for a minute's dance; slow dances were charged at a higher rate. Cleaners panning the bars' sawdust floors after hours were clearing $50 in gold dust a night. Rules of supply and demand also made Dawson an expensive town, with a single two-metre frontage fetching as much in rent in a month as a four-bedroom apartment in New York cost for two years.

Only a few of the many intact **heritage buildings** around the town date from the earliest days of the rush, dozens having been lost to fire and to permafrost, whose effects are seen in some of the most appealing of the older buildings: higgledy-piggledy collapsing ruins of rotting wood, weeds and rusting corrugated iron. Most of these, thankfully, have been deliberately preserved in their tumbledown state. Elsewhere, almost overzealous restoration projects are in full flow, partly financed by profits from the town casino. Permafrost precluded the construction of brick buildings with deep foundations, so restoration engineers have had to work doubly hard to save what are generally all-wood buildings, most notably the **Palace Grand Theatre** on the corner of 3rd Ave and King St (1899). The theatre was originally built from the hulks of two beached paddle steamers, and but for the intervention of the Klondike Visitors Association would have been pulled down for scrap timber in 1960. Tours run daily in summer ($5) and every night in summer (except Tues). There's a performance of *Gaslight Follies* (mid-May to mid-Sept daily 8pm; $15 on the main floor, $17 in the balcony; ☎867/993-5575, ⓦwww.dawsoncity .org), a predictable medley of cancan, frilly knickers and gold-rush cabaret, though this is among the best of several such shows around the country.

Nearby, on the corner of King St and 3rd Ave, there's the working 1901 **post office** (June–Aug daily noon–6pm); opposite is **Madame Tremblay's Store**. On 3rd Ave and Princess St, **Harrington's Store** has a "Dawson as They Saw It" exhibition of photos arranged by Parks Canada (June–Aug daily 9am–5pm; free); near the same junction stands **Billy Bigg's Blacksmith Shop**; elsewhere is the cream-and-brown clapboard **Anglican Church**, built in 1902 with money collected from the miners. At 4th Ave and Queen St is **Diamond Tooth Gertie's Gambling House**, founded by one of the town's more notorious characters, and still operating as the first legal casino in Canada (opened after restoration in 1971) – it's also the world's northernmost casino (for details, see "Nightlife" below).

Also check out the **Firefighters Museum** in City Hall (under restoration at time of writing) where a guide takes you on a tour of old fire tenders, water pumps and other old firefighting equipment. In a town built almost entirely of wood these were once vital to Dawson's survival: the town all but burnt to the ground twice in the space of a year in 1898–99. So far you can't visit one of the town's more obvious old wooden constructions, the **SS Keno** riverboat, moored on the river just down from the visitor centre – it's been under restoration for several years. It was built in 1922 and ran up and down the Stewart River carrying ore from the mines around Mayo. At the Yukon River the ore was unloaded for collection by larger boats and the journey to Whitehorse and the railway. Not all boats were as lucky as the *Keno*, and a good short hike just out of town will take you to a **ships' graveyard**. The improvements to transport links, chiefly the completion of the Klondike Hwy, made many riverboats redundant. Some were beached downstream, where their overgrown carcasses can still be seen with a little effort. Cross the river on the free George Black ferry on Front Street and walk through the campsite and then a farther ten minutes along the waterfront to reach the ruins.

The Dawson City Museum

The **Dawson City Museum & Historical Society**, 595 5th Ave and Church St (mid-May or June to Sept daily 10am–6pm; $5), has an adequate historical run-through of the gold rush from the first finds, though you get more out of the displays if you have some background to the period. Fascinating old diaries and newspaper cuttings vividly document the minutiae of pioneer life and events such as the big winter freeze of 1897–98 when temperatures reputedly touched -86°C, and of the summer heat wave of 1898 when the sun shone unbroken for almost 23 hours daily, bringing temperatures up to the upper thirties centigrade. The museum also shows some of the hundreds of old films that were discovered under the floorboards of a Dawson building a few years back. Its highlight – in fact, one of Dawson's highlights – is the wistful, award-winning, black-and-white film *City of Gold*, a wonderful documentary which first drew the attention of the federal government to Dawson's decline in the 1950s. The museum also holds interesting touring exhibitions in the wood-framed rooms upstairs that once housed the council offices. You might also take a **tour** of the museum building (summer daily 11am, 1pm & 5pm), the former Territorial Administration Building (1901), during which you're shown the old court chambers (still occasionally used), the resource library and archive, the Visible Storage area (with some 6000 of the museum's 30,000 artefacts) and (outside) a view of the Victory Gardens (1910). The locomotives outside the museum, incidentally, ran to Dawson from the gold fields between 1906 and 1914.

The Robert Service and Jack London cabins

The cabins of Dawson's two literary lions, Robert Service and Jack London, are only about 100m apart on 8th Ave, about ten minutes' walk from Front Street. Parks Canada offer tours of these and a third home, that of local writer Pierre Berton, but they are just as easily seen on your own.

Most Canadians hold **Robert Service** (1874–1958) in high esteem – despite his regularly execrable verse – and he has a place, deserved or not, in the pantheon of Canadian literature. Verses like *The Shooting of Dan McGrew* and *The Cremation of Sam McGee* (see "Contexts", p.1090) combine strong narrative and broad comedy to evoke the myth of the North. Born in Preston, England, in 1874, the poet wrote most of his gold-rush verse before he'd even set foot in the Yukon: he was posted by his bank employers to Whitehorse in 1904 and only made Dawson in 1908. He retired a rich man on the proceeds of his writing – he outsold Kipling and was one of the biggest-selling poets of his time – spending his last years mainly in France, where he died in 1958. His **cabin** (June–Sept daily 9am–noon & 1–5pm; free) is probably cosier and better decorated than it was, but it still gives an idea of how most people must have lived once Dawson was reasonably established. During the summer people come here to pay homage and join a **tour** which includes a short reading of one or two Service poems (July & Aug daily 10am & 3pm; $6 for cabin and recital). An actor, Irish-born Tom Byrne, dressed and mannered as the "Bard of the Yukon", once performed in front of the cabin, but the recitations became so popular that he now performs readings in summer on a small theatre at Front St between Queen and Princess (3pm & 8pm; $8).

The unexceptional-looking **Berton House Writers' Retreat** almost opposite the Service cabin was built in 1901, and bought by mining recorder, Frank Berton, for $500 in 1920. It was the Berton family home until they left Dawson, with son and future writer Pierre, in 1932. It was acquired by the Yukon Arts Council with a donation of $50,000 from Pierre Berton himself, and was restored and reopened in 1996 as a private retreat for Canadian writers.

Jack London's Cabin home two blocks south on 8th Ave at Grant is an unpersuasive piece of reconstruction, little more than a bleak, blank-walled and incomplete hut (logs from the original were separated and half of them used to build a cabin in Jack London Square in Oakland, California). London knew far more than Service of the real rigours of northern life, having spent time in 1897 as a ferryman on Whitehorse's Mile's Canyon before moving north to spend about a year holed up on Henderson's Creek above the Klondike River. He returned home to California penniless, but loaded with a fund of material that was to find expression in books like *The Call of the Wild*, *White Fang* and *A Daughter of the Snows*. Alongside the hut there's a good little museum of pictures and memorabilia, presided over by an amiable and knowledgeable curator (hut and museum mid-May or June to mid-Sept daily 10am–6pm; donation). Readings of London's work are presented here in summer (noon & 2.30pm).

Eating, drinking and nightlife

For **eating** there are numerous cafés around town, including several good snack places on Front Street – probably the most popular is *River West Cappuccino Bistro*, a place with some health-food options. The excellent *Klondike Kate's* (May–Sept daily 7am–11pm), at 3rd and King, is the friendliest and most laid-back place in town for staples like breakfasts and straightforward dinners (and has an outdoor patio). Otherwise, most dining goes on in the restaurants attached to the town's bigger hotels: three of the best are the *Jack London Grill* (☎867/993-5346) in the *Downtown Hotel* at 2nd and Queen; the *Bonanza Dining Room* in the Eldorado at 3rd and Princess; and *TJ's* in the *Triple J Hotel* at 5th and Queen. *Madame Zoom's*, at 2nd and King, has good ice cream and frozen yogurts, and for picnic goodies and **self-catering** supplies, there's the Dawson General Store on Front St at the corner of Queen as well as the Farmer's Market on 2nd near Princess.

Nightlife revolves around drinking in the main hotel bars, or an hour or so at *Diamond Tooth Gertie's* at 4th and Queen, Canada's only legal gambling hall (mid-May to mid-Sept daily 7pm–2am; $6); you need to be over 19 to gamble and all proceeds from here and several other town sights go to the restoration of Dawson. You can also catch the almost equally touristy period-costume melodramas and vaudeville acts held at the Palace Grand Theatre (June–Sept daily 8pm; $16–18). If you want a taste of a real northern **bar**, try the *Westminster* on 2nd Ave: it's full of grizzled characters and most certainly not the place for a quiet drink or the faint-hearted. It hosts live music most nights. Other hotel bars provide more sedate alternatives, among which the lounge at *Bombay Peggy's* hotel on 2nd and Princess stands out for its fine atmosphere. The *Sourdough Saloon* at the *Downtown Hotel*, 2nd and Queen, is also passable: popular with locals and visitors alike, and known for a cocktail that involves a real pickled human toe.

Listings

Books and guides Maximilian's ☎867/993-5486, on the corner of Front & Queen.

Car rental To rent a car or 4x4 for the Dempster Hwy (see p.1026), contact Budget, 451 Craig St ☎867/993-5644, ⊛www.budgetyukon.com.

Exchange and ATM At the CIBC bank ☎867/993-5447, on Queen St, between Front & 2nd.

Internet access Klondike Infotech, opposite the liquor store on 3rd Ave ☎867/993-5539.

Maps From the mining recorder's office alongside the post office.

Post office On 5th St between Harper & Princess (Mon–Fri 8.30am–5.30pm; ☎867/993-5342).

Taxis In Dawson, call Dawson City Courier & Taxi ☎867/993-6687.

Around Dawson

While in Dawson, make a point of seeing the two creeks where it all started and where most of the gold was mined – **Bonanza and Eldorado**, both over 20km away from the town site along rough roads to the southeast. These days, no big working mine survives in the region, though most of the claims are still owned and definitely out of bounds to amateurs. However, it's still possible to see some of the huge dredges that supplanted the individual prospectors, once the easily reached gold had been taken out. Another popular local excursion is to **Midnight Dome**, the gouged-out hill behind the town, while farther afield numerous RVs, cyclists and hitchhikers follow the **Top of the World Hwy**, which runs on beyond the Alaskan border to link with the Alaska Hwy at Tetlin Junction.

Bonanza and Eldorado creeks

To reach **Bonanza Creek**, follow the Klondike Hwy – the continuation of Front St – for 4km to the junction with Bonanza Creek Road. The road threads through scenes of apocalyptic piles of boulders and river gravel for some 12km until it comes to a simple cairn marking **Discovery Claim**, the spot staked by George Carmack after pulling out a nugget the size of his thumb, or so the story goes. Every 150m along the creek in front of you – the width of a claim – was to yield some 3000kg of gold, or about $25 million worth at 1900 prices. Exact amounts of gold taken out are difficult to establish because it was in miners' interests to undervalue their takings to the authorities, but most estimates suggest that around $600 million-worth left the creeks between 1897 and 1904. Given a claim's huge value they were often subdivided and sold as "fractions": one miner pulled out over 100kg of gold (worth almost $1 million) in eight hours from a fraction.

At Discovery Claim the road forks again, one spur running east up **Eldorado Creek**, if anything richer than Bonanza, the other following Upper Bonanza Road to the summit of **King Solomon's Dome**, where you can look down over smaller scarred rivulets like Hunker and Dominion creeks, before returning in a loop to the Klondike Hwy via Hunker Road.

As time went by and the easily reached gold was exploited, miners increasingly consolidated claims, or sold out to large companies who installed dredges capable of clawing out the bedrock and gravel. Numerous examples of these industrial dinosaurs litter the creeks, but the largest and most famous is the 1912 **No. 4 Dredge** at Claim 17 BD ("Below Discovery") off Bonanza Creek Road, an extraordinary piece of industrial archeology that from the start of operations in 1913 until 1966 dug up as much as 25kg of gold a day. Modern mines are lucky to produce a quarter of that amount in a week.

Without a car you'll have to rent a bike or join up with one of the various **gold-field tours** (from about $40 for a 3hr 30min tour) run by Gold City Tours, on Front Street (☏867/993-5175, ⓦwww.goldencitytours.com), either to see the dredges and creeks or to **pan for gold** yourself, at a price. Only three small fractions on Claim 6 can currently be panned free of charge – but enquire at the reception centre for latest locations: for $5 you can pan with a guarantee of finding gold (because it's been put there) on Claim 33.

Midnight Dome and Top of the World Highway

The **Midnight Dome** is the distinctive hill that rears up behind Dawson City, half-covered in stunted pines and half-eaten away by landslips. It's named because from its summit at midnight on June 21 you can watch the sun dip to the horizon before rising again straight away – Dawson being only 300km south of the Arctic Circle. The Midnight Dome Road runs 8km to its summit (884m) from the Klondike Hwy just out of the town proper. Without a car it's an extremely steep haul (ask at the visitor centre for details of the well-worn and partially signed trail), but more than worth the slog for the massive views over Dawson, the gold fields, the Yukon's broad meanders and the ranks of mountains stretching away in all directions. At the summer solstice there's a race to the top and lots of drink-sodden and fancy-dress festivities down in Dawson. Gold City Tours also runs regular daytime and evening tours up here.

You can snatch further broad vistas from the **Top of the World Hwy** (Hwy 9), a good summer-only gravel road reached by the *George Black* **ferry** from Front St across the Yukon (mid-May to mid-Sept daily 24hr; rest of year 7am–11pm, depending on weather conditions and whether or not the river is frozen; every 45min; free; ☏867/993-5441). After only 5km the road unfolds a great panorama over the area, and after 14km another **viewpoint** looks out over the Yukon Valley and the **Ogilvie Mountains** straddling the Arctic Circle. Thereafter the road runs above the tree line as a massive belvedere and can be seen switchbacking over barren ridges way into the distance. It hits the **Alaska border** 108km from Dawson, where you can cross only when the customs post is open (May–Sept 9am–9pm). Unlike the Dempster Hwy, there's no bus on this route, but you should be able to hitch easily in summer because it's much-travelled as a neat way of linking with the Alaska Hwy at Tok for the roads to Fairbanks and Anchorage or the loop back to Whitehorse. Be prepared to do only about 50kph, and enquire about local difficulties and fuel availability at the Dawson Visitor Reception Centre.

The Dempster Highway

Begun in 1959 to service northern oilfields, and completed over twenty years later – by which time all the accessible oil had been siphoned off – the 741-kilometre **Dempster Highway** between Dawson City and Inuvik in the

Northwest Territories is the only road in Canada to cross the **Arctic Circle**, offering a tremendous journey through a superb and ever-changing spectrum of landscapes. It's hard to resist the temptation of crossing into the Arctic 445km north of Dawson City, a section that takes you over the most captivating stretch of the highway. However, the Dempster is a **gravel road** and the journey north to Inuvik takes anything between twelve and fifteen hours by car in good conditions. It's an increasingly travelled route – which locals say means four cars an hour – but is not a journey to be undertaken lightly. Inuvik, too, is an ugly disappointment, but then this road is very much about the journey rather than the arriving.

For much of its course the road follows the path of the dog patrols operated by the Mounties in the first half of the twentieth century, taking its name from a Corporal W.J.D. Dempster, who in March 1922 was sent to look for a patrol lost between Fort McPherson and Dawson. He found their frozen bodies just 26 miles from where they had set off. They were buried on the banks of the Peel River and there's a monument to their memory at Fort McPherson.

Note that all distances given below (unless stated) are from **Kilometre 0** of the highway, which is at the junction of the North Klondike Hwy 40km east of Dawson City, almost the only way to locate things on the road.

Dempster Hwy practicalities

We've given **accommodation** options in the account below. If you're **cycling** or motorbiking – both increasingly popular ways of doing the trip – you need to be prepared for rough camping, and should call at the **Western Arctic-NWT Information Centre** on Front St in Dawson City (mid-May to mid-Sept 9am–7pm; ☏867/993-6167 or 1-800/661-0750) for invaluable practical as well as anecdotal information from the staff. If you're without your own transport you might pick up a **lift** here, or take the twelve-hour **Dempster Highway Bus Service** run by Dawson City Courier (see p.1012).

The first **fuel** is at the start of the highway at the Klondike River Lodge – the next is 365km north at the year-round *Eagle Plains Hotel* at Eagle Plains. Then it's Fort McPherson, 193km beyond Eagle Plains; thereafter there's nothing until Inuvik, so for emergencies take a jerrycan (you rent them at the *Klondike River Lodge* at the start of the highway) and make sure that you have two spare tyres and your car's mechanics are sound – the only maintenance facilities are at Eagle Plains. It's worth checking on ☏1-800/661-0752 that the two **ferry** services on the route at Peel River (539km; generally free on demand, spring to late autumn daily 9am–1am, then ice bridge) and Tsiigehtchic, formerly Arctic Red River (609km; same details) are running.

Just as important, make sure you have lots of **drinking water**: the only place you'll find any that isn't out of a stream is at Eagle Plains.

To the Arctic Circle and beyond

After the millions of lodgepole pines in this part of the world, it's almost time for a celebration when you pass what are reputedly Canada's most northerly pines (8km). Beyond them you'll see occasional trappers' cabins: the hunting of mink, wolverine and lynx is still lucrative, providing the Yukon's 700 or so full-time trappers with a $1.5-million annual income.

Some 72km north of Dawson is one of the highway's three rudimentary Yukon government campsites (shelter only), at **Tombstone Mountain** (31 RV/tent sites; $12), where, in July and August, there's usually a trailer information kiosk with details of good trails from the campsite.

At **Hart River** (80km) you may see part of the 1200-strong Hart River Woodland **caribou herd**; unlike the barren-ground herds farther north these caribou have sufficient fodder to graze one area instead of making seasonal migrations. Golden eagles and ptarmigan are also common on willow-lined streams like Blackstone River (93km), as are tundra birds like Lapland longspurs, lesser golden plovers, mew gulls and long-tailed jaegers. At Moose Lake (105km), **moose** can often be seen feeding, along with numerous species of waterfowl such as northern shoveller, American widgeon and the arctic tern, whose Arctic to Antarctic migration is the longest of any bird.

Chapman Lake (120km) marks the start of the northern **Ogilvie Mountains**, a region that has never been glaciated and so preserves numerous relic species of plant and insect, as well as providing an important early wintering range for the Porcupine Caribou Herd; as many as 40,000 caribou cross the highway in mid-October – they take four days and have right of way. The road crosses the Ogilvie Mountains at **North Fork Pass** (1289m), the highest elevation on the highway, at 139km. Unique butterfly species breed at Butterfly Ridge (155km), close to some obvious caribou trails which cross the region, and it should also be easy to spot Dall sheep, cliff swallows and bald eagles.

Beyond, the highway drops down to **Eagle Plain** and almost unparalleled access to the subarctic **tundra**, which in summer and autumn is a beautiful medley of colours, the vegetation having been coaxed to riotous life by hours of perpetual daylight. At **Engineer Creek** (194km) is another basic Yukon-government-run campsite (fifteen RV/tent sites; $12), but the only orthodox accommodation on the Dempster within YK is the 32-room **EAGLE PLAINS HOTEL** at 369km (T 867/993-2453, E eagleplains@yknet.yk.ca; ⑤; camping $12; year-round). It has fuel, a garage with mechanic, tyres, lounge and a restaurant.

The **Arctic Circle** (405km) is marked on the Dempster by a battered roadside cairn, and the occasional summer home of one of the north's premier eccentrics, one Harry Waldron, the self-proclaimed "Keeper of the Arctic Circle". In his late 60s, Harry was wont to sit in a rocking chair in a tuxedo with a glass of champagne and regale all-comers with snippets of Robert Service, facts about the Arctic and some fairly unimpeachable views on the environment. An ex-highway worker, he started his act of his own accord, but proved so popular that he was paid by the Yukon government to sit and do his spiel.

After here and a Yukon government-run campsite at **Rock River** (447km; seventeen RV sites/three tent sites; $12), the road climbs into the **Richardson Mountains** to meet the border of the NWT (465km) before the less-than-arresting flats of the Peel Plateau and Mackenzie River and the run to Inuvik. Note the **time change** at the Yukon–NWT border: NWT time is one hour ahead of Yukon time.

The tiny Gwich'in Dene village of **FORT MCPHERSON** is at 574km, or 115km south of Inuvik, soon after crossing the Peel River. Here, the lodgings amount to the *Bell River Bedrooms* (T 867/952-2465, F 867/952-2212; ④), with showers, laundry, cable TV and self-serve breakfast; and the *Tetlichi B&B* (T 867/952-2356; ④), just one double room with use of kitchen and laundry. It's essential to call ahead to check that these are still operating. Fort McPherson also has a small summer-only **visitor centre** in the log building by the monument to Dempster's "Lost Patrol". Nearby is also the unserviced NWT government **campsite**, the *Nutuiluie Territorial Campground*, 10km south of Fort McPherson (23 sites; shelter, toilets and water; $12; June–Sept). It has a small **infocentre** (daily June to early Sept).

The minuscule settlement of **TSIIGEHTCHIC** (formerly Arctic Red River), at 609km and 80km south of Inuvik, was founded as a mission in 1868 – a red-roofed mission church from 1931 still stands – acquiring a Hudson's Bay post soon after. Since 1996 it has been known by its Dene aboriginal name, which means "mouth of the red-coloured river". On the (relatively) short run on to Inuvik (see below), there's another eleven-site campsite at **VADZAIH VAN TSHIK**, at 692km ($12; water, shelter and toilets).

The Western Arctic

The **Western Arctic** region centres on the planned government-built town of **Inuvik**, embracing the mighty delta of the **Mackenzie River**, North America's second longest river, and reaching across the Beaufort Sea to the border with Nunavut, part of Victoria Island and Banks Island, the most westerly of Canada's Arctic islands. The delta ranks as one of the continent's great **bird** habitats, with swans, cranes and big raptors amongst the many hundreds of species that either nest or overfly the region during the spring and autumn migration cycles. It also offers the chance of seeing pods of **beluga whales** and other big sea mammals, while local **Inuit** guides on Banks Island should be able to lead you to possible sightings of musk ox, white fox and polar bears.

After Inuvik and the two villages on the short NWT section of the Dempster – Fort McPherson and Tsiigehtchic – the area's other four settlements are **fly-in communities** reached from Inuvik. Two of them, **Aklavik** and **Tuktoyaktuk**, are near – at least, by NWT standards – and are the places to fly out to if you want a comparatively accessible taste of aboriginal northern culture. **Sachs Harbour** (on Banks Island) and **Paulatuk** lie much farther afield, and are bases for more arduous tours into the delta and Arctic tundra. Inuvik, along with Yellowknife and Fort Smith, is one of the key centres of the accessible north, and one of the main places from which to make, take or plan tours farther afield. Two major – and several minor – **tour companies** run a wide variety of boat and plane tours to all four destinations (see box p.1030), varying from reasonably priced day-trips to full-on expeditions. Having come this far it's well worth taking one of the shorter tours to the fly-in communities for a taste of Arctic life, and to enjoy the superb bird's-eye view of the delta and surrounding country from the air.

Inuvik

INUVIK – "the place of man" – is the farthest north you can drive on a public highway in North America, unless, that is, you wait for the winter freeze and follow the ice road carved across the frozen sea to the north. Canada's first planned town north of the Arctic Circle, Inuvik is a battered spot begun in 1954 as an administrative centre to replace Aklavik, a settlement to the west wrongly thought to be doomed to envelopment by the Mackenzie's swirling waters and shifting mud flats. Finished in 1961, it's a strange melting pot of around 3000 people, with Dene, Métis and Inuvialuit living alongside the trappers, pilots, scientists and frontier entrepreneurs drawn here in the 1970s when a boom followed the oil exploration in the delta. Falling oil prices and the rising cost of exploitation, however, soon toppled the delta's vast rigs and it seems the oil is destined to remain largely untapped until well into this century. Today the local economy also relies on government jobs, services and the town's role as a supply and communication centre for much of the western Arctic.

Tours from Inuvik

Most people who come to Inuvik take a **tour** of some description, and despite the remoteness of the Northwest Territories and the isolated nature of its communities, it is remarkably simple – if occasionally rather expensive – to find **tour operators** who offer a wide range of cultural, natural history and other trips. We have listed some of the larger operators, but a full list can be found in the *Explorers' Guide to Canada's Northwest Territories* or by visiting the excellent ⊛ www.nwttravel.nt.ca. You can call for further information on ☏ 1-800/661-0788.

Inuvik's tour operators are well worth investigating, as most run a selection of similar and affordable daily boat and plane tours as well as longer full-blown tours and expeditions. **Day-trips** include tours to the tundra, to Hershel Island, to a traditional bush camp, boat tours on the Mackenzie River, beluga whale-watching and trips to Aklavik by boat or plane; **longer tours** include three- to five-day trips to Bank's Island and Sachs Harbour to watch wildlife (notably musk ox); whale-watching trips; and a nine-day Mackenzie River trip to Yellowknife. **Arctic Nature Tours** (☏ 867/777-3300 or 1-866/TOUR-TUK, ⊛ www.arcticnaturetours.com), with over forty years' experience of the region, runs excellent trips, and have a special bias towards wildlife: trips include tours to view Dall's sheep in the Richardson Mountains, Arctic safaris, Barrenlands photography tours, boat and plane trips to view the Porcupine Caribou Herd, and bird and wildlife visits to Hershel Island. Both these and other companies such as **Midnight Express** (☏ 867/777-4829) and **Western Arctic Adventures & Equipment** (☏ 867/777-2594) also offer guided and independent trips to all the fly-in communities.

Wandering the town provides an eye-opening introduction to the vagaries of northern life, from the strange stilted buildings designed to prevent their heat melting the **permafrost** (which would have disastrous effects on foundations, assuming any could be dug), to the strange pipes, or "utilidors", which snake round the streets carrying water, power and sewage lines – again, to prevent problems with permafrost (the average temperature here is a very chilly -9.7°C). There are also the all-too-visible signs of the **alcoholism** that affects this and many northern communities – a problem rarely alluded to outside them, partly because the region's aboriginal groups seem to be disproportionately afflicted: suicides here are four times the national average for groups of aboriginal people.

On a happier note, the influence of Inuvialuit people in local political and economic life has increased, to the extent that the **Western Claims Settlement Act** of 1984 saw the government cede titles to various lands in the area, returning control that had been lost to the fur trade, the church, oil companies and national government. A potent symbol of the church's local role in particular resides in the town's most-photographed building, the **Igloo Church**, or Our Lady of Victory, a rather incongruous cultural mix. It's on Mackenzie Road, the main street which runs west to east through town, but isn't always open; ask at the rectory for a glimpse inside and for the paintings of local Inuvialuit artist, Mona Thrasher. Much farther west on Mackenzie Road you might also want to take a look at the **Ingamo Hall**, a three-storey building built almost entirely from one thousand white-spruce logs brought up the Mackenzie River (local trees, such as there are, don't grow sufficiently to provide the timber required for building).

Practicalities

Flights from Whitehorse, Dawson City, Old Crow, Fairbanks and other points south (see box p.1012) operate to Inuvik's **Mike Zubko airport** (☏ 867/777-

2467), 12km south of town. Additionally, First Air (☎1-800/267-1247, ⓦwww.firstair.com) has numerous northern connections, including four flights weekly from Edmonton. Smaller local airlines also use the airport for flights to the "fly-in" communities around Inuvik (see p.1032). As elsewhere in Canada and the NWT, the cheapest way of getting to Inuvik may be to buy an Air Canada pass before arriving in Canada (see Basics, pp.35–36). When talking to airlines about onward flights to the fly-in communities or elsewhere, remember that local tour companies often use their scheduled flights, and may be able to offer better flight-only deals than the airlines; for more, see below for details of tour companies. A **taxi** run by United, 175 Mackenzie Rd (☎867/777-5050; open 24hr), to or from the airport, should cost around $25–30. If you've flown here and want to **rent a car** or truck to take you back to Dawson, then contact Norcan, 60 Franklin Rd (☎867/777-2346 or 1-877/298-1338, ⓔnorcan@permafrost.com) or Delta Auto Rentals, 25 Carn St (☎867/777-3535 or 777-4443). In summer a **bus** service operates to Inuvik from Dawson (see p.1013); the **Dempster Hwy** is open year-round except for brief periods during the November freeze and April thaw.

For information on Inuvik and the region, contact the **Western Arctic Visitor Centre** (daily: July & Aug 9am–8pm; mid-May or June to early Sept 10am–6pm; ☎867/777-4727, ⓦwww.nwttravel.nt.ca), located near the entrance to town at the eastern end of Mackenzie Road at the junction with Loucheux, a ten-minute walk from the centre. For town information, visit 2 Firth St (☎867/777-4321, ⓦwww.town.inuvik.nt.ca). For information on parks and protected areas in the region, contact Parks Canada (☎867/777-8800, ⓦwww.parkscanada.gc.ca). In town you can also dig out more background to the area and access the Internet at the **Inuvik Centennial Library** on Mackenzie Road west of the Igloo church (Mon & Fri 2–5pm, Tues–Thurs 10am–9pm; ☎867/777-2749, ⓦwww.inuvik.net/icl), and pick up **maps**, guides, books and charts at the Boreal Bookstore (☎867/777-3748), located almost opposite the church at the Arctic Tour Company office, 181 Mackenzie Rd. The **post office** is at 187 Mackenzie Rd (☎867/777-2749), and the **hospital** (☎867/777-2955) is at the eastern end of town on the Inuvik Access Rd close to the visitor centre. For the **police**, call ☎867/777-2935.

Accommodation and eating

There are three co-owned **hotels** in town, and all are almost identically pricey: the big *Eskimo Inn* (☎867/777-2801; ❻), in central downtown at 133 Mackenzie Rd; the *Finto Motor Inn* (☎867/777-2647 or 1-800/661-0843; ❻), to the east at 288 Mackenzie Rd next door to the Western Arctic Visitor Centre, with a good restaurant; and the central *Mackenzie Hotel* (☎867/777-2861; ❻) at 185 Mackenzie Rd. All are at ⓦwww.inuvikhotels.com. Two rival hotels are *Frosty's Arctic Pub & Suite Hotel*, 88 Tununuk Place (☎867/777-5194, ⓔfrostys@permafrost.com; ❺), south off Mackenzie Rd opposite Chief Koe Park and the town's baseball diamond; and *Arctic Chalet*, a set of cabins with kitchenettes 3km from town off the approach road at 25 Carn St (☎867/777-3535 or 777-4443, ⓔjudi@arcticchalet.com; ❺). There are also usually one or two B&B options in town, but these open and close with alarming regularity: check with the visitor centre for latest details. The nearest local **campsite**, the *Happy Valley*, overlooks the delta and Twin Lakes at the northwest end of town on Franklin Rd off Mackenzie Rd; the simple and peaceful *Chuk Park* (or *Juk Park*) site (☎867/777-3613; from $15; June–Oct) is quieter but 6km out of town on the way to the airport.

Eating possibilities are largely confined to hotel dining rooms, where (at a price) you can gorge on char, caribou and musk ox; the best is probably *The Peppermill* at the *Finto Motor Inn*, 288 Mackenzie Rd, followed by the *Green Briar Dining Room* (☎867/777-2414) in the *Mackenzie Hotel*, whose coffee shop is also a good place for breakfast. The *Back Room*, 108 Mackenzie Rd, is famed for its stuffed polar bear, and serves the usual steaks, fish, fries, Chinese, and won't break the bank. For the best and busiest **bar**, head for the *Zoo* in the *Mackenzie Hotel*, a gathering place for an eclectic mix of locals, backpackers and assorted out-of-towners. The *Cabin Lounge* in the *Finto* is more relaxed and cosy, and *The Mad Trapper Pub* (Mon–Fri 10am–2am) almost opposite the *Eskimo Inn* at 124 Mackenzie Rd is a locals' hangout with house bands playing country and rock and roll.

The fly-in communities

Accessible only by air except in winter, when incredible snow roads are ploughed across the frozen delta, the region's four **fly-in communities** are close to some fascinating and relatively accessible Arctic landscapes, wildlife and cultures. All are served by Inuvik-based **Aklak Air** (☎867/777-3777, ⓦwww.inuvialuit.com/aklak) or **BeauDel Air** (☎867/777-2333, ⓔbeaudel@permafrost.com). All also have simple stores, though their prices make it wise to take in at least some of your own supplies. Some have hotels, but you should be able to camp close to all four; ask permission first at the village head office. The best way to see them is with a tour company from Inuvik (see box p.1030), but even if you're going under your own steam it's still worth checking with the tour companies for discounted flight-only deals.

Aklavik

AKLAVIK (pop. 800), 50km west of Inuvik on the western bank of the Mackenzie delta, means "Place of the Barren Lands Grizzly Bear". A Hudson's Bay post aimed at the trade in muskrat fur was established here in 1918, though for generations before the region had been the home of Inuvialuit families who once traded and frequently clashed with the Gwich'in of Alaska and the Yukon. Today both live together in a town that melds modern and traditional, and whose inhabitants are proud not to have jumped ship when they were invited to leave their sinking town for Inuvik in the 1950s. Most are happy to regale you with stories of the mysterious "Mad Trapper of Rat River", a crazed drifter (supposedly a former Chicago gangster) who reputedly killed trappers for the gold in their teeth. Questions should really have been asked when he arrived in Fort McPherson and purchased – with suspiciously vast amounts of cash – unusually large numbers of guns and ammunition. He then built a cabin-cum-fortress on the delta and shot the constable sent to figure out what was going on. A seven-man posse armed with guns and fistfuls of dynamite were then forced to retreat after a fifteen-hour siege. After fleeing and shooting a Mountie, he grabbed world headlines briefly in 1931 as he managed to elude capture for forty days in the dead of a brutal winter. To this day no one knows who he was, where he came from or why he embarked on his killing spree. He was eventually shot on the Eagle River, surrounded by seventeen men and buzzed by a bomb-carrying light plane; he's buried in town in unconsecrated ground. The Hudson's Bay post is still around, together with a former mission church, now a small museum, but there's no restaurant and only one shop.

Arctic Wings and Aklak Air **flights** from Inuvik operate daily except Sunday. A one-day tour with stunning twenty-minute flight and an hour in town from one of Inuvik's big tour companies should cost around $140; for a few dollars more you can fly in and boat out, probably the best way of doing things. There's a store in town – but no restaurant – and a seven-room B&B boarding house (two shared bathrooms), *Bessie's* (☎867/978-2461; ❹). You can prepare your own meals here, or pay extra for half or full board.

Tuktoyaktuk

TUKTOYAKTUK, or simply Tuk (pop. around 1000), sits on a sandspit on the Beaufort coast about 137km north of Inuvik. It acts as a springboard for oil workers and tourists, both considered outsiders who have diluted the traditional ways of the whale-hunting Karngmalit (or Mackenzie Inuit), who have lived and hunted in small family groups on this fascinating but inhospitable shore for centuries. The settlements name means "Looks Like Caribou", as this was once a hunting ground for *tuktu*, or caribou. Half the families were wiped out in the early twentieth century by an influenza epidemic introduced by outsiders. The Hudson's Bay Company, inevitably, arrived in 1937. Many locals still hunt, fish and trap, but government, tourism and the oil business now pay most wages. This is the most popular tour outing from Inuvik, with trips starting at about $140, a sum worth paying just to enjoy the scenic low-altitude flight up here. Most casual visitors come to see pods of beluga and great bowhead whales, or to look at the world's largest concentration of **pingos**, 1400 volcano-like hills thrown up by frost heaves across the delta's otherwise treeless flats. This is among the world's largest grouping of these strange features, and includes the world's largest pingo, Ibyuk, a mound 30m high and 1.5km in circumference visible from the village.

Tuk's only **hotels** – booking is essential – are the *Hotel Tuk Inn* (☎867/977-2381; ❻), on the main street near the ocean, and the *Pingo Park Lodge* (☎867/977-2155; ❻); both have eighteen rooms and dining rooms open to nonresidents. The Northern supermarket sells groceries. You should be able to **camp** near the beach, but ask first. **Flights** from Inuvik operate daily (upwards of $200 return). Inuvik's main tour companies come out here, but if you want a local operator contact ookpik Tours & Adventures (☎867/777-3300, ☏arctic@permafrost.com) for naturalist, fishing, camping, hiking, activitiy or wildlife-watching tours in summer or winter. For further **information** on the settlement, contact the community office (☎867/977-2286).

Paulatuk and Ikahuk

PAULATUK (pop. 110), 400km east of Inuvik, is one of NWT's smallest permanent communities. Situated on a spur between the Beaufort and an inland lake, the settlement was started by the Roman Catholic Mission in 1935 as a communal focus for the semi-nomadic Karngmalit, who despite such paternalism have fought off the adverse effects of missionaries and trader-introduced alcoholism to hang on to some of their old ways. Hunting, fishing and trapping still provide their economic staples, along with handicrafts aimed at the tourists out here mainly for the chance to watch or hunt big game. Key sites for the former activity are the cliffs of the Cape Parry Bird Sanctuary and the **Tuktut National Park** on the Parry Peninsula to the west, a gathering place for the migrating Bluenose caribou herd. Local operators will take you out to both areas, and in spring run trips to look for polar bears on the Amundsen Gulf. The village's name means "place of coal", a reference to the coal seams to the northeast, where the (literally) Smoking Hills take their name from the smouldering coal ignited years ago and still burning. Aklak Air **flights** operate twice weekly from Inuvik. There is one place to **stay**: the ten rooms in the recently built *Parks Canada Visitor Centre Hotel* (℡867/580-3051 or 580-3054; ❹), with a small store and common kitchen facilities. For further **information** on the settlement, contact the General Delivery office (℡867/580-3531).

The only settlement on Bank's Island, 520km northeast of Inuvik, is **IKAHUK** ("Place Where One Crosses Over") or **SACHS HARBOUR** (pop. 150–200). It was only permanently settled in the late 1920s, and only then by just three Inuvialuit families. Today it supports a handful of self-sufficient Inuit families who survive largely by outfitting hunters and trapping musk ox for food and underfur (*qiviut*), which is spun and woven into clothes on sale locally. For generations the island has been known as one of the north's finest trapping areas, the abundance of white foxes in particular having long attracted the Inuit and other hunters. Today there's still an abundance of wildlife, including the world's largest grouping of musk ox. Five double **rooms** are available at *Kuptana's Guest House* (℡867/690-4151; ❼ including meals), with shared facilities. Ask first and you should be able to **camp** by the beach. Be warned: there is no restaurant in the town, just a small grocery store. Two Aklak Air **flights** operate from Inuvik weekly (from $350 one-way), though for a little more you can join an all-inclusive Arctic Nature Tours trip from Inuvik. For further **information** on the settlement, contact the community office (℡867/690-4351).

The Sahtu

The **Sahtu** embraces the Mackenzie River south of its delta as far as Fort Norman and the tranche of land across to and including **Great Bear Lake** to the east, the world's eighth largest lake. There's no year-round road access: you either fly in here, canoe the Mackenzie – no mean feat – or sign up with **fishing** and hunting charters that boat or fly you into the backcountry, home to some of North America's finest fishing lodges and lakes. Great Bear Lake, to name but one, holds world records for most classes of arctic char and for *every* class of lake trout going (the top trout overall – weighing in at 30kg – was caught in 1991). In 1994 a road was built to Wrigley, 225km northwest of Fort Simpson, with plans to push it through to Inuvik, but it'll be a long while before this becomes reality. In the meantime, most tours operate out of the area's nominal capital at **Norman Wells**, or its near neighbour **Tulita** (formerly Fort Norman), both on the Mackenzie in the lee of the Franklin Mountains, which separate the river and Great Bear Lake. The area has just three other lonely communities: **Fort Good Hope** on the Mackenzie north of Norman Wells; **Déline** (formerly Fort Franklin) on Great Bear Lake, a self-sufficient Dene community of hunters and trappers; and **Colville Lake**, north of Great Bear Lake, a spot which amounts to little more than a few log cabins in the woods.

For **flights**, Canadian North (℡867/587-2361 in Norman Wells or 1-800/661-1505, ⓦwww.canadiannorth.com) flies daily to Norman Wells from Inuvik, Yellowknife and Edmonton. Within the area North-Wright Air links all main communities from Norman Wells and flies to Yellowknife and Inuvik (℡867/587-2288 or 1-800/661-0702, ⓦwww.north-wrightairways.com) as well as offering sightseeing flights.

Norman Wells and Tulita

Ramshackle **NORMAN WELLS** (pop. 550) once owed its economic well-being to **oil**: the local Dene long knew this region as Le Gohlini – "where the oil is". The black gold was first noticed by an outsider as a yellow liquid seeping from the rocks by the explorer Alexander Mackenzie as early as 1789, but only rediscovered in 1919 after Dene locals had led geologists to the same spot. Production began in 1932 and was boosted during World War II when the American government sponsored the building of the **Canol Pipeline** to supply the Alaska Hwy – now long abandoned, though for a while the town continued to pump about 30,000 barrels a day through a pipeline to Zama, Alberta. At one time 160 wells pushed out 10 million barrels a year from the field. Economic disaster struck the region in 1996, when it was announced that the wells and refinery were to close. The only glimmer of hope is that the works and wells are likely to remain intact for a possible new lease of life sometime in the future. You can follow the oil and Canol story in the **Norman Wells Historical Centre** (July–Aug daily 10am–10pm, but check current opening; ℡867/587-2415), filled with photographs, modest displays and oddments of memorabilia. Alongside, the settlement's uniquely ecumenical **church** does double duty: Catholics sit on one side, Protestants on the other. These days the Canol's old route is becoming an increasingly popular **long-distance footpath**, a tough three- or four-week 372-kilometre wilderness trail from Norman Wells to the Canol Road above Ross River in the Yukon. Logistics are a problem, but if you want one of the world's tougher treks, this one's up there with the toughest. The mountains east of the town contain some of the NWT's bleaker and more spectacular ranges, but good outdoor skills are a must unless you sign up for a tour.

The **airport** is a twenty-minute walk from the centre of the village, which runs to a bank, post office, a trio of motels, supermarket and plenty of tumbledown housing. The local **visitor centre** is on the corner of Forestry Road and Mackenzie Drive (℡867/587-2054). There are three **hotels** in town: the *Mackenzie Valley Hotel* (℡867/587-2511, ✉jhan68@hotmail.com; ⑤), the *Yamouri Inn* (℡867/587-2744 or 1-800/661-0841; ⑥) and the *Rayuka Inn* (℡867/587-2354, ✉rayukainn@nt.sympatico.ca; ⑤). A touch cheaper is the intermittently open (call first) *Log Home B&B*, 5km out of town, with a 160-kilometre view from its front porch and weekly and monthly room deals (℡867/587-2784; ④). If you want to spend time on the river, try Mountain River Outfitters (℡867/587-2698, ⓦwww.mountainriver.nt.ca), which runs **day-trips** to Fort Good Hope and the Arctic Circle (mid-June to mid-Sept), provides support for hikers on the Canol trail and also **rents canoes** and other outdoor equipment. For details of the many fishing-charter companies, enquire locally or obtain the *Explorers' Guide* (see box p.976) from Canadian national tourist offices before you leave home.

TULITA (pop. 300), formerly known as Fort Norman, some 60km to the south, owes its long history to a strategic position at the junction of the Mackenzie and Great Bear rivers (its Dene name means "where the two rivers meet"). Long a Dene aboriginal settlement, it first acquired a trading post in 1810. Today it's an ethnically mixed community that looks to trapping and fishing for its livelihood: many houses have tepees out back for drying and smoking fish. It boasts just a riverfront mid-nineteenth-century church and old Hudson's Bay Company post as "attractions". Most visitors use the settlement to outfit canoe and boat trips downstream to Norman Wells or the Great Bear Lake, the latter lying 128km away on the easily navigable **Great Bear River**, a popular canoe trip with one simple portage. The four-room *Two Rivers Hotel* (℡867/588-3320; ⑥) is the only accommodation base; reservations are essential and meals can be arranged.

Nahanni-Ram

The **Nahanni-Ram**, or Deh Cho, area in the southwestern corner of the NWT centres on **Fort Simpson**, which is accessible by two long gravel roads: from the west, the **Liard Hwy** follows the Liard Valley from close to Fort Nelson, BC on the Alaska Hwy; from the east, the **Mackenzie Hwy** follows the Mackenzie Valley from close to Fort Providence and Hay River. Both roads offer drives through a fairly mundane wilderness of boreal forest and muskeg bog, but neither penetrates beyond Fort Simpson to offer ordinary travellers access to the **Nahanni National Park**, the area's jewel (see box below).

Fort Simpson

All means of access and facilities – including tour operators and outfitters – for the Nahanni National Park reside in busy **FORT SIMPSON** (pop. 1000), a

Nahanni National Park

With gorges deeper than the Grand Canyon and waterfalls twice the height of Niagara, the vast **Nahanni National Park** ranks as one of the finest national parks in North America and one of the most rugged wilderness areas anywhere in the world. Located close to the Yukon border in the heart of the Mackenzie Mountains, it surrounds the **South Nahanni River**, a renowned 322-kilometre stretch of water whose white-water torrents, pristine mountains and 1200-metre-deep canyons have attracted the world's most eminent explorers and the ultimate thrill-seeking canoeists (the river ranks as one of the best white-water runs in the world). Unless you fit one of these categories, however, or can afford to fork out for **guided trips** by boat or sightseeing by air – well worth the money, even if you're only out in the wilderness for a short time – there's no way of getting close to the best areas, even by backpacking: the park is totally roadless and totally wild. Also note that the popularity of trips means that a **reservation** and **fee** system have been instigated for people wishing to use the river: the day-use fee is $10 and there are strict quotas on numbers visiting the park, so check the latest details whether you intend to visit independently or with a tour. For full information, contact the **Nahanni National Park Reserve Office** (☎867/695-2310 or 695-3151) or visitor centre in Fort Simpson.

As for **tours**, the sky's the limit, and you should be able to organize just about any sort and length of trip into the National Park or elsewhere. Operators in Fort Simpson cater to all levels of demand, from day-trippers wanting air tours of the big set-pieces to self-contained canoeists and walkers off on month-long expeditions who require no more than a drop-off or pick-up by air. Even self-sufficient explorers should note that it can still save considerable time, hassle and money to take a three- or four-week tour with a licensed outfitter in Fort Simpson.

For day-trips to the spectacular **Virginia Falls**, one of the most popular day outings in the park (usually with 2 or 3hr on the ground), contact Deh Cho Air (☎867/770-4103) based in Fort Liard, which also rents canoes, plans fishing charters and organizes all manner of other flights and canoe or hiking drop-offs and pick-ups. For trips on the rivers, including day-trips and overnight trips or trips by traditional wooden scows (aboriginal canoes), contact North Nahanni River Tours (☎867/695-2116 or 1-888/880-6665, ⌨www.nnnlodge.com). Another outfit that caters to day and half-day visitors wanting to sightsee in the National Park is Nahanni Mountain Lodge (☎867/695-2505, ℱ695-2925). Most of the town's other operators offer full-scale expeditions that run into thousands of dollars; full details are available in Fort Simpson or from the *Explorers' Guide* (see p.976), which you can obtain from national tourist offices before you leave.

perfect base 150km to the east at the confluence of the Liard and Mackenzie, two of North America's greatest rivers. This spot has been inhabited for 9000 years by the Slavey peoples and their ancestors, making this the longest continually inhabited region in the NWT. The North West Company established a fur post here in 1804 at the so-called "Fort of the Forks" (after the river junction). This was renamed Fort Simpson in 1821, but the settlement became as important as much for its role as a staging point for supply boats using the Mackenzie as for its fur-trading potential. Later the inevitable missions arrived – in 1858 and 1894 – so often the bane of indigenous communities. Latterly the area has been an important base for oil exploration projects up and down the Mackenzie, a major regional administrative centre, and a bustling summer base for visitors renting camping equipment or booking onto tours and charter flights to the interior. Most of what you want in town is situated along the main street, **100th Street**, effectively a continuation of the main road through the town. Before this highway was built the main street was the almost parallel Mackenzie Drive on the lake waterfront, at the southern end of which you'll find the site of the old Hudson's Bay Company post and an area known as the "Flat" or the Papal Grounds, the latter an area whose tepee and other development dates from the papal visit here on September 20, 1987 (this area was inhabited until disastrous floods in 1963). A light plane and float-plane airstrip lies just to the northwest of the downtown area, while the bulk of the outfitters' offices are gathered north of the strip at the top of Mackenzie Drive.

You can get to Fort Simpson by **bus** using Frontier Coachlines (☎867/874-2566), which currently runs once weekly between Hay River, Fort Simpson and Yellowknife. By **air** you need to take a connecting flight from Yellowknife with Buffalo Airways (☎867/873-3333 or 1-877/269-8299, ⓦwww .buffaloairways.com) or use links from other Canadian cities and northern centres provided by First Air (☎613/839-3340 or 1-800/267-1247, ⓦwww .firstair.ca) or Air Tindi (☎867/669-8260, ⓦwww.airtindi.com). The **airport** is 12km south of town. The **visitor centre** (May–Sept daily 9am–6pm, July & Aug until 9pm; ☎867/695-3182, off-season ☎867/695-2253, ⓦwww .fortsimpson.com) lies at the south entrance to town close to the intersection of 100th St with Antoine Drive and 93rd Ave (which leads to the Papal Grounds). There are also summer **infocentres** at Fort Liard (☎867/770-4141) and Wrigley (☎867/581-3321).

If you're hoping to **stay** in town, be sure to book ahead. In town there are three major hotels on or just off 100th St. The more northerly, on the junction with 101st Ave, is the 29-room *Nahanni Inn* (☎867/695-2201, ⓔnahanmar @cancom.net; ❻), which also has a coffee shop and dining room; a couple of blocks south is the smaller *Maroda Motel* (☎867/695-2602; ❻), half of whose units have fully equipped kitchenettes. Finally, there's the even smaller seven-room *Bannockland Inn* (☎867/695-3337, ⓔbannockl@cancom.net; ❺). To **eat**, try the dining room of the *Nahanni Inn*, or the *Sub-Arctic* opposite the visitor centre. The local **campsite** is just to the southwest of the Papal Grounds with lots of space, showers and firewood, charging $15 nightly for tent sites, $20 for electrical hook-ups.

South Slave

The **South Slave** region covers the country, stretching north from Alberta to the south shore of the Great Slave Lake, and embraces several rivers, including large parts of the Mackenzie and Slave watersheds, and several of the territories' most accessible towns. **Hay River**, near the head of the Mackenzie Hwy from Alberta, is the area's hub and provides a gateway both to the **Great Slave Lake**, the third largest in North America, and to Fort Smith and the upper reaches of the mainly Albertan Wood Buffalo National Park. Unless you're headed for the park, however, or are prepared to drive east to **Fort Resolution** to see one of the most southerly examples of living Dene culture, most of this region and its seemingly limitless ridges of boreal forest is not the most rewarding zone of the north for scenery. However, if you do want to explore, it's relatively easy to get around under your own steam: Greyhound **buses** run to Hay River (Sun–Fri) – contact the Greyhound office in Hay River ☎867/874-6966 or 1-800/661-8747 (🌐www.greyhound.ca). Here they connect three times weekly with Frontier Coachlines, 16 102nd St (☎867/874-2566), which runs buses to Fort Providence, Yellowknife and connections to Fort Smith.

Hay River

HAY RIVER (pop. 3100) is a typical no-nonsense northern town designed for practicalities rather than sightseeing self-indulgence. Long a strategic site, it's been inhabited for thousands of years by Slavey Dene people attracted by its position on Great Slave Lake at the mouth of the Hay River. White settlers had put it on the map by 1854, but the inevitable Hudson's Bay Company trading post arrived only in 1868, and it wasn't until recently – with the completion of the Mackenzie Hwy, oil and gas exploration, and the arrival of a railway to carry zinc ore from local mines – that the town became an important transport centre. It's now also one of the most important **ports** in the north, shipping freight up the Mackenzie in huge barges to provide a precarious lifeline for High Arctic communities as far away as Inuvik and Tuktoyaktuk. If you're stuck in town, the best way to kill time is to wander the wharves where piles of supplies compete for space with tugs, barges, huge dredges and the town's big fishing fleet.

The town divides into the New Town on the west bank of the Hay River – home to most of the motels, restaurants and key buildings – and the somewhat moribund Vale Island across a bridge to the north; in the latter, which centres on Mackenzie Drive, you'll find the wharves, airport, the remnants of the old town (badly damaged by flooding in 1963), the campsite and a series of passable and popular **beaches** (the last a total of 7km from the centre of New Town). The best sand is near the campsite on the northeast side of the island at the end of 106th Avenue. The **bus depot** is on the right immediately over the bridge: cross back over for the New Town.

The **visitor centre** (mid-May to mid-Sept daily 9am–9pm; ☎867/874-3180) is on Hwy 2 south of the New Town centre on the corner with McBryan Drive. There's ample **accommodation**, much of it less expensive than elsewhere in the north. Most reasonable is the pretty downbeat ten-room *Cedar Rest Motel* (☎867/874-3732; ❸) on the main Hwy 2 south of the New Town downtown area (rooms have kitchenettes). Just north of downtown, on the right between New Town and the Vale Island bridge, is the *Migrator Hotel* (☎867/874-6792; ❹), five minutes' walk from the town centre. The best if you want comfort after a long haul is the downtown *Ptarmigan Inn*, 10 J. Gagnier St (☎867/874-6781 or 1-800/661-0842, 🌐www.ptarmiganinn.com; ❺); the **restaurant** here, *The Keys*, is popular. You can **camp** near the beach on Vale Island at the *Hay River Campground* ($15; mid-May to mid-Sept) or to the south of the New Town off Hwy 2 at the private *Paradise Gardens Campground* (☎867/874-4422; $10).

North Slave

The **North Slave** region is the broad sweep of lake-spotted barren land between the Great Slave and Great Bear lakes, and is largely the playground of canoeists and naturalists, or of hunters on the trail of the region's 400,000-strong herd of caribou. At its heart lies **Yellowknife**, Canada's most northerly big town and until 1999 the capital of the NWT (see also "Nunavut", p.1041). Despite its surreal inappropriateness in a region of virtual wilderness, it's not worth making a special trip to see – though you may find yourself passing through, as it's the main transport hub for movement throughout the territories.

Yellowknife

Nothing about **YELLOWKNIFE** – named after the copper knives of Slavey aboriginal people – can hide the fact that it's a city that shouldn't really be here. Its high-rise core of offices and government buildings exists to administer the NWT and support a workforce whose service needs to keep a population of some 18,500 occupied in a region whose resources – despite the recent discovery of diamonds to the north – should by rights support only a small town. Even the Hudson's Bay Company closed its trading post here as early as 1823 on the grounds of economics and except, for traces of gold found by prospectors on the way to the Klondike in 1898, the spot was a forgotten backwater until the advent of commercial gold and uranium mining in the 1930s. This prompted the growth of the **Old Town** on an island and rocky peninsula on Great Slave Lake, and then in 1947 the **New Town** on the sandy plain behind it. In 1967, the year a road to the outside world was completed (Edmonton is 1524km away by car), Yellowknife replaced Ottawa as the seat of government for the NWT. Oiled by bureaucratic profligacy and the odd gold mine, the city has blossomed ever since, if that's the word for so dispersed and unprepossessing a place. Today, the chances are you'll only be here en route for somewhere else, for this is the hub of many airline routes across the NWT and parts of Nunavut.

Arrival, information and accommodation

There are regular Canadian North and NWT Air **flights** from all major Canadian cities, as well as numerous smaller airline connections from most NWT destinations. Yellowknife's **airport** is 5km west of the city on Hwy 3. **Car rental** companies at or near the airport include Budget, 20 Old Airport Rd (☎867/920-2776); elsewhere try National, downtown at 5118-50th St (☎867/873-3424). **Taxis** to downtown from the airport cost around $14: call City Cab (☎867/873-4444) or Diamond (☎867/873-6666). Three **buses** run weekly by Frontier Coachlines (☎867/874-2556) shuttle from Hay River via Fort Smith (around $90 one-way).

The **Northern Frontier Regional Visitors Centre** is on the edge of Frame Lake just north of the Northern Heritage Centre at 4807 49th St (June to Aug daily 8.30am–6pm; rest of year Mon–Fri 9am–5pm, Sat & Sun noon–4/5pm; ☎867/873-4262 or 1-877/881-4262, ⓦwww.northernfrontier.com). The **post office** is at 4902 50th St and the **Stanton Regional Hospital** is off Old Airport Road at Range Lake Road (☎867/920-4111). For the **police**, call ☎867/669-1111. To rent camping gear, canoes, snowmobiles, fishing tackle and other **outdoor equipment**, contact Narwhal Northern Adventures, 101 5103-51st Ave (☎867/873-6443, Ⓔnarwal@ssimicro.com), canoe-trip and rental experts for over 25 years. The visitors centre has **bike rentals** (June–Aug only; $5/hr, $12/half-day, $20/day). Yellowknife is, along with Inuvik and Fort Smith, the headquarters of most of the far north's **outfitters and tour operators**. Many outfits run fishing, wildlife, Arctic sightseeing, canoeing, kayaking, boating and other trips, most ranging from one- or two-day outings up to full-blown three-week mini-expeditions to unimaginably wild areas. You'll find a comprehensive listing in the *Explorers' Guide* brochure (see p.976), which should be obtainable from national tourist offices before you go. If you decide you want adventure on the spur of the moment, contact the regional visitors centre.

Hotels in the city have plenty of rooms, but prices are high, and it can be worth looking up one of the dozen or so **B&Bs** if you're on a tight budget: try the three-room *Back Bay Boat B&B* at Ingraham drive on the shore of Back Bay in the Old Town (☎867/873-4080, ✉backbay@canada.com; ❸); the lakeshore *Captain Ron's B&B* near the *Wildcat Café*, also in the Old Town at 8 Lessard Drive (☎867/873-3746; ❸); or the *Blue Raven B&B*, 37b Otto Drive (☎867/873-6328, ✉tmacfoto@internorth.com; ❹). The *Igloo Inn*, 4115 Franklin Ave between the Old Town and downtown (☎867/873-8511 or 873-5547, ✉iglooin@internorth.com; ❹), is the cheapest of the **hotels** proper – pay a bit more and you can have a kitchenette – closely followed by the downtown *Northern Lites Motel* (☎867/873-6023; ❹). If you want something more salubrious try the simply appointed *Discovery Inn*, 4701 Franklin Ave (☎867/873-4151, ✉discovery2@arcticdata.nt.ca; ❻); the facility-laden and smart high-rise *Regency Explorer*, 49th Ave and 48th St (☎867/873-3531 or 1-800/661-0892, ⊕www.explorerhotel.nt.ca; ❻); or the swish *Yellowknife Inn*, downtown at 50th St and 49th St (☎867/873-2601 or 1-800/661-0580, ⊕www.yellowknifeinn.com; ❻). The only **campsite** is the fully serviced *Fred Henne Territorial Park* (☎867/920-2472; $13) by Long Lake off Hwy 3 north of the airport. Trails run to town from here via Frame Lake: allow about an hour – or you can follow the Prospectors' Trail north from the site, a good way to get a taste of the wilderness that encircles Yellowknife.

The City

Visitors are steered carefully down the main street, Franklin Avenue (50th Ave), and the long hill from the New Town to quaint Old Town cabins such as the still-operating **Wildcat Café**, 3904 Wiley Rd (June–Sept daily), an atmospheric and endlessly busy little café opened in 1937. Elsewhere the old town is a shakedown of pitted and buckled roads (the result of permafrost) and a few quaintly battered buildings on the aptly named Ragged Ass Road and Willow Road. These are more or less the only remnants of the old times – though if you venture to the outskirts you'll find shanty settlements and scenes of poverty that take the lustre off the high-rises of the city centre. This lends some irony to one of the city's promotional tags – "Where Yesterday Rubs Shoulders with Tomorrow" – coined to underline the city's undeniably striking juxtaposition of the old and new.

Just west of New Town's core lies the **Prince of Wales Northern Heritage Centre** (June to early Sept 10.30am–5.30pm; rest of year Tues–Fri 10.30am–5pm, Sat & Sun noon–5pm; free), three blocks from downtown on Frame Lake. Yellowknife's key sight, the modern centre peddles a more sanitized view of northern history and aboriginal culture than is on offer in parts of the Old Town, offering extensive displays of northern artefacts, Inuit carvings and persuasive dioramas of local wildlife and habitats. Shops around town also sell a variety of northern aboriginal crafts, still expensive, but cheaper than you'll find in southerly cities; most are beautiful products of a living culture – even if the culture is not at its healthiest in the city itself. The centre's South Gallery deals with displays on aboriginal people, the North Gallery with life in the north after the arrival of Europeans; there's also an Aviation Gallery, devoted to the planes and pilots who for years played (and play) a vital part in keeping the north alive. The centre also houses the NWT Archives, a collection of maps, books, photographs and documents devoted to the region. Just northwest of the centre, also on Frame Lake, stands the $25-million **Northwest Territories Legislative Assembly**, opened in 1993 to house the Territories' 24-strong Legislative Assembly. It's an impressive piece of architecture, much of it open to public view (tours June–Aug Mon–Fri 10.30am, 1.30pm & 3.30pm, Sun 1.30pm; rest of year Mon–Fri 10.30am; free).

Otherwise the only thing to do close to town is walk the trails around Frame Lake and from the campsite on Long Lake (see above). Or you can drive out on the **Ingraham Trail**, an 81-kilometre highway that was to be the start of a major NWT "Road to Resources" but which was abandoned in the 1960s. There are plenty of boat launches, picnic sites and campsites en route, as well as short walking trails like the **Cameron River Falls** (48km from Yellowknife) and lakeside beaches where the hardier of the city's population brave the water.

Eating, drinking and festivals

For **food**, join the locals and curious sightseers in the Old Town's *Wildcat Café*, 3904 Wiley Rd (see above). For a more unusual treat, head for *Office*, 4915 50th St (T867/873-3750), a fine place to sample northern specialities such as Arctic char. The excellent café-restaurant at the Prince of Wales Northern Heritage Centre also offers northern dishes, along with more conventional Italian cooking. Most of the hotels have good dining rooms and much of the **nightlife** revolves around their lounges, notably the plush nightclub at the *Explorer* – though you'll meet far more interesting and dubious types at the rough and raucous *Gold Range Hotel*, 5010 50th St. This is one of the greatest northern **bars**, and claims to sell the second-largest amount of beer per customer of any bar in Canada. For a gentle drink, the *Black Knight Pub* at 4910 49th St, is a popular spot and has great range of malts.

You'll also have an interesting time if you can contrive to be in town during one of Yellowknife's **festivals**; one of the most intriguing (check it's still running) is the **Caribou Carnival** in March, whose attractions include dog-sled racing, bingo on ice, igloo building, flour packing and – best of all – "ugliest truck" competitions. **Raven Mad Daze**, a midsummer celebration taking place each June 21, is celebrated with lots of street events, drinking and high spirits through 24 hours of daylight. More cerebral and fascinating is **Folk on the Rocks** (3rd weekend of July), when folk singers from across Canada and the US meet Inuit and Dene folk singers, folk dancers and the famous Inuit "throat singers" in an amazing medley of world music.

Nunavut

Home to only around 26,500 people, **Nunavut** (meaning "Our Land" in the **Inuit** language) covers almost two million square kilometres – a fifth of Canada's land surface and an area five times the size of California, stretching west from Hudson Bay then north through the great "Barrenlands" of the interior to the Arctic islands in the north. From its western edge to the tip of Baffin

Island in the east is 2000km (the distance from Washington DC to Denver). From north to south it's even farther – 2500km, or the distance from London to Moscow.

Long an amorphous political entity administered not as a semi-autonomous province but by the federal government, the Northwest Territories was formally superseded on April 1, 1999 by a land treaty which divided the old territories in two and created a new central and eastern Arctic territory termed Nunavut. A preliminary division took place as far back as January 1, 1996 (the talking had been going on for decades), and Nunavut is now firmly established as a political and physical entity. The new land deal – the largest in Canadian history – gave their homeland (valued at $1.15 billion) back to the Inuit, who in return renounced their claim to the remainder of the NWT. The deal followed fifteen years of low-profile but effective negotiating and campaigning.

This is the land of vast caribou migrations, musk ox, polar bears and endless empty horizons of fish-filled lakes and rivers. Most of the region's communities are formed of indigenous Inuit people and lie on the arc of Hudson Bay's western coast, from **Arviat** in the south through **Whale Cove** (Tikirarjuaq, "long point"), **Rankin Inlet** (Kangiqtinq, "deep bay") – the area's main transport and administrative centre – to **Chesterfield Inlet** (Igluligaarjuk, "place with a few igloos") and **Coral Harbour** (Salliq, "large flat island") in the north. In all of these you will find an almost unchanged way of life; the local arts and handicrafts are outstanding, and in places you can hear the old drummers and "throat singers" traditionally responsible for handing down the stories and myths of the Inuit. The entire region has just 21km of highway, with the capital at **Iqaluit** on Baffin Island home to nearly one-fifth of the province's population.

Exploring this region is hugely rewarding, but far from easy. The landscapes are sublime – huge expanses of flower-filled tundra, ice fields, open sea, frozen sea, deep valleys and beautiful vast horizons – but often inhospitable. Access is invariably by plane and therefore expensive, and often the best way to see the region, whatever your chosen interest or activity, is with a tour company (of which there are many). Besides breathtaking landscapes, there's also wildlife, fishing, whale-watching and a plethora of often exotic or high-adventure outdoor activities, not to mention a wide spectrum of cultural interests – anything from Inuit printmakers and carvers to traditional drummers and "throat" singers.

The region's major centres are covered below, but it's as well to know **flight details** and where **accommodation** is available in the smaller communities. Note that **hotel prices** in the north are invariably per person, not per room, so double all rates if you are two people sharing a double room. Rates sometimes include meals, so are not as steep as they first appear.

Kangiqtinq (Rankin Inlet) and around

Although you'll find an old way of life and sublime Arctic scenery in the region, don't expect much in the way of prettiness in the villages:

For comprehensive **information**, Nunavut puts out its own heavyweight visitors' guide, the annual *Canada's Arctic Nunavut Travel Planner* (free), an essential accessory to any visit, full of all the information you are likely to need for casual visits or fully fledged expeditions with tour operators and outfitters (all of whom are listed). Information is also available at ☏1-866/NUNAVUT, ⓦwww .nunavuttourism.com.

communities are often poor, roads pitted, houses strung out and battered, and the streets festooned with telephone and electric cables. The region currently has just one paved road – from the airport at **KANGIQTINQ** (pop. 2189) to the settlement's "downtown". And remember that villages often aren't communities at all in the accepted sense: Rankin Inlet, for example, was only founded in 1955 when the North Rankin Nickel Mine opened. Three years later the government, shocked at conditions of local Inuit, "moved" people here from their nomadic homes in the wilderness; the resulting settlement, **Itivia** (now all but vanished), 1km from Rankin, was a disaster, that was made worse by the closure of the nickel mine in 1962. Only a craft-producing initiative and recent tourism saved the day. Things to see and do include trails, fishing and bird-watching in the Ijiraliq (Meliadine) river valley 5km from the settlement, and a Thule site with stone tent rings, meat caches, kayak racks and underground winter houses.

First Air (☎1-800/267-1247, ⓦwww.firstair.ca) has direct **flights** to Rankin Inlet from Iqaluit via Coral Harbour and connecting services from Ottawa and Montréal via Iqaluit on Baffin Island. Calm Air (☎1-800/839-2256, ⓦwww.calmair.com) flies scheduled services from Churchill in Manitoba to Rankin Inlet and most other Keewatin villages. Outfitters and small charter firms here and in all the communities are available to fly or guide you into the interior or out into Hudson Bay for fishing and naturalist trips. Rankin Inlet boasts the small regional **Kivalliq Regional Visitor Centre**, housed at the airport, and a post office at the 65-room *Siniktarvik Hotel & Conference Centre* (☎867/645-2807; ❼ per person). The only other accommodation is *Tara's Bed & Breakfast* (☎867/645-3478, ⓔtarasbb@arctic.ca; ⓖ per person).

Coral Harbour or **SALLIQ** ("a large flat island in front of the mainland"; pop. 759) is the only settlement on Southampton Island and one of the best places to see walrus (on nearby Goats Island), as well as the beautiful Kirchoffer Falls and Thule archeological sites at "Native Point". To stay, it has the small *Leonie's Place* (☎867/925-9751 or 925-8810, ⓕ925-8606; ❼ per person with all meals) or the occasionally open (call to check) *Esungark Hotel* at the Katudgevik Co-op (☎867/925-9926 or 925-9969, ⓕ925-8308; ❼ per person). There are **flights** here on Calm Air three times weekly, and on First Air once weekly, from Iqaluit via Rankin Inlet.

ARVIAT (pop. 1676), 240km southwest of Rankin Inlet (connected by daily Calm Air flights from Rankin Inlet), means the "place of the bowhead whale" and is particularly known for its crafts and the McConnell River Migratory Bird Sanctuary, home to thousands of nesting waterfowl. For more information on the community call the summer-only Margaret Aniksak Visitors' Centre (☎867/857-2698). The settlement's **accommodation** comprises the *Padlei Inns North* (☎867/857-2919, ⓦwww.innsnorth.com or ⓦwww.arviathotel .com; ❼ per person) and *The Bayside B&B* (☎867/857-2653, ⓔbayside2@attcanada.ca; ❼); rates at the latter include three meals a day, though a kitchen facility is available.

At Whale Cove or **TIKIRARJUAQ** ("long point"; pop. 331), a traditional hunting, crafts and fishing community 80km south of Rankin Inlet, there's the six-room *Issatik Hotel Inns North* (☎867/896-9956 or 1-888-866-6784, ⓦwww.innsnorth.com or ⓦwww.whalecovehotel.com; ❼ per person with all meals). The similar Chesterfield Inlet, or **IGLULIGAARJUK** ("place with a few igloos"; pop. 364), is the oldest settlement in the region; it has daily flights from Rankin Inlet to the south, and one hotel, the *Tangmavik* (☎867/898-9190 or 1-888/866-6784, ⓦwww.innsnorth.com or ⓦwww.chesterfieldinlet .com; ❼ per person with all meals).

The Inuit

"They be like to Tartars, with long blacke haire, broad faces, and flatte noses, and tawnie in colour, wearing Seale skinnes... The women are marked in the faces with blewe streakes downe the cheekes, and round about the eies."
An officer on Frobisher's 1576 search for the Northwest Passage

Distinct from all other Canadian aboriginal peoples by virtue of their culture, language and Asiatic physical features, the **Inuit** are the dominant people of a **territory** that extends all the way from northern Alaska to Greenland. Nowadays increasingly confined to reserves, they once led a **nomadic** existence in one of the most hostile environments on earth, dwelling in domed **igloos** during the winter and **skin tents** in the summer, and moving around using **kayaks** (*umiaks*) or **dog sleds** (*komatik*). The latter were examples of typical Inuit adaptability – the runners were sometimes made from frozen fish wrapped in sealskin and, in the absence of wood, caribou bones were used for crossbars.

Their prey – caribou, musk ox, seals, walruses, narwhals, beluga whales, polar bears, birds and fish – provided oil for heating and cooking, hides for clothing and tents, harpoon lines, ivory and dog harnesses. Using harpoons, bows and arrows and spears, ingenious hunting methods were devised; to catch caribou, for example, huge **inuksuits**, piles of rocks resembling the human form, were used to steer the herd into a line of armed hunters.

The Inuit **diet** was composed totally of flesh, and every part of the animal was eaten, usually raw, from the eyeballs to the heart. Delicacies included the plaited and dried intestines of seals and whole sealskins stuffed with small birds and left to putrefy until the contents had turned to the consistency of cheese. All food was shared and the successful hunter had to watch his catch being distributed amongst other families in the group, in accordance with specific relationships, before his own kin were allowed the smallest portion. **Starvation** was common – it was not unusual for whole villages to perish in the winter – and consequently **infanticide**, particularly of females, was employed to keep population sizes down. Elderly people who could not keep up with the travelling group were abandoned, a fate that also befell some offenders against the social code, though the usual way of resolving conflict was the **song-duel**, whereby the aggrieved would publicly ridicule the behaviour of the other, who was expected to accept the insults with good grace.

Making **clothes**, most often of caribou hide, was a task assigned to women and was as essential to survival as a man's ability to hunt. Older women also **tattooed** the faces of the younger ones by threading a sinew darkened with soot through the face to make lines that radiated from the nose and mouth. Women were usually betrothed at birth and married at puberty, and both polygamy and polyandry were frequent – though female infanticide made it rare for a man to have more than two spouses.

Qamanit'uaq (Baker Lake)

Some 260km west of Rankin Inlet at the mouth of the Thelon River lies **QAMANIT'UAQ** (formerly Baker Lake; pop. 1453), the Arctic's only inland Inuit community (*Qamanit'uaq* means "far inland" or "huge widening of a river"), which marks both Canada's geographic centre – it has long been a meeting place for members of different Inuit groups – and provides a point of access into the **tundra** that characterizes the vastness of the region. This is a subtle landscape that's worth more than its "Barrenland" label suggests, particularly in summer, when the thaw brings to life thousands of tiny streams and lakes, and some three hundred species of wild flowers amidst the lichens and grasses that provide fodder for huge herds of musk ox and caribou. Millions of

Communion with supernatural spirits was maintained by a **shaman** or *angakok*, who was often a woman, and the deity who features most regularly in Inuit myth is a goddess called **Sedna**, who was mutilated by her father. Her severed fingers became seals and walruses and her hands became whales, while Sedna lived on as the mother and protector of all sea life, capable of withholding her bounty if strict taboos were not adhered to. These taboos included keeping land and sea products totally separate – and so seals could never be eaten with caribou and all caribou clothing had to be made before the winter seal hunt.

Sporadic **European contact** dates back to the Norse settlement of Greenland, and some Inuit were visited by early missionaries, but it wasn't until the early nineteenth century that the two cultures met in earnest. By 1860 commercial **whalers** had begun wintering around the north of Hudson Bay, employing Inuit as crew and hunters for their food in return for European goods. Even then, the impact on the Inuit was not really deleterious until the arrival of **American whalers** in Canadian waters in 1890, when the liberal dispensing of alcohol and diseases such as smallpox and VD led to a drastic decline in population.

By the early decades of the twentieth century **fur traders** were encouraging the Inuit to stop hunting off the coast and turn inland using firearms and traps. The accompanying **missionaries** brought welcome medical help and schools, but put an end to multiple marriages, shamanism and other traditional practices. More changes came when Inuit were employed to build roads, airfields and other military facilities during World War II and to construct the line of radar installations known as Distant Early Warning during the Cold War era. As well as bringing new jobs, this also focused government attention on the plight of the Inuit.

The consequent largesse was not wholly beneficial: subsidized housing and welfare payments led many Inuit to abandon their hunting camps and settle in **permanent communities**, usually located in places strategic to Canada's sovereignty in the Arctic. Without knowledge of the English and French languages, these Inuit were left out of all decision-making and often lived in a totally separate part of towns that were administered by outsiders. Old values and beliefs were all but eroded by television and radio, and high levels of depression, alcoholism and violence became the norm. The 1982 ban on European imports of sealskins created mass **unemployment**, and although hunting still provides the basics of subsistence, the high cost of ammunition and fuel makes commercial-scale hunting uneconomical.

All is not gloom, however. Inuit co-operatives are increasingly successful and the production of **soapstone carvings** – admittedly a commercial adulteration of traditional Inuit ivory art – is very profitable. Having organized themselves into politically active groups and secured such **land claims** as Nunavut, the Inuit are slowly rebuilding an ancient culture that was shattered in under half a century.

wildfowl can also be seen, and the huge skies and flat horizons are also one of the best places in Canada to see the **aurora borealis** (see box p.974). Also be sure to take in the **Inuit Camp,** which includes a demonstration by Inuit families of the activities, such as hunting, trapping and weaving, that might have taken place in a Caribou Inuit camp.

Calm Air has daily flights here from Rankin Inlet. For **accommodation** there's the *Iglu Hotel* (☎867/793-2801, ⓦwww.innsnorth.com & ⓦwww.bakerlakehotel.com; ❼ per person with all meals); the *Baker Lake Lodge* (☎867/793-2905; ❺ per person), a group of rooms and cabins sleeping a total of twenty (call and they will pick you up from the airport); and *Nunamuit Lodge* (☎867/793-2127; ❻), an Inuit-owned lodge sleeping fourteen with pretty lake views. There's also a small community campsite for campers. The summer-only Akumalik **visitors' centre** (☎867/793-2456) occupies a reconstructed 1936 Hudson's Bay Company post in the original building, successor to the 1916 post that originally brought about the settlement's development. There is also an **Inuit Heritage Centre** (July & Aug Mon–Fri 9am–noon & 1–5pm; ☎867/793-2598).

The Arctic Coast

Canada's last frontier, the **Arctic Coast** encompasses the country's northern mainland coast from the Mackenzie to Baffin Island, and – as "coast" is a relative term in a region where the sea is often frozen – numerous islands too, most notably a large part of Victoria Island. It is barren, ice-carved country, comprising a wind-scoured landscape of chill lakes and low hills with not a tree to be seen: it's also nearly completely dark and frozen for nine months of the year, yet still boasts a permanent population of a few hundred. It is home to **Inuit** (see box p.1044) who as recently as fifty years ago had known little or no

The Northwest Passage

Traversed in its entirety fewer than fifty times, the fabled **Northwest Passage** around the American continent exerts a continuing romantic allure – and, in the wake of oil discoveries in the far north, an increasing economic attraction too. The world's most severe maritime challenge, it involves a 1500-kilometre traverse from north of Baffin Island to the Beaufort Sea above Alaska. Some 50,000 icebergs constantly line the eastern approaches and thick pack ice covers the route for nine months of the year, with temperatures rising above freezing only in July and August. Perpetual darkness reigns for four months of the year, and thick fog and blizzards can obscure visibility for the remaining eight months. Even with modern technology navigation is almost impossible: a magnetic compass is useless as the magnetic north lies in the passage, and a gyro compass is unreliable at high latitudes; little is known of Arctic tides and currents; sonar is confused by submerged ice; and the featureless tundra of the Arctic islands provides the only few points of visual or radar reference.

John Cabot can hardly have been happy with his order from Henry VII in 1497 to blaze the northwest trail, the first recorded instance of such an attempt. The elusive passage subsequently excited the imagination of the world's greatest adventurers, men such as Sir Francis Drake, Jacques Cartier, Sir Martin Frobisher, James Cook and **Henry Hudson** – cast adrift by his mutinous crew in 1611 when the Hudson Bay turned out to be an icebound trap rather than the passage.

Details of a possible route were pieced together over the centuries, though many paid with their lives in the process, most famously **Sir John Franklin**, who vanished into the ice with 129 men in 1845. Many rescue parties set out to find Franklin's vessels, HMS *Erebus* and HMS *Terror*, and it was one searcher, **Robert McClure**, who – in the broadest sense – made the first northwest passage in 1854. Entering the passage from the west, he was trapped for two winters, and then sledged to meet a rescue boat coming from the east. The **first sea crossing** was achieved by the Norwegian **Roald Amundsen** in 1906, but only after a three-year voyage. The first single-season traverse was made by a Canadian Mountie, **Henry Larsen**, in 1944 – his schooner, the *St Roch*, is now enshrined in Vancouver's Maritime Museum. More recently huge ice-breakers have explored the potential of cracking a commercial route through the ice mainly for the export of oil from the Alaskan and Beaufort fields and for the exploitation of minerals in Canada's Arctic north.

contact with the outside world. Few explorers encountered them, and even the most determined of Western agencies – the church and the trading companies – have failed to compromise a people who are still extraordinarily isolated by climate, distance and culture. Today, however, few of the Inuit live according to the ways of popular myth. Except on the odd trapping party, for example, igloos have been replaced by government-built homes, and the bone tools, sledges and kayaks of a generation ago have been superseded by rifles, snow bikes and light aircraft.

You still have to be fairly determined, however, to reach any of the region's eight communities (five on the coast, three on islands), let alone explore the hauntingly beautiful ice fields and tundra. People up here are usually looking to spot wildlife, fish, or, more dubiously, to hunt for musk ox, caribou and polar bears, a practice the government defends by claiming "It's done the Inuit way, using dog teams, on a demanding safari over land and sea ice". It also provides much-needed income for the Inuit, who have the right to sell the limited number of permits. Most visitors base themselves either at **Kugluktuk** (formerly **Coppermine**) or at Victoria Island's **Ikaluktutiak** (formerly **Cambridge Bay**), the transport and service capital. Each main Arctic coast community, remarkably, has **accommodation**, but reservations are vital and prices predictably steep. You need to come prepared: in some cases meals must be booked in advance. Basic groceries are usually available at stores, but there are no banks. As ever, various **tour operators** run trips to and from the main centres; for information, send for the *Nunavut Travel Planner* before you go (see p.976).

Ikaluktutiak (Cambridge Bay)

IKALUKTUTIAK (pop.1413) – the "fair fishing place" – formerly known as Cambridge Bay, lies to the north of the Arctic Circle on the barren southern shore of **Victoria Island**, Canada's second largest island. As ever in the high Arctic, you need a special reason to come here, for accommodation, food and flights are all hideously expensive. Today it's the regional centre for the Kitikmeot communities and an important staging point for visitors making tours or heading still deeper into the hinterland. It also operates as the administrative focus for the region's western lands, despite being a full 1300km from Nunavut's capital at Iqaluit. Over the centuries the region was a summer gathering place for the Copper Inuit (so called by the whites because they made many of their tools and weapons from copper), attracted here by the abundance of good hunting, notably seals, caribou and arctic char. The last two are local staples to this day, and still provide work and income, Kitikmeot Meats processing caribou and musk for export, Ikaluktutiak Co-op running a fishery that supplies arctic char nationwide (both concerns are open to the public for direct sales). The Hudson's Bay Company arrived in 1921, late by Canadian standards, and purchased the *Maud*, explorer Roald Amundsen's schooner, for use as a supplies and trading ship. This little piece of Arctic history was used for years before being left to sink into disrepair and ultimately into the harbour, where its hulk can still be seen in the bay.

The region's main **tourist office** is the Arctic Coast Visitors Centre (year-round Mon–Fri 9am–5pm, extended hours in summer and on request at other times; ☎867/983-2842 or 983-2224). It's located in an attractive modern building overlooking the bay, and has displays on the art, history and culture of the Copper and Netsilik Inuit, as well as exhibits of maps and documents that shed light on the age-old search for the Northwest Passage (see box). A library of northern books and videos is also available, and there are pamphlets on self-guided walks around the community. **Scheduled flights** arrive on Canadian North (☎867/979-6828 or 1-800/661-1505, Ⓦwww.canadian.com) from Calgary and Edmonton; Aklak Air (☎867/777-3555) from Inuvik and Western Arctic towns; and First Air (☎1-800/267-1247) from Yellowknife and Baffin Island. Within the Arctic Coast area itself, First Air flies between all the settlements except Bathurst Inlet and Umingmaktok, which can be reached by charter aircraft only.

As regards **accommodation**, there's the 21-room *Ikaluktutiak Hotel Inns North* (☎867/983-2215, Ⓦwww.innsnorth.com & Ⓦwww.cambridgebayhotel .com; ❻ per person), where meals – which you're almost bound to have to buy – cost around $50–60 a head. There are also one- and two-bedroom apartments, a coffee shop and restaurant. Then there is the smaller *Green Row Executive Suites* (☎867/983-3456, Ⓦwww.greenrow.ca; ❻), which has eighteen central, self-contained suites with kitchenettes. The *Arctic Islands Lodge Inns North* (☎867/983-2345, Ⓦwww.innsnorth.com & Ⓦwww.cambridgebayhotel .com; ❼ per person with all meals) has 25 upscale rooms, a restaurant, coffee shop and laundry, and also offers weekly and monthly rates. You can **camp** at Freshwater Creek, 5km away, and – if you're self-catering – buy supplies at the Northern store. You should also be able to camp on the shoreline of the bay, but ask first, and make sure you are well away from, and out of sight of, any houses.

Kugluktuk (Coppermine)

KUGLUKTUK (pop. 1267) lies west of Ikaluktutiak on the Canadian "mainland", sitting astride the **Coppermine River** close to the westernmost point of Nunavut (the river lends Kugluktuk its name, which means "place of rapids"). Yellowknife is 600km away to the south. A relatively narrow sea passage, the Coronation Gulf, separates the mainland coast from Victoria Island at this point, a vital through-route on the Northwest Passage. The river has long been of primary importance in the region. Copper Inuit, so called because they fashioned tools and weapons from copper, converged at its mouth for a millennium to fish and hunt. In the twentieth century, as the numbers of caribou in the interior have declined, the Inuit have increasingly abandoned their semi-nomadic ways to settle on the coast. Today hunting and fishing still play a part in generating local income, though latterly tourism and oil and gas exploration have also contributed to local coffers. The river, which rises in the wilderness 360km north of Yellowknife, has also provided a "convenient" way of accessing the far north. It was used by Samuel Hearne, for example, the first white to reach the region, who paddled here on the orders of the Hudson's Bay Company to seek out the source of the copper being traded by the Inuit at company posts to the south. Today the river provides one of the continent's great **canoe trips**, most canoeists (or rafters) joining tours or chartering a plane from Yellowknife to the river's headwaters. The 325-kilometre trip downstream takes around ten days. The trip, among other things, offers sensational opportunities for watching wildlife, but you should also strike lucky with wildlife by walking or taking short tours from Kugluktuk itself. The most popular walk (20km one-way) is to the **Bloody Falls**, so called because a party of Inuit were massacred here following an argument with a group of Dene guides accompanying Hearne (relations between the two aboriginal groups were traditionally poor). If you don't fancy the walk – and it's tough going in places – you can pick up a boat trip up the river to the same point.

Access by **air** is provided through First Air (☎1-800/267-1247) from Yellowknife and other "local" communities. **Information** is available in summer from the Heritage Visitors Centre (July & Aug daily 8.30am–5pm, other times on request; ☎867/982-3232). There are two **accommodation** options. The central *Coppermine Inn* (☎867/982-3333, ⨍867/982-3340; ❼ per person) has motel rooms or self-contained units; breakfast, lunch and dinner if you want them should be reserved in advance (you can take meals individually). Alternatively, there's the smaller *Enokhok Inn* (☎867/982-3197, ⨍867/982-4291; ❼ per person including meals). **Camping** is possible at Kukluktuk Park. As for **eating**, nonresidents can use the *Coppermine Inn*, but you need to book meals a day in advance.

Uluqsaqtuuq (Holman)

One of the region's more northerly communities, **ULUQSAQTUUQ**, or Holman (pop. 300), lies across Coronation Gulf on Victoria Island from Cambridge Bay – strictly speaking just outside Nunavut's borders. Most people are here to fish for trout and arctic char or, remarkably, for the novelty of playing golf on one of the world's most northerly courses. The settlement is situated in a scenic open cove, the half-moon Queen's Bay, backed by massive two-metre bluffs and escarpments. It developed almost by default, when a Hudson's Bay Company post was moved here from Prince Albert Sound in 1939. Inuit had previously summered here in the search for caribou, but the post encouraged some to settle and sell white-fox furs with the Hudson's Bay traders. Today two groups of Inuit – the Copper and Inuvialuit – live here, the region forming part of a designated Inuvialuit settlement area. The community has become particularly well-known for its crafts, notably clothing and traditional tools, but most particularly prints and silk-screened items, a tradition that goes back fifty years, to when an Oblate missionary, the Reverend Henri Tardi, came here and taught locals various printing techniques.

You can buy crafts around the settlement, or at the gift shop in the hamlet's only **accommodation**, the *Arctic Char Inn* (☎867/396-3501 or 396-3531, ⨍867/396-3705; ❼ per person), which has just eight rooms at $185 per person per night. You can **camp** at Okpilik Lake, but should be able to pitch a tent just about anywhere if you ask at the hamlet office. The *Arctic Char Inn* is the only place to **eat**, but there is a Northern groceries store almost opposite for supplies.

Baffin Island

Baffin Island comprises half a million square kilometres of Arctic vastness, whose main attraction is **Auyuittuq National Park Reserve** on the Cumberland Peninsula, Canada's northernmost accessible national park. With a treeless landscape, mountains towering over 1500m, icy glacial streams and 24-hour daylight from May to July, hiking in Auyuittuq offers one of the most majestic experiences in Canada. However, with temperatures rising to a mere 6°C from June to August, it's a brutal environment that will appeal only to the truly adventurous; expensive though they are, **package tours** are definitely recommended if this is your first venture into such a forbidding place. Be sure to bring all necessary gear with you, as the island supplies arrive just once a year.

Iqaluit

The main gateway to Baffin Island – and capital of Nunavut – is the rapidly growing **IQALUIT** (formerly Frobisher Bay), whose name means simply "fish" and whose population of four thousand plus is predominantly Inuit. The Nunavut Tourism office is here (℡867/979-6551 or 1-866/686-2888, ⓦwww.nunavuttourism.com), as is the Unikkaarvik (Baffin Regional) **Visitor Centre** (July & Aug daily 9am–5pm, other times on request; ℡867/979-4636). So, too, are many of the **tour operators** who run trips into the interior. Things to see include the St Jude's Anglican church – an igloo-shaped affair like the one in Inuvik – and the collection of Inuit art and artefacts in the **Nunatta Sunakkutaangit Museum** (call for latest times; ℡867/979-5537).

Getting to Baffin Island is only feasible by **air**. First Air (℡1-800/267-1247 or 613/839-3340, ⓦwww.firstair.ca) and Canadian North (℡1-800/661-1505 or 867/979-6828, ⓦwww.canadiannorth.com) make the trip from Montréal (1–2 daily; 3hr) and from Ottawa (4 weekly; 4hr). Ticket **prices** can get as low as $400 return, but are usually nearer $700. First Air also links Yellowknife to Iqaluit (5 weekly; 3hr 50min) for around $700 return. Remember to ask about cheap pass deals and other prebooked flight deals if you're making international flights into Canada: these are often much cheaper bought beforehand in conjunction with the carrier you're using to fly to the country. Consult the *Nunavut Travel Planner* or website (see p.976) or contact the Iqaluit visitor centre for details of flights and other **information** on outfitters, guides and accommodation. However, hiking maps should be bought in advance from The Canada Map Office, 615 Booth St, Ottawa, ON K1A 0E9.

In summer many of the Inuit families of Iqaluit abandon their homes in favour of tents, and your best bet may well be to join them, although there are no fixed campsites. Iqaluit has around eight **accommodation** options, including B&B choices which tend to open and close from year to year. The big main **hotels** charge more or less similar rates – around $145 per person per night – for similar facilities: *The Navigator Inn* (℡867/979-6201, ⓔnavinn @nunanet.com; ⑥), *Discovery Lodge* (℡867/979-4433, ⓦwww.discoverylodge .com; ⑥) and the recently renovated *Frobisher Inn* (℡867/979-2222, ⓦwww.frobisherinn.com; ⑥).

In addition to flights to Pangnirtung (for the Auyuittuq park; see below), there are scheduled flights on First Air from Iqaluit to Baffin Island's various small communities, as well as chartered sightseeing flights. Each of the following remoter settlements has single and highly expensive hotels: Arctic Bay, Cape Dorset, Clyde River, Grise Ford, Hall Beach, Igloolik, Pond Inlet, Resolute and Sanikiluak.

Auyuittuq National Park Reserve

Straddling the Arctic Circle in the northeast of Baffin Island, **Auyuittuq National Park Reserve** is one of the most spectacular destinations in the Canadian north. The heart of the park is the massive **Penney Ice Cap**, a remnant of the ice sheet that extended over most of Canada east of the Rockies about 18,000 years ago, and the major **hiking route** is the 110-kilometre Pangnirtung/Aksayuk Pass, which cuts through the mountains between Cumberland Sound and the Davis Strait. *Auyuittuq* is Inuit for "the land that never melts", but despite the unrelenting cold there is abundant life here: in summer the sparse tundra plants burst into green, the wild flowers are blooming and the amazing array of wildlife includes lemmings, polar bears, caribou, arctic hares and foxes, snow geese, peregrines, narwhals, walruses, bowhead and beluga whales, as well as harp, ringed and bearded seals.

There is a daily one-hour First Air flight during the summer from Iqaluit to **PANGNIRTUNG**, the gateway to Auyuittuq National Park. In Pangnirtung there is an established free **campsite**, *Pisuktinee Tungavik*, and a church that occasionally lets you sleep on the floor for a donation if you are desperate. The only commercial **places to stay** are the 25-room *Auyuittuq Lodge* (☏867/473-8955, ⓔpang.lodge@nunanet.ca; ⓖ) and newer two-room *Kilabuk Lodge* (☏867/473-8229; ⓞ), where you can take meals or cook your own. The former has good but expensive meals and they usually allow exhausted hikers to use their showers for a few dollars.

The only transport for the 25km from Pangnirtung to the south entrance of the park is by **freighter canoe**, which the Inuit also charter for fishing, whale-watching and sightseeing trips. The rates on these "canoes" – which are like small fishing boats with outboard motors – are set by the Inuit co-operative, and work out at around $130 for two people one-way, plus $35–60 for each additional person. The boats can only pass through the Pangnirtung Fjord after the ice break-up in July; at other times you have to walk. Arrangements for a canoe pick-up should be possible by radio from the few emergency shelters in the park, but be warned that one summer all the batteries were stolen, so you may have to arrange your pick-up before being dropped off.

Services within the park are extremely limited and the **weather** is highly unpredictable. Snowstorms, high wind and rain occur frequently, and deaths from hypothermia have been known even in the height of summer. All-weather hiking gear is essential, and a walking stick or ski pole is necessary to assist you with the ice-cold stream crossings which occur every 200–300m and can still be waist-high in July. There is no wood for fuel, as the park is located kilometres north of the tree line, so a camping stove is also essential. You can get **information** from Auyuittuq National Park Reserve, Pangnirtung, NT, X0A 0R0 (☏867/473-8828, ⓦwww.pc.gc.ca).

Travel details

Trains

Prince George to: Edmonton via Jasper (3 weekly; 8hr 15min); Prince Rupert (3 weekly; 13hr); Vancouver (mid-June to Oct 1 daily; rest of year 3 weekly; 13hr 30min).
Prince Rupert to: Prince George (3 weekly; 13hr).

Buses

Dawson City to: Inuvik (mid-June to early Sept 2–3 weekly; 12hr); Whitehorse (late June to Sept 3 weekly; Oct & March to early June 2 weekly; rest of year 1 weekly; 7hr 30min).
Dawson Creek to: Edmonton (2 daily; 9hr); Prince George (2 daily; 6hr 30min); Whitehorse (mid-May to mid-Oct 1 daily except Sun; rest of year 3 weekly; 21hr).

Hay River to: Fort Resolution (3 weekly; 6hr); Fort Smith (3 weekly; 7hr); Peace River (daily except Mon; connections for Edmonton and Grande Prairie; 8hr); Yellowknife (3 weekly; 12hr).
Prince George to: Dawson Creek (2 daily; 6hr 30min); Edmonton via Jasper (2 daily; 9hr 45min); Prince Rupert (2 daily; 11hr); Vancouver via Williams Lake and Cache Creek (2 daily; 13hr).
Whitehorse to: Dawson City (June–Sept 3 weekly; Oct & March to early June 2 weekly; rest of year 1 weekly; 7hr 30min); Dawson Creek (mid-May to mid-Oct 1 daily except Sun; rest of year 3 weekly; 21hr); Skagway (mid-May to mid-June 1 daily except Wed & Sun; 4hr).

Flights

Listed below are only the main direct scheduled flights operated by the big carriers; for details on the vast range of small provincial companies operating within the north, turn to each relevant town account.

To Inuvik from: Yellowknife (1 daily; 2hr 35min).

To Iqaluit from: Montréal (1–2 daily; 3hr); Ottawa (4 weekly; 4hr); Yellowknife (5 weekly; 3hr 50min).

To Whitehorse from: Vancouver (3 daily; 2hr 20min).

To Yellowknife from: Cambridge Bay (1 weekly; 1hr 30min); Edmonton (3 daily; 1hr 35min); Fort Smith (1 daily; 1hr 30min); Inuvik (1 daily; 2hr 35min); Norman Wells (1 daily; 1hr 15min); Resolute (2 weekly; 3hr 20min).

Contexts

Contexts

The historical framework

Fully unified only since 1949, **Canada** is a country of intertwining histories rather than a single national thread. Not only does each of its provinces maintain a considerable degree of autonomy, but each grouping of native peoples can claim a heritage that cannot be fully integrated into the story of white Canada. Such a complex mosaic militates against generalization, although Canadians themselves continue to grapple with the nature of their own identity. What follows is an attempt to identify key events and themes.

The beginnings

The ancestors of the **aboriginal peoples** of North America first entered the continent around 25,000 years ago, when vast glaciers covered most of the northern continents, keeping the sea level far below that of today. It seems likely that North America's first human inhabitants crossed the land bridge linking Asia with present-day Alaska – they were probably Siberian hunter-nomads travelling in pursuit of mammoths, hairy rhinos, bison, wild horses and sloths, the Ice Age animals that made up their diet. These people left very little to mark their passing, apart from some simple graves and the grooved, chipped-stone spear-heads that earned them the name **Fluted Point People**. In successive waves the Fluted Point People moved down through North America, across the isthmus of Panama, until they reached the southernmost tip of South America. As they settled, so they slowly developed distinctive cultures and languages, whose degree of elaboration depended on the resources of their environment.

About 3000 BC another wave of migration passed over from Asia to North America. This wave was made up of the first group of **Inuit** migrants who – because the sea level had risen and submerged the land bridge under today's Bering Strait – made their crossings either in skin-covered boats or on foot over the winter ice. Within the next thousand years the Inuit occupied the entire northern zone of the continent, moving east as far as Greenland and displacing the earlier occupants. These first Inuits – called the **Dorset Eskimos** after Cape Dorset, on Baffin Island in the Northwest Territories, where archeologists first identified their remains in the 1920s – were assimilated or wiped out by the next wave of Inuit. These crossed into the continent 3000 years ago, creating the **Thule** culture – so called after the Greek word for the world's northernmost extremity. The Thule people were the direct ancestors of today's Inuit.

The aboriginal peoples

Before the Europeans arrived, the aboriginal peoples – numbering around 300,000 – were divided into three main language groups: **Algonkian**, **Athapascan** (principally in the north and west) and **Inuktitut** (Inuit). Within these groups existed a multitude of cultures. None of these people had a written language, the wheel was unknown to them and their largest draught animal, prior to the introduction of the horse, was the dog. However, over the centuries, each of the tribes developed techniques that enabled them to cope with the problems of survival posed by their environments.

Immediately prior to the arrival of the Europeans, Canada was divided into a number of cultural zones. In the extreme north lived the nomadic **Inuit** (see box p.1044), whose basic unit was the family group, small enough to survive in the precarious conditions. The necessarily small-scale nature of Inuit life meant that they developed no political structures and gathered together in larger groups only if the supply of food required it – when, for example, the arctic char were running upriver from the sea to spawn, or the caribou were migrating. Immediately to the south of the Inuit, in a zone stretching from the Labrador coast across the Canadian Shield to northern British Columbia, lived the tribes of the **northern forests**. This was a harsh environment, too, and consequently these peoples spent most of their time in small nomadic bands following the game on which they depended. Indeed, variations between the tribes largely resulted from the type of game they pursued: the **Naskapi** fished and hunted seals on the Labrador coast; the **Chipewyan**, occupying the border country between the tundra and forest to the west of Hudson Bay, mainly hunted caribou; the **Wood Cree**, to the south of the Chipewyan, along the Churchill River, hunted deer and moose; and the **Tahltan** of British Columbia combined hunting with seasonal fishing. Like the Inuit, the political structures of these tribes were rudimentary and, although older men enjoyed a certain respect, there were no "chiefs" in any European sense of the term. In fact, decisions were generally made collectively with the opinions of successful hunters – the guarantors of survival – carrying great weight, as did those of their shaman, whose main function was to satisfy the spirits that they believed inhabited every animate and inanimate object around them.

The southern zone of Canada, stretching from the St Lawrence River along the northern shores of the Great Lakes to southern British Columbia was climatically much kinder, and it's in this region that Canada's native peoples developed their most sophisticated cultures. Here, along the banks of the St Lawrence and the shores of the Great Lakes, lived the **Iroquois-speaking** peoples, divided into three tribal confederacies: the **Five Nations**, the **Huron** (see p.151) and the **Neutrals**. All three groups cultivated corn (maize), beans and squash in an agricultural system that enabled them to lead a settled life – often in communities of several hundreds. Iroquois society was divided into matriarchal clans, whose affairs would be governed by a female elder. The clan shared a long house and when a man married (always outside his own clan), he would go to live in the long house of his wife. Tribal chiefs (*sachems*) were male, but they were selected by the female elders of the tribe and they also had to belong to a lineage through which the rank of *sachem* descended. Once selected a *sachem* had to have his rank confirmed by the federal council of the inter-tribal league: in the case of the Five Nations this consisted of *sachems* from the Seneca, Cayuga, Onondaga, Oneida and Mohawk tribes. Iroquoian society had its bellicose side, too. An assured winter supply of food enabled the Iroquois to indulge in protracted inter-tribal warfare: in particular, the Five Nations were almost always at war with the Hurons.

To the west of the Iroquois, between lakes Superior and Winnipeg, lived the **Ojibwa**, forest hunters who learned to cultivate maize from the Iroquois and also harvested the wild rice that grew on the fringes of the region's lakes. Further west still, on the prairies, lived the peoples of the **Blackfoot Confederation**: the **Piegan**, **Blackfoot** and **Blood** tribes. The economy of this latter grouping was based on the buffalo (or bison): its flesh was eaten; its hide provided clothes and shelter; its bones were made into tools; its sinews were ideal for bow strings; and its hooves were melted down to provide glue. In the late seventeenth century, the hunting techniques of these prairie peoples were transformed by the arrival of the horse, which had made its way – either wild or by trade – from Mexico, where it had been introduced by the Spanish conquistadors. The horse made the bison easy prey and, as with the Iroquois, a ready food supply spawned the development of a militaristic culture centred on the prowess of the tribes' young braves.

On the **Pacific coast**, tribes such as the **Tlingit** and **Salish** were dependent on the ocean, which provided them with a plentiful supply of food. There was, however, little cohesion within tribes and people from different villages – even though of the same tribe – would at times be in conflict with each other. Yet these tribes had a rich ceremonial and cultural life, as exemplified by the excellence of their woodcarvings, whose most conspicuous manifestations were the **totem poles** (or house posts), which reached colossal sizes in the nineteenth century.

The coming of the Europeans

The first recorded contact between Europeans and the native peoples of North America occurred in around 1000 AD, when a **Norse** expedition sailing from Greenland landed somewhere on the Atlantic seaboard, probably in Newfoundland (see p.508 for more). It was a fairly short-lived stay – according to the Icelandic sagas, the Norse were forced to withdraw from the area they called Vinland because of the hostility of the natives.

In 1492 Ferdinand and Isabella of Spain were finally persuaded to underwrite **Christopher Columbus**'s expedition in search of the westward route to Asia. Columbus bumped into the West Indies instead, but his "discovery" of islands that were presumed to lie off India encouraged other European monarchs to sponsor expeditions of their own. In 1497 **John Cabot**, supported by the English king Henry VII, sailed west and sighted Newfoundland and Cape Breton. On his return, Cabot reported seeing multitudes of cod off Newfoundland, and his much-publicized comments effectively started the **Newfoundland** cod fishery. In less than sixty years, up to four hundred **fishing** vessels from Britain, France and Spain were making annual voyages to the Grand Banks fishing grounds around the island. Soon some of the fishermen established shore bases to cure their catch in the sun, and then they started to over-winter here – which was how settlement of the island began.

By the end of the sixteenth century the cod trade was largely controlled by the British and French, and Newfoundland became an early cockpit of English–French rivalries, a colonial conflict that continued until England secured control of the island in the 1713 Treaty of Utrecht.

New France

Meanwhile, in 1535, **Jacques Cartier**, on a voyage paid for by the French crown, made his way down the St Lawrence, also hoping to find Asia. Instead he stumbled upon the Iroquois, first at Stadacona, on the site of Québec City, and later at Hochelaga, today's Montréal. At both places the Frenchman had a friendly reception, but the Iroquois attitude changed after Cartier seized one of their *sachems* and took him to France. For a time the Iroquois were a barrier to further exploration up the St Lawrence, but subsequently they abandoned their riverside villages (possibly as a result of an epidemic brought about by contact with Europeans diseases), enabling French traders to move up the river buying **furs**, an enterprise pioneered by seasonal fishermen.

The development of this trade aroused the interest of the French king, who in 1603 commissioned **Samuel de Champlain** to chart the St Lawrence. Two years later Champlain founded **Port Royal** in today's Nova Scotia, which became the capital of **Acadie** (Acadia), a colony whose agricultural preoccupations were soon far removed from the main thrust of French colonialism along the St Lawrence. It was here, on a subsequent expedition in 1608, that Champlain established the settlement of Québec City at the heart of **New France**, and, to stimulate the fur trade, allied the French with those tribes he identified as likely to be his principal suppliers. In practice this meant siding with the Huron against the Five Nations, a decision that intensified their traditional hostility. Furthermore, the fur trade destroyed the balance of power between the tribes: first one and then another would receive, in return for their pelts, the latest type of musket as well as iron axes and knives, forcing enemies back to the fur trade to redress the military balance. One terrible consequence of such European intervention was the **extermination of the Huron people** in 1648 by the Five Nations, armed by the Dutch merchants of the Hudson River.

As pandemonium reigned among the native peoples, the pattern of life in **New France** was becoming well established. On the farmlands of the St Lawrence a New World feudalism was practised by the land-owning seigneurs and their *habitant* tenants, while the fur territories – entered at Montréal – were extended deep into the interior. Many of the fur traders adopted native dress, learnt aboriginal languages, and took wives from the tribes through which they passed, spawning the mixed-race people known as the **Métis**. The furs they brought back to Montréal were shipped downriver to Québec City whence they were shipped to France. But the white population in the French colony remained relatively small – there were only 18,000 New French in 1713. In the context of a growing British presence, this represented a dangerous weakness.

The rise of the British

In 1670 Charles II of England had established the **Hudson's Bay Company** and given it control of a million and a half square miles adjacent to its namesake bay, a territory named Rupert's Land, after the king's uncle. Four years later the British captured the Dutch possessions of the Hudson River Valley – thereby trapping New France. Slowly the British closed the net: in 1713, they took control of Acadia, renaming it **Nova Scotia** (New Scotland), and in 1755 they deported its French-speaking farmers. When the Seven Years War broke out in 1756, the French attempted to outflank the British by using the Great Lakes route to occupy the area to the west of the British colonies and then, with the help of their native allies, pin them to the coast. In the event the British won the war by exploiting their naval superiority: a large force under the command of **General James Wolfe** sailed up the St Lawrence in 1759 and, against all expectations, successfully scaled the Heights of Abraham to capture Québec City. Montréal fell a few months later – and at that point the French North American empire was effectively finished, though they held onto Louisiana until Napoleon sold it off in 1803.

For the native peoples the ending of the Anglo–French conflict was a mixed blessing. If the war had turned the tribes into sought-after allies, it had also destroyed the traditional inter-tribal balance of power and subordinated native to European interests. A recognition of the change wrought by the end of the war inspired the uprising of the Ottawas in 1763, when **Pontiac**, their chief, led an unsuccessful assault on Detroit, hoping to restore the French position and halt the progress of the English settlers. Moved largely by a desire for a stable economy, the response of the British Crown was to issue a proclamation which confirmed the legal right of the natives to their lands and set aside the territory to the west of the Appalachian Mountains and the Great Lakes as "**Indian Territory**". Although colonial governors were given instructions to remove trespassers on "Indian Land", in reality the proclamation had little practical effect until the twentieth century, when it became a cornerstone of the native peoples' attempts to seek compensation for the illegal confiscation of their land.

The other great problem the British faced in the 1760s was how to deal with the French-speaking **Canadiens** of the defunct New France – the term *Canadiens* used to distinguish local settlers from those born in France, most of whom left the colony after the British conquest. Initially the British government hoped to anglicize the province, swamping the French-speaking population with English-speaking Protestants. In the event large-scale migration failed to materialize immediately, and the second English governor of Québec, **Sir Guy Carleton**, realized that – as discontent grew in the American colonies – the loyalty of the *Canadiens* was of vital importance.

Carleton's plan to achieve this was embodied in the 1774 **Québec Act**, which made a number of concessions to the region's French speakers: Catholics were permitted to hold civil appointments, the seigneurial system was maintained, and the Roman Catholic Church allowed to collect tithes. Remarkably, all these concessions were made at a time when Catholics in Britain were not politically emancipated.

The migrations

The success of this policy was seen during the **American War of Independence** (1775–83) and the Anglo-American War of 1812. The Canadiens refused to volunteer for the armed forces of the Crown, but equally they failed to respond to the appeals of the Americans – no doubt calculating that their survival as a distinctive cultural group was more likely under the British than in an English-speaking United States.

In the immediate aftermath of the American War of Independence, the population of what was left of British North America expanded rapidly, both in "Canada" – which then covered the present-day provinces of Québec and Ontario – and in the separate colonies of New Brunswick, Nova Scotia, Prince Edward Island and Newfoundland. The first large wave of migration came from the United States as 40,000 **United Empire Loyalists** (see p.437 for more on this group) made their way north to stay within British jurisdiction. Of these, all but 8000 moved to Nova Scotia and New Brunswick, the rest going to the western edge of Québec, where they laid the foundations of the future province of Ontario. Between 1783 and 1812 the population of Canada, as defined at the time, trebled to 330,000, with a large part of the increase being the product of *revanche du berceau* (revenge of the cradle) – an attempt, encouraged by the Catholic clergy, to outbreed the English-speaking population.

However, tensions between Britain and the United States still deterred potential colonists, a problem resolved by the **War of 1812**. Neither side was strong enough to win, but by the Treaty of Ghent in 1814 the Americans recognized the legitimacy of British North America, whose border was established along the **49th parallel** west from Lake of the Woods to the Rockies. Immigration now boomed, especially in the 1840s, when economic crises and shortages in Britain as well as the Irish famine pushed it up to levels that even the fertile *Canadiens* could not match. Between 1815 and 1850 over 800,000 immigrants poured into British North America. Most headed for "Upper Canada", later called Ontario, which received 66,000 in the 1832 alone.

Faced with this human tide the surveyors charted new townships as quickly as possible, but they simply couldn't not keep pace with demand. The result was that many native peoples were dispossessed in direct contravention of the 1763 proclamation. By 1806 the region's native peoples had lost 4.5 million acres.

The division and union of Canada

Throughout this period economic expansion was largely generated by the English-speaking merchants who now controlled the Montréal-based fur trade, organized as the **North West Company**. Seeking political changes that would enhance their economic power, they wanted their own legislative assembly and the universal application of English law, which of course would not have been acceptable to the French-speakers.

In 1791, through the **Canada Act**, the British government imposed a compromise, dividing the region into **Upper** and **Lower Canada**, which broadly separated the two groups along the line of the Ottawa River. In Lower Canada, the French-based legal system was retained, as was the right of the Catholic Church to collect tithes, while in Upper Canada, English common law was introduced. Each of the new provinces had an elective assembly, though these shared their limited powers with an appointed assembly and executive councils appointed by the governor of each province. This arrangement allowed the assemblies to become the focal points for vocal opposition, but ultimately condemned them to impotence. At the same time, the merchant elite built up chains of influence and power around the appointed provincial governments: in Upper Canada this grouping was called the "**Family Compact**", in Lower Canada the "**Château Clique**".

By the late 1830s considerable opposition had developed to these cliques. In Upper Canada the **Reform Movement** led by **William Lyon Mackenzie** demanded a government accountable to a broad electorate, and the expansion of credit facilities for small farmers. In 1837 both Mackenzie and **Louis-Joseph Papineau**, the reform leader in Lower Canada, were sufficiently frustrated to attempt open rebellion. Neither was successful and both were forced into exile in the United States, but the rebellions did bring home to the British Government the need for effective reform, prompting the **Act of Union** of 1840, which united Lower and Upper Canada with a single assembly.

The rationale for this arrangement was the belief that the French-Canadians were incapable of handling elective government without Anglo-Saxon guidance. Nevertheless, the assembly provided equal representation for Canada East and West – in effect the old Lower and Upper Canadas. A few years later, this new assembly achieved **responsible government** almost accidentally. In 1849 the Reform Party, which had a majority of the seats, passed an Act compensating those involved in the 1837 rebellions. The Governor-General, Lord Elgin, disapproved, but he didn't exercise his veto – so, for the first time, a Canadian administration acted on the vote of an elected assembly, rather than imperial sanction.

The Reform Party, which pushed through the compensation scheme, included both French- and English-speakers and mainly represented small farmers and businessmen opposed to the power of the cliques. In the 1850s this grouping became the Canadian **Liberal Party**, but the coalition fell apart in the 1860s with the emergence of "Clear Grit" Liberals in Canada West. The Grits argued for "Representation by Population" – in other words, instead of equal representation for the two halves of Canada, they wanted constituencies based on the total population. As the English-speakers outnumbered the French, the "Rep by Poppers" slogan seemed a direct threat to many of the institutions of French Canada. As a consequence, many French-Canadians transferred their support to the **Conservative Party**, while the radicals of Canada East, the **Rouges**, developed a more nationalist creed.

The Conservative Party comprised a number of elements, including the rump of the merchant elite who were so infuriated by their loss of control that they burnt the Montréal parliament building to the ground in 1849. Some of this group campaigned to break the imperial tie and join the United States, but, when the party fully emerged in 1854, the old "Compact Tories" were much less influential than a younger generation of moderate conservatives. The lynchpin of this younger group was **John A. Macdonald**, who was to form the first federal government in 1868. Such moderates sought, by overcoming the democratic excesses of the "Grits" and the nationalism of the "Rouges", to weld together an economic and political state that would not be absorbed into the increasingly powerful United States.

Confederation

In the mid-1860s "Canada" had achieved responsible party government, but British North America was still a collection of **self-governing colonies**. In the east, Newfoundland was almost entirely dependent on its cod fishery, Prince Edward Island had a prosperous agricultural economy, and both Nova Scotia and New Brunswick had boomed on the backs of the shipbuilding industry. Far to the west, on the Pacific coast, lay fur-trading British Columbia, which had just beaten off American attempts to annex the region during the Oregon crisis, finally resolved in 1846, when the international frontier was fixed along a westward extension of the original 49th parallel. Not that this was the end of British Columbia's problems: in 1858 gold was discovered beside the Fraser River and, in response to the influx of American prospectors, British Columbia was hastily designated a Crown Colony – a process that was repeated in 1895 when gold was discovered in the Yukon's Klondike. Between Canada West and British Columbia stretched thousands of miles of prairie and forest, the old Rupert's Land that was still under the extremely loose authority of the Hudson's Bay Company.

The American Civil War raised fears of a US invasion of the incoherently structured British North America, at the same time as "Rep by Poppers" agitation was making the status of the French-speaking minority problematic. These issues prompted a series of conferences to discuss the issue of **Confederation**, and after three years of debate the British Parliament passed the British North America Act of 1867. In effect this was a constitution for the new **Dominion of Canada**, providing for a federal parliament to be established at Ottawa; for Canada East and West to become the provinces of Québec and Ontario respectively; and for each province to retain a regional government and assembly. All of the existing colonies joined the Confederation except British Columbia, which waited until 1871; Prince Edward Island, till 1873; and Newfoundland, which remained independent until 1949.

The consolidation of the west

Having settled the question of a constitution, the Dominion turned its attention to the west. In 1869, the territory of the Hudson's Bay Company was bought for £300,000 and the **Northwest Territories**, as the area then became known, reverted to the Crown until Canada was ready to administer them. Predictably, the wishes of its population – primarily Plains Indians and 5000 **Métis** – were given no heed. The Métis, whose main settlement was near the site of modern-day Winnipeg, were already alarmed by the arrival of Ontario settlers and were even more alarmed when government land surveyors arrived to divide the land into lots that cut right across their holdings. Fearful of their land rights, the Métis formed a provisional government under the leadership of **Louis Riel** and prepared to resist the federal authorities (see p.602).

In the course of the rebellion, Riel executed a troublesome Ontario Orangeman by the name of Thomas Scott, an action which created uproar in Ontario. Despite this, the federal government negotiated with a Métis delegation and appeared to meet all their demands, although Riel was obliged to go into exile in the States. As a result of the negotiations, Ottawa created the new province of **Manitoba** to the west of Ontario in 1870, and set aside 140 acres per person for the Métis – though land speculators and lawyers ensured that fewer than twenty percent of those eligible actually got their land.

Dispossession was also the fate of the **Plains Indians**. From 1871 onwards a series of treaties were negotiated, offering native families 160-acre plots and a whole range of goods and services if they signed. By 1877 seven treaties had been agreed (eventually there were eleven), handing over to the government all of the southern prairies. However, the promised aid did not materialize and the native peoples found themselves confined to small, infertile reservations.

The federal government's increased interest in the area – spurred by the **Cypress Hills Massacre** of Assiniboine natives in 1873 (see p.583) – was underlined by the arrival in 1874 of the first 275 members of the newly formed Northwest Mounted Police, the **Mounties** (for more, see p.569). One of their first actions was to expel the American whiskey traders who had earned the region the nickname Whoop-up Country. Once the police had taken charge, Ottawa passed the **Second Indian Act** of 1880, making a Minister of Indian Affairs responsible for the native peoples. The minister and his superintendents exercised a near dictatorial control, so that almost any action that a native person might wish to take, from building a house to making a visit off the reservation, had to be approved by the local official, and often the ministry in Ottawa too. The Act laid down that every aboriginal applicant for "enfranchisement" as an ordinary Canadian citizen had to pass through a three-year probation period. They were also to be examined to see if they had attained a sufficient level of "civilization". If "enfranchised," the individual was counted as a so-called "non-status Indians", as opposed to the "status Indians" of the reservations.

Meanwhile, during the 1870s, most of the **Métis** had moved west into the territory that would become the province of **Saskatchewan** in 1905. Here they congregated along the Saskatchewan River in the vicinity of Batoche, but once again federal surveyors caught up with them and, in the 1880s, began to divide the land into the familiar gridiron pattern. In 1885, the Métis again rose in **revolt** and, after the return of Riel, formed a provisional government. In March they successfully beat off a detachment of Mounted Police, encouraging the neighbouring Cree to raid a Hudson's Bay Company Store. It seemed that a general native insurrection might follow, born of the desperation that accompanied the treaty system, the starvation which went with the disappearance of the buffalo, and the ravages of smallpox. The government dispatched a force of 7000 with Gatling guns and an armed steamer, and after two preliminary skirmishes the Métis and the Cree were crushed absolutely. Riel, despite his obvious insanity, was found guilty of treason and hanged in November 1885.

The defeat of the Métis opened a new phase in the development of the west. In 1886 the first **train** ran **from Montréal to Vancouver** and settlers swarmed onto the prairies, pushing the population up from 250,000 in 1890 to 1,300,000 in 1911. Clifford Sifton, Minister of the Interior, encouraged the large-scale immigration from Eastern Europe of what he called "stalwart peasants in sheepskin coats". These Ukrainians, Poles, Czechs and Hungarians ploughed up the grasslands and turned central Canada into a vast granary, leading the Dominion into the "wheat boom" of the early twentieth century.

Native peoples today

For the **native peoples** the opening of the twentieth century ushered in a far from happy time. Herded onto small reservations under the authoritarian control of the ministry, they were subjected to a concerted campaign of Europeanization – ceremonies such as the sun dance and the potlatch were banned, and they were obliged to send their children to boarding schools for ten months of the year. Deprived of their traditions and independence, they lapsed into poverty, alcoholism and apathy. In the late 1940s, the academic Frederick Tisdall estimated that no fewer than 65,000 reservation aboriginals were "chronically sick" from starvation. In addition, the Inuit were drawn into increasing dependence on the Hudson's Bay Company, who encouraged them to concentrate on hunting for furs rather than food, while the twin agencies of the Christian missions and the Royal Canadian Mounted Police worked to incorporate the Inuit into white culture. All over Canada, a major consequence of the disruption of the traditional way of life was the spread of disease, especially TB, which was fifteen to twenty times more prevalent amongst the aboriginal population than amongst whites.

In 1951 a new **Indian Act** increased both the autonomy of tribal bands and federal subsidies, but nevertheless aboriginal people remained well behind the rest of Canadian society in all the key economic indicators. In 1969, the average income of a Canadian family was $8874, whilst 88 percent of aboriginal families earned $3000 or less, with fifty percent earning less than $1000. In recent years, however, native peoples have begun to assert their identity. "Status Indians" are now represented by the **Assembly of First Nations** (AFN), which has, since its foundation in the early 1980s, sponsored a number of legal actions over treaty rights. Many of these cases are based on breaches of the 1763 proclamation, whose terms stated that native land rights could only be taken away by direct negotiation with the Crown. One recent Grand Chief of the AFN, **Ovide Mercredi** – a lawyer and former human-rights commissioner – announced that the objective of the AFN was to secure an equal status with the provincial governments, a stance indicative of the growth in native self-confidence, despite the continuing impoverishment of the reservations. The political weight of the AFN was made clear in the constitutional talks that took place over the establishment of an **Inuit homeland** in the Northwest Territories, a complex negotiation resulting in an agreement to create two self-governing territories in 1999 (see p.975). But not all of Canada's natives see negotiation as their salvation: the action of armed Mohawks to prevent a golf course being built on tribal burial grounds at **Oka** in Québec (p.265) displayed an almost uncontainable anger against the dominant whites, and divided sympathies across the country. In the event, the Oka militants paved the way for more conciliatory voices to hold sway in the AFN, but the balance of power between those native peoples committed to negotiation as distinct from those favouring direct action is delicate. As a result, the AFN ploughs on with negotiations that rarely hit the headlines against a backdrop lit by occasional bursts of unrestrained native rage, often to do with fishing rights.

Québec and the future of Canada

Just as Canada's native peoples drew inspiration from the worldwide national liberation movements of the late 1950s and 1960s, so did the **Québecois**. Ever since the conquest of 1760, francophones had been deeply concerned about *la survivance*, the continuation of their language and culture. Periodically this anxiety had been heightened, notably during both world wars, when the Québecois opposed the introduction of conscription because it seemed to subordinate their interests to those of Britain. Nevertheless, despite these difficulties, the essentially conservative Québecois political–religious establishment almost always recommended accommodation with the British and later the federal authorities. This same establishment upheld the traditional values of Catholic rural New France, a consequence of which was that Québec's industry and commerce developed under anglophone control. Thus, in early twentieth-century Montréal, a francophone proletariat worked in the factories of anglophone owners, an anglophone dominance that was compounded by the indifference of Canada's other provinces to French-Canadian interests, spurring the development of a new generation of Québec **separatists**.

Held in Montréal, **Expo '67** was meant to be a confirmation of Canada's arrival as an industrial power of the first rank. However, when France's President de Gaulle used the event as a platform to announce his advocacy of a "free Québec", he ignited a row that has dominated the political agenda ever since. That same year, **René Lévesque** formed the **Parti Québécois** (PQ), with the ultimate goal of full independence, hence the slogan *Maîtres chez nous* ("masters in our own house"), but in 1968 this was offset by the election of a determinedly federalist French-Canadian, **Pierre Trudeau**, as prime minister: the scene was set for a showdown.

The PQ represented the constitutional wing of a social movement that, at its most militant extreme, embraced the activities of the short-lived **Front de la Libération du Québec** (FLQ). In 1970 the FLQ kidnapped and murdered Pierre Laporte, the province's Minister of Labour, an action which provoked Trudeau into putting the troops onto the streets of Montréal. This reaction was to benefit the PQ, a modernizing party of the social-democratic left, which came to power in 1976 and set about using state resources to develop economic interests such as the Québec hydroelectric plant on James Bay. It also reformed education – including controversial legislation to make Québec unilingual – and pressed ahead with plans for a referendum on secession. But when the referendum came, in 1980, sixty percent of Québec's electorate voted "*non*" to separation, partly because the 1970s had witnessed a closing of the opportunity gap between the francophone and anglophone communities. This did not, however, end the affair.

In 1985, Québec's PQ government was defeated by **Robert Bourassa**'s Liberals, not so much reflecting a shift in francophone feeling but more Bourassa's espousal of the bulk of the nationalist agenda and what many felt to be the PQ's poor economic track record. The Liberals held power in Québec until 1994, when the PQ bounced back into office, promising to hold another independence referendum. They seemed well set. Polls regularly rated support at around sixty percent, but in 1995 the PQ lost again in a **second referendum** that rejected independence by just 50,000 votes. Despite all the subsequent bluster, this was a political disaster for the PQ, and, with the momentum lost, subsequent polls have indicated that the separatist bubble has wel and truly burst. If this is indeed the case, one of the key reasons is the PQ's failure to define the precise nature of Québec sovereignty and how future relations with the rest of Canada would be conducted.

Into the twenty-first century

To say that the rest of Canada became exasperated with the interminable discussions over the future of Québec would be an understatement – and never more so than during the **Meech Lake** conference of 1990, which conspicuously failed to agree on a new decentralized constitution. The conference was convened by the Conservative **Brian Mulroney**, who had become the country's premier in 1984. Mulroney had other pressing problems, too, though nothing as fractious as Québec. To begin with, the NAFTA free trade agreement between the US and Canada, which Mulroney pushed through parliament, came into effect in 1989, destroying the country's protective tariffs and thereby exposing its industries to undercutting and causing thousands of redundancies. There was also the collapse of the North Atlantic cod fishery, which brought Nova Scotia and Newfoundland to the brink of economic ruin, whilst falls in wheat prices hurt the Prairies. Efforts were made to deal with these issues, but few were satisfied and during Mulroney's second term (1988–93), the premier became a byword for incompetence, his party commonly accused of large-scale corruption. As a result, the 1993 federal elections almost wiped out the Conservatives and, equipped with a huge majority, the new Liberal administration, under **Jean Chrétien**, once Trudeau's Minister of Finance, set about rebuilding federal prestige. A cautious politician, Chrétien had some success, his pragmatic approach to politics proving sufficiently popular to see him re-elected for a second term in 1997 and a third in 2000, albeit with reduced majorities. However, much of Chrétien's electoral success was down to the balkanization of the Canadian political scene. The Liberals were the only party with any claim to a national presence – with the right-wing Canadian Alliance (formerly the Reform Party), for instance, dominating much of the west, but simply failing to show in the east. Neither were Canadians as a whole politically enthused: in the 2000 federal election, only sixty percent turned out to vote and of these the Liberals only secured the support of 39 percent.

In 2003, Chrétien announced his retirement, and his Liberals appointed a new leader, the politically formidable and very competent **Paul Martin**. Facing the prospect of another defeat in the federal elections of 2004, Canada's two rightist parties – the Canadian Alliance and the Progressive Conservatives – belatedly managed to swallow their differences, uniting to form the **Conservative Party** in December 2003. Whether this will be enough to stop the Martin bandwagon remains to be seen.

Canada's aboriginal peoples

At the last census (in 2001) 976,305 Canadians claimed at least partial **aboriginal** ancestry (defined as North American Indian, Métis and Inuit), in an overall population of 29,639,030. Aboriginal populations continue to increase, and interest in their cultural heritage, by aboriginals and nonaboriginals alike, continues to grow.

(The term "aboriginal" does not indicate a common or shared culture, only descent from groups of people who arrived on the continent long before Europeans. The term "Indian" is now recognized as a misnomer, but other attempts to be more specific, such as "Amerindians", "First Peoples" or "Native Canadians", have been only partially successful and you're likely to hear several different terms on your travels. The terms "First Nations" and "aboriginals" are in vogue, but there is a good chance that new terms will be coined.)

Long treated as wards of the federal government, the Indians were put in a different legal category from all other Canadians by the Indian Acts in the nineteenth century. Modern legal distinctions divide this group further into those who are recognized as "Indian" by the federal government – a status bestowed on 608,850 Canadians (all figures here and below are from 2001) – and those who are denied this recognition, the so-called "non-status Indians". Amongst status Indians there are 633 **aboriginal bands** (the term "tribe" has also become outmoded) across Canada. Some communities number fewer than 100 inhabitants and others more than 5000. Status enables rights to fishing, hunting and living on a reservation, while nonstatus denies these rights but allows a person to vote, buy property and alcohol. Status can be lost and gained through marriage, an act of parliament or even a band taking a vote on the matter.

Later, as Canada's attention turned to its vast northern regions, the **Inuit** were also recognized as falling under federal jurisdiction. The Inuit have a separate

Aboriginal population figures

Population in Canada defining itself as aboriginal (2001 census).

	Aboriginal pop.	N. Am. Indian	Métis	Inuit
Alberta	156,225	84,995	66,060	1,090
British Columbia	170,025	118,295	44,265	800
Manitoba	150,045	90,340	56,800	340
New Brunswick	16,990	11,495	4,290	155
NF & Labrador	18,775	7,040	5,480	4,560
Northwest Terr	18,730	10,615	3,580	3,910
Nova Scotia	17,010	12,920	3,135	350
Nunavut	22,720	95	55	22,560
Ontario	188,315	131,560	48,340	1,375
Prince Edward Is	1,345	1,035	220	20
Québec	79,400	51,125	15,855	9,530
Saskatchewan	130,185	83,745	43,695	235
Yukon Territory	6,540	5,600	535	140
Total	**976,305**	**608,850**	**292,305**	**45,070**

origin, arriving much later to North America and inhabiting the inhospitable lands of Arctic Canada. The term Inuit totally replaced use of the derogatory term "**Eskimo**" in the 1970s. (Eskimo is an Algonkian word for "eaters of raw meat".) The Inuit share a common origin and a single language and at present number 45,070.

With a current population of 292,305, the **Métis** are the product of the unions between male fur traders, usually French-Canadians, and native women, particularly Cree. For centuries they were not recognized as Canadians or aboriginals, and with no rights many wandered the country, unable to settle. After a failed rebellion in 1885 (see p.602), they almost disappeared from social and political life and became "the forgotten people", largely poverty-stricken squatters on Crown land. Finally, in 1982, they were recognized as a First Nation in the Constitution.

Because of the distances separating them, each nation and even each community has its own characteristics. Their personalities and cultures are fashioned by history, the environment and by their surrounding neighbours. A large part of the aboriginal people live in relatively close contact with nonaboriginal people and interact on a daily basis with cultures that have a determining influence on their way of life. If there is any thread linking these groups, it is the cultural revival experienced over the last forty years. Under the banner of national political movements, all of these groups have renewed their commitment to organizing their social world, to re-establishing legal relationships to the land, and to maintaining and revitalizing their cultures and languages.

Colonization

When Europeans first arrived in northern North America they saw it as a *terra nullius* (empty land), but in reality it was a complex environment containing many cultures and communities. On the west coast the peoples had built societies of wealth and sophistication with plentiful resources from the sea and forest; in the prairies and northern tundra, the aboriginals lived off the vast herds of buffalo and caribou; in central Canada the forests were home to peoples who harvested wild rice from the marshes and grew corn, squash and beans by the rivers, supplementing their harvest with fishing and hunting; on the east coast and in the far north, the sea and land supplied their needs, and with incredible ingenuity enabled the inhabitants to survive harsh conditions.

Encounters between aboriginal and nonaboriginal people began to increase in number and complexity in the 1500s. There was an increased exchange of goods, trade deals, friendships and intermarriage as well as military and trade alliances. For at least two hundred years, the newcomers would not have been able to survive the rigours of the climate, succeed in their businesses (fishing, whaling, fur trading), or dodge each other's bullets, without aboriginal help.

Meanwhile **diseases** (typhoid, influenza, diptheria, plague, measles, tuberculosis, venereal disease and scarlet fever) killed tens of thousands – it is estimated that within a 200-year period aboriginal populations were reduced by as much as 95 percent.

As the fur trade intensified, the animal populations were wiped out in certain areas. This not only removed the traditional hunting practices but sparked off **inter-tribal wars**, all the more bloody now firearms were involved.

During this period, the French and British were few in number, the land seemed inhospitable and they feared attack from the aboriginal nations surrounding them. They were also fighting wars for trade and dominance –

they needed alliances with Indian nations, so many **treaties** were consequently negotiated. The treaties seemed to recognize the nationhood of aboriginal peoples and their equality but also demanded the authority of the monarch and, increasingly, the ceding of large tracts of land (particularly to British control for settlement and protection from seizure by the French and Americans). Usually what was agreed orally differed from what actually appeared in the treaties. The aboriginals did accept the monarch, but only as a kind of kin figure, a distant "protector" who could be called on to safeguard their interests and enforce treaty agreements. They had no notion of giving up their land, a concept foreign to aboriginal cultures; Chief François Paulette said: "In my language, there is no word for 'surrender'. I cannot describe 'surrender' to you in my language, so how do you expect my people to [have] put their X on 'surrender'?"

In 1763, the **Royal Proclamation** was a defining document in the relationship between the natives and the newcomers. Issued in the name of the king, it summarized the rules and regulations that were to govern British dealings with the aboriginal peoples – especially in relation to the question of land. It stated that aboriginal people were not to be "molested or disturbed" on their lands. Transactions involving aboriginal land were to be negotiated properly between the Crown and "assemblies of Indians". Aboriginal lands were to be acquired only by fair dealing: treaty, or purchase by the Crown. The aboriginal nations were portrayed as autonomous political entities, with their own internal political authority. Allowing for British settlement, it still safeguarded the rights of the aboriginals.

By the 1800s, the relationship between aboriginal and nonaboriginal people began to tilt on its foundation of rough equality. Through immigration the number of settlers was swelling, while disease and poverty continued to diminish aboriginal populations – by 1812, whites outnumbered indigenous people in Upper Canada by ten to one. The fur trade, which was established on a solid economic partnership between traders and trappers, was a declining industry. The new economy was based on timber, mining and agriculture and it needed land from the natives, who began to be seen as "impediments to progress". Colonial governments in Upper and Lower Canada no longer needed military allies, the British were victors in Canada, and the USA had won its independence. There was also a new attitude of European superiority over all other peoples and policies of domination and assimilation slowly replaced those of partnership.

Ironically, the transformation from respectful coexistence to **domination** by nonaboriginal laws and institutions began with the main instruments of the partnership: the treaties and the Royal Proclamation of 1763. These documents offered aboriginal people not only peace and friendship, respect and approximate equality, but also "protection". Protection was the leading edge of domination. At first, it meant preservation of aboriginal lands and cultural integrity from encroachment by settlers. Later, it meant "assistance", a code word implying an encouragement to stop being a part of aboriginal society and merge into the settler society.

Protection took the form of compulsory education, economic adjustment programmes, social and political control by federal agents, and much more. These policies, combined with missionary efforts to civilize and convert, tore wide holes in aboriginal cultures, autonomy and identity.

Reserves

In 1637, with a Jesuit settlement at Sillery in New France, the establishment of "**reserves**" of land for aboriginal peoples (usually of inadequate size and resources) began. Designed to "protect", they instead led to isolation and impoverishment. In 1857 the Province of Canada passed an act to "Encourage the Gradual Civilization of the Indian tribes": Indians of "good character" could be declared "non-Indian" by a panel of whites. Only one man, a Mohawk, is known to have accepted the invitation.

Confederation in 1867 was negotiated without reference to aboriginal nations. Indeed, newly elected Prime Minister John A. Macdonald announced that it would be his government's goal to "do away with the tribal system, and assimilate the Indian people in all respects with the inhabitants of the Dominion".

The **British North America Act**, young Canada's new constitution, made "Indians, and Lands reserved for the Indians" a subject for government regulation, like mines or roads. Indians became wards of the federal government and Parliament took on the job with vigour – passing laws to replace traditional aboriginal governments with band councils who had insignificant powers, taking control of valuable resources located on reserves, taking charge of reserve finances, imposing an unfamiliar system of land tenure, and applying nonaboriginal concepts of marriage and parenting.

These and other laws were codified in the main **Indian Acts** of 1876, 1880 and 1884. The Department of the Interior (later, Indian Affairs) sent Indian agents to every region to see that the laws were obeyed. In 1884, the **potlatch ceremony**, central to the cultures of west-coast aboriginal nations, was outlawed. A year later the **sun dance**, central to the cultures of prairie aboriginal nations, was outlawed. Participation was a criminal offence.

In 1885, the Department of Indian Affairs instituted a **pass system**. No outsider could come onto a reserve to do business with an aboriginal resident without permission from the Indian agent (a sort of government official with law-enforcement powers). Occasionally all aboriginal persons could not *leave* the reserve without permission from the Indian agent, either. Reserves were beginning to resemble prisons.

In 1849, the first of what would become a network of residential schools for aboriginal children was opened in Alderville, Ontario. Church and government leaders had come to the conclusion that the problem (as they saw it) of aboriginal independence and "savagery" could be solved by taking children from their families at an early age and instilling the ways of the dominant society during eight or nine years of residential schooling far from home. Attendance was compulsory. Aboriginal languages, customs and native skills were suppressed. The bonds between many hundreds of aboriginal children, their families and whole nations were broken.

During this stage Canadian governments moved aboriginal communities from one place to another at will. If aboriginal people were thought to have too little food, they could be relocated where game was more plentiful or jobs might be found. If they were suffering from illness, they could be sent to new communities where health services, sanitary facilities and permanent housing might be provided. If they were in the way of expanding agricultural frontiers, or in possession of land needed for settlement, they could be removed "for their own protection". If their lands contained minerals to be mined, forests to be cut, or rivers to be dammed, they could be displaced "in the national interest".

The result of centuries of mistreatment is that by almost every statistical indicator the aboriginal population is highly **disadvantaged** compared with all other Canadians. The problems affecting aboriginal peoples are grim, as alcoholism, drug use and sexual abuse continue to plague reserves. Infant mortality is twice as high among natives than non-natives, suicide rates among young people are five times higher among Indians than other Canadians, and life expectancy is seven years less for natives. Native peoples are also vastly overrepresented in jails across the country.

Resurgence

The 1940s were the beginning of a new era. Around 3000 aboriginals and unrecorded numbers of Métis and nonstatus Indians had fought for their country in both **World Wars**, and although accepted on the battlefield they were still badly treated at home. Aboriginal leaders emerged, forcefully expressing their people's desire to gain their rightful position of equality with other Canadians and maintain their cultural heritage, and in British Columbia, Alberta, Saskatchewan and Ontario, aboriginals formed provincially based organizations to protect and advance their interests. The Canadian public became more aware of the shocking way native society was being treated and how far their living standards had fallen behind all other groups of citizens. The **1951 Indian Act** rescinded the laws banning the potlatch and other ceremonies and aboriginal members were given the freedom to enter public bars to consume alcohol. But, on the whole, government oppression remained formidable. The **right to vote** in federal elections was granted only in 1960.

The rebirth of Canada's indigenous people can be traced to 1969, when a federal **"white paper"** proposed the elimination of Indian status. The result was a native backlash that forced the Trudeau Government to retreat and led to the creation of the **National Indian Brotherhood**, the forerunner of today's **Assembly of First Nations**.

Also in 1969, all Indian agents were withdrawn from reserves, and aboriginal political organizations started receiving government funding. Increasingly, these organizations focused on the need for full recognition of their aboriginal rights and renegotiation of the treaties. They believed that only in this way could they rise above their disadvantaged position in Canadian society. By 1973, aboriginals had local control of education and today more than half of all aboriginal students who live on reserves attend their own community schools.

Reclaiming the land

Land reserved for aboriginal people was steadily whittled away after its original allocation. Until recently, almost two-thirds of it had "disappeared" by various means since Confederation. In some cases, the government failed to deliver as much land as specified in a treaty. In other cases, it expropriated or sold reserved land, rarely with aboriginals as willing vendors. Once in a while, outright fraud took place. Even when aboriginals were able to keep hold of reserved land, the government sometimes sold its resources to outsiders. Some aboriginal nations have gone to court to force governments to recognize their rights to land and resources, and some have been successful. A series of court decisions in the 1970s confirmed that aboriginal peoples have more than a strong moral case for redress on land and resource issues – they have legal rights.

In recent years, Canada has come to a few new treaty-like **agreements**. The Innu and Cree took Québec to court in 1973, to stop a major hydroelectric project that threatened to decimate their traditional hunting grounds. The consequent **James Bay and Northern Québec Agreement**, signed in 1975, gave Innu and Crees (and later the Naskapi) $225m over twenty years in return for 981,610 square kilometres of territory. They were also given lands with exclusive hunting and trapping rights, native-controlled education and health authorities. With their funds the Cree have set up successful businesses such as Air Creebec and the Cree Construction Company. The **Cree-Naskapi Act**, passed in 1984, followed and enabled the Cree and Naskapi to establish their own forms of self-government – the first such legislation in Canada.

In 1973, the Supreme Court of Canada's decision on the Haida Indians led the federal government to establish a negotiating process to resolve **land claims** by recognizing two broad classes of claims – comprehensive and specific. Comprehensive claims are based on the recognition that there are continuing aboriginal rights to lands and natural resources and have a wide scope including such things as land title, fishing and trapping rights, financial compensation and other social and economic benefits. Specific claims deal with specific grievances that aboriginals may have regarding the fulfilment of treaties. In 1982, the government's recognition of land claims was renewed by a constitutional change, which touched off further favourable court decisions leading to new treaties with the Inuit of the Northwest Territories (1984 and 1993), the Yukon First Nations (1993) and the Nisga'a in BC (1996).

From the early 1970s until 1996, the government provided aboriginal groups with approximately $380 million to prepare their claims. This money enabled aboriginal peoples to conduct research into **treaties and rights** and to research, develop and negotiate their claims. But the negotiations have been notoriously long and painstaking, and until 1990 there was a limit of no more than six comprehensive claims at one time.

Enterprise

The ownership of land and control over funding have brought opportunities for economic self-sufficiency and expansion previously unavailable to aboriginal groups. This last decade has seen the rapid growth of a **free-enterprise** economy among Canada's aboriginals, especially in the cities. In 1995 there were an estimated 18,000 aboriginal-owned businesses across Canada. About 66 percent of aboriginal businesses were in the service sector; 13 percent were in construction and related sectors. Another 12 percent were in the primary industries such as mining and forestry, and 9 percent were businesses related to food processing, clothing, furniture, publishing and other manufacturing. One fast-growing area is aboriginal tourism, where an insight is given into culture and environment. However, employment and subsequent social problems (particularly among the growing young population) are still rampant.

Each year the oil-rich aboriginals get $32m in petroleum revenues. This upsurge in revenue would seem to bode well, but migration from the still impoverished reserves to the city (which began three decades ago) is on the increase, resulting in an unskilled and impoverished underclass of aboriginals in Canadian cities and a subsequent increase in social fragmentation, greater unrest and increased crime. Most of the aboriginal newcomers to the cities are young, and they are increasingly angry with the federal government and their own leaders. With 60 percent of aboriginal populations now city-based, there has also been the formation of young **street gangs**. Such gangs have made a mark in Winnipeg, which has the nation's biggest aboriginal urban population.

The **anger** that the street gangs epitomize has risen across native communities. Gang members complain about financial and political corruption by their leaders; young people, who make up more than half of the native population, say they are being ignored by an uncaring federal government and by ineffectual elders. As a young native activist said recently, "Most of us have nothing to lose, so we will do what we have to to have our voices heard." **Violence** is inevitable, and flared up most notoriously with an armed stand-off between Mohawk militants and the Canadian military at Oka in 1990 (see p.265). Five years later there was trouble again at Gustafsne Lake in the British Columbia interior and Ipperwash Provincial Park on the shores of Lake Huron. Meanwhile, the white attitude to militancy has hardened. Tough prison sentences are passed out to native protesters who break the law, yet there is little punishment for police officers who overstep the mark – in 1997, an Ontario Provincial policeman was given two years of community service after he was found guilty of criminal negligence in the fatal shooting of an aboriginal demonstrator at Ipperwash Provincial Park.

Change

The showdowns attracted much media attention and after Oka the government funded a $60m exhaustive **Royal Commission on Aboriginal Peoples**, which was finally published six years later in 1996 and called for fundamental change and self-government for aboriginals. The document presented a devastating account of the everyday struggle facing Canada's aboriginal peoples, including a catalogue of deprivation, mistreatment and official neglect suffered by native children in the residential schools. The report went on to recommend the creation of an aboriginal parliament to decide on land claims, establish a native university and steer an ambitious twenty-year multimillion dollar programme of economic aid to counter native unemployment and poor housing and health conditions. The majority of the recommendations seem to have been totally ignored by the present Liberal government – they've made it clear that broad structural change, particularly anything connected with the Constitution, is simply not on its agenda.

In 1998, the government did, however, formally apologize to the aboriginal peoples for the way they had been mistreated and offered compensation to those abused in the school system.

On April 1, 1999, after decades of negotiations and planning, came one of the most dramatic changes in the history of aboriginal land change. The creation of a new province, **Nunavut**, redrew Canada's borders and gave one-fifth of its landmass to Canada's smallest native population, the Inuit. Known as "our land" in Inuktitut, the two million square kilometres of Nunavut is home to a self-governed population of 27,000, 85 percent of which is Inuit. See p.975 for more on the region and its evolution. More recently, in 2000, the Supreme Court of British Columbia upheld the Nisga'a land treaty as constitutionally valid. This came after Liberals in British Columbia tried to quash the $487m deal, which gives 2000 square kilometres of land, $170m fishing and logging rights and a significant degree of self-government to the Nisga'a.

For their part the formerly fractured **Assembly of First Nations**, which represents "status Indians", enjoyed three years of relative calm under its national chief, Phil Fontaine, who lifted the AFN out of its debt, inherited from his predecessor, Ovide Mercredi, who had taken a much more hardline approach to aboriginal sovereignty. Fontaine also signed a co-operation agreement, in 1999, with the Washington-based National Congress of American Indians, America's largest Indian organization, to expand trade and cultural exchanges.

For all his achievements, Fontaine was seen as being too cosy with the government in Ottawa and in 2000, Mathew Coon Come, a tough-talking Cree leader from northern Québec, was elected the new national chief, signalling a return to more confrontational politics between Canada's natives and the federal government. His period in office, however, did not produce the results some might have hoped for, and in 2003 Fontaine was again returned as National Chief of First Nations with almost 61 percent of the vote.

Cultural revival

Beyond this volatile scenario there have been dramatic improvements secured since World War II that have led to a revival of interest in their own culture for many aboriginal people. Ceremonies, like the summer powwow celebrations, and art forms that have been almost forgotten, are being revived through research and reconstruction. There are aboriginal theatre groups that reinterpret the legends for modern audiences, aboriginal authors and poets who are publishing works that present unique and indigenous viewpoints; and aboriginal painters and sculptors who are using a mix of traditional and modern techniques to produce vivid and exciting works of art. A public television channel for indigenous people – the **Aboriginal Peoples Television Network** (APTN) – has been on the air since 1999. However, the optimism engendered by the creation of Nunavut has been tempered by the ever-present possibility of violent confrontation with the federal government and its agents as aboriginals seek redress for perceived ills. Employment figures hint at the problem: of the 652,345 aboriginal population, only 167,135 worked full time in 2001. Average annual income was $33,416 – against $43,298 for nonaboriginal population. As Coon Come declared before his fall, "Behaving like good little Indians never got us anywhere. There is a social time bomb that is ticking in the many Indian communities throughout Canada."

The natural environment

Canada has just about every **natural habitat** going, from ice-bound polar islands in the far north to sun-drilled pockets of desert along the US border. Between these extremes the country's mountains, forests and grasslands support an incredible variety and profusion of wildlife – any brief account can only scratch the surface of what it's possible to see. National and provincial parks offer the best starting places, and we've listed some of the outstanding sites for spotting particular species. However, don't expect to see the big attractions like bears and wolves easily; despite the enthusiasm of guides and tourist offices, these are encountered only rarely.

Flora and fauna checklist

This is by no means an exhaustive list of all Canada's flora and fauna – simply an indication of the places and the seasons that you are most likely to see certain species and types of wildlife.

Bears Black bears: Glacier National Park, BC and Banff, Jasper and Kananaskis Country, AB. Grizzlies: Glacier National Park, BC and Khutzeymateen Estuary, north of Prince Rupert, BC. *August.*

Bison Wood Buffalo National Park, AB.

Butterfly migrations Point Pelee and Long Point, Lake Erie, ON. *Spring and autumn.*

Caribou Dempster Hwy, YT. *Autumn.*

Cranes and pelicans Last Mountain Lake, SK. *Late August.*

Dall's sheep Sheep Mountain, Kluane National Park, YT. *Summer.*

Desert species Cacti, sagebrush, rattlesnakes and kangaroo rats: around Osoyoos, BC. *Summer.*

Eagles and owls Boundary Bay, south of Vancouver, BC. *Winter.*

Elk Banff, Jasper and Kananaskis Country, AB. *Summer.*

Orchids Bruce Peninsula National Park, ON. *Spring and summer.*

Polar bears Near Churchill, MB. *Autumn.*

Prairie species Hawks, coyotes and rattlesnakes: in the Milk River region, AB. *May and June.*

Salmon Adams River sockeye salmon run near Salmon Arm, BC. *October.*

Sea birds Gannets, murres and black kittiwakes around Cape St Mary's, NL. Waterfowl and sea birds in the Queen Charlotte Islands, BC. Northern gannets on Bonaventure Island, Gaspé Peninsula, QC. *June and July.*

Sea otters and sea lions Off Pacific Rim National Park, Vancouver Island, BC. *Spring and summer.*

Seals Queen Charlotte Islands, BC. *Summer.*

Snow geese Cap-Tourmente, QC. *Autumn.*

Whales Beluga, fin, humpback, blue and minke whales: near Tadoussac, QC. Killer whales (orcas): Robson Bight in Johnstone Strait, Vancouver Island, BC. *All in summer.* Grey whales: Pacific Rim National Park, Vancouver Island, BC. *Spring and summer.*

Wild flowers Numerous woodland species on Vancouver Island and the Gulf Islands, BC and at Mount Revelstoke National Park, BC. *Late spring to summer.*

Eastern forests

Canada's **eastern forests** divide into two main groups – the Carolinian forest of southwestern Ontario, and the Great Lakes-St Lawrence forest extending from the edge of the Carolinian forest to Lake Superior and the Gulf of St Lawrence.

The **Carolinian forest** forms a narrow belt of largely deciduous hardwood trees similar to the broad-leaved woodlands found over much of the eastern United States. Trees are often typical of more southerly climes – Kentucky coffee tree, tulip tree, sassafras, sycamore, chinquapin oak, shagbark hickory and more ordinary staples like beech, sugar maple, basswood and swamp oak. None of these is rare in the US, but in Canada they grow only here, thanks to the region's rich soils and relatively warm, sheltered climate.

A good deal of the Carolinian flora and fauna is coming under increasing threat from southern Ontario's urban and agricultural sprawl. These days much of the original forest has shrunk to a mosaic of fragments protected by national and provincial parks. The forests are most often visited by tourists for the astounding October colours, but if you're looking for **wildlife** you might also catch Canada's only marsupial, the **opossum**; or other southern species like the **fox squirrel** (introduced on Lake Erie's Pelee Island); the **eastern mole**, which occurs only in Essex County on Lake Erie's north shore; and the **eastern vole**, found only in a narrow band around Lake Erie.

Naturalists are equally drawn here for the **birds**, many of which are found nowhere else in Canada, especially during seasonal migrations, when up to one hundred species can easily be seen in a day. Most noteworthy of the more unusual species is the golden swamp warbler, a bird of almost unnaturally colourful plumage. More common visitors are hooded and Kentucky warblers, blue-winged and golden-winged warblers, gnatcatchers and virtually every species of eastern North American hawk. Sharp-shin hawks are common, and during autumn migrations of up to 70,000 broad-winged hawks might be seen in a single day near Port Stanley on Lake Erie's north shore.

In the wetlands bordering the forests, particularly at Long Point on Lake Erie, you can search out **reptiles** found nowhere else in the country. Most impressive is the water-loving fox snake, a harmless animal that often reaches well over a metre in length, but is often killed because of its resemblance to the rattlesnake and venomous copperhead – neither of which is found in the region. Also present, but in marked decline, are several **turtle** species, especially Blanding's, wood, spotted and spiny softshell.

Occurring in one of the most densely populated parts of Canada, the mixed conifer forests of the **Great Lakes-St Lawrence** area have been heavily logged and severely affected by urbanization. Most of the trees are southern species – beech and sugar maple, red and white pines – but are mixed with the eastern hemlock, spruce, jack pine, paper birch and balsam fir typical of more northerly forests. Ironically, widespread human disturbance has, if anything, created a greater diversity of forest types, which makes this region second only to southern British Columbia in the number of bird species it supports. It also provides for large numbers of **white-tailed deer**, a rare beneficiary of logging as it prefers to browse along the edges of clearings. In the evergreen stands on the north shore of the St Lawrence there are also large numbers of Canada's smallest mammal, the **pygmy shrew**. These tiny animals must eat their own weight in food daily and can't rest for more than an hour or so – they'd starve to death if they tried to sleep through the night.

Grassland

Contrary to the popular image of Canada's interior as a huge prairie of waving wheat, true **grassland** covers only ten percent of the country. Most is concentrated in the southernmost reaches of Alberta and Saskatchewan, with tiny spillovers in Manitoba and British Columbia – areas which lie in the Rockies' rain shadow and are too dry to support forest.

Two grassland belts once thrived in the region, tall-grass prairie in the north and shortgrass in the south. Farming has now not only put large areas of each under crops, but also decimated most of the large mammals that roamed the range – pronghorns, mule deer, white-tailed deer and elk – not to mention their predators, such as wolves, grizzlies, coyotes, foxes, bobcats and cougars.

The most dramatic loss from the grasslands, though, has been **bison** (or buffalo), the continent's largest land mammal. Once numbering an estimated 45 million, bison are now limited to just a few free-roaming herds in Canada. They're extraordinarily impressive animals – the average bull stands six feet at the shoulder and weighs over a ton – and early prairie settlers were so struck with their size that they believed bison, not the climate, had been responsible for clearing the grasslands.

Once almost as prevalent as the bison, but now almost as rare, is the **pronghorn**, a beautiful tawny-gold antelope species. Capable of speeds of over 100kph, it's the continent's swiftest land mammal, so you'll generally see nothing but its distinctive white rump disappearing at speed. Uniquely adapted for speed and stamina, the pronghorn has long legs, a heart twice the size of similar-sized animals, and an astonishingly wide windpipe. It also complements its respiratory machinery by running with its mouth open to gulp maximum amounts of air. Though only the size of a large dog, it has larger eyes than those of a horse, a refinement that spots predators several kilometres away. These days, however, wolves and coyotes are more likely to be after the prairie's new masters – countless small rodents such as gophers, ground squirrels and jackrabbits.

Birds have had to adapt not only to the prairie's dryness but also, of course, to the lack of extensive tree cover, and most species nest on the ground; many are also able to survive on reduced amounts of water and rely on seed-centred diets. Others confine themselves to occasional ponds, lakes and "sloughs", which are important breeding grounds for ducks, grebes, herons, pelicans, rails and many more. Other birds typical of the grassland in its natural state are the marbled godwit, the curlew and raptors such as the **prairie falcon**, a close relation of the peregrine falcon that's capable of diving speeds of up to 290kph.

Boreal forest

The **boreal forest** is Canada's largest single ecosystem, bigger than all the others combined. Stretching in a broad belt from Newfoundland to the Yukon, it fills the area between the eastern forests, grasslands and the northern tundra, occupying a good slice of every province except British Columbia. Only certain **trees** thrive in this zone of long, cold winters, short summers and acidic soils: although the cover is not identical countrywide, expect to see billions of white and black spruce (plus red spruce in the east), balsam fir, tamarack (larch) and jack pine, as well as such deciduous species as birch, poplar and aspen – all of which are ideal for wood pulp, making the boreal forest the staple resource of the country's **lumber industry**.

If you spend any time in the backcountry you'll also come across **muskeg**: neither land nor water, this porridge-like bog is the breeding ground of choice for pestilent hordes of mosquitoes and blackflies – and Canada has 1.3 million square kilometres of it. It also harbours mosses, scrub willow, pitcher plant, leatherleaf, sundew, cranberry and even the occasional orchid.

The boreal forest supports just about every animal recognized as distinctively Canadian: moose, beaver, black bear, wolf and lynx, plus a broad cross-section of small mammals and creatures such as deer, caribou and coyote from transitional forest-tundra and aspen-parkland habitats to the north and south. **Wolves** are still numerous in Canada, but hunting and harassment has pushed them to the northernmost parts of the boreal forest. Their supposed ferocity is more myth than truth; intelligent and elusive creatures, they rarely harm humans, and it's unlikely you'll see any – though you may well hear their howling if you're out in the sticks. **Lynx** are even more elusive. One of the northern forest's most elegant animals, this big cat requires a 150- to 200-square-kilometre range, making Canada's northern wilderness one of the world's few regions capable of sustaining a viable population. Nocturnal hunters, lynx feed on deer and moose but favour the hare, a common boreal creature that is to the forest's predators what the lemming is to the carnivores of the tundra.

Beavers, on the other hand, are commonly seen all over Canada. You may catch them at dawn or dusk, heads just above the water as they glide across lakes and rivers. Signs of their legendary activity include log jams across streams and ponds, stumps of felled saplings resembling sharpened pencils, and dens which look like domed piles of mud and sticks.

Lakes, streams and marshy muskeg margins are all favoured by **moose**. A lumbering animal with magnificent spreading antlers, it is the largest member of the deer family and is found over most of Canada, but especially near swampy ground, where it likes to graze on mosses and lichens. It's also a favourite with hunters, and few northern bars are without their moose head – perhaps the only place you'll see this solitary and reclusive species.

Forest wetlands also offer refuge for **ducks and geese**, with loons, grebes and songbirds attracted to their surrounding undergrowth. Canada's three species of ptarmigan – willow, rock and white-tailed – are also common, and you'll see plenty of big **raptors**, including the great grey owl, Canada's largest owl. Many boreal birds migrate, and even those that don't, such as hawks, jays, ravens and grouse, tend to move a little way south, sometimes breaking out into southern Canada in mass movements known as "irruptions". Smaller birds, like chickadees, waxwings and finches, are particularly fond of these sporadic forays.

Mountain forests

Mountain forests cover much of western Canada and, depending on location and elevation, divide into four types: West Coast, Columbia, montane and sub-alpine.

The **West Coast**'s torrential rainfall, mild maritime climate, deep soils and long growing season produce Canada's most impressive forests and its biggest trees. Swaths of luxuriant temperate **rainforest** cover much of Vancouver Island and the Pacific coast, dominated by Sitka spruce, western red cedar, Pacific silver fir, western hemlock, western yew and, biggest of all, **Douglas fir**, some of which tower 90 metres high and are 1200 years old. However, these conifers make valuable timber, and much of this forest is under severe threat from logging. Some of the best stands – a fraction of the original – have been preserved on the Queen Charlotte Islands and in Vancouver Island's Pacific Rim National Park. Below the luxuriant, dripping canopy of the big trees lies an **undergrowth** teeming with life. Shrubs and bushes such as salal, huckleberry, bunchberry, salmonberry and twinberry thrive alongside mosses, ferns, lichens, liverworts, skunk cabbage and orchids. All sorts of animals can be found here, most notably the **cougar** and its main prey, the Columbian blacktail **deer**, a subspecies of the mule deer. **Birds** are legion, and include a wealth of woodland species such as the Townsend's warbler, Wilson's warbler, orange-crowned warbler, junco, Swainson's thrush and golden-crowned kinglet. Rarer birds include the rufous **hummingbird**, which migrates from its wintering grounds in Mexico to feed on the forest's numerous nectar-bearing flowers.

The **Columbia forest** covers the lower slopes (400–1400m) of British Columbia's interior mountains and much of the Rockies. **Trees** here are similar to those of the West Coast's warmer and wetter rainforest – western red cedar, western hemlock and Douglas fir – with Sitka spruce, which rarely thrives away from the coast, the notable exception. The undercover, too, is similar, with lots of devil's club (a particularly vicious thorn), azaleas, black and red twinberry, salmonberry and redberry alder. Mountain lily, columbine, bunchberry and heart-leaf arnica are among the common flowers. Few mammals live exclusively in the forests with the exception of the **red squirrel**, which makes a meal of conifer seeds, and is in turn preyed on by hawks, owls, coyotes and weasels, among others. Bigger predators roam the mountain forest, however, most notably the **brown bear**, a western variant of the ubiquitous **black bear**. Aside from the coyote, the tough, agile black bear is one of the continent's most successful carnivores and the one you're most likely to see around campsites and rubbish dumps. Black bears have adapted to a wide range of habitats and food sources, and their only natural enemies – save wolves, which may attack young cubs – are hunters, who bag some 30,000 annually in North America. Scarcer but still hunted is the famous **grizzly bear**, a far larger and potentially dangerous creature distinguished by its brownish fur and the ridged hump on its back. Now extinct in many of its original habitats, the grizzly is largely confined to the remoter slopes of the Rockies and West Coast ranges, where it feeds mainly on berries and salmon. Like other bears, grizzlies are unpredictable and readily provoked – see p.686 for tips on avoiding unpleasant encounters.

Montane forest covers the more southerly and sheltered reaches of the Rockies and the dry plateaux of interior British Columbia, where spindly Douglas fir, western larch, ponderosa pine and the **lodgepole pine** predominate. Like its eastern counterpart, the jack pine, the lodgepole requires intense heat before opening and releasing its seeds, and huge stands of these trees grew in the aftermath of the forest fires which accompanied the building and running of the railways. Plentiful voles and small rodents attract **coyotes**, whose yapping – an announcement of territorial claims – you'll often hear at night close to small towns. Coyotes are spreading northwards into the Yukon and Northwest Territories and eastwards into Ontario and Québec, a proliferation that continues despite massive extermination campaigns, prompted by the coyotes' taste for livestock. Few predators have the speed to keep up with coyotes – only the stealthy **cougar**, or wolves hunting in tandem, can successfully bring them down. Cougars are now severely depleted in Canada, and the British Columbia interior and Vancouver Island are the only regions where they survive in significant numbers. Among the biggest and most beautiful of the carnivores, they seem to arouse the greatest bloodlust in hunters. Ponderosa and lodgepole pines provide fine cover for **birds** like goshawks, Swainson's hawks and lesser species such as ruby-crowned kinglets, warblers, pileated woodpeckers, nuthatches and chickadees. In the forest's lowest reaches the vegetation and birds are those of the southern prairies – semi-arid regions of sagebrush, prickly pear and bunch grasses, dotted with lakes full of common **ducks** such as mallard, shoveler and widgeon. You might also see the cinnamon teal, a red version of the more common green-wing teal, a bird whose limited distribution draws bird-watchers to British Columbia on its own account.

Subalpine forest covers mountain slopes from 1300m to 2200m throughout the Rockies and much of British Columbia, supporting lodgepole, whitebark and limber pines, alpine fir and Engelmann spruce. It also contains a preponderance of **alpine larch**, a deciduous conifer whose vivid autumnal yellows dot the mountainsides to beautiful effect. One of the more common animals of this zone is the **elk**, or **wapiti**, a powerful member of the deer family which can often be seen summering in large herds above the tree line. Elk court and mate during the autumn, making a thin nasal sound called "bugling". Respect their privacy, as rutting elk have notoriously unpredictable temperaments. Small herds of **mule deer** migrate between forests and alpine meadows, using small glands between their hooves to leave a scent for other herd members to follow. They're named after their distinctive ears, designed to provide early warning of predators. Other smaller animals which are also attracted to the subalpine forest include the golden-mantled ground squirrel, and birds such as Clark's nutcracker, both tame and curious creatures which often gather around campsites in search of scraps.

Alpine zones

Alpine zones occur in mountains above the tree line, which in Canada means parts of the Rockies, much of British Columbia and large areas of the Yukon. Plant and animal life varies hugely between summer and winter, and according to terrain and exposure to the elements – sometimes it resembles that of the tundra, at others it recalls the profile of lower forest habitats.

In spring, alpine meadows are carpeted with breathtaking displays of **wild flowers**: clumps of Parnassus grass, lilies, anemones, Indian paintbrushes, lupins and a wealth of yellow flowers such as arnica, cinquefoil, glacier lily and wood betony. These meadows make excellent pasture, attracting elk and mule deer in summer, as well as full-time residents such as **Dall's sheep**, the related **bighorn** and the incredible **mountain goat**, perhaps the hardiest of Canada's bigger mammals. Staying close to the roughest terrain possible, mountain goats are equipped with short, stolid legs, flexible toes and nonskid soles, all designed for clambering over near-vertical slopes, grazing well out of reach of their less agile predators.

Marmots, resembling hugely overstuffed squirrels, take things easier and hibernate through the worst of the winter and beyond. In a good year they can sleep for eight months, prey only to grizzly bears, which are strong enough and have the claws to dig down into their dens. In their waking periods they can be tame and friendly, often nibbling contentedly in the sunnier corners of campsites. When threatened, however, they produce a piercing and unearthly whistle. (They can also do a lot of damage: some specialize in chewing the radiator hoses of parked cars.) The strange little **pika**, a relative of the rabbit, is more elusive but keeps itself busy throughout the year, living off a miniature haystack of fodder which it builds up during the summer.

Birds are numerous in summer, and include rosy finches, pipits and blue grouse, but few manage to live in the alpine zone year-round. One which does is the white-tailed **ptarmigan**, a plump, partridge-like bird which, thanks to its heavily feathered feet and legs, is able to snowshoe around deep drifts of snow; its white winter plumage provides camouflage. Unfortunately, ptarmigans can be as slow-moving and stupid as barnyard chickens, making them easy targets for hunters and predators.

Coastlines

Canada has three coastlines: the Atlantic, the Pacific and the Arctic (dealt with under "Tundra"). Each boasts a profusion of maritime, dunal and intertidal life; the Pacific coast, warmed by the Japanese current, actually has the greatest number of species of any temperate shore. Few people are very interested in the small fry, however – most come for the big mammals, and **whales** in particular.

Grey whales are most common in the Pacific, and are often easily spotted from mainland headlands in the February to May and September to October periods as they migrate between the Arctic and their breeding grounds off Mexico. Once hunted close to the point of extinction, they've now returned in large numbers, and most West Coast harbours have charter companies offering whale-watching tours. **Humpback whales** are another favourite, largely because they're curious and follow sightseeing boats, but also because of their surface acrobatics and long, haunting "songs". They too were hunted to near-extinction, and though protected by international agreement since 1966 they still number less than ten percent of their original population. Vancouver Island's inner coast supports one of the world's most concentrated populations of **killer whales** or **orcas**. These are often seen in family groups or "pods" travelling close to shore, usually on the trail of large fish – which on the West Coast means **salmon**. The orca, however, is the only whale whose diet also runs to warm-blooded animals – hence the "killer" tag – and it will gorge on walrus, seal and even minke, grey and beluga whales.

Another West Coast inhabitant, the **sea otter**, differs from most marine mammals in that it keeps itself warm with a thick soft coat of fur rather than with blubber. This brought it to the attention of early Russian and British fur traders, and by the beginning of the twentieth century it was virtually extinct. Reintroduced in 1969 to Vancouver Island's northwest coast, they are now breeding successfully at the heart of their original range. With binoculars, it's often easy to spot these charming creatures lolling on their backs, cracking open sea urchins or mussels with a rock and using their stomachs as anvils; they often lie bobbing asleep, entwined in kelp to stop them floating away. Northern **fur seals** breed on Alaska's Pribilof Islands but are often seen off the British Columbian coast during their migrations. Like their cousin, the northern **sea lion**, a year-round resident, they are "eared seals", who can manage rudimentary shuffling on land thanks to short rear limbs which can be rotated for forward movement. They also swim with strokes from front flippers, as opposed to the slithering, fishlike action of true seals.

The **Atlantic's** colder waters nurture fewer overall species than the Pacific coast, but many birds and larger mammals – especially **whales** – are common to both. One of the Atlantic region's more distinctive creatures is the **harp seal** (or saddleback), a true seal species that migrates in late winter to breeding grounds off Newfoundland and in the Greenland and White seas. Most pups are born on the pack ice, and for about two weeks sport fluffy white coats that have been highly prized by the fur trade for centuries. Until the late 1960s tens of thousands of young seals died annually in an unsupervised slaughter whose methods – clubbing and skinning alive – brought about outrage on an international scale (see p.480).

Tundra

Tundra extends over much of northern Yukon, the Northwest Territories and Nunavut, stretching between the boreal forest and the polar seas. Part grassland and part wasteland, it's a region distinguished by high winds, bitter cold and **permafrost**, a layer of perpetually frozen subsoil which covers over thirty percent of Canada. The tundra is not only the domain of ice and emptiness, however: long hours of summer sunshine and the melting of topsoil nurture a carpet of wild flowers and many species of birds and mammals have adapted to the vagaries of climate and terrain.

Vegetation is uniformly stunted by poor drainage, acidic soils and permafrost, which prevents the formation of deep roots and locks nutrients in the ice. **Trees** like birch and willow can grow, but they spread their branches over a wide area, rarely rising over a metre in height. Over 99 percent of the remaining vegetation consists of perennials like **grasses** and sedges, small flowering annuals, mosses, lichens and shrubs. Most have evolved ingenious ways of protecting themselves against the elements: Arctic cotton grass, for example, grows in large insulated hummocks in which the interior temperature is higher than the air outside; others have large, waxy leaves to conserve moisture or catch as much sunlight as possible. **Wild flowers** during the short, intense spring can be superlative, covering seemingly inert ground in a carpet of purple mountain saxifrage, yellow Arctic poppy, indigo clusters of Arctic forget-me-not and the pink buds of Jacob's ladder.

Tundra grasses provide some of the first links in the food chain, nourishing mammals such as white **Arctic ground squirrels**, also known as parkas, as their fur is used by the Inuit to make parka jackets. Vegetation also provides the staple diet of **lemmings**, amongst the most remarkable of the Arctic fauna. Instead of hibernating these creatures live under the snow, busily tucking away on shoots in order to double their weight daily – the intake they need merely to survive. They also breed almost continuously, which is just as well for they are the mainstay of a long list of predators. Chief of these are **Arctic white foxes**, ermines and weasels, though birds, bears and Arctic wolves may also hunt them in preference to larger prey. Because they provide a staple diet to so many, lemming populations have a marked effect on the life cycles of numerous creatures.

A notable exception is the **caribou**, a member of the reindeer family and the most populous of the big tundra mammals. Caribou are known above all for their epic migrations, frequently involving thousands of animals, which start in March when the herds leave their wintering grounds on the fringes of the boreal forest for calving grounds to the north. The exact purpose of these migrations is still a matter of conjecture. They certainly prevent the overgrazing of the tundra's fragile mosses and lichens, and probably also enable the caribou to shake off some of the wolves that would otherwise shadow the herd (wolves have to find southerly dens at this time to bear their own pups). The timing of treks also means that calving takes place before the arrival of biting insects, which can claim as many calves as predators – an adult caribou can lose as much as a litre of blood a week to insects.

The tundra's other large mammal is the **musk ox**, a vast, shaggy herbivore and close cousin of the bison. The musk ox's Achilles' heel is a tendency to form lines or circles when threatened – a perfect defence against wolves, but not against rifle-toting hunters, who until the introduction of conservation measures threatened to be their undoing. Canada now has some of the world's largest free-roaming herds, although – like the caribou – they're still hunted for food and fur by the Inuit.

Tundra **birds** number about a hundred species and are mostly migratory. Three-quarters of these are waterfowl, which arrive first to take advantage of streams, marshes and small lakes created by surface meltwater: Arctic wetlands provide nesting grounds for numerous swans, geese and ducks, as well as the loon, which is immortalized on the back of the Canadian dollar coin. The red-necked **phalarope** is a particularly specialized visitor, able to feed on aquatic insects and plankton, though not as impressive in its abilities as the migratory **Arctic tern**, whose 32,000-kilometre round trip from the Antarctic is the longest annual migration of any creature on the planet. The handful of nonmigratory birds tend to be scavengers like the raven, or predators like the **gyrfalcon**, the world's largest falcon, which preys on Arctic hares and ptarmigan. Jaegers, gulls, hawks and owls largely depend on the lemming: the snowy owl, for example, synchronizes its returns to southern Canada with four-year dips in the lemming population.

Fauna on the Arctic **coast** has a food chain that starts with plankton and algae, ranging up through tiny crustaceans, clams and mussels, sea cucumbers and sea urchins, cod, ringed and bearded seals, to beluga whales and **polar bears** – perhaps the most evocative of all tundra creatures, but still being killed in their hundreds for "sport" despite almost thirty years of hunting restrictions. Migrating **birds** are especially common here, notably near Nunaluk Spit on the Yukon coast, which is used as a corridor and stopover by millions of loons, swans, geese, plovers, sandpipers, dowitchers, eagles, hawks, guillemots and assorted songbirds.

Books

Most of the following **books** should be readily available, though you may have a little more difficulty tracking down those few titles we mention which are currently out of print (signified o/p). The same caution applies to those books which are only published in Canada and in these cases we've given the name of the publisher in brackets after the title. Titles marked with a star are especially recommended.

Travel and guides

P. Browning *The Last Wilderness*. An engrossing description of a harsh and lonely canoe journey through the Northwest Territories.

Ranulph Fiennes *The Headless Valley*. Tales of derring-do from noted adventurer, white-water rafting down the South Nahanni and Fraser rivers of British Columbia and the old NWT.

Anna Jameson *Winter Studies and Summer Rambles in Canada*. Originally published in 1839, these tart observations of early Toronto's colonial society are marked by a sense of wonderment at the vastness of Canada's untamed wilderness.

★ **Paul Kane** *Wanderings of an Artist among the Indians of North America*. Kane, one of Canada's better-known landscape artists, spent two and a half years travelling from Toronto to the Pacific Coast and back in the 1840s. His witty, racy account of his wanderings makes a delightful read.

David McFadden *Trip Around Lake Ontario*. Part of a trilogy detailing the author's circumnavigation of lakes Ontario, Erie and Huron written in a deceptively simple style.

Gary and Joannie McGuffin *Canoeing Across Canada*. Reflections on a 6000-mile journey through the country's rivers and backwaters.

Susanna Moodie *Roughing It in the Bush, or Forest Life in Canada* (McClelland & Stewart, Canada). Intriguing narrative written in 1852, describing an English couple's slow ruin as they attempt to create a new life in southeastern Ontario.

Jan Morris *O Canada: Travels in an Unknown Country* (o/p) Musings from this well-known travel writer after a coast-to-coast Canadian trip.

Grey Owl *Three Complete & Unabridged Works – Men of the Last Frontier; Pilgrims of the Wild & The Adventures of Sajo and Her Beaver People*. First published in the 1930s, these three books – now packaged in one volume – romantically describe life in the wilds of Canada at the time when exploitation was changing the land forever. Grey Owl's love of animals and the wilderness are inspiring and his forward-thinking, ecological views are particularly startling. Also in print is Grey Owl's *Tales of an Empty Cabin*.

Duncan Pryde *Nununga: Ten Years of Eskimo Life*. Less a travel book than a social document from a Glaswegian who left home at eighteen to spend ten years with the Inuit.

Constance Rooke *Writing Home: a PEN Anthology*. A handful of Canada's leading contemporary authors muse on the idea of home.

Though more an insight into the inner workings of writers' minds than Canadian culture, this book's "sampler" style makes it a welcome partner on cross-country journeys.

⊠ **Elizabeth Simcoe** (ed. Mary Innis) *Mrs Simcoe's Diary*. The wife of Upper Canada's first lieutenant governor and an early resident of York (Toronto), not only did Mrs Simcoe provide detailed observations of the landscape and the city's way of life, but she was also an astute political observer, offering portraits of major historical figures like the Mohawk chief, Joseph Brant.

Natural history

Richard Chandler *The Macmillan Field Guide to North Atlantic Shorebirds* (o/p). Well-illustrated and comprehensive handbook.

Lyall Watson *Sea Guide to Whales of the World* (o/p). Encyclopedic and lavishly illustrated guide to the whale.

Specialist guides

Darryl Bray *Kluane National Park Hiking Guide* (Travel Vision, Canada, o/p). A much-needed guide to long and short walks in a park where the trail network is still in its infancy.

Neil G. Carey *A Guide to the Queen Charlotte Islands* (Group West, o/p). An authoritative guide to islands which are difficult to explore and ill-served by back-up literature.

John Dodd and Gail Helgason *The Canadian Rockies Access Guide*. Descriptions of 115 day-hikes, with degrees of difficulty, time needed, sketch maps of routes, wildlife descriptions and numerous photos.

David Dunbar *The Outdoor Traveller's Guide to Canada* (o/p). Too bulky to be a useful guide in the field, but a lavishly illustrated introduction to the outdoor pursuits, wildlife and geology of 37 of the country's best national and provincial parks.

Doug Eastcott *Backcountry Biking in the Canadian Rockies*. The essential and definitive guide to all things mountain-bike in the Rockies, with over 200 trails accompanied by accurate sketch maps and helpful elevation profiles.

Heather Elton *Banff's Best Day Hikes*. Good selection of walks in and around Banff town and national park with adequate maps and tempting photos.

Ben Gadd *A Handbook of the Canadian Rockies* (Corax). Widely available in western Canada's larger bookshops, this is a lovingly produced and painstakingly detailed account of walks, flora, fauna, geology and anything else remotely connected with the Rockies.

The Lost Moose Catalogue (Lost Moose Publishing, Canada). Highly entertaining and iconoclastic magazine-style guide and commentary on the contemporary mores of the Yukon and far north.

Teri Lydiard *The British Columbia Bicycling Guide* (o/p). Small but extremely detailed pointer to some tempting routes, backed up with good maps.

Brian Patton and Bart Robinson *The Canadian Rockies Trail Guide*. An essential guide for anyone wishing to do more than simply scratch the surface of the Rockies' walking possibilities.

Archie Shutterfield *The Chilkoot Trail: a Hiker's Historical Guide* (o/p). A pithy accompaniment to the Chilkoot Trail that should be read in conjunction with Pierre Berton's *Klondike*.

Sierra Club of West Canada *The West Coast Trail* (Douglas & McIntyre, Canada). Probably the best of several guides to Vancouver Island's popular but demanding long-distance footpath.

Culture and society

John Bently-Mays *Emerald City: Toronto Visited* (o/p). Thoughtful critical essays about Toronto, its architecture and its inhabitants.

Hugh Brody *Maps and Dreams* (o/p). Brilliantly written account of the lives and lands of the Beaver natives of northwest Canada. For further acute insights into the ways of the far north see also the same author's *Living Arctic* (o/p) and *The People's Land: Eskimos and Whites in the Eastern Arctic* (o/p).

David Cruise & Alison Griffiths *The Great Adventure: How the Mounties conquered the West.* Contemporary accounts of the Mounties' first major expedition into the West from the strange assortment of men who made up this legendary force.

Beatrice Culleton *April Raintree* (Pemmican, Canada). Heart-rending account of the enforced fostering of Métis children in Manitoba during the 1950s.

Don Dumond *The Eskimos and Aleuts.* Anthropological and archeological tour de force on the prehistory, history and culture of northern peoples: backed up with fine maps, drawings and photographs.

Christian F. Feest *Native Arts of North America.* This attractively illustrated book covers every aspect of North American native art in revealing detail. Everything you've ever wanted to know – and probably a good bit more.

Paul Fleming *The North American Indians in Early Photographs* (o/p). Stylized poses don't detract from a plaintive record of a way of life that has all but vanished.

Glenn Gould *The Solitude Trilogy.* These CDs comprise three extraor-dinary sound documentaries made by Gould for CBC (who also recorded his music) concerning life in the extreme parts of Canada. A fascinating insight into harsh lifestyles in the words of the people themselves.

Glenn Gould (ed. Tim Page) *The Glenn Gould Reader.* Sometimes chatty, sometimes pompous, Gould's voice and erudition shine through this collection of essays, articles and letters written from early adulthood to the end of his short life.

★ **Mark Kurlansky** *Cod: A Biography of the Fish that Changed the World.* This fascinating book tracks the life and times of the cod and the generations of fishermen who have lived off it. There are sections on over-fishing and the fish's breeding habits along with cod recipes. Naturally enough, the Newfoundland cod fishery features prominently and you won't get a more balanced view as to what went wrong – and why the fishery was closed.

Barry Lopez *Arctic Dreams: Imagination and Desire in a Northern Landscape.* Extraordinary, award-winning book combining natural history, physics, poetry, earth sciences and philosophy in a dazzling portrait of the far north.

Alan D. McMillan *Native Peoples and Cultures of Canada.* Comprehensive account of Canada's native groups from prehistory to current issues of self-government and land claims. Well written, though more an academic textbook than a leisure-time read. Published in 1995.

Dennis Reid *A Concise History of Canadian Painting.* Not especially concise, but a thorough trawl through Canada's leading artists, with bags of biographical detail and lots of black-and-white (and a few colour) illustrations of major works. Goes as far as the early 1980s.

Mike Tooby (ed) *The True North – Canadian Landscape Painting 1896–1939*. A fascinating and well-illustrated book exploring how Canadian artists have treated the country's challenging landscapes.

Harold Towne and David P. Silcox *Tom Thomson: The Silence in the Storm* (McClelland & Stewart, Canada). A study of the career and inspirations of Tom Thomson, one of Canada's best-known artists.

William White (ed) *The Complete Toronto Dispatches, 1920–1924* (Charles Scribners Sons, o/p). Ernest Hemingway's first professional writing job was with *The Toronto Star* as both a local reporter and as a European correspondent. This is a collection of his dispatches for the paper.

Biography

Anahareo *Grey Owl and I* (P. Davies, o/p). The story of Grey Owl's Iroquois wife, their fight to save the beaver from extinction and her shock at discovering that her husband was in fact an Englishman. Good insights into the changing life of Canada's natives in the twentieth century.

★ **Lovat Dickson** *Wilderness Man*. The fascinating story of Archie Belaney, the Englishman who became famous as his adopted persona, Grey Owl. Written by his English publisher and friend, who was one of many that did not discover the charade until after Grey Owl's death.

Richard Gwyn *Smallwood: the Unlikely Revolutionary* (McClelland & Stewart, o/p). Detailed biography of Joey Smallwood, the Newfoundland premier who pushed his island into Confederation in 1949. Gwyn's exploration of island corruption and incompetence is incisive and intriguing in equal measure.

James MacKay *Robert Service: Vagabond of Verse*. Not the first, but certainly the most substantial biography discussing this prominent Canadian poet's life and work. Published in 1995.

Peter F. Ostwald *Glenn Gould: The Ecstasy and Tragedy of Genius*. A biography by a psychiatrist (100% Freud-free) of Canada's most famous musician. The eccentric pianist comes across as a rather inhuman egotist but with a talent to make this sufferable to many of his followers.

History

Fred Anderson *Crucible of War: The Seven Years' War and the Fate of the British Empire in British North America, 1754–1766*. Lucid and extraordinarily well-researched account of this crucial period in the development of North America. At 800-odd pages, it's perhaps a little too detailed for many tastes, but it's a fascinating read. Included is the story of the fall of Fort William Henry, as celebrated in the film, *The Last of the Mohicans*.

Owen Beattie and John Geiger *The Fate of the Franklin Expedition 1845–48*. An account both of the doomed expedition to find the Northwest Passage and the discovery of artefacts and bodies still frozen in the northern ice; worth buying for the extraordinary photos.

Carl Benn *The Iroquois in the War of 1812*. In 1812 the United States, at war with Canada, invaded and briefly occupied York (Toronto). The role played by the Five Nations and Iroquois peoples in the war was pivotal in Canada's survival, and the ramifications of the War of 1812 affected the aboriginal people of Ontario for years to come.

⭐ **Pierre Berton** *Klondike: the Last Great Goldrush 1896–1899*. Exceptionally readable account from one of Canada's finest and most approachable writers of the characters and epic episodes of the Yukon gold rush. Other Berton titles include *The Arctic Grail*, describing the quest for the North Pole and the Northwest Passage from 1818 to 1919; *The Last Spike: the Great Railway 1881–1885*, an account of the history and building of the transcontinental railway; *Flames across the Border*, a detailed account of the US attack on Canada in 1813–1814; and *Vimy*, an account of the World War I battle fought mainly by Canadians which Berton sees as a turning point in the nation's history.

Gerald Friesen *The Canadian Prairies: a History*. Stunningly well-researched and detailed account of the development of Central Canada. A surprisingly entertaining book that's particularly good on the culture of the Métis and Plains Indians. First published in 1984.

Harold Innis *The Fur Trade in Canada: An Introduction to Canadian Economic History*. The words "dra-matic, sweeping and engaging" are not usually associated with books on economic history, but in this case they fit the bill. Innis's study is invaluable for the insight it gives to pre-European Canada, and its trading customs with Ontario's native peoples.

Kenneth McNaught *The Penguin History of Canada*. Concise analysis of the country's economic, social and political history. First published in 1970 and updated in 1988.

Peter Neary and Patrick O'Flaherty *Part of the Main: an Illustrated History of Newfoundland and Labrador* (Breakwater, Canada). Lively text and excellent illustrations make this the best account of the province's history, though it's short of contemporary information.

Peter C. Newman *Caesars of the Wilderness*. Highly acclaimed and readable account of the rise and fall of the Hudson's Bay Company.

⭐ **George Woodcock** *A Social History of Canada*. Erudite and incisive book about the peoples of Canada and the country's development. Woodcock is the most perceptive of Canada's historians and his work has the added advantage of being very readable. Also by the author is *The Canadians*, a lavishly illustrated and brilliantly lucid attempt to summarize the Canadian experience.

Fiction

Margaret Atwood *Surfacing*. Canada's most eminent novelist is not always easy reading, but her analysis, particularly of women and society, is invariably witty and penetrating. In *Surfacing* the remote landscape of northern Québec plays an instrumental part in an extreme voyage of self-discovery. Regeneration through exploration of the past is also the theme of *Cat's Eye* and *Lady Oracle*, while the collection of short stories *Wilderness Tips* sees women ruminating over the bastards in their lives. *Alias Grace* is a dark and sensual tale centred around the true story of one of Canada's most notorious female criminals of the 1840s. Atwood's *The Blind Assassin* is a

"Canadian dynastic epic" and won the UK's prestigious Booker Prize in 2000. Her latest work is the futuristic nightmare of *Oryx and Crake*.

Lynn Coady *Saints of Big Harbour*. Forceful novel set in rural Nova Scotia dealing with a dysfunctional family – all alcohol and violence. Hardly cheerful stuff, but the characters are immaculately portrayed.

★ **Robertson Davies** For many years the leading figure of Canada's literary scene, Davies died in 1995 at the age of 82. Amongst his considerable output are big, dark and complicated webs of familial and social history which include wonderful evocations of the semi-rural Canada of his youth. A good place to start is *What's Bred in the Bone*, part of *The Cornish Trilogy*, whose other titles are *The Rebel Angels* and *The Lyre of Orpheus*. Similarly intriguing is *Fifth Business*, the first part of *The Deptford Trilogy*.

Timothy Findley *Headhunter*. A sombre novel that brings aspects of Conrad's *Heart of Darkness* to contemporary Rosedale, a haute bourgeois Toronto neighbourhood.

William Gibson *Virtual Light* and *Idoru* are arguably the best books from the master of cyberdom. The impact of technologies on human experience and the overlapping of artifice and reality are his significant themes.

Hammond Innes *Campbell's Kingdom*. A melodrama of love and oil-drilling in the Canadian Rockies – though the landscape's less well evoked than in *The Land God Gave to Cain*, the story of one man's search for "gold and truth" in Labrador.

Margaret Laurence *A Jest of God* and *The Stone Angel*. Manitoba-born Laurence epitomized the new vigour that swept through the country's literature during the Sixties – though the best of her fiction was written in England. Most of her books are set in the fictional prairie backwater of Manawaka, and explore the loneliness and frustration of women within an environment of stifling small-town conventionality. Always highly revered at home, Laurence's reputation is on the increase abroad.

Stephen Leacock *Sunshine Sketches of a Little Town*. Whimsical tale of Ontario small-town life; the best of a series based on the author's summertime stays in Orillia.

Jack London *Call of the Wild* and *White Fang*. London spent over a year in the Yukon gold fields during the Klondike gold rush. Many of his experiences found their way into his vivid – if sometimes overwrought – tales of the northern wilderness. These are the pick.

Malcolm Lowry *Hear Us O Lord from Heaven thy Dwelling Place*. Lowry spent almost half his writing life (1939–54) in log cabins and beach houses he built for himself around Vancouver. *Hear Us O Lord* is a difficult read to say the least: a fragmentary novella which, amongst other things, describes a disturbing sojourn on Canada's wild Pacific coast.

Ann-Marie MacDonald *Fall on Your Knees*. Entertaining, epic-style family saga from this Toronto-based writer with an astute eye for characters and a fine storytelling touch. The novel follows the fortunes of four sisters from Halifax, against a backdrop which sweeps from World War II to the New York jazz scene.

★ **Alistair MacLeod** *No Great Mischief*. This forceful, evocative novel tells the tale of a family of Gaelic-speaking Nova Scotians from Cape Breton. Some of the episodes are brilliantly written – others less so – but it is still one of the best Canadian novels of the 1990s.

Anne Michaels *Fugitive Pieces*. This debut novel from an award-winning poet concerns survivors from the

Nazis who emigrate to Canada. Their relationship deepens but memory and the past are never far away. A beautiful work.

W.O. Mitchell *Who Has Seen the Wind*. Canada's equivalent of *Huckleberry Finn* is a folksy story of a young boy coming of age in small-town Saskatchewan, with great off-beat characters and fine evocations of prairie life.

★ **L.M. Montgomery** *Anne of Green Gables*. Growing pains and bucolic bliss in a children's classic from 1908. Bound to appeal to little girls of all ages.

Brian Moore *Black Robe*. Moore emigrated to Canada from Ireland in 1948 and stayed long enough to gain citizenship before moving on to California. *Black Robe* – the story of a missionary's journey into native territory – is typical of the author's preoccupations with Catholicism, repression and redemption.

★ **Alice Munro** *Lives of Girls and Women; The Progress of Love; The Beggar Maid; Friend of My Youth; Dance of the Happy Shades; Who Do You Think You Are?; Something I've Been Meaning to Tell You; The Moons of Jupiter;* and *Hateship, Friendship, Courtship, Loveship and Marriage*. Amongst the world's finest living short-story writers, Munro deals primarily with the lives of women in the semi-rural and Protestant backcountry of southwest Ontario. Unsettling emotions are never far beneath the surface. Among her more recent works, *Open Secrets* focuses on stories set in two small Ontario towns from the days of the early settlers to the present. Otherwise, start with *Who Do You Think You Are?*

New Oxford Book of Canadian Short Stories in English (ed. Margaret Atwood and Robert Weaver). A broad selection which delves beyond the better-known names of Alice Munro and Margaret Atwood, with space being given to diaspora writers. While the intention is to celebrate Canadian writing, some of the works offer a distinctly negative view of the country.

Howard Norman *The Haunting of L*. Curious novel of psychosis, deception and sexual shenanigans mostly set in the far north – Churchill, Manitoba to be exact. The writing is a tad patchy, but the best sections are disconcerting and effecting in equal measure.

Michael Ondaatje *In the Skin of a Lion*. This is the novel that introduces readers to the characters that appear in the more famous *The English Patient*. It's a highly charged work spanning the period between the end of World War I and the Great Depression in Toronto.

Oxford Book of Canadian Ghost Stories (ed. Alberto Manguel o/p). Over twenty stories, including W.P. Kinsella's *Shoeless Joe Jackson Comes to Iowa* – the inspiration for the fey *Field of Dreams*.

Oxford Companion to Canadian Literature (ed. William Toye & Eugene Benson, o/p). At almost 1200 pages, this is the last word on the subject, though it is more useful as a work of reference than as a primer for the country's literature. Published 1998.

E. Annie Proulx *The Shipping News*. The 1994 Pulitzer Prize-winner is a rambling, inconclusive narrative of a social misfit who finds love and happiness of sorts in small-town Newfoundland. Superb descriptions of sea, weather and all things fishy (as distinct from some very average characterization) make it a possible primer for a visit to the province.

Nino Ricci *Where Has She Gone?* The third in a trilogy that began with *The Book of Saints*, this book is about an Italian-Canadian family's sometimes tragic attempts to find its identity.

Mordecai Richler French-Canadian, working-class and Jewish – Yiddishkeit is Richler's bag. He is the laureate of the minority within a minority within a minority. All his novels explore this relation with broad humour and pathos. In *The Apprenticeship of Duddy Kravitz*, his best-known work, Richler uses his early experiences of Montréal's working-class Jewish ghetto in an acerbic and slick cross-cultural romance built around the ambivalent but tightly drawn figure of Kravitz. Richler's pushy and ironic prose is not to all tastes, but you might also try *Solomon Gursky Was Here* or his later *Barney's Version*, a rip-roaring comic portrait of a reckless artist *manqué*.

Carol Shields *Happenstance*; *The Stone Diaries*; *Larry's Party*. Winner of the Pulitzer Prize, Shields is much lauded for the detail she finds in the everyday. There are moments of great beauty and sensitivity in these books which chronicle the experiences of bourgeois North American suburbia with unnerving frankness.

Elizabeth Smart *By Grand Central Station I Sat Down and Wept*. A cult masterpiece which lyrically details the writer's love affair with the English poet George Barker.

Susan Swan *The Wives of Bath*. At a Toronto girls' school in the Sixties, the protagonist, Mouse, struggles with notions of feminine beauty as her best friend struggles with gender identity. A wry novel written in a genre the author described as "sexual gothic".

Audrey Thomas *The Wild Blue Yonder*. A collection of witty tales about male–female relationships by a renowned Canadian short-story writer.

Jane Urquhart *The Underpainter*. A painful book concerning the life of a narcissistic painter who uses and leaves his muse but ultimately finds the demands of art destroy his humanity.

Guy Vanderhaeghe *The Last Crossing*. A thoroughly researched account of the last of the Canadian Wild West, largely set in Saskatchewan and cleverly told from several points of view.

John Wyndham *The Chrysalids*. A science-fiction classic built around a group of telepathic children and their adventures in post-Holocaust Labrador.

Poetry

Elizabeth Bishop *The Complete Poems*. Though American by birth, Bishop spent much of her youth in Nova Scotia. Many of her early poems feed off her Canadian childhood and her fascination with the country's rough landscapes.

Leonard Cohen *Stranger Music: Selected Poems & Songs*. A fine collection from a Sixties survivor who enjoyed high critical acclaim as a poet before emerging as a husky-throated crooner of bedsit ballads. See also his *Beautiful Losers*, one of the most aggressively experimental Canadian novels of the Sixties.

New Oxford Book of Canadian Verse (ed. Margaret Atwood). Canadian poets are increasingly finding a distinctive voice, but few (except Atwood herself) have made much impact outside their native country. Atwood's own sharp, witty examinations of nationality and gender are among the best in this anthology, though there is much more of merit too.

Robert Service *The Best of Robert Service*. Service's Victorian ballads of pioneer and gold-rush life have a certain charm and they capture the essence of the gold-rush period. Amongst them the *Songs of a Sourdough* collection of 1907 is perhaps the most memorable.

Language

Language

Language

C anada has two official **languages** – English and French – though there are numerous native tongues as well. Tensions between the two main language groups play a prominent part in the politics of Canada, but the native languages are more or less ignored except in the country's more remote areas, particularly in the Northwest Territories and Nunavut, where **Inuktitut**, the language of the Inuit, is spoken widely. The Inuit are the only native population with their own-language TV channel and the only other group afforded comparable attention are the Montagnais: Montagnais-Naskapi translations appear in northern Québec and Labrador official publications.

In a brief glossary such as this there is no space to get to grips with the complexities of aboriginal languages, and very few travellers would have any need of them anyway: most natives (including those in Québec) have a good knowledge of English, especially if they deal with tourists in any capacity.

Québecois French

Québecois French differs from its European source in much the same way as North American English differs from British English. Thus, although Québecois French vocabulary, grammar and syntax are very near European French, speech can pose a few problems. If you plan to be spending much time in French-speaking Canada, consider investing in the *Rough Guide to French*, a pocket guide in a handy A–Z format.

Tracing its roots back to seventeenth-century vernacular French, Québecois has preserved features that disappeared long ago in France itself and it has also been affected by its close contact with English. The end result is a dialect that – frankly – is a source of amusement to many French people and bafflement for those educated in the French language back in Europe, not to mention other parts of Canada. Within Québec itself there are marked regional differences of pronunciation, so much so that Montréalers find it hard to understand northern Québecois.

The Québecois are extremely sympathetic when visiting English-speakers make the effort to speak French – and most are much more forthcoming with their knowledge of English when talking to a Briton or American than to a Canadian. Similarly easy-going is the attitude towards the formal *vous* (you), which is used less often in Québec; you may even be corrected when saying *S'il vous plaît* with the suggestion that *S'il te plaît* is more appropriate. Another popular phrase that you are likely to come across is *pas de tout* ("not at all") which in Québec is pronounced *pan toot*, completely different from the French *pa du too*. The same goes for *c'est tout?* ("is that all?"), pronounced *say toot*; you're likely to hear this when buying something in a shop.

With **pronunciation** there's little point trying to mimic the local dialect – generally, just stick to the classic French rules.

French pronunciation

French isn't an easy language for English-speakers to **pronounce**, despite the number of words shared with English, but learning the bare essentials is not difficult. Differentiating words is the initial problem in understanding spoken French; it's very hard to get people to slow down. If, as a last resort, you get them to write it down, you may find you can identify half the words anyway.

Vowels

a as in h**a**t

au as in **o**ver

e as in g**e**t

é between g**e**t and g**a**te

è between g**e**t and g**u**t

eu as in h**u**rt

i as in mach**i**ne

o as in h**o**t

ô as in **o**ver

ou as in f**oo**d

u is a pursed-lip version of tr**u**e

The following are extra-tricky nasal sounds:

an/am and *en/em* like **Don**caster said through your nose

in/im like **an**xious

on/om like **Don**caster said with a heavy cold

un/um like **un**derstand

Consonants

Consonants are pronounced much as in English, except:

ç is an English **s**

ch is an English **sh**

h is silent

ll as in ba**y**onet

r is growled rather than trilled

th is like an English **t**

w is an English **v**

French words and phrases

The basics

good morning/ afternoon/hello	**bonjour**	Do you speak English?	**Parlez-vous anglais?**
good evening	**bonsoir**	I don't speak French	**Je ne parle pas français**
good night	**bonne nuit**		
goodbye	**au revoir**	I don't understand	**Je ne comprends pas**
yes	**oui**		
no	**non**	I don't know	**Je ne sais pas**
please	**s'il vous/te plaît**	Excuse me (in a crowd)	**Excusez-moi**
		Sorry	**Pardon/désolé(e)**
thank you (very much)	**merci (beaucoup)**	I'm English	**Je suis anglais(e)**
you're welcome	**bienvenue/de rien/je vous en prie**	Scottish/Welsh	**écossais(e)/ gallois(e)**
		Irish/American	**irlandais(e)/ américain(e)**
OK	**d'accord**		
How are you?	**Comment allez-vous?/Ça va?**	Australian	**australian(e)**
		I live in…	**Je demeure à…**
		Wait a minute!	**Un instant!**
Fine, thanks	**Très bien, merci**	here/there	**ici/là**

good/bad	**bon/mauvais**	loudly/quietly	**bruyant/**
big/small	**grand/petit**		**tranquille**
cheap/expensive	**bon marché/cher**	with/without	**avec/sans**
early/late	**tôt/tard**	more/less	**plus/moins**
hot/cold	**chaud/froid**	enough/no more	**assez/ça suffit**
near/far	**près (pas loin)/loin**	Mr	**Monsieur**
vacant/occupied	**libre/occupé**	Mrs	**Madame**
quickly/slowly	**vite/lentement**	Miss	**Mademoiselle**

Numbers

1	**un/une**	19	**dix-neuf**
2	**deux**	20	**vingt**
3	**trois**	21	**vingt-et-un**
4	**quatre**	22	**vingt-deux**
5	**cinq**	30	**trente**
6	**six**	40	**quarante**
7	**sept**	50	**cinquante**
8	**huit**	60	**soixante**
9	**neuf**	70	**soixante-dix**
10	**dix**	80	**quatre-vingts**
11	**onze**	90	**quatre-vingt-dix**
12	**douze**	100	**cent**
13	**treize**	101	**cent-et-un**
14	**quatorze**	110	**cent-dix**
15	**quinze**	200	**deux cents**
16	**seize**	1000	**mille**
17	**dix-sept**	2000	**deux milles**
18	**dix-huit**		

Days and times

Monday	**lundi**	hour	**heure**
Tuesday	**mardi**	day	**jour**
Wednesday	**mercredi**	week	**semaine**
Thursday	**jeudi**	month	**mois**
Friday	**vendredi**	year	**année**
Saturday	**samedi**	now	**maintenant**
Sunday	**dimanche**	later	**plus tard**
morning	**le matin**	What time is it?	**Quelle heure est-il?**
afternoon	**l'après-midi**	It's 9.00	**Il est neuf heures**
evening	**le soir**	1.05	**une heure cinq**
night	**la nuit**	2.15	**deux heures et quart**
yesterday	**hier**	5.45	**six heures moins quart**
today	**aujourd'hui**	9.40	**dix heures moins vingt**
tomorrow	**demain**	10.30	**dix heures et demie**
tomorrow morning	**demain matin**	noon	**midi**
minute	**minute**	midnight	**minuit**

Questions and directions

Where?	Où?	Can you give me a lift to…?	Pouvez-vous me conduire jusqu'à…?
When?	Quand?		
What?	Quoi?		
What is it?	Qu'est-ce que c'est?	Can you tell me when to get off?	Pouvez-vous me dire quand descendre?
How much/many?	Combien?		
Why?	Pourquoi?	What time does it open?	À quelle heure ça ouvre?
It is/there is	C'est/Il y a		
Is it/is there…?	Est-ce que/ Y a-t-il…?	How much does it cost?	Combien cela coûte-t-il?
How do I get to…?	Où se trouve…?	How do you say it in French?	Comment ça se dit en français?
How far is it to…?	À quelle distance est-il à…?		

Accommodation

Is there a campsite nearby?	Y a-t-il un camping près d'ici?
tent	tente
cabin	chalet
hostel	auberge de jeunesse
hotel	hôtel
Do you have anything cheaper?	Avez-vous quelque chose de meilleur marché?
full board	tout compris
Can I see the room?	Puis-je peux voir la chambre?
I'll take this one	Je vais prendre celle-ci
I'd like to book a room	J'aimerais réserver une chambre
I have a booking	J'ai une réservation
Can we camp here?	Pouvons-nous camper ici?
How much is it?	C'est combien?
It's expensive	C'est cher
Is breakfast included?	Est-ce que le petit déjeuner est compris?
I'm looking for a nearby hotel	Je cherche un hôtel près d'ici
Do you have a room?	Avez-vous une chambre?
for one/two/three people	pour une/deux/trois personne(s)
for one/two/three nights	pour une/deux/trois nuit(s)
for one week	pour une semaine
with a double bed	avec un lit double
with a shower/bathtub	avec douche/salle de bain
hot/cold water	eau chaude/froide

Travelling

bus	autobus	bicycle	vélo
train	train	ferry	traversier
plane	avion	ship	bâteau
car	voiture	hitch-hiking	faire du pouce
taxi	taxi	on foot	à pied

bus station	terminus d'autobus	Do I have to change?	Dois-je transférer?
train station	gare centrale	Where does it leave from?	D'où est-ce qu'il part?
ferry terminal	quai du traversier		
port	port	How many kilometres?	Combien de kilomètres?
A ticket to...	Un billet pour...		
one-way/return	aller-simple/ aller-retour	How many hours?	Combien d'heures?
Can I book a seat?	Puis-je réserver un siège?	Which bus do I take to get to...?	Quel autobus dois-je prendre pour aller à...?
What time does it leave?	Il part à quelle heure?		
When is the next train to...?	Quand est le prochain train pour...?	Next stop	Le prochain arrêt
		Where's the road to...?	Où est la route pour...?

Some signs

Entrance/Exit	Entrée/Sortie	Platform	Voie
Free admission	Entrée Libre	Cash desk	Caisse
Gentlemen/Ladies	Messieurs/Dames	Go/Walk	Marchez
WC	Toilette	Stop	Arrêtez
Vacant/Engaged	Libre/Occupé	Customs	Douanes
Open/Closed	Ouvert/Fermé	Do not touch!	Défense de toucher!
Arrivals/Departures	Arrivées/Départs		
Closed for holidays	Fermé pour les vacances	Danger!	Danger!
		Beware!	Attention!
Pull/Push	Tirez/Poussez	First aid	Premiers soins
Out of order	Hors d'usage/Brisé	Ring the bell	Sonnez
To let	À louer	No smoking	Défense de fumer

Driving

turn to the left/right	tournez à gauche/droite	no overtaking	défense de dépasser
		passing lane only	voie réservée au dépassement
straight ahead	tout droit		
car park	terrain de stationnement	speed	vitesse
		self-service	libre-service
no parking	défense de stationner/ stationnement interdit	full service	service complet
		Fill the tank with...	Faîtes le plein avec...
		...regular	...de l'essence ordinaire
tow-away zone	zone de remorquage		
cars towed at owner's expense	remorquage à vos frais	...super	...du super
		...unleaded	...du sans plomb
one-way street	sens unique	Check the oil	Vérifiez l'huile
dead end	cul-de-sac	battery	la batterie
no entry	défense d'entrer	radiator	le radiateur
slow down	ralentir	plugs	bougies d'allumage
proceed on flashing green light	attendez le feu vert clignotant	tyre pressure	pression des pneus
		Pump up the tyres	Gonflez les pneus
turn on headlights!	allumez vos phares!		

A French menu reader

Basic terms and ingredients

beurre	butter	pain	bread
chaud	hot	poisson	fish
crème fraiche	sour cream	poivre	pepper
dessert	dessert	salade	salad
frappé	iced	sel	salt
froid	cold	sucre	sugar
fromage	cheese	tourte	tart or pie
hors d'oeuvre	starters	tranche	a slice
legumes	vegetables	viande	meat
oeufs	eggs		

Snacks

un sandwich/une baguette...	a sandwich...	oeufs au plat	fried eggs
		oeufs à la coque	boiled eggs
...de jambon	...with ham	oeufs durs	hard-boiled eggs
...de fromage	...with cheese	oeufs brouillés	scrambled eggs
...de saucisson	...with sausage	omelette nature	plain omelette
à l'ail	with garlic	omelette au fromage	cheese omelette
au poivre	with pepper		
croque-monsieur	grilled cheese and ham sandwich		

Soups and starters

assiette anglaise	plate of cold meats	crudités	raw vegetables with dressing
bisque	shellfish soup		
bouillabaisse	fish soup	potage	thick soup, usually vegetable
bouillon	broth or stock		
consommé	clear soup		

Meat and poultry

agneau	lamb	foie	liver
bifteck	steak	gibiers	game
boeuf	beef	gigot	leg of venison
canard	duck	jambon	ham
cheval	horsemeat	lard	bacon
côtelettes	cutlets	porc	pork
cuisson	leg of lamb	poulet	chicken
dindon	turkey	saucisse	sausage
escargots	snails	veau	veal

Fish and seafood

anchois	anchovies	maquereau	mackerel
anguilles	eels	morue	cod
carrelet	plaice	moules	mussels
cervettes roses	prawns	saumon	salmon
hareng	herring	sole	sole
homard	lobster	truite	trout
lotte de mer	monkfish		

Cooking methods

saignant	rare (steak)	fumé	smoked
a point	medium done (steak)	grillé	grilled
bien cuit	well done (steak)	mijoté	stewed
au four	baked	pané	breaded
bouilli	boiled	rôti	roasted
frit/friture	fried/deep fried	sauté	lightly cooked in butter

Vegetables and grains

ail	garlic	oignons	onions
asperges	asparagus	petits pois	peas
carottes	carrots	poireau	leek
champignons	mushrooms	pommes (de terre)	potatoes
choufleur	cauliflower	riz	rice
concombre	cucumber	tomate	tomato
laitue	lettuce		

Fruit and nuts

amandes	almonds	noisette	hazelnut
ananas	pineapple	pamplemousse	grapefruit
cacahouète	peanut	poire	pear
cérises	cherries	pomme	apple
citron	lemon	prune	plum
fraises	strawberries	pruneau	prune
framboises	raspberries	raisins	grapes
marrons	chestnuts		

Sweets and desserts

crêpes au sucre	pancakes with sugar	glace	ice cream
crêpes au citron	pancakes with lemon	madeleine	small, shell-shaped sponge cake
crêpes au miel	pancakes with honey		
crêpes à la confiture	pancakes with jam/jelly	parfait	frozen mousse, sometimes ice cream
crêpes suzettes	thin pancakes with orange juice and liqueur	petits fours	bite-sized cakes or pastries

Drinks

café	coffee	**vin blanc**	white wine
thé	tea	**brut**	very dry
lait	milk	**sec**	dry
jus d'orange	orange juice	**demi-sec**	sweet
citron pressé	sweetened lemon juice	**doux**	very sweet
bière	beer	**eaux de vie**	fruit spirit/liquor
vin rouge	red wine		

...music & reference

Also! More than 120 Rough Guide music CDs are available from all good book
and record stores. Listen in at www.worldmusic.net

1104

small print and

Index

A Rough Guide to Rough Guides

In the summer of 1981, Mark Ellingham, a recent graduate from Bristol University, was travelling round Greece and couldn't find a guidebook that really met his needs. On the one hand there were the student guides, insistent on saving every last cent, and on the other the heavyweight cultural tomes whose authors seemed to have spent more time in a research library than lounging away the afternoon at a taverna or on the beach.

In a bid to avoid getting a job, Mark and a small group of writers set about creating their own guidebook. It was a guide to Greece that aimed to combine a journalistic approach to description with a thoroughly practical approach to travellers' needs – a guide that would incorporate culture, history and contemporary insights with a critical edge, together with up-to-date, value-for-money listings. Back in London, Mark and the team finished their Rough Guide, as they called it, and talked Routledge into publishing the book.

That first *Rough Guide to Greece*, published in 1982, was a student scheme that became a publishing phenomenon. The immediate success of the book – with numerous reprints and a Thomas Cook prize shortlisting – spawned a series that rapidly covered dozens of destinations. Rough Guides had a ready market among low-budget backpackers, but soon also acquired a much broader and older readership that relished Rough Guides' wit and inquisitiveness as much as their enthusiastic, critical approach. Everyone wants value for money, but not at any price.

Rough Guides soon began supplementing the "rougher" information about hostels and low-budget listings with the kind of detail on restaurants and quality hotels that independent-minded visitors on any budget might expect, whether on business in New York or trekking in Thailand.

These days the guides – distributed worldwide by the Penguin group – offer recommendations from shoestring to luxury and cover more than 200 destinations around the globe, including almost every country in the Americas and Europe, more than half of Africa and most of Asia and Australasia. Our ever-growing team of authors and photographers is spread all over the world, particularly in Europe, the USA and Australia.

In 1994, we published the *Rough Guide to World Music* and *Rough Guide to Classical Music*; and a year later the *Rough Guide to the Internet*. All three books have become benchmark titles in their fields – which encouraged us to expand into other areas of publishing, mainly around popular culture. Rough Guides now publish:

- Travel guides to more than 200 worldwide destinations
- Dictionary phrasebooks for 22 major languages
- History guides ranging from Ireland to Islam
- Maps printed on rip-proof and waterproof Polyart™ paper
- Music guides running the gamut from Opera to Elvis
- Restaurant guides to London, New York and San Francisco
- Reference books on topics as diverse as the Weather and Shakespeare
- Sports guides from Formula 1 to Man Utd
- Pop culture books from *Lord of the Rings* to Cult TV
- World Music CDs in association with World Music Network

Visit **www.roughguides.com** to see our latest publications.

Rough Guide credits

Editor: Matthew Teller
Layout: Umesh Aggarwal, Ajay Verma
Cartography: Rajesh Chhibber, Ashutosh Bharti, Rajesh Mishra, Animesh Pathak
Picture research: Jj Luck
Proofreader: Susannah Wight
Editorial: London Martin Dunford, Kate Berens, Helena Smith, Claire Saunders, Geoff Howard, Ruth Blackmore, Gavin Thomas, Polly Thomas, Richard Lim, Lucy Ratcliffe, Clifton Wilkinson, Alison Murchie, Fran Sandham, Sally Schafer, Alexander Mark Rogers, Karoline Densley, Andy Turner, Ella O'Donnell, Keith Drew, Andrew Lockett, Joe Staines, Duncan Clark, Peter Buckley, Matthew Milton; **New York** Andrew Rosenberg, Richard Koss, Yuki Takagaki, Hunter Slaton, Chris Barsanti, Thomas Kohnstamm, Steven Horak
Design & Layout: London Dan May, Diana Jarvis; **Delhi** Madhulita Mohapatra, Umesh Aggarwal, Ajay Verma

Production: Julia Bovis, John McKay, Sophie Hewat
Cartography: London Maxine Repath, Ed Wright, Katie Lloyd-Jones, Miles Irving; **Delhi** Manish Chandra, Rajesh Chhibber, Jai Prakash Mishra, Ashutosh Bharti, Rajesh Mishra, Animesh Pathak
Cover art direction: Louise Boulton
Picture research: Mark Thomas, Jj Luck
Online: New York Jennifer Gold, Cree Lawson, Suzanne Welles, Benjamin Ross; **Delhi** Manik Chauhan, Amarjyoti Dutta, Narender Kumar
Marketing & Publicity: London Richard Trillo, Niki Smith, David Wearn, Chloë Roberts, Demelza Dallow, Kristina Pentland; **New York** Geoff Colquitt, David Wechsler, Megan Kennedy
Finance: Gary Singh
Manager India: Punita Singh
Series editor: Mark Ellingham
PA to Managing Director: Julie Sanderson
Managing Director: Kevin Fitzgerald

Publishing information

This fifth edition published June 2004 by
Rough Guides Ltd,
80 Strand, London WC2R 0RL.
345 Hudson St, 4th Floor,
New York, NY 10014, USA.
Distributed by the Penguin Group
Penguin Books Ltd,
80 Strand, London WC2R 0RL
Penguin Putnam, Inc,
375 Hudson Street, NY 10014, USA
Penguin Books Australia Ltd,
487 Maroondah Highway, PO Box 257,
Ringwood, Victoria 3134, Australia
Penguin Books Canada Ltd,
10 Alcorn Avenue, Toronto, Ontario,
Canada M4V 1E4
Penguin Books (NZ) Ltd,
182–190 Wairau Road, Auckland 10,
New Zealand
Typeset in Bembo and Helvetica to an original design by Henry Iles.

Printed in Italy by LegoPrint S.p.A

© Tim Jepson, Phil Lee, Tania Smith and Christian Williams

1136 pp includes index
A catalogue record for this book is available from the British Library

ISBN 1-84353-266-2

The publishers and authors have done their best to ensure the accuracy and currency of all the information in **The Rough Guide to Canada**; however, they can accept no responsibility for any loss, injury, or inconvenience sustained by any traveller as a result of information or advice contained in the guide.

3   5   7   9   8   6   4

Help us update

We've gone to a lot of effort to ensure that the fifth edition of **The Rough Guide to Canada** is accurate and up to date. However, things change – places get "discovered", opening hours are notoriously fickle, restaurants and rooms raise prices or lower standards. If you feel we've got it wrong or left something out, we'd like to know, and if you can remember the address, the price, the time, the phone number, so much the better.

We'll credit all contributions, and send a copy of the next edition (or any other Rough Guide if you prefer) for the best letters. Everyone who writes to us and isn't already a subscriber will receive a copy of our full-colour thrice-yearly newsletter. Please mark letters: "**Rough Guide to Canada Update**" and send to: Rough Guides, 80 Strand, London WC2R 0RL, or Rough Guides, 4th Floor, 345 Hudson St, New York, NY 10014.
Or send an email to **mail@roughguides.com**

Have your questions answered and tell others about your trip at **www.roughguides.atinfopop.com**

Readers' letters and emails

Many thanks to all those readers who took the time to write or email with comments on the last edition, new discoveries in Canada or just an account of their travels (apologies if we've misspelt or misunderstood anyone's name):

Juan Abad, Xavier Balducci, John Batey, G. Battersby, Xavier Brebion, Tom Brownlee, Chris Clayton, Sean Connelly, Kelly Cross, Marcus Dale, Brad Darch, Dan Driscoll, Matthew Ellis, Tony Francis, Monica Germana, Aleasha Gilpin, Rubye Grady, Denise Grant, Nina Hansen, Janne Hansen, Greg Harper, Sharon Harris, Gavin Hawe, Stephen Hayward, David Heller, Ann Heymans, David R. Howe, Jane King, Lori Johnson, Gilles Laberge, Simone Meixner, Michael Mersereau, Mike Metcalfe,

S.B. Morris, Jacqueline de Nooy, John D. Norman, Judy Nunn, Genevieve Paiement, Celine Palmer, Jeanette Potter, Nathan Powell, Rebecca Power, Otto Reid, Joanne Ross, Jayne Russell, Steve Sanna, Nicole & Kai Sauerbier, Benno Schummer, Eden Smith, Steve Smith, Erick Sodhi, Aidan Topping, Andrew Tzembelicos, Kyle Upton, Paul D. Wadsley, Alan Weeks, Suzanne Wells, Caroline Wright, D. Wright, Peter W. White, Andrew Young.

Acknowledgements

Tim Jepson would like to thank his editor, Matthew Teller; Lucy Hyslop; James and Vicky Ballentyne; Air Canada; Charlotte Fraser and Fairmont Hotels; Claire Griffin and Four Seasons hotels; and Kathleen Eccles.
Phil Lee would like to extend a special thanks to Diane Helinksi of Ontario Tourism; Kathleen Crotty and Ed Kirby of Newfoundland & Labrador Tourism; Valerie Kidney of New Brunswick Tourism; Randy Brooks of Nova Scotia Tourism; Carol Horne of PEI Tourism; Darlene Scott of Newfoundland's East Coast Trail Association; Diane Houston from Ottawa Tourism; Heather Gregg from Kingston Economic Development Corporation; and Paul & Carol Buer of Toronto.
John Watson says a big thank you to Gilles Bengle, Yves Pelletier and Jean-François Perrier at Tourisme Montréal, Richard Séguin and the staff at the Greater Québec Area Tourism and Convention Bureau, Roselyne Hébert and Bard Nordby at Tourisme Québec, Ronald Poiré and Élyse Busque for informative city tours, and to the folks at VIA, Air Canada and Les Dauphins de St-Laurent for assistance in getting there and around. Thanks also to Richard Burnett, Brett Shymanski, Pierre-Yves Legault, Charlie McKee, Robert Stewart, and especially Darren Henriet, Angela Songui and Stephanie Halley for specific advice and wholehearted support in Montréal.

Christian Williams thanks the people of Québec for their sense of fun and excellent cheeses, the CBC for making journeys in the prairies seem shorter and the parks service for keeping fires in the Rockies at bay. In particular praise is due for the assistance of Isabelle and Dominique in Québec; Heidi for stoic work in the prow of a Manitoban canoe; Nabby Frye for suffering fuel shortages in the prairies and Lisa for making me visit the 8th and 8th time and again and – together with Jessie and Randy – for hospitality in Calgary. Also thanks to Jocelyn for paying me in seaweed to carry her pack. In the UK thanks to Pop for keeping the flat in shape and Raymond for lending an ear. At Rough Guides credit goes to Martin Dunford and Andrew Rosenberg for letting me loose on Canada once again and to Matthew Teller for stepping in at the last minute to pull this book together.
The editor thanks the pre-press and cartography team: in Delhi Punita Singh, Madhu Mohapatra, Umesh Aggarwal, Ajay Verma, Manish Chandra, Jai Prakash Mishra, Rajesh Chhibber, Ashutosh Bharti, Rajesh Mishra and Animesh Pathak; and in London Katie Lloyd-Jones, Ed Wright, Miles Irving, Helen Prior, Julia Bovis and Karoline Densley; Sharon Martins, J.J. Luck and Louise Boulton for picture research; Susannah Wight for proofreading; and in the New York office Richard Koss and Andrew Rosenberg.

SMALL PRINT

Photo credits

Cover credits
Front main: Lobster traps, Nova Scotia © Getty
Front small top: Newfoundland © Robert Harding
Front small lower: Stanley Park, Vancouver © Robert Harding
Back top: Moraine Lake © Robert Harding
Back lower: Château Frontenac, Québec City © Robert Harding

Introduction
Canoe on Moraine Lake © Chris Coe/Axiom
Horse riding in Banff National Park © Chris Coe/Axiom
Traffic sign near Prince George, BC © Paul A. Souders/CORBIS
Canoes in autumn © Daryl Benson/Masterfile
Dempster Highway © Chris Coe/Axiom
Banff © Robert Harding
Inuit parka and gloves © Chris Coe/Axiom
Blueberry pancakes with maple syrup © Michael Kohn/Masterfile
Rock formation on Flower-Pot Island © Ron Watts/CORBIS
Polar bear, Churchill © Mike Macri/Masterfile
Climbers, Milk River Valley, AB © Daryl Benson/Masterfile
Café in Montréal © Chris Coe/Axiom

Things not to miss
01 Yoho National Park © Robert Harding
02 Stanley Park, Vancouver © Nick Hanmer
03 Ice climber in Maligne Canyon, Jasper © Chris Coe/Axiom
04 PEI National Park © Phil Lee
05 Burntcoat Head, Bay of Fundy, NS © Brian Sytnyk/Masterfile
06 Moraine Lake, Banff © Chris Coe/Axiom
07 Biosphere, Montréal © Tourisme Montréal, Stéphan Poulin
08 Mt Robson Provincial Park © G. Renner/Robert Harding
09 Museum of Civilizations, Ottawa © Chris Cole/Axiom
10 Niagara Falls © Miles Ertman/Masterfile
11 Polar bear with cub, Churchill © Mike Macri/Masterfile
12 Queen Charlotte Island, BC © J.A. Kraulis/Masterfile
13 Emily Carr, *Totem Poles, Kitseukla 1912*, oil on canvas, Vancouver Art Gallery, Founders Fund, VAG 37.2 (photo: Trevor Mills)
14 Café, Québec City © Chris Coe/Axiom
15 Lunenburg, NS © Phil Lee
16 Dawson City, Yukon © Chris Coe/Axiom
17 Calgary Stampede © Toby Rankin/Masterfile
18 Pod of orcas, Johnston Straits, BC © Joel W. Rogers/CORBIS
19 Iceberg, Calvert, Avalon Peninsula, Newfoundland © Greg Stott/Masterfile
20 Ice skating at New City Hall, Toronto © Corbis/Lowell Georgia
21 Boathouse on Lac Manitou, The Laurentians, QC © Mark Tomalty/Masterfile
22 Kaskawulsh Glacier, Kluane National Park, Yukon © Chris Coe/Axiom
23 Helmcken Canyon, Wells Gray Provincial Park, BC © Daryl Benson/Masterfile
24 Whistler © Ed Gifford/Masterfile
25 Brown bear with salmon © B&C Alexander
26 Empress Hotel, Victoria, BC © Mike Dobel/Masterfile
27 Kayaker on a whitewater river © Greg Stott/Masterfile
28 Aurora borealis, Churchill, MB © Mike Macri/Masterfile
29 Long Beach, Vancouver Island © Philip Rostron/Masterfile
30 Skiing in the Rockies © H. Elton/Axiom
31 The Narrows, Signal Hill, St John's © Phil Lee
32 Moose, Algonquin National Park, ON © Chris Coe/Axiom

Black and white photos
Yorkville Ave, Toronto © Trip/T. Bognar (p.68)
Henry Moore sculptures, AGO, Toronto © Bob Krist/CORBIS (p.89)
Niagara Falls © Michael S. Yamashita/CORBIS (p.124)
Algonquin Provincial Park © J. David Andrews/Masterfile (p.155)
Parliament Buildings, Ottawa © Chris Coe/Axiom (p.184)
Montréal houses © John Shandy Watson (p.218)
Montréal mural © John Shandy Watson (p.240)
Alley in Québec City © John Shandy Watson (p.290)
Hautes-Gorges © Christian Williams (p.346)
Harbour, Blue Rocks, NS © Chris Coe/Axiom (p.372)
Church at Mahone Bay, NS © Chris Coe/Axiom (p.408)
Trinity, NL © Phil Lee (p.468)
Puffin at Witless Bay © Garry Black/Masterfile (p.497)
Pick-your-own Saskatoon berries © Christian Williams (p.528)
Grain elevator on prairies © Christian Williams (p.580)
Emperor Falls in Mt Robson park © Christian Williams (p.620)
Calgary Stampede © Peter Christopher/Masterfile (p.650)
Lake Louise © Shaun Opperman (p.690)
Johnston Canyon © Nick Hanmer (p.741)
Vancouver skyline © Chris Coe/Axiom (p.772)
Skater on Vancouver waterfront © Chris Coe/Axiom (p.803)
Ferry on Inside Passage © Pat O'Hara/CORBIS (p.852)
Skiers at Whistler © Karl Weatherly/CORBIS (p.906)
"Kootenay" City Hall, Nelson, BC © Gunter Marx/CORBIS (p.957)
Gold store, Dawson City © Chris Coe/Axiom (p.970)
Dawson during the Klondike Gold Rush © Bettmann/CORBIS (p.1011)

Index

Map entries are in **colour**.

INDEX

INDEX

1123

Q

INDEX

INDEX

1134

I NDEX

Map symbols

Maps are listed in the full index using coloured text.

-----	International border	â	Monastery
--..--	Province/U.S. State border	⛩	Picnic Site
---	Chapter division boundary	P	Parking
=⑮=	Expressway	Ⓗ	Helijet
=✦=	Trans-Canada Highway	⚊	Dam
=⑯=	Yellowhead Highway	⚐	Ski area
=⑧⓪=	U.S. Interstate	▣	Restaurant
=㉚=	U.S. Highway	◉	Accommodation
=①=	Highway	⚠	Campsite
══	Secondary Highway	✈	Airport
═══	Local Road	⊠—⊠	Gate
▬▬	Pedestrianised Road	⊞	Hospital/medical centre
▥▥▥	Steps	ⓘ	Tourist Information
-----	Path	⊠	Post office
═══	Railway	☩	Church (regional maps)
— —	Ferry route	)(	Bridge
●----●	Cable car	♦	Point of interest
▪▪▪▪▪	Wall	⚑	Golf course
⊕	Subway station	★	Bus stop
—	River	⚓	Boat
⋀⋀	Mountain range	⊙	Statue
▲	Mountain peak	▮	Building
⚜	Waterfall	⊞	Church (town maps)
⚘	Viewpoint	⁺⁺⁺	Cemetery
⚲	Lighthouse	▓	Park
⏛	Monument	⬚	Forest
■	Tower	⬚	Beach